BASEBALL PROSPECTUS 2020

The Essential Guide to the 2020 Season

Edited by R.J. Anderson, Craig Goldstein and Bret Sayre

Lucas Apostoleris, Jorge Arangure, Darius Austin, Emma Baccellieri, Mark Barry, Jordan Bastian, Demetrius Bell, Sydney Bergman, J.P. Breen, Grant Brisbee, Ben Carsley, Ben Clemens, Zach Crizer, Spring Marie Cullen, Bradford William Davis, Russell Dorsey, Patrick Dubuque, Drew Fairservice, James Fegan, Anthony Fenech, Ken Funck, Brendan Gawlowski, Mike Gianella, Bryan Grosnick, Jon Hegglund, Christina Kahrl, Wilson Karaman, Justin Klugh, David Lee, Graham MacAree, Rob Mains, Allison McCague, Kelsey McKinney, Jon Meoli, Ian Miller, Jack Moore, Chad Moriyama, Zack Moser, Marc Normandin, Sara Nović, Eric Nusbaum, Robert O'Connell, Jeffrey Paternostro, Tommy Rancel, Manny Randawaha, David Roth, Nick Schaefer, Gerald Schifman, Ginny Searle, Jarrett Seidler, Jordan Shusterman, Matt Snyder, Adam Sobsey, Ben Spanier, Tyler Stafford, Linda Surovich, Matt Sussman, Jon Tayler, Matt Trueblood, Levi Weaver, Holly Wendt, Collin Whitchurch, Jeff Wiser, Clarissa Young

Craig Brown, Associate Editor
Robert Au, Harry Pavlidis and Amy Pircher, Statistics Editors

Library of Congress Cataloging-in-Publication Data:
paperback
ISBN-10: 1949332608
ISBN-13: 978-1949332605

Project Credits
Cover Design: Michael Byzewski at Aesthetic Apparatus
Interior Design and Production: Jeff Pease, Dave Pease
Layout: Jeff Pease, Dave Pease

Cover Photos
Front Cover: Jacob deGrom. © David Kohl-USA TODAY Sports

Baseball icon courtesy of Uberux, from https://www.shareicon.net/author/uberux

Manufactured in the United States of America
10 9 8 7 6 5 4 3 2 1

This book is dedicated to our friend Rob McQuown.

Thanks for the research, and for everything else.

Table of Contents

MLB Teams

Foreword

by Jason Benetti

If you've watched a telecast I've been on, whether it be a White Sox game with the incomparable Steve Stone or an ESPN Statcast broadcast with my wonderful compatriots Eduardo Pérez and Mike Petriello (and star producer Andy Jacobson), you may have noticed the fact that I'm not looking directly at you when the camera shows us in the booth. While choosing which households I want to make eye contact with would be an awesome trick, I sadly cannot do so. I have cerebral palsy, which affects the way I walk and also makes one of my eyes drift.

Based on American norms, I shouldn't be on television. The only main character I can distinctly recall with any disability from my childhood in the late 80s and early 90s was Corky (who had Down Syndrome) from a show called *Life Goes On*. We have made substantial strides since then, what with R.J. Mitte's Walt Jr. on the sensationally wicked *Breaking Bad*, and the recently-canceled *Speechless*, which aired on network TV and focused on a young man who uses assistive technology to speak.

Whether I or you, dear reader, like it or not, it took courage for my employers to place me on television and in front-facing roles. That courage took to the form of an affirmative choice to embrace and love what's different.

In part because of that backdrop, I'm pretty certain that there's room for different and deeper stats in baseball broadcasting. When a reliever comes in, the first thing we see at the top of some telecasts' graphics—including ours with the White Sox—is the pitcher's win-loss record. In my experience, the most common response to why the win-loss record remains is, "We've always done it that way." When I hear that phrase, which is common in the baseball world, I quickly think about how people had always "done it that way" by not hiring people who looked like me. There is a place for change. I'm proof of it.

Our Statcast telecasts—the brainchild of ESPN and lovingly nurtured by Phil Orlins and Tom Archer, among others—are further proof.

One of the knocks on advanced stats—or as new Mets manager Carlos Beltrán empowers them, "information"—is that they muck up the storytelling of baseball. Absolutely, baseball touches the most people when the human nature of the game makes fans laugh or cry. The first 90 seconds of the old Disney classic *Oliver and Company* make you care deeply about Oliver because he doesn't get picked out of the box of kittens and has to spend the night in a New York City downpour. The connection wouldn't be as powerful if there was a narrator discussing the downward angle of the raindrops onto the little guy's fur.

That's a straw man, though. The more deeply we delve into the information, the more specifically we can ask questions of players to learn about what they do and who they see themselves as, drawing out the human nature of competition, which appeals to wide swaths of people.

In 2018, the White Sox and I did a video chat with lefty reliever Jace Fry. We showed him numbers about his performance from Baseball Savant and asked him questions based on those numbers. When presented with his batting average against zone chart versus lefties, he said this:

> "I moved over to the first base side of the rubber and with my curveball having lateral movement and depth I think that is kind of changing their eye level and making it difficult to see pitches that are coming out of a completely different tunnel after that first pitch. One's sinking and running in and the other one's sliding away."

We chose batting average for that chart because we compromised in an effort to avoid explaining xBA in a short video setting. New stats can animate the game beautifully as long as we consider the audience in how we present them.

Ten years ago, a hyper-intelligent friend of mine suggested that I read the book Infinite Jest by David Foster Wallace. When I looked it up, I saw that it "featured" (if torture can "feature" anything) more than 1000 pages. So, I put it off. I waited for a vacation three years later even to start it.

And now a word about Infinite Jest substantively: The first 100 pages are confusing, sometimes nonsensical, and generally serve to puree the reader's brain. It's a slog without a compass. It's a sea of superscript and slang and esoterica.

I got to page 300 or so at the end of my vacation and felt both accomplished and exhausted. I wrote my friend an email to thank him for both introducing me to DFW's dazzling vocabulary (one passage refers to an obese person's backside as "two bulldogs in a bag") and also for hitting me over the head with a literary mallet. He wrote back:

"Two bookmarks? Reading the endnotes in full right when directed? Don't take any shortcuts, since the jumping around is an important part of the total immersion."

Gulp.[1]

Having done it wrong, I mulled my options:

1. Chuck the book into a toilet at LAX.
2. Chuck the book into some other final grave at LAX.
3. Keep going without reading the endnotes (while branding myself a cheater for the rest of my life).
4. Spend most of the cross-country flight going all the way back through the first 300 pages.

Against my instincts of hilarious book disposal in coastal air transit hubs, I chose option four and spent the plane ride re-reading the book with a second bookmark. I'm truly glad I did. The book is beautiful, to me.

I can't stress enough how little I wanted to re-read. Seriously, I was demoralized. I'd spent SO much mental energy convincing myself to push past difficult passages that seemed meaningless. Now, I was being told *I DID IT WRONG*. There aren't enough Lewis Black YouTube clips to sincerely express my anger.

Some people will push through the book, some won't. I personally will drive through some difficult situations, others I won't see through. Some readers will think I'm ridiculous for not wanting to go back, some will think I'm ridiculous for even starting the book in the first place. Others will think this a repulsive first-world problem. The way you think about this situation and what you'd have done is a product of grit and circumstance and encouragement, among other factors.

We, as broadcasters, researchers, lovers of baseball, thinkers, scientists and general purveyors of baseball information have a duty to communicate what we've learned about the game in an accessible, engaging, and easy-to-learn way for people who don't know it.

There was a day we all learned WAR. And BABIP. And OPS+. And wRC+. And xFIP. There was a first day for all of us.

For folks who've never experienced advanced stats, I believe it's very much like my experience with Infinite Jest. I felt warped after reading the first 300 pages. When fans are introduced to a wheelbarrow of new stats—or even one new stat, maybe—they can feel tired or get defensive about what they don't know. If the hobby is draining, some people might simply quit.

Then, sometimes even accidentally, we the analytically-minded are telling them that they're doing baseball wrong, just like I felt like I'd done David Foster Wallace incorrectly. That can be defeating absent encouragement.

The sentiment above is not meant to be a reprimand. For those of us who read the book that follows, it can be absolutely frustrating book when people would rather see batting average on the screen instead of wRC+. We know in our hearts that those people don't know as much as they COULD know, and that's somehow melancholic.

It's our job as people who study the game for a living and for deep enjoyment to remember that the way we present the information can be the difference between someone going back to read the first 300 pages or throwing the book in the toilet.

The way we name stats, the way we introduce stats, the way we make it clear why stats are important—every one of those moments matters. Our tone matters. I encourage you to be helpful, not condescending, even if you're irritated.

We are a group, all of us who care about this game in our own ways—whether we currently love in-depth information or might in the future. As you dive deeper into this book and the wondrous examples of thorough, glorious research inside of it, think about how you can bring its nuance into someone else's life. Mull over how you can help them know what we know—that the depth and beauty of baseball is unmatched. ∎

—Jason Benetti is the play-by-play announcer for the Chicago White Sox.

---

1. The writer was not "reading the endnotes in full right when directed."

Thanks to Rob McQuown for Research Assistance

by Ben Lindbergh

This essay was adapted from episode 1405 of the Effectively Wild podcast, which was published at FanGraphs on July 17, 2019.

The online baseball community got some sad news on Tuesday, and I want to tell you about the man that I and many others are mourning.

This is sort of a strange and solitary job—a good job, but an unusual one—and people like me and Sam Miller and Meg Rowley, who are lucky enough to do this thing full-time, we work from home, and whatever coworkers we have are typically people we interact with via Slack or Gchat or Twitter, maybe the occasional phone call. Of course, sometimes we meet up at conferences or the odd event. But it can be kind of a lonely life for part of the day. My wife's at work, I'm here with my dog, typing away…that's one of the reasons I value this podcast community so much—emails from listeners, and the Facebook group. And the constants in my life, from a professional perspective, are people I just Gchat with throughout the day. And there are people I've been talking to in this community, people I worked with at BP and elsewhere on a daily or near-daily basis now for about a decade, and a few of them I haven't met!

Most of them I've at least talked to, but you develop strong bonds with these people you've never actually seen in person because you talk to them constantly, and they're part of this world and your problems are often the problems they're facing and vice versa. One of those constants in my life, for the last decade or so, and someone who has been as helpful to me in my professional life as almost anyone, is Rob McQuown, who was the Director of Operations for Baseball Prospectus. And that title—Director of Operations—sounds like it could mean almost anything, and in Rob's case it did. It meant almost anything and everything. He was involved in every aspect of Baseball Prospectus, and whether you know it or not he probably had an impact on your life if you've been consuming any internet baseball content of a sabermetric slant over the last 10 years. Rob had a *bit* of a baseball background. He worked for STATS, Inc. for a few years in the '90s, but then he went to other internet and tech companies until he wound up at a site called Baseball Daily Digest, which was run by Joe Hamrahi. Joe later became the CEO and President of Baseball Prospectus, and Rob came over with him. So, he sort of entered BP's orbit in late 2008, which was also when I entered BP's orbit.

He started writing there occasionally in the spring of 2009, and by 2010 he was not only writing some fantasy stuff for the site but he was doing a lot of behind-the-scenes work, too. By 2011 he had taken over most of the website's operations, and a couple years later, Colin Wyers left to join the Astros, and Rob took over PECOTA and most of the stat generation for the site. He was just the go-to guy all the time that I was at BP, and ever since. He was the one who knew where everything was, because BP's back-end was sort of a tangle of byzantine databases and artifacts of the tenures of Keith Woolner and Clay Davenport and Colin, and Rob was the only one who knew where *every*thing was. If the site went down, we'd tell Rob and he'd know exactly what to kick to get it started again. If a stat looked wonky, we'd tell Rob and he'd be able to dive into the code and figure out what was wrong. He was involved in building so many of the tools that are available at Baseball Prospectus—various leaderboards and utilities, and the team tracker, and the scoresheet draft aid. The list goes on and on.

Rob was not only the one who would put out fires, but he was endlessly helpful to anyone and everyone, and probably *particularly* me. Rob was a SQL wizard. He could query a database like no one I've ever known—and I'm somewhat notorious at Baseball Prospectus for sending a lot of stat requests. As I've mentioned many times, I'm an English major. I didn't enter this line of work with any great background in math or computer science or programming. So, I've had to rely on the kindness of others over the years to help answer the questions that I've posed. And Rob has been the one answering those questions more than anyone else.

Part of my value as a writer, as a researcher, has been figuring out the right questions to ask. And that's nice, but it doesn't go a long way without being able to dig up the answers. And sometimes that's beyond my abilities. But it was almost never beyond Rob's. Right up until June, in fact—I wrote about Mike Trout and the Angels and how the Angels have hovered around .500 the last few years, and I wanted to know which teams in history have stayed the closest to .500 the longest. I think I mentioned that on this podcast, too. That was a stat request I sent Rob! And I knew he'd have no trouble with it, and he didn't. At times I've felt bad about bugging Rob with these things, especially after I left Baseball Prospectus and he had no real obligation to help me with anything. I tried to spare him when I could, but there were times I knew if I wanted to answer a question, there was no way I could do it without Rob.

He was tireless and endlessly patient and would always respond to requests. Sometimes he would say "I'm swamped" and "I'm fielding a dozen requests and this is going wrong and that's going wrong and I just can't possibly get to this anytime soon," but nine times out of ten after he said that and I said "OK, don't worry about it," he would get around to it after all, and he'd send me the answer and he would say, "actually this didn't take nearly as long as I thought it would." Because he was that good. I was so happy the odd time when I could help *him* with something. He'd ask for my opinion, or I'd report a bug that I'd found on the site, or something I had asked him to help search for *me* had helped him uncover some other issue that he was able to fix. I felt like I was working off my debt a little bit, but I knew I would never work it all off, because I was so deeply in his debt, so dependent on him.

And in fact when I left Baseball Prospectus for Grantland, one of the things that I fretted about was losing access to Rob, because he was such an integral part of my process. One of the reasons it was important to me to keep doing this podcast, which of course was started at Baseball Prospectus, was so that I could maintain some sort of connection to the site, so that I could have some reason to keep sending stat requests to Rob. Because when I got to Grantland and started sending stat requests to ESPN's Stats & Info, I was somewhat shocked to learn that there were many requests that would have been a cakewalk for Rob that when I sent them to ESPN—the biggest sports media company there is—no one there would know how to answer them, or no one would have the data that was needed to answer them. So I would end up asking Rob anyway, even though I'd left. I told him at the time, "If you wanted to go to ESPN, you could be running that place, because you can answer questions that this entire department is having trouble answering."

And it wasn't just that Rob could answer any question—although he could. I almost never stumped him. If I did, it was just because the data didn't exist, not because he couldn't query it. But it was more than that. It's very valuable to find someone who can answer questions, but he would also make the questions *better*. He would see how your question could be improved, how maybe you were overlooking something that would affect the answer. And he would talk it through with you and say, "Well, have you considered this?" and, "What about that?" and, "These results might not look the way that you want them to because of X and Y," and then you could craft the query together.

I developed a reputation for sending these stat requests and then after I got the results, saying, "One more thing!" and often "one more thing" would turn out to be two or three more things. I was worried about whether I was a pain, whether Rob wished I would go away and leave him alone. But he told me he enjoyed working with me, and others have told me he enjoyed working with me because he liked the questions I asked, and I would be very curious about them and he'd get curious about them and often they were sort of meaty topics, and he was excited to contribute to that research.

I really think if you did an audit of all of my baseball writing from the past decade, you would probably find at the bottom of 20 percent of those articles, "Thanks to Rob McQuown of Baseball Prospectus for research assistance." There were many articles I've written that wouldn't have been as good without Rob's input. There were others I might not have even *attempted* to write without knowing that Rob could supply whatever I wanted. It's not just me; I think I've probably been the one who's pestered him with the most stat requests, but he was a resource for the entire staff at Baseball Prospectus, for people who've left BP and went on to other sites and would still send stat requests. He was always happy to help if he had the time, and he always seemed to make the time, even if he didn't have it.

He was always generous when it came to trying to impart the skills he had to others. Many of the stat people that he worked with, and in some cases tutored at Baseball Prospectus, have gone on to work for teams. People like Bradley Ankrom and Andrew Koo, who are with the Rangers now, and of course Colin, and John Choiniere, and Ryan Lind, and Dan Turkenkopf with the Brewers—he had an impact on all of them. And if you've used Baseball Prospectus, if you've read anything at the site over the past decade, it's almost certain that Rob had a hand in some of those things.

Even when we started Effectively Wild, Rob was the one who submitted the podcast to iTunes and tinkered with the RSS feed and handled all of those things. I don't know if he knew anything about them, but we asked him to help, and he did. You may not know the name Rob McQuown if you haven't been reading to the bottom of all of my articles and seeing me thank him, because as far as I could tell he had no interest in getting credit. He certainly didn't seek the attention. I have no idea whether he ever looked at my articles to make sure that I had acknowledged him. He certainly never said so if he did. He was in it entirely to get to the answer and to help someone with whatever they were doing. He was so, so good at it. Sometimes I would see the queries he wrote and they seemed to go on for dozens, hundreds of lines, and I would just marvel at how he had written it and how quickly he had done it and how clever he was at answering questions that seemed so difficult to tease out the truth of.

The reason I mentioned at the beginning of this tribute that a lot of people we haven't met in person come to play a big role in our lives is that Rob was that person for many of us in this little world. I never met Rob. I talked to him on a few conference calls, but other than that, it was text only. And it was *so much* text. I just searched my email for his email address, and I found more than 5,000 threads that I was on with Rob, whether emails or Gchats, and to my knowledge *no one* at Baseball Prospectus ever met him in person. Even people who lived in some proximity to him in the Chicago area never met him. He was a private person. He certainly could have gone on to work for a bigger company or for a team, but I think he valued being able to keep to himself the way he could at BP. So he was something of a mystery man in that respect, and yet you felt like he was a constant presence, like you were interacting with him all the time because you *were* in one way or another.

People sometimes say *I* don't sleep, and I thought *Rob* didn't sleep. Clearly, I think he did sleep, but he slept at odd times, as I tend to do. So there was many a night or many an early morning when I would look at my Gchat list of contacts at 3 AM or some other ungodly hour, and the only green dot signifying that someone else was available and active was Rob McQuown. And there were many nights when we chatted about something or another, maybe some stat request I had sent him, but often just baseball or something else. And we kind of kept each other company. It's one of those things where, even though I never met the man, it's incomprehensible to me that I won't be able to talk to him again, because he's been there for as long as I've been doing this.

Even to the end, he wasn't very forthcoming about his personal life, and I don't think anyone knew the severity of the health issues he was facing. It's come as a shock to many of us that he's gone. He's been an unsung hero for so long, and he's had a huge impact on a lot of us in this line of work. If you've enjoyed anything I've written over the years, there's a good chance that Rob McQuown made it better. If you've read almost any BP research over the past decade, that is *certainly* true. So, my best to any family or friends in his life who probably knew Rob in a different way than we did. But even though the way we knew him was somewhat unusual, he meant so much to us, and he will be greatly, greatly missed.

So, sadly, for the last time: Thanks to Rob McQuown for research assistance. ▪

—*Ben Lindbergh is a staff writer for The Ringer.*

Statistical Introduction

by Bryan Grosnick

Sports are, fundamentally, a blend of athletic endeavor and storytelling. Baseball, like any other sport, tells its stories in so many ways: in the arc of a game from the stands or a season from the box scores, in photos, or even in numbers. At Baseball Prospectus, we understand that statistics don't replace observation or any of baseball's stories, but complement everything else that makes the game so much fun.

What stats help us with is with patterns and precision, variance and value. This book can help you learn things you may not see from watching a game or hundred, whether it's the path of a career over time or the breadth of the entire MLB. We'd also never ask you to choose between our numbers and the experience of viewing a game from the cheap seats or the comfort of your home; our publication combines running the numbers with observations and wisdom from some of the brightest minds we can find. But if you *do* want to learn more about the numbers beyond what's on the backs of player jerseys, let us help explain.

Offense

We've revised our methodology for determining batting value. Long-time readers of the book will notice that we've retired True Average in favor of a new metric: Deserved Runs Created Plus (DRC+). Developed by Jonathan Judge and our stats team, this statistic measures everything a player does at the plate–reaching base, hitting for power, making outs, and moving runners over–and puts it on a scale where 100 equals league-average performance. A DRC+ of 150 is terrific, a DRC+ of 100 is average and a DRC+ of 75 means you better be an excellent defender.

DRC+ also does a better job than any of our previous metrics in taking contextual factors into account. The model adjusts for how the park affects performance, but also for things like the talent of the opposing pitcher, value of different types of batted-ball events, league, temperature and other factors. It's able to describe a player's expected offensive contribution than any other statistic we've found over the years, and also does a better job of predicting future performance as well.

There's a lot more to DRC+'s story, and you can read all about it in greater depth near the end of this book.

The other aspect of run-scoring is baserunning, which we quantify using Baserunning Runs. BRR not only records the value of stolen bases (or getting caught in the act), but also accounts for all the stuff that doesn't show up on the back of a baseball card: a runner's ability to go first to third on a single, or advance on a fly ball.

Defense

Where offensive value is *relatively* easy to identify and understand, defensive value is...not. Over the past dozen years, the sabermetric community has focused mostly on stats based on zone data: a real-live human person records the type of batted ball and estimated landing location, and models are created that give expected outs. From there, you can compare fielders' actual outs to those expected ones. Simple, right?

Unfortunately, zone data has two major issues. First, zone data is recorded by commercial data providers who keep the raw data private unless you pay for it. (All the statistics we build in this book and on our website use public data as inputs.) That hurts our ability to test assumptions or duplicate results. Second, over the years it has become apparent that there's quite a bit of "noise" in zone-based fielding analysis. Sometimes the conclusions drawn from zone data don't hold up to scrutiny, and sometimes the different data provided by different providers don't look anything alike, giving wildly different results. Sometimes the hard-working professional stringers or scorers might unknowingly inflict unconscious bias into the mix: for example good fielders will often be credited with more expected outs despite the data, and ballparks with high press boxes tend to score more line drives than ones with a lower press box.

Enter our Fielding Runs Above Average (FRAA). For most positions, FRAA is built from play-by-play data, which allows us to avoid the subjectivity found in many other fielding metrics. The idea is this: count how many fielding plays are made by a given player and compare that to expected plays for an average fielder at their position (based on pitcher ground ball tendencies and batter handedness). Then we adjust for park and base-out situations.

When it comes to catchers, our methodology is a little different thanks to the laundry list of responsibilities they're tasked with beyond just, well, catching and throwing the ball.

By now you've probably heard about "framing" or the art of making umpires more likely to call balls outside the strike zone for strikes. To put this into one tidy number, we incorporate pitch tracking data (for the years it exists) and adjust for important factors like pitcher, umpire, batter and home-field advantage using a mixed-model approach. This grants us a number for how many strikes the catcher is personally adding to (or subtracting from) his pitchers' performance...which we then convert to runs added or lost using linear weights.

Framing is one of the biggest parts of determining catcher value, but we also take into account blocking balls from going past, whether a scorer deems it a passed ball or a wild pitch. We use a similar approach—one that really benefits from the pitch tracking data that tells us what ends up in the dirt and what doesn't. We also include a catcher's ability to prevent stolen bases and how well they field balls in play, and *finally* we come up with our FRAA for catchers.

Pitching

Both pitching and fielding make up the half of baseball that isn't run scoring: run prevention. Separating pitching from fielding is a tough task, and most recent pitching analysis has branched off from Voros McCracken's famous (and controversial) statement, "There is little if any difference among major-league pitchers in their ability to prevent hits on balls hit in the field of play." The research of the analytic community has validated this to some extent, and there are a host of "defense-independent" pitching measures that have been developed to try and extract the effect of the defense behind a hurler from the pitcher's work.

Our solution to this quandary is Deserved Run Average (DRA), our core pitching metric. DRA looks like earned run average (ERA), the tried-and-true pitching stat you've seen on every baseball broadcast or box score from the past century, but it's very different. To start, DRA takes an event-by-event look at what the pitchers does, and adjusts the value of that event based on different environmental factors like park, batter, catcher, umpire, base-out situation, run differential, inning, defense, home field advantage, pitcher role and temperature. That mixed model gives us a pitcher's expected contribution, similar to what we do for our DRC+ model for hitters and FRAA model for catchers. (Oh, and we also consider the pitcher's effect on basestealing and on balls getting past the catcher.)

It's important to note that DRA is set to the scale of runs allowed per nine innings (RA9) instead of ERA, which makes DRA's scale slightly higher than ERA's. The reason for this is because ERA tends to overrate three types of pitchers:

1. Pitchers who play in parks where scorers hand out more errors. Official scorers differ significantly in the frequency at which they assign errors to fielders.
2. Ground-ball pitchers, because a substantial proportion of errors occur on groundballs.

3. Pitchers who aren't very good. Better pitchers often allow fewer unearned runs than bad pitchers, because good pitchers tend to find ways to get out of jams.

Since the last time you picked up an edition of this book, we've also made a few minor changes to DRA to make it better. Recent research into "tunneling"—the act of throwing consecutive pitches that appear similar from a batter's point of view until after the swing decision point–data has given us a new contextual factor to account for in DRA: plate distance. This refers to the distance between successive pitches as they approach the plate, and while it has a smaller effect than factors like velocity or whiff rate, it still can help explain pitcher strikeout rate in our model.

New Pitching Metrics for 2020

We're including a few "new" pitching metrics in the book for the 2020 edition, though unlike last year, these numbers may be a little bit more familiar to those of you who have spent some time investigating baseball statistics.

Fastball Percentage

Our fastball percentage (FB%) statistic measures how frequently a pitcher throws a pitch classified as a "fastball," measured as a percentage of overall pitches thrown. We qualify three types of fastballs:

1. The traditional four-seam fastball;
2. The two-seam fastball or sinker;
3. "Hard cutters," which are pitches that have the movement profile of a cut fastball and are used as the pitcher's primary offering or in place of a more traditional fastball.

For example, a pitcher with a FB% of 67 throws any combination of these three pitches about two-thirds of the time.

Whiff Rate

Everybody loves a swing and a miss, and whiff rate (WHF) measures how frequently pitchers induce a swinging strike. To calculate WHF, we add up all the pitches thrown that ended with a swinging strike, then divide that number by a pitcher's total pitches thrown. Most often, high whiff rates correlate with high strikeout rates (and overall effective pitcher performance).

Called Strike Probability

Called Strike Probability (CSP) is a number that represents the likelihood that all of a pitcher's pitches will be called a strike while controlling for location, pitcher and batter handedness, umpire and count. Here's how it works: on each pitch, our model determines how many times (out of 100) that a similar pitch was called for a strike given those factors mentioned above, and when normalized for each batter's strike zone. Then we average the CSP for all pitches thrown by a pitcher in a season, and that gives us the yearly CSP percentage you see in the stats boxes.

As you might imagine, pitchers with a higher CSP are more likely to work in the zone, where pitchers with a lower CSP are likely locating their pitches outside the normal strike zone, for better or for worse.

Projections

Many of you aren't turning to this book just for a look at what a player has done, but for a look at what a player is going to do: the PECOTA projections. PECOTA, initially developed by Nate Silver (who has moved on to greater fame as a political analyst), consists of three parts:

1. Major-league equivalencies, which use minor-league statistics to project how a player will perform in the major leagues;

2. Baseline forecasts, which use weighted averages and regression to the mean to estimate a player's current true talent level; and

3. Aging curves, which uses the career paths of comparable players to estimate how a player's statistics are likely to change over time.

With all those important things covered, let's take a look at what's in the book this year.

Team Prospectus

Most of this book is composed of team chapters, with one for each of the 30 major-league franchises. On the first page of each chapter, you'll see a box that contains some of the key statistics for each team as well as a very inviting stadium diagram. (You can see an example of this for the Milwaukee Brewers on this very page!)

We start with the team name, their unadjusted 2019 win-loss record, and their divisional ranking. Beneath that are a host of other team statistics. **Pythag** presents an adjusted 2019 winning percentage, calculated by taking runs scored per game (**RS/G**) and runs allowed per game (**RA/G**) for the team, and running them through a version of Bill James' Pythagorean formula that was refined and improved by David Smyth and Brandon Heipp. (The formula is called "Pythagenpat," which is equally fun to type and to say.)

Next up is **DRC+**, described earlier, to indicate the overall hitting ability of the team either above or below league-average. Run prevention on the pitching side is covered by **DRA** (also mentioned earlier) and another metric: Fielding Independent Pitching (**FIP**), which calculates another ERA-like statistic based on strikeouts, walks, and home runs recorded. Defensive Efficiency Rating (**DER**) tells us the percentage of balls in play turned into outs for the team, and is a quick fielding shorthand that rounds out run prevention.

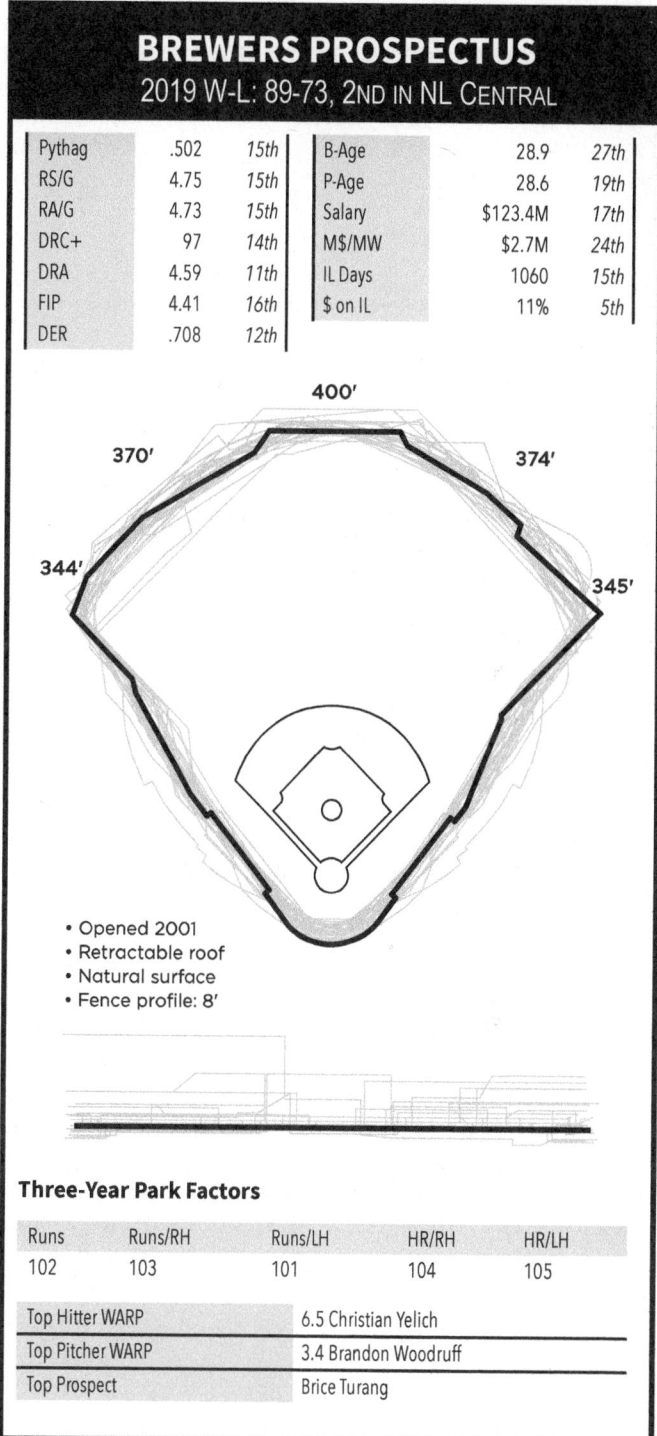

BREWERS PROSPECTUS
2019 W-L: 89-73, 2ND IN NL CENTRAL

Pythag	.502	15th	B-Age	28.9	27th
RS/G	4.75	15th	P-Age	28.6	19th
RA/G	4.73	15th	Salary	$123.4M	17th
DRC+	97	14th	M$/MW	$2.7M	24th
DRA	4.59	11th	IL Days	1060	15th
FIP	4.41	16th	$ on IL	11%	5th
DER	.708	12th			

400'
370'　374'
344'　345'

- Opened 2001
- Retractable roof
- Natural surface
- Fence profile: 8'

Three-Year Park Factors

Runs	Runs/RH	Runs/LH	HR/RH	HR/LH
102	103	101	104	105

Top Hitter WARP	6.5 Christian Yelich
Top Pitcher WARP	3.4 Brandon Woodruff
Top Prospect	Brice Turang

After that, we have several measures related to roster composition, as opposed to on-field performance. **B-Age** and **P-Age** tell us the average age of a team's batters and pitchers, respectively. **Salary** is the combined team payroll for all on-field players, and Doug Pappas' Marginal Dollars per Marginal Win (**M$/MW**) tells us how much money a team spent to earn production above replacement level.

Ending this batch of statistics is the number of disabled list days a team had over the season (**IL Days**) and the amount of salary paid to players on the disabled list (**$ on IL**); this final number is expressed as a percentage of total payroll.

Juan Soto LF Born: 10/25/98 Age: 21 Bats: L Throws: L Height: 6'1" Weight: 185 Origin: International Free Agent, 2015

YEAR	TEAM	LVL	AGE	PA	R	2B	3B	HR	RBI	BB	K	SB	CS	AVG/OBP/SLG	DRC+	VORP	BABIP	BRR	FRAA	WARP
2017	NAT	RK	18	27	3	1	1	0	4	2	1	0	0	.320/.370/.440	135	1.5	.333	0.0	RF(9): -1.1	0.0
2017	HAG	A	18	96	15	5	0	3	14	10	8	1	2	.360/.427/.523	181	8.0	.373	1.0	RF(19): -1.9, LF(2): -0.3	0.9
2018	HAG	A	19	74	12	5	3	5	24	14	13	2	0	.373/.486/.814	222	14.5	.405	0.3	RF(14): 1.1, CF(2): 0.2	1.2
2018	POT	A+	19	73	17	3	1	7	18	11	8	0	1	.371/.466/.790	260	15.4	.340	1.4	RF(14): 1.0, LF(1): 0.0	1.6
2018	HAR	AA	19	35	4	2	0	2	10	4	7	1	0	.323/.400/.581	113	3.6	.364	0.0	LF(4): 0.6, RF(4): -0.5	0.1
2018	WAS	MLB	19	494	77	25	1	22	70	79	99	5	2	.292/.406/.517	125	40.5	.338	-0.5	LF(114): 2.7	3.0
2019	WAS	MLB	20	659	110	32	5	34	110	108	132	12	1	.282/.401/.548	136	49.0	.312	1.4	LF(150): -0.8	4.9
2020	*WAS*	*MLB*	*21*	*630*	*92*	*30*	*3*	*35*	*102*	*85*	*123*	*5*	*2*	*.284/.382/.543*	*133*	*43.6*	*.310*	*-0.1*	*LF 3*	*4.8*

Comparables: Ronald Acuña Jr., Mike Trout, Tony Conigliaro

Next to each of these stats, we've listed each team's MLB rank in that category from first to 30th. In this, first always indicates a positive outcome and 30th a negative outcome, except in the case of salary—first is highest.

After the franchise statistics, we share a few items about the team's home ballpark. There's the aforementioned diagram of the park's dimensions (including distances to the outfield wall), a graphic showing the height of the wall from the left-field pole to the right-field pole, and a table showing three-year park factors for the stadium. The park factors are displayed as indexes where 100 is average, 110 means that the park inflates the statistic in question by 10 percent, and 90 means that the park deflates the statistic in question by 10 percent.

On the second page of each team chapter, you'll find three graphs. The first is the **2019 Hit List Ranking**. This shows our Hit List Rank for the team on each day of the 2019 season and is intended to give you a picture of the ups and downs of the team's season. Hit List Rank measures overall team performance and drives the Hit List Power Rankings at the baseballprospectus.com website.

The second graph is **Committed Payroll** and helps you see how the team's payroll has compared to the MLB and divisional average payrolls over time. Payroll figures are current as of January 1, 2020; with so many free agents still unsigned as of this writing, the final 2020 figure will likely be significantly different for many teams. (In the meantime, you can always find the most current data at Baseball Prospectus' Cot's Baseball Contracts page.)

The third graph is **Farm System Ranking** and displays how the Baseball Prospectus prospect team has ranked the organization's farm system since 2007.

After the graphs, we have a **Personnel** section that lists many of the important decision-makers and upper-level field and operations staff members for the franchise, as well as any former Baseball Prospectus staff members who are currently part of the organization. (In very rare circumstances, someone might be on both lists!)

Position Players

After all that information and a thoughtful bylined essay covering each team, we present our player comments. These are also bylined, but due to frequent franchise shifts during the offseason, our bylines are more a rough guide than a perfect accounting of who wrote what.

Each player is listed with the major-league team that employed him as of early January 2020. If a player changed teams after that point via free agency, trade, or any other method, you'll be able to find them in the chapter for their previous squad.

As an example, take a look at the player comment for Nationals outfielder Juan Soto: the stat block that accompanies his written comment is at the top of this page. First we cover biographical information (age is as of June 30, 2020) before moving onto the stats themselves. Our statistic columns include standard identifying information like **YEAR**, **TEAM**, **LVL** (level of affiliated play) and **AGE** before getting into the numbers. Next, we provide raw, untranslated numbers like you might find on the back of your dad's baseball cards: **PA** (plate appearances), **R** (runs), **2B** (doubles), **3B** (triples), **HR** (home runs), **RBI** (runs batted in), **BB** (walks), **K** (strikeouts), **SB** (stolen bases) and **CS** (caught stealing).

Next, we have unadjusted "slash" statistics: **AVG** (batting average), **OBP** (on-base percentage) and **SLG** (slugging percentage). Following the slash line is **DRC+** (Deserved Runs Created Plus), which we described earlier as total offensive expected contribution compared to the league average.

One of our oldest active metrics, **VORP** (Value Over Replacement Player), considers offensive production, position and plate appearances. In essence, it is the number of runs contributed beyond what a replacement-level player at the same position would contribute if given the same percentage of team plate appearances. VORP does not consider the quality of a player's defense.

BABIP (batting average on balls in play) tells us how often a ball in play fell for a hit, and can help us identify whether a batter may have been lucky or not...but note that high BABIPs also tend to follow the great hitters of our time, as well as speedy singles hitters who put the ball on the ground.

The next item is **BRR** (Baserunning Runs), which covers all of a player's baserunning accomplishments including (but not limited to) swiped bags and failed attempts. Next is **FRAA**

(Fielding Runs Above Average), which also includes the number of games previously played at each position noted in parentheses. Multi-position players have only their two most frequent positions listed here, but their total FRAA number reflects all positions played.

Our last column here is **WARP** (Wins Above Replacement Player). WARP estimates the total value of a player, which means for hitters it takes into account hitting runs above average (calculated using the DRC+ model), BRR and FRAA. Then, it makes an adjustment for positions played and gives the player a credit for plate appearances based upon the difference between "replacement level"—which is derived from the quality of players added to a team's roster after the start of the season–and the league average.

The final line just below the stats box is **PECOTA** data, which is discussed further in a following section.

Catchers

Catchers are a special breed, and thus they have earned their own separate box which displays some of the defensive metrics that we've built just for them. As an example, let's check out J.T. Realmuto.

The **YEAR** and **TEAM** columns match what you'd find in the other stat box. **P. COUNT** indicates the number of pitches thrown while the catcher was behind the plate, including swinging strikes, fouls and balls in play. **FRM RUNS** is the total run value the catcher provided (or cost) his team by influencing the umpire to call strikes where other catchers did not. **BLK RUNS** expresses the total run value above or below average for the catcher's ability to prevent wild pitches and passed balls. **THRW RUNS** is calculated using a similar model as the previous two statistics, and it measures a catcher's ability to throw out basestealers but also to dissuade them from testing his arm in the first place. It takes into account factors like the pitcher (including his delivery and pickoff move) and baserunner (who could be as fast as Billy Hamilton or as slow as Yonder Alonso). **TOT RUNS** is the sum of all of the previous three statistics.

Pitchers

Let's give our pitchers a turn, using 2019 AL Cy Young winner Justin Verlander as our example. Take a look at his stat block: the first line and the **YEAR**, **TEAM**, **LVL** and **AGE** columns are the same as in the position player example earlier.

Here too, we have a series of columns that display raw, unadjusted statistics compiled by the pitcher over the course of a season: **W** (wins), **L** (losses), **SV** (saves), **G** (games pitched), **GS** (games started), **IP** (innings pitched), **H** (hits allowed) and **HR** (home runs allowed). Next we have two statistics that are rates: **BB/9** (walks per nine innings) and **K/9** (strikeouts per nine innings), before returning to the unadjusted K (strikeouts).

Next up is **GB%** (ground ball percentage), which is the percentage of all batted balls that were hit on the ground, including both outs and hits. Remember, this is based on observational data and subject to human error, so please approach this with a healthy dose of skepticism.

BABIP (batting average on balls in play) is calculated using the same methodology as it is for position players, but it often tells us more about a pitcher than it does a hitter. With pitchers, a high BABIP is often due to poor defense or bad luck, and can often be an indicator of potential rebound, and a low BABIP may be cause to expect performance regression. (A typical league-average BABIP is close to .290-.300.)

The metrics **WHIP** (walks plus hits per inning pitched) and **ERA** (earned run average) are old standbys: WHIP measures walks and hits allowed on a per-inning basis, while ERA measures earned runs on a nine-inning basis. Neither of these stats are translated or adjusted.

DRA (Deserved Run Average) was described at length earlier, and measures how many runs the pitcher "deserved" to allow per nine innings. Please note that since we lack all the data points that would make for a "real" DRA for minor-league events, the DRA displayed for minor league partial-seasons is based off of different data. (That data is a modified version of our cFIP metric, which you can find more information about on our website.)

Just like with hitters, **WARP** (Wins Above Replacement Player) is a total value metric that puts pitchers of all stripes on the same scale as position players. We use DRA as the primary input for our calculation of WARP. You might notice that relief pitchers (due to their limited innings) may have a lower WARP than you were expecting or than you might see in other WARP-like metrics. WARP does not take leverage into account, just the actions a pitcher performs and the expected value of those actions...which ends up judging high-leverage relief pitchers differently than you might imagine given their prestige and market value.

Justin Verlander RHP Born: 02/20/83   Age: 37   Bats: R   Throws: R   Height: 6'5"   Weight: 225   Origin: Round 1, 2004 Draft (#2 overall)

YEAR	TEAM	LVL	AGE	W	L	SV	G	GS	IP	H	HR	BB/9	K/9	K	GB%	BABIP	WHIP	ERA	DRA	WARP	MPH	FB%	WHF	CSP
2017	DET	MLB	34	10	8	0	28	28	172	153	23	3.5	9.2	176	34%	.283	1.28	3.82	4.03	3.0	97.7	58	11	47.8
2017	HOU	MLB	34	5	0	0	5	5	34	17	4	1.3	11.4	43	32%	.194	0.65	1.06	3.08	0.9	97.5	59.6	15.1	49.9
2018	HOU	MLB	35	16	9	0	34	34	214	156	28	1.6	12.2	290	31%	.272	0.90	2.52	2.33	7.3	97.5	61.2	16.2	51.6
2019	HOU	MLB	36	21	6	0	34	34	223	137	36	1.7	12.1	300	36%	.219	0.80	2.58	2.51	7.9	96.8	49.9	17.5	48.3
2020	HOU	MLB	37	15	6	0	29	29	184	138	28	2.3	12.1	248	35%	.274	1.01	2.75	2.95	5.3	95.8	54.6	15.1	48.2

Comparables: Zack Greinke, A.J. Burnett, Aníbal Sánchez

MPH gives you the pitcher's 95th percentile velocity for the noted season, in order to give you an idea of what the *peak* fastball velocity a pitcher possesses. Since this comes from our pitch-tracking data, it is not publicly available for minor-league pitchers.

Finally, we display the three new pitching metrics we described earlier. **FB%** (fastball percentage) gives you the percentage of fastballs thrown out of all pitches. **WHF** (whiff rate) tells you the percentage of swinging strikes induced out of all pitches. **CSP** (called strike probability) expresses the likelihood of all pitches thrown to result in a called strike, after controlling for factors like handedness, umpire, pitch type, count and location.

PECOTA

All players have PECOTA projections for 2020, as well as a set of other numbers that describe the performance of comparable players according to PECOTA. All projections for 2020 are for the player at the date we went to press in early January and are projected into the league and park context as indicated by the team abbreviation. (Note that players at very low levels of the minors are too unpredictable to assess using these numbers.) All PECOTA projected statistics represent a player's projected major-league performance.

Below the projections are the player's three highest-scoring comparable players as determined by PECOTA. All comparables represent a snapshot of how the listed player was performing at the same age as the current player, so if a 23-year-old pitcher is compared to Bartolo Colón, he's actually being compared to a 23-year-old Colón, not the version that pitched for the Rangers in 2018, nor to Colón's career as a whole.

A few points about pitcher projections. First, we aren't yet projecting peak velocity, so that column will be blank in the PECOTA lines. Second, projecting DRA is trickier than evaluating past performance, because it is unclear how deserving each pitcher will be of his anticipated outcomes. However, we know that another DRA-related statistic–contextual FIP or cFIP–estimates future run scoring very well. So for PECOTA, the projected DRA figures you see are based on the past cFIPs generated by the pitcher and comparable players over time, along with the other factors described above.

Lineouts

In each chapter's Lineouts section, you'll find abbreviated text comments, as well as all the same information you'd find in our full player comments. The only difference is that we limit the stats boxes in this section to only including the 2019 information for each player.

Managers

After all those wonderful team chapters, we've got statistics for each big-league manager, all of whom are organized by alphabetical order. Here you'll find a block including an extraordinary amount of information collected from each manager's entire career. For more information on the acronyms and what they mean, please visit the Glossary at www.baseballprospectus.com.

There is one important metric that we'd like to call attention to, and you'll find it next to each manager's name: **wRM+** (weighted reliever management plus). Developed by Rob Arthur and Rian Watt, wRM+ investigates how good a manager is at using their best relievers during the moments of highest leverage, using both our proprietary DRA metric as well as Leverage Index. wRM+ is scaled to a league average of 100, and a wRM+ of 105 indicates that relievers were used approximately five percent "better" than average. On the other hand, a wRM+ of 95 would tell us the team used its relievers five percent "worse" than the average team.

While wRM+ does not have an extremely strong correlation with a manager, it is statistically significant; this means that a manager is not *entirely* responsible for a team's wRM+, but does have some effect on that number.

PECOTA Leaderboards

If you're familiar with PECOTA, then you'll have noticed that the projection system often appears bullish on players coming off a bad year and bearish on players coming off a good year. (This is because the system weights several previous seasons, not just the most recent one.) In addition, we publish the 50th percentile projections for each player–which is smack in the middle of the range of projected production—which tends to mean PECOTA stat lines don't often have extreme results like 40 home runs or 250 strikeouts in a given season. In essence, PECOTA doesn't project very many extreme seasons.

At the end of the book, we've ranked the top players at each position based on their PECOTA projections. This might help you visualize just how a given player's projection compares to that of their peers, so that even if a dramatic stat line isn't projected, you can still imagine how they stack up against the rest of the league.

ARIZONA DIAMONDBACKS

Essay by Jeff Wiser

Player comments by Collin Whitchurch and BP staff

Watching the Washington Nationals win the World Series must have been a lonely feeling for the Arizona Diamondbacks. No, the D-backs didn't lose to the Nats in the NLCS—the Snakes didn't even make the playoffs. But there were sure a lot of familiar faces on the field as the 2019 season came to its close. Many of those faces were celebrating while a few hung their heads in improbable defeat. For D-backs fans, watching the World Series seemed like a kind of Bizzaro World straight out of a Seinfeld episode. Minus the funny stuff, obviously.

Long-time Diamondback Daniel Hudson threw that final strike for the Nationals while Game 7 starter Max Scherzer was a Diamondbacks draftee and debuted in the desert. Former rotation stalwart Patrick Corbin provided three innings of important relief and 2010 draftee Adam Eaton got on base twice and scored a run, while a homegrown Gerardo Parra cheered on from the bench. On the losing side, Zack Greinke pitched marvelously for the Astros following his midseason trade to Houston and former D-backs reliever Will Harris played a pivotal role as he surrendered a lead that would not be regathered. Even the coaches got in on the action—Chip Hale, Alex Cintrón and Henry Blanco were all either former Diamondbacks players and/or coaches.

Arizona wasn't the only franchise to have former players on the field, of course, but the sheer bulk of them underscores a trend that's been persistent for much of the team's short history: The organization has been rather good at procuring talent. The trouble has come from the franchise's inability to capitalize on and/or retain the talent they've acquired.

A public spat ran its course before Justin Upton was shipped out of town, the team surrendered Scherzer before he was really given a chance to become Mad Max, first-round pick Trevor Bauer didn't mesh and was traded abruptly, the late Tyler Skaggs was traded for and then dealt before he could gain much traction (for Mark Trumbo, no less) and first-overall pick Dansby Swanson was sent packing along with homespun talent Ender Inciarte in what is probably baseball's worst trade of the last five years (see: Miller, Shelby). The returns weren't always bad and there were plenty of other trades that were just fine. The results from *these* transactions, however, indicate that the Diamondbacks

DIAMONDBACKS PROSPECTUS
2019 W-L: 85-77, 2ND IN NL WEST

Pythag	.542	12th	B-Age	28.8	24th
RS/G	5.02	10th	P-Age	28.6	19th
RA/G	4.59	12th	Salary	$123.8M	16th
DRC+	95	16th	M$/MW	$3M	22nd
DRA	4.84	14th	IL Days	1034	13th
FIP	4.35	14th	$ on IL	13%	10th
DER	.705	13th			

407'

376'   376'

330'   335'

- Opened 1998
- Retractable roof
- Synthetic surface
- Fence profile: 7'6" to 25'

Three-Year Park Factors

Runs	Runs/RH	Runs/LH	HR/RH	HR/LH
103	102	107	100	101

Top Hitter WARP	4.5 Ketel Marte
Top Pitcher WARP	4.3 Zack Greinke
Top Prospect	Kristian Robinson

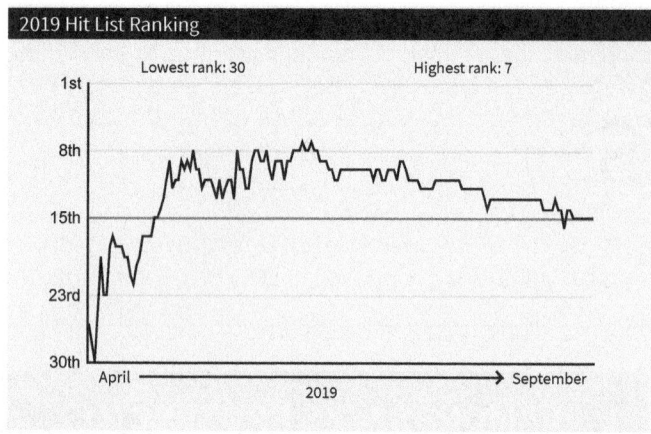

2019 Hit List Ranking

Lowest rank: 30   Highest rank: 7

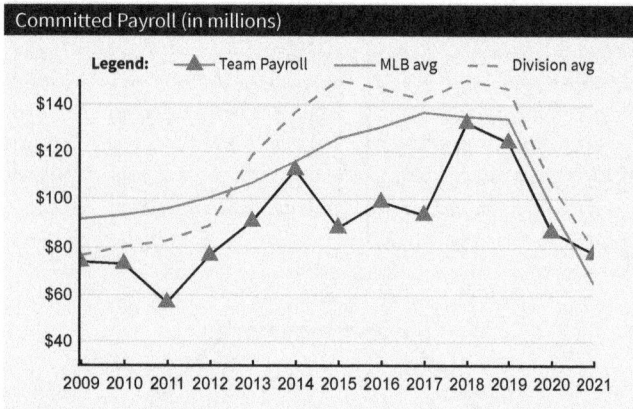

Committed Payroll (in millions)

Legend: — Team Payroll — MLB avg - - - Division avg

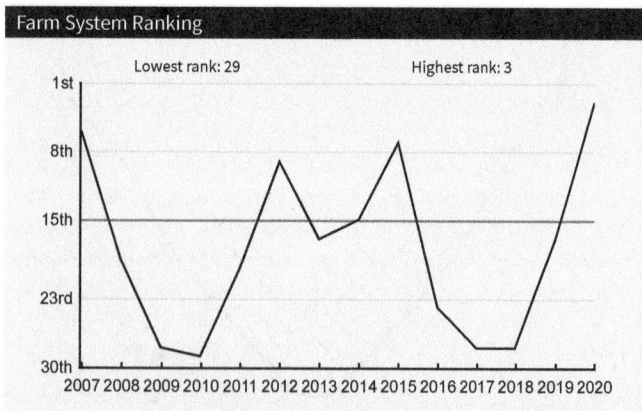

Farm System Ranking

Lowest rank: 29   Highest rank: 3

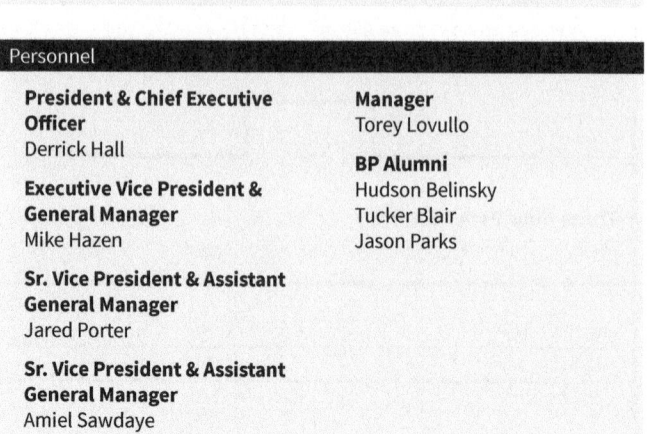

Personnel

President & Chief Executive Officer
Derrick Hall

Executive Vice President & General Manager
Mike Hazen

Sr. Vice President & Assistant General Manager
Jared Porter

Sr. Vice President & Assistant General Manager
Amiel Sawdaye

Manager
Torey Lovullo

BP Alumni
Hudson Belinsky
Tucker Blair
Jason Parks

frequently forwent premium production from the talent they collected, and in an attempt to hang on to relevance, often pushing their chips in further to their own detriment.

⚾   ⚾   ⚾

At the conclusion of the 2018 season, General Manager Mike Hazen faced a familiar line of questioning. Patrick Corbin and A.J. Pollock were set to hit free agency. Paul Goldschmidt was in the final year of his deal and hadn't signed a long-term extension. Zack Greinke was eating nearly a third of the team's payroll. Were the Diamondbacks going to join several other clubs in tearing down their roster and rebuild? Their history of selling short made rebuilding sound somewhat appealing. Wipe the slate clean, start over. The historic value left on the table wasn't Hazen's doing, but the idea was en vogue across baseball.

Instead, the Diamondbacks bucked the trend and didn't go down the path of a full rebuild simply because they didn't have to.

⚾   ⚾   ⚾

When Hazen took over the role of GM in October of 2016, he had a clear mission: build a more sustainable winner. When asked about his perception of the organization's collection of talent prior to taking the job, Hazen summarized the situation neatly.

"Looking back on it, I think it's hard to tell what you really have. You can evaluate things from afar, but it's hard to know without really being involved on the day-to-day how much talent you have. I think the general consensus was (that) the major league team was fairly talented and underperformed in 2016. They had spent quite a few of their resources to put that team together. The Shelby Miller trade being one where they had traded a number of young players in that deal. And then, the farm system—same. Using young players to make trades like that to bolster the major-league team, I just think that's naturally going to impact your general level of depth. I think a lot of our talent was aggregated at the major-league level and I think shared the responsibility for us getting to the playoffs in 2017. I think when we came in we knew and were told that building something sustainable from the ground level up was important and we have certainly spent a lot of our time doing that over the last three years."

Those three years have been remarkably focused. When other teams were lining up to zig (rebuild), the Diamondbacks zagged (re-tooled). And rather than make a familiar mistake in trying to recapture the magic, the team made bold moves in trading Goldschmidt and Greinke while making no major push (at least publicly) to re-sign the players they had made qualifying offers to in Corbin and Pollock. The trade returns were surprisingly good considering Goldschmidt had just one year left on his deal and Greinke was still owed a massive sum as an aging pitcher with diminished stuff. The QOs turned into extra draft picks as the D-backs boasted seven selections in the top 75 last June and nine inside the top 100. Those subtractions also freed up plenty of capital that could be reinvested.

That sounds an awful lot like a team that's trying to tank, but the Diamondbacks never saw it that way. The organization plays in a market full of transplants, and given the franchise's relative youth, there's no storied history to pull generational fans into the fold. Competing in earnest on the diamond year after year is the only way to keep the team relevant in their own home territory, something other franchises don't have to worry about so acutely. And compete they did in 2019—without many of the household names—to the tune of an 85-win season, one in which they remained in the playoff hunt until the final two weeks.

Recapturing organizational value while simultaneously trying to win is a difficult balance to strike, but that's a line that Hazen and his deputies continued to walk in 2019.

> "Well, when we were making most of our deals, one of the things we kept reminding ourselves was, because we were trying to compete, was we were trying to both satisfy the current and future in most deals. So we didn't end up doing a lot of deals that returned lower A-ball players. Maybe we yielded some upside in that thought process, but we tried to get younger as much as we could, but close to the big leagues in order to bring back guys that could help our major league team. We haven't gotten back to the playoffs, but we have tried to remain competitive because we thought that was important. So, when we were making a lot of these deals, that was one of the things we focused on was trying to both improve ourselves in the long term and also improve ourselves in the short term."

Rather than make a play for the deep rebuild, the team's biggest trades all brought back players that were either big leaguers or right on the cusp of their debuts. Goldschmidt turned into Luke Weaver and Carson Kelly. Greinke turned into Seth Beer, Corbin Martin, J.B. Bukauskas and Josh Rojas. They even flipped top prospect Jazz Chisholm for Zac Gallen. Kelly, Weaver, Gallen and Rojas have already paid dividends. Beer and Bukauskas are nearly ready and when Martin's elbow is healed, he'll factor heavily into the rotation discussion. None of those players compare to a Goldschmidt or a Greinke right now in terms of perennial value, but they sure can help bolster a roster for pennies on the dollar.

While the organization could spend more money, Hazen has done a tremendous job of working within his constraints to put a winner on the field despite subtracting some marquee talent. Because, even after those subtractions, there was still an enviable amount of talent to draw from. Things have to break right, but it helps when Ketel Marte signs a long-term extension and plays like an MVP candidate. It helps when Eduardo Escobar inks a team-friendly deal and has his best season while wearing Sedona Red. It helps when a young starter with six years of team control (Gallen) is made available by the Marlins. It helps when Carson Kelly takes full advantage of real, legitimate playing time and becomes the type of player he was forecast to be three or four years ago. Each of these moves—and dozens of others—are still bets at the end of the day. But those bets are working out consistently in Hazen's favor.

While formalizing important deals with Marte and Escobar, and acquiring about half a dozen current and future big league pieces, Hazen's organization has also gotten their hands on an intriguing mashup of amateur-turned-pro talent. The Diamondbacks have scored big over the past three drafts, finding talents like Daulton Varsho, Alek Thomas and Corbin Carroll. They've supplemented the domestic draftees with guys like Kristian Robinson, Liover Peguero, Wilderd Patino and Jeferson Espinal. The organization has also seen inherited international players like Geraldo Perdomo and Luis Frias take big steps forward. A minor-league system that was very recently near or at the bottom of the heap is now in the discussion for a top-five system in baseball, something Hazen and his staff deserve the lion's share of the credit for.

⚾   ⚾   ⚾

The Diamondbacks were able to avoid the rebuild because they still had quality contributors in place at the major-league level, an improving farm system established, a boatload of draft picks on the horizon, and more international bonus money to play with. They have proven capable of cashing in some their current chips for future ones while developing the ones they held onto. They played their cards right with impending free agents and received additional draft picks. They moved key pieces and got back enough talent to justify the moves. The easy perception is that, under Hazen's direction, the organization has made real progress in adding talent, value and depth to a system that didn't have nearly as much of those things just a few years ago. When asked if he feels accomplished to any degree in this work, Hazen's response was binary and straightforward.

> "No, not really. I think our job is, at a basic level, to be improving the talent of our organization. I think that's an expectation of all of the 30 teams. So saying that you're doing that to any degree is, I think, just a prerequisite for the job. I think how teams turn that into wins at the major league level is the separator. We haven't done that to a good enough degree to make the playoffs and we want to compete next year. We don't know what next year is going to bring."

It's a results-oriented business, after all. And it's unclear if the D-backs are going to be able to turn a healthy portion of their newfound talent into major league wins. That's something that previous Diamondbacks regimes have often failed to do. Fans of the team have been down this road before and will again approach the idea of the franchise building serious momentum with a healthy dose of skepticism. But if the current indicators are to be trusted at all, it appears that brighter days are ahead. Whether they come in 2020 or not is debatable. But the long-term forecast is more encouraging than it has been in quite some time. ▪

—*Jeff Wiser is an author of Baseball Prospectus.*

HITTERS

Nick Ahmed SS Born: 03/15/90 Age: 30 Bats: R Throws: R Height: 6'2" Weight: 195 Origin: Round 2, 2011 Draft (#85 overall)

YEAR	TEAM	LVL	AGE	PA	R	2B	3B	HR	RBI	BB	K	SB	CS	AVG/OBP/SLG	DRC+	VORP	BABIP	BRR	FRAA	WARP
2017	ARI	MLB	27	178	24	8	1	6	21	10	39	3	4	.251/.298/.419	80	1.5	.295	-0.8	SS(48): 3.9	0.7
2018	ARI	MLB	28	564	61	33	5	16	70	40	109	5	4	.234/.290/.411	89	17.5	.265	-0.4	SS(148): 15.1	3.3
2019	ARI	MLB	29	625	79	33	6	19	82	52	113	8	2	.254/.316/.437	93	24.4	.280	2.4	SS(158): 6.0	3.2
2020	ARI	MLB	30	630	60	29	4	16	67	47	124	8	5	.224/.286/.373	77	5.5	.259	0.7	SS 10	1.6

Comparables: Didi Gregorius, Greg Gagne, Dale Berra

UrbanDictionary.com eloquently defines the phrase "Get you a man who can do both" as "To be in a relationship when your boyfriend is classy, kind, and deep but thug'n it at the same time." For years, the Diamondbacks couldn't get that phrase out of their heads in regards to their six spot—staring longingly at other shortstops who could do both, while they were stuck with their nice guy without an ounce of "bad boy" in his body. Ahmed heard this and underwent a transformation akin to DJ Qualls in "The New Guy," finally pairing his usual sterling defense with palatable offensive production. Nobody will ever confuse Ahmed with Francisco Lindor or Young Thug, but a shortstop who can do both makes you reconsider the relationship altogether instead of saying "on to the next one."

Seth Beer 1B Born: 09/18/96 Age: 23 Bats: L Throws: R Height: 6'3" Weight: 195 Origin: Round 1, 2018 Draft (#28 overall)

YEAR	TEAM	LVL	AGE	PA	R	2B	3B	HR	RBI	BB	K	SB	CS	AVG/OBP/SLG	DRC+	VORP	BABIP	BRR	FRAA	WARP
2018	TCV	A-	21	51	9	3	0	4	7	6	10	0	0	.293/.431/.659	188	7.7	.296	-0.8	LF(7): -1.0, 1B(4): -0.1	0.3
2018	QUD	A	21	132	15	7	0	3	16	15	17	1	0	.348/.443/.491	166	11.6	.391	-1.2	RF(10): -0.9, LF(9): -1.1	0.8
2018	BCA	A+	21	114	15	4	0	5	19	4	22	0	1	.262/.307/.439	110	1.1	.288	-2.2	LF(13): -1.4, 1B(6): -0.2	-0.1
2019	BCA	A+	22	152	24	8	0	9	34	14	30	0	3	.328/.414/.602	189	14.6	.359	-1.6	1B(16): 0.0, LF(15): -0.7	1.3
2019	WTN	AA	22	101	8	7	0	1	17	8	25	0	1	.205/.297/.318	74	-0.2	.270	0.0	1B(14): -0.7, LF(9): -0.4	-0.2
2019	CCH	AA	22	280	40	9	0	16	52	24	58	0	0	.299/.407/.543	177	21.5	.333	-3.1	1B(46): 0.8, LF(8): -0.1	2.1
2020	ARI	MLB	23	42	6	2	0	2	7	3	11	0	0	.268/.347/.505	122	2.3	.320	-0.1	LF 0	0.2

Comparables: Nate Lowe, Anthony Santander, Ryan O'Hearn

It's not just that Beer didn't keep chugging along after a midseason trade sent him from Houston to Arizona, it's that his production fell flat entirely. Beer couldn't tap into the power he showed during the first half of the season after the move, and given his lack of defensive versatility, he really needs to hit for his team to be in good spirits about his future. To be clear, Beer should hit, and his stout frame possesses enough power to leave scouts frothing at the mouth when he makes contact. But the bar for prospects who offer no utility elsewhere is so high that hiccups such as Beer's second half are enough to leave you feeling bitter about his future potential.

Kole Calhoun RF Born: 10/14/87 Age: 32 Bats: L Throws: L Height: 5'10" Weight: 215 Origin: Round 8, 2010 Draft (#264 overall)

YEAR	TEAM	LVL	AGE	PA	R	2B	3B	HR	RBI	BB	K	SB	CS	AVG/OBP/SLG	DRC+	VORP	BABIP	BRR	FRAA	WARP
2017	LAA	MLB	29	654	77	23	2	19	71	71	134	5	1	.244/.333/.392	99	11.6	.284	-0.6	RF(154): 10.0	2.3
2018	LAA	MLB	30	552	71	18	2	19	57	53	133	6	2	.208/.283/.369	85	-3.3	.241	-0.2		-0.2
2019	LAA	MLB	31	632	92	29	1	33	74	70	162	4	1	.232/.325/.467	110	23.5	.265	0.6		3.1
2020	ARI	MLB	32	560	70	23	2	28	80	56	145	4	2	.240/.322/.461	102	13.1	.283	-0.3	RF 1	1.5

Comparables: Cody Ross, Kevin Kiermaier, Andruw Jones

Nothing typifies the offensively-addled fever dream of the 2019 season than waking up on a random September morning, looking over box scores and player updates, and seeing that Calhoun—Kole Calhoun? really?—has surpassed the 30-home run milestone. In the present era of fast, cheap, and out-of-control offense, it's easy to wave away this benchmark, but it's harder to dismiss the all-around player Calhoun has become. In the three categories that make up WARP for position players—hitting, baserunning, and fielding—Calhoun enjoyed the first full season in which he earned positive marks in all categories. He's not a great player, but he's a good player, and probably better than you think.

Jarrod Dyson CF Born: 08/15/84 Age: 35 Bats: L Throws: R Height: 5'10" Weight: 165 Origin: Round 50, 2006 Draft (#1475 overall)

YEAR	TEAM	LVL	AGE	PA	R	2B	3B	HR	RBI	BB	K	SB	CS	AVG/OBP/SLG	DRC+	VORP	BABIP	BRR	FRAA	WARP
2017	SEA	MLB	32	390	56	13	3	5	30	28	55	28	7	.251/.324/.350	80	2.7	.285	0.0	CF(96): 5.6, LF(12): 3.2	1.2
2018	ARI	MLB	33	237	29	4	2	2	12	27	34	16	3	.189/.282/.257	70	-3.6	.216	2.6	CF(41): 3.3, RF(18): 0.0	0.6
2019	ARI	MLB	34	452	65	11	2	7	27	47	86	30	4	.230/.313/.320	77	2.0	.275	6.3	CF(103): -3.7, RF(21): 4.0	0.8
2020	ARI	MLB	35	251	24	9	2	3	22	22	49	17	4	.233/.308/.340	74	0.7	.283	1.2	CF 1, RF 0	0.1

Comparables: John Moses, Mookie Wilson, Omar Moreno

Dyson has lasted 10 years in the majors for two incredibly obvious reasons: speed and defense. The former continued to hold even in his age-34 season, as he stole 30 bases and posted the fourth-best BRR mark in the league. The latter, though, took a step back. Dyson's skill set is well suited for a fourth outfielder, but if his defense continues to decline as he enters his mid-30s, so too will his opportunities for work.

Eduardo Escobar 3B Born: 01/05/89 Age: 31 Bats: B Throws: R Height: 5'10" Weight: 185 Origin: International Free Agent, 2006

YEAR	TEAM	LVL	AGE	PA	R	2B	3B	HR	RBI	BB	K	SB	CS	AVG/OBP/SLG	DRC+	VORP	BABIP	BRR	FRAA	WARP
2017	MIN	MLB	28	499	62	16	5	21	73	33	98	5	1	.254/.309/.449	100	15.4	.279	2.3	3B(79): -5.1, SS(16): -0.5	1.3
2018	MIN	MLB	29	408	45	37	3	15	63	34	91	1	3	.274/.338/.514	115	26.4	.325	-0.1	3B(77): -2.1, SS(21): 0.0	2.1
2018	ARI	MLB	29	223	30	11	0	8	21	18	35	1	1	.268/.327/.444	114	12.3	.281	0.5	3B(54): -4.9	0.8
2019	ARI	MLB	30	699	94	29	10	35	118	50	130	5	1	.269/.320/.511	116	41.4	.283	-0.6	3B(144): -8.4, SS(33): 1.1	3.3
2020	ARI	MLB	31	595	69	27	7	26	83	41	116	4	2	.254/.310/.469	97	17.8	.280	0.6	2B 2, 3B -3	1.8

Comparables: Freddy Galvis, Marwin Gonzalez, Alex Gonzalez

The Diamondbacks rewarded the late-blooming Escobar with a three-year extension prior to the season and he, in turn, showed that his breakout was no fluke. Long valued for his defensive utility, Escobar emerged as Arizona's primary third baseman and, while his defense at the hot corner leaves a lot to be desired, he made up for it with the stick by topping his career-high in dingers by a dozen and leading the league in three-baggers. Escobar would likely still be better utilized as a multi-positional player, given that he can handle many spots on defense but doesn't excel at any, but there's no question at this point that his bat can play anywhere.

Wilmer Flores INF Born: 08/06/91 Age: 28 Bats: R Throws: R Height: 6'3" Weight: 205 Origin: International Free Agent, 2007

YEAR	TEAM	LVL	AGE	PA	R	2B	3B	HR	RBI	BB	K	SB	CS	AVG/OBP/SLG	DRC+	VORP	BABIP	BRR	FRAA	WARP
2017	NYN	MLB	25	362	42	17	1	18	52	17	54	1	1	.271/.307/.488	112	15.8	.270	-0.6	3B(55): 0.2, 1B(29): -0.2	1.5
2018	NYN	MLB	26	429	43	25	0	11	51	29	42	0	0	.267/.319/.417	106	13.3	.269	-3.2	1B(83): -2.6, 2B(13): 0.1	0.4
2019	ARI	MLB	27	285	31	18	0	9	37	15	31	0	0	.317/.361/.487	117	15.5	.332	-0.2	2B(64): -5.4, 1B(16): 0.1	1.0
2020	ARI	MLB	28	251	29	12	0	10	33	14	34	1	0	.270/.317/.448	100	7.4	.281	-0.7	1B 0, 2B -1	0.6

Comparables: Cal Ripken Jr., Jay Bell, Jim Fregosi

Flores hit well in his part-time role with the Diamondbacks, spelling Christian Walker at first base and playing second when Ketel Marte was in center. He also got hurt, missing about two months with a broken foot. He was a poor defender at both spots, and it turns out breaking a foot doesn't help one's already declining defensive prowess. Flores would likely be better served playing for an American League club where he can primarily DH and play the field in a pinch. It's not clear that his bat can justify that type of role without the BABIP-infused progress it made in 2019. Somehow just 28, Flores feels more like he's exiting his prime than entering it.

Adam Jones RF Born: 08/01/85 Age: 34 Bats: R Throws: R Height: 6'2" Weight: 215 Origin: Round 1, 2003 Draft (#37 overall)

YEAR	TEAM	LVL	AGE	PA	R	2B	3B	HR	RBI	BB	K	SB	CS	AVG/OBP/SLG	DRC+	VORP	BABIP	BRR	FRAA	WARP
2017	BAL	MLB	31	635	82	28	1	26	73	27	113	2	1	.285/.322/.466	106	29.2	.312	3.4	CF(147): -4.7	2.6
2018	BAL	MLB	32	613	54	35	0	15	63	24	93	7	1	.281/.313/.419	99	12.4	.311	1.0	CF(106): -11.8, RF(33): 2.0	1.0
2019	ARI	MLB	33	528	66	25	1	16	67	31	101	2	1	.260/.313/.414	90	6.0	.296	1.0	RF(130): -6.2, CF(1): 0.0	0.1
2020	ARI	MLB	34	251	26	11	0	8	30	12	51	1	0	.251/.297/.407	84	3.6	.289	0.6	CF -3, RF 0	0.0

Comparables: Rondell White, Vernon Wells, Larry Herndon

The Baltimore franchise icon struggled to find work and was forced to settle for a one-year pact with Arizona late in the offseason. It was fair to wonder if Jones had enough left in the tank to reinvigorate his career in a new locale after a precipitous dip in power and lagging defense forced a move to the corner. The answer was, in a word, no. After a second straight sub-par offensive season, Jones is now firmly in the decline phase of his once-stellar career, and name recognition and his strong locker room reputation will only take him so far. He will play 2020 and 2021 with NPB's Orix Buffaloes.

Carson Kelly C Born: 07/14/94 Age: 25 Bats: R Throws: R Height: 6'2" Weight: 220 Origin: Round 2, 2012 Draft (#86 overall)

YEAR	TEAM	LVL	AGE	PA	R	2B	3B	HR	RBI	BB	K	SB	CS	AVG/OBP/SLG	DRC+	VORP	BABIP	BRR	FRAA	WARP
2017	MEM	AAA	22	280	37	13	0	10	41	33	40	0	2	.283/.375/.459	127	22.1	.304	-1.9	C(68): 10.8	3.2
2017	SLN	MLB	22	75	5	3	0	0	6	5	11	0	0	.174/.240/.217	73	-4.0	.207	0.7	C(31): 3.0	0.5
2018	MEM	AAA	23	349	38	14	1	7	41	48	48	0	0	.269/.378/.395	112	24.7	.299	-0.6	C(83): 10.1, 1B(1): 0.0	3.3
2018	SLN	MLB	23	42	1	0	0	0	3	3	7	0	0	.114/.205/.114	74	-3.2	.143	-0.2	C(16): -0.9	0.0
2019	ARI	MLB	24	365	46	19	0	18	47	48	79	0	0	.245/.348/.478	115	26.4	.271	-1.2	C(101): -0.1, 3B(1): 0.0	2.5
2020	ARI	MLB	25	434	50	21	0	17	55	46	93	1	0	.234/.323/.421	101	20.8	.267	-0.3	C 4	2.6

Comparables: Hank Conger, Enrique Hernández, Ronald Guzmán

"We Got Next" was a memorable marketing slogan used by the WNBA in the lead-up to the league's inaugural season in 1997, a way to indicate they were next in line for viewers' attention following the completion of the NBA season. It was also plastered across Kelly's forehead for the better part of the last half-decade as St. Louis' "catcher in waiting" bid his time in the minors behind stalwart Yadier Molina. Kelly's opportunity finally came in 2019, but not where he thought it would be, as he was sent to the Arizona in a deal that brought Paul Goldschmidt to the Cardinals. A desert rose, Kelly flourished in the arid climate, emerging as one of the best offensive catchers in the National League. While scouts had long touted his work behind the plate, defensive metrics weren't so in love with his glove.

YEAR	TEAM	P. COUNT	FRM RUNS	BLK RUNS	THRW RUNS	TOT RUNS
2017	MEM	9388	11.5	1.2	-0.1	12.2
2017	SLN	2565	2.5	0.4	0.1	3.2
2018	MEM	11582	9.0	0.5	0.7	9.9
2018	SLN	1715	-0.8	-0.3	0.0	-1.1
2019	ARI	13168	-0.9	2.6	0.3	1.9
2020	ARI	16275	3.4	1.2	0.9	5.4

Still, Kelly topped Molina in just about every relevant offensive statistic, proving his emergence from understudy was worth the wait.

Jake Lamb CI
Born: 10/09/90   Age: 29   Bats: L   Throws: R   Height: 6'3"   Weight: 215   Origin: Round 6, 2012 Draft (#213 overall)

YEAR	TEAM	LVL	AGE	PA	R	2B	3B	HR	RBI	BB	K	SB	CS	AVG/OBP/SLG	DRC+	VORP	BABIP	BRR	FRAA	WARP
2017	ARI	MLB	26	635	89	30	4	30	105	87	152	6	4	.248/.357/.487	119	44.2	.287	2.0	3B(144): -10.8	2.9
2018	ARI	MLB	27	238	34	8	0	6	31	26	65	1	2	.222/.307/.348	80	10.5	.286	1.6	3B(52): -3.7	0.0
2019	RNO	AAA	28	46	5	2	0	1	7	7	12	0	0	.179/.304/.308	71	-1.4	.231	0.0	3B(6): -0.8, 1B(5): 0.0	-0.1
2019	ARI	MLB	28	226	26	8	2	6	30	32	55	1	0	.193/.323/.353	94	5.2	.234	2.3	3B(36): -1.6, 1B(24): -1.3	0.4
2020	ARI	MLB	29	462	53	20	4	16	57	55	127	4	2	.227/.326/.420	93	9.9	.290	2.3	3B -6, 1B -1	0.3

Comparables: Shane Andrews, Pedro Álvarez, Evan Longoria

The All-Star first half Lamb put together in 2017 is looking more and more distant, and it's not just the passage of time. It's more likely that the player Lamb is going to be is the player he's been the last two seasons: an injury-prone platoon bat. Lamb has fewer than 500 plate appearances to his name the last two seasons combined, as a shoulder injury ended his 2018 season early and a quad injury derailed his 2019. During the rare healthy times, he's struggled to keep his batting average north of the Mendoza line, was moved off of third base because of defensive woes, and struggled to adjust to his new home at the cold corner. Lamb has enough utility against right-handed pitchers that he's probably not headed to slaughter yet, but that fleece isn't exactly white as snow anymore.

Tim Locastro OF
Born: 07/14/92   Age: 27   Bats: R   Throws: R   Height: 6'1"   Weight: 200   Origin: Round 13, 2013 Draft (#385 overall)

YEAR	TEAM	LVL	AGE	PA	R	2B	3B	HR	RBI	BB	K	SB	CS	AVG/OBP/SLG	DRC+	VORP	BABIP	BRR	FRAA	WARP
2017	TUL	AA	24	420	69	21	4	8	31	22	56	22	5	.285/.366/.429	131	31.2	.317	5.4	CF(46): -2.3, SS(31): -3.9	2.5
2017	OKL	AAA	24	115	18	10	0	2	9	6	12	12	2	.388/.443/.544	161	15.9	.422	1.7	2B(22): -2.0, LF(8): 0.0	1.2
2017	LAN	MLB	24	1	0	0	0	0	0	0	0	1	0	.000/.000/.000	95	-0.3	.000	0.0	LF(2): -0.1	0.0
2018	OKL	AAA	25	356	61	23	2	4	25	28	52	18	2	.279/.389/.409	119	29.2	.327	4.2	CF(46): -3.7, 2B(30): -1.8	2.0
2018	LAN	MLB	25	14	6	1	0	0	0	2	5	4	0	.182/.357/.273	77	1.4	.333	0.4	CF(4): -0.1, LF(1): 0.0	0.0
2019	RNO	AAA	26	143	35	11	2	8	21	10	24	9	1	.301/.394/.618	117	12.8	.319	1.9	CF(20): -1.4, RF(7): -0.2	0.7
2019	ARI	MLB	26	250	38	12	2	1	17	14	44	17	0	.250/.357/.340	85	2.6	.310	0.3	LF(34): 1.6, RF(25): 0.0	0.2
2020	ARI	MLB	27	287	30	12	1	6	29	16	52	12	3	.236/.329/.367	93	6.3	.275	-1.0	CF -4, LF 1	0.4

Comparables: Cord Phelps, Cliff Pennington, Scott Sizemore

On May 24, Locastro came to bat six times in the Diamondbacks' 18-2 win over the Giants. He reached base four of those times in the blowout, with three free passes via the HBP. This was nothing new for Locastro, who has been hit by a pitch at least 25 times in every season (majors and minors) since his first year in full-season ball in 2014. Since reaching the majors, first with cups of coffee in LA and continuing in 2019 with Arizona, Locastro's HBP rate is 8.7 percent, the highest rate in league history. As a part-time outfielder who will likely continue to ride the bus between Triple-A and the big leagues whenever a need arises, Locastro is unlikely to sniff deadballer Hughie Jennings' career record of 287, nor modern day specialist Craig Biggio's 285, but he clearly has a knack for getting on base in an unconventional way.

Ketel Marte CF
Born: 10/12/93   Age: 26   Bats: B   Throws: R   Height: 6'1"   Weight: 165   Origin: International Free Agent, 2010

YEAR	TEAM	LVL	AGE	PA	R	2B	3B	HR	RBI	BB	K	SB	CS	AVG/OBP/SLG	DRC+	VORP	BABIP	BRR	FRAA	WARP
2017	RNO	AAA	23	338	62	23	7	6	41	25	34	7	2	.338/.391/.514	124	31.9	.365	3.8	SS(59): 2.1, CF(5): 1.6	3.3
2017	ARI	MLB	23	255	30	11	2	5	18	29	37	3	1	.260/.345/.395	100	13.9	.290	1.5	SS(64): -0.1, 3B(3): 0.1	1.3
2018	ARI	MLB	24	580	68	26	12	14	59	54	79	6	1	.260/.332/.437	102	28.0	.282	0.6	2B(131): 4.5, SS(28): 1.8	2.9
2019	ARI	MLB	25	628	97	36	9	32	92	53	86	10	2	.329/.389/.592	141	56.4	.342	1.9	CF(96): -8.3, 2B(83): -2.9	4.5
2020	ARI	MLB	26	630	75	31	9	22	84	49	93	13	4	.290/.348/.491	114	36.2	.313	1.0	CF -6, 2B 0	3.2

Comparables: Francisco Lindor, Orlando Arcia, Jorge Polanco

When Jonah Hill played an E-Bay Store customer trying to buy a pair of bedazzled boots in *The 40-Year-Old Virgin*, it's unlikely anybody looked at him and said "that guy's going to be an Academy Award nominee one day." Similarly, when Marte was a light-hitting middle infielder for the Mariners, it's unlikely anybody looked at him and said "that guy's going to be an All-Star one day." Acting is an unforgiving profession, but one in which the perfect role, the perfect script, or the ideal director-actor relationship can lead to stardom. Hill found his in 2011's *Moneyball* and went from fat kid who makes sex jokes to svelte dude in action movies. Baseball can be an unforgiving profession, but it's easy to forget distinguishing oneself in the majors isn't about having talent—every major leaguer has talent. It's building on that talent and making meaningful changes that sets the stars apart.

Marte found the right recipe to do just that. He joined the Launch Angle Revolution, increased his hard hit rate, and transformed himself into an All-Star. What's more, he did it while undergoing a position change, becoming the first player in major-league history to hit 25 or more home runs while playing 75 or more games at two up-the-middle spots, splitting time between second base and center field. Hill has become a perennial Oscar contender since his 2011 rise to stardom, and went from jokester to serious actor seemingly overnight. Marte, at still just 26, is coming off the best season of his career and is hoping for a similar run of sustained success.

Jake McCarthy OF
Born: 07/30/97   Age: 22   Bats: L   Throws: L   Height: 6'2"   Weight: 195   Origin: Round 1, 2018 Draft (#39 overall)

YEAR	TEAM	LVL	AGE	PA	R	2B	3B	HR	RBI	BB	K	SB	CS	AVG/OBP/SLG	DRC+	VORP	BABIP	BRR	FRAA	WARP
2018	YAK	A-	20	241	33	17	3	3	18	22	40	20	8	.288/.378/.442	143	20.4	.341	-0.5	CF(44): 8.0, LF(11): -2.3	2.2
2019	VIS	A+	21	214	29	13	3	2	30	17	52	18	2	.277/.341/.405	104	15.2	.369	5.0	CF(53): -0.6	1.2
2020	ARI	MLB	22	251	23	13	1	5	24	15	71	9	4	.227/.283/.352	70	-0.7	.308	0.9	CF 2, LF 0	0.1

Comparables: Zoilo Almonte, Kirk Nieuwenhuis, Kyle Lewis

"The past cannot be changed. The future is in your power." That unattributed quote is doubly true for the Diamondbacks' second first-round pick in 2018 following a season mostly lost to injuries, in which he didn't show the power potential many believe he has. McCarthy has good wheels and projects to stick in center field, but a couple of injuries—including one to his ankle that shut him down for the season in July—limited him to just 53 games. In the games he did play, he handled the stick about as well as hoped, he just couldn't lift the danged ball over the fence. The injuries are troubling, especially given his aggressive play in the field, but his potential is still that of a solid regular, given some luck in the health department.

Liover Peguero SS   Born: 12/31/00   Age: 19   Bats: R   Throws: R   Height: 6'1"   Weight: 160   Origin: International Free Agent, 2017

YEAR	TEAM	LVL	AGE	PA	R	2B	3B	HR	RBI	BB	K	SB	CS	AVG/OBP/SLG	DRC+	VORP	BABIP	BRR	FRAA	WARP
2018	DDI	RK	17	90	14	3	3	1	16	6	12	4	1	.309/.356/.457	128	8.4	.343	-0.3	SS(21): 0.9	0.7
2018	DIA	RK	17	71	8	0	0	0	5	5	17	3	2	.197/.254/.197	76	-4.5	.265	-0.9	SS(19): 2.2	0.3
2019	MSO	RK+	18	156	34	7	3	5	27	12	34	8	1	.364/.410/.559	154	22.1	.448	1.7		1.6
2019	YAK	A-	18	93	13	4	2	0	11	8	17	3	1	.262/.333/.357	104	3.5	.328	0.1	SS(18): -0.1	0.4
2020	ARI	MLB	19	251	21	11	2	3	23	16	71	3	1	.239/.291/.343	70	-1.8	.328	0.0	SS 1	0.0

Comparables: Amed Rosario, Enrique Hernández, Willi Castro

The Diamondbacks are chock full of toolsy, young shortstop prospects and Peguero is the newest of the bunch, but might have as much upside as any of them. He's got a good shot to stick at the six, and he projects to have potential plus power that he can get to in games. Geraldo Perdomo gets most of the attention when it comes to up-and-coming shortstop prospects in the Arizona system, but don't sleep on Peguero, whose advanced barrel control and explosive bat speed give him a lofty ceiling.

David Peralta LF   Born: 08/14/87   Age: 32   Bats: L   Throws: L   Height: 6'1"   Weight: 210   Origin: International Free Agent, 2005

YEAR	TEAM	LVL	AGE	PA	R	2B	3B	HR	RBI	BB	K	SB	CS	AVG/OBP/SLG	DRC+	VORP	BABIP	BRR	FRAA	WARP
2017	ARI	MLB	29	577	82	31	3	14	57	43	94	8	4	.293/.352/.444	103	24.0	.333	-0.9	RF(78): 10.0, LF(50): 2.2	2.7
2018	ARI	MLB	30	614	75	25	5	30	87	48	124	4	0	.293/.352/.516	121	40.7	.328	1.2	LF(138): -11.0, RF(5): -0.5	2.1
2019	ARI	MLB	31	423	48	29	3	12	57	35	87	0	0	.275/.343/.461	97	9.9	.327	-2.8	LF(93): 13.4	2.0
2020	ARI	MLB	32	560	64	30	6	19	72	45	120	6	2	.273/.337/.467	105	18.1	.325	-0.9	LF 3	2.2

Comparables: Jermaine Dye, Hunter Pence, Brennan Boesch

Peralta is far from the most common surname in the majors, but it's certainly on the rise. Since Jhonny debuted with the Indians in 2003, we've had Joel (2005), Wily (2012), Wandy (2016), and Freddy (2018) debut with varying degrees of notoriety. David (10.3) passed Joel (8.6) for second place on the all-time Peralta WARP leaderboard, despite missing a third of the campaign with injury. A late bloomer, it's unlikely David will surpass Jhonny (31.8) for all-time Peralta Prowess, but you can do a whole lot worse than his consistent offensive production from a corner outfield spot. Eat your heart out, Wily.

───────── ★ ★ ★ *2020 Top 101 Prospect* **#91** ★ ★ ★ ─────────

Geraldo Perdomo SS   Born: 10/22/99   Age: 20   Bats: B   Throws: R   Height: 6'3"   Weight: 184   Origin: International Free Agent, 2016

YEAR	TEAM	LVL	AGE	PA	R	2B	3B	HR	RBI	BB	K	SB	CS	AVG/OBP/SLG	DRC+	VORP	BABIP	BRR	FRAA	WARP
2017	DDI	RK	17	278	42	3	2	1	11	60	37	16	8	.238/.410/.285	135	18.4	.282	1.4	SS(63): 11.9	3.5
2018	DIA	RK	18	101	20	4	2	1	8	14	17	14	1	.314/.416/.442	168	14.9	.382	2.6	SS(14): 2.6, 2B(8): 0.5	1.6
2018	MSO	RK	18	29	3	0	1	0	2	7	4	1	1	.455/.586/.545	248	6.6	.556	0.4	SS(5): 0.3, 2B(2): -0.2	0.5
2018	YAK	A-	18	127	20	3	2	3	14	18	23	9	4	.301/.421/.456	149	16.1	.359	1.4	SS(30): 3.9	1.7
2019	KNC	A	19	385	48	16	3	2	36	56	56	20	8	.268/.394/.357	127	25.7	.318	-2.2	SS(80): 2.1, 2B(11): -0.1	2.7
2019	VIS	A+	19	114	15	5	0	1	11	14	11	6	5	.301/.407/.387	128	7.8	.325	-0.2	SS(25): -1.0	0.6
2020	ARI	MLB	20	251	25	10	1	4	23	27	51	6	3	.237/.329/.346	84	2.9	.291	0.0	SS 2, 2B 0	0.5

Comparables: Victor Robles, J.P. Crawford, Jorge Polanco

Perdomo is somewhat unique for an up-the-middle prospect, especially one with his youth and skills. Namely, he already has a solid grasp of the strike zone and there's little swing-and-miss in his game. Across two levels, he walked more than he struck out and never had an issue putting the bat on the ball. The question for Perdomo is whether or not he'll ever develop any power, as it's been virtually nonexistent throughout his career, although he does project for average raw as he continues to fill out. Perdomo is likely to stick at short but if a move to third becomes necessary, the power will become a bigger factor in his long-term success.

★ ★ ★ *2020 Top 101 Prospect* **#16** ★ ★ ★

Kristian Robinson OF Born: 12/11/00 Age: 19 Bats: R Throws: R Height: 6'3" Weight: 190 Origin: International Free Agent, 2017

YEAR	TEAM	LVL	AGE	PA	R	2B	3B	HR	RBI	BB	K	SB	CS	AVG/OBP/SLG	DRC+	VORP	BABIP	BRR	FRAA	WARP
2018	DIA	RK	17	182	35	11	0	4	31	16	46	7	5	.272/.341/.414	126	9.5	.351	1.3	CF(26): -5.3, LF(6): -0.9	0.7
2018	MSO	RK	17	74	13	1	0	3	10	11	21	5	3	.300/.419/.467	119	6.0	.405	0.5	CF(10): -2.3, LF(7): 0.4	0.0
2019	YAK	A-	18	189	29	10	1	9	35	23	47	14	3	.319/.407/.558	208	24.4	.398	-0.1	CF(21): 1.6, RF(18): 3.8	2.8
2019	KNC	A	18	102	14	3	1	5	16	8	30	3	2	.217/.294/.435	91	3.0	.263	-0.3	CF(18): 0.6, RF(5): 0.2	0.2
2020	*ARI*	*MLB*	*19*	*251*	*25*	*11*	*1*	*7*	*27*	*22*	*85*	*5*	*3*	*.227/.301/.370*	*81*	*1.7*	*.332*	*-0.1*	*CF 1, RF 1*	*0.4*

Comparables: Ronald Acuña Jr., Fernando Tatis Jr., Yorman Rodriguez

In another universe, Robinson would have spent parts of 2019 touring the Northwest looking at college campuses, weighing where to continue his education, before ultimately deciding to go to Northwestern. In this universe, the 18-year-old went to many of the same places, only instead of touring campuses he was torturing opposing pitchers in the Northwest League. Speaking of another universe, Robinson seemingly defies physics; he's imposing in the box and explosive outside of it. In one reality, he ended up in Northwestern (Medicine Field); in this one, he received his first dose of higher education in full-season ball. There's a steep learning curve, but Robinson has every tool available to him to aid in his success. He ranked No. 100 on our 2019 list entering the season. Will he rank higher this year? You can check the back of the book and find out, but really, it's academic.

Josh Rojas UT Born: 06/30/94 Age: 26 Bats: L Throws: R Height: 6'1" Weight: 185 Origin: Round 26, 2017 Draft (#781 overall)

YEAR	TEAM	LVL	AGE	PA	R	2B	3B	HR	RBI	BB	K	SB	CS	AVG/OBP/SLG	DRC+	VORP	BABIP	BRR	FRAA	WARP
2017	QUD	A	23	219	33	5	5	10	40	15	43	0	0	.256/.306/.487	106	13.6	.268	0.1	3B(30): 0.7, 2B(18): -0.8	1.0
2018	BCA	A+	24	105	20	11	2	1	10	15	13	12	0	.311/.410/.511	158	12.9	.355	0.1	2B(10): 1.0, 1B(7): 0.0	0.9
2018	CCH	AA	24	451	64	23	4	7	45	53	76	26	14	.251/.338/.385	108	17.4	.291	1.0	LF(36): 2.2, 3B(16): 2.3	2.2
2019	CCH	AA	25	195	29	13	2	8	30	22	28	13	6	.322/.405/.561	180	16.6	.348	0.0	2B(30): 0.6, 1B(12): 0.8	2.1
2019	ROU	AAA	25	244	49	16	3	12	39	30	36	19	4	.310/.402/.586	149	27.1	.325	2.1	2B(15): -1.5, SS(15): 0.9	2.8
2019	RNO	AAA	25	40	11	4	1	3	14	5	6	1	0	.514/.575/.943	153	8.3	.577	-0.3	LF(2): 0.0, SS(2): -0.4	1.9
2019	ARI	MLB	25	157	17	7	0	2	16	18	41	4	2	.217/.312/.312	76	-0.7	.295	-1.7	LF(33): 2.7, RF(6): 0.0	0.0
2020	*ARI*	*MLB*	*26*	*210*	*24*	*10*	*2*	*7*	*26*	*20*	*48*	*7*	*3*	*.249/.326/.438*	*98*	*5.5*	*.297*	*0.6*	*RF -1, LF 0*	*0.5*

Comparables: Bob Nieman, Mitch Haniger, Tyler Austin

A player of Rojas' ilk has plenty of utility in today's game, given his ability to adequately handle every infield position and the corners in the outfield. His move, in the Zack Greinke blockbuster, from Houston's loaded organization to Arizona's more arid clime helped propel him to his first cup of coffee. He didn't quite play *every*where, seeing time in left field, right field, and at second base, but was serviceable enough in a little more than 100 plate appearances to get a prolonged look at some point in the future. A superstar Rojas will never be, but with rosters expanding to 26 players next year, he should be able to log plenty of time in the big leagues.

Pavin Smith 1B Born: 02/06/96 Age: 24 Bats: L Throws: L Height: 6'2" Weight: 210 Origin: Round 1, 2017 Draft (#7 overall)

YEAR	TEAM	LVL	AGE	PA	R	2B	3B	HR	RBI	BB	K	SB	CS	AVG/OBP/SLG	DRC+	VORP	BABIP	BRR	FRAA	WARP
2017	YAK	A-	21	223	34	15	2	0	27	27	24	2	1	.318/.401/.415	162	15.3	.363	-1.8	1B(42): 1.0	1.5
2018	VIS	A+	22	504	63	25	1	11	54	57	65	3	2	.255/.343/.392	112	9.5	.275	-1.1	1B(109): 9.0, RF(1): -0.1	2.0
2019	WTN	AA	23	507	62	29	6	12	67	59	61	2	1	.291/.370/.466	142	25.1	.310	-5.9	1B(78): 2.5, RF(28): -2.6	2.5
2020	*ARI*	*MLB*	*24*	*251*	*26*	*13*	*1*	*7*	*29*	*22*	*43*	*0*	*0*	*.249/.317/.409*	*92*	*5.3*	*.278*	*-0.4*	*1B 2, RF 0*	*0.8*

Comparables: Matt Thaiss, Yonder Alonso, Alex Hassan

The flaws in Smith's profile were apparent from the moment he was drafted: He was defensively limited to first base and had a flat bat path that didn't generate a lot of power. All of that coalesced into a powerless first full season in the California League. Smith showed signs of a swing change in 2019 and combined his keen eye and bat control with a little bit of pop, finishing with the sixth-best slugging percentage in the Southern League. There's little question that Smith will hit in the majors, but the development of his power will be the difference between whether as a solid regular or someone who hits enough to keep his job but consistently leaves employers wanting.

Steven Souza Jr. OF Born: 04/24/89 Age: 31 Bats: R Throws: R Height: 6'4" Weight: 225 Origin: Round 3, 2007 Draft (#100 overall)

YEAR	TEAM	LVL	AGE	PA	R	2B	3B	HR	RBI	BB	K	SB	CS	AVG/OBP/SLG	DRC+	VORP	BABIP	BRR	FRAA	WARP
2017	TBA	MLB	28	617	78	21	2	30	78	84	179	16	4	.239/.351/.459	116	27.3	.302	-1.9	RF(138): -6.8, CF(3): -0.5	1.6
2018	ARI	MLB	29	272	21	15	3	5	29	28	75	6	1	.220/.309/.369	77	-0.3	.298	0.1	RF(65): -5.9, CF(1): 0.0	-0.8
2020	*ARI*	*MLB*	*31*	*251*	*30*	*10*	*1*	*10*	*32*	*27*	*82*	*6*	*2*	*.225/.317/.414*	*97*	*6.5*	*.308*	*-0.8*	*RF -3, CF 0*	*0.3*

Comparables: George Springer, Scott Van Slyke, Aaron Altherr

After a 2018 season that could be described subjectively as "bad" and objectively as "injury-shortened," Souza—who the Diamondbacks undoubtedly envisioned anchoring right field for the foreseeable future when they acquired him that spring—never left the runway in 2019. A horrifying injury sustained stepping on home plate on the eve of the season, in which he tore his ACL, LCL, PCL and posterior lateral capsule, ended his tenure before it ever got started. Counting on a return to form after something like that is a risky proposition—one the Diamondbacks were unwilling to take on when they non-tendered him in December.

★ ★ ★ *2020 Top 101 Prospect* **#54** ★ ★ ★

Alek Thomas OF Born: 04/28/00 Age: 20 Bats: L Throws: L Height: 5'11" Weight: 175 Origin: Round 2, 2018 Draft (#63 overall)

YEAR	TEAM	LVL	AGE	PA	R	2B	3B	HR	RBI	BB	K	SB	CS	AVG/OBP/SLG	DRC+	VORP	BABIP	BRR	FRAA	WARP
2018	DIA	RK	18	138	24	3	5	0	10	13	18	8	2	.325/.394/.431	162	15.2	.381	1.6	CF(13): -2.1, LF(11): -2.4	0.8
2018	MSO	RK	18	134	26	11	1	2	17	11	19	4	3	.341/.396/.496	160	7.9	.392	-1.0	CF(21): 0.1, LF(7): 0.5	0.8
2019	KNC	A	19	402	63	21	7	8	48	43	72	11	6	.312/.393/.479	153	32.4	.372	0.4	CF(75): -10.1, RF(7): 0.8	2.5
2019	VIS	A+	19	104	13	2	0	2	7	9	33	4	5	.255/.327/.340	90	3.7	.373	0.4	CF(23): 2.6	0.6
2020	ARI	MLB	20	251	25	12	2	6	27	20	64	3	1	.256/.320/.393	90	4.8	.332	-0.2	CF -2, LF 0	0.3

Comparables: Victor Robles, Billy McKinney, Byron Buxton

You go to the hardware store and see a display for a beautiful new barbecue pit. You picture that pit in your backyard and know it's gonna be the best Summer ever. Hosting get-togethers for birthdays, anniversaries, or just because the weather's nice. The sun is shining, a cool breeze is blowing, and the cooler is filled with ice cold beer. You buy it and bring the box home, only to find complicated instructions on how to build the pit. This is the moment of truth. To realize your dream, you've got to follow the instructions perfectly. One misstep—a screw too loose or slotting Part J into Part Q instead of Part R—and your perfect barbecue-filled Summer will come crashing down. Thomas has everything you want in an above-average major league outfielder—a smooth swing, good speed, an athletic frame, and a good feel for the strike zone. But Thomas is still in the box. He aced his first look at full-season ball, torching Low-A and holding his own upon promotion. There's plenty there to envision a top-of-the-order hitter, it just all needs to be put together correctly. Any variance and the barbecue pit falls apart and that starter becomes a fourth outfielder, and you find yourself glancing over at your neighbor's young outfielder saying "why doesn't mine look like that?"

Yasmany Tomás OF/1B Born: 11/14/90 Age: 29 Bats: R Throws: R Height: 6'2" Weight: 250 Origin: International Free Agent, 2014

YEAR	TEAM	LVL	AGE	PA	R	2B	3B	HR	RBI	BB	K	SB	CS	AVG/OBP/SLG	DRC+	VORP	BABIP	BRR	FRAA	WARP
2017	ARI	MLB	26	180	19	11	1	8	32	13	50	0	0	.241/.294/.464	82	5.7	.294	-0.3	LF(42): -7.1	-0.7
2018	RNO	AAA	27	371	42	22	4	14	65	11	101	2	0	.262/.280/.465	72	-3.3	.322	-3.4	LF(44): -5.9, 1B(9): -0.3	-1.4
2019	RNO	AAA	28	431	63	24	3	29	82	22	110	2	0	.301/.341/.590	98	6.9	.348	-2.6	1B(46): 2.3, LF(44): -2.8	0.5
2019	ARI	MLB	28	6	0	0	0	0	0	0	3	0	0	.000/.000/.000	78	0.0	.000	0.0		0.0
2020	ARI	MLB	29	251	29	11	1	12	35	12	76	1	1	.243/.281/.451	88	3.8	.304	-0.2	LF -5, 1B 0	-0.1

Comparables: Hunter Pence, Avisaíl García, Laynce Nix

In the fifth year of an ill-fated six-year contract, Tomás accomplished something he failed to do a year prior: He made it back to the majors, albeit for four games and six hitless plate appearances. Tomás also mashed in the hitter-friendly Pacific Coast League, something he likewise failed to do in the past, though credit can likely be shared with a livelier baseball. It's anyone but Tomás' fault that the previous Arizona regime guaranteed him $68.5 million all those years ago, and the 29-year-old will most likely play out the final year of the contract in Reno once more, working to hit his way back to Arizona while raking in a cool $17 million.

Ildemaro Vargas 2B Born: 07/16/91 Age: 28 Bats: B Throws: R Height: 6'0" Weight: 170 Origin: International Free Agent, 2008

YEAR	TEAM	LVL	AGE	PA	R	2B	3B	HR	RBI	BB	K	SB	CS	AVG/OBP/SLG	DRC+	VORP	BABIP	BRR	FRAA	WARP
2017	RNO	AAA	25	535	87	35	4	10	65	30	40	8	3	.312/.355/.462	108	34.5	.319	1.3	2B(93): 11.8, SS(8): -1.6	3.2
2017	ARI	MLB	25	13	4	1	0	0	4	0	3	0	0	.308/.308/.385	85	-0.1	.400	0.1	2B(3): 0.0, 3B(2): -0.1	0.0
2018	RNO	AAA	26	572	78	31	10	7	54	30	46	10	4	.311/.348/.445	100	19.8	.329	-3.8	SS(107): -6.0, 2B(17): -0.1	1.5
2018	ARI	MLB	26	20	2	0	0	1	4	1	4	1	0	.211/.250/.368	93	0.5	.214	0.2	3B(3): 0.3, 2B(2): 0.1	0.1
2019	RNO	AAA	27	137	20	9	3	2	24	11	5	1	1	.403/.453/.573	144	14.9	.407	1.9	SS(13): 0.8, 3B(12): 0.3	1.6
2019	ARI	MLB	27	211	25	9	1	6	24	9	24	1	0	.269/.299/.413	88	4.0	.279	0.4	2B(48): 2.4, 3B(14): -1.1	0.6
2020	ARI	MLB	28	189	18	8	1	4	20	10	23	2	1	.268/.311/.394	83	2.9	.289	0.1	2B 2, SS 0	0.5

Comparables: Yangervis Solarte, Kevin Frandsen, Tony Kemp

A car needs oil, a painter needs paint, Kate Winslet needs an American-accented Oscar-bait role, and a major-league roster in 2020 needs a player like Vargas. An additional roster spot this season could create room for the more one-dimensional types, but Vargas' ability to play all over will serve him well. The Venezuelan native played primarily at second base, but saw time at shortstop, third base, and in both outfield corners in 2019, and that kind of utility should help him keep finding roles in the majors going forward. Now, if he could just handle the bat...

★ ★ ★ *2020 Top 101 Prospect* **#87** ★ ★ ★

Daulton Varsho C Born: 07/02/96 Age: 23 Bats: L Throws: R Height: 5'10" Weight: 190 Origin: Round 2, 2017 Draft (#68 overall)

YEAR	TEAM	LVL	AGE	PA	R	2B	3B	HR	RBI	BB	K	SB	CS	AVG/OBP/SLG	DRC+	VORP	BABIP	BRR	FRAA	WARP
2017	YAK	A-	20	212	36	16	3	7	39	17	30	7	2	.311/.368/.534	156	24.2	.338	2.4	C(36): 0.8	2.3
2018	VIS	A+	21	342	44	11	3	11	44	30	71	19	3	.286/.363/.451	131	30.5	.341	2.5	C(55): 1.4	2.7
2019	WTN	AA	22	452	85	25	4	18	58	42	63	21	5	.301/.378/.520	156	52.6	.317	5.9	C(75): -5.7, CF(4): -1.2	4.3
2020	ARI	MLB	23	70	9	4	1	3	10	5	15	1	0	.271/.332/.498	112	4.3	.304	0.2	C -1, CF 0	0.3

Comparables: Max Stassi, Kyle Lewis, Nate Lowe

YEAR	TEAM	P. COUNT	FRM RUNS	BLK RUNS	THRW RUNS	TOT RUNS
2019	WTN	10022	-4.0	0.0	-3.5	-7.1
2020	ARI	1280	-0.6	-0.1	-0.2	-0.9

Teams are finding it increasingly tough to develop catchers who provide value on both sides of the ball. Like so many other young catchers, Varsho has one side of that proposition covered, having battered the Southern League in his first look at Double-A pitching. The question, though, resides with his defense, and if it takes a little longer than expected for him to reach the majors, that'll be the reason. Catcher development is weird, though, so when Varsho turns out to be a Gold Glove backstop with a fringy bat, don't blame us.

Stephen Vogt C   Born: 11/01/84   Age: 35   Bats: L   Throws: R   Height: 6'0"   Weight: 225   Origin: Round 12, 2007 Draft (#365 overall)

YEAR	TEAM	LVL	AGE	PA	R	2B	3B	HR	RBI	BB	K	SB	CS	AVG/OBP/SLG	DRC+	VORP	BABIP	BRR	FRAA	WARP
2017	OAK	MLB	32	174	12	8	1	4	20	16	31	0	1	.217/.287/.357	92	-0.3	.244	-1.7	C(43): -0.9, LF(1): -0.1	0.3
2017	MIL	MLB	32	129	13	7	0	8	20	5	25	0	0	.254/.281/.508	92	6.9	.256	-1.8	C(38): 0.0	0.3
2019	SAC	AAA	34	72	9	3	0	4	7	14	11	0	0	.241/.389/.500	122	3.1	.233	-0.7	C(9): -0.3, 1B(6): -0.4	0.3
2019	SFN	MLB	34	280	30	24	2	10	40	20	66	3	1	.263/.314/.490	106	15.5	.311	-0.2	C(60): -1.0, LF(7): -0.2	1.4
2020	ARI	MLB	35	259	29	13	1	11	35	21	58	1	0	.240/.305/.446	92	8.5	.273	-1.0	C -6	0.2

Comparables: Adrián González, Wes Covington, Adam Rosales

YEAR	TEAM	P. COUNT	FRM RUNS	BLK RUNS	THRW RUNS	TOT RUNS
2017	OAK	5443	5.3	0.2	-1.6	3.8
2017	MIL	4322	4.3	1.4	-2.4	3.3
2019	SAC	1361	-0.2	-0.1	-0.2	-0.7
2019	SFN	7684	-1.6	-0.6	-0.5	-3.7
2020	ARI	14501	-4.4	-0.6	-1.6	-6.6

Shoulder surgery derailed this journeyman backstop's age-33 season, so a minor-league contract brought him back to the part of the country where he'd once found success, if not precisely within the same city limits. When he got the call to the bigs, he was asked to back up the team's signature star; he responded by out-hitting Buster Posey, filling in around the diamond, and re-establishing himself as a quality backup, despite not putting up the same numbers he did during his two All-Star seasons in the middle of the decade. His skillset includes moderate power, mediocre defense, versatility, and the ability to lighten the mood in the clubhouse, which dovetails nicely with his stated goal to find a team that contends for the World Series in 2020. Best cast as a premium backup catcher or a second-division starter, the Arizona Diamondbacks plan to use him in exactly that role next year.

Christian Walker 1B   Born: 03/28/91   Age: 29   Bats: R   Throws: R   Height: 6'0"   Weight: 220   Origin: Round 4, 2012 Draft (#132 overall)

YEAR	TEAM	LVL	AGE	PA	R	2B	3B	HR	RBI	BB	K	SB	CS	AVG/OBP/SLG	DRC+	VORP	BABIP	BRR	FRAA	WARP
2017	RNO	AAA	26	592	104	34	9	32	114	61	104	5	2	.309/.382/.597	134	40.6	.327	2.1	1B(119): -6.2, 3B(9): 0.4	2.9
2017	ARI	MLB	26	15	2	1	0	2	2	1	5	0	0	.250/.400/.833	92	2.4	.200	0.0	1B(1): 0.0	0.0
2018	RNO	AAA	27	359	68	25	4	18	71	26	86	1	0	.299/.354/.568	116	15.8	.351	-1.3	1B(64): 3.4, LF(18): -0.9	1.4
2018	ARI	MLB	27	53	6	2	0	3	6	3	22	1	0	.163/.226/.388	59	-1.1	.208	0.2	1B(7): 0.2, LF(1): -0.1	-0.1
2019	ARI	MLB	28	603	86	26	1	29	73	67	155	8	1	.259/.348/.476	112	19.4	.312	1.7	1B(142): 10.8	3.1
2020	ARI	MLB	29	567	70	27	2	27	81	53	157	2	1	.247/.326/.466	110	19.0	.305	0.5	1B 4	2.4

Comparables: Bryan LaHair, Danny Dorn, Nick Evans

Wait a minute, Walker is how old? Despite accruing service time as early as 2013, Walker entered 2019 with just 99 career plate appearances, serving instead as minor-league depth over the past five seasons, first behind Chris Davis in Baltimore and then Paul Goldschmidt in Arizona. Thus, it wasn't until his age-28 season that Walker finally got a chance to see regular playing time. The power played, he walked enough to make up for hefty strikeout numbers, and he emerged as one of the better defensive first basemen in the game. The problem is that you wonder if what we saw in 2019 is his ceiling.

PITCHERS

Matt Andriese RHP   Born: 08/28/89   Age: 30   Bats: R   Throws: R   Height: 6'2"   Weight: 225   Origin: Round 3, 2011 Draft (#112 overall)

YEAR	TEAM	LVL	AGE	W	L	SV	G	GS	IP	H	HR	BB/9	K/9	K	GB%	BABIP	WHIP	ERA	DRA	WARP	MPH	FB%	WHF	CSP
2017	TBA	MLB	27	5	5	1	18	17	86	90	16	2.9	8.0	76	46%	.296	1.37	4.50	4.10	1.4	93.8	44.3	11.8	48.2
2018	TBA	MLB	28	3	4	0	27	4	59²	55	7	2.7	8.9	59	52%	.291	1.22	4.07	4.89	0.1	94.5	46.1	12.8	48.5
2018	ARI	MLB	28	0	3	0	14	1	19	29	8	3.3	9.0	19	44%	.382	1.89	9.00	5.20	0.0	94.0	46.1	14.3	48
2019	ARI	MLB	29	5	5	1	54	0	70²	72	8	3.4	10.1	79	51%	.333	1.40	4.71	3.62	1.3	94.2	50.4	11.9	48.6
2020	ARI	MLB	30	3	3	0	58	0	61	57	9	2.7	8.9	61	48%	.292	1.23	3.78	4.01	0.9	93.4	47.1	12.3	48.3

Comparables: Chase Whitley, Cody Martin, Jake Buchanan

Sometimes, less is more. That's what both the Diamondbacks and Andriese learned during a 2019 season that can confidently be described as the best of his career. The right-hander seemed, for most of his career, to be nothing more than your prototypical swing-man. Last season he settled in as a reliable middle reliever who misses enough bats to survive in today's game and generates enough ground balls to thrive. He did so by simplifying his repertoire, ditching his cutter almost entirely for a fastball-changeup combo that has always been tough for hitters to differentiate between. Control issues still limit his ceiling, but Andriese seems to have found a recipe that allows him to stick around as a valuable piece of the bullpen.

Archie Bradley RHP   Born: 08/10/92   Age: 27   Bats: R   Throws: R   Height: 6'4"   Weight: 225   Origin: Round 1, 2011 Draft (#7 overall)

YEAR	TEAM	LVL	AGE	W	L	SV	G	GS	IP	H	HR	BB/9	K/9	K	GB%	BABIP	WHIP	ERA	DRA	WARP	MPH	FB%	WHF	CSP
2017	ARI	MLB	24	3	3	1	63	0	73	55	4	2.6	9.7	79	49%	.276	1.04	1.73	3.88	1.1	98.3	75.6	10.9	52.7
2018	ARI	MLB	25	4	5	3	76	0	71²	62	9	2.5	9.4	75	50%	.282	1.14	3.64	4.48	0.4	97.7	81.7	10	51.3
2019	ARI	MLB	26	4	5	18	66	1	71²	67	5	4.5	10.9	87	47%	.337	1.44	3.52	4.60	0.6	97.4	69.6	10.8	46.9
2020	ARI	MLB	27	3	3	32	58	0	61	57	7	4.1	9.9	67	48%	.311	1.39	4.24	4.29	0.8	97.2	75.9	10.7	50.4

Comparables: José Berríos, Aaron Sanchez, Lucas Giolito

Ever since being converted to the bullpen after the 2016 season, Bradley has been the Diamondbacks' Closer Of The Future. The only problem was that the future never seemed to arrive. It took three years and a Greg Holland implosion, but the future finally turned into the present in the second half of 2019. From the time he took over the job and earned his first save on July 30 through the end of the season, Bradley converted 18 of 19 save opportunities and allowed just six earned runs in 25 appearances. Bradley has always had The Stuff to be an elite, lockdown closer, but that swing-and-miss stuff was stymied by far too many walks. Indeed, Bradley's walk rate for the season was still too high, but those final two months brought a much more palatable figure to go along with the normal bat-missing stuff and a high ground ball rate. It took longer than many expected, but it appears Bradley finally fulfilled his prophecy as The Closer Who Was Promised.

J.B. Bukauskas RHP   Born: 10/11/96   Age: 23   Bats: R   Throws: R   Height: 6'0"   Weight: 196   Origin: Round 1, 2017 Draft (#15 overall)

YEAR	TEAM	LVL	AGE	W	L	SV	G	GS	IP	H	HR	BB/9	K/9	K	GB%	BABIP	WHIP	ERA	DRA	WARP	MPH	FB%	WHF	CSP
2017	TCV	A-	20	0	0	0	2	2	6	4	0	6.0	9.0	6	53%	.267	1.33	4.50	5.10	0.0				
2018	TCV	A-	21	0	0	0	3	3	8¹	8	0	2.2	9.7	9	46%	.364	1.20	0.00	4.27	0.1				
2018	QUD	A	21	1	2	0	4	4	15	15	0	4.2	12.6	21	55%	.395	1.47	4.20	3.95	0.2				
2018	BCA	A+	21	3	0	0	5	5	28	13	1	4.2	10.0	31	59%	.194	0.93	1.61	2.72	0.9				
2018	CCH	AA	21	0	0	0	1	1	6	1	0	3.0	12.0	8	60%	.100	0.50	0.00	2.56	0.2				
2019	CCH	AA	22	2	4	1	20	14	85²	81	8	5.7	10.3	98	48%	.332	1.58	5.25	6.11	-1.3				
2019	WTN	AA	22	0	1	0	2	2	7	10	0	6.4	14.1	11	39%	.556	2.14	7.71	7.33	-0.2				
2020	ARI	MLB	23	1	1	0	11	0	11	11	2	3.7	8.8	11	44%	.299	1.38	4.34	4.50	0.1				

Comparables: Logan Webb, Jorge Alcala, Nick Tropeano

One year after reportedly being included in a trade proposal that would've sent Bryce Harper to the Houston Astros, Bukauskas was instead shipped to Arizona in the Zack Greinke swap. Bukauskas has perhaps the highest ceiling of any of the players the Diamondbacks acquired for their erstwhile ace, but counters that ceiling with significant bullpen risk. His fastball sits 92-94 and he can get it into the mid-90s when he really amps it up. He has a nasty, wipeout slider with depth, and a cutter and changeup that could yet develop into above-average offerings. Far too often he isn't sure where any of those pitches are going, as evidenced by a walk rate that sat above six. Arizona bet a lot on Bukauskas, so they'll likely give him every opportunity to fail as a starter before going down the relief route.

Madison Bumgarner LHP   Born: 08/01/89   Age: 30   Bats: R   Throws: L   Height: 6'4"   Weight: 242   Origin: Round 1, 2007 Draft (#10 overall)

YEAR	TEAM	LVL	AGE	W	L	SV	G	GS	IP	H	HR	BB/9	K/9	K	GB%	BABIP	WHIP	ERA	DRA	WARP	MPH	FB%	WHF	CSP
2017	SJO	A+	27	0	1	0	2	2	10	11	4	1.8	11.7	13	29%	.292	1.30	8.10	4.24	0.1				
2017	SFN	MLB	27	4	9	0	17	17	111	101	17	1.6	8.2	101	42%	.272	1.09	3.32	3.66	2.4	93.1	43	11.1	46
2018	SFN	MLB	28	6	7	0	21	21	129²	118	14	3.0	7.6	109	43%	.274	1.24	3.26	4.47	1.3	92.4	34.4	10.1	49
2019	SFN	MLB	29	9	9	0	34	34	207²	191	30	1.9	8.8	203	37%	.289	1.13	3.90	4.47	2.9	93.1	43.1	12.5	48.6
2020	ARI	MLB	30	11	9	0	28	28	168	159	27	2.3	8.9	166	38%	.290	1.20	3.92	4.19	3.0	92.2	40.5	11.5	48

Comparables: Félix Hernández, Clayton Kershaw, Frank Tanana

After two injury-riddled years, Bumgarner reached the end of his Giants career doing what he does best: performing well when it means the most. Only this time, instead of dialing up his performance as his team rallies in the playoffs, Bumgarner rose to a more lucrative occasion: he made 34 solid starts in his contract year. He proved that despite all the mileage on his arm and the softening of his fastball, he's still an exceptional workhorse starter with command and strikeout stuff. Perhaps the biggest issue from last season was the ability of the opposing hitters to put his cutter into the air, leading to a career-high 30 home runs allowed and a career-low ground ball rate. Hitters appear to be squaring him up better than ever, but that didn't stop Arizona from bringing him across the division to be their new rotation cornerstone on a five-year contract.

Andrew Chafin LHP   Born: 06/17/90   Age: 30   Bats: R   Throws: L   Height: 6'2"   Weight: 225   Origin: Round 1, 2011 Draft (#43 overall)

YEAR	TEAM	LVL	AGE	W	L	SV	G	GS	IP	H	HR	BB/9	K/9	K	GB%	BABIP	WHIP	ERA	DRA	WARP	MPH	FB%	WHF	CSP
2017	ARI	MLB	27	1	0	0	71	0	51¹	48	5	3.7	10.7	61	58%	.326	1.34	3.51	3.51	0.9	95.4	61.2	11.9	41.8
2018	ARI	MLB	28	1	6	0	77	0	49¹	41	0	4.6	9.7	53	51%	.313	1.34	3.10	4.23	0.4	95.7	56.6	14.7	42.7
2019	ARI	MLB	29	2	2	0	77	0	52²	52	6	3.1	11.6	68	44%	.351	1.33	3.76	3.88	0.8	95.6	61.1	16.6	45.6
2020	ARI	MLB	30	3	3	2	53	0	56	49	6	3.7	10.8	67	48%	.311	1.30	3.68	3.80	1.0	94.8	59.5	14.7	43.6

Comparables: Neftalí Feliz, Luis Avilán, Jeremy Jeffress

Chafin faced two batters or fewer in nearly half of his 77 appearances in 2019, a stat that is only now relevant given the upcoming rule change requiring pitchers to face at least three batters or end a half-inning before being removed. There's hope for Chafin despite this, however: While he has primarily been used against lefties throughout his career, his splits aren't so extreme that facing the occasional right-handed bat will sap his value entirely. It's a good thing, too, as we could all use a little more of the mustachioed man nicknamed The Sheriff in our lives.

Jon Duplantier RHP   Born: 07/11/94   Age: 25   Bats: L   Throws: R   Height: 6'4"   Weight: 225   Origin: Round 3, 2016 Draft (#89 overall)

YEAR	TEAM	LVL	AGE	W	L	SV	G	GS	IP	H	HR	BB/9	K/9	K	GB%	BABIP	WHIP	ERA	DRA	WARP	MPH	FB%	WHF	CSP
2017	KNC	A	22	6	1	0	13	12	72²	45	4	1.9	9.7	78	52%	.240	0.83	1.24	2.23	2.6				
2017	VIS	A+	22	6	2	0	12	12	63¹	46	2	3.8	12.4	87	53%	.324	1.15	1.56	3.49	1.3				
2018	DIA	RK	23	0	0	0	2	2	7	5	0	2.6	11.6	9	44%	.312	1.00	1.29	3.05	0.2				
2018	WTN	AA	23	5	1	0	14	14	67	52	4	3.8	9.1	68	56%	.282	1.19	2.69	3.79	1.2				
2019	RNO	AAA	24	1	2	0	13	11	38	31	1	6.6	10.4	44	47%	.323	1.55	5.21	2.93	1.4				
2019	ARI	MLB	24	1	1	1	15	3	36²	39	2	4.4	8.3	34	44%	.356	1.55	4.42	5.73	-0.1	94.3	59	9.2	47.9
2020	ARI	MLB	25	2	2	0	30	3	42	44	6	4.5	7.5	35	46%	.299	1.54	5.22	5.14	0.2	94.0	60.4	9.4	49

Comparables: Yefry Ramírez, Alex Meyer, Jordan Montgomery

TINSTAAPP, thy name is Duplantier. The right-hander has been ticketed for a spot in the middle of Arizona's rotation ever since they took him in the second round in 2016, and he has certainly progressed according to plan when healthy. As expected, though, "when healthy" is the rub. Duplantier has shoulder, elbow, and biceps injuries in his past, and after debuting for the Diamondbacks in 2019 he again missed time with right shoulder inflammation, which cost him about a month of the season. Thus, instead of demonstrating that he could reliably hold down a spot in the rotation, Duplantier rode the Reno shuttle, making a spot start here and there, but mostly pitching out of the bullpen. Even as a former top pitching prospect in the system, Duplantier's ceiling was never much beyond "future rotation piece who could peak higher if everything went right." Injury concerns, however, could relegate him to more of a "swingman who we never know if we can rely on" type of role.

Zac Gallen RHP   Born: 08/03/95   Age: 24   Bats: R   Throws: R   Height: 6'2"   Weight: 191   Origin: Round 3, 2016 Draft (#106 overall)

YEAR	TEAM	LVL	AGE	W	L	SV	G	GS	IP	H	HR	BB/9	K/9	K	GB%	BABIP	WHIP	ERA	DRA	WARP	MPH	FB%	WHF	CSP
2017	PMB	A+	21	5	2	0	9	9	55²	44	1	1.6	9.1	56	48%	.283	0.97	1.62	3.31	1.3				
2017	SFD	AA	21	4	5	0	13	13	71¹	76	8	2.4	5.3	42	42%	.292	1.33	3.79	4.43	0.6				
2017	MEM	AAA	21	1	1	0	4	4	20²	18	2	2.6	10.0	23	47%	.314	1.16	3.48	3.24	0.6				
2018	NWO	AAA	22	8	9	0	25	25	133¹	148	14	3.2	9.2	136	41%	.351	1.47	3.64	5.03	0.8				
2019	NWO	AAA	23	9	1	0	14	14	91¹	48	10	1.7	11.0	112	48%	.197	0.71	1.77	0.79	5.2				
2019	ARI	MLB	23	2	3	0	8	8	43²	37	5	3.7	10.9	53	44%	.305	1.26	2.89	3.43	1.1	95.5	50.7	14	45.6
2019	MIA	MLB	23	1	3	0	7	7	36¹	25	3	4.5	10.7	43	34%	.259	1.18	2.72	4.34	0.6	94.7	48.3	12.7	45.1
2020	ARI	MLB	24	7	6	0	21	21	112	95	14	3.3	10.5	130	41%	.293	1.22	3.48	3.67	2.6	94.9	51.1	13.8	46.7

Comparables: Erasmo Ramírez, Rafael Montero, Jake Odorizzi

Gallen's season was fascinating. He entered the year as your run-of-the-mill, command over stuff, polished former college arm profile that teams appreciate but hardly covet. He had four offerings that could qualify as "solid" but none that would be described as a true put-away pitch. Then his fastball went from the low to mid-90s, he started throwing more strikes than ever, dominated the PCL and got an early summer call-up to the bigs. That's interesting already! But wait, there's more. Gallen was flipped by the Marlins to the Diamondbacks at the trade deadline for Jazz Chisholm in one of those rare prospect-for-prospect challenge trades that harkens memories of Matt Garza and Delmon Young. He continued to shove in Arizona, and now looks the part of a solid No. 3 in a good rotation, with a shot to climb even higher. What a difference a year can make.

Kevin Ginkel RHP   Born: 03/24/94   Age: 26   Bats: L   Throws: R   Height: 6'4"   Weight: 210   Origin: Round 22, 2016 Draft (#659 overall)

YEAR	TEAM	LVL	AGE	W	L	SV	G	GS	IP	H	HR	BB/9	K/9	K	GB%	BABIP	WHIP	ERA	DRA	WARP	MPH	FB%	WHF	CSP
2017	YAK	A-	23	0	1	0	20	0	33²	26	1	2.9	13.1	49	38%	.347	1.10	3.48	3.90	0.4				
2017	KNC	A	23	1	1	0	6	0	6²	8	1	12.1	6.8	5	35%	.318	2.55	14.85	8.20	-0.3				
2018	VIS	A+	24	1	1	4	20	0	27¹	20	2	1.0	13.2	40	38%	.305	0.84	0.99	1.92	1.0				
2018	WTN	AA	24	5	0	5	34	0	42²	26	3	1.9	12.7	60	40%	.258	0.82	1.69	2.30	1.3				
2019	WTN	AA	25	1	2	5	14	0	16²	9	2	2.7	14.0	26	52%	.226	0.84	2.16	2.42	0.4				
2019	RNO	AAA	25	1	0	6	15	0	16²	10	2	4.3	19.4	36	39%	.381	1.08	1.62	1.51	0.8				
2019	ARI	MLB	25	3	0	2	25	0	24¹	15	2	3.3	10.4	28	34%	.232	0.99	1.48	3.80	0.4	95.3	54	15.4	42.5
2020	ARI	MLB	26	2	2	2	47	0	50	43	7	3.9	10.6	59	37%	.287	1.28	3.90	4.07	0.7	94.9	55	15.7	43.3

Comparables: Sergio Romo, AJ Ramos, Bobby Poyner

A 22nd-round pick, Ginkel never registered on even the keenest prospect radar. In 2017, he posted a 5.36 ERA in A-ball and was undoubtedly closer to finding work in Indy ball than the majors. But Ginkel went to work that offseason and emerged with an entirely new setup and release point. He spent the next two seasons laying waste to minor league hitters and was called up to the majors in August. The finished product is someone with a future in a major-league bullpen.

Junior Guerra RHP   Born: 01/16/85   Age: 35   Bats: R   Throws: R   Height: 6'0"   Weight: 205   Origin: International Free Agent, 2001

YEAR	TEAM	LVL	AGE	W	L	SV	G	GS	IP	H	HR	BB/9	K/9	K	GB%	BABIP	WHIP	ERA	DRA	WARP	MPH	FB%	WHF	CSP
2017	CSP	AAA	32	2	2	0	6	6	30	27	0	3.6	6.0	20	47%	.303	1.30	2.10	3.55	0.7				
2017	MIL	MLB	32	1	4	0	21	14	70¹	61	18	5.5	8.6	67	36%	.236	1.48	5.12	6.31	-0.6	94.3	64.8	11.8	41.4
2018	MIL	MLB	33	6	9	0	31	26	141	143	19	3.5	8.7	136	45%	.313	1.40	4.09	4.50	1.3	95.4	69	11.6	46.5
2019	MIL	MLB	34	9	5	3	72	0	83²	58	11	3.9	8.3	77	46%	.218	1.12	3.55	4.04	1.2	96.4	60.2	12	45.1
2020	ARI	MLB	35	3	3	0	53	0	56	50	9	4.0	8.7	54	46%	.276	1.34	4.21	4.34	0.7	94.3	64	11.6	43.9

Comparables: Pat Venditte, Cory Gearrin, Aquilino Lopez

Guerra's career continues to be a testament to the value of versatility. He ate critical innings out of the Milwaukee bullpen in 2019, just a year after starting 26 times. This wasn't your standard starter-to-middle-reliever conversion tale, either. Sometimes the Brewers would call on him to get past one right-hander, but more often he provided length: he recorded at least four outs 23 times, and finished two-plus innings 12 times. His reliability was critical for a Brewers bullpen that suffered injury after injury. Guerra has shown he will do anything to stick around, and that's an important attribute for any player—particularly a pitcher—to have. What'll grant him senior status is his ability to maintain his high-spin fastball and pair of swing-and-miss secondaries. Unfortunately, it'll have to come with the Diamondbacks organization, as the Brewers non-tendered Guerra after the season.

Yoshihisa Hirano RHP   Born: 03/08/84   Age: 36   Bats: R   Throws: R   Height: 6'1"   Weight: 185   Origin: International Free Agent, 2017

YEAR	TEAM	LVL	AGE	W	L	SV	G	GS	IP	H	HR	BB/9	K/9	K	GB%	BABIP	WHIP	ERA	DRA	WARP	MPH	FB%	WHF	CSP
2018	ARI	MLB	34	4	3	3	75	0	66¹	49	6	3.1	8.0	59	51%	.250	1.09	2.44	4.47	0.3	93.7	53.7	13.5	42.4
2019	ARI	MLB	35	5	5	1	62	0	53	51	7	3.7	10.4	61	46%	.314	1.38	4.75	4.58	0.4	92.8	47.9	15.1	40.9
2020	ARI	MLB	36	2	2	0	33	0	35	31	5	3.5	9.5	37	48%	.283	1.27	3.90	4.03	0.5	91.9	49.6	14	40.7

Comparables: Jason Motte, Joe Smith, Dan Miceli

Hirano took a step back in his second season. While his ERA rose by more than two runs, his rate stats stayed mostly the same and DRA suggests he was a bit unlucky—he increased his strikeout rate and continued to generate plenty of grounders. Hirano will never be confused for the kind of lights-out reliever who seems to grow on trees these days, but he's pretty much the poster child of "serviceable middle reliever."

Merrill Kelly RHP
Born: 10/14/88   Age: 31   Bats: R   Throws: R   Height: 6'2"   Weight: 190   Origin: Round 8, 2010 Draft (#251 overall)

YEAR	TEAM	LVL	AGE	W	L	SV	G	GS	IP	H	HR	BB/9	K/9	K	GB%	BABIP	WHIP	ERA	DRA	WARP	MPH	FB%	WHF	CSP
2019	ARI	MLB	30	13	14	0	32	32	183¹	184	29	2.8	7.8	158	43%	.293	1.31	4.42	4.97	1.6	94.2	46.2	10.5	48.5
2020	ARI	MLB	31	8	9	0	24	24	139	142	22	2.9	7.7	118	43%	.298	1.35	4.51	4.66	1.8	93.4	45.9	10.4	48.2

Comparables: Brandon Cumpton, Asher Wojciechowski, Taylor Jungmann

The Diamondbacks signed Kelly out of the KBO to a deal akin to what a back-end starter makes. He performed as advertised. He ate innings, didn't miss many bats, gave up a lot of hits, and kept his team in games but didn't come close to dominating. That he allows so many balls in play leaves his production in the hands of the Diamondbacks defense—a defense that ranked 18th in Park Adjusted Defensive Efficiency. Kelly was serviceable last year, but could look better if the Diamondbacks could provide more consistent glovework behind him.

Mike Leake RHP
Born: 11/12/87   Age: 32   Bats: R   Throws: R   Height: 5'10"   Weight: 170   Origin: Round 1, 2009 Draft (#8 overall)

YEAR	TEAM	LVL	AGE	W	L	SV	G	GS	IP	H	HR	BB/9	K/9	K	GB%	BABIP	WHIP	ERA	DRA	WARP	MPH	FB%	WHF	CSP
2017	SLN	MLB	29	7	12	0	26	26	154	169	19	2.0	6.0	103	55%	.306	1.32	4.21	4.20	2.4	92.1	58.1	8.5	48.8
2017	SEA	MLB	29	3	1	0	5	5	32	32	1	0.6	7.6	27	50%	.323	1.06	2.53	3.64	0.7	92.3	58.1	9.7	47.9
2018	SEA	MLB	30	10	10	0	31	31	185²	207	23	1.6	5.8	119	50%	.306	1.30	4.36	4.46	1.8	91.0	59.4	8.3	50.7
2019	SEA	MLB	31	9	8	0	22	22	137	153	26	1.2	6.6	100	48%	.297	1.26	4.27	5.87	-0.2	90.4	57.5	9.2	51.2
2019	ARI	MLB	31	3	3	0	10	10	60	74	15	1.2	4.1	27	46%	.291	1.37	4.35	9.04	-2.1	90.5	57.5	9.2	50.9
2020	ARI	MLB	32	6	7	0	19	19	103	118	18	1.8	5.8	66	47%	.300	1.34	4.92	5.09	0.9	90.1	57.8	8.7	49.9

Comparables: Bill Monbouquette, Mike Mussina, Frank Castillo

On July 21, 2010, the Cleveland Cavaliers signed forward Samardo Samuels, an undrafted free agent rookie out of Louisville who would appear in 36 games for the Cavs that year. It's a notable transaction because it came 13 days after The Decision, and was the franchise's first transaction after LeBron James rocked the sports world by announcing his intention to sign with the Miami Heat. On July 31, 2019, within the same hour that the Arizona Diamondbacks traded their ace, Zack Greinke, to the Houston Astros, they made a deal to acquire Leake from the Seattle Mariners. Leake proceeded to post a 2.33 ERA over his final seven starts for the D-backs after a rocky introduction. The point here is that there are worse ways to replace a departed star.

Corbin Martin RHP
Born: 12/28/95   Age: 24   Bats: R   Throws: R   Height: 6'2"   Weight: 200   Origin: Round 2, 2017 Draft (#56 overall)

YEAR	TEAM	LVL	AGE	W	L	SV	G	GS	IP	H	HR	BB/9	K/9	K	GB%	BABIP	WHIP	ERA	DRA	WARP	MPH	FB%	WHF	CSP
2017	TCV	A-	21	0	1	1	8	3	27²	20	1	2.6	12.4	38	63%	.297	1.01	2.60	2.42	0.8				
2018	BCA	A+	22	2	0	1	4	3	19	4	0	3.3	12.3	26	64%	.111	0.58	0.00	1.74	0.8				
2018	CCH	AA	22	7	2	0	21	18	103	84	7	2.4	8.4	96	48%	.277	1.09	2.97	3.34	2.3				
2019	ROU	AAA	23	2	1	0	9	8	37¹	33	2	4.3	10.8	45	42%	.341	1.37	3.13	3.00	1.3				
2019	HOU	MLB	23	1	1	0	5	5	19¹	23	8	5.6	8.8	19	43%	.283	1.81	5.59	7.18	-0.3	97.3	62.6	9.4	43.8
2020	ARI	MLB	24	1	2	0	14	3	24	27	5	4.2	8.1	22	42%	.314	1.60	6.03	5.88	-0.1	97.1	64.5	9.7	45.2

Comparables: Jess Todd, Aaron Blair, Andrew Moore

Martin went from fringe starting pitching prospect to a cup of coffee in the bigs rather quickly, as he repeated his success at Double-A in 2018 in the hitter-friendly PCL. Though he struggled in his five mid-season big-league starts, Martin showed enough promise to maintain his projected role as a future mid-rotation piece. Once he returns in 2021 from Tommy John surgery, that is. Factor in his move from the Pitcher Factory that is Houston to Arizona and Martin's future goes from "high floor" to "well, he's a pitcher" all too quickly.

Robbie Ray LHP
Born: 10/01/91   Age: 28   Bats: L   Throws: L   Height: 6'2"   Weight: 195   Origin: Round 12, 2010 Draft (#356 overall)

YEAR	TEAM	LVL	AGE	W	L	SV	G	GS	IP	H	HR	BB/9	K/9	K	GB%	BABIP	WHIP	ERA	DRA	WARP	MPH	FB%	WHF	CSP
2017	ARI	MLB	25	15	5	0	28	28	162	116	23	3.9	12.1	218	42%	.267	1.15	2.89	3.06	4.6	96.5	59.3	15.3	44.2
2018	ARI	MLB	26	6	2	0	24	24	123²	97	19	5.1	12.0	165	41%	.292	1.35	3.93	3.99	1.9	96.2	53.9	13.8	44.8
2019	ARI	MLB	27	12	8	0	33	33	174¹	150	30	4.3	12.1	235	41%	.306	1.34	4.34	4.09	3.2	94.6	52.8	14.8	45.4
2020	ARI	MLB	28	9	8	0	26	26	137	113	21	4.2	11.8	180	40%	.293	1.29	3.85	3.98	2.8	95.0	55	14.7	45.2

Comparables: Eduardo Rodriguez, Gio Gonzalez, A.J. Cole

Ray continues to be an enigma. If you look up the league leaders in K/9, you'll find him in third place, just behind Gerrit Cole and Max Scherzer and just ahead of Justin Verlander. That is elite, bat-missing stuff. Now, check out the league leaders in BB/9. There's Ray again! Second place, right behind Dakota Hudson and in front of Julio Teheran. That is elite, no-idea-where-the-hell-the-ball-is-going stuff. You generally don't hear about Three True Outcome pitchers, but Ray is making a case for the title after he surrendered a career-high in home runs to go along with those whiffs and walks. Ray's pure stuff is tantalizing, but his lack of control takes him from a top-of-the-rotation arm to frustrating-but-still-valuable mid-rotation type.

Héctor Rondón RHP
Born: 02/26/88   Age: 32   Bats: R   Throws: R   Height: 6'3"   Weight: 230   Origin: International Free Agent, 2004

YEAR	TEAM	LVL	AGE	W	L	SV	G	GS	IP	H	HR	BB/9	K/9	K	GB%	BABIP	WHIP	ERA	DRA	WARP	MPH	FB%	WHF	CSP
2017	CHN	MLB	29	4	1	0	61	0	57¹	50	10	3.1	10.8	69	48%	.292	1.22	4.24	3.29	1.2	98.6	61.6	13	47.7
2018	HOU	MLB	30	2	5	15	63	0	59	58	4	3.1	10.2	67	48%	.340	1.32	3.20	2.81	1.4	99.2	61.7	14.7	48.9
2019	HOU	MLB	31	3	2	0	62	1	60²	56	10	3.0	7.1	48	51%	.263	1.25	3.71	5.72	-0.2	98.4	60.1	10.8	47.3
2020	ARI	MLB	32	2	2	0	33	0	35	32	5	3.0	8.4	33	49%	.283	1.26	4.01	4.11	0.4	97.7	60.4	12.5	47.5

Comparables: Bryan Shaw, Fernando Salas, Greg McMichael

Did you see the J.T. Realmuto eye roll gif? That's essentially what A.J. Hinch's soul was doing every time he went to put Rondón in the game in 2019. It's hard to blame him, as his double-digit K/9 rates of years past completely vanished. Oddly, his overall performance didn't suffer much, ending the season with essentially the same number of walks, runs, and innings as he did when he was the Astros closer in 2018. Maybe Hinch saw something we didn't, or maybe Rondón said something mean about pitching coach Brent Strom's shoes and never recovered. Regardless, he'll just take his fastball-slider combo to the next team that wants him and we'll be left to wonder why perfectly good relievers are so hard to appreciate.

Bo Takahashi RHP   Born: 01/23/97   Age: 23   Bats: R   Throws: R   Height: 6'0"   Weight: 197   Origin: International Free Agent, 2014

YEAR	TEAM	LVL	AGE	W	L	SV	G	GS	IP	H	HR	BB/9	K/9	K	GB%	BABIP	WHIP	ERA	DRA	WARP	MPH	FB%	WHF	CSP
2017	KNC	A	20	0	2	0	4	4	16¹	16	3	2.8	7.7	14	42%	.260	1.29	3.86	4.45	0.2				
2017	VIS	A+	20	7	10	0	20	20	109²	107	13	3.0	7.6	93	37%	.294	1.31	5.33	4.63	0.8				
2018	VIS	A+	21	3	3	0	9	9	47²	45	4	1.9	10.0	53	44%	.331	1.15	3.02	4.28	0.6				
2018	WTN	AA	21	3	3	0	14	14	73	65	12	2.5	9.5	77	35%	.286	1.16	4.68	4.30	0.9				
2019	WTN	AA	22	9	7	0	23	23	118²	108	12	2.9	7.9	104	42%	.294	1.23	3.72	5.07	-0.2				
2020	ARI	MLB	23	1	1	0	11	0	11	12	2	3.7	7.4	9	39%	.291	1.45	5.20	5.32	0.0				

Comparables: Jonathan Hernández, Sean Reid-Foley, Robert Gsellman

Throughout the course of major-league history, there have been countless players who have toiled away in the minor leagues waiting for a shot that never came. "It was like coming this close to your dreams...and then watching them brush past," said Burt Lancaster as Moonlight Graham in "Field of Dreams." Takahashi spent 5 1/2 years in the Diamondbacks' organization after signing as an international free agent as a 17-year-old in 2013. On August 18 he was called up from Double-A only to be sent back down two days later without making an appearance. The Brazilian has never much registered on the prospect radar, but has been a solid organizational soldier, one who managed a fine season in Double-A. Here's to his next major-league opportunity.

Taijuan Walker RHP   Born: 08/13/92   Age: 27   Bats: R   Throws: R   Height: 6'4"   Weight: 235   Origin: Round 1, 2010 Draft (#43 overall)

YEAR	TEAM	LVL	AGE	W	L	SV	G	GS	IP	H	HR	BB/9	K/9	K	GB%	BABIP	WHIP	ERA	DRA	WARP	MPH	FB%	WHF	CSP
2017	ARI	MLB	24	9	9	0	28	28	157¹	148	17	3.5	8.4	146	50%	.291	1.33	3.49	4.90	1.2	95.9	59.1	9.7	46.7
2018	ARI	MLB	25	0	0	0	3	3	13	15	1	3.5	6.2	9	45%	.341	1.54	3.46	5.15	0.0	96.5	70.5	7.1	53.8
2019	ARI	MLB	26	0	0	0	1	1	1	1	0	0.0	9.0	1	33%	.333	1.00	0.00			94.3	66.7	13.3	43.8
2020	ARI	MLB	27	2	2	0	33	0	35	36	5	3.6	7.2	28	39%	.296	1.41	4.74	4.80	0.2	95.5	61	9.6	48.4

Comparables: Julio Teheran, Tyler Skaggs, Matt Cain

The "most hyped finale" award of 2019 goes to *Game of Thrones*. Coming in second place was the final game of the Diamondbacks' season, in which they trotted out Walker to make his first start since undergoing Tommy John surgery in early 2018. Like the show, Walker continues to entice both fans with his "what's going to happen next?" potential. Also like the show, given years of unfulfilled hype, it seems increasingly likely we'll be left scratching our heads and wondering what the hell happened. Something we do know? Walker's time with the Diamondbacks and *Game of Thrones* both came to an unsatisfying close in 2019.

Luke Weaver RHP   Born: 08/21/93   Age: 26   Bats: R   Throws: R   Height: 6'2"   Weight: 170   Origin: Round 1, 2014 Draft (#27 overall)

YEAR	TEAM	LVL	AGE	W	L	SV	G	GS	IP	H	HR	BB/9	K/9	K	GB%	BABIP	WHIP	ERA	DRA	WARP	MPH	FB%	WHF	CSP
2017	MEM	AAA	23	10	2	0	15	15	77²	63	3	2.2	8.8	76	46%	.291	1.06	2.55	2.48	2.7				
2017	SLN	MLB	23	7	2	0	13	10	60¹	59	7	2.5	10.7	72	51%	.335	1.26	3.88	3.19	1.6	95.8	60.2	10.8	50
2018	SLN	MLB	24	7	11	0	30	25	136¹	150	19	3.6	8.0	121	44%	.318	1.50	4.95	4.62	1.1	96.2	57.7	10.4	48.9
2019	ARI	MLB	25	4	3	0	12	12	64¹	55	6	2.0	9.7	69	42%	.292	1.07	2.94	3.56	1.5	96.3	52.1	12.2	47.3
2020	ARI	MLB	26	7	7	0	21	21	116	113	16	3.0	9.3	119	42%	.306	1.31	4.15	4.32	1.9	95.8	57.5	11.2	49.4

Comparables: Rafael Montero, Clay Buchholz, Kevin Gausman

The Diamondbacks bet big on Weaver's future as a starter when they made him one of the primary returns in an offseason trade that sent Paul Goldschmidt to St. Louis. Weaver looked every bit the part through 11 starts. Two new pitches aided that resurgence—a cutter and curveball gave him the well-rounded repertoire necessary for surviving multiple trips through the order—and through late May he looked more like a potential front-line starter than he ever did in St. Louis. The problem being that those 11 starts is all we got. Weaver went down with strains to his flexor pronator and UCL. After an initial scare, Weaver avoided the dreaded TJ fate that befalls so many and, with an expected return to health, the Diamondbacks have every reason to keep their chips in the middle of the table when it comes to their new emerging ace.

Taylor Widener RHP   Born: 10/24/94   Age: 25   Bats: L   Throws: R   Height: 6'0"   Weight: 195   Origin: Round 12, 2016 Draft (#368 overall)

YEAR	TEAM	LVL	AGE	W	L	SV	G	GS	IP	H	HR	BB/9	K/9	K	GB%	BABIP	WHIP	ERA	DRA	WARP	MPH	FB%	WHF	CSP
2017	TAM	A+	22	7	8	0	27	27	119¹	87	5	3.8	9.7	129	45%	.273	1.15	3.39	3.05	3.1				
2018	WTN	AA	23	5	8	0	26	25	137¹	99	12	2.8	11.5	176	37%	.275	1.03	2.75	3.01	3.7				
2019	RNO	AAA	24	6	7	0	23	23	100	133	23	3.7	9.8	109	32%	.381	1.74	8.10	6.72	0.0				
2020	ARI	MLB	25	1	1	0	11	0	11	11	2	3.6	8.8	11	34%	.305	1.42	4.77	4.84	0.1				

Comparables: Jake Arrieta, Dean Deetz, Tyler Thornburg

Pitching is hard. Pitching with a rabbit/juiced/rocket ball is harder. Pitching in the notoriously hitter-friendly PCL with a juiced baseball? Good freaking luck. Widener, 2018's big riser, is still very much a pitching prospect, but his Triple-A ERA looks like a Central Michigan area code. It looked like Widener was destined for a mid-season call-up to the big club when the year began, but an early-season swoon put that thought to rest quickly. He rebounded to put together a solid second half, but the initial carnage left an unsightly final line in its wake. Consider it a setback, but not one so harmful as to keep him out of the Diamondbacks' future plans.

Alex Young LHP Born: 09/09/93 Age: 26 Bats: L Throws: L Height: 6'2" Weight: 205 Origin: Round 2, 2015 Draft (#43 overall)

YEAR	TEAM	LVL	AGE	W	L	SV	G	GS	IP	H	HR	BB/9	K/9	K	GB%	BABIP	WHIP	ERA	DRA	WARP	MPH	FB%	WHF	CSP
2017	WTN	AA	23	9	9	0	27	24	137	125	12	3.8	6.8	103	47%	.275	1.34	3.68	5.04	0.2				
2018	WTN	AA	24	5	1	0	9	9	50²	49	3	2.8	8.5	48	40%	.319	1.28	3.91	4.45	0.5				
2018	RNO	AAA	24	5	4	0	20	12	80	99	12	2.6	6.9	61	44%	.339	1.52	5.96	5.66	-0.1				
2019	RNO	AAA	25	4	3	0	20	8	54²	66	6	4.3	10.5	64	52%	.375	1.68	6.09	4.35	1.1				
2019	ARI	MLB	25	7	5	0	17	15	83¹	72	14	2.9	7.7	71	50%	.249	1.19	3.56	4.32	1.3	90.7	36.5	13	45
2020	ARI	MLB	26	3	3	0	24	8	58	55	9	3.2	8.1	52	48%	.280	1.30	4.24	4.46	0.8	90.3	37.1	13.2	45.8

Comparables: Taylor Rogers, Matt Hall, David Buchanan

Once considered a potential fast-moving starting pitching prospect, Young had all but fallen off the prospect radar when the Diamondbacks called him up to make what was presumed to be a spot start in late June. He was walking more than four batters per nine in Reno at the time, after all. Young wound up making 15 starts for the Snakes down the stretch and looked damn serviceable doing so, even spinning a 12-strikeout gem against the Reds in early September. Aside from that start, Young didn't miss a whole lot of bats and doesn't have the type of stuff that portends a future in the rotation, but at the very least he proved over half of a season that he can get major-league hitters out. And in doing so, he put himself back on the map as a multi-inning bullpen guy or rotational depth piece.

LINEOUTS

Hitters

HITTER	POS	TEAM	LVL	AGE	PA	R	2B	3B	HR	RBI	BB	K	SB	CS	AVG/OBP/SLG	DRC+	VORP	BABIP	BRR	FRAA	WARP
Blaze Alexander	SS	KNC	A	20	406	56	12	4	7	47	42	89	14	4	.262/.355/.382	120	24.8	.324	0.2	SS(49): 1.9, 2B(31): -0.5	2.5
Abraham Almonte	CF	ARI	MLB	30	38	11	3	1	1	4	7	8	0	0	.290/.421/.548	94	0.7	.364	2.1	RF(9): 0.2, CF(3): -0.2	0.3
	CF	RNO	AAA	30	382	78	33	4	17	59	60	70	12	3	.270/.382/.558	120	24.3	.294	0.5	CF(58): -2.9, RF(31): -1.6	1.8
Jorge Barrosa	OF	YAK	A-	18	252	25	12	2	1	26	21	32	8	4	.251/.335/.336	95	8.7	.289	-2.2	CF(37): 1.6, RF(19): 1.7	0.7
Corbin Carroll	OF	YAK	A-	18	49	13	3	4	0	6	5	12	2	0	.326/.408/.581	116	6.4	.452	0.8	CF(11): 0.0	0.3
	OF	DIA	Rk	18	137	23	6	3	2	14	24	29	16	1	.288/.409/.450	161	22.7	.366	2.7	CF(23): -0.1, LF(5): -0.6	1.3
Kevin Cron	1B	ARI	MLB	26	78	12	4	0	6	16	4	28	0	1	.211/.269/.521	83	0.0	.237	-0.1	1B(12): -0.4, 3B(1): 0.0	0.0
	1B	RNO	AAA	26	377	81	20	1	38	105	61	77	1	2	.331/.449/.777	178	42.8	.328	-2.3	1B(68): 8.2, 3B(15): -0.3	4.5
Tristin English	1B	YAK	A-	22	216	32	12	2	7	30	13	24	1	0	.290/.356/.482	139	16.5	.299	1.5	3B(21): -1.8, RF(15): -0.4	1.1
Jeferson Espinal	CF	DIA	Rk	17	43	6	1	0	0	7	8	11	4	1	.286/.419/.314	127	4.3	.417	0.7	CF(7): 0.7, LF(2): -0.2	0.4
Dominic Fletcher	OF	KNC	A	21	239	33	14	1	5	28	22	50	1	1	.318/.389/.463	145	21.1	.396	2.3	CF(25): -2.1, RF(22): 4.0	2.2
Glenallen Hill Jr.	SS	DIA	Rk	18	181	22	4	6	3	18	17	63	19	5	.206/.289/.363	53	-1.8	.316	-1.3	2B(39): 3.2	-0.1
Caleb Joseph	C	ARI	MLB	33	41	5	2	0	0	3	1	10	0	0	.211/.250/.263	72	0.6	.286	-0.4	C(16): 0.5, P(2): 0.0	0.1
	C	RNO	AAA	33	179	29	12	1	7	26	13	44	0	0	.265/.324/.481	74	10.7	.319	-0.8	C(42): -3.6, 1B(2): 0.0	0.0
Domingo Leyba	2B	RNO	AAA	23	498	85	37	3	19	77	32	78	0	2	.300/.351/.519	92	23.9	.325	2.9	SS(66): -4.0, 2B(42): 2.9	1.7
	2B	ARI	MLB	23	30	6	2	1	0	5	4	9	0	0	.280/.367/.440	84	0.4	.412	0.0	2B(8): 0.4, SS(2): 0.1	0.1
Wyatt Mathisen	3B	DIA	Rk	25	31	4	3	0	0	3	6	3	1	0	.348/.516/.478	201	6.1	.400	0.3	3B(4): 0.2, 2B(1): 0.2	0.4
	3B	RNO	AAA	25	345	72	19	1	23	61	39	84	1	0	.283/.403/.601	122	30.9	.318	0.1	3B(59): 0.2, 2B(20): 0.6	2.2
Wilderd Patino	OF	MSO	Rk+	17	40	6	1	2	0	4	2	14	1	1	.229/.300/.371	43	1.2	.364	0.1		-0.1
	OF	DIA	Rk	17	125	18	4	3	1	21	11	32	13	3	.349/.440/.472	147	13.3	.462	1.0	CF(22): 1.1, RF(5): -0.3	1.1
Andy Yerzy	1B	YAK	A-	20	272	30	11	0	6	34	37	61	1	1	.220/.331/.345	92	3.5	.271	-2.2	1B(55): 0.9	-0.1
	1B	KNC	A	20	136	8	5	0	0	5	9	39	0	0	.104/.176/.144	5	-16.3	.151	-0.9	C(17): 0.3, 1B(14): -1.8	-1.2
Andy Young	INF	WTN	AA	25	263	36	15	2	8	28	18	53	1	1	.260/.363/.453	128	18.2	.305	-0.3	2B(47): -2.5, SS(8): -1.1	1.2
	INF	RNO	AAA	25	277	53	10	3	21	53	24	68	2	2	.280/.373/.611	110	21.2	.305	0.9	SS(25): 1.3, 3B(23): -1.0	1.5

Blaze Alexander is fast (yes, really), touts a big arm and has a solid glove that should stick at short. How his bat progresses as he moves up the ladder will be the key to the former 11th-round pick going from being an intriguing prospect to a legitimate one. ⓧ **Abraham Almonte**'s nickname is, according to Baseball Reference, "El Varon," which translates to The Man. After playing for five teams in seven major league seasons, he should consider becoming "The Emergency Plan." ⓧ **Jorge Barrosa** held his own in Low-A and has the defensive prowess and on-base skill to project as solid regular down the road. ⓧ **Corbin Carroll** was one of the better prep bats in this year's draft and hit the snot out of the ball in his professional debut. He has a pure and advanced stroke and can take the ball to all fields, and has the tools to stick in center. ⓧ **Kevin Cron** got his first taste of big-league action and promptly struck out in nearly half of his plate appearances. At age 26, he's likely to shed the "C.J.'s brother" label, which is considerably less impressive than, say, being Corey Seager's brother. ⓧ A third-round pick out of the Georgia Institute of Technology, **Tristin English** didn't put any particular spin on his professional debut. He straight waxed the Northwest League. ⓧ Precocious slash-and-burn outfield prospect **Jeferson Espinal** arrived stateside just two months after his 17th birthday, where he showed enough tools to receive the prized "helium prospect" tag. ⓧ **Dominic Fletcher** does virtually everything well but has no real standout tool. The fourth-round pick out of Arkansas and brother of David can play all three outfield positions. He projects as a likely fourth outfielder at the next level. ⓧ The Diamondbacks inked **Alvin Guzmán** to a $1.85M deal during the 2018 international signing period. He's yet to play stateside, but is pretty much your prototypical raw, toolsy, J2 outfielder who is two years away from being two years away. ⓧ The Diamondbacks selected **Glenallen Hill Jr.** in the fourth round of the 2019 draft, and the 19-year-old shortstop shares his father's name, but at 5-foot-9, 160 pounds, literally nothing else. ⓧ **Caleb Joseph** has hung around the bigs thanks to his sterling reputation as a defender behind the plate, but even that can't salvage an increasingly bleak batting line. ⓧ The shine has faded a bit on **Domingo Leyba**'s star after injuries plagued the former top prospect, but he acquitted himself well in a cup of coffee at the majors and could stick as a backup infielder. ⓧ He might have spent the last year in Reno kicking all around the dirt and knocking guys around, but **Wyatt Mathisen** is less a old west gunslinger (despite his name) and more an up-and-down guy who benefitted from a crazy offensive environment. ⓧ Stop if you've heard this one before: **Wilderd Patino** is a tooled up, up-the-middle prospect who was born after the turn of the century and could be the Next Big Prospect. ⓧ Something weird happened on **Andy Yerzy**'s way toward becoming one of those bat-first catching prospects with questions about whether he'd stick behind the plate: He stopped hitting. ⊗ The quaternary piece of the Diamondbacks' return for Paul Goldschmidt, **Andy Young** acquitted himself well at the upper levels of the minors. He plays all over the dirt and as a 37th-round pick a brief summation of his scouting report must have read something like "Young, Andy: Restless."

Pitchers

PITCHER	TEAM	LVL	AGE	W	L	SV	G	GS	IP	H	HR	BB/9	K/9	K	GB%	BABIP	WHIP	ERA	DRA	WARP	MPH	FB%	WHF	CSP
Taylor Clarke	VIS	A+	26	1	0	0	1	1	6	3	0	0.0	4.5	3	71%	.176	0.50	0.00	2.88	0.2				
	RNO	AAA	26	3	1	0	8	8	36²	41	6	4.2	6.9	28	36%	.312	1.58	6.63	4.95	0.6				
	ARI	MLB	26	5	5	1	23	15	84²	86	23	3.2	7.2	68	40%	.264	1.37	5.31	6.46	-0.7	95.3	53.2	11.1	45.4
Stefan Crichton	RNO	AAA	27	4	3	1	36	0	57¹	52	4	2.4	8.2	52	58%	.300	1.17	3.61	2.45	2.1				
	ARI	MLB	27	1	0	0	28	0	30¹	23	3	2.4	9.8	33	52%	.260	1.02	3.56	3.72	0.5	94.6	63.6	11.1	49.9
Luis Frias	YAK	A-	21	3	3	0	10	10	49²	36	0	3.1	13.0	72	42%	.340	1.07	1.99	3.56	0.9				
	KNC	A	21	3	1	0	6	6	26²	22	1	4.1	9.8	29	37%	.300	1.27	4.39	4.78	0.1				
Josh Green	VIS	A+	23	9	1	0	14	14	78	69	1	1.5	8.0	69	67%	.324	1.05	1.73	3.94	1.0				
	WTN	AA	23	2	4	0	8	8	48¹	61	2	1.5	6.0	32	67%	.371	1.43	4.28	6.09	-0.7				
Greg Holland	HAR	AA	33	1	0	0	8	0	9	4	0	3.0	9.0	9	41%	.182	0.78	0.00	3.44	0.1				
	ARI	MLB	33	1	2	17	40	0	35²	25	5	6.1	10.3	41	45%	.244	1.37	4.54	4.46	0.3	94.0	47.3	12.5	42.3
Drey Jameson	YAK	A-	21	0	0	0	8	8	11²	14	1	6.9	9.3	12	42%	.371	1.97	6.17	7.64	-0.3				
Levi Kelly	KNC	A	20	5	1	0	22	22	100¹	72	4	3.5	11.3	126	48%	.292	1.11	2.15	3.17	2.4				
Matt Koch	RNO	AAA	28	5	10	0	21	17	100	135	21	2.7	7.3	81	42%	.345	1.65	7.38	5.55	1.1				
	ARI	MLB	28	0	0	0	9	0	20²	29	8	1.7	3.9	9	36%	.300	1.60	9.15	8.69	-0.7	94.2	48.1	6.6	46.4
Yoan López	ARI	MLB	26	2	7	1	70	0	60²	52	11	2.5	6.2	42	44%	.233	1.14	3.41	5.17	0.1	98.2	57.1	10.2	47.9
Brennan Malone	DIA	Rk	18	1	2	0	6	3	7	4	0	6.4	9.0	7	29%	.176	1.29	5.14	3.32	0.2				
Ryne Nelson	YAK	A-	21	0	1	0	10	7	18²	15	1	4.8	12.5	26	46%	.382	1.34	2.89	4.32	0.2				
Joel Payamps	WTN	AA	25	3	4	0	7	7	40²	40	2	0.4	8.6	39	49%	.325	1.03	2.88	3.76	0.6				
	RNO	AAA	25	2	2	0	8	8	38	41	6	3.8	7.1	30	43%	.307	1.50	4.97	4.45	0.8				
	ARI	MLB	25	0	0	0	2	0	4	4	0	6.8	6.8	3	18%	.364	1.75	4.50	5.68	0.0	95.1	59.1	7.6	51.4
Robby Scott	RNO	AAA	29	3	0	1	41	0	48	42	10	6.6	11.4	61	30%	.278	1.60	6.94	4.39	0.9				
	ARI	MLB	29	1	0	0	11	0	7¹	8	1	8.6	11.0	9	33%	.350	2.05	4.91	4.86	0.0	89.1	50.6	11	48.1
Jimmie Sherfy	RNO	AAA	27	2	3	12	35	0	35	32	2	5.4	12.6	49	41%	.361	1.51	3.60	3.22	1.0				
	ARI	MLB	27	1	0	1	17	0	18¹	23	4	2.5	10.8	22	22%	.373	1.53	5.89	5.90	-0.1	94.9	37.3	12.3	47.3
Riley Smith	WTN	AA	24	4	4	0	13	13	71¹	65	6	2.0	7.8	62	51%	.296	1.14	2.27	3.90	0.9				
	RNO	AAA	24	2	2	0	12	12	62²	85	15	2.9	6.9	48	44%	.348	1.68	6.89	6.89	-0.1				
Matt Tabor	KNC	A	20	5	4	0	21	21	95¹	79	6	1.5	9.5	101	44%	.290	1.00	2.93	3.30	2.1				
Emilio Vargas	DIA	Rk	22	0	2	0	3	3	10¹	9	1	1.7	10.5	12	36%	.333	1.06	4.35	2.36	0.4				
	WTN	AA	22	5	3	0	17	17	85²	74	10	2.4	7.4	70	44%	.261	1.13	3.78	4.52	0.5				
Blake Walston	YAK	A-	18	0	0	0	3	3	6	6	0	3.0	9.0	6	41%	.353	1.33	3.00	5.95	-0.1				

Silvino Bracho avoided yet another season of riding the bus between Phoenix and Reno, but unfortunately it was because Tommy John surgery cost him all of it. ⊗ **Taylor Clarke** is pretty much the epitome of a sixth starter, and given his nondescript name and role you'd be forgiven for forgetting he exists. If you did, though, you'd also be forgetting his wife, whose name is Taylor Clarke. ⊗ **Stefan Crichton** was called up to Arizona six different times during the season and until rosters expanded in September, never spent more than eight consecutive days there. ⊗ **Luis Frias** burst onto the scene with a dominating performance in the Northwest League and looks the part of a future starter if he can develop another offering to go with his plus-fastball and plus-curve. ⊗ Arizona transitioned **Josh Green** from a reliever to a starter this year and he promptly dominated High-A and held his own in a late-season audition at Double-A. The former 14th-round pick doesn't miss a ton of bats, but his sinking fastball induces a lot of grounders. ⊗ **Tommy Henry** grew up in Michigan and, unlike Derek Jeter, honored his commitment to play collegiately at the University of Michigan. He has an 80-grade pitch face and the type of stuff that will likely confine him to a bullpen role long term. ⊗ Baseball Reference shows **Greg Holland**'s nickname as "The Dirty South." He earned the moniker last season as his 16 percent walk rate meant there were few clean innings, and as a result, his numbers went south. ⊗ **Drey Jameson** was taken as a comp pick first-rounder and signed under-slot after some reported issues with his physical. He's an undersized right-hander with a busy delivery who has a lot to overcome to stick as a starter. ⊗ **Levi Kelly** took a step forward by missing a whole lotta bats in the Midwest League. He has three potential above-average offerings but might end up in the bullpen. ⊗ **Matt Koch's** surname is pronounced "cook," as in the present verb form of "cooked"—or, the answer to the question: "how'd Koch look today?" ⊗ Making the majors meant **Yoan López** could finally transition from the "Dave Stewart gave this dude $8.25 million?!" phase of his career to the "fairly anonymous middle reliever" phase. At least he throws real hard. ⊗ **Brennan Malone** has the look, velocity, and wipeout breaker of a future starter. There's a ton of development and projection left for the first-rounder. ⊗ **Ryne Nelson** was taken in the second round out of Oregon and looks like the second coming of Tyler Clippard, both in terms of his delivery and his specs. ⊗ **Joel Payamps** was added to the Diamondbacks' 40-man roster last offseason and seemed a good candidate to factor into their bullpen plans, but a broken foot limited him to just 17 appearances total between the minors and majors. ⊗ **Robby Scott** went from major-league caliber arm dominating Triple-A for a World Series champion to someone who not only couldn't crack the bullpen in Arizona, but couldn't find the plate in Reno, either. ⊗ **Jimmie Sherfy** has never been able to harness his funky delivery enough to deliver consistent results. Plus, his name sounds like a clothing brand for surfers. ⊗ LSU draftees finished second and fourth in AL MVP voting in 2019. No pressure, **Riley Smith**. Then again, as a 24th-round pick, just making the majors might be a comparable achievement for the right-hander. ⊗ **Matt Tabor** throws strikes, which is important because none of his offerings are considered above-average. ⊗ **Emilio Vargas** emerged as a viable starting pitching prospect in 2018 and picked up where he left off in his second go at Double-A. He has an electric fastball and could work his way into a rotation if he continues to develop his secondaries. ⊗ **Blake Walston** is a tall lefty with a clean arm action and the type of athleticism you expect from a former quarterback and first-round pick.

ATLANTA BRAVES

Essay by Robert O'Connell

Player comments by Demetrius Bell, David Lee and BP staff

Trying to sum up a season with a play is daffy. It requires swapping out nuance and accuracy for narrative tidiness, giving into the convenient logic of turning points and crucial moments. In baseball—162 games, some 300 pitches in each of them, countless veers of defense and decision-making and baserunning—the impulse is even more ridiculous. In no game is a player less reducible to a moment.

So—well, here goes.

The moment of Ronald Acuña, Jr.'s spectacular second season that sticks in my mind came in early May, during a game at Dodger Stadium. The Braves trailed 3-0 when Clayton Kershaw threw Acuña a lumpy curve, low but not low enough. Acuña waited on it, barreled it, held a one-handed—*that's f***ing right*—follow-through as it went backspinning over the right field wall. It was his seventh home run of the season, just the 33rd of his career.

The homer didn't end up much mattering; the Braves lost, 9-4. Nor was it all that stylistically distinct. Just eight months into his big-league career, Acuña was by last spring already known for his all-fields power and his ability to get to pitches in the depths of the strike zone. He had already hit six homers on the season, emerging as the most promising young player, production-wise and entertainment-value-wise, in the sport. He stole bases and laced doubles and cracked moonshots and let go of throws that sprouted rocket-boosters. He had all five tools and a baby face. He dropped his bat coolly and ran out from under his helmet even more coolly.

Still, there was something about the homer off Kershaw. Part of it, to be sure, was the generational aspect, the immortal-for-now kid versus the now-mortal legend. But the greater part was the basic visible makeup of the play. A hanging curve, especially one presented to a slugger in the heady environment of the late-2010s, is a chance to pull the ball, to get the swing started early and the hips involved heavily. But Acuña had waited on it. He'd held his hands back, kept his weight from spilling out over the plate, made hitting coaches swoon. *Then* he became the dynamo. The ball went over the opposite-field wall about as fast and hard

BRAVES PROSPECTUS
2019 W-L: 97-65, 1ST IN NL EAST

Pythag	.567	9th	B-Age	27.9	19th
RS/G	5.28	7th	P-Age	27.1	5th
RA/G	4.59	12th	Salary	$128.2M	14th
DRC+	104	7th	M$/MW	$2.4M	27th
DRA	4.39	10th	IL Days	947	9th
FIP	4.34	13th	$ on IL	16%	18th
DER	.698	21st			

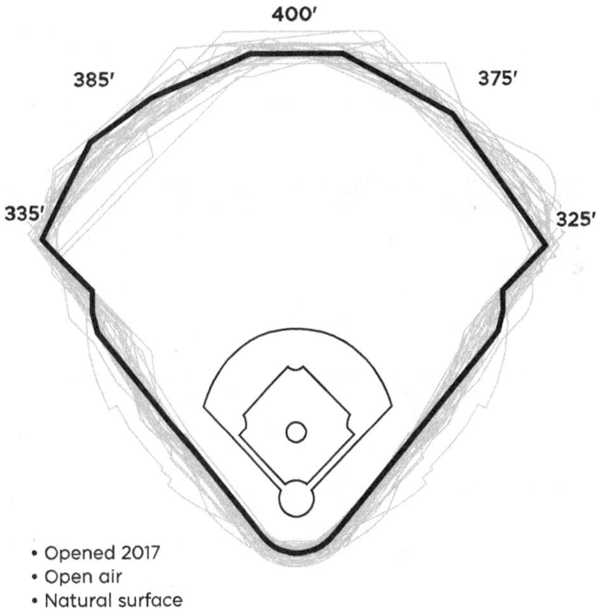

400'
385' 375'
335' 325'

- Opened 2017
- Open air
- Natural surface
- Fence profile: 6' to 16'

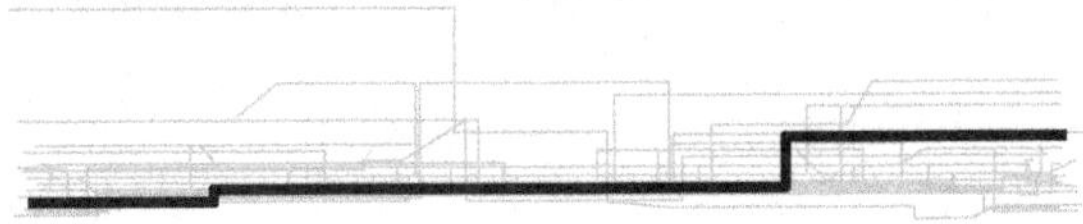

Three-Year Park Factors

Runs	Runs/RH	Runs/LH	HR/RH	HR/LH
102	101	105	94	100

Top Hitter WARP	6.1 Ronald Acuña Jr.
Top Pitcher WARP	4.8 Mike Soroka
Top Prospect	Cristian Pache

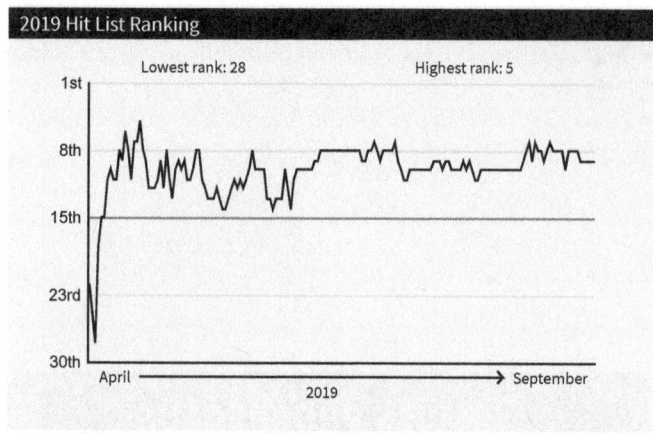

2019 Hit List Ranking

Lowest rank: 28   Highest rank: 5

1st
8th
15th
23rd
30th

April   2019   September

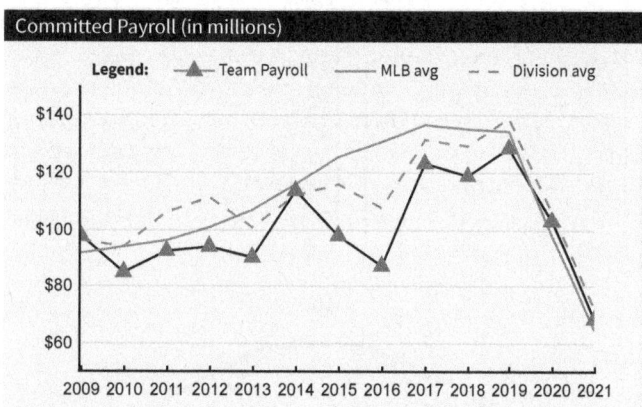

Committed Payroll (in millions)

Legend: —▲— Team Payroll   —— MLB avg   - - - Division avg

$140
$120
$100
$80
$60

2009 2010 2011 2012 2013 2014 2015 2016 2017 2018 2019 2020 2021

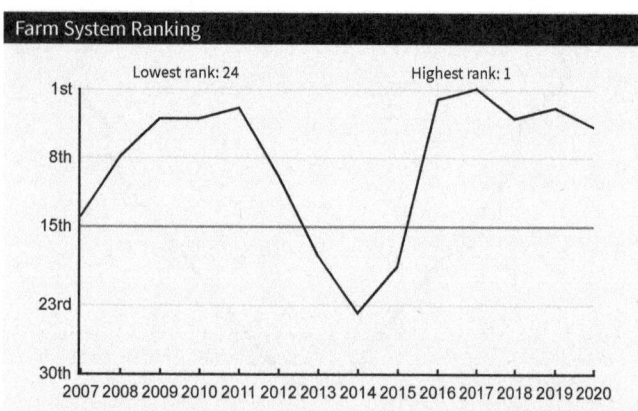

Farm System Ranking

Lowest rank: 24   Highest rank: 1

1st
8th
15th
23rd
30th

2007 2008 2009 2010 2011 2012 2013 2014 2015 2016 2017 2018 2019 2020

Personnel

Executive Vice President, General Manager
Alex Anthopoulos

Vice President, Baseball Operations & Assistant General Manager
Perry Minasian

Assistant General Manager, Research and Development
Jason Paré

Assistant General Manager, Major League Operations
Alex Tamin

Special Assistant to the General Manager
Mike Fast

Manager
Brian Snitker

BP Alumni
Mike Fast
Jason Paré
Ronit Shah
Noah Woodward
Smith Brickner

as any baseball goes anywhere. It was an instance of fundamentals-as-performance, a kind of flashy citation. He did it because he could.

Acuña, of course, serves as the centerpiece for a resurgent Braves franchise stocked well with young power arms and position players, and seasoned tastefully with veteran presence. He's the best reason Atlanta fans have to hope for another stretch atop the NL East. To baseball at large, he's something more interesting: that player who comes along every now and again with the ability to do very nearly whatever he wants. He ended up hitting 41 homers last year, and he swiped 37 bases. He persistently nudged the daily possibilities of baseball a little outward. All-Star games await him as a matter of course; MVPs seem almost inevitable.

Fans have the unavoidable tendency, with a player like Acuña, to forecast. As he gets stronger and his swing gets even sharper, as he sees more pitches and hones his approach, potential will harden into consistency. He remains, for now and by the coldest calculations, a smidge overenthusiastic about the spectacular play and bored by the routine one. His production can tip toward the highlight. But if the Braves' realization of their goals rests in large part on Acuña's maturation, their supporters would do well to enjoy another year of the version they get to watch now. Growing up, in baseball as in everything else, means giving something of yourself away.

⚾   ⚾   ⚾

Last October, in Game 1 of the Division Series against the St. Louis Cardinals, Acuña put another lovely swing on another not-good-enough breaking ball, sending it more than 350 feet down the right field line. Acuña thought it was gone and broke into a home-run trot, but it pulled up short and bounced off the wall, and the lack of an out-of-the-box sprint kept him to a single.

The dreaded accusation—a lack of hustle—had landed on Acuña before, most notably following a similar play in a loss to the Dodgers in August. "The name on the front is a lot more important than the name on the back of that jersey," Atlanta manager Brian Snitker had said then, and Acuña had concurred: "There's no excuse for it." After the Cardinals capped their Game 1 NLDS win, despite a ninth-inning bomb from Acuña making things more interesting, the tsk-ing repeated. "It's kind of beating a dead horse after that if you keep having the same conversation over and over again," first baseman Freddie Freeman said after the game. "You have to know that was a mistake." "He probably scores in that inning if he's on second base," second baseman Ozzie Albies said. "It's a big deal. He knows he needs to do better there."

The Braves had a reasonable enough gripe, of course; you'd be hard-pressed to find anyone in professional baseball who would shrug at leaving runs on the table in the middle of the summer, much less October. Still, there was something arch and archetypal to the messaging, a shared lineage with evil headmasters and draconian wardens. As the

Braves went on to lose the series in five games, Acuña was a rare bright spot; the 21-year-old tallied eight hits, five of them going for extra bases, for a 1.454 OPS. He had made a young player's mistake in Game 1, but he'd spent the rest of the series playing with a young player's fearlessness.

Hustle—like strike-zone discipline and solid baserunning and commitment to scouting-report preparation—is commonly understood to be a straightforward positive. It costs nothing but effort. What if this isn't the case? What if the youthful impulse that has Acuña occasionally lollygagging it out of the batter's box is the same one that lets him risk allowing a triple to dive for the ball in the gap? That lets him bring a slow pulse to the biggest games of the year? That lets him not only plaster a future Hall of Famer's signature pitch but decide exactly how he wants to plaster it, with what combination of approach and discipline and all-out style, to what part of the park?

⚾   ⚾   ⚾

It's more or less a sure thing that Acuña will improve in the aforementioned areas. The *Journal-Constitution* will run a story in March on his commitment to sprinting out every grounder. In May, people will be tracking a climbing OBP and a more reasonable strikeout-to-walk rate. Television announcers will take care to note his hitting the cutoff man. The data points and anecdotes will be presented as benchmarks along the trajectory linking phenom to franchise player. The word that will be invoked is "consistency," another of those uncomplicatedly good baseball values.

It's the way of things. Baseball seasons are long, and for good players, there are a lot of them. Habits build; they may as well be useful ones.

Soon enough, Acuña will be a constant. His statistical profile will have changed; there will be fewer steals (unneeded risk), more bases on balls (better pitch recognition), and lengthier plate appearances (improved discipline). His attention will shift toward the grind and away from the moment. The talk of a 40-40 season—the kind he might have had last year but for an injury that had him sitting the last week—will go away, but no matter. In all corners, he'll be a new-and-improved Ronald Acuña, Jr., a player whose promise is being cashed in. He'll sit in the middle of the Braves' lineup, and, if everyone else does their part, Atlanta will win a lot of games.

There's some sadness here. It's something like the sadness of a young pitcher dropping a dizzying but inconsistent breaking ball to hone his other pitches, or of a hitter succumbing to a career of platoon duties, or of Mike Trout, former all-everything wonder, stealing only 11 bases last season. There are no uncomplicated positives in baseball. They all come at the cost of something: immediacy, personality, hope, ideas of one's best self. They affirm that the reasons to play baseball and the ways of playing winning baseball are not always quite the same thing.

For now, Acuña still sits in that point in his career where things are not yet fully habitual. Even given his young age—what is it about reaching the big leagues that blots out all other context?—this is a source of some frustration to his fans and teammates. It is also the best reason to watch him. Soon enough, he'll run out all his grounders, and soon enough, when he gets a hanging breaking ball, he'll do just what all of the other great hitters around the game do: Pull it to left, drop his bat, and get around the bases. ∎

—Robert O'Connell is a freelance sportswriter whose work has appeared in The Athletic and Deadspin.

HITTERS

Ronald Acuña Jr. OF   Born: 12/18/97   Age: 22   Bats: R   Throws: R   Height: 6'0"   Weight: 180   Origin: International Free Agent, 2014

YEAR	TEAM	LVL	AGE	PA	R	2B	3B	HR	RBI	BB	K	SB	CS	AVG/OBP/SLG	DRC+	VORP	BABIP	BRR	FRAA	WARP
2017	BRV	A+	19	126	21	3	5	3	19	8	40	14	3	.287/.336/.478	111	7.7	.411	1.2	CF(19): -1.8, RF(9): 0.1	0.4
2017	MIS	AA	19	243	29	14	1	9	30	18	56	19	11	.326/.374/.520	153	21.0	.396	0.6	CF(34): -1.0, RF(14): -1.4	1.8
2017	GWN	AAA	19	243	38	14	2	9	33	17	48	11	6	.344/.393/.548	161	17.1	.404	0.0	CF(20): 1.7, RF(20): 2.8	2.5
2018	GWN	AAA	20	101	9	2	0	1	3	11	25	5	1	.211/.297/.267	74	-2.2	.281	1.0	LF(18): -3.1, CF(2): -0.6	-0.3
2018	ATL	MLB	20	487	78	26	4	26	64	45	123	16	5	.293/.366/.552	137	48.6	.352	3.1	LF(101): -10.8, CF(13): 1.0	2.9
2019	ATL	MLB	21	715	127	22	2	41	101	76	188	37	9	.280/.365/.518	129	51.1	.337	8.6	CF(100): -3.2, LF(46): 5.0	6.1
2020	ATL	MLB	22	595	84	27	3	31	92	54	155	23	9	.283/.355/.519	125	37.9	.343	3.4	RF -2, CF -1	3.5

Comparables: Mike Trout, Ozzie Albies, Bryce Harper

Roles play an extremely important part in the success of any group effort, and especially so in baseball. Just because someone has the skills for one role doesn't mean that it's the best one for them or for the group as a whole. In the case of Acuña, he started out the 2019 season as a cleanup hitter since he led the Braves in home runs during 2018. While Acuña is a dynamic enough talent to succeed in that role, the team wasn't playing at the same level as before. On May 10, Acuña was put back in the leadoff spot. By June 10, the Braves were at the top of their division and never looked back.

Acuña serves as a tone-setter. He is the straw that stirs the drink. He is the drummer who brings rhythm to the rest of the lineup. He's just as electrifying on defense as he is on offense, and serious flirtation with a 40/40 season goes a long way towards showing what the young Venezuelan is like at the plate and on the basepaths. Atlanta has a superstar talent on their hands, and Acuña is now very comfortable in his role at the top of the lineup.

Ozzie Albies 2B   Born: 01/07/97   Age: 23   Bats: B   Throws: R   Height: 5'8"   Weight: 165   Origin: International Free Agent, 2013

YEAR	TEAM	LVL	AGE	PA	R	2B	3B	HR	RBI	BB	K	SB	CS	AVG/OBP/SLG	DRC+	VORP	BABIP	BRR	FRAA	WARP
2017	GWN	AAA	20	448	67	21	8	9	41	28	90	21	2	.285/.330/.440	109	27.2	.342	3.3	2B(82): 3.8, SS(14): -2.0	2.3
2017	ATL	MLB	20	244	34	9	5	6	28	21	36	8	1	.286/.354/.456	109	14.2	.316	0.6	2B(57): -2.9	0.8
2018	ATL	MLB	21	684	105	40	5	24	72	36	116	14	3	.261/.305/.452	106	33.1	.285	5.9	2B(157): 7.0	4.0
2019	ATL	MLB	22	702	102	43	8	24	86	54	112	15	4	.295/.352/.500	119	41.3	.325	4.4	2B(158): -0.4	4.4
2020	ATL	MLB	23	595	66	33	6	19	74	40	98	17	5	.269/.324/.455	101	27.8	.297	2.8	2B 2	3.0

Comparables: Rougned Odor, Ted Lepcio, Carlos Correa

After hitting more homers in 2018 than he had in his entire pro career (majors and minors) to that point, the big question was whether Albies' power was here to stay. It turns out that the diminutive second baseman answered "yes" to a different question: Could he keep some of the power gains while showcasing the batting average and on-base skills he demonstrated in the minors? Albies still swings a lot—his 56 percent swing rate was eighth in the majors last season—but that's here to stay and it's a feature, not a bug. The next frontier for the Curacao native is not a small one: improving against right-handed pitching. For the second straight year, Albies showed a massive split and his overall numbers in 2019 were buoyed by a staggering .389/.414/.685 line against southpaws. Still just 23 for the entire 2020 season, there's plenty of time to continue providing answers for the things standing between Albies and stardom.

Johan Camargo UT   Born: 12/13/93   Age: 26   Bats: B   Throws: R   Height: 6'0"   Weight: 195   Origin: International Free Agent, 2010

YEAR	TEAM	LVL	AGE	PA	R	2B	3B	HR	RBI	BB	K	SB	CS	AVG/OBP/SLG	DRC+	VORP	BABIP	BRR	FRAA	WARP
2017	GWN	AAA	23	142	17	9	1	4	20	8	22	1	0	.295/.340/.473	112	8.6	.324	-0.2	SS(31): -6.4, 3B(2): 0.2	0.1
2017	ATL	MLB	23	256	30	21	2	4	27	12	51	0	0	.299/.331/.452	86	16.1	.364	3.0	3B(43): -0.4, SS(26): 0.6	0.8
2018	GWN	AAA	24	36	6	2	0	3	7	3	9	0	0	.303/.361/.636	134	3.5	.333	0.3	SS(4): -0.5, 3B(3): -0.2	0.2
2018	ATL	MLB	24	524	63	27	1	19	76	51	108	1	1	.272/.349/.457	116	34.2	.315	-1.6	3B(114): -9.8, SS(18): -1.5	1.6
2019	GWN	AAA	25	64	10	6	0	2	15	5	12	0	0	.483/.531/.690	186	11.1	.591	-1.9	3B(7): -0.6, SS(4): 0.3	0.6
2019	ATL	MLB	25	248	31	12	1	7	32	15	43	1	0	.233/.279/.384	80	3.0	.258	0.2	SS(25): 0.5, 3B(18): -0.2	0.3
2020	ATL	MLB	26	399	41	21	2	12	47	25	76	1	0	.252/.303/.415	86	4.8	.287	0.5	3B -3, 2B 0	0.1

Comparables: Lonnie Chisenhall, Didi Gregorius, Cody Asche

During rebuilds, you always hear about prospects as it can be hard for fans to get it up for the players who are actively contributing to the poor major-league product. Much less attention is paid to the young players who weren't fawned over on prospect lists but still play their way into a role with that first-wave contender. Such was the case with Camargo, who rose out of anonymity and into the starting lineup with the Braves more out of necessity than anything else. The arrival of Josh Donaldson indeed pushed Camargo back to the fringes and he returned to the role of utilityman, playing every non-pitching position in 2019 except for centerfield and catcher. Unfortunately, as Camargo went back to a reduced role, his bat returned to its pre-2018 form. Still a force against lefties on a team without a natural platoon partner, Camargo will need to continue to evolve in order to keep a defined role on this now-contending team.

William Contreras C   Born: 12/24/97   Age: 22   Bats: R   Throws: R   Height: 6'0"   Weight: 180   Origin: International Free Agent, 2015

YEAR	TEAM	LVL	AGE	PA	R	2B	3B	HR	RBI	BB	K	SB	CS	AVG/OBP/SLG	DRC+	VORP	BABIP	BRR	FRAA	WARP
2017	DNV	RK	19	198	29	10	1	4	25	24	30	1	0	.290/.379/.432	133	19.2	.326	-0.4	C(35): -0.5	1.4
2018	ROM	A	20	342	54	17	1	11	39	29	73	1	1	.293/.360/.463	138	23.3	.351	-0.9	C(43): -0.3	2.2
2018	BRV	A+	20	90	3	7	0	0	10	6	16	0	0	.253/.300/.337	103	2.5	.309	-0.3	C(20): -0.4	0.3
2019	BRV	A+	21	207	26	11	0	3	22	14	44	0	0	.263/.324/.368	112	6.6	.329	-0.2	C(43): -0.8	1.0
2019	MIS	AA	21	209	24	9	0	3	17	15	40	0	0	.246/.306/.340	99	8.4	.295	0.8	C(52): -1.1	0.9
2020	ATL	MLB	22	251	24	13	1	6	27	15	64	0	0	.245/.296/.383	76	-0.2	.312	-0.4	C -3	-0.3

Comparables: Abiatal Avelino, Meibrys Viloria, Jacob Nottingham

YEAR	TEAM	P. COUNT	FRM RUNS	BLK RUNS	THRW RUNS	TOT RUNS
2019	MIS	6064	-0.2	0.0	0.0	0.6
2020	ATL	9182	-2.2	-0.3	0.1	-2.3

Contreras did about as well as one could expect from a raw, 21-year-old catcher getting assigned to Double-A. He showed glimpses of the talent that put him on the prospect map at lower levels last year while reminding everyone that most catchers simply take longer to develop. The younger brother of Willson continues to boast impressive physical abilities behind the plate for potential above-average to plus defensive tools, including a cannon arm. It'll take time to mold those natural abilities, especially as he works on quieting his receiving and shoring up his blocking, but it's the type of clay that any development staff would love to have. Same deal at the plate, where he's raw but has the eye and swing to develop into an average hitter with above-average pop. Treat him right with his assignments and the final product has exciting, everyday potential.

Charlie Culberson 3B   Born: 04/10/89   Age: 31   Bats: R   Throws: R   Height: 6'0"   Weight: 200   Origin: Round 1, 2007 Draft (#51 overall)

YEAR	TEAM	LVL	AGE	PA	R	2B	3B	HR	RBI	BB	K	SB	CS	AVG/OBP/SLG	DRC+	VORP	BABIP	BRR	FRAA	WARP
2017	OKL	AAA	28	414	37	13	4	4	32	26	68	7	3	.250/.299/.336	68	-3.8	.294	-0.6	SS(97): 0.8, 3B(7): 0.9	0.4
2017	LAN	MLB	28	15	0	1	0	0	1	2	4	0	0	.154/.267/.231	84	-1.2	.222	0.0	SS(11): 0.2, 2B(2): 0.0	0.0
2018	ATL	MLB	29	322	47	18	2	12	45	21	85	4	2	.270/.326/.466	101	22.2	.340	2.3	LF(29): -2.1, SS(20): -2.6	0.5
2019	ATL	MLB	30	144	14	5	2	5	20	6	44	0	1	.259/.294/.437	75	0.2	.345	-0.2	LF(35): 1.9, RF(11): 1.1	0.3
2020	ATL	MLB	31	259	25	11	1	7	28	15	73	3	1	.237/.287/.379	73	-1.0	.312	0.8	3B -1, 2B 0	-0.3

Comparables: Danny Santana, Leury García, Aaron Boone

By day, the unassuming Culberson spends his time performing rudimentary utility duties and sending chills of slight disappointment down the spines of fans who walked up to him expecting an autograph from Dansby Swanson. However, the onset of night calls for Culberson to don the mask and become "Charlie Clutch." While the numbers suggest that he is just as unassuming as his alter ego, it is not Culberson who is out there making a game-winning defensive play by throwing across his body from the outfield to punch out a runner at home plate. Culberson is not the man who has a knack for coming through with a big pinch hit from time to time. Culberson is not the guy who has a 92-mph fastball in his shockingly live arm. The figure in the night accomplishing these unlikely feats is Charlie Clutch, and there's no telling what his next feat of legend will be.

Travis d'Arnaud C Born: 02/10/89 Age: 31 Bats: R Throws: R Height: 6'2" Weight: 210 Origin: Round 1, 2007 Draft (#37 overall)

YEAR	TEAM	LVL	AGE	PA	R	2B	3B	HR	RBI	BB	K	SB	CS	AVG/OBP/SLG	DRC+	VORP	BABIP	BRR	FRAA	WARP
2017	NYN	MLB	28	376	39	19	1	16	57	23	59	0	0	.244/.293/.443	99	15.8	.250	-2.2	C(93): 11.5, 2B(1): 0.0	2.7
2018	NYN	MLB	29	16	1	0	0	1	3	1	5	0	0	.200/.250/.400	80	0.7	.222	-0.1	C(4): 1.0	0.1
2019	LAN	MLB	30	1	0	0	0	0	0	0	0	0	0	.000/.000/.000	105	0.0	.000	0.0		0.0
2019	TBA	MLB	30	365	50	16	0	16	67	30	80	0	1	.263/.323/.459	104	17.6	.295	0.4	C(76): -2.2, 1B(21): -1.6	1.4
2019	NYN	MLB	30	25	2	0	0	0	2	2	5	0	0	.087/.160/.087	70	0.4	.111	0.4	C(9): 0.1	0.1
2020	ATL	MLB	31	294	32	14	0	11	37	23	61	0	0	.248/.313/.422	91	10.1	.285	-0.3	C 10	2.0

Comparables: Gary Carter, Bill Freehan, Jim Pagliaroni

YEAR	TEAM	P. COUNT	FRM RUNS	BLK RUNS	THRW RUNS	TOT RUNS
2017	NYN	13404	11.2	0.9	-3.1	9.0
2018	NYN	689	1.0	0.1	0.0	1.0
2019	NYN	899	0.2	0.0	0.0	0.2
2019	TBA	9678	1.8	-2.4	0.1	-0.8
2020	ATL	13793	9.5	-0.3	0.1	9.3

It was quite the year for d'Arnaud. He started another season with the Mets before they designated him for assignment out of frustration in late April after a 2-for-23 start at the plate. Los Angeles took a flier on him; though he wore Dodger blue just once before the Rays came calling for help. At the time, he looked like a temporary fix for a team that lost both of its catchers to injury at the same time. Meanwhile, a hot streak at the plate and the collapse of Mike Zunino, allowed for a larger role. The LBC native took advantage of the opportunity and became Tampa Bay's primary backstop for most of the season. He even hit his way into a platoon at first base, handling the cold corner and leadoff position against southpaws. The resurgence took him from a potential minor-league contract this winter to two-year deal with the Braves for $16 million.

Josh Donaldson 3B Born: 12/08/85 Age: 34 Bats: R Throws: R Height: 6'1" Weight: 210 Origin: Round 1, 2007 Draft (#48 overall)

YEAR	TEAM	LVL	AGE	PA	R	2B	3B	HR	RBI	BB	K	SB	CS	AVG/OBP/SLG	DRC+	VORP	BABIP	BRR	FRAA	WARP
2017	TOR	MLB	31	496	65	21	0	33	78	76	111	2	2	.270/.385/.559	141	44.8	.289	1.3	3B(105): -5.9, SS(4): -0.2	3.8
2018	TOR	MLB	32	159	22	11	0	5	16	21	44	2	0	.234/.333/.423	106	4.1	.303	-0.4	3B(26): -0.9, 1B(1): 0.1	0.5
2018	CLE	MLB	32	60	8	3	0	3	7	10	10	0	0	.280/.400/.520	106	3.5	.297	-0.8	3B(12): -0.9	0.1
2019	ATL	MLB	33	659	96	33	0	37	94	100	155	4	2	.259/.379/.521	130	51.6	.292	-1.0	3B(148): 1.2	5.1
2020	ATL	MLB	34	600	83	26	1	31	90	85	145	5	1	.249/.364/.490	124	16.1	.287	-0.2	3B -1, SS 0	3.9

Comparables: Todd Frazier, José Bautista, Howard Johnson

In the immediate aftermath of signing a one-year deal with the Braves for the 2019 season, Donaldson told anybody who doubted bringing him into the fold to look at the back of his baseball card. It would all come down to whether or not the former AL MVP could stay on the field and the Bringer of Rain answered that completely, playing in 155 games for the first time since 2016. It wasn't quite the OBP or slugging of his peak, but Donaldson certainly reminded everyone why he could have enough audacity to cite the credentials of his peak as enough reason to bet on himself. The torrential downpours from the 34-year-old, however, only came in the friendly confines of SunTrust Park—his 1.037 OPS there far eclipsing his .785 OPS on the road. Guess it's a good thing for Donaldson they still don't show splits on the back of a baseball card.

Adam Duvall OF Born: 09/04/88 Age: 31 Bats: R Throws: R Height: 6'1" Weight: 215 Origin: Round 11, 2010 Draft (#348 overall)

YEAR	TEAM	LVL	AGE	PA	R	2B	3B	HR	RBI	BB	K	SB	CS	AVG/OBP/SLG	DRC+	VORP	BABIP	BRR	FRAA	WARP
2017	CIN	MLB	28	647	78	37	3	31	99	39	170	5	3	.249/.301/.480	99	24.4	.290	-2.2	LF(151): 6.7, 1B(3): 0.0	2.0
2018	CIN	MLB	29	370	40	19	0	15	61	34	100	2	2	.205/.286/.399	81	3.3	.244	-0.6	LF(89): 6.9, 1B(10): 0.3	0.7
2018	ATL	MLB	29	57	8	1	0	0	0	3	17	0	0	.132/.193/.151	83	-4.2	.194	0.6	LF(12): 0.0, RF(2): 0.0	0.1
2019	GWN	AAA	30	429	74	20	4	32	93	48	86	1	0	.266/.364/.602	135	30.3	.261	0.2	LF(51): 4.7, RF(26): 1.5	3.1
2019	ATL	MLB	30	130	17	4	1	10	19	7	39	0	0	.267/.315/.567	105	4.4	.306	0.4	LF(31): 1.8, RF(2): -0.5	0.6
2020	ATL	MLB	31	210	28	10	1	13	34	16	59	2	1	.236/.304/.502	106	7.0	.268	-0.1	RF 0, LF 1	0.8

Comparables: Steve Balboni, Cecil Fielder, Al Ferrara

It was a banner year at the plate for Duvall in 2019, as he crushed fastball after fastball on his way to setting a team single-season record for home runs. Duvall even got to represent his team at the All-Star Game and the team duly rewarded him by naming him as their Most Valuable Player. That's an amazing year for anybody, but the fine print shows that it was done for the Gwinnett Stripers and not the Atlanta Braves. That's not where anybody expects to be for their age-30 season after putting three full seasons under their belt, but that's the situation Duvall found himself in after a career-worst 2018 season. Based on his strong close to the season in the majors, he's probably left the buses behind for good. That's great news for both his career and the careers of all those southpaws he demoralized throughout International League parks.

Tyler Flowers C Born: 01/24/86 Age: 34 Bats: R Throws: R Height: 6'4" Weight: 260 Origin: Round 33, 2005 Draft (#1007 overall)

YEAR	TEAM	LVL	AGE	PA	R	2B	3B	HR	RBI	BB	K	SB	CS	AVG/OBP/SLG	DRC+	VORP	BABIP	BRR	FRAA	WARP
2017	ATL	MLB	31	370	41	16	0	12	49	31	82	0	1	.281/.378/.445	115	35.3	.342	-0.2	C(85): 29.5	5.5
2018	ATL	MLB	32	296	34	9	0	8	30	35	76	0	0	.227/.341/.359	100	14.5	.292	0.3	C(76): 13.2	2.9
2019	ATL	MLB	33	310	36	11	3	11	34	31	105	0	0	.229/.319/.413	79	8.0	.325	-3.7	C(83): 10.3	1.4
2020	ATL	MLB	34	322	35	14	1	10	37	28	108	1	0	.235/.321/.390	87	9.0	.342	-0.8	C 12	2.2

Comparables: Jarrod Saltalamacchia, Ramon Castro, Ron Karkovice

There are certain species of exotic flowers that are known for taking years, even decades, to bloom. The Giant Himalayan Lily has been known to take seven years before blooming. The Century Plant is actually a misnomer in that it can take as few as ten years before it reaches full bloom. As far as the baseball version goes, it took Flowers around nine seasons to bloom, as he put up a career year in 2017 at age 31. But comparing something beautiful against it's visual peak is the easiest way to lose sight of the fact that there's something you should treasure right in front of you. Yes, the DRC+ and FRAA are well down from his

YEAR	TEAM	P. COUNT	FRM RUNS	BLK RUNS	THRW RUNS	TOT RUNS
2017	ATL	12424	32.0	-0.8	-1.1	30.1
2018	ATL	10185	13.7	-0.4	-0.2	13.0
2019	ATL	11720	15.3	-3.8	-0.6	10.7
2020	ATL	14576	15.2	-2.2	-0.6	12.4

breakout, but an above-average catcher is hard to find. With a little positive regression in his contact within the strike zone—he dropped from above 70 percent in each of the last three seasons to a paltry 63 percent in 2019—Flowers could prove again to be worthy of admiration.

Freddie Freeman 1B
Born: 09/12/89   Age: 30   Bats: L   Throws: R   Height: 6'5"   Weight: 220   Origin: Round 2, 2007 Draft (#78 overall)

YEAR	TEAM	LVL	AGE	PA	R	2B	3B	HR	RBI	BB	K	SB	CS	AVG/OBP/SLG	DRC+	VORP	BABIP	BRR	FRAA	WARP
2017	ATL	MLB	27	514	84	35	2	28	71	65	95	8	5	.307/.403/.586	145	52.9	.335	2.7	1B(105): -1.2, 3B(16): -2.4	3.7
2018	ATL	MLB	28	707	94	44	4	23	98	76	132	10	3	.309/.388/.505	137	53.7	.358	-1.7	1B(161): 3.5	4.4
2019	ATL	MLB	29	692	113	34	2	38	121	87	127	6	3	.295/.389/.549	141	47.9	.318	0.6	1B(158): -7.5	4.0
2020	ATL	MLB	30	595	84	33	2	30	92	75	117	6	2	.285/.382/.529	135	39.5	.317	0.6	1B 0	4.1

Comparables: Paul Goldschmidt, Pat Burrell, Jason Thompson

In early 2014, an ice storm hit the Atlanta metro area and Freeman had the bad luck of being out in the middle of it. Chipper Jones rescued him from the Atlanta traffic armageddon and the picture of a grateful and gleeful Freeman clutching onto Chipper's back as they rode into a garage was immortalized with a bobblehead promotion. Freeman's look of gratefulness also reflects how he must feel batting in a lineup with weapons all around him. However, for the analogy to truly hold, Chipper would had to have floated in on a UH-60 Black Hawk. Freeman has had four consecutive elite offensive seasons and there are no signs of him slowing down anytime soon. In his age-30 season, there will be plenty more cold nights on the horizon for opposing pitchers and Freeman will be the one clearing the traffic on the bases with ease.

Billy Hamilton CF
Born: 09/09/90   Age: 29   Bats: B   Throws: R   Height: 6'0"   Weight: 160   Origin: Round 2, 2009 Draft (#57 overall)

YEAR	TEAM	LVL	AGE	PA	R	2B	3B	HR	RBI	BB	K	SB	CS	AVG/OBP/SLG	DRC+	VORP	BABIP	BRR	FRAA	WARP
2017	CIN	MLB	26	633	85	17	11	4	38	44	133	59	13	.247/.299/.335	66	4.2	.313	6.6	CF(137): 5.1	0.7
2018	CIN	MLB	27	556	74	16	9	4	29	46	132	34	10	.236/.299/.327	70	8.5	.309	8.3	CF(150): 4.2	1.2
2019	ATL	MLB	28	48	9	2	0	0	3	7	13	4	1	.268/.375/.317	83	0.7	.393	0.5	CF(24): -2.7	-0.2
2019	KCA	MLB	28	305	32	12	2	0	12	25	74	18	5	.211/.275/.269	56	-6.4	.286	4.0	CF(90): -2.9	-0.5
2020	ATL	MLB	29	251	22	8	2	3	19	20	62	21	5	.218/.281/.301	55	-3.9	.286	2.6	CF 0	-0.4

Comparables: Brian McRae, Dave Martinez, Jerome Walton

For most games at SunTrust Park, a local sprinter known as "The Freeze" takes on a random fan from that night's Braves game in a foot race where the fan gets a head start. This normally results in The Freeze still taking the victory, but there was finally some intrigue about The Freeze getting a formidable opponent once the Braves traded for Hamilton. The race never happened during the 2019 season, so Atlanta had to settle for Hamilton coming off the bench to deliver blazing speed and capable defense when needed. Those two attributes are just about all you're going to get from Hamilton at this point, as it's clear that he's never going to do enough damage at the plate to be considered a real threat with the bat. Still, the advent of the 26th roster spot increases the chances that there is a place for Hamilton and the two definitive things he offers—well, three if you include potential between-innings hijinks.

Michael Harris RF
Born: 03/07/01   Age: 19   Bats: L   Throws: L   Height: 6'0"   Weight: 195   Origin: Round 3, 2019 Draft (#98 overall)

YEAR	TEAM	LVL	AGE	PA	R	2B	3B	HR	RBI	BB	K	SB	CS	AVG/OBP/SLG	DRC+	VORP	BABIP	BRR	FRAA	WARP
2019	BRA	RK	18	119	15	6	3	2	16	9	20	5	2	.349/.403/.514	138	11.3	.414	0.3	CF(19): 1.4, RF(3): -0.5	0.8
2019	ROM	A	18	93	11	2	1	0	11	9	22	3	0	.183/.269/.232	58	-4.5	.246	-0.7	RF(18): 5.1, CF(4): 0.8	0.4
2020	ATL	MLB	19	251	22	11	1	3	22	23	72	3	1	.229/.304/.335	73	-0.8	.321	0.0	CF 1, RF 1	0.2

Comparables: Justin Williams, J.P. Crawford, David Dahl

They say patience is a virtue because it sometimes produces solid major leaguers out of raw prep players. Pretty sure that's how the saying goes. It certainly applies to Harris, who is an above-average athlete with a cannon arm but will need time to develop the bat. He passed on the chance to be a two-way college player by signing with the Braves after being taken in the third round, and they liked what they saw on the position-player side. He's not a burner but has average speed and above-average range, which he'll need to use in center field to maximize his value. He could grow into above-average raw power. The question is how much Harris will hit, and it'll remain the question for some time as he needs to cut down the swing and find a more consistent bat path. Hit development would give Harris potential average or better tools across the board, and that's worth being patient.

Adeiny Hechavarría INF Born: 04/15/89 Age: 31 Bats: R Throws: R Height: 6'0" Weight: 195 Origin: International Free Agent, 2010

YEAR	TEAM	LVL	AGE	PA	R	2B	3B	HR	RBI	BB	K	SB	CS	AVG/OBP/SLG	DRC+	VORP	BABIP	BRR	FRAA	WARP
2017	JUP	A+	28	27	1	0	0	0	1	3	1	1	1	.304/.407/.304	156	1.5	.318	-0.6	SS(8): 1.0	0.3
2017	MIA	MLB	28	67	8	2	1	1	6	1	9	0	0	.277/.288/.385	83	0.6	.309	-0.9	SS(19): -1.1	0.0
2017	TBA	MLB	28	281	29	12	4	7	24	12	58	4	1	.257/.289/.411	85	5.9	.302	-1.3	SS(77): 3.4	1.0
2018	TBA	MLB	29	237	29	7	0	3	26	12	37	1	0	.258/.289/.332	89	6.5	.290	1.5	SS(61): -1.3	0.8
2018	PIT	MLB	29	47	2	4	0	1	3	3	11	0	0	.233/.277/.395	88	-1.1	.281	-1.3	SS(15): -1.1	-0.1
2018	NYA	MLB	29	37	3	0	0	2	2	1	10	1	0	.194/.216/.361	88	-0.2	.208	0.1	SS(16): -1.4, 3B(4): -0.3	-0.1
2019	SYR	AAA	30	102	15	9	0	0	17	6	14	2	1	.348/.382/.446	123	7.4	.395	0.3	SS(14): 1.9, 3B(13): -1.1	0.8
2019	ATL	MLB	30	70	14	5	1	4	15	6	15	0	0	.328/.400/.639	132	6.1	.372	0.4	SS(12): -0.2, 2B(3): -0.4	0.6
2019	NYN	MLB	30	151	20	7	0	5	18	8	33	3	1	.204/.252/.359	73	0.4	.231	-1.8	2B(26): -1.6, SS(15): -0.2	-0.4
2020	ATL	MLB	31	251	22	10	1	5	25	14	49	2	1	.232/.278/.355	66	-3.7	.273	-0.8	SS 0, 2B 0	-0.5

Comparables: Mark Lewis, Hubie Brooks, Mike Lamb

Hechavarría has become a rolling stone, and wherever he flips his bat and lays down his glove is his home. The streets of New York were clearly too cold for him, as stints with both the Yankees and Mets ended up becoming disastrous, with the latter releasing him one day before he was set to receive a $1 million bonus. Hechavarría responded by signing with the Braves, publicly thanking God that he was released by the Mets, and then hitting two home runs as a visitor at Citi Field in the final game of the season. In the words of the wise sage Andre 3000, "what's cooler than being cool? Ice cold."

Ender Inciarte CF Born: 10/29/90 Age: 29 Bats: L Throws: L Height: 5'11" Weight: 190 Origin: International Free Agent, 2008

YEAR	TEAM	LVL	AGE	PA	R	2B	3B	HR	RBI	BB	K	SB	CS	AVG/OBP/SLG	DRC+	VORP	BABIP	BRR	FRAA	WARP
2017	ATL	MLB	26	718	93	27	5	11	57	49	94	22	9	.304/.350/.409	98	34.8	.339	5.4	CF(156): 10.4	3.9
2018	ATL	MLB	27	660	83	27	6	10	61	49	86	28	14	.265/.325/.380	95	25.7	.293	2.3	CF(155): 9.6	3.1
2019	GWN	AAA	28	30	5	1	0	0	1	4	3	0	1	.231/.333/.269	86	-0.4	.261	0.3	CF(5): 0.1	0.1
2019	ATL	MLB	28	230	30	11	2	5	24	26	41	7	1	.246/.343/.397	95	7.1	.286	0.4	CF(63): 4.5	1.2
2020	ATL	MLB	29	504	48	22	3	8	48	40	82	15	7	.252/.315/.368	81	8.3	.291	2.0	CF 8	1.7

Comparables: Coco Crisp, Melky Cabrera, Michael Brantley

Whenever Inciarte takes the field, he's going to produce. Being known as a defensive specialist who hits just enough to justify being an everyday player may not be a glamorous profile, but it's a useful one to have in your team's toolbox. Sadly, Inciarte wasn't able to get a lot of time on the field last season, as a back injury and a hamstring injury limited him to just 230 plate appearances. But even a smaller sample size than normal did nothing to diminish the incredible consistency that the lefty has shown, as he's settled in as just below average by DRC+ every season of his career. Given the Braves' roster construction and the 100-point dip he takes when facing a same-side arm, Inciarte continues to make the perfect platoon center fielder and remains under contract for another three years at a very reasonable $24 million (assuming his 2022 option is picked up).

Greyson Jenista OF Born: 12/07/96 Age: 23 Bats: L Throws: R Height: 6'3" Weight: 210 Origin: Round 2, 2018 Draft (#49 overall)

YEAR	TEAM	LVL	AGE	PA	R	2B	3B	HR	RBI	BB	K	SB	CS	AVG/OBP/SLG	DRC+	VORP	BABIP	BRR	FRAA	WARP
2018	DNV	RK	21	47	10	1	0	3	7	6	9	0	1	.250/.348/.500	128	2.2	.250	0.0	RF(7): 2.6, LF(2): 0.6	0.5
2018	ROM	A	21	130	20	5	3	1	23	10	17	4	1	.333/.377/.453	143	7.5	.373	0.2	RF(30): -0.4	0.8
2018	BRV	A+	21	74	3	3	1	0	4	7	15	0	0	.152/.230/.227	33	-5.8	.192	-0.6	RF(14): -0.8, CF(1): 0.0	-0.5
2019	BRV	A+	22	231	24	14	1	4	29	27	70	1	4	.223/.312/.361	100	1.5	.315	-3.1	RF(40): -1.6, CF(8): -0.1	-0.1
2019	MIS	AA	22	256	18	4	1	5	26	27	75	2	4	.243/.324/.338	98	5.8	.333	-2.9	LF(30): -4.4, RF(27): 0.4	-0.3
2020	ATL	MLB	23	251	23	11	1	6	25	19	83	2	1	.219/.281/.351	68	-2.9	.314	-0.4	RF 1, LF -1	-0.3

Comparables: Bubba Starling, Michael Hermosillo, Joe Benson

Jenista is an enigma wrapped in a conundrum. His build and profile are made for a corner masher who doesn't clog the bases and offers value across all five tools. The problem is that he isn't tapping into the plus-or-better raw power because his swing isn't allowing it. He entered the pro ranks with a long, flat bat path and tons of moving parts, which he was able to get away with in his initial full-season taste just like he did in college. Swing tinkering and better competition has caught up to him as he's progressed, but he's far from being a lost cause and the Braves continue to show how much they like him by moving him up the ranks. Jenista still has the chance to be a low-end regular or platoon type. Those tweaks just need to start taking root.

Matt Joyce RF Born: 08/03/84 Age: 35 Bats: L Throws: R Height: 6'2" Weight: 200 Origin: Round 12, 2005 Draft (#360 overall)

YEAR	TEAM	LVL	AGE	PA	R	2B	3B	HR	RBI	BB	K	SB	CS	AVG/OBP/SLG	DRC+	VORP	BABIP	BRR	FRAA	WARP
2017	OAK	MLB	32	544	78	33	0	25	68	66	113	4	1	.243/.335/.473	108	19.0	.263	1.9	RF(115): 0.6, LF(24): 2.4	2.3
2018	NAS	AAA	33	35	4	3	0	0	3	3	5	0	0	.281/.343/.375	102	1.6	.333	-0.3	LF(6): 0.0	0.1
2018	OAK	MLB	33	246	34	9	0	7	15	35	53	0	2	.208/.322/.353	98	4.4	.242	0.1	LF(49): 2.0, RF(6): -0.3	0.7
2019	ATL	MLB	34	238	32	10	0	7	23	38	45	0	0	.295/.408/.450	124	13.8	.351	1.4	RF(33): 0.7, LF(4): -0.6	1.5
2020	ATL	MLB	35	251	30	11	0	9	30	35	58	2	1	.235/.345/.411	103	9.7	.282	0.7	RF 1, LF 1	1.2

Comparables: Barry Bonds, Gary Roenicke, Jeromy Burnitz

Pour out a little liquor for both San Francisco and Cleveland. Both of those teams could have absolutely used a corner outfielder who could come off the bench to provide capable defense and potent offense against right-handed pitching. That's exactly what Joyce ended up giving Atlanta, as the outfielder has now fully embraced his journeyman status at this late stage in his career. He has also entered into bench player territory, though he made that transition about as gracefully as you could dream of. There's always room on a major league roster for a lefty bat off the bench—here's hoping that two more teams don't make the same mistake that the Giants and Indians did.

─────────── ★ ★ ★ *2020 Top 101 Prospect* **#77** ★ ★ ★ ───────────

Shea Langeliers C Born: 11/18/97 Age: 22 Bats: R Throws: R Height: 6'0" Weight: 190 Origin: Round 1, 2019 Draft (#9 overall)

YEAR	TEAM	LVL	AGE	PA	R	2B	3B	HR	RBI	BB	K	SB	CS	AVG/OBP/SLG	DRC+	VORP	BABIP	BRR	FRAA	WARP
2019	ROM	A	21	239	27	13	0	2	34	17	55	0	0	.255/.310/.343	100	4.9	.325	-1.3	C(41): 0.8	0.9
2020	ATL	MLB	22	251	21	12	1	4	23	15	76	2	1	.219/.270/.330	60	-4.9	.303	0.0	C 0	-0.5

Comparables: Eddy Rodriguez, Tomás Nido, Elias Díaz

Let's get the obvious part out of the way first: Langeliers is a major-league defensive catcher with at least an above-average glove and a plus arm. He was probably the best defender behind the plate in the entire organization, majors included, the day he was drafted. The question is how much he'll hit. (How many times do we say that about prospects?) He has a surprisingly quick stroke and makes loud contact on the barrel. He's also over-aggressive at times. Developing an eye at the plate is the task going forward, as that would allow the above-average raw power to play in games. Improvements in that area would make Langeliers a standout everyday catcher in the big leagues, but he's a major-league quality backstop based on defense alone.

Nick Markakis RF Born: 11/17/83 Age: 36 Bats: L Throws: L Height: 6'1" Weight: 210 Origin: Round 1, 2003 Draft (#7 overall)

YEAR	TEAM	LVL	AGE	PA	R	2B	3B	HR	RBI	BB	K	SB	CS	AVG/OBP/SLG	DRC+	VORP	BABIP	BRR	FRAA	WARP
2017	ATL	MLB	33	670	76	39	1	8	76	68	110	0	2	.275/.354/.384	95	20.1	.324	2.1	RF(156): -9.0	0.3
2018	ATL	MLB	34	705	78	43	2	14	93	72	80	1	1	.297/.366/.440	116	34.4	.318	-1.6	RF(158): 6.9, LF(3): -0.4	3.5
2019	ATL	MLB	35	469	61	25	2	9	62	47	59	2	0	.285/.356/.420	106	14.9	.310	-2.8	RF(103): -11.5, LF(9): 3.4	0.4
2020	ATL	MLB	36	560	56	33	1	10	57	53	83	1	1	.267/.341/.395	95	10.4	.304	-0.5	LF 1, RF 0	1.1

Comparables: Denard Span, Al Cowens, Claudell Washington

After delivering a shockingly good contract year in which he outproduced the first three years of his four-year pact with the Braves, Markakis had earned a shot to show that his one season of glory wasn't a flash in the pan. Break out your best Ron Howard voice because it was. His value to a clubhouse is still extremely high and if you ask any of his teammates or casual fans about him, they will speak about him in wistful tones. That kind of clout goes a long way and while Markakis may not do much to separate himself from replacement level as he barrels towards his late 30s, he's still immaculate when it comes to intangibles.

Brian McCann C Born: 02/20/84 Age: 36 Bats: L Throws: R Height: 6'3" Weight: 225 Origin: Round 2, 2002 Draft (#64 overall)

YEAR	TEAM	LVL	AGE	PA	R	2B	3B	HR	RBI	BB	K	SB	CS	AVG/OBP/SLG	DRC+	VORP	BABIP	BRR	FRAA	WARP
2017	HOU	MLB	33	399	47	12	1	18	62	38	58	1	0	.241/.323/.436	106	19.5	.237	-0.2	C(95): -2.6	2.0
2018	HOU	MLB	34	216	22	3	0	7	23	19	40	0	1	.212/.301/.339	96	3.9	.229	-1.5	C(62): -3.4	0.5
2019	ATL	MLB	35	316	28	9	0	12	45	31	53	0	0	.249/.323/.412	100	16.8	.261	-3.7	C(83): 5.0	1.8
2020	ATL	MLB	36	251	28	10	0	9	31	23	48	1	0	.235/.315/.407	91	4.1	.261	-1.1	C -2	0.3

Comparables: Lance Parrish, Johnny Edwards, Mike Macfarlane

YEAR	TEAM	P. COUNT	FRM RUNS	BLK RUNS	THRW RUNS	TOT RUNS
2017	HOU	13673	1.4	-0.4	-2.5	-1.7
2018	HOU	7671	-3.0	-1.4	0.1	-4.5
2019	ATL	11106	5.3	-0.9	-0.7	3.4
2020	ATL	11770	-0.9	-0.3	-0.8	-2.0

In 2005, the Braves were at the end of their divisional dynasty that started in the early 1990s and stretched until a 21-year-old McCann was ready to make his debut, compiling 59 appearances as a rookie. By the time 2019 rolled around, McCann was back with the Braves for one last run at a division. All of his teammates from that 2005 team were now on the sidelines and one of them (namely, Jeff Francoeur) was in the press box to watch McCann play the final 85 games of his career for the Braves. McCann started his career as part of an Atlanta team that won their division and he finished it as part of an Atlanta team that won their division. It may not have been the Hollywood ending of another World Series championship that McCann had wanted, but ending a fantastic career with your baseball life coming full circle in the postseason isn't a bad note to end on. To top it all off, he even posted the exact same DRC+ in both his first and final seasons. Time is a flat circle and nobody can tell you that better than McCann.

─────────── ★ ★ ★ *2020 Top 101 Prospect* **#22** ★ ★ ★ ───────────

Cristian Pache CF Born: 11/19/98 Age: 21 Bats: R Throws: R Height: 6'2" Weight: 185 Origin: International Free Agent, 2015

YEAR	TEAM	LVL	AGE	PA	R	2B	3B	HR	RBI	BB	K	SB	CS	AVG/OBP/SLG	DRC+	VORP	BABIP	BRR	FRAA	WARP
2017	ROM	A	18	514	60	13	8	0	42	39	104	32	14	.281/.335/.343	100	22.0	.360	5.8	CF(116): 27.8, RF(2): 0.0	5.2
2018	BRV	A+	19	387	46	20	5	8	40	15	69	7	6	.285/.311/.431	114	14.7	.330	-1.1	CF(93): 3.9	2.1
2018	MIS	AA	19	109	10	3	1	1	7	5	28	0	2	.260/.294/.337	69	-0.6	.347	-0.5	CF(28): 1.3	0.1
2019	MIS	AA	20	433	50	28	8	11	53	34	104	8	11	.278/.340/.474	139	30.2	.351	-1.7	CF(57): 1.6, RF(23): 3.3	3.3
2019	GWN	AAA	20	105	13	8	1	1	8	9	18	0	0	.274/.337/.411	90	1.2	.329	-0.9	CF(23): -3.2, RF(3): 3.3	0.2
2020	ATL	MLB	21	154	15	8	1	4	17	9	39	3	2	.251/.299/.401	81	0.8	.320	-0.2	CF 1, RF 1	0.3

Comparables: Ronald Acuña Jr., Jake Bauers, Freddie Freeman

Pache's tools outside the box are so good, he can fall short of his hitting potential and still be a star at the highest level. Think about that. The guy can fall short of expectations at perhaps the most important tool for position players and he can still produce star-level WARP. That's because his center field defense nearly breaks the scouting scale and he's not even done there. He pairs it with a double-plus arm for a huge weapon up the middle, and he uses double-plus speed to range better than almost anyone in the game at any level. As for the hitting part he might fail at, he's made big strides there by solidifying his lower half, adding lift and creating a more optimal bat path to meet the ball out front and tap into his above-average raw power. At this point, it's a fairly decent bet that his aggressiveness and swing-and-miss will limit his hit utility, but as long as he stays above water at the plate, he's going to make more highlight-reel plays than MLB producers know what to do with. It's about to happen, too.

Austin Riley 3B/OF   Born: 04/02/97   Age: 23   Bats: R   Throws: R   Height: 6'3"   Weight: 220   Origin: Round 1, 2015 Draft (#41 overall)

YEAR	TEAM	LVL	AGE	PA	R	2B	3B	HR	RBI	BB	K	SB	CS	AVG/OBP/SLG	DRC+	VORP	BABIP	BRR	FRAA	WARP
2017	BRV	A+	20	339	43	10	1	12	47	23	74	0	2	.252/.310/.408	111	13.6	.289	-0.4	3B(80): -2.5	1.1
2017	MIS	AA	20	203	28	9	1	8	27	20	50	2	0	.315/.389/.511	156	20.0	.393	-0.5	3B(47): -1.6	1.6
2018	MIS	AA	21	109	17	10	3	6	20	8	28	0	0	.333/.394/.677	179	19.1	.415	1.0	3B(27): 1.2	1.5
2018	GWN	AAA	21	324	41	17	0	12	47	26	95	1	0	.282/.346/.464	127	24.1	.374	1.1	3B(71): -0.3	2.0
2019	GWN	AAA	22	194	39	13	0	15	41	20	39	0	0	.293/.366/.626	139	15.8	.300	0.2	3B(30): -0.9, LF(7): -0.8	1.3
2019	ATL	MLB	22	297	41	11	1	18	49	16	108	0	2	.226/.279/.471	89	3.9	.293	-0.4	LF(58): 2.0, 1B(6): -0.8	0.4
2020	ATL	MLB	23	539	69	25	1	31	85	36	178	1	0	.243/.301/.487	100	13.8	.311	0.5	3B -1, LF -1	1.3

Comparables: Clint Frazier, Javier Báez, Mike Moustakas

Imagine being a kid and being told two things. First, you get to go to a candy store. Next, you get to do whatever you want in that candy store for a limited amount of time but then the grown-ups will have to come in and take care of you once your time is up. The kid probably wouldn't care about anything that was said to them after "whatever you want in that candy store," and they would just proceed to run as wild as humanly possible. That's what Riley did for his 30 games in the bigs, as he hit .298/.336/.628 with 11 home runs and a whopping 32 RBI. He was grabbing all of the sweets and tearing through each bag with little regard for himself or others in his path. Then the alarm went off. The grown-ups found out that he had trouble with anything other than a fastball and that was the end, for now. When he's older and figures out how to hit breaking balls, the whole league will be his candy store.

Braden Shewmake SS   Born: 11/19/97   Age: 22   Bats: L   Throws: R   Height: 6'4"   Weight: 190   Origin: Round 1, 2019 Draft (#21 overall)

YEAR	TEAM	LVL	AGE	PA	R	2B	3B	HR	RBI	BB	K	SB	CS	AVG/OBP/SLG	DRC+	VORP	BABIP	BRR	FRAA	WARP
2019	ROM	A	21	226	37	18	2	3	39	21	29	11	3	.318/.389/.473	162	25.7	.359	3.5	SS(38): 0.0	2.5
2019	MIS	AA	21	52	7	0	0	0	1	4	11	2	0	.217/.288/.217	58	-0.9	.278	0.7	SS(14): 1.8	0.3
2020	ATL	MLB	22	251	22	12	1	4	24	15	54	2	1	.233/.288/.350	70	-1.6	.286	0.0	SS 2	0.1

Comparables: Darnell Sweeney, Donovan Solano, Gift Ngoepe

Atlanta's selection of Shewmake 21st overall in the 2019 draft came out of left field. Well, not literally—he's an infielder. The surprises weren't over when he went to Rome and showed potential average or better tools in all areas except power, boosting his post-draft stock and flying into the organization's top 10 prospects. The lanky Aggie is fluid at shortstop with enough arm for the left side, and he's equally fluid at the plate with a flat plane and contact approach. The ceiling is limited because there's no standout tool, but he squeezes the last drop out of every tool, including what could be an above-average bat. That will send him to the majors in at least a utility role in short order.

Dansby Swanson SS   Born: 02/11/94   Age: 26   Bats: R   Throws: R   Height: 6'1"   Weight: 190   Origin: Round 1, 2015 Draft (#1 overall)

YEAR	TEAM	LVL	AGE	PA	R	2B	3B	HR	RBI	BB	K	SB	CS	AVG/OBP/SLG	DRC+	VORP	BABIP	BRR	FRAA	WARP
2017	GWN	AAA	23	45	5	1	0	1	5	6	9	1	0	.237/.356/.342	97	1.5	.286	-0.9	SS(9): -0.9, 2B(2): -0.2	0.0
2017	ATL	MLB	23	551	59	23	2	6	51	59	120	3	3	.232/.312/.324	77	12.8	.292	3.2	SS(142): -10.1	0.2
2018	ATL	MLB	24	533	51	25	4	14	59	44	122	10	4	.238/.304/.395	91	23.1	.290	0.9	SS(136): 5.4	2.5
2019	ATL	MLB	25	545	77	26	3	17	65	51	124	10	5	.251/.325/.422	97	24.5	.300	1.6	SS(126): 1.3	2.7
2020	ATL	MLB	26	595	64	27	3	17	68	56	139	7	3	.244/.320/.403	90	17.1	.298	2.1	SS -1	1.6

Comparables: Eugenio Suárez, Everth Cabrera, Rico Petrocelli

When the universe conspires to give someone like Swanson a series of events that includes the honor of being the first overall pick in his draft class, getting traded to his hometown team and building a stadium that casts a shadow on your stomping grounds, exterior expectations can go through the roof. The fans were sold on a player who could be the star of a bright future while in a dark and murky present. His handsome face was on billboards and commercials across the metro area. In actuality, Swanson had the profile of a shortstop who could be a steady rock in the middle of the diamond and a calming presence in the lower third of the lineup. In short, he's a good everyday player who you can trust not to disappoint or overwhelm you. The bright lights of hometown fame may have dimmed a bit but if anybody is proof that you can always go home and lead a steady life, it's Swanson.

────────────── ★ ★ ★ *2020 Top 101 Prospect* **#42** ★ ★ ★ ──────────────

Drew Waters OF   Born: 12/30/98   Age: 21   Bats: B   Throws: R   Height: 6'2"   Weight: 183   Origin: Round 2, 2017 Draft (#41 overall)

YEAR	TEAM	LVL	AGE	PA	R	2B	3B	HR	RBI	BB	K	SB	CS	AVG/OBP/SLG	DRC+	VORP	BABIP	BRR	FRAA	WARP
2017	BRA	RK	18	58	13	3	1	2	10	7	11	2	1	.347/.448/.571	126	7.9	.417	0.8	CF(9): -1.6, RF(3): 0.7	0.2
2017	DNV	RK	18	166	20	11	1	2	14	16	59	4	2	.255/.331/.383	84	5.9	.409	-1.3	CF(35): -4.6	-0.3
2018	ROM	A	19	365	58	32	6	9	36	21	72	20	5	.303/.353/.513	143	31.6	.362	3.9	CF(83): -0.6	3.2
2018	BRV	A+	19	133	14	7	3	0	3	8	33	3	0	.268/.316/.374	92	4.6	.363	0.0	CF(30): -1.5, RF(1): -0.1	0.2
2019	MIS	AA	20	454	63	35	9	5	41	28	121	13	6	.319/.366/.481	143	36.7	.436	-3.3	LF(54): 6.3, CF(38): 7.0	4.2
2019	GWN	AAA	20	119	17	5	0	2	11	11	43	3	0	.271/.336/.374	79	-1.1	.429	0.7	RF(16): 2.1, LF(7): 0.4	0.3
2020	ATL	MLB	21	251	25	16	2	6	28	15	84	4	1	.258/.310/.417	88	4.2	.380	0.1	CF 2, LF 2	0.8

Comparables: Jorge Bonifacio, Travis Snider, Andrew Lambo

Those driving the Waters train have likely echoed the old saying, "hitters gonna hit," a few times already. It's understandable, because Waters is super aggressive at the plate and relies heavily on finding the barrel at an extremely high rate. And it's worked at every stop so far—including a brief taste of Triple-A before he could legally drink. Waters has the glove and range to play center field but hasn't done it in the Braves organization because of center fielder extraordinaire Cristian Pache, and while he's not a burner, he'll steal some bases to boot. He's a line-drive dude with the occasional eye-popping exit velocity, so the home run numbers won't match the raw power unless a tweak is made and he tones back the approach. Even so, put it all together and this is the profile of an above-average regular in the bigs. Braves scouting won't stop, can't stop.

PITCHERS

★ ★ ★ *2020 Top 101 Prospect* **#38** ★ ★ ★

Ian Anderson RHP   Born: 05/02/98   Age: 22   Bats: R   Throws: R   Height: 6'3"   Weight: 170   Origin: Round 1, 2016 Draft (#3 overall)

YEAR	TEAM	LVL	AGE	W	L	SV	G	GS	IP	H	HR	BB/9	K/9	K	GB%	BABIP	WHIP	ERA	DRA	WARP	MPH	FB%	WHF	CSP
2017	ROM	A	19	4	5	0	20	20	83	69	0	4.7	11.0	101	50%	.345	1.35	3.14	3.80	1.4				
2018	BRV	A+	20	2	6	0	20	20	100	73	2	3.6	10.6	118	47%	.282	1.13	2.52	2.75	3.0				
2018	MIS	AA	20	2	1	0	4	4	19¹	14	0	4.2	11.2	24	48%	.304	1.19	2.33	3.29	0.5				
2019	MIS	AA	21	7	5	0	21	21	111	82	8	3.8	11.9	147	46%	.287	1.16	2.68	3.80	1.6				
2019	GWN	AAA	21	1	2	0	5	5	24²	23	5	6.6	9.1	25	39%	.277	1.66	6.57	4.87	0.4				
2020	*ATL*	*MLB*	*22*	*3*	*4*	*0*	*22*	*11*	*57*	*55*	*7*	*3.6*	*9.9*	*62*	*42%*	*.316*	*1.37*	*4.14*	*4.23*	*0.9*				

Comparables: Alex Reyes, Archie Bradley, Jake Thompson

Atlanta's prep-pitching-heavy 2016 draft crop is collectively knocking on the door to consistent major-league production, which is a feat to behold considering the risk of popping prep arms early. Anderson was the headliner of that group and remains the face of it with three major-league offerings in his pocket. Does he have the high spin rates that the kids are buzzing about these days? Not really, but his stuff plays because of a tough arm angle and the ability to pair a plus changeup with a hard, sinking fastball. He doesn't have much room for error because his raw stuff isn't elite, but the successful Double-A jump showed he has enough command to live with what he's got, which is likely in the mid-rotation range.

Mike Foltynewicz RHP   Born: 10/07/91   Age: 28   Bats: R   Throws: R   Height: 6'4"   Weight: 200   Origin: Round 1, 2010 Draft (#19 overall)

YEAR	TEAM	LVL	AGE	W	L	SV	G	GS	IP	H	HR	BB/9	K/9	K	GB%	BABIP	WHIP	ERA	DRA	WARP	MPH	FB%	WHF	CSP
2017	ATL	MLB	25	10	13	0	29	28	154	169	20	3.4	8.4	143	42%	.324	1.48	4.79	5.52	0.1	98.3	60.7	10.3	46.6
2018	ATL	MLB	26	13	10	0	31	31	183	130	17	3.3	9.9	202	44%	.251	1.08	2.85	3.44	3.9	99.1	56.3	11.1	49
2019	GWN	AAA	27	5	1	0	10	10	51¹	49	1	3.0	7.9	45	40%	.316	1.29	3.86	3.67	1.5				
2019	ATL	MLB	27	8	6	0	21	21	117	109	23	2.8	8.1	105	39%	.265	1.25	4.54	4.36	1.8	97.4	52.2	11.4	50.4
2020	*ATL*	*MLB*	*28*	*9*	*9*	*0*	*26*	*26*	*145*	*139*	*23*	*3.2*	*8.6*	*139*	*39%*	*.289*	*1.31*	*4.17*	*4.34*	*2.4*	*97.7*	*56.6*	*11.1*	*49.3*

Comparables: Kevin Gausman, A.J. Cole, Joe Ross

There are few pitchers who had a more polarizing season than Foltynewicz. Just one year after seemingly breaking out and being on his way to becoming a viable frontline starter, his one step forward in 2018 resulted in 22 steps backward last season. A combination of limited spring training reps, poor performance and an equally poor in-game mentality resulted in Folty going from the penthouse of a major-league rotation to the outhouse of Triple-A baseball. Once he returned to the bigs with a new mindset—he would often let a single or a walk signal the end of the world—Foltynewicz's performance was more like the 2018 version rather than the 2019 version. Of course he didn't quite end the season on the best note, putting up the worst start in franchise playoff history (ex Tom Glavine division) in the NLDS winner-take-all game against the Cardinals. Sometimes your greatest enemy is yourself, and nobody knows that better than Foltynewicz now does.

Max Fried LHP   Born: 01/18/94   Age: 26   Bats: L   Throws: L   Height: 6'4"   Weight: 190   Origin: Round 1, 2012 Draft (#7 overall)

YEAR	TEAM	LVL	AGE	W	L	SV	G	GS	IP	H	HR	BB/9	K/9	K	GB%	BABIP	WHIP	ERA	DRA	WARP	MPH	FB%	WHF	CSP
2017	MIS	AA	23	2	11	0	19	19	86²	88	8	4.5	8.8	85	53%	.331	1.51	5.92	6.11	-1.0				
2017	GWN	AAA	23	0	0	0	2	2	6	1	0	3.0	9.0	6	67%	.083	0.50	0.00	2.51	0.2				
2017	ATL	MLB	23	1	1	0	9	4	26	30	3	4.2	7.6	22	65%	.338	1.62	3.81	4.79	0.2	95.5	63	9.2	45.4
2018	MIS	AA	24	1	0	0	2	2	11¹	4	0	3.2	12.7	16	67%	.190	0.71	0.00	1.80	0.5				
2018	GWN	AAA	24	2	6	0	13	13	66¹	66	4	4.1	9.6	71	58%	.343	1.45	4.61	4.93	0.5				
2018	ATL	MLB	24	1	4	0	14	5	33²	26	3	5.3	11.8	44	53%	.315	1.37	2.94	3.31	0.7	96.7	58.7	14.4	48.1
2019	ATL	MLB	25	17	6	0	33	30	165²	174	21	2.6	9.4	173	55%	.336	1.33	4.02	3.42	4.2	96.3	56.9	12.2	48.2
2020	*ATL*	*MLB*	*26*	*8*	*8*	*0*	*24*	*24*	*134*	*133*	*15*	*3.4*	*9.8*	*145*	*54%*	*.324*	*1.37*	*4.06*	*4.15*	*2.5*	*95.9*	*58.7*	*12.5*	*48.3*

Comparables: Blake Snell, Felix Doubront, Chris Archer

The story of Fried has long been one of being the bridesmaid and not the bride. When he was the seventh-overall pick out of the draft in 2012, he was the second-best prospect taken in his high school rotation. And when Fried finally had his breakout season in 2019, it was far less heralded than the one his former teammate Lucas Giolito had on the South Side of Chicago. After making more than 60 percent of his MLB appearances between 2017 and 2018 out of the bullpen, Fried was a rock for the Braves, finishing second on the team behind Julio Teheran with 30 starts last season. And when he pitched, he excelled as his DRA and WARP were both second among starters on the team behind fellow youngster Mike Soroka. The two biggest reasons for his expanded success in 2019 was the development of his slider, which gave him a second bat-missing breaker to go with his curve that was fawned over as an amateur, and the fact that he held his velocity gains as he moved back into a full-time starter role. If that sounds like a pitcher who shouldn't play second fiddle to anyone, you're not wrong, but at least Fried is used to it.

Shane Greene RHP   Born: 11/17/88   Age: 31   Bats: R   Throws: R   Height: 6'4"   Weight: 197   Origin: Round 15, 2009 Draft (#465 overall)

YEAR	TEAM	LVL	AGE	W	L	SV	G	GS	IP	H	HR	BB/9	K/9	K	GB%	BABIP	WHIP	ERA	DRA	WARP	MPH	FB%	WHF	CSP
2017	DET	MLB	28	4	3	9	71	0	67²	50	6	4.5	9.7	73	49%	.265	1.24	2.66	4.56	0.5	96.8	56.2	9.8	52
2018	DET	MLB	29	4	6	32	66	0	63¹	68	12	2.7	9.2	65	42%	.311	1.37	5.12	3.94	0.7	96.4	50.8	9.9	51.1
2019	ATL	MLB	30	0	1	1	27	0	24²	25	3	1.8	7.7	21	38%	.314	1.22	4.01	4.37	0.3	93.5	43.3	12.6	49.3
2019	DET	MLB	30	0	2	22	38	0	38	21	5	2.8	10.2	43	55%	.178	0.87	1.18	3.19	0.9	94.6	43.3	11.6	52.5
2020	*ATL*	*MLB*	*31*	*2*	*2*	*6*	*48*	*0*	*51*	*50*	*8*	*3.1*	*9.2*	*52*	*45%*	*.303*	*1.32*	*4.26*	*4.40*	*0.6*	*94.7*	*49*	*10.6*	*51.1*

Comparables: Roenis Elías, Joe Kelly, Neftalí Feliz

It was only a matter of time before Greene would be getting high-leverage opportunities in games that actually mattered after spending 2017 and 2018 racking up saves for the rebuilding Tigers. Sure enough, Greene found himself moving from the relative anonymity of pitching with nothing on the line in August to being thrust into a pennant race with the Braves. In professional wrestling, wrestlers who are still new to the big time and can't yet be trusted with a big match are considered to be green. After two blown saves and a loss in his first five appearances with Atlanta, you may have heard some rumblings of Greene being exactly this. However, in his final 22 games with the Braves, he pitched like the player Alex Anthopolous thought he was acquiring with a 2.61 ERA and proper ownership of the eighth inning. Not everybody can handle the main event role of the ninth inning, and Greene won't he asked to do so in 2020, but it's certainly premature to take the Proven Closer sticker off his post-2020 free agent spec sheet.

Cole Hamels LHP Born: 12/27/83   Age: 36   Bats: L   Throws: L   Height: 6'4"   Weight: 205   Origin: Round 1, 2002 Draft (#17 overall)

YEAR	TEAM	LVL	AGE	W	L	SV	G	GS	IP	H	HR	BB/9	K/9	K	GB%	BABIP	WHIP	ERA	DRA	WARP	MPH	FB%	WHF	CSP
2017	FRI	AA	33	1	0	0	2	2	8²	3	1	2.1	8.3	8	50%	.105	0.58	1.04	2.44	0.3				
2017	TEX	MLB	33	11	6	0	24	24	148	125	18	3.2	6.4	105	48%	.251	1.20	4.20	5.41	0.3	93.8	66.4	10	45.7
2018	TEX	MLB	34	5	9	0	20	20	114¹	115	23	3.3	9.0	114	45%	.296	1.37	4.72	5.17	0.2	93.7	67.8	13	45.7
2018	CHN	MLB	34	4	3	0	12	12	76¹	61	6	2.7	8.7	74	49%	.286	1.10	2.36	3.46	1.6	94.6	67.8	12.6	46.3
2019	CHN	MLB	35	7	7	0	27	27	141²	141	17	3.6	9.1	143	47%	.316	1.39	3.81	4.87	1.4	93.3	66.3	12.9	47.6
2020	ATL	MLB	36	10	9	0	28	28	157	154	24	3.4	9.1	158	46%	.302	1.36	4.39	4.48	2.3	92.4	65.5	12	45.6

Comparables: David Price, Mickey Lolich, Jon Lester

Hamels had an up-and-down '19. He was in the midst of a high-quality run when he injured his oblique in June. Upon returning, he just never seemed right. After signing with the Braves, Hamels conceded he came back too soon. Obviously the days of Hamels being considered an ace are far in the past, but he probably still has enough left in the tank to serve as a mid-rotation to back-end type. With a strong final act, he might even be able to pitch himself into Hall of Fame consideration. We'll save that conversation for another year.

Luke Jackson RHP   Born: 08/24/91   Age: 28   Bats: R   Throws: R   Height: 6'2"   Weight: 210   Origin: Round 1, 2010 Draft (#45 overall)

YEAR	TEAM	LVL	AGE	W	L	SV	G	GS	IP	H	HR	BB/9	K/9	K	GB%	BABIP	WHIP	ERA	DRA	WARP	MPH	FB%	WHF	CSP
2017	GWN	AAA	25	0	3	1	9	4	24¹	26	2	5.9	8.5	23	34%	.338	1.73	6.29	6.72	-0.3				
2017	ATL	MLB	25	2	0	0	43	0	50²	55	4	3.4	5.9	33	43%	.311	1.46	4.62	5.36	-0.1	96.8	51.1	11.5	43
2018	GWN	AAA	26	2	1	0	10	1	21¹	11	0	4.2	14.3	34	45%	.289	0.98	1.69	2.42	0.7				
2018	ATL	MLB	26	1	2	1	35	0	40²	41	3	4.6	10.2	46	50%	.339	1.52	4.43	5.79	-0.4	96.3	41.7	11.7	42.7
2019	ATL	MLB	27	9	2	18	70	0	72²	76	10	3.2	13.1	106	60%	.386	1.40	3.84	3.21	1.7	97.5	37.9	18	42
2020	ATL	MLB	28	2	2	0	43	0	45	43	5	4.1	12.0	60	53%	.346	1.41	3.95	4.02	0.7	96.5	41.7	15.2	42.8

Comparables: Jeremy Jeffress, Fernando Nieve, Nate Adcock

Following the 2018 season, all hope seemed to be lost for the unassuming reliever after two seasons in Atlanta. Jackson was destined to float through life in the major leagues as a hard-tosser who could never quite reach the level of reliability. Then on one fateful day between October 2018 and March 2019, Luke felt the bite of a radioactive slider. From that day forward, his life changed forever and he became your friendly neighborhood Slider-Man. With great power came great (high-leverage) responsibility. Jackson's slider—which he threw over 53 percent of the time—propelled him into the closer role for the Braves, but a tough July when he was done in by an unlikely foe saw him slide into middle relief. That unlikely foe? Right-handed hitters who patiently waded through breakers to tee off on his fastball. As the Braves continue to infuse talent into their bullpen, Jackson will have plenty of help in keeping foes off the basepaths at SunTrust Park and far from home.

Chris Martin RHP   Born: 06/02/86   Age: 34   Bats: R   Throws: R   Height: 6'8"   Weight: 215   Origin: Round 21, 2005 Draft (#627 overall)

YEAR	TEAM	LVL	AGE	W	L	SV	G	GS	IP	H	HR	BB/9	K/9	K	GB%	BABIP	WHIP	ERA	DRA	WARP	MPH	FB%	WHF	CSP
2018	TEX	MLB	32	1	5	0	46	0	41²	46	5	1.1	8.0	37	41%	.323	1.22	4.54	5.29	-0.2	97.0	72.4	10.1	50.9
2019	ATL	MLB	33	1	1	0	20	0	17²	17	1	0.5	11.2	22	52%	.356	1.02	4.08	2.88	0.5	96.8	82.4	15.7	49.6
2019	TEX	MLB	33	0	2	4	38	0	38	35	8	0.9	10.2	43	50%	.293	1.03	3.08	3.22	0.9	97.7	82.4	13.6	54.8
2020	ATL	MLB	34	2	2	0	43	0	45	45	6	2.0	9.6	49	49%	.315	1.21	3.59	3.83	0.8	96.1	77.2	12.4	51.3

Comparables: Rob Wooten, Casey Janssen, Chris Hatcher

After selling out shows across the world and taking a shine to Japan in particular, it's interesting to see Chris Martin eventually settle down and eventually enter the lane of Southern Relief Rock. After doing some shows across the Dallas-Fort Worth area for a little bit, he finally managed to pick up a residency gig in Atlanta where he could continue to play the hits. As a matter of fact, he had a show during this past September that could have been described as being "immaculate." The crowd was reportedly left speechless after Martin delivered nine consecutive classic tunes before making his exit. It was a quick performance, but it was all the people needed to remember the reason why Atlanta went out of their way to get him to perform in their city.

Mark Melancon RHP Born: 03/28/85 Age: 35 Bats: R Throws: R Height: 6'2" Weight: 215 Origin: Round 9, 2006 Draft (#284 overall)

YEAR	TEAM	LVL	AGE	W	L	SV	G	GS	IP	H	HR	BB/9	K/9	K	GB%	BABIP	WHIP	ERA	DRA	WARP	MPH	FB%	WHF	CSP
2017	SFN	MLB	32	1	2	11	32	0	30	37	3	1.8	8.7	29	54%	.374	1.43	4.50	2.75	0.8	93.5	74.7	10.6	43.9
2018	SFN	MLB	33	1	4	3	41	0	39	48	2	3.2	7.2	31	52%	.365	1.59	3.23	3.62	0.6	93.4	68.3	10.6	46.2
2019	ATL	MLB	34	1	0	11	23	0	21	22	1	0.9	10.3	24	62%	.339	1.14	3.86	2.21	0.7	93.6	68.8	12.6	44.2
2019	SFN	MLB	34	4	2	1	43	0	46¹	49	3	3.1	8.5	44	60%	.354	1.40	3.50	4.41	0.5	93.6	68.8	11.1	44.3
2020	ATL	MLB	35	3	3	18	54	0	57	56	6	2.5	8.6	54	57%	.310	1.27	3.59	3.77	1.0	92.3	68.3	11	44

Comparables: Fernando Salas, Luke Gregerson, Mike Adams

While conventional reasoning would suggest that there are two sides to every story, there are three when it comes to Melancon: San Francisco's story, Atlanta's story, and the actual truth. If you hear it from Giants fans, you'll hear a cautionary tale of the dangers of being the team that decides to give an aging reliever such a hefty average annual value contract. If you hear it from Braves fans, you'll hear about Melancon being just what Atlanta needed to stabilize their bullpen—even if that comes with a $14 million price tag. The version of Melancon that showed up in Atlanta and recorded 11 saves with a resurgently low DRA was a throwback to the simpler days before the contract entered every conversation about the 34-year-old. In reality, the expensive truth lies somewhere in the middle, but as long as Melancon continues to rack up grounders and saves, the focus will be on his performance and not his salary.

A.J. Minter LHP Born: 09/02/93 Age: 26 Bats: L Throws: L Height: 6'0" Weight: 215 Origin: Round 2, 2015 Draft (#75 overall)

YEAR	TEAM	LVL	AGE	W	L	SV	G	GS	IP	H	HR	BB/9	K/9	K	GB%	BABIP	WHIP	ERA	DRA	WARP	MPH	FB%	WHF	CSP
2017	GWN	AAA	23	1	2	0	17	0	15¹	15	1	5.9	10.0	17	30%	.326	1.63	4.70	6.10	-0.1				
2017	ATL	MLB	23	0	1	0	16	0	15	13	1	1.2	15.6	26	34%	.387	1.00	3.00	2.15	0.5	97.6	50.8	19.5	43
2018	ATL	MLB	24	4	3	15	65	0	61¹	57	3	3.2	10.1	69	39%	.329	1.29	3.23	3.42	1.1	98.7	49	15.8	48
2019	GWN	AAA	25	2	2	5	20	0	22²	24	4	1.2	11.9	30	38%	.351	1.19	3.57	2.67	0.8				
2019	ATL	MLB	25	3	4	5	36	0	29¹	36	3	7.1	10.7	35	40%	.388	2.01	7.06	5.95	-0.2	97.6	39.3	15.3	45.3
2020	ATL	MLB	26	1	1	0	21	0	23	19	3	3.6	10.2	26	39%	.284	1.24	3.42	3.62	0.4	97.8	46.4	16.3	46.4

Comparables: Paul Fry, Steven Okert, Hung-Chih Kuo

Part of the chorus to the album-ending breakup tune "Stay Together" by The Neptunes has Pharrell crooning out "Never dreamt I'd speak the phrase, now what the [bleep] just happened?" That's the question a lot of Braves fans were asking with Minter during the 2019 season. How in the world did it come to this? How did a reliever who was being hailed as a mini-Craig Kimbrel go from pitching high-leverage innings one season to completely falling off a cliff and spending significant time in Triple-A the following season? A minor car accident in spring training started the year off on uneasy footing, but it was his fastball command that let him down in the end. He not only had trouble throwing strikes with it—leading to a walk rate more than double his 2018 figure—but even when he threw it for strikes, it found too much of the zone and too many barrels because of that. His .692 slugging percentage allowed on fastballs was almost twice as high as it was the year prior. Sometimes it's difficult to explain how that command dies out. This isn't to assume that all is lost for Minter, but he's going to have to figure out "what the [bleep] just happened" if he wants to pitch in high-leverage situations again.

★ ★ ★ *2020 Top 101 Prospect* **#60** ★ ★ ★

Kyle Muller LHP Born: 10/07/97 Age: 22 Bats: R Throws: L Height: 6'6" Weight: 225 Origin: Round 2, 2016 Draft (#44 overall)

YEAR	TEAM	LVL	AGE	W	L	SV	G	GS	IP	H	HR	BB/9	K/9	K	GB%	BABIP	WHIP	ERA	DRA	WARP	MPH	FB%	WHF	CSP
2017	DNV	RK	19	1	1	0	11	11	47²	43	5	3.4	9.3	49	40%	.284	1.28	4.15	3.39	1.4				
2018	ROM	A	20	3	0	0	6	6	30	24	3	2.4	6.9	23	54%	.253	1.07	2.40	4.18	0.4				
2018	BRV	A+	20	4	2	0	14	14	80²	80	2	3.6	8.8	79	42%	.350	1.39	3.24	4.91	0.4				
2018	MIS	AA	20	4	1	0	5	5	29	22	3	1.9	8.4	27	40%	.244	0.97	3.10	3.48	0.6				
2019	MIS	AA	21	7	6	0	22	22	111²	81	5	5.5	9.7	120	41%	.284	1.33	3.14	4.85	0.1				
2020	ATL	MLB	22	1	1	0	3	3	16	16	2	3.8	8.4	15	39%	.302	1.43	4.61	4.69	0.2				

Comparables: Eduardo Rodriguez, Jake Thompson, Génesis Cabrera

Muller was a dude when the Braves picked him in the second round a few years back, but he turned himself into a Dude after a velocity training program upped his fastball by several ticks to sit mid-90s and bump higher. He's always had that kind of velocity in him, as Muller is massive and physical on the mound. He found that extra oomph and saw his fastball bump to plus potential to pair with a changeup that can boast the same projection. Muller won't command his way to a front-end starter future though, and that's what has evaluators thinking of him as a dominant reliever. The way starters are handled these days, though, one could envision Muller shoving for four or five innings at the time. Either way, he's going to throw impactful major-league innings with live stuff from the left side.

Sean Newcomb LHP   Born: 06/12/93   Age: 27   Bats: L   Throws: L   Height: 6'5"   Weight: 255   Origin: Round 1, 2014 Draft (#15 overall)

YEAR	TEAM	LVL	AGE	W	L	SV	G	GS	IP	H	HR	BB/9	K/9	K	GB%	BABIP	WHIP	ERA	DRA	WARP	MPH	FB%	WHF	CSP
2017	GWN	AAA	24	3	3	0	11	11	57²	45	3	5.2	11.5	74	41%	.304	1.35	2.97	3.62	1.3				
2017	ATL	MLB	24	4	9	0	19	19	100	100	10	5.1	9.7	108	46%	.327	1.57	4.32	4.61	1.1	96.8	63.4	12.7	42.8
2018	ATL	MLB	25	12	9	0	31	30	164	137	18	4.4	8.8	160	44%	.273	1.33	3.90	3.83	2.8	95.8	62.4	11	46.3
2019	GWN	AAA	26	2	1	0	4	3	20²	14	1	2.2	8.7	20	47%	.241	0.92	2.18	2.22	0.9				
2019	ATL	MLB	26	6	3	1	55	4	68¹	61	8	3.8	8.6	65	50%	.282	1.32	3.16	4.13	1.0	96.8	65.2	10.4	48.8
2020	*ATL*	*MLB*	*27*	*5*	*5*	*0*	*38*	*11*	*85*	*79*	*11*	*4.1*	*9.0*	*85*	*46%*	*.292*	*1.38*	*4.08*	*4.19*	*1.4*	*95.8*	*64.1*	*11.4*	*47*

Comparables: Nick Pivetta, Cody Reed, Jordan Montgomery

On August 10, Newcomb faced two batters with the game tied in the tenth inning after the Braves blew a 6-2 lead against the Marlins in the bottom of the ninth. Newcomb proceeded to lose the game after allowing a hit, committing a throwing error and giving up a sacrifice fly in what felt like the blink of an eye. In his postgame rage, Newcomb kicked a trash can into a fire extinguisher. The fire extinguisher exploded and covered the entire visitors locker room with powder. If you're expecting this to be some sort of story that ends with Newcomb and the Braves going on a tear from that point forward, then you're in for a swerve. While Atlanta went 28-15 from that point on and comfortably clinched the division, Newcomb continued to blend in with the rest of the Braves bullpen. It's a far cry from where he started the season—as a burgeoning member of a young starting rotation—to a faceless member of the relief corps. The good news is that the hard-throwing left-hander has no discernible splits so he can be brought in to extinguish any kind of fire.

Darren O'Day RHP   Born: 10/22/82   Age: 37   Bats: R   Throws: R   Height: 6'4"   Weight: 220   Origin: Undrafted Free Agent, 2006

YEAR	TEAM	LVL	AGE	W	L	SV	G	GS	IP	H	HR	BB/9	K/9	K	GB%	BABIP	WHIP	ERA	DRA	WARP	MPH	FB%	WHF	CSP
2017	BAL	MLB	34	2	3	2	64	0	60¹	41	8	3.6	11.3	76	48%	.256	1.08	3.43	3.14	1.4	89.4	53.8	11.8	42.5
2018	BAL	MLB	35	0	2	2	20	0	20	18	3	1.8	12.1	27	26%	.326	1.10	3.60	3.67	0.3	88.8	52.3	13.2	51.7
2019	ATL	MLB	36	0	0	0	8	0	5¹	3	0	1.7	10.1	6	23%	.231	0.75	1.69	5.03	0.0	88.4	55.1	17.9	48.4
2020	*ATL*	*MLB*	*37*	*1*	*1*	*0*	*27*	*0*	*28*	*26*	*6*	*2.7*	*9.4*	*30*	*38%*	*.268*	*1.20*	*4.17*	*4.44*	*0.3*	*87.8*	*52.2*	*12.4*	*46.9*

Comparables: Mariano Rivera, Rafael Soriano, J.J. Putz

It would be understandable if casual Braves fans figured that O'Day was just a rumor or a myth—one of those players who was doomed to remember some guys status while actually still being active. However, injuries can't keep a good pitcher down forever and O'Day returned to the mound just in time to get a handful of innings in during September and the playoffs. Even though he only made a cameo, it was the type of cameo that makes you want to lock up said player swiftly at the start of the offseason. He'll no longer be talked about in hushed tones as if he's a spirit that is still lurking, although opposing left-handed batters may still question his existence as they're unlikely to see him much.

Will Smith LHP   Born: 07/10/89   Age: 30   Bats: R   Throws: L   Height: 6'5"   Weight: 248   Origin: Round 7, 2008 Draft (#229 overall)

YEAR	TEAM	LVL	AGE	W	L	SV	G	GS	IP	H	HR	BB/9	K/9	K	GB%	BABIP	WHIP	ERA	DRA	WARP	MPH	FB%	WHF	CSP
2018	SFN	MLB	28	2	3	14	54	0	53	37	3	2.5	12.1	71	41%	.281	0.98	2.55	3.34	1.0	94.8	46.1	15.8	50.7
2019	SFN	MLB	29	6	0	34	63	0	65¹	46	10	2.9	13.2	96	44%	.277	1.03	2.76	2.84	1.8	94.5	47	16.4	45.3
2020	*ATL*	*MLB*	*30*	*3*	*2*	*16*	*54*	*0*	*57*	*45*	*7*	*3.2*	*12.8*	*81*	*42%*	*.307*	*1.15*	*2.86*	*3.14*	*1.4*	*93.9*	*46.5*	*16.1*	*47.6*

Comparables: Jake McGee, Brad Hand, Rafael Soriano

This fall has been a big one for Will Smith vs. Will Smith confrontations. But where October's release of *Gemini Man* was forgettable, the September 5 game between the Dodgers and Giants had the Hollywood drama. The elder Will M. Smith faced off against Dodgers rookie catcher Will D. Smith. Naturally it had to be part of one of the game's fiercest rivalries, with everything boiling down to two outs, bottom of the ninth, just like a screenwriter would craft it.

The broad themes were there too: after all, the veteran southpaw reliever had just reached the promised peak of his career; ensconced as the team's closer and named to his first All-Star Game, the strikeout artist was in the middle of his best season. The tyro facing him had the advantages of youth, raw athleticism, and was playing for a superior Dodgers team—all the benefits of Junior over Henry Brogan—but the elder Smith set down the younger with a strikeout to end the game.

The curtains closed on the 2019 season, and the Giants reliever would be just slightly overtaken by his rookie counterpart, 1.9 WARP to his own 1.8. But that fraction is well within the error bars, and the All-Star appearance pushes favor to the veteran lefty, at least for this season. It's likely that this Will Smith will have to be every bit as good as he was last season in order to stave off his doppelgänger for one more year, lest he be resigned to the role of second-best player with his famous name.

Mike Soroka RHP   Born: 08/04/97   Age: 22   Bats: R   Throws: R   Height: 6'5"   Weight: 225   Origin: Round 1, 2015 Draft (#28 overall)

YEAR	TEAM	LVL	AGE	W	L	SV	G	GS	IP	H	HR	BB/9	K/9	K	GB%	BABIP	WHIP	ERA	DRA	WARP	MPH	FB%	WHF	CSP
2017	MIS	AA	19	11	8	0	26	26	153²	133	10	2.0	7.3	125	49%	.275	1.09	2.75	3.54	3.0				
2018	GWN	AAA	20	2	1	0	5	5	27	20	0	2.0	10.3	31	70%	.299	0.96	2.00	2.73	0.9				
2018	ATL	MLB	20	2	1	0	5	5	25²	30	1	2.5	7.4	21	45%	.345	1.44	3.51	4.64	0.2	95.3	68.9	10.4	48.9
2019	GWN	AAA	21	1	0	0	2	2	9¹	5	1	1.0	9.6	10	73%	.190	0.64	3.86	2.20	0.4				
2019	ATL	MLB	21	13	4	0	29	29	174²	153	14	2.1	7.3	142	53%	.280	1.11	2.68	3.24	4.8	94.7	63.3	10.9	47.8
2020	*ATL*	*MLB*	*22*	*11*	*9*	*0*	*29*	*29*	*172*	*174*	*20*	*2.6*	*7.7*	*147*	*53%*	*.303*	*1.30*	*3.84*	*4.02*	*3.4*	*94.8*	*66.6*	*11.3*	*50.3*

Comparables: Jordan Lyles, Taijuan Walker, Tyler Skaggs

When you look at Soroka's body of work on paper, it's eye-popping. It's magisterial. It's truly a work of art. That is in stark contrast to what you see when he's pitching and he's on his A-game. Time seems to speed up and he lulls you into a false sense of complacency. He's not a boring pitcher, but he's not going to blow you away with his velocity or movement. Instead, he just spends his time casually painting the corners of the strike zone and inducing a pop fly every now and then until you look up and seven innings have passed in the blink of an eye. It's similar to how avid painters could lose an hour or two simply by watching Bob Ross calmly paint happy trees on a blank easel. Soroka has yet to paint a true masterpiece but if (and when) it happens, it'll happen before you realize what's really going on and you'll appreciate what he's done once he's finished.

Anthony Swarzak RHP Born: 09/10/85 Age: 34 Bats: R Throws: R Height: 6'4" Weight: 215 Origin: Round 2, 2004 Draft (#61 overall)

YEAR	TEAM	LVL	AGE	W	L	SV	G	GS	IP	H	HR	BB/9	K/9	K	GB%	BABIP	WHIP	ERA	DRA	WARP	MPH	FB%	WHF	CSP
2017	CHA	MLB	31	4	3	1	41	0	48¹	37	2	2.4	9.7	52	40%	.294	1.03	2.23	2.92	1.2	96.1	48.8	15.5	47.3
2017	MIL	MLB	31	2	1	1	29	0	29	21	4	2.8	12.1	39	51%	.270	1.03	2.48	3.37	0.6	96.6	48.2	15.3	46.8
2018	NYN	MLB	32	0	2	4	29	0	26¹	28	6	4.8	10.6	31	31%	.344	1.59	6.15	5.71	-0.2	96.3	53.5	9.8	46.9
2019	ATL	MLB	33	1	2	1	44	0	39²	38	6	4.3	7.9	35	49%	.291	1.44	4.31	5.48	-0.1	94.9	39.8	12.2	39.9
2019	SEA	MLB	33	2	2	3	15	0	13²	14	6	5.3	11.2	17	44%	.242	1.61	5.27	5.45	0.0	95.6	42.9	13.1	43.7
2020	ATL	MLB	34	2	2	0	33	0	35	35	6	3.6	8.7	34	43%	.301	1.41	4.66	4.86	0.2	94.6	45.2	12.8	43.8

Comparables: Brandon Lyon, Jeanmar Gómez, Tommy Hunter

At the three-and-a-half-week mark of the 2019 season, Swarzak had come out of the gate firing on all cylinders and making six consecutive scoreless appearances in a row for the Mariners—who added the righty as a cash balancer in the trade that sent Edwin Díaz and Robinson Canó to New York. He then had seven appearances in a row in which he allowed at least one run, and found himself pushed out of Seattle befor Memorial Day.

At the three-and-a-half month mark of the 2019 season, Swarzak was fully on the path to redemption and pitching high-leverage innings for a playoff team. He leaned heavily on his slider and held opposing hitters to a .129/.200/.214 line in his first two months in Atlanta, bringing his seasonal ERA down to 2.31. He then saw a drop in velocity down the stretch and gave up nearly a run an inning until his season ended by being unceremoniously left off the NLDS roster.

At the three-and-a-half decade mark in his time on Earth, Swarzak is inconsistent, unreliable and has gotten the last big payday of his career. That 2017 miracle of a season is a relic of a shoulder that cannot find the strike zone consistently enough to function as anything more than bullpen depth.

Josh Tomlin RHP Born: 10/19/84 Age: 35 Bats: R Throws: R Height: 6'1" Weight: 190 Origin: Round 19, 2006 Draft (#581 overall)

YEAR	TEAM	LVL	AGE	W	L	SV	G	GS	IP	H	HR	BB/9	K/9	K	GB%	BABIP	WHIP	ERA	DRA	WARP	MPH	FB%	WHF	CSP
2017	CLE	MLB	32	10	9	0	26	26	141	166	23	0.9	7.0	109	42%	.329	1.28	4.98	4.44	1.8	89.4	71.8	9.6	49.1
2018	COH	AAA	33	0	1	0	3	3	9¹	19	3	0.0	7.7	8	37%	.457	2.04	6.75	8.32	-0.3				
2018	CLE	MLB	33	2	5	0	32	9	70¹	92	25	1.5	5.9	46	32%	.286	1.48	6.14	6.87	-1.4	89.8	72.7	9.4	49.9
2019	ATL	MLB	34	2	1	2	51	1	79¹	82	14	0.8	5.8	51	35%	.274	1.12	3.74	5.27	0.1	90.6	74.1	10.1	47.3
2020	ATL	MLB	35	2	2	0	33	0	35	42	10	1.6	6.2	24	36%	.295	1.39	5.77	5.98	-0.2	88.8	71.5	9.5	47.7

Comparables: Tommy Hunter, Yohan Pino, Doug Fister

Going into the 2019 season, Tomlin had a clear reputation: He hated walks like your dog hated the vacuum cleaner. It seemed like he was pitching as if he was trying to avoid walking the batter at all costs. As it turned out, his walk-averse ways on the mound ended up transforming him from a waning starter to a somewhat reliable middle reliever. What's intriguing is that he managed to cut his home-run rate in half and did so without impeding on his strike-throwing proclivities. He's not someone you want for a high-leverage situation, but he's easy on the eyes and regardless of whether it works or not, you know it'll be over quickly.

Touki Toussaint RHP Born: 06/20/96 Age: 24 Bats: R Throws: R Height: 6'3" Weight: 185 Origin: Round 1, 2014 Draft (#16 overall)

YEAR	TEAM	LVL	AGE	W	L	SV	G	GS	IP	H	HR	BB/9	K/9	K	GB%	BABIP	WHIP	ERA	DRA	WARP	MPH	FB%	WHF	CSP
2017	BRV	A+	21	3	9	0	19	19	105¹	101	8	3.6	10.5	123	45%	.324	1.36	5.04	4.84	0.5				
2017	MIS	AA	21	3	4	0	7	7	39²	30	3	5.0	10.0	44	38%	.276	1.31	3.18	4.37	0.4				
2018	MIS	AA	22	4	6	0	16	16	86	66	7	3.8	11.2	107	48%	.284	1.19	2.93	3.46	1.9				
2018	GWN	AAA	22	5	0	0	8	8	50¹	35	0	3.0	10.0	56	44%	.280	1.03	1.43	2.75	1.6				
2018	ATL	MLB	22	2	1	0	7	5	29	18	1	6.5	9.9	32	47%	.254	1.34	4.03	4.69	0.2	95.9	53.4	9.9	43.6
2019	GWN	AAA	23	1	6	0	10	10	39²	51	5	6.4	10.0	44	43%	.393	1.99	7.49	6.83	0.0				
2019	ATL	MLB	23	4	0	0	24	1	41²	44	5	5.6	9.7	45	44%	.339	1.68	5.62	4.80	0.3	95.8	49.2	12.4	41.2
2020	ATL	MLB	24	4	4	0	20	10	60	56	8	4.8	9.5	63	43%	.301	1.46	4.61	4.56	0.8	95.6	52.1	11.9	43.6

Comparables: Sean Reid-Foley, Zack Littell, Jake Faria

It might sound absurd to say that a guy who's about to turn 24 is going into a make-or-break season, but that could indeed be the case for Toussaint in 2020. It's one thing to take a step back when it comes to making progress as a major leaguer, but it's a completely different thing to take a bit of a step back in Triple-A on top of that, as Touki didn't fare too much better while wearing a Stripers jersey. If and when the 2014 draft pick carves out a role in the majors, it's likely going to be in the bullpen, but he's going to need some semblance of control in order for his plus stuff to be useful in-game. That fearsome curveball still flashes under the surface and his split would be a weapon against lefties if he knew where it was going. Instead, left-handed batters waited on his fastball and tattooed him for a 1.205 OPS. On a team with less pitching depth, he'd have more opportunity to work through these issues, but that's not the situation at hand here.

Victor Vodnik RHP Born: 10/09/99 Age: 20 Bats: R Throws: R Height: 6'0" Weight: 200 Origin: Round 14, 2018 Draft (#412 overall)

YEAR	TEAM	LVL	AGE	W	L	SV	G	GS	IP	H	HR	BB/9	K/9	K	GB%	BABIP	WHIP	ERA	DRA	WARP	MPH	FB%	WHF	CSP
2019	ROM	A	19	1	3	3	23	3	67¹	55	1	3.2	9.2	69	53%	.303	1.17	2.94	4.44	0.4				
2020	ATL	MLB	20	2	2	0	33	0	35	34	5	3.9	7.8	30	48%	.289	1.41	4.43	4.70	0.3				

Comparables: Eduardo Sanchez, Edgar Garcia, Dustin Antolin

Vodnik was more whisper and legend than real human after getting drafted in the 14th round in 2018. A poor spring dropped his draft stock and the Braves pounced on the lottery ticket, immediately reaping benefits when his stuff shot upward in instructs. That drew the whispers about what this guy, with the name that's fun to say, could do in full-season ball. Vodnik didn't disappoint in Rome, pumping mid-90s heat, consistently touching 97 and 98 and flashing a solid breaking ball. Atlanta limited his innings and he missed all of July because of injury, but he came back strong and should see slight increases in usage as he goes level by level. He comes from a high slot that limits his movement, but the fastball is live and he has the stuff to thrive in an impactful relief role.

Jacob Webb RHP   Born: 08/15/93   Age: 26   Bats: R   Throws: R   Height: 6'1"   Weight: 200   Origin: Round 18, 2014 Draft (#553 overall)

YEAR	TEAM	LVL	AGE	W	L	SV	G	GS	IP	H	HR	BB/9	K/9	K	GB%	BABIP	WHIP	ERA	DRA	WARP	MPH	FB%	WHF	CSP
2017	BRV	A+	23	2	1	2	22	0	41^1	29	1	4.8	10.5	48	43%	.289	1.23	1.74	3.42	0.7				
2017	MIS	AA	23	3	1	0	16	0	24	17	1	5.2	9.8	26	36%	.276	1.29	2.62	4.15	0.2				
2018	MIS	AA	24	1	2	7	21	0	22^2	16	4	4.8	13.9	35	45%	.255	1.24	3.18	3.09	0.5				
2018	GWN	AAA	24	2	2	11	30	0	31^2	20	3	3.1	9.7	34	42%	.218	0.98	3.13	2.76	0.9				
2019	GWN	AAA	25	0	1	1	10	0	10^1	9	1	7.8	10.5	12	50%	.296	1.74	6.97	4.45	0.2				
2019	ATL	MLB	25	4	0	2	36	0	32^1	24	4	3.3	7.8	28	40%	.233	1.11	1.39	4.91	0.2	96.4	54.5	13.3	46.5
2020	ATL	MLB	26	1	1	0	21	0	23	21	4	4.2	9.1	23	40%	.290	1.40	4.38	4.48	0.2	96.0	55.5	13.5	47.3

Comparables: Mark Worrell, Ian Gibaut, Sam Tuivailala

As far as coverage of aspiring minor leaguers go, we're in a bit of a golden age. It's not particularly hard to find information on plenty of prospects, so there's less mystery and intrigue surrounding the arrival of young players in the major leagues. However, some guys can still fall through the cracks to make an anonymous arrival and Webb falls into that category. Even when he was actually showing up on prospect lists, he still elicited a reaction of "Who?" from casual fans when he made it to Atlanta. He continued to toil in obscurity while he racking up productive relief appearances for the Braves. An elbow impingement cut his season short, but it's clear that Webb does indeed have what it takes to stick around as a reliever at this level, even if his ERA overstates the impact.

Patrick Weigel RHP   Born: 07/08/94   Age: 25   Bats: R   Throws: R   Height: 6'6"   Weight: 240   Origin: Round 7, 2015 Draft (#210 overall)

YEAR	TEAM	LVL	AGE	W	L	SV	G	GS	IP	H	HR	BB/9	K/9	K	GB%	BABIP	WHIP	ERA	DRA	WARP	MPH	FB%	WHF	CSP
2017	MIS	AA	22	3	0	0	7	7	37^1	32	2	2.7	9.2	38	37%	.300	1.15	2.89	4.26	0.4				
2017	GWN	AAA	22	3	2	0	8	8	41	42	5	3.7	6.6	30	44%	.301	1.44	5.27	5.28	0.2				
2019	MIS	AA	24	0	1	0	7	7	15^2	8	0	5.2	9.2	16	54%	.205	1.09	1.72	3.21	0.3				
2019	GWN	AAA	24	6	1	0	21	11	63^1	42	9	4.5	7.8	55	40%	.208	1.17	2.98	3.03	2.2				
2020	ATL	MLB	25	1	2	0	14	3	28	28	4	3.9	7.9	24	40%	.300	1.47	5.12	5.09	0.2				

Comparables: Keyvius Sampson, Stephen Gonsalves, Ryan Helsley

Congratulations are in order for Weigel, who made it to the major leagues in 2019 after losing most of his 2018 season due to Tommy John surgery. It'll be hard to find video evidence of Weigel in the big leagues since he didn't make a single appearance (despite being called up twice), but he got to put the uniform on and realize a lifelong dream. After getting through 2019 with a clean bill of health while being guided through most of the season on a pitch limit, the next step for Weigel is to break those chains and show what he can really do with his high-octane fastball and biting slider. The next time he makes the big leagues, you won't have to look hard to find video of him being there—he'll be the center of attention.

Bryse Wilson RHP   Born: 12/20/97   Age: 22   Bats: R   Throws: R   Height: 6'1"   Weight: 225   Origin: Round 4, 2016 Draft (#109 overall)

YEAR	TEAM	LVL	AGE	W	L	SV	G	GS	IP	H	HR	BB/9	K/9	K	GB%	BABIP	WHIP	ERA	DRA	WARP	MPH	FB%	WHF	CSP
2017	ROM	A	19	10	7	0	26	26	137	105	8	2.4	9.1	139	54%	.272	1.04	2.50	3.33	3.1				
2018	BRV	A+	20	2	0	0	5	5	26^2	16	0	2.4	8.8	26	60%	.229	0.86	0.34	2.48	0.9				
2018	MIS	AA	20	3	5	0	15	15	77	77	3	3.0	10.4	89	44%	.347	1.34	3.97	4.63	0.6				
2018	GWN	AAA	20	3	0	0	5	3	22	20	6	1.2	11.5	28	45%	.280	1.05	5.32	3.38	0.5				
2018	ATL	MLB	20	1	0	0	3	1	7	8	0	7.7	7.7	6	29%	.381	2.00	6.43	5.37	0.0	97.0	71.1	15.6	45.4
2019	GWN	AAA	21	10	7	0	21	21	121	120	12	1.9	8.8	118	46%	.316	1.21	3.42	3.27	4.0				
2019	ATL	MLB	21	1	1	0	6	4	20	26	5	4.5	7.2	16	34%	.339	1.80	7.20	7.30	-0.3	96.6	71.9	9.5	47.6
2020	ATL	MLB	22	3	3	0	37	5	58	60	10	2.9	7.9	51	40%	.294	1.35	4.61	4.77	0.5	96.7	74.7	11.4	48.6

Comparables: Lucas Giolito, Jaime Barria, Jake Thompson

Wilson ended up starting the 2019 season with the Braves, but it was pretty evident by his subsequent cameo appearances across the rest of the season that he was not ready for the majors. The good news is that the Braves weren't counting on him being ready and are continuing to be patient with the 22-year-old. While the new balls were flying all over the International League, Wilson did a great job of keeping the ball in the yard and limiting unnecessary baserunners by posting the best walk rate of his pro career. And despite a step back in his strikeout rate, it allowed him to pitch deeper into games as he made it through at least six innings in 13 of his 21 starts, including his final eight in a row in Gwinnett. Wilson is going to get plenty of time to figure out whether his future is in the rotation.

★　★　★ *2020 Top 101 Prospect* **#89** ★　★　★

Kyle Wright RHP Born: 10/02/95 Age: 24 Bats: R Throws: R Height: 6'4" Weight: 200 Origin: Round 1, 2017 Draft (#5 overall)

YEAR	TEAM	LVL	AGE	W	L	SV	G	GS	IP	H	HR	BB/9	K/9	K	GB%	BABIP	WHIP	ERA	DRA	WARP	MPH	FB%	WHF	CSP
2017	BRV	A+	21	0	1	0	6	6	11¹	8	0	3.2	7.9	10	61%	.258	1.06	3.18	3.01	0.3				
2018	MIS	AA	22	6	8	0	20	20	109¹	103	6	3.5	8.6	105	56%	.311	1.34	3.70	4.12	1.6				
2018	GWN	AAA	22	2	1	0	7	4	28²	15	2	2.5	8.8	28	51%	.183	0.80	2.51	2.15	1.1				
2018	ATL	MLB	22	0	0	0	4	0	6	4	2	9.0	7.5	5	41%	.133	1.67	4.50	4.98	0.0	95.8	51.6	10.2	37.6
2019	GWN	AAA	23	11	4	0	21	21	112¹	107	13	2.8	9.3	116	48%	.313	1.26	4.17	3.54	3.4				
2019	ATL	MLB	23	0	3	0	7	4	19²	24	4	5.9	8.2	18	43%	.351	1.88	8.69	6.33	-0.1	96.6	54.4	9.7	42.6
2020	*ATL*	*MLB*	*24*	*4*	*5*	*0*	*37*	*10*	*78*	*83*	*12*	*3.7*	*7.8*	*68*	*47%*	*.308*	*1.48*	*5.10*	*5.06*	*0.5*	*96.3*	*55.4*	*10.1*	*41.6*

Comparables: Reynaldo López, Zack Wheeler, Zack Littell

For a prospect who ended up making the Opening Day roster for a playoff contender, there weren't really too many accompanying expectations for Wright in 2019. If anything, he just happened to be in the right place at the right time during the first week of the season. This was more of a learning year for Wright than anything else with two of the most common issues to tackle among upper-level prospects: fastball command and some sort of reliable third pitch to go with his mid-90s fastball and hard slider. He simplified his approach tremendously when he made a few relief appearances in September and looked excellent while doing so. While having their second-highest draft pick of the century turn out to be a potential impact reliever isn't the outcome the Braves were hoping for, that may just be what they get in the former Vanderbilt ace if Wright can't solve at least one of those two lingering issues.

LINEOUTS

Hitters

HITTER	POS	TEAM	LVL	AGE	PA	R	2B	3B	HR	RBI	BB	K	SB	CS	AVG/OBP/SLG	DRC+	VORP	BABIP	BRR	FRAA	WARP
CJ Alexander	INF	MIS	AA	22	78	6	1	0	2	7	8	25	0	0	.103/.195/.206	39	-2.9	.119	0.5	3B(10): -0.3, 1B(5): -0.2	-0.2
	INF	BRV	A+	22	74	4	1	0	0	1	14	18	3	1	.133/.297/.150	102	0.7	.190	0.0	3B(11): 1.8, 1B(4): -0.6	0.3
Mahki Backstrom	1B	BRA	Rk	17	82	8	5	0	2	8	12	27	1	0	.300/.402/.457	113	4.7	.463	0.1	1B(22): 0.5	0.2
Bryce Ball	1B	DNV	Rk+	20	173	37	12	0	13	38	22	30	0	0	.324/.410/.676	173	25.5	.321	0.3		1.5
	1B	ROM	A	20	90	14	6	0	4	14	4	20	0	0	.337/.367/.547	154	5.2	.403	-0.7	1B(11): -1.3	0.4
Justin Dean	CF	ROM	A	22	503	85	18	9	9	46	62	115	47	10	.284/.386/.431	141	43.9	.368	2.8	CF(101): 3.7, RF(3): -0.2	4.3
Lucas Duda	1B	OMA	AAA	33	46	6	3	0	1	4	4	13	0	0	.286/.348/.429	75	-1.4	.393	-1.0	1B(3): 0.3	-0.1
	1B	GWN	AAA	33	68	3	1	0	1	5	6	21	0	0	.140/.235/.211	43	-7.0	.184	-0.4	1B(7): 0.5	-0.3
	1B	KCA	MLB	33	119	7	4	0	4	15	11	32	0	0	.171/.252/.324	78	-1.5	.197	-0.7	1B(19): 0.6	-0.2
Trey Harris	OF	ROM	A	23	230	38	14	4	8	44	20	32	4	4	.366/.437/.594	207	32.3	.405	1.3	RF(27): -1.4, LF(17): -2.1	2.7
	OF	MIS	AA	23	156	15	7	3	2	12	4	33	1	2	.281/.318/.411	91	6.7	.351	-1.1	RF(36): -1.3	-0.1
	OF	BRV	A+	23	139	20	5	0	4	17	12	26	3	0	.303/.388/.443	145	5.6	.359	-2.5	RF(20): 1.4, LF(9): -0.4	0.7
Alex Jackson	C	ATL	MLB	23	15	0	0	0	0	0	1	5	0	0	.000/.133/.000	77	0.4	.000	0.0	C(4): 0.5	0.1
	C	GWN	AAA	23	345	52	9	0	28	65	20	118	1	0	.229/.313/.533	106	13.6	.261	-2.8	C(78): 17.9	3.1
John Ryan Murphy	C	GWN	AAA	28	50	5	0	0	1	3	2	13	0	0	.170/.220/.234	31	-5.3	.212	0.1	C(13): 0.2	-0.1
	C	RNO	AAA	28	136	26	7	0	9	26	12	34	0	0	.250/.316/.524	92	6.5	.272	1.4	C(31): -1.7	0.5
	C	ARI	MLB	28	69	9	3	0	4	7	6	28	0	0	.177/.250/.419	68	0.8	.233	0.3	C(18): 1.4, P(2): 0.0	0.2
	C	ATL	MLB	28	1	0	0	0	0	0	0	0	0	0	.000/.000/.000	143	0.0	.000	0.0	C(1): 0.0	0.0
Rafael Ortega	LF	GWN	AAA	28	493	83	34	3	21	58	59	95	14	7	.285/.373/.524	121	29.7	.323	2.8	CF(60): 4.0, RF(29): 3.2	3.3
	LF	ATL	MLB	28	96	7	3	0	2	10	8	22	3	0	.205/.271/.307	75	-0.4	.250	0.8	LF(20): -1.0, RF(6): 0.0	-0.1
Beau Philip	SS	DNV	Rk+	20	239	27	6	0	4	20	26	51	5	5	.193/.297/.280	72	-0.3	.235	0.2		0.3
Jefrey Ramos	LF	BRV	A+	20	498	49	16	4	9	56	30	99	1	1	.241/.291/.352	94	6.1	.287	-1.7	LF(114): -14.7	-1.0

You'll be hard pressed to find a more unlucky, injury-plagued 2019 season than **CJ Alexander**'s, but maybe the baseball gods were angry for how easy he was making the sport look in the lower levels in 2018. ⊗ **Mahki Backstrom** is the poster child for Atlanta's 2019 draft strategy of late-round fliers on athletes with long developmental roads ahead of them. It's fun when one of these lands, especially when they're accompanied by an 80-grade name. ⊗ The biggest question surrounding **Bryce Ball**, who already boasted the biggest power in Atlanta's system after the 2019 draft, isn't his ultimate future but why he was picked so low. The kid is huge, hits tanks and is going to rocket up prospect lists, defense be damned. ⊗ **Justin Dean**'s feet on the basepaths are hotter than an overheated microwave sausage biscuit. Unlike the breakfast sandwich, Dean, a speedy fourth outfielder type, can potentially live up to expectations. ⊗ At a time in this country when most elected officials think leadership is a boat, we say good on **Lucas Duda** for extending his big-league career by another year on the strength of his vibes. ⊗ **Trey Harris** just won't stop hitting and maximizing his prospect value, which is fun to watch from a 32nd-round pick and senior sign with what's now a major-league future and fewer doubters by the day. ⊗ If you want a prime example of what the juiced baseball was like in Triple-A last season, **Alex Jackson** hit 28 homers in just 345 plate appearances. It'll be a miracle if he can ever replicate that at the major league level. ⊗ The man of many first names is a solid defensive catcher who can be trusted behind the plate. When it comes to what **John Ryan Murphy** can do for you at the plate with a bat in his hand, it's a completely different story and explains why he's in third-catcher purgatory. ⊗ If someone ever asks you who hit a game-winning grand slam on August 19, 2019 to defeat the Los Angeles Dodgers, you can now say that it was **Rafael Ortega**. Do with that information what you will. ⊗ **Beau Philip** became Atlanta's second-round beau in 2019 and offers some pop up the middle, but his hand path to the zone might necessitate a future tweak to get to that power more efficiently. ⊗ **Jefrey Ramos**, a bat-first corner prospect with diminishing value, ended up lost while trying to navigate through Florida, which has probably happened to a lot of us at some point.

Pitchers

PITCHER	TEAM	LVL	AGE	W	L	SV	G	GS	IP	H	HR	BB/9	K/9	K	GB%	BABIP	WHIP	ERA	DRA	WARP	MPH	FB%	WHF	CSP
Jerry Blevins	LVG	AAA	35	0	0	0	7	0	10²	9	2	3.4	13.5	16	12%	.318	1.22	1.69	3.23	0.3				
	ATL	MLB	35	1	0	1	45	0	32¹	25	5	4.5	10.3	37	29%	.247	1.27	3.90	4.98	0.1	90.2	42.7	11.6	43.5
Thomas Burrows	MIS	AA	24	1	3	1	16	0	21	16	2	2.6	10.3	24	47%	.264	1.05	3.86	3.56	0.3				
	GWN	AAA	24	1	1	6	27	0	36	31	3	4.5	9.8	39	41%	.298	1.36	4.75	3.51	0.9				
Tucker Davidson	MIS	AA	23	7	6	0	21	21	110²	88	5	3.7	9.9	122	51%	.304	1.20	2.03	4.43	0.7				
	GWN	AAA	23	1	1	0	4	4	19	20	0	4.3	5.7	12	51%	.339	1.53	2.84	5.48	0.2				
Grant Dayton	GWN	AAA	31	0	1	0	22	0	26²	20	6	1.4	13.8	41	40%	.275	0.90	3.04	2.52	1.0				
	ATL	MLB	31	0	1	0	14	0	12	12	4	3.0	10.5	14	39%	.276	1.33	3.00	4.01	0.2	92.8	76.5	13.2	49.8
Jasseel De La Cruz	ROM	A	22	0	1	0	4	4	18	19	1	2.5	11.0	22	53%	.391	1.33	2.50	4.67	0.1				
	BRV	A+	22	3	1	0	4	4	28	12	0	2.2	8.4	26	52%	.174	0.68	1.93	2.44	0.9				
	MIS	AA	22	4	7	0	17	16	87	71	7	3.8	7.6	73	46%	.262	1.24	3.83	4.67	0.3				
Daysbel Hernandez	BRV	A+	22	5	2	7	35	0	52²	34	2	3.9	12.0	70	38%	.264	1.08	1.71	2.88	1.1				
Jake Higginbotham	ROM	A	23	4	4	4	33	0	58²	52	5	4.0	9.7	63	49%	.311	1.33	3.07	4.94	-0.1				
Philip Pfeifer	BRV	A+	26	4	6	0	16	14	92	81	7	2.2	10.8	110	42%	.315	1.13	3.23	3.86	1.3				
	MIS	AA	26	1	2	0	11	4	34	25	2	4.2	9.5	36	40%	.264	1.21	2.38	4.09	0.3				
	GWN	AAA	26	1	0	0	3	0	7¹	7	1	3.7	16.0	13	53%	.333	1.36	2.45	1.44	0.3				
Trey Riley	ROM	A	21	2	7	0	17	12	58²	71	4	7.1	6.3	41	47%	.354	1.99	7.67	8.24	-2.2				
Chad Sobotka	GWN	AAA	25	2	1	2	17	0	20²	23	3	1.7	13.9	32	48%	.426	1.31	4.79	3.14	0.6				
	ATL	MLB	25	0	0	0	32	0	29	28	6	5.9	11.8	38	45%	.324	1.62	6.21	4.51	0.3	98.1	56.6	16.2	41.7
Freddy Tarnok	BRA	Rk	20	0	1	0	3	3	8	3	1	1.1	10.1	9	50%	.118	0.50	3.38	1.00	0.4				
	BRV	A+	20	3	7	0	19	19	98	105	6	3.3	7.5	82	38%	.329	1.44	4.87	6.06	-1.2				
Jeremy Walker	MIS	AA	24	1	6	6	21	1	58²	56	2	0.8	8.7	57	57%	.316	1.04	2.45	3.81	0.6				
	GWN	AAA	24	2	1	1	11	0	22²	20	1	2.4	9.9	25	50%	.339	1.15	3.97	2.87	0.7				
	ATL	MLB	24	0	0	0	6	0	9¹	9	0	3.9	5.8	6	57%	.321	1.39	1.93	5.49	0.0	94.1	63.4	9.1	41
Huascar Ynoa	BRV	A+	21	0	1	0	3	3	11	10	0	4.9	13.1	16	59%	.370	1.45	3.27	3.91	0.2				
	MIS	AA	21	1	2	1	6	0	13²	17	2	3.3	9.9	15	67%	.366	1.61	5.27	5.49	-0.1				
	GWN	AAA	21	3	5	0	17	14	72²	80	14	4.2	9.8	79	43%	.332	1.57	5.33	5.06	1.1				
	ATL	MLB	21	0	0	0	2	0	3	6	1	3.0	9.0	3	42%	.455	2.33	18.00	6.70	0.0	99.2	60.6	10.6	40.8

Being a LOOGY in 2020 means that **Jerry Blevins** spent much of the offseason workshopping some new skills like faking an arm injury, throwing a punch or disappearing into a puff of smoke. ⊗ **Thomas Burrows** is running out of time to find the strike zone and a major-league relief role—which will have to come in that order—but he's a lefty with a plus slider so opportunities will most assuredly come. ⊗ Texas high school Tascosa's **Tucker Davidson** has a titillating, tailing heater, a tilting breaker and a teasing changeup, all of which took a step forward to put him at the doorstep to a major-league role. ⊗ If anybody can tell you the dangers of playing catch, it's **Grant Dayton**. He came out of one with a fractured big toe. The unfortunate miss cost him a month of what turned out to be a very underwhelming season. ⊗ For **Jasseel De La Cruz**, it was simply a matter of staying healthy for his lively stuff and major-league (relief) ability to shine through in a breakout prospect season, which is the case for many but actually happened for him. ⊗ **Daysbel Hernández** is a quick-armed, physical Cuban with a lively two-pitch mix that wasn't even close to tested in A-ball, but a trip to the Arizona Fall League should mean his plus name appears on a more suitable roster going forward. ⊗ **Jake Higginbotham** flashes a two-pitch mix from the left side that shows major-league potential, which makes the fact that he was relegated to the depths of the minors at 23 years old even more taxing on the brain than saying his last name. ⊗ Despite limiting runs fairly successfully, disturbing walk rates have always lain beneath the surface of **Philip Pfeifer**'s line. That changed in 2019 as a significant uptick in control meant that he was no longer flirting dangerously with too many baserunners and the ERA improved further as a result. ⊗ Safe to say that **Trey Riley**'s full-season debut—full of inconsistent stuff and injured list stints—could go in the trash and no one would miss it, but the potential for upper-90s heat and a sharp slider in short bursts will keep prospect hounds on his trail. ⊗ The good news is that **Chad Sobotka** got the opportunity to throw twice as many innings in 2019 than he did in 2018. Unfortunately, every single one of his stats went in the wrong direction. ⊗ **Freddy Tarnok**'s development journey toward a big-league staff is going to be long and arduous, but what's the fun in getting there easily? ⊗ **Jeremy Walker** spent 2019 making some serious improvement at both the Double-A and Triple-A levels. He was rewarded with a handful of big league appearances in 2019 and he'll be aiming for a steady bullpen role soon. ⊗ **Huascar Ynoa** was called up in 2019 for the first three major league innings of his career. That was enough time for him to give up a grand slam to Christian Yelich. Good morning, good afternoon and good night until we see you again, Huascar.

BALTIMORE ORIOLES

Essay by Allison McCague

Player comments by Jon Meoli and BP staff

I remember standing in the upper deck at Camden Yards on May 11, 2015. The stadium was packed and the crowd swelled with anticipation ahead of the first home game since the protests against police brutality that brought Baltimore to its knees. I still get emotional about that day, and how it transported me back to my post-9/11 New Jersey childhood, when I first learned what a baseball team can mean to a place—how it can stitch together a city torn apart at the seams.

Along with many other residents instructed to remain indoors, I watched the April 29th game on television. You might recall that game as the empty-stadium contest played by the Orioles and Chicago White Sox. Even then, as each bat crack and slapped mitt echoed around the ballpark, I thought I was experiencing something I would never see again.

Over the intervening years, I went to countless Orioles games. The team and the open arms of Camden Yards kept me company during my time in graduate school. During one otherwise forgettable weekday game in June of 2019—one of the last games I would attend before leaving Baltimore—a thought passed through my mind: "This place is a ghost town." The stadium was almost as quiet as it had been on that April afternoon.

Just as the city had attempted to rebuild years prior, now its baseball team has to as well.

⚾   ⚾   ⚾

Of the players on those 2015 Orioles, only Chris Davis and Mychal Givens remain. Gone are the days of Adam Jones and Manny Machado, as the franchise has sped away from the Buck Showalter era. This is instead Mike Elias and Brandon Hyde's time to...well, not shine, not yet.

I don't want to dwell too much on the negative aspects of the 2019 Orioles—and there were many, to be clear, including yielding a record amount of home runs. Every season, even a 108-loss effort, contains within it nuggets of joy. To wit: John Means' star rose bright across the night sky that was the majors' worst pitching staff; Jonathan Villar, Trey Mancini and Hanser Alberto all gave fans reasons to keep watching when the Orioles were at the dish; Stevie Wilkerson recorded

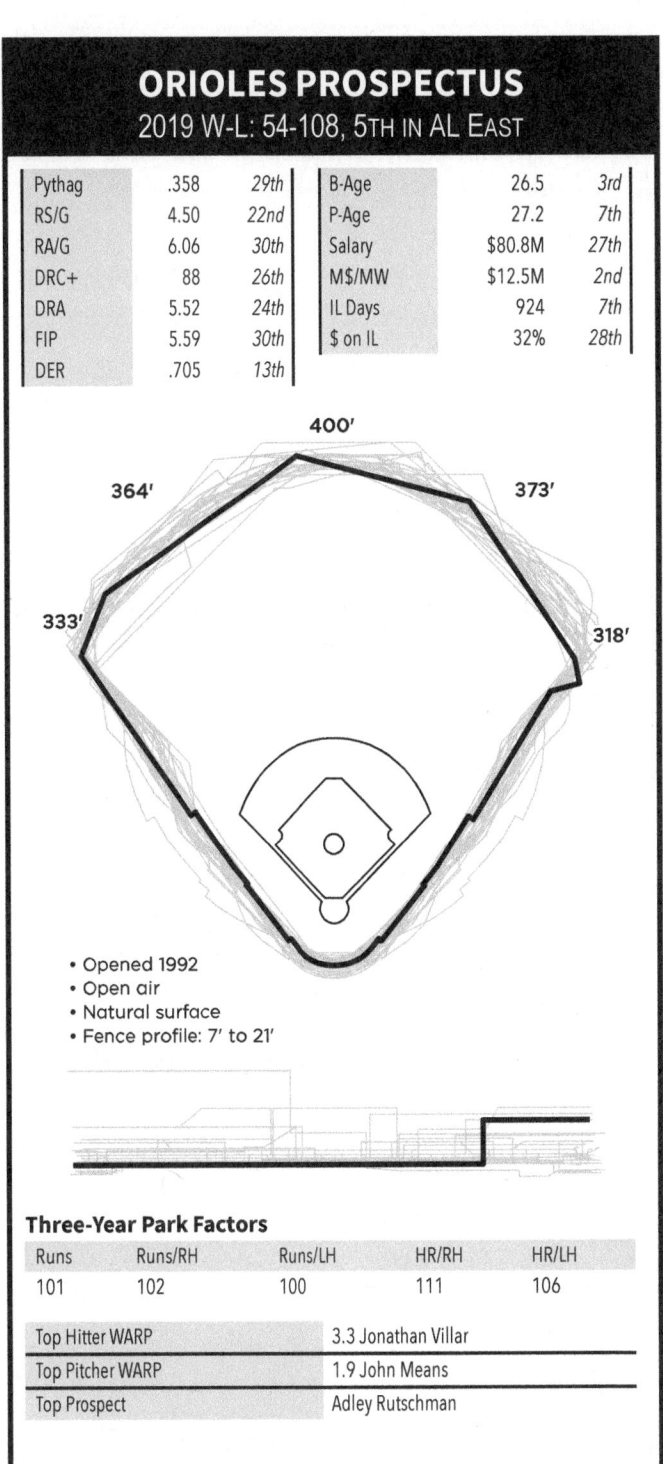

ORIOLES PROSPECTUS
2019 W-L: 54-108, 5TH IN AL EAST

Pythag	.358	29th	B-Age	26.5	3rd
RS/G	4.50	22nd	P-Age	27.2	7th
RA/G	6.06	30th	Salary	$80.8M	27th
DRC+	88	26th	M$/MW	$12.5M	2nd
DRA	5.52	24th	IL Days	924	7th
FIP	5.59	30th	$ on IL	32%	28th
DER	.705	13th			

400'
364'   373'
333'   318'

- Opened 1992
- Open air
- Natural surface
- Fence profile: 7' to 21'

Three-Year Park Factors

Runs	Runs/RH	Runs/LH	HR/RH	HR/LH
101	102	100	111	106

Top Hitter WARP	3.3 Jonathan Villar
Top Pitcher WARP	1.9 John Means
Top Prospect	Adley Rutschman

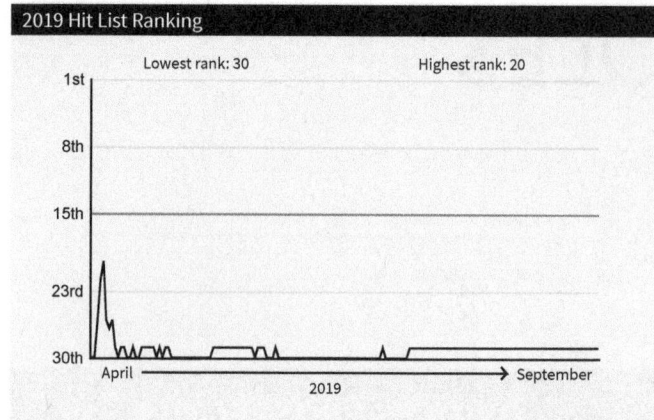

2019 Hit List Ranking

Lowest rank: 30   Highest rank: 20

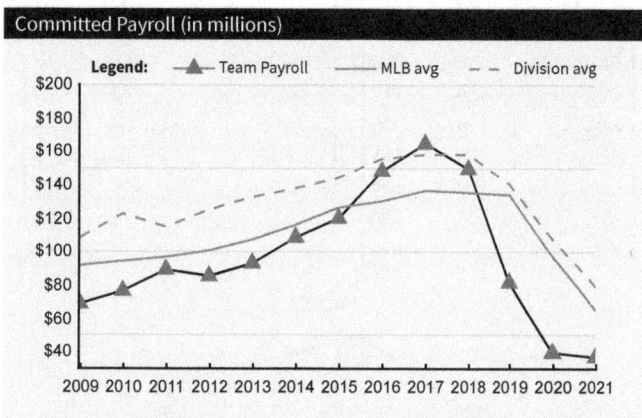

Committed Payroll (in millions)

Legend: ▲ Team Payroll   — MLB avg   - - Division avg

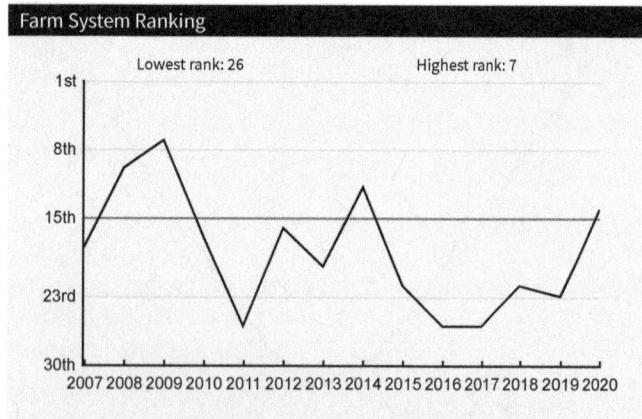

Farm System Ranking

Lowest rank: 26   Highest rank: 7

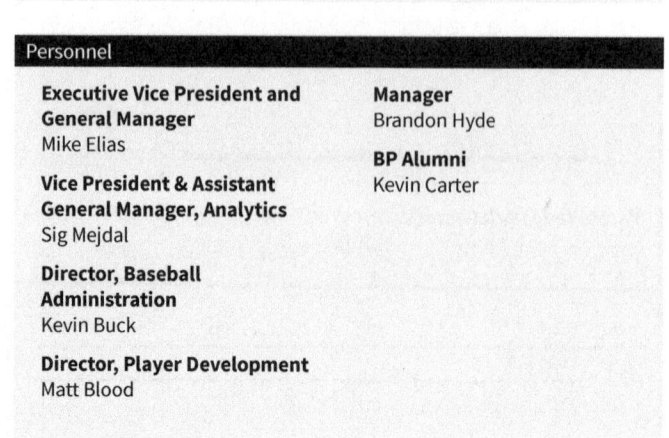

Personnel

Executive Vice President and General Manager
Mike Elias

Vice President & Assistant General Manager, Analytics
Sig Mejdal

Director, Baseball Administration
Kevin Buck

Director, Player Development
Matt Blood

Manager
Brandon Hyde

BP Alumni
Kevin Carter

the first save by a position player in the history of the game, and then recorded arguably the best catch of the year during the season finale. (It was an exciting game, for those who didn't watch it. The Orioles lost, which you probably guessed. So it goes.)

It's eternally tempting to lean into those negative aspects because of the circumstances at play. After all, as the Orioles suffered through their second consecutive 100-loss season in 2019, their Beltway rivals celebrated their first World Series victory—and did so while embracing a player who had come up short during his time in Baltimore. But hey, Gerardo Parra, cult hero, was simply a dash of salt in the protracted wound for most Orioles fans.

The reality is that this is not the upstart team down the road in the nation's capital—still a fledgling in baseball years. This is not the headline-grabbing, All-American championship squad. This is standing resolute, with a chip on your shoulder and knowing the difficult road ahead. This is Birdland. And right now, Birdland is a tough place to be—partially by design.

The Orioles continued to dismantle their old core over the winter, trading Dylan Bundy and non-tendering Jonathan Villar. Heading into 2020, there's a tacit agreement in place: play well, and you'll probably find yourself traded—especially if you make more than the league-minimum salary. That could mean the likes of Mancini and—yes—Givens go next.

Were it not for Chris Davis' immovable deal, the Orioles payroll would likely sit well below its current $60 million projection.

⚾   ⚾   ⚾

"I want to see a playoff team at Camden Yards, and we want to see a playoff team at Camden Yards," Elias said in the aftermath of the Villar and Bundy moves. "There's only one way to get there, given where we're at, where we're starting from. We all know the strategy, the process. This is not easy. This is not something we want to happen again, but coming into the organization in late 2018, with the roster construction what it was, where the talent base was, where we were in the standings—this was the only path."

The only path.

When Elias says that a full teardown is "the only path," he's not offering a valid premise. Of course it wasn't the only path; tanking never is, not in an industry that prints money—not for a team that made three postseason appearances over a five-year span over the last decade. It is, however, the path that Elias—who comes direct from Houston—opted for, and it is now the path that the fan base, along with the rest of the organization, has to endure. There's no going back.

During the last homestand of the 2019 season, Orioles players wrote thank you notes to some randomly selected season ticket holders. The catharsis in the exercise was obvious. Much is made—rightly so—of the toll tanking takes on a fanbase. But it's not easy for the players either. They didn't have a choice in the matter—and still don't. They still have to show up to the ballpark every day and play, knowing that they're part of a grand exercise where their chance of signing another lease in Baltimore hinges on how well they perform—too well, and they'll find themselves on the first plane out of BWI. It could be worse; they could become known for not being good enough for a team punting the foreseeable future.

The cruel reality of a full-fledged rebuild is that it is not only the players who are perpetually on the block. The Orioles are in the midst of an organizational shakeup from top to bottom, punctuated by the firing of nearly a dozen people in the scouting department in late August, including some of whom had been with the team for decades. In a time when it feels like Moneyball has been stretched to its furthest conclusion across the sport, this is far from the most prominent or even the most cynical example of bald cost-cutting measures. But, when lifelong members of the team's community depart, a thread of Baltimore's fabric is given a gentle tug.

Ask anyone in the new Orioles regime and they will tell you there is still a lot of work to be done. Adley Rutschman, who instantly became the best prospect in the organization when the Orioles selected him with the first pick in the 2019 draft, is the first glimpse of what the future can hold. He is a switch-hitting, defensively gifted catcher who may just be everything Matt Wieters never quite was. But one top prospect, even if he develops into a superstar, does not a successful rebuild make. True, there are other reasons for optimism: Grayson Rodriguez is a promising prep pitcher with mid-rotation potential and Ryan Mountcastle posted a 115 DRC+ in Triple-A in 2019. Beyond (and arguably even including) them, many questions remain.

Look no further than last season for evidence of how quickly youngsters can see their stock collapse. Cedric Mullins ended his 2018 as Jones's heir apparent, but struggled mightily last season to remain in the plans. Yusniel Díaz, the centerpiece of the Manny Machado trade, also took a step back in 2019, as he was stymied by injury. There's a faint light at the end of the Harbor Tunnel, but it's still at the stage where you have to really squint to see it.

⚾   ⚾   ⚾

A baseball team can mean a lot to a place and to a person—in good times, and in bad, but maybe especially in bad. At its best, doing a doctorate is challenging and rewarding. It can also be incredibly isolating. When science was often fickle, baseball was always there. Camden Yards, with its gorgeous sightlines and wonderful aesthetics, was always there. Losing myself in the cadence of a game was precisely what meant the most to me when I was stretched to my mental and emotional limits.

When we discuss "meaningful" games, we almost always mean games that have implications for the postseason. But that premise operates under the basic assumption that

meaning is derived solely from winning. Rejecting that premise is smiling when you see the Orioles run out onto the field donning their weird and beautiful Maryland flag alternate jerseys. Rejecting that premise is yelling the "O!" extra loudly during the Star Spangled Banner, befuddling all of the visiting fans in the building. Rejecting that premise is sprinkling a little extra Old Bay on those crab fries. Rejecting that premise is seeking refuge at the ballpark as your city tries to heal itself, remembering that there is so much more to loving a team and loving a game than winning.

What much of the public consumes about Baltimore—the city and its baseball team—is what rises to the national headlines, much of which has been ugly. Yet the small moments embedded in the seams, from pitches thrown during a lost season, can be woven into a tapestry that tells you the story of a city lying underneath those headlines.

It can tell you the story of a city that even prior to those headlines has been decimated by systemic racism, crumbling housing and infrastructure, wage stagnation and violence. These things are unbearably isolating for those affected by them and often the only antidote is something, anything, that fosters a sense of community and supplies a rallying cry. Baltimore's communities have always been its strength. It is, after all, a city of neighborhoods, each with its own flavor and character. The cold, calculated commodification of the game and players that could have provided that sense of community and rallying cry turns baseball into a reminder of that trauma, rather than the escape it was for me all those summer nights at Camden Yards.

But I suppose baseball has always been a game that favors the journey over the destination. It meanders. It calls on you to crack open a Natty Boh and stay awhile. Baltimore is like that too. It's a rough-around-the-edges sort of place, always living in the shadow of its presently-celebrating close neighbor to the south. The longer you stay in Charm City, sitting on its stoops and walking its neighborhoods, the more apparent the aptness of the moniker becomes. Sure, investing emotionally takes work, but it is a labor of love, an exercise in passionate dedication that breeds the resilience required of an Orioles fan.

It's a bitter pill to swallow, knowing that Baltimore is a stepping stone on the way to something better. If he pitches well enough, he'll get traded to a contender. If he gets a decent enough job and starts a family, he'll leave Baltimore to live in the surrounding suburbs. What's left behind is an empty ballpark, the question hanging in the silent rows of seats: What if they stayed instead? I finished my graduate degree and I moved away from the city I had come to call home, just as the Orioles began their own journey towards something better. But just as Elias hopes to bring playoff baseball back to Baltimore, I hope I will return someday, too.

On October 15, 2014, I was finishing up an evening of experiments in the lab, listening on the radio as the Orioles were eliminated in the ALCS, bringing my first full baseball season in Baltimore to an end. It had been storming all day, but when I looked out the window next to my desk I saw a bright, beautiful rainbow arcing across the sky—a reminder that after a storm, there is hope, even if it can be fragile and fleeting.

It's a rebuild. We understand that. This was, we're told, the only path. ▪

—Allison McCague is an author of Baseball Prospectus.

HITTERS

Hanser Alberto INF Born: 10/17/92 Age: 27 Bats: R Throws: R Height: 5'11" Weight: 215 Origin: International Free Agent, 2009

YEAR	TEAM	LVL	AGE	PA	R	2B	3B	HR	RBI	BB	K	SB	CS	AVG/OBP/SLG	DRC+	VORP	BABIP	BRR	FRAA	WARP
2018	ROU	AAA	25	384	45	17	3	7	58	9	28	0	3	.330/.346/.452	111	18.4	.337	-0.8	SS(44): 7.1, 1B(43): -3.5	2.1
2018	TEX	MLB	25	30	0	2	0	0	0	2	4	0	1	.185/.241/.259	88	-1.3	.217	-0.4	SS(5): 0.1, 2B(4): -0.1	0.0
2019	BAL	MLB	26	550	62	21	2	12	51	16	50	4	4	.305/.329/.422	98	18.2	.318	1.6	2B(90): -5.0, 3B(66): 5.3	2.0
2020	BAL	MLB	27	595	58	25	2	14	65	18	68	5	3	.275/.303/.400	84	11.6	.292	1.4	2B -4, 3B 1	0.9

Comparables: Luis Sardiñas, Donovan Solano, Gio Urshela

While Alberto is an absolute delight and more-than-capable defender at three infield positions, the reason he was most useful to the Orioles will be the reason he'll be in the league for another decade if he wants to: he rakes against left-handed pitching. The only batter this century with over 200 plate appearances against southpaws to have a higher batting average against lefties than Alberto's .398 was Ichiro Suzuki in 2004. Alberto's 88 hits off lefties were the most of any player in a season, ever. After being waived by four organizations (including by the Orioles) between the end of 2018 and Opening Day 2019, a season like this will forever make Alberto a player who has a singular, exploitable skill coveted by every team, especially around playoff time. In an era of walks over hits and power over contact, Alberto's brand of late-blooming infielder is a fun throwback.

Chris Davis 1B Born: 03/17/86 Age: 34 Bats: L Throws: R Height: 6'3" Weight: 230 Origin: Round 5, 2006 Draft (#148 overall)

YEAR	TEAM	LVL	AGE	PA	R	2B	3B	HR	RBI	BB	K	SB	CS	AVG/OBP/SLG	DRC+	VORP	BABIP	BRR	FRAA	WARP
2017	BAL	MLB	31	524	65	15	1	26	61	61	195	1	1	.215/.309/.423	88	-1.4	.301	-2.0	1B(125): 4.2, 3B(2): -0.1	0.2
2018	BAL	MLB	32	522	40	12	0	16	49	41	192	2	0	.168/.243/.296	56	-28.7	.237	-4.6	1B(116): -5.4	-3.2
2019	BAL	MLB	33	352	26	9	0	12	36	39	139	0	0	.179/.276/.326	65	-1.6	.270	0.7	1B(97): -4.6, P(1): 0.0	-1.5
2020	BAL	MLB	34	315	37	12	0	14	41	36	124	1	0	.206/.306/.403	84	-2.7	.311	-1.1	1B -2	-0.4

Comparables: Ryan Howard, Carlos Pena, Jonny Gomes

There was a wraparound stretch across 2018 and 2019 during which Davis set a major-league record, going 62 consecutive plate appearances without a hit. Something like that doesn't happen without very bad luck, but striking out in 30 of those trips to the plate surely didn't help. Since he signed his miserable seven-year, $161 million contract ahead of the 2016 season, 96 players have at least 2,000 plate appearances and Davis has the eighth-lowest soft contact rate among them. It's just that his 36.1 percent strikeout rate is miles ahead of anyone else, culminating in a 39.5 percent strikeout rate last season—another major-league record (min 350 PA) that he will wear. Another year and Davis will have been known as "Crush" longer for his impact on the Orioles' payroll than on opposing pitchers' fastballs.

Cadyn Grenier SS Born: 10/31/96 Age: 23 Bats: R Throws: R Height: 5'11" Weight: 188 Origin: Round 1, 2018 Draft (#37 overall)

YEAR	TEAM	LVL	AGE	PA	R	2B	3B	HR	RBI	BB	K	SB	CS	AVG/OBP/SLG	DRC+	VORP	BABIP	BRR	FRAA	WARP
2018	DEL	A	21	183	23	12	2	1	13	17	53	3	2	.216/.297/.333	84	9.9	.312	-0.5	SS(39): 2.7	0.7
2019	DEL	A	22	364	49	18	3	7	39	48	107	5	1	.253/.360/.399	123	29.3	.360	3.0	SS(54): 6.1, 2B(26): -2.2	2.9
2019	FRD	A+	22	92	11	4	1	1	4	11	31	2	1	.208/.337/.325	72	2.4	.333	0.9	SS(22): 2.7	0.5
2020	BAL	MLB	23	251	22	12	1	6	25	17	93	1	0	.208/.271/.342	62	-4.7	.321	-0.3	SS 4, 2B 0	-0.1

Comparables: Michael Perez, Jeremy Hazelbaker, Jaylin Davis

The 2018 College World Series winners from Oregon State had plenty of offensive firepower that has translated into early pro success, perhaps most notably with the Orioles' top pick in 2019, Adley Rutschman. But as infielder Nick Madrigal put himself on the cusp of a major-league call with the White Sox and outfielder Trevor Larnach tore it up at the plate with the Twins system, Grenier barely lived up to his billing as a standout defender and excelled at little else in a difficult full-season debut. The 2018 competitive balance pick has a decent approach but no fluidity or power in his swing, and unless the Orioles can change that, it will have been a lot of draft capital spent on the type of player that can be had as a low-cost free agent or Rule 5 pick. They'd know. They grabbed a half-dozen last year.

Austin Hays CF Born: 07/05/95 Age: 24 Bats: R Throws: R Height: 6'1" Weight: 195 Origin: Round 3, 2016 Draft (#91 overall)

YEAR	TEAM	LVL	AGE	PA	R	2B	3B	HR	RBI	BB	K	SB	CS	AVG/OBP/SLG	DRC+	VORP	BABIP	BRR	FRAA	WARP
2017	FRD	A+	21	280	42	15	3	16	41	12	40	4	6	.328/.364/.592	149	25.5	.337	0.7	CF(57): 8.1, RF(4): -0.6	3.1
2017	BOW	AA	21	283	39	17	2	16	54	13	45	1	1	.330/.367/.594	157	31.3	.345	3.2	CF(32): -3.3, RF(29): -0.4	2.4
2017	BAL	MLB	21	63	4	3	0	1	8	2	16	0	0	.217/.238/.317	70	-3.3	.273	-0.4	RF(14): -1.6, CF(8): -1.3	-0.4
2018	ABE	A-	22	39	6	2	0	0	3	2	7	0	0	.189/.231/.243	92	-2.9	.233	0.0	RF(5): -0.6	0.0
2018	BOW	AA	22	288	34	12	2	12	43	12	59	6	3	.242/.271/.432	89	8.3	.263	0.9	RF(36): 6.7, LF(16): -0.3	1.1
2019	FRD	A+	23	40	3	0	0	2	6	1	11	0	0	.162/.200/.324	41	-1.0	.160	0.2	CF(7): -0.7	-0.2
2019	BOW	AA	23	61	9	5	0	3	11	5	11	3	1	.268/.328/.518	142	3.2	.286	-1.1	RF(7): 1.2, CF(4): 0.0	0.4
2019	NOR	AAA	23	257	43	16	1	10	27	11	61	6	4	.254/.304/.454	93	10.1	.302	4.2	CF(38): 4.8, RF(16): 0.0	1.3
2019	BAL	MLB	23	75	12	6	0	4	13	7	13	2	0	.309/.373/.574	111	3.9	.333	0.8	CF(20): 2.3	0.7
2020	BAL	MLB	24	350	43	19	1	19	54	16	85	2	1	.253/.293/.490	98	11.9	.283	-0.4	CF 4	1.6

Comparables: Christian Yelich, Nomar Mazara, Tyler Colvin

Since Hays became the first 2016 draftee to make his debut in September 2017, his career has been a Netflix series where you just keep waiting for something to happen. And once it finally does at the end, it doesn't really connect with anything you've seen before. Hays was summoned to the majors again last September and showed that not only can he play an impressive center field despite limited experience, but that he took the organization's advice to be more selective to heart as well. In order for the new approach to work, Hays will have to figure out how to be discerning without becoming too passive, but his season finale set him up for an anticipated premiere as the Orioles' presumptive center fielder in 2020.

José Iglesias SS   Born: 01/05/90   Age: 30   Bats: R   Throws: R   Height: 5'11"   Weight: 194   Origin: International Free Agent, 2009

YEAR	TEAM	LVL	AGE	PA	R	2B	3B	HR	RBI	BB	K	SB	CS	AVG/OBP/SLG	DRC+	VORP	BABIP	BRR	FRAA	WARP
2017	DET	MLB	27	489	56	33	1	6	54	21	65	7	4	.255/.288/.369	72	4.8	.285	3.7	SS(130): -4.8	0.4
2018	DET	MLB	28	464	43	31	3	5	48	19	47	15	6	.269/.310/.389	93	18.0	.291	1.6	SS(122): 4.7	2.3
2019	CIN	MLB	29	530	62	21	3	11	59	20	70	6	6	.288/.318/.407	86	16.2	.315	3.0	SS(144): 6.5	2.5
2020	BAL	MLB	30	525	49	25	1	10	52	24	69	10	5	.265/.306/.379	79	8.3	.292	2.5	SS 2	1.1

Comparables: Jean Segura, Erick Aybar, Angel Berroa

If it feels like Iglesias has been around forever, it's because he has—he's an immortal shapeshifter who has taken many faces and names over the years. No, no, we're just kidding about that … it's because he first debuted on the 2011 Red Sox, a team that featured Kevin Youkilis, Daisuke Matsuzaka and Mike Cameron, among others. And yet Iglesias will play this season at the ripe age of 30 following a solid season in 2019 that saw him slug over .400 for the first time in his career. He remains a plus defensive shortstop, but one interesting change within his profile is that he's increased his swing rate to career-high levels in each of the past three seasons. Walking was never something Iglesias cared to do, so we applaud him leaning into it.

Trey Mancini OF/1B   Born: 03/18/92   Age: 28   Bats: R   Throws: R   Height: 6'4"   Weight: 215   Origin: Round 8, 2013 Draft (#249 overall)

YEAR	TEAM	LVL	AGE	PA	R	2B	3B	HR	RBI	BB	K	SB	CS	AVG/OBP/SLG	DRC+	VORP	BABIP	BRR	FRAA	WARP
2017	BAL	MLB	25	586	65	26	4	24	78	33	139	1	0	.293/.338/.488	106	22.6	.352	0.9	LF(88): 0.9, 1B(45): -2.1	1.6
2018	BAL	MLB	26	636	69	23	3	24	58	44	153	0	1	.242/.299/.416	92	2.5	.285	0.5	LF(98): 4.5, 1B(47): 2.7	1.5
2019	BAL	MLB	27	679	106	38	2	35	97	63	143	1	0	.291/.364/.535	120	31.8	.326	-0.9	RF(87): -3.6, 1B(56): 1.7	2.8
2020	BAL	MLB	28	525	71	25	2	29	83	42	115	1	0	.277/.342/.519	119	23.5	.310	0.2	1B 0, RF -1	2.4

Comparables: Brant Brown, Rico Brogna, Mitch Moreland

There's a bit of a misnomer about Mancini around Baltimore that he's a young player still, but at age 27, he's finally hitting arbitration around the time that actual young stars are nearing free agency. No matter. Put a player of his experience as the only legitimate threat in a lineup made to lose 100 games, and all you can ask is he takes as many steps forward as Mancini did in 2019. He was among the most productive outfielders in the American League, and all of it was backed up by legitimate underlying improvements from his inconsistent 2018. If you could pick any three stats for a power hitter to improve, it would be raising his walk rate and lowering both his strikeout and groundball rates—and Mancini did all three. So, despite no opposing pitcher having any real reason to pitch to him, Mancini still got his. While he was jobbed a bit in not being an All-Star in 2019, that's his ceiling. He might be miscast as a franchise face, and definitely is miscast as an outfielder, but this is a player who is capable of hitting in the middle of any order in baseball.

Richie Martin SS   Born: 12/22/94   Age: 25   Bats: R   Throws: R   Height: 5'11"   Weight: 190   Origin: Round 1, 2015 Draft (#20 overall)

YEAR	TEAM	LVL	AGE	PA	R	2B	3B	HR	RBI	BB	K	SB	CS	AVG/OBP/SLG	DRC+	VORP	BABIP	BRR	FRAA	WARP
2017	STO	A+	22	103	16	2	3	1	6	8	21	1	1	.266/.330/.383	98	3.3	.333	0.0	SS(14): 0.3	0.3
2017	MID	AA	22	325	43	11	3	3	27	24	57	12	3	.224/.306/.315	64	9.0	.266	3.3	SS(86): -8.2	-0.2
2018	MID	AA	23	509	68	29	8	6	42	44	86	25	10	.300/.368/.439	120	28.4	.357	-0.3	SS(96): 9.1, 2B(21): 1.0	4.1
2019	BAL	MLB	24	309	29	8	3	6	23	14	83	10	1	.208/.260/.322	50	-5.2	.272	-0.9	SS(117): -0.8	-0.7
2020	BAL	MLB	25	70	6	3	0	1	7	4	19	1	1	.212/.274/.329	60	-1.3	.278	-0.3	SS 0	-0.2

Comparables: Danny Worth, Yadiel Rivera, Erick Mejia

Even if there's an extremely low bar for success when the subject is a Rule 5 pick on a team that's just looking to get talent in the organization, Martin's rookie year could not have been less conclusive. He hit well enough in the second half, but really only against lefties. He looked the part at shortstop, but the team combats the public-facing metrics that don't flatter him by saying their internal ones rate him well. The overall package of a speedy infielder who can lay down a bunt, make all the plays at shortstop and literally run into an extra-base hit is a valuable one. Martin's rookie season just didn't make it clear that's what he actually is.

Ryan McKenna OF   Born: 02/14/97   Age: 23   Bats: R   Throws: R   Height: 5'11"   Weight: 185   Origin: Round 4, 2015 Draft (#133 overall)

YEAR	TEAM	LVL	AGE	PA	R	2B	3B	HR	RBI	BB	K	SB	CS	AVG/OBP/SLG	DRC+	VORP	BABIP	BRR	FRAA	WARP
2017	DEL	A	20	530	62	33	2	7	42	43	128	20	2	.256/.331/.380	117	28.3	.336	-0.2	CF(124): -7.6	1.8
2018	FRD	A+	21	301	60	18	2	8	37	37	45	5	6	.377/.467/.556	218	46.2	.436	2.5	CF(64): -6.2, LF(2): -0.2	4.1
2018	BOW	AA	21	250	35	8	2	3	16	29	56	4	1	.239/.341/.338	90	10.7	.312	2.6	CF(55): 3.4, RF(3): 2.1	1.4
2019	BOW	AA	22	567	78	26	6	9	54	59	121	25	11	.232/.321/.365	112	21.5	.287	1.9	CF(98): -4.1, LF(18): 0.6	2.3
2020	BAL	MLB	23	175	17	9	1	4	18	14	47	2	1	.226/.299/.367	76	0.8	.294	0.1	CF 0, LF 1	0.1

Comparables: Brandon Nimmo, Brett Phillips, Rey Fuentes

McKenna took a massive step forward in 2018, but the indicators behind a 2019 in which he didn't make much progress aren't the kind that lend themselves to an undersized center fielder leaning into his skillset. McKenna bulked up last offseason and saw his fly ball rate jump to 40.3 percent, the highest it has been in full-season ball, while pulling the ball more than ever. That approach has led to unprecedented success for many, but McKenna strayed too far from the profile that has propelled him to the upper minors and onto prospect lists. There's no shame in being a plus defender at a premium position with a hose for an arm, who makes his bones offensively on his speed and ability to drive the ball into the gaps.

★ ★ ★ *2020 Top 101 Prospect* **#57** ★ ★ ★

Ryan Mountcastle 1B   Born: 02/18/97   Age: 23   Bats: R   Throws: R   Height: 6'3"   Weight: 195   Origin: Round 1, 2015 Draft (#36 overall)

YEAR	TEAM	LVL	AGE	PA	R	2B	3B	HR	RBI	BB	K	SB	CS	AVG/OBP/SLG	DRC+	VORP	BABIP	BRR	FRAA	WARP
2017	FRD	A+	20	379	63	35	1	15	47	14	61	8	2	.314/.343/.542	137	28.3	.343	1.5	SS(82): -12.1	1.8
2017	BOW	AA	20	159	18	13	0	3	15	3	35	0	0	.222/.239/.366	56	-0.4	.265	0.5	3B(37): -1.1	-0.3
2018	BOW	AA	21	428	63	19	4	13	59	26	79	2	0	.297/.341/.464	119	22.2	.339	-1.5	3B(81): -4.9	1.6
2019	NOR	AAA	22	553	81	35	1	25	83	24	130	2	1	.312/.344/.527	115	18.2	.370	-0.9	1B(84): -6.1, LF(25): 2.1	1.3
2020	BAL	MLB	23	385	44	22	1	17	54	15	104	2	1	.266/.299/.472	93	4.2	.326	-0.6	3B -2, 1B 0	0.2

Comparables: Brendan Rodgers, Richard Ureña, Justin Williams

Drafted as a shortstop in 2015 before tumbling down the defensive spectrum, Mountcastle has been held to a standard that often overlooks what he was taken 36th overall for: he can absolutely mash. The fact that he has loose, quick hands that can get to anything and has grown into significant power gets lost as he's penalized for his defensive outlook and whether he walks enough. Those concerns are legitimate, but they are also not going to be wished away by another tour in Norfolk. Look for the Orioles to talk them up following spring training as a defense (ha ha) of why Mountcastle isn't in Baltimore until all relevant service time and free agency dates have passed.

Cedric Mullins CF   Born: 10/01/94   Age: 25   Bats: B   Throws: L   Height: 5'8"   Weight: 175   Origin: Round 13, 2015 Draft (#403 overall)

YEAR	TEAM	LVL	AGE	PA	R	2B	3B	HR	RBI	BB	K	SB	CS	AVG/OBP/SLG	DRC+	VORP	BABIP	BRR	FRAA	WARP
2017	BOW	AA	22	350	53	19	1	13	37	27	58	9	7	.265/.319/.460	101	15.6	.283	0.9	CF(57): 7.2, LF(8): 1.1	2.0
2018	BOW	AA	23	218	36	12	5	6	28	15	28	9	1	.313/.362/.512	136	22.8	.339	2.4	CF(43): 0.4, LF(3): 0.5	1.8
2018	NOR	AAA	23	269	41	17	3	6	19	22	39	12	0	.269/.333/.438	122	15.0	.298	2.2	CF(60): 0.2	1.7
2018	BAL	MLB	23	191	23	9	0	4	11	17	37	2	3	.235/.312/.359	82	1.6	.279	-0.6	CF(45): -3.8, LF(1): 0.0	-0.2
2019	BOW	AA	24	226	35	11	0	5	18	22	31	20	3	.271/.341/.402	127	16.5	.293	2.8	CF(30): 0.9, LF(19): 0.1	1.7
2019	NOR	AAA	24	306	40	8	2	5	24	25	51	13	4	.205/.272/.306	50	-9.3	.231	1.8	CF(56): 4.1, LF(6): -0.6	-0.3
2019	BAL	MLB	24	74	7	0	2	0	4	4	14	1	0	.094/.181/.156	57	-1.5	.118	0.5	CF(22): 1.4	0.0
2020	BAL	MLB	25	210	20	10	1	6	23	15	44	5	2	.222/.281/.379	69	-0.5	.258	0.3	CF 3	0.2

Comparables: Mallex Smith, Gary Geiger, Oddibe McDowell

When the Orioles worried near the end of the Adam Jones era that replacing him in center field would be a tougher task on the field than off it, even the most cynical couldn't envision Mullins being demoted to Double-A while trying. Conan O'Brien thinks his run at the Tonight Show went well by comparison. That return to Double-A Bowie for the North Carolina native seemed to allow him to not only reset as a player, but reset expectations. Maybe now, a speedy slasher type who can patrol center field but tops out as a bench outfielder will be an outcome all parties will take.

Renato Núñez DH   Born: 04/04/94   Age: 26   Bats: R   Throws: R   Height: 6'1"   Weight: 220   Origin: International Free Agent, 2010

YEAR	TEAM	LVL	AGE	PA	R	2B	3B	HR	RBI	BB	K	SB	CS	AVG/OBP/SLG	DRC+	VORP	BABIP	BRR	FRAA	WARP
2017	NAS	AAA	23	533	74	27	2	32	78	47	141	2	1	.249/.319/.518	113	24.5	.279	-1.5	LF(48): -7.0, 3B(44): -4.7	0.9
2017	OAK	MLB	23	16	1	0	0	1	3	1	8	0	0	.200/.250/.400	70	-0.5	.333	-0.2	LF(3): -0.2, 3B(1): 0.2	0.0
2018	NAS	AAA	24	30	3	0	0	0	4	2	6	0	0	.357/.400/.357	101	1.4	.455	-0.5	3B(2): -0.2, LF(2): -0.5	0.0
2018	NOR	AAA	24	228	25	14	1	5	25	23	49	1	0	.289/.361/.443	134	12.2	.356	0.8	3B(38): 0.1, 1B(6): 0.6	1.6
2018	TEX	MLB	24	41	2	1	0	1	2	3	12	0	0	.167/.244/.278	94	-0.8	.208	-0.2	3B(8): 0.9, LF(4): -0.2	0.2
2018	BAL	MLB	24	220	26	13	0	7	20	16	50	0	0	.275/.336/.445	95	8.4	.333	-0.8	3B(59): -4.0	0.2
2019	BAL	MLB	25	599	72	24	0	31	90	44	143	1	1	.244/.311/.460	99	9.8	.272	-2.1	1B(24): -1.9, 3B(9): 0.0	0.6
2020	BAL	MLB	26	525	66	20	1	29	79	37	131	1	0	.241/.305/.468	95	2.0	.270	-1.3	3B 0, 1B 0	0.2

Comparables: Wilson Betemit, Michael Cuddyer, Adrián González

Summoned from the minors to take over as the Orioles' everyday third baseman after they traded Manny Machado, Núñez coming to Baltimore was modern-day baseball equivalent of replacing Vin Diesel in the Fast franchise with Billy Zane because they're both bald. The shine they share in a baseball sense is raw power in games (and nice smiles off them), with Núñez being one of 61 players to reach the 30-homer plateau this season. Only three of them—Rougned Odor, José Abreu and Randal Grichuk—had lower a WARP than Núñez, who became an emergency-only third baseman and is far down the Orioles' first base depth chart. He's a power-hitting designated hitter in an era when power has never come cheaper, but there's value to the Orioles as long as that power is literally as cheap as it comes.

José Rondón INF   Born: 03/03/94   Age: 26   Bats: R   Throws: R   Height: 6'1"   Weight: 195   Origin: International Free Agent, 2011

YEAR	TEAM	LVL	AGE	PA	R	2B	3B	HR	RBI	BB	K	SB	CS	AVG/OBP/SLG	DRC+	VORP	BABIP	BRR	FRAA	WARP
2017	SAN	AA	23	234	30	12	3	4	28	16	43	2	1	.293/.343/.433	106	17.0	.349	1.4	SS(32): 4.4, 2B(11): -1.2	1.5
2017	ELP	AAA	23	91	9	8	0	1	14	6	16	1	0	.282/.330/.412	89	2.9	.338	0.4	SS(18): 0.3, 2B(3): -0.3	0.3
2018	CHR	AAA	24	336	41	15	4	18	38	16	82	5	6	.249/.290/.495	100	14.6	.278	0.9	SS(78): 10.9, 3B(2): 0.0	2.7
2018	CHA	MLB	24	107	15	6	0	6	14	7	30	2	1	.230/.280/.470	94	2.3	.266	-1.0	SS(10): -0.4, 3B(8): 0.5	0.2
2019	NOR	AAA	25	83	9	4	0	2	12	10	22	1	0	.219/.313/.356	87	1.3	.286	0.9	SS(14): 0.8, 3B(3): -0.2	0.3
2019	CHA	MLB	25	156	10	3	0	3	9	11	38	0	0	.197/.265/.282	67	-0.6	.248	-0.8	2B(18): -0.1, SS(15): -1.3	-0.5
2019	BAL	MLB	25	1	0	0	0	0	0	0	0	0	0	.000/.000/.000	185	0.1	.000	0.0	3B(1): 0.0	0.0
2020	BAL	MLB	26	251	26	11	1	9	30	14	63	4	2	.232/.280/.397	76	-0.5	.281	-0.9	SS 3, 2B 0	0.3

Comparables: Roy Smalley, Johan Camargo, Yairo Muñoz

Before he can settle into his future role as a utility infielder for hire, the few days Rondón spent with the Orioles were typical of their 2019 season. He was run through his paces all over the outfield and, perhaps deemed unfit to be a makeshift outfielder, was sent down to the minors. Rondón could be in a large category of players kept from doing what they're best at by the Orioles' constant experimenting; it's just unclear what he's actually best at.

Rio Ruiz 3B Born: 05/22/94 Age: 26 Bats: L Throws: R Height: 6'1" Weight: 215 Origin: Round 4, 2012 Draft (#129 overall)

YEAR	TEAM	LVL	AGE	PA	R	2B	3B	HR	RBI	BB	K	SB	CS	AVG/OBP/SLG	DRC+	VORP	BABIP	BRR	FRAA	WARP
2017	GWN	AAA	23	432	48	25	2	16	56	42	110	1	2	.247/.322/.446	116	13.2	.304	-0.2	3B(91): 2.0, 1B(5): 0.2	2.3
2017	ATL	MLB	23	173	22	5	0	4	19	19	41	1	0	.193/.283/.307	76	-0.9	.231	0.9	3B(41): 0.6, 1B(2): 0.0	0.3
2018	GWN	AAA	24	541	72	25	4	9	72	40	90	2	1	.269/.322/.390	96	9.9	.311	1.8	3B(49): 2.3, 1B(35): 1.5	1.2
2018	ATL	MLB	24	15	1	0	0	0	0	2	5	0	0	.083/.267/.083	78	0.3	.143	-0.1	3B(1): -0.2	0.0
2019	BAL	MLB	25	413	35	13	2	12	46	40	88	0	1	.232/.306/.376	81	5.3	.272	-1.4	3B(114): 2.3, 1B(12): 0.3	0.6
2020	BAL	MLB	26	280	29	12	1	9	32	27	64	1	0	.232/.307/.392	80	-0.5	.276	-0.1	3B 1	0.0

Comparables: Lonnie Chisenhall, Andy Marte, Nicky Delmonico

Is Dad Strength a real thing? Consider the case of Ruiz, who spent a few weeks in the minors from late July into August that coincided with the birth of his son, Luca, and hit the O's only walk-off home run of the season against the Houston Astros (the team that drafted him) in his first start back. Ruiz hit seven home runs in 124 plate appearances following his August 10 return, after hitting nine in 484 career plate appearances leading up to that. There's literally nothing to explain it, except *perhaps* a better approach. His contact rates didn't change in a way to lend itself to more power. His exit velocity stayed flat most of the year. It didn't even seem to be a matter of luck. So, by process of elimination, it has to be the Dad Strength. With it, Ruiz had a .779 OPS and just enough pop to make his standout defense play at third base. Without it, he's a glove-first third baseman with too much swing-and-miss. And he's very much with it so far.

★ ★ ★ 2020 Top 101 Prospect **#4** ★ ★ ★

Adley Rutschman C Born: 02/06/98 Age: 22 Bats: B Throws: R Height: 6'2" Weight: 216 Origin: Round 1, 2019 Draft (#1 overall)

YEAR	TEAM	LVL	AGE	PA	R	2B	3B	HR	RBI	BB	K	SB	CS	AVG/OBP/SLG	DRC+	VORP	BABIP	BRR	FRAA	WARP
2019	ABE	A-	21	92	11	7	1	1	15	12	16	0	0	.325/.413/.481	177	11.5	.387	-0.1	C(9): -0.2	0.8
2019	DEL	A	21	47	5	1	0	2	8	6	9	0	0	.154/.261/.333	85	1.2	.138	0.1	C(6): 0.1	0.1
2020	BAL	MLB	22	251	24	12	1	7	27	18	65	2	1	.219/.281/.363	73	-0.7	.275	0.0	C 0	-0.1

Comparables: Lucas Duda, Chris McGuiness, Christian Walker

Someone goes 1-1 in the MLB draft every year, but few arrive with the expectations that Rutschman did as the Orioles' top pick in 2019. Not only is he the franchise savior and a second chance at a perennial All-Star catcher in Baltimore this century, but he gets to make nearly every stop of his minor league journey inside the state of Maryland, meaning there's no hiding any bumps in the road. Luckily for him, the Orioles don't expect there to be. He's an advanced defensive catcher with a plus arm and good receiving; he can be a 70 hitter with pop, and won't get himself out at the plate; one of his college coaches promised the local newspaper that he'd feed the hungry in Baltimore while extolling his virtues. It might be a couple years before he gets that chance, but rarely are there easier picks than the one the Orioles made in June.

Anthony Santander OF Born: 10/19/94 Age: 25 Bats: B Throws: R Height: 6'2" Weight: 190 Origin: International Free Agent, 2011

YEAR	TEAM	LVL	AGE	PA	R	2B	3B	HR	RBI	BB	K	SB	CS	AVG/OBP/SLG	DRC+	VORP	BABIP	BRR	FRAA	WARP
2017	BOW	AA	22	59	13	5	0	5	14	7	9	0	0	.380/.458/.780	193	8.4	.378	-0.7	RF(6): 0.0, LF(4): -0.2	0.6
2017	BAL	MLB	22	31	1	3	0	0	2	0	8	0	0	.267/.258/.367	74	-0.1	.348	0.1	RF(8): 0.7, LF(4): -0.2	0.0
2018	ABE	A-	23	31	6	5	0	1	5	2	5	2	0	.286/.355/.571	133	4.3	.318	0.2	RF(5): -0.2	0.1
2018	BOW	AA	23	222	26	9	3	5	22	10	32	4	1	.258/.293/.402	87	4.8	.282	0.7	RF(35): -3.6, LF(14): -1.4	-0.3
2018	NOR	AAA	23	47	3	3	0	2	7	2	9	0	0	.182/.213/.386	81	-1.7	.176	-0.1	RF(8): 1.1, LF(2): -0.3	0.1
2018	BAL	MLB	23	108	8	5	1	1	6	6	21	1	0	.198/.250/.297	75	-5.9	.241	0.0	RF(29): 0.8, LF(1): 0.0	0.0
2019	NOR	AAA	24	209	30	15	0	5	28	13	38	3	2	.259/.311/.415	85	-0.8	.298	1.1	RF(35): 1.8, LF(8): -0.9	0.2
2019	BAL	MLB	24	405	46	20	1	20	59	19	86	1	2	.261/.297/.476	98	10.0	.285	-0.5	RF(50): -4.8, LF(40): 8.3	1.6
2020	BAL	MLB	25	525	59	29	1	23	72	27	120	3	1	.248/.293/.453	86	3.7	.283	0.0	LF 10, RF 0	1.3

Comparables: Paul Householder, Jake Marisnick, Nomar Mazara

A front office with the Orioles' data-driven predilections operates under the assumption that they know what a player will become with enough minor-league experience. That said, the Orioles weren't banking on the kind of production they got from Santander when he was summoned from Triple-A Norfolk in June. His power showed through in a way it hadn't since 2016 - before he was taken in the Rule 5 draft and dealt with shoulder and elbow injuries - and even pitched in as a center fielder. His production only depreciated because he overdrafted his health and hid injuries in September, batting .155 in the final month of the season. Before that? He made a real statement, and showed the skills to be a capable defender and a useful bat off the bench if the Orioles ever transition back to being a first-division club. That's quite the return on investment for a Rule 5 pick.

Pedro Severino C Born: 07/20/93 Age: 26 Bats: R Throws: R Height: 6'1" Weight: 219 Origin: International Free Agent, 2010

YEAR	TEAM	LVL	AGE	PA	R	2B	3B	HR	RBI	BB	K	SB	CS	AVG/OBP/SLG	DRC+	VORP	BABIP	BRR	FRAA	WARP
2017	SYR	AAA	23	227	17	4	0	5	29	15	43	1	1	.242/.291/.332	86	3.1	.280	-0.4	C(58): 5.1	1.2
2017	WAS	MLB	23	31	0	1	0	0	3	2	10	0	0	.172/.226/.207	60	-2.4	.263	-0.5	C(10): 0.3	0.0
2018	SYR	AAA	24	136	14	5	1	6	13	5	23	0	0	.269/.294/.462	93	7.3	.284	-2.1	C(32): 1.1	0.4
2018	WAS	MLB	24	213	14	9	0	2	15	18	47	1	0	.168/.254/.247	61	-6.9	.211	-0.1	C(67): 0.0	0.0
2019	BAL	MLB	25	341	37	13	0	13	44	29	73	3	1	.249/.321/.420	91	13.3	.285	-2.4	C(89): -13.8	-0.3
2020	BAL	MLB	26	315	33	12	0	11	38	22	67	1	1	.233/.293/.395	78	4.7	.266	-1.2	C -3	0.2

Comparables: Chris Snyder, Austin Hedges, Wilson Ramos

Head injuries are no joke, and even if they're not specifically called concussions, they can be hidden inflection points in a player's season that explain what look like a sudden downturn in production. When home plate umpire Brian O'Nora called the Orioles' medical staff out to check on Severino after a foul tip to the face on June 5 in Texas, he was batting .286 with a .929 OPS, mostly thanks to a three-homer game the night before. He was back in the lineup two games later and hit .230 with a .640 OPS in 61 games the rest of the way. None of this takes away from the fact that Severino is a fine, if not often focused, defender who can hit left-handed pitching as the short side of a platoon but is asked to do far more in Baltimore. Here's hoping he has a restful offseason.

YEAR	TEAM	P. COUNT	FRM RUNS	BLK RUNS	THRW RUNS	TOT RUNS
2017	SYR	8269	8.1	-2.3	0.3	5.2
2017	WAS	939	0.7	-0.4	0.0	0.3
2018	SYR	4103	1.4	0.0	0.0	1.4
2018	WAS	8290	0.3	0.2	0.1	0.5
2019	BAL	12950	-9.6	-4.1	-0.2	-13.9
2020	*BAL*	*12899*	*0.2*	*-1.2*	*-0.5*	*-1.5*

Chance Sisco C Born: 02/24/95 Age: 25 Bats: L Throws: R Height: 6'2" Weight: 195 Origin: Round 2, 2013 Draft (#61 overall)

YEAR	TEAM	LVL	AGE	PA	R	2B	3B	HR	RBI	BB	K	SB	CS	AVG/OBP/SLG	DRC+	VORP	BABIP	BRR	FRAA	WARP
2017	NOR	AAA	22	388	47	23	0	7	47	32	99	2	2	.267/.340/.395	117	22.2	.351	1.9	C(94): 3.2	3.0
2017	BAL	MLB	22	22	3	2	0	2	4	3	7	0	0	.333/.455/.778	94	3.8	.444	-0.3	C(10): -0.7	0.0
2018	NOR	AAA	23	151	22	5	0	3	12	16	36	0	0	.242/.344/.352	114	5.4	.308	-1.1	C(37): -2.8	0.5
2018	BAL	MLB	23	184	13	8	0	2	16	13	66	1	0	.181/.288/.269	58	-3.5	.293	-1.3	C(55): -2.8	-0.5
2019	NOR	AAA	24	196	31	10	0	10	37	20	44	0	0	.292/.388/.530	131	16.8	.339	0.1	C(35): -3.3	1.2
2019	BAL	MLB	24	198	29	7	0	8	20	22	61	0	1	.210/.333/.395	92	7.7	.276	0.1	C(52): -11.1, 1B(1): 0.0	-0.3
2020	*BAL*	*MLB*	*25*	*315*	*35*	*13*	*0*	*11*	*38*	*29*	*91*	*1*	*0*	*.234/.325/.404*	*90*	*10.1*	*.307*	*-0.5*	*C -11*	*-0.1*

Comparables: Gary Sánchez, Dominic Smith, J.P. Crawford

YEAR	TEAM	P. COUNT	FRM RUNS	BLK RUNS	THRW RUNS	TOT RUNS
2017	BAL	653	-0.6	-0.2	-0.1	-1.1
2017	NOR	13196	5.9	1.1	-1.7	4.6
2018	BAL	6491	-2.2	0.3	-0.1	-2.1
2018	NOR	5151	-1.3	0.0	-0.8	-2.0
2019	BAL	6712	-9.6	-0.7	-0.5	-11.8
2019	NOR	4944	-1.8	0.3	-0.8	-2.5
2020	*BAL*	*11846*	*-8.5*	*-0.6*	*-1.1*	*-10.1*

There was a lot of risk in Sisco's profile coming up by virtue of his crude defensive skills and well-below average throwing arm, but as fate would have it, there's a possibility that the offensive profile that was supposed to mask over that is gone. He still has pitch recognition skills and cut down on his swing-and-miss while making much better contact in his third major-league season, though the all-fields approach that made him a top prospect is gone. There might be more room for a bat-first catcher if robots take over behind the plate, but sometimes you can't just wait for Skynet to take control.

Dwight Smith Jr LF Born: 10/26/92 Age: 27 Bats: L Throws: R Height: 6'0" Weight: 210 Origin: Round 1, 2011 Draft (#53 overall)

YEAR	TEAM	LVL	AGE	PA	R	2B	3B	HR	RBI	BB	K	SB	CS	AVG/OBP/SLG	DRC+	VORP	BABIP	BRR	FRAA	WARP
2017	BUF	AAA	24	449	56	21	1	8	46	47	71	8	8	.273/.350/.392	117	14.8	.313	0.6	RF(67): -4.0, LF(32): -0.6	1.2
2017	TOR	MLB	24	29	2	2	0	0	1	1	10	1	0	.370/.414/.444	69	2.8	.588	0.9	LF(9): -1.8, CF(1): 0.0	-0.2
2018	BUF	AAA	25	361	39	25	1	6	42	44	53	9	3	.268/.358/.413	131	11.4	.302	-0.3	LF(62): 1.2, RF(14): -0.1	1.9
2018	TOR	MLB	25	75	9	8	0	2	8	7	13	0	0	.262/.347/.477	99	3.7	.294	-0.4	LF(19): -1.5, RF(6): 0.7	0.1
2019	NOR	AAA	26	49	9	2	0	3	12	3	8	0	0	.311/.367/.556	117	3.7	.324	-0.1	LF(5): -0.3, RF(2): 0.1	0.2
2019	BAL	MLB	26	392	46	16	3	13	53	26	82	5	1	.241/.297/.412	82	1.0	.274	-0.1	LF(86): -0.7	0.0
2020	*BAL*	*MLB*	*27*	*315*	*34*	*15*	*1*	*11*	*38*	*25*	*65*	*3*	*2*	*.241/.306/.411*	*84*	*1.1*	*.278*	*-0.2*	*LF -1, RF -1*	*-0.1*

Comparables: Bob Nieman, Stephen Piscotty, Aaron Cunningham

Acquired in a DFA trade from the Toronto Blue Jays, Smith essentially went from spending two years on a really talented Triple-A team with the likes of Vladimir Guerrero Jr., Rowdy Tellez and Danny Jansen to a more talented Triple-A team in big-league clothes. But what began as a possible breakout for Smith with a hot April ultimately cooled, and his OPS never got back above .800 after the end of May. Without the chance to make much defensive impact, Smith will need to start driving the ball more in order to keep getting opportunities in a crowded Orioles outfield at the corners. They moved Trey Mancini to right field to accommodate Smith in 2019; it's more likely Smith will move on to accommodate someone younger in left field in 2020 and beyond.

DJ Stewart OF Born: 11/30/93 Age: 26 Bats: L Throws: R Height: 6'0" Weight: 230 Origin: Round 1, 2015 Draft (#25 overall)

YEAR	TEAM	LVL	AGE	PA	R	2B	3B	HR	RBI	BB	K	SB	CS	AVG/OBP/SLG	DRC+	VORP	BABIP	BRR	FRAA	WARP
2017	BOW	AA	23	540	80	26	2	21	79	65	87	20	4	.278/.378/.481	134	37.2	.299	2.1	LF(113): -0.6, RF(4): 0.7	3.5
2018	NOR	AAA	24	490	59	24	2	12	55	54	103	11	4	.235/.329/.387	107	14.3	.278	4.7	RF(88): -14.1, LF(24): 1.9	0.5
2018	BAL	MLB	24	47	8	3	0	3	10	4	12	2	1	.250/.340/.550	88	3.2	.269	0.5	LF(9): 4.4, RF(6): -0.4	0.5
2019	NOR	AAA	25	277	42	19	2	12	47	38	51	5	4	.291/.396/.548	131	18.6	.324	-2.1	LF(30): -1.2, RF(22): 1.6	1.4
2019	BAL	MLB	25	142	15	6	0	4	15	14	26	1	2	.238/.317/.381	84	0.4	.268	-0.3	RF(26): -1.8, LF(11): -0.5	-0.2
2020	*BAL*	*MLB*	*26*	*455*	*54*	*20*	*1*	*19*	*59*	*46*	*101*	*9*	*3*	*.229/.317/.425*	*91*	*3.9*	*.258*	*-0.2*	*RF -9*	*-0.6*

Comparables: Alex Hassan, Preston Tucker, Nicky Delmonico

First-round picks are fun to have, but the wrong kind can be like a talented band that gets radio play early and has the fanbase they're trying to play for resent them for it. Enter Stewart, the Orioles' top pick in 2015. If he was a senior-sign who: played a reckless outfield to his own detriment; never saw a ball he didn't think he could hit or a throw he didn't think he could make; could work a walk and run into some power, even if it's a one-plane swing; who has won all his life, and wasn't afraid to swipe a base? He'd be every scout's sneaky favorite. Instead, he's all that with a first-rounder's mentality and expectations. It doesn't change what he actually is, which is a corner bat with an approach and a bench profile on a better team than his current one.

Jesús Sucre C Born: 04/30/88 Age: 32 Bats: R Throws: R Height: 6'0" Weight: 200 Origin: International Free Agent, 2005

YEAR	TEAM	LVL	AGE	PA	R	2B	3B	HR	RBI	BB	K	SB	CS	AVG/OBP/SLG	DRC+	VORP	BABIP	BRR	FRAA	WARP
2017	TBA	MLB	29	192	20	6	0	7	29	7	35	2	0	.256/.289/.409	93	6.8	.275	0.2	C(61): 3.1, P(1): 0.0	1.1
2018	TBA	MLB	30	198	9	5	0	1	17	9	29	1	0	.209/.247/.253	73	-9.1	.240	-1.8	C(71): -4.2, P(2): 0.0	-0.3
2019	NOR	AAA	31	198	20	15	0	0	19	12	29	0	0	.283/.333/.364	101	0.6	.335	0.2	C(37): -3.8, 1B(2): 0.2	0.5
2019	BAL	MLB	31	67	3	2	0	0	3	4	13	0	0	.210/.269/.242	78	1.5	.265	0.1	C(18): -1.1, P(1): 0.0	0.0
2020	BAL	MLB	32	251	20	10	0	4	22	12	48	1	0	.221/.264/.316	54	-7.8	.263	-0.6	C 0, 1B 0	-0.8

Comparables: Pete Daley, Greg Myers, Pat Borders

YEAR	TEAM	P. COUNT	FRM RUNS	BLK RUNS	THRW RUNS	TOT RUNS
2017	TBA	7812	4.1	0.9	-0.4	5.7
2018	TBA	7931	-4.9	0.7	0.4	-3.8
2019	BAL	2494	-0.9	-0.4	0.1	-1.1
2019	NOR	5325	-3.6	0.0	0.9	-2.7
2020	BAL	10097	0.0	0.1	1.5	1.6

Sucre might not have survived a season of catching this Orioles' pitching staff, so it's probably best that he didn't get the chance. A well-respected defender who throws out runners at an above-average clip and knows how to call a game, Sucre barely made it to April before every opposing home run he watched fly off the bat brought out a visceral—and visible—reaction of disgust. But if the Orioles' new front office could watch after being used to the Houston Astros' stellar arms, Sucre could have sucked it up after two years with the Tampa Bay Rays. Instead, he was outrighted before May and never seen again.

Mark Trumbo DH Born: 01/16/86 Age: 34 Bats: R Throws: R Height: 6'4" Weight: 225 Origin: Round 18, 2004 Draft (#533 overall)

YEAR	TEAM	LVL	AGE	PA	R	2B	3B	HR	RBI	BB	K	SB	CS	AVG/OBP/SLG	DRC+	VORP	BABIP	BRR	FRAA	WARP
2017	BAL	MLB	31	603	79	22	0	23	65	42	149	1	0	.234/.289/.397	87	-8.4	.278	-2.3	RF(31): -4.6, 3B(2): 0.0	-0.7
2018	BAL	MLB	32	358	41	12	0	17	44	24	87	0	0	.261/.313/.452	102	6.2	.303	0.9	RF(19): -1.4, 1B(3): 0.2	0.6
2019	NOR	AAA	33	48	5	3	0	4	10	6	15	0	0	.214/.313/.571	121	2.3	.217	0.0	RF(2): -0.3, 1B(1): 0.0	0.2
2019	BAL	MLB	33	31	1	3	0	0	3	2	5	0	0	.172/.226/.276	80	-0.3	.208	0.1		0.0
2020	BAL	MLB	34	251	28	11	0	11	33	19	71	0	0	.230/.290/.422	86	3.3	.284	-0.2	RF -6, 1B 0	-0.2

Comparables: Dick Stuart, David Ortiz, Adrián González

Trumbo was somewhat unfairly moved to the outfield when Chris Davis was re-signed in 2016 and hit 47 home runs to lead the majors anyway. He was then unfairly lumped in with that disastrous $161-million Davis contract when he never matched that 2016 production over his own three-year, $37.5 million pact that concluded after 2019. He was duty-bound by that contract to come back in September after a complicated cartilage replacement surgery in his knee, the same that has ruined Dustin Pedroia's career. He did it, and wasn't himself. Here's hoping wherever he ends up in his future isn't close enough to Davis to remain in his gravitational pull.

Pat Valaika INF Born: 09/09/92 Age: 27 Bats: R Throws: R Height: 5'11" Weight: 208 Origin: Round 9, 2013 Draft (#259 overall)

YEAR	TEAM	LVL	AGE	PA	R	2B	3B	HR	RBI	BB	K	SB	CS	AVG/OBP/SLG	DRC+	VORP	BABIP	BRR	FRAA	WARP
2017	ABQ	AAA	24	50	6	2	1	1	11	4	11	0	0	.267/.327/.422	77	1.3	.333	0.5	SS(9): 0.3, 1B(2): 0.0	0.2
2017	COL	MLB	24	195	28	11	0	13	40	7	53	0	0	.258/.284/.533	96	10.8	.291	2.1	SS(22): -0.6, 3B(19): -0.1	0.7
2018	ABQ	AAA	25	147	13	4	1	8	20	7	30	1	1	.216/.252/.432	67	-2.2	.216	-0.6	2B(9): 0.1, SS(9): 0.4	-0.1
2018	COL	MLB	25	133	8	5	0	2	5	9	30	0	0	.156/.214/.246	63	-8.0	.189	0.3	2B(17): -0.6, 1B(15): -0.4	-0.3
2019	ABQ	AAA	26	383	60	26	1	22	75	27	90	5	1	.320/.364/.589	118	24.8	.370	1.0	2B(35): 1.1, SS(18): -1.4	2.3
2019	COL	MLB	26	86	11	5	1	1	4	7	34	0	0	.190/.256/.316	60	-1.5	.318	0.0	2B(13): -0.8, SS(7): 0.1	-0.2
2020	BAL	MLB	27	105	11	4	0	5	14	6	32	1	1	.221/.266/.417	70	-0.1	.276	0.3	2B 0, 3B 0	0.0

Comparables: Gil McDougald, Cody Asche, Will Middlebrooks

Patty Barrels lived up to his nickname in the PCL, even if Statcast wasn't available to tell us how many of his 22 dingers were verified barrels of the MLBAM variety. That did nothing to help him improve upon his woeful 2018 showing at the major-league level, where he met the bare minimum required to keep that nickname. With a second straight sub-replacement performance, he dropped dangerously close to surrendering the Valaika family WARP title to brother Chris, who is now just 0.3 WARP behind Pat's plummeting mark despite last appearing in the majors five years ago.

Stevie Wilkerson OF Born: 01/11/92 Age: 28 Bats: B Throws: R Height: 6'1" Weight: 195 Origin: Round 8, 2014 Draft (#241 overall)

YEAR	TEAM	LVL	AGE	PA	R	2B	3B	HR	RBI	BB	K	SB	CS	AVG/OBP/SLG	DRC+	VORP	BABIP	BRR	FRAA	WARP
2017	FRD	A+	25	180	29	10	0	2	15	19	40	2	3	.323/.407/.426	143	11.1	.425	1.0	2B(26): -0.5, 3B(8): 0.6	1.5
2017	BOW	AA	25	273	34	13	0	6	30	20	53	5	2	.294/.354/.420	110	11.5	.351	-0.5	3B(37): -0.6, 2B(28): 0.8	1.2
2018	NOR	AAA	26	86	13	5	0	4	13	5	15	0	1	.270/.329/.500	122	6.0	.276	0.2	2B(10): 2.7, 3B(6): 0.3	0.8
2018	BAL	MLB	26	49	2	3	0	0	3	3	16	1	0	.174/.224/.239	64	-3.7	.267	-0.6	2B(9): 0.9, 3B(6): 0.2	0.0
2019	NOR	AAA	27	67	13	0	1	2	10	3	9	3	0	.323/.354/.452	92	2.1	.353	0.2	2B(10): 0.6, 3B(3): 0.1	0.2
2019	BAL	MLB	27	361	41	18	2	10	35	22	108	3	3	.225/.286/.383	66	-3.5	.300	-1.9	CF(72): -8.3, LF(29): -3.5	-1.6
2020	BAL	MLB	28	210	20	9	1	5	22	13	60	2	1	.228/.285/.364	67	-1.6	.302	-0.6	2B 3, SS -1	0.1

Comparables: Danny Klassen, Jonathan Schoop, Tommy Manzella

The pre-2019 edition of Wilkerson played all over the infield dirt and was groomed to be a homegrown utility solution on a team that spent most of the decade overpaying bad ones. The 2019 edition never played center field as a pro but started there a team-high 52 times for the Orioles; had never pitched as a pro but made four appearances off the mound. He even earned the first ever save recorded by a position player on July 25 against the Angels. His manager called him "Dr. Poo Poo." Who said rebuilds aren't fun?

PITCHERS

Keegan Akin LHP   Born: 04/01/95   Age: 25   Bats: L   Throws: L   Height: 6'0"   Weight: 225   Origin: Round 2, 2016 Draft (#54 overall)

YEAR	TEAM	LVL	AGE	W	L	SV	G	GS	IP	H	HR	BB/9	K/9	K	GB%	BABIP	WHIP	ERA	DRA	WARP	MPH	FB%	WHF	CSP
2017	FRD	A+	22	7	8	0	21	21	100	89	12	4.1	10.0	111	38%	.307	1.35	4.14	3.96	1.5				
2018	BOW	AA	23	14	7	0	25	25	137²	114	16	3.8	9.3	142	32%	.278	1.25	3.27	3.76	2.5				
2019	NOR	AAA	24	6	7	0	25	24	112¹	109	10	4.9	10.5	131	34%	.331	1.51	4.73	4.36	2.6				
2020	BAL	MLB	25	4	5	0	16	16	68	71	12	3.7	9.1	68	34%	.310	1.45	5.29	4.88	0.5				

Comparables: Matt Hall, Brad Mills, Taylor Hearn

In his yard in Sumner, Michigan, Akin turned a pole barn into his own pitching facility to train in during the offseason, with mounds, a strike zone painted on a tarp, some weights and enough heat and electricity so that none of it's very spartan. It's enough to create easy solutions in Michigan winters, but might not be enough to turn him into the modern pitcher the Orioles want him to be. Perhaps an Edgertronic camera or Rapsodo system will help develop the inconsistent changeup and slider he'll need to be a backend starter for the Orioles. It's a role that his "invisiball" heater—sitting at 89-93 mph and eluding barrels—has him on the cusp of for 2020 and beyond.

Shawn Armstrong RHP   Born: 09/11/90   Age: 29   Bats: R   Throws: R   Height: 6'2"   Weight: 225   Origin: Round 18, 2011 Draft (#548 overall)

YEAR	TEAM	LVL	AGE	W	L	SV	G	GS	IP	H	HR	BB/9	K/9	K	GB%	BABIP	WHIP	ERA	DRA	WARP	MPH	FB%	WHF	CSP
2017	COH	AAA	26	1	1	10	28	0	29¹	27	3	3.4	11.0	36	48%	.324	1.30	3.07	3.82	0.5				
2017	CLE	MLB	26	1	0	0	21	0	24²	23	5	3.6	7.3	20	40%	.250	1.34	4.38	5.02	0.0	95.1	63.5	11.6	50.9
2018	TAC	AAA	27	2	5	15	49	0	56	38	3	4.2	13.2	82	35%	.294	1.14	1.77	2.45	1.7				
2018	SEA	MLB	27	0	1	1	14	0	14²	9	1	1.8	9.2	15	44%	.229	0.82	1.23	4.40	0.1	95.7	39.2	12.7	52.1
2019	BAL	MLB	28	1	0	4	51	0	54¹	58	7	4.3	9.9	60	31%	.336	1.55	5.13	5.43	0.0	95.4	58.8	12.7	50.4
2019	SEA	MLB	28	0	1	0	4	0	3²	8	1	7.4	7.4	3	25%	.467	3.00	14.73	7.26	-0.1	94.5	57.8	16.7	54.5
2020	BAL	MLB	29	2	2	0	48	0	51	48	9	3.9	8.9	50	34%	.286	1.38	4.92	4.54	0.4	94.7	57.5	12.8	51.2

Comparables: Santiago Casilla, Sam Tuivailala, J.J. Hoover

Mike Wright was an East Carolina product with a big fastball who got a million chances with the Orioles and was finally cut loose in April. Armstrong, his college teammate and close friend, was cut by the Mariners that same weekend. They switched places, switched numbers (43) and Armstrong continued on with Wright's work. He became the new Mike Wright, right down to the ERA that started with a five. The stuff, however, is better than Wright's and Armstrong spent most of the year as the Orioles' top set-up man before struggling down the stretch.

Ty Blach LHP   Born: 10/20/90   Age: 29   Bats: R   Throws: L   Height: 6'1"   Weight: 213   Origin: Round 5, 2012 Draft (#178 overall)

YEAR	TEAM	LVL	AGE	W	L	SV	G	GS	IP	H	HR	BB/9	K/9	K	GB%	BABIP	WHIP	ERA	DRA	WARP	MPH	FB%	WHF	CSP
2017	SFN	MLB	26	8	12	0	34	24	163²	179	17	2.4	4.0	73	48%	.290	1.36	4.78	4.75	1.5	91.9	60.1	7	50.5
2018	SFN	MLB	27	6	7	0	47	13	118²	133	8	3.1	5.7	75	55%	.323	1.47	4.25	4.79	0.5	92.0	57.6	7.9	50.3
2019	SAC	AAA	28	3	4	0	17	15	91	121	14	2.5	6.4	65	50%	.346	1.60	5.93	5.69	0.9				
2019	BAL	MLB	28	1	3	0	5	5	20²	32	6	5.7	7.4	17	34%	.388	2.18	11.32	10.61	-1.1	91.9	55.5	8.1	49.1
2019	SFN	MLB	28	0	0	0	2	0	6¹	14	2	5.7	4.3	3	34%	.444	2.84	14.21	9.42	-0.3	92.5	60.6	3.9	47.4
2020	BAL	MLB	29	2	2	0	33	0	35	42	5	2.9	5.8	23	46%	.316	1.51	5.61	5.31	0.0	91.3	58.5	7.4	49.7

Comparables: Tom Urbani, T.J. McFarland, Ryan Weber

There are plenty of ways for pitchers to be successful; few, if any, involve a 6.3 percent swinging strike rate. Blach has spent over three years as a swingman/fifth starter type after his debut in September 2016. Since then, no pitcher who has thrown as many innings as Blach has posted a lower strikeout rate (4.9 per nine and 12.7 percent of plate appearances). His innate inability to miss bats didn't stop the Orioles from taking a shot on him in 2019 because he was a living, breathing pitcher with serviceable Triple-A stats. But his hard and soft contact rates are going in the wrong directions, and the way opposing hitters square him up, those lasers are hard to, ahem, block.

Richard Bleier LHP   Born: 04/16/87   Age: 33   Bats: L   Throws: L   Height: 6'3"   Weight: 215   Origin: Round 6, 2008 Draft (#183 overall)

YEAR	TEAM	LVL	AGE	W	L	SV	G	GS	IP	H	HR	BB/9	K/9	K	GB%	BABIP	WHIP	ERA	DRA	WARP	MPH	FB%	WHF	CSP
2017	NOR	AAA	30	0	0	1	8	0	14²	9	0	0.0	9.2	15	70%	.243	0.61	0.61	2.17	0.5				
2017	BAL	MLB	30	2	1	0	57	0	63¹	62	6	1.8	3.7	26	69%	.259	1.18	1.99	5.01	0.1	91.2	62.8	10	52.7
2018	BAL	MLB	31	3	0	0	31	0	32²	36	0	1.1	4.1	15	58%	.319	1.22	1.93	5.09	-0.1	90.2	61.2	10	53.6
2019	BAL	MLB	32	3	0	4	53	1	55¹	65	6	1.3	4.9	30	60%	.321	1.32	5.37	5.22	0.1	90.9	64.7	8.8	53.1
2020	BAL	MLB	33	3	3	3	54	0	57	64	8	1.8	5.2	33	60%	.297	1.32	4.82	4.59	0.4	89.8	62.6	9.4	52.5

Comparables: Chris Rusin, Steven Wright, Blaine Hardy

Chris Davis got all the attention for starting the Orioles' major dugout altercation of the season with manager Brandon Hyde, but Bleier's a few weeks later was far more effective. All Davis got for his dust-up was a cut in his playing time. Bleier let third base coach José David Flóres know he didn't appreciate the Orioles' infield positioning on a single through the right side that had double-play potential, but instead contributed to a three-run inning on Aug. 28 against Washington. The consequence? Bleier got a straight-up defense the last month of the season, and allowed three runs and just eight baserunners in 11 appearances the rest of the way. The batted-ball misfortune of the preceding five months is reflected above.

Aaron Brooks RHP Born: 04/27/90 Age: 30 Bats: R Throws: R Height: 6'4" Weight: 230 Origin: Round 9, 2011 Draft (#276 overall)

YEAR	TEAM	LVL	AGE	W	L	SV	G	GS	IP	H	HR	BB/9	K/9	K	GB%	BABIP	WHIP	ERA	DRA	WARP	MPH	FB%	WHF	CSP
2017	IOW	AAA	27	8	9	0	24	24	138	181	27	1.8	6.8	105	50%	.345	1.51	6.20	6.16	-0.7				
2017	CSP	AAA	27	0	1	0	2	2	7²	11	2	1.2	2.3	2	50%	.300	1.57	4.70	6.04	0.0				
2018	CSP	AAA	28	9	4	0	26	15	99¹	100	8	2.5	6.7	74	56%	.307	1.29	3.35	2.96	2.8				
2018	OAK	MLB	28	0	0	0	3	0	2²	1	0	6.8	3.4	1	71%	.143	1.12	0.00	4.72	0.0	94.4	45.2	0	43.4
2019	BAL	MLB	29	4	5	0	14	12	59²	69	9	3.0	5.9	39	47%	.311	1.49	6.18	5.87	-0.1	93.9	50.3	8.5	47.9
2019	OAK	MLB	29	2	3	0	15	6	50¹	49	12	2.5	7.7	43	41%	.261	1.25	5.01	6.35	-0.4	94.6	58.4	9.5	47.6
2020	BAL	MLB	30	2	2	0	33	0	35	37	6	2.6	6.5	25	47%	.293	1.35	4.92	4.82	0.1	93.5	53.6	8.8	45.7

Comparables: Tyler Wilson, Zach Neal, Justin Haley

Brooks was an opener, a starter, a bulk reliever and a short reliever in a unique year spent between Oakland and Baltimore, but none of those roles really address what the otherwise-useful sinkerballer truly struggled with: getting outs right as he entered a game. Brooks allowed a .310 average with a .918 OPS in his first 25 pitches of an outing, and after he settled in, it was a .248 average with a .780 OPS. He was far better coming out of the bullpen, whether the expectation was to pitch one inning or seven. Yet, the KIA Tigers are likely to use him as one of their top starters as Brooks inked a deal to give the KBO a whirl in 2020.

Miguel Castro RHP Born: 12/24/94 Age: 25 Bats: R Throws: R Height: 6'7" Weight: 205 Origin: International Free Agent, 2012

YEAR	TEAM	LVL	AGE	W	L	SV	G	GS	IP	H	HR	BB/9	K/9	K	GB%	BABIP	WHIP	ERA	DRA	WARP	MPH	FB%	WHF	CSP
2017	BOW	AA	22	3	0	0	6	0	24¹	23	1	2.2	4.1	11	49%	.275	1.19	4.44	4.38	0.1				
2017	BAL	MLB	22	3	3	0	39	1	66¹	53	8	3.8	5.2	38	50%	.227	1.22	3.53	5.51	-0.2	98.7	61.4	10.5	45.9
2018	BAL	MLB	23	2	7	0	63	1	86¹	75	9	5.2	5.9	57	49%	.259	1.45	3.96	6.49	-1.5	98.7	58.1	10.4	47.8
2019	BAL	MLB	24	1	3	2	65	0	73¹	63	10	5.0	8.7	71	48%	.269	1.42	4.66	4.02	1.1	99.5	49.1	12.2	45.7
2020	BAL	MLB	25	3	3	0	60	0	64	60	9	4.5	8.3	59	48%	.288	1.44	4.69	4.32	0.6	98.7	56.4	11.4	47.6

Comparables: Gary Ross, Brad Keller, Aaron Sanchez

Hard as it is to consistently throw a fastball in the upper 90s and hit triple-digits in a big-league game—Castro was one of 37 pitchers to do in 2019—it is apparently much harder to be convinced not to throw it as often. Castro's two-seamer was touched up to the tune of a .346 average and a .583 slugging percentage in 2019, accounting for 70 percent of his homers allowed and 75 percent of his doubles. Meanwhile, his slider and change languished with 37.5 and 39.8 percent whiff rates, respectively. He doesn't command either terribly consistently—mechanics are hard when you're 6-foot-7—and fastball counts typically result in loud sounds when fastballs are thrown. It seems like there's a usage issue that can help Castro become the reliever his stuff has always teased.

Alex Cobb RHP Born: 10/07/87 Age: 32 Bats: R Throws: R Height: 6'3" Weight: 205 Origin: Round 4, 2006 Draft (#109 overall)

YEAR	TEAM	LVL	AGE	W	L	SV	G	GS	IP	H	HR	BB/9	K/9	K	GB%	BABIP	WHIP	ERA	DRA	WARP	MPH	FB%	WHF	CSP
2017	TBA	MLB	29	12	10	0	29	29	179¹	175	22	2.2	6.4	128	49%	.282	1.22	3.66	4.07	3.0	93.5	51.5	7.5	47
2018	BAL	MLB	30	5	15	0	28	28	152¹	172	24	2.5	6.0	102	51%	.303	1.41	4.90	5.50	-0.3	93.6	51.5	8	47.6
2019	BAL	MLB	31	0	2	0	3	3	12¹	21	9	1.5	5.8	8	48%	.293	1.86	10.95	8.27	-0.3	94.0	47.8	11.4	43.4
2020	BAL	MLB	32	8	10	0	26	26	143	176	26	3.0	6.4	102	51%	.324	1.57	6.37	5.73	-0.2	92.6	50.8	7.9	45.3

Comparables: Erik Hanson, John Lackey, Jered Weaver

The former Ray didn't get a spring training after signing his four-year, $57 million contract a week before the 2018 season, instead using the first two months of the season to find his form. He wasn't going to let that happen in 2019, and had command and feel for his vaunted split-change (FKA "The Thing"). He was three good months away from getting out of Baltimore; who wouldn't want a motivated veteran starter whose deferred money was another team's problem? But alas, a groin injury became a back injury, which was traced to a femoroacetabular impingement in his right hip. Just Google it. That was corrected by surgery, so provided his split-change comes back after a long layoff—which didn't happen after his 2015 Tommy John surgery—literally all of that will be the script again.

Paul Fry LHP Born: 07/26/92 Age: 27 Bats: L Throws: L Height: 6'0" Weight: 190 Origin: Round 17, 2013 Draft (#507 overall)

YEAR	TEAM	LVL	AGE	W	L	SV	G	GS	IP	H	HR	BB/9	K/9	K	GB%	BABIP	WHIP	ERA	DRA	WARP	MPH	FB%	WHF	CSP
2017	BOW	AA	24	0	0	1	7	0	12	7	0	3.8	13.5	18	54%	.292	1.00	0.75	2.17	0.4				
2017	NOR	AAA	24	3	2	0	25	3	46¹	47	6	5.1	10.3	53	49%	.333	1.58	4.66	5.56	-0.1				
2018	BOW	AA	25	3	0	2	15	0	19	10	2	5.2	13.3	28	68%	.229	1.11	2.84	1.87	0.7				
2018	NOR	AAA	25	0	1	0	13	1	23¹	22	2	1.5	11.2	29	53%	.345	1.11	3.47	3.97	0.3				
2018	BAL	MLB	25	1	2	2	35	0	37²	33	1	3.6	8.6	36	58%	.311	1.27	3.35	4.17	0.3	93.3	56.5	10.8	44.6
2019	BAL	MLB	26	1	9	3	66	0	57¹	54	7	4.6	8.6	55	59%	.297	1.45	5.34	4.75	0.4	92.8	52.3	10.9	47.1
2020	BAL	MLB	27	2	2	3	42	0	44	42	7	3.6	8.2	41	55%	.284	1.34	4.57	4.27	0.4	92.5	54.3	11	46.5

Comparables: Steven Okert, Eury De La Rosa, Tyler Johnson

The looming three-batter minimum for relievers is, in theory, meant to shake left-handers like Fry out of the majors; though he might be an exception to that rule. The Orioles spent most of the year using him against left-handed hitters, and especially in the second half they ended up greasing him. Five homers in 56 batters will do that. But he struck out a quarter of the righties he faced this year, so maybe there's a little extra mustard on his slider when he backdoors it. Maybe lefties know to avoid that sauce at all costs. Maybe the Orioles' bullpen will be better equipped to put the likes of Fry in better position in 2020 as, eventually, their focus will be on competing as opposed to just running out the clock. Maybe their own data still needs to catch up to this observation. It stands to reason, however, that a lefty reliever who can get righties out will be worth his weight in salt.

Mychal Givens RHP Born: 05/13/90 Age: 30 Bats: R Throws: R Height: 6'0" Weight: 210 Origin: Round 2, 2009 Draft (#54 overall)

YEAR	TEAM	LVL	AGE	W	L	SV	G	GS	IP	H	HR	BB/9	K/9	K	GB%	BABIP	WHIP	ERA	DRA	WARP	MPH	FB%	WHF	CSP
2017	BAL	MLB	27	8	1	0	69	0	78²	57	10	2.9	10.1	88	43%	.251	1.04	2.75	3.69	1.3	98.0	72.2	13.1	50.3
2018	BAL	MLB	28	0	7	9	69	0	76²	61	4	3.5	9.3	79	38%	.284	1.19	3.99	4.84	0.1	97.8	76.8	12.5	53.1
2019	BAL	MLB	29	2	6	11	58	0	63	49	13	3.7	12.3	86	39%	.271	1.19	4.57	3.08	1.6	98.0	70.3	17.1	50.4
2020	BAL	MLB	30	3	3	14	54	0	57	47	8	3.6	11.4	73	40%	.293	1.24	3.89	3.69	0.9	97.1	72.9	14.4	51.1

Comparables: Vinnie Pestano, Arodys Vizcaíno, Tommy Kahnle

Fifty pitchers had at least 25 appearances in save situations in 2019. Only two—Colin Poche and Edwin Díaz—had a higher ERA than Givens' 5.90 in such situations, and two—Josh Hader and Emilio Pagán—allowed more than his eight home runs in them. Simply put, Givens has not been one when it comes to locking down saves. He had a 1.67 ERA before the ninth inning, and a 6.75 ERA in and after it. He's murder on righties, and lefties come calling with the receipts. It's an electric arsenal that will probably make an All-Star team the second he leaves Baltimore and gets to set-up somewhere else, but it's hard to showcase that when he has to pitch in situations he's shown aren't for him.

DL Hall LHP Born: 09/19/98 Age: 21 Bats: L Throws: L Height: 6'2" Weight: 195 Origin: Round 1, 2017 Draft (#21 overall)

YEAR	TEAM	LVL	AGE	W	L	SV	G	GS	IP	H	HR	BB/9	K/9	K	GB%	BABIP	WHIP	ERA	DRA	WARP	MPH	FB%	WHF	CSP
2017	ORI	RK	18	0	0	0	5	5	10¹	10	1	8.7	10.5	12	58%	.360	1.94	6.97	6.58	-0.1				
2018	DEL	A	19	2	7	0	22	20	94¹	68	6	4.0	9.5	100	46%	.262	1.17	2.10	3.80	1.5				
2019	FRD	A+	20	4	5	1	19	17	80²	53	3	6.0	12.9	116	36%	.299	1.33	3.46	3.72	1.3				
2020	BAL	MLB	21	2	2	0	33	0	35	35	5	4.2	10.5	41	39%	.327	1.47	5.16	4.89	0.1				

Comparables: Jeremy Jeffress, Alex Reyes, Jesse Biddle

It's hard to figure what offseason development ahead of the 2019 season benefitted Hall more: the change in nomenclature that transformed the disabled list and its abbreviation to injured list, or the regime change in Baltimore that installed a staff with a background in bringing along young pitching. They have a great piece to work with in the 2017 first-round pick, whose fastball was up to 97 mph in a walk-laden year at High-A Frederick. He's still trying to get back the feel for his plus curveball he came out of high school with, but has developed an above-average changeup in the meantime. Fortunately for the Orioles, he went to the Futures Game and realized his stuff was too good to not throw in the zone. Hall re-affirmed his top-end rotation potential by throwing down a 2.67 ERA with 36 strikeouts against 12 walks between that appearance and an oblique injury that prematurely ended his season.

Hunter Harvey RHP Born: 12/09/94 Age: 25 Bats: R Throws: R Height: 6'3" Weight: 175 Origin: Round 1, 2013 Draft (#22 overall)

YEAR	TEAM	LVL	AGE	W	L	SV	G	GS	IP	H	HR	BB/9	K/9	K	GB%	BABIP	WHIP	ERA	DRA	WARP	MPH	FB%	WHF	CSP
2017	DEL	A	22	0	1	0	3	3	8²	4	0	3.1	14.5	14	31%	.250	0.81	2.08	2.21	0.3				
2018	BOW	AA	23	1	2	0	9	9	32¹	36	3	2.5	8.4	30	36%	.351	1.39	5.57	5.07	0.1				
2019	BOW	AA	24	2	5	1	14	11	59	63	14	3.2	9.3	61	40%	.316	1.42	5.19	6.42	-1.1				
2019	NOR	AAA	24	1	1	0	12	0	16²	13	2	2.7	11.9	22	43%	.275	1.08	4.32	2.97	0.5				
2019	BAL	MLB	24	1	0	0	7	0	6¹	3	1	5.7	15.6	11	55%	.200	1.11	1.42	3.70	0.1	99.8	69.6	12.6	48.2
2020	BAL	MLB	25	3	3	10	54	0	57	49	8	3.6	10.1	64	39%	.286	1.26	4.08	3.84	0.8	99.5	71.3	12.9	49.3

Comparables: Keury Mella, Michael Blazek, Wilfredo Boscan

Harvey's long-awaited major-league debut was a bright moment for the 2019 Orioles, considering he'd been injured for all but fleeting spells from July 2014 to this spring. It was only made sweeter by a mullet/mustache combination straight out of "Road House." But he finally made it in a new relief role where his fastball bumped triple digits, his dad's splitter fell out of the zone and his breaking ball flashed. All his presence did was make the miserable Orioles bullpen instantly different. His first outing was low-leverage; his last was 10 days after the preceding one, and then he was shut down for typical September reasons. In between, he was the high-leverage reliever Brandon Hyde never had. The Orioles' bullpen ERA in that two-week span with Harvey pitching the seventh and eighth was 2.58, third-best in the majors. It was 5.98 outside that span. Maybe the mullet is magic.

David Hess RHP Born: 07/10/93 Age: 26 Bats: R Throws: R Height: 6'2" Weight: 180 Origin: Round 5, 2014 Draft (#151 overall)

YEAR	TEAM	LVL	AGE	W	L	SV	G	GS	IP	H	HR	BB/9	K/9	K	GB%	BABIP	WHIP	ERA	DRA	WARP	MPH	FB%	WHF	CSP
2017	BOW	AA	23	11	9	0	27	26	154¹	137	16	3.1	7.2	123	32%	.269	1.23	3.85	3.60	2.9				
2018	NOR	AAA	24	3	2	0	9	9	45²	38	3	3.7	8.7	44	29%	.285	1.25	3.15	4.40	0.6				
2018	BAL	MLB	24	3	10	0	21	19	103¹	106	22	3.2	6.4	74	35%	.268	1.38	4.88	7.38	-2.5	94.6	58.7	9.1	47.9
2019	NOR	AAA	25	3	2	1	13	4	41¹	41	7	2.6	10.2	47	45%	.312	1.28	4.57	4.18	0.9				
2019	BAL	MLB	25	1	10	0	23	14	80	94	28	3.4	7.7	68	34%	.278	1.55	7.09	8.46	-2.4	95.2	59.2	9.5	47.1
2020	BAL	MLB	26	2	3	0	35	5	49	57	13	3.5	7.3	39	35%	.304	1.57	6.65	5.89	-0.3	94.5	60	9.5	48.3

Comparables: Zeke Spruill, Myles Jaye, Allen Webster

The quiet thing left unsaid when a pitcher is removed late in a no-hitter is that he might not be good enough to ever get that close again. Hess, on the first of April, took one into the seventh on short rest against the Blue Jays but was removed after just 82 pitches and watched from the dugout as Elvis Araujo surrendered a homer two batters later. The strong performance was ultimately just a cruel April Fool's joke, as Hess went on to allow the most home runs of any pitcher in major-league history with 80 innings or fewer.

Nate Karns RHP   Born: 11/25/87   Age: 32   Bats: R   Throws: R   Height: 6'3"   Weight: 225   Origin: Round 12, 2009 Draft (#352 overall)

YEAR	TEAM	LVL	AGE	W	L	SV	G	GS	IP	H	HR	BB/9	K/9	K	GB%	BABIP	WHIP	ERA	DRA	WARP	MPH	FB%	WHF	CSP
2017	KCA	MLB	29	2	2	0	9	8	45¹	41	9	2.6	10.1	51	48%	.283	1.19	4.17	4.94	0.3	95.4	49.4	13.6	47.7
2019	BAL	MLB	31	0	1	0	4	2	5¹	7	0	5.1	8.4	5	75%	.438	1.88	0.00	4.38	0.1	93.8	65.9	11	45.5
2020	BAL	MLB	32	2	2	0	33	0	35	33	7	4.1	7.3	28	40%	.263	1.40	5.13	4.94	0.1	94.2	51.7	13	45.9

Comparables: Tyson Ross, Mike Bolsinger, Blake Treinen

In the Year of the Home Run, no team allowed more than the Orioles, who broke the previous record of 256 allowed in August and ended the season with a grueling 305. The league as a whole saw 6,776 of them hit. On the Orioles alone, 36 pitchers allowed home runs—and three of them weren't even actual pitchers. But Karns stood alone having not allowed a home run in any of his four appearances. That he made just four appearances, as he dealt with forearm soreness all year and was released in August, means the Orioles' only offseason major-league free agent didn't do much to help any of their causes whether good or evil. That said, he made himself into the answer to the saddest trivia question ever conceived.

Branden Kline RHP   Born: 09/29/91   Age: 28   Bats: R   Throws: R   Height: 6'3"   Weight: 210   Origin: Round 2, 2012 Draft (#65 overall)

YEAR	TEAM	LVL	AGE	W	L	SV	G	GS	IP	H	HR	BB/9	K/9	K	GB%	BABIP	WHIP	ERA	DRA	WARP	MPH	FB%	WHF	CSP
2018	FRD	A+	26	1	0	2	12	0	20²	20	0	1.3	10.0	23	36%	.357	1.11	1.31	3.65	0.3				
2018	BOW	AA	26	4	4	15	32	0	45	32	3	3.0	9.6	48	45%	.254	1.04	1.80	2.43	1.3				
2019	NOR	AAA	27	1	1	2	18	0	21	27	4	5.6	11.6	27	43%	.404	1.90	6.86	6.70	-0.1				
2019	BAL	MLB	27	1	4	0	34	0	41	44	9	4.2	7.5	34	40%	.294	1.54	5.93	6.10	-0.3	98.8	57.5	11	46.4
2020	BAL	MLB	28	1	1	0	18	0	19	20	3	3.8	8.0	17	41%	.299	1.45	5.32	4.92	0.1	98.2	57.8	11.1	46.6

Comparables: J.R. Graham, Luis Cessa, Steven Wright

Before the Orioles' young pitchers played catch on the outfield grass every afternoon, they circled up and played hacky sack. And boy oh boy, were they good at hacky sack. Once 7:05 p.m. comes, they all have the raw ingredients to be successful in the majors, if not the consistency. Kline's mid-90s fastball and swing-and-miss slider put him in that category. He, like the rest, could grow into a qualified major-league reliever with experience and refinement. Right now, it's important to note that they are all very, very good at hacky sack.

John Means LHP   Born: 04/24/93   Age: 27   Bats: L   Throws: L   Height: 6'3"   Weight: 230   Origin: Round 11, 2014 Draft (#331 overall)

YEAR	TEAM	LVL	AGE	W	L	SV	G	GS	IP	H	HR	BB/9	K/9	K	GB%	BABIP	WHIP	ERA	DRA	WARP	MPH	FB%	WHF	CSP
2017	BOW	AA	24	9	9	0	26	24	142¹	158	16	2.3	7.8	124	38%	.322	1.36	4.11	4.83	0.5				
2018	BOW	AA	25	1	4	0	8	7	46	43	6	2.5	8.0	41	41%	.276	1.22	4.30	3.84	0.8				
2018	NOR	AAA	25	6	5	0	20	19	111¹	123	9	1.5	7.2	89	35%	.324	1.28	3.48	4.97	0.7				
2018	BAL	MLB	25	0	0	0	1	0	3¹	6	1	0.0	10.8	4	25%	.455	1.80	13.50	9.83	-0.2	91.7	37.9	12.1	41.7
2019	BAL	MLB	26	12	11	0	31	27	155	138	23	2.2	7.0	121	32%	.256	1.14	3.60	4.61	1.9	94.0	50.8	10.6	47.1
2020	BAL	MLB	27	10	9	0	28	28	151	141	29	2.3	7.1	120	33%	.259	1.19	4.25	4.10	2.5	93.5	51.1	10.8	45.2

Comparables: Zach Neal, Tyler Wilson, Joel Payamps

Means was sitting on his couch watching football in September 2018 when he lied and told the Orioles he'd still been throwing and could build back up to possibly make his major-league debut. That was about the only time he was dishonest about his career; he thought he'd be the first spring training cut and bide his time in the minors, but instead, the fruits of a career-changing offseason took hold. He went to a specialized performance center and added three ticks of velocity to his fastball while learning the benefits of locating it up in the zone; then, in spring training, he worked with new pitching guru Chris Holt on developing a changeup that got 13 swinging strikes in his 2019 debut. Means never looked back. He was an All-Star because the changeup punished teams for stacking right-handers against him, and he had enough fastball to trick hitters who looked for the fade. He started throwing a shorter slider that can be a weapon against both sides late in the season.

For an organization that's so committed to player development—more specifically, having those players develop legitimate major-league skills and tools—having someone like Means do what he did as a rookie is a bastion of hope and an example that all this can work. It takes commitment. It takes a willingness to change everything about yourself as a player. It takes a little bit of fortune. And it takes a consistent plan to bring all those things about and put yourself in position to make Giancarlo Stanton whiff so hard it ruined his season. Means went from a fringe minor leaguer to a legitimate major-league starter who could be one of the few players still on the Orioles the next time they're competitive.

Luis Ortiz RHP   Born: 09/22/95   Age: 24   Bats: R   Throws: R   Height: 6'3"   Weight: 230   Origin: Round 1, 2014 Draft (#30 overall)

YEAR	TEAM	LVL	AGE	W	L	SV	G	GS	IP	H	HR	BB/9	K/9	K	GB%	BABIP	WHIP	ERA	DRA	WARP	MPH	FB%	WHF	CSP
2017	BLX	AA	21	4	7	0	22	20	94¹	79	12	3.5	7.5	79	36%	.258	1.23	4.01	4.45	0.8				
2018	BLX	AA	22	3	4	2	16	11	68	63	7	2.4	8.6	65	48%	.289	1.19	3.71	4.10	0.9				
2018	NOR	AAA	22	2	1	0	6	6	31²	34	4	2.3	6.0	21	40%	.297	1.33	3.69	5.47	0.0				
2018	BAL	MLB	22	0	1	0	2	1	2¹	7	0	11.6	0.0	0	53%	.467	4.29	15.43	7.94	-0.1	94.3	59.1	9.1	41.8
2019	NOR	AAA	23	3	7	0	14	14	66¹	77	15	4.2	6.4	47	47%	.294	1.63	6.38	5.88	0.5				
2019	BAL	MLB	23	0	1	0	1	1	3¹	4	2	13.5	8.1	3	30%	.250	2.70	10.80	6.61	0.0	96.4	52.5	1.7	44.3
2020	BAL	MLB	24	2	2	0	33	0	35	38	6	3.8	5.6	22	43%	.289	1.51	5.58	5.27	0.0	95.5	57.3	5.3	44.5

Comparables: Zach Lee, Jake Thompson, David Holmberg

Ortiz's fall from being the Texas Rangers' first-round pick in 2014 to where he ended 2019 can be summed up in Brandon Hyde's six-word response when asked about the big righty making a spot start in June. "I have no idea what to expect," Hyde said, though that was only because he couldn't say what everyone has come to expect: a fastball that bumps up in the mid-90s but is imminently hittable, and nothing really to keep hitters off it. Until that changes, the answer to the question posed to Hyde won't be one the big right-hander wants to hear.

Evan Phillips RHP   Born: 09/11/94   Age: 25   Bats: R   Throws: R   Height: 6'2"   Weight: 215   Origin: Round 17, 2015 Draft (#510 overall)

YEAR	TEAM	LVL	AGE	W	L	SV	G	GS	IP	H	HR	BB/9	K/9	K	GB%	BABIP	WHIP	ERA	DRA	WARP	MPH	FB%	WHF	CSP
2017	MIS	AA	22	1	1	1	15	0	21	22	5	4.7	10.3	24	47%	.321	1.57	8.14	5.85	-0.3				
2017	GWN	AAA	22	2	3	2	25	1	30¹	30	1	6.8	8.6	29	46%	.345	1.75	4.75	5.97	-0.2				
2018	GWN	AAA	23	4	4	8	31	0	40²	28	1	3.1	13.1	59	51%	.325	1.03	1.99	3.10	0.9				
2018	NOR	AAA	23	0	2	0	8	0	10²	6	1	2.5	11.0	13	32%	.208	0.84	3.38	5.31	0.0				
2018	ATL	MLB	23	0	0	0	4	0	6¹	6	3	5.7	4.3	3	41%	.158	1.58	8.53	5.71	-0.1	96.0	62.5	11.5	47.6
2018	BAL	MLB	23	0	1	0	5	1	5¹	7	2	10.1	8.4	5	39%	.312	2.44	18.56	9.68	-0.3	95.8	73	7	44.8
2019	NOR	AAA	24	1	2	1	27	0	39²	35	2	3.9	10.0	44	50%	.324	1.31	3.86	3.82	0.9				
2019	BAL	MLB	24	0	1	0	25	0	28	32	2	6.4	12.9	40	40%	.411	1.86	6.43	4.63	0.2	96.2	66.3	13.2	47.3
2020	BAL	MLB	25	1	1	0	24	0	25	25	4	4.3	9.9	28	42%	.310	1.45	5.10	4.69	0.1	95.8	68.3	12.5	47.9

Comparables: Eduardo Paredes, Andrew Bellatti, Jake Newberry

One of the most frequent shuttle-riders between Triple-A Norfolk and Baltimore, Phillips was called up eight different times, and pitched on seven of those occasions. Here is how he re-introduced himself with his first batter. April 9: walk. May 26: walk. June 7: pop fly, (followed immediately by a walk). June 20: strikeout! But, then an RBI-single July 27: lineout! But, then a home run. August 12: three-run home run. Sept. 7: lineout, then two strikeouts. September was a good month because he attacked the strike zone far more often, and didn't give up a run until the last day of the season. The 2020 roster changes will eliminate the chance for these types to pitch well knowing they don't need to fear being sent down in September, and that's a shame. How will we know which 95-and-a-slider reliever might turn the corner?

★ ★ ★ *2020 Top 101 Prospect* **#45** ★ ★ ★

Grayson Rodriguez RHP   Born: 11/16/99   Age: 20   Bats: L   Throws: R   Height: 6'5"   Weight: 220   Origin: Round 1, 2018 Draft (#11 overall)

YEAR	TEAM	LVL	AGE	W	L	SV	G	GS	IP	H	HR	BB/9	K/9	K	GB%	BABIP	WHIP	ERA	DRA	WARP	MPH	FB%	WHF	CSP
2018	ORI	RK	18	0	2	0	9	8	19¹	17	0	3.3	9.3	20	43%	.321	1.24	1.40	2.89	0.7				
2019	DEL	A	19	10	4	0	20	20	94	57	4	3.4	12.4	129	45%	.262	0.99	2.68	2.69	2.8				
2020	BAL	MLB	20	2	2	0	33	0	35	34	5	3.5	10.1	39	42%	.317	1.37	4.66	4.51	0.3				

Comparables: Tyler Glasnow, Clayton Kershaw, Lucas Giolito

When the Houston Astros brass that turned around that franchise took over ahead of the 2012 season, they already had a few gems in their farm system to jump-start it. If Mike Elias and company do the same in Baltimore, the first-round pick from the year before they arrived will be regarded as one of those. Rodriguez posted the highest strikeout-per-nine rate of any teenager in full-season ball with at least 90 innings, and only five pitchers in all the minors at that threshold had a higher strikeout rate than his 34.2 percent. His big fastball—which was up to 98 mph and sits easily in the mid-90s—is a major reason why. But combine his fantastic starter's frame with the fact that he was able to develop a future plus changeup after learning it this spring, and there are many reasons the Orioles see a frontline starter in Rodriguez.

Tanner Scott LHP   Born: 07/22/94   Age: 25   Bats: R   Throws: L   Height: 6'2"   Weight: 220   Origin: Round 6, 2014 Draft (#181 overall)

YEAR	TEAM	LVL	AGE	W	L	SV	G	GS	IP	H	HR	BB/9	K/9	K	GB%	BABIP	WHIP	ERA	DRA	WARP	MPH	FB%	WHF	CSP
2017	BOW	AA	22	0	2	0	24	24	69	45	2	6.0	11.3	87	54%	.281	1.32	2.22	3.24	1.6				
2017	BAL	MLB	22	0	0	0	2	0	1²	2	0	10.8	10.8	2	20%	.400	2.40	10.80	2.36	0.1	100.2	70.3	10.8	29.6
2018	NOR	AAA	23	0	1	0	10	0	12	10	0	6.8	9.8	13	62%	.345	1.58	0.75	5.27	0.0				
2018	BAL	MLB	23	3	3	0	53	0	53¹	55	6	4.7	12.8	76	49%	.380	1.56	5.40	2.85	1.3	99.1	55.3	18	43.3
2019	NOR	AAA	24	3	4	7	30	0	45¹	35	2	3.0	11.3	57	56%	.303	1.10	2.98	2.44	1.7				
2019	BAL	MLB	24	1	1	0	28	0	26¹	28	4	6.5	12.6	37	52%	.400	1.78	4.78	4.52	0.2	98.2	58.8	15.5	42.8
2020	BAL	MLB	25	2	2	0	42	0	44	39	4	4.7	12.3	61	50%	.329	1.41	4.45	4.07	0.5	98.5	58.2	17.4	40.6

Comparables: Rex Brothers, Hunter Wood, Edwin Díaz

"Just when they think they have the answers, I change the questions," said the late, iconic professional wrestler Roddy Piper. Minus the kilt, that about sums up Scott's 2019 season. He's still got a downhill fastball that topped out at 99 mph and a swing-and-miss slider on its day. And yet all he's ever been instructed to do is limit the walks and pitch in the zone. He did in his time at Triple-A this year, but opponents hit .479 with four home runs on pitches in the zone once he got to the big leagues, and of the 545 pitchers with at least 20 innings this year, only 19 walked more per inning. So Scott will enter his final option year with as much knowledge as anyone of the difference between just throwing it over and throwing quality strikes. It's just that not many of them throw 99 from the left side.

Tayler Scott RHP   Born: 06/01/92   Age: 28   Bats: R   Throws: R   Height: 6'3"   Weight: 185   Origin: Round 5, 2011 Draft (#159 overall)

YEAR	TEAM	LVL	AGE	W	L	SV	G	GS	IP	H	HR	BB/9	K/9	K	GB%	BABIP	WHIP	ERA	DRA	WARP	MPH	FB%	WHF	CSP
2017	BLX	AA	25	4	6	2	42	0	61²	57	3	5.1	9.2	63	48%	.321	1.49	2.34	5.20	-0.3				
2017	ROU	AAA	25	0	1	1	12	0	13	17	3	3.5	9.0	13	52%	.341	1.69	7.62	5.59	0.0				
2018	ROU	AAA	26	5	5	1	44	0	60²	60	4	3.7	7.7	52	59%	.324	1.40	3.26	4.62	0.4				
2019	TAC	AAA	27	3	2	1	20	0	35	32	4	4.9	12.1	47	56%	.350	1.46	6.43	3.61	0.9				
2019	NOR	AAA	27	0	0	6	13	0	16	11	0	1.7	11.8	21	59%	.324	0.88	0.56	1.80	0.7				
2019	SEA	MLB	27	0	0	0	5	2	7²	11	1	7.0	8.2	7	65%	.400	2.22	9.39	5.65	0.0	96.7	51	13.8	44
2019	BAL	MLB	27	0	0	0	8	0	8²	20	5	5.2	7.3	7	50%	.455	2.88	18.69	8.89	-0.3	96.1	61.2	7.2	45.4
2020	BAL	MLB	28	2	2	0	33	0	35	41	6	4.0	7.3	28	53%	.319	1.60	6.17	5.67	-0.2	95.8	57.4	9.9	45.1

Comparables: Marcus Hatley, Yacksel Ríos, Reed Garrett

If it isn't more complicated than this, then the rising sea levels will overtake Camden Yards before the Orioles are good again. It just seems like the team's driving force in major league player acquisition in 2019 was based on Triple-A stats, and the South African right-hander showed just how tenuous those can be. Scott didn't allow a run at Triple-A Norfolk from the time he was claimed on waivers to the last day of the season, spanning 13 appearances. In between, he made eight appearances for the Orioles and allowed runs in six of them for a double-digit ERA. On a major-league roster full of Triple-A pitchers, he showed that mostly drastically. But he did it with the best accent in the room.

Dillon Tate RHP Born: 05/01/94 Age: 26 Bats: R Throws: R Height: 6'2" Weight: 195 Origin: Round 1, 2015 Draft (#4 overall)

YEAR	TEAM	LVL	AGE	W	L	SV	G	GS	IP	H	HR	BB/9	K/9	K	GB%	BABIP	WHIP	ERA	DRA	WARP	MPH	FB%	WHF	CSP
2017	TAM	A+	23	6	0	0	9	9	58¹	48	4	2.3	7.1	46	61%	.262	1.08	2.62	3.46	1.2				
2017	TRN	AA	23	1	2	0	4	4	25	23	3	3.2	6.1	17	56%	.270	1.28	3.24	4.34	0.2				
2018	TRN	AA	24	5	2	0	15	15	82²	67	7	2.7	8.2	75	48%	.263	1.11	3.38	4.77	0.6				
2018	BOW	AA	24	2	3	0	7	7	40²	48	3	2.0	4.6	21	63%	.324	1.40	5.75	5.57	-0.1				
2019	BOW	AA	25	2	3	5	17	2	33²	28	4	2.4	8.0	30	50%	.261	1.10	3.48	4.60	0.0				
2019	NOR	AAA	25	2	0	2	4	0	9	7	1	1.0	7.0	7	65%	.240	0.89	2.00	3.06	0.3				
2019	BAL	MLB	25	0	2	0	16	0	21	18	3	3.9	8.6	20	61%	.268	1.29	6.43	4.65	0.2	96.0	56.6	8.6	49.8
2020	BAL	MLB	26	1	1	0	18	0	19	20	3	3.3	7.7	16	54%	.301	1.43	5.29	4.83	0.1	95.6	57.6	8.7	50.7

Comparables: Yohan Pino, Zach Neal, John Means

How necessary was the move to the bullpen that Tate asked the Orioles' brass to give him after two starts this season? He allowed eight earned runs over those two starts, and allowed seven earned runs in 36 minor-league relief innings the rest of the way. His major-league debut wasn't a disaster, but his 93-96 mph sinker still doesn't miss bats. More consistent command of his slider and changeup could make Tate a viable middle reliever—an outcome that would seem like a success were he not drafted fourth overall in 2015 and traded twice before reaching it. Of course, the four pitchers the Orioles have selected with the fourth-overall pick this century have a median WARP barely north of one, so it's a low bar in Baltimore.

Alex Wells LHP Born: 02/27/97 Age: 23 Bats: L Throws: L Height: 6'1" Weight: 190 Origin: International Free Agent, 2015

YEAR	TEAM	LVL	AGE	W	L	SV	G	GS	IP	H	HR	BB/9	K/9	K	GB%	BABIP	WHIP	ERA	DRA	WARP	MPH	FB%	WHF	CSP
2017	DEL	A	20	11	5	0	25	25	140	118	16	0.6	7.3	113	43%	.251	0.91	2.38	3.48	2.9				
2018	FRD	A+	21	7	8	0	24	24	135	142	19	2.2	6.7	101	36%	.301	1.30	3.47	5.21	0.2				
2019	BOW	AA	22	8	6	0	24	24	137¹	123	10	1.6	6.9	105	43%	.274	1.07	2.95	4.56	0.7				
2020	BAL	MLB	23	2	2	0	33	0	35	35	6	3.2	6.2	24	41%	.274	1.37	4.92	4.83	0.1				

Comparables: Gabriel Ynoa, José Ureña, Paul Blackburn

Wells, a left-hander signed for $350,000 out of Australia in 2015 who has graduated from projectable to perplexingly effective with a fastball that tops out at 90 mph and impeccable command. He is one of 29 pitchers with at least 400 innings in the minors the last three years. He's in the top-five in WHIP (1.09), walks per nine (1.46), batting average against (.240) and ERA (2.92) among them. If you're going to put someone in the "prove it at every level" basket, there isn't much more one can do to prove it, though a fly-ball rate near 50 percent could be a dangerous proposition once he reaches Triple-A and the big leagues with the current baseball construction.

Asher Wojciechowski RHP Born: 12/21/88 Age: 31 Bats: R Throws: R Height: 6'4" Weight: 235 Origin: Round 1, 2010 Draft (#41 overall)

YEAR	TEAM	LVL	AGE	W	L	SV	G	GS	IP	H	HR	BB/9	K/9	K	GB%	BABIP	WHIP	ERA	DRA	WARP	MPH	FB%	WHF	CSP
2017	LOU	AAA	28	2	0	0	8	5	30²	24	2	2.3	10.3	35	28%	.275	1.04	2.05	2.15	1.2				
2017	CIN	MLB	28	4	3	0	25	8	62¹	71	14	2.7	9.2	64	32%	.324	1.44	6.50	6.98	-1.1	94.2	61.8	11.3	48.9
2018	NOR	AAA	29	5	4	0	19	12	84²	68	14	3.4	9.5	89	31%	.255	1.18	3.51	5.22	0.3				
2018	CHR	AAA	29	0	5	0	6	6	34²	40	12	1.3	9.6	37	26%	.308	1.30	7.01	5.75	-0.1				
2019	COH	AAA	30	8	2	0	15	15	84²	67	19	3.3	8.7	82	28%	.227	1.16	3.61	4.32	2.0				
2019	BAL	MLB	30	4	8	0	17	16	82¹	80	17	3.1	8.7	80	30%	.278	1.31	4.92	5.44	0.3	93.4	53.9	12.7	45.4
2020	BAL	MLB	31	7	9	0	35	23	126	124	29	3.1	8.2	116	29%	.275	1.34	5.35	4.96	0.8	92.8	56	12.2	46.4

Comparables: William Cuevas, André Rienzo, Chris Stratton

Considering that Wojcieshowski was a prospect coming up with the Houston Astros during the lean years of their rebuild, his coming full-circle as a 30-year-old, cash-purchased starter in this second-generation rebuild is being told to expect a four-course meal, only getting the salad, then being forced to do the dishes. It's not as though he didn't benefit from the modern game, though. Wojciechowski honed a breaking ball that looks like it was developed in a lab with the Cleveland Indians in spring training, embraced a long-toss program and pitched himself into a regular role in a major-league rotation. It will be his until the Orioles find someone homegrown to take it.

Gabriel Ynoa RHP Born: 05/26/93 Age: 27 Bats: R Throws: R Height: 6'2" Weight: 205 Origin: International Free Agent, 2009

YEAR	TEAM	LVL	AGE	W	L	SV	G	GS	IP	H	HR	BB/9	K/9	K	GB%	BABIP	WHIP	ERA	DRA	WARP	MPH	FB%	WHF	CSP
2017	NOR	AAA	24	6	9	0	21	21	106¹	129	8	2.0	6.1	72	44%	.333	1.44	5.25	6.21	-0.6				
2017	BAL	MLB	24	2	3	0	9	4	34²	39	5	2.1	6.8	26	39%	.318	1.36	4.15	5.82	-0.2	95.8	55.7	10.2	47.4
2018	BOW	AA	25	0	0	0	2	2	7	6	1	0.0	7.7	6	45%	.263	0.86	2.57	4.09	0.1				
2019	NOR	AAA	26	1	0	0	3	3	17	13	3	3.2	6.9	13	59%	.208	1.12	4.76	2.65	0.7				
2019	BAL	MLB	26	1	10	0	36	13	110²	126	29	2.1	5.4	67	47%	.273	1.37	5.61	6.72	-1.4	95.5	56.5	10.1	48.9
2020	BAL	MLB	27	2	2	0	33	0	35	39	6	2.6	6.2	24	47%	.297	1.41	5.45	5.28	0.0	95.1	57	10.2	48.9

Comparables: Justin Nicolino, Enrique Gonzalez, José Ureña

As these pages have often noted, Ynoa can be pretty interesting. He joined the Orioles in April in a long-relief role and pitched well enough over the first few weeks that the local media essentially wanted him to transition into being a starter or the closer. A few more outings and he would have been in line to be the manager, or maybe even the mayor. Alas, he kept up what's been a career of inconsistency and somehow managed to throw 110 2/3 innings without a single one of them meaning anything. He was outrighted a second time this offseason, and you know the old saying. Outright me once, shame on you. Outright me twice, I'm going to pitch in Japan.

LINEOUTS

Hitters

HITTER	POS	TEAM	LVL	AGE	PA	R	2B	3B	HR	RBI	BB	K	SB	CS	AVG/OBP/SLG	DRC+	VORP	BABIP	BRR	FRAA	WARP
Rylan Bannon	3B	NOR	AAA	23	90	18	10	0	3	17	3	14	0	1	.317/.344/.549	119	6.1	.338	-0.3	3B(20): 3.1	0.7
	3B	BOW	AA	23	444	45	22	4	8	42	47	72	8	4	.255/.345/.394	124	19.4	.294	-0.4	3B(68): 1.8, 2B(38): 1.4	2.8
Yusniel Díaz	OF	FRD	A+	22	25	0	0	0	0	2	3	7	0	0	.273/.360/.273	88	-0.7	.400	-0.6	CF(5): -0.4	-0.1
	OF	BOW	AA	22	322	45	19	4	11	53	32	67	0	3	.262/.335/.472	150	19.7	.303	0.6	RF(53): 1.4, CF(5): 0.3	2.5
Adam Hall	SS	DEL	A	20	534	78	22	4	5	45	45	117	33	9	.298/.385/.395	140	52.3	.387	3.1	SS(79): 0.4, 2B(39): 0.2	4.5
Gunnar Henderson	SS	ORI	Rk	18	121	21	5	2	1	11	11	28	2	2	.259/.331/.370	65	2.7	.338	0.4	SS(21): -1.6	0.0
Kyle Stowers	OF	ABE	A-	21	228	19	13	1	6	23	20	53	5	1	.216/.289/.377	88	2.5	.259	-0.6	RF(20): 1.7, LF(20): -0.7	0.5
Mason Williams	OF	NOR	AAA	27	494	62	15	3	18	67	46	86	4	7	.308/.371/.477	113	21.3	.346	2.6	RF(48): 7.2, CF(40): -3.2	2.8
	OF	BAL	MLB	27	34	4	1	0	0	2	3	6	1	0	.267/.324/.300	93	0.9	.320	0.5	CF(7): -0.4, LF(2): -0.1	0.1
Austin Wynns	C	NOR	AAA	28	230	26	5	0	3	25	25	35	0	0	.264/.351/.335	91	5.2	.302	-0.7	C(54): 5.8	1.2
	C	BAL	MLB	28	74	8	1	0	1	5	3	14	0	0	.214/.247/.271	72	1.2	.255	0.7	C(25): -2.3	0.0

The wide-open stance that **Rylan Bannon** came to the Orioles with is now closed, but the equally-large gap in the bat-first infielder's defensive resume isn't. Bannon can play second base and third base and might have the pop to make an offensive impact at each, but the modern utility profile demands more. ⚾ **Yusniel Díaz**, the crown jewel of the Orioles' trade for Manny Machado in 2018, is entering Year Two of a staring match between a player whose fantastic tools seem destined to really only show themselves on a major-league stage and a front office who won't promote a player to said stage unless he's absolutely ready. ⚾ No player born in the Bahamas was ever selected in the MLB Draft before **Adam Hall** went in the second round of 2017, though he'd moved to Canada to pursue baseball long before that. It's not like there are many Canadian middle-infielders, either, but Hall's average-everything ceiling could change that as well. ⚾ There are three Gunnars ahead of 2019 second-round pick **Gunnar Henderson** in the race to be the first of his name to play in the big leagues, and three shortstops more advanced on the Orioles' depth chart for him to overtake to get there. The Orioles will be far more concerned with him accomplishing the latter than being the No. 1 Gunnar. ⚾ It's simple to get drafted on the first day when you are in the top five percent of average exit velocity for college hitters. **Kyle Stowers** will have to show he can get his bat on the ball enough for that easy plus raw power to be useful in right field. ⚾ There was a running joke around the Dan Duquette-led Orioles about his affinity for New England-born players and the sons of former Patriots (Hello, John Andreoli). **Mason Williams** joined the Orioles after Duquette was run out of town, and what's worse, he's actually useful as a spare outfielder. ⚾ Give credit where it's due: **Austin Wynns** has reached his ceiling as an up-and-down backup catcher with the Orioles. If he ever moves on from this organization, he can try to do it with a major-league team.

Pitchers

PITCHER	TEAM	LVL	AGE	W	L	SV	G	GS	IP	H	HR	BB/9	K/9	K	GB%	BABIP	WHIP	ERA	DRA	WARP	MPH	FB%	WHF	CSP
Brandon Bailey	CCH	AA	24	4	5	0	22	17	92²	72	12	4.0	10.0	103	37%	.271	1.22	3.30	4.18	0.8				
Michael Baumann	FRD	A+	23	1	4	0	11	11	54	40	2	4.0	12.8	77	46%	.314	1.19	3.83	3.79	0.8				
	BOW	AA	23	6	2	1	13	11	70	45	2	2.7	8.4	65	43%	.229	0.94	2.31	2.79	1.8				
Marcos Diplan	PEN	AA	22	0	1	0	8	2	11	10	1	5.7	8.2	10	20%	.310	1.55	4.09	6.38	-0.2				
	BLX	AA	22	3	4	3	30	5	57²	47	6	5.8	9.8	63	44%	.279	1.46	4.99	5.55	-0.6				
Ryan Eades	ROC	AAA	27	4	3	3	29	2	50²	59	7	2.8	11.2	63	39%	.385	1.48	5.51	5.16	0.5				
	MIN	MLB	27	0	0	0	2	0	3²	4	0	4.9	12.3	5	44%	.444	1.64	0.00	5.23	0.0	95.3	58.9	8.2	56.5
	BAL	MLB	27	0	1	0	6	0	7²	7	2	4.7	5.9	5	46%	.227	1.43	3.52	5.74	0.0	92.5	42.6	10.8	42.7
Tom Eshelman	REA	AA	25	0	3	0	6	6	28²	43	4	1.9	8.2	26	44%	.402	1.71	6.28	7.01	-0.7				
	NOR	AAA	25	2	1	0	7	6	38¹	43	6	1.6	6.6	28	45%	.298	1.30	4.70	4.51	0.8				
	LEH	AAA	25	1	1	0	4	4	26	23	3	1.7	8.0	23	49%	.282	1.08	2.77	5.01	0.4				
	BAL	MLB	25	1	2	0	10	4	36	47	12	2.8	5.5	22	33%	.297	1.61	6.50	8.73	-1.2	87.6	45.8	7.2	51.3
Eric Hanhold	BIN	AA	25	2	0	2	9	0	14²	9	1	3.1	11.0	18	50%	.242	0.95	1.23	3.53	0.2				
	SYR	AAA	25	3	4	0	39	0	48²	59	5	3.9	6.7	36	49%	.344	1.64	4.62	6.27	0.0				
Dean Kremer	FRD	A+	23	0	0	0	2	2	9²	6	0	3.7	13.0	14	20%	.300	1.03	0.00	3.56	0.2				
	BOW	AA	23	9	4	0	15	15	84²	75	9	3.1	9.2	87	42%	.297	1.23	2.98	4.68	0.3				
	NOR	AAA	23	0	2	0	4	4	19¹	30	2	1.9	9.8	21	38%	.459	1.76	8.84	7.58	-0.2				
Zac Lowther	BOW	AA	23	13	7	0	26	26	148	102	8	3.8	9.4	154	41%	.259	1.11	2.55	4.16	1.4				
Josh Rogers	NOR	AAA	24	2	6	0	11	11	55	86	18	1.6	5.4	33	40%	.356	1.75	8.51	8.40	-0.9				
	BAL	MLB	24	0	1	0	5	0	14¹	18	7	3.8	3.1	5	24%	.234	1.67	8.79	11.14	-0.9	92.1	53.2	6.1	49.8
Cody Sedlock	FRD	A+	24	4	1	0	13	10	61	38	4	3.8	9.7	66	42%	.238	1.05	2.36	3.13	1.4				
	BOW	AA	24	1	2	1	9	6	34	30	3	5.3	9.0	34	33%	.300	1.47	3.71	5.75	-0.4				
Chandler Shepherd	NOR	AAA	26	3	5	0	14	12	72¹	75	8	2.9	9.1	73	46%	.322	1.35	4.60	6.19	0.3				
	PAW	AAA	26	0	5	0	8	7	29²	53	11	4.9	9.1	30	37%	.416	2.33	10.01	5.94	0.2				
	BAL	MLB	26	0	0	0	5	3	19	23	5	2.8	8.1	17	36%	.333	1.53	6.63	7.27	-0.3	93.6	47.2	9.1	52.6
Kohl Stewart	ROC	AAA	24	8	6	0	20	19	91	90	10	4.4	7.9	80	53%	.299	1.47	5.14	4.52	1.9				
	MIN	MLB	24	2	2	0	9	2	25¹	29	5	2.8	3.6	10	49%	.282	1.46	6.39	6.70	-0.3	94.1	53	9.1	45.1
Cole Sulser	DUR	AAA	29	6	3	2	49	4	66	51	4	3.3	12.1	89	32%	.307	1.14	3.27	2.56	2.4				
	TBA	MLB	29	0	0	0	7	0	7¹	5	0	3.7	11.0	9	35%	.294	1.09	0.00	4.26	0.1	95.0	63.9	12.3	42
Bruce Zimmermann	BOW	AA	24	5	3	0	18	17	101¹	88	9	3.0	9.0	101	41%	.283	1.20	2.58	4.38	0.7				
	NOR	AAA	24	2	3	0	7	7	38²	44	3	4.2	7.7	33	49%	.352	1.60	4.89	5.69	0.4				

Swiped from the Astros with the second pick in the Rule 5 draft, right-hander **Brandon Bailey** is an undersized starter who relies on a deep pitch mix and a solid changeup to survive. He'll also get you a third of the way to an Irish Car Bomb—something anyone watching the 2020 Orioles rotation figures to need. ⓧ No pitcher in the Orioles' system benefited more from their new philosophies than **Michael Baumann**, who threw a no-hitter a month into his time at Double-A Bowie. He has the makings of a plus slider and above-average changeup to go with his four-seam fastball that runs up to 99 mph. ⓧ If **Cody Carroll**'s back issue is resolved, he and his mid-to-upper-90s fastball might have avoided a fate worse than injury: pitching for the 2019 Orioles. ⓧ Teams seem to want **Marcos Diplan** enough to acquire him but not sufficiently so to keep him on their roster—he bounced from Milwaukee to Minnesota to Detroit and finally Baltimore within five months. A combination of prospect pedigree and the absence of any clear minor league progress may explain why. ⓧ It's easy to mock the Orioles for taking on everyone else's detritus, but former second-rounders like **Ryan Eades** are the types of risks Baltimore should be taking. ⓧ The statistics for **Tom Eshelman** are the product of an 85-mph fastball, fringe-average command, and an organization starved for any kind of pitching depth. ⓧ The Orioles' computer told them **Eric Hanhold**'s mid-90s fastball and ability to miss bats with his slider was worth a waiver claim, and that may prove to be true. The fact that they claimed him and sent him home rather than have him help a depleted pitching staff in September suggests otherwise. ⓧ **Dean Kremer** led the minors in strikeouts in 2018 with 178, and still struck out over a batter per inning in a 2019 shortened by a spring oblique strain. His plus curveball, fastball command and pitchability could make him one of the more successful young pitchers in the early phase of the Orioles rebuild when he debuts in 2020. ⓧ One of three pitchers with at least 150 strikeouts in the last two minor league seasons, **Zac Lowther** does it with a fastball in the 88-91 mph and a plus changeup. His elite extension makes everything play up. ⓧ **Josh Rogers** had UCL revision surgery—essentially a second Tommy John—in June. The whole arm contraption that came with it really took away from the drip. ⓧ Before the new Orioles' staff resurrected 2016 first-round pick **Cody Sedlock**'s career, it was laying on the operating table surrounded by the ghosts of Brian Matusz, Matt Hobgood and the cadre of Orioles' ruined pitching prospects. But for now, his career and fastball still have some life left. ⓧ Outrighting **Chandler Shepherd** the day after he started the final game of the season for the Orioles must have felt like a cigarette after an extremely regrettable romp. ⓧ **Kohl Stewart** is now 25, and he still hasn't figured out how to strike out anyone. It's ... it's not an ideal outcome for the former fourth-overall pick. ⓧ **Cole Sulser** was a useful, two-pitch middle reliever in the Rays' organization in 2019. That means he will be a member of the Los Angeles Dodgers or the Milwaukee Brewers by the time the 2021 Annual goes to print. ⓧ Who has two thumbs, four pitches, a killer mustache and could arrive in Baltimore in 2020 to pitch in his hometown, saving the local media from writing about actual Orioles games for a week or so? **Bruce Zimmermann**.

BOSTON RED SOX

Essay by Jon Tayler

Player comments by Ben Carsley and BP staff

Just over 18 years ago, the Red Sox changed ownership. For nearly seven decades, the franchise had been in the hands (and then the family) of Tom Yawkey, who had bought the club in 1933 for $1.25 million—about $24 million in today's money—and ran it until his death in 1977. Under Yawkey, the Red Sox were sporadically good, mixing long stretches of mediocrity and outright awfulness with transcendent bursts of contention that inevitably ended in excruciating World Series losses. (Yawkey also threw in some racism that was egregious even by the standards of the time: Boston was the last team to integrate, doing so in 1959, and only grudgingly, having famously passed on a chance to sign Jackie Robinson in 1945.)

After Yawkey's death, his wife Jean took over until she passed away in 1992, at which point the team was run by a trust set up in the family name. They carried on Yawkey's legacy of blending intermittent highs with a smooth paste of third-place finishes and 81-win seasons. But no matter the Hall-of-Fame talents who passed through Fenway Park—Ted Williams, Carl Yastrzemski, Carlton Fisk, Pedro Martínez, the four weeks of the season during which Brian Daubach hit like peak Barry Bonds—the end result was always the same: no championship.

By the end of the 2001 season, the Red Sox hadn't won a pennant in 15 years or a World Series in nearly a century. A miasma of bad feelings created by petty, internecine squabbles and ill-considered moves (or non-moves, occasionally) hung over the team, broken up only by Martínez's starts. At the same time, there were persistent rumors that the club was going to tear down Fenway—the lyrical little bandbox of John Updike's prose that nonetheless fit only 35,000 people and was about as comfortable to sit in as a porta-potty—and leave Boston proper. The present was uninspiring; the future was bleak.

Then along came John W. Henry. Tall, thin and nearly translucent, Henry made his millions as a commodities trader but always harbored a dream of owning a baseball team. He managed to gain sole control of the then-Florida Marlins in the late 1990s, but that was the equivalent of buying a gutted house. A better opportunity presented itself in 2001, when the Red Sox went on the block.

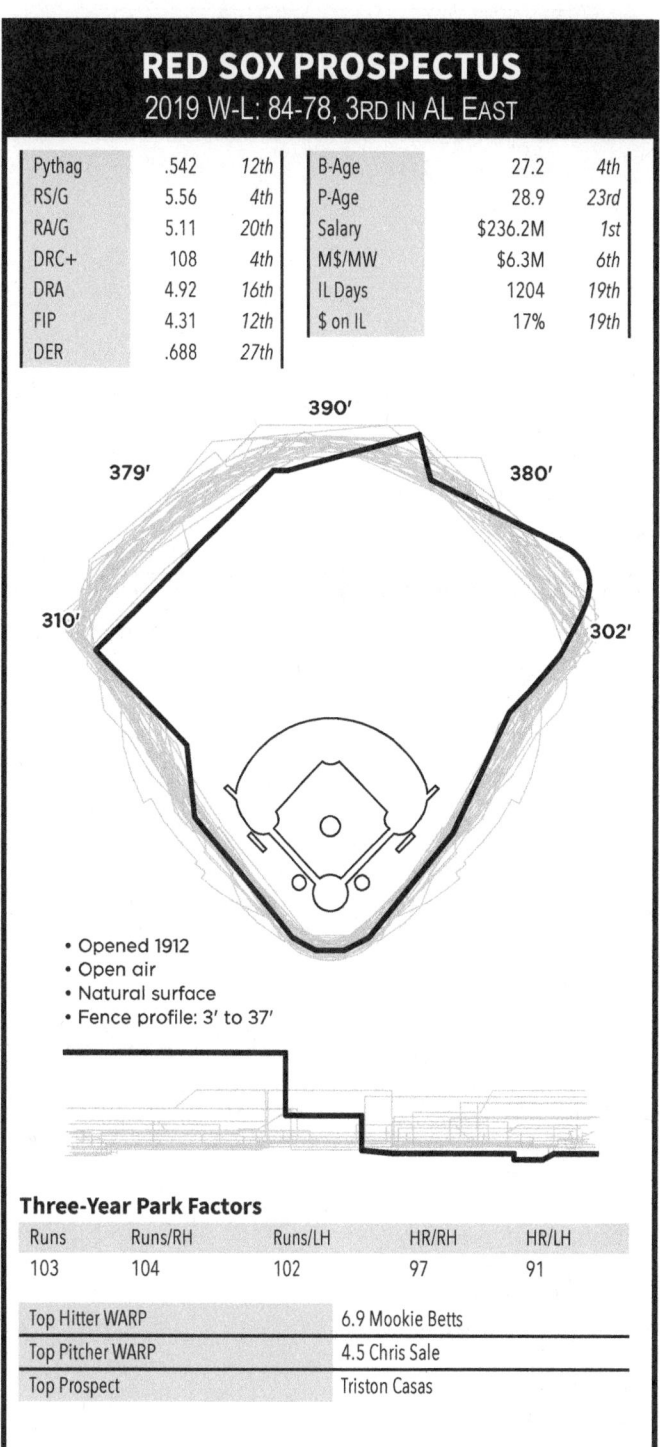

RED SOX PROSPECTUS
2019 W-L: 84-78, 3RD IN AL EAST

Pythag	.542	12th	B-Age	27.2	4th
RS/G	5.56	4th	P-Age	28.9	23rd
RA/G	5.11	20th	Salary	$236.2M	1st
DRC+	108	4th	M$/MW	$6.3M	6th
DRA	4.92	16th	IL Days	1204	19th
FIP	4.31	12th	$ on IL	17%	19th
DER	.688	27th			

390'
379'
380'
310'
302'

- Opened 1912
- Open air
- Natural surface
- Fence profile: 3' to 37'

Three-Year Park Factors

Runs	Runs/RH	Runs/LH	HR/RH	HR/LH
103	104	102	97	91

Top Hitter WARP	6.9 Mookie Betts
Top Pitcher WARP	4.5 Chris Sale
Top Prospect	Triston Casas

2019 Hit List Ranking

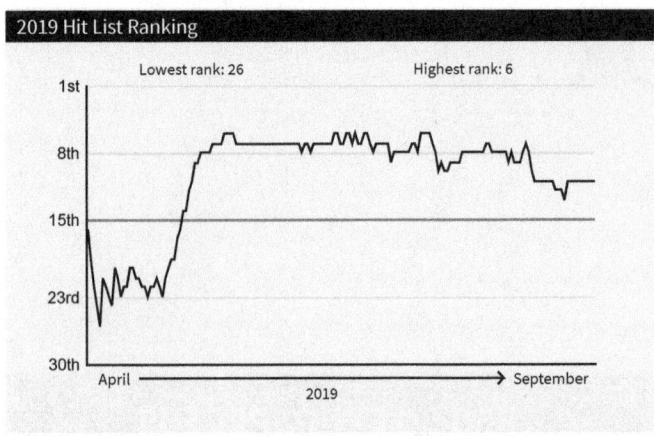

Lowest rank: 26   Highest rank: 6

1st
8th
15th
23rd
30th
April ————— 2019 ————→ September

Committed Payroll (in millions)

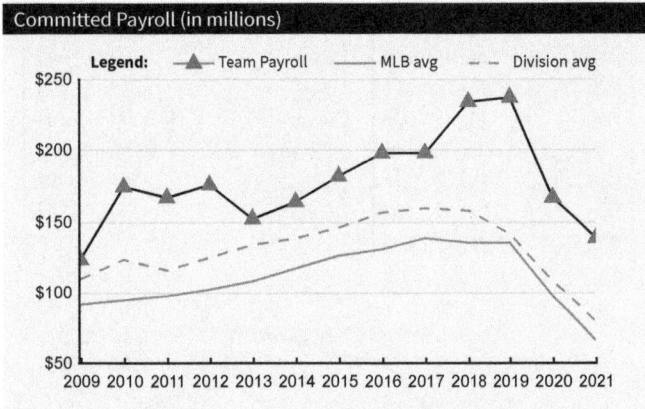

Legend: ▲ Team Payroll   — MLB avg   - - - Division avg

$250
$200
$150
$100
$50
2009 2010 2011 2012 2013 2014 2015 2016 2017 2018 2019 2020 2021

Farm System Ranking

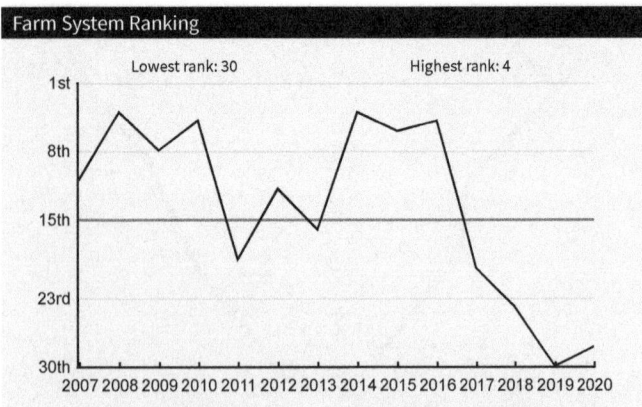

Lowest rank: 30   Highest rank: 4

1st
8th
15th
23rd
30th
2007 2008 2009 2010 2011 2012 2013 2014 2015 2016 2017 2018 2019 2020

Personnel

Chief Baseball Officer
Chaim Bloom

**Executive Vice President/
Assistant General Manager**
Zack Scott

**Executive Vice President/
Assistant General Manager**
Raquel Ferreira

**Vice President, Player
Development**
Ben Crockett

Manager
Alex Cora

BP Alumni
Chaim Bloom
Todd Gold
Tyler Oringer

Joining former Padres CEO Larry Lucchino and television producer Tom Werner, Henry became the money man for a group who, before he jumped on board, was a relative long shot to purchase the team. (The favorite at the time was Frank McCourt, who went on to buy and almost destroy the Dodgers; I think about the alternate universe where he takes over the Red Sox at least four times a week.) With Henry footing the majority of the bill, the new group took over on Dec. 20, 2001, for a price tag of $695 million, and committed to staying in the city and Fenway.

Within three years of taking over, Henry and company built the Red Sox into something most fans in New England figured the team would never be: a world champion. A second title followed in 2007, then another in '13, and a fourth in '18. Almost overnight, baseball's perpetual bridesmaid became this millennium's version of the Yankees, in the process (and along with the Patriots) turning Boston from America's most insufferable sports city into America's most insufferable and successful sports city.

All the while, as the team took its place among MLB's elite, Henry kept footing the bill, spending millions upon millions of dollars to ensure a winning club and also to establish the Red Sox as a money-making machine. The two went hand-in-hand: No one will repeatedly spend their hard-earned paychecks to watch a loser, so Henry had to spend his to make sure that never came to pass. Beyond that, though, he understood that the club needed as many revenue streams as possible, and ideally for said streams to be diverse. So, he poured money not just into the roster but also into Fenway, the team's cable network NESN, the *Boston Globe* (which he purchased in 2013) and a sports consortium who bought Liverpool F.C. in the English Premier League and half of Roush Racing, a NASCAR team. As Henry told ESPN in 2011: "You can't win in any sport without concentrating on revenue generation. You have to be relentless in that regard if you are going to be able to afford the kind of players you need to compete at the highest level. There is simply no way around that."

Which brings us to 2019, and the apparent end of the John Henry gravy train. The architect of Boston's last championship club was Dave Dombrowski, a man renowned in baseball for his ability to spend other people's money to build a winner. He did that in Florida; came within a whisker of doing so several times in Detroit; and, just three years after being appointed the president of baseball operations for the Red Sox, pulled off the feat once more. The 2018 team was one of the best in franchise history, steamrolling all comers en route to 108 wins, a pennant and a World Series. Yet all that bought Dombrowski was another 11 months: With the 2019 team struggling to repeat the previous year's dominance, he was fired in September.

Six weeks later, the Red Sox hired his replacement: Chaim Bloom, late of the Rays. With Tampa Bay, Bloom had established himself as a forward thinker, helping the team develop a reputation as a Silicon Valley-style disruptor. What was likely more important to Henry and company, though, was Bloom's environment—which is to say, that Tampa Bay won despite running payrolls that barely cracked $60 million. For a club who had spent $240 million in exchange for 84 wins and a third-place finish behind Bloom's Rays, the idea of winning without spending probably held plenty of appeal.

So it is that the 2020 Red Sox, with Bloom at the forefront, will join the rest of baseball in worshipping at the altar of Sustainability and Financial Flexibility, and all the other buzzwords dragged in from the finance world that now acts as a pipeline to front offices. In theory and in the press conferences, that's presented as a kind of ideal contention state in which a team is composed entirely of 26-year-old players putting up 8-WARP seasons for no more than $2 million per person. It's a farm system that never stops producing; prospects who never fail; free-agent and trade decisions that never go wrong because they're made with minimal emotion and maximum attention to the cold, hard reality of aging curves and predictive models.

That's the dream, anyway. The reality is far simpler: less spending. The teams who preach sustainability are selling a dressed-up version of belt-tightening, in which free agency is more or less ignored and contract extensions done only if a player is willing to take 75 percent of his value. The majority of the money a team makes is no longer poured into payroll, in part because the majority of the money a team makes now is no longer tied to anything affected by payroll. Like Henry, MLB and its teams have spent the last decade or so diversifying their revenue streams, and in the process, they've largely divorced profit from the actual games being played on the field. Cable networks, streaming packages, stadium deals, corporate sponsorships: Those are what bring in the money, and those stay steady whether a team wins 100 games or 60. Ticket sales, meanwhile, continue to shrink in each club's pie chart of revenues—even as, ironically enough, ticket prices keep increasing.

The end result is a team who can now make money without spending as much of it. Like America's richest individuals and families, teams have reached a level of wealth wherein the faucet never goes dry. And like that same group firmly ensconced in the country's top 1 percent of earners, teams have committed to making sure as much of that money stays with them as is possible. Hence, the aversion to giving it to players, or at least, the aversion to giving it to players if they don't have to. That's all been helped along by the data showing the most productive years of a player's career come in his early to mid-20s; by pure coincidence, those also happen to be the cheapest years of a player's career.

The Dombrowski Red Sox weren't built with that in mind; if the linchpins of a champion happened to be earning 1/10th of what they were worth, that was a happy accident. Spending in free agency (and a willingness to trade those desirable cheap prospects for expensive stars) was the key to their success. The future of the Bloom Red Sox, though, is one wherein as much of the roster as possible is being underpaid relative to the value created. It's why rumors of

a Mookie Betts trade persisted all offseason long (and will likely continue throughout the year), despite the fact that a Red Sox team without him is a Red Sox team who won't win anything at all. Betts will be a free agent after the season, and he's a lock to score $300 million-plus on the open market; a team already on the hook for nearly a quarter billion dollars in payroll this year isn't eager to add more numbers to that tally. It's also why, if Betts survives the winter still with the team who drafted him, he almost certainly won't re-sign there. Those kinds of expenditures don't fit with the concept of financial flexibility.

Sustainability promises perpetual contention. But what it amounts to is your favorite players turned into numbers, or into chess pieces to be sacrificed if necessary: Picture an Excel spreadsheet stamping on a Mookie Betts jersey, forever. Winning—a thing the Red Sox did only every now and then, and incompletely at that, before Henry became Boston's biggest sugar daddy—becomes secondary to bottom lines. This doesn't benefit the fans, who should care more about trophies than luxury tax payments. It exists for the owners—to take Henry's investment and give it a positive yield.

This is the tack many teams have taken, but for a good long while, the Red Sox resisted the siren song of spending less to win...uh, less. You don't hire Dave Dombrowski to clip coupons. And what's been admirable about Red Sox ownership under Henry, even amid the apparently universe-mandated directive that whoever's in charge of the team has to be weirdly and dismissively pissy about departing managers, GMs, players and just about everyone else, is that they've spent willingly and spent big. They shelled out $160 million for Manny Ramirez and $210 million for David Price. They acquired big-name players via trade, contract be damned. Henry easily and understandably could've snapped his checkbook shut for good after deals that went sour, like Carl Crawford and Adrián González and Hanley Ramírez and Pablo Sandoval. But he kept the dollars flowing, and for it, he's been rewarded with four championships in 18 years. The 2013 and '18 titles, in particular, don't happen unless Boston throws its financial weight around.

That's the advantage Boston is supposed to have and supposed to use. Few if any teams can match the Red Sox dollar for dollar. It's their bad luck that one of those teams so happens to reside in their division (and splurged heavily this winter for the best pitcher on the market in Gerrit Cole), but otherwise, they exist within their own layer of the atmosphere. Owning a sports team of any real sort in America is a license to print money; if you happen to be one of the lucky saps who controls a titanic, historic franchise like the Red Sox, you're basically in charge of Baseball Disneyland.

Yet that won't be the path going forward—at least, that seems like a safe bet given the hiring of Bloom and an offseason so quiet that Boston was outspent by the likes of the Blue Jays and White Sox. The track has already been laid for a pivot toward spending less. Despite the prospect of losing Betts and despite the window he helped create inching further shut, there's been no push to build the best team possible while he's still under contract. Where that ends up leaving Red Sox fans, so used to champagne and parades and lording it over Yankees fans as the most successful team of this century, remains to be seen. Maybe it works. But one thing is certain: The true beneficiary in all this is the man who, nearly two decades ago, put down more money than anyone reading this will make in 10 lifetimes to own a baseball team.

By the way, in case you were wondering, the present-day value of Fenway Sports Group—the Red Sox, Liverpool, Roush Racing, NESN, Fenway Park and much more—is $6.6 billion. Even with all the money spent on players, John Henry has more than made his money back and then some. The question going forward is what the fans are going to get out of his newfound turn toward austerity. ▪

—Jon Tayler is a former staff writer at Sports Illustrated.

HITTERS

Andrew Benintendi LF   Born: 07/06/94   Age: 25   Bats: L   Throws: L   Height: 5'10"   Weight: 170   Origin: Round 1, 2015 Draft (#7 overall)

YEAR	TEAM	LVL	AGE	PA	R	2B	3B	HR	RBI	BB	K	SB	CS	AVG/OBP/SLG	DRC+	VORP	BABIP	BRR	FRAA	WARP
2017	BOS	MLB	22	658	84	26	1	20	90	70	112	20	5	.271/.352/.424	107	18.1	.301	1.4	LF(123): -0.6, CF(30): 0.0	2.5
2018	BOS	MLB	23	661	103	41	6	16	87	71	106	21	3	.290/.366/.465	118	33.3	.328	-1.1	LF(129): 8.2, CF(24): -2.6	3.7
2019	BOS	MLB	24	615	72	40	5	13	68	59	140	10	3	.266/.343/.431	95	12.9	.333	0.8	LF(131): -5.7, CF(12): 1.5	0.9
2020	BOS	MLB	25	595	67	39	4	17	71	58	129	13	4	.266/.343/.449	104	19.2	.323	-0.6	LF -3, CF -1	1.6

Comparables: Carl Yastrzemski, Christian Yelich, Roger Cedeno

Do we never hear about "junior slumps" because they're rarer than their sophomore counterpart, or simply because they're less alliterative? In his third full season, Benintendi set career worsts in just about every category that matters. Despite the hitter-friendly balls, his slugging percentage dropped. Despite an improved BABIP, he posted his worst batting average. He walked less and struck out more, as he chased more pitches out of the zone. He didn't run as much. And for the turd cherry on top of this poop sundae (scouting term), he even had a bad year in the field, per FRAA. If you're looking for a silver lining or two, Benny still hit the ball hard and didn't post big platoon splits. Plus, there was absolutely nothing in Benintendi's profile to suggest this type of decline in performance was around the corner, which could mean a bounce back is in store. Then again, there's no one injury, event or major change that can explain away Benintendi's poor showing either. That's got to make the Red Sox at least a little uneasy.

Mookie Betts RF   Born: 10/07/92   Age: 27   Bats: R   Throws: R   Height: 5'9"   Weight: 180   Origin: Round 5, 2011 Draft (#172 overall)

YEAR	TEAM	LVL	AGE	PA	R	2B	3B	HR	RBI	BB	K	SB	CS	AVG/OBP/SLG	DRC+	VORP	BABIP	BRR	FRAA	WARP
2017	BOS	MLB	24	712	101	46	2	24	102	77	79	26	3	.264/.344/.459	115	31.1	.268	6.2	RF(153): 23.9	5.9
2018	BOS	MLB	25	614	129	47	5	32	80	81	91	30	6	.346/.438/.640	178	76.5	.368	3.8	RF(120): 10.7, CF(14): 0.4	8.9
2019	BOS	MLB	26	706	135	40	5	29	80	97	101	16	3	.295/.391/.524	137	51.7	.309	5.7	RF(132): 11.9, CF(17): 1.6	6.9
2020	BOS	MLB	27	630	85	38	3	27	91	76	90	22	5	.286/.375/.514	134	45.1	.300	3.3	RF 16	6.3

Comparables: Ellis Burks, Chet Lemon, Jim Delsing

What continues to make Betts so special is that he's so damn good at *everything*. He was the game's 16th-best hitter, per DRC+. He was its ninth-best fielder (non-catcher division), per FRAA. He was its sixth-best baserunner, per BRR. And yet, you could call 2019 a down year by his nearly unparalleled standards, as he fell from first in the majors in WARP all the way down to sixth(!) among hitters. That's where we are with Betts; when anyone other than that Mike Trout guy outperforms him, it's a letdown. Now entering his walk year in his age-27 season, Betts is justly poised to threaten the record books with his next contract. He deserves whatever asking price he sets, and if the Red Sox refuse to give it to him, they should be criticized for decades to come. Every franchise only gets a few shots to draft, develop and retain a Hall-of-Fame talent like Betts. Letting one get away is baseball's highest crime, and anyone who tells you otherwise is prioritizing profit margins over fielding the best team possible.

Xander Bogaerts SS   Born: 10/01/92   Age: 27   Bats: R   Throws: R   Height: 6'1"   Weight: 210   Origin: International Free Agent, 2009

YEAR	TEAM	LVL	AGE	PA	R	2B	3B	HR	RBI	BB	K	SB	CS	AVG/OBP/SLG	DRC+	VORP	BABIP	BRR	FRAA	WARP
2017	BOS	MLB	24	635	94	32	6	10	62	56	116	15	1	.273/.343/.403	98	31.9	.327	5.5	SS(146): -9.2	2.4
2018	BOS	MLB	25	580	72	45	3	23	103	55	102	8	2	.288/.360/.522	130	49.6	.317	-0.2	SS(136): 1.5	4.9
2019	BOS	MLB	26	698	110	52	0	33	117	76	122	4	2	.309/.384/.555	134	65.2	.338	-0.1	SS(153): -20.8	4.3
2020	BOS	MLB	27	595	74	37	1	23	81	56	107	9	3	.285/.358/.488	123	41.2	.320	0.9	SS -9	3.4

Comparables: Alex Gonzalez, Derek Jeter, Starlin Castro

Only two factors prevent our metrics from indicating that Bogaerts was the best shortstop in baseball in 2019. The first is that Marcus Semien used some *Space Jam*-ass magic to post a vintage Alex Rodríguez season, and if you can explain that, well, we're all ears. The second equally mysterious but perhaps more digestible reason: Bogaerts went from an average defender to one of the league's worst overnight, per FRAA. That doesn't jive with the eye test, and if you take Bogey to a net even defender, our metrics suddenly say he's a down-ballot MVP candidate on the strength of his potent bat. The X-Man lived up to expectations and then some following his six-year contract extension, pacing the Sox in RBI and OPS while growing into more of a leadership role in the clubhouse—of particular note is his mentorship of Rafael Devers, which gives baseball its spiritual successor to the Adrián Beltré/Elvis Andrus buddy cop comedy. Now entering just his age-27 season, Bogaerts remains a foundational piece for the Sox and one of the best middle infielders in the game; a true stabilizing force for an otherwise turbulent franchise.

Jackie Bradley Jr. CF Born: 04/19/90 Age: 30 Bats: L Throws: R Height: 5'10" Weight: 200 Origin: Round 1, 2011 Draft (#40 overall)

YEAR	TEAM	LVL	AGE	PA	R	2B	3B	HR	RBI	BB	K	SB	CS	AVG/OBP/SLG	DRC+	VORP	BABIP	BRR	FRAA	WARP
2017	BOS	MLB	27	541	58	19	3	17	63	48	124	8	3	.245/.323/.402	96	19.3	.294	3.8	CF(132): -7.4	1.3
2018	BOS	MLB	28	535	76	33	4	13	59	46	137	17	1	.234/.314/.403	88	14.9	.299	2.5	CF(135): 6.1, RF(15): 0.3	1.9
2019	BOS	MLB	29	567	69	28	3	21	62	56	155	8	6	.225/.317/.421	86	10.8	.281	0.9	CF(144): 0.9, RF(3): 0.4	1.3
2020	BOS	MLB	30	560	61	29	3	19	67	53	157	8	3	.226/.313/.410	87	13.0	.292	1.8	CF 0	1.3

Comparables: Ray Lankford, Aaron Hicks, Peter Bourjos

Few things in baseball cause more cognitive dissonance than what the eye test tells you about Bradley's defense and what defensive metrics would have you to believe. For the second year in a row, FRAA hasn't been overly impressed by his defense in center field. But for the seventh straight season, he sure looked like a natural out there en route to yet *another* Gold Glove nomination. Now entering his walk year, Bradley has to view this discrepancy in defensive valuation as a major threat to his future earnings. It's been three years since he's offered a better than league-average bat, and as he enters his age-30 season, it's probably safe to stop waiting for a breakout. If he's still the Gold Glover many think he is, Bradley has plenty to offer as a run-saver and professional down-the-order hitter. If not, we're fast approaching a time when Bradley offers far more name value than actual value.

Cameron Cannon SS Born: 10/16/97 Age: 22 Bats: R Throws: R Height: 5'10" Weight: 196 Origin: Round 2, 2019 Draft (#43 overall)

YEAR	TEAM	LVL	AGE	PA	R	2B	3B	HR	RBI	BB	K	SB	CS	AVG/OBP/SLG	DRC+	VORP	BABIP	BRR	FRAA	WARP
2019	LOW	A-	21	180	17	12	0	3	21	12	37	1	0	.205/.289/.335	101	2.6	.248	0.2	2B(19): 1.8, SS(18): -0.8	0.7
2020	BOS	MLB	22	251	22	12	1	6	25	14	76	2	1	.204/.260/.343	59	-5.3	.274	0.0	SS 0, 2B 0	-0.5

Comparables: David Adams, Taylor Featherston, Sheldon Neuse

There are other places in the multiverse in which a character named Cameron Cannon is the main protagonist of a series of Young Adult novels, or Brandi Maxxxx's understudy or the new Spider-Man. In our timeline, he's Boston's first selection from the 2019 draft. That fact alone may overstate Cannon's upside—the Sox didn't pick until the second round thanks to luxury tax penalties, and Cannon doesn't have a ton to offer in the way of splashy tools. Still, he's a bat-first middle infielder with plenty of athleticism who scouts think will probably move fairly quickly towards a long-term home at second base. The last time the Sox popped a guy with that profile out of an Arizona school, it worked out okay.

Triston Casas 1B Born: 01/15/00 Age: 20 Bats: L Throws: R Height: 6'4" Weight: 238 Origin: Round 1, 2018 Draft (#26 overall)

YEAR	TEAM	LVL	AGE	PA	R	2B	3B	HR	RBI	BB	K	SB	CS	AVG/OBP/SLG	DRC+	VORP	BABIP	BRR	FRAA	WARP
2019	GRN	A	19	493	64	25	5	19	78	58	116	3	2	.254/.349/.472	145	24.1	.300	-0.9	1B(94): -4.7, 3B(8): -1.2	2.1
2020	BOS	MLB	20	251	26	12	1	9	30	20	74	3	1	.219/.289/.395	81	1.6	.282	-0.4	1B -2, 3B 0	0.0

Comparables: Matt Olson, Mike Carp, Trayce Thompson

Boston's first-round pick in 2018, Casas has taken the leap from "best prospect in a terrible system" to "potential legitimate top-100 dude." After his debut professional season was cut short by a torn UCL in his thumb, Casas got off to a very slow start in 2019, hitting just .208/.384/.364 in April. He adjusted as you'd expect a first-round talent would, hitting .264/.363/.469 the rest of the way in Low A en route to being named the Red Sox's Minor League Offensive Player of the Year. Casas has already moved to first base full-time and is a poor bet to contend for future batting titles. But he's got plenty of pop, better makeup than a Sephora outlet and a good idea what he's doing at the plate. "What if Eric Hosmer, but slower" isn't the sexiest ceiling in the world, but it's nothing to shake a stick at, either.

Michael Chavis INF Born: 08/11/95 Age: 24 Bats: R Throws: R Height: 5'10" Weight: 216 Origin: Round 1, 2014 Draft (#26 overall)

YEAR	TEAM	LVL	AGE	PA	R	2B	3B	HR	RBI	BB	K	SB	CS	AVG/OBP/SLG	DRC+	VORP	BABIP	BRR	FRAA	WARP
2017	SLM	A+	21	250	50	17	2	17	55	19	57	1	0	.318/.388/.641	174	28.2	.360	1.3	3B(27): -1.6	2.4
2017	PME	AA	21	274	39	18	0	14	39	20	56	1	0	.250/.310/.492	103	11.8	.265	0.1	3B(43): -0.5, SS(1): 0.0	0.8
2018	PME	AA	22	139	23	7	0	6	17	13	35	3	1	.303/.388/.508	146	13.3	.383	0.5	3B(18): 1.5, 1B(11): -0.5	1.2
2018	PAW	AAA	22	34	8	3	0	2	7	1	12	0	0	.273/.294/.545	90	4.7	.368	0.2	3B(4): -1.2, 1B(1): 0.0	-0.1
2019	PAW	AAA	23	79	11	4	0	7	11	8	21	0	0	.257/.329/.614	143	8.0	.256	-0.7	3B(7): -0.6, 2B(7): 1.6	0.7
2019	BOS	MLB	23	382	46	10	1	18	58	31	127	2	1	.254/.322/.444	93	5.8	.347	0.0	1B(49): 2.4, 2B(45): -0.9	0.7
2020	BOS	MLB	24	595	71	26	1	28	83	45	194	3	1	.237/.303/.446	96	12.3	.314	0.1	1B 1, 2B 0	1.4

Comparables: Shed Long, Trevor Story, Jeimer Candelario

For a brief while, it looked like Chavis might save the 2019 Red Sox. Pressed into duty in late April when the Sox were already struggling, the rookie briefly took the league by storm. The short, stocky slugger hit .290/.389/.570 through his first 25 games, providing the club with the type of spark it sorely lacked for a majority of the season. Unfortunately, the league adjusted—primarily by pitching him up and in with hard stuff—and as is often the case with rookies, Chavis couldn't fully adjust back. He hit just .240/.296/.398 for the remainder of his debut season, which was cut short by a sprained AC joint in mid-August. Chavis revealed plenty of MLB-caliber skills, though. He can sock some majestic taters, he's a passable defender on the right side of the infield, and he can absolutely serve as a team's most adorable celebrator, but it's still unclear if he can hit enough to play every day for a first-division team. At least 2019 revealed he belongs on one in some capacity.

Bobby Dalbec 3B Born: 06/29/95 Age: 25 Bats: R Throws: R Height: 6'4" Weight: 225 Origin: Round 4, 2016 Draft (#118 overall)

YEAR	TEAM	LVL	AGE	PA	R	2B	3B	HR	RBI	BB	K	SB	CS	AVG/OBP/SLG	DRC+	VORP	BABIP	BRR	FRAA	WARP
2017	RSX	RK	22	32	3	1	0	0	2	5	9	1	0	.259/.375/.296	62	-0.1	.389	0.7	3B(4): -0.5	0.0
2017	GRN	A	22	329	48	15	0	13	39	36	123	4	5	.246/.345/.437	113	13.2	.383	-2.0	3B(67): -2.3	1.0
2018	SLM	A+	23	419	59	27	2	26	85	60	130	3	1	.256/.372/.573	161	44.2	.318	0.9	3B(91): 5.2, SS(1): 0.0	4.5
2018	PME	AA	23	124	14	8	1	6	24	6	46	0	0	.261/.323/.514	96	7.1	.377	-0.1	3B(18): -3.9, 1B(2): -0.3	-0.2
2019	PME	AA	24	439	57	15	2	20	57	68	110	6	4	.234/.371/.454	151	31.4	.278	-2.2	3B(90): 7.2, 1B(13): 0.9	4.2
2019	PAW	AAA	24	123	12	4	0	7	16	5	29	0	2	.257/.301/.478	83	3.8	.278	0.3	3B(17): 2.0, 1B(11): -1.3	0.2
2020	BOS	MLB	25	350	39	17	1	14	45	32	113	1	0	.220/.304/.415	91	1.1	.296	-0.6	1B -2, 3B 0	0.0

Comparables: Jabari Blash, Josh Bell, Taylor Teagarden

For several seasons now any praise for Dalbec has been balanced with the caveat that he whiffs more than often than the New York Times Op-Ed team. It's true that Dalbec's game will always feature plenty of swing-and-miss, but in 2019 he surprised by cutting back on the Ks to a significant degree. Yes, he still struck out a quarter of the time, but hey, progress is progress. All of Dalbec's other strengths remain. He's a good defender at third and first, has a rocket arm, and will have 40-homer power even if the balls become de-juiced. Mark Reynolds has been the butt of many a joke (as well as the best Baseball Prospectus article of all time), but he's also been in the majors for 12 seasons and counting. Dalbec is close enough and does enough things well that he can reasonably dream of enjoying such a future.

Rafael Devers 3B Born: 10/24/96 Age: 23 Bats: L Throws: R Height: 6'0" Weight: 237 Origin: International Free Agent, 2013

YEAR	TEAM	LVL	AGE	PA	R	2B	3B	HR	RBI	BB	K	SB	CS	AVG/OBP/SLG	DRC+	VORP	BABIP	BRR	FRAA	WARP
2017	PME	AA	20	320	48	19	3	18	56	31	55	0	3	.300/.369/.575	153	26.5	.316	-0.7	3B(64): 4.6	3.3
2017	PAW	AAA	20	38	6	1	0	2	4	3	8	0	0	.400/.447/.600	151	5.5	.480	0.1	3B(8): -2.1	0.1
2017	BOS	MLB	20	240	34	14	0	10	30	18	57	3	1	.284/.338/.482	106	11.6	.342	0.2	3B(56): 4.9	1.6
2018	BOS	MLB	21	490	59	24	0	21	66	38	121	5	2	.240/.298/.433	94	13.3	.281	1.7	3B(116): 11.2	2.8
2019	BOS	MLB	22	702	129	54	4	32	115	48	119	8	8	.311/.361/.555	125	50.0	.339	0.2	3B(152): 7.2, SS(1): 0.0	5.6
2020	BOS	MLB	23	595	73	40	2	27	87	41	111	5	2	.278/.332/.505	112	25.1	.306	1.1	3B 8	3.4

Comparables: Rougned Odor, Carlos Correa, Gleyber Torres

What were you doing when you were 22? Maybe you took a year off to find yourself. Maybe you headed straight to grad school. Maybe you moved back home for a bit to find your footing. Or maybe you became one of the dozen-or-so best hitters in baseball. No? Guess that's just Devers, then. It's funny to say about someone who's younger than 7th Heaven, but for years now, scouts have hinted at potential greatness in Devers' bat. He'd shown glimpses here and there, but was also prone to months-long stretches where he looked utterly overmatched. Not so in 2019. Devers finished 11th overall in WARP among hitters. He finished first in the majors in total bases, second in doubles and second in hits. Better yet, Devers' dominance looks sustainable, as he significantly lowered his strikeout rate while offering insane plate coverage and boasting the 16th best average exit velocity in the game. The middle-of-the-order masher scouts have long prophesied has arrived.

While Devers' progress at the plate was dramatic, it's perhaps not all that surprising given his reputation and resume. More stunning were the physical and defensive transformations Devers enjoyed. He showed up in spring training with a noticeably reshaped body, improving his conditioning in the hopes of avoiding more soft tissue injuries. He also made tremendous defensive strides at third, and though it's unlikely any Gold Gloves are in his future, he looks capable of manning the hot corner for the next several seasons. Add it all together, and while Devers' face may say "hello I am a harmless baby"—his nickname is Carita, after all—his performance and contract combine to tell a different story: he's now the Red Sox's most valuable player.

Jarren Duran OF Born: 09/05/96 Age: 23 Bats: L Throws: R Height: 6'2" Weight: 200 Origin: Round 7, 2018 Draft (#220 overall)

YEAR	TEAM	LVL	AGE	PA	R	2B	3B	HR	RBI	BB	K	SB	CS	AVG/OBP/SLG	DRC+	VORP	BABIP	BRR	FRAA	WARP
2018	LOW	A-	21	168	28	5	10	2	20	11	26	12	4	.348/.393/.548	177	19.6	.406	0.4	2B(20): 4.9, CF(15): 0.1	2.2
2018	GRN	A	21	134	24	9	1	1	15	5	22	12	6	.367/.396/.477	167	12.2	.438	1.6	RF(30): 0.0	1.3
2019	SLM	A+	22	226	49	13	3	4	19	23	44	18	5	.387/.456/.543	201	30.5	.480	3.4	CF(50): 0.2	3.3
2019	PME	AA	22	352	41	11	5	1	19	23	84	28	8	.250/.309/.325	76	9.9	.335	5.1	CF(79): -3.3	0.5
2020	BOS	MLB	23	251	24	11	2	4	24	13	67	11	6	.264/.309/.380	81	3.1	.355	1.1	CF -1, RF 0	0.2

Comparables: Jedd Gyorko, Andrew Stevenson, Eddie Rosario

A seventh-round pick out of Long Beach State in 2018, Duran has emerged in short order as one of the more intriguing prospects on *Planet Earth*. Armed with plus-plus speed, great bat-to-ball ability and *The Reflex*(es) needed to succeed at the plate, Duran rode his skills and a ludicrous BABIP to flirt with a .400 average in High A. After a midseason promotion to Portland, things started to *Come Undone*, but Duran still acquitted himself reasonably well for a dude who was in college about 12 months earlier. Despite the impressive start to his career, there are holes in Duran's game. He's got a *Notorious*-ly weak arm that could limit him to left field, and he offers very little in the way of power at present; he'll have to do most of his damage between the *White Lines*. Still, scouts say Duran is *Hungry (Like The Wolf)* to get better, and if the hit tool ticks up a half-grade we're looking at a potential everyday regular.

Marco Hernández MI Born: 09/06/92 Age: 27 Bats: L Throws: R Height: 6'0" Weight: 200 Origin: International Free Agent, 2009

YEAR	TEAM	LVL	AGE	PA	R	2B	3B	HR	RBI	BB	K	SB	CS	AVG/OBP/SLG	DRC+	VORP	BABIP	BRR	FRAA	WARP
2017	BOS	MLB	24	60	7	3	0	0	2	1	15	0	1	.276/.300/.328	68	-1.0	.372	-0.3	3B(9): 0.0, 2B(6): 1.7	0.1
2019	SLM	A+	26	91	15	7	0	0	9	8	9	1	1	.295/.374/.385	132	4.4	.324	-1.1	SS(11): -2.3, 2B(6): -1.7	0.0
2019	PAW	AAA	26	146	23	12	0	2	11	6	32	3	2	.285/.308/.416	92	1.1	.349	-0.1	2B(24): 0.3, SS(8): -0.7	0.3
2019	BOS	MLB	26	155	18	7	0	2	11	3	42	1	2	.250/.279/.338	60	-3.0	.337	-0.6	2B(48): 0.1, SS(2): 0.0	-0.3
2020	BOS	MLB	27	175	15	9	1	3	17	7	43	1	0	.243/.280/.360	65	-1.5	.310	0.0	2B -1, 3B 0	-0.2

Comparables: Charlie Culberson, Danny Santana, Edmundo Sosa

A full 1,112 days: that's how long Hernández went in between his first two major-league home runs. Both came against the same pitcher—Mychal Givens—and both came as Hernández vied for playing time on disappointing Red Sox teams. But while the opponent he victimized and the circumstances he faced were similar, Hernández himself had been through a world of change. After the promising start to his career was cut short by a dislocated shoulder early in 2017, Hernández had to battle through three surgeries to the joint that left him unable to swing consistently for nearly 18 months. It's a real triumph, then, that Hernández looks to be much the same guy we saw way back in 2016; a good hitter against righties who can capably man second base, and who can step in at third or at short in a pinch. Now with a Red Sox team that could potentially lose Brock Holt to free agency and has no real plan at the keystone at present, Hernández's perseverance could land him a significant role.

Brock Holt INF   Born: 06/11/88   Age: 32   Bats: L   Throws: R   Height: 5'10"   Weight: 180   Origin: Round 9, 2009 Draft (#265 overall)

YEAR	TEAM	LVL	AGE	PA	R	2B	3B	HR	RBI	BB	K	SB	CS	AVG/OBP/SLG	DRC+	VORP	BABIP	BRR	FRAA	WARP
2017	PAW	AAA	29	77	9	1	0	3	9	6	14	0	0	.214/.286/.357	82	0.5	.226	0.1	LF(7): 1.3, 3B(4): 0.1	0.2
2017	BOS	MLB	29	164	20	6	0	0	7	19	34	2	1	.200/.305/.243	69	-3.1	.259	0.6	2B(31): 0.1, LF(10): 0.7	0.0
2018	BOS	MLB	30	367	41	18	2	7	46	37	73	7	7	.277/.362/.411	101	13.4	.337	-1.9	2B(56): -5.3, SS(23): -2.0	0.1
2019	PAW	AAA	31	37	7	2	0	1	3	8	12	1	0	.250/.432/.429	108	2.8	.400	0.0	SS(3): 1.1, 2B(2): -0.3	0.2
2019	BOS	MLB	31	295	38	14	2	3	31	28	57	1	0	.297/.369/.402	98	8.6	.365	-1.1	2B(60): 3.7, 1B(11): 1.7	1.3
2020	BOS	MLB	32	251	25	11	1	4	24	24	54	4	2	.254/.335/.368	89	4.5	.317	-0.2	2B 0, SS 0	0.5

Comparables: Josh Harrison, Hubie Brooks, Matt Tolbert

On the surface, Holt might just appear as a decent utility player who's getting a bit long in the tooth. But to the Red Sox, Holt has been much more than that. He was the only thing that made them watchable way back in 2015. He hit for the cycle against the dreaded Yankees in the 2018 ALCS. He's huge in the Boston philanthropy scene. And he's Andrew Benintendi's sidekick. Holt's free agency, then, should provide an interesting litmus test for new Chief Baseball Officer Chaim Bloom. Will Bloom and company throw a few million Holt's way to ensure he keeps serving as the organization's safety blanket, potentially earning a few points with Red Sox fans along the way? Or will value dictate that some combination of Marco Hernández, Tzu-Wei Lin and C.J. Chatham can take his job on the cheap? If Bloom picks door number two, expect the loss of Holt to hit Sox fans a lot harder than you'd think it ought to.

Gilberto Jimenez OF   Born: 07/08/00   Age: 19   Bats: B   Throws: R   Height: 5'11"   Weight: 160   Origin: International Free Agent, 2017

YEAR	TEAM	LVL	AGE	PA	R	2B	3B	HR	RBI	BB	K	SB	CS	AVG/OBP/SLG	DRC+	VORP	BABIP	BRR	FRAA	WARP
2018	DRS	RK	17	284	42	10	8	0	22	19	40	16	14	.319/.384/.420	146	25.1	.378	-1.0	CF(64): 3.4	2.5
2019	LOW	A-	18	254	35	11	3	3	19	13	38	14	6	.359/.393/.470	191	30.7	.413	1.2	CF(57): -9.8, RF(1): -0.1	1.9
2020	BOS	MLB	19	251	23	11	2	3	23	15	57	6	5	.271/.321/.369	86	3.3	.349	-0.2	CF -3, RF 0	0.0

Comparables: Victor Robles, Harold Ramirez, Enrique Hernández

The Red Sox's farm system is perhaps less desolate than a season ago, but it's still fairly bereft of high-upside talent. Jimenez serves as an exception. A blazingly fast center fielder who the Sox signed out of the Dominican as an IFA in 2017, Jimenez made quick work of the New York-Penn League as an 18-year-old. While power isn't a part of his game, he's a potential plus switch-hitter who's already showing impressive bat-to-ball skills from the left side despite just starting to hit from there in 2017. Defensively, speed is Jimenez's primary calling card, but he also offers above-average arm strength, giving him all the ingredients of a potential impact center fielder. If you're counting at home, that's four average-or-better tools Jimenez flashes at present, which a year ago may have been more than the rest of Boston's farm offered collectively. He's another good season away from entering the national prospect consciousness.

J.D. Martinez DH   Born: 08/21/87   Age: 32   Bats: R   Throws: R   Height: 6'3"   Weight: 220   Origin: Round 20, 2009 Draft (#611 overall)

YEAR	TEAM	LVL	AGE	PA	R	2B	3B	HR	RBI	BB	K	SB	CS	AVG/OBP/SLG	DRC+	VORP	BABIP	BRR	FRAA	WARP
2017	DET	MLB	29	232	38	13	2	16	39	29	54	2	0	.305/.388/.630	162	18.3	.338	-1.5	RF(53): -6.3	1.5
2017	ARI	MLB	29	257	47	13	1	29	65	24	74	2	0	.302/.366/.741	158	26.4	.315	-2.4	RF(60): -3.9	1.8
2018	BOS	MLB	30	649	111	37	2	43	130	69	146	6	1	.330/.402/.629	167	57.2	.375	-3.9	LF(32): -0.9, RF(25): 2.4	6.3
2019	BOS	MLB	31	657	98	33	2	36	105	72	138	2	0	.304/.383/.557	139	45.3	.342	-6.2	RF(24): 3.8, LF(15): 0.5	4.2
2020	BOS	MLB	32	630	90	37	2	37	105	63	150	4	2	.290/.365/.555	140	38.3	.337	-4.6	LF -1, RF 0	3.9

Comparables: Cliff Floyd, Geoff Jenkins, Ryan Braun

In Martinez's 2019 *Annual* comment, we remarked that giving the best players a lot of money leads to good results. Yet a popular narrative in Boston this offseason centered on how Martinez handicapped the suddenly cost-conscious Red Sox by declining to opt out of his contract. In many ways, that's ridiculous. While Martinez took a slight step back from his otherworldly 2018 campaign, he still paced the Sox in slugging percentage, homers and DRC+. Per WARP, he was one of the best 30-or-so hitters in the game. Any offense would be lucky to have him. And yet, there's an argument to be made that he no longer represents Boston's best allocation of resources, given their self-imposed financial bind. Mookie Betts, Xander Bogaerts and Rafael Devers all provided more offensive value while also playing important positions in the field, and for all of the Red Sox's woes last season, they finished fourth in team DRC+. It's wildly unfair that Martinez can be one of the 20-or-so most feared hitters on the planet, make just $22 million a year and be viewed as a liability rather than an asset, but welcome to how the owners have conditioned many to think in 2020. Don't fall for it; Martinez remains a stud.

Mitch Moreland 1B   Born: 09/06/85   Age: 34   Bats: L   Throws: L   Height: 6'2"   Weight: 230   Origin: Round 17, 2007 Draft (#530 overall)

YEAR	TEAM	LVL	AGE	PA	R	2B	3B	HR	RBI	BB	K	SB	CS	AVG/OBP/SLG	DRC+	VORP	BABIP	BRR	FRAA	WARP
2017	BOS	MLB	31	576	73	34	0	22	79	57	120	0	1	.246/.326/.443	103	3.3	.278	-2.7	1B(138): 5.7, P(1): 0.0	1.3
2018	BOS	MLB	32	459	57	23	4	15	68	50	102	2	0	.245/.325/.433	103	3.4	.288	-2.5	1B(116): 2.4	0.8
2019	BOS	MLB	33	335	48	17	1	19	58	34	74	1	0	.252/.328/.507	111	10.3	.271	-2.6	1B(85): 4.3	1.2
2020	BOS	MLB	34	350	40	15	1	15	45	32	86	1	0	.225/.301/.416	88	3.0	.262	-1.6	1B 2	0.7

Comparables: Eric Hinske, Adam LaRoche, Derrek Lee

On a rate basis, Moreland was actually better last season than he was in 2018, when he played a complementary but important role on the World Series champs. The problem in 2019 was that Moreland spent nearly as much time hurt as he did on the diamond. The lumbering lefty struggled with back and quad injuries en route to appearing in his fewest games in a season since 2014, which was bad news for a Sox squad forced to start all sorts of riffraff at first base during his absence. Though his ceiling is lower than a priest hole's, Moreland still has some value to offer on a one-year contract as a platoon bat and capable defender at first base. Unfortunately, he exists in a timeline in which half the orgs in baseball would rather be cheap than good.

Eduardo Núñez INF   Born: 06/15/87   Age: 33   Bats: R   Throws: R   Height: 6'0"   Weight: 195   Origin: International Free Agent, 2004

YEAR	TEAM	LVL	AGE	PA	R	2B	3B	HR	RBI	BB	K	SB	CS	AVG/OBP/SLG	DRC+	VORP	BABIP	BRR	FRAA	WARP
2017	SFN	MLB	30	318	37	21	0	4	31	12	29	18	5	.308/.334/.417	104	18.3	.328	4.4	3B(49): -0.1, LF(19): 2.3	1.8
2017	BOS	MLB	30	173	23	12	0	8	27	6	25	6	2	.321/.353/.539	105	11.9	.341	-1.2	2B(26): -0.8, SS(5): 0.0	0.5
2018	BOS	MLB	31	502	56	23	3	10	44	16	69	7	2	.265/.289/.388	84	-1.3	.290	-2.6	2B(74): -2.0, 3B(45): 1.2	0.2
2019	BOS	MLB	32	174	13	7	0	2	20	4	27	5	1	.228/.243/.305	59	-3.9	.257	1.7	2B(31): 1.3, 3B(8): -0.5	-0.2
2020	BOS	MLB	33	251	24	12	1	5	26	10	41	9	3	.254/.289/.381	76	0.4	.287	0.2	2B -1, 3B 0	0.0

Comparables: Charlie Hayes, Hubie Brooks, Martín Prado

Harken back to the halcyon days of Núñez's career. What comes to mind? Perhaps it's speed; Núñez stole 24 bases as recently as 2017. Maybe it's versatility? Núñez has more than 150 appearances each at second base, third base and shortstop in his career, as well as 50-plus more in the outfield. Maybe you recall the way Núñez's bat would randomly catch fire, especially against left-handed pitching? It's best to cling to those happy memories, because the Núñez of the present—the one whom the Sox released in July and whom no other team even took a flier on—looks cooked. He can't run. He hit .200/.240/.313 against southpaws. And let's be real, he could never really field. Rumors of Núñez's demise have been greatly exaggerated before, but they've never come as Núñez was a 32-year-old with a long history of leg injuries.

Chris Owings SS   Born: 08/12/91   Age: 28   Bats: R   Throws: R   Height: 5'10"   Weight: 185   Origin: Round 1, 2009 Draft (#41 overall)

YEAR	TEAM	LVL	AGE	PA	R	2B	3B	HR	RBI	BB	K	SB	CS	AVG/OBP/SLG	DRC+	VORP	BABIP	BRR	FRAA	WARP
2017	ARI	MLB	25	386	41	25	1	12	51	17	87	12	2	.268/.299/.442	85	14.5	.318	-0.6	SS(54): 4.2, RF(25): 1.5	1.2
2018	RNO	AAA	26	92	15	4	2	1	11	1	17	1	2	.286/.293/.407	67	-0.6	.342	1.4	2B(10): -0.2, 3B(6): 0.3	0.1
2018	ARI	MLB	26	309	34	15	0	4	22	24	75	11	4	.206/.272/.302	70	-6.2	.265	0.8	RF(43): -1.1, CF(16): 1.2	-0.4
2019	PAW	AAA	27	183	26	11	0	11	34	15	50	6	4	.325/.385/.595	140	22.8	.404	-1.0	SS(18): 0.3, 2B(10): 1.5	1.4
2019	KCA	MLB	27	145	9	4	1	2	9	8	55	4	1	.133/.193/.222	35	-7.2	.205	0.9	2B(13): -1.8, 3B(12): 1.4	-0.7
2019	BOS	MLB	27	51	4	2	0	1	5	6	23	1	1	.156/.255/.267	29	-2.8	.286	-1.0	2B(12): 0.2, SS(7): 0.7	-0.3
2020	BOS	MLB	28	251	21	10	1	5	23	15	81	7	2	.199/.251/.316	48	-9.0	.281	-0.1	SS 1, 2B 0	-0.9

Comparables: Alex Gonzalez, Granny Hamner, Leo Cardenas

Excluding the members of the Astros PR department, you'd be hard pressed to find someone who had a worse 2019 than Owings. He wasn't good enough for the 2019 Royals, who finished 12th in the AL in team DRC+. He wasn't good enough for the 2019 Red Sox, who showed about as much life down the stretch as a taxidermied possum. The exhaustive list of hitters who received as many plate appearances as Owings and who performed worse is as follows: Colin Moran, Wellington Castillo, Christin Stewart, John Hicks, Chris Davis and Stevie Wilkerson. We're now two seasons out from Owings providing any semblance of value at the major-league level. It's beginning to look like, just maybe, the Diamondbacks should've kept Didi Gregorius instead.

Steve Pearce 1B   Born: 04/13/83   Age: 37   Bats: R   Throws: R   Height: 5'11"   Weight: 200   Origin: Round 8, 2005 Draft (#241 overall)

YEAR	TEAM	LVL	AGE	PA	R	2B	3B	HR	RBI	BB	K	SB	CS	AVG/OBP/SLG	DRC+	VORP	BABIP	BRR	FRAA	WARP
2017	TOR	MLB	34	348	38	17	1	13	37	27	68	0	0	.252/.319/.438	100	7.5	.281	0.3	LF(85): 3.3, 1B(10): -0.4	1.2
2018	TOR	MLB	35	86	16	6	0	4	16	7	14	0	0	.291/.349/.519	130	5.1	.311	0.7	LF(9): -1.4, 1B(3): 0.4	0.5
2018	BOS	MLB	35	165	19	8	1	7	26	22	27	0	0	.279/.394/.507	133	10.6	.298	-1.4	1B(31): -1.0, LF(2): -0.1	0.7
2019	PAW	AAA	36	29	3	1	0	0	2	3	10	0	0	.167/.310/.208	68	-0.3	.286	0.3	1B(4): 1.0	0.0
2019	BOS	MLB	36	99	9	4	0	1	9	7	31	0	0	.180/.245/.258	60	-3.3	.259	-0.3	1B(19): 0.9, LF(4): 0.6	-0.2
2020	BOS	MLB	37	251	27	12	1	9	30	22	69	1	0	.234/.312/.411	91	5.0	.297	-0.2	LF 1, 1B 0	0.7

Comparables: Brian Giles, Dwight Evans, Shin-Soo Choo

"The Patriot Way" is code for lots of things—image rehabilitation, disdain for the media, the dehumanization of players, etc—but one of its more useful tenets is that it's better to get out on a dude a year too early than a year too late. With Pearce, it looks like the Sox should have borrowed their football brethren's playbook. Sure, you can understand why the Boston brass wanted a reunion with the reigning World Series MVP. He only cost $6.25 million, he made a good platoon partner with Mitch Moreland on paper and did we mention that he'd just improbably won World Series MVP? Then again, the Sox likely outbid themselves for a 36-year-old short-side platoon bat's services, and Pearce was unable to reward their loyalty. A miserable start gave way to a back injury that put him on the IL, and while rehabbing that particular booboo, he partially tore his PCL. Hindsight is 20/20 and all that, but it looks like Pearce missed his chance to go out a conquering hero, and is instead headed toward a less distinguished end.

Dustin Pedroia 2B   Born: 08/17/83   Age: 36   Bats: R   Throws: R   Height: 5'9"   Weight: 175   Origin: Round 2, 2004 Draft (#65 overall)

YEAR	TEAM	LVL	AGE	PA	R	2B	3B	HR	RBI	BB	K	SB	CS	AVG/OBP/SLG	DRC+	VORP	BABIP	BRR	FRAA	WARP
2017	BOS	MLB	33	463	46	19	0	7	62	49	48	4	3	.293/.369/.392	109	9.2	.315	-5.7	2B(98): -0.1	1.3
2018	BOS	MLB	34	13	1	0	0	0	0	2	1	0	0	.091/.231/.091	97	-1.3	.100	-0.1	2B(3): -0.4	0.0
2019	BOS	MLB	35	21	1	0	0	0	1	1	2	0	0	.100/.143/.100	87	0.1	.111	-0.1	2B(4): -0.2	0.0
2020	BOS	MLB	36	35	3	2	0	1	3	3	5	0	0	.255/.321/.371	86	0.5	.291	-0.2	2B 0	0.1

Comparables: Adam Kennedy, Steve Sax, Ramon Martinez

At its best, baseball rewards perseverance, celebrates its unique talents and sends its heroes out with honor and dignity. At its worst, the game is unforgiving and cruel, forcing its stars to limp undignified to the finish line. Pedroia has now played in just nine games over the last two seasons because of his left knee. The experimental "cartilage restoration procedure" he had during the 2017-2018 offseason has not worked, or at least not well enough to withstand the rigors that come with being a professional athlete. At a May press conference, Pedroia admitted as such for the first time—perhaps as much to himself as to the rest of us—and while he's stopped short of officially retiring to date, there's a good chance he will have by the time this book is in your hands. That's a damn shame for many reasons, not least of which because it means Pedroia, long one of the game's best pure hitters when healthy, will finish with a career batting average of .299. In reality, his legacy is already set—a three-time World Series winner, MVP and franchise icon whose serious bid for Hall-of-Fame consideration ended four or five years ago—but it's sad the game won't provide him with a more poetic ending. Few players of his generation have loved baseball quite so obviously as Pedroia has, but in the end it's proving it can't love him back.

José Peraza UT   Born: 04/30/94   Age: 26   Bats: R   Throws: R   Height: 6'0"   Weight: 196   Origin: International Free Agent, 2010

YEAR	TEAM	LVL	AGE	PA	R	2B	3B	HR	RBI	BB	K	SB	CS	AVG/OBP/SLG	DRC+	VORP	BABIP	BRR	FRAA	WARP
2017	CIN	MLB	23	518	50	9	4	5	37	20	70	23	8	.259/.297/.324	76	-0.4	.293	0.6	2B(77): 2.3, SS(55): 0.6	0.7
2018	CIN	MLB	24	683	85	31	4	14	58	29	75	23	6	.288/.326/.416	101	31.7	.307	2.4	SS(156): -3.4, RF(1): 0.0	3.1
2019	CIN	MLB	25	403	37	18	2	6	33	17	58	7	6	.239/.285/.346	79	3.8	.268	2.7	2B(78): 1.0, SS(39): 0.3	0.5
2020	BOS	MLB	26	350	32	16	2	6	33	15	51	14	5	.255/.295/.367	75	3.1	.287	0.8	2B 2, LF 0	0.5

Comparables: Donovan Solano, Jose Lopez, José Altuve

Peraza's at-bats should be sponsored by Bumble because the intention for each is to connect with a single. He doesn't walk, he doesn't bop and he didn't even steal efficiently (or often) last season. If we didn't know any better, we'd say he was auditioning for a gig with the Royals. First, though, he'll take a tour of Boston. Peraza will turn 26 in April, meaning he's likely to get at least a few more chances to live up to his old promise and/or replicate his solid 2018. He won't; not unless he hits .280 or better.

Kevin Plawecki C   Born: 02/26/91   Age: 29   Bats: R   Throws: R   Height: 6'2"   Weight: 220   Origin: Round 1, 2012 Draft (#35 overall)

YEAR	TEAM	LVL	AGE	PA	R	2B	3B	HR	RBI	BB	K	SB	CS	AVG/OBP/SLG	DRC+	VORP	BABIP	BRR	FRAA	WARP
2017	LVG	AAA	26	275	37	17	1	9	45	16	38	0	0	.328/.375/.514	125	22.9	.350	-1.4	C(63): 10.7	3.1
2017	NYN	MLB	26	118	11	5	0	3	13	14	17	1	0	.260/.364/.400	101	8.5	.284	-0.3	C(29): -3.3, 1B(2): 0.0	0.2
2018	NYN	MLB	27	277	33	13	2	7	30	28	65	0	1	.210/.315/.370	92	11.5	.257	-1.2	C(71): -2.0, 1B(3): 0.0	0.8
2019	CLE	MLB	28	174	13	10	0	3	17	12	31	0	1	.222/.287/.342	79	4.5	.256	-1.3	C(57): 7.8, P(2): 0.0	1.1
2020	BOS	MLB	29	140	13	6	0	3	14	11	29	0	0	.215/.289/.346	71	0.9	.253	-0.3	C 4	0.5

Comparables: Hank Conger, Derek Norris, Andy Etchebarren

When you're coming up in an organization that has a fancier catching prospect, sometimes opportunities can be limited. Plawecki found that out the hard way during his time alongside Travis d'Arnaud in the Mets system. Traded to Cleveland over the winter, he looked in line to replace Yan Gomes. Yet, Plawecki once again disappointed, serving as the backup behind the dish to Roberto Perez and struggling to crack a .600 OPS. His defensive numbers rebounded, per our metrics, but that's the formula for a dependable backup, not someone who deserves a greater opportunity.

YEAR	TEAM	P. COUNT	FRM RUNS	BLK RUNS	THRW RUNS	TOT RUNS
2017	LVG	9115	8.7	0.8	-0.4	8.6
2017	NYN	3842	-3.2	0.7	-0.6	-3.3
2018	NYN	9839	-4.6	2.0	0.0	-2.7
2019	CLE	6773	6.6	2.2	-0.3	8.4
2020	BOS	6352	3.2	0.9	-0.3	3.8

Sam Travis OF/1B   Born: 08/27/93   Age: 26   Bats: R   Throws: R   Height: 6'0"   Weight: 205   Origin: Round 2, 2014 Draft (#67 overall)

YEAR	TEAM	LVL	AGE	PA	R	2B	3B	HR	RBI	BB	K	SB	CS	AVG/OBP/SLG	DRC+	VORP	BABIP	BRR	FRAA	WARP
2017	PAW	AAA	23	342	40	14	0	6	24	37	57	6	2	.270/.351/.375	117	-0.1	.315	-3.5	1B(58): -0.1	0.6
2017	BOS	MLB	23	83	13	6	0	0	1	6	23	1	0	.263/.325/.342	68	-3.8	.377	-1.0	1B(21): 0.2	-0.3
2018	PAW	AAA	24	398	35	13	0	8	43	29	89	1	2	.258/.317/.360	94	9.1	.317	1.3	1B(45): 0.5, LF(36): -2.7	0.3
2018	BOS	MLB	24	38	5	3	0	1	7	2	10	0	0	.222/.263/.389	80	-0.4	.280	0.0	LF(6): 0.0, 1B(3): -0.1	0.0
2019	PAW	AAA	25	268	36	14	1	7	33	31	62	5	1	.275/.362/.432	114	11.8	.347	-0.3	LF(31): -2.3, 1B(26): -0.1	0.6
2019	BOS	MLB	25	157	17	4	1	6	16	11	36	2	0	.215/.274/.382	83	-0.2	.243	-0.1	1B(29): 0.1, LF(18): 0.5	0.0
2020	BOS	MLB	26	35	3	2	0	1	4	3	8	0	0	.231/.299/.369	78	-0.5	.288	-0.1	1B 0	-0.1

Comparables: Brandon Snyder, Nick Evans, Chris Marrero

It wasn't supposed to be the hit tool. Travis was never projected to hit for power, and he's never been known for his glove. But the hit tool was supposed to be safe. Well, he's got nearly 300 major-league plate appearances under his belt now and that small but not insignificant sample tells us Travis kinda stinks. There were 49 first basemen who recorded as many plate appearances as the 2014 draft pick did last season and among them he ranked 40th in DRC+, ahead of Cheslor Cuthbert and Justin Bour, to his eternal credit, but also behind Neil Walker's ambulatory remains. Travis's ceiling at this point is as the short-side platoon guy on a weak roster, and he should *never* be allowed to face same-side pitching. Honestly, he's so useless against righties it's a wonder Nancy Pelosi isn't his hitting coach. Travis is a fine organizational depth piece, but if you're seeing a lot of him after March and before September, something's gone wrong.

Christian Vázquez C   Born: 08/21/90   Age: 29   Bats: R   Throws: R   Height: 5'9"   Weight: 195   Origin: Round 9, 2008 Draft (#292 overall)

YEAR	TEAM	LVL	AGE	PA	R	2B	3B	HR	RBI	BB	K	SB	CS	AVG/OBP/SLG	DRC+	VORP	BABIP	BRR	FRAA	WARP
2017	BOS	MLB	26	345	43	18	2	5	32	17	64	7	2	.290/.330/.404	93	6.7	.348	-3.3	C(95): 16.4, 3B(2): 0.0	2.7
2018	BOS	MLB	27	269	24	10	0	3	16	13	41	4	1	.207/.257/.283	71	-5.4	.237	-0.4	C(75): 8.3, 3B(2): 0.0	1.2
2019	BOS	MLB	28	521	66	26	1	23	72	33	101	4	2	.276/.320/.477	106	28.3	.305	-0.3	C(119): 7.0, 1B(10): 1.0	3.5
2020	BOS	MLB	29	560	56	26	1	16	62	36	115	6	2	.246/.299/.390	82	10.6	.289	-1.7	C 16, 1B 0	2.7

Comparables: Tom Pagnozzi, Brent Mayne, Francisco Cervelli

One season after producing less offensive value than peers like Chris Iannetta, Manny Piña and Austin Romine, Vázquez outhit Buster Posey, Gary Sánchez and Yadier Molina. He hit the ball harder, struck out and walked more, rode some positive BABIP regression and was likely helped quite a bit by the bouncy balls. Vázquez's emergence as an offensive threat is well-timed, because he's trending from elite to merely very good as a defender; one that figures to continue as he enters his 30s. That being said, what he's losing in catching prowess he may learn to compensate for in defensive versatility. In an effort to keep

YEAR	TEAM	P. COUNT	FRM RUNS	BLK RUNS	THRW RUNS	TOT RUNS
2017	BOS	13558	15.5	1.0	2.4	19.6
2018	BOS	10330	9.0	0.1	0.1	9.0
2019	BOS	16455	12.3	-5.3	0.8	7.7
2020	BOS	23520	18.5	-2.6	1.6	17.4

Vázquez's bat in the lineup—a sentence that we can't believe we're typing either—the Red Sox gave him some major-league reps at first, second, third, and yes, even DH. Essentially, this is a drawn-out way of telling you Vázquez has become the player we all though Blake Swihart would be. Catchers, man.

PITCHERS

Matt Barnes RHP   Born: 06/17/90   Age: 30   Bats: R   Throws: R   Height: 6'4"   Weight: 210   Origin: Round 1, 2011 Draft (#19 overall)

YEAR	TEAM	LVL	AGE	W	L	SV	G	GS	IP	H	HR	BB/9	K/9	K	GB%	BABIP	WHIP	ERA	DRA	WARP	MPH	FB%	WHF	CSP
2017	BOS	MLB	27	7	3	1	70	0	69²	57	7	3.6	10.7	83	50%	.298	1.22	3.88	3.30	1.5	97.1	55	13.2	42.7
2018	BOS	MLB	28	6	4	0	62	0	61²	47	5	4.5	14.0	96	53%	.321	1.26	3.65	2.21	1.9	98.7	54.8	15	42.7
2019	BOS	MLB	29	5	4	4	70	0	64¹	51	8	5.3	15.4	110	48%	.341	1.38	3.78	2.75	1.8	98.4	47.3	16	38.8
2020	BOS	MLB	30	3	3	11	61	0	65	53	7	4.8	13.8	99	49%	.333	1.35	3.66	3.76	1.0	97.4	51.3	14.9	40.9

Comparables: Cody Martin, Justin Grimm, Tommy Kahnle

For better and for worse, nothing about Barnes' 2019 can be considered surprising. He missed a ton of bats; among pitchers with at least 50 innings he ranked second in the league in K/9 behind only Josh Hader. He also walked too many—he had the 14th worst BB/9 in baseball—and gave up his fair share of taters. That's Barnes in a nutshell, a fireman who's equally as capable of shutting down the heart of an order as he is walking the opposing team's pitcher or serving up a spicy meatball to, like, Bubba Starling. (Seriously, he did this.) By WARP, Barnes has proven to be one of the most valuable 20-or-so relievers in the game over the past two seasons—he's in the same range as Aroldis Chapman, Kenley Jansen and Héctor Neris—but that's at least in part because he throws a lot of innings. Both for their own good and for Barnes' sake, the Red Sox need to get him some help.

Ryan Brasier RHP   Born: 08/26/87   Age: 32   Bats: R   Throws: R   Height: 6'0"   Weight: 225   Origin: Round 6, 2007 Draft (#208 overall)

YEAR	TEAM	LVL	AGE	W	L	SV	G	GS	IP	H	HR	BB/9	K/9	K	GB%	BABIP	WHIP	ERA	DRA	WARP	MPH	FB%	WHF	CSP
2018	PAW	AAA	30	2	5	13	34	0	40¹	29	1	1.8	8.9	40	43%	.277	0.92	1.34	3.13	0.9				
2018	BOS	MLB	30	2	0	0	34	0	33²	19	2	1.9	7.8	29	43%	.198	0.77	1.60	3.57	0.5	98.4	62.6	17.3	45.8
2019	PAW	AAA	31	2	0	0	10	0	9¹	6	1	1.0	12.5	13	45%	.263	0.75	0.96	2.26	0.4				
2019	BOS	MLB	31	2	4	7	62	0	55²	51	9	3.4	9.9	61	33%	.286	1.29	4.85	5.38	0.0	97.7	59.3	16.5	44.2
2020	BOS	MLB	32	2	2	0	45	0	47	42	7	3.1	9.9	52	37%	.288	1.23	3.79	4.04	0.6	96.9	59.7	16.6	44.5

Comparables: Miguel Socolovich, Kevin Quackenbush, Justin Miller

Brasier's fall from grace was fairly dramatic even by 2019's lofty standards among hard-ass righties. The big Texan became a cult hero during the 2018 World Series run when he barked at Gary Sánchez to "get his ass back in the box," and he entered 2019 as one of the front-runners to earn saves for the Craig Kimbrel-less Red Sox. Instead, Brasier was back in Pawtucket by July. That'll happen when your walk, homer and contact allowed rates all skyrocket. Brasier was always a long shot to repeat his breakout season, but it's hard to pinpoint exactly why he regressed so quickly; while his command wavered, he still featured plus velocity and his pitch mix didn't change much. The optimists may say that points toward a potential rebound, but realists are more likely to acknowledge Brasier's 2018 as the fun fluke it was.

Colten Brewer RHP   Born: 10/29/92   Age: 27   Bats: R   Throws: R   Height: 6'4"   Weight: 230   Origin: Round 4, 2011 Draft (#122 overall)

YEAR	TEAM	LVL	AGE	W	L	SV	G	GS	IP	H	HR	BB/9	K/9	K	GB%	BABIP	WHIP	ERA	DRA	WARP	MPH	FB%	WHF	CSP
2017	TAM	A+	24	0	0	2	6	0	9¹	3	0	1.0	14.5	15	78%	.167	0.43	0.00	1.57	0.4				
2017	TRN	AA	24	3	1	11	29	0	41¹	37	0	2.4	9.4	43	64%	.314	1.16	1.31	3.39	0.7				
2017	SWB	AAA	24	0	0	1	6	0	10	17	2	3.6	9.9	11	60%	.417	2.10	11.70	7.16	-0.2				
2018	ELP	AAA	25	3	4	3	37	0	48	40	3	2.8	11.8	63	56%	.330	1.15	3.75	2.56	1.4				
2018	SDN	MLB	25	1	0	0	11	0	9²	15	0	6.5	9.3	10	50%	.469	2.28	5.59	2.71	0.2	95.7	68.6	10.8	48.6
2019	PAW	AAA	26	2	3	0	9	0	11	14	2	5.7	8.2	10	57%	.343	1.91	4.91	6.54	0.0				
2019	BOS	MLB	26	1	2	0	58	0	54²	59	6	5.6	8.6	52	53%	.333	1.70	4.12	5.20	0.1	95.8	44	11.7	43.7
2020	BOS	MLB	27	2	2	0	39	0	41	41	5	4.5	8.7	40	53%	.308	1.48	4.65	4.64	0.2	95.3	47.8	11.7	46.5

Comparables: Dovydas Neverauskas, Marcus Hatley, Yacksel Ríos

Tree House. Nightshift. Trillium. Aeronaut. Lord Hobo. Notch. And yes, even Harpoon. There are no shortage of outstanding purveyors of craft beer in Greater Boston, but in Colten, the area finally hosted a Brewer that fell flat. While Brewer missed his fair share of bats, he also walked too many batters and gave up too many home runs, which helps to explain why DRA tells us his ERA overstates his effectiveness by more than a full run. Most teams don't run five or six elite relievers deep, but it says plenty about the 2019 Red Sox bullpen that Brewer was its fifth-most used option. Odds are Boston will look to have better options on tap, which means Brewer may find himself back with the Narragansetts of the world in Rhode Island.

Andrew Cashner RHP Born: 09/11/86 Age: 33 Bats: R Throws: R Height: 6'6" Weight: 235 Origin: Round 1, 2008 Draft (#19 overall)

YEAR	TEAM	LVL	AGE	W	L	SV	G	GS	IP	H	HR	BB/9	K/9	K	GB%	BABIP	WHIP	ERA	DRA	WARP	MPH	FB%	WHF	CSP
2017	TEX	MLB	30	11	11	0	28	28	166²	156	15	3.5	4.6	86	49%	.266	1.32	3.40	5.58	0.0	96.3	65.1	6.7	49.6
2018	BAL	MLB	31	4	15	0	28	28	153	177	25	3.8	5.8	99	42%	.311	1.58	5.29	6.69	-2.4	95.5	60.2	7.5	46.7
2019	BAL	MLB	32	9	3	0	17	17	96¹	86	11	2.7	6.2	66	50%	.256	1.19	3.83	4.74	1.0	96.2	50.4	9.3	47.1
2019	BOS	MLB	32	2	5	1	25	6	53²	58	8	4.9	7.0	42	49%	.325	1.62	6.20	5.71	0.0	96.9	50.4	11.8	44.1
2020	BOS	MLB	33	2	2	0	33	0	35	38	5	3.6	6.6	26	47%	.299	1.48	5.03	5.05	0.1	95.0	56.8	8.3	46.5

Comparables: Tyson Ross, Daniel Hudson, Dillon Gee

Perhaps nothing better encapsulates the difficulties the 2019 Red Sox faced on the mound than their need to trade for Cashner in mid-July. To be fair, Cashner was in the midst of his best season since 2015, what with his ERA south of 4.00 and his one WARP. His supposed evolution was attributed to a newfound ability to limit walks, and a changing pitch mix that saw Cashner favor his changeup over his sinker. But this is (Chris Traeger voice) *literally* Andrew Cashner we're talking about. It can't be that surprising that he bombed in six starts with Boston before facing relegation to the bullpen. A look at his first half in Baltimore and there is hope that league-average production can be squeezed out of him for a bit, but that's a best-case scenario at this point.

Jhoulys Chacín RHP Born: 01/07/88 Age: 32 Bats: R Throws: R Height: 6'3" Weight: 215 Origin: International Free Agent, 2004

YEAR	TEAM	LVL	AGE	W	L	SV	G	GS	IP	H	HR	BB/9	K/9	K	GB%	BABIP	WHIP	ERA	DRA	WARP	MPH	FB%	WHF	CSP
2017	SDN	MLB	29	13	10	0	32	32	180¹	157	19	3.6	7.6	153	50%	.272	1.27	3.89	4.50	2.2	93.7	54.1	8.6	48.2
2018	MIL	MLB	30	15	8	0	35	35	192²	153	18	3.3	7.3	156	44%	.250	1.16	3.50	4.51	1.8	92.5	48.1	9.1	48.9
2019	BOS	MLB	31	0	2	0	6	5	14²	16	6	4.3	12.9	21	38%	.303	1.57	7.36	3.83	0.3	91.7	44.3	10	46.5
2019	MIL	MLB	31	3	10	0	19	19	88²	99	19	4.0	8.1	80	38%	.308	1.56	5.79	6.96	-1.2	92.1	44.3	8.6	47.4
2020	BOS	MLB	32	2	2	0	33	0	35	34	6	3.6	7.8	30	41%	.287	1.38	4.55	4.68	0.2	91.8	48.2	8.8	47.6

Comparables: Clay Buchholz, Trevor Cahill, Aaron Sele

One season after serving as the de facto ace of an exciting Brewers team, Chacín performed so poorly that he earned a DFA in late August. Sometimes it can be difficult to pinpoint exactly why pitchers see their performance fluctuate so wildly, but in the case of Chacín, it's pretty simple: too many damn homers. His home-run rate nearly *tripled*, and while Rob Manfred would probably look at that stat and give you his best Bernard Lowe—"this doesn't look like anything to me"—it's fairly obvious what's to blame. Chacín didn't lose velocity. He didn't substantially alter his pitch mix. He wasn't hurt. We're just to believe that he turned into a JUGS machine overnight. If MLB ever does come clean about whatever baseball shenanigans occurred in 2019, Chacín should file a grievance. Considering he ended the year as a Red Sox starter, perhaps he should sue for emotional damages, too.

Nathan Eovaldi RHP Born: 02/13/90 Age: 30 Bats: R Throws: R Height: 6'2" Weight: 225 Origin: Round 11, 2008 Draft (#337 overall)

YEAR	TEAM	LVL	AGE	W	L	SV	G	GS	IP	H	HR	BB/9	K/9	K	GB%	BABIP	WHIP	ERA	DRA	WARP	MPH	FB%	WHF	CSP
2018	PCH	A+	28	0	0	0	3	3	6	6	2	0.0	10.5	7	47%	.267	1.00	4.50	3.80	0.1				
2018	TBA	MLB	28	3	4	0	10	10	57	48	11	1.3	8.4	53	48%	.245	0.98	4.26	3.19	1.4	99.0	38.2	12.7	54.7
2018	BOS	MLB	28	3	3	0	12	11	54	57	3	2.0	8.0	48	46%	.325	1.28	3.33	3.28	1.3	99.4	38.2	10.9	51.7
2019	BOS	MLB	29	2	1	0	23	12	67²	72	16	4.7	9.3	70	45%	.315	1.58	5.99	6.37	-0.5	99.7	43.3	11.8	46.8
2020	BOS	MLB	30	9	7	0	24	24	134	136	19	3.4	9.0	133	46%	.314	1.40	4.54	4.62	1.4	98.6	40.5	11.8	49.5

Comparables: Trevor Cahill, Jair Jurrjens, Randall Delgado

It's entirely possible that Eovaldi is the man who got Dave Dombrowski fired. If you squint, you can sort of see why Dombo backed up the Brinks truck for Eovaldi. The flame-throwing righty was just off his best season, came up huge for the Red Sox in October and was likely seen as Rick Porcello's replacement for 2020 and beyond. Still, there's no way to sugarcoat the fact that Dombrowski chose to give nearly $70 million to a dude with as many Tommy John surgeries as 2-WARP seasons. Sure enough, Eovaldi missed a ton of time in 2019 after undergoing a procedure to remove loose bodies from his elbow. When on the mound, he displayed all the command and accuracy of a Bob Nightengale tweet, embarrassing himself in a very short stint as Boston's closer. For a Red Sox team that's suddenly crying poor, Eovaldi's albatross of a contract is an utter disaster; one new head honcho Chaim Bloom may either try to get out from under or, at the very least, avoid replicating.

Durbin Feltman RHP Born: 04/18/97 Age: 23 Bats: R Throws: R Height: 6'0" Weight: 205 Origin: Round 3, 2018 Draft (#100 overall)

YEAR	TEAM	LVL	AGE	W	L	SV	G	GS	IP	H	HR	BB/9	K/9	K	GB%	BABIP	WHIP	ERA	DRA	WARP	MPH	FB%	WHF	CSP
2018	GRN	A	21	0	1	3	7	0	7	6	0	1.3	18.0	14	43%	.429	1.00	2.57	2.65	0.2				
2018	SLM	A+	21	1	0	1	11	0	12¹	12	0	2.9	10.9	15	58%	.364	1.30	2.19	3.68	0.2				
2019	PME	AA	22	2	3	5	43	0	51¹	42	8	5.4	9.5	54	43%	.266	1.42	5.26	5.14	-0.3				
2020	BOS	MLB	23	2	2	0	33	0	35	35	6	3.7	8.7	34	41%	.302	1.41	4.72	4.87	0.1				

Comparables: Shawn Armstrong, Evan Phillips, Trevor Gott

Coming out of the draft in 2018, Feltman was considered about as safe a reliever prospect as could be. For the umpteenth time, "safe reliever prospect" has turned out to be quite the oxymoron. Feltman struggled mightily in Double-A, coughing up walks and homers at such a rate that one wonders if he was performing some sort of masochistic tribute to late-career Daniel Bard. Feltman still owns the type of high-velocity fastball/wipeout slider combo that many of the game's high-leverage relievers feature, but he'll need to hit the strike zone far more often if he wants a chance at deploying said weapons in Boston.

Jay Groome LHP Born: 08/23/98 Age: 21 Bats: L Throws: L Height: 6'6" Weight: 220 Origin: Round 1, 2016 Draft (#12 overall)

YEAR	TEAM	LVL	AGE	W	L	SV	G	GS	IP	H	HR	BB/9	K/9	K	GB%	BABIP	WHIP	ERA	DRA	WARP	MPH	FB%	WHF	CSP
2017	LOW	A-	18	0	2	0	3	3	11	5	0	4.1	11.5	14	58%	.208	0.91	1.64	2.65	0.3				
2017	GRN	A	18	3	7	0	11	11	44¹	44	6	5.1	11.8	58	55%	.355	1.56	6.70	4.49	0.4				
2020	BOS	MLB	21	2	2	0	33	0	35	35	6	4.1	9.0	35	47%	.304	1.47	4.97	5.06	0.1				

Comparables: Lewis Thorpe, Jordan Lyles, Mike Soroka

Folks, we haven't seen a Groome get abandoned like this since *The Princess Bride*. Our protagonist was a consensus top-three pitcher in the 2016 draft and top-100 prospect in the game as recently as 2017. But since Groome has been largely out of sight, out of mind for 15 months as he recovered from Tommy John surgery, it seems as though his prospect luster has faded. It's entirely possible that Groome will serve as example number 23,542 as to why the TINSTAAPP acronym was invented. It's also possible that Groome, who looked great once he climbed back on a mound in August, is about to remind us all why he generated so many Jon Lester comps to begin with.

Heath Hembree RHP Born: 01/13/89 Age: 31 Bats: R Throws: R Height: 6'4" Weight: 210 Origin: Round 5, 2010 Draft (#168 overall)

YEAR	TEAM	LVL	AGE	W	L	SV	G	GS	IP	H	HR	BB/9	K/9	K	GB%	BABIP	WHIP	ERA	DRA	WARP	MPH	FB%	WHF	CSP
2017	BOS	MLB	28	2	3	0	62	0	62	72	10	2.6	10.2	70	42%	.360	1.45	3.63	3.39	1.2	97.7	53.1	15.2	45.3
2018	BOS	MLB	29	4	1	0	67	0	60	53	10	4.1	11.4	76	40%	.295	1.33	4.20	3.87	0.7	96.8	54.9	15.5	45.3
2019	BOS	MLB	30	1	0	2	45	0	39²	34	7	4.1	10.4	46	24%	.273	1.31	3.86	6.54	-0.5	96.0	69.9	13.3	45.5
2020	BOS	MLB	31	2	2	0	45	0	47	40	8	3.5	9.7	51	32%	.269	1.25	3.98	4.21	0.5	95.9	58.8	14.6	45.1

Comparables: Kevin Quackenbush, Chase Whitley, Jeremy Accardo

June 14 might not have been a very memorable day for you, but for Hembree, it marked the beginning of the end. Up until that point, he owned a 2.51 ERA, had only allowed a run in six of his 31 appearances and had been especially dominant since May 1 (0.60 ERA). Unfortunately, Hembree's season was derailed by an extensor strain in his right elbow, which knocked him out until July 5. He was never the same upon his return, allowing nine earned runs in nine innings over his next 12 appearances before returning to the IL on August 2. Hembree got a PRP injection in his balky joint and reappeared at the very end of the year for two final appearances, but by then it was far too late to save either his season or Boston's. DRA tells us Hembree was getting lucky even during his hot stretch, and as such he remains nothing more than a serviceable arm who can soak up low-to-moderate leverage innings. When his arm is healthy, that is.

Darwinzon Hernandez LHP Born: 12/17/96 Age: 23 Bats: L Throws: L Height: 6'2" Weight: 245 Origin: International Free Agent, 2013

YEAR	TEAM	LVL	AGE	W	L	SV	G	GS	IP	H	HR	BB/9	K/9	K	GB%	BABIP	WHIP	ERA	DRA	WARP	MPH	FB%	WHF	CSP
2017	GRN	A	20	4	5	0	23	23	103¹	85	8	4.3	10.1	116	50%	.292	1.30	4.01	4.11	1.4				
2018	SLM	A+	21	9	5	0	23	23	101	80	1	5.3	11.0	124	46%	.326	1.39	3.56	4.15	1.4				
2018	PME	AA	21	0	0	0	5	0	6	6	0	9.0	15.0	10	36%	.429	2.00	3.00	4.27	0.0				
2019	PME	AA	22	1	4	0	10	9	40¹	33	2	7.1	13.2	59	39%	.337	1.61	5.13	5.03	-0.1				
2019	PAW	AAA	22	1	2	0	7	3	17	10	2	8.5	10.6	20	38%	.229	1.53	4.76	4.70	0.3				
2019	BOS	MLB	22	0	1	0	29	1	30¹	27	1	7.7	16.9	57	44%	.433	1.75	4.45	3.04	0.8	97.7	74.2	14.7	47.3
2020	BOS	MLB	23	3	3	0	38	5	55	40	7	5.1	12.5	76	39%	.280	1.29	3.58	3.70	1.0	97.6	76.9	15.2	49

Comparables: Touki Toussaint, Enny Romero, Mitch Atkins

Thirty innings is often too small a sample size from which to derive anything meaningful, but in his first 30 frames in the big leagues, Hernandez told us *exactly* who he was. No one with as many innings pitched—not Josh Hader, nor Edwin Díaz nor Nick Anderson—struck out more batters per inning. At the same time, only one pitcher with as many innings—José Alvarado—issued walks at a higher rate. That's Hernandez to a tee; a chonky, flamethrowing lefty who can strike out any hitter on the planet, but who could also find a way to give a windmill first base. There's a chance this is as good as it'll ever get for Hernandez, but if he can improve his command even just a little, we might be looking at the new poster child for Effectively Wild. Fortunately, his first name suggests he should be open to evolving.

Tanner Houck RHP Born: 06/29/96 Age: 24 Bats: R Throws: R Height: 6'4" Weight: 210 Origin: Round 1, 2017 Draft (#24 overall)

YEAR	TEAM	LVL	AGE	W	L	SV	G	GS	IP	H	HR	BB/9	K/9	K	GB%	BABIP	WHIP	ERA	DRA	WARP	MPH	FB%	WHF	CSP
2017	LOW	A-	21	0	3	0	10	10	22¹	21	0	3.2	10.1	25	49%	.333	1.30	3.63	4.91	0.1				
2018	SLM	A+	22	7	11	0	23	23	119	110	11	4.5	8.4	111	50%	.298	1.43	4.24	4.96	0.5				
2019	PME	AA	23	8	6	0	17	15	82²	86	4	3.5	8.7	80	50%	.346	1.43	4.25	5.45	-0.5				
2019	PAW	AAA	23	0	0	1	16	2	25	19	3	5.0	9.7	27	48%	.250	1.32	3.24	3.52	0.7				
2020	BOS	MLB	24	1	1	0	3	3	15	14	2	4.0	7.7	12	46%	.292	1.44	4.85	4.88	0.1				

Comparables: Reed Garrett, Hansel Robles, Corey Kluber

Houck was a first-round pick back in 2017 and that comes with certain expectations, but if you're waiting for him to front a rotation some day it's time to recalibrate. Houck's lack of a reliable third pitch and spotty command are likely to preclude him from dominating as a starter at the next level, and may prevent him from starting there at all. The good news? Houck's fastball/slider combo can miss major-league bats right now, and if that third pitch ever does click, he's got the frame and athleticism to soak up lots of innings. Houck mostly pitched in relief after a promotion to Pawtucket but was featured as a starter in the AFL, so some ambiguity as to his future role remains. For 2020, it's easiest to envision him contributing out of the bullpen with the Red Sox, even if he's only used against righties early in his career. In other words, prepare yourself for lots of "Houck: A ROOGY" jokes next June.

Bryan Mata RHP Born: 05/03/99 Age: 21 Bats: R Throws: R Height: 6'3" Weight: 160 Origin: International Free Agent, 2016

YEAR	TEAM	LVL	AGE	W	L	SV	G	GS	IP	H	HR	BB/9	K/9	K	GB%	BABIP	WHIP	ERA	DRA	WARP	MPH	FB%	WHF	CSP
2017	GRN	A	18	5	6	0	17	17	77	75	3	3.0	8.6	74	53%	.333	1.31	3.74	4.67	0.5				
2018	SLM	A+	19	6	3	0	17	17	72	58	1	7.2	7.6	61	59%	.292	1.61	3.50	5.71	-0.3				
2019	SLM	A+	20	3	1	0	10	10	51¹	38	1	3.2	9.1	52	67%	.268	1.09	1.75	3.68	0.8				
2019	PME	AA	20	4	6	0	11	11	53²	54	6	4.0	9.9	59	54%	.340	1.45	5.03	5.42	-0.3				
2020	BOS	MLB	21	2	2	0	33	0	35	34	5	3.7	7.9	31	47%	.292	1.39	4.55	4.68	0.2				

Comparables: Carlos Martínez, Junior Fernandez, David Holmberg

To be fair to Mata, he's always been kinda young for his levels. Unfortunately, he's also always been kinda bad for his levels. Ok, that's not *quite* true. Mata was dominant in his half-season of repeat work at High A, but following a promotion to Portland the hard-throwing righty's impressive stuff didn't lead to impressive results. For the most part, that's been the story of Mata's career: aggressive assignments, promising scouting reports and lackluster box scores. It seems as though the Red Sox are still grooming Mata as a potential mid-rotation starter, but he pitched out of the bullpen in the AFL and some scouts think his future may lie in relief, where his mid-90s fastball and power slider/curve figure to miss bats. Either way, history tells us Mata won't be young forever, and it's time for his results to start matching his talent.

Josh Osich LHP Born: 09/03/88 Age: 31 Bats: L Throws: L Height: 6'3" Weight: 232 Origin: Round 6, 2011 Draft (#207 overall)

YEAR	TEAM	LVL	AGE	W	L	SV	G	GS	IP	H	HR	BB/9	K/9	K	GB%	BABIP	WHIP	ERA	DRA	WARP	MPH	FB%	WHF	CSP
2017	SAC	AAA	28	1	1	2	9	0	9¹	12	0	2.9	7.7	8	55%	.364	1.61	7.71	4.35	0.1				
2017	SFN	MLB	28	3	2	0	54	0	43¹	48	7	5.6	8.9	43	46%	.333	1.73	6.23	5.62	-0.2	97.5	54.7	10	46.7
2018	SAC	AAA	29	0	0	0	37	2	45¹	56	2	3.6	8.3	42	47%	.365	1.63	4.96	5.10	0.0				
2018	SFN	MLB	29	0	0	0	12	0	12	20	2	5.2	7.5	10	45%	.450	2.25	8.25	6.64	-0.2	97.4	48.5	14.1	49.6
2019	CHA	MLB	30	4	0	0	57	0	67²	62	15	2.0	8.1	61	42%	.260	1.14	4.66	4.49	0.6	95.6	16.9	13.4	48.3
2020	BOS	MLB	31	1	1	0	17	0	18	17	3	3.4	9.0	18	45%	.297	1.36	4.48	4.63	0.1	95.4	30.3	12.5	48

Comparables: Bobby LaFromboise, Sam Freeman, Javy Guerra

For about five seconds each time Josh Osich jogged out from the bullpen during White Sox home games, fans had to wonder what was going on as the delicate opening licks of Fleetwood Mac's "The Chain" aired on the Guaranteed Rate Field speaker system. By the time the longtime Giant, oft-time Triple-A River Cat arrived in White Sox camp in the middle of March, he was on his third organization of the spring, and being allowed five seconds in the majors to set the mood didn't seem like something that was in his future. Osich certainly didn't do anything in 2019 to make any team reserve a place for him in their future plans. But for the first time in four years, the burly, hard-throwing lefty, didn't make everyone wonder what he was doing in the big leagues in the first place, either. He doesn't throw that hard anymore, but more by choice as he's flipped to a cutter-heavy approach that strangely has improved his strike-throwing. Far too many of those strikes still wound up in the seats, but it feels like an accomplishment these days when a guy gets cut by the Orioles and it's not the end of his career.

Martín Pérez LHP Born: 04/04/91 Age: 29 Bats: L Throws: L Height: 6'0" Weight: 200 Origin: International Free Agent, 2007

YEAR	TEAM	LVL	AGE	W	L	SV	G	GS	IP	H	HR	BB/9	K/9	K	GB%	BABIP	WHIP	ERA	DRA	WARP	MPH	FB%	WHF	CSP
2017	TEX	MLB	26	13	12	0	32	32	185	221	23	3.1	5.6	115	48%	.328	1.54	4.82	7.09	-3.1	95.4	58.7	8	41.1
2018	FRI	AA	27	1	0	0	1	1	6	2	0	4.5	6.0	4	65%	.118	0.83	0.00	3.02	0.2				
2018	ROU	AAA	27	1	0	0	1	1	6¹	6	1	0.0	8.5	6	72%	.294	0.95	1.42	3.41	0.2				
2018	TEX	MLB	27	2	7	0	22	15	85¹	116	16	3.8	5.5	52	52%	.344	1.78	6.22	7.31	-2.0	95.5	67.3	8.2	48.8
2019	MIN	MLB	28	10	7	0	32	29	165¹	184	23	3.6	7.3	135	49%	.316	1.52	5.12	6.32	-1.0	96.2	42.3	10.5	46.1
2020	BOS	MLB	29	7	6	0	23	23	98	108	13	3.6	7.2	78	50%	.314	1.50	4.89	4.89	0.8	95.1	52.5	9.2	45.8

Comparables: Jordan Lyles, Matt Harrison, Chris Haney

Left-handed pitchers have career paths that don't end until the last pasta bowl hits an Olive Garden table. And when one of 'em shows up in March of their age-28 season with a couple extra ticks on an already-fast fastball as well as a shiny new cutter? Well, they're upgraded to the Lifetime Pasta Pass. Pérez is going to need all the carbs he can get to land future opportunities. The seemingly turbo-charged four-seamer was bashed by hitters, who slugged .729 against it. Predictably, he posted his fifth consecutive negative-WARP season; an impressive run of mediocrity, to be sure, but one that's not going to cut it for a team with 100-win aspirations. Pérez signed a one-year deal with Boston, where he'll try to avoid the clam chowder bowl.

David Price LHP Born: 08/26/85 Age: 34 Bats: L Throws: L Height: 6'5" Weight: 215 Origin: Round 1, 2007 Draft (#1 overall)

YEAR	TEAM	LVL	AGE	W	L	SV	G	GS	IP	H	HR	BB/9	K/9	K	GB%	BABIP	WHIP	ERA	DRA	WARP	MPH	FB%	WHF	CSP
2017	BOS	MLB	31	6	3	0	16	11	74²	65	8	2.9	9.2	76	40%	.278	1.19	3.38	5.04	0.4	96.1	58.3	13.1	44.1
2018	BOS	MLB	32	16	7	0	30	30	176	151	25	2.6	9.1	177	41%	.274	1.14	3.58	3.72	3.2	94.6	46.5	10.8	49.9
2019	BOS	MLB	33	7	5	0	22	22	107¹	109	15	2.7	10.7	128	42%	.336	1.31	4.28	4.68	1.3	94.3	52	12.4	49.9
2020	BOS	MLB	34	11	7	0	26	26	150	136	23	2.5	10.0	167	40%	.294	1.18	3.59	3.86	2.8	93.6	49.7	11.6	47.7

Comparables: Cole Hamels, Jon Lester, Gio Gonzalez

With Chris Sale and Nathan Eovaldi hurt, and Rick Porcello having one of his off years, the Red Sox turned to Price for an assist in carrying their rotation. He clearly misheard them, as the veteran lefty threw the second-fewest innings of his career thanks in large part to a cyst in his left wrist. If you're a Red Sox apologist, you could argue that 2019 was a lost season anyway, and that the Sox saved themselves from putting another 100-or-so innings on an arm to which they owe in excess of $60 million over the next three years. If you're more of a realist, you may point out that it's been three full seasons since the now 34-year-old Price has able to throw 200 innings. Price pitched quite well before the cyst started to limit his effectiveness in early July, and he had offseason surgery to remove the troublesome growth, so theoretically he should be at 100 percent come spring training. Yet, at this point even a Price who enters the year healthy can't be relied upon for 30-plus starts.

Eduardo Rodriguez LHP   Born: 04/07/93   Age: 27   Bats: L   Throws: L   Height: 6'2"   Weight: 220   Origin: International Free Agent, 2010

YEAR	TEAM	LVL	AGE	W	L	SV	G	GS	IP	H	HR	BB/9	K/9	K	GB%	BABIP	WHIP	ERA	DRA	WARP	MPH	FB%	WHF	CSP
2017	PAW	AAA	24	0	1	0	2	2	10¹	10	0	4.4	10.5	12	38%	.385	1.45	4.35	4.35	0.2				
2017	BOS	MLB	24	6	7	0	25	24	137¹	126	19	3.3	9.8	150	36%	.299	1.28	4.19	4.37	1.8	95.4	65.3	12.4	44
2018	PME	AA	25	0	0	0	2	2	8	3	0	4.5	15.8	14	69%	.231	0.88	0.00	1.74	0.3				
2018	BOS	MLB	25	13	5	0	27	23	129²	119	16	3.1	10.1	146	39%	.301	1.26	3.82	3.77	2.3	95.3	51.6	12.4	46.4
2019	BOS	MLB	26	19	6	0	34	34	203¹	195	24	3.3	9.4	213	50%	.317	1.33	3.81	4.46	2.9	94.9	54.6	12.7	43.9
2020	BOS	MLB	27	11	8	0	28	28	157	151	22	3.5	9.7	169	46%	.308	1.35	4.18	4.32	2.2	94.6	56.7	12.7	45.3

Comparables: Robbie Ray, Aaron Sanchez, Brad Hand

The 2019 Red Sox enjoyed relatively few bright spots on the mound, but Rodriguez served as a welcome exception. It's hard to find a pitching category in which Rodriguez did not post a career-best mark, from strikeout rate to ERA to WARP to ground-ball rate to innings pitched. That last stat is particularly telling, as E-Rod finally went a full season without succumbing to the leg injuries that have derailed many of his previous attempts at putting it all together. Rodriguez was a top-40 overall starting pitcher, besting more celebrated AL-East arms like Marcus Stroman, James Paxton and even Blake Snell. Given that the Sox still have Chris Sale and David Price on payroll, they must hope Rodriguez doesn't need to front their rotation. But it's awfully nice to know that, health permitting, he can if he needs to.

Chris Sale LHP   Born: 03/30/89   Age: 31   Bats: L   Throws: L   Height: 6'6"   Weight: 180   Origin: Round 1, 2010 Draft (#13 overall)

YEAR	TEAM	LVL	AGE	W	L	SV	G	GS	IP	H	HR	BB/9	K/9	K	GB%	BABIP	WHIP	ERA	DRA	WARP	MPH	FB%	WHF	CSP
2017	BOS	MLB	28	17	8	0	32	32	214¹	165	24	1.8	12.9	308	40%	.301	0.97	2.90	2.51	7.3	97.7	50.5	15.8	48.3
2018	BOS	MLB	29	12	4	0	27	27	158	102	11	1.9	13.5	237	45%	.283	0.86	2.11	2.24	5.6	99.2	50.1	16.9	49.4
2019	BOS	MLB	30	6	11	0	25	25	147¹	123	24	2.3	13.3	218	44%	.309	1.09	4.40	2.93	4.5	96.9	46.3	15.1	50.2
2020	BOS	MLB	31	13	6	0	26	26	168	130	21	2.3	12.7	237	42%	.297	1.02	2.63	3.00	4.8	97.0	48.5	15.8	49.2

Comparables: Pedro Martinez, Johan Santana, Sandy Koufax

Sale is lucky that David Benioff and D.B. Weiss exist because otherwise he'd serve as 2019's most disastrous example of subverting expectations. Fresh off of signing a five-year, $145 million contract extension, Sale had his worst season since 2011. He still missed plenty of bats, and yes, he became the fastest pitcher ever to 2,000 strikeouts, but his homer and walk rates jumped while his velocity diminished. That alone would be troubling enough, but to make matters much, much worse, Sale hit the IL in mid-August with left elbow inflammation, necessitating a trip to the equally esteemed and dreaded Dr. James Andrews. The silver lining here is that Sale was *not* found to require Tommy John surgery, received a PRP injection instead, and is reportedly expected to be all systems go once spring training rolls around. People have doubted Sale's ability to stay healthy his entire career, and for the most part, they've been wrong. But he'll start this season as a 31-year-old with recent elbow and shoulder injuries who hasn't been at his best in about 18 months. If you think this has a happy ending…

Noah Song RHP   Born: 05/28/97   Age: 23   Bats: R   Throws: R   Height: 6'4"   Weight: 200   Origin: Round 4, 2019 Draft (#137 overall)

YEAR	TEAM	LVL	AGE	W	L	SV	G	GS	IP	H	HR	BB/9	K/9	K	GB%	BABIP	WHIP	ERA	DRA	WARP	MPH	FB%	WHF	CSP
2019	LOW	A-	22	0	0	0	7	7	17	10	0	2.6	10.1	19	42%	.244	0.88	1.06	2.49	0.5				
2020	BOS	MLB	23	2	2	0	33	0	35	35	5	3.5	7.9	31	40%	.293	1.39	4.52	4.68	0.2				

Comparables: Troy Scribner, Jesse Hahn, Daniel Ponce de Leon

You might not find a more intriguing prospect than Song, who the Red Sox popped in the fourth round for a cool $100,000 in last year's draft. Not just because he went from relative unknown to a Golden Spikes Award finalist, nor because on talent alone Song may be the best pitching prospect in Boston's system, but because Song was drafted out of the Naval Academy. That muddles Song's immediate future, as it's equally plausible he could miss the next five years fulfilling his military service commitment as it is he could petition to serve in the reserves after two years, or be granted a waiver that allows him to play baseball full-time. On the mound, Song features a mid-90s fastball, a potent slider and a developing changeup. Add that to his ideal pitcher's build and you've got the ingredients of a solid mid-rotation starter. It's anyone's guess as to when and if Song will be allowed to use those talents in the minors, but at the end of the day we shouldn't be surprised that a guy named "Noah Song" figures to have an interesting career arc.

Josh Taylor LHP   Born: 03/02/93   Age: 27   Bats: L   Throws: L   Height: 6'5"   Weight: 225   Origin: Undrafted Free Agent, 2014

YEAR	TEAM	LVL	AGE	W	L	SV	G	GS	IP	H	HR	BB/9	K/9	K	GB%	BABIP	WHIP	ERA	DRA	WARP	MPH	FB%	WHF	CSP
2017	WTN	AA	24	4	7	1	33	14	97	115	7	4.3	8.4	91	50%	.371	1.66	5.01	7.15	-2.4				
2018	VIS	A+	25	1	2	5	14	0	16	16	1	2.8	11.2	20	45%	.366	1.31	2.81	4.36	0.1				
2018	PME	AA	25	2	5	8	33	0	35²	42	1	4.5	9.3	37	54%	.376	1.68	3.79	6.09	-0.5				
2019	PAW	AAA	26	1	1	3	20	0	23¹	18	2	4.2	12.3	32	53%	.314	1.24	2.70	2.94	0.7				
2019	BOS	MLB	26	2	2	0	52	1	47¹	40	5	3.0	11.8	62	46%	.321	1.18	3.04	3.94	0.7	96.5	60.4	16.2	42.3
2020	BOS	MLB	27	2	2	0	45	0	47	40	6	4.0	12.0	63	47%	.307	1.28	3.62	3.79	0.7	96.0	61.1	16.4	42.8

Comparables: Sandy Baez, Jake Jewell, Reed Garrett

Sure, it may not be the trade for a southpaw that Dave Dombrowski is best remembered by, but acquiring Taylor for Deven Marrero back in 2018 is starting to look like a pretty shrewd move. Taylor finally improved his command enough to let his plus fastball/slider combo play up in the majors and initial results were quite promising. Taylor held lefties to a .203/.247/.304 line, proving to be a devastating weapon against same-side hitters. But he also held his own against righties and in high-leverage situations en route to finishing fifth among Red Sox relievers in DRA. Taylor will already be 27 when next season starts and his upside is capped by his touch-and-go control, but barring a massive influx of talent, he's earned a spot in Boston's bullpen.

Hector Velázquez RHP   Born: 11/26/88   Age: 31   Bats: R   Throws: R   Height: 6'0"   Weight: 180   Origin: International Free Agent, 2017

YEAR	TEAM	LVL	AGE	W	L	SV	G	GS	IP	H	HR	BB/9	K/9	K	GB%	BABIP	WHIP	ERA	DRA	WARP	MPH	FB%	WHF	CSP
2017	PAW	AAA	28	8	4	0	19	19	102	78	7	2.1	7.0	79	45%	.251	1.00	2.21	2.95	3.1				
2017	BOS	MLB	28	3	1	0	8	3	24²	21	4	2.6	6.9	19	44%	.258	1.14	2.92	4.88	0.1	92.2	68.9	8.6	51.2
2018	BOS	MLB	29	7	2	0	47	8	85	97	7	2.8	5.6	53	50%	.325	1.45	3.18	5.61	-0.5	93.6	59.2	9	46.7
2019	PAW	AAA	30	0	0	1	12	0	16¹	11	3	6.1	7.7	14	46%	.211	1.35	3.31	4.99	0.2				
2019	BOS	MLB	30	1	4	0	34	8	56¹	58	7	4.5	7.8	49	37%	.319	1.53	5.43	6.56	-0.6	94.0	50.7	10.8	44.8
2020	*BOS*	*MLB*	*31*	*3*	*3*	*0*	*34*	*6*	*55*	*58*	*8*	*3.6*	*7.1*	*44*	*44%*	*.297*	*1.45*	*4.88*	*4.93*	*0.3*	*92.8*	*56.2*	*9.6*	*46.8*

Comparables: Josh Tomlin, Vinnie Chulk, Jose Cabrera

Velázquez's best ability is availability, and in 2019 he was too often unable to deliver. Back-to-back back strains strained Velázquez's ability to serve as Boston's primary swingman, leading to a marked decrease in innings and appearances. But it wasn't just Velázquez's durability that faltered; his performance did, too. Career-worst marks in DRA, homer rate and walk rate led to Velázquez performing in the bottom 50 among all pitchers who threw at least 50 innings. He's cheap enough that the Red Sox could decide to keep him around for another go, but when your ceiling is "well, he's available," you're always in the DFA danger zone.

Marcus Walden RHP   Born: 09/13/88   Age: 31   Bats: R   Throws: R   Height: 6'0"   Weight: 195   Origin: Round 9, 2007 Draft (#295 overall)

YEAR	TEAM	LVL	AGE	W	L	SV	G	GS	IP	H	HR	BB/9	K/9	K	GB%	BABIP	WHIP	ERA	DRA	WARP	MPH	FB%	WHF	CSP
2017	PAW	AAA	28	10	6	0	29	15	105²	102	4	3.1	7.3	86	54%	.312	1.31	3.92	4.04	1.8				
2018	PAW	AAA	29	0	4	2	18	5	32²	44	2	4.7	6.6	24	53%	.365	1.87	4.96	6.66	-0.5				
2018	BOS	MLB	29	0	0	1	8	0	14²	14	0	1.8	8.6	14	58%	.341	1.16	3.68	3.18	0.3	96.1	45.1	12.7	49
2019	BOS	MLB	30	9	2	2	70	0	78	61	6	3.7	8.8	76	56%	.264	1.19	3.81	3.83	1.3	95.8	34.7	14.1	42.9
2020	*BOS*	*MLB*	*31*	*3*	*3*	*0*	*61*	*0*	*65*	*60*	*8*	*4.0*	*9.4*	*68*	*54%*	*.300*	*1.37*	*4.21*	*4.30*	*0.6*	*95.0*	*35.7*	*13.9*	*45.3*

Comparables: Murphy Smith, Drew Gagnon, Steven Wright

The Red Sox faced plenty of warranted criticism for deciding to replace Craig Kimbrel and Joe Kelly with a collection of largely anonymous dudes, but don't blame Walden for any shortcomings in that strategy. Only 12 pitchers in the big leagues threw more innings in relief, and of that dozen, only three—Liam Hendriks, Michael Lorenzen and Seth Lugo—had lower DRAs. Walden was also the fourth-best Red Sox reliever, as well as their third-most valuable fireman by WARP. He doesn't have closer stuff and isn't suited to serve in the type of super-reliever role that's currently en vogue, but Walden can eat some medium-leverage innings at an above league-average rate while making a below-market salary. For a team facing (self-imposed) payroll limitations, that's a bigger deal than it may seem.

Thad Ward RHP   Born: 01/16/97   Age: 23   Bats: R   Throws: R   Height: 6'3"   Weight: 182   Origin: Round 5, 2018 Draft (#160 overall)

YEAR	TEAM	LVL	AGE	W	L	SV	G	GS	IP	H	HR	BB/9	K/9	K	GB%	BABIP	WHIP	ERA	DRA	WARP	MPH	FB%	WHF	CSP
2018	LOW	A-	21	0	3	0	11	11	31	33	2	3.5	7.8	27	54%	.337	1.45	3.77	5.89	-0.2				
2019	GRN	A	22	5	2	0	13	13	72¹	51	2	3.1	10.8	87	48%	.280	1.05	1.99	3.25	1.7				
2019	SLM	A+	22	3	3	0	12	12	54	38	4	5.3	11.7	70	48%	.296	1.30	2.33	4.35	0.5				
2020	*BOS*	*MLB*	*23*	*2*	*2*	*0*	*33*	*0*	*35*	*35*	*5*	*4.2*	*9.3*	*36*	*45%*	*.309*	*1.47*	*4.99*	*4.96*	*0.1*				

Comparables: Parker Bridwell, Dinelson Lamet, Tyler Thornburg

Few systems in baseball were in as much need of a breakout arm as Boston, and Ward obliged. A fifth-round pick by the Sox in 2018, Ward dominated in his first full professional season between Greenville and Salem, including a stretch from May 14 through June 6 in which he did not allow an earned run. Ward has always had a funky, three-quarters delivery that makes his pitches hard to pick up, but the real reason for his ascension may be a new cutter, which Ward used to follow the time-honored South Carolina tradition of marginalizing lefties. Positive developments aside, it's worth pointing out that Ward was old for his levels and awfully wild, especially after he got the bump to High A. A test against more advanced hitters should tell us whether Ward is a flash-in-the-pan or on the path toward becoming Boston's first good homegrown starter in what feels like several decades.

Brandon Workman RHP   Born: 08/13/88   Age: 31   Bats: R   Throws: R   Height: 6'5"   Weight: 235   Origin: Round 2, 2010 Draft (#57 overall)

YEAR	TEAM	LVL	AGE	W	L	SV	G	GS	IP	H	HR	BB/9	K/9	K	GB%	BABIP	WHIP	ERA	DRA	WARP	MPH	FB%	WHF	CSP
2017	PAW	AAA	28	4	1	2	18	0	29	16	1	4.0	10.9	35	46%	.234	1.00	1.55	2.48	0.9				
2017	BOS	MLB	28	1	1	0	33	0	39²	37	7	2.5	8.4	37	44%	.283	1.21	3.18	3.68	0.7	94.9	51.4	11.3	45.9
2018	PAW	AAA	29	2	1	1	17	0	30	21	3	1.5	10.2	34	40%	.247	0.87	3.90	2.93	0.8				
2018	BOS	MLB	29	6	1	0	43	0	41¹	34	6	3.5	8.1	37	46%	.259	1.21	3.27	6.21	-0.6	93.3	38.9	11.1	48.1
2019	BOS	MLB	30	10	1	16	73	0	71²	29	1	5.7	13.1	104	53%	.209	1.03	1.88	2.86	1.9	94.8	33.6	13.6	41.2
2020	*BOS*	*MLB*	*31*	*3*	*3*	*34*	*61*	*0*	*65*	*54*	*8*	*4.4*	*11.5*	*83*	*49%*	*.300*	*1.32*	*3.63*	*3.78*	*1.0*	*93.6*	*37.7*	*12.5*	*44.4*

Comparables: Justin Grimm, Tyler Duffey, A.J. Griffin

Why choose between being lucky or good when you can be both? Workman was Boston's best reliever in 2019. An uptick in velocity and increased reliance on his nasty curveball led to a drastic increase in strikeouts; he earned whiffs at a rate commensurate with big-name relievers like Will Smith, Brad Hand and José Leclerc. Workman was durable, performed well in high-leverage situations and ended up leading the Sox in saves. It was quite the redemption story for a dude who got bumped from the 2018 World Series roster in favor of Drew Pomeranz, but it's fair to question how sustainable Workman's performance will prove to be. Among pitchers who threw at least 50 innings, he had the eighth-highest walk rate. He led all of baseball in suppressing homers, despite allowing them at an above average rate throughout his career. And he held opposing batters to a BABIP near the Mendoza Line. DRA tells us this wasn't all luck and that Workman can be a solid reliever moving forward. But if the Sox enter 2020 with him poised to serve as their best bullpen option, they'll be asking for trouble.

Steven Wright RHP   Born: 08/30/84   Age: 35   Bats: R   Throws: R   Height: 6'2"   Weight: 215   Origin: Round 2, 2006 Draft (#56 overall)

YEAR	TEAM	LVL	AGE	W	L	SV	G	GS	IP	H	HR	BB/9	K/9	K	GB%	BABIP	WHIP	ERA	DRA	WARP	MPH	FB%	WHF	CSP
2017	BOS	MLB	32	1	3	0	5	5	24	40	9	1.9	4.9	13	43%	.365	1.88	8.25	8.93	-0.9	87.6	8.2	7.2	48.3
2018	PAW	AAA	33	0	0	0	5	3	16²	20	0	2.2	4.9	9	48%	.333	1.44	3.78	5.91	-0.1				
2018	BOS	MLB	33	3	1	1	20	4	53²	41	5	4.4	7.0	42	54%	.243	1.25	2.68	2.72	1.5	88.0	7.5	10	52.3
2019	PAW	AAA	34	1	0	0	5	1	9²	6	1	2.8	3.7	4	53%	.172	0.93	1.86	3.66	0.2				
2019	BOS	MLB	34	0	1	0	6	0	6¹	11	3	5.7	7.1	5	35%	.400	2.37	8.53	7.78	-0.2	83.4	6.1	9.2	52.1
2020	BOS	MLB	35	2	2	0	33	0	35	36	8	2.9	5.3	21	43%	.261	1.36	5.10	5.28	0.0	86.3	7.4	9.1	50.3

Comparables: George Kontos, Jeff Manship, Fernando Salas

Wright has gone from an intriguing underdog story to an All-Star to an oft-injured arm who can't stay on the mound even when healthy—in the span of about 12 months, he was suspended for PED use and, more seriously, a violation of the league's domestic violence policy. Released by the Red Sox in October, Wright paired that career development with Tommy John surgery, which means the earliest he figures to see another major-league mound is 2021. Once he's healthy, perhaps some team will recall the effectiveness Wright displayed in a limited stint in 2018 and try to use him for some innings on the cheap. But overall, it's tough to find anything the 35-year-old has done on or off the field over the past three years that indicates he should be given additional chances.

LINEOUTS

Hitters

HITTER	POS	TEAM	LVL	AGE	PA	R	2B	3B	HR	RBI	BB	K	SB	CS	AVG/OBP/SLG	DRC+	VORP	BABIP	BRR	FRAA	WARP
Jonathan Arauz	SS	CCH	AA	20	119	12	3	2	3	13	10	19	1	1	.241/.311/.389	118	4.0	.267	-0.8	2B(14): -1.7, SS(7): 0.4	0.4
	SS	BCA	A+	20	354	41	19	0	8	42	30	69	5	4	.252/.322/.388	111	13.1	.296	-2.5	SS(62): -2.3, 3B(18): 0.8	1.3
Rusney Castillo	OF	PAW	AAA	31	493	63	25	1	17	64	25	63	5	9	.278/.321/.448	102	8.4	.291	-1.3	RF(82): 1.9, CF(25): 1.2	1.3
Juan Centeno	C	BOS	MLB	29	18	0	0	0	0	2	2	2	1	0	.133/.278/.133	90	0.6	.154	0.0	C(5): -1.1	-0.1
	C	PAW	AAA	29	301	27	15	0	4	40	24	47	2	0	.248/.321/.350	84	4.7	.284	0.1	C(80): -29.6	-1.6
C.J. Chatham	SS	PAW	AAA	24	91	11	5	0	2	10	4	21	0	0	.302/.330/.430	109	3.2	.375	0.3	SS(15): -0.6, 2B(5): -0.7	0.4
	SS	PME	AA	24	376	39	26	1	3	36	18	66	7	1	.297/.333/.403	126	18.1	.354	-2.2	SS(77): -1.4, 2B(7): 2.3	2.3
Nick Decker	OF	LOW	A-	19	197	23	10	5	6	25	21	59	4	5	.247/.328/.471	121	13.3	.333	1.7	RF(50): -5.1, CF(2): -0.2	0.4
Danny Diaz	3B	RSX	Rk	18	113	15	11	0	1	12	5	30	0	0	.210/.257/.343	70	-2.1	.280	-0.6	3B(21): -0.9, 1B(1): 0.0	-0.1
Tyler Esplin	OF	GRN	A	19	436	52	26	3	5	43	40	107	6	3	.253/.326/.375	111	8.6	.333	-2.1	RF(92): -3.7, CF(1): -0.2	0.6
Antoni Flores	SS	LOW	A-	18	208	14	4	1	0	12	25	59	1	3	.193/.293/.227	84	-2.5	.285	-1.9	SS(47): 4.8, 2B(6): -0.1	0.8
Gorkys Hernández	CF	PAW	AAA	31	504	75	14	3	16	53	62	146	20	6	.219/.319/.377	77	2.8	.285	1.9	CF(101): -4.9, RF(14): 0.7	0.1
	CF	BOS	MLB	31	57	5	1	2	0	2	5	14	1	0	.143/.218/.245	71	-0.7	.194	-0.2	RF(7): 0.9, LF(6): 0.1	0.0
Brandon Howlett	3B	GRN	A	19	465	48	23	1	8	35	56	144	1	5	.231/.341/.356	110	17.5	.337	-0.9	3B(105): -13.5	0.4
Tzu-Wei Lin	2B	BOS	MLB	25	22	3	2	0	0	1	2	6	1	1	.200/.273/.300	71	0.0	.286	0.0	2B(8): -0.3, SS(2): 0.0	0.0
	2B	PAW	AAA	25	250	30	11	1	4	22	21	58	6	2	.246/.308/.357	84	0.8	.311	1.5	SS(26): 4.6, 2B(15): 1.7	1.2
Nick Longhi	LF	LOU	AAA	23	424	51	28	3	12	51	30	102	0	1	.283/.336/.463	103	4.7	.354	1.9	1B(50): 1.1, LF(49): -1.9	0.9
Matthew Lugo	SS	RSX	Rk	18	157	19	5	1	1	12	15	36	3	0	.257/.342/.331	125	6.0	.340	1.0	SS(30): 1.7	1.2
Jhon Nunez	C	PME	AA	24	233	26	11	1	5	21	13	39	5	3	.280/.333/.412	116	14.6	.323	-0.3	C(62): -3.4, LF(1): -0.1	1.1
Josh Ockimey	1B	PAW	AAA	23	468	64	17	2	25	57	82	139	0	2	.204/.353/.459	113	10.1	.241	-3.4	1B(82): -3.5	0.6
Austin Rei	C	PME	AA	25	90	4	5	0	1	9	6	29	0	0	.157/.213/.253	40	-4.6	.226	-0.6	C(25): -0.2	-0.2
Marcus Wilson	OF	SLM	A+	22	167	26	12	1	8	29	18	47	4	3	.342/.413/.603	212	18.7	.452	-2.2	CF(25): -1.9, RF(14): 1.7	1.9
	OF	PME	AA	22	238	35	14	0	8	22	28	82	6	0	.223/.319/.408	101	7.2	.322	-1.5	RF(30): 3.9, CF(24): -4.9	0.3
	OF	WTN	AA	22	40	4	2	1	2	7	5	13	3	1	.235/.350/.529	121	3.1	.316	-0.7	CF(6): -0.1, RF(3): 0.3	0.2

Good news: **Jonathan Arauz** posted a career-best OPS in 2019. Bad news: It was .707. The glove is nice, though, and the world is always ready for another glove-first shortstop. ⊕ Forgotten outfielder **Rusney Castillo** continues to prove that he's too good for Triple-A, but too expensive for the majors. In exercising his player option for 2020, Castillo has ensured that he'll get $13.5 million, but also that he'll be spending another full season in Pawtucket. ⊕ Probably the only thing you need to know about career backup catcher **Juan Centeno** at this point is that the Red Sox didn't think he'd be an upgrade over Sandy León. ⊕ Future backup infielder **C.J. Chatham** has proven definitively in both Portland and Pawtucket that he can hit for decent averages and zero power. By his sixth major-league game, he'll have been compared to Brock Holt four thousand times. ⊕ 2018 second-round pick **Nick Decker** may only look like a potential fourth outfielder with pop, but as a cold-weather prep bat we can get away with projecting more for at least another five or six seasons. ⊕ Potential slugging third baseman **Danny Diaz** crushed the DSL but got crushed by the GCL, which means he's SOL if he wanted to appear on any top prospect lists this offseason. ⊕ **Jhonathan Diaz** signed for $1.5 million dollars as an international free agent. The teenage outfielder receives high marks for speed and defense with potential to add with the bat. ⊕ This is probably the first time you've heard of potential lefty slugger **Tyler Esplin**, but if he wasn't full of promise why would Boston have already named that big area right by the Charles River after him? ⊕ Promising teenage shortstop prospect **Antoni Flores** faced lots of older competition as an 18-year-old in the New York-Penn League. Even so, he was probably hoping to hit above the Mendoza Line. ⊕ It's unfortunate that as soon as **Gorkys Hernández** learned a new trick—hitting for power—baseball made it so that the rest of the world could easily follow suit. As such, Hernández remains more remarkable for his first name than for anything he can do on the diamond. ⊕ If third base prospect **Brandon Howlett** is going to insist on developing into a Three True Outcomes guy, he'd better increase the frequency with which he provides the best of the outcome trio. ⊕ In missing much of 2019 with a litany of injuries, speedy utility man **Tzu-Wei Lin** took his role as Brock Holt's understudy a bit too literally. ⊕ You could describe **Nick Longhi**'s seven years in the minors with a .736 OPS at unimportant defensive positions as a slow burn—or, you could say Longhi's playing days will soon journey into night. Either way. ⊕ He may have been Boston's second-round pick, but it's easy to argue that speedy shortstop prospect **Matthew Lugo** was the highest-upside hitter they popped in the 2019 draft. Red Sox fans can relax: he's not related to Julio. ⊕ **Jhon Nunez** is a small, athletic backstop with a good arm who should be thrilled if he has Juan Centeno's career. ⊕ Three True Outcomes lord **Josh Ockimey** keeps proving he can really hit for power and can't really do much else as he climbs the ladder. ⊕ **Austin Rei** (pronounced "Ray") wasn't in last year's book, when his PECOTA comparable was Petey Paramore. Of course, Paramore is also the name of a band signed to the Fueled by Ramen label. These facts are as loosely connected as the Red Sox will be to the playoff race if Rei gets significant burn. ⊕ Acquired for the low, low price of one Blake Swihart last April, **Marcus Wilson** made the 40-man roster this past offseason thanks to his speed and defense.

Pitchers

PITCHER	TEAM	LVL	AGE	W	L	SV	G	GS	IP	H	HR	BB/9	K/9	K	GB%	BABIP	WHIP	ERA	DRA	WARP	MPH	FB%	WHF	CSP
Yoan Aybar	GRN	A	21	1	3	0	40	0	51^2	34	1	7.0	11.7	67	53%	.266	1.43	4.88	4.37	0.3				
Kyle Hart	PME	AA	26	3	6	0	9	9	55^2	39	3	2.7	9.7	60	39%	.219	1.01	2.91	3.58	0.9				
	PAW	AAA	26	9	7	0	18	15	100^1	91	8	3.2	7.2	80	41%	.293	1.27	3.86	4.38	2.2				
Brian Johnson	PME	AA	28	0	1	0	3	2	6	11	1	4.5	10.5	7	44%	.455	2.33	10.50	7.91	-0.2				
	PAW	AAA	28	1	0	0	6	3	14^2	13	1	4.9	11.7	19	48%	.375	1.43	3.68	4.71	0.3				
	BOS	MLB	28	1	3	0	21	7	40^1	53	6	5.1	6.9	31	43%	.353	1.88	6.02	8.15	-1.1	91.7	38.2	9.1	44.2
Travis Lakins	PAW	AAA	25	3	4	6	40	1	45	46	4	4.6	8.4	42	42%	.323	1.53	4.60	5.26	0.4				
	BOS	MLB	25	0	1	0	16	3	23^1	23	1	3.9	6.9	18	48%	.306	1.41	3.86	6.06	-0.2	95.3	40	11.3	43.6
Chris Mazza	BIN	AA	29	0	2	0	4	4	23^2	26	0	3.0	8.0	21	51%	.356	1.44	3.42	5.80	-0.2				
	SYR	AAA	29	3	3	0	14	13	76	65	6	2.1	7.3	62	59%	.278	1.09	3.67	2.78	2.9				
	NYN	MLB	29	1	1	0	9	0	16^1	21	0	2.8	6.1	11	41%	.389	1.59	5.51	7.73	-0.4	93.6	50.7	8.5	46.3
Jenrry Mejia	LOW	A-	29	0	1	1	6	0	6^1	7	1	1.4	11.4	8	63%	.333	1.26	4.26	3.91	0.1				
	PAW	AAA	29	2	7	7	42	0	48	52	9	3.0	9.2	49	42%	.321	1.42	6.38	5.27	0.4				
Chris Murphy	LOW	A-	21	0	1	0	10	10	33^1	23	1	1.9	9.2	34	45%	.257	0.90	1.08	3.40	0.7				
Bobby Poyner	PAW	AAA	26	2	5	6	43	1	57^1	47	9	4.2	11.0	70	22%	.271	1.29	3.77	3.76	1.4				
	BOS	MLB	26	1	0	0	13	1	11^2	10	2	3.9	8.5	11	28%	.267	1.29	6.94	6.55	-0.1	91.3	65.8	12.4	47.9
Aldo Ramirez	LOW	A-	18	2	3	0	14	13	61^2	59	5	2.3	9.2	63	48%	.309	1.22	3.94	4.78	0.3				
Erasmo Ramírez	PAW	AAA	29	6	8	0	27	24	125^1	125	18	3.1	6.8	95	48%	.285	1.34	4.74	4.61	2.5				
	BOS	MLB	29	0	0	0	1	0	3	4	2	3.0	3.0	1	50%	.200	1.67	12.00	7.01	-0.1	93.0	53.7	9.8	47.4
Denyi Reyes	PME	AA	22	8	12	0	26	26	151^1	142	14	2.2	6.9	116	33%	.281	1.18	4.16	4.52	0.8				
Mike Shawaryn	PAW	AAA	24	1	2	0	26	14	89^2	76	13	4.9	7.6	76	43%	.264	1.39	4.52	4.40	1.9				
	BOS	MLB	24	0	0	0	14	0	20^1	26	5	5.8	12.8	29	32%	.412	1.92	9.74	6.94	-0.3	93.8	42.7	16.1	39.4
Ryan Weber	PAW	AAA	28	1	5	0	16	16	78	86	9	2.9	7.3	63	55%	.325	1.42	4.50	4.90	1.4				
	BOS	MLB	28	2	4	0	18	3	40^2	48	5	1.8	6.4	29	50%	.316	1.38	5.09	4.98	0.2	90.8	52.7	6.5	50.5
Ryan Zeferjahn	LOW	A-	21	0	2	0	12	12	22	24	2	4.9	12.7	31	40%	.415	1.64	4.50	6.45	-0.3				

Converted outfielder **Yoan Aybar** has relatively little idea where the ball is going when he releases it, but as an athletic lefty who can hit the mid-90s with his fastball, he'll be given plenty of time to figure it out. ⊕ Now that he's reached Pawtucket, it's time for 27-year-old potential LOOGY **Kyle Hart** to take a big sip out of his "I love getting pulled after just one important batter" mug and read about the upcoming rule changes... ⊕ Whether used as a starter or in relief, former first-rounder **Brian Johnson** was wholly ineffective even by his relatively modest standards. It's clear at this point he does not belong on a first-division club, which made him a perfect fit for the 2019 Red Sox. ⊕ Don't let his ERA fool you; righty **Travis Lakins** walked too many hitters, allowed too many hits and missed too few bats in his first MLB stint. In Boston bullpen terms, his results may scream "Marcus Walden," but his performance more suggests "Colten Brewer." ⊕ After bouncing around the minors for his entire career, **Chris Mazza** finally got the call-up to the big leagues and it did not go well. His stuff was mostly underwhelming, but his story (including a stopover in the Pacific Association of *The Only Rule Is It Has To Work* fame) was anything but. ⊕ We'll say this about **Jenrry Mejia**'s ill-fated comeback; if he's still taking PEDs, he should get his money back for the whole P and E parts. ⊕ A sixth-rounder who shares a name with 30 percent of the population of South Boston, **Chris Murphy** is left-handed enough to warrant some attention as a potential big league reliever. ⊕ Quad-A LOOGY **Bobby Poyner** continued to miss bats in Pawtucket, but his brief major-league stints have proven he's got about as much upside as penny stocks. ⊕ Mexican right-hander **Aldo Ramirez** might not love getting the standard "back-end starting pitcher prospect" tag, but if the (accessibly-priced) shoe fits... ⊕ **Erasmo Ramírez** kept his consecutive years appearing in the majors streak alive on April 16, when he allowed four earned runs in three innings against the Yankees. The rest is better left unsaid. ⊕ What if Dennys Reyes ate at Denny's less often? He might look something like righty **Denyi Reyes**, who makes up for what he lacks in velocity, upside and girth with impressive command and control. ⊕ Fire-hydrant-shaped right-hander **Michael Shawaryn** missed lots of bats in his first 20 major-league innings. He found lots of them too en route to surrendering more than an earned run per inning. ⊕ Once-promising sidewinder **Carson Smith** had one of the best 2019 seasons among all Red Sox relievers, as he was released by the team in mid-June while still recovering from labrum surgery. ⓧ There are lots of ways to say "the 2019 Red Sox had a mediocre bullpen," but none are quite so succinct as "**Ryan Weber** set a new career-high in innings pitched." ⓧ Boston's third-round pick in the 2019 draft, **Ryan Zeferjahn** is your typical hard-throwing righty with a good fastball and few other discernible skills. Let's hope he makes it to the bigs, because we need to hear Jerry Remy try to pronounce his name (Ze-fuh-jun?).

CHICAGO CUBS

Essay by Jordan Bastian

Player comments by Matt Snyder and BP staff

For more than a century, Cubs fans were conditioned to be fatalistic. Sure, there was the annual optimistic refrain of, "Wait 'til next year," but there was also an underlying pain that existed when those words were inevitably uttered each September or October.

At the foundation of this sentiment were a series of events that programmed the Cubs Fan DNA.

Maybe you don't believe that Babe Ruth *actually* called his shot at Wrigley Field in the 1932 World Series—historic accounts have rendered that a myth—but there it is, smack in the middle of Cubs lore. Ditto the legend of tavern owner Bill Sianis cursing the Cubs when his pet goat was not allowed in the ballpark during the 1945 Fall Classic. Cubs fans also had the black cat roaming in front of their team's dugout in September of 1969, when the club famously collapsed down the stretch; the ball that rolled through Leon Durham's legs in the '84 playoffs; and the ball that clanked off the glove of Brant Brown in September of '98. Oh, and the gut punch of them all: the Bartman Game in 2003, when Moisés Alou slammed his glove in frustration after a fan reached for the same, ill-fated foul ball. You know that story.

Back in '03, I was at Michigan State University working on a journalism degree. A Chicago kid, I still had fandom flowing through my veins in those days, and we watched Game 6 of the National League Championship Series at The Riv on M.A.C. Avenue. My friend reminded me, as Bartman was being escorted out of the ballpark, that there was still a Game 7 to be played.

No, I explained, that was the moment. It was over. The baseball gods had intervened. Every time it felt like the demons of 1908 were going to be exorcised, some moment or another would occur, prolonging the so-called curse.

Sixteen years later, I'm now a reporter chronicling the Cubs whose fandom has been stripped away in the name of objectivity. As a writer, however, you remain on the hunt for these moments—the fans do, too, although the sense of fatalism has mostly been subdued since the 2016 World Series victory. Rather, the moments that Cubs fans search for now are the ones that fuel the belief that this dynastic

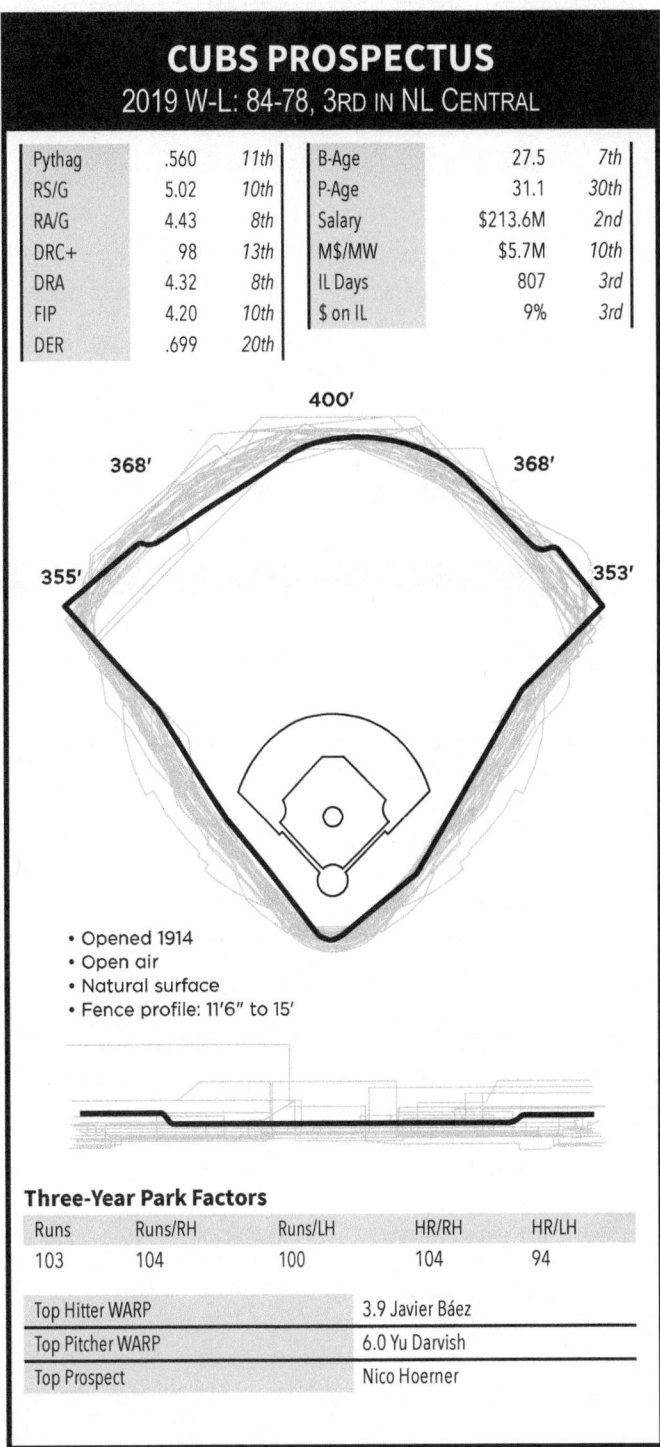

CUBS PROSPECTUS
2019 W-L: 84-78, 3RD IN NL CENTRAL

Pythag	.560	11th	B-Age		27.5	7th
RS/G	5.02	10th	P-Age		31.1	30th
RA/G	4.43	8th	Salary		$213.6M	2nd
DRC+	98	13th	M$/MW		$5.7M	10th
DRA	4.32	8th	IL Days		807	3rd
FIP	4.20	10th	$ on IL		9%	3rd
DER	.699	20th				

400'

368'   368'

355'   353'

- Opened 1914
- Open air
- Natural surface
- Fence profile: 11'6" to 15'

Three-Year Park Factors

Runs	Runs/RH	Runs/LH	HR/RH	HR/LH
103	104	100	104	94

Top Hitter WARP	3.9 Javier Báez
Top Pitcher WARP	6.0 Yu Darvish
Top Prospect	Nico Hoerner

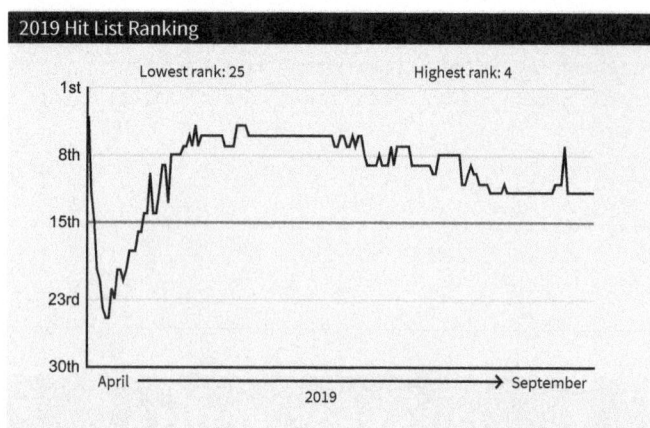

2019 Hit List Ranking
Lowest rank: 25   Highest rank: 4
1st
8th
15th
23rd
30th
April
2019
September

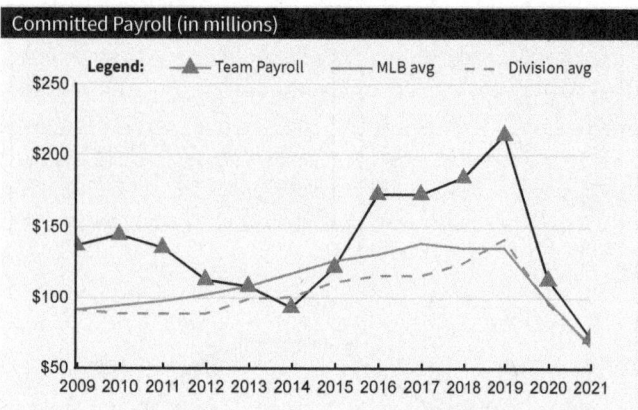

Committed Payroll (in millions)
Legend: —▲— Team Payroll —— MLB avg – – – Division avg
$250
$200
$150
$100
$50
2009 2010 2011 2012 2013 2014 2015 2016 2017 2018 2019 2020 2021

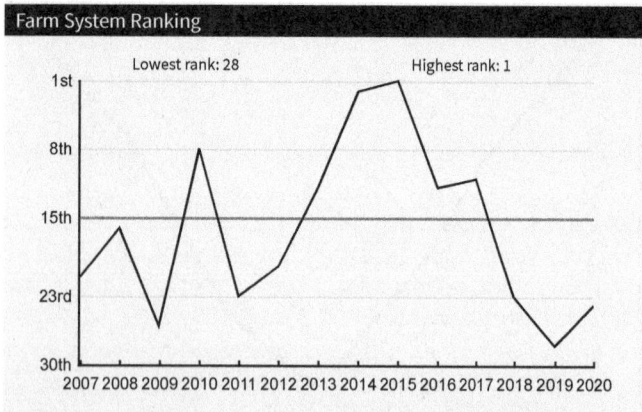

Farm System Ranking
Lowest rank: 28   Highest rank: 1
1st
8th
15th
23rd
30th
2007 2008 2009 2010 2011 2012 2013 2014 2015 2016 2017 2018 2019 2020

Personnel

President, Baseball Operations
Theo Epstein

Executive Vice President, General Manager
Jed Hoyer

Assistant General Manager
Randy Bush

Director, Pro Scouting and Baseball Operations
Jeff Greenberg

Senior Vice President, Player Personnel
Jason McLeod

Manager
David Ross

BP Alumni
Bryan Cole
Jeremy Greenhouse

locomotive is still very much roaring down the tracks. An example of this arrived last season at 5:49 p.m. CT on September 19 at Wrigley Field.

Four days after collapsing on the infield with a severely sprained ankle, first baseman Anthony Rizzo was in full uniform out in left field, going through some running drills. He had been in a walking boot a day earlier and needed the help of a medical scooter to move around the clubhouse the day before that. Now, with the St. Louis Cardinals in town and the Cubs' season in the balance, Rizzo was having his Willis Reed moment. Here's a brief timeline of events:

5:51 p.m.: Rizzo did some stutter steps. He zigged and zagged while jogging. Manager Joe Maddon watched and talked things over with the first baseman.

5:55 p.m.: The Cubs announce in the press box that the lineup has been changed. Rizzo was in as the leadoff man.

6:08 p.m.: The public address announcer reads the batting order to the Wrigley Field crowd, which roars upon the mention of "No. 44" at the top.

In the third inning, Rizzo launched a game-tying home run off St. Louis ace Jack Flaherty, who was in the midst of a historic second half. This was it. This was the moment. The flaws exposed all season were going to be erased through pure determination by this Cubs roster still chock-full of stars. That was the hope, anyway. It was not, ultimately, the reality.

Matt Carpenter delivered a game-deciding homer in the 10th inning that night and St. Louis dealt the Cubs a season-crushing four-game sweep. That was part of a nine-game losing streak in the final weeks, sending the Cubs from two back of the division lead to eight back and facing a long winter. The Cubs missed the playoffs for the first time in five years, giving away to a franchise-altering offseason.

Those fatalistic feelings, dormant for years, started permeating again through the fan base. This was supposed to be a dynasty complete with multiple World Series titles. What happened? That was one of the questions that Theo Epstein, the Cubs president of baseball operations, had to answer in the 2019 postmortem, one day after he announced that Maddon's contract would not be extended for 2020. "Looking back," Epstein said, "I had this belief that this group of players who won the World Series at 22 and 23 years old, many of them, were going to grow into an unstoppable set of players if we could continue to supplement them and show faith in them."

This is where it is important to note that Epstein's initial vision worked. He arrived to the Cubs ahead of the 2012 season and strategically stripped the franchise down to a base layer. As the major-league team piled up the losses, the Cubs' front office went about building its future core through the draft and trades. Financial might would help on the pitching front in due time.

When Kris Bryant (the No. 2 pick in the 2013 Draft) fired the baseball to Rizzo (acquired from the Padres in January of '12) for the final out of the '16 World Series, it was the embodiment of the new Cubs Way. Kyle Hendricks (acquired from the Rangers in '12) started Game 7. Jon Lester (signed to a six-year, $155 million free-agent contract before the '15 season) appeared in relief. Everything about that season validated Epstein and company's approach.

For one glorious season, it worked. At the same time, ownership was transforming Wrigley Field and the neighborhood surrounding the old ballpark. The team was also inching closer to creating its own regional network—another vision that will be realized in 2020 with the launch of Marquee Sports Network. The baseball budget kept climbing. The only thing missing from this well-oiled business machine in the time since that fateful October has been multiple trophies.

So, how did the Cubs get here? In part by chasing those titles. In the name of winning, Epstein and crew invested heavily in free-agent deals to supplement the core, and shipped away prospect capital to add impact-caliber pieces to the roster.

To wit, the current hole at second base might not feel so vacuous if Gleyber Torres (dealt in the Aroldis Chapman trade in '16) were still around. At least Chapman helped the Cubs win a title. The same is not true of José Quintana, who the Cubs acquired in exchange for Dylan Cease and Eloy Jiménez in a deal that fans have developed a growing discontent toward. Meanwhile, the large free-agent deals and the core's rising arbitration costs have strangled the budget, limiting the team's flexibility. And, as the rotation ages, the position-player focus of the past has resulted in a lack of homegrown arms to supplement and/or replace underachievers.

What's happening now for the Cubs perhaps should have taken place after the '18 campaign, when some of the issues were already surfacing. A year ago, though, the Cubs could look at all of the flaws and then chase it with a look at the win column. For all the cracks starting to form in the foundation, the Cubs still won 95 games. They could lean hard on that win total when responding to criticism, and keep expressing a firm faith in their group of players.

As an example, the Cubs' offense fell off a cliff in the second half of '18, hitting .249/.316/.389 overall. No question, Chicago should have expected positive regression there. But, the underlying areas of concern were the strikeout rate (22.6 percent), swinging-strike rate (11.9 percent), contact rate (74.9 percent) and ground-ball rate (48.6 percent). With little financial wiggle room, the Cubs' front office essentially stood pat in the offseason. The overall season slash line in '19 (.252/.331/.452) was much better than the second-half tailspin of the previous fall. But, those other areas remained problematic. Last year, the Cubs had a 23.6 percent strikeout rate, 12.3 percent swinging-strike rate, 73.9 percent contact rate and 45.8 percent ground-ball rate.

Along the same lines, the Cubs touted their National League-leading 3.35 bullpen ERA in the wake of the '18 season, but the ERA was not the issue. The group had an 11 percent walk rate (14th in the NL) and an average four-seam velocity of 94.4 mph, per Pitch Info (10th in the NL).

The bullpen was ball-in-play focused and reliant on stout defense. In '19, the Cubs' defense took a step back and the relief corps was a big issue before undergoing an in-season overhaul.

Maybe it was just a case of having too much faith in the aftermath of '18. Epstein found a more headline-grabbing way to sum it up in '19 by saying the organization fell into a "winner's trap" in the years after winning the World Series. What Epstein meant was that the decision-makers continued to focus on methods that worked in building the '16 team, when new strategies were probably necessary. "If I could do it over again," Epstein said, "as a leader, I'd try to find a way to be more objective and more critical and more open-minded to various different ways to do it. I think that's got us in trouble, if you look at the amount of resources that have gone out the door while trying to supplement this group."

At the start of this past offseason, Epstein said the challenge for his front office was to look at their operation like they did when they arrived ahead of the 2012 season. The time had come to do an assessment of all departments, finding things they would change if they were coming in and examining the franchise for the first time.

At the big-league level, the Cubs hired David Ross to be their new manager, with "accountability" serving as the buzzword for 2020. As Chicago's stars have matured, there has been a feeling behind the scenes that the players have become more individualized with their routines. Ross and his revamped coaching staff will try to foster more unity among the group.

The Cubs also altered the leadership landscape of their scouting and player development departments, taking steps to modernize the team's processes. Beyond some internal promotions—including the hiring of a director of pitching (Craig Breslow) and director of hitting (Justin Stone)—the Cubs made an external hire for their new vice president of scouting position, tabbing former Oakland Athletics executive Dan Kantrovitz for the role. The Cubs have to start planning for the next wave of core players. And, while they could come via trades, the organization improving in the draft is also going to be critical. Epstein lauded Kantrovitz's ability to blend traditional scouting with a model-driven approach to the draft.

The goal here is, essentially, to stop those fatalistic feelings from taking over again—and to get the Cubs back on track. That 2016 World Series triumph—even with 108 years of drought before it—feels further and further away for Cubs fans. Likewise, 2021 doesn't feel so far off anymore—that's when core players like Bryant, Rizzo, Javier Báez and Kyle Schwarber can file for free agency. It's also when Epstein's contract expires.

Undoubtedly, with so much potential change looming on the horizon, there will be moments throughout the 2020 season that reveal which direction the Cubs are headed.

"If you look at it," Epstein said at the end of the '19 season, "the five-year rebuild was just about perfect. It was probably one of the best in history, if not the best. And, why? It wasn't because it was a grand strategy or any new paradigm of how to run a baseball operation. It was because we performed at an extraordinarily high level. We hit on an incredible amount of deals and got impact players back in deals where we shouldn't have.

"We haven't performed at that level since then. So, that's an easy area of self-criticism, too. So you question, you ask, 'What are we doing differently to adjust our approaches a little bit?' But, stay aggressive and know that we're the right group to build the next Cubs championship team."

—Jordan Bastian is a Cubs beat reporter for MLB.com.

HITTERS

Jim Adduci OF/1B
Born: 05/15/85   Age: 35   Bats: L   Throws: L   Height: 6'2"   Weight: 210   Origin: Round 42, 2003 Draft (#1252 overall)

YEAR	TEAM	LVL	AGE	PA	R	2B	3B	HR	RBI	BB	K	SB	CS	AVG/OBP/SLG	DRC+	VORP	BABIP	BRR	FRAA	WARP
2017	TOL	AAA	32	239	32	13	1	4	27	20	59	10	3	.288/.343/.414	101	10.4	.372	2.8	RF(24): -0.8, LF(15): -1.1	0.7
2017	DET	MLB	32	93	14	6	2	1	10	10	27	1	1	.241/.323/.398	72	0.2	.345	-0.9	RF(26): 1.1	-0.1
2018	TOL	AAA	33	296	39	22	1	7	44	22	60	8	1	.309/.358/.474	140	18.8	.372	1.1	RF(45): -2.4, 1B(10): 0.8	1.6
2018	DET	MLB	33	185	19	8	2	3	21	6	45	1	0	.267/.290/.386	75	-2.7	.341	-0.6	1B(48): -4.7	-0.9
2019	IOW	AAA	34	386	59	23	0	12	58	21	89	9	4	.301/.338/.465	95	11.4	.366	-1.3	1B(87): -4.2, LF(7): 0.0	-0.2
2019	CHN	MLB	34	5	0	0	0	0	0	0	3	0	0	.000/.000/.000	66	0.0	.000	0.0	RF(1): 0.2	0.0
2020	CHN	MLB	35	251	24	9	1	6	26	15	73	4	1	.232/.279/.360	69	-2.7	.309	-0.6	1B -1, RF 0	-0.4

Comparables: Ángel Pagán, Paulo Orlando, Melvin Mora

Did you know that Adduci is a legacy player? His dad, also named Jim Adduci, appeared in 70 big-league games. Baseball-Reference says the younger Adduci, a marginally better veteran of more than 150 big-league games, is nicknamed "Deuce," which is more clever than it seems—short for both, "Adduci" and "Two," as in the second Jim Adduci. If the trend holds then Jim Adduci Three (Addu-tre?) will appear in about 300 big-league games, and be almost good enough to hold down a bench spot.

Albert Almora Jr. CF
Born: 04/16/94   Age: 26   Bats: R   Throws: R   Height: 6'2"   Weight: 190   Origin: Round 1, 2012 Draft (#6 overall)

YEAR	TEAM	LVL	AGE	PA	R	2B	3B	HR	RBI	BB	K	SB	CS	AVG/OBP/SLG	DRC+	VORP	BABIP	BRR	FRAA	WARP
2017	CHN	MLB	23	323	39	18	1	8	46	19	53	1	0	.298/.338/.445	93	16.2	.338	3.2	CF(104): -1.1, LF(1): 0.0	1.0
2018	CHN	MLB	24	479	62	24	1	5	41	24	83	1	3	.286/.323/.378	85	11.0	.337	-0.1	CF(137): 2.5, LF(2): -0.1	1.0
2019	IOW	AAA	25	54	6	3	1	0	2	4	7	2	1	.224/.283/.327	57	-2.0	.262	0.0	CF(12): 2.0	0.1
2019	CHN	MLB	25	363	41	11	1	12	32	16	62	2	1	.236/.271/.381	72	0.4	.255	-0.4	CF(125): 2.0	0.2
2020	CHN	MLB	26	189	17	9	1	4	19	9	34	2	1	.244/.284/.373	73	1.0	.279	0.4	CF 1	0.2

Comparables: Coco Crisp, Rocco Baldelli, Larry Herndon

Did Almora have dirt on Joe Maddon? That might be the most reasonable explanation for how often he played in 2019. The only hitters with more plate appearances and a worse DRC+ were Nicky Lopez and Brandon Drury—and those two played for tanking teams, not contenders. To Maddon's credit, he used Almora in a more fitting role late in the season—as a defensive sub—but even then we find his reputation with the glove to be overstated, the product of highlight-reel catches made toward the start of the 2018 season. Almora is good out there, but not so good as to be worth this much burn. The best way forward for him seems to be tightening his zone and prioritizing a contact-over-power approach. If he can do that, he just might make it to free agency.

──────────── ★ ★ ★ *2020 Top 101 Prospect* **#78** ★ ★ ★ ────────────

Miguel Amaya C
Born: 03/09/99   Age: 21   Bats: R   Throws: R   Height: 6'1"   Weight: 185   Origin: International Free Agent, 2015

YEAR	TEAM	LVL	AGE	PA	R	2B	3B	HR	RBI	BB	K	SB	CS	AVG/OBP/SLG	DRC+	VORP	BABIP	BRR	FRAA	WARP
2017	EUG	A-	18	244	21	14	1	3	26	11	49	1	0	.228/.266/.338	69	1.6	.274	-1.5	C(43): -0.5, 1B(8): -0.4	-0.1
2018	SBN	A	19	479	54	21	2	12	52	50	91	1	0	.256/.349/.403	119	31.5	.298	0.6	C(95): 2.5, 1B(9): -0.7	3.1
2019	MYR	A+	20	410	50	24	0	11	57	54	69	2	0	.235/.351/.402	124	20.9	.259	-3.6	C(90): 2.8	2.7
2020	CHN	MLB	21	251	24	12	0	7	27	18	57	1	0	.211/.278/.362	71	-1.9	.250	-0.5	C 0, 1B 0	-0.2

Comparables: Francisco Mejía, Victor Robles, Manuel Margot

One of the top catching prospects in baseball, Amaya improved his stock by making appearances in the Futures Game and the Arizona Fall League. On the regular circuit, he spent the season in High-A, where he cut down on his strikeouts and continued to get on base. There's some untapped thunder in his bat, too, even if his power is presently of the gap variety. Amaya will likely be tasked with Double-A in 2020. He's not too far away from the majors, where he could become the Cubs' best homegrown backstop since…Willson Contreras. Hey, usually that construct is more fun.

Javier Báez SS
Born: 12/01/92   Age: 27   Bats: R   Throws: R   Height: 6'0"   Weight: 190   Origin: Round 1, 2011 Draft (#9 overall)

YEAR	TEAM	LVL	AGE	PA	R	2B	3B	HR	RBI	BB	K	SB	CS	AVG/OBP/SLG	DRC+	VORP	BABIP	BRR	FRAA	WARP
2017	CHN	MLB	24	508	75	24	2	23	75	30	144	10	3	.273/.317/.480	94	30.1	.345	4.4	2B(80): -1.3, SS(73): -6.6	1.3
2018	CHN	MLB	25	645	101	40	9	34	111	29	167	21	9	.290/.326/.554	120	55.4	.347	3.2	2B(104): -0.6, SS(65): 1.3	4.6
2019	CHN	MLB	26	561	89	38	4	29	85	28	156	11	7	.281/.316/.531	102	28.3	.345	4.3	SS(129): 7.2, 3B(1): 0.1	3.9
2020	CHN	MLB	27	630	78	30	4	31	92	34	177	15	5	.262/.307/.483	105	32.1	.323	3.9	SS 1	3.4

Comparables: Jonathan Villar, Corey Seager, Trevor Story

While it remains possible that 2018 was the career year for Báez, his performance in 2019 should quell any concern that it was a total outlier. He was hitting .319/.359/.595 before a heel injury in May, and a thumb injury later ended his season. Any concerns about his BABIP being too high are misplaced, since he hits the ball hard and gets down the line quickly. He's a star, not a one-hit wonder. With that established, it is worth wondering if he can take yet another step and improve his approach at the dish. Báez is basically guessing up there; he'll take fastballs right down the middle for strike three (assuming he's getting something outside the zone), or flail helplessly at breaking stuff that bounces three feet outside. We're probably being too greedy by asking a player who does almost everything to do even more, but watch out if he develops a better concept of the zone—he almost won MVP without.

David Bote   INF   Born: 04/07/93   Age: 27   Bats: R   Throws: R   Height: 6'1"   Weight: 210   Origin: Round 18, 2012 Draft (#554 overall)

YEAR	TEAM	LVL	AGE	PA	R	2B	3B	HR	RBI	BB	K	SB	CS	AVG/OBP/SLG	DRC+	VORP	BABIP	BRR	FRAA	WARP
2017	TEN	AA	24	536	65	30	3	14	59	49	101	5	2	.272/.353/.438	125	30.0	.318	1.0	2B(107): 5.7, RF(9): 1.2	3.6
2018	IOW	AAA	25	263	34	10	2	13	41	26	63	3	1	.268/.342/.494	127	16.4	.313	-0.2	2B(38): -2.9, SS(15): 1.3	1.7
2018	CHN	MLB	25	210	23	9	2	6	33	19	60	3	4	.239/.319/.408	77	7.5	.314	-1.0	3B(56): 2.4, 2B(13): -0.6	0.2
2019	CHN	MLB	26	356	47	17	0	11	41	44	93	5	1	.257/.362/.422	97	11.9	.333	3.7	3B(67): -1.0, 2B(50): 2.0	1.6
2020	CHN	MLB	27	343	40	15	1	12	43	34	89	2	1	.245/.332/.424	102	12.9	.307	1.4	3B 0, 2B 0	1.4

Comparables: Evan Longoria, Willie Jones, Aaron Altherr

Bote will never, ever, ever, ever do anything on a baseball field more impressive than hitting a walkoff grand slam in 2018. Still, he's now established himself as a quality utility infielder, and better yet, as a multimillionaire. Bote nearly retired before the 2018 season, but has since signed a five-year deal worth a guaranteed $15 million. It's a bargain for the Cubs, of course. He's streaky, yet he gets on base and can play good defense at multiple infield positions. That's a handy player to have around.

Kris Bryant   3B/OF   Born: 01/04/92   Age: 28   Bats: R   Throws: R   Height: 6'5"   Weight: 230   Origin: Round 1, 2013 Draft (#2 overall)

YEAR	TEAM	LVL	AGE	PA	R	2B	3B	HR	RBI	BB	K	SB	CS	AVG/OBP/SLG	DRC+	VORP	BABIP	BRR	FRAA	WARP
2017	CHN	MLB	25	665	111	38	4	29	73	95	128	7	5	.295/.409/.537	137	69.6	.334	1.9	3B(144): -3.9, RF(7): 0.2	5.3
2018	CHN	MLB	26	457	59	28	3	13	52	48	107	2	4	.272/.374/.460	109	31.8	.342	-2.2	3B(86): 0.8, RF(15): 0.0	1.9
2019	CHN	MLB	27	634	108	35	1	31	77	74	145	4	0	.282/.382/.521	125	43.1	.331	2.2	3B(115): -14.3, RF(27): -2.2	2.7
2020	CHN	MLB	28	595	80	28	2	27	85	71	147	7	4	.264/.369/.486	127	36.0	.321	0.8	3B -2, RF 1	3.5

Comparables: Troy Glaus, Pedro Álvarez, Mark Reynolds

It seems like just yesterday that the Cubs were suppressing Bryant's service time. Now, he's nearly on his way out of town. He has two more years of team control remaining, yet over the winter rumors surfaced about his perceived availability through trade. It's a shame that the two sides are heading for a split, because a healthy Bryant remains one of the better players in the game. He can hit for average and power; he walks; and he can play a number of defensive positions. Someone is going to get a heck of a player; let's just hope they treat him as he deserves to be treated.

Victor Caratini   C   Born: 08/17/93   Age: 26   Bats: B   Throws: R   Height: 6'1"   Weight: 215   Origin: Round 2, 2013 Draft (#65 overall)

YEAR	TEAM	LVL	AGE	PA	R	2B	3B	HR	RBI	BB	K	SB	CS	AVG/OBP/SLG	DRC+	VORP	BABIP	BRR	FRAA	WARP
2017	IOW	AAA	23	326	50	27	3	10	61	27	48	1	0	.342/.393/.558	141	34.0	.375	1.4	C(50): -3.9, 1B(30): 0.7	2.6
2017	CHN	MLB	23	66	6	3	0	1	2	4	13	0	0	.254/.333/.356	76	0.5	.311	-0.4	C(12): -0.6, 1B(8): 0.1	-0.1
2018	IOW	AAA	24	137	13	7	0	4	22	18	25	0	0	.313/.409/.478	136	12.3	.364	-0.6	C(18): -2.2, 1B(12): 1.6	1.0
2018	CHN	MLB	24	200	21	7	0	2	21	12	42	0	0	.232/.293/.304	70	-1.3	.290	-0.6	C(37): -0.8, 1B(20): 0.5	0.0
2019	CHN	MLB	25	279	31	11	0	11	34	29	59	1	0	.266/.348/.447	103	13.3	.305	-1.4	C(59): 3.7, 1B(23): -0.5	1.5
2020	CHN	MLB	26	294	31	13	1	8	33	27	62	0	0	.247/.323/.391	92	6.7	.295	-0.8	C -1, 1B 0	0.6

Comparables: Travis Lee, Aaron Cunningham, Jesus Montero

The possessor of an 80-grade last name, Caratini broke through last season and proved himself to be a quality backup catcher. Everyone wants to be a starter, or at least a most-days option, but that just isn't in the cards for most players. Good backup catchers, however, have a long shelf life. There's plenty of money to be made in that role, too. If Caratini doubts us, he should just go ask his new manager. Be cheerful, be studious, be ready. Do all that consistently and you just might earn a full pension.

YEAR	TEAM	P. COUNT	FRM RUNS	BLK RUNS	THRW RUNS	TOT RUNS
2017	CHN	1182	-1.0	0.5	0.0	-0.6
2017	IOW	7230	-3.9	0.6	0.1	-3.6
2018	CHN	4929	-1.0	0.3	0.1	-1.1
2018	IOW	2828	-1.9	0.0	-0.1	-1.5
2019	CHN	6891	3.4	0.9	-0.1	4.6
2020	CHN	6327	-0.7	0.6	-0.1	-0.1

Nicholas Castellanos   RF   Born: 03/04/92   Age: 28   Bats: R   Throws: R   Height: 6'4"   Weight: 203   Origin: Round 1, 2010 Draft (#44 overall)

YEAR	TEAM	LVL	AGE	PA	R	2B	3B	HR	RBI	BB	K	SB	CS	AVG/OBP/SLG	DRC+	VORP	BABIP	BRR	FRAA	WARP
2017	DET	MLB	25	665	73	36	10	26	101	41	142	4	5	.272/.320/.490	110	23.2	.313	-2.6	3B(129): -7.7, RF(21): -6.0	1.4
2018	DET	MLB	26	678	88	46	5	23	89	49	151	2	1	.298/.354/.500	124	46.9	.361	3.4	RF(142): -2.8	3.5
2019	CHN	MLB	27	225	43	21	0	16	36	10	47	0	1	.321/.356/.646	141	17.7	.347	0.1	RF(48): 0.9, LF(11): -0.6	1.8
2019	DET	MLB	27	439	57	37	3	11	37	31	96	2	1	.273/.328/.462	105	12.6	.332	-1.7	RF(89): 0.9	1.1
2020	CHN	MLB	28	600	73	36	4	28	88	40	134	3	2	.268/.321/.496	112	12.1	.307	0.1	RF -1, 3B -1	2.9

Comparables: Jim Presley, Felipe Lopez, Butch Hobson

Figuring out the root of Castellanos' breakout with the Cubs is harder than it appears. He didn't hit the ball in the air more often, nor did he pull it more frequently. He didn't show a greater feel for contact, or demonstrably improve his strike-zone judgement, either. What Castellanos did do was get away from cavernous Comerica Park and a poorly performing team. How much either of those factors, and especially the second one, should be held against him is up to the jury.

Willson Contreras C   Born: 05/13/92   Age: 28   Bats: R   Throws: R   Height: 6'1"   Weight: 210   Origin: International Free Agent, 2009

YEAR	TEAM	LVL	AGE	PA	R	2B	3B	HR	RBI	BB	K	SB	CS	AVG/OBP/SLG	DRC+	VORP	BABIP	BRR	FRAA	WARP
2017	CHN	MLB	25	428	50	21	0	21	74	45	98	5	4	.276/.356/.499	116	34.6	.319	-3.9	C(108): 0.7, 1B(5): 0.0	2.6
2018	CHN	MLB	26	544	50	27	5	10	54	53	121	4	1	.249/.339/.390	90	27.5	.313	0.6	C(133): -14.6, LF(5): -0.8	0.5
2019	CHN	MLB	27	409	57	18	2	24	64	38	102	1	2	.272/.355/.533	110	26.7	.314	-1.9	C(99): -8.7, 1B(2): 0.0	1.7
2020	CHN	MLB	28	497	62	23	2	21	69	48	122	4	2	.260/.345/.468	115	31.9	.313	-1.4	C -2	3.1

Comparables: Rick Wilkins, Stan Lopata, Alex Avila

YEAR	TEAM	P. COUNT	FRM RUNS	BLK RUNS	THRW RUNS	TOT RUNS
2017	CHN	14005	-2.8	0.6	-1.1	-1.1
2018	CHN	18508	-17.8	1.9	0.4	-15.0
2019	CHN	13897	-9.4	0.0	-0.3	-9.7
2020	CHN	19618	-4.6	1.1	-0.4	-3.9

We're at the point with Contreras where it's acceptable to believe his body is fed up. In 2017, he missed most of August and some of September due to a hamstring injury; in 2019, he missed most of August and some of September due to a hamstring injury. (Sense a pattern?) There's a chicken-or-egg situation to behold here: does Contreras seems to break down because of his body, or because of how Joe Maddon deploys him? After all, other teams seem to be shying away from the workhorse catcher model, with Contreras ranking sixth in appearances since 2017 despite the aforementioned injuries. Whatever the case, Contreras has a cannon behind the plate and is an elite bat for his position. Even so, his shaky framing and injury history are concerns that will continue to linger—and could, in due time—force him out of the squat and to a more forgiving defensive home.

★ ★ ★ *2020 Top 101 Prospect* **#92** ★ ★ ★

Brennen Davis OF   Born: 11/02/99   Age: 20   Bats: R   Throws: R   Height: 6'4"   Weight: 175   Origin: Round 2, 2018 Draft (#62 overall)

YEAR	TEAM	LVL	AGE	PA	R	2B	3B	HR	RBI	BB	K	SB	CS	AVG/OBP/SLG	DRC+	VORP	BABIP	BRR	FRAA	WARP
2018	CUT	RK	18	72	9	2	0	0	3	10	12	6	1	.298/.431/.333	156	4.4	.370	0.0	CF(10): 0.6, RF(4): -0.6	0.5
2019	SBN	A	19	204	33	9	3	8	30	18	38	4	1	.305/.381/.525	155	19.9	.346	-0.6	LF(23): -1.2, CF(23): -2.1	1.4
2020	CHN	MLB	20	251	27	11	1	8	30	19	64	5	1	.245/.315/.409	92	5.6	.306	-0.1	CF 0, LF 0	0.6

Comparables: Trent Grisham, Trayce Thompson, Abraham Almonte

Since being taken in the second round in 2018, Davis has added at least 20 pounds of bulk to his lanky frame and has made some tweaks to his swing. The result was an excellent 50-game stint with Low-A South Bend. He'll surely begin 2020 with High-A Myrtle Beach in his age-20 season, and while the Cubs haven't had much success in drafting past the first round in recent years, he's one to monitor. He's also the son of former NBA player Reggie Theus. Get used to hearing about that.

Taylor Davis C   Born: 11/28/89   Age: 30   Bats: R   Throws: R   Height: 5'10"   Weight: 200   Origin: Round 49, 2008 Draft (#1456 overall)

YEAR	TEAM	LVL	AGE	PA	R	2B	3B	HR	RBI	BB	K	SB	CS	AVG/OBP/SLG	DRC+	VORP	BABIP	BRR	FRAA	WARP
2017	IOW	AAA	27	406	41	27	1	6	62	37	45	0	3	.297/.357/.429	109	19.5	.318	-2.0	C(59): 11.9, 1B(26): -1.3	2.8
2017	CHN	MLB	27	13	1	1	0	0	1	0	4	0	0	.231/.231/.308	68	-0.8	.333	-0.2	3B(2): 0.0, 1B(2): 0.0	0.0
2018	IOW	AAA	28	409	38	18	0	4	41	40	57	0	2	.275/.348/.360	105	13.8	.315	-2.7	C(67): 8.1, 1B(24): -1.3	2.3
2018	CHN	MLB	28	6	0	0	0	0	2	0	1	0	0	.400/.333/.400	90	0.5	.400	0.0	C(3): 0.1, 1B(1): 0.0	0.0
2019	IOW	AAA	29	241	21	4	0	5	23	31	38	0	0	.235/.338/.328	82	1.7	.265	-2.4	C(51): 3.0, 1B(6): 1.1	0.8
2019	CHN	MLB	29	20	2	0	0	1	4	2	4	0	0	.167/.250/.333	80	0.7	.154	0.1	C(6): -0.4, 1B(1): 0.0	0.1
2020	CHN	MLB	30	251	22	10	0	4	23	22	48	0	0	.222/.293/.327	68	-2.8	.265	-0.6	C 1, 1B 0	-0.3

Comparables: David Freitas, Jason Jaramillo, Manny Piña

Davis seemed destined to be remembered as the random minor-league backstop whose career-defining moment involved him staring at the camera a lot. We're delighted to report that changed in 2019, when he delivered an early-season grand slam to tie a contest against the Cardinals. The Cubs would then go on to win that game. We have to imagine Davis felt pretty good afterward. It'll have to last him, because he's probably not going to find himself on the glorious side of many more big-league moments.

YEAR	TEAM	P. COUNT	FRM RUNS	BLK RUNS	THRW RUNS	TOT RUNS
2017	CHN	70	0.0	0.1	0.0	1.0
2017	IOW	8301	12.7	0.0	-0.9	12.4
2018	CHN	51	0.0	0.0	0.0	1.5
2018	IOW	9120	9.8	0.3	-0.6	10.1
2019	CHN	702	0.5	-0.7	-0.1	-0.4
2019	IOW	7225	4.2	0.1	-0.8	3.5
2020	CHN	6850	2.6	-1.4	-0.3	0.9

Daniel Descalso 2B   Born: 10/19/86   Age: 33   Bats: L   Throws: R   Height: 5'10"   Weight: 190   Origin: Round 3, 2007 Draft (#112 overall)

YEAR	TEAM	LVL	AGE	PA	R	2B	3B	HR	RBI	BB	K	SB	CS	AVG/OBP/SLG	DRC+	VORP	BABIP	BRR	FRAA	WARP
2017	ARI	MLB	30	398	47	16	5	10	51	48	89	4	0	.233/.332/.395	96	5.5	.283	-3.2	2B(45): 0.9, LF(36): -4.8	0.1
2018	ARI	MLB	31	423	54	22	4	13	57	64	110	0	1	.238/.353/.436	106	23.4	.300	-0.7	2B(52): 3.2, 3B(37): -0.8	1.8
2019	IOW	AAA	32	33	5	0	0	2	4	5	8	0	0	.148/.303/.370	74	-1.9	.118	-0.3	2B(5): 0.0, 3B(4): -0.6	-0.1
2019	CHN	MLB	32	194	20	5	1	2	15	23	57	2	1	.173/.271/.250	59	-4.0	.245	-0.5	2B(45): 2.1, 3B(3): -0.1	-0.2
2020	CHN	MLB	33	238	24	10	2	5	24	29	66	2	1	.213/.314/.353	79	1.1	.285	-0.8	2B 2, 3B -1	0.2

Comparables: Tony Phillips, Stephen Drew, Jose Valentin

Descalso had the makings of a sneaky good signing. He'd proved to be a decent hitter against right-handed pitching in recent seasons, and his defensive versatility made him ideal for a Cubs team that likes its protean actors. Yet for whatever reason—and an early-season ankle injury probably deserves some blame—he was one of the worst position players in baseball over the course of the year. He still walked, but he struck out more often and when he made contact he hit the ball softer and at a lower angle than the season prior. That, plus him celebrating his 33rd birthday in October, makes for a bad combination. We're betting against the Cubs picking up their club option for the 2021 season.

Robel Garcia 2B Born: 03/28/93 Age: 27 Bats: B Throws: R Height: 6'0" Weight: 168 Origin: International Free Agent, 2010

YEAR	TEAM	LVL	AGE	PA	R	2B	3B	HR	RBI	BB	K	SB	CS	AVG/OBP/SLG	DRC+	VORP	BABIP	BRR	FRAA	WARP
2019	TEN	AA	26	92	12	5	0	6	26	12	22	1	1	.295/.391/.590	172	10.5	.333	-0.7	3B(18): 0.4, 2B(4): 0.6	1.1
2019	IOW	AAA	26	296	51	12	2	21	52	30	98	3	3	.281/.361/.585	125	26.7	.364	2.8	2B(29): 0.8, LF(21): 2.9	2.1
2019	CHN	MLB	26	80	8	2	2	5	11	7	35	0	0	.208/.275/.500	71	-0.5	.303	-0.4	2B(18): -1.0, LF(5): -0.2	-0.2
2020	CHN	MLB	27	70	7	3	0	3	8	6	26	1	1	.215/.287/.392	80	0.4	.315	-0.1	2B 0, LF 0	0.1

Comparables: Steven Souza Jr., Travis d'Arnaud, Drew Robinson

Prior to last season, Garcia had never played above Low-A in the minors. He wasn't even in organized, professional baseball from 2014-18. Rather, he had been playing in Italy, as part of the national team. A Cubs scout noticed Garcia's raw power during a spring-training scrimmage against the A's, and that was enough to land him in the system. He tore through the minors en route to the majors, where he continued to showcase a swing-at-all-costs approach that will likely limit him to up-and-down duty. He has a good story though.

Carlos González OF Born: 10/17/85 Age: 34 Bats: L Throws: L Height: 6'1" Weight: 220 Origin: International Free Agent, 2002

YEAR	TEAM	LVL	AGE	PA	R	2B	3B	HR	RBI	BB	K	SB	CS	AVG/OBP/SLG	DRC+	VORP	BABIP	BRR	FRAA	WARP
2017	COL	MLB	31	534	72	34	0	14	57	56	119	3	0	.262/.339/.423	87	9.5	.318	1.1	RF(125): -5.0	-0.1
2018	COL	MLB	32	504	71	32	4	16	64	37	113	5	2	.276/.329/.467	99	18.6	.332	4.0	RF(117): 7.7	2.3
2019	COH	AAA	33	29	1	1	0	1	3	6	5	0	0	.348/.483/.522	120	2.3	.412	-0.2	RF(5): 0.8, LF(1): 0.2	0.2
2019	CHN	MLB	33	49	8	2	0	1	3	8	19	0	0	.175/.306/.300	59	-1.7	.286	-0.2	RF(13): -1.1, LF(4): -0.3	-0.3
2019	CLE	MLB	33	117	13	1	0	2	7	10	33	0	1	.210/.282/.276	69	-1.7	.282	2.2	LF(16): 2.4, RF(4): -0.1	0.3
2020	CHN	MLB	34	251	27	12	1	9	31	22	70	1	1	.245/.314/.416	91	6.6	.316	1.3	RF 0, LF 1	0.7

Comparables: Geoff Jenkins, Al Martin, Jim Rice

The night comes for us all—even three-time All Stars with pretty swings. González lasted only 30 games with a Cleveland team desperate for outfield help, and didn't get even that many appearances with the Cubs. If this is the end, pretend he went down swinging like a titan—not on strikes against Bryse Wilson.

Ian Happ UT Born: 08/12/94 Age: 25 Bats: B Throws: R Height: 6'0" Weight: 205 Origin: Round 1, 2015 Draft (#9 overall)

YEAR	TEAM	LVL	AGE	PA	R	2B	3B	HR	RBI	BB	K	SB	CS	AVG/OBP/SLG	DRC+	VORP	BABIP	BRR	FRAA	WARP
2017	IOW	AAA	22	116	21	6	0	9	25	11	27	2	1	.298/.362/.615	139	13.8	.319	0.0	2B(16): 1.2, CF(6): 1.0	1.2
2017	CHN	MLB	22	413	62	17	3	24	68	39	129	8	4	.253/.328/.514	106	25.5	.316	3.1	CF(54): 0.7, 2B(44): 0.1	1.5
2018	CHN	MLB	23	462	56	19	2	15	44	70	167	8	4	.233/.353/.408	88	23.5	.362	2.0	CF(63): -7.9, LF(59): -2.5	-0.1
2019	IOW	AAA	24	429	66	18	1	16	53	65	113	9	2	.242/.364/.432	99	30.1	.307	1.2	CF(79): -4.0, 2B(20): 3.1	1.5
2019	CHN	MLB	24	156	25	7	1	11	30	15	39	2	0	.264/.333/.564	113	7.6	.286	1.7	LF(15): -0.4, 2B(13): -0.9	1.0
2020	CHN	MLB	25	539	63	23	2	22	69	61	166	8	3	.228/.319/.421	98	20.5	.302	3.0	CF -4, LF -1	1.6

Comparables: Oswaldo Arcia, Yoán Moncada, Brett Jackson

Happ was surprisingly demoted to the minors prior to the start of the season and languished in Triple-A until July 26. The New Happ resembled the old one, albeit with some tweaks. He posted the lowest strikeout percentage of his career (granted, 25 percent isn't good, but it was 36.1 percent the year prior) while posting the highest ISO of his career. If those tweaks are sustainable—for the most part, anyway—Happ will again prove to be a valuable big-league player. If he goes back to fanning nearly 40 percent of the time, then it's probably time to start the egg timer on his big-league career.

Jason Heyward OF Born: 08/09/89 Age: 30 Bats: L Throws: L Height: 6'5" Weight: 240 Origin: Round 1, 2007 Draft (#14 overall)

YEAR	TEAM	LVL	AGE	PA	R	2B	3B	HR	RBI	BB	K	SB	CS	AVG/OBP/SLG	DRC+	VORP	BABIP	BRR	FRAA	WARP
2017	CHN	MLB	27	481	59	15	4	11	59	41	67	4	4	.259/.326/.389	86	9.0	.284	1.9	RF(120): 10.0, CF(13): 1.0	1.6
2018	CHN	MLB	28	489	67	23	4	8	57	42	60	1	1	.270/.335/.395	94	16.4	.297	3.0	RF(118): 11.5, CF(25): -2.7	2.0
2019	CHN	MLB	29	589	78	20	4	21	62	68	110	8	3	.251/.343/.429	104	21.4	.281	-0.4	RF(105): -11.3, CF(84): -1.5	0.8
2020	CHN	MLB	30	595	64	26	3	15	65	63	107	10	4	.251/.335/.398	96	12.5	.289	1.7	RF 2, CF -1	1.5

Comparables: Travis Buck, Tom Brunansky, Mike Marshall

We're not saying Heyward homering 21 times is definitive proof that the ball was juiced, but it does make for some compelling evidence. We're kidding—sort of. Heyward is a big, strong lad who has always had the potential to offer more power than he has. He made some adjustments to his swing, and that, plus the altered ball and a willingness to trade contact for power, led to him nearly doubling the amount of home runs he'd hit in his previous seasons in Chicago. Now halfway through his contract, he's essentially a league-average player. There are worse fates.

★ ★ ★ *2020 Top 101 Prospect* **#41** ★ ★ ★

Nico Hoerner SS Born: 05/13/97 Age: 23 Bats: R Throws: R Height: 5'11" Weight: 200 Origin: Round 1, 2018 Draft (#24 overall)

YEAR	TEAM	LVL	AGE	PA	R	2B	3B	HR	RBI	BB	K	SB	CS	AVG/OBP/SLG	DRC+	VORP	BABIP	BRR	FRAA	WARP
2018	EUG	A-	21	28	6	0	1	1	2	5	3	4	1	.318/.464/.545	170	4.1	.333	-0.5	SS(5): -0.4	0.2
2019	TEN	AA	22	294	37	16	3	3	22	21	31	8	4	.284/.344/.399	104	16.5	.311	1.6	SS(44): -2.6, 2B(15): 0.5	1.5
2019	CHN	MLB	22	82	13	1	1	3	17	3	11	0	0	.282/.305/.436	95	3.3	.292	0.3	SS(17): 0.6, CF(1): -0.1	0.4
2020	CHN	MLB	23	420	42	19	3	10	46	24	64	7	3	.260/.310/.403	89	10.5	.287	0.0	2B 3, SS 0	1.4

Comparables: Andrelton Simmons, Willi Castro, Milt Bolling

Hoerner was unexpectedly thrown into the pennant race in September due to injuries to all three of the Cubs ahead of him on the shortstop depth chart. He hit the ground running before tapering off by swinging at everything without hitting much hard. There's a decent chance Hoerner, who is well-regarded as a diamond rat, is going to spend the bulk of the next six seasons as Chicago's second baseman. There is some risk in his game, however, as he's highly dependent on hitting for average. If his hit tool doesn't play above average, he might have to settle for being an extra infielder.

Tony Kemp UT Born: 10/31/91 Age: 28 Bats: L Throws: R Height: 5'6" Weight: 165 Origin: Round 5, 2013 Draft (#137 overall)

YEAR	TEAM	LVL	AGE	PA	R	2B	3B	HR	RBI	BB	K	SB	CS	AVG/OBP/SLG	DRC+	VORP	BABIP	BRR	FRAA	WARP
2017	FRE	AAA	25	554	95	23	9	10	62	35	43	24	7	.329/.375/.470	112	40.4	.344	0.4	2B(97): -10.2, CF(10): -0.2	1.4
2017	HOU	MLB	25	39	6	1	0	0	4	1	5	1	0	.216/.256/.243	91	-1.7	.250	0.9	LF(10): -0.4, CF(4): -0.2	0.1
2018	FRE	AAA	26	183	33	6	5	0	19	19	15	13	2	.335/.407/.435	110	14.6	.367	3.5	2B(25): -0.5, CF(14): -1.4	1.0
2018	HOU	MLB	26	295	37	15	0	6	30	32	44	9	3	.263/.351/.392	105	9.4	.296	-0.5	LF(61): -2.8, CF(32): 0.3	0.7
2019	HOU	MLB	27	186	23	6	2	7	17	16	29	4	3	.227/.308/.417	100	5.7	.233	-1.1	2B(29): -0.9, LF(14): 0.7	0.4
2019	CHN	MLB	27	93	8	3	2	1	12	7	18	0	1	.183/.258/.305	67	-1.2	.215	0.8	2B(14): 0.0, LF(6): 0.5	0.0
2020	CHN	MLB	28	168	16	7	1	3	16	15	29	5	2	.232/.308/.363	79	1.6	.268	0.0	CF 0, 2B 0	0.1

Comparables: Johnny Giavotella, Adam Frazier, Jemile Weeks

Kemp is, at best, a handy end-of-bench utility type. We can all agree to that, and to him authoring one of the strangest sequences of the season in late September. If you missed it, he appeared to have struck out against Giovanny Gallegos…except Gallegos had been called for a balk, voiding the pitch result. On the next pitch—yes, the very next one—Kemp hit a go-ahead home run. We can't remember anything like it happening, which is to say, baseball is a cool game.

Jonathan Lucroy C Born: 06/13/86 Age: 34 Bats: R Throws: R Height: 6'0" Weight: 200 Origin: Round 3, 2007 Draft (#101 overall)

YEAR	TEAM	LVL	AGE	PA	R	2B	3B	HR	RBI	BB	K	SB	CS	AVG/OBP/SLG	DRC+	VORP	BABIP	BRR	FRAA	WARP
2017	TEX	MLB	31	306	27	15	0	4	27	19	32	1	0	.242/.297/.338	95	0.1	.259	1.0	C(66): -0.7, 1B(1): 0.0	1.2
2017	COL	MLB	31	175	18	6	3	2	13	27	19	0	0	.310/.429/.437	93	13.4	.341	-0.2	C(44): 0.6	0.8
2018	OAK	MLB	32	454	41	21	1	4	51	29	65	0	0	.241/.291/.325	82	2.2	.273	-2.5	C(125): -9.7	0.0
2019	CHN	MLB	33	60	2	2	0	1	6	6	12	0	0	.189/.283/.283	65	0.3	.225	-0.5	C(20): 0.4, 1B(4): 0.0	0.0
2019	LAA	MLB	33	268	28	8	1	7	30	21	39	0	0	.242/.310/.371	88	9.5	.259	-2.5		-0.2
2020	CHN	MLB	34	251	25	11	1	6	26	22	42	1	0	.242/.315/.375	85	2.3	.274	-0.7	C -7, 1B 0	-0.5

Comparables: Don Slaught, Damon Berryhill, Brian Schneider

It's remarkable how quickly things fell apart for Lucroy. He was the best hitting catcher in baseball in 2014, and even finished fourth in NL MVP voting due to his contributions at the dish and behind it. In 2016, he was a hot commodity at the trade deadline for the same reasons. And, in the years since? His bat has been downright offensive as he's lost power and no longer is a big enough threat to draw walks. Lucroy keeps cashing checks due to a defensive reputation that our metrics suggest he no longer merits, and he figures to hang around for at least a couple more seasons as a backup. But Lord, it appears his days as a meaningful contributor are here, and far sooner than expected.

YEAR	TEAM	P. COUNT	FRM RUNS	BLK RUNS	THRW RUNS	TOT RUNS
2017	TEX	9640	-11.1	-1.2	0.6	-12.2
2017	COL	5958	-6.8	-1.8	0.1	-8.8
2018	OAK	16900	-3.7	-3.7	0.3	-7.3
2019	LAA	9556	-3.1	-5.5	0.4	-8.4
2019	CHN	2272	-0.7	0.0	-0.2	-1.0
2020	CHN	12446	-4.9	-2.0	0.4	-6.5

Hernán Pérez UT Born: 03/26/91 Age: 29 Bats: R Throws: R Height: 6'1" Weight: 215 Origin: International Free Agent, 2007

YEAR	TEAM	LVL	AGE	PA	R	2B	3B	HR	RBI	BB	K	SB	CS	AVG/OBP/SLG	DRC+	VORP	BABIP	BRR	FRAA	WARP
2017	MIL	MLB	26	458	47	19	3	14	51	20	79	13	4	.259/.289/.414	83	9.0	.286	2.4	LF(53): 2.5, 3B(31): 3.4	1.0
2018	MIL	MLB	27	334	36	11	2	9	29	17	71	11	3	.253/.290/.386	92	10.0	.300	0.6	2B(51): -0.9, RF(27): 0.4	0.7
2019	SAN	AAA	28	121	18	10	0	5	19	14	23	6	0	.290/.372/.523	127	8.8	.329	0.8	1B(9): 1.0, 2B(8): -0.3	0.8
2019	MIL	MLB	28	246	29	11	0	8	18	11	66	5	1	.228/.262/.379	69	-0.9	.283	-1.7	2B(45): 3.4, SS(21): -1.9	0.1
2020	CHN	MLB	29	251	25	11	1	7	28	13	63	9	3	.235/.276/.382	71	-1.0	.288	0.2	2B 0, LF 0	-0.1

Comparables: Brandon Phillips, Asdrúbal Cabrera, Scooter Gennett

Positional versatility can carry you only so far, as Pérez learned after a dismal 2019 season that saw him outrighted off Milwaukee's 40-man roster at the conclusion of the campaign. His versatility was enough to carry him as far as it can carry anyone, though. Over his career, Pérez has at least 25 appearances at every position but pitcher and catcher (and he does have seven career pitching appearances). Alas, he has a woeful approach and shouldn't be regarded as anything more than an end-of-the-bench option.

Anthony Rizzo 1B Born: 08/08/89 Age: 30 Bats: L Throws: L Height: 6'3" Weight: 240 Origin: Round 6, 2007 Draft (#204 overall)

YEAR	TEAM	LVL	AGE	PA	R	2B	3B	HR	RBI	BB	K	SB	CS	AVG/OBP/SLG	DRC+	VORP	BABIP	BRR	FRAA	WARP
2017	CHN	MLB	27	691	99	32	3	32	109	91	90	10	4	.273/.392/.507	126	36.8	.273	-3.2	1B(157): 14.4, 2B(10): -0.3	4.3
2018	CHN	MLB	28	665	74	29	1	25	101	70	80	6	4	.283/.376/.470	128	28.6	.287	-5.8	1B(153): 14.4, P(1): 0.0	4.1
2019	CHN	MLB	29	613	89	29	3	27	94	71	86	5	2	.293/.405/.520	135	37.9	.306	-4.9	1B(146): 4.4	3.7
2020	CHN	MLB	30	595	80	28	2	25	83	70	90	8	4	.273/.386/.484	132	32.8	.290	-3.8	1B 8	4.2

Comparables: John Mayberry, Ike Davis, Frank Thomas

The word "quiet" doesn't often come to mind with Rizzo. He never shuts up at first base, even when it's not occupied (there is, after all, a first-base umpire he can chat up). Nearly every shot of Rizzo in the dugout, meanwhile, includes him chewing off a teammate's ear. He isn't shy to offer up his opinions in the clubhouse, either, and when he pitched in 2018 it was presumably a ploy on Maddon's part to get Rizzo off his back about it. And yet, Rizzo somehow quietly posted career-highs in average and on-base percentage in 2019, and nobody seemed to notice. What Ross and the Cubs should notice is how good Rizzo's strike-zone command is these days (though he remains streaky). Maybe it's time to let the Greatest Leadoff Hitter of All Time out of the garage?

Addison Russell MI   Born: 01/23/94   Age: 26   Bats: R   Throws: R   Height: 6'0"   Weight: 200   Origin: Round 1, 2012 Draft (#11 overall)

YEAR	TEAM	LVL	AGE	PA	R	2B	3B	HR	RBI	BB	K	SB	CS	AVG/OBP/SLG	DRC+	VORP	BABIP	BRR	FRAA	WARP
2017	CHN	MLB	23	385	52	21	3	12	43	29	91	2	1	.239/.304/.418	85	13.8	.289	-0.3	SS(101): 3.4	1.4
2018	CHN	MLB	24	465	52	21	1	5	38	40	99	4	0	.250/.317/.340	81	13.6	.314	-0.8	SS(129): 1.2	1.0
2019	IOW	AAA	25	119	25	6	0	7	26	14	25	1	2	.281/.387/.563	114	14.6	.294	-0.1	SS(17): 0.4, 2B(7): 1.7	0.8
2019	CHN	MLB	25	241	25	4	1	9	23	20	58	2	0	.237/.308/.391	84	4.0	.280	0.0	2B(63): 3.4, SS(21): -0.2	0.7
2020	CHN	MLB	26	251	26	10	1	8	29	21	63	2	1	.227/.301/.384	82	2.0	.280	-0.4	SS 2, 2B 2	0.6

Comparables: Rougned Odor, Nick Franklin, Corey Seager

The 24-hour national domestic violence hotline number is 800-799-7233.

Kyle Schwarber LF   Born: 03/05/93   Age: 27   Bats: L   Throws: R   Height: 6'0"   Weight: 235   Origin: Round 1, 2014 Draft (#4 overall)

YEAR	TEAM	LVL	AGE	PA	R	2B	3B	HR	RBI	BB	K	SB	CS	AVG/OBP/SLG	DRC+	VORP	BABIP	BRR	FRAA	WARP
2017	IOW	AAA	24	44	9	1	0	4	9	8	12	0	0	.343/.477/.714	158	6.8	.421	-0.1	LF(9): -1.5	0.3
2017	CHN	MLB	24	486	67	16	1	30	59	59	150	1	1	.211/.315/.467	95	15.3	.244	0.6	LF(110): 2.7, C(4): 0.0	1.2
2018	CHN	MLB	25	510	64	14	3	26	61	78	140	4	3	.238/.356/.467	111	21.8	.288	-3.4	LF(120): 2.7	1.9
2019	CHN	MLB	26	610	82	29	3	38	92	70	156	2	3	.250/.339/.531	121	33.5	.276	-5.0	LF(140): -0.6, C(1): 0.1	2.7
2020	CHN	MLB	27	532	75	22	2	32	86	66	139	4	2	.244/.343/.509	123	28.3	.277	-1.9	LF -1	2.9

Comparables: Michael Conforto, Dave Nicholson, Kyle Blanks

Let's have a discussion about perception, shall we? It's a powerful thing.

In the 2015 playoffs, Schwarber had several embarrassing episodes in left field. He was then branded a DH trying to play left field. In the years since, he hasn't been nearly as bad. Rather, he's been passable, if below-average. Every once in a while he makes a great play that seems to go unnoticed by the masses. Every once in a while he has a terrible play and people go nuts. Rinse. Repeat.

Also in 2015, Schwarber was the Incredible Hulk in the playoffs. He then tore his ACL in the third game of the 2016 season. Then he was amazing in the World Series in a surprise return. It was inevitable that he would become vastly overrated and that's what happened.

Schwarber's career has been a nonstop perception battle, with each camp having more than enough evidence to justify their position. What's the perception now, after a monster season that saw him post new career-bests in most of the important categories? Is it that he just had a hot streak that coincided with the rabbit ball, and that he's the streaky hitter he's always been? Or is it that he made adjustments and has tapped into his well-rounded potential at the dish people always expected?

The safe answer is that Schwarber is somewhere in the middle. Our guess is there's a fair chance of him being better due to his makeup and the fact he's now in his statistical prime.

Ben Zobrist UT   Born: 05/26/81   Age: 39   Bats: B   Throws: R   Height: 6'3"   Weight: 210   Origin: Round 6, 2004 Draft (#184 overall)

YEAR	TEAM	LVL	AGE	PA	R	2B	3B	HR	RBI	BB	K	SB	CS	AVG/OBP/SLG	DRC+	VORP	BABIP	BRR	FRAA	WARP
2017	CHN	MLB	36	496	58	20	3	12	50	54	71	2	2	.232/.318/.375	87	5.4	.251	-1.3	2B(81): -2.0, LF(36): -0.2	0.1
2018	CHN	MLB	37	520	67	28	3	9	58	55	60	3	4	.305/.378/.440	118	36.5	.331	3.0	2B(63): 4.2, RF(61): 6.1	3.6
2019	CHN	MLB	38	176	24	5	0	1	17	23	24	0	0	.260/.358/.313	91	3.0	.299	-2.8	2B(32): 1.4, RF(13): -0.7	0.2
2020	CHN	MLB	39	251	25	11	1	5	25	30	40	2	1	.241/.336/.364	90	5.0	.277	0.0	2B 1, RF 1	0.7

Comparables: Ernie Banks, Stephen Drew, Tony Phillips

On May 7, Zobrist took a leave from the Cubs to deal with a personal matter—later revealed to be a divorce from his wife. He returned on September 7 wearing his wedding band and sporting his wife's song as his walk-up music. He would hit .284 with a .377 on-base percentage the rest of the way (albeit with fading power and defensive utility). Here's hoping the Zobrists—especially the children of the family—can find peace and happiness no matter what comes next. If this is the end of the line for Ben as a player, then he'll go down as one of the most underrated performers of his generation.

PITCHERS

Adbert Alzolay RHP   Born: 03/01/95   Age: 25   Bats: R   Throws: R   Height: 6'0"   Weight: 179   Origin: International Free Agent, 2012

YEAR	TEAM	LVL	AGE	W	L	SV	G	GS	IP	H	HR	BB/9	K/9	K	GB%	BABIP	WHIP	ERA	DRA	WARP	MPH	FB%	WHF	CSP
2017	MYR	A+	22	7	1	0	15	15	81²	65	8	2.4	8.6	78	39%	.263	1.07	2.98	3.26	1.9				
2017	TEN	AA	22	0	3	0	7	7	32²	27	0	3.3	8.3	30	36%	.297	1.19	3.03	3.58	0.6				
2018	IOW	AAA	23	2	4	0	8	8	39²	43	4	2.9	6.1	27	37%	.307	1.41	4.76	5.29	0.1				
2019	IOW	AAA	24	2	4	0	15	15	65¹	53	10	4.3	12.5	91	32%	.295	1.29	4.41	2.70	2.5				
2019	CHN	MLB	24	1	1	0	4	2	12¹	13	4	6.6	9.5	13	32%	.273	1.78	7.30	5.52	0.0	95.7	57.3	12	42.8
2020	CHN	MLB	25	5	5	0	47	10	88	89	16	4.3	9.0	87	34%	.301	1.49	5.22	5.28	0.4	95.4	58.7	12.3	43.8

Comparables: John Gant, Jakob Junis, Corbin Burnes

The Cubs do not have the best track record of developing arms under the Epstein-Hoyer regime. When Alzolay impressed in his big-league debut in late June, there was much rejoicing by the Wrigley faithful. Maybe, they collectively thought, maybe this is the turning of the tide. Alas, the water retracted quicker than expected. Alzolay made just three more big-league appearances the rest of the way, and was limited by injury to fewer than 100 innings for a second consecutive season. He has the stuff to be an effective reliever, and that seems like his most likely destination given his health and command woes. That isn't the outcome the Cubs or their fans wanted, but it's a pretty good one relative to their other recent attempts.

Tyler Chatwood RHP Born: 12/16/89 Age: 30 Bats: R Throws: R Height: 6'0" Weight: 185 Origin: Round 2, 2008 Draft (#74 overall)

YEAR	TEAM	LVL	AGE	W	L	SV	G	GS	IP	H	HR	BB/9	K/9	K	GB%	BABIP	WHIP	ERA	DRA	WARP	MPH	FB%	WHF	CSP
2017	COL	MLB	27	8	15	1	33	25	147²	136	20	4.7	7.3	120	59%	.283	1.44	4.69	5.28	0.4	96.7	63.7	10.6	43.2
2018	IOW	AAA	28	0	1	0	2	2	6²	5	0	13.5	5.4	4	61%	.278	2.25	9.45	8.22	-0.2				
2018	CHN	MLB	28	4	6	0	24	20	103²	92	9	8.2	7.4	85	55%	.286	1.80	5.30	7.28	-2.4	95.3	58.9	8.6	43.4
2019	CHN	MLB	29	5	3	2	38	5	76²	65	8	4.3	8.7	74	54%	.285	1.33	3.76	3.88	1.3	97.8	71	10.7	44.5
2020	CHN	MLB	30	7	8	0	46	19	125	126	16	5.5	8.9	123	56%	.313	1.62	5.26	5.12	0.9	95.8	63.9	9.9	43.7

Comparables: Jaret Wright, Kyle Davies, Chris Tillman

In Chatwood's first season in Chicago, he recorded more walks than strikeouts. His second take was almost guaranteed to be an improvement—and it was, as he provided some quality work out of the bullpen in a multi-inning role. Chatwood doesn't have the command to go deep into games without risking overexposure—for his career he's averaged 5.3 innings per start—so tasking him with working in bursts seems like the best possible arrangement. Expect the Cubs to do that more in year three—and provided his results are similar to what he put forth in 2019, his stint in Chicago just might be viewed favorably after all.

Yu Darvish RHP Born: 08/16/86 Age: 33 Bats: R Throws: R Height: 6'5" Weight: 220 Origin: International Free Agent, 2012

YEAR	TEAM	LVL	AGE	W	L	SV	G	GS	IP	H	HR	BB/9	K/9	K	GB%	BABIP	WHIP	ERA	DRA	WARP	MPH	FB%	WHF	CSP
2017	TEX	MLB	30	6	9	0	22	22	137	115	20	3.0	9.7	148	42%	.275	1.17	4.01	3.95	2.5	96.9	67.4	12.7	49.3
2017	LAN	MLB	30	4	3	0	9	9	49²	44	7	2.4	11.1	61	45%	.308	1.15	3.44	2.47	1.7	96.7	67.4	14	46.6
2018	SBN	A	31	0	0	0	2	2	6	4	1	1.5	9.0	6	38%	.200	0.83	1.50	3.56	0.1				
2018	CHN	MLB	31	1	3	0	8	8	40	36	7	4.7	11.0	49	42%	.293	1.42	4.95	4.73	0.3	96.7	69.1	11.3	50.4
2019	CHN	MLB	32	6	8	0	31	31	178²	140	33	2.8	11.5	229	46%	.266	1.10	3.98	2.69	6.0	96.9	39.8	14.4	47.5
2020	CHN	MLB	33	10	7	0	26	26	150	125	21	3.3	11.4	191	44%	.294	1.20	3.48	3.71	3.5	95.8	52	13.5	48.1

Comparables: Kerry Wood, Hideo Nomo, Max Scherzer

The seasonal line above hides the real story of Darvish's year—him turning into his old ace self at the midway point. From the All-Star Break onward, he posted a 2.76 ERA in 81 innings while fanning 118 and walking seven batters—yes, he recorded 111 more strikeouts than walks. The only issue plaguing Darvish was the long ball, as he coughed up a league-leading number. How can a pitcher be so effective yet prone to the gopher ball? The best theory we've seen is that hitters are willing to gamble against Darvish, who has so many bat-missing weapons that defeat always seems imminent. That, plus Darvish's unwillingness to work up, allow hitters to keyhole fastballs down. So long as he limits them to the solo variety, he'll be just fine.

Kyle Hendricks RHP Born: 12/07/89 Age: 30 Bats: R Throws: R Height: 6'3" Weight: 190 Origin: Round 8, 2011 Draft (#264 overall)

YEAR	TEAM	LVL	AGE	W	L	SV	G	GS	IP	H	HR	BB/9	K/9	K	GB%	BABIP	WHIP	ERA	DRA	WARP	MPH	FB%	WHF	CSP
2017	TEN	AA	27	0	0	0	2	2	8¹	2	0	1.1	5.4	5	41%	.091	0.36	1.08	2.24	0.3				
2017	CHN	MLB	27	7	5	0	24	24	139²	126	17	2.6	7.9	123	52%	.281	1.19	3.03	3.45	3.3	87.9	64.1	9	46.7
2018	CHN	MLB	28	14	11	0	33	33	199	184	22	2.0	7.3	161	49%	.281	1.15	3.44	3.13	5.0	88.9	61.8	9.7	50.4
2019	CHN	MLB	29	11	10	0	30	30	177	168	19	1.6	7.6	150	44%	.287	1.13	3.46	3.89	3.6	89.0	62.2	10.8	50.1
2020	CHN	MLB	30	12	9	0	29	29	172	163	26	2.1	7.5	143	45%	.278	1.18	3.65	3.99	3.5	88.0	62.3	10	49.2

Comparables: Matt Harvey, Danny Salazar, Garrett Richards

A little-known Chicago law states that, whenever one is discussing Hendricks, they must invoke Greg Maddux before the conversation ends or face a steep fine. Hendricks is not Maddux, but he is quite good. He has one of the best changeups in baseball, and he clearly knows what he's doing on the mound—hence his nickname, "The Professor." We can't help but think about Maddux in a different regard whenever we praise a pitcher's intelligence, for Mad Dog once (supposedly) told a group of youngsters that what made him look so smart was locating his fastball. If command is a proxy for IQ points, then Hendricks is indeed a bright one—even if he isn't, you know, Maddux.

Derek Holland LHP Born: 10/09/86 Age: 33 Bats: B Throws: L Height: 6'2" Weight: 213 Origin: Round 25, 2006 Draft (#748 overall)

YEAR	TEAM	LVL	AGE	W	L	SV	G	GS	IP	H	HR	BB/9	K/9	K	GB%	BABIP	WHIP	ERA	DRA	WARP	MPH	FB%	WHF	CSP
2017	CHA	MLB	30	7	14	0	29	26	135	156	31	5.0	6.9	104	39%	.307	1.71	6.20	8.59	-4.6	93.4	55.1	7.8	45.1
2018	SFN	MLB	31	7	9	0	36	30	171¹	154	19	3.5	8.9	169	42%	.288	1.29	3.57	3.80	2.9	93.8	56.9	11.2	49.5
2019	CHN	MLB	32	0	1	0	20	1	15²	14	3	5.7	6.3	11	38%	.250	1.53	6.89	2.52	0.5	95.3	67.4	9.6	46.4
2019	SFN	MLB	32	2	4	0	31	7	68²	68	17	4.6	9.3	71	45%	.282	1.50	5.90	6.96	-1.1	94.7	60.9	12.5	47.8
2020	CHN	MLB	33	2	2	0	33	0	35	36	6	3.9	8.6	33	42%	.305	1.46	5.04	5.03	0.2	92.9	57.1	10.3	47

Comparables: John Danks, Brett Cecil, Sterling Hitchcock

Holland is about as friendly to lefties as Mitch McConnell. Last season, he held same-handed batters to a .192/.286/.242 slash line, suggesting he has promise as a specialist of some kind—whatever that does or doesn't look like in the new world. That's about the long and short of the positives we have to note here. Otherwise, his season was so poor as to endanger his chances of a sustained big-league career. His impersonation of a big-league starter was particularly poor—arguably worse than his impersonation of Harry Caray, or, at least, Will Ferrell's impersonation of Harry Caray, because that's all it really is.

Danny Hultzen LHP Born: 11/28/89 Age: 30 Bats: L Throws: L Height: 6'3" Weight: 210 Origin: Round 1, 2011 Draft (#2 overall)

YEAR	TEAM	LVL	AGE	W	L	SV	G	GS	IP	H	HR	BB/9	K/9	K	GB%	BABIP	WHIP	ERA	DRA	WARP	MPH	FB%	WHF	CSP
2018	CUB	RK	28	0	0	0	8	3	6²	6	1	2.7	20.2	15	27%	.500	1.20	5.40	1.30	0.3				
2019	IOW	AAA	29	0	1	3	14	0	14¹	4	0	5.7	14.4	23	46%	.167	0.91	1.26	0.94	0.7				
2019	CHN	MLB	29	0	0	0	6	0	3¹	4	0	5.4	13.5	5	50%	.400	1.80	0.00	4.77	0.0	95.1	58.9	13.7	50.2
2020	CHN	MLB	30	2	2	0	33	0	35	33	5	3.5	8.1	32	45%	.278	1.32	4.25	4.48	0.4	94.3	58.7	13.7	50.1

Comparables: Cesar Jimenez, Matt Magill, Neil Ramírez

Hultzen finally reached the majors in 2019, and not just as part of a PR stunt. It was a great story. For those unfamiliar with his background, he was the second overall pick in a draft that featured Trevor Bauer, Dylan Bundy, Anthony Rendon, Francisco Lindor, Javier Báez, George Springer and—well, we can just stop there, right? Hultzen pitched fine as a professional; he just couldn't stay healthy. Given an opportunity and a rare streak of good health, he reeled off six appearances with the Cubs and looked the part of a big-league pitcher. It's a small sample and who knows if his body will permit him to hang around for long, but we're rooting for him.

Craig Kimbrel RHP Born: 05/28/88 Age: 32 Bats: R Throws: R Height: 6'0" Weight: 210 Origin: Round 3, 2008 Draft (#96 overall)

YEAR	TEAM	LVL	AGE	W	L	SV	G	GS	IP	H	HR	BB/9	K/9	K	GB%	BABIP	WHIP	ERA	DRA	WARP	MPH	FB%	WHF	CSP
2017	BOS	MLB	29	5	0	35	67	0	69	33	6	1.8	16.4	126	37%	.260	0.68	1.43	1.94	2.5	100.1	68.5	21	47.8
2018	BOS	MLB	30	5	1	42	63	0	62¹	31	7	4.5	13.9	96	30%	.216	0.99	2.74	2.58	1.7	99.0	64.5	18.5	40.7
2019	CHN	MLB	31	0	4	13	23	0	20²	21	9	5.2	13.1	30	29%	.279	1.60	6.53	6.05	-0.2	98.0	66.6	15.1	40.9
2020	CHN	MLB	32	3	3	36	53	0	56	41	8	4.4	14.0	87	33%	.297	1.22	3.51	3.69	1.1	98.2	65.7	18.5	42.2

Comparables: Kenley Jansen, Aroldis Chapman, Dellin Betances

It's tough to get a read on Kimbrel. He's been a great closer, but he's shown some worrisome signs dating back to the 2018 postseason. The question is, how many of his issues are excusable? He was good during the 2018 regular season, for starters. He then went unsigned into June, which presumably contributed to his troubles with the Cubs. It's easy to say someone kept in shape, yet there isn't a genuine substitute for the in-game experience—especially when it pertains to an adrenaline-soaked role like closer. We're willing to give Kimbrel a mulligan for last season. Another rough year and we might have to reconsider.

Brandon Kintzler RHP Born: 08/01/84 Age: 35 Bats: R Throws: R Height: 6'0" Weight: 194 Origin: Round 40, 2004 Draft (#1182 overall)

YEAR	TEAM	LVL	AGE	W	L	SV	G	GS	IP	H	HR	BB/9	K/9	K	GB%	BABIP	WHIP	ERA	DRA	WARP	MPH	FB%	WHF	CSP
2017	MIN	MLB	32	2	2	28	45	0	45¹	41	3	2.2	5.4	27	54%	.273	1.15	2.78	4.76	0.2	95.2	80.9	6.5	46.9
2017	WAS	MLB	32	2	1	1	27	0	26	25	2	1.7	4.2	12	57%	.267	1.15	3.46	5.84	-0.2	95.1	83.2	4.8	54.7
2018	WAS	MLB	33	1	2	2	45	0	42²	40	2	2.7	6.5	31	49%	.302	1.24	3.59	6.36	-0.7	94.4	83.6	7.4	48.9
2018	CHN	MLB	33	2	1	0	25	0	18	27	3	4.5	6.0	12	53%	.381	2.00	7.00	6.40	-0.3	94.6	85.8	8.4	45.4
2019	CHN	MLB	34	3	3	1	62	0	57	46	5	2.1	7.6	48	56%	.261	1.04	2.68	3.81	1.0	94.5	73.3	8.3	49.2
2020	CHN	MLB	35	2	2	0	33	0	35	38	5	2.4	6.7	26	54%	.307	1.37	4.64	4.75	0.3	93.4	78.1	7.3	47.9

Comparables: Luis Ayala, Matt Guerrier, Mark Huismann

Kintzler's past two seasons are a good example of what we mean when we talk about bullpen volatility. The Cubs acquired him at the 2018 deadline hopeful that he could give them a late-inning boost. He didn't, instead posting a 7.00 ERA in 18 innings. That performance cratered his perspective market, resulting in him exercising his player option and handcuffing Chicago (due to its self-imposed budget restrictions). Kintzler, then unwanted, went out in 2019 was about as productive as ever, all the while remaining antithetical to the modern reliever, who more than ever believes in throwing hard and missing bats. Relief pitchers, y'all.

Jon Lester LHP Born: 01/07/84 Age: 36 Bats: L Throws: L Height: 6'4" Weight: 240 Origin: Round 2, 2002 Draft (#57 overall)

YEAR	TEAM	LVL	AGE	W	L	SV	G	GS	IP	H	HR	BB/9	K/9	K	GB%	BABIP	WHIP	ERA	DRA	WARP	MPH	FB%	WHF	CSP
2017	CHN	MLB	33	13	8	0	32	32	180²	179	26	3.0	9.0	180	48%	.310	1.32	4.33	3.71	3.8	92.9	50.6	11.3	42
2018	CHN	MLB	34	18	6	0	32	32	181²	174	24	3.2	7.4	149	40%	.290	1.31	3.32	4.44	1.8	92.8	50.3	8.9	47
2019	CHN	MLB	35	13	10	0	31	31	171²	205	26	2.7	8.7	165	44%	.347	1.50	4.46	5.59	0.3	92.1	38.8	9.6	45.5
2020	CHN	MLB	36	9	9	0	26	26	143	149	23	2.9	8.3	131	43%	.308	1.37	4.58	4.73	1.7	91.2	44.7	9.6	44.2

Comparables: Gio Gonzalez, Aníbal Sánchez, Justin Verlander

You can, in a sense, trace the Cubs' rise to the moment when Theo Epstein and crew convinced Lester to join their upstart roster rather than take his talents to Boston or San Francisco. His was a symbolic signing: the Cubs were done rebuilding and were ready to shift into contention. If it seems like we're talking a lot about the Meaning of Lester's deal, it's because we are. He's now entering the final season of the guaranteed portion of his contract, and last year was arguably the worst of his tenure. He's 36 years old with reduced velocity, and there's enough mileage on his arm to suspect it's all downhill from here.

Dillon Maples RHP Born: 05/09/92 Age: 28 Bats: R Throws: R Height: 6'2" Weight: 230 Origin: Round 14, 2011 Draft (#429 overall)

YEAR	TEAM	LVL	AGE	W	L	SV	G	GS	IP	H	HR	BB/9	K/9	K	GB%	BABIP	WHIP	ERA	DRA	WARP	MPH	FB%	WHF	CSP
2017	MYR	A+	25	4	0	3	21	0	31¹	21	2	4.3	12.6	44	65%	.288	1.15	2.01	2.94	0.7				
2017	TEN	AA	25	1	1	6	14	0	13²	11	0	7.2	18.4	28	64%	.440	1.61	3.29	3.80	0.2				
2017	IOW	AAA	25	1	2	4	17	.0	18¹	12	1	5.4	13.7	28	63%	.297	1.25	1.96	2.60	0.5				
2017	CHN	MLB	25	0	0	0	6	0	5¹	6	0	10.1	18.6	11	50%	.600	2.25	10.12	1.81	0.2	98.3	43.1	12.8	48.9
2018	IOW	AAA	26	2	3	10	41	0	38²	22	1	9.1	17.5	75	57%	.350	1.58	2.79	2.53	1.1				
2018	CHN	MLB	26	1	0	0	9	0	5¹	7	2	8.4	15.2	9	38%	.455	2.25	11.81	4.86	0.0	98.3	23.9	6.3	47.5
2019	IOW	AAA	27	4	4	7	38	0	43	21	1	7.5	16.5	79	63%	.303	1.33	3.77	1.32	2.0				
2019	CHN	MLB	27	1	0	0	14	0	11²	6	2	7.7	13.9	18	68%	.200	1.37	5.40	4.02	0.2	98.0	33.3	15.6	45.5
2020	CHN	MLB	28	1	1	0	21	0	22	18	3	6.7	12.9	32	54%	.306	1.54	4.73	4.56	0.2	97.5	32.5	12.7	47.3

Comparables: Drew Steckenrider, Juan Jaime, Gerardo Reyes

One of last season's most amusing scenes saw Maples ejected for hitting an opposing batter. Sure, the benches had been warned. But you had to wonder, was the umpire familiar with Maples' work? This is someone who, when it comes to command, makes Tyler Chatwood look like Greg Maddux. Maples' strikes seem to be the product of accident rather than intelligent design, and that's why he seems to yo-yo between Chicago and Iowa every other week. On the bright side, Maples is likely to continue getting opportunities due to his big arm, and his capturing of baseball's zeitgeist—59 percent of the batters he faced in 2019 either walked, were hit by the pitch, or struck out.

───────────────── ★ ★ ★ *2020 Top 101 Prospect* **#84** ★ ★ ★ ─────────────────

Brailyn Marquez LHP Born: 01/30/99 Age: 21 Bats: L Throws: L Height: 6'4" Weight: 185 Origin: International Free Agent, 2015

YEAR	TEAM	LVL	AGE	W	L	SV	G	GS	IP	H	HR	BB/9	K/9	K	GB%	BABIP	WHIP	ERA	DRA	WARP	MPH	FB%	WHF	CSP
2017	CUB	RK	18	2	1	0	11	9	44	50	3	2.5	10.6	52	52%	.367	1.41	5.52	4.75	0.6				
2018	EUG	A-	19	1	4	0	10	10	47²	46	5	2.6	9.8	52	52%	.333	1.26	3.21	4.75	0.3				
2018	SBN	A	19	0	0	0	2	2	7	7	0	2.6	9.0	7	33%	.333	1.29	2.57	5.06	0.0				
2019	SBN	A	20	5	4	0	17	17	77¹	64	4	5.0	11.9	102	51%	.335	1.38	3.61	5.25	-0.1				
2019	MYR	A+	20	4	1	0	5	5	26¹	21	1	2.4	8.9	26	44%	.282	1.06	1.71	3.98	0.3				
2020	CHN	MLB	21	2	2	0	33	0	35	35	5	3.7	8.8	34	45%	.302	1.40	4.64	4.77	0.3				

Comparables: Brad Keller, Justus Sheffield, Jesse Biddle

Marquez could well be a Guy. He's listed at 6-foot-4, and he's certain to fill out as he gets into his 20s. That's exciting in part because his fastball already qualifies as a plus-plus offering. He's shown an ability to miss bats, too—look no further than a 14-K effort in late July. (Beginning with that outing in question, he struck out 48 batters over his next 38 innings, even with a promotion to High-A mixed in.) Marquez will see Double-A at some point next year. He's definitely a rising star in the organization.

Alec Mills RHP Born: 11/30/91 Age: 28 Bats: R Throws: R Height: 6'4" Weight: 190 Origin: Round 22, 2012 Draft (#673 overall)

YEAR	TEAM	LVL	AGE	W	L	SV	G	GS	IP	H	HR	BB/9	K/9	K	GB%	BABIP	WHIP	ERA	DRA	WARP	MPH	FB%	WHF	CSP
2017	MYR	A+	25	0	1	0	2	2	9	8	0	1.0	7.0	7	68%	.320	1.00	3.00	4.12	0.1				
2017	IOW	AAA	25	2	0	0	3	3	14	12	0	1.9	4.5	7	47%	.255	1.07	3.21	3.30	0.4				
2018	IOW	AAA	26	5	12	0	23	23	124²	121	10	3.0	7.8	108	42%	.303	1.30	4.84	4.31	1.7				
2018	CHN	MLB	26	0	1	0	7	2	18	11	1	3.5	11.5	23	51%	.250	1.00	4.00	2.42	0.6	92.7	58.9	12	47.1
2019	IOW	AAA	27	6	4	0	19	18	104	116	17	2.6	8.3	96	41%	.325	1.40	5.11	4.42	2.3				
2019	CHN	MLB	27	1	0	1	9	4	36	31	5	2.8	10.5	42	49%	.299	1.17	2.75	3.70	0.7	91.5	54.3	13.4	43.6
2020	CHN	MLB	28	7	6	0	55	13	111	98	15	3.1	9.7	120	43%	.287	1.22	3.65	3.90	2.1	91.3	56	13	45.5

Comparables: Austin Voth, William Cuevas, Chris Stratton

Originally a 22nd-round pick, Mills received his most big-league burn to date last season with the Cubs, missing more bats than expected over a nine-game cameo. He doesn't average so much as 90 mph with his heater, which has caused obvious (and misplaced) comparisons to Kyle Hendricks, but his secondary stuff (including a slow curve) showed some evasive qualities. Mills lacks Hendrick's changeup and command, but there's at least some hope he can settle in as a big-league pitcher now, which is more than most thought at this time last year.

David Phelps RHP Born: 10/09/86 Age: 33 Bats: R Throws: R Height: 6'3" Weight: 200 Origin: Round 14, 2008 Draft (#440 overall)

YEAR	TEAM	LVL	AGE	W	L	SV	G	GS	IP	H	HR	BB/9	K/9	K	GB%	BABIP	WHIP	ERA	DRA	WARP	MPH	FB%	WHF	CSP
2017	MIA	MLB	30	2	4	0	44	0	47	42	5	4.0	9.8	51	49%	.308	1.34	3.45	3.36	1.0	96.1	47.3	10.1	50.4
2017	SEA	MLB	30	2	1	0	10	0	8²	9	0	5.2	11.4	11	42%	.375	1.62	3.12	3.99	0.1	96.2	47.3	11.5	46.2
2019	TOR	MLB	32	0	0	0	17	1	17¹	14	3	3.6	9.3	18	31%	.262	1.21	3.63	5.90	-0.1	93.3	39.7	6.1	43
2019	CHN	MLB	32	2	1	1	24	0	17	17	2	5.3	9.5	18	46%	.326	1.59	3.18	4.87	0.1	94.7	39.7	10.5	44.4
2020	CHN	MLB	33	2	2	2	33	0	35	35	5	3.9	8.1	31	41%	.297	1.43	4.62	4.65	0.3	94.0	42.8	9.2	45.4

Comparables: Ramon E Ramirez, Adam Warren, Bobby Parnell

Phelps returned from Tommy John surgery in June and split his season between the Blue Jays and the Cubs, facing 70-something batters for each. The ERA looks better than the rest of his components, but the most interesting aspect of his season was the shift in approach. Phelps leaned into being a flyball pitcher, tossing more cutters and curves at the cost of his sinker. The Cubs declined his option, sending him to the free-agent market at a peculiar time.

José Quintana LHP Born: 01/24/89 Age: 31 Bats: R Throws: L Height: 6'1" Weight: 220 Origin: International Free Agent, 2006

YEAR	TEAM	LVL	AGE	W	L	SV	G	GS	IP	H	HR	BB/9	K/9	K	GB%	BABIP	WHIP	ERA	DRA	WARP	MPH	FB%	WHF	CSP
2017	CHA	MLB	28	4	8	0	18	18	104¹	98	14	3.5	9.4	109	45%	.301	1.32	4.49	4.59	1.1	93.7	62.2	9.3	44.7
2017	CHN	MLB	28	7	3	0	14	14	84¹	72	9	2.2	10.5	98	48%	.300	1.10	3.74	3.94	1.5	94.2	63.7	9.3	46.4
2018	CHN	MLB	29	13	11	0	32	32	174¹	162	25	3.5	8.2	158	45%	.282	1.32	4.03	4.93	0.8	93.6	68.3	8.8	49
2019	CHN	MLB	30	13	9	0	32	31	171	191	20	2.4	8.0	152	45%	.328	1.39	4.68	4.51	2.3	93.2	61.8	9.2	47.3
2020	CHN	MLB	31	9	9	0	26	26	143	153	22	2.8	7.8	124	45%	.310	1.38	4.69	4.85	1.6	92.7	63.8	9	47.1

Comparables: Jaime García, Andrew Heaney, Wade Miley

Few things are relitigated more often in Chicago baseball than the trade that landed Quintana on the Cubs in exchange for Eloy Jiménez and Dylan Cease. Those who thumb their nose at the Cubs' side of the deal often forget how Quintana helped the Cubs win the division in 2017. That matters—even if they fell short in their efforts to repeat. Truthfully, it's been the seasons since that have caused second- and third-guessing about the deal's merits. Quintana has been amazingly inconsistent. The last two months of 2019 illustrated that well: he had a 2.02 ERA in August, then an 11.09 ERA in September. Yes, it's just ERA, but that's a jarring split. As he heads to his age-31 season, it's hard to envision him being an above-average member of a rotation without some adjustments.

Kyle Ryan LHP Born: 09/25/91 Age: 28 Bats: L Throws: L Height: 6'5" Weight: 215 Origin: Round 12, 2010 Draft (#373 overall)

YEAR	TEAM	LVL	AGE	W	L	SV	G	GS	IP	H	HR	BB/9	K/9	K	GB%	BABIP	WHIP	ERA	DRA	WARP	MPH	FB%	WHF	CSP
2017	TOL	AAA	25	3	1	0	48	0	45¹	55	5	5.4	7.7	39	54%	.365	1.81	4.96	6.80	-0.7				
2017	DET	MLB	25	0	0	0	8	0	5²	9	0	11.1	1.6	1	52%	.429	2.82	7.94	7.94	-0.2	93.0	63.1	8.1	39.2
2018	IOW	AAA	26	1	2	0	22	8	66	48	9	2.5	8.3	61	62%	.236	1.00	2.86	3.05	1.7				
2019	CHN	MLB	27	4	2	0	73	0	61	55	5	4.3	8.6	58	57%	.301	1.38	3.54	4.03	0.9	91.1	46.6	10.3	47.7
2020	CHN	MLB	28	3	3	2	53	0	56	57	7	3.4	7.7	48	55%	.302	1.39	4.34	4.46	0.6	90.7	47.9	10.2	44.8

Comparables: Kyle Lobstein, T.J. McFarland, Brian Flynn

They say never trust a person with two first names. It worked out for the Cubs with Ryan, who had quietly spent the previous season as part of the organization as well. By luck or skill, he permitted just 16 of his 44 inherited runners to score, a little better than the league-average rate, making him a reliable hand for Maddon to insert in a jam. He had a rough September—who didn't on this roster?—to the extent that he saw his ERA increase from 2.79 to 3.54 over his final three outings. Ouch. Ryan's best role on a roster is as a second lefty.

Pedro Strop RHP Born: 06/13/85 Age: 35 Bats: R Throws: R Height: 6'1" Weight: 220 Origin: International Free Agent, 2002

YEAR	TEAM	LVL	AGE	W	L	SV	G	GS	IP	H	HR	BB/9	K/9	K	GB%	BABIP	WHIP	ERA	DRA	WARP	MPH	FB%	WHF	CSP
2017	CHN	MLB	32	5	4	0	69	0	60¹	45	4	3.9	9.7	65	61%	.270	1.18	2.83	3.23	1.3	97.6	55.7	16.3	43.1
2018	CHN	MLB	33	6	1	13	60	0	59²	38	4	3.2	8.6	57	48%	.222	0.99	2.26	3.67	0.9	96.7	38.6	17	42.7
2019	CHN	MLB	34	2	5	10	50	0	41²	33	6	4.3	10.6	49	54%	.276	1.27	4.97	3.66	0.8	95.3	36.7	14.5	40.5
2020	CHN	MLB	35	2	2	0	33	0	35	28	4	4.1	11.0	43	50%	.283	1.24	3.52	3.65	0.7	95.2	42.3	15.6	41.1

Comparables: Brad Brach, Tyler Clippard, David Aardsma

Coughlin's law states that everything ends poorly—otherwise, it wouldn't end. Strop was one of the best relievers in Cubs history, up there with Bruce Sutter, Lee Smith and Carlos Marmol. Yet for whatever reason—perhaps his crooked hat, which angers some for whatever silly or malicious reason, or his high-profile meltdowns against the Cardinals early in his Wrigley residency—he had an uneven reputation in the fan base. Strop had a poor 2019 and it's at least possible his productive days are behind him. Regardless, he was perhaps the unsung hero of the Maddon era.

Ryan Tepera RHP Born: 11/03/87 Age: 32 Bats: R Throws: R Height: 6'1" Weight: 195 Origin: Round 19, 2009 Draft (#580 overall)

YEAR	TEAM	LVL	AGE	W	L	SV	G	GS	IP	H	HR	BB/9	K/9	K	GB%	BABIP	WHIP	ERA	DRA	WARP	MPH	FB%	WHF	CSP
2017	TOR	MLB	29	7	1	2	73	0	77²	57	7	3.6	9.4	81	43%	.260	1.13	3.59	4.85	0.3	96.5	59	14.2	43.9
2018	TOR	MLB	30	5	5	7	68	0	64²	55	9	3.3	9.5	68	44%	.291	1.22	3.62	4.92	0.0	96.8	61.3	14.8	43.3
2019	TOR	MLB	31	0	2	0	23	1	21²	20	5	3.3	5.8	14	44%	.234	1.29	4.98	5.98	-0.1	95.2	57.1	13.5	41.1
2020	CHN	MLB	32	2	2	0	42	0	45	40	7	3.6	7.9	39	43%	.268	1.30	4.22	4.44	0.5	95.4	59.1	14.2	42.1

Comparables: Miguel Socolovich, Blake Treinen, Sam Freeman

Tepera has been a DRA-beater his entire career, it's just that prior to last season it was DRAs starting with a four that he consistently outshone. In 2019, the deserved mark was up near six and injuries—including a May surgery to alleviate elbow impingement—limited the longtime Jay to merely 21 2/3 innings. Unfortunately, his velocity dipped nearly as much as his workload and the Texan was given his walking papers as opposed to his arbitration dollars. Having lost the confidence of the only organization for which he has appeared professionally, an enlivened fastball will be key to Tepera building on his five-year MLB career in Chicago.

Rowan Wick **RHP** Born: 11/09/92 Age: 27 Bats: L Throws: R Height: 6'3" Weight: 235 Origin: Round 9, 2012 Draft (#300 overall)

YEAR	TEAM	LVL	AGE	W	L	SV	G	GS	IP	H	HR	BB/9	K/9	K	GB%	BABIP	WHIP	ERA	DRA	WARP	MPH	FB%	WHF	CSP
2017	SFD	AA	24	0	0	5	16	0	21²	16	1	4.6	7.1	17	36%	.246	1.25	2.08	3.65	0.3				
2017	MEM	AAA	24	2	1	1	14	0	16²	16	2	3.8	9.2	17	53%	.286	1.38	5.40	2.87	0.4				
2018	SAN	AA	25	2	4	5	29	0	31¹	22	0	6.0	12.1	42	58%	.310	1.37	3.16	3.98	0.4				
2018	ELP	AAA	25	2	0	9	20	0	22²	16	3	4.0	8.7	22	48%	.224	1.15	1.99	3.28	0.5				
2018	SDN	MLB	25	0	1	0	10	0	8¹	13	1	1.1	7.6	7	43%	.414	1.68	6.48	4.10	0.1	96.8	67.7	12	56
2019	IOW	AAA	26	1	0	6	27	0	35	25	3	2.3	11.3	44	49%	.272	0.97	1.80	1.82	1.5				
2019	CHN	MLB	26	2	0	2	31	0	33¹	22	0	4.3	9.4	35	55%	.256	1.14	2.43	3.84	0.5	97.4	66.4	12.8	49
2020	CHN	MLB	27	3	3	4	53	0	56	49	7	3.4	8.8	54	49%	.279	1.25	3.52	3.76	1.0	96.8	67.4	12.8	52.7

Comparables: A.J. Achter, Zach Putnam, Pedro Strop

How's this for a glow-up: Wick had an ERA higher than his 6-foot-3 listed height during his brief big-league stint with the Padres. He was sent packing to Chicago in exchange for a minor-league player you've never heard of during the offseason, and emerged as a reliable relief option following a tour of the Cubs' so-called "pitching lab." One key difference? More curveballs, fewer cutters. We'll see what he looks like when he gives up a home run—something he didn't do in 31 appearances in 2019.

Brad Wieck **LHP** Born: 10/14/91 Age: 28 Bats: L Throws: L Height: 6'9" Weight: 255 Origin: Round 7, 2014 Draft (#205 overall)

YEAR	TEAM	LVL	AGE	W	L	SV	G	GS	IP	H	HR	BB/9	K/9	K	GB%	BABIP	WHIP	ERA	DRA	WARP	MPH	FB%	WHF	CSP
2017	SAN	AA	25	2	1	7	31	0	30²	21	1	3.8	15.0	51	57%	.333	1.11	2.64	2.80	0.7				
2017	ELP	AAA	25	0	0	0	9	0	7	11	1	12.9	10.3	8	42%	.435	3.00	10.29	8.34	-0.2				
2018	SAN	AA	26	1	2	10	27	0	28	20	1	2.6	11.6	36	29%	.279	1.00	1.93	2.20	0.9				
2018	ELP	AAA	26	3	0	2	17	0	18¹	16	2	4.4	16.7	34	50%	.389	1.36	3.44	1.73	0.7				
2018	SDN	MLB	26	0	0	0	5	0	7	3	1	0.0	12.9	10	29%	.154	0.43	1.29	2.68	0.2	94.1	64.5	12.9	55.2
2019	ELP	AAA	27	1	1	2	14	0	17²	16	5	3.1	17.3	34	29%	.379	1.25	6.11	2.83	0.6				
2019	SDN	MLB	27	0	1	0	30	0	24²	26	7	3.3	11.3	31	33%	.306	1.42	6.57	5.55	-0.1	95.8	79.9	11.9	46.5
2019	CHN	MLB	27	2	1	0	14	0	10	2	1	3.6	16.2	18	21%	.077	0.60	3.60	0.66	0.5	95.3	71.1	15.6	49.6
2020	CHN	MLB	28	2	2	0	37	0	39	35	6	3.6	11.1	48	34%	.298	1.28	4.05	4.26	0.5	94.9	76.5	13	51.2

Comparables: Andrew Vasquez, Emilio Pagán, D.J. Snelten

Another apparent win for the Cubs' newly minted pitching factory, the gigantic Wieck was terrible for the Padres, but posted a ridiculous strikeout rate with the Cubs. He ascended to high-leverage work quickly—a statement on his quality, as well as the rest of the bullpen's—and was recording important outs down the stretch. Wieck lacks the big-time velocity you'd expect from someone of his size, but the threat of his curveball and the depth of his release point permit his fastball to play firmer than the radar gun suggests.

LINEOUTS

Hitters

HITTER	POS	TEAM	LVL	AGE	PA	R	2B	3B	HR	RBI	BB	K	SB	CS	AVG/OBP/SLG	DRC+	VORP	BABIP	BRR	FRAA	WARP
Aramis Ademan	SS	MYR	A+	20	422	40	10	8	5	39	48	92	16	9	.221/.318/.334	94	10.3	.282	-4.4	SS(101): -8.7, 2B(7): -0.1	0.1
Trent Giambrone	UT	IOW	AAA	25	478	66	27	0	23	66	42	131	17	4	.241/.314/.464	81	12.7	.292	1.1	2B(43): 1.9, 3B(25): -0.6	0.8
Pedro Martinez	INF	CUB	Rk	18	121	12	6	3	2	17	12	27	8	5	.352/.417/.519	144	11.0	.456	-0.2	SS(16): -0.4, 2B(9): -2.1	0.7
	INF	EUG	A-	18	112	15	2	3	0	7	12	36	11	5	.265/.357/.347	83	3.8	.419	1.1	2B(14): 1.7, SS(11): -1.2	0.4
Christopher Morel	UT	SBN	A	20	278	36	15	7	6	31	11	60	9	6	.284/.320/.467	113	16.3	.345	0.2	3B(72): 2.2, LF(1): 0.4	1.6
Cole Roederer	OF	SBN	A	19	448	45	19	4	9	60	52	112	16	5	.224/.319/.365	91	13.6	.285	1.6	CF(94): 3.3, LF(9): -0.7	1.4
Zack Short	INF	IOW	AAA	24	160	22	9	0	6	17	21	50	2	1	.211/.338/.414	76	3.3	.282	-1.9	SS(27): 1.2, 2B(13): -0.1	0.1
	INF	TEN	AA	24	74	7	3	2	0	5	9	18	0	1	.250/.338/.359	86	4.3	.340	0.4	SS(13): -0.7, 2B(2): -0.2	0.2
	INF	CUB	Rk	24	25	5	2	0	0	3	8	4	0	0	.375/.600/.500	180	3.4	.500	-0.7	SS(3): 0.5, 2B(2): 0.1	0.2
Chase Strumpf	MI	EUG	A-	21	111	17	8	0	2	14	15	28	2	0	.292/.405/.449	151	9.9	.387	-1.3	2B(24): -3.4	0.3
	MI	CUT	Rk	21	32	5	3	0	0	1	7	7	0	0	.182/.406/.318	116	2.1	.250	0.2	2B(5): 0.4	0.2
	MI	SBN	A	21	28	3	1	0	1	2	1	7	0	0	.125/.214/.292	50	-0.9	.118	0.0	2B(6): 0.2	-0.1
Mark Zagunis	RF	CHN	MLB	26	40	2	3	0	0	5	4	16	0	0	.250/.325/.333	60	-0.9	.450	-0.5	RF(6): -0.7, LF(2): -0.1	-0.2
	RF	IOW	AAA	26	285	35	26	1	6	43	24	94	6	3	.294/.361/.475	95	13.2	.439	0.5	RF(33): -0.6, LF(20): -0.9	0.4

That's two straight full seasons in Myrtle Beach without much apparent progress for shortstop prospect **Aramis Ademan**, who is so young that he was born on the same 1998 day that Sammy Sosa hit his 61st and 62nd home runs. ⓧ **Trent Giambrone** is on the older side, the shorter side and the strikeout-prone side. He has more pop than you'd think and experience at every position but catcher and center field, meaning he could come in handy as a super-utility player. ⓧ The toughest player in the system to Google, **Pedro Martinez** is a raw infielder who can rake. The original Pedro hit .099 with a .256 OPS for his career; this Pedro, then, has a good chance to be better in one regard. ⓧ **Christopher Morel** is a 20-year-old infielder with a wide range of potential outcomes. He could be a power-hitting third baseman, or he could be an outfielder with a disqualifying strikeout-to-walk ratio. ⓧ **Cole Roederer**, the Cubs' second-round pick in 2018, likely needs another year in South Bend. He has a long way to go, in other words, if he's going to surpass James Shields as the most successful player from William S. Hart High School. ⓧ **Zack Short** is indeed diminutive and is indeed a shortstop. He needs to get more length out of his bat if he's going to start in the bigs, but his defense and baserunning should lift him. ⓧ The Cubs popped **Chase Strumpf** in the second round out of UCLA with the hope that he'll outperform Ryan Schimpf, so far as infielders with crustacean-sounding surnames go. ⓧ **Mark Zagunis** has a career .385 OBP in 330 Triple-A games. He's hit .200/.313/.273 in 64 big-league plate appearances. We're not saying his name should be spelled with four A's, but we're preparing to say it.

Pitchers

PITCHER	TEAM	LVL	AGE	W	L	SV	G	GS	IP	H	HR	BB/9	K/9	K	GB%	BABIP	WHIP	ERA	DRA	WARP	MPH	FB%	WHF	CSP
Cory Abbott	TEN	AA	23	8	8	0	26	26	146²	112	15	3.2	10.2	166	38%	.274	1.12	3.01	4.19	1.4				
Xavier Cedeño	IOW	AAA	32	1	0	0	9	0	7	8	0	9.0	3.9	3	38%	.333	2.14	3.86	7.54	-0.1				
	CHN	MLB	32	0	0	0	5	0	2	4	0	13.5	4.5	1	44%	.444	3.50	0.00	6.76	0.0	87.4	76.7	7	41.6
Jharel Cotton	STO	A+	27	1	1	0	4	2	9	7	3	2.0	9.0	9	23%	.174	1.00	6.00	4.64	0.0				
	LVG	AAA	27	0	2	0	14	1	18²	23	5	4.8	11.6	24	44%	.370	1.77	7.71	5.22	0.2				
Yovanny Cruz	CUT	Rk	19	0	0	0	4	4	9	7	0	7.0	7.0	7	65%	.269	1.56	4.00	5.49	0.1				
	EUG	A-	19	1	2	0	5	3	14²	13	3	7.4	12.9	21	52%	.270	1.70	7.98	7.08	-0.4				
Oscar De La Cruz	MYR	A+	24	1	0	0	3	3	15	14	0	3.0	10.2	17	37%	.341	1.27	1.20	4.40	0.1				
	TEN	AA	24	4	5	2	31	8	81¹	65	8	3.2	9.7	88	39%	.275	1.16	4.09	4.01	0.8				
Richard Gallardo	CUB	Rk	17	0	2	0	11	9	30¹	32	1	3.6	6.8	23	55%	.316	1.45	4.15	4.16	0.6				
Ryan Jensen	EUG	A-	21	0	0	0	6	6	12	7	0	10.5	14.2	19	68%	.318	1.75	2.25	6.90	-0.2				
Michael McAvene	EUG	A-	21	0	0	0	6	6	12²	5	0	2.8	14.2	20	29%	.238	0.71	1.42	2.28	0.4				
Tyson Miller	TEN	AA	23	4	3	0	15	15	88	70	6	1.8	8.2	80	35%	.272	1.00	2.56	3.58	1.5				
	IOW	AAA	23	3	5	0	11	11	48²	62	13	4.6	8.0	43	34%	.331	1.79	7.58	6.73	0.0				
James Norwood	IOW	AAA	25	3	2	6	45	0	57²	40	9	4.8	12.6	81	36%	.265	1.23	4.21	2.79	1.9				
	CHN	MLB	25	0	1	0	9	0	9¹	9	1	7.7	10.6	11	40%	.333	1.82	3.98	4.70	0.1	98.1	64.1	12.1	42.2
CD Pelham	FRI	AA	24	1	3	0	29	0	21²	32	4	12.0	12.5	30	46%	.452	2.82	12.05	8.84	-1.1				
	NAS	AAA	24	0	1	0	13	0	10²	16	2	9.3	5.9	7	48%	.368	2.53	11.81	8.87	-0.3				
Colin Rea	IOW	AAA	28	14	4	0	26	26	148	142	17	3.6	7.3	120	46%	.293	1.36	3.95	4.06	3.8				
Manuel Rodriguez	MYR	A+	22	1	3	2	35	0	47	43	1	3.3	12.4	65	55%	.378	1.28	3.45	5.02	-0.2				
Justin Steele	TEN	AA	23	0	6	0	11	11	38²	45	3	4.7	9.8	42	45%	.404	1.68	5.59	6.70	-0.8				
Riley Thompson	SBN	A	22	8	6	0	21	21	94	85	9	3.0	8.3	87	45%	.290	1.23	3.06	4.77	0.5				
Duane Underwood Jr.	IOW	AAA	24	3	7	0	33	10	81²	84	8	4.5	10.5	95	48%	.342	1.53	5.07	3.85	2.1				
	CHN	MLB	24	0	0	0	12	0	11²	13	2	2.3	10.0	13	53%	.344	1.37	5.40	3.69	0.2	96.8	59.5	12.9	46.6
Allen Webster	CHN	MLB	29	0	0	1	12	0	11	14	2	4.1	7.4	9	60%	.343	1.73	4.91	3.90	0.2	96.7	43.3	17.5	48
Dan Winkler	GWN	AAA	29	0	1	2	18	0	16²	16	1	9.7	10.8	20	41%	.333	2.04	4.86	5.74	0.1				
	SAC	AAA	29	0	1	0	12	0	14	6	1	3.2	5.8	9	57%	.139	0.79	0.64	2.19	0.5				
	ATL	MLB	29	3	1	0	27	0	21²	18	5	4.6	9.1	22	30%	.241	1.34	4.98	6.20	-0.2	94.0	33.9	16	42.6

Riding his plus-cutter, **Cory Abbott** continued his ascent in 2019 with a quality season in Double-A. Might the Cubs have developed a big-league hurler? ⦻ **Xavier Cedeño's** long-term prospects were already dim by virtue of him being a left-handed specialist. He's now been limited to single-digit appearances in two of three seasons, which ain't gonna help him. ⦻ The saddest lineout is of a good prospect gone bad, but it's now been more than three years since **Jharel Cotton**'s Bugs Bunny changeup captivated the internet. ⦻ **Yovanny Cruz** was more than two years younger than his average competition last season, making his results easier to forgive. His plus fastball has the same balm-like effect on his anti-plus control. ⦻ **Oscar De La Cruz's** surname translates to "Of The Cross" but his profile has always read more like "Of The Bullpen." The Cubs moved him there last season and he fared much better in his second Double-A go-round. ⦻ Spindly teen **Richard Gallardo** still needs to grow into his frame. We'll see what he looks like when he gets there, but he might have the highest ceiling of any Cubs pitching prospect. ⦻ Surprise first-round pick **Ryan Jensen** comes close to triple digits with his heater and is working to develop his slider and change. There's a non-zero chance he develops into a quality starter; there's also a higher probability he's just a reliever due to his size and arm action. ⦻ **Michael McAvene** went viral due to a nonsense ejection while serving as the University of Louisville's closer last summer. The Cubs picked him in the third round and his next notable ejection could be from the farm system to the bigs. ⦻ If not for the Cubs' inability to develop pitchers, **Tyson Miller** is another one we'd be more excited about. Should he keep improving with the slider and change, he'll land in a major-league rotation someday. ⦻ **James Norwood** misses bats and the zone with such regularity that you'd think his middle name was Findsplate. (If that joke sailed wide left then pretend we quipped about Scott Norwood instead.) ⦻ **CD Pelham** made it to the big leagues in 2018 and then went full Bruce Banner in 2019. The Cubs need him to remember how to hulk out in 2020, since an upper-90s fastball is of no use if you're not willing to intimidate batters with it. ⦻ Remember when **Colin Rea** was traded to the Marlins, but the Padres had to take him back because he was injured when the deal went down? (You know who was sent back the Marlins? Luis Castillo. Oops.) Anyway, Rea is relevant once again, as he was added to the 40-man roster at season's end. ⦻ Signed out of the Mexican League after the 2016 season, **Manuel Rodriguez** took a big step forward with his control in the Florida State League last year and rode it all the way to a 40-man roster spot. ⦻ **Justin Steele** might be a superhero's alias. Moonlighting as a crime fighter might explain why he has such trouble throwing strikes. ⦻ **Riley Thompson** displays a plus fastball and a plus curve, but he's had Tommy John surgery and has battled shoulder injuries as well. ⦻ The Cubs have given up any hope of having **Duane Underwood Jr.** start. He could still carve out a role as a quality bullpen piece, but that's been the expectation for a minute and we're still waiting. ⦻ **Allen Webster** was once ranked by us as the 69th-best prospect in the game. That was the last nice thing this book said about him. ⦻ After walking more than a batter per inning in Gwinnett, **Dan Winkler**'s stock dropped from potential setup man to secondary piece in the Mark Melancon trade. A nice rebound in Sacramento means he'll likely get another chance at a big-league 'pen.

CHICAGO WHITE SOX

Essay by Russell Dorsey

Player comments by James Fegan and BP staff

Long before the creation of online tracking services, waiting for a package to arrive was an exercise of excitement and expectation. Your loving grandma would call and tell you she was shipping a package of delicious baked goods and that they would be delivered to your doorstep. She couldn't give an exact date, but she let you know it would be coming soon.

Over the last four years, White Sox general manager Rick Hahn has served as the fan base's grandma. Instead of promising cookies made with love, he would declare that better days were ahead—some that might even include playoff games. He couldn't give a precise timeline, either, of course, and at times he appeared more likely to kick the can down the road than deliver. But last season's progress and this past winter suggest Hahn is ready to make good on his pledge.

Unlike teams with plans of immediate contention, the success of the 2019 White Sox couldn't be measured in wins and losses. Rather, that club became defined by the development of their young, inexperienced players—players they hope will be part of their next playoff team. That was a good thing, too, considering the year started inauspiciously with failed pursuits of superstar free-agent hitters Bryce Harper and Manny Machado.

But the 2019 White Sox were able to salvage the year—and separate themselves from previous editions—by launching Lucas Giolito, Tim Anderson and Yoán Moncada to new heights. Add in Eloy Jiménez's introduction to the majors, and White Sox fans could hear the faint rumblings of a delivery truck.

It's rare for a player to catapult from average (or worse) production to being top-five at their position within a single season. Not only did the Sox have that happen once, but they had it happen with three different players. Giolito, Anderson and Moncada ended the 2018 season with a combined 1.1 Wins Above Replacement Player, a major disappointment for a team expecting growth from its cabal of formerly well-regarded prospects.

The most shocking of the three was Giolito, whose resurgence from a historically poor 2018 came with an adjustment to his arm action and his mindset. Always well-

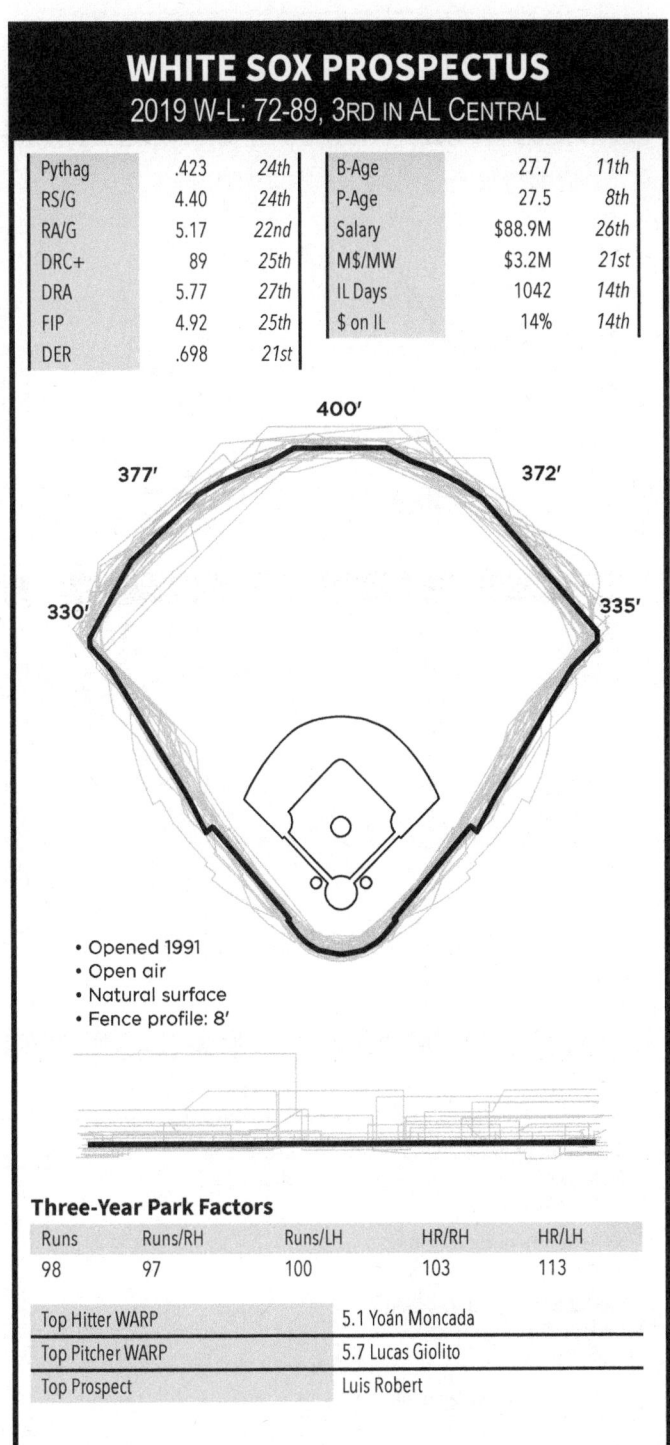

WHITE SOX PROSPECTUS
2019 W-L: 72-89, 3RD IN AL CENTRAL

Pythag	.423	24th	B-Age	27.7	11th
RS/G	4.40	24th	P-Age	27.5	8th
RA/G	5.17	22nd	Salary	$88.9M	26th
DRC+	89	25th	M$/MW	$3.2M	21st
DRA	5.77	27th	IL Days	1042	14th
FIP	4.92	25th	$ on IL	14%	14th
DER	.698	21st			

400'

377'   372'

330'   335'

- Opened 1991
- Open air
- Natural surface
- Fence profile: 8'

Three-Year Park Factors

Runs	Runs/RH	Runs/LH	HR/RH	HR/LH
98	97	100	103	113

Top Hitter WARP	5.1 Yoán Moncada
Top Pitcher WARP	5.7 Lucas Giolito
Top Prospect	Luis Robert

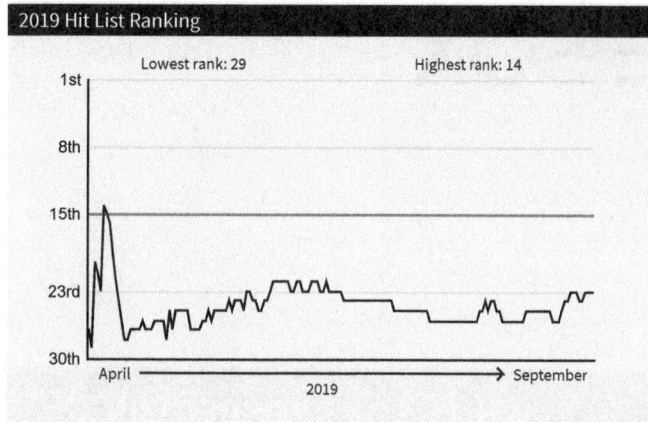

2019 Hit List Ranking

Lowest rank: 29   Highest rank: 14

April   2019   September

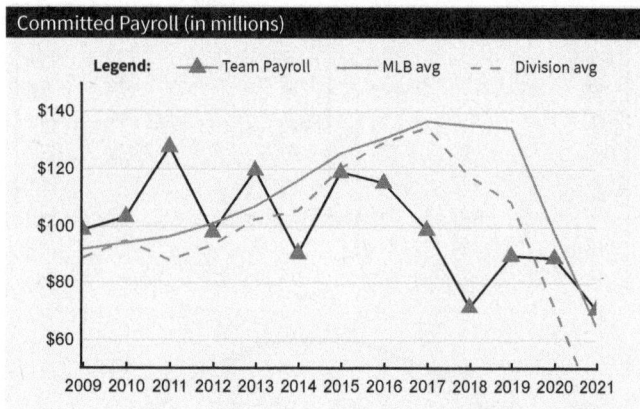

Committed Payroll (in millions)

Legend: ▲ Team Payroll   — MLB avg   - - Division avg

2009 2010 2011 2012 2013 2014 2015 2016 2017 2018 2019 2020 2021

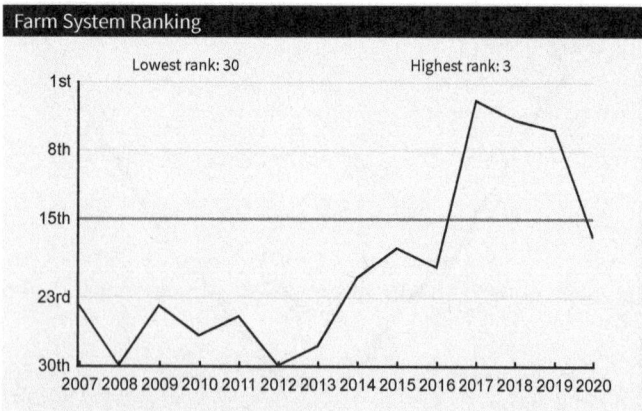

Farm System Ranking

Lowest rank: 30   Highest rank: 3

2007 2008 2009 2010 2011 2012 2013 2014 2015 2016 2017 2018 2019 2020

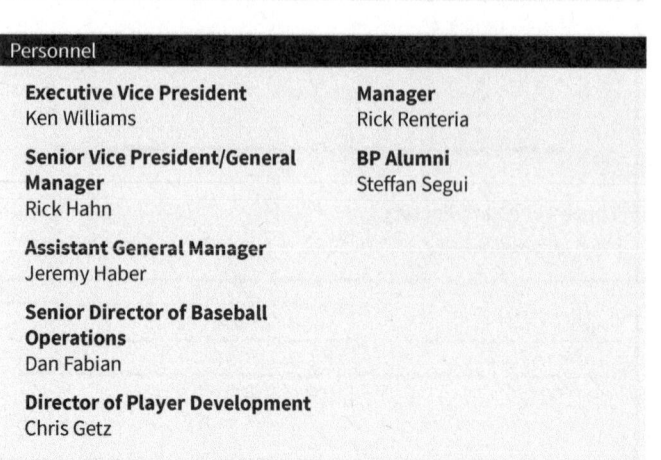

Personnel

Executive Vice President
Ken Williams

Senior Vice President/General Manager
Rick Hahn

Assistant General Manager
Jeremy Haber

Senior Director of Baseball Operations
Dan Fabian

Director of Player Development
Chris Getz

Manager
Rick Renteria

BP Alumni
Steffan Segui

spoken and thought-provoking, the cerebral right-hander seemingly reached enlightenment after a winter of reflection and evolution. His confidence grew and that, combined with his shortened arm swing, allowed him early success and a sprouting presence on the mound. The pitcher who led MLB in both walks and earned runs the year prior was no more present than yesterday's breeze.

The White Sox have lacked a legitimate ace since Chris Sale was traded to the Red Sox in winter 2016. Giolito seems up for the task as serving as the face and anchor of a rotation with little experience but ample upside. The White Sox's only focus for Giolito should be ensuring he stays healthy enough to post the first 200-inning, 200-strikeout season of his career—a feat that could well enable him to rank higher than seventh in Cy Young Award voting.

For Anderson and Moncada, the adjustments were different, but just as effective.

Many hitting coaches would have tried to force Anderson into a box, getting him away from his natural strengths and free-swinging approach. The Sox took the scenic route, letting him grow and become a big-league hitter at his own pace. Their patience was rewarded in 2019, as he no longer wasted at-bats en route to the American League batting title.

Anderson won't have to repeat as champion to showcase his maturity in 2020. His ability to put the barrel on the ball has made him a dangerous hitter who is nearly impossible to retire within the zone. It's also allowed him to tap into his pop. Though Anderson is perhaps better known for his speed—he has swiped at least 15 bags in each of the past three years—power is part of his game. Were it not for an ankle injury that sidelined him for a month, he would've eclipsed both the 20-homer and 200-hit marks—making him the third White Sox hitter ever to do so.

As for Moncada, his breakout season began with an adjustment to his approach at the plate. The 24-year-old third baseman started attacking pitches earlier in counts, allowing him to cut down his strikeouts by six percentage points (from 33.4 percent in '18 to 27.5 percent in '19). His other results followed as he set career-highs in almost every notable offensive category.

Moncada has always had elite plate discipline, but it became more of a hindrance prior to last season as he would often take borderline pitches for strikes. Because of his increased aggressiveness, his walk rate dipped, falling to 7.2 percent. The drop in walks helped Moncada find his swing, but finding a new balance between that controlled aggressiveness and his superior eye at the plate took him from a good player to an elite player.

Should the gains stick, Moncada could lead the Sox in every offensive category in 2020. The question for Moncada is: how do you top a 5.7 WAR season?

Jiménez's arrival, meanwhile, should have brought a sparkle to the eye of White Sox fans. He produced in a big way, with an .828 OPS and a 105 DRC+. If not for a litany of freak injuries, Jiménez could have shown even more growth.

Despite playing in just 122 games, he finished the season leading all American League rookies with 31 homers. Should he continue his ascend, he could live up to expectations of becoming one of the game's elite hitters over the next decade. (It doesn't hurt that he has star-caliber charisma, either.)

Soon enough, Jiménez and company will be joined by another phenom: Luis Robert. Robert captivated the baseball world in 2019, recording an impressive 30-30 season combined across three levels in his first full professional campaign. Not only is Robert's superstar potential undeniable; the opportunity to put him together with Jiménez for the next seven years should—at the very least—give the White Sox one of the most-formidable young duos in baseball.

In past years, this is the part of the White Sox essay where Nick Madrigal and Andrew Vaughn and other prospects would get name dropped and presented as the other great hopes for the club.

But unlike in those previous years, this time around Hahn added some legitimate outside help by signing one of the game's premier catchers, Yasmani Grandal, to give the White Sox a boost. Grandal is, in addition to being perhaps the best framing catcher in baseball, also a quality hitter no matter the position. Including 2019, he's posted a DRC+ over 100 in five of his six full-time seasons. For as good of a year as James McCann had, Grandal is a clear, substantive upgrade.

The White Sox, then, have the makings of a roster that is not only interesting, but brimming with the potential to end what has been a miserable 12-year period of baseball on the South Side. Still, there should be no pats on the back for Hahn and company until the wins come.

Since Hahn took over as general manager in 2013, the White Sox have the second-most losses in baseball (642), ahead of only the Miami Marlins (646). While high-end prospect acquisitions—like Jiménez, Moncada, Giolito, Reynaldo López and Dylan Cease—have contributed at the highest level, others—Micker Adolfo, Blake Rutherford, Jake Burger, Luis Alexander Basabe and Zack Burdi—have served as high-profile disappointments or busts. To add insult to injury, the White Sox have experienced a run of bad luck with pitchers needing Tommy John surgery. Five have undergone the knife in the last year, including Michael Kopech and Carlos Rodón.

Whether those development and injury woes are the result of bad luck or organizational deficiencies is impossible to suss out. What's certain is that turning around a franchise, from a rebuilding loser to a contending winner, takes more than a single successful offseason. It takes successful trades—for prospects and veterans; smart free-agent signings; continued player growth; and maintained health. All are easier said than done. Nevertheless, the White Sox will have to figure it all out—something they couldn't do during their previous years on the upswing, when they had Sale, José Quintana, Adam Eaton and others in town.

Will Hahn be up for the task? He better hope. The time has come when the word "rebuild," or any other cute synonyms non-competitive teams hide behind, should be removed from the White Sox's vocabulary. To sit at the big kids' table to get taken seriously requires acting the part. No more promises, no more lectures about the future or the importance of patience and flexibility. The White Sox have many of the pieces, now they need the wins.

Fortunately for fans, package tracking exists these days. And it looks an upgraded product—albeit not yet as delightful as grandma's cookies—will be delivered to the corner of 35th and Shields as soon as this season. ■

—Russell Dorsey is a Chicago reporter for MLB.com.

HITTERS

José Abreu 1B Born: 01/29/87 Age: 33 Bats: R Throws: R Height: 6'3" Weight: 255 Origin: International Free Agent, 2013

YEAR	TEAM	LVL	AGE	PA	R	2B	3B	HR	RBI	BB	K	SB	CS	AVG/OBP/SLG	DRC+	VORP	BABIP	BRR	FRAA	WARP
2017	CHA	MLB	30	675	95	43	6	33	102	35	119	3	0	.304/.354/.552	130	34.1	.330	0.8	1B(139): 5.5	4.1
2018	CHA	MLB	31	553	68	36	1	22	78	37	109	2	0	.265/.325/.473	114	14.7	.294	0.0	1B(114): 4.9	2.3
2019	CHA	MLB	32	693	85	38	1	33	123	36	152	2	2	.284/.330/.503	108	18.0	.320	-5.1	1B(125): -10.5	0.2
2020	CHA	MLB	33	595	74	31	1	28	86	36	135	2	1	.271/.329/.484	111	18.5	.313	-1.3	1B 0	1.9

Comparables: Andres Galarraga, Michael Cuddyer, Mo Vaughn

Abreu is as strong as an ox and, especially in our current era of ball juiciness, capable of leaving the park just about any way he pleases. It's just that doing as he pleases, or as he feels he musts, is such an overriding principle in his plate approach that he will expand the zone frequently. Maybe if he could always step into a situation where the opposing pitcher felt the need to challenge him in the zone to stave off disaster, he would have something. With this in mind, Abreu will enter 2020 as the reigning American League RBI champion, thanks to him reserving all of his remaining vestiges of his 2014 form for the 190 plate appearances he strode up with runners in scoring position in 2019. It's a method, or at least a split, that he's repeatedly employed throughout his undeniably productive career, and might have even more success with as the White Sox offense expands beyond its previous setup of Abreu and eight guys until Abreu gets to hit again. But, as much as we always search for the loophole, the exception, the ingenious fix; he's still an aging right-handed first baseman, and he's getting steadily worse.

Tim Anderson SS   Born: 06/23/93   Age: 27   Bats: R   Throws: R   Height: 6'1"   Weight: 185   Origin: Round 1, 2013 Draft (#17 overall)

YEAR	TEAM	LVL	AGE	PA	R	2B	3B	HR	RBI	BB	K	SB	CS	AVG/OBP/SLG	DRC+	VORP	BABIP	BRR	FRAA	WARP
2017	CHA	MLB	24	606	72	26	4	17	56	13	162	15	1	.257/.276/.402	78	11.1	.328	2.1	SS(145): -11.7	0.1
2018	CHA	MLB	25	606	77	28	3	20	64	30	149	26	8	.240/.281/.406	92	19.5	.289	6.5	SS(151): 9.1	3.8
2019	CHA	MLB	26	518	81	32	0	18	56	15	109	17	5	.335/.357/.508	113	33.8	.399	4.3	SS(122): 1.7	3.9
2020	CHA	MLB	27	595	66	29	2	20	74	20	133	24	6	.284/.313/.447	98	24.3	.341	3.3	SS 0	2.5

Comparables: Billy Hunter, Chris Owings, Josh Rutledge

In 2018, Anderson and locker neighbor Daniel Palka posted identical .240 batting averages. In 2019, Palka batted .107, was optioned to the minors twice, and didn't launch his first home run until the final week of the season; Anderson batted .335, the highest qualified average of anyone in the majors. Casual observers will not struggle to conclude Palka, with his cartoonishly large leg kick and hand load and hyper-violent stroke, is even worse than a .240 hitter. Concluding that Anderson—a silky-smooth athlete with lightning-quick hands, a more upright stance than ever before and something bordering on a newfound compulsion to spray the ball to all fields—has radically improved is something we're all a bit more judicious about accepting. With two straight years of rangy but error-prone defense at short, consistent but average power and a lifelong aversion to walks, determining where he falls between a viable starting shortstop and a fringe All-Star is really just about his batting average—even in our statistically vibrant era. To that end, there were material improvements in contact rate and Anderson's ability to stay with and drive breaking pitches that will serve him well in years where he doesn't post the second-highest BABIP in the league. He just probably doesn't need to set aside space on his wall for more than one batting title plaque. (They do they get plaques, right?)

Luis Alexander Basabe OF   Born: 08/26/96   Age: 23   Bats: B   Throws: R   Height: 6'0"   Weight: 160   Origin: International Free Agent, 2012

YEAR	TEAM	LVL	AGE	PA	R	2B	3B	HR	RBI	BB	K	SB	CS	AVG/OBP/SLG	DRC+	VORP	BABIP	BRR	FRAA	WARP
2017	WNS	A+	20	435	52	12	5	5	36	49	104	17	6	.221/.320/.320	85	9.6	.292	4.4	CF(92): 0.1, RF(12): -0.4	1.1
2018	WNS	A+	21	245	36	12	5	9	30	34	64	7	8	.266/.370/.502	144	19.7	.341	-2.0	CF(28): 2.2, LF(16): 1.5	2.0
2018	BIR	AA	21	270	41	9	3	6	26	30	76	9	4	.251/.340/.394	108	13.3	.344	2.1	CF(42): -1.9, RF(15): 0.3	1.1
2019	BIR	AA	22	291	31	12	1	3	30	29	85	9	4	.246/.324/.336	92	3.3	.355	1.4	CF(25): 0.3, LF(22): -2.7	0.6
2020	CHA	MLB	23	105	11	4	1	3	12	9	35	2	1	.217/.286/.370	73	-0.3	.307	0.2	LF 0, CF 0	0.0

Comparables: Daniel Fields, Lewis Brinson, Jeimer Candelario

Basabe already invoked the "bad due to injury" provision in 2017, before rebounding with a Carolina League All-Star and Futures Game appearance in 2018 after offseason knee surgery. When he broke his right hamate bone in February, most hope of any kind of normal season went out the door. Sure enough, the power that lifts Basabe's profile onto the level of a potential everyday player was absent for most of 2019. Between that and a pair of quad strains, his most impressive accomplishment was managing to not have his game go significantly backward. Basabe is still just 23 years old, so treading water in Double-A is not the worst place to be. Alas, the smooth path he needed to transcend a fourth-outfielder destiny does not seem in the stars.

Welington Castillo C   Born: 04/24/87   Age: 33   Bats: R   Throws: R   Height: 5'10"   Weight: 220   Origin: International Free Agent, 2004

YEAR	TEAM	LVL	AGE	PA	R	2B	3B	HR	RBI	BB	K	SB	CS	AVG/OBP/SLG	DRC+	VORP	BABIP	BRR	FRAA	WARP
2017	BAL	MLB	30	365	44	11	0	20	53	22	97	0	0	.282/.323/.490	114	21.0	.336	-0.7	C(88): 10.8	3.4
2018	CHR	AAA	31	40	2	1	0	0	3	3	11	0	0	.189/.250/.216	60	-2.3	.269	-0.3	C(8): -0.5	-0.1
2018	CHA	MLB	31	181	17	7	0	6	15	9	46	1	0	.259/.304/.406	93	4.6	.322	0.2	C(43): -6.5	0.0
2019	CHA	MLB	32	251	19	12	0	12	41	16	74	0	0	.209/.267/.417	78	3.5	.247	-3.1	C(48): -13.7	-1.3
2020	CHA	MLB	33	251	27	10	0	10	32	17	75	1	0	.223/.282/.402	79	0.4	.282	-0.8	C -10	-1.0

Comparables: Martín Maldonado, Miguel Montero, Jeff Mathis

YEAR	TEAM	P. COUNT	FRM RUNS	BLK RUNS	THRW RUNS	TOT RUNS
2017	BAL	13481	6.8	1.3	3.2	12.4
2018	CHA	6226	-5.5	-0.8	0.1	-6.4
2019	CHA	6939	-10.5	-3.1	-0.3	-14.0
2020	CHA	14147	-7.5	-1.6	-0.8	-9.8

Having secured more than half his career earnings in the past two years, Castillo probably won't look back on his time on the South Side entirely with disdain. Most everyone else will. And, since the worst offensive results of his career, a blizzard of passed balls and a complete collapse of his framing performance were all scattered amid a bizarre PED suspension, a concussion, a pulled oblique that cost him a month, shoulder inflammation and a sore elbow (for good measure), it wasn't really a joyful run for anyone involved. He can still run into a dinger, but runs into too much other trouble along the way,

Zack Collins C   Born: 02/06/95   Age: 25   Bats: L   Throws: R   Height: 6'3"   Weight: 220   Origin: Round 1, 2016 Draft (#10 overall)

YEAR	TEAM	LVL	AGE	PA	R	2B	3B	HR	RBI	BB	K	SB	CS	AVG/OBP/SLG	DRC+	VORP	BABIP	BRR	FRAA	WARP
2017	WNS	A+	22	426	63	18	3	17	48	76	118	0	2	.223/.365/.443	119	21.9	.282	-2.6	C(76): 1.5	2.4
2017	BIR	AA	22	45	7	2	0	2	5	11	11	0	0	.235/.422/.471	164	4.7	.286	-0.1	C(11): -2.4	0.2
2018	BIR	AA	23	531	58	24	1	15	68	101	158	5	0	.234/.382/.404	126	33.7	.329	-3.2	C(74): -14.4	1.5
2019	CHR	AAA	24	367	56	19	1	19	74	62	98	0	0	.282/.403/.548	134	27.1	.346	0.8	C(50): -4.6, 1B(19): -1.6	2.1
2019	CHA	MLB	24	102	10	3	1	3	12	14	39	0	0	.186/.307/.349	79	0.3	.295	0.0	C(10): -3.0, 1B(1): -0.1	-0.3
2020	CHA	MLB	25	140	16	6	0	6	17	19	48	0	0	.209/.320/.397	89	1.0	.295	-0.3	1B -1, C -1	-0.1

Comparables: Will Smith, Ryan O'Hearn, Derek Norris

With Collins off to a strong offensive start to 2019 in Triple-A, the White Sox gave him an early big-league cameo. It wasn't just a reward; they brought him up with the hopes that the Show would kick his butt and humble him into a new approach on both sides of the ball—especially offensively, where he'd ideally control the zone rather than just punish mistakes. The Sox are touting incremental progress from Collins as evidence the 25-year-old will soon arrive at the final destination of an impact player. A reliable platoon DH is a more reasonable goal.

YEAR	TEAM	P. COUNT	FRM RUNS	BLK RUNS	THRW RUNS	TOT RUNS
2017	BIR	1559	-1.8	-0.3	0.0	-2.5
2018	BIR	10814	-12.2	-0.9	-0.7	-14.5
2019	CHA	1653	-1.8	-1.1	0.0	-2.9
2019	CHR	6858	-3.9	-0.1	-0.3	-4.6
2020	CHA	1308	-1.0	-0.3	0.0	-1.3

Ryan Cordell OF Born: 03/31/92 Age: 28 Bats: R Throws: R Height: 6'4" Weight: 195 Origin: Round 11, 2013 Draft (#340 overall)

YEAR	TEAM	LVL	AGE	PA	R	2B	3B	HR	RBI	BB	K	SB	CS	AVG/OBP/SLG	DRC+	VORP	BABIP	BRR	FRAA	WARP
2017	CSP	AAA	25	292	49	18	5	10	45	25	65	9	4	.284/.349/.506	100	12.4	.339	1.6	RF(29): 0.0, LF(15): 0.2	0.9
2018	CHR	AAA	26	193	15	9	2	3	22	11	44	7	2	.239/.281/.364	79	-0.1	.293	0.4	CF(22): -0.2, RF(13): -0.4	0.5
2018	CHA	MLB	26	40	3	1	0	1	4	0	15	0	0	.108/.125/.216	61	-3.4	.130	0.4	RF(9): -0.3, CF(7): -0.6	-0.1
2019	CHR	AAA	27	55	8	5	1	1	6	4	17	1	1	.275/.327/.471	74	-3.3	.394	-2.9	RF(8): 0.5, CF(3): -0.1	-0.3
2019	CHA	MLB	27	247	22	8	0	7	24	19	69	3	1	.221/.290/.355	68	-3.6	.287	-0.5	RF(72): 1.5, CF(19): 2.6	0.0
2020	CHA	MLB	28	251	26	10	1	9	30	16	72	5	2	.220/.278/.390	74	-0.6	.279	-0.1	RF 1, CF 1	0.2

Comparables: Matthew den Dekker, Scott Cousins, Johnny Field

"That's a goshdang ballplayer," several scouts have surely exclaimed while laying eyes upon Cordell, an idyllically long and lean, athletic and fleet-footed outfielder. Blessed with plus speed and raw power, everything looks perfect when he's gliding at full-tilt toward a sinking flare, or when he squares up a fastball. Unfortunately, he doesn't do the latter often enough. Cordell spins off the ball in his swing and is slow to make adjustments to how he's attacked at the plate. Those would be acceptable sins six years ago given his innate physical characteristics. These days? He'll turn 28 right after Opening Day 2020, and it's time for him to become a fourth outfielder or not.

Cheslor Cuthbert CI Born: 11/16/92 Age: 27 Bats: R Throws: R Height: 6'1" Weight: 210 Origin: International Free Agent, 2009

YEAR	TEAM	LVL	AGE	PA	R	2B	3B	HR	RBI	BB	K	SB	CS	AVG/OBP/SLG	DRC+	VORP	BABIP	BRR	FRAA	WARP
2017	OMA	AAA	24	68	10	3	1	4	9	7	11	0	0	.271/.353/.559	109	4.7	.267	0.0	3B(10): 0.6, 1B(2): -0.2	0.3
2017	KCA	MLB	24	153	10	7	0	2	18	9	39	0	0	.231/.275/.322	77	-1.5	.301	0.2	3B(44): 0.6, 1B(6): 0.0	0.1
2018	KCA	MLB	25	117	11	2	0	3	7	11	23	0	1	.194/.282/.301	88	-3.7	.218	0.6	3B(12): 0.1, 1B(10): -0.9	0.1
2019	OMA	AAA	26	219	25	17	1	8	35	17	46	0	0	.310/.370/.528	114	9.6	.366	0.9	1B(27): 0.0, 3B(9): -0.6	0.8
2019	KCA	MLB	26	330	24	14	0	9	40	19	67	1	0	.246/.294/.379	82	1.2	.288	-1.7	1B(46): 0.2, 3B(40): -2.9	-0.3
2020	CHA	MLB	27	251	25	12	1	7	28	17	55	1	0	.248/.304/.397	84	2.8	.297	-0.1	3B -1, 1B -1	0.1

Comparables: Lonnie Chisenhall, Matt Dominguez, Brandon Drury

Sometimes prospects just stop being prospects without really becoming anything else. Cuthbert just kept playing baseball in 2019, without any real indication of what purpose it served; a utility infielder without utility who suffered through a 1-for-40 stretch in August. The thing is, thanks to injury and baseball's modern aversion to baseline competence, the one-time champion earned playing time in keeping with a full annual comment, and thus, we're compelled to keep writing. And writing. Reading this comment, in fact, is exactly what it feels like to watch Cuthbert play on a regular basis.

Edwin Encarnación DH Born: 01/07/83 Age: 37 Bats: R Throws: R Height: 6'1" Weight: 230 Origin: Round 9, 2000 Draft (#274 overall)

YEAR	TEAM	LVL	AGE	PA	R	2B	3B	HR	RBI	BB	K	SB	CS	AVG/OBP/SLG	DRC+	VORP	BABIP	BRR	FRAA	WARP
2017	CLE	MLB	34	669	96	20	1	38	107	104	133	2	0	.258/.377/.504	142	28.9	.271	-5.2	1B(23): -0.6	3.8
2018	CLE	MLB	35	579	74	16	1	32	107	63	132	3	0	.246/.336/.474	125	12.4	.265	-5.1	1B(23): 0.8	2.1
2019	SEA	MLB	36	289	48	7	0	21	49	41	55	0	1	.241/.356/.531	135	17.2	.220	0.6	1B(45): -0.6, 2B(1): 0.0	1.7
2019	NYA	MLB	36	197	33	11	0	13	37	17	48	0	0	.249/.325/.531	128	10.6	.267	-1.7	1B(12): -0.4	0.8
2020	CHA	MLB	37	525	75	20	0	34	87	60	118	2	1	.241/.337/.509	118	15.5	.250	-3.0	1B 0	1.6

Comparables: Jason Giambi, Eric Chavez, Albert Pujols

Everything about Encarnación aligned with the Yankees' team structure: A big bomber who's more of a designated hitter than a position player sporting an all-or-nothing approach. Though perhaps his biggest selling point at the trade deadline was acquiring him meant their divisional rivals, who were more in need of his thunder, could not. His veteran presence was welcomed on the young team, as were the stuffed parrots fans and teammates started displaying. But no matter how much excitement Encarnación's addition initially brought, his performance in the ALCS tarnished any positive impact he had in New York. His bat suddenly went ice cold and the parrot got a head start flying south for the winter, leaving Encarnación with just one hit in 18 at-bats while falling short to the Astros. The once-fun home-run race between him and Gary Sánchez earlier in the season turned into a strikeout race in the postseason. Encarnación still has a few more 30-homer seasons in him, something the White Sox are hoping to take advantage of in the short term.

Adam Engel CF Born: 12/09/91 Age: 28 Bats: R Throws: R Height: 6'2" Weight: 210 Origin: Round 19, 2013 Draft (#573 overall)

YEAR	TEAM	LVL	AGE	PA	R	2B	3B	HR	RBI	BB	K	SB	CS	AVG/OBP/SLG	DRC+	VORP	BABIP	BRR	FRAA	WARP
2017	CHR	AAA	25	192	20	12	2	8	19	19	51	4	3	.218/.312/.461	92	10.0	.262	1.8	CF(33): -0.3, LF(13): 1.9	0.8
2017	CHA	MLB	25	336	34	11	3	6	21	19	117	8	1	.166/.235/.282	46	-9.0	.247	1.4	CF(95): 7.9, LF(1): 0.0	-0.2
2018	CHA	MLB	26	463	49	17	4	6	29	18	129	16	8	.235/.279/.336	68	-1.3	.322	1.5	CF(140): 10.0	1.0
2019	CHR	AAA	27	277	43	13	4	9	29	22	62	13	3	.270/.347/.464	92	9.2	.328	4.0	CF(58): 7.4, LF(5): -0.4	1.6
2019	CHA	MLB	27	248	26	10	2	6	26	14	78	3	3	.242/.304/.383	65	-2.1	.343	0.6	CF(86): 0.8	-0.1
2020	CHA	MLB	28	210	20	8	1	5	21	13	65	10	3	.214/.277/.350	68	-0.4	.295	0.6	CF 4	0.3

Comparables: Drew Stubbs, Jordan Danks, Aaron Hicks

In 2019, the White Sox seemed to have gotten fed up with Engel's brand of athletic and increasingly instinctual center-field defense paired with, at most, bimonthly outbursts of offensive impact. They optioned him to Triple-A in early May amid a wave of reassignments to try to jolt a struggling roster—and it sort of worked? Engel toiled in Charlotte for over two months, hit as well there as every single human being in that ballpark did in 2019 and returned to Chicago not, like, transformed or anything, but capable of running into the occasional meatball with his deceptive raw strength. The starting center fielder job on the South Side is about to be reserved for the next several years, which could be convenient since Engel is showing glimpses of being able to hit enough to be a fourth outfielder.

Leury García UT Born: 03/18/91 Age: 29 Bats: B Throws: R Height: 5'8" Weight: 180 Origin: International Free Agent, 2007

YEAR	TEAM	LVL	AGE	PA	R	2B	3B	HR	RBI	BB	K	SB	CS	AVG/OBP/SLG	DRC+	VORP	BABIP	BRR	FRAA	WARP
2017	CHA	MLB	26	326	41	15	2	9	33	13	69	8	5	.270/.316/.423	82	7.5	.321	0.5	CF(51): 3.4, LF(24): 0.2	0.8
2018	CHA	MLB	27	275	23	7	4	4	32	9	69	12	1	.271/.303/.376	74	4.9	.355	1.8	LF(40): 1.4, CF(26): -0.8	0.3
2019	CHA	MLB	28	618	93	27	3	8	40	21	139	15	5	.279/.310/.378	78	3.6	.353	7.9	CF(80): -5.4, RF(45): -2.7	0.3
2020	CHA	MLB	29	385	36	14	2	7	38	16	94	15	6	.255/.295/.366	76	2.5	.325	2.1	2B 1, RF -2	0.1

Comparables: Jeff Bianchi, Charlie Culberson, George Kell

García was surprised when he was told two days prior to the game that he was going to be the White Sox Opening Day leadoff man and center fielder. One can only imagine what he would have thought of the idea seven years ago, when he was a glove-first shortstop. Not every avant garde idea is a great one. After two seasons shortened by nagging injuries, García finally showed he could navigate the travails of full-season play, but in doing that, strongly supported the conclusion that he's ideally a part-time player. His batting line crested at .301/.335/.405 after a four-hit night on Independence Day, and given what became of his second half, someone might consider cutting him off at exactly 327 plate appearances in 2020. García's helter-skelter approach produces a good average, but not good enough to counter the disparities everywhere else. He can run, but not quite fast enough to counter the lack of other weapons. He can play everywhere, but not well enough to be a net positive at somewhere specific. Four-hit nights like July 4 are in him, just don't come around asking for the same thing on July 5.

Luis González OF Born: 09/10/95 Age: 24 Bats: L Throws: L Height: 6'1" Weight: 195 Origin: Round 3, 2017 Draft (#87 overall)

YEAR	TEAM	LVL	AGE	PA	R	2B	3B	HR	RBI	BB	K	SB	CS	AVG/OBP/SLG	DRC+	VORP	BABIP	BRR	FRAA	WARP
2017	KAN	A	21	277	26	13	4	2	12	38	50	2	3	.245/.356/.361	116	10.9	.302	-0.2	CF(31): -2.9, LF(18): -0.1	0.8
2018	KAN	A	22	255	35	16	2	8	26	21	57	7	2	.300/.358/.491	147	19.8	.365	-0.6	CF(39): -1.0, RF(13): -1.9	1.6
2018	WNS	A+	22	288	50	24	3	6	45	27	46	3	5	.313/.376/.504	150	26.8	.354	5.8	CF(31): 3.9, LF(14): 0.2	3.1
2019	BIR	AA	23	535	63	18	4	9	59	47	89	17	9	.247/.316/.359	103	13.0	.281	1.0	CF(60): 0.7, RF(29): 1.1	2.1
2020	CHA	MLB	24	251	24	12	1	6	27	18	57	1	1	.234/.293/.380	78	0.7	.284	-0.3	CF 1, RF 0	0.3

Comparables: Gary Brown, Danny Ortiz, Lane Adams

González hasn't so much as dominated a Google search of his own name since he started playing baseball. But not dominating Double-A will put the 24-year-old González on a time crunch, as the first taste of Southern League pitching is often a separating year for mid-tier position prospects. His tweener profile prompts a lot of questions about his future home and utility if there aren't shiny numbers sitting next to it at all times. (Can he stick in center or can he hit enough to play right? Does he have enough pop despite his lack of size? Does his open stance give up too much of the outer half while enabling pull-side pop?) There's probably a future big-leaguer in some fashion in there, but you'll have to get more specific in your search bar entry if you want to get more details on him than that.

Yasmani Grandal C Born: 11/08/88 Age: 31 Bats: B Throws: R Height: 6'1" Weight: 235 Origin: Round 1, 2010 Draft (#12 overall)

YEAR	TEAM	LVL	AGE	PA	R	2B	3B	HR	RBI	BB	K	SB	CS	AVG/OBP/SLG	DRC+	VORP	BABIP	BRR	FRAA	WARP
2017	LAN	MLB	28	482	50	27	0	22	58	40	130	0	1	.247/.308/.459	93	25.2	.298	-2.6	C(117): 27.7	4.5
2018	LAN	MLB	29	518	65	23	2	24	68	72	124	2	1	.241/.349/.466	113	36.6	.278	-4.4	C(135): 17.7, 1B(2): 0.0	4.7
2019	MIL	MLB	30	632	79	26	2	28	77	109	139	5	1	.246/.380/.468	124	50.1	.279	-7.5	C(137): 19.9, 1B(20): 0.2	6.1
2020	CHA	MLB	31	560	76	21	1	28	81	88	131	3	1	.235/.359/.460	113	29.5	.266	-4.3	C 28, 1B 0	6.0

Comparables: Carlos Santana, Chris Iannetta, Duke Sims

YEAR	TEAM	P. COUNT	FRM RUNS	BLK RUNS	THRW RUNS	TOT RUNS
2017	LAN	16211	26.2	-1.4	1.3	26.2
2018	LAN	16615	15.7	0.8	0.1	16.3
2019	MIL	18727	19.4	1.8	-0.1	20.9
2020	CHA	21509	27.4	0.4	0.0	27.8

Grandal bet on himself the winter before last by foregoing at least one reported multi-year offer in favor of a one-year deal with the Brewers. After a fourth-straight 20-dinger season, Grandal's wager paid off as he signed a four-year deal worth $73 million with the White Sox. It was a smart signing on GM Rick Hahn's part, as there aren't many backstops who are elite framers in addition to being high-quality hitters—he was one of just four backstops in 2019 to slug better than .450 and reach base more than 35 percent of the time. Grandal has, for whatever reason, been an underrated player throughout his career. It's time for that to change.

Jon Jay OF Born: 03/15/85 Age: 35 Bats: L Throws: L Height: 5'11" Weight: 195 Origin: Round 2, 2006 Draft (#74 overall)

YEAR	TEAM	LVL	AGE	PA	R	2B	3B	HR	RBI	BB	K	SB	CS	AVG/OBP/SLG	DRC+	VORP	BABIP	BRR	FRAA	WARP
2017	CHN	MLB	32	433	65	18	3	2	34	37	80	6	2	.296/.374/.375	94	16.8	.368	2.4	LF(64): -3.6, CF(54): -4.8	0.2
2018	KCA	MLB	33	266	28	9	2	1	18	19	39	3	2	.307/.363/.374	80	5.9	.360	-0.5	LF(27): 1.2, CF(15): 1.8	0.3
2018	ARI	MLB	33	320	46	10	5	2	22	14	56	1	1	.235/.304/.325	80	-3.7	.284	-0.1	RF(45): 1.9, LF(14): -1.9	-0.1
2019	CHR	AAA	34	55	8	2	0	0	6	2	10	1	0	.358/.382/.396	93	-1.1	.442	0.0	RF(11): -1.4	-0.1
2019	CHA	MLB	34	182	12	8	0	0	9	8	30	0	0	.267/.311/.315	78	-0.9	.324	0.3	RF(33): -4.6, LF(13): -1.6	-0.7
2020	CHA	MLB	35	251	22	11	1	2	21	15	49	2	1	.261/.324/.346	81	2.4	.324	0.4	RF -1, LF -1	-0.1

Comparables: Denard Span, Nick Markakis, Troy O'Leary

The White Sox *seemed* to place a lot of unreasonable expectations at the feet of Jay when they signed him to a $4 million deal a year ago. As most immediately centered on, they *seemed* to expect him to play a role in recruiting Manny Machado to Chicago. Jay, a respected teammate and Machado's longtime friend, would be forced to recommend a summer at a home stadium that plays Fall Out Boy after victories—one presumes the White Sox won't actually stop wearing black when they make a darker color, but nevertheless—over a decade of fish tacos, a jarring disavowal of personal values. They *seemed* to expect Jay, at age 34, to return to his existence as a slap-hitting/spark-plug on-base machine that had defined his 10-year career, rather than read into the collapse of his offense in the second half of 2018 as a relevant indicator of his capabilities going forward. But, most reasonably of all, they *seemed* to expect him to have two working hips...which, between a three-month absence to start the season, three weeks of pretty good ball, six weeks of pretty awful ball, some very slow if still spirited baserunning and a season-ending surgery, he pretty clearly did not have. At least Machado *seems* happy.

Eloy Jiménez LF Born: 11/27/96 Age: 23 Bats: R Throws: R Height: 6'4" Weight: 205 Origin: International Free Agent, 2013

YEAR	TEAM	LVL	AGE	PA	R	2B	3B	HR	RBI	BB	K	SB	CS	AVG/OBP/SLG	DRC+	VORP	BABIP	BRR	FRAA	WARP
2017	MYR	A+	20	174	23	6	2	8	32	18	35	0	0	.271/.351/.490	158	9.5	.304	-0.3	LF(17): 0.3, RF(7): -0.1	2.0
2017	WNS	A+	20	122	20	11	1	8	26	12	21	0	2	.345/.410/.682	158	13.6	.370	0.4	RF(21): -0.6	1.9
2017	BIR	AA	20	73	11	5	0	3	7	5	16	1	1	.353/.397/.559	170	8.5	.429	0.1	RF(15): -1.1	0.5
2018	BIR	AA	21	228	36	15	2	10	42	18	39	0	0	.317/.368/.556	161	23.9	.344	-1.3	LF(30): -3.6, RF(13): -1.8	1.2
2018	CHR	AAA	21	228	28	13	1	12	33	14	30	0	1	.355/.399/.597	181	19.9	.371	-1.8	LF(41): -0.2, RF(6): 0.0	2.1
2019	CHA	MLB	22	504	69	18	2	31	79	30	134	0	0	.267/.315/.513	105	17.1	.308	1.0	LF(114): -0.7	1.7
2020	CHA	MLB	23	595	80	25	1	37	98	34	155	1	1	.271/.316/.519	114	27.2	.312	0.8	LF-1	2.7

Comparables: Maikel Franco, Clint Frazier, Manuel Margot

Jiménez kind of stunk for much of a full rookie season (enabled by a late-spring contract extension to head off service-time games). He waved at sliders out of the zone, which were flung at him at the league's-highest rate. He flopped around and slammed into objects both stationary and in motion while playing left field—frequently at his own physical peril. And so on. For the baseball writing world, who declared Jiménez was big-league ready—eminently so—early in 2018, it was pretty awkward. Just imagine how Eloy felt! But the thing about near-elite hit and power tools working in concert, is that eventually they synced up, leaving him with respectable end-of-season numbers. He'll need to figure out how to play defense and how to stay healthy, but the bat is there.

───────────────── ★ ★ ★ *2020 Top 101 Prospect* **#13** ★ ★ ★ ─────────────────

Nick Madrigal 2B Born: 03/05/97 Age: 23 Bats: R Throws: R Height: 5'7" Weight: 165 Origin: Round 1, 2018 Draft (#4 overall)

YEAR	TEAM	LVL	AGE	PA	R	2B	3B	HR	RBI	BB	K	SB	CS	AVG/OBP/SLG	DRC+	VORP	BABIP	BRR	FRAA	WARP
2018	KAN	A	21	49	9	3	0	0	6	1	0	2	2	.341/.347/.409	145	5.3	.319	1.1	2B(12): 0.9	0.6
2018	WNS	A+	21	107	14	4	0	0	9	5	5	6	3	.306/.355/.347	121	2.7	.319	0.0	2B(25): -1.8	0.3
2019	WNS	A+	22	218	20	10	2	2	27	17	6	17	4	.272/.346/.377	114	11.5	.269	3.6	2B(41): 3.4	1.6
2019	BIR	AA	22	180	30	11	2	1	16	14	5	14	6	.341/.400/.451	154	14.0	.348	0.3	2B(39): 0.1	1.6
2019	CHR	AAA	22	134	26	6	1	1	12	13	5	4	3	.331/.398/.424	103	6.0	.336	0.5	2B(27): 1.5	0.6
2020	CHA	MLB	23	420	39	20	1	6	38	26	29	12	6	.259/.315/.359	83	7.9	.268	0.2	2B 2	1.0

Comparables: Kevin Newman, Dixon Machado, Steve Clevenger

For the plurality of the season, Madrigal was in the Carolina League. He ran extremely hard, made lightning quick transfers and, due to a lack of power, was not much better than the average hitter playing High-A baseball on the east coast—that despite possessing insanely distinct contact skills. From there on out, he hit .337/.399/.440 while playing the rest of the season at two higher levels. That's an overtly more impressive testament to Madrigal's abilities, but really a more extreme form of what had already been demonstrated. He unleashes blizzards of singles that look like BABIP-fueled hot streaks until they stretch on for months and seasons rather than weeks. His well-rounded game full of up-the-middle defense and plus running raises the floor around his offense, and his biggest advocates tout that there's more ability to drive the ball with authority than the simple numbers game of putting every single ball in play would immediately indicate. He's one of the oddest prospects in the game, and therefore one of the most interesting.

Nomar Mazara RF Born: 04/26/95 Age: 25 Bats: L Throws: L Height: 6'4" Weight: 215 Origin: International Free Agent, 2011

YEAR	TEAM	LVL	AGE	PA	R	2B	3B	HR	RBI	BB	K	SB	CS	AVG/OBP/SLG	DRC+	VORP	BABIP	BRR	FRAA	WARP
2017	TEX	MLB	22	616	64	30	2	20	101	55	127	2	2	.253/.323/.422	91	0.5	.293	-2.4	RF(92): -6.2, LF(47): 0.8	-0.1
2018	TEX	MLB	23	536	61	25	1	20	77	40	116	1	0	.258/.317/.436	98	5.2	.298	-1.2	RF(113): -10.2, LF(2): -0.2	-0.2
2019	TEX	MLB	24	469	69	27	1	19	66	28	108	4	1	.268/.318/.469	95	7.6	.312	-1.4	RF(101): -5.1	0.1
2020	CHA	MLB	25	455	54	20	1	20	62	33	103	1	1	.255/.315/.451	98	7.5	.293	-1.2	RF-9	-0.1

Comparables: Jeremy Hermida, Jose Tabata, Shawn Green

It's not exactly Khris Davis' penchant for hitting .247, but it should be fairly easy to project Mazara's offensive output for 2020. Mazara was pegged as a mega-prospect, so his numbers are obviously underwhelming thus far, but the consistency is truly amazing given how Mazara's proclivity towards streaks. Looking at Mazara's season-end numbers is like assessing a room containing only NBA centers and second-grade children and surmising that the average height of people in the room is 5-foot-10. Mazara is never a 5-foot-10 baseball player. He's either hitting monster home runs in bunches or mired in a month-long slump. He's still just 24 (he'll be 25 in April) so there's time yet for him to have a fully healthy, fully consistent season, but the Rangers have decided it won't be in Texas. The White Sox are simply hoping it happens at all, and paid a small price in prospect Steele Walker to find out.

James McCann C   Born: 06/13/90   Age: 30   Bats: R   Throws: R   Height: 6'3"   Weight: 225   Origin: Round 2, 2011 Draft (#76 overall)

YEAR	TEAM	LVL	AGE	PA	R	2B	3B	HR	RBI	BB	K	SB	CS	AVG/OBP/SLG	DRC+	VORP	BABIP	BRR	FRAA	WARP
2017	DET	MLB	27	391	39	14	2	13	49	26	89	1	0	.253/.318/.415	96	13.7	.300	-0.9	C(103): -20.9	-0.5
2018	DET	MLB	28	457	31	16	0	8	39	26	116	0	3	.220/.267/.314	72	-5.0	.282	-4.2	C(114): -5.0	-0.3
2019	CHA	MLB	29	476	62	26	1	18	60	30	137	4	1	.273/.328/.460	96	20.7	.359	-0.1	C(106): -10.2	1.0
2020	*CHA*	*MLB*	*30*	*210*	*22*	*8*	*1*	*7*	*25*	*13*	*61*	*1*	*0*	*.242/.296/.405*	*84*	*3.5*	*.313*	*-0.6*	*C -4*	*0.0*

Comparables: Gerald Laird, Chad Moeller, Austin Romine

YEAR	TEAM	P. COUNT	FRM RUNS	BLK RUNS	THRW RUNS	TOT RUNS
2017	DET	14626	-13.2	-3.4	-0.8	-18.6
2018	DET	16526	-2.3	-1.4	1.1	-2.9
2019	CHA	15318	-8.0	-0.9	0.9	-7.6
2020	*CHA*	*8154*	*-3.3*	*-0.3*	*0.6*	*-3.0*

Cutting loose their former second-round pick and longtime veteran backstop to save a couple million after a career-worst offensive year is not the reason the Tigers went from 98 losses to 114 in 2019. But it doesn't seem to have been a positive maneuver, either—not after McCann rode a magic carpet to a shocking All-Star appearance with the team five hours away while the Tigers got a .186/.234/.321 slash line from their backstops in his stead. To be fair, even during a good season there were some clear deficiencies with his game. He's upfront about valuing blocking and throwing over framing—a position backed up by our metrics—and his on-base skills are light, to say the least of it. Whatever can be said about the value of a personable and thoughtful game-caller and clubhouse chairman, those words wound up getting said about McCann. Now that he's hitting his weight again, there's reason to listen.

Danny Mendick MI   Born: 09/28/93   Age: 26   Bats: R   Throws: R   Height: 5'10"   Weight: 189   Origin: Round 22, 2015 Draft (#652 overall)

YEAR	TEAM	LVL	AGE	PA	R	2B	3B	HR	RBI	BB	K	SB	CS	AVG/OBP/SLG	DRC+	VORP	BABIP	BRR	FRAA	WARP
2017	WNS	A+	23	305	45	18	4	7	30	31	40	11	4	.289/.373/.468	139	24.8	.315	1.3	2B(45): 5.8, SS(25): -1.6	2.8
2017	BIR	AA	23	165	14	5	0	3	21	17	27	1	2	.197/.280/.293	79	1.0	.222	0.4	SS(34): 5.3, 2B(7): -0.8	0.9
2018	BIR	AA	24	529	62	25	0	14	59	57	90	20	10	.247/.340/.395	110	34.3	.275	1.4	SS(131): -4.2	2.7
2019	CHR	AAA	25	558	75	26	1	17	64	66	96	19	8	.279/.368/.444	102	14.7	.313	0.3	2B(48): 4.2, SS(41): 2.4	2.8
2019	CHA	MLB	25	40	6	0	0	2	4	1	11	0	0	.308/.325/.462	88	1.0	.385	0.0	SS(5): 0.0, 3B(3): 0.7	0.1
2020	*CHA*	*MLB*	*26*	*315*	*33*	*14*	*0*	*9*	*34*	*27*	*71*	*4*	*2*	*.236/.309/.381*	*84*	*4.0*	*.285*	*-0.4*	*2B 2, 3B 1*	*0.8*

Comparables: Billy Hunter, Kelby Tomlinson, Cliff Pennington

Mendick made his major-league debut before he made his BP Annual debut—and not because of some sort of unforeseeable crisis of White Sox infield depth, either. To trudge through the minors on merit-based promotions and sneak below the radar, Mendick needed to have it all. He's small—generously listed at 5-foot-10—which pushes any notion of even average raw power aside. Unlike the similarly diminutive Madrigal, Mendick doesn't have a standout tool to speak of, getting by on average straight-line speed and making a typical hit tool play up with a mature approach. Additionally, Mendick's big-league plate appearance total only surpassed his advanced age (26) in the final week of the 2019 season, and he has been tasked with proving he was more than just an old guy whipping up on youngsters his entire career. After two years at junior college, Mendick spent two years at Massachusetts-Lowell before he was picked as a 22nd-round senior signing, and then spent another year as an org soldier bouncing between affiliates, emphasizing the primary reason he took this long to get a book comment: no one ever thought he was good enough to make it this far.

Yoán Moncada 3B   Born: 05/27/95   Age: 25   Bats: B   Throws: R   Height: 6'2"   Weight: 205   Origin: International Free Agent, 2015

YEAR	TEAM	LVL	AGE	PA	R	2B	3B	HR	RBI	BB	K	SB	CS	AVG/OBP/SLG	DRC+	VORP	BABIP	BRR	FRAA	WARP
2017	CHR	AAA	22	361	57	9	3	12	36	49	102	17	8	.282/.377/.447	130	16.4	.379	-0.1	2B(80): 1.4	2.2
2017	CHA	MLB	22	231	31	8	2	8	22	29	74	3	2	.231/.338/.412	92	4.5	.325	-0.7	2B(54): 5.8	1.0
2018	CHA	MLB	23	650	73	32	6	17	61	67	217	12	6	.235/.315/.400	89	15.1	.344	-0.4	2B(149): -12.7	-0.2
2019	CHA	MLB	24	559	83	34	5	25	79	40	154	10	3	.315/.367/.548	123	38.5	.406	3.5	3B(129): 10.3	5.1
2020	*CHA*	*MLB*	*25*	*595*	*76*	*25*	*3*	*27*	*83*	*53*	*170*	*22*	*8*	*.263/.334/.473*	*108*	*21.3*	*.336*	*0.9*	*3B 4*	*2.6*

Comparables: Gil McDougald, Evan Longoria, Willie Greene

Chances are, the White Sox would have figured out a way to make Manny Machado and Yoán Moncada work in the same infield in some fashion. (What a harrowing challenge that would've been for manager Rick Renteria.) In the meantime, the Sox responded to their failed Machado bid by moving Moncada to Machado's position and watching him outplay the former All-Star. After fetishizing patience to the point of passivity (and a near-record setting number of strikeouts), Moncada turned his in-zone aggression all the way up in 2019. He partly unlocked elite hand speed and plus raw power that was lying fallow as he stared at two-strike fastballs on the outside corner in large quantities, and he was partly rewarded with some of the nuttiest batted-ball luck seen this decade. Think of it as the universe winking at Moncada for embracing the approach that was always best for him—and man, think of how good it would have been to flank him with Machado.

Daniel Palka RF   Born: 10/28/91   Age: 28   Bats: L   Throws: L   Height: 6'2"   Weight: 220   Origin: Round 3, 2013 Draft (#88 overall)

YEAR	TEAM	LVL	AGE	PA	R	2B	3B	HR	RBI	BB	K	SB	CS	AVG/OBP/SLG	DRC+	VORP	BABIP	BRR	FRAA	WARP
2017	ROC	AAA	25	362	47	13	3	11	42	27	80	1	2	.274/.329/.431	105	9.4	.329	1.2	RF(61): 3.5, LF(25): 0.1	1.3
2018	CHR	AAA	26	73	11	3	0	3	7	10	21	1	2	.286/.384/.476	123	3.7	.385	0.1	RF(15): 0.5	0.4
2018	CHA	MLB	26	449	56	15	3	27	67	30	153	2	1	.240/.294/.484	100	11.4	.308	-0.8	RF(43): -3.0, LF(26): -0.5	0.4
2019	CHR	AAA	27	471	83	23	0	27	72	72	109	2	0	.263/.374/.527	124	9.9	.293	-6.1	RF(62): -5.9, 1B(13): -0.4	0.9
2019	CHA	MLB	27	93	4	0	0	2	4	8	35	0	1	.107/.194/.179	50	-4.0	.149	0.1	RF(23): -4.0, 1B(1): -0.1	-0.8
2020	*CHA*	*MLB*	*28*	*251*	*31*	*9*	*1*	*14*	*37*	*24*	*83*	*3*	*1*	*.220/.298/.446*	*88*	*4.2*	*.279*	*-0.2*	*RF -2, LF -1*	*0.1*

Comparables: Tyler Austin, Jonny Gomes, Jerry Sands

There's never a good situation for a major-league player to forget how to hit, but it's probably significantly more inconvenient for a lumbering...er, lumberjack-type build slugger like Palka. Possessing no true defensive home (and quickly contributing negative defensive value at any spot he lays his hat), an 0-for-32 slump to start the year sent him from Opening Day right fielder to playing right field in Charlotte within the first month of the season. Either comfortably or confoundingly or both, Palka retained the ability to produce offensively in Triple-A, where he was exiled for most of 2019. He'll probably do the same in 2020, when he'll be a 28-year-old platoon bat who has suddenly cast a lot more doubt on how reliable that description remains.

★ ★ ★ *2020 Top 101 Prospect* **#6** ★ ★ ★

Luis Robert CF Born: 08/03/97 Age: 22 Bats: R Throws: R Height: 6'3" Weight: 185 Origin: International Free Agent, 2017

YEAR	TEAM	LVL	AGE	PA	R	2B	3B	HR	RBI	BB	K	SB	CS	AVG/OBP/SLG	DRC+	VORP	BABIP	BRR	FRAA	WARP
2017	DWS	RK	19	114	17	8	1	3	14	22	23	12	3	.310/.491/.536	203	20.6	.397	2.5	CF(19): -0.5	1.7
2018	KAN	A	20	50	5	3	1	0	4	4	12	4	2	.289/.360/.400	105	3.0	.394	-0.2	CF(10): 0.0	0.1
2018	WNS	A+	20	140	21	6	1	0	11	8	37	8	2	.244/.317/.309	83	2.7	.341	0.5	CF(27): 3.1, RF(4): -0.4	0.5
2019	WNS	A+	21	84	21	5	3	8	24	4	20	8	2	.453/.512/.920	273	18.3	.553	-1.2	CF(13): 1.9	1.6
2019	BIR	AA	21	244	43	16	3	8	29	13	54	21	6	.314/.362/.518	128	20.2	.384	2.5	CF(36): 1.9, RF(7): -0.8	1.8
2019	CHR	AAA	21	223	44	10	5	16	39	11	55	7	3	.297/.341/.634	114	13.2	.324	1.2	CF(46): 6.5	1.7
2020	CHA	MLB	22	595	74	30	4	29	86	30	175	18	6	.262/.315/.487	109	28.6	.333	1.9	CF 8, RF 0	3.8

Comparables: Brett Phillips, Lewis Brinson, Greg Golson

Robert's plate discipline and offensive performance dipped precipitously with every promotion during his three-level dash through the minors in 2019, to the point where he was striking out five times as often as he took a free pass in Triple-A. (That stint in Charlotte also saw him launch 16 home runs in 47 games, which is a pretty metal, even in the rarified mania that was 2019 Triple-A baseball.) Robert was sold as an impossibly physically gifted toolshed who dominated the best professional competition in Cuba at a young age, and finally healthy in 2019, a 30-30 (and more) season displayed all the physical gifts. As for the level of polish in his game, there's likely a myriad of approach adjustments he will need in the majors, but those clearly aren't going to be forced at any level of competition below that. Where he ultimately falls between world-conquering stardom and limitlessly talented but somewhat frustrating regular contributor will get hashed out sometime over the next decade.

Blake Rutherford OF Born: 05/02/97 Age: 23 Bats: L Throws: R Height: 6'2" Weight: 210 Origin: Round 1, 2016 Draft (#18 overall)

YEAR	TEAM	LVL	AGE	PA	R	2B	3B	HR	RBI	BB	K	SB	CS	AVG/OBP/SLG	DRC+	VORP	BABIP	BRR	FRAA	WARP
2017	CSC	A	20	304	41	20	2	2	30	25	55	9	4	.281/.342/.391	98	10.8	.341	-2.6	CF(39): -5.6, LF(13): -0.5	-0.3
2017	KAN	A	20	136	11	5	0	0	5	13	21	1	0	.213/.289/.254	98	-4.9	.257	-0.1	CF(13): -1.3, LF(10): -0.3	0.1
2018	WNS	A+	21	487	67	25	9	7	78	34	90	15	8	.293/.345/.436	121	18.7	.351	1.1	RF(74): -2.5, LF(15): -2.7	1.4
2019	BIR	AA	22	480	50	17	3	7	49	37	118	9	2	.265/.319/.365	95	7.1	.343	2.4	RF(67): 1.7, LF(29): -1.7	1.0
2020	CHA	MLB	23	251	23	11	1	5	25	16	72	3	1	.237/.289/.363	74	-0.5	.318	-0.1	RF -1, LF -1	-0.5

Comparables: Destin Hood, Sócrates Brito, Eddie Rosario

YOU, UNFEELING MONSTER WHO REVELS IN THE PAIN OF OTHERS: Rutherford is a future corner guy whose polish was supposed to carry a profile that lacks standout tools, specifically the typical impact power of a corner outfielder, and the speed that would make sticking in center field or adding a ton of value on defense realistic. As for that polish, he has hit .280/.337/.400 in four professional seasons, with the most damage coming when he was in rookie ball. There's just not much reason to expect a big-league regular if you didn't see one already.

US, SHAMELESS OPTIMISTS: Rutherford will be 22 on Opening Day with time yet to show more pitch recognition and ability to adjust, has pretty much not played against competition that was his same age since rookie ball, and just flashed standout contact ability during a strong finish to an otherwise nightmarish 2019 season. Surely not *every* team that put first-round grades on him out of high school were suffering from madness.

Yolmer Sánchez 2B Born: 06/29/92 Age: 28 Bats: B Throws: R Height: 5'11" Weight: 185 Origin: International Free Agent, 2009

YEAR	TEAM	LVL	AGE	PA	R	2B	3B	HR	RBI	BB	K	SB	CS	AVG/OBP/SLG	DRC+	VORP	BABIP	BRR	FRAA	WARP
2017	CHA	MLB	25	534	63	19	8	12	59	35	111	8	9	.267/.319/.413	93	13.8	.321	0.9	2B(78): -0.3, 3B(52): 3.2	1.6
2018	CHA	MLB	26	662	62	34	10	8	55	49	138	14	6	.242/.306/.372	80	11.4	.300	0.7	3B(141): -1.2, 2B(9): 0.2	0.7
2019	CHA	MLB	27	555	59	20	4	2	43	44	117	5	4	.252/.318/.321	78	2.3	.324	0.2	2B(149): 19.0	2.1
2020	CHA	MLB	28	251	23	10	2	5	24	17	54	4	2	.235/.295/.352	75	0.3	.289	0.4	2B 2, 3B 1	0.3

Comparables: Asdrúbal Cabrera, Rubén Tejada, Bret Boone

The balls were pretty juicy back in 2017, when Sánchez's stilted uncoil of a swing produced a career-high 12 home runs and he flirted with league-average offensive production. Two years later, they were even juicier, and...he posted the lowest ISO of any qualified hitter in the game. Hmph. To his credit, he's leaned in hard to both sides of his light-hitting, nimble glove profile over the last three years—his Gold Glove win was legitimate, in our estimation. All jokes are funnier when you're hitting 20 bombs per year, which is a shame because Sánchez ambushing random teammates and coaches who aren't looking with Gatorade baths during walk-off dogpiles is one of baseball's best running bits.

Gavin Sheets 1B Born: 04/23/96 Age: 24 Bats: L Throws: L Height: 6'4" Weight: 230 Origin: Round 2, 2017 Draft (#49 overall)

YEAR	TEAM	LVL	AGE	PA	R	2B	3B	HR	RBI	BB	K	SB	CS	AVG/OBP/SLG	DRC+	VORP	BABIP	BRR	FRAA	WARP
2017	KAN	A	21	218	16	10	0	3	25	20	34	0	0	.266/.346/.365	112	2.1	.308	-2.4	1B(50): -2.1	0.0
2018	WNS	A+	22	497	58	28	2	6	61	52	81	1	0	.293/.368/.407	134	10.5	.344	-3.9	1B(108): -4.3	1.4
2019	BIR	AA	23	527	56	18	1	16	83	54	99	3	1	.267/.345/.414	129	10.4	.305	-6.3	1B(109): 3.8	1.9
2020	CHA	MLB	24	251	26	12	0	8	29	20	58	0	0	.249/.314/.402	90	4.2	.303	-0.5	1B 0	0.5

Comparables: Russ Canzler, Matt Thaiss, David Cooper

Tasked with the solemn task of cranking more rocking dingers as a complement to his admirable contact and plate discipline, Sheets recovered from an ugly start in Double-A to fulfill his central purpose. His 16 homers were top-10 in the category in the pitching-friendly Southern League, even if everyone ahead of him among the league leaders did it in fewer than his 527 plate appearances in Birmingham. That continued a trend for him, as he's never pushed aside all the doubts about his game—he's a bat-only prospect without an elite bat—by laying waste to opposing pitching. Sheets will almost surely play in the Show, but it's unclear for how long.

Charles Tilson OF Born: 12/02/92 Age: 27 Bats: L Throws: L Height: 6'0" Weight: 185 Origin: Round 2, 2011 Draft (#79 overall)

YEAR	TEAM	LVL	AGE	PA	R	2B	3B	HR	RBI	BB	K	SB	CS	AVG/OBP/SLG	DRC+	VORP	BABIP	BRR	FRAA	WARP
2018	CHR	AAA	25	292	27	12	0	0	25	16	52	10	2	.244/.288/.289	67	-5.1	.301	1.4	CF(49): -3.1, LF(17): -0.7	-0.3
2018	CHA	MLB	25	121	7	1	1	0	11	10	20	2	3	.264/.331/.292	72	-0.7	.322	0.7	LF(32): -0.3, CF(5): -0.2	-0.1
2019	CHR	AAA	26	258	36	13	2	3	34	19	43	4	3	.288/.345/.398	87	2.3	.340	1.5	LF(35): 1.0, CF(23): -3.7	0.2
2019	CHA	MLB	26	157	16	5	0	1	12	10	38	4	0	.229/.293/.285	68	-2.3	.305	2.3	RF(30): 2.7, LF(19): -0.9	0.3
2020	CHA	MLB	27	251	21	10	1	3	21	16	54	9	3	.238/.293/.324	65	-1.9	.300	1.3	CF 1, LF 0	-0.1

Comparables: Ezequiel Carrera, Rey Fuentes, Dalton Pompey

Surely more than a few people noticed that within days of colliding with left fielder and White Sox rebuild centerpiece Eloy Jiménez (thus sending him to the injured list), Tilson was on a plane back to Charlotte, where he spent the final six weeks of the minor-league season. Of course, eight hits over his last month-plus in Chicago was also possibly a culprit in his demise. Tilson was never supposed to make a living hitting for power, but save for a wacky moment in Houston where he turned around a 98-mph Josh James fastball for a grand slam, he's lived up to the advertising too well. Tilson will enter 2020 out of options, which means he could get the chance to climb his way up another club's totem pole of light-hitting, fleet-footed outfielders. If given the opportunity, next time he should use his speed to dodge the franchise cornerstone—you know, just in case.

———————————— ★ ★ ★ *2020 Top 101 Prospect* **#31** ★ ★ ★ ————————————

Andrew Vaughn 1B Born: 04/03/98 Age: 22 Bats: R Throws: R Height: 6'0" Weight: 214 Origin: Round 1, 2019 Draft (#3 overall)

YEAR	TEAM	LVL	AGE	PA	R	2B	3B	HR	RBI	BB	K	SB	CS	AVG/OBP/SLG	DRC+	VORP	BABIP	BRR	FRAA	WARP
2019	KAN	A	21	103	14	7	0	2	11	14	18	0	0	.253/.388/.410	137	6.0	.297	1.2	1B(19): -0.5	0.6
2019	WNS	A+	21	126	16	8	0	3	21	16	17	0	1	.252/.349/.411	140	6.0	.270	-0.3	1B(15): -0.3	0.5
2020	CHA	MLB	22	251	24	12	0	6	26	19	56	3	1	.222/.294/.360	76	0.2	.270	0.0	1B -2	-0.2

Comparables: Ty France, Mike Ford, Patrick Wisdom

In the rare instances where Vaughn rolls over a ball and chops a slow roller to third base, it's hard not to think of *Star Wars* as he digs in to beat out the throw. Specifically, it's that scene in *The Empire Strikes Back* where Han Solo pulls the handle for the hyperdrive, expecting the stars to streak in the sky as his ship leaps into light speed, only for the engine to whine as the Millenium Falcon keeps chugging along at the same unsuitable pace. Vaughn has a throwing arm strong enough that he was recruited out of high school as a two-way player and dutifully works on his glove. But, in general, there's not the oozing athleticism present to provide some extra value to his game outside his bat. That, in the end, could just be another compliment for his truly exceptional bat: plus power to all-fields as well as a plate approach so disciplined that every at-bat takes on the feeling that the opposing pitcher is being audited after three years of not self-paying taxes on his freelance income. This is as advanced and polished as a young hitter gets—it's a good thing, too, because there's not a fallback option if flaws emerge.

Seby Zavala C Born: 08/28/93 Age: 26 Bats: R Throws: R Height: 5'11" Weight: 215 Origin: Round 12, 2015 Draft (#352 overall)

YEAR	TEAM	LVL	AGE	PA	R	2B	3B	HR	RBI	BB	K	SB	CS	AVG/OBP/SLG	DRC+	VORP	BABIP	BRR	FRAA	WARP
2017	KAN	A	23	207	32	8	0	13	34	13	52	0	0	.259/.327/.514	133	17.2	.289	0.9	C(43): -1.5	1.5
2017	WNS	A+	23	228	31	13	0	8	38	24	52	1	0	.302/.376/.485	141	20.1	.373	3.0	C(34): 0.9	2.1
2018	BIR	AA	24	232	32	7	0	11	31	27	65	0	0	.271/.358/.472	133	18.4	.339	0.0	C(31): 4.0	2.0
2018	CHR	AAA	24	191	18	15	0	2	20	6	44	0	2	.243/.267/.359	81	-2.6	.304	-1.2	C(35): -3.0	-0.1
2019	CHR	AAA	25	331	49	14	0	20	45	26	116	1	1	.222/.296/.471	78	-3.2	.282	-1.7	C(52): 6.8, 1B(18): -0.3	0.7
2019	CHA	MLB	25	12	1	0	0	0	0	0	9	0	0	.083/.083/.083	52	-0.1	.333	0.0	C(3): 0.2	0.0
2020	CHA	MLB	26	251	22	9	0	7	26	16	97	0	0	.191/.252/.328	52	-8.1	.289	-0.5	C 4, 1B 0	-0.4

Comparables: Cameron Rupp, Adam Engel, JaCoby Jones

Your defensive-minded, game-managing catching prospect clubbing 20 home runs in Triple-A just isn't the coup it was before the top levels of professional baseball started using glorified racquetballs in games. The gritty and weathered Zavala has overcome waiting until the third day of the draft to hear his name called and a wealth of nagging injuries to get to this point. He posted the highest home-run total and second-highest ISO of his professional career at Charlotte in 2019, but looked overmatched and overwhelmed against big-league pitching during two cups of coffee in Chicago. With decent power production being easier to find than ever, and the White Sox more interested in squeezing offense from the catching position than most, the White Sox might end up saying bye to Seby.

YEAR	TEAM	P. COUNT	FRM RUNS	BLK RUNS	THRW RUNS	TOT RUNS
2018	BIR	4264	3.3	0.1	0.4	4.0
2018	CHR	4728	-2.6	0.0	-0.1	-2.3
2019	CHA	345	0.1	0.1	0.0	0.2
2019	CHR	7180	5.4	-0.1	0.4	5.6
2020	CHA	8438	2.8	1.2	-0.3	3.6

PITCHERS

Manny Bañuelos LHP Born: 03/13/91 Age: 29 Bats: R Throws: L Height: 5'10" Weight: 215 Origin: International Free Agent, 2008

YEAR	TEAM	LVL	AGE	W	L	SV	G	GS	IP	H	HR	BB/9	K/9	K	GB%	BABIP	WHIP	ERA	DRA	WARP	MPH	FB%	WHF	CSP
2017	SLC	AAA	26	5	6	0	39	9	95	107	4	4.6	8.1	85	48%	.350	1.64	4.93	5.13	0.3				
2018	OKL	AAA	27	9	7	0	31	18	108²	109	10	3.5	10.5	127	45%	.349	1.39	3.73	4.35	1.4				
2019	WNS	A+	28	0	0	0	2	2	8²	14	1	4.2	10.4	10	48%	.464	2.08	4.15	6.85	-0.2				
2019	CHA	MLB	28	3	4	0	16	8	50²	60	12	5.9	7.8	44	37%	.331	1.84	6.93	8.41	-1.5	93.9	47.4	10.6	47
2020	CHA	MLB	29	2	2	0	33	0	35	37	7	4.1	7.6	29	39%	.296	1.52	5.53	5.43	-0.1	93.2	47.4	10.6	47

Comparables: Chris Seddon, John Lamb, Greg Smith

For every Rich Hill—a formerly ballyhooed prospect lefty beset by injuries and setbacks, who really just needed a prolonged break to get healthy, an opportunity and maybe a tweak or two to unlock their dormant talent—there are a legion of stories like Manny Bañuelos. Tommy John surgery, subsequent setbacks and a myriad of other elbow ailments that put many years between the baseball world and the last time they saw him at the height of his powers. Finally afforded the opportunity to rehab by the Angels, and after quietly thriving in Triple-A for a loaded Dodgers organization that didn't need to take a chance on him, the White Sox figured they'd give Bañuelos some run in a rebuilding year. In return they got what they probably should have expected based on his track record. There were some brief glimpses of ability, multiple trips to the injured list for his throwing shoulder, and some true stat-destroying shellackings in moments where he seemed less than 100 percent—all making for a fairly infuriating total package. There's talent in there, though, and with any luck he'll find himself on the Rich side of the hill.

Aaron Bummer LHP Born: 09/21/93 Age: 26 Bats: L Throws: L Height: 6'3" Weight: 200 Origin: Round 19, 2014 Draft (#558 overall)

YEAR	TEAM	LVL	AGE	W	L	SV	G	GS	IP	H	HR	BB/9	K/9	K	GB%	BABIP	WHIP	ERA	DRA	WARP	MPH	FB%	WHF	CSP
2017	WNS	A+	23	0	2	2	8	0	11	10	2	2.5	12.3	15	59%	.296	1.18	4.91	3.40	0.2				
2017	BIR	AA	23	1	3	3	17	1	33	29	2	4.4	9.3	34	56%	.318	1.36	3.00	4.87	0.0				
2017	CHA	MLB	23	1	3	0	30	0	22	13	4	6.1	7.0	17	57%	.167	1.27	4.50	5.95	-0.2	95.1	61	11.1	42.1
2018	CHR	AAA	24	2	3	0	31	0	30²	27	0	3.2	8.8	30	67%	.310	1.24	2.64	3.82	0.5				
2018	CHA	MLB	24	0	1	0	37	0	31²	40	1	2.8	9.9	35	62%	.402	1.58	4.26	3.71	0.4	95.2	65.9	10.5	48.5
2019	CHR	AAA	25	0	0	0	5	0	7²	7	0	2.3	7.0	6	96%	.304	1.17	2.35	3.49	0.2				
2019	CHA	MLB	25	0	0	1	58	0	67²	43	4	3.2	8.0	60	71%	.228	0.99	2.13	2.99	1.7	97.5	76.1	11.4	50.8
2020	CHA	MLB	26	3	3	4	59	0	62	56	6	3.6	8.9	61	68%	.293	1.30	3.58	3.81	0.9	96.3	72.6	11.3	48.7

Comparables: Jerry Blevins, Paul Fry, Eric Stout

Scrolling through an article at his locker about rising batting averages against fastballs during his breakout season, Bummer smirked and quipped that it seemed like great news for him: someone who throws a heater around 80 percent of the time. Prompted by an ugly spring, Bummer mostly ditched his slider for a cutter that he could more consistently locate. He then went through entire innings doing nothing but pounding sinkers. He struck out fewer hitters, walked more, and basically tried to do every outmoded pitching tactic all at once. It worked amazingly well, perhaps because all the cautionary notions about throwing sinkers and striving for weak contact apply to pitchers who are throwing inferior versions of the 95-mph bowling ball Bummer tosses from a lefty slinging motion. Like the best years of Matt Thornton on the South Side a decade before him, if your fastball is good enough—and maybe if you throw it from the left side—then predictability and trends mean about as much as a pot of beans on a Sunday.

Dylan Cease RHP Born: 12/28/95 Age: 24 Bats: R Throws: R Height: 6'2" Weight: 190 Origin: Round 6, 2014 Draft (#169 overall)

YEAR	TEAM	LVL	AGE	W	L	SV	G	GS	IP	H	HR	BB/9	K/9	K	GB%	BABIP	WHIP	ERA	DRA	WARP	MPH	FB%	WHF	CSP
2017	SBN	A	21	1	2	0	13	13	51²	39	2	4.5	12.9	74	46%	.339	1.26	2.79	3.65	1.0				
2017	KAN	A	21	0	8	0	9	9	41²	35	1	3.9	11.2	52	43%	.330	1.27	3.89	4.00	0.6				
2018	WNS	A+	22	9	2	0	13	13	71²	52	5	3.5	10.3	82	50%	.273	1.12	2.89	3.34	1.7				
2018	BIR	AA	22	3	0	0	10	10	52¹	30	3	3.8	13.4	78	50%	.273	0.99	1.72	2.52	1.7				
2019	CHR	AAA	23	5	2	0	15	15	68¹	75	4	4.2	9.6	73	55%	.370	1.57	4.48	4.50	1.5				
2019	CHA	MLB	23	4	7	0	14	14	73	78	15	4.3	10.0	81	46%	.326	1.55	5.79	5.28	0.4	98.4	51.5	11.6	42.3
2020	CHA	MLB	24	6	5	0	16	16	86	82	13	4.4	9.5	91	47%	.302	1.44	4.56	4.59	0.9	98.2	53.1	11.9	43.6

Comparables: Hunter Wood, Kyle McGowin, John Gant

It's rare that a pitcher's major-league debut comes in a season where he never seems to get hot for any stretch of time. But such was Cease's 2019, in which his promotion to Chicago was preordained and continued apace despite control and fastball spin issues that never seemed conquered for a period longer than two weeks. He still threw hard, still spun offspeed pitches that fell off the table, and still remained well-regarded. Now that he's a big leaguer, Cease's days of being evaluated for potential—for flashing the look of an upper-90s fastball with three swing-and-miss secondaries—are over; heading forward, it's all about track record. Heretofore, he's proven he can dominate the Tigers, which, since they promoted him from Triple-A, seems like something the White Sox already knew.

Steve Cishek RHP Born: 06/18/86 Age: 34 Bats: R Throws: R Height: 6'6" Weight: 215 Origin: Round 5, 2007 Draft (#166 overall)

YEAR	TEAM	LVL	AGE	W	L	SV	G	GS	IP	H	HR	BB/9	K/9	K	GB%	BABIP	WHIP	ERA	DRA	WARP	MPH	FB%	WHF	CSP
2017	SEA	MLB	31	1	1	1	23	0	20	13	3	3.2	6.8	15	61%	.185	1.00	3.15	4.78	0.1	92.3	51.5	8.2	46.5
2017	TBA	MLB	31	2	1	0	26	0	24²	13	0	2.6	9.5	26	52%	.220	0.81	1.09	3.41	0.5	92.8	49.5	13.7	44.3
2018	CHN	MLB	32	4	3	4	80	0	70¹	45	5	3.6	10.0	78	49%	.238	1.04	2.18	4.68	0.2	92.7	61.6	12	46.7
2019	CHN	MLB	33	4	6	7	70	0	64	48	7	4.1	8.0	57	50%	.246	1.20	2.95	4.08	0.9	92.7	59.2	9.8	44.3
2020	CHA	MLB	34	2	2	0	48	0	51	44	8	3.5	8.8	50	48%	.268	1.26	3.87	4.16	0.7	91.6	57.7	10.7	44.7

Comparables: Brad Brach, Rafael Soriano, Brian Wilson

In the era of power-armed strikeout pitchers, Cishek has found a home in the bigs as a rubber-armed, quirky, change-of-pace pitcher. One problem: His command is becoming an issue, as his walk rate has gone from 8.1 percent to 9.7 percent, to 10.9 percent over the last three years. He still gets loads of groundballs, but he'll need to stop putting runners on base as he ages and (presumably) misses fewer bats. Can he reverse the trend?

Alex Colomé RHP Born: 12/31/88   Age: 31   Bats: R   Throws: R   Height: 6'1"   Weight: 220   Origin: International Free Agent, 2007

YEAR	TEAM	LVL	AGE	W	L	SV	G	GS	IP	H	HR	BB/9	K/9	K	GB%	BABIP	WHIP	ERA	DRA	WARP	MPH	FB%	WHF	CSP
2017	TBA	MLB	28	2	3	47	65	0	66²	57	4	3.1	7.8	58	50%	.275	1.20	3.24	3.97	0.9	96.2	32.7	12.4	46.8
2018	TBA	MLB	29	2	5	11	23	0	21²	24	1	3.3	9.6	23	55%	.354	1.48	4.15	3.91	0.3	96.3	36.8	16	48.9
2018	SEA	MLB	29	5	0	1	47	0	46¹	35	6	2.5	9.5	49	42%	.254	1.04	2.53	3.97	0.5	96.8	36.8	15	45.5
2019	CHA	MLB	30	4	5	30	62	0	61	42	7	3.4	8.1	55	45%	.215	1.07	2.80	3.99	0.9	95.7	29	14.5	45.6
2020	CHA	MLB	31	3	3	36	59	0	62	54	9	3.1	8.8	61	45%	.273	1.22	3.56	3.80	0.9	95.3	32.5	14.2	46

Comparables: Cody Martin, Adam Warren, Aaron Blair

In the three seasons since his deserved 2016 trip to the All-Star Game, Colomé's strikeout rates have yo-yo'd, his sweeping and diving cutter has and hasn't racked up harmless ground balls for various stretches, and he's bounced in and out of a closer role that's highly coveted for someone whose salary is at least partially mapped out by arbitration projections.)DRA, to its credit, has seen the same guy three years running.) There's decent, but not exceptional control, he's not a wormkiller, but more likely to get someone to roll-over than most. Colomé doesn't get hammered, but is no wizard of weak contact. He's a bit better than your typical reliever, which means when he's rolling, he can get high-leverage outs. It also means that the ideal bullpen would task him with getting only medium-leverage ones, putting him in a position to overperform rather than disappoint. The White Sox bullpen is not that ideal bullpen.

Jimmy Cordero RHP Born: 10/19/91   Age: 28   Bats: R   Throws: R   Height: 6'4"   Weight: 222   Origin: International Free Agent, 2012

YEAR	TEAM	LVL	AGE	W	L	SV	G	GS	IP	H	HR	BB/9	K/9	K	GB%	BABIP	WHIP	ERA	DRA	WARP	MPH	FB%	WHF	CSP
2017	HAR	AA	25	2	6	0	41	0	51¹	52	7	6.7	7.0	40	53%	.290	1.75	6.84	6.89	-1.3				
2018	SYR	AAA	26	4	1	6	41	0	46	43	0	4.3	10.4	53	55%	.333	1.41	1.96	4.55	0.3				
2018	WAS	MLB	26	1	2	0	22	0	19	23	2	5.7	5.7	12	57%	.318	1.84	5.68	6.42	-0.3	100.4	61.8	12.3	43.8
2019	CHR	AAA	27	3	1	4	13	0	17²	14	0	1.0	7.1	14	72%	.275	0.91	0.51	2.16	0.7				
2019	FRE	AAA	27	0	1	3	12	0	15	17	3	5.4	10.2	17	53%	.333	1.73	6.00	4.27	0.3				
2019	CHA	MLB	27	1	0	0	30	0	36	24	3	2.8	7.8	31	62%	.226	0.97	2.75	3.47	0.7	99.8	68.6	15.4	49.8
2019	TOR	MLB	27	0	1	0	1	0	1¹	2	1	0.0	0.0	0	40%	.250	1.50	6.75	6.21	0.0	98.2	53.3	6.7	57.9
2020	CHA	MLB	28	1	1	0	27	0	28	26	3	3.8	9.0	28	58%	.292	1.32	3.84	3.99	0.4	99.3	66.5	14.3	47.5

Comparables: Kyle Martin, Branden Pinder, Tayler Scott

Cordero has huge biceps, a pathological hatred of sleeves (he rolls them up when he pitches), and (very) easily touches 98 mph with a sinker that generates heaps of ground balls. That he's changed teams six times in his young career (three times in 2019 alone) seems like a flagrant display of ignorance of how cool it is to watch a pitcher huck high-90s heaters with his guns out. But given how often Cordero was re-gifted (and whom he was re-gifted by), you would have expected a more arduous reclamation project than he proved to be. He was…fine. He torched Triple-A like legit big leaguers tend to do, and threw enough strikes at high enough speeds to balance out how non-particular he was about where in the zone he located them. If he continues to do that, he should remain in the majors, tease some possibility of more, and never have to wear his sleeves down again.

Dylan Covey RHP Born: 08/14/91   Age: 28   Bats: R   Throws: R   Height: 6'1"   Weight: 220   Origin: Round 4, 2013 Draft (#131 overall)

YEAR	TEAM	LVL	AGE	W	L	SV	G	GS	IP	H	HR	BB/9	K/9	K	GB%	BABIP	WHIP	ERA	DRA	WARP	MPH	FB%	WHF	CSP
2017	CHR	AAA	25	0	0	0	2	0	6	5	1	1.5	4.5	3	58%	.222	1.00	3.00	4.55	0.0				
2017	CHA	MLB	25	0	7	0	18	12	70	83	20	4.4	5.3	41	49%	.296	1.67	7.71	7.88	-1.9	95.0	60.5	6.8	45.5
2018	CHR	AAA	26	3	1	0	7	7	38²	32	3	3.5	8.1	35	57%	.282	1.22	2.33	3.98	0.7				
2018	CHA	MLB	26	5	14	0	27	21	121²	129	13	3.8	6.7	91	56%	.302	1.49	5.18	5.15	0.2	96.3	61.4	7.8	49.6
2019	CHR	AAA	27	2	1	0	13	11	51	59	6	1.6	8.1	46	56%	.342	1.33	2.82	3.83	1.4				
2019	CHA	MLB	27	1	8	0	18	12	58²	75	12	4.3	6.3	41	44%	.321	1.76	7.98	7.92	-1.4	96.5	49.8	8.3	49.3
2020	CHA	MLB	28	4	4	0	13	13	65	77	13	3.5	6.4	46	49%	.312	1.58	5.98	5.76	-0.1	95.5	58.1	7.8	48.8

Comparables: Kevin McGowan, Tyler Wilson, Rob Scahill

It's not ideal that exhortations about Covey's movement and velocity—and how they should result in better numbers—are more necessary now, years into his big-league career, than they were when he was selected in the Rule 5 out of Double-A. Covey has the necessary arm strength (he barely even dips below 95 mph anymore) and has added a four-seam fastball to his arsenal. Yet he's done little but get relentlessly shelled at the major-league level for three years now, and has dealt with his share of injury woes. Many a big-league reliever has had the origin story of "always threw hard with movement" and still self-actualized somehow. For Covey, his awakening may require that the White Sox stop having him start.

Odrisamer Despaigne RHP Born: 04/04/87 Age: 33 Bats: R Throws: R Height: 6'0" Weight: 200 Origin: International Free Agent, 2014

YEAR	TEAM	LVL	AGE	W	L	SV	G	GS	IP	H	HR	BB/9	K/9	K	GB%	BABIP	WHIP	ERA	DRA	WARP	MPH	FB%	WHF	CSP
2017	NWO	AAA	30	2	4	2	20	10	70	62	6	3.1	6.3	49	52%	.271	1.23	3.09	3.39	1.7				
2017	MIA	MLB	30	2	3	1	18	8	58¹	57	3	3.7	4.8	31	38%	.280	1.39	4.01	5.17	0.2	94.4	84.3	8	47.5
2018	NWO	AAA	31	2	3	2	13	4	43¹	52	0	2.5	8.3	40	44%	.380	1.48	4.36	4.74	0.3				
2018	LAA	MLB	31	0	3	0	8	4	18²	30	3	5.3	8.2	17	44%	.415	2.20	8.20	6.74	-0.4	95.3	67.4	9.7	48.9
2018	MIA	MLB	31	2	0	0	11	1	20¹	22	1	3.5	8.0	18	41%	.333	1.48	5.31	4.61	0.1	94.6	67.4	14.6	43.2
2019	CHR	AAA	32	5	4	0	16	14	83	83	6	3.0	9.1	84	50%	.333	1.34	3.25	4.42	1.8				
2019	LOU	AAA	32	3	2	0	8	8	41¹	40	5	3.5	8.7	40	53%	.310	1.35	3.92	5.14	0.6				
2019	CHA	MLB	32	0	2	0	3	3	13¹	24	3	4.7	4.7	7	28%	.420	2.33	9.45	10.03	-0.6	94.9	74.8	5.9	45.9
2020	CHA	MLB	33	2	2	0	33	0	35	40	6	3.7	5.8	23	43%	.300	1.55	5.73	5.58	-0.1	93.7	74.6	9.2	45.9

Comparables: Alex Wilson, Eric O'Flaherty, Chris Rusin

If you need someone to be an innings-eating lynchpin of a Triple-A rotation, serving as both a key figure in an International League playoff drive and providing a small thrill to fans as guy who does a vaguely convincing El Duque impersonation, Odrisamer is your man. If you want someone to perplex your major-league roster and coaching staff with an oddly lax pregame warmup routine that seems to make everyone ask "My God, does he know what time it is?" before unleashing an astonishingly wide arsenal of poorly commanded and eminently hittable pitches, Odrisamer, regrettably, is also your man. Teams never seem to truly need the former, and so quickly grow weary of the latter, that Despaigne's professional future figures to be at least as transient as his already fairly wacky 2019.

Bernardo Flores LHP Born: 08/23/95 Age: 24 Bats: L Throws: L Height: 6'2" Weight: 190 Origin: Round 7, 2016 Draft (#206 overall)

YEAR	TEAM	LVL	AGE	W	L	SV	G	GS	IP	H	HR	BB/9	K/9	K	GB%	BABIP	WHIP	ERA	DRA	WARP	MPH	FB%	WHF	CSP
2017	KAN	A	21	8	4	0	14	14	78	73	5	1.5	8.1	70	50%	.308	1.10	3.00	4.16	1.0				
2017	WNS	A+	21	2	3	0	9	9	40¹	43	5	4.2	7.4	33	41%	.309	1.54	4.24	5.44	-0.1				
2018	WNS	A+	22	5	4	0	12	12	77²	75	5	2.0	6.7	58	56%	.294	1.18	2.55	4.43	0.8				
2018	BIR	AA	22	3	5	0	13	13	78¹	79	5	1.6	5.4	47	52%	.301	1.19	2.76	4.80	0.5				
2019	WSX	RK	23	0	0	0	4	4	12	17	2	0.8	9.8	13	54%	.455	1.50	3.75	5.77	0.0				
2019	BIR	AA	23	3	8	0	15	15	78¹	74	10	1.7	7.9	69	55%	.282	1.14	3.33	4.40	0.5				
2020	CHA	MLB	24	2	1	0	14	3	26	25	5	3.3	6.6	19	49%	.271	1.35	4.46	4.67	0.2				

Comparables: Jayson Aquino, Jarlin García, Josh Rogers

Flores is a bespectacled baseball nerd who got lost somewhere on the path of becoming an amiable presence on Baseball Twitter and transformed into a full-on baseball player. (To wit, he hoards '80s ballcaps and '90s Starter jackets, and wanders the grounds of Negro League stadiums in his spare time.) True to the genre, the lanky Californian's knowledge of baseball history and pitchability outpace the raw power of his low-90s heater and three-pitch arsenal. Were his share of oblique pulls not as impressive as his memorabilia collection, he would have gotten his shot by now to explore his back-end starter/swingman potential in the majors.

Jace Fry LHP Born: 07/09/93 Age: 26 Bats: L Throws: L Height: 6'1" Weight: 190 Origin: Round 3, 2014 Draft (#77 overall)

YEAR	TEAM	LVL	AGE	W	L	SV	G	GS	IP	H	HR	BB/9	K/9	K	GB%	BABIP	WHIP	ERA	DRA	WARP	MPH	FB%	WHF	CSP
2017	BIR	AA	23	2	1	3	33	0	45¹	36	1	4.8	10.3	52	59%	.307	1.32	2.78	4.14	0.4				
2017	CHA	MLB	23	0	0	0	11	0	6²	12	1	6.8	4.1	3	39%	.407	2.55	10.80	5.83	0.0	95.8	68.2	10.8	41.1
2018	CHR	AAA	24	0	0	0	5	0	6²	3	1	0.0	14.9	11	54%	.167	0.45	1.35	1.69	0.3				
2018	CHA	MLB	24	2	3	4	59	1	51¹	37	4	3.5	12.3	70	47%	.277	1.11	4.38	2.96	1.2	95.4	34.2	15.3	43.7
2019	CHA	MLB	25	3	4	0	68	0	55	44	7	7.0	11.1	68	58%	.292	1.58	4.75	4.06	0.8	95.0	25.1	14.7	40.4
2020	CHA	MLB	26	3	3	0	53	0	57	46	7	4.6	10.8	68	52%	.285	1.32	3.64	3.83	0.8	94.8	31	15.1	42.4

Comparables: Rex Brothers, Tony Sipp, Antonio Bastardo

It's seldom fair to compare a pitcher like Fry—a mercurial second-year lefty reliever in a rebuilding team's bullpen—to a future Hall of Famer like Zack Greinke, but humor us for a moment. That Fry threw about a quarter as many innings as Greinke did in 2019, yet issued a good deal more walks than Greinke (along with 12 other qualified starters) is a good encapsulation of his sophomore struggles. Fry's best pitch is a cutter, and part of his appeal is having a five-pitch mix of which no offering moves in a straight line. Seeing as how no pitcher with more than 50 frames walked a higher rate, that liveliness may double as his downfall.

Carson Fulmer RHP Born: 12/13/93 Age: 26 Bats: R Throws: R Height: 6'0" Weight: 195 Origin: Round 1, 2015 Draft (#8 overall)

YEAR	TEAM	LVL	AGE	W	L	SV	G	GS	IP	H	HR	BB/9	K/9	K	GB%	BABIP	WHIP	ERA	DRA	WARP	MPH	FB%	WHF	CSP
2017	CHR	AAA	23	7	9	0	25	25	126	132	18	4.6	6.9	96	46%	.297	1.56	5.79	6.04	-0.5				
2017	CHA	MLB	23	3	1	0	7	5	23¹	16	4	5.0	7.3	19	31%	.190	1.24	3.86	7.31	-0.5	94.9	51.8	9.6	46.1
2018	CHR	AAA	24	5	6	0	25	9	67²	70	10	5.5	8.2	62	40%	.316	1.64	5.32	6.24	-0.6				
2018	CHA	MLB	24	2	4	0	9	8	32¹	37	8	6.7	8.1	29	34%	.296	1.89	8.07	8.06	-1.0	94.8	55.3	7.3	44.8
2019	CHR	AAA	25	1	2	1	24	0	34	31	2	5.6	13.5	51	32%	.372	1.53	4.76	3.42	0.9				
2019	CHA	MLB	25	1	2	0	20	2	27¹	26	5	6.6	8.2	25	47%	.262	1.68	6.26	6.60	-0.4	95.2	43.9	11.7	45.7
2020	CHA	MLB	26	4	4	0	29	8	64	64	11	5.3	7.8	56	39%	.288	1.59	5.51	5.31	0.1	94.6	50.8	9.7	46.3

Comparables: Miguel Almonte, Lucas Sims, Chase De Jong

Two of the sharpest innings Fulmer threw in 2019, and maybe even his entire career, came in the 12th and 13th innings of an August victory in Philadelphia that was mostly marked by the unyielding chaos of the five-and-a-half hour affair. Rather than build off of it, he would not pitch in the majors for another month, as he pulled his hamstring trying to run out a would-be infield single while batting for himself in the 14th. This isn't the most telling moment of Fulmer's inability to gain traction since being drafted eighth overall in 2015, just the most recent. He's changed roles, moving to the bullpen; he's changed residencies, moving to Washington so he can train at Driveline's facility during the offseason; but he hasn't yet changed teams. He will. Likely soon.

Lucas Giolito RHP   Born: 07/14/94   Age: 25   Bats: R   Throws: R   Height: 6'6"   Weight: 245   Origin: Round 1, 2012 Draft (#16 overall)

YEAR	TEAM	LVL	AGE	W	L	SV	G	GS	IP	H	HR	BB/9	K/9	K	GB%	BABIP	WHIP	ERA	DRA	WARP	MPH	FB%	WHF	CSP
2017	CHR	AAA	22	6	10	0	24	24	128²	122	17	4.1	9.4	134	45%	.312	1.41	4.48	4.89	1.1				
2017	CHA	MLB	22	3	3	0	7	7	45¹	31	8	2.4	6.8	34	47%	.189	0.95	2.38	4.27	0.7	94.3	59.8	11.1	46.2
2018	CHA	MLB	23	10	13	0	32	32	173¹	166	27	4.7	6.5	125	45%	.268	1.48	6.13	6.58	-2.5	95.0	59.5	9.2	46.8
2019	CHA	MLB	24	14	9	0	29	29	176²	131	24	2.9	11.6	228	36%	.273	1.06	3.41	2.81	5.7	96.7	55	16.1	50.3
2020	CHA	MLB	25	12	8	0	28	28	165	141	26	3.6	11.1	204	39%	.290	1.25	3.76	3.93	3.0	95.5	58.6	13.1	49.3

Comparables: Archie Bradley, José Berríos, Jake Thompson

If you're a 0.9er who listened to his dad get interviewed, or just the type of casual fan who watches enough baseball to hear mention of the top-10 prospects in baseball on a year-to-year basis, Lucas Giolito's ascent to greatness has felt like an inevitability. When it's all said and done, Giolito's 2018 season, where he briefly fashioned himself a sinkerballer as he toggled through different mechanics in a desperate search for a fix, will eventually read as an aberrant blip entirely. That would be a shame because Giolito's dedicated efforts to overhaul his delivery and his mindset—and emerge from inconsistency and uncertainty as a relentless barrage of high-riding four-seamers and unshakable confidence—is the sort of straightforward tale of determined self-improvement that draws us to sports. They provide an easy story that anything is possible if we dedicate ourselves to making it happen. The hard part is actually doing it.

Gio Gonzalez LHP   Born: 09/19/85   Age: 34   Bats: R   Throws: L   Height: 6'0"   Weight: 205   Origin: Round 1, 2004 Draft (#38 overall)

YEAR	TEAM	LVL	AGE	W	L	SV	G	GS	IP	H	HR	BB/9	K/9	K	GB%	BABIP	WHIP	ERA	DRA	WARP	MPH	FB%	WHF	CSP
2017	WAS	MLB	31	15	9	0	32	32	201	158	21	3.5	8.4	188	48%	.258	1.18	2.96	3.60	4.4	91.8	56.8	9.4	42.3
2018	WAS	MLB	32	7	11	0	27	27	145²	153	15	4.3	7.8	126	47%	.319	1.53	4.57	4.33	1.7	92.0	56.4	9.8	45.8
2018	MIL	MLB	32	3	0	0	5	5	25¹	14	2	3.6	7.8	22	46%	.182	0.95	2.13	3.27	0.6	92.2	58.2	12.6	41.2
2019	SWB	AAA	33	2	1	0	3	3	15	19	1	3.6	11.4	19	48%	.439	1.67	6.00	5.44	0.2				
2019	MIL	MLB	33	3	2	0	19	17	87¹	76	9	3.8	8.0	78	47%	.277	1.29	3.50	4.41	1.3	91.1	51.9	11.2	37.1
2020	CHA	MLB	34	8	6	0	23	23	116	105	18	3.9	7.8	101	47%	.271	1.34	4.10	4.26	1.7	90.6	54.7	10	40.5

Comparables: Jon Lester, Francisco Liriano, David Price

Gonzalez is a good example of how the Brewers profit off the league-wide aversion to 30-something-year-olds. Yes, last year was his age-33 season; yes, his peripherals were decidedly mediocre; and yes, he has middling control at best and a waning fastball. But can you imagine a pitcher like Gonzalez—a longtime, left-handed veteran with his year-to-year consistency—receiving a piddling $2 million in free agency just a decade ago? There's risk management and then there's playing yourself. Gonzalez had some injury problems, but he delivered more value for the Brewers than what they deposited into his bank account. The White Sox took note, signing him to a one-year, $4.5 million contract with an option for 2021.

Tayron Guerrero RHP   Born: 01/09/91   Age: 29   Bats: R   Throws: R   Height: 6'8"   Weight: 210   Origin: International Free Agent, 2009

YEAR	TEAM	LVL	AGE	W	L	SV	G	GS	IP	H	HR	BB/9	K/9	K	GB%	BABIP	WHIP	ERA	DRA	WARP	MPH	FB%	WHF	CSP
2017	JAX	AA	26	0	1	0	17	0	16	14	3	7.9	12.4	22	41%	.306	1.75	3.38	4.80	0.0				
2017	NWO	AAA	26	3	2	0	13	0	15¹	12	2	7.0	6.5	11	44%	.217	1.57	5.87	5.41	0.0				
2018	MIA	MLB	27	1	3	0	60	0	58	64	8	4.7	10.6	68	45%	.354	1.62	5.43	4.80	0.1	102.0	79.2	12.4	49.4
2019	MIA	MLB	28	1	2	0	52	0	46	42	7	7.0	8.4	43	44%	.282	1.70	6.26	6.04	-0.3	101.8	79.2	14.1	44.8
2020	CHA	MLB	29	1	1	0	11	0	11	12	2	5.7	10.1	13	44%	.325	1.67	5.72	5.41	0.0	101.2	79.2	13.3	46.9

Comparables: Gregory Infante, Ryne Harper, Hunter Cervenka

There are relievers with dubious command, and then there is Guerrero. That he managed a painful-to-watch walk rate and a pedestrian strikeout rate, all while hurling his 99-mph fastball somewhere in the vicinity of home plate, is a modern marvel. Among relievers who threw at least 40 innings in 2019, Guerrero had the third-highest walk rate and second-worst K/BB percentage. Seemingly the only thing that kept Guerrero on the mound—besides Miami's dearth of solid relievers—was the non-alarming rate at which he surrendered homers, limiting the significance of the walks to merely "very damaging." The 6-foot-8 righty will continue to get more opportunities to harness that fastball for as long as it maintains its radar gun readings, but the Marlins do have more capable arms in the pipeline. Guerrero's time in one of the NL's worst bullpens was short-lived, but he'll always have those highlights for the Wide, Wide, Wide World of Sports.

Ian Hamilton RHP   Born: 06/16/95   Age: 25   Bats: R   Throws: R   Height: 6'0"   Weight: 200   Origin: Round 11, 2016 Draft (#326 overall)

YEAR	TEAM	LVL	AGE	W	L	SV	G	GS	IP	H	HR	BB/9	K/9	K	GB%	BABIP	WHIP	ERA	DRA	WARP	MPH	FB%	WHF	CSP
2017	WNS	A+	22	3	3	6	30	0	52²	33	1	1.4	8.9	52	46%	.241	0.78	1.71	2.40	1.5				
2017	BIR	AA	22	1	3	1	14	0	19	26	0	3.8	10.4	22	52%	.419	1.79	5.21	6.63	-0.4				
2018	BIR	AA	23	2	1	12	21	0	25¹	20	0	4.3	12.1	34	47%	.323	1.26	1.78	3.34	0.5				
2018	CHR	AAA	23	1	1	10	22	0	26¹	18	2	1.4	9.6	28	49%	.254	0.84	1.71	2.54	0.8				
2018	CHA	MLB	23	1	2	0	10	0	8	6	2	2.2	5.6	5	48%	.174	1.00	4.50	3.37	0.1	98.4	70.1	12	46.3
2019	CHR	AAA	24	0	2	3	16	0	16¹	28	4	1.7	11.0	20	53%	.471	1.90	9.92	6.53	0.0				
2020	CHA	MLB	25	1	1	0	16	0	17	18	3	3.6	8.0	15	46%	.294	1.44	5.14	5.16	0.0	98.1	71.8	12.3	47.4

Comparables: Chase Whitley, Alejandro Chacin, Jimmy Herget

Hard-throwing reliever Ian, as prominent Hamiltons are seemingly wont to do, took a life-altering shot to the face this past year. He wasn't dueling with a rival or anything like that; instead, he was chilling in the Charlotte dugout when a wayward baseball made a lopsided trade with his face, taking with it several teeth in exchange for a handful of facial fractures that he was allowed to keep for months afterward. And whereas Alexander's shot to the face cut short a government career that at least had more confidently-written documents left in it, the blow to Ian's face could be construed as an act of mercy for a season that had already turned into a nightmare by mid-May. A scary car crash effectively canceled his spring training, a stiff shoulder briefly sapped his velocity, the juiced ball thrashed his hopes of a palatable Triple-A ERA, and that foul ball ended his season. Christmas still proceeded as scheduled.

Kelvin Herrera RHP Born: 12/31/89   Age: 30   Bats: R   Throws: R   Height: 5'10"   Weight: 200   Origin: International Free Agent, 2006

YEAR	TEAM	LVL	AGE	W	L	SV	G	GS	IP	H	HR	BB/9	K/9	K	GB%	BABIP	WHIP	ERA	DRA	WARP	MPH	FB%	WHF	CSP
2017	KCA	MLB	27	3	3	26	64	0	59¹	60	9	3.0	8.5	56	47%	.295	1.35	4.25	3.82	0.9	99.7	66.5	13.2	48.6
2018	KCA	MLB	28	1	1	14	27	0	25²	19	2	0.7	7.7	22	39%	.246	0.82	1.05	3.88	0.3	99.0	64.9	15.7	48.3
2018	WAS	MLB	28	1	2	3	21	0	18²	24	4	3.9	7.7	16	36%	.333	1.71	4.34	4.20	0.2	98.9	62.6	12.9	46.6
2019	CHA	MLB	29	3	3	1	57	0	51¹	60	8	4.0	9.3	53	39%	.347	1.62	6.14	5.21	0.1	98.3	55.9	13	47.1
2020	*CHA*	*MLB*	*30*	*2*	*2*	*0*	*32*	*0*	*34*	*31*	*5*	*3.1*	*9.2*	*35*	*38%*	*.288*	*1.27*	*3.93*	*4.15*	*0.4*	*98.1*	*60.9*	*13.4*	*47.5*

Comparables: Huston Street, Drew Storen, Bruce Sutter

Our 20s are such a fleeting, treasured time. So, then, it was a powerful gesture that Herrera dedicated his 29th year to acting out a telling lesson about the interconnected nature of the human body. After tearing the Lisfranc ligament in his left foot—the plant foot!—to end his 2018 season, Herrera was not able to build up strength in his left leg during his winter, resulting in reduced velocity during the spring. He was making due until all of his careful compensation for his leg led to him tweaking his back (in his 20s!) and spending almost the rest of the season accumulating the worst results of his life—and, oh, tweaking his oblique at one point for good measure. Rationalizing that his April served as his offseason, Herrera looked like his old self for the last couple weeks of the year. His contract assured he'd get another chance either way.

Dallas Keuchel LHP Born: 01/01/88   Age: 32   Bats: L   Throws: L   Height: 6'3"   Weight: 205   Origin: Round 7, 2009 Draft (#221 overall)

YEAR	TEAM	LVL	AGE	W	L	SV	G	GS	IP	H	HR	BB/9	K/9	K	GB%	BABIP	WHIP	ERA	DRA	WARP	MPH	FB%	WHF	CSP
2017	HOU	MLB	29	14	5	0	23	23	145²	116	15	2.9	7.7	125	68%	.256	1.12	2.90	3.64	3.1	90.8	68.2	12.3	38.9
2018	HOU	MLB	30	12	11	0	34	34	204²	211	18	2.6	6.7	153	55%	.300	1.31	3.74	3.87	3.4	91.3	69.1	8.9	45
2019	ROM	A	31	0	0	0	1	1	7	1	0	1.3	11.6	9	77%	.077	0.29	0.00						
2019	MIS	AA	31	0	0	0	1	1	7	11	0	1.3	5.1	4	46%	.423	1.71	3.86	7.02	-0.2				
2019	ATL	MLB	31	8	8	0	19	19	112²	115	16	3.1	7.3	91	60%	.298	1.37	3.75	4.25	1.9	89.9	74	9.5	40.8
2020	*CHA*	*MLB*	*32*	*12*	*8*	*0*	*29*	*29*	*172*	*169*	*22*	*3.0*	*7.0*	*133*	*58%*	*.285*	*1.31*	*3.96*	*4.17*	*2.7*	*89.8*	*69.8*	*9.8*	*41.3*

Comparables: Chris Short, Wade Miley, Dillon Gee

On September 29, 2018, Keuchel threw his final pitch of that regular season. He wouldn't throw another regular season pitch until almost nine months later. Was there some sort of injury that ended up costing him a big chunk of 2019? Did he do something awful during the offseason sending him into baseball exile as part of his punishment? Well, sort of. He made the mistake of choosing to decline a qualifying offer and test the free agent waters. Even when the Braves finally signed him in June, he only agreed to a one-year deal. Despite the fact that he delivered more of the same production that we're used to seeing from him on the mound, his streak of three-win seasons ended at five. With a more normal offseason, Keuchel will look to start a new streak on the South Side in 2020.

──────── ★ ★ ★ *2020 Top 101 Prospect* **#20** ★ ★ ★ ────────

Michael Kopech RHP Born: 04/30/96   Age: 24   Bats: R   Throws: R   Height: 6'3"   Weight: 205   Origin: Round 1, 2014 Draft (#33 overall)

YEAR	TEAM	LVL	AGE	W	L	SV	G	GS	IP	H	HR	BB/9	K/9	K	GB%	BABIP	WHIP	ERA	DRA	WARP	MPH	FB%	WHF	CSP
2017	BIR	AA	21	8	7	0	22	22	119¹	77	6	4.5	11.7	155	42%	.272	1.15	2.87	3.15	2.9				
2017	CHR	AAA	21	1	1	0	3	3	15	15	0	3.0	10.2	17	35%	.375	1.33	3.00	4.18	0.3				
2018	CHR	AAA	22	7	7	0	24	24	126¹	101	9	4.3	12.1	170	40%	.316	1.27	3.70	3.75	2.6				
2018	CHA	MLB	22	1	1	0	4	4	14¹	20	4	1.3	9.4	15	28%	.381	1.53	5.02	6.84	-0.3	97.7	62.5	10.9	50.9
2020	*CHA*	*MLB*	*24*	*5*	*5*	*0*	*38*	*11*	*83*	*89*	*18*	*4.2*	*7.8*	*71*	*36%*	*.294*	*1.54*	*5.99*	*5.73*	*-0.2*	*97.5*	*64.4*	*11.3*	*52.5*

Comparables: Tyler Glasnow, Eric Hurley, Logan Allen

A surprise torn UCL (there was no "blow out" moment, just a dispiriting MRI) transformed 2019 from a first full season in the majors for Kopech into a poncho-clad vision quest full of hikes through the desert and self-reflection while he rehabbed in Arizona. For a top pitching prospect who claims his midseason struggles in 2018 were the product of anxiety and even used the term "yips" to describe his Triple-A struggles, a step back from the endless chug of baseball might not be what Kopech ordered, but he wouldn't send it back to the kitchen, either. From more of a purely physical perspective, Kopech was back to throwing his typical upper-90s fastball in instructs by October, albeit with appropriately rusty command, and will be another long, lanky body in spring camp with a curious pink scar running along his underarm by the time February rolls around. He'll just be the strongest one.

Jimmy Lambert RHP Born: 11/18/94   Age: 25   Bats: R   Throws: R   Height: 6'2"   Weight: 190   Origin: Round 5, 2016 Draft (#146 overall)

YEAR	TEAM	LVL	AGE	W	L	SV	G	GS	IP	H	HR	BB/9	K/9	K	GB%	BABIP	WHIP	ERA	DRA	WARP	MPH	FB%	WHF	CSP
2017	KAN	A	22	7	2	0	12	12	74	77	1	1.3	5.2	43	57%	.315	1.19	2.19	4.78	0.4				
2017	WNS	A+	22	5	4	0	14	14	76	86	10	3.4	7.0	59	50%	.326	1.51	5.45	6.08	-0.7				
2018	WNS	A+	23	5	7	0	13	13	70²	57	5	2.7	10.2	80	46%	.292	1.10	3.95	3.67	1.4				
2018	BIR	AA	23	3	1	0	5	5	25	20	2	2.2	10.8	30	40%	.286	1.04	2.88	3.07	0.7				
2019	BIR	AA	24	3	4	0	11	11	59¹	62	11	4.1	10.6	70	38%	.338	1.50	4.55	5.57	-0.4				
2020	*CHA*	*MLB*	*25*	*2*	*2*	*0*	*33*	*0*	*35*	*35*	*6*	*3.4*	*8.8*	*34*	*38%*	*.299*	*1.38*	*4.64*	*4.81*	*0.1*				

Comparables: Dylan Covey, Brandon Woodruff, Travis Lakins

After a year of waning effectiveness as an uninspiring and ignored sinker-slider type, Lambert transformed into a different pitcher thanks to Trackman-inspired tweaks. A shift to a high-fastball, 12-to-6-curveball diet led to swing-and-miss numbers befitting someone with real rotation potential. Alas, not all went well for Lambert. When he went down for Tommy John surgery in June, general manager Rick Hahn tabbed the lanky right-hander as someone who would have gotten a major-league look in 2019 had he stayed healthy, which is like raaaaaaaaaaaaaiiiiiiiiiiiinnnnnn on your wedding day. It's a free riiiiiiiiiiiiiide, when you've already paid. It's the good adviiiiiiiiiiiiiice, that you just didn't take, and who would have thought, he's Peter's brotherrrrrrr.

Reynaldo López RHP Born: 01/04/94 Age: 26 Bats: R Throws: R Height: 6'1" Weight: 200 Origin: International Free Agent, 2012

YEAR	TEAM	LVL	AGE	W	L	SV	G	GS	IP	H	HR	BB/9	K/9	K	GB%	BABIP	WHIP	ERA	DRA	WARP	MPH	FB%	WHF	CSP
2017	CHR	AAA	23	6	7	0	22	22	121	101	16	3.6	9.7	131	38%	.270	1.24	3.79	3.90	2.4				
2017	CHA	MLB	23	3	3	0	8	8	47²	49	7	2.6	5.7	30	30%	.271	1.32	4.72	6.40	-0.4	97.8	60.9	9	48.8
2018	CHA	MLB	24	7	10	0	32	32	188²	165	25	3.6	7.2	151	34%	.260	1.27	3.91	5.65	-0.7	98.2	60.9	10	49.2
2019	CHA	MLB	25	10	15	0	33	33	184	203	35	3.2	8.3	169	35%	.316	1.46	5.38	7.06	-2.6	98.2	58.6	12	51.2
2020	CHA	MLB	26	7	6	0	19	19	109	109	19	3.5	8.2	99	34%	.293	1.39	4.69	4.78	1.0	97.8	60.8	11.1	50.9

Comparables: Robert Gsellman, Tyler Mahle, Jake Faria

In a sense, López has made an absurd amount of progress in his development as a pitcher. It wasn't long ago he was a skinny Dominican 16-year-old who was not only without a professional contract, but catching for a lightly scouted youth team near San Pedro de Macorís. In another sense, his progress seems to have slackened in the past two years. He's continued to touch the upper-90s and pile up healthy innings despite his unusual looking delivery, yet has done little else to reward the White Sox's devotion to starting him. A team with less patience and more alternatives would have challenged him by now to throw as many 100 mph fastballs as he could out of the bullpen. The White Sox were rewarded for their unique patience by López's longtime teammate Lucas Giolito in 2019, but López will need a similarly stark turnaround to remain a starter past 2020. We think, anyway.

Evan Marshall RHP Born: 04/18/90 Age: 30 Bats: R Throws: R Height: 6'2" Weight: 225 Origin: Round 4, 2011 Draft (#124 overall)

YEAR	TEAM	LVL	AGE	W	L	SV	G	GS	IP	H	HR	BB/9	K/9	K	GB%	BABIP	WHIP	ERA	DRA	WARP	MPH	FB%	WHF	CSP
2017	TAC	AAA	27	1	0	1	13	1	21²	28	4	2.9	10.8	26	61%	.400	1.62	4.15	5.56	-0.1				
2017	SEA	MLB	27	0	0	0	6	0	7²	12	1	5.9	4.7	4	34%	.393	2.22	9.39	8.07	-0.2	95.7	65.6	7.4	46.6
2018	COH	AAA	28	1	1	4	20	0	24	18	1	1.1	7.9	21	68%	.254	0.88	1.12	2.78	0.6				
2018	CLE	MLB	28	0	0	0	10	0	7	12	0	5.1	11.6	9	56%	.522	2.29	7.71	3.65	0.1	95.5	54.7	17.3	43.1
2019	CHR	AAA	29	3	0	2	9	0	10	8	0	0.9	11.7	13	52%	.348	0.90	0.00	2.28	0.4				
2019	CHA	MLB	29	4	2	0	55	0	50²	42	5	4.3	7.3	41	52%	.266	1.30	2.49	5.08	0.2	95.2	43.9	11.7	40.1
2020	CHA	MLB	30	3	3	3	53	0	57	54	7	3.9	8.4	53	52%	.294	1.38	4.19	4.33	0.5	94.5	46.5	12.1	42.6

Comparables: Javy Guerra, Gregory Infante, JC Ramírez

Both before and after he exchanged texts with him—mostly discussing his "Forgetting Sarah Marshall"-themed Players' Weekend jersey—Marshall was clear about wanting actor Jason Segel to portray him in a movie about his life. There's certainly ample material for such a film, meaning it's a question of what tone the biopic would take. Maybe a more family-oriented movie would focus on Marshall's near-death experience after being struck by a line drive in 2015, and how the presence of his beloved pet dog roused him from a coma. An Oscar-bait type of approach would focus more on the draining grind to find a big-league home Marshall has faced over the last four seasons, as sympathy for his suffering gave way to scrutiny at his ability to match his pre-injury form, until he remade himself as a yeoman-like weak contact-hunting sinkerballer in an age of riding four-seam strikeout artists. Or they could make a divisive, dark-toned film loved only by movie snobs who appreciate the ambiguous ending where below-average peripheral stats suggest that trouble is always lurking around the corner for Marshall, even after successful year in the White Sox bullpen.

Iván Nova RHP Born: 01/12/87 Age: 33 Bats: R Throws: R Height: 6'5" Weight: 250 Origin: International Free Agent, 2004

YEAR	TEAM	LVL	AGE	W	L	SV	G	GS	IP	H	HR	BB/9	K/9	K	GB%	BABIP	WHIP	ERA	DRA	WARP	MPH	FB%	WHF	CSP
2017	PIT	MLB	30	11	14	0	31	31	187	203	29	1.7	6.3	131	48%	.299	1.28	4.14	4.71	1.8	95.1	68.1	9	49.5
2018	PIT	MLB	31	9	9	0	29	29	161	171	26	2.0	6.4	114	47%	.288	1.28	4.19	4.60	1.3	95.3	66.9	9.7	46.6
2019	CHA	MLB	32	11	12	0	34	34	187	225	30	2.3	5.5	114	47%	.322	1.45	4.72	7.54	-3.6	94.6	54.2	9	47
2020	CHA	MLB	33	2	2	0	33	0	35	42	6	2.4	5.9	23	47%	.309	1.46	5.45	5.46	-0.1	93.9	60.7	9.1	46.9

Comparables: Jason Hammel, Pat Hentgen, Jhoulys Chacín

Tucking his t-shirt into his jeans for postgame interviews is probably the most superficial of the many ways Nova is trending away from the rest of the league. In an era of fastball carry and breaking balls, Nova pounds sinkers in the zone relentlessly with a small set of variations on the margins. As strikeout rates accelerate across the game, Nova is unapologetically racing in the other direction. As teams focus on youth, Nova is progressively getting older—seemingly every year! Despite producing the same functionally average-ish results four years-running, there's a cost to being an iconoclast. A strong second half brought Nova even to the pack in 2019, but getting the rope—even from a rebuilding team—to work his way back is not a given when every statistical indicator says his next slump is just as likely to be the end of the line as it is to be the standard rough patch that his contact-heavy approach invites.

Carlos Rodón LHP Born: 12/10/92 Age: 27 Bats: L Throws: L Height: 6'3" Weight: 235 Origin: Round 1, 2014 Draft (#3 overall)

YEAR	TEAM	LVL	AGE	W	L	SV	G	GS	IP	H	HR	BB/9	K/9	K	GB%	BABIP	WHIP	ERA	DRA	WARP	MPH	FB%	WHF	CSP
2017	CHR	AAA	24	0	3	0	3	3	13²	17	0	4.6	7.2	11	50%	.354	1.76	9.22	6.53	-0.1				
2017	CHA	MLB	24	2	5	0	12	12	69¹	64	12	4.0	9.9	76	45%	.297	1.37	4.15	5.13	0.3	96.6	61.2	11.1	47.9
2018	CHR	AAA	25	1	0	0	3	3	12²	10	0	3.6	15.6	22	56%	.435	1.18	1.42	3.18	0.3				
2018	CHA	MLB	25	6	8	0	20	20	120²	97	15	4.1	6.7	90	42%	.243	1.26	4.18	6.57	-1.8	96.1	59.8	9.7	47.6
2019	CHA	MLB	26	3	2	0	7	7	34²	33	4	4.4	11.9	46	43%	.322	1.44	5.19	4.05	0.6	94.7	51.9	13.1	46.8
2020	CHA	MLB	27	2	2	0	21	5	39	35	6	4.0	9.2	39	39%	.276	1.34	4.30	4.41	0.4	95.5	59	10.9	47.9

Comparables: Daniel Norris, Eduardo Rodriguez, Henry Owens

Rodón finally had a healthy (and full) spring training for the first time in years, which simultaneously seems like: 1) an irrelevant trifle and 2) a reason to vault his strikeout rate up 10 percentage points. His career has been frustrating but he's too talented to do anything but let it play out.

His strikeout rate actually vaulted by 11.5 percentage points despite a precipitous loss of velocity. He compensated for that loss by throwing just *so* many more sliders. Maybe it means he's not healthy, but his is an elite slider and if Patrick Corbin can do it, why not Rodón?

So it turns out Rodón was *definitely* not healthy, and he will be churning through Tommy John rehab instead of enjoying a healthy and full 2020 spring training. It is not good to tear a UCL, but perhaps it explains the precipitous velocity loss and certainly would explain getting torched by the dang Tigers and Orioles in his last two starts.

Maybe at some point he'll encounter all three—being healthy, flipping that nasty slider a ton, and throwing hard again—at the same time. Why not? His career has been frustrating but he's too talented to do anything but let it play out.

José Ruiz RHP Born: 10/21/94 Age: 25 Bats: R Throws: R Height: 6'1" Weight: 190 Origin: International Free Agent, 2011

YEAR	TEAM	LVL	AGE	W	L	SV	G	GS	IP	H	HR	BB/9	K/9	K	GB%	BABIP	WHIP	ERA	DRA	WARP	MPH	FB%	WHF	CSP
2017	LEL	A+	22	1	2	2	44	0	49²	57	7	4.5	8.2	45	33%	.345	1.65	5.98	5.93	-0.6				
2017	SDN	MLB	22	0	0	0	1	0	1	0	0	9.0	9.0	1	50%	.000	1.00	0.00	9.17	0.0	96.6	80	6.7	49.2
2018	WNS	A+	23	0	0	2	10	0	13¹	6	2	3.4	14.9	22	33%	.182	0.82	2.70	2.36	0.4				
2018	BIR	AA	23	3	1	14	33	0	45¹	33	2	3.8	10.9	55	41%	.290	1.15	3.18	3.37	0.8				
2018	CHA	MLB	23	0	0	0	6	0	4¹	5	1	6.2	12.5	6	42%	.364	1.85	4.15	2.40	0.1	98.0	58.4	16.9	44.7
2019	CHR	AAA	24	0	0	7	11	0	14¹	9	0	4.4	9.4	15	34%	.257	1.12	1.26	2.50	0.5				
2019	CHA	MLB	24	1	4	0	40	1	40	56	6	5.4	7.9	35	37%	.377	2.00	5.62	8.13	-1.2	98.8	61.6	12	47.3
2020	CHA	MLB	25	1	1	0	16	0	17	17	3	4.4	8.1	15	37%	.288	1.47	4.94	4.94	0.0	98.4	63	12.6	48

Comparables: Ian Gibaut, Shawn Armstrong, Jaye Chapman

Ruiz was optioned six times during the course of last season, and averaged fewer than three innings per assignment before being rocketed back to the majors. For a converted ex-catcher who throws hard and does little else well, the White Sox's scattershot usage of him seems telling. Most good relievers have been treated as if they were functionally worthless for some stretch of their career, yet Ruiz will require a quantum leap of development—not unlike going from light-hitting A-ball catcher to the ninth-best reliever in a bad bullpen—if he's going to achieve a reoccurring presence in this book.

Jonathan Stiever RHP Born: 05/12/97 Age: 23 Bats: R Throws: R Height: 6'2" Weight: 205 Origin: Round 5, 2018 Draft (#138 overall)

YEAR	TEAM	LVL	AGE	W	L	SV	G	GS	IP	H	HR	BB/9	K/9	K	GB%	BABIP	WHIP	ERA	DRA	WARP	MPH	FB%	WHF	CSP
2018	GRF	RK	21	0	1	0	13	13	28	23	3	2.9	12.5	39	48%	.323	1.14	4.18	2.71	1.0				
2019	KAN	A	22	4	6	0	14	14	74	88	10	1.7	9.4	77	46%	.361	1.38	4.74	6.02	-0.7				
2019	WNS	A+	22	6	4	0	12	12	71	56	7	1.6	9.8	77	41%	.278	0.97	2.15	3.11	1.7				
2020	CHA	MLB	23	2	2	0	33	0	35	36	6	3.4	8.2	32	41%	.297	1.40	4.81	4.94	0.1				

Comparables: Trent Thornton, Felix Jorge, Jordan Smith

Stiever has been someone worth throwing into a big book of baseball players for all of 12 professional starts, which is indicative of them being pretty good. Upon getting promoted to High-A, Stiever got told to "let it eat" up in the zone, and to pair his curve and slider off of that plane. It went at least as well for him as it has gone for the seemingly 5,000 others who have toyed with those levers in the last five years. There's still the whole issue of a changeup that could use more tumble so that lefties are less of an ordeal. But Stiever, originally a Trackman transformation project, now serves as an actual prospect.

LINEOUTS

Hitters

HITTER	POS	TEAM	LVL	AGE	PA	R	2B	3B	HR	RBI	BB	K	SB	CS	AVG/OBP/SLG	DRC+	VORP	BABIP	BRR	FRAA	WARP
Micker Adolfo	OF	BIR	AA	22	95	5	7	0	0	9	14	36	0	3	.205/.337/.295	95	-2.7	.372	-3.3		-0.3
	OF	WSX	Rk	22	58	8	5	0	2	3	7	21	0	0	.260/.362/.480	86	-0.2	.407	-3.1		-0.3
James Beard	CF	WSX	Rk	18	138	19	4	1	2	12	8	54	9	3	.213/.270/.307	40	-2.3	.352	0.7	CF(31): -9.0	-1.1
Nicky Delmonico	LF	CHR	AAA	26	76	13	7	0	3	10	10	12	1	0	.286/.382/.540	131	3.8	.300	-0.8	LF(9): -2.0, 1B(4): -0.2	0.1
	LF	CHA	MLB	26	68	6	2	0	1	6	4	25	0	1	.206/.265/.286	57	-1.9	.324	0.0	LF(21): 1.2, 1B(1): 0.0	-0.1
Alcides Escobar	SS	CHR	AAA	32	405	52	28	0	10	70	32	64	6	2	.286/.343/.444	96	6.2	.320	-0.9	SS(49): 2.5, 3B(41): 0.4	1.5
Yermin Mercedes	C	CHR	AAA	26	220	35	12	0	17	62	24	42	0	0	.310/.386/.647	143	16.5	.306	-2.4	C(23): 3.2, 1B(4): -0.6	1.6
	C	BIR	AA	26	167	19	7	0	6	18	17	25	2	0	.327/.389/.497	166	18.3	.353	-0.8	C(34): 6.7	2.5
AJ Reed	1B	CHA	MLB	26	49	1	0	0	1	4	4	21	0	0	.136/.204/.205	62	-1.5	.217	-0.1	1B(4): 0.5, P(1): 0.0	-0.1
	1B	ROU	AAA	26	225	33	11	0	12	35	27	67	0	0	.224/.329/.469	92	0.7	.270	1.3	1B(40): -3.0	0.0
	1B	CHR	AAA	26	42	3	1	0	1	2	2	17	0	0	.179/.238/.282	31	-5.9	.286	-1.8	1B(8): 0.7	-0.4
Matt Skole	1B	CHR	AAA	29	392	65	15	0	21	56	70	99	0	0	.248/.384/.497	115	4.5	.286	-2.6	1B(64): -1.9, 3B(10): 0.7	0.9
	1B	CHA	MLB	29	80	7	2	0	0	6	7	31	0	0	.208/.275/.236	58	-3.1	.357	0.0	1B(9): -1.5	-0.4

Six seasons into his pro career, **Micker Adolfo** is yet to put together a full campaign, most recently because of surgery to clean up his elbow following Tommy John in 2018. The return of a strikeout rate more gargantuan than his raw power adds to the concern that the big outfielder will never live up to his tools. ⓧ Outside of the Royals organization, it's only acceptable to have the profile of "fast but raw in every other baseball aspect" for about a year as a professional. Hopefully **James Beard** enjoys this while it lasts. ⓧ Two Achilles tears have not only kept the former 11th overall pick out of an affiliated game for two seasons, but also made us all too sad to sink our teeth into these juicy burger puns. It's hard to keep the sizzle for **Jake Burger** sticking at third going after such an absence, and even though the raw hitting talent was supposed to be enough to play at first, that's a tall order at this point...a tall order of burgers. His name is Burger. ⓧ There is no official point at which an organization exits a rebuild and enters a contention cycle, but "stops giving playing time to **Nicky Delmonico** seems like a fairly good benchmark. ⚾ It turns out that signing on to be minor-league depth for a rebuilding team that has the AL batting champion at your position locked in through 2024 is *not* a viable route to big-league playing time. Lesson learned for **Alcides Escobar**, who hit okay in Triple-A, saw that it was not going to lead him to a call-up, demanded his release in August, and wasn't heard from again. ⚾ No one is quite sure what defensive position he's capable of manning at the major-league level, or why his massive hand load and ultra-aggressive approach at the plate have not been exploited, or how much upside to assume from a very thickly-built 27-year-old...but dang, *look* at **Yermin Mercedes**' minor league numbers. ⚾ In 2015, we wrote that "Scouting is strange business," as it pertained to **AJ Reed** falling out of the first round despite being a highly productive collegiate. In 2018, we expected that someone would give "this hulk the chance to prove he's either the second coming of Russell Branyan or the second coming of Matt LaPorta." In 2021, we'll concede the scouts were right to have concerns. ⚾ Maybe light-hitting, slick-fielding middle infielders aren't the sexiest profile to be the jewel of your international class. But the Cuban-born **Yolbert Sanchez** got a $2.5 million bonus because he's supposed to be ready to field well (and not hit) in the majors relatively soon. ⚾ Five years in, **Matt Skole** has gotten pretty good—not great—at this whole veteran Triple-A masher lifestyle. This past August, the White Sox took Skole out of his natural habitat. Hijinks ensued, extra-base hits did not.

Pitchers

PITCHER	TEAM	LVL	AGE	W	L	SV	G	GS	IP	H	HR	BB/9	K/9	K	GB%	BABIP	WHIP	ERA	DRA	WARP	MPH	FB%	WHF	CSP
Zack Burdi	BIR	AA	24	0	3	3	17	0	19²	24	5	5.9	11.0	24	30%	.345	1.88	6.41	6.59	-0.5				
Ryan Burr	CHA	MLB	25	1	1	0	16	1	19²	17	3	3.7	9.2	20	47%	.255	1.27	4.58	4.82	0.1	96.9	58.1	10.3	52.3
Ross Detwiler	CHR	AAA	33	1	2	0	8	8	43	44	11	2.3	7.3	35	52%	.287	1.28	3.98	3.71	1.2				
	CHA	MLB	33	3	5	0	18	12	69²	86	20	3.5	5.9	46	52%	.301	1.62	6.59	8.06	-1.8	93.1	51.5	7.7	51.1
Matt Foster	BIR	AA	24	0	0	1	6	0	9²	3	0	1.9	11.2	12	32%	.158	0.52	0.00	2.26	0.3				
	CHR	AAA	24	4	1	4	37	0	55	46	9	3.1	10.1	62	37%	.278	1.18	3.76	2.93	1.8				
Caleb Frare	CHR	AAA	25	2	1	1	21	0	22¹	22	5	7.7	13.7	34	42%	.354	1.84	7.66	5.04	0.3				
	CHA	MLB	25	0	0	0	5	0	2²	2	1	13.5	10.1	3	29%	.167	2.25	10.12	4.33	0.0	95.5	60.4	11.3	36.7
Alec Hansen	WNS	A+	24	1	0	0	9	0	12²	1	0	5.0	14.9	21	63%	.053	0.63	2.13	1.95	0.4				
	BIR	AA	24	1	2	1	30	1	39²	43	5	8.4	10.2	45	38%	.362	2.02	5.45	7.21	-1.3				
Codi Heuer	WNS	A+	22	4	1	2	20	0	38¹	34	0	1.9	10.1	43	63%	.324	1.10	2.82	3.59	0.5				
	BIR	AA	22	2	3	9	22	0	29¹	25	0	2.1	6.8	22	66%	.280	1.09	1.84	3.78	0.3				
Tyler Johnson	WNS	A+	23	0	1	0	7	0	10	6	1	3.6	13.5	15	73%	.238	1.00	1.80	2.85	0.2				
	BIR	AA	23	2	0	0	12	0	18¹	10	3	2.9	11.3	23	36%	.179	0.87	3.44	2.85	0.4				
Kodi Medeiros	BIR	AA	23	4	8	0	28	9	83	80	11	5.5	8.1	75	37%	.296	1.58	5.10	6.12	-1.4				
Juan Minaya	CHR	AAA	28	4	3	6	24	0	34	32	4	4.0	10.9	41	49%	.326	1.38	3.71	3.47	0.9				
	CHA	MLB	28	0	0	0	22	0	27²	31	4	3.9	8.8	27	29%	.333	1.55	3.90	6.12	-0.2	95.5	62.6	10.9	49.1
Konnor Pilkington	KAN	A	21	1	0	0	6	6	33¹	15	2	3.0	11.3	42	35%	.186	0.78	1.62	2.18	1.2				
	WNS	A+	21	4	9	0	19	19	95²	99	7	3.7	9.0	96	38%	.341	1.44	4.99	5.69	-0.8				
Héctor Santiago	CHR	AAA	31	1	4	0	7	7	37	45	9	2.2	8.0	33	37%	.343	1.46	5.84	5.47	0.4				
	SYR	AAA	31	3	1	0	8	7	43	32	5	4.8	8.0	38	42%	.235	1.28	3.35	5.07	0.7				
	CHA	MLB	31	0	1	0	11	2	25²	32	7	6.0	11.9	34	35%	.373	1.91	6.66	7.43	-0.5	94.5	59.3	13.1	51
	NYN	MLB	31	1	0	0	8	0	8	10	1	5.6	6.8	6	22%	.346	1.88	6.75	8.61	-0.3	93.6	63.4	10.5	49.1
Thyago Vieira	CHR	AAA	25	6	4	8	39	0	47¹	53	7	4.2	9.7	51	52%	.357	1.58	5.70	4.97	0.6				
	CHA	MLB	25	1	0	0	6	0	7	11	0	6.4	10.3	8	38%	.458	2.29	9.00	6.86	-0.1	101.0	68.1	13.6	46.8

Some control problems aside, **Zack Burdi** (the younger brother of Nick) was pushing for a big-league call-up barely a year after being drafted when his elbow blew out in July 2017. Between an extended Tommy John rehab, a lat strain, and now knee surgery, that fire-breathing form has yet to be seen since. ⚾ White Sox relievers Ian Hamilton and **Ryan Burr** played up their historic namesakes for laughs in a spring training skit. But in keeping with the theme, Hamilton's spring training was derailed by a car crash and a foul ball to the face, and Burr keeps photoshopping googly eyes over Instagram posts of his Tommy John scar. Duels are bad, kids. ⚾ Unless you were so good at something in high school that you asked for $2 million to skip college and turn professional, you cannot relate to **Andrew Dalquist**, whose senior-year velocity jump matched up with the excitement his easy delivery inspired in scouts. As a lauded high-school pitching prospect, Dalquist probably cannot relate to his peers in a college-heavy Sox system, but maybe he can pass them up. ⚾ It seems like a bygone era when **Ross Detwiler** was drafted sixth overall. Judging by the way hitters treated his sinker in 2019—.338 batting average, .636 slugging percentage, and 6.9 percent whiff rate—it was. ⚾ Safe, reliable strike-throwing from a tall, sturdy frame with consistent success into the upper minors are soothing qualities for a pitching prospect profile. A season and a half of inaction due to elbow troubles and eventual Tommy John surgery are less so, but such is life for **Dane Dunning**, who will likely continue rehabbing until midway through 2020. ⚾ Alabama has been good to right-handed reliever **Matt Foster** from his illustrious high school career at Valley to his impressive junior season in Tuscaloosa to his scoreless streak to start the 2019 season in Birmingham, and he now finds himself knocking on the door to the White Sox bullpen. ⚾ **Caleb Frare** got himself to the majors by ceasing to worry about control and just throwing the ball as hard as he could. But despite winning an Opening Day roster spot, his velocity backing up only made everyone worry about his flighty control even more. The three-batter minimum won't be good news for his career even if some mid-90s juice returns. ⚾ **Alec Hansen** had an outstanding pro debut. He's struggled since, resulting in a shift to the 'pen. It didn't help, given he walked 103 batters in 103 innings. We're optimistic about his prospects. It's three truths and a lie, folks —here's a hint: they're in order. ⚾ With the White Sox having spent only a half-season wasting time on the illusion that **Codi Heuer's** control issues would get worked out as a starter, they will likely will have to wait only that much longer for him to reach the majors. The plus life on his fastball weighs just as heavily on his profile as any concerns about the strikeout dip in Double-A. ⚾ **Tyler Johnson's** crossfiring ways finally caught up with him last season in the form of a lat strain that swallowed half of his year. When he played, there were no signs yet that platoon issues will limit him to middle relief. ⚾ Minor-league pitcher wins and losses are the only thing dumber than the major-league version, but it sure is something that former first rounder **Kodi Medeiros** managed to drop 10 decisions in a row after being traded to the White Sox. It wasn't like he was secretly pitching well while his team lost before the Sox converted him to relief, just as it's not like that switch led him to throw more strikes. ⚾ To get outrighted and go unclaimed on waivers is a dispiriting career low-point. To battle back to the majors in the same season is a demonstration of determination. To get outrighted and go unclaimed on waivers twice in the same season is the sort of oddity that makes its way into a year-end comment. Here's to you, **Juan Minaya**. ⚾ The burly left-hander's selling points after a decorated career at Mississippi State were polish and deception rather than raw stuff. Therefore **Konnor Pilkington** racking up big strikeout numbers while barely cracking 90 mph, but struggling to stanch big innings in High-A, is more odd than encouraging. ⚾ Given the progression of the printing industry and human society, we have to prepare for the strong possibility that **Héctor Santiago** will be making a small collection of valiant but ineffective spot starts years after the discontinuance of this publication. It will probably be for the White Sox, as he remains the most successful member of their 2006 draft class, despite being taken in the 30th round. ⚾ A 2019 draft light on college

www.baseballprospectus.com

pitching finally nudged the White Sox into the prep market. Once there, they swung big to land **Matthew Thompson**, a multi-sport star in Houston (he can sing too) who has all the athleticism and projection you would want in a teenage pitcher, as well as the strike-throwing consistency issues you would expect.

⚘ **Thyago Vieira** hit a legit 102 mph on the radar gun at Triple-A Charlotte in August. His post-save celebrations answer the hypothetical of what the "Ace Ventura" movies would be like if they were remade starring a 230-pound Brazilian man wearing rec specs. Other than that, he's a drag to watch.

CINCINNATI REDS

Essay by Lucas Apostoleris

Player comments by Nick Schaefer and BP staff

When spring training commenced last year, it marked the first time since the Dusty Baker era that the Cincinnati Reds stretched and played long toss in an optimistic air. The Reds' front office, led by Dick Williams and Nick Krall, had spent the winter completing a series of deals that signaled a "win-now" mentality. There was Tanner Roark, and Yasiel Puig, and Matt Kemp, and Alex Wood and Sonny Gray. (Jose Iglesias and Derek Dietrich were also added, and played larger-than-expected roles.) In an era of constant fretting over the luxury tax, club control and financial flexibility, the Reds emerged as the iconoclast—the team who wanted to win, even if it meant spending more money and punting away potential league-minimum labor.

The Reds' investment in their on-the-field product was rewarded in a sense—attendance improved for the first time in years—and not in another. Improving by 10 wins, to a 75-87 mark, was enough to net them fourth place. It was not enough to end their playoff drought (now the sixth longest in the majors) or their streak of consecutive losing seasons (six and counting). Some teams would have hit the reset button and conformed in response, thinking to themselves, "Ah, well, that didn't work." The Reds, though, doubled down.

The most obvious sign of this was Cincinnati's continued willingness to do deals others would bristle at as inefficient. Hence Krall's decision to sign infielder Mike Moustakas to a four-year deal worth $64 million, and left-hander Wade Miley to a two-year pact worth $15 million. Neither seemed like the cleanest fit on a roster that already had a third baseman (and required its top infield prospect to move to the outfield a year ago) and a loaded rotation. Yet both could pay off.

Last season, Cincinnati's various second basemen combined to hit .221/.288/.390 with 23 home runs. Moustakas, comparatively, has averaged 34 home runs over the past three years. The Reds were tied for 18th in the majors in DRC+, a mark that placed them in the same ballpark as bottom feeders like the Toronto Blue Jays, Colorado Rockies, Kansas City Royals and Pittsburgh Pirates. They needed the offensive help, in other words, and that should make Moustakas a welcomed addition—at least offensively.

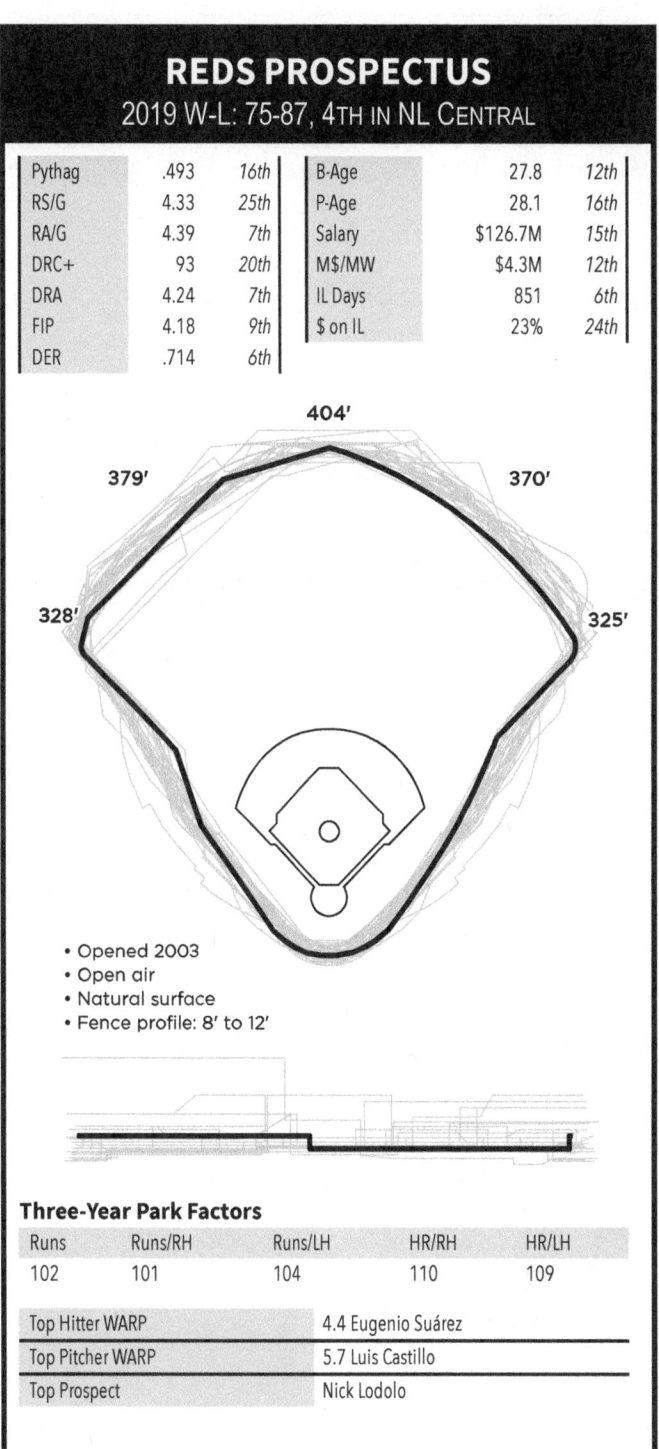

REDS PROSPECTUS
2019 W-L: 75-87, 4TH IN NL CENTRAL

Pythag	.493	16th	B-Age	27.8	12th
RS/G	4.33	25th	P-Age	28.1	16th
RA/G	4.39	7th	Salary	$126.7M	15th
DRC+	93	20th	M$/MW	$4.3M	12th
DRA	4.24	7th	IL Days	851	6th
FIP	4.18	9th	$ on IL	23%	24th
DER	.714	6th			

404'

379'

370'

328'

325'

- Opened 2003
- Open air
- Natural surface
- Fence profile: 8' to 12'

Three-Year Park Factors

Runs	Runs/RH	Runs/LH	HR/RH	HR/LH
102	101	104	110	109

Top Hitter WARP	4.4 Eugenio Suárez
Top Pitcher WARP	5.7 Luis Castillo
Top Prospect	Nick Lodolo

2019 Hit List Ranking

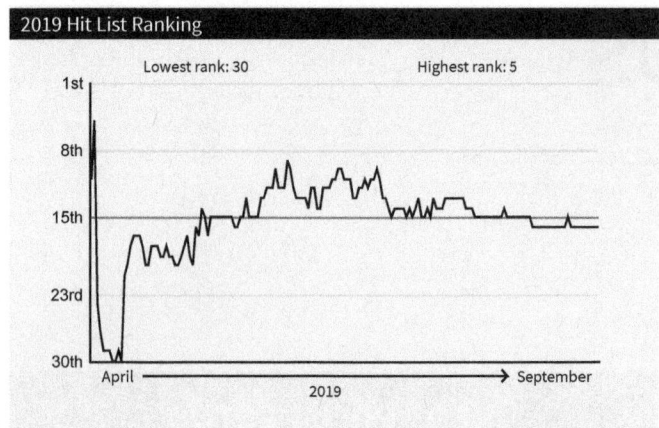

Lowest rank: 30   Highest rank: 5

Committed Payroll (in millions)

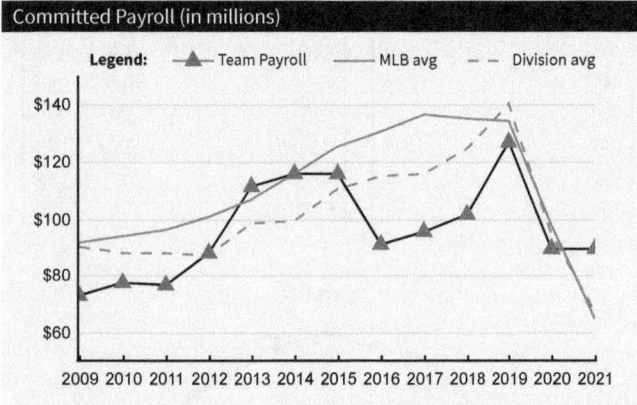

Legend: ▲ Team Payroll   — MLB avg   - - Division avg

Farm System Ranking

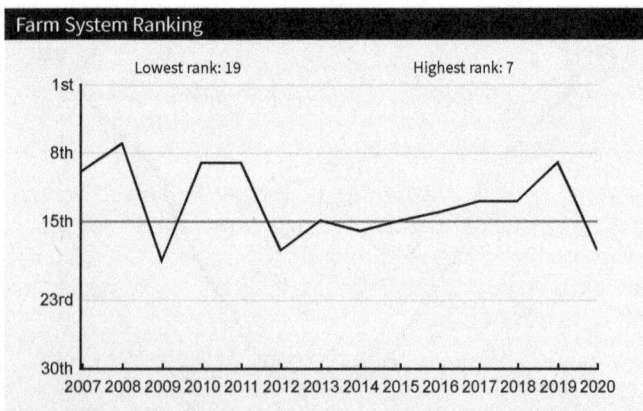

Lowest rank: 19   Highest rank: 7

Personnel

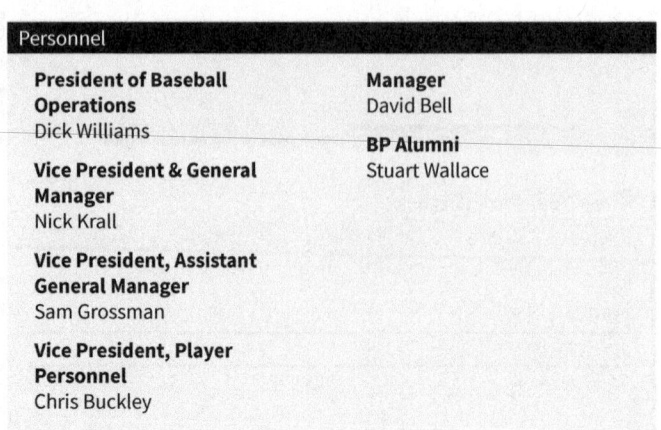

President of Baseball Operations
Dick Williams

Vice President & General Manager
Nick Krall

Vice President, Assistant General Manager
Sam Grossman

Vice President, Player Personnel
Chris Buckley

Manager
David Bell

BP Alumni
Stuart Wallace

Miley seemed well on his way to a richer multi-year deal before the All-Star Game. He entered the Midsummer Classic with a 3.28 ERA and 2.61 strikeout-to-walk ratio in 18 starts. The second half was considerably less kind to Miley, however, and he ended the year with an atrocious September—and we mean atrocious. Miley yielded 28 hits and 21 runs in 11 innings across five starts. The Reds can only hope Miley experiences a bounce-back season now that he's reunited with an old pitching coach.

The more interesting aspect of the Reds' winter was how they went all-in on eschewing pitching tradition. The transformation started last offseason when the team hired well-respected pitching coach Derek Johnson from the Milwaukee Brewers. Unlike with their win-now trades, the Reds saw nothing but positive results from Johnson's hiring.

Johnson's mystique dated back to his time at Vanderbilt University, where he coached from 2002 to 2012 and worked with countless future professionals, including David Price, Mike Minor and Gray. For as often as he brushed shoulders with blue chippers while overseeing the Commodores, he proved his touch was as effective with the at-times ragtag Brewers' staffs.

Under Johnson's instruction, Brewers pitchers had exceeded expectations in each of the past two seasons, even coming within a win of the 2018 World Series. There were countless anecdotes about how Johnson massaged the Brewers' unique staff—devoid of a front-line starter and often resorted to bullpen games in the postseason—to success. Some choice cuts included him helping Miley command a new cutter; aiding Jhoulys Chacin with the hunt for a changeup grip; and assisting Corbin Burnes adapt to a new role. No matter who and no matter what, Johnson always seems to have the ability to connect and correct.

"I don't think he has a secret potion of a formula or like, everyone's glove side is doing this or everyone's arm action has to do this," Gray told The Athletic last season. "It's everyone. I mean, he obviously teaches those things, but he teaches guys about themselves and what they need to do...he lets guys kind of be themselves, and helps them be the best version of themselves."

The numbers validate Gray's assertion. In Johnson's first year at the helm, Reds starters pitched to a runs-per-nine rate of 4.39, the ninth-best in baseball and a stark improvement over their previous mark (5.45, which ranked 26th). We can, of course, go deeper than that. The Reds' 4.05 rotational DRA was sixth in baseball, behind a quintet of teams with much better records: the Los Angeles Dodgers, Washington Nationals, New York Mets, Houston Astros, and Tampa Bay Rays. Their 1.39-run improvement in DRA was the largest in the sport.

But, while Gray said there's no set formula, it seemed like Johnson did instill in the Reds a predilection for the high fastball.

Throwing high fastballs is a tactic that has grown in popularity for obvious reasons: high heaters are harder to make contact with, leading to more whiffs and more weak contact. The league as a whole last season threw 40.4 percent of its four-seam fastballs in the upper-third of the strike zone or higher. (For reference, in 2018 that percentage was 37.8.) Johnson's pitching philosophy helped contribute to the trend. Don't believe us? Take a look at the table below, which shows team-wide rates for four-seam fastballs thrown in the upper third of the strike zone (or higher) since 2008. The 2019 Reds, as well as three other teams from last year, are in the top 10:

Rank	Team	High Fastball Rate
1	2019 Red Sox	52.7%
2	2017 Red Sox	51.8%
3	2018 Red Sox	51.7%
4	2019 Rays	48.5%
5	2016 Rays	47.0%
6	2016 Red Sox	46.3%
7	2019 Reds	45.7%
8	2019 Marlins	45.4%
9	2016 Tigers	45.4%
1	2014 Nationals	44.9%

The Boston Red Sox, with a similar overhaul of their pitching strategy in the latter half of the decade, have been in a league of their own with only the Rays posing a threat. The Reds weren't too far off, though, at seventh out of the 360 individual team seasons since 2008.

To be clear, this wasn't a case where the Reds were already into high fastballs before Johnson took over the reins, either. Going back as far as we have pitch tracking data, the only increase larger than the Reds' last year (just shy of 12 percent) was actually from another 2019 team: the Marlins, at 13.1 percentage points. Predictably, a number of mainstay Reds pitchers saw large jumps in their high fastball rate from the previous year: Anthony DeSclafani (20 percentage points), Michael Lorenzen (18) and Luis Castillo (16) included. (Even Gray, Johnson's former pupil in college, had his go up by 10 percentage points.) In turn, the fastball whiffs-per-swing rates for DeSclafani, Lorenzen and Castillo were all substantially higher last year than in 2018—in other words, the strategy had a direct benefit for those who bought in.

Keep in mind, that's just one detectable philosophical shift imparted by Johnson during his season in town—one that suggests, of course, that his hiring has already been a fruitful one. Perhaps those results emboldened the Reds to go all-in on a new approach this winter, as they altered their organizational pitching philosophy in an unprecedented way.

Former big-league pitcher and Johnson study Caleb Cotham, who had served as the team's assistant pitching coach for a year, was given a new title right after the season ended: director of pitching. The Reds also hired Kyle Boddy, founder of the Driveline Baseball facility, as their director of pitching initiatives and pitching coordinator. Boddy was brought on to help provide what he described as a "unified decision-making model from top to bottom." Accordingly, the Reds then hired countless coaches and instructors with Driveline ties.

Clearly the Reds are heavily invested in creating a pitching development pipeline informed by the latest methods and techniques. Whether or not it pays off is to be seen. But there's something to be said about committing to a vision. These days the view of teams is the same as airplane seats: the worst spot is in the middle. That can apply to strategies, too. The Reds could have continued to operate like every other franchise. But it's more interesting (and potentially rewarding, for all we know at this point) that they've deviated from the norm in a significant way.

On paper, the Reds don't match up with the favorites of the division. Their roster has its pluses: Eugenio Suárez is a hidden gem; Nick Senzel could win a batting title someday; we're not quite ready to write off Joey Votto; and so on. But this is a group that needs to be aggressive and to approach things from a different vantage point in order to succeed. Based on the last two offseasons, it seems like the Reds are willing to do both.

Now, it's time for the record to match the boldness. ∎

—Lucas Apostoleris is an author of Baseball Prospectus.

HITTERS

Shogo Akiyama CF Born: 04/16/88 Age: 32 Bats: L Throws: R Height: 6'0" Weight: 187 Origin: International Free Agent, 2019

In the 50-plus years since Masanori Murakami debuted, every team except one—the Reds, naturally—has employed a big-league player of Japanese nationality. That'll change come Opening Day, as the Reds struck a deal to land Akiyama and his well-rounded collection of average-to-plus tools. Not only does he have the speed to play center field, but his combination of above-average bat-to-ball skills and a keen eye should help him get on base at a respectable clip—making him a nice change of pace from the days of Billy Hamilton and Drew Stubbs. Akiyama is more of a gap hitter, though he could post better power numbers than expected thanks to the Great American Ballpark's shallow dimensions. Being on the wrong side of 30 at the start of a three-year contract is concerning, but there's enough here to think he will remain an average or better regular for the duration.

Aristides Aquino   RF   Born: 04/22/94   Age: 26   Bats: R   Throws: R   Height: 6'4"   Weight: 220   Origin: International Free Agent, 2011

YEAR	TEAM	LVL	AGE	PA	R	2B	3B	HR	RBI	BB	K	SB	CS	AVG/OBP/SLG	DRC+	VORP	BABIP	BRR	FRAA	WARP
2017	PEN	AA	23	504	54	20	6	17	56	39	145	9	3	.216/.282/.397	73	-2.2	.274	-0.9	RF(128): 8.9	0.7
2018	PEN	AA	24	445	49	20	2	20	55	35	112	4	5	.240/.306/.448	103	8.2	.282	-1.3	RF(108): 7.7	1.7
2018	CIN	MLB	24	1	0	0	0	0	0	0	1	0	0	.000/.000/.000	87	-0.9	--	-0.7	RF(1): 0.1	-0.1
2019	LOU	AAA	25	323	56	13	1	28	53	23	81	5	1	.299/.356/.636	149	22.7	.321	0.2	RF(64): 3.4, CF(5): 1.8	2.9
2019	CIN	MLB	25	225	31	8	0	19	47	16	60	7	0	.259/.316/.576	114	9.5	.266	0.3	RF(54): 0.9	1.0
2020	CIN	MLB	26	462	68	19	2	35	86	28	134	4	2	.255/.308/.555	118	19.5	.285	-1.3	RF 3	2.3

Comparables: Lane Adams, Aaron Altherr, Kennys Vargas

Aquino is an extreme example of how modern player development can frustrate prospect evaluation. He produced just middling results after two tries in Double-A, with power appearing to be his only plus tool. Accordingly, we had him outside of the Reds' top 10 list coming into 2019 (although he did get an honorable mention). After a swing change, Aquino laid waste to Triple-A and didn't look back, hitting 11 home runs in his first 16 major-league games following an August call-up. It was a dramatic showing, and one that all but forced us to recalibrate our expectations for him moving forward. Still, we feel it's worth noting that he slowed down from his initial historic run (how could he not?), and that his profile remains that of a high-strikeout/low-walk slugger who's a little older than you'd think. There's volatility in them there mountains, in other words, even if the peaks are taller than we originally estimated.

Tucker Barnhart   C   Born: 01/07/91   Age: 29   Bats: L   Throws: R   Height: 5'11"   Weight: 192   Origin: Round 10, 2009 Draft (#299 overall)

YEAR	TEAM	LVL	AGE	PA	R	2B	3B	HR	RBI	BB	K	SB	CS	AVG/OBP/SLG	DRC+	VORP	BABIP	BRR	FRAA	WARP
2017	CIN	MLB	26	423	26	24	2	7	44	42	68	4	0	.270/.347/.403	90	20.6	.312	-1.6	C(110): 0.7	1.5
2018	CIN	MLB	27	522	50	21	3	10	46	54	96	0	4	.248/.328/.372	86	12.4	.291	-3.3	C(118): -9.6, 1B(11): -0.7	0.2
2019	CIN	MLB	28	364	32	14	0	11	40	44	83	1	0	.231/.328/.380	90	13.8	.278	-3.7	C(102): 15.3, 1B(3): 0.0	2.5
2020	CIN	MLB	29	350	36	16	1	9	37	37	77	2	1	.241/.325/.379	87	8.9	.294	-1.7	C 3	1.2

Comparables: Mike Fitzgerald, Rube Walker, Chris Turner

The light-hitting Barnhart has scratched and clawed his way to become an everyday catcher. He's done that despite an odd twist that has seen his bat—again, the weaker aspect of his game—prove to be a more stable quality than his mitt. Consider that Barnhart's arm has declined from great to merely okay over the years, and that his framing has improved from a liability to a clear asset in 2019. Consider also that his DRC+ has finished within a tight 85-90 window in all five of his full seasons. There's something to be said about consistency, even if the area of consistency is substandard. Put another way, if Barnhart's bat were predictably less predictable, he'd probably still be a backup.

YEAR	TEAM	P. COUNT	FRM RUNS	BLK RUNS	THRW RUNS	TOT RUNS
2017	CIN	15640	-8.2	2.7	4.9	-0.9
2018	CIN	16826	-11.5	3.6	-0.3	-8.4
2019	CIN	12997	10.1	4.9	-0.3	14.7
2020	CIN	16840	-0.3	2.3	-0.2	1.8

Mariel Bautista   OF   Born: 10/15/97   Age: 22   Bats: R   Throws: R   Height: 6'3"   Weight: 194   Origin: International Free Agent, 2014

YEAR	TEAM	LVL	AGE	PA	R	2B	3B	HR	RBI	BB	K	SB	CS	AVG/OBP/SLG	DRC+	VORP	BABIP	BRR	FRAA	WARP
2017	CIN	RK	19	157	29	9	1	0	20	5	24	16	1	.320/.353/.395	119	14.8	.379	3.5	LF(24): -1.7, CF(10): 3.2	1.1
2018	BIL	RK	20	233	43	12	4	8	37	16	29	16	3	.330/.386/.541	139	28.0	.349	2.3	CF(40): -4.4, LF(6): -1.3	0.6
2019	DYT	A	21	433	43	10	2	8	33	28	88	19	11	.233/.303/.332	88	5.5	.278	1.9	LF(42): -3.0, RF(36): 0.9	0.2
2020	CIN	MLB	22	251	22	11	1	4	23	12	66	4	2	.227/.276/.340	64	-3.6	.298	0.1	LF -1, CF -1	-0.5

Comparables: Victor Robles, Aristides Aquino, Michael Hermosillo

The phrase that always gets used to excuse so-so performances from athletic youngsters is "don't scout the stat line." Applying it to Bautista makes sense, given he shows the potential for five tools that grade as average or better—with the hit, power and speed comprising the "better" part. At some point projection has to materialize; otherwise, it's just phantom potential. Unfortunately, Bautista is nearing *that* point while remaining raw enough to threaten salmonella poisoning. He's too old for rookie ball, but not mature enough as a player to succeed in A-ball, let alone higher up. Something's going to have to give—either he's going to make The Jump, or he's going to fall into the non-prospect void. Check back in a year for the conclusion.

Alex Blandino   INF   Born: 11/06/92   Age: 27   Bats: R   Throws: R   Height: 6'0"   Weight: 190   Origin: Round 1, 2014 Draft (#29 overall)

YEAR	TEAM	LVL	AGE	PA	R	2B	3B	HR	RBI	BB	K	SB	CS	AVG/OBP/SLG	DRC+	VORP	BABIP	BRR	FRAA	WARP
2017	PEN	AA	24	236	31	22	0	6	31	32	49	3	4	.259/.374/.462	137	12.7	.315	-1.6	2B(39): 1.8, 3B(18): 2.1	1.8
2017	LOU	AAA	24	237	29	14	1	6	20	32	37	1	3	.270/.390/.444	141	12.0	.305	-2.8	2B(29): -1.8, 3B(26): 0.5	1.4
2018	CIN	MLB	25	147	14	4	0	1	8	13	41	0	0	.234/.324/.289	79	2.8	.337	2.3	2B(21): -1.4, 3B(15): -1.2	0.0
2019	LOU	AAA	26	293	36	13	1	5	24	40	73	1	3	.247/.386/.372	108	6.8	.335	-3.2	2B(34): -1.6, SS(18): -1.1	0.8
2019	CIN	MLB	26	50	6	1	0	1	3	10	14	0	0	.250/.420/.361	91	1.0	.348	-0.3	2B(10): 0.1, 3B(4): 0.0	0.1
2020	CIN	MLB	27	112	12	5	0	3	12	12	32	1	1	.229/.335/.379	92	3.0	.311	-0.3	SS 0, 2B -1	0.3

Comparables: Stan Hollmig, Greg Garcia, Hunter Dozier

Branzino: A popular dinner fish, especially at Italian restaurants. Blonde Eno: Brian in a killer wig. Blandino: a walk-heavy minor-league second baseman. Originally a first-round pick, it seems more likely with each passing month that he'll top out as organizational depth. Blandino's patient, disciplined approach is the extent of his plus traits. Otherwise, he's not much of an athlete and he lacks even average arm strength or power potential, limiting his value as a utility infielder. We're the publication that once hyped up Jackie Rexrode, so take it from us: there's more to life than walk rate.

Curt Casali C   Born: 11/09/88   Age: 31   Bats: R   Throws: R   Height: 6'3"   Weight: 225   Origin: Round 10, 2011 Draft (#317 overall)

YEAR	TEAM	LVL	AGE	PA	R	2B	3B	HR	RBI	BB	K	SB	CS	AVG/OBP/SLG	DRC+	VORP	BABIP	BRR	FRAA	WARP
2017	DUR	AAA	28	343	36	10	0	5	48	37	65	0	0	.263/.351/.347	104	8.8	.320	-0.4	C(53): -2.1	1.1
2017	TBA	MLB	28	13	2	0	0	1	3	3	3	0	0	.333/.462/.667	94	3.0	.333	0.3	C(8): 0.6	0.2
2018	DUR	AAA	29	104	13	5	0	4	20	7	19	0	0	.274/.327/.453	112	4.5	.301	-0.1	C(26): 1.0	0.7
2018	CIN	MLB	29	156	15	10	0	4	16	12	32	0	2	.293/.355/.450	101	9.3	.352	0.1	C(38): -4.1, 1B(6): 0.1	0.3
2019	CIN	MLB	30	236	24	9	0	8	32	25	59	0	0	.251/.331/.411	102	12.8	.308	0.1	C(67): 6.0, 1B(4): 0.0	1.8
2020	CIN	MLB	31	287	34	13	0	11	37	30	77	1	0	.239/.328/.423	98	13.3	.300	0.6	C 5	1.9

Comparables: David Ross, Chris Gimenez, Tony Sanchez

YEAR	TEAM	P. COUNT	FRM RUNS	BLK RUNS	THRW RUNS	TOT RUNS
2017	DUR	7761	2.3	-3.0	-1.0	-1.7
2017	TBA	486	0.6	-0.1	0.0	0.8
2018	CIN	4795	-2.1	-1.3	-0.2	-3.0
2018	DUR	3527	1.8	0.3	-0.3	1.9
2019	CIN	8388	4.5	1.8	-0.3	6.0
2020	CIN	15231	5.7	-0.3	-0.3	5.1

There's nothing remarkable about Casali's game. He's a good framer and a below-average thrower; a disciplined hitter with pull-side power who strikes out a fair amount and would probably be overexposed if asked to play daily. But it's neat whenever a 10th-round pick beats the odds and makes it all the way to the arbitration phase of their career. For that, we tip our collective caps to you, Mr. Casali. May you continue to be a perfectly respectable reserve.

Christian Colón INF   Born: 05/14/89   Age: 31   Bats: R   Throws: R   Height: 5'10"   Weight: 195   Origin: Round 1, 2010 Draft (#4 overall)

YEAR	TEAM	LVL	AGE	PA	R	2B	3B	HR	RBI	BB	K	SB	CS	AVG/OBP/SLG	DRC+	VORP	BABIP	BRR	FRAA	WARP
2017	NWO	AAA	28	177	17	8	1	1	13	16	26	6	3	.302/.379/.376	106	9.9	.358	-1.5	3B(17): -2.0, 2B(16): 0.4	0.3
2017	KCA	MLB	28	19	1	0	0	0	0	1	3	0	0	.176/.222/.176	66	-2.1	.214	0.1	2B(6): 0.8	0.1
2017	MIA	MLB	28	38	3	1	0	0	0	4	7	0	0	.152/.243/.182	64	-2.1	.192	0.4	3B(10): 0.7, 2B(4): 0.3	0.1
2018	GWN	AAA	29	55	3	0	0	0	3	4	8	1	0	.204/.278/.204	56	-3.4	.244	-0.5	2B(14): 1.1	0.0
2018	LVG	AAA	29	313	44	22	1	6	38	36	30	11	5	.304/.396/.459	122	14.9	.323	-0.9	2B(43): 4.5, 3B(25): 0.9	2.2
2019	LOU	AAA	30	582	63	37	2	10	70	57	58	24	13	.300/.372/.443	110	28.6	.315	-2.4	3B(104): 12.6, SS(15): -1.7	3.4
2019	CIN	MLB	30	8	1	0	0	0	1	0	0	0	0	.500/.625/.500	92	0.2	.500	-0.4	2B(3): 0.0	0.0
2020	CIN	MLB	31	251	23	9	0	4	23	20	38	5	2	.230/.300/.328	70	-2.0	.260	-0.3	3B 1, 2B 1	0.0

Comparables: Adam Kennedy, Marlon Anderson, Mickey Morandini

Colón joined his fifth organization in 2019, making him fit for the "journeyman" title. Along the way, he's piled up thousands of professional plate appearances that suggest he's a slap-hitting, up-and-down infielder who is useful only in an emergency. The Reds have had some successes coaxing power out of unexpected places—Eugenio Suárez, Scooter Gennett and Zack Cozart come to mind—so you never want to say never. Even so, we're comfortable in our assessment that he's just a depth piece, his draft pedigree serving as little more than a trivial footnote.

Derek Dietrich 2B   Born: 07/18/89   Age: 30   Bats: L   Throws: R   Height: 6'0"   Weight: 205   Origin: Round 2, 2010 Draft (#79 overall)

YEAR	TEAM	LVL	AGE	PA	R	2B	3B	HR	RBI	BB	K	SB	CS	AVG/OBP/SLG	DRC+	VORP	BABIP	BRR	FRAA	WARP
2017	MIA	MLB	27	464	56	22	5	13	53	36	98	0	1	.249/.334/.424	96	22.3	.294	0.5	3B(103): -7.6, 2B(10): 0.3	0.7
2018	MIA	MLB	28	551	72	26	2	16	45	29	140	2	0	.265/.330/.421	100	25.2	.336	1.7	LF(97): -8.4, 1B(33): -1.9	0.4
2019	CIN	MLB	29	306	41	8	2	19	43	28	74	1	1	.187/.328/.462	113	14.1	.176	1.5	2B(58): -3.1, 1B(21): -0.7	1.1
2020	CIN	MLB	30	251	32	10	1	11	35	19	61	1	0	.234/.341/.450	111	12.3	.272	0.6	3B -1, LF -1	1.0

Comparables: Rickie Weeks Jr., Danny Espinosa, Jedd Gyorko

Bill James once riffed that it's better to start hot than finish hot. The reason is straightforward: a player who has a good April and May will have better-looking statistics than the player who is cold until, say, June rolls around—even if their production ends up being the same when all is sand and dust. Dietrich is a good example of this in motion. He hit .254/.364/.720 with 17 home runs through May 28th, at which point everyone labeled him a smart get by the Reds. With that decided, people stopped checking in and instead used their time to monitor teams in playoff races or virtual ant farms or whatever. They missed that Dietrich hit .128/.297/.233 with two home runs the rest of the way before undergoing shoulder surgery in September. Despite it all, he still finished as an above-average hitter thanks to those hot months. It didn't matter though. When Dietrich was made available on waivers after the season, before being set free, every team quoted a different Jamesism—the one from the *New Historical Abstract* when he wrote, of Jeff Bagwell, "Pass."

Phillip Ervin OF   Born: 07/15/92   Age: 27   Bats: R   Throws: R   Height: 5'10"   Weight: 207   Origin: Round 1, 2013 Draft (#27 overall)

YEAR	TEAM	LVL	AGE	PA	R	2B	3B	HR	RBI	BB	K	SB	CS	AVG/OBP/SLG	DRC+	VORP	BABIP	BRR	FRAA	WARP
2017	LOU	AAA	24	408	46	20	2	7	40	37	83	23	6	.256/.328/.380	99	7.7	.315	0.6	LF(56): 8.7, CF(40): -3.1	1.6
2017	CIN	MLB	24	64	8	2	0	3	10	4	15	4	1	.259/.317/.448	96	4.7	.300	1.1	CF(9): -0.6, RF(5): -0.4	0.2
2018	LOU	AAA	25	202	25	12	4	5	38	20	39	10	7	.289/.373/.491	136	14.7	.341	-0.8	LF(37): 5.2, CF(8): -0.5	1.6
2018	CIN	MLB	25	247	27	10	1	7	31	20	60	6	1	.252/.324/.404	96	6.4	.310	1.0	LF(39): 0.2, RF(33): -2.7	0.3
2019	LOU	AAA	26	172	27	8	1	6	26	19	34	6	6	.290/.384/.483	135	14.7	.333	2.0	CF(25): 0.9, LF(10): 1.2	1.5
2019	CIN	MLB	26	260	30	11	7	7	23	18	63	4	3	.271/.331/.466	94	6.1	.339	1.0	LF(61): -5.5, CF(25): 1.1	0.2
2020	CIN	MLB	27	91	11	4	1	3	11	8	22	4	1	.240/.319/.422	96	2.8	.289	0.2	CF 0, RF 0	0.3

Comparables: Tyler Collins, Mo Vaughn, Desmond Jennings

Ervin has been on prospect radars since he was drafted 27th in 2013—or, a handful of spots ahead of a different right-handed collegiate outfielder named Aaron Judge. Whoops. While Judge has since solidified himself as one of the best hitters in the game, Ervin is still trying to establish a foothold on a roster spot. His time is coming. He's hit .313/.371/.536 in his first 200 plate appearances against lefties, and no longer has minor-league options remaining. Presuming teams don't do something ridiculous with the 26-player roster—like, say, carry 14 pitchers at a time—Ervin should spend at least a few seasons on bench.

TJ Friedl OF   Born: 08/14/95   Age: 24   Bats: L   Throws: L   Height: 5'10"   Weight: 180   Origin: Undrafted Free Agent, 2016

YEAR	TEAM	LVL	AGE	PA	R	2B	3B	HR	RBI	BB	K	SB	CS	AVG/OBP/SLG	DRC+	VORP	BABIP	BRR	FRAA	WARP
2017	DYT	A	21	292	47	20	6	5	25	29	46	14	8	.284/.378/.472	138	25.6	.328	4.1	RF(22): 0.7, CF(18): -3.0	1.9
2017	DAY	A+	21	199	15	6	2	2	13	10	39	2	1	.257/.313/.346	80	3.3	.317	0.0	CF(20): -1.3, RF(18): -2.5	0.2
2018	DAY	A+	22	274	40	10	4	3	35	38	44	11	4	.294/.405/.412	138	23.4	.350	4.7	LF(39): 2.0, CF(19): -1.0	2.3
2018	PEN	AA	22	296	47	10	3	2	16	28	56	19	5	.276/.359/.360	112	12.7	.345	3.3	LF(53): 5.1, CF(9): -1.0	1.9
2019	CHT	AA	23	269	38	11	4	5	28	29	50	13	4	.235/.347/.385	113	9.4	.277	1.3	RF(42): 2.4, LF(14): -1.4	1.1
2020	CIN	MLB	24	251	24	11	2	5	25	20	60	6	2	.227/.305/.363	79	1.6	.286	0.4	LF 2, CF -2	0.2

Comparables: Matt Szczur, Ty France, Zoilo Almonte

Friedl, who signed in 2016 as an undrafted free agent out of University of Nevada-Reno, has since outplayed plenty of players who were more highly thought of as amateurs. You can probably guess what kind of skill set he has based on that alone. If you said some combination of "fourth outfielder," "high-motor," "good eye," "good speed" and/or "no power," then congratulations—you win. He didn't hit as well as one might hope in a second look at Double-A. But, as we like to say around here, once you've made it to Double-A you're only a phone call away from the majors. For a player with Friedl's background, making it this far is already a win.

Freddy Galvis SS   Born: 11/14/89   Age: 30   Bats: B   Throws: R   Height: 5'10"   Weight: 185   Origin: International Free Agent, 2006

YEAR	TEAM	LVL	AGE	PA	R	2B	3B	HR	RBI	BB	K	SB	CS	AVG/OBP/SLG	DRC+	VORP	BABIP	BRR	FRAA	WARP
2017	PHI	MLB	27	663	71	29	6	12	61	45	111	14	5	.255/.309/.382	85	25.9	.292	1.6	SS(155): 1.7, LF(1): 0.0	2.2
2018	SDN	MLB	28	656	62	31	5	13	67	45	147	8	6	.248/.299/.380	82	19.0	.304	-1.2	SS(160): -8.9, 2B(5): -0.5	0.4
2019	CIN	MLB	29	116	12	4	0	5	16	7	33	0	1	.234/.284/.411	88	2.2	.286	-0.6	2B(27): -1.4, SS(7): -0.5	0.0
2019	TOR	MLB	29	473	55	24	1	18	54	21	112	4	1	.267/.299/.444	92	17.4	.318	-1.8	SS(103): -2.0, 2B(5): -0.2	1.3
2020	CIN	MLB	30	595	60	25	2	18	68	33	140	11	4	.248/.292/.397	79	5.9	.300	-0.3	SS -3	0.3

Comparables: Greg Gagne, Eduardo Escobar, Luis Rivera

The Reds entered last season with competitive aspirations thanks to a remade pitching staff, a number of rental vets and some up-and-coming homegrown talent. It didn't work out. A good microcosm of their season came in late August, when they were swept in a three-game series by the Pirates, who played like a 55-win team during the second half. Galvis batted second in each of those contests. Cincinnati's troubles went far beyond him, but it makes for a nice comment construct, right? Anyway, Galvis resides in an awkward space: he's not good enough to start on a contender, yet he's too good to be a reserve. Recently, that's left him bouncing from team to team, where he's tolerated for his defense and good vibes until an upgrade can be acquired. That process figures to play out once more in Cincinnati, after which Galvis might be far enough on the downswing to slot in as someone's well-liked fifth infielder.

Jonathan India 3B   Born: 12/15/96   Age: 23   Bats: R   Throws: R   Height: 6'0"   Weight: 200   Origin: Round 1, 2018 Draft (#5 overall)

YEAR	TEAM	LVL	AGE	PA	R	2B	3B	HR	RBI	BB	K	SB	CS	AVG/OBP/SLG	DRC+	VORP	BABIP	BRR	FRAA	WARP
2018	GRV	RK	21	62	11	2	1	3	12	15	12	1	0	.261/.452/.543	150	6.3	.290	0.6	3B(12): -0.6, SS(2): -0.2	0.5
2018	DYT	A	21	112	17	7	0	3	11	13	28	5	0	.229/.339/.396	104	7.0	.292	1.5	3B(21): 2.4, SS(4): -0.1	0.8
2019	DAY	A+	22	367	50	15	5	8	30	37	84	7	5	.256/.346/.410	130	18.1	.319	-1.8	3B(74): -9.2, 2B(5): 0.0	1.0
2019	CHT	AA	22	145	24	3	0	3	14	22	26	4	0	.270/.414/.378	141	11.0	.314	0.2	3B(31): -0.4	1.1
2020	CIN	MLB	23	251	28	11	1	8	29	25	70	4	1	.231/.326/.399	95	6.5	.303	-0.1	3B -2, SS 0	0.4

Comparables: Alex Blandino, Hunter Dozier, Kyle Kubitza

The Reds were evidently so happy with Nick Senzel that they took the Coke Zero version, in India, two drafts later at No. 5. Like Senzel, India has a slick glove at third with enough athleticism to cover short or second in a pinch; he also has a contact-over-power offensive profile, and so on and so forth. We could keep going, but you get the point: it's similar, just less of. Teams have done worse with higher draft picks than what India projects to become, which is a totally fine third baseman who could reach the majors in 2020.

Travis Jankowski OF   Born: 06/15/91   Age: 29   Bats: L   Throws: R   Height: 6'2"   Weight: 185   Origin: Round 1, 2012 Draft (#44 overall)

YEAR	TEAM	LVL	AGE	PA	R	2B	3B	HR	RBI	BB	K	SB	CS	AVG/OBP/SLG	DRC+	VORP	BABIP	BRR	FRAA	WARP
2017	ELP	AAA	26	157	20	5	1	0	11	18	28	8	1	.266/.350/.317	75	1.4	.333	0.1	CF(22): -1.7, LF(7): -0.3	-0.2
2017	SDN	MLB	26	87	10	2	0	0	1	9	28	4	0	.187/.282/.213	53	-3.1	.298	0.9	LF(19): -0.4, CF(4): 0.3	-0.2
2018	ELP	AAA	27	94	17	4	0	1	11	11	21	4	3	.363/.452/.450	112	8.8	.483	1.5	CF(20): 2.5	0.9
2018	SDN	MLB	27	387	45	12	3	4	17	37	73	24	4	.259/.332/.346	79	8.6	.319	4.5	RF(58): 3.3, CF(34): -1.7	0.4
2019	ELP	AAA	28	183	27	6	0	0	12	21	32	7	2	.313/.393/.350	92	2.4	.388	0.8	CF(18): -2.2, RF(10): -0.5	0.2
2019	SDN	MLB	28	24	4	0	0	0	0	2	4	2	2	.182/.250/.182	78	0.2	.222	0.7	CF(5): 0.5, RF(5): -0.1	0.1
2020	CIN	MLB	29	77	7	2	0	1	6	7	18	4	1	.241/.317/.314	72	-0.6	.319	0.5	RF 2	0.2

Comparables: Dexter Fowler, Herm Winningham, A.J. Pollock

There isn't much to say about Jankowski's lost 2019 season, as the fleet outfielder with the flowing blond locks missed much of it with a fractured wrist suffered when attempting a diving catch in March, then ping-ponged between San Diego and El Paso while the Friars sorted through their outfield logjam. You already know his game (serious speed, reasonable center field defense, high energy, no power) and his optimal role (fifth outfielder and pinch runner).

But did you know his nickname is "Freddy" due to his daily childhood dose of *Mister Rogers' Neighborhood*? Makes you wonder whether every time Jankowski swipes a bag or runs down a gapper he hears a voice in his head repeating "Speedy Delivery!" Jankowski will compete for a big-league bench role with Cincinnati this spring.

Nick Martini LF Born: 06/27/90 Age: 30 Bats: L Throws: L Height: 5'11" Weight: 205 Origin: Round 7, 2011 Draft (#230 overall)

YEAR	TEAM	LVL	AGE	PA	R	2B	3B	HR	RBI	BB	K	SB	CS	AVG/OBP/SLG	DRC+	VORP	BABIP	BRR	FRAA	WARP
2017	SFD	AA	27	110	13	5	0	2	15	11	16	1	0	.263/.336/.374	113	5.4	.296	0.9	LF(16): 1.9, RF(3): 0.7	0.7
2017	MEM	AAA	27	426	60	20	5	6	55	55	77	5	1	.303/.394/.436	121	29.6	.363	1.2	LF(53): -0.3, RF(24): 0.6	2.3
2018	NAS	AAA	28	330	44	12	2	6	40	51	68	5	1	.297/.406/.420	128	23.3	.373	2.5	1B(41): 2.8, LF(22): 0.2	2.4
2018	OAK	MLB	28	179	26	9	3	1	19	21	36	0	0	.296/.397/.414	104	14.0	.379	1.1	LF(47): 2.1, CF(2): 0.2	0.9
2019	LVG	AAA	29	329	57	18	0	8	42	49	51	0	0	.328/.432/.482	122	18.8	.376	-1.3	LF(51): -8.8	0.8
2019	SDN	MLB	29	96	7	4	1	0	5	12	21	0	0	.244/.344/.317	80	0.1	.323	-0.4	LF(23): 0.6	0.0
2019	OAK	MLB	29	13	1	0	0	1	2	2	5	0	0	.091/.231/.364	79	0.1	.000	0.0	LF(3): 0.1, P(1): 0.0	0.0
2020	CIN	MLB	30	7	1	0	0	0	1	1	2	0	0	.247/.342/.367	92	0.2	.310	0.0	LF 0, 1B 0	0.0

Comparables: David Freitas, Robbie Grossman, Darin Mastroianni

If you read *Moneyball*, you might well have thought Martini and his on-base-centric approach was the Platonic ideal of a *Moneyball* player. And when Billy Beane's Athletics released him last August, you would have been shocked, since you clearly misunderstood both *Moneyball* and the concept of a Platonic ideal. Martini caught on with the Padres and provided them with his usual mix of punchless patience and competent defense in an outfield corner, making him perfectly suited for a big-league bench role. He's the heir apparent to another factory second from the St. Louis assembly line, Jon Jay, whose similar lefty on-base skills and reputation for professional at-bats has kept him hitting white balls for batting practice well into his mid-30s.

Braylin Minier SS Born: 06/11/03 Age: 17 Bats: L Throws: R Height: 6'0" Weight: 160 Origin: International Free Agent, 2019

A Dominican-born shortstop, Minier turned 16 about three weeks before signing with the Reds for a $1.8 million bonus on July 2. Seeing as how he's years away from playing stateside, we could write just about anything here and have it fly. We'll pass on abusing your trust in us to offer the truth: we have no idea at this point if Minier will stick at shortstop, grow into his frame enough to hit for power, or hit on 16 during a friendly clubhouse game of blackjack. In four years, we'll know a little more.

Mike Moustakas 2B Born: 09/11/88 Age: 31 Bats: L Throws: R Height: 6'0" Weight: 225 Origin: Round 1, 2007 Draft (#2 overall)

YEAR	TEAM	LVL	AGE	PA	R	2B	3B	HR	RBI	BB	K	SB	CS	AVG/OBP/SLG	DRC+	VORP	BABIP	BRR	FRAA	WARP
2017	KCA	MLB	28	598	75	24	0	38	85	34	94	0	0	.272/.314/.521	121	27.0	.263	-1.6	3B(127): -7.4	2.7
2018	KCA	MLB	29	417	46	21	1	20	62	30	63	3	0	.249/.309/.468	109	13.9	.247	-2.6	3B(76): 11.3, 1B(4): -0.2	2.7
2018	MIL	MLB	29	218	20	12	0	8	33	19	40	1	1	.256/.326/.441	107	8.3	.282	-2.6	3B(52): 0.5	0.8
2019	MIL	MLB	30	584	80	30	1	35	87	53	98	3	0	.254/.329/.516	118	35.6	.250	-2.8	3B(105): -0.7, 2B(47): -1.9	2.9
2020	CIN	MLB	31	595	78	28	1	34	93	48	101	2	1	.254/.322/.496	111	29.3	.255	-2.9	2B -7, 3B 0	2.4

Comparables: Larry Parrish, Ryan Zimmerman, Edwin Encarnación

It took a few tries, but Moustakas finally landed that ever-elusive multi-year deal. Obviously, he's a flawed player in a few regards; there can be no arguing that, especially in the face of four consecutive seasons with an OBP under .330, poor base running and middling defense. But *sheesh*. In past editions, we might have dunked on the Reds for the potential overpay. These days, with the state of baseball being what it is, we're just glad that we can use the term "potential overpay."

Scott Schebler OF Born: 10/06/90 Age: 29 Bats: L Throws: R Height: 6'0" Weight: 228 Origin: Round 26, 2010 Draft (#802 overall)

YEAR	TEAM	LVL	AGE	PA	R	2B	3B	HR	RBI	BB	K	SB	CS	AVG/OBP/SLG	DRC+	VORP	BABIP	BRR	FRAA	WARP
2017	CIN	MLB	26	531	63	25	2	30	67	39	125	5	3	.233/.307/.484	95	20.3	.248	-0.2	RF(120): -4.8, CF(15): 0.9	0.5
2018	PEN	AA	27	28	2	1	0	0	1	2	4	0	0	.154/.214/.192	47	-2.0	.182	0.0	RF(6): -1.0, LF(1): -0.1	-0.2
2018	LOU	AAA	27	31	3	1	0	1	2	5	6	0	0	.231/.355/.385	100	1.1	.263	0.0	LF(1): 0.1, RF(1): 0.1	0.1
2018	CIN	MLB	27	430	55	19	0	17	49	39	99	4	2	.255/.337/.439	101	15.3	.301	-1.4	RF(86): -2.4, CF(16): 0.5	0.7
2019	LOU	AAA	28	212	18	6	0	5	17	12	51	0	1	.216/.274/.325	52	-11.9	.264	-1.7	CF(33): -0.9, LF(9): 1.5	-0.6
2019	CIN	MLB	28	95	11	2	0	2	7	14	27	0	0	.123/.253/.222	67	-0.6	.154	0.1	CF(24): 0.8, LF(3): -0.1	0.0
2020	CIN	MLB	29	70	8	3	0	3	9	5	19	1	0	.226/.300/.412	85	0.1	.281	-0.1	RF -1	-0.1

Comparables: Eric Munson, Carlos Pena, Justin Smoak

Schebler has virtues, but each comes with a caveat: he can start most days, yet he needs to sit against lefties; he can cover center adequately for periods of time, even if he's not great at it; he's a decent hitter, though his DRC+ has topped 100 just once; and so on. Fifteen years ago, he would've enjoyed a decade-long run as a bench type. In this era, where teams are obsessive about carrying as many relievers as possible? Schebler is probably another underwhelming effort away from permanent residence in Triple-A. Season-ending shoulder surgery last August doesn't help his chances of avoiding that fate. For Schebler's sake, here's hoping he comes back hearty and hale.

Nick Senzel CF Born: 06/29/95   Age: 25   Bats: R   Throws: R   Height: 6'1"   Weight: 205   Origin: Round 1, 2016 Draft (#2 overall)

YEAR	TEAM	LVL	AGE	PA	R	2B	3B	HR	RBI	BB	K	SB	CS	AVG/OBP/SLG	DRC+	VORP	BABIP	BRR	FRAA	WARP
2017	DAY	A+	22	272	41	26	2	4	31	23	54	9	2	.305/.371/.476	161	24.7	.378	1.3	3B(60): 5.1	3.0
2017	PEN	AA	22	235	40	14	1	10	34	26	43	5	4	.340/.413/.560	179	26.6	.391	-0.5	3B(56): 1.7	2.8
2018	LOU	AAA	23	193	23	12	2	6	25	19	39	8	2	.310/.378/.509	156	19.5	.367	1.9	2B(28): -0.8, 3B(14): 0.8	1.8
2019	LOU	AAA	24	38	7	1	0	1	2	3	13	0	0	.257/.316/.371	66	2.2	.381	0.4	CF(8): -1.2	-0.1
2019	CIN	MLB	24	414	55	20	4	12	42	30	101	14	5	.256/.315/.427	88	8.6	.319	-0.1	CF(96): -4.6, 2B(1): 0.0	0.4
2020	CIN	MLB	25	511	56	22	2	18	62	40	128	10	5	.242/.307/.412	88	8.0	.296	-0.4	LF, CF -3	0.5

Comparables: Bill Tuttle, Ryan Ludwick, Ryan Lavarnway

Senzel has generally lived up to expectations since being drafted second overall a few years back. He pairs plus contact skills with good but not great power and a mature enough understanding of the zone. On paper, he profiles as a well-rounded, safe big-league starter at whatever position the Reds choose to stick him at—that being center field, for now, anyway. Unfortunately, Senzel has dealt with one injury after another since hitting pro ball, losing chunks of 2018 to finger and elbow injuries, and then having his 2019 end early due to right shoulder surgery. Provided he can stay on the field—and who knows anymore—he has a chance to hit .300 while playing a position on the valuable side of the defensive spectrum. Good player.

Michael Siani CF Born: 07/16/99   Age: 20   Bats: L   Throws: L   Height: 6'1"   Weight: 188   Origin: Round 4, 2018 Draft (#109 overall)

YEAR	TEAM	LVL	AGE	PA	R	2B	3B	HR	RBI	BB	K	SB	CS	AVG/OBP/SLG	DRC+	VORP	BABIP	BRR	FRAA	WARP
2018	GRV	RK	18	205	24	6	3	2	13	16	35	6	4	.288/.351/.386	115	10.8	.342	-0.1	CF(45): 6.5	1.6
2019	DYT	A	19	531	75	10	6	6	39	46	109	45	15	.253/.333/.339	96	22.0	.318	7.4	CF(111): 24.7, RF(5): -0.7	4.8
2020	CIN	MLB	20	251	22	10	1	4	22	16	65	4	2	.231/.289/.329	66	-2.6	.306	0.4	CF 6, RF 0	0.3

Comparables: Kyle Tucker, Abraham Almonte, Xavier Avery

The good: Siani won't turn 21 until July and hit .350/.412/.483 over his final 15 games of the season. The bad: he had a disappointing season overall and looks like a fourth outfielder at best. The worst: his brother, Sammy, was drafted 70-something picks earlier this year—ruining Thanksgiving by ensuring that he doesn't even have family bragging rights to fall back on.

Jose Siri CF Born: 07/22/95   Age: 24   Bats: R   Throws: R   Height: 6'2"   Weight: 175   Origin: International Free Agent, 2012

YEAR	TEAM	LVL	AGE	PA	R	2B	3B	HR	RBI	BB	K	SB	CS	AVG/OBP/SLG	DRC+	VORP	BABIP	BRR	FRAA	WARP
2017	DYT	A	21	552	92	24	11	24	76	33	130	46	12	.293/.341/.530	137	50.5	.349	7.4	CF(103): 15.7, RF(9): 1.5	6.4
2018	DAY	A+	22	126	15	9	2	1	9	4	32	9	1	.261/.280/.395	89	2.2	.341	1.1	CF(26): 0.4	0.4
2018	PEN	AA	22	283	42	8	9	12	34	24	91	14	5	.229/.300/.474	91	15.0	.301	2.2	CF(59): -3.9	0.5
2019	CHT	AA	23	405	46	15	1	11	50	33	126	21	6	.251/.313/.388	84	8.0	.349	-0.1	CF(98): 22.8, RF(1): 0.0	3.2
2019	LOU	AAA	23	112	10	4	1	0	3	9	39	5	2	.186/.252/.245	42	-6.0	.302	1.6	CF(26): 2.3, RF(4): -0.1	0.0
2020	CIN	MLB	24	35	4	2	0	1	4	2	13	1	1	.224/.272/.389	70	0.0	.332	0.1	CF 1	0.1

Comparables: Zoilo Almonte, Jeremy Moore, Aristides Aquino

A center fielder with power and speed is one of the most exciting archetypes in baseball. When it clicks, the profile can result in all-star or all-time great levels of production. Siri has plenty of athleticism and physicality to burn but almost zero production to show for it all. Put simply, he strikes out too often to leverage his gifts. He's tried to adjust and it hasn't worked. The Reds have promoted him and that hasn't worked, either. Siri will probably get big-league burn and, who knows, maybe somehow he'll unlock his immense potential. Based on everything we know about Siri and his career, Houdini himself would find that to be a trick beyond comprehension.

Tyler Stephenson C Born: 08/16/96   Age: 23   Bats: R   Throws: R   Height: 6'4"   Weight: 225   Origin: Round 1, 2015 Draft (#11 overall)

YEAR	TEAM	LVL	AGE	PA	R	2B	3B	HR	RBI	BB	K	SB	CS	AVG/OBP/SLG	DRC+	VORP	BABIP	BRR	FRAA	WARP
2017	DYT	A	20	348	39	22	0	6	50	44	58	2	1	.278/.374/.414	138	20.4	.322	-2.6	C(53): -4.0	2.0
2018	DAY	A+	21	450	60	20	1	11	59	45	98	1	0	.250/.338/.392	118	24.3	.301	0.2	C(97): -3.3	2.4
2019	CHT	AA	22	363	47	19	1	6	44	37	60	0	0	.285/.372/.410	128	23.3	.331	-2.1	C(85): -11.8	1.3
2020	CIN	MLB	23	251	26	13	0	7	29	19	63	0	0	.240/.309/.396	86	3.0	.300	-0.5	C -8	-0.5

Comparables: Christian Vázquez, Victor Caratini, Meibrys Viloria

YEAR	TEAM	P. COUNT	FRM RUNS	BLK RUNS	THRW RUNS	TOT RUNS
2019	CHT	11672	-11.5	0.0	-1.2	-12.5
2020	CIN	9182	-6.8	-0.5	-0.5	-7.8

The Reds have had a lot of high first-round picks in recent years, and they've used them on a variety of different player types. There's Senzel and India (safe collegiate hitters), Lodolo (a stud lefty from a major conference) and Greene (an explosive prep arm). There's also Stephenson, who hails from perhaps the riskiest pool of them all as a prep catcher. Extremely tall and injury prone, Stephenson still grades well as a defender. He also, as an added bonus, just posted a strong effort showing in Double-A last season. There's obvious attrition potential here—he might get hurt some more, or he might prove unable to hit big-league pitching—but there's also a real chance he's going to be at least a reserve backstop. All things considered, that's a win.

Eugenio Suárez 3B   Born: 07/18/91   Age: 28   Bats: R   Throws: R   Height: 5'11"   Weight: 213   Origin: International Free Agent, 2008

YEAR	TEAM	LVL	AGE	PA	R	2B	3B	HR	RBI	BB	K	SB	CS	AVG/OBP/SLG	DRC+	VORP	BABIP	BRR	FRAA	WARP
2017	CIN	MLB	25	632	87	25	2	26	82	84	147	4	5	.260/.367/.461	119	38.0	.309	-4.7	3B(153): -1.9, SS(1): 0.0	3.2
2018	CIN	MLB	26	606	79	22	2	34	104	64	142	1	1	.283/.366/.526	136	46.2	.322	-3.5	3B(143): -7.6, SS(3): 0.0	3.8
2019	CIN	MLB	27	662	87	22	2	49	103	70	189	3	2	.271/.358/.572	132	53.3	.312	-7.9	3B(158): 0.1	4.4
2020	CIN	MLB	28	630	94	25	2	42	109	63	180	6	3	.269/.353/.544	130	35.6	.323	-4.4	3B -3	3.4

Comparables: Chris Taylor, Jonathan Villar, Brad Miller

The Reds haven't enjoyed a winning season since 2013. You can empathize with any Cincy fan, then, who considers the franchise's biggest victory during this period to be the trade that netted the club Suárez in exchange for a year of Alfredo Simon. Top prospect lists gravitate toward recent first-round draft picks and J2 bonus babies, but sometimes players like Suárez—who was neither—end up more valuable by virtue of constant, reliable improvement. We'd tsk-tsk ourselves for never thinking Suárez would be this good, yet the truth is we believe these stories are part of what makes the game so great.

Michel Triana INF   Born: 11/23/99   Age: 20   Bats: L   Throws: R   Height: 6'3"   Weight: 230   Origin: International Free Agent, 2019

One thinks of July 2nd signings as all belonging to the same archetype: incredibly raw, athletic 16-year-olds. Triana received a $1.3 million bonus, but the above description doesn't apply to him. Rather, this season will represent his age-20 campaign, and he's likely to end up at first base over the long haul—suggesting he's going to have to hit to make up for his lacking physicality and reach the majors. The odds are, of course, very much against him. In that sense, Triana *is* a typical July 2nd signing.

Josh VanMeter UT   Born: 03/10/95   Age: 25   Bats: L   Throws: R   Height: 5'11"   Weight: 165   Origin: Round 5, 2013 Draft (#148 overall)

YEAR	TEAM	LVL	AGE	PA	R	2B	3B	HR	RBI	BB	K	SB	CS	AVG/OBP/SLG	DRC+	VORP	BABIP	BRR	FRAA	WARP
2017	PEN	AA	22	538	45	29	1	5	54	53	100	15	3	.255/.326/.352	103	8.0	.308	-0.5	3B(48): -2.5, 2B(41): 0.0	1.1
2018	PEN	AA	23	121	13	10	0	1	14	23	19	5	2	.284/.420/.421	150	11.3	.342	-0.4	LF(15): -0.9, 2B(9): -0.4	0.7
2018	LOU	AAA	23	362	40	25	6	11	45	28	73	5	3	.253/.309/.464	113	11.3	.292	-2.7	2B(47): -3.8, LF(23): -1.3	0.8
2019	LOU	AAA	24	211	43	14	1	14	43	24	37	8	3	.348/.429/.669	160	27.7	.371	0.2	2B(22): 0.1, 1B(13): 0.4	2.0
2019	CIN	MLB	24	260	33	13	1	8	23	29	56	9	3	.237/.327/.408	99	7.0	.279	-1.2	LF(47): 2.3, 2B(18): 0.2	0.8
2020	CIN	MLB	25	238	28	11	1	10	31	22	52	3	1	.242/.316/.432	95	5.1	.277	-0.6	1B 2, 2B 0	0.6

Comparables: Tzu-Wei Lin, Ehire Adrianza, Jeimer Candelario

Prior to this edition, VanMeter had made the Annual only one time: back in 2017, when we noted he had shown "plus power and strong plate discipline," in High-A. He struggled in a subsequent promotion to Double-A, and was later traded from the Padres to the Reds. A few years have passed, yet VanMeter made his big-league debut in 2019 after a redesigned swing permitted him to scorch Triple-A pitching. He couldn't continue his Manny Ramirez impersonation in the majors, but he was roughly a league-average hitter who filled in at all four corners and the keystone. Sounds like a useful enough player to us—and a healthy reminder that sometimes Role 3s turn into Role 4s and earn a partial pension in the process.

Joey Votto 1B   Born: 09/10/83   Age: 36   Bats: L   Throws: R   Height: 6'2"   Weight: 220   Origin: Round 2, 2002 Draft (#44 overall)

YEAR	TEAM	LVL	AGE	PA	R	2B	3B	HR	RBI	BB	K	SB	CS	AVG/OBP/SLG	DRC+	VORP	BABIP	BRR	FRAA	WARP
2017	CIN	MLB	33	707	106	34	1	36	100	134	83	5	1	.320/.454/.578	159	69.0	.321	-6.9	1B(162): 9.5	6.5
2018	CIN	MLB	34	623	67	28	2	12	67	108	101	2	0	.284/.417/.419	124	29.2	.333	-2.6	1B(139): 11.6	3.7
2019	CIN	MLB	35	608	79	32	1	15	47	76	123	5	0	.261/.357/.411	108	16.2	.313	-4.3	1B(133): 4.6	1.6
2020	CIN	MLB	36	560	68	25	1	17	67	79	117	4	1	.264/.374/.428	114	17.3	.317	-3.7	1B 11	2.9

Comparables: David Ortiz, Mark Teixeira, Travis Hafner

It's probably fair to observe that most people have a dimmer view of the world now than they did five years ago. That Votto might be on the downside of his career plays absolutely no role in that perception shift, but it does make baseball less enjoyable. Votto has had a bad season before—in 2014, he played in 62 games before he was shelved with a left knee/quad injury. He was injured again last year, this time it was his back ailing him. Back injuries, obviously, can be debilitating and they don't tend to improve as you age. The argument for optimism is a short one: normal rules don't apply to Hall of Fame-caliber players. Pick your favorite hitting metric and Votto has been one of the 30 or 40 best bats of all-time, ranking somewhere in the vicinity of say, Willie McCovey, Willie Stargell and David Ortiz—who, it should be noted, recovered from what proved to be a premature funeral in 2009 and turned in another seven good seasons. Maybe Votto can pull off the same trick. Hopefully he does. We've already lost the Zac Brown Band to mediocrity, let us have some more Votto excellence, cruel world. Please?

Jesse Winker OF   Born: 08/17/93   Age: 26   Bats: L   Throws: L   Height: 6'3"   Weight: 215   Origin: Round 1, 2012 Draft (#49 overall)

YEAR	TEAM	LVL	AGE	PA	R	2B	3B	HR	RBI	BB	K	SB	CS	AVG/OBP/SLG	DRC+	VORP	BABIP	BRR	FRAA	WARP
2017	LOU	AAA	23	347	33	22	0	2	41	38	46	2	4	.314/.395/.408	133	14.9	.359	-3.2	RF(70): 2.7, LF(3): 0.4	1.8
2017	CIN	MLB	23	137	21	7	0	7	15	15	24	1	1	.298/.375/.529	112	9.5	.322	-0.6	RF(25): -1.4, LF(2): -0.3	0.3
2018	CIN	MLB	24	334	38	16	0	7	43	49	46	0	0	.299/.405/.431	118	17.5	.336	-2.6	RF(47): -1.0, LF(34): -3.5	0.8
2019	CIN	MLB	25	384	51	17	2	16	38	38	60	0	2	.269/.357/.473	115	18.6	.286	0.6	LF(72): 1.4, CF(21): 0.0	2.2
2020	CIN	MLB	26	357	43	18	0	12	44	41	59	2	1	.270/.361/.442	113	15.1	.301	-0.6	LF -2	1.3

Comparables: Andruw Jones, Max Kepler, Ben Grieve

The book on Winker was always that his hit tool and strike-zone judgement would have to atone for his lacking power and defensive utility. Through his age-25 season, that's mostly been the case—and he's been quite productive, as an above-average hitter. So why then has his career felt underwhelming? Likely because of unforeseen injury woes. Winker had to undergo shoulder surgery during the 2018-19 offseason and just missed the second half of the season due to a newly developed back issue. That's a bad combination, to say the least, and one that has limited him to 202 games over the past two seasons. Now 26, it's about time Winker had a healthy season.

PITCHERS

Trevor Bauer RHP   Born: 01/17/91   Age: 29   Bats: R   Throws: R   Height: 6'1"   Weight: 205   Origin: Round 1, 2011 Draft (#3 overall)

YEAR	TEAM	LVL	AGE	W	L	SV	G	GS	IP	H	HR	BB/9	K/9	K	GB%	BABIP	WHIP	ERA	DRA	WARP	MPH	FB%	WHF	CSP
2017	CLE	MLB	26	17	9	0	32	31	176^1	181	25	3.1	10.0	196	47%	.337	1.37	4.19	3.95	3.2	96.4	49.3	10.1	44
2018	CLE	MLB	27	12	6	1	28	27	175^1	134	9	2.9	11.3	221	45%	.297	1.09	2.21	2.48	5.7	96.8	42.2	14.2	44.3
2019	CLE	MLB	28	9	8	0	24	24	156^2	127	22	3.6	10.6	185	40%	.276	1.21	3.79	4.67	1.9	96.8	45.3	13.2	44.2
2019	CIN	MLB	28	2	5	0	10	10	56^1	57	12	3.0	10.9	68	36%	.315	1.35	6.39	5.53	0.1	96.0	45.3	13.5	44.2
2020	CIN	MLB	29	10	10	0	29	29	172	150	24	3.6	10.6	202	40%	.294	1.27	3.92	3.99	3.5	95.9	45.3	12.8	44.2

Comparables: Edinson Vólquez, Shelby Miller, Ubaldo Jiménez

For all the coverage concerning Bauer, we now have a lot of data—1,117 innings' worth—suggesting he's a mid-rotation starter.

Brad Boxberger RHP   Born: 05/27/88   Age: 32   Bats: R   Throws: R   Height: 6'2"   Weight: 205   Origin: Round 1, 2009 Draft (#43 overall)

YEAR	TEAM	LVL	AGE	W	L	SV	G	GS	IP	H	HR	BB/9	K/9	K	GB%	BABIP	WHIP	ERA	DRA	WARP	MPH	FB%	WHF	CSP
2017	TBA	MLB	29	4	4	0	30	0	29^1	23	4	3.4	12.3	40	46%	.292	1.16	3.38	2.89	0.7	94.6	65.6	14.3	49.4
2018	ARI	MLB	30	3	7	32	60	0	53^1	44	9	5.4	12.0	71	48%	.287	1.42	4.39	5.11	-0.1	93.8	66.3	11.5	46.7
2019	HAR	AA	31	1	1	1	8	0	8^2	6	0	3.1	11.4	11	38%	.286	1.04	1.04	3.48	0.1				
2019	KCA	MLB	31	1	3	1	29	0	26^2	25	3	5.7	9.1	27	40%	.297	1.58	5.40	6.17	-0.2	92.2	47	12.9	45.6
2020	CIN	MLB	32	2	2	0	33	0	35	30	7	4.3	9.9	38	39%	.268	1.34	4.36	4.51	0.3	92.5	59.6	12.4	46.5

Comparables: Ernesto Frieri, Kirby Yates, Carlos Marmol

"The Death of a Closer."

Stuff contracts and designation is expected,
As in a season in limbo.
The closer falls.

He does not become a three-outs personage,
Imposing his domination,
Calling for pomp.

Designation is absolute and without memorial,
As in a season of autumn,
When the wind stops,

When the wind stops and, over the heavens,
The dingers go, nevertheless,
In their direction.

Luis Castillo RHP   Born: 12/12/92   Age: 27   Bats: R   Throws: R   Height: 6'2"   Weight: 190   Origin: International Free Agent, 2012

YEAR	TEAM	LVL	AGE	W	L	SV	G	GS	IP	H	HR	BB/9	K/9	K	GB%	BABIP	WHIP	ERA	DRA	WARP	MPH	FB%	WHF	CSP
2017	PEN	AA	24	4	4	0	14	14	80^1	68	5	1.5	9.1	81	42%	.293	1.01	2.58	3.47	1.6				
2017	CIN	MLB	24	3	7	0	15	15	89^1	64	11	3.2	9.9	98	60%	.247	1.07	3.12	3.41	2.2	99.1	62.1	13.5	47.9
2018	CIN	MLB	25	10	12	0	31	31	169^2	158	28	2.6	8.8	165	48%	.282	1.22	4.30	4.76	1.1	98.2	57.2	14.2	48.9
2019	CIN	MLB	26	15	8	0	32	32	190^2	139	22	3.7	10.7	226	56%	.262	1.14	3.40	3.02	5.7	98.3	50.6	16.7	40.1
2020	CIN	MLB	27	11	10	0	29	29	175	142	22	3.8	10.9	212	55%	.286	1.23	3.35	3.48	4.5	97.9	55.3	15.5	45.6

Comparables: Vince Velasquez, Brandon Woodruff, Nick Pivetta

It used to be that every pitcher had to follow the same approach: establish the fastball, then deploy your secondary stuff as needed. In recent times, we've seen pitchers adapt a different line of thinking—one that states they should throw their best pitch no matter what. Have an awesome change? Throw the awesome change and enjoy the easy outs. Although Castillo's results have oscillated from year to year, he continued a steady trend of throwing fewer and fewer four-seam fastballs (from roughly half his pitches in 2017 all the way down to less than a third in 2019) and throwing more and more of his elite changeup—to the extent that he threw the cambio more often than he threw the heat. Based on the results, we'd say it's an effective framework.

José De León RHP   Born: 08/07/92   Age: 27   Bats: R   Throws: R   Height: 6'1"   Weight: 220   Origin: Round 24, 2013 Draft (#724 overall)

YEAR	TEAM	LVL	AGE	W	L	SV	G	GS	IP	H	HR	BB/9	K/9	K	GB%	BABIP	WHIP	ERA	DRA	WARP	MPH	FB%	WHF	CSP
2017	RAY	RK	24	1	0	0	3	2	12	4	1	0.8	9.0	12	30%	.115	0.42	0.75	0.66	0.7				
2017	PCH	A+	24	1	0	0	4	3	14^1	11	0	5.7	11.3	18	39%	.333	1.40	1.88	3.93	0.2				
2017	DUR	AAA	24	0	2	0	3	3	12	14	1	4.5	10.5	14	38%	.394	1.67	6.75	5.31	0.1				
2017	TBA	MLB	24	1	0	0	1	0	2^2	4	1	10.1	6.8	2	60%	.333	2.62	10.12	6.15	0.0	93.3	60.3	8.8	47.1
2019	DUR	AAA	26	2	1	1	17	13	51^1	41	4	4.7	12.8	73	30%	.330	1.32	3.51	3.80	1.4				
2019	TBA	MLB	26	1	0	0	3	0	4	3	0	6.8	15.8	7	44%	.333	1.50	2.25	3.10	0.1	94.8	57.5	21.3	49
2020	CIN	MLB	27	2	2	0	42	0	44	37	7	3.9	8.5	42	35%	.259	1.27	3.95	4.05	0.7	93.9	59.1	17.3	48.9

Comparables: Rafael Montero, Ryan Helsley, Dan Straily

Turn ahead a few chapters and read most of what was written about Anthony Banda. Go ahead, take a minute. Oh, hey! Welcome back. Much of the same can be said for De León, who also returned from Tommy John surgery with minimal impact to the Rays. He still has a low-90s fastball that he backs with a very good off-speed pitch in his change. De León also figures to be in that hybrid mix of probably not good enough for 200 innings, but more talented than 50 standard reliever frames. He is certainly worth the flier the Reds took on him this winter.

Anthony DeSclafani RHP Born: 04/18/90 Age: 30 Bats: R Throws: R Height: 6'1" Weight: 195 Origin: Round 6, 2011 Draft (#199 overall)

YEAR	TEAM	LVL	AGE	W	L	SV	G	GS	IP	H	HR	BB/9	K/9	K	GB%	BABIP	WHIP	ERA	DRA	WARP	MPH	FB%	WHF	CSP
2018	PEN	AA	28	0	1	0	2	2	8	5	0	1.1	13.5	12	59%	.294	0.75	2.25	2.42	0.3				
2018	LOU	AAA	28	0	2	0	2	2	11¹	15	5	1.6	7.9	10	43%	.312	1.50	6.35	6.91	-0.2				
2018	CIN	MLB	28	7	8	0	21	21	115	118	24	2.3	8.5	108	43%	.294	1.29	4.93	5.16	0.2	96.0	57.9	10.7	49.8
2019	CIN	MLB	29	9	9	0	31	31	166²	151	29	2.6	9.0	167	44%	.273	1.20	3.89	3.95	3.3	96.4	55.4	11.3	46.2
2020	CIN	MLB	30	7	8	0	23	23	125	125	22	2.8	8.9	123	43%	.301	1.31	4.39	4.49	1.8	95.5	56.1	11	47.7

Comparables: Erasmo Ramírez, Charles Brewer, Jesse Hahn

The Reds have had myriad pitching-related "what if" scenarios to ponder during their lean years. Presumably, DeSclafani staying healthy was one of those. The Reds received an answer of sorts in 2019, when he made 30-plus starts for just the second time in his career. Granted, he didn't throw 200 innings (or even 180), but he did his usual thing: a fair amount of strikeouts, good control and a concerning tendency to give up home runs. If you know how to prevent home runs and/or chronic pitcher injuries in otherwise capable mid-rotation starters, please reach out to the Reds—or, better yet, to this author.

Zach Duke LHP Born: 04/19/83 Age: 37 Bats: L Throws: L Height: 6'2" Weight: 210 Origin: Round 20, 2001 Draft (#594 overall)

YEAR	TEAM	LVL	AGE	W	L	SV	G	GS	IP	H	HR	BB/9	K/9	K	GB%	BABIP	WHIP	ERA	DRA	WARP	MPH	FB%	WHF	CSP
2017	MEM	AAA	34	0	0	0	6	0	6	2	0	1.5	9.0	6	71%	.143	0.50	0.00	2.22	0.2				
2017	SLN	MLB	34	1	1	0	27	0	18¹	13	3	2.9	5.9	12	52%	.196	1.04	3.93	5.47	-0.1	89.8	57.3	13	47.9
2018	MIN	MLB	35	3	4	0	45	0	37¹	44	0	3.6	9.4	39	60%	.370	1.58	3.62	3.73	0.5	90.2	47.2	10.9	45.8
2018	SEA	MLB	35	2	1	0	27	0	14²	13	1	3.7	7.4	12	60%	.286	1.30	5.52	3.65	0.2	90.8	53.9	11	43.7
2019	CIN	MLB	36	3	1	0	30	0	23¹	21	4	6.9	6.9	18	50%	.266	1.67	5.01	7.13	-0.5	91.0	56	9.3	41.7
2020	CIN	MLB	37	2	2	0	33	0	35	33	4	4.0	8.0	31	56%	.285	1.38	4.32	4.38	0.4	89.1	51	10.5	43.3

Comparables: Jason Vargas, Joe Saunders, Jamie Moyer

When humans first arrived on the islands of what is now New Zealand in the late 13th century, scientists estimate it was populated by 60,000 flightless birds called "moa." These ostrich-like beasts presented in a variety of species, and ranged anywhere from 25 to nearly 600 pounds and some were as tall as 6-foot-5. Recent studies indicate they went extinct abruptly (rather than gradually) because of human hunting, and the last moa perished around 1400 CE. It is appropriate, then, that Duke - released by the Reds in July - has signed to pitch for the Auckland Tuatara for the 2019-2020 season (with the seasons reversed in the Southern Hemisphere and all that). Duke, who hasn't been able to get right-handed batters out for some time now, may want to read up on the moa during his stay. He and his LOOGY peers are about to become the baseball equivalent with the three-batter minimum rule in place.

Amir Garrett LHP Born: 05/03/92 Age: 28 Bats: R Throws: L Height: 6'5" Weight: 228 Origin: Round 22, 2011 Draft (#685 overall)

YEAR	TEAM	LVL	AGE	W	L	SV	G	GS	IP	H	HR	BB/9	K/9	K	GB%	BABIP	WHIP	ERA	DRA	WARP	MPH	FB%	WHF	CSP
2017	LOU	AAA	25	2	4	0	14	14	67²	79	7	3.2	8.1	61	41%	.346	1.52	5.72	5.69	0.0				
2017	CIN	MLB	25	3	8	0	16	14	70²	74	23	5.1	8.0	63	44%	.264	1.61	7.39	7.46	-1.5	94.9	62.1	9.1	47.7
2018	CIN	MLB	26	1	2	0	66	0	63	56	8	3.6	10.1	71	39%	.306	1.29	4.29	4.41	0.4	97.6	63.1	14.8	47.5
2019	CIN	MLB	27	5	3	0	69	0	56	44	7	5.6	12.5	78	55%	.303	1.41	3.21	3.35	1.2	97.5	42	17	42
2020	CIN	MLB	28	3	3	3	52	0	55	50	8	4.9	12.0	74	51%	.324	1.45	4.43	4.34	0.7	96.2	55.1	14	45.5

Comparables: Jefry Rodriguez, William Cuevas, Cody Reed

Yasiel Puig's brief tenure with the Reds included a brawl with the Pirates during which he struck a pose reminiscent of Tintoretto's "Massacre of the Innocents" or Michelangelo's "Battle of Cascina" while battling the entire roster. Garrett, somehow, topped Puig in July when he charged the Pirates dugout by himself mid-mound visit. That act drew attention away from an otherwise excellent season. Garrett shifted to a slider-heavy approach and made the two-seamer his main fastball. The result was a delightful combination of grounders and strikeouts. Moving forward, opponents won't want to hit against him or, um, be hit by him.

Sonny Gray RHP Born: 11/07/89 Age: 30 Bats: R Throws: R Height: 5'10" Weight: 192 Origin: Round 1, 2011 Draft (#18 overall)

YEAR	TEAM	LVL	AGE	W	L	SV	G	GS	IP	H	HR	BB/9	K/9	K	GB%	BABIP	WHIP	ERA	DRA	WARP	MPH	FB%	WHF	CSP
2017	OAK	MLB	27	6	5	0	16	16	97	84	8	2.8	8.7	94	58%	.285	1.18	3.43	4.22	1.5	95.3	63.7	13.1	45.5
2017	NYA	MLB	27	4	7	0	11	11	65¹	55	11	3.7	8.1	59	48%	.246	1.26	3.72	4.04	1.1	95.0	63.7	12	41.8
2018	NYA	MLB	28	11	9	0	30	23	130¹	138	14	3.9	8.5	123	52%	.326	1.50	4.90	5.00	0.4	95.4	57.2	10.8	45.2
2019	CIN	MLB	29	11	8	0	31	31	175¹	122	17	3.5	10.5	205	53%	.255	1.08	2.87	2.98	5.3	95.2	50.5	11.7	42.8
2020	CIN	MLB	30	10	10	0	29	29	163	144	20	3.7	10.2	185	52%	.297	1.29	3.70	3.77	3.7	94.5	55.6	11.7	43.7

Comparables: Jake Odorizzi, Chris Archer, Danny Salazar

Baseball is a funny game. Take Gray's past couple seasons. He performed so poorly with the Yankees that they shipped him to the Reds, where he was reunited with Derek Johnson, who was previously his pitching coach at Vanderbilt. Gray made a point of blaming his struggles in New York on their instruction to throw more sliders. So, what did he do to correct his pitch-usage issues? Why, he threw even more sliders, as well as more curveballs, of course. And how did that work out for him? Quite well, actually, as he had the best season of his career. Obviously the issues that were at play with the Yankees are more complicated than we're presenting here. But doesn't this whole mess read like a John Mulaney bit? What a sport. What. A. Sport.

Hunter Greene RHP Born: 08/06/99   Age: 20   Bats: R   Throws: R   Height: 6'4"   Weight: 215   Origin: Round 1, 2017 Draft (#2 overall)

YEAR	TEAM	LVL	AGE	W	L	SV	G	GS	IP	H	HR	BB/9	K/9	K	GB%	BABIP	WHIP	ERA	DRA	WARP	MPH	FB%	WHF	CSP
2018	DYT	A	18	3	7	0	18	18	68¹	66	6	3.0	11.7	89	43%	.353	1.30	4.48	4.58	0.5				
2020	CIN	MLB	20	2	2	0	33	0	35	36	6	4.2	9.1	35	40%	.310	1.49	5.13	5.13	0.1				

Comparables: Jordan Lyles, Roberto Osuna, Mike Soroka

Greene arrived in professional baseball as one of the most hyped prep prospects in recent memory. A dazzling two-way talent with a big-time arm who probably would've been picked in the first round as a shortstop had he played only that side of the ball. Yet in the time since he was drafted, he's encountered all the snags that tend to derail young pitching prospects—beginning with struggles based on his limited, fastball-heavy arsenal, and extending to health woes that culminated in Tommy John surgery. Greene should be back on the mound come 2020 and here's hoping that his arm strength, athleticism and aptitude will get his stock moving in the right direction. We're certainly not ready to move on from or dismiss him as a bust.

Vladimir Gutierrez RHP Born: 09/18/95   Age: 24   Bats: R   Throws: R   Height: 6'0"   Weight: 190   Origin: International Free Agent, 2016

YEAR	TEAM	LVL	AGE	W	L	SV	G	GS	IP	H	HR	BB/9	K/9	K	GB%	BABIP	WHIP	ERA	DRA	WARP	MPH	FB%	WHF	CSP
2017	DAY	A+	21	7	8	0	19	19	103	108	10	1.7	8.2	94	42%	.320	1.23	4.46	3.84	1.7				
2018	PEN	AA	22	9	10	0	27	27	147	139	18	2.3	8.9	145	46%	.298	1.20	4.35	4.18	2.0				
2019	LOU	AAA	23	6	11	0	27	27	137	144	26	3.2	7.7	117	41%	.291	1.40	6.04	4.93	2.4				
2020	CIN	MLB	24	2	2	0	33	0	35	37	7	3.6	6.9	27	41%	.287	1.45	5.32	5.34	0.0				

Comparables: José Ureña, Hunter Wood, Jackson Stephens

Gutierrez stands at 6-foot even and has a gigantic spider tattooed on his throat. Those two tidbits should be all you need to know in order to guess he's probably headed for the bullpen. (Hey, you have to be wired a little differently to succeed in relief.) Sure enough, that outcome seems more likely following his struggles in Triple-A with the rabbit ball (his home run rate spiked and his ERA went with it). The fastball sits in the 92-94 mph range and his main putaway pitch is a curveball that he can manipulate to different effects. He's likely to be a fine middle-relief type, just nothing special. In a sense, then, Gutierrez almost feels like something of a throwback. He would have been a dominant sensation if he had arrived in the '90s, but will probably be just another pitcher these days—albeit just another pitcher who has an enormous spider guarding his windpipe.

Raisel Iglesias RHP Born: 01/04/90   Age: 30   Bats: R   Throws: R   Height: 6'2"   Weight: 188   Origin: International Free Agent, 2014

YEAR	TEAM	LVL	AGE	W	L	SV	G	GS	IP	H	HR	BB/9	K/9	K	GB%	BABIP	WHIP	ERA	DRA	WARP	MPH	FB%	WHF	CSP
2017	CIN	MLB	27	3	3	28	63	0	76	57	5	3.2	10.9	92	43%	.287	1.11	2.49	3.34	1.6	99.1	57.1	15.1	50.2
2018	CIN	MLB	28	2	5	30	66	0	72	52	12	3.1	10.0	80	40%	.233	1.07	2.38	3.48	1.2	98.3	50.2	16.5	47.9
2019	CIN	MLB	29	3	12	34	68	0	67	61	12	2.8	12.0	89	31%	.316	1.22	4.16	3.82	1.1	97.9	47.8	16.6	46.1
2020	CIN	MLB	30	3	2	30	52	0	55	45	8	3.3	11.2	69	37%	.286	1.19	3.40	3.55	1.1	97.6	50.9	16.1	47.6

Comparables: Jeurys Familia, Erik Goeddel, Héctor Neris

The consistently effective relief ace is one of the rarest treasures in baseball. Think Mariano Rivera, or even peak Craig Kimbrel. Iglesias had been that prior to 2019. He then experienced some turbulence—by which we mean his propeller and wings fell off—following his initial ascent into the new year. Iglesias was charged with four losses in April and dropped 12 overall. The loss isn't a particularly useful statistic when evaluating anyone, but it does suggest he was giving up runs in late-and-close situations. The more pressing matter as it pertained to the rest of his season had to do with his home-run rate—he yielded a career-worst 1.6 per nine. There's no telling what the ball is going to be like heading forward, yet a career-best strikeout-to-walk ratio suggests Iglesias will probably return to being his normally consistently effective self in 2020.

Joel Kuhnel RHP Born: 02/19/95   Age: 25   Bats: R   Throws: R   Height: 6'5"   Weight: 260   Origin: Round 11, 2016 Draft (#318 overall)

YEAR	TEAM	LVL	AGE	W	L	SV	G	GS	IP	H	HR	BB/9	K/9	K	GB%	BABIP	WHIP	ERA	DRA	WARP	MPH	FB%	WHF	CSP
2017	DYT	A	22	2	4	11	48	0	64	78	6	1.4	7.6	54	54%	.353	1.38	4.36	5.10	-0.1				
2018	DAY	A+	23	1	4	17	44	0	53¹	54	2	1.9	9.4	56	54%	.340	1.22	3.04	3.84	0.7				
2019	CHT	AA	24	3	2	10	25	0	35²	26	5	2.0	7.6	30	39%	.212	0.95	2.27	3.23	0.6				
2019	LOU	AAA	24	2	1	4	16	0	18	13	1	4.0	10.0	20	38%	.273	1.17	2.00	3.41	0.5				
2019	CIN	MLB	24	1	0	0	11	0	9²	8	1	4.7	8.4	9	54%	.259	1.34	4.66	4.37	0.1	98.4	61.5	14.5	42.7
2020	CIN	MLB	25	2	2	0	42	0	44	42	7	3.8	9.9	49	42%	.303	1.38	4.33	4.36	0.5	98.1	62.9	14.8	43.7

Comparables: Chasen Bradford, Dan Slania, Sam Tuivailala

Kuhnel, who was drafted in the 11th round in 2016, is making his book debut. Consider that a statement on how many power arms are floating around, because 20 years ago we would've been all over a 6-foot-5, 260-pound pitcher with a 96-mph fastball. Consider it another sign of the times that Kuhnel is probably more solid than elite. He should see ample big-league duty in 2020.

───────── ★ ★ ★ *2020 Top 101 Prospect* **#59** ★ ★ ★ ─────────

Nick Lodolo LHP Born: 02/05/98   Age: 22   Bats: L   Throws: L   Height: 6'6"   Weight: 202   Origin: Round 1, 2019 Draft (#7 overall)

YEAR	TEAM	LVL	AGE	W	L	SV	G	GS	IP	H	HR	BB/9	K/9	K	GB%	BABIP	WHIP	ERA	DRA	WARP	MPH	FB%	WHF	CSP
2019	BIL	RK+	21	0	1	0	6	6	11¹	12	1	0.0	16.7	21	36%	.458	1.06	2.38	2.41	0.5				
2019	DYT	A	21	0	0	0	2	2	7	6	0	0.0	11.6	9	50%	.333	0.86	2.57	3.40	0.1				
2020	CIN	MLB	22	2	2	0	33	0	35	35	5	3.6	8.2	32	43%	.295	1.39	4.64	4.82	0.2				

Comparables: Josh Rogers, Devin Smeltzer, Eric Surkamp

The first pitcher selected in June's draft, Lodolo hails from TCU and possesses an alluring frame (he's tall and lanky) and arsenal (led mid-90s heat and a potential breaking ball). As is often the case with very good, not elite pitching prospects, he needs to continue to refine his command and his changeup. All pitchers carry a certain amount of risk, and Lord knows the Reds have whiffed more than they've hit on pitchers, but Lodolo looks like he could be a quality one—and a fast-moving one, at that.

Michael Lorenzen RHP Born: 01/04/92 Age: 28 Bats: R Throws: R Height: 6'3" Weight: 217 Origin: Round 1, 2013 Draft (#38 overall)

YEAR	TEAM	LVL	AGE	W	L	SV	G	GS	IP	H	HR	BB/9	K/9	K	GB%	BABIP	WHIP	ERA	DRA	WARP	MPH	FB%	WHF	CSP
2017	CIN	MLB	25	8	4	2	70	0	83	78	9	3.7	8.7	80	57%	.295	1.35	4.45	4.37	0.7	98.2	51.3	11.3	47.8
2018	CIN	MLB	26	4	2	1	45	3	81	78	6	3.8	6.0	54	52%	.291	1.38	3.11	5.87	-0.8	97.3	51.5	7.6	48.6
2019	CIN	MLB	27	1	4	7	73	0	83¹	68	9	3.0	9.2	85	46%	.269	1.15	2.92	3.78	1.4	98.3	36.1	15.2	44.2
2020	CIN	MLB	28	3	3	4	58	0	61	58	8	3.9	9.1	62	48%	.301	1.37	4.15	4.16	0.8	97.4	45.4	11.8	46.8

Comparables: Trevor Gott, Drew VerHagen, José Ureña

Once upon a time, the Reds dreamed for a rotation fronted by Homer Bailey, Robert Stephenson and Lorenzen. Perhaps there's another timeline where those three became this generation's Zito, Mulder and Hudson, but this reality has seen Lorenzen develop into an intriguing quantity. In addition to being a rubber-armed reliever with three consecutive 80-plus inning seasons under his belt, he's now leaning into his potential as a two-way player. In September, he became the only player other than Babe Ruth to ever homer, earn the win and play the field in a single game. Lorenzen has .180 career OPS points on Madison Bumgarner, and has retained the athleticism that allowed him to be a legitimate two-way draft prospect as a youngster. We're intrigued by how the Reds will experiment with Lorenzen heading forward, because it could come to serve as a blueprint.

Tyler Mahle RHP Born: 09/29/94 Age: 25 Bats: R Throws: R Height: 6'3" Weight: 210 Origin: Round 7, 2013 Draft (#225 overall)

YEAR	TEAM	LVL	AGE	W	L	SV	G	GS	IP	H	HR	BB/9	K/9	K	GB%	BABIP	WHIP	ERA	DRA	WARP	MPH	FB%	WHF	CSP
2017	PEN	AA	22	7	3	0	14	14	85	57	5	1.8	9.2	87	42%	.245	0.87	1.59	2.65	2.6				
2017	LOU	AAA	22	3	4	0	10	10	59¹	52	4	2.0	7.7	51	42%	.281	1.10	2.73	3.25	1.6				
2017	CIN	MLB	22	1	2	0	4	4	20	19	0	4.9	6.3	14	56%	.302	1.50	2.70	5.48	0.0	95.9	65.8	7.9	47.2
2018	LOU	AAA	23	2	1	0	5	5	29²	22	4	3.3	6.1	20	39%	.209	1.11	2.73	3.89	0.6				
2018	CIN	MLB	23	7	9	0	23	23	112	125	22	4.3	8.8	110	41%	.324	1.59	4.98	6.30	-1.3	96.0	67.8	11.4	49.6
2019	LOU	AAA	24	1	2	0	3	3	9	8	0	3.0	13.0	13	65%	.400	1.22	4.00	3.37	0.3				
2019	CIN	MLB	24	3	12	0	25	25	129²	136	25	2.4	9.0	129	48%	.307	1.31	5.14	4.82	1.3	96.1	56.7	10.7	49.3
2020	CIN	MLB	25	4	5	0	16	16	70	72	11	3.0	9.0	70	47%	.312	1.37	4.52	4.54	1.0	95.8	63.3	11.1	50.1

Comparables: Jake Faria, Jake Odorizzi, Nick Kingham

Although Mahle missed time with a hamstring injury, and on the surface it looked like he had the same season in 2019 that he did in 2018, there were signs of progress below. His peripherals were vastly improved, as he cut his walks and dialed up his groundball rate. He also made significant changes to his pitching arsenal, ditching his slider and his change for a curve and a split to go along with his low-to-mid 90s heat. Mahle will always have to tinker and get by on guile rather than sheer stuff, but last season suggests the young northpaw is up for it.

Wade Miley LHP Born: 11/13/86 Age: 33 Bats: L Throws: L Height: 6'0" Weight: 220 Origin: Round 1, 2008 Draft (#43 overall)

YEAR	TEAM	LVL	AGE	W	L	SV	G	GS	IP	H	HR	BB/9	K/9	K	GB%	BABIP	WHIP	ERA	DRA	WARP	MPH	FB%	WHF	CSP
2017	BAL	MLB	30	8	15	0	32	32	157¹	179	25	5.3	8.1	142	51%	.332	1.73	5.61	7.20	-2.9	93.7	53.4	9	36.9
2018	BLX	AA	31	1	2	0	7	7	25¹	27	3	1.4	9.9	28	59%	.393	1.22	3.55	4.87	0.1				
2018	MIL	MLB	31	5	2	0	16	16	80²	71	3	3.0	5.6	50	54%	.269	1.21	2.57	4.13	1.1	93.0	20	9.9	42.5
2019	HOU	MLB	32	14	6	0	33	33	167¹	164	23	3.3	7.5	140	50%	.288	1.34	3.98	5.42	0.6	92.3	21.9	10.4	42.4
2020	CIN	MLB	33	6	8	0	23	23	116	119	17	3.5	7.4	95	50%	.298	1.42	4.61	4.60	1.6	91.8	31.2	9.7	40.6

Comparables: Tommy Milone, Dallas Keuchel, Pete Schourek

If you went into a coma just before the season started and woke up at the end, you would probably have a lot of questions like "How much did everyone love the ending of *Game of Thrones*?" and "What is an Old Town Road?" Once you figured that out, you might hug your friends and family and catch up and tell them what happens in the afterlife. Then you would immediately head to Miley's player card and think "Wow, not bad!" But you would be a silly goose for thinking that (Note: You also missed a thing with an Untitled Goose Game). In early August, Astros manager A.J. Hinch called his starting rotation "Wade Miley and the Famous Guys" and he was right at that point. But then, like a senior in high school, his last six weeks derailed an otherwise exceptional year.

Cody Reed LHP Born: 04/15/93 Age: 27 Bats: L Throws: L Height: 6'5" Weight: 230 Origin: Round 2, 2013 Draft (#46 overall)

YEAR	TEAM	LVL	AGE	W	L	SV	G	GS	IP	H	HR	BB/9	K/9	K	GB%	BABIP	WHIP	ERA	DRA	WARP	MPH	FB%	WHF	CSP
2017	LOU	AAA	24	4	9	0	21	20	106¹	105	7	5.2	8.6	102	50%	.328	1.56	3.55	5.43	0.3				
2017	CIN	MLB	24	1	1	1	12	1	17²	11	3	9.7	8.7	17	65%	.200	1.70	5.09	4.82	0.1	96.8	51.2	13.9	40.4
2018	LOU	AAA	25	4	8	0	18	17	105²	109	13	2.6	8.9	105	46%	.325	1.32	3.92	5.42	0.1				
2018	CIN	MLB	25	1	3	0	17	7	43	45	5	3.1	8.8	42	63%	.323	1.40	3.98	4.36	0.4	95.4	50.2	11	48.1
2019	LOU	AAA	26	1	2	0	18	0	20²	13	1	3.5	10.9	25	70%	.267	1.02	2.61	2.81	0.7				
2019	CIN	MLB	26	0	0	0	3	0	6¹	6	0	1.4	9.9	7	76%	.353	1.11	1.42	3.17	0.2	96.6	55.2	15.5	55.6
2020	CIN	MLB	27	2	2	0	42	0	44	48	7	3.4	7.9	39	61%	.312	1.45	4.97	4.92	0.2	95.4	51.4	12.2	49.9

Comparables: Brian Flynn, John Gant, Aaron Blair

The Reds finally gave up the ghost on Reed as a starter. Fortunately, he seemed to take well to life in short spurts by better leveraging his best pitches and…yes, this reads like a half-dozen other comments in this chapter. What can we say? Cincinnati hasn't done much to develop quality starters, but if 2019 is any indication they should have a small fleet of cheap relievers. There's some value in that.

Sal Romano RHP Born: 10/12/93 Age: 26 Bats: L Throws: R Height: 6'5" Weight: 255 Origin: Round 23, 2011 Draft (#715 overall)

YEAR	TEAM	LVL	AGE	W	L	SV	G	GS	IP	H	HR	BB/9	K/9	K	GB%	BABIP	WHIP	ERA	DRA	WARP	MPH	FB%	WHF	CSP
2017	LOU	AAA	23	1	4	0	10	10	49¹	49	1	3.1	5.8	32	50%	.298	1.34	3.47	4.73	0.5				
2017	CIN	MLB	23	5	8	0	16	16	87	91	9	3.8	7.6	73	53%	.314	1.47	4.45	4.55	1.0	97.6	62.7	9.6	46.6
2018	CIN	MLB	24	8	11	0	39	25	145²	155	23	3.3	6.5	105	47%	.288	1.43	5.31	5.76	-0.8	96.4	65.6	8.6	49.1
2019	LOU	AAA	25	4	8	1	43	5	69¹	72	6	3.4	9.9	76	47%	.349	1.41	4.28	4.84	1.0				
2019	CIN	MLB	25	1	0	2	12	0	16¹	22	4	4.4	8.8	16	38%	.375	1.84	7.71	6.07	-0.1	97.4	64.2	7.5	48.7
2020	CIN	MLB	26	3	3	0	40	3	55	62	9	3.4	7.2	44	46%	.314	1.51	5.40	5.29	0.2	96.4	65.8	9	49.2

Comparables: Robert Gsellman, Jackson Stephens, Nate Adcock

"We constantly joke about this being the era where you can find a 95-and-a-slider pitcher under the cushions of your couch," we wrote as part of Romano's comment a few books ago. Technically, Romano is more of a 96-and-a-cutter guy, but his results have been indistinguishable from generic sofa detritus since a surprisingly solid rookie effort. He's 6-foot-5 and throws hard, so he'll get another look or two over the coming years. Eventually, Romano will be vacuumed into a different plane of existence—same as us all—and that'll be that.

Justin Shafer RHP Born: 09/18/92 Age: 27 Bats: R Throws: R Height: 6'2" Weight: 195 Origin: Round 8, 2014 Draft (#234 overall)

YEAR	TEAM	LVL	AGE	W	L	SV	G	GS	IP	H	HR	BB/9	K/9	K	GB%	BABIP	WHIP	ERA	DRA	WARP	MPH	FB%	WHF	CSP
2017	DUN	A+	24	0	0	0	5	0	9¹	7	0	1.9	12.5	13	62%	.333	0.96	0.00	3.53	0.1				
2017	NHP	AA	24	5	2	1	37	0	58	45	6	4.0	7.4	48	51%	.244	1.22	3.41	3.32	1.0				
2018	NHP	AA	25	2	2	1	13	0	17¹	12	1	2.6	8.8	17	58%	.262	0.98	0.52	2.99	0.4				
2018	BUF	AAA	25	3	3	15	34	0	38¹	27	0	3.8	7.5	32	45%	.252	1.12	1.41	3.58	0.7				
2018	TOR	MLB	25	0	0	0	6	0	8¹	6	1	7.6	2.2	2	45%	.179	1.56	3.24	7.96	-0.3	94.6	68.5	7.5	43.3
2019	BUF	AAA	26	0	2	7	24	0	30²	29	3	2.3	10.3	35	34%	.317	1.21	3.52	3.36	0.8				
2019	TOR	MLB	26	2	1	1	34	0	39²	41	6	5.7	8.8	39	32%	.315	1.66	3.86	7.46	-0.9	95.8	51.6	12.6	44.6
2020	CIN	MLB	27	1	1	0	21	0	22	22	4	4.3	8.5	21	36%	.294	1.49	5.17	5.08	0.1	95.1	54.6	12	44.5

Comparables: Kevin McGowan, Jimmy Yacabonis, Damien Magnifico

if you're a sinkerballer, you get outs on the ground. To borrow a phrase from Geico's latest ad campaign—as with each new campaign from them, raising concerns about the brand mascot's whereabouts and the lifespan of a gecko—it's what you do. Unfortunately for Shafer, he couldn't get enough ground balls on his sinker to hack it in the majors, so he nearly excised the pitch from his mix in his Jays call back. By traditional metrics, the experiment went swimmingly, though his DRA quite objects to the word choice there. Whether his new approach, which relies heavily on his four-seamer and a new cutter, sticks in 2020 with Derek Johnson now in his ear really just depends on how much all involved believe in Santa Claus.

Lucas Sims RHP Born: 05/10/94 Age: 26 Bats: R Throws: R Height: 6'2" Weight: 225 Origin: Round 1, 2012 Draft (#21 overall)

YEAR	TEAM	LVL	AGE	W	L	SV	G	GS	IP	H	HR	BB/9	K/9	K	GB%	BABIP	WHIP	ERA	DRA	WARP	MPH	FB%	WHF	CSP
2017	GWN	AAA	23	7	4	0	20	19	115¹	95	19	2.8	10.3	132	35%	.275	1.14	3.75	3.81	2.4				
2017	ATL	MLB	23	3	6	0	14	10	57²	64	9	3.6	6.9	44	40%	.314	1.51	5.62	6.13	-0.4	94.4	46.5	9	46.7
2018	GWN	AAA	24	4	3	0	15	14	73	66	6	4.2	10.2	83	44%	.330	1.37	2.84	4.53	0.8				
2018	LOU	AAA	24	0	2	0	5	5	28¹	20	5	1.6	10.2	32	29%	.224	0.88	3.81	5.48	0.0				
2018	ATL	MLB	24	0	0	0	6	0	10¹	12	2	7.0	8.7	10	42%	.323	1.94	7.84	6.38	-0.2	95.1	55.7	10	37.4
2018	CIN	MLB	24	0	0	0	3	0	5¹	3	1	8.4	10.1	6	23%	.167	1.50	6.75	3.59	0.1	94.3	55	15.3	49.3
2019	LOU	AAA	25	5	0	0	16	16	79	69	9	4.1	11.6	102	34%	.321	1.33	4.56	3.48	2.5				
2019	CIN	MLB	25	2	1	0	24	4	43	31	8	4.0	11.9	57	26%	.253	1.16	4.60	4.30	0.6	95.2	50.6	16	40.9
2020	CIN	MLB	26	3	3	0	36	5	58	51	10	4.2	10.8	69	32%	.292	1.35	4.44	4.44	0.7	94.5	50.7	13	43.3

Comparables: Robert Stephenson, Jake Faria, A.J. Cole

Fans of teams who go years without ample pitching can develop some odd tics. For example, an irrational fondness of competent hurlers—or, even, those who show potential to become as much. Sims is the latter. As with some other of Cincy's failed starter prospects, he found himself in relief last year and posted the best numbers of his career (though that's damning him with faint praise). Sims' velocity improved to the 93-94 mph range and he struck out nearly 12 batters per nine, yet there were some red flags worth acknowledging—namely, that his command remained poor and his extreme flyball tendencies didn't play nice with the rabbit ball. There's some potential value here is as a multi-inning reliever—perhaps a hair more if the hare ball goes away—but let's not get too overzealous about what he is or what he's likely to become.

Robert Stephenson RHP Born: 02/24/93 Age: 27 Bats: R Throws: R Height: 6'3" Weight: 215 Origin: Round 1, 2011 Draft (#27 overall)

YEAR	TEAM	LVL	AGE	W	L	SV	G	GS	IP	H	HR	BB/9	K/9	K	GB%	BABIP	WHIP	ERA	DRA	WARP	MPH	FB%	WHF	CSP
2017	LOU	AAA	24	1	2	0	8	7	40¹	27	8	2.9	10.0	45	40%	.200	0.99	3.79	2.89	1.2				
2017	CIN	MLB	24	5	6	1	25	11	84²	81	12	5.6	9.1	86	41%	.300	1.58	4.68	5.98	-0.5	96.6	54.2	13.5	43
2018	LOU	AAA	25	11	6	0	20	20	113	74	12	4.5	10.8	135	38%	.239	1.16	2.87	3.52	2.6				
2018	CIN	MLB	25	0	2	0	4	3	11²	17	2	9.3	8.5	11	32%	.395	2.49	9.26	6.50	-0.2	95.2	36.4	11.3	47.2
2019	CIN	MLB	26	3	2	0	57	0	64²	43	9	3.3	11.3	81	33%	.231	1.04	3.76	3.76	1.1	96.7	36.2	19.4	43.6
2020	CIN	MLB	27	3	3	0	52	0	55	48	9	4.8	11.7	72	35%	.300	1.40	4.33	4.31	0.7	96.1	44.3	16.3	45.2

Comparables: Jake Thompson, A.J. Cole, Lucas Sims

It's a classic tale: an ambitious crew collects the best talent available to them and sets sail for what they think is a gilded future. Conflict arises, and the group faces what looks like certain doom. A resourceful soul in the company then solves the riddle. Stephenson has always had huge stuff but not enough command to start. Someone, perhaps pitching coach Derek Johnson, finally figured out that the "X" on his treasure map was located in the Reds bullpen. Predictably, Stephenson broke out when deployed in shorter spurts—he ditched his curveball and changeup in favor of leaning more on his upped fastball and mid-80s slider. The majors are treacherous waters, but as Stephenson's 2019 shows, there's often plunder to be had if you keep at it.

Alex Wood LHP Born: 01/12/91 Age: 29 Bats: R Throws: L Height: 6'4" Weight: 215 Origin: Round 2, 2012 Draft (#85 overall)

YEAR	TEAM	LVL	AGE	W	L	SV	G	GS	IP	H	HR	BB/9	K/9	K	GB%	BABIP	WHIP	ERA	DRA	WARP	MPH	FB%	WHF	CSP
2017	LAN	MLB	26	16	3	0	27	25	152^1	123	15	2.2	8.9	151	54%	.267	1.06	2.72	2.89	4.5	94.1	50.4	12.5	45.1
2018	LAN	MLB	27	9	7	0	33	27	151^2	143	14	2.4	8.0	135	50%	.293	1.21	3.68	3.41	3.3	91.9	43.1	11.6	47.2
2019	CIN	MLB	28	1	3	0	7	7	35^2	41	11	2.3	7.6	30	39%	.294	1.40	5.80	6.31	-0.2	91.3	50.3	12.1	45
2020	CIN	MLB	29	2	2	0	33	0	35	35	6	2.7	8.1	32	45%	.289	1.29	4.27	4.43	0.4	92.0	46.7	12	45.7

Comparables: *David Price, Kevin Gausman, Gerrit Cole*

People watch sports for different reasons. Some people love the puzzles of strategy and roster-building. Some people love that anything can happen at any time, no matter how unlikely. Others enjoy watching individual players overcome adversity and hearing those stories. Some just like the aesthetic splendor of seeing players with otherworldly physical gifts, mental acuity and work ethic perform almost absurd feats of skill and strength. Sadly, sometimes those physical gifts are bestowed on a body that can't hold up to the task of doing the very thing it is better than basically everyone else at doing it.

Wood's career isn't over by any means, but so far it has been a frustrating story. Wood flashes brilliance and uncorks multi-month stretches of dominance, only to break down from the repeated and unnatural act of pitching—a decay perhaps exacerbated by his unusual delivery. While in the past, Wood has muddled through to still wind up with strong numbers at the end of a mostly-complete season, 2019 was a lost year. He barely pitched and when he did he got smoked before getting shut down with a back injury. He continued to rehab but setbacks and the Reds' disappointing season kept him on the shelf. Hopefully an offseason to rest and heal will get Wood back to his effective self in 2020, so that we can enjoy his brilliance instead of the frustrating downside of his absence.

LINEOUTS

Hitters

HITTER	POS	TEAM	LVL	AGE	PA	R	2B	3B	HR	RBI	BB	K	SB	CS	AVG/OBP/SLG	DRC+	VORP	BABIP	BRR	FRAA	WARP
Tyler Callihan	2B	GRV	Rk+	19	217	27	10	5	5	26	9	46	9	3	.250/.286/.422	86	3.9	.297	-0.4		0.3
Stuart Fairchild	CF	DAY	A+	23	281	32	17	2	8	37	25	60	3	5	.258/.335/.440	148	16.5	.306	-1.1	CF(39): -3.3, LF(15): 3.5	1.9
	CF	CHT	AA	23	179	25	12	1	4	17	19	23	3	2	.275/.380/.444	132	11.4	.302	-1.1	CF(28): 0.2, RF(10): 1.6	1.2
Kyle Farmer	UT	CIN	MLB	28	197	22	6	0	9	27	10	59	4	1	.230/.279/.410	76	0.8	.284	-1.5	2B(41): -1.0, 1B(18): -0.1	-0.2
Jose Garcia	SS	DAY	A+	21	452	58	37	1	8	55	25	83	15	2	.280/.343/.436	143	27.5	.329	-0.8	SS(99): 0.7	3.8
Juan Graterol	C	CIN	MLB	30	18	1	0	0	0	1	0	4	0	0	.222/.222/.222	75	0.3	.286	-0.6	C(5): 0.0	0.0
	C	LOU	AAA	30	226	19	8	1	2	26	14	18	0	1	.249/.301/.325	68	-7.4	.263	-3.2	C(58): -10.2, 1B(1): 0.0	-0.9
Jameson Hannah	CF	STO	A+	21	414	48	25	3	2	31	29	88	6	7	.283/.341/.381	111	12.7	.361	-3.2	RF(49): -0.8, CF(41): -2.4	0.7
	CF	DAY	A+	21	78	6	3	1	0	6	9	16	2	1	.224/.325/.299	70	-1.4	.294	-0.3	CF(13): -0.3, RF(2): 0.1	-0.1
Alfredo Rodriguez	MI	CHT	AA	25	436	50	18	2	1	25	22	62	13	9	.286/.325/.347	93	6.9	.334	1.8	SS(98): -2.3, 3B(2): -0.1	1.6
	MI	LOU	AAA	25	88	5	4	0	0	9	7	13	3	0	.169/.261/.221	56	-5.3	.200	0.6	SS(23): 0.5	0.1
Andy Sugilio	OF	DAY	A+	22	485	57	11	5	3	39	24	92	23	11	.294/.331/.360	115	13.4	.361	1.2	RF(78): -3.7, CF(31): 0.7	1.5

A name for the deepest of dynasty players, July 2nd signing **Deivid Alcantara** is a teenage outfielder who can really run. We may see him in the majors in 2025 or so. We probably won't. ⓧ Drafted in the third round but paid a second-round signing bonus, **Tyler Callihan** is a big and (somewhat older) prep infielder who is already flashing serious power and swing-and-miss potential in rookie ball. ⓧ Typically, guys who float through the minors doing a little bit of everything offensively without any standout carrying tool are playing with fire. **Stuart Fairchild** distinguishes himself from that group with his ability to play a good center field. ⓧ A product of these bullpen-laden times, C/1B/2B/3B **Kyle Farmer** is about as exciting and necessary as a quarter-rest in a musical score. You may look at his production and come away underwhelmed, but then, you may also have tried playing rec-league softball with a team of eight players. ⓧ For a minute it looked like **Jose Garcia**, a $5 million Cuban signing, was going to be only a slick-fielding shortstop and nothing more. He broke out in 2019, hitting for surprisingly decent power in a tough environment in High-A. ⓧ **Juan Graterol** has appeared in 10 major-league games across the last two seasons and serves as an answer to the question, "What is a replacement-level catcher?" The Twins will find out for themselves. ⓧ Find yourself someone who loves you as much as the Reds love hit-over-power fourth outfielders who can handle center. On a related note, Cincy made sure to grab **Jameson Hannah** from the Athletics as the return on Tanner Roark. ⓧ Technically drafted as a shortstop, **Rece Hinds** played in three professional games after signing - each as a third baseman. His calling card is a whole lot of power, but it's anyone's guess as to how much he'll tap into. ⓧ The Reds like to find good defensive infielders and teach them how to access some power. Pulling that trick with **Alfredo Rodriguez** has thus far proved to be beyond their reach. ⓧ The FSL is a tough place to hit, meaning **Andy Sugilio**'s 2019 was better than it looks. He'll try again to break out in 2020, just like the Baha Men will keep searching for another hit record.

Pitchers

PITCHER	TEAM	LVL	AGE	W	L	SV	G	GS	IP	H	HR	BB/9	K/9	K	GB%	BABIP	WHIP	ERA	DRA	WARP	MPH	FB%	WHF	CSP
R.J. Alaniz	TAC	AAA	28	2	1	2	10	0	12²	18	3	5.0	16.3	23	42%	.500	1.97	6.39	4.08	0.3				
	LOU	AAA	28	1	2	4	25	0	27²	25	1	3.6	10.1	31	50%	.320	1.30	2.93	3.18	0.8				
	SEA	MLB	28	0	0	0	4	0	4	11	3	6.8	13.5	6	44%	.615	3.50	20.25	5.84	0.0	96.2	51.8	14.5	49.5
	CIN	MLB	28	1	0	0	8	0	11²	8	0	3.1	5.4	7	46%	.229	1.03	5.40	5.55	0.0	94.5	49.7	8.4	48.5
Tejay Antone	CHT	AA	25	7	4	0	13	13	74²	63	4	2.7	7.6	63	60%	.274	1.14	3.38	4.21	0.7				
	LOU	AAA	25	4	8	0	14	13	71²	93	7	3.9	8.8	70	52%	.402	1.73	4.65	6.51	0.1				
Matt Bowman	LOU	AAA	28	1	1	4	29	0	39	28	1	4.2	8.1	35	55%	.273	1.18	2.08	3.78	0.9				
	CIN	MLB	28	2	0	0	27	0	32	27	2	3.7	7.0	25	56%	.258	1.25	3.66	4.92	0.2	94.5	53.9	8.4	45.8
Ryan Hendrix	CHT	AA	24	3	0	2	16	0	19¹	14	0	3.7	10.7	23	46%	.292	1.14	2.33	4.00	0.1				
Keury Mella	LOU	AAA	25	8	14	0	27	27	142²	160	22	3.5	6.4	102	53%	.307	1.51	5.05	5.38	1.8				
	CIN	MLB	25	0	0	0	2	0	3²	5	0	4.9	9.8	4	33%	.417	1.91	7.36	4.87	0.0	97.1	77.4	16.1	41.2
Packy Naughton	DAY	A+	23	5	2	0	9	9	51¹	49	2	1.6	8.8	50	45%	.320	1.13	2.63	4.20	0.5				
	CHT	AA	23	6	10	0	19	19	105²	109	8	2.2	6.9	81	40%	.299	1.28	3.66	4.91	0.1				
Lyon Richardson	DYT	A	19	3	9	0	26	26	112²	126	10	2.6	8.5	106	41%	.340	1.41	4.15	5.70	-0.7				
Tony Santillan	CHT	AA	22	2	8	0	21	21	102¹	110	8	4.7	8.1	92	37%	.333	1.60	4.84	5.75	-1.0				
Josh D. Smith	COH	AAA	29	8	1	6	41	0	52²	32	7	4.1	12.6	74	39%	.231	1.06	2.73	2.43	1.9				
	CLE	MLB	29	0	0	0	8	0	8¹	8	0	8.6	13.0	12	38%	.381	1.92	5.40	5.06	0.0	92.8	62.8	8.2	48.8
	MIA	MLB	29	0	0	0	6	0	4¹	3	0	6.2	4.2	2	27%	.200	1.38	8.31	7.83	-0.1	91.7	61.8	9	54.4
Jackson Stephens	LOU	AAA	25	8	4	0	47	2	84	93	6	4.0	8.6	80	52%	.347	1.55	5.14	4.46	1.5				
Tyler Thornburg	PAW	AAA	30	0	2	0	11	1	10²	17	5	7.6	11.0	13	29%	.364	2.44	12.66	8.52	-0.2				
	OKL	AAA	30	0	0	0	12	0	12	11	3	6.8	11.2	15	26%	.280	1.67	6.00	3.95	0.3				
	BOS	MLB	30	0	0	0	16	0	18²	21	4	4.8	10.6	22	30%	.347	1.66	7.71	6.51	-0.2	95.5	55	9.4	43.4

It's really, really cool that **R.J. Alaniz** - an undrafted free-agent in 2010 - made his major-league debut in 2019 at age 28. He got knocked around pretty hard and doesn't have surplus heat so it's going to take all he has to stick around. ⓧ The only thing that righty reliever prospect **Tejay Antone** loves more than spelling names phonetically is inducing ground balls—something he did more than half the time between Double- and Triple-A. ⓧ No. You're thinking of Michael Baumann, the prospect. No, not that one either, that's Michael Bowden, the old Red Sox prospect. Matt Barnes? Nah, he misses way more bats. This is **Matt Bowman**. He's pretty good. ⓧ **Ryan Hendrix** didn't pitch much in 2019, but he missed bats and allowed zero homers in Double-A. That's a recipe to get into the Reds house over yonder. ⓧ The Reds used **Keury Mella** as a starter throughout the minors, but he looks to have hit his head in Triple-A. He turns 27 in August and a transition to the bullpen may be necessary. ⓧ Former ninth-round pick **Packy Naughton** has added a little extra heat to his otherwise "soft-tossing southpaw with a change" profile, but feel for the curve remains on his to-do list. His name is Packy Naughton. ⓧ **Lyon Richardson** is a raw, athletic prospect with a ferocious delivery. He befuddled Low-A hitters as if Truthful Richardson was also on the mound with him and opponents could ask only one question. ⓧ [Pitcher Name] is a [insert year] [insert high round] Reds draft pick whose command isn't good enough to stick in the rotation but the big [right/left]-hander could become a contributor with a transition to the bullpen. We'll let you fill in those fields for **Tony Santillan**. ⓧ Thirty-year-old lefty relievers often end up stashed in Triple-A, and luckily for **Josh Smith** that means he can still occasionally hit the college bars he frequented at Wichita State. ⓧ After pitching in the majors two years in a row, the Reds left **Jackson Stephens** in Triple-A all year, where he threw 80 innings primarily as a reliever. Consider that a bad sign for his long-term job prospects. ⓧ It sure looks like **Tyler Thornburg**'s shoulder injuries have killed his career, but at least the Reds didn't have to give up Travis Shaw to find out.

CLEVELAND INDIANS

Essay by Christina Kahrl

Player comments by Mark Barry and BP staff

If we're going to talk about the Indians, the legend of Sisyphus seems like as good a place to start as any. You probably know the basic outline: Dude has to push a very big rock up a hill for eternity; when he gets close to the top, the rock rolls to the bottom and he has to start all over again.

In the broad strokes, as a metaphor for Cleveland's legacy of title-free competitiveness goes, it isn't particularly tortured. But when you drill down to the original root of the legend, Sisyphus was being punished for being crafty and deceitful, greedy beyond avarice, controlling and murderous, opaque and ingenuine about his motives. In death, the rolling stone was Zeus's eternal punishment for how Sisyphus had used these qualities in life.

Looking at their recent run of competitiveness, you can understand a certain sense of frustration in this vein. They've averaged 91 wins per season over the last seven years, all of them above-.500 campaigns, winning three AL Central titles and a league pennant. That hardly seems like cause for celebration after a year in which they took their 93-win season straight to the links, no later than the epically awful Tigers or Royals. Heck, during that same seven-year stretch, the Royals—Ned Yost's Royals!—won a World Series.

Perhaps the most frustrating thing about 2019 was the sense that a window—of opportunity, to contend and to win with a roster built around Francisco Lindor—is closing. Some of that might be the product of recognizing that the Twins' agglomeration of talent is finally reaching critical mass at a time when Minnesota's profiting from smart management. Some of that may also be fear that something similar is on the way from the White Sox. The Age of Lindor in the Land, with just two years left to tick down before the star shortstop heads into free agency with a chance to make Harper or Machado money, is already clouded over.

Exacerbating that sense of frustration was the front office's failure to add anything approaching adequate outfield help last winter, effectively frittering away a Lindor-enabled season with division rivals on the rise. But to be fair, the decade just ending saw the Giants win three titles with strong starting pitching and cobbled-together outfields. Knowing

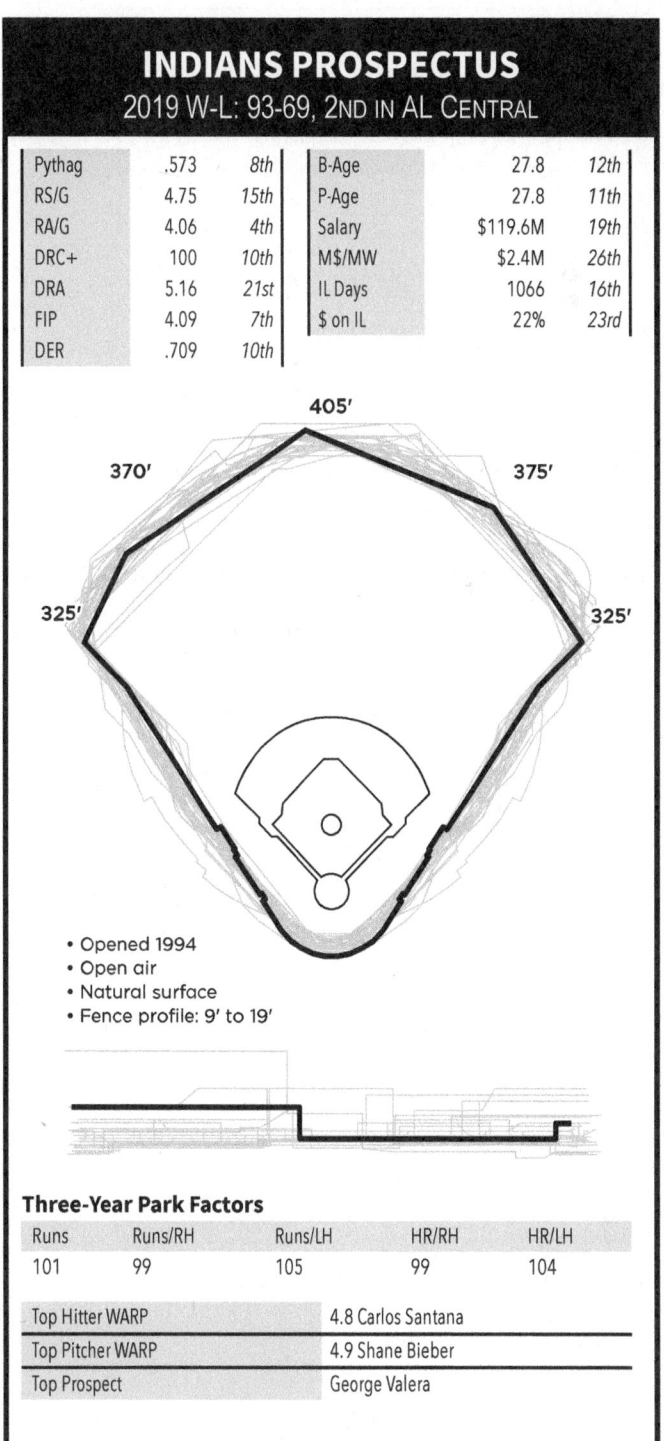

INDIANS PROSPECTUS
2019 W-L: 93-69, 2ND IN AL CENTRAL

Pythag	.573	8th	B-Age	27.8	12th
RS/G	4.75	15th	P-Age	27.8	11th
RA/G	4.06	4th	Salary	$119.6M	19th
DRC+	100	10th	M$/MW	$2.4M	26th
DRA	5.16	21st	IL Days	1066	16th
FIP	4.09	7th	$ on IL	22%	23rd
DER	.709	10th			

- Opened 1994
- Open air
- Natural surface
- Fence profile: 9' to 19'

Three-Year Park Factors

Runs	Runs/RH	Runs/LH	HR/RH	HR/LH
101	99	105	99	104

Top Hitter WARP	4.8 Carlos Santana
Top Pitcher WARP	4.9 Shane Bieber
Top Prospect	George Valera

2019 Hit List Ranking

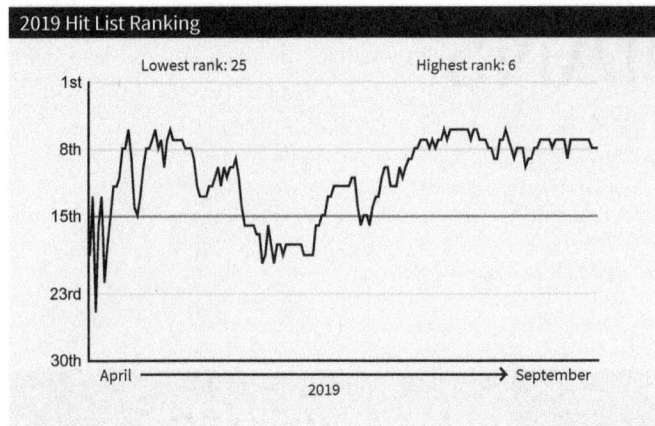

Lowest rank: 25   Highest rank: 6

Committed Payroll (in millions)

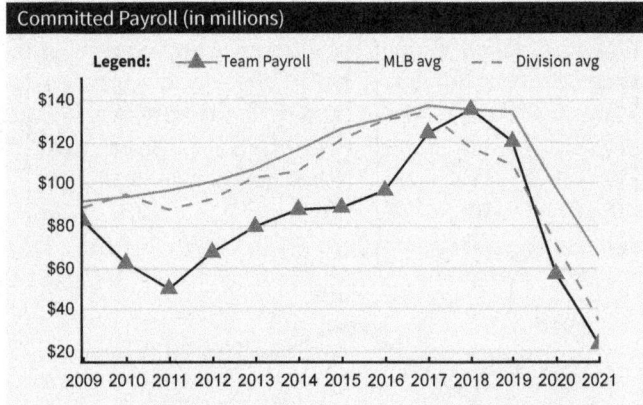

Legend: ▲ Team Payroll   — MLB avg   - - Division avg

Farm System Ranking

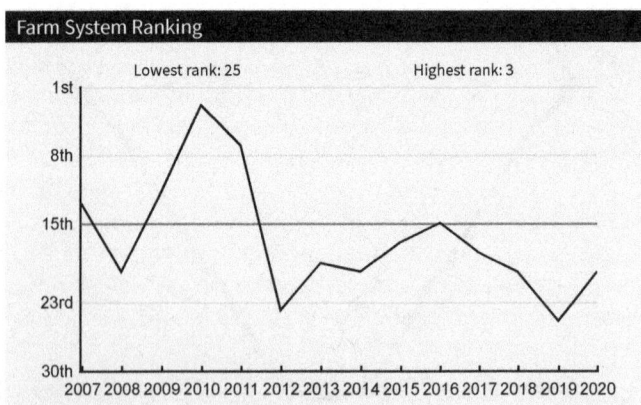

Lowest rank: 25   Highest rank: 3

Personnel

President, Baseball Operations
Chris Antonetti

General Manager
Mike Chernoff

Assistant General Manager
Carter Hawkins

Assistant General Manager
Matt Forman

Assistant General Manager
Sky Andrecheck

Manager
Terry Francona

BP Alumni
Max Marchi
Ethan Purser
Keith Woolner

that Oscar Mercado was on the way up, can you blame the Indians for giving that a shot last year after letting Michael Brantley walk away?

We can and should, of course, especially in light of their modest in-season trade for outfield reinforcements—with a strategically precise Trevor Bauer-ectomy, no less. Failing to give Brantley a qualifying offer was the big mistake; failing to get anyone in the vicinity of his value multiplied it. But, in fairness, let's remember that Franmil Reyes and Yasiel Puig didn't really outperform the Tyler Naquins or Jordan Luplows of the world. The problem wasn't quantitative as much as it was qualitative—the failure to acquire a premium outfield asset, Brantley-level or better—and evaluative, because Leonys Martín and Jake Bauers and Greg Allen didn't come close to cutting it, not in any offensive role.

Admittedly, getting players Brantley-grade good isn't easy. On the open market those guys can usually choose their own employers, and in trade they generally don't come cheap. Failing to get Brantley while—again—seeing Jason Kipnis continue to crumble and José Ramírez get off to a slow start exacerbated the sense that the Indians had been reduced to Frankie Lindor and the Smilettes. And the failure to adequately anticipate the scale of the problem bodes ill for a long-term future that may not have Lindor in it.

Getting 93 wins out of this roster despite Corey Kluber's injury or Carlos Carrasco's cancer or Ramírez's slow start might sound like a tremendous, brag-worthy accomplishment. It isn't. It's a Lindor year wasted. With just two of those left, Cleveland should consider the 2019 season a disaster.

Consider the value Lindor represents. Among shortstops through their age-25 seasons, Lindor ranks fifth all-time in WARP:

Shortstop	PA	WARP	Years in the Postseason
Alex Rodriguez	4247	40.2	3
Cal Ripken	3562	29.7	1 (won WS)
Francisco Lindor	3244	25.1	3 (lost WS x1)
Arky Vaughan	3712	24.0	0
Jim Fregosi	3487	21.0	0
Hanley Ramirez	2753	20.6	0
Robin Yount	4553	20.5	1
Nomar Garciaparra	2074	20.3	2
Troy Tulowitzki	2368	19.3	2 (lost WS x1)
Chris Speier	3086	17.9	1

The lone guy in the top five who never got as much as a pennant was Fregosi, whose career was a byword for tough luck. (Ramirez, Garciaparra and Speier join him when the bottom half of the list is considered.) Expand the scope to the top 20 and we can note that Derek Jeter won yet another title in his age-26 season, while Yount and Joe Cronin won AL pennants in theirs. Lou Boudreau, whose career predated free agency, would ultimately win the World Series. And on that note, by his age-26 season A-Rod was in his second season of cashing checks from the Rangers after his record-setting deal for a quarter of a billion dollars. Other notables in the top 20 include Xander Bogaerts, José Reyes and Carlos Correa—franchise players, in short, who powered postseason runs very early on in their careers.

The lesson, as far as it goes, is that you're supposed to build around players of this caliber, not cash them in for prospects' prospects. So the proposition that the Indians might flip Frankie Lindor for prospects, at a time when the industry is historically reticent to yield value, would be historically remarkable, and downright disappointing almost any way you look at it.

In this particular pageant, nobody cares or should care about who wins Ms. Sabermetrically Savvy, even when the competition for it is fierce. It isn't the Indians who are on Sisyphus' eternal hamster wheel; their fans are, telling themselves stories about Andrew Miller or Rajai Davis or José Mesa or the Curse of Rocky Colavito or even Willie Mays if they can remember the heartbreak of the 1954 World Series. Terry Francona wouldn't be the first manager in Indians history to never put up a losing season without winning a World Series title, just the most famous since Al Lopez.[1]

Trading Bauer and subsequently Corey Kluber represent choices to convert the perishability of pitching prowess into future value (and rid themselves of the dubious charms of Bauer's insufferable *je ne sais quoi* while they were at it). There's a measure of irony in dispensing with both pitchers within a few months of one another; they have been held up as very different exemplars. As a matter of pitching instruction and inspiration, Indians coaches and instructors pointed to Kluber as the perfect possibility model, a man who had not merely mastered the daily preparatory routines of his craft with a robotic zen quality, but who had demonstrated how far that mastery can take a pitcher who, as a farmhand, had never been an idealized prospect. Broadly speaking, Bauer pursues an identical quest to be the best he can be, but his combination of conviction in and proselytization for his more tech-savvy process appears to have made him even more of a pain in the ass than just his picking fights on the internet.

Which is why what they do with Francisco Lindor is the defining choice for the organization. And this is where the legend of Sisyphus fails us as a metaphor, as grubby reality intrudes. Because like Sisyphus, the Indians are not stupid, and they reap the full measure of their ambition and actions. They haven't reached the top since that last World Series title in 1948. But it isn't like they're losing money, not when baseball is making more than $10 billion in a season while the Indians' payroll might be found in the majors' bottom third. Money should not be a problem, not when there's more money sloshing around the industry than ever before.

The Indians are welcome to open their books and show us otherwise, of course. But until they do, it seems as if we can count on their ability to afford Lindor now, and afford the talent to put around him as well. Shedding the salaries of Kipnis and Kluber (not to mention Bauer) should buy Cleveland more than just Lindor's arbitration-fueled pay raise and second-base adequacy in the form of César Hernández. Much more. The Indians' ambitions embrace higher goals than adequacy on the cheap or cleverly buying back Carlos Santana on a fraction of his market price.

To make good on the two years left with Lindor, they will need more. The Twins and White Sox are threats, but beatable threats for the next two seasons. Pinching pennies during the final Lindor years the Indians have left to them would be a mistake; once he's gone, they won't be able to replace him. Once he scrams for 2022, the Indians could very well find themselves mired with the Royals and Tigers in Rust Belt ignominy and irrelevance.

That's in the uncertain future, a future that is beyond their control. The next two years, however, are theirs to win with. To try selling a Lindor deal to their fans, any time between now and his filing for free agency, instead of embracing the chance to actually get over their historic hump, would be as bleak a confession of "higher" priorities than winning within the industry as any that could be made. It would come at a time when tanking in the standings is tanking the entertainment value of multiple franchises. It's up to the Indians to rise above the temptation to accept they've won what they could with a Lindor-led roster, and embrace the privilege of employing him with all that entails—including spending to win. ▪

—Christina Kahrl is a senior writer at ESPN.

---

1. Yes, Joe Gordon and Birdie Tebbetts also achieved this in their multi-year stints, though without winning at least an AL pennant as Lopez and Francona did. Heck, even Ossie Vitt of "Cleveland Crybabies" infamy never had a losing season.

HITTERS

Greg Allen OF
Born: 03/15/93   Age: 27   Bats: B   Throws: R   Height: 6'0"   Weight: 185   Origin: Round 6, 2014 Draft (#188 overall)

YEAR	TEAM	LVL	AGE	PA	R	2B	3B	HR	RBI	BB	K	SB	CS	AVG/OBP/SLG	DRC+	VORP	BABIP	BRR	FRAA	WARP
2017	AKR	AA	24	303	37	16	1	2	24	22	55	21	2	.264/.344/.357	93	12.7	.319	1.5	CF(67): -6.4, RF(1): -0.1	0.3
2017	CLE	MLB	24	39	7	1	0	1	6	2	8	1	0	.229/.282/.343	75	0.6	.259	0.7	CF(21): -0.9, LF(5): -0.1	0.0
2018	COH	AAA	25	205	31	13	0	2	14	19	44	12	6	.298/.395/.409	129	13.1	.389	0.3	CF(42): 2.3, LF(5): -0.4	1.5
2018	CLE	MLB	25	291	36	11	3	2	20	14	58	21	4	.257/.310/.343	79	4.0	.320	3.4	CF(78): 2.8, RF(16): -0.4	0.8
2019	COH	AAA	26	226	37	9	3	5	17	20	44	10	5	.268/.358/.419	95	9.5	.322	0.6	CF(25): 1.6, LF(15): 1.4	0.8
2019	CLE	MLB	26	256	30	9	3	4	27	11	53	8	2	.229/.290/.346	74	-1.1	.280	0.8	LF(60): 6.0, CF(18): -1.6	0.4
2020	CLE	MLB	27	280	27	13	1	5	27	18	57	12	4	.234/.307/.355	79	-0.1	.283	0.9	RF -3, CF 0	-0.2

Comparables: *Johnny Groth, Herm Winningham, Ruben Mateo*

We've all had the pleasure of dining at the fine establishment known as McDonald's. It's fine. It's usually very fast. It's rarely offensive. Coincidentally, these adjectives can also sum up Allen's 2019 campaign, as the 26-year-old leaned on his speed to play passable outfield defense. The problem for Allen, however, was his production at the plate, where he hit like a decent pitcher as opposed to someone in the mix for everyday reps on a team with playoff aspirations. It's fair to assume that his existence as a starter might go the way of the Arch Deluxe, as opposed to the steady, reliability of the Big Mac.

Jake Bauers OF/1B
Born: 10/06/95   Age: 24   Bats: L   Throws: L   Height: 6'1"   Weight: 195   Origin: Round 7, 2013 Draft (#208 overall)

YEAR	TEAM	LVL	AGE	PA	R	2B	3B	HR	RBI	BB	K	SB	CS	AVG/OBP/SLG	DRC+	VORP	BABIP	BRR	FRAA	WARP
2017	DUR	AAA	21	575	79	31	1	13	63	78	112	20	3	.263/.368/.412	124	22.1	.314	0.5	LF(55): 4.7, 1B(52): -1.0	2.8
2018	DUR	AAA	22	222	31	14	0	5	24	23	47	10	6	.279/.357/.426	128	12.0	.345	0.9	1B(46): -0.4, LF(4): 0.3	0.9
2018	TBA	MLB	22	388	48	22	2	11	48	54	104	6	6	.201/.316/.384	86	8.2	.252	2.5	1B(76): -2.4, LF(16): 0.5	0.0
2019	COH	AAA	23	103	13	7	0	3	15	14	26	8	2	.247/.350/.427	96	0.9	.317	0.1	LF(15): 2.1, 1B(6): 0.1	0.3
2019	CLE	MLB	23	423	46	16	1	12	43	45	115	3	3	.226/.312/.371	85	0.5	.290	0.7	LF(53): 0.1, 1B(31): -2.2	-0.1
2020	CLE	MLB	24	455	49	19	1	15	52	50	120	7	3	.219/.310/.381	84	2.7	.275	2.0	LF 4, 1B 0	0.6

Comparables: *Jon Singleton, Wayne Belardi, Freddie Freeman*

The following takes place from March to September, 2019.

FADE IN: Our secret weapon, Jake Bauers (24), wipes sweat from his brow as he works tirelessly and deliberately to diffuse the bomb. Tick, tock. Tick, tock. He's speedy, to be sure, but has difficulty utilizing the power to effectively finish the task. He waits. And waits. And ultimately his patience, a calling card that separates him from other agents...uh, hitters, is used against him. The bomb explodes and he strikes out, leaving the debris of a 2019 season in its wake.

Boop Beep Boop Beep

Will Benson OF
Born: 06/16/98   Age: 22   Bats: L   Throws: L   Height: 6'5"   Weight: 225   Origin: Round 1, 2016 Draft (#14 overall)

YEAR	TEAM	LVL	AGE	PA	R	2B	3B	HR	RBI	BB	K	SB	CS	AVG/OBP/SLG	DRC+	VORP	BABIP	BRR	FRAA	WARP
2017	MHV	A-	19	236	29	8	5	10	36	31	80	7	1	.238/.347/.475	108	11.6	.339	0.1	RF(56): -2.5	0.3
2018	LKC	A	20	506	54	11	1	22	58	82	152	12	6	.180/.324/.370	89	5.6	.218	-0.4	RF(113): 5.4, CF(4): -0.2	0.9
2019	LKC	A	21	259	44	12	3	18	55	37	78	18	2	.272/.371/.604	140	25.6	.325	1.5	RF(21): -0.8, LF(20): 0.7	1.6
2019	LYN	A+	21	255	29	9	2	4	23	31	73	9	2	.189/.290/.304	79	1.3	.255	3.5	LF(37): -3.0, RF(15): -1.1	-0.1
2020	CLE	MLB	22	251	23	10	1	7	26	21	94	2	1	.180/.253/.332	54	-6.9	.264	0.2	RF -1, LF 0	-0.8

Comparables: *Jamie Romak, Derek Norris, Tommy Pham*

Sometimes potential and promise can be a double-edged sword. The first season of HBO's *Game of Thrones* (ever heard of it?) peaked with over three million U.S. viewers, garnering rave reviews both critically and commercially. The sky was the limit for the fantasy series, and by the eighth and final season, almost 14 million Americans were glued to the television, awaiting the fate of Westeros. Then it ended, and all the hope for an epic finish was dashed by a rushed, careless finale. Anyway, Will Benson was drafted in the first round, with his scouting reports brimming with glowing descriptors about his tools, projection and power. He tore up Lake County in the first half of 2019, finally flashing the power and speed combo that was so tantalizing at draft time. Unfortunately, Benson struggled after a promotion and failed to maintain his breakout. Just 21 years old, the end isn't in sight for Benson. Yet, he will need to curb his strikeout issues if he's to avoid the wrong side of a different sword—that of Damocles.

Aaron Bracho 2B
Born: 04/24/01   Age: 19   Bats: B   Throws: R   Height: 5'11"   Weight: 175   Origin: International Free Agent, 2017

YEAR	TEAM	LVL	AGE	PA	R	2B	3B	HR	RBI	BB	K	SB	CS	AVG/OBP/SLG	DRC+	VORP	BABIP	BRR	FRAA	WARP
2019	CLT	RK	18	137	25	10	2	6	29	23	21	4	1	.296/.416/.593	186	22.8	.306	0.9	2B(22): 1.0	1.5
2019	MHV	A-	18	32	5	1	0	2	4	5	8	0	0	.222/.344/.481	93	2.3	.235	0.3	2B(8): -1.4	0.0
2020	CLE	MLB	19	251	25	12	1	5	25	30	69	3	1	.210/.310/.346	81	2.1	.281	0.0	2B 0	0.2

Comparables: *Joey Gallo, Daniel Robertson, Logan Morrison*

When Cleveland landed Bracho for $1.5 million in July 2017, they saw an infielder who had a good idea at the plate and could even add a little pop. And that's pretty much exactly what the 18-year-old switch hitter has been, recording Votto-like walk rates in two stops in 2019, culminating with a late-season cup of coffee in Mahoning Valley. There's still some swing-and-miss in his game, but it's not too hard to envision a 20-25 homer profile with a glove that permits him to play up-the-middle.

Bobby Bradley 1B   Born: 05/29/96   Age: 24   Bats: L   Throws: R   Height: 6'1"   Weight: 225   Origin: Round 3, 2014 Draft (#97 overall)

YEAR	TEAM	LVL	AGE	PA	R	2B	3B	HR	RBI	BB	K	SB	CS	AVG/OBP/SLG	DRC+	VORP	BABIP	BRR	FRAA	WARP
2017	AKR	AA	21	532	66	25	3	23	89	55	122	3	3	.251/.331/.465	120	17.4	.287	-2.6	1B(125): -6.3	0.9
2018	AKR	AA	22	421	49	19	3	24	64	45	105	1	0	.214/.304/.477	109	17.0	.226	-2.3	1B(97): 1.4	0.8
2018	COH	AAA	22	128	11	7	2	3	19	11	43	0	0	.254/.323/.430	101	2.8	.377	0.3	1B(29): 1.5	0.3
2019	COH	AAA	23	453	65	23	0	33	74	46	153	0	0	.264/.344/.567	124	16.7	.336	-2.5	1B(97): 1.9	1.7
2019	CLE	MLB	23	49	4	5	0	1	4	4	20	0	0	.178/.245/.356	54	-2.2	.292	-0.1	1B(5): -0.2	-0.2
2020	*CLE*	*MLB*	*24*	*105*	*11*	*5*	*0*	*4*	*13*	*8*	*39*	*0*	*0*	*.200/.271/.385*	*72*	*-2.4*	*.285*	*-0.2*	*1B 0*	*-0.3*

Comparables: Dick Gernert, Tyler O'Neill, Ryan McMahon

In the last two seasons, Bradley has been referred to as bulky, a large adult son and the usher of BIG BOY SZN in Cleveland. It's hard to argue with much of that, but there's not a whole lot else to say. Bradley's skill set is a little like putting a Charger engine in a go-kart: there's power, for sure, but it's mostly wasted. In a 15-game cameo with the big club this season, Bradley forgot to bring two of the Three True Outcomes—the "good" two, as it were. He struck out in over 40 percent of his trips to the dish while managing all of one home run. There's obviously still time for Bradley to shape himself into a productive big-league hitter—he did smack 33 homers in Triple-A, after all—but his contact woes are a legitimate threat to him becoming more than a Quad-A type.

Yu Chang INF   Born: 08/18/95   Age: 24   Bats: R   Throws: R   Height: 6'1"   Weight: 180   Origin: International Free Agent, 2013

YEAR	TEAM	LVL	AGE	PA	R	2B	3B	HR	RBI	BB	K	SB	CS	AVG/OBP/SLG	DRC+	VORP	BABIP	BRR	FRAA	WARP
2017	AKR	AA	21	508	72	24	5	24	66	52	134	11	4	.220/.312/.461	102	33.9	.254	2.3	SS(122): 20.3	4.8
2018	COH	AAA	22	518	56	28	2	13	62	44	144	4	3	.256/.330/.411	104	16.6	.341	-3.3	SS(94): -7.3, 3B(23): -0.7	1.1
2019	COH	AAA	23	283	45	15	1	9	39	26	67	4	1	.253/.322/.427	93	8.2	.306	0.9	SS(22): 0.2, 2B(22): 0.4	0.8
2019	CLE	MLB	23	84	8	2	1	1	6	11	22	0	0	.178/.286/.274	77	0.7	.240	-0.9	3B(25): -0.3, SS(8): -0.1	-0.1
2020	*CLE*	*MLB*	*24*	*140*	*14*	*6*	*1*	*5*	*16*	*11*	*39*	*1*	*0*	*.205/.277/.371*	*69*	*-1.4*	*.257*	*0.0*	*SS 1, 3B -1*	*-0.1*

Comparables: Gil McDougald, Jonathan Villar, Daniel Robertson

Chang debuted in 2019, making him just the fifth Taiwanese-born position player in big-league history. The results weren't great, as his strikeout problems followed him to the Show, but he displayed an aptitude for walking and playing defense on the left side of the infield. His ultimate landing spot (at least in Cleveland) will likely be at second base, which should help his chances for everyday reps.

Delino DeShields CF   Born: 08/16/92   Age: 27   Bats: R   Throws: R   Height: 5'9"   Weight: 200   Origin: Round 1, 2010 Draft (#8 overall)

YEAR	TEAM	LVL	AGE	PA	R	2B	3B	HR	RBI	BB	K	SB	CS	AVG/OBP/SLG	DRC+	VORP	BABIP	BRR	FRAA	WARP
2017	TEX	MLB	24	440	75	15	2	6	22	44	109	29	8	.269/.347/.367	86	13.8	.358	7.6	LF(60): 4.3, CF(51): -0.5	1.7
2018	FRI	AA	25	26	2	0	0	0	0	8	2	2	2	.278/.500/.278	176	0.6	.313	-0.9	CF(5): -0.5	0.1
2018	TEX	MLB	25	393	52	14	1	2	22	43	83	20	4	.216/.310/.281	73	1.0	.280	3.4	CF(102): 10.3	1.5
2019	NAS	AAA	26	75	10	3	0	3	11	8	17	8	0	.258/.338/.439	93	5.8	.304	1.6	CF(13): 1.1, LF(1): 0.8	0.5
2019	TEX	MLB	26	408	42	15	4	4	32	38	100	24	6	.249/.325/.347	77	2.9	.333	4.9	CF(112): 6.9	1.4
2020	*CLE*	*MLB*	*27*	*280*	*27*	*11*	*1*	*4*	*24*	*28*	*69*	*14*	*4*	*.226/.311/.329*	*75*	*3.5*	*.296*	*2.4*	*CF 4*	*0.8*

Comparables: Herm Winningham, Roy Sievers, Milton Bradley

It's coming to the point in DeShields' career that he's going to have to take the Ferrell/Carrey split. Both actors were known early in their career for doing one thing really well. Ferrell yelled at the camera in nearly the same voice as a step-brother, a racecar driver, an anchorman and numerous other roles. Carrey was the rubber-faced over-actor, gesturing wildly as he contorted his face into impossibly emotive shapes. As each actor hit the saturation point, they had to make a decision. Carrey adjusted, carrying such chops-forward films as Truman Show, 23 and the heavy-but-quirky Eternal Sunshine of the Spotless Mind. Ferrell did try that one weird Spanish movie, but largely just kept yelling in the same way he always had. How does this have anything to do with Delino DeShields? He's been a speedster his entire life. It's the first thing anyone says about him: he's fast. So far, that's been enough to make up for any other deficiencies in his game. But now he's entering his late 20s, meaning his legs will start to let him down within the next few years. If he can keep adding improvements—as he did with his defense a couple of years ago—he'll be able to retire on his own terms and get as weird as he wants. If not, the turn of the decade might be less "Good Guys" and more "Holmes and Watson."

Mike Freeman UT   Born: 08/04/87   Age: 32   Bats: L   Throws: R   Height: 6'0"   Weight: 195   Origin: Round 11, 2010 Draft (#331 overall)

YEAR	TEAM	LVL	AGE	PA	R	2B	3B	HR	RBI	BB	K	SB	CS	AVG/OBP/SLG	DRC+	VORP	BABIP	BRR	FRAA	WARP
2017	TAC	AAA	29	67	12	3	1	1	9	7	10	2	0	.350/.418/.483	99	6.9	.408	0.7	2B(9): 0.5, 3B(6): -0.1	0.4
2017	OKL	AAA	29	139	17	4	2	0	16	13	31	5	0	.306/.384/.372	100	5.6	.407	1.5	SS(14): 1.7, 3B(14): -0.1	0.8
2017	IOW	AAA	29	88	10	3	0	2	6	7	19	3	0	.273/.345/.390	101	4.0	.333	-0.6	SS(11): -0.1, 3B(7): -1.3	0.2
2017	SEA	MLB	29	34	3	0	0	1	1	4	9	0	0	.067/.176/.167	57	-3.4	.050	0.2	2B(3): -0.2, 1B(3): 0.3	-0.1
2017	LAN	MLB	29	5	0	0	0	0	0	0	2	0	0	.000/.000/.000	57	-1.3	.000	0.0	3B(1): 0.0	0.0
2017	CHN	MLB	29	27	3	2	0	0	0	2	8	0	0	.160/.222/.240	58	-1.7	.235	-0.1	SS(10): 0.0, 2B(3): 0.0	0.0
2018	IOW	AAA	30	331	51	15	2	6	38	25	66	6	6	.274/.330/.396	101	21.2	.332	1.8	SS(55): 2.7, 2B(16): -0.1	1.9
2018	CHN	MLB	30	1	0	0	0	0	0	0	0	0	0		91	0.0	--	0.0	2B(1): 0.0	0.0
2019	COH	AAA	31	33	6	0	0	3	3	9	7	1	0	.208/.424/.583	147	2.6	.143	0.0	SS(4): 0.2, 3B(2): 0.2	0.3
2019	CLE	MLB	31	213	27	8	0	4	24	22	61	1	2	.277/.362/.390	78	1.7	.388	1.3	2B(33): 2.1, 3B(18): -0.1	0.4
2020	*CLE*	*MLB*	*32*	*35*	*3*	*1*	*0*	*1*	*3*	*3*	*10*	*0*	*0*	*.218/.295/.318*	*66*	*0.0*	*.297*	*0.1*	*2B 0*	*0.0*

Comparables: Collin Cowgill, Ferris Fain, Alex Presley

Freeman strode to the plate more times last season than the rest of his big-league career *combined*, and would you believe he looked the part of a useful utility player? Heck, he was even called upon for mop-up duty during a 13-0 drubbing against the Orioles. Freeman was an intimidating presence on the bump, ranging from 64-76 mph with his "fastball" and breaking off a curveball that certainly had the intent of being a curveball. He immediately induced a groundout, but ran into some turbulence that ruined his perfect ERA. He did cruise to another scoreless inning afterward, though, and should get a chance to replicate what he actually gets paid to do—hitting, but mostly being able to defend multiple positions—in 2020.

Tyler Freeman SS Born: 05/21/99   Age: 21   Bats: R   Throws: R   Height: 6'0"   Weight: 170   Origin: Round 2, 2017 Draft (#71 overall)

YEAR	TEAM	LVL	AGE	PA	R	2B	3B	HR	RBI	BB	K	SB	CS	AVG/OBP/SLG	DRC+	VORP	BABIP	BRR	FRAA	WARP
2017	CLE	RK	18	144	19	9	0	2	14	7	12	5	1	.297/.364/.414	117	12.9	.313	1.8	SS(29): -0.1, 2B(4): -0.9	0.9
2018	MHV	A-	19	301	49	29	4	2	38	8	22	14	3	.352/.405/.511	189	37.7	.372	3.5	SS(52): -0.1, 2B(10): -0.2	3.7
2019	LKC	A	20	272	51	16	3	3	24	18	28	11	4	.292/.382/.424	142	25.1	.320	2.6	SS(57): 0.5, 2B(3): -0.2	2.6
2019	LYN	A+	20	275	38	16	2	0	20	8	25	8	1	.319/.354/.397	129	16.7	.350	1.2	SS(56): -1.0, 2B(3): 0.1	1.9
2020	*CLE*	*MLB*	*21*	*251*	*24*	*14*	*1*	*3*	*24*	*14*	*35*	*4*	*1*	*.267/.331/.380*	*91*	*5.3*	*.304*	*0.0*	*SS 1, 2B 0*	*0.6*

Comparables: Isiah Kiner-Falefa, Thairo Estrada, José Altuve

Freeman's ability to make contact is such that he's a legitimate prospect despite not doing much else at the dish. He posted the second-highest average in the Carolina League as a 20-year-old, which is something, and he did so while playing passable defense at the six. It's not your typical profile, and there's obviously a good deal of downside in the profile—his hit tool has to play well-above-average to give him a chance to start—but it's working for now and that's the best any of us can aspire to.

César Hernández 2B Born: 05/23/90   Age: 30   Bats: B   Throws: R   Height: 5'10"   Weight: 160   Origin: International Free Agent, 2006

YEAR	TEAM	LVL	AGE	PA	R	2B	3B	HR	RBI	BB	K	SB	CS	AVG/OBP/SLG	DRC+	VORP	BABIP	BRR	FRAA	WARP
2017	PHI	MLB	27	577	85	26	6	9	34	61	104	15	5	.294/.373/.421	103	35.8	.353	4.2	2B(127): -2.4, SS(1): 0.0	2.2
2018	PHI	MLB	28	708	91	15	3	15	60	95	155	19	6	.253/.356/.362	101	30.7	.315	2.0	2B(154): 3.7	2.9
2019	PHI	MLB	29	667	77	31	3	14	71	45	100	9	2	.279/.333/.408	90	13.7	.313	-1.2	2B(157): -4.7	0.8
2020	*CLE*	*MLB*	*30*	*560*	*57*	*23*	*3*	*11*	*56*	*49*	*100*	*14*	*6*	*.264/.333/.384*	*94*	*19.2*	*.312*	*0.7*	*2B -1*	*1.9*

Comparables: Jerome Walton, Herm Winningham, Dave Martinez

For the last few years, Hernández has been profiled in this space as a good player who was underrated and misunderstood by the talk-radio airheads on both sides of the telephone. Score one for the airheads last year, as Hernandez slipped significantly on both sides of the ball. Hernández took a far more free-swinging approach than ever, and while the strikeouts didn't increase, he lost more with the lack of walks than he gained with additional weakly batted balls in play. The mental miscues that have always been part of the package with Hernández are easier to overlook when he's having a three-WARP campaign than when he's hovering barely over replacement level. Even on a team of players who generally underperformed, Hernández's slippage stood out. He'll try to regroup in Cleveland.

Daniel Johnson OF Born: 07/11/95   Age: 24   Bats: L   Throws: L   Height: 5'10"   Weight: 200   Origin: Round 5, 2016 Draft (#154 overall)

YEAR	TEAM	LVL	AGE	PA	R	2B	3B	HR	RBI	BB	K	SB	CS	AVG/OBP/SLG	DRC+	VORP	BABIP	BRR	FRAA	WARP
2017	HAG	A	21	364	61	16	4	17	52	22	70	12	9	.300/.361/.529	142	30.7	.333	-0.5	RF(51): -1.1, CF(15): 0.3	2.3
2017	POT	A+	21	185	22	13	0	5	20	13	30	10	2	.294/.346/.459	119	10.2	.331	1.7	CF(30): -3.2, RF(9): 3.5	1.1
2018	HAR	AA	22	391	48	19	7	6	31	23	90	21	4	.267/.321/.410	96	7.6	.338	-2.3	RF(54): 6.3, CF(33): -2.9	0.9
2019	AKR	AA	23	167	25	7	2	10	33	16	39	6	3	.253/.337/.534	122	12.0	.276	-2.3	CF(24): -2.3, RF(10): -0.3	0.2
2019	COH	AAA	23	380	51	27	5	9	44	34	79	6	7	.306/.371/.496	123	18.0	.370	-1.5	RF(47): 6.4, CF(21): 1.2	2.4
2020	*CLE*	*MLB*	*24*	*105*	*11*	*5*	*1*	*4*	*13*	*7*	*27*	*3*	*1*	*.245/.305/.425*	*92*	*2.2*	*.304*	*-0.1*	*CF -1, RF 0*	*0.2*

Comparables: Zoilo Almonte, Cedric Mullins, Austin Hays

It was a good year for Johnson, who was traded from the Nationals to Cleveland as part of the Yan Gomes swap. How good? He played in the second-most games of his career, and posted a new career-high OPS. There are some hit-tool concerns here, and not all of his power followed him to his stint in Columbus. But he has a big-time arm and louder tools than he's shown for most of his minor-league career. Johnson should receive a big-league opportunity in 2020, and in time could look like a savvy pick-up.

──────────── ★ ★ ★ *2020 Top 101 Prospect* **#66** ★ ★ ★ ────────────

Nolan Jones 3B Born: 05/07/98   Age: 22   Bats: L   Throws: R   Height: 6'2"   Weight: 185   Origin: Round 2, 2016 Draft (#55 overall)

YEAR	TEAM	LVL	AGE	PA	R	2B	3B	HR	RBI	BB	K	SB	CS	AVG/OBP/SLG	DRC+	VORP	BABIP	BRR	FRAA	WARP
2017	MHV	A-	19	265	41	18	3	4	33	43	60	1	0	.317/.430/.482	182	28.6	.417	1.7	3B(53): 0.0	2.8
2018	LKC	A	20	389	46	12	0	16	49	63	97	2	1	.279/.393/.464	155	33.5	.347	-0.9	3B(77): -4.1	2.9
2018	LYN	A+	20	130	23	9	0	3	17	26	34	0	0	.298/.438/.471	159	12.7	.418	0.1	3B(28): -0.3	1.1
2019	LYN	A+	21	324	48	12	1	7	41	65	85	5	3	.286/.435/.425	172	28.7	.399	-1.4	3B(72): -3.4	2.8
2019	AKR	AA	21	211	33	10	2	8	22	31	63	2	0	.253/.370/.466	150	17.0	.346	0.8	3B(43): 0.0	1.8
2020	*CLE*	*MLB*	*22*	*251*	*28*	*12*	*1*	*8*	*29*	*29*	*85*	*0*	*0*	*.240/.333/.405*	*97*	*6.8*	*.352*	*-0.3*	*3B -1*	*0.6*

Comparables: Drew Robinson, Lewis Brinson, Shed Long

An appropriate response to Jones's minor-league career is that Larry David GIF. You know the one. On one hand, Jones has incrementally tapped into his raw power over the last couple seasons, a skill that pairs beautifully with his plus plate discipline. On the other, he struck out almost a third of the time at Double-A this season, which is too frequently to feel good about. It doesn't help that Jones's defense is nearly as polarizing. He has more than enough arm for the hot corner, yet his actions there are likely to cap his ceiling around "tolerable." Back and forth, back and forth. Jones is a solid prospect, but he's also a liquid one.

Jason Kipnis 2B   Born: 04/03/87   Age: 33   Bats: L   Throws: R   Height: 5'11"   Weight: 200   Origin: Round 2, 2009 Draft (#63 overall)

YEAR	TEAM	LVL	AGE	PA	R	2B	3B	HR	RBI	BB	K	SB	CS	AVG/OBP/SLG	DRC+	VORP	BABIP	BRR	FRAA	WARP
2017	CLE	MLB	30	373	43	25	0	12	35	28	71	6	2	.232/.291/.414	85	7.2	.256	-0.7	2B(75): 1.0, CF(11): -1.1	0.4
2018	CLE	MLB	31	601	65	28	1	18	75	60	112	7	1	.230/.315/.389	94	10.8	.258	-1.2	2B(131): -0.5, CF(14): -2.0	1.1
2019	CLE	MLB	32	511	52	23	1	17	65	40	88	7	2	.245/.304/.410	94	12.7	.265	0.2	2B(117): 0.0	1.3
2020	CLE	MLB	33	300	31	14	1	9	34	26	59	5	2	.233/.304/.390	83	2.3	.267	-0.5	2B 0, CF 0	0.2

Comparables: Gordon Beckham, Jeff Kent, Cliff Pennington

The stage was set. It was the bottom of the ninth in Game 7 of the 2016 World Series. Kipnis strode to the plate while Joe Buck touted the second baseman as the "heart and soul" of the Cleveland team. He smoked a 1-1 slider from Aroldis Chapman deep into right field, and off the bat it appeared to be a title-winner. The ball hooked foul, and fell just short of the wall. Kipnis would strike out four pitches later, and Cleveland would go on to lose. The line between franchise hero and good player is thinner than we'd like to believe. But Kipnis is evidence of how our fates can sway with the wind. He was so close to being immortalized forever. And then? Less than four years later Cleveland declined Kipnis's $16.5 million option following three substandard seasons at the dish. It wasn't a surprise nor was it a sad occasion for Cleveland fans; it just was, and, because of the home run that wasn't, that's all it ever will be.

Sandy León C   Born: 03/13/89   Age: 31   Bats: B   Throws: R   Height: 5'10"   Weight: 225   Origin: International Free Agent, 2007

YEAR	TEAM	LVL	AGE	PA	R	2B	3B	HR	RBI	BB	K	SB	CS	AVG/OBP/SLG	DRC+	VORP	BABIP	BRR	FRAA	WARP
2017	BOS	MLB	28	301	32	14	0	7	39	25	74	0	0	.225/.290/.354	74	-2.0	.280	-5.2	C(84): 10.8	1.1
2018	BOS	MLB	29	288	30	12	0	5	22	15	75	1	0	.177/.232/.279	58	-1.4	.226	-0.7	C(87): 11.7	1.1
2019	BOS	MLB	30	191	14	3	0	5	19	13	47	0	0	.192/.251/.297	65	1.4	.231	-0.2	C(65): 2.9, 1B(1): 0.0	0.4
2020	CLE	MLB	31	245	22	9	0	6	24	18	63	1	0	.210/.275/.334	63	-1.8	.265	-1.4	C 1	-0.1

Comparables: Miguel Montero, Brandon Inge, Randy Knorr

YEAR	TEAM	P. COUNT	FRM RUNS	BLK RUNS	THRW RUNS	TOT RUNS
2017	BOS	11373	9.7	0.4	2.0	10.7
2018	BOS	11107	11.6	0.1	0.1	11.7
2019	BOS	8115	4.8	-1.0	-0.2	3.5
2020	CLE	11942	2.0	-0.3	0.5	2.2

Any marketer knows that brand loyalty is among the most difficult concepts to measure, maintain and instill in a consumer base. Perhaps they should all consult León, who continued to convince the Red Sox to use his services despite the many superior options on the market. Defense has long been León's *raison d'etre*, but he is declining as a receiver, framer and thrower at this point. Offensively, well, the most polite thing we can say is that León hasn't posted a DRC+ north of 100 since 2016. (If one wished to be impolite, one could point out that the remains of Carlos González, Mark Reynolds and *literally Gordon Beckham* all provided more value as hitters in 2019.) Even León's familiarity with the underperforming Boston pitching staff didn't carry enough weight to keep him around in the end, but he'll function as a better backup in Cleveland than Kevin Plawecki.

Francisco Lindor SS   Born: 11/14/93   Age: 26   Bats: B   Throws: R   Height: 5'11"   Weight: 190   Origin: Round 1, 2011 Draft (#8 overall)

YEAR	TEAM	LVL	AGE	PA	R	2B	3B	HR	RBI	BB	K	SB	CS	AVG/OBP/SLG	DRC+	VORP	BABIP	BRR	FRAA	WARP
2017	CLE	MLB	23	723	99	44	4	33	89	60	93	15	3	.273/.337/.505	118	49.8	.275	2.1	SS(158): 3.8	5.5
2018	CLE	MLB	24	745	129	42	2	38	92	70	107	25	10	.277/.352/.519	128	57.9	.279	-0.5	SS(157): 5.9	6.5
2019	CLE	MLB	25	654	101	40	2	32	74	46	98	22	5	.284/.335/.518	117	45.7	.291	-2.3	SS(137): -4.8	3.8
2020	CLE	MLB	26	630	80	35	2	30	92	49	96	15	5	.273/.333/.495	117	36.0	.282	-0.6	SS 1	3.8

Comparables: Ketel Marte, Orlando Arcia, Jorge Polanco

Let's talk smiles. Mona Lisa's? Classic. Sly, yet alluring. She knows something, but she's not telling. Jack Nicholson? No wait, the Joker—eh, no, let's just do regular Jack, because then we get "The Shining" Jack and "A Few Good Men" Jack. It's mischievous, but somehow also warm and exciting. What about Magic Johnson? Excellence and confidence. Julia Roberts, more specifically, Julia in "Pretty Woman"—it was an announcement, an arrival. How good of a smile do you have to have in order to wear "Mr. Smile" on your back for Players' Weekend? As it turns out, a pretty good one.

Lindor's smile is the absolute perfect encapsulation of him as a player. His smile is sheer joy and authority. It's pure. Lots of young stars start their careers this way, sure, but somehow Lindor has managed to maintain that exuberance on his ascent to superstardom. Despite missing roughly the first month of the campaign, he still smacked 30 homers and snagged 15 bags for the third consecutive season.

During the extension-happy portion offseason, Cleveland's owner Paul Dolan was asked about signing Lindor for the long term. Dolan's response: "Enjoy him." It was unnecessary, frustrating and ominous. Smiles don't last, but turning a smile into a frown is dastardly. It was, in a sense, the exact opposite of why people love Lindor and the game—and the reason why smiles seem to be harder to come by in baseball, be it on the field or in the stands, where happy faces have been replaced by empty seatbacks.

Jordan Luplow OF   Born: 09/26/93   Age: 26   Bats: R   Throws: R   Height: 6'1"   Weight: 195   Origin: Round 3, 2014 Draft (#100 overall)

YEAR	TEAM	LVL	AGE	PA	R	2B	3B	HR	RBI	BB	K	SB	CS	AVG/OBP/SLG	DRC+	VORP	BABIP	BRR	FRAA	WARP
2017	ALT	AA	23	288	45	15	0	16	37	29	45	1	3	.287/.368/.535	149	25.9	.294	1.5	LF(65): 4.3, 3B(1): 0.0	2.8
2017	IND	AAA	23	182	29	7	1	7	19	16	36	4	1	.325/.401/.513	163	18.0	.381	-0.8	LF(27): 3.4, RF(15): 0.9	1.9
2017	PIT	MLB	23	87	6	3	1	3	11	6	22	0	1	.205/.276/.385	77	-1.4	.241	-0.4	RF(14): 0.1, LF(10): 0.7	0.0
2018	IND	AAA	24	357	41	25	3	8	49	39	64	7	2	.287/.367/.462	146	20.4	.336	-1.7	LF(41): 4.3, RF(38): 1.4	2.8
2018	PIT	MLB	24	103	16	1	3	3	7	10	18	2	2	.185/.272/.359	85	-2.7	.197	-0.4	LF(16): 5.4, RF(11): -0.3	0.6
2019	COH	AAA	25	57	12	3	0	2	7	10	14	2	1	.311/.456/.511	126	3.3	.414	-0.5	LF(10): 1.5, RF(2): -0.2	0.4
2019	CLE	MLB	25	261	42	15	1	15	38	33	61	3	2	.276/.372/.551	126	15.5	.313	0.3	RF(42): 3.4, LF(34): 0.3	1.9
2020	CLE	MLB	26	175	23	8	1	9	26	18	41	1	1	.240/.328/.472	107	5.8	.269	0.2	RF -1, LF 2	0.7

Comparables: Mike Young, Jeff Burroughs, Matt Joyce

When Cleveland acquired Luplow, a reasonable goal was to strengthen their lineup against left-handers by being better than Brandon Guyer. He checked off both boxes by hitting southpaws to the tune of a .320/.439/.742 slash line in 128 trips to the plate. Unfortunately, thanks to a dearth of big-league quality outfielders in Cleveland this season, he also played against righties. That didn't go as well. Still, he finished as a well-above-average hitter overall and looks like a savvy pickup and useful player.

Oscar Mercado CF Born: 12/16/94 Age: 25 Bats: R Throws: R Height: 6'2" Weight: 197 Origin: Round 2, 2013 Draft (#57 overall)

YEAR	TEAM	LVL	AGE	PA	R	2B	3B	HR	RBI	BB	K	SB	CS	AVG/OBP/SLG	DRC+	VORP	BABIP	BRR	FRAA	WARP
2017	SFD	AA	22	523	76	20	4	13	46	32	112	38	19	.287/.341/.428	114	35.1	.348	5.7	CF(108): -2.1, LF(7): -0.7	2.7
2018	MEM	AAA	23	427	73	21	1	8	42	36	64	31	8	.285/.351/.408	108	32.6	.323	8.1	CF(89): -2.6, LF(7): -0.5	2.4
2018	COH	AAA	23	119	12	5	1	0	5	13	23	6	4	.252/.342/.320	93	-2.3	.325	-2.2	CF(24): -0.8, RF(7): 0.3	0.0
2019	COH	AAA	24	140	24	10	1	4	15	16	32	14	3	.294/.396/.496	129	11.6	.373	1.1	CF(19): 5.4, LF(5): 1.1	1.5
2019	CLE	MLB	24	482	70	25	3	15	54	28	84	15	4	.269/.318/.443	97	15.0	.300	2.3	CF(82): 8.3, LF(24): -1.6	2.2
2020	CLE	MLB	25	560	59	28	2	15	61	37	111	29	13	.241/.301/.389	81	3.5	.281	0.3	CF 2, LF -1	0.4

Comparables: Roy Sievers, Rip Repulski, Rondell White

In a sense, Mercado had a typical rookie season, complete with stretches of brilliance (usually on defense) and bouts of frustration. Oddly, his trademark patience didn't make the trip to the big leagues. He did maintain an above-average contact rate that helped him eschew strikeouts and showcase his plus speed. Although never known for his power, he took full advantage of the rabbit ball to hit 15 home runs. Mercado looks a bit like the Ender Inciarte starter kit, and that should be enough for him to remain a starting center fielder.

Tyler Naquin RF Born: 04/24/91 Age: 29 Bats: L Throws: R Height: 6'2" Weight: 195 Origin: Round 1, 2012 Draft (#15 overall)

YEAR	TEAM	LVL	AGE	PA	R	2B	3B	HR	RBI	BB	K	SB	CS	AVG/OBP/SLG	DRC+	VORP	BABIP	BRR	FRAA	WARP
2017	COH	AAA	26	330	42	14	4	10	51	30	71	5	2	.298/.359/.475	122	18.3	.358	0.9	CF(49): 10.7, RF(23): -1.1	2.6
2017	CLE	MLB	26	40	4	2	0	0	1	2	9	0	1	.216/.250/.270	73	-1.4	.276	-0.2	CF(11): -0.4, RF(8): -0.5	-0.1
2018	CLE	MLB	27	183	22	7	0	3	23	6	42	1	1	.264/.295/.356	79	1.3	.331	1.0	RF(39): 5.2, CF(19): 0.2	0.6
2019	CLE	MLB	28	294	34	19	0	10	34	14	66	4	2	.288/.325/.467	93	4.6	.345	-0.3	RF(68): 12.2, LF(15): 4.1	2.0
2020	CLE	MLB	29	280	31	15	1	10	35	19	72	4	2	.261/.318/.438	98	6.3	.327	0.3	LF 5, RF 5	1.6

Comparables: Abraham Almonte, Lorenzo Cain, Roger Bernadina

Dinner rolls are good; sometimes they're even great. You just don't want to have an entire meal comprised of dinner rolls. It's kind of like Naquin's involvement in the Cleveland outfield. He's fine to have around, but he's at his best when he's the third or fourth most important part of the experience. A team can get into trouble if they need him to provide more than that. A shift to a corner-outfield spot has helped Naquin defensively, as he led all outfielders in FRAA. That value helps offset his bat—he's now been a below-average hitter for three consecutive seasons. He's best when warm and dipped in gravy.

Bo Naylor C Born: 02/21/00 Age: 20 Bats: L Throws: R Height: 6'0" Weight: 195 Origin: Round 1, 2018 Draft (#29 overall)

YEAR	TEAM	LVL	AGE	PA	R	2B	3B	HR	RBI	BB	K	SB	CS	AVG/OBP/SLG	DRC+	VORP	BABIP	BRR	FRAA	WARP
2018	CLT	RK	18	139	17	3	3	2	17	21	28	5	1	.274/.381/.402	124	12.2	.341	0.3	C(19): -0.4, 3B(5): -0.7	0.7
2019	LKC	A	19	453	60	18	10	11	65	43	104	7	5	.243/.313/.421	98	20.9	.296	0.9	C(85): 3.4	2.2
2020	CLE	MLB	20	251	23	11	2	6	26	22	72	1	0	.216/.289/.359	74	-0.5	.290	-0.1	C 0, 3B 0	0.0

Comparables: Rio Ruiz, Kyle Skipworth, Joe Benson

A year after being selected in the first round, Naylor has assuaged initial concerns about his likelihood of sticking behind the plate. There are still some questions about his arm strength, but quick hands and athleticism have righted a lot of wrongs so far. Offensively, Naylor gave back some of his usefulness with both average and walk rate, yet the uptick in power production was encouraging. He's still years away from factoring into Cleveland's big-league plans. But there's plenty to like here.

Roberto Pérez C Born: 12/23/88 Age: 31 Bats: R Throws: R Height: 5'11" Weight: 220 Origin: Round 33, 2008 Draft (#1011 overall)

YEAR	TEAM	LVL	AGE	PA	R	2B	3B	HR	RBI	BB	K	SB	CS	AVG/OBP/SLG	DRC+	VORP	BABIP	BRR	FRAA	WARP
2017	CLE	MLB	28	248	22	12	0	8	38	26	71	0	1	.207/.291/.373	80	4.0	.266	-0.6	C(71): 19.8	2.5
2018	CLE	MLB	29	210	16	9	1	2	19	21	70	1	0	.168/.256/.263	52	-4.5	.257	-0.2	C(58): 11.1	0.9
2019	CLE	MLB	30	449	46	9	1	24	63	45	127	0	0	.239/.321/.452	100	24.0	.285	-1.1	C(118): 25.7	4.7
2020	CLE	MLB	31	420	47	15	1	16	51	46	122	1	1	.212/.303/.390	82	9.2	.268	-0.6	C 25	3.5

Comparables: Sal Fasano, Alex Avila, Chris Herrmann

If Francisco Lindor is the face of the Indians, Pérez might be the heart. The long-time backup backstop finally got a chance for regular reps last season, and emerged as a no-doubt starter. Pérez notched 449 trips to the plate, over 200 more than any previous season of his career, and more than doubled his career home-run total in the process. On the other side of the plate, Pérez was the second-best defender in baseball, per FRAA, behind only Austin Hedges. He led the league in blocking runs, and finished in the top three for runs saved via framing and throwing. Pérez, who signed a four-year, $9 million extension with two club options in 2017, was one of the 25 most valuable position players in baseball according to WARP. That's not an outcome anyone saw coming, but it's a welcomed one all the same.

YEAR	TEAM	P. COUNT	FRM RUNS	BLK RUNS	THRW RUNS	TOT RUNS
2017	CLE	9658	17.6	2.2	0.4	19.7
2018	CLE	7861	10.9	1.6	-0.2	12.1
2019	CLE	16272	15.5	8.8	1.5	25.6
2020	CLE	18552	18.2	4.6	2.5	25.2

Yasiel Puig RF Born: 12/07/90 Age: 29 Bats: R Throws: R Height: 6'2" Weight: 240 Origin: International Free Agent, 2012

YEAR	TEAM	LVL	AGE	PA	R	2B	3B	HR	RBI	BB	K	SB	CS	AVG/OBP/SLG	DRC+	VORP	BABIP	BRR	FRAA	WARP
2017	LAN	MLB	26	570	72	24	2	28	74	64	100	15	6	.263/.346/.487	119	27.1	.274	-4.3	RF(145): 9.0	3.1
2018	LAN	MLB	27	444	60	21	1	23	63	36	87	15	5	.267/.327/.494	120	23.7	.286	2.4	RF(118): -4.5	1.9
2019	CLE	MLB	28	207	25	15	1	2	23	21	44	5	2	.297/.377/.423	101	5.3	.380	-1.5	RF(48): 2.7	0.6
2019	CIN	MLB	28	404	51	15	1	22	61	23	89	14	5	.252/.302/.475	101	10.1	.272	-2.8	RF(98): 2.1	0.9
2020	*CLE*	*MLB*	*29*	*575*	*70*	*27*	*2*	*24*	*77*	*48*	*130*	*12*	*5*	*.260/.330/.457*	*106*	*9.3*	*.305*	*-2.3*	*RF 0*	*2.2*

Comparables: Travis Buck, Justin Upton, Jay Bruce

Just when you think you've seen everything Puig has to offer—an exciting play, a humorous celebration, a bewildering gaffe—he goes and delivers something like his Cleveland stint. Puig homered 24 times in 2019, the second-most of his career. Yet 22 of those came with the Reds; in 49 games with Cleveland, he cleared the fences twice, and instead prioritized hitting for average and getting on base. It was an odd, presumably intentional shift for someone heading to free agency—and one that, frankly, leaves us wondering what's coming next. That Puig, he's baseball's best at keeping us engaged.

José Ramírez 3B Born: 09/17/92 Age: 27 Bats: B Throws: R Height: 5'9" Weight: 190 Origin: International Free Agent, 2009

YEAR	TEAM	LVL	AGE	PA	R	2B	3B	HR	RBI	BB	K	SB	CS	AVG/OBP/SLG	DRC+	VORP	BABIP	BRR	FRAA	WARP
2017	CLE	MLB	24	645	107	56	6	29	83	52	69	17	5	.318/.374/.583	137	58.5	.319	0.2	3B(88): 6.0, 2B(71): -0.1	5.8
2018	CLE	MLB	25	698	110	38	4	39	105	106	80	34	6	.270/.387/.552	146	69.9	.252	5.2	3B(137): -3.5, 2B(16): -0.7	6.6
2019	CLE	MLB	26	542	68	33	3	23	83	52	74	24	4	.255/.327/.479	115	31.8	.256	2.6	3B(126): 2.4	3.6
2020	*CLE*	*MLB*	*27*	*560*	*71*	*33*	*2*	*25*	*79*	*54*	*75*	*18*	*5*	*.259/.334/.482*	*113*	*24.4*	*.261*	*1.0*	*3B -2*	*2.3*

Comparables: Zoilo Versalles, Francisco Lindor, Wilmer Flores

There's an urban legend contained within Cleveland's fan base that Ramírez, world-renowned Mario Kart stud, went into a tailspin after suffering a shocking defeat at the hands of Shane Bieber. If that's true—and Lord knows it's probably not—he wasn't over the loss by the start of the 2019 campaign, as the former-All Star limped to a .212/.323/.349 line from August 1, 2018 to July 1, 2019. Yet Ramírez must've had a blue shell handy, because from that point forward he resumed pulling the ball and producing like an elite hitter—he slashed .321/.356/.722, and even returned late in the season from a broken hamate bone to homer twice in his first game back. We're not buying into the idea that Ramírez's play is connected with his pay ... but, just to be safe, Cleveland should institute a Yoshi court fine for anyone who makes an earnest attempt to defeat Ramírez.

Franmil Reyes DH Born: 07/07/95 Age: 24 Bats: R Throws: R Height: 6'5" Weight: 275 Origin: International Free Agent, 2012

YEAR	TEAM	LVL	AGE	PA	R	2B	3B	HR	RBI	BB	K	SB	CS	AVG/OBP/SLG	DRC+	VORP	BABIP	BRR	FRAA	WARP
2017	SAN	AA	21	566	79	27	1	25	102	48	134	4	4	.258/.322/.464	120	27.8	.298	-1.1	RF(89): 3.2	2.3
2018	ELP	AAA	22	250	50	11	1	16	52	37	59	0	0	.324/.428/.614	162	20.3	.382	1.9	RF(46): -2.2	2.3
2018	SDN	MLB	22	285	36	9	0	16	31	24	80	0	0	.280/.340/.498	112	14.8	.345	0.3	RF(75): -7.1	0.3
2019	SDN	MLB	23	354	43	9	0	27	46	29	93	0	0	.255/.314/.536	114	15.0	.268	0.4	RF(83): 1.4	1.6
2019	CLE	MLB	23	194	26	10	0	10	35	18	63	0	0	.237/.304/.468	106	4.7	.301	-0.8	RF(3): 0.6	0.4
2020	*CLE*	*MLB*	*24*	*525*	*73*	*24*	*1*	*34*	*89*	*45*	*147*	*1*	*1*	*.258/.323/.527*	*115*	*16.4*	*.299*	*-0.1*	*RF 0*	*1.7*

Comparables: Yorman Rodriguez, Randal Grichuk, Ronald Guzmán

It took Reyes 11 games to launch his first dinger after being shipped from San Diego to Cleveland. From that point on, he homered around once every three games, flirting with a .900 OPS down the stretch. Despite spreading out 37 home runs over two leagues, Reyes's huge power numbers didn't come with a side of sunshine and rainbows. Of 140 qualified hitters, nobody made less contact than he did, and only Javier Báez swung and missed more frequently. It's an issue that Reyes will need to address if he's ever going to make the leap to stardom. On the bright side, his hop to the AL will likely correspond with entry into the hallowed Full-Time DH Club, which is a positive for humanity.

───────────────── ★ ★ ★ *2020 Top 101 Prospect* **#98** ★ ★ ★ ─────────────────

Brayan Rocchio SS Born: 01/13/01 Age: 19 Bats: B Throws: R Height: 5'10" Weight: 150 Origin: International Free Agent, 2017

YEAR	TEAM	LVL	AGE	PA	R	2B	3B	HR	RBI	BB	K	SB	CS	AVG/OBP/SLG	DRC+	VORP	BABIP	BRR	FRAA	WARP
2018	DIN	RK	17	111	19	2	3	1	12	5	14	8	5	.323/.391/.434	136	9.7	.369	-1.0	SS(15): -0.2, 2B(8): 0.6	0.8
2018	CLT	RK	17	158	21	10	1	1	17	10	17	14	8	.343/.389/.448	161	15.0	.378	1.2	SS(26): 5.2, 3B(8): -1.1	2.0
2019	MHV	A-	18	295	33	12	3	5	27	20	40	14	8	.250/.310/.373	107	12.8	.276	-1.8	SS(62): 5.5, 2B(6): 0.6	1.8
2020	*CLE*	*MLB*	*19*	*251*	*24*	*11*	*1*	*5*	*25*	*17*	*53*	*9*	*5*	*.242/.301/.367*	*79*	*1.1*	*.293*	*-0.1*	*SS 2, 2B 0*	*0.3*

Comparables: Enrique Hernández, Amed Rosario, Juniel Querecuto

Rocchio was born just five months before the release of *The Fast and the Furious*, which is astounding because there's a decent chance those films continue to be made into his retirement—and that isn't a knock on his career prospects. A nitrous oxide boost for Rocchio's bat would be nice, as the Venezuelan's lumber is a little light on the pop, but even if the power doesn't come, he'll still be a top-flight defender with plus hit and run tools. It's definitely a profile worthy of a Corona at the family barbecue, or a public spat between Dwayne "The Rock" Johnson and Tyrese.

Carlos Santana 1B Born: 04/08/86 Age: 34 Bats: B Throws: R Height: 5'11" Weight: 210 Origin: International Free Agent, 2004

YEAR	TEAM	LVL	AGE	PA	R	2B	3B	HR	RBI	BB	K	SB	CS	AVG/OBP/SLG	DRC+	VORP	BABIP	BRR	FRAA	WARP
2017	CLE	MLB	31	667	90	37	3	23	79	88	94	5	1	.259/.363/.455	114	18.7	.274	-1.9	1B(140): 6.2, RF(7): 0.7	2.6
2018	PHI	MLB	32	679	82	28	2	24	86	110	93	2	1	.229/.352/.414	108	26.1	.231	0.2	1B(149): -0.7, 3B(19): 0.6	1.8
2019	CLE	MLB	33	686	110	30	1	34	93	108	108	4	0	.281/.397/.515	138	44.3	.293	1.1	1B(135): 3.9	4.8
2020	*CLE*	*MLB*	*34*	*595*	*80*	*28*	*1*	*26*	*82*	*94*	*104*	*5*	*2*	*.256/.376/.470*	*125*	*30.4*	*.276*	*-0.4*	*1B 1*	*3.3*

Comparables: Chris Iannetta, Duke Sims, Mike Napoli

Santana's one-year sabbatical in Philly was a typical Santana season. He smacked 24 homers, walked a ton and played solid defense at the cold corner. One distinguishing scene, however, was Santana destroying a television after seeing teammates playing Fortnite during the final series of the year. We know that virtual reality is the next big thing in training, but that entails swinging in front of a screen to improve—not swinging *at* it. Nonetheless, the act of destruction transferred new electricity to Santana's bat, and in 2019 he enjoyed the best offensive season of his career. He came out of the gates hot, slashing .297/.418/.540 before the break, permitting him his first All-Star Game appearance and the honor of starting in his home ballpark. Our guess is that Santana will fall back in line with his usual output: a good on-base percentage, 20-plus homers and zero destroyed televisions.

Ka'ai Tom OF Born: 05/29/94 Age: 26 Bats: L Throws: R Height: 5'9" Weight: 190 Origin: Round 5, 2015 Draft (#154 overall)

YEAR	TEAM	LVL	AGE	PA	R	2B	3B	HR	RBI	BB	K	SB	CS	AVG/OBP/SLG	DRC+	VORP	BABIP	BRR	FRAA	WARP
2017	LYN	A+	23	529	68	31	7	10	65	59	100	23	6	.254/.340/.418	120	31.8	.299	2.8	CF(47): -1.8, RF(35): -0.2	2.6
2018	AKR	AA	24	484	60	21	4	12	64	46	102	13	10	.245/.329/.399	108	26.3	.291	-0.3	CF(54): -1.4, RF(35): 9.5	2.7
2019	AKR	AA	25	343	50	12	6	14	42	43	73	3	2	.285/.386/.512	149	31.7	.335	2.2	RF(32): -3.0, CF(31): -6.2	1.7
2019	COH	AAA	25	211	33	15	4	9	44	21	53	2	3	.298/.370/.564	131	14.6	.370	0.7	LF(19): -0.6, RF(16): 0.5	1.4
2020	CLE	MLB	26	251	29	12	2	10	33	23	68	5	2	.245/.322/.444	102	8.7	.309	0.0	CF -1, RF 0	0.9

Comparables: Andy Parrino, Melky Mesa, Skye Bolt

Here's a cool story about Tom. He was born in Hawaii and played both baseball and football in high school. It was on the gridiron that he was teammates with former Heisman Trophy winner Marcus Mariota. Another cool story about Tom: Ka'ai is his middle name and his given name is actually Blaze. One more cool story about Tom: he tore through two minor-league levels last season, smacking more homers than all but three other Cleveland minor leaguers while playing strong center-field defense. Provided he can keep his swing-and-miss in check, he's likely to debut in 2020.

★ ★ ★ *2020 Top 101 Prospect* **#58** ★ ★ ★

George Valera OF Born: 11/13/00 Age: 19 Bats: L Throws: L Height: 5'10" Weight: 160 Origin: International Free Agent, 2017

YEAR	TEAM	LVL	AGE	PA	R	2B	3B	HR	RBI	BB	K	SB	CS	AVG/OBP/SLG	DRC+	VORP	BABIP	BRR	FRAA	WARP
2019	MHV	A-	18	188	22	7	1	8	29	29	52	6	2	.236/.356/.446	132	11.8	.296	-0.3	CF(25): 0.7, RF(11): -3.5	1.1
2019	LKC	A	18	26	1	0	1	0	3	2	9	0	2	.087/.192/.174	35	-3.4	.143	-1.0	RF(3): 1.2, LF(2): 1.6	0.0
2020	CLE	MLB	19	251	24	11	1	7	26	22	85	3	2	.202/.278/.344	68	-2.7	.290	-0.5	CF -1, RF -1	-0.5

Comparables: Ronald Acuña Jr., Carson Kelly, Victor Robles

You know the adage, about how development isn't linear? Good, because Valera is evidence of that. His 2019 statistics were—to be charitable—not what you want. It mostly doesn't matter though because of his physical traits. Scouts rave about his projectible hit tool and his chances of posting a .300 average with 25 or so home runs at maturity. Oftentimes potential is never realized, or is lost to the heavens through injury or other reasons beyond our understanding—call it the angel's share if you'd like. But it's too early to say that will be the case here. As such, keep an eye on Valera—just not while driving.

Bradley Zimmer CF Born: 11/27/92 Age: 27 Bats: L Throws: R Height: 6'5" Weight: 220 Origin: Round 1, 2014 Draft (#21 overall)

YEAR	TEAM	LVL	AGE	PA	R	2B	3B	HR	RBI	BB	K	SB	CS	AVG/OBP/SLG	DRC+	VORP	BABIP	BRR	FRAA	WARP
2017	COH	AAA	24	144	22	11	2	5	14	14	43	9	3	.294/.371/.532	129	9.9	.405	-0.6	CF(26): 3.6, RF(8): 0.5	1.2
2017	CLE	MLB	24	332	41	15	2	8	39	26	99	18	1	.241/.307/.385	70	7.3	.328	1.6	CF(97): 9.5	1.0
2018	COH	AAA	25	28	1	0	0	1	1	1	11	1	0	.148/.179/.259	8	-2.4	.200	0.1	CF(5): -0.2	-0.2
2018	CLE	MLB	25	114	14	5	0	2	9	7	44	4	1	.226/.281/.330	49	-0.7	.367	1.4	CF(34): 5.4	0.4
2019	COH	AAA	26	26	5	1	1	1	2	3	6	2	0	.364/.440/.636	112	4.5	.467	0.6	CF(6): -0.1	0.2
2019	CLE	MLB	26	14	1	0	0	0	0	1	7	0	0	.000/.071/.000	71	-0.1	.000	0.3	RF(4): -0.4, CF(2): 0.2	0.0
2020	CLE	MLB	27	105	11	4	0	3	12	9	35	5	1	.219/.303/.373	83	1.2	.314	0.2	CF 2, RF 0	0.3

Comparables: Jordan Danks, Kirk Nieuwenhuis, Dexter Fowler

Zimmer's injury woes the past few seasons would not fit comfortably within the allotted run time of a "House" episode. He wedged his way into Cleveland's long-term plans with a pretty good, if not awe-inspiring, rookie campaign, before having since succumbed to several maulings by the injury bug. There was a bruised rib, then shoulder surgery, then recovery from shoulder surgery. He's appeared in just 43 games over the past two years as a result, and hasn't rapped a hit since June 2018—even Vanilla Ice is like, c'mon, buddy. The tools for Zimmer are still there, it's really all about the durability.

PITCHERS

Logan Allen LHP Born: 05/23/97 Age: 23 Bats: R Throws: L Height: 6'3" Weight: 200 Origin: Round 8, 2015 Draft (#231 overall)

YEAR	TEAM	LVL	AGE	W	L	SV	G	GS	IP	H	HR	BB/9	K/9	K	GB%	BABIP	WHIP	ERA	DRA	WARP	MPH	FB%	WHF	CSP
2017	FTW	A	20	5	4	0	13	13	68¹	49	1	3.4	11.2	85	43%	.294	1.10	2.11	2.52	2.2				
2017	LEL	A+	20	2	5	0	11	10	56²	60	2	2.9	9.1	57	50%	.352	1.38	3.97	3.95	0.9				
2018	SAN	AA	21	10	6	0	20	19	121	89	7	2.8	9.3	125	43%	.269	1.05	2.75	3.22	3.0				
2018	ELP	AAA	21	4	0	0	5	5	27²	21	4	4.2	8.5	26	38%	.236	1.23	1.63	3.24	0.7				
2019	ELP	AAA	22	4	3	0	13	13	57²	61	8	3.4	9.8	63	47%	.338	1.44	5.15	3.84	1.6				
2019	COH	AAA	22	1	1	0	5	5	22¹	31	6	4.8	7.3	18	24%	.362	1.93	7.66	8.48	-0.4				
2019	SDN	MLB	22	2	3	0	8	4	25¹	33	4	4.6	5.0	14	54%	.341	1.82	6.75	6.71	-0.3	95.2	48.7	10	46.6
2019	CLE	MLB	22	0	0	0	1	0	2¹	3	0	0.0	11.6	3	17%	.500	1.29	0.00	8.06	-0.1	96.0	42.5	12.5	52.4
2020	CLE	MLB	23	5	6	0	41	11	88	99	14	3.8	6.9	68	43%	.310	1.54	5.47	5.39	0.1	95.2	49.8	10.6	48.8

Comparables: Brett Cecil, Peter Lambert, Stephen Gonsalves

Replacing an outspoken righty is always a tall task. Ask Logan Roy. Another Logan, Sr. Allen, was faced with that challenge after being acquired as part of a three-team deal that also involved Trevor Bauer and Yasiel Puig. Allen's rookie exploits didn't go well, but it could've been worse. It should get better, too. He pairs a mid-90s heater with a plus changeup and more than enough strike-throwing ability to profile as at least at No. 4 type. Cleveland has gotten more mileage than most out of that type—he just needs to cruise on the mound and not off somewhere with Waystar Royco.

Shane Bieber RHP Born: 05/31/95 Age: 25 Bats: R Throws: R Height: 6'3" Weight: 200 Origin: Round 4, 2016 Draft (#122 overall)

YEAR	TEAM	LVL	AGE	W	L	SV	G	GS	IP	H	HR	BB/9	K/9	K	GB%	BABIP	WHIP	ERA	DRA	WARP	MPH	FB%	WHF	CSP
2017	LKC	A	22	2	3	0	5	5	29	34	1	0.3	9.6	31	45%	.375	1.21	3.10	3.93	0.5				
2017	LYN	A+	22	6	1	0	14	14	90	95	5	0.4	8.2	82	50%	.340	1.10	3.10	3.99	1.3				
2017	AKR	AA	22	2	1	0	9	9	54¹	56	2	0.8	8.1	49	50%	.331	1.12	2.32	3.49	1.1				
2018	AKR	AA	23	3	0	0	5	5	31	26	1	0.3	8.7	30	48%	.278	0.87	1.16	2.40	1.1				
2018	COH	AAA	23	3	1	0	8	8	48²	30	3	1.1	8.7	47	56%	.225	0.74	1.66	2.30	1.8				
2018	CLE	MLB	23	11	5	0	20	19	114²	130	13	1.8	9.3	118	46%	.356	1.33	4.55	3.32	2.6	94.8	57.4	12.3	51.2
2019	CLE	MLB	24	15	8	0	34	33	214¹	186	31	1.7	10.9	259	45%	.296	1.05	3.28	3.68	4.9	94.6	45.8	14.7	45.1
2020	CLE	MLB	25	12	8	0	29	29	178	162	24	2.2	10.8	213	45%	.310	1.16	3.26	3.60	3.9	94.4	50.5	14.3	49

Comparables: Danny Salazar, Joe Musgrove, Yonny Chirinos

Everyone missed on Bieber, in a sense. He was pegged as a control-over-stuff pitcher as a prospect, a fancy way of saying "potential back-end starter." Cleveland even seemed open to trading him shortly after his big-league debut, only to have at least one offer for a young outfielder rebuked. Yet Bieber added to his heater, chucked his slider a little harder and recast himself as a 200-inning ace in 2019. His finished second in the league in innings, and third in strikeouts. That's decent. Bieber even won All-Star Game MVP honors—pleasing the hometown crowd. If 2019 is any indication, Bieber might well follow in Corey Kluber's footsteps as a late-bloomer who exceeds expectations. He seems well on his way.

Carlos Carrasco RHP Born: 03/21/87 Age: 33 Bats: R Throws: R Height: 6'4" Weight: 224 Origin: International Free Agent, 2003

YEAR	TEAM	LVL	AGE	W	L	SV	G	GS	IP	H	HR	BB/9	K/9	K	GB%	BABIP	WHIP	ERA	DRA	WARP	MPH	FB%	WHF	CSP
2017	CLE	MLB	30	18	6	0	32	32	200	173	21	2.1	10.2	226	47%	.307	1.10	3.29	2.79	6.2	96.7	48.9	14.5	47.5
2018	CLE	MLB	31	17	10	0	32	30	192	173	21	2.0	10.8	231	48%	.315	1.12	3.38	2.91	5.3	95.8	44.9	16.5	45.9
2019	CLE	MLB	32	6	7	1	23	12	80	92	18	1.8	10.8	96	42%	.354	1.35	5.29	5.44	0.2	96.0	46	16.2	46.4
2020	CLE	MLB	33	9	6	0	23	23	129	119	18	2.3	10.6	153	45%	.308	1.18	3.46	3.78	2.6	95.1	45.9	15.6	46

Comparables: Curt Schilling, Michael Bowden, Collin McHugh

It's not always about baseball; in fact, it shouldn't be. After sputtering to start the year, Carrasco complained of sluggishness and fatigue—something just wasn't right. He was subsequently shut down in late May, due to a blood condition that was later revealed to be leukemia. His early-season struggles were placed in perspective as he entered his next battle, with a more fearsome foe than big-league hitters.

In July, MLB featured Carrasco as part of the All-Star festivities in Cleveland, where the hometown fans and the baseball world, as well as humans with heart could show their support during the All-Star Game's annual "Stand Up to Cancer" showcase in a fitting tribute to a beloved teammate and player. Awards are generally silly, but Carrasco's humanitarianism earned him the 2019 Roberto Clemente Award, an honor bestowed upon the player that "best exemplifies the game of baseball, sportsmanship, community involvement and the individual's contribution to his team." It's hard to imagine a more suitable champion for the cause. To wit, Carrasco spent time during his recovery helping underprivileged families in need.

On a more trivial note, Carrasco was even able to follow through on his promise to return to the bump in 2019, hitting 99 mph on the gun with regularity in a handful of September relief appearances. It wasn't vintage Carrasco by any stretch, as he had spotty control and struggled to keep the ball in the yard—in retrospect giving high-leverage, playoff-chasing innings to someone who had been preoccupied with fighting for his life may have not been the best strategy—but that's hardly the point.

It's difficult to predict his 2020 outlook with any certainty, but it doesn't really matter, because it's not always about baseball, and Carrasco's 2019 season can only be considered a rousing triumph.

Adam Cimber RHP Born: 08/15/90 Age: 29 Bats: R Throws: R Height: 6'4" Weight: 195 Origin: Round 9, 2013 Draft (#268 overall)

YEAR	TEAM	LVL	AGE	W	L	SV	G	GS	IP	H	HR	BB/9	K/9	K	GB%	BABIP	WHIP	ERA	DRA	WARP	MPH	FB%	WHF	CSP
2017	SAN	AA	26	1	1	1	12	0	16	12	1	1.1	7.3	13	48%	.244	0.88	2.81	3.26	0.3				
2017	ELP	AAA	26	4	1	4	37	2	64²	51	10	1.1	7.2	52	55%	.233	0.91	2.92	1.99	2.4				
2018	SDN	MLB	27	3	5	0	42	0	48¹	42	2	1.9	9.5	51	53%	.315	1.08	3.17	3.92	0.6	89.2	75.8	12.7	59.1
2018	CLE	MLB	27	0	3	0	28	0	20	26	3	3.2	3.2	7	68%	.324	1.65	4.05	6.17	-0.3	89.4	73.5	7.4	50.4
2019	CLE	MLB	28	6	3	1	68	0	56²	56	6	3.0	6.5	41	56%	.287	1.32	4.45	5.26	0.1	88.0	67.8	10.3	49.7
2020	CLE	MLB	29	3	3	2	55	0	58	64	12	2.3	6.7	43	55%	.290	1.35	4.97	5.15	0.0	88.0	71.3	10.6	52.6

Comparables: Chasen Bradford, Nick Wittgren, Robby Scott

If you're playing limbo, don't invite Cimber. If you're in an argument, be careful—Cimber won't take the high road. If you find low-hanging fruit delicious, you better pick it quickly because…well, you get it. The other reliever acquired in the Brad Hand-Francisco Mejía trade, Cimber has overcome a mediocre strikeout rate to become a trusted high-leverage specialist. Just don't ask him to grab something off the top shelf—or face a left-handed batter.

Aaron Civale RHP Born: 06/12/95 Age: 25 Bats: R Throws: R Height: 6'2" Weight: 215 Origin: Round 3, 2016 Draft (#92 overall)

YEAR	TEAM	LVL	AGE	W	L	SV	G	GS	IP	H	HR	BB/9	K/9	K	GB%	BABIP	WHIP	ERA	DRA	WARP	MPH	FB%	WHF	CSP
2017	LKC	A	22	2	4	0	10	10	57	64	2	0.8	8.4	53	55%	.358	1.21	4.58	4.73	0.4				
2017	LYN	A+	22	11	2	0	17	17	107²	96	11	0.8	7.4	88	49%	.276	0.98	2.59	3.53	2.2				
2018	AKR	AA	23	5	7	0	21	21	106¹	115	12	1.8	6.6	78	49%	.308	1.28	3.89	5.03	0.4				
2019	AKR	AA	24	4	0	0	5	5	30¹	26	3	1.8	7.1	24	42%	.264	1.05	2.67	4.88	0.0				
2019	COH	AAA	24	3	1	0	8	8	42¹	38	4	1.9	9.8	46	40%	.296	1.11	2.13	3.01	1.5				
2019	CLE	MLB	24	3	4	0	10	10	57²	44	4	2.5	7.2	46	42%	.250	1.04	2.34	5.13	0.4	94.1	38.5	9.7	41.8
2020	CLE	MLB	25	8	7	0	23	23	125	126	21	3.0	7.3	102	42%	.286	1.34	4.43	4.64	1.3	93.8	39.5	9.9	42.8

Comparables: Tyler Wilson, Anthony DeSclafani, Dario Agrazal

Civale went 10 starts before giving up more than two earned runs in an outing, but he didn't truly enter the zeitgeist until an umpire tweeted a poorly spelled attempt at "civil." Ah, well. While Civale might not have been anyone's first choice to help prop up a patchwork rotation, he led Cleveland's starters in ERA. How? By leaning heavily on an über-spinny breaking ball and a keen knack for evading loud contact. Whether or not that proves sustainable, Civale has displayed a stinginess on baserunners via the walk, which should help keep him in the mix as a back-end starter for the foreseeable future.

Emmanuel Clase RHP Born: 03/18/98 Age: 22 Bats: R Throws: R Height: 6'2" Weight: 206 Origin: International Free Agent, 2015

YEAR	TEAM	LVL	AGE	W	L	SV	G	GS	IP	H	HR	BB/9	K/9	K	GB%	BABIP	WHIP	ERA	DRA	WARP	MPH	FB%	WHF	CSP
2017	SDP	RK	19	2	4	0	9	6	35²	40	4	5.6	10.6	42	48%	.360	1.74	5.30	6.12	-0.1				
2018	SPO	A-	20	1	1	12	22	0	28¹	16	0	1.9	8.6	27	62%	.222	0.78	0.64	2.25	0.9				
2019	DEB	A+	21	2	0	1	6	0	7	4	0	1.3	14.1	11	77%	.308	0.71	0.00	2.98	0.1				
2019	FRI	AA	21	1	2	11	33	1	37²	34	1	1.9	9.3	39	62%	.314	1.12	3.35	3.70	0.4				
2019	TEX	MLB	21	2	3	1	21	1	23¹	20	2	2.3	8.1	21	59%	.281	1.11	2.31	3.91	0.4	101.1	78.8	12.2	49.4
2020	CLE	MLB	22	2	2	4	45	0	48	46	7	3.5	8.8	47	55%	.296	1.34	4.09	4.29	0.5	101.1	82.2	12.7	51.5

Comparables: Yennsy Diaz, Jake Newberry, Michael Feliz

Question: how did Clase learn to throw a 102 mph cutter? Allow us to answer your question with a question: How did Beethoven learn to compose melody? How did Superman learn to fly? How did Elvis Presley learn to do that thing with his hips? How did Bob Beamon learn to… also fly? How did Jason Giambi learn to apply hair gel? How did that one lady from the memes learn to make her eyes pop out like that? How did shows like NCIS or Criminal Minds or House become so popular despite having more or less the exact same plot every week? What we're saying here is that an answer definitely exists, but we remain unconvinced that knowing the answer at the expense of the mystery would add to the enjoyment in any material way. Another mystery: will Emmanuel Clase…close? (that pun only works in print; Clase is pronounced Clah-SAY, so if you say it out loud, you have to say it like "will Clah-SAY … CLOH-ZAY?!" and you have to make dad-joke face when you do it.)

Mike Clevinger RHP Born: 12/21/90 Age: 29 Bats: R Throws: R Height: 6'4" Weight: 215 Origin: Round 4, 2011 Draft (#135 overall)

YEAR	TEAM	LVL	AGE	W	L	SV	G	GS	IP	H	HR	BB/9	K/9	K	GB%	BABIP	WHIP	ERA	DRA	WARP	MPH	FB%	WHF	CSP
2017	COH	AAA	26	3	2	0	7	7	34	28	3	3.7	10.1	38	40%	.298	1.24	2.65	3.48	0.8				
2017	CLE	MLB	26	12	6	0	27	21	121²	92	13	4.4	10.1	137	40%	.274	1.25	3.11	3.61	2.6	94.7	53.5	13.1	42.7
2018	CLE	MLB	27	13	8	0	32	32	200	164	21	3.0	9.3	207	41%	.280	1.15	3.02	3.52	4.1	96.2	52.9	12.8	48.8
2019	CLE	MLB	28	13	4	0	21	21	126	96	10	2.6	12.1	169	41%	.306	1.06	2.71	3.32	3.3	97.7	51.2	16.1	45.9
2020	CLE	MLB	29	11	8	0	28	28	162	136	21	3.7	12.1	219	42%	.308	1.24	3.34	3.57	3.6	95.7	52.4	14	46.1

Comparables: Domingo Germán, Mike Hauschild, Chad Green

To paraphrase Led Zeppelin, Cleveland sings loud for the sunshine while their opponents pray hard for the rain. Clevinger had his finest season as a big-leaguer, twirling 99-mph heaters and swing-and-miss sliders; setting new career-bests in ERA and strikeout-to-walk ratio. The only blemish was the fact he was limited to 21 starts due to a pair of trips to the injured list: once for a sprained ankle, another for a strained back. Otherwise? Nary a cloud in the sky.

Daniel Espino RHP Born: 01/05/01 Age: 19 Bats: R Throws: R Height: 6'2" Weight: 205 Origin: Round 1, 2019 Draft (#24 overall)

YEAR	TEAM	LVL	AGE	W	L	SV	G	GS	IP	H	HR	BB/9	K/9	K	GB%	BABIP	WHIP	ERA	DRA	WARP	MPH	FB%	WHF	CSP
2019	CLE	RK	18	0	1	0	6	6	13²	7	1	3.3	10.5	16	50%	.207	0.88	1.98	1.65	0.6				
2019	MHV	A-	18	0	2	0	3	3	10	9	1	4.5	16.2	18	32%	.381	1.40	6.30	2.96	0.3				
2020	CLE	MLB	19	2	2	0	33	0	35	36	6	3.7	9.3	36	38%	.311	1.43	4.75	4.93	0.1				

Comparables: Pedro Avila, Jake Thompson, Jenrry Mejia

Espino was Cleveland's first pick in June's draft and the proud recipient of a $2.5 million signing bonus (enough shells to convince him he didn't really want to have to find his way around LSU's campus). He's on the smaller side, but makes up for it with extreme flexibility and arm speed. In the past, Espino has touched triple digits with his heater. In the future, he might pair the fastball with two high-quality secondary offerings. Expect the slow-and-low treatment, but Espino is otherwise one to know.

Brad Hand LHP   Born: 03/20/90   Age: 30   Bats: L   Throws: L   Height: 6'3"   Weight: 220   Origin: Round 2, 2008 Draft (#52 overall)

YEAR	TEAM	LVL	AGE	W	L	SV	G	GS	IP	H	HR	BB/9	K/9	K	GB%	BABIP	WHIP	ERA	DRA	WARP	MPH	FB%	WHF	CSP
2017	SDN	MLB	27	3	4	21	72	0	79¹	54	9	2.3	11.8	104	46%	.263	0.93	2.16	3.03	1.9	95.5	51.1	14.1	46.1
2018	SDN	MLB	28	2	4	24	41	0	44¹	33	5	3.0	13.2	65	48%	.298	1.08	3.05	3.15	0.9	96.4	44.2	13.6	50
2018	CLE	MLB	28	0	1	8	28	0	27²	19	3	4.2	13.3	41	44%	.286	1.16	2.28	3.47	0.5	95.7	48.1	13.2	52.7
2019	CLE	MLB	29	6	4	34	60	0	57¹	53	6	2.8	13.2	84	28%	.362	1.24	3.30	4.24	0.7	95.0	45.8	14.6	49.6
2020	CLE	MLB	30	3	3	34	55	0	58	51	9	3.2	12.0	78	36%	.310	1.22	3.58	3.84	0.9	94.8	47.1	14	49

Comparables: Randall Delgado, Brett Cecil, Drew Pomeranz

In July 2018, Cleveland pondered, "How do we get the hand?" Just once in their existence, they wanted hand—but they had no hand. No hand at all. And let us tell you something, a team without a hand is not a team. Upon acquiring Hand, the team enjoyed a few months of dominant relief work and seemed set at closer for a few seasons longer. Cleveland enjoyed Hand through the first half of 2019, too, as he punched out 55 batters in 37 innings of work en route to his third consecutive All-Star Game appearance. Cleveland had so much hand, they were coming out of their gloves. The second half, however, was far less kind. The strikeout numbers remained lofty, but his walk rate shot up. Hand also served up twice as many dingers in the second half than the first half—despite having thrown nearly half as many innings—and hitters slashed .310/.383/.512 against him. (Yoán Moncada hit .315/.367/.548, for reference.) Hand was then limited to two appearances in Cleveland's last 20 appearances due to arm fatigue. He has up to two years remaining of team control, but for the first time in a while there's reason for skepticism about what those seasons will entail.

Ethan Hankins RHP   Born: 05/23/00   Age: 20   Bats: R   Throws: R   Height: 6'6"   Weight: 200   Origin: Round 1C, 2018 Draft (#35 overall)

YEAR	TEAM	LVL	AGE	W	L	SV	G	GS	IP	H	HR	BB/9	K/9	K	GB%	BABIP	WHIP	ERA	DRA	WARP	MPH	FB%	WHF	CSP
2019	MHV	A-	19	0	0	0	9	8	38²	23	1	4.2	10.0	43	61%	.232	1.06	1.40	3.30	0.8				
2019	LKC	A	19	0	3	0	5	5	21¹	20	3	5.1	11.8	28	49%	.340	1.50	4.64	5.49	-0.1				
2020	CLE	MLB	20	2	2	0	33	0	35	35	6	3.7	8.4	33	49%	.297	1.41	4.67	4.87	0.1				

Comparables: Pedro Avila, Joe Ross, Jake Thompson

Bringing along a starting pitching prospect is a little like teaching a kid how to ride a bike: the main goal is to prevent injury. Hankins was a candidate for the top spot in the 2018 draft before a shoulder injury cost him a couple ticks of velocity and his chance at going first overall. Cleveland scooped him up later in the first round and has kept on his training wheels thus far, permitting him to just 63 innings in his first season two seasons as a pro. Hankins exceeded five innings of work just once in 2019, but gaudy strikeout numbers bode well for his future prospects as a potential top-end starter (though not his, well, gaudy walk totals). With linear progression, next season should see him pedaling furiously with GM Mike Chernoff running beside the bike and steadying the back of his seat before finally letting go. In baseball terms, that means we should get to see Hankins pump a high-90s heater while also baffling hitters with a pair of strong secondaries.

★   ★   ★   *2020 Top 101 Prospect* **#101** ★   ★   ★

James Karinchak RHP   Born: 09/22/95   Age: 24   Bats: R   Throws: R   Height: 6'3"   Weight: 230   Origin: Round 9, 2017 Draft (#282 overall)

YEAR	TEAM	LVL	AGE	W	L	SV	G	GS	IP	H	HR	BB/9	K/9	K	GB%	BABIP	WHIP	ERA	DRA	WARP	MPH	FB%	WHF	CSP
2017	MHV	A-	21	2	2	0	10	6	23¹	30	1	3.5	12.0	31	30%	.468	1.67	5.79	7.07	-0.5				
2018	LKC	A	22	3	0	1	7	0	11¹	8	0	5.6	15.9	20	55%	.400	1.32	0.79	3.41	0.2				
2018	LYN	A+	22	1	1	13	25	0	27	14	1	5.7	15.0	45	40%	.295	1.15	1.00	2.77	0.7				
2018	AKR	AA	22	0	1	0	10	0	10¹	7	1	10.5	13.9	16	29%	.300	1.84	2.61	5.59	-0.1				
2019	AKR	AA	23	0	0	6	10	0	10	2	0	1.8	21.6	24	56%	.222	0.40	0.00	1.80	0.3				
2019	COH	AAA	23	1	1	2	17	0	17¹	14	2	6.8	21.8	42	48%	.571	1.56	4.67	2.12	0.7				
2019	CLE	MLB	23	0	0	0	5	0	5¹	3	0	1.7	13.5	8	38%	.231	0.75	1.69	3.89	0.1	97.7	56.4	18.1	47.8
2020	CLE	MLB	24	2	2	0	45	0	48	42	7	4.5	8.3	44	42%	.270	1.38	4.08	4.27	0.5	97.5	58.1	18.6	49.2

Comparables: Jensen Lewis, Rogelio Armenteros, Aaron Blair

In 1998, Irvine Welsh wrote *Filth*, a crime novel that was later turned into a film starring James McAvoy. The book was about a hallucinating misanthrope who solved crimes. The title, however, would be apt for a book (probably a novella) about Karinchak's curveball—an offering who has already been featured plenty on the smallest screen via Pitching Ninja's acclaimed Twitter account. He used the curveball to great success in 2019, punching out 74 guys in just over 30 innings of minor-league work and earning a late-season promotion to the majors. His strikeout numbers weren't as prodigious in Cleveland, albeit in a small sample, but they were still super good. Something that bodes well for him should it continue: his 16 percent swinging-strike rate would have placed him among the league's best.

Triston McKenzie RHP   Born: 08/02/97   Age: 22   Bats: R   Throws: R   Height: 6'5"   Weight: 165   Origin: Round 1, 2015 Draft (#42 overall)

YEAR	TEAM	LVL	AGE	W	L	SV	G	GS	IP	H	HR	BB/9	K/9	K	GB%	BABIP	WHIP	ERA	DRA	WARP	MPH	FB%	WHF	CSP
2017	LYN	A+	19	12	6	0	25	25	143	105	14	2.8	11.7	186	43%	.283	1.05	3.46	3.21	3.5				
2018	AKR	AA	20	7	4	0	16	16	90²	63	8	2.8	8.6	87	34%	.234	1.00	2.68	3.05	2.4				
2020	CLE	MLB	22	2	2	0	33	0	35	35	6	3.2	8.9	35	36%	.303	1.37	4.51	4.72	0.2				

Comparables: Adrian Morejon, Chris Tillman, Arodys Vizcaíno

Everything is skinny these days—jeans, margaritas, even pitchers. McKenzie is charitably listed at 165 pounds despite a 6-foot-5 frame. His lithe nature has caused concerns in the past about his viability as a starter—scouts tend to like to see pitchers with broad shoulders and developed frames, believing those pitchers are better equipped to handle a rigorous workload. Those worries aren't going anyway anytime soon. He was shut down with a back injury in early March, and never returned to make a start, giving him two consecutive injury-plagued years. He's still just 22, so there's plenty of book left to be written. But another thin year will leave him with slim chances of remaining a starter.

Tyler Olson LHP   Born: 10/02/89   Age: 30   Bats: R   Throws: L   Height: 6'3"   Weight: 205   Origin: Round 7, 2013 Draft (#207 overall)

YEAR	TEAM	LVL	AGE	W	L	SV	G	GS	IP	H	HR	BB/9	K/9	K	GB%	BABIP	WHIP	ERA	DRA	WARP	MPH	FB%	WHF	CSP
2017	COH	AAA	27	2	0	2	34	0	42	28	7	2.6	11.6	54	43%	.241	0.95	3.21	2.27	1.4				
2017	CLE	MLB	27	1	0	1	30	0	20	13	0	2.7	8.1	18	54%	.250	0.95	0.00	3.90	0.3	90.6	39.8	10.7	49.2
2018	COH	AAA	28	2	1	1	17	0	12¹	8	0	2.2	13.1	18	42%	.308	0.89	3.65	2.60	0.4				
2018	CLE	MLB	28	2	1	0	43	0	27¹	26	4	4.0	13.2	40	42%	.355	1.39	4.94	2.74	0.7	90.8	47.6	15.3	45.5
2019	CLE	MLB	29	1	1	0	39	0	30²	34	3	4.7	8.2	28	47%	.341	1.63	4.40	6.40	-0.3	88.8	44.9	11.5	51.7
2020	CLE	MLB	30	2	2	0	33	0	35	32	6	2.8	8.3	32	43%	.275	1.23	3.81	4.14	0.4	89.1	44.8	12.6	48.8

Comparables: Robby Scott, Sam Freeman, Buddy Baumann

Olson achieved perfection in 2017, when he maintained a 0.00 ERA through 20 innings of work. Rather than walk away at the peak of his profession, he chose to pitch on. You can probably guess how things have gone for him since—hint: worse. Olson is an effective specialist, but with Oliver Pérez in tow he was used against considerably more right-handers. Hence, ugly surface-level numbers. To make matters worse, he was shut down in August with a case of shingles. In honor of Olson's vintage fastball, we'll snark here and say we haven't seen a two-year fall from grace like this since Buster Douglas.

Oliver Pérez LHP   Born: 08/15/81   Age: 38   Bats: L   Throws: L   Height: 6'3"   Weight: 225   Origin: International Free Agent, 1999

YEAR	TEAM	LVL	AGE	W	L	SV	G	GS	IP	H	HR	BB/9	K/9	K	GB%	BABIP	WHIP	ERA	DRA	WARP	MPH	FB%	WHF	CSP
2017	WAS	MLB	35	0	0	1	50	0	33	32	4	3.3	10.6	39	32%	.333	1.33	4.64	6.18	-0.4	94.8	57.3	11	53.6
2018	SWB	AAA	36	1	0	0	16	0	14	17	1	1.9	9.6	15	33%	.421	1.43	2.57	5.58	-0.1				
2018	CLE	MLB	36	1	1	0	51	0	32¹	17	1	1.9	12.0	43	46%	.239	0.74	1.39	2.61	0.9	94.1	50.9	16	52.2
2019	CLE	MLB	37	2	4	1	67	0	40²	38	5	2.7	10.6	48	46%	.314	1.23	3.98	4.28	0.5	94.2	51	13.8	51.5
2020	CLE	MLB	38	2	2	0	45	0	48	38	6	2.7	10.4	55	40%	.274	1.10	3.01	3.36	1.0	92.8	51.2	13.3	50.9

Comparables: Al Leiter, Francisco Liriano, Scott Kazmir

On October 23, 2001, Apple revolutionized the music industry—and, probably, the world—when the company released the first generation of the iPod. Pérez made his big-league debut eight months later. In the 18-plus years since, the two have appeared linked in some way. He had a "classic" run as a hotshot young starter; he "shuffled" around after repeated failure; and so on. Since 2012, he's had his "mini" phase as a left-handed specialist—an effective one, too; the kind left-handed hitters' moms warn them about. So solid is Pérez that Cleveland permitted his option to vest despite impending rule changes devaluing LOOGY. Much like the iPod you gifted your younger sibling, Pérez has survived a lot to get here—but he still works.

Zach Plesac RHP   Born: 01/21/95   Age: 25   Bats: R   Throws: R   Height: 6'3"   Weight: 220   Origin: Round 12, 2016 Draft (#362 overall)

YEAR	TEAM	LVL	AGE	W	L	SV	G	GS	IP	H	HR	BB/9	K/9	K	GB%	BABIP	WHIP	ERA	DRA	WARP	MPH	FB%	WHF	CSP
2017	MHV	A-	22	0	1	0	8	7	26	14	0	2.8	10.7	31	46%	.246	0.85	1.38	2.53	0.8				
2017	LKC	A	22	1	1	0	6	6	25	19	2	2.2	6.8	19	38%	.236	1.00	3.60	3.84	0.4				
2018	LYN	A+	23	8	5	0	22	22	122²	124	8	2.4	8.1	111	45%	.327	1.28	4.04	4.34	1.4				
2018	AKR	AA	23	3	1	0	4	4	22	19	1	1.6	8.6	21	30%	.300	1.05	2.45	3.44	0.5				
2019	AKR	AA	24	1	1	0	6	6	37¹	23	0	1.4	8.2	34	50%	.237	0.78	0.96	2.58	1.1				
2019	COH	AAA	24	3	1	0	4	4	26¹	19	2	1.0	10.6	31	31%	.270	0.84	2.73	2.31	1.1				
2019	CLE	MLB	24	8	6	0	21	21	115²	102	19	3.1	6.8	88	40%	.255	1.23	3.81	6.29	-0.6	95.7	50.6	10.3	49.8
2020	CLE	MLB	25	8	8	0	33	23	133	131	23	3.0	7.1	105	39%	.278	1.32	4.39	4.59	1.4	95.4	51.8	10.5	51

Comparables: Michael King, Erick Fedde, Tyler Duffey

In an ode to fellow Ball State University alumnus David Letterman, we were going to present the top 10 fun facts about Plesac's rookie year. Space limitations and self-respect led us to cut it down to three. Let's go. No. 1: Despite being thought of as a fastball-changeup pitcher coming up, the righty's slider generated his best whiff rate. No. 2: This is his first Annual appearance, in his fourth attempt. And No. 3: Yes, he's still Dan's nephew. This was nothing less than what it was. Pretend we just threw a pencil.

Jefry Rodriguez RHP   Born: 07/26/93   Age: 26   Bats: R   Throws: R   Height: 6'6"   Weight: 232   Origin: International Free Agent, 2012

YEAR	TEAM	LVL	AGE	W	L	SV	G	GS	IP	H	HR	BB/9	K/9	K	GB%	BABIP	WHIP	ERA	DRA	WARP	MPH	FB%	WHF	CSP
2017	POT	A+	23	4	3	0	12	10	57	44	2	3.0	8.1	51	53%	.278	1.11	3.32	3.38	1.3				
2018	HAR	AA	24	5	3	0	13	13	68	55	6	3.7	9.5	72	53%	.280	1.22	3.31	3.62	1.4				
2018	SYR	AAA	24	2	2	0	6	6	32²	32	0	4.1	8.3	30	47%	.333	1.44	3.58	4.56	0.4				
2018	WAS	MLB	24	3	3	0	14	8	52	43	8	6.4	6.8	39	46%	.240	1.54	5.71	7.35	-1.3	97.8	65	9.2	46.1
2019	COH	AAA	25	1	0	0	5	3	21²	16	1	4.6	6.6	16	54%	.250	1.25	4.15	4.21	0.5				
2019	CLE	MLB	25	1	5	0	10	8	46²	48	5	4.1	6.4	33	49%	.299	1.48	4.63	7.00	-0.6	96.7	70	8.7	46.9
2020	CLE	MLB	26	3	4	0	37	6	64	68	11	4.3	6.7	48	48%	.294	1.55	5.38	5.31	0.1	96.8	68.8	9.1	47.4

Comparables: Elvin Ramirez, Michael Blazek, Brad Peacock

Rodriguez was the first line of defense after Cleveland's rotation was chomped by the injury bug. He started eight games before succumbing to his own malady, a strained shoulder that sidelined him for most of the summer. The highlight of his year was likely his first three-start stretch where he gave up just five runs in 18 2/3 innings against the Royals, Marlins and White Sox—it's clear that he can succeed against Triple-A talent, is what we're saying. Rodriguez is likely to end up in the bullpen once he reaches the majors on a full-time basis due to a thin arsenal and a thinner feel for throwing quality strikes.

Danny Salazar RHP Born: 01/11/90 Age: 30 Bats: R Throws: R Height: 6'0" Weight: 195 Origin: International Free Agent, 2006

YEAR	TEAM	LVL	AGE	W	L	SV	G	GS	IP	H	HR	BB/9	K/9	K	GB%	BABIP	WHIP	ERA	DRA	WARP	MPH	FB%	WHF	CSP
2017	COH	AAA	27	1	1	0	2	2	9¹	6	3	4.8	12.5	13	37%	.188	1.18	2.89	3.79	0.2				
2017	CLE	MLB	27	5	6	0	23	19	103	94	14	3.8	12.7	145	39%	.343	1.34	4.28	3.54	2.3	97.5	59.7	17.3	45.8
2019	AKR	AA	29	0	1	0	5	4	8¹	8	1	6.5	7.6	7	58%	.280	1.68	5.40	6.07	-0.1				
2019	COH	AAA	29	0	0	0	2	2	7¹	4	0	2.5	13.5	11	40%	.267	0.82	0.00	2.14	0.3				
2019	CLE	MLB	29	0	1	0	1	1	4	4	2	6.8	4.5	2	42%	.200	1.75	4.50	7.32	-0.1	88.5	31.8	4.5	38.4
2020	CLE	MLB	30	1	2	0	33	0	35	42	16	4.4	8.1	32	37%	.270	1.68	8.22	6.87	-0.6	96.2	57.9	16.6	41.1

Comparables: Chris Archer, Rogelio Armenteros, Sonny Gray

Six years ago, the world was a vastly different place. Apple's earbuds had cords; reality TV game-show hosts stuck to reality TV game shows; and Mike Trout was getting robbed of MVP Awards (okay, maybe not *everything* has changed). Salazar, then a 23-year-old rookie, was chucking gas, punching out almost 31 percent of batters faced and starting the Wild Card Game. He was, in so many words, establishing himself as one of the most exciting young starters in the game. Now 29 years old, Salazar's body has failed him. He's thrown four innings the last two seasons, and he sat in the mid-80s in his most recent outing. Afterward, he requested time off to consider his career. If this is it for Salazar, it went by quickly—too quickly—but boy, oh boy, was he fun.

Nick Wittgren RHP Born: 05/29/91 Age: 29 Bats: R Throws: R Height: 6'2" Weight: 216 Origin: Round 9, 2012 Draft (#287 overall)

YEAR	TEAM	LVL	AGE	W	L	SV	G	GS	IP	H	HR	BB/9	K/9	K	GB%	BABIP	WHIP	ERA	DRA	WARP	MPH	FB%	WHF	CSP
2017	MIA	MLB	26	3	1	0	38	0	42¹	46	5	2.8	9.1	43	32%	.339	1.39	4.68	4.40	0.4	94.4	72.8	12	52.5
2018	NWO	AAA	27	0	5	2	25	0	29¹	34	4	2.5	10.4	34	46%	.353	1.43	5.22	4.24	0.3				
2018	MIA	MLB	27	2	1	0	32	0	33²	29	1	4.0	8.3	31	46%	.280	1.31	2.94	3.81	0.4	94.4	70	10.7	49
2019	CLE	MLB	28	5	1	4	55	0	57²	47	10	2.3	9.4	60	40%	.253	1.08	2.81	4.91	0.3	94.2	66.4	10.8	48.6
2020	CLE	MLB	29	3	3	2	55	0	58	55	9	2.8	8.6	56	39%	.287	1.26	3.89	4.13	0.7	93.6	68.8	11.1	49.7

Comparables: Chase Whitley, Preston Guilmet, Evan Scribner

Cleveland pulled a neat trick last February when it convinced the Marlins to take Jordan Milbrath in exchange for Wittgren. Why Miami agreed to the deal is beyond us. Milbrath is about 60 days younger, and has zero big-league experience to his credit. Conversely, Wittgren has now accumulated 185 innings of quality relief work. Sure, he's not impressive to watch—he mostly spams the opposition with his low-90s fastball—but there's something to be said about valuing results to aesthetics, especially when those results come this cheap.

Hunter Wood RHP Born: 08/12/93 Age: 26 Bats: R Throws: R Height: 6'1" Weight: 175 Origin: Round 29, 2013 Draft (#878 overall)

YEAR	TEAM	LVL	AGE	W	L	SV	G	GS	IP	H	HR	BB/9	K/9	K	GB%	BABIP	WHIP	ERA	DRA	WARP	MPH	FB%	WHF	CSP
2017	MNT	AA	23	4	4	0	12	12	70	68	7	3.1	8.7	68	38%	.319	1.31	4.76	4.66	0.4				
2017	DUR	AAA	23	3	1	0	19	6	53¹	54	8	3.4	7.9	47	46%	.299	1.39	4.39	5.25	0.2				
2017	TBA	MLB	23	0	0	0	1	0	0¹	0	0	0.0	0.0	0	0%	.000	0.00	0.00	4.12	0.0	89.9	40	0	38.2
2018	DUR	AAA	24	2	2	3	24	2	42	26	4	2.1	13.5	63	46%	.262	0.86	3.00	2.44	1.3				
2018	TBA	MLB	24	1	1	0	29	8	41	42	4	4.0	9.2	42	44%	.330	1.46	3.73	2.97	1.0	96.5	52.7	14.4	45.6
2019	DUR	AAA	25	1	0	1	8	0	10²	16	3	4.2	11.8	14	26%	.419	1.97	7.59	6.25	0.0				
2019	CLE	MLB	25	0	0	0	17	0	16¹	20	3	2.8	8.3	15	38%	.327	1.53	3.86	4.32	0.2	95.7	58.9	13	39.9
2019	TBA	MLB	25	1	1	1	19	2	29	26	4	2.2	7.4	24	31%	.265	1.14	2.48	6.59	-0.4	95.3	58.9	12.5	48
2020	CLE	MLB	26	2	2	0	40	0	42	42	8	3.3	8.9	42	35%	.292	1.35	4.56	4.73	0.2	95.5	57.2	13.6	44.3

Comparables: John Gant, Nick Tropeano, Luis Cessa

Wood is similar to Wittgren in two regards: 1) his results also don't match his aesthetics; and 2) he too was acquired for pennies from a Florida-based team. Both fit in fine, as Cleveland's bullpen finished third in ERA and last in average fastball velocity. It's worth wondering if there's a connection there. Velocity matters—we're not suggesting otherwise—but there are bargains to be had if teams are going to approach every low-to-mid-90s hurler with the indifference that the Rays and Marlins had toward Wood and Wittgren. Luck is said to be the residue of design, so credit Cleveland for being there to take advantage of other teams' biases.

LINEOUTS

Hitters

HITTER	POS	TEAM	LVL	AGE	PA	R	2B	3B	HR	RBI	BB	K	SB	CS	AVG/OBP/SLG	DRC+	VORP	BABIP	BRR	FRAA	WARP
Christian Arroyo	3B	DUR	AAA	24	134	21	9	1	8	29	12	26	1	0	.314/.381/.603	144	14.4	.345	1.2	3B(20): 0.3, SS(9): -0.1	1.3
	3B	TBA	MLB	24	57	8	2	0	2	7	5	18	0	0	.220/.304/.380	73	0.1	.300	0.1	3B(13): -0.4, 2B(1): 0.0	0.0
Christian Cairo	SS	CLE	Rk	18	179	26	3	1	0	9	25	40	7	3	.178/.324/.212	75	2.0	.243	2.3	3B(23): -0.4, SS(15): -1.8	0.3
Ernie Clement	SS	AKR	AA	23	437	46	15	3	1	24	26	33	16	10	.261/.314/.322	116	17.1	.279	-2.5	SS(89): 11.6, 2B(3): -0.5	3.5
Joe Naranjo	1B	CLE	Rk	18	200	25	5	2	1	21	22	44	1	0	.266/.345/.333	102	0.3	.346	0.9	1B(36): 2.1	0.5
Hanley Ramirez	SS	CLE	MLB	35	57	4	1	0	2	8	8	17	0	0	.184/.298/.327	79	-0.7	.233	0.4		0.0
Gabriel Rodriguez	SS	CLE	Rk	17	73	7	3	0	0	10	4	22	1	1	.215/.288/.262	40	-2.4	.318	0.6	SS(10): -1.4, 3B(6): -0.8	-0.3
Yordys Valdes	SS	CLE	Rk	17	181	17	3	1	2	11	16	53	15	4	.179/.251/.247	34	-9.1	.250	-0.5	SS(32): -0.5, 2B(10): 0.7	-0.3
Andrew Velazquez	UT	COH	AAA	24	46	5	4	1	0	5	0	9	1	1	.244/.261/.378	79	-1.8	.306	0.3	CF(6): 0.2, SS(4): -0.2	-0.3
	UT	DUR	AAA	24	141	20	9	1	4	16	10	30	2	4	.271/.329/.450	75	0.0	.326	-1.0	CF(22): 3.5, SS(10): -1.1	0.1
	UT	CLE	MLB	24	12	1	1	0	0	0	1	7	1	0	.091/.167/.182	25	-0.7	.250	0.3	2B(3): 0.0, CF(2): -0.1	-0.1
	UT	TBA	MLB	24	12	2	1	0	0	0	0	6	0	0	.083/.083/.167	67	-0.1	.167	-0.5	3B(4): -0.6, 2B(2): 0.0	-0.1

Christian Arroyo spent time near bays on both coasts before finding himself dumped on Cleveland at the deadline. He struggled at the plate before a barking elbow shut him down for good in June. ⓧ The Indians gave 2019 fourth rounder **Christian Cairo** more than twice his slot value to lure him away from a scholarship at LSU, proving once again that the "stay in school" messaging works only when the alternative isn't a boatload of cash. ⓧ **Ernie Clement**, who struck out a measly seven times his junior year, could be bringing his high-contact bat and flexible glove to Cleveland in short order. ⓧ A Google search for **Luis Durango Jr.** returns hits mostly concerning his father, who played in the majors for two different organizations. The magic number for bragging rights is 40 games. ⓧ Cleveland went overslot to coax **Joseph Naranjo** away from Cal State Fullerton, betting on a little extra pop from an otherwise James Loney-esque first-base prospect. ⓧ It was a long short year for **Hanley Ramirez**. He scored Cleveland's first run of the season with a homer, but limped (both figuratively and literally) to a sub-Mendoza line average before receiving a late-April release. This might be the end. ⓧ Cleveland clearly followed their own instructions for finding toolsy, flexible middle infielders when they signed **Gabriel Rodriguez** for a cool $2.1 million in July 2018. The 17-year-old flashed a little pop and a little speed, but will require a lot more time in the oven. ⓧ **Yordys Valdes** spurned Florida State with Tebow-like precision when he traded in his commitment to join Cleveland for a cool mil. Valdes then hit .179/.251/.247 with Tebow-like precision in his first taste of pro ball. ⓧ Though **Andrew Velazquez** is from the Bronx, he hasn't been a bomber during his big-league career—not in a good way, at least. His positional flexibility could come in handy off the bench, but he needs to make more contact.

Pitchers

PITCHER	TEAM	LVL	AGE	W	L	SV	G	GS	IP	H	HR	BB/9	K/9	K	GB%	BABIP	WHIP	ERA	DRA	WARP	MPH	FB%	WHF	CSP
Cody Anderson	COH	AAA	28	0	2	0	6	6	23²	25	3	2.7	8.0	21	54%	.344	1.35	4.56	5.05	0.4				
	CLE	MLB	28	0	1	0	5	2	8²	12	1	8.3	9.3	9	29%	.407	2.31	9.35	7.60	-0.2	96.3	43	11.9	42.7
Jon Edwards	COH	AAA	31	6	1	3	41	0	49	43	7	4.8	11.4	62	40%	.295	1.41	4.22	3.70	1.2				
	CLE	MLB	31	2	0	0	9	0	8	5	2	6.8	5.6	5	44%	.143	1.38	2.25	9.19	-0.3	95.7	50.7	14.1	39.3
Sam Hentges	AKR	AA	22	2	13	0	26	26	128²	148	11	4.5	8.8	126	36%	.358	1.65	5.11	7.13	-3.4				
James Hoyt	COH	AAA	32	2	0	4	40	2	42	46	3	4.3	10.3	48	53%	.384	1.57	3.43	5.02	0.5				
	CLE	MLB	32	0	0	0	8	0	8¹	6	2	2.2	10.8	10	45%	.222	0.96	2.16	5.12	0.0	95.6	42.3	17.9	43.8
Phil Maton	ELP	AAA	26	2	1	2	13	0	18²	17	2	2.9	14.5	30	59%	.395	1.23	2.89	1.80	0.8				
	COH	AAA	26	0	1	3	9	0	10²	5	1	3.4	14.3	17	44%	.235	0.84	2.53	1.91	0.4				
	CLE	MLB	26	0	0	0	9	0	12¹	4	1	4.4	9.5	13	46%	.111	0.81	2.92	2.67	0.4	92.4	59.8	11.6	50
	SDN	MLB	26	0	0	0	21	0	24¹	34	6	2.2	7.4	20	47%	.341	1.64	7.77	5.69	-0.1	93.5	59.8	12.9	49.3
Jean Carlos Mejía	LYN	A+	22	3	1	0	8	8	33	28	0	2.5	9.8	36	57%	.318	1.12	4.09	3.76	0.5				
Eli Morgan	LYN	A+	23	3	1	0	6	6	33²	19	3	1.3	10.7	40	25%	.219	0.71	1.87	2.43	1.1				
	AKR	AA	23	6	4	0	19	18	102	100	12	2.9	9.2	104	33%	.315	1.30	3.79	5.23	-0.4				
Scott Moss	CHT	AA	24	6	5	0	20	20	102	84	7	5.0	10.9	123	39%	.313	1.38	3.44	4.51	0.6				
	AKR	AA	24	2	0	0	2	2	10	3	0	4.5	11.7	13	35%	.150	0.80	0.00	2.83	0.3				
	COH	AAA	24	2	1	0	4	4	18²	12	1	3.9	11.1	23	29%	.250	1.07	1.93	2.41	0.8				
Dan Otero	COH	AAA	34	0	0	0	11	0	12¹	5	1	0.7	5.8	8	74%	.121	0.49	0.73	1.70	0.5				
	CLE	MLB	34	0	0	0	25	0	29²	42	6	0.9	4.9	16	53%	.343	1.52	4.85	7.09	-0.6	91.0	67.2	6.1	49.8
Luis Oviedo	LKC	A	20	6	6	0	19	19	87	80	6	4.1	7.4	72	43%	.294	1.38	5.38	4.98	0.2				
Adam Plutko	COH	AAA	27	1	3	0	4	4	15²	21	1	2.3	9.2	16	22%	.408	1.60	7.47	6.59	0.0				
	CLE	MLB	27	7	5	0	21	20	109¹	115	22	2.1	6.4	78	32%	.280	1.29	4.86	7.76	-2.4	92.6	54.1	9.3	46.9
Nick Sandlin	AKR	AA	22	0	0	2	15	0	17¹	13	2	4.2	14.0	27	49%	.314	1.21	1.56	4.22	0.1				
	COH	AAA	22	1	0	0	9	0	9	5	2	7.0	11.0	11	53%	.176	1.33	4.00	3.56	0.2				
Carlos Vargas	MHV	A-	19	6	4	0	15	15	77²	73	4	2.8	8.2	71	48%	.312	1.25	4.52	4.82	0.3				

It was a tough acronym year for **Cody Anderson**. After missing most of the last two seasons due to TJS, he returned to the bigs and posted ugly ERA and DRA before requiring another trip to the IL. His next acronym will be "AAA" or "DFA." ⓧ If you need someone to take your dog for a stroll around the block, you might want to consider **Jon Edwards** for the job. Because he's good at walks, you see. Unfortunately, that's not a great trait for a professional pitcher. ⓧ **Sam Hentges** is a 6-foot-8 lefty who pumps 95 mph fastballs. That's great. He also walked nearly five dudes per nine innings in Double-A, which, uh, is not. ⓧ **James Hoyt** has at times over the years looked like a legit relief option, pairing a mid-90s sinker with a wipeout slider that gets an obscene number of swinging strikes. He turned 33 in September, so we're getting near now-or-never territory. ⓧ The Maton family has produced three MLB draftees. **Phil Maton**, the elder of the trio, has more than 120 big-league innings to his name. He has an uptempo delivery and a high-spin fastball, but there's a chance he ends up the Cooper Manning of the bunch. ⓧ **Juan Carlos Mejía** was on the rise thanks to his mid-90s sinker and high groundball rate. His season ended after eight starts due to hernia surgery, delaying his ascent. ⓧ Contrary to popular belief, **Eli Morgan** is not an investment bank out of the movie *Boiler Room*. Rather, he's a changeup artist who jumped three levels in 2019, striking out more than a batter per inning along the way. ⓧ A rolling stone gathers no moss, but Cleveland picked up **Scott Moss** in the Trevor Bauer trade and he started rocking right afterward. He gave up four runs and accumulated 36 strikeouts in 28 innings with his new organization. ⓧ **Dan Otero** had an arm. O-T-E-R-O. And with that arm he gave up many homers. O-T-E-uh-oh. ⓧ **Luis Oviedo** gave back most of his gains from Mahoning Valley, making his story a relatable one for local gamblers. ⓧ In theory, **Adam Plutko** is a replacement-level pitcher. In practice, he was about two wins below replacement, according to DRA, suggesting any number of random Triple-A pitchers would have performed better. ⓧ If you're going to be a relief prospect, you'd better strike out a ton of batters. Luckily for **Nick Sandlin**, he does just that (36 percent for his career). His spotty command cost him a late-season cup of coffee. ⓧ **Lenny Torres** underwent Tommy John surgery in May. He was the 41st pick in the 2018 draft, so Cleveland has every reason to be patient as he rehabs. ⓧ The crown jewel of Cleveland's 2016 July 2 signing class, **Carlos Vargas** has started filling out his frame and pumping high-90s fastballs. His chance of remaining in a rotation hinges on the development his changeup.

COLORADO ROCKIES

Essay by Grant Brisbee

Player comments by Darius Austin and BP staff

When you check into a two-star hotel room, the odds are still decent that there will be an alarm clock with an iPod dock next to the bed. There are probably features included with this clock, like the ability to wake up to whatever hot new Fall Out Boy song is on your iPod. At one point, this bold, new technology was the future. It prompted hotel managers around the country to think, yes, this is an investment that will last. This is what people will need. We should spend money on this…because it will help us *make* money.

Cut to a few years later, and that clock-radio might as well be a cassette player. No one is jamming iPods into those things in 2020. Entire generations of dust mites have come and gone, from mite cavemen to mite Mesopotamians to mite Americans, without anyone using them. Technology has advanced too far, too fast.

This is what's happened in baseball. A front office from 2010 is one of those iPod clock radios. A front office from 2020 is a phone that can stream the entire Fall Out Boy catalog to a wireless speaker at the same time you're playing *Civilization VI*. It's the future, and it makes the recent past look like the distant past.

And in 2030, when *Civilization X* is beamed directly to our brains, today's technology will seem even quainter. The front offices of 2030 will laugh at the spin-rate fetish. They'll have proprietary statistics that will prove that Yadier Molina was always more valuable than Mike Trout, and we'll just have to fall in line, shuffling and looking down at our feet, saying, "I guess this is just how baseball is now."

Baseball is hard, in other words. This ain't a game, it's a gosh dang arms race. In ten years, teams will sink if they use nothing but 2020 information. You have to keep up with the Astroses.

With that established, let's take a look at the Rockies. Not the 2020 Rockies. Not the 2019 Rockies. The Rockies as a franchise. The whole thing. If we're going to draw out the analogy even further, we have to assume that the Rockies are forever trying to figure out what the newest iPhone will be, just like the rest of baseball.

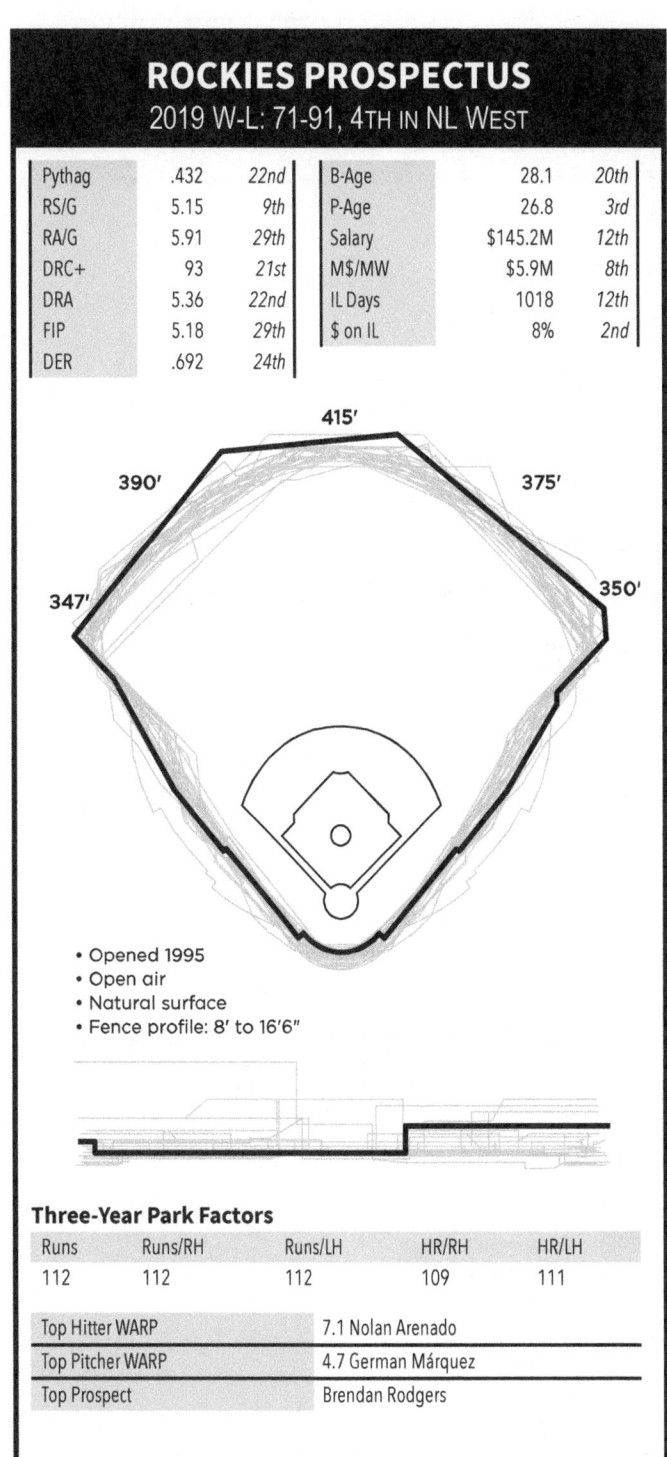

ROCKIES PROSPECTUS
2019 W-L: 71-91, 4TH IN NL WEST

Pythag	.432	22nd	B-Age	28.1	20th
RS/G	5.15	9th	P-Age	26.8	3rd
RA/G	5.91	29th	Salary	$145.2M	12th
DRC+	93	21st	M$/MW	$5.9M	8th
DRA	5.36	22nd	IL Days	1018	12th
FIP	5.18	29th	$ on IL	8%	2nd
DER	.692	24th			

415'
390'
375'
347'
350'

- Opened 1995
- Open air
- Natural surface
- Fence profile: 8' to 16'6"

Three-Year Park Factors

Runs	Runs/RH	Runs/LH	HR/RH	HR/LH
112	112	112	109	111

Top Hitter WARP	7.1 Nolan Arenado
Top Pitcher WARP	4.7 German Márquez
Top Prospect	Brendan Rodgers

2019 Hit List Ranking

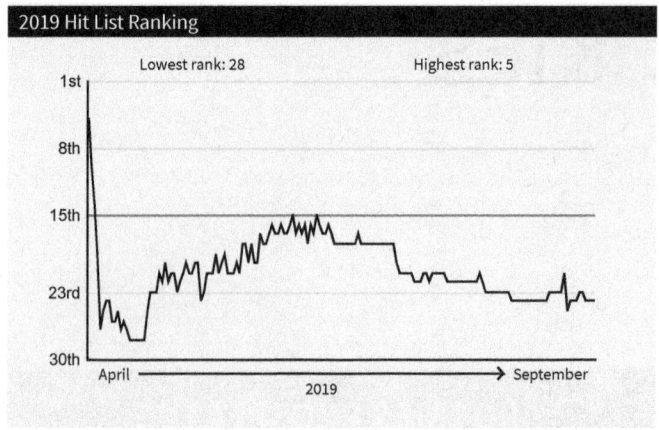

Lowest rank: 28   Highest rank: 5

Committed Payroll (in millions)

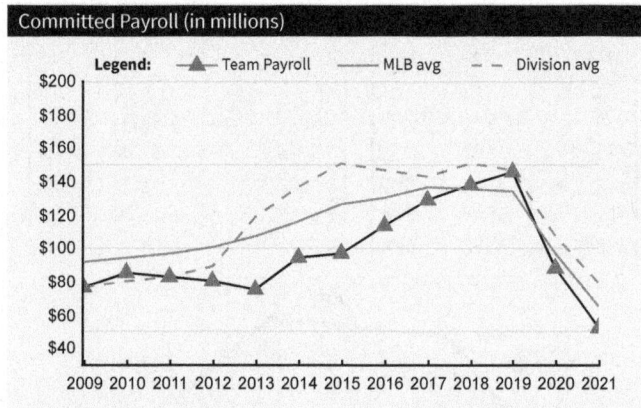

Legend: ▲ Team Payroll   — MLB avg   – – Division avg

Farm System Ranking

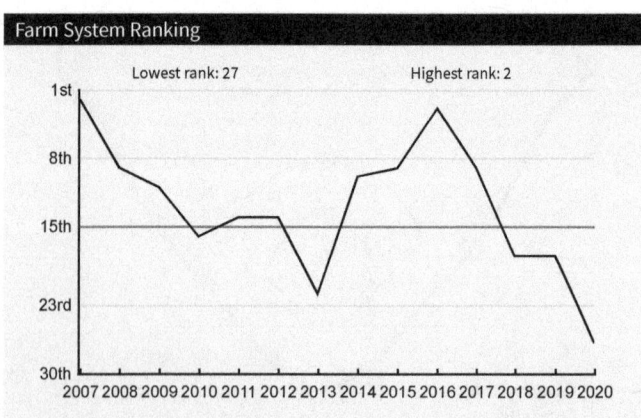

Lowest rank: 27   Highest rank: 2

Personnel

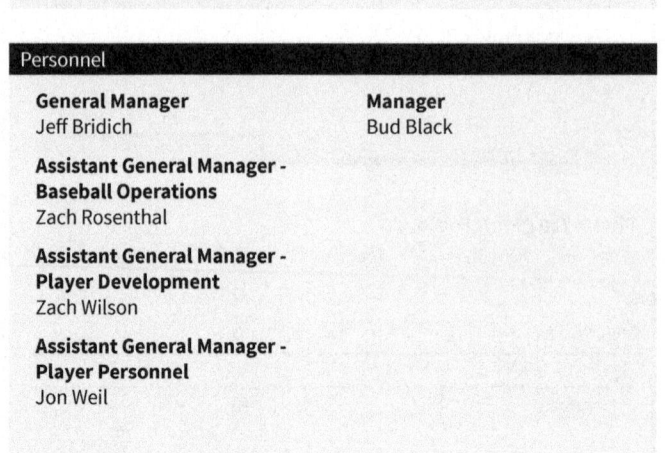

General Manager
Jeff Bridich

Manager
Bud Black

**Assistant General Manager -
Baseball Operations**
Zach Rosenthal

**Assistant General Manager -
Player Development**
Zach Wilson

**Assistant General Manager -
Player Personnel**
Jon Weil

But being the only team that plays at altitude means that they're doing it all without high-speed internet. While the other 29 teams are downloading schematics and hour-long HD presentations, the Rockies are forced to listen to the connection scrrrrkkkkkhhzzzz of the 56k modem and take their chances. It's not that they're behind in the brain race. It's that they're starting with more of a disadvantage than any other team in baseball, and it's not even close.

If you think this is an unfair description, it is not. It's the Rockies' difficulty setting on this particular video game that is unfair. Baseball is hard enough, but the Rockies are forced to figure out a new branch of physics on the fly. They have to conquer something that's just as hard to conquer as baseball *at the same time they're supposed to be conquering baseball.*

That something is how to adjust for playing baseball 5,200 feet above the ocean, and it's a problem that's tormented the franchise since they've existed. They're no closer to solving it. The Rockies—the entire franchise—is the Riemann hypothesis of baseball.

The early history of the Rockies was that of an entire league realizing that hitting was very, very different at altitude. Vinny Castilla and Dante Bichette became stars and MVP candidates. Double-digit slugfests from both teams were happening once a homestand, at least. But the Rockies continually allowed more runs than they scored.

"A-ha!", someone in the Rockies' front office thought. "We need to *buy* our pitchers!"

So they tried. Mike Hampton and Denny Neagle might not have been the best test cases for this experiment—the eight years, $121 million given to Hampton would still be a huge contract for a pitcher almost 20 years later—but it's refreshing in retrospect to see an ownership group apply their profits in an effort to build a better team. Those were the days.

Didn't work.

Then there was the fascination with sinkerballers, which also made sense. Keep the ball on the ground, keep the ball in the park.

Didn't work.

Then there was a strange period where the Rockies seemed to be acquiring pitchers who didn't strike batters out on purpose. Didn't work. They tried piggy-back starters, which was almost forward-thinking, considering how baseball started experimenting with openers and Johnny Wholestaff games shortly after. Didn't work.

Then the Rockies realized that the money-in-the-banana-stand theory of baseball actually was in the bullpen, so they pumped a whole mess of money into name-brand relievers at retail prices.

Didn't work.

So, congratulations, you're the GM of the Rockies. You get to build this team. First thing you have to do is, uh, build this team. To do that, you'll need to come up with a strategy.

I have an idea. Free of charge. Build the entire team out of fastball-first starters. Breaking balls don't spin as much in the low air resistance of Denver, so build a team of pitchers who can throw a fastball three-quarters of the time and be successful. That way, the other (dumb) teams are coming in and throwing breaking balls like they always do, and you (smart) have a rotation of pitchers who don't need bendy pitches. Lance Lynn just had one of the best pitching seasons in Rangers history throwing a fastball 71.4 percent of the time, for example.

Great. Sold. Here are the 10 starting pitchers who threw the fastball most often in 2019:

- Lance Lynn
- Brad Keller
- Julio Teheran
- Mike Soroka
- Kyle Hendricks
- José Quintana
- Dakota Hudson
- Walker Buehler
- Noah Syndergaard
- Zack Wheeler

Here's the part where I guess you're supposed to smack Jeff Bridich on the butt and say, "Go get 'em!"

Except those pitchers aren't exactly available, at least not all of them. And, really, once you get past Lynn, it's not like the other pitchers are that extreme. They're almost closer to 30th place in fastball percentage than first.

Got it. So maybe the plan should be for the Rockies to develop their own pitchers. When they won the pennant in 2007, it was with the help of Jeff Francis (1st-round draft pick), Aaron Cook (2nd round) and Ubaldo Jiménez (international free agent).

Except a team should…*always* develop their own pitchers, if possible? They're cheaper, and they're more likely to have their best seasons while under team control. This is a strategy for all 30 teams, not some sort of Coors-buster. Besides, the current iteration of the Rockies is already doing this. When they made the postseason in 2018, it was because they had a rotation filled with homegrown pitchers having tremendous seasons.

Then the pitchers got all squirrely and weird and hurt. As pitchers do. There's at least proof that pitching-first teams will work in Denver, especially with homegrown pitchers who spend their entire minor-league development time adjusting to altitude, though. So far, it's been the franchise's only path to success.

This also highlights the inherent disadvantage the Rockies face, though. Other teams can slap a free agent starter at the back of their rotation for cheap. Or they can go big and allocate a chunk of their payroll for an ace-type free agent starter. Even if those pitchers would consider the Rockies, it's

not like anyone would feel especially confident when they're acquired. You want to be excited about the pitchers acquired for millions of dollars, not scrunch up like a human shrug emoji and wait a few months for evidence. So the Rockies are forced to focus on a development-first staff, without fail and regardless of circumstances, which is like forcing the Diamondbacks to ignore left-handed hitters entirely. The Diamondbacks could still find success with an entirely right-handed lineup, sure, but the disadvantage would be immense.

Then, even when there's a thriving, homegrown pitching staff in place, there's the problem of the Coors hangover effect, which is unmistakable and absolutely horrifying. Rockies hitters hit far worse on the road than their talent level suggests they should. This was true in 2019, it was true in 2009, and it was true in 1999. It'll almost certainly be true in 2029.

tOPS+ is a stat that measures the difference between a team's splits, which means you can use it to measure the difference between the Rockies at home and on the road. Here are the 15 worst road tOPS+ marks in baseball history, courtesy of Baseball-Reference:

Rank	Team	Year	Road tOPS+
1	Rockies	1996	59
2	Rockies	2014	66
3	Rockies	2000	69
4	Rockies	2002	70
T5	Phillies	1932	72
T5	Rockies	1995	72
T5	Rockies	1999	72
T8	Rockies	2010	73
T8	Rockies	2012	73
T10	Rockies	1993	74
T10	Rockies	2019	74
12	Rockies	2015	75
T13	Red Sox	1950	76
T13	Red Sox	1955	76
T13	Rockies	2001	76

Again, that's baseball history. Twelve out of the 15 teams with the lowest road tOPS+ all-time are Rockies teams. Before you bring up Coors Field, note that tOPS+ is park adjusted. Even after adjusting for the boost of thin air, the Rockies are especially awful on the road, every year. If you want to use raw OPS, the Rockies still have three of the 10 worst road OPS since 1993 (when they entered the league.) They have six of the 20 worst. That's out of a pool of 800 possible seasons.

So now you have to grow your own pitchers, and you'll also have to figure out how to help your hitters acclimate to sea level for every road trip. Uh, hyperbaric chambers? I don't even know what those are, but I think I remember them from a movie. Maybe there are, uh, you know, *brain implants* that could help the hitters recognize the sharper breaking balls on the road sooner. It's like that famous maxim that neuroscientists use all the time, "Cybernetic implants are the humidor of the brain." Or, no, maybe some sort of virtual reality program that helps rewire the brains of Rockies hitters, that's the ticket.

Also, don't forget about figuring out baseball. You'll have to figure out the game of baseball while doing all of these experiments. It's still extremely hard for the normal teams to figure out baseball, remember.

This, all of this, is why the Rockies have won 90 games or more just three times in 27 seasons. It's why they've finished over .500 just eight times. It's why they've never won a division title. And danged if there's an accessible answer to be found.

In the end, fixing the Rockies isn't as simple as using piggyback starters or building the whole airplane out of expensive relievers, and it never was. The real solution is something totally outlandish, whether it's the aid of a technology that hasn't been invented yet, or MLB somehow putting their thumb on the scale to help them out. If they're wholly reliant on homegrown pitching, how's about an extra draft pick or three? They give extra draft picks to the freaking Cardinals, for crying out loud, just because nobody wants to adjust for the difference between "small market" and "established brand that sweeps across huge swaths of the Midwest," so why not boost their chances of getting another Francis or Freeland?

That'll never happen, of course, so the Rockies will have to juggle more chainsaws than the other 29 teams, and they'll fail more often than they'll succeed. The franchise will be at a crossroads soon, with Trevor Story and Jon Gray being free agents after the 2021 season (and Nolan Arenado able to opt out of his contract), so if the front office and ownership group haven't discussed strip-mining the team for prospects yet, they will soon.

At the same time, their 2020 season shouldn't be so hopeless. If you want to fix *those* Rockies, fix Kyle Freeland. Keep developing Gray. Hope for German Márquez to become the Cy Young contender he absolutely can be. And, sweet mercy, get some hitters around Arenado, Story and Charlie Blackmon. If you can't sign pitchers, at least throw the door open for the hitters, and don't be a bunch of weirdos and sign a shortstop to play first base this time. There is still a window here. Even after the dreadful 2019 season, there is still a window worth chasing.

Because if that window shuts, the Rockies will be at the bottom of the mountain range, rubble all around them. They'll look to the left and see a team with carabiners and Prusik cords. They'll look to the right and see a team with an ice axe, a harness, and an assortment of ropes. Then they'll have to dust themselves off, armed with nothing but a spork and some superglue, and start climbing that mountain all over again. ∎

—Grant Brisbee is an author at The Athletic Bay Area.

HITTERS

Yonder Alonso 1B Born: 04/08/87 Age: 33 Bats: L Throws: R Height: 6'1" Weight: 230 Origin: Round 1, 2008 Draft (#7 overall)

YEAR	TEAM	LVL	AGE	PA	R	2B	3B	HR	RBI	BB	K	SB	CS	AVG/OBP/SLG	DRC+	VORP	BABIP	BRR	FRAA	WARP
2017	OAK	MLB	30	371	52	17	0	22	49	50	88	1	0	.266/.369/.527	123	17.8	.301	-0.2	1B(96): -2.7	1.3
2017	SEA	MLB	30	150	20	5	0	6	18	18	30	1	0	.265/.353/.439	125	2.3	.302	-0.1	1B(39): -2.8	0.4
2018	CLE	MLB	31	574	64	19	0	23	83	51	123	0	0	.250/.317/.421	96	7.6	.283	1.1	1B(138): -0.6	0.6
2019	ABQ	AAA	32	38	7	3	1	2	12	5	6	0	0	.419/.500/.774	145	4.1	.458	-1.5	1B(8): -0.2	0.1
2019	COL	MLB	32	84	11	7	0	3	10	10	17	0	0	.260/.357/.479	102	2.2	.302	0.3	1B(11): -1.1	0.1
2019	CHA	MLB	32	251	23	6	0	7	27	29	53	0	1	.178/.275/.301	79	-3.0	.199	0.1	1B(21): -0.1	-0.3
2020	COL	MLB	33	251	26	11	0	8	28	26	52	1	1	.225/.310/.382	84	3.0	.261	0.1	1B -2	0.1

Comparables: Paul Konerko, Torii Hunter, Michael Cuddyer

As revolutions go, Alonso's personal launch angle overhaul has proven to be more 1979 Nicaragua than 1789 France. Explosive initial change gave way to mediocrity that looked awfully like the old version, with a slightly different batted-ball mix producing essentially the same results. If 2018 was evidence that nothing had really changed, 2019 suggested that the new Alonso might be worse than the old. A disastrous half-season with the White Sox saw him booted out of Chicago in favor of...well, anyone who could swing a bat, including most of their catchers and Matt Skole. The Rockies picked him up and used him tremendously sparingly, with starts in just 10 of his 54 games. The line improved a great deal in Colorado, albeit only to his typical career league-average mark. Alonso needs another transformation if he's going to convince teams he isn't just following the path of many revolutionaries before him: clinging on to his position long after it's clear a change is needed.

Nolan Arenado 3B Born: 04/16/91 Age: 29 Bats: R Throws: R Height: 6'2" Weight: 215 Origin: Round 2, 2009 Draft (#59 overall)

YEAR	TEAM	LVL	AGE	PA	R	2B	3B	HR	RBI	BB	K	SB	CS	AVG/OBP/SLG	DRC+	VORP	BABIP	BRR	FRAA	WARP
2017	COL	MLB	26	680	100	43	7	37	130	62	106	3	2	.309/.373/.586	136	61.5	.320	-0.5	3B(157): 5.0	6.0
2018	COL	MLB	27	673	104	38	2	38	110	73	122	2	2	.297/.374/.561	138	48.3	.314	-2.9	3B(152): 9.1	6.2
2019	COL	MLB	28	662	102	31	2	41	118	62	93	3	2	.315/.379/.583	136	56.8	.312	2.0	3B(154): 14.2	7.1
2020	COL	MLB	29	630	93	35	4	38	110	55	100	4	2	.308/.373/.587	133	41.8	.318	-0.3	3B 6	5.0

Comparables: Aramis Ramirez, Adrián Beltré, Lonnie Chisenhall

The Rockies rewarded Arenado for his stellar production with an eight-year, $260 million deal. He repaid them in kind with a fifth-straight season of at least six WARP, 660 plate appearances, 127 DRC+ and 37 homers. It had little impact on a team that utterly failed to build on its trip to the playoffs. Arenado may grow impatient without significant team improvement, if he isn't already. Impatience was certainly in evidence at the plate, despite the consistent slash line. Arenado saw his fewest pitches per plate appearance since 2015 and swung at a career-high 35.4 percent of first pitches. Fortunately, Jeff Bridich insisted on inserting an opt-out in that deal after 2021. That may not fill Arenado with confidence that the front office will maneuver their way back into playoff contention, but it does mean his patience will only have to last another two years rather than seven.

Charlie Blackmon RF Born: 07/01/86 Age: 33 Bats: L Throws: L Height: 6'3" Weight: 220 Origin: Round 2, 2008 Draft (#72 overall)

YEAR	TEAM	LVL	AGE	PA	R	2B	3B	HR	RBI	BB	K	SB	CS	AVG/OBP/SLG	DRC+	VORP	BABIP	BRR	FRAA	WARP
2017	COL	MLB	30	725	137	35	14	37	104	65	135	14	10	.331/.399/.601	144	77.3	.371	1.6	CF(158): -0.1	6.7
2018	COL	MLB	31	696	119	31	7	29	70	59	134	12	4	.291/.358/.502	123	38.4	.329	-0.6	CF(151): -21.7	2.1
2019	COL	MLB	32	634	112	42	7	32	86	40	104	2	5	.314/.364/.576	129	39.1	.334	0.4	RF(135): -8.8	3.0
2020	COL	MLB	34	595	78	33	7	26	88	41	109	16	7	.301/.360/.530	123	31.1	.337	0.3	RF -6	2.6

Comparables: Alex Rios, Jon Jay, Denard Span

Concerns that Blackmon's contract extension might have been poorly-timed were assuaged with a performance that was close to, if not quite at, Blackmon's offensive peak at the plate. Colorado addressed his disastrous defensive 2018 in center field by fully embracing a logical move to a corner, with one hundred percent of Blackmon's defensive innings coming in right field. Unfortunately, it seems that Chuck's Nazty-ness with the glove has outpaced that move as he still rated as one of the worst defensive outfielders in the game, even at the easier position. Blackmon no longer needs to worry about what he'll do after leaving Coors, since his extension keeps him there through 2023 if he so desires. Given that he now has the largest home-road OPS split of any player in history, the 33-year-old may not have any interest in finding out how he'd fare with another club, as much as playing a smaller outfield would compensate for his loss of speed.

Drew Butera C Born: 08/09/83 Age: 36 Bats: R Throws: R Height: 6'1" Weight: 205 Origin: Round 5, 2005 Draft (#149 overall)

YEAR	TEAM	LVL	AGE	PA	R	2B	3B	HR	RBI	BB	K	SB	CS	AVG/OBP/SLG	DRC+	VORP	BABIP	BRR	FRAA	WARP
2017	KCA	MLB	33	177	18	4	1	3	14	12	41	0	0	.227/.284/.319	84	1.3	.286	-0.1	C(74): -3.4, 1B(4): -0.2	0.2
2018	KCA	MLB	34	166	11	9	0	2	18	13	37	0	0	.188/.259/.289	80	-0.4	.232	1.2	C(48): -6.9, 1B(2): 0.9	-0.1
2018	COL	MLB	34	16	2	0	0	1	3	2	2	0	0	.214/.313/.429	78	0.5	.182	0.1	C(6): -0.9, 1B(4): 0.0	-0.1
2019	ABQ	AAA	35	262	38	16	2	9	40	33	55	2	0	.300/.389/.511	108	17.5	.356	0.3	C(64): -5.7	1.1
2019	COL	MLB	35	49	6	3	0	0	3	4	14	0	0	.163/.229/.233	63	0.0	.233	0.5	C(14): 0.2, 1B(3): 0.0	0.1
2020	COL	MLB	36	35	3	2	0	1	4	3	10	0	0	.232/.300/.378	69	0.3	.304	0.1	C -1	0.0

Comparables: Chris Cannizzaro, Matt Treanor, Jim Sundberg

Butera has made a career out of hanging on to a major-league spot as a backup catcher. His tenuous grip on a job at the highest level started to slip in 2019 as he was forced to don the tools of ignorance in the minor leagues for the first time in six years. Triple-A suited him rather well, as he supplied just his second pro season of positive production at the plate, a phenomenon not seen since his stint at High-A in 2007. It made no difference at all to his big-league numbers when he finally clambered back onto the 40-man in September, with the 35-year-old recording just four hits all month. While Butera's batting performance has never had much impact on his roster status, he's not going to be able to keep clinging on for much longer.

YEAR	TEAM	P. COUNT	FRM RUNS	BLK RUNS	THRW RUNS	TOT RUNS
2017	KCA	7350	-4.2	2.0	-0.2	-3.0
2018	KCA	6521	-6.4	0.0	-0.2	-6.8
2018	COL	730	-0.7	-0.1	0.0	-0.9
2019	ABQ	9577	-7.5	-0.2	0.4	-7.5
2019	COL	1969	-1.3	1.2	0.0	-0.1
2020	COL	1750	-1.1	0.3	0.1	-0.7

David Dahl OF Born: 04/01/94 Age: 26 Bats: L Throws: R Height: 6'2" Weight: 200 Origin: Round 1, 2012 Draft (#10 overall)

YEAR	TEAM	LVL	AGE	PA	R	2B	3B	HR	RBI	BB	K	SB	CS	AVG/OBP/SLG	DRC+	VORP	BABIP	BRR	FRAA	WARP
2017	ABQ	AAA	23	74	12	2	2	2	14	3	17	1	1	.243/.274/.414	56	0.4	.294	0.7	CF(6): -0.3, LF(6): -0.2	-0.2
2018	ABQ	AAA	24	78	7	7	0	2	9	1	19	1	0	.286/.295/.455	85	-0.4	.357	-0.6	RF(6): 0.2, CF(6): 0.4	0.2
2018	COL	MLB	24	271	31	11	3	16	48	19	68	5	3	.273/.325/.534	112	8.7	.311	-1.3	LF(34): 2.9, RF(30): -1.4	1.1
2019	COL	MLB	25	413	67	28	5	15	61	28	110	4	4	.302/.353/.524	103	14.4	.386	2.1	CF(40): 1.3, LF(39): 0.2	1.3
2020	COL	MLB	26	462	53	22	5	18	61	27	125	12	4	.271/.317/.467	96	12.6	.344	0.9	CF 0, LF 3	1.6

Comparables: Eddie Rosario, Junior Lake, Jake Marisnick

It was going so well for Dahl in his battle with the injury-prone tag. Even with a slight core issue, Dahl appeared in 100 of the first 110 contests, making his first All-Star game in the process. Then disaster struck once again: In an August 2nd game against the Giants, the 25-year-old was tracking down a line drive when his foot got caught in the Coors Field turf and his ankle moved in ways it's certainly not supposed to. Dahl made the catch; he also missed the remaining two months of the season with a high ankle sprain. He therefore once again managed to fuel the injury-prone narrative with a different ailment from those that had sidelined him previously. It's theoretically encouraging that Dahl doesn't have a chronic problem, and yet with every passing year it's becoming harder to shake the notion that he simply can't play every day without sustaining an injury at some point. This was the first time he'd reached triple-digit games since 2014 and also one of his most mediocre offensive performances, by DRC's reckoning. One can argue that a fully healthy season will also lead to better production with the bat. Let's hope that argument doesn't remain purely theoretical.

Ian Desmond OF Born: 09/20/85 Age: 34 Bats: R Throws: R Height: 6'3" Weight: 220 Origin: Round 3, 2004 Draft (#84 overall)

YEAR	TEAM	LVL	AGE	PA	R	2B	3B	HR	RBI	BB	K	SB	CS	AVG/OBP/SLG	DRC+	VORP	BABIP	BRR	FRAA	WARP
2017	COL	MLB	31	373	47	11	1	7	40	24	87	15	4	.274/.326/.375	74	3.3	.345	2.7	LF(66): -2.8, 1B(27): -2.5	-0.6
2018	COL	MLB	32	619	82	21	8	22	88	53	146	20	6	.236/.307/.422	90	4.8	.279	0.8	1B(138): -2.6, LF(18): 0.8	0.2
2019	COL	MLB	33	482	64	31	4	20	65	34	119	3	3	.255/.310/.479	86	7.3	.304	0.4	CF(74): -12.8, LF(44): -2.9	-0.8
2020	COL	MLB	34	336	37	14	3	12	41	24	91	8	3	.245/.305/.424	78	2.5	.309	0.6	CF -5, LF -1	-0.3

Comparables: Jhonny Peralta, Troy Tulowitzki, Alex Gonzalez

Desmond's arrival in Colorado three years ago coincided with their most competitive period in a decade. It's unfortunate, then, that he has done virtually nothing to contribute to that success. The Rockies moved away from the baffling first base plan in 2019 with an even more baffling move up the defensive spectrum to center field. While FRAA is a little kinder to Desmond than other defensive metrics, that only serves to make him around replacement-level rather than clearly below when combined with his thoroughly subpar performance at the plate. After almost 400 games of futility, the team has relented a little: Desmond only appeared in 140 contests rather than 160. There are two years left on his deal, so there's plenty more time for the Rockies to show that they understand sunk cost better than we understand any of their Desmond-related decisions.

Garrett Hampson 2B Born: 10/10/94 Age: 25 Bats: R Throws: R Height: 5'11" Weight: 188 Origin: Round 3, 2016 Draft (#81 overall)

YEAR	TEAM	LVL	AGE	PA	R	2B	3B	HR	RBI	BB	K	SB	CS	AVG/OBP/SLG	DRC+	VORP	BABIP	BRR	FRAA	WARP
2017	LNC	A+	22	603	113	24	12	8	70	56	77	51	14	.326/.387/.462	128	41.5	.364	7.5	2B(71): -0.4, SS(56): 7.3	5.4
2018	HFD	AA	23	172	28	8	2	4	15	21	17	19	1	.304/.391/.466	136	18.7	.323	3.5	SS(18): 0.4, 2B(17): 1.7	1.9
2018	ABQ	AAA	23	332	53	17	4	6	25	30	58	17	4	.314/.377/.459	110	16.9	.372	0.9	2B(44): -0.1, SS(23): -2.3	1.6
2018	COL	MLB	23	48	3	3	1	0	4	7	12	2	0	.275/.396/.400	81	3.6	.393	1.1	SS(8): 0.2, 2B(7): 0.6	0.2
2019	ABQ	AAA	24	117	15	9	1	2	9	5	25	7	2	.266/.310/.422	63	0.8	.329	1.0	2B(15): 0.3, SS(10): -1.5	-0.1
2019	COL	MLB	24	327	40	9	4	8	27	24	88	15	3	.247/.302/.385	71	-0.5	.322	3.5	2B(50): -1.1, CF(31): -0.8	0.1
2020	COL	MLB	25	350	35	14	5	7	35	26	90	17	4	.256/.314/.392	73	3.6	.337	2.3	CF 0, 2B 0	0.4

Comparables: Roy McMillan, Joe Demaestri, Pete Runnels

What looked like a complicated path to playing time for the speedy Hampson turned into a golden chance right out of the blocks as both Ryan McMahon and Daniel Murphy got hurt inside the first 10 games of the season. Hampson didn't run, either with the opportunity or on the basepaths, stumbling to one of the worst offensive months in Rockies history. That false start followed by several more disqualified him from a regular role until the season's final month. Hampson made up for lost time with a .903 OPS in September, dazzling on the bases and adding five homers for good measure. The complicated playing time situation remains going into 2020, but it's a marathon, not a sprint.

Sam Hilliard OF Born: 02/21/94 Age: 26 Bats: L Throws: L Height: 6'5" Weight: 238 Origin: Round 15, 2015 Draft (#437 overall)

YEAR	TEAM	LVL	AGE	PA	R	2B	3B	HR	RBI	BB	K	SB	CS	AVG/OBP/SLG	DRC+	VORP	BABIP	BRR	FRAA	WARP
2017	LNC	A+	23	597	95	23	7	21	92	50	154	37	17	.300/.360/.487	121	25.1	.384	3.9	RF(85): 6.6, LF(30): 5.1	4.1
2018	HFD	AA	24	484	58	22	3	9	40	41	151	23	14	.262/.327/.389	97	9.1	.379	0.3	RF(70): 3.5, LF(29): -1.8	1.1
2019	ABQ	AAA	25	559	109	29	7	35	101	54	164	22	5	.262/.335/.558	98	17.0	.316	0.5	RF(82): -0.2, CF(33): 5.2	1.8
2019	COL	MLB	25	87	13	4	2	7	13	9	23	2	0	.273/.356/.649	109	3.8	.298	0.7	CF(17): 0.6, RF(6): 1.7	0.5
2020	COL	MLB	26	154	16	7	1	5	17	12	51	4	2	.222/.285/.388	70	-0.8	.311	0.4	CF 2, LF 0	0.1

Comparables: Jared Walsh, Aristides Aquino, Donald Lutz

No Hilliard had ever made the majors before Sam—not unless one includes 1930s infielder Meredith Hilliard Hopkins, who hardly counts, not least because he went by Marty. Sam's monster raw power showed up in a big way in 2019, with a near-.300 ISO at Albuquerque, and then a mark over 80 points higher in his big-league debut. Questions still need to be answered about his ability to regularly get that power into games given his pitch recognition issues and accompanying high strikeout rate. His platoon problems seem to have faded, however, and if he can hit for remotely this much power, then he won't need to keep playing center, where he is rather stretched. Even for Hilliard fun fact sticklers, there's no doubt that Sam is the best of all time: he has already passed Marty in both WARP and home runs, with barely a sixth of the playing time.

Ryan McMahon INF Born: 12/14/94 Age: 25 Bats: L Throws: R Height: 6'2" Weight: 208 Origin: Round 2, 2013 Draft (#42 overall)

YEAR	TEAM	LVL	AGE	PA	R	2B	3B	HR	RBI	BB	K	SB	CS	AVG/OBP/SLG	DRC+	VORP	BABIP	BRR	FRAA	WARP
2017	HFD	AA	22	205	28	16	2	6	32	20	39	7	0	.326/.390/.536	141	15.7	.381	0.0	1B(25): 0.4, 2B(15): 2.1	1.7
2017	ABQ	AAA	22	314	46	23	2	14	56	21	53	4	3	.374/.411/.612	150	26.3	.416	-2.9	1B(36): 1.1, 2B(24): 2.4	2.6
2017	COL	MLB	22	24	2	1	0	0	1	5	5	0	0	.158/.333/.211	76	0.3	.214	1.4	1B(7): 0.2, 2B(4): 0.0	0.1
2018	ABQ	AAA	23	242	40	15	3	11	48	15	61	3	2	.290/.339/.531	107	5.6	.353	1.9	1B(43): -1.9, 2B(10): -1.0	0.5
2018	COL	MLB	23	202	17	9	1	5	19	18	64	1	0	.232/.307/.376	74	0.0	.327	0.9	1B(31): -1.1, 3B(17): 0.1	-0.1
2019	COL	MLB	24	539	70	22	1	24	83	56	160	5	1	.250/.329/.450	92	11.6	.323	-0.1	2B(113): 6.9, 3B(22): -0.5	1.7
2020	COL	MLB	25	539	63	21	2	22	70	48	163	5	3	.247/.319/.434	91	15.4	.326	0.5	2B 7, 1B 0	2.3

Comparables: Tommy Brown, Byron Buxton, Clint Frazier

The Rockies *almost* committed to McMahon as an everyday option, employing him as their primary second baseman with a smattering of appearances at both infield corners. He played the keystone reasonably well while improving, if not excelling, with the bat. There are still a lot of whiffs in this profile, and McMahon hasn't yet been able to find the level of power that would make them palatable. Sure, the loud contact is there, but too much of it sends the ball into the ground rather than the thin Denver air. Every now and then, McMahon launches one way beyond the center field fence to remind us the ability is there. Now he just has to figure out how to get to it more often. He might need to in order to fight off the queue of alternatives waiting to take infield time away from him. from him.

Daniel Murphy 1B Born: 04/01/85 Age: 35 Bats: L Throws: R Height: 6'1" Weight: 221 Origin: Round 13, 2006 Draft (#394 overall)

YEAR	TEAM	LVL	AGE	PA	R	2B	3B	HR	RBI	BB	K	SB	CS	AVG/OBP/SLG	DRC+	VORP	BABIP	BRR	FRAA	WARP
2017	WAS	MLB	32	593	94	43	3	23	93	52	77	2	0	.322/.384/.543	133	51.4	.341	1.2	2B(139): 3.8	4.8
2018	HAR	AA	33	44	8	2	0	2	7	6	4	0	0	.243/.364/.459	121	3.6	.226	0.5	2B(8): -0.6, 1B(2): 0.3	0.2
2018	WAS	MLB	33	205	17	9	0	6	29	13	17	1	0	.300/.341/.442	114	8.3	.302	-1.0	2B(38): -2.9, 1B(14): -0.6	0.4
2018	CHN	MLB	33	146	23	6	0	6	13	7	23	2	0	.297/.329/.471	112	8.1	.318	0.7	2B(33): -1.1	0.6
2019	COL	MLB	34	478	56	35	1	13	78	32	74	1	1	.279/.328/.452	97	6.2	.307	0.0	1B(110): 5.9, 2B(3): 0.4	1.2
2020	COL	MLB	35	511	55	30	2	15	61	35	80	3	1	.277/.331/.442	96	7.4	.307	0.1	1B 5	1.3

Comparables: Juan Rivera, Elston Howard, Omar Infante

Murphy heading to Coors looked like a batting title waiting to happen. It worked for Justin Morneau and Michael Cuddyer in their mid-thirties. Instead, we got an extremely Mets Murphy line, one that was almost identical to his final year in New York. That's not a good sign given the respective contexts in which those two seasons were played. There were mitigating circumstances. A broken index finger put his season on hold before it even got started and continued to bother him long after he returned. Murphy will get another shot at that batting title in the second year of his deal. It's about time a Rockie won one.

Tyler Nevin 1B Born: 05/29/97 Age: 23 Bats: R Throws: R Height: 6'4" Weight: 200 Origin: Round 1, 2015 Draft (#38 overall)

YEAR	TEAM	LVL	AGE	PA	R	2B	3B	HR	RBI	BB	K	SB	CS	AVG/OBP/SLG	DRC+	VORP	BABIP	BRR	FRAA	WARP
2017	BOI	A-	20	30	4	3	0	1	5	0	9	0	1	.233/.233/.433	55	0.1	.300	0.1	3B(3): 0.0, 1B(2): -0.2	-0.1
2017	ASH	A	20	335	45	18	3	7	47	27	56	10	5	.305/.364/.456	133	18.5	.349	1.3	1B(32): 1.6, 3B(23): -2.5	1.8
2018	LNC	A+	21	417	59	25	1	13	62	34	77	4	3	.328/.386/.503	139	15.1	.383	-4.4	1B(67): -0.7, 3B(17): 1.0	1.9
2019	HFD	AA	22	540	60	26	2	13	61	65	90	6	2	.251/.345/.399	120	9.5	.283	1.9	1B(97): 2.8, 3B(12): 0.1	2.4
2020	COL	MLB	23	251	26	14	1	7	29	22	58	1	1	.253/.324/.413	84	2.4	.311	-0.4	1B 1, 3B 0	0.3

Comparables: David Cooper, Rangel Ravelo, Dalton Pompey

Every year, Nevin plays a little more cold corner than hot, making evaluators lukewarm on his chances of being a regular in the majors. Some of that is based on circumstance rather than Nevin's talent, but he's also not a good third baseman, and if he's going to become an everyday player, the bat really needs to heat up. The performance was better than the slash line looks given how difficult it is to hit in the Eastern League. Even with a late-season homer surge, the power has not yet developed enough to make this profile work at first.

Dom Nuñez C Born: 01/17/95 Age: 25 Bats: L Throws: R Height: 6'0" Weight: 175 Origin: Round 6, 2013 Draft (#169 overall)

YEAR	TEAM	LVL	AGE	PA	R	2B	3B	HR	RBI	BB	K	SB	CS	AVG/OBP/SLG	DRC+	VORP	BABIP	BRR	FRAA	WARP
2017	HFD	AA	22	364	37	10	1	11	28	53	83	7	1	.202/.335/.354	93	15.2	.238	0.0	C(88): 12.2	2.7
2018	HFD	AA	23	377	34	12	0	9	42	46	73	8	6	.222/.320/.343	90	6.3	.257	-1.0	C(70): 5.8	1.7
2019	ABQ	AAA	24	257	43	14	1	17	42	35	69	2	0	.244/.362/.559	112	19.2	.269	-0.3	C(60): 7.6	2.3
2019	COL	MLB	24	43	4	3	0	2	4	3	17	0	0	.179/.233/.410	74	0.8	.238	1.0	C(14): 0.9	0.3
2020	COL	MLB	25	245	25	10	0	8	28	25	72	2	1	.207/.294/.369	70	1.6	.268	-0.4	C 6	0.7

Comparables: Bill Sarni, Austin Dean, Jake Smolinski

A premature nickname can be more of a curse than a blessing. Case in point: the Rockies' Twitter account dubbed their 24-year-old catcher 'Bomb Nuñez' when he homered in his very first major-league game. That blew up in their faces over the next month and a half, as Nuñez did nothing but bomb at the plate. On the very final day of the season, he ensured that the moniker-making homer was not his only blast of 2019 and helped Colorado to finish a single game ahead of the basement-dwelling Padres in the process. The social media team wasted no time in rolling out the nickname again. As long as it doesn't catch on when he strikes out, they've probably gotten away with this one.

YEAR	TEAM	P. COUNT	FRM RUNS	BLK RUNS	THRW RUNS	TOT RUNS
2017	HFD	5592	11.6	0.5	0.5	12.3
2018	HFD	9227	6.6	0.7	0.4	7.9
2019	ABQ	9193	5.2	0.1	-0.9	4.3
2019	COL	1637	0.3	0.6	0.0	1.2
2020	COL	9102	3.9	1.4	-0.2	5.1

★ ★ ★ *2020 Top 101 Prospect* **#56** ★ ★ ★

Brendan Rodgers 2B Born: 08/09/96 Age: 23 Bats: R Throws: R Height: 6'0" Weight: 180 Origin: Round 1, 2015 Draft (#3 overall)

YEAR	TEAM	LVL	AGE	PA	R	2B	3B	HR	RBI	BB	K	SB	CS	AVG/OBP/SLG	DRC+	VORP	BABIP	BRR	FRAA	WARP
2017	LNC	A+	20	236	44	21	3	12	47	6	35	2	1	.387/.407/.671	173	26.5	.413	0.9	SS(47): -5.6, 2B(4): -0.6	2.2
2017	HFD	AA	20	164	20	5	0	6	17	8	36	0	2	.260/.323/.413	100	6.5	.306	-0.5	SS(33): -1.2, 2B(6): 0.3	0.5
2018	HFD	AA	21	402	49	23	2	17	62	30	76	12	3	.275/.342/.493	112	27.4	.301	0.6	SS(58): -6.7, 2B(21): -2.1	1.5
2018	ABQ	AAA	21	72	5	4	0	0	5	1	16	0	0	.232/.264/.290	52	-2.8	.302	-0.3	SS(11): -1.8, 3B(4): -0.2	-0.4
2019	ABQ	AAA	22	160	34	10	1	9	21	14	27	0	0	.350/.413/.622	130	20.2	.380	2.0	2B(27): -1.9, SS(6): -0.1	1.2
2019	COL	MLB	22	81	8	2	0	0	7	4	27	0	0	.224/.272/.250	47	-2.7	.347	1.5	2B(16): 1.1, SS(9): -1.1	-0.1
2020	COL	MLB	23	154	17	7	1	6	20	9	41	1	0	.258/.310/.436	84	2.2	.323	-0.1	2B 0, SS -1	0.1

Comparables: Jonathan Villar, Alen Hanson, Richard Ureña

After helping Celtic to become the first team in Scottish football history to win the treble in consecutive seasons, Rodgers departed for Leicester City in February, where he quickly ... what? Baseball? Oh, you mean the *other* Brendan Rodgers. His 2019 didn't go as well as his namesake's across the pond. The Rockies infielder got his first shot at the big leagues but whiffed a ton and displayed almost no power. While a Colorado prospect's failing to make an impact in their first taste of the bigs is nothing new, the torn labrum that ended his season gives Rodgers another obstacle to a successful sophomore season on top of adjusting to the Show and finding time in a crowded infield. It probably won't be much consolation for him to learn that Leicester look terrific this season.

Trevor Story SS Born: 11/15/92 Age: 27 Bats: R Throws: R Height: 6'2" Weight: 214 Origin: Round 1, 2011 Draft (#45 overall)

YEAR	TEAM	LVL	AGE	PA	R	2B	3B	HR	RBI	BB	K	SB	CS	AVG/OBP/SLG	DRC+	VORP	BABIP	BRR	FRAA	WARP
2017	COL	MLB	24	555	68	32	3	24	82	49	191	7	2	.239/.308/.457	92	27.6	.332	4.2	SS(142): -0.4	2.4
2018	COL	MLB	25	656	88	42	6	37	108	47	168	27	6	.291/.348/.567	128	52.7	.345	-0.8	SS(156): -2.0	5.0
2019	COL	MLB	26	656	111	38	5	35	85	58	174	23	8	.294/.363/.554	118	47.3	.361	3.5	SS(144): -0.3	4.9
2020	COL	MLB	27	595	82	32	6	32	95	52	165	16	5	.280/.349/.542	115	35.9	.347	1.4	SS -2	3.5

Comparables: Javier Báez, Jonathan Villar, Junior Lake

You've heard all the Story puns by now, so let's make it through this without one. His performance has been worthy of far more than a quip in any case. Story consolidated his success from 2018, demonstrating the kind of high-end consistency for his neighbor at third base has become known. That osmosis hasn't quite extended to the defensive side of the game, but Story's no joke with the glove either. He was a worthy All-Star for the second season running, and while he's a tier below the true MVP candidates, he's knocking on the door to that club. Even though there are still plenty of strikeouts, the Rockies shortstop has made a mockery of the notion that the swing-and-miss issues in his game were too much to overcome. Two more years remain before Story hits the open market, as much as fans might wish his tenure was never-ending (almost made it).

Raimel Tapia LF Born: 02/04/94 Age: 26 Bats: L Throws: L Height: 6'3" Weight: 185 Origin: International Free Agent, 2010

YEAR	TEAM	LVL	AGE	PA	R	2B	3B	HR	RBI	BB	K	SB	CS	AVG/OBP/SLG	DRC+	VORP	BABIP	BRR	FRAA	WARP
2017	ABQ	AAA	23	277	45	20	8	2	30	13	42	12	2	.369/.397/.529	121	20.0	.432	-0.1	CF(48): 0.0, LF(5): -0.6	1.5
2017	COL	MLB	23	171	27	12	2	2	16	8	36	5	2	.288/.329/.425	80	3.7	.361	1.6	RF(22): -3.0, LF(18): -1.3	-0.3
2018	ABQ	AAA	24	473	81	33	9	11	62	32	85	21	3	.302/.352/.495	99	16.1	.354	1.4	CF(65): -5.2, RF(24): 0.0	0.8
2018	COL	MLB	24	27	6	2	1	1	6	2	7	0	0	.200/.259/.480	87	0.7	.235	0.7	CF(6): -0.4, LF(1): 0.0	0.1
2019	COL	MLB	25	447	54	23	5	9	44	21	100	9	3	.275/.309/.415	80	0.9	.341	-0.4	LF(91): 1.7, CF(13): -0.4	0.1
2020	COL	MLB	26	413	40	20	5	8	43	21	95	12	5	.266/.307/.403	79	0.9	.334	0.6	LF -2, CF 0	-0.1

Comparables: Victor Reyes, Brandon Drury, Sócrates Brito

Naturally, Tapia hit for average in 2019, even if it wasn't the .300-plus he managed in the minors. With his options exhausted, he got to stick around on the major-league roster all season. The continued exposure didn't give Tapia the chance to show what he can do as much as demonstrate what he can't: hit for power. The ball simply doesn't come off the bat that hard, whether in the air or on the ground. Given that he also doesn't take a ton of walks or play a particularly impressive outfield, Tapia's chances of making it as an everyday player hinge even more on his ability to hit for average. In truth, even hitting .300 might not get him there if he can't squeeze out more production elsewhere.

Ryan Vilade SS Born: 02/18/99 Age: 21 Bats: R Throws: R Height: 6'2" Weight: 194 Origin: Round 2, 2017 Draft (#48 overall)

YEAR	TEAM	LVL	AGE	PA	R	2B	3B	HR	RBI	BB	K	SB	CS	AVG/OBP/SLG	DRC+	VORP	BABIP	BRR	FRAA	WARP
2017	GJR	RK	18	146	23	3	2	5	21	27	31	5	5	.308/.438/.496	130	14.0	.378	0.4	SS(30): -2.1	0.6
2018	ASH	A	19	533	77	20	4	5	44	49	96	17	13	.274/.353/.368	114	25.8	.333	-1.9	SS(116): -6.3	2.1
2019	LNC	A+	20	587	92	27	10	12	71	56	95	24	7	.303/.367/.466	118	33.5	.342	2.5	SS(82): -4.0, 3B(46): -4.3	2.6
2020	COL	MLB	21	251	23	11	2	4	23	23	56	4	2	.238/.314/.348	79	1.2	.302	0.0	SS -2, 3B 0	-0.1

Comparables: Gavin Lux, Daniel Robertson, Carlos Rivero

Vilade's offensive development continued smoothly at High-A, where he demonstrated a strong all-fields approach with power to boot. The road has been a little more bumpy defensively, where his 37 errors speak to the issues he's had throwing the ball. Vilade spent more time at third base as the season went on and could yet develop into a plus defender given his athleticism. He's also an excellent baserunner despite not having top-end speed. The components are all here for an above-average player on all sides of the ball, and Vilade has given every indication that he'll be able to realize that potential.

Colton Welker 3B Born: 10/09/97 Age: 22 Bats: R Throws: R Height: 6'1" Weight: 195 Origin: Round 4, 2016 Draft (#110 overall)

YEAR	TEAM	LVL	AGE	PA	R	2B	3B	HR	RBI	BB	K	SB	CS	AVG/OBP/SLG	DRC+	VORP	BABIP	BRR	FRAA	WARP
2017	ASH	A	19	279	32	18	1	6	33	18	42	5	7	.350/.401/.500	156	19.4	.399	-1.6	3B(52): -7.3	1.5
2018	LNC	A+	20	509	74	32	0	13	82	42	103	5	1	.333/.383/.489	138	30.1	.395	1.1	3B(92): -9.3, 1B(6): -0.7	2.6
2019	HFD	AA	21	394	37	23	1	10	53	32	68	2	1	.252/.313/.408	113	6.9	.281	-2.8	3B(63): -1.5, 1B(27): 2.2	1.3
2020	COL	MLB	22	251	24	13	0	6	27	16	57	1	0	.245/.296/.384	79	0.6	.298	-0.5	3B -4, 1B 0	-0.4

Comparables: Renato Núñez, Nolan Arenado, Gabriel Guerrero

Welker started out hot at Double-A and looked as though he would breeze through the level like every other assignment he's had. Then, he ran into his first signs of adversity. A lifeless June dropped his batting average well below .300 for the first time as a pro, and he was on the injured list by mid-July with a left shoulder impingement. That cost him a month, and Welker headed to the Arizona Fall League to make up for lost time, where he continued to struggle. If Welker can adjust against higher-level pitching, the bat speed and concurrent raw power will be thrilling to see in game action. For the first time in affiliated ball, however, he has thrown up questions about whether he'll be able to take that final step.

Tony Wolters C Born: 06/09/92 Age: 28 Bats: L Throws: R Height: 5'10" Weight: 197 Origin: Round 3, 2010 Draft (#87 overall)

YEAR	TEAM	LVL	AGE	PA	R	2B	3B	HR	RBI	BB	K	SB	CS	AVG/OBP/SLG	DRC+	VORP	BABIP	BRR	FRAA	WARP
2017	ABQ	AAA	25	58	6	5	1	2	9	3	15	0	1	.259/.310/.500	90	3.8	.324	0.3	C(13): 1.9	0.4
2017	COL	MLB	25	266	30	8	1	0	16	33	55	0	1	.240/.341/.284	75	0.6	.316	0.5	C(77): -0.9, 2B(4): 0.1	0.4
2018	COL	MLB	26	216	19	4	4	3	27	26	33	2	0	.170/.292/.286	76	1.1	.189	2.5	C(64): 10.7, LF(2): 0.0	1.8
2019	COL	MLB	27	411	42	17	2	1	42	36	68	0	1	.262/.337/.329	85	13.2	.314	3.4	C(112): -4.5, 2B(8): 0.0	1.2
2020	COL	MLB	28	427	39	20	3	5	38	39	80	3	2	.246/.326/.351	78	10.0	.299	2.4	C 10	2.0

Comparables: Tucker Barnhart, Smoky Burgess, Omar Narváez

YEAR	TEAM	P. COUNT	FRM RUNS	BLK RUNS	THRW RUNS	TOT RUNS
2017	ABQ	1747	2.3	0.0	0.1	2.6
2017	COL	9693	-2.7	-0.6	1.1	-3.0
2018	COL	7924	10.2	-0.6	0.2	9.6
2019	COL	15038	-8.8	1.4	1.1	-6.4
2020	COL	19233	6.9	0.3	1.6	8.8

Wolters stood out in 2019. In the most home run-friendly environment in major-league history—in terms of both park and league—he managed just one in over 400 trips to the plate. That was dead last among players with that many plate appearances and only Billy Hamilton (zero in 353 PA) saved him from being last among players with 300-plus. Wolters also joined a group of just four other Rockies to have a season with just a single homer in at least 300 opportunities. The converted catcher has never had power, of course, with a mere six homers over his previous three seasons in Colorado. That helps to explain how his offensive performance actually improved, with his batting average resurgence aided by a bunch of ground balls traded for line drives. With his more useful stand-out tool (his framing) going in the wrong direction, Wolters needs to reverse that decline to be anything more than the wrong end of a Rockies fun fact.

PITCHERS

Yency Almonte RHP Born: 06/04/94 Age: 26 Bats: B Throws: R Height: 6'5" Weight: 217 Origin: Round 17, 2012 Draft (#537 overall)

YEAR	TEAM	LVL	AGE	W	L	SV	G	GS	IP	H	HR	BB/9	K/9	K	GB%	BABIP	WHIP	ERA	DRA	WARP	MPH	FB%	WHF	CSP
2017	HFD	AA	23	5	3	0	14	14	76¹	58	4	3.7	8.4	71	45%	.267	1.17	2.00	3.19	1.8				
2017	ABQ	AAA	23	3	1	0	8	7	35	41	7	5.4	5.7	22	50%	.321	1.77	4.89	6.92	-0.5				
2018	ABQ	AAA	24	3	5	1	18	10	43²	44	8	2.9	7.0	34	45%	.283	1.33	5.56	4.44	0.5				
2018	COL	MLB	24	0	0	0	14	0	14²	15	1	2.5	8.6	14	48%	.341	1.30	1.84	4.37	0.1	97.3	63	13.5	45.8
2019	ABQ	AAA	25	2	3	5	30	0	30	29	2	7.8	9.6	32	49%	.318	1.83	4.20	4.88	0.4				
2019	COL	MLB	25	0	1	0	28	0	34	39	7	3.7	7.7	29	34%	.302	1.56	5.56	6.39	-0.4	97.4	56.8	12.1	45.2
2020	COL	MLB	26	2	2	0	33	0	35	38	6	4.3	8.5	33	40%	.317	1.57	5.67	5.07	0.1	97.0	59.4	12.7	46.3

Comparables: Chase De Jong, Hunter Wood, Brad Peacock

Like many of his colleagues, Almonte suffered some serious regression after a promising 2018. While the fastball still touches 98, that helps very little when it is frequently returned with significant interest. The 25-year-old simply stopped missing bats with the heater as the season went on and finished the year with opponents slugging .781 against the pitch. The slider is still a real weapon: Almonte now has 39 strikeouts to just one walk with the pitch since his debut, with a .146 batting average allowed. The question is whether he will get enough opportunities to use it if the four-seam remains this ineffective. By the end of the year, this contrast appeared to have some material effects on his usage, as September represented the first month of his career in which Almonte threw more sliders than fastballs.

Chad Bettis RHP Born: 04/26/89 Age: 31 Bats: R Throws: R Height: 6'0" Weight: 201 Origin: Round 2, 2010 Draft (#76 overall)

YEAR	TEAM	LVL	AGE	W	L	SV	G	GS	IP	H	HR	BB/9	K/9	K	GB%	BABIP	WHIP	ERA	DRA	WARP	MPH	FB%	WHF	CSP
2017	ABQ	AAA	28	0	3	0	4	4	18²	22	2	2.9	5.3	11	55%	.312	1.50	4.82	5.17	0.1				
2017	COL	MLB	28	2	4	0	9	9	46¹	52	8	2.1	5.8	30	50%	.293	1.36	5.05	4.39	0.6	92.9	51.9	9.7	43
2018	ABQ	AAA	29	0	0	0	3	3	14	16	2	1.9	6.4	10	51%	.311	1.36	5.14	4.37	0.2				
2018	COL	MLB	29	5	2	0	27	20	120¹	121	18	3.5	6.0	80	51%	.280	1.40	5.01	5.74	-0.6	93.5	41.4	9.2	46.9
2019	COL	MLB	30	1	6	1	39	3	63²	78	10	3.0	5.9	42	61%	.325	1.55	6.08	5.22	0.2	95.6	39.1	9.7	49.1
2020	COL	MLB	31	2	2	0	33	0	35	39	5	3.2	7.0	27	57%	.314	1.48	5.05	5.13	0.1	93.3	41.9	9.4	46.6

Comparables: Joe Kelly, Wily Peralta, Jeff Manship

After three starts, Bettis had allowed 13 runs in the same number of innings. He didn't get to make any more in 2019. Moving to relief can often bring a clear velocity bump, and Reliever Bettis was no exception: he gained almost two full ticks on his fastball on average and nearly three by mid-season. What he failed to gain was strikeouts. A brief whiff surge in May gave way to a worse strikeout rate than Starter Bettis', as the 30-year-old punched out just 17 of the 139 batters he faced from the start of June onwards. The impingements that ended his season and led to surgery on both hips may have had something to do with that.

Ben Bowden LHP Born: 10/21/94 Age: 25 Bats: L Throws: L Height: 6'4" Weight: 235 Origin: Round 2, 2016 Draft (#45 overall)

YEAR	TEAM	LVL	AGE	W	L	SV	G	GS	IP	H	HR	BB/9	K/9	K	GB%	BABIP	WHIP	ERA	DRA	WARP	MPH	FB%	WHF	CSP
2018	ASH	A	23	3	0	0	15	0	15¹	17	2	2.9	14.7	25	43%	.429	1.43	3.52	3.64	0.2				
2018	LNC	A+	23	4	2	0	34	0	36²	35	6	3.7	13.0	53	35%	.337	1.36	4.17	3.48	0.6				
2019	HFD	AA	24	0	0	20	26	0	25²	8	1	2.5	14.7	42	38%	.171	0.58	1.05	1.94	0.8				
2019	ABQ	AAA	24	1	3	1	22	0	26	29	4	5.9	12.8	37	34%	.379	1.77	5.88	4.49	0.4				
2020	COL	MLB	25	1	1	0	11	0	12	13	2	3.4	12.1	16	38%	.365	1.47	5.13	4.67	0.1				

Comparables: Paul Fry, Andrew Vasquez, James Pazos

Bowden appeared to be racing to the majors over the first half of the season. After giving up three runs in his third appearance at Double-A, he recorded 23 consecutive scoreless appearances with 39 strikeouts and just five walks to practically force the Rockies to promote him to Albuquerque. The second-round pick failed to bend the team to his will once he got there, as he struggled with control and proved far more hittable. He also came to wider prominence for the wrong reason, surrendering the Futures Game-tying home run to Rangers prospect Sam Huff. DRA still considered Bowden an above-average pitcher, and with three pitches, including a sinker with plenty of run, he is better-equipped than many relievers to deal with life in Colorado. His major-league bow isn't far off.

Wade Davis RHP Born: 09/07/85 Age: 34 Bats: R Throws: R Height: 6'5" Weight: 227 Origin: Round 3, 2004 Draft (#75 overall)

YEAR	TEAM	LVL	AGE	W	L	SV	G	GS	IP	H	HR	BB/9	K/9	K	GB%	BABIP	WHIP	ERA	DRA	WARP	MPH	FB%	WHF	CSP
2017	CHN	MLB	31	4	2	32	59	0	58²	39	6	4.3	12.1	79	42%	.262	1.14	2.30	2.78	1.6	96.4	47.6	16	41.8
2018	COL	MLB	32	3	6	43	69	0	65¹	43	8	3.6	10.7	78	42%	.238	1.06	4.13	3.90	0.8	95.9	49	12.7	40.1
2019	COL	MLB	33	1	6	15	50	0	42²	51	7	6.1	8.9	42	40%	.349	1.88	8.65	6.31	-0.4	95.0	46.3	11.1	41
2020	COL	MLB	34	3	2	9	50	0	52	49	8	4.5	9.9	58	41%	.301	1.43	4.53	4.16	0.7	94.6	46.9	12.8	40.3

Comparables: Jason Isringhausen, Daniel Hudson, Jim Gott

The warning signs have been there for Davis since his year in Chicago, when his velocity was starting to dip and he began nibbling around the zone to compensate. Now the demoted closer isn't throwing any harder than when he was a starter, and the results were much, much worse. No longer able to challenge hitters in the zone with his fastball at all, Davis has seen his secondary pitches lose effectiveness too. The loss in velocity hasn't helped his walk rate either. A violent reversal of his BABIP fortune from 2018 completed this run-per-inning recipe for disaster. A move to the bullpen once rejuvenated Davis, but there's no transition the 34-year-old could make that would have remotely the same effect. At this point, the Rockies will have to hope for respectable middle reliever and brace themselves for worse.

Jairo Díaz RHP Born: 05/27/91 Age: 29 Bats: R Throws: R Height: 6'0" Weight: 200 Origin: International Free Agent, 2007

YEAR	TEAM	LVL	AGE	W	L	SV	G	GS	IP	H	HR	BB/9	K/9	K	GB%	BABIP	WHIP	ERA	DRA	WARP	MPH	FB%	WHF	CSP
2017	ABQ	AAA	26	0	1	3	20	0	18	16	1	3.5	8.5	17	56%	.306	1.28	5.00	3.18	0.4				
2017	COL	MLB	26	0	0	0	4	0	5	12	0	9.0	3.6	2	59%	.545	3.40	9.00	7.96	-0.2	100.1	77.3	5	43.2
2019	ABQ	AAA	28	1	0	6	16	0	20	12	0	2.7	9.9	22	65%	.250	0.90	0.45	1.54	0.9				
2019	COL	MLB	28	6	4	5	56	0	57²	56	7	3.0	9.8	63	50%	.318	1.30	4.53	3.49	1.2	98.8	56	15.2	47.7
2020	COL	MLB	29	3	3	3	55	0	58	61	8	3.7	10.3	67	52%	.340	1.47	4.77	4.33	0.7	98.2	57.6	14.5	46

Comparables: Jose A. Valdez, Hansel Robles, Kevin Jepsen

After a long and complicated road back from Tommy John surgery, Díaz emphatically turned the corner to open 2019 with just a single earned run given up over 20 Triple-A innings. That earned him the call back to the majors in mid-May, and he would stick around for the rest of the year. With his fastball touching 99, wipeout slider in full effect, and control finally harnessed, Díaz earned the trust of Bud Black and became the closer in September. A few bad outings inflated his ERA, but his overall park-adjusted performance was well above-average. Whether he gets another shot at closing likely depends on Wade Davis and Scott Oberg more than Díaz himself, but he's clearly next in line.

Phillip Diehl LHP Born: 07/16/94 Age: 25 Bats: L Throws: L Height: 6'2" Weight: 180 Origin: Round 27, 2016 Draft (#818 overall)

YEAR	TEAM	LVL	AGE	W	L	SV	G	GS	IP	H	HR	BB/9	K/9	K	GB%	BABIP	WHIP	ERA	DRA	WARP	MPH	FB%	WHF	CSP
2017	CSC	A	22	9	3	2	28	5	85¹	76	4	2.7	10.7	101	49%	.329	1.20	3.16	4.13	0.9				
2018	TAM	A+	23	2	2	3	25	0	48²	37	2	2.2	14.6	79	43%	.357	1.01	3.14	2.57	1.3				
2018	TRN	AA	23	0	1	1	14	0	26²	18	2	3.7	9.8	29	35%	.254	1.09	1.35	3.70	0.4				
2019	HFD	AA	24	0	0	0	11	0	13¹	5	0	2.0	8.1	12	58%	.161	0.60	0.00	2.88	0.3				
2019	ABQ	AAA	24	2	1	0	39	0	45¹	54	16	3.0	10.3	52	37%	.333	1.52	6.75	6.17	0.0				
2019	COL	MLB	24	0	0	0	10	0	7¹	10	1	2.5	9.8	8	21%	.391	1.64	7.36	6.25	-0.1	91.8	44.9	18.1	41.8
2020	COL	MLB	25	1	1	0	22	0	23	24	5	3.7	10.7	28	35%	.317	1.43	5.19	4.77	0.2	91.5	46	18.6	42.8

Comparables: James Pazos, Steven Matz, Kevin Chapman

Traded to Colorado last offseason for Mike Tauchman, Diehl cruised through his assignment to Double-A Hartford without giving up a single run to earn a promotion to Albuquerque. Meanwhile, Tauchman had a .641 OPS in his first month filling in for the injury-riddled Yankees. Diehl and his low-90s fastball didn't take so well to pitching at altitude: he allowed 41 runs in his next 49 appearances across Triple-A and the majors. As for Tauchman's season...let's just say it went in the opposite direction.

Carlos Estévez RHP Born: 12/28/92 Age: 27 Bats: R Throws: R Height: 6'6" Weight: 275 Origin: International Free Agent, 2011

YEAR	TEAM	LVL	AGE	W	L	SV	G	GS	IP	H	HR	BB/9	K/9	K	GB%	BABIP	WHIP	ERA	DRA	WARP	MPH	FB%	WHF	CSP
2017	ABQ	AAA	24	1	4	4	33	0	33²	23	2	2.7	9.1	34	60%	.253	0.98	1.34	1.93	1.2				
2017	COL	MLB	24	5	0	0	35	0	32¹	39	3	3.9	8.6	31	47%	.360	1.64	5.57	5.06	0.0	99.2	74.5	11.7	50
2018	ABQ	AAA	25	0	1	1	28	0	28¹	37	6	3.5	11.1	35	39%	.397	1.69	6.35	5.00	0.0				
2019	COL	MLB	26	2	2	0	71	0	72	70	12	2.9	10.1	81	39%	.304	1.29	3.75	4.09	1.0	99.6	69.3	15.1	52.7
2020	COL	MLB	27	3	3	0	55	0	58	57	9	3.3	10.5	68	40%	.319	1.34	4.29	3.97	0.9	99.0	71.3	14.5	52.3

Comparables: Jake Barrett, Michael Tonkin, John Gant

Estévez rebounded from a lost season in style by leading the team in appearances and relief innings to go along with a distinctly un-Coors ERA. A drop in his release point and increased reliance on his slider led to more strikeouts, fewer walks and a DRA 15 percent better than league-average. A flawless September was ruined in his very last appearance of the year as an Evan Longoria homer represented the only run he gave up all month. By that point, his case for a higher-leverage role was already well-made.

Kyle Freeland LHP Born: 05/14/93 Age: 27 Bats: L Throws: L Height: 6'4" Weight: 201 Origin: Round 1, 2014 Draft (#8 overall)

YEAR	TEAM	LVL	AGE	W	L	SV	G	GS	IP	H	HR	BB/9	K/9	K	GB%	BABIP	WHIP	ERA	DRA	WARP	MPH	FB%	WHF	CSP
2017	COL	MLB	24	11	11	0	33	28	156	169	17	3.6	6.2	107	56%	.308	1.49	4.10	5.91	-0.6	94.1	64.5	8.2	46.1
2018	COL	MLB	25	17	7	0	33	33	202¹	182	17	3.1	7.7	173	48%	.285	1.25	2.85	3.89	3.3	94.1	52.5	9.9	47.9
2019	ABQ	AAA	26	0	4	0	6	6	29²	40	4	4.9	8.5	28	60%	.379	1.89	8.80	6.44	0.1				
2019	COL	MLB	26	3	11	0	22	22	104¹	126	25	3.4	6.8	79	48%	.308	1.58	6.73	6.30	-0.6	93.8	52.1	10.3	47
2020	COL	MLB	27	7	9	0	24	24	122	140	19	3.5	7.3	98	49%	.322	1.54	5.40	4.86	1.3	93.5	56.2	9.7	47.7

Comparables: Brian Flynn, Ricky Romero, Wade LeBlanc

Buffy the Vampire Slayer introduced us to the term Big Bad, the overarching villain that the season-long plot ultimately revolved around. For Rockies pitchers, Coors Field is the Big Bad, and Freeland defeated it in 2018. In true supervillain fashion, Coors refused to simply roll over and quit, and instead plotted monstrous revenge. The memory of the best ERA by a starter in Coors history quickly faded as the new season started and dinger after dinger soared over the outfield wall. By the time he was demoted to the minors at the end of May, Freeland was just one round-tripper shy of tying his 17 homers allowed in 2018, a total accumulated over more than 200 innings. Essentially everything Freeland throws was hit harder, with the cutter, so effective last season, responsible for 10 homers alone, while the changeup lost separation in terms of both velocity and movement. A slightly reduced homer rate upon his return did little to improve the overall results. By the end of the year, his Coors ERA stood at 9.25, almost seven runs higher than it was in 2018. Buffy always eventually defeated the Big Bad for good. There's no real way to slay Coors Field—at least as long as the Rockies remain in Denver.

Chi Chi González RHP Born: 01/15/92 Age: 28 Bats: R Throws: R Height: 6'3" Weight: 215 Origin: Round 1, 2013 Draft (#23 overall)

YEAR	TEAM	LVL	AGE	W	L	SV	G	GS	IP	H	HR	BB/9	K/9	K	GB%	BABIP	WHIP	ERA	DRA	WARP	MPH	FB%	WHF	CSP
2019	ABQ	AAA	27	4	5	0	16	15	87	105	15	3.7	7.9	76	52%	.342	1.62	6.10	4.82	1.6				
2019	COL	MLB	27	2	6	0	14	12	63	59	11	4.7	6.6	46	45%	.257	1.46	5.29	6.16	-0.3	93.9	54.9	8.9	46.6
2020	COL	MLB	28	7	8	0	23	23	113	126	18	3.9	6.6	83	47%	.304	1.54	5.37	4.84	1.3	93.3	55.2	9	46.9

Comparables: Drew VerHagen, Kyle Ryan, Allen Webster

Following many years of development, salmon must undergo a grueling, dangerous journey to reach their ultimate goal. They need to swim upstream against the current, in some cases for hundreds of miles, while evading both natural predators and fishermen, in order to reach their spawning grounds. Many of them die during the journey, and even those that make it usually pass away not long after arrival, sometimes before they're even able to reproduce. González's journey back from Tommy John surgery was also long, challenging, and culminated at much higher ground without much success. He did ultimately put together some promising starts in September with signs of a rejuvenated changeup, and, unlike the salmon, he gets to come back next season and have another go.

Jon Gray RHP Born: 11/05/91 Age: 28 Bats: R Throws: R Height: 6'4" Weight: 227 Origin: Round 1, 2013 Draft (#3 overall)

YEAR	TEAM	LVL	AGE	W	L	SV	G	GS	IP	H	HR	BB/9	K/9	K	GB%	BABIP	WHIP	ERA	DRA	WARP	MPH	FB%	WHF	CSP
2017	ABQ	AAA	25	0	0	0	2	2	9¹	10	2	4.8	12.5	13	48%	.348	1.61	1.93	4.67	0.1				
2017	COL	MLB	25	10	4	0	20	20	110¹	113	10	2.4	9.1	112	49%	.336	1.30	3.67	3.32	2.8	98.0	57.4	9.9	49.8
2018	COL	MLB	26	12	9	0	31	31	172¹	180	27	2.7	9.6	183	49%	.323	1.35	5.12	4.45	1.7	97.4	49.7	13.3	48.7
2019	COL	MLB	27	11	8	0	26	25	150	147	19	3.4	9.0	150	52%	.314	1.35	3.84	3.97	2.9	98.0	52.7	12.4	48.6
2020	COL	MLB	28	9	9	0	26	26	156	163	21	3.4	9.7	167	50%	.330	1.43	4.64	4.24	2.7	97.2	52.7	12.3	49.2

Comparables: Vince Velasquez, Kevin Gausman, Dan Straily

Fifty might be too many shades even for a pitcher as inconsistent as Gray. Nonetheless, 2019 presented yet another version—or versions—of the starter who at various points in the last four years has looked like everything from the team's ace to back-of-the-rotation fodder with a cloudy future. By comparison to the rest of the rotation, this Gray was a bright spot, going deeper into games more consistently than ever before and simply keeping the team in them more often than anyone else. Yes, there were starts where he was simply off, and this wasn't the shining example of a rotation-leading workhorse we once hoped for. The hard contact alone also paints a dim picture of Gray's chance of ever truly reaching his ceiling. Still, while this season wasn't brilliant, it was still tinged with far more hope than the previous campaign.

Jeff Hoffman RHP Born: 01/08/93 Age: 27 Bats: R Throws: R Height: 6'5" Weight: 227 Origin: Round 1, 2014 Draft (#9 overall)

YEAR	TEAM	LVL	AGE	W	L	SV	G	GS	IP	H	HR	BB/9	K/9	K	GB%	BABIP	WHIP	ERA	DRA	WARP	MPH	FB%	WHF	CSP
2017	ABQ	AAA	24	3	3	0	10	10	49²	44	3	3.4	8.5	47	46%	.285	1.27	4.71	2.51	1.7				
2017	COL	MLB	24	6	5	0	23	16	99¹	106	15	3.6	7.4	82	42%	.304	1.47	5.89	6.08	-0.6	97.0	67	8.9	50.7
2018	ABQ	AAA	25	6	8	0	21	21	105²	105	9	4.0	8.7	102	46%	.331	1.44	4.44	4.24	1.6				
2018	COL	MLB	25	0	0	0	6	1	8²	15	0	7.3	5.2	5	53%	.469	2.54	9.35	7.23	-0.2	95.0	53.9	8.9	42.8
2019	ABQ	AAA	26	6	8	0	17	16	85¹	105	19	3.2	10.3	98	44%	.361	1.58	7.70	5.54	1.0				
2019	COL	MLB	26	2	6	0	15	15	70	77	21	4.4	8.7	68	37%	.298	1.59	6.56	6.93	-0.9	95.7	58.8	10	47.8
2020	COL	MLB	27	6	8	0	32	21	113	128	22	3.8	8.0	101	41%	.316	1.56	5.85	5.23	0.7	95.8	62.6	9.6	47.4

Comparables: Aaron Blair, André Rienzo, Daniel Mengden

Hoffman spent three years as a consensus top-100 prospect, and it has been three years since his last appearance on such a list. That's long enough that the shine of that prospect pedigree has faded and been replaced by doubt—not just about whether Hoffman can ever live up to that pedigree, but about whether he can even cut it as a major leaguer. His four-seam fastball was one of the worst pitches in baseball, with Hoffman allowing extra-base hits more often than he struck hitters out. Every now and then, the stuff shows up and a hitter swings wildly over a curveball or fails to catch up to a heater that explodes past them. That only serves to make it more maddening when the command fails Hoffman so badly later in the game, if not that very same inning. At 27, with a 6.11 ERA in over 200 big-league innings, he's running out of chances to show he can start. A full-time move to the bullpen might both ameliorate his command issues and allow him to get back to pumping 99 with the fastball.

DJ Johnson RHP Born: 08/30/89 Age: 30 Bats: L Throws: R Height: 6'4" Weight: 230 Origin: Undrafted Free Agent, 2010

YEAR	TEAM	LVL	AGE	W	L	SV	G	GS	IP	H	HR	BB/9	K/9	K	GB%	BABIP	WHIP	ERA	DRA	WARP	MPH	FB%	WHF	CSP
2017	HFD	AA	27	1	1	4	43	0	64¹	53	4	3.4	7.1	51	59%	.265	1.20	2.80	3.33	1.1				
2018	ABQ	AAA	28	3	5	18	50	0	55¹	56	5	2.4	13.7	84	44%	.398	1.28	3.90	3.09	1.3				
2018	COL	MLB	28	1	0	0	7	0	6¹	6	0	2.8	12.8	9	38%	.375	1.26	4.26	4.70	0.0	95.4	44.8	16.2	44.8
2019	ABQ	AAA	29	4	1	3	40	0	48	62	8	3.0	12.6	67	48%	.429	1.62	5.62	4.78	0.7				
2019	COL	MLB	29	0	2	0	28	0	25	23	1	6.8	8.6	24	46%	.319	1.68	5.04	5.94	-0.2	94.9	58.3	11.9	48.2
2020	COL	MLB	30	2	2	0	33	0	35	32	5	3.3	8.9	34	45%	.285	1.28	3.83	4.07	0.5	94.2	56.1	12.5	46.5

Comparables: Kevin Shackelford, Andrew Kittredge, Jacob Barnes

An appearance in the 2018 postseason after an epic journey to the majors proved to be the biggest splash Johnson made in a Rockies uniform. He added opening day roster to his list of firsts, but failed to get enough hitters to bite on his slider and ended up with far too many walks on his line. Before he got the hook from the Colorado roster, Johnson seized the opportunity to pitch elsewhere in late October, crossing the Pacific to join the Hiroshima Carp.

Peter Lambert RHP Born: 04/18/97 Age: 23 Bats: R Throws: R Height: 6'2" Weight: 185 Origin: Round 2, 2015 Draft (#44 overall)

YEAR	TEAM	LVL	AGE	W	L	SV	G	GS	IP	H	HR	BB/9	K/9	K	GB%	BABIP	WHIP	ERA	DRA	WARP	MPH	FB%	WHF	CSP
2017	LNC	A+	20	9	8	0	26	26	142¹	147	18	1.9	8.3	131	43%	.321	1.24	4.17	4.10	1.9				
2018	HFD	AA	21	8	2	0	15	15	92²	80	6	1.2	7.3	75	50%	.282	0.99	2.23	3.19	2.3				
2018	ABQ	AAA	21	2	5	0	11	11	55¹	72	5	2.4	5.0	31	52%	.345	1.57	5.04	5.67	-0.1				
2019	ABQ	AAA	22	2	2	0	11	11	60¹	63	10	2.4	7.6	51	53%	.294	1.31	5.07	3.19	2.1				
2019	COL	MLB	22	3	7	0	19	19	89¹	119	18	3.6	5.7	57	48%	.333	1.74	7.25	7.43	-1.6	94.3	53	7.5	47.2
2020	COL	MLB	23	5	6	0	37	15	90	115	16	3.2	5.7	57	48%	.324	1.62	6.13	5.40	0.3	94.2	54.9	7.7	48.9

Comparables: Jarrod Parker, Héctor Rondón, Eric Hurley

Deserved Run Average is designed to isolate a pitcher's contribution from other factors like defense (the Rockies were dead last in Park Adjusted Defensive Efficiency) and park (enough said). This can have the effect of suggesting that Rockies pitcher seasons aren't nearly as bad as their ERA indicates. It is therefore particularly disheartening that Lambert, who ranked dead last in ERA among all pitchers with at least 70 innings, in fact had a worse DRA. It's no coincidence that the rookie had the second-worst swinging strike rate and sixth-worst strikeout rate among that same group. Lambert's lack of bat-missing stuff might play elsewhere given his strong command profile. At Coors, all it meant was that he deserved every bit of that 7.25 ERA, and then some.

German Márquez RHP Born: 02/22/95 Age: 25 Bats: R Throws: R Height: 6'1" Weight: 225 Origin: International Free Agent, 2011

YEAR	TEAM	LVL	AGE	W	L	SV	G	GS	IP	H	HR	BB/9	K/9	K	GB%	BABIP	WHIP	ERA	DRA	WARP	MPH	FB%	WHF	CSP
2017	ABQ	AAA	22	0	0	0	3	2	10	8	2	0.0	16.2	18	53%	.353	0.80	2.70	1.00	0.5				
2017	COL	MLB	22	11	7	0	29	29	162	174	25	2.7	8.2	147	47%	.316	1.38	4.39	5.08	0.9	97.9	65.5	10	53.7
2018	COL	MLB	23	14	11	0	33	33	196	179	24	2.6	10.6	230	48%	.312	1.20	3.77	3.23	4.7	97.9	54.9	13.4	49.9
2019	COL	MLB	24	12	5	0	28	28	174	174	29	1.8	9.1	175	50%	.304	1.20	4.76	3.26	4.7	97.7	52.1	13.2	50.5
2020	COL	MLB	25	10	9	0	26	26	161	176	23	2.6	9.7	172	49%	.339	1.38	4.63	4.22	2.8	97.5	57.7	12.8	52.3

Comparables: Lucas Giolito, Phil Hughes, Luis Severino

What a player deserved is at the heart at a lot of advanced metrics. When it comes to DRA, the notion of what is deserved rests on a player's expected contribution to each play. No play is made in isolation, and no player should get the entirety of the outcome credited to them.

How, then, should we process the fact that DRA considers Márquez to have been one of the top 20 starters in baseball once again? It is clear that he pitched more or less as well at home as he did on the road in terms of strikeouts, walks, and even home runs. It is also clear that he gave up two and a half more runs per nine innings in Colorado than he did everywhere else, and that over 150 points of BABIP separated his home performance from away.

Should we then consider Márquez to have been essentially the same pitcher regardless of whether he was in Denver or not? Should we think that Márquez was just as good as he was in 2018 (slightly better, in fact), when all the talk was of his mastering Coors? We probably should, and yet even with all the context the stats provide, it's hard to believe it. Knowing that he deserved certain results isn't quite the same as understanding that in an alternative universe, there's a Márquez that repeated his 2018 ERA, just as there was a Márquez last season that struggled badly at Coors.

When we get to the real outliers, we just have to try that little bit harder to accept what the underlying stats are telling us. It is one thing to say that a player gave up a few extra home runs and just got unlucky. It's another to believe that Márquez allowed almost twice as many runs as he deserved to at home based on his own expected contribution.

Or maybe this isn't difficult to accept at all. Maybe the issue is simply that Márquez made a seemingly convincing case that a good enough starter *could* reliably overcome Coors, and then that case was thoroughly dismissed. The deserved numbers tell us that the Rockies' ace did effectively pitch like one, if not of the very highest quality then certainly of the tier below. What happens after the ball leaves his hand is not in his control, and sometimes we get an unpleasant reminder that Coors, like life, doesn't always give you what you deserve.

Jake McGee LHP Born: 08/06/86 Age: 33 Bats: L Throws: L Height: 6'4" Weight: 237 Origin: Round 5, 2004 Draft (#135 overall)

YEAR	TEAM	LVL	AGE	W	L	SV	G	GS	IP	H	HR	BB/9	K/9	K	GB%	BABIP	WHIP	ERA	DRA	WARP	MPH	FB%	WHF	CSP
2017	COL	MLB	30	0	2	3	62	0	57¹	47	4	2.5	9.1	58	40%	.287	1.10	3.61	4.26	0.6	97.6	93.4	10.2	51.9
2018	COL	MLB	31	2	4	1	61	0	51¹	59	10	2.8	8.2	47	42%	.322	1.46	6.49	6.15	-0.7	96.6	86.3	11.1	53.2
2019	COL	MLB	32	0	2	0	45	0	41¹	47	11	2.4	7.6	35	37%	.300	1.40	4.35	6.33	-0.4	95.7	80.4	9.4	51.5
2020	COL	MLB	33	2	3	0	50	0	52	60	11	2.9	8.3	48	37%	.318	1.46	5.65	5.10	0.2	95.5	85.3	10.1	51.5

Comparables: Rafael Soriano, Jonathan Papelbon, Sean Doolittle

Rockies hurlers are used to their environment's making them look worse. In McGee's case, he had some company that made him seem better, as his ERA compared rather favorably to the other two expensive arms that were supposed to make up the back end of the Colorado bullpen. That's not to say that 2019 was a success, nor did it appear that the veteran southpaw deserved that number. The signs were encouraging early on, when McGee came out of the spring sitting 95 and touching 97 with his four-seamer. Then he sustained a knee sprain, never quite got the heat back when he returned, and suffered a second, more debilitating velocity drop mid-season that coincided with a truly brutal stretch over which hitters slugged .867 against the once-vaunted fastball. It was so bad that McGee actually started leaning on his second pitch, a hitherto unprecedented strategy. He either needs to incorporate the slider even more or figure out how to sustain the higher velo over a full season, because he simply can't compare to his former self without it.

Tim Melville RHP   Born: 10/09/89   Age: 30   Bats: R   Throws: R   Height: 6'4"   Weight: 225   Origin: Round 4, 2008 Draft (#115 overall)

YEAR	TEAM	LVL	AGE	W	L	SV	G	GS	IP	H	HR	BB/9	K/9	K	GB%	BABIP	WHIP	ERA	DRA	WARP	MPH	FB%	WHF	CSP
2017	ROC	AAA	27	4	3	0	11	10	66²	48	5	3.1	8.6	64	36%	.246	1.07	2.70	2.86	2.1				
2017	ELP	AAA	27	1	0	0	2	2	9²	7	0	9.3	7.4	8	36%	.250	1.76	4.66	5.35	0.0				
2017	MIN	MLB	27	0	1	0	1	1	3¹	4	1	8.1	10.8	4	50%	.333	2.10	13.50	6.36	0.0	96.0	59.8	8.5	36.6
2017	SDN	MLB	27	0	0	0	2	0	2¹	3	0	11.6	11.6	3	17%	.500	2.57	7.71	8.47	-0.1	96.3	67.3	7.7	42.7
2018	NOR	AAA	28	9	6	4	40	14	104²	115	15	3.6	7.1	82	39%	.311	1.50	5.33	6.19	-0.9				
2019	ABQ	AAA	29	10	5	0	18	17	96¹	113	24	3.7	8.8	94	42%	.320	1.59	5.42	5.12	1.5				
2019	COL	MLB	29	2	3	0	7	7	33¹	34	9	3.8	6.5	24	45%	.263	1.44	4.86	6.21	-0.2	91.0	33.4	11.9	44.6
2020	COL	MLB	30	2	2	0	33	0	35	37	7	4.0	7.4	29	40%	.285	1.49	5.41	5.46	0.0	90.7	36.9	11.4	42.4

Comparables: Matt Magill, Drew Gagnon, Josh A. Smith

Melville's indy-league-to-the-majors tale didn't turn out all that well in 2017 beyond the fact that he simply made the majors, so he rebooted the story in 2019. Once again, Melville went from the Long Island Ducks to Triple-A and, after a three-month wait, was back in the big leagues for his first truly successful major league start: seven innings of one-run ball against the Diamondbacks. He continued the fairytale by shutting out the Braves over five innings in his next start. That was as good as it got for the one-time top draft prospect. Given the frequency with which the entertainment industry recycles former projects, Melville might yet get another run at spinning this yarn into something even better than the first two versions.

Scott Oberg RHP   Born: 03/13/90   Age: 30   Bats: R   Throws: R   Height: 6'2"   Weight: 203   Origin: Round 15, 2012 Draft (#468 overall)

YEAR	TEAM	LVL	AGE	W	L	SV	G	GS	IP	H	HR	BB/9	K/9	K	GB%	BABIP	WHIP	ERA	DRA	WARP	MPH	FB%	WHF	CSP
2017	COL	MLB	27	0	1	0	66	0	58¹	70	4	3.7	8.5	55	58%	.367	1.61	4.94	4.89	0.2	98.4	56.4	12.2	50.5
2018	ABQ	AAA	28	1	0	3	13	0	15¹	14	1	1.2	8.2	14	62%	.333	1.04	1.76	3.36	0.3				
2018	COL	MLB	28	8	1	0	56	0	58²	45	4	1.8	8.7	57	58%	.270	0.97	2.45	3.49	1.0	97.4	55.1	14.7	48.1
2019	COL	MLB	29	6	1	5	49	0	56	39	5	3.7	9.3	58	51%	.248	1.11	2.25	3.31	1.2	96.1	52.2	13.2	47.2
2020	COL	MLB	30	3	3	19	55	0	58	58	8	3.4	9.6	62	52%	.316	1.37	4.26	3.97	0.9	96.3	54.1	13.4	48.2

Comparables: Kevin Quackenbush, Darren O'Day, Neftalí Feliz

In early August, Oberg finally got his reward for being the best reliever in the Rockies 'pen: He was promoted to closer at the expense of Wade Davis. Two weeks later, his season came to an abrupt end in scary fashion when he was hospitalized with blood clots in his pitching arm. While it was the second time Oberg suffered from a problem with clots, the 29-year-old is confident the underlying cause has now been treated. As long as the issue is truly past, Bud Black desperately needs Oberg in his bullpen. He was the team's highest-leverage option in 2019 even though his run as closer was so quickly curtailed. That status was deserved too, as the right-hander's season ranked as one of the top 10 all-time Rockies pitching seasons by not only ERA, but also DRA-. Regardless of how he is deployed in 2020, it will simply be good to see Oberg back on the mound.

Riley Pint RHP   Born: 11/06/97   Age: 22   Bats: R   Throws: R   Height: 6'5"   Weight: 225   Origin: Round 1, 2016 Draft (#4 overall)

YEAR	TEAM	LVL	AGE	W	L	SV	G	GS	IP	H	HR	BB/9	K/9	K	GB%	BABIP	WHIP	ERA	DRA	WARP	MPH	FB%	WHF	CSP
2017	ASH	A	19	2	11	0	22	22	93	96	3	5.7	7.6	79	60%	.325	1.67	5.42	5.67	-0.4				
2018	BOI	A-	20	0	2	0	3	3	8	4	0	10.1	9.0	8	47%	.235	1.62	1.12	5.39	0.0				
2019	ASH	A	21	0	1	0	21	3	17²	12	0	15.8	11.7	23	50%	.316	2.43	8.66	7.50	-0.6				
2020	COL	MLB	22	2	2	0	33	0	35	34	5	4.5	7.2	28	51%	.285	1.48	4.90	4.99	0.2				

Comparables: Sal Romano, Nate Adcock, Tyrell Jenkins

Saying that Pint has control problems is like saying the Titanic had iceberg problems. It's *technically* accurate while barely scratching the surface of the issue. Pint walked an astounding 31 of the 98 batters he faced for Asheville before going down with yet another injury, this time a shoulder strain. Any evaluator will tell you that Pint's stuff is so electric that his ceiling is as high as that of almost any pitching prospect in the game. At this point, however, the possibility that the control issues sink his career before he even reaches the majors looms disturbingly large underneath the veneer of that gaudy stuff.

Ryan Rolison LHP   Born: 07/11/97   Age: 22   Bats: R   Throws: L   Height: 6'2"   Weight: 195   Origin: Round 1, 2018 Draft (#22 overall)

YEAR	TEAM	LVL	AGE	W	L	SV	G	GS	IP	H	HR	BB/9	K/9	K	GB%	BABIP	WHIP	ERA	DRA	WARP	MPH	FB%	WHF	CSP
2018	GJR	RK	20	0	1	0	9	9	29	15	2	2.5	10.6	34	66%	.200	0.79	1.86	0.65	1.7				
2019	ASH	A	21	2	1	0	3	3	14²	8	0	1.2	8.6	14	40%	.216	0.68	0.61	2.43	0.5				
2019	LNC	A+	21	6	7	0	22	22	116¹	129	22	2.9	9.1	118	46%	.320	1.44	4.87	4.61	0.6				
2020	COL	MLB	22	2	2	0	33	0	35	36	6	3.5	7.5	29	42%	.288	1.41	4.76	5.02	0.2				

Comparables: Josh Rogers, Devin Smeltzer, Scott Diamond

Rolison came into the season as BP's top pitching prospect in the Rockies organization and left with more questions than answers. While his four-pitch mix and high degree of polish helped him make short work of Low-A, the same couldn't be said of his lengthier stint at the level above. The command wavered frequently, and the underlying stuff simply didn't flash enough to compensate for it. His curveball leads the way when the command is on, but with the fastball struggling to get out of the low 90s and a slider and change that have a long way to go to catch up with the curve, more than a little extra polish is needed to make this package play at the higher levels.

Antonio Senzatela RHP   Born: 01/21/95   Age: 25   Bats: R   Throws: R   Height: 6'1"   Weight: 246   Origin: International Free Agent, 2011

YEAR	TEAM	LVL	AGE	W	L	SV	G	GS	IP	H	HR	BB/9	K/9	K	GB%	BABIP	WHIP	ERA	DRA	WARP	MPH	FB%	WHF	CSP
2017	COL	MLB	22	10	5	0	36	20	134²	128	18	3.1	6.8	102	50%	.280	1.30	4.68	4.63	1.3	97.4	71.8	7.6	52.2
2018	ABQ	AAA	23	3	1	0	8	8	37²	29	1	2.9	10.0	42	48%	.298	1.09	2.15	2.73	1.2				
2018	COL	MLB	23	6	6	0	23	13	90¹	94	10	3.0	6.9	69	47%	.302	1.37	4.38	5.10	0.1	96.6	64.1	8.9	47.5
2019	ABQ	AAA	24	1	1	0	7	7	34¹	45	7	2.6	3.1	12	50%	.314	1.60	5.77	5.63	0.4				
2019	COL	MLB	24	11	11	0	25	25	124²	161	19	4.1	5.5	76	55%	.333	1.75	6.71	7.14	-1.9	96.1	63.7	8	48
2020	COL	MLB	25	7	9	0	24	24	122	152	18	3.5	5.9	80	52%	.329	1.64	5.91	5.19	0.9	96.3	67.6	8.3	50.1

Comparables: Zach Eflin, Jake Thompson, Reynaldo López

Living at extremes becomes a fact of life for Colorado starters. Senzatela had dealt admirably with that in his first two major-league seasons, which defied the environment with solid, respectable production. This year, when Coors saw the fifth-most home runs of any park in major-league history, Senzatela also veered towards the extreme in a number of areas. The good: Only three pitchers with as many starts had a higher ground ball rate in 2019. The bad: He also fell behind 3-0 more often than all but one of those starters, and none of them gave up more hits per inning than the young right-hander. Senzatela would be very happy with falling back to the middle ground, as long as the same also happened to his ERA.

Bryan Shaw RHP   Born: 11/08/87   Age: 32   Bats: B   Throws: R   Height: 6'1"   Weight: 232   Origin: Round 2, 2008 Draft (#73 overall)

YEAR	TEAM	LVL	AGE	W	L	SV	G	GS	IP	H	HR	BB/9	K/9	K	GB%	BABIP	WHIP	ERA	DRA	WARP	MPH	FB%	WHF	CSP
2017	CLE	MLB	29	4	6	3	79	0	76²	71	5	2.6	8.6	73	57%	.311	1.21	3.52	2.73	2.1	96.8	88.2	13.1	48.4
2018	COL	MLB	30	4	6	0	61	0	54²	70	9	4.6	8.9	54	49%	.370	1.79	5.93	4.07	0.5	96.5	84.8	12.5	43.8
2019	COL	MLB	31	3	2	1	70	0	72	69	12	3.6	7.2	58	50%	.275	1.36	5.38	5.05	0.2	94.8	75.4	11.6	44.7
2020	COL	MLB	32	2	3	0	50	0	52	55	8	3.7	8.0	46	50%	.308	1.47	4.96	4.54	0.5	94.9	80.9	12.2	44.9

Comparables: Greg McMichael, Kevin Jepsen, Juan Rincon

The $106 million the Rockies spent on their bullpen two offseasons ago was met with a lot of head-scratching. If one studied their comments for long enough to figure out this mystery, it appeared that they greatly valued durability, as well as the benefit of a pitcher's having an extended period of time in which to adjust to pitching at Coors. Well, Shaw has largely lived up to the durability part; he appeared in another 70 games in 2019. Only Tyler Clippard has made more pitching appearances since Shaw first appeared in the majors in 2011. As for adjusting to Coors, suffice it to say that that these past two seasons have, by a comfortable margin, been the worst of his career. Shaw's got at least one more season to prove that theory right, and likely two: in order for his 2021 option to vest, he just has to appear in 40 games. That's a mark he's topped by more than 20 games every year but his rookie season, when he only arrived in mid-June. Colorado might not be so pleased about that durability after all.

LINEOUTS

Hitters

HITTER	POS	TEAM	LVL	AGE	PA	R	2B	3B	HR	RBI	BB	K	SB	CS	AVG/OBP/SLG	DRC+	VORP	BABIP	BRR	FRAA	WARP
Julio Carreras	3B	GJR	Rk+	19	307	51	14	8	5	38	25	63	14	8	.294/.369/.466	115	24.4	.362	3.6		1.8
Yonathan Daza	LF	COL	MLB	25	105	7	1	1	0	3	7	21	1	0	.206/.257/.237	60	-1.8	.260	1.2	CF(24): -0.5, RF(3): 0.1	0.0
	LF	ABQ	AAA	25	418	67	30	4	11	48	25	52	12	9	.364/.404/.548	122	29.4	.399	-1.2	CF(86): 4.1, LF(2): 0.0	2.8
Eddy Diaz	SS	GJR	Rk+	19	177	32	12	3	0	10	8	33	20	9	.331/.366/.440	131	13.4	.414	2.4		1.3
Brenton Doyle	RF	GJR	Rk+	21	215	42	11	3	8	33	31	47	17	3	.383/.477/.611	198	38.0	.484	7.1		3.1
Josh Fuentes	3B	COL	MLB	26	56	8	1	0	3	7	1	20	1	0	.218/.232/.400	73	-0.8	.281	0.1	1B(11): -0.3, 3B(2): 0.0	-0.1
	3B	ABQ	AAA	26	437	66	23	2	17	64	25	118	1	1	.254/.298/.448	67	-2.4	.314	0.2	3B(95): 10.3, 2B(1): 0.0	0.8
Chris Iannetta	C	COL	MLB	36	164	20	10	0	6	21	18	54	0	0	.222/.311/.417	82	4.5	.306	1.5	C(45): -6.3	0.0
Grant Lavigne	1B	ASH	A	19	526	52	19	0	7	64	68	129	8	9	.236/.347/.327	87	-9.0	.314	-4.4	1B(111): 0.9	-0.5
Roberto Ramos	1B	ABQ	AAA	24	503	77	27	0	30	105	61	141	0	1	.309/.400/.580	124	28.6	.390	-1.3	1B(103): -7.8, 3B(2): -0.1	1.4
Mark Reynolds	1B	COL	MLB	35	162	13	7	0	4	20	22	57	2	0	.170/.290/.311	66	-3.7	.247	-0.7	1B(32): -2.5, P(1): 0.0	-0.7
Aaron Schunk	3B	BOI	A-	21	192	31	12	2	6	23	14	25	4	1	.306/.370/.503	138	14.4	.329	1.8	3B(37): 7.4	2.2
Eric Stamets	SS	CLE	MLB	27	48	4	1	0	0	2	5	24	0	0	.049/.149/.073	38	-1.6	.111	-1.1	SS(15): -0.8	-0.3
	SS	COH	AAA	27	327	40	10	5	6	38	27	83	14	1	.244/.312/.373	65	2.2	.317	1.4	SS(51): 2.5, 2B(22): -1.3	0.2
Michael Toglia	1B	BOI	A-	20	176	25	7	0	9	26	28	45	1	1	.248/.369/.483	132	10.2	.290	0.3	1B(38): -0.2	0.6
Terrin Vavra	SS	ASH	A	22	453	79	32	1	10	52	62	62	18	9	.318/.409/.489	152	33.2	.350	0.4	SS(53): -1.4, 2B(40): 2.7	4.0

A 2017 international signee, **Julio Carreras** made some noise in the Dominican Summer League and continued to do so in his stateside debut. There's speed, athleticism, and, if he can iron out his approach at the plate, an exciting future ahead. He's got plenty of time to do it. ⊗ **Yonathan Daza**'s run at the PCL batting title was a promising chapter in his quest to be more than just a fourth outfielder. The next installment may prove to be rather more challenging, as he needs to pass several other options on a team that rarely hands rookies a starring role. ⊗ **Eddy Diaz** loves to run, but he found catchers in the Pioneer League to be a tougher assignment than those he had succeeded against at an 86 percent rate in the Dominican Republic. His blazing speed and contact skills still helped him to excel at the plate before a knee injury cut short his season. ⊗ Fourth-rounder **Brenton Doyle** couldn't be stopped in the Pioneer League. That even proved to be the case when a foul ball into the dugout broke his cheekbone: Doyle was only out for three weeks and marched to a batting title upon his return. ⊗ Now that the upper levels of pro ball have silenced his bat, you'd be hard-pressed to convince people **Josh Fuentes** wasn't a generic OOTP regen, particularly considering the suspicious proximity between his pro debut and the retirement of namesake Brian. ⊗ They say you can't ever go home again, but as **Chris Iannetta** proved, it's really easy to go home. You just can't ever be young or hopeful or happy ever again. ⊗ Following up on an incredible debut in Rookie ball, **Grant Lavigne** acted like somebody else entirely with Asheville. He needs to start taking what he gets and turning it into something other than ground balls, as he can't even fake it anywhere but first base. Oh Grant. Why'd you have to go and make things so complicated? ⊗ That **Roberto Ramos**' near-1.000 OPS at Triple-A was only good for a 124 DRC+ spoke volumes about both the swing-and-miss in his game and what the major-league ball has done to the Triple-A run environment. ⓧ If you weren't already convinced that **Mark Reynolds** is blind, his 2019 stat line aught to prove it. The Chandrayaan-2 made better contact. ⓧ Schunk is one of the words that appears when Batman hits a villain. Reports that the same happens when a ball hits **Aaron Schunk**'s bat have yet to be confirmed. ⓧ **Eric Stamets** spent the first two weeks of the season filling in for Francisco Lindor, which would be a little like trying to replace *Veep*'s Julia Louis-Dreyfuss with baseball's Eric Stamets. ⓧ The Rockies drafted switch-hitting slugger **Michael Toglia** 23rd overall and signed him for $2.7 million. Turning Colorado down for UCLA as a 35th-rounder back in 2016 was the right call. ⓧ Remarkably, **Terrin Vavra** is not the protagonist of an interstellar sci-fi novel. If one wanted to make the case he is from another planet, however, his numbers with Asheville would be an excellent starting point.

Pitchers

PITCHER	TEAM	LVL	AGE	W	L	SV	G	GS	IP	H	HR	BB/9	K/9	K	GB%	BABIP	WHIP	ERA	DRA	WARP	MPH	FB%	WHF	CSP
Ryan Castellani	ABQ	AAA	23	2	5	0	10	10	43^1	54	14	6.2	9.8	47	46%	.333	1.94	8.31	8.02	-0.5				
Mike Dunn	COL	MLB	34	1	0	0	28	0	17^2	17	4	3.1	7.6	15	41%	.260	1.30	7.13	4.24	0.2	93.1	47	12.4	47.6
Rico Garcia	HFD	AA	25	8	2	0	13	13	68	41	4	3.0	11.5	87	49%	.261	0.94	1.85	2.95	1.7				
	ABQ	AAA	25	2	4	0	13	13	61^1	77	14	4.1	7.5	51	37%	.330	1.71	6.90	5.95	0.5				
	COL	MLB	25	0	1	0	2	1	6	9	3	7.5	3.0	2	44%	.300	2.33	10.50	7.29	-0.1	93.2	61.6	6.1	46.3
Ashton Goudeau	HFD	AA	26	3	3	0	16	16	78^1	60	4	1.4	10.5	91	45%	.292	0.92	2.07	3.18	1.7				
Alexander Guillen	HFD	AA	23	2	2	1	37	0	76^2	50	4	2.5	10.7	91	44%	.251	0.93	1.53	2.50	2.0				
Joe Harvey	ABQ	AAA	27	0	1	1	9	0	8^2	12	5	5.2	10.4	10	21%	.304	1.96	10.38	7.88	-0.1				
	SWB	AAA	27	0	1	9	22	0	26	15	4	5.2	13.2	38	23%	.212	1.15	3.12	2.80	0.9				
	NYA	MLB	27	1	0	0	9	0	10	11	1	6.3	9.9	11	48%	.357	1.80	4.50	5.45	0.0	97.2	80.5	10.9	43.5
	COL	MLB	27	0	0	0	9	0	8	7	2	6.8	6.8	6	44%	.238	1.62	5.62	7.87	-0.2	96.1	70.9	11.3	42.6
Mitchell Kilkenny	GJR	Rk+	22	2	3	0	12	12	42	44	3	2.1	7.9	37	56%	.328	1.29	4.50	4.21	0.9				
Tyler Kinley	NWO	AAA	28	0	1	2	14	0	15^2	4	1	4.0	10.9	19	36%	.100	0.70	1.72	1.76	0.7				
	MIA	MLB	28	3	1	1	52	0	49^1	43	5	6.6	8.4	46	39%	.286	1.60	3.65	5.84	-0.3	96.7	42.3	13.8	42.7
Justin Lawrence	HFD	AA	24	0	4	0	30	0	26^2	35	1	6.8	8.8	26	51%	.412	2.06	8.77	7.75	-1.0				
	ABQ	AAA	24	1	1	0	8	0	10^1	12	3	7.8	5.2	6	53%	.290	2.03	8.71	7.04	-0.1				
Harrison Musgrave	ABQ	AAA	27	0	2	0	21	1	24	51	5	4.5	8.6	23	41%	.505	2.62	10.12	10.41	-1.0				
	COL	MLB	27	0	0	0	10	0	10	9	0	6.3	10.8	12	25%	.321	1.60	3.60	4.48	0.1	93.5	51.2	9.3	48.3
Seunghwan Oh	COL	MLB	36	3	1	0	21	0	18^1	29	6	2.9	7.9	16	38%	.383	1.91	9.33	6.27	-0.2	92.6	42.3	14.6	46.9
Wes Parsons	GWN	AAA	26	2	3	4	27	0	56^2	58	1	3.3	8.6	54	57%	.358	1.39	2.86	4.09	1.2				
	ATL	MLB	26	1	2	0	17	0	15^1	11	2	7.6	7.0	12	45%	.250	1.57	3.52	6.77	-0.2	95.4	62.1	7.9	42.2
	COL	MLB	26	0	0	0	15	0	19^1	21	4	7.4	6.5	14	48%	.293	1.91	6.98	7.61	-0.5	95.8	53.3	10.8	46
James Pazos	ABQ	AAA	28	1	3	1	39	0	44	69	8	4.7	8.6	42	48%	.422	2.09	8.80	6.91	-0.3				
	LEH	AAA	28	0	1	2	7	0	7^1	8	0	8.6	4.9	4	42%	.308	2.05	6.14	6.96	-0.1				
	COL	MLB	28	0	0	0	12	0	10^1	7	1	3.5	8.7	10	60%	.250	1.06	1.74	4.62	0.1	95.8	68.5	14.8	50.4
Chris Rusin	HFD	AA	32	1	0	0	3	0	7	8	0	3.9	6.4	5	39%	.348	1.57	5.14	5.58	-0.1				
	ABQ	AAA	32	3	4	0	22	10	65^2	83	7	2.9	5.8	42	55%	.335	1.58	4.93	4.50	1.3				
	COL	MLB	32	0	0	0	2	0	1	5	1	9.0	0.0	0	12%	.571	6.00	36.00	8.43	0.0	89.9	56	8	47.7
Antonio Santos	LNC	A+	22	3	6	0	18	18	99^1	116	11	1.6	8.7	96	42%	.348	1.35	4.35	5.17	-0.2				
	HFD	AA	22	3	3	0	8	8	45^2	47	3	2.0	8.7	44	41%	.342	1.25	4.93	5.09	-0.1				
Jesus Tinoco	ABQ	AAA	24	3	1	1	29	0	34	33	4	4.8	6.1	23	55%	.293	1.50	3.97	4.15	0.7				
	COL	MLB	24	0	3	1	24	0	36	36	12	5.5	7.0	28	44%	.245	1.61	4.75	6.83	-0.6	96.1	62.3	9.9	44.2

A solid AFL showing in 2018 did enough to earn **Ryan Castellani** the call to Triple-A. There he got lit up, then sidelined with bone fragments in his elbow. He returned to the AFL, where an excellent ERA masked more mixed performance. If his work in Arizona impressed the team again, a major-league debut is imminent. ⓧ Pretty much all you need to know about **Mike Dunn**'s unsightly Rockies career is that now all three of his corresponding Annual comments mention the phrase "sunk cost." ⓧ An utterly dominant half-season at Double-A Hartford must feel a very long way off now for **Rico Garcia**. The 30th-round pick joined a long list of pitchers who would rather they hadn't toured the PCL and capped that off by getting crushed in his major-league debut. ⓧ **Ashton Goudeau** just recorded his best season as a professional pitcher thanks to an ERA approaching 2.00. Drafted way back in 2012, it's been a long time coming—and at 26 and only in Double-A, the Rockies may spend a few years yet waiting for Goudeau. ⓧ **Alexander Guillen** dazzled in a multi-inning relief role throughout the minor league season and maintained his dominance in the Arizona Fall League. ⓧ **Joe Harvey**'s results have been anything but average. A string of exceptionally good ratios was snapped by a rough introduction to the majors and an even more unpleasant trip to Albuquerque after his trade to Colorado. As a major-leaguer, he'd settle for being just an average Joe. ⓧ After leading Michigan all the way to the College World Series, Wolverines ace **Karl Kauffmann** fell at the final hurdle in the decider. His next challenge is to prove he can complement his lively sinker with enough secondaries to stick at the back end of the rotation. ⓧ Crushed? Sure. Mauled? It works. Trampled? Possibly. Spontaneously combusted? Plausible, if unconventional. Electrocuted? Back to the drawing board. **Mitchell Kilkenny** survived Tommy John surgery and made a solid pro debut, but every time he gets lit up, the only saving grace will be that some of Kenny's myriad *South Park* demises are just not going to fit in a headline. ⓧ You've heard of the Kinsey Scale, yeah? Well here's the Kinley Scale: it's just **Tyler Kinley**'s walk rate, and it ranges from 14 to 16 percent. ⓧ An aggressive assignment didn't work for sidearmer **Justin Lawrence**, as his command disappeared, along with the high-90s heat from his unusual slot. ⓧ A long-time Rays' farmhand, **José Mujica**, was finally on the front step of the majors in 2019 when Tommy John opened the door and tossed him back so hard he landed in Colorado. ⓧ When you pitch in the Rockies organization, posting a near-5.00 ERA on the road isn't ideal. It wouldn't have mattered regardless for **Harrison Musgrave**, who was attempting to offset an 11.21 ERA at home. ⓧ A common convention in video games is for the difficult boss of an early level to return as a normal enemy in some later stage. The idea is to feel empowering for the player, but when you consider **Seunghwan Oh**, it's kind of depressing from the boss' point of view. ⓧ The Rockies took a gamble on **Wes Parsons** after he showed decent run prevention skills in Atlanta's org. That didn't pay off, as Parson's peripherals got the best of him in Colorado. ⓧ **James Pazos** was one of the worst relievers in the minors before the Phillies designated him for assignment and one of the worst relievers in the minors after the Rockies picked him up, but gave up just one run in 12 games when he was recalled in September. Small sample size can be a wonderful thing. ⓧ **Chris Rusin** allowed six of the nine major-league batters he faced to reach base and wasn't all that much better in the minors. Somehow, that resulted in his finishing the minor-league season in the rotation for the first time since 2016. ⓧ **Antonio Santos** has a playable fastball and a bunch of unremarkable secondaries. His delivery screams "reliever," but the Rockies keep whispering "no" in response. Maybe that'll change this year. ⚾

Jesus Tinoco pitched entirely out of the bullpen, but maintained a five-pitch starter's repertoire. Results suggest he might be better off focusing on just two or three of those pitches.

DETROIT TIGERS

Essay by Anthony Fenech

Player comments by Matt Sussman, Jarrett Seidler and BP staff

The first time Justin Verlander said my name, I took it as a compliment. It was October 2015 and the final day of my rookie year on the Tigers beat for the *Detroit Free Press*, as I stood near the back of the since-renovated visitors' clubhouse at the since-renamed U.S. Cellular Field.

A week earlier, as my long limp to the finish line entered the home stretch, one of my editors levied a challenge: Could I score an interview with the Tigers' resurgent ace and write it up for next Sunday's paper?

The write-up—a story about how Verlander bounced back from core muscle surgery to re-establish himself as one of the better pitchers in baseball—was apparently read by the subject, who pulled up to his locker stall close by.

"About time you wrote a good article, Anthony," he said.

After an eight-month struggle to establish myself in the veteran-laden Tigers clubhouse as a mostly anonymous, sometimes sarcastic, occasionally immature mid-20's beat writer, I had a name.

Following the game, a Tigers loss that cemented the first of three last-place seasons in my five years on the beat, I made my first uncomfortable final-day foray into the clubhouse. The task at hand: Bid adieu to players, coaches and other clubhouse staff with a handshake, and collect as many personal cell phone numbers as possible—"In case I need to get a hold of you in the offseason."

Most players complied. A couple offered their email addresses instead. J.D. Martinez wondered why I decided to ask while he was naked.

But I knew better than to ask Verlander, the celebrity-status face of the Tigers' franchise who had long since directed reporters to get in touch with his agent if they needed anything. I knew better than to overstep my bounds, lest I turn his sweet, sarcastic comment earlier into a sour season-ender for one of my more important relationships.

Relationships. In a word, relationships are what baseball reporting is all about. Relationships are where scoops come from. How the best stories are found. What any reporter worth their salt is judged by, the best of them standing the test of time, much longer than nearly all of us will be writing about baseball.

TIGERS PROSPECTUS
2019 W-L: 47-114, 5TH IN AL CENTRAL

Pythag	.298	30th	B-Age	27.5	7th
RS/G	3.61	30th	P-Age	27.9	14th
RA/G	5.68	28th	Salary	$115.7M	22nd
DRC+	80	29th	M$/MW	$100M	1st
DRA	5.59	25th	IL Days	1222	21st
FIP	4.87	23rd	$ on IL	19%	22nd
DER	.683	30th			

420'
370'
365'
345'
330'

- Opened 2000
- Open air
- Natural surface
- Fence profile: 6'10" to 14'

Three-Year Park Factors

Runs	Runs/RH	Runs/LH	HR/RH	HR/LH
102	104	99	102	97

Top Hitter WARP	1.6 Niko Goodrum
Top Pitcher WARP	3.7 Matthew Boyd
Top Prospect	Casey Mize

2019 Hit List Ranking

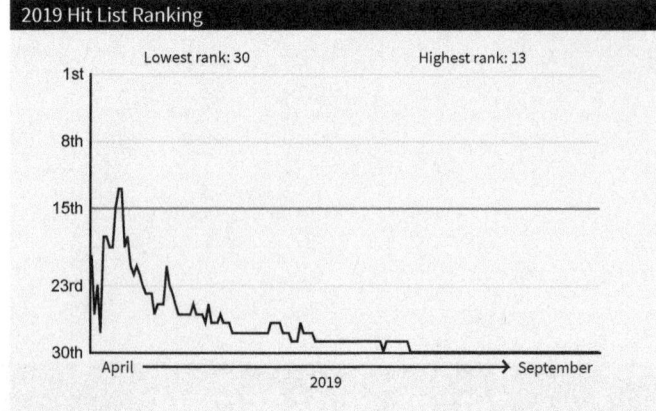

Committed Payroll (in millions)

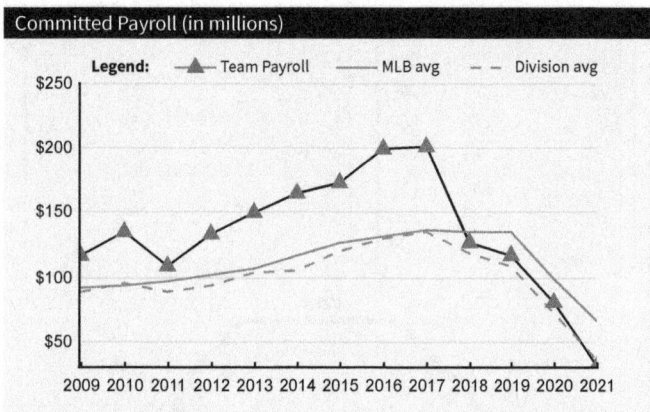

Farm System Ranking

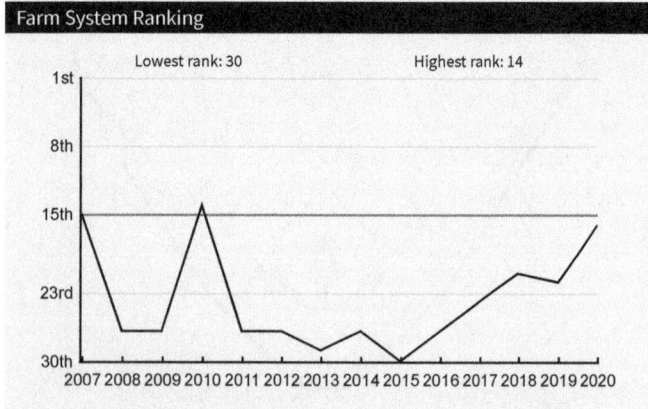

Personnel

Executive Vice President of Baseball Operations and General Manager
Al Avila

Vice President, Assistant General Manager
David Chadd

Vice President, Player Personnel
Scott Bream

Vice President, Player Development
Dave Littlefield

Manager
Ron Gardenhire

But as these relationships form, an inherent give-and-take is woven into the fabric between reporters and agents, executives, scouts, media relations officials and yes, players, too. It is not a spoken quid-pro-quo, rather an understanding of everyone's role in baseball's information ecosystem, a respect for what each sector needs and an appreciation when help is afforded.

Verlander willingly handed over his agent's personal cell phone number that day. A year later, after probably a dozen failed attempts, he made contact with me on it.

He texted me in early November, well past the due date for submitting ballots. I was a seasoned veteran then—or, so I thought—with two years under my belt and plenty of confidence after breaking big news earlier that offseason about the Tigers picking up the contract option of righty Joakim Soria.

A few of the many, awkward cold calls I placed to agents in laying the groundwork on the beat that first off-season were paying off. But this guy—probably a young, hotshot agent, I imagined—had never returned a call or text. Now, one of Verlander's agents was asking for a favor. In what figured to be a close American League Cy Young Award race, he wanted to get his client some publicity, as if it could change anything—ballots for Baseball Writers' Association of America awards are due before the postseason starts; disclosing them prior to announcement is frowned upon.

To make matters more complicated, I was an AL Cy Young voter. But this opportunity to give—building a relationship with a key person—was too much to pass up.

After hassling him for never answering my correspondence, I wrote up something about the historical perspective of Verlander winning a second Cy Young, which served as a Cooperstown clearinghouse of sorts. With the writing of a future rebuilding process on the wall—one which could send Verlander elsewhere—I was playing the long game, giving to take in the future.

"JV says thanks," he texted.

Although you likely can't notice it with the naked eye, the give-and-take in the reporting process is everywhere, showing up on your Twitter feeds constantly.

It's agents leaking information about teams interested in their clients; executives leaking teams' trade interest in their players to influence leverage; smokescreens sent through willing channels—I've certainly been willing before—and narratives pushed by those with agendas.

On a more grassroots level, it's finding out pitching assignments for a traveling scout. Providing them with injury updates and inside opinions on what your team may do. Writing a column when an agent keeps you up all night to convince you that your team should sign their client.

Through these exchanges, trust is built, with the information you give and what you do with the information you take: Nearly two months before the Tigers traded Verlander to the Astros right at the non-waiver trade deadline in 2017, a deal which looks more favorable as the years go on, a top scout from an interested team cornered me with questions about his clubhouse personality.

I didn't do anything with that information, hoping to build trust in the case something did, indeed, go down in the future. Trust waters relationships, helping them grow: Not only do the national reporters work harder than the vast majority of baseball writers, but they've been doing it for quite some time.

And those reporters—unlike the beat writers—have a huge audience, endearing them to agents and executives: "sources" who can communicate their message to the masses with one tweet.

Additionally, some of those national reporters are represented by agents who represent many players. In those cases, it's not hard to trace how certain reporters get scoops.

But for as big as scoops are—and I'd argue they've become less important as the speed of technology has increased—perhaps where beat writers have the biggest influence is locally, with their coverage.

Players read. Executives read. They want good coverage in their own backyard, where they too are trying to build a sense of community with their fans. It's one thing for a national reporter to tweet something out; it's another for a story to be in the newspaper in the clubhouse the next day.

⚾　　⚾　　⚾

The last time Verlander said my name, it was "Fenech," as in, "I told you guys, I'm not talking with Fenech here." I did not take it as a compliment.

This was not unexpected; Verlander was not happy that I wrote a story a season earlier about his claim that the Tigers misdiagnosed his injury years earlier. I was a bad guy. The only one to go ask him about it when he returned to Detroit. Also, a couple solar eclipse tweets years earlier made him feel like a nerd.

I told him that I didn't have much of a choice in the deal—that my editor had told me to come over here and talk to him about it. Plus, there were Tigers folks upset that he had thrown the medical staff under the bus.

But, as a reporter, I did have a choice. Perhaps, I never saw Verlander at his locker. Maybe he blew me off. "I just missed him," I could have told my editors, invoking an executive privilege as part of the give-and-take relationship that is at the core of baseball's information exchange.

There are many players who, in the same boat, had earned that privilege.

But from that Cy Young story—which didn't so much as trigger a response from his agent as the clock ticked down on his time with the Tigers—to the puff pieces and charity stories, the "Justin Verlander is a great guy, just like me and you" narrative I had willfully pedaled in exchange for the smallest kind of take at some point, the imbalanced scales were too much to ignore.

Verlander commented on the injury diagnosis that day. He said a lot more than what I wrote. Then, he deemed the story unnecessary. Then, he said we were off-the-record. Then, in our final comments before that fateful day last season which had me standing outside the clubhouse, I explained to him what was once explained to me, about how you break news in this industry. "I understand you don't want this story written," I told him. "But there's a give-and-take with all of this; you, agents, executives, everybody. And I've been giving for five years now, and, look...."

Verlander took my business card. I told him my deadline. That if he wanted to add anything to the quote, text me. That I'd love to keep in touch, that he's an important guy in Tigers history. He never gave me a text. ▪

—Anthony Fenech is a Tigers beat reporter for the Detroit Free Press.

HITTERS

Gordon Beckham INF Born: 09/16/86 Age: 33 Bats: R Throws: R Height: 6'0" Weight: 190 Origin: Round 1, 2008 Draft (#8 overall)

YEAR	TEAM	LVL	AGE	PA	R	2B	3B	HR	RBI	BB	K	SB	CS	AVG/OBP/SLG	DRC+	VORP	BABIP	BRR	FRAA	WARP
2017	TAC	AAA	30	355	37	16	0	9	45	20	58	3	2	.262/.313/.393	85	8.2	.293	1.4	2B(63): -4.5, 3B(7): -0.8	0.0
2017	SEA	MLB	30	18	2	0	0	0	0	1	2	1	0	.176/.222/.176	87	-1.9	.200	0.2	2B(5): 0.0, SS(4): -0.8	0.0
2018	TAC	AAA	31	425	64	24	1	10	51	57	52	6	2	.302/.400/.458	125	28.9	.326	1.6	2B(32): -0.6, SS(27): -0.5	3.1
2018	SEA	MLB	31	50	3	1	0	0	1	4	11	1	0	.182/.250/.205	82	-1.6	.242	0.3	2B(13): 1.4, 3B(6): 0.2	0.3
2019	DET	MLB	32	240	29	13	2	6	15	13	68	3	1	.215/.271/.372	66	-1.9	.282	0.0	2B(39): 0.3, SS(18): -1.6	-0.3
2020	DET	MLB	33	251	22	12	1	6	25	18	64	2	1	.208/.276/.337	63	-4.0	.263	0.1	2B 0, SS 0	-0.4

Comparables: Cliff Pennington, Vance Law, Terry Shumpert

Beckham is the type of player who looks and feels like he'll be in the league until he's 40, in part because he'll basically accept any pittance of playing time you have for him. (That, and he already plays like that age.) He's the quintessential soft-spoken infielder gallivanting about from team to team, as long as he's somewhere on the diamond. Triple-A is fine, too, because it beats the alternative. He broke camp with the Tigers last year because most of his middle-infield competition was still on the vine, making him an upgrade due to the fact that he's not going to make "rookie mistakes." He just won't hit or make highlight plays. His extant march into Bloomquistian status does not have an ending in sight.

Miguel Cabrera   DH   Born: 04/18/83   Age: 37   Bats: R   Throws: R   Height: 6'4"   Weight: 249   Origin: International Free Agent, 1999

YEAR	TEAM	LVL	AGE	PA	R	2B	3B	HR	RBI	BB	K	SB	CS	AVG/OBP/SLG	DRC+	VORP	BABIP	BRR	FRAA	WARP
2017	DET	MLB	34	529	50	22	0	16	60	54	110	0	1	.249/.329/.399	103	-9.8	.292	-6.6	1B(115): -1.7	0.1
2018	DET	MLB	35	157	17	11	0	3	22	22	27	0	0	.299/.395/.448	108	7.0	.352	0.5	1B(32): 0.0	0.4
2019	DET	MLB	36	549	41	21	0	12	59	48	108	0	0	.282/.346/.398	100	8.6	.336	-4.4	1B(26): -1.5	0.3
2020	DET	MLB	37	525	60	26	1	15	63	51	110	1	0	.286/.358/.440	108	8.1	.346	-3.4	1B 0	0.8

Comparables: Cliff Floyd, Matt Holliday, Jim Rice

We knew it would happen eventually. Cabrera's body has finally designated him to be a hitter. He's working with one good knee—which most orthopedic specialists will tell you is 50 percent of the optimal amount of good knees to play sports—and is learning to slug with just upper body brawn, which you might remember was sapped a bit from his ruptured biceps in 2018. Hitting double-digit dingers might be a chore for him from here on out. His biggest value to the Tigers remains being *Miguel freaking Cabrera* and rare is the opportunity to be a young player batting alongside an active future Hall of Famer. Of course, they're just going to see him churn out more sad singles than a Kraft factory.

Daz Cameron   CF   Born: 01/15/97   Age: 23   Bats: R   Throws: R   Height: 6'2"   Weight: 195   Origin: Round 1, 2015 Draft (#37 overall)

YEAR	TEAM	LVL	AGE	PA	R	2B	3B	HR	RBI	BB	K	SB	CS	AVG/OBP/SLG	DRC+	VORP	BABIP	BRR	FRAA	WARP
2017	QUD	A	20	511	79	29	8	14	73	45	108	32	12	.271/.349/.466	132	38.5	.323	3.1	CF(110): 1.8, LF(4): -0.7	3.9
2018	LAK	A+	21	246	35	9	3	3	20	25	69	10	4	.259/.346/.370	119	9.9	.366	2.5	CF(38): 1.9, RF(18): 0.9	1.7
2018	ERI	AA	21	226	32	12	5	5	35	25	53	12	5	.285/.367/.470	126	11.4	.366	3.4	CF(34): -7.0, RF(16): 1.5	1.1
2018	TOL	AAA	21	62	8	4	1	0	6	2	15	2	2	.211/.246/.316	52	-1.1	.279	0.7	CF(14): 0.3, RF(1): 0.0	0.0
2019	TOL	AAA	22	528	68	22	6	13	43	62	152	17	8	.214/.330/.377	86	13.1	.291	2.4	CF(92): -1.0, RF(19): 5.4	1.3
2020	DET	MLB	23	251	24	12	2	5	25	22	84	9	4	.215/.297/.356	72	-0.7	.318	0.4	CF 0, RF 1	0.0

Comparables: Brett Phillips, Alex Jackson, Rymer Liriano

You have to think the Tigers envisioned Cameron developing into a player like his All-Star father, Mike, when they acquired him in the Verlander deal, right? They certainly have broadly similar skill sets: outfielders light on the hit tool and extremely loud on the other tools. Cameron *père* was only a career .249 hitter, and never hit .270 in a season where he qualified for the batting title. Yet he consistently hit for just enough average to let his potent power/speed/ glove combination carry the day. After a season-plus of brutal struggles against Triple-A arms, Cameron *fils* needs to substantially improve his bat-to-ball skills to even make it to "just enough." His pops didn't establish himself as a major-league regular until he was 24, so there's a little time left to get back on track, but the sand is starting to pile up at the bottom of the hourglass.

Roberto Campos   OF   Born: 06/14/03   Age: 17   Bats: R   Throws: R   Height: 6'3"   Weight: 200   Origin: International Free Agent, 2019

When the Tigers signed Campos last summer for $2.85 million, it was one of the few genuine surprises in the July 2nd international free agent market. Seven-figure July 2nd signees are often publicly "connected" to teams (read: in agreement on early and illegal deals) months to years in advance of becoming official, and deals involving players at this bonus level are almost always known ahead of time. Yet, when the Tigers announced the Campos signing, few knew who he was at all, as he didn't make any of the top July 2 prospect lists. We know he defected from Cuba to the Dominican Republic during a youth baseball tournament in 2016 and trained thereafter with former Tiger-turned-buscone Alex Sánchez, but that's about it. Check back in two or three years to see if he's a real prospect, because we don't have the slightest clue right now.

Jeimer Candelario   CI   Born: 11/24/93   Age: 26   Bats: B   Throws: R   Height: 6'1"   Weight: 221   Origin: International Free Agent, 2010

YEAR	TEAM	LVL	AGE	PA	R	2B	3B	HR	RBI	BB	K	SB	CS	AVG/OBP/SLG	DRC+	VORP	BABIP	BRR	FRAA	WARP
2017	IOW	AAA	23	330	39	27	3	12	52	41	72	0	0	.266/.361/.507	125	22.9	.315	-4.5	3B(70): 5.0, 1B(16): -0.7	2.1
2017	TOL	AAA	23	128	13	9	1	3	19	5	32	1	0	.264/.297/.430	79	1.1	.333	-1.9	3B(28): -1.5	-0.2
2017	CHN	MLB	23	36	2	2	0	1	3	1	12	0	0	.152/.222/.303	98	-1.1	.200	0.2	3B(9): 0.9, 1B(1): 0.0	0.2
2017	DET	MLB	23	106	16	7	0	2	13	12	18	0	0	.330/.406/.468	95	7.0	.392	0.2	3B(27): -2.4	0.1
2018	DET	MLB	24	619	78	28	3	19	54	66	160	3	2	.224/.317/.393	91	16.4	.279	-2.4	3B(140): -4.1	0.9
2019	TOL	AAA	25	178	30	10	2	9	33	22	35	0	0	.320/.416/.588	154	18.5	.367	-1.4	3B(30): 0.1, 1B(7): -0.4	1.5
2019	DET	MLB	25	386	33	17	2	8	32	43	99	3	1	.203/.306/.337	78	2.0	.262	-1.0	3B(69): -1.0, 1B(20): -0.2	0.0
2020	DET	MLB	26	525	56	23	3	16	61	55	130	1	1	.224/.314/.394	88	3.3	.276	-1.0	3B 0, 1B 0	0.3

Comparables: Mat Gamel, Matt Tuiasosopo, Rio Ruiz

In a Tigers lineup filled with more hackers than an audition line for the 1995 box office smash thriller *The Net*, Candelario was expected to be one of the rare batsmen to hold his own. And he began with a bang, recording the entire league's first five-hit game of 2019. But his summer was marred with demotions, primarily because of his bat, and even when he crawled his way back up he lost the third base job to Dawel Lugo. Candelario struggled from both sides of the plate, especially on pitches up in the zone—an aspect of his game that doesn't bode well, given the northern drift of fastballs across the league. At 26, we've yet to see results from the "one sure thing" the Tigers had to offer, further proving nothing is what it seems, which was also the point in *The Net*. (Probably.)

Harold Castro UT   Born: 11/30/93   Age: 26   Bats: L   Throws: R   Height: 6'0"   Weight: 180   Origin: International Free Agent, 2011

YEAR	TEAM	LVL	AGE	PA	R	2B	3B	HR	RBI	BB	K	SB	CS	AVG/OBP/SLG	DRC+	VORP	BABIP	BRR	FRAA	WARP
2017	LAK	A+	23	33	3	2	1	0	3	0	3	2	0	.364/.364/.485	132	0.0	.400	-0.2	2B(6): 0.6, SS(1): 0.2	0.2
2017	ERI	AA	23	449	51	16	4	1	30	18	53	20	9	.290/.325/.355	84	6.2	.326	1.0	CF(44): -2.9, 2B(42): 0.3	0.4
2018	ERI	AA	24	116	10	5	0	0	10	4	21	2	1	.282/.310/.327	78	-0.6	.344	0.1	2B(14): -1.6, 3B(8): 0.9	0.0
2018	TOL	AAA	24	251	24	8	0	2	19	5	47	3	3	.257/.270/.315	65	-5.4	.309	1.0	3B(30): -0.1, SS(22): -1.7	-0.4
2018	DET	MLB	24	10	2	0	0	0	0	0	2	1	0	.300/.300/.300	79	-0.1	.375	-0.1	SS(4): 0.1, 2B(2): 0.0	0.0
2019	TOL	AAA	25	134	20	5	1	4	25	9	26	1	3	.328/.371/.484	123	10.1	.387	1.6	2B(23): -1.0, 1B(2): 0.1	0.9
2019	DET	MLB	25	369	30	10	4	5	38	9	86	4	2	.291/.305/.384	77	1.6	.367	-2.8	2B(34): -2.1, CF(30): 0.0	-0.4
2020	DET	MLB	26	245	21	10	2	3	22	8	55	6	3	.265/.293/.362	72	-2.5	.335	-1.4	3B 1, CF 0	-0.3

Comparables: Humberto Arteaga, Alvaro Espinoza, Rey Navarro

Now there's a batting line out of another era. Castro BABIP'd his way to a perfectly respectable batting average despite taking a walk only about twice a month and rarely hitting the ball hard. Suffice to say, we're extremely skeptical this offensive success, such as it is, was anything other than a random fluke. He can play every position except pitcher and catcher, so you can do worse for a 26th man on a bad team, but it's hard to see much upside here.

Willi Castro SS   Born: 04/24/97   Age: 23   Bats: B   Throws: R   Height: 6'1"   Weight: 205   Origin: International Free Agent, 2013

YEAR	TEAM	LVL	AGE	PA	R	2B	3B	HR	RBI	BB	K	SB	CS	AVG/OBP/SLG	DRC+	VORP	BABIP	BRR	FRAA	WARP
2017	LYN	A+	20	510	69	24	3	11	58	28	90	19	9	.290/.337/.424	119	33.6	.336	1.6	SS(122): 5.0	3.9
2018	AKR	AA	21	410	55	20	2	5	39	28	84	13	4	.245/.303/.350	97	17.4	.304	1.3	SS(96): 7.5	2.6
2018	ERI	AA	21	114	12	9	2	4	13	6	25	4	1	.324/.366/.562	99	10.0	.395	-0.8	SS(10): 0.7, 2B(9): -0.2	0.4
2019	TOL	AAA	22	525	75	28	8	11	62	37	110	17	4	.301/.366/.467	111	37.4	.369	0.3	SS(110): -15.3, 2B(7): 0.2	1.6
2019	DET	MLB	22	110	10	6	1	1	8	6	34	0	1	.230/.284/.340	69	0.8	.333	0.9	SS(29): 1.1	0.3
2020	DET	MLB	23	175	15	7	2	3	16	9	46	4	2	.229/.280/.348	65	-1.1	.300	0.3	SS 0	-0.1

Comparables: Cole Tucker, Jonathan Villar, Richard Ureña

Rebuilds offer opportunities for teams to look at players who might otherwise never get a clean shot at starting time. Castro has projected as a utility infielder dating back to his time in the Cleveland system. He's a switch-hitter with a bit of pop who can play shortstop, so he has some things going for him—just not enough that you would usually make room for him in the lineup. The outcome of Tigers games late last season were in no way meaningful to the future of the Tigers, so they took advantage by giving Castro a run at shortstop. He was neither good enough to guarantee future opportunities nor bad enough to foreclose them. He'll probably get some more shots as a result. Because the Tigers don't rate to be competitive anytime soon, they can afford to hope for the outside chance that he's more than a utility player.

C.J. Cron 1B   Born: 01/05/90   Age: 30   Bats: R   Throws: R   Height: 6'4"   Weight: 235   Origin: Round 1, 2011 Draft (#17 overall)

YEAR	TEAM	LVL	AGE	PA	R	2B	3B	HR	RBI	BB	K	SB	CS	AVG/OBP/SLG	DRC+	VORP	BABIP	BRR	FRAA	WARP
2017	SLC	AAA	27	96	11	6	0	4	23	7	15	1	0	.268/.344/.488	99	3.2	.273	0.0	1B(19): 0.9	0.2
2017	LAA	MLB	27	373	39	14	1	16	56	22	96	3	2	.248/.305/.437	99	2.7	.296	-2.1	1B(98): 4.1	0.7
2018	TBA	MLB	28	560	68	28	1	30	74	37	145	1	2	.253/.323/.493	118	17.6	.293	-3.5	1B(61): 2.6	1.9
2019	MIN	MLB	29	499	51	24	0	25	78	29	107	0	0	.253/.311/.469	101	8.3	.277	-2.6	1B(117): 8.0	1.3
2020	DET	MLB	30	525	62	22	1	24	72	31	117	3	2	.244/.302/.445	91	1.0	.275	-2.3	1B 7	0.8

Comparables: Matt Adams, Mitch Moreland, Brett Wallace

"Modesty inspires good will and confidence," Dale Carnegie once wrote. We're pretty sure Cron is familiar with the text. His career 107 DRC+ and 1.5 WARP per 162 games are the definition of replaceable-yet-acceptable production for a big-league first baseman. Certainly he's managed to win enough friends and influence enough people to remain employed throughout his 20s as a most-days regular in the Show—despite weak-side platoon traits and below-average on-base skills. Detroit will be his fourth team in four years; there's no reason to think he'll ever spend more than a season with a team again.

Travis Demeritte RF   Born: 09/30/94   Age: 25   Bats: R   Throws: R   Height: 6'0"   Weight: 180   Origin: Round 1, 2013 Draft (#30 overall)

YEAR	TEAM	LVL	AGE	PA	R	2B	3B	HR	RBI	BB	K	SB	CS	AVG/OBP/SLG	DRC+	VORP	BABIP	BRR	FRAA	WARP
2017	MIS	AA	22	511	62	21	6	15	45	49	134	5	7	.231/.306/.402	97	19.5	.293	1.8	2B(77): 7.8, 3B(43): 1.4	2.7
2018	MIS	AA	23	494	69	22	5	17	63	57	140	6	2	.222/.316/.416	104	19.5	.284	-2.2	LF(119): -5.9, 3B(1): 0.1	0.6
2019	GWN	AAA	24	399	68	28	2	20	73	51	106	4	3	.286/.387/.558	136	29.7	.358	0.0	LF(38): 0.1, RF(36): -2.0	2.3
2019	DET	MLB	24	186	24	7	2	3	10	14	63	3	0	.225/.286/.343	62	-5.0	.337	1.7	RF(47): 3.8	0.0
2020	DET	MLB	25	385	38	17	3	11	42	35	135	4	2	.211/.288/.369	69	-7.3	.309	0.1	RF 2	-0.5

Comparables: Trayce Thompson, Lewis Brinson, Teoscar Hernández

Demeritte traveled a long path to the majors from being a Rangers first-rounder way back in 2013, and lost most of his hype along the way. He never quite developed much of a hit tool, and a year ago looked like he might be stalling out in Double-A. But things turned around when his all-or-nothing power game turned out to be particularly well-suited for the launch-a-ball bonanza known as 2019 Triple-A baseball. He showed enough there that the Tigers inserted him straight into the major-league lineup after plucking him out of Atlanta's farm at the trade deadline. Things trended more toward "nothing" after he was called up, but he could certainly smash a bunch of dingers if conditions remain friendly.

Brandon Dixon UT Born: 01/29/92 Age: 28 Bats: R Throws: R Height: 6'2" Weight: 215 Origin: Round 3, 2013 Draft (#92 overall)

YEAR	TEAM	LVL	AGE	PA	R	2B	3B	HR	RBI	BB	K	SB	CS	AVG/OBP/SLG	DRC+	VORP	BABIP	BRR	FRAA	WARP
2017	LOU	AAA	25	491	58	31	3	16	64	37	125	18	8	.264/.327/.457	115	22.5	.328	1.0	3B(93): 5.2, 1B(17): -0.3	2.8
2018	LOU	AAA	26	193	28	18	2	6	23	12	54	9	3	.346/.389/.570	164	23.0	.467	2.9	2B(14): -2.3, 1B(14): 0.1	1.7
2018	CIN	MLB	26	124	14	6	0	5	10	6	43	0	0	.178/.218/.356	68	-5.3	.229	-0.5	1B(27): 0.0, RF(17): -1.1	-0.5
2019	TOL	AAA	27	46	6	0	0	1	3	0	16	0	0	.174/.174/.239	27	-5.3	.241	0.5	1B(11): 0.9	-0.2
2019	DET	MLB	27	420	41	20	4	15	52	21	136	5	1	.248/.290/.435	78	-3.3	.336	-0.9	1B(61): -3.7, LF(26): -0.9	-0.7
2020	DET	MLB	28	350	37	15	2	13	43	18	115	9	3	.232/.277/.409	73	-5.3	.314	-0.8	LF 0, 1B -1	-0.6

Comparables: Russ Canzler, Aaron Altherr, Keon Broxton

It's a bit generous to refer to Dixon as bright spot in a dark season; he was more like a bike reflector in a black hole. Dixon's 15 home runs were the fewest for a team leader since the Padres in 2014, a year in which dingers were way down and definitely not a year where the persons sitting on either side of you somehow hit 27 of them for the Minnesota Twins. His strikeout rate (32.4 percent) does not come close to justifying having him run into one every 10 days, and to top it off, his best position is first base. Dixon had a dismal finish to the season, so keeping him in Triple-A until he hits a hot streak could be the correct way to turn him into a bright spot.

Niko Goodrum UT Born: 02/28/92 Age: 28 Bats: B Throws: R Height: 6'3" Weight: 218 Origin: Round 2, 2010 Draft (#71 overall)

YEAR	TEAM	LVL	AGE	PA	R	2B	3B	HR	RBI	BB	K	SB	CS	AVG/OBP/SLG	DRC+	VORP	BABIP	BRR	FRAA	WARP
2017	ROC	AAA	25	499	71	25	5	13	66	30	119	11	7	.265/.309/.425	100	17.0	.326	4.4	RF(47): 3.3, 2B(37): -4.2	1.6
2017	MIN	MLB	25	18	1	0	0	0	0	1	10	0	0	.059/.111/.059	48	-2.9	.143	0.2	2B(8): -0.4, RF(1): 0.0	-0.1
2018	DET	MLB	26	492	55	29	3	16	53	42	132	12	4	.245/.315/.432	98	11.9	.312	-1.3	2B(64): 1.0, 1B(37): -0.8	0.9
2019	DET	MLB	27	472	61	27	5	12	45	46	138	12	3	.248/.322/.421	87	7.9	.338	3.4	SS(38): 3.6, 2B(22): -1.9	1.6
2020	DET	MLB	28	525	55	22	5	16	60	46	152	14	5	.225/.296/.393	79	3.9	.295	0.4	SS 8, LF -1	1.2

Comparables: Pedro Florimón, Lane Adams, Aaron Altherr

What's it like to be able to play any position and hold your own at the plate? It's sort of like having the birth name Cartier and the middle name Niko and getting to pick which one people call you. Most would trade their childhood blanket for just one of those. The extremely versatile Goodrum was one of five players who started a game last year at every position except pitcher and catcher. He also switch hits. "Utilityman" gets thrown around a lot, both in conversation and the lineup, but he's an overachiever in the category such that he makes regular utilitymen look like mere Schwarbers. He also has a bit of power, a bit of speed and a really huge bit of swings and misses. Remember, when you strive to do *everything*, that includes the bad stuff.

★ ★ ★ *2020 Top 101 Prospect* **#49** ★ ★ ★

Riley Greene CF Born: 09/28/00 Age: 19 Bats: L Throws: L Height: 6'3" Weight: 200 Origin: Round 1, 2019 Draft (#5 overall)

YEAR	TEAM	LVL	AGE	PA	R	2B	3B	HR	RBI	BB	K	SB	CS	AVG/OBP/SLG	DRC+	VORP	BABIP	BRR	FRAA	WARP
2019	TGW	RK	18	43	9	3	0	2	8	5	12	0	0	.351/.442/.595	165	4.9	.478	-1.6	CF(9): -1.9	0.1
2019	ONE	A-	18	100	12	3	1	1	7	11	25	1	0	.295/.380/.386	128	5.7	.403	-1.5	CF(21): 3.5	0.7
2019	WMI	A	18	108	13	2	2	2	13	6	26	4	0	.219/.278/.344	62	1.9	.268	0.8	CF(20): 1.9, RF(4): 0.0	0.2
2020	DET	MLB	19	251	21	11	1	4	22	19	79	3	1	.221/.287/.326	66	-3.1	.322	0.0	CF 3, RF 0	0.0

Comparables: Addison Russell, Harold Ramirez, Anthony Gose

Nothing is more enticing than limitless potential. The Tigers were locked in on Greene with the No. 5 pick early in the process, ensorceled by his sweet lefty swing and a high offensive ceiling. He struggled some after an August promotion to Low-A, but also good Lord the kid made full-season ball at 18 in his draft summer. He might grow out of center field as he fills out, and the power is currently more projection than reality—he also might be one of baseball's best prospects in a year or two's time.

Grayson Greiner C Born: 10/11/92 Age: 27 Bats: R Throws: R Height: 6'6" Weight: 239 Origin: Round 3, 2014 Draft (#99 overall)

YEAR	TEAM	LVL	AGE	PA	R	2B	3B	HR	RBI	BB	K	SB	CS	AVG/OBP/SLG	DRC+	VORP	BABIP	BRR	FRAA	WARP
2017	ERI	AA	24	371	34	20	1	14	42	38	72	0	0	.241/.323/.436	106	13.8	.266	-3.0	C(93): 27.5	4.6
2018	TOL	AAA	25	180	12	8	1	4	23	21	42	0	0	.266/.350/.405	118	10.9	.336	0.3	C(44): 11.2	2.3
2018	DET	MLB	25	116	9	6	0	0	12	17	32	0	1	.219/.328/.281	79	3.5	.313	0.3	C(30): -0.5	0.3
2019	TOL	AAA	26	53	8	1	0	2	4	4	16	0	0	.250/.321/.396	90	2.0	.333	0.5	C(9): 1.1	0.3
2019	DET	MLB	26	224	18	5	1	5	19	13	70	0	0	.202/.251/.308	56	-1.0	.276	-0.9	C(58): -2.9	-0.5
2020	DET	MLB	27	245	22	9	1	6	24	18	75	0	0	.212/.277/.336	59	-1.8	.291	0.0	C -2	-0.4

Comparables: Michael Perez, Martín Maldonado, José Osuna

It's the scene from *Animal House*, except Dean Wormer is just reading off the batting statistics of the 2019 Tigers catchers, who went a combined .176/.226/.300—the most offensively challenged set of baseball squatters since the '15 Mariners. Greiner, the presumptive starter and thus the Robert Hoover of the pack, had the most PAs (despite a 60-day IL trip) and the highest OBP. While he floundered in the first half, he found a September boon after his back injury in the form of a .321 average, albeit with no walks or power. He otter earn himself a roster spot this year, if not a starting role, but either way he's damn glad to meet you.

YEAR	TEAM	P. COUNT	FRM RUNS	BLK RUNS	THRW RUNS	TOT RUNS
2017	ERI	12250	22.4	5.5	0.2	27.3
2018	DET	4428	-0.6	-0.2	0.0	-0.9
2018	TOL	6014	9.5	0.5	0.3	10.0
2019	DET	8618	-2.4	0.3	0.2	-1.8
2019	TOL	1168	1.2	0.0	0.0	1.7
2020	DET	7919	-1.5	-0.1	0.2	-1.4

John Hicks C   Born: 08/31/89   Age: 30   Bats: R   Throws: R   Height: 6'2"   Weight: 230   Origin: Round 4, 2011 Draft (#123 overall)

YEAR	TEAM	LVL	AGE	PA	R	2B	3B	HR	RBI	BB	K	SB	CS	AVG/OBP/SLG	DRC+	VORP	BABIP	BRR	FRAA	WARP
2017	TOL	AAA	27	218	21	10	1	7	35	4	54	5	3	.269/.281/.428	84	5.9	.325	-0.5	C(37): 3.4, 1B(11): -0.8	0.5
2017	DET	MLB	27	190	25	12	0	6	22	13	51	2	1	.266/.326/.439	80	1.1	.342	-1.0	1B(26): -0.4, C(18): 0.8	-0.1
2018	DET	MLB	28	312	35	12	1	9	32	22	84	0	1	.260/.312/.403	91	1.6	.337	-1.3	1B(59): 0.3, C(21): -2.3	0.0
2019	DET	MLB	29	333	29	15	0	13	35	13	109	1	1	.210/.240/.379	63	-2.8	.273	-1.6	C(60): -8.1, 1B(29): -1.5	-1.4
2020	*DET*	*MLB*	*30*	*251*	*25*	*15*	*0*	*8*	*30*	*13*	*79*	*3*	*1*	*.238/.282/.411*	*79*	*0.6*	*.321*	*-0.7*	*C -2, 1B -1*	*-0.2*

Comparables: René Rivera, James McCann, Carlos Corporán

YEAR	TEAM	P. COUNT	FRM RUNS	BLK RUNS	THRW RUNS	TOT RUNS
2017	DET	2077	0.9	-0.1	0.0	1.2
2017	TOL	4951	2.8	0.5	0.0	3.6
2018	DET	2984	-0.9	-0.9	-0.1	-1.9
2019	DET	8575	-7.4	-1.3	0.2	-8.6
2020	*DET*	*4854*	*-1.5*	*-0.4*	*0.1*	*-1.8*

Hicks is a one-dimensional swing-happy fellow whose ability to crouch behind home plate, wear protective padding and flash an array of fingers between his knees will extend his career. He did clout more than his appropriate share of "big" home runs, such as an extra-innings walk-off grand slam and two go-ahead-for-good home runs in ninth innings (one of them off Justin Verlander). He can rise to the occasion though he can't sustain the occasion for the first eight innings. You could do worse with a backup catcher/pinch hitter, but you should probably do better.

JaCoby Jones CF   Born: 05/10/92   Age: 28   Bats: R   Throws: R   Height: 6'2"   Weight: 201   Origin: Round 3, 2013 Draft (#87 overall)

YEAR	TEAM	LVL	AGE	PA	R	2B	3B	HR	RBI	BB	K	SB	CS	AVG/OBP/SLG	DRC+	VORP	BABIP	BRR	FRAA	WARP
2017	TOL	AAA	25	393	57	19	2	9	44	33	104	12	4	.245/.314/.387	93	15.8	.322	3.6	CF(76): 3.2, LF(7): 0.2	1.6
2017	DET	MLB	25	154	14	3	1	3	13	9	65	6	2	.170/.240/.270	43	-7.9	.288	1.1	CF(51): 2.3, RF(1): 0.0	-0.2
2018	DET	MLB	26	467	54	22	6	11	34	24	142	13	5	.207/.266/.364	67	-1.4	.281	4.3	CF(67): 4.0, LF(55): 2.7	0.7
2019	DET	MLB	27	333	39	19	3	11	26	27	94	7	2	.235/.310/.430	87	6.9	.304	1.2	CF(85): -7.8	0.0
2020	*DET*	*MLB*	*28*	*490*	*50*	*22*	*4*	*14*	*54*	*36*	*151*	*13*	*4*	*.220/.290/.383*	*74*	*3.9*	*.299*	*2.4*	*CF 4*	*0.8*

Comparables: Matthew den Dekker, Johnny Field, Andy Sheets

Jones, a rangy and athletic center fielder, made terrific strides at the plate last year. The adjustment that seemed to help him the most was laying his bat against his shoulder, as if to calm a previously feral barrel, or store potential energy, or align the chakras or soothe it like an infant who is going through teething (you parents out there know what we're talking about). Whatever the reason, the adjustment showed up in his peripherals: his exit velocity jumped up three mph, his swing and chase rates went down and his contact rates went up. Because he was near the caboose in several batting categories, he's still not your first choice for an everyday center fielder, or second or even 15th, but thanks to his top-level speed, he's gaining ground.

Dawel Lugo 3B   Born: 12/31/94   Age: 25   Bats: R   Throws: R   Height: 6'0"   Weight: 220   Origin: International Free Agent, 2012

YEAR	TEAM	LVL	AGE	PA	R	2B	3B	HR	RBI	BB	K	SB	CS	AVG/OBP/SLG	DRC+	VORP	BABIP	BRR	FRAA	WARP
2017	WTN	AA	22	369	40	21	4	7	43	21	51	1	0	.282/.325/.428	109	13.7	.310	-1.7	3B(77): 4.5, SS(10): -0.4	2.0
2017	ERI	AA	22	188	18	6	1	6	22	12	21	2	1	.269/.314/.417	97	3.4	.275	-1.5	3B(29): -1.1, 2B(13): 0.6	0.4
2018	TOL	AAA	23	523	56	26	3	3	59	9	66	12	4	.269/.283/.350	80	1.8	.302	-1.1	2B(80): -6.0, 3B(43): -2.0	-0.4
2018	DET	MLB	23	101	10	4	1	1	8	7	20	0	0	.213/.267/.309	77	-1.1	.260	-0.2	2B(27): -3.2	-0.3
2019	TOL	AAA	24	303	46	21	4	5	41	15	52	6	3	.333/.370/.489	119	16.5	.390	-1.0	3B(61): -3.7, 2B(6): 0.9	1.3
2019	DET	MLB	24	288	28	11	4	6	26	8	59	0	0	.245/.271/.381	71	0.2	.288	-0.1	3B(73): -3.7	-0.4
2020	*DET*	*MLB*	*25*	*140*	*12*	*6*	*1*	*3*	*14*	*5*	*30*	*1*	*0*	*.251/.283/.374*	*68*	*-2.1*	*.303*	*-0.1*	*3B 0, 2B 0*	*-0.3*

Comparables: Eduardo Escobar, Luis Sardiñas, Miguel Andújar

Lugo was traded twice as a prospect for two players who could not possibly be more different: Cliff Pennington and J.D. Martinez. Through parts of two seasons, his career is trending more towards Pennington, with the caveat that Lugo lacks the ability to play shortstop that kept Pennington in the majors for more than a decade. He's had three separate opportunities to stake a claim on a job during the last season-plus, and keeps failing to do so. There's latent hitting ability and raw power here, and if you want to be insanely optimistic you can even point to Martinez himself, who didn't get it going until he was older than this. Except you really shouldn't pin player development hopes on one-in-a-thousand outcomes; not when the likelier outcome is that Lugo is forgotten by all except those who look at the transactions portions of Pennington and/or Martinez's Baseball-Reference page.

Jordy Mercer SS   Born: 08/27/86   Age: 33   Bats: R   Throws: R   Height: 6'3"   Weight: 210   Origin: Round 3, 2008 Draft (#79 overall)

YEAR	TEAM	LVL	AGE	PA	R	2B	3B	HR	RBI	BB	K	SB	CS	AVG/OBP/SLG	DRC+	VORP	BABIP	BRR	FRAA	WARP
2017	PIT	MLB	30	558	52	24	5	14	58	51	88	0	4	.255/.326/.406	96	21.3	.284	-1.2	SS(144): -18.7	0.3
2018	PIT	MLB	31	436	43	29	2	6	39	32	87	2	0	.251/.315/.381	87	10.9	.306	-1.0	SS(117): -3.0	0.9
2019	TOL	AAA	32	50	11	3	0	0	4	5	6	0	0	.233/.340/.302	90	0.9	.270	0.9	SS(7): -0.3	0.1
2019	DET	MLB	32	271	24	16	0	9	22	13	57	0	0	.270/.310/.438	91	8.6	.316	-1.1	SS(59): -0.5, 2B(8): 1.9	0.9
2020	*DET*	*MLB*	*33*	*251*	*23*	*12*	*1*	*5*	*25*	*18*	*52*	*1*	*1*	*.233/.295/.355*	*73*	*-1.1*	*.281*	*-0.4*	*SS -3, 2B 0*	*-0.4*

Comparables: Zack Cozart, J.J. Hardy, Ian Desmond

Mercer's persistent blandness has been much discussed on these pages, so in an attempt to add a dash of flavor to this portion: for the first time since his rookie season in 2012, he finished a year with more home runs than intentional walks. This was to be expected since he no longer batted eighth for a National League side. (Although he did bat in a 2019 Tigers lineup, so, six of one....) While his seasonal line blended in with much of his Pirates campaigns, he hit .292/.323/.479 over three months after convalescing from back-to-back quad strains, adding a bit of punch to an otherwise vacuous lineup. Definitely not enough to lift a team, but enough to cleanse the palate. Mercer can definitely keep hanging onto a lineup and do this, and we'll certainly scrounge up something interesting to say about him next year—one of these statements is a lie.

Chace Numata C Born: 08/14/92 Age: 27 Bats: B Throws: R Height: 6'0" Weight: 200 Origin: Round 14, 2010 Draft (#441 overall)

YEAR	TEAM	LVL	AGE	PA	R	2B	3B	HR	RBI	BB	K	SB	CS	AVG/OBP/SLG	DRC+	VORP	BABIP	BRR	FRAA	WARP
2017	REA	AA	24	340	32	17	1	4	28	30	37	0	1	.249/.318/.351	83	2.8	.270	-0.7	C(83): -7.9	0.1
2018	TAM	A+	25	32	7	2	1	1	4	3	4	0	0	.286/.375/.536	76	4.2	.304	0.7	C(8): -0.1	0.2
2018	TRN	AA	25	135	6	6	1	0	8	7	25	1	1	.180/.222/.242	35	-6.6	.223	0.2	C(38): 1.3	-0.1
2019	ERI	AA	26	258	30	11	2	4	26	16	48	0	0	.239/.291/.355	82	4.1	.278	-2.7	C(69): 1.2, P(1): 0.0	0.6

"A life is not important except in the impact it has on other lives." — Jackie Robinson

YEAR	TEAM	P. COUNT	FRM RUNS	BLK RUNS	THRW RUNS	TOT RUNS
2017	REA	11602	-3.3	-3.6	0.3	-6.6
2018	TRN	5509	2.1	0.4	-0.7	1.8
2019	ERI	8840	1.0	0.0	1.5	2.4

Chace Numata was selected out of a Hawaiian high school by the Phillies in the 14th round of the 2010 Draft. He kicked around their farm system for the better part of this decade before moving along in minor-league free agency to the Yankees and then the Tigers. He finally made the Triple-A level just this past April, in his 10th pro season. He called games in 2019 for Casey Mize, Matt Manning, Alex Faedo and Tarik Skubal—all of whom are headed toward the big leagues, and soon. He never made one of our prospect lists, and he's never been in this book before. But none of that is important anymore.

Numata passed away in September following a skateboarding accident. He was remembered around baseball as a beloved teammate and friend with an infectious and ever-present smile. He touched many lives around the game and beyond. And in death, he touched five more by giving the gift of life as an organ donor. Rest in peace, Numi.

Isaac Paredes 3B Born: 02/18/99 Age: 21 Bats: R Throws: R Height: 5'11" Weight: 225 Origin: International Free Agent, 2015

YEAR	TEAM	LVL	AGE	PA	R	2B	3B	HR	RBI	BB	K	SB	CS	AVG/OBP/SLG	DRC+	VORP	BABIP	BRR	FRAA	WARP
2017	SBN	A	18	384	49	25	0	7	49	29	54	2	1	.264/.343/.401	111	18.2	.294	-1.0	SS(70): -2.7, 3B(7): 2.5	1.9
2017	WMI	A	18	133	16	3	0	4	21	13	13	0	0	.217/.323/.348	111	0.3	.214	-0.5	SS(22): -2.4, 3B(5): 1.4	1.1
2018	LAK	A+	19	347	50	19	2	12	48	32	54	1	0	.259/.338/.455	130	24.2	.274	0.3	SS(59): 3.2, 2B(22): 0.5	2.8
2018	ERI	AA	19	155	20	9	0	3	22	19	22	1	0	.321/.406/.458	145	13.7	.358	0.3	3B(18): 0.6, SS(15): 0.9	1.5
2019	ERI	AA	20	552	63	23	1	13	66	57	61	5	3	.282/.368/.416	138	33.2	.298	-2.3	3B(81): -3.4, SS(31): 0.1	3.4
2020	DET	MLB	21	35	4	2	0	1	4	3	6	0	0	.250/.332/.395	91	0.9	.282	-0.1	SS 0	0.1

Comparables: Jake Bauers, Ozzie Albies, Cheslor Cuthbert

Welcome to Defensive Spectrum Press Your Luck, baseball's most competitive game. Let's meet today's player, Isaac. He's a 21-year-old with plus bat speed and a knack for hitting who has put up excellent numbers relative to age/league context. He's short and his frame is maxed out, so his range in the infield isn't so hot, and he's already been bouncing around the Big Board trying to find the right home. If Isaac's spin for a long-term position lands on third base or better, he wins an all-expenses paid trip to the majors as a potential first-division regular. If not...well, let's think positive thoughts! Big bucks, no whammies!

Victor Reyes OF Born: 10/05/94 Age: 25 Bats: B Throws: R Height: 6'5" Weight: 215 Origin: International Free Agent, 2011

YEAR	TEAM	LVL	AGE	PA	R	2B	3B	HR	RBI	BB	K	SB	CS	AVG/OBP/SLG	DRC+	VORP	BABIP	BRR	FRAA	WARP
2017	WTN	AA	22	516	59	29	5	4	51	27	80	18	9	.292/.332/.399	112	9.8	.342	0.1	RF(83): 4.9, CF(57): 10.8	3.7
2018	DET	MLB	23	219	35	5	3	1	12	5	46	9	1	.222/.239/.288	63	-7.9	.277	0.1	LF(34): -3.2, CF(21): 2.2	-0.6
2019	TOL	AAA	24	308	50	19	1	10	58	14	50	10	6	.304/.334/.481	105	9.2	.335	0.4	RF(36): 0.8, CF(31): -0.4	1.0
2019	DET	MLB	24	292	29	16	5	3	25	14	64	9	3	.304/.336/.431	89	5.2	.384	-0.4	CF(37): -0.1, LF(21): 2.0	0.6
2020	DET	MLB	25	490	43	22	6	7	47	21	107	9	4	.263/.296/.383	76	-3.0	.327	-1.0	RF 3, CF 2	0.2

Comparables: Dawel Lugo, Raimel Tapia, Sócrates Brito

Another delayed Rule 5 success story, Reyes was a nightlight in the supermassive black hole that was last year's Tigers offense. He vastly improved from an outfielder constantly running into his teammates on fly balls to one who, uh, didn't do that as often. Being able to play against his own kind for a few Triple-A months after being tethered to the 25-player roster due to Rule 5 restrictions certainly helped, too. His greatest strides came at the plate, showing improved line-drive power and a bit more patience. He can play all three outfield positions but ultimately projects to patrol either of the corners.

Jake Rogers C Born: 04/18/95 Age: 25 Bats: R Throws: R Height: 6'1" Weight: 205 Origin: Round 3, 2016 Draft (#97 overall)

YEAR	TEAM	LVL	AGE	PA	R	2B	3B	HR	RBI	BB	K	SB	CS	AVG/OBP/SLG	DRC+	VORP	BABIP	BRR	FRAA	WARP
2017	QUD	A	22	116	17	7	1	6	15	9	28	1	0	.255/.336/.520	130	10.3	.290	0.3	C(21): 0.9	1.0
2017	BCA	A+	22	367	43	18	3	12	55	44	72	13	8	.265/.357/.457	135	29.4	.302	-0.8	C(63): 1.4	2.8
2018	ERI	AA	23	408	57	15	1	17	56	41	112	7	1	.219/.305/.412	88	20.8	.261	2.7	C(98): 29.4, 1B(1): 0.0	4.9
2019	ERI	AA	24	112	17	3	1	5	21	19	26	0	0	.302/.429/.535	164	13.6	.356	-1.7	C(21): 2.3	1.2
2019	TOL	AAA	24	191	29	10	1	9	31	18	53	0	0	.223/.321/.458	88	6.0	.269	-2.7	C(48): 9.5	1.3
2019	DET	MLB	24	128	11	3	0	4	8	13	51	0	0	.125/.222/.259	53	-1.3	.175	-0.4	C(34): -4.0	-0.6
2020	DET	MLB	25	70	7	3	0	2	8	6	24	1	0	.197/.281/.362	67	0.2	.271	-0.1	C 0	0.0

Comparables: Will Smith, Tom Murphy, Johnny Field

YEAR	TEAM	P. COUNT	FRM RUNS	BLK RUNS	THRW RUNS	TOT RUNS
2018	ERI	13801	20.3	-0.4	7.2	28.0
2019	DET	5368	-1.4	-2.2	0.2	-3.1
2019	ERI	2716	2.1	0.0	0.7	2.6
2019	TOL	6978	7.3	0.0	1.2	9.0
2020	DET	2740	0.1	-0.4	0.2	-0.2

Rogers is one of the best throwing catchers in the game. That would've been quite exciting in past decades of baseball, and yet seems trivial as we enter the 2020s. We know enough now to know that throwing simply isn't that valuable compared to, say, framing. Rogers also excelled at the latter in the upper-minors, but struggled in his brief stint in the majors. His reputation is strong enough that he'll get a few more chances (and then a few more chances after that). Even if the framing does translate, a new foe awaits on the horizon in Robo Ump, a threat that could undermine the value of catch-and-throw types.

Austin Romine C Born: 11/22/88 Age: 31 Bats: R Throws: R Height: 6'1" Weight: 220 Origin: Round 2, 2007 Draft (#94 overall)

YEAR	TEAM	LVL	AGE	PA	R	2B	3B	HR	RBI	BB	K	SB	CS	AVG/OBP/SLG	DRC+	VORP	BABIP	BRR	FRAA	WARP
2017	NYA	MLB	28	252	19	9	1	2	21	16	57	0	0	.218/.272/.293	66	-5.2	.277	-1.8	C(67): 4.5, 1B(12): 0.7	0.4
2018	NYA	MLB	29	265	30	12	0	10	42	17	67	1	0	.244/.295/.417	85	4.3	.292	-3.1	C(76): 6.8	1.2
2019	NYA	MLB	30	240	29	12	0	8	35	10	50	1	1	.281/.310/.439	90	9.5	.327	-1.0	C(70): -2.5, P(1): 0.0	0.6
2020	DET	MLB	31	385	35	17	1	8	39	22	86	1	0	.236/.283/.356	65	-1.7	.287	-2.1	C 2	0.1

Comparables: Gerald Laird, Sandy Martinez, Bryan Holaday

Romine's role has stayed remarkably constant over the last three years as the reliable catcher who is occasionally forced into short bursts of regular duty. What he lacks in terms of controlling the running game, he makes up with competent blocking and framing skills. He also smelled his impending free agency like a shark smells blood in the water and brought his offensive game to a new level in the second half, hitting .325/.364/.550 in 129 plate appearances. The understudy has longed to be a star, and it's about time he got it, it was just never going to be in New York. A career-high workload in Detroit awaits.

YEAR	TEAM	P. COUNT	FRM RUNS	BLK RUNS	THRW RUNS	TOT RUNS
2017	NYA	8705	6.3	-0.3	-1.3	4.3
2018	NYA	10341	4.2	2.2	0.0	6.3
2019	NYA	9502	-2.2	0.9	0.1	-1.6
2020	DET	17397	0.9	0.8	0.3	2.1

Jonathan Schoop 2B Born: 10/16/91 Age: 28 Bats: R Throws: R Height: 6'1" Weight: 225 Origin: International Free Agent, 2008

YEAR	TEAM	LVL	AGE	PA	R	2B	3B	HR	RBI	BB	K	SB	CS	AVG/OBP/SLG	DRC+	VORP	BABIP	BRR	FRAA	WARP
2017	BAL	MLB	25	675	92	35	0	32	105	35	142	1	0	.293/.338/.503	115	38.6	.330	4.2	2B(159): 8.2, SS(5): 0.8	4.7
2018	BAL	MLB	26	367	45	18	1	17	40	12	74	0	1	.244/.273/.447	83	5.4	.262	-0.6	2B(85): 7.9, SS(2): 0.0	1.1
2018	MIL	MLB	26	134	16	4	0	4	21	7	41	1	0	.202/.246/.331	83	-1.0	.259	1.0	2B(31): 1.4, SS(15): 1.1	0.5
2019	MIN	MLB	27	464	61	23	1	23	59	20	116	1	1	.256/.304/.473	93	11.1	.298	-1.8	2B(113): -5.8	0.3
2020	DET	MLB	28	525	57	24	1	22	69	21	135	2	1	.247/.289/.431	82	9.5	.296	0.8	2B 3	1.3

Comparables: Asdrúbal Cabrera, Yolmer Sánchez, Rubén Tejada

Schoop recorded a terrible trifecta in what was supposed to be a redemption year. He posted below-average offensive, defensive and baserunning marks, with his new city serving as the backdrop for a frustratingly familiar story. His bat ate garbage-time pitching for lunch, but shrunk consistently in big moments. That, plus his empty slugging profile, left him on the outs by the time the postseason rolled around for a second consecutive fall. Schoop is still in his prime and might get a few more starting opportunities; he's almost certain to never repeat his 2017.

Christin Stewart LF Born: 12/10/93 Age: 26 Bats: L Throws: R Height: 6'0" Weight: 205 Origin: Round 1, 2015 Draft (#34 overall)

YEAR	TEAM	LVL	AGE	PA	R	2B	3B	HR	RBI	BB	K	SB	CS	AVG/OBP/SLG	DRC+	VORP	BABIP	BRR	FRAA	WARP
2017	ERI	AA	23	555	67	29	3	28	86	56	138	3	0	.256/.335/.501	115	31.2	.294	-0.8	LF(124): -10.6	1.0
2018	TOL	AAA	24	522	69	21	3	23	77	67	108	0	0	.264/.364/.480	141	36.1	.296	0.8	LF(97): 9.8, RF(12): -0.7	4.3
2018	DET	MLB	24	72	7	1	1	2	10	10	13	0	0	.267/.375/.417	107	3.3	.304	-0.3	LF(15): -0.9	0.1
2019	LAK	A+	25	25	2	1	0	1	5	3	3	0	0	.350/.400/.550	145	3.3	.333	0.2	LF(3): -0.4	0.1
2019	TOL	AAA	25	102	14	2	0	4	14	18	25	1	0	.289/.422/.458	139	7.4	.370	-0.1	LF(16): -3.4	0.4
2019	DET	MLB	25	416	32	25	1	10	40	34	103	0	1	.233/.305/.388	86	3.3	.290	-4.1	LF(89): -12.5	-1.3
2020	DET	MLB	26	490	57	20	2	20	64	46	124	1	0	.230/.314/.428	95	6.6	.273	-2.4	LF -2	0.5

Comparables: Jackie Jensen, Jackie Mayo, Ryan O'Hearn

Quite often there are rookies who don't get the requisite publicity but nonetheless perform well and carry it into the next season. If you're looking for such stories, you're in the wrong paragraph. Stewart was basically gift-wrapped the left field job in 2019 because there were few who can rival his raw power. Save for an Opening Day game-winning home run in the 10th inning, Stewart's struggles were the antithesis of Detroit's youth movement (though, perhaps, more true to the story of Detroit's season). Without a correction in 2020, major-league-quality breaking stuff will leave him skipping down Brennan Boesch Boulevard.

PITCHERS

Dario Agrazal RHP Born: 12/28/94 Age: 25 Bats: R Throws: R Height: 6'2" Weight: 240 Origin: International Free Agent, 2012

YEAR	TEAM	LVL	AGE	W	L	SV	G	GS	IP	H	HR	BB/9	K/9	K	GB%	BABIP	WHIP	ERA	DRA	WARP	MPH	FB%	WHF	CSP
2017	BRD	A+	22	5	3	0	14	13	80¹	73	4	1.1	7.1	63	56%	.289	1.03	2.91	3.69	1.5				
2018	BRD	A+	23	0	0	0	2	2	8	3	0	0.0	4.5	4	57%	.143	0.38	0.00	2.99	0.2				
2018	ALT	AA	23	5	6	0	15	14	85²	91	9	1.4	5.5	52	50%	.298	1.21	3.99	4.88	0.4				
2019	ALT	AA	24	1	1	0	4	4	25	29	3	0.0	6.8	19	48%	.342	1.16	3.60	5.20	-0.1				
2019	IND	AAA	24	4	4	0	12	12	64	62	8	1.7	7.7	55	52%	.298	1.16	4.78	3.79	1.8				
2019	PIT	MLB	24	4	5	0	15	14	73¹	82	15	2.2	5.0	41	42%	.283	1.36	4.91	5.99	-0.2	93.0	67	7.2	50.4
2020	DET	MLB	25	4	6	0	39	10	79	99	19	2.6	5.3	47	45%	.305	1.54	6.46	6.01	-0.5	92.7	68.6	7.4	51.6

Comparables: Rookie Davis, Corey Oswalt, Jordan Smith

Agrazal is in for a tightrope act. His minor-league résumé is heavy on soft contact and striked outs (not to be confused with strikeouts) and light on balls four. In the majors last year, only one other dude threw more innings with a thinner strikeout rate—Brett Anderson. When it comes to the Three True Outcomes, Agrazal is a ruthless contrarian, whatabouting the outcomes that sees fielders closing the at-bat's loop. When it comes to his realistic projection, he should get a chance at the back of a rotation for now given his array of pitches and their tendency to inspire more mindless chasing than a Benny Hill closing scene. As tends to be the case with tightrope artists, it's possible (if not probable) that Agrazal isn't around for long.

Tyler Alexander LHP   Born: 07/14/94   Age: 25   Bats: R   Throws: L   Height: 6'2"   Weight: 200   Origin: Round 2, 2015 Draft (#65 overall)

YEAR	TEAM	LVL	AGE	W	L	SV	G	GS	IP	H	HR	BB/9	K/9	K	GB%	BABIP	WHIP	ERA	DRA	WARP	MPH	FB%	WHF	CSP
2017	ERI	AA	22	8	9	0	27	26	138¹	178	20	1.5	7.8	120	41%	.356	1.45	5.07	5.97	-1.4				
2018	ERI	AA	23	3	2	0	9	9	48	64	7	1.7	6.6	35	45%	.358	1.52	3.75	6.92	-0.9				
2018	TOL	AAA	23	3	6	0	17	15	92	120	9	1.3	5.9	60	47%	.354	1.45	4.79	6.27	-0.8				
2019	TOL	AAA	24	5	10	0	20	16	98¹	112	18	2.1	9.9	108	40%	.344	1.37	5.13	5.40	1.2				
2019	DET	MLB	24	1	4	0	13	8	53²	68	9	1.2	7.9	47	37%	.347	1.40	4.86	5.98	-0.2	92.6	54.6	9.6	51.5
2020	DET	MLB	25	6	8	0	51	16	116	133	23	2.2	7.0	90	39%	.307	1.39	5.36	5.25	0.3	92.3	55.9	9.8	52.7

Comparables: Kyle Lobstein, Justin Nicolino, Jake Buchanan

When you're a soft-tossing lefty and you meet the riddle deities—the same set who quiz people on if they'd rather fight a horse-sized duck or 100 duck-sized horses—and they ask whether you'd prefer to have a lot of strikeouts or few walks…well, you can guess how Alexander answered. He walked seven dudes in his first eight big-league starts, and it wasn't a fluke. In college, a time when most of us are feral, he averaged one free pass per nine innings. Why isn't Alexander a bigger deal? Because velocity is the new black, and he is a modest taupe. His heat barely registers 90, which is hardly summer in Texas. Alexander isn't going to overpower anyone; rather, he is going to make his coin by mixing those secondaries like a Sherwin-Williams sales rep taking their job way too seriously. His ceiling is uncomfortably low but the floor is solid steel, and he ought to latch onto the end of a rotation by taking a cue from the gods and asking the batters a riddle of his own: namely, which of his five pitches is next.

Matthew Boyd LHP   Born: 02/02/91   Age: 29   Bats: L   Throws: L   Height: 6'3"   Weight: 234   Origin: Round 6, 2013 Draft (#175 overall)

YEAR	TEAM	LVL	AGE	W	L	SV	G	GS	IP	H	HR	BB/9	K/9	K	GB%	BABIP	WHIP	ERA	DRA	WARP	MPH	FB%	WHF	CSP
2017	TOL	AAA	26	3	3	0	8	8	51	35	7	2.3	9.4	53	39%	.224	0.94	2.82	2.56	1.8				
2017	DET	MLB	26	6	11	0	26	25	135	157	18	3.5	7.3	110	40%	.330	1.56	5.27	6.46	-1.3	94.6	50.7	11	48
2018	DET	MLB	27	9	13	0	31	31	170¹	146	27	2.7	8.4	159	30%	.258	1.16	4.39	5.22	0.2	93.8	48.9	10.9	49
2019	DET	MLB	28	9	12	0	32	32	185¹	178	39	2.4	11.6	238	36%	.308	1.23	4.56	3.93	3.7	94.5	53.9	15.6	49.9
2020	DET	MLB	29	10	10	0	29	29	169	160	30	2.9	10.9	204	34%	.309	1.27	4.23	4.23	2.5	93.6	51.5	13	49.1

Comparables: Tyler Duffey, Brian Johnson, Drew Pomeranz

"And you, my friend, would be da' belle of da' ball." Prison Mike would never convince anyone that prison is better than a season on a 114-loss team, however Boyd spent the summer as the breakout starting pitcher and the most discussed trade target. His refined slider has supplanted his changeup as his go-to gambit, feeding the opponents nothing but gruel. Not a bad progression for someone whose second career start featured seven runs and zero outs. That doesn't mean he's an ace—he led the league in home runs and failed to go past seven innings all but once in his final 10 tries. The rumors will inevitably begin again this summer, provided he gets back on track, and some opposing general manager—realizing they don't have a solid left-handed starter on their potential playoff roster—will be scared straight into a trade.

Beau Burrows RHP   Born: 09/18/96   Age: 23   Bats: R   Throws: R   Height: 6'2"   Weight: 215   Origin: Round 1, 2015 Draft (#22 overall)

YEAR	TEAM	LVL	AGE	W	L	SV	G	GS	IP	H	HR	BB/9	K/9	K	GB%	BABIP	WHIP	ERA	DRA	WARP	MPH	FB%	WHF	CSP
2017	LAK	A+	20	4	3	0	11	11	58²	45	3	1.7	9.5	62	45%	.298	0.95	1.23	3.38	1.3				
2017	ERI	AA	20	6	4	0	15	15	76¹	79	5	3.9	8.8	75	40%	.339	1.47	4.72	5.12	0.0				
2018	ERI	AA	21	10	9	0	26	26	134	126	12	3.8	8.5	127	32%	.310	1.36	4.10	4.58	1.2				
2019	TOL	AAA	22	2	6	0	15	15	65¹	68	12	4.4	8.4	61	34%	.303	1.53	5.51	5.70	0.6				
2020	DET	MLB	23	1	1	0	3	3	15	15	2	3.8	7.6	12	35%	.296	1.45	4.94	4.84	0.1				

Comparables: Luis Ortiz, Lucas Giolito, Zach Lee

You're going to read a lot about shoulder problems in this section of this chapter. This comment will be no different; Burrows missed almost two months in 2019 with shoulder and biceps inflammation. His fastball wasn't all the way back when he returned, continuing a troubling trend of velocity bleed that started in 2018. Any chance of a September call-up to jump start the engines ended with an August oblique strain. His development has stalled out since he made our top 101 list two years ago. It's not what you want, but it's not irreversible.

Jose Cisnero RHP   Born: 04/11/89   Age: 31   Bats: R   Throws: R   Height: 6'3"   Weight: 245   Origin: International Free Agent, 2007

YEAR	TEAM	LVL	AGE	W	L	SV	G	GS	IP	H	HR	BB/9	K/9	K	GB%	BABIP	WHIP	ERA	DRA	WARP	MPH	FB%	WHF	CSP
2019	TOL	AAA	30	1	2	7	32	2	40	36	3	4.7	11.0	49	43%	.324	1.42	2.70	4.31	0.8				
2019	DET	MLB	30	0	4	0	35	0	35¹	35	5	4.8	10.2	40	39%	.316	1.53	4.33	5.35	0.0	98.5	60.8	13.5	48.9
2020	DET	MLB	31	3	3	2	58	0	61	57	9	4.0	9.5	64	39%	.292	1.37	4.44	4.39	0.5	97.6	60.4	13.4	48.6

Comparables: Justin Grimm, Ethan Martin, Gregory Infante

On May 6, 2014, Cisnero, then an Astro, battled the heart of the Tigers order: Kinsler, Hunter, Cabrera, and both Martinezes. It was his last major league outing for 1,874 days—a sabbatical that included Tommy John surgery, a failed spring training, the Mexican League, the Can-Am League, a Dominican summer league completely off the Baseball-Reference grid and a couple rounds of winter ball. That last leg is where he was spotted by a Tigers scout, setting in motion his return to the Show. For years he didn't exactly go where he wanted (also an apt description for his mid-90s heater), but the comeback story is complete.

Alex Faedo RHP Born: 11/12/95 Age: 24 Bats: R Throws: R Height: 6'5" Weight: 230 Origin: Round 1, 2017 Draft (#18 overall)

YEAR	TEAM	LVL	AGE	W	L	SV	G	GS	IP	H	HR	BB/9	K/9	K	GB%	BABIP	WHIP	ERA	DRA	WARP	MPH	FB%	WHF	CSP
2018	LAK	A+	22	2	4	0	12	12	61	49	3	1.9	7.5	51	33%	.263	1.02	3.10	3.20	1.5				
2018	ERI	AA	22	3	6	0	12	12	60	54	15	3.3	8.9	59	28%	.250	1.27	4.95	5.14	0.1				
2019	ERI	AA	23	6	7	0	22	22	115¹	104	17	2.0	10.5	134	33%	.293	1.12	3.90	3.75	1.7				
2020	DET	MLB	24	2	2	0	33	0	35	37	7	3.3	9.1	35	33%	.311	1.41	5.06	5.14	0.0				

Comparables: Matt Harvey, Jakob Junis, Robert Dugger

Faedo has gotten lost in the shuffle for various reasons. An early candidate to go in the first few picks of the 2017 draft, he slid all the way to No. 18—making him the first-round pitcher chosen by the Tigers a year after Matt Manning and a year before Casey Mize. Faedo isn't in that class of prospect: he doesn't quite throw as hard as he did at the University of Florida; he's been just fine as a pro, neither spectacular enough to gain hype nor bad enough to lose it; and he was the forgotten man in an Erie rotation that was loaded. Yet Faedo is still a cromulent pitching prospect in his own right, with plenty of indicators for future success. He might be flying under the radar now, but the coordinates are still aimed squarely at a rotation spot, and he's closing in fast.

Buck Farmer RHP Born: 02/20/91 Age: 29 Bats: L Throws: R Height: 6'4" Weight: 232 Origin: Round 5, 2013 Draft (#156 overall)

YEAR	TEAM	LVL	AGE	W	L	SV	G	GS	IP	H	HR	BB/9	K/9	K	GB%	BABIP	WHIP	ERA	DRA	WARP	MPH	FB%	WHF	CSP
2017	TOL	AAA	26	6	4	0	21	21	123²	133	9	2.3	8.3	114	43%	.343	1.33	3.93	4.48	1.7				
2017	DET	MLB	26	5	5	0	11	11	48	55	9	3.8	9.2	49	34%	.336	1.56	6.75	5.85	-0.1	94.2	61.2	11.7	45.7
2018	DET	MLB	27	3	4	0	66	1	69¹	67	6	5.3	7.4	57	41%	.300	1.56	4.15	5.49	-0.4	96.5	57.6	12	45.3
2019	DET	MLB	28	6	6	0	73	1	67²	62	8	3.2	9.7	73	49%	.303	1.27	3.72	3.92	1.1	96.7	49	13.6	44.3
2020	DET	MLB	29	3	3	3	64	0	67	63	9	3.7	9.4	70	45%	.300	1.36	4.27	4.23	0.7	95.5	54.6	12.6	45

Comparables: Bryan Mitchell, Brad Peacock, Erik Johnson

It's time for the annual crop report—and for once it's promising. Farmer yielded one of the league's top sliders, getting swings and misses more than half the time last season—not bad for a pitch he didn't start throwing until 2017, replacing his bargain-bin curve. That third major-league quality pitch could be his ticket back to the rotation, though he hasn't been stretched out in two seasons and seemed perfectly fine as the torchbearer for the bullpen after Shane Greene left. That Farmer is being trusted with higher leverage innings means he's likely found his green acres.

Michael Fulmer RHP Born: 03/15/93 Age: 27 Bats: R Throws: R Height: 6'3" Weight: 246 Origin: Round 1, 2011 Draft (#44 overall)

YEAR	TEAM	LVL	AGE	W	L	SV	G	GS	IP	H	HR	BB/9	K/9	K	GB%	BABIP	WHIP	ERA	DRA	WARP	MPH	FB%	WHF	CSP
2017	DET	MLB	24	10	12	0	25	25	164²	150	13	2.2	6.2	114	51%	.273	1.15	3.83	3.75	3.4	98.1	59.4	10.5	48.6
2018	LAK	A+	25	0	0	0	2	2	6	1	0	0.0	16.5	11	38%	.125	0.17	0.00	1.71	0.3				
2018	DET	MLB	25	3	12	0	24	24	132¹	128	19	3.1	7.5	110	47%	.288	1.31	4.69	4.66	1.0	98.3	61	11.7	48.6
2020	DET	MLB	27	5	7	0	19	19	99	102	17	3.2	8.1	90	46%	.298	1.38	4.81	4.73	0.9	97.7	61	11.3	49.2

Comparables: Joe Ross, Jered Weaver, Aaron Sanchez

Fulmer should have been prone to an incessant cascade of trade rumors, constantly looking over his shoulder to check the runner as well as the latest tweets suggesting he's drawing interest. Tommy John surgery is a weird way to get out of all that (and unload the uncertainty on to Matthew Boyd in the process) but Fulmer has been a lightning rod of transaction wishcasting ever since being named Rookie of the Year (and subsequently an All-Star), so the long respite might've helped in a weird/bad way. He should be ready for some sweet mound action by the upcoming trade deadline, so he'll miss another season of scuttlebutt and focus on the confidence to throw that slider again.

Zack Godley RHP Born: 04/21/90 Age: 30 Bats: R Throws: R Height: 6'3" Weight: 240 Origin: Round 10, 2013 Draft (#288 overall)

YEAR	TEAM	LVL	AGE	W	L	SV	G	GS	IP	H	HR	BB/9	K/9	K	GB%	BABIP	WHIP	ERA	DRA	WARP	MPH	FB%	WHF	CSP
2017	RNO	AAA	27	2	1	0	5	3	28	14	0	5.5	9.3	29	68%	.222	1.11	2.57	1.97	1.1				
2017	ARI	MLB	27	8	9	0	26	25	155	124	15	3.1	9.6	165	58%	.280	1.14	3.37	3.69	3.3	93.3	56.9	13.7	42.3
2018	ARI	MLB	28	15	11	0	33	32	178¹	177	16	4.1	9.3	185	50%	.324	1.45	4.74	4.78	1.1	92.0	54.4	12.2	43.4
2019	ARI	MLB	29	3	5	2	27	9	76	81	12	4.1	6.9	58	44%	.303	1.53	6.39	6.70	-1.0	91.8	65.3	11.1	44.8
2019	TOR	MLB	29	1	0	0	6	0	16	15	2	3.9	6.8	12	43%	.277	1.38	3.94	5.26	0.0	91.6	65.3	12.4	39.5
2020	DET	MLB	30	2	2	0	33	0	35	34	5	3.9	8.0	31	47%	.294	1.42	4.70	4.70	0.2	91.6	58	12.3	43.2

Comparables: Justin Grimm, Seth Lugo, Calvin Schiraldi

They say cleanliness is next to godliness, in which case Godley may have entered into apostasy after a terrible 2019. Before being moved to the bullpen in late April, he posted a 1.72 WHIP across his first six starts. Things weren't much better as a bullpen piece; Godley had just a single clean inning all year, coincidentally against the team who would take him when the D-backs moved on. As a long reliever for Toronto, Godley was tolerable, but even after arresting the velocity drop-off of 2018 he posted a career-worst strikeout rate, providing little solace that he might be one of those starters enlivened by a move to relief. A three-win campaign is still in memory, though, giving reason to hope he might return to grace in his age-30 season.

Edwin Jackson RHP Born: 09/09/83 Age: 36 Bats: R Throws: R Height: 6'2" Weight: 215 Origin: Round 6, 2001 Draft (#190 overall)

YEAR	TEAM	LVL	AGE	W	L	SV	G	GS	IP	H	HR	BB/9	K/9	K	GB%	BABIP	WHIP	ERA	DRA	WARP	MPH	FB%	WHF	CSP
2017	NOR	AAA	33	0	0	2	12	1	20¹	20	1	4.4	7.5	17	33%	.339	1.48	3.10	4.83	0.2				
2017	SYR	AAA	33	2	0	0	5	4	20¹	9	0	4.4	9.7	22	51%	.191	0.93	0.44	4.80	0.2				
2017	BAL	MLB	33	0	0	0	3	0	5	11	2	7.2	3.6	2	30%	.429	3.00	7.20	8.81	-0.2	93.9	76.9	8.3	42.3
2017	WAS	MLB	33	5	6	0	13	13	71	75	18	3.2	7.4	58	40%	.273	1.41	5.07	6.39	-0.7	95.8	76.9	10.9	48
2018	SYR	AAA	34	4	2	0	10	10	55²	51	4	3.6	7.6	47	42%	.285	1.31	3.40	4.50	0.7				
2018	NAS	AAA	34	0	1	0	3	3	15²	12	1	4.6	9.2	16	41%	.256	1.28	4.02	3.45	0.4				
2018	OAK	MLB	34	6	3	0	17	17	92	75	12	3.6	6.7	68	38%	.240	1.22	3.33	5.23	0.1	95.7	67	9.7	44.4
2019	LVG	AAA	35	0	0	0	2	2	9²	9	3	6.5	9.3	10	54%	.240	1.66	8.38	5.85	0.1				
2019	TOL	AAA	35	0	2	0	2	2	7²	11	1	4.7	2.3	2	38%	.385	1.96	5.87	5.73	0.1				
2019	TOR	MLB	35	1	5	0	8	5	28¹	49	12	4.1	6.0	19	44%	.378	2.19	11.12	10.20	-1.4	95.8	64.9	9.6	45
2019	DET	MLB	35	2	5	0	10	8	39¹	56	11	4.3	7.6	33	43%	.352	1.91	8.47	9.31	-1.5	95.6	64.9	11.8	47.3
2020	DET	MLB	36	2	2	0	33	0	35	40	7	4.2	7.2	28	42%	.308	1.61	6.24	5.93	-0.3	94.3	67	10.2	45

Comparables: Ervin Santana, Homer Bailey, Gavin Floyd

At this point the reason to watch Jackson is to see if he'll end up representing half the league. He broke Octavio Dotel's record for teams played with last year by suiting up for the Blue Jays. Following a midseason release, he double-dipped with the Tigers, the org with which he earned his lone All-Star nod, rather than latching on with team No. 15. This could be the year, though, and the more words reserved for describing his uniform quantity, the less needed to describe his pitching quality.

Joe Jiménez RHP Born: 01/17/95 Age: 25 Bats: R Throws: R Height: 6'3" Weight: 272 Origin: Undrafted Free Agent, 2013

YEAR	TEAM	LVL	AGE	W	L	SV	G	GS	IP	H	HR	BB/9	K/9	K	GB%	BABIP	WHIP	ERA	DRA	WARP	MPH	FB%	WHF	CSP
2017	TOL	AAA	22	1	1	4	26	0	25	19	1	4.3	13.0	36	43%	.340	1.24	1.44	2.78	0.7				
2017	DET	MLB	22	0	2	0	24	0	19	31	4	4.3	8.1	17	37%	.403	2.11	12.32	5.25	0.0	97.8	63.1	12.8	52
2018	DET	MLB	23	5	4	3	68	0	62²	53	5	3.2	11.2	78	36%	.304	1.20	4.31	3.05	1.4	97.9	67.2	14.7	47.3
2019	DET	MLB	24	4	7	9	66	0	59²	56	13	3.5	12.4	82	30%	.319	1.32	4.37	4.01	0.9	97.4	68.3	15.7	51.4
2020	DET	MLB	25	3	3	26	64	0	67	56	10	3.3	11.6	86	32%	.293	1.20	3.64	3.73	1.1	97.4	68.9	15.3	51.4

Comparables: Chris Perez, Carter Capps, Stephen Pryor

The career arc of a power-armed reliever can resemble a heart murmur in that both can be volatile. Jiménez demonstrated as much last year, though there appears to be a clean demarcation between the two acts, in that he settled down and got better once he moved into the [checks notes] ninth inning, of course. (Maybe he was one of those kids who did poorly at school because they were bored with the coursework?) Shane Greene's departure from the foreground had his eighth-inning ERA above six switch to a ninth-inning ERA below three (and the component measures to back it up). The fastball was lively and the slider was unfair the entire time. If he gets more ninth inning opportunities, and he should, then strap in. It will probably work out. Probably.

★ ★ ★ *2020 Top 101 Prospect* **#47** ★ ★ ★

Matt Manning RHP Born: 01/28/98 Age: 22 Bats: R Throws: R Height: 6'6" Weight: 215 Origin: Round 1, 2016 Draft (#9 overall)

YEAR	TEAM	LVL	AGE	W	L	SV	G	GS	IP	H	HR	BB/9	K/9	K	GB%	BABIP	WHIP	ERA	DRA	WARP	MPH	FB%	WHF	CSP
2017	ONE	A-	19	2	2	0	9	9	33¹	27	0	3.8	9.7	36	31%	.310	1.23	1.89	4.32	0.4				
2017	WMI	A	19	2	0	0	5	5	17²	14	0	5.6	13.2	26	49%	.341	1.42	5.60	3.60	0.3				
2018	WMI	A	20	3	3	0	11	11	55²	47	3	4.5	12.3	76	43%	.344	1.35	3.40	3.77	0.9				
2018	LAK	A+	20	4	4	0	9	9	51¹	32	4	3.3	11.4	65	47%	.241	0.99	2.98	2.71	1.6				
2018	ERI	AA	20	0	1	0	2	2	10²	11	0	3.4	11.0	13	46%	.393	1.41	4.22	4.39	0.1				
2019	ERI	AA	21	11	5	0	24	24	133²	93	7	2.6	10.0	148	48%	.259	0.98	2.56	2.75	3.6				
2020	DET	MLB	22	2	2	0	33	0	35	34	5	3.6	9.4	37	44%	.307	1.36	4.27	4.41	0.3				

Comparables: José Berríos, Jake Thompson, Dustin May

When you draft a tall, projectable prep pitcher in the top 10, this is about where you're hoping he is four years down the line. At that point, Manning was an athletic kid with a fastball and curveball that flashed big. It took him awhile to truly get going as a pro—to learn the finer points of command and control, to hone repeatability in his delivery, to sharpen his changeup, all of those small things that separate first-round picks from frontline starters. Things came together quite well in 2019, as Manning was one of the best pitchers in Double-A all season long. He's still a bit of changeup development and more consistency away from being one of the *very* best pitching prospects in the game, but he's in the next tier down. That No. 2 starter outcome is looking quite attainable.

★ ★ ★ *2020 Top 101 Prospect* **#12** ★ ★ ★

Casey Mize RHP Born: 05/01/97 Age: 23 Bats: R Throws: R Height: 6'3" Weight: 220 Origin: Round 1, 2018 Draft (#1 overall)

YEAR	TEAM	LVL	AGE	W	L	SV	G	GS	IP	H	HR	BB/9	K/9	K	GB%	BABIP	WHIP	ERA	DRA	WARP	MPH	FB%	WHF	CSP
2018	LAK	A+	21	0	1	0	4	4	11²	13	2	1.5	7.7	10	44%	.344	1.29	4.63	5.08	0.0				
2019	LAK	A+	22	2	0	0	6	6	30²	11	0	1.5	8.8	30	48%	.155	0.52	0.88	1.83	1.2				
2019	ERI	AA	22	6	3	0	15	15	78²	69	5	2.1	8.7	76	42%	.294	1.11	3.20	4.17	0.8				
2020	DET	MLB	23	2	2	0	33	0	35	35	5	3.0	7.9	31	40%	.292	1.32	4.33	4.53	0.3				

Comparables: Jackson Stephens, Brett Kennedy, Robert Dugger

Behold, the agony and the ecstasy of the heralded pitching prospect. The No. 1 overall pick in the 2018 draft showed up last spring as a fully-formed good MLB pitcher. He proceeded to decimate batters at the High-A and Double-A levels to the tune of a 0.78 ERA and 2.43 DRA over 78 innings in the first half. By June, he'd emerged into one of the best prospects in the entire sport…just in time to be pulled from a start with a pitcher's most dreaded foe: shoulder inflammation. The injury ultimately cost him only a month of time, but our bigger concern is that he wasn't the same pitcher when he came back. He showed reduced stuff and command, and ran up a 6.61 ERA and 5.86 DRA in 31 innings before being shut down in mid-August. The ultimate fate of Detroit's rebuild may turn on whether the future ace version of Mize resurfaces this year.

Matt Moore LHP Born: 06/18/89 Age: 31 Bats: L Throws: L Height: 6'3" Weight: 210 Origin: Round 8, 2007 Draft (#245 overall)

YEAR	TEAM	LVL	AGE	W	L	SV	G	GS	IP	H	HR	BB/9	K/9	K	GB%	BABIP	WHIP	ERA	DRA	WARP	MPH	FB%	WHF	CSP
2017	SFN	MLB	28	6	15	0	32	31	174¹	200	27	3.5	7.6	148	39%	.320	1.53	5.52	5.34	0.4	94.1	51.7	9.4	49.7
2018	TEX	MLB	29	3	8	0	39	12	102	128	19	3.6	7.6	86	39%	.341	1.66	6.79	7.00	-2.2	94.7	58.7	10.7	52.5
2019	DET	MLB	30	0	0	0	2	2	10	3	0	0.9	8.1	9	61%	.130	0.40	0.00	4.48	0.1	95.0	53.9	16.2	52.6
2020	DET	MLB	31	2	2	0	33	0	35	33	5	3.2	8.0	31	41%	.286	1.31	4.12	4.26	0.4	93.5	54.5	10.2	51.5

Comparables: Danny Duffy, Jhoulys Chacín, Barry Zito

Much can be said about the "team-friendly extension" and why players should/shouldn't take it, but one unintended consequence is at the completion of the contract, the pitcher is not overpaid and thus very fashionable to sign again. Moore was an All-Star pitcher at the beginning and ended it a hanger-on. After a disappointing turn of events with the Giants, he was dumped on the Rangers with slot money like a single grandmother. Then, on his first year post-Friedman contract, he had two decent starts in Detroit before becoming more like Matt Less thanks to season-ending knee surgery. The lefty was all set for a Something To Prove contract, Take Two even though it's No, Really, I Can Do It This Time, Year Four. Instead, he got a Can't Believe This Guy Is Open To Playing In Asia contract with the Softbank Hawks as he looks to rebuild his value abroad.

Daniel Norris LHP Born: 04/25/93 Age: 27 Bats: L Throws: L Height: 6'2" Weight: 185 Origin: Round 2, 2011 Draft (#74 overall)

YEAR	TEAM	LVL	AGE	W	L	SV	G	GS	IP	H	HR	BB/9	K/9	K	GB%	BABIP	WHIP	ERA	DRA	WARP	MPH	FB%	WHF	CSP
2017	TOL	AAA	24	0	4	0	6	6	14	22	3	10.3	11.6	18	50%	.442	2.71	12.21	9.01	-0.5				
2017	DET	MLB	24	5	8	0	22	18	101²	120	12	3.9	7.6	86	40%	.344	1.61	5.31	6.48	-1.1	95.5	55	10	45.1
2018	DET	MLB	25	0	5	0	11	8	44¹	46	8	3.9	10.4	51	33%	.317	1.47	5.68	5.12	0.1	92.5	52.7	11.4	49.4
2019	DET	MLB	26	3	13	0	32	29	144¹	154	25	2.4	7.8	125	44%	.309	1.33	4.49	5.18	0.9	93.1	51.6	10.9	50.1
2020	DET	MLB	27	7	10	0	26	26	130	141	22	3.3	8.4	121	41%	.317	1.45	5.15	4.97	0.9	93.2	53.3	10.9	49.2

Comparables: Aaron Sanchez, Eduardo Rodriguez, Matt Wisler

You're looking at Injured Starter Patient Zero. Norris, a way-too-oft-injured lefty, actually went the entire year without a lengthy respite—a rarity on the 2019 Tigers, so much that he was nearly shut down manually due to an innings limit. He finagled his way into tossing three-inning starts instead of getting the heave ho into an early offseason, and performed well in nine pseudo-starts by posting a 3.33 ERA, a strikeout-to-walk ratio nearing 4.00, and a .683 OPS against. That type of workload suits him well, but he will likely be asked to again pitch five or six (okay five and five-plus) innings to conform to tradition. Maybe one day, when everyone has forgotten he was the centerpiece of the David Price trade or that he lived in a van, Norris will be able to fill the multi-inning relief role that seems to suit him best. Just make sure you check the rest of the relievers for symptoms regularly.

Franklin Perez RHP Born: 12/06/97 Age: 22 Bats: R Throws: R Height: 6'3" Weight: 197 Origin: International Free Agent, 2014

YEAR	TEAM	LVL	AGE	W	L	SV	G	GS	IP	H	HR	BB/9	K/9	K	GB%	BABIP	WHIP	ERA	DRA	WARP	MPH	FB%	WHF	CSP
2017	BCA	A+	19	4	2	2	12	10	54¹	38	4	2.7	8.8	53	38%	.236	0.99	2.98	2.76	1.6				
2017	CCH	AA	19	2	1	1	7	6	32	33	2	3.1	7.0	25	35%	.316	1.38	3.09	4.89	0.1				
2018	TGR	RK	20	0	1	0	3	3	8	3	0	0.0	5.6	5	27%	.136	0.38	4.50	1.08	0.4				
2018	LAK	A+	20	0	1	0	4	4	11¹	15	2	6.4	7.1	9	43%	.371	2.03	7.94	7.67	-0.3				
2019	LAK	A+	21	0	0	0	2	2	7²	7	1	5.9	7.0	6	46%	.286	1.57	2.35	6.15	-0.1				
2020	DET	MLB	22	2	2	0	33	0	35	35	5	3.6	7.0	27	38%	.287	1.40	4.59	4.62	0.2				

Comparables: Francis Martes, Brady Lail, Mike Soroka

Perez moved from Houston to Detroit in the Verlander deal, which happened right at the end of the 2017 minor-league season. He was a great get for a waiver trade, or so it seemed at the time, and we ranked him as the No. 53 prospect in baseball that offseason. Since then, he's pitched in a grand total of nine games over two seasons while battling chronic shoulder problems. Meanwhile, as you may already know, Verlander has been the best pitcher in the American League. It seems just a bit less good now, in the same way that *Rocky V* was just a bit less good than the rest of the series.

Nick Ramirez LHP Born: 08/01/89 Age: 30 Bats: L Throws: L Height: 6'3" Weight: 240 Origin: Round 4, 2011 Draft (#131 overall)

YEAR	TEAM	LVL	AGE	W	L	SV	G	GS	IP	H	HR	BB/9	K/9	K	GB%	BABIP	WHIP	ERA	DRA	WARP	MPH	FB%	WHF	CSP
2017	BLX	AA	27	7	4	3	48	0	79	56	4	2.7	6.4	56	49%	.230	1.01	1.37	3.26	1.4				
2018	BLX	AA	28	8	0	1	19	0	30²	17	2	3.8	9.7	33	55%	.205	0.98	1.76	2.97	0.7				
2018	CSP	AAA	28	3	3	0	20	2	37²	44	3	5.0	4.3	18	52%	.308	1.73	5.73	5.87	-0.3				
2019	ERI	AA	29	1	0	0	3	3	14¹	11	1	1.3	12.6	20	55%	.312	0.91	2.51	2.98	0.3				
2019	TOL	AAA	29	0	1	0	2	2	9	12	1	3.0	10.0	10	45%	.393	1.67	2.00	5.17	0.1				
2019	DET	MLB	29	5	4	0	46	0	79²	76	11	4.0	8.4	74	47%	.286	1.39	4.07	4.52	0.7	91.6	30.1	13.2	41.2
2020	DET	MLB	30	2	2	0	33	0	35	32	5	3.7	8.2	32	47%	.277	1.32	4.08	4.26	0.4	90.9	30	13.2	41.1

Comparables: Gregory Infante, Tanner Scheppers, Matt Buschmann

Ramirez is a multi-inning relief option who took the Sean Doolittle scenic route to the big leagues, converting to the mound in 2017 after seven years of tepid slugging. The ex-first baseman lefty ascended to a major league long relief role thanks to a dynamite changeup in the high-70s that offsets a high-80s fastball. His outgoing exit velocity was among the best in the league and as a result he paced a desolate Tigers team in relief innings. Mileage on Ramirez's arm isn't a concern, but a second year of the league seeing him might be.

★　★　★　*2020 Top 101 Prospect* **#76**　★　★　★

Tarik Skubal LHP   Born: 11/20/96   Age: 23   Bats: L   Throws: L   Height: 6'3"   Weight: 215   Origin: Round 9, 2018 Draft (#255 overall)

YEAR	TEAM	LVL	AGE	W	L	SV	G	GS	IP	H	HR	BB/9	K/9	K	GB%	BABIP	WHIP	ERA	DRA	WARP	MPH	FB%	WHF	CSP
2018	ONE	A-	21	0	0	1	4	0	12	8	0	1.5	12.8	17	46%	.333	0.83	0.75	3.08	0.2				
2018	WMI	A	21	2	0	1	3	0	7¹	5	0	1.2	13.5	11	29%	.357	0.82	0.00	2.52	0.2				
2019	LAK	A+	22	4	5	0	15	15	80¹	62	5	2.1	10.9	97	40%	.292	1.01	2.58	3.31	1.7				
2019	ERI	AA	22	2	3	0	9	9	42¹	25	2	3.8	17.4	82	41%	.343	1.02	2.13	2.40	1.3				
2020	DET	MLB	23	2	2	0	33	0	35	34	5	3.4	11.8	46	40%	.341	1.36	4.35	4.45	0.3				

Comparables: Taylor Rogers, Adam Morgan, Dylan Cease

If you love lefties who throw gorgeous curveballs—and who doesn't?—meet your new favorite artist. Skubal had just a little buzz coming into 2019 as a lefty with good stuff whose college career was marred by Tommy John surgery. After a true breakout campaign, he's emerged as a top prospect, with a full four-pitch mix fronted by a mid-90s heater. The true star of the band is his curve, which has a chance to be one of Detroit's best hooks since the heyday of Motown. Because of the injury history and all the usual questions about pitching prospects, we don't know whether the final cut will be starter or reliever as of yet. We think it'll be a great album either way.

Gregory Soto LHP   Born: 02/11/95   Age: 25   Bats: L   Throws: L   Height: 6'1"   Weight: 240   Origin: International Free Agent, 2012

YEAR	TEAM	LVL	AGE	W	L	SV	G	GS	IP	H	HR	BB/9	K/9	K	GB%	BABIP	WHIP	ERA	DRA	WARP	MPH	FB%	WHF	CSP
2017	WMI	A	22	10	1	0	18	18	96	70	3	5.1	10.9	116	45%	.295	1.29	2.25	3.73	1.7				
2017	LAK	A+	22	2	1	0	5	5	28	27	1	3.5	9.0	28	56%	.351	1.36	2.25	5.35	0.0				
2018	LAK	A+	23	8	8	0	25	23	113¹	101	4	5.6	9.1	115	47%	.306	1.51	4.45	5.53	-0.3				
2019	ERI	AA	24	0	1	0	3	3	13¹	10	2	2.7	8.1	12	54%	.229	1.05	2.03	3.70	0.2				
2019	TOL	AAA	24	0	3	0	6	5	23¹	25	2	5.0	11.6	30	48%	.371	1.63	6.94	5.19	0.3				
2019	DET	MLB	24	0	5	0	33	7	57²	74	9	5.2	7.0	45	49%	.344	1.86	5.77	7.65	-1.3	98.1	70.7	9.1	51.5
2020	DET	MLB	25	2	2	0	35	0	37	42	6	4.5	6.9	28	48%	.318	1.66	6.00	5.53	-0.1	97.8	72.4	9.3	52.8

Comparables: Matt Hall, Ryan Carpenter, Rob Rasmussen

It would seem to be an inopportune time in baseball history to be a Soto unless you're the Juan and only. But did you know that Gregory led all Sotos in batting average (minimum, ahem, two at-bats)? To be serious: this Soto has a decent slider but lacks fastball command to get to that good pitch, and for that reason all the batters he faces end up producing like Juan—a condition likely to sentence him to low-leverage pen work, at best. Fastball command is one of those career-long enigmas that can shatter potential into a million tiny ball fours and will remain his nemesis alongside everyone asking him to do the Shuffle.

Spencer Turnbull RHP   Born: 09/18/92   Age: 27   Bats: R   Throws: R   Height: 6'3"   Weight: 215   Origin: Round 2, 2014 Draft (#63 overall)

YEAR	TEAM	LVL	AGE	W	L	SV	G	GS	IP	H	HR	BB/9	K/9	K	GB%	BABIP	WHIP	ERA	DRA	WARP	MPH	FB%	WHF	CSP
2017	TGW	RK	24	0	0	0	2	2	9	8	0	2.0	16.0	16	65%	.471	1.11	4.00	2.21	0.4				
2017	LAK	A+	24	7	3	0	15	15	82²	68	3	2.7	7.0	64	52%	.280	1.12	3.05	4.41	0.8				
2017	ERI	AA	24	0	3	0	4	4	20¹	22	1	3.5	9.7	22	58%	.356	1.48	6.20	4.47	0.2				
2018	ERI	AA	25	4	7	0	19	19	98²	92	4	3.6	9.6	105	56%	.332	1.34	4.47	4.22	1.3				
2018	TOL	AAA	25	1	1	0	2	2	13¹	8	0	2.0	12.8	19	57%	.267	0.82	2.03	2.90	0.4				
2018	DET	MLB	25	0	2	0	4	3	16¹	17	1	2.2	8.3	15	48%	.327	1.29	6.06	4.99	0.1	96.5	63.5	9.9	49.3
2019	DET	MLB	26	3	17	0	30	30	148¹	154	14	3.6	8.9	146	49%	.333	1.44	4.61	5.21	0.9	96.2	64.8	11.6	45.3
2020	DET	MLB	27	7	9	0	26	26	130	131	16	3.8	8.9	127	48%	.314	1.43	4.72	4.55	1.5	95.7	65.5	11.6	47.7

Comparables: Brock Stewart, Tyler Cloyd, Mark Leiter Jr.

Rookie years are supposed to be learning experiences, not sensory deprivation chambers. Turnbull wasn't awful, in fact he was arguably above average, but by happenstance became the second pitcher in the last 40 years to lose at least 17 as a rookie. (Jeremy Bonderman dropped 19 in 2003, further proof something is afoot in Michigan.) He has several good pitches but none were clicking especially in the second half, battling a befuddling combination of arm and brain fatigue. With the catharses behind him thanks to months of wintertime rest, the crimson-chinned chucker ought to be back as a reliable mid-rotation starter.

Drew VerHagen RHP   Born: 10/22/90   Age: 29   Bats: R   Throws: R   Height: 6'6"   Weight: 230   Origin: Round 4, 2012 Draft (#154 overall)

YEAR	TEAM	LVL	AGE	W	L	SV	G	GS	IP	H	HR	BB/9	K/9	K	GB%	BABIP	WHIP	ERA	DRA	WARP	MPH	FB%	WHF	CSP
2017	TOL	AAA	26	7	7	0	19	19	97¹	108	7	4.0	6.4	69	46%	.329	1.55	4.90	5.74	0.0				
2017	DET	MLB	26	0	3	0	24	2	34¹	42	10	2.4	6.6	25	51%	.317	1.49	5.77	4.95	0.1	95.8	60.5	9.6	50.2
2018	TOL	AAA	27	2	1	0	10	6	32²	18	0	2.8	14.1	51	52%	.273	0.86	1.65	2.11	1.2				
2018	DET	MLB	27	3	3	0	41	1	56¹	46	6	3.0	8.5	53	48%	.263	1.15	4.63	3.79	0.8	96.4	54	12.7	46.8
2019	TOL	AAA	28	4	2	0	11	11	53	61	5	2.2	8.7	51	41%	.350	1.40	4.42	4.62	1.1				
2019	DET	MLB	28	4	3	0	22	4	58	70	9	3.6	7.9	51	52%	.357	1.60	5.90	5.80	-0.2	95.3	52.9	10.2	49.8
2020	DET	MLB	29	2	2	0	33	0	35	39	6	3.3	8.2	32	48%	.319	1.47	5.31	5.09	0.0	95.1	54.5	11	48.9

Comparables: Chris Beck, Chris Stratton, Matt Magill

The second-best pitcher in Tigers history whose last name starts with "Ver" spent parts of six major-league seasons with an impressive four-pitch mix and a lack of lasting success. He's been bandied about the pitching staff, struggling at each role: long relief, late-inning and especially his preference, the rotation. He lost his 40-man roster spot each of the last two seasons, but found modest success with an overly specific role: relieving Daniel Norris for eight of his shortened starts in the last two months, going about four to five innings per gig. His 4.18 ERA in such situations means either: (a) he's possibly suited for a primary reliever role, or (b) he can get a ride in Norris's van any time he wants.

Joey Wentz   LHP   Born: 10/06/97   Age: 22   Bats: L   Throws: L   Height: 6'5"   Weight: 210   Origin: Round 1, 2016 Draft (#40 overall)

YEAR	TEAM	LVL	AGE	W	L	SV	G	GS	IP	H	HR	BB/9	K/9	K	GB%	BABIP	WHIP	ERA	DRA	WARP	MPH	FB%	WHF	CSP
2017	ROM	A	19	8	3	0	26	26	131²	99	4	3.1	10.4	152	41%	.293	1.10	2.60	2.78	3.9				
2018	BRV	A+	20	3	4	0	16	16	67	49	3	3.2	7.1	53	46%	.250	1.09	2.28	3.46	1.5				
2019	MIS	AA	21	5	8	0	20	20	103	90	13	3.9	8.7	100	35%	.280	1.31	4.72	5.50	-0.7				
2019	ERI	AA	21	2	0	0	5	5	25²	20	3	1.4	13.0	37	19%	.315	0.94	2.10	3.28	0.5				
2020	DET	MLB	22	2	2	0	33	0	35	35	5	3.7	8.4	33	34%	.300	1.40	4.54	4.65	0.2				

Comparables: Danny Duffy, Giovanni Soto, Alex Torres

Wentz was one of the best prospects moved at the 2019 trade deadline. It was a slow deadline and everyone hugged top prospects like their favorite childhood stuffed animal, true, yet the Tigers nabbed this promising and touted young southpaw for Shane Greene's extremely shiny and totally unsustainable ERA. Sure enough, Greene went back to being a decent if unspectacular reliever the moment he landed with Atlanta, and Wentz ripped off one of the best months of his career in his new system. This is the type of sneaky deal that can separate successful rebuilds from perpetual mediocrity.

Jordan Zimmermann   RHP   Born: 05/23/86   Age: 34   Bats: R   Throws: R   Height: 6'2"   Weight: 225   Origin: Round 2, 2007 Draft (#67 overall)

YEAR	TEAM	LVL	AGE	W	L	SV	G	GS	IP	H	HR	BB/9	K/9	K	GB%	BABIP	WHIP	ERA	DRA	WARP	MPH	FB%	WHF	CSP
2017	DET	MLB	31	8	13	0	29	29	160	204	29	2.5	5.8	103	35%	.330	1.55	6.07	6.90	-2.4	93.9	54.2	8.8	51.3
2018	DET	MLB	32	7	8	0	25	25	131¹	140	28	1.8	7.6	111	37%	.288	1.26	4.52	4.76	0.8	93.0	45.3	9.9	48.2
2019	DET	MLB	33	1	13	0	23	23	112	145	19	2.0	6.6	82	43%	.339	1.52	6.91	6.74	-1.2	91.9	47	9.5	46.5
2020	DET	MLB	34	6	11	0	26	26	130	161	28	2.3	6.8	98	41%	.322	1.49	6.15	5.76	-0.2	91.8	47.9	9.3	47.6

Comparables: Ricky Nolasco, Kevin Millwood, Erik Hanson

It's funny, Zimmermann's most memorable appearance to date might've been an NLDS start in which Matt Williams pulled him a batter too soon. Now, he's spent the last four years in there too long. (Note that nothing funny ever follows "it's funny.") Zimmermann pressing his ink on a Tigers contract was equivalent to drinking from the wrong grail; the Old English D has been a parasite on his fastball, slowly sucking the usefulness away until all that was left was a modest changeup. Zimmermann's time in Detroit hasn't gone well, is what we're saying. Entering the finale of his $110 million agreement, it seems inevitable he will be jettisoned from the rotation soon, assuming he even makes it past camp. He had the worst ERA in a season, minimum 100 innings, since Hideo Nomo *and* José Lima overstayed their major league welcome for the Devil Rays and Royals, respectively, in 2005. This is a rough denouement to his otherwise honorable career.

LINEOUTS

Hitters

HITTER	POS	TEAM	LVL	AGE	PA	R	2B	3B	HR	RBI	BB	K	SB	CS	AVG/OBP/SLG	DRC+	VORP	BABIP	BRR	FRAA	WARP
Sergio Alcántara	SS	ERI	AA	22	378	46	10	0	2	27	48	71	7	6	.247/.346/.296	101	10.3	.308	0.1	SS(73): 4.4, 2B(29): 1.8	2.2
Jorge Bonifacio	RF	KCA	MLB	26	21	3	3	0	0	3	1	7	0	0	.350/.381/.500	67	-0.4	.538	-0.3	RF(4): -0.3, LF(1): 0.0	-0.1
	RF	OMA	AAA	26	500	67	18	5	20	62	38	121	6	4	.222/.284/.417	74	-3.8	.252	0.4	LF(55): 9.6, RF(42): 3.7	0.8
Eric Haase	C	CLE	MLB	26	17	1	0	0	1	3	1	8	0	0	.063/.118/.250	72	0.1	.000	0.0	C(8): -1.1	-0.1
	C	COH	AAA	26	401	67	12	3	28	60	42	142	1	1	.226/.315/.517	93	19.8	.279	0.1	C(92): 3.8	1.9
Derek Hill	OF	ERI	AA	23	526	78	19	5	14	45	38	147	21	13	.243/.311/.394	92	16.3	.321	0.7	CF(79): 1.4, RF(37): 7.8	2.2
Pete Kozma	SS	TOL	AAA	31	322	44	17	2	7	51	32	49	2	0	.263/.340/.414	99	16.1	.288	1.0	2B(58): 6.9, SS(24): 1.3	1.9
Parker Meadows	CF	WMI	A	19	504	52	15	2	7	40	47	113	14	8	.221/.296/.312	78	3.6	.277	-1.1	CF(100): -2.3, RF(16): 0.8	0.0
Wenceel Perez	SS	WMI	A	19	516	59	16	6	3	30	45	87	21	13	.233/.299/.314	78	12.7	.279	0.8	SS(118): -13.2	-0.4
Dustin Peterson	RF	DET	MLB	24	47	3	4	0	0	6	2	14	1	0	.227/.277/.318	62	-1.0	.333	-0.1	LF(9): -0.1, RF(2): 0.0	-0.2
	RF	TOL	AAA	24	319	31	13	0	11	49	14	78	1	1	.286/.317/.439	91	-7.8	.349	-3.1	1B(74): -4.9	-0.7
Nick Quintana	3B	WMI	A	21	162	14	5	1	1	13	13	51	3	1	.158/.228/.226	37	-4.3	.229	0.6	3B(38): 3.4	-0.1
	3B	ONE	A-	21	98	12	7	0	1	4	12	31	1	0	.256/.347/.372	130	4.5	.389	0.4	3B(25): -2.9	0.3
Jacob Robson	OF	TOL	AAA	24	473	61	21	3	9	52	53	132	25	10	.267/.352/.399	97	7.7	.368	-0.2	LF(46): 0.0, RF(35): 0.5	0.8
Frank Schwindel	1B	ERI	AA	27	188	21	8	0	5	23	11	27	0	0	.257/.309/.392	98	2.8	.275	-3.1	1B(21): 0.0	-0.1
	1B	OMA	AAA	27	76	8	4	0	1	10	4	13	0	1	.186/.237/.286	36	-5.7	.211	0.0	1B(13): -0.7	-0.5
	1B	TOL	AAA	27	119	21	7	0	9	33	6	19	0	0	.327/.361/.628	150	9.4	.329	-0.4	1B(25): 0.0, RF(2): 0.2	0.8
	1B	KCA	MLB	27	15	0	0	0	0	0	0	2	0	0	.067/.067/.067	83	-0.1	.077	0.0	1B(5): -0.4	0.0
Troy Stokes Jr.	LF	SAN	AAA	23	381	50	22	0	9	40	47	87	14	3	.233/.341/.385	90	11.4	.287	2.4	LF(76): -6.9, RF(10): -1.5	0.1
Bobby Wilson	C	TOL	AAA	36	101	12	2	0	5	10	11	25	0	0	.244/.327/.433	101	2.7	.283	-1.3	C(25): 10.6, 3B(1): 0.0	1.3
	C	DET	MLB	36	47	2	1	0	0	2	2	11	0	0	.091/.130/.114	60	0.1	.121	0.0	C(15): 1.9	0.2

Here's our annual reminder that **Sergio Alcántara** is still on track for a career as a glove-first utility player. ⓧ **Jorge Bonifacio** started 122 games during the 2019 season; granted, 117 of them were at Triple-A, but statistically it still seems fairly damning. ⓧ The good: **Eric Haase** socked 28 dingers in Triple-A, tied for fifth in the International League. The bad: Despite the pop, he hit .226 and really struggled framing behind the dish. The ugly: In a 10-game cup of coffee, the backup backstop fell to strikes almost half the time. Maybe he should go by Haaaase? ⓧ Now five years removed from his one and presumably only appearance on the BP 101, former first-rounder **Derek Hill** keeps hitting *just* enough to maintain a slight bit of prospect relevancy. ⓧ In November 2018, the Perth Heat of the Australian Baseball League announced the signing of "MLB star **Pete Kozma**" for the winter campaign. In the Northern Hemisphere, he continues to be "Quad-A utility man who inexplicably was the starting shortstop for the Cards that one year Pete Kozma." ⓧ **Parker Meadows** shares a sweet lefty swing and a big set of athletic tools with older brother Austin. Whether he also got any of the family hitting ability is still unclear. ⓧ **Wenceel Perez** had a rough offensive campaign as a teenager in Low-A, and yet playing the entire summer as a teenager in full-season ball is a significant accomplishment in and of itself. He still has quite a bit of time for the offensive tools to pull together. ⓧ **Dustin Peterson** opened the season as a semi-regular in Detroit for a hot second, and might eventually stick somewhere as a fourth outfielder. ⓧ Second-rounder **Nick Quintana** struggled so badly at the Low-A level after signing that he was demoted to short-season ball in August. He'll get something of a pass for being at the end of a long college campaign, but it wasn't encouraging for someone advertised as a polished college power bat. ⓧ **Jacob Robson** grew up a Tigers fan in neighboring Windsor, Ontario. He didn't quite get to Detroit this year, but his old-school leadoff profile should play in the majors soon. ⓧ Trivia note for future generations: the Opening Day first baseman for the 2019 Royals was **Frank Schwindel**, making his major-league debut. He was sent down by Tax Day and released in May, ending up on an odyssey that included stops at four levels in two organizations. ⓧ **Troy Stokes** has an intriguing basket of tools that includes both power and speed. His home-run production sharply dipped in 2019, even though he was moving to the new power-mad environment in Triple-A, and he was claimed off waivers in September. If you write his name out in full—Troy Stokes Junior—it doubles as a sentence. ⓧ If you're going to spend the twilight of a long, occasionally successful career hoping for an emergency call-up while hanging around Triple-A as a backup catcher, it's important to pick the right organization. **Bobby Wilson**—or "BMW," per his chest protector—now has a two-year streak of choosing wisely.

Pitchers

PITCHER	TEAM	LVL	AGE	W	L	SV	G	GS	IP	H	HR	BB/9	K/9	K	GB%	BABIP	WHIP	ERA	DRA	WARP	MPH	FB%	WHF	CSP
Austin Adams	ROC	AAA	32	1	1	1	11	1	18	16	3	3.0	14.0	28	60%	.333	1.22	4.50	5.41	0.2				
	TOL	AAA	32	0	2	1	18	1	25²	26	6	3.5	7.0	20	46%	.263	1.40	6.66	5.37	0.2				
	MIN	MLB	32	0	0	0	2	0	2²	4	2	10.1	16.9	5	43%	.400	2.62	16.88	5.32	0.0	97.7	73	8.1	42.7
	DET	MLB	32	0	0	0	13	0	14	14	2	6.4	5.8	9	41%	.273	1.71	5.14	7.80	-0.4	98.7	49.4	11.3	45.1
Victor Alcántara	TOL	AAA	26	0	0	0	13	2	18¹	17	3	2.9	7.9	16	59%	.271	1.25	5.89	4.07	0.4				
	DET	MLB	26	3	2	0	46	0	42²	45	8	3.2	5.1	24	55%	.278	1.41	4.85	5.62	-0.1	95.1	75.8	10.8	45.2
Sandy Baez	TOL	AAA	25	1	0	0	18	0	22	27	1	5.7	7.4	18	34%	.356	1.86	7.36	6.72	-0.1				
	DET	MLB	25	0	0	0	1	0	1	2	0	0.0	0.0	0	40%	.400	2.00	9.00	5.90	0.0	94.6	50	10	66.7
Ryan Carpenter	TOL	AAA	28	5	7	0	14	14	77	77	11	3.0	8.9	76	42%	.310	1.34	5.26	4.74	1.5				
	DET	MLB	28	1	6	0	9	9	40²	61	12	2.9	5.5	25	38%	.338	1.82	9.30	9.03	-1.4	92.2	45.2	8	51.8
Anthony Castro	ERI	AA	24	5	3	1	27	18	102¹	75	9	5.7	10.2	116	45%	.273	1.37	4.40	4.78	0.2				
José Manuel Fernández	ERI	AA	26	1	3	1	11	3	26	30	4	2.4	6.6	19	27%	.310	1.42	4.15	5.84	-0.3				
	TOL	AAA	26	1	1	0	27	1	34²	40	5	4.2	6.2	24	39%	.318	1.62	5.97	6.58	-0.1				
	DET	MLB	26	0	0	0	4	0	3²	6	1	12.3	4.9	2	20%	.357	3.00	17.18	8.35	-0.1	94.6	54.7	6.7	50.6
Kyle Funkhouser	ERI	AA	25	3	1	0	4	4	23²	16	2	1.1	11.0	29	45%	.275	0.80	1.90	2.81	0.6				
	TOL	AAA	25	3	7	0	18	18	63¹	79	3	7.7	9.2	65	54%	.396	2.10	8.53	7.79	-0.7				
Bryan Garcia	TOL	AAA	24	3	0	0	31	0	33¹	26	4	3.8	8.9	33	46%	.253	1.20	2.97	3.79	0.8				
	DET	MLB	24	0	0	0	7	0	6²	9	1	6.8	9.4	7	62%	.400	2.10	12.15	4.83	0.0	95.8	51.9	14.7	45.5
Rony Garcia	TAM	A+	21	0	2	0	5	4	25	21	2	2.5	9.0	25	34%	.288	1.12	2.16	4.03	0.3				
	TRN	AA	21	4	11	0	20	20	105¹	94	14	3.2	8.9	104	35%	.281	1.25	4.44	5.52	-0.7				
Carlos Guzman	WMI	A	21	2	2	0	7	7	33	23	3	4.9	7.4	27	47%	.227	1.24	2.73	3.89	0.5				
Matt Hall	TOL	AAA	25	5	4	0	25	13	86²	102	16	3.2	11.0	106	50%	.369	1.53	5.30	5.72	0.7				
	DET	MLB	25	0	1	0	16	0	23¹	28	4	5.8	10.4	27	39%	.364	1.84	7.71	5.71	-0.1	92.5	66.3	9.8	44.7
Wilkel Hernandez	WMI	A	20	9	7	0	21	21	101¹	97	5	2.3	8.0	90	40%	.302	1.21	3.73	4.05	1.4				
Eduardo Jiménez	TOL	AAA	24	4	3	2	41	0	54²	39	5	3.0	8.4	51	47%	.239	1.04	2.96	3.00	1.7				
	DET	MLB	24	0	0	0	8	0	10²	12	1	4.2	6.8	8	39%	.314	1.59	5.91	6.14	-0.1	95.2	57.1	7.9	45.9
Alex Lange	MYR	A+	23	1	9	0	11	11	47²	58	4	4.9	9.6	51	52%	.372	1.76	7.36	7.04	-1.2				
	TEN	AA	23	2	3	0	7	7	39	36	4	4.4	6.5	28	47%	.283	1.41	3.92	5.82	-0.5				
	ERI	AA	23	2	1	0	9	0	15²	13	0	4.6	8.6	15	47%	.342	1.34	3.45	5.46	-0.1				
David McKay	TAC	A+	24	3	1	1	30	0	43²	31	4	6.4	14.6	71	32%	.321	1.42	5.15	2.88	1.4				
	SEA	MLB	24	0	0	0	7	0	7	5	1	10.3	6.4	5	33%	.200	1.86	5.14	8.22	-0.2	94.6	56.8	7.7	45.8
	DET	MLB	24	0	0	0	18	0	19¹	15	2	4.2	13.5	29	26%	.325	1.24	5.59	3.59	0.4	95.7	65.6	10.8	50.1
Zac Reininger	TOL	AAA	26	4	3	0	34	4	57¹	65	7	4.1	8.0	51	44%	.337	1.59	4.08	5.55	0.5				
	DET	MLB	26	0	3	0	25	1	28	44	11	5.1	5.5	17	38%	.344	2.14	8.68	9.91	-1.4	96.1	59.1	7.7	45.7
Paul Richan	MYR	A+	22	10	5	0	17	17	93	96	10	1.7	8.3	86	40%	.315	1.23	3.97	4.90	0.1				
	LAK	A+	22	2	2	0	5	5	30²	39	2	0.6	8.5	29	43%	.398	1.34	4.11	6.73	-0.6				
Elvin Rodriguez	LAK	A+	21	11	9	0	24	23	133²	113	12	3.0	7.5	112	37%	.267	1.17	3.77	4.88	0.2				
John Schreiber	ERI	AA	25	0	0	0	5	0	7	4	1	3.9	15.4	12	57%	.231	1.00	2.57	2.92	0.1				
	TOL	AAA	25	6	4	4	48	0	59¹	39	4	3.2	10.6	70	42%	.250	1.01	2.28	2.40	2.2				
	DET	MLB	25	2	0	0	13	0	13	16	3	2.8	13.2	19	37%	.406	1.54	6.23	5.02	0.0	93.8	61.9	12.8	47.4
Daniel Stumpf	TOL	AAA	28	2	1	4	14	0	15¹	8	0	2.3	14.1	24	32%	.258	0.78	0.59	1.39	0.7				
	DET	MLB	28	1	1	0	48	0	29	35	5	4.7	8.7	28	37%	.345	1.72	4.34	7.22	-0.6	94.1	52.7	11.3	49.2
Alex Wilson	SAN	AAA	32	4	1	2	29	0	38	33	8	1.7	7.3	31	51%	.236	1.05	2.13	3.91	0.9				
	IOW	AAA	32	1	2	1	10	0	12¹	12	2	1.5	8.0	11	51%	.303	1.14	5.11	5.50	0.1				
	MIL	MLB	32	1	1	1	13	0	11¹	15	3	7.1	10.3	13	40%	.375	2.12	9.53	5.14	0.0	93.0	45.5	9.9	39

Austin Adams still approaches 100 mph on the radar gun despite being well into his 30s. He also still gets clobbered every time he makes it back to the majors. It's nice when people stay true to their roots. ⊗ Sinkerballer **Victor Alcántara** had injured list stints in 2019 for a wisdom tooth extraction and a finger contusion. There's a third condition that isn't health related that's a bigger threat to his place on the active roster: his stuff doesn't fool MLB hitters. ⊗ **Sandy Baez** provides a slightly different spin on the generic 95-and-a-slider up-and-down reliever by mixing in a foshball, an old-timey name for a split-change. ⊗ Fringe southpaw **Ryan Carpenter**'s career 8.57 ERA is the eighth worst in MLB history, minimum 60 innings. Conversely, Ryan Baseball is one of the worst-rated contractors in the metro area, minimum one-and-a-half Yelp stars. ⊗ Not to be confused with the other Castro in the Tigers system, or the other-other Castro in the Tigers system, **Anthony Castro** is a pitcher. Like the other Castro's, his fringy stuff has the floor to reach the big leagues and that's about it. ⊗ This **José Fernández** shares a name and an approximate velocity band with the late Marlins ace but little else. He's a lefty reliever who needs some things to break right to get a steady LOOGY paycheck. The three-batter minimum rule is an extinction-level threat to his career. ⊗ **Kyle Funkhouser** has battled a long string of injuries encompassing everything from vague shoulder soreness to a broken foot from bad concrete on a sidewalk. The stuff still flashes enough to have a bit of hope, but it's fading fast. ⊗ Former University of Miami closer **Bryan Garcia** had a successful return from 2018 Tommy John surgery, earning a September call-up. As relief prospects go, he's mildly interesting. ⊗ Converted infielder **Carlos Guzman** was just starting to make waves as a pitching prospect when he went down with an elbow injury in May and missed the rest of the season. His athleticism and changeup make him one worth watching. ⊗ Were the late poet Donald Hall to write a lineout concerning soft-tossing lefty **Matt Hall**, he might go with something like: "It's almost relaxing to know he'll be designated for assignment fairly soon, as it's a comfort not to obsess about his next failed big-league stint." ⊗ One of two live arms acquired in a 2017 trade with the Angels for Ian Kinsler, **Wilkel Hernandez** has a starter's frame and worked all season at High-A to decent results. How the secondaries develop as he progresses through the system will determine if he can stick in a rotation. ⊗ "It's just a dream. I still do not believe that I am finally here," reliever **Eduardo Jiménez** told Chris McCosky of *The Detroit News* after he was called up in May. "Since I was a kid I dreamed about this." We should always remember that making the majors is the culmination of a lifetime of dreams and hard work, even for an up-and-down reliever. ⊗ Former Cubs first-rounder **Alex Lange** moved to the Tigers system in the Nicholas Castellanos trade; he was the more famous of the two prospects moved, but the lesser one by the time of the deal. Detroit converted him to relief after acquiring him, and he pitched much better in that role. ⊗ Curveball specialist and Florida Atlantic alum **David McKay** was an August waiver claim by the Tigers from the Mariners, which is about as depressing as a 2019 baseball transaction can get. Roll Owls. ⊗ **Zac Reininger** has the same initials and letter count as *Final Sacrifice* antihero Zap Rowsdower, and both prove you need more than decent mechanics and questionable '90s stuff. ⊗ **Paul Richan**, the better prospect from the Castellanos deal, is one of the best command-and-control pitching prospects in the minors. Some guys with this profile turn into good major league starters, and some of them turn into human JUGS machines. ⊗ Once upon a time, **Elvin Rodriguez** was an interesting but very skinny pitching prospect traded for Justin Upton. He's older now—aren't we all—but remains an interesting prospect who is as thick as a bow string. He'll face the Double-A test in 2020. ⊗ The stars of *I Love Lucy* and *The Six Million Dollar Man* share a hometown of Wyandotte, Michigan with Downriver Detroit denizen **John Schreiber**. That explains why his deceptive sidearm delivery got him a callup to play Ball in the Majors. ⊗ **Daniel Stumpf** has built a career of not being able to handle righties at all, which explains spending much of his spare time volunteering for the Hillary Clinton campaign. ⊗ **Alex Wilson** has reached the "gotta sign a minor-league deal with the Tigers" portion of his unremarkable but solid career. We don't feel the need to pile on further.

HOUSTON ASTROS

Essay by Ian Miller

Player comments by Tyler Stafford and BP staff

All 30 of the team essays in this book are, by definition, failures.

I say this in part, of course, to abnegate responsibility for my own personal failure on these pages, but also because it's true. Each author is trying to impose order on utter randomness, which is futile.

This is a normal human impulse. Consciousness—even the limbic-cortex-level sort—depends on this. Look at those trees: Is there a threat lurking? Is there one of those Pleistocene-era megafauna sloths hiding behind that dumpster? Why didn't A.J. Hinch go to Gerrit Cole in the 7th inning of Game 7 of the World Series?

The idea that our existence is nothing more than a series of random events and has no meaning is too terrifying to contemplate, and so we set about distracting ourselves. We mate and raise children, we watch sports, we go to work; we expend terrific amounts of energy to add structure to our lives. We are meaning-making beings.

"Moneyball," to the extent that term still has any meaning, is rooted in the same impulse. Front offices do their best to reduce variance; they stack marginal improvement on marginal improvement to increase their odds of winning. The "best" teams develop new metrics to quantify the previously unquantifiable in an effort to wring every iota of certitude from the available data. What started as a scrappy, under-resourced team looking for an edge has developed into a bloodless business of consultants willing to win at virtually any cost. Call it the McKinsey-fication of baseball.

The Astros, headed by ex-McKinsey consultant Jeff Luhnow, have proven better at this than most. Luhnow has proven willing to make marginal moves that other GMs aren't, from overseeing a genuine tanking effort early in his tenure to risking PR disaster by acquiring distressed assets (see Osuna, Roberto). Despite missing on a No. 1 overall pick or two, Luhnow has overseen a remarkable transformation of the Astros, shepherding them through their transition to the AL to a World Series win in 2017 and another appearance this past year.

But even Luhnow's level of ISO 9001-level scientifically derived certitude wasn't enough. In 2017, the Astros players set out to determine what would happen before it happened.

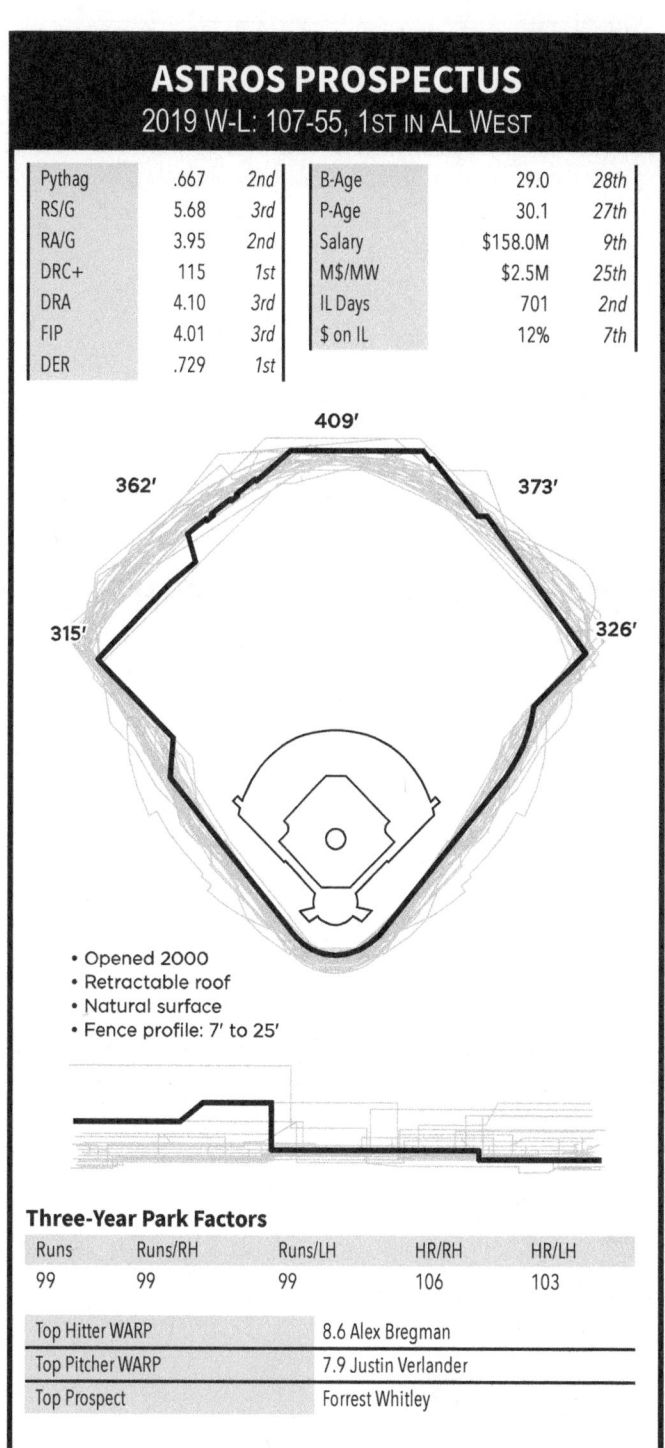

ASTROS PROSPECTUS
2019 W-L: 107-55, 1ST IN AL WEST

Pythag	.667	2nd	B-Age	29.0	28th
RS/G	5.68	3rd	P-Age	30.1	27th
RA/G	3.95	2nd	Salary	$158.0M	9th
DRC+	115	1st	M$/MW	$2.5M	25th
DRA	4.10	3rd	IL Days	701	2nd
FIP	4.01	3rd	$ on IL	12%	7th
DER	.729	1st			

409'

362' 373'

315' 326'

- Opened 2000
- Retractable roof
- Natural surface
- Fence profile: 7' to 25'

Three-Year Park Factors

Runs	Runs/RH	Runs/LH	HR/RH	HR/LH
99	99	99	106	103

Top Hitter WARP	8.6 Alex Bregman
Top Pitcher WARP	7.9 Justin Verlander
Top Prospect	Forrest Whitley

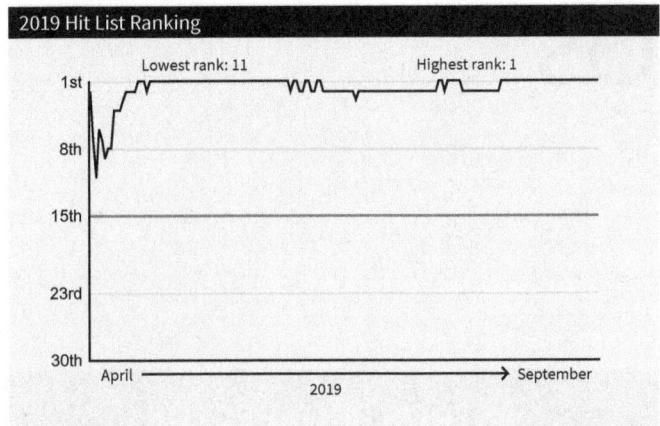

2019 Hit List Ranking

Lowest rank: 11   Highest rank: 1

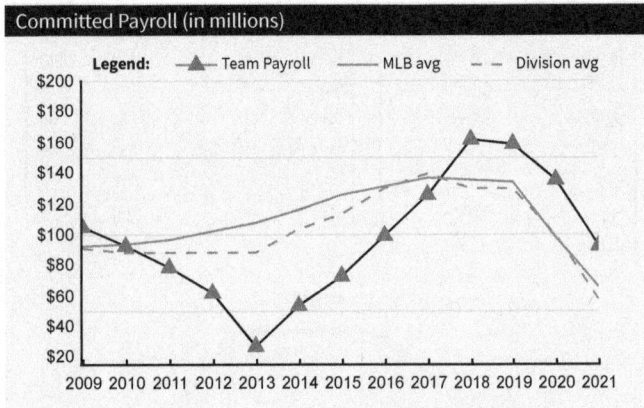

Committed Payroll (in millions)

Legend: Team Payroll — MLB avg - - Division avg

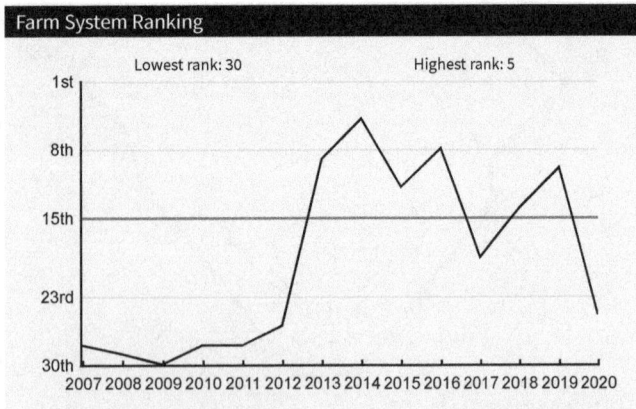

Farm System Ranking

Lowest rank: 30   Highest rank: 5

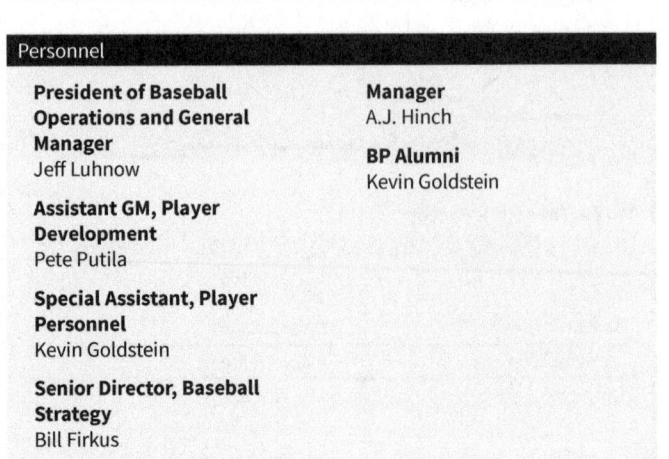

Personnel

President of Baseball Operations and General Manager
Jeff Luhnow

Assistant GM, Player Development
Pete Putila

Special Assistant, Player Personnel
Kevin Goldstein

Senior Director, Baseball Strategy
Bill Firkus

Manager
A.J. Hinch

BP Alumni
Kevin Goldstein

They melded high tech with low to relay the signs of the opposing battery to hitters by using cameras in the stands and a trash can in the clubhouse. This scheme appears to have worked remarkably well before it was exposed. What we know about the sign-stealing scheme maps pretty well to a substantial drop in team strikeouts in 2017, and may have continued through 2019, when they boat raced the AL West and finished the season with the best record in baseball.

We're still processing what we know about the Astros' cheating; new information is coming to light, and Major League Baseball has not yet leveled any penalties on the team, players, or staff. But it very well may be that cameras and trash cans will be the legacy of the 2019 Astros.

One imagines Brandon Taubman was thrilled when the Astros' cheating efforts came to light. This new scandal blew his scandal completely out of the news cycle. But for a minute there, after the Astros lost the World Series but before allegations of cheating became the focus, some Houston fans were compelled to blame him for the loss. After all, following the Taubman incident, the Astros dropped games 1 and 2 of the World Series at home, where they were all but unbeatable. Then, they mitigated in the most mild of terms the PR disaster they created by proffering a marginally satisfactory apology about Taubman's repugnant behavior, and won the next three games. How could this be anything other than karmic retribution?

Well, because it's just not, that's how. Shit doesn't work like that. That's the meaning-making impulse at its worst and most misleading.

The Astros didn't lose because Brandon Taubman did something awful or because the Astros picked up Roberto Osuna as a distressed asset. (Osuna's poor pitching in the World Series absolutely was a factor, however.) The way this game (and this society) is structured, front offices have perverse incentives to acquire people like Osuna; this is baseball under late capitalism, our national pastime in the early 21st century. As long as the PR blowback is less detrimental than the cost-savings is beneficial, teams will sign perpetrators of domestic violence. (We can have a discussion about the concept of punishment and forgiveness elsewhere, but I'll remind you that Osuna faced no real legal punishment for his actions; the charges against him were dropped when Osuna agreed to submit to the equivalent of a restraining order and undergo counseling. He also, of course, received a 75-game suspension and was sent packing by the Blue Jays, which is how we got here.)

No, the Astros lost the World Series because the Nationals beat them in seven weird and hard-fought games. Before the World Series, though, the Astros were golden gods.

When the regular season ended on September 29, 2019, the Astros had the best record in baseball and were the prohibitive favorites to win the World Series. The Astros had:

- The AL Cy Young winner and runner-up
- The probable AL MVP runner-up

- The AL Rookie of the Year
- The best record in baseball
- The best home record in baseball and home-field advantage throughout the playoffs

and still managed to lose to the Nationals (an extremely good team, despite the narrative some writers have overlaid onto their weird and circuitous journey to a World Series championship, but on paper not nearly the generationally good club the Astros were).

So why look at 180 random events—in this case, baseball games—and attempt to craft a narrative? Some of us hope that a postmortem of the season will help us understand what went well, what went poorly, and how this might inform what happens in 2020. Or perhaps you don't follow this club closely, and you're looking to these pages for an abstract, a summary, a story. See chaos; impose order. Normal human impulse.

A 107-win season was the result of a painstaking rebuild orchestrated primarily by Jeff Luhnow. Luhnow was retained as GM in 2011 and the Astros moved from the NL Central to the AL West in 2013. They lost 111 games that year and secured yet another number one draft pick—their third in three years—which Luhnow spent on Carlos Correa. Mark Appel and Brady Aiken were also drafted during Luhnow's tenure, which serves to remind us that number-one picks are anything but a lock.

Luhnow and staff hit paydirt with Alex Bregman in 2015, whom the Astros were able to select because they failed to sign Aiken the previous year. All Bregman did last year was mount an MVP campaign that logged him 8.6 BWARP, second only to some guy who patrols the outfield in Anaheim. Houston also picked Kyle Tucker at no. 5 overall that year, who did much better last season than in his 2018 call-up. Tucker showed glimpses of what his future could be, with the kind of stringy power that, if you squint, looks something like Cody Bellinger's. But Tucker's contributions would likely be getting a lot more adulation if it weren't for another 22-year-old rookie who's made an even bigger splash.

Yordan Alvarez, whom Houston got from the Dodgers for Josh Fields in 2016, has been a revelation. He made his debut in early June and appeared in 87 games and quickly amassed 2.8 WARP. He looked overmatched in the DS and CS playoff rounds, but found his footing again in the World Series against the Nationals, hitting a bomb to help his team win Game 5 and showing a veteran eye at the plate, spitting on pitches from some of the most devious hurlers in the game. He was the Astros' first rookie of the year to win the award unanimously.

Most fanbases would jump at the chance to have either a legit starter or a ROY power-hitting corner infielder emerge from their minor-league chain in a single season; in Alvarez and Jose Urquidy, the Astros had both.

Urquidy came out of nowhere, starting the season at Double-A Corpus Christi and ending up taking the ball to start game 4 of the World Series. The 24-year-old's pitch mix, command and control, and unflappableness on the mound means he'll likely slide into the rotation in 2020.

The Astros system is so deep, in fact, that they weathered IL stints by some of their superstars—George Springer and José Altuve missed 31 and 39 days, respectively, and Correa was out for 87—and they still won 107 games. Of course, it helps when you have Bregman to slide over to shortstop when your All-Star starter goes down. Eight pitchers also spent time on the IL, notably Lance McCullers and Collin McHugh. None of this is 2019 Yankees-level injury-bug stuff, but not every org can paper over these kinds of losses, much less fill those gaps and post the best record in baseball.

In fact, it's probably only possible if instead of a starting rotation you have a Cerberus comprising three of the greatest pitchers in the game. The Astros let Dallas Keuchel walk and filled the void with an unholy amalgamation of guys like Framber Valdez and Corbin Martin, plus a third of a season of Zack Greinke.

Adding Greinke to a rotation that already included a resurgent Justin Verlander and a peak Gerrit Cole seemed borderline unfair. Cole inked a record-setting deal to suit up for the Yankees, today, tomorrow, and forever, but Greinke and Verlander will still be in blue and orange for the next two years. Add a healthy Brad Peacock, the aforementioned Urquidy, and a fifth starter TBD—Valdez, or, dare to dream, a functional Forrest Whitley?—and the Astros rotation looks as fearsome as any in baseball though 2021.

The only obvious hole is at catcher. Martín Maldonado and Robinson Chirinos were adequate behind the dish last season in their walk years. Maldonaldo returns on a two-year deal, but Chirinos departs as a free agent. With Yasmani Grandal off the board early, the pickins were slim. But the Astros are nothing if not resourceful.

The Astros likely could've made a run at Grandal. Had they made a competitive offer, one assumes he would've jumped at the chance to play in Houston, handle an elite pitching staff, and play half his games in the shadow of the Crawford Boxes. The only thing that stopped them from signing Grandal (or re-signing Cole, for that matter) is money. But it's not just the salaries and the competitive balance surtax we're talking about here. There's also the…see, this is difficult to talk about, because we all know it's happening, but no one is quite sure what to call it. Let's try, instead of a capital strike, a capital slowdown. The competitive balance tax functionally acts as a salary cap, giving cover to any owner inclined to plead poverty. And even as team profits and valuations have exploded, the CBT hasn't remotely kept pace. Since 2009, the average franchise's value has increased 300 percent; during that same time, the CBT has increased 27 percent.

According to Forbes, the average MLB team is worth $1.78B, and no team is worth less than a billion dollars. The Marlins could have, at the dawn of 2019 free agency, gone out and signed Rendon, Cole, and Grandal and they'd still be worth a billion dollars. Hell, they might be worth *more* considering people might even buy tickets to see that team. There were no objective financial factors stopping your favorite team from signing Gerrit Cole; the austerity is coming from inside the ownership group. This is why we'll almost certainly have a "work stoppage" in 2021, when the current collective bargaining agreement expires. The first-year player draft, the arbitration process, and free agency (especially compensation picks) all function to depress player salaries. What kinds of concessions the Players Association under Tony Clark will be able to extract from ownership remains to be seen. What, if anything, will a union called the *Major* League Baseball Players Association do to address the staggering exploitation occurring throughout the minor leagues?

Ultimately no one knows what will happen in 2020 or beyond. Hell, we don't really even know what happened in 2019. There's no objective truth anywhere, but especially not here. All we have are the narratives we've constructed, replete with our blind spots, biases, and misinterpretations. Give typewriters to an infinite number of baseball fans and ask them to craft a narrative about the Astros season, and you'd get an infinite number of different responses, each one trying to make meaning where no such thing exists. Or, as I like to call it, the internet. ▪

—Ian Miller is half of Productive Outs and a quarter of Puig Destroyer.

HITTERS

José Altuve 2B Born: 05/06/90 Age: 30 Bats: R Throws: R Height: 5'6" Weight: 165 Origin: International Free Agent, 2007

YEAR	TEAM	LVL	AGE	PA	R	2B	3B	HR	RBI	BB	K	SB	CS	AVG/OBP/SLG	DRC+	VORP	BABIP	BRR	FRAA	WARP
2017	HOU	MLB	27	662	112	39	4	24	81	58	84	32	6	.346/.410/.547	140	65.0	.370	2.7	2B(149): -0.1	5.6
2018	HOU	MLB	28	599	84	29	2	13	61	55	79	17	4	.316/.386/.451	126	41.4	.352	2.4	2B(130): -7.9	3.2
2019	HOU	MLB	29	548	89	27	3	31	74	41	82	6	5	.298/.353/.550	119	31.8	.303	-0.5	2B(121): -0.6, SS(1): 0.0	3.0
2020	HOU	MLB	30	595	77	28	2	25	83	44	91	21	7	.292/.351/.490	119	38.2	.312	0.6	2B -4	3.5

Comparables: Rennie Stennett, Alexi Casilla, Rod Carew

Good Financial Cents dot com says the best way to invest $10,000 is to play it safe and put it in a High Yielding Savings Account. Baseball Prospectus dot com encourages you to simply give it to an undersized, but scrappy child who will one day become a superstar. Still hampered by a knee issue sustained halfway through 2018, Altuve looked decidedly not himself to start last season. There were whispers in Houston that perhaps the Astros would regret the 7-year, $163.5 million extension inked with him. When he went to the IL in early May, he was hitting .243. Turns out having a healthy knee is one of the things required to succeed at the big-league level, because Altuve finished the season slashing .320/.363/.581. One of the easiest people in the game to root for, Altuve remains an elite talent.

Yordan Alvarez OF/1B Born: 06/27/97 Age: 23 Bats: L Throws: R Height: 6'5" Weight: 225 Origin: International Free Agent, 2016

YEAR	TEAM	LVL	AGE	PA	R	2B	3B	HR	RBI	BB	K	SB	CS	AVG/OBP/SLG	DRC+	VORP	BABIP	BRR	FRAA	WARP
2017	QUD	A	20	139	26	6	0	9	33	23	36	2	0	.360/.468/.658	190	18.1	.449	-1.6	LF(13): -1.5, 1B(7): 0.0	1.3
2017	BCA	A+	20	252	19	11	3	3	36	19	41	6	1	.277/.329/.393	117	6.6	.316	-0.2	LF(28): 2.6, 1B(15): -0.4	1.1
2018	CCH	AA	21	190	39	13	0	12	46	19	45	5	2	.325/.389/.615	172	21.5	.377	0.2	LF(31): 3.6, 1B(5): -0.1	2.1
2018	FRE	AAA	21	189	24	8	0	8	28	23	47	1	0	.259/.349/.452	110	5.3	.315	-2.0	LF(34): -6.3	-0.2
2019	ROU	AAA	22	253	50	16	0	23	71	38	50	2	1	.343/.443/.742	176	36.1	.355	-2.3	LF(27): 0.3, 1B(9): -1.1	2.4
2019	HOU	MLB	22	369	58	26	0	27	78	52	94	0	0	.313/.412/.655	149	29.9	.366	-0.5	LF(10): -0.5	2.8
2020	HOU	MLB	23	595	93	28	1	42	108	70	151	4	1	.279/.367/.576	140	38.9	.314	-0.4	LF -1	3.9

Comparables: Austin Riley, Austin Meadows, Clint Frazier

Conveying how terrifying Alvarez is at the plate is simultaneously a laughably simple and incredibly complex task. His frame fills the entire batter's box and he moves with a silence that borders on imposing. A mere lift of his bat portends future harm to an innocent baseball. On the one hand, it's a text, no subtext. He hits 474-foot homers. He's a Michael Bay movie at the plate, complete with the necessary explosions followed by a slow-motion trot around the bases. On the other hand, there's far more nuance. Much like jazz, Alvarez's success is in the swings he doesn't take. It feels like he knows what pitch is coming (*Editor's note: Uhhhh*). His ability to lay off pitches just outside the zone is almost as fun to watch as him launching dingers. Almost.

It's not true that he takes away in the field what he brings to the plate, but it is closer than you'd like. He's a left fielder in the same way that going to the dentist is fun. More of a natural first baseman, he's not going to displace Yuli Gurriel until at least 2021. He'll enter his age-23 season as a unanimous Rookie of the Year. He's not the most decorated player in the Astros lineup, but he might just be the most captivating at-bat.

Michael Brantley LF Born: 05/15/87 Age: 33 Bats: L Throws: L Height: 6'2" Weight: 200 Origin: Round 7, 2005 Draft (#205 overall)

YEAR	TEAM	LVL	AGE	PA	R	2B	3B	HR	RBI	BB	K	SB	CS	AVG/OBP/SLG	DRC+	VORP	BABIP	BRR	FRAA	WARP
2017	CLE	MLB	30	375	47	20	1	9	52	31	50	11	1	.299/.357/.444	106	14.5	.325	-0.6	LF(87): 5.2	1.7
2018	CLE	MLB	31	631	89	36	2	17	76	48	60	12	3	.309/.364/.468	118	31.3	.319	1.4	LF(134): -3.4	2.8
2019	HOU	MLB	32	637	88	40	2	22	90	51	66	3	2	.311/.372/.503	122	34.1	.320	0.0	LF(120): -7.4, RF(9): -0.8	2.5
2020	HOU	MLB	33	560	66	29	1	19	71	47	65	11	3	.283/.349/.456	112	23.1	.295	-0.1	LF -3	2.1

Comparables: Johnny Damon, Darin Erstad, Melky Cabrera

"Uncle Mike" was a steady presence both on and off the field for an Astros team that saw many of its best hitters miss time with injuries. Suffice it to stay "steady" and "on the field" haven't been used together often for Brantley, which is probably why Cleveland failed to dispense a qualifying offer following 2018. Defying the odds, Brantley put together a second straight season of over 140 games played, improving his walk rate and ISO in the process. He has the skill set to turn into a Launch Angle Guy and add some power as he continues to thicken out through the end of his prime, but he seems content to lash line drives to the gap and ring up 35-40 doubles per year. It's not a bad gig if you can get it.

Alex Bregman   3B   Born: 03/30/94   Age: 26   Bats: R   Throws: R   Height: 6'0"   Weight: 180   Origin: Round 1, 2015 Draft (#2 overall)

YEAR	TEAM	LVL	AGE	PA	R	2B	3B	HR	RBI	BB	K	SB	CS	AVG/OBP/SLG	DRC+	VORP	BABIP	BRR	FRAA	WARP
2017	HOU	MLB	23	626	88	39	5	19	71	55	97	17	5	.284/.352/.475	114	35.5	.311	-1.5	3B(132): 8.7, SS(30): -2.9	3.9
2018	HOU	MLB	24	705	105	51	1	31	103	96	85	10	4	.286/.394/.532	150	71.7	.289	-1.6	3B(136): 5.4, SS(28): -0.4	7.4
2019	HOU	MLB	25	690	122	37	2	41	112	119	83	5	1	.296/.423/.592	157	80.6	.281	-3.8	3B(99): 6.6, SS(65): 4.7	8.6
2020	HOU	MLB	26	630	97	36	2	36	106	92	87	12	5	.292/.404/.572	152	57.7	.292	-2.2	3B 5, SS 0	6.6

Comparables: Evan Longoria, Bob Horner, Jim Ray Hart

There's no shame in being second-best to Mike Trout. Bregman was nothing short of phenomenal in 2019, walking more than he struck out for the second straight season, flashing additional value by filling in capably at shortstop when he wasn't manning third base. He overcame a slow start to the season (five homers through May 1st) to come a few votes away from giving the Astros a clean sweep in the major award voting. For whatever being the Face of Baseball means to both the sport and the player, Bregman seems ready and willing to take on that mantle. He's cocky, right up to, and sometimes past, the point of annoyance, but he's spent his whole career backing it up.

Carlos Correa   SS   Born: 09/22/94   Age: 25   Bats: R   Throws: R   Height: 6'4"   Weight: 215   Origin: Round 1, 2012 Draft (#1 overall)

YEAR	TEAM	LVL	AGE	PA	R	2B	3B	HR	RBI	BB	K	SB	CS	AVG/OBP/SLG	DRC+	VORP	BABIP	BRR	FRAA	WARP
2017	HOU	MLB	22	481	82	25	1	24	84	53	92	2	1	.315/.391/.550	140	48.2	.352	-3.0	SS(108): -1.4	4.1
2018	HOU	MLB	23	468	60	20	1	15	65	53	111	3	0	.239/.323/.405	98	20.4	.282	0.8	SS(109): 7.2	2.8
2019	HOU	MLB	24	321	42	16	1	21	59	35	75	1	0	.279/.358/.568	126	26.5	.303	-0.6	SS(75): -2.3	2.3
2020	HOU	MLB	25	525	72	24	1	28	81	56	122	9	3	.266/.349/.503	122	33.7	.303	-1.0	SS 1	3.6

Comparables: Corey Seager, Rougned Odor, Freddie Freeman

Since his debut in 2015 as a 20-year-old, Correa has been one of the best shortstops in baseball. A string of injuries have limited his time on the field, but there is no arguing that when he's healthy, Correa is a generational talent. He leads all shortstops in DRC+ during his career with a healthy gap between him and Francisco Lindor in second place (123 to 117). His arm belongs in the museum at the NASA Space Center alongside all of Houston's other famous rockets, and his 6-foot-4 frame allows him to make up for whatever he lacks in agility. Everything about him screams superstardom and every year feels like it could be the year that vaults him firmly into the upper echelon of major-leaguers.

Aledmys Díaz   INF   Born: 08/01/90   Age: 29   Bats: R   Throws: R   Height: 6'1"   Weight: 195   Origin: International Free Agent, 2014

YEAR	TEAM	LVL	AGE	PA	R	2B	3B	HR	RBI	BB	K	SB	CS	AVG/OBP/SLG	DRC+	VORP	BABIP	BRR	FRAA	WARP
2017	MEM	AAA	26	187	19	9	1	4	26	10	30	3	3	.253/.305/.388	77	4.9	.281	-1.2	SS(28): 2.3, 3B(9): -0.6	0.5
2017	SLN	MLB	26	301	31	17	0	7	20	13	42	4	1	.259/.290/.392	80	2.4	.282	-1.3	SS(68): -10.6, 3B(4): -0.2	-0.6
2018	TOR	MLB	27	452	55	26	0	18	55	23	62	3	4	.263/.303/.453	108	18.9	.269	-1.8	SS(95): -5.8, 3B(38): -0.5	1.5
2019	HOU	MLB	28	247	36	12	1	9	40	26	28	2	0	.271/.356/.467	109	10.1	.268	1.9	1B(26): -0.8, 2B(25): 0.6	1.1
2020	HOU	MLB	29	280	32	14	1	10	35	20	44	3	2	.252/.316/.433	95	6.6	.269	-0.3	2B 1, 3B -1	0.5

Comparables: Stephen Drew, Jordy Mercer, Johnny Logan

When the Astros acquired Díaz, it was clear he was to fill the Marwin González role of plug-and-play utility man who was not expected to dazzle or disappoint. Through the end of May, he filled that role admirably, playing in 60 percent of Houston's games at six different positions. Unfortunately, hamstring and foot injuries limited him to 69 games. All in all, though, he looked comfortable serving as a human Swiss Army Knife. With Yordan Alvarez locking up the DH spot for the foreseeable future, the Astros will need to find other ways to spell their starters and Díaz certainly seems capable of doing just that.

Dustin Garneau   C   Born: 08/13/87   Age: 32   Bats: R   Throws: R   Height: 6'2"   Weight: 205   Origin: Round 19, 2009 Draft (#571 overall)

YEAR	TEAM	LVL	AGE	PA	R	2B	3B	HR	RBI	BB	K	SB	CS	AVG/OBP/SLG	DRC+	VORP	BABIP	BRR	FRAA	WARP
2017	ABQ	AAA	29	144	24	9	2	10	26	13	22	0	1	.281/.347/.617	124	14.7	.265	0.2	C(36): -1.9	1.0
2017	COL	MLB	29	74	5	7	0	1	6	4	24	0	0	.206/.260/.353	68	0.9	.302	0.8	C(22): -0.1	0.1
2017	OAK	MLB	29	52	5	1	0	1	3	8	12	0	0	.159/.288/.250	69	-0.9	.194	-0.3	C(18): 0.0	0.0
2018	NAS	AAA	30	80	8	3	0	2	9	5	10	0	0	.208/.263/.333	70	-2.1	.210	-1.3	C(18): -2.2	-0.3
2018	CHR	AAA	30	160	19	9	0	7	22	16	38	0	2	.252/.340/.468	118	8.8	.295	-0.3	C(39): -0.9, LF(1): -0.2	0.8
2018	CHA	MLB	30	3	0	0	0	0	1	1	0	0	0	.500/.667/.500	98	0.7	.500	0.0	C(1): -0.3	0.0
2019	LVG	AAA	31	32	2	2	1	1	3	3	9	0	0	.308/.387/.577	99	1.6	.412	-1.0	C(7): -0.1, 1B(1): 0.0	0.1
2019	SLC	AAA	31	98	16	8	0	6	13	11	28	0	0	.229/.347/.542	91	3.7	.265	-0.6	C(26): 8.7	1.1
2019	LAA	MLB	31	82	11	3	0	2	7	8	18	0	0	.232/.346/.362	88	2.9	.286	-0.5		0.2
2019	OAK	MLB	31	19	3	2	0	1	7	2	4	0	0	.294/.368/.588	109	1.2	.333	-0.2	C(7): 0.0	0.1
2020	HOU	MLB	32	210	24	9	0	10	28	18	58	1	0	.214/.296/.420	87	6.3	.253	0.0	C -6	0.0

Comparables: Ron Karkovice, Chris Herrmann, Tim Spehr

On September 9, 2015, Hillary Clinton made the first of many apologies for her email server. Kim Davis spent most of the day in jail for refusing to issue a marriage license to a same sex couple. Queen Elizabeth became Britain's longest serving monarch. President Obama sought additional Senate support for his Iran deal. Also, Dustin Garneau homered that night, his first dinger in the major leagues. People forget that.

YEAR	TEAM	P. COUNT	FRM RUNS	BLK RUNS	THRW RUNS	TOT RUNS
2017	ABQ	5165	-3.2	0.2	0.7	-2.7
2017	COL	2719	-1.3	-1.0	0.0	-2.6
2017	OAK	2146	-1.0	-0.6	0.3	-1.5
2018	CHA	154	0.0	0.1	0.0	1.5
2018	NAS	2347	-2.1	-0.2	0.7	-0.9
2018	CHR	5299	0.0	0.0	0.4	1.3
2019	LAA	3366	0.4	0.0	0.0	0.4
2019	SLC	3832	7.2	0.1	0.6	7.7
2019	OAK	690	0.1	-0.2	0.0	0.4
2020	HOU	9423	-5.8	-0.2	0.1	-5.8

Yuli Gurriel CI Born: 06/09/84 Age: 36 Bats: R Throws: R Height: 6'0" Weight: 190 Origin: International Free Agent, 2016

YEAR	TEAM	LVL	AGE	PA	R	2B	3B	HR	RBI	BB	K	SB	CS	AVG/OBP/SLG	DRC+	VORP	BABIP	BRR	FRAA	WARP
2017	HOU	MLB	33	564	69	43	1	18	75	22	62	3	2	.299/.332/.486	109	18.6	.308	-1.7	1B(131): 8.4, 3B(7): -0.3	2.1
2018	HOU	MLB	34	573	70	33	1	13	85	23	63	5	1	.291/.323/.428	109	20.3	.306	1.1	1B(109): 1.5, 3B(21): 1.2	2.0
2019	HOU	MLB	35	612	85	40	2	31	104	37	65	5	3	.298/.343/.541	119	29.0	.289	-1.5	1B(110): 7.3, 3B(42): 0.4	3.4
2020	HOU	MLB	36	595	69	33	1	25	82	28	75	4	2	.274/.315/.469	102	12.5	.280	-0.6	1B 9	2.2

Comparables: Ray Knight, Bill Madlock, Charlie Hayes

The way he torques his arms and twists all of his body weight to his front foot is wholly unique to Gurriel. Nothing about his approach seems like it should work. He swings at everything. His 37 walks were by far a career-best and it just feels like there should not be any power in his bat, but from the middle of July to the end of the season, he sustained an OPS above 1.000. And he is a very good defender at first base to boot, specifically when it comes to backhanded picks that he perfected early in his career as a third baseman. In November, the Astros and Gurriel avoided arbitration by inking a $8.3 million contract giving him the option of free agency at the end of the 2020 season.

Martín Maldonado C Born: 08/16/86 Age: 33 Bats: R Throws: R Height: 6'0" Weight: 230 Origin: Round 27, 2004 Draft (#803 overall)

YEAR	TEAM	LVL	AGE	PA	R	2B	3B	HR	RBI	BB	K	SB	CS	AVG/OBP/SLG	DRC+	VORP	BABIP	BRR	FRAA	WARP
2017	LAA	MLB	30	471	43	19	1	14	38	15	119	0	2	.221/.276/.368	73	2.2	.273	-2.4	C(137): 32.1, 1B(1): 0.0	3.8
2018	LAA	MLB	31	290	24	14	0	5	32	13	73	0	1	.223/.284/.332	74	3.1	.287	-0.1		0.6
2018	HOU	MLB	31	114	15	4	1	4	12	3	25	0	0	.231/.257/.398	75	-0.3	.263	-0.6	C(40): 2.0	0.4
2019	KCA	MLB	32	263	26	15	0	6	17	17	55	0	0	.227/.291/.366	76	5.9	.270	-4.6	C(73): 1.8	0.3
2019	CHN	MLB	32	13	0	0	0	0	0	2	5	0	0	.000/.154/.000	-25	-1.5	.000	-0.1	C(4): -0.2	-0.2
2019	HOU	MLB	32	98	20	4	0	6	10	13	26	0	0	.202/.316/.464	97	4.6	.212	0.0	C(26): 0.1, 1B(1): 0.0	0.5
2020	HOU	MLB	33	350	35	13	0	11	38	27	89	1	1	.205/.282/.353	67	-0.2	.249	-1.5	C 4	0.4

Comparables: Miguel Montero, Welington Castillo, Jeff Mathis

It's like the old saying goes: If you love someone, let them go ... and just trade for them again next year. Maldonado left in free agency after the Astros acquired him for the 2018 stretch run. When they were again in need of a backup in 2019, they went back to the well, sending a DFA'd Tony Kemp to the Cubs in exchange for "El Machete." In a testament to just how juiced the 2019 baseball was, Maldonado somehow hit 12 home runs in 374 plate appearances. An owner of a 36 percent career caught stealing rate, runners have poorly donated outs to Maldonado.

YEAR	TEAM	P. COUNT	FRM RUNS	BLK RUNS	THRW RUNS	TOT RUNS
2017	LAA	18609	27.2	1.0	3.2	32.0
2018	LAA	11256	4.1	-0.8	0.3	4.0
2018	HOU	4686	1.7	-0.3	0.2	2.5
2019	KCA	10448	-1.4	3.3	0.3	2.1
2019	CHN	571	-0.1	-0.3	0.0	0.1
2019	HOU	3404	-0.5	0.9	-0.3	0.6
2020	HOU	15936	3.1	1.0	0.2	4.3

Jack Mayfield MI Born: 09/30/90 Age: 29 Bats: R Throws: R Height: 5'11" Weight: 190 Origin: Undrafted Free Agent, 2013

YEAR	TEAM	LVL	AGE	PA	R	2B	3B	HR	RBI	BB	K	SB	CS	AVG/OBP/SLG	DRC+	VORP	BABIP	BRR	FRAA	WARP
2017	CCH	AA	26	291	39	16	2	14	44	17	57	7	2	.289/.330/.519	121	22.0	.317	1.3	2B(43): -1.8, SS(20): 0.9	1.6
2017	FRE	AAA	26	165	28	12	0	6	23	10	30	3	0	.273/.321/.468	95	8.0	.305	2.1	3B(17): 2.5, 2B(14): -1.6	0.7
2018	FRE	AAA	27	479	66	31	1	16	66	33	92	5	4	.270/.324/.457	110	21.1	.304	-0.2	2B(62): -6.3, SS(48): -8.9	0.7
2019	ROU	AAA	28	431	78	26	1	26	79	37	78	7	1	.287/.350/.566	118	41.7	.291	0.0	SS(42): -1.5, 2B(33): 2.9	2.5
2019	HOU	MLB	28	65	8	5	0	2	5	1	16	0	0	.156/.169/.328	73	0.7	.174	-0.6	SS(21): 0.2, 2B(5): -0.2	0.0
2020	HOU	MLB	29	35	4	2	0	2	5	2	9	0	0	.232/.285/.444	87	0.8	.262	0.0	2B 0	0.0

Comparables: Tommy Field, Tommy Manzella, Mike Yastrzemski

In 2013, 1,216 players were chosen in the June draft, including Mark Appel at No. 1 overall by the Astros. Mayfield was not one of them. He finished his senior season at Oklahoma with a .711 OPS and the Astros signed him, undoubtedly with the assumption that he would help round out a lineup card in the lower levels of the minors. But then he started hitting. And hitting. And suddenly you look up to see him with a .916 OPS at Triple-A. Injuries to essentially the entire infield meant Mayfield was needed in the majors. He hit a double off Cole Hamels in his first at-bat, but that was the highlight of a season where he looked very overwhelmed at the plate. Still, he played in the big leagues and proved that you should never give up on your dreams, and more importantly, you should never try to predict baseball.

Josh Reddick   RF   Born: 02/19/87   Age: 33   Bats: L   Throws: R   Height: 6'2"   Weight: 195   Origin: Round 17, 2006 Draft (#523 overall)

YEAR	TEAM	LVL	AGE	PA	R	2B	3B	HR	RBI	BB	K	SB	CS	AVG/OBP/SLG	DRC+	VORP	BABIP	BRR	FRAA	WARP
2017	HOU	MLB	30	540	77	34	4	13	82	43	72	7	3	.314/.363/.484	119	34.1	.339	2.5	RF(102): -1.6, LF(48): -1.2	2.4
2018	HOU	MLB	31	487	63	13	2	17	47	49	77	7	2	.242/.318/.400	106	10.3	.258	-1.0	RF(111): -2.0, LF(43): 0.4	1.2
2019	HOU	MLB	32	550	57	19	3	14	56	36	66	5	2	.275/.319/.409	97	11.6	.288	-2.2	RF(119): 5.2, LF(29): -1.1	1.3
2020	HOU	MLB	33	420	46	17	2	14	51	32	60	6	2	.265/.323/.424	97	7.7	.284	-0.2	RF 0, CF 0	0.7

Comparables: Dwight Evans, Bubba Trammell, Trot Nixon

WOOOOOO Reddick's offensive production WOOOOOO has started to fall off. You hope WOOOOOO it is fixable, but the dip in power and loss of bat speed WOOOOOOOO is almost always a sure sign of a guy in decline. He still has the WOOOOOOOOO defensive prowess to rob some dingers from Minute Maid WOOOOOO Park's short right field fence and can make any third base coach sweat with his arm WOOOOOOOO so there's definitely still value there. However, WOOOOO with Kyle Tucker waiting in the wings, Houston may let that value (and his $13 million contract) find WOOOOOO a home elsewhere.

George Springer   CF   Born: 09/19/89   Age: 30   Bats: R   Throws: R   Height: 6'3"   Weight: 215   Origin: Round 1, 2011 Draft (#11 overall)

YEAR	TEAM	LVL	AGE	PA	R	2B	3B	HR	RBI	BB	K	SB	CS	AVG/OBP/SLG	DRC+	VORP	BABIP	BRR	FRAA	WARP
2017	HOU	MLB	27	629	112	29	0	34	85	64	111	5	7	.283/.367/.522	130	41.6	.297	0.5	CF(84): 2.6, RF(78): 0.6	4.5
2018	HOU	MLB	28	620	102	26	0	22	71	64	122	6	4	.265/.346/.434	114	30.1	.303	1.5	CF(80): -2.8, RF(77): 2.6	2.9
2019	HOU	MLB	29	556	96	20	3	39	96	67	113	6	2	.292/.383/.591	141	46.6	.305	2.5	CF(75): 2.4, RF(59): 4.1	5.4
2020	HOU	MLB	30	595	90	22	1	37	100	70	129	9	5	.278/.373/.540	136	48.9	.305	1.3	CF -1, RF 1	5.1

Comparables: Tim Salmon, Mike Young, Jay Bruce

A beloved clubhouse presence, Springer finally harnessed his raw talent into the MVP-caliber season of which he always seemed capable. Despite missing a month with a hamstring injury, Springer finished 7th on a loaded American League ballot. One of the game's most dangerous leadoff hitters, he set a franchise record with 10 leadoff home runs in 2019 and now has 36 in his young career, putting him well within striking distance of franchise legend Craig Biggio's National League record of 53. He's not as fast as you would think he is given his above-average glove in center field [he finished outside the top 100 in Statcast's sprint speed leaderboard in 2019]. At some point even that speed will leave him relegated to the corner outfield, but the Astros will cross that bridge when they get to it.

He's gone to great lengths to put together competitive at-bats, something that was a real struggle when he posted a 33 percent strikeout rate in his rookie year. Time flies when you're having fun and somehow Springer is already set to be a free agent at the end of the 2020 season unless an extension is agreed to. His departure would signal the closing of no doubt the greatest chapter in Astros history.

Myles Straw   UT   Born: 10/17/94   Age: 25   Bats: R   Throws: R   Height: 5'10"   Weight: 180   Origin: Round 12, 2015 Draft (#349 overall)

YEAR	TEAM	LVL	AGE	PA	R	2B	3B	HR	RBI	BB	K	SB	CS	AVG/OBP/SLG	DRC+	VORP	BABIP	BRR	FRAA	WARP
2017	BCA	A+	22	533	81	17	7	1	41	87	70	36	9	.295/.412/.373	152	52.8	.347	5.5	CF(72): 6.9, RF(31): 7.2	6.6
2017	CCH	AA	22	54	9	0	0	0	3	7	9	2	0	.239/.340/.239	92	1.8	.297	0.6	CF(11): -1.1, LF(2): 0.7	0.2
2018	CCH	AA	23	294	47	7	3	1	17	35	42	35	6	.327/.414/.390	142	24.5	.386	4.4	CF(58): 6.0, RF(6): 2.0	3.4
2018	FRE	AAA	23	304	48	10	3	0	14	38	60	35	3	.257/.349/.317	96	8.1	.330	3.8	CF(43): 4.9, RF(25): 1.4	1.8
2018	HOU	MLB	23	10	4	0	0	1	1	1	0	2	0	.333/.400/.667	108	1.8	.250	0.7	RF(5): -0.1, CF(3): 0.0	0.1
2019	ROU	AAA	24	313	46	11	3	1	33	32	50	19	4	.321/.391/.394	105	20.2	.386	2.5	CF(31): 4.9, SS(30): -1.1	1.9
2019	HOU	MLB	24	128	27	4	2	0	7	19	24	8	1	.269/.378/.343	92	4.0	.345	3.5	SS(26): 1.4, CF(11): -0.8	0.8
2020	HOU	MLB	25	245	24	11	2	2	21	24	52	12	4	.274/.348/.366	94	8.0	.350	0.8	CF 4, SS 0	1.3

Comparables: David Dellucci, Mallex Smith, Denard Span

A man stops you at a fork in the road and offers you two choices. Go right and you are destined to the life of a fifth-outfielder, forever doomed to be a light-hitting speedster representing nothing more than a pinch runner in your wildest playoff dreams. To the left is career-ending embarrassment as you attempt to play shortstop for the first time at the second-highest level of competition the sport has to offer. In 2019, Straw chose to punch that man in the face and run away so fast no one could catch him. Straw finished with a Top-5 average sprint speed, according to Statcast, coming in just behind Trea Turner and Byron Buxton. But like the old saying goes, you can't steal first base unless you're in the Atlantic League where you can apparently do whatever you want.

Garrett Stubbs   C   Born: 05/26/93   Age: 27   Bats: L   Throws: R   Height: 5'10"   Weight: 175   Origin: Round 8, 2015 Draft (#229 overall)

YEAR	TEAM	LVL	AGE	PA	R	2B	3B	HR	RBI	BB	K	SB	CS	AVG/OBP/SLG	DRC+	VORP	BABIP	BRR	FRAA	WARP
2017	CCH	AA	24	300	36	13	0	4	25	32	44	8	0	.236/.324/.331	94	10.9	.269	2.3	C(64): 8.8	2.3
2017	FRE	AAA	24	91	11	5	0	0	12	11	15	3	0	.221/.341/.286	80	1.8	.274	1.9	C(19): 0.5	0.4
2018	FRE	AAA	25	340	60	19	6	4	38	35	53	6	0	.310/.382/.455	116	30.6	.361	3.0	C(75): 10.5, RF(2): -0.2	3.6
2019	ROU	AAA	26	235	33	11	0	7	23	24	38	12	2	.240/.332/.397	85	9.8	.261	0.7	C(54): 8.8, 2B(5): -0.8	1.5
2019	HOU	MLB	26	39	8	3	0	0	2	4	7	1	0	.200/.282/.286	79	0.8	.250	0.2	C(11): -1.5, LF(7): -0.1	-0.1
2020	HOU	MLB	27	140	14	7	0	3	14	13	26	2	0	.225/.303/.361	77	2.3	.258	0.0	C -3	-0.1

Comparables: Joe Ginsberg, John Jaso, Chris Herrmann

Stubbs is a guy who might be fine/
He also might be a bust-a/
Always talking about Triple-A/
And Twenty-Eighteen stats/

No, I don't want no Stubbs/
Stubbs is a guy that can't get no starts from me/
A catcher on the shorter side, with a bat so light/
Trying to holla at me/

YEAR	TEAM	P. COUNT	FRM RUNS	BLK RUNS	THRW RUNS	TOT RUNS
2017	CCH	8443	4.5	2.1	0.5	6.5
2017	FRE	2836	0.3	0.3	-0.1	0.3
2018	FRE	10886	7.8	0.2	1.5	9.5
2019	HOU	1145	-0.5	-0.9	0.0	-1.4
2019	ROU	7765	8.2	0.1	0.6	8.6
2020	HOU	5150	-1.6	-1.6	-0.1	-3.3

Abraham Toro 3B Born: 12/20/96 Age: 23 Bats: B Throws: R Height: 6'1" Weight: 190 Origin: Round 5, 2016 Draft (#157 overall)

YEAR	TEAM	LVL	AGE	PA	R	2B	3B	HR	RBI	BB	K	SB	CS	AVG/OBP/SLG	DRC+	VORP	BABIP	BRR	FRAA	WARP
2017	TCV	A-	20	128	21	8	0	6	16	19	21	1	3	.292/.414/.538	190	14.2	.316	-2.1	3B(25): -2.5, C(6): -0.1	0.9
2017	QUD	A	20	158	25	3	2	9	17	21	30	2	0	.209/.323/.463	113	11.2	.198	1.1	3B(17): 0.8, C(9): -0.2	0.9
2018	BCA	A+	21	349	54	20	1	14	56	45	62	5	1	.257/.361/.473	156	31.2	.278	1.7	3B(81): 3.4	3.6
2018	CCH	AA	21	202	16	15	2	2	22	17	46	3	3	.230/.317/.371	89	1.1	.298	-2.6	3B(43): -0.7	0.1
2019	CCH	AA	22	435	65	22	4	16	70	48	77	4	1	.306/.393/.513	161	40.4	.346	-0.6	3B(85): 6.3, 2B(11): 0.2	4.6
2019	ROU	AAA	22	79	17	9	0	1	10	10	5	0	1	.424/.506/.606	174	15.3	.443	1.9	3B(7): -0.7, 2B(4): -0.2	1.0
2019	HOU	MLB	22	89	13	3	2	2	9	9	19	1	1	.218/.303/.385	79	1.0	.259	-0.1	3B(24): -0.8, 1B(1): 0.0	0.0
2020	HOU	MLB	23	105	12	4	1	4	14	9	23	0	0	.241/.314/.433	95	1.8	.273	0.0	3B 1	0.3

Comparables: Andy LaRoche, Dalton Pompey, Ryan Kalish

A multi-hyphenated player, this Venezuelan-Canadian former-catcher switch-hitter who now plays as many positions (first, second, and third) as languages spoken (English, Spanish and French) can add another hyphen to his resume: no-hitter hero. With Justin Verlander eight innings deep in a no-hitter, Toro broke a scoreless tie in the top of the ninth—in Toronto no less—to allow Verlander to finish off the deed.

He's 23 with a catcher's arm, and while he's still getting comfortable on the infield, he has the athleticism to potentially stick at the hot corner. Toro is a better hitter from the left side, which was even more apparent when he faced big-league southpaws. But there's no rush in Houston. The infield is set in stone in the majors and Aledmys Díaz is currently serving in the utility role Toro seems best suited for one day. Not surprisingly scouts are, uh, bullish on Toro after a really strong year in the upper levels of the minors.

Kyle Tucker OF Born: 01/17/97 Age: 23 Bats: L Throws: R Height: 6'4" Weight: 190 Origin: Round 1, 2015 Draft (#5 overall)

YEAR	TEAM	LVL	AGE	PA	R	2B	3B	HR	RBI	BB	K	SB	CS	AVG/OBP/SLG	DRC+	VORP	BABIP	BRR	FRAA	WARP
2017	BCA	A+	20	206	31	12	4	9	43	24	45	13	5	.288/.379/.554	146	20.6	.336	-3.1	RF(19): -1.8, CF(17): 1.2	1.1
2017	CCH	AA	20	318	39	21	1	16	47	22	64	8	4	.265/.325/.512	137	20.8	.286	1.2	CF(37): -5.3, RF(18): -1.4	1.4
2018	FRE	AAA	21	465	86	27	3	24	93	48	84	20	4	.332/.400/.590	156	52.9	.364	1.7	RF(54): 0.3, LF(32): -0.4	4.3
2018	HOU	MLB	21	72	10	2	1	0	4	6	13	1	1	.141/.236/.203	73	-5.7	.176	-0.4	LF(20): -2.1, RF(3): 0.2	-0.3
2019	ROU	AAA	22	536	92	26	3	34	97	60	116	30	5	.266/.354/.555	114	36.6	.280	1.3	RF(60): 3.2, LF(39): -0.3	2.4
2019	HOU	MLB	22	72	15	6	0	4	11	4	20	5	0	.269/.319/.537	87	0.6	.326	0.6	LF(11): -0.4, RF(11): 0.9	0.2
2020	HOU	MLB	23	420	54	19	2	24	64	32	104	11	4	.236/.302/.479	98	8.8	.261	1.0	RF 1, LF -2	0.9

Comparables: Anthony Rizzo, Wil Myers, Victor Robles

One of the most important things for a batter to do is to make good contact. Tucker does that as well as anyone, sandwiching himself between J.D. Martinez and Freddie Freeman in Statcast's Barrels Per Plate Appearance. He finished tied for 24th in the league with unanimous Rookie of the Year Yordan Alvarez in Hard Hit Percentage (48.9). The next trick for Tucker to learn is to hit it where they ain't. His long, lanky frame allows him to crush pitches middle-out, but teams have learned to feed him a steady diet of elevated fastballs and back-foot breaking balls to neutralize his power. In what we're calling a Reverse Springer, Tucker is a major threat on the basepaths while providing next to no defensive value in the outfield. He has fallen down the defensive spectrum so much that it's not out of the realm of possibility that he and Yordan Alvarez will fight to back up Yuli Gurriel at first base in 2020. The Astros made Tucker a full-time outfielder starting on September 13th and he proceeded to slash .268/.333/.561 from that point forward. The potential for a breakout is there, but this is probably the last time we say that with confidence.

PITCHERS

Bryan Abreu RHP Born: 04/22/97 Age: 23 Bats: R Throws: R Height: 6'1" Weight: 204 Origin: International Free Agent, 2013

YEAR	TEAM	LVL	AGE	W	L	SV	G	GS	IP	H	HR	BB/9	K/9	K	GB%	BABIP	WHIP	ERA	DRA	WARP	MPH	FB%	WHF	CSP
2017	GRV	RK	20	1	3	0	8	6	29¹	29	4	6.4	12.3	40	38%	.357	1.70	7.98	5.52	0.2				
2018	TCV	A-	21	2	0	0	4	2	16	11	2	3.4	12.4	22	35%	.281	1.06	1.12	2.93	0.4				
2018	QUD	A	21	4	1	3	10	5	38¹	22	2	4.0	16.0	68	50%	.312	1.02	1.64	1.89	1.4				
2019	BCA	A+	22	1	0	0	3	3	14²	9	2	3.7	15.3	25	38%	.292	1.02	3.68	3.09	0.3				
2019	CCH	AA	22	6	2	2	20	13	76²	60	6	5.6	11.9	101	43%	.309	1.41	5.05	4.24	0.6				
2019	HOU	MLB	22	0	0	0	7	0	8²	4	0	3.1	13.5	13	50%	.250	0.81	1.04	4.66	0.1	96.8	32.2	19.9	42.3
2020	HOU	MLB	23	4	3	0	47	3	61	45	7	4.5	13.2	89	42%	.300	1.25	3.49	3.49	1.2	96.7	33.3	20.6	43.8

Comparables: Dylan Cease, Jorge Alcala, Victor Alcántara

Call him Jonah Hill because he skates on mid-90s stuff. Abreu left enough of an impression in 8 2/3 September innings to earn a spot on the ALCS roster. He has elite spin on both his slider and curveball and got whiffs on over half of swings against those pitches which is...hang on, calculating...good. The command is decidedly Not Good, which means any dreams of Abreu starting in the majors are gone for now, but he has already shown he can be successful in a very short big-league stint.

Rogelio Armenteros RHP   Born: 06/30/94   Age: 26   Bats: R   Throws: R   Height: 6'1"   Weight: 215   Origin: International Free Agent, 2014

YEAR	TEAM	LVL	AGE	W	L	SV	G	GS	IP	H	HR	BB/9	K/9	K	GB%	BABIP	WHIP	ERA	DRA	WARP	MPH	FB%	WHF	CSP
2017	CCH	AA	23	2	3	1	14	10	65¹	49	3	2.6	10.2	74	42%	.284	1.04	1.93	3.08	1.6				
2017	FRE	AAA	23	8	1	0	10	10	58¹	42	5	2.9	11.1	72	50%	.276	1.05	2.16	2.24	2.2				
2018	FRE	AAA	24	8	1	1	22	21	118	106	15	3.7	10.2	134	38%	.301	1.31	3.74	3.97	2.1				
2019	ROU	AAA	25	6	7	0	19	18	84¹	90	14	3.3	9.1	85	35%	.325	1.43	4.80	4.61	1.7				
2019	HOU	MLB	25	1	1	1	5	2	18	17	1	2.5	9.0	18	38%	.314	1.22	4.00	5.23	0.1	94.3	48.4	11.7	43.2
2020	*HOU*	*MLB*	*26*	*5*	*4*	*0*	*32*	*10*	*70*	*68*	*13*	*3.5*	*8.1*	*63*	*36%*	*.280*	*1.36*	*4.80*	*4.72*	*0.6*	*93.9*	*49.2*	*11.9*	*44*

Comparables: Nick Tropeano, Aaron Blair, Dan Straily

It seems like having Arm 'n' Tear in your last name would be a bad sign for a pitcher, but all Armenteros has done since signing for $40,000 out of Cuba is get dudes out. This last one was a year of ups and downs for him. The Good: He made his major-league debut without looking overmatched. The Bad: His walk and strikeout and ground ball rates all were worse than in 2018, and unsurprisingly, so was his ERA. Still, he's big league ready and will have a chance to earn a back-end spot in the rotation come Spring Training. His low-90s sinking fastball lets him miss barrels with regularity and his changeup and curve lets him miss bats when he needs to. He throws them all in any location in any count (most of the times on purpose) and he evokes the energy of a wily 37-year-old veteran.

Joe Biagini RHP   Born: 05/29/90   Age: 30   Bats: R   Throws: R   Height: 6'5"   Weight: 235   Origin: Round 26, 2011 Draft (#807 overall)

YEAR	TEAM	LVL	AGE	W	L	SV	G	GS	IP	H	HR	BB/9	K/9	K	GB%	BABIP	WHIP	ERA	DRA	WARP	MPH	FB%	WHF	CSP
2017	BUF	AAA	27	1	1	0	4	4	17¹	13	2	3.1	7.3	14	58%	.239	1.10	3.12	3.50	0.4				
2017	TOR	MLB	27	3	13	1	44	18	119²	125	15	3.2	7.3	97	56%	.305	1.40	5.34	3.98	2.0	95.9	52.9	9	47.1
2018	BUF	AAA	28	0	3	0	4	4	21²	19	1	3.3	5.4	13	45%	.257	1.25	4.57	5.96	-0.1				
2018	TOR	MLB	28	4	7	0	50	4	72	96	14	3.0	6.6	53	49%	.355	1.67	6.00	5.72	-0.6	96.6	60.8	9.5	45.6
2019	TOR	MLB	29	3	1	1	50	0	50	50	8	3.1	9.0	50	45%	.309	1.34	3.78	4.73	0.3	95.5	48.5	14.3	43
2019	HOU	MLB	29	0	1	0	13	0	14²	21	6	5.5	6.1	10	50%	.341	2.05	7.36	11.80	-1.0	95.0	48.5	9.3	42.9
2020	*HOU*	*MLB*	*30*	*2*	*2*	*0*	*44*	*0*	*47*	*47*	*7*	*3.5*	*7.8*	*40*	*49%*	*.299*	*1.41*	*4.74*	*4.62*	*0.3*	*95.2*	*53.6*	*10.5*	*44.8*

Comparables: Burke Badenhop, Logan Ondrusek, Chris Leroux

Well, it turns out the Astros can't fix everybody. When asked what he was looking forward to upon learning of his trade to Houston, Biagini said going to space. He may have stayed earthside, but his ERA did not. He's under team control through 2023, so the Astros will continue to hope he can find that 2016 magic. His curveball spin rate and movement is still well above-average, though he did not throw it often in 2019 and it got hit hard when he did. The Astros will have an offseason to tinker with his arsenal to try to squeeze a last bit of success out of the former 28th-round pick. If not, he seems destined to shuttle between Triple-A and mop up duty in the big leagues.

Chris Devenski RHP   Born: 11/13/90   Age: 29   Bats: R   Throws: R   Height: 6'3"   Weight: 210   Origin: Round 25, 2011 Draft (#771 overall)

YEAR	TEAM	LVL	AGE	W	L	SV	G	GS	IP	H	HR	BB/9	K/9	K	GB%	BABIP	WHIP	ERA	DRA	WARP	MPH	FB%	WHF	CSP
2017	HOU	MLB	26	8	5	4	62	0	80²	50	11	2.9	11.2	100	41%	.220	0.94	2.68	3.09	1.9	95.9	39.7	17.7	45.9
2018	HOU	MLB	27	2	3	2	50	1	47¹	42	9	2.5	9.7	51	37%	.275	1.16	4.18	3.61	0.7	96.2	41.6	15.2	46.7
2019	HOU	MLB	28	2	3	0	61	1	69	69	13	2.7	9.4	72	35%	.296	1.30	4.83	5.49	-0.1	96.7	44.1	13.7	46.6
2020	*HOU*	*MLB*	*29*	*3*	*3*	*0*	*55*	*0*	*58*	*51*	*9*	*2.9*	*10.2*	*66*	*35%*	*.286*	*1.20*	*3.76*	*3.81*	*0.9*	*95.7*	*42.1*	*15.3*	*46.5*

Comparables: Fernando Salas, Derek Law, Huston Street

In the first half of the 2015 Texas League season, Devenski was the clear ace on a team that included names like McCullers, Hader, Feliz, Appel and Velasquez. He started the All-Star Game with a 1.16 ERA. Two starts before, he gave up four runs in six innings and got so mad that he did pull-ups from a giant pipe under the stadium until his arms were bruised. He would run around the stadium with one of those Bane masks that restrict your breathing, sometimes even on days he was pitching. He's a crazy person, is the point here. It's not easy to bounce back from a 5.49 DRA season, but if anyone can do it, it would be a maniacal worker like Devenski.

Zack Greinke RHP   Born: 10/21/83   Age: 36   Bats: R   Throws: R   Height: 6'2"   Weight: 200   Origin: Round 1, 2002 Draft (#6 overall)

YEAR	TEAM	LVL	AGE	W	L	SV	G	GS	IP	H	HR	BB/9	K/9	K	GB%	BABIP	WHIP	ERA	DRA	WARP	MPH	FB%	WHF	CSP
2017	ARI	MLB	33	17	7	0	32	32	202¹	172	25	2.0	9.6	215	48%	.285	1.07	3.20	2.77	6.3	92.6	48.4	13.4	40.9
2018	ARI	MLB	34	15	11	0	33	33	207²	181	28	1.9	8.6	199	46%	.272	1.08	3.21	3.09	5.3	91.8	48.7	11.7	45.1
2019	HOU	MLB	35	8	1	0	10	10	62²	58	6	1.3	7.5	52	52%	.289	1.07	3.02	3.52	1.5	92.2	47.7	11.7	46.7
2019	ARI	MLB	35	10	4	0	23	23	146	117	15	1.3	8.3	135	44%	.263	0.95	2.90	3.06	4.3	91.9	47.7	11	47.5
2020	*HOU*	*MLB*	*36*	*14*	*6*	*0*	*29*	*29*	*175*	*158*	*27*	*1.9*	*8.6*	*166*	*46%*	*.277*	*1.11*	*3.33*	*3.48*	*4.0*	*90.8*	*47.2*	*11.7*	*44*

Comparables: Javier Vazquez, Justin Verlander, Mike Mussina

Greinke is a work of art. He throws changeups faster than his fastball. He throws curveballs so slow he makes you believe you, too, could be in the big leagues. His grunts keep you on the edge of your seat. He's not going to strike out a ton of hitters, but he's going to throw all five of his pitches exactly where he wants to. He still plays Gold Glove defense, and it's an absolute shame he plays in the AL where we will be deprived of 36-year-old Greinke dingers. Houston could, and probably would, have been World Series favorites with or without Greinke, but that ring was too enticing not to go for it. When the Astros traded for him it signaled two things: Number 1, they were not content to simply be among the best teams in baseball this year, they wanted to be the clear-cut favorites. And the Number 2 should always be followed by washing your hands.

Josh James RHP Born: 03/08/93 Age: 27 Bats: R Throws: R Height: 6'3" Weight: 206 Origin: Round 34, 2014 Draft (#1006 overall)

YEAR	TEAM	LVL	AGE	W	L	SV	G	GS	IP	H	HR	BB/9	K/9	K	GB%	BABIP	WHIP	ERA	DRA	WARP	MPH	FB%	WHF	CSP
2017	CCH	AA	24	4	8	3	21	11	76	79	1	3.8	8.5	72	53%	.338	1.46	4.38	5.11	-0.1				
2018	CCH	AA	25	0	0	1	6	4	21²	17	1	4.2	15.8	38	58%	.364	1.25	2.49	2.93	0.6				
2018	FRE	AAA	25	6	4	0	17	17	92²	62	8	3.8	12.9	133	41%	.278	1.09	3.40	2.47	3.2				
2018	HOU	MLB	25	2	0	0	6	3	23	15	3	2.7	11.3	29	42%	.240	0.96	2.35	3.20	0.5	100.2	59.9	14.6	46.7
2019	HOU	MLB	26	5	1	1	49	1	61¹	46	10	5.1	14.7	100	35%	.308	1.32	4.70	3.36	1.3	99.3	63.3	16.6	46.4
2020	HOU	MLB	27	7	5	0	63	13	100	79	14	4.3	13.7	153	38%	.312	1.26	3.76	3.68	1.9	99.0	63.4	16.4	47.1

Comparables: Sean Poppen, Wander Suero, Brad Boxberger

A true breakout candidate after a phenomenal end to the 2018 season, James never really put it together in 2019. He tweaked his mechanics in the offseason but missed spring training and the first month of the season due to a quad injury. Inconsistency and a nagging shoulder injury added to his struggles. Though he routinely touches triple digits, the pitch he loves the most is his changeup, which he throws 20% of the time to both sides of the plate. Batters hit just .138 on the upper-80s offering. He threw his slider more last season, losing a tick of velocity in exchange for a few more inches of horizontal movement.

When he's on, that three-pitch mix is borderline unhittable. The problem is he hasn't shown the consistency needed to be a starter. He's got the raw stuff of a top of the rotation guy, but the command of a middle reliever. Whether that means he ends up as a back-of-the-rotation guy or a back-of-the-bullpen guy or something in between remains to be seen. There's a hole after the top three in the Astros rotation, so James will have his shot, but either way the Astros have a live arm they found in the 34th round.

Francis Martes RHP Born: 11/24/95 Age: 24 Bats: R Throws: R Height: 6'1" Weight: 225 Origin: International Free Agent, 2012

YEAR	TEAM	LVL	AGE	W	L	SV	G	GS	IP	H	HR	BB/9	K/9	K	GB%	BABIP	WHIP	ERA	DRA	WARP	MPH	FB%	WHF	CSP
2017	FRE	AAA	21	0	2	0	8	8	32¹	40	5	7.8	10.6	38	39%	.380	2.10	5.29	6.61	-0.3				
2017	HOU	MLB	21	5	2	0	32	4	54¹	51	7	5.1	11.4	69	44%	.328	1.51	5.80	4.39	0.6	98.3	55.4	13.5	46.7
2018	FRE	AAA	22	0	1	0	4	4	18²	25	2	8.2	7.7	16	40%	.397	2.25	6.75	7.97	-0.5				
2020	HOU	MLB	24	1	1	0	28	0	29	26	5	4.6	10.9	35	40%	.297	1.41	4.74	4.55	0.2	98.1	57.1	13.9	48.1

Comparables: Tyler Danish, Casey Kelly, Taijuan Walker

It's hard to believe just three years ago Martes was the Astros No. 1 prospect. He toiled in the bullpen in 2017 before losing most of 2018 and 2019 to elbow discomfort as a prerequisite to Tommy John surgery. He's thrown just 25 innings over the last two seasons. Still, he's only 24 years old with the fastball-slider-curveball-changeup mix to be a legitimate starter in the big leagues. The only problem is the Astros might be too good to let him fail as he builds back his strength, relegating him to the bullpen for the time being.

Lance McCullers Jr. RHP Born: 10/02/93 Age: 26 Bats: L Throws: R Height: 6'1" Weight: 205 Origin: Round 1, 2012 Draft (#41 overall)

YEAR	TEAM	LVL	AGE	W	L	SV	G	GS	IP	H	HR	BB/9	K/9	K	GB%	BABIP	WHIP	ERA	DRA	WARP	MPH	FB%	WHF	CSP
2017	HOU	MLB	23	7	4	0	22	22	118²	114	8	3.0	10.0	132	62%	.330	1.30	4.25	4.13	1.9	96.9	40.4	12.8	45.4
2018	HOU	MLB	24	10	6	0	25	22	128¹	100	12	3.5	10.0	142	56%	.278	1.17	3.86	3.30	3.0	96.6	37.4	14.3	43.9
2020	HOU	MLB	26	9	6	0	41	19	126	118	20	4.2	10.5	147	54%	.305	1.40	4.66	4.47	1.5	96.3	39.3	13.9	45.3

Comparables: Luis Severino, Alex Reyes, Aaron Sanchez

A quick-Twitch athlete—in that he has raw athleticism and streams himself playing Fortnite—McCullers spent 2019 recovering from Tommy John surgery. His breaking ball, whatever you want to call it, is a performance art piece. Sometimes it's a 12-6 loop, sometimes it's Turn 3 at Daytona. It's so lethal, he doesn't even practice it in his bullpens, choosing to save its magic and his fingernail for when he needs it in a game. It will be interesting to see what fastball he pairs it with, having gone with a four-seam in the past before switching to a two-seam in 2018, though the velocity stayed the same at 93-95. He found a changeup grip he liked from scrolling through the Pitching Ninja's Twitter feed and used it to dominate in 2018, to the tune of a .136 batting average against, even better than his famous curve. He's a rescue animal advocate, a great follow on social media, and a healthy season away from being a household name.

Collin McHugh RHP Born: 06/19/87 Age: 33 Bats: R Throws: R Height: 6'2" Weight: 190 Origin: Round 18, 2008 Draft (#554 overall)

YEAR	TEAM	LVL	AGE	W	L	SV	G	GS	IP	H	HR	BB/9	K/9	K	GB%	BABIP	WHIP	ERA	DRA	WARP	MPH	FB%	WHF	CSP
2017	CCH	AA	30	0	0	0	4	4	15	18	1	2.4	6.6	11	57%	.340	1.47	3.60	5.78	-0.1				
2017	HOU	MLB	30	5	2	0	12	12	63¹	62	7	2.8	8.8	62	33%	.312	1.29	3.55	4.58	0.7	92.1	50.6	13.2	48.4
2018	HOU	MLB	31	6	2	0	58	0	72¹	45	6	2.6	11.7	94	35%	.248	0.91	1.99	2.70	1.9	93.8	49.6	14.1	47.1
2019	HOU	MLB	32	4	5	0	35	8	74²	62	12	3.6	9.9	82	40%	.265	1.23	4.70	4.94	0.5	92.7	33.4	12.2	46.8
2020	HOU	MLB	33	2	2	0	33	0	35	31	6	3.2	9.5	37	38%	.278	1.23	4.00	4.09	0.4	91.9	42.1	12.9	46.7

Comparables: Kris Medlen, Carlos Carrasco, Mike Bolsinger

McHugh was set up perfectly to choose what kind of journey he took into the sunset of his career. After a career revitalization when the Astros picked him off the waiver wire heap in 2014, he had shown success as a starter and received a solid four days of All-Star buzz as a reliever in 2018. With 60% of Houston's rotation leaving due to injury or free agency, McHugh could show other teams he was still a viable starter, or if that didn't work, he could still be a lockdown reliever like he was in 2018. Unfortunately for him, none of that happened. He ditched his spin-rate-darling curveball for a sidearm slider that backfired all year. His K:BB rate plummeted and he lost a tick and a half of fastball velocity. He'll still get to play baseball in 2020, which I'm sure would have been thrilling to know back in 2013 with a double-digit ERA, but it seems he hit free agency one year too late.

Roberto Osuna RHP Born: 02/07/95 Age: 25 Bats: R Throws: R Height: 6'2" Weight: 215 Origin: International Free Agent, 2011

YEAR	TEAM	LVL	AGE	W	L	SV	G	GS	IP	H	HR	BB/9	K/9	K	GB%	BABIP	WHIP	ERA	DRA	WARP	MPH	FB%	WHF	CSP
2017	TOR	MLB	22	3	4	39	66	0	64	46	3	1.3	11.7	83	47%	.285	0.86	3.38	2.41	2.0	96.4	48	17.6	41.9
2018	TOR	MLB	23	0	0	9	15	0	15¹	16	0	0.6	7.6	13	40%	.340	1.11	2.93	3.97	0.2	97.5	67.7	13.4	50.5
2018	HOU	MLB	23	2	2	12	23	0	22²	17	1	1.2	7.5	19	44%	.258	0.88	1.99	3.54	0.4	96.9	67.7	16.9	48.3
2019	HOU	MLB	24	4	3	38	66	0	65	45	8	1.7	10.1	73	40%	.234	0.88	2.63	3.53	1.3	98.6	49.3	18.4	46.6
2020	HOU	MLB	25	3	3	44	61	0	64	50	8	2.4	10.7	76	40%	.275	1.05	2.78	2.96	1.6	97.3	54.2	17.9	47.4

Comparables: Huston Street, Kelvin Herrera, Neftalí Feliz

Still just 24, Osuna became the youngest player ever to record 150 saves. Interestingly, he does it without striking out an absurd amount of hitters, finishing 61st among qualified relievers in strikeout rate.

But that's not really the story, is it? Last season, he served a 75-game suspension under the Joint Domestic Violence, Sexual Assault and Child Abuse policy, the second-longest suspension administered under the policy since its implementation in 2015. Then, moments after he blew a save in an eventual ALCS Game 6 win that would send the Astros to the World Series, *Sports Illustrated* writer Stephanie Apstein reported that assistant general manager Brandon Taubman "turned to a group of three female reporters, including one wearing a purple domestic-violence awareness bracelet, and yelled, half a dozen times, "Thank God we got Osuna! I'm so f- - - glad we got Osuna!" After increasingly pathetic attempts to deny or downplay the events, the Astros eventually fired Taubman.

www.hawc.org/donate

Brad Peacock RHP Born: 02/02/88 Age: 32 Bats: R Throws: R Height: 6'1" Weight: 210 Origin: Round 41, 2006 Draft (#1231 overall)

YEAR	TEAM	LVL	AGE	W	L	SV	G	GS	IP	H	HR	BB/9	K/9	K	GB%	BABIP	WHIP	ERA	DRA	WARP	MPH	FB%	WHF	CSP
2017	HOU	MLB	29	13	2	0	34	21	132	100	10	3.9	11.0	161	44%	.286	1.19	3.00	2.91	3.8	94.3	51.3	12.9	47.8
2018	HOU	MLB	30	3	5	3	61	1	65	56	11	2.8	13.3	96	37%	.317	1.17	3.46	2.54	1.8	94.9	54.6	13.9	45.4
2019	HOU	MLB	31	7	6	0	23	15	91²	78	15	3.0	9.4	96	38%	.267	1.19	4.12	5.11	0.6	94.1	58.5	9.4	47.7
2020	HOU	MLB	32	8	6	0	55	16	123	117	22	3.8	10.1	138	39%	.300	1.37	4.81	4.70	1.0	93.4	54.5	11.6	46.5

Comparables: P.J. Walters, Fernando Nieve, Cody Martin

Peacock's past few seasons have mirrored his two-seam and slider pitch mix, yo-yoing back and forth from the rotation to the bullpen. It's too bad Jake Mintz of the Céspedes Family BBQ already has dibs on "America's ROOGY" because Peacock would be in the running with his utter dominance of same-handed foes—he finished with the second-best batting average allowed (.179) to righties in 2019. Last year, we said his days as a starting pitcher are over; then he went out and started 15 games so what do we know? He'll probably [side eyes the 2019 Annual] never replicate his 2017 season when he became the de facto Staff Ace for a good chunk of the season, but there's still value in his arm, no matter what inning he's pitching in.

Cionel Pérez LHP Born: 04/21/96 Age: 24 Bats: L Throws: L Height: 5'11" Weight: 170 Origin: International Free Agent, 2016

YEAR	TEAM	LVL	AGE	W	L	SV	G	GS	IP	H	HR	BB/9	K/9	K	GB%	BABIP	WHIP	ERA	DRA	WARP	MPH	FB%	WHF	CSP
2017	QUD	A	21	4	3	2	12	9	55¹	52	2	2.8	8.9	55	51%	.331	1.25	4.39	4.34	0.6				
2017	BCA	A+	21	2	1	0	5	4	25¹	27	1	1.8	6.4	18	46%	.325	1.26	2.84	4.80	0.1				
2017	CCH	AA	21	0	0	0	4	3	13	15	1	3.5	6.9	10	33%	.341	1.54	5.54	5.70	-0.1				
2018	CCH	AA	22	6	1	1	16	11	68¹	54	3	2.9	10.9	83	47%	.304	1.11	1.98	3.36	1.5				
2018	HOU	MLB	22	0	0	0	8	0	11¹	6	3	5.6	9.5	12	58%	.130	1.15	3.97	4.58	0.0	97.3	63.2	11.8	41.6
2019	ROU	AAA	23	2	1	0	13	10	47	53	6	4.6	8.2	43	54%	.343	1.64	5.36	4.89	0.8				
2019	HOU	MLB	23	1	1	0	5	0	9	11	3	2.0	7.0	7	48%	.286	1.44	10.00	6.79	-0.1	97.3	61.5	10.6	41.7
2020	HOU	MLB	24	1	1	0	11	0	12	13	3	4.8	9.7	13	48%	.334	1.67	6.56	5.95	-0.1	97.1	64.2	11.6	42.9

Comparables: Ranger Suárez, Touki Toussaint, Zack Littell

Look, we're not here to judge, but Pérez's stat line is already trending towards "May Have Peaked At 18" and that mullet/goatee combo isn't exactly helping to dispel that notion. After shredding the Cuban league as a teenager, Pérez has not been able to find that same success in Houston's organization. A forearm injury limited him to 63 2/3 innings in 2019, and they were not particularly exciting ones, either. He threw his slider a tick-and-a-half slower this year, which got him shredded at the big-league level. He's still young. He's still left-handed. He still sits in the mid-90s. But next year is going to tell us a lot about his potential. The Astros chose not to carry a single lefty in their bullpen for most of the year and postseason, which theoretically gives him ample opportunity to prove himself.

Ryan Pressly RHP Born: 12/15/88 Age: 31 Bats: R Throws: R Height: 6'3" Weight: 210 Origin: Round 11, 2007 Draft (#354 overall)

YEAR	TEAM	LVL	AGE	W	L	SV	G	GS	IP	H	HR	BB/9	K/9	K	GB%	BABIP	WHIP	ERA	DRA	WARP	MPH	FB%	WHF	CSP
2017	ROC	AAA	28	2	0	4	7	0	10	5	0	4.5	13.5	15	55%	.250	1.00	0.90	2.81	0.3				
2017	MIN	MLB	28	2	3	0	57	0	61¹	52	10	2.8	9.0	61	52%	.264	1.16	4.70	3.48	1.2	97.8	55	13.4	49.4
2018	MIN	MLB	29	1	1	0	51	0	47²	46	5	3.6	13.0	69	50%	.363	1.36	3.40	1.97	1.6	98.1	48.6	19.4	47.2
2018	HOU	MLB	29	1	0	2	26	0	23¹	11	1	1.2	12.3	32	62%	.213	0.60	0.77	1.73	0.9	97.6	34.7	17.7	47.6
2019	HOU	MLB	30	2	3	3	55	0	54¹	37	6	2.0	11.9	72	52%	.258	0.90	2.32	2.60	1.6	97.3	35.7	18.3	46.7
2020	HOU	MLB	31	3	3	8	61	0	64	55	8	3.0	11.9	85	50%	.312	1.19	3.30	3.33	1.3	96.8	43.6	17.2	47.3

Comparables: Kevin Jepsen, Mel Rojas, Mike Adams

How good does one have to be that a season in which they make an All-Star team and have a 2.32 ERA feels like a disappointment? Apparently Pressly-level good. He didn't even give up a run until his 20th appearance of the season. A freak knee injury limited him to just 10 appearances after July and he was clearly a shell of himself in the postseason, but even "bad" Pressly held opponents scoreless in nine of those ten outings. He lost a tick and a half of velo on all of his pitches down the stretch and at one point during the ALCS looked like his knee came unglued from his thigh, only for him to say post-game he had been expecting that for weeks and he would be good to go for the World Series. Professional athletes are crazy. Assuming he's healthy in 2020, look for him to spin hitters dizzy with his hammer curve and power slider. He has quickly blossomed into one of the game's upper-echelon relievers.

Aaron Sanchez RHP Born: 07/01/92 Age: 27 Bats: R Throws: R Height: 6'4" Weight: 210 Origin: Round 1, 2010 Draft (#34 overall)

YEAR	TEAM	LVL	AGE	W	L	SV	G	GS	IP	H	HR	BB/9	K/9	K	GB%	BABIP	WHIP	ERA	DRA	WARP	MPH	FB%	WHF	CSP
2017	TOR	MLB	24	1	3	0	8	8	36	42	6	5.0	6.0	24	48%	.310	1.72	4.25	7.30	-0.7	97.3	76.9	6.5	44.7
2018	TOR	MLB	25	4	6	0	20	20	105	106	11	5.0	7.4	86	50%	.304	1.56	4.89	5.97	-0.8	96.4	64.5	10.5	44.9
2019	HOU	MLB	26	2	0	0	4	4	18²	14	5	4.3	7.7	16	47%	.180	1.23	4.82	2.89	0.6	94.1	53.8	10.8	46.1
2019	TOR	MLB	26	3	14	0	23	23	112²	131	15	4.7	7.9	99	48%	.341	1.69	6.07	7.40	-2.0	96.2	58.3	9.6	46.9
2020	HOU	MLB	27	2	2	0	33	0	35	37	5	4.6	7.9	31	49%	.311	1.58	5.56	5.17	0.0	95.7	62.5	9.9	46.2

Comparables: Randall Delgado, Eduardo Rodriguez, Archie Bradley

It's got to be jarring for a team to make a trade with the Astros and the entire world to nod their head in unison while saying that player is going to get better immediately just by virtue of not being on your team anymore. It can't help when that pitcher is part of a combined no-hitter in his very first start. But hot takes that burn brightest burn out the fastest as Sanchez struggled to command, well, anything, and then had season-ending shoulder surgery. From the looks of it, he will be out for a good chunk of next season, too. If and when he does return, he will have just a few months to try and recoup his value before heading into free agency.

Joe Smith RHP Born: 03/22/84 Age: 36 Bats: R Throws: R Height: 6'2" Weight: 205 Origin: Round 3, 2006 Draft (#94 overall)

YEAR	TEAM	LVL	AGE	W	L	SV	G	GS	IP	H	HR	BB/9	K/9	K	GB%	BABIP	WHIP	ERA	DRA	WARP	MPH	FB%	WHF	CSP
2017	TOR	MLB	33	3	0	0	38	0	35²	30	3	2.5	12.9	51	44%	.342	1.12	3.28	3.28	0.8	91.0	67.7	13.4	52.8
2017	CLE	MLB	33	0	0	1	21	0	18¹	16	1	0.0	9.8	20	60%	.306	0.87	3.44	3.54	0.3	90.4	64.2	10.6	53.2
2018	HOU	MLB	34	5	1	0	56	0	45²	34	7	2.4	9.1	46	45%	.239	1.01	3.74	4.49	0.2	89.9	65.1	11.2	50.5
2019	HOU	MLB	35	1	0	0	28	0	25	19	2	1.8	7.9	22	49%	.254	0.96	1.80	4.25	0.3	90.1	57.6	9.9	56.4
2020	HOU	MLB	36	2	2	0	44	0	47	49	8	2.1	8.5	44	48%	.307	1.29	4.70	4.69	0.3	89.0	62.4	11.1	52.4

Comparables: Javy Guerra, Jeremy Jeffress, Hector Carrasco

After recovering from an offseason Achilles injury, Smith returned with enough side-arm arrows to prove he could still miss Styx at the big-league level. Though he appeared in less than half the season, Smith was lights out during the regular and postseason, especially in the ALCS where he had a higher WPA than any Astros pitcher not named Gerrit Cole. Thirteen seasons in, you know what you're getting—an upper-80s fastball and a big, sweeping slider with a delivery inversely proportional to how boring his name is.

Cy Sneed RHP Born: 10/01/92 Age: 27 Bats: R Throws: R Height: 6'4" Weight: 215 Origin: Round 3, 2014 Draft (#85 overall)

YEAR	TEAM	LVL	AGE	W	L	SV	G	GS	IP	H	HR	BB/9	K/9	K	GB%	BABIP	WHIP	ERA	DRA	WARP	MPH	FB%	WHF	CSP
2017	CCH	AA	24	9	5	1	22	14	97	117	12	3.1	7.5	81	47%	.345	1.55	5.01	5.76	-0.8				
2017	FRE	AAA	24	1	1	0	4	4	17²	25	4	3.6	7.1	14	40%	.362	1.81	11.21	6.00	-0.1				
2018	FRE	AAA	25	10	6	0	26	20	127	120	6	3.8	8.1	114	46%	.315	1.36	3.83	4.13	2.0				
2019	ROU	AAA	26	7	6	1	19	9	81²	71	13	2.6	7.8	71	41%	.261	1.16	4.19	2.89	2.9				
2019	HOU	MLB	26	0	1	0	8	0	21¹	26	5	2.1	9.7	23	48%	.350	1.45	5.48	5.23	0.0	94.8	69.8	11.6	50.7
2020	HOU	MLB	27	3	3	0	32	5	50	52	10	2.9	8.1	45	42%	.297	1.37	4.93	4.82	0.3	94.3	70.6	11.8	51.3

Comparables: Charles Brewer, Logan Verrett, Tyler Wilson

There are 143 anonymous, bearded American men who throw 94 miles an hour with a slider and a changeup. They can be found across the land, shuttling back and forth between Triple-A and the majors whenever an injury occurs, or the bullpen is overworked, or there is a doubleheader, or no one can find the remote to the TV. You might see them in the wild. Maybe they were your waiter on Thursday night at Outback Steakhouse, maybe they helped you with your taxes, maybe they are making the league minimum. Sneed is the one that plays for the Astros.

★ ★ ★ *2020 Top 101 Prospect* **#82** ★ ★ ★

Jose Urquidy RHP Born: 05/01/95 Age: 25 Bats: R Throws: R Height: 6'0" Weight: 180 Origin: International Free Agent, 2015

YEAR	TEAM	LVL	AGE	W	L	SV	G	GS	IP	H	HR	BB/9	K/9	K	GB%	BABIP	WHIP	ERA	DRA	WARP	MPH	FB%	WHF	CSP
2018	TCV	A-	23	0	0	0	4	4	11¹	15	0	1.6	7.9	10	42%	.395	1.50	2.38	5.83	-0.1				
2018	BCA	A+	23	2	2	0	9	7	46	40	2	1.6	7.4	38	52%	.281	1.04	2.35	3.26	1.1				
2019	CCH	AA	24	2	2	0	7	6	33	28	2	1.4	10.9	40	43%	.302	1.00	4.09	3.07	0.7				
2019	ROU	AAA	24	5	3	0	13	12	70	67	15	2.1	12.1	94	34%	.311	1.19	4.63	2.87	2.6				
2019	HOU	MLB	24	2	1	0	9	7	41	38	6	1.5	8.8	40	38%	.281	1.10	3.95	4.33	0.6	95.4	47.3	13	49.8
2020	HOU	MLB	25	9	5	0	21	21	112	101	17	2.6	9.0	112	37%	.282	1.20	3.73	3.81	2.2	95.1	48.5	13.3	51

Comparables: Domingo Germán, Jharel Cotton, Rafael Montero

In October of 2018, Urquidy was named Hernández, playing in the Mexican Winter League, unprotected in the Rule 5 Draft and had never thrown a pitch above A-ball. In October of 2019, he was handed the ball to start Game 4 of the World Series where he earned a win with five scoreless innings. His rise to prominence lies in his changeup, a firm mid-80s offering he throws a quarter of the time that teleports into the catcher's mitt after 55 feet of convincing the hitter it's a fastball. The changeup causes his nothing-special fastball to play up and he'll mix in a slider and a curveball from time to time, though the former is much better as of now.

Framber Valdez LHP Born: 11/19/93 Age: 26 Bats: L Throws: L Height: 5'11" Weight: 170 Origin: International Free Agent, 2015

YEAR	TEAM	LVL	AGE	W	L	SV	G	GS	IP	H	HR	BB/9	K/9	K	GB%	BABIP	WHIP	ERA	DRA	WARP	MPH	FB%	WHF	CSP
2017	BCA	A+	23	2	3	1	13	9	61¹	41	3	4.3	10.7	73	57%	.257	1.14	2.79	3.23	1.4				
2017	CCH	AA	23	5	5	0	12	9	49	60	4	4.2	9.7	53	60%	.394	1.69	5.88	6.60	-0.9				
2018	CCH	AA	24	4	5	1	20	13	94¹	92	7	2.8	11.4	120	58%	.363	1.28	4.10	4.04	1.3				
2018	FRE	AAA	24	2	0	0	2	1	8²	8	0	3.1	9.3	9	48%	.348	1.27	4.15	4.03	0.1				
2018	HOU	MLB	24	4	1	0	8	5	37	22	3	5.8	8.3	34	71%	.213	1.24	2.19	6.12	-0.4	94.8	69	8.9	43.9
2019	ROU	AAA	25	5	2	1	10	7	44¹	29	3	3.5	14.0	69	76%	.299	1.04	3.25	1.35	2.3				
2019	HOU	MLB	25	4	7	0	26	8	70²	74	9	5.6	8.7	68	62%	.319	1.67	5.86	5.70	-0.1	95.6	61.5	11.2	48.4
2020	HOU	MLB	26	6	5	0	44	11	86	87	11	4.8	8.7	83	63%	.314	1.55	5.13	4.83	0.6	95.0	64.9	10.6	47.2

Comparables: Thomas Pannone, Matt Hall, Erick Fedde

What do you do with a command pitcher's arsenal equipped to a pitcher with no command? A big lefty with a bowling ball sinker, Valdez could not find enough consistency to be effective at the big league level. His curveball is nasty, with .186 and .188 xwOBAs allowed the past two years, respectively, but every other offering gets hammered due to his propensity to carefully place them directly down the middle of the plate. If there's any organization that would tell someone to throw their best pitch until they're beaten by it, though, it's the Astros.

Justin Verlander RHP Born: 02/20/83 Age: 37 Bats: R Throws: R Height: 6'5" Weight: 225 Origin: Round 1, 2004 Draft (#2 overall)

YEAR	TEAM	LVL	AGE	W	L	SV	G	GS	IP	H	HR	BB/9	K/9	K	GB%	BABIP	WHIP	ERA	DRA	WARP	MPH	FB%	WHF	CSP
2017	DET	MLB	34	10	8	0	28	28	172	153	23	3.5	9.2	176	34%	.283	1.28	3.82	4.03	3.0	97.7	58	11	47.8
2017	HOU	MLB	34	5	0	0	5	5	34	17	4	1.3	11.4	43	32%	.194	0.65	1.06	3.08	0.9	97.5	59.6	15.1	49.9
2018	HOU	MLB	35	16	9	0	34	34	214	156	28	1.6	12.2	290	31%	.272	0.90	2.52	2.33	7.3	97.5	61.2	16.2	51.6
2019	HOU	MLB	36	21	6	0	34	34	223	137	36	1.7	12.1	300	36%	.219	0.80	2.58	2.51	7.9	96.8	49.9	17.5	48.3
2020	HOU	MLB	37	15	6	0	29	29	184	138	28	2.3	12.1	248	35%	.274	1.01	2.75	2.95	5.3	95.8	54.6	15.1	48.2

Comparables: Zack Greinke, A.J. Burnett, Aníbal Sánchez

In the same way he will often leave a little something extra for late in the game, Verlander found a little something extra late in his career, winning his first Cy Old, er, Young award since he was a flamethrowing 28-year-old in 2011. It was a year of milestones for the future Hall of Famer, eclipsing 3,000 career strikeouts, registering his first-ever 300-K season, and became just the sixth pitcher in baseball history to throw three no-hitters. Astoundingly, you could argue he has never looked better than he has the past two years. Here's a fact so crazy we had to check three times just to make sure it is true: 21 percent of his career strikeouts have come in an Astros uniform.

—————— ★ ★ ★ *2020 Top 101 Prospect* **#26** ★ ★ ★ ——————

Forrest Whitley RHP Born: 09/15/97 Age: 22 Bats: R Throws: R Height: 6'7" Weight: 195 Origin: Round 1, 2016 Draft (#17 overall)

YEAR	TEAM	LVL	AGE	W	L	SV	G	GS	IP	H	HR	BB/9	K/9	K	GB%	BABIP	WHIP	ERA	DRA	WARP	MPH	FB%	WHF	CSP
2017	QUD	A	19	2	3	0	12	10	46¹	42	2	4.1	13.0	67	37%	.388	1.36	2.91	3.98	0.7				
2017	BCA	A+	19	3	1	0	7	6	31¹	28	2	2.6	14.4	50	40%	.394	1.18	3.16	3.17	0.8				
2017	CCH	AA	19	0	0	0	4	2	14²	8	1	2.5	16.0	26	48%	.292	0.82	1.84	2.28	0.5				
2018	CCH	AA	20	0	2	0	8	8	26¹	15	2	3.8	11.6	34	39%	.220	0.99	3.76	2.29	0.9				
2019	BCA	A+	21	1	0	0	2	2	8¹	4	0	1.1	11.9	11	44%	.222	0.60	2.16	2.27	0.3				
2019	CCH	AA	21	2	2	0	6	6	22²	18	2	7.5	14.3	36	47%	.372	1.63	5.56	5.46	-0.1				
2019	ROU	AAA	21	0	3	0	8	5	24¹	35	9	5.5	10.7	29	32%	.394	2.05	12.21	7.64	-0.2				
2020	HOU	MLB	22	2	2	0	33	0	35	36	6	4.0	10.9	42	38%	.332	1.46	5.12	4.96	0.1				

Comparables: Lucas Sims, Clayton Kershaw, Alex Reyes

This Forrest is getting dangerously close to becoming a MarkAppelago. The list of successful, much less impactful, big leaguers with ERAs hovering around 8 for an entire season in the minors is not very long. But Whitley's arsenal is just too good to not find success eventually...right? He led the Arizona Fall League in strikeouts for the second straight year and despite getting knocked around, he had double-digit strikeout rates in every uniform he put on (five teams from levels spanning Rookie Ball to Triple-A).

LINEOUTS

Hitters

HITTER	POS	TEAM	LVL	AGE	PA	R	2B	3B	HR	RBI	BB	K	SB	CS	AVG/OBP/SLG	DRC+	VORP	BABIP	BRR	FRAA	WARP
Ross Adolph	OF	QUD	A	22	288	45	15	5	6	24	37	99	9	8	.223/.354/.403	114	17.9	.351	2.1	CF(51): -3.3, LF(9): 1.8	1.4
	OF	BCA	A+	22	172	24	5	1	1	16	24	43	2	1	.236/.360/.306	112	4.4	.330	1.2	CF(20): -0.2, LF(15): -0.9	0.6
Colin Barber	CF	AST	Rk	18	119	19	5	1	2	6	19	29	2	1	.263/.387/.394	139	4.5	.353	-2.4	CF(13): -2.5, LF(10): -2.2	0.0
Jordan Brewer	OF	TCV	A-	21	56	5	0	0	1	3	2	6	2	0	.130/.161/.185	31	-4.3	.128	-0.3	RF(8): -0.9, CF(3): -0.4	-0.3
Ronnie Dawson	OF	ROU	AAA	24	39	1	1	0	0	3	3	11	1	0	.147/.231/.176	26	-3.5	.208	0.1	CF(6): -0.5, RF(4): 0.0	-0.2
	OF	CCH	AA	24	459	71	20	2	17	50	47	141	13	10	.212/.320/.403	98	18.8	.281	1.1	CF(78): -2.6, RF(10): -0.7	1.3
Taylor Jones	1B	ROU	AAA	25	531	86	28	0	22	84	68	112	0	1	.291/.388/.501	123	30.5	.336	-1.7	1B(67): 6.3, LF(27): 0.5	2.9
Grae Kessinger	INF	QUD	A	21	201	25	6	0	2	17	26	32	8	2	.224/.333/.294	105	3.9	.261	0.2	SS(23): -2.5, 3B(18): 2.4	0.8
	INF	TCV	A-	21	45	5	4	0	0	3	3	4	1	1	.268/.333/.366	136	2.9	.297	-0.2	SS(10): 0.9, 3B(1): 0.0	0.4
Korey Lee	C	TCV	A-	20	259	31	6	4	3	28	28	49	8	5	.268/.359/.371	140	18.8	.328	2.5	C(30): 0.7, LF(5): -0.9	1.8
J.J. Matijevic	OF	CCH	AA	23	312	41	21	1	9	35	27	97	8	0	.246/.314/.423	107	5.6	.339	2.3	1B(48): -0.2, LF(21): 2.4	1.2
Freudis Nova	INF	QUD	A	19	299	35	20	1	3	29	15	68	10	7	.259/.301/.369	105	8.6	.332	-0.4	SS(31): -3.0, 2B(23): 0.0	0.8
Jeremy Pena	SS	QUD	A	21	289	44	8	4	5	41	35	57	17	6	.293/.389/.421	154	33.9	.357	3.3	SS(60): -2.1, 2B(2): -0.3	2.9
	SS	BCA	A+	21	185	28	13	3	2	13	12	33	3	4	.317/.378/.467	144	16.6	.383	1.8	SS(29): -0.2, 2B(11): 0.1	1.7
Luis Santana	SS	CCH	AA	19	66	5	2	0	0	2	6	9	0	0	.228/.333/.263	93	0.5	.271	-0.3	2B(17): -2.0, 3B(1): 0.2	-0.1
	SS	TCV	A-	19	186	19	8	0	2	15	14	24	4	2	.267/.339/.352	139	13.1	.298	0.2	2B(37): -2.2, 3B(15): -0.6	0.9

Acquired in the J.D. Davis trade, **Ross Adolph** walked half as often as he struck out this year, which isn't bad until you realize he struck out 142 times. ⓧ Comb through his resume, and you'll see **Collin Barber** got a million dollars as a fourth-round pick out of high school. He keeps his hands high and tight which leads to a cut that buzzes through the strike zone. ⓧ Recruited by major programs as a wide receiver, **Jordan Brewer** couldn't catch a break in his first stint in pro ball. ⓧ A tantalizing tools-heavy prospect, **Ronnie Dawson** struggled mightily in the upper levels of the minors, striking out almost a third of the time. ⓧ **Taylor Jones** is 6-foot-7, went to Gonzaga and managed not to play basketball, instead opting to pitch and play first base. After refining his strike zone defense at the plate in 2019, he could see the majors in 2020. ⓧ A second-round pick with a first-round name, **Graeber Crawley Kessinger** wasn't known for his bat until he broke out as a junior at Ole Miss. It hasn't translated to pro ball yet, but there's a lot of potential in his 6'2" frame. ⓧ With an above-average arm and a huge junior season at Cal, **Korey Lee** came off the board earlier than some expected. With no one blocking him in the system and a solid pro debut, he could arrive in the majors quickly. ⓧ A former Cape Cod League darling, **J.J. Matijevic** missed 50 games after a suspension, then struck out almost 10 times for every home run he hit in 2019. It's not what you want. ⓧ He may not stay at shortstop, but **Freudis Nova** still has all the tools to become a big leaguer. You could look at his 2019 stat line and call him a bust, but that would be psycho analysis. ⓧ His father Geronimo played in the big leagues, which provided **Jeremy Pena** with a solid jumping off point. He looked over-matched in the AFL, but that can't dampen his otherwise stellar first full pro season. ⓧ A stocky second baseman with solid bat-to-ball skills, **Luis Santana** resupplied the #Beef lost when J.D. Davis went to the Mets in the same transaction.

Pitchers

PITCHER	TEAM	LVL	AGE	W	L	SV	G	GS	IP	H	HR	BB/9	K/9	K	GB%	BABIP	WHIP	ERA	DRA	WARP	MPH	FB%	WHF	CSP
Brandon Bielak	CCH	AA	23	3	0	0	8	6	36	29	3	3.5	8.2	33	53%	.268	1.19	3.75	4.03	0.4				
	ROU	AAA	23	8	4	0	15	14	85²	69	10	3.8	9.0	86	44%	.269	1.23	4.41	2.73	3.3				
Hunter Brown	TCV	A-	20	2	2	0	12	6	23²	13	0	6.8	12.5	33	53%	.277	1.31	4.56	3.88	0.3				
Humberto Castellanos	QUD	A	21	3	0	4	14	0	36¹	29	4	1.5	11.4	46	47%	.278	0.96	3.22	3.37	0.6				
	BCA	A+	21	1	1	3	15	0	25²	30	1	2.1	9.5	27	64%	.367	1.40	3.16	5.92	-0.4				
	ROU	AAA	21	0	1	0	5	0	12²	4	1	2.1	7.1	10	57%	.103	0.55	1.42	2.52	0.5				
Brett Conine	QUD	A	22	3	2	0	6	5	33	19	3	1.6	10.9	40	61%	.216	0.76	1.91	2.78	0.9				
	BCA	A+	22	4	2	0	15	8	63¹	52	3	2.4	11.4	80	55%	.320	1.09	2.42	3.62	1.0				
	CCH	AA	22	1	0	0	4	2	18	20	1	3.0	7.0	14	53%	.339	1.44	2.00	6.13	-0.3				
Cody Deason	QUD	A	22	5	3	0	14	11	60¹	42	3	4.6	11.3	76	41%	.281	1.21	3.28	3.75	1.0				
	BCA	A+	22	4	3	1	9	6	40¹	34	0	3.1	9.8	44	50%	.312	1.19	3.57	3.75	0.6				
Dean Deetz	ROU	AAA	25	2	0	2	24	0	34	32	8	9.8	13.5	51	41%	.358	2.03	7.15	5.72	0.2				
Kent Emanuel	ROU	AAA	27	8	2	1	28	7	101²	98	9	2.0	7.2	81	57%	.299	1.19	3.90	2.49	3.9				
Tyler Ivey	CCH	AA	23	4	0	0	11	8	46	28	5	3.1	11.9	61	39%	.228	0.96	1.57	2.84	1.1				
Cristian Javier	BCA	A+	22	2	0	1	7	5	28²	15	1	5.0	12.6	40	33%	.226	1.08	0.94	2.87	0.7				
	CCH	AA	22	6	3	3	17	11	74	31	5	4.7	13.9	114	31%	.197	0.95	2.07	2.11	2.5				
	ROU	AAA	22	0	0	0	2	2	11	5	1	3.3	13.1	16	17%	.182	0.82	1.64	2.66	0.4				
Enoli Paredes	BCA	A+	23	3	1	0	10	6	44	21	3	4.3	12.1	59	45%	.205	0.95	1.64	2.60	1.2				
	CCH	AA	23	2	3	1	12	6	50	29	1	3.8	12.4	69	38%	.267	1.00	3.78	2.86	1.2				
Jose Alberto Rivera	QUD	A	22	5	5	1	18	11	75²	61	2	4.3	11.3	95	44%	.322	1.28	3.81	4.14	0.8				
Nivaldo Rodriguez	QUD	A	22	3	1	0	6	6	31	23	2	1.2	11.3	39	0%	.284	0.87	1.16						
	BCA	A+	22	3	5	2	18	9	74	46	5	3.8	9.1	75	0%	.222	1.04	2.92						
Jayson Schroeder	AST	Rk	19	1	0	0	3	1	6¹	3	0	7.1	7.1	5	29%	.214	1.26	0.00	4.97	0.1				
	TCV	A-	19	0	4	0	6	4	12²	19	1	16.3	7.8	11	51%	.391	3.32	8.53						
	QUD	A	19	0	1	0	3	1	6	7	0	13.5	13.5	9	19%	.438	2.67	12.00	7.67	-0.2				
Peter Solomon	BCA	A+	22	0	0	0	2	2	7²	7	1	4.7	16.4	14	33%	.429	1.43	2.35	4.03	0.1				
Blake Taylor	SLU	A+	23	2	2	7	21	0	27¹	24	1	4.0	9.5	29	67%	.307	1.32	2.63	4.95	-0.1				
	BIN	AA	23	0	1	3	18	0	39	25	2	2.8	10.4	45	53%	.240	0.95	1.85	3.31	0.6				

After flying up prospect lists in 2018, **Brandon Bielak** failed to replicate his success last season. It seems his early K/9s were all bark and no bite. ⊗ The star of the reality show *Sister Wives* shares a surname with Houston's latest fifth-round pick, **Hunter Brown**. They both have eye-popping SO (strikeout and significant other) numbers. ⊗ He won't overpower you, but he sure as hell won't walk you either. **Humberto Castellanos** keeps getting dudes out no matter what level you put him at. ⊗ A less-than-stellar ERA his junior year caused **Brett Conine** to slip to the 11th round where the Astros were waiting. He's a breakout star with back-to-back years with double digit strikeout rates. Call him Brett K/9. ⊗ The walks are concerning, but **Cody Deason** posted a double-digit strikeout rate and paired it with mid-3 ERAs across two levels. More like Cody Decent. ⊗ 2019 was a crazy year for **Dean Deetz**. Nuts that he fell off so much, walking almost a batter per inning after a 2018 season that held so much promise. ⊗ It's got to be hard being a low-ceiling pitching prospect in a system like Houston's, as **Kent Emanuel** has spent five years in the upper minors, perfecting his averageness. The reward: He was added to the 40-man roster this winter to protect him from Rule 5. Another five years and he might make the 25-man. ⊗ **Tyler Ivey** doesn't throw particularly hard, but he does fill up the strike zone. So far, that's led to a ton of success. Whether it can be done against big leaguers remains to be seen. ⊗ There's not much left for **Cristian Javier** to prove, having just been named the Astros Minor League Pitcher of the Year with a 1.74 ERA across the top three levels. His fastball sits in the low 90s, but his breaking ball is a thing of beauty. ⊗ You're not going to believe this but the Astros have a pitcher in their system that is getting a ton of strikeouts without walking anyone. **Enoli Paredes** continues to blow through the lower levels. The diminutive righty sits in the mid-90s but it's not hard to imagine him flirting with triple digits out of the 'pen. ⊗ **Jose Alberto Rivera** is from a city in the Dominican Republic called San Cristóbal. He's hovered around a 3.50 ERA at every level of the minor leagues, but it's impossible to tell if that success will continue in the future, sans crystal ball. ⊗ **Nivaldo Rodriguez** has found success at every level by using a low-90s fastball up, and curve and change down. Call it the Paul Giamatti profile: it's not sexy but it works. ⊗ Until you open the box score, you can't know if **Jayson Schroeder**'s prospect status is alive or dead. Once you do, though, you see a young, second-round pick who issued multiple free passes in all but one of his appearances in 2019. ⊗ **Jairo Solis** missed all of last season while recovering from Tommy John surgery, but showed a tantalizing live arm in 2018. ⊗ Drafted in the fourth round out of Notre Dame, **Peter Solomon** has had double digit K/9s at every level. He had Tommy John during the summer. The real story here is his Twitter account consists almost entirely of quotes from *The Office*. Here's one to tryout after his next punchout, "Fool me once, strike one. But fool me twice, strike three." ⊗ The Mets got then-lived armed prep lefty **Blake Taylor** way back in June 2014 for Ike Davis. Taylor's time in the Mets' system outlasted Davis' professional career, but came to an end when he was traded to the Astros for Jake Marisnick in December. He's now a semi-interesting relief prospect.

KANSAS CITY ROYALS

Essay by David Roth

Player comments by Patrick Dubuque and BP staff

Over the last two decades, the Kansas City Royals have been a very unsuccessful team. During that time, the Royals have finished a season within seven games of first place in their division four times; they won it once, in 2015, which was also the year they won the World Series. Over that same period, they've finished more than 30 games out seven times and lost more than 100 games six times. Both tallies include the last two years and, at the risk of losing more results-oriented readers of this essay before the end of its fourth sentence, are likely to continue into the next one. The pitching is bad, the hitting is not what you could call "good" and the farm system is...well, it's hard to be as definitive here, but it's also unlikely to make much difference this season. They'll be bad in the same ways and for more or less the same reasons.

None of this is new, in short. The Royals are recursive in terms of their broader approach and their results, to the point where the organization appears to have lapped itself; as it happens, they already have another three-year stretch of 100 or more losses, between 2004 and 2006, on the ledger in recent memory. There are only so many ways a team can lose a game, but while the Royals tend to lock into grooves that last for whole presidential administrations at a time, the way in which they lose now is not the same way that they have always lost over the last 20 years. It's happening for the same fundamental reasons that it always has, which is that the organization is cheap and reactionary. But there are different ways for a team to be bad. Some of those ways of failing can be seen as pointing or building towards success. Some of them are just plain failure. The Royals have chosen, actively or passively, to lose during their decades of doing nothing but. The question is what they might someday get out of it.

Before tanking became a recognizable concept, let alone a process that could be spun as a tactical choice toward a competitive end, the Royals made it into something of an ethos. The futility of the worst Royals teams was visible in their records and some exceptionally rude stats—this is neither here nor there, but the 2005 and 2006 Royals were both 47 runs worse by run differential than any team in baseball—and in a deeper sense that was profound, unique,

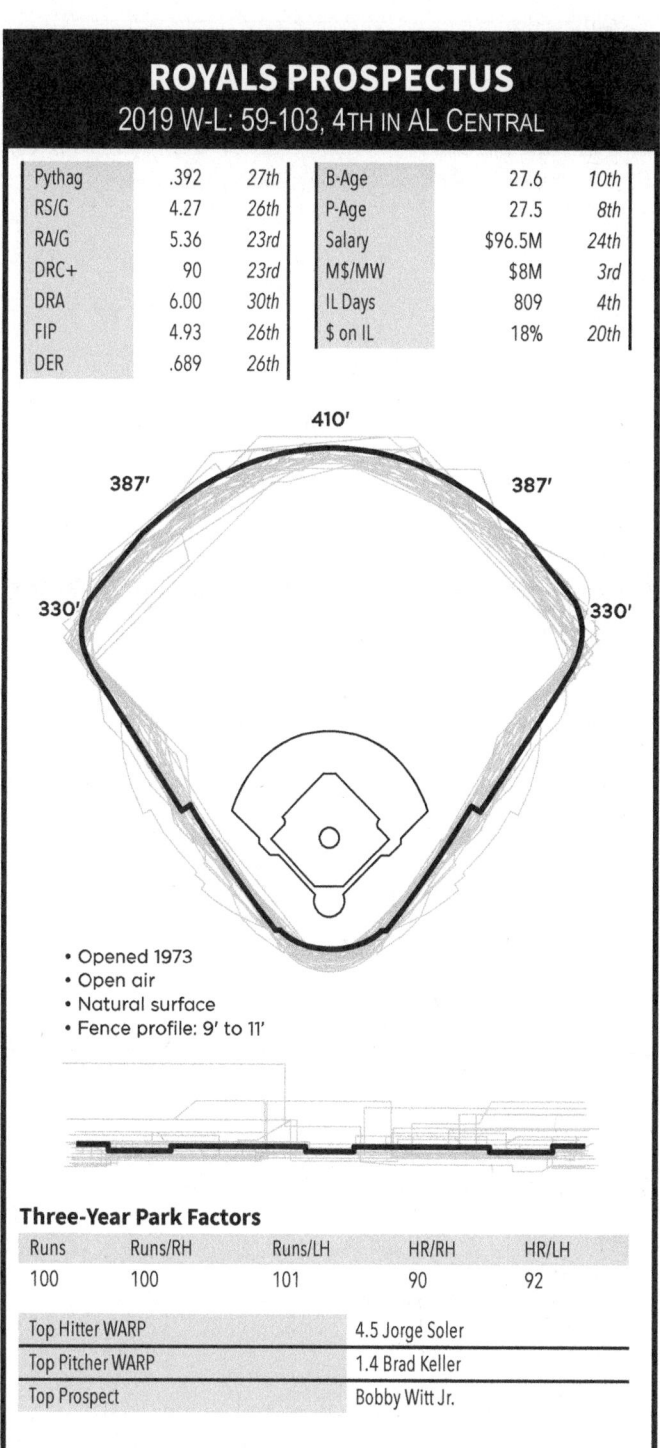

ROYALS PROSPECTUS
2019 W-L: 59-103, 4TH IN AL CENTRAL

Pythag	.392	27th	B-Age	27.6	10th
RS/G	4.27	26th	P-Age	27.5	8th
RA/G	5.36	23rd	Salary	$96.5M	24th
DRC+	90	23rd	M$/MW	$8M	3rd
DRA	6.00	30th	IL Days	809	4th
FIP	4.93	26th	$ on IL	18%	20th
DER	.689	26th			

- Opened 1973
- Open air
- Natural surface
- Fence profile: 9' to 11'

Three-Year Park Factors

Runs	Runs/RH	Runs/LH	HR/RH	HR/LH
100	100	101	90	92

Top Hitter WARP	4.5 Jorge Soler
Top Pitcher WARP	1.4 Brad Keller
Top Prospect	Bobby Witt Jr.

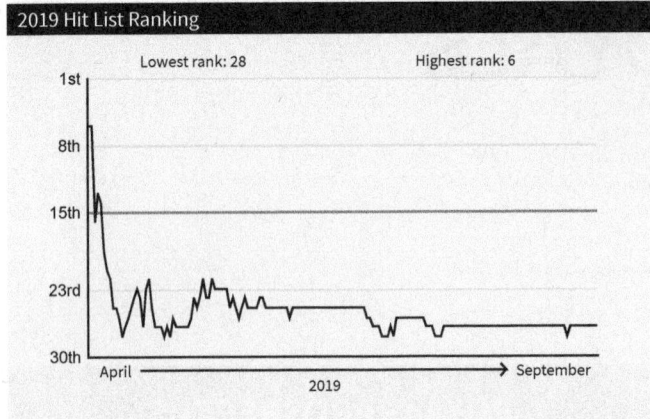

2019 Hit List Ranking

Lowest rank: 28   Highest rank: 6

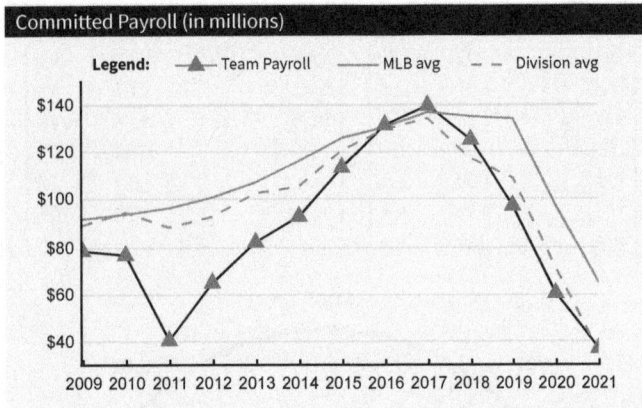

Committed Payroll (in millions)

Legend: ▲ Team Payroll   — MLB avg   – – Division avg

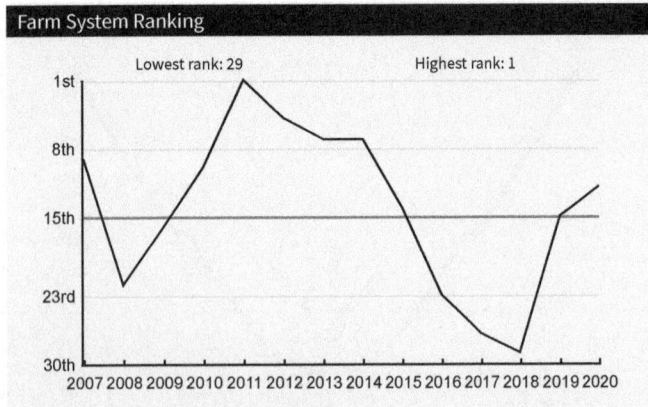

Farm System Ranking

Lowest rank: 29   Highest rank: 1

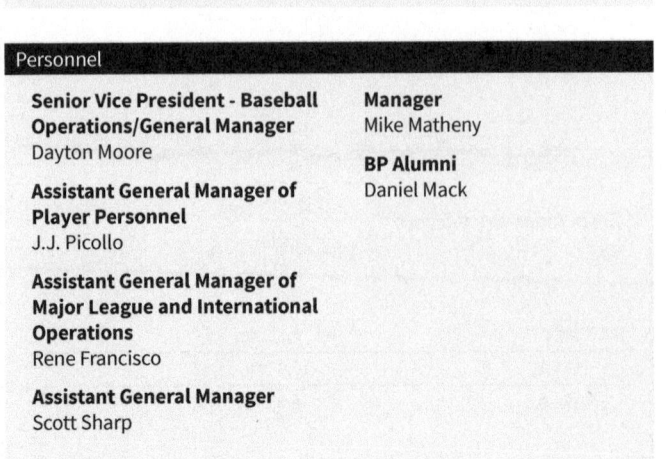

Personnel

Senior Vice President - Baseball Operations/General Manager
Dayton Moore

Assistant General Manager of Player Personnel
J.J. Picollo

Assistant General Manager of Major League and International Operations
Rene Francisco

Assistant General Manager
Scott Sharp

Manager
Mike Matheny

BP Alumni
Daniel Mack

somehow almost spiritual. There was a deep and abiding purposelessness to those teams: a sense that they were rudderless, more or less by design.

The system intermittently delivered some rising stars, and they showed out without any apparent attempt being made to build around them; budgets were stable, but static. Some free agents came aboard every year into a career hospice, and there enjoyed a quiet last turn or two around the league. Those odd stars the system produced squandered their early primes in Kansas City, generally with dignity and distinction, and then left in free agency without the team putting up much of a fight, or in deadline deals for the kind of interchangeable prospects the team developed on its own—corner infielders near the majors with plate discipline but no pop, or pop but no plate discipline and/or some live-armed, bullpen-bound pitchers named Mike or Luke. There was one flukey 83-win year in 2003, a false dawn that baseball historians may someday call the Randaissance, after the team's mainstay third baseman (although we should all hope they won't). Otherwise all that aimless futility went on for 13 years.

⚾   ⚾   ⚾

It wasn't just that the team didn't get better during that period (split roughly evenly between the GM tenures of Allard Baird and Dayton Moore), although they assuredly did not. It was that every move seemed to have been made with the intention of getting the team as close as possible to 95 losses without going over. Weird things happened in the purgatory that the team furnished for itself at the bottom of the American League Central. Ken Harvey made an All-Star team, then played just 12 more games in the bigs when that season was over. Ángel Berroa was Rookie of the Year, somehow. There was a lot of Bruce Chen on the monitors, just in general. A striking number of the names that filled out the rosters over that lost decade-and-a-half sound like characters from Charles Portis novels—Jimmy Gobble, Calvin Pickering, Tug Hulett, Everett Teaford, Runelvys Hernandez, Ross Gload.

It was never clear what Baird was trying to do during his years at the helm, but Moore, who was hired in 2006, is and was different. Moore has notched only three winning seasons in 13 years, but he has always given the impression that things were happening for a reason, even when that reason has been difficult to discern. "Let's just trust the process," Moore told the *Kansas City Star* in 2009. "If other people don't want to trust the process, that's fine. If other people want to abandon the process, then abandon it. I'm not abandoning the process. I believe in the process. You get a good group of people together. You work hard together. You trust in one another. You go through the difficult times. You work hard to make good decisions. You keep guys together and, eventually, it will happen."

Moore had overseen three awful seasons by that point and the Royals would lose 95, 91 and 90 games before they broke .500, but he also wasn't wrong. It really did happen, and then it ended. Moore got through the miserable years before and after because he made it seem as if there was some process to trust and because he made moves that, however well they fit with the relentless cheapness that was the team's core corporate value under previous ownership, did seem to be building toward some goal. He found value in the favorable draft positions that those miserable seasons afforded the team and also in later rounds—stealing Greg Holland in the 10th, Whit Merrifield in the ninth, Jarrod Dyson in the 50th—for a few years, and then went right back to missing as egregiously as Baird ever had.

When all those small wins prised open a competitive window in the middle of the decade, Moore pushed through it. He nailed every big move he made when the team made a push for 2015, some of which were quite risky. The championship team was sui generis, and a testament to both Moore's vision and ownership's patience and, when the time came, willingness to jump. They put exquisite and sadistic pressure on every team they played through their refusal to make mistakes, and every one of those teams eventually relented under that assault. All of this is true, which is to say that, albeit on the most generous timetable, Moore was right.

But it is also true that the team hasn't finished above .500 once in the four seasons since they won the dang World Series. It is true, too, that fans showed up in droves when the team was good, and continued to turn out in dwindling numbers as the on-field product faded toward mediocrity, but they stopped turning out once the gradual burial of the championship roster was complete. A million fewer people attended Royals games in 2019 than came to watch the 2016 club; the 2019 figure was nearly half as many as during the team's World Series run. This stands to reason, but all of it points back to the same question that Moore used to answer with "trust the process," and it amounts to what are you trying to do here. You may not be surprised to learn the answer.

"You ask if this year is different," Moore told MLB.com before the 2018 season. "It isn't. It really isn't. The purpose doesn't change. You hold true to the things you believe in and the things you've learned...If we play the game for the right reasons and we do it together, we'll compete. We'll win. That formula doesn't change." That team lost 104 games, and lost 103 the year after that. There is no reason to think that Moore's answer has changed. It is difficult to imagine what would change it.

⚾   ⚾   ⚾

The competitive justification for a team choosing to stink for years, on purpose, is complicated without being complex. It boils down to the fact that baseball is extremely hard, and that building a winning baseball team is difficult. It takes a long time to replenish a farm system, and even brilliant youngsters can bust for various reasons; bodies break and owners don't want to spend money even though they're making it hand over fist, and so on. There is no real parity in baseball beyond this stubborn and fundamental truth, but the difficulty of it all does level the playing field. It is inherent not just to the game but to the broader business and study of the game that everyone involved is going to fail often, and fail badly.

There are ways to deal with this, or at least try to mitigate it. Teams that can afford to do so take the same approach that venture capitalists do: spraying a bunch of money at an impossible problem in the understanding that most of the bets will necessarily be losers, but that the ones that hit (or even push) might be instructive going forward. In point of fact, "teams that can afford to do so" includes basically every MLB team; the Royals were owned by the billionaire Walmart scion David Glass until the very end of 2019, at which point they were sold, for a clean $1 billion, to Kansas City businessman John Sherman.

That approach works, generally, but because it's expensive and because it's considered gauche to pay retail in baseball owner circles, most teams prefer the model of minimizing costs where it's expensive—or, "the players who actually play the games"—and spending that money to figure out ways to get more for less, or more from less. What this means, for our purposes as people who care about baseball, is that owners are trying to figure out the least they can spend and still make money at the volume and rate to which they've become accustomed. There are all kinds of ways to make this seem more complex than it is, and various obfuscatory bits of jargon pass into and out of vogue, but all those faddish terms and tortured justifications obscure the same fact, which is that some teams don't try very hard to win the World Series.

Some owners do want to win a World Series, for the natural and healthy reasons that everyone that cares about baseball would like to win a World Series, which is that it's an extremely cool and very difficult thing to do. Many of them don't want it all that much, or anyway don't want it enough to jeopardize the profitability built into owning a franchise by spending money on players that could otherwise just not be spent at all. In the crudest bottom-line sense, it can be difficult to tell the difference between a rebuilding team—one that's swapping expensive veteran assets for cheaper and more volatile ones and letting green rookies flounder in games that count in the standings because they believe it will help them flourish under similar circumstances in due time—and one that is just losing games because it doesn't know what it's about, or because its priors and principles are off, or because it isn't really trying that hard to do anything in particular beyond kick the can down the road. Not every losing team is rebuilding. Some of them are just like that.

This is where The Dayton Moore Experience and the broader Royals gambit becomes difficult to assess. Moore knows what he knows and believes what he believes, and he has gotten some important things right. But, whether because of how little ownership gave him or how little ownership asked of him, he has also been allowed to go on failing righteously—in the same ways, and for the same reasons—for far longer than would seem justified or even justifiable. It might not have been Moore's preference to draft the more-signable Luke Hochevar over Clayton Kershaw and Max Scherzer and literally every other player drafted in 2006, but he did it all the same; Hochevar has his World Series ring, but he is out of baseball and Kershaw and Scherzer are...not, let's just say. Drafting and player development are hard, but when Moore stopped hitting on important picks—when he took Aaron Crow 13 picks before Mike Trout in 2009; or Christian Colón instead of Chris Sale and Yasmani Grandal in 2010; or Bubba Starling ahead of Anthony Rendon, Francisco Lindor, Javy Báez and George Springer a year later—he put more pressure on his belief in what it means to build and be a baseball team. It's difficult to trust a process when it stops delivering desirable outcomes.

Theoretically, anyway. Colón delivered the decisive hit in that 2015 World Series and hasn't done much else, but he has a co-starring role in millions of happy memories. Starling, who finally made it to the bigs in 2019 after remaking everything that once made him a prodigy, doesn't look like someone likely to have a long career, but he's having one now. Kyle Zimmer, whom the team made the fifth pick of the 2012 draft, clawed his way to the majors in 2019 at age 27; he was hit hard, but he saw his dream through. They are not the future of the Royals, and look unlikely to be integral parts of the next good Royals team, whenever that might arrive. They are proof of Moore's belief that people who play the game for the right reasons and value their opportunity and never quit can indeed make it, but they are also, relative to their peers, compelling proof that a more capacious or forward-thinking organizational approach might yield better on-field results. All the values that Moore has centered as part of his perpetual process are laudable enough, but they're not enough on their own to get the Royals anywhere in particular. If the goal is simply to Do The Right Things per a certain definition, then the Royals are indeed doing just fine. If the goal is something more pedestrian and concrete like Improve Baseball Outcomes In The Near Term, they are not. Once again, it's far from clear what the Royals are doing, or trying to do.

And yet there's no reason to think they're going to stop doing it. Faith and patience and fellowship are important, and, while those are also words politicians tend to use to conceal various craven cynicisms, there's no reason to think Moore is insincere in his belief. Getting a good group of people together and working hard together and trusting each other and all the rest is not a bad idea when it comes to building a baseball team, or a shed or anything else, but it is also not sufficient on its own. At some point, if this shed is ever going to get built, some of the good and faithful men called to the task are going to have to show up with tools.

—*David Roth is a former editor at Deadspin.*

HITTERS

Humberto Arteaga SS   Born: 01/23/94   Age: 26   Bats: R   Throws: R   Height: 6'1"   Weight: 160   Origin: International Free Agent, 2010

YEAR	TEAM	LVL	AGE	PA	R	2B	3B	HR	RBI	BB	K	SB	CS	AVG/OBP/SLG	DRC+	VORP	BABIP	BRR	FRAA	WARP
2017	NWA	AA	23	490	47	12	3	1	35	25	65	4	4	.258/.300/.305	61	0.3	.297	-3.1	SS(96): 2.6, 2B(19): -1.9	-0.1
2018	OMA	AAA	24	445	42	19	1	6	49	21	73	2	3	.292/.322/.386	84	9.8	.337	-0.6	3B(51): -1.7, SS(31): -2.4	0.4
2019	OMA	AAA	25	302	39	10	1	5	26	12	34	11	5	.299/.333/.394	79	1.4	.325	-3.7	SS(26): 4.8, 2B(22): 1.7	0.9
2019	KCA	MLB	25	135	11	4	0	0	4	8	28	1	1	.197/.258/.230	68	0.9	.255	0.4	SS(36): -2.4, 2B(2): -0.1	-0.1
2020	KCA	MLB	26	251	19	12	1	2	21	10	51	3	2	.242/.278/.326	58	-5.9	.299	-0.3	SS 0, 3B 0	-0.5

Comparables: Tom Upton, Harold Castro, Yadiel Rivera

Arteaga repeated every level of the minor leagues and still managed to reach the majors at 25, which is kind of impressive in its own right. To be fair, his promotion could be described as a result of suction: Whit Merrifield's move to right forced Nicky Lopez to second, and when Adelberto Mondesi got hurt and Chris Owings imploded, Arteaga got sucked into the wake of the collective misery. It shouldn't happen again; the Venezuelan shortstop simply cannot hit, and also cannot stop himself from trying to hit. Instead, his major league career will serve as an example of the New Order of roster management, when teams start rebuilding before they have the necessary materials, and are forced to assemble baseball games out of spackle, tarp, and Humberto Arteagas.

Hunter Dozier 3B/OF   Born: 08/22/91   Age: 28   Bats: R   Throws: R   Height: 6'4"   Weight: 220   Origin: Round 1, 2013 Draft (#8 overall)

YEAR	TEAM	LVL	AGE	PA	R	2B	3B	HR	RBI	BB	K	SB	CS	AVG/OBP/SLG	DRC+	VORP	BABIP	BRR	FRAA	WARP
2017	OMA	AAA	25	96	11	6	1	4	12	9	37	1	1	.226/.313/.464	75	3.9	.341	-0.3	RF(10): -0.1, 3B(7): -0.3	-0.2
2018	OMA	AAA	26	143	18	7	0	1	11	24	43	2	1	.254/.385/.339	114	5.4	.392	-0.2	3B(19): 0.6, RF(13): 1.2	0.8
2018	KCA	MLB	26	388	36	19	4	11	34	24	109	2	3	.229/.278/.395	80	-4.9	.296	-0.3	1B(51): -7.5, 3B(37): -5.9	-1.5
2019	KCA	MLB	27	586	75	29	10	26	84	55	148	2	2	.279/.348/.522	118	33.4	.339	-1.8	3B(100): -0.3, RF(20): 0.4	3.0
2020	KCA	MLB	28	595	65	25	5	21	73	52	164	4	2	.237/.308/.418	92	6.2	.301	-0.4	RF 4, 3B -1	1.0

Comparables: Sherman Obando, Josh Fields, Jake Marisnick

Everyone sings of March and October, those two magnetic poles of the baseball season. Perhaps the most underrated month is May, the time when the shadows recede from the field, the games grow comfortable, and the clatter and bombast of April dies down. In May we have a moment to breathe, and to ask ourselves: *Is it real?* In Dozier's case, the answer was an emphatic yes. After a lengthy delay, it all came together for the hope of the post-championship youth movement, as he cut down on balls out of the zone and put more of his batted balls in the air. Yet another cause for optimism: amidst the team's post-deadline shakeup, Dozier moved to right field, and the results passed all the tests, both qualitative and quantitative. Persistent injuries are the biggest concern, as a June chest injury seemed to nag at him even after he returned to the lineup, but he finished strong. Having conquered spring, hopefully he'll get to find out what this fall thing is all about.

Maikel Franco 3B   Born: 08/26/92   Age: 27   Bats: R   Throws: R   Height: 6'1"   Weight: 215   Origin: International Free Agent, 2010

YEAR	TEAM	LVL	AGE	PA	R	2B	3B	HR	RBI	BB	K	SB	CS	AVG/OBP/SLG	DRC+	VORP	BABIP	BRR	FRAA	WARP
2017	PHI	MLB	24	623	66	29	1	24	76	41	95	0	0	.230/.281/.409	82	1.2	.234	-1.8	3B(144): -9.2, 1B(2): -0.1	-0.3
2018	PHI	MLB	25	465	48	17	1	22	68	29	62	1	0	.270/.314/.467	109	22.1	.270	1.5	3B(117): -2.7	2.1
2019	LEH	AAA	26	46	5	2	1	2	6	5	7	0	0	.175/.283/.425	84	-0.5	.161	-0.3	3B(11): 0.9	0.1
2019	PHI	MLB	26	428	48	17	0	17	56	36	61	0	0	.234/.297/.409	88	9.9	.236	-1.0	3B(110): 2.5, 1B(2): 0.0	1.1
2020	KCA	MLB	27	455	49	21	1	17	57	33	71	1	0	.237/.295/.413	87	2.3	.248	-0.4	3B -2	0.0

Comparables: Mike Moustakas, Brett Lawrie, Lonnie Chisenhall

One of the most enduring images in American sports isn't something that happened but rather an ingenious fiction: the timeless illustration of Charlie Brown trying and failing to kick a football as Lucy Van Pelt yanks it away at the last second. Franco's four-and-a-half-year tenure with the Phillies had its moments was mostly been an exercise in briefly resplendent flashes of greatness surrounded by extreme disappointment. A seven-homer April would have been exciting coming from a different player, but Phillies fans had been down this road with Franco too many times. Sure enough, when the calendar flipped to May, Franco disappeared, hitting a woeful .227/.281/.374 from that point forward. The problems that plagued Franco in 2019—a long swing, poor mechanics, trouble driving pitches, difficulty elevating balls—have been present ever since his debut in 2014. Franco and the Phillies both diligently attempted to fix these issues, but hitting coaches aren't magicians and some flaws are just fatal. Philadelphia demoted him in August and while he returned in September, it was a taste of what 2020 would be like: Franco tantalizing a new fan base with his potential before yanking away the proverbial pigskin once pitchers reacquaint themselves with his weaknesses.

Cam Gallagher C   Born: 12/06/92   Age: 27   Bats: R   Throws: R   Height: 6'3"   Weight: 230   Origin: Round 2, 2011 Draft (#65 overall)

YEAR	TEAM	LVL	AGE	PA	R	2B	3B	HR	RBI	BB	K	SB	CS	AVG/OBP/SLG	DRC+	VORP	BABIP	BRR	FRAA	WARP
2017	OMA	AAA	24	282	26	13	0	5	37	18	33	0	1	.292/.336/.400	94	5.1	.317	-4.1	C(71): 11.8	2.0
2017	KCA	MLB	24	27	2	1	0	1	5	3	4	0	0	.250/.333/.417	93	0.4	.263	-0.4	C(13): -0.2	0.0
2018	OMA	AAA	25	303	28	13	0	4	42	26	38	1	0	.265/.334/.358	86	11.3	.294	-2.0	C(72): 11.9	2.0
2018	KCA	MLB	25	69	5	3	0	1	7	3	15	0	0	.206/.250/.302	84	-1.9	.250	-1.6	C(20): 2.4	0.3
2019	KCA	MLB	26	142	14	7	0	3	12	11	28	0	1	.238/.312/.365	92	6.0	.281	-0.6	C(44): 3.8	0.9
2020	KCA	MLB	27	175	16	8	0	4	17	14	34	0	0	.230/.296/.352	71	1.0	.270	-0.7	C 2	0.3

Comparables: Johnny Edwards, Bob Melvin, Sal Fasano

You rarely get experiences like Gallagher outside of sports. The longtime backup stumbled into playing time when franchise icon/living statue Salvador Perez was lost for the season, and proceeded to play exactly how you would expect: good defense, lots of lazy flyballs to left. In other areas of life, it's generally easy to avoid such predictable mediocrity. Gallagher is the movie you scroll past without thinking in the Netflix queue, the music at the supermarket you don't actually notice is even playing. He's the can of cream of mushroom you never have to actually open. But all this sounds too negative; in the world, and especially the 2019 Royals, mediocrity can be a blessing. Think of Gallagher, then, as the cartoon your kid makes you watch that doesn't make you cringe. Think of him as

YEAR	TEAM	P. COUNT	FRM RUNS	BLK RUNS	THRW RUNS	TOT RUNS
2017	KCA	1026	-0.2	0.2	-0.1	0.6
2017	OMA	9981	11.1	1.6	1.0	14.1
2018	KCA	2387	1.5	1.0	0.0	2.6
2018	OMA	9812	11.3	0.3	0.1	11.4
2019	KCA	5498	3.7	0.9	-0.3	4.3
2020	KCA	6619	-2.2	1.1	-0.4	2.9

Octonauts. You won't think about it when your kids get older, but there's a lot worse you could do in the world than Octonauts.

Michael Gigliotti CF   Born: 02/14/96   Age: 24   Bats: L   Throws: L   Height: 6'1"   Weight: 180   Origin: Round 4, 2017 Draft (#120 overall)

YEAR	TEAM	LVL	AGE	PA	R	2B	3B	HR	RBI	BB	K	SB	CS	AVG/OBP/SLG	DRC+	VORP	BABIP	BRR	FRAA	WARP
2017	BNC	RK	21	191	30	8	3	3	30	32	21	15	5	.329/.442/.477	168	27.2	.361	0.7	CF(39): -5.8	1.5
2017	LEX	A	21	100	14	5	1	1	8	8	20	7	5	.302/.378/.419	131	6.3	.379	0.3	CF(18): 1.7	0.8
2019	LEX	A	23	279	42	19	1	1	23	27	49	29	7	.309/.394/.411	148	27.8	.381	2.0	CF(59): 1.4	2.5
2019	WIL	A+	23	99	8	2	1	0	5	8	23	5	3	.184/.268/.230	40	-2.5	.250	1.5	CF(16): -1.6, RF(6): 1.1	-0.2
2020	KCA	MLB	24	251	23	12	1	3	21	21	62	9	5	.234/.306/.333	73	-0.5	.309	0.4	CF 1, RF 0	0.0

Comparables: Taylor Motter, Adam Engel, Lane Adams

Sometimes it's easy to look at a prospect and envision them at the major league level. Gigliotti, for example, feels like a perfect fit for Kauffman Stadium: the spacious greens, the tempered expectations. The fleet-footed former fourth-rounder lost a season to an ACL tear in 2018, leaving many with concerns not only over development but also damage to his very essence as a ballplayer. He answered them all, flashing untarnished speed, defense and well-in-front-of-the-outfielders power on his way to the South Atlantic League All-Star Game. Then he went on to provide new ones after his midseason promotion. At his age and with his profile, there's exactly one type of major-league player Gigliotti could end up being, and it's not a given that he achieves it. But in the meantime, it's hard to blame Royals fans if they close their eyes and dream of a rangy center fielder who steals bases *and* takes walks.

Alex Gordon LF   Born: 02/10/84   Age: 36   Bats: L   Throws: R   Height: 6'1"   Weight: 225   Origin: Round 1, 2005 Draft (#2 overall)

YEAR	TEAM	LVL	AGE	PA	R	2B	3B	HR	RBI	BB	K	SB	CS	AVG/OBP/SLG	DRC+	VORP	BABIP	BRR	FRAA	WARP
2017	KCA	MLB	33	541	52	20	2	9	45	45	126	7	4	.208/.293/.315	69	-8.5	.261	-0.2	LF(140): 2.7, CF(15): -0.9	-0.5
2018	KCA	MLB	34	568	56	24	0	13	54	50	124	12	2	.245/.324/.370	90	4.0	.299	-1.9	LF(125): 3.3, CF(11): -0.9	0.8
2019	KCA	MLB	35	633	77	31	1	13	76	51	100	5	3	.266/.345/.396	97	14.8	.301	0.6	LF(146): -2.7, P(2): 0.0	1.2
2020	KCA	MLB	36	251	26	10	0	6	25	22	49	3	1	.235/.321/.360	84	2.5	.279	-0.3	LF 0, CF 0	0.3

Comparables: Ryan Zimmerman, Eduardo Perez, Ed Sprague

One of the reasons that there aren't many good sports movies is that sports are really the opposite of the movies. Exhibit A: Gordon slew the dragon four years ago and has spent half the film strolling through his denouement, the credits crawling up the screen. Also unlike the movies, it works just fine; narrative structure, it turns out, is overrated. Though the glory years recede into the distance, Gordon serves not only as a mentor, but as an absolutely vital source of esteem. As baseball slides further into asset management, we need fan favorites, especially in dark times. We need a reason to feel romantic. The former three-time All-Star was undecided about retirement as the season ended; certainly, from a story standpoint, it makes the most sense. But if the team deigns to throw him a few bucks and a few hundred plate appearances in an otherwise meaningless 2020 Royals season, we're all better off. Let the kids wait a little bit.

Kelvin Gutierrez 3B   Born: 08/28/94   Age: 25   Bats: R   Throws: R   Height: 6'3"   Weight: 215   Origin: International Free Agent, 2013

YEAR	TEAM	LVL	AGE	PA	R	2B	3B	HR	RBI	BB	K	SB	CS	AVG/OBP/SLG	DRC+	VORP	BABIP	BRR	FRAA	WARP
2017	NAT	RK	22	37	6	3	1	0	1	4	7	2	0	.212/.297/.364	65	0.5	.269	0.8	3B(8): -1.1	0.0
2017	POT	A+	22	245	34	10	6	2	16	19	59	3	0	.288/.347/.414	121	12.5	.380	2.0	3B(57): 6.4	2.2
2018	HAR	AA	23	249	36	6	3	5	26	16	62	10	1	.274/.321/.391	96	9.3	.352	1.0	3B(56): 12.7, SS(1): 0.1	2.2
2018	NWA	AA	23	264	29	8	3	6	40	20	46	10	3	.277/.337/.409	103	9.8	.321	1.3	3B(62): -0.7, SS(2): -0.2	1.0
2019	OMA	AAA	24	327	41	9	2	9	43	35	71	12	1	.287/.367/.427	97	13.9	.349	2.3	3B(62): -3.3, 1B(7): -0.7	0.8
2019	KCA	MLB	24	79	4	2	1	1	11	5	24	1	0	.260/.304/.356	67	-0.4	.367	-0.8	3B(18): -0.1	-0.1
2020	KCA	MLB	25	70	6	3	0	1	7	5	19	1	0	.249/.306/.359	76	-0.6	.340	0.1	3B 0, 1B -1	-0.1

Comparables: Erik González, Brent Morel, Zoilo Almonte

It's not easy to imagine a player on the low end of a middling prospect list on a bad team and think "investment opportunity," but Gutierrez may just qualify. He offers a very rare combination of strengths and weaknesses: solid defense and arm at third, a relatively short swing and all the power of a Richard Marx album. It's not often you see a combination of that BABIP, a 68 percent groundball rate and average-at-best footspeed. But before you shout "regression," take a shot, and turn the page, Gutierrez pulled this trick off with not just luck but a 90.2 mph exit velocity on groundballs, good for 30th in baseball. The bat speed is there, it's just pointing the wrong direction. A broken toe thwarted a September callup and a chance at confirming any progress, and with Hunter Dozier entrenched at third, some enterprising, confident team might consider Gutierrez a fixer-upper worth putting some elbow grease into.

Kyle Isbel CF   Born: 03/03/97   Age: 23   Bats: L   Throws: R   Height: 5'11"   Weight: 183   Origin: Round 3, 2018 Draft (#94 overall)

YEAR	TEAM	LVL	AGE	PA	R	2B	3B	HR	RBI	BB	K	SB	CS	AVG/OBP/SLG	DRC+	VORP	BABIP	BRR	FRAA	WARP
2018	IDA	RK	21	119	27	10	1	4	18	14	17	12	3	.381/.454/.610	195	18.0	.429	-0.8	CF(19): 4.5, RF(2): 1.1	1.6
2018	LEX	A	21	174	30	12	1	3	14	12	43	12	3	.289/.345/.434	111	7.0	.377	2.8	CF(27): 0.8, LF(11): -0.5	1.0
2019	ROY	RK	22	27	9	2	0	2	7	2	5	3	1	.360/.407/.680	155	5.4	.389	1.0	CF(6): 1.6	0.5
2019	WIL	A+	22	214	26	7	3	5	23	15	44	8	3	.216/.282/.361	86	5.5	.253	1.8	CF(32): -2.3, RF(11): 0.5	0.2
2020	KCA	MLB	23	251	23	12	1	5	24	16	67	9	3	.222/.276/.348	65	-2.8	.291	0.6	CF 0, RF 0	-0.2

Comparables: Andrew Toles, Alex Presley, Clete Thomas

Isbel is the platonic ideal of the fan favorite prospect: he does everything well, as defined by being slightly above average at every tool. He hits well for a center fielder, has a plus arm for someone out in left and demonstrates excellent range for a guy in front of the right field wall. Plus, he runs the bases pretty well for someone who might possibly get shifted down to second base. He plays hard, puts on a show at BP and generally throws out a stat line that entices one to scout. The last of these didn't quite work out in 2019, though even this can be explained away by emphasizing his hot start and solid AFL performance, and noting the broken hamate that ruined the span in between. This comment may seem like damning with faint praise, but it really isn't: Isbel is the kind of prospect you enjoy watching as he tries to put it together. He's also the kind who often magically transforms, five years later, into a forgettable fourth outfielder, the way we all wake up one morning to find we look like our parents.

Khalil Lee OF   Born: 06/26/98   Age: 22   Bats: L   Throws: L   Height: 5'10"   Weight: 170   Origin: Round 3, 2016 Draft (#103 overall)

YEAR	TEAM	LVL	AGE	PA	R	2B	3B	HR	RBI	BB	K	SB	CS	AVG/OBP/SLG	DRC+	VORP	BABIP	BRR	FRAA	WARP
2017	LEX	A	19	532	71	24	6	17	61	65	171	20	18	.237/.344/.430	109	19.6	.338	-2.2	CF(67): -6.2, RF(52): 4.3	1.5
2018	WIL	A+	20	301	42	13	4	4	41	48	75	14	3	.270/.402/.406	142	26.4	.371	2.2	CF(57): 3.8, RF(9): 0.3	2.8
2018	NWA	AA	20	118	15	5	0	2	10	11	28	2	2	.245/.330/.353	81	1.2	.319	0.6	CF(17): 0.3, LF(9): 0.7	0.3
2019	NWA	AA	21	546	74	21	3	8	51	65	154	53	12	.264/.363/.372	117	26.4	.374	3.7	RF(54): -6.0, CF(45): -5.7	1.2
2020	KCA	MLB	22	251	23	11	1	4	23	24	86	5	3	.220/.307/.336	73	-0.5	.340	0.2	CF -3, RF -1	-0.4

Comparables: Clint Frazier, Byron Buxton, Jaff Decker

The phrase "Swiss Army Knife" might be the worst cliche when it comes to prospect writing, but Lee might also be the best example of them—because in reality, they only really work when you only have one or two tools out at a time. Every new season, seemingly every new look, the talented and amorphous outfielder looks like something different: one day demonstrating raw power, the next hitting everything on the ground, then looking awkward and sluggish in center, then carving up the basepaths. It's a little frustrating from a scouting perspective, but there are two important takeaways. One, regardless of which Lee shows up on a given team, they all average out to be pretty good, and two, there's always the chance that he figures out how to do everything at once. Even if he doesn't, and the 2019 version of Lee is actually his final form, it's one worth getting excited about.

Nicky Lopez **MI**   Born: 03/13/95   Age: 25   Bats: L   Throws: R   Height: 5'11"   Weight: 175   Origin: Round 5, 2016 Draft (#163 overall)

YEAR	TEAM	LVL	AGE	PA	R	2B	3B	HR	RBI	BB	K	SB	CS	AVG/OBP/SLG	DRC+	VORP	BABIP	BRR	FRAA	WARP
2017	WIL	A+	22	324	42	12	7	2	27	36	23	14	8	.295/.376/.407	127	25.3	.315	0.8	SS(66): 4.4	2.8
2017	NWA	AA	22	253	26	6	1	0	11	16	29	7	4	.259/.312/.293	70	5.2	.296	2.2	SS(33): -2.9, 2B(25): 2.5	0.4
2018	NWA	AA	23	325	42	8	5	2	27	33	23	9	4	.331/.397/.416	123	25.9	.351	2.8	SS(58): -4.8, 2B(14): 0.4	1.9
2018	OMA	AAA	23	256	33	6	2	7	26	27	29	6	2	.278/.364/.417	119	19.5	.294	0.0	SS(36): -1.0, 2B(18): 1.7	1.7
2019	OMA	AAA	24	138	27	6	1	3	13	20	5	9	3	.353/.457/.500	140	15.1	.352	-1.3	SS(17): 3.5, 2B(14): 1.0	1.5
2019	KCA	MLB	24	402	44	22	2	2	30	18	51	1	1	.240/.276/.325	61	-5.4	.273	2.5	2B(76): 1.3, SS(33): 1.2	0.0
2020	KCA	MLB	25	595	53	31	3	6	53	42	75	12	5	.258/.316/.360	75	6.5	.290	2.1	2B 7, SS 0	1.4

Comparables: Dustin Pedroia, Mike Richardt, Lenny Harris

Fans love prospects like Lopez, but in 2019 he proved, in the best and worst possible ways, why the David Fletcher role is such a difficult act to pull off. It's not about being good at one thing; you have to be good at so many things. Lopez was able to put up quality numbers in the minors in no small part thanks to his excellent batting eye. But there's a problem: major league pitchers knew they could force-feed strikes (Lopez led the league in pitches seen in the zone). Lopez had a solution: he'd just hit everything in the zone, ranking eighth in contact rate. But there's a problem: when he did put the bat on the ball, he had one of the worst exit velocities in the league. Lopez had a solution: he put everything on the ground, ranking second in baseball, and tried to run everything out. But there's a problem: he just wasn't fast enough to beat those grounders out, hitting .246 on them, 10 points above the league average. There's just always another roadblock, and while there's plenty of reason for optimism (especially in terms of defense), it just goes to show you what rare little diamonds the Fletchers and Ecksteins are: the league-average hitters who can't really hit. Treasure them, and root for Lopez to join them.

Seuly Matias **RF**   Born: 09/04/98   Age: 21   Bats: R   Throws: R   Height: 6'3"   Weight: 198   Origin: International Free Agent, 2015

YEAR	TEAM	LVL	AGE	PA	R	2B	3B	HR	RBI	BB	K	SB	CS	AVG/OBP/SLG	DRC+	VORP	BABIP	BRR	FRAA	WARP
2017	BNC	RK	18	246	27	13	3	7	36	16	72	2	1	.243/.297/.423	84	7.4	.318	0.7	RF(52): 9.0	1.0
2018	LEX	A	19	376	62	13	1	31	63	24	131	6	0	.231/.303/.550	97	18.8	.264	0.7	RF(75): -2.1	0.4
2019	WIL	A+	20	221	23	10	4	4	22	25	98	2	4	.148/.259/.307	48	-4.5	.270	-0.6	RF(51): 5.6	-0.2
2020	KCA	MLB	21	251	17	11	1	3	19	17	117	0	0	.156/.223/.258	28	-15.7	.295	-0.3	RF 1	-1.5

Comparables: Miguel Sanó, Lewis Brinson, Tyler O'Neill

As bad as it looks, it was even worse. Matias hit four home runs in three games between April 13-15; from then on he shambled through a .118/.229/.203 slash line, trying to play through a broken hand that ultimately ended his season in mid-June. If there's any positive to spin here, it's that the excruciating pain of swinging the bat may have forced Matias to watch more pitches; for all the infinite Joey Gallo comps that have been made since his debut, he's never shown the selectivity of so many of his all-or-nothing colleagues. But even that's probably reading too much. The more prudent takeaway would be to dismiss the whole debacle as a lost year, and wait and see if the homers migrate back in the spring. And remember: always feel like you can tell people when you're hurting, whether it's your heart or your metacarpal.

Brady McConnell **SS**   Born: 05/24/98   Age: 22   Bats: R   Throws: R   Height: 6'3"   Weight: 195   Origin: Round 2, 2019 Draft (#44 overall)

YEAR	TEAM	LVL	AGE	PA	R	2B	3B	HR	RBI	BB	K	SB	CS	AVG/OBP/SLG	DRC+	VORP	BABIP	BRR	FRAA	WARP
2019	IDA	RK+	21	169	25	12	1	4	22	14	66	5	3	.211/.286/.382	58	0.2	.341	0.5		0.0
2020	KCA	MLB	22	251	18	12	1	4	20	15	114	2	1	.176/.230/.278	35	-13.2	.322	0.0		-1.4

Comparables: Brandon Hicks, Steve Tolleson, Jerry Sands

McConnell swings the bat the way one tries to kill a spider: a sharp, short slap followed by an almost instant recoil. The generically beautiful swings are languid, smooth, effortless, but there's something equally pleasing about his stapler gun trigger at the plate. Considered to be a first rounder out of high school, McConnell honored his commitment to Florida, suffered nerve damage in his hand, then rebounded in his senior year to become the Royals' second-round pick. He'll probably move off short before long, given that the team's best position player and best prospect stand in his way, which will make it vital that he unearth some plate discipline on one of those bus trips through the heartland.

MJ Melendez **C**   Born: 11/29/98   Age: 21   Bats: L   Throws: R   Height: 6'1"   Weight: 185   Origin: Round 2, 2017 Draft (#52 overall)

YEAR	TEAM	LVL	AGE	PA	R	2B	3B	HR	RBI	BB	K	SB	CS	AVG/OBP/SLG	DRC+	VORP	BABIP	BRR	FRAA	WARP
2017	ROY	RK	18	198	25	8	3	4	30	26	60	4	2	.262/.374/.417	113	11.7	.385	0.1	C(30): 0.5	1.0
2018	LEX	A	19	472	52	26	9	19	73	43	143	4	6	.251/.322/.492	103	24.5	.327	-1.7	C(73): 1.4	1.7
2019	WIL	A+	20	419	34	23	2	9	54	44	165	7	5	.163/.260/.311	51	-2.7	.259	-0.9	C(71): 2.4	-0.4
2020	KCA	MLB	21	251	20	12	1	6	24	19	107	0	0	.175/.244/.312	46	-9.8	.298	-0.3	C 0	-1.0

Comparables: Austin Riley, Bobby Bradley, Lewis Brinson

It's been 18 years since a first- or second-round high school catcher panned out, in Brian McCann. (J.T. Realmuto was a third-rounder.) Melendez is targeted for an ETA of 2022, so by then it might be 20 years. Unlike many young backstops, assigned to the dish because of their general shape more than their fancy catching, the 20-year-old was comparatively lithe by the standards of his age. He's filled out in the intervening time, however, and FRAA so far rates him a talent, if hardly a prodigy. (Admittedly, there are limitations to all catching defensive metrics, especially on the minor-league side.) Meanwhile, his tendency to sell out for power in the batter's box appears to have suffered from a dip in the conversion rate. It's probably not as bad as it looks; Wilmington might be one of the toughest hitter's parks in the country, and he's only just now old enough to drink. Still, there's a lot of Zunino in the profile, and as underwhelming as that might sound to certain fanbases, a Zunino career would be a pretty fortunate outcome.

Whit Merrifield 2B   Born: 01/24/89   Age: 31   Bats: R   Throws: R   Height: 6'0"   Weight: 195   Origin: Round 9, 2010 Draft (#269 overall)

YEAR	TEAM	LVL	AGE	PA	R	2B	3B	HR	RBI	BB	K	SB	CS	AVG/OBP/SLG	DRC+	VORP	BABIP	BRR	FRAA	WARP
2017	OMA	AAA	28	37	6	4	0	3	9	1	4	1	1	.412/.432/.794	169	5.5	.393	-1.3	2B(6): 0.3, RF(1): -0.1	0.3
2017	KCA	MLB	28	630	80	32	6	19	78	29	88	34	8	.288/.324/.460	113	27.2	.308	1.7	2B(132): -0.2, RF(10): -1.9	2.9
2018	KCA	MLB	29	707	88	43	3	12	60	61	114	45	10	.304/.367/.438	119	38.3	.352	3.5	2B(108): 2.3, RF(30): 1.4	4.4
2019	KCA	MLB	30	735	105	41	10	16	74	45	126	20	10	.302/.348/.463	110	30.8	.350	-1.9	2B(82): 6.2, RF(61): -6.4	3.0
2020	KCA	MLB	31	595	62	31	5	12	63	38	104	28	8	.279/.329/.418	95	17.9	.326	0.1	CF 7, 2B 1	2.6

Comparables: Adam Kennedy, Orlando Hudson, Howie Kendrick

Here's one of those situations where the numbers actually *don't* tell the whole story, or at least, they tell only the actual story. Merrifield was not a three-win player last year, despite the fact that he produced three wins in value; he was a four-win player forced to play like a three-win player. Stocked with young infield talent and cursed with Jorge Soler in right, the Royals moved Whit out there for most of the summer, where he could charitably be described as doing his best. He's a fine second baseman, and he will be again next year for whichever team trades for him; everything about his offense is as consistent as it is exemplary, given that no one in the game is better at hitting line drives. And for concerned fantasy owners: sure, he's thirty and it makes sense for him to slow down, but the invisible eyes that lace each stadium still think he's one of the faster runners in the game, so factor that into all the other ways that Merrifield remains underrated going into 2020.

Adalberto Mondesi SS   Born: 07/27/95   Age: 24   Bats: B   Throws: R   Height: 6'1"   Weight: 190   Origin: International Free Agent, 2011

YEAR	TEAM	LVL	AGE	PA	R	2B	3B	HR	RBI	BB	K	SB	CS	AVG/OBP/SLG	DRC+	VORP	BABIP	BRR	FRAA	WARP
2017	OMA	AAA	21	357	52	20	8	13	52	18	86	21	3	.305/.340/.539	107	30.5	.373	1.3	SS(71): 2.2, 2B(10): 0.1	2.2
2017	KCA	MLB	21	60	4	1	0	1	3	3	22	5	2	.170/.214/.245	50	-5.8	.267	-1.4	2B(14): 0.1, SS(9): 0.1	-0.3
2018	OMA	AAA	22	133	19	8	3	5	21	8	30	10	0	.250/.295/.492	75	7.6	.291	1.2	SS(18): 0.6, 2B(6): 0.8	0.4
2018	KCA	MLB	22	291	47	13	3	14	37	11	77	32	7	.276/.306/.498	104	18.4	.335	0.3	SS(61): 1.2, 2B(12): 0.9	1.6
2019	OMA	AAA	23	37	5	1	1	1	3	4	13	2	1	.242/.324/.424	67	1.0	.368	0.5	SS(6): 0.1	0.0
2019	KCA	MLB	23	443	58	20	10	9	62	19	132	43	7	.263/.291/.424	75	7.0	.357	3.1	SS(100): 6.3	1.6
2020	KCA	MLB	24	525	53	23	7	15	59	25	160	32	7	.242/.281/.407	74	2.0	.326	-0.2	SS 6	0.8

Comparables: Rougned Odor, Ted Lepcio, Javier Báez

As BP author Zach Crizer pointed out, 2019 PECOTA projected Mondesi to hit 15+ home runs, steal 40+ bases and post an OBP below .300, something that no baseball player had ever done before. They still haven't, but only because Mondesi lost time to a groin pull and two shoulder injuries, the second of which has a chance to push back his 2020 debut past Opening Day. It's a credit to the game of baseball and its core design, that despite the flaws and the misfortune Mondesi was still a very good baseball player despite being very bad at certain parts of it. Certainly, the team has to hope that it can introduce some level of restraint in his offensive game—among players with 300 plate appearances, only Jorge Alfaro whiffed more often than Mondesi—his speed, defense and raw power make him a special player, albeit not a perfect one.

Ryan O'Hearn 1B   Born: 07/26/93   Age: 26   Bats: L   Throws: L   Height: 6'3"   Weight: 200   Origin: Round 8, 2014 Draft (#243 overall)

YEAR	TEAM	LVL	AGE	PA	R	2B	3B	HR	RBI	BB	K	SB	CS	AVG/OBP/SLG	DRC+	VORP	BABIP	BRR	FRAA	WARP
2017	NWA	AA	23	76	7	1	1	4	11	10	20	0	0	.258/.355/.485	128	3.3	.310	0.1	1B(8): 0.3, LF(5): -0.6	0.3
2017	OMA	AAA	23	463	48	26	1	18	53	45	119	1	0	.252/.325/.450	95	4.9	.309	-2.5	1B(75): -1.2, RF(5): -0.2	0.0
2018	OMA	AAA	24	406	47	21	1	11	52	45	97	2	0	.232/.322/.391	91	6.0	.286	3.9	1B(69): -6.3, LF(13): -2.1	-0.2
2018	KCA	MLB	24	170	23	10	2	12	30	20	45	0	0	.262/.353/.597	130	8.9	.293	-3.6	1B(31): 0.4, LF(1): -0.1	0.5
2019	OMA	AAA	25	149	20	10	1	9	28	17	31	0	0	.295/.383/.597	130	12.8	.322	0.5	1B(25): 0.0	0.8
2019	KCA	MLB	25	370	32	13	1	14	38	39	99	0	1	.195/.281/.369	80	-3.9	.230	-1.0	1B(94): -5.0, LF(2): -0.1	-1.0
2020	KCA	MLB	26	490	54	23	1	19	62	48	134	1	0	.221/.301/.412	83	-4.0	.271	-2.4	1B -4	-0.8

Comparables: Brandon Allen, Greg Bird, Nick Evans

More contact isn't always better contact. It's rare to see a player add five percent to their contact rate and struggle mightily, but O'Hearn was never able to recapture the unexpected brilliance of his 2018 autumn, leading to a midsummer exile. He took out his frustrations on Triple-A pitchers but also left them there, improving only slightly on his return. His downfall was a sudden inability to lay off pitches out of the zone, something he'd done well to avoid the prior year. Instead of striking out on bad pitches, however, he actually got the bat on them, which was even worse. The result was a spike in ground balls, many of them into the teeth of the shift, eroding his power and, with it, his offensive value. If he'd just missed those pitches, he could have at least fought back in some of those counts. If he wants to stick around, O'Hearn will need to learn to take those bad pitches, or miss them, or figure out a way to hit them in the air. Any of those would be an improvement.

Salvador Perez C   Born: 05/10/90   Age: 30   Bats: R   Throws: R   Height: 6'4"   Weight: 240   Origin: International Free Agent, 2006

YEAR	TEAM	LVL	AGE	PA	R	2B	3B	HR	RBI	BB	K	SB	CS	AVG/OBP/SLG	DRC+	VORP	BABIP	BRR	FRAA	WARP
2017	KCA	MLB	27	499	57	24	1	27	80	17	95	1	0	.268/.297/.495	112	19.7	.280	-1.3	C(115): -10.2	1.9
2018	KCA	MLB	28	544	52	23	0	27	80	17	108	1	1	.235/.274/.439	104	9.1	.245	-3.7	C(96): -8.1, 1B(3): 0.0	1.3
2020	KCA	MLB	30	525	59	25	1	25	74	20	109	1	0	.245/.283/.449	92	14.0	.267	-1.9	C -7, 1B 0	0.7

Comparables: Terry Kennedy, Wilson Ramos, Joe Oliver

There are things we're supposed to be able to count on. Perez was given a day to recover from elbow soreness at the beginning of training camp in 2019, and then was given several hundred more after an MRI revealed damage to his ulnar collateral ligament. Expectations are that he'll enter 2020 with fewer limitations and return to catching duties eventually, a relief for everyone in Kansas City who had to watch his understudies. (He will likely see

YEAR	TEAM	P. COUNT	FRM RUNS	BLK RUNS	THRW RUNS	TOT RUNS
2017	KCA	15629	-10.0	1.5	0.1	-8.4
2018	KCA	14052	-9.9	-0.6	0.8	-9.5
2020	KCA	22129	-9.0	0.4	1.2	-7.4

time at first base and designated hitter, for some reason, while fully recovering.) When healthy, Perez is one of the most consistent performers in baseball, and it should be noted that for all the sabermetric shade cast upon him during the Royals' glory days, DRC+ appreciates his bat-to-ball and ball-beyond-fence skills more than other offensive metrics.

Blake Perkins CF Born: 09/10/96 Age: 23 Bats: B Throws: R Height: 5'11" Weight: 181 Origin: Round 2, 2015 Draft (#69 overall)

YEAR	TEAM	LVL	AGE	PA	R	2B	3B	HR	RBI	BB	K	SB	CS	AVG/OBP/SLG	DRC+	VORP	BABIP	BRR	FRAA	WARP
2017	HAG	A	20	572	105	27	4	8	48	72	118	31	8	.255/.354/.378	119	34.8	.318	7.4	CF(118): 8.4, LF(10): 0.9	4.7
2018	POT	A+	21	305	39	11	0	1	21	42	67	12	5	.234/.344/.290	100	7.9	.307	2.7	CF(62): -6.6, LF(1): 0.1	0.6
2018	WIL	A+	21	291	48	11	1	2	18	50	67	17	4	.240/.381/.322	101	11.3	.329	0.4	CF(61): 11.9, LF(1): -0.1	2.2
2019	WIL	A+	22	352	43	11	4	6	22	52	79	18	7	.226/.345/.354	104	16.6	.286	0.2	CF(48): 4.1, RF(27): -3.7	1.1
2019	NWA	AA	22	122	10	2	2	2	12	9	30	4	1	.218/.287/.327	62	-0.2	.278	-0.2	LF(15): -0.6, CF(12): 2.0	0.2
2020	KCA	MLB	23	251	20	11	1	4	21	19	71	4	2	.200/.265/.303	53	-7.3	.272	0.1	CF 3, RF 0	-0.5

Comparables: Aaron Hicks, Tommy Pham, Shawn O'Malley

The good news is that Perkins got his slugging percentage above his on-base percentage; the bad news is how. Double-A pitchers challenged the athletic center fielder with pitches in the zone, and suddenly his patience was no longer the carrying offensive tool it used to be. Sometimes, a low-effort swing just creates low-effort exit velocity. The hope was that a late conversion to switch hitting would offer just enough value to warrant the ninth spot in the order, or at least an inning or two of strong defensive replacement. Alas, unless baseball goes the football route and demands full specialization between offense and defense, Perkins' shot at the majors is looking grim.

Brett Phillips OF Born: 05/30/94 Age: 26 Bats: L Throws: R Height: 6'0" Weight: 185 Origin: Round 6, 2012 Draft (#189 overall)

YEAR	TEAM	LVL	AGE	PA	R	2B	3B	HR	RBI	BB	K	SB	CS	AVG/OBP/SLG	DRC+	VORP	BABIP	BRR	FRAA	WARP
2017	CSP	AAA	23	432	79	23	10	19	78	45	129	9	1	.305/.377/.567	125	30.9	.412	2.1	RF(52): -3.2, CF(49): 3.9	2.9
2017	MIL	MLB	23	98	9	3	0	4	12	9	34	5	0	.276/.351/.448	90	6.5	.408	0.3	CF(26): 4.8, RF(9): -0.3	0.7
2018	CSP	AAA	24	299	42	12	7	6	25	36	94	11	0	.240/.331/.411	77	10.7	.346	1.1	RF(34): 2.9, CF(20): -1.8	0.2
2018	MIL	MLB	24	24	2	0	1	0	4	2	11	0	0	.182/.250/.273	43	-1.0	.364	0.0	RF(7): -0.6, CF(5): 0.5	-0.1
2018	KCA	MLB	24	123	13	4	2	2	7	9	50	1	1	.188/.252/.313	46	-1.8	.311	0.3	CF(23): 4.4, RF(9): 0.3	0.1
2019	OMA	AAA	25	414	75	8	13	18	54	72	118	22	1	.240/.378/.505	108	28.8	.312	3.0	RF(63): 9.4, CF(32): -1.1	2.5
2019	KCA	MLB	25	79	7	2	0	2	6	10	23	3	0	.138/.247/.262	77	0.5	.167	1.2	CF(23): 1.0, RF(3): 2.0	0.5
2020	KCA	MLB	26	455	48	19	6	12	50	53	151	9	3	.219/.316/.389	85	6.0	.318	0.9	LF 2, CF 3	1.1

Comparables: Teoscar Hernández, Byron Buxton, Lewis Brinson

The novelty of the two-way player is, admittedly, starting to wear off. It's really just the newest form of the same old lazy swipe at reinvention: move to a new town, quit your job and try acting, change up your batting stance, join the Peace Corps, take pottery classes, learn a new pitch. It's clearly a mark of desperation when your friends try it, but you look at Phillips and…well, he's already hitting like a pitcher anyway, right? And he has that arm. And he could swap out into the outfield if a lefty came up between righties! What other choice is there? Sure, the Royals could just give him time in center field and see if he develops, but if learning just came from making mistakes, Phillips would have already been improving forty percent of the time.

Nick Pratto 1B Born: 10/06/98 Age: 21 Bats: L Throws: L Height: 6'1" Weight: 195 Origin: Round 1, 2017 Draft (#14 overall)

YEAR	TEAM	LVL	AGE	PA	R	2B	3B	HR	RBI	BB	K	SB	CS	AVG/OBP/SLG	DRC+	VORP	BABIP	BRR	FRAA	WARP
2017	ROY	RK	18	230	25	15	3	4	34	24	58	10	4	.247/.330/.414	108	5.0	.319	-0.8	1B(51): 5.2	0.8
2018	LEX	A	19	537	79	33	2	14	62	45	150	22	5	.280/.343/.443	111	14.4	.375	1.4	1B(125): -0.6	1.3
2019	WIL	A+	20	472	48	21	1	9	46	49	164	17	7	.191/.278/.310	64	-7.1	.286	0.5	1B(122): 5.2	-0.5
2020	KCA	MLB	21	251	21	13	1	5	24	18	98	4	1	.199/.259/.329	54	-6.7	.317	0.2	1B 2	-0.5

Comparables: Trevor Story, Cody Bellinger, Willy García

Everyone wants answers. You bought a book on the pretense that it would explain, in part, why Kansas City's best hitting prospect collapsed so badly last season. The Royals' organization would like to know why. Pratto himself would love to know more than anyone. And yet, sometimes there are no answers: There are no clues here, no brush strokes in the painting, no tea leaves, no magic eye puzzle. Pratto slumped early in the season, then slumped through the middle and ended on a slump. He lost his ability to hit for power and his ability to make contact. He probably got worse at Pop-A-Shot, too. In one interview he blamed the length of the grass for slowing down his hard-hit ground balls, and not the fact that he was hitting lots of ground balls. But what else could he say? This is how it is. Sometimes you work hard at something, and you do exactly what you're supposed to do and nothing happens. If you're really unlucky, they calculate the results to the third decimal point.

Jorge Soler RF Born: 02/25/92 Age: 28 Bats: R Throws: R Height: 6'4" Weight: 230 Origin: International Free Agent, 2012

YEAR	TEAM	LVL	AGE	PA	R	2B	3B	HR	RBI	BB	K	SB	CS	AVG/OBP/SLG	DRC+	VORP	BABIP	BRR	FRAA	WARP
2017	OMA	AAA	25	327	49	9	0	24	59	50	82	1	0	.267/.388/.564	140	24.9	.293	-2.0	RF(39): -0.4, LF(23): 3.0	2.4
2017	KCA	MLB	25	110	7	5	0	2	6	12	36	0	0	.144/.245/.258	64	-8.6	.203	-0.3	RF(15): -1.6, LF(7): 0.8	-0.4
2018	KCA	MLB	26	257	27	18	0	9	28	28	69	3	1	.265/.354/.466	101	11.6	.340	-0.5	RF(52): -1.0	0.4
2019	KCA	MLB	27	679	95	33	1	48	117	73	178	3	1	.265/.354/.569	142	49.5	.294	-4.3	RF(56): 0.4	4.5
2020	KCA	MLB	28	595	81	27	1	33	92	66	159	3	1	.249/.340/.493	122	21.9	.293	-2.3	RF 0	2.2

Comparables: Jay Bruce, Wil Myers, Yasiel Puig

Calendars are wonderful things. Not just because they allow us to time our harvests and arrange our business meetings, but because they carve up the endless parade of afternoons into something digestible, relatable, easy to celebrate. Soler's career has been checkered by hamstring injuries and expectations, but for one calendar year, one brief six-month moment, he stood among the best in baseball and was everything Jorge Soler could be all at once. If Mike Moustakas overcame the Curse of Balboni in 2017 with the aid of the rabbit ball, Soler erased it from history, clubbing baseballs deep into the bleachers seemingly every other night. He may never be quite this again—he almost certainly won't start 162 games again, a number almost as unthinkable as the 48—though the gradual transition toward full-time DH is a wise choice for both safety and value. But regardless, for a franchise as deep in winter as the Royals, fans will have the fortune of remembering Soler when they think of 2019, and not a faceless reliever warming up in the fourth.

Bubba Starling CF Born: 08/03/92 Age: 27 Bats: R Throws: R Height: 6'4" Weight: 215 Origin: Round 1, 2011 Draft (#5 overall)

YEAR	TEAM	LVL	AGE	PA	R	2B	3B	HR	RBI	BB	K	SB	CS	AVG/OBP/SLG	DRC+	VORP	BABIP	BRR	FRAA	WARP
2017	OMA	AAA	24	303	35	14	1	7	21	19	65	5	4	.248/.303/.381	81	1.3	.301	-2.2	RF(40): 7.7, CF(37): 3.4	1.0
2018	OMA	AAA	25	41	5	2	0	0	2	5	6	1	0	.257/.350/.314	88	0.8	.310	-0.2	CF(10): -0.7, RF(1): -0.1	0.0
2019	OMA	AAA	26	285	34	11	2	7	38	21	59	9	3	.310/.358/.448	101	14.2	.374	0.0	CF(51): 3.1, RF(18): 2.2	1.4
2019	KCA	MLB	26	197	26	7	0	4	12	9	56	2	0	.215/.255/.317	63	-3.1	.286	3.8	CF(36): 5.8, RF(23): -0.4	0.5
2020	KCA	MLB	27	455	40	17	1	10	43	27	131	6	3	.217/.271/.332	59	-10.8	.291	0.0	LF -4, CF 1	-1.3

Comparables: Jake Marisnick, Slade Heathcott, Daniel Fields

The hero's journey is meant to be about an everyman who receives the call, overcomes obstacles and tragedy, and returns home a superman. Starling started his path as the superhero and came out the other side an ordinary man. After years of setbacks and struggles, the former fifth-overall pick finally made the majors, and the outcome was anything but storybook. His athleticism never translated at the plate, either in contact or power, and now he's a spare outfielder, a minor barrier between some other young man and glory. That's just how it is: Not every boy thrown to the wolves becomes a hero. Most of them just become wolves.

Meibrys Viloria C Born: 02/15/97 Age: 23 Bats: L Throws: R Height: 5'11" Weight: 220 Origin: International Free Agent, 2013

YEAR	TEAM	LVL	AGE	PA	R	2B	3B	HR	RBI	BB	K	SB	CS	AVG/OBP/SLG	DRC+	VORP	BABIP	BRR	FRAA	WARP
2017	LEX	A	20	398	42	25	0	8	52	25	79	4	3	.259/.313/.394	104	8.2	.310	-0.4	C(92): -0.4	1.8
2018	WIL	A+	21	407	34	16	1	6	44	40	75	2	1	.260/.342/.360	107	11.0	.313	-2.8	C(88): 2.8	2.1
2018	KCA	MLB	21	29	4	2	0	0	4	1	9	0	0	.259/.286/.333	74	0.2	.389	0.1	C(10): -1.0	0.0
2019	NWA	AA	22	248	21	12	0	1	24	24	60	2	0	.264/.344/.332	97	9.2	.358	0.9	C(58): -6.3	0.5
2019	KCA	MLB	22	148	7	7	0	1	15	10	44	0	1	.211/.259/.286	59	-0.1	.293	-0.5	C(41): -3.6	-0.4
2020	KCA	MLB	23	105	9	5	0	1	9	8	30	0	0	.226/.288/.318	58	-1.1	.311	-0.2	C -2	-0.3

Comparables: Tony Wolters, Abiatal Avelino, Raimel Tapia

Exhibit A for the argument that baseball games are actually detrimental to rebuilding franchises, Viloria was once again thrust into major-league playing time thanks to a rash of catching injuries in the organization, this time forced to devote a quarter of his season to getting battered around by pitchers he had no business facing. It's frustrating because Viloria could really use the development time: he has a strong arm and rapport with his pitchers, but his framing desperately needs work and he relies on the always-capricious hit tool to provide offensive value. For most players, being in the majors is the short- and long-term goal; in Viloria's case, he and the Royals would both be better off if we didn't hear from him, at least for a little while.

YEAR	TEAM	P. COUNT	FRM RUNS	BLK RUNS	THRW RUNS	TOT RUNS
2018	KCA	1167	0.0	-0.8	0.0	-0.1
2019	KCA	5921	-4.0	0.0	0.3	-3.2
2019	NWA	8242	-7.7	0.0	0.3	-7.7
2020	KCA	4022	-1.4	-0.4	0.3	-1.5

★ ★ ★ *2020 Top 101 Prospect* **#29** ★ ★ ★

Bobby Witt Jr. SS Born: 06/14/00 Age: 20 Bats: R Throws: R Height: 6'1" Weight: 190 Origin: Round 1, 2019 Draft (#2 overall)

YEAR	TEAM	LVL	AGE	PA	R	2B	3B	HR	RBI	BB	K	SB	CS	AVG/OBP/SLG	DRC+	VORP	BABIP	BRR	FRAA	WARP
2019	ROY	RK	19	180	30	2	5	1	27	13	35	9	1	.262/.317/.354	94	4.2	.323	-0.1	SS(26): 3.3	0.8
2020	KCA	MLB	20	251	19	10	1	3	20	16	72	2	1	.216/.270/.305	56	-6.3	.302	0.0	SS 1	-0.5

Comparables: Humberto Arteaga, Niko Goodrum, Leury García

Sometimes in the draft there's isn't a clear No. 1 draft pick; this year, there wasn't only one, but a clear number two as well. The son of 16-year veteran Bobby Witt, Witt the Younger's scouting profile begins with athleticism: He has the frame of a guy who's not quite too big to play shortstop, and he makes plays and throws with the elan of George Clooney playing Danny Ocean. Some scouts do worry that the contact skills will limit his total power, and that he'll never hit enough to be a true star; he does use the opposite field, but he was inconsistent during his showcase last summer. Still, given the legs and arm and glove, the floor appears to be solid regular, and that's some good floor.

PITCHERS

Chance Adams RHP Born: 08/10/94 Age: 25 Bats: R Throws: R Height: 6'1" Weight: 225 Origin: Round 5, 2015 Draft (#153 overall)

YEAR	TEAM	LVL	AGE	W	L	SV	G	GS	IP	H	HR	BB/9	K/9	K	GB%	BABIP	WHIP	ERA	DRA	WARP	MPH	FB%	WHF	CSP
2017	TRN	AA	22	4	0	0	6	6	35	23	2	3.9	8.2	32	43%	.228	1.09	1.03	2.84	1.0				
2017	SWB	AAA	22	11	5	0	21	21	115¹	81	9	3.4	8.0	103	42%	.236	1.08	2.89	2.90	3.5				
2018	SWB	AAA	23	4	5	0	27	23	113	101	16	4.6	9.0	113	42%	.282	1.41	4.78	4.86	0.9				
2018	NYA	MLB	23	0	1	0	3	1	7²	8	3	4.7	4.7	4	38%	.217	1.57	7.04	7.07	-0.2	94.4	66.7	5.2	41.6
2019	SWB	AAA	24	4	4	1	18	15	81²	77	11	4.2	8.8	80	37%	.291	1.41	4.63	4.19	2.0				
2019	NYA	MLB	24	1	1	1	13	0	25¹	39	7	3.9	8.2	23	31%	.395	1.97	8.53	8.77	-0.9	93.6	58.8	8.3	43.5
2020	KCA	MLB	25	2	2	0	33	0	35	39	7	4.0	6.1	24	35%	.293	1.57	5.98	5.89	-0.3	93.5	61.7	7.9	43.7

Comparables: Jake Faria, Stephen Gonsalves, Anthony Banda

Once upon a time, Adams was a promising prospect. That time has long since passed, and Adams has just about run out of chances. A spot in the starting rotation was his for the taking and he let it slip through his hands as his diminished velocity and a propensity for allowing fly balls made for uncomfortable bedfellows. With a new batch of hard-throwing minor leaguers ready to pitch him into oblivion, Adams has become little more than necessary depth for the Yankees. A change of scenery might be just what he needs, as sometimes goodbye is a second chance.

Scott Barlow RHP   Born: 12/18/92   Age: 27   Bats: R   Throws: R   Height: 6'3"   Weight: 215   Origin: Round 6, 2011 Draft (#194 overall)

YEAR	TEAM	LVL	AGE	W	L	SV	G	GS	IP	H	HR	BB/9	K/9	K	GB%	BABIP	WHIP	ERA	DRA	WARP	MPH	FB%	WHF	CSP
2017	TUL	AA	24	6	3	0	19	19	107¹	60	9	3.1	10.4	124	45%	.211	0.90	2.10	2.57	3.3				
2017	OKL	AAA	24	1	3	0	7	7	32¹	37	6	6.4	10.0	36	37%	.333	1.86	7.24	5.39	0.1				
2018	OMA	AAA	25	1	4	1	13	10	45²	54	9	4.1	9.9	50	38%	.357	1.64	6.11	5.78	-0.1				
2018	KCA	MLB	25	1	1	0	6	0	15	16	2	1.8	9.0	15	40%	.311	1.27	3.60	3.69	0.2	93.6	53	11.9	50.8
2019	OMA	AAA	26	0	0	1	3	0	6	3	0	4.5	7.5	5	21%	.214	1.00	0.00	4.01	0.1				
2019	KCA	MLB	26	3	3	1	61	0	70¹	64	6	4.7	11.8	92	41%	.337	1.44	4.22	4.20	0.9	96.6	43.5	15.7	44.4
2020	KCA	MLB	27	3	3	3	60	0	63	54	7	4.1	11.4	80	41%	.307	1.31	3.85	3.84	0.9	95.7	45.2	15.4	47.8

Comparables: Chris Ellis, Paul Clemens, Adrian Houser

Between May 25 and a short demotion at the end of June, Barlow gave up 20 earned runs in 14 innings. Basic arithmetic will provide you with how the rest of the season went. The former minor league free agent found extra life on all his pitches in 2019, wearing down only slightly in June and September despite a heavy workload. At this point, he's the best reliever on the Royals not making eight figures, and the only issues keeping him from closer-in-waiting status are flickering command and some struggles against lefties with the slider. He'll probably be first in line to close anyway, once Ian Kennedy gets shipped off or becomes Ian Kennedy again.

Jacob Barnes RHP   Born: 04/14/90   Age: 30   Bats: R   Throws: R   Height: 6'2"   Weight: 220   Origin: Round 14, 2011 Draft (#431 overall)

YEAR	TEAM	LVL	AGE	W	L	SV	G	GS	IP	H	HR	BB/9	K/9	K	GB%	BABIP	WHIP	ERA	DRA	WARP	MPH	FB%	WHF	CSP
2017	MIL	MLB	27	3	4	2	73	0	72	57	8	4.1	10.0	80	54%	.272	1.25	4.00	3.67	1.2	99.3	54.2	16.5	41.8
2018	CSP	AAA	28	1	0	2	11	0	11²	5	0	6.2	7.7	10	64%	.161	1.11	1.54	2.83	0.3				
2018	MIL	MLB	28	0	1	2	49	0	48²	51	4	4.3	8.7	47	51%	.329	1.52	3.33	3.54	0.8	98.0	50.5	14.6	44.6
2019	SAN	AAA	29	2	0	1	14	0	14	14	3	1.3	9.6	15	52%	.282	1.14	4.50	2.95	0.4				
2019	KCA	MLB	29	0	4	0	15	0	13	14	4	7.6	6.9	10	50%	.250	1.92	8.31	7.18	-0.3	96.2	50.4	9.7	41
2019	MIL	MLB	29	1	1	0	18	1	19²	22	3	5.0	10.1	22	47%	.322	1.68	6.86	5.54	0.0	95.9	46.4	9.4	41.9
2020	KCA	MLB	30	2	2	0	33	0	35	31	5	3.9	9.3	36	48%	.286	1.33	4.13	4.18	0.4	97.1	50.9	13.6	42.5

Comparables: Josh Lueke, Erik Goeddel, Félix Peña

There are three easy methods to make time fly by: sleep, consume alcohol or pitch in relief. It was two scant years ago that Barnes was an important member of one of the best relief corps in the game; this fall he was making bus trips to Omaha and serving up free passes to Billy Hamilton. It made sense for the Royals to take a flier, but his fastball and slider appear to be damaged goods, and his control, never a strong suit, has grown increasingly perilous. Entering arbitration, he'll probably find himself in Triple-A next year, searching for a way to make time move backward. Unfortunately for Barnes, that's a lot harder.

Jonathan Bowlan RHP   Born: 12/01/96   Age: 23   Bats: R   Throws: R   Height: 6'6"   Weight: 262   Origin: Round 2, 2018 Draft (#58 overall)

YEAR	TEAM	LVL	AGE	W	L	SV	G	GS	IP	H	HR	BB/9	K/9	K	GB%	BABIP	WHIP	ERA	DRA	WARP	MPH	FB%	WHF	CSP
2018	IDA	RK	21	1	4	0	9	9	35	51	6	2.3	5.9	23	52%	.354	1.71	6.94	6.63	-0.2				
2019	LEX	A	22	6	2	1	13	11	69²	55	4	1.3	9.6	74	50%	.280	0.93	3.36	3.60	1.3				
2019	WIL	A+	22	5	3	0	13	12	76¹	66	5	1.5	9.0	76	43%	.305	1.03	2.95	3.38	1.5				
2020	KCA	MLB	23	2	2	0	33	0	35	35	6	3.3	7.7	30	43%	.289	1.37	4.73	4.78	0.2				

Comparables: Cy Sneed, P.J. Walters, Rookie Davis

It's not impossible for the Royals to have built their entire 2022 starting rotation in the first two rounds of the 2018 draft. Singer, Lynch, Kowar and Bubic have garnered most of the attention from that promising class, but Bowlan recovered nicely from a rough pro start to follow along in their footsteps. The imposing right-hander out of Memphis remains the longshot of the group, mostly because his secondaries are the farthest away, but if he can find consistency, the Royals organization has shown they can make good material out of live arms. Perhaps most interesting is that so far, more than 20 percent of Bowlan's flyballs failed to leave the infield; either he's got some of that ol' Matt Cain magic in him, or there's a touch of regression coming his way as he climbs the ladder. Odds are still good that he ends up relieving, since those are almost always the odds. It's a fun story to root for, though.

★ ★ ★ *2020 Top 101 Prospect* **#96** ★ ★ ★

Kris Bubic LHP   Born: 08/19/97   Age: 22   Bats: L   Throws: L   Height: 6'3"   Weight: 220   Origin: Round 1, 2018 Draft (#40 overall)

YEAR	TEAM	LVL	AGE	W	L	SV	G	GS	IP	H	HR	BB/9	K/9	K	GB%	BABIP	WHIP	ERA	DRA	WARP	MPH	FB%	WHF	CSP
2018	IDA	RK	20	2	3	0	10	10	38	38	2	4.5	12.6	53	47%	.379	1.50	4.03	4.28	0.7				
2019	LEX	A	21	4	1	0	9	9	47²	27	3	2.8	14.2	75	49%	.270	0.88	2.08	2.40	1.6				
2019	WIL	A+	21	7	4	0	17	17	101²	76	3	2.4	9.7	110	43%	.286	1.01	2.30	3.52	1.9				
2020	KCA	MLB	22	2	2	0	33	0	35	35	5	3.7	10.1	39	42%	.318	1.40	4.64	4.60	0.2				

Comparables: Andrew Faulkner, Anthony Banda, Nestor Cortes Jr.

Well, that went fairly well. Most of the attention given to Bubic in his rookie season went to his delivery, with a windup like an exasperated sixth tug on a lawn mower, and the rather pedestrian fastball that emerged from the effort. The changeup was always going to be his best pitch, but it was the discovery of a second offering, in the form of a quality curveball, that forced opposing hitters back on their heels. There's still room for skepticism: It's not easy getting by in the majors without a decent fastball. But the wonderful thing about baseball is that no one needs to be able to do everything well, and if Bubic can continue hold his newfound velocity (91-94 mph) while throwing both breaking pitches for strikes, as he did in 2019, he should provide a welcome reinforcement for the initial pitching prospect sortie of Brady Singer and Jackson Kowar.

Danny Duffy LHP   Born: 12/21/88   Age: 31   Bats: L   Throws: L   Height: 6'3"   Weight: 205   Origin: Round 3, 2007 Draft (#96 overall)

YEAR	TEAM	LVL	AGE	W	L	SV	G	GS	IP	H	HR	BB/9	K/9	K	GB%	BABIP	WHIP	ERA	DRA	WARP	MPH	FB%	WHF	CSP
2017	OMA	AAA	28	0	1	0	2	2	7¹	6	1	1.2	9.8	8	30%	.263	0.95	3.68	3.18	0.2				
2017	KCA	MLB	28	9	10	0	24	24	146¹	143	13	2.5	8.0	130	41%	.309	1.26	3.81	3.87	2.8	95.2	47.3	12.3	50.6
2018	KCA	MLB	29	8	12	0	28	28	155	161	23	4.1	8.2	141	36%	.304	1.49	4.88	5.54	-0.4	95.8	55.7	10.8	49.6
2019	NWA	AA	30	1	0	0	2	2	10¹	8	1	0.0	9.6	11	46%	.280	0.77	0.87	3.24	0.2				
2019	KCA	MLB	30	7	6	0	23	23	130²	125	21	3.2	7.9	115	36%	.285	1.31	4.34	5.35	0.6	94.8	53	11.4	51
2020	KCA	MLB	31	9	9	0	26	26	148	150	24	3.3	8.1	133	35%	.298	1.38	4.81	4.78	1.3	94.4	52.4	11.3	50.1

Comparables: Drew Pomeranz, Matt Moore, Jhoulys Chacín

Warren Spahn once said: "Hitting is timing. Pitching is upsetting timing." In the case of Duffy, however, it was the timing itself that was upsetting, as the Royals' ace struggled all year to find his rhythm. After losing most of April to a bum shoulder, Duffy was struck by comebackers three times, as well as losing a few weeks to a hamstring pull. It's impossible to extricate exactly how much shrapnel from those blow-ups caused—the four runs he gave up on July 12 after getting struck on the hand, for example, tacked a quarter of a run onto his season ERA—but he looked more himself in September, or at least the post-2017 version of himself. The question then becomes whether new manager Mike Matheny and the Royals keep Duffy, signed through 2021, on board for his veteran leadership, or whether they trade him to make room for the new wave. It may come down to his value, and the timing.

Carlos Hernandez RHP   Born: 03/11/97   Age: 23   Bats: R   Throws: R   Height: 6'4"   Weight: 175   Origin: International Free Agent, 2016

YEAR	TEAM	LVL	AGE	W	L	SV	G	GS	IP	H	HR	BB/9	K/9	K	GB%	BABIP	WHIP	ERA	DRA	WARP	MPH	FB%	WHF	CSP
2017	BNC	RK	20	1	4	0	12	11	62¹	64	6	3.9	9.0	62	44%	.322	1.46	5.49	5.12	0.6				
2018	LEX	A	21	6	5	0	15	15	79¹	71	7	2.6	9.3	82	44%	.298	1.18	3.29	4.24	0.9				
2019	ROY	RK	22	0	2	0	5	5	11	14	1	2.5	9.8	12	41%	.387	1.55	7.36	2.90	0.4				
2019	BNC	RK+	22	0	0	0	3	3	10²	11	1	10.1	11.0	13	33%	.345	2.16	9.28	6.11	0.0				
2019	LEX	A	22	3	3	0	7	7	36	34	5	2.2	10.8	43	40%	.326	1.19	3.50	4.19	0.4				
2020	KCA	MLB	23	2	2	0	33	0	35	37	6	3.9	8.4	33	39%	.308	1.49	5.31	5.22	0.0				

Comparables: Scott Barlow, Seranthony Domínguez, Alec Mills

Ignore the ugly rookie-ball lines: Hernandez suffered a stress fracture in his rib cage before the season, and it took him half the year and some rookie-ball rehab to get back into playing shape. Signed out of Venezuela for a pittance at the autumn age of 19, the young man has expanded both his potential and mass over the past few years. While much of the latter has found its way to his midsection, the rest was channeled into his right arm, and he now sits in the mid-90s with his fastball. He's also equipped with a decent, if overly direct, slider and an inconsistent changeup as a third pitch. If you read that last sentence and thought, "Hey, that sounds like a reliever," well, congratulations. Hernandez is probably going to be a reliever, and he could end up a very good one. There's just enough time, as he avoids breaking bones and moving up the ranks, to roll the dice and find out if a third pitch magically reveals itself on the way.

Tim Hill LHP   Born: 02/10/90   Age: 30   Bats: R   Throws: L   Height: 6'2"   Weight: 200   Origin: Round 32, 2014 Draft (#963 overall)

YEAR	TEAM	LVL	AGE	W	L	SV	G	GS	IP	H	HR	BB/9	K/9	K	GB%	BABIP	WHIP	ERA	DRA	WARP	MPH	FB%	WHF	CSP
2017	NWA	AA	27	1	2	4	36	0	69	76	2	2.5	9.8	75	62%	.372	1.38	4.17	4.24	0.5				
2018	KCA	MLB	28	1	4	2	70	0	45²	46	4	2.8	8.3	42	64%	.309	1.31	4.53	5.00		93.5	76.4	9.5	55.6
2019	OMA	AAA	29	1	1	3	27	0	29²	26	2	1.8	9.1	30	55%	.308	1.08	2.12	2.15	1.2				
2019	KCA	MLB	29	2	0	1	46	0	39²	31	4	2.9	8.8	39	58%	.267	1.11	3.63	3.64	0.7	92.3	75.3	9.7	54.3
2020	KCA	MLB	30	3	3	0	54	0	57	59	9	2.6	7.6	48	57%	.298	1.32	4.53	4.59	0.4	92.1	75.6	9.6	54.7

Comparables: Josh Osich, Ryan Kelly, Grant Dayton

Let's take a moment to lament the sidearmer. It's a shame that physics works the way it does, and reduces the majority of sidearmers to platoon pitchers, because every single pitch looks terrifying and unhittable, from the whiplike arm action to the cartoon parabola as it rises toward the plate, screaming with improbability. It looks like what every pitcher would dream of throwing, not a last gasp for late-twenties left-handed non-prospects. So it's delightful that Hill, in what began as another year of promotions and demotions, mastered the art and became one of the team's most consistent arms after the break. He did it the exact way we're taught he shouldn't: by striking out righthanders (29.2 percent), evenly mixing his three slippery pitches (fastball, sinker, slider) in equal measure. Quiz would be proud.

Jakob Junis RHP   Born: 09/16/92   Age: 27   Bats: R   Throws: R   Height: 6'2"   Weight: 225   Origin: Round 29, 2011 Draft (#876 overall)

YEAR	TEAM	LVL	AGE	W	L	SV	G	GS	IP	H	HR	BB/9	K/9	K	GB%	BABIP	WHIP	ERA	DRA	WARP	MPH	FB%	WHF	CSP
2017	OMA	AAA	24	3	5	0	12	12	71	61	6	1.9	10.9	86	37%	.307	1.07	2.92	1.95	2.9				
2017	KCA	MLB	24	9	3	0	20	16	98¹	101	15	2.3	7.3	80	42%	.294	1.28	4.30	4.88	0.7	93.5	55.3	9.9	51.8
2018	KCA	MLB	25	9	12	0	30	30	177	182	32	2.2	8.3	164	43%	.298	1.27	4.37	5.53	-0.4	93.5	53.3	10.3	49.2
2019	KCA	MLB	26	9	14	0	31	31	175¹	192	31	3.0	8.4	164	43%	.318	1.43	5.24	5.91	-0.3	93.7	50.8	10.3	47.6
2020	KCA	MLB	27	8	10	0	26	26	145	160	24	2.9	8.4	136	42%	.323	1.43	5.23	5.10	0.8	93.1	53.1	10.4	49.7

Comparables: Luis Cessa, Esmil Rogers, Nick Pivetta

It's almost as if Junis' 2018 and 2019 seasons were part of a science experiment crafted in a lab. The young righty posted nearly identical seasons: same fastball-slider mix, same velocity, same batted-ball profile, same strikeout rate. What the scientists learned from all this: It's pretty important to be able to place your breaking ball. Junis stopped being able to locate the slider that was his bread-and-butter, and it all went downhill from there. It's not that his control was *awful* so much as it was vital, given that his fastball has always been relatively stiff. Any time he fell behind in the count with errant sliders, he couldn't trust his fastball to get him back into the at-bat. In essence, every two-ball count felt like a three-ball count, and every three-ball count was as good as a walk; it's hard for anyone to pitch like that. The nice thing about mysterious disappearances is that they allow for mysterious reappearances; the team has no reason not to give Junis a chance to lodge the keystone back in place and pitch another set of competent starts.

Brad Keller   RHP   Born: 07/27/95   Age: 24   Bats: R   Throws: R   Height: 6'5"   Weight: 230   Origin: Round 8, 2013 Draft (#240 overall)

YEAR	TEAM	LVL	AGE	W	L	SV	G	GS	IP	H	HR	BB/9	K/9	K	GB%	BABIP	WHIP	ERA	DRA	WARP	MPH	FB%	WHF	CSP
2017	WTN	AA	21	10	9	0	26	26	130²	142	7	3.9	7.6	111	51%	.339	1.52	4.68	6.07	-1.4				
2018	KCA	MLB	22	9	6	0	41	20	140¹	133	7	3.2	6.2	96	56%	.294	1.30	3.08	4.87	0.6	96.5	69.8	9.8	46.5
2019	KCA	MLB	23	7	14	0	28	28	165¹	154	15	3.8	6.6	122	51%	.282	1.35	4.19	5.01	1.4	96.2	66.7	9.1	45.7
2020	KCA	MLB	24	8	9	0	24	24	141	152	16	3.7	6.9	108	51%	.310	1.49	5.00	4.77	1.3	96.1	69.9	9.6	47.5

Comparables: Antonio Senzatela, Jason Adam, German Márquez

In an era when so many teams aren't trying to win, we need new statistics. Twenty years ago, the casual fan would have glanced at Keller's win-loss record (he led the league in the latter at the point where he was shut down at the end of August) and dismissed him out of hand. Five years ago, that WARP number might have earned a respectful nod. But now we're forced to think in terms of arcs, and Keller, who sports the lowest of all possible ceilings with his "throw it at the heels and hope they swing" strategy, probably isn't good enough to be part of the next Royals dynasty. But that doesn't mean he's worthless; rather, for the poor souls tricked into attending Kauffman Stadium in these dark times, he's a godsend. That's why we need a new metric to celebrate Keller's ability, not to win games, but to make them tolerable. "Keller's starting today," you might note. "We might get seven innings out of this game before it gets out of hand." Let's put that on the back of a baseball card.

Ian Kennedy   RHP   Born: 12/19/84   Age: 35   Bats: R   Throws: R   Height: 6'0"   Weight: 205   Origin: Round 1, 2006 Draft (#21 overall)

YEAR	TEAM	LVL	AGE	W	L	SV	G	GS	IP	H	HR	BB/9	K/9	K	GB%	BABIP	WHIP	ERA	DRA	WARP	MPH	FB%	WHF	CSP
2017	KCA	MLB	32	5	13	0	30	30	154	143	34	3.6	7.7	131	36%	.257	1.32	5.38	6.18	-1.0	93.9	61.7	10.2	50.2
2018	KCA	MLB	33	3	9	0	22	22	119²	125	20	3.0	7.9	105	31%	.298	1.38	4.66	5.32	0.0	94.2	58.7	9	49.2
2019	KCA	MLB	34	3	2	30	63	0	63¹	64	6	2.4	10.4	73	46%	.343	1.28	3.41	3.52	1.3	96.2	67.5	11.7	51.6
2020	KCA	MLB	35	3	3	27	60	0	63	63	10	3.0	9.4	66	39%	.308	1.33	4.41	4.45	0.5	93.4	60.9	9.9	49.6

Comparables: Aníbal Sánchez, Clay Buchholz, Matt Garza

A while back, the cutesy idea spread through certain circles that baseball teams should go around tearing elbow ligaments, given the success of Tommy John surgery. Perhaps the wiser inoculation should have been to force every Triple-A starter to throw a month in relief and see how much their stuff plays up. After three years of middling rotation work, the Royals assigned Kennedy closer duty almost out of necessity, and the results were both immediate and spectacular. The veteran saw his velocity jump from 91 to 95 mph, allowing him to abandon his change and cram fastballs down batters' throats. "It's fun to be good at something again and contribute," Kennedy told reporters in July, a quote equal parts pleasant and depressing; three months more, and he'll likely find additional pleasure in some contending team's pennant run.

Jackson Kowar   RHP   Born: 10/04/96   Age: 23   Bats: R   Throws: R   Height: 6'5"   Weight: 180   Origin: Round 1C, 2018 Draft (#33 overall)

YEAR	TEAM	LVL	AGE	W	L	SV	G	GS	IP	H	HR	BB/9	K/9	K	GB%	BABIP	WHIP	ERA	DRA	WARP	MPH	FB%	WHF	CSP
2018	LEX	A	21	0	1	0	9	9	26¹	19	2	4.1	7.5	22	59%	.239	1.18	3.42	3.71	0.5				
2019	WIL	A+	22	5	3	0	13	13	74	68	4	2.7	8.0	66	46%	.305	1.22	3.53	4.72	0.3				
2019	NWA	AA	22	2	7	0	13	13	74¹	73	8	2.5	9.4	78	46%	.323	1.26	3.51	4.67	0.3				
2020	KCA	MLB	23	2	2	0	33	0	35	35	5	3.8	7.5	29	43%	.288	1.43	4.93	4.92	0.1				

Comparables: Michael Ynoa, Esmil Rogers, Victor Alcántara

It's pretty impressive how we trick ourselves into enjoying mainstream movies. We sit down to a summer blockbuster, and enjoy a popular action hero play him or herself for the twentieth time while a different setting trembles and explodes behind them. And even though we know how it's going to end, how the hero is going to save the day, how they always save the day every single time because of some unforeseen and poorly signaled *deus ex machina*, we thrill as everything turns out okay. And then it wraps up, because of course it does, because it always does. The lava can be diverted. The salt does kill the aliens. And we leave the theater entertained, knowing that Kowar was fine all along, that he always going to have a good hard fastball with decent command, a rough curveball that'll go missing some nights, and he was always, always going to be a fourth starter. It never could have ended any other way.

Jorge López   RHP   Born: 02/10/93   Age: 27   Bats: R   Throws: R   Height: 6'3"   Weight: 195   Origin: Round 2, 2011 Draft (#70 overall)

YEAR	TEAM	LVL	AGE	W	L	SV	G	GS	IP	H	HR	BB/9	K/9	K	GB%	BABIP	WHIP	ERA	DRA	WARP	MPH	FB%	WHF	CSP
2017	BLX	AA	24	8	8	7	39	13	103²	92	7	3.3	9.1	105	49%	.301	1.25	4.25	4.47	0.7				
2017	MIL	MLB	24	0	0	0	1	0	2	4	0	4.5	0.0	0	44%	.444	2.50	4.50	9.45	-0.1	96.5	74.3	5.7	42.2
2018	CSP	AAA	25	3	3	5	24	0	28²	33	3	3.1	7.2	23	63%	.333	1.50	5.65	4.22	0.3				
2018	OMA	AAA	25	1	0	0	2	2	9	8	2	1.0	11.0	11	26%	.286	1.00	4.00	5.79	-0.1				
2018	MIL	MLB	25	0	1	0	10	0	19²	16	1	5.9	6.9	15	56%	.268	1.47	2.75	3.84	0.3	96.1	53.5	11.5	43.8
2018	KCA	MLB	25	2	4	0	7	7	34	41	5	2.4	6.1	23	40%	.324	1.47	6.35	5.08	0.0	95.8	50.8	7.4	51.1
2019	KCA	MLB	26	4	9	1	39	18	123²	140	27	3.1	7.9	109	47%	.314	1.47	6.33	6.64	-1.3	96.3	54.3	9.5	47.3
2020	KCA	MLB	27	7	9	0	52	19	136	153	21	3.5	7.8	118	48%	.323	1.52	5.54	5.29	0.3	95.7	54.5	9.4	47

Comparables: *Chase De Jong, Rob Whalen, Alberto Cabrera*

A little glimpse inside the comment-writing process: At some point when you write a bunch of Kansas City Royals, you're going to get to a guy like López. The first thing you'll do is look at the pitch mix, check the velocity, see if anything shouts elbow injury. Then you'll go through the splits, looking for some ray of light, some potential building block or a better use of their talents. Once you have all that, you find some piece of media to serve as a metaphor, and you've got yourself a comment. Unfortunately with López, there's no split, no angle that looks better than the others: He struggled against lefties, righties, starting, relieving, home, away, every time through the order. It's all bad. We don't like to toss around comps like this lightly, but 2019 Jorge López was the James Fenimore Cooper of pitchers. At this point, if he can get the gopher problems under control, he might work his way up to Theodore Dreiser, but that's the limit to our optimism.

Richard Lovelady   LHP   Born: 07/07/95   Age: 24   Bats: L   Throws: L   Height: 6'0"   Weight: 175   Origin: Round 10, 2016 Draft (#313 overall)

YEAR	TEAM	LVL	AGE	W	L	SV	G	GS	IP	H	HR	BB/9	K/9	K	GB%	BABIP	WHIP	ERA	DRA	WARP	MPH	FB%	WHF	CSP
2017	WIL	A+	21	1	0	7	21	0	33¹	18	0	1.1	11.1	41	70%	.237	0.66	1.08	1.86	1.2				
2017	NWA	AA	21	3	2	3	21	0	33¹	28	1	3.5	9.7	36	50%	.310	1.23	2.16	3.28	0.6				
2018	OMA	AAA	22	3	3	9	46	0	73	53	3	2.6	8.8	71	51%	.262	1.01	2.47	2.32	2.3				
2019	OMA	AAA	23	1	2	4	24	0	26¹	26	1	2.4	9.9	29	57%	.342	1.25	3.08	1.86	1.1				
2019	KCA	MLB	23	0	3	0	25	0	20	30	2	3.6	7.7	17	53%	.412	1.90	7.65	5.62	-0.1	96.0	60.8	8.3	53
2020	KCA	MLB	24	1	1	0	11	0	11	13	2	2.8	6.4	8	50%	.305	1.43	5.04	4.96	0.0	95.8	62.6	8.5	54.6

Comparables: *Eduardo Paredes, José Quijada, Alex Claudio*

The Charlie Furbush of Our Times earned a major league promotion in spring and unearned it over the course of the summer, leading to a late-August demotion and an early winter break. The lesson for Lovelady is the same one often taught to small children: You can't control other people, but you can control how you respond to other people. Lovelady was the victim of some brutal BABIP, particularly for someone who draws so many groundballs. But he compounded his own troubles by losing faith and nibbling at the plate, upping both his walk rate and his out-of-zone contact rate to unnaturally high levels. Success in Triple-A both before and after the waking nightmare lead one to believe that a new year, and renewed confidence, can return Lovelady and his low-slot fastball/slider combo to the rare tier of left-handed relief prospectdom he so recently held.

★   ★   ★   *2020 Top 101 Prospect*   **#93**   ★   ★   ★

Daniel Lynch   LHP   Born: 11/17/96   Age: 23   Bats: L   Throws: L   Height: 6'6"   Weight: 190   Origin: Round 1C, 2018 Draft (#34 overall)

YEAR	TEAM	LVL	AGE	W	L	SV	G	GS	IP	H	HR	BB/9	K/9	K	GB%	BABIP	WHIP	ERA	DRA	WARP	MPH	FB%	WHF	CSP
2018	BNC	RK	21	0	0	0	3	3	11¹	9	0	1.6	11.1	14	59%	.310	0.97	1.59	3.08	0.4				
2018	LEX	A	21	5	1	0	9	9	40	35	1	1.4	10.6	47	51%	.343	1.02	1.58	3.37	0.9				
2019	ROY	RK	22	0	0	0	3	3	9	6	0	3.0	12.0	12	65%	.294	1.00	1.00	2.09	0.4				
2019	BNC	RK+	22	1	0	0	2	2	9	13	1	3.0	7.0	7	59%	.429	1.78	4.00	8.31	-0.2				
2019	WIL	A+	22	5	2	0	15	15	78¹	76	4	2.6	8.8	77	49%	.324	1.26	3.10	4.47	0.5				
2020	KCA	MLB	23	2	2	0	33	0	35	34	5	3.5	8.1	31	46%	.290	1.35	4.32	4.42	0.3				

Comparables: *Nick Maronde, Eric Skoglund, Taylor Rogers*

After a fine season in High-A, Lynch made the Arizona Fall League his personal scouting showcase, wielding an awl-punch of a fastball that touched 99 mph. He also demonstrated an out-pitch-quality slider and a stern reminder of a changeup, both plenty good enough to classify him as starter material. Given that he's already building up enough mass to drop the "lanky" adjective, and the fact that he's shown that the velocity plays up in bursts, it's easy to envision a closer here if the whole starting pitching thing doesn't work out. That said, Lynch also lost two months to deal with a bum shoulder, and you're well aware of the cliché about pitching prospects.

Kevin McCarthy RHP   Born: 02/22/92   Age: 28   Bats: R   Throws: R   Height: 6'3"   Weight: 215   Origin: Round 16, 2013 Draft (#474 overall)

YEAR	TEAM	LVL	AGE	W	L	SV	G	GS	IP	H	HR	BB/9	K/9	K	GB%	BABIP	WHIP	ERA	DRA	WARP	MPH	FB%	WHF	CSP
2017	OMA	AAA	25	1	1	2	25	0	32	32	3	2.5	4.8	17	58%	.296	1.28	3.09	4.29	0.4				
2017	KCA	MLB	25	1	0	0	33	0	45	50	4	2.6	5.4	27	55%	.303	1.40	3.20	5.36	-0.1	94.7	60.8	9.7	52.3
2018	KCA	MLB	26	5	4	0	65	0	72	70	7	2.5	5.8	46	65%	.289	1.25	3.25	4.46	0.4	93.9	67	10.1	49.4
2019	OMA	AAA	27	0	0	3	13	0	16²	19	0	2.7	8.1	15	64%	.380	1.44	3.78	3.41	0.5				
2019	KCA	MLB	27	4	2	1	56	0	60¹	68	4	3.1	5.7	38	59%	.315	1.48	4.48	4.95	0.3	93.0	59.8	10.9	49.4
2020	KCA	MLB	28	3	3	2	54	0	57	65	7	3.0	6.3	40	58%	.313	1.46	4.98	4.85	0.2	93.1	63.1	10.4	50.4

Comparables: Pedro Beato, Donovan Hand, Scott Alexander

After honing his skills on Broadway, McCarthy won a Golden Globe for "Most Promising Newcomer" for his role in the 1952 adaptation of "Death of a Salesman." He wasn't, really; he was just never going to be a star. If that award wasn't his peak, it was very near: best known for starring in "Invasion of the Body Snatchers," the actor worked in more than 200 television shows and films over 60 years, always happy to take on the thankless task of the sheriff, the doctor, the schoolmaster, the rich businessman who got his in the end. The kind of character actor whose name you couldn't place and whose face you can't quite remember, McCarthy was there, no matter how bad the movie, to deliver the necessary exposition and keep the plot moving forward, because every movie has to end. This comment has been a metaphor.

Mike Montgomery LHP   Born: 07/01/89   Age: 30   Bats: L   Throws: L   Height: 6'5"   Weight: 215   Origin: Round 1, 2008 Draft (#36 overall)

YEAR	TEAM	LVL	AGE	W	L	SV	G	GS	IP	H	HR	BB/9	K/9	K	GB%	BABIP	WHIP	ERA	DRA	WARP	MPH	FB%	WHF	CSP
2017	CHN	MLB	27	7	8	3	44	14	130²	103	10	3.8	6.9	100	59%	.253	1.21	3.38	4.31	1.6	94.5	53	8.9	44.6
2018	CHN	MLB	28	5	6	0	38	19	124	131	10	2.8	6.2	86	53%	.309	1.37	3.99	4.57	0.9	93.9	49.6	9.9	49.6
2019	IOW	AAA	29	1	1	0	2	2	10	3	0	3.6	7.2	8	59%	.111	0.70	2.70	1.69	0.5				
2019	KCA	MLB	29	2	7	0	13	13	64	78	12	3.0	7.2	51	52%	.346	1.55	4.64	7.16	-1.0	93.2	47.4	10	42.4
2019	CHN	MLB	29	1	2	0	20	0	27	35	6	4.3	6.0	18	44%	.341	1.78	5.67	8.83	-0.9	94.8	47.4	9.2	44.7
2020	KCA	MLB	30	7	9	0	24	24	124	138	15	3.8	7.2	99	52%	.319	1.53	5.26	5.00	0.8	93.2	49.6	9.5	45.5

Comparables: Roenis Elías, Sean Gilmartin, Brett Cecil

It made sense for everyone involved: the Cubs, fancying themselves championship contenders, couldn't afford to keep giving meaningful innings to a clearly malfunctioning pitcher. The Royals, at the price offered, could hardly say no to a once-promising arm, free to rehabilitate his trade value off (national) camera. And Montgomery himself understood the limitations of his current occupation, glorious as the World Series ring was, and that his best path forward was getting an opportunity to start. So all parties involved were pretty content. It didn't quite work out. In terms of peripherals, Montgomery improved in the starter's role, though it could be argued that regression did the bulk of the labor. The crafty lefty always had more of a starter's repertoire anyway, mixing four competent pitches, but the major change he made in his pitch mix heading south was to limit probably his best offering, the high-spin curveball that earned him a job in Chicago in the first place. Someone is contractually obligated to start baseball games for the 2020 Royals, so there's no harm in letting Montgomery see what he can do. (That last sentence was edited three times to supply the faintest praise measurable by science.)

Jake Newberry RHP   Born: 11/20/94   Age: 25   Bats: R   Throws: R   Height: 6'2"   Weight: 195   Origin: Round 37, 2012 Draft (#1123 overall)

YEAR	TEAM	LVL	AGE	W	L	SV	G	GS	IP	H	HR	BB/9	K/9	K	GB%	BABIP	WHIP	ERA	DRA	WARP	MPH	FB%	WHF	CSP
2017	NWA	AA	22	4	2	15	36	0	50²	45	3	3.4	5.9	33	38%	.268	1.26	2.13	3.55	0.8				
2017	OMA	AAA	22	2	2	0	7	0	11¹	10	1	5.6	8.7	11	33%	.257	1.50	4.76	4.73	0.1				
2018	NWA	AA	23	2	0	12	25	0	29²	29	2	2.4	11.2	37	32%	.360	1.25	2.12	3.90	0.4				
2018	OMA	AAA	23	3	0	3	16	0	20	13	1	2.7	7.2	16	51%	.231	0.95	0.90	3.44	0.4				
2018	KCA	MLB	23	2	0	0	14	0	13¹	13	3	6.1	7.4	11	32%	.270	1.65	4.72	5.64	-0.1	95.7	54.8	10.3	47.1
2019	OMA	AAA	24	2	2	0	22	0	28	29	3	4.5	9.6	30	41%	.333	1.54	3.86	3.85	0.6				
2019	KCA	MLB	24	1	0	0	27	0	31	29	7	4.6	8.4	29	34%	.262	1.45	3.77	7.42	-0.7	95.7	53.2	12.5	42.6
2020	KCA	MLB	25	1	1	0	22	0	23	23	4	4.1	8.4	22	36%	.296	1.44	4.91	4.82	0.1	95.4	54.9	12.2	45.7

Comparables: Jake Barrett, Fernando Romero, Eduardo Paredes

Newberry easily won the award for Most Royals Moment of 2019, when he threw a fastball more than a foot and a half inside, only to have Ronny Rodríguez turn on it and club it into the seats anyway. It certainly underscored the challenges for the former 37th-round draft pick, who struggled with the home run and the walk in nearly equal measure. The former tends to be the result of the low-90s fastball left up in the zone, while the latter results from a sharp, plunging slider that starts low and ends in a cloud of dust. Thanks to some luck with stranded runners, Newberry will likely get another shot to straighten things out, and if he can get that slider up and that fastball down, he might be able to tunnel his way out of that ugly DRA.

Trevor Rosenthal RHP   Born: 05/29/90   Age: 30   Bats: R   Throws: R   Height: 6'2"   Weight: 230   Origin: Round 21, 2009 Draft (#639 overall)

YEAR	TEAM	LVL	AGE	W	L	SV	G	GS	IP	H	HR	BB/9	K/9	K	GB%	BABIP	WHIP	ERA	DRA	WARP	MPH	FB%	WHF	CSP
2017	SLN	MLB	27	3	4	11	50	0	47²	37	3	3.8	14.3	76	40%	.337	1.20	3.40	2.65	1.3	101.0	74.6	17.1	49
2019	HAR	AA	29	0	1	0	10	0	9¹	9	2	6.8	10.6	11	50%	.292	1.71	5.79	6.03	-0.2				
2019	DET	MLB	29	0	0	0	10	0	9	3	0	11.0	12.0	12	56%	.167	1.56	7.00	6.12	-0.1	99.9	68.8	12.2	42.1
2019	WAS	MLB	29	0	1	0	12	0	6¹	8	0	21.3	7.1	5	35%	.400	3.63	22.74	7.56	-0.2	100.3	75.5	9.5	43.6
2020	KCA	MLB	30	1	1	0	16	0	17	15	2	6.7	10.7	21	43%	.297	1.59	5.04	4.67	0.1	99.9	73.3	14.4	45

Comparables: Jonathan Broxton, Scott Williamson, Keone Kela

BASEBALL PROSPECTUS 2020

A healthy, effective return from Tommy John surgery is taken for granted too often. Rosenthal was one of baseball's better relievers in the middle part of the decade, but missed all of 2018 after late-2017 surgery. The Nationals took a shot on a healthy recovery and guaranteed him $7 million for 2019. He came back simply unable to throw consistent strikes and was released in June. A stint with the Tigers went no better and lasted just ten appearances before they too gave up. The Yankees tried last, and Rosenthal walked three, hit a batter and threw a wild pitch over a third of an inning in his lone Triple-A outing. For Rosenthal's sake, hopefully these are merely steps in a troubled recovery and not the end of the line.

★ ★ ★ *2020 Top 101 Prospect* **#64** ★ ★ ★

Brady Singer RHP   Born: 08/04/96   Age: 23   Bats: R   Throws: R   Height: 6'5"   Weight: 210   Origin: Round 1, 2018 Draft (#18 overall)

YEAR	TEAM	LVL	AGE	W	L	SV	G	GS	IP	H	HR	BB/9	K/9	K	GB%	BABIP	WHIP	ERA	DRA	WARP	MPH	FB%	WHF	CSP
2019	WIL	A+	22	5	2	0	10	10	57²	51	1	2.0	8.3	53	56%	.325	1.11	1.87	5.14	-0.1				
2019	NWA	AA	22	7	3	0	16	16	90²	86	8	2.6	8.4	85	51%	.301	1.24	3.47	3.97	1.1				
2020	KCA	MLB	23	1	2	0	5	5	24	24	3	3.7	7.4	20	46%	.292	1.41	4.82	4.77	0.2				

Comparables: Jeff Hoffman, Zach Stewart, Jon Gray

When a movie or a book gets reviewed, its score tends to be based not on its brilliancies but its lack of flaws. Brilliance in art, after all, is unquantifiable; mistakes can be counted. It's why every Marvel movie gets the same review score, and why Singer is a top prospect. He's exactly the opposite of what you don't want: despite a relatively low ceiling from a stuff standpoint, he demonstrates advanced command and has shown excellent durability. It's the kind of profile that makes one stand back and just admire the reliability, like a big truck sitting on the edge of a canyon in a Chevrolet commercial. If there's one concern, it's his lower arm slot, and what that might mean for pitching against lefties: He didn't exactly struggle with them in 2019, but the higher walk rate was evidence that he was worried enough to start nibbling. Still, Singer is as good a bet as any to be near the top of the leaderboards in innings pitched five years from now, steady, dependable, formulaic. It's not what you don't want.

Eric Skoglund LHP   Born: 10/26/92   Age: 27   Bats: L   Throws: L   Height: 6'7"   Weight: 210   Origin: Round 3, 2014 Draft (#92 overall)

YEAR	TEAM	LVL	AGE	W	L	SV	G	GS	IP	H	HR	BB/9	K/9	K	GB%	BABIP	WHIP	ERA	DRA	WARP	MPH	FB%	WHF	CSP
2017	OMA	AAA	24	4	5	0	19	19	100²	110	14	2.6	9.1	102	42%	.331	1.38	4.11	4.09	1.8				
2017	KCA	MLB	24	1	2	0	7	5	18	30	2	6.0	7.0	14	39%	.431	2.33	9.50	8.05	-0.5	94.4	63.3	7.1	54
2018	NWA	AA	25	0	0	0	2	2	9	12	1	2.0	4.0	4	41%	.333	1.56	4.00	4.18	0.0				
2018	OMA	AAA	25	0	1	0	2	2	8¹	8	2	0.0	6.5	6	44%	.240	0.96	4.32	4.18	0.1				
2018	KCA	MLB	25	1	6	0	14	13	70	66	12	2.4	6.3	49	44%	.261	1.21	5.14	6.20	-0.7	93.9	60.2	8	49.2
2019	OMA	AAA	26	2	4	0	11	11	63	79	12	2.4	6.1	43	38%	.333	1.52	6.14	5.86	0.5				
2019	KCA	MLB	26	0	3	0	6	4	21	30	5	3.9	1.7	4	36%	.305	1.86	9.00	9.80	-0.9	91.7	61.8	5.6	49.5
2020	KCA	MLB	27	3	5	0	35	8	69	89	16	2.8	4.9	37	39%	.308	1.60	6.92	6.41	-0.7	93.0	61.8	7.3	51.1

Comparables: Erick Fedde, Jason Wheeler, Cole Irvin

Skoglund lost half the season after testing positive for Ostarine and Ligandrol, and then lost the other half of the season by showing back up to work afterward. The lanky lefthander struggled to rediscover his rhythm in Triple-A, only to be battered around in September like a seal in a pod of orcas. Each of his pitches lost between one and three ticks, and no pitcher with as many innings had a higher contact rate than Skoglund's 89 percent. It's not like he was terrifying the worms, either; the balls were getting hit hard, and they were getting hit upwards. It's probably just best for everyone to pretend this never happened, hypnotize him into thinking it's still 2018, and starting him off in Triple-A to get ready for his second shot at the big leagues.

Glenn Sparkman RHP   Born: 05/11/92   Age: 28   Bats: R   Throws: R   Height: 6'2"   Weight: 210   Origin: Round 20, 2013 Draft (#594 overall)

YEAR	TEAM	LVL	AGE	W	L	SV	G	GS	IP	H	HR	BB/9	K/9	K	GB%	BABIP	WHIP	ERA	DRA	WARP	MPH	FB%	WHF	CSP
2017	NHP	AA	25	1	1	0	2	2	8²	6	2	3.1	6.2	6	52%	.174	1.04	3.12	4.20	0.1				
2017	NWA	AA	25	0	0	0	3	2	10¹	11	0	4.4	4.4	5	47%	.306	1.55	2.61	4.80	0.0				
2017	BUF	AAA	25	1	2	1	4	1	8	7	1	1.1	3.4	3	38%	.240	1.00	2.25	4.27	0.1				
2017	TOR	MLB	25	0	0	0	2	0	1	9	0	9.0	9.0	1	20%	.900	10.00	63.00	9.33	0.0	95.8	63.6	3.6	46.8
2018	NWA	AA	26	3	2	0	6	6	33²	35	0	0.3	7.0	26	45%	.321	1.07	2.94	3.86	0.6				
2018	OMA	AAA	26	5	1	0	12	12	67¹	76	10	1.5	6.4	48	46%	.314	1.29	4.01	5.17	0.3				
2018	KCA	MLB	26	0	3	0	15	3	38¹	47	3	3.5	6.3	27	47%	.338	1.62	4.46	5.21	-0.1	96.0	56.6	10.6	48.9
2019	OMA	AAA	27	0	0	0	2	1	6¹	4	0	1.4	5.7	4	44%	.222	0.79	0.00	3.18	0.2				
2019	KCA	MLB	27	4	11	0	31	23	136	164	30	2.7	5.4	81	38%	.299	1.51	6.02	8.56	-4.2	95.9	60.9	8.2	49.2
2020	KCA	MLB	28	5	7	0	47	15	107	130	19	2.7	5.8	69	39%	.314	1.51	5.85	5.63	-0.2	95.3	60.5	8.6	48.8

Comparables: Justin Haley, Rookie Davis, Nick Kingham

In the courts of England and Spain, where social etiquette restricted women from verbal communication, women of court often used a coded language via a fan with a photograph of Glenn Sparkman to demonstrate their disinterest in a potential suitor.

Around the turn of the century, photographs of Glenn Sparkman were posted in factory break rooms, until the government shut down the practice in an attempt to improve working conditions.

In Victorian times, children were often punished by having to draw pictures of Glenn Sparkman and then write their own name over the chest.

Wealthy Icelandic families suffering from poor harvests would often select a random peasant, name them Glenn Sparkman, then drive them into the sea in hopes that the evil spirits would be drawn away with them.

Josh Staumont RHP Born: 12/21/93 Age: 26 Bats: R Throws: R Height: 6'3" Weight: 200 Origin: Round 2, 2015 Draft (#64 overall)

YEAR	TEAM	LVL	AGE	W	L	SV	G	GS	IP	H	HR	BB/9	K/9	K	GB%	BABIP	WHIP	ERA	DRA	WARP	MPH	FB%	WHF	CSP
2017	NWA	AA	23	3	4	0	10	10	48²	42	2	6.3	8.3	45	36%	.308	1.56	4.44	4.72	0.3				
2017	OMA	AAA	23	3	8	0	16	15	76	64	14	7.5	11.0	93	41%	.279	1.67	6.28	4.94	0.6				
2018	OMA	AAA	24	2	5	1	41	5	74¹	59	4	6.3	12.5	103	44%	.327	1.49	3.51	3.92	1.1				
2019	OMA	AAA	25	1	5	2	32	12	51¹	31	4	6.5	13.0	74	50%	.262	1.32	3.16	2.10	2.1				
2019	KCA	MLB	25	0	0	0	16	0	19¹	21	4	4.7	7.0	15	32%	.293	1.60	3.72	7.96	-0.5	98.3	69.6	9.2	46.8
2020	KCA	MLB	26	1	1	0	22	0	23	29	5	6.2	8.3	21	39%	.349	1.96	8.05	6.66	-0.4	97.9	70.9	9.4	47.6

Comparables: Chris Beck, Ethan Martin, Maikel Cleto

What we need is a metric for madness. Baseball lore is littered with slouching giants with cruel eyes and wild fastballs, men who stalked the mound and cursed into their gloves and terrified their opponents. But the Hraboskies of baseball largely worked in the twilight of the game's bronze age. We have no way of knowing how effective their intimidation tactics really were, whether batters froze at strikes imagined to be sailing headward. All this is to say that we ask a service of Staumont, who pairs a scorching fastball with a complete indifference to the strike zone. The latter doesn't seem like it's going to go away, so why not advertise it? Yell at the baseball, have arguments with spirits haunting the mound, do whatever it takes to strike fear into the hearts of mortals. Every little bit helps, and every little bit is probably going to be necessary.

Daniel Tillo LHP Born: 06/13/96 Age: 24 Bats: L Throws: L Height: 6'5" Weight: 215 Origin: Round 3, 2017 Draft (#90 overall)

YEAR	TEAM	LVL	AGE	W	L	SV	G	GS	IP	H	HR	BB/9	K/9	K	GB%	BABIP	WHIP	ERA	DRA	WARP	MPH	FB%	WHF	CSP
2017	BNC	RK	21	3	2	0	7	7	31	35	1	1.7	7.3	25	69%	.351	1.32	3.48	5.06	0.3				
2018	LEX	A	22	1	1	0	7	7	41¹	37	3	3.0	6.8	31	65%	.270	1.23	4.35	4.12	0.5				
2018	WIL	A+	22	3	5	0	19	19	93	99	3	4.9	6.7	69	59%	.333	1.61	4.94	6.17	-0.9				
2019	WIL	A+	23	7	8	0	20	20	107¹	95	5	3.6	5.4	64	64%	.265	1.29	3.77	5.26	-0.3				
2019	NWA	AA	23	1	1	0	9	3	23¹	22	1	4.2	8.1	21	62%	.323	1.41	3.47	4.81	0.0				
2020	KCA	MLB	24	2	2	0	33	0	35	34	5	4.0	5.1	20	48%	.262	1.41	4.71	4.71	0.2				

Comparables: Drake Britton, Jason Wheeler, Josh Butler

Sometimes life is less about how well you do and more about how you manage people's expectations. That's what makes life interesting; by the time you're an adult, you have a pretty good handle on what you're good at, how you're going to deal with the people and the obstacles you run into. And then the world rolls some dice at you, and you have to figure out how to respond. Tillo got a particularly unlucky break when, after getting promoted to Double-A, he got invited to the Arizona Fall League, and because of the AFL's roster restrictions, he had to pretend to be a reliever for a few months. A lefty with a good fastball and wayward secondaries, Tillo was put in a predicament: perform poorly, and fall out of the team's plans, or perform well, and reinforce the team's choice to make him a reliever. He chose the latter, relying on lefty-righty splits to markedly improve his command. He'll likely get another shot at starting next year, but if he struggles early, the memory of his late-inning successes may get him typecast.

Kyle Zimmer RHP Born: 09/13/91 Age: 28 Bats: R Throws: R Height: 6'3" Weight: 225 Origin: Round 1, 2012 Draft (#5 overall)

YEAR	TEAM	LVL	AGE	W	L	SV	G	GS	IP	H	HR	BB/9	K/9	K	GB%	BABIP	WHIP	ERA	DRA	WARP	MPH	FB%	WHF	CSP
2017	OMA	AAA	25	0	0	3	20	2	32²	35	4	4.4	9.4	34	28%	.337	1.56	5.79	4.48	0.3				
2019	OMA	AAA	27	2	4	1	37	12	54	46	6	5.5	8.7	52	46%	.276	1.46	4.33	3.53	1.5				
2019	KCA	MLB	27	0	1	0	15	0	18¹	28	2	9.3	8.8	18	42%	.413	2.56	10.80	8.52	-0.6	98.4	60.9	11.9	47
2020	KCA	MLB	28	2	2	0	33	0	34	32	4	4.8	8.5	33	41%	.286	1.45	4.51	4.43	0.3	97.8	61.3	12	47.3

Comparables: Jake Faria, Luis Santos, Brooks Pounders

The surprising thing about grief is its ridiculous longevity: eventually the pain gets overshadowed by embarrassment for still feeling that pain, long after it grows stale, then uninteresting, then actively dull. Then there are the lies about the stages of grief, as though any of them ever get completed, as if bargaining doesn't return every day, like a tax collector. Zimmer went from promise to tragedy to gallows humor to that strange brand of gallows antihumor, a password for the world weary and cynical. And then, finally, he made the major leagues. And now. What's left?

LINEOUTS

Hitters

HITTER	POS	TEAM	LVL	AGE	PA	R	2B	3B	HR	RBI	BB	K	SB	CS	AVG/OBP/SLG	DRC+	VORP	BABIP	BRR	FRAA	WARP
Gabriel Cancel	2B	NWA	AA	22	513	70	30	0	18	69	34	144	15	2	.246/.308/.427	96	17.8	.313	4.4	2B(82): -8.1, 1B(17): -0.6	0.5
Nick Dini	C	OMA	AAA	25	213	34	11	0	13	36	21	29	7	2	.296/.370/.565	124	22.2	.288	-0.8	C(56): -5.8, 3B(1): 0.0	1.1
	C	KCA	MLB	25	64	11	3	0	2	6	4	18	0	0	.196/.270/.357	80	1.7	.243	-0.2	C(20): -2.0	-0.1
Jeison Guzman	SS	LEX	A	20	490	51	23	5	7	48	29	98	15	13	.253/.296/.373	85	15.6	.308	1.4	SS(115): 10.6	2.6
Nick Heath	OF	NWA	AA	25	375	55	10	7	6	27	39	116	50	9	.255/.332/.382	87	20.4	.373	7.0	CF(62): -2.2, RF(9): -0.6	1.1
	OF	OMA	AAA	25	97	17	4	1	2	9	17	27	10	4	.256/.392/.410	100	4.3	.360	-0.7	CF(18): 1.6	0.4
Brewer Hicklen	OF	WIL	A+	23	494	70	13	7	14	51	55	140	39	14	.263/.363/.427	132	38.3	.358	4.6	LF(64): 4.1, CF(20): -3.8	3.3
Ryan McBroom	1B	SWB	AAA	27	482	87	29	0	26	66	58	100	2	2	.315/.402/.574	141	26.7	.356	-3.8	1B(62): -1.2, RF(37): -0.3	2.6
	1B	KCA	MLB	27	83	8	5	0	0	6	7	25	0	0	.293/.361/.360	73	-1.1	.440	0.1	RF(12): -1.5, 1B(6): -0.5	-0.3
Erick Mejia	2B	OMA	AAA	24	556	83	22	6	7	63	50	103	19	6	.271/.339/.382	75	12.9	.327	5.3	SS(34): 4.6, 2B(31): -1.1	1.6
	2B	KCA	MLB	24	27	3	1	0	0	4	4	7	0	0	.227/.333/.273	82	0.4	.313	0.2	CF(7): 0.3, 2B(1): 0.0	0.1
Emmanuel Rivera	3B	NWA	AA	23	534	59	18	2	7	57	25	77	6	2	.258/.297/.345	71	3.6	.289	0.1	3B(116): 0.5, 2B(1): -0.2	0.4

Gabriel Cancel moved up a level, and in so doing he became more Gabriel Cancel than ever before, enhancing both his strength and inaccuracy with the bat. At this rate he'll get to wear a major league uniform by 2021, and swing said bat a few times a week. ⑩ On September 15, Nick Dini accomplished something George Brett never did, when he doubled off Wade Miley. ⑩ Jeison Guzman isn't a name to remember yet, but put him down as a name to remember to remember. He's still fluid at short after having grown into his frame, and every once in a while, viewed in the right light, he looks like he can hit, too. ⑩ In any other chapter, a prospect like Nick Heath would probably go unmentioned, but Kansas City has a legacy of men like him, men who run with a blind fury and also hit with a blind fury, the emphasis slightly shifted. A toast, friends, to the Jarrod Dysons yet to come. ⑩ In the grand tradition of Ángel Pagán, Ranger Suárez and Rocky Gale, Brewer Hicklen hopes to translate his surfeit of raw athleticism into a spot on the wrong team's major-league roster. ⑩ The system works! The Yankees had no room for the Rule 5-eligible Ryan McBroom, so they sold him to a team with a little room. The Quad-A slugger got his shot, the Royals got to play the Luke Voit lottery for fairly cheap, and some meaningless September baseball became a little less meaningless, at least for the McBroom family. ⑩ Erick Mejia certainly is a baseball player. Capable of running and fielding, it's not impossible that he could develop into a utility infielder; it's also hard to imagine any team putting in the effort to find out. ⑩ The Royals had a surplus of international spending money, and they devoted a plurality of it to teenage outfielder Erick Pena, an athletic outfielder out of the Dominican Republic. Enjoy half a dozen years of Carlos Beltran comps, assuming everything goes well. ⑩ If you took all of the hitters in the Royals system and shoved their 2019 seasons into one man, you'd get Emmanuel Rivera, who took a step back with the bat and the eye in his first taste of Double-A. Or, he somehow instilled himself in all of them, and he's a villain who needs to be stopped.

Pitchers

PITCHER	TEAM	LVL	AGE	W	L	SV	G	GS	IP	H	HR	BB/9	K/9	K	GB%	BABIP	WHIP	ERA	DRA	WARP	MPH	FB%	WHF	CSP
Scott Blewett	NWA	AA	23	1	3	0	5	5	25¹	21	2	2.8	12.1	34	42%	.317	1.14	3.55	4.64	0.1				
	OMA	AAA	23	5	8	0	18	16	81¹	115	24	5.1	6.2	56	38%	.333	1.98	8.52	8.25	-1.2				
Austin Cox	LEX	A	22	5	3	0	13	13	75¹	59	5	2.6	9.2	77	42%	.262	1.08	2.75	3.86	1.2				
	WIL	A+	22	3	3	0	11	10	55¹	53	6	2.6	8.5	52	34%	.318	1.25	2.77	5.23	-0.2				
Heath Fillmyer	OMA	AAA	25	2	3	0	19	10	49¹	48	8	4.7	9.3	51	42%	.310	1.50	5.11	4.16	1.2				
	KCA	MLB	25	0	2	0	12	3	22¹	28	6	4.8	6.0	15	42%	.301	1.79	8.06	8.08	-0.6	94.6	51.9	8.2	45.1
Conner Greene	NWA	AA	24	3	9	1	21	16	97	101	11	3.5	7.9	85	46%	.311	1.43	5.29	5.53	-0.7				
	OMA	AAA	24	1	0	0	8	0	15¹	14	2	9.4	5.9	10	53%	.279	1.96	4.11	7.46	-0.2				
Foster Griffin	OMA	AAA	23	8	6	0	25	25	130²	134	20	4.4	7.6	111	50%	.295	1.52	5.23	4.38	3.0				
Zach Haake	LEX	A	22	4	6	0	18	18	75²	60	2	4.3	10.7	90	40%	.314	1.27	2.85	4.28	0.8				
Jesse Hahn	KCA	MLB	29	0	1	0	6	0	4²	7	1	11.6	13.5	7	43%	.462	2.79	13.50	5.64	0.0	96.9	62.6	13.1	50.2
Arnaldo Hernandez	NWA	AA	23	2	2	0	4	4	23	21	2	4.3	7.8	20	35%	.297	1.39	1.96	4.94	0.0				
	OMA	AAA	23	4	8	0	22	20	105²	142	24	3.5	5.5	65	38%	.334	1.73	6.39	7.24	-0.6				
Alec Marsh	IDA	Rk+	21	0	1	0	13	13	33¹	30	5	1.1	10.3	38	46%	.294	1.02	4.05	2.73	1.2				
Wily Peralta	KCA	MLB	30	2	4	2	42	0	40¹	45	7	4.2	5.4	24	45%	.306	1.59	5.80	7.94	-1.1	96.7	54.9	9.7	43.9
Randy Rosario	IOW	AAA	25	1	2	4	31	0	37²	46	5	3.3	7.4	31	61%	.325	1.59	3.11	4.79	0.5				
	KCA	MLB	25	1	0	0	6	0	3²	3	0	0.0	7.4	3	64%	.273	0.82	0.00	1.91	0.1	95.2	66.7	14.8	55.2
	CHN	MLB	25	1	0	0	13	0	10²	12	2	4.2	8.4	10	59%	.312	1.59	5.91	3.59	0.2	96.1	70.4	9.5	50.2
Gabe Speier	NWA	AA	24	1	1	5	17	0	22¹	20	2	3.6	11.3	28	41%	.305	1.30	2.42	3.93	0.2				
	OMA	AAA	24	0	4	1	30	0	40	41	10	3.8	10.1	45	35%	.301	1.45	5.62	4.55	0.7				
	KCA	MLB	24	0	0	0	9	0	7¹	5	2	7.4	12.3	10	29%	.200	1.50	7.36	4.78	0.0	96.1	61.4	10.5	45.7
Drew Storen	NWA	AA	31	0	1	0	9	0	10¹	15	1	4.4	10.5	12	45%	.467	1.94	7.84	7.05	-0.3				
Stephen Woods Jr.	PCH	A+	24	9	3	0	18	12	86¹	71	2	3.4	8.2	79	54%	.294	1.20	1.88	4.24	0.7				
Michael Ynoa	OMA	AAA	27	1	1	2	17	0	21²	19	3	5.8	10.8	26	36%	.291	1.52	4.57	3.51	0.6				

Look, it's never easy pitching in the PCL, especially with the new rabbit ball, but Scott Blewett managed to make it look nearly impossible. It's time to abandon hopes for that third pitch and see if there are some sixth-inning appearances to squeeze out of that 6-foot-6 frame. ⑩ Austin Cox only earns a lineout this year, because despite his posting strong performances at two levels in 2019, it's hard to come up with 130 words explaining how. As a low-velo college lefty, the chance of a breakout is slim, but give him credit for developing his secondary pitches thus far. ⑩ Biceps, day-to-day: Five-seventeenths of a haiku, and an encapsulation of the entire 2019 season for Yefri del Rosario. Given that his age was his greatest virtue, it was a particularly harsh blow, as the young Dominican has plenty of work left to do. ⑩ As the great Will Rogers once said, "We can't all be heroes, because somebody has to throw them belt-high sliders when their bats go by." In that sense, Heath Fillmyer really is a hero too, in his own way. ⑩ If you're a team with a surfeit of roster spots and a long road ahead, you could do far worse than Connor Greene, a blunderbuss of a reliever in search of one weird trick. ⑩ Foster Griffin is not one of the Royals' fleet of wunderkinds, but at least he had the good sense to precede them. To survive in the majors, he'll have to limit walks and keep the ball on the ground, and he hasn't done both concurrently since Low-A. ⑩ Here's a reward for digging this deep in the lineouts: Former sixth-rounder Zach Haake has an inconsistent slider and a telegraphed changeup, but when he has them right, he has some of the best stuff in the system. The fastball has enough life and run to make him a bullpen asset at the very least. Keep an eye on him. ⑩ The Jesse Hahn that staggered back to the majors after a grueling two-year recovery was almost unrecognizable, abandoning his entire arsenal for a traditional fastball-slider pairing. Still, you have to wonder if he printed out curveballer Rich Hill's stats page, highlighted those lean 2012-2014 seasons, and maintains a little shred of hope. ⑩ With the most "can I see you in my office for a moment" energy possible, let us say: perhaps it's time to see what Arnaldo Hernandez can do in relief. ⑩ Third-round pick Alec Marsh has five average pitches and a low-90s fastball, which is the kind of profile that works as long as you never walk anyone ever. He passed the test in year one; next year will be the real proving ground, as well as the one after that, and the one after that. ⑩ Wily Peralta lost two ticks off his fastball, 10 percentage points off his strikeout rate and, ultimately, lost his roster spot. ⑩ The Cubs liked Randy Rosario enough to use him in a high-leverage spot in the 2018 Wild Card Game. A year later he was throwing low-leverage pitches for the Royals. ⑩ Gabe Speier has been included in trades for Rick Porcello, Cameron Maybin, Dansby Swanson and Jon Jay. Sadly, there will likely never be an annual comment about being traded for Gabe Speier. ⑩ After a failed comeback attempt, Drew Storen's life as Closer of the Future is formally at an end. But there are still so many Drew Storens left: Kiwanis Club Vice President of the Future, Country Music Singer of the Future, Mid-Tier YouTube Celebrity of the Future…. ⑩ Careful with the numbers here: Stephen Woods Jr. dominated A-ball, but he did it at age 24, thanks to a torn labrum that slowed down his progress. He'll have to prove that he can throw strikes against real hitters this year, but the stuff was worth a Rule 5 flyer for a team with plenty of bullpen room. ⑩ Michael Ynoa earned one last shot at the majors last offseason, and as with so many of his attempts, it missed the mark. This is probably the end of his career, or perhaps to put it better, the second end; the first one ended after nine innings, nine years ago.

LOS ANGELES ANGELS

Essay by Ginny Searle

Player comments by Jon Hegglund and BP staff

If you were to wander the streets of some major city, claiming that Mike Trout played for the Seattle Pilots, how many people would believe it? It's not as outlandish a question as it might seem—Trout's abilities demand a generational legacy of his play, a legend in the same mold as Mantle or Williams. If baseball is still a going concern in decades, Trout's story will be an integral part of it. His team though? Not so much. The greatness of Trout underlines the core paradox of his team: No one cares about the Los Angeles Angels, and yet everyone watches them.

Erstwhile Angels manager Mike Scioscia was well-known for his box of sayings, with his most commonly used mantra at the end of his reign perhaps being "turn the page." The Angels have done lots of page-turning of late, so much that their second season post-Scioscia brings another new manager. Last season was the Angels' worst campaign of the century, whether mounted from Los Angeles, Anaheim or Los Angeles of Anaheim. The last time the Angels were worse than the 72-90 was 1999, when only a strong finish (19-10) under interim manager Joe Maddon brought them to 71 wins. The team has long been searching, increasingly frantically, for its next chapter, something worth remembering.

It's not meant pejoratively, but more as a matter of fact: Despite the presence of a true contender for baseball's "best ever" crown, continued futility has turned the team into an afterthought. Joke does not seem the harshest descriptor, given the prevalence of the "wasting Mike Trout" refrain that grows harder to deny each season the team is functionally eliminated by the trade deadline. The Angels have consciously courted the same media market as the Dodgers, who since 2013 have surpassed them by six division titles and 204 wins. While Commissioner Rob Manfred has criticized Trout for not cultivating his own legend, a much more obvious critique is of the failure of his organization to put talent around its homegrown superstar. The 2020 season is, as much as it is about winning, a challenge in relevance.

Things have to get better for the Angels, if almost by default, since they spent the latter half of the year eliminated from contention and embroiled in tragedy and scandal. The tragic death of Tyler Skaggs, and subsequent revelation of Angels employees with knowledge of and involvement in the

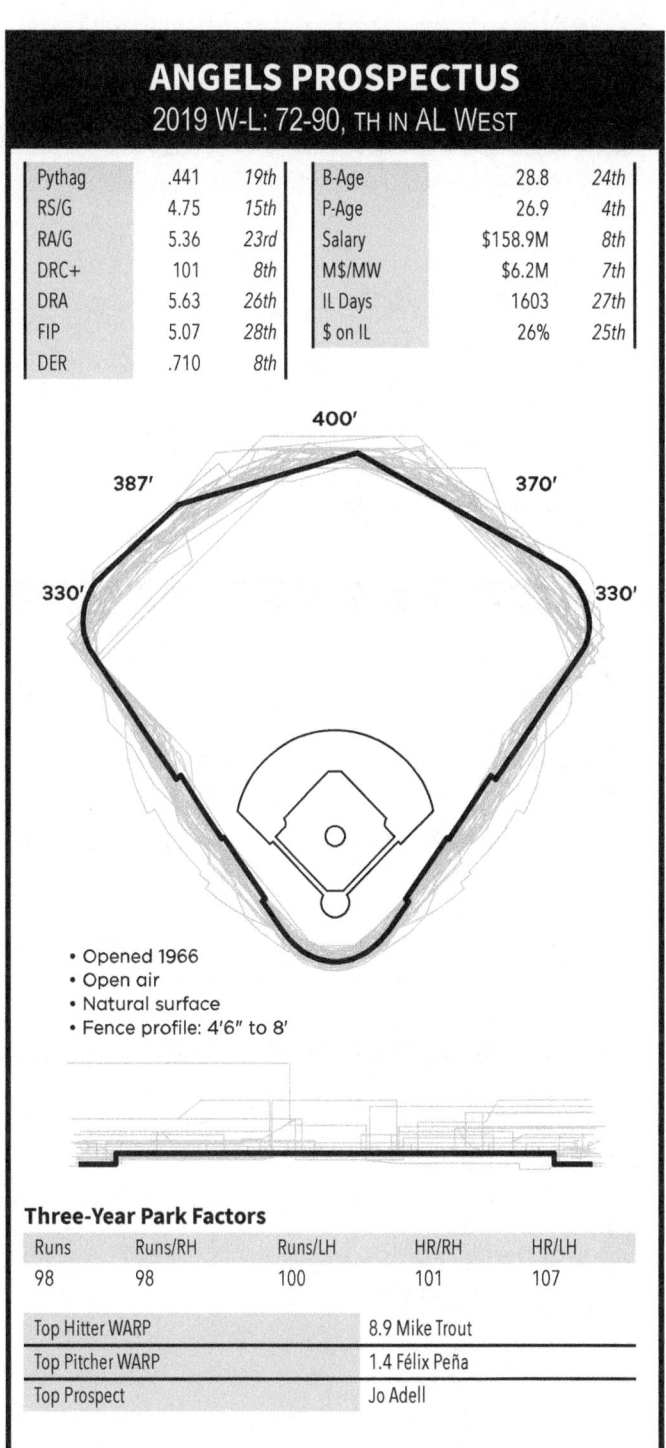

ANGELS PROSPECTUS
2019 W-L: 72-90, TH IN AL WEST

Pythag	.441	19th	B-Age	28.8	24th
RS/G	4.75	15th	P-Age	26.9	4th
RA/G	5.36	23rd	Salary	$158.9M	8th
DRC+	101	8th	M$/MW	$6.2M	7th
DRA	5.63	26th	IL Days	1603	27th
FIP	5.07	28th	$ on IL	26%	25th
DER	.710	8th			

- Opened 1966
- Open air
- Natural surface
- Fence profile: 4'6" to 8'

Three-Year Park Factors

Runs	Runs/RH	Runs/LH	HR/RH	HR/LH
98	98	100	101	107

Top Hitter WARP	8.9 Mike Trout
Top Pitcher WARP	1.4 Félix Peña
Top Prospect	Jo Adell

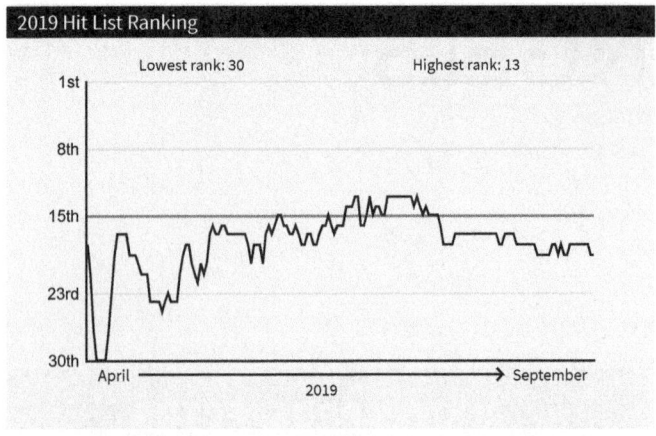

2019 Hit List Ranking

Lowest rank: 30   Highest rank: 13

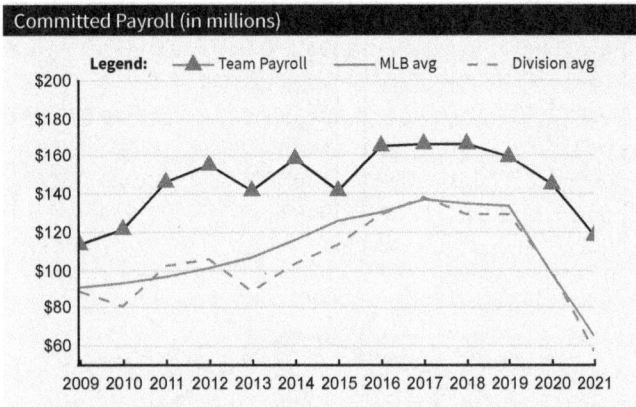

Committed Payroll (in millions)

Legend: ▲ Team Payroll   —— MLB avg   - - Division avg

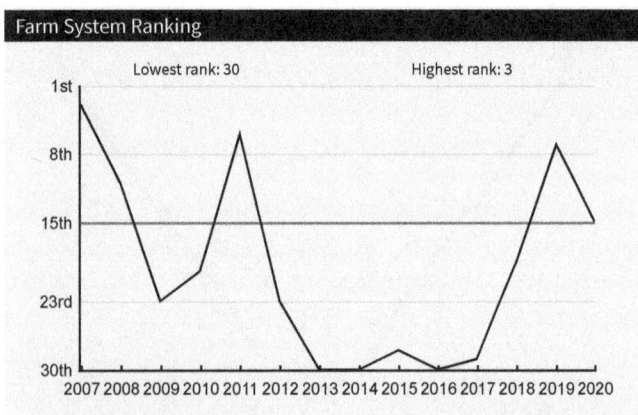

Farm System Ranking

Lowest rank: 30   Highest rank: 3

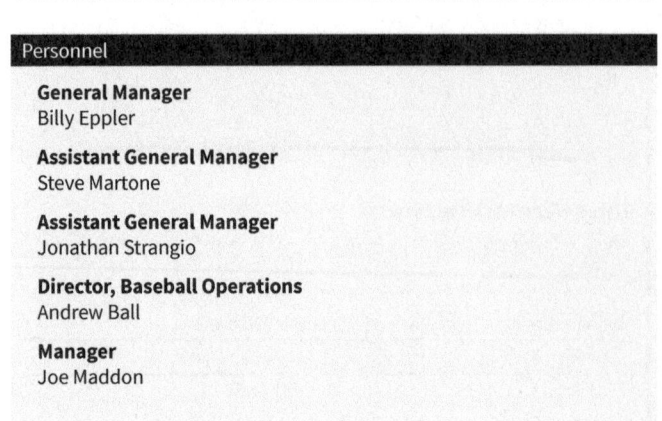

Personnel

General Manager
Billy Eppler

Assistant General Manager
Steve Martone

Assistant General Manager
Jonathan Strangio

Director, Baseball Operations
Andrew Ball

Manager
Joe Maddon

pitcher's opioid use, tinged everything that followed: a deeply emotional combined no-hitter, a freefall sans Trout to end the season, the firing of Brad Ausmus and installation of former bench coach Joe Maddon.

In spite of it all, some 3,019,012 people were reported as coming to see Trout & Co. The teams surrounding the Angels on the attendance list—the Cubs, Rockies and Red Sox—suggest a certain level of insularity from performance. The Angels' last game of the season was started by Dillon Peters. Brian Goodwin hit third! 34,693 arrived to bear witness, and were treated to a perfect encapsulation of their season: Peters failed to escape the fourth and the Angels never held the lead and were out of it by the seventh-inning stretch. For the 162nd time, the team showed up, the fans did too, but the positives ended there.

Last season was not the most injury-laden for Angels pitchers in recent memory, but, it might well have been the worst. Experiments with starters Matt Harvey and Trevor Cahill, and closer Cody Allen are better left as forgotten as the team's Disney phase, and their underperformance—plus the void left by Skaggs' passing—put a lot on rookie starters, and, more frequently, the bullpen. The Angels received a franchise record 761 2/3 relief innings, one of just four instances in league history where a team saw its bullpen rack up more frames than its rotation. None of the other entrants, the 2018-19 Rays and the 2019 Blue Jays, were known for playing a particularly alluring brand of baseball.

In contrast to the beleaguered pitchers, the Angels offense has long been fine. With Mike Trout consistently 75-plus percent above league average (and age-related decline hopefully years down the line), it'd take something truly putrid for the lineup as a whole to rest below. With Anthony Rendon likely hitting behind Trout most days, the ceiling is the league's best offense. The team has to lean on a lot of rebounds, however: No one's expecting Albert Pujols to be more than replacement-level at this point, but Shohei Ohtani, Andrelton Simmons and Justin Upton each struggled with injury and underperformance. The latter two sitting on the wrong side of 30 makes a return to form unassured. Top prospect Jo Adell waits in the wings, with space cleared for him by a declined Kole Calhoun option. It's unclear if he'll have to play the service-time waiting game. And, in any case, the underwhelming rookie season of Vladimir Guerrero Jr. gives a rejoinder against expecting every uber-prospect to perform immediately on the level of Ronald Acuña Jr.

It's clear Moreno wants the Angels to be more than an also-ran. The Rendon signing aligns with the Pujols and Josh Hamilton deals in more than its boundary-pushing AAV: While there were myriad factors that caused him to land in Southern California rather than Gerrit Cole and Stephen Strasburg, Rendon reaffirms a preference to spend on position players and their possibility for daily contributions, rather than the once-every-five-days model for starting pitchers. It's not that there's no logic there; the team's own track record of fragile starters underscores that, but the team's failure to make a big splash in the rotation puts a lot on a group reasonably described as Ohtani et al.

It's fair to argue that Rendon was the best player available in the offseason, but there are just as many reasons to think Angels fans have heard this story before. Rendon is coming off a 6.3 WARP season, and will be entering his age-30 season in 2020. Pujols recorded a 6.4 WARP campaign in his final year in St. Louis, and arrived in Anaheim for his age-31 season. Upton, meanwhile, was coming off a 4.9 WARP effort split between Detroit and Anaheim, before re-upping ahead of his age-30 season. Rendon, perhaps, combines the best of those two qualities, and therefore could be the best veteran teammate of Trout's tenure—but one can't blame the fanbase for feeling like Lucy is holding a football, saying this time it's different.

Meanwhile, Billy Eppler leaned hard into reliability for the rotation, ultimately winding up with a mostly durable group with shaky upside. If Andrew Heaney can put it all together in his walk year for a repeat of 2018, he's probably still a third starter. Ohtani is an aberration all his own, but a full healthy season would still represent a mutation of sorts for the flamethrower, entering his third year in the league. Julio Teherán and Dylan Bundy will probably help ensure the rotation again outstrips the bullpen in frames, if simultaneously pushing the group downwards in rate metrics. Collected together, it's hardly an intimidating list of names.

Here is the problem, however: The Angels are a team with little identity or attraction besides an archipelago of otherworldly players, going it in isolation. Trout's legacy will endure, as will those of Ohtani and even Pujols in this latter form, but the team they played for will be of little consequence or relevance. You may as well swap out the halos on the caps for the Pilots' long-neglected aerial motifs. In time, bereft of any memorable accomplishments or feats of their own, the Angels' significance to these stages of its stars' careers will be minimal. Trout, Ohtani, Pujols and now Rendon play in Anaheim. Outside of the Anaheim faithful (whose continued, obedient attendance suggests a Stockholm-lite Syndrome with their underperforming home team), who cares?

It would be easy to blame east coast bias for the neglect, or their also-ran status of late. They boast the game's brightest star, but Trout often rises to the occasion long after fans in earlier time zones have fallen asleep. Plus, those occasions of actual relevance are fewer and farther between than you'd like, given how little the Angels have mattered in the standings. Their efforts each year are undone by the type of unfortunate events fit for a children's series, but also by inadequacy; poor planning and poorer pitching. Causally the latter via the former. A never-ending slurry of disappointing, nondescript pitchers and middling supporting casts will earn you four consecutive sub-.500 seasons, certainly. But the question persists: Why do people keep showing up?

One answer is that, in some lights, the Angels are the most interesting team in baseball. Inadequacy might be at the forefront, but behind those failed efforts is, well, effort. That has been, in the last few seasons, a notable distinction from the rest of the league. Their 40-man payroll hasn't ended the season below $176 million since 2016. Their 26-man roster entering 2020 currently features four players earning more than $21 million (Trout, Pujols, Rendon, Upton), and a fifth (Simmons) at $15 million. They've amassed more singular talents than anyone else in the league: Trout is the best player in the game, possibly ever; Simmons is an ethereal defender and Ohtani is the premiere two-way player in baseball, whose prodigious talent on both sides of the ball demanded a rethinking of what is feasible within the modern game.

Framed a different way, it isn't as shocking as it might seem (based on their record) that a team who ranked in the top 10 in year-end payroll from 2004-13 has seen more than 3 million fans through their turnstiles every year since 2003. The Angels may be Lucy, but they can't be blamed for the fact that every fan is already, inherently, Charlie Brown. There's something virtuous in Charlie's hope, and so too in Lucy's determination to deny; even if Angels fans might have expected more coming into the season than another kick at the placed football, it still lingers, enticing the true believers.

The Angels, 3 million fans and all, are presently making no one care about a roster including Trout and Ohtani, Simmons and the remaining swings of Pujols. Even Rendon, with Trout's prime and his on the clock, might not be enough to quell the naysayers. Even so, they'll probably be entertained, even if they can't quite remember why. ▪

—Ginny Searle is an author of Baseball Prospectus.

HITTERS

───────────── ★ ★ ★ *2020 Top 101 Prospect* **#72** ★ ★ ★ ─────────────

Jordyn Adams **OF** Born: 10/18/99 Age: 20 Bats: R Throws: R Height: 6'2" Weight: 180 Origin: Round 1, 2018 Draft (#17 overall)

YEAR	TEAM	LVL	AGE	PA	R	2B	3B	HR	RBI	BB	K	SB	CS	AVG/OBP/SLG	DRC+	VORP	BABIP	BRR	FRAA	WARP
2018	ANG	RK	18	82	8	2	2	0	5	10	23	5	2	.243/.354/.329	84	2.3	.362	0.9	CF(14): -4.2, RF(1): 0.0	-0.2
2018	ORM	RK	18	40	5	4	1	0	8	4	7	0	1	.314/.375/.486	113	1.3	.379	-0.8	CF(8): 3.1	0.3
2019	BUR	A	19	428	52	15	2	7	31	50	94	12	5	.250/.346/.358	123	20.6	.316	2.4	CF(73): -1.2, LF(9): 2.5	2.6
2019	INL	A+	19	40	7	1	1	1	1	5	14	0	1	.229/.325/.400	94	2.0	.350	0.2	CF(4): 0.4, RF(2): -0.3	0.1
2020	LAA	MLB	20	251	23	11	1	5	24	20	76	3	1	.226/.292/.342	71	-1.6	.317	-0.2	CF 0, LF 0	-0.1

Comparables: Trent Grisham, Joe Benson, Victor Robles

You could do worse for an organizational philosophy than "draft athletes and worry about the rest later." Adams joins a swelling cohort of Angels position-player prospects who have plenty of tools with varying degrees of refinement. What opened eyes about the former North Carolina football recruit was a strong performance in the notoriously hitter-hostile Midwest League, earning him a late-season call-up to the friendlier offensive climes of the Cal League, where he looks to start in the coming season. If the power isn't quite there yet, the patience and speed are, and Adams' development will be an above-the-fold story for Angels prospect watchers in 2020.

───────────── ★ ★ ★ *2020 Top 101 Prospect* **#2** ★ ★ ★ ─────────────

Jo Adell **OF** Born: 04/08/99 Age: 21 Bats: R Throws: R Height: 6'3" Weight: 215 Origin: Round 1, 2017 Draft (#10 overall)

YEAR	TEAM	LVL	AGE	PA	R	2B	3B	HR	RBI	BB	K	SB	CS	AVG/OBP/SLG	DRC+	VORP	BABIP	BRR	FRAA	WARP
2017	ANG	RK	18	132	18	6	6	4	21	10	32	5	0	.288/.351/.542	117	13.4	.361	1.9		0.5
2017	ORM	RK	18	90	25	5	2	1	9	4	17	3	2	.376/.411/.518	133	7.3	.463	0.4		0.3
2018	BUR	A	19	108	23	7	1	6	29	11	26	4	1	.326/.398/.611	164	12.4	.391	1.2	CF(16): -0.4, RF(3): -0.9	1.0
2018	INL	A+	19	262	46	19	3	12	42	15	63	9	2	.290/.345/.546	142	21.9	.345	2.0	CF(36): -5.6, RF(8): -1.1	1.4
2018	MOB	AA	19	71	14	6	0	2	6	6	22	2	0	.238/.324/.429	100	4.5	.333	-0.3	CF(17): -1.9	0.0
2019	INL	A+	20	27	4	1	0	2	5	1	10	0	0	.280/.333/.560	115	3.0	.385	0.3	CF(3): 0.5, RF(2): -0.1	0.2
2019	MOB	AA	20	182	28	15	0	8	23	19	41	6	0	.308/.390/.553	168	14.6	.369	0.5	RF(19): -1.2, CF(17): -3.5	1.5
2019	SLC	AAA	20	132	22	11	0	0	8	10	43	1	0	.264/.321/.355	66	0.3	.410	2.5	RF(12): -0.5, LF(9): 0.6	0.0
2020	LAA	MLB	21	245	26	15	1	8	29	19	78	3	1	.248/.313/.424	93	2.9	.345	0.0	RF -6	-0.3

Comparables: Corey Seager, Ronald Acuña Jr., Austin Riley

According to the debut episode of BP's "Three-Quarters Delivery" podcast (cross-platform synergies, y'all!), Adell is an *icon*. Certainly, that's a weighty word for a dude who hasn't yet taken his first major-league licks. And if we're being honest, Adell's most recent minor-league stop, at Triple-A Salt Lake City, hints at some development yet to come for the 20-year-old (to be fair, he was never fully healthy after an early-season ankle/hammy injury). But one doesn't get "icon" from a stat line, however impressive. That title comes from qualitative, human observation—watching him calmly waggle his bat before uncorking a home-run swing, gracefully cover huge expanses of green as he tracks down a fly ball in center field, or conduct interviews and interact with fans with an easy charm and ready smile. In baseball terms, should the Angels and their fans be excited for Adell's arrival in 2020? Of course. But his iconic potential, particularly as a young black player in a sport with a dearth of African-American superstars, gives reason for those who simply root for baseball—its goodness, its relevance, its survival—to rejoice.

Anthony Bemboom **C** Born: 01/18/90 Age: 30 Bats: L Throws: R Height: 6'2" Weight: 200 Origin: Round 22, 2012 Draft (#687 overall)

YEAR	TEAM	LVL	AGE	PA	R	2B	3B	HR	RBI	BB	K	SB	CS	AVG/OBP/SLG	DRC+	VORP	BABIP	BRR	FRAA	WARP
2017	ABQ	AAA	27	160	20	8	2	4	20	24	30	0	0	.278/.390/.459	108	10.4	.330	-0.5	C(40): 6.7	1.6
2018	ABQ	AAA	28	249	25	10	0	5	29	32	49	0	0	.232/.339/.351	81	4.0	.277	1.9	C(52): 7.4, 1B(1): 0.0	1.5
2019	DUR	AAA	29	50	7	3	0	1	6	2	10	0	1	.213/.240/.340	62	-2.8	.243	0.3	C(8): 2.4	0.2
2019	SLC	AAA	29	64	7	1	2	2	10	7	9	0	0	.316/.391/.509	95	4.0	.348	-0.4	C(15): 0.1	0.3
2019	TBA	MLB	29	5	0	1	0	0	1	0	2	0	0	.400/.400/.600	79	0.2	.667	0.0	C(3): -0.6	0.0
2019	LAA	MLB	29	51	2	0	0	1	3	1	19	0	0	.102/.120/.163	59	-0.1	.138	-0.2		0.2
2020	LAA	MLB	30	70	6	2	0	2	7	5	20	0	0	.201/.267/.321	56	-0.9	.267	-0.1	C 2	0.1

Comparables: David Freitas, Mike Nickeas, Raffy Lopez

YEAR	TEAM	P. COUNT	FRM RUNS	BLK RUNS	THRW RUNS	TOT RUNS
2017	ABQ	5432	5.7	-0.4	0.2	5.3
2018	ABQ	7516	3.7	-0.1	0.3	3.7
2019	DUR	1141	2.6	0.0	0.0	2.6
2019	TBA	271	0.2	-1.1	0.3	-0.6
2019	LAA	2348	2.1	-0.1	0.0	2.0
2019	SLC	2161	0.0	0.0	0.2	0.2
2020	LAA	2717	1.9	-0.5	0.3	1.7

You struggle for eight years in three minor-league systems, you put in the work, you know you're not getting to the Show with your bat (you've never cracked double-digit homers or a .250 average outside the PCL), so you work with your pitchers, you work on your framing, your release—you just work. One day, you get to the show, and in your third game: it's the sixth inning, you've gone 2-for-2 with an RBI double, and what's more, you've piloted three pitchers through five shutout innings. You're most proud of that. Even the empty seats in Miami seem full of promise. Then, on a routine play, you tweak your knee and the brilliant night ends early. Your team? It signs a vet who goes on to an improbable comeback season. Good for him, you wish him nothing but the best. You? You get shipped to Anaheim, where you're the third catcher up, so: back to the minors, with some spot duty in September. There may not be many more extended stays in the show, but hey, you crossed the threshold. 2019 was a great year. You're a big-league catcher. Forever.

Justin Bour 1B Born: 05/28/88 Age: 32 Bats: L Throws: R Height: 6'4" Weight: 270 Origin: Round 25, 2009 Draft (#770 overall)

YEAR	TEAM	LVL	AGE	PA	R	2B	3B	HR	RBI	BB	K	SB	CS	AVG/OBP/SLG	DRC+	VORP	BABIP	BRR	FRAA	WARP
2017	MIA	MLB	29	429	52	18	0	25	83	47	95	1	0	.289/.366/.536	126	30.0	.322	-1.8	1B(102): -10.0	0.8
2018	MIA	MLB	30	447	43	10	1	19	54	69	111	1	0	.227/.347/.412	103	14.8	.267	-3.1	1B(103): -6.3	-0.2
2018	PHI	MLB	30	54	6	3	0	1	5	4	13	1	0	.224/.296/.347	103	-0.9	.286	0.2	1B(10): -0.5	0.1
2019	SLC	AAA	31	229	44	12	1	17	43	41	46	2	1	.316/.441/.663	157	20.3	.339	-1.4	1B(25): -2.8	1.4
2019	LAA	MLB	31	170	18	5	0	8	26	17	52	0	0	.172/.259/.364	77	-2.3	.196	-1.3		-0.4
2020	*LAA*	*MLB*	*32*	*251*	*33*	*9*	*0*	*13*	*37*	*29*	*67*	*1*	*0*	*.238/.330/.464*	*108*	*9.6*	*.279*	*-1.2*	*1B -4*	*0.6*

Comparables: Brandon Belt, Justin Smoak, Steve Balboni

There's a scene in *Multiplicity*, 1996's sci-fi/fantasy comedy starring Michael Keaton (x4) where the original Keaton walks into a room to find that his two clones have created yet another clone. As the original panics, he also wonders, "What's up with #4?" #2 explains, "You know when you make a copy of a copy, it's not quite as sharp as the original?" Well, Bour was a copy of a copy of C.J. Cron's Angels tenure—a poorly applied patch among many for a lineup that never stopped leaking production from multiple holes. At a time when empty power has never been a more plentiful resource (pending the State of the Ball, of course), Bour has become part of MLB's latest wave of exports to Japan, signing with the Hanshin Tigers in November. Still no word on the contract status of the other clones, though.

Jason Castro C Born: 06/18/87 Age: 33 Bats: L Throws: R Height: 6'3" Weight: 215 Origin: Round 1, 2008 Draft (#10 overall)

YEAR	TEAM	LVL	AGE	PA	R	2B	3B	HR	RBI	BB	K	SB	CS	AVG/OBP/SLG	DRC+	VORP	BABIP	BRR	FRAA	WARP
2017	MIN	MLB	30	407	49	22	0	10	47	45	108	0	0	.242/.333/.388	86	13.4	.318	-0.4	C(108): 7.7	2.1
2018	MIN	MLB	31	74	4	3	0	1	3	9	26	0	0	.143/.257/.238	57	-2.3	.216	-0.7	C(19): 2.5	0.2
2019	MIN	MLB	32	275	39	9	0	13	30	33	88	0	0	.232/.332/.435	100	14.7	.307	1.0	C(78): 3.5	1.9
2020	*LAA*	*MLB*	*33*	*350*	*39*	*14*	*1*	*13*	*42*	*37*	*116*	*1*	*0*	*.214/.305/.389*	*83*	*8.8*	*.295*	*0.0*	*C 6*	*1.5*

Comparables: Rick Wilkins, Jorge Posada, Ron Karkovice

Castro bounced back in the last act of his three-year deal, posting his sixth twoish win season in his last seven. His script for success has turned: his defense has settled into very-good-not-quite-great middle age, while he posted the best DRC+ of his career thanks to a flyball-orientated shift in line with the rest of the Twins roster. It remains to be seen if his offensive gains will stick, but he should at least open 2020 getting starts against most right-handed pitchers.

YEAR	TEAM	P. COUNT	FRM RUNS	BLK RUNS	THRW RUNS	TOT RUNS
2017	MIN	14556	8.3	0.3	-0.2	8.1
2018	MIN	3132	1.4	0.9	0.1	2.2
2019	MIN	10672	6.1	-1.9	-0.3	3.8
2020	*LAA*	*18622*	*8.3*	*-0.9*	*-0.9*	*6.5*

Trent Deveaux OF Born: 05/04/00 Age: 20 Bats: R Throws: R Height: 6'0" Weight: 160 Origin: International Free Agent, 2017

YEAR	TEAM	LVL	AGE	PA	R	2B	3B	HR	RBI	BB	K	SB	CS	AVG/OBP/SLG	DRC+	VORP	BABIP	BRR	FRAA	WARP
2018	ANG	RK	18	194	20	5	0	1	11	24	68	7	4	.199/.309/.247	67	-1.5	.327	1.4	CF(26): -6.1, RF(14): -0.3	-0.4
2019	ANG	RK	19	244	38	15	4	6	23	24	76	14	6	.247/.332/.437	105	13.6	.351	0.3	CF(28): -5.0, LF(14): 0.1	0.4
2019	ORM	RK+	19	31	4	1	0	1	2	2	15	1	0	.172/.226/.310	29	-1.7	.308	0.1		-0.1
2020	*LAA*	*MLB*	*20*	*251*	*20*	*12*	*1*	*4*	*22*	*19*	*108*	*2*	*1*	*.192/.259/.306*	*50*	*-8.2*	*.339*	*0.0*	*CF -2, RF 0*	*-1.1*

Comparables: Brett Phillips, Aristides Aquino, Derrick Robinson

One can easily level the charge of "lazy comp" in pairing Deveaux with fellow 2017 signee D'Shawn Knowles but, c'mon, it's practically unavoidable: both signed out of the Bahamas in the same year, both are speedy, athletic outfielders of similar size and build, both finished 2019 in the Pioneer League. It's difficult to say much more at this early point. Deveaux might have an edge in speed but Knowles has shown more power; Deveaux is older than Knowles but slightly below him on the organizational ladder. It's no sure thing that either player hits (in both literal and metaphorical senses), but 2020 will be a crucial year for this prospect's (oh please no...please don't do this) Deveaux-lopment.

David Fletcher UT Born: 05/31/94 Age: 26 Bats: R Throws: R Height: 5'9" Weight: 185 Origin: Round 6, 2015 Draft (#195 overall)

YEAR	TEAM	LVL	AGE	PA	R	2B	3B	HR	RBI	BB	K	SB	CS	AVG/OBP/SLG	DRC+	VORP	BABIP	BRR	FRAA	WARP
2017	MOB	AA	23	272	32	14	1	1	22	21	30	12	5	.276/.341/.354	115	9.6	.308	-1.5	2B(34): 1.0, SS(28): 0.0	1.3
2017	SLC	AAA	23	217	27	6	1	2	17	6	25	8	1	.254/.285/.322	63	0.3	.281	2.3	SS(26): 0.2, 2B(22): 0.2	0.1
2018	SLC	AAA	24	275	55	25	5	6	37	16	21	7	2	.350/.394/.559	135	24.4	.364	3.4	SS(31): 3.4, 2B(18): -1.6	3.0
2018	LAA	MLB	24	307	35	18	2	1	25	15	34	3	0	.275/.316/.363	91	6.5	.307	3.5		1.6
2019	LAA	MLB	25	653	83	30	4	6	49	55	64	8	3	.290/.350/.384	101	25.8	.317	-4.5		2.5
2020	*LAA*	*MLB*	*26*	*525*	*50*	*27*	*2*	*7*	*50*	*36*	*61*	*10*	*3*	*.277/.331/.387*	*91*	*13.1*	*.306*	*-0.5*	*2B 0, SS 0*	*1.6*

Comparables: Darwin Barney, Brent Butler, Aaron Hill

While The Beach Boys are a natural fit for Orange County's first professional sports team, Fletcher's jam isn't anything so obvious as "Surfin' USA" or "Wouldn't It Be Nice." No, you'll find the infielder sitting pensively by his locker, listening to *Pet Sounds* deep cut "I Just Wasn't Made for These Times." Fletcher, an OC native, would have been celebrated for his contact skills, excellent defense, and all-round grit in a bygone era. In the age of moonshots and megatools, he seems a quaint anachronism. But even if the skills are unfashionable, they propelled him to being the third-most valuable Angel in 2019. God only knows what the Angels will look like in 2020, but Fletcher's still bound to be giving his good vibrations.

Brian Goodwin OF Born: 11/02/90 Age: 29 Bats: L Throws: R Height: 6'0" Weight: 200 Origin: Round 1, 2011 Draft (#34 overall)

YEAR	TEAM	LVL	AGE	PA	R	2B	3B	HR	RBI	BB	K	SB	CS	AVG/OBP/SLG	DRC+	VORP	BABIP	BRR	FRAA	WARP
2017	SYR	AAA	26	103	9	4	0	2	11	10	29	2	1	.256/.327/.367	91	0.3	.350	-1.6	RF(9): 0.8, CF(8): 0.0	0.0
2017	WAS	MLB	26	278	41	21	1	13	30	23	69	6	0	.251/.313/.498	97	13.5	.291	0.1	CF(34): -1.2, LF(31): -0.2	0.8
2018	OMA	AAA	27	44	6	4	0	2	9	4	11	0	0	.225/.295/.475	91	2.6	.259	0.1	CF(3): -0.5, RF(2): -0.4	0.1
2018	WAS	MLB	27	79	9	1	0	3	12	10	26	3	1	.200/.321/.354	80	-0.6	.270	-1.8	LF(11): -0.2, RF(10): -0.7	-0.2
2018	KCA	MLB	27	101	11	5	0	3	13	6	31	1	1	.266/.317/.415	84	3.5	.367	0.2	CF(25): -0.7, LF(1): -0.1	0.1
2019	LAA	MLB	28	458	65	29	3	17	47	38	129	7	3	.262/.326/.470	100	13.7	.337	-1.3		0.9
2020	LAA	MLB	29	525	60	24	2	21	68	45	156	10	3	.236/.306/.428	92	6.1	.304	-1.5	RF 6, CF -2	1.1

Comparables: Jake Marisnick, Craig Wilson, Robbie Grossman

With the prolonged absence of Justin Upton and the occasional absence of Mike Trout, spring training waiver claim Goodwin used 2019 to demonstrate that he was just good enough in full-time run to earn a more stable role as a fourth outfielder, able to competently hold down starting duties as needs dictate. Every aspect of his offensive game—power, plate discipline, speed—was similar to, if slightly better than, his prior part-time work over three seasons with the Nats and Royals. His defense wasn't terrible, though the metrics dinged his overuse as a jack-of-all-outfield-positions. All of this added up to a season in which, by WARP's lights, Goodwin very nearly earned his last name.

Michael Hermosillo OF Born: 01/17/95 Age: 25 Bats: R Throws: R Height: 6'0" Weight: 205 Origin: Round 28, 2013 Draft (#847 overall)

YEAR	TEAM	LVL	AGE	PA	R	2B	3B	HR	RBI	BB	K	SB	CS	AVG/OBP/SLG	DRC+	VORP	BABIP	BRR	FRAA	WARP
2017	INL	A+	22	64	5	6	0	0	2	9	15	5	2	.321/.438/.434	161	4.3	.447	-1.3	CF(9): -2.3, LF(3): -0.3	0.2
2017	MOB	AA	22	340	40	13	2	4	26	40	73	21	9	.248/.361/.353	119	14.5	.316	-2.0	CF(52): -2.3, RF(13): 2.3	1.5
2017	SLC	AAA	22	129	20	6	1	5	16	7	28	9	2	.287/.341/.487	91	5.7	.337	0.3	LF(14): -0.1, CF(10): 0.6	0.4
2018	SLC	AAA	23	323	43	14	4	12	46	30	87	10	5	.267/.357/.480	91	11.6	.341	-0.4	CF(36): 5.5, RF(19): 0.3	1.4
2018	LAA	MLB	23	62	7	4	0	1	1	3	17	0	1	.211/.274/.333	61	-1.3	.282	-0.5		0.1
2019	SLC	AAA	24	296	51	8	3	15	43	26	88	6	4	.243/.331/.471	72	11.1	.304	0.4	CF(40): 3.4, RF(11): -0.3	0.4
2019	LAA	MLB	24	46	7	1	1	0	3	5	19	2	0	.139/.304/.222	62	-0.9	.278	0.8		0.0
2020	LAA	MLB	25	210	21	9	1	5	21	17	67	6	3	.214/.297/.351	73	-1.4	.303	0.0	CF 0, LF 0	0.0

Comparables: Mallex Smith, Brandon Nimmo, Billy McKinney

Biographically, Hermosillo is a one-man Proper Noun NAFTA, as the Ottawa, Illinois product shares a last name with a Mexican city and a hometown with the Canadian capital, all the while growing up in the Land of Lincoln. A high-school football standout, Hermosillo briefly occupied an Arizona Fall League dugout with fellow crossover Tim Tebow. It's not going too far on a limb to say that while Tebow unquestionably takes the gridiron honors, Hermosillo can easily claim supremacy on the diamond. You may think this is praise so faint as to be an ambient hum, so let's put a more positive spin on this: at least Hermosillo's athleticism got him to the majors, which is more than we can say for the other guy.

Jeremiah Jackson SS Born: 03/26/00 Age: 20 Bats: R Throws: R Height: 6'0" Weight: 165 Origin: Round 2, 2018 Draft (#57 overall)

YEAR	TEAM	LVL	AGE	PA	R	2B	3B	HR	RBI	BB	K	SB	CS	AVG/OBP/SLG	DRC+	VORP	BABIP	BRR	FRAA	WARP
2018	ANG	RK	18	91	13	4	2	5	14	7	25	6	1	.317/.374/.598	147	13.9	.396	1.3	SS(21): -1.3	0.8
2018	ORM	RK	18	100	13	6	3	2	9	8	34	4	1	.198/.260/.396	26	-1.4	.286	-0.3	SS(21): -1.7, 2B(1): 0.0	-0.7
2019	ORM	RK+	19	291	47	14	2	23	60	24	96	5	1	.266/.333/.605	111	22.4	.315	1.0		1.3
2020	LAA	MLB	20	251	20	12	1	5	22	18	102	5	2	.181/.245/.304	45	-9.6	.296	0.3	SS -1, 2B 0	-1.1

Comparables: Carter Kieboom, Lewis Brinson, Clint Frazier

Like a number of the Angels' top prospects, Jackson is a toolsy, athletic, but still quite raw outfiel—wait, I'm sorry (holding finger to ear)—I'm being told that Jackson is a *shortstop*. A shortstop, in fact, who socked 23 bombs in a mere 291 plate appearances at short-season Orem. The good news and bad news both stem from the same source: he's only 19 and looks to fill out physically over the next few years. While a bigger body will likely move him off shortstop, it bodes very well for the continued development of his already-legit power bat. To be clear, the good news is much, much better than the bad.

Jahmai Jones 2B Born: 08/04/97 Age: 22 Bats: R Throws: R Height: 5'11" Weight: 205 Origin: Round 2, 2015 Draft (#70 overall)

YEAR	TEAM	LVL	AGE	PA	R	2B	3B	HR	RBI	BB	K	SB	CS	AVG/OBP/SLG	DRC+	VORP	BABIP	BRR	FRAA	WARP
2017	BUR	A	19	387	54	18	4	9	30	32	63	18	7	.272/.338/.425	115	27.5	.309	5.7	CF(65): -3.4, LF(16): 0.5	2.1
2017	INL	A+	19	191	32	11	3	5	17	13	43	9	6	.302/.368/.488	124	17.9	.379	2.0	CF(37): -9.7, LF(3): -0.5	0.2
2018	INL	A+	20	347	47	10	5	8	35	43	63	13	3	.235/.338/.383	111	12.6	.272	1.5	2B(70): -6.9	0.8
2018	MOB	AA	20	212	33	10	4	2	20	24	51	11	1	.245/.335/.375	104	5.7	.323	-1.5	2B(45): -1.7	0.4
2019	MOB	AA	21	544	66	22	3	5	50	50	109	9	11	.234/.308/.324	79	2.8	.288	2.3	2B(108): 14.4, CF(7): 0.3	2.3
2020	LAA	MLB	22	251	24	12	1	5	25	19	62	6	2	.228/.292/.362	73	-0.7	.289	0.0	2B 1, CF -2	-0.1

Comparables: Victor Robles, Cole Tucker, Billy McKinney

For a few years, Jones was the pride of the Angels' farm system, but at some point reality outruns potential and you're a 22-year-old who just completed a first full year of Double-A with downturns in just about every aspect of your game. To be fair, Jones has learned a new position in the past couple of years, and well, maybe the upside was overplayed simply because there were no other prospects around to measure for scale. Now that the prospect fanfare has died down, the "post-hype sleeper" phase of his career is nicely teed up. Regardless of what the future holds, one never likes to see the hype train lose steam two stops before the big city.

Ty Kelly **2B** Born: 07/20/88 Age: 31 Bats: B Throws: R Height: 6'0" Weight: 180 Origin: Round 13, 2009 Draft (#386 overall)

YEAR	TEAM	LVL	AGE	PA	R	2B	3B	HR	RBI	BB	K	SB	CS	AVG/OBP/SLG	DRC+	VORP	BABIP	BRR	FRAA	WARP
2017	NYN	MLB	28	1	0	0	0	0	0	0	1	0	0	.000/.000/.000	62	-0.3	--	0.0		0.0
2017	PHI	MLB	28	104	11	7	0	2	14	8	24	0	0	.193/.260/.341	67	2.5	.231	0.9	2B(14): 0.3, LF(9): -1.0	0.2
2018	LVG	AAA	29	424	60	24	5	8	52	48	92	2	1	.259/.348/.416	91	9.6	.326	-2.8	2B(45): -2.9, SS(42): -1.5	0.4
2018	NYN	MLB	29	12	1	0	0	0	0	1	2	0	0	.091/.167/.091	82	-2.1	.111	0.1	2B(2): 0.0, 3B(1): 0.0	0.0
2019	SLC	AAA	30	317	37	12	3	1	22	32	80	3	2	.246/.325/.320	52	-7.1	.337	-0.4	2B(67): -10.0, RF(9): -2.0	-1.9
2020	LAA	MLB	31	251	22	11	1	3	21	25	66	1	1	.215/.298/.316	67	-3.0	.290	-0.3	2B -3, SS 0	-0.8

Comparables: Jemile Weeks, Mike Baxter, Earl Torgeson

Kelly announced his retirement in August 2019 after bouncing around between the Mets, Blue Jays, Phillies and Angels organizations. While he was never much more than a Quad-A bat, and perhaps barely that, he's showing some upside for a plus Twitter game in his post-baseball career. One such example: In his response to the Max Muncy-Madison Bumgarner kerfuffle, Kelly puts baseball beef in its proper perspective: "pimping home runs doesn't matter the planet is dying." Kelly may not be baseball's own Greta Thunberg, and he still has work to do to reach @BMcCarthy32 or @faridyu levels of tweet glory, but here's hoping that, in addition to his new role as third baseman for Team Israel, he finds time to keep tweeting about the larger contexts within which baseball—with its rituals, absurdities, and unwritten rules—is but a trivial pursuit.

★ ★ ★ *2020 Top 101 Prospect* **#99** ★ ★ ★

D'Shawn Knowles **OF** Born: 01/16/01 Age: 19 Bats: B Throws: R Height: 6'0" Weight: 165 Origin: International Free Agent, 2017

YEAR	TEAM	LVL	AGE	PA	R	2B	3B	HR	RBI	BB	K	SB	CS	AVG/OBP/SLG	DRC+	VORP	BABIP	BRR	FRAA	WARP
2018	ANG	RK	17	130	19	4	1	1	14	15	27	7	4	.301/.385/.381	132	9.6	.384	1.1	LF(13): -3.1, CF(9): -0.5	0.4
2018	ORM	RK	17	123	27	9	2	4	15	13	38	2	3	.321/.398/.550	123	8.7	.463	0.3	CF(17): -1.2, RF(9): 1.8	0.4
2019	ORM	RK+	18	290	38	11	4	6	28	26	76	5	4	.241/.310/.387	70	2.0	.307	-0.3		0.0
2020	LAA	MLB	19	251	22	11	1	4	22	24	89	3	2	.210/.291/.318	66	-3.3	.328	-0.4	CF 0, RF 0	-0.4

Comparables: Mike Trout, Anthony Santander, Juan Soto

Signed out of the Bahamas in 2017, Knowles did just fine in the Pioneer League in his age-18 season. Like fellow countryman and organizational mate Trent Deveaux, Knowles profiles as a speed-and-defense guy, but he also showed a soupçon of power in his rookie league stint, and room to further fill out portends a few more long balls in his future. Whether the Angels' organizational gambit of drafting and signing toolsy, speedy, athletic outfielders in bulk pays off, it certainly makes their lower-minors teams a lot more fun to watch.

Tommy La Stella **INF** Born: 01/31/89 Age: 31 Bats: L Throws: R Height: 5'11" Weight: 180 Origin: Round 8, 2011 Draft (#266 overall)

YEAR	TEAM	LVL	AGE	PA	R	2B	3B	HR	RBI	BB	K	SB	CS	AVG/OBP/SLG	DRC+	VORP	BABIP	BRR	FRAA	WARP
2017	IOW	AAA	28	121	14	2	0	1	6	10	22	0	1	.218/.281/.264	56	-3.5	.261	1.0	2B(22): 0.3, 3B(4): 0.0	-0.1
2017	CHN	MLB	28	151	18	8	0	5	22	20	18	0	0	.288/.389/.472	114	11.6	.298	-0.7	2B(21): -2.4, 3B(18): -0.5	0.4
2018	CHN	MLB	29	192	23	8	0	1	19	17	27	0	1	.266/.340/.331	84	3.1	.312	0.7	3B(26): -1.8, 2B(15): 0.3	0.2
2019	LAA	MLB	30	321	49	8	0	16	44	20	28	0	0	.295/.346/.486	119	19.2	.282	-1.0		1.5
2020	LAA	MLB	31	385	43	17	1	12	46	33	46	2	1	.265/.335/.422	101	10.7	.277	-0.3	1B -1, 2B -2	0.7

Comparables: Lou Whitaker, Luis Alicea, Phil Garner

Using *The Ball* as an explanation for an unexpected 2019 power breakout is fast becoming a tired, intellectually lazy argument. Forget the banality of everyday, materialist realism—we need myths to describe what happened to La Stella, who was an unassuming utility infielder with 10 career home runs and a .366 slugging percentage in over 900 major-league plate appearances coming into last season. He promptly went gonzo and jacked 16 bombs in a half-season until he launch-angled some extreme exit velocity off of his shin and succumbed to a broken tibia. Was the power a Faustian bargain? Icarus flying too close to the sun? While the Angels are filled to the brim with tantalizing storylines heading into 2020, one of the low-key more interesting ones will be the next installment of the myth of La Stella, even if *The Ball* ends up being the all-too-prosaic denouement to the tale.

Kevin Maitan **3B** Born: 02/12/00 Age: 20 Bats: B Throws: R Height: 6'2" Weight: 190 Origin: International Free Agent, 2016

YEAR	TEAM	LVL	AGE	PA	R	2B	3B	HR	RBI	BB	K	SB	CS	AVG/OBP/SLG	DRC+	VORP	BABIP	BRR	FRAA	WARP
2017	BRA	RK	17	37	5	3	0	0	3	2	10	1	0	.314/.351/.400	101	2.1	.440	0.3	SS(5): -1.7	0.0
2017	DNV	RK	17	139	10	5	1	2	15	9	39	1	0	.220/.273/.323	48	0.4	.295	-0.7	SS(30): 0.9	-0.2
2018	ORM	RK	18	284	42	13	1	8	26	19	66	1	2	.248/.306/.397	64	7.5	.303	1.1	3B(40): 3.3, SS(21): -3.1	-0.4
2019	BUR	A	19	532	56	11	3	12	46	39	164	7	4	.214/.278/.323	69	-5.5	.295	-1.9	3B(92): -6.9, 2B(21): -2.8	-1.4
2020	LAA	MLB	20	251	21	10	1	5	23	17	90	0	0	.204/.262/.319	54	-7.4	.307	-0.3	3B -1, SS -1	-0.9

Comparables: Miguel Andújar, Alex Liddi, Renato Núñez

Literally the only way to put a positive spin on the trendline of Maitan is to remind yourself that, in 2019, he was a 19-year-old in the offense-smothering Midwest League. And, while he was bad, he wasn't, like, *historically* bad. There's not much else to recommend the two-time bonus baby: the wide-eyed Miggy comps, along with any chance at playing shortstop, have long since left the building. Stranger things have happened, and an age-20 season is by no means a late date to make a great leap forward, but Maitan will have to battle heroically against the forces of entropy to become a chapter, or even a paragraph, in an Angels success story rather than a mere footnote to Atlanta's failures.

★ ★ ★ *2020 Top 101 Prospect* **#51** ★ ★ ★

Brandon Marsh **OF** Born: 12/18/97 Age: 22 Bats: L Throws: R Height: 6'4" Weight: 215 Origin: Round 2, 2016 Draft (#60 overall)

YEAR	TEAM	LVL	AGE	PA	R	2B	3B	HR	RBI	BB	K	SB	CS	AVG/OBP/SLG	DRC+	VORP	BABIP	BRR	FRAA	WARP
2017	ORM	RK	19	192	47	13	5	4	44	9	35	10	2	.350/.396/.548	120	18.4	.417	3.2	RF(26): -1.9, CF(11): 1.5	0.7
2018	BUR	A	20	154	26	12	1	3	24	21	40	4	0	.295/.390/.470	139	12.2	.400	2.9	CF(14): 1.2, RF(13): -1.3	1.4
2018	INL	A+	20	426	59	15	6	7	46	52	118	10	4	.256/.348/.385	107	21.3	.356	4.3	CF(50): -0.8, RF(33): 3.0	2.2
2019	MOB	AA	21	412	48	21	2	7	43	47	92	18	5	.300/.383/.428	141	27.8	.384	2.6	CF(54): -0.7, RF(19): 1.8	2.9
2020	LAA	MLB	22	251	24	13	1	5	25	19	77	3	1	.246/.307/.375	81	2.1	.347	0.0	CF 0, RF 1	0.4

Comparables: Tyler Austin, Jordan Schafer, Brett Jackson

We're not sure this is Billy Eppler's plan, but we need to be open to the possibility that the Angels GM has found the new market inefficiency in baseball: not enough football players—or at least players who could succeed at the other, lesser sport's skill positions. Along with the demonstrated gridiron success of D1-recruited high-school stars like Jordyn Adams and Michael Hermosillo, the Angels have the makings an up-and-coming backfield duo in the big-fast-strong combo of Jo Adell and the less-celebrated Marsh. With a frame that could bowl tacklers over at close range and speed that could lose them in the open field, Marsh has fortunately been able to translate his tools into the sport he actually plays. The full offensive package was on display in Double-A, which augurs well based on the tamer ball used at that level. Defensively, he'll probably end up in a corner, but has the tools to cover center if need be. Somewhat obscured by the luminous intensity of Adell's supernova, Marsh himself has enough light and energy to emerge as a minor star in his own constellation.

Shohei Ohtani **RHP** Born: 07/05/94 Age: 25 Bats: L Throws: R Height: 6'4" Weight: 210 Origin: International Free Agent, 2017

YEAR	TEAM	LVL	AGE	PA	R	2B	3B	HR	RBI	BB	K	SB	CS	AVG/OBP/SLG	DRC+	VORP	BABIP	BRR	FRAA	WARP
2018	LAA	MLB	23	367	59	21	2	22	61	37	102	10	4	.285/.361/.564	129	22.8	.350	-2.3		1.7
2019	LAA	MLB	24	425	51	20	5	18	62	33	110	12	3	.286/.343/.505	106	10.0	.354	-1.5		0.8
2020	LAA	MLB	25	420	53	18	2	20	60	35	113	11	4	.261/.326/.477	110	19.0	.320	0.0		2.0

Comparables: Dick Gernert, Gary Sánchez, Paul Goldschmidt

A mythical talent in a prosaic world, Ohtani is set to return to his full powers in 2020, once again bringing together what we only saw in fleeting glimpses during his 2018 debut: a pitcher virtually unhittable when he can command his high-90s cheese alongside his devastating splitter and slider, and ... *and* ... an offensive force with silly power to all fields and blazing speed to boot. There's a small sadness in the fact that, in a different age, Ohtani would have no such restrictions on the display of his talents: he could pitch every fifth day as long as he wants, roam the outfield on his off days, hit in the middle of the order every day, and have full rein to run wild on the bases. To imagine this alternate reality is to approach the Platonic ideal of a baseball player. In the real, imperfect world, we'll have to settle for the actual Ohtani, who still has a chance, even in a part-time, designated-hitting offensive role, to be a historically unique and generationally valuable talent. Lucky us.

Albert Pujols **1B** Born: 01/16/80 Age: 40 Bats: R Throws: R Height: 6'3" Weight: 235 Origin: Round 13, 1999 Draft (#402 overall)

YEAR	TEAM	LVL	AGE	PA	R	2B	3B	HR	RBI	BB	K	SB	CS	AVG/OBP/SLG	DRC+	VORP	BABIP	BRR	FRAA	WARP
2017	LAA	MLB	37	636	53	17	0	23	101	37	93	3	0	.241/.286/.386	90	-17.5	.249	-1.2	1B(6): -0.6	-0.1
2018	LAA	MLB	38	498	50	20	0	19	64	28	65	1	0	.245/.289/.411	101	0.9	.247	-1.9		1.0
2019	LAA	MLB	39	545	55	22	0	23	93	43	68	3	0	.244/.305/.430	98	7.2	.238	-5.0		0.2
2020	LAA	MLB	40	490	55	21	0	20	64	34	70	3	1	.241/.299/.423	87	-2.5	.245	-2.2	1B 0	-0.3

Comparables: Chipper Jones, Scott Rolen, Eric Chavez

It would be easy to add another pile of snark onto the mountain of derision that Pujols' contract with the Angels has garnered since months after ink was put to paper back in the first Obama administration. What Pujols' 2019 performance makes clear, however, is that the 40-year-old has no desire to hobble gently into that good night. 2019 both held an uptick in plate appearances and was the second year running that, by DRC+, he's bobbed within the standard deviation of a league-average bat. And while largely irrelevant to his team's (lack of) success, the fact that the oft-injured DH stole three bases at least suggests a fierce wish to inhabit his younger body, if only for a short moment likely to lead to a much longer pain. Watching a generational talent decline is no fun for anybody. But from these quarters, Pujols gets nothing but respect: both for a monumental career and an evident desire to do everything within his dwindling powers to end it as a productive player.

Anthony Rendon **3B** Born: 06/06/90 Age: 30 Bats: R Throws: R Height: 6'1" Weight: 200 Origin: Round 1, 2011 Draft (#6 overall)

YEAR	TEAM	LVL	AGE	PA	R	2B	3B	HR	RBI	BB	K	SB	CS	AVG/OBP/SLG	DRC+	VORP	BABIP	BRR	FRAA	WARP
2017	WAS	MLB	27	605	81	41	1	25	100	84	82	7	2	.301/.403/.533	139	63.4	.314	2.0	3B(145): -1.6	5.2
2018	WAS	MLB	28	597	88	44	2	24	92	55	82	2	1	.308/.374/.535	134	60.1	.323	2.9	3B(136): -5.7	4.4
2019	WAS	MLB	29	646	117	44	3	34	126	80	86	5	1	.319/.412/.598	150	67.8	.323	1.0	3B(146): -4.5, 2B(1): 0.0	6.3
2020	LAA	MLB	30	630	82	37	1	26	88	72	99	7	3	.279/.371/.493	125	36.9	.299	1.4	3B -3	3.5

Comparables: Steve Buechele, David Wright, Edwin Encarnación

The most "Rendon" moment of the season didn't come when he deposited a Zack Greinke center-cut changeup into the Crawford Boxes during Game 7 of the World Series. Or when he took Clayton Kershaw deep in Game 5 of the NLDS. Or any of the 44 league-leading doubles he slapped, as easy as you please, all over the field. Or any of the runs he drove in; in any of the walks that in aggregate nearly eclipsed his strikeout total. In any of the pitches he took in the shadow of the zone or incredible, league-leading side-eyes at called strikes that were well off the plate. If Rendon didn't swing at it, it probably wasn't a strike.

No, the most "Rendon" moment of the season came in an August sweep of the Cubs at Wrigley Field, Rendon entering the stadium in a plain white T-shirt and jeans, face buried in his phone. Cubs fans filed by him; no one pointed or commented or even did the elbow-whisper of, "Hey, isn't that ... ?" There's a point where being underrated is the same thing as being overlooked. Rendon will be neither after last season, an MVP candidate who lacks Harper's Vegas flash and showmanship but nevertheless commands attention, that fast, devastating, wrist-snapping swing of his seeming to run at odds with his easygoing, occasionally sardonic presence.

Perhaps the only room for improvement in his game is fielding, though zoned and unzoned rating systems appear to disagree about its quality. Rendon himself has joked that fielding behind Washington's strikeout-emphasizing pitching staff was "boring." He'll certainly face more challenges (and balls in play) in Anaheim over the next eight years, but one thing is guaranteed: watching him will be anything but.

Luis Rengifo 2B Born: 02/26/97 Age: 23 Bats: B Throws: R Height: 5'10" Weight: 195 Origin: International Free Agent, 2013

YEAR	TEAM	LVL	AGE	PA	R	2B	3B	HR	RBI	BB	K	SB	CS	AVG/OBP/SLG	DRC+	VORP	BABIP	BRR	FRAA	WARP
2017	CLN	A	20	450	65	24	4	11	44	33	80	29	14	.250/.318/.413	107	22.0	.285	4.3	SS(31): -2.8, 2B(25): 2.8	2.4
2017	BGR	A	20	104	14	3	1	1	8	8	17	5	3	.250/.308/.333	110	6.0	.295	0.4	SS(23): -1.5	0.9
2018	INL	A+	21	190	36	11	3	2	16	27	22	22	8	.323/.426/.466	173	28.1	.365	2.5	SS(36): 3.9, 2B(2): 0.0	2.8
2018	MOB	AA	21	181	37	10	5	2	21	23	22	13	2	.305/.420/.477	146	14.2	.346	-1.0	SS(30): -3.4, 2B(9): -0.8	1.1
2018	SLC	AAA	21	219	36	9	5	3	27	25	31	6	6	.274/.358/.421	112	12.0	.310	3.3	2B(31): -1.5, SS(16): 0.1	1.3
2019	SLC	AAA	22	122	16	4	1	5	14	11	24	3	3	.273/.336/.464	77	2.7	.305	-0.4	SS(12): 0.9, 2B(12): 3.6	0.5
2019	LAA	MLB	22	406	44	18	3	7	33	40	93	2	5	.238/.321/.364	84	5.8	.300	-0.4		0.5
2020	LAA	MLB	23	210	21	8	1	5	21	18	48	8	4	.228/.301/.360	78	2.2	.282	-0.1	2B 0, SS 0	0.2

Comparables: Dalton Pompey, Luis Urías, Jesmuel Valentín

If you're not a close follower of the Angels, you may not remember that, among the seemingly endless list of misfortunes suffered by the club in 2019, Rengifo was lost in the middle of September to a broken hamate bone in his left hand. Hamates can be a notoriously tricky rehab, and some players (looking at you, Pablo Sandoval) never fully get their mojo back. Assuming Rengifo can be ready to roll by spring, however, he'll be looking to build on a promising rookie season. The stat line doesn't wow, but he does a lot of things well, and it comes with a solid foundation: a patient plate approach and impressive athletic ability in the middle infield. Before we cast him into the "utility" bin, there's reason to hope for growth in power and some more game speed on the bases as well. The bat hinges on the hamate, however, so here's hoping Rengifo can benefit from some karmic redistribution for baseball's unluckiest 2019 club.

Andrelton Simmons SS Born: 09/04/89 Age: 30 Bats: R Throws: R Height: 6'2" Weight: 195 Origin: Round 2, 2010 Draft (#70 overall)

YEAR	TEAM	LVL	AGE	PA	R	2B	3B	HR	RBI	BB	K	SB	CS	AVG/OBP/SLG	DRC+	VORP	BABIP	BRR	FRAA	WARP
2017	LAA	MLB	27	647	77	38	2	14	69	47	67	19	6	.278/.331/.421	102	32.3	.291	2.7	SS(158): 16.1	5.0
2018	LAA	MLB	28	600	68	26	5	11	75	35	44	10	2	.292/.337/.417	107	35.1	.300	3.8		2.9
2019	LAA	MLB	29	424	47	19	0	7	40	24	37	10	2	.264/.309/.364	81	9.9	.277	-0.1		2.0
2020	LAA	MLB	30	595	56	28	2	10	58	37	59	10	3	.263/.313/.374	82	10.0	.279	1.4	SS 6	1.6

Comparables: Barry Larkin, Bill Russell, José Reyes

The perennial Gold Glover and Resident Fielding Wizard, Simmons once again returned to elite leather levels if you look at the metrics alone. But defensive stats are a tricky business, and even at their best they give only a partial, blinkered view. First of all, Simmons' 2018 down year, FRAA-ly speaking, was mainly due to a reduction of overall chances, not any downturn in fielding acumen. And 2019 was spoiled almost from the get-go by a nagging ankle sprain and related injuries to tendons and bone. Offensively, this made it hard for Simmons to take advantage of the funtime happyball, and he stepped back from the hitting gains of the previous two seasons. But let's not forget the fortitude of a player who, bum ankle and all, managed a fielding season that graded out (in only 103 games!) as the second-best among shortstops—oh, while stealing 10 bags, too. Health, and with it a rebound to league-average offense, should return Simmons to his rightful place as one of the most valuable shortstops in the league.

Kevan Smith C Born: 06/28/88 Age: 32 Bats: R Throws: R Height: 6'4" Weight: 240 Origin: Round 7, 2011 Draft (#231 overall)

YEAR	TEAM	LVL	AGE	PA	R	2B	3B	HR	RBI	BB	K	SB	CS	AVG/OBP/SLG	DRC+	VORP	BABIP	BRR	FRAA	WARP
2017	CHR	AAA	29	62	10	6	0	0	15	6	9	0	0	.377/.435/.491	164	5.4	.435	0.5	C(13): -0.2	0.7
2017	CHA	MLB	29	294	23	17	0	4	30	9	46	0	0	.283/.309/.388	80	6.8	.323	0.5	C(79): -6.2	0.1
2018	CHR	AAA	30	124	12	4	0	4	16	8	18	0	0	.268/.331/.411	102	2.6	.286	-1.0	C(22): -0.7	0.3
2018	CHA	MLB	30	187	21	6	0	3	21	10	18	1	0	.292/.348/.380	101	7.2	.311	0.2	C(47): 0.1	1.0
2019	LAA	MLB	31	211	21	12	0	5	20	16	37	2	0	.251/.318/.393	89	7.4	.287	-1.2		-0.2
2020	LAA	MLB	32	251	25	12	0	6	27	18	47	1	0	.246/.310/.381	83	2.3	.285	-0.2	C -5	-0.2

Comparables: Bryan Holaday, Jason Jaramillo, Chase d'Arnaud

You never go into a season with a catcher like Smith as your Plan A. He backed up Omar Narváez in Chicago in 2018, and began 2019 backing up Jonathan Lucroy in Anaheim. Still and all, Smith emerged with far more plate appearances than the Angels probably hoped he would, and the midseason acquisition of Max Stassi gives you a rough idea of what Eppler and Co. think of the 31-year-old. The hitting is just good enough to keep him from falling entirely out of the picture in the present, but the defense is just bad enough to shorten his shelf life as a backup deep into his 30s. Following a non-tender in December, Smith will likely spend 2020 as somebody's Plan B, it just won't be in the Big A.

YEAR	TEAM	P. COUNT	FRM RUNS	BLK RUNS	THRW RUNS	TOT RUNS
2017	CHA	10862	1.6	-1.6	-3.9	-4.5
2017	CHR	1944	0.1	-0.4	-0.1	-0.4
2018	CHA	6961	1.5	-0.9	-0.3	0.7
2018	CHR	2973	0.4	-0.8	-0.2	-0.5
2019	LAA	7453	-4.3	-2.0	-0.7	-6.9
2020	LAA	9904	-2.5	-0.4	-1.0	-3.9

Max Stassi C Born: 03/15/91 Age: 29 Bats: R Throws: R Height: 5'10" Weight: 200 Origin: Round 4, 2009 Draft (#123 overall)

YEAR	TEAM	LVL	AGE	PA	R	2B	3B	HR	RBI	BB	K	SB	CS	AVG/OBP/SLG	DRC+	VORP	BABIP	BRR	FRAA	WARP
2017	FRE	AAA	26	287	54	14	0	12	33	38	67	1	1	.266/.383/.473	125	27.0	.321	-0.2	C(65): 10.8	3.2
2017	HOU	MLB	26	31	5	1	0	2	4	6	4	0	0	.167/.323/.458	106	0.9	.105	0.0	C(11): 0.5, 1B(1): 0.0	0.2
2018	HOU	MLB	27	250	28	13	0	8	27	23	74	0	0	.226/.316/.394	86	9.6	.302	-0.1	C(82): 14.5	2.3
2019	HOU	MLB	28	98	4	1	0	1	3	7	34	0	0	.167/.235/.211	61	0.1	.255	-1.3	C(26): 6.1, 1B(3): 0.0	0.5
2019	LAA	MLB	28	49	3	0	0	0	2	5	15	0	0	.071/.163/.071	24	-2.3	.103	0.0		0.1
2020	*LAA*	*MLB*	*29*	*280*	*28*	*12*	*0*	*10*	*32*	*22*	*91*	*0*	*0*	*.207/.281/.370*	*72*	*2.3*	*.281*	*-0.5*	*C 5*	*0.7*

Comparables: Mike Carp, Jake Marisnick, John Ryan Murphy

YEAR	TEAM	P. COUNT	FRM RUNS	BLK RUNS	THRW RUNS	TOT RUNS
2017	FRE	9878	11.4	0.0	-0.8	10.1
2017	HOU	1029	0.2	0.4	0.0	0.5
2018	HOU	9540	13.9	0.1	-0.1	14.0
2019	HOU	3717	6.6	-0.2	-0.1	6.3
2019	LAA	2392	3.9	-0.5	-0.1	3.3
2020	*LAA*	*11239*	*4.7*	*0.3*	*-0.3*	*4.7*

For those of you hip to the Gen-Z catcher-framing metrics here at BP, you've probably had Stassi on your short list of crushes for a while: Last season, his framing saved more runs than J.T. Realmuto—in fewer than one-third as many chances. Somewhere, there's a TikTok montage of Stassi's framing going viral in a very niche way (are we doing this right?). If the framing is *au courant*, however, the bat is the equivalent of the Steve Buscemi character from *30 Rock*, skateboard slung over his shoulder, enthusiastically asking his "fellow" high school kids how they do. That is to say, awkward, out of place, and redolent of a 40-something desperately and unsuccessfully trying to keep up with the youngsters. The defense puts him on a Jeff Mathis-like career trajectory (forever young, or at least on a roster), while the bat looks to age as well as that MySpace background you thought was kind of edgy in 2005.

Matt Thaiss CI Born: 05/06/95 Age: 25 Bats: L Throws: R Height: 6'0" Weight: 215 Origin: Round 1, 2016 Draft (#16 overall)

YEAR	TEAM	LVL	AGE	PA	R	2B	3B	HR	RBI	BB	K	SB	CS	AVG/OBP/SLG	DRC+	VORP	BABIP	BRR	FRAA	WARP
2017	INL	A+	22	385	46	13	4	8	48	40	59	4	3	.265/.353/.399	120	13.7	.299	0.5	1B(78): 2.8	1.6
2017	MOB	AA	22	221	29	14	0	1	25	37	50	4	3	.292/.412/.388	158	11.5	.389	-1.2	1B(46): -1.5	1.2
2018	MOB	AA	23	176	24	10	2	6	25	16	35	2	1	.287/.352/.490	125	9.0	.331	-1.1	1B(36): 2.6	0.8
2018	SLC	AAA	23	400	54	24	6	10	51	28	68	6	3	.277/.328/.457	95	-0.6	.314	0.2	1B(77): 5.4	0.9
2019	SLC	AAA	24	372	63	17	2	14	49	59	64	1	0	.274/.390/.477	109	18.8	.303	1.3	3B(47): -2.5, 1B(23): -1.4	1.2
2019	LAA	MLB	24	164	17	7	0	8	23	17	52	0	0	.211/.293/.422	91	3.7	.264	-1.6		-0.1
2020	*LAA*	*MLB*	*25*	*105*	*12*	*4*	*0*	*4*	*13*	*11*	*27*	*1*	*0*	*.230/.314/.401*	*90*	*0.4*	*.283*	*-0.2*	*1B 1*	*0.1*

Comparables: Yonder Alonso, Max Muncy, Brett Wallace

Every once in a while a first base prospect without hammerhead power swims against the current of probability and makes it to the far shore of the majors. Thaiss reached that beachhead in 2019, though he floundered a bit once he came ashore. It remains to be seen if the hit tool will play enough to give him some oxygen, and if the power is enough to reach dry land. If his 2019 is any indication, we already know his approach has evolved enough for him walk just fine.

Mike Trout CF Born: 08/07/91 Age: 28 Bats: R Throws: R Height: 6'2" Weight: 235 Origin: Round 1, 2009 Draft (#25 overall)

YEAR	TEAM	LVL	AGE	PA	R	2B	3B	HR	RBI	BB	K	SB	CS	AVG/OBP/SLG	DRC+	VORP	BABIP	BRR	FRAA	WARP
2017	LAA	MLB	25	507	92	25	3	33	72	94	90	22	4	.306/.442/.629	176	69.9	.318	0.0	CF(108): -3.3	6.2
2018	LAA	MLB	26	608	101	24	4	39	79	122	124	24	2	.312/.460/.628	183	91.0	.346	1.5		8.2
2019	LAA	MLB	27	600	110	27	2	45	104	110	120	11	2	.291/.438/.645	177	81.5	.298	3.4		8.9
2020	*LAA*	*MLB*	*28*	*630*	*114*	*27*	*3*	*48*	*124*	*110*	*138*	*19*	*6*	*.298/.435/.645*	*177*	*85.6*	*.322*	*0.2*	*CF -3*	*8.6*

Comparables: Giancarlo Stanton, Bryce Harper, Rick Monday

It's hard to be mad at Mike Trout for being the most unassuming "greatest player of his generation" in baseball's (or really, any sport's) history. His performance continues to outclass virtually all of his peers, and any statistical variations (say, the reduction of steals) seem less like a cause for concern than an effortless toggling between different genres of perfection, a DJ of baseball godhead on the ones and twos. He even turned a potential free-agency circus into an acoustic set on a side stage, inking a 12-year, $430 million contract extension with little fanfare on a Wednesday in March, presumably making him a lifelong Angel. Trout also resists being a headliner among the league's impressive lineup of young stars: in its "Let the Kids Play" ad, an attempt to market its faces for a new generation, Trout recedes to the background, only speaking when hounded by "reporters," letting the gregarious swagger of Alex Bregman and Francisco Lindor take center stage. One could surmise that the only publicity Trout might feel comfortable with is hoisting a trophy with his Angels teammates. The generationally-talented centerpiece is firmly in place through the 2020s; it's now up to Moreno, Eppler and Co. to find the perfect ensemble.

Justin Upton LF Born: 08/25/87 Age: 32 Bats: R Throws: R Height: 6'1" Weight: 215 Origin: Round 1, 2005 Draft (#1 overall)

YEAR	TEAM	LVL	AGE	PA	R	2B	3B	HR	RBI	BB	K	SB	CS	AVG/OBP/SLG	DRC+	VORP	BABIP	BRR	FRAA	WARP
2017	LAA	MLB	29	115	19	7	0	7	15	17	33	4	0	.245/.357/.531	131	7.7	.293	1.1	LF(27): -2.6	0.6
2017	DET	MLB	29	520	81	37	0	28	94	57	147	10	5	.279/.362/.542	129	32.1	.351	-0.6	LF(124): 11.8	4.3
2018	LAA	MLB	30	613	80	18	1	30	85	64	176	8	2	.257/.344/.463	117	32.6	.321	-1.6		4.4
2019	LAA	MLB	31	256	34	8	0	12	40	32	78	1	1	.215/.309/.416	91	3.8	.261	0.5		0.1
2020	*LAA*	*MLB*	*32*	*560*	*76*	*24*	*1*	*31*	*86*	*62*	*173*	*10*	*4*	*.245/.334/.486*	*113*	*23.3*	*.310*	*-0.4*	*LF 10*	*3.5*

Comparables: Andruw Jones, Mike Cameron, Jay Bruce

At some point, almost imperceptibly, Upton went from being a young, promising player to a grizzled veteran. It probably happened somewhere in his odyssey to four different clubs in five years, between the 2013 viral image, riffing off of DMX, proclaiming a fraternal Atlanta outfield of "Upton here! Upton here!" and landing his last big payday to patrol left field and swat bombs in Anaheim through his age-34 season. Lest we write career eulogies too soon,

Upton's 2019 was a total write-off, as he battled toe and knee woes from the spring right through September. Upton is still young and talented enough to come back and enjoy a productive stretch through his mid-30s, and a now-broken track record of eight consecutive 600 PA seasons backs this up. He is also old enough that we'd be naïve to think that his hobbled 2019 doesn't remind us that even the sturdiest bodies can, and do, eventually break down.

Jared Walsh 1B Born: 07/30/93 Age: 26 Bats: L Throws: L Height: 6'0" Weight: 210 Origin: Round 39, 2015 Draft (#1185 overall)

YEAR	TEAM	LVL	AGE	PA	R	2B	3B	HR	RBI	BB	K	SB	CS	AVG/OBP/SLG	DRC+	VORP	BABIP	BRR	FRAA	WARP
2017	INL	A+	23	306	43	29	1	8	52	26	72	1	0	.331/.395/.531	157	20.5	.423	-1.9	1B(51): 1.5, RF(12): -1.7	2.0
2017	MOB	AA	23	74	7	3	0	3	9	3	29	1	0	.232/.274/.406	76	-0.5	.351	-0.7	1B(18): -1.1, RF(1): -0.1	-0.3
2018	INL	A+	24	178	28	8	1	13	36	24	50	0	1	.275/.365/.604	166	15.3	.308	-0.6	1B(26): 0.3, RF(5): 0.7	1.4
2018	MOB	AA	24	173	26	13	0	8	26	21	48	1	0	.289/.382/.537	132	9.6	.372	-0.8	1B(37): 2.0, P(2): 0.0	0.9
2018	SLC	AAA	24	198	32	13	0	8	37	16	56	0	0	.270/.333/.478	114	7.1	.345	1.8	RF(27): -5.7, LF(14): -1.7	0.2
2019	SLC	AAA	25	454	90	30	0	36	86	59	115	0	0	.325/.423/.686	145	45.4	.374	0.7	1B(58): 4.6, P(12): 0.5	3.6
2019	LAA	MLB	25	87	6	5	1	1	5	6	35	0	0	.203/.276/.329	59	-3.3	.349	-0.2		-0.3
2020	LAA	MLB	26	35	4	1	0	2	5	3	11	0	0	.237/.310/.454	97	0.4	.308	-0.1	1B 0	0.1

Comparables: Harry Agganis, Trey Mancini, Dale Long

Somewhere between the full-on two-way excellence of Shohei Ohtani and the wacky novelty of position players like, say, Stevie Wilkerson notching saves with 56 mph junk (against the Angels, no less!) exists a grayer area occupied by folks like Walsh. For all intents and purposes, he's an interesting corner-infield bat whose improved patience was overshadowed by out-of-nowhere, PCL-silly power numbers in 2019. Along the way the Angels have nurtured his pitching dreams, which are not completely crazy given his low-90s fastball and competent secondaries. At least there's some credible hope that he can serve a major-league roster in a mop-up role. None of this is to say that Walsh has much of a ceiling on either side of the ledger, and the cynical among us might foresee an increase in Walshes—players just good enough to fill out the ends of both benches—as teams bow to the gods Efficiency and Optimization. If Ohtani is the generational pitcher-hitter unicorn, then Walsh might be the workhorse, heralding a more realistic trend toward the two*ish*-way player.

PITCHERS

Justin Anderson RHP Born: 09/28/92 Age: 27 Bats: L Throws: R Height: 6'3" Weight: 230 Origin: Round 14, 2014 Draft (#419 overall)

YEAR	TEAM	LVL	AGE	W	L	SV	G	GS	IP	H	HR	BB/9	K/9	K	GB%	BABIP	WHIP	ERA	DRA	WARP	MPH	FB%	WHF	CSP
2017	MOB	AA	24	3	2	1	42	0	58²	56	7	4.4	5.5	36	49%	.266	1.45	5.06	6.04	-0.9				
2018	LAA	MLB	25	3	3	4	57	0	55¹	42	3	6.5	10.9	67	54%	.310	1.48	4.07	4.52	0.3	99.5	44.7	14.4	42.2
2019	LAA	MLB	26	3	0	1	54	0	47	42	6	6.1	11.5	60	36%	.305	1.57	5.55	4.86	0.3	96.3	47.1	12.8	42.4
2020	LAA	MLB	27	2	2	0	40	0	43	36	6	5.0	11.3	54	42%	.297	1.40	4.33	4.36	0.4	97.4	46.5	13.7	42.8

Comparables: Jake Jewell, Colten Brewer, Phillips Valdez

The hard-throwing righty began 2019 with five scoreless appearances in the season's first 10 days and was promptly rewarded with ... the closer's job, you say? Well, no, the Angels had to wait until the final frames of the Cody Allen disaster film before making the switch to Hansel Robles. No, Anderson's sterling start was rewarded with a head-scratching demotion to Triple-A Salt Lake City. Upon his return from a short stint at the foot of the Wasatch, the early-April magic dissipated in a fog of inconsistency, with poor command being the main culprit. Heading into his age-27 season, Anderson's time to become a late-inning fireballer, rather than cannon fodder, is rapidly approaching the zero hour.

Luke Bard RHP Born: 11/13/90 Age: 29 Bats: R Throws: R Height: 6'3" Weight: 200 Origin: Round 1, 2012 Draft (#42 overall)

YEAR	TEAM	LVL	AGE	W	L	SV	G	GS	IP	H	HR	BB/9	K/9	K	GB%	BABIP	WHIP	ERA	DRA	WARP	MPH	FB%	WHF	CSP
2017	CHT	AA	26	4	3	5	33	0	52¹	50	4	3.4	13.4	78	35%	.380	1.34	2.58	3.89	0.6				
2017	ROC	AAA	26	0	0	0	8	0	13	13	1	2.8	14.5	21	30%	.400	1.31	3.46	3.31	0.3				
2018	ROC	AAA	27	3	3	1	32	0	48¹	54	6	3.4	9.7	52	37%	.356	1.49	4.66	6.05	-0.5				
2018	LAA	MLB	27	0	0	0	8	0	11²	10	4	3.9	10.0	13	31%	.214	1.29	5.40	6.83	-0.3	94.5	55.4	9.9	46.1
2019	SLC	AAA	28	2	4	1	16	1	19	28	4	4.7	12.3	26	33%	.453	2.00	7.11	6.79	-0.1				
2019	LAA	MLB	28	3	3	0	32	3	49	41	8	2.4	7.3	40	37%	.248	1.10	4.78	4.81	0.3	96.1	44.1	13	47.1
2020	LAA	MLB	29	1	2	0	29	0	30	30	6	3.4	8.8	30	36%	.292	1.37	5.02	5.02	0.1	95.2	46.1	12.4	46.6

Comparables: B.J. Rosenberg, Luis Santos, Jose A. Valdez

More often than not, the life of a pitching prospect is filled with injury and woe. With a minor-league career full of pauses and detours since his comp-pick selection by the Twins in 2012, Bard is a living example of this principle. Despite a career of struggle, the former Rule 5 pick put together a four-game stretch in September—against the Yankees, Astros, and A's, no less—in which he retired 20 batters in a row, striking out eight of them. Will this be enough to keep him in the bullpen mix in 2020? Until we see what Bard brings to the table in the spring, this is a matter, as befits his name, for the prophets and the poets.

Jaime Barria   RHP   Born: 07/18/96   Age: 23   Bats: R   Throws: R   Height: 6'1"   Weight: 210   Origin: International Free Agent, 2013

YEAR	TEAM	LVL	AGE	W	L	SV	G	GS	IP	H	HR	BB/9	K/9	K	GB%	BABIP	WHIP	ERA	DRA	WARP	MPH	FB%	WHF	CSP
2017	INL	A+	20	4	3	0	11	11	65¹	48	6	1.8	7.9	57	35%	.236	0.93	2.48	2.54	2.1				
2017	MOB	AA	20	1	6	0	12	12	61²	62	8	2.2	6.9	47	29%	.284	1.25	3.21	5.23	0.0				
2017	SLC	AAA	20	2	0	0	3	3	14²	11	0	1.8	8.0	13	29%	.262	0.95	2.45	2.89	0.5				
2018	SLC	AAA	21	0	0	0	5	5	18	20	2	2.5	9.5	19	28%	.353	1.39	3.50	4.84	0.1				
2018	LAA	MLB	21	10	9	0	26	26	129¹	117	17	3.3	6.8	98	37%	.272	1.27	3.41	5.67	-0.5	93.2	49.6	11.2	45
2019	SLC	AAA	22	3	3	0	10	10	48¹	73	16	1.9	8.2	44	27%	.368	1.72	9.68	7.27	-0.3				
2019	LAA	MLB	22	4	10	0	19	13	82²	92	24	2.9	8.2	75	36%	.287	1.44	6.42	7.74	-1.9	93.3	36.9	9.8	47.2
2020	LAA	MLB	23	4	3	0	25	8	57	57	11	2.9	7.6	49	34%	.282	1.33	4.71	4.85	0.4	93.2	45.3	10.9	47.9

Comparables: Lucas Giolito, Bryse Wilson, Peter Lambert

If you have any doubts about whom the hyperball hurt in 2019, look no further than Barria. Over the last two seasons, Barria has been more or less the same pitcher in terms of pitch mix and velocity: he's a slider/four-seam guy whose fastball is accurate but pretty straight and eminently hittable. In 2018, this made him a fringy-but-usable piece at the end of the rotation. In 2019, it made him a batting practice tosser who was saved only by the existence of the Orioles' David Hess from leading the HR/9 charts for pitchers with at least 80 innings. Barria, more than most, will be eager to see what the primary tool of his trade looks, feels, and plays like in 2020.

Cam Bedrosian   RHP   Born: 10/02/91   Age: 28   Bats: R   Throws: R   Height: 6'1"   Weight: 225   Origin: Round 1, 2010 Draft (#29 overall)

YEAR	TEAM	LVL	AGE	W	L	SV	G	GS	IP	H	HR	BB/9	K/9	K	GB%	BABIP	WHIP	ERA	DRA	WARP	MPH	FB%	WHF	CSP
2017	LAA	MLB	25	6	5	6	48	0	44²	41	5	3.4	10.7	53	45%	.313	1.30	4.43	2.97	1.1	95.8	57.7	13.5	46.5
2018	LAA	MLB	26	5	4	1	71	0	64	63	7	3.7	8.0	57	50%	.315	1.39	3.80	4.21	0.5	95.6	55.5	8.6	47.9
2019	LAA	MLB	27	3	3	1	59	7	61¹	48	7	3.2	9.4	64	48%	.253	1.14	3.23	3.50	1.3	94.7	47.8	13.2	45.9
2020	LAA	MLB	28	3	3	0	52	0	55	52	8	3.8	9.3	56	48%	.296	1.36	4.32	4.36	0.5	94.7	52.9	11.7	47

Comparables: Arodys Vizcaíno, Chris Perez, Dominic Leone

Despite its ending with the always-ominous "forearm strain" diagnosis, Bedrosian's 2019 was far from a failure. Though his 2017 occupation of the closer throne was a brief one, he was more valuable to the Angels in both late-inning and occasional opener roles this past season. Even as his fastball has steadily, if slowly, declined into the high end of the low 90s, his slider is still devastating, with a down-and-in drop that makes him even more effective against lefties than same-sided hitters. If healthy, Bedrosian looks to be back in the high-leverage mix again, with a return to closing royalty unlikely, but, given the rabble of pretenders in the Halos' pen, not impossible.

Dylan Bundy   RHP   Born: 11/15/92   Age: 27   Bats: B   Throws: R   Height: 6'1"   Weight: 200   Origin: Round 1, 2011 Draft (#4 overall)

YEAR	TEAM	LVL	AGE	W	L	SV	G	GS	IP	H	HR	BB/9	K/9	K	GB%	BABIP	WHIP	ERA	DRA	WARP	MPH	FB%	WHF	CSP
2017	BAL	MLB	24	13	9	0	28	28	169²	152	26	2.7	8.1	152	33%	.273	1.20	4.24	4.93	1.2	94.4	53.8	12.3	46.4
2018	BAL	MLB	25	8	16	0	31	31	171²	188	41	2.8	9.6	184	35%	.316	1.41	5.45	5.34	-0.1	93.7	55.8	13.5	50.2
2019	BAL	MLB	26	7	14	0	30	30	161²	161	29	3.2	9.0	162	42%	.297	1.35	4.79	4.88	1.6	93.4	50	13.8	46.8
2020	LAA	MLB	27	10	8	0	26	26	137	131	26	3.3	9.1	139	39%	.287	1.32	4.57	4.67	1.4	93.3	53.6	13.5	48.4

Comparables: Chad Kuhl, Robert Gsellman, A.J. Cole

In the fifth inning of his May 11 start against the Los Angeles Angels, Bundy got a visit from pitching coach Doug Brocail asking if he was hurt. The one-time flamethrower wasn't even hitting 90 mph anymore, and it's not like the fastball he's carried the last few years was much better. From the start of 2017 until that day, Bundy allowed a league-high 45 home runs on his fastball. But that start was enough to wean himself off of it, and his higher frequency of secondary pitches made for…pretty much more of the same, except fewer home runs. On its day, Bundy's slider is still a swing-and-miss pitch. He grew more comfortable pitching with his curveball and changeup, and worked more on locating his fastball at the edges. The resulting pitcher was league-average in 2019, and a full transformation into the type of junk-baller he started to become might only slightly improve that going forward.

Ty Buttrey   RHP   Born: 03/31/93   Age: 27   Bats: L   Throws: R   Height: 6'6"   Weight: 240   Origin: Round 4, 2012 Draft (#151 overall)

YEAR	TEAM	LVL	AGE	W	L	SV	G	GS	IP	H	HR	BB/9	K/9	K	GB%	BABIP	WHIP	ERA	DRA	WARP	MPH	FB%	WHF	CSP
2017	PME	AA	24	1	4	4	30	0	46	39	1	4.5	11.0	56	50%	.339	1.35	3.72	3.58	0.7				
2017	PAW	AAA	24	1	1	0	10	0	17²	21	2	5.1	9.2	18	53%	.358	1.75	7.64	6.68	-0.3				
2018	PAW	AAA	25	1	1	1	32	0	44	36	4	2.9	13.1	64	45%	.320	1.14	2.25	3.06	1.0				
2018	LAA	MLB	25	0	1	4	16	0	16¹	15	0	2.8	11.0	20	58%	.333	1.22	3.31	2.90	0.4	98.6	58	14	47.3
2019	LAA	MLB	26	6	7	2	72	0	72¹	69	8	2.9	10.5	84	45%	.323	1.27	3.98	3.54	1.4	99.1	57.2	12.7	50.2
2020	LAA	MLB	27	3	3	9	63	0	67	62	9	3.3	10.3	77	46%	.308	1.29	3.95	4.10	0.8	98.5	58	13.1	49.5

Comparables: Marcus Hatley, Victor Alcántara, Dovydas Neverauskas

There was a minor scandal at the MLB offices in the midsummer of 2019. The league was approving nicknames for the Players' Weekend jerseys, and there was a mysterious text from the 714 area code. All it contained was two emojis: a peach, and a tree.

"Peachtree?" The confused intern who received the text looked perplexed. "Who is that?"

Over the intern's shoulder, another intern chimed in.

"It's not a peach. It's…a butt."

"Butt … tree … Butt-tree. I GET IT. Ty Buttrey! Could've sworn he was gonna go with some kind of 'butter' pun, but OK." There was a pause. "Wait, so you're telling me that we get our panties in a bunch about bat flips but we're OK having an icon of, well … a human ass … on our jerseys? I mean, who is Buttrey, anyway?"

The other intern sighed. "Big body reliever. Red Sox draft pick, went to the Angels in the Ian Kinsler trade, good heat, killer change, really cut down on his walks the last couple of years. Good pitcher. Bit unlucky in 2019, or he could've been the closer instead of Robles."
"No, I *knew* that. I meant, who does he *think* he is? Listen, I knew Box Burger. And Butt Tree is *no* Box Burger."

Trevor Cahill RHP   Born: 03/01/88   Age: 32   Bats: R   Throws: R   Height: 6'4"   Weight: 230   Origin: Round 2, 2006 Draft (#66 overall)

YEAR	TEAM	LVL	AGE	W	L	SV	G	GS	IP	H	HR	BB/9	K/9	K	GB%	BABIP	WHIP	ERA	DRA	WARP	MPH	FB%	WHF	CSP
2017	SDN	MLB	29	4	3	0	11	11	61	58	6	3.5	10.6	72	58%	.329	1.34	3.69	3.51	1.4	93.5	45.7	13.4	42.4
2017	KCA	MLB	29	0	0	0	10	3	23	33	10	8.2	5.9	15	54%	.319	2.35	8.22	6.61	-0.3	93.8	50	7.3	41.7
2018	NAS	AAA	30	0	1	0	3	3	13²	7	0	5.3	11.2	17	81%	.226	1.10	2.63	2.59	0.5				
2018	OAK	MLB	30	7	4	0	21	20	110	90	8	3.4	8.2	100	54%	.278	1.19	3.76	3.48	2.3	94.4	41.1	12.1	44.5
2019	LAA	MLB	31	4	9	0	37	11	102¹	111	25	3.4	7.1	81	46%	.283	1.47	5.98	5.97	-0.4	93.7	36.5	10.8	47.7
2020	*LAA*	*MLB*	*32*	*2*	*2*	*0*	*33*	*0*	*35*	*33*	*5*	*3.8*	*7.8*	*30*	*49%*	*.283*	*1.38*	*4.48*	*4.54*	*0.2*	*93.0*	*40.1*	*11.3*	*44.8*

Comparables: Jair Jurrjens, Jhoulys Chacín, Chris Volstad

While cats, as the myth holds, are afforded nine lives, pitchers seldom get more than one—and that's if they're lucky. Cahill's career has nonetheless taken a feline trajectory: His rise as a dependable ground-baller with the A's and Diamondbacks eventually stalled out, leaving him an itinerant reliever with five different clubs from 2015 to 2017. It took a return to Oakland to resuscitate his life as a starter, but his East Bay rejuvenation was subsequently squandered in Anaheim, where he signed a one-year deal. The sinker, his stock in trade, became the pitch *non grata* in the age of uppercutting hitters and the, ah ... enhanced offensive environment, and Cahill found himself in bullpen and bulk-pitcher purgatory by June. Cats have a preternatural ability to land on their feet; Cahill will have to make some fairly acrobatic contortions to do the same with a major-league staff in 2020.

Griffin Canning RHP   Born: 05/11/96   Age: 24   Bats: R   Throws: R   Height: 6'2"   Weight: 180   Origin: Round 2, 2017 Draft (#47 overall)

YEAR	TEAM	LVL	AGE	W	L	SV	G	GS	IP	H	HR	BB/9	K/9	K	GB%	BABIP	WHIP	ERA	DRA	WARP	MPH	FB%	WHF	CSP
2018	INL	A+	22	0	0	0	2	2	8²	4	0	3.1	12.5	12	56%	.222	0.81	0.00	2.44	0.3				
2018	MOB	AA	22	1	0	0	10	10	45²	27	2	3.7	9.7	49	48%	.229	1.01	1.97	2.75	1.4				
2018	SLC	AAA	22	3	3	0	13	13	59	68	6	3.4	9.8	64	42%	.376	1.53	5.49	4.78	0.5				
2019	SLC	AAA	23	1	0	0	3	3	16	13	0	1.1	9.6	17	42%	.317	0.94	0.56	2.06	0.7				
2019	LAA	MLB	23	5	6	0	18	17	90¹	80	14	3.0	9.6	96	39%	.280	1.22	4.58	4.50	1.2	95.8	42.1	14.6	44.5
2020	*LAA*	*MLB*	*24*	*9*	*6*	*0*	*23*	*23*	*120*	*103*	*18*	*3.4*	*9.8*	*131*	*39%*	*.279*	*1.24*	*3.81*	*3.98*	*2.1*	*95.6*	*43.3*	*15.1*	*45.8*

Comparables: Kevin Gausman, Zack Wheeler, Dylan Cease

With the untimely UCL injury to Shohei Ohtani and the inevitable ailment perpetually lurking around the corner for Andrew Heaney, the Angels have to walk a fine line with Canning, their most promising home-grown arm in years. On the one hand, it would make sense—especially given his injury history in both college and the minors—to keep him gently but tightly ensconced in bubble wrap in a climate-controlled safe room, the seal to be broken only when the time of contention arrives. On the other hand, the 23-year-old was plenty ready when the rotation sprung several leaks in midsummer and proved himself a worthy mid-rotation arm, with the upside for more. Unfortunately, with an air of inevitability, the dreaded "elbow inflammation" sidelined the promising rookie for the rest of the season, and health, more than ability, will be his primary question mark going forward.

Taylor Cole RHP   Born: 08/20/89   Age: 30   Bats: R   Throws: R   Height: 6'1"   Weight: 200   Origin: Round 29, 2011 Draft (#889 overall)

YEAR	TEAM	LVL	AGE	W	L	SV	G	GS	IP	H	HR	BB/9	K/9	K	GB%	BABIP	WHIP	ERA	DRA	WARP	MPH	FB%	WHF	CSP
2017	TOR	MLB	27	0	0	0	1	0	1	6	0	9.0	9.0	1	57%	.857	7.00	36.00	11.11	-0.1	95.8	58.5	9.8	43.2
2018	SLC	AAA	28	3	0	6	34	0	55¹	55	6	4.4	10.6	65	48%	.343	1.48	5.37	4.02	0.7				
2018	LAA	MLB	28	4	2	0	18	2	36	20	3	3.0	9.8	39	52%	.218	0.89	2.75	4.24	0.3	95.3	41	15.9	41.8
2019	SLC	AAA	29	3	0	3	16	0	20²	29	5	2.6	10.5	24	35%	.414	1.69	5.23	5.30	0.2				
2019	LAA	MLB	29	3	4	0	38	6	51²	58	2	4.2	8.7	50	48%	.366	1.59	5.92	5.09	0.2	95.6	42.2	12.4	44
2020	*LAA*	*MLB*	*30*	*2*	*2*	*0*	*40*	*0*	*43*	*38*	*5*	*3.7*	*9.2*	*44*	*46%*	*.290*	*1.30*	*3.81*	*3.92*	*0.6*	*94.7*	*41.9*	*13.5*	*42.9*

Comparables: Félix Peña, Darin Downs, Josh Ravin

In an alternate universe, "Cole Taylor" is a similarly anonymous pitcher as the pitcher whose profile you are reading—but "Cole Taylor" throws lefty instead of righty, and he's a bullpen piece for, let's say, the Reds. We could easily slip in a capsule, or at the very least a lineout, about this entirely-made-up doppelgänger. We could talk about his fringy arsenal, muse about how if he could fine-tune his command he might get some high-leverage looks, point out how it's players like him who should be especially thankful for that 26th roster spot next season. And we would be willing to bet that precisely none of you, not even the most rabid Reds fans, would write in to our editors and complain that we inserted an entirely fictitious pitcher into the book. Just like none of you probably knew who "Taylor Cole" was before his two-inning start of a combined no-hitter with Félix Peña in July. His part in a historic game saves Cole from oblivion, but it remains to be seen if it can save his job as a major-league reliever.

Luis García RHP   Born: 01/30/87   Age: 33   Bats: R   Throws: R   Height: 6'2"   Weight: 240   Origin: International Free Agent, 2017

YEAR	TEAM	LVL	AGE	W	L	SV	G	GS	IP	H	HR	BB/9	K/9	K	GB%	BABIP	WHIP	ERA	DRA	WARP	MPH	FB%	WHF	CSP
2017	PHI	MLB	30	2	5	2	66	0	71¹	61	3	3.3	7.6	60	57%	.282	1.22	2.65	3.26	1.5	99.0	63.3	12.8	49
2018	PHI	MLB	31	3	1	1	59	0	46	49	4	3.5	10.0	51	50%	.354	1.46	6.07	3.25	0.9	99.5	48.4	15.5	44.8
2019	LAA	MLB	32	2	1	1	64	2	62	61	13	4.8	8.3	57	49%	.282	1.52	4.35	5.87	-0.3	99.2	47	13.1	43.6
2020	*LAA*	*MLB*	*33*	*2*	*2*	*0*	*33*	*0*	*35*	*33*	*4*	*4.5*	*9.2*	*36*	*52%*	*.304*	*1.45*	*4.52*	*4.49*	*0.3*	*98.1*	*51.1*	*13.5*	*44.8*

Comparables: Sam Freeman, Blaine Hardy, Cory Gearrin

Current baseball discussions that mention the name "Luis García" are typically followed by a question: "The Phillies one or the Nationals one?" For the Angels, the answer was "neither," as their García is a journeyman reliever rather than a promising teenage shortstop. An up-and-down bullpen arm for the Phillies over several seasons, García spent virtually all of his 2019 in the Angels' 'pen, logging 62 largely forgettable innings. Like many fringy arms, García suffered from the Three True Outcomes tendencies of the game, with his strikeout ability not quite compensating for the plentiful walks and home runs. The Angels did their part to turn the Luis García question into an either/or, releasing theirs following the season.

Andrew Heaney LHP Born: 06/05/91 Age: 29 Bats: L Throws: L Height: 6'2" Weight: 200 Origin: Round 1, 2012 Draft (#9 overall)

YEAR	TEAM	LVL	AGE	W	L	SV	G	GS	IP	H	HR	BB/9	K/9	K	GB%	BABIP	WHIP	ERA	DRA	WARP	MPH	FB%	WHF	CSP
2017	ANG	RK	26	0	1	0	3	3	10¹	11	0	0.9	13.1	15	42%	.423	1.16	1.74	2.46	0.4				
2017	SLC	AAA	26	1	1	0	3	3	17¹	17	2	2.1	7.3	14	39%	.306	1.21	3.12	4.42	0.2				
2017	LAA	MLB	26	1	2	0	5	5	21²	27	12	3.7	11.2	27	34%	.283	1.66	7.06	5.71	0.0	94.5	61.6	14.6	44.5
2018	INL	A+	27	1	0	0	1	1	6¹	2	0	1.4	8.5	6	73%	.133	0.47	1.42	2.33	0.2				
2018	LAA	MLB	27	9	10	0	30	30	180	171	27	2.2	9.0	180	44%	.294	1.20	4.15	3.63	3.5	94.6	58.1	12.7	50.8
2019	LAA	MLB	28	4	6	0	18	18	95¹	93	20	2.8	11.1	118	34%	.312	1.29	4.91	5.31	0.5	94.7	58	15.2	49.6
2020	LAA	MLB	29	10	7	0	26	26	137	131	26	2.8	10.3	158	37%	.302	1.26	4.29	4.44	1.7	94.0	58.3	13.8	48.7

Comparables: Steven Matz, Wade LeBlanc, Jerad Eickhoff

Like a showy sports car notorious for mechanical breakdowns, Heaney looks and feels great on the road—but only for short stretches and always with the looming dread that a breakdown is just around the next bend. In 2018, he ran smoothly the entire year and showed the kind of performance that could land him near the top of a competitive team's rotation. But 2019 was more trouble under the hood, and even though he revved higher (to the tune of 11 strikeouts per nine), his shoulder couldn't take the redlining and he went back to the garage with shoulder inflammation in July. A late-season return showed him in need of a tune-up, and 2020 leaves the Angels happy to have him in the fleet, but sorely in need of more reliable vehicles to get them anywhere near the postseason.

Adalberto Mejía LHP Born: 06/20/93 Age: 27 Bats: R Throws: L Height: 6'3" Weight: 195 Origin: International Free Agent, 2011

YEAR	TEAM	LVL	AGE	W	L	SV	G	GS	IP	H	HR	BB/9	K/9	K	GB%	BABIP	WHIP	ERA	DRA	WARP	MPH	FB%	WHF	CSP
2017	ROC	AAA	24	1	1	0	6	6	28²	26	1	1.9	6.9	22	51%	.294	1.12	2.83	3.92	0.6				
2017	MIN	MLB	24	4	7	0	21	21	98	110	13	4.0	7.8	85	41%	.328	1.57	4.50	6.02	-0.5	94.4	56.3	11.2	43.6
2018	ROC	AAA	25	5	3	0	15	12	63¹	55	3	2.8	8.8	62	43%	.294	1.18	3.27	3.68	1.3				
2018	MIN	MLB	25	2	0	0	5	4	22¹	17	1	3.6	5.2	13	40%	.239	1.16	2.01	6.86	-0.4	95.0	59.1	9.5	48
2019	LAA	MLB	26	0	0	0	20	0	13	9	1	5.5	9.0	13	39%	.229	1.31	3.46	8.44	-0.4	94.8	55.4	11.9	46.4
2019	SLN	MLB	26	0	0	0	2	0	3	8	0	3.0	6.0	2	14%	.571	3.00	9.00	6.56	0.0	93.6	61.8	5.9	54.3
2019	MIN	MLB	26	0	2	0	13	0	15¹	16	3	7.0	8.8	15	25%	.317	1.83	8.80	8.19	-0.5	96.0	51	10.6	42.6
2020	LAA	MLB	27	1	1	0	12	0	12	12	2	3.7	7.6	10	36%	.290	1.40	4.49	4.58	0.1	94.3	56.6	10.9	46.4

Comparables: Jeff Hoffman, Felix Doubront, Robert Stephenson

The word "odyssey" conjures something cool and epic, but Mejía's 2019 voyage was something far less than an excellent adventure. DFAed by Minnesota after a rocky start to the season, he was claimed and quickly DFAed again by the Angels, picked up by the Cards, jettisoned shortly thereafter, and once again grabbed by the Halos, only to be outrighted to Triple-A in August. It's not that anything has drastically changed in Mejía's skills, but the talent was fringy to begin with, and while the future seems a bit hazy at the moment, the lefty should find himself stopping periodically in major-league ports of call.

Keynan Middleton RHP Born: 09/12/93 Age: 26 Bats: R Throws: R Height: 6'3" Weight: 215 Origin: Round 3, 2013 Draft (#95 overall)

YEAR	TEAM	LVL	AGE	W	L	SV	G	GS	IP	H	HR	BB/9	K/9	K	GB%	BABIP	WHIP	ERA	DRA	WARP	MPH	FB%	WHF	CSP
2017	SLC	AAA	23	0	0	2	10	0	12²	11	0	2.8	5.7	8	36%	.282	1.18	2.84	3.44	0.3				
2017	LAA	MLB	23	6	1	3	64	0	58¹	60	11	2.8	9.7	63	38%	.318	1.34	3.86	3.80	0.9	99.4	62.6	18.2	48.7
2018	LAA	MLB	24	0	0	6	16	0	17²	14	1	4.6	8.2	16	33%	.295	1.30	2.04	5.55	-0.1	98.8	64.4	11	44.7
2019	LAA	MLB	25	0	0	0	11	0	7²	4	0	8.2	7.0	6	35%	.200	1.43	1.17	5.25	0.0	96.5	57.3	10.5	43.5
2020	LAA	MLB	26	2	2	2	46	0	49	42	8	4.3	10.0	54	36%	.277	1.34	4.26	4.37	0.4	98.5	63.4	15.5	46

Comparables: Joe Musgrove, Chase Whitley, Dovydas Neverauskas

For a few weeks early in the 2018 season, Middleton had been bestowed with the mantle that all relief pitchers covet: The Closer. He'd earned that role through a strong 2017, an ability to get out lefties as well as righties, and a bullpen that was bereft of other options. Oh, he also got it by throwing major heat, which may or may not have been a proximate cause of a UCL tear. Middleton's September comeback was enough to feel good about, but not conclusive enough to know where he stands coming into 2020. Should the heat return to full boil, Middleton may again enter the end-game conversation. If not, the innings may come in a more nominatively appropriate way: in the middle, and by the ton.

Shohei Ohtani RHP Born: 07/05/94 Age: 25 Bats: L Throws: R Height: 6'4" Weight: 210 Origin: International Free Agent, 2017

YEAR	TEAM	LVL	AGE	W	L	SV	G	GS	IP	H	HR	BB/9	K/9	K	GB%	BABIP	WHIP	ERA	DRA	WARP	MPH	FB%	WHF	CSP
2018	LAA	MLB	23	4	2	0	10	10	51²	38	6	3.8	11.0	63	40%	.269	1.16	3.31	3.46	1.1	100.3	46.4	15.5	47.6
2020	LAA	MLB	25	8	6	0	21	21	116	98	19	4.3	12.3	158	41%	.303	1.32	4.13	4.22	1.7	100.0	47.5	15.8	48.8

Comparables: Matt Harvey, Chris Archer, Zac Gallen

A mythical talent in a prosaic world, Ohtani is set to return to his full powers in 2020, once again bringing together what we only saw in fleeting glimpses during his 2018 debut: a pitcher virtually unhittable when he can command his high-90s cheese alongside his devastating splitter and slider, and … *and* … an offensive force with silly power to all fields and blazing speed to boot. There's a small sadness in the fact that, in a different age, Ohtani would have no such restrictions on the display of his talents: he could pitch every fifth day as long as he wants, roam the outfield on his off days, hit in the middle of the order every day, and have full rein to run wild on the bases. To imagine this alternate reality is to approach the Platonic ideal of a baseball player. In the real, imperfect world, we'll have to settle for the actual Ohtani, who still has a chance, even in a part-time, designated-hitting offensive role, to be a historically unique and generationally valuable talent. Lucky us.

Félix Peña RHP Born: 02/25/90 Age: 30 Bats: R Throws: R Height: 6'2" Weight: 220 Origin: International Free Agent, 2009

YEAR	TEAM	LVL	AGE	W	L	SV	G	GS	IP	H	HR	BB/9	K/9	K	GB%	BABIP	WHIP	ERA	DRA	WARP	MPH	FB%	WHF	CSP
2017	IOW	AAA	27	2	1	6	24	0	39	42	6	3.2	10.6	46	42%	.346	1.44	5.54	4.47	0.4				
2017	CHN	MLB	27	1	0	0	25	0	34¹	35	8	4.7	9.7	37	35%	.300	1.54	5.24	5.46	-0.1	96.3	65.8	13.4	46.7
2018	SLC	AAA	28	1	2	0	10	9	33¹	30	2	4.3	10.3	38	39%	.346	1.38	3.51	3.84	0.6				
2018	LAA	MLB	28	3	5	0	19	17	92²	87	12	2.7	8.3	85	44%	.288	1.24	4.18	4.15	1.2	94.5	57.9	11.8	46.2
2019	LAA	MLB	29	8	3	0	22	7	96¹	80	16	3.2	9.4	101	45%	.256	1.18	4.58	4.11	1.4	94.0	49.2	13.2	46.3
2020	*LAA*	*MLB*	*30*	*3*	*2*	*0*	*28*	*5*	*46*	*42*	*7*	*3.4*	*9.3*	*48*	*43%*	*.286*	*1.29*	*4.22*	*4.34*	*0.5*	*93.7*	*54.2*	*12.7*	*46.2*

Comparables: Jacob Barnes, Josh Lueke, Paul Sewald

By WARP, Peña was the 108th most valuable pitcher in the majors in 2019. By WARP, Peña was the, uh, *first* most valuable pitcher on the Angels in 2019—and this while missing the final two months of the season after tearing his ACL. He gets by on a sinker-slider combo mainly because of the filthiness of the latter, though he shouldn't be seeing lineups a third time through. Peña's true talent is probably somewhere near the midpoint of two consecutive outings in July: In the first, he gave up a solitary walk to the Mariners over seven relief innings of a combined no-hitter in the first home game following the death of teammate Tyler Skaggs; in the next, he was chased in the fifth after giving up eight runs to the Astros. In other words, he's a better-than-average pitcher whose ideal role is near the back end of a competing team's rotation.

Dillon Peters LHP Born: 08/31/92 Age: 27 Bats: L Throws: L Height: 5'11" Weight: 190 Origin: Round 10, 2014 Draft (#287 overall)

YEAR	TEAM	LVL	AGE	W	L	SV	G	GS	IP	H	HR	BB/9	K/9	K	GB%	BABIP	WHIP	ERA	DRA	WARP	MPH	FB%	WHF	CSP
2017	MRL	RK	24	0	1	0	2	2	6²	3	0	5.4	8.1	6	65%	.176	1.05	1.35	3.05	0.2				
2017	JUP	A+	24	1	0	0	2	2	10²	5	0	1.7	7.6	9	59%	.185	0.66	0.00	2.60	0.3				
2017	JAX	AA	24	6	2	0	9	9	45²	33	1	2.2	7.9	40	46%	.258	0.96	1.97	3.11	1.1				
2017	MIA	MLB	24	1	2	0	6	6	31¹	32	3	5.5	7.8	27	63%	.330	1.63	5.17	3.98	0.6	93.6	49.9	10.8	44.5
2018	NWO	AAA	25	6	7	0	19	19	102²	129	15	2.5	7.5	85	46%	.355	1.54	5.61	6.44	-1.0				
2018	MIA	MLB	25	2	2	0	7	5	27²	34	4	4.9	5.5	17	45%	.326	1.77	7.16	5.69	-0.1	93.1	52.2	7.8	50.2
2019	SLC	AAA	26	4	1	0	13	11	57	74	11	2.7	8.7	55	50%	.366	1.60	6.47	4.72	1.1				
2019	LAA	MLB	26	4	4	0	17	12	72	85	18	3.2	6.9	55	41%	.300	1.54	5.38	7.68	-1.6	92.7	50.4	9.6	47
2020	*LAA*	*MLB*	*27*	*2*	*2*	*0*	*16*	*5*	*34*	*37*	*6*	*3.3*	*6.9*	*26*	*44%*	*.296*	*1.45*	*5.37*	*5.33*	*0.0*	*92.5*	*51.3*	*9.5*	*48*

Comparables: Erick Fedde, Jarlin García, Andrew Miller

This is a hypothesis that calls for empirical verification, but "Dylans" seem to come from the coasts while "Dillons" feel like they're more often found in the nation's interior. The lefty from Indianapolis confirms these hunches, though he has spent his major-league time bi-coastally: first in Miami, and now Anaheim. While offering a rotation tourniquet for the Halos late in the season, Peters showed that his fragile pitch-mix Jenga depends upon the structural stability of his changeup. Take that away, and the blocks fall quickly. Unfortunately for Peters, any 2020 plan that involves "trying to win" likely pushes him out of contention for a rotation spot on the Angels, or any playoff-credible team.

Noé Ramirez RHP Born: 12/22/89 Age: 30 Bats: R Throws: R Height: 6'3" Weight: 205 Origin: Round 4, 2011 Draft (#142 overall)

YEAR	TEAM	LVL	AGE	W	L	SV	G	GS	IP	H	HR	BB/9	K/9	K	GB%	BABIP	WHIP	ERA	DRA	WARP	MPH	FB%	WHF	CSP
2017	PAW	AAA	27	3	3	5	33	0	48²	40	7	3.0	10.5	57	35%	.284	1.15	3.51	3.51	1.0				
2017	LAA	MLB	27	0	0	0	10	0	8¹	3	0	4.3	10.8	10	65%	.176	0.84	2.16	3.65	0.1	91.7	25.9	14.7	42.4
2017	BOS	MLB	27	0	0	0	2	0	4²	3	2	1.9	7.7	4	23%	.091	0.86	3.86	9.83	-0.2	91.9	50.7	16.9	48.8
2018	LAA	MLB	28	7	5	1	69	1	83¹	75	15	3.2	10.3	95	44%	.290	1.26	4.54	3.36	1.5	92.0	41.9	12.3	46.4
2019	LAA	MLB	29	5	4	0	51	7	67²	59	9	2.7	10.5	79	38%	.299	1.17	3.99	3.87	1.1	91.0	28.4	14	47
2020	*LAA*	*MLB*	*30*	*3*	*3*	*0*	*52*	*0*	*55*	*49*	*10*	*3.1*	*10.4*	*63*	*37%*	*.287*	*1.24*	*4.14*	*4.30*	*0.5*	*90.8*	*35*	*13.2*	*46*

Comparables: Heath Hembree, Michael Mariot, Juan Minaya

Trying to match up Ramirez's stat line with his pitches is something of a conundrum. You'd think that a sinker barely scraping 90 mph, thrown nearly half the time, wouldn't set up a pitcher for either a double-digit K/9 nor, in 2019, an ability to keep the ball in the yard at a reasonable rate. And yet, here we have Ramirez. When you see the filthy change you sort of get it: It tumbles startlingly out of the zone like a roller coaster's stomach-churning, accelerating descent—a Noé's Arc, if you will. Ramirez parlayed this successful pairing into a boatload of multi-inning turns, along with some spot-work as an opener. The limited arsenal will leave him open to some leaky outings, so more middle innings are likely what keeps him seaworthy in 2020.

Hansel Robles RHP Born: 08/13/90 Age: 29 Bats: R Throws: R Height: 6'0" Weight: 220 Origin: International Free Agent, 2008

YEAR	TEAM	LVL	AGE	W	L	SV	G	GS	IP	H	HR	BB/9	K/9	K	GB%	BABIP	WHIP	ERA	DRA	WARP	MPH	FB%	WHF	CSP
2017	LVG	AAA	26	0	1	4	18	0	23¹	27	5	5.4	8.5	22	36%	.319	1.76	5.79	6.41	-0.3				
2017	NYN	MLB	26	7	5	0	46	0	56²	47	10	4.6	9.5	60	35%	.259	1.34	4.92	5.63	-0.3	97.5	66.6	9.8	48
2018	LVG	AAA	27	0	0	2	8	0	7²	7	1	5.9	8.2	7	61%	.273	1.57	3.52	4.86	0.0				
2018	LAA	MLB	27	0	1	2	37	0	36¹	32	2	3.7	8.9	36	40%	.300	1.29	2.97	4.90	0.0	99.0	67.5	12.5	49.5
2018	NYN	MLB	27	2	2	0	16	0	19²	21	7	4.6	10.5	23	28%	.298	1.58	5.03	3.75	0.3	97.5	69.1	11.6	50.7
2019	LAA	MLB	28	5	1	23	71	1	72²	58	6	2.0	9.3	75	40%	.280	1.02	2.48	3.67	1.3	99.3	56.3	13.5	49.8
2020	*LAA*	*MLB*	*29*	*3*	*3*	*34*	*63*	*0*	*67*	*61*	*9*	*3.4*	*10.0*	*75*	*38%*	*.297*	*1.29*	*3.92*	*4.05*	*0.8*	*98.0*	*62.3*	*12.3*	*49.4*

Comparables: Arodys Vizcaíno, Bruce Rondón, Justin Grimm

If you're reading this comment, you're probably the type of fan who has pondered what walk-up or entrance music you would choose, should you ever have the opportunity. It's perhaps the most relatable thing that players do (even if we sometimes look down our collective noses at their questionable taste). Robles was one of us for many years, knowing his potential entrance music—the ominous, funereal theme of WWE's The Undertaker—but never getting quite to the closer's role, when he could blast his music from a stadium-sized PA to tens of thousands of fans. He spent a few years in Flushing, but Jeurys Familia would not yield. He waited. In 2018, he became part of a the Anaheim pen but couldn't get into the closing mix. Still he waited: dreaming, planning. By the time he took over for the deposed Cody Allen in May, Robles had an entire multimedia experience to accompany his entrance—the music, yes, but also a short film featuring a white horse, rose petals falling in slow motion through smoke, streaks of lightning. It lasts about two minutes and feels like outtakes from some obscure epic. It's a good thing Robles' production in the studio was matched by his production on the mound: The development of a dominant changeup helped him gallop away with the closer's job like the wild horse in his video. Now with some security in his role, we await the next development of the Hansel Robles Experience ... Holograms? Flash mobs? Interpretive dance? May all our dreams be as fully realized as the moment in which Robles makes his way from the 'pen to the mound.

Patrick Sandoval LHP Born: 10/18/96 Age: 23 Bats: L Throws: L Height: 6'3" Weight: 190 Origin: Round 11, 2015 Draft (#319 overall)

YEAR	TEAM	LVL	AGE	W	L	SV	G	GS	IP	H	HR	BB/9	K/9	K	GB%	BABIP	WHIP	ERA	DRA	WARP	MPH	FB%	WHF	CSP
2017	TCV	A-	20	1	1	0	4	4	19	19	0	2.8	13.3	28	47%	.404	1.32	3.79	3.86	0.3				
2017	QUD	A	20	2	2	1	9	7	40	38	1	3.6	10.8	48	48%	.333	1.35	3.83	4.65	0.3				
2018	QUD	A	21	7	1	1	14	10	65	58	4	1.5	9.8	71	48%	.305	1.06	2.49	3.25	1.4				
2018	BCA	A+	21	2	0	1	5	3	23	12	1	1.6	10.2	26	46%	.216	0.70	2.74	2.28	0.8				
2018	INL	A+	21	1	0	0	3	3	14²	6	0	3.7	12.9	21	47%	.200	0.82	0.00	2.30	0.5				
2018	MOB	AA	21	1	0	0	4	4	19²	12	0	3.7	12.4	27	40%	.286	1.02	1.37	2.89	0.6				
2019	MOB	AA	22	0	3	0	5	4	20	14	1	3.2	14.4	32	52%	.302	1.05	3.60	2.55	0.6				
2019	SLC	AAA	22	4	4	0	15	15	60¹	84	7	5.2	9.8	66	47%	.401	1.97	6.41	6.86	-0.1				
2019	LAA	MLB	22	0	4	0	10	9	39¹	35	6	4.3	9.6	42	50%	.287	1.37	5.03	4.35	0.6	94.8	46.5	14.3	45
2020	LAA	MLB	23	6	4	0	36	13	83	70	11	4.2	9.9	91	46%	.282	1.31	3.79	3.88	1.4	94.7	48.2	14.8	46.6

Comparables: Hunter Wood, Jake Faria, Mitch Keller

Had everything gone according to plan, Sandoval would have likely remained in Salt Lake until September, and even then would have probably only been pressed into the odd relief or "opener" outing in Anaheim. Needless to say, the Angels needed him sooner, and as a starter. He managed to tread water in this role, with a tumbling curveball his strongest offering. Now with some major-league seasoning, Sandoval should get the chance to work on limiting walks and home runs, the main barrier for him (and most fringe-types) to overcome on the path to major-league value.

Tyler Skaggs LHP Born: 07/13/91 Age: 28 Bats: L Throws: L Height: 6'4" Weight: 225 Origin: Round 1, 2009 Draft (#40 overall)

YEAR	TEAM	LVL	AGE	W	L	SV	G	GS	IP	H	HR	BB/9	K/9	K	GB%	BABIP	WHIP	ERA	DRA	WARP	MPH	FB%	WHF	CSP
2017	SLC	AAA	25	0	1	0	3	3	10	14	0	5.4	6.3	7	54%	.400	2.00	8.10	7.48	-0.2				
2017	LAA	MLB	25	2	6	0	16	16	85	90	13	3.0	8.0	76	42%	.318	1.39	4.55	5.12	0.4	94.3	60.2	8.6	45.9
2018	LAA	MLB	26	8	10	0	24	24	125¹	127	14	2.9	9.3	129	45%	.328	1.33	4.02	3.86	2.1	94.3	58.6	12	48.9
2019	LAA	MLB	27	7	7	0	15	15	79²	73	9	3.2	8.8	78	38%	.294	1.27	4.29	5.20	0.5	94.0	50.5	10	49

Skaggs died in a Southlake, Texas, hotel room in the early-morning hours of July 1, 2019, as his team was set to begin a four-game series with the Rangers. The coroner's report revealed that the Angels pitcher died of asphyxia while under the influence of fentanyl, oxycodone and alcohol. He was having an uneven but solid season as a starter, and had become a mainstay of the Angels rotation in his age-27 season. He and his wife, Carli, were married on New Year's Eve, 2018.

It would be a small comfort if we could leave Skaggs' tragic death in the realm of the personal, here grieving the loss of ballplayer while those who knew him grieve the loss of a friend, teammate, husband, brother, son. But in October of last year, reporting by ESPN's T.J. Quinn revealed that Skaggs had been sold opioids by a team employee, Eric Kay, and that team officials were aware of Skaggs' use. Kay also stated that he had provided drugs to five other players while they were with the Angels. Kay claims he did not provide the opioids that contributed to Skaggs' death.

In December, MLB introduced a new policy that includes opioid and cocaine testing, but most importantly, prioritizes treatment over punishment, only disciplining players who test positive after the violation of a prescribed treatment plan. One hopes this is a first step toward a drug testing and enforcement philosophy focused on empathy and care for those in need rather than punitive measures that scapegoat and criminalize individual users. Addressing this crisis on a systemic level, with intelligence and compassion, would be the best and most lasting tribute that could be paid to Skaggs.

Jose Suarez LHP Born: 01/03/98 Age: 22 Bats: L Throws: L Height: 5'10" Weight: 225 Origin: International Free Agent, 2014

YEAR	TEAM	LVL	AGE	W	L	SV	G	GS	IP	H	HR	BB/9	K/9	K	GB%	BABIP	WHIP	ERA	DRA	WARP	MPH	FB%	WHF	CSP
2017	ANG	RK	19	1	0	0	3	3	14	10	1	2.6	12.2	19	40%	.310	1.00	1.93	1.37	0.7				
2017	BUR	A	19	5	1	0	12	12	54²	49	7	3.0	11.7	71	48%	.333	1.23	3.62	4.84	0.3				
2018	INL	A+	20	0	1	0	2	2	9	6	0	1.0	18.0	18	67%	.400	0.78	2.00	1.72	0.4				
2018	MOB	AA	20	2	1	0	7	7	29²	34	0	2.4	15.5	51	37%	.500	1.42	3.03	4.91	0.1				
2018	SLC	AAA	20	1	4	0	17	17	78¹	81	5	4.0	8.4	73	48%	.336	1.48	4.48	4.26	1.1				
2019	SLC	AAA	21	2	1	0	7	6	32¹	24	3	4.7	8.6	31	46%	.247	1.27	3.62	2.58	1.3				
2019	LAA	MLB	21	2	6	0	19	15	81	100	23	3.7	8.0	72	38%	.325	1.64	7.11	8.98	-2.9	93.4	47.2	11.5	47.2
2020	LAA	MLB	22	3	2	0	8	8	38	40	7	3.8	7.7	33	39%	.291	1.46	5.40	5.31	0.1	93.4	49.2	11.9	49.2

Comparables: Bryse Wilson, Jaime Barria, Lucas Giolito

Just because Suarez wasn't ready for prime time in 2019 doesn't mean he'll never be ready. Pressed into service in June, subsequent crises kept him in Anaheim for the bulk of the season. His four-seamer has some natural sink, which ran smack into plenty of uppercutting bats, frequently sending the balls into faraway, irretrievable places. Some more Triple-A time might be the best way forward for the 22-year-old in the hopes that the second run goes a little more smoothly than the messy debut.

Julio Teheran RHP Born: 01/27/91 Age: 29 Bats: R Throws: R Height: 6'2" Weight: 205 Origin: International Free Agent, 2007

YEAR	TEAM	LVL	AGE	W	L	SV	G	GS	IP	H	HR	BB/9	K/9	K	GB%	BABIP	WHIP	ERA	DRA	WARP	MPH	FB%	WHF	CSP
2017	ATL	MLB	26	11	13	0	32	32	188¹	186	31	3.4	7.2	151	41%	.281	1.37	4.49	5.07	1.1	94.0	64.3	10	46.3
2018	ATL	MLB	27	9	9	0	31	31	175²	122	26	4.3	8.3	162	40%	.217	1.17	3.94	4.06	2.5	92.7	61.9	12.3	44
2019	ATL	MLB	28	10	11	0	33	33	174²	148	22	4.3	8.3	162	40%	.267	1.32	3.81	4.59	2.2	92.0	63.8	10.1	45.5
2020	LAA	MLB	29	10	8	0	28	28	140	127	25	3.8	8.4	131	39%	.269	1.33	4.42	4.52	1.6	92.1	63.3	10.8	45.2

Comparables: Ramon Martinez, Matt Cain, Michael Wacha

There aren't too many players in baseball who can be considered a crafty veteran by their age-28 season. Such was the case for Teheran entering the 2019 campaign, as his precipitous drop in velocity coincided with a similarly precipitous drop in prominence in Atlanta's rotation. Sure enough, he made one big adjustment to fight off Father Time's obscenely early attempt to reel him in. Teheran spent the 2019 season pitching exclusively from the stretch and it paid off—as the consistency allowed him to coerce more batters to meet him on his turf: just outside the strike zone. His velocity has continued to drop, which certainly played a role in Atlanta's decision to decline his 2020 option, but he's showing that young dogs can in fact learn some new tricks.

LINEOUTS

Hitters

HITTER	POS	TEAM	LVL	AGE	PA	R	2B	3B	HR	RBI	BB	K	SB	CS	AVG/OBP/SLG	DRC+	VORP	BABIP	BRR	FRAA	WARP
Kaleb Cowart	INF	MOB	AA	27	42	4	1	0	1	2	2	11	0	0	.179/.214/.282	50	-2.5	.214	0.4	P(4): 0.4, 1B(3): 0.4	0.0
	INF	SLC	AAA	27	317	42	15	4	8	60	25	55	3	4	.289/.345/.453	86	10.3	.330	1.6	3B(42): -5.2, SS(18): 2.1	0.4
	INF	LAA	MLB	27	26	1	3	0	0	1	1	7	1	0	.160/.192/.280	76	0.2	.222	-0.1		0.0
Orlando Martinez	OF	INL	A+	21	422	55	21	4	12	49	36	79	5	4	.263/.325/.434	111	20.7	.299	1.4	CF(41): 3.4, LF(20): 1.6	1.9
Adrian Rondon	3B	ORM	Rk+	20	122	19	7	2	5	19	10	21	2	0	.315/.369/.550	132	9.9	.349	-1.8		0.6
	3B	BUR	A	20	168	10	4	0	0	8	8	45	3	3	.231/.280/.256	70	-3.7	.321	-1.1	2B(24): -2.9, SS(12): -0.8	-0.5
Livan Soto	SS	ANG	Rk	19	29	4	2	0	0	1	1	4	0	2	.214/.241/.286	87	0.2	.250	0.2	2B(4): 0.0, SS(3): 0.0	0.1
	SS	BUR	A	19	282	24	5	0	1	20	32	40	6	2	.220/.311/.253	82	-0.9	.257	-0.6	SS(45): -3.0, 2B(15): -1.5	-0.1
Wilfredo Tovar	SS	SLC	AAA	27	349	53	17	6	4	57	19	45	3	6	.321/.355/.446	81	8.7	.359	1.0	SS(76): -9.6, 2B(7): 0.5	0.1
	SS	LAA	MLB	27	88	5	5	0	0	5	5	15	0	0	.193/.239/.253	64	0.2	.235	1.1		0.2
Taylor Ward	3B	SLC	AAA	25	512	102	34	1	27	71	80	101	11	5	.306/.427/.584	139	45.9	.347	3.0	LF(74): 8.9, 3B(17): -0.6	4.6
	3B	LAA	MLB	25	48	4	3	0	1	2	6	23	0	0	.190/.292/.333	60	-1.2	.389	-0.2		-0.2

"Utility" is often used in a quietly pejorative way: the player so designated is not good but can at least be average in diverse ways and at multiple positions. **Kaleb Cowart** dipped below that standard in 2019, revealing the precise moment at which "utility" adds an "f" as its first letter. ⓧ **Orlando Martinez**, a 22-year-old 2017 signee out of Cuba is, in keeping with organizational type, a toolsy, athletic outfielder. Unlike some of his organizational counterparts, he has good shot to be useful in a fourth-outfielder role sooner, rather than later thanks to an advanced approach. ⓧ A second-round pick who chose the dream of playing in Anaheim over the certainty of college ball in Berkeley, **Kyren Paris** has a first name that shares two of three syllables with a recent Star Wars villain. With his slick glove and slight frame, it remains to be seen if the force can awaken his bat. ⓧ Acquired from the Rays for cash, former high-profile J2 signee **Adrian Rondon** has been on a similarly disappointing path as new org-mate Kevin Maitan. Rondon did what he was supposed to do as a 20-year-old in rookie ball, but was flummoxed after a mid-season promotion to Low-A. Without significant growth in the bat, Rondon will be a lot closer to being Ron-done. ⓧ The fact that feather-hitting shortstop **Livan Soto** may have passed the more celebrated prospect-also-stripped-from-Atlanta, Kevin Maitan, will mean very little to future baseball historians when both players top out at Double-A in 2022. ⓧ A shortstop who, before last June, had most recently appeared in the majors in 2014, **Wilfredo Tovar**—somehow—parlayed five subpar hitting seasons in Triple-A into a mid-season call-up to Anaheim. This speaks well of Tovar's persistence, but less well of the Angels organizational depth. ⓧ After two cups of coffee that were more Yuban than Yirgacheffe, it's easy to dismiss **Taylor Ward** as a Quad-A superstar. Yet, that advanced plate approach calls us back to the urn again, hoping that, when we weren't looking, someone brewed up a fresh pot of the good stuff.

Pitchers

PITCHER	TEAM	LVL	AGE	W	L	SV	G	GS	IP	H	HR	BB/9	K/9	K	GB%	BABIP	WHIP	ERA	DRA	WARP	MPH	FB%	WHF	CSP
Stiward Aquino	ANG	Rk	20	0	4	0	8	8	21	27	1	4.3	11.1	26	39%	.448	1.76	7.71	7.50	-0.3				
	ORM	Rk+	20	0	1	0	4	4	15²	19	3	3.4	13.2	23	43%	.410	1.60	5.74	5.50	0.1				
Kyle Bradish	INL	A+	22	6	7	0	24	18	101	90	9	4.7	10.7	120	45%	.312	1.42	4.28	4.85	0.1				
Jesus Castillo	MOB	AA	23	6	6	2	38	12	99²	100	4	2.3	7.2	80	51%	.319	1.26	2.71	4.80	0.0				
William Holmes	ANG	Rk	18	0	2	0	7	6	17¹	15	2	8.3	13.0	25	38%	.351	1.79	5.71	5.89	0.0				
	ORM	Rk+	18	0	0	0	2	2	7	4	2	5.1	16.7	13	33%	.286	1.14	3.86	5.53	0.1				
Aaron Hernandez	INL	A+	22	1	4	0	20	15	72²	75	6	5.7	10.0	81	40%	.352	1.67	4.46	6.07	-1.0				
Jake Jewell	SLC	AAA	26	4	4	8	34	0	37²	42	3	4.1	9.8	41	50%	.371	1.57	5.26	4.12	0.8				
	LAA	MLB	26	0	0	0	18	0	26¹	28	8	2.7	7.9	23	62%	.278	1.37	6.84	4.89	0.1	96.2	49.9	13.9	47
Kyle Keller	NWO	AAA	26	2	3	10	37	0	54	44	8	3.5	12.2	73	35%	.295	1.20	4.50	3.14	1.6				
	MIA	MLB	26	0	0	0	10	0	10²	5	3	6.8	9.3	11	24%	.091	1.22	3.38	5.88	-0.1	96.1	68.4	13.5	44.7
Luis Madero	INL	A+	22	1	0	0	4	3	16	15	0	3.9	12.9	23	40%	.395	1.38	1.12	4.98	0.0				
	MOB	AA	22	5	11	0	20	19	89²	117	11	2.4	7.5	75	49%	.362	1.57	5.72	6.41	-1.6				
Parker Markel	ARK	AA	28	2	0	1	5	0	7²	2	0	2.3	21.1	18	29%	.286	0.52	0.00	1.42	0.3				
	IND	AAA	28	1	0	0	4	0	6	0	0	4.5	19.5	13	100%	.000	0.50	0.00	1.16	0.3				
	TAC	AAA	28	2	0	8	22	0	27²	13	3	6.8	14.3	44	44%	.204	1.23	2.60	1.71	1.2				
	SEA	MLB	28	0	0	0	5	0	4²	10	3	7.7	5.8	3	25%	.412	3.00	15.43	9.53	-0.2	97.0	48	11.4	42.3
	PIT	MLB	28	0	1	0	15	0	17¹	16	3	6.8	10.9	21	41%	.302	1.67	5.71	5.42	0.0	97.1	47.8	11	41.7
Isaac Mattson	INL	A+	23	3	0	0	8	0	20¹	8	1	4.0	13.3	30	46%	.194	0.84	0.89	2.15	0.6				
	MOB	AA	23	3	3	0	24	0	43²	30	3	2.7	12.6	61	52%	.287	0.98	2.68	3.04	0.8				
	SLC	AAA	23	0	0	1	5	0	9¹	9	0	4.8	18.3	19	39%	.500	1.50	3.86	1.62	0.4				
Mike Mayers	MEM	AAA	27	0	1	6	20	1	20	21	4	3.2	10.8	24	55%	.333	1.40	3.15	4.23	0.4				
	SLN	MLB	27	0	1	0	16	0	19	21	3	5.2	7.6	16	22%	.316	1.68	6.63	8.02	-0.5	97.1	53.2	12.1	43.7
JC Ramírez	INL	A+	30	0	1	0	4	2	7	8	3	2.6	9.0	7	43%	.278	1.43	6.43	4.25	0.1				
	SLC	AAA	30	1	2	0	12	8	41	49	7	4.0	5.7	26	43%	.318	1.63	6.59	5.48	0.5				
	LAA	MLB	30	0	0	0	5	0	8	8	1	1.1	4.5	4	50%	.259	1.12	4.50	5.26	0.0	92.6	54.2	11.2	51.5
Neil Ramírez	COH	AAA	30	2	1	2	25	0	29¹	28	7	3.4	13.8	45	28%	.328	1.33	4.91	3.60	0.7				
	CLE	MLB	30	0	1	0	16	0	16²	18	5	4.9	9.7	18	25%	.302	1.62	5.40	7.97	-0.5	96.6	58	15	46.6
	TOR	MLB	30	0	0	0	6	1	8¹	8	2	6.5	6.5	6	20%	.261	1.68	5.40	8.66	-0.3	95.5	51	13.6	39.3
Chris Rodriguez	INL	A+	20	0	0	0	3	3	9¹	6	0	3.9	12.5	13	68%	.316	1.07	0.00	3.14	0.2				
Jose Rodriguez	MOB	AA	23	0	2	0	5	5	17¹	24	2	3.1	12.5	24	51%	.449	1.73	7.27	5.16	0.0				
	SLC	AAA	23	3	3	2	18	2	44¹	48	7	4.5	9.1	45	41%	.325	1.58	6.29	4.57	0.7				
	LAA	MLB	23	0	1	0	9	1	19²	17	5	5.0	5.9	13	40%	.218	1.42	2.75	6.62	-0.3	94.8	46.2	10.9	45.7
Jose Soriano	BUR	A	20	5	6	0	17	15	77²	53	5	5.6	9.7	84	55%	.261	1.30	2.55	4.40	0.7				
Hector Yan	BUR	A	20	4	5	1	26	20	109	74	5	4.3	12.2	148	41%	.298	1.16	3.39	3.76	1.7				

Described by one of BP's prospect analysts as "goofy-long," **Stiward Aquino** came back from TJ surgery with a few more ticks on his fastball. 2020 will be the year to watch for command and refinement, and if both arrive, Stiward will be headed skyward. ⊗ Maybe it was growing up in the thin, desert air of the Phoenix area, and going to college in similar climes at New Mexico State, but **Kyle Bradish** handled the pitcher's nightmare of the Cal League respectably well in his first season of pro ball. He's likely a relief arm, but one that could move quickly. ⊗ In his second full year at Double-A, former Cubs prospect **Jesus Castillo** began to fulfill the prophecy: he shall be a reliever, and he shall induce ground balls, but it will be a small miracle if he saves. ⊗ Formerly William English, now **William Holmes**, the two-way player from Detroit lost most of 2019 to injury, and 2020 will see him try to pump up the volume on both tracks of his stereophonic game. ⊗ 2018 third-round draftee **Aaron Hernandez** held serve in his first pro season, impressing with strikeouts and disappointing with spotty command. 2020 could be the fork in the road for his future role, and he's likely to take a relief path. ⊗ Unless he can develop more facets to his game, **Jake Jewell** can hope to shine only in low-leverage relief settings. Otherwise, it all looks pretty dull for the 26-year-old. ⊗ **Kyle Keller** pitched his way into the Marlins bullpen by the end of 2019 by striking out more than 12 batters per nine with the Baby Cakes; however, he struggled to find the zone in any consistent manner during his cup of coffee in Miami and bullpen slots are getting harder to come by with increasing organizational depth. ⊗ **Luis Madero** does a good job of throwing strikes, but he's going to need to stop allowing so many hits if he wants to make his big-league debut in 2020. ⊗ Late-bloomer **Parker Markel** and his mid-90s gas went from the American Association in 2018 to an array of teams plucking him from waivers in 2019. Hopping from org to org sure beats the alternative. ⊗ Though great things were not expected from college righty **Isaac Mattson**, he had himself a great year, with two promotions, a dominant stint in the Arizona Fall League, and a strikeout rate that makes you think there's more upside than his passable three-pitch mix actually holds. ⊗ **Mike Mayers** lost nearly two miles per hour off his fastball from 2018 to 2019, reducing his outings from pleasant enough to a horror show. His name is pronounced "Myers" and he passed through waivers before later being re-added to the 40-man roster—meaning he reappears just when you think he's history. If he ends up in Peoria we'll begin to wonder if Dr. Loomis is required. ⊗ As recently as 2017, **JC Ramírez** was an unlikely rotation piece for the Angels. Since then, it's all gone to pieces: working back from UCL surgery, Ramirez only logged 14 2/3 major-league innings over the last two years—not enough for the Angels to keep him around for 2020. ⊗ After what looked like a much-delayed breakout in 2018, **Neil Ramírez** found himself with a ground-ball rate in the low 20s and a lot more spare time on his hands in September. ⊗ Dogged by a back injury that has allowed him to pitch only nine innings over the past two seasons, **Chris Rodriguez** is a righty with a major-league arsenal, which is why the Angels will practice all the patience necessary to get him back on the mound—hopefully for a full 2020. ⊗ If you *only* let opponents score on home runs, maybe you can get away with allowing more than two per nine, or barely striking out more than you walk - or both. Somehow, it seems unlikely the **Jose Rodriguez** Method will catch on. ⊗ The big body and raw stuff alone could power **Jose Soriano**'s path to major-league relevance. Developing a consistent repeatable motion will be key in making that relevance happen sooner and in a starter's role. ⊗ Who can strike out north of 12 hitters per nine while firing mid-90s with movement from the left side? Why, **Hector Yan** can. His smaller frame points toward a relief role, which could jump the 20-year-old up the ladder quickly.

LOS ANGELES DODGERS

Essay by Patrick Dubuque

Player comments by Chad Moriyama and BP staff

It was an ugly swing, a swing like a rough shove in a bar fight, and as Cody Bellinger ranged back he looked up every two steps, as if expecting it to die. His long stride stretched into an elope, as if his feet were caught in the slow-motion of the moment, as if he would keep running halfway to the wall forever, as in a dream. And then his hands slapped the blue vinyl just as the ball sailed overhead and, in an instant, the work of eight months, of 106 wins, of perhaps the most talented Dodgers team in history dissolved on camera, a supercut of hollow stares into some other timeline before fading into black. The fans pulsed up the aisles as though the stadium itself were bleeding out blue.

Baseball is designed to be fair and unfair. The physics of the bat and ball generates, more than any other action in professional sports, pure chaos; it bends but does not break to the strongest manipulation of reason and strategy. It's the mythology that rejects mythology, propping up nobodies and felling heroes. It cuts down demigods like Clayton Kershaw and props up the likes of Howie Kendrick. It gives us teams like the Los Angeles Dodgers, winners of more games this decade than any other NL franchise, perched alongside such dynasties as the 1960s Giants, the 1970s Red Sox, and the 1990s Mariners, the incomplete elite.

After the loss, after destiny swept their opponents to their ensuing championship, the message was clear: Something had to change. The Nationals, as the symbol for modern postseason futility, are no more; now, the Dodgers are the Nationals. Seven years of beautiful summers and grisly autumns were enough. As of printing, that change hasn't happened yet. The team's transactions as of the end of the year amounted to signing one reliever on a bounce-back contract, even as they suffered the loss of Hyun-Jin Ryu and Rich Hill. On offense, there are more reinforcements than holes to patch, as Will Smith, Gavin Lux and Alex Verdugo demonstrated that the machine is still firing on all cylinders. And yet for a fanbase in need of postseason heroics, there are no new heroes, no deck chairs to shuffle. The Dodgers were never designed to change, but then, they weren't designed to lose.

It's difficult to evaluate a ballclub so consistently successful and disappointing; it resists traditional analysis. Besides, number crunching always fails to capture the

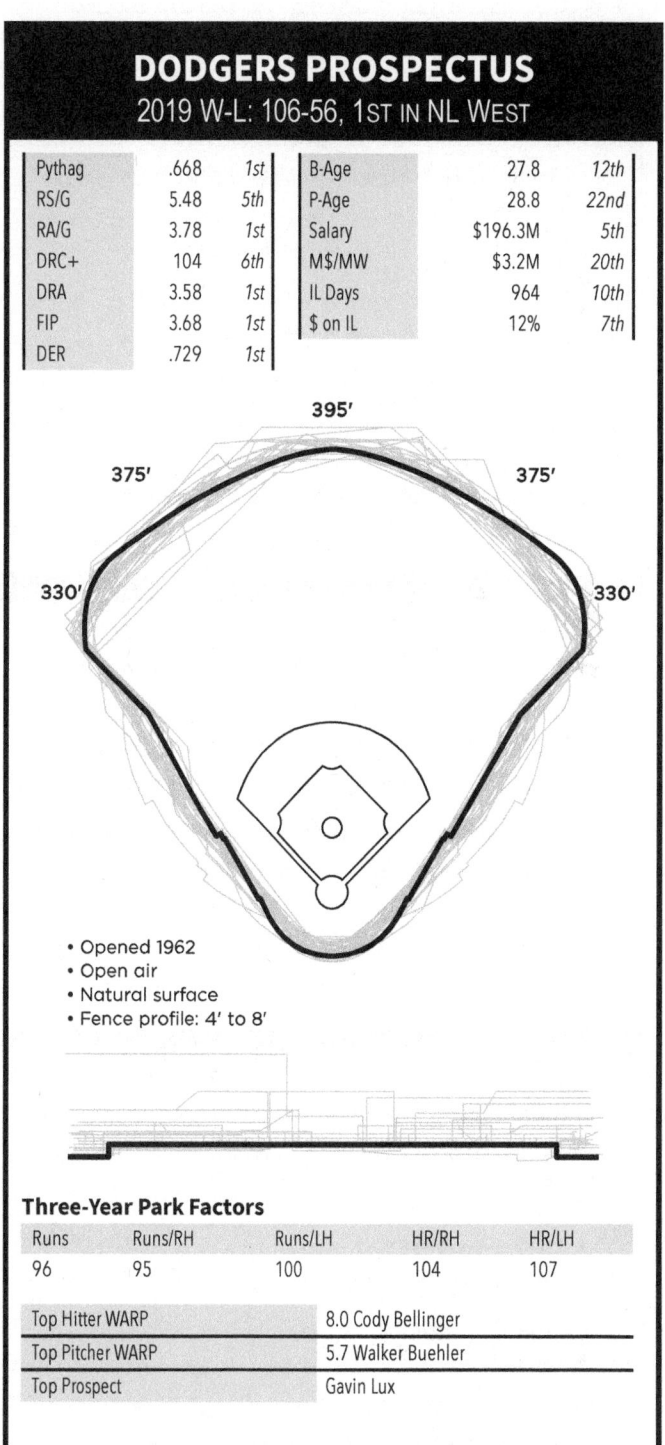

DODGERS PROSPECTUS
2019 W-L: 106-56, 1st in NL West

Pythag	.668	1st	B-Age	27.8	12th
RS/G	5.48	5th	P-Age	28.8	22nd
RA/G	3.78	1st	Salary	$196.3M	5th
DRC+	104	6th	M$/MW	$3.2M	20th
DRA	3.58	1st	IL Days	964	10th
FIP	3.68	1st	$ on IL	12%	7th
DER	.729	1st			

375' 395' 375'
330'   330'

- Opened 1962
- Open air
- Natural surface
- Fence profile: 4' to 8'

Three-Year Park Factors

Runs	Runs/RH	Runs/LH	HR/RH	HR/LH
96	95	100	104	107

Top Hitter WARP	8.0 Cody Bellinger
Top Pitcher WARP	5.7 Walker Buehler
Top Prospect	Gavin Lux

2019 Hit List Ranking

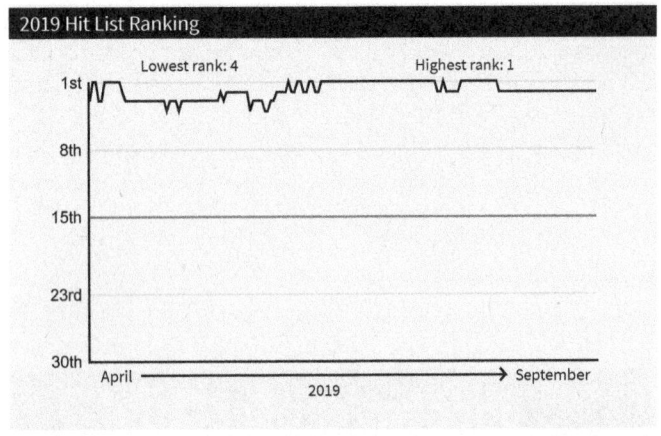

Committed Payroll (in millions)

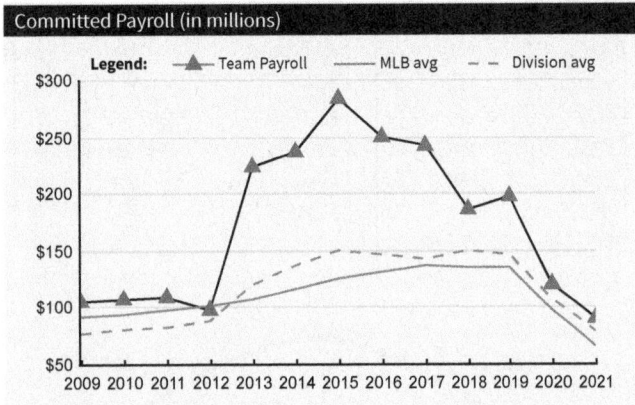

Farm System Ranking

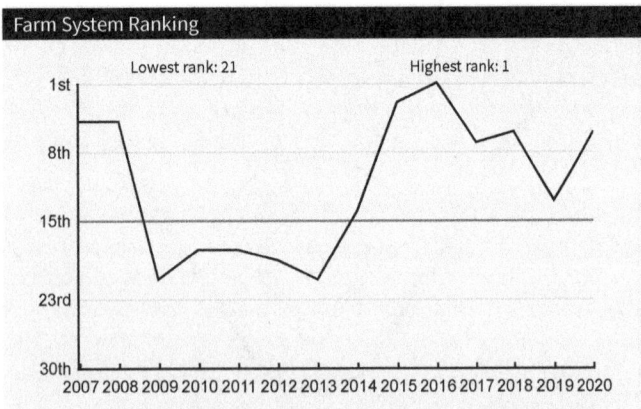

Personnel

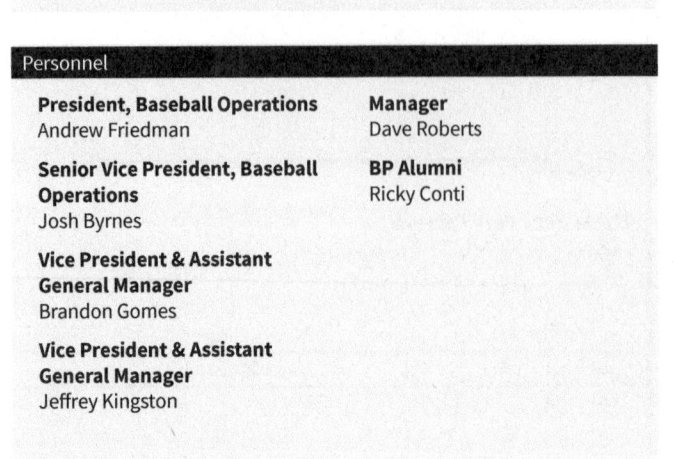

President, Baseball Operations
Andrew Friedman

Senior Vice President, Baseball Operations
Josh Byrnes

Vice President & Assistant General Manager
Brandon Gomes

Vice President & Assistant General Manager
Jeffrey Kingston

Manager
Dave Roberts

BP Alumni
Ricky Conti

dualism of the sport, thirty nation-states that act as both teams and corporations. So instead we'll apply the lens of military philosophy. In his book *Just and Unjust Wars*, professor Henry Walzer divides the ethics of war into two categories: *jus in bello* and *jus ad bellum*. The first belongs to the hemisphere of justice within war: what is considered acceptable behavior during battle. This includes the war convention and its rules: don't use mustard gas, don't shoot soldiers after they've surrendered, leave the ambulance drivers alone. The second centers on the justice of going to war, or when it's acceptable to bear arms at all, to invade, to strike first. The goal of the exercise is not to grade a particular team, but to prove that ethics are both possible and attainable, that wars can be limited, and games can be played fair.

And in a strange way, the story of the 2019 Dodgers isn't even about the 2019 season. Stories always begin before their beginnings. This one starts half a century ago on the other side of the country, and marches toward its resolution in the ruins of a recent battlefield: The hollow irregular timpani ring of a trash can that not one person heard, and now echoes everywhere.

⚾   ⚾   ⚾

Baseball is hardly war, and we're spared the worst of the clichés so often anointed upon the ugly phalanx thrust that is football. Like any sport, though, baseball isn't totally divorced from war, either: The *Iliad* caps its history of the Trojan War not with the death of Hektor or the retrieval of Helen, but with a postwar chariot race that mends the alliances of the victorious army. Athletic contest has always served as both a training ground and a psychological substitute for armed conflict, a channeling of social aggression. In an America that grows increasingly culturally homogenous in the age of the internet and Amazon, professional sports hold as one of the last remaining vestiges of localized nationalism, even in Los Angeles, the city that exports so much of that homogeneity to the world.

The Spartans employed sports to train their warriors, get them used to grappling and spears, but they also served as their cultural indoctrination, a rite of passage. Today, sports take on a more moderate application of these same ideals, the intent being to build character, discipline, teamwork and sportsmanship. Baseball, at its heart, is a code of ethics: It's an amalgam of intricate, incomprehensible rules specifying human conduct to an inhuman degree, rivaling Leviticus, with another invisible code laid on top of it by the tradition of the players themselves. One of its core tenets is the shared, level playing field, the equal opportunity it provides each man. The game is at heart a contract, a social construct, and it only works when everyone adheres to its values in good faith.

Justice within war, *jus in bello*, maps onto baseball's rules, written and unwritten: Don't run too far outside the lines. Don't gamble on your sport. Don't throw the ball at a batter's head, and don't hit John Roseboro in the head with a bat. The Dodgers have generally, since their arrival in Los Angeles, taken on the aura of good-natured, clean-playing young men, almost as if the climate were baked into them. It took shape in the '70s, with Rick Monday saving the flag and imperturbable Steve Garvey fielding reporters; it carried through the officious and efficient Orel Hershiser and holds today, despite the bat flips of Yasiel Puig and the blood drawn by the errant cleats of Chase Utley and Manny Machado. It's not an ethos of grit, no Cardinals Way, but rather just the languorous ease of conspicuous talent. The Dodgers have three losing seasons in a quarter of a century, almost despite themselves at times. They ascend beyond grit.

After the installation of Andrew Friedman as President of Baseball Operations, the destiny of the Dodgers seemed almost foregone. It culminated in a 2017 team that fell a game shy of ending the team's three-decade championship drought. It was perhaps the most exciting, evenly-matched final in memory, the battle of two model franchises at the peak of their power. The Astros won, because in sports, unlike war, someone has to win. They also, as it turns out, cheated.

The news came out just this offseason, by way of the testimony of four people, including former Astro Mike Fiers: An intricate and institutional system for stealing and relaying signs was in place for the entire 2017 season. The Astros used a camera in center field to read the catcher's signs, and employees and players in the clubhouse tunnel deciphered them, and banged on a nearby trash can to tell the batter that an offspeed was coming. As Rob Arthur analyzed at Baseball Prospectus, the correlation of trash can signals and strikeouts at Minute Maid on pitches in the dirt was decisive. MLB has begun an investigation into the accusations, though video and correspondence have already demonstrated a damning level of proof. As the book heads to print, MLB's decision, and its potential punishment, have not been established.

One takeaway seems safe to publish: Rob Manfred may make the Astros organization regret the choices they made, but it will be of little use to fans in Los Angeles. Even in the NCAA, a vacated title doesn't find a new home; it just never happened. But such a result is itself unthinkably drastic, and it's more likely to result in fines, draft pick forfeitures, and/or suspensions. The flag will fly forever, no matter how blackened. Such is war; chemical weapons are prohibited by the war convention, but the world has no real commissioner. Tribunals are powerless to bring back the dead, and mournful bells can't be unrung.

⚾   ⚾   ⚾

So the Dodgers were victims of a violation of the rules of engagement in 2017. More meaningful to the current roster is the other half of the equation. *Jus ad bellum* is the trickier aspect to translate to baseball, because it regards the justice of when to go to war, when to make a political act guaranteed

to kill people. There are no such aggressions in baseball because it's a sport that exists in continual (mock) conflict. So perhaps the better way to define the justice of baseball, as nation-states rather than individual combatants, is to examine whether a team is acting ethically based on the customs of the sport itself: Are the Dodgers behaving the way that a baseball team ought to behave?

There are two ways to answer this question, because baseball is an interconnected relationship between three parties: the team, the players, and the fans. In terms of the team's conduct with its players, the record isn't quite as sun-dappled as its on-field reputation. The team remains under investigation by the U.S. Department of Justice for its documented involvement in the shady world of international scouting, including official interaction with *buscones*, local agents whose interests often align with human trafficking and organized crime. It's a widespread issue across the league, but the Dodgers figure prominently because of the existence of an internal document, a "crimes.xlsx," that lists the names of team employees and an estimation—on a scale of 1 to 5—how their behavior ranks, from "innocent bystander" to "criminal."

Also unresolved is the conduct of former head of player development and current San Francisco Giants manager Gabe Kapler, who in 2015 was notified of sexual assault committed by a Dodgers minor leaguer against a 17-year-old. Kapler insisted that he hadn't been made aware of the incident. It was later revealed via a *Sports Illustrated* report that this was not true; not only had he chosen not to notify the police of the crime, he failed to enlist any professional help in his attempt to resolve the matter internally. The situation speaks to a lack of institutional control, and accountability, over the conditions of the team's employees.

Assessing the ethics of the Dodgers' conduct toward its fans is a more difficult task. One of the primary causes for concern in the modern era of baseball is the transition of its revenue, away from ticket sales toward a greater influence of broadcast media and merchandising. The sport is, in a way, too popular for its own good, and it is too easy for corporations in this strange, restricted trust to extract money from its fans. For a century, baseball teams had two ways to profit: win, or develop players and sell them to winners. True, social mobility was often nonexistent, and the bottom feeders of the league could never quite get ahead. But profit was tied to winning, and winning meant selling tickets. Today, that correlation no longer holds true: baseball teams no longer have to sell out to make money. They make money, as each new sale proves, just by existing, as the last money market accounts on earth.

The Dodgers do draw—half a million more than the second-place Cardinals, and five times as many fans as the Marlins—and they do offer a product worth watching. The team understands this, of course, and has responded by raising prices to meet demand. Bill Shaikin of the *Los Angeles Times* recently reported that, a family of four will pay, on average, around $150 for the privilege of sitting in the cheap seats. That's half of the median L.A. family's discretionary spending for the entire month, devoted to a single Rockies game. Sports franchises across the country have been converting the stadium experience of baseball into a luxury event, and in so doing have priced out its poorer, and younger, audience. Couple that with the ongoing price war over cable television that has left half the city unable to watch a Dodgers game, and it's easy to see why the team feels so isolated and foreign to even its hometown fans.

The other violation of the contract between the Dodgers and their fans, however, is the allocation of those revenues. Despite its massive income, for the third straight offseason the team refused to go over the luxury tax threshold, despite public statements that the decision was not a mandate from ownership. There are plenty of terms for explaining this kind of fiscal conservatism—payroll flexibility is in vogue—but they're meaningless. The Dodgers have chosen to enter the 2020 season with a roster that, especially on the pitching side, appears weaker than the one that lost to the Nationals. The rotation depth that has marked the Andrew Friedman era has been worn away, and an injury or two could leave the 2020 Dodgers in perilous condition. Given their resources, it's an unjustifiable risk. Unless you're a shareholder.

⚾   ⚾   ⚾

This, then, is the Dodgers' crime, every bit as great as the one laid against them by Houston. We expect sportsmanship out of players, but we must demand equal sportsmanship out of teams. The violation of *jus in bello* on the level of the Houston Astros is something that should and will be punished, severely. But the Dodgers, as an organization, are hardly without guilt. On the level of *jus ad bellum*, this means that every team must try not just to profit, but to win, and must use all the resources available to them in order to do so.

Cheating has been a part of baseball since its inception, and the way in which the game governs itself and interprets its lawbreakers is a strange and obscure process. Stealing signs from second is fine, if done subtly, while doing it through binoculars or cameras or watches is not. What matters isn't the law itself, it's the unquestionable faith of everyone involved, players and teams and fans, that the process is fair, and conducted in good faith. It's the same as war; nations avoid committing atrocities because they don't want the global repercussions, but also because they don't want to have those same atrocities committed against them later. Everyone benefits from fair, limited war, and fair baseball.

Somewhere along the path from childhood to adulthood, sportsmanship evaporates from organized baseball. In fact, the intricate moral system created to house baseball does the opposite of instilling values in its players. Instead, it frees it from them entirely. No professional athlete, after a questionable call comes down in their favor, turns to the umpire and admits, "Actually, I'm pretty sure I was out." It's the umpire's job to make the call, and thus the player is freed from all obligation. And by extension, all cheating is the responsibility of the judges to catch. "It's only cheating if you get caught" is a worn baseball cliché, but what it fails to explain is: if you do get caught, so what?

The what, ultimately, is that the entire sport suffers. The Los Angeles Dodgers, with their legacy, their fanbase and their player development, are perhaps the league's model franchise, for good and for ill. It's easy to imagine them, one year from now, the champions of baseball; it's equally easy to envision them tarnishing the league. Ultimately it will come down to how they fight, and what they fight for. ◼

—Patrick Dubuque is an author of Baseball Prospectus.

HITTERS

Matt Beaty OF/1B
Born: 04/28/93   Age: 27   Bats: L   Throws: R   Height: 6'0"   Weight: 215   Origin: Round 12, 2015 Draft (#372 overall)

YEAR	TEAM	LVL	AGE	PA	R	2B	3B	HR	RBI	BB	K	SB	CS	AVG/OBP/SLG	DRC+	VORP	BABIP	BRR	FRAA	WARP
2017	TUL	AA	24	481	61	31	1	15	69	35	54	3	3	.326/.378/.505	158	32.6	.343	0.2	1B(55): 2.3, 3B(49): -0.7	3.9
2018	OKL	AAA	25	120	13	10	0	1	12	12	17	0	0	.277/.378/.406	109	5.3	.321	-0.3	1B(16): -0.3, LF(5): 1.0	0.5
2019	OKL	AAA	26	135	17	7	1	3	18	10	12	0	0	.306/.378/.455	92	6.9	.321	-0.4	1B(11): -0.9, 3B(11): 1.4	0.3
2019	LAN	MLB	26	268	36	19	1	9	46	17	33	5	0	.265/.317/.458	94	4.5	.275	1.1	1B(35): -0.7, LF(34): 0.6	0.5
2020	LAN	MLB	27	84	9	5	0	3	10	5	12	0	0	.259/.313/.421	93	1.8	.277	0.1	LF 1	0.3

Comparables: Gordy Coleman, José Osuna, Tim Locastro

Batt Meaty started out as a convenient spoonerism, but ended up being an appropriate description of his breakout 2019. Drafted out of college, Beaty was 24 when he made it to Double-A and he was never ranked as a relevant prospect by any publication. Yet he continued to hit, putting up a .309/.367/.447 slash line in the minors, and injuries to the veteran Dodgers gave him a chance to prove he could do it in the majors as well. After a scorching start, Beaty cooled off and finished the year with a below-average DRC+ over 268 plate appearances. It won't wow anyone, but to get a credible utility man from a 12th-round pick—who earned starts in the NLDS—speaks to the job the organization's player development program has done. Normally Beaty would be a candidate for regression back towards something like organizational depth, but betting against a Dodgers hitter who has shown quality development comes with a warning label at this point.

Cody Bellinger OF/1B Born: 07/13/95   Age: 24   Bats: L   Throws: L   Height: 6'4"   Weight: 203   Origin: Round 4, 2013 Draft (#124 overall)

YEAR	TEAM	LVL	AGE	PA	R	2B	3B	HR	RBI	BB	K	SB	CS	AVG/OBP/SLG	DRC+	VORP	BABIP	BRR	FRAA	WARP
2017	OKL	AAA	21	77	15	4	0	5	15	9	22	7	0	.343/.429/.627	138	8.8	.450	0.8	1B(16): 1.0, CF(2): -0.5	0.6
2017	LAN	MLB	21	548	87	26	4	39	97	64	146	10	3	.267/.352/.581	129	47.9	.299	-0.2	1B(93): 0.7, LF(39): -2.5	2.9
2018	LAN	MLB	22	632	84	28	7	25	76	69	151	14	1	.260/.343/.470	113	39.6	.313	3.3	1B(110): -0.9, CF(78): 2.0	2.8
2019	LAN	MLB	23	661	121	34	3	47	115	95	108	15	5	.305/.406/.629	158	66.2	.302	0.4	RF(115): 13.3, 1B(36): 1.9	8.0
2020	LAN	MLB	24	595	91	27	2	40	105	76	113	10	3	.271/.367/.562	141	47.9	.275	0.5	1B 0, CF 3	5.4

Comparables: Wayne Belardi, Giancarlo Stanton, Anthony Rizzo

Following his breakout 2017, Bellinger was more solid than superstar in 2018, ending the season as a platoon bat. So perhaps nothing better showcases his ascent in 2019 than his OPS boost from .681 to .982 against southpaws, powering his overall 1.035 OPS. But that's just the start, as his walk rate improved (10.9 percent to 14.4 percent), his strikeout rate plummeted (23.9 percent to 16.4 percent) and his power busted loose (60 XBH to 84 XBH). Combine that with a Gold Glove win in right field (he could've won one at first base as well) and the ability to play center, and he very much earned his NL MVP. Bellinger not only cemented himself as a regular in the Dodgers lineup no matter who was pitching, but also signified the rise to stardom that seemed like would come after 2017.

Of course, whenever 2017 comes up, so does his disastrous World Series against the Astros—in which he struck out 17 times in 29 plate appearances. To Bellinger's credit, he's made the necessary adjustments to get to where he is today. Unfortunately, production when it matters most for the Dodgers has not followed. For as much as people made of his .565 OPS in that series, he has since posted just one series better, coming in the NLCS last year with a whopping .591. The team's NLDS exit in 2019 will be blamed on Clayton Kershaw or Dave Roberts, but the offense let the team down for the third year in a row and their MVP's three singles and a double in 21 trips to the plate certainly didn't help the cause. Still, he's only had 145 plate appearances in the playoffs, so there's time for him to turn it around. But if the Dodgers ever hope to break their now 31-year World Series drought, they're likely going to need him to get hot when it matters in order to do it.

Michael Busch 2B Born: 11/09/97   Age: 22   Bats: L   Throws: R   Height: 6'0"   Weight: 207   Origin: Round 1, 2019 Draft (#31 overall)

YEAR	TEAM	LVL	AGE	PA	R	2B	3B	HR	RBI	BB	K	SB	CS	AVG/OBP/SLG	DRC+	VORP	BABIP	BRR	FRAA	WARP
2020	LAN	MLB	22	251	23	11	1	6	25	19	68	2	1	.210/.283/.345	71	-1.4	.271	0.0	2B 0	-0.1

Comparables: Wilmer Difo, Josh Prince, Lane Adams

Busch was selected with one of the two first-round picks the Dodgers had in 2019. Despite playing mostly first base in college, the organization will try him at second base with an eye on getting the most out of his bat. While he had just 35 plate appearances split between Rookie and A levels (.496 OPS) this year, Busch was pushed to the Arizona Fall League where he put up a 1.007 OPS in 22 plate appearances. Reports on Busch's bat are promising, as he controls the strike zone well and makes a lot of quality contact to all fields thanks to his smooth left-handed stroke. The biggest question is whether he can actually handle the keystone in the majors. Early returns have been positive and he seems primed to become a part of the next wave in the Dodgers' talent pipeline.

Diego Cartaya C Born: 09/07/01   Age: 18   Bats: R   Throws: R   Height: 6'2"   Weight: 199   Origin: International Free Agent, 2018

YEAR	TEAM	LVL	AGE	PA	R	2B	3B	HR	RBI	BB	K	SB	CS	AVG/OBP/SLG	DRC+	VORP	BABIP	BRR	FRAA	WARP
2019	DOD	RK	17	150	25	10	0	3	13	11	31	1	0	.296/.353/.437	126	12.3	.359	1.9	C(28): -0.2	1.1
2020	LAN	MLB	18	251	22	12	1	4	23	18	79	3	1	.225/.288/.339	68	-2.3	.322	0.0	C 0	-0.2

Comparables: Francisco Mejía, Chris Marrero, Cheslor Cuthbert

Cartaya is 18 and hasn't made it out of the complex leagues, but he is starting to make it clear why the Dodgers signed him for $2.5 million in 2018. Cartaya's bat came alive in 2019, and most importantly scouts see him developing nicely behind the plate while having a mature feel for hitting. It's difficult to project Cartaya at his tender age, but the Dodgers are treating him like a potential starter. He'll likely be promoted next year, perhaps even to A-ball. Although his breakout as a prospect is likely a couple years off, it wouldn't surprise if he made the Dodgers reconsider their schedule.

Jeter Downs SS Born: 07/27/98   Age: 21   Bats: R   Throws: R   Height: 5'11"   Weight: 180   Origin: Round 1, 2017 Draft (#32 overall)

YEAR	TEAM	LVL	AGE	PA	R	2B	3B	HR	RBI	BB	K	SB	CS	AVG/OBP/SLG	DRC+	VORP	BABIP	BRR	FRAA	WARP
2017	BIL	RK	18	209	31	3	3	6	29	27	32	8	5	.267/.370/.424	97	12.8	.288	-1.5	SS(50): -4.5	-0.1
2018	DYT	A	19	524	63	23	2	13	47	52	103	37	10	.257/.351/.402	124	23.2	.306	-1.6	2B(73): -2.9, SS(43): -9.3	1.6
2019	RCU	A+	20	479	78	33	4	19	75	54	97	23	8	.269/.354/.507	127	44.3	.304	4.1	SS(90): -4.0, 2B(10): -1.1	2.9
2019	TUL	AA	20	56	14	2	0	5	11	6	10	1	0	.333/.429/.688	167	7.9	.333	0.8	SS(11): -0.4, 2B(1): 0.0	0.6
2020	LAN	MLB	21	251	30	12	1	11	34	20	63	7	3	.236/.306/.445	96	7.3	.276	0.4	SS -4, 2B -1	0.3

Comparables: Gavin Lux, Carter Kieboom, Alen Hanson

It's been about five years now since a shortstop named Jeter commanded the attention of the baseball world, but Downs is on a mission to change that, turning more and more heads with every game he plays. Only some guy named Gavin Lux kept him from winning the Minor League Player Of The Year for the Dodgers, following his breakout 2019. Acquired in an unpopular trade at the time due to fan favorite Yasiel Puig being dealt, Downs validated the faith of the Dodgers by showing on-base and power skills in High-A, then flexing his muscles even more in a 12-game stint in Double-A. He ended up posting a 20/20 season on the year and forced his way into Top 100 lists everywhere. While it appears Downs is blocked by Corey Seager and/or Lux, the Dodgers value versatility, and Downs has experience at second base, with enough athleticism to try the outfield. He could force his way into a Dodgers debut, but the most likely scenario at this point is he's dealt within the next couple seasons for an impact player.

David Freese   1B   Born: 04/28/83   Age: 37   Bats: R   Throws: R   Height: 6'2"   Weight: 213   Origin: Round 9, 2006 Draft (#273 overall)

YEAR	TEAM	LVL	AGE	PA	R	2B	3B	HR	RBI	BB	K	SB	CS	AVG/OBP/SLG	DRC+	VORP	BABIP	BRR	FRAA	WARP
2017	PIT	MLB	34	503	44	16	0	10	52	58	116	0	1	.263/.368/.371	96	16.8	.336	-4.7	3B(116): 5.3, 1B(3): 0.0	1.6
2018	PIT	MLB	35	265	29	10	1	9	42	18	56	0	0	.282/.336/.444	109	11.6	.330	-0.9	3B(55): 1.7, 1B(15): 1.0	1.3
2018	LAN	MLB	35	47	9	2	1	2	9	6	16	0	0	.385/.489/.641	111	7.1	.619	-0.5	1B(14): -0.4, 3B(3): 0.0	0.0
2019	LAN	MLB	36	186	35	13	0	11	29	23	44	0	0	.315/.403/.599	128	10.3	.374	-0.8	1B(50): -1.6, 3B(2): 0.0	0.8
2020	LAN	MLB	37	251	30	11	0	10	33	23	68	1	0	.261/.341/.444	107	9.4	.332	-1.2	3B 2, 1B 0	1.1

Comparables: Kevin Young, Wes Helms, Kevin Millar

Freese hung up his cleats following the conclusion of the 2019 season. The reliable team dad (Chase Utley) retired, so Freese stepped in as the cool step-dad and was a standout, both in the clubhouse and on the field. While PECOTA pegged him for a .720 OPS, understandably assuming age-related decline, Freese annihilated the ball, outperforming his projection by nearly 300 points of OPS. The only signs of age were the injuries that cost him a couple months of playing time. Even then, he returned down the stretch and continued to add to his postseason legacy by going 4-for-8 with a double in the NLDS. It is remarkable that Freese had so many moments with the Dodgers that eclipsed his 2011 World Series Game 6 heroics with the Cardinals and yet he did, repeatedly.

Kyle Garlick   OF   Born: 01/26/92   Age: 28   Bats: R   Throws: R   Height: 6'1"   Weight: 210   Origin: Round 28, 2015 Draft (#852 overall)

YEAR	TEAM	LVL	AGE	PA	R	2B	3B	HR	RBI	BB	K	SB	CS	AVG/OBP/SLG	DRC+	VORP	BABIP	BRR	FRAA	WARP
2017	TUL	AA	25	305	45	9	0	17	42	30	78	1	0	.239/.321/.463	113	8.0	.267	0.9	LF(43): -1.2, RF(23): 3.8	1.4
2018	TUL	AA	26	85	11	4	0	5	14	6	33	0	0	.282/.329/.526	77	3.3	.415	0.6	RF(8): -0.2, LF(8): 1.7	0.2
2018	OKL	AAA	26	341	49	18	2	17	46	14	105	2	0	.253/.287/.478	83	9.2	.320	-1.2	RF(58): 3.9, LF(26): -1.4	0.2
2019	OKL	AAA	27	304	54	25	2	23	59	25	84	2	1	.314/.382/.675	139	29.1	.373	-0.8	RF(47): -0.2, LF(23): -3.6	1.6
2019	LAN	MLB	27	53	8	4	0	3	6	5	19	0	0	.250/.321/.521	87	0.6	.346	0.2	LF(12): 0.3, RF(5): -0.2	0.1
2020	LAN	MLB	28	42	4	2	0	2	5	3	14	0	0	.218/.276/.400	75	-0.2	.293	-0.1	LF 0	0.0

Comparables: Andrew Brown, Brad Glenn, Keon Broxton

It's a testament to both Garlick himself and the Dodgers player development machine that he gets more than a lineout in this book. Most 27-year-old organizational depth pieces get a cursory nod and nothing more. Of course, Garlick proved to be something more than that, slugging nearly 100 points better than league average in limited time. Most organizational depth pieces don't lead the majors in any category, but Garlick again proved something more by averaging 245 feet in batted ball distance (Joey Gallo eat your heart out). The Dodgers didn't really need another random player to turn into a viable major leaguer, but it just goes to show that a little bit of Garlick can enhance just about anything.

Enrique Hernández   UT   Born: 08/24/91   Age: 28   Bats: R   Throws: R   Height: 5'11"   Weight: 192   Origin: Round 6, 2009 Draft (#191 overall)

YEAR	TEAM	LVL	AGE	PA	R	2B	3B	HR	RBI	BB	K	SB	CS	AVG/OBP/SLG	DRC+	VORP	BABIP	BRR	FRAA	WARP
2017	LAN	MLB	25	342	46	24	2	11	37	41	80	3	0	.215/.308/.421	89	14.1	.254	2.6	CF(34): 5.8, LF(28): 0.7	1.7
2018	LAN	MLB	26	462	67	17	3	21	52	50	78	3	0	.256/.336/.470	112	29.4	.266	1.9	CF(63): -0.8, 2B(41): -0.3	2.2
2019	LAN	MLB	27	460	57	19	1	17	64	36	97	4	0	.237/.304/.411	91	10.4	.266	1.3	2B(85): 1.1, CF(20): -1.4	1.1
2020	LAN	MLB	28	231	27	9	1	10	31	20	51	1	1	.231/.303/.425	90	5.6	.259	0.6	2B 0, CF 0	0.6

Comparables: Rick Monday, Andrew McCutchen, Mack Jones

This was supposed to be the year Hernández was going to hold down a starting role. He has always been keenly aware of his place on the 25-man hierarchy and has always strived for something more. When the curtains were drawn in 2019, the human meme, the constant jokester, the man who always had something to say … went silent. Or his bat did, anyway. Hernández found himself once again contributing from the edges of the stage rather than the center of it, but contributing all the same. An up-and-down year culminating with some lead-role-worthy performances, notching a major hit in Game 3 of the NLDS and a home run in Game 5. A crowded roster makes it unlikely that he gets another run at a starting role, but Hernández has made clear how valuable he is the top understudy for just about every spot.

Kody Hoese   3B   Born: 07/13/97   Age: 22   Bats: R   Throws: R   Height: 6'4"   Weight: 200   Origin: Round 1, 2019 Draft (#25 overall)

YEAR	TEAM	LVL	AGE	PA	R	2B	3B	HR	RBI	BB	K	SB	CS	AVG/OBP/SLG	DRC+	VORP	BABIP	BRR	FRAA	WARP
2019	DOD	RK	21	68	14	5	1	3	13	10	11	1	0	.357/.456/.643	185	11.1	.395	1.9	3B(6): -0.5	0.8
2019	GRL	A	21	103	15	3	1	2	16	8	14	0	0	.264/.330/.385	103	3.6	.286	-0.2	3B(11): 0.7	0.3
2020	LAN	MLB	22	251	22	11	1	5	24	16	60	2	1	.226/.283/.344	68	-2.4	.285	0.0	3B 0	-0.3

Comparables: Matt Thaiss, Hunter Dozier, Erik Komatsu

Until further notice, "Hoese" is pronounced "Hoe-Say" because quite frankly that is what we all deserve. Name aside, Hoese was one of the two first-round draft picks the Dodgers had in 2019. While Hoese is never going to be the rangiest third baseman, reports indicate that he has the athleticism and arm to stick at the position. Of course, the draw is his offensive upside, where he pairs a disciplined approach with usable power to all fields. Expect him to start 2020 at A-ball again, but given that he's already 22, the Dodgers will likely push him aggressively if he gets out of the blocks quickly.

Connor Joe 1B Born: 08/16/92 Age: 27 Bats: R Throws: R Height: 6'0" Weight: 205 Origin: Round 1, 2014 Draft (#39 overall)

YEAR	TEAM	LVL	AGE	PA	R	2B	3B	HR	RBI	BB	K	SB	CS	AVG/OBP/SLG	DRC+	VORP	BABIP	BRR	FRAA	WARP
2017	ALT	AA	24	282	29	11	4	5	30	34	40	2	4	.240/.338/.380	100	7.9	.266	1.5	RF(33): 0.5, 1B(24): 2.6	1.0
2017	MIS	AA	24	61	2	1	0	0	4	6	18	0	1	.135/.233/.154	20	-4.2	.200	0.2	RF(11): 0.5, 1B(4): 0.4	-0.2
2018	TUL	AA	25	248	35	16	1	11	30	38	57	1	2	.304/.425/.554	160	24.4	.375	1.2	3B(34): -1.7, 1B(21): -1.3	1.8
2018	OKL	AAA	25	188	34	10	2	6	25	22	31	2	0	.294/.385/.494	127	10.7	.328	-0.2	1B(41): 0.5, 3B(4): -0.1	0.9
2019	OKL	AAA	26	446	82	26	1	15	68	72	81	1	2	.300/.426/.503	137	33.8	.347	0.1	1B(78): -1.1, LF(10): -0.2	2.4
2019	SFN	MLB	26	16	1	0	0	0	0	1	5	0	0	.067/.125/.067	59	-0.4	.100	0.0	LF(5): 2.2	0.2
2020	*LAN*	*MLB*	*27*	*251*	*27*	*9*	*1*	*7*	*28*	*28*	*59*	*1*	*0*	*.221/.319/.367*	*86*	*3.1*	*.268*	*-0.4*	*1B 2, RF 0*	*0.5*

Comparables: Mike Ford, Tim Locastro, Mitch Haniger

The reigning king of having two traditionally first names made his major-league debut in 2019 following his 2018 breakout in the minors. Joe was selected in the Rule 5 Draft by the Reds from the Dodgers and then traded to the Giants. However, he was quickly designated for assignment and returned to the Dodgers after just 16 plate appearances in which he at least got his first (and only) big-league hit. Joe seemed undeterred as he put up another quality season in Triple-A as he waits in the wings for another cup of—no, we're not going to do it to you.

★ ★ ★ *2020 Top 101 Prospect* **#3** ★ ★ ★

Gavin Lux SS Born: 11/23/97 Age: 22 Bats: L Throws: R Height: 6'2" Weight: 190 Origin: Round 1, 2016 Draft (#20 overall)

YEAR	TEAM	LVL	AGE	PA	R	2B	3B	HR	RBI	BB	K	SB	CS	AVG/OBP/SLG	DRC+	VORP	BABIP	BRR	FRAA	WARP
2017	GRL	A	19	501	68	14	8	7	39	56	88	27	10	.244/.331/.362	97	20.4	.288	3.4	SS(65): 3.8, 2B(43): 4.0	2.8
2018	RCU	A+	20	404	64	23	7	11	48	43	68	11	7	.324/.396/.520	144	34.4	.374	-1.8	SS(66): -0.6, 2B(17): 0.8	3.2
2018	TUL	AA	20	120	21	4	1	4	9	14	20	2	2	.324/.408/.495	153	11.6	.370	1.3	SS(26): -0.6	1.2
2019	TUL	AA	21	291	45	7	4	13	37	28	60	7	3	.313/.375/.521	166	28.9	.358	-2.6	SS(55): -3.0, 2B(7): 0.5	2.4
2019	OKL	AAA	21	232	54	18	4	13	39	33	42	3	3	.392/.478/.719	176	41.2	.451	-1.2	SS(35): -2.8, 2B(12): -0.3	2.7
2019	LAN	MLB	21	82	12	4	1	2	9	7	24	2	0	.240/.305/.400	75	0.1	.327	0.1	2B(22): -0.9	-0.1
2020	*LAN*	*MLB*	*22*	*392*	*46*	*18*	*3*	*14*	*51*	*34*	*100*	*6*	*3*	*.267/.333/.454*	*107*	*19.2*	*.334*	*-0.1*	*2B 0*	*2.0*

Comparables: Corey Seager, Brendan Rodgers, Dilson Herrera

It seems like eons ago that Lux struggled mightily to hit in A-ball, but that it was just a couple years back proves the mantra that development isn't linear. After his breakout last year, Lux continued to cement his lofty prospect status in Double-A. Lux burned brightest following his promotion to Oklahoma City, when he went all Barry Bonds on the PCL, a performance that propelled him to becoming Dodgers Minor League Player Of The Year, a consensus top-five overall prospect ranking, and a big-league debut. The team appeared reluctant to promote him ahead of schedule, but Lux forced their hand. His overall line in the majors was unimpressive, but he demonstrated flashes of the star quality that has the team so optimistic about his future. Most importantly, he looks like the antagonist jock of every heartwarming teen movie, which will only increase the entertainment value of everything he does.

Max Muncy INF Born: 08/25/90 Age: 29 Bats: L Throws: R Height: 6'0" Weight: 218 Origin: Round 5, 2012 Draft (#169 overall)

YEAR	TEAM	LVL	AGE	PA	R	2B	3B	HR	RBI	BB	K	SB	CS	AVG/OBP/SLG	DRC+	VORP	BABIP	BRR	FRAA	WARP
2017	OKL	AAA	26	379	62	20	1	12	44	54	84	3	6	.309/.414/.491	136	35.0	.387	2.0	3B(53): 0.3, 1B(22): 1.9	3.0
2018	OKL	AAA	27	38	7	2	0	2	4	6	5	0	0	.313/.421/.563	127	4.6	.320	0.7	1B(7): 0.1, 3B(3): 0.2	0.3
2018	LAN	MLB	27	481	75	17	2	35	79	79	131	3	0	.263/.391/.582	146	50.2	.299	2.3	1B(84): -0.5, 3B(38): 0.3	3.9
2019	LAN	MLB	28	589	101	22	1	35	98	90	149	4	1	.251/.374/.515	131	40.9	.283	4.1	2B(70): -0.1, 1B(65): 4.2	5.1
2020	*LAN*	*MLB*	*29*	*595*	*85*	*22*	*1*	*34*	*94*	*86*	*159*	*3*	*1*	*.245/.361/.496*	*125*	*38.5*	*.287*	*2.4*	*1B 1, 2B -2*	*3.9*

Comparables: Matt Tuiasosopo, Ji-Man Choi, Mike Epstein

After coming out of nowhere to get MVP votes in 2018, Muncy wasn't in the mood for a letdown as 2019 marked his first year as an All-Star. His production with the bat (.889 OPS) did take a step back from his ridiculous breakout showing, but he compensated for this by coming into the year in better shape and ended up being a plus defender at three positions (1B/2B/3B). That's all wonderful, but it's even better when paired with Muncy's surprisingly unlimited swag. Between pimping massive dongs with bat drops and telling Madison Bumgarner to go get his homer out of the ocean, Muncy has already cemented himself as a fan favorite. And as one of the key cogs that shows up in the playoffs, hopefully he'll be able to elevate himself to team legend status when all is said and done.

Joc Pederson OF   Born: 04/21/92   Age: 28   Bats: L   Throws: L   Height: 6'1"   Weight: 220   Origin: Round 11, 2010 Draft (#352 overall)

YEAR	TEAM	LVL	AGE	PA	R	2B	3B	HR	RBI	BB	K	SB	CS	AVG/OBP/SLG	DRC+	VORP	BABIP	BRR	FRAA	WARP
2017	OKL	AAA	25	71	8	1	0	3	9	5	14	1	0	.169/.225/.323	45	-4.0	.163	-0.2	LF(10): 3.7, CF(4): 0.8	0.1
2017	LAN	MLB	25	323	44	20	0	11	35	39	68	4	3	.212/.331/.407	89	13.8	.241	1.8	CF(92): -9.1, CF(4): -0.4	-0.1
2018	LAN	MLB	26	443	65	27	3	25	56	40	85	1	5	.248/.321/.522	118	26.9	.253	0.9	LF(116): -1.3, CF(32): -2.4	1.9
2019	LAN	MLB	27	514	83	16	3	36	74	50	111	1	1	.249/.339/.538	123	28.3	.249	2.6	LF(84): 0.5, RF(39): 0.0	3.0
2020	LAN	MLB	28	476	69	22	1	30	79	57	110	5	3	.244/.346/.521	124	29.6	.259	2.0	LF -1, RF 0	3.0

Comparables: Harmon Killebrew, Mark McGwire, Kyle Blanks

Pederson was much the same player that he's always been (don't let that OBP bump fool you, it was buoyed by 12 HBPs). What he's always been has been pretty good, too: a strong-side platoon bat that murderizes righties. Pederson benefited from the rabbit ball, turning 11 fewer doubles into 11 more home runs. He's effective at the dish thanks to a violent swing that is the antithesis of the traditional picturesque lefty stroke. It remains aesthetically pleasing though; the visual version of onomatopoeia, where it *looks* like he's hitting the ball as far as it actually ends up flying. He's got one year of team control remaining, and considering the fringe-average to average skill set he provides everywhere other than the plate, it shouldn't surprise to see him on the trade block. The Dodgers emphasis on players with multiple tools generally makes sense as an approach, but they shouldn't overlook the fact that sometimes you just need a sledgehammer.

DJ Peters CF   Born: 12/12/95   Age: 24   Bats: R   Throws: R   Height: 6'6"   Weight: 225   Origin: Round 4, 2016 Draft (#131 overall)

YEAR	TEAM	LVL	AGE	PA	R	2B	3B	HR	RBI	BB	K	SB	CS	AVG/OBP/SLG	DRC+	VORP	BABIP	BRR	FRAA	WARP
2017	RCU	A+	21	587	91	29	5	27	82	64	189	3	3	.276/.372/.514	118	43.2	.385	0.9	CF(80): -3.5, LF(18): -1.0	2.3
2018	TUL	AA	22	559	79	23	3	29	60	45	192	1	2	.236/.320/.473	97	20.6	.316	-3.6	CF(96): -3.1, RF(29): 1.4	0.9
2019	TUL	AA	23	288	31	10	1	11	42	28	93	1	0	.241/.331/.422	104	15.7	.331	-0.6	CF(48): -1.2, RF(20): 1.1	0.9
2019	OKL	AAA	23	255	40	10	1	12	39	33	75	1	1	.260/.388/.490	120	19.6	.341	0.0	CF(55): -0.9	1.4
2020	LAN	MLB	24	251	25	10	1	7	27	21	91	0	0	.209/.293/.355	74	-0.8	.316	-0.3	CF -1, RF 0	-0.1

Comparables: Ryan O'Hearn, Joe Benson, Brett Jackson

At 6-foot-6 and 230 pounds, Peters looks the part of a top prospect, with a beefier Jayson Werth an understandable comp for dreamers. The raw power is the athletic outfielder's calling card and the Dodgers are working hard to find him a swing that can tap into that as often as possible. Peters flashed big power in 2018 but was otherwise too easy of an out at the plate, racking up monster strikeout totals without the walks to balance them. He made progress this year, cutting down on the whiffs and upping the walks, with only a slight reduction in his home run totals. He'll need that trend to continue in the right direction to attain a big-league future, with his contact rate representing a significant hurdle to overcome. He'll head back to Triple-A as he continues to iron out the kinks in his swing, and consistently produce more quality plate appearances.

A.J. Pollock CF   Born: 12/05/87   Age: 32   Bats: R   Throws: R   Height: 6'1"   Weight: 212   Origin: Round 1, 2009 Draft (#17 overall)

YEAR	TEAM	LVL	AGE	PA	R	2B	3B	HR	RBI	BB	K	SB	CS	AVG/OBP/SLG	DRC+	VORP	BABIP	BRR	FRAA	WARP
2017	ARI	MLB	29	466	73	33	6	14	49	35	71	20	6	.266/.330/.471	100	28.0	.291	0.7	CF(109): 0.3	1.7
2018	ARI	MLB	30	460	61	21	5	21	65	31	100	13	2	.257/.316/.484	106	23.9	.284	1.1	CF(109): -7.6	1.3
2019	LAN	MLB	31	342	49	15	1	15	47	23	74	5	1	.266/.327/.468	98	10.9	.300	-0.3	CF(62): -8.6, LF(18): -0.1	0.2
2020	LAN	MLB	32	455	55	21	2	19	62	34	98	17	5	.258/.321/.460	103	18.3	.294	0.2	CF -5, LF 0	1.3

Comparables: Milton Bradley, Fred Lynn, Carlos Gómez

If you squinted at Pollock this past offseason, you might've seen a true center fielder that produced at an All-Star level when healthy, who possessed the tantalizing upside of the down-ballot MVP showing back in 2017. Well, the Dodgers might have been squinting too hard, deciding to give the frequently-injured outfielder four years and a player option for a fifth. That faith was rewarded with the worst season of Pollock's career. It wasn't a surprise to anyone when he missed over two months of the season, but that "produced when healthy" angle went missing, *and* he struggled so much in the field that Cody Bellinger had to take over center field duties. It feels like we've hit rock bottom in this sordid tale, but Pollock came equipped with a diamond-tipped drill of despair. As poorly as the regular season went, Pollock's NLDS performance stands alone: 0-13, one walk, 11 strikeouts and a benching in favor of Matt Beaty. Juan Uribe's transformation from a vitriol-inducing player to a fan favorite lends some optimism for Pollock going forward. At 32, though, it will be an uphill battle to remain healthy and productive, especially as a shift to the corner outfield puts more pressure on his bat. It's unlikely Pollock is as bad going forward as he was in 2019, but only because he'd be hard-pressed to be worse.

Edwin Ríos CI   Born: 04/21/94   Age: 26   Bats: L   Throws: R   Height: 6'3"   Weight: 220   Origin: Round 6, 2015 Draft (#192 overall)

YEAR	TEAM	LVL	AGE	PA	R	2B	3B	HR	RBI	BB	K	SB	CS	AVG/OBP/SLG	DRC+	VORP	BABIP	BRR	FRAA	WARP
2017	TUL	AA	23	332	47	21	0	15	62	17	69	1	1	.317/.358/.533	144	24.9	.363	0.9	3B(38): -4.1, 1B(28): 1.8	2.0
2017	OKL	AAA	23	190	23	13	0	9	29	18	42	0	1	.296/.368/.533	121	8.6	.345	-2.6	1B(33): 0.6, 3B(9): -1.0	0.6
2018	OKL	AAA	24	341	45	25	0	10	55	23	110	0	1	.304/.355/.482	116	16.6	.433	-2.4	3B(38): -4.2, 1B(28): -1.3	0.6
2019	OKL	AAA	25	444	72	23	2	31	91	37	153	2	2	.270/.340/.575	106	24.4	.349	-2.6	3B(66): 1.7, 1B(25): 0.6	1.8
2019	LAN	MLB	25	56	10	2	1	4	8	9	21	0	0	.277/.393/.617	87	0.5	.409	-0.2	1B(12): -0.4, 3B(5): -0.5	-0.1
2020	LAN	MLB	26	77	8	4	0	3	10	5	29	0	0	.227/.287/.414	81	-0.1	.337	-0.2	LF 1, 1B 0	0.1

Comparables: Chris Shaw, Ryan O'Hearn, Tyler Austin

Seemingly destined to be a bat-only Quad-A type, Ríos got his shot with the Dodgers towards the end of June and ran with it. He put an exclamation point on his season by smashing the longest home run by a Dodger (473 feet) on a team that led the NL in homers by a significant margin. Any GM of a rebuilding club watching the endless parade of bats breaking out for the Dodgers has to try and pry a guy like Ríos away with the idea of giving him a shot at being a regular, right? The Dodgers don't have room for him, and the elevated strikeout rates make him a risk, but there's no reason he couldn't have a late breakout like other Dodgers before him.

Luis Rodriguez OF   Born: 09/16/02   Age: 17   Bats: R   Throws: R   Height: 6'2"   Weight: 175   Origin: International Free Agent, 2019

Rodriguez is a 17-year-old outfielder from Venezuela who has yet to play an inning of professional baseball but was highly ranked in the 2019 July 2nd market. At 6-foot-2, Rodriguez has a lot of projection and pairs that with athleticism and instincts to provide a foundation for evaluators to dream on. Whether he's able to stick in center field will depend on how he fills out, but one thing that's agreed upon is his ability with a bat in his hand. He pairs impressive bat speed with an ability to consistently find the sweet spot. Wild speculation and dreaming big are always fun, but the basic report provided above has been written about any number of prospect shortly after they signed as teenagers. A little caution would be the prudent approach as it pertains to his prospect status.

★ ★ ★ *2020 Top 101 Prospect* **#79** ★ ★ ★

Keibert Ruiz C   Born: 07/20/98   Age: 21   Bats: B   Throws: R   Height: 6'0"   Weight: 200   Origin: International Free Agent, 2015

YEAR	TEAM	LVL	AGE	PA	R	2B	3B	HR	RBI	BB	K	SB	CS	AVG/OBP/SLG	DRC+	VORP	BABIP	BRR	FRAA	WARP
2017	GRL	A	18	251	34	16	1	2	24	18	30	0	0	.317/.372/.423	127	16.2	.355	-3.2	C(49): -0.9	1.3
2017	RCU	A+	18	160	24	7	1	6	27	7	23	0	0	.315/.344/.497	127	13.2	.333	0.0	C(37): -0.3	1.2
2018	TUL	AA	19	415	44	14	0	12	47	26	33	0	1	.268/.328/.401	91	8.3	.266	-3.8	C(86): 3.5	1.4
2019	TUL	AA	20	310	33	9	0	4	25	28	21	0	0	.254/.329/.330	105	4.1	.261	-3.5	C(61): 0.5	1.1
2019	OKL	AAA	20	40	6	0	0	2	9	2	1	0	0	.316/.350/.474	87	-0.5	.286	0.9	C(8): -0.5	0.2
2020	LAN	MLB	21	35	4	2	0	1	4	2	5	0	0	.259/.311/.394	86	0.9	.279	-0.1	C 0	0.1

Comparables: Jake Bauers, Jose Tabata, Wilmer Flores

Was there a trade package involving the Dodgers for the last year or so that Ruiz was not a part of? That must've been mighty annoying for a player who was once the prize of the system and was assumed to be the future starter. With Will Smith's ascendance, Ruiz is in a bit of a no man's land within the organization. Ruiz has stagnated in the upper minors. Still just 20 years old, he's struggled to turn his sub-seven percent whiff rate into useful production. The offensive bar for catchers is essentially resting on the floor, but the promise that Ruiz once showed in his ability to marry power with contact his dissipated. Reports still indicate that a top prospect's tools reside within Ruiz's frame, but descriptive words being used are a bit more muted and hesitant than they were in recent memory.

YEAR	TEAM	P. COUNT	FRM RUNS	BLK RUNS	THRW RUNS	TOT RUNS
2018	TUL	11928	5.3	-0.6	-0.4	3.9
2019	OKL	1280	-0.3	0.0	0.0	0.4
2019	TUL	8565	3.3	0.0	-2.2	1.0
2020	LAN	1280	-0.2	0.0	-0.1	-0.3

Corey Seager SS   Born: 04/27/94   Age: 26   Bats: L   Throws: R   Height: 6'4"   Weight: 215   Origin: Round 1, 2012 Draft (#18 overall)

YEAR	TEAM	LVL	AGE	PA	R	2B	3B	HR	RBI	BB	K	SB	CS	AVG/OBP/SLG	DRC+	VORP	BABIP	BRR	FRAA	WARP
2017	LAN	MLB	23	613	85	33	0	22	77	67	131	4	2	.295/.375/.479	115	57.6	.352	2.2	SS(138): -1.8	4.0
2018	LAN	MLB	24	115	13	5	1	2	13	11	17	0	0	.267/.348/.396	104	7.4	.301	0.8	SS(25): 0.3	0.7
2019	LAN	MLB	25	541	82	44	1	19	87	44	98	1	0	.272/.335/.483	106	30.4	.303	0.7	SS(132): 1.2	3.1
2020	LAN	MLB	26	595	70	36	1	24	80	49	117	3	1	.265/.332/.467	108	30.3	.300	1.4	SS -1	3.1

Comparables: Carlos Correa, Javier Báez, Cal Ripken Jr.

Seager's first two full seasons with the Dodgers established him as a four-plus win player and perennial All-Star at shortstop, while his third was lost after a mere 26 games thanks to elbow and hip surgeries. Last year brought about some more missed time due to a balky hamstring, and it seemed every time he was getting right at the plate, a muscle would strain or a ligament would tweak. Still, he produced a solid, if not vintage, season and the further removed he is from those major surgeries the better he figures to be. How much he can distance himself from the injury bug remains to be seen, however, and it's possible the 2019 version of Seager is the new normal. Health isn't the only black mark on his ledger either, as a .605 OPS in 31 playoff games hangs over his Dodgers tenure like a dark cloud.

There have been some trade rumblings with Seager's name included, which serves as a convenient representation of his current career crossroads: Is he still a franchise cornerstone or is he just another piece of the puzzle? Seager likely goes nowhere and puts up another quality season, the quality of which will go a long way towards determining his future with the team beyond just the years of team control.

Will Smith C   Born: 03/28/95   Age: 25   Bats: R   Throws: R   Height: 5'10"   Weight: 195   Origin: Round 1, 2016 Draft (#32 overall)

YEAR	TEAM	LVL	AGE	PA	R	2B	3B	HR	RBI	BB	K	SB	CS	AVG/OBP/SLG	DRC+	VORP	BABIP	BRR	FRAA	WARP
2017	RCU	A+	22	305	38	15	3	11	43	37	71	6	2	.232/.355/.448	105	16.7	.273	-2.0	C(55): 2.7, 3B(6): -1.0	1.4
2018	TUL	AA	23	307	48	14	0	19	53	36	75	4	0	.264/.358/.532	137	25.5	.295	-1.8	C(33): 7.4, 3B(33): -1.3	2.7
2018	OKL	AAA	23	98	9	4	0	1	6	7	37	1	0	.138/.206/.218	14	-3.8	.216	1.4	C(16): 1.4, 3B(10): 0.3	-0.3
2019	OKL	AAA	24	270	48	11	2	20	54	40	49	1	0	.268/.381/.603	138	30.4	.253	0.9	C(52): -0.1, 3B(1): -0.1	2.5
2019	LAN	MLB	24	196	30	9	0	15	42	18	52	2	0	.253/.337/.571	123	16.0	.264	-0.6	C(46): 4.5	1.9
2020	LAN	MLB	25	455	64	19	1	29	75	45	118	2	1	.240/.330/.509	117	30.0	.265	-0.5	C 10, 3B 0	4.1

Comparables: Jake Rogers, Gene Tenace, Carlos Santana

The only thing more tired than puns of Will Smith's name is other teams asking for him in trade talks, so rest easy, you won't find any here. You're welcome, everyone. It's hard to believe now, but just four years ago Smith put up a .665 OPS in college with only two homers. Thankfully he took to the Dodgers instruction, adding loft to his swing, and he's never looked back. Smith completed his meteoric rise to prominence in 2019, supplanting both Austin Barnes and Russell Martin to become the starting catcher, and also leaping

YEAR	TEAM	P. COUNT	FRM RUNS	BLK RUNS	THRW RUNS	TOT RUNS
2018	OKL	2087	1.2	0.0	0.0	2.1
2018	TUL	4187	7.0	0.1	0.6	8.4
2019	LAN	6644	2.1	1.2	-0.1	4.1
2019	OKL	7280	0.5	0.0	-1.0	-0.2
2020	LAN	15190	8.3	0.9	-0.3	8.9

over fellow top prospect Keibert Ruiz entirely. Of course, there are always concerns with breakout rookie stars, like the 26.5 strikeout rate or posting a .582 OPS in September. But even assuming regression, he looks like an above-average present regular with All-Star potential and that's why the Dodgers are already penciling him in as the 2020 starter.

Chris Taylor UT Born: 08/29/90 Age: 29 Bats: R Throws: R Height: 6'1" Weight: 196 Origin: Round 5, 2012 Draft (#161 overall)

YEAR	TEAM	LVL	AGE	PA	R	2B	3B	HR	RBI	BB	K	SB	CS	AVG/OBP/SLG	DRC+	VORP	BABIP	BRR	FRAA	WARP
2017	OKL	AAA	26	49	8	2	2	1	5	5	5	1	2	.233/.327/.442	89	2.9	.243	0.6	SS(5): 0.5, CF(3): 0.2	0.3
2017	LAN	MLB	26	568	85	34	5	21	72	50	142	17	4	.288/.354/.496	114	49.7	.361	4.4	CF(49): -2.2, LF(48): 6.6	3.9
2018	LAN	MLB	27	604	85	35	8	17	63	55	178	9	6	.254/.331/.444	103	35.6	.345	0.9	SS(81): 3.7, CF(50): -4.5	2.7
2019	LAN	MLB	28	414	52	29	4	12	52	37	115	8	0	.262/.333/.462	92	11.0	.344	3.0	LF(56): 0.8, SS(39): -4.6	0.8
2020	LAN	MLB	29	294	32	13	2	9	34	26	84	7	3	.238/.313/.405	90	6.1	.317	1.0	SS 0, LF 2	0.8

Comparables: Roy Smalley, Eugenio Suárez, Brad Miller

Taylor remained productive, if less so, in 2018 despite leading the National League in strikeouts. His propensity for whiffitude didn't engender much love among the fanbase, and an ice-cold April (.171 batting average) led to many suggestions that he go warm up on the face of the sun. Taylor took it all in stride, and proceeded to post a .860 OPS the rest of the way. Pair that with solid defense at six different positions, and you'll find a lot of people pretending they liked him just fine all along. Taylor will get a deserved pay raise this off-season in arbitration and then resume his marauding around the field in a utility role while bringing a quality bat to the plate.

Justin Turner 3B Born: 11/23/84 Age: 35 Bats: R Throws: R Height: 5'11" Weight: 202 Origin: Round 7, 2006 Draft (#204 overall)

YEAR	TEAM	LVL	AGE	PA	R	2B	3B	HR	RBI	BB	K	SB	CS	AVG/OBP/SLG	DRC+	VORP	BABIP	BRR	FRAA	WARP
2017	LAN	MLB	32	543	72	32	0	21	71	59	56	7	1	.322/.415/.530	149	62.8	.326	-3.2	3B(121): -5.5	4.4
2018	LAN	MLB	33	426	62	31	1	14	52	47	54	2	1	.312/.406/.518	146	44.3	.334	0.3	3B(96): 11.1	5.1
2019	LAN	MLB	34	549	80	24	0	27	67	51	88	2	0	.290/.372/.509	134	45.2	.304	-1.3	3B(124): 2.2, 2B(1): 0.0	4.5
2020	LAN	MLB	35	560	72	27	1	24	79	50	98	5	2	.277/.359/.481	122	27.9	.302	-1.5	3B 4	3.3

Comparables: Chase Utley, Bill Doran, Bernie Allen

Turner ending his career with the Dodgers without winning a World Series ring would be a travesty. After building himself into an All-Star with the club, JT has been one of the few stars for the team who have performed in the playoffs (.931 OPS). While he may look like a character from a fantasy series, he's not immortal and one has to ask when the breaking point will come. He will be 35 next year and the slow signs of decline are creeping in, especially on defense. Before free agency even officially began, there was already talk about him moving across the diamond to first base. Turner arrived on the team one year into their seven-year run atop the NL West, but he, as much as any player, defines their rise. An early adopter of the swing change that gripped the league, Turner's steady presence and potent bat has driven the Dodgers lineup since he arrived. It would be a shame if his time on the team ends without him hoisting a World Series trophy.

──────────── ★ ★ ★ *2020 Top 101 Prospect* **#65** ★ ★ ★ ────────────

Miguel Vargas 3B Born: 11/17/99 Age: 20 Bats: R Throws: R Height: 6'3" Weight: 205 Origin: International Free Agent, 2017

YEAR	TEAM	LVL	AGE	PA	R	2B	3B	HR	RBI	BB	K	SB	CS	AVG/OBP/SLG	DRC+	VORP	BABIP	BRR	FRAA	WARP
2018	DOD	RK	18	37	6	3	1	0	2	5	3	1	0	.419/.514/.581	196	4.6	.464	-0.7	1B(5): 0.8, 3B(4): 1.1	0.5
2018	OGD	RK	18	103	25	11	1	2	22	8	13	6	1	.394/.447/.596	203	13.0	.443	1.2	3B(13): 0.5, 1B(6): -0.4	1.2
2018	GRL	A	18	89	4	1	1	0	6	10	20	0	0	.213/.307/.253	66	-1.0	.281	-0.5	3B(19): 3.1	0.2
2019	GRL	A	19	323	53	20	2	5	45	35	43	9	1	.325/.399/.464	162	27.6	.363	-2.5	3B(59): 2.2, 1B(2): 0.4	3.1
2019	RCU	A+	19	236	23	18	1	2	32	20	40	4	3	.284/.353/.408	127	8.9	.341	-2.3	3B(43): -1.9, 1B(6): 0.4	0.8
2020	LAN	MLB	20	251	25	14	1	5	26	20	51	1	0	.259/.324/.393	91	5.0	.314	-0.3	3B 0, 1B 0	0.5

Comparables: Jeimer Candelario, Delino DeShields, J.P. Crawford

Vargas defected from Cuba in 2015 and signed with the Dodgers in 2017 for $300,000. He quickly proved a wise investment for the team, as he impressed between Low-A and High-A with a combined .308/.380/.440 slash line. Vargas will likely be assigned back to Rancho Cucamonga in 2020 with an eye on a promotion to Tulsa if he starts out well. Scouts report Vargas is in possession of a discerning eye and an exceptional hit tool. While he doesn't show present power there's certainly room in his frame for him to develop some thump. Whether he sticks at third or not isn't yet clear, but his future will mostly be determined by the development of his bat.

Alex Verdugo OF Born: 05/15/96 Age: 24 Bats: L Throws: L Height: 6'0" Weight: 212 Origin: Round 2, 2014 Draft (#62 overall)

YEAR	TEAM	LVL	AGE	PA	R	2B	3B	HR	RBI	BB	K	SB	CS	AVG/OBP/SLG	DRC+	VORP	BABIP	BRR	FRAA	WARP
2017	OKL	AAA	21	495	67	27	4	6	62	52	50	9	3	.314/.389/.436	113	31.4	.340	3.1	CF(59): -5.5, RF(46): 3.1	2.3
2017	LAN	MLB	21	25	1	0	0	1	1	2	4	0	1	.174/.240/.304	86	-1.2	.167	-0.1	CF(6): -0.7, RF(3): 0.0	0.0
2018	OKL	AAA	22	379	44	19	0	10	44	34	47	8	2	.329/.391/.472	128	24.0	.359	-0.5	CF(45): 2.0, RF(31): 2.4	2.8
2018	LAN	MLB	22	86	11	6	0	1	4	8	14	0	0	.260/.329/.377	85	3.3	.306	1.5	RF(16): -0.1, LF(12): 0.2	0.1
2019	LAN	MLB	23	377	43	22	2	12	44	26	49	4	1	.294/.342/.475	102	13.7	.309	1.4	CF(61): -1.2, RF(25): 1.2	1.7
2020	LAN	MLB	24	504	55	24	1	15	59	38	73	4	2	.263/.324/.419	96	10.7	.284	1.8	RF 9, CF 0	1.9

Comparables: Paul Konerko, Joe Torre, Jose Tabata

For most other teams, Verdugo would've been given a shot to start two years ago, but only this past offseason did the Dodgers clear enough of their outfield logjam to give him a spot on the Opening Day roster. He took immediate advantage, posting an .817 OPS along with plus defense in the outfield, playing at a borderline All-Star level while healthy. Not many rookies have the ability to accomplish that, so it was a surprise that he became a bit of a forgotten man down the stretch following the oblique and back injuries that put him out of sight as the Dodgers rolled to 106 wins. Unfortunately, his importance came back to prominence in a hurry in the postseason when he wasn't around to supplant A.J. Pollock, and his bat-to-ball skills were especially missed as Dodger after Dodger struck out in crucial situations. Barring a trade, Verdugo will compete for a job with Pollock in 2020 and, despite the latter's contract, there's no reason Verdugo shouldn't find plenty of playing time available to him.

Connor Wong C Born: 05/19/96 Age: 24 Bats: R Throws: R Height: 6'1" Weight: 181 Origin: Round 3, 2017 Draft (#100 overall)

YEAR	TEAM	LVL	AGE	PA	R	2B	3B	HR	RBI	BB	K	SB	CS	AVG/OBP/SLG	DRC+	VORP	BABIP	BRR	FRAA	WARP
2017	GRL	A	21	107	19	6	0	5	18	7	26	1	1	.278/.336/.495	125	7.4	.328	0.0	C(27): 0.2	0.8
2018	RCU	A+	22	431	64	20	2	19	60	38	138	6	2	.269/.350/.480	113	27.8	.372	0.9	C(71): 0.7, 2B(11): -0.5	2.4
2019	RCU	A+	23	302	39	15	6	15	51	21	93	9	2	.245/.306/.507	102	22.6	.310	1.3	C(59): 0.7, 2B(10): 1.3	1.7
2019	TUL	AA	23	163	17	9	1	9	31	11	50	2	1	.349/.393/.604	163	18.1	.467	0.3	C(23): 0.1, 3B(10): -0.8	1.5
2020	LAN	MLB	24	251	25	12	1	9	30	15	91	1	0	.226/.281/.400	77	0.2	.331	-0.2	C -3, 2B 0	-0.2

Comparables: Xavier Scruggs, Eric Haase, Jamie Romak

YEAR	TEAM	P. COUNT	FRM RUNS	BLK RUNS	THRW RUNS	TOT RUNS
2019	TUL	3251	-0.8	0.0	1.3	0.5
2020	LAN	7805	-3.3	-0.5	1.1	-2.8

Buried behind the likes of Austin Barnes, Will Smith, Keibert Ruiz and even Diego Cartaya is Wong, who has flown under the radar and has stealthily turned himself into a legitimate prospect. An athletic backstop that played shortstop in college and can play both second and third, Wong handled advanced pitching well in 2019 and bumped his stock significantly by doing so. He has pop, but it comes along with a 31 percent strikeout rate that has to improve if he wants to take the next step. To Wong's credit, he has been working on a bat path that will generate more consistent contact, and if it sticks then the Dodgers may envision him as a unique type of super-utility player.

PITCHERS

Scott Alexander LHP Born: 07/10/89 Age: 30 Bats: L Throws: L Height: 6'2" Weight: 195 Origin: Round 6, 2010 Draft (#179 overall)

YEAR	TEAM	LVL	AGE	W	L	SV	G	GS	IP	H	HR	BB/9	K/9	K	GB%	BABIP	WHIP	ERA	DRA	WARP	MPH	FB%	WHF	CSP
2017	OMA	AAA	27	1	0	0	7	0	7²	9	1	3.5	4.7	4	78%	.308	1.57	4.70	4.46	0.1				
2017	KCA	MLB	27	5	4	4	58	0	69	62	3	3.7	7.7	59	73%	.306	1.30	2.48	4.64	0.4	95.3	93.9	14.3	45.6
2018	LAN	MLB	28	2	1	3	73	1	66	57	4	3.7	7.6	56	72%	.296	1.27	3.68	5.33	-0.3	95.4	85.6	12.4	46.5
2019	LAN	MLB	29	3	2	0	28	0	17¹	17	2	3.6	4.7	9	61%	.263	1.38	3.63	5.52	0.0	94.5	88.9	10.1	44.2
2020	LAN	MLB	30	2	2	0	37	0	39	38	4	4.0	8.2	36	66%	.300	1.40	4.01	4.26	0.5	94.5	89	12.7	45.1

Comparables: Dan Jennings, Sam Freeman, Kevin Chapman

Hyped as a potential Zack Britton-lite when he was acquired in 2018, Alexander ended up as more like a literally lighter Ray King for the Dodgers. After a rough 2019 in which he couldn't seem to miss any bats, Alexander made his last appearance on June 5 and then started a seemingly endless state of rehab until he suddenly and ominously posted a picture of himself after surgery (for a nerve issue) on September 12. Guess that's one way of announcing your season is over.

Walker Buehler RHP Born: 07/28/94 Age: 25 Bats: R Throws: R Height: 6'2" Weight: 185 Origin: Round 1, 2015 Draft (#24 overall)

YEAR	TEAM	LVL	AGE	W	L	SV	G	GS	IP	H	HR	BB/9	K/9	K	GB%	BABIP	WHIP	ERA	DRA	WARP	MPH	FB%	WHF	CSP
2017	RCU	A+	22	0	0	0	5	5	16¹	8	0	2.8	14.9	27	57%	.267	0.80	1.10	1.53	0.7				
2017	TUL	AA	22	2	2	0	11	11	49	40	5	2.8	11.8	64	52%	.315	1.12	3.49	3.22	1.1				
2017	OKL	AAA	22	1	1	1	12	3	23¹	19	1	4.2	13.1	34	62%	.333	1.29	4.63	1.43	1.0				
2017	LAN	MLB	22	1	0	0	8	0	9¹	11	2	7.7	11.6	12	67%	.409	2.04	7.71	4.10	0.1	99.8	69.8	11.5	47.9
2018	OKL	AAA	23	1	0	0	3	3	13	10	0	2.8	11.1	16	61%	.303	1.08	2.08	2.21	0.5				
2018	LAN	MLB	23	8	5	0	24	23	137¹	95	12	2.4	9.9	151	50%	.248	0.96	2.62	3.21	3.3	98.5	59.6	12.6	49.5
2019	LAN	MLB	24	14	4	0	30	30	182¹	153	20	1.8	10.6	215	43%	.290	1.04	3.26	2.89	5.7	98.5	60.2	13.4	49.8
2020	LAN	MLB	25	13	8	0	29	29	178	155	23	2.6	10.6	210	44%	.298	1.16	3.08	3.47	4.6	98.2	61.6	13.4	50.4

Comparables: Matt Harvey, Rafael Montero, Max Scherzer

It says a lot about Buehler's talent that not being in the top five for NL Cy Young Award voting this year was surprising, but that's just how far expectations have risen for the 25-year-old. In his defense, Buehler was a top-five level pitcher for much of the season after starting slowly in April (5.22 ERA) following missing most of spring training due to not feeling right. Following the ominous start to the year, he settled down beginning in May, and turned in a 2.88 ERA the rest of the season.

Despite his age, Buehler has already taken the torch from Clayton Kershaw as the Dodgers ace and is running with it. It was Buehler who the Dodgers have trusted in big games of late, and aside from his playoff debut he's repaid their trust with excellent results. Ending 31 years of futility is a lot of pressure to heap on Buehler's wiry frame, but the 2020 hopes of the Dodgers will in large part rest on his shoulders and his expected ascent to perennial Cy Young Award candidate.

Gerardo Carrillo RHP Born: 09/13/98 Age: 21 Bats: R Throws: R Height: 5'10" Weight: 154 Origin: International Free Agent, 2016

YEAR	TEAM	LVL	AGE	W	L	SV	G	GS	IP	H	HR	BB/9	K/9	K	GB%	BABIP	WHIP	ERA	DRA	WARP	MPH	FB%	WHF	CSP
2017	DDG	RK	18	5	2	0	14	10	48¹	44	1	2.6	6.0	32	58%	.277	1.20	2.79	5.23	0.4				
2018	DOD	RK	19	2	0	1	4	1	11	6	0	1.6	10.6	13	58%	.231	0.73	0.82	1.71	0.5				
2018	GRL	A	19	2	1	0	9	9	49	35	3	2.8	6.8	37	50%	.235	1.02	1.65	3.26	1.1				
2019	RCU	A+	20	5	9	0	23	21	86	87	3	5.3	9.0	86	54%	.338	1.60	5.44	5.22	-0.2				
2020	LAN	MLB	21	2	2	0	33	0	35	34	5	3.8	7.0	27	48%	.283	1.41	4.63	4.85	0.2				

Comparables: Jeanmar Gómez, Lance McCullers Jr., German Márquez

Carrillo is all about velocity, which only popped up in recent years and has led to his sudden ascent as a prospect. When the 21-year-old Mexican is right, he's in the mid-90s with sink and velocity that has touched triple digits. His slider is his best secondary option and his curve flashes usable but lags behind. All of this makes relieving a realistic fallback option, especially when combined with his (lack of) height. Despite struggling to a mid-5s ERA in High-A, scouts remain high on his potential. Carrillo showcased his upside in the Arizona Fall League recently, posting a 2.22 ERA in 24 1/3 innings with 25 strikeouts against much more advanced competition. Based on results, he seems like an unlikely candidate to be a fast mover, but it wouldn't be surprising to see Carrillo get time in Tulsa next year as the Dodgers appear impressed.

Caleb Ferguson LHP Born: 07/02/96 Age: 23 Bats: R Throws: L Height: 6'3" Weight: 226 Origin: Round 38, 2014 Draft (#1149 overall)

YEAR	TEAM	LVL	AGE	W	L	SV	G	GS	IP	H	HR	BB/9	K/9	K	GB%	BABIP	WHIP	ERA	DRA	WARP	MPH	FB%	WHF	CSP
2017	RCU	A+	20	9	4	0	25	24	122¹	113	6	4.0	10.3	140	46%	.335	1.37	2.87	3.90	1.9				
2018	TUL	AA	21	3	0	0	8	8	39	31	2	2.3	9.2	40	42%	.284	1.05	1.38	2.73	1.2				
2018	OKL	AAA	21	0	0	0	2	2	8	6	0	7.9	13.5	12	21%	.316	1.62	2.25	4.02	0.1				
2018	LAN	MLB	21	7	2	2	29	3	49	43	8	2.2	10.8	59	47%	.292	1.12	3.49	3.17	1.0	96.3	71.9	12.5	54.7
2019	OKL	AAA	22	0	0	1	13	1	15¹	9	1	2.9	15.8	27	50%	.333	0.91	1.76	1.28	0.7				
2019	LAN	MLB	22	1	2	0	46	2	44²	39	7	5.4	10.9	54	40%	.291	1.48	4.84	4.92	0.2	96.4	78	11.3	49.3
2020	LAN	MLB	23	2	2	0	32	0	34	31	5	3.8	9.5	36	41%	.286	1.34	4.11	4.35	0.4	96.3	78	12.3	53.5

Comparables: Jack Flaherty, Michael Kirkman, Logan Allen

After emerging as a viable starting pitching prospect, Ferguson was moved to the 'pen for the Dodgers last year and excelled in the role. While the Dodgers claimed they still wanted to develop him as a starter, he eventually returned to relief and his future seemed primed to be at the back-end of a bullpen. A strong initial performance didn't augur a repeat performance, however. Through mid-August, Ferguson was a disaster, posting a 6.04 ERA. Thanks to an adjustment pitching coach Rick Honeycutt made to his curve grip, Ferguson seemed to regain his old form down the stretch, finishing with a 2.76 ERA over his final 16 1/3 innings. With the relief corps still a question mark going into 2020, the Dodgers will need Ferguson to replicate his late-season form over a whole year.

Dylan Floro RHP Born: 12/27/90 Age: 29 Bats: L Throws: R Height: 6'2" Weight: 203 Origin: Round 13, 2012 Draft (#422 overall)

YEAR	TEAM	LVL	AGE	W	L	SV	G	GS	IP	H	HR	BB/9	K/9	K	GB%	BABIP	WHIP	ERA	DRA	WARP	MPH	FB%	WHF	CSP
2017	IOW	AAA	26	3	2	1	25	2	48²	54	9	1.5	4.8	26	63%	.274	1.27	3.88	4.89	0.2				
2017	OKL	AAA	26	0	1	1	8	0	11¹	18	0	2.4	9.5	12	58%	.474	1.85	5.56	5.67	0.0				
2017	CHN	MLB	26	0	0	0	3	0	9²	15	2	1.9	5.6	6	53%	.382	1.76	6.52	6.19	-0.1	93.5	67.7	9.8	54.8
2018	CIN	MLB	27	3	2	0	25	0	36¹	39	2	3.0	6.7	27	57%	.314	1.40	2.72	5.25	-0.1	95.3	62.4	9.8	48.1
2018	LAN	MLB	27	3	1	0	29	0	27²	18	1	3.6	10.1	31	55%	.250	1.05	1.63	3.14	0.6	95.8	64.8	15.3	45
2019	LAN	MLB	28	5	3	0	50	0	46²	46	4	2.7	8.1	42	52%	.302	1.29	4.24	4.56	0.4	95.6	67.5	13.4	50.9
2020	LAN	MLB	29	2	2	0	32	0	34	33	4	2.4	8.3	31	53%	.300	1.26	3.65	4.01	0.5	94.8	65.5	12.6	50.5

Comparables: Chasen Bradford, Matt Bowman, Shane Carle

Floro was a revelation after coming over in a trade from the Reds in 2018, using his hard sinker to miss a surprising amount of at-bats while performing like a quality back-end relief arm. However, he struggled to repeat his success in 2019, ending the year with an ERA over 4.00 and missing out on the playoff roster. Whether his year was typical reliever variation or evidence of why he's been with four teams in four years will be an important factor in determining whether he's a solid middle relief option going forward.

★ ★ ★ *2020 Top 101 Prospect* **#81** ★ ★ ★

Tony Gonsolin **RHP** Born: 05/14/94 Age: 26 Bats: R Throws: R Height: 6'3" Weight: 205 Origin: Round 9, 2016 Draft (#281 overall)

YEAR	TEAM	LVL	AGE	W	L	SV	G	GS	IP	H	HR	BB/9	K/9	K	GB%	BABIP	WHIP	ERA	DRA	WARP	MPH	FB%	WHF	CSP
2017	GRL	A	23	0	1	1	3	0	8	8	2	0.0	13.5	12	38%	.316	1.00	3.38	3.29	0.2				
2017	RCU	A+	23	7	5	5	39	0	62	61	5	2.6	10.6	73	43%	.344	1.27	3.92	3.30	1.2				
2018	RCU	A+	24	4	2	0	17	17	83²	72	5	2.8	11.4	106	38%	.319	1.17	2.69	2.72	2.5				
2018	TUL	AA	24	6	0	0	9	9	44¹	32	3	3.2	9.9	49	39%	.261	1.08	2.44	3.00	1.2				
2019	OKL	AAA	25	2	4	0	13	13	41¹	41	4	4.6	10.9	50	37%	.327	1.50	4.35	2.98	1.5				
2019	LAN	MLB	25	4	2	1	11	6	40	26	4	3.4	8.3	37	43%	.208	1.02	2.92	4.19	0.6	95.4	48.3	12.5	43.1
2020	LAN	MLB	26	6	5	0	30	15	90	79	13	3.7	8.7	86	39%	.275	1.29	3.72	4.04	1.7	95.0	49.2	12.8	43.9

Comparables: John Curtiss, Brock Stewart, Trevor Richards

The guy best known for breaking out the cat meme shirts during spring training earned notoriety for a lot more than that. Gonsolin broke out, himself, in 2018, running amok in Tulsa. He opened 2019 at Triple-A before making his big-league debut, throwing 40 innings of sub-3.00 ERA ball split between starting and relieving. With a fastball sitting in the 92-95 mph range, Gonsolin effectively uses a four-pitch mix, and even if things don't work out in the rotation, his fastball and split combo should find a place in the 'pen. The long-locked righty was on the outside looking in when it came to the playoff roster, but figures to factor in heavily as the Dodgers once again rely on their depth heading into 2020.

★ ★ ★ *2020 Top 101 Prospect* **#61** ★ ★ ★

Josiah Gray **RHP** Born: 12/21/97 Age: 22 Bats: R Throws: R Height: 6'1" Weight: 190 Origin: Round 2, 2018 Draft (#72 overall)

YEAR	TEAM	LVL	AGE	W	L	SV	G	GS	IP	H	HR	BB/9	K/9	K	GB%	BABIP	WHIP	ERA	DRA	WARP	MPH	FB%	WHF	CSP
2018	GRV	RK	20	2	2	0	12	12	52¹	29	1	2.9	10.1	59	38%	.219	0.88	2.58	0.91	2.9				
2019	GRL	A	21	1	0	0	5	5	23¹	13	0	2.7	10.0	26	41%	.241	0.86	1.93	2.26	0.8				
2019	RCU	A+	21	7	0	0	12	12	67¹	52	3	1.7	10.7	80	40%	.292	0.97	2.14	2.29	2.2				
2019	TUL	AA	21	3	2	0	9	8	39¹	33	0	2.5	9.4	41	35%	.314	1.12	2.75	3.27	0.8				
2020	LAN	MLB	22	1	1	0	11	0	11	11	2	3.2	8.9	11	38%	.302	1.33	3.97	4.36	0.1				

Comparables: Chance Adams, Rafael Montero, Jorge Alcala

The other half of the prospect haul acquired for Yasiel Puig, Gray ended up as the team's Minor League Pitcher Of The Year. He plowed through three levels in 2019, ending his season in Double-A, posting a combined 2.28 ERA along the way. In 130 innings, he struck out an impressive 147 and walked just 31. While he can top out at 97 mph, he generally works in the low-to-mid 90s, adding to his swing-and-miss slider with a curve and change, both of which he's still trying to develop into legit third offerings. Gray is also a strike thrower, and both his relative inexperience (converted shortstop) and athleticism bode well for his fine command to come along eventually. It wouldn't be surprising if he makes himself relevant to the Dodgers bullpen in the second half of 2020.

Michael Grove **RHP** Born: 12/18/96 Age: 23 Bats: R Throws: R Height: 6'3" Weight: 200 Origin: Round 2, 2018 Draft (#68 overall)

YEAR	TEAM	LVL	AGE	W	L	SV	G	GS	IP	H	HR	BB/9	K/9	K	GB%	BABIP	WHIP	ERA	DRA	WARP	MPH	FB%	WHF	CSP
2019	RCU	A+	22	0	5	0	21	21	51²	61	7	3.3	12.7	73	30%	.412	1.55	6.10	5.38	-0.2				
2020	LAN	MLB	23	2	2	0	33	0	35	36	6	4.2	10.0	39	32%	.323	1.50	4.99	5.18	0.1				

Comparables: Mike Mayers, Taylor Williams, Zach Stewart

The Dodgers took a risk on Grove in 2018, selecting him in the second round despite the fact that he missed the whole year with Tommy John surgery. From a results perspective, the outcome hasn't paid off yet as he was assigned to High-A, where he struggled mightily in terms of surface stats. His peripherals fared much better, as he missed bats with frequency and recorded a solid walk rate. One thing to keep an eye on: The Cal League is a hitter's haven, Grove operates as a fly ball pitcher—it's possible he'll see markedly different topline stats in a more neutral environment. Perhaps most importantly, reports on Grove are that he's healthy again. He's once again seeing his pre-surgery velocity and stuff, sitting 92-94 mph with an above-average slider. The changeup still needs work, but given that he missed a year of development, that's not surprising. Still, he'll be 23 next year so the Dodgers likely want to push him to the upper minors with hopes that everything will come together. Being two years removed from the injury sets Grove up nicely for a breakout year.

Kenley Jansen **RHP** Born: 09/30/87 Age: 32 Bats: B Throws: R Height: 6'5" Weight: 265 Origin: International Free Agent, 2004

YEAR	TEAM	LVL	AGE	W	L	SV	G	GS	IP	H	HR	BB/9	K/9	K	GB%	BABIP	WHIP	ERA	DRA	WARP	MPH	FB%	WHF	CSP
2017	LAN	MLB	29	5	0	41	65	0	68¹	44	5	0.9	14.4	109	40%	.291	0.75	1.32	1.90	2.5	96.0	92	19.8	51.8
2018	LAN	MLB	30	1	5	38	69	0	71²	54	13	2.1	10.3	82	36%	.234	0.99	3.01	2.56	2.0	95.2	94.2	14.6	49
2019	LAN	MLB	31	5	3	33	62	0	63	51	9	2.3	11.4	80	36%	.273	1.06	3.71	3.51	1.3	94.4	87.7	17.2	47.7
2020	LAN	MLB	32	3	2	41	53	0	56	42	9	2.4	11.1	69	35%	.257	1.01	2.54	3.03	1.5	94.1	90.2	16.7	48.7

Comparables: Craig Kimbrel, Francisco Rodríguez, David Robertson

Jansen has had a remarkable career, starting off with a ridiculous eight-year run from his debut in 2010 to 2017. He was effectively the best reliever in baseball over that stretch, posting a 2.08 ERA in 477 innings and striking out an unreal 741 against just 126 walks. Unfortunately, all good things must come to an end, and in the past two seasons, his mortality has been laid bare as his strikeouts have dipped and his walks ticked up. Kenley ended 2019 with a career-high 3.71 ERA, almost a full run higher than any other year in his career. Perhaps no other stat illustrates his newfound hittability better than having surrendered 35 homers over his first eight years and 22 homers in his last two. A lot of ink has been spilled on trying to figure out what's wrong with Jansen and how to get him back to his old form, but he's now 32 and it seems fairly obvious that turning back the clock is unlikely. Still, the Dodgers need him to find a way—whether it be increased use of his slider and/or two-seamer—to become a viable first-division closer again because their 'pen doesn't work without one. As it is, 1988 continues to drift further into the rear-view mirror.

Joe Kelly RHP Born: 06/09/88 Age: 32 Bats: R Throws: R Height: 6'1" Weight: 174 Origin: Round 3, 2009 Draft (#98 overall)

YEAR	TEAM	LVL	AGE	W	L	SV	G	GS	IP	H	HR	BB/9	K/9	K	GB%	BABIP	WHIP	ERA	DRA	WARP	MPH	FB%	WHF	CSP
2017	BOS	MLB	29	4	1	0	54	0	58	42	3	4.2	8.1	52	51%	.252	1.19	2.79	4.00	0.8	101.4	64.3	11.6	45.2
2018	BOS	MLB	30	4	2	2	73	0	65²	57	4	4.4	9.3	68	49%	.301	1.36	4.39	4.56	0.3	100.4	55.4	11.4	45.8
2019	LAN	MLB	31	5	4	1	55	0	51¹	49	6	3.9	10.9	62	63%	.323	1.38	4.56	3.27	1.2	99.7	50.9	11.1	48.4
2020	LAN	MLB	32	2	2	4	48	0	50	48	6	3.9	9.7	54	56%	.312	1.39	4.05	4.27	0.6	99.4	55.5	11.2	46.3

Comparables: Jeff Manship, Chad Bettis, Anthony Bass

Can someone help us off this ride? Sure, yes, "Joe Kelly has great stuff" is a meme built around his inconsistency of results despite his ability, but nothing could've prepared us for his 2019. He began his Dodgers career by attempting to become the most hated member of the team, giving up a 10.13 ERA in around a month and was responsible for ~25 percent of the team's losses to that point. Then something clicked and Kelly started pitching like an elite setup man, putting up a 1.69 ERA over a four-month stretch in the middle of the season. Just when it seemed like he would be the answer to the Dodgers bullpen problems, he surrendered a 7.50 ERA in about the final month. Worse yet he pitched just once after mid-September due to vague soreness that still hasn't been explained. But wait! There's more! Kelly then gave up six runs in 2 1/3 innings in the NLDS, including surrendering the series-losing grand slam in Game 5. All in all, he was a replacement-level relief option, which isn't an ideal outcome from the team's big free agent addition. The hope going forward is that Kelly will be more like he was the middle of last year and not like the bookends, but at this point hope is all it is. At least he has great stuff.

Clayton Kershaw LHP Born: 03/19/88 Age: 32 Bats: L Throws: L Height: 6'4" Weight: 226 Origin: Round 1, 2006 Draft (#7 overall)

YEAR	TEAM	LVL	AGE	W	L	SV	G	GS	IP	H	HR	BB/9	K/9	K	GB%	BABIP	WHIP	ERA	DRA	WARP	MPH	FB%	WHF	CSP
2017	LAN	MLB	29	18	4	0	27	27	175	136	23	1.5	10.4	202	49%	.267	0.95	2.31	2.24	6.5	94.8	47.8	15.3	46.5
2018	LAN	MLB	30	9	5	0	26	26	161¹	139	17	1.6	8.6	155	50%	.274	1.04	2.73	3.11	4.1	92.9	41.2	11.8	50.6
2019	LAN	MLB	31	16	5	0	29	28	178¹	145	28	2.1	9.5	189	49%	.264	1.04	3.03	3.33	4.7	91.9	43.9	14.3	46.4
2020	LAN	MLB	32	13	7	0	28	28	171	143	24	2.1	9.7	183	49%	.273	1.07	2.69	3.18	5.0	92.0	43.6	13.6	47.4

Comparables: Sid Fernandez, Madison Bumgarner, Stephen Strasburg

Kershaw seems to be stuck in his own personal "Groundhog Day" except over the course of a baseball season. While he's no longer invincible during the regular season, he's still continued to prove that betting against him finding a way to be effective is for fools. His 2019 ERA was his highest since 2008 and he surrendered 28 homers. He once again managed to stave off any *precipitous* decline despite his fastball now sitting around 90 mph and his slider struggling to find separation. Tragically, like in past years, Kershaw's postseason was worse than expected. He lost a close Game 2 and then was pushed into the decisive Game 5 by Dave Roberts, blowing a two-run lead in the seventh inning on back-to-back pitches via the home-run ball, once again reliving his October nightmare.

In the aftermath, Kershaw seemed a bit broken by it, admitting that the playoff talk surrounding him was less a narrative and more a truth. It's difficult to argue with him. To be fair, things likely would've been less miserable for him by now if it wasn't for the Astros playing the "In The Air Tonight" drum fill on a dugout trash can in Game 5 of the 2017 World Series, but we can't travel back in time or undo wrongs. All Kershaw can do next year is what he admirably does every year: give it another go and hope this time he'll be able to break his personal time loop.

Adam Kolarek LHP Born: 01/14/89 Age: 31 Bats: L Throws: L Height: 6'3" Weight: 215 Origin: Round 11, 2010 Draft (#332 overall)

YEAR	TEAM	LVL	AGE	W	L	SV	G	GS	IP	H	HR	BB/9	K/9	K	GB%	BABIP	WHIP	ERA	DRA	WARP	MPH	FB%	WHF	CSP
2017	DUR	AAA	28	3	4	2	41	0	43²	37	0	3.3	9.5	46	74%	.311	1.21	1.65	3.84	0.7				
2017	TBA	MLB	28	1	0	0	12	0	8¹	9	2	4.3	4.3	4	61%	.269	1.56	6.48	8.19	-0.3	92.3	88.2	7.4	49.6
2018	DUR	AAA	29	5	1	4	31	1	44²	35	1	2.4	10.5	52	64%	.306	1.05	1.61	2.91	1.1				
2018	TBA	MLB	29	1	0	2	31	0	34¹	38	0	1.3	5.0	19	59%	.328	1.25	3.93	4.25	0.3	93.2	63.7	10.1	53.4
2019	TBA	MLB	30	4	3	1	54	0	43¹	39	6	2.9	7.5	36	65%	.264	1.22	3.95	3.78	0.7	92.5	80.9	10.4	46.3
2019	LAN	MLB	30	2	0	0	26	0	11²	9	1	1.5	6.9	9	74%	.242	0.94	0.77	3.81	0.2	91.4	83.2	16.8	47
2020	LAN	MLB	31	2	2	0	48	0	50	53	8	2.9	7.3	41	63%	.298	1.37	4.43	4.71	0.4	91.7	75.8	10.9	49.3

Comparables: Hunter Cervenka, Kevin Chapman, Bobby LaFromboise

Kolarek quickly proved his worth to the Dodgers following his mid-season acquisition. While he had an unremarkable 3.95 ERA with a Rays team that let him face righties, the Dodgers promptly deployed him as their LOOGY and the results were amazing. Kolarek posted a 0.77 ERA in 11 2/3 innings, limiting lefties to a .370 OPS. Most importantly, in the biggest moments of his career, Kolarek dominated Juan Soto in the NLDS: facing the Nationals wunderkind three times, Kolarek didn't flinch, inducing a comebacker to go along with two strikeouts. Their fourth potential matchup (in Game 5) remains one of the greatest "what ifs" of the 2019 season, as the Nationals burned Clayton Kershaw twice and went on to win the series and the Series. On the strength of his excellent turn as a LOOGY, Kolarek should be an easy choice for the 2020 'pen. However, a likely rule change will force pitchers to face at least three hitters or end a half inning, making his roster spot (and career) and pretty big question mark unto itself.

Kenta Maeda RHP Born: 04/11/88 Age: 32 Bats: R Throws: R Height: 6'1" Weight: 184 Origin: International Free Agent, 2016

YEAR	TEAM	LVL	AGE	W	L	SV	G	GS	IP	H	HR	BB/9	K/9	K	GB%	BABIP	WHIP	ERA	DRA	WARP	MPH	FB%	WHF	CSP
2017	LAN	MLB	29	13	6	1	29	25	134¹	121	22	2.3	9.4	140	40%	.278	1.15	4.22	3.53	3.0	93.5	43.4	13	47.1
2018	LAN	MLB	30	8	10	2	39	20	125¹	115	13	3.1	11.0	153	42%	.321	1.26	3.81	2.78	3.6	93.9	44.4	15.8	46.1
2019	LAN	MLB	31	10	8	3	37	26	153²	114	22	3.0	9.9	169	41%	.243	1.07	4.04	3.28	4.1	93.8	37.3	15.7	45.4
2020	LAN	MLB	32	10	7	0	44	23	143	118	22	3.0	10.2	162	41%	.274	1.17	3.17	3.57	3.4	92.8	40.5	14.9	45.6

Comparables: Robb Nen, Eric Gagne, John Wetteland

Maeda's story in the majors has been essentially the same every year now. He spends most of the year as an average starter before converting to relief to patch an otherwise leaky bullpen. It's recently emerged that Maeda is tired of that cycle and it's hard to blame him; a significant portion of his contract is based on incentives awarded for innings accumulated and starts made. It's hard to do those things when one's time in the rotation is cut short each year. For that reason though, the Dodgers are unlikely to change much in regards to Maeda's seasonal pattern. The Dodgers are unlikely to trade him, so the only way for Maeda to change his future is to ensure he is one of their three starters come playoff time. While somewhat unlikely, it's definitely possible because his problem is clear: he dominates righties (.590 OPS) and struggles against lefties (.766 OPS). Maeda has the stuff to handle the split as his changeup is a plus offering, but he's never been able to do it consistently. Until he does, it's difficult to predict a different story for him in 2020.

★　★　★　*2020 Top 101 Prospect* **#8** ★　★　★

Dustin May RHP Born: 09/06/97 Age: 22 Bats: R Throws: R Height: 6'6" Weight: 180 Origin: Round 3, 2016 Draft (#101 overall)

YEAR	TEAM	LVL	AGE	W	L	SV	G	GS	IP	H	HR	BB/9	K/9	K	GB%	BABIP	WHIP	ERA	DRA	WARP	MPH	FB%	WHF	CSP
2017	GRL	A	19	9	6	0	23	23	123	121	8	1.9	8.3	113	52%	.306	1.20	3.88	4.28	1.4				
2017	RCU	A+	19	0	0	0	2	1	11	6	0	0.8	12.3	15	60%	.240	0.64	0.82	1.81	0.4				
2018	RCU	A+	20	7	3	0	17	17	98¹	91	9	1.6	8.6	94	58%	.294	1.10	3.29	2.98	2.7				
2018	TUL	AA	20	2	2	0	6	6	34¹	27	0	3.1	7.3	28	54%	.267	1.14	3.67	3.50	0.7				
2019	TUL	AA	21	3	5	0	15	15	79¹	71	5	2.3	9.8	86	52%	.307	1.15	3.74	3.84	1.1				
2019	OKL	AAA	21	3	0	0	5	5	27¹	21	0	3.0	7.9	24	60%	.276	1.10	2.30	1.90	1.3				
2019	LAN	MLB	21	2	3	0	14	4	34²	33	2	1.3	8.3	32	46%	.316	1.10	3.63	4.55	0.4	98.1	57.2	9.7	52.1
2020	LAN	MLB	22	7	6	0	30	19	112	114	15	2.7	7.7	97	50%	.300	1.31	4.10	4.39	1.7	98.1	59.6	10.1	54.3

Comparables: José Berríos, Jake Thompson, Lucas Giolito

Some guy named Craig once said that May has extreme Waluigi energy, which is a perfect description of the gangly mannerisms of the top Dodgers pitching prospect. We knew about the glorious mane of red hair, but weren't prepared for how animated he is, portending aesthetic promise on top of athletic. Shuffling between 'pen and starting roles, May impressed with a 3.63 ERA and 2.90 FIP, while perhaps the most impressive thing about his debut was his walk rate of just 3.6 percent. He leans heavily on a sinker that moves like a mid-to-upper-90s changeup. His cutter, curve, and change all show signs of being usable pitches, but if he hopes to achieve his upside May will have to develop one of them into a consistent strikeout offering. That's easier said than done, but even in his current form his floor is a worthy rotation option, and May is an adjustment away from being a Dodgers mainstay. WAHHH!

Jimmy Nelson RHP Born: 06/05/89 Age: 31 Bats: R Throws: R Height: 6'6" Weight: 250 Origin: Round 2, 2010 Draft (#64 overall)

YEAR	TEAM	LVL	AGE	W	L	SV	G	GS	IP	H	HR	BB/9	K/9	K	GB%	BABIP	WHIP	ERA	DRA	WARP	MPH	FB%	WHF	CSP
2017	MIL	MLB	28	12	6	0	29	29	175¹	171	16	2.5	10.2	199	51%	.340	1.25	3.49	3.32	4.4	95.9	61.2	12.3	50.7
2019	SAN	AAA	30	3	2	0	16	4	40¹	33	4	5.4	12.7	57	43%	.322	1.41	4.69	2.71	1.5				
2019	MIL	MLB	30	0	2	0	10	3	22	25	4	7.0	10.6	26	35%	.375	1.91	6.95	7.15	-0.4	94.8	52.1	10.4	44
2020	LAN	MLB	31	2	2	0	33	0	35	35	5	4.2	8.6	33	42%	.299	1.46	4.83	5.02	0.2	94.8	59.1	11.9	46.2

Comparables: Rubby De La Rosa, Shane Greene, Joe Kelly

Nelson's 2019 season is why people push back against the tough guy culture that plagues baseball (and all professional sports). Nelson is known as one of the most competitive people in Milwaukee's organization, and he was itching to return as soon as possible after missing the entirety of 2018 due to a shoulder injury (suffered, of all things, running the bases). He was supposed to be healthy by spring training 2019, but setback after setback pushed his debut into June, and after three awful starts and a swift demotion to the bullpen, it was revealed that he had aggravated an elbow issue he had been dealing with since spring training. He obviously wasn't ready, but whether through his own bullheadedness or the Brewers' desperation for a top-flight starter, he was pushed through regardless. Nelson pitched all of 22 innings for the 2019 Brewers as a result of his boneheaded handling, and was non-tendered afterward.

Dennis Santana   RHP   Born: 04/12/96   Age: 24   Bats: R   Throws: R   Height: 6'2"   Weight: 190   Origin: International Free Agent, 2013

YEAR	TEAM	LVL	AGE	W	L	SV	G	GS	IP	H	HR	BB/9	K/9	K	GB%	BABIP	WHIP	ERA	DRA	WARP	MPH	FB%	WHF	CSP
2017	RCU	A+	21	5	6	0	17	14	85²	87	5	2.3	9.7	92	50%	.340	1.27	3.57	3.88	1.3				
2017	TUL	AA	21	3	1	0	7	7	32²	32	2	6.3	10.2	37	52%	.337	1.68	5.51	4.93	0.1				
2018	TUL	AA	22	0	2	0	8	8	38²	26	3	3.3	11.9	51	56%	.258	1.03	2.56	2.44	1.3				
2018	OKL	AAA	22	1	1	0	2	2	11	10	0	1.6	11.5	14	45%	.345	1.09	2.45	2.93	0.3				
2018	LAN	MLB	22	1	0	0	1	0	3²	6	0	2.5	9.8	4	31%	.462	1.91	12.27	3.78	0.0	95.9	54.3	14.3	44.3
2019	OKL	AAA	23	5	9	0	27	17	93¹	111	16	5.1	10.1	105	44%	.364	1.76	6.94	6.51	0.1				
2019	LAN	MLB	23	0	0	0	3	0	5	6	1	7.2	10.8	6	47%	.357	2.00	7.20	5.24	0.0	94.6	56.7	13.5	39
2020	LAN	MLB	24	3	2	0	17	6	44	38	6	4.5	9.5	46	43%	.281	1.38	4.14	4.33	0.7	94.9	57.6	14.2	42.6

Comparables: Touki Toussaint, Rob Whalen, Miguel Almonte

It was only 2018 when Santana seemed like the next pitcher up in the Dodgers system, popping up onto radars everywhere with an uptick in velocity and his swing-and-miss stuff. It seemed like 2019 would be the year to look for his true arrival in the majors. Instead, disaster struck: He maintained his ability to induce whiffs, but lost the strikezone entirely. Santana did make a cameo in the big leagues but did himself no favors there, either. Rather, he seemed to cement a relief role for himself if he was to return to the 25-man roster. That's a lot of negativity, but it's important to remember that he will be just 24 next season, so there's still time for him to right the ship. The Dodgers need relief help in 2020 and with an off-season to focus on his new role, they have to be hoping that Santana is one of the names that emerges.

Josh Sborz   RHP   Born: 12/17/93   Age: 26   Bats: R   Throws: R   Height: 6'3"   Weight: 215   Origin: Round 2, 2015 Draft (#74 overall)

YEAR	TEAM	LVL	AGE	W	L	SV	G	GS	IP	H	HR	BB/9	K/9	K	GB%	BABIP	WHIP	ERA	DRA	WARP	MPH	FB%	WHF	CSP
2017	TUL	AA	23	8	8	0	24	24	116²	106	8	4.3	6.2	81	46%	.275	1.39	3.86	4.74	0.6				
2018	TUL	AA	24	3	1	6	13	0	16¹	11	1	2.8	13.2	24	35%	.303	0.98	2.76	1.88	0.6				
2018	OKL	AAA	24	1	1	0	33	0	37	38	0	3.6	11.4	47	43%	.388	1.43	4.38	3.88	0.5				
2019	OKL	AAA	25	4	3	3	46	0	50	56	2	2.5	12.2	68	40%	.409	1.40	4.68	2.27	1.9				
2019	LAN	MLB	25	0	1	0	7	0	9	10	2	4.0	7.0	7	38%	.296	1.56	8.00	6.99	-0.2	96.4	64.3	10.8	44.9
2020	LAN	MLB	26	1	1	0	16	0	17	17	3	3.6	7.1	13	39%	.285	1.42	4.78	5.04	0.1	96.0	65.5	11	45.7

Comparables: Jacob Rhame, Hunter Wood, Tony Zych

The reality facing Sborz at the moment is that his results have never been all that good. He's relevant because over his minor-league career he's struck out around 12 and walked just three per nine. Add in a fastball that works from 94-96 mph and a slider and curve that both flash above-average, and there always seems to be a middle relief option in there. However, at 26, it does feel like Sborz needs to turn that promise into results sooner than later if he's to establish himself in a big-league pen, because the growing sample size of results is talking louder by the inning.

Ross Stripling   RHP   Born: 11/23/89   Age: 30   Bats: R   Throws: R   Height: 6'2"   Weight: 220   Origin: Round 5, 2012 Draft (#176 overall)

YEAR	TEAM	LVL	AGE	W	L	SV	G	GS	IP	H	HR	BB/9	K/9	K	GB%	BABIP	WHIP	ERA	DRA	WARP	MPH	FB%	WHF	CSP
2017	LAN	MLB	27	3	5	2	49	2	74¹	69	10	2.3	9.0	74	51%	.294	1.18	3.75	3.23	1.6	94.8	38.4	12	44.1
2018	LAN	MLB	28	8	6	0	33	21	122	123	18	1.6	10.0	136	47%	.322	1.19	3.02	2.94	3.3	94.3	41.1	12.5	47.3
2019	LAN	MLB	29	4	4	0	32	15	90²	84	11	2.0	9.2	93	51%	.299	1.15	3.47	3.47	2.2	93.0	39	11.2	46.7
2020	LAN	MLB	30	7	5	0	37	16	103	101	16	2.4	9.2	105	49%	.302	1.24	3.73	4.12	1.8	93.1	39.7	11.9	46.1

Comparables: Mike Fiers, Marco Estrada, Fernando Salas

It's easy to forget that the man nicknamed Chicken Strip was an All-Star as a starting pitcher in 2018, mainly because by the end of the year he was not only out of the rotation but off the playoff roster entirely. That early-'18 run represents his considerable upside, though, and his relegation to a swingman is more a testament to the Dodgers considerable depth than to Stripling's talents. Stripling has always been a good pitcher regardless of role, and nothing changed in that regard for 2019. It's easy to understand the team's reluctance to deal him given that he essentially functions as an insurance plan, but if another team correctly values him as a quality rotation arm, his best use to the Dodgers may be as a trade chip.

Blake Treinen   RHP   Born: 06/30/88   Age: 32   Bats: R   Throws: R   Height: 6'5"   Weight: 225   Origin: Round 7, 2011 Draft (#226 overall)

YEAR	TEAM	LVL	AGE	W	L	SV	G	GS	IP	H	HR	BB/9	K/9	K	GB%	BABIP	WHIP	ERA	DRA	WARP	MPH	FB%	WHF	CSP
2017	WAS	MLB	29	0	2	3	37	0	37²	48	3	3.1	7.6	32	62%	.381	1.62	5.73	4.79	0.2	99.2	72.6	13.1	46.9
2017	OAK	MLB	29	3	4	13	35	0	38	32	3	2.8	9.9	42	60%	.299	1.16	2.13	3.96	0.5	99.4	61.8	14.3	48.3
2018	OAK	MLB	30	9	2	38	68	0	80¹	46	2	2.4	11.2	100	53%	.232	0.83	0.78	2.22	2.5	99.6	67.1	19.2	47.7
2019	OAK	MLB	31	6	5	16	57	0	58²	58	9	5.7	9.1	59	45%	.306	1.62	4.91	5.64	-0.2	98.7	67.1	12.8	43.6
2020	LAN	MLB	32	3	3	2	53	0	56	51	6	3.9	9.7	61	50%	.302	1.35	3.72	3.98	0.9	98.2	66.5	15.2	45.5

Comparables: Jeremy Jeffress, Ryan Tepera, Sam Dyson

For years, everyone wondered how batters could possibly touch Treinen's cocktail of wicked 99 mph two-seamers and vanishing offspeed pitches. For one year, they could not. In 2018, Treinen's sinker darted around and under barrels, he assumed the job as Oakland's closer and posted one of the best seasons we've seen out of a reliever in recent memory. The thing about cocktails is they can leave you with quite the hangover. In 2019, the right-hander battled through a couple minor ailments and lost a tick or two on his fastball, explaining his descent from Cy Young contender to replacement-level reliever as well as anything else. Rather than swing over sinking fastballs, hitters mostly laid off; in turn, Treinen's walk rate more than doubled and when he did come into the strike zone, opponents pounced, homering seven more times than they did a year ago. What awaits him in 2020? "Relievers are volatile" feels like a very 2015 bit of analysis, but it's a useful and truthful hedge in this case.

Julio Urías LHP Born: 08/12/96 Age: 23 Bats: L Throws: L Height: 6'0" Weight: 225 Origin: International Free Agent, 2012

YEAR	TEAM	LVL	AGE	W	L	SV	G	GS	IP	H	HR	BB/9	K/9	K	GB%	BABIP	WHIP	ERA	DRA	WARP	MPH	FB%	WHF	CSP
2017	OKL	AAA	20	3	0	0	6	6	31¹	20	1	4.3	9.2	32	47%	.253	1.12	2.59	2.99	0.9				
2017	LAN	MLB	20	0	2	0	5	5	23¹	23	1	5.4	4.2	11	43%	.293	1.59	5.40	5.35	0.1	95.4	52	10.2	43.2
2018	RCU	A+	21	0	0	0	4	4	7¹	6	3	4.9	16.0	13	46%	.300	1.36	4.91	5.02	0.0				
2018	LAN	MLB	21	0	0	0	3	0	4	1	0	0.0	15.8	7	50%	.167	0.25	0.00	1.89	0.1	95.3	69	22.4	58.6
2019	LAN	MLB	22	4	3	4	37	8	79²	59	7	3.1	9.6	85	39%	.257	1.08	2.49	3.39	1.8	97.1	60.3	15.3	45.7
2020	LAN	MLB	23	7	5	0	21	21	101	82	13	3.6	9.7	109	40%	.270	1.21	3.17	3.51	2.6	96.7	61.4	15.2	51.1

Comparables: Clayton Kershaw, Tyler Skaggs, Jose Rijo

Urías quickly became a fan favorite with the Dodgers, initially due to his phenom status after a meteoric rise through the minors to his big-league debut at 19, then due to his serious shoulder injury and journey back to the majors. But while the story of his 2019 should've been one of triumph over what could've been a career-derailing injury, one cannot talk about Urías in 2019 without mentioning his domestic violence suspension. The details are unfortunately still murky, but MLB saw fit to suspend him for 20 games and some wrongdoing on his part isn't in doubt. The Dodgers and Urías have thus far handled it reasonably well, but only time will tell if their actions will back up their words.

Mitchell White RHP Born: 12/28/94 Age: 25 Bats: R Throws: R Height: 6'3" Weight: 210 Origin: Round 2, 2016 Draft (#65 overall)

YEAR	TEAM	LVL	AGE	W	L	SV	G	GS	IP	H	HR	BB/9	K/9	K	GB%	BABIP	WHIP	ERA	DRA	WARP	MPH	FB%	WHF	CSP
2017	DOD	RK	22	0	0	0	3	3	7	2	0	2.6	10.3	8	53%	.133	0.57	0.00	0.72	0.4				
2017	RCU	A+	22	2	1	0	9	9	38²	26	0	3.7	11.4	49	64%	.286	1.09	3.72	2.41	1.3				
2017	TUL	AA	22	1	1	0	7	7	28	17	2	4.2	10.0	31	51%	.217	1.07	2.57	2.83	0.8				
2018	TUL	AA	23	6	7	0	22	22	105¹	114	12	2.9	7.5	88	49%	.317	1.41	4.53	5.57	-0.3				
2019	TUL	AA	24	1	0	0	7	7	30	18	3	2.1	11.1	37	43%	.217	0.83	2.10	2.97	0.7				
2019	OKL	AAA	24	3	6	0	16	13	63²	73	13	3.4	9.6	68	43%	.349	1.52	6.50	4.94	1.0				
2020	LAN	MLB	25	2	2	0	15	5	33	33	6	3.7	8.9	33	43%	.302	1.41	4.55	4.84	0.3				

Comparables: Hunter Wood, Ben Lively, Jerad Eickhoff

White's upside continue to allure, as the 24-year-old can show a mid-90s fastball with movement, a wipeout slider that locks in strikeouts, and can really spin a curve. While not the most consistent strike-thrower, White finds the zone when necessary as well. Yet, in four years, he's thrown under 300 innings and carries an unremarkable 3.97 career ERA, so something has to give. After a promising start to the season in Double-A, he was promoted to Triple-A and struggled with the juiced ball. Through it all, White's peripherals have remained promising, which is what keeps the Dodgers clinging to a potential quality mid-rotation arm. However, given issues fighting his delivery, bouts with inconsistency, and injury woes, White fits the profile of a future relief arm and likely finds his calling there at some point.

LINEOUTS

Hitters

HITTER	POS	TEAM	LVL	AGE	PA	R	2B	3B	HR	RBI	BB	K	SB	CS	AVG/OBP/SLG	DRC+	VORP	BABIP	BRR	FRAA	WARP
Jacob Amaya	SS	RCU	A+	20	89	14	3	2	1	13	7	15	1	3	.250/.307/.375	99	5.3	.292	0.3	SS(14): -2.1, 2B(4): 1.0	0.2
	SS	GRL	A	20	470	68	25	4	6	58	74	83	4	4	.262/.381/.394	146	41.0	.314	-0.5	SS(50): -3.8, 2B(49): 1.9	3.6
Austin Barnes	C	OKL	AAA	29	104	19	6	0	6	17	14	20	1	1	.264/.375/.540	104	5.9	.274	-0.1	C(13): 2.1, 2B(5): -0.3	0.6
	C	LAN	MLB	29	242	28	12	1	5	25	23	56	3	0	.203/.293/.340	78	5.8	.248	2.4	C(64): 8.4, 2B(1): 0.1	1.6
Omar Estevez	2B	TUL	AA	21	336	34	24	0	6	36	31	70	0	2	.291/.352/.431	118	15.5	.355	-0.2	2B(50): -2.6, SS(23): -0.4	1.3
Jedd Gyorko	3B	LAN	MLB	30	39	1	1	0	0	2	3	10	0	0	.139/.205/.167	53	-1.2	.192	-0.3	3B(9): 0.3, 1B(7): -0.8	-0.1
	3B	SLN	MLB	30	62	5	0	0	2	7	6	14	2	0	.196/.274/.304	78	0.6	.225	-0.1	3B(12): 0.5, 2B(2): 0.1	0.1
	3B	OKL	AAA	30	26	5	1	0	1	5	3	5	0	0	.273/.385/.455	90	-0.3	.313	-0.8	1B(4): -0.2, 3B(2): -0.1	-0.1
Jeren Kendall	CF	RCU	A+	23	412	51	11	10	19	63	51	147	24	7	.219/.319/.469	81	22.9	.304	2.2	CF(77): 0.4, RF(5): -0.6	0.7
Russell Martin	C	LAN	MLB	36	249	29	5	0	6	20	30	60	1	0	.220/.337/.330	85	7.8	.276	-1.6	C(60): 6.0, 3B(7): 0.3	1.2
Zach McKinstry	SS	OKL	AAA	24	95	17	8	2	7	26	6	18	0	1	.382/.421/.753	152	13.7	.422	-0.4	SS(17): -0.1, 2B(3): 0.6	1.0
	SS	TUL	AA	24	384	53	16	4	12	52	37	74	8	8	.279/.352/.455	147	25.6	.323	-0.5	2B(49): -2.7, SS(28): 1.8	2.7
Kristopher Negrón	UT	LAN	MLB	33	57	9	1	0	2	7	3	17	0	1	.259/.298/.389	68	-0.4	.343	-2.2	CF(7): -0.7, RF(6): -0.3	-0.4
	UT	TAC	AAA	33	356	62	15	4	12	61	41	91	11	3	.310/.396/.503	109	27.5	.401	3.1	1B(25): -0.4, SS(18): -1.8	2.1
	UT	SEA	MLB	33	25	3	0	0	0	1	2	9	1	0	.217/.280/.217	77	0.0	.357	0.8	RF(6): -0.4, LF(4): 0.0	0.0
Andy Pages	OF	OGD	Rk+	18	279	57	22	2	19	55	26	79	7	6	.298/.398/.651	173	33.8	.364	-0.2		2.6
Cristian Santana	3B	TUL	AA	22	413	45	22	1	10	57	10	88	0	0	.301/.320/.436	96	13.8	.363	-2.6	3B(82): -2.1, 1B(14): -0.7	0.5
Tyler White	1B	LAN	MLB	28	26	2	0	0	0	2	4	4	0	0	.045/.192/.045	-11	-3.3	.056	-0.1	1B(8): -0.6	-0.4
	1B	HOU	MLB	28	253	16	14	0	3	21	32	74	0	0	.225/.320/.330	86	-0.2	.319	-3.2	1B(48): -1.5, P(4): 0.0	-0.5

On December 31, 2019, **Jacob Amaya** tweeted "showers w the light off be hitting different !" Hitting different at High-A Rancho Cucamonga could double as a New Year's Resolution for the middle infield prospect, who struggled upon a late-season promotion. ⓧ A once-promising athletic catcher, **Austin Barnes** walked a lot and framed exceptionally well, but has now been reduced to the note that he had a 69 OPS+ over the last two seasons before he singled in his final at-bat of 2019 to bump it up to 70. Not-so-nice. ⓧ Signed for $6 million in 2015, Cuban-import **Omar Estevez** was billed as a pure hitter with questionable pop. While that evaluation has proved true, expectations were set a bit higher when he signed, making him yet another disappointing Estevez when it comes to sheen. ⓧ **Jedd Gyorko** put up a .416 OPS as a Dodger belying his true contribution to the team: a 'Jerk-Store' Dodgers jersey during Players' Weekend. ⓧ **Jeren Kendall**'s potential upside was the reason for his first-round selection and continues to be the carrot on the stick that the Dodgers desperately chase, but those Boston Dynamics robots are less mechanical than his swing. ⓧ A reunion with the team he began his career with didn't end in fairy tale fashion for **Russell Martin**, though that's likely because the Dodgers didn't use his prowess on the mound—now the all-time MLB ERA leader (minimum four innings)—in the playoffs. For shame. ⓧ A defensive maestro, **Zach McKinstry** orchestrated a virtuoso offensive performance in a 26-game sample at Triple-A, earning himself a standing ovation—and a spot on the 40-man roster. ⓧ The self-proclaimed "Negrón James" put up dominance worthy of the moniker in his first week after being acquired by the Dodgers with a 1.069 OPS. He then regressed to being **Kristopher Negrón** with a .354 OPS the rest of the way. ⓧ Signed out of Cuba for $300,000 in the 2018 international free agent period, **Andy Pages** gives the Dodgers a bat-first, high-OBP outfield prospect, and more pages than George R. R. Martin. ⓧ First, the good news: Since graduating from rookie ball, **Cristian Santana** has homered four more times than he's walked. Now, the bad news: He's walked four fewer times than he's homered. ⓧ Acquired for a literal (Andre) Scrubb, **Tyler White** quickly proved why his job security in Houston evaporated, going an almost impressive 1-for-22 with the Dodgers before hitting the 60-day IL with a trapezius strain.

Pitchers

PITCHER	TEAM	LVL	AGE	W	L	SV	G	GS	IP	H	HR	BB/9	K/9	K	GB%	BABIP	WHIP	ERA	DRA	WARP	MPH	FB%	WHF	CSP
Pedro Báez	LAN	MLB	31	7	2	1	71	0	69²	43	6	3.0	8.9	69	37%	.213	0.95	3.10	3.68	1.3	97.5	50.7	16.4	42
JT Chargois	OKL	AAA	28	1	2	4	27	0	32²	27	3	4.4	10.2	37	59%	.308	1.32	2.76	2.53	1.2				
	LAN	MLB	28	1	0	0	21	0	21¹	21	4	2.1	11.8	28	47%	.347	1.22	6.33	3.66	0.4	97.5	41.6	16.4	49.3
Brett de Geus	GRL	A	21	4	2	4	19	0	30²	17	0	1.8	10.6	36	49%	.239	0.75	2.35	2.22	0.9				
	RCU	A+	21	2	0	4	20	0	31	28	0	2.0	10.5	36	65%	.341	1.13	1.16	3.23	0.5				
Victor Gonzalez	RCU	A+	23	2	1	0	8	5	27¹	17	0	4.6	11.9	36	52%	.262	1.13	1.65	2.96	0.6				
	TUL	AA	23	3	1	2	15	8	48¹	48	4	2.6	8.2	44	54%	.314	1.28	2.23	4.59	0.2				
	OKL	AAA	23	0	0	0	15	0	14	16	3	2.6	8.4	13	55%	.317	1.43	3.86	4.83	0.2				
Melvin Jimenez	OGD	Rk+	19	5	0	0	10	1	20	8	0	2.7	19.4	43	27%	.308	0.70	2.25	1.40	0.9				
	RCU	A+	19	2	0	2	19	0	30²	24	5	5.6	13.5	46	35%	.279	1.40	3.52	3.70	0.4				
Marshall Kasowski	TUL	AA	24	4	3	2	27	0	29¹	17	1	4.9	14.1	46	43%	.267	1.12	2.45	3.13	0.5				
Kevin Quackenbush	OKL	AAA	30	2	5	11	54	0	58²	59	9	2.5	13.0	85	37%	.348	1.28	5.06	3.07	1.8				
Edubray Ramos	LEH	AAA	26	2	0	6	10	0	10	6	1	3.6	7.2	8	36%	.208	1.00	1.80	3.77	0.2				
	PHI	MLB	26	1	0	0	20	0	15	19	5	4.2	6.6	11	28%	.311	1.73	5.40	5.61	0.0	93.7	42.1	10.2	44.6
Casey Sadler	OKL	AAA	28	0	0	1	2	1	6	8	1	1.5	13.5	9	56%	.467	1.50	6.00	2.03	0.3				
	DUR	AAA	28	1	1	1	11	3	32²	30	5	1.4	12.1	44	40%	.312	1.07	2.76	2.92	1.1				
	TBA	MLB	28	0	0	0	9	0	19¹	16	2	2.3	5.1	11	55%	.233	1.09	1.86	5.35	0.0	94.9	44.3	10	44.5
	LAN	MLB	28	4	0	1	24	1	27	25	3	2.7	6.7	20	52%	.272	1.22	2.33	4.96	0.1	95.1	44.3	10.6	44.4
Edwin Uceta	RCU	A+	21	4	0	0	10	10	50¹	47	6	2.9	11.6	65	36%	.323	1.25	2.15	3.72	0.8				
	TUL	AA	21	7	2	0	16	14	73	62	5	4.1	9.4	76	44%	.303	1.30	3.21	4.93	0.0				

Three years ago, **Yadier Álvarez** was a consensus Top 50 prospect with a Zeusian arm. Now he's coming off a year in which he threw just a handful of innings due to injuries and a suspension for disciplinary issues, that make it seem like he's using that arm to throw his career away. ⓧ **Pedro Báez** is an above-average reliever who is frequently miscast as a great reliever to be used in key moments, which leads to predictably mixed results. ⓧ On a scale of 1-10, **JT Chargois**' handsomeness is probably about a 9. Unfortunately, he seems to believe the higher the number the better applies to ERA as well. ⓧ A transition to the bullpen came with a huge strikeout boost for **Brett de Geus**, which bodes well for his future as a high-leverage reliever as well as the opportunities for De Geus Ex Machina jokes for his bases loaded, no-out appearances. ⓧ Though he hasn't tossed a pitch above Triple-A, **Victor Gonzalez** could soon be joining Randy Choate, Adam Kolarek and Boone Logan in the anti-LOOGY class action lawsuit after having his big-prospects potentially diminished despite leaving a trail of left-handed hitters in his wake. ⓧ Right-hander **Melvin Jimenez** has a fairly classic scouting profile in that he misses lots of bats, allows too many walks, coughs up too many homers and probably used to go by "B.J." ⓧ **Marshall Kasowski** misses a ton of bats with a fastball that touches the upper 90s with ride and deception. Everything else, including his control, is iffy. ⓧ Named for the sound a duck makes after falling into shrubbery, **Kevin Quackenbush** also has trouble escaping jams; that's part of why he spent the whole year in Triple-A despite a flashy strikeout rate. ⓧ It was another injury-riddled campaign for **Edubray Ramos**, who missed significant chunks of time with shoulder injuries and lost nearly two miles an hour off both his fastball and slider when he was healthy enough to trudge to the mound in relief. ⓧ Let us hope that teenage righty pitching prospect **Jerming Rosario** never finds himself in the employ of one Joe Girardi, lest he forever become known as "Jermy." ⓧ Acquired midseason from Tampa Bay, **Casey Sadler** earned the Dodgers' 2019 Sword of Damocles award, as his shiny surface stats (ERA) outpaced his concerning peripherals (FIP, DRA) and fans waited for disaster to strike with every outing. ⓧ Striking out over a batter per inning is good. Also good, **Edwin Uceta**'s name anagrams perfectly to CA We United, which, you know, really provides some extra juice to endear the righty to his future west coast fanbase.

MIAMI MARLINS

Essay by Justin Klugh

Player comments by Zack Moser and BP staff

If you're the type of person who is about to settle in and read 2,500 words on the 2020 Miami Marlins, I'm going to assume you are also the type of person who has at least once thought about faking your death. So I see immediately what this team's appeal is to you.

> *Things haven't been good for a long time. You've become distant and strange. Might as well cut ties with the familiar. Tear it all down. Start over. Inform everyone you haven't been feeling so hot. Announce a sudden interest in an uncharacteristically life-threatening hobby. Disappear in some kind of mountain-unicycling accident. Make yourself unrecognizable. Resurface as another, better you. Begin a new life with a fresh identity. Forget everything that's happened to this point. This is how it's always been.*

What you need to fake your death is a plan. An old man in Florida once tried to stage his own murder by tying a gun to a weather balloon. He succeeded in dying, but not in fooling investigators, who, according to the *Tampa Bay Times*, discovered a list of internet searches on his phone like "How to commit Suicide" and "Undetectable suicide methods" and "How many cubic feet of helium do you need to raise one pound?" So you need a better plan than that.

And it seems like the Marlins have one. As of now, their rebuild has moved beyond "no body was recovered among the wreckage" and has reached a phase closer to "shaving in a gas station bathroom and nodding in approval at the altered reflection staring back at them."

More baseball fans than ever are familiar with the "rebuild" process and have become sickened by the term, knowing exactly what it includes, but having long-ago surrendered to its inevitable protocol. And like faking your death, rebuilds are complex and contain multitudes of X-factors. Maybe the people you were basing your plan around aren't as valuable as you thought or some flawed analysis gets your money invested in the wrong thing. Or maybe some long lost neighbor recognizes you on the street and, when they shout your old name, you instinctively turn and look and there's a horrific moment of recognition in which you

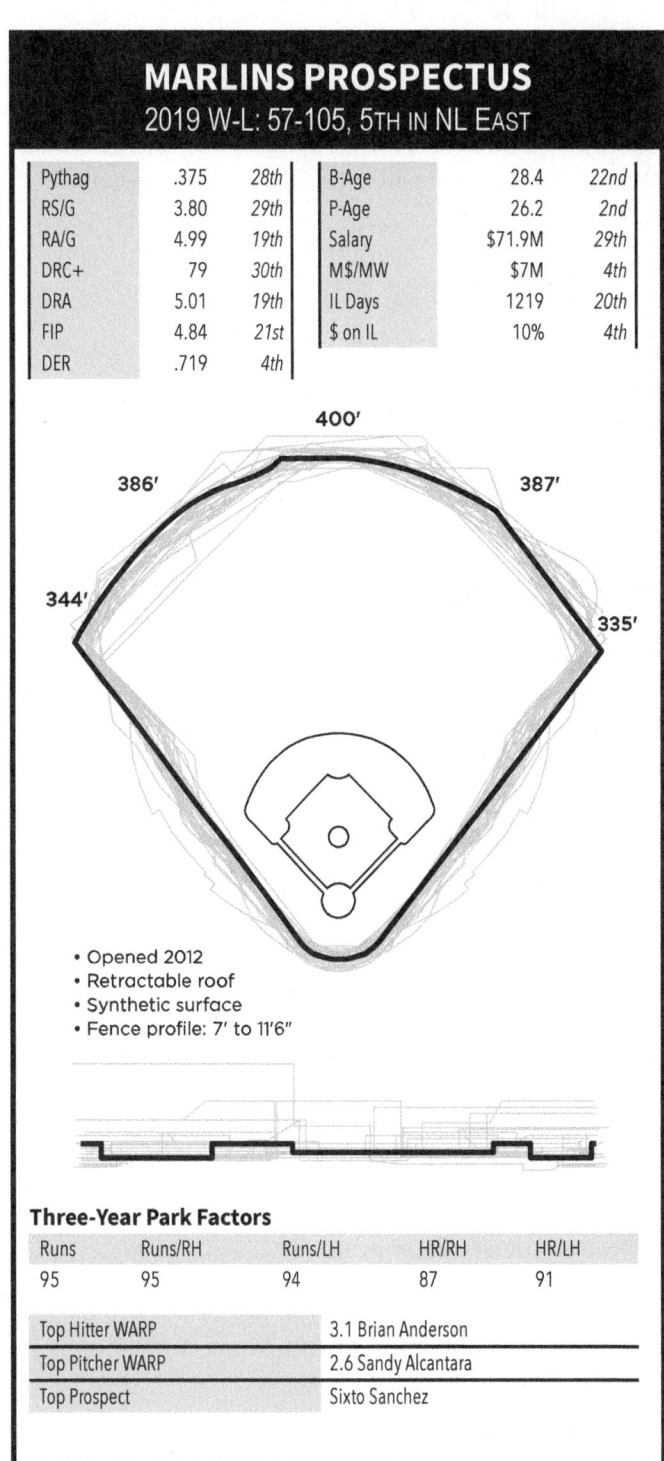

MARLINS PROSPECTUS
2019 W-L: 57-105, 5TH IN NL EAST

Pythag	.375	28th	B-Age	28.4	22nd
RS/G	3.80	29th	P-Age	26.2	2nd
RA/G	4.99	19th	Salary	$71.9M	29th
DRC+	79	30th	M$/MW	$7M	4th
DRA	5.01	19th	IL Days	1219	20th
FIP	4.84	21st	$ on IL	10%	4th
DER	.719	4th			

- Opened 2012
- Retractable roof
- Synthetic surface
- Fence profile: 7' to 11'6"

Three-Year Park Factors

Runs	Runs/RH	Runs/LH	HR/RH	HR/LH
95	95	94	87	91

Top Hitter WARP	3.1 Brian Anderson
Top Pitcher WARP	2.6 Sandy Alcantara
Top Prospect	Sixto Sanchez

2019 Hit List Ranking

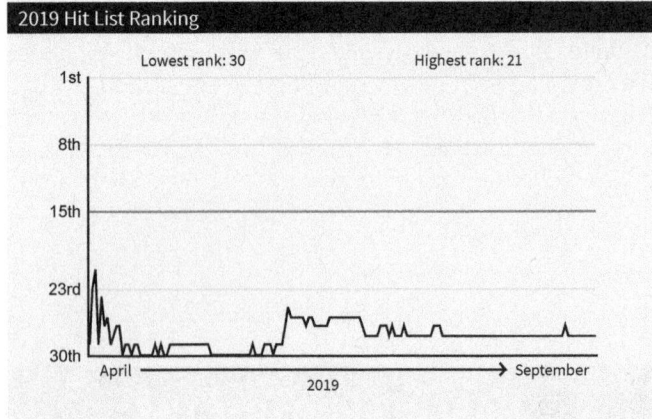

Lowest rank: 30   Highest rank: 21

Committed Payroll (in millions)

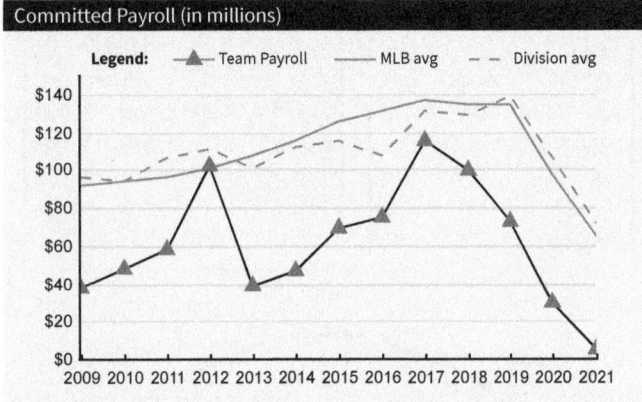

Legend: ▲ Team Payroll — MLB avg --- Division avg

Farm System Ranking

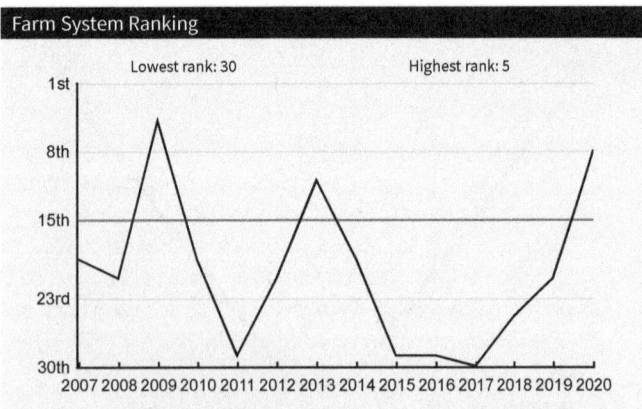

Lowest rank: 30   Highest rank: 5

Personnel

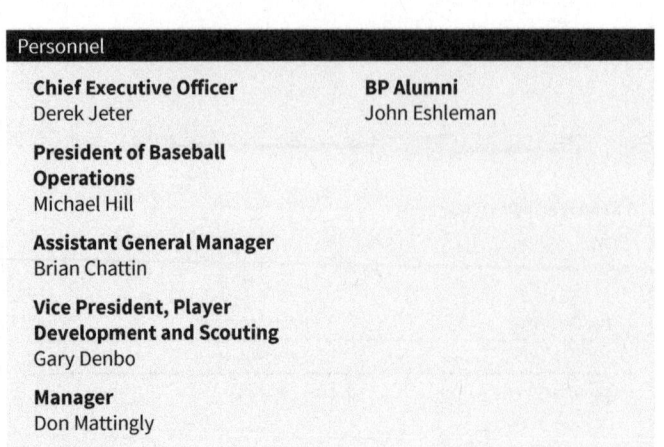

Chief Executive Officer
Derek Jeter

BP Alumni
John Eshleman

President of Baseball Operations
Michael Hill

Assistant General Manager
Brian Chattin

Vice President, Player Development and Scouting
Gary Denbo

Manager
Don Mattingly

both know that it's you, and you have to decide, there and now, if your plan can survive with a witness out there saying they spotted you in Puerto Christo without your beard.

The point is, rebuilding and faking your death are both some of the toughest challenges we'll face in life, but *unlike* faking your death, when you're rebuilding a baseball team, everybody's watching.

Well, not really. Not in South Florida. You will be unsurprised to learn that the Marlins attracted more people than absolutely no one in 2019, with the lowest average attendance by far (just over 10,000). They were the only team in the major leagues to have a total attendance number lower than 1 million for the season, and it wasn't even close (811,302). They will once again have some work to do in getting fans into the stadium, sitting them down, and pointing their heads toward Marlins baseball and saying, "This is a sport some people like. Do you like it? No, you can't leave. This won't end for three and a half hours." Marlins CEO and part-owner Derek Jeter even moved the home run sculpture outside. God forbid the Marlins be known for something other than not having fans.

Just to provide you some context for cost of the Marlins' current roster ($27 million) it's about the price of a mansion in San Francisco, or a large-scale money laundering conspiracy, or the amount that was awarded to a man released from prison after serving 27 years for a murder he didn't commit. The 2020 season will be all about the Yankees, who made a big free agent signing and will be the top story of the league, at least until Rob Manfred announces that MLB is abandoning its attempts to market itself to children and will simply ride out its popularity with upper middle-aged sourpusses until they've all died out. Regardless of what people are talking about in baseball, no one really talks about a team constructed so inexpensively that it costs, in total, about 1/12th of what the Yankees paid Gerrit Cole.

If you're a follower of this team, and if you're reading this I assume you must be—either that or you read all of the other essays already and you're some kind of deranged completist—then you might be sick of sentiments like, "The Marlins? They're bad," or "The Marlins? No thanks," or "The Marlins? They make me want to fake my own death!"

You're likely sick of these sentiments because they're the only things most people have had to say about Miami for years. Every division has its filthy basement, and other than occasional check-ins on how poorly everything is going, the teams inhabiting that basement spend most of the season totally ignored. Miami knew where it was headed when it traded away all of its realest talent a couple of years ago, and everyone watching knew it, too: They held a town hall, and Jeter had to sit there while a line of people took turns insulting him into a microphone. It was the greatest moment in sports history.

Reporters found Jeter again in late August of 2019 at a team event in an elementary school. Jeter said he was frustrated, being a real competitor and all, that the Marlins were still only in this early phase of the rebuild, in which they would lose a ton of games and not have a lot of good players. Later in the off-season, Jeter handed out meals to the community for Thanksgiving in a continuance of his rebrand from "overwhelmed rich person who thought this would be easier" to "benevolent millionaire about town." One can only assume this was *his* attempt at faking his own death and starting over, only without the staged helicopter crash, because let's face it, setting all *that* up probably wound up seeming like *way* too much work, so he settled for some media spin.

When the press talked to him around Thanksgiving, Jeter made it clear through brazen pronouncements and the cutting off of questions that if the Marlins saw a player they *wanted* in free agency, they would *get* him. The question is, *who* did the Marlins, a team early in its construction and far from contention, *want* in free agency? Why *didn't* they want *the best* players? And are they really ready to get *better*?

Because, you know, the Marlins *are* a tanking team, and that means for now, the *best* players available are still invisible to them. So, what have the Marlins gained by spending the last decade as an unwatched franchise under .500? As far as people you know who've put on the famous Midnight Black, Miami Blue, and Caliente Red uniforms, Martin Prado, Curtis Granderson and Neil Walker have been phased out. Wei-Yin Chen's contract is finally disintegrating, and they bought out Starlin Castro's deal.

If you are a Marlins fan, this is very scary! Not because of who these players are, but because of the fun 2019 baseball activity of saying the names of players who aren't on the Marlins anymore: Giancarlo Stanton. Christian Yelich. J.T. Realmuto. Marcell Ozuna. Dee Gordon. For a few weeks at the beginning of 2019, it seemed like it was going to be the Year of Derek Dietrich during which the former Marlins second baseman would do things that no one on the *current* Marlins could do, like hit three home runs in a game and extremely piss off Chris Archer. Dietrich returned to being a random infielder who hits .187 eventually, but for a while, it looked like the best thing that could happen to a major-league ball player in 2019 was to no longer play for the Marlins.

Every plan, whether a meandering franchise rebuild or burning your apartment down and moving into a shack in the local swamp, has a final phase. When will the Marlins reach theirs? If this past winter is any indication, they're still stroking their chins at mid-range free agent options, signing outfielder Corey Dickerson and checking in on Kole Calhoun and Yasiel Puig. They also acquired infielder Jonathan Villar, who instantly went from being the best player on the Orioles to being the best player on the Marlins, via trade. They locked up manager Don Mattingly with an extension, despite a record almost a hundred games under .500 over four years. Whatever you want to see from a manager in his situation, Miami has seen it. Maybe they want an expert on-hand who has experience in shaving a signature mustache and is aware of how effective it was in remaking himself.

And there are players *currently* on the team to contribute to their future, more successful persona of their franchise; they just had to cycle through a few identities to get here. The Marlins turned Marcell Ozuna into Zac Gallen and turned Zac Gallen into toolsy prospect, Jazz Chisholm. Now, instead of waiting out another will-he-or-won't-he pitching prospect, the Marlins have a potent, harefooted shortstop of the future. Sandy Alcantara, Caleb Smith and Pablo Lopez are all young pitchers who have had their names mentioned in earnest this past season, with Alcantara and his high-90s fastball serving as Miami's annual obligatory All-Star. Brian Anderson was one of the few pistons firing on the Marlins offense in 2019, and when he came up with the bases loaded against the Phillies on August 23, the hope was that he would improve on his already impressive numbers. Instead, he was hit in the hand with a 93 mph fastball, and his season was over.

As key young players heal, the perception of Jeter, too, is on the mend—that is, if you consider iconic Yankees shortstop Derek Jeter and bumbling Marlins part-owner Derek Jeter the same person. His name being on the Hall of Fame ballot this winter ended the novelty of Jeter-as-owner critiques and reminded writers why they got into this business in the first place: to vote Derek Jeter into the Hall of Fame. In some cases, they intend to do so while voting for absolutely no one else, out of fear of tarnishing Jeter's induction. And just look at the places you can find Jeter in his adopted hometown of Miami: An elementary school. A holiday food drive. Infielder Miguel Rojas bothered to say of Jeter and owner Bruce Sherman, "They are always going to tell you the truth from day one." Finally, some *good* press for the guy, and he didn't even have to remote crash his private jet in the Everglades and start wearing a fake beard.

So there's a little bit going on for the Marlins, but a key part of a rebuild, and of faking your death, is patience. Patience to bide your time. To wait for your moment. To watch things develop until you can resurface. That's asking a lot of everyone involved. And until that time comes, all you can do is hide in the basement while the authorities embark on a fruitless search for your corpse and be sure to never go outside in the same outfit.

The Marlins' scheme to fake their death over the last few years has an ironically fatal flaw: Sure, they've worn two sets of new uniforms and tried to destroy evidence of their existence by dragging the home run sculpture out to the dumpster, but we still know it's them. There are at least a couple of fans waiting for them to resurface—think of them like investigators scrolling through internet searches, formulating theories as to what exactly the Marlins are up to, and watching their every move to see if their theories were correct. The Marlins have got to know how to distract them in the short-term so they can keep changing their long-term appearance.

On September 20, Marlins outfielder Austin Dean threw a ball into the stands and knocked an empty can off the top of a pile of other cans. We can talk about the future all we want, but the team and its dwindling fan base still has to survive the present. Rebuilds are not fun and should not be celebrated, but the team will still exist whether it's making an effort to win or not. There will be players on it and, presumably, the whole mess they've put together will develop a little more in 2020. It may seem like inconsequential social media fodder, but the Marlins will need many, many little moments, like a career minor leaguer sniping a tin can from the grass, to help remind people at a Marlins game that they are still alive. You have to be able to

look in the mirror and, though you are now quite altered, still be able to recognize yourself; to see past all of the changes and secrets and lies and know that the team you want to be is still in there, under the tilted brim of a soiled ball cap. Because that's the trick with faking your death—the main part of it, really: You're not actually supposed to die. ■

—Justin Klugh is an author of Baseball Prospectus.

HITTERS

Jesús Aguilar 1B   Born: 06/30/90   Age: 30   Bats: R   Throws: R   Height: 6'3"   Weight: 250   Origin: International Free Agent, 2007

YEAR	TEAM	LVL	AGE	PA	R	2B	3B	HR	RBI	BB	K	SB	CS	AVG/OBP/SLG	DRC+	VORP	BABIP	BRR	FRAA	WARP
2017	MIL	MLB	27	311	40	15	2	16	52	25	94	0	0	.265/.331/.505	101	12.4	.337	0.4	1B(77): 1.2, 3B(1): 0.0	0.7
2018	MIL	MLB	28	566	80	25	0	35	108	58	143	0	0	.274/.352/.539	135	35.6	.309	-1.1	1B(132): 3.6, 3B(5): 0.0	3.6
2019	MIL	MLB	29	262	26	9	0	8	34	31	59	0	0	.225/.320/.374	94	2.5	.264	-1.9	1B(60): 0.1, 3B(2): 0.0	0.1
2019	TBA	MLB	29	107	13	3	0	4	16	12	22	0	0	.261/.336/.424	104	2.3	.290	-1.7	1B(15): 0.0	0.1
2020	MIA	MLB	30	518	60	21	1	20	66	52	131	1	0	.239/.323/.421	96	6.5	.290	-1.4	1B 2	0.9

Comparables: Travis Shaw, Brett Wallace, Chris Davis

For the 813rd season in a row, the Rays attempted to buy low on a struggling offensive player that had success the year prior. In 2018, it was Tommy Pham. That worked out really well. In 2019, it was Aguilar. It worked out...less well. An All-Star selection in 2018 when he smashed 60 extra-base hits—including 35 home runs—he collected just seven of them with Tampa Bay after a trade from Milwaukee. Though his exit velocity remained the same, he did not barrel the ball as often and his launch angle dropped nearly three degrees. With three years left until free agency, Aguilar will look to bring the thunder back as the Marlins' starting first baseman.

Jorge Alfaro C   Born: 06/11/93   Age: 27   Bats: R   Throws: R   Height: 6'2"   Weight: 225   Origin: International Free Agent, 2010

YEAR	TEAM	LVL	AGE	PA	R	2B	3B	HR	RBI	BB	K	SB	CS	AVG/OBP/SLG	DRC+	VORP	BABIP	BRR	FRAA	WARP
2017	LEH	AAA	24	350	34	13	2	7	43	16	113	1	1	.241/.291/.358	71	4.0	.345	-1.4	C(77): 4.8	0.9
2017	PHI	MLB	24	114	12	6	0	5	14	3	33	0	0	.318/.360/.514	93	10.3	.420	-1.5	C(28): -2.5, 1B(2): 0.1	0.1
2018	PHI	MLB	25	377	35	16	2	10	37	18	138	3	0	.262/.324/.407	84	24.6	.406	0.5	C(104): 12.2, 3B(1): 0.0	2.5
2019	MIA	MLB	26	465	44	14	1	18	57	22	154	4	4	.262/.312/.425	86	16.0	.364	-2.1	C(118): -2.0, 1B(1): 0.0	1.1
2020	MIA	MLB	27	385	40	14	1	12	45	18	126	1	1	.248/.301/.400	84	9.1	.349	-0.8	C 1	1.0

Comparables: Josh Phelps, Junior Lake, Jake Marisnick

A positive 2018 season during which Alfaro significantly improved his framing gave way to a somewhat middling 2019, during which he had to catch the illustrious Marlins pitching staff. Alfaro still graded out well on the defensive end, but the latent raw power that prospectniks have ogled over for years didn't materialize even with the juiced ball. He'll have many opportunities to stick behind the plate and garner enough plate appearances to adjust in the majors, but as he ages, the odds only increase that Alfaro will max out as a league-average backstop. Then again, catchers are weird and someone with legendary tools as a teenager can turn into a post-hype darling as fast as one of his fabled pop times.

YEAR	TEAM	P. COUNT	FRM RUNS	BLK RUNS	THRW RUNS	TOT RUNS
2017	LEH	10516	2.0	-0.5	0.3	0.9
2017	PHI	4051	-2.6	0.2	-0.1	-2.9
2018	PHI	14100	12.3	-2.4	0.0	10.2
2019	MIA	16910	-1.7	-3.5	0.1	-5.2
2020	MIA	14686	1.6	-2.9	0.0	-1.2

Brian Anderson 3B/OF   Born: 05/19/93   Age: 27   Bats: R   Throws: R   Height: 6'3"   Weight: 185   Origin: Round 3, 2014 Draft (#76 overall)

YEAR	TEAM	LVL	AGE	PA	R	2B	3B	HR	RBI	BB	K	SB	CS	AVG/OBP/SLG	DRC+	VORP	BABIP	BRR	FRAA	WARP
2017	JAX	AA	24	361	53	14	3	14	55	36	71	1	1	.251/.341/.450	115	19.5	.277	-1.3	3B(82): 9.0	2.7
2017	NWO	AAA	24	137	21	7	0	8	26	12	27	0	1	.339/.416/.602	163	20.4	.376	-0.4	3B(30): 1.5	1.7
2017	MIA	MLB	24	95	11	7	1	0	8	10	28	0	0	.262/.337/.369	66	4.5	.386	1.0	3B(25): -2.2	-0.2
2018	MIA	MLB	25	670	87	34	4	11	65	62	129	2	4	.273/.357/.400	109	43.9	.332	2.3	RF(91): -1.1, 3B(71): -9.0	1.8
2019	MIA	MLB	26	520	57	33	1	20	66	44	114	5	1	.261/.342/.468	108	22.1	.305	2.0	3B(67): 1.1, RF(55): 6.3	3.1
2020	MIA	MLB	27	595	67	28	2	20	73	51	131	2	1	.248/.328/.423	99	15.2	.294	2.3	RF 1, 3B 0	1.7

Comparables: Willie Jones, Gil McDougald, Craig Worthington

Water… water… Your mouth is parched. You've stumbled across the desert for three days, your canteen's precious few drops long since dried up under the unforgiving sun. *Water…* Three days of sunburn and sand, the hallucinations setting in—you've begun to question yourself, how exactly you got here. What could have damned you to such a fate? Was it the white flag trades you made before the season even started the past two years? The ignominious heel turn of a precious baseball icon? Have the gods finally smote you for removing their favorite home run sculpture? *Water...*

Wait. What's that on the horizon? Slightly above-average production at a premium defensive position? You scramble toward the oasis, praying it's not a cartoon mirage. You arrive, and Brian Anderson greets you. You kiss his feet. Sweet, sweet Brian Anderson.

Will Banfield C   Born: 11/18/99   Age: 20   Bats: R   Throws: R   Height: 6'0"   Weight: 200   Origin: Round 2, 2018 Draft (#69 overall)

YEAR	TEAM	LVL	AGE	PA	R	2B	3B	HR	RBI	BB	K	SB	CS	AVG/OBP/SLG	DRC+	VORP	BABIP	BRR	FRAA	WARP
2018	MRL	RK	18	94	7	8	1	0	14	7	28	0	1	.256/.330/.378	82	1.8	.375	-0.9	C(22): 1.2	0.3
2018	GRB	A	18	52	5	0	0	3	4	4	15	0	0	.208/.269/.396	76	0.7	.233	0.1	C(14): 0.1	0.1
2019	CLN	A	19	433	44	13	2	9	55	25	121	0	0	.199/.252/.310	53	-1.4	.256	-1.7	C(91): 5.5	0.2
2020	MIA	MLB	20	251	21	11	1	5	24	16	88	1	0	.197/.256/.321	53	-7.8	.291	-0.3	C 0	-0.8

Comparables: Kyle Skipworth, Justin Williams, Deivy Grullon

After pushing 2018's 69th overall pick into full-season ball for his first pro season at 18, Miami made the wise decision to have Banfield repeat a level at new Low-A affiliate Clinton in 2019, where he struggled to hit his weight. Banfield is a polished backstop, which explains the aggressive assignments. His high strikeout and low walk rates are no fluke, however. The good thing is that he's only going to be 20 this season, and the Marlins can afford to be as patient as needed with his development. A good defensive catcher who hunts fastballs at the plate isn't a bad thing—just look at Banfield's senior, Jorge Alfaro—but developing Banfield's hit tool into something...nicer...will be his and Miami's priority as he ascends in the system.

Jon Berti UT   Born: 01/22/90   Age: 30   Bats: R   Throws: R   Height: 5'10"   Weight: 195   Origin: Round 18, 2011 Draft (#559 overall)

YEAR	TEAM	LVL	AGE	PA	R	2B	3B	HR	RBI	BB	K	SB	CS	AVG/OBP/SLG	DRC+	VORP	BABIP	BRR	FRAA	WARP
2017	BUF	AAA	27	237	26	8	4	3	20	20	53	23	4	.205/.271/.321	62	-4.3	.256	1.9	2B(47): 9.9, LF(13): -0.5	0.9
2018	NHP	AA	28	316	55	13	7	8	42	29	46	21	9	.314/.399/.498	157	28.7	.354	0.6	3B(27): -0.8, 2B(20): -0.1	2.8
2018	COH	AAA	28	73	10	1	0	0	3	9	13	8	1	.217/.333/.233	75	-3.1	.271	-0.5	LF(11): -1.5, 2B(6): -0.2	-0.3
2018	TOR	MLB	28	15	2	1	1	0	2	0	4	1	0	.267/.267/.467	85	0.7	.364	0.6	2B(4): -0.6	0.0
2019	NWO	AAA	29	79	14	1	0	4	8	15	11	5	0	.290/.430/.500	132	9.3	.292	1.2	3B(9): -0.4, CF(6): 1.2	0.8
2019	MIA	MLB	29	287	52	14	1	6	24	24	73	17	3	.273/.348/.406	87	7.3	.360	5.0	SS(32): -1.4, CF(21): -1.2	1.1
2020	MIA	MLB	30	385	40	19	3	7	39	32	96	20	6	.253/.328/.388	89	10.5	.331	2.9	CF -1, SS -1	0.8

Comparables: Tyler Ladendorf, David Adams, Quintin Berry

The man who calls himself "Jonny Hustle" (let's hope Berti doesn't get traded to San Diego anytime soon) earned his fins in the final two months of 2019. Seeing time all over the diamond, Berti broke out in a minor mood after spending the better part of the last decade in Toronto's farm system. His combination of speed and versatility is perhaps more attractive to fantasy players than an actual major league team these days, but he nabbed a regular spot in Miami's lineup by August and put his speed to use. Sure, he's scrappy—there's little about "career minor leaguer with legs and glove" that would decry that characterization—but he can slap it, spray it and bop it like an annoying '90s toy hawked on Nickelodeon. As Don Mattingly said, Berti is a "true piece."

──────────── ★ ★ ★ *2020 Top 101 Prospect* **#35** ★ ★ ★ ────────────

JJ Bleday OF   Born: 11/10/97   Age: 22   Bats: L   Throws: L   Height: 6'3"   Weight: 205   Origin: Round 1, 2019 Draft (#4 overall)

YEAR	TEAM	LVL	AGE	PA	R	2B	3B	HR	RBI	BB	K	SB	CS	AVG/OBP/SLG	DRC+	VORP	BABIP	BRR	FRAA	WARP
2019	JUP	A+	21	151	13	8	0	3	19	11	29	0	0	.257/.311/.379	105	2.1	.306	-1.1	RF(32): -0.9	0.1
2020	MIA	MLB	22	251	23	12	1	6	25	16	66	2	1	.224/.277/.355	68	-2.3	.287	0.0	RF -5	-0.7

Comparables: Yangervis Solarte, Rymer Liriano, Abraham Almonte

The top-of-the-first-round college outfielder is a relatively rare specimen these days, but Bleday sports the sort of mature approach that compels a team to snag such a player that early. He can adjust mid-swing to get the barrel to the ball even when beaten, and he has good power, evidenced by his Division-I leading home run total in 2019. While already a corner outfielder, which may give some pause, he has a strong arm and average speed/acceleration on the grass that should allow him to stick in right field for a while. Miami assigned him somewhat aggressively to High-A Jupiter, and his profile—lefty power hitter with an advanced approach—gives the organization the type of player they've been starved for, as they stockpile role-55 arms and toolsy infielders. Marrying his bat-to-ball skills with his penchant for power is key to Bleday's success, and he'll get to work on that union in his first full season of pro ball in 2020.

Lewis Brinson CF   Born: 05/08/94   Age: 26   Bats: R   Throws: R   Height: 6'3"   Weight: 195   Origin: Round 1, 2012 Draft (#29 overall)

YEAR	TEAM	LVL	AGE	PA	R	2B	3B	HR	RBI	BB	K	SB	CS	AVG/OBP/SLG	DRC+	VORP	BABIP	BRR	FRAA	WARP
2017	CSP	AAA	23	340	66	22	4	13	48	32	62	11	5	.331/.400/.562	126	27.1	.377	1.6	CF(61): 1.1, LF(6): 3.2	2.8
2017	MIL	MLB	23	55	2	0	1	2	3	7	17	1	0	.106/.236/.277	73	-3.4	.107	-0.5	LF(8): -0.1, CF(8): 0.4	0.0
2018	JAX	AA	24	26	1	0	0	1	1	3	5	1	0	.130/.231/.261	55	-1.3	.118	-0.1	CF(8): -1.0	-0.1
2018	NWO	AAA	24	27	0	1	1	0	3	0	6	0	0	.222/.222/.333	64	-1.9	.286	0.0	CF(5): -1.6	-0.2
2018	MIA	MLB	24	406	31	10	5	11	42	17	120	2	1	.199/.240/.338	64	-5.0	.257	-0.9	CF(106): 3.3	-0.1
2019	NWO	AAA	25	339	56	15	4	16	56	32	100	16	5	.270/.361/.510	106	18.7	.356	2.3	CF(49): 4.4, RF(27): 5.1	2.2
2019	MIA	MLB	25	248	15	9	1	0	15	13	74	1	1	.173/.236/.221	42	-1.0	.255	1.5	CF(60): 6.4, RF(11): 0.7	-0.1
2020	MIA	MLB	26	217	20	9	2	5	23	14	70	4	2	.213/.276/.362	64	-2.0	.298	0.0	CF 4	0.2

Comparables: Travis Snider, Clint Frazier, Aaron Hicks

A player with a batting average in the .100s is said to be "on the interstate." Brinson must be going for his learner's permit: He finished his third straight season with a major-league batting average under .200, and he even threatened to take his slugging percentage for a drive. Ranting about Brinson's tools is almost as much a cliché as singing the praises of Joe Kelly's "great stuff," and we've reached the point where major league reps might not help the 25-year-old outfielder. Tearing up the PCL at 25 is encouraging, if not particularly impressive, and it's unclear if the Marlins will be able to develop Brinson in Wichita. If he has any remaining virtues, it's that youth—the Marlins aren't exactly pressed to give other outfielders the reps from which Brinson might benefit. Manager Don Mattingly has a difficult choice to make, though, as the power-and-defense combo Brinson is supposed to possess has manifested in the most half-baked fashion to this point.

Francisco Cervelli C   Born: 03/06/86   Age: 34   Bats: R   Throws: R   Height: 6'1"   Weight: 210   Origin: International Free Agent, 2003

YEAR	TEAM	LVL	AGE	PA	R	2B	3B	HR	RBI	BB	K	SB	CS	AVG/OBP/SLG	DRC+	VORP	BABIP	BRR	FRAA	WARP
2017	PIT	MLB	31	304	31	13	2	5	31	32	65	0	2	.249/.342/.370	91	11.7	.311	-2.9	C(78): -5.6	0.3
2018	PIT	MLB	32	404	39	15	3	12	57	51	84	2	3	.259/.378/.431	116	33.7	.308	0.7	C(94): -3.9, 1B(5): -0.1	2.4
2019	PIT	MLB	33	123	11	3	0	1	5	9	31	1	0	.193/.279/.248	73	2.2	.260	-0.3	C(32): 0.3, 1B(1): 0.0	0.2
2019	ATL	MLB	33	37	4	5	1	2	7	4	10	0	0	.281/.378/.688	95	1.4	.350	0.8	C(9): -0.6, 1B(2): -0.1	0.1
2020	MIA	MLB	34	217	22	8	1	4	21	23	54	1	1	.238/.339/.362	89	5.9	.314	-0.1	C 0, 1B 0	0.6

The injury bug has been buzzing around Cervelli's career for a some time now, and 2019 was the year when it went from being pesky to a full-on nuisance for the well-regarded catcher. The 34-year-old went through the ringer last season, with concussion symptoms being the biggest culprit—to the point where there were rumors that Cervelli was going to give up catching in an effort to extend his career. As it turns out, he did continue catching, just with another team as the Pirates released him and the Braves brought him on as depth behind their own oft-injured starter. If catching is still in Cervelli's future, it'll have to come on a part-time basis, as both the bat and the once-elite framing skills have been reduced by both age and that unrelenting bug.

Comparables: Brian Schneider, Jonathan Lucroy, Chad Moeller

YEAR	TEAM	P. COUNT	FRM RUNS	BLK RUNS	THRW RUNS	TOT RUNS
2017	PIT	10368	-6.0	0.5	-1.0	-6.8
2018	PIT	13072	-5.8	-1.1	0.6	-6.5
2019	PIT	4324	0.0	-1.1	0.1	-1.0
2019	ATL	824	0.0	-0.7	0.1	-0.6
2020	MIA	8414	-0.2	-1.2	0.4	-1.1

───────────── ★ ★ ★ *2020 Top 101 Prospect* **#52** ★ ★ ★ ─────────────

Jazz Chisholm SS   Born: 02/01/98   Age: 22   Bats: L   Throws: R   Height: 5'11"   Weight: 165   Origin: International Free Agent, 2015

YEAR	TEAM	LVL	AGE	PA	R	2B	3B	HR	RBI	BB	K	SB	CS	AVG/OBP/SLG	DRC+	VORP	BABIP	BRR	FRAA	WARP
2017	KNC	A	19	125	14	5	2	1	12	10	39	3	0	.248/.325/.358	92	6.4	.371	0.7	SS(29): 0.8	0.6
2018	KNC	A	20	341	52	17	4	15	43	30	97	8	2	.244/.311/.472	102	17.7	.303	-1.4	SS(75): -0.3	1.3
2018	VIS	A+	20	160	27	6	2	10	27	9	52	9	2	.329/.369/.597	139	21.1	.443	0.5	SS(36): -0.7	1.3
2019	WTN	AA	21	364	51	6	5	18	44	41	123	13	4	.204/.305/.427	108	19.9	.261	2.9	SS(88): -5.8	1.7
2019	JAX	AA	21	94	6	4	2	3	10	11	24	3	0	.284/.383/.494	104	10.2	.370	-0.5	SS(21): -1.8	0.4
2020	MIA	MLB	22	35	3	1	0	1	4	3	13	1	0	.205/.278/.366	70	-0.1	.311	0.0	SS 0	0.0

Comparables: Yu Chang, Michael Chavis, Trevor Story

Double-A can be a reckoning for players like Chisholm. The plus-everything in the field remains plus, but the bat—with its surprising pop but high potential for swing-and-miss—faces perhaps its first real challenge. For Chisholm, the reckoning came while still in Arizona's system, when he barely managed to crack a .200 batting average and .300 OBP in Jackson. It may appear that the titillating Chisholm-for-Zac Gallen swap at the trade deadline energized the Bahamian shortstop, but in reality, Chisholm was making adjustments in the weeks prior to the trade, and manifested in a nice stat line when he added the "ville" to his chest. Most importantly, he cut his 34 percent strikeout rate down to a manageable 25 percent; for a player who exhibits a rather violent approach, gaining that much contact has outsized benefit.

Garrett Cooper OF/1B   Born: 12/25/90   Age: 29   Bats: R   Throws: R   Height: 6'6"   Weight: 230   Origin: Round 6, 2013 Draft (#182 overall)

YEAR	TEAM	LVL	AGE	PA	R	2B	3B	HR	RBI	BB	K	SB	CS	AVG/OBP/SLG	DRC+	VORP	BABIP	BRR	FRAA	WARP
2017	CSP	AAA	26	320	64	29	0	17	82	33	48	0	0	.366/.428/.652	173	26.6	.386	-2.3	1B(73): 4.3	3.5
2017	NYA	MLB	26	45	3	5	1	0	6	1	12	0	0	.326/.333/.488	80	1.3	.438	0.0	1B(13): 0.0	0.0
2018	NWO	AAA	27	34	2	1	0	1	5	3	5	0	0	.300/.382/.433	115	2.5	.333	-0.5	1B(5): 0.3, LF(4): 0.5	0.1
2018	MIA	MLB	27	38	2	1	0	0	2	4	12	0	0	.212/.316/.242	67	0.3	.333	0.4	LF(6): 0.7, 1B(4): 1.1	0.1
2019	MIA	MLB	28	421	52	16	1	15	50	33	110	0	0	.281/.344/.446	101	8.4	.357	-0.4	1B(73): -0.2, RF(31): 5.1	1.2
2020	MIA	MLB	29	308	34	13	1	9	37	24	82	1	0	.267/.331/.421	98	6.7	.346	0.0	1B 1, RF 1	0.9

Comparables: Dee Fondy, Adam Rosales, Brandon Barnes

"Is the Quad-A player extinct?"

The greatest thread in the history of baseball forums, locked after only a few comments because someone remembered Cooper. He mashed in Double-A. He mashed in Triple-A. He's 28 and *thriving*. Cooper's 2019 was his first full season in the majors, and he was an unexpected bright spot for a dismal Marlins club. The first baseman/corner outfielder smokes the ball with regularity and he hit better versus righties than lefties in 2019, despite losing the platoon advantage. Cooper faltered a bit in the second half, but a torrid September before being shut down due to a knee injury suggests that he's currently the Marlins' best in-house option for first base.

Isan Díaz 2B   Born: 05/27/96   Age: 24   Bats: L   Throws: R   Height: 5'10"   Weight: 185   Origin: Round 2, 2014 Draft (#70 overall)

YEAR	TEAM	LVL	AGE	PA	R	2B	3B	HR	RBI	BB	K	SB	CS	AVG/OBP/SLG	DRC+	VORP	BABIP	BRR	FRAA	WARP
2017	CAR	A+	21	455	59	20	0	13	54	62	121	9	3	.222/.334/.376	105	13.8	.283	0.1	2B(70): -1.9, SS(32): -4.8	0.9
2018	JAX	AA	22	356	44	19	1	10	42	53	95	10	3	.245/.365/.418	124	22.5	.325	0.0	2B(82): 2.1	2.2
2018	NWO	AAA	22	155	19	4	4	3	14	15	45	4	0	.204/.281/.358	69	-2.0	.278	0.8	2B(35): -1.6	-0.2
2019	NWO	AAA	23	435	89	21	2	26	70	49	96	5	4	.305/.395/.578	132	44.6	.349	0.7	2B(98): 0.8	3.1
2019	MIA	MLB	23	201	17	5	2	5	23	19	59	0	3	.173/.259/.307	63	-3.2	.224	0.1	2B(48): 0.0	-0.3
2020	MIA	MLB	24	455	48	18	3	16	54	42	133	4	2	.214/.293/.389	82	8.4	.275	1.1	2B 0	0.8

Comparables: Shed Long, Drew Robinson, Lane Thomas

Díaz's lack of power in his 2019 debut might dull his prospect shine a bit, but it really shouldn't. He still wielded a loud bat with authority in the superball-enhanced PCL and walked a ton. Now fully ensconced at second, Díaz is a good bet to fill into a profile not dissimilar to former Fish second-sacker Dan Uggla. The biggest questions for Díaz are whether he'll make enough contact for the power to show up at the major-league level, and if he'll come into spring training with biceps the size of cement mixers. This sort of power from the left side, even with Díaz's high prospective strikeout rate, is appealing to a team that finished dead last in homers during 2019. Here's to Díaz getting ripped and hitting second-deck shots over the newly-moved walls at Pro Player...er, Marlins Park.

Corey Dickerson LF Born: 05/22/89 Age: 31 Bats: L Throws: R Height: 6'1" Weight: 210 Origin: Round 8, 2010 Draft (#260 overall)

YEAR	TEAM	LVL	AGE	PA	R	2B	3B	HR	RBI	BB	K	SB	CS	AVG/OBP/SLG	DRC+	VORP	BABIP	BRR	FRAA	WARP
2017	TBA	MLB	28	629	84	33	4	27	62	35	152	4	3	.282/.325/.490	109	25.0	.338	-1.9	LF(93): 13.4	3.2
2018	PIT	MLB	29	533	65	35	7	13	55	21	80	8	3	.300/.330/.474	106	17.2	.333	-4.1	LF(124): 10.7	2.4
2019	IND	AAA	30	38	4	1	0	0	4	3	8	0	0	.182/.237/.212	61	-3.2	.222	0.2	LF(7): 0.6	0.0
2019	PHI	MLB	30	137	13	10	2	8	34	3	33	0	0	.293/.307/.579	105	4.7	.333	-3.1	LF(32): -1.2	0.0
2019	PIT	MLB	30	142	20	18	0	4	25	13	23	1	0	.315/.373/.551	107	5.4	.353	-0.1	LF(33): -0.7	0.5
2020	MIA	MLB	31	504	52	30	4	17	63	30	110	3	2	.250/.296/.437	92	5.4	.292	-2.6	LF 9	1.5

Comparables: Geoff Jenkins, Adam Lind, Jim Rice

Dickerson's season was bookended by injuries: he missed slightly over two months of action at the beginning of 2019 with a posterior shoulder strain and ended it with a fractured left foot in mid-September. The meat in between that injury bread was another productive campaign. Dickerson is a slightly above average major league outfielder, and while the shape of his contribution varies from year to year his DRC+ has remained remarkably consistent since 2015. The cozy dimensions of Citizens Bank Park were too enticing for C-Dick to ignore after the Pirates traded him across the Keystone State at the deadline; he returned to the free swinging style that was a hallmark of his pre-Pirate career and smacked twice as many home runs as a result. Dickerson isn't ready to be mentioned in the same breath as death and taxes yet, but another steady season is on the horizon in 2020.

Curtis Granderson LF Born: 03/16/81 Age: 39 Bats: L Throws: R Height: 6'1" Weight: 200 Origin: Round 3, 2002 Draft (#80 overall)

YEAR	TEAM	LVL	AGE	PA	R	2B	3B	HR	RBI	BB	K	SB	CS	AVG/OBP/SLG	DRC+	VORP	BABIP	BRR	FRAA	WARP
2017	NYN	MLB	36	395	58	22	3	19	52	53	90	4	2	.228/.334/.481	107	26.0	.251	1.5	CF(59): -8.4, RF(30): 1.9	1.0
2017	LAN	MLB	36	132	16	2	0	7	12	18	33	2	0	.161/.288/.366	107	2.7	.153	0.2	LF(26): -3.2, RF(8): 0.2	0.2
2018	TOR	MLB	37	349	48	21	1	11	35	42	96	2	1	.245/.342/.430	100	8.0	.321	-2.3	LF(41): 0.5, RF(31): -1.9	0.4
2018	MIL	MLB	37	54	12	1	1	2	3	12	10	0	0	.220/.407/.439	100	3.4	.241	-0.5	RF(14): -0.5, LF(3): -0.1	0.0
2019	MIA	MLB	38	363	44	17	1	12	34	41	98	0	3	.183/.281/.356	83	2.5	.220	-1.1	LF(85): 4.7, RF(6): -0.2	0.6
2020	MIA	MLB	39	251	27	11	1	9	29	29	69	2	1	.203/.303/.379	81	1.8	.254	-0.2	LF 1, RF 0	0.1

Comparables: Kirk Gibson, Dexter Fowler, Rick Monday

For the first time since his first full season in the majors, deep in those halcyon mid-2000s now gauzy with the soft light of Remembering Some Guys, Granderson turned in a below-average offensive season while healthy. It's tough to quantify which act of his career this is, but the eminently likable outfielder exhibited some pennant-race savoir faire as recently as his 2018 stint with Milwaukee. Would that it were another era for Mr. Granderson, who might prolong his career for several more seasons if free agency (and many teams' lust for wins) hadn't been smothered by the ownership class.

But Granderson's career twilight, like contemporaries (Ichiro, CC Sabathia, Joe Mauer), isn't defined by his on-field performance. Rather, we remember his outsized generosity: He donated a large sum to the University of Illinois-Chicago, his alma mater, to build a baseball stadium. His idiosyncrasies: In 2015, when prompted to say "something controversial," he posited that the moon landing might have been faked. His obvious love for baseball: While he didn't get picked up for a stretch run in 2019, he did saddle up in the broadcast booth for the playoffs. His efforts on and off the field didn't go unrecognized, either, as Granderson won the Marvin Miller Man of the Year Award four times for his remarkable career. On the day he chooses to retire, the game will be slightly dimmer without his smile.

Monte Harrison OF Born: 08/10/95 Age: 24 Bats: R Throws: R Height: 6'3" Weight: 220 Origin: Round 2, 2014 Draft (#50 overall)

YEAR	TEAM	LVL	AGE	PA	R	2B	3B	HR	RBI	BB	K	SB	CS	AVG/OBP/SLG	DRC+	VORP	BABIP	BRR	FRAA	WARP
2017	WIS	A	21	261	32	12	1	11	32	29	70	11	3	.265/.359/.475	132	22.1	.333	1.3	CF(62): 1.6	2.1
2017	CAR	A+	21	252	41	16	1	10	35	14	69	16	1	.278/.341/.487	127	20.5	.358	3.3	CF(32): -1.8, RF(24): 2.1	1.8
2018	JAX	AA	22	583	85	20	3	19	48	44	215	28	9	.240/.316/.399	96	28.5	.368	3.6	CF(121): -8.0, RF(14): 0.4	1.3
2019	NWO	AAA	23	244	41	7	2	9	24	25	73	20	2	.274/.357/.451	94	12.5	.373	3.2	CF(32): 2.6, RF(19): -2.4	0.9
2020	MIA	MLB	24	112	10	5	1	2	11	8	41	3	1	.215/.288/.343	67	-0.9	.332	0.3	CF 0, RF 0	-0.1

Comparables: Lane Thomas, Brett Phillips, Teoscar Hernández

Harrison owns one of 2019's most bizarre seasons for any top prospect. His obscene number of strikeouts in Double-A in 2018 were enough to tarnish his prospect shine, but he came out mashing in New Orleans last year with a strikeout rate below 30 percent and was selected to play in the Futures Game. He then injured his wrist in late June diving for a ball, tried to stay in the game and ultimately was pulled after setting up in the lefty batter's box, even though, like Inigo Montoyo, he's not left-handed. Harrison subsequently hit the IL, missed the Futures Game and got surgery on his wrist, missing most of the rest of the season. Whereas he had previously been ticketed for a September call-up and competition for an outfield spot this spring, he's now a 24-year-old coming off a significant injury needing to hold gains made by retooling his swing.

Bryan Holaday C   Born: 11/19/87   Age: 32   Bats: R   Throws: R   Height: 6'0"   Weight: 214   Origin: Round 6, 2010 Draft (#193 overall)

YEAR	TEAM	LVL	AGE	PA	R	2B	3B	HR	RBI	BB	K	SB	CS	AVG/OBP/SLG	DRC+	VORP	BABIP	BRR	FRAA	WARP
2017	TOL	AAA	29	347	31	20	0	12	50	22	54	0	3	.269/.325/.450	107	18.7	.286	-3.2	C(90): 3.8, 3B(3): 0.0	1.9
2017	DET	MLB	29	29	1	2	0	0	2	0	1	0	0	.241/.241/.310	87	-1.2	.250	0.5	C(11): -2.9, 2B(1): 0.0	-0.1
2018	MIA	MLB	30	166	7	5	0	1	16	10	29	0	0	.205/.261/.258	81	-4.9	.244	-1.5	C(50): 4.5, P(2): 0.0	0.7
2019	NWO	AAA	31	118	8	7	0	2	12	17	12	1	1	.247/.385/.387	108	8.2	.259	0.5	C(34): 4.1	1.1
2019	MIA	MLB	31	129	12	6	0	4	12	11	21	0	1	.278/.344/.435	97	6.3	.308	-2.3	C(38): -5.2, P(1): 0.0	-0.1
2020	MIA	MLB	32	251	23	11	0	6	25	17	48	1	0	.222/.288/.352	71	-2.6	.257	-1.2	C -10, 3B 0	-1.3

Comparables: Robert Machado, Brian Johnson, Yorvit Torrealba

YEAR	TEAM	P. COUNT	FRM RUNS	BLK RUNS	THRW RUNS	TOT RUNS
2017	DET	1073	-1.4	-1.4	0.0	-3.0
2017	TOL	12913	-3.0	3.9	2.5	2.7
2018	MIA	6233	2.8	0.9	0.4	4.0
2019	MIA	5153	-4.8	-0.1	0.0	-4.9
2019	NWO	4286	3.4	0.0	0.6	3.8
2020	MIA	12365	-9.0	-1.1	-0.3	-10.5

It's a luxury to have a backup catcher who can make some noise with the stick, and it's a downright excess for a cellar dweller like the Marlins to have enjoyed Holaday's 2019 season. After 600 plate appearances spread over his first seven seasons, Holaday "broke out" at the dish while backing up Jorge Alfaro, managing the third-best DRC+ of any Miami hitter, though that itself is more an indictment of the Marlins than praise for Holaday. Unfortunately, he swallowed those gains—giving it all back and then some on defense by being one of the league's 10 worst framers. On the bright side, Holaday did lower his career ERA to 7.36 after getting fellow backup backstop Russell Martin to ground out to end a meaningless 15-1 drubbing in August.

Víctor Víctor Mesa OF   Born: 07/20/96   Age: 23   Bats: R   Throws: R   Height: 5'10"   Weight: 165   Origin: International Free Agent, 2018

YEAR	TEAM	LVL	AGE	PA	R	2B	3B	HR	RBI	BB	K	SB	CS	AVG/OBP/SLG	DRC+	VORP	BABIP	BRR	FRAA	WARP
2019	JUP	A+	22	390	37	5	3	0	26	19	48	15	2	.252/.295/.283	90	1.2	.287	-0.9	CF(75): -3.3	0.3
2019	JAX	AA	22	113	8	2	0	0	3	3	16	3	0	.178/.200/.196	16	-6.9	.209	-0.4	CF(25): 6.0	0.1
2020	MIA	MLB	23	35	3	1	0	0	3	2	7	1	0	.227/.268/.300	49	-1.0	.275	0.0	CF 0	-0.1

Comparables: Rafael Bautista, Engelb Vielma, David Fletcher

The man often compared to Albert Almora has begun to hit like Albert Almora … except Mesa did it in Double-A during 2019, which does not bode well for the highly touted international signee. It was Mesa's first time back in game action after an extended layoff, which could be a blessing (he just needs to shake the rust) or a curse (he lost vital development time and likely won't recover). The elements that made him an attractive prospect remain, since he can still run very well and play a good center field with a strong arm, but Mesa's penchant for contact at the plate won't be much of an asset if it continues to result in less pop than a Whole Foods.

Kameron Misner CF   Born: 01/08/98   Age: 22   Bats: L   Throws: L   Height: 6'4"   Weight: 219   Origin: Round 1, 2019 Draft (#35 overall)

YEAR	TEAM	LVL	AGE	PA	R	2B	3B	HR	RBI	BB	K	SB	CS	AVG/OBP/SLG	DRC+	VORP	BABIP	BRR	FRAA	WARP
2019	MRL	RK	21	38	2	2	0	0	4	9	7	3	0	.241/.421/.310	139	3.7	.318	0.4	CF(5): -0.1, RF(3): -0.2	0.2
2019	CLN	A	21	158	25	7	0	2	20	21	35	8	0	.276/.380/.373	137	11.1	.357	2.2	CF(30): 7.1	2.0
2020	MIA	MLB	22	251	24	12	1	5	24	24	73	3	1	.225/.304/.345	76	0.3	.311	0.0	CF 7, RF 0	0.8

Comparables: Darrell Ceciliani, Mitch Haniger, Jacob May

Friends call me Kam Misner / Whatever I touch / Clears the fence in the clutch / I'm too much! Misner is a big boy with big power and big speed. He lofts the ball with the best of 'em, and he can play across the outfield or at first base. Misner's patience allows him to wait for pitches to drive, which he did with regularity at Mizzou, even if that power didn't show up during his abbreviated pro debut in 2019. More professional reps will give Misner the opportunity to display whether he is content to be a Three True Outcomes guy with ridiculous power or if he'll temper his approach in order to max out the hit tool. Regardless of his future shape of production, he's a remarkably attractive prospect with both a high floor and a high ceiling.

Martín Prado CI   Born: 10/27/83   Age: 36   Bats: R   Throws: R   Height: 6'0"   Weight: 215   Origin: International Free Agent, 2001

YEAR	TEAM	LVL	AGE	PA	R	2B	3B	HR	RBI	BB	K	SB	CS	AVG/OBP/SLG	DRC+	VORP	BABIP	BRR	FRAA	WARP
2017	JUP	A+	33	25	0	1	0	0	0	3	5	0	0	.273/.360/.318	124	1.5	.353	0.2	3B(8): -0.1	0.2
2017	MIA	MLB	33	147	13	9	0	2	12	6	22	0	0	.250/.279/.357	79	-2.3	.282	-1.0	3B(34): -1.2	-0.1
2018	JUP	A+	34	31	3	1	0	0	2	3	2	0	0	.250/.323/.286	116	0.3	.269	0.0	3B(10): 1.2	0.3
2018	MIA	MLB	34	209	16	9	0	1	18	11	35	1	1	.244/.287/.305	84	1.3	.292	0.4	3B(48): -4.5, 1B(1): 0.1	-0.1
2019	MIA	MLB	35	260	26	9	0	2	15	12	41	0	0	.233/.265/.294	70	-3.6	.268	-0.2	1B(40): -0.2, 3B(22): 0.5	-0.3
2020	MIA	MLB	36	251	22	12	1	3	23	15	42	1	0	.250/.300/.347	72	-1.1	.293	-0.1	3B 0, 1B 0	-0.1

Comparables: Ray Knight, Mike Lamb, Carney Lansford

Prado will be remembered partially as the last recipient of a bizarre Jeffrey Loria-blessed contract, one useful for soaking up a bit of payroll if not for acquiring an actually good player. Since signing his three-year extension before the 2017 season, Prado has come to the plate a mere 612 times and hit like he strode up to the plate carrying a pool noodle instead a wood bat, sporting a .240/.276/.308 line. He's 36 now, a far cry from his promising days as a utility guy in Atlanta, and he'll likely into the sunset with one All-Star appearance and a ninth-place MVP finish in his cap.

Harold Ramírez OF Born: 09/06/94 Age: 25 Bats: R Throws: R Height: 5'10" Weight: 220 Origin: International Free Agent, 2011

YEAR	TEAM	LVL	AGE	PA	R	2B	3B	HR	RBI	BB	K	SB	CS	AVG/OBP/SLG	DRC+	VORP	BABIP	BRR	FRAA	WARP
2017	NHP	AA	22	490	46	19	2	6	53	32	65	5	3	.266/.320/.358	84	-0.9	.296	-2.3	RF(73): 0.3, LF(25): -3.4	-0.5
2018	NHP	AA	23	505	60	37	0	11	70	27	88	16	2	.320/.365/.471	135	31.3	.371	2.5	RF(61): -2.7, LF(8): -0.5	2.7
2019	NWO	AAA	24	120	19	12	1	4	14	6	19	1	1	.355/.408/.591	122	12.2	.402	-2.3	LF(16): -0.2, RF(8): 0.1	0.4
2019	MIA	MLB	24	446	54	20	3	11	50	18	91	2	1	.276/.312/.416	84	3.3	.328	-0.2	LF(61): 4.1, RF(55): -2.5	0.7
2020	MIA	MLB	25	336	33	17	2	7	36	16	71	6	3	.274/.319/.408	89	5.6	.334	-0.3	CF 7, LF 1	1.5

Comparables: Gorkys Hernández, Victor Reyes, Tyrone Taylor

While they unfortunately didn't reunite with Hanley Ramírez after his unceremonious departures from both Boston and Cleveland, Miami did hand a boatload of plate appearances to a much younger "H. Ramírez." A year removed from an Eastern League playoff MVP award, Ramírez did little to stand out among a crowded Marlins outfield picture while making his major-league debut. He's been a high-average hitter for most of his extensive minor-league career, and Ramírez at least looked the part in that respect, posting the third-highest batting average on the team among players with at least 150 at-bats. However, his overall performance could cut one of two ways with this Miami club: Ramírez could have played acceptably enough to warrant a longer look and some development, or he could have bored the front office enough to find himself at the bottom of the depth chart in favor of some fresher faces with louder tools.

Miguel Rojas SS Born: 02/24/89 Age: 31 Bats: R Throws: R Height: 5'11" Weight: 195 Origin: International Free Agent, 2005

YEAR	TEAM	LVL	AGE	PA	R	2B	3B	HR	RBI	BB	K	SB	CS	AVG/OBP/SLG	DRC+	VORP	BABIP	BRR	FRAA	WARP
2017	JUP	A+	28	30	3	2	0	0	2	3	1	0	1	.308/.400/.385	143	2.7	.320	0.3	2B(3): -0.4, SS(2): 0.0	0.3
2017	MIA	MLB	28	306	37	16	2	1	26	27	32	2	1	.290/.361/.375	92	20.9	.324	4.6	SS(77): -0.2, 3B(15): -0.2	1.5
2018	MIA	MLB	29	527	44	13	0	11	53	24	69	6	3	.252/.297/.346	90	9.1	.272	-2.5	SS(83): 5.4, 1B(49): -0.3	1.6
2019	MIA	MLB	30	526	52	29	1	5	46	32	62	9	5	.284/.331/.379	93	20.6	.314	-1.7	SS(125): -4.8, 1B(16): -0.1	1.4
2020	MIA	MLB	31	560	51	26	2	8	52	34	72	5	3	.263/.316/.364	79	5.9	.293	0.1	SS 1, 2B 0	0.7

Comparables: Adam Everett, Denny Hocking, Abraham O. Nunez

The Marlins love their light-hitting, contact-oriented infielders, huh? Sometimes it seems like they want to field a whole team of Rojases. Rojasi? Rojasim? Maybe their plan is to assemble a Manny Alexander Voltron. To his credit, Rojas managed to boost his on-base skills while maintaining a superb contact rate, simply by laying off more pitches out of the zone. On a team full of role players and fifth infielders, Rojas is maybe the most role-player-ish, the most fifth-infielder-y, which means he'll likely log 500-plus plate appearances again in 2020.

───────────── ★ ★ ★ *2020 Top 101 Prospect* **#80** ★ ★ ★ ─────────────

Jesús Sánchez OF Born: 10/07/97 Age: 22 Bats: L Throws: R Height: 6'3" Weight: 230 Origin: International Free Agent, 2014

YEAR	TEAM	LVL	AGE	PA	R	2B	3B	HR	RBI	BB	K	SB	CS	AVG/OBP/SLG	DRC+	VORP	BABIP	BRR	FRAA	WARP
2017	BGR	A	19	512	81	29	4	15	82	32	91	7	2	.305/.348/.478	127	29.7	.349	3.4	LF(78): 14.0, RF(19): -0.5	4.3
2018	PCH	A+	20	378	56	24	2	10	64	15	71	6	3	.301/.331/.462	137	19.9	.350	-1.5	RF(78): 1.8, CF(7): -1.4	2.0
2018	MNT	AA	20	110	14	8	0	1	11	11	21	1	1	.214/.300/.327	92	-0.8	.263	0.7	RF(26): -0.8, CF(1): 0.0	0.1
2019	MNT	AA	21	316	32	11	1	8	49	24	65	5	4	.275/.332/.404	122	10.2	.327	0.1	RF(72): 0.0	1.4
2019	NWO	AAA	21	78	11	1	0	4	9	9	15	0	0	.246/.338/.446	74	-2.5	.250	0.3	CF(8): -1.6, RF(7): 3.6	0.2
2019	DUR	AAA	21	71	6	2	1	1	5	6	20	0	0	.206/.282/.317	52	-6.2	.279	-0.3	RF(15): 0.7	-0.2
2020	MIA	MLB	22	42	4	2	0	1	4	3	11	0	0	.239/.289/.379	78	-0.3	.308	-0.1	RF 0	0.0

Comparables: Jorge Bonifacio, Justin Williams, Gabriel Guerrero

Carrying his very consistent offensive profile from the Rays to the Marlins in the Nick Anderson trade, Sánchez hasn't really taken that next big step since tearing up the Midwest League in 2017 as a teenager. The big outfielder doesn't hurt you in the field or on the bases, but neither of those skills are the crux of his future value. That lies in his lumber, and most specifically his power. Only problem is that it hasn't shown up in games yet to the extent that is expected—the Dominican native has not eclipsed 15 homers in any of his full pro seasons. The bat-to-ball skills remain solid, but even exceptional barrel control and a top-50 prospect pedigree can't stave off worries that Sánchez has set up camp on a performance plateau as a 22-year-old knocking on the door to the majors.

Connor Scott OF Born: 10/08/99 Age: 20 Bats: L Throws: L Height: 6'4" Weight: 180 Origin: Round 1, 2018 Draft (#13 overall)

YEAR	TEAM	LVL	AGE	PA	R	2B	3B	HR	RBI	BB	K	SB	CS	AVG/OBP/SLG	DRC+	VORP	BABIP	BRR	FRAA	WARP
2018	MRL	RK	18	119	15	1	4	0	8	14	29	8	5	.223/.319/.311	90	0.5	.307	-1.2	CF(22): -1.6	0.0
2018	GRB	A	18	89	4	2	0	1	5	10	27	1	3	.211/.295/.276	56	-2.5	.300	-1.9	CF(22): -3.0	-0.7
2019	CLN	A	19	413	56	24	4	4	36	31	91	21	9	.251/.311/.368	98	12.6	.322	1.6	CF(85): -2.6, LF(1): -0.1	1.1
2019	JUP	A+	19	111	12	4	1	1	5	11	26	2	1	.235/.306/.327	85	3.0	.301	0.9	CF(24): -1.5	0.1
2020	MIA	MLB	20	251	21	11	1	3	21	20	73	4	3	.213/.280/.316	61	-4.9	.298	-0.2	CF -2, LF 0	-0.7

Comparables: Carlos Tocci, Anthony Gose, Joe Benson

You would prefer your high school position player draftees carry a higher ceiling than Scott, but the Marlins' 2018 first-rounder hit adequately enough for a teenager after an aggressive promotion to High-A in July; his acceleration parrying the doubters for at least one more season. Miami seems to have guys like Scott by the bushel, propped up by good outfield defense and athleticism, but many of them are older and at a more advanced level than he is. A 20-year-old ticketed for a return engagement in the Florida State League in 2020, he will need to rein in his sometimes hitchy, looped swing as he ascends through the minors.

Jonathan Villar MI Born: 05/02/91   Age: 29   Bats: B   Throws: R   Height: 6'1"   Weight: 215   Origin: International Free Agent, 2008

YEAR	TEAM	LVL	AGE	PA	R	2B	3B	HR	RBI	BB	K	SB	CS	AVG/OBP/SLG	DRC+	VORP	BABIP	BRR	FRAA	WARP
2017	MIL	MLB	26	436	49	18	1	11	40	30	132	23	8	.241/.293/.372	64	5.2	.330	1.6	2B(98): 2.7, CF(6): -0.1	-0.2
2018	MIL	MLB	27	279	26	10	1	6	22	19	80	14	2	.261/.315/.377	82	6.7	.355	0.5	2B(74): -6.1	-0.3
2018	BAL	MLB	27	236	28	4	0	8	24	22	58	21	3	.258/.336/.392	85	8.0	.319	2.4	2B(36): 1.0, SS(18): 0.5	0.8
2019	BAL	MLB	28	714	111	33	5	24	73	61	176	40	9	.274/.339/.453	94	23.6	.341	5.6	2B(111): 4.0, SS(97): 0.9	3.3
2020	MIA	MLB	29	595	64	23	4	15	63	52	158	38	11	.245/.315/.386	87	9.7	.320	2.0	3B 0, 2B 0	1.0

Comparables: *Jhonny Peralta, Bill Hall, Everth Cabrera*

It must be spectacularly motivating to think you're going to be traded away from one of the worst teams in baseball. Villar had 13 hits the week before the trade deadline, yet he ultimately stayed put. To his credit, he not only kept the party going, but shelved the act where he played like the squirrel in "Ice Age" in favor of a more focused game. That leaves a player who can be utterly dynamic, both on the bases and at the plate, though the perception is better than the reality with a glove on his hand. Villar, characterized aptly this year as the perfect rebuilding player, will soon graduate into a life of being underpaid on short-term contracts. It's just a matter of when that starts. After being traded to the worst team in the National League, he'll have to hope that motivation carries over to at least one more July.

Neil Walker CI Born: 09/10/85   Age: 34   Bats: B   Throws: R   Height: 6'3"   Weight: 210   Origin: Round 1, 2004 Draft (#11 overall)

YEAR	TEAM	LVL	AGE	PA	R	2B	3B	HR	RBI	BB	K	SB	CS	AVG/OBP/SLG	DRC+	VORP	BABIP	BRR	FRAA	WARP
2017	NYN	MLB	31	299	40	13	2	10	36	27	47	0	1	.264/.339/.442	107	12.3	.286	-1.5	2B(68): -5.0, 1B(3): 0.0	0.5
2017	MIL	MLB	31	149	19	8	0	4	13	28	30	0	1	.267/.409/.433	108	9.7	.326	-0.7	2B(27): -1.1, 1B(14): 0.0	0.4
2018	NYA	MLB	32	398	48	12	1	11	46	42	87	0	0	.219/.309/.354	89	-0.8	.257	-1.0	1B(42): 4.2, 2B(32): 0.7	0.7
2019	MIA	MLB	33	381	37	19	1	8	38	42	77	3	0	.261/.344/.395	95	5.8	.316	-0.3	1B(69): -2.2, 3B(26): -2.5	0.1
2020	MIA	MLB	34	251	26	9	1	6	26	25	54	1	1	.233/.317/.365	83	2.0	.280	-0.5	2B -1, 1B 1	0.1

Comparables: *Chase Utley, Gordon Beckham, Asdrúbal Cabrera*

"There are four million different kinds of animals and plants in the world," says David Attenborough. "Four million different solutions to the problems of staying alive." In the ecosystem of Major League Baseball, some of these different plants and animals, and the solutions they represent, are dying at an alarming rate. Is the veteran, bench-bat utility infielder going extinct? One could ask Walker, who rebounded slightly in 2019 from an abysmal season in the Bronx, although the switch-hitting Pirates legend seems to have forgotten his power stroke even with the advent of the juiced ball. Walker surely ascribes to the Attenboroughian mantra, "even here, there is life"—as long as "life" means league-average hitting.

PITCHERS

Sandy Alcantara RHP Born: 09/07/95   Age: 24   Bats: R   Throws: R   Height: 6'4"   Weight: 170   Origin: International Free Agent, 2013

YEAR	TEAM	LVL	AGE	W	L	SV	G	GS	IP	H	HR	BB/9	K/9	K	GB%	BABIP	WHIP	ERA	DRA	WARP	MPH	FB%	WHF	CSP
2017	SFD	AA	21	7	5	0	25	22	125¹	125	13	3.9	7.6	106	46%	.305	1.43	4.31	5.14	0.0				
2017	SLN	MLB	21	0	0	0	8	0	8¹	9	2	6.5	10.8	10	26%	.333	1.80	4.32	6.58	-0.1	100.5	66.5	16.8	44.3
2018	JUP	A+	22	0	0	0	3	3	11¹	10	0	4.0	6.4	8	62%	.294	1.32	3.97	4.15	0.2				
2018	NWO	AAA	22	6	3	0	19	19	115²	107	10	3.0	6.8	88	50%	.283	1.25	3.89	3.80	2.3				
2018	MIA	MLB	22	2	3	0	6	6	34	25	3	6.1	7.9	30	50%	.250	1.41	3.44	5.57	-0.1	98.4	60	11.8	45.2
2019	MIA	MLB	23	6	14	0	32	32	197¹	179	23	3.7	6.9	151	46%	.271	1.32	3.88	4.56	2.6	97.9	57	11.7	48.7
2020	MIA	MLB	24	9	11	0	29	29	172	163	21	4.0	7.5	143	45%	.284	1.39	4.23	4.39	2.7	97.8	59.3	12.2	47.8

Comparables: *Jhoulys Chacín, Enyel De Los Santos, Zach Davies*

Alcantara is a poster child for the high spin rate fastball, and in his first full season in the majors, he sank and ran that devastating pitch to some actual success. He throws his two- and four-seam flavors with sink, and while they generate some swings and misses, the ball-in-play results are disparate. If Alcantara wished to be a ground-ball pitcher in the juiced ball era, he could rely on the two-seamer that keeps the ball on the ground 60 percent of the time—yet he only threw it a quarter of the time. It wasn't the only unusual thing about Alcantara's season, which played out as a litany of nearly-fun fun facts. He played in a generous pitcher's park, yet his ERA at home was three-quarters of a run lower on the road. He played in a season full of increasing reliever usage, yet nearly threw 200 innings and finished seventh in the National League in the bulk category. The only pitcher who threw more innings and gave up fewer homers than Alcantara won the Cy Young Award. Yes, the walks are still concerning but at least he closed out the season with a strikeout-to-walk rate of 3.9 in September after not clearing 2.3 in any other month. Baseball history is littered with so many "but his September" guys though Alcantara doesn't need to be one of the exceptions to be Miami's nominal ace in 2020 - unless he wants to ditch the word "nominal."

Austin Brice RHP Born: 06/19/92   Age: 28   Bats: R   Throws: R   Height: 6'4"   Weight: 235   Origin: Round 9, 2010 Draft (#287 overall)

YEAR	TEAM	LVL	AGE	W	L	SV	G	GS	IP	H	HR	BB/9	K/9	K	GB%	BABIP	WHIP	ERA	DRA	WARP	MPH	FB%	WHF	CSP
2017	LOU	AAA	25	1	2	1	15	0	21¹	23	0	3.8	8.9	21	46%	.365	1.50	3.80	5.20	0.0				
2017	CIN	MLB	25	0	0	0	22	0	32²	33	6	1.9	7.2	26	50%	.284	1.22	4.96	4.76	0.2	96.1	62.4	11.9	51.1
2018	LOU	AAA	26	3	1	1	17	0	23¹	18	2	2.7	9.3	24	36%	.296	1.07	2.31	3.88	0.3				
2018	CIN	MLB	26	2	3	0	33	0	37¹	39	9	3.1	7.7	32	53%	.286	1.39	5.79	5.75	-0.4	96.0	68.4	10	50.1
2019	MIA	MLB	27	1	0	0	36	0	44²	37	7	3.6	9.3	46	42%	.248	1.23	3.43	4.51	0.4	94.9	51	12.5	48.1
2020	MIA	MLB	28	1	1	0	11	0	12	12	2	3.2	8.8	11	43%	.296	1.36	4.79	5.01	0.1	94.9	58.9	11.7	49.8

Comparables: *Jake Barrett, Victor Alcántara, Parker Bridwell*

In 2019, Brice partially exorcised the home run demon that has haunted him throughout his young major league career. Considering the bizarre ball aerodynamics, that's cause for minor celebration. His four-seam fastball velocity dipped below 95 mph, but it remains a weapon against righties because of its heavy sink and he hides the ball well behind his very low three-quarters delivery. While he set a career high for innings in 2019, he still hit the IL multiple times with right forearm issues and even his attractive top-line stats weren't enough for him to be used in high-leverage situations. The all-time leader in strikeouts among pitchers born in Hong Kong has solidified a bullpen spot for now—quite possibly as a result of the all-time leader in strikeouts from Taiwan, Wei-Yin Chen, getting DFA'd.

Jeff Brigham RHP Born: 02/16/92 Age: 28 Bats: R Throws: R Height: 6'0" Weight: 200 Origin: Round 4, 2014 Draft (#129 overall)

YEAR	TEAM	LVL	AGE	W	L	SV	G	GS	IP	H	HR	BB/9	K/9	K	GB%	BABIP	WHIP	ERA	DRA	WARP	MPH	FB%	WHF	CSP
2017	JUP	A+	25	4	2	0	11	11	59	49	2	3.1	8.1	53	44%	.287	1.17	2.90	3.93	0.9				
2018	JAX	AA	26	4	1	0	7	7	38	27	1	2.1	9.7	41	41%	.299	0.95	1.18	2.84	1.1				
2018	NWO	AAA	26	5	2	0	9	9	52¹	53	7	2.2	8.3	48	30%	.315	1.26	3.44	4.90	0.4				
2018	MIA	MLB	26	0	4	0	4	4	16¹	16	2	7.2	6.6	12	20%	.292	1.78	6.06	7.19	-0.4	95.2	61.1	8.9	47.4
2019	NWO	AAA	27	0	1	2	17	0	24	9	0	3.0	11.2	30	43%	.184	0.71	1.50	1.00	1.2				
2019	MIA	MLB	27	3	2	1	32	0	38¹	36	8	3.3	9.2	39	34%	.283	1.30	4.46	4.73	0.3	98.1	51.5	12.3	49.8
2020	MIA	MLB	28	2	3	0	49	0	52	51	9	3.3	8.7	50	33%	.295	1.35	4.52	4.74	0.4	96.8	54.4	11.5	49

Comparables: Luis Santos, Brock Stewart, Ryan Tepera

Possessing an electric arm, Brigham followed a disappointing and abbreviated 2018 campaign with a promising turn in shorter bursts last season. Possessing an eclectic medical history involving that arm, Brigham found success simply by being on the bump for nearly 40 innings last season. He made the most of those innings by getting strikeouts and limiting walks at almost exactly league-average rates. Unfortunately for Brigham, he was exceptional in two categories: fly-ball rate and home runs per fly ball. No, not the good kind of exceptional.

★ ★ ★ *2020 Top 101 Prospect* **#97** ★ ★ ★

Edward Cabrera RHP Born: 04/13/98 Age: 22 Bats: R Throws: R Height: 6'4" Weight: 175 Origin: International Free Agent, 2015

YEAR	TEAM	LVL	AGE	W	L	SV	G	GS	IP	H	HR	BB/9	K/9	K	GB%	BABIP	WHIP	ERA	DRA	WARP	MPH	FB%	WHF	CSP
2017	BAT	A-	19	1	3	0	13	6	35²	42	1	2.0	8.1	32	55%	.350	1.40	5.30	6.17	-0.4				
2018	GRB	A	20	4	8	0	22	22	100¹	105	11	3.8	8.3	93	44%	.329	1.47	4.22	5.33	-0.2				
2019	JUP	A+	21	5	3	0	11	11	58	37	1	2.8	11.3	73	49%	.277	0.95	2.02	3.04	1.4				
2019	JAX	AA	21	4	1	0	8	8	38²	28	6	3.0	10.0	43	50%	.242	1.06	2.56	3.43	0.7				
2020	MIA	MLB	22	2	2	0	29	2	37	37	6	3.9	9.3	38	44%	.313	1.45	4.81	4.95	0.2				

Comparables: Jake Faria, Yordano Ventura, Gerrit Cole

Tall, slight and nasty. Young, projectable and breaking out before our eyes. Cabrera ripped through his initial Florida State League assignment en route to Jacksonville, where he was more than three years younger than league average and continued to strike out hitters with his mid- to upper-90s fastball and whiff-inducing slider. Making the leap to Double A as a 21-year-old pitcher is a significant step, and Cabrera made marked improvements by flashing an average changeup and suppressing the walks that clouded his 2018 performance. Concerns about the long-term viability of his changeup and a violent delivery are salient, and he's still a riskier prospect because of those concerns, but Cabrera showed he has at least mid-rotation potential. The 2020 season will not only be important in terms of in-game development, but in workload; even by today's standards, a true starter needs to be able to throw more than 100 innings per season.

Wei-Yin Chen LHP Born: 07/21/85 Age: 34 Bats: R Throws: L Height: 6'0" Weight: 200 Origin: International Free Agent, 2012

YEAR	TEAM	LVL	AGE	W	L	SV	G	GS	IP	H	HR	BB/9	K/9	K	GB%	BABIP	WHIP	ERA	DRA	WARP	MPH	FB%	WHF	CSP
2017	MIA	MLB	31	2	1	0	9	5	33	25	3	2.5	6.8	25	39%	.234	1.03	3.82	4.28	0.5	92.8	65	9.5	48.5
2018	JUP	A+	32	1	0	0	2	2	7²	5	0	1.2	12.9	11	39%	.278	0.78	1.17	2.42	0.3				
2018	MIA	MLB	32	6	12	0	26	26	133¹	131	19	3.2	7.5	111	38%	.285	1.34	4.79	4.88	0.7	93.4	55.9	9.2	49.1
2019	MIA	MLB	33	0	1	0	45	0	68¹	87	15	2.4	8.3	63	38%	.350	1.54	6.59	6.36	-0.7	93.5	50.9	10.2	52.2
2020	MIA	MLB	34	2	2	0	33	0	35	37	7	2.3	7.4	29	38%	.295	1.31	4.50	4.82	0.2	92.3	54.1	9.4	49.5

Comparables: Tommy Milone, Jason Vargas, Wade Miley

You have a spare screw rolling around in your junk drawer. You know you kept it for some reason—there was a time when it went to something, right? Maybe it fit into a wall mount, or a kitchen chair, or...aw hell, it was probably a spare from some IKEA furniture you put together 90 percent correctly. It doesn't seem to fit anything you remember. The Marlins' vestigial screw is Chen. At one point, he must have been a useful addition, but heading into the final year of a five-year deal he signed to decamp from the wretched Baltimore pitching staff, it's hard to remember what Chen's utility was. Year Four of the regrettable contract gifted the lefty a full season of relief work after working as a starter almost exclusively, and Chen adapted poorly. While his walk and strikeout rates were perfectly cromulent for a Marlins pitcher, Chen gave up a ton of hits, and most of those hits were loud. Even louder still was the slam of the metal doors behind him, as the Marlins unceremoniously dumped Chen and his $22 million in guaranteed money, preventing him from screwing them any further in Year Five.

Adam Conley LHP Born: 05/24/90 Age: 30 Bats: L Throws: L Height: 6'3" Weight: 200 Origin: Round 2, 2011 Draft (#72 overall)

YEAR	TEAM	LVL	AGE	W	L	SV	G	GS	IP	H	HR	BB/9	K/9	K	GB%	BABIP	WHIP	ERA	DRA	WARP	MPH	FB%	WHF	CSP
2017	NWO	AAA	27	3	3	0	12	12	62¹	69	7	3.6	5.9	41	39%	.310	1.51	5.49	5.79	-0.1				
2017	MIA	MLB	27	8	8	0	22	20	102²	114	19	3.7	6.3	72	42%	.295	1.52	6.14	6.64	-1.2	92.2	64.4	10.6	47.7
2018	NWO	AAA	28	2	4	0	8	8	40	45	6	3.2	5.6	25	50%	.300	1.48	5.18	5.15	0.2				
2018	MIA	MLB	28	3	4	3	52	0	50²	37	5	3.2	8.9	50	45%	.250	1.09	4.09	3.58	0.8	97.6	56.9	15.6	46.9
2019	MIA	MLB	29	2	11	2	60	0	60²	76	10	4.3	7.9	53	40%	.353	1.73	6.53	6.87	-1.0	97.7	61.7	11.5	51
2020	MIA	MLB	30	3	3	2	54	0	58	57	8	3.5	8.2	53	42%	.300	1.38	4.30	4.47	0.6	94.8	61.4	12	48.7

Comparables: Mike Kickham, César Ramos, Brian Flynn

The honeymoon is over for Conley, who had submitted a pristine 2018 season immediately following his conversion to relief. Maybe he woke up on Opening Day 2019 in a cold sweat, wondering what he's done with his life to become a reliever for the Marlins, because last season was a step backwards in almost every aspect for the lefty. The changeup that he rode to great success in 2018 turned into a clunker, as Conley surrendered an ISO almost 200 points higher with that pitch in 2019. His breaking ball veered toward the slurvy end of the spectrum more often, and even his improved fastball showed signs of velocity decline toward the end of the season.

Robert Dugger RHP Born: 07/03/95 Age: 24 Bats: R Throws: R Height: 6'2" Weight: 180 Origin: Round 18, 2016 Draft (#537 overall)

YEAR	TEAM	LVL	AGE	W	L	SV	G	GS	IP	H	HR	BB/9	K/9	K	GB%	BABIP	WHIP	ERA	DRA	WARP	MPH	FB%	WHF	CSP
2017	CLN	A	21	4	1	2	22	9	72	55	4	2.0	8.6	69	51%	.263	0.99	2.00	2.87	1.9				
2017	MOD	A+	21	2	5	0	9	9	45²	49	4	3.2	9.3	47	40%	.341	1.42	3.94	5.40	-0.1				
2018	JUP	A+	22	3	1	0	7	7	41¹	40	2	1.5	7.4	34	57%	.306	1.14	2.40	3.83	0.7				
2018	JAX	AA	22	7	6	0	18	18	109¹	100	13	3.0	8.8	107	36%	.296	1.24	3.79	4.42	1.2				
2019	JAX	AA	23	6	6	0	13	13	70²	57	6	2.7	9.3	73	48%	.276	1.10	3.31	3.93	0.9				
2019	NWO	AAA	23	2	4	0	10	10	53¹	74	12	2.9	8.3	49	38%	.376	1.71	7.59	8.50	-0.9				
2019	MIA	MLB	23	0	4	0	7	7	34¹	33	6	4.5	6.6	25	39%	.262	1.46	5.77	6.38	-0.2	92.0	59.2	10.2	43.5
2020	MIA	MLB	24	4	6	0	15	15	74	79	15	3.5	6.7	55	40%	.285	1.45	5.25	5.39	0.4	91.8	60.9	10.5	44.8

Comparables: Hunter Wood, Justin Dunn, Jorge Alcala

Getting a polished righty starter (Nick Neidert) who was close to the majors in return for Dee Gordon was a savvy move by the Marlins, but getting such a player and another pitcher who projects to be very similar was a pretty damn good bonus. That's exactly who Miami received in Dugger, who projects as a back-end starter with a firm, cross-fired fastball and a good slider. The coup for Dugger in 2019 was developing his change, which is now a serviceable third offering. That said, seven lackluster starts between August and September show why his lack of fastball command could be enough to condemn him to relief. Still, the stuff is there, and he's only 24. Add him to the list of potential role-5 arms in the Marlins' stable.

Jarlin García LHP Born: 01/18/93 Age: 27 Bats: L Throws: L Height: 6'3" Weight: 215 Origin: International Free Agent, 2010

YEAR	TEAM	LVL	AGE	W	L	SV	G	GS	IP	H	HR	BB/9	K/9	K	GB%	BABIP	WHIP	ERA	DRA	WARP	MPH	FB%	WHF	CSP
2017	MIA	MLB	24	1	2	0	68	0	53¹	47	6	2.9	7.1	42	41%	.263	1.20	4.72	4.42	0.4	96.1	49.8	12.1	47.8
2018	NWO	AAA	25	2	2	0	10	9	48²	57	5	2.6	6.1	33	40%	.323	1.46	4.81	5.41	0.1				
2018	MIA	MLB	25	3	3	0	29	7	66	59	16	3.8	5.5	40	44%	.222	1.32	4.91	5.51	-0.3	94.2	52.5	8.4	49.3
2019	NWO	AAA	26	2	0	0	7	0	9¹	6	1	3.9	10.6	11	38%	.250	1.07	1.93	3.35	0.3				
2019	MIA	MLB	26	4	2	0	53	0	50²	40	4	2.8	6.9	39	48%	.248	1.11	3.02	3.92	0.8	95.1	39.8	9.8	51.8
2020	MIA	MLB	27	3	3	8	54	0	58	59	10	3.0	7.0	45	44%	.287	1.36	4.52	4.77	0.4	94.5	47.9	10	50.6

Comparables: Robbie Ross Jr., T.J. McFarland, Luis Cessa

García righted the ship in 2019 following an acutely disappointing sophomore effort, gaining velocity throughout the year and limiting the walks and homers that previously plagued him so. His unusually heavy four-seamer still didn't miss many bats, but García's ground-ball-oriented arsenal played up in the age of the gopher ball. Yet it was García's commitment to altering his pitch mix between righties and lefties combined with improved movement on both his fastball and slider that propelled him into high-leverage situations. Against righties, he deployed a much more democratic approach across all counts; against lefties, he almost stopped throwing his changeup altogether and instead went heavy on the slider. It's difficult to be a lefty reliever who relies on contact more than strikeouts, but García has found a path to success for now.

Braxton Garrett LHP Born: 08/05/97 Age: 22 Bats: L Throws: L Height: 6'3" Weight: 190 Origin: Round 1, 2016 Draft (#7 overall)

YEAR	TEAM	LVL	AGE	W	L	SV	G	GS	IP	H	HR	BB/9	K/9	K	GB%	BABIP	WHIP	ERA	DRA	WARP	MPH	FB%	WHF	CSP
2017	GRB	A	19	1	0	0	4	4	15¹	13	3	3.5	9.4	16	49%	.250	1.24	2.93	4.86	0.1				
2019	JUP	A+	21	6	6	0	20	20	105	92	13	3.2	10.1	118	54%	.294	1.23	3.34	4.85	0.2				
2020	MIA	MLB	22	2	2	0	33	0	35	36	6	4.1	8.5	33	42%	.300	1.48	4.97	5.15	0.1				

Comparables: Sal Romano, Kyle Ryan, Victor Arano

He's finally healthy! Garrett not only returned from Tommy John surgery in 2019 after almost two full years away from game action—he tossed over 100 innings, no small feat for the former first-rounder. The fastball-curveball combo that was fawned over in his amateur days mowed down High-A hitters, and he kept the ball down showing his mettle as a ground-ball pitcher. Asking any pitcher, even one as talented as Garrett, to work on regaining some fastball velocity and command in the wake of his extended absence while making the leap to the high minors is a tall order. A strong showing in the first half of the year would accelerate his timeline to Miami, but simply staying on the mound for the full season would be a win for the organization that has seen every Braxton in major-league history pass through its dimly-lit corridors.

Jorge Guzman   RHP   Born: 01/28/96   Age: 24   Bats: R   Throws: R   Height: 6'2"   Weight: 182   Origin: International Free Agent, 2014

YEAR	TEAM	LVL	AGE	W	L	SV	G	GS	IP	H	HR	BB/9	K/9	K	GB%	BABIP	WHIP	ERA	DRA	WARP	MPH	FB%	WHF	CSP
2017	STA	A-	21	5	3	0	13	13	66²	51	4	2.4	11.9	88	55%	.311	1.03	2.30	3.42	1.4				
2018	JUP	A+	22	0	9	0	21	21	96	84	7	6.0	9.5	101	40%	.303	1.54	4.03	5.77	-0.5				
2019	JAX	AA	23	7	11	0	25	24	138²	96	13	4.6	8.2	127	34%	.241	1.20	3.50	4.16	1.3				
2020	MIA	MLB	24	2	2	0	33	0	35	36	5	3.9	7.8	30	35%	.298	1.46	4.77	4.95	0.2				

Comparables: Matt Hall, Hansel Robles, André Rienzo

Maybe it was the weight of expectations sitting on him that led to Guzmán's disappointing 2018 season. "We got him for Stanton and he does this???," they cried. Those burdens seemed to have lifted for 2019; the young righty can still touch triple digits, and he improved his change and slider while getting stretched out at Double A last season. For Guzmán, though, enough concerns remain that he won't be making any global top prospect lists again soon. The free passes that doomed his 2018 campaign didn't entirely disappear, as he still posted a walk rate north of 12 percent. No matter how good the raw stuff is, the path to a major-league starting role is through the strike zone. As it is, the fireballer looks destined to be a three-pitch, late-inning reliever—a good outcome for a pitching prospect, but not what you want from the non-monetary headliner of the trade that sent the best power hitter in franchise history packing.

Elieser Hernandez   RHP   Born: 05/03/95   Age: 25   Bats: R   Throws: R   Height: 6'0"   Weight: 210   Origin: International Free Agent, 2011

YEAR	TEAM	LVL	AGE	W	L	SV	G	GS	IP	H	HR	BB/9	K/9	K	GB%	BABIP	WHIP	ERA	DRA	WARP	MPH	FB%	WHF	CSP
2017	AST	RK	22	1	0	0	3	2	10	6	0	0.9	12.6	14	62%	.286	0.70	1.80	0.95	0.5				
2017	BCA	A+	22	4	5	0	15	11	63¹	55	6	3.0	10.5	74	40%	.310	1.20	3.98	4.33	0.6				
2018	JUP	A+	23	0	1	0	2	2	6	9	2	6.0	7.5	5	68%	.350	2.17	6.00	7.03	-0.1				
2018	JAX	AA	23	0	0	0	2	2	9	7	3	4.0	10.0	10	23%	.211	1.22	4.00	4.76	0.1				
2018	MIA	MLB	23	2	7	0	32	6	65²	68	11	3.7	6.2	45	30%	.286	1.45	5.21	6.00	-0.7	93.2	62.1	9.3	49.7
2019	NWO	AAA	24	3	1	0	9	9	48	35	0	2.6	12.9	69	34%	.315	1.02	1.12	1.45	2.4				
2019	MIA	MLB	24	3	5	0	21	15	82¹	76	20	2.8	9.3	85	36%	.263	1.24	5.03	4.78	0.9	93.1	55.3	12.1	48.9
2020	MIA	MLB	25	3	4	0	45	6	69	70	14	3.4	8.7	67	33%	.289	1.38	4.96	5.13	0.4	92.9	59.3	11.3	50.4

Comparables: Wes Parsons, Dan Straily, Justin Dunn

The Marlins' most galaxy-brain move of the season was to stick Hernández—a poor reliever who they plucked in the Rule 5 draft and then rushed to the majors in 2018—into the rotation for 15 (!!!) starts last season. It worked about as well as you'd expect. A true millennial, Hernández gave out souvenirs as if they were participation trophies, which sapped any value from the solid walk and strikeout rates he managed. Maybe Marlins management has been afflicted with a terminally Panglossian mindset regarding Hernández...or maybe their options for the rotation have been so poor that Hernández actually did represent an improvement. But what's really the difference between self-inflicted lack of depth and a swift kick in the pants from the universe as far as pitching is concerned?

Pablo López   RHP   Born: 03/07/96   Age: 24   Bats: L   Throws: R   Height: 6'3"   Weight: 200   Origin: International Free Agent, 2012

YEAR	TEAM	LVL	AGE	W	L	SV	G	GS	IP	H	HR	BB/9	K/9	K	GB%	BABIP	WHIP	ERA	DRA	WARP	MPH	FB%	WHF	CSP
2017	MOD	A+	21	5	8	0	19	18	100	113	6	1.2	8.0	89	51%	.341	1.26	5.04	4.68	0.6				
2017	JUP	A+	21	0	3	0	8	6	45¹	42	0	1.4	6.4	32	59%	.307	1.08	2.18	4.38	0.4				
2018	JAX	AA	22	1	2	0	8	8	43²	30	3	1.6	10.5	51	42%	.245	0.87	0.62	2.58	1.4				
2018	NWO	AAA	22	1	1	0	4	4	18²	16	3	1.9	7.2	15	47%	.236	1.07	3.38	3.18	0.5				
2018	MIA	MLB	22	2	4	0	10	10	58²	56	8	2.8	7.1	46	50%	.281	1.26	4.14	4.58	0.5	95.1	60.4	11.7	46.5
2019	NWO	AAA	23	0	0	0	2	2	9¹	10	0	2.9	9.6	10	62%	.385	1.39	1.93	4.47	0.2				
2019	MIA	MLB	23	5	8	0	21	21	111¹	111	15	2.2	7.7	95	49%	.299	1.24	5.09	4.19	1.9	95.9	58.6	11.5	48.8
2020	MIA	MLB	24	7	8	0	24	24	129	123	17	2.4	7.5	107	48%	.285	1.22	3.71	4.03	2.6	95.5	60.9	11.9	49.2

Comparables: Jake Odorizzi, Reynaldo López, Kevin Gausman

Recently, it seems like every year the Marlins churn out a young, mid-rotation starter. This year's model was López, who just might be more than the kind of pitcher who gets lip service because he stands out in the bleak landscape of Marlins hurlers. The ERA belies a fine DRA, and López was living in paradise at home, where hitters managed a meager .638 OPS against him. As for the fastball, he can pump it up to 96 and it goes hand in hand with a decent change and curve to produce a bunch of grounders. López is a mature pitcher who feels comfortable using all his offerings versus both lefties and righties, even though he's a ripe 24 years old and was in High-A as recently as 2017. Although he missed two months in the middle of 2019 due to a right shoulder strain, López has the beat on a rotation spot for 2020 as the Marlins continue to take no action in the free agent market.

Brian Moran   LHP   Born: 09/30/88   Age: 31   Bats: L   Throws: L   Height: 6'4"   Weight: 230   Origin: Round 7, 2009 Draft (#203 overall)

YEAR	TEAM	LVL	AGE	W	L	SV	G	GS	IP	H	HR	BB/9	K/9	K	GB%	BABIP	WHIP	ERA	DRA	WARP	MPH	FB%	WHF	CSP
2017	TUL	AA	28	0	1	1	19	0	19	12	1	1.4	12.8	27	38%	.282	0.79	1.89	2.05	0.6				
2018	TUL	AA	29	1	1	3	22	0	26²	30	3	3.4	11.5	34	47%	.386	1.50	3.71	4.71	0.1				
2018	HFD	AA	29	0	1	0	19	0	22¹	15	1	2.8	12.9	32	44%	.286	0.99	2.42	2.38	0.7				
2018	OKL	AAA	29	1	1	0	9	0	11²	16	0	3.9	7.7	10	42%	.390	1.80	6.17	6.31	-0.2				
2019	NWO	AAA	30	2	3	0	43	1	60	45	6	3.9	11.6	77	49%	.289	1.18	3.15	2.65	2.1				
2019	MIA	MLB	30	1	0	0	10	0	6¹	6	1	2.8	14.2	10	47%	.357	1.26	4.26	3.82	0.1	86.3	56.3	14.3	48.7
2020	MIA	MLB	31	1	1	0	11	0	12	10	3	3.4	7.9	10	41%	.248	1.28	4.62	4.97	0.1	85.5	55.9	14.2	48.5

Comparables: Bobby LaFromboise, Buddy Baumann, Pat Venditte

After ten years cutting his (now long) teeth in the minors, Moran debuted with the Marlins and immediately had to face his brother, the bearded Pirate Colin Moran, whom he promptly struck out. He's been a Rule 5 pick, a Tommy John recipient, a Mariner. He's been everywhere, man: Clinton, West Tenn, High Desert, Oklahoma / Jackson, Peoria, Pulaski and Tacoma / Bakersfield, Gwinnett, Caguas, Bridgeport / Hartford, Tulsa, New Orleans. The trials of this Sisyphean, down-and-out lefty pluck those country-western, literary, Crash Davis strings. Moran's hardships are those of many others, compounded but spread over many years, and his strong 2019 is evidence enough that baseball's chaos and ruthlessness can still accidentally produce some poetic justice.

Nick Neidert RHP Born: 11/20/96 Age: 23 Bats: R Throws: R Height: 6'1" Weight: 202 Origin: Round 2, 2015 Draft (#60 overall)

YEAR	TEAM	LVL	AGE	W	L	SV	G	GS	IP	H	HR	BB/9	K/9	K	GB%	BABIP	WHIP	ERA	DRA	WARP	MPH	FB%	WHF	CSP
2017	MOD	A+	20	10	3	0	19	19	104¹	95	7	1.5	9.4	109	43%	.318	1.07	2.76	3.40	2.3				
2017	ARK	AA	20	1	3	0	6	6	23¹	33	4	1.9	5.0	13	47%	.341	1.63	6.56	6.40	-0.3				
2018	JAX	AA	21	12	7	0	26	26	152²	142	17	1.8	9.1	154	47%	.309	1.13	3.24	4.21	2.0				
2019	JUP	A+	22	0	1	0	2	2	9¹	10	1	3.9	5.8	6	29%	.300	1.50	4.82	5.38	0.0				
2019	NWO	AAA	22	3	4	0	9	9	41	45	4	4.8	8.1	37	25%	.336	1.63	5.05	5.70	0.4				
2020	MIA	MLB	23	3	3	0	28	6	52	54	8	3.4	7.3	42	36%	.292	1.40	4.63	4.89	0.4				

Comparables: Zach Lee, Luis Ortiz, Ronald Herrera

To reiterate that a major leaguer can be successful with the type of profile Neidert has is tired and rote: hang up a photo of Kyle Hendricks and call it a day. But Neidert offers a few wrinkles to the archetype, enough to both intrigue and befuddle. His changeup is a bit behind his other pitches in terms of its development, but in Neidert's recent AFL stint, it flashed plus. His fastball, despite sitting in the 89-91 band, has good life as Neidert can cut and run it on both sides of the plate. His breaking balls are what really shine, though, and he uses both a curve and a slider as out pitches—the former in particular can be dropped in for a strike or buried to get a hitter to chase. He'll be a candidate for the Marlins rotation as soon as 2020, but the separator between "fifth starter" and "mid-rotation stalwart" is the development of the change as more than a show-me pitch.

★ ★ ★ *2020 Top 101 Prospect* **#27** ★ ★ ★

Sixto Sanchez RHP Born: 07/29/98 Age: 21 Bats: R Throws: R Height: 6'0" Weight: 185 Origin: International Free Agent, 2015

YEAR	TEAM	LVL	AGE	W	L	SV	G	GS	IP	H	HR	BB/9	K/9	K	GB%	BABIP	WHIP	ERA	DRA	WARP	MPH	FB%	WHF	CSP
2017	LWD	A	18	5	3	0	13	13	67¹	46	1	1.2	8.6	64	49%	.251	0.82	2.41	2.72	2.0				
2017	CLR	A+	18	0	4	0	5	5	27²	27	1	2.9	6.5	20	42%	.295	1.30	4.55	4.83	0.1				
2018	CLR	A+	19	4	3	0	8	8	46²	39	1	2.1	8.7	45	52%	.295	1.07	2.51	3.48	1.0				
2019	JUP	A+	20	0	2	0	2	2	11	14	1	1.6	4.9	6	60%	.351	1.45	4.91	5.73	-0.1				
2019	JAX	AA	20	8	4	0	18	18	103	87	5	1.7	8.5	97	49%	.286	1.03	2.53	4.06	1.1				
2020	MIA	MLB	21	2	3	0	17	6	44	42	5	3.1	7.3	36	45%	.285	1.29	3.72	4.05	0.8				

Comparables: David Holmberg, Deolis Guerra, Mike Soroka

Following a 2018 mostly lost due to elbow inflammation and a Fall League stint cut short due to collarbone discomfort, Sánchez needed a healthy, productive 2019 to convince those who aren't true believers that he can remain in a starting rotation. Sánchez responded by pumping 101 at his season debut in High-A before tossing another hundred-plus innings between there and Double-A. The stuff speaks for itself, as he continues to pair his plus-plus fastball with several good secondary pitches: His bowling ball changeup is a weapon against both righties and lefties. His slight frame may still limit his ability to be a workhorse in any rotation, but Sánchez is likely to make his major league debut as a starter in the back half of 2020. And as pitcher usage continues to mutate, his durability might not cap his no. 2 potential as much as it would have in years past.

Caleb Smith LHP Born: 07/28/91 Age: 28 Bats: R Throws: L Height: 6'2" Weight: 205 Origin: Round 14, 2013 Draft (#434 overall)

YEAR	TEAM	LVL	AGE	W	L	SV	G	GS	IP	H	HR	BB/9	K/9	K	GB%	BABIP	WHIP	ERA	DRA	WARP	MPH	FB%	WHF	CSP
2017	SWB	AAA	25	9	1	0	18	17	98	75	7	2.6	8.9	97	42%	.264	1.05	2.39	2.68	3.2				
2017	NYA	MLB	25	0	1	0	9	2	18²	21	4	4.8	8.7	18	28%	.315	1.66	7.71	4.92	0.1	95.5	50.3	14.4	42.2
2018	MIA	MLB	26	5	6	0	16	16	77¹	63	10	3.8	10.2	88	31%	.276	1.24	4.19	4.05	1.1	94.8	59.1	13.3	48.7
2019	JAX	AA	27	0	0	0	2	2	9¹	7	4	1.9	18.3	19	25%	.250	0.96	5.79	2.83	0.2				
2019	MIA	MLB	27	10	11	0	28	28	153¹	128	33	3.5	9.9	168	28%	.251	1.23	4.52	4.55	2.0	93.9	53.7	13.8	47.3
2020	MIA	MLB	28	9	10	0	28	28	154	132	29	3.5	9.7	167	29%	.267	1.24	3.93	4.26	2.7	93.7	55.4	13.8	46.8

Comparables: Rob Zastryzny, Austin Voth, Austin Brice

The most intriguing pitcher in the Marlins rotation entering last season, Smith unleashed his slider on the National League and struck out 26 percent of hitters, four points above the major-league average for starters. That singular development is significant, but within the context of a real velocity drop on his fastball, it's rather surprising. The biggest impact from a results standpoint, as his top-line stats remained relatively similar to his 2018 season, was that Smith turned into a pitcher with a heavy platoon split. Out of the 33 homers he gave up last year, only four of them came against left-handed batters. A fly-ball pitcher in Marlins Park is generally a good thing though, even with the fences coming in, and Smith will once again be a key contributor in a still-developing Marlins rotation.

Ryne Stanek RHP Born: 07/26/91 Age: 28 Bats: R Throws: R Height: 6'4" Weight: 225 Origin: Round 1, 2013 Draft (#29 overall)

YEAR	TEAM	LVL	AGE	W	L	SV	G	GS	IP	H	HR	BB/9	K/9	K	GB%	BABIP	WHIP	ERA	DRA	WARP	MPH	FB%	WHF	CSP
2017	DUR	AAA	25	3	0	8	37	0	44²	26	0	3.2	12.1	60	40%	.268	0.94	1.21	2.33	1.5				
2017	TBA	MLB	25	0	0	0	21	0	20	26	6	5.4	13.1	29	33%	.417	1.90	5.85	2.67	0.6	100.3	67.1	16.3	44.4
2018	DUR	AAA	26	0	1	2	10	0	9²	5	1	5.6	15.8	17	59%	.250	1.14	1.86	2.65	0.3				
2018	TBA	MLB	26	2	3	0	59	29	66¹	45	8	3.7	11.0	81	32%	.253	1.09	2.98	3.34	1.4	99.9	60.1	16.9	44.1
2019	TBA	MLB	27	0	2	0	41	27	55²	44	7	3.2	9.9	61	33%	.264	1.15	3.40	4.92	0.4	99.5	57.4	16.7	42.4
2019	MIA	MLB	27	0	2	1	22	0	21¹	17	4	8.0	11.8	28	31%	.271	1.69	5.48	4.19	0.3	98.9	52	16.3	38.9
2020	MIA	MLB	28	3	3	13	65	0	69	58	10	4.6	11.5	88	34%	.296	1.35	3.89	4.12	1.0	99.0	58.8	16.8	43.3

Comparables: Wander Suero, Kevin McGowan, Tobi Stoner

A year after running him out as the poster child of the Opener movement, the Rays sent Stanek from Florida's Gulf Coast to its Atlantic Coast in a deal that also netted Miami top prospect Jesús Sánchez. Once he arrived in Miami, Stanek pitched exclusively in a legacy reliever role despite his splits: for his career, his 2.71 ERA when starting a game is more than two runs lower than when he enters a game in relief. On top of that, his walk rate after coming over to the senior circuit ballooned well beyond anything he'd posted in a reasonable pro sample due to a severe drop in fastball command. His slider and splitter have grown into solid out pitches, and his fastball is still top-flight when he controls it. That enough will keep Stanek in the mix for high-leverage spots in 2020 and his fly-ball tendencies, while not ideal in this era, make for a good fit in Marlins Park.

Drew Steckenrider RHP Born: 01/10/91 Age: 29 Bats: R Throws: R Height: 6'5" Weight: 215 Origin: Round 8, 2012 Draft (#257 overall)

YEAR	TEAM	LVL	AGE	W	L	SV	G	GS	IP	H	HR	BB/9	K/9	K	GB%	BABIP	WHIP	ERA	DRA	WARP	MPH	FB%	WHF	CSP
2017	NWO	AAA	26	0	1	5	26	0	33¹	18	3	2.2	11.9	44	43%	.217	0.78	1.62	1.26	1.5				
2017	MIA	MLB	26	1	1	1	37	0	34²	30	4	4.7	14.0	54	43%	.347	1.38	2.34	3.70	0.6	97.3	77.8	14.8	49.9
2018	MIA	MLB	27	4	4	5	71	0	64²	55	7	3.8	10.3	74	34%	.296	1.27	3.90	4.44	0.4	96.8	76.4	12.2	50.8
2019	MIA	MLB	28	0	2	0	15	0	14¹	9	6	3.1	8.8	14	32%	.094	0.98	6.28	5.93	-0.1	96.4	62	9.3	48.3
2020	MIA	MLB	29	2	2	0	44	0	46	44	8	3.6	9.6	49	35%	.292	1.35	4.50	4.75	0.3	96.2	74.6	12.5	49.5

Comparables: Brad Brach, Cody Carroll, Ryne Stanek

The dreaded "flexor strain" comes for us all, as long as "us all" is comprised of promising major league hurlers. For Steckenrider, the ghost of TINSTAAPP past visited his arm after only a handful of poor innings in 2019, and early optimism morphed into season-ending severity by August. For the Marlins, this means little; they still retain their precious team control for a few more seasons and Steckenrider should be in the mix for the back end of their bullpen. Barring catastrophe (i.e. Tommy John), his fastball-heavy approach should still play well in short bursts.

José Ureña RHP Born: 09/12/91 Age: 28 Bats: R Throws: R Height: 6'2" Weight: 200 Origin: International Free Agent, 2008

YEAR	TEAM	LVL	AGE	W	L	SV	G	GS	IP	H	HR	BB/9	K/9	K	GB%	BABIP	WHIP	ERA	DRA	WARP	MPH	FB%	WHF	CSP
2017	MIA	MLB	25	14	7	0	34	28	169²	152	26	3.4	6.0	113	44%	.249	1.27	3.82	5.25	0.5	97.6	56.2	9.1	45.2
2018	MIA	MLB	26	9	12	0	31	31	174	155	19	2.6	6.7	130	51%	.272	1.18	3.98	4.01	2.6	97.9	58.8	9.7	46.2
2019	MIA	MLB	27	4	10	3	24	13	84²	99	13	2.8	6.6	62	50%	.323	1.48	5.21	5.73	0.0	97.9	63.1	10.4	44.8
2020	MIA	MLB	28	7	10	10	58	19	141	157	20	3.0	7.0	111	50%	.314	1.45	4.89	4.99	1.1	97.2	59.4	9.7	45.6

Comparables: Zack Britton, Joe Kelly, Wade Davis

The list of excellent starting pitchers to wear a Marlins uniform is short. That list doesn't include Ureña, and after a disappointing, injury-addled 2019, Pat Rapp's mantle as the sixth-best starter in franchise history is safe. Ureña simply couldn't build on his solid 2018, when he rode a mid-90s fastball to a high ground-ball rate even as he failed to find any sort of strikeout pitch in his arsenal. While Ureña started the season by surrendering 14 runs in his first three starts, he righted the ship until a herniated disc in June relegated him to the IL for nearly three months, stalling any progress. When he returned, he slotted in as the Marlins' closer; and while his velocity ticked up, his performance declined as he allowed multiple runs in four of his September relief appearances. The righty's heater still has zip, and Ureña is likely to get another shot as a starter, but Don Mattingly has to decide if a 16 percent career strikeout rate belongs in even Miami's rotation. At some point, a pitching development machine needs to churn out one or two stars. The Marlins appear to have bought an aftermarket Joe Kelly mold.

Jordan Yamamoto RHP Born: 05/11/96 Age: 24 Bats: R Throws: R Height: 6'0" Weight: 185 Origin: Round 12, 2014 Draft (#356 overall)

YEAR	TEAM	LVL	AGE	W	L	SV	G	GS	IP	H	HR	BB/9	K/9	K	GB%	BABIP	WHIP	ERA	DRA	WARP	MPH	FB%	WHF	CSP
2017	CAR	A+	21	9	4	1	22	18	111	91	8	2.4	9.2	113	40%	.286	1.09	2.51	3.36	2.4				
2018	MRL	RK	22	1	0	0	3	3	11	5	1	1.6	12.3	15	64%	.190	0.64	2.45	0.90	0.6				
2018	JUP	A+	22	4	1	0	7	7	40²	26	0	1.8	10.4	47	44%	.268	0.84	1.55	2.46	1.4				
2018	JAX	AA	22	1	0	0	3	3	17	12	1	2.1	12.2	23	45%	.282	0.94	2.12	2.99	0.5				
2019	JAX	AA	23	3	5	0	12	12	65¹	53	7	3.4	8.8	64	47%	.275	1.19	3.58	4.53	0.3				
2019	MIA	MLB	23	4	5	0	15	15	78²	54	11	4.1	9.4	82	37%	.225	1.14	4.46	3.56	1.9	93.8	50.2	10.1	46.9
2020	MIA	MLB	24	7	9	0	26	26	135	123	20	3.7	8.3	124	39%	.276	1.32	4.10	4.36	2.2	93.6	51.7	10.5	48.3

Comparables: Hunter Wood, Yency Almonte, Pablo López

Yamamoto confused major league hitters well enough in his 2019 debut that they couldn't muster a run through 15 innings against the Hawaiian-born pitcher. Acquired from Milwaukee in the Christian Yelich trade, Yamamoto slotted into Miami's rotation shortly after José Ureña hit the IL in early June, and he shone despite his lack of flash—his DRA was tops among all Marlins starters by over half a run. Though he ran into some rough patches in July and August, he returned in September from an ominous forearm strain to finish a strong rookie campaign. He's a bit unusually built for a pitcher, with short legs and a long torso, and the margin for error with his control is slim, but Yamamoto's strong slider and workmanlike fastball may have already punched his ticket to fourth starterdom.

LINEOUTS

Hitters

HITTER	POS	TEAM	LVL	AGE	PA	R	2B	3B	HR	RBI	BB	K	SB	CS	AVG/OBP/SLG	DRC+	VORP	BABIP	BRR	FRAA	WARP
Wilkin Castillo	C	NWO	AAA	35	214	23	9	2	6	24	16	30	5	1	.250/.310/.408	78	6.4	.269	2.1	C(52): 8.0	1.4
	C	MIA	MLB	35	7	0	1	0	0	2	0	3	0	0	.143/.143/.286	84	0.2	.250	0.0	C(2): 0.2	0.0
Austin Dean	LF	MIA	MLB	25	189	17	14	0	6	21	9	47	0	2	.225/.261/.404	77	-0.6	.270	1.0	LF(44): -2.8, 1B(5): -0.1	-0.2
	LF	NWO	AAA	25	282	48	19	1	18	57	28	52	4	3	.337/.401/.635	148	32.8	.364	2.2	1B(26): 0.7, LF(22): 2.0	2.6
Lewin Diaz	1B	JAX	AA	22	129	16	6	0	8	14	11	28	0	1	.200/.279/.461	122	-0.5	.188	-0.2	1B(29): -2.2	0.5
	1B	FTM	A+	22	234	34	11	1	13	36	14	40	0	0	.290/.333/.533	157	15.5	.297	-1.3	1B(52): 4.9	2.0
	1B	PEN	AA	22	138	12	16	1	6	26	8	23	0	0	.302/.341/.587	130	10.2	.320	-0.6	1B(31): -0.2	0.9
Isaac Galloway	OF	MIA	MLB	29	54	6	1	0	0	1	0	17	2	0	.167/.167/.185	52	-1.5	.243	0.2	CF(13): 0.2, LF(4): -0.6	-0.1
	OF	NWO	AAA	29	108	19	5	0	7	16	2	41	3	1	.223/.252/.476	64	1.7	.291	1.7	LF(18): 1.4, CF(7): 0.6	0.2
Tyler Heineman	C	NWO	AAA	28	182	26	12	2	10	25	12	21	4	0	.341/.397/.622	131	21.6	.346	-1.5	C(44): 2.7, 1B(3): 0.1	2.0
	C	MIA	MLB	28	12	1	1	0	0	4	0	4	0	0	.273/.273/.636	82	0.4	.333	0.0	C(2): -0.1	0.0
	C	RNO	AAA	28	91	16	5	1	3	13	9	14	0	0	.325/.407/.525	126	7.0	.365	-0.3	C(21): 6.6	1.9
Matt Kemp	DH	CIN	MLB	34	62	4	2	0	1	5	1	19	0	0	.200/.210/.283	73	-0.4	.268	0.0	LF(17): -1.6	-0.2
	DH	SYR	AAA	34	36	3	0	0	1	3	2	7	0	0	.235/.278/.324	72	-3.1	.269	-0.5	LF(3): -0.7	-0.2
Deven Marrero	3B	NWO	AAA	28	431	55	16	2	15	42	43	100	10	1	.245/.322/.415	81	5.3	.294	-1.4	SS(49): 4.3, 3B(43): 4.1	1.2
	3B	MIA	MLB	28	5	0	0	0	0	0	0	3	0	0	.000/.000/.000	62	0.0	.000	0.0	SS(2): -0.1, 3B(1): 0.0	0.0
Victor Mesa Jr.	OF	MRL	Rk	17	207	39	9	4	1	24	24	29	7	4	.284/.366/.398	116	16.9	.327	2.1	CF(39): 1.2, RF(4): -0.2	1.2
Nasim Nunez	MI	MRL	Rk	18	214	37	5	1	0	12	34	43	28	2	.211/.340/.251	88	13.3	.276	3.2	SS(48): 1.7	1.2
Peter O'Brien	RF	MIA	MLB	28	47	2	1	0	1	4	4	19	1	0	.167/.255/.262	55	-1.7	.273	-0.3	RF(10): -1.4, LF(4): -0.6	-0.4
	RF	NWO	AAA	28	291	41	8	0	17	45	36	107	0	1	.220/.316/.451	90	0.5	.298	-0.1	1B(45): -4.1, RF(15): 1.5	0.0
César Puello	OF	LAA	MLB	28	50	6	3	0	3	12	3	8	0	0	.390/.500/.683	118	2.5	.433	0.3		0.3
	OF	SLC	AAA	28	167	25	7	0	7	27	22	37	2	1	.296/.431/.504	112	11.0	.363	-3.1	CF(15): -1.5, RF(15): -0.8	0.2
	OF	MIA	MLB	28	97	8	2	0	1	6	7	30	0	0	.179/.281/.238	63	-1.5	.264	0.3	CF(20): 5.0, RF(10): 0.1	0.4
JT Riddle	SS	MIA	MLB	27	139	15	6	0	6	12	5	42	0	0	.189/.230/.371	69	-0.2	.226	-1.6	CF(31): 2.8, SS(12): -1.5	0.0
	SS	NWO	AAA	27	131	22	10	1	4	19	6	20	3	0	.240/.277/.438	64	2.8	.253	1.0	SS(23): 3.4, CF(8): 2.4	0.6
Yadiel Rivera	3B	NWO	AAA	27	312	38	11	1	14	46	6	81	15	6	.293/.310/.477	92	9.1	.357	0.0	SS(35): 3.2, 3B(24): 0.6	1.2
	3B	MIA	MLB	27	66	8	2	0	0	3	6	20	2	0	.183/.258/.217	59	-1.2	.275	0.9	SS(8): -0.5, 3B(8): -0.3	0.0
Magneuris Sierra	CF	MIA	MLB	23	42	5	1	1	0	1	2	7	3	3	.350/.381/.425	82	0.5	.424	-0.7	CF(9): 3.3, RF(5): 0.4	0.3
	CF	JAX	AA	23	197	21	8	2	1	7	13	32	7	1	.282/.337/.365	110	9.1	.338	1.8	CF(21): 0.7, RF(15): 4.2	1.6
	CF	NWO	AAA	23	352	56	11	7	6	21	15	58	26	10	.271/.304/.399	62	-1.7	.313	3.7	CF(32): -0.7, RF(23): 1.5	-0.3
Yangervis Solarte	3B	NWO	AAA	31	55	7	2	1	1	9	3	7	0	0	.314/.345/.451	75	-0.8	.341	-0.7	1B(6): -0.3, 3B(5): 0.2	-0.1
	3B	SFN	MLB	31	78	9	5	0	1	7	4	16	0	0	.205/.247/.315	65	-0.9	.250	0.1	2B(10): -0.6, LF(9): 0.4	-0.1
Chad Wallach	C	MIA	MLB	27	54	4	3	0	1	3	6	12	0	0	.250/.333/.375	96	2.5	.314	-0.1	C(14): -0.7	0.2

After swearing off caffeine for a decade, **Wilkin Castillo** snagged another cup o' coffee after putting in yeoman's work for more than a half-dozen organizations and he jolted a go-ahead double in his first at-bat back for good measure. ⊕ Stare long enough at a photo of **Austin Dean** and you may start thinking he's Chris Taylor. Stare long enough at his stat line and you'll quickly be dispelled of that notion. ⊕ Three teams across two levels cashed in on **Lewin Díaz**'s materialized power in 2019, but he'll have to keep those slugging numbers afloat if he's to become a big league first sacker instead of a Quad-A disappointment. ⊕ In a story as cool as the word "rax," **Isaac Galloway** reached the majors in 2018 after more than a decade spent in the minors. Unfortunately, it looks like Galloway's big-league career will also have length in common with the word "rax." That's a verb meaning "to stretch oneself, as after sleeping," folks. Diction is important. ⊕ The defense is good and the bat has materialized enough in the minors for former UCLA catcher **Tyler Heineman**, who came over in June from the Arizona system, to hang around as a traditional type of backup. ⊕ If baseball is, at its heart, an elaborate work of symbolism, then **Matt Kemp** signing a minor-league contract with the Marlins is the most heavy-handed metaphor for death imaginable. ⊕ He still can't hit, and his sterling defense is likely to tarnish as he barrels towards his 30s, but that turn of phrase is the closest **Deven Marrero** might get to barreling anything. ⊕ With his older brother turning in a disappointing first season stateside, 17-year-old **Víctor Mesa Jr.** ditched switch-hitting and showed a penchant for getting on-base as in the Gulf Coast League. ⊕ He may only stand 1.05 Altuves tall, but **Nasim Nuñez** has a great middle infielder's glove and a set of wheels—products of his agile and quick-twitch athleticism—but he'll have to hit for more power than the "absolutely none" he showed off in the Gulf Coast League if he's to be any more than a defensive replacement. ⊕ The Quad-A Corner Guy is a tried and true archetype, and **Peter O'Brien** imitates it the best he can. ⊕ Ten years in the minors and a PED suspension didn't discourage **César Puello**, who finally put up solid on-base numbers in the majors after making a career out of it in Triple-A. ⊕ **JT Riddle** is still strong enough at the six and the eight to hold a roster spot, but the stick dwindled to nigh unplayable before a forearm strain in July spelled doom for the remainder of his season. ⊕ **Yadiel Rivera** hit the upper reaches of his PECOTA projection in 2019, which meant he was exactly replacement level. ⊕ **Magneuris Sierra** rebounded slightly from an abysmal 2018 campaign, but 23-year-old outfielders who can't hit in the PCL won't get a lot of chances, even in the Marlins organization. ⊕ Even good hitters can't endure three seasons in a row of double-digit decline in DRC+, so it was especially graphic to watch this happen to **Yangervis Solarte**, who found himself forced out of the Marlins' organization as a result. ⊕ **Chad Wallach** is once again following in the footsteps of his father by playing for a team that'll be relocated soon.

Pitchers

PITCHER	TEAM	LVL	AGE	W	L	SV	G	GS	IP	H	HR	BB/9	K/9	K	GB%	BABIP	WHIP	ERA	DRA	WARP	MPH	FB%	WHF	CSP
Yimi García	LAN	MLB	28	1	4	0	64	0	62¹	40	15	2.0	9.5	66	30%	.171	0.87	3.61	4.31	0.7	96.5	46	12.6	48.3
Jordan Holloway	JUP	A+	23	4	11	0	21	21	95	77	6	6.3	8.8	93	51%	.281	1.51	4.45	5.74	-0.8				
Tyler Kolek	CLN	A	23	0	0	0	9	0	8¹	6	0	21.6	11.9	11	25%	.300	3.12	9.72	8.56	-0.4				
Humberto Mejia	CLN	A	22	5	1	1	13	10	66²	42	4	2.6	9.2	68	34%	.228	0.92	2.03	2.71	1.9				
	JUP	A+	22	0	1	0	5	4	23²	15	2	1.9	8.0	21	47%	.210	0.85	2.28	3.07	0.5				
José Quijada	NWO	AAA	23	1	0	4	22	0	29¹	27	5	3.7	10.7	35	35%	.293	1.33	4.30	4.07	0.6				
	MIA	MLB	23	2	3	1	34	0	29²	27	10	7.9	13.3	44	34%	.283	1.79	5.76	5.10	0.1	95.8	71.7	15.3	44.9
Trevor Rogers	JUP	A+	21	5	8	0	18	18	110¹	97	7	2.0	10.0	122	44%	.303	1.10	2.53	3.93	1.5				
	JAX	AA	21	1	2	0	5	5	26	25	3	3.1	9.7	28	34%	.314	1.31	4.50	4.96	0.0				
Sterling Sharp	AUB	A-	24	0	1	0	2	2	7	4	0	1.3	6.4	5	76%	.235	0.71	1.29	4.83	0.0				
	HAR	AA	24	5	3	0	9	9	49²	56	1	2.5	8.2	45	64%	.362	1.41	3.99	5.91	-0.6				
Josh A. Smith	PAW	AAA	31	5	3	0	13	12	67¹	82	9	2.7	9.4	70	39%	.376	1.51	5.48	5.91	0.5				
	BOS	MLB	31	0	3	1	18	2	31	36	10	2.3	8.4	29	35%	.292	1.42	5.81	7.24	-0.6	93.1	38.8	13.2	44
Will Stewart	JUP	A+	21	6	12	0	23	21	129¹	137	13	2.9	6.7	96	53%	.313	1.38	5.43	6.78	-2.8				
Pat Venditte	SAC	AAA	34	6	2	0	25	1	47¹	31	5	3.2	11.2	59	34%	.243	1.01	2.85	1.92	2.0				
	SFN	MLB	34	0	0	0	2	0	3¹	4	1	5.4	5.4	2	42%	.273	1.80	16.20	4.74	0.0	88.7	52.4	7.9	38.4
Alex Vesia	CLN	A	23	1	2	3	19	1	31²	24	1	4.8	14.5	51	30%	.354	1.29	2.56	3.47	0.5				
	JUP	A+	23	4	0	1	10	0	18²	12	2	0.5	11.6	24	48%	.238	0.70	1.93	2.42	0.5				
	JAX	AA	23	2	0	1	9	0	16¹	8	0	0.6	13.8	25	46%	.286	0.55	0.00	2.62	0.4				

The fan experience of watching **Yimi García** pitch is essentially playing Press Your Luck, but instead of "no whammy" everybody is desperately chanting "no homer". An otherwise fine reliever, the ding-dong problem is always lurking like the villain in a horror movie waiting for a naive individual to put him into a high-leverage spot. ⓪ Even a selection to the Florida State League All-Star Game couldn't mask **Jordan Holloway**'s unseemly 16 percent walk rate, and the 23-year-old is running out of chances to show he's deserving of a starting role. ⓪ **Tyler Kolek** finally struck out more than a third of the hitters he faced. That's good! It was as a 23-year-old in barely five innings at short-season Batavia. That's bad! ⓪ After taming the lower minors with plus control and bat-missing curve, **Humberto Mejia** will have his otherwise pedestrian repertoire tested more quickly after being added to the 40-man roster in November. ⓪ **José Quijada** is a Three True Outcomes pitcher, which for him meant that 37 percent of hits he allowed flew over the fence. ⓪ Although he isn't the sexy prospect that fellow southpaw Braxton Garrett is, **Trevor Rogers** dominated the Florida State League before a promotion to Double-A and re-joined Miami's armada of projectable arms. ⓪ **Sterling Sharp** lived up to his name with as many strikeouts as innings pitched in the Arizona Fall League, based around an on-point sinker-changeup arsenal. He'll attempt to stick with the Marlins in 2020 after being selected from Washington in the Rule 5 Draft. ⓪ Someday a few years from now when you take the "2019 Red Sox" Sporcle quiz, **Josh Smith** will be the nondescript middle reliever you can't quite recall. ⓪ When you're the fourth piece in a blockbuster trade—the third was some international bonus pool cash—you can perform as poorly as **Will Stewart** did in High-A and still see your name in this book. ⓪ On the one hand, switch-pitcher **Pat Venditte** had a marvelous year closing games for the River Cats and making a PCL All-Star Game ... but on the other hand, he had an astonishingly bad pair of appearances at the big league-level. ⓪ **Alex Vesia** started his season in the Midwest League but finished with nine scoreless appearances in Jacksonville. The former Division II starter has rapidly ascended to a true left-handed relief prospect simply by striking out everyone and walking no one. (This is only a slight exaggeration.)

MILWAUKEE BREWERS

Essay by J.P. Breen

Player comments by Jack Moore and BP staff

We think about fandom as something static and binary: you either are or are not a baseball fan. But that's not really accurate. Fandom often waxes and wanes. In baseball, it is reconstituted every spring as people choose to become invested again and choose to expend time, money and emotional energy on their favorite team. As Major League Baseball continues to tinker with countless rules—to try and fix what's ostensibly wrong with baseball—in order to attract new fans, it often seems as if the current baseball fan is left unexplored or taken for granted.

What is it about baseball that refuses to allow millions of people to let the sport go? Instead of taking established fandom as an immutable given, Major League Baseball should talk and listen to current fans—in part to avoid losing their base, and in part because such efforts are likely helpful in MLB's commitment to growth. The things that current fans love about the game can be improved upon and/or better leveraged to incorporate more potential fans.

For example, baseball attracts the analytical types. Whether we talk about Strat-O-Matic debuting in the early 1960s, the emergence of Baseball Prospectus in 1996 or Sony Pictures bankrolling a $50 million movie in 2011 about the sabermetric revolution, it's almost banal at this point to point out how baseball fandom has long been correlated with those who harbor an affinity for numbers. It's clear that Major League Baseball is leaning into this appeal with Statcast and analytics-driven television broadcasts. They've even hired sabermetrically inclined writers, like Mike Petriello, to drive these types of fans to the league's website more often.

After interviewing roughly two dozen Milwaukee Brewers fans, though, a very different theme emerges regarding fandom: community. Diehard fans treasure the various kinds of personal connections that they find through baseball.

The desire for community stands out because Americans voluntarily come together in society less than ever before. Political scientist Robert Putnam famously wrote about the decline of social interaction in Bowling Alone (2000). In his study, Putnam charts less engagement in civic and religious organizations, and the title comes from the odd fact that the number of Americans who bowl has increased while activity

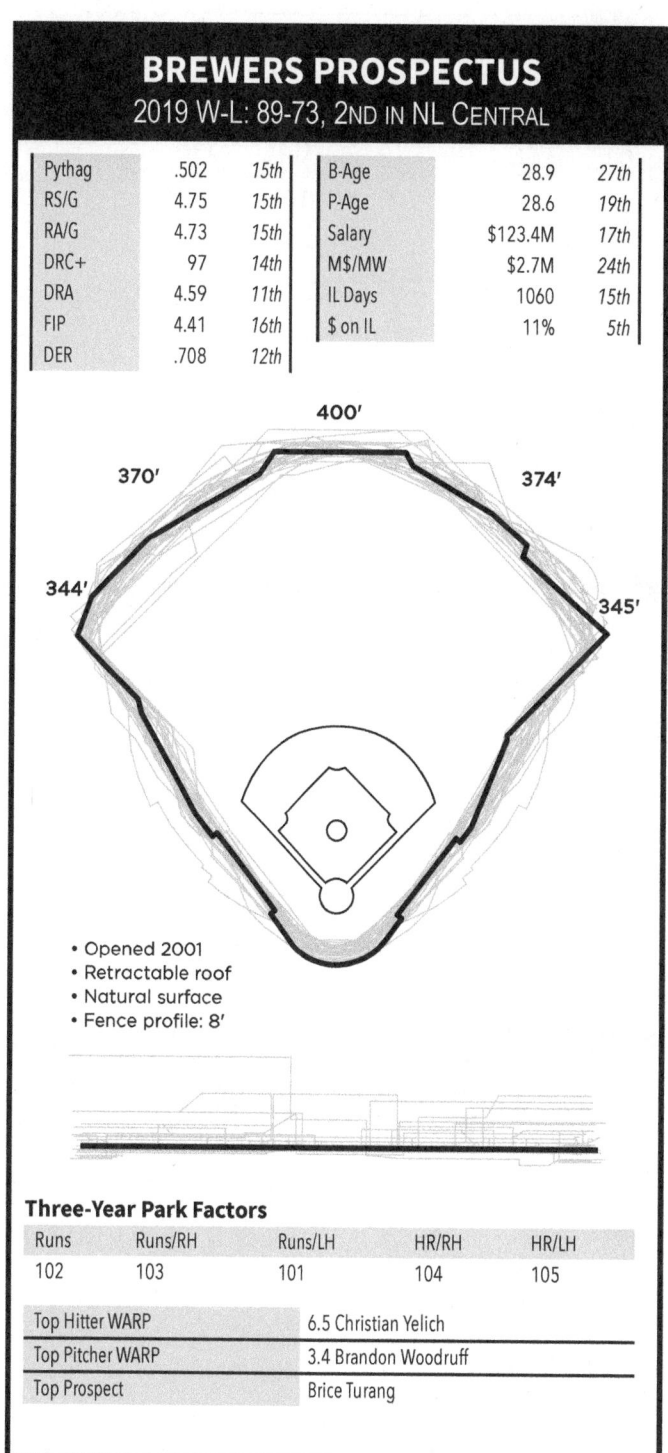

BREWERS PROSPECTUS
2019 W-L: 89-73, 2ND IN NL CENTRAL

Pythag	.502	15th	B-Age	28.9	27th
RS/G	4.75	15th	P-Age	28.6	19th
RA/G	4.73	15th	Salary	$123.4M	17th
DRC+	97	14th	M$/MW	$2.7M	24th
DRA	4.59	11th	IL Days	1060	15th
FIP	4.41	16th	$ on IL	11%	5th
DER	.708	12th			

400'
370'
374'
344'
345'

- Opened 2001
- Retractable roof
- Natural surface
- Fence profile: 8'

Three-Year Park Factors

Runs	Runs/RH	Runs/LH	HR/RH	HR/LH
102	103	101	104	105

Top Hitter WARP	6.5 Christian Yelich
Top Pitcher WARP	3.4 Brandon Woodruff
Top Prospect	Brice Turang

2019 Hit List Ranking

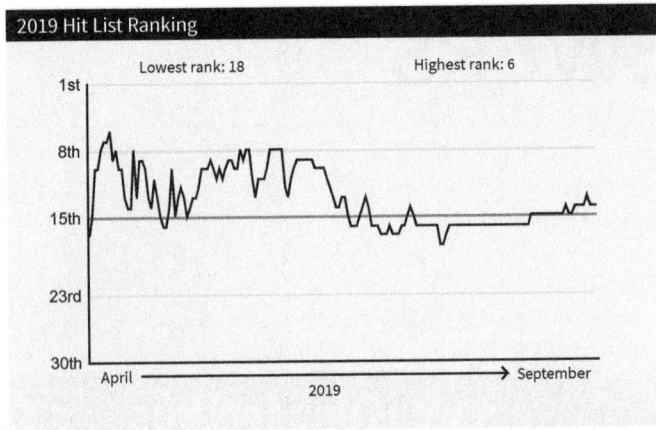

Committed Payroll (in millions)

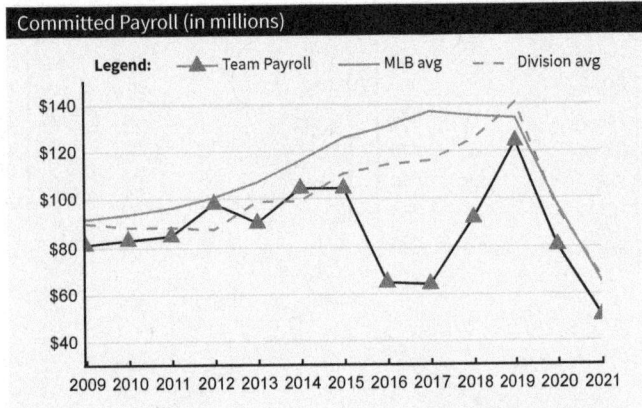

Farm System Ranking

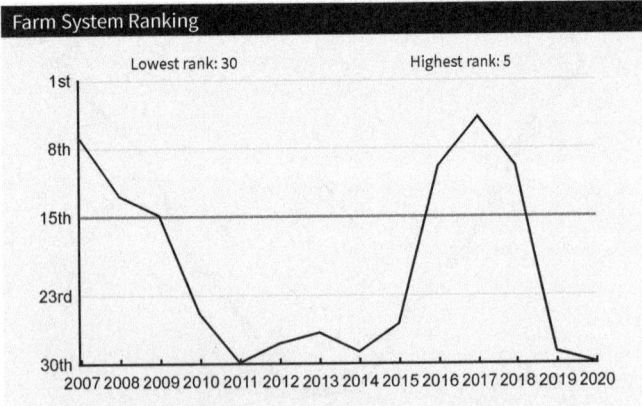

Personnel

President - Baseball Operations and General Manager
David Stearns

Senior Vice President and Assistant General Manager
Matt Arnold

Senior Vice President - Player Personnel
Karl Mueller

Manager
Craig Counsell

BP Alumni
James Fisher
Adam Hayes
Greg Goldstein
Mike Groopman
Shawn Hoffman
Matt Kleine
Dan Turkenkopf

in bowling leagues has dropped. American society, according to Putnam, has become more individualized. Historian Daniel Rodgers agrees with Putnam and argued that Americans' social and communal ways of understanding the world have been replaced over the last four or five decades with language and metaphors that stress individualism, agency, and choice. Rodgers calls this the Age of Fracture.[1]

In Wisconsin and beyond, the Milwaukee Brewers appear to help counter this age of fracture. "The second I find out another person is a Brewers fan," Brad Ford explained, "we immediately have a connection that makes it so easy to build a friendship." Relationships are built over an extended period of time, with small common experiences being stacked upon one another until there's something stable on which to stand. Baseball fandom provides a shortcut. As Jason Spitz told me, "I love feeling like I'm part of an experience that can't fully be grasped by outsiders." For many who love baseball, fandom is relational. No fan spoke to me about their love of the Brewers without mentioning how it tied them to other people, even (and sometimes especially) strangers.

If Putnam and Rodgers are correct that American society is fracturing and becoming more individualized, baseball and other sports might serve as one of the last widespread avenues for large-scale community engagement. And Brewers fans, at least, love the game for that fact.

Sometimes that community looks like throngs of people grilling brats, drinking beer and playing catch in the stadium parking lots. Though tailgating may be popular for football games across the country, it happens in earnest 81 times a year for baseball games in Wisconsin. Paul Noonan said, "With pace-of-play and the length of games being top of mind for everyone else, Milwaukeeans are happy to add a few extra hours to every game, and occasionally, not make it in until the third." In other words, going to a baseball game is often just an excuse to clear the schedule, leave work behind, and get both friends and family together at the ballpark.

Sometimes that community looks like 40,000-plus people cheering for the blue and gold inside Miller Park itself. For Aaron Sevedge, it "warms his soul" when he thinks of the strong local support the Brewers have, "even after 20 years in the playoff wilderness." It's an expression of civic pride, of communal support for something beyond the individual. Mike Treacy explained that his love for baseball developed when he was young and attended games at old County Stadium in Milwaukee. It wasn't the product on the field that attracted him, as the Brewers compiled a losing record in every season between 1993 and 2004, but the atmosphere drew him in. "At that age, I didn't care" about wins and losses, Treacy said, "baseball games were fun to go to." Talking to Brewers fans, it was common to learn that their love of baseball developed from physically attending games. There was something special and engrossing about sitting in the bleachers with thousands of like-minded individuals, cheering for the same outcome.

Sometimes, though, that community proved to be much smaller than thousands of strangers in a single stadium. The Brewers have knitted families together over time. Trenni Kusnierek, now an anchor and sports reporter for NBC Sports Boston, explained that being a Brewers fan was just part of growing up in her family. Even when the Brewers made the NLCS in 2018, Kusnierek said that she flew home to take her brother and sister to Game 6. She then went to Game 7 with her mom and dad. Supporting the Brewers was fundamentally a family affair. That is also true for Jason Spitz. He has always shared the Brewers with his family—first his dad and brother, now with his wife and kids.

That community regularly crosses generational lines, too. When Brewers fans told stories about their family, they involved parents, children, grandchildren, nieces, and nephews. It was never just about brothers, sisters or cousins. Beyond extended families, though, Sean Andrews explained that he enjoys being a part of a fanbase that can boast distinct generations with different experiences. The CC Sabathia trade in 2008 made Sean a supporter of the team, but he values the "older, hardcore crowd who were around for the '82 team." America has always dealt with intergenerational conflict—with the "OK Boomer" meme being its latest manifestation—but it's significant that baseball, in part, holds meaning for many Brewers fans because it brings together people of all ages.

Whether it centered on tailgating, attending games, uniting families or overcoming generational divides, the clearest common theme that emerged when talking to Brewers supporters about their fandom was community.

⚾   ⚾   ⚾

However, if what diehard Brewers fans cherish most about their fandom, and what often drew them into baseball in the first place, is the communal aspect of the game, both the league and its franchises appear to be shooting themselves in the foot.

According to the *New York Times*, Major League Baseball has suffered a 14-percent drop in ticket sales since 2007, which works out to roughly 11 million fewer tickets sold.[2] Part of this is because teams are diversifying their revenue streams and are less reliant on getting butts in seats to prop up their bottom line. Teams like the Los Angeles Angels, on the other hand, have also recognized that they can increase their profits, despite lower attendance numbers, as long as they attract the right kind of fan (i.e., a wealthier fan who can spend more money at the ballpark).[3] This latter trend of increasing ticket prices with an eye toward the economic quality of a baseball fan, rather than the quantity of fans, explains why teams may not be worried about the short-term consequences of decreased attendance.

What's undeniable, though, is that such trends are crippling the very thing that Brewers fans claim to value most.

Decreasing access to live baseball extends down to the minor leagues. Numerous reports have suggested that Major League Baseball and Minor League Baseball plan to contract up to 42 current minor-league affiliates.[4] The league has claimed that such streamlining will eliminate the organizations that have inadequate facilities, and it will also enable minor-league players to receive higher pay. Putting aside the various structural, economic and moral critiques that can be leveled at such an argument, slashing almost four dozen minor-league clubs will remove even more opportunities for baseball to attract new fans via the kinds of communal activities described above. This is especially true for potential baseball fans in less populated parts of the country, creating what could be described as more of an urban-rural divide in access to live baseball.

It is also important to ask for whom these baseballing communities have been built. Major League Baseball has catered to mostly cisgender, heterosexual white men throughout its history, including in the 21st century, and those cultural biases have often sheltered and sustained various kinds of abuse, harassment, discrimination, and disparate access. For baseball to truly be a positive communal force, as many Brewers fans suggest it could be, Major League Baseball must meaningfully address these prejudices and blindspots. There are positive steps being made on which MLB can build, such as the Play Ball initiative and MLB's partnership with mitú. And while commissioner Rob Manfred has pushed to grow the game among African-American communities, Latinx communities, women and younger generations, more effort must be concentrated in these directions and beyond.

There is a dissonance between Major League Baseball's perpetual desire to grow the game and access new markets, and their recent actions. They are eliminating its best chance at organic growth in the United States. The league is sometimes limiting access to games through higher prices and uneven support of diversity, while other times removing access to live baseball altogether. If sustained fandom is created through involvement in baseballing communities, it is difficult to see from where this engagement comes with the current trends. Even worse, it stands to figure that Major League Baseball might be pushing away current baseball fans by curtailing their favorite part of the game.

The Brewers are better off, in some respects, than many other teams when it comes to creating communities at Miller Park. They're consistently a top-half team in terms of attendance, despite being located in the league's smallest metropolitan market.[5] This is due to three reasons: (1) the team ranks in the league's top-10 most affordable stadiums;[6] (2) Miller Park's roof enables long-term planning for families; and (3) tailgating. The latter point deserves special mention. Multiple fans swore the tailgating experience couldn't be disentangled from the game itself; they were one and the same. Those people are saying something about what's important to them—being allowed to drink before noon for afternoon games, as one fan said, but also that baseball fandom is more meaningful with other people.

As Major League Baseball caters to what it thinks younger baseball fans want—better technology, more statistics, faster games, and more balls in play—it should also ask what attracted current fans in the first place. Growing the game is impossible if baseball is not able to retain its current fanbase. Listening to Brewers fans, the league should be accommodating and creating opportunities for physical community whenever possible, not limiting them. Major League Baseball may ultimately be chasing its own tail if it pursues higher profits and new markets by undercutting—and fracturing—what made it successful in the first place. ▪

—*J.P. Breen is an author of Baseball Prospectus.*

1. Robert D. Putnam, *Bowling Alone: The Collapse and Revival of American Community*. New York: Simon & Schuster Paperbacks, 2000; Daniel T. Rodgers, *Age of Fracture*. Cambridge, Mass.: Belknap Press of Harvard University Press, 2011.

2. https://www.nytimes.com/2019/09/29/sports/baseball/mlb-attendance.html

3. https://www.ocregister.com/2015/06/04/moura-angels-see-fewer-fans-but-revenue-rises-with-higher-ticket-prices/

4. https://www.baseballamerica.com/stories/mlb-floats-proposal-that-would-eliminate-42-minor-league-teams/

5. https://www.baseball-almanac.com/articles/baseball_markets.shtml

6. https://finance.yahoo.com/news/most-least-expensive-stadiums-mlb-090700815.html

HITTERS

Orlando Arcia SS
Born: 08/04/94　Age: 25　Bats: R　Throws: R　Height: 6'0"　Weight: 165　Origin: International Free Agent, 2010

YEAR	TEAM	LVL	AGE	PA	R	2B	3B	HR	RBI	BB	K	SB	CS	AVG/OBP/SLG	DRC+	VORP	BABIP	BRR	FRAA	WARP
2017	MIL	MLB	22	548	56	17	2	15	53	36	100	14	7	.277/.324/.407	94	26.1	.317	2.1	SS(152): 6.8	3.0
2018	CSP	AAA	23	96	16	5	1	2	8	10	15	2	1	.341/.417/.494	127	10.8	.397	2.3	SS(22): 3.9	1.4
2018	MIL	MLB	23	366	32	16	0	3	30	15	87	7	4	.236/.268/.307	59	-0.1	.305	2.0	SS(116): 3.8	0.4
2019	MIL	MLB	24	546	51	16	1	15	59	43	109	8	5	.223/.283/.350	74	7.9	.253	-0.7	SS(150): -2.3	0.5
2020	MIL	MLB	25	210	20	9	1	5	22	14	44	5	2	.234/.288/.371	74	0.9	.275	0.5	SS 2, 3B 0	0.3

Comparables: Pete Runnels, Ketel Marte, Francisco Lindor

There was a time when Arcia was projected to become a No. 2 hitter with a well-above-average glove at short. That hasn't happened, least of all on the offensive end. He continued to struggle at the plate last season—though he did improve his exit velocity and walked more often without seeing bottom-line improvement—and his glove grew more spotty as the season burned on—perhaps a sign he was taking his issues into the field with him. As a result, the Brewers benched Arcia in favor of Tyler Saladino, of all people. Arcia will probably get another chance to prove he's the cat's meow, but maybe not in Milwaukee—they acquired Luis Urías to slot in at short.

Ryan Braun LF
Born: 11/17/83　Age: 36　Bats: R　Throws: R　Height: 6'2"　Weight: 205　Origin: Round 1, 2005 Draft (#5 overall)

YEAR	TEAM	LVL	AGE	PA	R	2B	3B	HR	RBI	BB	K	SB	CS	AVG/OBP/SLG	DRC+	VORP	BABIP	BRR	FRAA	WARP
2017	MIL	MLB	33	425	58	28	2	17	52	38	76	12	4	.268/.336/.487	104	19.5	.292	0.5	LF(95): -3.7	1.0
2018	MIL	MLB	34	447	59	25	1	20	64	34	85	11	5	.254/.313/.469	108	17.8	.274	-0.8	LF(93): -4.9, 1B(18): -0.4	0.8
2019	MIL	MLB	35	508	70	31	2	22	75	34	105	11	1	.285/.343/.505	111	20.9	.325	0.7	LF(110): -7.1, RF(2): -0.2	1.4
2020	MIL	MLB	36	518	64	27	2	24	73	38	114	13	4	.262/.323/.475	107	18.0	.299	0.0	LF -4, 1B 0	1.5

Comparables: Cliff Floyd, Tim Wallach, George Hendrick

Braun isn't the hitter he was earlier in his career, but you have to admire his consistency. He's now played 13 full big-league seasons, delivering an above-average offensive performance in each. He's never batted lower than .250; he's reached base more often than 32 percent of the time all but once; and his lowest slugging percentage is .453. He's done all this while switching positions as often as the Brewers desired. The drug-test scandal is a permanent blemish on Braun's record, but as he enters the final guaranteed year of his contract, it's worth acknowledging that it's a mighty fine record, as far as ballplaying goes.

Keon Broxton CF
Born: 05/07/90　Age: 30　Bats: R　Throws: R　Height: 6'3"　Weight: 195　Origin: Round 3, 2009 Draft (#95 overall)

YEAR	TEAM	LVL	AGE	PA	R	2B	3B	HR	RBI	BB	K	SB	CS	AVG/OBP/SLG	DRC+	VORP	BABIP	BRR	FRAA	WARP
2017	CSP	AAA	27	34	4	2	0	1	7	7	8	4	0	.385/.500/.577	127	4.0	.500	0.5	CF(7): -0.8	0.2
2017	MIL	MLB	27	463	66	15	4	20	49	40	175	21	7	.220/.299/.420	76	16.9	.323	3.6	CF(139): -8.2	-0.2
2018	CSP	AAA	28	334	47	16	2	10	37	30	119	27	4	.254/.323/.421	83	10.2	.382	5.1	CF(61): -1.0, LF(8): 2.0	1.1
2018	MIL	MLB	28	89	15	2	2	4	11	11	28	5	1	.179/.281/.410	77	6.1	.217	2.3	CF(24): 1.5, RF(20): 0.6	0.5
2019	NYN	MLB	29	53	5	1	0	0	2	4	22	4	1	.143/.208/.163	48	-1.7	.259	-0.2	LF(18): 0.9, CF(9): 0.8	0.0
2019	BAL	MLB	29	112	14	3	0	4	9	8	49	4	1	.204/.261/.350	39	-4.9	.340	1.5	CF(36): 5.8	0.2
2019	SEA	MLB	29	63	5	0	0	2	5	8	33	2	4	.115/.238/.231	28	-3.7	.211	-0.2	CF(20): -0.6, LF(3): -0.2	-0.5
2020	MIL	MLB	30	35	4	1	0	1	4	3	15	2	1	.201/.286/.363	71	0.2	.340	0.2	CF 0	0.0

Comparables: Aaron Altherr, Larry Doby, Tommy Pham

Modern baseball teams may have an increased willingness to overlook a hitter's high strikeout totals if there are rosterable secondary skills present, but Broxton's astronomical whiff rates appear to be testing the league's patience. It took five months for the outfielder to go from "Acquired for Three Players By a Team Trying to Win" to "DFA'd by the Orioles," which is a pretty devastating case of life coming at you fast, even by baseball standards. The stellar outfield defense is still in place, but the elite exit velocity that once gave hope to peripheral-hunting analysts has all but vanished.

Lorenzo Cain CF Born: 04/13/86 Age: 34 Bats: R Throws: R Height: 6'2" Weight: 205 Origin: Round 17, 2004 Draft (#496 overall)

YEAR	TEAM	LVL	AGE	PA	R	2B	3B	HR	RBI	BB	K	SB	CS	AVG/OBP/SLG	DRC+	VORP	BABIP	BRR	FRAA	WARP
2017	KCA	MLB	31	645	86	27	5	15	49	54	100	26	2	.300/.363/.440	119	37.2	.340	2.4	CF(151): 19.4	6.0
2018	MIL	MLB	32	620	90	25	2	10	38	71	94	30	7	.308/.395/.417	121	53.6	.357	4.3	CF(138): 2.1	4.5
2019	MIL	MLB	33	623	75	30	0	11	48	50	106	18	8	.260/.325/.372	87	12.8	.301	1.0	CF(143): -1.6	1.2
2020	MIL	MLB	34	560	59	26	2	13	59	44	105	19	5	.264/.330/.395	94	18.0	.311	1.2	CF 8	2.6

Comparables: Michael Bourn, Roberto Kelly, Rondell White

It was downright painful to watch Cain play by the end of the 2019 season. It's not that he wasn't producing—Cain was reliable for incredible diving catches and an intelligent, gap-to-gap line-drive approach at the plate—but by September, he was playing through numerous ailments to the joints in both legs. A sprained ankle suffered in a collision with Rockies catcher Tony Wolters in a play at the plate during Game 161 added further insult to...well, injury. Nevertheless, when the Brewers took the field for the National League Wild Card Game, there was Cain out in center, hobbled but doing all he could do. You can't question Cain's effort, but as he enters the last three years of his contract with Milwaukee, it's fair to wonder if Father Time will take vengeance on his body sevenfold for all the miles he's racked up.

Lucas Erceg 3B Born: 05/01/95 Age: 25 Bats: L Throws: R Height: 6'3" Weight: 210 Origin: Round 2, 2016 Draft (#46 overall)

YEAR	TEAM	LVL	AGE	PA	R	2B	3B	HR	RBI	BB	K	SB	CS	AVG/OBP/SLG	DRC+	VORP	BABIP	BRR	FRAA	WARP
2017	CAR	A+	22	538	66	33	1	15	81	35	95	2	3	.256/.307/.417	100	11.3	.287	-1.6	3B(97): -0.6	1.3
2018	BLX	AA	23	508	52	21	1	13	51	37	82	3	1	.248/.306/.382	96	8.5	.274	-0.4	3B(117): -0.7	1.5
2019	SAN	AAA	24	406	55	17	1	15	52	44	102	2	2	.218/.305/.398	65	-1.6	.259	-2.0	3B(84): 7.9, 1B(18): 1.8	0.4
2020	MIL	MLB	25	251	26	12	1	9	30	19	69	0	0	.224/.285/.394	77	0.2	.279	-0.4	3B 1, 1B 0	0.2

Comparables: Kelvin Gutiérrez, Jordy Mercer, Jefry Marte

Even before the season, some scouts were ready to see Erceg and his near-elite arm switch from the infield to the mound. After a disappointing 2019 that suggested he might have peaked as a hitter, more and more evaluators are likely to join the chorus. Erceg doesn't have the mobility to play anywhere but a corner, and while he has the raw power to make it work, his plate discipline hampers his overall offensive upside. Perhaps another year of working with Driveline Baseball can help Erceg, but there's a real chance that this time next year he'll be working with them on his fastball-curveball combination.

Mario Feliciano C Born: 11/20/98 Age: 21 Bats: R Throws: R Height: 6'1" Weight: 195 Origin: Round 2, 2016 Draft (#75 overall)

YEAR	TEAM	LVL	AGE	PA	R	2B	3B	HR	RBI	BB	K	SB	CS	AVG/OBP/SLG	DRC+	VORP	BABIP	BRR	FRAA	WARP
2017	WIS	A	18	446	47	16	2	4	36	34	72	10	2	.251/.320/.331	88	11.2	.297	1.4	C(78): -2.8	0.9
2018	CAR	A+	19	165	20	7	1	3	12	13	59	2	0	.205/.282/.329	51	0.4	.318	0.5	C(25): -0.6	-0.2
2019	CAR	A+	20	482	62	25	4	19	81	29	139	2	1	.273/.324/.477	119	19.0	.351	-5.1	C(60): -0.4	1.7
2020	MIL	MLB	21	251	23	11	1	7	27	15	78	1	0	.223/.277/.368	70	-1.8	.304	-0.3	C -1	-0.3

Comparables: Cole Tucker, Gary Sánchez, Engel Beltre

Despite Feliciano being just 20 years old, 2019 was a critical season for him. The previous campaign had been a bust, as he had dealt with numerous injuries and had struggled in his sporadic appearances to adapt to High-A pitching. A second rough campaign in a row would have threatened his prospect status. Feliciano instead bounced back and reminded everyone why he merited a second-round selection in the first place, earning Carolina League MVP honors thanks to his budding home-run swing. Providing he can continue to hone his defensive skills—including an above-average arm—he has the potential to give the Brewers everything they want and need, baby: good glove and offensive projection. Make Feliciano your selection for Milwaukee's catcher of the future.

Ben Gamel OF Born: 05/17/92 Age: 28 Bats: L Throws: L Height: 5'11" Weight: 185 Origin: Round 10, 2010 Draft (#325 overall)

YEAR	TEAM	LVL	AGE	PA	R	2B	3B	HR	RBI	BB	K	SB	CS	AVG/OBP/SLG	DRC+	VORP	BABIP	BRR	FRAA	WARP
2017	TAC	AAA	25	75	6	1	1	1	8	12	11	1	1	.300/.427/.400	114	6.2	.347	0.6	RF(11): -0.2, CF(7): -0.9	0.2
2017	SEA	MLB	25	550	68	27	5	11	59	36	122	4	1	.275/.322/.413	90	12.9	.340	1.1	LF(85): -3.5, RF(50): 3.1	0.7
2018	TAC	AAA	26	94	19	8	3	1	16	10	12	4	0	.349/.415/.554	134	10.7	.394	2.5	LF(8): -0.7, CF(6): -0.1	0.8
2018	SEA	MLB	26	293	37	14	4	1	19	31	61	7	3	.272/.358/.370	98	12.2	.352	3.3	LF(48): -1.4, RF(40): -1.9	0.7
2019	MIL	MLB	27	356	47	18	0	7	33	40	104	2	2	.248/.337/.373	82	2.1	.347	0.5	LF(70): -1.6, RF(23): 0.0	0.1
2020	MIL	MLB	28	84	8	3	0	2	8	8	22	1	1	.237/.312/.367	83	0.7	.313	0.3	LF 0, RF 0	0.0

Comparables: Jake Marisnick, Alex Presley, Bob Borkowski

Gamel remains underwhelming—he's a tweener in more ways than one—when examined without context. But within the context of the 2019 Brewers it's fair to write he was a good fit. There, he could sub in as a defensive or baserunning upgrade over Ryan Braun or Eric Thames, and could do so without embarrassing himself at the plate, the way most fourth or fifth outfielders do. Force Gamel into an everyday role and everyone is going to be miserable; put him on the bench and ask him to play to his strengths and everyone is happy. Sometimes, it's just that simple.

Avisaíl García RF Born: 06/12/91 Age: 29 Bats: R Throws: R Height: 6'4" Weight: 250 Origin: International Free Agent, 2007

YEAR	TEAM	LVL	AGE	PA	R	2B	3B	HR	RBI	BB	K	SB	CS	AVG/OBP/SLG	DRC+	VORP	BABIP	BRR	FRAA	WARP
2017	CHA	MLB	26	561	75	27	5	18	80	33	111	5	3	.330/.380/.506	126	30.2	.392	-0.5	RF(132): 7.2	3.7
2018	CHR	AAA	27	28	5	3	0	3	9	3	9	0	0	.360/.429/.840	138	4.9	.462	-0.3	RF(5): -0.2	0.1
2018	CHA	MLB	27	385	47	11	2	19	49	20	102	3	1	.236/.281/.438	98	4.1	.271	-1.4	RF(87): 6.3	1.2
2019	TBA	MLB	28	530	61	25	2	20	72	31	125	10	4	.282/.332/.464	103	14.4	.340	-3.5	RF(92): -3.7, CF(12): 2.1	0.9
2020	MIL	MLB	29	392	47	18	1	16	53	24	99	4	2	.271/.326/.464	106	12.5	.331	-1.4	LF, CF 0	1.3

Comparables: Laynce Nix, Jeff Francoeur, Dave Parker

Much like Eminem or Ron Artest, García has matured since his time with Detroit. The 28-year-old was a bargain for the Rays as a free agent signing at a base salary of $3.5 million, and even as he earned another million in plate appearance bonuses. For that modest amount, the Rays received above-average offensive production, which allowed them to cover injuries in the outfield and rotate tired players through the designated hitter spot. Despite his large frame, García's 20 home runs in 2019 represented a career high. And despite putting up unexpected reverse splits last year, he will make his biggest mark as a hired gun versus southpaws. Though with an average-ish glove and no standout tool, he seems destined to be set up with short-term relationships for the next few years until his skills atrophy.

Keston Hiura 2B Born: 08/02/96 Age: 23 Bats: R Throws: R Height: 5'11" Weight: 190 Origin: Round 1, 2017 Draft (#9 overall)

YEAR	TEAM	LVL	AGE	PA	R	2B	3B	HR	RBI	BB	K	SB	CS	AVG/OBP/SLG	DRC+	VORP	BABIP	BRR	FRAA	WARP
2017	BRR	RK	20	72	18	3	5	4	18	6	13	0	2	.435/.500/.839	231	17.3	.500	0.5		1.0
2017	WIS	A	20	115	14	11	2	0	15	7	24	2	0	.333/.374/.476	138	10.4	.422	1.1	2B(3): -0.4	0.7
2018	CAR	A+	21	228	38	16	3	7	23	14	47	4	6	.320/.382/.529	163	20.8	.386	0.6	2B(15): 0.6	1.9
2018	BLX	AA	21	307	36	18	2	6	20	22	56	11	5	.272/.339/.416	118	13.9	.323	0.6	2B(64): -3.5	1.2
2019	SAN	AAA	22	243	44	16	1	19	46	23	64	7	2	.329/.407/.681	155	34.3	.389	0.0	2B(46): -1.6	2.1
2019	MIL	MLB	22	348	51	23	2	19	49	25	107	9	3	.303/.368/.570	115	18.2	.402	-0.5	2B(81): -4.9	1.3
2020	MIL	MLB	23	560	64	26	3	22	73	37	167	8	4	.251/.315/.444	98	20.5	.330	-0.7	2B -6	1.5

Comparables: Frank Bolling, Ian Happ, Ted Lepcio

The Brewers resisted calling up Hiura as long as they could—presumably in part to game his service-time clock—but the struggles of Travis Shaw forced their hand. Sometimes rookies stumble out of the gate, or require extra seasoning before living up to the scouting report. Not Hiura. When he made contact, he was about as productive as any hitter in the league, posting a .268 ISO that trailed only Derek Dietrich among second basemen with 300 or more plate appearances. He rifled line drives across the field and showed more power than any Brewers homegrown hitter since Ryan Braun. It may sound like he's bound for stardom, but there are two hurdles in his way: strikeouts and defense. Hiura's 30 percent strikeout rate was more Branyan than Braun, and a repeat of his batting average will be nigh impossible without improvement. More worryingly, Hiura was a disaster in the field; errors rarely tell a story, but 16, including six throwing errors from second base, says nothing good.

Omar Narváez C Born: 02/10/92 Age: 28 Bats: L Throws: R Height: 5'11" Weight: 220 Origin: International Free Agent, 2008

YEAR	TEAM	LVL	AGE	PA	R	2B	3B	HR	RBI	BB	K	SB	CS	AVG/OBP/SLG	DRC+	VORP	BABIP	BRR	FRAA	WARP
2017	CHA	MLB	25	295	23	10	0	2	14	38	45	0	0	.277/.373/.340	100	8.6	.330	-1.0	C(83): -9.5, 1B(1): 0.0	0.4
2018	CHA	MLB	26	322	30	14	1	9	30	38	65	0	2	.275/.366/.429	109	21.0	.330	0.0	C(85): -17.6	0.0
2019	SEA	MLB	27	482	63	12	0	22	55	47	92	0	0	.278/.353/.460	123	37.2	.306	-1.5	C(98): -12.3, 2B(1): 0.0	2.3
2020	MIL	MLB	28	490	57	21	0	17	61	49	90	1	0	.269/.345/.433	109	28.5	.304	-0.6	C -17	1.2

Comparables: Tucker Barnhart, Russell Martin, Yorvit Torrealba

A career-high 91 starts behind the dish further exposed Narváez as one of the shakiest backstops in the game, but his defensive transgressions were masked by his progression as one of baseball's best-hitting catchers. Narváez was one of the many beneficiaries of a livelier baseball in 2019, although pointing to the ball alone may undersell just how drastic of a power surge he experienced: His home run total in 132 games with Seattle outpaced the 19 he had hit in 680 career professional games previously. The result was the third-best

YEAR	TEAM	P. COUNT	FRM RUNS	BLK RUNS	THRW RUNS	TOT RUNS
2017	CHA	11422	-6.3	-1.5	-0.6	-9.3
2018	CHA	11231	-10.8	-4.6	-0.1	-15.7
2019	SEA	13756	-8.2	-4.3	-1.0	-13.7
2020	MIL	20469	-10.8	-3.6	-1.5	-15.8

DRC+ among catchers, making his defensive deficiencies more palatable. Still, defensive metrics suggest he upgraded from Probably The Worst to merely One of the Worst catchers in the league. Narváez's efforts to improve behind the plate weren't helped by seemingly catching someone new every day; Narváez set a major-league record for most different pitchers caught in a single season with 41. Forty-one! How many co-workers do you have to directly collaborate with on a regular basis? Is it 41? It's probably a smaller number than 41. For Narváez, meetings on the mound were often quite literally just that. And now, as a reward for his success, he'll get to memorize a new set of faces in Milwaukee.

Jacob Nottingham C Born: 04/03/95 Age: 25 Bats: R Throws: R Height: 6'2" Weight: 230 Origin: Round 6, 2013 Draft (#167 overall)

YEAR	TEAM	LVL	AGE	PA	R	2B	3B	HR	RBI	BB	K	SB	CS	AVG/OBP/SLG	DRC+	VORP	BABIP	BRR	FRAA	WARP
2017	BLX	AA	22	385	37	21	2	9	48	37	87	7	3	.209/.326/.369	104	11.9	.255	-3.0	C(83): 4.7, 1B(13): -0.8	2.0
2018	CSP	AAA	23	196	33	10	2	10	36	14	59	2	1	.281/.347/.528	96	10.7	.367	-0.6	C(32): -0.3, 1B(9): 0.0	0.6
2018	MIL	MLB	23	24	2	1	0	0	0	4	8	0	0	.200/.333/.250	71	0.7	.333	-0.1	C(8): -0.5	0.0
2019	SAN	AAA	24	332	40	21	0	5	40	28	95	6	1	.231/.313/.355	74	3.3	.318	-1.4	C(65): 11.7, 1B(8): 0.2	1.4
2019	MIL	MLB	24	7	1	0	0	1	4	0	2	0	0	.333/.429/.833	97	0.3	.333	0.0	C(6): -0.3, 1B(1): 0.0	0.0
2020	MIL	MLB	25	42	4	2	0	1	5	3	14	0	0	.217/.288/.379	76	0.6	.297	-0.1	C -1	0.0

Comparables: Gary Sánchez, Brett Phillips, Kyle Skipworth

Milwaukee's surprise Yasmani Grandal signing sealed Nottingham's assignment to Triple-A before he had a chance to win a big-league job. Grandal's one-year deal set the table for Nottingham to go back to the minors, dominate and position himself for a position in the 2020 startling lineup. Yet at a time when every other Triple-A hitter produced more power, Nottingham went counterculture. We're generally fans of subversion, but it's not a great idea when you're a bat-only catcher whose entire stock hinges on the one thing you're no longer doing. He'll try again in 2020, right along with the rest of us.

YEAR	TEAM	P. COUNT	FRM RUNS	BLK RUNS	THRW RUNS	TOT RUNS
2017	BLX	11440	7.2	-1.7	0.0	5.8
2018	CSP	4056	1.5	-1.1	-0.2	0.0
2018	MIL	937	-0.7	0.2	0.0	-0.5
2019	MIL	163	0.0	-0.1	0.0	0.4
2019	SAN	8544	12.0	0.0	-0.9	11.4
2020	MIL	1298	-0.7	0.0	-0.1	-0.8

Manny Piña   C   Born: 06/05/87   Age: 33   Bats: R   Throws: R   Height: 6'0"   Weight: 215   Origin: International Free Agent, 2004

YEAR	TEAM	LVL	AGE	PA	R	2B	3B	HR	RBI	BB	K	SB	CS	AVG/OBP/SLG	DRC+	VORP	BABIP	BRR	FRAA	WARP
2017	MIL	MLB	30	359	45	21	0	9	43	20	79	2	0	.279/.327/.424	93	16.4	.339	-0.6	C(102): 1.4	1.5
2018	MIL	MLB	31	337	39	13	2	9	28	21	62	2	0	.252/.307/.395	90	9.1	.285	-3.6	C(92): 7.0, 1B(1): 0.0	1.6
2019	MIL	MLB	32	179	10	8	0	7	25	16	50	0	0	.228/.313/.411	90	6.7	.284	-0.5	C(53): 8.3, 3B(1): 0.0	1.4
2020	MIL	MLB	33	189	20	8	0	6	23	14	47	1	0	.240/.306/.404	88	4.0	.294	-0.8	C 1, 1B 0	0.5

Comparables: Francisco Cervelli, Dioner Navarro, Martín Maldonado

YEAR	TEAM	P. COUNT	FRM RUNS	BLK RUNS	THRW RUNS	TOT RUNS
2017	MIL	12774	-2.9	0.7	2.0	3.0
2018	MIL	12411	4.8	1.3	0.5	6.3
2019	MIL	6195	6.4	2.0	-0.1	8.3
2020	MIL	5531	0.3	0.5	-0.3	0.5

Even with Piña on the wrong side of 30, and coming off his worst season at the plate since coming to Milwaukee in 2016, the Brewers continue to believe in his defensive chops. Baseball Prospectus co-founder Rany Jazayerli once suggested every backup catcher will hit .300 in a season given enough opportunity. The first half of Piña's 2017—when he hit .287/.328/.457—suggests Jazayerli had a point. Piña hasn't hit so well since, and that's all right given his defense and low cost. Much like that new song on the radio, the key to enjoying Piña is to avoid overexposure.

Corey Ray   OF   Born: 09/22/94   Age: 25   Bats: L   Throws: L   Height: 6'0"   Weight: 195   Origin: Round 1, 2016 Draft (#5 overall)

YEAR	TEAM	LVL	AGE	PA	R	2B	3B	HR	RBI	BB	K	SB	CS	AVG/OBP/SLG	DRC+	VORP	BABIP	BRR	FRAA	WARP
2017	CAR	A+	22	503	56	29	4	7	48	48	156	24	10	.238/.311/.367	96	7.1	.346	-2.5	CF(80): 5.5, RF(24): 0.9	1.6
2018	BLX	AA	23	600	86	32	7	27	74	60	176	37	7	.239/.323/.477	119	35.8	.303	0.5	CF(126): 1.8, LF(6): 1.4	3.6
2019	BLX	AA	24	46	5	3	0	0	0	6	14	3	2	.250/.348/.325	116	1.0	.385	0.1	CF(10): 1.6, LF(1): -0.2	0.4
2019	SAN	AAA	24	230	23	8	0	7	21	20	89	3	1	.188/.261/.329	45	-1.2	.283	-0.4	CF(40): -5.0, RF(8): -1.3	-1.2
2020	MIL	MLB	25	251	23	13	1	6	24	19	98	8	3	.197/.262/.336	58	-5.0	.313	0.5	CF 2, RF 0	-0.3

Comparables: Joe Benson, Michael A. Taylor, Anthony Alford

That whole "striking out 30 percent of the time" thing came back to bite Ray in a big way in 2019, as did Milwaukee's change of Triple-A venue, from Colorado Springs to San Antonio. The result was by far his worst season in the minors, including the ignominious accomplishment of accumulating more strikeouts than total bases. The power Ray showed in 2018 is impossible to ignore, and he will be just 25 in 2020. A time of reckoning (Ray-gnarök?) will come shortly if he can't patch the holes in his swing.

Ronny Rodríguez   INF   Born: 04/17/92   Age: 28   Bats: R   Throws: R   Height: 6'0"   Weight: 200   Origin: International Free Agent, 2011

YEAR	TEAM	LVL	AGE	PA	R	2B	3B	HR	RBI	BB	K	SB	CS	AVG/OBP/SLG	DRC+	VORP	BABIP	BRR	FRAA	WARP
2017	COH	AAA	25	483	60	18	2	17	64	23	92	15	5	.291/.324/.454	108	11.1	.329	-1.4	2B(62): 7.9, 3B(25): 1.6	3.2
2018	TOL	AAA	26	275	42	20	5	9	40	10	47	10	8	.338/.365/.558	163	30.8	.383	-1.8	3B(34): 2.1, SS(26): -0.9	2.7
2018	DET	MLB	26	206	17	7	0	5	20	10	42	2	0	.220/.256/.335	77	-4.4	.253	-0.3	SS(24): -2.3, 2B(17): 0.1	-0.3
2019	TOL	AAA	27	181	33	9	2	11	31	6	41	5	0	.320/.343/.587	136	13.3	.361	-1.0	2B(24): 3.2, 3B(7): -0.5	1.3
2019	DET	MLB	27	294	29	12	3	14	43	13	82	3	1	.221/.252/.438	72	-0.8	.254	-1.1	2B(31): 1.3, SS(20): -2.0	-0.3
2020	MIL	MLB	28	140	17	6	1	8	22	6	37	2	1	.249/.284/.490	96	3.2	.284	-0.4	2B 1, SS 0	0.4

Comparables: Trevor Plouffe, Jose Pirela, Jimmy Paredes

Rodríguez's game aspires to be that of a Quad-A cult favorite. His big personality fits in the game; his swing-and-miss penchant doesn't. (Or, given the recent trends, maybe it does?) He will always have a spot on a team due to his joie de vivre and his infield versatility, coupled with the fact that pitchers often throw fastballs and Rodríguez has a way of turning some of those fastballs into home runs. With his not-so-secret passion of being a musician, it would be nice to see El Felino have a complete season of 25-30 home runs then write music about how he once did that. You'd do the same thing.

Tyler Saladino   UT   Born: 07/20/89   Age: 30   Bats: R   Throws: R   Height: 6'0"   Weight: 200   Origin: Round 7, 2010 Draft (#218 overall)

YEAR	TEAM	LVL	AGE	PA	R	2B	3B	HR	RBI	BB	K	SB	CS	AVG/OBP/SLG	DRC+	VORP	BABIP	BRR	FRAA	WARP
2017	CHA	MLB	27	281	23	9	2	0	10	23	67	5	4	.178/.254/.229	57	-14.1	.242	1.1	2B(26): 1.2, 3B(22): 4.3	0.0
2018	CSP	AAA	28	154	23	4	3	3	19	21	28	10	0	.262/.370/.408	101	8.9	.310	1.6	SS(25): -2.6, 2B(9): -0.7	0.5
2018	CHA	MLB	28	9	2	1	0	0	0	0	3	0	0	.250/.250/.375	80	0.0	.400	0.0	3B(2): 0.2	0.0
2018	MIL	MLB	28	130	11	3	0	5	16	9	38	2	2	.246/.302/.398	88	3.9	.316	0.1	SS(28): 1.7, 2B(6): 0.0	0.5
2019	SAN	AAA	29	310	51	19	2	17	64	41	67	8	1	.287/.384/.566	137	26.5	.322	0.4	LF(18): -1.0, SS(18): -1.8	2.0
2019	MIL	MLB	29	71	7	0	0	2	8	5	26	2	0	.123/.197/.215	60	-0.9	.162	0.8	SS(13): -0.1, LF(7): -0.4	-0.1
2020	MIL	MLB	30	251	27	9	1	9	29	21	69	8	3	.221/.291/.384	78	1.9	.276	1.1	SS 0, 2B 1	0.3

Comparables: Aaron Boone, Brock Holt, Chris Truby

You've undoubtedly heard about the Peter principle. Allow us to introduce the Pete Kozma principle, which states that a career can be extended by unreal lengths just because somebody can kinda-sorta passably play shortstop. Despite reintroducing a leg kick in the minors, Saladino was one of baseball's worst hitters in his short time in the majors. To be clear: he's always been ineffectual at the dish, but this go around he fanned in nearly 40 percent of his plate appearances, making him even more of a black hole. Fortunately for Saladino, some team will always need a shortstop. For 2020, it's the Samsung Lions.

Justin Smoak 1B Born: 12/05/86 Age: 33 Bats: B Throws: L Height: 6'4" Weight: 220 Origin: Round 1, 2008 Draft (#11 overall)

YEAR	TEAM	LVL	AGE	PA	R	2B	3B	HR	RBI	BB	K	SB	CS	AVG/OBP/SLG	DRC+	VORP	BABIP	BRR	FRAA	WARP
2017	TOR	MLB	30	637	85	29	1	38	90	73	128	0	1	.270/.355/.529	135	27.4	.285	0.6	1B(151): -0.9	3.6
2018	TOR	MLB	31	594	67	34	0	25	77	83	156	0	1	.242/.350/.457	117	14.7	.297	-5.1	1B(134): -7.2	0.8
2019	TOR	MLB	32	500	54	16	0	22	61	79	106	0	0	.208/.342/.406	111	15.0	.223	-2.0	1B(89): -5.5	0.7
2020	MIL	MLB	33	399	50	16	0	18	54	54	97	1	0	.221/.332/.430	104	8.8	.253	-1.1	1B -3	0.6

Comparables: Brandon Belt, Franklin Stubbs, Pat Burrell

2019 marked a second consecutive season of decline for Smoak after he finally had that breakout year in 2017, long after anyone had hoped for it. The average fell though the patient approach established two seasons ago was maintained, resulting in a career-best strikeout-to-walk ratio. Though he fell just two plate appearances short of qualifying for a batting title he wasn't within kilometers of, the first baseman still provided presence and consistency to a club that had little of either. In fact, Smoak grew enough on Jays fans in his five years there to earn multiple standing ovations in what was potentially his last game at Rogers Centre. He wryly remarked, "Can you believe they do that for a .200 hitter?" The other two stints in which Smoak hit within ten points of .200 (2010 and 2014) both ended in him moving teams, so misleading batting average or not, it's possible the Smoak coming out of the Sistine Chapel to herald his next deal is not Blue.

Eric Sogard 2B Born: 05/22/86 Age: 34 Bats: L Throws: R Height: 5'10" Weight: 185 Origin: Round 2, 2007 Draft (#81 overall)

YEAR	TEAM	LVL	AGE	PA	R	2B	3B	HR	RBI	BB	K	SB	CS	AVG/OBP/SLG	DRC+	VORP	BABIP	BRR	FRAA	WARP
2017	CSP	AAA	31	107	30	8	0	3	17	15	12	5	0	.330/.421/.516	126	7.0	.351	-0.2	2B(15): -0.2, 3B(3): 0.0	0.6
2017	MIL	MLB	31	299	37	15	1	3	18	45	37	3	3	.273/.393/.378	105	13.4	.311	-2.9	2B(60): -2.1, SS(26): -0.2	0.7
2018	CSP	AAA	32	101	10	4	0	0	11	10	16	0	1	.225/.297/.270	65	-2.0	.267	1.6	2B(18): 1.2, SS(5): 1.2	0.3
2018	MIL	MLB	32	113	7	3	0	0	2	12	23	3	0	.134/.241/.165	72	-5.4	.173	0.3	SS(24): 0.0, 2B(22): 0.1	0.1
2019	BUF	AAA	33	38	7	2	0	1	6	7	4	0	0	.267/.395/.433	119	3.0	.269	0.7	3B(5): 0.6, 2B(2): 0.4	0.3
2019	TOR	MLB	33	323	45	17	2	10	30	29	47	6	0	.300/.363/.477	112	14.9	.326	3.0	2B(43): -1.4, RF(6): 0.3	1.7
2019	TBA	MLB	33	119	14	6	0	3	10	9	16	2	0	.266/.328/.404	104	4.6	.289	-0.1	2B(31): 0.7	0.5
2020	MIL	MLB	34	497	52	24	1	11	53	48	79	7	3	.257/.333/.391	96	10.5	.291	-0.1	3B 5, 2B 0	1.7

Comparables: Mark Ellis, Jim Morrison, Cliff Pennington

It is a giant upset that Sogard—the poster boy of "nerd power"—is also not the cover boy of the "nerd bible." A useful reserve for most of his career because of his defensive flexibility, Sogard did that thing where you change the angle of your launch and started hitting dingers. The 13 home runs he hit in 2019 represented 54 percent of his career total and were potentially career-saving. Without the new stick, Sogard offers little in tangible items. He has cool glasses and seems like a good dude but is average or below as a defender no matter where you put him. If he improves upon his 2019, he should probably be on the cover next year. If not, please direct all complaints to @cdgoldstein on Twitter.

Cory Spangenberg UT Born: 03/16/91 Age: 29 Bats: L Throws: R Height: 6'0" Weight: 195 Origin: Round 1, 2011 Draft (#10 overall)

YEAR	TEAM	LVL	AGE	PA	R	2B	3B	HR	RBI	BB	K	SB	CS	AVG/OBP/SLG	DRC+	VORP	BABIP	BRR	FRAA	WARP
2017	ELP	AAA	26	72	8	3	1	1	7	4	8	3	2	.348/.403/.470	104	3.4	.386	-0.2	3B(17): -3.3	0.0
2017	SDN	MLB	26	486	57	18	2	13	46	34	128	11	3	.264/.322/.401	82	28.5	.342	5.3	3B(96): -0.8, LF(32): -3.0	0.8
2018	ELP	AAA	27	95	14	8	2	4	16	6	30	3	0	.341/.383/.614	116	6.4	.481	-0.4	3B(13): 0.8, 2B(5): -0.9	0.4
2018	SDN	MLB	27	329	35	9	4	7	25	25	108	6	1	.235/.298/.362	64	4.6	.344	-0.1	2B(49): -2.8, 3B(44): 0.3	-0.7
2019	SAN	AAA	28	476	82	28	5	14	62	43	136	28	4	.309/.378/.498	103	41.3	.422	5.6	LF(29): -2.6, 2B(20): -2.1	1.5
2019	MIL	MLB	28	102	11	2	2	2	10	6	36	3	0	.232/.277/.358	47	-3.5	.351	-0.4	2B(22): 0.0, 3B(6): 0.4	-0.3
2020	MIL	MLB	29	251	24	9	2	6	26	17	82	5	2	.237/.295/.372	75	0.8	.340	0.8	3B 1, 2B -1	0.0

Comparables: Randy Jackson, Jim Presley, Craig Paquette

Questions commonly asked when watching Spangenberg: "Wait, he's still around?" followed by "Wait, the G is soft?" Yes, Spangenberg still got occasional at-bats in 2019, and yes, it's pronounced "Spange" as in "Sponge." One other question he inspires, that also has an affirmative answer, is: "Can't they do better?" Spangenberg's ability to make consistent contact against big-league pitchers has evaporated. He can theoretically play multiple infield positions, but so can dozens of minor leaguers. Perhaps Spangenberg's best attribute at this point is stimulating curiosity and marvel. That counts for something, just not enough. Perhaps that final question will have a different answer on another continent, as the former first-rounder signed with the Seibu Lions for 2020.

Tyrone Taylor OF Born: 01/22/94 Age: 26 Bats: R Throws: R Height: 6'0" Weight: 185 Origin: Round 2, 2012 Draft (#92 overall)

YEAR	TEAM	LVL	AGE	PA	R	2B	3B	HR	RBI	BB	K	SB	CS	AVG/OBP/SLG	DRC+	VORP	BABIP	BRR	FRAA	WARP
2017	BRR	RK	23	26	6	1	0	4	7	3	3	2	0	.435/.500/1.000	215	7.3	.375	0.3	CF(7): -0.8	0.3
2017	BLX	AA	23	95	15	6	1	1	6	8	18	2	1	.247/.316/.376	85	1.8	.299	1.1	LF(8): 0.7, RF(7): 2.5	0.5
2018	CSP	AAA	24	481	73	23	9	20	80	27	74	13	4	.278/.321/.504	99	17.6	.292	2.3	CF(56): 0.5, LF(39): 7.2	2.5
2019	SAN	AAA	25	375	44	20	1	14	59	28	85	5	0	.269/.334/.461	92	12.0	.317	0.3	RF(46): 1.6, CF(43): 8.5	1.7
2019	MIL	MLB	25	12	1	2	0	0	1	1	1	0	0	.400/.500/.600	89	0.3	.444	-0.4	RF(8): -0.1, CF(3): -0.3	0.0
2020	MIL	MLB	26	119	13	5	0	4	14	7	27	2	1	.231/.287/.401	81	0.8	.268	-0.1	CF 1, RF 0	0.2

Comparables: Rey Fuentes, Gorkys Hernández, Tzu-Wei Lin

Taylor's numbers look more or less the same from 2018 to 2019, but the context is key: Colorado Springs, the Brewers' 2018 Triple-A home, is arguably the most hitter-friendly park in professional baseball (or, at least, this side of High Desert). Taylor showed improved discipline and hardly suffered at all from a power perspective after the move to San Antonio. Consider those both good signs for his future. It can be easy with a player like Taylor to lament the fact that he hasn't reached the lofty heights his tools suggested he could, but he might be just what Milwaukee needs in 2020: a strong defensive outfielder capable of covering all three outfield spots.

Brice Turang MI Born: 11/21/99 Age: 20 Bats: L Throws: R Height: 6'0" Weight: 173 Origin: Round 1, 2018 Draft (#21 overall)

YEAR	TEAM	LVL	AGE	PA	R	2B	3B	HR	RBI	BB	K	SB	CS	AVG/OBP/SLG	DRC+	VORP	BABIP	BRR	FRAA	WARP
2018	BRR	RK	18	57	11	2	0	0	7	9	6	8	1	.319/.421/.362	153	4.5	.357	0.0	SS(12): 2.0	0.7
2018	HEL	RK	18	135	26	4	1	1	11	22	28	6	1	.268/.385/.348	119	9.8	.345	1.7	SS(23): -0.1, 2B(5): -0.1	0.6
2019	WIS	A	19	357	57	13	4	2	31	49	54	21	4	.287/.384/.376	142	25.1	.339	3.2	SS(43): 0.6, 2B(28): 0.9	3.2
2019	CAR	A+	19	207	25	6	2	1	6	34	47	9	1	.200/.338/.276	99	2.4	.268	1.6	SS(35): -2.6, 2B(5): -0.8	0.6
2020	MIL	MLB	20	251	23	10	1	4	23	25	60	5	1	.230/.310/.338	76	0.8	.297	0.4	SS -1, 2B -1	-0.1

Comparables: J.P. Crawford, Gavin Lux, Ehire Adrianza

Milwaukee's top prospect, Turang didn't respond well to a promotion to High-A. That's understandable, given he was three-plus years younger than the average competition he faced. His lack of pop and devotion to walking leaves us thinking about Cliff Pennington. That's supposed to be a compliment—Pennington had a long, and at times fruitful career—but we understand if you instead take it as an indictment of the Brewers' farm system.

Luis Urías SS Born: 06/03/97 Age: 23 Bats: R Throws: R Height: 5'9" Weight: 185 Origin: International Free Agent, 2013

YEAR	TEAM	LVL	AGE	PA	R	2B	3B	HR	RBI	BB	K	SB	CS	AVG/OBP/SLG	DRC+	VORP	BABIP	BRR	FRAA	WARP
2017	SAN	AA	20	526	77	20	4	3	38	68	65	7	5	.296/.398/.380	132	42.3	.340	2.6	SS(60): 4.7, 2B(55): -1.1	4.2
2018	ELP	AAA	21	533	83	30	7	8	45	67	109	2	1	.296/.398/.447	116	27.3	.373	1.4	2B(90): 10.2, SS(20): 3.4	4.5
2018	SDN	MLB	21	53	5	1	0	2	5	3	10	1	0	.208/.264/.354	85	0.6	.216	0.3	2B(12): -0.2	0.1
2019	ELP	AAA	22	339	62	19	4	19	50	36	62	7	2	.315/.398/.600	125	33.5	.343	2.5	SS(53): 8.5, 2B(21): 4.1	3.8
2019	SDN	MLB	22	249	27	8	1	4	24	25	56	0	1	.223/.329/.326	83	5.1	.284	0.0	SS(41): -5.4, 2B(26): -1.7	-0.2
2020	MIL	MLB	23	455	49	21	2	12	51	42	91	3	2	.251/.336/.401	98	16.4	.297	0.2	SS 2, 2B 0	2.0

Comparables: Luis Rengifo, Wilmer Flores, Orlando Arcia

Urías can hit. Urías *will* hit. Urías has *always* hit. His minor-league slash line is .308/.397/.433. His Triple-A slash line is .305/.403/.511. Numbers like those sometimes comprise a lot of seasons for players who have been old for their level, or describe Quad-A corner men in the PCL. Urías will be *22 years old* on opening day, and he's a *middle infielder*. He spent his age 20 and 21 seasons in the high minors, during which he batted .296 and got on base at a .398 clip. The power may never come, he may not be an everyday shortstop and at the keystone he's more steady than spectacular. But Urías can hit. Trust us on this one.

Christian Yelich RF Born: 12/05/91 Age: 28 Bats: L Throws: R Height: 6'3" Weight: 195 Origin: Round 1, 2010 Draft (#23 overall)

YEAR	TEAM	LVL	AGE	PA	R	2B	3B	HR	RBI	BB	K	SB	CS	AVG/OBP/SLG	DRC+	VORP	BABIP	BRR	FRAA	WARP
2017	MIA	MLB	25	695	100	36	2	18	81	80	137	16	2	.282/.369/.439	105	45.6	.336	0.8	CF(155): -17.3	1.2
2018	MIL	MLB	26	651	118	34	7	36	110	68	135	22	4	.326/.402/.598	143	79.0	.373	2.4	LF(90): -7.3, RF(75): 2.1	4.8
2019	MIL	MLB	27	580	100	29	3	44	97	80	118	30	2	.329/.429/.671	167	64.4	.355	3.7	RF(124): -1.6, LF(6): 0.5	6.5
2020	MIL	MLB	28	595	91	26	2	36	101	73	129	14	4	.295/.387/.563	149	51.1	.330	0.4	RF -1	5.2

Comparables: Greg Luzinski, Travis Snider, Stephen Piscotty

Milwaukee's glorious golden god, Yelich took his MVP 2018 season and made it better in every way in 2019; from surface counting stats like homers, stolen bases and RBI, to his entire triple-slash line, to peripherals like walk rate and isolated power. He's improved from a well-rounded hitter with the Marlins to elite in every facet of the game for the Brewers thanks to swing adjustments and an impeccable feel for hard contact—he finished fifth in exit velocity, behind a bunch of players who "look" more like sluggers. He has, essentially, become the closest thing we have to a left-handed Mike Trout. Despite the fact that Yelich's season ended with just 130 games played after he fouled a ball off his kneecap in September, his 53.4 DRAA trailed only Alex Bregman and, well, Trout. There have been 14 individual seasons in the past five years where a batter has topped 50 DRAA. Trout has four of those; Yelich will look for his second in 2020.

PITCHERS

Matt Albers RHP Born: 01/20/83 Age: 37 Bats: L Throws: R Height: 6'1" Weight: 225 Origin: Round 23, 2001 Draft (#686 overall)

YEAR	TEAM	LVL	AGE	W	L	SV	G	GS	IP	H	HR	BB/9	K/9	K	GB%	BABIP	WHIP	ERA	DRA	WARP	MPH	FB%	WHF	CSP
2017	WAS	MLB	34	7	2	2	63	0	61	35	6	2.5	9.3	63	52%	.203	0.85	1.62	3.93	0.8	95.6	67.7	10.1	49.5
2018	MIL	MLB	35	3	3	1	34	0	34¹	45	10	3.1	8.4	32	47%	.347	1.66	7.34	6.09	-0.5	94.5	64.6	11.6	44.1
2019	MIL	MLB	36	8	6	4	67	0	59²	53	8	4.4	8.6	57	52%	.280	1.37	5.13	4.79	0.4	95.0	56.7	10.1	40.7
2020	MIL	MLB	37	2	2	0	33	0	35	36	5	3.8	8.3	32	50%	.301	1.44	4.92	4.83	0.2	93.6	60.2	10.2	43

Comparables: David Weathers, Mike Fetters, Bob Wickman

For a second consecutive season, it was a story of first half versus second half. Albers struck out 38 and held opponents to a .216/.282/.358 batting line through 37 first-half innings, then collapsed after the break. He walked 18 batters in 22 ⅔ second-half innings and allowed a .402 on-base percentage. That was essentially the same story as 2018, when Albers was solid through the first half and was awful down the stretch. Albers will turn 37 years old in 2020. Another year probably won't help him retain a full season's worth of gas.

Brett Anderson LHP   Born: 02/01/88   Age: 32   Bats: L   Throws: L   Height: 6'4"   Weight: 230   Origin: Round 2, 2006 Draft (#55 overall)

YEAR	TEAM	LVL	AGE	W	L	SV	G	GS	IP	H	HR	BB/9	K/9	K	GB%	BABIP	WHIP	ERA	DRA	WARP	MPH	FB%	WHF	CSP
2017	TEN	AA	29	2	2	0	6	5	27¹	34	2	3.0	4.9	15	69%	.348	1.57	4.61	6.45	-0.4				
2017	BUF	AAA	29	1	1	0	2	2	9²	4	0	1.9	2.8	3	53%	.133	0.62	0.93	2.37	0.4				
2017	CHN	MLB	29	2	2	0	6	6	22	34	2	4.9	6.5	16	51%	.395	2.09	8.18	4.87	0.2	92.5	56.7	9	41.6
2017	TOR	MLB	29	2	2	0	7	7	33¹	39	3	2.4	5.9	22	50%	.340	1.44	5.13	5.88	-0.1	93.4	48.6	9.5	46.3
2018	NAS	AAA	30	2	1	0	7	7	32¹	32	0	1.7	10.0	36	60%	.333	1.18	2.78	3.21	0.9				
2018	OAK	MLB	30	4	5	0	17	17	80¹	90	10	1.5	5.3	47	57%	.307	1.28	4.48	3.98	1.2	93.1	49.5	8.1	49.2
2019	OAK	MLB	31	13	9	0	31	31	176	181	20	2.5	4.6	90	56%	.278	1.31	3.89	5.65	0.2	93.4	49.7	8.1	51.7
2020	MIL	MLB	32	8	8	0	23	23	129	145	19	2.5	5.1	74	56%	.295	1.40	4.89	4.97	1.2	92.4	49.5	8.2	48.5

Comparables: Trevor Cahill, John Danks, Jaime García

There aren't many starters who can survive without missing bats, but together Anderson and the A's found a formula. His elite ground ball rate, a cavernous yard and tremendous defense on the left side of the infield helped Oakland wring a 3.89 ERA out of the aging southpaw, which was nearly a run better than his DRA. And what a delightfully unexpected contribution it was: Anderson had topped 20 starts and 120 innings only once all decade so, sure, why wouldn't he fire 175 frames for a playoff team in the September of his career? The lefty's surprising durability was a shot in the arm for a staff otherwise battered by injuries and suspensions all year long. It's unlikely he gives them 30 starts, but the Brewers, perennially short on starters, inked him to a one-year deal in December.

Aaron Ashby LHP   Born: 05/24/98   Age: 22   Bats: R   Throws: L   Height: 6'2"   Weight: 181   Origin: Round 4, 2018 Draft (#125 overall)

YEAR	TEAM	LVL	AGE	W	L	SV	G	GS	IP	H	HR	BB/9	K/9	K	GB%	BABIP	WHIP	ERA	DRA	WARP	MPH	FB%	WHF	CSP
2018	HEL	RK	20	1	2	1	6	3	20¹	18	3	3.5	8.4	19	52%	.273	1.28	6.20	2.95	0.7				
2018	WIS	A	20	1	1	0	7	7	37¹	40	1	2.2	11.3	47	52%	.398	1.31	2.17	4.19	0.5				
2019	WIS	A	21	3	4	0	11	10	61	47	4	4.1	11.8	80	49%	.319	1.23	3.54	4.45	0.5				
2019	CAR	A+	21	2	6	0	13	13	65	54	1	4.4	7.6	55	50%	.283	1.32	3.46	4.81	0.2				
2020	MIL	MLB	22	2	2	0	33	0	35	34	5	4.1	8.1	32	46%	.293	1.43	4.79	4.81	0.2				

Comparables: Justin Wilson, Blake Snell, Yennsy Diaz

The nephew of Andy, who played 14 years for various National League squads, Aaron showed he wasn't just a nepotism pick in his first full season in professional baseball. Rather, he earned the organization's award for the top minor-league pitcher for his success across both A-ball levels. This Ashby can only hope that his control improves with age, the way his uncle's did. Should that happen, he might stick in the rotation. Otherwise, he's looking at life in the pen—but what a life it could be.

Ray Black RHP   Born: 06/26/90   Age: 30   Bats: R   Throws: R   Height: 6'5"   Weight: 225   Origin: Round 7, 2011 Draft (#237 overall)

YEAR	TEAM	LVL	AGE	W	L	SV	G	GS	IP	H	HR	BB/9	K/9	K	GB%	BABIP	WHIP	ERA	DRA	WARP	MPH	FB%	WHF	CSP
2018	RIC	AA	28	0	0	4	10	0	10	4	0	3.6	18.0	20	7%	.286	0.80	0.90	1.54	0.4				
2018	SAC	AAA	28	3	0	1	26	0	25²	15	2	2.8	16.1	46	25%	.310	0.90	3.16	1.79	1.0				
2018	SFN	MLB	28	2	2	0	26	0	23¹	17	4	3.9	12.7	33	41%	.277	1.16	6.17	2.66	0.6	100.5	64	17.1	45.7
2019	SAC	AAA	29	1	0	1	23	1	22²	19	4	5.2	14.3	36	38%	.349	1.41	5.16	3.72	0.6				
2019	SAN	AAA	29	0	0	1	6	0	6	1	0	3.0	13.5	9	60%	.100	0.50	1.50	5.93	0.0				
2019	SFN	MLB	29	0	0	0	2	0	2	4	1	4.5	22.5	5	0%	.750	2.50	4.50	3.61	0.0	101.5	71.2	17.3	57.1
2019	MIL	MLB	29	0	1	0	15	0	14	10	4	5.1	8.4	13	30%	.182	1.29	5.14	7.42	-0.3	99.8	76.3	13.7	46.6
2020	MIL	MLB	30	3	3	0	56	0	60	51	10	4.3	12.5	83	33%	.309	1.34	4.26	4.25	0.8	99.5	68.9	15.9	47.2

Comparables: Grant Dayton, Robert Coello, Leonel Campos

In a sense, it's remarkable Black has been a functional pitcher at any level, given that his only real tool is a fastball he locates as well and frequently as blindfolded children do the donkey's tail. That's the value—or allure, anyway—of velocity. He averaged 98.4 MPH on his fourseamer in 2019, ranking him ninth among relievers who threw at least one big-league pitch. Black was even ahead of some guy named Aroldis Chapman. Imagining what Black could do with marginally improved command is a fool's errand, but every pitching coach needs hope in their life, even if it proves to be misplaced—like, um, a certain right-hander's heater.

Corbin Burnes RHP   Born: 10/22/94   Age: 25   Bats: R   Throws: R   Height: 6'3"   Weight: 205   Origin: Round 4, 2016 Draft (#111 overall)

YEAR	TEAM	LVL	AGE	W	L	SV	G	GS	IP	H	HR	BB/9	K/9	K	GB%	BABIP	WHIP	ERA	DRA	WARP	MPH	FB%	WHF	CSP
2017	CAR	A+	22	5	0	0	10	10	60	37	1	2.4	8.4	56	54%	.243	0.88	1.05	2.37	2.0				
2017	BLX	AA	22	3	3	0	16	16	85²	66	2	2.1	8.8	84	51%	.279	1.00	2.10	3.23	2.0				
2018	CSP	AAA	23	3	4	0	19	13	78²	83	7	3.5	9.3	81	47%	.347	1.45	5.15	4.30	1.1				
2018	MIL	MLB	23	7	0	1	30	0	38	27	4	2.6	8.3	35	50%	.232	1.00	2.61	3.39	0.7	97.6	58.8	15.8	50.6
2019	SAN	AAA	24	0	1	0	8	7	22¹	29	2	3.6	10.1	25	50%	.409	1.70	8.46	3.70	0.6				
2019	MIL	MLB	24	1	5	1	32	4	49	70	17	3.7	12.9	70	46%	.414	1.84	8.82	4.99	0.3	98.0	56.8	18	45.7
2020	MIL	MLB	25	4	4	0	46	6	74	66	10	3.9	11.8	97	47%	.317	1.32	4.09	4.12	1.2	97.6	58.9	17.7	49.1

Comparables: John Gant, Cody Martin, Hunter Wood

Disaster. Calamity. Catastrophe. Debacle. Cataclysm. Tragedy. Fiasco. We're running out of synonyms here, but all of them perfectly describe Burnes' 2019. After giving up just four homers in 38 frames in 2018, batters teed off for 17 blasts in 48 innings in 2019—that's a ridiculous 3.1 per nine, for those without a calculator handy. His slider was still nasty, as it finished off a majority of his strikeouts, but he just couldn't get the fastball by hitters. That's a notable change from the previous season, when he held opponents to a .176 average and .250 slugging (those marks were up to .420 and .790 last season). The Brewers have to hope some time to reflect can help Burnes get back on track as a mid-rotation starter.

Alex Claudio LHP   Born: 01/31/92   Age: 28   Bats: L   Throws: L   Height: 6'3"   Weight: 180   Origin: Round 27, 2010 Draft (#826 overall)

YEAR	TEAM	LVL	AGE	W	L	SV	G	GS	IP	H	HR	BB/9	K/9	K	GB%	BABIP	WHIP	ERA	DRA	WARP	MPH	FB%	WHF	CSP
2017	TEX	MLB	25	4	2	11	70	1	82²	71	5	1.6	6.1	56	68%	.269	1.04	2.50	3.77	1.3	88.4	56.6	10.6	45.8
2018	TEX	MLB	26	4	2	1	66	1	68¹	91	4	1.7	5.4	41	64%	.366	1.52	4.48	4.69	0.2	88.1	52	12.3	45.1
2019	MIL	MLB	27	2	2	0	83	0	62	57	8	3.5	6.4	44	58%	.266	1.31	4.06	4.93	0.3	87.6	46.2	11.3	41.1
2020	MIL	MLB	28	3	3	2	56	0	60	55	7	2.6	6.5	43	60%	.269	1.21	3.64	3.83	1.0	87.5	51.3	11.5	43.9

Comparables: Jeremy Accardo, Brandon Maurer, Cla Meredith

In times where we practically expect relievers to bring 95-plus mph heat, Claudio feels like a relic from the past. Despite the fact that Claudio never once breached 89 mph in 2019, he was an above-replacement reliever for a fourth-straight season. His sinker is one of the heaviest in the league, as he induced nearly 2.5 grounders for every ball in the air, and he did that while allowing just one home run off the pitch all year. Not everything was golden for Claudio in his first season in Milwaukee, though, as hitters connected against his previously baffling changeup, a pitch that often clocks in the 60s. After allowing just a .296 slugging against the change in 2018, hitters connected for four homers and a .471 slugging percentage on the pitch in 2019. Given how the odds are stacked against him already based on his well-below-average velocity, he'll need to correct that in 2020 if he's to have a 2021.

Josh Hader LHP   Born: 04/07/94   Age: 26   Bats: L   Throws: L   Height: 6'3"   Weight: 185   Origin: Round 19, 2012 Draft (#582 overall)

YEAR	TEAM	LVL	AGE	W	L	SV	G	GS	IP	H	HR	BB/9	K/9	K	GB%	BABIP	WHIP	ERA	DRA	WARP	MPH	FB%	WHF	CSP
2017	CSP	AAA	23	3	4	0	12	12	52	49	14	5.4	8.8	51	37%	.265	1.54	5.37	4.82	0.5				
2017	MIL	MLB	23	2	3	0	35	0	47²	25	4	4.2	12.8	68	36%	.233	0.99	2.08	3.31	1.0	97.1	81.4	18.4	49.4
2018	MIL	MLB	24	6	1	12	55	0	81¹	36	9	3.3	15.8	143	31%	.220	0.81	2.43	2.00	2.7	97.4	79.1	20.5	51.7
2019	MIL	MLB	25	3	5	37	61	0	75²	41	15	2.4	16.4	138	22%	.232	0.81	2.62	2.20	2.6	97.9	84.1	24.4	51
2020	MIL	MLB	26	3	3	36	62	0	66	41	10	3.6	16.5	120	29%	.300	1.03	2.68	2.85	1.8	97.2	83.1	22.2	51.8

Comparables: Stephen Gonsalves, Touki Toussaint, Justus Sheffield

We're joking when we write that the altered baseball should be used whenever Hader is on the mound, but that might be the only way batters have a chance. Hitters made contact even less often against Hader last season, down to just 58.2 percent of swings (versus 60.5 percent in 2018). Yet 15 of the 41 hits he allowed were home runs—that works out to 21.4 percent of his flyballs. Woof. We can talk all we want about pitchers like Hader "providing the power" with the velocity on their fastballs, except that's been proven to be an overstated factor. The bigger factor, if we had to guess, was that batters are geared up to swing hard on his heater, which he threw roughly 80 percent of the time. May as well; it's not as though they're likely to make contact regardless.

Adrian Houser RHP   Born: 02/02/93   Age: 27   Bats: R   Throws: R   Height: 6'4"   Weight: 235   Origin: Round 2, 2011 Draft (#69 overall)

YEAR	TEAM	LVL	AGE	W	L	SV	G	GS	IP	H	HR	BB/9	K/9	K	GB%	BABIP	WHIP	ERA	DRA	WARP	MPH	FB%	WHF	CSP
2017	BRR	RK	24	0	1	0	6	6	8²	4	1	4.2	16.6	16	73%	.214	0.92	1.04	0.00	0.6				
2017	WIS	A	24	1	0	0	3	2	9	5	0	0.0	11.0	11	71%	.238	0.56	1.00	2.11	0.3				
2018	BLX	AA	25	0	1	0	8	8	26²	30	3	2.4	10.1	30	51%	.365	1.39	4.72	6.34	-0.3				
2018	CSP	AAA	25	2	3	0	13	13	52	66	6	3.1	6.4	37	54%	.357	1.62	5.19	5.89	-0.2				
2018	MIL	MLB	25	0	0	0	7	0	13²	13	0	4.6	5.3	8	40%	.302	1.46	3.29	5.04	0.0	96.7	66.4	11.1	44.7
2019	SAN	AAA	26	2	0	0	4	4	21¹	13	2	1.7	9.7	23	56%	.212	0.80	1.27	1.39	1.1				
2019	MIL	MLB	26	6	7	0	35	18	111¹	101	14	3.0	9.5	117	55%	.301	1.24	3.72	3.61	2.5	96.4	67.4	10.5	47.2
2020	MIL	MLB	27	8	8	0	26	26	122	117	16	3.3	9.2	124	54%	.305	1.33	4.27	4.32	2.0	95.9	68.1	10.7	46.6

Comparables: Jarlin García, Rookie Davis, Steven Shell

Believe it or not, Houser was part of the Carlos Gómez trade that also netted the Brewers Josh Hader, Domingo Santana and Brett Phillips. (Hey, three out of four ain't bad.) Houser showed aptitude for starting in the second half, fanning a batter per inning over his final 77 innings with a 4.02 ERA to boot. A strong offspeed pitch has eluded him thus far, but he's doing just fine with a 95 mph four-seamer that can leap over bats and a heavy sinker that generates grounders as need be. The Brewers will presumably give him a chance to continue along in the rotation. Worst-case: he can transition back into the multi-inning relief role that he was quite good in earlier in the season.

Corey Knebel RHP   Born: 11/26/91   Age: 28   Bats: R   Throws: R   Height: 6'4"   Weight: 220   Origin: Round 1, 2013 Draft (#39 overall)

YEAR	TEAM	LVL	AGE	W	L	SV	G	GS	IP	H	HR	BB/9	K/9	K	GB%	BABIP	WHIP	ERA	DRA	WARP	MPH	FB%	WHF	CSP
2017	MIL	MLB	25	1	4	39	76	0	76	48	6	4.7	14.9	126	39%	.311	1.16	1.78	3.09	1.8	99.2	71.8	15.4	47.4
2018	MIL	MLB	26	4	3	16	57	0	55¹	38	7	3.6	14.3	88	50%	.304	1.08	3.58	2.53	1.5	98.8	70.9	14.5	49.2
2020	MIL	MLB	28	2	2	2	34	0	36	31	6	4.1	12.4	49	44%	.308	1.31	4.20	4.22	0.5	98.4	71.8	15	48.7

Comparables: Carl Edwards Jr., Keone Kela, Bruce Rondón

Is a tired arm ever really just a tired arm? That was the diagnosis for Knebel on March 20th, just a few days after he pushed through his longest outing of spring training—a five-out appearance, the likes of which the Brewers were hoping to rely on long into the dog days of summer. "Just giving it a break," Knebel told reporters. He wouldn't throw a single major league inning in 2019, as that "tired arm" evolved in to a UCL issue, and he underwent Tommy John surgery later in the month. Perhaps we shouldn't be too surprised; Knebel's delivery is violent, and he threw more innings in 2017 and 2018 combined than any two-year stretch in his career, all while pumping his average fastball velocity up from 95 to over 97. Knebel's recovery was on track as of the end of the season, so he should be back sometime in 2020.

Eric Lauer LHP   Born: 06/03/95   Age: 25   Bats: R   Throws: L   Height: 6'3"   Weight: 205   Origin: Round 1, 2016 Draft (#25 overall)

YEAR	TEAM	LVL	AGE	W	L	SV	G	GS	IP	H	HR	BB/9	K/9	K	GB%	BABIP	WHIP	ERA	DRA	WARP	MPH	FB%	WHF	CSP
2017	LEL	A+	22	2	5	0	12	12	67²	65	4	2.5	11.2	84	42%	.351	1.24	2.79	3.93	1.1				
2017	SAN	AA	22	4	3	0	10	9	55	52	6	2.8	7.9	48	38%	.295	1.25	3.93	4.77	0.2				
2018	ELP	AAA	23	2	1	0	4	4	21¹	13	1	3.8	9.3	22	48%	.226	1.03	2.53	2.76	0.7				
2018	SDN	MLB	23	6	7	0	23	23	112	127	15	3.7	8.0	100	39%	.332	1.54	4.34	5.27	0.1	94.0	57.8	9.7	51.5
2019	SDN	MLB	24	8	10	0	30	29	149²	158	20	3.1	8.3	138	42%	.316	1.40	4.45	4.85	1.5	94.0	53	9.5	51.5
2020	MIL	MLB	25	9	9	0	26	26	137	140	22	3.0	7.9	121	41%	.297	1.35	4.60	4.66	1.8	93.7	56.1	9.8	52.7

Comparables: Antonio Bastardo, David Price, Derek Holland

Lauer earned the Opening Day nod last spring and showed improvement during his second year in the Padres rotation, pitching more efficiently and improving both his walk and strikeout rates. The young lefty doesn't throw hard, but he's always around the zone and shows solid command, with a wide assortment of curveballs, sliders, cutters and changeups. That mix helps his mundane four-seamer play up and keep him effective against righties. Lauer doesn't have a true swing-and-miss offering, isn't going to toss any shutouts and won't be a top jersey-seller. Instead, he'll hit his target, control the running game, post average numbers and keep his team in games more often than not, from a spot at the back of the rotation. That's a lot more valuable than most people think.

Josh Lindblom RHP   Born: 06/15/87   Age: 33   Bats: R   Throws: R   Height: 6'4"   Weight: 240   Origin: Round 2, 2008 Draft (#61 overall)

YEAR	TEAM	LVL	AGE	W	L	SV	G	GS	IP	H	HR	BB/9	K/9	K	GB%	BABIP	WHIP	ERA	DRA	WARP	MPH	FB%	WHF	CSP
2017	IND	AAA	30	0	2	0	17	4	37²	37	5	1.9	7.9	33	34%	.294	1.19	4.06	4.32	0.5				
2017	PIT	MLB	30	0	0	0	4	0	10¹	18	0	2.6	8.7	10	42%	.474	2.03	7.84	6.99	-0.2	92.4	53.8	11.3	46.1
2020	MIL	MLB	33	8	9	0	26	26	135	145	28	2.8	6.7	100	36%	.288	1.39	5.31	5.35	0.7	91.4	53.1	11.2	45.6

Comparables: Jeff Manship, Chaz Roe, Logan Kensing

Denis Johnson once suggested that the key to making a tree treat you as a friend was to leave it alone. "After the blade bit in," Johnson wrote, "you had yourself a war." The Brewers have, for years, gotten away with a so-so-looking rotation by leaving it alone, save for a late-season addition here and there. That changed over the winter winter. They shipped out Zach Davies and Chase Anderson and non-tendered Jimmy Nelson—all for financial reasons—only to eschew big-named replacements and instead add Eric Lauer, Brett Anderson and Lindblom, who performed nicely in his three seasons spent in Korea. He doesn't throw hard and he'll be doing well if he's a league-average starter, but the Brewers are used to courting war with their budget-saving maneuvers. Now that the blade has bit in, the Brewers are just hoping for a WARP.

Freddy Peralta RHP   Born: 06/04/96   Age: 24   Bats: R   Throws: R   Height: 5'11"   Weight: 175   Origin: International Free Agent, 2013

YEAR	TEAM	LVL	AGE	W	L	SV	G	GS	IP	H	HR	BB/9	K/9	K	GB%	BABIP	WHIP	ERA	DRA	WARP	MPH	FB%	WHF	CSP
2017	CAR	A+	21	1	0	0	12	8	56¹	39	6	5.0	12.5	78	39%	.268	1.24	3.04	2.81	1.6				
2017	BLX	AA	21	2	5	1	13	11	63²	38	2	4.4	12.9	91	46%	.267	1.08	2.26	2.78	1.8				
2018	CSP	AAA	22	6	2	0	13	13	61	49	1	4.1	12.8	87	48%	.343	1.26	3.10	2.80	1.9				
2018	MIL	MLB	22	6	4	0	16	14	78¹	49	8	4.6	11.0	96	33%	.237	1.14	4.25	5.21	0.1	94.3	77.6	12	49.2
2019	SAN	AAA	23	0	0	0	4	0	7	4	0	3.9	21.9	17	25%	.500	1.00	1.29	0.56	0.4				
2019	MIL	MLB	23	7	3	1	39	8	85	87	15	3.9	12.2	115	34%	.338	1.46	5.29	4.93	0.6	97.3	78.4	14.5	49.8
2020	MIL	MLB	24	6	5	2	47	13	97	83	14	4.1	11.2	121	36%	.296	1.31	4.09	4.12	1.7	95.8	80.4	13.9	51

Comparables: Jake Faria, Touki Toussaint, Enyel De Los Santos

Watching Peralta dominate the Reds in Cincinnati for eight innings on April 3rd, his second start of the campaign, it looked like he was the future of the Brewers rotation. He blew his electric fastball by Red after Red and even caught Joey Votto staring at a curveball for strike three. His 10th and final strikeout of the day came on a vicious biting curve spiked dead into the dirt to retire Yasiel Puig to end the eighth representing the go-ahead run at the plate. It's the stuff fans dream about. But Peralta lasted over five innings just once in six more starts before he was ultimately demoted to the bullpen in mid-June, where he was still mediocre at best. The curveball, so stunning that April afternoon, proved inconsistent; he couldn't locate it for a strike, and his poor control gave hitters no incentive to wave at the one in the dirt. A one-trick pony is fun to watch, but only for a little while.

Trey Supak RHP Born: 05/31/96 Age: 24 Bats: R Throws: R Height: 6'5" Weight: 240 Origin: Round 2, 2014 Draft (#73 overall)

YEAR	TEAM	LVL	AGE	W	L	SV	G	GS	IP	H	HR	BB/9	K/9	K	GB%	BABIP	WHIP	ERA	DRA	WARP	MPH	FB%	WHF	CSP
2017	WIS	A	21	2	2	0	8	7	41	21	1	2.2	11.6	53	36%	.235	0.76	1.76	2.08	1.5				
2017	CAR	A+	21	3	4	1	15	11	72¹	65	12	3.5	7.1	57	34%	.261	1.29	4.60	4.93	0.2				
2018	CAR	A+	22	2	1	0	9	9	51	37	2	2.8	8.5	48	38%	.269	1.04	1.76	3.14	1.3				
2018	BLX	AA	22	6	6	0	16	16	86²	74	4	2.9	7.8	75	45%	.286	1.18	2.91	4.05	1.3				
2019	BLX	AA	23	11	4	0	20	20	122²	84	6	1.7	6.7	91	47%	.226	0.87	2.20	3.19	2.6				
2019	SAN	AAA	23	1	2	0	7	7	30	41	6	2.7	8.1	27	37%	.387	1.67	9.30	8.27	-0.4				
2020	MIL	MLB	24	3	3	0	10	10	46	46	8	3.8	6.4	33	42%	.274	1.42	5.03	5.05	0.4				

Comparables: Jorge López, Ronald Bolaños, Chase De Jong

A rough introduction to the Pacific Coast League put to rest talk of Supak arriving in Milwaukee in 2019. How rough was it? Supak allowed just as many home runs in his 20 starts in Double-A as he did in seven starts in Triple-A. Woof. The altered baseball undoubtedly is a partial culprit, but Supak has long been considered a potential bullpen candidate due to merely average stuff. The Brewers originally acquired him (*and* Keon Broxton) for Jason Rogers, so whatever happens won't result in trader's remorse.

Brent Suter LHP Born: 08/29/89 Age: 30 Bats: L Throws: L Height: 6'5" Weight: 195 Origin: Round 31, 2012 Draft (#965 overall)

YEAR	TEAM	LVL	AGE	W	L	SV	G	GS	IP	H	HR	BB/9	K/9	K	GB%	BABIP	WHIP	ERA	DRA	WARP	MPH	FB%	WHF	CSP
2017	CSP	AAA	27	3	1	0	10	8	36²	42	5	2.0	9.3	38	46%	.359	1.36	4.42	3.79	0.8				
2017	MIL	MLB	27	3	2	0	22	14	81²	83	8	2.4	7.1	64	46%	.306	1.29	3.42	4.72	0.7	88.5	70.6	10.3	49
2018	MIL	MLB	28	8	7	0	20	18	101¹	102	18	1.7	7.5	84	36%	.281	1.19	4.44	5.01	0.3	89.0	68.9	11.1	50.1
2019	SAN	AAA	29	0	0	0	4	2	11²	4	0	1.5	13.9	18	46%	.182	0.51	0.00	0.37	0.7				
2019	MIL	MLB	29	4	0	0	9	0	18¹	10	1	0.5	7.4	15	53%	.188	0.60	0.49	4.11	0.2	89.4	78.1	14.6	52.5
2020	MIL	MLB	30	4	4	0	60	3	74	70	13	2.0	7.7	63	42%	.270	1.17	3.86	4.05	1.2	88.2	70.2	11.1	50.7

Comparables: Tyler Lyons, Scott Alexander, Sam Gaviglio

Suter's 2019 was assumed to be a lost year after he underwent Tommy John surgery in July 2018. Yet he made his way back to the majors for September, and turned out to be a vital performer for the Brewers down the stretch. The question moving forward is how Milwaukee will deploy him. Suter has had some success in a starting role, but he looked perfectly suited to pitch multiple innings out of the bullpen, too. With Josh Hader settling more into a traditional role, the Brewers could use another versatile, multi-inning threat in their bullpen. Suter might just be that guy.

Bobby Wahl RHP Born: 03/21/92 Age: 28 Bats: R Throws: R Height: 6'2" Weight: 210 Origin: Round 5, 2013 Draft (#161 overall)

YEAR	TEAM	LVL	AGE	W	L	SV	G	GS	IP	H	HR	BB/9	K/9	K	GB%	BABIP	WHIP	ERA	DRA	WARP	MPH	FB%	WHF	CSP
2017	NAS	AAA	25	1	1	3	11	0	13	13	3	3.5	15.2	22	23%	.357	1.38	4.15	2.91	0.3				
2017	OAK	MLB	25	0	0	0	7	0	7²	8	0	4.7	9.4	8	22%	.348	1.57	4.70	7.51	-0.2	97.4	78.6	11	51.2
2018	NAS	AAA	26	3	2	11	34	1	39²	17	2	3.9	14.7	65	42%	.224	0.86	2.27	1.91	1.5				
2018	NYN	MLB	26	0	1	0	7	0	5¹	9	2	6.8	11.8	7	17%	.438	2.44	10.12	4.11	0.0	98.3	72.3	14.3	51.7
2020	MIL	MLB	28	1	1	0	23	0	24	24	5	4.2	9.3	25	36%	.293	1.46	5.43	5.33	0.0	97.2	75.9	12.8	51.8

Comparables: Jimmie Sherfy, Colton Murray, Giovanny Gallegos

Ligaments are fickle beasts. It wasn't the UCL that doomed Wahl—as you might expect from a reliever capable of chucking 98 mph fastballs and biting mid-80s curveballs—instead, it was the ACL in his right knee, his push-off leg, that gave away as he delivered a pitch in a spring training game. If that sounds like a freak injury to you...well, history agrees: According to MLB's central injury database, Wahl is just the third player to suffer such an injury to his back knee as the direct result of throwing a pitch. It's too bad for various reasons, including the possibility that Wahl would have made for a nifty addition to the Brewers bullpen; his 42.7 percent strikeout rate and 20.7 percent whiff rate in Triple-A in 2018 made him one of the more enticing young relief arms out there. Provided he makes a full recovery, he should factor into their 2020 bullpen.

Devin Williams RHP Born: 09/21/94 Age: 25 Bats: R Throws: R Height: 6'3" Weight: 165 Origin: Round 2, 2013 Draft (#54 overall)

YEAR	TEAM	LVL	AGE	W	L	SV	G	GS	IP	H	HR	BB/9	K/9	K	GB%	BABIP	WHIP	ERA	DRA	WARP	MPH	FB%	WHF	CSP
2018	CAR	A+	23	0	3	0	14	14	34	40	2	5.8	9.3	35	38%	.380	1.82	5.82	6.33	-0.4				
2019	BLX	AA	24	7	2	4	31	0	53¹	34	3	4.9	12.8	76	48%	.279	1.18	2.36	3.88	0.5				
2019	MIL	MLB	24	0	0	0	13	0	13²	18	2	4.0	9.2	14	42%	.372	1.76	3.95	5.15	0.0	98.3	61	12.2	45.7
2020	MIL	MLB	25	2	2	0	39	0	42	41	8	3.9	8.6	40	44%	.292	1.42	4.98	4.93	0.2	98.0	62.5	12.5	46.8

Comparables: Elieser Hernandez, Domingo Germán, Jake Newberry

Williams had stagnated as a starter, but a move to the bullpen seems to have instilled new life. Looking at his profile, it's a move that makes perfect sense. Williams has posted huge strikeout numbers behind a two-pitch mix, yet struggled with wildness and endurance. The control issues, though present out of the bullpen, were less burdensome. Meanwhile, he's able to consistently air out a fastball that can touch into the upper-90s. Williams isn't going to be what the Brewers hoped he would turn into on draft day, but he might just become a high-quality reliever—and that's a win, all things considered.

Brandon Woodruff RHP Born: 02/10/93 Age: 27 Bats: L Throws: R Height: 6'4" Weight: 215 Origin: Round 11, 2014 Draft (#326 overall)

YEAR	TEAM	LVL	AGE	W	L	SV	G	GS	IP	H	HR	BB/9	K/9	K	GB%	BABIP	WHIP	ERA	DRA	WARP	MPH	FB%	WHF	CSP
2017	CSP	AAA	24	6	5	0	16	16	75¹	78	8	3.0	8.4	70	49%	.323	1.37	4.30	3.74	1.6				
2017	MIL	MLB	24	2	3	0	8	8	43	43	5	2.9	6.7	32	50%	.292	1.33	4.81	5.65	0.0	96.7	60.5	9.8	46.2
2018	CSP	AAA	25	3	2	0	17	17	71¹	67	8	4.0	8.6	68	50%	.296	1.39	4.04	3.59	1.6				
2018	MIL	MLB	25	3	0	1	19	4	42¹	36	4	3.0	10.0	47	54%	.294	1.18	3.61	3.16	0.9	97.9	64.1	11.3	50.1
2019	MIL	MLB	26	11	3	0	22	22	121²	109	12	2.2	10.6	143	46%	.320	1.14	3.62	3.23	3.4	98.4	64.1	13.1	49.3
2020	MIL	MLB	27	11	9	0	29	29	166	148	21	3.0	10.3	190	48%	.301	1.22	3.57	3.69	3.9	97.6	64.3	12.4	49.4

Comparables: Asher Wojciechowski, Trevor Oaks, Justin Grimm

Here's a stat for you. Woodruff's fastball coerced a whiff on 26 percent of the swings taken against it—that ranked 14th among all pitchers with 500-plus heaters thrown in 2019, right behind Max Scherzer and Jacob deGrom. Woodruff isn't Scherzer or deGrom, of course, but he looked like Milwaukee's best starter when he was healthy. The move to the rotation didn't dampen his strikeout ability, and he even added control. Woodruff will need to continue to refine his secondaries if he's going to make another All-Star Game, yet the real key to his game is going to be maintaining that top-notch fastball.

LINEOUTS

Hitters

HITTER	POS	TEAM	LVL	AGE	PA	R	2B	3B	HR	RBI	BB	K	SB	CS	AVG/OBP/SLG	DRC+	VORP	BABIP	BRR	FRAA	WARP
Pablo Abreu	OF	BRR	Rk	19	62	7	4	1	1	10	6	21	0	0	.226/.306/.396	50	1.6	.333	0.3	CF(2): -0.4	-0.2
	OF	WIS	A	19	113	13	4	1	0	11	9	35	3	0	.186/.248/.245	54	-2.4	.275	2.1	CF(13): 1.8, RF(11): 1.1	0.3
Micah Bello	OF	CSP	Rk+	18	198	30	9	3	6	20	18	47	5	4	.232/.308/.418	73	7.2	.280	2.4		0.2
Thomas Dillard	C	WIS	A	21	216	27	6	0	6	24	43	50	7	0	.246/.398/.386	144	9.9	.310	-1.8	1B(31): -0.3, LF(9): 1.7	1.2
Larry Ernesto	OF	BRR	Rk	18	132	15	3	0	2	9	7	59	5	1	.172/.229/.246	4	-4.1	.311	2.2	CF(24): 1.0, RF(3): -0.5	-0.6
David Freitas	C	SEA	MLB	30	4	1	0	0	0	1	1	0	0	0	.000/.250/.000	95	0.2	.000	0.0	C(1): 0.1	0.0
	C	TAC	AAA	30	25	4	2	0	0	5	5	6	0	0	.278/.480/.389	152	2.6	.417	-0.1	C(3): 0.7	2.5
	C	SAN	AAA	30	359	51	21	0	12	76	42	49	0	1	.387/.459/.571	161	43.1	.429	-2.0	C(47): -1.6, 1B(24): -1.9	3.4
	C	MIL	MLB	30	16	1	0	0	0	0	3	5	0	0	.077/.250/.077	82	0.2	.125	0.0		0.0
Ryon Healy	3B	SEA	MLB	27	187	24	16	0	7	26	13	40	0	0	.237/.289/.456	95	5.5	.262	-2.5	3B(44): -4.8, 1B(11): 0.7	-0.1
Payton Henry	C	CAR	A+	22	482	49	22	1	14	75	26	142	1	1	.242/.315/.395	98	6.6	.324	-2.5	C(67): 2.4	1.4
Nick Kahle	C	CSP	Rk+	21	163	25	11	1	6	25	20	36	2	1	.255/.350/.475	125	9.0	.300	-1.6		0.7
Tristen Lutz	OF	CAR	A+	20	477	62	24	3	13	54	46	137	3	2	.255/.335/.419	109	17.4	.343	-1.5	CF(70): -3.0, RF(39): -2.4	0.9
Mark Mathias	2B	COH	AAA	24	478	62	31	2	12	59	51	91	13	2	.269/.355/.442	105	25.9	.314	1.7	2B(52): 1.7, 3B(47): -1.8	1.8
Jace Peterson	2B	BAL	MLB	29	108	14	3	1	2	11	6	24	4	1	.220/.269/.330	80	0.6	.267	0.7	LF(18): 3.3, 3B(9): 0.0	0.5
	2B	NOR	AAA	29	377	58	25	5	10	46	46	56	13	3	.313/.398/.512	131	23.3	.350	-0.9	3B(38): 1.2, 1B(27): 1.8	2.7
Carlos Rodriguez	OF	CSP	Rk+	18	157	20	3	1	3	12	4	20	4	6	.331/.350/.424	120	8.9	.364	-0.5		0.7

Pablo Abreu, signed out of the Dominican Republic for $800,000 in 2016, has a good frame and power potential, but desperately needs to adjust his swing for the soft stuff. ⓧ When 19th century Californians found mica below, they were bummed about fool's gold. When the present day Brewers found **Micah Bello**, they hoped to unearth an eventual everyday outfielder. ⓧ One can only hope fifth-rounder **Thomas Dillard** is half as funny as former reliever Tim Dillard. This Dillard won't have all that free time in the bullpen to construct his routine—his future lies behind the plate or in the outfield. ⓧ Five-tool potential earned **Larry Ernesto** a $1.7 million signing bonus out of the Dominican Republic. You'll have a different job by the time he reaches the majors. ⓧ **David Freitas** appeared in 16 games with the Brewers, and every single time as a pinch-hitter. He's known more for his mitt than his stick, so you do the math on how that worked out. ⓧ The poorly named **Ryon Healy** had his season disrupted by nagging back and hip injuries, which led to season-ending surgery. The power is still there, but the only way you'll see "patient" and Healy in the same sentence is when discussing his medical records. ⓧ **Payton Henry** has a Russell Branyan-sized strikeout problem to solve, but any catcher with his kind of pop is worth keeping eyes on. He could be the next Sam Huff, or he could be the next Sam Hunt if this whole 'ball thing fails. ⓧ With many catchers, the question is if their defense will hold up as they climb the ladder; for **Nick Kahle**, the defense was what attracted the Brewers. The power and discipline the fourth-rounder showed in his first full season, then, are quite encouraging. ⓧ **Tristen Lutz** produced a near duplicate of his 2018 line, which is more impressive than it sounds given his advancement up the ladder. He has the physical tools to be a starting-caliber outfielder, so now we just have to wait for his contact or power to take the next step. Or for the tides to rise. That's an option, too. ⓧ Acquired from Cleveland in November, **Mark Mathias** joins a slew of infielders for whom major-league playing time would mean disaster in Milwaukee. ⓧ There's a three percent chance **Jace Peterson**'s next club will unlock something in his swing that adds some power and makes him a massive breakout slugger, and a 97 percent chance that club will also put off selecting his contract from Triple-A because he'll cost too much. ⓧ Big ticket 2017 international signing **Carlos Rodriguez** has hit for big average in the lowest levels of the minors over the last two years. He's got limited power, but has potential to be a nifty hit/speed/defense center fielder.

Pitchers

PITCHER	TEAM	LVL	AGE	W	L	SV	G	GS	IP	H	HR	BB/9	K/9	K	GB%	BABIP	WHIP	ERA	DRA	WARP	MPH	FB%	WHF	CSP
Zack Brown	SAN	AAA	24	3	7	0	25	23	116²	138	16	4.9	7.6	98	54%	.342	1.73	5.79	6.53	0.2				
Jake Faria	DUR	AAA	25	6	2	1	23	7	59²	55	8	3.9	11.2	74	37%	.331	1.36	4.07	4.10	1.3				
	SAN	AAA	25	1	1	0	6	0	7²	8	1	5.9	9.4	8	43%	.350	1.70	2.35	6.43	0.0				
	MIL	MLB	25	0	1	0	9	0	8²	18	3	5.2	8.3	8	41%	.484	2.65	11.42	6.62	-0.1	94.6	63	10.9	43.2
	TBA	MLB	25	0	0	0	7	0	10	10	2	6.3	9.9	11	45%	.296	1.70	2.70	5.89	-0.1	95.8	59.3	15.3	41.3
J.P. Feyereisen	SWB	AAA	26	10	2	7	40	0	61¹	37	6	4.5	13.8	94	38%	.261	1.11	2.49	2.08	2.5				
Deolis Guerra	SAN	AAA	30	4	0	0	45	1	66²	43	5	2.2	11.9	88	44%	.262	0.88	1.89	1.15	3.3				
	MIL	MLB	30	0	0	0	1	0	0²	4	1	0.0	0.0	0	0%	.600	6.00	54.00	5.29	0.0	93.1	35.3	17.6	55.2
Jay Jackson	SAN	AAA	31	5	2	8	34	0	40²	28	1	2.2	12.0	54	41%	.287	0.93	1.33	1.11	2.0				
	MIL	MLB	31	1	0	0	28	0	30¹	22	6	5.3	13.9	47	38%	.271	1.32	4.45	3.96	0.5	96.1	41.5	18.6	39.6
Jeremy Jeffress	MIL	MLB	31	3	4	1	48	0	52	54	5	2.9	8.0	46	49%	.322	1.37	5.02	4.80	0.3	96.0	64.3	10.1	47.2
Antoine Kelly	BRB	Rk	19	0	0	0	9	9	28²	21	0	1.6	12.9	41	47%	.333	0.91	1.26	1.57	1.4				
Shelby Miller	BRR	Rk	28	0	1	0	2	2	9	4	0	1.0	14.0	14	67%	.222	0.56	2.00	3.45	0.3				
	SAN	AAA	28	1	2	0	5	5	20²	17	1	7.0	8.7	20	44%	.296	1.60	4.79	4.36	0.5				
	TEX	MLB	28	1	3	0	19	8	44	58	8	5.9	6.1	30	41%	.336	1.98	8.59	9.08	-1.6	96.8	69.5	8.3	50.8
Angel Perdomo	BLX	AA	25	2	0	0	7	0	15¹	6	0	4.7	12.3	21	46%	.214	0.91	1.17	2.59	0.4				
	SAN	AAA	25	3	2	1	40	0	54	47	8	6.3	14.3	86	34%	.352	1.57	5.17	4.14	1.1				
Drew Rasmussen	CAR	A+	23	0	0	0	4	4	11¹	7	0	1.6	12.7	16	52%	.280	0.79	1.59	2.57	0.3				
	BLX	AA	23	1	3	0	22	18	61	49	4	4.3	11.4	77	48%	.317	1.28	3.54	4.29	0.5				
Ethan Small	WIS	A	22	0	2	0	5	5	18	11	0	2.0	15.5	31	32%	.286	0.83	1.00	2.50	0.6				
Braden Webb	BRR	Rk	24	0	1	0	5	5	8	1	0	5.6	14.6	13	46%	.077	0.75	2.25	0.94	0.4				
	CAR	A+	24	1	2	0	8	8	36²	23	6	6.1	7.6	31	35%	.226	1.31	3.44	3.69	0.6				
	BLX	AA	24	1	4	0	6	5	15	15	2	9.0	7.8	13	32%	.289	2.00	9.00	7.52	-0.5				
Aaron Wilkerson	SAN	AAA	30	8	2	0	17	17	76¹	62	10	3.4	9.6	81	38%	.271	1.19	3.42	2.44	3.2				
	MIL	MLB	30	0	0	0	8	0	16	25	4	5.1	6.2	11	38%	.375	2.12	7.31	8.11	-0.5	92.1	50.5	8.7	42.9
Taylor Williams	SAN	AAA	27	3	3	6	46	0	54	40	8	3.5	9.5	57	56%	.237	1.13	2.83	2.59	1.9				
	MIL	MLB	27	1	1	0	10	0	14²	22	1	4.3	9.2	15	61%	.438	1.98	9.82	4.96	0.1	97.0	63.3	12.7	44.7
Eric Yardley	ELP	AAA	28	0	2	7	43	0	63²	60	3	2.0	7.4	52	64%	.303	1.16	2.83	2.01	2.6				
	SDN	MLB	28	0	1	0	10	0	11²	12	1	2.3	5.4	7	66%	.275	1.29	2.31	4.37	0.1	87.7	67.4	11.1	44.8

Between "The Owl" and the combination of the altered ball and the PCL, it just wasn't a good year for anyone named **Zack Brown**. This one will try to regain some prospect shine in 2020. ⓧ **Jake Faria**'s lack of velocity forces him to nibble a bit, but there's a fine line between nibbling and lacking control. Faria vaulted over it at both Triple-A and the majors in 2019. ⓧ Milwaukee finally freed **J.P. Feyereisen** from the overstock of interesting Yankee arms just before the Rule 5 Draft. A long history of high-minors success (and nominative determinism) suggests he could be an effective Feyer Man if give a chance. ⓧ Dominating Triple-A (as a 30-year-old, mind you) landed **Deolis Guerra** back in the majors for the first time since 2017—for two outs, anyway. Still, that's more than Johan Santana, Kevin Mulvey, Carlos Gómez and Phil Humber did in 2019. ⓧ **Jay Jackson's** fastball-slider combination was fierce against right-handed batters, but he chose to return to Japan rather than follow the Joe Smith career path. ⓧ **Jeremy Jeffress'** food truck, JJ's Bread and Butter, served meals this year at Miller Park, which is odd because opposing batters seemed to prefer eating up his pitches. ⓧ Ever moths to the flames that are young, tall pitchers, the Brewers selected 6-foot-6 **Antoine Kelly** in the second round. He has a huge fastball, but Milwaukee's development team will be tasked with building up his nascent secondary offerings. ⓧ It's true what they say. Whether he was pitching for the Rangers or the San Antonio Missions, **Shelby Miller**'s FIP really was bigger in Texas. ⓧ The non-roster signing of **Angel Perdomo** continued the Brewers' obsession with tall pitchers—maybe they're scouting for the Bucks?—but he walked the baseline every time out and frankly didn't show much effort on the glass. ⓧ Two Tommy John surgeries later, **Drew Rasmussen** is still throwing absolute gas. The fact that he was able to complete 72 healthy innings was an accomplishment in itself, and he should reach the majors this year. ⓧ Even with just five pro starts under his belt, it's easy to see why **Ethan Small** was able to earn Pitcher of the Year honors. He finished his amateur career ranked third on the Mississippi State all-time strikeout leaderboard, and then showed his deceptive ways could miss minor-league bats just as easily. ⓧ Remember Brandon Webb? **Braden Webb** is of no relation beyond sharing a surname - a vague connection, sure, but a stronger one than the bond between his pitches and the strike zone. Webb has a mid-90s fastball and a solid curveball, yet walking seven per nine is good for nothing except getting people thinking and talking and writing about better pitchers. ⓧ **Aaron Wilkerson** went unclaimed on waivers in September, but the big guy can throw strikes and pitch long relief or spot start if needed. Now on the wrong side of 30 with a fastball too often on the wrong side of 90, it's hard to see glory in his future. ⓧ **Taylor Williams** has impressive raw stuff on paper. His fastball is a bit too straight, however, and batters hit .442 (and slugged .553) against it in 2019. ⓧ Longtime minor league ground ball savant **Eric Yardley** was finally given a chance to prove his low-velo sidearm sinker/slider routine can leave doubled-up big-leaguers slamming their helmets in frustration; it wasn't enough for him to stick with the prospect-rich Padres, but Yardley peddles a product every bullpen can use.

MINNESOTA TWINS

Essay by Matt Trueblood

Player comments by Wilson Karaman and BP staff

The 2019 Twins were the quintessential team for that season, in ways both very good and very bad. No single fact about the club better illustrates this than their home-run total, 307, which obliterated the old franchise and league records. On the other hand, and in the other valence, that home-run total was inflated by the aeroball, which permitted three other teams to hit what would also have been record-setting numbers of dingers, so it's hard to truly grasp what the record does and doesn't mean. The Twins were fun to watch, and in some senses, they were wildly successful: they won 101 games and cruised to the American League Central crown. After they were swept by the Yankees (yet again) in the Divisional Series, however, fans departed with a bitter taste in their mouths; the same sense of meaninglessness (perhaps even of artifice) that colored the home-run record settled over the team's won-lost record.

It's not just the aeroball distorting our understanding of the game as we embark on a new decade, however, and it's not only the Twins who were left buffeted by criss-crossing winds of change, and thus made to feel terrifyingly still, even as they make ample progress. The Statcast Era has had effects even more profound and far-reaching than most imagined when the system was first implemented in 2014. Off the big-league field and away from the Statcast cameras, other technological advancements have similarly thrown open new doors. A great many things we long believed to be fixed but largely unknowable have turned out to be knowable but highly fluid—from the aerodynamic properties of the baseball, to a player's individual talent level, to the interaction factors that make up a winning clubhouse.

That's set the game on its ear, and forced teams to adopt new philosophies based on a crucial premise: you have to work relentlessly to get ahead, but once there, you can't stop for even a moment. As teams prepare for 2020, the Twins exemplify that better than any other team.

Last year's Twins were not just a product of the aeroball. They were a team with talent in many places on the roster, and more importantly, they got more out of their talent than all but a few other teams in the majors. By replacing Paul Molitor (who was nobly open-minded about advanced information, given his age and background, but who wasn't the proactive conduit for that information the front office

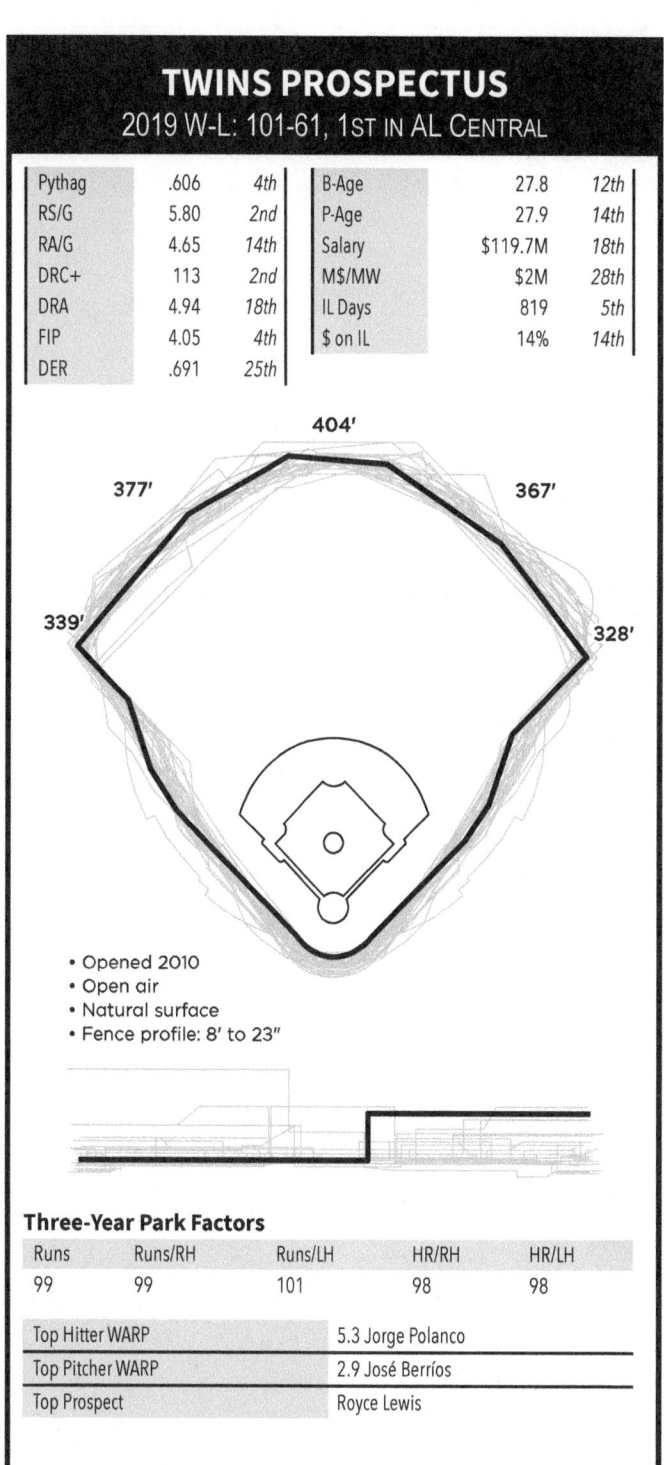

TWINS PROSPECTUS
2019 W-L: 101-61, 1ST IN AL CENTRAL

Pythag	.606	4th	B-Age	27.8	12th
RS/G	5.80	2nd	P-Age	27.9	14th
RA/G	4.65	14th	Salary	$119.7M	18th
DRC+	113	2nd	M$/MW	$2M	28th
DRA	4.94	18th	IL Days	819	5th
FIP	4.05	4th	$ on IL	14%	14th
DER	.691	25th			

404'
377'
367'
339'
328'

- Opened 2010
- Open air
- Natural surface
- Fence profile: 8' to 23"

Three-Year Park Factors

Runs	Runs/RH	Runs/LH	HR/RH	HR/LH
99	99	101	98	98

Top Hitter WARP	5.3 Jorge Polanco
Top Pitcher WARP	2.9 José Berríos
Top Prospect	Royce Lewis

277

2019 Hit List Ranking

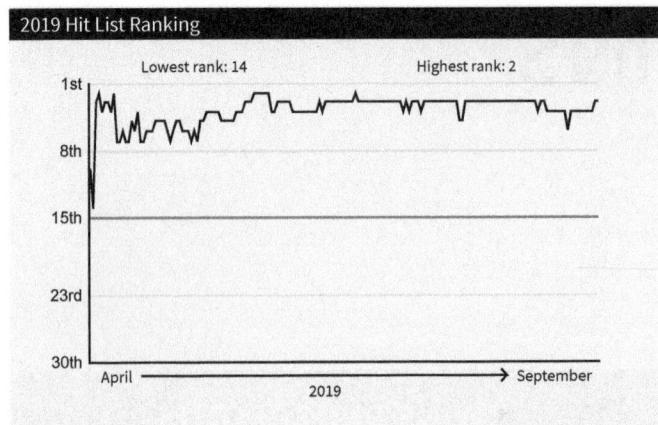

Lowest rank: 14   Highest rank: 2

1st · 8th · 15th · 23rd · 30th

April — 2019 → September

Committed Payroll (in millions)

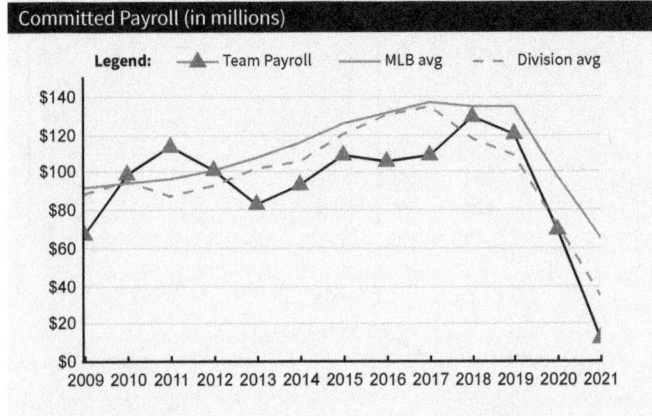

Legend: ▲ Team Payroll   —— MLB avg   - - - Division avg

$140 $120 $100 $80 $60 $40 $20 $0

2009 2010 2011 2012 2013 2014 2015 2016 2017 2018 2019 2020 2021

Farm System Ranking

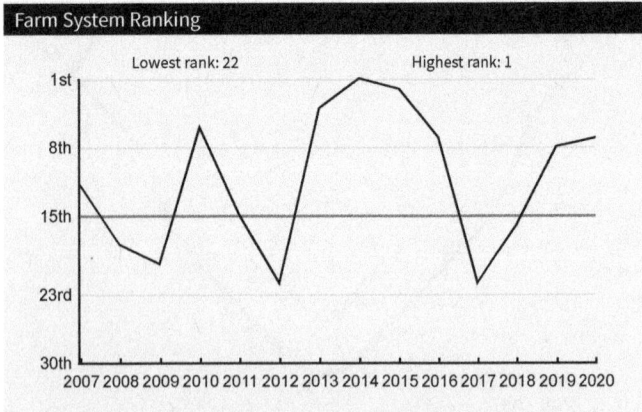

Lowest rank: 22   Highest rank: 1

1st · 8th · 15th · 23rd · 30th

2007 2008 2009 2010 2011 2012 2013 2014 2015 2016 2017 2018 2019 2020

Personnel

Executive Vice President, Chief Baseball Officer
Derek Falvey

Senior Vice President, General Manager
Thad Levine

Vice President, Assistant General Manager
Rob Antony

Vice President, Player Personnel
Mike Radcliff

Manager
Rocco Baldelli

BP Alumni
Ezra Wise

needed) with Rocco Baldelli, the team continued what was already an ongoing effort to better equip and develop their players. Baldelli and his coaching staff, led by bench coach Derek Shelton (who provided invaluable experience and organization to the man who beat him out for the job on the top step), altered everything about the way the Twins operated—even with regard to things that had already changed a lot over the previous seasons. Shelton quietly oversaw an increasingly aggressive array of defensive alignments, as the Twins stayed ahead of the sharply rising curve in shifts league-wide.

The front office hired Wes Johnson, a short guy from Arkansas who had spent the last decade instructing college pitchers and had never before held a job in pro ball, to be their pitching coach, making him the first person ever to make that jump directly. Under his tutelage, Trevor May and Tyler Duffey found the consistency and dominance that had long eluded them, taking the team's bullpen to a new level in the second half. They promoted advance scout Jeremy Hefner, an ex-pitcher in his early 30s, to assistant pitching coach, and Hefner helped implement informed changes that got multiple pitchers back on track at various points during the season.

They tethered emerging catcher Mitch Garver to catching coordinator Tanner Swanson, and Swanson reshaped Garver from a poor framer into an average-to-plus one. Meanwhile, the team's hitting infrastructure (which had been in place for a couple of years) found a new gear. If you want to find the secret of the Twins' success at the plate last year, don't look at the balls; look at the guys who flipped so many of them to Twins hitters. James Rowson and Rudy Hernandez had previously, though impermanently, fixed Byron Buxton and aided the impressive progress of Jorge Polanco and Max Kepler.

In 2019, they turned up the intensity, helping hitters find their optimal approaches, groove their swings to suit those approaches and consistently accomplish what the organization considered the most desirable outcome of a plate appearance: hard-hit balls, in the air, to the pull field. They even fixed Miguel Sanó on the fly, in the middle of the season, and helped him unlock his full power profile in the second half.

Meanwhile, organizational hitting coordinator Peter Fatse churned out players with the same focus and the same consistent success in the minor leagues. The Twins hit the ball hard, in the air, to the pull field, in 5.5 percent of their plate appearances; the league-average rate was 4 percent, and no team other than the Twins reached 5 percent. The A's, who were second-best at it, were as far behind the Twins as they were ahead of the 13th-place Orioles.

All that success couldn't go unnoticed, however, and even if the Twins were a half-step ahead in some aspects, the whole league is now immersed in similarly cooperative coaching and development superstructures. Right after the Twins' unceremonious playoff ouster, they fell victim to a shockingly rapid brain drain among the team's most well-known development people. Swanson and Fatse got jobs on the big-league coaching staffs of the Yankees and Red Sox, respectively; Rowson became the bench coach and offensive coordinator (title inflation is a trend more pervasive than heavy slider usage) for the Marlins; Hefner left for the Mets' pitching coach job; and Shelton was hired as the Pirates' new manager. That's enough to stagger a team, especially one that depended so much on the synergy between front office, field staff and players.

Pushing to stay ahead despite their losses, the Twins hired (if anything) even more aggressively. They coaxed Mike Bell, who had spent over a decade in the player-development department for the Diamondbacks, into replacing Shelton as the bench coach. They lured Tucker Frawley, the mastermind of recruitment, player development and strategy for Yale's program, into becoming their assistant field coordinator and coordinator of skill development. And they shelled out top dollar (for the position) to replace Fatse with Donegal Fergus, a highly-regarded collegiate hitting guru from the University of California, Santa Barbara.

On top of on-field, player development-focused hires, Minnesota hired Chris Mitchell, formerly of FanGraphs and the architect of a projection system for minor-league players, to join a front office that has been built out in ways that even a few years ago would have been unimaginable to any Twins fan. The team hired Daniel Adler to head their research and development department in late 2017, and ever since, they've been snatching up impressive and improbable talents to help them generate and manage as much useful information as possible. They've brought everyone from former Baseball-Reference.com developer Hans Van Slooten to PITCHf/x analyst-turned-Rays executive Josh Kalk to Baseball America head honcho John Manuel into their fold, stretching tendrils deep into the internet baseball community to find people with valuable perspectives, skills and relationships. There's some risk that the brain drain has become a money pit, but the team is still convinced it can spend both money and intellectual resources in ways that will augment their present and future ability to find and maximize talent.

How much of that work must they do, from moment to moment, as opposed to being able to count on the baseline levels of the players they've acquired? How much can players improve even without the organization's direct help, the way Jake Odorizzi did in 2019? After a winter at the Florida Baseball Ranch, Odorizzi had the breakout that multiple organizations had hoped to eventually extract from him. He was more mechanically efficient, leading to more velocity and more life on his stuff. He was more confident and consistent in using his full repertoire, locating to each

quadrant of the strike zone and inducing opponents to expand that zone. Johnson was a positive influence, but Odorizzi largely remade himself, and that's not uncommon in today's game. The trick is for teams to allow players to pursue options like the Ranch, outside their direct control, and to communicate openly and honestly enough to ensure players can get the full benefit from those options.

Odorizzi will be back in 2020, but it's no guarantee that all his improvements will hold, as the league adjusts to his new arsenal and style and forces him to adjust back.

On a team level, similar balancing acts are necessary, but they're trickier. The team can't abandon what it has done well, but must keep adapting and anticipating changes in trends and opponent strategies. After a disappointing 2018 in which they considered their clubhouse culture part of the problem, they assembled a perfect blend of personalities and backgrounds in 2019, with players and coaches working (mostly) harmoniously and teammates finding numerous ways to support and reinforce one another's success. Baldelli managed the depth the front office gave him with the savvy and deftness of a more veteran skipper. Reproducing that magic in 2020, however, will be hard, not only because of the coaching turnover, but because even the players and coaches in the room will be one year different, with different expectations, different ideas and different senses of their relative statuses.

The baseball itself is no more predictable. The league's self-investigation yielded few satisfying conclusions or plans of action, so it's unlikely big changes in the liveliness of the ball are forthcoming, but as we've seen, even small changes can have big consequences. That's the short version of much longer stories in many other aspects of baseball right now, and it's the scariest thing for Twins fans to ponder as a new season looms. The Twins haven't undergone small changes, but big ones, and the consequences of those could turn them back toward the middle of the pack, or catapult them into the class of the American League's elite.

In either case, Twins fans won't consider that much has changed unless one crucial thing does: Minnesota needs to win a playoff series. That can't happen until they win a whole lot of regular-season games again, and the front office's dedication to acquiring and preparing players who can do that is exciting and interesting.

But for all their data and technology-informed technique improvements—and for all of their redefinition and trailblazing in coaching, development and front-office hires—there's one thing these Twins can't reliably change: the dynamic of October. ▪

—*Matt Trueblood is an author of Baseball Prospectus.*

HITTERS

Ehire Adrianza INF Born: 08/21/89 Age: 30 Bats: B Throws: R Height: 6'1" Weight: 195 Origin: International Free Agent, 2006

YEAR	TEAM	LVL	AGE	PA	R	2B	3B	HR	RBI	BB	K	SB	CS	AVG/OBP/SLG	DRC+	VORP	BABIP	BRR	FRAA	WARP
2017	ROC	AAA	27	44	1	0	0	0	3	6	11	0	1	.216/.326/.216	72	-1.6	.308	-0.1	LF(4): 1.0, SS(2): 0.3	0.1
2017	MIN	MLB	27	186	30	9	2	2	24	16	25	8	1	.265/.324/.383	87	6.5	.291	1.6	SS(29): 3.0, LF(17): 1.5	1.1
2018	MIN	MLB	28	366	42	23	1	6	39	24	82	5	1	.251/.301/.379	82	7.4	.313	0.7	SS(64): -6.1, 3B(28): 0.6	0.0
2019	MIN	MLB	29	236	34	8	3	5	22	20	40	0	2	.272/.349/.416	101	8.2	.311	-1.2	SS(24): 1.4, 3B(24): 0.0	0.8
2020	MIN	MLB	30	315	31	13	1	7	32	24	60	6	2	.238/.306/.364	79	0.3	.279	0.0	1B -1, 2B 0	0.0

Comparables: Didi Gregorius, Stephen Drew, Andre Rodgers

Pitchers gifted Adrianza first-pitch balls at an abnormal rate, and a season after lifting and separating a little too often, he rediscovered his approach, found the opposite field and put together the first league-average offensive effort of his career. He did it at a career-high six different positions, too, as he added right field reps for the first time. He's creeping into his 30s now and he'll get a little pricey for the role in this, his fourth and final year of arbitration, so he's going to have to fight for his right to party with the 26-man Twins at every step of the way in 2020.

Luis Arraez 2B Born: 04/09/97 Age: 23 Bats: L Throws: R Height: 5'10" Weight: 177 Origin: International Free Agent, 2013

YEAR	TEAM	LVL	AGE	PA	R	2B	3B	HR	RBI	BB	K	SB	CS	AVG/OBP/SLG	DRC+	VORP	BABIP	BRR	FRAA	WARP
2018	FTM	A+	21	258	27	14	3	1	20	19	28	2	3	.320/.373/.421	134	14.2	.356	-2.4	2B(40): 1.7, 3B(6): 0.3	1.6
2018	CHT	AA	21	195	25	6	0	2	16	13	16	2	0	.298/.345/.365	112	6.2	.315	0.0	2B(27): -1.0, 3B(10): 0.3	0.9
2019	PEN	AA	22	164	18	6	1	0	14	18	13	3	3	.342/.415/.397	177	11.8	.376	-0.9	2B(15): -0.1, 3B(15): 4.2	2.2
2019	ROC	AAA	22	73	8	4	0	0	8	6	2	1	0	.348/.397/.409	130	3.5	.354	-0.9	SS(8): 0.4, 2B(4): 1.5	0.6
2019	MIN	MLB	22	366	54	20	1	4	28	36	29	2	2	.334/.399/.439	122	22.6	.355	2.9	2B(49): -2.8, LF(21): 1.5	2.3
2020	MIN	MLB	23	525	52	26	2	6	50	41	52	3	1	.303/.360/.397	103	25.4	.331	2.5	2B -1, 3B 0	2.5

Comparables: Abiatal Avelino, Odúbel Herrera, L.J. Hoes

"Taking an enemy on the battlefield is like a hawk taking a bird," Ghost Dog once said, "even though it enters into the midst of a thousand of them, it gives no attention to any bird other than the one that it has first marked." Watching Arraez shuffle and shake his head at a diving slider off the black, you get the sense he has that kind of monomaniacal focus. An impeccable eye and a samurai-worthy stroke propelled Arraez to the third-best batting average in baseball (minimum 300 at-bats), and he did that on the back of the best contact rate in the game. Emptiness is form; Arraez's bat shape-shifts to find pitches in all corners of the zone, and while he doesn't drive the ball against lefties, he sees 'em and leaves 'em plenty. The leather must come into accord with its own, but it should have its chance to grow over a full season of regular starts in 2020. A successful sequel would mean finding his Way into the starting nine for a long time to come.

Willians Astudillo C Born: 10/14/91 Age: 28 Bats: R Throws: R Height: 5'9" Weight: 225 Origin: International Free Agent, 2008

YEAR	TEAM	LVL	AGE	PA	R	2B	3B	HR	RBI	BB	K	SB	CS	AVG/OBP/SLG	DRC+	VORP	BABIP	BRR	FRAA	WARP
2017	RNO	AAA	25	128	22	14	0	4	22	4	5	0	1	.342/.370/.558	124	7.8	.330	-1.4	C(19): 0.9, 3B(14): 0.0	0.9
2018	ROC	AAA	26	307	30	17	1	12	38	10	14	7	4	.276/.314/.469	110	16.0	.255	-1.4	C(39): 2.5, 3B(28): 0.6	1.7
2018	MIN	MLB	26	97	9	4	1	3	21	2	3	0	0	.355/.371/.516	129	8.4	.341	0.4	C(16): 2.1, 3B(6): 0.0	1.0
2019	ROC	AAA	27	83	18	1	0	5	19	2	2	1	1	.423/.446/.628	169	14.2	.389	0.6	C(8): 1.3, 3B(5): 0.4	1.1
2019	MIN	MLB	27	204	28	9	0	4	21	5	8	0	0	.268/.299/.379	95	6.2	.258	-2.1	C(21): -0.4, 1B(15): -0.3	0.4
2020	MIN	MLB	28	245	27	12	0	8	31	7	15	1	1	.279/.315/.442	100	6.4	.270	-0.7	1B 0, C 1	0.6

Comparables: Ildemaro Vargas, Charles Silvera, Brayan Peña

To have loved and lost, or to have never loved at all? The poetry and prose of Astudillo's game turned sour in 2019, as inconsistent opportunity and an inability to replicate his magical production of 2018 conspired to drop the big man down to Triple-A before an oblique injury scuttled his efforts at a rebound. The baseball world was fortunate to catch a stray glimpse of his wonder after rosters expanded in September, but it wasn't enough to salvage his season. Tortugas are of course slow and steady types blessed with a steadfast persistence. All hope is not lost, then, that he plows on ahead and blossoms into a utility stalwart. We stand with just about every corner of the baseball-loving world in hoping for that outcome.

YEAR	TEAM	P. COUNT	FRM RUNS	BLK RUNS	THRW RUNS	TOT RUNS
2017	RNO	2571	1.4	0.0	-0.2	1.0
2018	MIN	2234	1.1	0.5	0.0	1.6
2018	ROC	5149	1.4	0.3	0.3	1.6
2019	MIN	2577	-0.3	0.0	-0.1	-0.4
2019	ROC	1130	1.5	0.0	0.0	1.4
2020	MIN	2526	0.6	0.0	-0.1	0.5

Alex Avila C Born: 01/29/87 Age: 33 Bats: L Throws: R Height: 5'11" Weight: 210 Origin: Round 5, 2008 Draft (#163 overall)

YEAR	TEAM	LVL	AGE	PA	R	2B	3B	HR	RBI	BB	K	SB	CS	AVG/OBP/SLG	DRC+	VORP	BABIP	BRR	FRAA	WARP
2017	DET	MLB	30	264	30	11	0	11	32	43	80	0	1	.274/.394/.475	107	16.6	.380	-1.5	C(50): -0.5, 1B(16): -0.9	1.0
2017	CHN	MLB	30	112	11	2	1	3	17	19	40	0	0	.239/.369/.380	107	5.6	.388	0.5	C(28): 0.2, 1B(3): 0.2	0.7
2018	ARI	MLB	31	234	13	6	0	7	20	37	90	0	0	.165/.299/.304	62	-0.1	.253	-1.4	C(61): 3.2, 1B(3): 0.0	0.2
2019	ARI	MLB	32	201	22	8	0	9	24	36	68	1	0	.207/.353/.421	96	9.4	.287	-1.1	C(54): 2.1, P(2): 0.0	1.0
2020	MIN	MLB	33	245	29	9	0	8	28	41	88	1	0	.218/.352/.380	101	10.0	.342	-0.8	C -4	0.6

Comparables: Jason Castro, Ron Karkovice, Geovany Soto

The list of pitchers Avila has caught is a Who's Who list of All-Star and Cy Young-caliber talent. Justin Verlander, Max Scherzer, David Price, Chris Sale, Jon Lester, Jake Arrieta and Zack Greinke all dot the veteran backstop's ledger. (Fine, we can throw Rick Porcello in there, too. He *did* win a Cy Young once). Avila's longevity in the league can mostly be attributed to the fact that pitchers seem to enjoy throwing to him, and while he's declined to the point where "serviceable backup" is his most ideal role, he's competent enough at the plate (for a catcher) to continue being worth rostering even if teams more or less know what they're going to get at this point.

YEAR	TEAM	P. COUNT	FRM RUNS	BLK RUNS	THRW RUNS	TOT RUNS
2017	DET	6716	-5.8	0.7	0.2	-4.8
2017	CHN	3507	-3.3	-0.2	0.0	-3.2
2018	ARI	7984	3.7	0.3	0.0	4.3
2019	ARI	7089	-0.1	2.3	0.7	2.8
2020	*MIN*	*9345*	*-4.8*	*0.5*	*1.1*	*-3.2*

Akil Baddoo OF   Born: 08/16/98   Age: 21   Bats: L   Throws: L   Height: 6'1"   Weight: 210   Origin: Round 2, 2016 Draft (#74 overall)

YEAR	TEAM	LVL	AGE	PA	R	2B	3B	HR	RBI	BB	K	SB	CS	AVG/OBP/SLG	DRC+	VORP	BABIP	BRR	FRAA	WARP
2017	TWI	RK	18	86	18	4	3	1	10	9	13	4	0	.267/.360/.440	143	4.9	.311	0.9	CF(8): -0.7	0.5
2017	ELZ	RK	18	157	39	15	2	3	19	27	19	5	4	.357/.478/.579	194	27.1	.400	0.8	CF(28): -4.2	1.7
2018	CDR	A	19	517	83	22	11	11	40	74	124	24	5	.243/.351/.419	117	30.7	.311	4.7	CF(97): -12.1, LF(3): 0.1	1.7
2019	FTM	A+	20	131	15	3	3	4	9	12	39	6	2	.214/.290/.393	90	4.5	.280	1.6	CF(21): -2.7, LF(6): -0.2	0.1
2020	*MIN*	*MLB*	*21*	*251*	*24*	*12*	*2*	*6*	*26*	*22*	*80*	*4*	*1*	*.210/.284/.361*	*71*	*-1.2*	*.294*	*0.3*	*CF -4, LF 0*	*-0.6*

Comparables: Victor Robles, Jason Martin, Dilson Herrera

Baddoo cracked our organizational top-10 list last offseason, albeit with warning bells ringing. What began as an uneven full-season debut evolved into a reasonably strong second half in the Midwest League, but he gained some density and blanched at the sight of better breaking balls often enough to inspire concern for both his offensive and defensive skill sets. Sure enough Baddoo's whiff and walk rates wandered in the wrong directions during his tour of the Florida State League before late-May Tommy John surgery put the kibosh on any hopes for another second-half rebound. He'll bring a new elbow ligament with him on a return trip to Fort Myers this spring, with plenty of tools remaining but a long and uncertain path ahead.

Byron Buxton CF   Born: 12/18/93   Age: 26   Bats: R   Throws: R   Height: 6'2"   Weight: 190   Origin: Round 1, 2012 Draft (#2 overall)

YEAR	TEAM	LVL	AGE	PA	R	2B	3B	HR	RBI	BB	K	SB	CS	AVG/OBP/SLG	DRC+	VORP	BABIP	BRR	FRAA	WARP
2017	MIN	MLB	23	511	69	14	6	16	51	38	150	29	1	.253/.314/.413	86	17.6	.339	7.4	CF(137): 25.4	4.2
2018	ROC	AAA	24	148	22	11	1	4	14	9	42	4	1	.272/.331/.456	103	8.8	.367	1.4	CF(28): 9.0	1.5
2018	MIN	MLB	24	94	8	4	0	0	4	3	28	5	0	.156/.183/.200	57	-7.6	.226	0.3	CF(27): 1.4	0.0
2019	MIN	MLB	25	295	48	30	4	10	46	19	68	14	3	.262/.314/.513	99	10.6	.314	4.4	CF(86): 14.2	2.9
2020	*MIN*	*MLB*	*26*	*490*	*52*	*23*	*6*	*18*	*60*	*34*	*131*	*15*	*3*	*.223/.283/.419*	*81*	*9.6*	*.274*	*3.4*	*CF 20*	*3.1*

Comparables: Cameron Maybin, Wil Myers, Clint Frazier

Buxton was doing it—he was doing *it!*—and then he met a familiar foe: the injury bug. There are few more electrifying players on the planet than a healthy Buxton, an impeccable athletic marvel on the field who streaks over grass and dirt alike with a churn that would make Karl Gustaf Patrik de Laval blush. But his all-out style of play giveth, and it taketh away. He was concussed on a diving catch, then had his campaign halted prematurely when he underwent shoulder surgery—the kind that entails a half-year of rehab. His cost control and talent capture the Twins in an awkward spot, and there are just a whole bunch of parallel universes where his career shakes out a whole bunch of different ways from here. The Twins exist only in this one, wherein Buxton seems cursed to perpetual disappointment.

Keoni Cavaco SS   Born: 06/02/01   Age: 19   Bats: R   Throws: R   Height: 6'2"   Weight: 195   Origin: Round 1, 2019 Draft (#13 overall)

YEAR	TEAM	LVL	AGE	PA	R	2B	3B	HR	RBI	BB	K	SB	CS	AVG/OBP/SLG	DRC+	VORP	BABIP	BRR	FRAA	WARP
2019	TWI	RK	18	92	9	4	0	1	6	4	35	1	1	.172/.217/.253	28	-6.0	.275	-0.6	SS(20): 0.5	-0.3
2020	*MIN*	*MLB*	*19*	*251*	*19*	*11*	*1*	*3*	*21*	*17*	*113*	*2*	*1*	*.194/.253/.291*	*46*	*-9.7*	*.359*	*0.0*	*SS 0*	*-1.0*

Comparables: Billy Hamilton, Isan Díaz, Gavin Cecchini

Heading into the draft, scouts questioned how Cavaco would fare against steeper competition. The Twins, evidently unbothered by those qualms, selected him 13th overall—only to see him whiff 38 percent of the time in his first exposure to professional pitching. Ouch. Of course, there's no sense giving up on Cavaco. His struggles were expected to some degree, and he has the tools and athleticism to project as a potential middle-of-the-order hitter. We do think, however, that his development will entail moving to a non-shortstop position, thereby putting more pressure on his stick and greater emphasis on him figuring out pro-level stuff sooner than later.

Jake Cave OF
Born: 12/04/92   Age: 27   Bats: L   Throws: L   Height: 6'0"   Weight: 200   Origin: Round 6, 2011 Draft (#209 overall)

YEAR	TEAM	LVL	AGE	PA	R	2B	3B	HR	RBI	BB	K	SB	CS	AVG/OBP/SLG	DRC+	VORP	BABIP	BRR	FRAA	WARP
2017	TRN	AA	24	140	19	13	2	5	18	10	33	1	0	.266/.317/.516	113	6.3	.319	-1.0	LF(17): 0.7, CF(7): -0.5	0.5
2017	SWB	AAA	24	297	47	13	3	15	38	18	82	1	3	.324/.367/.554	150	25.2	.414	0.5	CF(30): -1.8, RF(25): 2.2	2.2
2018	ROC	AAA	25	250	26	9	1	6	28	26	55	4	2	.269/.352/.403	115	12.9	.327	-0.1	RF(36): 5.4, CF(17): -0.6	1.6
2018	MIN	MLB	25	309	54	16	2	13	45	18	102	2	1	.265/.313/.473	93	18.0	.363	3.1	CF(70): -7.5, RF(11): 0.3	0.3
2019	ROC	AAA	26	214	37	18	4	7	39	15	50	5	0	.352/.393/.592	141	21.6	.437	1.1	CF(36): -3.5, RF(7): -0.8	1.3
2019	MIN	MLB	26	228	28	11	2	8	25	21	71	0	0	.258/.351/.455	89	3.2	.358	1.3	RF(45): -1.7, CF(23): 0.2	0.3
2020	MIN	MLB	27	245	26	11	2	7	29	18	74	2	1	.245/.307/.410	89	4.6	.332	1.3	RF 1, CF -1	0.4

Comparables: Duke Snider, Peter Bourjos, Tyler Austin

Cave continues to occupy that awkward space between being a fourth outfielder and being an up-and-down player. He scuffled out of the gate last season, suggesting he was unlikely to replicate his pleasant freshman efforts. His woes were such that he even found himself back in Triple-A in mid-May, the first in a series of demotions and recalls. From that point forward, Cave hit well enough to raise his numbers (relative to the league) close to what he produced the year prior. His versatility and sure-fine-adequate array of skills should allow him to continue receiving big-league at-bats. Cave's performance in 2020 will help dictate whether it's 300-plus annually, or something closer to half that.

Gilberto Celestino OF
Born: 02/13/99   Age: 21   Bats: R   Throws: L   Height: 6'0"   Weight: 170   Origin: International Free Agent, 2015

YEAR	TEAM	LVL	AGE	PA	R	2B	3B	HR	RBI	BB	K	SB	CS	AVG/OBP/SLG	DRC+	VORP	BABIP	BRR	FRAA	WARP
2017	GRV	RK	18	261	38	10	2	4	24	22	59	10	2	.268/.331/.379	102	14.1	.339	5.3	CF(43): 2.6, RF(8): 0.1	1.5
2018	ELZ	RK	19	117	13	4	1	1	13	6	16	8	2	.266/.308/.349	89	-0.8	.301	1.1	CF(23): -1.0	0.2
2018	TCV	A-	19	142	18	8	0	4	21	10	25	14	0	.323/.387/.480	175	15.2	.374	1.6	CF(16): 0.9, RF(12): 2.6	1.7
2019	CDR	A	20	503	52	24	3	10	51	48	81	14	8	.276/.350/.409	137	22.7	.317	-3.6	CF(82): 3.7, RF(25): -3.6	3.0
2019	FTM	A+	20	33	6	4	0	0	3	2	4	0	0	.300/.333/.433	124	3.5	.333	0.2	CF(4): -0.8, RF(3): -0.3	0.0
2020	MIN	MLB	21	251	23	13	1	5	25	17	59	5	1	.233/.290/.361	74	-0.4	.292	0.0	CF 1, RF 0	0.1

Comparables: Brett Phillips, Dalton Pompey, Victor Robles

Another year, another steady step forward in the development of young Mr. Celestino. A tough first couple months melted into an encouraging full-season debut for the 20-year-old, who rode a smoother leg kick and weight transfer to more pop than expected in the Midwest League—all while flashing plenty of other above-average tools. His strong arm profiles well anywhere on the grass, while solid speed and instincts have kept a future in center firmly on the table. His timeline won't be confused with fellow July 2nd classmate Juan Soto's, but he remains on a nice track toward eventual everyday play in the big leagues.

Nelson Cruz DH
Born: 07/01/80   Age: 39   Bats: R   Throws: R   Height: 6'2"   Weight: 230   Origin: International Free Agent, 1998

YEAR	TEAM	LVL	AGE	PA	R	2B	3B	HR	RBI	BB	K	SB	CS	AVG/OBP/SLG	DRC+	VORP	BABIP	BRR	FRAA	WARP
2017	SEA	MLB	36	645	91	28	0	39	119	70	140	1	1	.288/.375/.549	143	40.1	.315	-1.8	RF(5): -0.1	4.2
2018	SEA	MLB	37	591	70	18	1	37	97	55	122	1	0	.256/.342/.509	132	27.5	.264	-1.2	RF(4): 0.1	3.1
2019	MIN	MLB	38	521	81	26	0	41	108	56	131	0	1	.311/.392/.639	152	43.5	.351	-1.0		4.1
2020	MIN	MLB	40	560	84	26	1	38	99	54	148	2	1	.279/.358/.561	139	27.8	.323	-1.0	RF -1	2.8

Comparables: Manny Ramirez, Shin-Soo Choo, Donn Clendenon

Sure, Cruz was worth four wins (as a designated hitter!) and barreled balls at a higher rate than anyone else while anchoring the best homer-hitting team in baseball history...but have you seen him hit a golf ball? Somehow, Cruz's signature moment came well after the season ended, when he went viral for teeing off. While he can't be more than a couple years away from hitting the links more often, he has yet to show signs of mortality—save for, perhaps, a torn wrist tendon that cost him chunks of last season. Cruz will try for an encore performance in 2020 as part of a painfully team-friendly deal. The 40-year-old designated hitter is not a player type that tends to inspire confidence—Cruz is, safely, the exception.

Mitch Garver C
Born: 01/15/91   Age: 29   Bats: R   Throws: R   Height: 6'1"   Weight: 220   Origin: Round 9, 2013 Draft (#260 overall)

YEAR	TEAM	LVL	AGE	PA	R	2B	3B	HR	RBI	BB	K	SB	CS	AVG/OBP/SLG	DRC+	VORP	BABIP	BRR	FRAA	WARP
2017	ROC	AAA	26	372	56	29	0	17	45	50	85	2	0	.291/.387/.541	165	39.4	.347	0.2	C(67): 3.6, LF(14): 0.9	4.4
2017	MIN	MLB	26	52	5	1	3	0	3	6	15	0	0	.196/.288/.348	71	-1.0	.290	0.2	C(13): -1.1, 1B(3): 0.3	-0.1
2018	MIN	MLB	27	335	38	19	2	7	45	29	72	0	0	.268/.335/.414	100	14.1	.330	-1.3	C(86): -8.5, 1B(5): -0.1	0.5
2019	MIN	MLB	28	359	70	16	1	31	67	41	87	0	0	.273/.365/.630	149	41.1	.277	-0.7	C(82): 4.7, 1B(1): 0.0	4.4
2020	MIN	MLB	29	455	60	21	1	25	70	46	115	0	0	.244/.329/.489	115	28.4	.279	-0.8	C -8	2.1

Comparables: Jorge Posada, Kelly Shoppach, Yan Gomes

YEAR	TEAM	P. COUNT	FRM RUNS	BLK RUNS	THRW RUNS	TOT RUNS
2017	MIN	832	-0.9	-0.1	0.0	-1.0
2017	ROC	8976	3.3	-0.9	0.4	2.5
2018	MIN	11726	-8.2	0.2	-0.4	-8.5
2019	MIN	10997	4.2	-0.3	-0.4	3.3
2020	MIN	15381	-7.0	-0.8	-1.2	-9.0

If there's one theme to this chapter, it's that of players improving after working with the Twins' new coaches to alter their approach. No player reaped greater rewards in 2019 than Garver. His offensive potential intrigued scouts in the minors, particularly during a stellar Triple-A campaign in 2017 that pushed him into the bigs, and he atoned for a disappointing 2018 with a barrage of walks and home runs. Just as impressively, his previously mediocre defense took a step forward, as he learned to better settle in place and control the bottom of the zone. A year remains before Garver reaches arbitration, making him a bigger steal for the club than all those extra strikes he found last season.

Moises Gomez OF   Born: 02/08/97   Age: 23   Bats: R   Throws: R   Height: 6'1"   Weight: 215   Origin: International Free Agent, 2015

When a scouting type describes someone as having "Large Richard" or "Willy Bobo" power, they're talking about the type of power that Gomez has. After a breakout at the dish in 2018 in the Midwest League, the slugger stalled a bit playing in the organization's home state. The hit tool has always been in question as he does not recognize spin all that well and can sell out for power. A sub-.230 average validates those concerns, but the good news is the power held up despite the large ballparks and more advanced arms—he finished the year among the Florida State League's top-10 in homers, doubles and total bases. No matter where his development goes from here, Gomez is a scouting success considering he signed for just $40,000 out of his native Venezuela in 2015.

Marwin Gonzalez UT   Born: 03/14/89   Age: 31   Bats: B   Throws: R   Height: 6'1"   Weight: 205   Origin: International Free Agent, 2005

YEAR	TEAM	LVL	AGE	PA	R	2B	3B	HR	RBI	BB	K	SB	CS	AVG/OBP/SLG	DRC+	VORP	BABIP	BRR	FRAA	WARP
2017	HOU	MLB	28	515	67	34	0	23	90	49	99	8	3	.303/.377/.530	124	37.3	.343	-0.8	LF(47): -3.6, SS(38): -1.7	2.5
2018	HOU	MLB	29	552	61	25	3	16	68	53	126	2	3	.247/.324/.409	101	22.4	.301	1.5	LF(73): 0.7, SS(39): -2.7	1.6
2019	MIN	MLB	30	463	52	19	0	15	55	31	98	1	0	.264/.322/.414	92	7.9	.310	-1.2	RF(44): -4.8, 3B(40): 5.0	1.1
2020	MIN	MLB	31	560	60	28	1	17	65	39	122	8	4	.258/.317/.415	93	6.7	.308	-0.3	1B 0, 3B 2	0.8

Comparables: Eduardo Escobar, Alex Gonzalez, J.J. Hardy

Once Gonzalez got acclimated following a long free agency, he went on to do what he usually does at the dish. He missed some time with short-term injuries, but by the end of the year he'd cobbled together something approaching league-average offense while logging at least 18 games in each of the four corners. That fits Gonzalez's previous track record and scouting report, and the Twins more or less got what they paid for. One interesting twist worth keeping an eye on this season is how Gonzalez became far more aggressive in the zone in 2019, swinging nearly 68 percent of the time, or well above his career norm (around 60 percent).

Wander Javier SS   Born: 12/29/98   Age: 21   Bats: R   Throws: R   Height: 6'1"   Weight: 165   Origin: International Free Agent, 2015

YEAR	TEAM	LVL	AGE	PA	R	2B	3B	HR	RBI	BB	K	SB	CS	AVG/OBP/SLG	DRC+	VORP	BABIP	BRR	FRAA	WARP
2017	ELZ	RK	18	180	34	13	1	4	22	19	49	4	3	.299/.383/.471	127	17.2	.410	1.9	SS(36): -6.5	0.8
2019	CDR	A	20	342	43	9	1	11	37	35	116	2	0	.177/.278/.323	70	2.1	.243	-0.9	SS(65): 2.0	0.3
2020	MIN	MLB	21	251	20	11	1	5	23	18	98	1	0	.185/.252/.303	49	-8.9	.297	-0.3	SS 0	-0.9

Comparables: Lane Thomas, Carter Kieboom, Oscar Hernández

For a couple of years there, Minnesota had paid $4 million so Dusty from Colorado could badger us on the internet. That changed last season, as Javier stayed healthy enough to log substantial playing time. That's the good news; the bad news is that he didn't play well. The rust on his barrel weighed it down and he struggled to catch up to velocity or connect with A-ball secondaries; there's still a long way for his body to go in terms of filling out as well. Javier looks like a stone-cold six-spotter on the dirt, and that's always a good place to start. But he has a long way to go before we feel comfortable pegging him as a big-league lock.

Max Kepler RF   Born: 02/10/93   Age: 27   Bats: L   Throws: L   Height: 6'4"   Weight: 220   Origin: International Free Agent, 2009

YEAR	TEAM	LVL	AGE	PA	R	2B	3B	HR	RBI	BB	K	SB	CS	AVG/OBP/SLG	DRC+	VORP	BABIP	BRR	FRAA	WARP
2017	MIN	MLB	24	568	67	32	2	19	69	47	114	6	1	.243/.312/.425	90	2.0	.276	-2.2	RF(138): 5.1, CF(13): 0.3	0.9
2018	MIN	MLB	25	611	80	30	4	20	58	71	96	4	5	.224/.319/.408	102	16.0	.236	2.7	RF(117): 10.2, CF(55): -1.3	2.9
2019	MIN	MLB	26	596	98	32	0	36	90	60	99	1	5	.252/.336/.519	126	37.4	.244	-3.7	RF(84): 6.0, CF(60): -3.6	3.5
2020	MIN	MLB	27	595	75	30	3	28	86	61	104	7	3	.245/.329/.475	111	23.0	.256	-0.4	RF 6, CF 0	2.9

Comparables: Mike Marshall, Gregory Polanco, Travis Buck

Making steady, continual progress each year is Kepler's kink. He stayed true to it last season, finding the barrel more often and turning on pitches on the regular. He'll probably never run a high batting average on balls in play, but he makes plenty of contact for his power-hitting ways and has improved against left-handed pitchers. Add in a glove that can play in center, and you've got yourself a quality, prime-aged ballplayer. The five-year extension Kepler signed last off-season already looks like one of the bigger bargains in a sport increasingly defined by bargains.

—————————————— ★ ★ ★ *2020 Top 101 Prospect* **#86** ★ ★ ★ ——————————————

Alex Kirilloff OF   Born: 11/09/97   Age: 22   Bats: L   Throws: L   Height: 6'2"   Weight: 195   Origin: Round 1, 2016 Draft (#15 overall)

YEAR	TEAM	LVL	AGE	PA	R	2B	3B	HR	RBI	BB	K	SB	CS	AVG/OBP/SLG	DRC+	VORP	BABIP	BRR	FRAA	WARP
2018	CDR	A	20	281	36	20	5	13	56	24	47	1	1	.333/.391/.607	169	27.2	.364	-0.8	RF(53): -4.0, CF(1): 0.0	1.9
2018	FTM	A+	20	280	39	24	2	7	45	14	39	3	2	.362/.393/.550	169	26.9	.399	-0.8	RF(51): 0.4, CF(3): 0.3	2.3
2019	PEN	AA	21	411	47	18	2	9	43	29	76	7	6	.283/.343/.413	121	10.5	.333	-3.3	RF(41): -4.0, 1B(35): 0.3	0.6
2020	MIN	MLB	22	251	26	14	1	8	31	14	58	0	0	.268/.315/.435	95	6.3	.325	-0.4	RF -3, 1B 0	0.4

Comparables: Tyler Austin, Justin Williams, Gabriel Guerrero

The 15th pick in the 2016 draft, Kirilloff has experienced peaks and valleys throughout his pro career—accumulating displays of barrel work and injury issues alike. There's little doubt about his pure hitting ability, nor his size and strength; there's much doubt how the power translates, and whether enough will play to offset the penalties of a first-base-cum-corner-outfield defensive profile. Kirilloff didn't do a ton to answer those questions last year. That's not to take away from an impressive offensive effort as a 21-year-old in Double-A, nor is it to suggest he won't grow into a valuable player with the ability to anchor a lineup. He's capable of lifting his ceiling with a strong, healthy showing in the high minors this spring, and he could play his way firmly into the club's second-half plans.

★   ★   ★ *2020 Top 101 Prospect* **#85** ★   ★   ★

Trevor Larnach OF Born: 02/26/97   Age: 23   Bats: L   Throws: R   Height: 6'4"   Weight: 223   Origin: Round 1, 2018 Draft (#20 overall)

YEAR	TEAM	LVL	AGE	PA	R	2B	3B	HR	RBI	BB	K	SB	CS	AVG/OBP/SLG	DRC+	VORP	BABIP	BRR	FRAA	WARP
2018	ELZ	RK	21	75	10	5	0	2	16	10	11	2	0	.311/.413/.492	157	5.5	.340	-1.5	RF(14): 3.8	0.8
2018	CDR	A	21	102	17	8	1	3	10	11	17	1	0	.297/.373/.505	154	8.8	.338	0.7	RF(17): -1.5	0.7
2019	FTM	A+	22	361	33	26	1	6	44	35	74	4	1	.316/.382/.459	165	22.2	.389	-1.4	RF(59): -8.1, LF(9): -0.4	1.9
2019	PEN	AA	22	181	26	4	0	7	22	22	50	0	0	.295/.387/.455	146	13.9	.390	-0.3	RF(28): -2.2, LF(5): -0.1	0.8
2020	MIN	MLB	23	251	26	13	1	7	29	21	71	1	0	.258/.324/.409	95	6.2	.344	-0.3	RF -4, LF 0	0.2

Comparables: Zoilo Almonte, James Jones, Jordan Patterson

A year after signing underslot as the 20th-overall pick, Larnach was positively fine in his first full professional season. He split time between the Florida swamps, and in each place he hit the ball fine. The strikeout rate surged after his mid-season promotion to Double-A, but the game power started to play, so it was a fine trade-off. Scouts still see a defender who is entirely fine in either corner-outfield spot, too, as well a bat that should produce a bunch of dingers and an eye that should get him on base at an adequate rate. Franchise cornerstones are cool and all, but winning teams surround those types with ballplayers who can add value in various ways. Larnach appears that he's going to be fine in that role.

★   ★   ★ *2020 Top 101 Prospect* **#21** ★   ★   ★

Royce Lewis SS Born: 06/05/99   Age: 21   Bats: R   Throws: R   Height: 6'2"   Weight: 200   Origin: Round 1, 2017 Draft (#1 overall)

YEAR	TEAM	LVL	AGE	PA	R	2B	3B	HR	RBI	BB	K	SB	CS	AVG/OBP/SLG	DRC+	VORP	BABIP	BRR	FRAA	WARP
2017	TWI	RK	18	159	38	6	2	3	17	19	17	15	2	.271/.390/.414	159	18.1	.292	4.6	SS(32): -0.9	1.7
2017	CDR	A	18	80	16	2	1	1	10	6	16	3	1	.296/.363/.394	111	6.5	.364	1.0	SS(17): 1.9	0.7
2018	CDR	A	19	327	50	23	0	9	53	24	49	22	4	.315/.368/.485	156	31.3	.349	3.7	SS(67): 0.8	3.7
2018	FTM	A+	19	208	33	6	3	5	21	19	35	6	4	.255/.327/.399	107	11.6	.291	1.7	SS(45): -4.8	0.7
2019	FTM	A+	20	418	55	17	3	10	35	27	90	16	8	.238/.289/.376	97	15.0	.281	-1.5	SS(84): 4.0	1.8
2019	PEN	AA	20	148	18	9	1	2	14	11	33	6	2	.231/.291/.358	67	7.8	.287	2.0	SS(28): -2.6, CF(1): 1.7	0.3
2020	MIN	MLB	21	251	25	12	1	7	28	19	62	6	2	.231/.296/.383	81	2.1	.287	0.3	SS 0, CF 0	0.2

Comparables: Cole Tucker, Alen Hanson, Jonathan Schoop

Lewis turned in possibly the most divisive season in all the minor-league land last season—or at least it seemed that way inside the BP Prospect Team's Slack channel. He continued to drop jaws with his explosiveness and elite physicality, as he's an 80-grade athlete who can show off in rapid bursts of coordinated, dynamic action. The baseball-specific movements, however, can still appear puzzlingly unrefined. For one thing, his quick-twitch start-up and plus foot speed haven't translated yet to acceptable success on stolen-base attempts. His agility is an asset at short, but the game clock and consistency remain in development and he saw reps just about everywhere else on the diamond in the AFL. And then there's the swing: a stiff, unathletic leg kick that'd get him banished from Radio City contributed to timing issues and below-average performance across two levels. His season was salvaged, to some extent, by an MVP campaign in fall ball. In spite of the litany of present warts, there's so much to get excited about with Lewis that we're sweet on his future.

Ian Miller OF Born: 02/21/92   Age: 28   Bats: L   Throws: R   Height: 6'0"   Weight: 175   Origin: Round 14, 2013 Draft (#417 overall)

YEAR	TEAM	LVL	AGE	PA	R	2B	3B	HR	RBI	BB	K	SB	CS	AVG/OBP/SLG	DRC+	VORP	BABIP	BRR	FRAA	WARP
2017	ARK	AA	25	384	63	18	3	4	29	28	69	30	4	.326/.382/.430	146	39.6	.393	4.3	CF(80): 2.4	3.6
2017	TAC	AAA	25	177	22	4	2	0	6	5	33	13	1	.268/.297/.315	58	-2.6	.333	1.1	LF(27): -0.7, CF(15): 4.1	0.1
2018	TAC	AAA	26	478	60	16	3	2	41	43	89	33	9	.261/.333/.327	75	10.3	.322	3.1	CF(71): 0.4, LF(41): -1.8	0.3
2019	TAC	AAA	27	445	64	27	5	11	54	45	81	29	5	.269/.351/.449	94	18.5	.311	3.1	RF(45): 3.2, CF(44): -1.1	1.4
2019	ROC	AAA	27	69	8	3	1	0	4	6	8	6	2	.233/.319/.317	81	-0.1	.264	0.3	CF(15): -0.9	0.0
2019	MIN	MLB	27	17	2	1	0	0	1	0	3	0	0	.176/.176/.235	85	0.1	.214	0.1	CF(8): 0.5, LF(2): 0.1	0.1
2020	MIN	MLB	28	251	22	12	2	3	21	18	54	13	3	.223/.286/.328	65	-1.7	.278	1.6	CF 1, LF 0	0.0

Comparables: Darin Mastroianni, Kelby Tomlinson, Whit Merrifield

It's a tale of wonder as old as the game itself: a grinding, late-blooming rookie claws their way to the big-league roster after some 3,000-odd minor-league plate appearances, grounds one up the middle and stamps their name into the record books. The Twins acquired Miller as part of their September mix-and-match attempts to fill Byron Buxton's cleats, and his go-get-it defense and big wheels will likely keep him in the mix for a bench spot over the next few years. And after that? The story of that first big-league knock should keep him warm.

Jorge Polanco SS Born: 07/05/93   Age: 26   Bats: B   Throws: R   Height: 5'11"   Weight: 200   Origin: International Free Agent, 2009

YEAR	TEAM	LVL	AGE	PA	R	2B	3B	HR	RBI	BB	K	SB	CS	AVG/OBP/SLG	DRC+	VORP	BABIP	BRR	FRAA	WARP
2017	MIN	MLB	23	544	60	30	3	13	74	41	78	13	5	.256/.313/.410	90	17.7	.278	0.8	SS(130): -9.2	0.9
2018	MIN	MLB	24	333	38	18	3	6	42	25	62	7	7	.288/.345/.427	97	12.6	.345	-3.0	SS(76): -9.7	0.1
2019	MIN	MLB	25	704	107	40	7	22	79	60	116	4	3	.295/.356/.485	119	50.2	.328	4.9	SS(142): -0.7	5.3
2020	MIN	MLB	26	595	66	31	4	17	71	47	100	13	6	.273/.334/.440	104	26.5	.307	0.9	SS -5	2.2

Comparables: Ketel Marte, Francisco Lindor, Omar Infante

Polanco rewarded the faith the Twins showed when they signed him to a long-term extension during the spring with a strong offensive season. He nearly doubled his barrel rate and scaled way back on slapped contact the other way in favor of driving more balls up the middle and in the air. The adjustments catapulted him into a higher tier of shortstop offense, and better positioning even helped raise his suspect leather into a more passable range. How long he'll be able to stick at shortstop has been a career-dogging question, and it promises to remain a front-and-center concern after offseason ankle surgery. But one thing is for certain: his long, cheap deal will keep him anchored in Minnesota while he answers it.

Brent Rooker OF   Born: 11/01/94   Age: 25   Bats: R   Throws: R   Height: 6'3"   Weight: 215   Origin: Round 1, 2017 Draft (#35 overall)

YEAR	TEAM	LVL	AGE	PA	R	2B	3B	HR	RBI	BB	K	SB	CS	AVG/OBP/SLG	DRC+	VORP	BABIP	BRR	FRAA	WARP
2017	ELZ	RK	22	99	19	5	0	7	17	11	21	2	2	.282/.364/.588	134	10.3	.288	0.6	LF(17): 0.4	0.7
2017	FTM	A+	22	162	23	6	0	11	35	16	47	0	0	.280/.364/.552	171	13.3	.341	-1.5	LF(16): -2.6, 1B(11): -0.4	0.8
2018	CHT	AA	23	568	72	32	4	22	79	56	150	6	1	.254/.333/.465	117	13.2	.316	-4.7	1B(47): -5.7, LF(44): -8.2	0.0
2019	ROC	AAA	24	274	41	16	0	14	47	35	95	2	0	.281/.398/.535	123	22.6	.417	2.6	LF(56): -0.6	1.5
2020	MIN	MLB	25	70	7	4	0	2	8	6	26	0	0	.218/.298/.389	82	-0.5	.330	-0.1	LF -1	-0.1

Comparables: Chris Shaw, Joe Benson, Jake Lamb

Rooker likely would have debuted in the majors last season were it not for wrist and groin injuries. The story remains the same for the former 35th-overall pick: he'll need to mash, and he'll need to mash hard, if he's going to carve out a regular role at the highest level. Fortunately for him, he's now posted well above-average DRC+ numbers at every stop of his career, including last year's start-and-stop effort with the Triple-A moon ball. Rooker should get his first crack at the majors in 2020—he'll need to make the most of it, because his type is only a few hundred rough plate appearances from being tagged with the Quad-A label.

Eddie Rosario LF   Born: 09/28/91   Age: 28   Bats: L   Throws: R   Height: 6'1"   Weight: 180   Origin: Round 4, 2010 Draft (#135 overall)

YEAR	TEAM	LVL	AGE	PA	R	2B	3B	HR	RBI	BB	K	SB	CS	AVG/OBP/SLG	DRC+	VORP	BABIP	BRR	FRAA	WARP
2017	MIN	MLB	25	589	79	33	2	27	78	35	106	9	8	.290/.328/.507	107	18.9	.312	-1.6	LF(138): -2.7, RF(16): 0.2	1.6
2018	MIN	MLB	26	592	87	31	2	24	77	30	104	8	2	.288/.323/.479	112	29.4	.316	6.8	LF(125): 5.9, RF(5): -0.2	3.6
2019	MIN	MLB	27	590	91	28	1	32	109	22	86	3	1	.276/.300/.500	109	23.2	.273	0.9	LF(124): -8.8, RF(11): -0.5	1.5
2020	MIN	MLB	28	560	67	29	3	26	81	25	101	9	4	.273/.306/.485	104	19.6	.293	1.7	LF -5, RF 0	1.5

Comparables: Gerardo Parra, Aaron Rowand, Adam Lind

Whatever questions remained about the staying power of Rosario's offensive production quieted after a third consecutive solidly above-average campaign. You won't find his approach in an instruction manual, as he's among the freest of free-swingers the game has to offer. Yet he makes it work because he's also really good at getting his bat on the ball, as well as yanking it with authority. A midseason ankle injury seemed to stick with Rosario, and his work on both sides of the ball never quite recovered, with his lackluster glovework in particular taking a bite out of his overall value. Rosario will start to get expensive this year, as a solid in-prime player should, but his contact skills should keep him in-demand.

Miguel Sanó 3B   Born: 05/11/93   Age: 27   Bats: R   Throws: R   Height: 6'4"   Weight: 272   Origin: International Free Agent, 2009

YEAR	TEAM	LVL	AGE	PA	R	2B	3B	HR	RBI	BB	K	SB	CS	AVG/OBP/SLG	DRC+	VORP	BABIP	BRR	FRAA	WARP
2017	MIN	MLB	24	483	75	15	2	28	77	54	173	0	0	.264/.352/.507	119	23.1	.375	-2.0	3B(82): -5.9, 1B(9): 1.2	1.9
2018	FTM	A+	25	77	11	2	0	2	12	13	21	0	0	.328/.442/.453	169	7.8	.463	0.2	3B(10): 0.4	0.8
2018	ROC	AAA	25	36	2	1	0	2	5	6	8	0	0	.267/.389/.500	130	2.7	.300	0.2	3B(4): 1.5, 1B(1): 0.0	0.4
2018	MIN	MLB	25	299	32	14	0	13	41	31	115	0	0	.199/.281/.398	83	-0.5	.286	-1.0	3B(56): 0.1, 1B(11): 0.1	0.2
2019	MIN	MLB	26	439	76	19	2	34	79	55	159	0	1	.247/.346/.576	128	31.7	.319	-2.5	3B(91): -3.2, 1B(9): -0.6	2.5
2020	MIN	MLB	27	560	82	26	1	38	98	67	201	1	1	.247/.341/.540	130	32.5	.331	-1.9	3B -2, 1B 1	3.3

Comparables: Gary Sánchez, Brandon Allen, Randal Grichuk

In a make-or-break year, Sanó finally, mercifully made. An offseason heel injury delayed his seasonal debut, and a brutal six-week stretch as the weather warmed threatened his opportunity. But a two-homer outburst at the end of June begot a second-half onslaught the likes of which Twins fans have pined for. He broke out over the season's final three months, racking up elite exit velocities, dingers and signature moments. Our defensive metrics continued to like him a lot more than our eyes, but let's be clear: the Twins continue to employ him for his bat. And his bat seems on the upswing.

PITCHERS

Jorge Alcala RHP   Born: 07/28/95   Age: 24   Bats: R   Throws: R   Height: 6'3"   Weight: 205   Origin: International Free Agent, 2014

YEAR	TEAM	LVL	AGE	W	L	SV	G	GS	IP	H	HR	BB/9	K/9	K	GB%	BABIP	WHIP	ERA	DRA	WARP	MPH	FB%	WHF	CSP
2017	QUD	A	21	2	0	0	6	4	31	16	3	3.5	10.2	35	51%	.194	0.90	2.03	2.51	1.0				
2017	BCA	A+	21	5	6	0	16	14	78¹	55	7	3.8	6.9	60	40%	.223	1.12	3.45	3.70	1.4				
2018	BCA	A+	22	1	4	2	10	7	38²	25	2	4.2	10.5	45	48%	.256	1.11	3.03	3.28	0.9				
2018	CCH	AA	22	2	3	1	9	5	40²	36	1	3.8	8.2	37	42%	.307	1.30	3.54	3.91	0.6				
2018	CHT	AA	22	0	4	0	5	4	20	23	4	6.3	9.9	22	35%	.339	1.85	5.85	6.72	-0.3				
2019	PEN	AA	23	5	7	0	26	16	102²	114	12	3.2	9.2	105	40%	.351	1.47	5.87	6.31	-1.8				
2019	ROC	AAA	23	1	0	0	5	0	7²	4	0	2.3	12.9	11	60%	.267	0.78	0.00	1.89	0.3				
2019	MIN	MLB	23	0	0	0	2	0	1²	1	0	5.4	5.4	1	0%	.200	1.20	0.00	5.77	0.0	97.0	65.5	17.2	36.6
2020	MIN	MLB	24	3	3	0	27	5	48	47	8	5.2	7.5	40	38%	.285	1.57	5.54	5.27	0.1	96.8	67.5	17.8	37.7

Comparables: Hunter Wood, Robert Dugger, Brett Kennedy

We are all unique, but the human brain can't help but to order our natural world into patterns. No matter what anyone does, we all end up in buckets in other peoples' brains. There are worse baseball-related buckets than the "95-and-a-slider" one, even as it overflows. Alcala came one step closer to fulfilling that destiny in 2019, transitioning to the bullpen after his chuck-it command of four pitches torpedoed too many starts at Double-A. He promptly dominated in the role with a consolidated, short-burst arsenal that he rode all the way to the big-league debut that a lot of 95-and-a-slider prospects eventually enjoy. There's a little funk in his quick arm action, and therefore a little wiggle room with that loose command. If he can locate more consistently, he could land in Rocco Baldelli's "high-leverage" bucket sooner than later.

Cody Allen RHP Born: 11/20/88 Age: 31 Bats: R Throws: R Height: 6'1" Weight: 210 Origin: Round 23, 2011 Draft (#698 overall)

YEAR	TEAM	LVL	AGE	W	L	SV	G	GS	IP	H	HR	BB/9	K/9	K	GB%	BABIP	WHIP	ERA	DRA	WARP	MPH	FB%	WHF	CSP
2017	CLE	MLB	28	3	7	30	69	0	67¹	57	9	2.8	12.3	92	34%	.304	1.16	2.94	2.64	1.9	95.8	55.5	15.5	41.8
2018	CLE	MLB	29	4	6	27	70	0	67	58	11	4.4	10.7	80	31%	.292	1.36	4.70	3.61	1.0	95.3	60.3	13.9	43.1
2019	ROC	AAA	30	0	2	0	7	1	8	7	1	5.6	7.9	7	27%	.286	1.50	3.38	6.50	0.0				
2019	LAA	MLB	30	0	2	4	25	0	23	24	9	7.8	11.3	29	20%	.263	1.91	6.26	8.94	-0.9	94.3	53.7	10.6	41.8
2020	MIN	MLB	31	2	2	0	33	0	35	31	7	4.3	10.6	41	30%	.279	1.35	4.79	4.71	0.2	94.4	56.8	13.6	42

Comparables: Troy Percival, Francisco Rodríguez, Ugueth Urbina

Allen lost about a mile-and-a-half per hour off his heater from 2018 to 2019. Some pitchers can survive that kind of velocity loss by relying on their secondaries and de-emphasizing the importance of the fastball in their repertoire. Allen isn't that kind of guy, as his once simple-but-effective two-pitch arsenal left little room to maneuver. Hitters knew they could sit on the curveball and still catch up to his defanged fastball, leading Allen to nibble, leading to an increased walk rate. Add all that to a 65 percent fly ball rate amidst the year of the rocket ball, and you get the season Cody Allen just endured.

Homer Bailey RHP Born: 05/03/86 Age: 34 Bats: R Throws: R Height: 6'4" Weight: 223 Origin: Round 1, 2004 Draft (#7 overall)

YEAR	TEAM	LVL	AGE	W	L	SV	G	GS	IP	H	HR	BB/9	K/9	K	GB%	BABIP	WHIP	ERA	DRA	WARP	MPH	FB%	WHF	CSP
2017	DYT	A	31	1	0	0	1	1	6	1	0	0.0	9.0	6	54%	.077	0.17	0.00	2.38	0.2				
2017	CIN	MLB	31	6	9	0	18	18	91	112	11	4.2	6.6	67	46%	.346	1.69	6.43	7.38	-1.8	95.7	57	10.2	48
2018	LOU	AAA	32	2	2	0	7	6	37²	41	4	2.4	6.7	28	37%	.311	1.35	4.78	5.70	-0.1				
2018	CIN	MLB	32	1	14	0	20	20	106¹	141	23	2.8	6.3	75	44%	.327	1.64	6.09	6.03	-0.9	95.7	56	9.8	49.6
2019	OAK	MLB	33	6	3	0	13	13	73¹	73	9	1.8	8.3	68	44%	.300	1.20	4.30	3.72	1.6	95.2	52.5	12.2	50.2
2019	KCA	MLB	33	7	6	0	18	18	90	89	12	3.8	8.1	81	46%	.301	1.41	4.80	5.42	0.3	95.6	49.1	11.2	47
2020	MIN	MLB	34	9	7	0	24	24	129	137	19	3.1	8.1	116	44%	.312	1.40	4.86	4.77	1.2	94.4	52.5	10.7	48

Comparables: Ervin Santana, Matt Garza, Edwin Jackson

After watching Bailey implode yet again last April, it was easy to think "Does anyone get less out of good stuff than this guy?" When the A's acquired the always-talented, usually-lousy righty last July, the move had more than a whiff of "we're out of functional bodies" desperation to it. All of which is to say that Bailey's 13 starts with Oakland went better than anyone could have possibly expected. He halved his walk rate from recent years while limiting damage on contact, and he ultimately produced 1.6 very crucial WARP for the A's down the stretch. The abrupt turnaround stemmed from the kind of adjustments everyone else is making: fewer sinkers, more of his best secondary (an excellent split, in this case), and better location on his fastballs. It seems simple, but he isn't the first guy to post dramatically better results after a few modest changes. Provided that he returns to his new well, there's no reason to think he can't be a mid-rotation starter again. Nine lives, this cat.

Jordan Balazovic RHP Born: 09/17/98 Age: 21 Bats: R Throws: R Height: 6'5" Weight: 215 Origin: Round 5, 2016 Draft (#153 overall)

YEAR	TEAM	LVL	AGE	W	L	SV	G	GS	IP	H	HR	BB/9	K/9	K	GB%	BABIP	WHIP	ERA	DRA	WARP	MPH	FB%	WHF	CSP
2017	TWI	RK	18	1	3	0	10	3	40¹	47	5	4.5	6.5	29	37%	.331	1.66	4.91	8.77	-1.3				
2018	CDR	A	19	7	3	0	12	11	61²	54	5	2.6	11.4	78	48%	.327	1.17	3.94	3.53	1.2				
2019	CDR	A	20	2	1	0	4	4	20²	15	1	1.7	14.4	33	42%	.318	0.92	2.18	1.97	0.8				
2019	FTM	A+	20	6	4	0	15	14	73	52	3	2.6	11.8	96	45%	.283	1.00	2.84	3.23	1.6				
2020	MIN	MLB	21	2	2	0	33	0	35	35	5	3.4	10.2	40	43%	.320	1.38	4.77	4.70	0.2				

Comparables: German Márquez, Alex Reyes, Antonio Senzatela

A former fifth-rounder out of the relatively obscure Ontario prep ranks, Balazovic has blossomed into a big, highly projectable arm over the past couple years. He has an ideal frame with a steep release point, and he introduced himself to a lot of preference lists last year with dominant stretches of strikeout-heavy pitching across two levels of A-ball. There should be a couple more ticks to come as he continues filling out, which is an exciting proposition considering he's already advanced his secondaries. He should spend a good chunk of his age-21 season at Double-A, making him an arm to watch closely.

José Berríos RHP Born: 05/27/94 Age: 26 Bats: R Throws: R Height: 6'0" Weight: 205 Origin: Round 1, 2012 Draft (#32 overall)

YEAR	TEAM	LVL	AGE	W	L	SV	G	GS	IP	H	HR	BB/9	K/9	K	GB%	BABIP	WHIP	ERA	DRA	WARP	MPH	FB%	WHF	CSP
2017	ROC	AAA	23	3	0	0	6	6	39²	24	2	1.8	8.8	39	40%	.214	0.81	1.13	1.84	1.7				
2017	MIN	MLB	23	14	8	0	26	25	145²	131	15	3.0	8.6	139	41%	.289	1.23	3.89	4.29	2.1	96.0	61.5	10.5	46.4
2018	MIN	MLB	24	12	11	0	32	32	192¹	159	25	2.9	9.5	202	43%	.270	1.14	3.84	4.25	2.4	95.5	60.4	12.3	46.7
2019	MIN	MLB	25	14	8	0	32	32	200¹	194	26	2.3	8.8	195	43%	.299	1.22	3.68	4.44	2.9	95.2	55.2	11.4	48.4
2020	MIN	MLB	26	13	9	0	29	29	184	179	28	2.9	9.0	184	42%	.301	1.30	4.37	4.39	2.4	95.1	59.4	11.8	48.2

Comparables: Archie Bradley, Lucas Giolito, Eduardo Rodriguez

Berríos' signature curveball swept more than ever last season, but he paid for the longer movement trajectory with a reduced whiff rate. He left more of 'em hanging than usual, too. Berríos was able to offset his bendy losses with faded gains, however, as he dramatically improved his changeup performance. In the end, he left some whiffs on the table, but the eventual result was everything on the top lines remaining eerily in agreement with his prior seasons. Though he's not quite an ace (yet), he'll be 25 until the end of May, and it still feels like there's a next gear here. With his arbitration years hurtling closer, the Twins will hope that he finds it on the sooner side of later.

Matt Canterino RHP Born: 12/14/97 Age: 22 Bats: R Throws: R Height: 6'2" Weight: 222 Origin: Round 2, 2019 Draft (#54 overall)

YEAR	TEAM	LVL	AGE	W	L	SV	G	GS	IP	H	HR	BB/9	K/9	K	GB%	BABIP	WHIP	ERA	DRA	WARP	MPH	FB%	WHF	CSP
2019	CDR	A	21	1	1	0	5	5	20	6	0	3.2	11.2	25	49%	.146	0.65	1.35	2.03	0.7				
2020	MIN	MLB	22	2	2	0	33	0	35	35	5	3.6	9.1	35	43%	.306	1.39	4.76	4.78	0.2				

Comparables: Carl Edwards Jr., Michael Stutes, Jorge Alcala

The Twins saved a bit of money last June when they grabbed Canterino in the second round. A steady college performer at Rice, he signed for less than slot value to turn professional. Canterino then rode an above-average three-pitch mix to a stellar debut. The heater will tickle the mid-90s and features strong plane thanks to his higher arm slot, while both his bendy pitches receive solid reviews as potential bat-missers. He can(terino) dominate the low-minors, but don't be surprised if he can't(erino) succeed with similar aplomb against more mature hitters.

Tyler Clippard RHP Born: 02/14/85 Age: 35 Bats: R Throws: R Height: 6'3" Weight: 200 Origin: Round 9, 2003 Draft (#274 overall)

YEAR	TEAM	LVL	AGE	W	L	SV	G	GS	IP	H	HR	BB/9	K/9	K	GB%	BABIP	WHIP	ERA	DRA	WARP	MPH	FB%	WHF	CSP
2017	NYA	MLB	32	1	5	1	40	0	36¹	28	7	4.7	10.4	42	35%	.236	1.29	4.95	2.86	0.9	92.6	40.4	15.9	43.9
2017	CHA	MLB	32	1	1	2	11	0	10	8	0	4.5	10.8	12	30%	.296	1.30	1.80	2.76	0.3	93.2	32.9	14.5	41.2
2017	HOU	MLB	32	0	2	2	16	0	14	11	3	4.5	11.6	18	36%	.242	1.29	6.43	3.48	0.3	92.3	36.3	12.6	47.3
2018	TOR	MLB	33	4	3	7	73	1	68²	57	13	3.0	11.1	85	22%	.272	1.17	3.67	3.55	1.1	92.9	41.8	15.8	45.5
2019	CLE	MLB	34	1	0	0	53	3	62	38	8	2.2	9.3	64	33%	.204	0.85	2.90	4.14	0.8	91.4	40.8	14.2	46.1
2020	MIN	MLB	35	2	2	0	44	0	46	37	9	3.2	10.1	52	30%	.248	1.15	3.79	3.94	0.6	91.0	39.7	14.7	44.6

Comparables: Eric Gagne, Rafael Soriano, Juan Cruz

Did you know: Clippard added a ninth jersey to his collection in 2019 by pitching for Cleveland? In doing so, he passed Rich Hill for the third-most teams played for by an active player. More importantly, did you know: Clippard pitched *well*? He still gave up his share of home runs, but not as many as you'd suspect given the altered baseball and his history of gopheritis—heck, it's enough to make one wonder if the lobster, with its institutional knowledge of being boiled, might be the being best suited to survive climate change. Clippard is now 35 and the Twins will be his tenth major-league employer, but he'll need to try to extend his career much further if he wants to give Edwin Jackson a run for his wardrobe.

Randy Dobnak RHP Born: 01/17/95 Age: 25 Bats: R Throws: R Height: 6'1" Weight: 230 Origin: Undrafted Free Agent, 2017

YEAR	TEAM	LVL	AGE	W	L	SV	G	GS	IP	H	HR	BB/9	K/9	K	GB%	BABIP	WHIP	ERA	DRA	WARP	MPH	FB%	WHF	CSP
2017	ELZ	RK	22	2	0	1	5	3	26¹	19	3	2.1	7.5	22	46%	.225	0.95	2.39	1.91	1.1				
2017	CDR	A	22	0	0	0	1	1	7	6	0	1.3	1.3	1	56%	.240	1.00	2.57	4.57	0.1				
2018	CDR	A	23	10	5	0	24	20	129	138	6	1.7	5.9	84	47%	.314	1.26	3.14	4.44	1.1				
2019	FTM	A+	24	3	0	0	4	4	22¹	18	0	1.6	5.6	14	59%	.273	0.99	0.40	3.78	0.3				
2019	PEN	AA	24	4	2	0	11	10	66²	58	6	0.8	8.2	61	60%	.278	0.96	2.57	3.67	1.0				
2019	ROC	AAA	24	5	2	0	9	7	46	28	0	3.5	6.7	34	62%	.229	1.00	2.15	2.47	1.8				
2019	MIN	MLB	24	2	1	1	9	5	28¹	27	1	1.6	7.3	23	54%	.302	1.13	1.59	4.60	0.3	94.5	59	14	46.4
2020	MIN	MLB	25	4	3	0	21	10	63	61	7	3.1	8.3	58	56%	.299	1.31	4.08	4.08	1.0	94.2	60.4	14.4	47.5

Comparables: Taylor Jordan, Brock Stewart, Phil Irwin

You want a story for the silver screen? How about Dobnak's: undrafted D-II pitcher, independent league hustler, Uber driver, bespectacled horseshoe mustache wearer and now accomplished big-league starter. He began his year in High-A and ended it as Minnesota's Game 2 starter—an assignment that, when combined with his former side gig, casted simultaneous spotlights on both the obscenity of non-living wages paid to up-and-coming ballplayers and the insufferability of Yankees fans, who razzed him with "U-ber!" chants. Sinker-slider combinations aren't exactly en vogue right now, but Dobnak's is a solid one, and his results to date suggest a deserved spot in the rotation or (at least) in the bullpen to begin 2020.

Tyler Duffey RHP Born: 12/27/90 Age: 29 Bats: R Throws: R Height: 6'3" Weight: 220 Origin: Round 5, 2012 Draft (#160 overall)

YEAR	TEAM	LVL	AGE	W	L	SV	G	GS	IP	H	HR	BB/9	K/9	K	GB%	BABIP	WHIP	ERA	DRA	WARP	MPH	FB%	WHF	CSP
2017	MIN	MLB	26	2	3	1	56	0	71	79	9	2.3	8.5	67	50%	.326	1.37	4.94	3.65	1.2	94.0	59.4	11.8	48
2018	ROC	AAA	27	4	4	3	31	0	59	48	3	3.1	9.6	63	45%	.277	1.15	2.90	3.35	1.2				
2018	MIN	MLB	27	2	2	0	19	1	25	26	6	1.4	6.8	19	35%	.260	1.20	7.20	5.41	-0.1	95.4	61.2	11.3	48.5
2019	ROC	AAA	28	0	0	1	7	0	13²	8	0	3.3	14.5	22	48%	.320	0.95	1.32	2.36	0.5				
2019	MIN	MLB	28	5	1	0	58	0	57²	44	8	2.2	12.8	82	38%	.275	1.01	2.50	3.05	1.4	96.1	54	16.7	47
2020	MIN	MLB	29	3	3	0	60	0	64	58	9	2.6	10.7	76	40%	.307	1.20	3.75	3.80	1.0	94.6	57	14.1	47.8

Comparables: Zach McAllister, Jerad Eickhoff, Trevor Oaks

Minnesota's emphasis on pitch development paid huge dividends for Duffey, who transformed his breaking ball in-season—from a downer with too much hump into a hard, tight hook that devastated hitters in the second half. Long an electric arm without the consistency to stick in the rotation, or quite enough raw stuff to dominate in the pen, Duffey finally got the recipe right in 2019—and boy, did it result in a ton of empty swings. Provided his gains stick, he'll represent an analytic victory for the new regime—and a mighty fine late-inning reliever to boot.

Jhoan Duran RHP Born: 01/08/98 Age: 22 Bats: R Throws: R Height: 6'5" Weight: 230 Origin: International Free Agent, 2014

YEAR	TEAM	LVL	AGE	W	L	SV	G	GS	IP	H	HR	BB/9	K/9	K	GB%	BABIP	WHIP	ERA	DRA	WARP	MPH	FB%	WHF	CSP
2017	DIA	RK	19	0	2	0	3	3	11¹	19	0	3.2	10.3	13	64%	.452	2.03	7.15	7.31	-0.1				
2017	YAK	A-	19	6	3	0	11	11	51	44	5	3.0	6.4	36	54%	.253	1.20	4.24	4.19	0.6				
2018	KNC	A	20	5	4	0	15	15	64²	69	6	3.9	9.9	71	52%	.346	1.50	4.73	4.49	0.5				
2018	CDR	A	20	2	1	0	6	6	36	19	2	2.5	11.0	44	66%	.218	0.81	2.00	5.32	-0.1				
2019	FTM	A+	21	2	9	0	16	15	78	63	5	3.6	11.0	95	53%	.317	1.21	3.23	4.39	0.6				
2019	PEN	AA	21	3	3	0	7	7	37	34	2	2.2	10.0	41	64%	.349	1.16	4.86	6.27	-0.6				
2020	MIN	MLB	22	2	2	0	33	0	35	34	5	3.6	9.0	35	50%	.303	1.38	4.70	4.70	0.2				

Comparables: Huascar Ynoa, Joel Payamps, Alex Cobb

The enormous Duran—listed at 6-foot-5 and 230 pounds—finally saw his stuff catch up to his frame last year. His lively four-seamer now touches triple digits, while a hammer curve darts down south of the zone off the same steep plane. If you caught him on the right day last season—like that May day when he whiffed 14 in just six innings, or his second-to-last start when he punched out 11 across eight scoreless—then you left thinking he sure looked like a front-of-the-rotation starter in the making. That might just be the case if he can progress further. Look for Duran to debut this summer.

Sam Dyson RHP Born: 05/07/88 Age: 32 Bats: R Throws: R Height: 6'1" Weight: 212 Origin: Round 4, 2010 Draft (#126 overall)

YEAR	TEAM	LVL	AGE	W	L	SV	G	GS	IP	H	HR	BB/9	K/9	K	GB%	BABIP	WHIP	ERA	DRA	WARP	MPH	FB%	WHF	CSP
2017	TEX	MLB	29	1	6	0	17	0	16²	31	6	6.5	3.8	7	62%	.379	2.58	10.80	8.89	-0.7	96.9	73.8	6	47.2
2017	SFN	MLB	29	3	4	14	38	0	38	36	2	4.3	6.4	27	67%	.286	1.42	4.03	6.27	-0.5	96.9	73.8	10	48.3
2018	SFN	MLB	30	4	3	3	74	0	70¹	56	5	2.6	7.2	56	62%	.270	1.08	2.69	4.01	0.7	96.0	65.4	11.9	48.8
2019	MIN	MLB	31	1	0	0	12	0	11¹	14	3	4.8	6.4	8	51%	.306	1.76	7.15	6.37	-0.1	95.0	57.8	7	51.5
2019	SFN	MLB	31	4	1	2	49	0	51	39	3	1.2	8.3	47	58%	.265	0.90	2.47	3.18	1.2	95.6	57.8	9.6	49
2020	MIN	MLB	32	2	2	0	33	0	35	35	5	3.0	8.1	32	58%	.302	1.33	4.37	4.35	0.3	95.0	64	9.8	48.5

Comparables: Jeremy Jeffress, Brandon League, Blake Treinen

In November, MLB opened an investigation into two Instagram posts by Dyson's ex-girlfriend alleging physical and emotional abuse against her and acts of animal cruelty against the couple's cat. As of press time this investigation remains open.

Blayne Enlow RHP Born: 03/21/99 Age: 21 Bats: R Throws: R Height: 6'3" Weight: 170 Origin: Round 3, 2017 Draft (#76 overall)

YEAR	TEAM	LVL	AGE	W	L	SV	G	GS	IP	H	HR	BB/9	K/9	K	GB%	BABIP	WHIP	ERA	DRA	WARP	MPH	FB%	WHF	CSP
2017	TWI	RK	18	3	0	0	6	1	20¹	10	1	1.8	8.4	19	56%	.176	0.69	1.33	1.16	1.0				
2018	CDR	A	19	3	5	1	20	17	94	94	4	3.4	6.8	71	47%	.315	1.37	3.26	5.10	0.1				
2019	CDR	A	20	4	3	0	8	8	41¹	42	4	3.3	9.6	44	61%	.317	1.38	4.57	4.72	0.2				
2019	FTM	A+	20	4	4	0	13	12	69¹	61	4	3.0	6.6	51	46%	.275	1.21	3.38	4.76	0.2				
2020	MIN	MLB	21	2	2	0	33	0	35	34	5	3.5	6.1	24	46%	.272	1.37	4.72	4.75	0.2				

Comparables: Jonathan Hernández, Nate Adcock, Mike Foltynewicz

Enlow stayed relatively healthy and grew quite a bit, both literally and in his approach on the mound. He added a bunch of the necessary strength and polish a highly-drafted prep arm invariably lacks, along with a hard slider to round out what is now a stout four-pitch mix. His fastball jumped into the mid-90s, as well, and while the results were mixed (as they often are for a still-filling-out 20-year-old pitching well above his age class), the foundation of a mid-rotation starter is now present. Health permitting, he should continue a rapid advance this year.

——————————— ★ ★ ★ *2020 Top 101 Prospect* **#32** ★ ★ ★ ———————————

Brusdar Graterol RHP Born: 08/26/98 Age: 21 Bats: R Throws: R Height: 6'1" Weight: 265 Origin: International Free Agent, 2014

YEAR	TEAM	LVL	AGE	W	L	SV	G	GS	IP	H	HR	BB/9	K/9	K	GB%	BABIP	WHIP	ERA	DRA	WARP	MPH	FB%	WHF	CSP
2017	TWI	RK	18	2	0	0	5	2	19¹	10	1	1.9	9.8	21	58%	.205	0.72	1.40	1.12	1.0				
2017	ELZ	RK	18	2	1	0	5	5	20²	16	1	3.9	10.5	24	59%	.300	1.21	3.92	2.38	0.8				
2018	CDR	A	19	3	2	0	8	8	41¹	30	3	2.0	11.1	51	64%	.270	0.94	2.18	2.45	1.4				
2018	FTM	A+	19	5	2	0	11	11	60²	59	0	2.8	8.3	56	49%	.343	1.29	3.12	4.61	0.5				
2019	PEN	AA	20	6	0	1	12	9	52²	32	2	3.6	8.5	50	56%	.233	1.01	1.71	2.93	1.3				
2019	MIN	MLB	20	1	1	0	10	0	9²	10	1	1.9	9.3	10	52%	.346	1.24	4.66	3.44	0.2	100.4	67.4	9.7	53.1
2020	MIN	MLB	21	4	3	0	30	8	64	65	8	3.3	7.9	56	53%	.305	1.39	4.62	4.58	0.6	100.6	70.6	10.2	55.6

Comparables: Chris Tillman, Lucas Giolito, Jenrry Mejia

Graterol presents a proposition as old as baseball time: big boy, big stuff, big question marks about health and durability. Major-league hitters received a preview of coming attractions late last season, when he debuted and introduced his triple-digit heat. It's an elite two-way offering, with gnarly two-seam sink or four-seam ride, and it looked more than capable of paving the way. The way he loads his shoulder proved problematic, however, and he missed a chunk of the season with an impingement—a concerning development for a guy with a catastrophic arm injury already headlining his medical records. There's enough projection to his secondaries that he should force his way firmly into the team's short-term rotation plans, and there's also more than enough short-burst velocity to fall back on.

Blaine Hardy LHP Born: 03/14/87 Age: 33 Bats: L Throws: L Height: 6'2" Weight: 218 Origin: Round 22, 2008 Draft (#655 overall)

YEAR	TEAM	LVL	AGE	W	L	SV	G	GS	IP	H	HR	BB/9	K/9	K	GB%	BABIP	WHIP	ERA	DRA	WARP	MPH	FB%	WHF	CSP
2017	TOL	AAA	30	7	3	3	34	2	40²	32	1	1.1	10.0	45	48%	.304	0.91	3.10	2.35	1.3				
2017	DET	MLB	30	1	0	0	35	0	33¹	46	7	3.5	7.6	28	34%	.361	1.77	5.94	5.24	0.0	91.7	44.9	11.3	49.8
2018	TOL	AAA	31	3	0	0	9	4	26¹	14	0	1.4	11.6	34	39%	.250	0.68	1.03	2.40	0.9				
2018	DET	MLB	31	4	5	1	30	13	86	79	10	2.3	6.9	66	42%	.275	1.17	3.56	3.98	1.2	90.2	32.9	9.1	51.5
2019	DET	MLB	32	1	1	0	39	0	44¹	38	10	2.6	5.9	29	50%	.215	1.15	4.47	4.75	0.3	90.4	22.5	10.5	47.8
2020	MIN	MLB	33	2	2	0	33	0	35	35	7	2.8	6.6	26	46%	.275	1.32	4.59	4.78	0.2	89.5	31.2	9.8	48.9

Comparables: Dan Jennings, Sam Freeman, Luis García

Hardy is the inverse of a Clint Eastwood baseball movie: He has trouble with everything but the curve. The lefty was wrecked by, of all demographics, his own kind last year (seven HR in 59 plate appearances) before being medically wrecked by a flexor tendon strain. The curve remains his golden calf, and he began setting up more with a changeup rather than his upper-80s fastball. Hardy's experience overwhelming you with soft stuff should help him transition to a post-baseball career as a MyPillow spokesperson.

Ryne Harper RHP Born: 03/27/89 Age: 31 Bats: R Throws: R Height: 6'3" Weight: 215 Origin: Round 37, 2011 Draft (#1136 overall)

YEAR	TEAM	LVL	AGE	W	L	SV	G	GS	IP	H	HR	BB/9	K/9	K	GB%	BABIP	WHIP	ERA	DRA	WARP	MPH	FB%	WHF	CSP
2017	ARK	AA	28	1	0	0	4	0	7¹	2	0	0.0	12.3	10	50%	.143	0.27	0.00	1.76	0.3				
2017	TAC	AAA	28	3	2	3	37	0	46¹	42	5	4.1	8.7	45	48%	.296	1.36	3.88	4.06	0.6				
2018	CHT	AA	29	1	2	6	24	0	39	35	0	1.2	11.8	51	40%	.361	1.03	2.54	3.19	0.8				
2018	ROC	AAA	29	0	3	0	14	0	26	26	2	1.7	12.1	35	62%	.364	1.19	5.19	3.34	0.5				
2019	MIN	MLB	30	4	2	1	61	0	54¹	54	7	1.7	8.3	50	39%	.301	1.18	3.81	4.67	0.4	91.3	38.7	11.4	52.1
2020	MIN	MLB	31	2	2	0	44	0	46	45	7	2.3	7.8	40	42%	.289	1.23	3.99	4.11	0.5	90.5	38.5	11.3	51.7

Comparables: Rob Wooten, Colton Murray, Pat Venditte

Entering 2019, Harper was a 30-year-old who'd thrown over 350 innings in the high minors and had failed to appear in a single Annual despite reaching the majors for a brief promotion. He'd thrown well enough in the high minors to bounce around and earn some sweet, sweet projection-system love for his robust whiff-to-walk tendencies. Last season, he made good on his opportunity, turning in a perfectly average season of big-league middle relief. Sure, the league started to catch on to his shtick as they saw more of him, and he got passed over by other emergent bullpen talent down the stretch. Still, Harper will always have the summer of '19 and this Annual comment to hold onto, if not a firm spot in a big-league bullpen.

Rich Hill LHP Born: 03/11/80 Age: 40 Bats: L Throws: L Height: 6'5" Weight: 221 Origin: Round 4, 2002 Draft (#112 overall)

YEAR	TEAM	LVL	AGE	W	L	SV	G	GS	IP	H	HR	BB/9	K/9	K	GB%	BABIP	WHIP	ERA	DRA	WARP	MPH	FB%	WHF	CSP
2017	LAN	MLB	37	12	8	0	25	25	135²	99	18	3.3	11.0	166	39%	.261	1.09	3.32	3.35	3.4	91.0	54.8	12.7	49.2
2018	LAN	MLB	38	11	5	0	25	24	132²	108	20	2.8	10.2	150	40%	.268	1.12	3.66	3.92	2.1	91.6	58.8	11.6	54.5
2019	LAN	MLB	39	4	1	0	13	13	58²	48	10	2.8	11.0	72	52%	.275	1.12	2.45	3.39	1.5	92.6	52.6	12.3	56.1
2020	MIN	MLB	40	4	2	0	11	11	52	42	6	2.8	10.2	59	46%	.275	1.11	3.13	3.30	1.3	90.0	54.1	11.8	52.1

Comparables: Arthur Rhodes, Manny Parra, Mike Remlinger

Psycho Rich seems like a bizarre nickname for a guy who looks like any other suburban dad on first glance, but everything about his demeanor changes when he's scheduled to pitch—or when he's trying to enter Foxboro Stadium. That competitiveness on the field, along with his personality off the field, has endeared him to the organization, teammates, and fans alike. Due to knee and elbow issues, the oft-injured Hill only pitched about a third of the innings he'd have liked to, but was nonetheless effective when on the mound. After the season concluded, we found that he had to battle to pitch his final 6 2/3 innings due to a re-injured MCL in his knee and a detached UCL in his elbow that will cause him to miss at least half of next season. He gave up two runs and hit one double in that span. Soon to turn 40, his future is that of the Lakers in reverse as he'll leave behind the bright lights of L.A. for the polite tundra of Minnesota.

Zack Littell RHP Born: 10/05/95 Age: 24 Bats: R Throws: R Height: 6'4" Weight: 220 Origin: Round 11, 2013 Draft (#327 overall)

YEAR	TEAM	LVL	AGE	W	L	SV	G	GS	IP	H	HR	BB/9	K/9	K	GB%	BABIP	WHIP	ERA	DRA	WARP	MPH	FB%	WHF	CSP
2017	TAM	A+	21	9	1	0	13	11	71¹	65	4	1.9	7.2	57	55%	.302	1.12	1.77	3.61	1.4				
2017	TRN	AA	21	5	0	0	7	7	44	37	3	1.6	10.6	52	52%	.304	1.02	2.05	3.35	1.0				
2017	CHT	AA	21	5	0	0	7	7	41²	33	1	3.9	7.1	33	55%	.274	1.22	2.81	4.32	0.4				
2018	CHT	AA	22	0	3	0	5	5	23	28	3	2.7	12.5	32	38%	.431	1.52	5.87	5.36	0.0				
2018	ROC	AAA	22	6	6	0	19	15	106	100	5	3.4	8.3	98	40%	.310	1.32	3.57	4.26	1.5				
2018	MIN	MLB	22	0	2	0	8	2	20¹	25	3	4.9	6.2	14	44%	.319	1.77	6.20	6.71	-0.4	94.8	58.5	8	49.2
2019	ROC	AAA	23	3	3	1	20	7	63	55	11	3.6	9.7	68	49%	.278	1.27	3.71	3.32	2.0				
2019	MIN	MLB	23	6	0	0	29	0	37	34	4	2.2	7.8	32	39%	.297	1.16	2.68	5.42	0.0	96.4	49.1	14.4	50.7
2020	MIN	MLB	24	2	2	0	44	0	46	47	6	3.3	8.1	42	42%	.304	1.39	4.78	4.71	0.2	95.7	54.3	12.3	51.5

Comparables: Robert Gsellman, Jake Thompson, Touki Toussaint

Littell rode a mix-master profile to the majors in 2018, leaning on arsenal depth rather than any overwhelming quality to force an audition in a swing role. That didn't go well, so he consolidated things into a tidy fastball-slider package for his encore and provided a sneaky chunk of consistent value as an emergent middle man. Outside of taking an eight-run lump for the team in late May, he yielded just three earned runs in 28 appearances. The view under his hood painted a bit of a lucky picture: he didn't strike out a ton of batters, and when opponents made contact they tended to square 'em up at an uncomfortable rate. Still, he'll pitch as a 24-year-old for the entirety of 2020, and his breakout performance and remaining option should make him a valuable piece of the 40-man puzzle.

Trevor May RHP Born: 09/23/89 Age: 30 Bats: R Throws: R Height: 6'5" Weight: 240 Origin: Round 4, 2008 Draft (#136 overall)

YEAR	TEAM	LVL	AGE	W	L	SV	G	GS	IP	H	HR	BB/9	K/9	K	GB%	BABIP	WHIP	ERA	DRA	WARP	MPH	FB%	WHF	CSP
2018	ROC	AAA	28	0	4	2	13	4	27	24	2	5.3	8.3	25	40%	.293	1.48	4.00	4.45	0.3				
2018	MIN	MLB	28	4	1	3	24	1	25¹	21	4	1.8	12.8	36	41%	.298	1.03	3.20	2.98	0.6	95.7	59.2	15.6	46.7
2019	MIN	MLB	29	5	3	2	65	0	64¹	43	8	3.6	11.1	79	35%	.233	1.07	2.94	3.95	1.0	97.6	62.9	13.9	46.3
2020	MIN	MLB	30	3	3	4	60	0	64	56	9	3.8	10.9	77	36%	.296	1.30	4.14	4.16	0.7	96.4	61.8	14.3	46.3

Comparables: Jeremy Jeffress, Neftalí Feliz, Bobby Parnell

Last year in this space we suggested May lean a little less on a heretofore pedestrian fastball. Rather than listen to our advice, he instead went out and made his fastball better. Another year removed from a surgeon's knife, his velocity ticked up to touch 96 mph. Some in-season fiddling with his slider fueled a breakout effort— with that pitch and, accordingly, his pitching at large. By the second half May had morphed into the setup monster Minnesota needed. He'll be in line for a nice free-agent payday if he can repeat his efforts this season.

Bailey Ober RHP Born: 07/12/95 Age: 24 Bats: R Throws: R Height: 6'9" Weight: 260 Origin: Round 12, 2017 Draft (#346 overall)

YEAR	TEAM	LVL	AGE	W	L	SV	G	GS	IP	H	HR	BB/9	K/9	K	GB%	BABIP	WHIP	ERA	DRA	WARP	MPH	FB%	WHF	CSP
2017	ELZ	RK	21	2	2	0	6	4	28	24	2	1.0	11.2	35	45%	.319	0.96	3.21	2.09	1.2				
2018	CDR	A	22	7	1	0	14	14	75	71	7	1.1	10.6	88	44%	.337	1.07	3.84	3.39	1.6				
2019	TWI	RK	23	1	0	0	2	1	9	6	0	1.0	13.0	13	71%	.286	0.78	0.00	0.92	0.5				
2019	FTM	A+	23	4	0	0	8	8	45²	39	1	1.2	10.4	53	40%	.330	0.99	0.99	3.38	0.9				
2019	PEN	AA	23	3	0	0	4	4	24	10	1	0.8	12.8	34	40%	.191	0.50	0.38	2.00	0.9				
2020	MIN	MLB	24	2	2	0	33	0	35	35	5	2.9	10.2	40	40%	.318	1.30	4.30	4.36	0.3				

Comparables: Brandon Workman, Cody Stashak, JD Hammer

Any time a pitcher yields all of six earned runs across an entire season—one spanning nearly 80 innings and three minor-league levels—it's bound to catch an inquisitive eye or three. And when the pitcher doing it stands 6-foot-9? Interest tends to grow to a similar scale from there. Not so with Ober, as the scouting community remains unimpressed. He uses every inch of his extra-large frame to generate outrageous downhill plane with an over-the-top delivery, and it helps a good changeup perform great against minor-league hitters. Unfortunately, his fastball tops out around 87 mph, and there's only so far that tends to take a pitcher in this day and age. Nevertheless, he should get his chance to prove the critics wrong this season, and stranger things have happened than an unorthodox 12th-round reliever figuring out how to pull rabbits out of his hat.

Jake Odorizzi RHP Born: 03/27/90 Age: 30 Bats: R Throws: R Height: 6'2" Weight: 190 Origin: Round 1, 2008 Draft (#32 overall)

YEAR	TEAM	LVL	AGE	W	L	SV	G	GS	IP	H	HR	BB/9	K/9	K	GB%	BABIP	WHIP	ERA	DRA	WARP	MPH	FB%	WHF	CSP
2017	TBA	MLB	27	10	8	0	28	28	143¹	117	30	3.8	8.0	127	32%	.227	1.24	4.14	5.29	0.5	93.8	48.7	12.1	43.9
2018	MIN	MLB	28	7	10	0	32	32	164¹	151	20	3.8	8.9	162	31%	.290	1.34	4.49	5.62	-0.6	92.9	54.3	11.7	42.1
2019	MIN	MLB	29	15	7	0	30	30	159	139	16	3.0	10.1	178	37%	.302	1.21	3.51	4.23	2.7	94.6	57.8	13.8	45.4
2020	MIN	MLB	30	11	8	0	28	28	149	138	24	3.4	9.8	162	35%	.295	1.30	4.32	4.33	2.0	93.1	54.2	12.6	43.8

Comparables: Kevin Gausman, Ubaldo Jiménez, Enyel De Los Santos

Odorizzi is the poster child for both: adaptive analytics and the terrifying prospect of free agency in the year 2020. After seeking out restructured training and strategic approaches at a Florida performance institute last winter, Odorizzi added a couple ticks to his fastball and worked a little farther down in the zone. His performance with the pitch improved. Better gas was accompanied by a splitter that featured more drop than usual, which helped him rein in his longball tendencies, and permitted him to put together the kind of solidly above-average walk year that should absolutely get a 30-year-old mid-rotation starter paid. Alas, the poisoned waters of the free market kept him in Minnesota as he accepted the qualifying offer. He'll make his play for a multi-year deal next winter instead.

Michael Pineda RHP Born: 01/18/89 Age: 31 Bats: R Throws: R Height: 6'7" Weight: 280 Origin: International Free Agent, 2005

YEAR	TEAM	LVL	AGE	W	L	SV	G	GS	IP	H	HR	BB/9	K/9	K	GB%	BABIP	WHIP	ERA	DRA	WARP	MPH	FB%	WHF	CSP
2017	NYA	MLB	28	8	4	0	17	17	96¹	103	20	2.0	8.6	92	52%	.302	1.29	4.39	3.36	2.4	96.2	48.5	13.3	46.6
2018	FTM	A+	29	0	0	0	2	2	6	7	0	0.0	6.0	4	35%	.350	1.17	1.50	5.67	0.0				
2019	MIN	MLB	30	11	5	0	26	26	146	141	23	1.7	8.6	140	37%	.292	1.16	4.01	4.74	1.6	95.1	55.6	13.4	49
2020	MIN	MLB	31	7	5	0	18	18	100	96	17	2.2	8.9	99	39%	.292	1.21	4.16	4.30	1.4	94.6	53.2	13.3	47.8

Comparables: Brett Anderson, Ricky Nolasco, Tyson Ross

The recipient of a two-year deal on the front end of Tommy John recovery last winter, Pineda returned to the bump and more or less picked up where he'd left off. He threw a higher percentage of changeups in Minnesota than he'd ever thrown before, and he managed good results with the pitch, even seeing a jump in fastball effectiveness despite coming back from the knife with lighter velocity. Somewhere along the way he lost the feel for his slider, but it didn't seem to matter as his game remained the same: limited baserunners, loud contact and a wobbly relationship with Lady Luck. As the calendar flipped to September he found himself on pace for a solid season in the middle of a playoff-bound rotation. That's when it all came crashing down, as it turned out that his comeback performance had been at least partially bought and paid for by a banned diuretic. His season-ending suspension cost him the shine of October's lights and a healthier paycheck. Still, the Twins liked what they saw when they did see it, and it all sounded so nice they played twice, signing him to another two-year deal over the winter.

Taylor Rogers LHP Born: 12/17/90 Age: 29 Bats: L Throws: L Height: 6'3" Weight: 190 Origin: Round 11, 2012 Draft (#340 overall)

YEAR	TEAM	LVL	AGE	W	L	SV	G	GS	IP	H	HR	BB/9	K/9	K	GB%	BABIP	WHIP	ERA	DRA	WARP	MPH	FB%	WHF	CSP
2017	MIN	MLB	26	7	3	0	69	0	55²	52	6	3.4	7.9	49	46%	.291	1.31	3.07	4.63	0.3	94.9	62.3	9.3	50
2018	MIN	MLB	27	1	2	2	72	0	68¹	49	3	2.1	9.9	75	46%	.280	0.95	2.63	3.33	1.3	95.2	52.9	12.3	51.5
2019	MIN	MLB	28	2	4	30	60	0	69	58	8	1.4	11.7	90	53%	.307	1.00	2.61	2.79	1.9	96.5	50.1	11.9	53.5
2020	MIN	MLB	29	3	3	38	60	0	64	58	7	2.2	10.7	76	49%	.315	1.16	3.29	3.42	1.2	95.0	53.7	11.4	51.9

Comparables: Justin Grimm, Alex Young, Rafael Perez

It all came together for Rogers, as he completed his transformation from a former back-end control lefty, to a burgeoning LOOGY, to a dominant all-world reliever. The introduction of a slider in 2018 had fueled his breakout, and his work with pitching coach Wes Johnson resulted in another tick of fastball velocity to tie the whole package together. Righties and lefties struggled each struggled to find his stuff consistently at any point in the season, and he even got to check out his twin brother break into the bigs. It's been a fun rise for the former 11th-rounder, and he'll resume his role at the back end of the 'pen with another chance to rack up saves before entering an arbitration system that pays closers handsomely.

Fernando Romero RHP Born: 12/24/94 Age: 25 Bats: R Throws: R Height: 6'0" Weight: 215 Origin: International Free Agent, 2011

YEAR	TEAM	LVL	AGE	W	L	SV	G	GS	IP	H	HR	BB/9	K/9	K	GB%	BABIP	WHIP	ERA	DRA	WARP	MPH	FB%	WHF	CSP
2017	CHT	AA	22	11	9	0	24	23	125	124	4	3.2	8.6	120	54%	.328	1.35	3.53	4.99	0.2				
2018	ROC	AAA	23	5	6	0	16	13	90²	85	5	3.2	6.8	69	50%	.294	1.29	3.57	3.73	1.8				
2018	MIN	MLB	23	3	3	0	11	11	55²	60	6	3.1	7.3	45	48%	.318	1.42	4.69	6.13	-0.5	97.5	63.3	11.3	48.4
2019	ROC	AAA	24	2	4	4	35	1	57²	53	7	4.5	9.8	63	63%	.311	1.42	4.37	4.34	1.1				
2019	MIN	MLB	24	0	1	0	15	0	14	19	2	7.1	11.6	18	52%	.425	2.14	7.07	3.77	0.2	98.7	67.6	12.6	43.1
2020	MIN	MLB	25	2	2	0	33	0	35	35	5	4.2	8.5	33	54%	.306	1.47	5.04	4.85	0.1	97.5	66	11.9	46.5

Comparables: Duane Underwood Jr., Allen Webster, John Gant

Once a surefire rotation anchor in the making, Romero slid into a relief role last year as the club sought to harness his obscene stuff. The days changed but the song stayed the same, and he again stalled out against high-end hitters and failed to contribute meaningful innings to the big-league club. His 97-mph sinker and hard slider both miss a bunch of bats and get beat into the ground often, so it's far too early to give up on him. But he'll head into 2020 out of options, as a true wildcard for the Twins' pen planning.

Sergio Romo RHP Born: 03/04/83 Age: 37 Bats: R Throws: R Height: 5'11" Weight: 185 Origin: Round 28, 2005 Draft (#852 overall)

YEAR	TEAM	LVL	AGE	W	L	SV	G	GS	IP	H	HR	BB/9	K/9	K	GB%	BABIP	WHIP	ERA	DRA	WARP	MPH	FB%	WHF	CSP
2017	LAN	MLB	34	1	1	0	30	0	25	23	7	4.3	11.2	31	35%	.276	1.40	6.12	2.58	0.7	88.2	27.2	15.4	41.1
2017	TBA	MLB	34	2	0	0	25	0	30²	19	2	2.1	8.2	28	40%	.218	0.85	1.47	3.76	0.5	87.9	41.5	16.3	41.7
2018	TBA	MLB	35	3	4	25	73	5	67¹	65	11	2.7	10.0	75	38%	.309	1.26	4.14	2.80	1.7	88.1	30.1	14.6	44
2019	MIA	MLB	36	2	0	17	38	0	37²	33	4	3.1	7.9	33	36%	.274	1.22	3.58	5.76	-0.2	87.6	26.2	15	42.7
2019	MIN	MLB	36	0	1	3	27	0	22²	17	3	1.6	10.7	27	37%	.246	0.93	3.18	2.73	0.6	87.5	22	14.6	40.5
2020	MIN	MLB	37	3	3	5	55	0	58	50	12	2.7	9.6	62	37%	.264	1.17	3.96	4.16	0.7	86.5	28.1	14.6	41.4

Comparables: Trevor Hoffman, Tom Henke, Joakim Soria

A few years back psychology professor Frank Durgin ran a study about human perceptions of hill slant. He found (overwhelmingly) that younger, less experienced people tended to wildly exaggerate the angle of a steep hill, while his sample of older, more experienced participants made much more educated, accurate estimates. Wisdom comes from experience. Usually, humans apply the wisdom of our experiences to make adjustments and offset the decay of our physical skills and the degradation of our brain's processing speed as we age; most of us consolidate our strengths in order to overcome our growing weaknesses. And then there are the people who just never learn or grow or change in any way. Sometimes those people become President of the United States. Other times they throw a dozen seasons of excellent high-leverage relief in the major leagues.

An ugly April and some shaky control in May briefly jeopardized an impressive streak of career-long above-average (or better) DRA performance, but Romo just kept flipping sliders throughout a much more stable midsummer that eventually saw him closing games in Miami. He was really good against lefties in 2019, and that's a good thing to be when you're a free agent who'll be 37 on Opening Day. It's an uphill climb indeed to hold onto a bullpen seat at that age, but being able to spin it like Romo does makes that path a little less steep.

Devin Smeltzer LHP Born: 09/07/95 Age: 24 Bats: R Throws: L Height: 6'3" Weight: 195 Origin: Round 5, 2016 Draft (#161 overall)

YEAR	TEAM	LVL	AGE	W	L	SV	G	GS	IP	H	HR	BB/9	K/9	K	GB%	BABIP	WHIP	ERA	DRA	WARP	MPH	FB%	WHF	CSP
2017	GRL	A	21	2	3	0	10	10	52¹	40	6	2.1	9.8	57	49%	.266	0.99	3.78	2.93	1.4				
2017	RCU	A+	21	5	4	0	16	15	90	107	10	1.8	10.2	102	44%	.367	1.39	4.40	4.75	0.5				
2018	TUL	AA	22	5	5	0	23	14	83²	94	9	2.0	7.2	67	39%	.321	1.35	4.73	4.70	0.5				
2018	CHT	AA	22	0	0	4	10	0	12	14	0	1.5	12.0	16	36%	.389	1.33	3.00	3.60	0.2				
2019	PEN	AA	23	3	1	0	5	5	30	19	0	0.9	9.9	33	42%	.268	0.73	0.60	2.66	0.8				
2019	ROC	AAA	23	1	4	0	15	14	74¹	68	14	2.3	8.6	71	40%	.271	1.17	3.63	3.89	2.0				
2019	MIN	MLB	23	2	2	1	11	6	49	50	8	2.2	7.0	38	39%	.294	1.27	3.86	5.59	0.0	90.9	45.8	10.2	49.3
2020	MIN	MLB	24	4	4	0	11	11	60	66	12	2.7	7.0	46	38%	.297	1.40	5.41	5.33	0.2	90.7	47.1	10.6	50.8

Comparables: Josh Rogers, Ranger Suárez, Andrew Heaney

Smeltzer flew a curious course in his big-league debut as that rare left-hander who gets tuned up by his own kind. It wasn't a wholly surprising outcome: he'd dabbled in reverse-splitting at points in his minor-league career, and loitered around even at other times. His curveball too often strayed from its intended target, meeting barrels instead of mitts. Nonetheless, Smeltzer has a three-pitch mix that also includes a dandy of a changeup. He should remain useful in the majors—and he might even prove to be an asset if he can figure out how to retire lefties.

Cody Stashak RHP Born: 06/04/94 Age: 26 Bats: R Throws: R Height: 6'2" Weight: 169 Origin: Round 13, 2015 Draft (#380 overall)

YEAR	TEAM	LVL	AGE	W	L	SV	G	GS	IP	H	HR	BB/9	K/9	K	GB%	BABIP	WHIP	ERA	DRA	WARP	MPH	FB%	WHF	CSP
2017	FTM	A+	23	3	4	0	16	16	83¹	72	7	2.2	7.8	72	33%	.279	1.10	3.89	3.62	1.6				
2017	CHT	AA	23	0	0	0	3	0	6	4	0	0.0	15.0	10	17%	.333	0.67	0.00	2.55	0.2				
2018	CHT	AA	24	1	1	4	35	2	55²	47	4	2.1	11.2	69	32%	.321	1.08	2.75	3.42	1.0				
2019	PEN	AA	25	2	3	4	19	0	28¹	28	4	1.6	12.7	40	30%	.348	1.16	4.76	5.23	-0.2				
2019	ROC	AAA	25	5	0	0	14	2	25	17	1	1.4	12.2	34	41%	.276	0.84	1.44	2.29	1.0				
2019	MIN	MLB	25	0	1	0	18	1	25	29	3	0.4	9.0	25	25%	.351	1.20	3.24	5.85	-0.1	93.0	54	18	54.3
2020	*MIN*	*MLB*	*26*	*2*	*2*	*0*	*33*	*0*	*35*	*32*	*6*	*2.3*	*9.8*	*38*	*30%*	*.287*	*1.17*	*4.00*	*4.15*	*0.4*	*92.6*	*54.9*	*18.3*	*55.3*

Comparables: Adbert Alzolay, Wei-Chieh Huang, Tyler Wilson

A former 13th-round pick by way of Queens, Stashak makes this year's Annual after missing the cut last year. That'll happen when a pitcher whiffs eight for every walk he issues in the high minors, then goes out and drops a 25-to-1 ratio in his big-league stint. He doesn't throw a particularly fast fastball, but it plays up with sneakiness generated by his extension and backspin. His slider's a short little thing that off of barrels, and his mechanics are cleaner than any Dirty Money radio edit, too. He's an interesting candidate to fill a Yusmeiro Petit-like hybrid role as soon as 2020.

Lewis Thorpe LHP Born: 11/23/95 Age: 24 Bats: R Throws: L Height: 6'1" Weight: 218 Origin: International Free Agent, 2012

YEAR	TEAM	LVL	AGE	W	L	SV	G	GS	IP	H	HR	BB/9	K/9	K	GB%	BABIP	WHIP	ERA	DRA	WARP	MPH	FB%	WHF	CSP
2017	FTM	A+	21	3	4	0	16	15	77	62	3	3.6	9.8	84	39%	.304	1.21	2.69	4.02	1.1				
2017	CHT	AA	21	1	0	0	1	1	6	5	2	3.0	10.5	7	19%	.214	1.17	6.00	4.12	0.1				
2018	CHT	AA	22	8	4	0	22	21	108	105	13	2.5	10.9	131	38%	.327	1.25	3.58	4.14	1.5				
2018	ROC	AAA	22	0	3	0	4	4	21²	20	3	2.5	10.8	26	45%	.321	1.20	3.32	3.94	0.4				
2019	ROC	AAA	23	5	4	0	20	19	96¹	91	13	2.3	11.1	119	43%	.318	1.20	4.58	3.53	2.9				
2019	MIN	MLB	23	3	2	0	12	2	27²	38	3	3.3	10.1	31	35%	.438	1.73	6.18	5.36	0.0	93.7	50	13.2	48.9
2020	*MIN*	*MLB*	*24*	*4*	*3*	*0*	*30*	*8*	*64*	*60*	*9*	*3.0*	*8.7*	*62*	*38%*	*.289*	*1.28*	*4.15*	*4.20*	*0.9*	*93.5*	*51.5*	*13.6*	*50.4*

Comparables: Anthony Banda, Jake Odorizzi, Zack Littell

To label last season a success for Thorpe is to undersell it. The Aussie had previously lost two years of development to Tommy John surgery and recovery, as well as assorted complications therefrom. But, less than three years after his return to the bump, he found the rubber in Minnesota for a dozen appearances. Thorpe works across three velocity bands with a four-pitch mix, and has shown consistent, high-end strikeout ability throughout his minor-league career. That held true in his big-league debut, even if the results didn't. A couple clunkers in an unfamiliar relief role won't diminish the clear triumph of a fought-for debut, and he'll enter 2020 in line for a step up in quantity and quality.

Matt Wisler RHP Born: 09/12/92 Age: 27 Bats: R Throws: R Height: 6'3" Weight: 215 Origin: Round 7, 2011 Draft (#233 overall)

YEAR	TEAM	LVL	AGE	W	L	SV	G	GS	IP	H	HR	BB/9	K/9	K	GB%	BABIP	WHIP	ERA	DRA	WARP	MPH	FB%	WHF	CSP
2017	GWN	AAA	24	7	5	0	18	14	93²	101	7	1.9	6.1	64	44%	.310	1.29	3.56	4.74	1.0				
2017	ATL	MLB	24	0	1	0	20	1	32¹	43	5	3.6	6.1	22	33%	.342	1.73	8.35	7.24	-0.7	94.9	55.9	10.1	46.1
2018	GWN	AAA	25	4	4	0	13	13	70	79	6	1.8	8.4	65	48%	.348	1.33	4.37	4.73	0.6				
2018	LOU	AAA	25	1	1	0	8	2	19²	19	0	1.4	9.6	21	36%	.339	1.12	1.83	5.65	0.0				
2018	ATL	MLB	25	1	1	0	7	3	26²	30	6	1.7	7.1	21	28%	.300	1.31	5.40	3.99	0.3	94.9	53.4	10.2	49.5
2018	CIN	MLB	25	0	0	0	11	0	13¹	11	2	1.4	7.4	11	42%	.231	0.98	2.03	4.26	0.1	94.0	42.1	12.2	51.2
2019	SEA	MLB	26	1	2	0	23	8	22¹	22	5	2.4	11.7	29	27%	.309	1.25	6.04	4.54	0.2	94.5	29.8	14.9	44.8
2019	SDN	MLB	26	2	2	0	21	0	29	34	5	3.1	10.6	34	46%	.363	1.52	5.28	3.86	0.5	94.9	28.6	16.2	47.8
2020	*MIN*	*MLB*	*27*	*2*	*2*	*0*	*27*	*5*	*28*	*28*	*5*	*2.7*	*9.2*	*29*	*36%*	*.299*	*1.28*	*4.38*	*4.45*	*0.2*	*94.2*	*40.5*	*13.4*	*48.1*

Comparables: Erasmo Ramírez, Archie Bradley, Vin Mazzaro

Wisler is on a quest to become the first slider-only pitcher in baseball, hucking it 70 percent of the time in 2019. It's a good hard slider, a variant on the cutter-dominant approaches of other relievers, but it hasn't reflected in the ERA yet, primarily because he's a fly ball pitcher who gives up a lot of home runs on fly balls. The pieces are interesting, however, and you can see why Minnesota wanted a chance to try to put them together.

LINEOUTS

Hitters

HITTER	POS	TEAM	LVL	AGE	PA	R	2B	3B	HR	RBI	BB	K	SB	CS	AVG/OBP/SLG	DRC+	VORP	BABIP	BRR	FRAA	WARP
Travis Blankenhorn	UT	PEN	AA	22	410	50	18	2	18	51	18	93	11	0	.278/.312/.474	119	26.0	.323	2.7	2B(67): 3.2, LF(18): 0.1	2.5
	UT	FTM	A+	22	61	6	4	0	1	3	9	12	0	0	.269/.377/.404	133	2.6	.333	-0.3	LF(6): -1.1, 2B(5): -0.3	0.2
Nick Gordon	MI	ROC	AAA	23	319	49	29	3	4	40	18	65	14	4	.298/.342/.459	107	16.5	.364	-0.1	SS(40): 1.6, 2B(29): -1.4	1.5
Seth Gray	3B	ELZ	Rk+	21	257	34	15	0	11	36	30	53	4	1	.225/.336/.445	112	12.8	.245	1.3		1.3
Will Holland	SS	ELZ	Rk+	21	145	22	2	0	7	16	14	44	8	1	.192/.299/.376	72	5.3	.230	1.3		0.3
Ryan Jeffers	C	PEN	AA	22	99	13	5	0	4	9	9	19	0	0	.287/.374/.483	142	9.8	.328	1.4	C(16): -0.9	0.8
	C	FTM	A+	22	315	35	11	0	10	40	28	64	0	0	.256/.330/.402	122	15.0	.297	-2.7	C(57): 0.7	1.6
Ryan LaMarre	OF	GWN	AAA	30	455	55	24	8	9	53	38	118	19	9	.311/.380/.477	112	21.0	.416	4.5	CF(44): -0.5, RF(27): 4.7	2.4
	OF	MIN	MLB	30	26	3	0	0	2	3	3	5	1	1	.217/.308/.478	97	0.8	.188	0.7	CF(12): -0.9, RF(2): -0.1	0.0
Gabriel Maciel	OF	CDR	A	20	187	28	3	4	0	17	23	31	8	2	.309/.395/.377	135	15.6	.382	2.7	CF(24): -2.1, RF(16): -0.1	1.2
	OF	FTM	A+	20	229	29	6	2	3	17	21	30	14	7	.261/.342/.357	117	10.9	.290	0.5	CF(31): 2.5, RF(16): -0.9	1.2
Jose Miranda	INF	FTM	A+	21	478	48	25	1	8	55	24	54	0	0	.248/.299/.364	103	7.0	.264	-3.0	3B(71): -0.5, 2B(34): 0.5	1.3
Luke Raley	OF	ROC	AAA	24	138	28	6	0	7	21	7	42	4	0	.302/.362/.516	118	10.3	.403	2.0	RF(22): 2.3, CF(5): 0.0	0.9
Yunior Severino	INF	CDR	A	19	86	7	7	0	0	8	7	27	0	0	.244/.302/.333	95	2.3	.365	-0.2	2B(20): -0.3	0.1
Spencer Steer	INF	ELZ	Rk+	21	95	14	6	1	2	13	15	5	0	1	.325/.442/.506	165	12.7	.324	0.4		1.0
	INF	CDR	A	21	201	26	12	2	2	20	19	28	5	1	.260/.358/.387	129	11.5	.299	-1.0	3B(24): 0.3, 2B(13): -2.0	0.8
LaMonte Wade Jr	LF	MIN	MLB	25	69	10	2	1	2	5	11	9	0	1	.196/.348/.375	105	2.6	.200	0.0	CF(14): 0.9, LF(8): -0.6	0.2
	LF	ROC	AAA	25	334	47	12	1	5	24	56	48	7	2	.246/.392/.356	106	9.4	.280	0.8	RF(34): -6.5, LF(28): -1.4	0.3
Matt Wallner	OF	CDR	A	21	53	7	3	1	2	6	5	14	0	0	.205/.340/.455	114	1.9	.250	-0.4	RF(10): -1.8	-0.1
	OF	ELZ	Rk+	21	238	35	18	1	6	28	19	66	1	1	.269/.361/.452	133	12.2	.368	-0.8		1.2
Zander Wiel	1B	ROC	AAA	26	522	86	40	5	24	78	40	158	2	1	.254/.320/.514	101	10.4	.325	0.6	1B(107): 7.1, RF(4): -0.6	1.3

Not to be confused with a slow-footed mountain goat, **Travis Blankenhorn** is a slow-seasoning prospect whose inconsistencies of approach and leather have left the former third-rounder staring up a rocky slope to the majors. ⓧ **Nick Gordon** held his own when healthy at Triple-A last year, but these days he looks more like a depth-chart puzzle piece than a regular. ⓧ A good glove and plenty of pop got **Seth Gray** drafted in the fourth round. His bat will need to find some color if it's going to play at the highest levels ⓧ The Twins paid third-round money in the fifth for **Will Holland** and all they got was this crappy t-shirt and a 30-percent whiff rate in short-season ball. ⓧ **Ryan Jeffers** impressed on both sides in his first full pro season, showing power potential at the plate and making strides with his receiving behind it. After a successful cameo at Double-A, he looks to be the rare fast-moving catching prospect. Should everything go well, he might elbow his way onto the big-league depth chart at some point this season. ⓧ The Twins brought back **Ryan LaMarre** to fill some September at-bats, clearing the way for him to log big-league playing time for the fifth consecutive season. He'll look to keep that streak alive in 2020 despite being short on tools—and on time left in his prime. ⓧ So far, so good for **Gabriel Maciel**, a 20-year-old speed-and-leather prospect whose bat held serve after a midseason promotion to High-A. ⓧ A former second-rounder, **Jose Miranda** hung in there against Florida State League pitching. His stick will have to show it can do more than that after he shed his shortstop ambitions. ⓧ Ugly approach notwithstanding, **Luke Raley** raked at Triple-A before breaking his ankle in May. He has large muscles and some versatility, and he should be in the mix for big-league at-bats in 2020. ⓧ A casualty of the Braves' international signing scandal a couple years back, **Yunior Severino** resurfaced with Minnesota and appeared poised to take a leap in full-season ball last year before a broken thumb derailed him for two and a half months. He has some pop but a raw approach and hazy defensive future. ⓧ The club's third-rounder last June, **Spencer Steer** is a high-floor utility prospect with a solid hit tool and excellent defensive skills. The Twins will try to herd him up to Minnesota on a quicker timeline after his successful pro debut. ⓧ The centerpiece of Minnesota's 2018 international spending strategy, **Misael Urbina** looked great out of the gate in his Dominican debut and should see the American seashore this season. ⓧ **LaMonte Wade, Jr.** gets on base a lot, and the skill held after about 18 injuries cleared a path for him to big-league at-bats down the stretch. He'll need to find another defining trait (or three) if he's going to garner more playing time in 2020. ⓧ The 39th overall pick last June, **Matt Wallner** is a big boy with big-boy power, big-boy length to his swing, and a big-boy fastball in his back pocket in case the second thing torpedoes the first thing. ⓧ After spending decades as a famous Coney Island landmark **Zander Wiel** will shift gears and try his hand at supplanting C.J. Cron as a cheaper block of corner-masher wood for the Twins' fire.

Pitchers

PITCHER	TEAM	LVL	AGE	W	L	SV	G	GS	IP	H	HR	BB/9	K/9	K	GB%	BABIP	WHIP	ERA	DRA	WARP	MPH	FB%	WHF	CSP
Dakota Chalmers	TWI	Rk	22	1	0	0	4	4	13¹	8	0	5.4	12.8	19	68%	.320	1.20	4.05	2.34	0.5				
	FTM	A+	22	1	1	0	5	5	21¹	12	0	6.3	12.2	29	55%	.273	1.27	3.38	3.49	0.4				
Trevor Hildenberger	ROC	AAA	28	1	0	2	14	0	19	19	2	1.9	7.1	15	46%	.298	1.21	4.74	3.75	0.5				
	MIN	MLB	28	2	2	1	22	0	16¹	30	2	3.9	8.3	15	41%	.459	2.27	10.47	7.51	-0.4	91.8	37.2	10.8	43.8
Griffin Jax	PEN	AA	24	4	5	0	20	20	111¹	98	5	1.9	6.8	84	50%	.280	1.10	2.67	4.32	0.9				
	ROC	AAA	24	1	2	0	3	3	16	19	2	1.7	5.6	10	46%	.321	1.38	4.50	5.60	0.2				
Ryan O'Rourke	ROC	AAA	31	2	1	0	7	0	12	7	0	9.0	10.5	14	39%	.250	1.58	4.50	5.63	0.1				
	SYR	AAA	31	2	3	2	36	2	44	39	4	4.7	9.6	47	53%	.310	1.41	3.27	4.31	0.8				
	NYN	MLB	31	0	0	0	2	0	1¹	0	0	20.2	6.8	1	0%	.000	2.25	0.00	8.30	0.0	93.2	42.9	0	34.9
Sean Poppen	PEN	AA	25	2	3	0	8	7	28²	30	0	5.3	12.2	39	59%	.423	1.64	4.40	5.73	-0.3				
	ROC	AAA	25	5	1	0	12	9	61	53	4	4.0	10.0	68	58%	.306	1.31	3.84	3.69	1.7				
	MIN	MLB	25	0	0	0	4	0	8¹	10	1	5.4	9.7	9	46%	.429	1.80	7.56	5.83	0.0	96.4	57.5	10.5	49.1
Chris Vallimont	CLN	A	22	4	4	0	13	13	69¹	48	4	3.4	10.4	80	41%	.273	1.07	2.99	3.10	1.7				
	JUP	A+	22	2	3	0	6	6	36	31	3	2.8	10.5	42	30%	.308	1.17	3.50	4.71	0.1				
	FTM	A+	22	2	2	0	4	4	22¹	15	0	1.6	11.3	28	38%	.283	0.85	3.63	5.47	-0.1				

Oakland popped **Dakota Chalmers** in the third round in 2015. Then he couldn't throw strikes; then he popped his UCL; then he got shipped to the midwest; and now he's back to not throwing strikes. His misses can touch 97 mph and buckle knees, however. ⓧ **Trevor Hildenberger** was just okay at Triple-A before a catastrophic late-season return to the Show sealed his non-tender fate with the Twins. He'll look to recapture glory on someone else's Triple-A roster this year. ⓧ A former third-rounder, **Griffin Jax** has been fakin' his way through Double-A, leaning on good command of moving stuff to stymie Southern League hitters despite a concerning lack of whiffs. He'll be in the mix for rotation innings in the year ahead. ⓧ Dual Irish/American citizen **Ryan O'Rourke** went over to Bulgaria and closed a couple games for the Irish national team in the European Baseball Championships during a week of DFA limbo in the middle of last summer. ⓧ **Sean Poppen's** elbow didn't go full onomatopoeia, but it did bark loud enough to knock him out for the season a mere four games into his big-league career. It was an unfortunate injury, but his Engineering Sciences degree from Harvard should come in handy should his wing ever require structural reconfiguration. ⓧ A sneaky late-season grab for Sergio Romo's services, **Chris Vallimont** brings a legendary D-II pedigree and serious strikeout potential. He's not as good of a prospect as his numbers suggest, but he's one worth keeping tabs on.

NEW YORK METS

Essay by Sara Nović

Player comments by Linda Surovich and BP staff

Sorry About That: A Letter to My Son

First things first. I suppose I owe you an apology. Before you were even conceived your father and I had decided to split the (then hypothetical) baby—you could be an Eagles, Sixers and Flyers fan, just as long as we taught you to root for the Mets.

It's a difficult row to hoe, made harder by the fact that you're now growing up in the shadow of Citizens Bank Park. And these days the Phillies are trying very hard to be good. It didn't quite work this year, but if they buy all the remaining baseball players, something could really stick!

As a kid, I also spent most of my childhood a Mets fan in Phillies territory. Once, on a field trip to the Vet, the Phanatic gave me a noogie. On. The. Jumbotron. My introvert self has never quite recovered.

And yet. This is a fate I want—I've *bargained*—to pass on to you. Now that you're here, I feel a bit more conflicted. I hate seeing you sad, and should you be as emotionally invested in sports as your father, some tears over a lost baseball game are unavoidable should you follow the Mets. I wish I could promise you it will be worth it, that statistically speaking they have to be good again eventually. But as they well know in Sox and Cubs fiefdoms, it doesn't always play that way in baseball. And this is the Mets we're talking about.

Nevertheless, you deserve a look at some of the finer points of the team. In laying them out for you, I hope the argument for supporting them might yet reveal itself.

But first, a few caveats. A couple things we're definitely *not* rooting for:

- Fraud! Look, being suckered by Bernie Madoff is excusable, or at least it can be—many good people were. But once you start running your own insurance scam, being chummy with Madoff gives off more of a "takes one to know one" vibe. I'm not a conspiracy theorist; it's well known that the Wilpons keep the insurance payouts for injured players rather than invest that money back into the team. Did I mention that one of the Mets' more productive hitters missed the entire season

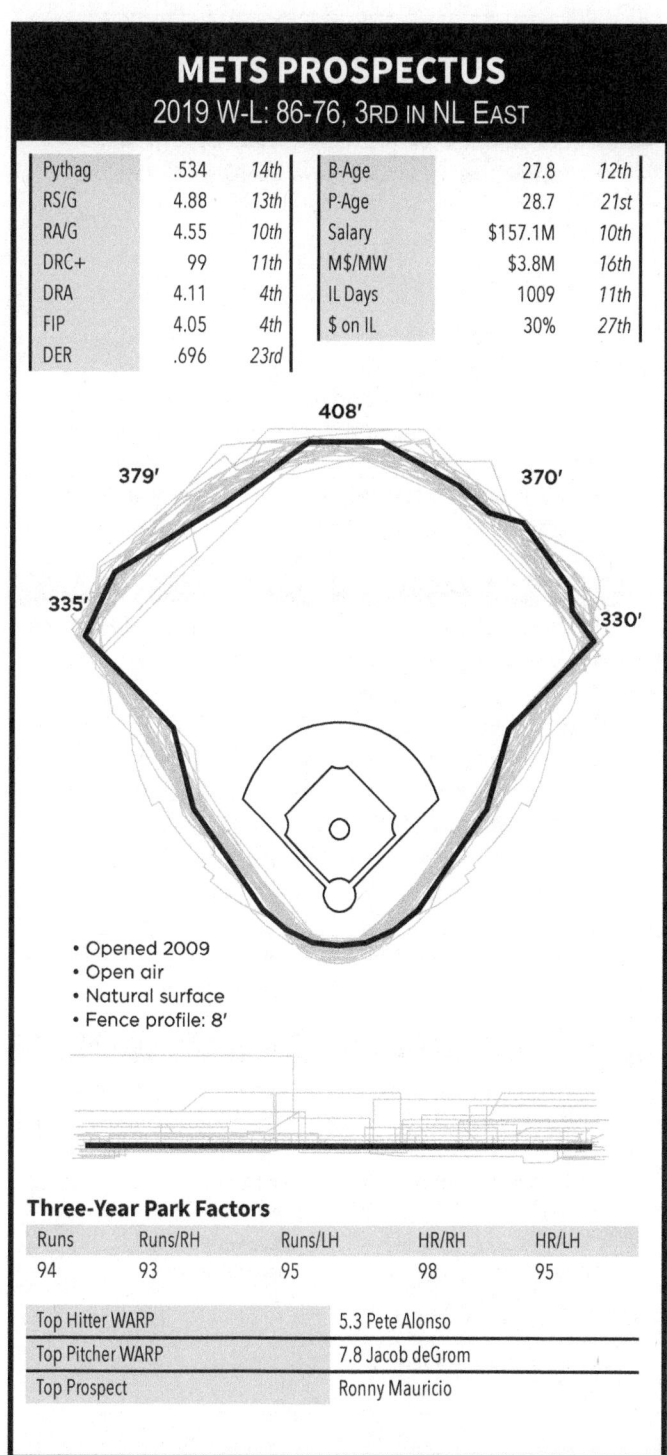

METS PROSPECTUS
2019 W-L: 86-76, 3RD IN NL EAST

Pythag	.534	14th	B-Age	27.8	12th
RS/G	4.88	13th	P-Age	28.7	21st
RA/G	4.55	10th	Salary	$157.1M	10th
DRC+	99	11th	M$/MW	$3.8M	16th
DRA	4.11	4th	IL Days	1009	11th
FIP	4.05	4th	$ on IL	30%	27th
DER	.696	23rd			

408'
379'   370'
335'   330'

- Opened 2009
- Open air
- Natural surface
- Fence profile: 8'

Three-Year Park Factors

Runs	Runs/RH	Runs/LH	HR/RH	HR/LH
94	93	95	98	95

Top Hitter WARP	5.3 Pete Alonso
Top Pitcher WARP	7.8 Jacob deGrom
Top Prospect	Ronny Mauricio

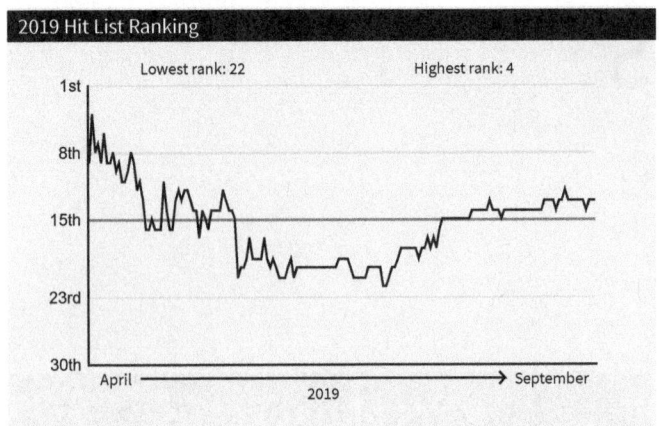

2019 Hit List Ranking

Lowest rank: 22   Highest rank: 4

1st
8th
15th
23rd
30th
April — 2019 → September

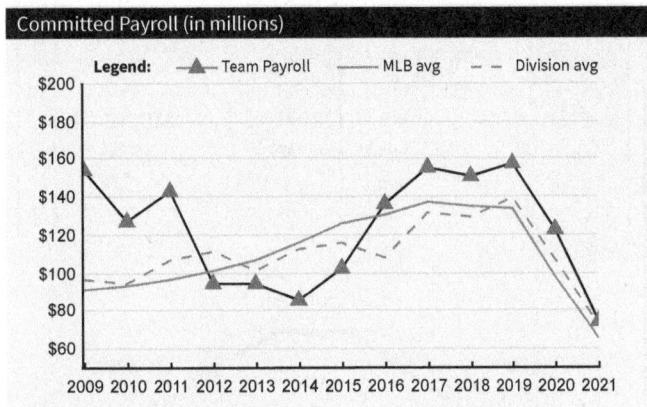

Committed Payroll (in millions)

Legend: ▲ Team Payroll — MLB avg -- Division avg

$200
$180
$160
$140
$120
$100
$80
$60

2009 2010 2011 2012 2013 2014 2015 2016 2017 2018 2019 2020 2021

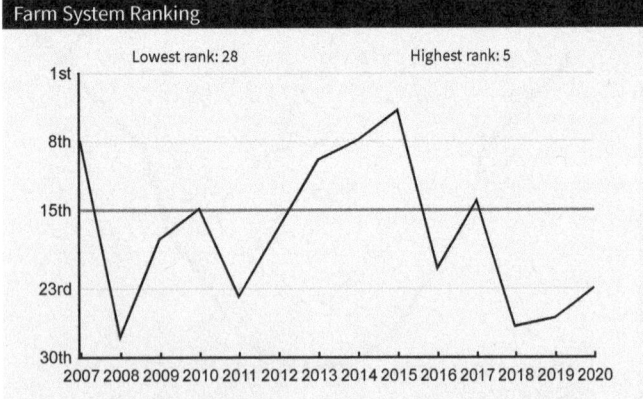

Farm System Ranking

Lowest rank: 28   Highest rank: 5

1st
8th
15th
23rd
30th
2007 2008 2009 2010 2011 2012 2013 2014 2015 2016 2017 2018 2019 2020

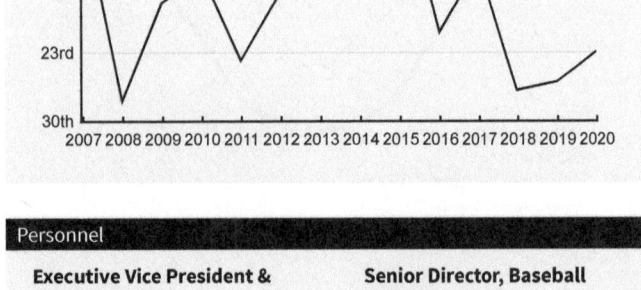

Personnel

Executive Vice President & General Manager
Brodie Van Wagenen

VP, Assistant General Manager, Scouting & Player Development
Allard Baird

Vice President, International & Amateur Scouting
Tommy Tanous

Assistant General Manager
Adam Guttridge

Senior Director, Baseball Operations
Ian Levin

Manager
Carlos Beltrán

BP Alumni
Russell Carleton
Josh Turner

because he fell in a hole? It's curious to me that the league doesn't enforce some sort of protocol or ethical code that would require a change of ownership, unless they, too, have something worth hiding. Alright, maybe I've got a touch of conspiracy theorist in me. Anyway, suffice it to say we're rooting for the players, not the Wilpons. With any luck, they'll be gone before you're conscious.

- Misogyny! It's hard to know why domestic violence is so prevalent amongst athletes. Could it be that those whose egos and livelihoods are reliant upon their physical prowess then turn erroneously to that strength in times of turmoil? Or are they, with lives lived in the public eye, simply getting caught more? Either way, I'd love to simply steer your gaze away from the Jose Reyeses of the world and back to the David Wrights and the Jacob deGroms, but as MLB may finally kind of, sort of, be realizing, ignoring the problem is not going to work. Your dad and I talk often about how to teach you to be a kind person—to be a feminist, attuned to your emotions, to get and give consent. From my perspective, part of that is offering up good role models. I hope as you grow there will be fewer and fewer moments where I'm forced to decide between a love of the sport and love for my son, because that will always mean turning the game off.

- Sloth! The Mets are always finding new and interesting ways to be bad, and this past year was no exception. Credit is largely due to the hiring of Brodie Van Wagenen, who your uncle (also torturing your cousins into Mets fandom, by the way) has very accurately dubbed "the Anthony Scaramucci of baseball." Besides Van Wagenen having only an ancillary knowledge of the sport, it came out midseason that he also couldn't be bothered to actually attend the games, and was attempting to manage from the comfort of his La-Z-Boy. You can't make this stuff up. But you shouldn't root for it, either.

So what exactly are we waving our foam fingers for? Well the talent, for one. Despite the Wilpons' best efforts, we managed to land the most powerful slugger in the league. The rookie Pete Alonso smashed Mets and major-league records alike, hitting a league-wide 2019 high of 53 home runs, and simultaneously breaking Aaron Judge's record for most home runs in a rookie season (52). Alonso won the Home Run Derby and was Rookie of the Year. If the Mets' signature yips don't overtake him, (and if the Wilpons will pay him), he'll be a powerhouse to enjoy for years to come.

Jeff McNeil also had a breakout season, slashing .318/.384/.531 with 25 homers and 75 RBI. And despite some speed bumps, deGrom and Thor remained largely dominant, even when they didn't have help to lock down the W.

But with the Mets, fandom isn't all about the win. (Let's face it: if it were, we fans wouldn't exist.) Fortunately, though, there are other bright spots:

- Sloth! You've come into the world too late to enjoy the sight of pitcher Bartolo Colón taking the mound (though weirdly, not *that* late). Though it looks as if Big Sexy's playing days are (finally) over, his accolades remain—he was, in 2018, the oldest active player and the last man standing to have played in the 90s or for the Montreal Expos, and holds the most wins by a Latino pitcher. And just a few years ago he was pitching for the Mets, sending the league's best and brightest down looking with his 90 MPH "fastball" in the NLCS, and catching comebackers with his gut. While Bartolo's beer belly might be evidence for the argument that baseball requires less athleticism than other sports, I think it's intensely charming, a reminder why baseball is America's pastime, a game for the everyfan. DeGrom, while opposite in body type, shares that down-to-earth aura—he keeps limber in the offseason by playing catch with his dad, and has a penchant for Big Macs and Mountain Dew. *Stars, they're just like us!* It's nice when even our most talented Cy Young winners don't have the ego and showboating you get in some other sports, or, say, up in the Bronx.
- Community! You know, Citi Field had a Shake Shack before it was cool.

  It takes a certain constitution to continue to love a team when that team's one true love is blowing a lead. But the people who stick around are ones you'd want to sit next to at a ball game. They find humor in despair; they are pot committed. Famous fans include Harper Lee, Jerry Seinfeld, Chris Rock, Hank Azaria, Itzhak Perlman, and Leonardo DiCaprio-while-getting-hit-in-the-head-with-a-volleyball, to name a few. Not to mention several generations of your own family. Your great-grandma, a diehard fan from the team's inaugural season, bought a tiny Mets hat before she died. Sure, it was probably an accident of online shopping by a near octogenarian. But I like to think she knew you were coming.

- Hope! This year is gonna be the year, I can feel it. Maybe Steve Cohen really will purchase the team and spend money to pay good players. Maybe the return of Carlos Beltrán to the team, this time as manager, will warm up the Mets bats so that poor deGrom can get a win once and a while. Maybe Alonso will continue to be an absolute stud and get a long, fat contract befitting of his talent and the large market team for which he plays. Maybe Yoenis Céspedes will climb out of that hole. Maybe, this time, they won't blow it.

The Mets are the poster team for being so close. They're not bad like, Orioles bad. They're always nearly good. It can be heartbreaking, these near misses, but it is also exhilarating. Watching the Mets reminds me that there's always a little bit of hope, even if it is against the odds. Maybe especially then. In these dark times, hope is a good thing to practice.

Do you want to know a secret? If, one day, after being humiliated in front of your friends by a man wearing a green shag carpet, you came to me and said you didn't want to root for the Mets anymore, I wouldn't press the issue. I might even take you out and buy you the gear for some other team (or at least send your dad to do it). But I hope that can I raise you to be the kind of person who *wants* to be a Mets fan, someone with the patience to see the diamond for the coal: that is, an optimist. ■

—*Sara Nović is an author of Baseball Prospectus.*

HITTERS

Pete Alonso 1B Born: 12/07/94 Age: 25 Bats: R Throws: R Height: 6'3" Weight: 245 Origin: Round 2, 2016 Draft (#64 overall)

YEAR	TEAM	LVL	AGE	PA	R	2B	3B	HR	RBI	BB	K	SB	CS	AVG/OBP/SLG	DRC+	VORP	BABIP	BRR	FRAA	WARP
2017	SLU	A+	22	346	45	23	0	16	58	25	64	3	4	.286/.361/.516	168	12.8	.314	-5.8	1B(78): 3.2	2.2
2017	BIN	AA	22	47	7	4	1	2	5	2	7	0	0	.311/.340/.578	104	3.2	.333	-0.1	1B(5): 0.1	0.1
2018	BIN	AA	23	273	42	12	0	15	52	43	50	0	2	.314/.440/.573	180	30.5	.344	-1.6	1B(51): 1.8	2.6
2018	LVG	AAA	23	301	50	19	1	21	67	33	78	0	1	.260/.355/.585	122	14.6	.284	1.2	1B(59): 5.0	1.8
2019	NYN	MLB	24	693	103	30	2	53	120	72	183	1	0	.260/.358/.583	141	47.7	.280	0.5	1B(156): 6.1	5.3
2020	NYN	MLB	25	630	98	28	1	48	118	63	169	1	1	.256/.349/.570	138	43.8	.280	0.2	1B 6	5.1

Comparables: AJ Reed, Ryan O'Hearn, Brandon Allen

For a franchise that seems to be cursed by the baseball gods, they were certainly blessed with a franchise cornerstone whose baseball abilities were equally matched by his off-the-field persona and leadership qualities. That person of course was David Wright but the team was gifted another player who perfectly lives up to that high blue and orange standard and this one is also a bear. From the pomp of starting a jersey-ripping tradition for walk-offs to the custom cleats that he bought his teammates to honor first responders and 9/11 victims, Alonso has attempted to check all of the makeup boxes in just a single endearing season.

The Mets bucked the trend of keeping rookies in the minors to start the season and were rewarded handsomely for their decision. April 12th could have been the date where the slugger made his debut had service time factored into the team's decision-making; between Opening Day and that date Alonso hit .378/.451/.911 with six homers, six doubles, 17 RBI and an eye-popping 1.362 OPS. It was a good move for all involved, except for the folks who have to rewrite the books. If Alonso was in the minors to start the year, he would not have broken the MLB rookie home run record or the franchise records for extra base hits, total bases and hits by a rookie in a single season. This past season was truly a special one both on and off the field for the National League Rookie of the Year and fans everywhere got to witness the birth of a star in the making.

★ ★ ★ *2020 Top 101 Prospect* **#88** ★ ★ ★

Francisco Alvarez **C** Born: 11/19/01 Age: 18 Bats: R Throws: R Height: 5'11" Weight: 220 Origin: International Free Agent, 2018

YEAR	TEAM	LVL	AGE	PA	R	2B	3B	HR	RBI	BB	K	SB	CS	AVG/OBP/SLG	DRC+	VORP	BABIP	BRR	FRAA	WARP
2019	MTS	RK	17	31	8	4	0	2	10	4	4	0	1	.462/.548/.846	224	7.7	.500	-0.3	C(4): 0.3	0.4
2019	KNG	RK+	17	151	24	6	0	5	16	17	33	1	1	.282/.377/.443	128	9.1	.344	-1.4		0.9
2020	NYN	MLB	18	251	24	12	1	5	25	24	75	3	1	.231/.313/.356	82	2.3	.325	0.0	C 0	0.2

Comparables: Oscar Hernández, Gary Sánchez, Jefry Marte

The Mets are a franchise whose catching situation has often been muddled ever since Mike Piazza left in 2005. Trying to rectify that, the team went all out and signed Alvarez out of Venezuela to a team record $2.9 million deal in 2018. To say the early returns have been promising for the teenager is an understatement as big as the teenager's arm. After obliterating complex-league pitchers so thoroughly that he was moved up to the Appy League after only 31 plate appearances, Alvarez was a well above-average hitter while being one of the youngest players in the league and getting his first experience catching pro pitchers. He remains a ways away from contributing in Queens, despite being advanced for his age. He's got work to do on his receiving behind the plate but getting the heightened attention of prospect hounds in your first stateside season is quite a feat.

Brett Baty **3B** Born: 11/13/99 Age: 20 Bats: L Throws: R Height: 6'3" Weight: 210 Origin: Round 1, 2019 Draft (#12 overall)

YEAR	TEAM	LVL	AGE	PA	R	2B	3B	HR	RBI	BB	K	SB	CS	AVG/OBP/SLG	DRC+	VORP	BABIP	BRR	FRAA	WARP
2019	MTS	RK	19	25	5	3	0	1	8	5	6	0	0	.350/.480/.650	148	4.1	.462	0.2	3B(4): -0.2	0.2
2019	KNG	RK+	19	186	30	12	2	6	22	24	56	0	0	.222/.339/.437	108	5.5	.302	-0.4		0.6
2020	NYN	MLB	20	251	21	12	1	4	21	25	92	2	1	.186/.276/.300	57	-5.9	.297	0.0	3B 0	-0.6

Comparables: Carlos Peguero, Chris Carter, José Altuve

Baty was old for a high school draftee, which may have led some teams to shy away from him in the first round of the 2019 draft but the Mets went for the then 19-and-a-half-year-old with the twelfth overall pick. At the plate, he showcases easy plus raw power and shows a discerning approach that in time should develop a shade more aggressiveness when appropriate. On the field, the Texan looks the part of someone who can hold down the hot corner until his body starts to turn—it's just a matter of when that might be. But for an organization that just graduated the NL Rookie of the Year and a fanbase that is ready for the next next big thing, expectations are going to be an issue. In fact, when he was selected, Harold Reynolds described Baty on the MLB Network broadcast as "Freddie Freeman with power." Freeman only hit *checks notes* 38 home runs last season, so no pressure, kid.

Robinson Canó **2B** Born: 10/22/82 Age: 37 Bats: L Throws: R Height: 6'0" Weight: 210 Origin: International Free Agent, 2001

YEAR	TEAM	LVL	AGE	PA	R	2B	3B	HR	RBI	BB	K	SB	CS	AVG/OBP/SLG	DRC+	VORP	BABIP	BRR	FRAA	WARP
2017	SEA	MLB	34	648	79	33	0	23	97	49	85	1	0	.280/.338/.453	108	22.6	.294	-2.0	2B(150): -7.3	1.7
2018	SEA	MLB	35	348	44	22	0	10	50	32	47	0	0	.303/.374/.471	125	23.2	.329	-0.4	2B(69): -2.5, 1B(14): 0.3	1.8
2019	NYN	MLB	36	423	46	28	0	13	39	25	69	0	0	.256/.307/.428	89	7.9	.280	-0.7	2B(99): -7.4	0.0
2020	NYN	MLB	37	525	57	26	0	18	65	35	91	2	1	.256/.312/.426	93	15.5	.281	-1.1	2B -6	1.0

Comparables: Brandon Phillips, Howie Kendrick, Adam Kennedy

Ask any ruffled Mets fan about Canó and they will probably respond with their best Comic Book Guy three-word diatribe. It wasn't always like this though. Opening Day was a simpler time, in which at least for a brief moment everything went the way it was supposed to. Canó took Max Scherzer deep and Edwin Díaz preserved the lead for Jacob deGrom, giving the Mets a victory to start the season. But happy stories are not the Mets' forte and over the remainder of the first half of the season, Canó had a paltry .628 OPS with eroding plate discipline and little-to-no power. The veteran second baseman came out of the break a new man (well, a rejuvenated one at least) and put up a second-half OPS of .896 until a torn hamstring sidelined him into September. Were he not making nearly $100 million over the next four years of his deal and were Jarred Kelenic not part of the return to get him, Canó might be talked about as an invaluable mentor in the clubhouse to Amed Rosario and gave Pete Alonso sound advice for the Home Run Derby. But if you think it's bad now, wait until you see the discourse in 2022.

Yoenis Céspedes **LF** Born: 10/18/85 Age: 34 Bats: R Throws: R Height: 5'10" Weight: 220 Origin: International Free Agent, 2012

YEAR	TEAM	LVL	AGE	PA	R	2B	3B	HR	RBI	BB	K	SB	CS	AVG/OBP/SLG	DRC+	VORP	BABIP	BRR	FRAA	WARP
2017	NYN	MLB	31	321	46	17	2	17	42	26	61	0	1	.292/.352/.540	123	23.6	.316	-1.1	LF(74): 2.9	1.9
2018	NYN	MLB	32	157	20	6	0	9	29	13	50	3	0	.262/.325/.496	99	11.3	.333	0.5	LF(35): 1.8	0.6
2020	NYN	MLB	34	217	28	9	1	13	34	16	55	2	1	.249/.310/.493	111	8.7	.280	-0.2	LF 2	1.1

Comparables: Willie Horton, Gene Oliver, Jeromy Burnitz

Nearly a decade after he burst onto the U.S. baseball scene with a workout video for the ages, La Potencia has captivated four different fanbases—well, maybe not the Red Sox—and flashed the talent that led Kevin Goldstein to call him the best all-around prospect to come out of Cuba in a generation. In New York, he's a legend both on the field and off, his hitting prowess from 2015 and 2016 nearly as memorable as his many spring training rides—both of the sports car and equine variety. Unfortunately, that fame has been stymied by unusual injuries that have conspired to limit him to 119 games over the last three years. This culminated with surgery to remove calcification on both heels in late 2018, followed by a severely broken ankle in May—quite possibly the only boar-related injury of the 2019 season. There's almost nothing Céspedes could do that would surprise anyone at this point, except possibly for returning as a middle-of-the-order thumper to lead the Mets in his final contract year.

Michael Conforto RF   Born: 03/01/93   Age: 27   Bats: L   Throws: R   Height: 6'1"   Weight: 215   Origin: Round 1, 2014 Draft (#10 overall)

YEAR	TEAM	LVL	AGE	PA	R	2B	3B	HR	RBI	BB	K	SB	CS	AVG/OBP/SLG	DRC+	VORP	BABIP	BRR	FRAA	WARP
2017	NYN	MLB	24	440	72	20	1	27	68	57	113	2	0	.279/.384/.555	133	47.7	.328	1.4	LF(52): 3.9, CF(43): -3.6	3.3
2018	NYN	MLB	25	638	78	25	1	28	82	84	159	3	4	.243/.350/.448	112	36.9	.289	-4.2	LF(84): 1.1, CF(58): -7.3	1.8
2019	NYN	MLB	26	648	90	29	1	33	92	84	149	7	2	.257/.363/.494	122	36.4	.290	-0.3	RF(132): 10.0, CF(39): -3.7	4.1
2020	NYN	MLB	27	595	83	24	1	33	93	73	138	3	2	.253/.355/.498	123	29.9	.282	-0.9	RF 9	4.1

Comparables: Kyle Schwarber, Bryce Harper, Matt Joyce

Conforto quietly had his best season in 2019, putting up career highs in home runs, RBI, hits, doubles and runs. He blasted the 100th home run of his career and his first walk-off was a memorable one when he survived a Polar Bear attack and ended up shirtless in front of a frenzied Citi Field crowd. That signature moment led to many walk-off, shirts-off celebrations from that point on. But the quiet star in Queens also took a different part of his game to a new level without any fanfare: his defense. Already known as someone who could fake it in center when needed, Conforto played his first full season in right field and was a top-five defender by FRAA in that corner. And with two years left until free agency, it's a good time to be showing off his well-roundedness.

J.D. Davis LF   Born: 04/27/93   Age: 27   Bats: R   Throws: R   Height: 6'3"   Weight: 225   Origin: Round 3, 2014 Draft (#75 overall)

YEAR	TEAM	LVL	AGE	PA	R	2B	3B	HR	RBI	BB	K	SB	CS	AVG/OBP/SLG	DRC+	VORP	BABIP	BRR	FRAA	WARP
2017	CCH	AA	24	388	49	18	0	21	60	31	90	5	2	.279/.340/.510	137	31.5	.317	-0.5	3B(73): 6.1, 1B(3): -0.2	3.2
2017	FRE	AAA	24	73	10	5	0	5	18	9	18	0	0	.295/.370/.623	138	8.0	.317	-0.4	3B(13): 2.1, 1B(4): 0.0	0.7
2017	HOU	MLB	24	68	8	4	0	4	7	4	20	1	1	.226/.279/.484	78	1.8	.256	-0.2	3B(22): 0.5, 1B(2): 0.0	0.1
2018	FRE	AAA	25	377	56	25	2	17	81	36	69	3	0	.342/.406/.583	158	39.5	.385	0.0	3B(51): 4.2, LF(11): -0.8	4.2
2018	HOU	MLB	25	113	9	2	0	1	5	10	29	0	0	.175/.248/.223	68	-7.4	.233	-0.5	3B(23): 0.9, 1B(13): 0.0	0.0
2019	NYN	MLB	26	453	65	22	1	22	57	38	97	3	0	.307/.369/.527	122	27.0	.355	0.4	LF(79): -4.9, 3B(31): -0.5	2.1
2020	NYN	MLB	27	455	58	19	1	23	67	36	108	1	1	.260/.325/.477	111	18.6	.298	-0.2	LF -6, 3B 2	1.5

Comparables: Eric Hinske, Will Middlebrooks, Josh Fields

The trade that brought Davis to Queens in January of 2019 was met with a resounding "why?" After all, they had just signed Jed Lowrie to shore up the infield, which freed up Jeff McNeil to play on the grass—so spending some of their precious prospect capital on a four-corners type to add to the mix seemed suspect. Of course, if Brodie didn't consult PECOTA on the matter, he can certainly pretend he did as Davis almost exactly hit the 122 DRC+ he was projected for heading into the 2019 season. The presumption in Murphy's Law didn't hurt either, as Davis turned quickly from a depth move to, plot twist, an actual offensive threat playing regularly for the Mets. In the second half of the year, Davis was brilliant at the plate and his .979 OPS made him one of the best offensive outfielders in the league. Defensively, he was not so brilliant, but his goofy celebrations made him must-see TV. Keep a camera on that man at all times.

Todd Frazier 3B   Born: 02/12/86   Age: 34   Bats: R   Throws: R   Height: 6'3"   Weight: 220   Origin: Round 1, 2007 Draft (#34 overall)

YEAR	TEAM	LVL	AGE	PA	R	2B	3B	HR	RBI	BB	K	SB	CS	AVG/OBP/SLG	DRC+	VORP	BABIP	BRR	FRAA	WARP
2017	CHA	MLB	31	335	41	15	0	16	44	48	71	4	3	.207/.328/.432	113	12.5	.214	-0.4	3B(67): 2.2, 1B(4): 0.5	1.9
2017	NYA	MLB	31	241	33	4	1	11	32	35	54	0	0	.222/.365/.423	113	9.9	.244	0.2	3B(66): 1.0	1.4
2018	NYN	MLB	32	472	54	18	0	18	59	48	112	9	4	.213/.303/.390	99	24.3	.241	2.5	3B(109): 5.9	2.5
2019	SLU	A+	33	43	3	0	0	1	8	6	8	0	1	.216/.326/.297	117	0.0	.250	0.1	3B(10): 1.1, 1B(5): -0.1	0.3
2019	NYN	MLB	33	499	63	19	2	21	67	40	106	1	2	.251/.329/.443	104	21.2	.284	0.0	3B(120): 6.5, 1B(3): 0.1	2.7
2020	NYN	MLB	34	400	47	15	1	17	52	36	94	7	3	.222/.305/.412	89	4.9	.251	0.5	3B 2, 1B 0	1.0

Comparables: Josh Donaldson, José Bautista, Troy Glaus

Did you know Frazier is from Toms River, New Jersey? The third baseman, along with Steven Matz, ushered in a brief era where the roster had quite a bit of local flavor. The New York area is not known for producing ballplayers but somehow they all ended up on the Mets last season. Matz and Stroman are of course from Long Island, Rajai Davis hails from Connecticut, Joe Panik the Hudson Valley region, and Brad Brach is from New Jersey—along with Frazier which is certainly news to everyone. True to form, most impending free agents in their mid-30s will spend the offseason fighting back against the system that artificially reduces their market but not Frazier. He spent the first part of the offseason fighting back against the wild turkey population in Toms River, which was damaging property and scaring off residents. You know, since he lives in Toms River. New Jersey.

─────────────── ★   ★   ★ *2020 Top 101 Prospect* **#90** ★   ★   ★ ───────────────

Andrés Giménez SS Born: 09/04/98   Age: 21   Bats: L   Throws: R   Height: 6'0"   Weight: 161   Origin: International Free Agent, 2015

YEAR	TEAM	LVL	AGE	PA	R	2B	3B	HR	RBI	BB	K	SB	CS	AVG/OBP/SLG	DRC+	VORP	BABIP	BRR	FRAA	WARP
2017	COL	A	18	399	50	9	4	4	31	28	61	14	8	.265/.346/.349	110	22.3	.310	0.7	SS(89): 6.6	2.9
2018	SLU	A+	19	351	43	20	4	6	30	22	70	28	11	.282/.348/.432	113	24.8	.343	3.4	SS(83): 14.2, 2B(2): -0.1	3.8
2018	BIN	AA	19	153	19	9	1	0	16	9	22	10	3	.277/.344/.358	102	8.4	.330	1.2	SS(36): -1.3, 2B(1): 0.2	0.7
2019	BIN	AA	20	479	54	22	5	9	37	24	102	28	16	.250/.309/.387	92	17.9	.306	-2.9	SS(111): -0.7	1.3
2020	NYN	MLB	21	35	3	1	0	1	3	2	9	1	0	.229/.287/.357	71	0.0	.289	0.0	SS 0	0.0

Comparables: Rougned Odor, Jake Bauers, Francisco Lindor

It was a year of return engagements for the 21-year-old shortstop, first in Binghamton and then in the Arizona Fall League. Giménez was the Mets' consensus top prospect in the organization once Pete Alonso graduated to the majors, but sputtered after a change to his swing—designed to get him to leverage his strength better—didn't take hold. While he's been passed in those pesky org rankings, the base package of defense at the six and speed still remain and will propel him to a major-league future. The difference between that future being an everyday starting spot or a utility role will ultimately come down to his hit tool, which was still somewhat evident when he took home the 2019 batting title in the AFL. Giménez is still young enough to get back to track as long as he isn't too Metsed up.

Carlos Gómez CF Born: 12/04/85   Age: 34   Bats: R   Throws: R   Height: 6'3"   Weight: 220   Origin: International Free Agent, 2002

YEAR	TEAM	LVL	AGE	PA	R	2B	3B	HR	RBI	BB	K	SB	CS	AVG/OBP/SLG	DRC+	VORP	BABIP	BRR	FRAA	WARP
2017	TEX	MLB	31	426	51	23	1	17	51	31	127	13	5	.255/.340/.462	101	16.8	.336	-0.7	CF(102): -2.3	1.2
2018	TBA	MLB	32	408	42	15	2	9	32	25	103	12	3	.208/.298/.336	84	-0.7	.266	3.6	RF(100): 5.4, CF(4): -0.1	1.0
2019	SYR	AAA	33	140	16	9	1	6	22	8	29	5	5	.270/.329/.500	102	7.0	.301	0.0	CF(23): 1.5, RF(1): -0.1	0.5
2019	NYN	MLB	33	99	10	3	0	3	10	7	30	4	1	.198/.278/.337	73	-0.2	.259	0.5	CF(22): 0.1, LF(13): -0.4	0.1
2020	NYN	MLB	34	251	27	10	1	8	28	17	73	7	3	.216/.292/.376	76	0.7	.279	0.4	CF 0, RF 1	0.2

Comparables: Milton Bradley, Cameron Maybin, Alejandro De Aza

Gómez completed his Mets circle of life when he returned to the team after being traded for Johan Santana in 2008. (He almost made his return earlier in the infamous Wilmer Flores Trade That Wasn't Made in 2015.) Injuries and underperformance opened up the door for him to have a memorable day against the Nationals where he lost a shoe and blasted a game-winning home run, causing fans to lose their minds. As it goes in baseball, the magic didn't last; he was designated for assignment in July, which finally closed the book on this Mets saga. For now.

Luis Guillorme SS Born: 09/27/94   Age: 25   Bats: L   Throws: R   Height: 5'10"   Weight: 195   Origin: Round 10, 2013 Draft (#296 overall)

YEAR	TEAM	LVL	AGE	PA	R	2B	3B	HR	RBI	BB	K	SB	CS	AVG/OBP/SLG	DRC+	VORP	BABIP	BRR	FRAA	WARP
2017	BIN	AA	22	558	70	20	0	1	43	72	55	4	3	.283/.376/.331	116	25.2	.316	3.4	2B(72): 4.1, SS(58): -2.1	3.6
2018	LVG	AAA	23	281	41	15	2	3	33	30	39	2	1	.304/.380/.417	107	12.3	.350	0.3	SS(54): 1.9, 2B(9): -1.4	1.7
2018	NYN	MLB	23	74	4	2	0	0	5	7	3	1	0	.209/.284/.239	92	-0.5	.219	0.7	3B(14): -1.8, 2B(8): -0.5	0.0
2019	SYR	AAA	24	278	33	12	0	7	32	39	42	4	4	.307/.412/.452	130	21.9	.346	0.7	2B(30): -0.3, SS(26): -0.9	1.9
2019	NYN	MLB	24	70	8	4	0	1	3	7	14	0	0	.246/.324/.361	85	1.4	.304	0.4	SS(8): -0.2, 2B(8): 0.0	0.2
2020	NYN	MLB	25	147	14	6	0	2	13	15	26	1	0	.249/.328/.345	85	1.4	.299	-0.3	SS 0, 3B -1	0.0

Comparables: Didi Gregorius, Tommy Brown, Johan Camargo

For an organization that successfully had Rey Ordoñez in its lineup for years, and for one that is currently significantly handicapped by its defense, one would think that Guillorme would get more of a look in the infield. Instead the organization steered into the skid, and he actually saw less action that the previous year despite putting up better numbers in Syracuse than he did in Las Vegas. *insert shrug emoji here*

Jed Lowrie INF Born: 04/17/84   Age: 36   Bats: B   Throws: R   Height: 6'0"   Weight: 180   Origin: Round 1, 2005 Draft (#45 overall)

YEAR	TEAM	LVL	AGE	PA	R	2B	3B	HR	RBI	BB	K	SB	CS	AVG/OBP/SLG	DRC+	VORP	BABIP	BRR	FRAA	WARP
2017	OAK	MLB	33	645	86	49	3	14	69	73	100	0	1	.277/.360/.448	114	27.0	.314	-2.4	2B(136): -3.5, 3B(1): 0.2	2.4
2018	OAK	MLB	34	680	78	37	1	23	99	78	128	0	0	.267/.353/.448	126	37.9	.304	-3.0	2B(136): -0.4, 3B(14): -0.5	3.9
2019	SYR	AAA	35	48	7	1	0	2	3	4	12	0	0	.250/.313/.409	92	0.6	.300	0.5	2B(5): -0.5, 3B(5): -0.9	0.0
2019	NYN	MLB	35	8	0	0	0	0	1	4	0	0	0	.000/.125/.000	71	-0.1	.000	0.1		0.0
2020	NYN	MLB	36	161	17	6	0	5	18	15	35	0	0	.231/.307/.384	84	1.5	.271	-0.5	2B 0, 3B -1	0.0

Comparables: Eddie Bressoud, Roy Smalley, Tony Phillips

Eight plate appearances. Eight. After two straight full seasons in Oakland, Lowrie found the point of demarcation between injury prone and having Mr. Burns's Three Stooges syndrome. Calf, hamstring, left side, right side, head, shoulders, knees and toes; you name it, he tweaked it. To his credit he worked his way back and even helped the Brooklyn Cyclones in their quest for a championship along the way, which ironically made Lowrie the only active Met to appear in the playoffs last season. Counting on Lowrie to provide anything in 2020 aside from a $10 million hit to the Wilpons' self-imposed salary cap is a fool's errand, but here's hoping he can at least go back to his simply injury prone days.

Jake Marisnick CF
Born: 03/30/91 Age: 29 Bats: R Throws: R Height: 6'4" Weight: 220 Origin: Round 3, 2009 Draft (#104 overall)

YEAR	TEAM	LVL	AGE	PA	R	2B	3B	HR	RBI	BB	K	SB	CS	AVG/OBP/SLG	DRC+	VORP	BABIP	BRR	FRAA	WARP
2017	HOU	MLB	26	259	50	10	0	16	35	20	90	9	4	.243/.319/.496	95	14.4	.320	1.4	CF(93): -5.2, LF(6): 0.3	0.4
2018	FRE	AAA	27	82	18	8	2	4	13	6	17	3	1	.342/.402/.671	164	10.2	.396	-0.5	CF(12): -2.3, RF(6): 0.9	0.6
2018	HOU	MLB	27	235	34	8	1	10	28	15	84	6	2	.211/.275/.399	80	5.9	.292	2.3	CF(96): -5.7, LF(1): 0.0	-0.1
2019	HOU	MLB	28	318	46	16	3	10	34	17	95	10	3	.233/.289/.411	68	-1.5	.310	0.8	CF(109): 7.7	0.7
2020	NYN	MLB	29	322	33	13	1	12	38	18	101	11	4	.208/.266/.380	71	0.8	.272	1.1	CF -1	0.0

Comparables: Marcell Ozuna, Gregory Polanco, Jeremy Hermida

Despite starting fewer than half of Houston's games this year, Marisnick finished first on the team and 11th in the league in Statcast's Outs Above Average metric. An elite defender with even elite-r hair, Marisnick glides through Minute Maid Park's spacious center field with ease. He *is* legally required to hit sometimes. This small quirk in the rulebook is what prevents him from being an above-average regular. Teammate Zack Greinke (.240/.281/.346) has an eerily similar line since Marisnick entered the league in 2013, something we can only hope Greinke has pointed out in an Astros group text. Acquired by the Mets in early December, Marisnick will be reunited with Carlos Beltrán as he seeks to take control of the center field job in Flushing.

★ ★ ★ *2020 Top 101 Prospect* **#48** ★ ★ ★

Ronny Mauricio SS
Born: 04/04/01 Age: 19 Bats: B Throws: R Height: 6'3" Weight: 166 Origin: International Free Agent, 2017

YEAR	TEAM	LVL	AGE	PA	R	2B	3B	HR	RBI	BB	K	SB	CS	AVG/OBP/SLG	DRC+	VORP	BABIP	BRR	FRAA	WARP
2018	MTS	RK	17	212	26	13	3	3	31	10	31	1	6	.279/.307/.421	125	10.1	.310	-0.3	SS(45): 0.3	1.3
2018	KNG	RK	17	35	6	3	0	0	4	3	9	1	0	.233/.286/.333	78	1.9	.304	0.5	SS(8): -0.1	0.1
2019	COL	A	18	504	62	20	5	4	37	23	99	6	10	.268/.307/.357	100	24.4	.330	2.9	SS(106): -0.1	2.3
2020	NYN	MLB	19	251	22	12	1	3	22	20	66	1	1	.239/.302/.343	74	-0.9	.321	-0.5	SS 1	0.0

Comparables: Amed Rosario, Andrew Velazquez, Leury García

While Andrés Giménez left an opening to be surpassed as the team's top prospect, Mauricio's strong full-season debut and collection of tools made sure the door slammed loudly behind him. A potential plus hit tool drives the soon-to-be-19-year-old's profile and with some added strength on his frame and loft in his bat path, he should be able to push plus power in the future to match it. The switch hitter was stronger when swinging from the left side in 2019—though at this point in his development that's more about reps than anything else. With smooth motions and a strong arm, Mauricio could end up an above-average defender at either shortstop or third base. If that sounds a little like Carlos Correa, you're both naturally optimistic and not entirely wrong. It's a fun profile.

Jeff McNeil 3B/OF
Born: 04/08/92 Age: 28 Bats: L Throws: R Height: 6'1" Weight: 195 Origin: Round 12, 2013 Draft (#356 overall)

YEAR	TEAM	LVL	AGE	PA	R	2B	3B	HR	RBI	BB	K	SB	CS	AVG/OBP/SLG	DRC+	VORP	BABIP	BRR	FRAA	WARP
2017	SLU	A+	25	116	13	7	0	3	15	7	19	2	2	.324/.388/.476	165	7.6	.373	-0.6	2B(18): -1.5, 3B(4): -0.3	0.7
2017	LVG	AAA	25	78	12	5	0	1	6	3	10	2	0	.254/.295/.366	74	0.5	.274	1.0	2B(17): 0.2, 3B(1): 0.6	0.2
2018	BIN	AA	26	241	49	16	3	14	43	22	23	3	0	.327/.402/.626	176	31.4	.316	1.7	2B(47): 3.9, 3B(9): -0.6	3.2
2018	LVG	AAA	26	143	23	10	2	5	28	14	19	3	0	.368/.427/.600	152	15.4	.394	0.4	2B(24): -3.3, 3B(3): -0.1	1.1
2018	NYN	MLB	26	248	35	11	6	3	19	14	24	7	1	.329/.381/.471	119	24.4	.359	0.8	2B(54): -2.6, 3B(4): 0.3	1.2
2019	NYN	MLB	27	567	83	38	1	23	75	35	75	5	6	.318/.384/.531	129	38.1	.337	-2.7	LF(71): -5.2, RF(42): -1.2	2.5
2020	NYN	MLB	28	595	72	28	3	22	79	38	83	8	3	.287/.352/.470	117	28.4	.306	-0.6	3B -1, 2B -1	2.5

Comparables: Joe Panik, Justin Turner, Vance Law

Two years ago, McNeil was about as far from being a major-league All-Star as a 25-year-old professional baseball player could be. He had barely played in 2016 and 2017 while battling injuries, and had little experience or success above A-ball. He had twice been left unprotected in the Rule 5 Draft and was passed over both times. A bad start in Double-A in 2018 might've gotten him released, but instead McNeil started mashing right out of the gate, hitting his way to the majors by the end of July. He continued mashing throughout 2019 while seeing significant time at four different positions, earning that first All-Star nod and establishing himself as one of baseball's most versatile stars. He even adopted an adorable new puppy, Willow, from a team event with the North Shore Animal League, and Willow McNeil's puppy power sparked newfound power at the plate from her human.

13/10 would let both play in the outfield.

Shervyen Newton INF
Born: 04/24/99 Age: 21 Bats: B Throws: R Height: 6'4" Weight: 180 Origin: International Free Agent, 2015

YEAR	TEAM	LVL	AGE	PA	R	2B	3B	HR	RBI	BB	K	SB	CS	AVG/OBP/SLG	DRC+	VORP	BABIP	BRR	FRAA	WARP
2017	MET	RK	18	303	51	11	9	1	31	50	57	10	4	.311/.433/.444	161	33.0	.398	-2.0	SS(60): 7.7, 3B(5): 0.8	3.7
2018	KNG	RK	19	266	50	16	2	5	41	46	84	4	0	.280/.408/.449	124	24.5	.421	2.2	SS(49): 10.8, 2B(3): 0.3	3.0
2019	COL	A	20	423	35	15	2	9	32	37	139	1	4	.209/.283/.330	86	3.9	.303	-2.0	2B(53): -0.4, SS(27): -2.0	0.2
2020	NYN	MLB	21	251	22	11	1	5	23	23	96	0	0	.203/.282/.327	64	-4.2	.330	-0.4	SS 1, 2B 0	-0.3

Comparables: Luis Rengifo, Drew Robinson, Teoscar Hernández

At every level of the organization, the Mets' cup seemingly runneth over at the shortstop position. In addition to Andrés Giménez and Ronny Mauricio, Newton is a worthy inclusion in the intriguing prospects category—though he bounced mostly between second and third last season in deference to Mauricio. A tall, switch-hitter, Newton has serious power potential that can bend the laws of physics, especially as he continues to grow. But for every action there is an equal and opposite reaction, and for how much pop is in his bat, the physics of a pitched ball can be equally confounding to the youngster.

Tomás Nido C Born: 04/12/94   Age: 26   Bats: R   Throws: R   Height: 6'0"   Weight: 210   Origin: Round 8, 2012 Draft (#260 overall)

YEAR	TEAM	LVL	AGE	PA	R	2B	3B	HR	RBI	BB	K	SB	CS	AVG/OBP/SLG	DRC+	VORP	BABIP	BRR	FRAA	WARP
2017	BIN	AA	23	404	41	19	1	8	60	30	63	0	0	.232/.287/.354	68	4.0	.255	2.4	C(85): 28.4	3.7
2017	NYN	MLB	23	10	0	1	0	0	3	0	2	0	0	.300/.300/.400	89	0.2	.375	-0.1	C(3): 0.3	0.1
2018	BIN	AA	24	228	23	18	1	5	30	7	36	0	0	.274/.298/.437	112	6.1	.303	-2.0	C(30): 3.4	2.0
2018	NYN	MLB	24	90	10	3	0	1	9	4	27	0	0	.167/.200/.238	58	-3.7	.224	0.2	C(30): 3.4	0.3
2019	SYR	AAA	25	40	3	1	0	0	4	1	13	0	0	.289/.300/.316	79	-0.8	.423	-1.2	C(11): 1.4	0.1
2019	NYN	MLB	25	144	9	5	0	4	14	7	37	0	0	.191/.231/.316	58	-0.4	.232	-1.5	C(48): 5.1	0.3
2020	NYN	MLB	26	210	19	11	0	6	22	11	57	0	0	.223/.265/.365	66	0.1	.284	-0.5	C 7	0.7

Comparables: John Hicks, A.J. Jimenez, Tucker Barnhart

YEAR	TEAM	P. COUNT	FRM RUNS	BLK RUNS	THRW RUNS	TOT RUNS
2017	BIN	10148	27.4	2.3	0.6	30.8
2017	NYN	379	0.1	0.3	0.0	1.7
2018	BIN	6337	7.7	0.0	0.5	8.2
2018	NYN	3444	3.5	-0.1	0.0	3.3
2019	NYN	5589	5.3	0.4	-0.6	5.1
2019	SYR	1196	1.2	0.1	0.1	1.3
2020	NYN	8113	6.5	1.0	-0.4	7.0

The Mets saw a need at catcher, addressed it, made a mess of it, forced Devin Mesoraco to retire and ended up with Nido on the Opening Day roster in 2019. For his young major-league career, he has not shown much offensively, and last season was no different. As the season wore on, however, Nido became Noah Syndergaard's personal safety net—which would ultimately become quite the point of consternation down the stretch as the Mets worked their way back into nominal contention. Eventually Mickey Callaway threw everyone for a loop when he cited "catcher wins" as a stat and as a reason Nido lost playing time, even when Syndergaard was pitching. With Callaway gone, Carlos Beltrán and company will have to find their own balance between comfort and contact.

Brandon Nimmo CF Born: 03/27/93   Age: 27   Bats: L   Throws: R   Height: 6'3"   Weight: 207   Origin: Round 1, 2011 Draft (#13 overall)

YEAR	TEAM	LVL	AGE	PA	R	2B	3B	HR	RBI	BB	K	SB	CS	AVG/OBP/SLG	DRC+	VORP	BABIP	BRR	FRAA	WARP
2017	LVG	AAA	24	198	23	12	1	3	17	33	49	0	0	.227/.364/.368	96	5.6	.306	-1.0	CF(31): -4.8, RF(12): 2.2	0.2
2017	NYN	MLB	24	215	26	11	1	5	21	33	60	2	0	.260/.379/.418	92	12.3	.360	-0.9	LF(32): 3.0, CF(12): 0.5	0.6
2018	NYN	MLB	25	535	77	28	8	17	47	80	140	9	6	.263/.404/.483	123	57.0	.351	5.1	RF(62): 0.1, CF(44): -0.9	3.6
2019	SYR	AAA	26	44	10	2	0	1	6	8	8	3	0	.200/.364/.343	101	2.1	.231	0.2	CF(8): 0.4, LF(2): -0.2	0.2
2019	NYN	MLB	26	254	34	11	1	8	29	46	71	3	0	.221/.375/.407	100	8.5	.293	1.0	CF(43): 0.0, LF(37): -0.8	0.9
2020	NYN	MLB	27	490	59	21	3	15	58	71	129	6	3	.238/.362/.415	111	25.5	.310	1.7	CF -1, LF 2	2.9

Comparables: Dalton Pompey, Aaron Cunningham, Desmond Jennings

The overall season numbers hide a dynamic return for the Happiest Man in Baseball after missing a good chunk of the year with a neck injury. Being wary of September stats is a tried and true tradition, but if you're going to show up once the kids go back to school, you might as well make the most of it. Nimmo certainly did just that with a .430 on-base percentage, five homers and a nearly square strikeout-to-walk rate. It turns out having a healthy neck is instrumental in being able to turn while swinging a bat. His return was an instant boost to the lineup down the stretch, and he worked his way back into the leadoff role where he should return in 2020. As an exclamation point, he walked off a game in the final week of the season in the most Nimmo way possible, with a bases-loaded walk, a signature sprint to first, a bright smile and a plea to Pete Alonso to not rip the jersey. Request denied.

Joe Panik 2B Born: 10/30/90   Age: 29   Bats: L   Throws: R   Height: 6'1"   Weight: 200   Origin: Round 1, 2011 Draft (#29 overall)

YEAR	TEAM	LVL	AGE	PA	R	2B	3B	HR	RBI	BB	K	SB	CS	AVG/OBP/SLG	DRC+	VORP	BABIP	BRR	FRAA	WARP
2017	SFN	MLB	26	573	60	28	5	10	53	46	54	4	1	.288/.347/.421	100	26.3	.301	0.9	2B(137): -7.5	1.1
2018	SFN	MLB	27	392	38	14	1	4	24	26	30	4	2	.254/.307/.332	86	1.6	.265	1.0	2B(94): 4.3, 1B(1): 0.1	1.1
2019	SFN	MLB	28	388	33	17	1	3	27	36	38	4	2	.235/.310/.317	86	5.9	.254	-0.5	2B(90): 5.0	1.0
2019	NYN	MLB	28	103	17	4	1	2	12	7	9	0	0	.277/.333/.404	91	2.3	.289	-0.1	2B(28): -1.4	0.1
2020	NYN	MLB	29	251	24	11	1	5	25	21	28	2	1	.248/.317/.367	83	2.6	.266	0.2	2B -1, 1B 0	0.2

Comparables: Rich Rollins, Johnny Giavotella, Justin Turner

The former Giant second baseman finally fulfilled Sandy Alderson's "Panic City" proclamation from 2015 when he came over to the Mets in August and turned New York into Panik Citi by hitting .342 and scoring 10 runs over his first 12 games with the team. It was a really fun homecoming at first as Panik had been drafted out of St. John's University—just a few miles or 45 minutes of traffic up the Grand Central—but the party was short-lived, as he returned to the bench once Robinson Canó returned to the lineup in early September. All in all, he was and is a perfectly cromulent bench piece who should not be stretched into everyday work again.

Wilson Ramos C Born: 08/10/87   Age: 32   Bats: R   Throws: R   Height: 6'1"   Weight: 245   Origin: International Free Agent, 2004

YEAR	TEAM	LVL	AGE	PA	R	2B	3B	HR	RBI	BB	K	SB	CS	AVG/OBP/SLG	DRC+	VORP	BABIP	BRR	FRAA	WARP
2017	DUR	AAA	29	30	4	2	0	2	5	2	1	0	0	.250/.300/.536	109	0.9	.200	-0.2	C(6): 0.3	0.1
2017	TBA	MLB	29	224	19	6	0	11	35	10	36	0	0	.260/.290/.447	101	4.1	.262	-3.4	C(62): -3.1	0.5
2018	TBA	MLB	30	315	30	14	0	14	53	22	61	0	0	.297/.346/.488	121	15.6	.335	-4.4	C(73): -0.8	1.8
2018	PHI	MLB	30	101	9	8	1	1	17	10	19	0	0	.337/.396/.483	123	8.4	.408	-2.6	C(23): 0.0	0.5
2019	NYN	MLB	31	524	52	19	0	14	73	44	69	1	0	.288/.351/.416	100	27.2	.310	-4.6	C(124): -6.7	1.6
2020	NYN	MLB	32	483	51	21	0	15	57	33	78	1	0	.263/.316/.412	95	14.4	.290	-5.0	C -4	1.1

Comparables: Rod Barajas, Ramon Hernandez, Josh Bard

The Mets had an uncertain-at-best catching situation develop prior to the 2019 season with Travis d'Arnaud recovering from Tommy John surgery and their two backups, Kevin Plawecki and Tomás Nido, barely owning bats. GM Brodie Van Wagenen addressed the problem when he signed Ramos to be their primary backstop. Offensively, the signing ended up working out well after it was touch-and-go for the first few months. Defensively, the signing was a mess. Ramos threw himself fully into bad framer territory, the final chapter of a precipitous decline from his early-decade peak. Despite losing the confidence of some of the starting staff and sitting on a .709 OPS at the end of July, Mickey Callaway stuck with him and he subsequently went on a tear. During the Mets charge back into the Wild Card race, Ramos had a 26-game hit streak and hit .347/.392/.485 between August and September. In fact, he was playing with so much house money that he even stole the first base of his career off former Met Anthony Swarzak.

YEAR	TEAM	P. COUNT	FRM RUNS	BLK RUNS	THRW RUNS	TOT RUNS
2017	TBA	8203	1.4	-3.9	-0.8	-4.1
2018	TBA	9850	0.2	0.3	-0.2	0.6
2018	PHI	3106	0.1	-0.3	0.2	0.3
2019	NYN	17231	-4.7	-0.5	-3.3	-8.6
2020	*NYN*	*22300*	*0.1*	*-1.4*	*-3.1*	*-4.3*

Amed Rosario SS   Born: 11/20/95   Age: 24   Bats: R   Throws: R   Height: 6'2"   Weight: 189   Origin: International Free Agent, 2012

YEAR	TEAM	LVL	AGE	PA	R	2B	3B	HR	RBI	BB	K	SB	CS	AVG/OBP/SLG	DRC+	VORP	BABIP	BRR	FRAA	WARP
2017	LVG	AAA	21	425	66	19	7	7	58	23	67	19	6	.328/.367/.466	115	31.3	.377	1.4	SS(88): 2.0, 3B(6): -0.2	3.0
2017	NYN	MLB	21	170	16	4	4	4	10	3	49	7	3	.248/.271/.394	69	0.6	.330	1.0	SS(45): -0.3	0.2
2018	NYN	MLB	22	592	76	26	8	9	51	29	119	24	11	.256/.295/.381	83	22.6	.310	2.8	SS(146): -6.6	1.0
2019	NYN	MLB	23	655	75	30	7	15	72	31	124	19	10	.287/.323/.432	96	28.2	.338	1.5	SS(152): -6.0, LF(1): -0.1	2.3
2020	*NYN*	*MLB*	*24*	*595*	*57*	*27*	*5*	*12*	*62*	*29*	*119*	*16*	*6*	*.259/.300/.392*	*86*	*14.1*	*.309*	*2.2*	*SS -4*	*1.0*

Comparables: Chris Owings, Wilmer Flores, Orlando Arcia

After whispers of "bust" followed Rosario as he scuffled for most of his sophomore season, he took major steps forward offensively in his third campaign. Unfortunately for the 24-year-old, it still left him as a below-average hitter despite leading all National League shortstops in hits. A player's WARP is supposed to be the sum of his strengths, but for Rosario it sits as a reminder of what stands between him and the stardom that was promised when he was a prospect. He hits for contact, but is overaggressive at the plate and is nearly allergic to walks. He plays a premium defensive position, but he can't do it at a high enough level to ward off talks of a move to center field. He uses his speed to steal bases, but he also gets caught nearly a third of the time. The transition from what Rosario could do to what he can't do is approaching, and his assignment is laid bare in front of him.

Dominic Smith 1B   Born: 06/15/95   Age: 25   Bats: L   Throws: L   Height: 6'0"   Weight: 239   Origin: Round 1, 2013 Draft (#11 overall)

YEAR	TEAM	LVL	AGE	PA	R	2B	3B	HR	RBI	BB	K	SB	CS	AVG/OBP/SLG	DRC+	VORP	BABIP	BRR	FRAA	WARP
2017	LVG	AAA	22	500	77	34	2	16	76	39	87	1	1	.330/.386/.519	128	24.0	.380	-2.4	1B(107): 6.6	2.8
2017	NYN	MLB	22	183	17	6	0	9	26	14	49	0	0	.198/.262/.395	80	-3.3	.218	0.3	1B(46): -5.5	-0.7
2018	LVG	AAA	23	375	52	21	1	6	41	34	76	3	0	.258/.328/.380	83	3.6	.315	1.9	1B(53): 6.5, LF(22): -0.2	1.0
2018	NYN	MLB	23	149	14	11	1	5	11	4	47	0	0	.224/.255/.420	77	1.1	.297	0.3	1B(28): -0.5, LF(13): -1.9	-0.4
2019	NYN	MLB	24	197	35	10	0	11	25	19	44	1	2	.282/.355/.525	112	8.3	.320	2.8	1B(36): -0.6, LF(32): -1.0	0.9
2020	*NYN*	*MLB*	*25*	*175*	*19*	*7*	*0*	*7*	*22*	*14*	*41*	*0*	*0*	*.241/.304/.416*	*89*	*3.1*	*.284*	*0.9*	*LF 0, 1B 1*	*0.4*

Comparables: Ronald Guzmán, Steve Bilko, Cecil Fielder

Smith and his injured foot became legendary whenever he was spotted taking his scooter for a ride on the field after big wins. His presence may have still been felt in the clubhouse while he was out with a stress reaction in his foot, but his lefty bat in the midst of a breakout season was missed off the bench. Finding a cure for sleep apnea helped contribute to his meteoric rise with the bat, yet Smith had trouble finding a spot on the field with a soon-to-be Rookie of the Year entrenched at his natural position. Left field was a bridge too far, even for a team that openly sacrificed defense for offense throughout the year. However, he took his legend to a new level on the final day of the regular season. After not being able to play for two months, he strode to the plate with two out in the bottom of the 11th inning and the Mets down two. A three-run homer and complete pandemonium at Citi Field ensued.

Rubén Tejada INF   Born: 10/27/89   Age: 30   Bats: R   Throws: R   Height: 5'11"   Weight: 200   Origin: International Free Agent, 2006

YEAR	TEAM	LVL	AGE	PA	R	2B	3B	HR	RBI	BB	K	SB	CS	AVG/OBP/SLG	DRC+	VORP	BABIP	BRR	FRAA	WARP
2017	SWB	AAA	27	148	22	7	0	6	21	15	17	0	2	.269/.345/.462	128	7.4	.266	0.8	3B(14): -0.3, SS(12): -1.1	1.0
2017	NOR	AAA	27	51	9	3	0	0	2	4	4	0	0	.311/.392/.378	132	3.2	.341	0.0	SS(10): 0.5, 3B(4): -0.2	0.8
2017	BAL	MLB	27	124	17	6	0	0	5	8	15	0	0	.230/.293/.283	87	-3.3	.265	-0.1	SS(36): -2.4, 3B(6): -0.5	0.1
2018	NOR	AAA	28	392	34	18	0	2	34	24	69	5	0	.230/.291/.298	77	-3.2	.277	2.6	2B(53): -2.8, SS(27): 1.1	0.4
2019	SYR	AAA	29	314	54	20	1	6	42	30	53	3	3	.326/.404/.471	136	26.0	.385	0.7	3B(44): 0.5, SS(18): -0.8	2.5
2019	NYN	MLB	29	9	1	0	0	0	0	0	3	0	0	.000/.000/.000	63	-0.1	.000	0.0	SS(2): -0.1, 2B(2): -0.2	0.0
2020	*NYN*	*MLB*	*30*	*251*	*23*	*11*	*0*	*4*	*24*	*21*	*51*	*1*	*0*	*.233/.309/.345*	*76*	*-0.1*	*.283*	*-0.5*	*SS -1, 3B 0*	*-0.2*

Comparables: Terry Shumpert, Gordon Beckham, Asdrúbal Cabrera

Tejada joined Carlos Gómez as familiar faces who made their return to the team last season, after unwittingly changing baseball when he got his leg broken by Chase Utley in the 2015 NLDS. He hit quite well in Triple-A, which included a cycle, and simply making his way back to the majors was a major accomplishment for the 30-year-old. He failed to pick up a hit in his short stint back with the Mets but as always #winforruben.

PITCHERS

Matthew Allan **RHP** Born: 04/17/01 Age: 19 Bats: R Throws: R Height: 6'3" Weight: 225 Origin: Round 3, 2019 Draft (#89 overall)

YEAR	TEAM	LVL	AGE	W	L	SV	G	GS	IP	H	HR	BB/9	K/9	K	GB%	BABIP	WHIP	ERA	DRA	WARP	MPH	FB%	WHF	CSP
2019	MTS	RK	18	1	0	0	5	4	8¹	5	0	4.3	11.9	11	32%	.263	1.08	1.08	2.36	0.3				
2020	NYN	MLB	19	2	2	0	33	0	35	35	5	3.8	8.2	32	41%	.296	1.42	4.74	4.82	0.2				

Comparables: Jake Thompson, Tyler Glasnow, Neftalí Feliz

If there was any team in the league who would draft a prized arm and then not be able to sign him it would be the Mets. Especially since they had a rookie GM in his first draft with a revamped front office. While other teams shied away from Allan's asking price, it seemed the Mets got a steal when they drafted Allan 89th overall, especially since he was regarded as one of the best prep pitchers in the class. After drafting inexpensive college seniors in the following rounds, the Mets not only managed to avoid egg on their face by signing Allan, but inked him for a less-than-expected $2.5 million signing bonus. With a mid-90's fastball, a curve that flashes easy plus and the makings of a solid change, Allan immediately became the best pitching prospect in the system.

Luis Avilán **LHP** Born: 07/19/89 Age: 30 Bats: L Throws: L Height: 6'2" Weight: 220 Origin: International Free Agent, 2005

YEAR	TEAM	LVL	AGE	W	L	SV	G	GS	IP	H	HR	BB/9	K/9	K	GB%	BABIP	WHIP	ERA	DRA	WARP	MPH	FB%	WHF	CSP
2017	LAN	MLB	27	2	3	0	61	0	46	42	2	4.3	10.2	52	56%	.342	1.39	2.93	3.33	0.9	94.6	41.7	15.1	33
2018	CHA	MLB	28	2	1	2	58	0	39²	40	2	3.2	10.4	46	37%	.352	1.36	3.86	4.83	0.0	92.9	35.5	10.8	42.3
2018	PHI	MLB	28	0	0	0	12	0	5²	4	1	6.4	7.9	5	38%	.200	1.41	3.18	5.26	0.0	92.3	41.8	13.3	43.6
2019	NYN	MLB	29	4	0	0	45	0	32	33	5	3.9	8.4	30	45%	.315	1.47	5.06	5.10	0.1	91.9	29.5	11.7	37.7
2020	NYN	MLB	30	2	2	0	33	0	35	30	5	3.9	8.9	35	45%	.276	1.29	3.87	3.95	0.6	92.3	35.3	12.4	38

Comparables: Eric O'Flaherty, Neftalí Feliz, Robbie Ross Jr.

Avilán's overall numbers don't look pretty for the year, but he more than accomplished what was tasked of him when the Mets penned him to a modest one-year deal last offseason. After all, lefties hit just .102/.185/.184 off him. Yet 62 percent of the batters he faced during 2019 were right-handed, which was highly questionable decision making by Mickey Callaway given that Avilán's OPS when hitters were allowed the platoon advantage was nearly 700 points higher than without. Yes, that's not a typo. Seven hundred. The new rule changes are not going to be his friend.

Dellin Betances **RHP** Born: 03/23/88 Age: 32 Bats: R Throws: R Height: 6'8" Weight: 265 Origin: Round 8, 2006 Draft (#254 overall)

YEAR	TEAM	LVL	AGE	W	L	SV	G	GS	IP	H	HR	BB/9	K/9	K	GB%	BABIP	WHIP	ERA	DRA	WARP	MPH	FB%	WHF	CSP
2017	NYA	MLB	29	3	6	10	66	0	59²	29	3	6.6	15.1	100	49%	.252	1.22	2.87	3.04	1.4	100.3	46.2	13.3	44.1
2018	NYA	MLB	30	4	6	4	66	0	66²	44	7	3.5	15.5	115	46%	.311	1.05	2.70	2.15	2.1	99.9	47.8	16	47.1
2019	NYA	MLB	31	0	0	0	1	0	0²	0	0	0.0	27.0	2	0%	.000	0.00	0.00	10.17	0.0	95.4	62.5	0	56
2020	NYN	MLB	32	3	2	7	50	0	53	32	5	2.9	12.2	72	46%	.245	0.92	1.60	2.38	1.8	99.0	46.8	14.7	49.6

Comparables: Craig Kimbrel, Aroldis Chapman, Kenley Jansen

Despite a record-breaking number of injuries during the Yankees' 2019 season, Brian Cashman called Betances' "the most heart-breaking of the year." The big righty's frustration was palpable as he went through countless setbacks while trying to get back in fighting shape, struggling through a shoulder impingement before being slowed by a lat strain. But finally, on September 15, Betances toed the rubber in Toronto and struck out the first two batters he faced—for a second, all of the hard work in a lost season was going to pay off and he'd reprise a key role for a playoff-bound squad. Instead, he partially tore his Achilles and is now questionable for the start of the 2020 season. He managed two strikeouts in his lone appearance. Fate can be so cruel.

Brad Brach **RHP** Born: 04/12/86 Age: 34 Bats: R Throws: R Height: 6'6" Weight: 215 Origin: Round 42, 2008 Draft (#1275 overall)

YEAR	TEAM	LVL	AGE	W	L	SV	G	GS	IP	H	HR	BB/9	K/9	K	GB%	BABIP	WHIP	ERA	DRA	WARP	MPH	FB%	WHF	CSP
2017	BAL	MLB	31	4	5	18	67	0	68	51	7	3.4	9.3	70	42%	.256	1.13	3.18	3.39	1.3	96.8	62.9	12.9	46.6
2018	BAL	MLB	32	1	2	11	42	0	39	50	4	4.4	8.8	38	48%	.371	1.77	4.85	4.28	0.3	95.6	61.4	14	44.5
2018	ATL	MLB	32	1	2	1	27	0	23²	22	1	3.4	8.4	22	47%	.296	1.31	1.52	3.37	0.4	96.2	52.4	13.7	41.6
2019	CHN	MLB	33	4	3	0	42	0	39²	42	3	6.4	10.2	45	39%	.375	1.76	6.13	5.36	0.0	95.8	59.5	13.1	44.5
2019	NYN	MLB	33	1	1	0	16	0	14²	15	1	1.8	9.2	15	40%	.333	1.23	3.68	3.78	0.2	95.5	59.5	12.9	53.8
2020	NYN	MLB	34	2	2	0	40	0	43	38	6	3.9	9.8	47	42%	.295	1.32	3.90	4.11	0.6	94.9	59	13.1	44.8

Comparables: Steve Cishek, Pedro Strop, Nate Jones

Brach was a sweet addition to the bullpen after he was released by the Cubs in August. He immediately endeared himself to the Queens faithful when he said he grew up a Mets fan and was present at Citi Field for David Wright's home run in the 2015 World Series. After joining the team, he significantly cut down on the walks that plagued him in Chicago and it helped him establish himself as a key member of the bullpen down the stretch. He didn't totally rediscover his All-Star form that he had with the Orioles though, and he continued to get rocked by lefties—his 1.139 OPS against was more of a cry for help than a baseball stat. Much like the candy corn whose name he bears, Brach is good only in small doses. Also, he rocks the orange.

Jacob deGrom **RHP** Born: 06/19/88 Age: 32 Bats: L Throws: R Height: 6'4" Weight: 180 Origin: Round 9, 2010 Draft (#272 overall)

YEAR	TEAM	LVL	AGE	W	L	SV	G	GS	IP	H	HR	BB/9	K/9	K	GB%	BABIP	WHIP	ERA	DRA	WARP	MPH	FB%	WHF	CSP
2017	NYN	MLB	29	15	10	0	31	31	201¹	180	28	2.6	10.7	239	48%	.305	1.19	3.53	3.02	5.7	97.7	55.5	14.5	49.5
2018	NYN	MLB	30	10	9	0	32	32	217	152	10	1.9	11.2	269	48%	.281	0.91	1.70	2.09	8.0	98.5	52.1	16.3	48.4
2019	NYN	MLB	31	11	8	0	32	32	204	154	19	1.9	11.2	255	45%	.282	0.97	2.43	2.27	7.8	98.9	49.3	16.9	46.5
2020	NYN	MLB	32	13	8	0	29	29	187	145	21	2.4	11.3	235	45%	.285	1.05	2.52	2.90	6.0	97.5	51.3	16	47.5

Comparables: Corey Kluber, Collin McHugh, Mike Bolsinger

The combination of David Wright's influence as a new front office member, Noah Syndergaard's public plea and 7-Eleven taquitos helped deGrom sign a contract extension, fresh off a Cy Young-winning season. Regression was expected after the cheat code numbers deGrom put up in 2018, but he was almost the exact same pitcher on the whole. After the All-Star Break, deGrom pitched to a 1.44 ERA and a 0.83 WHIP after ramping up the usage of his devastating slider to great effect. His signature consistency, combined with an uptick in velocity on his entire arsenal, left many batters walking away from the box shaking their heads in disbelief. Ultimately, the right-hander became the first pitcher in franchise history to bring home the Cy Young hardware in consecutive seasons—although that's only because Dwight Gooden was completely hosed in 1984.

Edwin Díaz RHP   Born: 03/22/94   Age: 26   Bats: R   Throws: R   Height: 6'3"   Weight: 165   Origin: Round 3, 2012 Draft (#98 overall)

YEAR	TEAM	LVL	AGE	W	L	SV	G	GS	IP	H	HR	BB/9	K/9	K	GB%	BABIP	WHIP	ERA	DRA	WARP	MPH	FB%	WHF	CSP
2017	SEA	MLB	23	4	6	34	66	0	66	44	10	4.4	12.1	89	41%	.236	1.15	3.27	3.20	1.5	100.0	68.4	16.7	46
2018	SEA	MLB	24	0	4	57	73	0	73¹	41	5	2.1	15.2	124	47%	.281	0.79	1.96	1.77	2.7	99.8	62.4	20.7	48.4
2019	NYN	MLB	25	2	7	26	66	0	58	58	15	3.4	15.4	99	37%	.377	1.38	5.59	2.95	1.5	99.9	66.1	19.5	47.1
2020	NYN	MLB	26	3	2	30	50	0	53	38	7	3.4	14.6	87	40%	.305	1.09	2.84	3.10	1.3	99.5	66.6	19.5	48.1

Comparables: Dennis Santana, Nick Kingham, Touki Toussaint

Every great magic trick consists of three parts or acts. The first part is called "The Pledge." The magician shows you something ordinary: an elite strikeout rate, a fastball that touched triple digits or a devastating slider. He shows you these objects. Perhaps he uses them to lead the league in saves to see if it is indeed real, unaltered, normal. But of course...it probably isn't. The second act is called "The Turn." The magician takes the ordinary something and makes it do something extraordinary. Now you're looking for the reasons...but you won't find them, because of course you're not really looking. You don't really want to know. You want to be fooled. But you wouldn't clap yet. Because making something disappear isn't enough; you have to bring it back. That's why every magic trick has a third act, the hardest part, the part we call "The Prestige."

Jeurys Familia RHP   Born: 10/10/89   Age: 30   Bats: R   Throws: R   Height: 6'3"   Weight: 240   Origin: International Free Agent, 2007

YEAR	TEAM	LVL	AGE	W	L	SV	G	GS	IP	H	HR	BB/9	K/9	K	GB%	BABIP	WHIP	ERA	DRA	WARP	MPH	FB%	WHF	CSP
2017	NYN	MLB	27	2	2	6	26	0	24²	21	1	5.5	9.1	25	61%	.290	1.46	4.38	6.48	-0.4	98.4	82.5	10.8	46.6
2018	NYN	MLB	28	4	4	17	40	0	40²	36	1	3.1	9.5	43	52%	.315	1.23	2.88	4.62	0.1	98.3	70.2	12.6	49.6
2018	OAK	MLB	28	4	2	1	30	0	31¹	24	2	4.0	11.5	40	40%	.293	1.21	3.45	3.06	0.7	98.9	66.8	17.5	47.3
2019	NYN	MLB	29	4	2	0	66	0	60	62	7	6.3	9.4	63	52%	.346	1.73	5.70	5.87	-0.3	98.0	66.5	11.9	46.5
2020	NYN	MLB	30	2	2	0	45	0	48	41	5	4.2	9.8	52	52%	.288	1.31	3.63	3.82	0.8	97.5	69	13	47.1

Comparables: Kelvin Herrera, Jeremy Jeffress, Luis Avilán

The Mets and Familia reunited in 2019 and it did not feel so good. Unfairly blamed for the 2015 World Series, the right-hander did nothing to alleviate the anxiety from those ill-fated appearances and put together the worst full season of his career. A shoulder injury sidelined him twice in the first half of the season, but his 3.90 ERA after returning from his second IL trip looked a lot less ghastly even if his walk rate was as terrible as ever. When he was traded away in 2018, the return was underwhelming to say the least (sorry, Will Toffey) but at least he was gone. With two years and over $23 million remaining on his contract, the Mets have to be counting down the days until he is once again.

Chris Flexen RHP   Born: 07/01/94   Age: 25   Bats: R   Throws: R   Height: 6'3"   Weight: 250   Origin: Round 14, 2012 Draft (#440 overall)

YEAR	TEAM	LVL	AGE	W	L	SV	G	GS	IP	H	HR	BB/9	K/9	K	GB%	BABIP	WHIP	ERA	DRA	WARP	MPH	FB%	WHF	CSP
2017	SLU	A+	22	0	0	0	3	3	12²	12	1	2.1	9.2	13	54%	.306	1.18	2.13	4.21	0.2				
2017	BIN	AA	22	6	1	0	7	7	48²	28	4	1.3	9.2	50	55%	.203	0.72	1.66	2.03	1.8				
2017	NYN	MLB	22	3	6	0	14	9	48	62	11	6.6	6.8	36	42%	.342	2.02	7.88	7.82	-1.2	95.1	60.5	8.8	45.9
2018	LVG	AAA	23	6	7	0	18	17	92	109	11	3.0	7.6	78	43%	.354	1.52	4.40	4.75	0.8				
2018	NYN	MLB	23	0	2	0	4	1	6¹	14	2	8.5	4.3	3	40%	.429	3.16	12.79	7.44	-0.2	94.6	62.3	6	45
2019	SYR	AAA	24	5	3	0	26	14	78²	94	11	2.4	10.5	92	46%	.379	1.46	4.46	5.34	1.0				
2019	NYN	MLB	24	0	3	0	9	1	13²	15	1	8.6	6.6	10	34%	.304	2.05	6.59	6.03	-0.1	96.8	61.7	8.4	46.8
2020	NYN	MLB	25	2	2	0	33	0	35	36	6	3.7	6.1	24	41%	.278	1.44	5.00	5.16	0.1	95.2	62.5	8.5	47.1

Comparables: Jackson Stephens, Raúl Alcántara, Zack Littell

Flexen came into camp 30 pounds lighter and tried to flex his muscles out of the bullpen to varying degrees of effectiveness with the big-league club. It is a small sample but a 4.82 ERA as a reliever was actually an improvement for him, compared with a 10.38 ERA as a starter, and if given more of a chance he would have been in higher standing than some of the other Quad-A arms the Mets paraded through the beleaguered bullpen. Instead, he will look to shrink that ERA for the Doosan Bears in the KBO.

Robert Gsellman RHP   Born: 07/18/93   Age: 26   Bats: R   Throws: R   Height: 6'4"   Weight: 205   Origin: Round 13, 2011 Draft (#402 overall)

YEAR	TEAM	LVL	AGE	W	L	SV	G	GS	IP	H	HR	BB/9	K/9	K	GB%	BABIP	WHIP	ERA	DRA	WARP	MPH	FB%	WHF	CSP
2017	BIN	AA	23	1	0	0	4	4	12¹	15	0	3.6	6.6	9	76%	.366	1.62	2.92	5.67	-0.1				
2017	LVG	AAA	23	0	0	0	1	1	6	10	1	4.5	4.5	3	50%	.391	2.17	7.50	7.78	-0.1				
2017	NYN	MLB	23	8	7	0	25	22	119²	138	17	3.2	6.2	82	51%	.303	1.50	5.19	5.77	-0.3	95.2	63.4	8.1	45.7
2018	NYN	MLB	24	6	3	13	68	0	80	76	8	3.2	7.9	70	52%	.291	1.30	4.28	4.38	0.5	96.6	62.8	10.8	49.3
2019	NYN	MLB	25	2	3	1	52	0	63²	64	7	3.3	8.5	60	45%	.315	1.37	4.66	4.85	0.3	97.3	51.8	12.3	47
2020	NYN	MLB	26	3	3	0	55	0	59	55	7	3.3	8.0	52	49%	.284	1.30	4.01	4.24	0.8	95.9	60.5	10.5	48.3

Comparables: Sal Romano, Zack Littell, Wade Davis

Gsellman was one of the few relievers who unequivocally gained entry into Mickey Callaway's circle of trust, which led to both a mixed bag of results and heavy usage that ultimately led to a season-ending injury. He also ended 2019 with one of the most bizarre home/road splits. Gsellman gave up six of his seven homers on road, and yet he pitched to a 2.29 ERA. On the other hand, the former top prospect got absolutely BABIP'd to death at Citi Field and that .449 mark led to a brutal 8.51 ERA at home. Gsellman remains as much of an enigma as that split, someone who is capable of appearing dominant at times but is just as likely to be a low-key adventure on the mound.

Seth Lugo RHP Born: 11/17/89 Age: 30 Bats: R Throws: R Height: 6'4" Weight: 225 Origin: Round 34, 2011 Draft (#1032 overall)

YEAR	TEAM	LVL	AGE	W	L	SV	G	GS	IP	H	HR	BB/9	K/9	K	GB%	BABIP	WHIP	ERA	DRA	WARP	MPH	FB%	WHF	CSP
2017	SLU	A+	27	0	1	0	2	1	6²	9	2	1.4	5.4	4	48%	.304	1.50	8.10	5.83	-0.1				
2017	BIN	AA	27	1	1	0	2	2	13	14	1	1.4	10.4	15	54%	.382	1.23	2.77	3.77	0.2				
2017	NYN	MLB	27	7	5	0	19	18	101¹	114	13	2.2	7.5	85	43%	.325	1.37	4.71	5.26	0.3	94.3	56.8	9.7	50.3
2018	NYN	MLB	28	3	4	3	54	5	101¹	81	9	2.5	9.1	103	47%	.269	1.08	2.66	3.82	1.4	97.0	48.8	10.8	50
2019	NYN	MLB	29	7	4	6	61	0	80	56	8	1.8	11.7	104	44%	.265	0.90	2.70	2.71	2.3	96.9	56.7	12.2	51.3
2020	NYN	MLB	30	3	3	9	55	0	59	51	8	2.4	10.2	67	44%	.292	1.14	3.24	3.55	1.2	95.5	53.7	11	50.4

Comparables: Chase Whitley, Chris Leroux, Andrew Triggs

After coming down with an illness early in the season, Lugo came back more dominant than ever and morphed into Seth Flugo, the man with downright nasty stuff and poor puns. Known for his sick curveball and its dizzying spin rate, it caused quite a few headaches for batters last season. With a UCL on double-secret probation, his usage had to be monitored, but he was able to both stay healthy for a full season and turn into an otherworldly force in the second half of the season. From July 1 on, Lugo had a 1.80 ERA, 0.60 WHIP and a preposterous 51 strikeouts against only four walks, all while pitching in the most high-leverage situations possible during a playoff run. The self-proclaimed Quarterrican (in honor of his paternal grandfather) was one of the few bright spots in the infectious disaster that was the Mets' 2019 bullpen, and he looked so out of place that the Mets once again are discussing a potential move into the rotation.

Steven Matz LHP Born: 05/29/91 Age: 29 Bats: R Throws: L Height: 6'2" Weight: 200 Origin: Round 2, 2009 Draft (#72 overall)

YEAR	TEAM	LVL	AGE	W	L	SV	G	GS	IP	H	HR	BB/9	K/9	K	GB%	BABIP	WHIP	ERA	DRA	WARP	MPH	FB%	WHF	CSP
2017	LVG	AAA	26	0	1	0	3	3	13¹	13	3	1.4	11.5	17	35%	.323	1.12	6.75	2.73	0.4				
2017	NYN	MLB	26	2	7	0	13	13	66²	83	12	2.6	6.5	48	49%	.329	1.53	6.07	6.03	-0.3	94.8	59.1	7.9	48.4
2018	NYN	MLB	27	5	11	0	30	30	154	134	25	3.4	8.9	152	50%	.267	1.25	3.97	3.62	3.0	95.5	60	10	52.6
2019	NYN	MLB	28	11	10	0	32	30	160¹	163	27	2.9	8.6	153	48%	.301	1.34	4.21	4.39	2.4	95.1	50.7	10.6	50.5
2020	NYN	MLB	29	7	6	0	21	21	107	102	17	2.7	8.3	99	48%	.283	1.25	4.07	4.34	1.8	94.5	55.3	10	50.7

Comparables: Drew Smyly, Andrew Heaney, Jordan Montgomery

"I learned to recognise the thorough and primitive duality of man; I saw that, of the two natures that contended in the field of my consciousness, even if I could rightly be said to be either, it was only because I was radically both." Robert Louis Stevenson's words described the main character(s) in his famous novel, *The Strange Case of Dr. Jekyll and Mr. Hyde*, but he might as well have written it about the enigmatic Matz. Nobody had more pronounced and prolonged home/road splits than the southpaw. At home, he had a lower ERA than Jacob deGrom. On the road, he had a higher ERA than Jeurys Familia. After holding him back to face the Marlins at home rather than the Reds on the road with a week left in the regular season and barely a thread of hope alive for a playoff spot, Matz's potion finally ran out, as he gave up six runs to the hapless Jeters. Two days later, the Mets were eliminated from postseason contention. Still, he managed to stay healthy enough to make 30 starts for the second season in a row, which was a major accomplishment for the lefty, even if his shocking transformations on the road were difficult to watch.

Corey Oswalt RHP Born: 09/03/93 Age: 26 Bats: R Throws: R Height: 6'5" Weight: 250 Origin: Round 7, 2012 Draft (#230 overall)

YEAR	TEAM	LVL	AGE	W	L	SV	G	GS	IP	H	HR	BB/9	K/9	K	GB%	BABIP	WHIP	ERA	DRA	WARP	MPH	FB%	WHF	CSP
2017	BIN	AA	23	12	5	0	24	24	134¹	118	9	2.7	8.0	119	49%	.290	1.18	2.28	3.44	2.8				
2018	LVG	AAA	24	4	4	0	11	11	52¹	58	9	3.4	8.9	52	45%	.331	1.49	6.02	4.21	0.8				
2018	NYN	MLB	24	3	3	0	17	12	64²	69	14	2.8	6.3	45	43%	.276	1.38	5.85	5.73	-0.4	92.9	67	8	47.8
2019	BRO	A-	25	0	0	0	2	2	6	6	0	4.5	10.5	7	28%	.333	1.50	1.50	5.24	0.0				
2019	SYR	AAA	25	10	4	0	16	16	86²	84	9	1.6	8.2	79	45%	.304	1.14	2.91	3.17	3.0				
2019	NYN	MLB	25	0	1	0	2	0	6²	9	1	8.1	6.8	5	35%	.364	2.25	12.15	5.63	0.0	94.0	65.7	6.6	42
2020	NYN	MLB	26	1	2	0	5	5	23	26	5	3.1	5.3	14	42%	.277	1.45	5.52	5.64	0.1	92.7	68	8	45.4

Comparables: Luis Cessa, Brandon Woodruff, Jarlin García

After making his major-league debut in 2018, Oswalt had an arm up on the competition and was the first reinforcement called up when the Mets needed a fresh arm early in the season. Of course, the act of needing a fresh arm on April 10 was a portent of things to come for this team and perhaps even more fitting was when that fresh arm walked more batters than he struck out and gave up more than a run per inning. Without overpowering stuff, Oswalt was not seen in the majors after late April, but he did go on to become one of the best pitchers at Triple-A Syracuse.

David Peterson LHP Born: 09/03/95 Age: 24 Bats: L Throws: L Height: 6'6" Weight: 240 Origin: Round 1, 2017 Draft (#20 overall)

YEAR	TEAM	LVL	AGE	W	L	SV	G	GS	IP	H	HR	BB/9	K/9	K	GB%	BABIP	WHIP	ERA	DRA	WARP	MPH	FB%	WHF	CSP
2018	COL	A	22	1	4	0	9	9	59¹	46	1	1.7	8.6	57	68%	.283	0.96	1.82	3.45	1.2				
2018	SLU	A+	22	6	6	0	13	13	68²	74	1	2.5	7.6	58	64%	.335	1.35	4.33	4.89	0.4				
2019	BIN	AA	23	3	6	0	24	24	116	119	9	2.9	9.5	122	54%	.340	1.34	4.19	5.65	-1.0				
2020	NYN	MLB	24	2	2	0	6	6	32	30	4	3.6	8.0	29	49%	.282	1.34	4.20	4.47	0.5				

Comparables: Nick Margevicius, Matt Hall, Matt Bowman

Peterson's slider usage increased last season leading to a rise in strikeouts; however, it did not lead to a corresponding increase in his prospect status. The 2017 first-rounder entered the organization with the floor of a back-end starter who can miss enough bats and kill enough worms to see at least a trial run in a major-league rotation, and he's still that now. He'll head to the International League to start 2020 and sits on the cusp of a call-up due to the lack of pitching depth the Mets have in the upper minors.

Rick Porcello RHP   Born: 12/27/88   Age: 31   Bats: R   Throws: R   Height: 6'5"   Weight: 205   Origin: Round 1, 2007 Draft (#27 overall)

YEAR	TEAM	LVL	AGE	W	L	SV	G	GS	IP	H	HR	BB/9	K/9	K	GB%	BABIP	WHIP	ERA	DRA	WARP	MPH	FB%	WHF	CSP
2017	BOS	MLB	28	11	17	0	33	33	203¹	236	38	2.1	8.0	181	40%	.322	1.40	4.65	4.84	1.7	94.3	59.4	10.4	49.1
2018	BOS	MLB	29	17	7	0	33	33	191¹	177	27	2.3	8.9	190	45%	.285	1.18	4.28	4.02	2.8	93.2	50	9.6	48.9
2019	BOS	MLB	30	14	12	0	32	32	174¹	198	31	2.3	7.4	143	39%	.308	1.39	5.52	6.06	-0.5	92.8	56.5	8.9	49.1
2020	NYN	MLB	31	7	7	0	21	21	107	112	21	2.4	7.4	88	39%	.289	1.31	4.73	4.98	1.0	92.5	54.8	9.5	48.7

Comparables: Rick Wise, Mike Witt, Alex Fernandez

In *A Storm of Swords*, Ser Barristan Selmy tells Daenerys Targaryen, "Every time a Targaryen is born, the gods toss a coin in the air and the world holds its breath to see how it will land." Well, every time Porcello started a season, the Red Sox were left in a similar state of respiratory suspense. The Sox didn't win the coin toss in 2019, as Porcello not only had the worst showing of his turbulent stint in Boston, but of his entire career. Porcello was a bottom-25 starter by DRA and a bottom-20 starter by ERA. He finished 11th in the majors in home runs allowed. In a stark reversal of his recent trends, he threw his slider less and his sinker more as the season went on, but to no avail. Maybe the new baseballs killed Porcello, but it's tough to give the benefit of the doubt to a player who rises and falls like bitcoin value. Porcello ended his Red Sox tenure having won a Cy Young and a World Series, but also having provided two truly terrible years and a third so-so one in the middle. He's too young, too durable and too talented not to rebound, but come April a new fanbase in Queens will be the ones holding their breath.

Jacob Rhame RHP   Born: 03/16/93   Age: 27   Bats: R   Throws: R   Height: 6'1"   Weight: 215   Origin: Round 6, 2013 Draft (#184 overall)

YEAR	TEAM	LVL	AGE	W	L	SV	G	GS	IP	H	HR	BB/9	K/9	K	GB%	BABIP	WHIP	ERA	DRA	WARP	MPH	FB%	WHF	CSP
2017	OKL	AAA	24	0	2	2	41	0	48	52	6	1.9	10.3	55	34%	.351	1.29	4.31	3.65	0.9				
2017	LVG	AAA	24	0	1	0	4	0	6	2	0	0.0	16.5	11	44%	.222	0.33	1.50	5.82	0.0				
2017	NYN	MLB	24	1	1	0	9	0	9	12	2	7.0	7.0	7	39%	.345	2.11	9.00	7.37	-0.2	96.9	61.6	11.9	49.5
2018	LVG	AAA	25	1	2	11	25	0	32¹	22	4	2.2	11.4	41	32%	.250	0.93	3.06	2.19	1.1				
2018	NYN	MLB	25	1	2	1	30	0	32¹	38	8	2.2	7.8	28	30%	.316	1.42	5.85	4.84	0.0	97.8	68.5	15.2	50.9
2019	SYR	AAA	26	3	2	3	20	0	19²	19	4	2.7	11.4	25	35%	.312	1.27	5.49	4.15	0.4				
2019	NYN	MLB	26	0	1	0	5	0	6¹	3	1	12.8	7.1	5	38%	.133	1.89	4.26	6.95	-0.1	97.5	67.8	8.3	45.2
2020	NYN	MLB	27	1	1	0	25	0	27	24	6	3.3	8.7	26	32%	.258	1.27	4.41	4.70	0.2	97.1	68	13.5	48.7

Comparables: Nick Rumbelow, Heath Hembree, Silvino Bracho

Rhame's reign of terror ended in August after he underwent ulnar nerve surgery. He gained notoriety earlier in the season when he threw near the head of Rhys Hoskins, leading to an inevitable home run and a trot that was slower than Bartolo Colón's. Rhame routinely had control issues so it was legitimately possible he did not mean to throw near the slugger's head. Still he was suspended, sent to the minors and appeared in only two more games at the major-league level before undergoing surgery. All-in-all, a very Metsian year for the reliever.

Paul Sewald RHP   Born: 05/26/90   Age: 30   Bats: R   Throws: R   Height: 6'3"   Weight: 207   Origin: Round 10, 2012 Draft (#320 overall)

YEAR	TEAM	LVL	AGE	W	L	SV	G	GS	IP	H	HR	BB/9	K/9	K	GB%	BABIP	WHIP	ERA	DRA	WARP	MPH	FB%	WHF	CSP
2017	LVG	AAA	27	1	0	4	8	0	8²	7	1	2.1	12.5	12	27%	.286	1.04	2.08	2.14	0.3				
2017	NYN	MLB	27	0	6	0	57	0	65¹	58	8	2.9	9.5	69	35%	.287	1.21	4.55	3.59	1.2	93.6	64	12.3	50.4
2018	LVG	AAA	28	3	0	1	7	0	8	7	0	1.1	7.9	7	62%	.292	1.00	1.12	2.87	0.2				
2018	NYN	MLB	28	0	7	2	46	0	56¹	62	8	3.7	9.3	58	32%	.331	1.51	6.07	4.24	0.4	92.6	63.4	10.3	50.6
2019	SYR	AAA	29	3	3	3	41	0	51	56	6	2.6	9.2	52	40%	.357	1.39	3.35	4.02	1.1				
2019	NYN	MLB	29	1	1	1	17	0	19²	18	3	1.4	10.1	22	17%	.294	1.07	4.58	5.31	0.0	93.6	70.6	10	55.4
2020	NYN	MLB	30	1	1	0	15	0	16	14	3	2.4	8.2	15	32%	.258	1.17	4.04	4.39	0.2	92.4	64.7	11	52.4

Comparables: Emilio Pagán, Richard Rodríguez, Josh Lueke

At one point during The LEGO Movie, one of Lord Business' robot minions says Emmet's face "is so generic it matches every other face in our database." That was Sewald in the Mets bullpen. Aside from the fact that he looks like a plain-faced LEGO man, nothing about Sewald or his stuff distinguished him from a bevy of Quad-A relievers in the Mets system. This was Sewald's third year in the league and he has tried everything from changing arm angles to the Tom Brady diet, which seemed to work for a bit but it evaporated faster than a 28-3 lead. At this point, if Sewald is in the game you know everything is not awesome.

Marcus Stroman RHP   Born: 05/01/91   Age: 29   Bats: R   Throws: R   Height: 5'7"   Weight: 180   Origin: Round 1, 2012 Draft (#22 overall)

YEAR	TEAM	LVL	AGE	W	L	SV	G	GS	IP	H	HR	BB/9	K/9	K	GB%	BABIP	WHIP	ERA	DRA	WARP	MPH	FB%	WHF	CSP
2017	TOR	MLB	26	13	9	0	33	33	201	201	21	2.8	7.3	164	63%	.310	1.31	3.09	4.18	3.1	95.2	62.2	10.6	46.7
2018	TOR	MLB	27	4	9	0	19	19	102¹	115	9	3.2	6.8	77	64%	.326	1.48	5.54	4.19	1.3	93.9	49.3	9.8	47.3
2019	TOR	MLB	28	6	11	0	21	21	124²	118	10	2.5	7.1	99	56%	.293	1.23	2.96	3.74	2.8	94.1	44.1	10.8	45.1
2019	NYN	MLB	28	4	2	0	11	11	59²	65	8	3.5	9.1	60	49%	.337	1.47	3.77	3.91	1.2	93.3	44.1	11.6	43.6
2020	NYN	MLB	29	10	9	0	28	28	162	162	21	3.0	7.7	140	55%	.298	1.34	4.09	4.31	2.7	93.6	50.6	10.7	46

Comparables: Kevin Gausman, Sonny Gray, Alex Cobb

Stroman didn't get traded to the New York team he expected when the Mets made a stunning move at the deadline, but he was a quality addition to the rotation in Queens. The Mets won his first four starts, helping to draw them back into an ultimately unsuccessful playoff chase, and were 8-3 overall when he toed the rubber. He even threw in seven scoreless innings at Coors Field for good measure. His charm and personality drew fans in from the get-go, especially compared with his more reserved rotation-mates, and a slightly more fastball-heavy approach once he got to Queens elevated both his strikeout and home-run rates—an extremely 2019 thing to do. With one more year left until free agency, Stroman will line up as the Mets' third starter in 2020 and his extended run of above-average performance will help solidify an already strong rotation.

Noah Syndergaard RHP Born: 08/29/92   Age: 27   Bats: L   Throws: R   Height: 6'6"   Weight: 240   Origin: Round 1, 2010 Draft (#38 overall)

YEAR	TEAM	LVL	AGE	W	L	SV	G	GS	IP	H	HR	BB/9	K/9	K	GB%	BABIP	WHIP	ERA	DRA	WARP	MPH	FB%	WHF	CSP
2017	NYN	MLB	24	1	2	0	7	7	30¹	29	0	0.9	10.1	34	59%	.337	1.05	2.97	2.54	1.0	100.6	51.3	14.9	47
2018	NYN	MLB	25	13	4	0	25	25	154¹	148	9	2.3	9.0	155	50%	.320	1.21	3.03	2.47	5.0	99.9	53.7	14.4	47.5
2019	NYN	MLB	26	10	8	0	32	32	197²	194	24	2.3	9.2	202	48%	.313	1.23	4.28	3.40	5.1	99.6	59.2	13.7	50.1
2020	NYN	MLB	27	12	8	0	28	28	168	148	18	2.4	9.5	178	48%	.293	1.14	3.07	3.41	4.5	99.3	57.5	14.2	49

Comparables: Carlos Martínez, Aaron Nola, Gerrit Cole

A desolate, abandoned Citi Field was the result of *spoiler alert* Thanos turning half of humanity into ash. Thor made a valiant attempt to avoid the disaster but it was too late. The god of thunder spiraled pretty quickly from his mistake and wasn't the same hero everyone came to expect. Life imitated art a little too closely when Syndergaard struggled on the top-line in 2019, having the worst season of his MLB career and leading the league in earned runs allowed. Despite that, Thor still finished had a top-20 DRA among the 69 pitchers who threw at least 150 innings last season—further highlighting that "worst" is awfully relative. More troubling was that he backed off his devastating slider that early in the year he had zero confidence in and throughout the year carried diminished velocity. With a new manager and new pitching coach in town for 2020, Syndergaard will look to regain his elite form, and rediscovering his best offspeed pitch is tantamount. In fact, a hard turn into a pitch mix that features it more often at the expense of his fastball would help avenge his trend of diminishing strikeouts.

Thomas Szapucki LHP Born: 06/12/96   Age: 24   Bats: R   Throws: L   Height: 6'2"   Weight: 181   Origin: Round 5, 2015 Draft (#149 overall)

YEAR	TEAM	LVL	AGE	W	L	SV	G	GS	IP	H	HR	BB/9	K/9	K	GB%	BABIP	WHIP	ERA	DRA	WARP	MPH	FB%	WHF	CSP
2017	COL	A	21	1	2	0	6	6	29	24	0	3.1	8.4	27	44%	.304	1.17	2.79	4.34	0.3				
2019	COL	A	23	0	0	0	11	8	21²	14	1	4.2	10.8	26	37%	.260	1.11	2.08	3.62	0.4				
2019	SLU	A+	23	1	3	0	9	9	36	33	1	3.8	10.5	42	48%	.314	1.33	3.25	4.69	0.1				
2020	NYN	MLB	24	2	2	0	33	0	35	34	5	3.5	8.5	33	40%	.293	1.35	4.42	4.65	0.3				

Comparables: Domingo Germán, Jarlin García, Brad Mills

Szapucki successfully returned to action in 2019 after undergoing Tommy John surgery and missing all of the previous season. The organization very carefully managed his usage as evidenced by the lefty averaging only slightly more than three innings per start. Despite some initial rust, Szapucki put together a successful season across two different leagues and will have a more normal workload as he gets his first taste of the upper minors in 2020.

Michael Wacha RHP Born: 07/01/91   Age: 28   Bats: R   Throws: R   Height: 6'6"   Weight: 215   Origin: Round 1, 2012 Draft (#19 overall)

YEAR	TEAM	LVL	AGE	W	L	SV	G	GS	IP	H	HR	BB/9	K/9	K	GB%	BABIP	WHIP	ERA	DRA	WARP	MPH	FB%	WHF	CSP
2017	SLN	MLB	25	12	9	0	30	30	165²	170	17	3.0	8.6	158	50%	.327	1.36	4.13	3.83	3.2	97.5	52.8	10.9	49.9
2018	SLN	MLB	26	8	2	0	15	15	84¹	68	9	3.8	7.6	71	47%	.249	1.23	3.20	3.98	1.3	96.3	43.1	10.4	46.2
2019	SLN	MLB	27	6	7	0	29	24	126²	143	26	3.9	7.4	104	50%	.313	1.56	4.76	6.25	-0.7	95.5	50.8	10.1	46.3
2020	NYN	MLB	28	6	6	0	33	18	103	102	15	3.4	7.5	86	47%	.288	1.36	4.37	4.56	1.4	95.8	50	10.5	47.5

Comparables: Julio Teheran, Shelby Miller, Mat Latos

Wacha might never recapture his transcendent 2013 form, but you have to admit: 2019 felt like a logical end to a riches-to-rags story arc. After years of bouncing between good and hurt, the cumulative toll of injuries caught up to him; not only has his fastball has never been slower than it was in 2019, it's never featured less rise, either. Wacha has always leaned heavily on his fastball and changeup, and losing one of those two pillars of his game was simply too much to withstand. He looked a bit better in the second half of the season in two-to-four-inning spurts, and that ought to be his role going forward. That his fastball didn't seem to perk up in shorter outings could be a sign that he's just not going to find sustainable success again.

Justin Wilson LHP Born: 08/18/87   Age: 32   Bats: L   Throws: L   Height: 6'2"   Weight: 205   Origin: Round 5, 2008 Draft (#144 overall)

YEAR	TEAM	LVL	AGE	W	L	SV	G	GS	IP	H	HR	BB/9	K/9	K	GB%	BABIP	WHIP	ERA	DRA	WARP	MPH	FB%	WHF	CSP
2017	DET	MLB	29	3	4	13	42	0	40¹	22	5	3.6	12.3	55	38%	.210	0.94	2.68	3.24	0.9	97.8	64.3	16	49.2
2017	CHN	MLB	29	1	0	0	23	0	17²	18	0	9.7	12.7	25	37%	.391	2.09	5.09	6.03	-0.2	97.2	64.3	9.2	46.5
2018	CHN	MLB	30	4	5	0	71	0	54²	45	5	5.4	11.4	69	37%	.310	1.43	3.46	4.65	0.2	96.3	75.4	13.4	51.9
2019	NYN	MLB	31	4	2	4	45	0	39	33	4	4.4	10.2	44	52%	.299	1.33	2.54	3.51	0.8	96.5	52.4	12.6	49
2020	NYN	MLB	32	2	2	0	45	0	48	39	6	4.0	9.7	52	44%	.271	1.26	3.46	3.71	0.9	95.8	64.1	13	49.3

Comparables: Jeremy Jeffress, Brian Wilson, Randy Myers

Despite being injured for a good chunk of the year, Wilson's signing was one of Brodie Van Wagenen's best moves of last offseason. That statement sounds like an indictment, but in this case it's not. Wilson's elbow inflammation helped to descend the bullpen into chaos, but they relied on that appendage heavily in the second half of the season. In fact, between the start of the All-Star Break and when Wilson was shut down after the Mets were eliminated from the playoffs, the southpaw pitched in 52 percent of the team's games—a higher rate than Alex Claudio, who led baseball in appearances. Wilson was even tasked with closing four games out in September when the bullpen was in full-on committee mode and his lack of a platoon split—thanks to a cutter than holds righties in check—made him a valuable late-inning weapon. If his elbow holds up after such heavy use, he'll assume the same bullpen role in 2020.

Josh Wolf   RHP   Born: 09/01/00   Age: 19   Bats: R   Throws: R   Height: 6'3"   Weight: 170   Origin: Round 2, 2019 Draft (#53 overall)

YEAR	TEAM	LVL	AGE	W	L	SV	G	GS	IP	H	HR	BB/9	K/9	K	GB%	BABIP	WHIP	ERA	DRA	WARP	MPH	FB%	WHF	CSP
2019	MTS	RK	18	0	1	0	5	5	8	9	0	1.1	13.5	12	40%	.450	1.25	3.38	3.77	0.2				
2020													No projection											

The organization huffed and puffed and blew a good amount of their draft pool allocation on Wolf when they took him in the second round of the 2019 draft and signed him to a $2.15 million bonus—nearly $800,000 over slot. They scraped the bottom of the barrel with senior signs from the fourth through tenth rounds so they could sign both Wolf and third-rounder Matthew Allan to add two promising arms to their system. Wolf's fastball saw a jump in velocity his senior year that he coupled with an above-average curve, making him instantly one of the top pitching prospects in a starved system.

LINEOUTS

Hitters

HITTER	POS	TEAM	LVL	AGE	PA	R	2B	3B	HR	RBI	BB	K	SB	CS	AVG/OBP/SLG	DRC+	VORP	BABIP	BRR	FRAA	WARP
Aaron Altherr	OF	NYN	MLB	28	35	6	1	0	1	2	2	15	0	0	.129/.200/.258	43	-1.6	.188	0.0	LF(13): -0.5, CF(8): -0.1	-0.2
	OF	PHI	MLB	28	30	2	1	0	0	1	1	9	0	0	.034/.067/.069	59	-0.4	.050	0.0	CF(8): -0.3, RF(4): 0.2	-0.1
	OF	SYR	AAA	28	88	9	5	1	4	13	10	16	3	2	.270/.375/.527	115	2.1	.291	-0.8	RF(11): 2.1, CF(11): -0.7	0.5
	OF	SFN	MLB	28	1	0	0	0	0	0	0	1	0	0	.000/.000/.000	29	-0.1	--	0.0		0.0
Rajai Davis	LF	SYR	AAA	38	337	47	8	3	8	28	17	72	20	6	.287/.334/.410	91	12.2	.349	3.6	CF(48): 3.3, LF(20): -0.1	1.2
	LF	NYN	MLB	38	26	4	2	0	1	8	1	5	0	1	.200/.231/.400	83	0.2	.211	-1.2	LF(11): -0.6, RF(3): 0.3	-0.1
Sam Haggerty	UT	NYN	MLB	25	4	2	0	0	0	0	0	3	0	0	.000/.000/.000	58	-0.1	.000	0.5	2B(1): 0.0, RF(1): 0.0	0.0
	UT	BIN	AA	25	292	39	8	5	2	13	40	78	19	4	.259/.370/.356	118	17.8	.369	4.2	CF(25): 0.2, 2B(23): -1.2	1.7
	UT	BRO	A-	25	25	5	3	0	0	4	4	8	0	0	.333/.440/.476	118	3.7	.538	0.8	3B(2): 0.1, LF(1): -0.1	0.2
	UT	SYR	AAA	25	49	9	4	1	1	9	4	10	4	0	.310/.383/.524	106	3.1	.387	-0.6	2B(7): -0.4, LF(5): -0.5	0.0
Juan Lagares	CF	NYN	MLB	30	285	38	12	1	5	27	22	75	4	1	.213/.279/.326	62	-3.7	.279	3.3	CF(125): -5.7	-0.6
Jake Mangum	CF	BRO	A-	23	210	29	5	2	0	18	15	26	17	5	.247/.337/.297	128	14.9	.287	2.3	CF(40): -0.3, RF(10): -0.1	1.3
Max Moroff	SS	CLE	MLB	26	35	3	1	0	1	4	2	16	1	0	.125/.176/.250	53	-0.7	.200	0.5	SS(10): 0.1, 2B(9): -0.5	0.0
	SS	COH	AAA	26	136	20	4	0	4	8	26	34	1	2	.213/.375/.361	107	3.0	.271	0.0	SS(14): 0.5, 2B(11): -0.2	0.6
Jarrett Parker	LF	LAA	MLB	30	15	1	0	0	0	0	3	8	0	0	.000/.200/.000	81	0.1	.000	0.4		0.0
	LF	SLC	AAA	30	424	71	19	1	24	75	72	125	2	1	.266/.394/.535	114	19.7	.340	-0.6	RF(59): 1.4, 1B(14): -0.7	1.5
René Rivera	C	SYR	AAA	35	396	53	13	0	25	73	31	103	0	0	.254/.319/.501	105	16.2	.281	-2.0	C(80): 5.1, 1B(2): -0.1	2.2
	C	NYN	MLB	35	20	2	0	0	1	3	3	4	0	0	.235/.350/.412	91	0.7	.250	0.0	C(8): -0.6	0.0
Ali Sanchez	C	SYR	AAA	22	65	5	4	0	0	3	5	11	0	1	.179/.277/.250	57	-1.9	.217	-0.5	C(19): 1.2	0.1
	C	BIN	AA	22	294	28	13	0	1	30	23	52	1	0	.278/.337/.337	116	7.5	.341	-1.9	C(65): 1.2	1.7
Mark Vientos	3B	COL	A	19	454	48	27	1	12	62	22	110	1	4	.255/.300/.411	122	16.3	.311	-5.2	3B(98): -3.0	1.5

Aaron Altherr's whirlwind tour across three National League teams in 2019 ended with a .300 OPS and an oversized neck brace. ⓧ **Rajai Davis**' debut with the Mets was a memorable day that started with an epic Uber ride from Lehigh Valley and ended with a pinch-hit home run off Sean Doolittle that became one of the more unique highlights of the season. ⓧ **Sam Haggerty** came over in the Kevin Plawecki trade and didn't pick up a hit in four big league at-bats, but his speed made him an ideal pinch-runner. ⓧ **Juan Lagares** had his worst season both at the plate and in the field, which was a troubling development for a team relying on him as one of the few who knew how to play defense. ⓧ **Jake Mangum** is the Mets' fourth-round pick from the 2019 draft. Jeff Mangum is the singer and songwriter from Neutral Milk Hotel. The Dodge Magnum is a two-door coupe produced by Chrysler in the late 1970s. Thomas Magnum is a former navy officer turned private investigator who lives on the island of Oahu. Any questions? ⓧ The Tribe decided they wanted Minimum Moroff after **Max Moroff** logged four hits in 32 at-bats through May 1. ⓧ As an Angel in 2019, **Jarrett Parker** had exactly half as many plate appearance (15) as his age. In baseball's math system, those numbers equate to four—as in Quad-A. ⓧ The Mets have had success with infielders on the international market throughout the decade, but far less so on the grass. They'll look to buck that trend after inking **Alexander Ramirez** to a $2.1 million bonus last summer. He checks a lot of the right boxes as a potential five-tool prospect, but so did Alex Ochoa and Fernando Martínez. ⓧ With the Mets' catching situation so desperate they may as well have lived on Wisteria Lane, it was inevitable that **René Rivera** would be a Met once again after he was released by the Giants. Yet when your homers in Triple A outflank your plate appearances in the majors, it can't really be considered a homecoming. ⓧ **Ali Sanchez** is a defense-first catcher, but offensively he neither floats like a butterfly nor stings like a bee. ⓧ **Mark Vientos** took home the organizational award for the minor-league hitter of the year, and it was well-earned as his offense was 20 percent above league average despite being one of the small group of teenagers in full-season ball.

Pitchers

PITCHER	TEAM	LVL	AGE	W	L	SV	G	GS	IP	H	HR	BB/9	K/9	K	GB%	BABIP	WHIP	ERA	DRA	WARP	MPH	FB%	WHF	CSP
Tyler Bashlor	SYR	AAA	26	3	2	8	33	0	37	29	3	3.6	9.0	37	34%	.277	1.19	3.41	3.36	1.0				
	NYN	MLB	26	0	3	0	24	0	22	21	6	7.0	8.2	20	33%	.250	1.73	6.95	7.90	-0.6	98.0	62.2	11.3	49.2
Tony Dibrell	SLU	A+	23	8	4	0	17	16	90¹	73	2	3.6	7.6	76	41%	.285	1.21	2.39	3.95	1.2				
	BIN	AA	23	0	8	0	9	8	38²	51	10	4.9	8.6	37	35%	.350	1.86	9.31	8.30	-1.6				
Drew Gagnon	SYR	AAA	29	6	5	0	15	15	88²	78	12	1.7	7.3	72	43%	.255	1.07	2.33	2.98	3.2				
	NYN	MLB	29	3	1	0	18	0	23²	34	11	2.7	6.5	17	40%	.287	1.73	8.37	7.38	-0.5	94.1	54.4	12	51
Ryley Gilliam	SLU	A+	22	0	0	2	7	0	10²	8	0	1.7	13.5	16	33%	.333	0.94	2.53	2.66	0.3				
	BIN	AA	22	3	0	1	12	0	18²	15	1	3.4	13.5	28	42%	.350	1.18	4.34	3.40	0.3				
	SYR	AAA	22	2	0	0	10	0	9¹	19	3	8.7	11.6	12	26%	.516	3.00	13.50	10.07	-0.3				
Stephen Gonsalves	TWI	Rk	24	0	1	0	5	5	9	6	2	0.0	16.0	16	35%	.267	0.67	2.00	0.42	0.5				
Harol Gonzalez	BIN	AA	24	6	4	0	17	16	97¹	83	12	2.1	8.2	89	46%	.269	1.09	3.14	4.26	0.8				
	SYR	AAA	24	6	0	0	8	7	40¹	33	8	2.2	5.1	23	44%	.214	1.07	2.68	3.69	1.2				
Donnie Hart	SAN	AAA	28	4	3	3	40	0	37¹	43	3	3.1	7.2	30	57%	.325	1.50	4.10	4.10	0.8				
	SYR	AAA	28	0	0	0	8	0	7¹	11	2	1.2	3.7	3	47%	.321	1.64	6.14	5.43	0.1				
	MIL	MLB	28	0	0	0	4	0	6²	4	0	5.4	4.1	3	68%	.211	1.20	0.00	5.30	0.0	88.6	61.1	12.6	38.6
	NYN	MLB	28	0	0	0	1	0	1	0	0	0.0	0.0	0	100%	.000	0.00	0.00	3.35	0.0	88.2	66.7	22.2	37.9
Walker Lockett	SLU	A+	25	1	0	0	2	2	7	8	1	0.0	7.7	6	52%	.318	1.14	5.14	4.15	0.1				
	SYR	AAA	25	3	3	0	11	10	59	75	5	1.7	5.9	39	56%	.343	1.46	3.66	4.44	1.3				
	NYN	MLB	25	1	1	0	9	4	22²	33	6	2.4	6.4	16	42%	.365	1.72	8.34	4.96	0.2	94.7	54.4	7.6	51.6
Stephen Nogosek	BIN	AA	24	0	0	1	11	0	19	13	0	5.7	9.5	20	35%	.283	1.32	0.95	4.57	0.0				
	SYR	AAA	24	3	0	2	24	0	31¹	12	1	3.7	8.6	30	38%	.155	0.80	1.15	1.83	1.3				
	NYN	MLB	24	0	1	0	7	0	6²	12	2	2.7	8.1	6	38%	.417	2.10	10.80	6.23	-0.1	96.7	66.7	6.4	48.2
Pedro Payano	FRI	AA	24	3	1	0	8	8	42²	30	3	3.8	10.3	49	43%	.270	1.12	4.43	3.32	0.9				
	NAS	AAA	24	2	3	0	11	10	41¹	42	8	6.1	9.6	44	38%	.304	1.69	5.44	6.97	-0.1				
	TEX	MLB	24	1	2	0	6	4	22	26	3	6.1	7.0	17	47%	.343	1.86	5.73	7.39	-0.4	95.6	46.5	11.3	43.5
Tim Peterson	SYR	AAA	28	2	6	9	41	0	55	42	7	2.1	8.8	54	33%	.243	1.00	2.95	2.66	1.9				
	NYN	MLB	28	0	0	0	6	0	7¹	7	1	8.6	3.7	3	25%	.261	1.91	4.91	5.40	-0.1	92.1	54.9	9.9	42
Brooks Pounders	COH	AAA	28	2	1	1	24	0	35	19	4	2.8	11.8	46	42%	.217	0.86	2.31	4.64	0.5				
	SYR	AAA	28	1	2	0	19	1	21¹	29	4	3.8	8.4	20	30%	.373	1.78	7.59	4.96	0.3				
	NYN	MLB	28	1	0	0	7	0	7¹	9	1	2.5	6.1	5	42%	.320	1.50	6.14	6.19	-0.1	93.7	34.8	11.1	49.6
Nick Rumbelow	SYR	AAA	27	0	0	0	5	0	6¹	11	1	2.8	8.5	6	44%	.455	2.05	4.26	6.10	0.0				
	TAC	AAA	27	3	2	0	19	0	25¹	37	5	5.3	7.8	22	47%	.381	2.05	8.17	7.62	-0.3				
	SEA	MLB	27	0	0	1	3	0	1¹	3	2	6.8	13.5	2	17%	.250	3.00	27.00	6.52	0.0	95.5	47.4	5.3	55.8
Ervin Santana	SLU	A+	36	1	1	0	3	3	13	15	2	2.1	7.6	11	58%	.317	1.38	4.85	5.55	-0.1				
	SYR	AAA	36	4	4	0	15	15	82	97	11	3.5	5.9	54	39%	.321	1.57	5.38	5.98	0.6				
	CHA	MLB	36	0	2	0	3	3	13¹	19	6	4.1	3.4	5	32%	.277	1.88	9.45	9.25	-0.5	92.7	52	6	48.1
Junior Santos	KNG	Rk+	17	0	5	0	14	14	40²	46	4	5.5	8.0	36	31%	.333	1.75	5.09	7.00	-0.3				
Kevin Smith	SLU	A+	22	5	5	0	17	17	85²	83	5	2.5	10.7	102	45%	.359	1.25	3.05	4.32	0.7				
	BIN	AA	22	3	2	0	6	6	31¹	25	1	4.3	8.0	28	40%	.289	1.28	3.45	5.60	-0.2				
Daniel Zamora	SYR	AAA	26	2	1	4	29	0	30	26	1	2.1	10.8	36	47%	.342	1.10	4.20	2.70	1.0				
	NYN	MLB	26	0	1	0	17	0	8²	10	1	5.2	8.3	8	30%	.346	1.73	5.19	7.63	-0.2	90.7	25	11.2	45.6

For a person with "bash" in their last name **Tyler Bashlor** couldn't help but become a self-fulfilling prophecy last season by allowing nearly 2.5 homers per nine innings. It's not what you want. ⊕ **Tony Dibrell** pitched effectively enough to earn a promotion to Double-A, but the walks that had plagued him throughout his young career found him again in Binghamton, adding up to disastrous results for the 23-year-old. ⊕ After a few good outings, **Drew Gagnon** was mistakenly placed in manager Mickey Callaway's circle of trust only for it to blow up spectacularly. This is also a summary for how his appearances went after May. ⊕ **Ryley Gilliam** was a fast riser through the system, features an above-average fastball and sports an 80-grade baseball name. ⊕ A year after losing his fastball location and any semblance of bat-missing, **Stephen Gonsalves** missed just about the entire season with a strained elbow. ⊕ **Harol Gonzalez** was a borderline non-prospect heading into the season after struggling in Double-A without overpowering stuff, but he was significantly better the second time around, participated in a combined no-hitter and continued to thrive after getting a promotion to Syracuse. ⊕ **Donnie Hart** doesn't wear his sunglasses at night because he is Donnie and not Corey. He also throws sidearm and pitched exactly one inning for the Mets last season. ⊕ **Jordan Humphreys** has missed most of the last two-and-a-half seasons due to things related to Tommy John surgery. He was emerging into a pretty good prospect before he was felled back in 2017, and the Mets saw enough in the Arizona Fall League to add him to the 40-man roster in November. ⊕ The Mets seemingly made a shrewd move when they acquired **Franklyn Kilome** for Asdrúbal Cabrera in 2018, so naturally he underwent Tommy John and missed the entire 2019 season. ⊕ **Walker Lockett** was traded for catcher Kevin Plawecki and pitched to an 8.34 ERA for the Mets whereas Plawecki had an elite 0.00 ERA in relief for Cleveland. So who won the trade? It's hard to say really. ⊕ **Stephen Nogosek** had an amazing year if you ignore everything he did at the major-league level. ⊕ **Pedro Payano** pairs a low-to-mid-90s sinker with a slider that generated whiffs on more than half the swings taken against it during his big-league cameo. So far as minor-league signings go, he's one worth watching. ⊕ Homer-prone **Tim Peterson** is the kind of generic Triple-A relief arm that has gotten pressed into up-and-down duty as pitching staffs have expanded and teams have gotten aggressive about cycling optionable pitchers. ⊕ Between his great name and stout frame, **Brooks Pounders** is a BIG BOY SZN meme waiting to happen, if only he could pitch well enough to hang around in the majors for a bit. It didn't happen in 2019 and it probably won't in 2020. ⊕ If history proves any guide, **Nick Rumbelow**'s signing with a New York franchise in the winter augurs a trade to Seattle by the next offseason for a prospect who the Mariners will pay more to reacquire in two years' time. ⊕ Signing a player with the last name of Santana who had thrown a no-hitter in his career seemed like a good idea at the time, but **Ervin Santana** struggled mightily in the minors and luckily for the Mets the veteran was never needed to plug holes. ⊕ **Junior Santos** stood head and shoulders above his competition last season. At 6-foot-8 and 218 pounds he had a commanding presence on the mound coupled with a fastball that sat in the mid-90s. As a teen, he still has room to grow which is a terrifying thought for opposing batters. ⊕ **Drew Smith** remains the most promising arm the Mets managed to get back at the 2017 trade deadline, and he was sidelined all season after undergoing Tommy John surgery. ⊕ **Kevin Smith** won the organization's award for pitcher of the year after becoming a full-time starter last season, and did not give up a home run to a lefty despite pitching nearly 120 innings. ⊕ **Daniel Zamora** once threw only sliders in a nine-pitch at-bat that ended in a walk.

NEW YORK YANKEES

Essay by Bradford William Davis

Player comments by Spring Marie Cullen and BP staff

Right as the playoffs began, Major League Baseball lugged its skateboard behind its back, turned its bent brim cap backward, snuck into the local middle school with its finest unlicensed band tee and unveiled a string of snappy hashtags for the postseason—surely enough to draw fellow kids to America's Pastime.

#WePlayLoud was one slogan, mixing in black and white footage of baseball games with young stars like Alex Bregman pimping out home-run trots. (Bregman would apologize for staring down a World Series Game 6 home run.) The others were team-specific hashtags of varying quality. As a baseball fan who, though no longer all that young has attempted to remain youthful—I use moisturizer and occasionally clean my sneakers (try it, dads)—I had opinions on how well the hashtagged slogans seized the essence of the team and its supporters.

Some captured its fanbase but failed to endear them to young people, or, Lord willing, anyone else. For example, the Braves' #ChopOn rendered the essence of fans who pack their Cobb County stadium to perform demeaning caricature in unison. But, as the organization learned when Cherokee Nation citizen and Cardinals reliever Ryan Helsley expressed his frustrations, their atonal and tone-deaf gesture just don't slap as hard when sharing the field with the object of your mimicry.

Other slogans deserve as much scrutiny as effort put into them by the league. Even if Toby Hall, Jorge Cantu and Dewon Brazelton jointly requested a 2,000-word essay on the meaning of #RaysUp, sorry to say, I could not oblige.

Then there's the Yankees' #NextManUp. It's not an artful turn of phrase, but it sure as hell represented the Yankees, who succeeded by cycling through retreads and late bloomers, even if forging a deep team came at the expense of fielding a complete one.

The Yankees came into 2019 with a 100-win Wild Card team and more than a few superstars like Aaron Judge, 2017 NL MVP Giancarlo Stanton and Luis Severino, each comfortably recognized among the inner circle of the best players alive. All of them spent time on the shelf.

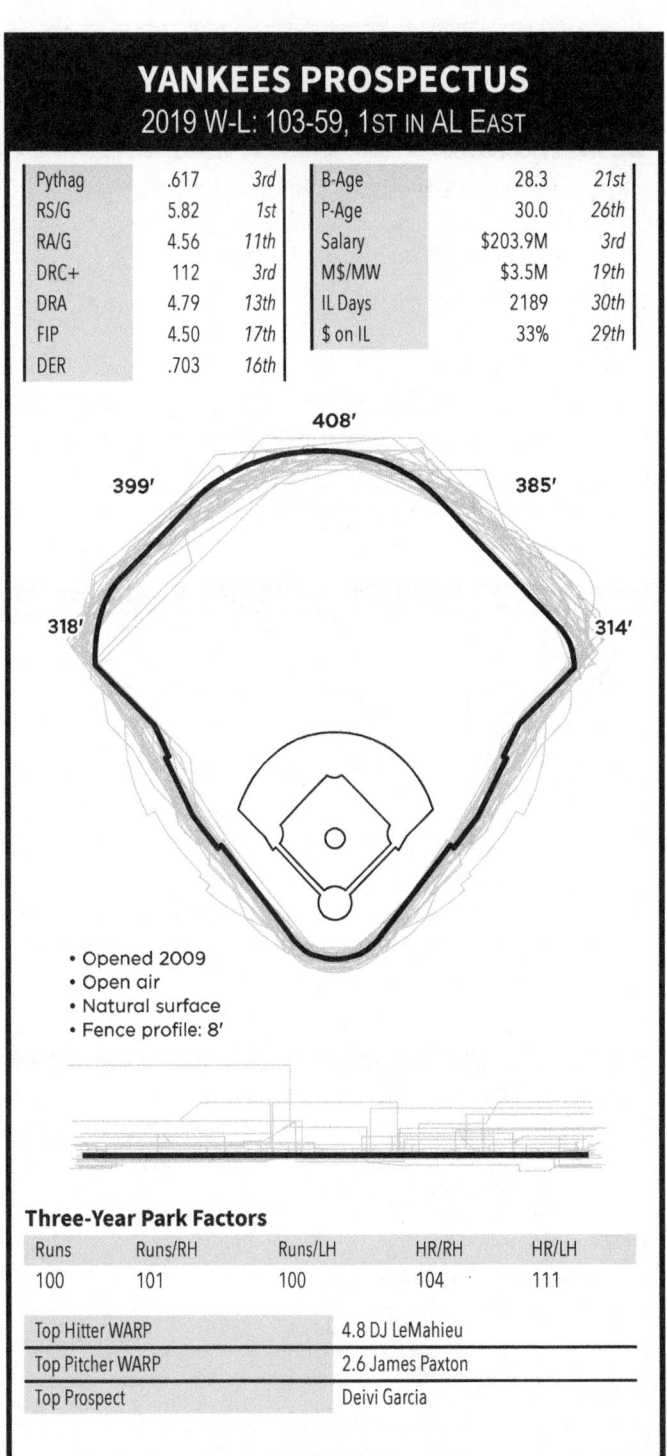

YANKEES PROSPECTUS
2019 W-L: 103-59, 1ST IN AL EAST

Pythag	.617	3rd	B-Age	28.3	21st
RS/G	5.82	1st	P-Age	30.0	26th
RA/G	4.56	11th	Salary	$203.9M	3rd
DRC+	112	3rd	M$/MW	$3.5M	19th
DRA	4.79	13th	IL Days	2189	30th
FIP	4.50	17th	$ on IL	33%	29th
DER	.703	16th			

408'
399'
385'
318'
314'

- Opened 2009
- Open air
- Natural surface
- Fence profile: 8'

Three-Year Park Factors

Runs	Runs/RH	Runs/LH	HR/RH	HR/LH
100	101	100	104	111

Top Hitter WARP	4.8 DJ LeMahieu
Top Pitcher WARP	2.6 James Paxton
Top Prospect	Deivi Garcia

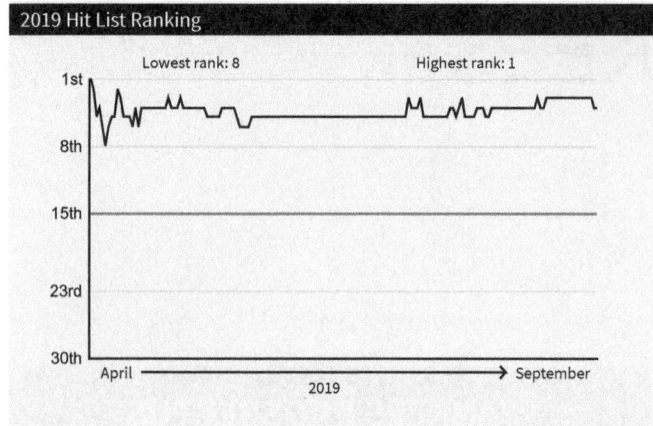

2019 Hit List Ranking

Lowest rank: 8   Highest rank: 1

1st
8th
15th
23rd
30th

April — 2019 → September

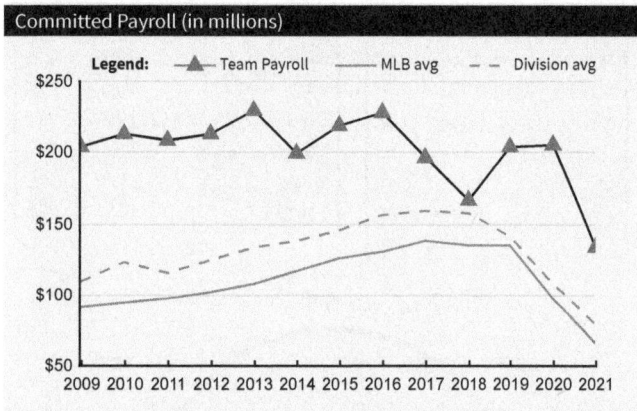

Committed Payroll (in millions)

Legend: ▲ Team Payroll   — MLB avg   - - Division avg

$250
$200
$150
$100
$50

2009 2010 2011 2012 2013 2014 2015 2016 2017 2018 2019 2020 2021

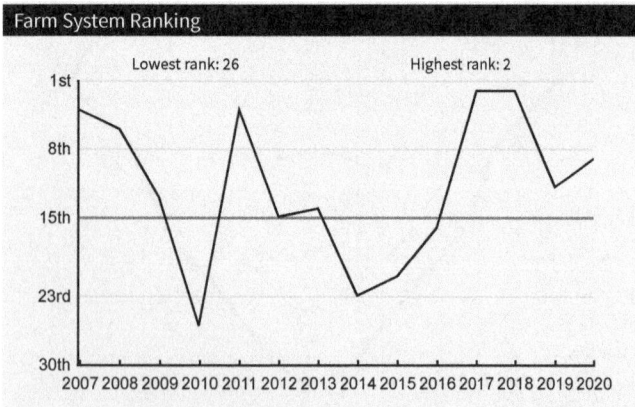

Farm System Ranking

Lowest rank: 26   Highest rank: 2

1st
8th
15th
23rd
30th

2007 2008 2009 2010 2011 2012 2013 2014 2015 2016 2017 2018 2019 2020

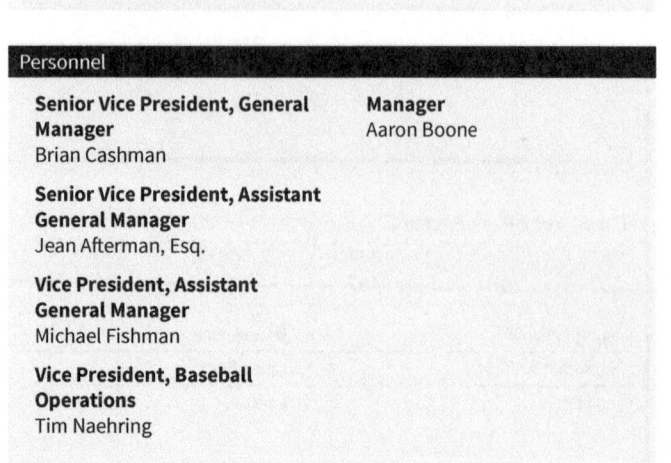

Personnel

Senior Vice President, General Manager
Brian Cashman

Senior Vice President, Assistant General Manager
Jean Afterman, Esq.

Vice President, Assistant General Manager
Michael Fishman

Vice President, Baseball Operations
Tim Naehring

Manager
Aaron Boone

Severino and Aaron Hicks, both recipients of owner-friendly extensions before the season began, lost significant time to injuries suffered in spring training. Severino and relief ace Dellin Betances, in particular, were in injury sync, battling shoulder and lat issues that almost wiped out their entire year. Stanton led the team in games played the year prior, his first in New York, but managed just 72 plate appearances in 2019. So, injuries bested the staff ace, relief ace, heart-of-the-order-slugger, starting shortstop and $70-million dollar center fielder—that's enough significant injuries for one year right? Heh.

Miguel Andújar, who was a Rookie of the Year Award runner-up in 2018, needed season-ending shoulder surgery. Greg Bird has more or less made his nest on the injured list since 2016. Luke Voit, acquired in a minor (at the time) deal for Giovanny Gallegos, was detected by their analytics department and did nothing but hit as the primary first baseman in 2018. He was going almost as strong until a sports hernia derailed his second half. This is but a taste of the 2019 Yankees' injury problems—they sent a record 30 players to the IL over the course of the season, resulting in 600 more days lost to injury than any other team, per Spotrac. So, why didn't they suck? All those #NextManUps, of course.

DJ LeMahieu was acquired as a high-usage utility player, but the 30-year-old became one of the Yankees' primary infielders, and then their first baseman throughout the playoffs. He was the first and greatest #NextManUp. LeMahieu alone couldn't run away with the division, not with all the injuries.

Gio Urshela was DFA'd by the Blue Jays last summer, and pressed into duty with Andújar's injury. He responded with outstanding work on both sides of the ball, challenging for the batting title late into the season while slugging .539 (his career OPS was .589 before he donned pinstripes).

There was Cameron Maybin, once a super prospect traded for Miguel Cabrera, who was a journeyman cut by the Giants before the season began and traded to the Yankees after hitting .229/.397/.292 for Triple-A Columbus. Marcus Thames told Maybin to "use his good swing," and "hit the ball hard." Sounds too simple, but the 32-year-old added four degrees to his launch angle and slugged a career-high .496.

And then there's Mike Tauchman, a 27-year-old Rockies outfielder with brief, stale cups of coffee in Colorado. He blew Statcast's Outs Above Average metric out the water, and did it while slugging 13 home runs in half a season of work. (Tauchman got with the program and ended his season on the IL, too.)

When Voit got hurt, 26-year-old rookie Mike Ford did what so many whiff-heavy, older minor-league first baseman do—he brought his impressive Triple-A numbers to the Show, helping ensure the Yankees didn't skip a beat.

Oh, and of course, there's Clint Frazier, a young outfielder who hit real good, fielded real bad and, worst of all, ducked reporters after a few ugly misplays amounted to the worst game of his life. Then, he complained about what he perceived to be unfair media treatment to ESPN's Coley Harvey via text. In fairness to everyone frustrated with him, from beat reporters to Yankees brass, it's much easier to discuss a player's struggles when the player can account for them, as Frazier should have. But, whether it's violence against an intimate partner or parading slurs against blacks and gays on Twitter, all sins can be forgiven—except blaspheming the Holy Press. (Frazier's apparent persona non grata status inside the Yankees organization left him in Triple-A for much of the summer and off the playoff roster.)

And so on.

The impressive stand-ins weren't the only reason the Yankees were good—Brett Gardner went from looking washed to belting a career-high 28 home runs; Masahiro Tanaka and offseason trade acquisition James Paxton were up and down but the former pitched well enough to make his second All-Star team, while the latter finished the season 10-0 with a 2.25 ERA; Aaron Judge missed significant time, worked through an Aaron Judge slump and ended with an Aaron Judge streak; Gary Sánchez bounced back on offense; and the super bullpen, which included a full season of Zack Britton and new signee Adam Ottavino, locked down the game in late innings.

⚾　　⚾　　⚾

If there is a pixie dust capable of turning Quad-A flotsam into 2.7 WARP position players, the dust was gathered with an old Metrocard into fine lines and wantonly snorted throughout the Yankee Stadium front office. But, like a blogger mixing in hackneyed metaphors into his first Baseball Prospectus essay, each one more convoluted than the last, the Yankees got high on their own supply—to the point where they may have acted unwisely.

All these Next Men Up and none—save for 27-year-old Domingo Germán, filling in for Severino—were able to take the ball every fifth day in the rotation. And Germán's ebbs and flows with his fastball velocity, combined with his leap in innings from 2018 (he had a 4.93 ERA from May 24 onward), left him as more of a five-and-dive pitcher, not the guy you'd ideally stack up against Justin Verlander. They were already experimenting with him in long relief before the playoffs, with all those concerns coalescing before a domestic violence allegation ended his season in September.

So, what did the Yankees do at the deadline for an ailing rotation, no certainty that Severino would return healthy, if at all, with Paxton and Tanaka pitching through the worst stretches of their careers? Nothing. They waited on the next man.

The only trade of note Brian Cashman made was for Edwin Encarnación—a proven hitter, but one who did nothing to address their glaring weakness. "The best play was we did nothing," Cashman said moments after the July 31 deadline, in his attempt to deflect criticism about their lack of success pursuing the top-end of the free agent market. He wasn't

done inspiring confidence. "We did nothing for a good reason because we felt everything that was in front of me was really not attainable."

(Incidentally, Cashman would later tell Yahoo's Wallace Matthews he doubted Marcus Stroman, who was absolutely attainable, "would be a difference-maker" for their team, adding that the 2019 All-Star would likely fail to crack the Yankees rotation. Stroman was attained by the other New York team, the Mets, with whom he put the finishing touches on a 3.22 ERA/4 WARP season; no Yankees starter crossed 3 WARP.)

Naturally, Cashman was asked about getting outbid for top-flight pitching, like Patrick Corbin, during the previous offseason, to which he told reporters "There's a lot of guys currently sitting in (the Yankees') locker room that wouldn't be here because, again, all that money would have gone in one direction."

You could debate the merits of choosing one dollar versus four quarters, then teaching each scrappy coin about launch angle, but we're not going to legitimize Cashman's false premise that the New York Yankees did not, in fact, have a second dollar bill.

Cashman's inactive deadline didn't matter much during the regular season. The Yankees kept a 103-win pace behind their merry collection of Next Man Ups, from LeMahieu to Tauchman, and by beating the teams in front of them. This is to the players' credit and to the league's shame.

For example, the Yankees went 17-2 against the Orioles. Gleyber Torres hit .394 with 13 of his 38 home runs against a pitching staff that amounted to facing the computer in Triple Play Baseball '99 set to rookie difficulty. It's not his fault, but we all knew he was playing two-player mode with the DualShock controller plugged into the second port—everyone was, really, when it came to facing the Orioles and other tanking teams.

In 2019, four teams won 100-plus games because four teams lost 100-plus games. When planned obsolescence is guiding the long-term strategies of a third of the league, juggernauts just aren't what they used to be. Like 20 home runs, a 4.00 ERA, 200 innings pitched or a 10-strikeout performance, 100 wins is a round number that may be a useful shorthand for excellence in another era. But not ours, not anymore.

When talent is consciously drained from the league, teams like the Yankees can not only hide behind their inaction at the top end of baseball's talent pool—they, and the league, can brand it in the hopes that some fans root for baseball like they're auditioning for a Pirates front office gig. Bob Nutting's not gonna hire you, bro.

The Yankees were fine in the regular season. They were always going to be fine. But, flash forward to the postseason, specifically Game 6 of the ALCS, when Jose Altuve ended a closely contested series with a walk-off home run against Aroldis Chapman, and the Yankees were considerably less fine.

Even though there was supposedly nothing attainable on the starting-pitcher market, except the non-difference-making Stroman, the Yankees probably would've liked a mulligan after losing a planned bullpen game. Relievers like Britton, echoing comments made by Green, told reporters he felt "uber-exposed" by pitching so frequently, in lieu of high level starters, during a short series. Their top three starters, Tanaka, Paxton and Severino, combined for 23 2/3 innings in their five starts. The Yankees' bullpen-heavy strategy almost worked—their series ERA was 3.13—but they stretched it too far.

"That's why we're relievers, not starters," said Britton. "You overexpose guys, it's inevitable that eventually, they're going to get got a little bit."

As of press time, the Yankees haven't rationalized their premature exit by blaming banging trash cans and espionage. Instead, they signed Gerrit Cole to a nine-year, $324 million contract—the largest length, average annual value and dollar amount awarded to any pitcher ever. Cole offers many luxuries, including the ability to piece together elite production while consistently throwing over 200 innings, a league-wide rarity and function no one on the current staff has shown the capacity for. Slotting Severino, Paxton and Tanaka into the two through four slots gives a playoff rotation few teams can expect to match.

Cole is the ace the Yankees finally decided to splurge on after passing on Stroman, Corbin and others over the past couple deadlines and winters. In a sense, the ultimate next man up.

⚾   ⚾   ⚾

The concept of #NextManUp is unlikely to go away, even after the Yankees behaved like...well, the Yankees. Cashman also allowed mainstays, like Betances and fan-favorite shortstop Didi Gregorius, to walk in free agency. (Didi to the Phillies, Betances to the Mets.) Both players had down years

due to injury (or age?) at positions where the Yankees had strong depth, making the moves defensible. Elongated Orioles jokes aside, Gleyber is a stud who looks more comfortable playing his natural position. Meanwhile, Britton, Ottavino, Green, Tommy Kahnle and Chapman—who tacked on another year to his contract after winning the AL Reliever of the Year Award—are perhaps the only set of relievers that could possibly make Betances redundant.

Still, those planned redundancies sustained the Yankees, and enabled them to overcome an absurd rash of injuries in 2019. The Yankees are betting their uncanny and unprecedented injury bug won't return. (They also fired their director of strength and conditioning after six years on the job, so maybe the organization doesn't find it totally uncanny.) If it does, New York might not have the depth to combat the losses now that, as Cashman said, "all that money is going in one direction."

Of course, the Yankees could have kept everyone—such a plan would have complicated their desire to remain under the highest luxury-tax tier, where few teams dare to tread. (As of press time, there were rumors of the Yankees dumping J.A. Happ's contract to reduce their number. Plans can change, so kudos to the Yankees if they decided to go all-in on leveraging their financial might.) If the Yankees are allowing the tax to drive their roster situations, surprising as it may be to some after making Cole the richest pitcher alive, it would absolutely fit into the team's recent history of permitting external forces to guide their hand.

The Yankees shouldn't rob Peter to pay Paul when they're wealthy enough to keep both around and pay the relative pittance of a luxury tax, even if the 2020 team may be strong enough relative to their peers that it won't matter anyway. But, I don't have a snappy hashtag for that. ▪

—Bradford William Davis is an author at the New York Daily News.

HITTERS

Miguel Andújar 3B   Born: 03/02/95   Age: 25   Bats: R   Throws: R   Height: 6'0"   Weight: 215   Origin: International Free Agent, 2011

YEAR	TEAM	LVL	AGE	PA	R	2B	3B	HR	RBI	BB	K	SB	CS	AVG/OBP/SLG	DRC+	VORP	BABIP	BRR	FRAA	WARP
2017	TRN	AA	22	272	30	23	1	7	52	12	38	2	3	.312/.342/.494	126	18.8	.338	-1.6	3B(58): -4.5	1.0
2017	SWB	AAA	22	250	36	13	1	9	30	17	33	3	0	.317/.364/.502	142	20.3	.333	0.3	3B(57): -1.4	1.7
2017	NYA	MLB	22	8	0	2	0	0	4	1	0	1	0	.571/.625/.857	96	2.0	.571	0.0	3B(3): 0.0	0.0
2018	NYA	MLB	23	606	83	47	2	27	92	25	97	2	1	.297/.328/.527	120	37.5	.316	-0.1	3B(136): -15.2	2.0
2019	NYA	MLB	24	49	1	0	0	0	1	1	11	0	0	.128/.143/.128	63	-1.3	.162	0.2	3B(4): -0.8	-0.2
2020	*NYA*	*MLB*	*25*	*455*	*51*	*25*	*2*	*20*	*62*	*22*	*87*	*2*	*1*	*.257/.299/.459*	*101*	*8.4*	*.281*	*0.0*	*3B-4*	*0.4*

Comparables: Brandon Drury, Jeimer Candelario, Cheslor Cuthbert

As the Rookie of the Year runner-up in 2018, there was more pressure on Andújar than anyone to carry that success across calendar years. Yet a season almost entirely lost to injury did little to answer the long-term questions that surround the 25-year-old. In the shadow of a presumed move to another corner (or designated hitter) coming, and a new breakout third baseman playing Ringo Starr to his Pete Best, Andújar enters 2020 with less pressure but a lot more uncertainty—starting with whether he'll even be ready to head north with the team on Opening Day after undergoing surgery to repair a torn labrum in his right shoulder last May.

Greg Bird 1B Born: 11/09/92   Age: 27   Bats: L   Throws: R   Height: 6'4"   Weight: 220   Origin: Round 5, 2011 Draft (#179 overall)

YEAR	TEAM	LVL	AGE	PA	R	2B	3B	HR	RBI	BB	K	SB	CS	AVG/OBP/SLG	DRC+	VORP	BABIP	BRR	FRAA	WARP
2017	SWB	AAA	24	59	12	4	0	3	7	11	9	0	0	.298/.424/.574	161	4.5	.306	-1.0	1B(10): 0.9	0.4
2017	NYA	MLB	24	170	20	7	0	9	28	19	42	0	0	.190/.288/.422	99	0.6	.194	-1.0	1B(46): -1.1	0.0
2018	NYA	MLB	25	311	23	16	1	11	38	30	78	0	0	.199/.286/.386	84	-7.9	.230	-1.8	1B(74): 1.4	-0.2
2019	NYA	MLB	26	41	6	0	0	1	1	6	16	0	0	.171/.293/.257	73	-0.9	.278	0.5	1B(10): 0.5	0.0
2020	NYA	MLB	27	251	31	10	0	13	36	29	74	0	0	.222/.318/.443	100	7.6	.271	-0.7	1B 0	0.7

Comparables: Brandon Nimmo, Daniel Vogelbach, Ryan O'Hearn

An exciting spring training competition with Luke Voit promised great things for Bird's 2019 season. He was back to his true form; with a vengeance; with something to prove. In a lineup that lacked enough of a left-handed presence, Bird's beautiful swing could have been a serious game changer, and he came out of the cage showcasing just that. Unfortunately, Bird has a long resume of could have beens. After a strong burst out of the gate in his rookie season, a shoulder injury cost him all of 2016. Then it was his ankle that sidelined him for most of 2017. A healthy (at least for him) Bird struggled in 2018 and left the door open for Voit to make his way into the Yankees' long-term plans. This time around he tore his left plantar fascia, limiting him to just a handful of at-bats in his age-26 season. The broken tissue acted as final straw for the organization, as they designated him for assignment in November. Bird remains, as always, with everything left to prove once again.

─────────────── ★ ★ ★ *2020 Top 101 Prospect* **#46** ★ ★ ★ ───────────────

Jasson Dominguez CF Born: 02/07/03   Age: 17   Bats: B   Throws: R   Height: 5'10"   Weight: 190   Origin: International Free Agent, 2019

Talent takes human form in Dominguez. He's the Regina George of international signings; everyone wants him and those that don't, want to be him. The Yankees love dipping their toes in the international market, spending over $5 million on the switch-hitting outfielder from the Dominican Republic. He may be shorter than 6-foot but his tools have caused scouts to call him The Martian, as his skill set is not from this planet. Dominguez was named after former MVP and Yankee slugger Jason Giambi (seriously), but the comps so far have touched on such untouchable names as Mike Trout, Mickey Mantle and Bo Jackson. That gives you a pretty good sense of his power, speed and defensive upside. Dominguez is as far away as can be from the majors—he was born in 2003 for god's sake—but he's nearly a lock to make his stateside debut this summer, which will be must-watch viewing for the entire baseball world.

Thairo Estrada MI Born: 02/22/96   Age: 24   Bats: R   Throws: R   Height: 5'10"   Weight: 190   Origin: International Free Agent, 2012

YEAR	TEAM	LVL	AGE	PA	R	2B	3B	HR	RBI	BB	K	SB	CS	AVG/OBP/SLG	DRC+	VORP	BABIP	BRR	FRAA	WARP
2017	TRN	AA	21	542	72	19	4	6	48	34	56	8	11	.301/.353/.392	117	32.7	.327	-2.2	SS(90): -0.3, 2B(23): -0.5	2.8
2018	TAM	A+	22	47	4	2	0	0	5	0	9	0	0	.222/.234/.267	48	-2.9	.270	-0.6	SS(8): -0.2	-0.2
2018	SWB	AAA	22	34	1	1	0	0	3	0	8	0	0	.152/.176/.182	20	-3.9	.200	-0.3	SS(5): 0.0, 2B(3): 0.9	-0.1
2019	SWB	AAA	23	259	39	17	2	8	32	14	50	3	1	.266/.313/.452	86	4.0	.304	-1.1	SS(32): 1.7, 2B(24): -0.9	0.5
2019	NYA	MLB	23	69	12	3	0	3	12	3	15	4	0	.250/.294/.438	87	1.3	.283	1.0	2B(17): -1.1, SS(9): 0.3	0.1
2020	NYA	MLB	24	105	10	5	0	3	11	5	22	1	1	.236/.280/.373	75	0.5	.276	-0.2	SS 0, 2B -1	0.0

Comparables: Yairo Muñoz, Abiatal Avelino, Richard Ureña

After missing most of the 2018 season after being shot during a robbery attempt in Venezuela before spring training, Estrada returned to showcase a truly endearing 25th-man profile. In his MLB debut, Estrada laid down a textbook sacrifice bunt as a pinch hitter. A week later, the natural infielder started in left. Estrada's an athlete who will give you whatever you need from him—as long as you don't need him to do it with flare or stand out in any particular way. Come up big with bases loaded? He's got you. Learn a new position in three days? He's got you. This guy just delivers in the most W.B. Mason style possible. You know, a few cases of Keurig cups here, a few boxes of pens there and maybe even the occasional 50-pound bag of rock salt for those front steps.

Estevan Florial CF Born: 11/25/97   Age: 22   Bats: L   Throws: R   Height: 6'1"   Weight: 185   Origin: International Free Agent, 2015

YEAR	TEAM	LVL	AGE	PA	R	2B	3B	HR	RBI	BB	K	SB	CS	AVG/OBP/SLG	DRC+	VORP	BABIP	BRR	FRAA	WARP
2017	CSC	A	19	389	64	21	5	11	43	41	124	17	7	.297/.373/.483	134	31.8	.431	-0.7	CF(62): -2.1, LF(13): 2.9	2.4
2017	TAM	A+	19	87	13	2	2	2	14	9	24	6	1	.303/.368/.461	125	7.4	.404	0.7	CF(18): 0.4	0.6
2018	TAM	A+	20	339	45	16	3	3	27	44	87	11	10	.255/.354/.361	103	10.5	.353	-0.9	CF(59): 1.8, RF(6): -0.2	1.1
2019	TAM	A+	21	301	38	10	3	8	38	24	98	9	5	.237/.297/.383	92	4.2	.335	1.0	CF(62): 2.9	1.1
2020	NYA	MLB	22	35	3	2	0	1	4	3	13	1	0	.222/.280/.370	74	0.1	.344	0.0	CF 0	0.0

Comparables: Lewis Brinson, Byron Buxton, Daniel Fields

Florial's injuries continue to disrupt crucial development time, as he's yet to get a full, healthy season in High-A under his belt. He still has the same four standout tools he showed up stateside with a few years ago—plus speed, plus power, a strong arm and reliable centerfield glove—but still hasn't racked up enough at-bats to correct his pitch recognition and general plate discipline issues. His ceiling remains high, though so do those strikeout rates.

Mike Ford 1B Born: 07/04/92   Age: 27   Bats: L   Throws: R   Height: 6'0"   Weight: 225   Origin: Undrafted Free Agent, 2013

YEAR	TEAM	LVL	AGE	PA	R	2B	3B	HR	RBI	BB	K	SB	CS	AVG/OBP/SLG	DRC+	VORP	BABIP	BRR	FRAA	WARP
2017	TRN	AA	24	417	61	19	1	13	65	76	56	1	0	.272/.410/.451	158	26.5	.291	-1.8	1B(55): -0.5, 3B(1): 0.0	2.9
2017	SWB	AAA	24	115	19	5	0	7	21	18	16	0	0	.266/.383/.543	142	7.2	.247	0.1	1B(19): -0.2	0.6
2018	SWB	AAA	25	410	48	21	0	15	52	37	70	1	0	.253/.327/.433	116	2.5	.275	-0.9	1B(57): -0.2	1.0
2019	SWB	AAA	26	349	59	20	0	23	60	46	55	0	1	.303/.401/.605	141	24.5	.300	0.3	1B(44): -3.2, 3B(5): 0.0	1.8
2019	NYA	MLB	26	163	30	7	0	12	25	17	28	0	0	.259/.350/.559	125	8.3	.243	-0.6	1B(29): -0.2, P(1): 0.0	0.7
2020	NYA	MLB	27	210	30	10	0	13	35	23	39	0	0	.259/.346/.525	130	11.3	.263	-0.5	1B -1	1.1

Comparables: Ji-Man Choi, Jesús Aguilar, Tyler White

Ford is a shorter, stockier Luke Voit with better plate discipline and defense around the cold corner. He doesn't have the "wow" factor of his counterpart and lacks similar power, but there's a lot to like about his approach, and the fact that he's left-handed certainly doesn't hurt at Yankee Stadium. He made a two-inning relief appearance in a blowout loss, and former Princeton pitcher or not, he did about what you'd expect from a position player pitching. Yet, somehow his smiling while giving up five runs didn't make Yankees fans angry and instead made him more endearing to them. That only happens to the underdoggiest of underdogs, and the Jersey native even has the local ties to cement that status.

Clint Frazier OF
Born: 09/06/94 Age: 25 Bats: R Throws: R Height: 6'1" Weight: 190 Origin: Round 1, 2013 Draft (#5 overall)

YEAR	TEAM	LVL	AGE	PA	R	2B	3B	HR	RBI	BB	K	SB	CS	AVG/OBP/SLG	DRC+	VORP	BABIP	BRR	FRAA	WARP
2017	SWB	AAA	22	320	46	19	2	12	42	37	69	9	2	.256/.344/.473	118	14.8	.291	1.8	LF(38): 1.2, RF(29): -1.3	1.4
2017	NYA	MLB	22	142	16	9	4	4	17	7	43	1	0	.231/.268/.448	82	0.8	.307	0.8	LF(30): -3.1, RF(7): 0.4	-0.2
2018	TAM	A+	23	26	6	1	0	1	3	4	3	2	0	.250/.385/.450	96	2.0	.235	0.3	LF(3): -0.3	0.0
2018	SWB	AAA	23	216	38	14	3	10	21	23	52	4	2	.311/.389/.574	143	20.4	.380	0.9	CF(26): -2.9, LF(16): -0.3	1.3
2018	NYA	MLB	23	41	9	3	0	0	1	5	13	0	0	.265/.390/.353	76	0.6	.429	0.2	LF(9): -0.7, CF(1): -0.2	-0.1
2019	SWB	AAA	24	269	35	20	1	8	26	17	56	1	2	.247/.305/.433	80	-5.2	.288	-0.8	LF(51): -0.1, CF(7): -1.3	-0.2
2019	NYA	MLB	24	246	31	14	0	12	38	16	70	1	2	.267/.317/.489	99	5.4	.329	-0.6	RF(36): -1.7, LF(17): 0.5	0.4
2020	NYA	MLB	25	175	20	8	1	8	24	13	51	2	1	.233/.297/.437	94	2.7	.291	0.2	LF -1, RF 0	0.1

Comparables: Michael Saunders, Byron Buxton, Travis Snider

Frazier opened the year declaring he was gunning for a starting job, then proceeded to show off his lumber while filling in for Giancarlo Stanton in April by hitting .324 with six homers. Unfortunately, over the remainder of the season he did everything to prove himself undeserving. His impressive bat slumped and was overshadowed by defensive woes and the apparent need for an attitude adjustment. Does he spend more time worrying about custom cleats and his red-hot shoe game than he does practicing? No. But butchering routine plays while wearing Jordans, then refusing to talk to the media afterwards doesn't exactly invoke confidence. Air Force Ones only look good when you can catch a simple pop up. To quote one of Frazier's own passive-aggressive tweets: "guys a DH". He may believe he's earned his pinstripes, but his usage says otherwise.

Brett Gardner OF
Born: 08/24/83 Age: 36 Bats: L Throws: L Height: 5'11" Weight: 195 Origin: Round 3, 2005 Draft (#109 overall)

YEAR	TEAM	LVL	AGE	PA	R	2B	3B	HR	RBI	BB	K	SB	CS	AVG/OBP/SLG	DRC+	VORP	BABIP	BRR	FRAA	WARP
2017	NYA	MLB	33	682	96	26	4	21	63	72	122	23	5	.264/.350/.428	107	24.4	.300	1.4	LF(122): 12.5, CF(22): 0.2	3.8
2018	NYA	MLB	34	609	95	20	7	12	45	65	107	16	2	.236/.322/.368	90	11.9	.272	4.1	LF(107): 11.8, CF(34): 0.0	2.6
2019	NYA	MLB	35	550	86	26	7	28	74	52	108	10	2	.251/.325/.503	109	25.9	.265	1.4	CF(98): 1.7, LF(45): -1.9	2.6
2020	NYA	MLB	36	525	59	21	3	18	63	49	112	12	3	.234/.313/.409	95	14.2	.270	1.0	LF 6, CF 0	2.1

Comparables: Alejandro De Aza, Bernie Williams, Fred Lynn

Gardner was supposed to be a fourth outfielder. He was signed for depth, to provide veteran presence in the dugout and partially because, as the longest-tenured Yankee, he earned a courtesy signing. The 2019 season was supposed to mark a turning point in Gardner's career where he'd pass the torch onto the next batch of hopeful prospects. He'd come in as a late inning defensive replacement and share war stories about life before they let iPads in the dugouts. A lot was supposed to happen this season, and it didn't. Gardner is gusty, gritty and a grinder. He's John McClane. This old, bald guy has no business scaling skyscrapers, walking through glass barefoot or having a career year during his age-36 season, but he's doing it anyway. He became the lefty power bat the Yankees were lost without. He was the starting center fielder for months. He reached a career high with 28 home runs, outdingering Aaron Judge. Grandpa Gardner's out here stealing bases and stretching triples. He's always been a streaky hitter and he picked the wrong time to go cold, sinking to a .528 OPS and 39 percent strikeout rate in the postseason. But for the most part, in posting the highest DRC+ of his career, Gardner said thank you to New York in style. Goodbye, however, will have to wait at least another year. Yippee-ki-yay, [redacted].

Aaron Hicks CF
Born: 10/02/89 Age: 30 Bats: B Throws: R Height: 6'1" Weight: 202 Origin: Round 1, 2008 Draft (#14 overall)

YEAR	TEAM	LVL	AGE	PA	R	2B	3B	HR	RBI	BB	K	SB	CS	AVG/OBP/SLG	DRC+	VORP	BABIP	BRR	FRAA	WARP
2017	NYA	MLB	27	361	54	18	0	15	52	51	67	10	5	.266/.372/.475	114	21.2	.290	2.0	CF(52): -0.8, LF(22): 0.8	1.8
2018	NYA	MLB	28	581	90	18	3	27	79	90	111	11	2	.248/.366/.467	121	35.9	.264	2.3	CF(131): -8.6	2.9
2019	NYA	MLB	29	255	41	10	0	12	36	31	72	1	2	.235/.325/.443	100	9.4	.286	0.3	CF(58): -6.8	0.3
2020	NYA	MLB	30	280	34	11	1	12	37	34	69	5	2	.234/.330/.428	105	12.9	.278	0.8	CF -4	0.9

Comparables: Jackie Bradley Jr., Colby Rasmus, Matthew den Dekker

Bottom of the tenth. Up by two. Bases loaded. Two outs. Max Kepler at the plate. One team was going home disappointed, and Hicks hopped on his horse to ensure it'd be his former one. Air Hicks was born that night, ending the game on the flashiest of plays and justifying his contract extension with one diving catch. On the other side of the ball, months later, Hicks mashed a highlight reel home run off of Cy Young winner Justin Verlander in Game 5 of the ALCS, giving the Yankees the lead in the first inning of an elimination game. He spent the majority of the season shelved, ultimately leading to offseason Tommy John surgery, so he won't be present for the first half of 2020 either, but he's gone out of his way to make sure that he won't be forgotten while he's recovering.

Kyle Higashioka C   Born: 04/20/90   Age: 30   Bats: R   Throws: R   Height: 6'1"   Weight: 205   Origin: Round 7, 2008 Draft (#230 overall)

YEAR	TEAM	LVL	AGE	PA	R	2B	3B	HR	RBI	BB	K	SB	CS	AVG/OBP/SLG	DRC+	VORP	BABIP	BRR	FRAA	WARP
2017	SWB	AAA	27	57	5	4	0	2	11	4	7	0	0	.264/.316/.453	103	2.2	.273	-0.2	C(14): 4.5	0.7
2017	NYA	MLB	27	20	2	0	0	0	0	2	6	0	0	.000/.100/.000	59	-1.7	.000	-0.1	C(8): 1.6	0.2
2018	SWB	AAA	28	211	16	10	1	5	22	17	44	2	0	.202/.276/.346	55	-0.9	.234	-0.7	C(49): 6.6	0.6
2018	NYA	MLB	28	79	6	2	0	3	6	6	16	0	0	.167/.241/.319	98	-2.6	.170	-0.7	C(27): 3.8	0.7
2019	SWB	AAA	29	270	42	13	0	20	56	24	53	0	0	.278/.348/.581	122	19.1	.276	-3.2	C(64): 15.2	3.0
2019	NYA	MLB	29	57	8	5	0	3	11	0	26	0	0	.214/.211/.464	62	0.2	.321	0.6	C(18): 2.1	0.3
2020	NYA	MLB	30	175	22	6	0	11	27	12	51	0	0	.223/.280/.462	94	6.4	.254	-0.4	C 8	1.5

Comparables: Tommy Pham, Lane Adams, Curt Casali

YEAR	TEAM	P. COUNT	FRM RUNS	BLK RUNS	THRW RUNS	TOT RUNS
2017	NYA	813	1.7	-0.1	0.0	1.5
2017	SWB	2153	4.3	-0.3	-0.1	3.8
2018	NYA	3384	3.2	0.8	-0.1	4.4
2018	SWB	6908	7.2	0.6	-0.2	7.6
2019	NYA	2271	1.9	0.1	-0.1	1.7
2019	SWB	8880	15.4	0.0	-0.1	15.1
2020	NYA	6833	7.8	0.3	-0.1	8.0

The backup to the backup, Higashioka's time in the big leagues has been contingent on Gary Sánchez's health. He made the Triple-A All-Star team this year, which was sadly the highlight of his season, but perhaps a big step in the right direction as he bounced back nicely from a season that undersold his offensive potential. Higashioka's combination of power and strong receiving skills are enough to earn him a promotion to a singular understudy role. He also plays guitar, so rain delay entertainment is always at his fingertips.

Aaron Judge RF   Born: 04/26/92   Age: 28   Bats: R   Throws: R   Height: 6'7"   Weight: 282   Origin: Round 1, 2013 Draft (#32 overall)

YEAR	TEAM	LVL	AGE	PA	R	2B	3B	HR	RBI	BB	K	SB	CS	AVG/OBP/SLG	DRC+	VORP	BABIP	BRR	FRAA	WARP
2017	NYA	MLB	25	678	128	24	3	52	114	127	208	9	4	.284/.422/.627	166	66.6	.357	-0.1	RF(141): 4.4	7.5
2018	NYA	MLB	26	498	77	22	0	27	67	76	152	6	3	.278/.392/.528	137	32.7	.368	1.0	RF(90): 12.6, CF(1): -0.1	4.7
2019	NYA	MLB	27	447	75	18	1	27	55	64	141	3	2	.272/.381/.540	132	28.7	.360	0.2	RF(92): 8.3	3.6
2020	NYA	MLB	28	560	83	21	1	35	93	78	179	6	2	.256/.366/.523	135	37.7	.332	0.5	RF 6	4.6

Comparables: Adam Dunn, George Springer, Giancarlo Stanton

Stature can be measured in a multitude of ways. The most obvious is physicality, but the most significant is through earned respect. Judge checks all of those boxes and more: He's a Gold-Glove-caliber defender in right, an elite slugger, even potentially the new captain in the Bronx. He's one of just a handful of players in baseball who is recognizable off the field and has single-handedly driven up usage of the number 99 in youth baseball and softball leagues across the Tri-State Area by roughly 2000% (probably). Well, all of the boxes except for durability as he's lost significant portions of each of the last two seasons—the 2019 culprit being a strained oblique that cost him much of May and June. Judge is also the shining exemplar of why you don't need to be fast to put up elite BABIPs, and 2019 marked the third season in a row leading all of baseball in measured exit velocity. In a league that seemingly enjoys stamping out of the individuality of its players, Judge is uniquely...well, unique.

DJ LeMahieu 2B   Born: 07/13/88   Age: 31   Bats: R   Throws: R   Height: 6'4"   Weight: 215   Origin: Round 2, 2009 Draft (#79 overall)

YEAR	TEAM	LVL	AGE	PA	R	2B	3B	HR	RBI	BB	K	SB	CS	AVG/OBP/SLG	DRC+	VORP	BABIP	BRR	FRAA	WARP
2017	COL	MLB	28	682	95	28	4	8	64	59	90	6	5	.310/.374/.409	102	26.7	.351	3.4	2B(153): 20.5	4.7
2018	COL	MLB	29	581	90	32	2	15	62	37	82	6	5	.276/.321/.428	98	17.6	.298	4.5	2B(128): 20.1	4.2
2019	NYA	MLB	30	655	109	33	2	26	102	46	90	5	2	.327/.375/.518	128	44.5	.349	-2.1	2B(75): 4.5, 3B(52): 0.7	4.8
2020	NYA	MLB	31	595	70	27	3	18	74	46	89	10	4	.303/.360/.462	119	39.3	.336	1.8	2B 16, 3B 0	5.7

Comparables: Howie Kendrick, Joaquin Arias, Robinson Canó

M-V-P! M-V-P! M-V-P! LeMahieu was so awe-inspiring that a discourse on what it really meant to be the most valuable player broke out. His signing, which baffled the masses at the time because of the mere existence of Manny Machado, turned out to be the gift that keeps on giving. A calm and unshakable demeanor was the perfect addition to a pressure-filled New York team, and his ability to play three infield positions at an above-average level gave the Yankees an incredible amount of flexibility when dealing with their slew of injuries. As for what LeMahieu means, it's French for clutch hitting, as evidenced by his 1.162 OPS with two out and runners in scoring position. It's French for hanging tough, as he hit an incredible .274/.297/.491 after being down 0-2 in the count. It's French for holy shit we're tied at four. (That one is self-explanatory.) He may not have taken home the hardware, but it turns out that niveau de la mer suits the 31-year-old sparkplug just fine.

Cameron Maybin OF   Born: 04/04/87   Age: 33   Bats: R   Throws: R   Height: 6'3"   Weight: 215   Origin: Round 1, 2005 Draft (#10 overall)

YEAR	TEAM	LVL	AGE	PA	R	2B	3B	HR	RBI	BB	K	SB	CS	AVG/OBP/SLG	DRC+	VORP	BABIP	BRR	FRAA	WARP
2017	LAA	MLB	30	387	57	19	1	6	22	48	78	29	5	.235/.333/.351	88	10.0	.289	4.9	LF(45): 2.6, CF(42): 1.5	1.4
2017	HOU	MLB	30	63	6	1	1	4	13	3	16	4	3	.186/.226/.441	87	-0.1	.179	-0.4	CF(15): -0.4, LF(5): -0.3	-0.1
2018	MIA	MLB	31	287	20	12	1	3	20	32	55	8	5	.251/.338/.343	89	8.1	.308	-2.7	LF(44): 2.1, CF(30): -0.7	0.3
2018	SEA	MLB	31	97	12	2	1	1	8	6	20	2	0	.242/.289/.319	88	-0.6	.300	-0.2	CF(20): -1.6, LF(12): 0.4	0.0
2019	COH	AAA	32	67	4	3	0	0	5	13	20	1	2	.216/.388/.275	128	-1.6	.344	-1.9	CF(5): -0.3, LF(4): -0.2	0.2
2019	NYA	MLB	32	269	48	17	0	11	32	30	72	9	6	.285/.364/.494	106	9.1	.365	-1.0	LF(46): -0.5, RF(36): 0.7	0.9
2020	NYA	MLB	33	251	28	11	1	7	28	26	65	9	3	.249/.332/.397	96	6.7	.324	-0.1	LF 2, CF 0	0.9

Comparables: Carlos Gómez, Lee Walls, Peter Bourjos

Wham bam thank you Cam was the actual plan when the Yankees acquired Maybin from the Indians. A major leaguer treading water in Triple A for months, he was prepared to fight tooth and nail to stay in the big leagues, if only he had the chance. When Bombers started dropping like they were filming a Top Gun remake, he got his chance and made the most of it. Maybin was meant to be temporary, a depth piece during a dire time of need. Then he became the

Wolf of Wall Street "I'm not leaving" meme. He forced the Yankees hands, playing in a way that made it impossible for the club to jettison him even as the team returned to health. During his audition stretch, he homered in four consecutive games, hit three doubles and drove in seven runs, all while playing quality defense at either corner outfield spot and starting the cutest home run dugout celebration of all time. #HugSZN

Gary Sánchez C Born: 12/02/92 Age: 27 Bats: R Throws: R Height: 6'2" Weight: 230 Origin: International Free Agent, 2009

YEAR	TEAM	LVL	AGE	PA	R	2B	3B	HR	RBI	BB	K	SB	CS	AVG/OBP/SLG	DRC+	VORP	BABIP	BRR	FRAA	WARP
2017	NYA	MLB	24	525	79	20	0	33	90	40	120	2	1	.278/.345/.531	127	43.8	.304	2.3	C(104): 5.4, 1B(2): 0.0	4.9
2018	SWB	AAA	25	28	4	0	0	4	4	0	10	0	0	.179/.179/.607	83	0.3	.071	0.0	C(5): 0.0	0.1
2018	NYA	MLB	25	374	51	17	0	18	53	46	94	1	0	.186/.291/.406	94	5.4	.197	-1.4	C(76): -1.4	1.1
2019	NYA	MLB	26	446	62	12	1	34	77	40	125	0	1	.232/.316/.525	121	33.6	.244	-2.5	C(90): -6.3	2.4
2020	NYA	MLB	27	525	75	20	1	36	90	46	140	3	1	.240/.316/.515	118	35.3	.260	-0.4	C -1	3.6

Comparables: Anthony Rizzo, Randal Grichuk, Tommy Joseph

YEAR	TEAM	P. COUNT	FRM RUNS	BLK RUNS	THRW RUNS	TOT RUNS
2017	NYA	14363	7.4	-3.1	2.3	7.2
2018	NYA	10822	3.3	-4.3	0.2	-1.0
2019	NYA	12670	-5.1	-0.8	-0.2	-6.1
2020	NYA	18452	2.8	-2.3	-0.2	0.3

The gap between a ball and a strike can be as small as a quarter of an inch or as large as a couple of wins, and Sánchez was guilty of letting that differentiation hold him back on both sides of the ball in 2019. On offense, the power returned but it was mitigated by a poor swing decision rate—the gap between his swing percentage inside the zone and outside the zone was the fourth smallest among all major-league hitters with 300 at-bats. As a result, he saw the fifth-fewest strikes—both due to his elevated chase rate and the damage he would do the balls that he came into contact with. On defense, Sánchez finally veered into a borderline poor framer as his focus from game-to-game continued to come under fire—though an improvement in his blocking and a notable reduction in passed balls helped recover some of his overall defensive value. The skills are still those of a perennial All-Star catcher, but it's now been two full seasons since the game of inches has pulled the curtain back on him.

Giancarlo Stanton OF Born: 11/08/89 Age: 30 Bats: R Throws: R Height: 6'6" Weight: 245 Origin: Round 2, 2007 Draft (#76 overall)

YEAR	TEAM	LVL	AGE	PA	R	2B	3B	HR	RBI	BB	K	SB	CS	AVG/OBP/SLG	DRC+	VORP	BABIP	BRR	FRAA	WARP
2017	MIA	MLB	27	692	123	32	0	59	132	85	163	2	2	.281/.376/.631	155	76.5	.288	-0.1	RF(149): 8.3	7.1
2018	NYA	MLB	28	705	102	34	1	38	100	70	211	5	0	.266/.343/.509	117	29.4	.333	0.0	RF(37): -1.1, LF(36): 0.0	2.6
2019	NYA	MLB	29	72	8	3	0	3	13	12	24	0	0	.288/.403/.492	87	0.5	.424	-0.3	LF(10): -1.3, RF(3): -0.4	-0.2
2020	NYA	MLB	30	595	93	25	1	43	109	72	191	3	1	.261/.357/.563	141	43.2	.324	-0.3	LF -5, RF 0	4.0

Comparables: Darryl Strawberry, Adam Dunn, Reggie Jackson

The bigger they are, the harder they fall. Staying healthy has been an issue for Stanton throughout his career, something about a guy so big and made of 120 percent muscle always seems to lead to time on the injured list. He only played in 23 games, including the postseason, and despite what irrationally angry Yankees fans think they know, no one was more frustrated by that than Stanton himself. His road to recovery was equally frustrating. When he solved one injury, three more popped up in its place. He struggled with strains, sprains and tears; his biceps, knees and shoulders betraying him throughout the year until a quad strain during the ALCS finally ended his season. It's a testament to Stanton's talent, and what a game changer he can be, that the Yankees kept him on the postseason roster despite an injury adhering him on the bench. Even hurt, he was the best option.

It's very easy to get up in arms about his contract, and boy do people love complaining about every type of price tag attached to him. But the real tragedy is a player like Stanton, an All-Star and former MVP, having a season like this. Imagine the majesty and pure terror of a full season of Stanton with 2019's juiced balls. Baseball fans were robbed. Stanton suffering multiple injuries shouldn't be a punchline. Big time competitors like him are great for the game, and the entirety of the Bronx should be rooting for him to come back and crush it.

Mike Tauchman **OF** Born: 12/03/90 Age: 29 Bats: L Throws: L Height: 6'2" Weight: 220 Origin: Round 10, 2013 Draft (#289 overall)

YEAR	TEAM	LVL	AGE	PA	R	2B	3B	HR	RBI	BB	K	SB	CS	AVG/OBP/SLG	DRC+	VORP	BABIP	BRR	FRAA	WARP
2017	ABQ	AAA	26	475	82	30	8	16	80	40	73	16	7	.331/.386/.555	125	38.1	.361	2.5	CF(62): 1.3, LF(34): 5.7	3.7
2017	COL	MLB	26	32	2	0	1	0	2	5	10	1	2	.222/.344/.296	64	-1.1	.353	-0.5	RF(3): -0.1, CF(3): -0.3	-0.2
2018	ABQ	AAA	27	471	84	26	7	20	81	60	70	12	10	.323/.408/.571	144	39.6	.345	3.5	CF(65): 4.2, LF(30): 6.1	5.5
2018	COL	MLB	27	37	5	1	0	0	0	4	15	1	0	.094/.194/.125	52	-3.5	.176	0.1	CF(5): -0.1, LF(3): -0.9	-0.2
2019	SWB	AAA	28	114	22	10	3	2	16	16	16	4	0	.274/.386/.505	115	6.7	.308	1.2	CF(15): 0.4, LF(7): 1.4	0.8
2019	NYA	MLB	28	296	46	18	1	13	47	34	71	6	0	.277/.361/.504	112	13.1	.333	2.4	LF(59): 5.3, RF(19): -0.5	1.9
2020	NYA	MLB	29	245	27	9	1	8	29	24	60	6	3	.233/.311/.397	91	5.2	.283	0.3	CF 2, RF 0	0.9

Comparables: Collin Cowgill, Darin Mastroianni, Jamie Hoffmann

Aside from maybe Gio Urshela, no player benefited from the historic Yankee injury parade more than Tauchman. When Aaron Hicks hit the injured list before the start of the season, suddenly the outfield depth that supposedly prevented them from getting involved in the Bryce Harper sweepstakes didn't feel so deep. Enter Tauchman. A three-year veteran of the International League, he came over to New York with the fanfare of a regional theater actor trying to make the big time. Tauchman was described as speedy with a great glove who raked in Triple-A so...basically, he was Tyler Wade: Outfield Version. Tauchman lived in minor league/major league limbo with the Yankees, much like he did in Colorado, until he faced his former team and a fire lit under him.

Tauchman's numbers were decent, not great, but his glove was worth what little offensive impact he brought to the table. Playing the Rockies, who never really gave Tauchman a true shot at cracking their roster, set him off. Maybe it was all the purple. On July 19th, he recorded his first three hit game of the year, including a double and a stolen base. Was he simply overperforming against the team that traded him away? Possibly, but it continued long after they left the opposing locker room. His batting average climbed over .300 on multiple occasions while he continued making Gold-Glove-worthy plays in left field, adding an exciting element to the team as if he were a touted outfield prospect and not a 28-year-old discard. The height of Tauchman's season involved some serious discussion about his eligibility for Rookie of the Year and minor outrage when it was revealed he was not. Tauchman made the most of his opportunity and on any other team should be the starting left fielder going forward, at least against right-handed pitchers (though he actually hit lefties better in a small sample). But on this team, in this season, he'll have to bide his time for another opening.

Gleyber Torres **MI** Born: 12/13/96 Age: 23 Bats: R Throws: R Height: 6'1" Weight: 200 Origin: International Free Agent, 2013

YEAR	TEAM	LVL	AGE	PA	R	2B	3B	HR	RBI	BB	K	SB	CS	AVG/OBP/SLG	DRC+	VORP	BABIP	BRR	FRAA	WARP
2017	TRN	AA	20	139	22	10	1	5	18	17	21	5	4	.273/.367/.496	138	15.3	.295	1.3	SS(19): 2.2, 3B(6): 0.8	1.5
2017	SWB	AAA	20	96	9	4	1	2	16	13	26	2	2	.309/.406/.457	127	7.1	.426	-1.8	SS(9): 1.0, 3B(9): 1.8	0.7
2018	SWB	AAA	21	56	6	3	1	1	11	5	10	1	1	.347/.393/.510	119	4.7	.400	0.1	3B(8): 0.6, 2B(3): 0.0	0.4
2018	NYA	MLB	21	484	54	16	1	24	77	42	122	6	2	.271/.340/.480	121	23.9	.321	0.8	2B(109): 5.4, SS(21): 1.5	3.7
2019	NYA	MLB	22	604	96	26	0	38	90	48	129	5	2	.278/.337/.535	124	43.8	.296	-1.0	SS(77): -1.4, 2B(65): -1.0	3.9
2020	NYA	MLB	23	595	77	23	2	31	88	49	134	11	6	.259/.325/.479	111	30.4	.291	-0.8	SS 2, 2B 0	3.4

Comparables: Carlos Correa, Rougned Odor, Rafael Devers

Webster's Dictionary defines a beneficiary owner as "one who enjoys the benefit of a property of which another is the legal owner." Peter Angelos may be the most famous legal owner of the Baltimore Orioles franchise, but Torres established his own control over the organization in 2019. In 18 games against his moribund division foe, the sophomore shortstop hit .394/.467/1.045 with 13 of his team-leading 38 homers, each one slowly destroying the professional brain of Orioles' television announcer Gary Thorne. The 13th and final homer on August 12th—his third of the day, spanning both ends of a doubleheader—caused the MASN broadcaster to just exasperatedly yell "You've got to be kidding me!"

Thorne wasn't the only one to throw that phrase at the budding star. Whether it's the stepped-up power or the ability to play any position on the infield without missing a beat, Torres has become a core tenet of this great Yankees team. And in an effort to be appreciated outside of New York as well, his 1.078 OPS in the 2019 postseason put an exclamation point on his season. The infield will now, and likely for the next decade, be built around Torres playing his natural shortstop. Alongside Aaron Judge, Torres is the future of the franchise.

Troy Tulowitzki **SS** Born: 10/10/84 Age: 35 Bats: R Throws: R Height: 6'3" Weight: 205 Origin: Round 1, 2005 Draft (#7 overall)

YEAR	TEAM	LVL	AGE	PA	R	2B	3B	HR	RBI	BB	K	SB	CS	AVG/OBP/SLG	DRC+	VORP	BABIP	BRR	FRAA	WARP
2017	TOR	MLB	32	260	16	10	0	7	26	17	40	0	1	.249/.300/.378	85	0.7	.272	-3.0	SS(64): 2.4	0.7
2019	NYA	MLB	34	13	1	1	0	1	1	2	4	0	0	.182/.308/.545	74	0.2	.167	0.0	SS(4): 0.7	0.1
2020	NYA	MLB	35	251	31	10	0	11	34	22	57	1	0	.252/.326/.448	104	8.3	.288	-1.1	SS 1	0.9

Comparables: Jhonny Peralta, J.J. Hardy, Jay Bell

Seemingly on track for a Hall-of-Fame induction during his prime, the last few seasons of Tulowitzki's playing career were bizarre and fairly heartbreaking. The All-Star caliber player he was during his time in Colorado could never fight his way back from the injuries to reemerge again, despite how badly he wanted to stick it to the doubters. Luckily, he defied the odds long enough to sneak in a swan song before retiring for good. Tulo's first and only home run as a Yankee was an emotional one, as he rounded the bases with an expression on his face that looks to say "I'm finally back", and he's a bit choked up about it. The injury bug bit him once again shortly thereafter, and after years of pushing himself, he just couldn't anymore. Tulo's presence will be missed, but it's a fitting end to his story. He grew up idolizing Derek Jeter and he got to spend his last games on the field playing shortstop in pinstripes. How can you not be romantic about baseball?

Gio Urshela 3B Born: 10/11/91 Age: 28 Bats: R Throws: R Height: 6'0" Weight: 220 Origin: International Free Agent, 2008

YEAR	TEAM	LVL	AGE	PA	R	2B	3B	HR	RBI	BB	K	SB	CS	AVG/OBP/SLG	DRC+	VORP	BABIP	BRR	FRAA	WARP
2017	COH	AAA	25	325	34	12	1	6	34	20	45	0	0	.266/.321/.374	97	1.3	.294	-3.5	3B(60): 0.3, SS(16): 1.0	0.8
2017	CLE	MLB	25	165	14	7	0	1	15	8	22	0	0	.224/.262/.288	79	-5.8	.256	-0.5	3B(60): 0.9, SS(5): -0.1	0.2
2018	COH	AAA	26	42	6	4	0	0	7	5	9	0	0	.324/.405/.432	101	3.1	.429	0.3	2B(4): 0.3, 3B(4): 0.3	0.2
2018	BUF	AAA	26	91	7	3	0	0	5	4	9	0	0	.244/.275/.279	105	-3.4	.269	-0.1	3B(14): -1.4, 1B(7): 0.2	0.3
2018	SWB	AAA	26	107	14	7	2	2	12	4	13	0	0	.307/.340/.475	104	5.2	.337	0.0	3B(20): 1.1, SS(8): -1.0	0.5
2018	TOR	MLB	26	46	7	1	0	1	3	2	10	0	0	.233/.283/.326	82	-1.4	.281	-0.2	3B(10): -0.8, SS(8): -0.3	-0.1
2019	NYA	MLB	27	476	73	34	0	21	74	25	87	1	1	.314/.355/.534	121	31.2	.349	-1.8	3B(123): 5.8, LF(1): 0.0	3.4
2020	NYA	MLB	28	455	49	23	1	16	57	24	89	1	0	.265/.309/.435	98	8.5	.301	-1.0	3B 2	1.1

Comparables: Danny Valencia, Leury García, Donovan Solano

It may not have been a bastion of stardom, but Urshela was quite the unlikely candidate to finish the decade with the highest single-season OPS of any Yankee third baseman. After all, he came into the 2019 season with a career .589 mark and a minor-league assignment. In his age-27 season, everything changed. Urshela had a full-on breakout, filling the hole left by Miguel Andújar with ease and likely stealing the starting spot for good. His defense has always been top notch, flashy and highlight reel worthy, but desperately waiting for his bat to catch up. Well, it's here. The juiced balls certainly played a factor in the power jump, but to go from a hitter who had never broken .300 in the minors, aside from two small-sample Triple-A appearances, to the fifth-best batting average in the American League is a substantial improvement. With a newfound aggressiveness at the plate, and a distinct defensive advantage over his competition, Urshela has the all-around skill to man the position well into the next decade.

Luke Voit 1B Born: 02/13/91 Age: 29 Bats: R Throws: R Height: 6'3" Weight: 225 Origin: Round 22, 2013 Draft (#665 overall)

YEAR	TEAM	LVL	AGE	PA	R	2B	3B	HR	RBI	BB	K	SB	CS	AVG/OBP/SLG	DRC+	VORP	BABIP	BRR	FRAA	WARP
2017	MEM	AAA	26	307	35	23	1	13	50	29	53	1	1	.327/.407/.565	155	29.6	.368	-3.6	1B(62): 4.3	2.6
2017	SLN	MLB	26	124	18	9	0	4	18	7	31	0	0	.246/.306/.430	88	0.8	.304	-0.3	1B(31): 1.6	0.2
2018	MEM	AAA	27	271	35	16	2	9	36	31	49	0	1	.299/.391/.500	133	17.0	.345	-1.3	1B(56): 2.1, LF(1): -0.1	1.5
2018	SWB	AAA	27	32	2	2	0	1	3	3	7	0	0	.310/.375/.483	114	1.3	.381	-0.1	1B(3): 0.2	0.1
2018	SLN	MLB	27	13	2	0	0	1	3	2	4	0	0	.182/.308/.455	159	1.4	.167	0.1	1B(3): 0.3	0.2
2018	NYA	MLB	27	148	28	5	0	14	33	15	39	0	0	.333/.405/.689	155	18.2	.380	1.1	1B(32): -2.7	1.1
2019	NYA	MLB	28	510	72	21	1	21	62	71	142	0	0	.263/.378/.464	118	20.1	.345	-3.2	1B(83): -3.2	1.3
2020	NYA	MLB	29	560	75	22	2	28	83	62	156	1	0	.264/.356/.486	125	27.4	.332	-1.1	1B 1	2.9

Comparables: Tyler White, Justin Bour, Craig Wilson

Frankie Valli voice
You're not too good to be true
Can't take my eyes off of you.
Oh God, I think you're so clutch
I wanna hold you so much.

Was Luke a fluke? Not at all. With a delicate skip and a jump, Voit's plus power and infectious energy complemented the Bronx Bomber line up perfectly. Questions about whether or not he could play up to the standards he set in his abbreviated torching of the American League down the stretch in 2018 lingered throughout the offseason, but he played a huge role in carrying the team through a first half marred by injury. His overall numbers were soured by an abdominal injury that turned into a sports hernia and required offseason surgery, as he was hitting .280/.393/.503 when it struck and .228/.348/.368 afterwards. Once he's back 100 percent health wise? Oh, what a night.

Anthony Volpe SS Born: 04/28/01 Age: 19 Bats: R Throws: R Height: 5'11" Weight: 180 Origin: Round 1, 2019 Draft (#30 overall)

YEAR	TEAM	LVL	AGE	PA	R	2B	3B	HR	RBI	BB	K	SB	CS	AVG/OBP/SLG	DRC+	VORP	BABIP	BRR	FRAA	WARP
2019	PUL	RK+	18	150	19	7	2	2	11	23	38	6	1	.215/.349/.355	100	8.5	.289	0.3		0.7
2020	NYA	MLB	19	251	24	11	1	5	24	28	87	3	1	.209/.306/.338	78	1.0	.321	0.0		0.1

Comparables:

Nothing captivates the attention of New York baseball fans like a local boy who grew up rooting for the team making good on the promise of his future. There are quite a number of years standing between the introduction and the outcome with Volpe, but the New Jersey native and Yankee fan was bought out of a strong commitment to Vanderbilt after being taken towards the end of the first round in the 2019 draft. It's not the flashiest of profiles, but Volpe substitutes a dreamy upside for a steady hand across the board. In other words, you won't find any tools on his scouting report that start with a three or four, but you won't find any that start with a six or seven either.

Tyler Wade INF Born: 11/23/94 Age: 25 Bats: L Throws: R Height: 6'1" Weight: 185 Origin: Round 4, 2013 Draft (#134 overall)

YEAR	TEAM	LVL	AGE	PA	R	2B	3B	HR	RBI	BB	K	SB	CS	AVG/OBP/SLG	DRC+	VORP	BABIP	BRR	FRAA	WARP
2017	SWB	AAA	22	388	68	22	4	7	31	38	75	26	5	.310/.382/.460	130	30.4	.375	3.0	SS(54): -2.3, 2B(13): 2.8	3.4
2017	NYA	MLB	22	63	7	4	0	0	2	5	19	1	1	.155/.222/.224	65	-3.3	.231	0.7	2B(15): -0.8, SS(7): 0.0	-0.1
2018	SWB	AAA	23	408	46	18	4	4	27	37	82	11	8	.255/.328/.360	97	8.5	.318	-2.1	SS(51): -0.2, LF(12): 2.1	1.7
2018	NYA	MLB	23	70	8	4	0	1	5	4	23	1	0	.167/.214/.273	55	-2.9	.238	1.7	2B(26): -0.6, RF(5): -0.1	-0.1
2019	SWB	AAA	24	335	51	19	4	4	38	23	76	13	5	.296/.352/.425	92	13.8	.381	1.6	SS(43): 2.6, 2B(28): 0.7	1.4
2019	NYA	MLB	24	108	16	3	1	2	11	11	28	7	0	.245/.330/.362	73	-0.3	.328	0.5	2B(18): 1.8, LF(14): 0.1	0.1
2020	NYA	MLB	25	175	16	7	1	3	16	13	49	5	2	.226/.290/.334	69	0.2	.306	0.6	SS 0, 2B 2	0.2

Comparables: Jerry Snyder, Jonathan Villar, Tim Beckham

Wade experienced a bit of a rollercoaster throughout the season, from thinking he had earned a spot on the Opening Day roster only to be left off in the final hour to spending more time traveling to and from Scranton than on the playing field. His versatility came in handy as the natural infielder racked up innings at all three outfield positions, second, third and shortstop. Speed on the basepaths remains his strongest tool. While he often looks outmatched at the plate, he's a constant threat to steal once he reaches base and scoring from first is never off the table. He's in Quad-A limbo, but makes a good case for himself as a bench player. He's the perfect pinch runner or late inning defensive replacement, though a second-division team would be happy enough to play him every day.

PITCHERS

Zack Britton LHP Born: 12/22/87 Age: 32 Bats: L Throws: L Height: 6'3" Weight: 195 Origin: Round 3, 2006 Draft (#85 overall)

YEAR	TEAM	LVL	AGE	W	L	SV	G	GS	IP	H	HR	BB/9	K/9	K	GB%	BABIP	WHIP	ERA	DRA	WARP	MPH	FB%	WHF	CSP
2017	BAL	MLB	29	2	1	15	38	0	37¹	39	1	4.3	7.0	29	75%	.336	1.53	2.89	5.91	-0.3	97.6	94.7	12.4	42.2
2018	BAL	MLB	30	1	0	4	16	0	15²	11	1	5.7	7.5	13	64%	.263	1.34	3.45	7.71	-0.5	96.6	94.4	14.5	42.3
2018	NYA	MLB	30	1	0	3	25	0	25	18	2	4.0	7.6	21	78%	.229	1.16	2.88	6.55	-0.5	96.7	93.1	12.3	42.8
2019	NYA	MLB	31	3	1	3	66	0	61¹	38	3	4.7	7.8	53	77%	.224	1.14	1.91	3.47	1.2	96.3	86.4	11.5	42.5
2020	NYA	MLB	32	3	3	5	56	0	60	47	5	4.1	9.2	61	74%	.272	1.24	2.90	3.27	1.2	95.7	89.3	12.1	42.1

Comparables: Brett Cecil, Brian Matusz, Eric O'Flaherty

In another world, Britton would be the Yankees closer. In many worlds, he should be. He was the team's most consistent reliever, turning in another extremely strong year, both in the regular season and playoffs—his highest ERA in an individual month was 3.60. Speaking of consistency, in a surprise to absolutely no one, Britton had the highest ground-ball rate among relievers at 77 percent, combating the juiced ball with ease. One of the Yankees' Four Horsemen of the Apocalypse, Britton's trot from the bullpen invoked fear in his opponents, his sinker's as deadly as ever and it shows no real signs of stopping.

Luis Cessa RHP Born: 04/25/92 Age: 28 Bats: R Throws: R Height: 6'0" Weight: 210 Origin: International Free Agent, 2008

YEAR	TEAM	LVL	AGE	W	L	SV	G	GS	IP	H	HR	BB/9	K/9	K	GB%	BABIP	WHIP	ERA	DRA	WARP	MPH	FB%	WHF	CSP
2017	SWB	AAA	25	4	6	0	14	13	78¹	75	7	3.0	7.7	67	48%	.304	1.29	3.45	4.57	1.0				
2017	NYA	MLB	25	0	3	0	10	5	36	36	7	4.2	7.5	30	46%	.282	1.47	4.75	4.72	0.3	97.7	41.8	11.5	44.5
2018	TRN	AA	26	0	1	0	2	2	10	6	0	0.9	10.8	12	50%	.250	0.70	2.70	2.96	0.3				
2018	SWB	AAA	26	3	0	0	6	5	26¹	19	1	1.4	8.5	25	40%	.250	0.87	2.73	2.52	0.9				
2018	NYA	MLB	26	1	4	2	16	5	44²	51	5	2.6	7.9	39	48%	.333	1.43	5.24	3.23	1.0	97.1	41.6	12.6	45.7
2019	NYA	MLB	27	2	1	1	43	0	81	75	14	3.4	8.3	75	48%	.282	1.31	4.11	4.82	0.5	96.5	41.9	13.8	44
2020	NYA	MLB	28	3	3	0	51	0	54	52	9	3.2	8.7	52	47%	.291	1.32	4.19	4.51	0.4	96.3	42.1	13.2	45

Comparables: Héctor Noesi, Jake Buchanan, Jakob Junis

Patience is a virtue. Brian Cashman stuck with Cessa when the whole world was screaming for him to be DFA'd and he quietly put together a solid year. In the new age of the bullpen, Cessa has real value—he eats innings and can bridge the gap between starters and elite bullpen arms, all while keeping the game within reach. His slider is easily his best offering and he relied on it heavily this season, throwing the pitch more than 50 percent of the time. His most notable performance came in the ALCS, where he pitched a pair of scoreless innings in each of his appearances. In a bullpen with much bigger names, Cessa has finally figured it out and turned himself into a trusted arm.

Aroldis Chapman LHP Born: 02/28/88 Age: 32 Bats: L Throws: L Height: 6'4" Weight: 212 Origin: International Free Agent, 2010

YEAR	TEAM	LVL	AGE	W	L	SV	G	GS	IP	H	HR	BB/9	K/9	K	GB%	BABIP	WHIP	ERA	DRA	WARP	MPH	FB%	WHF	CSP
2017	NYA	MLB	29	4	3	22	52	0	50¹	37	3	3.6	12.3	69	48%	.298	1.13	3.22	3.50	0.9	102.5	76.8	15.2	48.5
2018	NYA	MLB	30	3	0	32	55	0	51¹	24	2	5.3	16.3	93	46%	.268	1.05	2.45	2.13	1.7	102.4	73.8	16.8	45.8
2019	NYA	MLB	31	3	2	37	60	0	57	38	3	3.9	13.4	85	42%	.292	1.11	2.21	2.57	1.7	101.5	68.8	14.9	49.2
2020	NYA	MLB	32	3	3	46	56	0	60	40	6	4.1	14.1	93	43%	.291	1.12	2.51	2.90	1.5	101.0	71.6	15.4	47.5

Comparables: Craig Kimbrel, Kenley Jansen, Dellin Betances

Chapman's still a fireballer, despite a consistent, albeit minor, dip in velocity the last few seasons. The subtle decline is a blessing in disguise, causing Chapman to utilize his slider more often—the mix making both pitches more effective. Fewer strikeouts and stare downs, but more outs and still the same amount of sweat and turtlenecks. He's an elite closer and even if he no longer tops the velocity leaderboards, he has the formula to repeat this season's success as he ages. Clearly the Yankees agree as Chapman was able to leverage the opt-out clause in his contract to get an extra year and $18 million from the team; extending his stay in New York at least through the end of the 2022 season.

Gerrit Cole RHP Born: 09/08/90 Age: 29 Bats: R Throws: R Height: 6'4" Weight: 225 Origin: Round 1, 2011 Draft (#1 overall)

YEAR	TEAM	LVL	AGE	W	L	SV	G	GS	IP	H	HR	BB/9	K/9	K	GB%	BABIP	WHIP	ERA	DRA	WARP	MPH	FB%	WHF	CSP
2017	PIT	MLB	26	12	12	0	33	33	203	199	31	2.4	8.7	196	47%	.298	1.25	4.26	3.84	3.9	98.4	60	10.1	49.5
2018	HOU	MLB	27	15	5	0	32	32	200¹	143	19	2.9	12.4	276	38%	.286	1.03	2.88	2.55	6.4	99.0	56.3	15.3	49.8
2019	HOU	MLB	28	20	5	0	33	33	212¹	142	29	2.0	13.8	326	41%	.275	0.89	2.50	2.36	7.9	99.4	54	18.5	48.8
2020	NYA	MLB	29	16	6	0	31	31	200	152	24	2.7	13.6	255	41%	.309	1.06	2.52	2.99	5.7	98.3	56.3	15.4	49.3

Comparables: Roger Clemens, Josh Johnson, Tommy Hanson

To give you a sense of just how dominant Cole was down the stretch in 2019, here is a stat for you: he was 5-5 with a 4.02 ERA at the end of May, then he finished second in the AL Cy Young race. In his final 21 starts, he had a 1.73 ERA, allowing 30 walks and 27 earned runs over 140 2/3 innings while striking out 214. Two hundred fourteen! It was like he turned the calendar to June and had the thought, "Hey why don't I try to just humiliate every single person that comes into the batter's box?" and it worked. He set a major-league record by striking out double-digit batters in nine straight appearances to end the season. Then he went and did it in his first two postseason appearances. He set a new record for a single season K/9.

He throws upper-90s heat with ease, and much like the guy he lost the Cy Young to, teammate Justin Verlander, he saves an extra gear for when he needs it most. His slider doesn't so much fall off the table as it breaks the table in half and then laughs at you for putting a silly table in its way. When he gets bored and wants to play around, he'll throw an 88 mph change up to lefties and when he really feels like slowing it down he'll casually toss in an 82 mph curveball. He's unhittable. He's not even 30. He's going to make the Yankees very happy for a long time. And all it took was money.

───────────────── ★ ★ ★ *2020 Top 101 Prospect* **#24** ★ ★ ★ ─────────────────

Deivi Garcia **RHP** Born: 05/19/99 Age: 21 Bats: R Throws: R Height: 5'9" Weight: 163 Origin: International Free Agent, 2015

YEAR	TEAM	LVL	AGE	W	L	SV	G	GS	IP	H	HR	BB/9	K/9	K	GB%	BABIP	WHIP	ERA	DRA	WARP	MPH	FB%	WHF	CSP
2017	DYA	RK	18	1	1	0	3	3	15¹	10	1	1.2	10.6	18	58%	.281	0.78	1.17	1.77	0.7				
2017	YAT	RK	18	3	0	0	4	2	16²	9	3	2.2	13.0	24	32%	.194	0.78	3.24	1.42	0.8				
2017	PUL	RK	18	2	1	0	6	5	28	23	3	4.2	13.8	43	32%	.370	1.29	4.50	3.01	0.9				
2018	CSC	A	19	2	4	0	8	8	40²	31	5	2.2	13.9	63	31%	.302	1.01	3.76	3.14	1.0				
2018	TAM	A+	19	2	0	0	5	5	28¹	19	0	2.5	11.1	35	37%	.292	0.95	1.27	2.69	0.9				
2019	TAM	A+	20	0	2	0	4	4	17²	14	0	4.1	16.8	33	50%	.438	1.25	3.06	3.55	0.3				
2019	TRN	AA	20	4	4	0	11	11	53²	43	2	4.4	14.6	87	44%	.360	1.29	3.86	4.30	0.4				
2019	SWB	AAA	20	1	3	0	11	6	40	39	8	4.5	10.1	45	38%	.307	1.48	5.40	5.12	0.6				
2020	NYA	MLB	21	2	2	0	15	5	30	30	5	3.5	11.6	39	40%	.339	1.39	4.71	4.96	0.2				

Comparables: Sean Reid-Foley, David Holmberg, Alex Reyes

New York's farm system revolved around the rise of Garcia, who shot up the ranks and became their top prospect without much debate. The diminutive righty was exciting enough when he simply featured a fastball and curve that could each draw plus-plus grades. However, the 2019 season saw the continued development of his change and the addition of a suddenly plus slider to boot. Garcia would have likely made a late-season appearance in the big leagues, but an innings limit held him back—after all, his 111 1/3 innings were by far a career high. A smaller frame gives the impression his body won't hold up to the grueling workload of a starter, and he's going to need to cut back on the walks in order to get deep enough into games, but it's hard to argue with dominance.

Cory Gearrin **RHP** Born: 04/14/86 Age: 34 Bats: R Throws: R Height: 6'1" Weight: 205 Origin: Round 4, 2007 Draft (#138 overall)

YEAR	TEAM	LVL	AGE	W	L	SV	G	GS	IP	H	HR	BB/9	K/9	K	GB%	BABIP	WHIP	ERA	DRA	WARP	MPH	FB%	WHF	CSP
2017	SFN	MLB	31	4	3	0	68	0	68	50	4	4.6	8.5	64	49%	.263	1.25	1.99	5.60	-0.3	94.0	54.9	12.5	48.6
2018	SFN	MLB	32	1	1	1	35	0	30	33	5	3.9	9.3	31	34%	.329	1.53	4.20	4.57	0.1	94.3	48.9	12.2	44.3
2018	TEX	MLB	32	1	0	0	21	0	21¹	13	2	2.5	8.4	20	52%	.212	0.89	2.53	4.97	0.0	93.6	49	12.4	46.6
2018	OAK	MLB	32	0	0	0	6	0	6	10	0	3.0	3.0	2	50%	.417	2.00	6.00	3.91	0.1	93.7	60	7.6	51.4
2019	SEA	MLB	33	0	2	0	48	2	41¹	38	3	4.6	8.5	39	47%	.310	1.43	3.92	4.95	0.2	93.4	46.1	10.3	46
2019	NYA	MLB	33	1	1	0	18	0	14	17	2	2.6	5.1	8	43%	.319	1.50	4.50	6.84	-0.2	93.5	40	5	52.2
2020	NYA	MLB	34	2	2	0	33	0	35	35	5	3.8	8.5	33	45%	.302	1.41	4.67	4.70	0.2	92.6	48.5	10.7	46.6

Comparables: Ricky Bottalico, Al Reyes, David Aardsma

Imagine the "guy tapping his temple" meme for a second. Good. Now picture Gearrin. If you're always balking, you can never be charged with a balk. The most interesting aspect of his season was the weird toe tap he does before every pitch, which at one point was okay, then it was illegal, then it was allowed again. Riveting stuff. It's not just movement on the rubber that has people's heads spinning though—Gearrin has now made his way through five teams in the last two seasons.

Domingo Germán **RHP** Born: 08/04/92 Age: 27 Bats: R Throws: R Height: 6'2" Weight: 175 Origin: International Free Agent, 2009

YEAR	TEAM	LVL	AGE	W	L	SV	G	GS	IP	H	HR	BB/9	K/9	K	GB%	BABIP	WHIP	ERA	DRA	WARP	MPH	FB%	WHF	CSP
2017	TRN	AA	24	1	4	0	6	6	33	32	4	2.7	10.4	38	50%	.318	1.27	3.00	4.74	0.2				
2017	SWB	AAA	24	7	2	0	14	13	76¹	59	5	2.6	9.6	81	46%	.274	1.06	2.83	2.79	2.4				
2017	NYA	MLB	24	0	1	0	7	0	14¹	11	1	5.7	11.3	18	54%	.294	1.40	3.14	3.15	0.3	98.5	50.4	12.7	40
2018	TAM	A+	25	0	0	0	2	2	6	3	0	3.0	12.0	8	23%	.231	0.83	0.00	2.54	0.2				
2018	NYA	MLB	25	2	6	0	21	14	85²	81	15	3.5	10.7	102	39%	.300	1.33	5.57	4.36	0.9	96.7	46.9	15.5	46.9
2019	NYA	MLB	26	18	4	0	27	24	143	125	30	2.5	9.6	153	38%	.259	1.15	4.03	4.27	2.3	95.8	44.9	13.9	47.3
2020	NYA	MLB	27	4	3	0	34	8	68	59	11	3.0	10.0	75	38%	.280	1.20	3.74	4.16	0.9	95.7	46.3	14.6	45.9

Comparables: Mike Clevinger, Brock Stewart, Alec Mills

Germán was placed on administrative leave under the MLB-MLBPA Joint Domestic Violence Policy on September 19, and will miss the first 63 games of the 2020 season as part of an 81-game suspension handed down by Major League Baseball. The National Coalition Against Domestic Violence reports that more than 10 million people a year are physically abused by an intimate partner, and that 1-in-4 women and 1-in-7 men have been victims of severe physical violence by an intimate partner. Even if you don't know it, survivors are all around you. It is far bigger than baseball. Please consider donating to a local women's shelter or charity. If you need help, the 24-hour National Domestic Violence Hotline can be reached at 800-799-7233.

Chad Green RHP   Born: 05/24/91   Age: 29   Bats: L   Throws: R   Height: 6'3"   Weight: 210   Origin: Round 11, 2013 Draft (#336 overall)

YEAR	TEAM	LVL	AGE	W	L	SV	G	GS	IP	H	HR	BB/9	K/9	K	GB%	BABIP	WHIP	ERA	DRA	WARP	MPH	FB%	WHF	CSP
2017	SWB	AAA	26	2	1	0	5	5	26²	32	1	3.7	11.1	33	53%	.397	1.61	4.72	5.48	0.1				
2017	NYA	MLB	26	5	0	0	40	1	69	34	4	2.2	13.4	103	28%	.236	0.74	1.83	2.42	2.1	97.6	69.4	16.4	50.3
2018	NYA	MLB	27	8	3	0	63	0	75²	64	9	1.8	11.2	94	33%	.307	1.04	2.50	3.38	1.3	97.8	86.6	14.9	52.6
2019	SWB	AAA	28	0	0	0	3	3	7¹	5	0	2.5	17.2	14	31%	.385	0.95	2.45	2.06	0.3				
2019	NYA	MLB	28	4	4	2	54	15	69	66	10	2.5	12.8	98	36%	.346	1.23	4.17	3.71	1.3	98.1	77.3	15	50.5
2020	NYA	MLB	29	3	3	0	61	0	65	53	9	2.8	12.1	87	35%	.301	1.12	3.02	3.48	1.2	97.2	78.6	15.3	51.1

Comparables: *Mike Clevinger, Gonzalez Germen, Mike Hauschild*

Sometimes a trip down to Triple-A is crucial and beneficial for everyone involved. No one's a better example of that than Green. After allowing an eighth-inning grand slam to Justin Bour on April 23, his ERA was a whopping 16.43. Calling it a rough start would be offensive to rough starts. Outside of the big stage, he was able to zero in on his issues—a balance adjustment and relocating his fastball helped Green find his rhythm again, and expanded his role to the Yankees' go-to opener. Relying heavily on his four-seamer again, but mixing in his slider more frequently than last season turned out to be the key to his success. Whether he's used as an opener or a more traditional reliever in 2020, Green will once again be a key cog in the Yankee bullpen.

David Hale RHP   Born: 09/27/87   Age: 32   Bats: R   Throws: R   Height: 6'2"   Weight: 210   Origin: Round 3, 2009 Draft (#87 overall)

YEAR	TEAM	LVL	AGE	W	L	SV	G	GS	IP	H	HR	BB/9	K/9	K	GB%	BABIP	WHIP	ERA	DRA	WARP	MPH	FB%	WHF	CSP
2017	TUL	AA	29	3	0	0	6	5	29	36	3	2.2	6.5	21	52%	.344	1.48	3.72	5.58	-0.2				
2017	OKL	AAA	29	2	4	0	9	9	52²	64	4	1.2	6.7	39	45%	.347	1.35	4.27	4.34	0.8				
2018	SWB	AAA	30	3	2	0	11	11	55²	58	5	2.7	7.1	44	48%	.306	1.35	4.20	4.57	0.6				
2018	MIN	MLB	30	0	0	0	1	0	3	4	1	12.0	6.0	2	40%	.333	2.67	12.00	5.89	0.0	93.7	49.1	10.5	38.3
2018	NYA	MLB	30	0	0	0	3	0	10²	12	2	0.8	5.1	6	42%	.278	1.22	2.53	6.08	-0.1	94.0	49.1	12.4	48.6
2019	SWB	AAA	31	3	2	0	7	7	32²	36	3	2.8	8.3	30	54%	.330	1.41	4.13	4.39	0.7				
2019	NYA	MLB	31	3	0	2	20	0	37²	39	2	1.7	5.5	23	51%	.298	1.22	3.11	4.60	0.3	95.2	60.5	8.5	47.9
2020	NYA	MLB	32	2	2	0	33	0	35	36	5	2.9	6.5	25	49%	.289	1.36	4.55	4.72	0.2	94.0	57.4	9.2	46.6

Comparables: *Chris Rusin, Stephen Fife, Jason Berken*

The 32-year-old minor-league vet has been through a Hale of a ride. He's been DFA'd so many times the 'D' may as well stand for David, but his dream never faltered. That dedication led him to a resurgent season in the Bronx where he pitched surprisingly well in almost entirely low-leverage situations, but the second half of the year was less kind to the former Princeton Tiger. A combination of lumbar and knee injuries sidelined him for most of August and September, only to come back and be DFA'd in the middle of the playoffs to make room for Aaron Hicks on the ALCS roster. On top of all that, his Google search results tanked as David Hale, the diplomat and the U.S. Under Secretary of State for Political Affairs, testified in Donald Trump's impeachment inquiry in November.

J.A. Happ LHP   Born: 10/19/82   Age: 37   Bats: L   Throws: L   Height: 6'5"   Weight: 205   Origin: Round 3, 2004 Draft (#92 overall)

YEAR	TEAM	LVL	AGE	W	L	SV	G	GS	IP	H	HR	BB/9	K/9	K	GB%	BABIP	WHIP	ERA	DRA	WARP	MPH	FB%	WHF	CSP
2017	TOR	MLB	34	10	11	0	25	25	145¹	145	18	2.8	8.8	142	48%	.302	1.31	3.53	4.07	2.4	94.4	71.3	10.5	43.8
2018	TOR	MLB	35	10	6	0	20	20	114	99	17	2.8	10.3	130	45%	.285	1.18	4.18	3.89	1.9	94.7	74.2	11.7	48
2018	NYA	MLB	35	7	0	0	11	11	63²	51	10	2.3	8.9	63	33%	.250	1.05	2.69	4.00	1.0	94.0	72.3	11.1	48.3
2019	NYA	MLB	36	12	8	0	31	30	161¹	160	34	2.7	7.8	140	41%	.281	1.30	4.91	6.00	-0.4	93.6	68.3	11.3	47.3
2020	NYA	MLB	37	9	6	0	23	23	113	110	20	2.9	8.0	101	41%	.280	1.29	4.24	4.61	1.2	92.7	69.2	10.9	45.6

Comparables: *Jorge De La Rosa, Chuck Finley, Ted Lilly*

Happ is a Dodge Neon. Not the car you want, but one that will get you from Point A to Point B. Just when the tank seems empty, he keeps chugging along, somehow, someway. He's dependable, good never great, and can take a beating. Nearly 200,000 miles on him, and Happ's still going. The squad's biggest victim of the juiced ball, he's a fifth starter these days, and he's okay with that. Neons are underrated.

Jonathan Holder RHP   Born: 06/09/93   Age: 27   Bats: R   Throws: R   Height: 6'2"   Weight: 235   Origin: Round 6, 2014 Draft (#182 overall)

YEAR	TEAM	LVL	AGE	W	L	SV	G	GS	IP	H	HR	BB/9	K/9	K	GB%	BABIP	WHIP	ERA	DRA	WARP	MPH	FB%	WHF	CSP
2017	SWB	AAA	24	0	0	1	12	0	16	15	1	4.5	11.8	21	40%	.359	1.44	1.69	3.91	0.2				
2017	NYA	MLB	24	1	1	0	37	0	39¹	45	5	1.8	9.2	40	42%	.348	1.35	3.89	3.11	0.9	93.7	37.2	13.2	47.9
2018	SWB	AAA	25	1	0	0	4	1	6	5	1	1.5	12.0	8	53%	.286	1.00	3.00	2.94	0.2				
2018	NYA	MLB	25	1	3	0	60	1	66	53	4	2.6	8.2	60	31%	.261	1.09	3.14	4.33	0.5	94.4	55.4	11.5	47.5
2019	SWB	AAA	26	1	1	2	9	0	12¹	13	1	1.5	10.9	15	49%	.353	1.22	2.92	3.21	0.4				
2019	NYA	MLB	26	5	2	0	34	1	41¹	43	8	2.4	10.0	46	38%	.307	1.31	6.31	4.72	0.3	93.9	54.5	12.7	49.6
2020	NYA	MLB	27	1	1	0	20	0	22	19	3	2.4	8.7	21	37%	.278	1.17	3.47	3.95	0.3	93.6	51.9	12.4	49

Comparables: *Sam Tuivailala, Jensen Lewis, Michael Tonkin*

In the world of situational comedies, sometimes actors get replaced and the show in question doesn't comment on it. At all. They rarely look anything like the previous portrayer of the character, and viewers are simply forced to accept it. Every time Aaron Boone made a call to the bullpen for Holder in a high-leverage situation, the replacement came out. The Holder of the last two seasons was no more, instead an inferior one whose timing never quite clicked. A slight downtick in velocity from both his fastball and slider, the pitches he throws most often, paired with more pitches in the zone made for a dangerous combination—especially with such a homer-prone ball. Holder spent some time in Triple-A attempting to fix his issues, before an injury ended his season. Recasts never work out.

Tommy Kahnle RHP   Born: 08/07/89   Age: 30   Bats: R   Throws: R   Height: 6'1"   Weight: 235   Origin: Round 5, 2010 Draft (#175 overall)

YEAR	TEAM	LVL	AGE	W	L	SV	G	GS	IP	H	HR	BB/9	K/9	K	GB%	BABIP	WHIP	ERA	DRA	WARP	MPH	FB%	WHF	CSP
2017	CHA	MLB	27	1	3	0	37	0	36	28	3	1.8	15.0	60	43%	.352	0.97	2.50	2.10	1.2	100.2	72.6	18.2	51.3
2017	NYA	MLB	27	1	1	0	32	0	26²	25	1	3.4	12.1	36	40%	.364	1.31	2.70	2.05	0.9	99.4	58.9	17.2	46.6
2018	SWB	AAA	28	2	2	1	25	0	24²	23	2	4.0	13.5	37	40%	.375	1.38	4.01	4.05	0.3				
2018	NYA	MLB	28	2	0	1	24	0	23¹	23	3	5.8	11.6	30	39%	.339	1.63	6.56	4.03	0.2	97.2	54.3	15.2	46
2019	NYA	MLB	29	3	2	0	72	0	61¹	45	9	2.9	12.9	88	51%	.279	1.06	3.67	2.41	2.0	98.6	44.1	18.6	46.6
2020	NYA	MLB	30	3	3	0	56	0	60	46	6	4.0	12.5	83	47%	.299	1.21	2.95	3.30	1.2	98.0	52.6	17.7	46.9

Comparables: Jordan Jankowski, Chasen Shreve, J.J. Hoover

Tommy thunder thighs. Tommy tight pants. Tommy two times. Tommy throwing straight fire. Kahnle's a lunatic, in a great way. A former Red-Bull-chugging, would-tackle-a-bear-for-an-out, crazy man who turned things around after a mess of a previous season. The righty reliever quickly returned to his 2017 form, becoming a vital piece in the bullpen when injuries and ineffectiveness plagued his teammates. The secret to Kahnle's success was relying heavily on his changeup, which he threw 52 percent of the time, allowing him to almost eliminate his slider completely. Regaining a tick on his fastball after watching the pitch fall flat in 2018 didn't hurt either. He was at home in the late innings, his aggressive sprints from the bullpen and dousing of himself in bottled water added much needed dramatic effect to his game. Kahnle's going to stay in the exact same late-inning role for at least another two years.

Jordan Montgomery LHP   Born: 12/27/92   Age: 27   Bats: L   Throws: L   Height: 6'6"   Weight: 225   Origin: Round 4, 2014 Draft (#122 overall)

YEAR	TEAM	LVL	AGE	W	L	SV	G	GS	IP	H	HR	BB/9	K/9	K	GB%	BABIP	WHIP	ERA	DRA	WARP	MPH	FB%	WHF	CSP
2017	NYA	MLB	24	9	7	0	29	29	155¹	140	21	3.0	8.3	144	42%	.275	1.23	3.88	4.51	1.8	93.6	41.8	12.7	43
2018	NYA	MLB	25	2	0	0	6	6	27¹	25	3	4.0	7.6	23	46%	.282	1.35	3.62	5.86	-0.2	92.3	41.1	11	45.3
2019	NYA	MLB	26	0	0	0	2	1	4	7	1	0.0	11.2	5	21%	.462	1.75	6.75	6.11	0.0	93.4	50	13.4	49
2020	NYA	MLB	27	5	3	0	13	13	65	59	9	3.1	7.4	53	41%	.268	1.26	3.75	4.19	1.0	92.9	42.5	12.5	46.8

Comparables: Sean Manaea, Steven Matz, Dan Straily

Recovering from Tommy John surgery was Montgomery's one and only goal in 2019. He was never expected to contribute to the team, in the postseason or otherwise, and if he didn't make it back in time for September call-ups no one would have cared. He made a couple appearances, threw some good pitches, mostly bad ones, and no real weight should be placed on either aside from his velocity staying intact. Montgomery will be competing for a spot in the rotation this year, and how quickly his command comes back will determine how successful that campaign is.

Adam Ottavino RHP   Born: 11/22/85   Age: 34   Bats: B   Throws: R   Height: 6'5"   Weight: 220   Origin: Round 1, 2006 Draft (#30 overall)

YEAR	TEAM	LVL	AGE	W	L	SV	G	GS	IP	H	HR	BB/9	K/9	K	GB%	BABIP	WHIP	ERA	DRA	WARP	MPH	FB%	WHF	CSP
2017	COL	MLB	31	2	3	0	63	0	53¹	48	8	6.6	10.6	63	40%	.310	1.63	5.06	6.10	-0.6	96.6	50.2	9.9	46.3
2018	COL	MLB	32	6	4	6	75	0	77²	41	5	4.2	13.0	112	44%	.242	0.99	2.43	3.02	1.7	96.3	43.1	13	47.9
2019	NYA	MLB	33	6	5	2	73	0	66¹	47	5	5.4	11.9	88	41%	.286	1.31	1.90	3.63	1.2	95.7	41.6	11.8	48.5
2020	NYA	MLB	34	3	3	3	61	0	65	51	9	4.2	11.4	82	43%	.281	1.25	3.45	3.71	1.0	95.0	43.4	11.6	47

Comparables: David Hernandez, Kyle Farnsworth, Al Reyes

Superstitions are a major part of baseball, like hot dogs and the seventh inning stretch; the game is equally linked to the occasionally insane superstitious actions of its players. Avoiding the chalk lines, refusing to change articles of clothing after a win, slump-busting facial hair. Ottavino's personal superstition involves switching Gatorade colors if he's having trouble. It's time to add "don't insult baseball legends" to his list. When Ottavino shared a story in which he claimed he'd strike out Babe Ruth every time, he got himself in hot water and picked up some serious bad juju. Sure, it was taken out of context. And yes, it makes sense with the way the game has evolved that someone who played in the olden times wouldn't be able to handle the harsh movement of Ottavino's sweeping slider. But it's Babe Ruth. Ottavino was a dominant bullpen arm throughout the regular season because the Great Bambino let him be. But once October hit, he lost all effectiveness and Yankees fans went from cheering in support to screaming Ottavino get off the mound-o. During four of his postseason appearances, he failed to record a single out. You don't mess with the Colossus of Clout, and the hard throwing righty paid the price when it hurt the most.

James Paxton LHP   Born: 11/06/88   Age: 31   Bats: L   Throws: L   Height: 6'4"   Weight: 235   Origin: Round 4, 2010 Draft (#132 overall)

YEAR	TEAM	LVL	AGE	W	L	SV	G	GS	IP	H	HR	BB/9	K/9	K	GB%	BABIP	WHIP	ERA	DRA	WARP	MPH	FB%	WHF	CSP
2017	SEA	MLB	28	12	5	0	24	24	136	113	9	2.4	10.3	156	46%	.300	1.10	2.98	2.63	4.5	98.1	65.6	13.5	49.5
2018	SEA	MLB	29	11	6	0	28	28	160¹	134	23	2.4	11.7	208	41%	.299	1.10	3.76	2.67	4.9	98.0	63.7	15.8	53
2019	NYA	MLB	30	15	6	0	29	29	150²	138	23	3.3	11.1	186	40%	.313	1.28	3.82	4.18	2.6	97.6	60	15.3	47
2020	NYA	MLB	31	11	6	0	26	26	143	123	19	3.3	11.0	174	41%	.301	1.23	3.38	3.73	2.9	97.0	62.1	15	49.3

Comparables: David Price, Kyle Lobstein, Jaime García

The Big Maple takes the Big Apple. It sounds like a Mary-Kate and Ashley movie, which is fitting for Paxton's first season in the Bronx because the majority of his starts included what must have been a zany twin switch between the first and second innings. Mary-Kate was running late, so Ashley threw on the uniform to stall. Paxton's first-inning ERA was a whopping 9.00, giving up 12 of his 23 homers on the entire season during that frame. Thankfully, Mary-Kate always made it there in time for the second and dominated the way that was expected throughout the rest of the start. With one year left until the 31-year-old hits free agency, he'll look to build on his strong close to the season—opposing hitters scratched out a .177/.248/.298 line against the left-hander during August and September—in 2020 to try to bring in that Olsen-level cash.

CC Sabathia LHP Born: 07/21/80   Age: 39   Bats: L   Throws: L   Height: 6'6"   Weight: 300   Origin: Round 1, 1998 Draft (#20 overall)

YEAR	TEAM	LVL	AGE	W	L	SV	G	GS	IP	H	HR	BB/9	K/9	K	GB%	BABIP	WHIP	ERA	DRA	WARP	MPH	FB%	WHF	CSP
2017	NYA	MLB	36	14	5	0	27	27	148²	139	21	3.0	7.3	120	51%	.276	1.27	3.69	3.92	2.7	93.0	53.2	9.6	45.3
2018	NYA	MLB	37	9	7	0	29	29	153	150	19	3.0	8.2	140	45%	.295	1.31	3.65	4.40	1.6	92.0	59.1	11.8	45.7
2019	NYA	MLB	38	5	8	0	23	22	107¹	112	27	3.3	9.0	107	41%	.292	1.41	4.95	6.41	-0.7	90.9	57.6	11.9	45.3
2020	NYA	MLB	39	2	2	0	33	0	35	35	7	3.2	8.7	34	42%	.294	1.36	4.77	4.87	0.1	90.3	55.3	10.9	44

Comparables: Steve Carlton, Frank Tanana, Kevin Millwood

A future first-ballot Hall of Famer, Sabathia's final season was somewhat of a victory lap. If there was ever any doubt about whether deserves the highest honor in the game, reaching 3,000 strikeouts, getting 250 wins and literally pitching until his arm gave out put them to rest. Sabathia's the last of his kind, a dying breed of pitchers who'd put their neck on the line for their team, who used his voice for those who couldn't use theirs. The player he was on the mound—a leader, a fighter—was the same man he was off the field. Sabathia's season wasn't perfect by any statistical standard. He gave up too many home runs and he didn't pitch deep enough in games. For Sabathia, what he meant to his communities, to the game and to the Bronx was bigger than baseball too.

Luis Severino RHP Born: 02/20/94   Age: 26   Bats: R   Throws: R   Height: 6'2"   Weight: 215   Origin: International Free Agent, 2011

YEAR	TEAM	LVL	AGE	W	L	SV	G	GS	IP	H	HR	BB/9	K/9	K	GB%	BABIP	WHIP	ERA	DRA	WARP	MPH	FB%	WHF	CSP
2017	NYA	MLB	23	14	6	0	31	31	193¹	150	21	2.4	10.7	230	50%	.272	1.04	2.98	2.68	6.2	99.6	51.4	13.7	49.4
2018	NYA	MLB	24	19	8	0	32	32	191¹	173	19	2.2	10.3	220	42%	.314	1.14	3.39	2.79	5.6	99.7	50.5	13.3	51.2
2019	NYA	MLB	25	1	1	0	3	3	12	6	0	4.5	12.8	17	38%	.250	1.00	1.50	4.05	0.2	98.0	56.6	12.8	47.3
2020	NYA	MLB	26	12	6	0	26	26	156	130	20	3.0	10.6	184	43%	.288	1.17	3.12	3.52	3.5	99.2	52	13.7	50

Comparables: Yovani Gallardo, Tommy Hanson, Carlos Martínez

First, the bad news. The young ace didn't make his first start of the season until September 17th, after being sidelined first with shoulder inflammation, and then a grade-two lat strain. The good news? The version of Severino who made his triumphant return looked a lot like the elite starter they severely missed during the majority of the regular season. The Yankees kept him on a strict pitch count, never letting him go more than five innings. His high-90s velocity was there from the jump, topping out at 98 in his first start back. The lone laggard was the command of his secondary pitches, which was the driver of his elevated walk rate over the small sample, but you can excuse a pitcher for being a touch rusty after missing over six months of action. Expect a repeat of the All-Star-caliber Severino come 2020.

T.J. Sikkema LHP Born: 07/25/98   Age: 21   Bats: L   Throws: L   Height: 6'0"   Weight: 221   Origin: Round 1, 2019 Draft (#38 overall)

YEAR	TEAM	LVL	AGE	W	L	SV	G	GS	IP	H	HR	BB/9	K/9	K	GB%	BABIP	WHIP	ERA	DRA	WARP	MPH	FB%	WHF	CSP
2019	STA	A-	20	0	0	0	4	4	10²	6	0	0.8	11.0	13	52%	.240	0.66	0.84	2.02	0.4				
2020	NYA	MLB	21	2	2	0	33	0	35	35	5	4.0	8.5	33	43%	.300	1.45	4.85	4.94	0.1				

Comparables: Tyler Alexander, Brett Cecil, Clay Buchholz

Sikkema was selected in the supplemental round of the 2019 amateur draft—an additional pick coming via the Sonny Gray trade—after dominating at Missouri to the tune of a 1.32 ERA during his junior season. He made four abbreviated appearances with Staten Island, and was thoroughly dominant by being stingy with the walks and plentiful with the grounders. The 20-year-old southpaw profiles as a likely reliever due to both his size and his non-ideal delivery, with potential to be a shutdown closer, though a future as a starter isn't completely off the table.

Masahiro Tanaka RHP Born: 11/01/88   Age: 31   Bats: R   Throws: R   Height: 6'3"   Weight: 215   Origin: International Free Agent, 2014

YEAR	TEAM	LVL	AGE	W	L	SV	G	GS	IP	H	HR	BB/9	K/9	K	GB%	BABIP	WHIP	ERA	DRA	WARP	MPH	FB%	WHF	CSP
2017	NYA	MLB	28	13	12	0	30	30	178¹	180	35	2.1	9.8	194	50%	.306	1.24	4.74	3.91	3.3	94.3	37.6	15.8	41.7
2018	NYA	MLB	29	12	6	0	27	27	156	141	25	2.0	9.2	159	49%	.284	1.13	3.75	3.95	2.5	93.9	31.5	14.8	44
2019	NYA	MLB	30	11	9	0	32	31	182	186	28	2.0	7.4	149	48%	.293	1.24	4.45	4.94	1.6	93.6	32.5	11.7	46.8
2020	NYA	MLB	31	11	7	0	28	28	151	149	28	2.3	8.0	135	48%	.282	1.24	4.13	4.55	1.7	93.0	33.3	13.6	44.3

Comparables: Michael Pineda, Matt Harvey, Ricky Nolasco

Tanaka is a big-game pitcher, and when the Yankees need him to show up, he goes to heroic lengths to do so. His postseason numbers are ridiculous, with an ERA of 1.76 across eight starts, and he had never given up more than two runs in a single one of them until Game 4 of last year's ALCS against the Astros. However, his domination of the division-rival Rays also helped the Yankees wrap up their first AL East title since 2012. In his four starts against them, Tanaka had a 1.59 ERA and 28 strikeouts against just three walks, including a June complete-game shutout. Going into his age-31 season and the final year of his $155-million contract, Tanaka may be overshadowed by the Gerrit Cole signing but is a strong leader in his own right and poised to take that mantle after CC Sabathia's retirement.

Adam Warren RHP Born: 08/25/87   Age: 32   Bats: R   Throws: R   Height: 6'1"   Weight: 224   Origin: Round 4, 2009 Draft (#135 overall)

YEAR	TEAM	LVL	AGE	W	L	SV	G	GS	IP	H	HR	BB/9	K/9	K	GB%	BABIP	WHIP	ERA	DRA	WARP	MPH	FB%	WHF	CSP
2017	NYA	MLB	29	3	2	1	46	0	57¹	35	4	2.4	8.5	54	44%	.208	0.87	2.35	3.01	1.4	94.3	38.9	10.7	42.5
2018	NYA	MLB	30	0	1	0	24	0	30	26	3	3.6	11.1	37	37%	.307	1.27	2.70	3.27	0.6	93.5	39	12	38.6
2018	SEA	MLB	30	3	1	0	23	0	21²	22	3	3.3	6.2	15	39%	.279	1.38	3.74	5.44	-0.1	94.0	41.7	10.4	44.2
2019	SDN	MLB	31	4	1	0	25	0	28²	28	9	3.8	7.8	25	44%	.247	1.40	5.34	5.02	0.1	93.2	30.8	10.3	39.7
2020	NYA	MLB	32	2	2	0	33	0	35	34	6	3.7	8.1	31	42%	.281	1.37	4.75	4.72	0.3	92.8	36.7	10.7	40.4

Comparables: Jeremy Jeffress, David Phelps, Ramon E Ramírez

Last year in this space we posited a wild theory that Warren's suckitude in any uniform other than Yankee pinstripes was due to a sinister plot involving androids. This year, we're lowering the android threat level from "Hmmmmm" to "Yeah, right," as Warren's most recent west coast clunker ended after 29 innings (and nine home runs) when his elbow went *sproing*. Tommy John surgery ensued in September, and Warren will likely be out until the 2021 season. Androids don't have elbow ligaments, of course. Or do they? Hmmmmm.

LINEOUTS

Hitters

HITTER	POS	TEAM	LVL	AGE	PA	R	2B	3B	HR	RBI	BB	K	SB	CS	AVG/OBP/SLG	DRC+	VORP	BABIP	BRR	FRAA	WARP
Kevin Alcantara	CF	YAN	Rk	16	128	19	5	2	1	13	3	27	3	3	.260/.289/.358	108	2.0	.326	0.5	CF(27): -1.3	0.4
Ezequiel Duran	2B	STA	A-	20	277	49	12	4	13	37	25	77	11	4	.256/.329/.496	160	21.3	.314	0.6	2B(56): 7.6	3.0
Terrance Gore	OF	SWB	AAA	28	69	8	3	1	0	1	12	17	3	0	.164/.324/.255	64	-1.6	.237	0.3	CF(19): -1.8	-0.2
	OF	KCA	MLB	28	58	13	2	1	0	1	6	18	13	5	.275/.362/.353	68	-0.7	.424	-0.5	RF(10): -1.3, LF(9): 0.4	-0.2
Zack Granite	CF	NAS	AAA	26	541	66	18	8	3	37	31	45	25	13	.290/.331/.375	76	6.0	.311	3.7	LF(43): 2.3, CF(42): -2.0	0.5
Rosell Herrera	UT	NWO	AAA	26	180	21	11	1	5	24	14	32	2	1	.309/.367/.479	115	9.9	.359	0.5	3B(21): -1.4, LF(12): 0.0	0.7
	UT	MIA	MLB	26	119	10	6	0	2	11	11	27	4	1	.200/.288/.314	72	-0.5	.250	0.9	CF(25): -2.0, RF(15): -1.9	-0.3
Erik Kratz	C	SFN	MLB	39	36	1	2	0	1	3	2	6	0	0	.125/.222/.281	73	0.6	.120	-1.2	C(11): 1.2	0.1
	C	SWB	AAA	39	176	27	10	0	7	31	17	21	1	0	.299/.375/.500	123	10.4	.305	1.2	C(37): 2.9, 1B(2): -0.2	1.5
	C	TBA	MLB	39	17	0	0	0	0	0	0	8	0	0	.059/.059/.059	37	-0.6	.111	-0.1	C(6): -0.7	-0.1
Kendrys Morales	1B	NYA	MLB	36	75	7	1	0	1	5	12	6	0	0	.177/.320/.242	83	-0.6	.182	-1.4	1B(7): -0.2	-0.2
	1B	OAK	MLB	36	126	9	1	1	1	7	14	20	0	0	.204/.310/.259	87	0.2	.239	-1.2	1B(26): -0.4, P(1): 0.0	-0.1
Everson Pereira	CF	STA	A-	18	74	9	3	0	1	3	4	26	3	0	.171/.216/.257	35	-2.5	.256	0.5	CF(15): -0.3, RF(1): -0.1	-0.1
Anthony Seigler	C	CSC	A	20	120	10	3	0	0	6	20	28	1	0	.175/.328/.206	73	1.1	.246	-0.2	C(23): 0.4	0.2
Canaan Smith	LF	CSC	A	20	528	67	32	3	11	74	74	108	16	4	.307/.405/.465	182	45.0	.381	-2.0	LF(97): 4.1, RF(2): 0.1	5.4
Josh Smith	SS	STA	A-	21	141	17	6	1	3	15	25	17	6	3	.324/.450/.477	207	15.3	.355	0.7	SS(24): -1.3	1.7

Kevin Alcantara made his stateside debut at 16 years old and brings a plus arm, plus speed and above average raw power to potential otherworldly upside, which is fitting since the week he was born, Men In Black II was the top-grossing movie in the United States. ⊗ **Ezequiel Duran** is full of potential, with no present defensive weakness and loads of raw talent. His plate approach needs some polishing, but he led the New York-Penn League in home runs and flashes impressive bat speed to make up for it. ⊗ With due respect to **Terrance Gore**, whose pinch-running prowess has been a fun October subplot over the past half-decade, you can tell it was a lost season for the Royals because they gave him 58 plate appearances. Oh, and because they sent him to the Yankees in July for cash considerations. ⊗ **Zack Granite** once hit .470 during the month of June (in 2017), encompassing 117 at-bats at Triple-A Rochester. However, that fun fact might have more staying power than the speed-and-contact lefty. ⊗ Ever bought a pair of sunglasses that looked better on the model than they did on you? **Rosell Herrera** knows how you feel. He upped his launch angle and walked more often last season, but instead of a breakout all he got was a pink slip from the Marlins. The Yankees signed Herrera in January in a move that can be described only as a heat check. ⊗ An organizational guy who provides depth and is well-liked by fans and teammates alike, **Erik Kratz**, is a solid insurance policy. There if you need him, but you silently hope you never do. ⊗ Few players in recent memory have had such Late Career A's Energy as **Kendrys Morales**, but the former slugger couldn't hack it in Oakland or New York. MLB would need to add more than just a 26th roster spot for him to stick at this point. ⊗ His offensive numbers aren't pretty and he's been knocked out of the Yankees top 20 prospects, but **Everson Pereira** still utilizes his plus speed in center. The Yankees have been aggressive with his assignments and he's plenty young enough to grow into some power. ⊗ In keeping with the trend of the Yankees season, **Anthony Seigler** spent ample time out due to injury. The young athletic catcher appeared in only 30 games throughout his first full professional season, but still showed off his plus-plus arm that pairs well with a quick release that will dominate the running game. ⊗ **Canaan Smith** is a pure hitter, with raw power and advanced barrel control. A doubles machine, he currently lacks the ability to tap into his full power potential in-game and the big parks of the Florida State League in 2020 won't help there. ⊗ When your name is **Josh Smith** you have to be really good to stand out, and a .450 on-base percentage in his pro debut allowed him to do just that.

Pitchers

PITCHER	TEAM	LVL	AGE	W	L	SV	G	GS	IP	H	HR	BB/9	K/9	K	GB%	BABIP	WHIP	ERA	DRA	WARP	MPH	FB%	WHF	CSP
Albert Abreu	TRN	AA	23	5	8	0	23	20	96²	103	9	4.9	8.5	91	43%	.336	1.61	4.28	6.77	-2.2				
Jake Barrett	SWB	AAA	27	0	1	1	10	0	15¹	10	0	2.3	11.7	20	49%	.286	0.91	1.17	2.38	0.6				
	NYA	MLB	27	0	0	0	2	0	3²	6	2	4.9	9.8	4	8%	.364	2.18	14.73	7.79	-0.1	94.7	47.1	11.4	45.1
Roansy Contreras	CSC	A	19	12	5	0	24	24	132¹	105	10	2.4	7.7	113	42%	.255	1.07	3.33	3.94	1.9				
Frank German	TAM	A+	21	4	4	0	16	15	76	70	9	4.1	9.7	82	46%	.314	1.38	3.79	5.94	-0.9				
Luis Gil	CSC	A	21	4	5	0	17	17	83	60	1	4.2	12.1	112	50%	.304	1.19	2.39	3.89	1.3				
	TAM	A+	21	1	0	0	3	3	13	11	0	5.5	7.6	11	40%	.297	1.46	4.85	5.60	-0.1				
Yoendrys Gomez	PUL	Rk+	19	4	2	0	6	6	29²	26	1	3.0	8.5	28	45%	.309	1.21	2.12	3.68	0.8				
	CSC	A	19	0	3	0	6	6	26²	28	2	3.0	8.4	25	43%	.353	1.39	6.07	5.78	-0.2				
Ben Heller	SWB	AAA	27	0	0	1	9	4	11	5	0	2.5	10.6	13	55%	.227	0.73	0.82	1.77	0.5				
	NYA	MLB	27	0	0	0	6	0	7¹	6	1	3.7	11.0	9	50%	.333	1.23	1.23	5.06	0.0	95.2	49	13.7	37.9
Michael King	TRN	AA	24	0	1	0	3	2	12²	20	1	1.4	5.7	8	51%	.396	1.74	9.95	6.92	-0.3				
	SWB	AAA	24	3	1	0	4	3	23²	20	3	2.3	10.6	28	48%	.293	1.10	4.18	2.99	0.8				
	NYA	MLB	24	0	0	0	1	0	2	2	0	0.0	4.5	1	38%	.250	1.00	0.00	5.19	0.0	93.1	65.9	2.4	44.3
Brooks Kriske	TAM	A+	25	1	1	1	7	0	12	4	0	3.8	12.0	16	43%	.190	0.75	0.00	2.61	0.3				
	TRN	AA	25	2	2	11	36	0	48²	30	3	4.3	11.8	64	32%	.257	1.09	2.59	3.88	0.4				
Brady Lail	TRN	AA	25	3	1	1	14	1	31	18	1	3.5	13.6	47	45%	.279	0.97	1.74	2.73	0.7				
	SWB	AAA	25	1	1	0	11	0	15²	19	3	1.7	9.8	17	40%	.356	1.40	7.47	4.91	0.2				
	NYA	MLB	25	0	0	0	1	0	2¹	2	1	3.4	6.8	2	57%	.167	1.12	10.12	6.01	0.0	92.7	45.7	13	35
Jonathan Loaisiga	SWB	AAA	24	0	2	0	5	4	15²	14	3	2.9	10.9	19	49%	.275	1.21	6.32	3.20	0.5				
	NYA	MLB	24	2	2	0	15	4	31²	31	6	4.5	10.5	37	46%	.316	1.48	4.55	5.33	0.1	99.0	56.4	14.9	44.3
Tyler Lyons	IND	AAA	31	4	3	3	35	0	45²	34	4	3.2	10.8	55	40%	.286	1.09	3.35	3.31	1.3				
	PIT	MLB	31	1	1	0	3	0	4	6	1	6.8	11.2	5	33%	.455	2.25	11.25	5.17	0.0	91.9	45.7	11.4	45.7
	NYA	MLB	31	0	1	0	11	0	8²	7	3	2.1	12.5	12	32%	.250	1.04	4.15	4.91	0.0	91.0	37.2	19	47.3
Luis Medina	CSC	A	20	1	8	0	20	20	93	86	9	6.5	11.1	115	47%	.339	1.65	6.00	7.09	-2.1				
	TAM	A+	20	0	0	0	2	2	10²	7	0	2.5	10.1	12	71%	.250	0.94	0.84	3.52	0.2				
Nick Nelson	TRN	AA	23	7	2	0	13	12	65	48	4	4.8	11.5	83	31%	.308	1.28	2.35	4.62	0.3				
	SWB	AAA	23	1	1	0	4	4	21	20	2	3.0	10.3	24	45%	.321	1.29	4.71	2.75	0.8				
Clarke Schmidt	TAM	A+	23	4	5	0	13	12	63¹	59	2	3.4	9.8	69	57%	.331	1.31	3.84	4.13	0.7				
	TRN	AA	23	2	0	0	3	3	19	14	1	0.5	9.0	19	45%	.260	0.79	2.37	3.84	0.3				
Stephen Tarpley	SWB	AAA	26	5	1	3	18	2	31²	25	3	3.7	9.7	34	66%	.268	1.20	3.13	2.90	1.0				
	NYA	MLB	26	1	0	2	21	1	24²	34	6	5.5	12.4	34	36%	.444	1.99	6.93	4.15	0.3	94.7	51.1	13.1	43.4
Nick Tropeano	SLC	AAA	28	4	6	0	17	15	79²	90	12	3.5	9.6	85	36%	.351	1.52	5.87	4.25	1.9				
	LAA	MLB	28	0	1	0	3	1	13²	18	6	4.0	6.6	10	25%	.286	1.76	9.88	9.14	-0.5	92.6	46.5	12.1	45.8
Miguel Yajure	TAM	A+	21	8	6	0	22	18	127²	110	5	2.0	8.6	122	55%	.296	1.08	2.26	3.82	1.8				
	TRN	AA	21	1	0	0	2	2	11	9	0	1.6	9.0	11	36%	.290	1.00	0.82	5.08	0.0				

Albert Abreu still comes with quite a bit of risk. And while questions of his long-term durability and a history of injuries cast a shadow, a fastball that can scrape 99 makes him more than worth it. ⊗ **Jake Barrett** gave up five runs to the Mariners in one of his two major-league appearances of the season. There's no joke here. How do you give up five runs to the Mariners? ⊗ Currently on track to become a mid-rotation/back-end starter, **Roansy Contreras** is another Yankee arm already flashing major-league level stuff, but durability is the biggest question mark given his frame. ⊗ **Frank German** wields a mid-90's fastball alongside a pair of solid secondary offerings. Sound familiar? The Yankees are practically creating these guys from thin air and hoarding them. ⊗ **Luis Gil** is a big strikeout guy. His fastball sits at 95-97 mph from a seemingly effortless delivery, but his other pitches aren't quite there yet largely due to lack of command. ⊗ At 6-foot-3, 175 pounds with room to add onto the frame, **Yoendrys Gomez**'s physical presence on the mound is a daunting one, as is his rapidly improving changeup. ⊗ **Ben Heller** worked his way back from Tommy John surgery in September and even got to be on the postseason roster for a few days after he replaced CC Sabathia on the ALCS roster when he went down. ⊗ **Michael King** has a fairly impressive mix of average pitches in his arsenal. A four-seamer, cutter, change and slider all play second fiddle to his best offering: a sinker. King could be a back-end starter, but his best hope is to get close to Zack Britton and pick his brain. ⊗ **Brooks Kriske** entered 2019 as an afterthought, a senior sign reliever from 2016 that hadn't pitched much as a pro due to ill-timed Tommy John surgery. After a season of minors dominance off a fastball up to 98 MPH, a plus slider and an interesting new splitter, he exited it as a 40-man roster member and real prospect. ⊗ In his major-league debut, **Brady Lail** recorded his first strikeout with his family excitedly cheering him on from the stands. He was immediately sent back down to Triple-A following the outing, never to return. ⊗ Former top prospect **Jonathan Loaisiga** didn't seem nearly as sharp or promising this season. The stuff is there as he flirted with triple digits, but location is everything and neither his current level of command nor his inability to stay healthy will separate him in a system full of ripe, young arms. ⊗ **Luis Medina** has all the raw stuff of a future star—a plus-plus fastball that frequents 98, and two plus off-speed pitches to go along with it—none of which will matter if he can't throw them for strikes. ⊗ **Nick Nelson**'s high-quality curve is both a set-up and putaway pitch, his mid-90's fastball garners swings and misses with late life and his changeup and slider are each solid enough to round out his repertoire. ⊗ While it's likely he ends up as a reliever, **Clarke Schmidt** is slowly but surely working up to his full potential. His strikeout numbers are impressive, and pitched into the seventh inning in three of his last four starts; not too shabby for his first season of work after Tommy John surgery. ⊗ **Stephen Tarpley** is just a LOOGY in a world where they're becoming obsolete and righties have anagrammed his name into El Party via a career .378/.474/.634 line against him. ⊗ In another era and with different elbow ligaments, **Nick Tropeano** might have been something. As it is, both his pre- and post-TJ selves gave up a few too many walks, and way too many fly balls. In 2019, these traits led, first, to Salt Lake City, and ultimately, out of the organization altogether. ⊗ **Miguel Yajure** has flown under the radar in a Yankees system deep with pitching of all sorts, but he's a potential future rotation piece, now up to the mid-90s with command and good feel for a changeup. He was protected from Rule 5 despite a crowded 40-man situation.

OAKLAND ATHLETICS

Essay by Clarissa Young

Player comments by Brendan Gawlowski and BP staff

One of the more offbeat plays of the 2019 season happened on a Thursday afternoon in Kansas City, on August 29th. The Oakland A's held an 8-7 lead in the top of the ninth with runners on second and third when Royals third baseman Cheslor Cuthbert chased a pop-up into foul territory, making a leaning catch on the top step of the visitor's dugout before momentum carried him the rest of the way down.

It was a good catch and a bad play. The batter, Corban Joseph, was retired on the foul out, but umpire Chris Segal, either anticipating confusion or just generally emphatic as umpires are, vigorously motioned for the runner on third to score. Cuthbert stopped dead in his tracks; Seth Brown trotted home and was received with noncommittal high fives.

The rule behind this sequence of events, 5.06(b)(3)(C), states: "If a fielder, after having made a legal catch, should step or fall into any out-of-play area, the ball is dead and each runner shall advance one base, without liability to be put out, from his last legally touched base at the time the fielder entered such out-of-play area." The A's got an insurance run out of the deal, and they needed it, since the Royals later scored what would have been the tying run in the bottom of the ninth.

It's important that this game happened in Kansas City. Had it been played in Oakland, Cuthbert might have gone the rest of his career unaware of Rule 5.06(b)(3)(C). He might have made the equivalent catch fully upright with several steps to go before meeting the dugout, thanks to the Oakland Coliseum's generous foul territory.

Happily tangled in the spirit of the game is the romantic notion, unique to baseball among sports, that architecture can and should wield influence. You can see it at field level in Fenway's Green Monster, Yankee Stadium's short porch, the catwalks and white roof at The Trop, and Oakland's foul ground. While Major League Baseball's rule book is firm on the sacred 90-foot sides of the diamond, it offers only rough suggestions when it comes to perimeter dimensions and miscellaneous park quirks. It follows that architecture also impacts baseball on a tactical level, as coaches and front

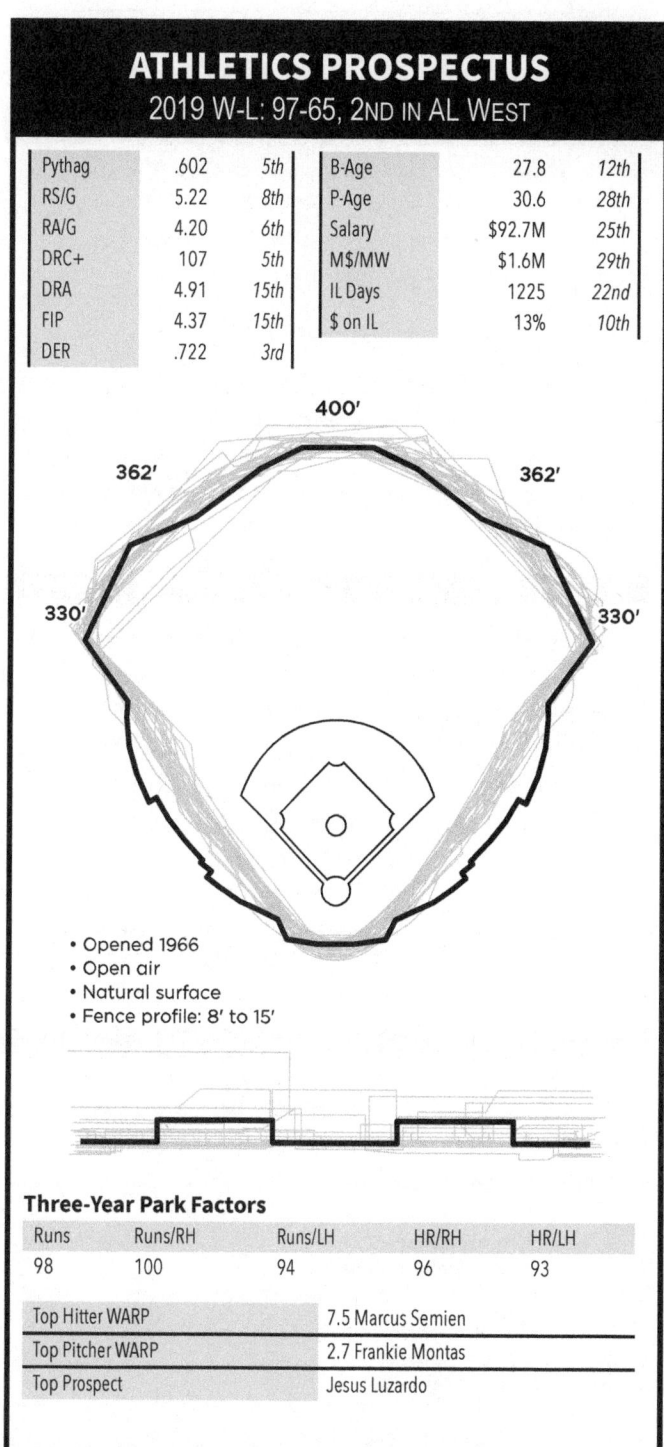

ATHLETICS PROSPECTUS
2019 W-L: 97-65, 2ND IN AL WEST

Pythag	.602	5th	B-Age	27.8	12th
RS/G	5.22	8th	P-Age	30.6	28th
RA/G	4.20	6th	Salary	$92.7M	25th
DRC+	107	5th	M$/MW	$1.6M	29th
DRA	4.91	15th	IL Days	1225	22nd
FIP	4.37	15th	$ on IL	13%	10th
DER	.722	3rd			

400'

362'   362'

330'   330'

- Opened 1966
- Open air
- Natural surface
- Fence profile: 8' to 15'

Three-Year Park Factors

Runs	Runs/RH	Runs/LH	HR/RH	HR/LH
98	100	94	96	93

Top Hitter WARP	7.5 Marcus Semien
Top Pitcher WARP	2.7 Frankie Montas
Top Prospect	Jesus Luzardo

2019 Hit List Ranking

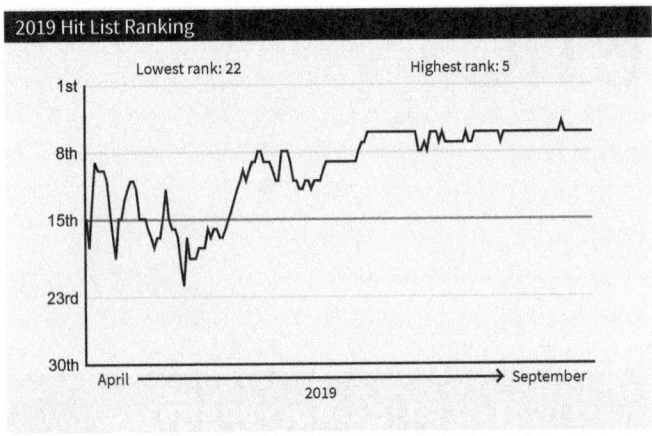

Lowest rank: 22   Highest rank: 5

Committed Payroll (in millions)

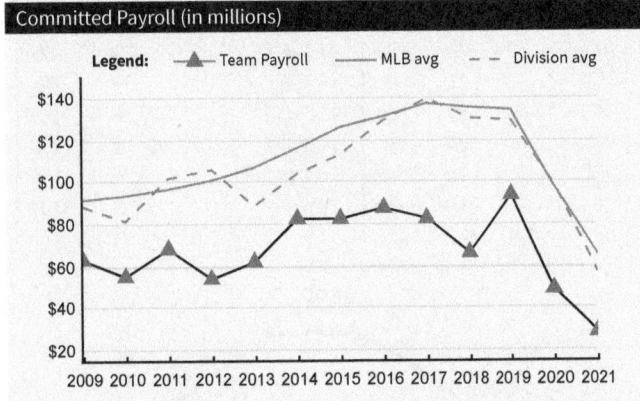

Legend: ▲ Team Payroll —— MLB avg – – Division avg

Farm System Ranking

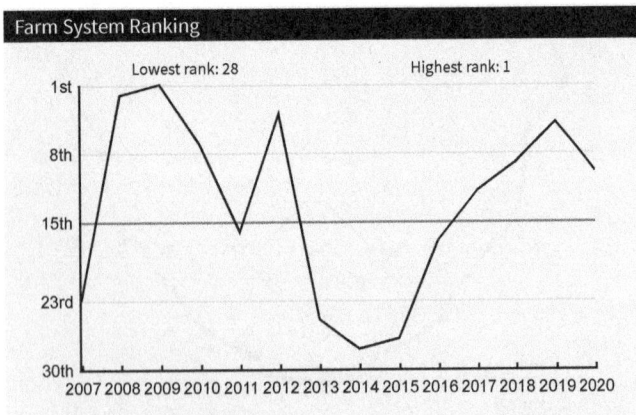

Lowest rank: 28   Highest rank: 1

Personnel

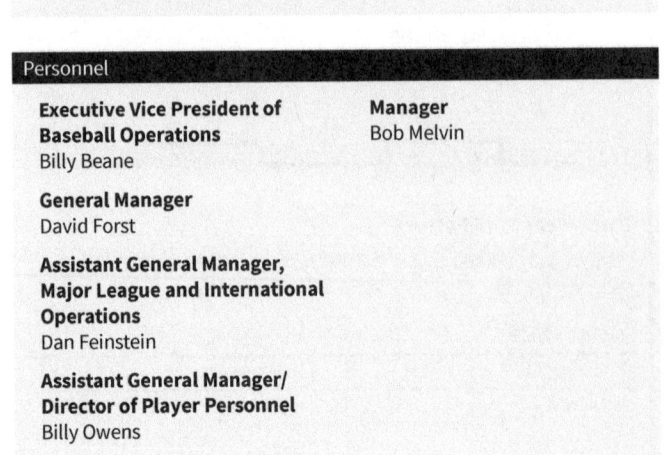

Executive Vice President of Baseball Operations
Billy Beane

General Manager
David Forst

Assistant General Manager, Major League and International Operations
Dan Feinstein

Assistant General Manager/ Director of Player Personnel
Billy Owens

Manager
Bob Melvin

office staff must decide which players' skills are a match for their own confines or potentially disastrous in those they encounter on the road.

The win at Kauffman Stadium was one of 97 on the year, and it looms significant—as all unlikely wins tend to—given the single-game margin that kept the A's above the Tampa Bay Rays in the final American League Wild Card standings. Over 54,000 fans gathered in the Coliseum for the play-in game, setting a major-league record for Wild Card game attendance. They even spilled over into Mount Davis, that aftermarket eye-sore that wooed the Raiders back to town in 1995, obscured a wide view of the Oakland hills, and now remains mostly tarped in the name of "intimacy," a softer quality invoked because it's more appealing than "artificial scarcity."

This night held all the conditions for home-field advantage when it's been relentlessly hammered home what a disadvantage the Coliseum is and how shaky the team's presence in Oakland is as a result. Plans, renderings, stalled talks, and even lawsuits surrounding the pursuit of a new stadium landed as syncopated drum beats throughout the season. Although the A's lost their third Wild Card game that evening, the atmosphere was devout and defiant, a realization of the building's original premise with acknowledgment of all it's been through along the way.

The Oakland–Alameda County Coliseum complex was completed in 1966, garnering praise for its elegant geometry and sensible, multi-sport functionality. Its raw concrete exterior was an extension of the earnest post-war spirit of renewal seen in other Brutalist buildings of the era. You can watch old black and white news footage of a local reporter comparing it to the Roman Colosseum "if you look quickly as you drive by it," a load-bearing caveat that does nothing to detract from the apparent optimism.

Equally relevant to the design, concrete was cheap. Publicly financed for $25 million (still a bargain at roughly $213 million in today's dollars), the complex comprising both the Coliseum and the adjacent arena was designed by Myron Goldsmith from Skidmore, Owings & Merrill, the firm responsible for skyscrapers including the Willis Tower (previously Sears Tower) in Chicago, One World Trade Center in New York, and the Burj Khalifa in Dubai, currently the tallest structure in the world.

The Coliseum was designed with a modest profile, sunken into the earth below grade, literally rooted in Oakland, if you will. Just over 50 years later, with the Coliseum as the last remaining "concrete doughnut" replete with unpredictable plumbing, sparse attendance, and an unknown number of resident possums, the A's have had to find new ways to embrace that grounded quality and draw on the community they're nestled in.

One of the main elements distinguishing architecture from fine art is function. A structure can't simply be beautiful; it must be engineered and designed for practical use. In changing the prescribed function, you also change the criteria by which the structure is assessed. An office building does not make for a good church sanctuary, no matter how ardently capitalism tries to convince us otherwise.

By 2019, the A's had replaced traditional season ticket plans with "A's Access" membership, a natural fit for a team with seats to spare and an audience accustomed to subscription models. For a reasonable price, benefits include general admission to all home games plus discounts on concessions and merchandise. Where the Coliseum lacked the bevy of dining options surrounding other urban stadiums, the A's invited local food trucks to be part of "Championship Plaza," a pre-game gathering spot just outside the park.

All of this, coupled with the everyday nature of baseball's schedule, made it possible and desirable to spend a lot more time at the ballpark. In this way, the A's altered the Coliseum's function; by making the game-going experience something less lofty and precious, they relaxed the standards one might otherwise apply to the built environment. This is to say: it's harder to complain when you've paid $7 for a hot dog and beer, get to watch a 97-win team, and will be back later in the week (if not the very next day).

"The Coliseum is baseball's last dive bar," wrote Jack Nicas in a *New York Times* essay. Neighborhood bars, along with rec centers, places of worship, and barbershops, are common examples of what the urban sociologist Ray Oldenburg termed the "third place": "a setting beyond home and work (the 'first' and 'second' places, respectively) in which people relax in good company and do so on a regular basis." As a widely-accessible home away from home, why not add the Coliseum to that list?

These informal meeting places, Oldenburg argues, are essential for building community and even for maintaining the grass roots of democracy. Anchored by central figures the urbanist Jane Jacobs called "public characters" (e.g. the outfield bleacher regulars with their drums, banners, and bells), people of different backgrounds can share in a common purpose and cultivate a sense of ownership. In this environment it's easy to become fiercely protective of the Coliseum, to love the humble surroundings and wear them as a badge of pride. "I like that it's not glamorized," Khris Davis told the *San Francisco Chronicle's* John Shea in 2016. "You've got to change your attitude, you've got to come with the right attitude here every day to perform."

It's especially easy to feel this way when the team is playing well. Despite the Coliseum's reputation as a pitcher's park, seven Athletics hit 20 or more home runs in 2019: Matt Olson, Matt Chapman, Marcus Semien, Mark Canha, Ramón Laureano, Davis, and Jurickson Profar. Olson and Chapman won Gold Gloves as part of an indispensable defense. Semien had a banner year with 7.5 WARP and finished third in AL MVP voting. All-Star Liam Hendriks offered late-inning security with a 1.80 ERA, and Jesus Luzardo was a crystalline vision of the future in a handful of electric appearances.

But in worse times, say, in the immediate aftermath of a Wild Card loss, the Coliseum seems like an emblem of this franchise's inability to break into the league's upper tier, if not partly the cause of it. Architecture's influence is not only physical and tactical but emotional. Baseball is a game played and watched by humans, and it's difficult to feel like a first-rate club when the ceiling is leaking, when your surroundings feel fragile, irrelevant or impermanent.

In *The Architecture of Happiness*, Alain de Botton writes, "Belief in the significance of architecture is premised on the notion that we are, for better or for worse, different people in different places—and on the conviction that it is architecture's task to render vivid to us who we might ideally be."

First shared in November 2018 and since modified according to public feedback, renderings of the A's proposed waterfront park at Howard Terminal are boldly contemporary, fitting for a franchise that has always identified as audacious and a bit different. Designed by Bjarke Ingels Group, the plans are a welcome departure from the now-ubiquitous "retro" stadiums, some of which paired red brick and steel with so many custom amenities and motifs that they ironically appear postmodern rather than classic.

It's an open design, playing foil to the Coliseum's walled fortress, and its airiness also symbolizes what architecture critic Paul Goldberger observes as "the current trend of extending a team's sphere of influence out beyond the ballpark gates and of trying to create a new neighborhood in which the ballpark can sit." To that end, the plans include surrounding high-rises and other businesses. "Bigger than baseball," is how the team described it.

All of this is nice enough, but is it really the design itself, the cosmetic upgrades and touted features like an elevated rooftop park that has stoked fans' desires? Or is it powerful because it grants permission to dream of deep playoff runs, contract extensions and free agent signings; a vision of the actualized self, as de Botton describes?

It's both, and it's more. Architecture's final realm of influence is financial, particularly so when it comes to sports stadiums. Without a good dose of luck, the A's actually can't succeed without the revenue a new stadium brings. This became a pressing concern when the CBA introduced a schedule of revenue sharing restrictions for the team in 2016, and in 2020, the A's will be fully disqualified from revenue sharing. Anticipated contract extensions wait in the wings.

The prolific Bay Area architect and teacher William Wurster saw architecture as "the picture frame, not the picture." With top prospects ready to hit the majors next season and a foundation of home-grown talent already soaring, the "picture" for the Oakland Athletics is fine indeed, though it longs for some gilding around the edges.

—*Clarissa Young is a former author of Baseball Prospectus.*

HITTERS

Austin Allen C   Born: 01/16/94   Age: 26   Bats: L   Throws: R   Height: 6'2"   Weight: 220   Origin: Round 4, 2015 Draft (#117 overall)

YEAR	TEAM	LVL	AGE	PA	R	2B	3B	HR	RBI	BB	K	SB	CS	AVG/OBP/SLG	DRC+	VORP	BABIP	BRR	FRAA	WARP
2017	LEL	A+	23	516	71	31	1	22	81	44	109	0	1	.283/.353/.497	139	31.0	.326	-5.5	C(85): -5.4, 1B(1): 0.0	2.8
2018	SAN	AA	24	498	59	31	0	22	56	37	97	0	3	.290/.351/.506	142	34.8	.325	-2.1	C(91): 14.6, 1B(19): -1.5	5.2
2019	ELP	AAA	25	298	52	27	0	21	67	22	56	0	0	.330/.379/.663	128	25.1	.345	-2.5	C(60): 7.2, 1B(2): -0.1	2.8
2019	SDN	MLB	25	71	4	4	0	0	3	6	21	0	0	.215/.282/.277	62	-0.1	.318	0.0	C(19): -0.2, 1B(2): 0.1	0.0
2020	OAK	MLB	26	245	27	10	0	10	32	15	64	0	0	.238/.292/.419	90	7.8	.286	-0.5	C 0	0.8

Comparables: Trey Mancini, Ryan Cordell, Bruce Maxwell

YEAR	TEAM	P. COUNT	FRM RUNS	BLK RUNS	THRW RUNS	TOT RUNS
2018	SAN	12612	8.3	1.0	3.0	12.0
2019	ELP	8806	6.9	0.0	-1.2	5.5
2019	SDN	2293	-0.1	-0.4	0.0	-0.5
2020	OAK	9269	-0.3	-0.5	-0.1	-0.9

Joan Jett can afford not to give a damn about her bad reputation, but in Allen's case his may wind up costing him millions. After all, what's not to like about a lefty-hitting catcher with a career minor-league batting line of .296/.354/.490? The fact that he's considered a lefty-hitting "catcher," that's what. The scare quotes come courtesy of scouts who have long questioned Allen's abilities behind the dish, a reputation that the young slugger certainly earned but has worked hard to change, without getting much traction. Despite showing well in our framing, blocking and overall fielding metrics over his last two seasons in the high minors, Allen is still branded a Doumit-class catcher/DH rather than a Pierzynski-class bat-first receiver. Given a fair shot, he'd likely zoom past the collective .237/.308/.406 line posted by big-league catchers last year, and with even sub-par defense Allen would be an improvement for many teams.

Nick Allen SS   Born: 10/08/98   Age: 21   Bats: R   Throws: R   Height: 5'9"   Weight: 166   Origin: Round 3, 2017 Draft (#81 overall)

YEAR	TEAM	LVL	AGE	PA	R	2B	3B	HR	RBI	BB	K	SB	CS	AVG/OBP/SLG	DRC+	VORP	BABIP	BRR	FRAA	WARP
2017	ATH	RK	18	154	26	3	2	1	14	13	28	7	3	.254/.322/.326	99	6.8	.312	1.1	SS(33): 2.5	1.0
2018	BLT	A	19	512	51	17	6	0	34	34	85	24	8	.239/.301/.302	74	15.2	.289	3.7	SS(121): 5.2	1.8
2019	STO	A+	20	328	45	22	5	3	25	28	52	13	5	.292/.363/.434	135	17.6	.348	-4.4	SS(45): 4.7, 2B(24): -1.6	2.1
2020	OAK	MLB	21	251	20	11	1	3	21	15	56	5	2	.222/.277/.319	60	-5.0	.281	0.2	SS 3, 2B 0	-0.2

Comparables: Ehire Adrianza, Tyler Wade, Jose Pirela

Allen took a step forward last year, which is something to savor now because you won't be reading many more happy stories from this farm system. Already one of the best defenders in the minors, Allen had a surprisingly productive year at the plate. He hit nearly .300 as a 20-year-old in the Cal League, with respectable plate discipline and even a few homers. Scouts are still concerned that advanced pitchers will knock the bat out of his hands, but he looks more likely to crack a big-league lineup now than he did at this time last year. If he can, the A's will have a good player on their hands, because Allen is the total package at shortstop. He has above-average range, a plus arm, good instincts, and excellent hands. He'll have no trouble staying at the position, and he could be a 70 defender at maturity. Don't be too concerned if he struggles at Double-A in 2020: he's moving fast and is ahead of schedule.

Lazaro Armenteros OF   Born: 05/22/99   Age: 21   Bats: R   Throws: R   Height: 6'0"   Weight: 182   Origin: International Free Agent, 2016

YEAR	TEAM	LVL	AGE	PA	R	2B	3B	HR	RBI	BB	K	SB	CS	AVG/OBP/SLG	DRC+	VORP	BABIP	BRR	FRAA	WARP
2017	DAT	RK	18	26	6	0	0	0	1	3	9	2	2	.167/.385/.167	39	1.8	.300	0.9	CF(6): 1.5	0.2
2017	ATH	RK	18	181	24	9	4	4	22	16	48	10	1	.288/.376/.474	110	14.5	.387	2.8	LF(28): 4.2, CF(2): -0.5	1.1
2018	BLT	A	19	340	43	8	2	8	39	36	115	8	6	.277/.374/.401	121	21.6	.427	2.1	LF(69): -0.7	1.6
2019	STO	A+	20	538	65	22	5	17	61	73	227	22	6	.222/.336/.403	102	18.0	.395	2.4	LF(112): -1.3, CF(7): -0.1	1.4
2020	OAK	MLB	21	251	20	10	1	4	21	19	113	2	1	.191/.264/.295	49	-8.5	.357	0.0	LF 1, CF 0	-0.7

Comparables: Tyler O'Neill, Ryan McMahon, Nick Williams

Armenteros is a tooled-up 20-year-old from Cuba with obvious raw power, good speed, and a 25 percent whiff rate in the soft toss drill. Pedro Serrano comps fly thick and fast around this type of player, but in Armenteros, we may have found a case where it's unfair *to Serrano*. A big hack, poor pitch recognition and an utter inability to hit bendy things neutralized a man who did plenty of damage when he did connect. He hit 17 bombs and was actually a tick better than league average at the plate—not too shabby at his age in High-A. Still, even as a youngin', even in this boom-or-bust era of baseball, you can't strike out 42 percent of the time and project as a big leaguer. The tools are tantalizing, but short of an intervention from Jobu, he'll get carved by upper-level arms.

Franklin Barreto 2B   Born: 02/27/96   Age: 24   Bats: R   Throws: R   Height: 5'10"   Weight: 200   Origin: International Free Agent, 2012

YEAR	TEAM	LVL	AGE	PA	R	2B	3B	HR	RBI	BB	K	SB	CS	AVG/OBP/SLG	DRC+	VORP	BABIP	BRR	FRAA	WARP
2017	NAS	AAA	21	510	63	19	7	15	54	27	141	15	8	.290/.339/.456	104	34.7	.384	0.3	SS(83): -3.3, 2B(25): -2.6	1.9
2017	OAK	MLB	21	76	10	1	2	2	6	5	33	2	0	.197/.250/.352	55	0.4	.333	0.7	SS(11): 0.3, 2B(10): 0.2	0.0
2018	NAS	AAA	22	333	54	16	1	18	46	39	106	5	2	.259/.357/.514	127	35.6	.337	3.5	2B(60): -2.2, SS(11): 0.4	2.3
2018	OAK	MLB	22	75	10	4	0	5	16	1	29	0	0	.233/.253/.493	76	-0.8	.308	-1.1	2B(26): -1.7, SS(2): 0.0	-0.3
2019	LVG	AAA	23	424	88	29	5	19	65	42	113	15	1	.295/.374/.552	108	31.7	.374	2.2	2B(47): -5.1, SS(30): 0.1	1.8
2019	OAK	MLB	23	58	6	2	0	2	5	1	23	1	0	.123/.138/.263	50	-1.6	.156	0.5	2B(17): -0.2, SS(5): -0.2	-0.1
2020	OAK	MLB	24	455	46	20	2	14	52	30	149	10	4	.220/.281/.383	75	2.7	.304	-0.5	2B -5, SS 0	-0.2

Comparables: Javier Báez, Adalberto Mondesi, Roy McMillan

It seems an age since the A's shipped Josh Donaldson to Toronto for a package headlined by Baretto and Brett Lawrie. Normally, we could toss on another sentence about how sad it is to see a young buck's career come to this and move on to the next blurb, but this is supposed to be about Barreto. Even though he's been in the public consciousness for five years, he's still just 24, and he's never really had an extended audition at the highest level. You'd rather be a top prospect than a post-hype sleeper, but the tools seem mostly intact and Barreto's career still has a pulse. He does himself no favors with auditions like he gave in Oakland last summer, but he needs to get a few months of sustained playing time before we can write him off entirely.

Austin Beck CF   Born: 11/21/98   Age: 21   Bats: R   Throws: R   Height: 6'1"   Weight: 200   Origin: Round 1, 2017 Draft (#6 overall)

YEAR	TEAM	LVL	AGE	PA	R	2B	3B	HR	RBI	BB	K	SB	CS	AVG/OBP/SLG	DRC+	VORP	BABIP	BRR	FRAA	WARP
2017	ATH	RK	18	174	23	7	4	2	28	17	51	7	1	.211/.293/.349	59	2.7	.294	1.8	CF(33): 1.2	0.2
2018	BLT	A	19	534	58	29	4	2	60	30	117	8	6	.296/.335/.383	105	14.9	.377	-4.8	CF(113): 2.0	1.6
2019	STO	A+	20	367	40	22	4	8	49	24	126	2	2	.251/.302/.411	92	7.5	.372	-0.1	CF(69): -0.3, RF(10): 2.7	1.1
2020	OAK	MLB	21	251	20	12	1	3	22	16	95	1	1	.216/.270/.324	57	-6.2	.347	-0.3	CF -2, RF 0	-0.8

Comparables: Willy García, Trayvon Robinson, Gabriel Guerrero

More than most teams, the A's draft for upside. Sometimes that gamble lands you Sonny Gray; sometimes your first-rounder quits to play football instead. Beck, Oakland's top pick in 2017, fits the general pattern. As an amateur, a knee injury initially kept him below the radar as a draft prospect, but his stock surged when he finally got healthy and terrorized overmatched North Carolina high schoolers as a senior. There's plenty of risk in any late-bloomer, but with huge bat speed and an athletic, powerful frame, Beck offered enticing potential in a draft largely lacking it.

Two-and-a-half years later though, the selection seems like a reach. Beck had a bumpy transition to pro ball, and the 20-year-old has yet to hit for power in games. There's plenty of time for things to turn around, and this profile—toolsy, light amateur resume—is often a slow burn. As it is though, Beck was a below-average hitter in the Cal League last summer and he's probably more of a corner guy than a center fielder. He needs a big 2020 to avoid the dreaded tweener label.

Marcos Brito SS   Born: 03/06/00   Age: 20   Bats: B   Throws: R   Height: 6'0"   Weight: 165   Origin: International Free Agent, 2016

YEAR	TEAM	LVL	AGE	PA	R	2B	3B	HR	RBI	BB	K	SB	CS	AVG/OBP/SLG	DRC+	VORP	BABIP	BRR	FRAA	WARP
2017	DAT	RK	17	62	3	1	0	0	8	13	8	5	0	.178/.339/.200	134	1.7	.195	0.3	2B(6): -0.6, SS(5): -0.9	0.2
2017	ATH	RK	17	194	30	4	2	1	17	21	42	4	1	.234/.320/.298	64	0.2	.302	1.2	2B(34): -4.9, SS(5): -1.0	-0.5
2018	VER	A-	18	241	29	5	1	1	20	27	50	7	6	.241/.325/.288	108	-0.9	.309	-3.6	2B(52): -0.6, SS(1): -0.4	0.4
2019	BLT	A	19	228	21	8	0	2	13	22	67	3	4	.181/.260/.250	62	-4.1	.257	0.6	SS(60): -7.6	-0.7
2020	OAK	MLB	20	251	20	10	1	3	20	24	82	2	1	.199/.279/.289	55	-6.9	.297	-0.2	2B -1, SS -2	-1.0

Comparables: Deivy Grullon, Willi Castro, Juniel Querecuto

Billed as a second baseman who could hit, Brito was signed out of the Dominican Republic for $1.1 million back in 2016. Three years later, he's still a second baseman but he hasn't fulfilled the second part of the bargain. The switch-hitter struggled badly in 2019: He didn't hit lefties, didn't hit righties, didn't hit for power and, well, looking at the strikeout totals, it doesn't appear he hit much of anything at all. Brito won't turn 20 until Spring Training, so he has time to turn things around, but he was overmatched in A-ball and it's a long row to hoe from there.

Mark Canha OF   Born: 02/15/89   Age: 31   Bats: R   Throws: R   Height: 6'2"   Weight: 212   Origin: Round 7, 2010 Draft (#227 overall)

YEAR	TEAM	LVL	AGE	PA	R	2B	3B	HR	RBI	BB	K	SB	CS	AVG/OBP/SLG	DRC+	VORP	BABIP	BRR	FRAA	WARP
2017	NAS	AAA	28	317	52	25	3	12	50	34	62	4	0	.283/.373/.529	136	33.0	.323	3.3	RF(61): -2.7, CF(8): 0.9	2.3
2017	OAK	MLB	28	187	16	13	1	5	14	7	56	2	0	.208/.262/.382	67	-2.8	.274	0.3	RF(22): -1.0, LF(20): -0.9	-0.6
2018	OAK	MLB	29	411	60	22	0	17	52	34	88	1	2	.249/.328/.449	115	18.8	.282	-0.3	CF(62): -5.9, LF(51): 1.4	1.5
2019	OAK	MLB	30	497	80	16	3	26	58	67	107	3	2	.273/.396/.517	135	36.9	.308	1.3	CF(56): -3.8, RF(27): 1.9	3.5
2020	OAK	MLB	31	595	76	25	2	27	83	61	138	6	2	.244/.343/.460	113	26.4	.282	0.8	LF 7, CF -1	3.1

Comparables: Franklin Stubbs, Lee May, Mike Laga

Canha is presumably too busy enjoying life in The Show to give two rips about his Baseball Prospectus card. Nonetheless, it's unfortunate that all of his Annual comments reference the occasion Oakland took him in the Rule 5 draft, as that legacy seemingly defines every twist and turn in his career. Each milestone is thus a surprise (he was a Rule 5 guy once, you know!) and each setback explained away by a nod to his prior fungibility. It all feels reductive and unfair, and has no place in any discussion about his 3.5 WARP breakout 2019 season. Another thing Canha has no control of: the ball. Its disproportionately positive impact on players like him—those with middling power who put the ball in the air frequently—will be used as a justification for his career-high in home runs, slugging, DRC+, and a slew of other offensive categories. It belies an improvement that occurred that was very much in Canha's control, though: his walk rate. A five percentage point increased established a career high. A livelier ball can explain a lot, but Canha's improvement was as much internal as it was external, and whether the ball retains its 2019 traits or not, Canha's new normal is pretty good.

Matt Chapman 3B   Born: 04/28/93   Age: 27   Bats: R   Throws: R   Height: 6'0"   Weight: 220   Origin: Round 1, 2014 Draft (#25 overall)

YEAR	TEAM	LVL	AGE	PA	R	2B	3B	HR	RBI	BB	K	SB	CS	AVG/OBP/SLG	DRC+	VORP	BABIP	BRR	FRAA	WARP
2017	NAS	AAA	24	204	30	6	2	16	30	25	63	5	4	.257/.348/.589	130	20.8	.293	-0.1	3B(49): 7.2	2.2
2017	OAK	MLB	24	326	39	23	2	14	40	32	92	0	3	.234/.313/.472	97	14.9	.290	-1.0	3B(84): 12.6	2.2
2018	OAK	MLB	25	616	100	42	6	24	68	58	146	1	2	.278/.356/.508	125	47.9	.338	3.8	3B(145): 15.6	6.2
2019	OAK	MLB	26	670	102	36	3	36	91	73	147	1	1	.249/.342/.506	120	43.8	.270	-3.2	3B(156): 12.9	5.2
2020	OAK	MLB	27	630	80	33	3	33	94	64	146	4	2	.235/.321/.481	108	22.3	.259	0.4	3B 17	4.1

Comparables: Pedro Álvarez, Jake Lamb, Troy Glaus

The best player you never see on Sunday Night Baseball, Chapman again topped the five-WARP mark in 2019. The game is remarkably flush in third basemen these days, and while it's easy to lose a good one in the shuffle, it shouldn't be Chapman. At the plate, he's a formidable hitter, and he pressed through a July swoon to notch his second straight season of a 120 DRC+ or better. Defensively, he's developed a signature all to his own, stretching out into an exaggerated, wide-legged crouch as the pitch comes in and efficiently leaping out of it in whatever direction the ball travels. He's a star, full stop, and the kind of player who can make a kid really *want* to play baseball.

The nagging question A's fans won't want to consider is how much longer their star will stay in town. He's entering his third full season, and with a competitive team and a salary barely over the minimum, he's not going anywhere in 2020. But the A's almost religiously make a habit of observing Branch Rickey's wisdom of preferring to trade a man a year too early rather than a year too late; there's a decent chance Chapman's Oakland career is more than half over. A's fans should enjoy their man while they can.

Logan Davidson SS   Born: 12/26/97   Age: 22   Bats: B   Throws: R   Height: 6'3"   Weight: 185   Origin: Round 1, 2019 Draft (#29 overall)

YEAR	TEAM	LVL	AGE	PA	R	2B	3B	HR	RBI	BB	K	SB	CS	AVG/OBP/SLG	DRC+	VORP	BABIP	BRR	FRAA	WARP
2019	VER	A-	21	238	42	7	0	4	12	31	55	5	0	.239/.345/.332	133	16.0	.308	1.5	SS(49): 11.8	3.0
2020	OAK	MLB	22	251	22	11	0	5	24	16	80	2	1	.214/.268/.333	61	-4.6	.300	0.0	SS 4	-0.1

Comparables: Tyler Greene, Taylor Featherston, Trea Turner

Oakland's first-round pick last summer, Davidson is a modern, bat-first shortstop. At 6-foot-3, he's a big guy for the position, and both his arm and range suggest that he'll be competent, if not exactly Gold Glove material at the six. If everything clicks at the plate though, he could bloom into a Silver Slugger candidate. Davidson is a switch-hitter with pop from both sides. There's a lot of swing and miss in his game, but he posted double-digit homer totals all three seasons at Clemson and he takes his share of walks too. There's 25-homer upside in the bat, and if he hits enough of those, probably an average or better hit tool to go with them. He acquitted himself well enough in a pitcher-friendly short-season league after signing, and should be ready for High-A out of the gate in 2020.

Khris Davis LF   Born: 12/21/87   Age: 32   Bats: R   Throws: R   Height: 5'11"   Weight: 203   Origin: Round 7, 2009 Draft (#226 overall)

YEAR	TEAM	LVL	AGE	PA	R	2B	3B	HR	RBI	BB	K	SB	CS	AVG/OBP/SLG	DRC+	VORP	BABIP	BRR	FRAA	WARP
2017	OAK	MLB	29	652	91	28	1	43	110	73	195	4	0	.247/.336/.528	123	34.1	.290	-0.2	LF(116): -8.9	2.5
2018	OAK	MLB	30	654	98	28	1	48	123	59	175	0	0	.247/.326/.549	139	33.3	.261	-4.6	LF(11): -1.9	3.4
2019	OAK	MLB	31	533	61	11	0	23	73	47	146	0	0	.220/.293/.387	91	2.5	.264	-1.6	LF(4): -0.3	0.1
2020	OAK	MLB	32	525	66	20	1	29	78	46	151	3	1	.230/.306/.457	100	0.8	.274	-1.8	LF -2	-0.1

Comparables: Matt Joyce, Don Lock, Lucas Duda

The run of .247 batting averages couldn't last forever, and unfortunately the end came with too many other red flags to be glib about it. In a year everyone else homered like crazy, Davis fell back to the pack, cracking a mere 23 while slugging below .400. Alongside, both his exit velocity and hard-hit rate were much worse than normal. If there's good news, it's that Davis spent 2019 battling through a hand injury, which provides a reasonable explanation for the power outage. Still, there's reason to worry. As a DH with limited on-base skills, Davis only does one thing well. If the injury proves chronic or his pop doesn't return entirely, it's hard to justify his spot in the lineup—a troubling state of affairs for someone on the wrong side of 30. Hopefully 2019 was just a blip. The jaw-dropping bombs his merry-go-round swing produces are a true joy; baseball is simply better when Khrush Davis is on top of his game.

Jordan Diaz 3B   Born: 08/13/00   Age: 19   Bats: R   Throws: R   Height: 5'10"   Weight: 175   Origin: International Free Agent, 2016

YEAR	TEAM	LVL	AGE	PA	R	2B	3B	HR	RBI	BB	K	SB	CS	AVG/OBP/SLG	DRC+	VORP	BABIP	BRR	FRAA	WARP
2017	ATH	RK	16	28	2	0	0	0	2	0	4	1	0	.185/.179/.185	46	-2.0	.208	0.2	3B(8): -0.5	-0.1
2017	DAT	RK	16	149	14	7	0	0	18	6	22	2	0	.255/.295/.307	93	0.9	.297	0.7	3B(33): 0.8, 3B(7): 0.8	0.5
2018	ATH	RK	17	186	23	11	2	1	25	19	22	0	2	.277/.371/.390	147	10.7	.312	-0.9	3B(44): -2.5, 2B(1): 0.0	1.1
2019	VER	A-	18	300	31	17	1	9	47	18	46	2	2	.264/.307/.430	144	16.8	.283	-0.9	3B(61): -2.5	1.7
2020	OAK	MLB	19	251	23	13	1	6	26	15	54	0	0	.226/.277/.362	69	-2.5	.270	-0.4	3B -2, C 0	-0.4

Comparables: Maikel Franco, Eloy Jiménez, Harold Ramirez

Diaz has a bunch of 45s and 50s on the scouting report, but if he has upside, it's in the one area it matters. Just a teenager, Diaz took well to short-season ball, making plenty of contact and hitting for enough thump to suggest above-average power down the line if he leans into that part of his game. He'll need to hit, because he's just an okay third basemen and there aren't a whole lot of enticing secondary skills. Oakland farmhands have made a habit of crashing in the Midwest League recently, and the cold weather and jump in competition should challenge the Colombian in 2020. Should he pass the test, he'll be on our Top 10 A's prospects for 2021.

Jeremy Eierman SS   Born: 09/10/96   Age: 23   Bats: R   Throws: R   Height: 6'0"   Weight: 205   Origin: Round 2, 2018 Draft (#70 overall)

YEAR	TEAM	LVL	AGE	PA	R	2B	3B	HR	RBI	BB	K	SB	CS	AVG/OBP/SLG	DRC+	VORP	BABIP	BRR	FRAA	WARP
2018	VER	A-	21	267	36	8	2	8	26	13	70	10	4	.235/.283/.381	74	5.6	.294	-0.1	SS(56): 0.3, 2B(2): 0.9	0.6
2019	STO	A+	22	552	57	22	7	13	64	39	177	11	3	.208/.270/.357	68	11.5	.289	3.7	SS(90): -8.6, 2B(33): 1.1	0.1
2020	OAK	MLB	23	251	23	11	1	8	27	15	95	4	2	.202/.254/.355	60	-5.0	.301	0.0	SS -2, 2B 0	-0.7

Comparables: Jaycob Brugman, Kevin Cron, Chase d'Arnaud

School teachers often offer a simple guideline in regards to books: You can put them down, but you should give one 25-30 pages first. Fortunately for Eierman, the same principle applies to early draftees. Eierman is a bat-first shortstop who needed to show he could rake in the Cal League last summer. Instead, he hit .208 with big strikeout totals and without enough thump to compensate. Even worse, he played about a third of his games at second or third. A weak stick with occasional pop is tolerable in a great gloveman or backup catcher, but unusable pretty much anywhere else. We're still only 20 pages into this story, but thus far it's not looking promising.

Robbie Grossman OF Born: 09/16/89 Age: 30 Bats: B Throws: L Height: 6'0" Weight: 215 Origin: Round 6, 2008 Draft (#174 overall)

YEAR	TEAM	LVL	AGE	PA	R	2B	3B	HR	RBI	BB	K	SB	CS	AVG/OBP/SLG	DRC+	VORP	BABIP	BRR	FRAA	WARP
2017	MIN	MLB	27	456	62	22	1	9	45	67	79	3	1	.246/.361/.380	99	5.5	.287	-1.9	RF(35): -1.6, LF(18): -1.2	0.3
2018	MIN	MLB	28	465	50	27	1	5	48	60	83	0	1	.273/.367/.384	105	12.8	.329	-4.9	RF(52): -2.6, LF(34): 1.2	0.6
2019	OAK	MLB	29	482	57	21	3	6	38	59	86	9	4	.240/.334/.348	97	11.2	.288	-4.3	LF(112): 3.2, RF(20): -1.3	0.9
2020	OAK	MLB	30	280	28	12	1	5	26	36	56	3	1	.228/.331/.342	87	0.3	.278	-1.9	LF 3, RF -1	0.3

Comparables: Chase Headley, Travis Buck, Aaron Hicks

After 68 competent but hardly spectacular games with the 2013 Astros, Houston tried to lock Grossman up to a long-term deal that would have bought out his arbitration years and early free agency. The $13 million offer raised eyebrows at the time, and offered a hint at the direction baseball's marketplace was heading. In a depressing twist, Grossman has both been a better player than $13 million over six years should buy, and been paid less than that for his trouble. In any case, Grossman is a pretty easy guy to peg these days: He's a decent hitter characterized by an extremely patient approach that makes him a useful player, even though he's never put up the kind of counting numbers that leads to a big raise.

Ramón Laureano CF Born: 07/15/94 Age: 25 Bats: R Throws: R Height: 5'11" Weight: 200 Origin: Round 16, 2014 Draft (#466 overall)

YEAR	TEAM	LVL	AGE	PA	R	2B	3B	HR	RBI	BB	K	SB	CS	AVG/OBP/SLG	DRC+	VORP	BABIP	BRR	FRAA	WARP
2017	CCH	AA	22	513	65	21	6	11	55	40	110	24	5	.227/.298/.369	80	12.7	.273	6.3	RF(95): 7.8, CF(31): -1.7	1.6
2018	NAS	AAA	23	284	44	12	1	14	35	31	70	11	2	.297/.380/.524	142	24.2	.358	1.7	RF(45): 6.2, CF(19): -0.5	2.9
2018	OAK	MLB	23	176	27	12	1	5	19	16	50	7	1	.288/.358/.474	93	16.0	.388	1.4	CF(47): 3.0	0.9
2019	OAK	MLB	24	481	79	29	0	24	67	27	123	13	2	.288/.340/.521	115	26.9	.342	2.2	CF(110): 9.0, RF(13): 5.1	4.2
2020	OAK	MLB	25	595	74	30	3	27	83	43	163	21	6	.259/.325/.471	110	30.1	.323	1.6	CF 3, RF 1	3.4

Comparables: Chris Young, Brett Phillips, Aaron Cunningham

In an early-season episode of Effectively Wild, Ben Lindbergh declared that Laureano is as watchable of a player as there is—"for a non-star player." The first part held up, as he again dazzled with a sublime collection of moonshots, lasers, and tremendous catches, including a memorable home run robbery that preserved a no-hitter for Mike Fiers. But Laureano isn't just a ballplayer who shines occasionally anymore: He's a star in his own right. And in an era where big bashers run amok, Laureano's well-rounded game makes him a rare five-tool player. Oakland was somehow able to acquire this guy for a minor-league starter named Brandon Bailey, and it's turned into one of the low-key steals of the decade.

Jorge Mateo SS Born: 06/23/95 Age: 25 Bats: R Throws: R Height: 6'0" Weight: 192 Origin: International Free Agent, 2012

YEAR	TEAM	LVL	AGE	PA	R	2B	3B	HR	RBI	BB	K	SB	CS	AVG/OBP/SLG	DRC+	VORP	BABIP	BRR	FRAA	WARP
2017	TAM	A+	22	297	39	16	8	4	11	16	79	28	3	.240/.288/.400	87	15.6	.321	7.6	SS(42): 2.9, CF(22): -0.8	1.8
2017	TRN	AA	22	140	26	9	3	4	26	15	32	11	7	.300/.381/.525	127	16.7	.372	1.6	SS(17): 1.1, CF(7): -0.4	1.3
2017	MID	AA	22	147	25	5	7	4	20	9	33	13	3	.292/.333/.518	105	14.8	.356	2.2	SS(30): 0.8	1.0
2018	NAS	AAA	23	510	50	17	16	3	45	29	139	25	10	.230/.280/.353	61	3.7	.316	1.1	SS(123): -0.8, 2B(4): -0.5	-0.1
2019	LVG	AAA	24	566	95	29	14	19	78	29	145	24	11	.289/.330/.504	81	27.8	.366	3.2	SS(100): 16.6, 2B(14): -0.2	2.9
2020	OAK	MLB	25	105	10	5	1	2	10	5	31	6	2	.228/.273/.372	68	0.2	.312	0.5	CF 0, 2B 0	0.1

Comparables: Abiatal Avelino, Andrew Velazquez, Yairo Muñoz

Mateo has long been a mercurial prospect, and at a glance, his numbers imply he made progress after a disappointing 2018 season. With Jorge though, surprises lurk at every turn. In this era of PCL baseball, a .289/.330/.504 slash line is below par; his slugging percentage was actually one of the lowest marks on the team. That leaves Mateo more or less where we found him this time last year. He's still the fastest guy on the field, but he strikes out too often, probably won't hit enough to make an impact and ultimately projects as a utility man.

★ ★ ★ *2020 Top 101 Prospect* **#44** ★ ★ ★

Sean Murphy C Born: 10/10/94 Age: 25 Bats: R Throws: R Height: 6'3" Weight: 232 Origin: Round 3, 2016 Draft (#83 overall)

YEAR	TEAM	LVL	AGE	PA	R	2B	3B	HR	RBI	BB	K	SB	CS	AVG/OBP/SLG	DRC+	VORP	BABIP	BRR	FRAA	WARP
2017	STO	A+	22	178	22	11	0	9	26	11	33	0	0	.297/.343/.527	132	15.1	.323	0.2	C(40): -0.3	1.3
2017	MID	AA	22	217	25	7	0	4	22	21	34	0	0	.209/.288/.309	58	2.1	.232	0.6	C(51): 3.8	0.6
2018	MID	AA	23	289	51	26	2	8	43	23	47	3	0	.288/.358/.498	137	22.5	.324	2.1	C(65): 14.5	4.2
2019	AGO	RK	24	32	8	2	0	1	1	4	4	0	0	.214/.313/.393	122	0.0	.217	0.2	C(8): -0.1	0.2
2019	LVG	AAA	24	140	25	6	1	10	30	15	31	0	1	.308/.386/.625	122	13.4	.329	-1.3	C(27): 1.5	1.0
2019	OAK	MLB	24	60	14	5	0	4	8	6	16	0	0	.245/.333/.566	98	2.9	.273	1.1	C(18): -1.6	0.2
2020	OAK	MLB	25	385	43	18	1	16	50	31	98	1	0	.227/.297/.421	90	11.1	.268	-0.6	C -4	0.7

Comparables: J.T. Realmuto, Chris Parmelee, Ty France

Oakland's catcher of the future managed to stay just healthy enough to become the catcher of the present in the season's final month. A strong defender with a rocket arm, above-average power and a plan at the plate, Murphy is one of the best young backstops in baseball. There is some injury risk here: Murphy has broken both hamate bones and he had to battle through two knee injuries last season, one of which required surgery after the campaign. That's more dings than you'd like on anybody, much less one who dons the tools of ignorance. We obviously can't forecast a clean bill of health here, but Murphy's 2016 third-round selection is already looking like quite the smart investment.

YEAR	TEAM	P. COUNT	FRM RUNS	BLK RUNS	THRW RUNS	TOT RUNS
2017	MID	7267	3.6	-0.5	0.2	2.7
2018	MID	8864	13.6	1.4	0.6	15.6
2019	LVG	3998	1.1	0.2	-0.5	0.6
2019	OAK	2051	-0.2	-1.2	0.0	-1.4
2020	OAK	12807	-1.4	-2.8	0.1	-4.1

Kyler Murray OF/QB Born: 08/07/97 Age: 22 Bats: R Throws: R Height: 5'11" Weight: 195 Origin: Round 1, 2018 Draft (#9 overall)

When asked "how can we jazz up baseball," the game's gatekeepers can't help but amend the question by tacking on "and how will it save us money?" When your only tool is a hammer and all that. Look, maybe Murray was always going to play football. He was a better prospect on the gridiron, and that seems to be where his heart lies. But money talks and baseball's push to muzzle signing bonuses has always been penny-wise, pound-stupid and this is the clearest example why. Murray is a unicorn, an athlete with crossover appeal who had the potential to attract eyeballs in a way that no current big leaguer possibly can. That player is insanely valuable to a league that cashed in most of its mainstream cultural appeal decades ago. Or, at least he should be. There's a cap on signing bonuses now, you know, and MLB just couldn't figure out how to raise the ceiling enough to change Murray's destiny without—gasp!—creating a precedent. In the end, the league saved a few bucks up front. I'm sure A's fans were delighted by the austerity; Arizona Cardinals fans sure are.

Sheldon Neuse 3B Born: 12/10/94 Age: 25 Bats: R Throws: R Height: 6'0" Weight: 218 Origin: Round 2, 2016 Draft (#58 overall)

YEAR	TEAM	LVL	AGE	PA	R	2B	3B	HR	RBI	BB	K	SB	CS	AVG/OBP/SLG	DRC+	VORP	BABIP	BRR	FRAA	WARP
2017	HAG	A	22	321	40	19	3	9	51	25	66	12	5	.291/.349/.469	147	26.7	.347	-1.9	SS(43): -2.9, 3B(33): 6.6	3.0
2017	STO	A+	22	94	21	3	0	7	22	9	25	2	0	.386/.457/.675	217	17.0	.490	0.4	3B(10): -1.5, SS(8): -0.4	1.3
2017	MID	AA	22	75	9	4	0	0	6	6	21	0	0	.373/.427/.433	142	4.9	.532	0.3	3B(18): 1.4, 1B(1): -0.4	0.7
2018	NAS	AAA	23	537	48	26	3	5	55	32	172	4	1	.263/.304/.357	77	11.4	.385	-0.4	3B(130): -3.1, 2B(1): 0.0	0.2
2019	LVG	AAA	24	560	99	31	2	27	102	56	132	3	3	.317/.389/.550	117	39.2	.384	0.3	3B(96): 12.3, 2B(15): 0.6	4.4
2019	OAK	MLB	24	61	3	3	0	0	7	4	19	0	0	.250/.295/.304	70	-0.4	.368	0.3	2B(20): -1.4, 3B(5): -0.3	-0.2
2020	OAK	MLB	25	245	24	11	1	7	27	17	73	1	1	.245/.302/.388	82	3.2	.333	-0.3	2B -2, SS 0	0.2

Comparables: Cody Asche, Preston Tucker, Trea Turner

The A's found out that when you bring Neuse to Oakland, you might also bring a funk. While the 25-year-old produced in the high-octane environs of the PCL (and particularly Las Vegas), he struggled upon arriving in the majors, failing to display the raw power he's known for. He's got the arm and body for the hot corner, but there's a Matt Chapman-sized roadblock there. The defense wouldn't be pretty at second base, if his bat can state his case for it. After all, this is the organization well-known for not selling jeans.

Matt Olson 1B Born: 03/29/94 Age: 26 Bats: L Throws: R Height: 6'5" Weight: 230 Origin: Round 1, 2012 Draft (#47 overall)

YEAR	TEAM	LVL	AGE	PA	R	2B	3B	HR	RBI	BB	K	SB	CS	AVG/OBP/SLG	DRC+	VORP	BABIP	BRR	FRAA	WARP
2017	NAS	AAA	23	343	56	16	1	23	60	45	83	3	0	.272/.367/.568	139	29.8	.298	-0.1	1B(73): -0.8, 3B(1): -0.2	2.0
2017	OAK	MLB	23	216	33	2	0	24	45	22	60	0	0	.259/.352/.651	146	16.1	.238	0.3	1B(43): 4.7, RF(12): 2.7	2.4
2018	OAK	MLB	24	660	85	33	0	29	84	70	163	2	1	.247/.335/.453	114	20.6	.292	-2.6	1B(162): 3.8	2.2
2019	OAK	MLB	25	547	73	26	0	36	91	51	138	0	0	.267/.351/.545	134	32.7	.300	-1.9	1B(127): 11.7	4.1
2020	OAK	MLB	26	595	81	25	0	35	94	64	155	1	0	.240/.332/.491	121	26.5	.272	-1.4	1B 5	3.3

Comparables: Randal Grichuk, Kyle Blanks, Tyler O'Neill

Olson anchored the Athletics order in a breakout season reminiscent of his torrid debut. It's fair to say that he's one of the American League's best hitters now (11th in DRC+ among qualifying hitters), and he would have made his first All-Star team if he hadn't missed 30-odd games after breaking his hamate bone in Japan. For an injury that often saps a player's power for months, Olson looked no worse for wear, finishing near the top of the charts in wOBA, exit velocity, hard hit percentage, muscle density... That last one may sound irrelevant, but it's actually part of the charm here: He's just a massive person who wields his bat like an axe as he gets ready to hit, and then whacks the crap out of the ball on its way in. What's not to love?

Josh Phegley C Born: 02/12/88 Age: 32 Bats: R Throws: R Height: 5'10" Weight: 225 Origin: Round 1, 2009 Draft (#38 overall)

YEAR	TEAM	LVL	AGE	PA	R	2B	3B	HR	RBI	BB	K	SB	CS	AVG/OBP/SLG	DRC+	VORP	BABIP	BRR	FRAA	WARP
2017	NAS	AAA	29	34	2	2	0	1	4	2	5	0	0	.310/.382/.483	111	3.1	.333	-0.8	C(6): -0.7	0.0
2017	OAK	MLB	29	161	14	11	0	3	10	9	26	0	1	.201/.255/.336	80	-1.4	.223	0.0	C(56): 3.2	0.7
2018	NAS	AAA	30	139	12	6	3	3	18	15	31	0	0	.235/.331/.412	101	7.8	.287	-0.1	C(19): 2.8	0.8
2018	OAK	MLB	30	102	13	7	0	2	15	6	27	0	0	.204/.255/.344	75	0.8	.258	-0.1	C(39): -1.3	0.1
2019	OAK	MLB	31	342	44	18	0	12	62	15	63	0	1	.239/.282/.411	91	13.8	.258	-3.0	C(106): -14.3	-0.3
2020	OAK	MLB	32	251	25	13	1	8	29	15	51	1	0	.222/.281/.385	75	-0.6	.252	-0.6	C -6	-0.7

Comparables: Martín Maldonado, Adam Moore, Miguel Montero

YEAR	TEAM	P. COUNT	FRM RUNS	BLK RUNS	THRW RUNS	TOT RUNS
2017	OAK	6653	3.4	-1.0	1.1	2.7
2018	NAS	2352	2.4	-0.2	0.3	2.5
2018	OAK	3948	-0.9	-1.5	0.0	-2.3
2019	OAK	13296	-7.1	-5.5	1.0	-11.6
2020	OAK	10982	-4.2	-2.3	0.4	-6.1

Generally, the backup catcher gig is a job for a placeholder until someone better, younger, or cheaper comes along. Phegley defies the natural order. He's been a reliable reserve for the better part of seven years now, all without really changing much as a player: still a competent defender, still not much of a bat. An early-season hot streak and lack of compelling alternatives put him in the lineup more than usual, but rest assured, he's still the oatmeal breakfast you're accustomed to. If all goes well, he'll be safely tucked behind Sean Murphy on the depth chart soon.

Chad Pinder UT Born: 03/29/92 Age: 28 Bats: R Throws: R Height: 6'2" Weight: 207 Origin: Round 2, 2013 Draft (#71 overall)

YEAR	TEAM	LVL	AGE	PA	R	2B	3B	HR	RBI	BB	K	SB	CS	AVG/OBP/SLG	DRC+	VORP	BABIP	BRR	FRAA	WARP
2017	NAS	AAA	25	71	3	2	1	1	2	6	23	2	1	.266/.338/.375	77	0.7	.400	-1.5	2B(8): 0.1, SS(4): -0.3	-0.2
2017	OAK	MLB	25	309	36	15	1	15	42	18	92	2	1	.238/.292/.457	97	7.6	.292	-1.8	RF(35): -0.5, SS(22): 1.6	0.8
2018	OAK	MLB	26	333	43	12	1	13	27	27	88	0	2	.258/.332/.436	110	15.4	.325	0.8	LF(64): 4.8, 2B(21): -1.3	1.8
2019	OAK	MLB	27	370	45	21	0	13	47	20	88	0	1	.240/.290/.416	82	2.0	.284	0.9	LF(46): 2.4, RF(34): 4.2	0.7
2020	OAK	MLB	28	175	19	8	0	7	22	10	44	1	0	.232/.289/.410	84	1.9	.278	0.1	2B -1, LF 2	0.3

Comparables: Danny Espinosa, Jedd Gyorko, Jason Kipnis

Pinder is perhaps the game's most versatile utility man these days, a bit of an odd role for someone with a .432 career slugging percentage. He again saw time at every position besides catcher and pitcher, starting at least once everywhere except short. His career trajectory appears set now, as he's basically baseball's Jonathan Isaac: not quite reliable enough on offense for a starring role, but too valuable and versatile defensively to get traded. There are worse fates a man could have.

Stephen Piscotty RF Born: 01/14/91 Age: 29 Bats: R Throws: R Height: 6'4" Weight: 205 Origin: Round 1, 2012 Draft (#36 overall)

YEAR	TEAM	LVL	AGE	PA	R	2B	3B	HR	RBI	BB	K	SB	CS	AVG/OBP/SLG	DRC+	VORP	BABIP	BRR	FRAA	WARP
2017	MEM	AAA	26	38	7	3	0	4	7	6	7	0	0	.313/.421/.781	180	7.0	.286	0.0	RF(6): -0.2	0.4
2017	SLN	MLB	26	401	40	16	1	9	39	52	87	3	6	.235/.342/.367	95	1.9	.286	-2.5	RF(99): -0.9	0.3
2018	OAK	MLB	27	605	78	41	0	27	88	42	114	2	0	.267/.331/.491	120	28.0	.290	-1.4	RF(151): -9.3	1.7
2019	OAK	MLB	28	393	46	17	1	13	44	29	84	2	0	.249/.309/.412	95	6.5	.289	1.1	RF(90): -3.7	0.4
2020	OAK	MLB	29	455	53	24	1	17	59	38	101	4	2	.253/.324/.444	103	10.8	.296	-0.6	RF -2	0.9

Comparables: Greg Luzinski, Ryan Klesko, Mike Shannon

After his second subpar season at the plate in three tries, Piscotty's career is at an early crossroads. There've been extenuating circumstances, including a melanoma scare and a bad ankle sprain last year, but at the end of the day he has only notched 2.7 WARP over the last three years combined. Twenty-nine now, he's not much of a defender, and he's at risk of falling down Oakland's pecking order in the outfield. The tradeoff of more swing-and-miss for additional power is one a lot of players have made, but Piscotty's extra whiffs brought about a decline in ISO. If there's a positive here, it's that Piscotty has shown more stick in the past, and is not yet at an age where you'd think he's seriously declining. But for someone who hit the ground running when he debuted in 2015, Piscotty's career has been more turbulent than we'd have guessed three years ago.

Robert Puason SS Born: 09/11/02 Age: 17 Bats: B Throws: R Height: 6'3" Weight: 165 Origin: International Free Agent, 2019

Puason was one of the top-rated J2 signees last summer, and the A's paid him more than $5 million to sign on the dotted line. If you have to buy a 16-year-old player, you might as well take the twitchy shortstop who can hit a ball nearly 400 feet. But for crying out loud, Puason is sixteen. The Latin American market has long been little more than an exploitative dart throw, and if you don't believe us about that last point, take a look at Baseball America's top prospects for the international signing period from 10 years ago. Miguel Sanó ranked first and Gary Sánchez featured two spots behind him—familiar, successful names. But sandwiched in between was Wagner Mateo, who became infamous in prospecting circles for having his signing bonus voided once the Cardinals discovered he had terrible eyesight. Later in the top 10, you'll find luminaries like Guillermo Pimentel, Juan Urbina, and Jose Sanchez. Puason looks like a nice player, but let's wait until he's an adult before we start speculating on his ceiling.

Marcus Semien SS Born: 09/17/90 Age: 29 Bats: R Throws: R Height: 6'0" Weight: 195 Origin: Round 6, 2011 Draft (#201 overall)

YEAR	TEAM	LVL	AGE	PA	R	2B	3B	HR	RBI	BB	K	SB	CS	AVG/OBP/SLG	DRC+	VORP	BABIP	BRR	FRAA	WARP
2017	OAK	MLB	26	386	53	19	1	10	40	38	85	12	1	.249/.325/.398	94	19.0	.300	3.9	SS(85): -1.5	1.7
2018	OAK	MLB	27	703	89	35	2	15	70	61	131	14	6	.255/.318/.388	99	37.5	.296	5.4	SS(159): 16.2	5.4
2019	OAK	MLB	28	747	123	43	7	33	92	87	102	10	8	.285/.369/.522	135	70.6	.294	1.8	SS(161): 4.2	7.5
2020	OAK	MLB	29	595	72	31	3	23	78	62	103	11	4	.258/.337/.455	109	32.6	.281	3.0	SS 6	4.0

Comparables: Edwin Encarnación, Anthony Rendon, David Wright

As Semien hung near the top of the WARP leaderboard throughout the summer, a narrative emerged: He was last year's breakout player, the man who had sprouted from the minors as a feeble hitter and worse fielder only to bloom into a star late in his prime. The sentiment is mostly right, particularly defensively where he's transformed into one of the league's finest fielders at an age most shortstops begin warily eyeing third base. But while 2019 might be his statistical summit, Semien's ascendency to stardom has been far more linear than most assume. At the plate, he's shown a Troutian ability to enhance his game with each passing year. Power and patience came first, and now he's hitting for average and making more contact, too. Whether he's done growing or not—short of a BABIP spike, he's running out of things to get batter at—he's an MVP candidate now, and the key to any potential for a passing of the torch at the top of the AL West.

PITCHERS

Chris Bassitt RHP Born: 02/22/89 Age: 31 Bats: R Throws: R Height: 6'5" Weight: 220 Origin: Round 16, 2011 Draft (#501 overall)

YEAR	TEAM	LVL	AGE	W	L	SV	G	GS	IP	H	HR	BB/9	K/9	K	GB%	BABIP	WHIP	ERA	DRA	WARP	MPH	FB%	WHF	CSP
2017	STO	A+	28	0	1	0	7	7	13	9	0	2.8	9.7	14	64%	.273	1.00	2.77	3.02	0.3				
2017	NAS	AAA	28	4	2	0	17	2	37²	41	3	3.8	7.4	31	36%	.336	1.51	6.21	5.05	0.1				
2018	NAS	AAA	29	5	5	0	18	14	81²	86	6	2.8	9.1	83	44%	.348	1.36	4.30	4.15	1.2				
2018	OAK	MLB	29	2	3	0	11	7	47²	40	4	3.6	7.7	41	44%	.265	1.24	3.02	5.24	0.0	94.7	57.4	7.6	51.8
2019	LVG	AAA	30	0	0	0	2	2	8	8	2	2.2	10.1	9	58%	.273	1.25	4.50	2.60	0.3				
2019	OAK	MLB	30	10	5	0	28	25	144	125	21	2.9	8.8	141	42%	.267	1.19	3.81	4.45	2.0	95.8	64.9	9.7	51.9
2020	OAK	MLB	31	6	5	0	16	16	84	82	12	3.3	8.4	79	43%	.296	1.35	4.50	4.69	0.8	94.7	62.9	9.2	51.6

Comparables: Erik Davis, Jeff Manship, Chad Bettis

In a relic from the Moneyball days, the A's remain proficient at squeezing magic from obscure 30-year-olds. Bassitt is the latest rabbit out of the hat. He only appeared 18 times from 2016-2018 but started 25 games last year, riding a velocity boost to a breakout season. There's not much mystery about how Bassitt conducts his business: gas, gas, more gas and the occasional slow curve just to keep hitters honest. Opponents had a typically difficult time with the fastball: statistically, it's the pitch that most batters hit hardest but Bassitt both missed bats and limited hard contact with the ol' number one. That's a nice trick if you can pull it off; we'll need to see him do it again before comfortably calling him a mid-rotation arm going forward.

Tyler Baum RHP Born: 01/14/98 Age: 22 Bats: R Throws: R Height: 6'2" Weight: 195 Origin: Round 2, 2019 Draft (#66 overall)

YEAR	TEAM	LVL	AGE	W	L	SV	G	GS	IP	H	HR	BB/9	K/9	K	GB%	BABIP	WHIP	ERA	DRA	WARP	MPH	FB%	WHF	CSP
2019	VER	A-	21	0	3	0	11	11	30²	29	4	2.1	10.0	34	40%	.306	1.17	4.70	4.42	0.3				
2020	OAK	MLB	22	2	2	0	33	0	35	35	6	3.3	8.0	31	38%	.294	1.38	4.66	4.82	0.1				

Comparables: Joel Carreno, Pat Light, Jensen Lewis

With a low-90s fastball and a chance to have four average pitches, Baum spent most of his college career looking like a solid, if unspectacular, prospect—the kind usually ticketed for the fifth round. But humans tend to value small samples of exciting, recently absorbed information more favorably than a larger but older collection of less impressionable material. That worked in Baum's favor when a late-season velocity spike sent his fastball into the mid-90s and propelled him to a second-round selection. Whether that extra heat tangibly alters his career trajectory or was simply the baseball equivalent of pulling an all-nighter before the final will be for time and the Athletics player development staff to sort out.

Ryan Buchter LHP Born: 02/13/87 Age: 33 Bats: L Throws: L Height: 6'4" Weight: 232 Origin: Round 33, 2005 Draft (#984 overall)

YEAR	TEAM	LVL	AGE	W	L	SV	G	GS	IP	H	HR	BB/9	K/9	K	GB%	BABIP	WHIP	ERA	DRA	WARP	MPH	FB%	WHF	CSP
2017	SDN	MLB	30	3	3	1	42	0	38¹	28	7	4.2	11.0	47	33%	.239	1.20	3.05	5.03	0.1	94.8	72.1	12.7	47.3
2017	KCA	MLB	30	1	0	0	29	0	27	16	3	2.7	6.0	18	32%	.173	0.89	2.67	5.67	-0.2	94.4	72.1	10.3	49.8
2018	OAK	MLB	31	6	0	0	54	0	39¹	32	4	3.4	9.4	41	28%	.272	1.19	2.75	3.60	0.6	94.6	65.7	12.2	48.1
2019	OAK	MLB	32	1	1	0	64	0	45¹	42	8	4.6	9.9	50	29%	.296	1.43	2.98	5.94	-0.3	94.7	64.1	12.3	46.4
2020	OAK	MLB	33	2	2	0	33	0	35	29	6	4.1	8.9	35	29%	.262	1.29	4.00	4.24	0.4	93.6	66.4	11.9	46.9

Comparables: Sam Freeman, Clay Rapada, Dan Runzler

Though not quite as one-dimensional as A's legend Mike Holtz, Buchter has averaged less than an inning per outing every year of his career. He's here to get lefties out and, to his credit, he's done just that: Over the past four years, lefties have produced a sub-.600 OPS and only 10 homers in nearly 400 plate appearances against Buchter. He's not so good against righties, though, and that's troubling since he can no longer come in to face just one batter. Buchter leaned less on his cutter and more on his curve last year as compared to 2018, and to good results: Batters couldn't manage an extra-base hit in 170 chances against his yellow hammer. That's good news for Buchter going forward, as curves show less of a platoon split than most offerings.

Jake Diekman LHP Born: 01/21/87 Age: 33 Bats: L Throws: L Height: 6'4" Weight: 200 Origin: Round 30, 2007 Draft (#923 overall)

YEAR	TEAM	LVL	AGE	W	L	SV	G	GS	IP	H	HR	BB/9	K/9	K	GB%	BABIP	WHIP	ERA	DRA	WARP	MPH	FB%	WHF	CSP
2017	TEX	MLB	30	0	0	1	11	0	10²	4	1	8.4	11.0	13	59%	.143	1.31	2.53	7.02	-0.2	97.8	68.1	12.2	37.4
2018	TEX	MLB	31	1	1	2	47	0	39	31	2	5.3	11.1	48	48%	.302	1.38	3.69	6.34	-0.6	97.2	62.4	11.4	45.4
2018	ARI	MLB	31	0	1	0	24	0	14¹	18	2	5.0	11.3	18	57%	.400	1.81	7.53	6.25	-0.2	97.6	67.9	13.5	46.8
2019	OAK	MLB	32	1	1	0	28	0	20¹	16	0	7.1	9.3	21	46%	.296	1.57	4.43	4.81	0.1	97.5	59.1	12.2	46.8
2019	KCA	MLB	32	0	6	0	48	0	41²	33	3	5.0	13.6	63	49%	.330	1.34	4.75	2.69	1.2	97.9	51	17.7	47.5
2020	OAK	MLB	33	3	2	0	49	0	52	41	5	4.7	11.5	66	48%	.295	1.32	3.78	3.91	0.7	96.5	57.7	14	43.8

Comparables: Sam Freeman, Mike Dunn, Kevin Chapman

In a league where a fair number of pitchers have cooked better meals with worse ingredients, Diekman's overall numbers look mediocre for a guy throwing 98 with a plus slider. The problem, of course, is that neither of those weapons winds up in the strike zone all that often. His career BB/9 ratio is north of five, which is surprisingly rare air: There are only 13 pitchers this century who have walked so many while throwing at least 300 innings. That makes Diekman a bit like your printer: usually effective, but often frustrating and always stressful in high-leverage situations.

Parker Dunshee RHP Born: 02/12/95 Age: 25 Bats: R Throws: R Height: 6'0" Weight: 215 Origin: Round 7, 2017 Draft (#201 overall)

YEAR	TEAM	LVL	AGE	W	L	SV	G	GS	IP	H	HR	BB/9	K/9	K	GB%	BABIP	WHIP	ERA	DRA	WARP	MPH	FB%	WHF	CSP
2017	VER	A-	22	1	0	0	12	9	38¹	15	0	1.9	10.6	45	46%	.185	0.60	0.00	1.86	1.5				
2018	STO	A+	23	6	2	0	12	10	70	61	7	2.2	10.5	82	35%	.314	1.11	2.70	3.03	1.8				
2018	MID	AA	23	7	4	0	12	12	80²	59	5	1.6	9.0	81	34%	.266	0.90	2.01	2.47	2.7				
2019	MID	AA	24	2	2	0	6	6	38	26	1	2.6	8.1	34	38%	.255	0.97	1.89	3.29	0.8				
2019	LVG	AAA	24	4	5	1	20	19	92	86	21	3.6	8.8	90	35%	.261	1.34	5.38	3.64	2.7				
2020	OAK	MLB	25	2	2	0	25	3	38	38	6	3.3	8.2	34	35%	.299	1.39	4.79	4.97	0.2				

Comparables: Michael King, Brandon Workman, Erick Fedde

Twenty-four is roughly the age at which spending time in Las Vegas stops being any fun, as Dunshee himself discovered last summer. Sure, the glitz and the lights are novel at first, and the occasional free drink can make anyone feel like a VIP. In time though, everyone realizes that the decks are stacked the wrong way, the water tastes salty, the free gin and tonic actually costs forty bucks and the baseballs carry deep into the night. That last one particularly applies to our beleaguered right-hander. Dunshee's command-n-control, low-90s profile ran smack into the juiced ball and desert climes of the PCL, and the results were as ugly as hitting on 17. If you can look past the garishly flashy home run rate, there's a functional pitcher here, so long as he can clear the last Vegas obstacle: leaving.

Mike Fiers RHP Born: 06/15/85 Age: 35 Bats: R Throws: R Height: 6'2" Weight: 202 Origin: Round 22, 2009 Draft (#676 overall)

YEAR	TEAM	LVL	AGE	W	L	SV	G	GS	IP	H	HR	BB/9	K/9	K	GB%	BABIP	WHIP	ERA	DRA	WARP	MPH	FB%	WHF	CSP
2017	HOU	MLB	32	8	10	0	29	28	153¹	157	32	3.6	8.6	146	43%	.300	1.43	5.22	5.82	-0.4	91.9	47.5	9.9	46.6
2018	DET	MLB	33	7	6	0	21	21	119	121	20	2.0	6.6	87	39%	.277	1.24	3.48	4.87	0.6	91.6	51.4	8.8	49.1
2018	OAK	MLB	33	5	2	0	10	9	53	45	12	1.9	8.8	52	43%	.246	1.06	3.74	4.02	0.8	92.5	51.4	10.1	50.9
2019	OAK	MLB	34	15	4	0	33	33	184²	166	30	2.6	6.1	126	40%	.254	1.19	3.90	5.06	1.4	92.6	51.8	8.6	49.8
2020	OAK	MLB	35	10	9	0	29	29	152	157	31	2.8	6.8	114	40%	.280	1.35	4.89	5.12	0.8	91.0	49.7	8.9	48

Comparables: Marco Estrada, Jeff Samardzija, Collin McHugh

There are 35 pitchers in MLB history who have thrown multiple no-hitters. Tossing out the Dead Ball guys, the remaining 25 or so break down into two camps: Guys with insanely dominant stuff and everyone else. The former group contains luminaries like Sandy Koufax, Nolan Ryan, and Randy Johnson, with room for folks who burned brightly but quickly: Jim Maloney, Jake Arrieta, etc. Fiers belongs to the latter cohort, a soft-tosser for his day, and not one too adept at suppressing hits normally. That isn't to say he isn't good: Whether you place more faith in his ho-hum DRA's or moderately better ERA figures in recent years, he clearly can get people out. But the no-hitters are as shocking as they seem, a wonderfully bizarre example of baseball's ceaseless capacity to surprise. And while we're on surprises: Who would have guessed that Fiers, a member of the Astros' 2017 World Series team, would go on record about his discomfort with Houston's sign stealing system? His public account did much to spur MLB's investigation into Houston; we don't know the full ramifications of that investigation or how it will affect Fiers and his legacy, but the guess at press time is that the fallout will be substantial.

Matt Harvey RHP Born: 03/27/89 Age: 31 Bats: R Throws: R Height: 6'4" Weight: 220 Origin: Round 1, 2010 Draft (#7 overall)

YEAR	TEAM	LVL	AGE	W	L	SV	G	GS	IP	H	HR	BB/9	K/9	K	GB%	BABIP	WHIP	ERA	DRA	WARP	MPH	FB%	WHF	CSP
2017	BIN	AA	28	0	0	0	2	2	7²	9	1	2.3	5.9	5	33%	.308	1.43	5.87	4.85	0.0				
2017	NYN	MLB	28	5	7	0	19	18	92²	110	21	4.6	6.5	67	46%	.307	1.69	6.70	6.63	-1.1	96.4	59.3	8.6	47
2018	NYN	MLB	29	0	2	0	8	4	27	33	6	3.0	6.7	20	43%	.310	1.56	7.00	4.18	0.3	95.3	61.2	8.2	49.7
2018	CIN	MLB	29	7	7	0	24	24	128	132	21	2.0	7.8	111	46%	.296	1.25	4.50	4.79	0.7	96.7	58.7	10.4	53
2019	LVG	AAA	30	1	0	0	5	3	17	13	2	2.6	11.1	21	37%	.282	1.06	3.18	5.35	0.2				
2019	LAA	MLB	30	3	5	0	12	12	59²	63	13	4.4	5.9	39	44%	.275	1.54	7.09	7.62	-1.2	95.7	47.6	9.9	48.2
2020	OAK	MLB	31	2	2	0	33	0	35	38	7	3.3	7.0	27	43%	.297	1.45	5.37	5.38	-0.1	95.4	56.1	9.6	49

Comparables: Chris Archer, Kyle Hendricks, Tyson Ross

Poor Matt Harvey. It can't be easy to peak at 26, much less to have both your finest hour and the subsequent free-fall broadcast on national television and plastered all over the New York Post. It's easy to say, four years on from Harvey's last productive season in Queens, that this was the inevitable path for a talented but cocky young star who relied on the powerful but fleeting strength of his right arm to roast National League lineups. It didn't have to be that way: When he first looked mortal, he was still throwing pretty hard and still getting a lot of bite on his curve. Harvey maintains an average fastball if you're grading on velocity alone, but it's trending in the wrong direction. His heater fell another tick in 2019, when he was more or less the worst pitcher in the league over 12 starts until the Angels finally threw in the towel. The A's picked him up as Homer Bailey insurance, in a sentence that would have made as much sense while invoking a lot less sadness back in 2013. The stuff is mediocre now, the execution is far worse and the trajectory is not promising. A dark night, indeed.

Liam Hendriks RHP Born: 02/10/89 Age: 31 Bats: R Throws: R Height: 6'0" Weight: 225 Origin: International Free Agent, 2007

YEAR	TEAM	LVL	AGE	W	L	SV	G	GS	IP	H	HR	BB/9	K/9	K	GB%	BABIP	WHIP	ERA	DRA	WARP	MPH	FB%	WHF	CSP
2017	OAK	MLB	28	4	2	1	70	0	64	57	7	3.2	11.0	78	41%	.303	1.25	4.22	3.45	1.2	96.7	74.1	13.6	46.7
2018	NAS	AAA	29	4	1	6	23	1	25¹	21	1	1.4	15.3	43	41%	.364	0.99	2.84	2.03	0.9				
2018	OAK	MLB	29	0	1	0	25	8	24	25	3	3.8	8.2	22	41%	.324	1.46	4.12	4.70	0.1	97.7	70.1	12.1	47.1
2019	OAK	MLB	30	4	4	25	75	2	85	61	5	2.2	13.1	124	32%	.311	0.96	1.80	2.73	2.4	98.8	70.6	18.7	48.6
2020	OAK	MLB	31	3	3	38	60	0	63	52	7	2.3	11.9	84	35%	.303	1.07	2.70	3.13	1.4	97.2	71.1	16.1	47.3

Comparables: Brett Cecil, Tommy Hunter, Zach McAllister

Always a solid reliever, Hendriks notched a career year in 2019 and emerged as Oakland's closer by the end of June. Key for him was the slider, now thrown harder and more often. Opponents could barely touch it, hitting just .114 with no power and an absurdly high 29% whiff rate on the pitch. If he can maintain his newfound arm strength, there's no reason he can't be filthy again next year, although there are a couple of reasons to be cautious. The first is that he's never pitched nearly this well before; as with Blake Treinen and Lou Trivino last season, it's best to see the goods twice before we expect them as a matter of course. The second is that he worked quite hard, appearing 75 times while throwing 20 more innings than normal. Perhaps he has the stamina for it, but that's a lot of miles for a guy in his 30s. That isn't to say Hendriks won't be good again this season, of course: Just don't be shocked if 2019 was the peak.

Daulton Jefferies RHP   Born: 08/02/95   Age: 24   Bats: L   Throws: R   Height: 6'0"   Weight: 182   Origin: Round 1, 2016 Draft (#37 overall)

YEAR	TEAM	LVL	AGE	W	L	SV	G	GS	IP	H	HR	BB/9	K/9	K	GB%	BABIP	WHIP	ERA	DRA	WARP	MPH	FB%	WHF	CSP
2017	STO	A+	21	0	0	0	2	1	7	7	0	1.3	7.7	6	67%	.292	1.14	2.57	4.07	0.1				
2019	STO	A+	23	1	0	0	5	3	15	10	1	1.2	12.6	21	44%	.273	0.80	2.40	2.57	0.4				
2019	MID	AA	23	1	2	0	21	12	64	63	7	1.0	10.1	72	42%	.327	1.09	3.66	3.39	1.1				
2020	OAK	MLB	24	1	1	0	22	0	23	23	3	3.0	9.4	24	40%	.308	1.32	4.27	4.61	0.1				

Comparables: Michael King, Daniel Gossett, Brandon Workman

Jefferies has battled injury problems throughout his career—broken pitchers grow on oak trees—and the 64 innings he threw last summer account for the lion's share of his professional workload. Fortunately for all parties, Jefferies looked little worse for wear in his return from an extended absence. At his best, he combines an above-average fastball with a firm but effective change that projects as a plus offering. Those weapons were intact, albeit in short stints: His workload was spread across 21 outings and he never finished the fourth in any one game. Still, he managed to whiff more than a batter per inning across two levels, and looked sharp at Double-A. The A's will understandably try to stretch him out more next summer, but if the club ever decides the juice isn't quite worth the squeeze there, he would be very effective in short stints or a multi-inning relief role.

James Kaprielian RHP   Born: 03/02/94   Age: 26   Bats: R   Throws: R   Height: 6'3"   Weight: 210   Origin: Round 1, 2015 Draft (#16 overall)

YEAR	TEAM	LVL	AGE	W	L	SV	G	GS	IP	H	HR	BB/9	K/9	K	GB%	BABIP	WHIP	ERA	DRA	WARP	MPH	FB%	WHF	CSP
2019	STO	A+	25	2	2	0	11	10	36¹	35	6	2.0	10.7	43	32%	.319	1.18	4.46	4.47	0.2				
2019	MID	AA	25	2	1	0	7	5	27²	18	2	2.6	8.5	26	41%	.232	0.94	1.63	3.01	0.6				
2020	OAK	MLB	26	3	3	0	32	5	52	51	8	3.1	8.7	50	39%	.301	1.34	4.46	4.71	0.4				

Comparables: Joe Musgrove, Glenn Sparkman, David Phelps

There comes a time when a minor-league pitcher simply has too many injuries on the ledger to be taken seriously as a prospect. For Kaprielian, who battled flexor issues and then separately needed Tommy John surgery, that point may well have been three years ago. Just when all hope seemed lost, the right-hander turned in a pretty healthy season, though one that brought fresh concerns. At his peak Kaprielian had an electric arm, and between that and his injury history, it made all the sense in the world for Oakland to push him aggressively in 2019. So when the A's both played it safe—he averaged less than four innings per appearance—and opted not to promote him to the bigs for the stretch run, well, that and diminished velocity suggests the former second-rounder isn't all the way back. There's still upside here, but the No. 2 starter ceiling from draft day seems like a pipe dream.

★ ★ ★ *2020 Top 101 Prospect* **#9** ★ ★ ★

Jesus Luzardo LHP   Born: 09/30/97   Age: 22   Bats: L   Throws: L   Height: 6'0"   Weight: 209   Origin: Round 3, 2016 Draft (#94 overall)

YEAR	TEAM	LVL	AGE	W	L	SV	G	GS	IP	H	HR	BB/9	K/9	K	GB%	BABIP	WHIP	ERA	DRA	WARP	MPH	FB%	WHF	CSP
2017	NAT	RK	19	1	0	0	3	3	13²	14	1	0.0	9.9	15	33%	.342	1.02	1.32	3.00	0.4				
2017	ATH	RK	19	0	1	0	4	3	11²	9	0	0.8	10.0	13	58%	.290	0.86	1.54	2.17	0.5				
2017	VER	A-	19	1	0	0	5	5	18	12	1	2.0	10.0	20	53%	.250	0.89	2.00	2.75	0.5				
2018	STO	A+	20	2	1	0	3	3	14²	6	0	3.1	15.3	25	56%	.240	0.75	1.23	1.88	0.6				
2018	MID	AA	20	7	3	0	16	16	78²	58	5	2.1	9.8	86	46%	.268	0.97	2.29	2.70	2.4				
2018	NAS	AAA	20	1	1	0	4	4	16	25	2	3.9	10.1	18	51%	.469	2.00	7.31	7.75	-0.4				
2019	STO	A+	21	1	0	0	3	1	10	6	1	0.0	16.2	18	50%	.294	0.60	0.90	2.19	0.3				
2019	LVG	AAA	21	1	1	0	7	7	31	29	3	2.3	9.9	34	56%	.302	1.19	3.19	2.57	1.2				
2019	OAK	MLB	21	0	0	2	6	0	12	5	1	2.2	12.0	16	42%	.160	0.67	1.50	3.32	0.3	98.5	48.5	15.2	45
2020	OAK	MLB	22	9	7	0	43	21	128	109	18	3.7	11.0	156	48%	.294	1.26	3.73	4.00	2.1	98.5	50.6	15.8	46.9

Comparables: Luiz Gohara, Alex Reyes, Tyler Skaggs

If there are better pitching prospects than Luzardo, you wouldn't need more than five fingers to count them. In many ways, he's the Platonic ideal of what a pitching prospect should look like. He's 22, athletic, left-handed, throws 100 mph and he misses bats with both a sharp curve and a delightful fading changeup. The ingredients are great, but Luzardo is also very polished for someone so young and naturally gifted. He can move the ball around the zone, and is able to attack both lefties and righties with his curve. He even generates ground balls: The two-seamer may be falling out of fashion, but if yours sits in the high-90s with vicious tail, you can still chew threw a lot of bats pretty quickly. If there's a concern here, it's health. Luzardo has Tommy John on his resume, he's missed starts each of the past two seasons with small ailments, and the A's have been loathe to stretch him out. If he stays healthy, look out. He's one of the very few minor leaguers with legitimate No. 1 upside, and a guy Oakland fans will surely cherish—at least until he hits arbitration.

Sean Manaea LHP   Born: 02/01/92   Age: 28   Bats: R   Throws: L   Height: 6'5"   Weight: 245   Origin: Round 1, 2013 Draft (#34 overall)

YEAR	TEAM	LVL	AGE	W	L	SV	G	GS	IP	H	HR	BB/9	K/9	K	GB%	BABIP	WHIP	ERA	DRA	WARP	MPH	FB%	WHF	CSP
2017	OAK	MLB	25	12	10	0	29	29	158²	167	18	3.1	7.9	140	44%	.318	1.40	4.37	5.17	0.7	94.1	58.3	12.1	46
2018	OAK	MLB	26	12	9	0	27	27	160²	141	21	1.8	6.0	108	46%	.247	1.08	3.59	4.04	2.4	93.1	56.2	10.2	53.4
2019	STO	A+	27	0	2	0	3	3	8¹	14	1	4.3	10.8	10	43%	.481	2.16	9.72	9.37	-0.4				
2019	LVG	AAA	27	3	1	0	5	5	28	16	5	1.9	13.8	43	48%	.224	0.79	3.21	1.24	1.5				
2019	OAK	MLB	27	4	0	0	5	5	29²	16	3	2.1	9.1	30	41%	.194	0.78	1.21	4.00	0.6	92.4	63.5	13.5	46.1
2020	OAK	MLB	28	10	7	0	24	24	146	134	23	2.8	8.2	133	42%	.274	1.23	3.87	4.20	2.2	92.8	58.2	11.4	48.8

Comparables: Jordan Montgomery, Tyler Duffey, Steven Matz

Manaea returned from Tommy John surgery in time to push Oakland over the top in their playoff quest, throwing five excellent ballgames in September and drawing the start in the Wild Card round against Tampa. Unfortunately for him, folks will remember his disappointing playoff outing far more than anything else, particularly the two misplaced pitches to Yandy Díaz. Regardless, 2019 was a success for Manaea. He's back in the majors, he's pitching effectively, and he'll be ready to go in 2020. His velocity hasn't come *all* the way back yet, and that's legitimate cause for concern: Manaea sat below 91 mph for the first time in his career, and rested three ticks off his average velocity when he entered the league. September proved he could succeed without premium heat, but it was a five-start sample, with four coming against Detroit, Texas, and Seattle. If he can find that missing oomph, he could again be a solid No. 2/3 starter sooner rather than later.

T.J. McFarland LHP Born: 06/08/89 Age: 31 Bats: L Throws: L Height: 6'3" Weight: 220 Origin: Round 4, 2007 Draft (#137 overall)

YEAR	TEAM	LVL	AGE	W	L	SV	G	GS	IP	H	HR	BB/9	K/9	K	GB%	BABIP	WHIP	ERA	DRA	WARP	MPH	FB%	WHF	CSP
2017	RNO	AAA	28	0	0	1	7	0	11	6	0	3.3	7.4	9	81%	.231	0.91	0.00	2.90	0.3				
2017	ARI	MLB	28	4	5	0	43	1	54	65	4	2.8	4.8	29	69%	.323	1.52	5.33	5.89	-0.4	93.0	73.1	7.7	43.7
2018	ARI	MLB	29	2	2	1	47	0	72	64	4	2.8	5.2	42	68%	.268	1.19	2.00	4.72	0.2	92.1	72.7	8.8	41.6
2019	ARI	MLB	30	0	0	0	51	0	56	71	6	3.2	5.6	35	62%	.346	1.62	4.82	6.54	-0.7	90.8	68.6	10.8	42.8
2020	OAK	MLB	31	1	1	0	16	0	17	19	2	2.8	5.5	11	62%	.297	1.39	4.34	4.55	0.1	91.0	70.7	9.3	42.4

Comparables: Chris Rusin, Kyle Lobstein, Duane Below

DRA said McFarland's 2018 breakout was the product of quite a bit of BABIP luck, and DRA is not to be messed with. Indeed, McFarland's run prevention the previous year was not duplicated and the long-man reverted back to the sub-standard reliever he had been for the majority of his career. A contact-oriented, ground ball pitcher, McFarland's best path to success is generating soft contact that can be gobbled up by his infielders, but his hard-hit rate ballooned and his ERA expanded right alongside it, putting his future as a big league-caliber reliever in doubt.

Frankie Montas RHP Born: 03/21/93 Age: 27 Bats: R Throws: R Height: 6'2" Weight: 245 Origin: International Free Agent, 2009

YEAR	TEAM	LVL	AGE	W	L	SV	G	GS	IP	H	HR	BB/9	K/9	K	GB%	BABIP	WHIP	ERA	DRA	WARP	MPH	FB%	WHF	CSP
2017	NAS	AAA	24	0	2	0	9	8	29¹	25	4	2.1	11.4	37	53%	.296	1.09	5.22	2.53	1.0				
2017	OAK	MLB	24	1	1	0	23	0	32	39	10	5.6	10.1	36	36%	.349	1.84	7.03	6.69	-0.5	100.6	66.3	12.3	49.9
2018	NAS	AAA	25	4	5	0	15	15	71²	69	7	3.3	7.7	61	48%	.300	1.33	4.65	4.42	0.9				
2018	OAK	MLB	25	5	4	0	13	11	65	74	5	2.9	6.0	43	44%	.325	1.46	3.88	5.59	-0.2	98.1	72.5	9.4	51.3
2019	OAK	MLB	26	9	2	0	16	16	96	84	8	2.2	9.7	103	50%	.297	1.11	2.62	3.16	2.7	98.9	56.8	12.7	49.3
2020	OAK	MLB	27	12	9	0	29	29	175	163	22	3.3	9.3	181	47%	.299	1.30	3.84	4.11	2.8	98.4	63.6	11.8	50.7

Comparables: Jake Faria, John Gant, Robert Gsellman

For three months, Montas was one of the game's best pitchers. For all the world, it looked like Frustrating Frankie had turned the corner from talented, oft-injured pitcher into one of the game's finest hurlers. Through 15 starts and 90 innings, the righty punched out 97 hitters with excellent peripherals; his ERA was near the top of the league, and he looked like a shoe-in for the All-Star game.

On June 21st, one day after tossing eight innings of one run ball in a win over the Rays, Montas was suspended 80 games for testing positive for ostarine, a banned substance. News of his transgression struck like a thunderbolt, an uncomfortable flashback to the mid-aughts when we first learned to treat every breakout with cynical suspicion. Montas returned in September in time to make one final start, a good outing that did as much to highlight how much Oakland missed their ace in the one-game playoff as anything else. If there's a bright side here for Montas, it's that the baseball community has become much more tolerant of its PED users over time; Nelson Cruz's name is in better shape than many guys listed in the infamous Mitchell Report. If last year's breakout was real, and it's not clear why it wouldn't be, last year's suspension will soon become a footnote in his career.

Yusmeiro Petit RHP Born: 11/22/84 Age: 35 Bats: R Throws: R Height: 6'1" Weight: 255 Origin: International Free Agent, 2001

YEAR	TEAM	LVL	AGE	W	L	SV	G	GS	IP	H	HR	BB/9	K/9	K	GB%	BABIP	WHIP	ERA	DRA	WARP	MPH	FB%	WHF	CSP
2017	LAA	MLB	32	5	2	4	60	1	91¹	69	9	1.8	10.0	101	34%	.267	0.95	2.76	2.83	2.4	91.4	47.8	11.6	48.5
2018	OAK	MLB	33	7	3	0	74	0	93	76	13	1.7	7.4	76	36%	.241	1.01	3.00	3.74	1.3	91.4	47.5	10	51.1
2019	OAK	MLB	34	5	3	0	80	0	83	57	11	1.1	7.7	71	32%	.213	0.81	2.71	3.93	1.3	90.8	45.8	12.4	49
2020	OAK	MLB	35	3	3	2	60	0	63	59	13	1.9	7.9	56	33%	.266	1.14	3.80	4.29	0.6	90.0	46.1	11.1	48.7

Comparables: Dan Wheeler, Tim Stauffer, Brandon McCarthy

Petit is a righty with an 88 mph fastball, extremely low spin rates and... (double-checks notes) solid whiff rates and elite contact management numbers? This is not generally a skillset that plays well in 2019. But Petit does all of the little things right: His arm slot is a little funky. He has elite control. He's sneaky fast. While he doesn't get much spin on the ball, his hook moves like crazy and his change flops off the deck on its way to the plate. This may all be witchcraft: perhaps Petit has the ability to freeze time and uses his power to subtly tweak the location and trajectory of his pitches on their way to the plate. It would be a questionable use of such powers, to be sure, but one we're lucky to enjoy all the same.

★ ★ ★ *2020 Top 101 Prospect* **#17** ★ ★ ★

A.J. Puk LHP Born: 04/25/95 Age: 25 Bats: L Throws: L Height: 6'7" Weight: 238 Origin: Round 1, 2016 Draft (#6 overall)

YEAR	TEAM	LVL	AGE	W	L	SV	G	GS	IP	H	HR	BB/9	K/9	K	GB%	BABIP	WHIP	ERA	DRA	WARP	MPH	FB%	WHF	CSP
2017	STO	A+	22	4	5	0	14	11	61	44	1	3.4	14.5	98	42%	.336	1.10	3.69	2.35	2.0				
2017	MID	AA	22	2	5	0	13	13	64	64	2	3.5	12.1	86	48%	.380	1.39	4.36	3.51	1.3				
2019	STO	A+	24	0	0	0	3	3	6	5	2	6.0	13.5	9	33%	.300	1.50	6.00	5.31	0.0				
2019	MID	AA	24	0	0	0	6	1	8¹	9	2	3.2	14.0	13	58%	.412	1.44	4.32	5.92	-0.1				
2019	LVG	AAA	24	4	1	0	9	0	11	7	3	2.5	13.1	16	45%	.222	0.91	4.91	2.25	0.4				
2019	OAK	MLB	24	2	0	0	10	0	11¹	10	1	4.0	10.3	13	45%	.321	1.32	3.18	3.44	0.2	99.2	63.9	14.4	52.1
2020	OAK	MLB	25	7	6	0	43	16	110	97	17	3.3	10.4	127	44%	.292	1.25	3.79	4.11	1.7	98.9	65.4	14.7	53.4

Comparables: José De León, Sean Newcomb, Brian Matusz

The X-factor in Oakland's farm system, Puk returned from 2018 Tommy John surgery in time to fortify the A's bullpen in September. And what a debut it was, as he struck out 13 hitters in 11 very effective innings, showing off legitimately nasty stuff along the way. He missed bats with all three of his primary offerings, and sat above 97 mph with the fastball. It's not entirely clear whether he's returned to his pre-injury form: He threw only 36 innings across four levels last year, all of them in relief or at least very short starting stints. He still needs to get stretched out, didn't use the curve much, and he may not be all the way past the lingering command problems most TJ returnees have to battle through. But anyone worried about his long term future after the surgery has to be encouraged at this point. Puk is again one of the game's top pitching prospects and he should challenge for big league starts right out of the chute.

Joakim Soria RHP Born: 05/18/84 Age: 36 Bats: R Throws: R Height: 6'3" Weight: 200 Origin: International Free Agent, 2001

YEAR	TEAM	LVL	AGE	W	L	SV	G	GS	IP	H	HR	BB/9	K/9	K	GB%	BABIP	WHIP	ERA	DRA	WARP	MPH	FB%	WHF	CSP
2017	KCA	MLB	33	4	3	1	59	0	56	49	1	3.2	10.3	64	58%	.329	1.23	3.70	3.62	1.0	95.1	49.3	13.5	46.6
2018	CHA	MLB	34	0	3	16	40	0	38²	35	2	2.3	11.4	49	35%	.324	1.16	2.56	2.35	1.1	94.5	63	15.4	45.8
2018	MIL	MLB	34	3	1	0	26	0	22	18	2	2.5	10.6	26	48%	.286	1.09	4.09	2.94	0.5	94.8	71.2	14.2	50.1
2019	OAK	MLB	35	2	4	1	71	1	69	51	9	2.6	10.3	79	39%	.251	1.03	4.30	3.48	1.4	94.9	68.2	14.1	51.3
2020	OAK	MLB	36	3	3	4	55	0	58	50	8	2.7	10.0	64	41%	.285	1.16	3.28	3.64	1.0	93.5	61.7	13.9	47.8

Comparables: Luke Gregerson, John Wetteland, Jonathan Papelbon

You can infer a lot from looking at a player's collection of BP Annual comments, particularly if they have 14 of them, as Soria does. He marked his arrival to the Annual as a Rule 5 pick, a perceived nifty acquisition based on our new understanding of Mexican League park effects. From there, there's a mention of "adjusted runs prevented," apparently a proprietary pitching metric of some years ago. We also see a mention of "Mexicutioner" before Soria begged off the nickname given the level of violence in his native country. Reflecting on more recent entries, such as the note about how the slider fueled Soria's late career renaissance, and you see that these comments are symbiotically telling the story of a player and the game itself. So, if you're wondering why you found this book in the anthropology section, well, here's your answer.

Lou Trivino RHP Born: 10/01/91 Age: 28 Bats: R Throws: R Height: 6'5" Weight: 240 Origin: Round 11, 2013 Draft (#341 overall)

YEAR	TEAM	LVL	AGE	W	L	SV	G	GS	IP	H	HR	BB/9	K/9	K	GB%	BABIP	WHIP	ERA	DRA	WARP	MPH	FB%	WHF	CSP
2017	MID	AA	25	7	1	1	23	0	33¹	31	0	2.7	9.2	34	57%	.333	1.23	2.43	3.92	0.3				
2017	NAS	AAA	25	1	2	4	25	0	35	33	0	2.8	8.0	31	54%	.308	1.26	3.60	3.10	0.8				
2018	OAK	MLB	26	8	3	4	69	1	74	53	8	3.8	10.0	82	47%	.256	1.14	2.92	3.10	1.6	99.4	53.7	15.1	47.8
2019	OAK	MLB	27	4	6	0	61	0	60	61	7	4.7	8.6	57	47%	.316	1.53	5.25	4.67	0.4	98.9	50.8	13.3	46.3
2020	OAK	MLB	28	3	3	0	60	0	63	58	9	4.2	9.7	69	46%	.294	1.37	4.21	4.34	0.6	98.6	52.5	14.3	47.3

Comparables: Josh Roenicke, Colton Murray, Jacob Barnes

Asked about Oakland's dominant 'pen in 2018, Robinson Canó specifically highlighted Trivino: "For me, the nastiest of all is Trivino... You can't tell if it's going to be a cutter or a sinker and (all his pitches) move." What a difference a year makes. In 2019, his velocity dropped slightly, he stopped missing bats, started walking people, saw his BABIP spike, his strand rate plummet, and his role on the team diminish. Look, relievers are a volatile species: Trivino's step back wasn't even the biggest or most surprising dip among relievers with surnames starting with "T-r" in his own bullpen. His electric stuff ensures he'll get chances, even if his limited track record implies that we shouldn't expect a return to peak form.

LINEOUTS

Hitters

HITTER	POS	TEAM	LVL	AGE	PA	R	2B	3B	HR	RBI	BB	K	SB	CS	AVG/OBP/SLG	DRC+	VORP	BABIP	BRR	FRAA	WARP
Luis Barrera	CF	MID	AA	23	240	35	9	11	4	24	12	48	9	7	.321/.357/.513	136	19.5	.393	-1.0	CF(36): -5.5, RF(14): 3.0	1.1
Skye Bolt	OF	OAK	MLB	25	11	1	1	0	0	0	1	3	0	0	.100/.182/.200	77	0.0	.143	-0.1	CF(3): 0.0, RF(1): 0.0	0.0
	OF	LVG	AAA	25	347	57	19	3	11	61	37	94	7	5	.269/.350/.459	81	4.8	.351	-0.3	RF(39): 8.5, CF(37): 1.1	1.1
Seth Brown	1B	OAK	MLB	26	83	11	8	2	0	13	7	23	1	0	.293/.361/.453	83	0.3	.423	1.0	LF(23): 0.3, 1B(4): -0.7	0.1
	1B	LVG	AAA	26	500	101	29	6	37	104	38	127	8	1	.297/.352/.634	112	26.3	.330	-0.2	1B(63): 0.6, LF(17): 1.0	1.6
Greg Deichmann	OF	MID	AA	24	340	42	10	2	11	36	34	103	19	5	.219/.300/.375	91	4.6	.289	2.7	RF(69): 0.0, CF(3): 0.2	0.7
Dustin Fowler	OF	LVG	AAA	24	606	98	22	7	25	89	42	145	12	4	.277/.333/.477	82	15.8	.332	0.8	CF(88): -3.5, RF(30): 1.3	0.5
Ryan Goins	2B	CHA	MLB	31	163	13	6	1	2	10	17	44	0	1	.250/.333/.347	75	1.0	.347	-0.5	3B(23): 1.1, SS(14): -0.5	0.1
	2B	CHR	AAA	31	316	47	23	2	10	48	39	77	3	3	.322/.406/.531	130	24.3	.415	2.4	2B(56): 3.2, SS(28): 2.8	2.9
Jonah Heim	C	MID	AA	24	208	20	12	0	5	34	24	27	0	1	.282/.370/.431	137	12.9	.307	-1.6	C(43): 7.7	2.3
	C	LVG	AAA	24	119	22	9	0	4	19	11	18	0	0	.358/.412/.557	125	10.0	.395	-0.5	C(28): 2.2	1.0
Chris Herrmann	C	LVG	AAA	31	58	14	3	1	4	13	6	18	0	0	.333/.397/.667	113	7.3	.433	0.1	C(8): -1.3	0.2
	C	OAK	MLB	31	94	9	3	0	1	8	9	29	0	0	.202/.280/.274	64	0.4	.296	0.1	C(25): -3.1, LF(3): -0.2	-0.3
Kyle McCann	C	AGO	Rk	21	25	10	2	2	2	7	5	6	0	0	.400/.520/1.000	169	6.5	.500	0.0	C(3): 0.2, 1B(1): -0.1	0.2
	C	VER	A-	21	225	23	7	1	7	25	25	81	0	0	.192/.289/.343	85	-0.3	.282	-0.2	1B(19): -1.6, C(18): -0.5	0.0
Marcus Smith	OF	AGO	Rk	18	119	21	6	1	0	14	20	29	1	1	.361/.466/.443	164	12.9	.507	0.9	CF(20): -5.1, LF(7): 0.6	0.6

Be careful not to scout the stat line with **Luis Barrera**, who always posts solid numbers but doesn't project to have the bat or the power to start full-time. He's fast as heck with a 70 arm though, so he should have a big-league role, possibly as early as 2020. ⓧ **Skye Bolt** recorded his first and heretofore only career hit last May. On that occasion, the bat boy took the unusual step of handing Bolt a letterman's jacket, at which point the exuberant batsman donned the coat, flexed his biceps, raised his arms and exclaimed "SKYE BOLT!" ⓧ **Seth Brown** arrived out of nowhere to run an .815 OPS over nearly 100 plate appearances in the season's final month, strong enough play to deserve an honorable mention in BP's Vogelsong Awards. The guess here is that the power doesn't translate well enough for him to be more of an up-and-down guy over the long haul. ⓧ Nine homers in 23 Fall League games rescued an otherwise disappointing season for **Greg Deichmann**, a positionless power hitter with a, uh, *whiff* of up-and-down guy to him. ⓧ **Dustin Fowler** was a top-100 prospect at the time of his debut, when he crashed into a wall and tore his patellar tendon. Grim as it is to say, he hasn't looked like the same player since. ⓧ **Ryan Goins** hit his last extra-base hit of the 2019 season on August 24, and ended his year with a 75 DRC+ that propelled him right back into the light-hitting veteran minor-league deal market from whence he emerged. A brief sign of offensive life will keep him within firing range of drawing a major league check in 2020, which was the goal all along. ⓧ **Jonah Heim** had a backup catcher starter kit when he was drafted six years ago. After a good season in the high minors, it appears that Oakland will assemble the final pieces sometime in 2020. ⓧ On Pentecost Island in Vanuatu, there is a custom where men climb a wooden tower, attach their limbs to vines, and leap toward the ground below. Those whose chests scrape the dirt earn the utmost respect for their daring and bravery; rumors that the one furthest from the ground is forced to wear the community's **Chris Herrmann** shirsey for an entire calendar year were unsubstantiated at press time. ⓧ **Kyle McCann** was drafted as a catcher, but he's likely a first basemen, and he'll head to Beloit next spring. For a metaphor on how Oakland's bat-first prospects have coped with that assignment lately, please direct your attention to the burning pile of tires adjacent to Harry C. Pohlman Field. ⓧ Oakland's 2018 third-rounder, **Marcus Smith** was a nifty find out of a Kansas City high school. Scouts weren't sure how he'd fare against professional pitching, but he looked surprisingly advanced in the AZL, showing off a feel for the barrel alongside 70 speed. He's young but promising.

Pitchers

PITCHER	TEAM	LVL	AGE	W	L	SV	G	GS	IP	H	HR	BB/9	K/9	K	GB%	BABIP	WHIP	ERA	DRA	WARP	MPH	FB%	WHF	CSP
Paul Blackburn	LVG	AAA	25	11	3	0	24	22	132²	133	18	2.3	6.2	92	54%	.293	1.26	4.34	3.24	4.4				
	OAK	MLB	25	0	2	0	4	1	11	19	3	3.3	6.5	8	55%	.390	2.09	10.64	5.60	0.0	92.5	51.3	10.7	42.6
Marco Estrada	STO	A+	35	0	1	0	3	3	6²	9	3	1.4	10.8	8	36%	.316	1.50	8.10	6.09	-0.1				
	OAK	MLB	35	0	2	0	5	5	23²	23	7	3.0	4.2	11	20%	.208	1.31	6.85	8.89	-0.8	89.1	52.7	8.4	49.3
Grant Holmes	MID	AA	23	6	5	0	22	16	81²	71	9	3.0	8.4	76	52%	.281	1.20	3.31	4.78	0.1				
Brian Howard	MID	AA	24	8	8	0	23	23	130	137	7	2.7	8.2	118	42%	.348	1.35	3.25	5.50	-0.9				
	LVG	AAA	24	0	1	0	4	4	14¹	28	4	5.0	10.0	16	36%	.471	2.51	13.81	9.27	-0.4				
Jhenderson Hurtado	VER	A-	23	3	0	1	7	0	23¹	12	1	3.9	13.1	34	42%	.262	0.94	0.77	2.79	0.6				
	BLT	A	23	1	1	1	7	5	31	22	1	3.8	11.0	38	32%	.269	1.13	2.61	3.61	0.5				
Aiden McIntyre	BLT	A	23	3	10	1	27	22	112²	99	5	6.1	12.0	150	42%	.332	1.55	4.15	5.94	-1.1				
Daniel Mengden	LVG	AAA	26	4	3	0	13	10	64	56	8	2.8	8.6	61	53%	.268	1.19	4.22	2.41	2.6				
	OAK	MLB	26	5	2	1	13	9	59²	59	7	4.1	6.3	42	38%	.283	1.44	4.83	7.47	-1.1	94.0	52.6	6.5	48.5
Miguel Romero	LVG	AAA	25	4	1	3	45	1	72²	65	11	4.5	10.0	81	49%	.284	1.39	3.96	3.31	2.1				
Jaime Schultz	OKL	AAA	28	2	3	4	47	1	47²	52	3	5.1	11.7	62	49%	.386	1.66	5.85	2.99	1.5				
	LAN	MLB	28	0	0	0	4	0	5	6	1	5.4	5.4	3	25%	.333	1.80	7.20	6.85	-0.1	97.4	51	11.5	50.2
Chasen Shreve	MEM	AAA	28	2	2	3	51	0	60	45	6	3.9	10.2	68	32%	.275	1.18	3.45	2.54	2.1				
	SLN	MLB	28	1	0	0	3	0	2	2	0	4.5	9.0	2	0%	.333	1.50	9.00	5.93	0.0	91.8	66.7	4.8	34.9
Gus Varland	STO	A+	22	2	1	0	5	4	26¹	23	3	2.7	9.2	27	37%	.294	1.18	2.39	4.20	0.2				
J.B. Wendelken	LVG	AAA	26	6	3	3	30	1	38²	47	8	4.4	10.0	43	46%	.365	1.71	5.59	5.60	0.2				
	OAK	MLB	26	3	1	0	27	0	32²	21	2	2.5	9.4	34	38%	.226	0.92	3.58	4.12	0.4	96.9	60.6	13	49.7

Paul Blackburn's 4.34 ERA was the eighth-best mark in the PCL among hurlers who made at least 15 starts, which says all you need to know about both Blackburn and the PCL last season. ⓧ We have a deep field for the "That guy was an All-Star four years ago?" award this spring, but my money is on **Marco Estrada**. ⓧ **Daniel Gossett** posted a 5.91 ERA in 25 starts in 2017-18, and after missing all of last year with an injury, he'll seek to recapture that form in 2020. ⓧ The best thing about **Grant Holmes** is his hair. That could be true even if he was still a big-time prospect, but it's a more damning statement than it used to be. ⓧ **Brian Howard** is probably just a No. 5 starter, but he's a fun one. He's 6-foot-9 and has some natural deception in his delivery. Between that and surprisingly good control for such a lanky dude, he's awkward to face and that helps him survive with fringy stuff. ⓧ **Jhenderson Hurtado** was assigned to and subsequently scratched from the Arizona Fall League. That was disappointing: After a breakout season, it would have been fun to see how Hurtado's sharp curve and unconventional delivery would have fared against good competition. ⓧ In Little League, you'll sometimes see a big kid who throws too hard—not just for the batter, but also the catcher, umpire, and strike zone. **Aiden McIntyre** is the A-ball equivalent. ⓧ Right ho! Saw this young sport called **Daniel Mengden** take the box for his debut against the Red Stockings in '16. Wrote down 'None too impressed,' in the ol' diary that very evening, 'this yannigan will never make good.' Three years on and he's yet to prove that proclamation incorrect. Shame, really; nice fellow with a delightful handlebar." ⓧ **Miguel Romero** throws a knuckle changeup, a charming detail that separates him from the rest of the right-handed minor league relievers with control problems. ⓧ **Jaime Schultz** is anonymous enough as a baseball player that you're more likely to call to mind Charles Schulz. Allow us to merge the two: Schultz struggled so badly that he was about one hard-hit ball away from getting undressed by those rockets whizzing around him, not unlike Charlie Brown himself. ⓧ **Chasen Shreve** is the rare pitcher who causes both dataheads (spin rate) and batters (home-run rate) to drool over him. That combination should make him popular on the waiver wire—and in opposing dugouts. ⓧ **Gus Varland** entered 2019 as a sleeper, and after making only five appearances in the Cal League, he's now a sleeper with a history of arm trouble. When healthy he hits the mid-90s with two usable breaking balls, and he may be able to start. ⓧ **J.B. Wendelken** isn't a flight attendant on the route between Oakland and Las Vegas, but he's taken the trip enough to know the job pretty well by now. He's pitched well enough to get a full-time shot in the bullpen, and now out of options, 2020 may be his best chance to do so.

PHILADELPHIA PHILLIES

Essay by Holly Wendt

Player comments by Mike Gianella and BP staff

Most everyone who might be reading this is familiar with the story of Romeo and Juliet, if not through a required high school reading of William Shakespeare's play, then through the sprawling net of imaginings and re-imaginings that have been cast over the past 400 years. Everyone knows it's a tragedy—the very prologue of the play announces it:

> From forth the fatal loins of these two foes
> A pair of star-cross'd lovers take their life;
> Whose misadventured piteous overthrows
> Do with their death bury their parents' strife.
> (I.i.5-8)[1]

To call a baseball season—any season, no matter how bad—a tragedy makes no sense, not in the context of the wide world in which we live. A baseball season is a tally of won games and lost games, that's all. Those wins and losses break hearts, sure. But a tragedy in the more common, less theatrical definition of the word? No. And yet, here is "Romeo and Juliet" in the Phillies essay, or rather *Romeo + Juliet*, Baz Luhrmann's garish, extravagant 1996 tumble through Shakespeare's text, and that is because *Romeo + Juliet* is a baseball movie.

In Luhrmann's iteration, Romeo's banishment from Verona for killing Juliet's cousin Tybalt takes Romeo to a dust-swept RV park, and as bad news speeds toward him and good news blows away on a missed package notice come unstuck from his door, Romeo stands out back, hitting stones with a bat made of a broken branch. As far as baseball film tropes go, the image is iconic, even though it's anguish and rage and probably boredom that toss the stone up and crank the stick forward in this iteration, not the yard-bound dreams of youth. Romeo has a whole bucket of stones, but the viewer only watches him hit one. It sounds like he makes good contact.

⚾   ⚾   ⚾

The ending of "Romeo and Juliet" is so wrenching because it almost works out. With Friar Lawrence's help, Juliet fakes death to escape another marriage and is given a perfect

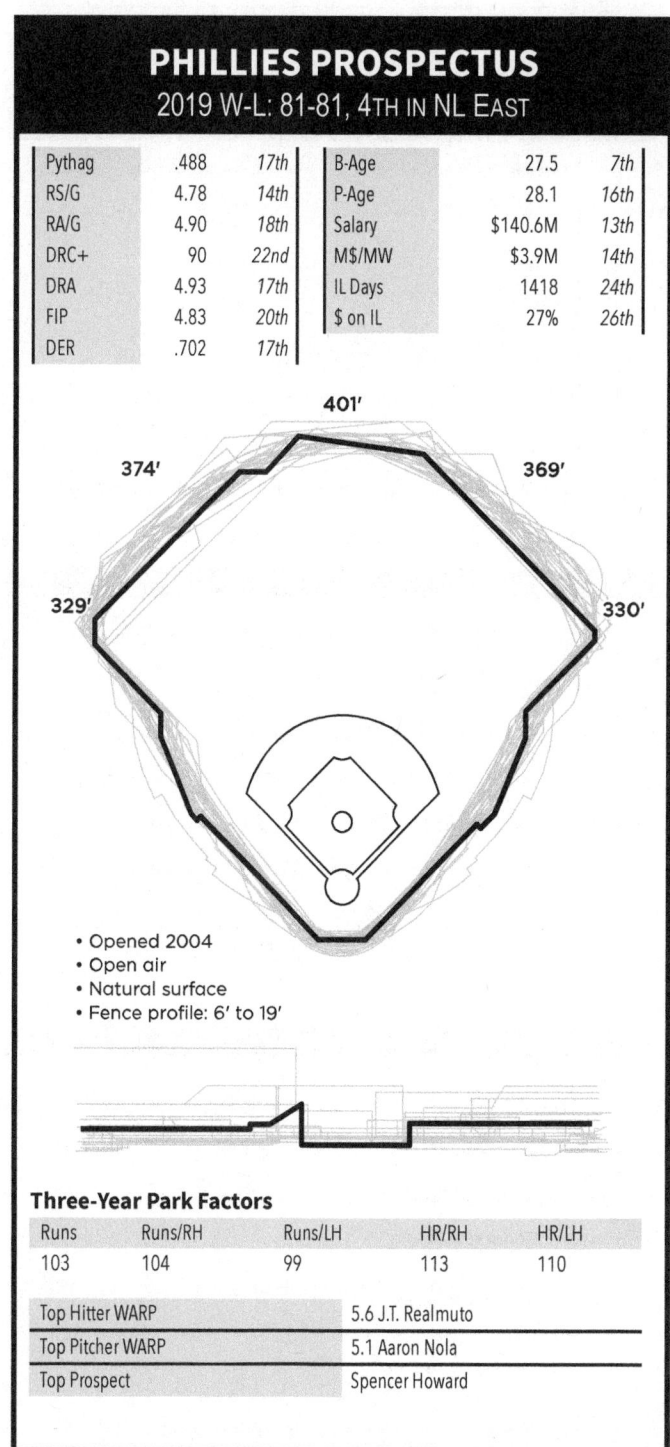

PHILLIES PROSPECTUS
2019 W-L: 81-81, 4TH IN NL EAST

Pythag	.488	17th	B-Age	27.5	7th
RS/G	4.78	14th	P-Age	28.1	16th
RA/G	4.90	18th	Salary	$140.6M	13th
DRC+	90	22nd	M$/MW	$3.9M	14th
DRA	4.93	17th	IL Days	1418	24th
FIP	4.83	20th	$ on IL	27%	26th
DER	.702	17th			

401'
374'   369'
329'   330'

- Opened 2004
- Open air
- Natural surface
- Fence profile: 6' to 19'

Three-Year Park Factors

Runs	Runs/RH	Runs/LH	HR/RH	HR/LH
103	104	99	113	110

Top Hitter WARP	5.6 J.T. Realmuto
Top Pitcher WARP	5.1 Aaron Nola
Top Prospect	Spencer Howard

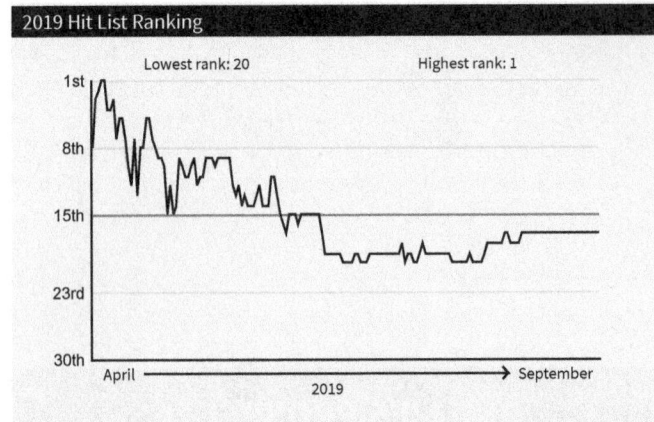

2019 Hit List Ranking

Lowest rank: 20   Highest rank: 1

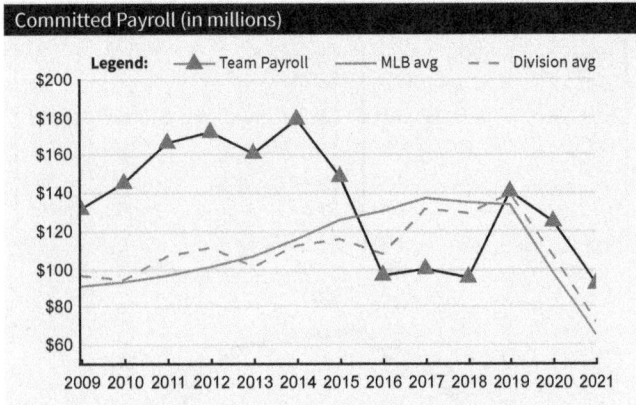

Committed Payroll (in millions)

Legend: Team Payroll — MLB avg — Division avg

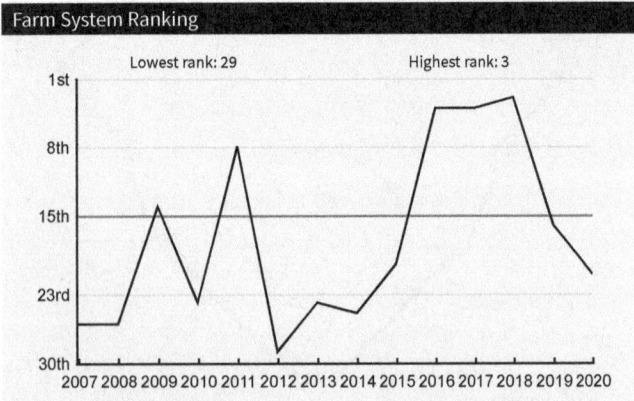

Farm System Ranking

Lowest rank: 29   Highest rank: 3

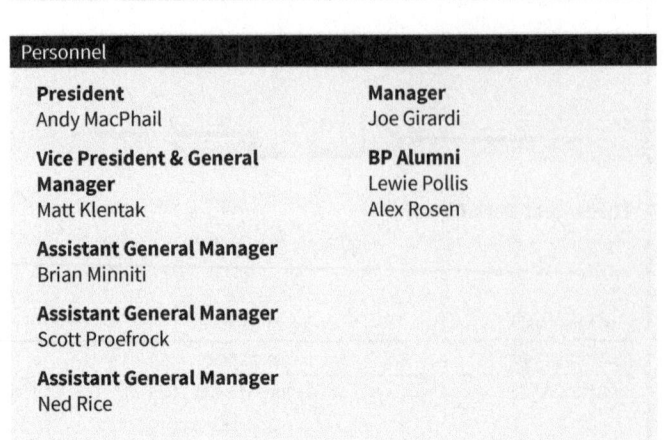

Personnel

President
Andy MacPhail

Vice President & General Manager
Matt Klentak

Assistant General Manager
Brian Minniti

Assistant General Manager
Scott Proefrock

Assistant General Manager
Ned Rice

Manager
Joe Girardi

BP Alumni
Lewie Pollis
Alex Rosen

hiding place in the Capulet vault to wait for Romeo and their future together. If Romeo gets the right message, sleeping Juliet can be spirited from the tomb and the two young lovers have the promise of happily ever after. But Romeo gets only the message of the appearance—Juliet's death—and he goes to the tomb bearing poison. He kills himself a moment before Juliet wakes, and she, in despair, takes up his dagger. Many stagings of the play toy with the nearness of the miss: Juliet's hand moves while Romeo looks elsewhere or the actor gives some other signal that happiness could be mere seconds away, until it isn't. Luhrmann's iteration of the scene is so striking because they're both conscious at the same time. A poisoned Romeo watches Juliet wake. They speak their last lines to each other, not to the dark air of the tomb, and it's still too late. By seconds, by a knife's edge, still too late.

The 2019 Phillies season did not come down to any kind of tenterhooked almost. Instead, the 2019 Phillies enacted their slow-motion collapse as Atlanta and, more meteorically, Washington, climbed. But the Phillies might have been chasing real success. If the admittedly thin rotation had performed at least to expectation—if Aaron Nola hadn't opened and closed the year with uncharacteristic hittableness; if Jake Arrieta's elbow hadn't developed another bone spur. If the front office had done more to bolster pitching altogether; if the one splashy offseason bullpen addition—David Robertson—hadn't found himself hurt and in Dr. James Andrews's office and facing more than the loss of one season. If Andrew McCutchen hadn't been waylaid by a knee injury a mere third of the way through. If Rhys Hoskins hadn't fallen into a slump so deep it might have been a grave. If Pat Neshek, if Tommy Hunter—

How many *ifs* can one narrative sustain?

If, in Shakespeare's play, the messenger hadn't been obstructed by plague quarantine. If, in Luhrmann's film, the package delivery notice hadn't blown away. If, in all versions, Romeo had arrived five minutes later. If only.

⚾   ⚾   ⚾

Though what most remember of Romeo's friend Mercutio in *Romeo + Juliet* is Harold Perrineau in a glittering silver skirt and crimson lipstick passing out ecstasy, all iterations of Mercutio attempt to bring reason to the play. Mercutio, as neither Montague nor Capulet, feels no reflexive obligation toward the central blood feud. Mercutio is playful where others are serious, which is to say, Mercutio treats the cycle of insult and honor as only so much puffery. Though the play doesn't openly acknowledge as much, an ounce of the same attitude from both the warring families would make this a comedy, not a tragedy. Instead, the play forces Mercutio's hand and pulls him into the violence, too. As he's dying, fatally wounded in an attempt to protect Romeo from Juliet's cousin Tybalt, he curses the Capulets and the Montagues for both houses' inability to see sense and make peace.

Earlier in the play, Mercutio even questions Romeo's impulsive, youthful passions (which are the same passions that lead to a double suicide at the story's close). Mercutio does this in the famous Queen Mab speech, in which the fairies' midwife manipulates dreams and makes mischief. This speech is often presented as sheer fancy (in Luhrmann's film, Mercutio is literally on drugs at the time), but in context, it serves as a reality check. Mercutio uses whimsy to mock Romeo's hyperbolic, melancholic mooning over Rosaline, the girl for whom Romeo is sick with love at the play's opening and the girl for whom Romeo spares not a thought the moment he sees Juliet. Mercutio derides the extremity of Romeo's sentiment, and, when Romeo begins to convey what is sure to be a melodramatic portent, Mercutio, sagely, has no patience for it:

> ROMEO
> I dreamt a dream tonight.
> MERCUTIO
> And so did I.
> ROMEO
> Well, what was yours?
> MERCUTIO
> That dreamers often lie. (I.iv.53-56)[2]

Later in the same scene, while Romeo protests the veracity of his feelings (which are soon to be revealed as easily dismissed), Mercutio says,

> True, I talk of dreams,
> Which are the children of an idle brain,
> Begot of nothing but vain fantasy,
> Which is as thin of substance as the air.
> (I.iv.103-106)[3]

See reason, Mercutio says. But reason isn't romantic. Pragmatism doesn't sell tissues or tickets, and pragmatism flew out the window on Thursday, August 15, when, with the bases loaded, in the bottom of the ninth, Bryce Harper muscled Derek Holland's 2-2 sinker hand over hand into the second deck for the single most satisfying moment of the season. There's your balcony scene, Philadelphia. But you know how this play ends. Don't get your hopes up when Juliet's eyelids flutter.

⚾   ⚾   ⚾

It's the contemplation of what might have been that is so wrenching, the heady heights of the early acts. The team spent sixty spring days in first place in the NL East, but a terrible conclusion to June—one marked by a centerpiece of a seven-game skid—kicked into motion that steady decline. Though it would take until September's six-game losing streak to echo June's particular awfulness, the more damning piece was that the Phillies couldn't conjure success on a similar scale, not once all season. The team enjoyed a handful of four-game win streaks over the course of the

season, but only one of those came in the second half. They did not find a way to "go on a tear." What they found was a way to infuriatingly replicate too many of the worst parts of 2018, despite real and reasonable improvements in the offseason. The 2019 Phillies roster was significantly, objectively better than 2018's, and yet the tangible effects of that improvement equaled one additional win.

Definitions of tragedy, in their theatrical or literary sense, generally hinge on the question of hamartia, which most take to signify the protagonist's fatal flaw. The source of the flaw in this sense is within the character's control: it's an excess of pride, ambition, indecision, suggestibility, jealousy. The literary world has a tragedy for every season, and it's easy enough to map any of those onto baseball and to add a few more: miserliness, naivete, moral bankruptcy. But what if it's not so easy to point a specific finger? (Or what if there are simply too many things at which to point?)

Scholar Jules Brody offers an older definition of the word:

> Hamartia is a morally neutral non-normative term, derived from the verb hamartano, meaning "to miss the mark," "to fall short of an objective." And by extension: to reach one destination rather than the intended one; to make a mistake, not in the sense of a moral failure, but in the nonjudgmental sense of taking one thing for another, taking something for its opposite. Hamartia may betoken an error of discernment due to ignorance, to the lack of an essential piece of information. Finally, hamartia may be viewed simply as an act which, for whatever reason, ends in failure rather than success.[4]

Herein lie the 2019 Phillies in the only way I can understand them, which is not especially illuminating. Injury is the purview of chance, especially as it pertains to players like McCutchen and Robertson, two players who have heretofore enjoyed the lion's share of luck and durability in relation to their bodies and their work. There is no model against the cruel and curious whims of the universe. But if it's hard to pinpoint a sole cause—or even a small group of them—what can be corrected? If, beyond chance, the vast majority of the players on the team perform below expectations—even and especially the ones for whom a team has the highest hopes—in concert, what is to be done?

Well, one thing that was done was to relieve some people of their duties. If it's difficult to make something tangibly better, at least make it different. Hitting coach John Mallee was replaced by Charlie Manuel (in interim capacity) in August and pitching coach Chris Young was let go at season's end. Though much beloved in Philadelphia, Charlie had no swift resolution for the quiet bats (Harper's near-immediate moonshot notwithstanding). No reverse Friar Lawrence here, bearing a potion for waking. And, as seemed inevitable as the regular season ended, Gabe Kapler, whose managerial stint in Philadelphia died amid the accumulated wreckage of two dismal Septembers, has been replaced. The Phillies chose Joe Girardi.

"Romeo and Juliet" ends with a nod toward peace between the Montagues and Capulets, a peace born of the ugliest kind of failure, but the failure in the play is easy enough to name: vengefulness, pride, and those occasional caprices of the author's hand that move in the guise of chance. Here is the thesis of a thousand sophomore-year essays: success—which is to say peace, harmony, happiness—might have been one interaction away for Juliet and her Romeo. What peace in Philadelphia?

When last Joe Girardi stood meaningfully in a dugout in Citizens Bank Park, it was as the manager of the New York Yankees, en route to a 4-2 triumph in the 2009 World Series. When the Phillies announced Girardi's hiring in October, former Phillies outfielder Shane Victorino welcomed him, saying he was still mad about '09, but he'd forgive him if Girardi could get the current Phillies another championship.[5] It's a joke, and it isn't. The Phillies 2009 World Series loss stands as the edge of a steep downward slope. Not even the frighteningly impressive rotation including Roy Halladay,

Cliff Lee, Cole Hamels, and Roy Oswalt could spur the team back to championship play, and there've been no trips to the playoffs at all since 2011.

One may erase a handful of those fruitless years with the word *rebuild*. Those years had a different destination than the one the team declared by signing Harper and McCutchen and acquiring Realmuto an offseason ago. (One may argue that declaring one particular destination—playoff-bound—with an expected rotation of Nola, Arrieta, and a lot of *hope* regarding a handful of pitchers who have never quite managed to execute success for any particular duration, is another oft-cited source of hamartia: hubris. But, as Jules Brody writes, let's call it "failure for whatever reason.")

Regardless of signings and the absence of such, it's the players on the field, the actors on the wide, green stage under so many lights, who have to see the story through. It's going to take a lot of good contact. It's going to take Fortune's favors. It's going to take success, which is to say the cumulative effect of 162 games, which, for whatever reason, end in success, rather than failure. That, and only that, will bury this decade of strife. ◼

—Holly Wendt is an author of Baseball Prospectus.

---

1. William Shakespeare, "Romeo and Juliet," in The Riverside Shakespeare, 2nd ed. (New York: Houghton Mifflin, 1997), 1104-1139.

2. Ibid.

3. Ibid.

4. Jules Brody, "Fate, Philology, Freud," Philosophy and Literature 38 (2014): 1-29.

5. Philadelphia Phillies, "Photo of Joe Girardi." Instagram, 28 October 2019. Accessed 3 November 2019. https://www.instagram.com/p/B4LYuFzJBmA/?igshid=93486k06b4vj

Hitters

★ ★ ★ *2020 Top 101 Prospect* **#40** ★ ★ ★

Alec Bohm **3B** Born: 08/03/96 Age: 23 Bats: R Throws: R Height: 6'5" Weight: 225 Origin: Round 1, 2018 Draft (#3 overall)

YEAR	TEAM	LVL	AGE	PA	R	2B	3B	HR	RBI	BB	K	SB	CS	AVG/OBP/SLG	DRC+	VORP	BABIP	BRR	FRAA	WARP
2018	PLL	RK	21	27	8	1	1	0	3	2	0	2	0	.391/.481/.522	147	2.1	.391	-1.6	3B(5): 1.3	0.2
2018	WPT	A-	21	121	9	5	1	0	12	10	19	1	0	.224/.314/.290	89	-0.4	.273	-0.9	3B(20): -2.7	-0.2
2019	LWD	A	22	93	13	9	0	3	11	12	14	3	0	.367/.441/.595	213	14.3	.406	-0.8	3B(14): -0.8, 1B(5): -0.1	1.1
2019	CLR	A+	22	177	25	10	3	4	27	17	21	1	2	.329/.395/.506	173	18.1	.358	0.8	3B(25): 1.1, 1B(7): 0.6	2.0
2019	REA	AA	22	270	38	11	1	14	42	28	38	2	2	.269/.344/.500	154	16.4	.265	-0.7	3B(43): 0.0, 1B(12): -0.8	2.1
2020	PHI	MLB	23	280	31	13	1	10	35	21	54	1	0	.256/.317/.433	96	4.9	.290	-0.4	3B -1	0.5

Comparables: Matt Antonelli, Carlos Asuaje, Adam Duvall

Bohm's prospect status entering 2019 was based far more on projection than performance. The third-overall pick in the 2018 draft missed a month with a knee injury, didn't play in a full-season league and couldn't even clear the fences once in his first taste of pro ball. Yet, he put those concerns to rest with a strong season across three levels, looking like the hitter everyone thought the Phillies drafted: a future stud with the rare combination of plus power and contact. Bohm's glove is another story. He has worked hard on improving his defense, but his slow footwork and lack of instincts at the hot corner are evident. He's going to be an offensive mainstay in Philadelphia regardless of where he plays, but Rhys Hoskins v2.0 at a corner outfield slot or the hot corner isn't optimal for an organization that has struggled to put quality defenders on the diamond of late.

Jay Bruce **RF**   Born: 04/03/87   Age: 33   Bats: L   Throws: L   Height: 6'3"   Weight: 225   Origin: Round 1, 2005 Draft (#12 overall)

YEAR	TEAM	LVL	AGE	PA	R	2B	3B	HR	RBI	BB	K	SB	CS	AVG/OBP/SLG	DRC+	VORP	BABIP	BRR	FRAA	WARP
2017	NYN	MLB	30	448	61	20	2	29	75	39	102	0	1	.256/.321/.520	115	25.6	.271	0.1	RF(92): 2.3, 1B(11): -0.1	2.0
2017	CLE	MLB	30	169	21	9	2	7	26	18	37	1	0	.248/.331/.477	114	6.9	.283	0.4	RF(41): -2.7, 1B(1): 0.0	0.4
2018	SLU	A+	31	27	3	1	0	1	2	2	6	0	0	.360/.407/.520	139	2.3	.444	0.0	RF(3): -0.4, 1B(3): 0.2	0.1
2018	NYN	MLB	31	361	31	18	1	9	37	41	75	2	3	.223/.310/.370	91	2.2	.263	-1.8	RF(64): -0.6, 1B(21): -0.2	0.0
2019	SEA	MLB	32	184	27	11	0	14	28	16	53	1	0	.212/.283/.533	115	7.2	.210	0.6	RF(24): -1.5, 1B(16): 0.5	1.0
2019	PHI	MLB	32	149	16	6	0	12	31	3	29	0	0	.221/.235/.510	97	3.7	.190	0.1	LF(31): 3.6	0.7
2020	PHI	MLB	33	238	29	10	1	14	36	19	62	2	1	.212/.278/.453	85	1.5	.228	0.0	LF 1, 1B 0	0.3

Comparables: Jesse Barfield, Justin Upton, Wil Myers

Bruce's last two seasons have been so injury riddled that BP's lawyers had to carefully review this comment to make sure it wasn't committing a HIPAA violation. Initially, a change of scenery and leagues seemed to light a fire under Bruce, as he hit seven home runs in his first 12 games for the Mariners, but only two hits of the non-dong variety led to a bizarre .204/.298/.673 line. Before his BABIP could get right, his left Achilles went wrong on April 12, setting off a series of maladies that marred Bruce's season. Traded to the Phillies in early June, he missed time with hamstring, elbow and Achilles (again) injuries before finally landing on the IL on July 17 with a right oblique strain. Upon returning, he lasted exactly one day before a new injury - a left flexor strain for those playing Bruce malady bingo at home - put him back on the shelf and rendered him a 1990's-style pinch hitter the rest of the way. Only 32 on Opening Day, Bruce has what Bill James once described as "old player skills" and while Bruce can still put a charge into the ball, that alone won't allow him to hang around well into his 30s.

Luis Garcia **MI**   Born: 10/01/00   Age: 19   Bats: B   Throws: R   Height: 5'11"   Weight: 170   Origin: International Free Agent, 2017

YEAR	TEAM	LVL	AGE	PA	R	2B	3B	HR	RBI	BB	K	SB	CS	AVG/OBP/SLG	DRC+	VORP	BABIP	BRR	FRAA	WARP
2018	PLL	RK	17	187	33	11	3	1	32	15	21	12	8	.369/.433/.488	196	22.6	.418	-0.1	SS(43): -2.1	2.2
2019	LWD	A	18	524	36	14	3	4	36	44	132	9	8	.186/.261/.255	58	-9.8	.247	-5.0	SS(71): -0.2, 2B(55): -5.3	-1.4
2020	PHI	MLB	19	251	20	11	1	3	21	18	71	4	2	.208/.271/.304	55	-6.8	.284	-0.3	SS -1, 2B -1	-0.9

Comparables: Jefry Marte, Carson Kelly, Cheslor Cuthbert

Garcia struggled mightily in his first taste of full-season ball. He looked overmatched most of the year, his diminutive size serving to his disadvantage as even when Garcia made contact, he had difficulty making it count. All this means little if anything in terms of Garcia's long-term outlook. He has solid barrel control and bat speed, is still a good-looking defender up the middle and is eventually going to grow into that gangly frame of his. He was also one of only four 18-year-old players who logged significant time in the Sally League. All Garcia's poor 2019 means is that he is on a longer developmental path; he has plenty of time to break out and live up to the hype that made him such a prized signing in 2017.

Didi Gregorius **SS**   Born: 02/18/90   Age: 30   Bats: L   Throws: R   Height: 6'3"   Weight: 205   Origin: International Free Agent, 2007

YEAR	TEAM	LVL	AGE	PA	R	2B	3B	HR	RBI	BB	K	SB	CS	AVG/OBP/SLG	DRC+	VORP	BABIP	BRR	FRAA	WARP
2017	NYA	MLB	27	570	73	27	0	25	87	25	70	3	1	.287/.318/.478	115	38.4	.287	1.9	SS(135): 4.9	4.4
2018	NYA	MLB	28	569	89	23	5	27	86	48	69	10	6	.268/.335/.494	121	40.3	.259	2.3	SS(132): 0.4	4.4
2019	NYA	MLB	29	344	47	14	2	16	61	17	53	2	1	.238/.276/.441	96	14.9	.237	1.0	SS(80): -7.3	0.8
2020	PHI	MLB	30	560	61	25	2	21	71	32	92	6	2	.243/.294/.421	87	13.0	.258	1.8	SS 1, 2B 0	1.4

Comparables: Marwin Gonzalez, Freddy Galvis, Eduardo Escobar

Sir Didi, The Knight in shining pinstripes, spent his last year donning the iconic uniform and he went out, not with a bang, but a whimper. Fighting back from Tommy John surgery, it was an open question as to whether or not Gregorius would be the same player he was before: a smooth-fielding shortstop with newly acquired lefty power. And while the power still flashed, it was an unfortunate façade as his approach returned to its pre-2018 days and his defense unraveled. The truncated recovery time and lack of spring training certainly played a role in his lackluster performance, but with Gleyber Torres locked into the six, there was no need for the Yankees to find out exactly how much positive regression can be expected first-hand.

Bryce Harper **RF**   Born: 10/16/92   Age: 27   Bats: L   Throws: R   Height: 6'3"   Weight: 220   Origin: Round 1, 2010 Draft (#1 overall)

YEAR	TEAM	LVL	AGE	PA	R	2B	3B	HR	RBI	BB	K	SB	CS	AVG/OBP/SLG	DRC+	VORP	BABIP	BRR	FRAA	WARP
2017	WAS	MLB	24	492	95	27	1	29	87	68	99	4	2	.319/.413/.595	147	47.2	.356	-1.3	RF(110): -3.4	3.5
2018	WAS	MLB	25	695	103	34	0	34	100	130	169	13	3	.249/.393/.496	126	53.0	.289	-3.2	RF(116): -12.1, CF(63): -0.1	2.5
2019	PHI	MLB	26	682	98	36	1	35	114	99	178	15	3	.260/.372/.510	122	36.0	.313	-1.4	RF(152): 3.7	3.7
2020	PHI	MLB	27	595	86	27	1	32	91	92	149	9	4	.254/.374/.502	127	31.9	.298	-2.3	RF -7	2.6

Comparables: Boog Powell, Matt Joyce, Willie Horton

Year One of the Bryce Harper Era in The City of Brotherly Love felt like an anticlimax, an inaugural season that was somehow very good yet simultaneously unremarkable. Even the press conference in early March anointing of the next great face of the franchise played like the end of a reality television show that had been on the air far too long and provided its disinterested audience a clumsy, ham-handed and disappointing ending. Baseball isn't dying (even though the constant chirping of the nattering nabobs might make some believe otherwise), but it also isn't the preeminent and dominant sport it was a generation ago. It isn't his fault, but Harper is a superstar who belongs in a different age, an era that would have had a greater appreciation for his personality and a fanbase unaware of WARP and DRC+ that could instead marvel at what he is instead of nitpicking what he isn't.

Even this milquetoast "what Bryce Harper is" qualifier is more than a little disingenuous. He isn't a slice of stinky cheese sitting atop a slice of moldy, day old bread; since his debut in 2012 Harper is sixth in runs scored, eighth in on-base percentage and ninth in home runs across the majors. He's even one the clutchest hitters there is, with a WPA that's sixth-best in baseball over that span. But even if you are adamant about using a nerd stat like WARP as Harper's definitive yardstick, he's still pretty damn good, the 29th best age 26 and under hitter since integration, ranked mostly behind a bushel of Hall of Famers, active or recently retired players who will be Hall of Famers and PED or alleged PED users who will never be enshrined. Harper is sometimes painted with a harsh brush that says he's a lousy teammate, a malcontent or a player who doesn't try hard enough. But he is none of those things. What he is is a player who is incessantly penalized for not being Mantle, A-Rod, Griffey, Aaron or even his own generation's version of those guys: Mike Trout.

There is a parallel universe where baseball still reigns supreme, kids gush over boxscores, and Harper is part of a lively discussion among ardent fans over where he belongs in the game's pantheon. It's the jaded world that surrounds Harper - and not his accomplishments on the field - that have reduced him into someone who recedes into the background and is blamed for what he isn't instead of celebrated for everything that he is.

Josh Harrison 2B Born: 07/08/87 Age: 32 Bats: R Throws: R Height: 5'8" Weight: 185 Origin: Round 6, 2008 Draft (#191 overall)

YEAR	TEAM	LVL	AGE	PA	R	2B	3B	HR	RBI	BB	K	SB	CS	AVG/OBP/SLG	DRC+	VORP	BABIP	BRR	FRAA	WARP
2017	PIT	MLB	29	542	66	26	2	16	47	28	90	12	4	.272/.339/.432	105	31.8	.303	1.7	2B(83): -2.6, 3B(49): 2.6	2.2
2018	PIT	MLB	30	374	41	13	1	8	37	18	68	3	0	.250/.293/.363	87	3.2	.286	0.5	2B(87): -5.6, 3B(2): 0.0	0.0
2019	TOL	AAA	31	29	2	1	0	0	3	6	4	0	0	.174/.345/.217	105	-1.5	.211	-0.9	2B(3): -0.1	0.0
2019	DET	MLB	31	147	10	7	1	1	8	6	27	4	2	.175/.218/.263	63	-2.2	.207	-1.1	2B(34): 2.7	-0.1
2020	PHI	MLB	32	294	27	13	1	6	29	15	56	6	2	.234/.285/.360	70	-1.4	.272	0.1	2B -1, 3B 0	-0.2

Comparables: Luis Salazar, Terry Pendleton, Brock Holt

Everybody knows Achilles had one weakness and it was a spot on his heel. What mythologians rarely discuss is the Greek hero of Hamstring, one of the fastest and most energetic warriors who suddenly missed significant time on the battlefield because he pulled up lame one day. Thousands of years later, Harrison suffered a similar injury during a bizarre 2019 season that saw him signed during spring training and released at the end of his rehab assignment because his position had been filled. Never one for walking and seldom one for bopping, his on-field contributions are tied to his energy, defensive flexibility and mobility—and, if he hits a snag and loses any of those attributes, then he's just another tragedy. Have you read the essay at the beginning of this chapter? He'll fit in perfectly with the Phillies.

Adam Haseley CF Born: 04/12/96 Age: 24 Bats: L Throws: L Height: 6'1" Weight: 195 Origin: Round 1, 2017 Draft (#8 overall)

YEAR	TEAM	LVL	AGE	PA	R	2B	3B	HR	RBI	BB	K	SB	CS	AVG/OBP/SLG	DRC+	VORP	BABIP	BRR	FRAA	WARP
2017	WPT	A-	21	158	18	9	0	2	18	14	28	5	3	.270/.350/.380	134	12.9	.321	2.6	CF(31): 0.1	1.2
2017	LWD	A	21	74	15	3	1	1	6	6	13	0	1	.258/.315/.379	108	5.9	.302	1.6	LF(12): 1.3, CF(4): 0.8	0.6
2018	CLR	A+	22	354	54	13	5	5	38	19	54	7	3	.300/.343/.415	109	15.2	.346	2.9	LF(39): -2.5, CF(30): -2.2	1.4
2018	REA	AA	22	159	23	4	0	6	17	16	19	0	1	.316/.403/.478	135	13.1	.327	-0.5	CF(28): -2.3, RF(5): -0.5	0.7
2019	REA	AA	23	190	30	8	2	8	21	21	35	4	2	.267/.353/.485	120	15.2	.290	2.1	RF(23): 1.3, CF(19): -1.8	1.0
2019	LEH	AAA	23	78	8	6	0	2	9	8	14	1	1	.294/.377/.471	116	4.1	.346	-0.8	CF(12): -0.4, LF(5): 0.1	0.3
2019	PHI	MLB	23	242	30	14	0	5	26	14	60	4	0	.266/.324/.396	71	-1.4	.344	1.1	CF(40): -3.9, LF(22): 2.0	-0.2
2020	PHI	MLB	24	364	36	16	1	10	39	26	87	2	1	.241/.305/.380	82	4.0	.299	0.3	CF -4, RF 1	0.1

Comparables: Cedric Mullins, Preston Tucker, Carlos González

Haseley is a solid defender and a good contact hitter with a discerning eye but one can't help thinking he'd be better served by a DeLorean and an eccentric scientist from Hill Valley. Haseley's heavy ground-ball profile isn't a great fit in a version of the game where balls are escaping the yard at a prodigious rate. To his credit, he has worked arduously with the Phillies' coaching staff at multiple levels of the organization to adjust his swing, but this is a tough trick to turn on the fly, particularly when the plan was for Haseley to spend all of 2019 at Lehigh Valley before injuries forced the team's hand. The former first-rounder was an adequate hitter out of the gate before he became too pull happy, resulting in even more grounders. He's young enough to believe tangible improvement is possible, but one can't help thinking Haseley is an anachronism in a game where 20-25 home run power is a prerequisite for a starting outfielder without game breaking speed.

Odúbel Herrera CF Born: 12/29/91 Age: 28 Bats: L Throws: R Height: 5'11" Weight: 205 Origin: International Free Agent, 2008

YEAR	TEAM	LVL	AGE	PA	R	2B	3B	HR	RBI	BB	K	SB	CS	AVG/OBP/SLG	DRC+	VORP	BABIP	BRR	FRAA	WARP
2017	PHI	MLB	25	563	67	42	3	14	56	31	126	8	5	.281/.325/.452	90	21.3	.345	-1.8	CF(133): 10.5	2.1
2018	PHI	MLB	26	597	64	19	3	22	71	38	122	5	2	.255/.310/.420	93	21.3	.290	0.8	CF(133): -1.1, RF(9): -1.2	1.4
2019	PHI	MLB	27	139	12	10	1	1	16	11	33	2	2	.222/.288/.341	70	-0.3	.290	-1.2	CF(37): -2.1	-0.3
2020	PHI	MLB	28	119	12	5	1	3	14	9	29	2	1	.248/.308/.401	86	2.2	.307	-0.1	CF 1	0.3

Comparables: Milton Bradley, Carlos Beltrán, Carlos Gómez

On May 27, 2019, Herrera was arrested and charged with assault in Atlantic City after allegedly attacking his then 20-year-old girlfriend. A criminal assault case was dropped by the District Attorney's office in early July because the victim decided not to press charges. After conducting their own investigation of the incident, Major League Baseball suspended Herrera for 85 games, retroactive to June 24, ending his season. This spring, scribes might wax poetic about Herrera's return to the baseball diamond. A few may even misguidedly opine about his difficult road, idiotically conflating his return from a justified, deserved suspension with overcoming personal adversity. Herrera could have a great or awful year on the diamond. It will be meaningless compared to the damage he did to the health and well-being of his victim, something that is all too easily and quickly forgotten. This happens far too frequently where domestic violence is concerned.

Rhys Hoskins 1B Born: 03/17/93 Age: 27 Bats: R Throws: R Height: 6'4" Weight: 225 Origin: Round 5, 2014 Draft (#142 overall)

YEAR	TEAM	LVL	AGE	PA	R	2B	3B	HR	RBI	BB	K	SB	CS	AVG/OBP/SLG	DRC+	VORP	BABIP	BRR	FRAA	WARP
2017	LEH	AAA	24	475	78	24	4	29	91	64	75	4	2	.284/.385/.581	162	36.4	.281	-0.6	1B(105): -9.8, LF(3): 0.2	2.5
2017	PHI	MLB	24	212	37	7	0	18	48	37	46	2	0	.259/.396/.618	151	26.5	.241	-0.1	LF(30): -0.8, 1B(27): -0.3	1.6
2018	PHI	MLB	25	660	89	38	0	34	96	87	150	5	3	.246/.354/.496	129	48.1	.272	0.2	LF(135): -0.7, 1B(17): 0.2	3.9
2019	PHI	MLB	26	705	86	33	5	29	85	116	173	2	2	.226/.364/.454	115	24.3	.267	-2.3	1B(158): 2.6	2.4
2020	PHI	MLB	27	595	82	26	2	31	89	88	143	3	1	.237/.360/.483	120	26.4	.268	-0.6	1B 0	2.8

Comparables: Michael Conforto, Brandon Allen, Mike Olt

Like Walt Whitman in his Leaves of Grass anthology, Hoskins contained multitudes. After posting a blistering .931 OPS before the All-Star break (good for 14th overall among qualifiers), Hoskins cratered, posting a woeful .180/.318/.361 line in the second half. Hoskins' contact rate didn't change much, but his quality of contact was far poorer after the break. He had trouble getting around on fastballs and the pull approach that was such a significant part of Hoskins' game gave way to a more straightaway swing that didn't serve him well. A hand injury in August might have had an impact, but the slump started in mid-July well before the malady occurred. Hoskins didn't drop off the way some of his teammates did in 2019, but the Phillies lack right-handed power and need him to show up in 2020 with all his laser beams full-dazzling.

Scott Kingery CF Born: 04/29/94 Age: 26 Bats: R Throws: R Height: 5'10" Weight: 180 Origin: Round 2, 2015 Draft (#48 overall)

YEAR	TEAM	LVL	AGE	PA	R	2B	3B	HR	RBI	BB	K	SB	CS	AVG/OBP/SLG	DRC+	VORP	BABIP	BRR	FRAA	WARP
2017	REA	AA	23	317	62	18	5	18	44	28	51	19	3	.313/.379/.608	147	33.9	.324	2.7	2B(59): 1.7	3.0
2017	LEH	AAA	23	286	41	11	3	8	21	13	58	10	2	.294/.337/.449	111	9.7	.348	-1.2	2B(54): 0.9, 3B(4): 0.3	1.2
2018	PHI	MLB	24	484	55	23	2	8	35	24	126	10	3	.226/.267/.338	70	4.5	.291	2.1	SS(119): -3.9, 3B(10): -0.2	0.2
2019	PHI	MLB	25	500	64	34	4	19	55	34	147	15	4	.258/.315/.474	93	14.9	.337	3.1	CF(65): -2.2, 3B(41): 1.4	1.9
2020	PHI	MLB	26	532	54	23	3	18	62	31	151	12	3	.228/.282/.392	74	0.1	.292	2.1	3B 4, CF -1	0.4

Comparables: Eddie Miksis, Tom Upton, Don Zimmer

There was nowhere to go but up after a miserable rookie campaign, so by this admittedly low bar, Kingery's sophomore season was a rousing success. The former Arizona Wildcat took a more aggressive approach in his second go-round, swinging earlier in the count and attacking pitchers instead of falling behind and taking defensive swings. On the other side of the ball, Kingery adapted well to a super utility role, playing multiple positions capably and giving the Phillies an opportunity to give several veterans a breather throughout the season. The downside of Kingery's year is while he did show marked improvement, he was merely a two-win player who was slightly below average offensively. Kingery is likely to be a fixture for years to come, but the excitement fueled by a strong season in an extremely hitter-friendly minor league environment appears to have been overblown.

Andrew McCutchen LF Born: 10/10/86 Age: 33 Bats: R Throws: R Height: 5'11" Weight: 195 Origin: Round 1, 2005 Draft (#11 overall)

YEAR	TEAM	LVL	AGE	PA	R	2B	3B	HR	RBI	BB	K	SB	CS	AVG/OBP/SLG	DRC+	VORP	BABIP	BRR	FRAA	WARP
2017	PIT	MLB	30	650	94	30	2	28	88	73	116	11	5	.279/.363/.486	124	48.7	.305	1.0	CF(139): -10.4, RF(13): -0.8	3.1
2018	SFN	MLB	31	568	65	28	2	15	55	73	123	13	6	.255/.357/.415	116	22.9	.309	-3.7	RF(128): -4.9	1.4
2018	NYA	MLB	31	114	18	2	1	5	10	22	22	1	3	.253/.421/.471	121	8.9	.279	0.3	RF(15): -1.9, LF(12): 0.0	0.4
2019	PHI	MLB	32	262	45	12	1	10	29	43	55	2	1	.256/.378/.457	108	10.3	.299	0.0	LF(52): -0.8, CF(15): -0.7	0.9
2020	PHI	MLB	33	490	62	19	2	19	63	69	110	8	4	.250/.364/.438	113	21.0	.298	-0.6	LF -3	1.9

Comparables: Chris Young, Colby Rasmus, Ken Griffey Jr.

It's impossible to talk about Cutch's 2019 without mentioning the horrific injury that abruptly ended his season on June 3; the torn ACL suffered in a rundown that wouldn't have happened if teammate Jean Segura hadn't slipped in the batter's box. Entering the year, McCutchen was the only player in baseball to play at least 146 games in all nine seasons from 2010 to 2018. Even as his performance had somewhat given ground to Father Time, he had managed to stay on the field and soldier on as a productive mainstay. The Phillies missed McCutchen's on-base ability in the second half, but also missed his quiet leadership on and off the field. Cutch is expected to be back at full strength by Opening Day. While he's a long way removed from his halcyon days of MVP, Silver Slugger and Gold Glove awards, Cutch is set to resume his role as table setter and mentor up where the Delaware hits the Schuylkill in 2020.

Brad Miller UT Born: 10/18/89 Age: 30 Bats: L Throws: R Height: 6'2" Weight: 215 Origin: Round 2, 2011 Draft (#62 overall)

YEAR	TEAM	LVL	AGE	PA	R	2B	3B	HR	RBI	BB	K	SB	CS	AVG/OBP/SLG	DRC+	VORP	BABIP	BRR	FRAA	WARP
2017	TBA	MLB	27	407	43	13	3	9	40	63	110	5	3	.201/.327/.337	84	7.8	.265	-1.3	2B(98): -1.3	0.1
2018	CSP	AAA	28	31	4	0	0	1	2	3	9	1	0	.185/.258/.296	52	-2.2	.222	-0.7	SS(6): 0.2, 2B(1): 0.1	-0.1
2018	TBA	MLB	28	174	16	10	1	5	21	16	51	0	0	.256/.322/.429	81	4.6	.343	-0.6	1B(35): -2.1, 2B(6): 0.2	-0.4
2018	MIL	MLB	28	80	5	3	1	2	8	6	31	0	0	.230/.288/.378	83	-1.0	.366	-0.7	2B(15): 0.1, SS(6): -0.4	0.0
2019	SWB	AAA	29	163	31	9	1	10	29	24	40	1	3	.294/.399/.596	133	14.9	.341	-0.7	2B(13): -0.9, LF(11): 0.6	0.8
2019	PHI	MLB	29	130	22	3	1	12	21	11	35	1	0	.263/.331/.610	128	9.1	.268	0.3	3B(19): 0.4, LF(16): 1.3	1.1
2019	CLE	MLB	29	40	4	3	0	1	4	4	10	1	0	.250/.325/.417	82	0.4	.320	0.7	2B(13): 0.4	0.1
2020	PHI	MLB	30	251	30	10	1	11	34	26	69	3	1	.232/.314/.440	97	6.7	.282	-0.4	2B -1, 1B 0	0.6

Comparables: Chris Taylor, Tom Tresh, Dick McAuliffe

Finding something symbolic of the 2019 Phillies' futility isn't hard, but perhaps nothing was more fitting than Miller's two-homer, four-RBI outburst on September 24. Not only had they been eliminated from the playoffs earlier that day after losing the first game of a doubleheader against the streaking Nationals, but Miller's performance couldn't even net them a meaningless win in the night cap. Picked up off the scrap heap after Philadelphia purchased him from the Yankees minor league system in June, Miller became a vital piece of the Phillies' thwarted playoff drive as the team around him collapsed. None of this was Miller's fault. He is a useful piece, a versatile player who can cover multiple positions and provide left-handed pop off the bench. However, if he's starting for your favorite team down the stretch, you've got a big problem regardless of what one day's worth of results suggested.

Mickey Moniak CF Born: 05/13/98 Age: 22 Bats: L Throws: R Height: 6'2" Weight: 185 Origin: Round 1, 2016 Draft (#1 overall)

YEAR	TEAM	LVL	AGE	PA	R	2B	3B	HR	RBI	BB	K	SB	CS	AVG/OBP/SLG	DRC+	VORP	BABIP	BRR	FRAA	WARP
2017	LWD	A	19	509	53	22	6	5	44	28	109	11	7	.236/.284/.341	84	12.6	.292	-0.1	CF(115): -9.8	-0.3
2018	CLR	A+	20	465	50	28	3	5	55	22	100	6	5	.270/.304/.383	84	6.5	.334	-0.1	CF(99): -7.3, LF(9): -0.3	-0.1
2019	REA	AA	21	504	63	28	13	11	67	33	111	15	3	.252/.303/.439	97	20.9	.307	1.4	CF(93): -2.2, RF(24): 0.5	1.3
2020	PHI	MLB	22	251	21	13	2	5	25	14	68	2	1	.221/.269/.358	63	-4.0	.289	0.0	CF -2, RF 0	-0.7

Comparables: Xavier Avery, Dustin Fowler, Rey Fuentes

If Moniak wasn't a first-overall pick who took home a $6 million signing bonus, he'd be likely be lumped in with all the lineouts at the end of this chapter. He wasn't overmatched or completely out of his element at Double-A Reading but the hitch in his swing, the poor pitch recognition on high spin offerings and his difficulties with same-side hurlers led to another nondescript season. Moniak's most probable path to the majors is as a fourth outfielder, and while he is only 21 there is nothing buried in either his stat line or the intense scouting of the last three and a half years that provide any legitimate hope that he can live up to the expectations that should go along with the 1-1 pick in the draft. For the faceless, nameless version of Moniak, however, a potential everyday role in the outfield would be a realistically achievable success.

Roman Quinn OF Born: 05/14/93 Age: 27 Bats: B Throws: R Height: 5'10" Weight: 170 Origin: Round 2, 2011 Draft (#66 overall)

YEAR	TEAM	LVL	AGE	PA	R	2B	3B	HR	RBI	BB	K	SB	CS	AVG/OBP/SLG	DRC+	VORP	BABIP	BRR	FRAA	WARP
2017	LEH	AAA	24	197	24	8	3	2	13	18	49	10	4	.274/.344/.389	91	9.9	.368	3.8	CF(38): -0.4, LF(4): -0.2	0.7
2018	LEH	AAA	25	107	14	2	3	2	11	8	19	13	1	.296/.349/.439	104	6.7	.351	3.5	CF(21): 0.3, RF(2): -0.2	0.7
2018	PHI	MLB	25	143	13	6	4	2	12	10	35	10	4	.260/.317/.412	82	4.0	.340	-0.9	CF(30): 0.9, RF(5): 1.3	0.3
2019	CLR	A+	26	25	6	3	0	1	1	3	6	2	0	.500/.565/.800	198	6.2	.692	0.3	CF(5): 0.3	0.4
2019	PHI	MLB	26	122	18	3	1	4	11	12	34	8	0	.213/.298/.370	68	-0.3	.271	0.3	CF(34): -0.6, P(2): 0.0	-0.1
2020	PHI	MLB	27	224	22	8	2	5	22	18	63	13	4	.231/.300/.358	77	1.3	.311	-0.5	CF 2	0.4

Comparables: Dick Kokos, Ben Gamel, Dalton Pompey

Quinn has two problems: he can't stay healthy and on the rare occasions he manages to stay healthy he isn't very good. This is somewhat hyperbolic and unfair. The speedster has shown flashes of the ability that made him a second-round pick by the Phillies in 2011, but he doesn't have enough pop to survive the contemporary version of the game, unless one wants to really buy into his 1.139 August OPS. (Small sample sizes can have severe side effects like vomiting, nausea and overdrafting in fantasy leagues.) Quinn might be helped by baseball's newly expanded rosters in 2020 but it's more likely he'll be a fringe bench player who spends most of his time bouncing between the majors, Triple-A and the injured list yet again.

J.T. Realmuto C Born: 03/18/91 Age: 29 Bats: R Throws: R Height: 6'1" Weight: 210 Origin: Round 3, 2010 Draft (#104 overall)

YEAR	TEAM	LVL	AGE	PA	R	2B	3B	HR	RBI	BB	K	SB	CS	AVG/OBP/SLG	DRC+	VORP	BABIP	BRR	FRAA	WARP
2017	MIA	MLB	26	579	68	31	5	17	65	36	106	8	2	.278/.332/.451	101	37.5	.318	1.0	C(126): 15.8, 1B(9): 0.3	4.5
2018	MIA	MLB	27	531	74	30	3	21	74	38	104	3	2	.277/.340/.484	122	51.7	.312	4.1	C(112): 3.7, 1B(13): 0.6	4.8
2019	PHI	MLB	28	593	92	36	3	25	83	41	123	9	1	.275/.328/.493	106	35.3	.309	2.1	C(133): 19.5, 1B(4): 0.0	5.6
2020	PHI	MLB	29	560	66	29	3	23	76	37	119	7	3	.267/.322/.467	104	30.1	.306	1.7	C 9, 1B 1	4.1

Comparables: Tucker Barnhart, Mike Macfarlane, Miguel Montero

The Phillies 2019 season was a story of minor frustrations multiplied to the nth degree, death by a million microscopic cuts, a season that should have and could have been great but instead was decidedly mediocre. Within the framework of several decisions that didn't quite work out or blew up entirely, Realmuto stands out as a gigantic victory. Acquired from the Marlins last February for the considerable cost of Jorge Alfaro and Sixto Sánchez, all he did his first year in the City of Brotherly Love was have a season for the ages, providing elite value behind the dish while also providing strong contributions with the stick. Already a

YEAR	TEAM	P. COUNT	FRM RUNS	BLK RUNS	THRW RUNS	TOT RUNS
2017	MIA	18959	5.3	1.7	1.0	9.1
2018	MIA	16399	-0.4	0.9	0.1	0.4
2019	PHI	19166	10.5	4.8	4.7	20.4
2020	PHI	23851	-0.5	1.8	4.8	6.1

very good player with Miami, Realmuto took it to the next level, putting together a top-10 season among NL hitters and positioning himself for down-ballot MVP votes. The cost of Alfaro and Sanchez might be lamented by Phillies fans half a decade from now but it's difficult if not impossible to kvetch about the short-term impact of a player who delivered in spades by elevating his game to an even higher level.

Jean Segura SS Born: 03/17/90 Age: 30 Bats: R Throws: R Height: 5'10" Weight: 205 Origin: International Free Agent, 2007

YEAR	TEAM	LVL	AGE	PA	R	2B	3B	HR	RBI	BB	K	SB	CS	AVG/OBP/SLG	DRC+	VORP	BABIP	BRR	FRAA	WARP
2017	SEA	MLB	27	566	80	30	2	11	45	34	83	22	8	.300/.349/.427	104	27.4	.339	2.1	SS(124): -8.9	2.2
2018	SEA	MLB	28	632	91	29	3	10	63	32	69	20	11	.304/.341/.415	105	35.5	.327	-1.0	SS(144): 3.4	3.5
2019	PHI	MLB	29	618	79	37	4	12	60	30	73	10	2	.280/.323/.420	86	19.0	.302	2.5	SS(142): -3.8	1.7
2020	PHI	MLB	30	595	59	31	3	12	62	30	83	20	7	.273/.317/.405	90	16.7	.304	1.1	2B 0, SS -1	1.6

Comparables: Angel Berroa, Jack Wilson, Elvis Andrus

In a year where balls flew out of the yard at a record pace, Segura slipped significantly by standing still. Never a patient hitter, Segura chased more offerings out of the zone while taking more pitches in it, which predictably led to poorer quality of contact and worse outcomes on balls in play. He also slipped defensively, although it was difficult to discern how much of this was Segura's fault as opposed to being a product of playing next to Maikel Franco and subsequently a parade of out-of-position third basemen. Always a durable player, Segura seemed to wear down as the season progressed, running less and losing what little power he had. He remains a decent enough option at short, but there's some risk the stagnation is real as he enters his 30s at a physically demanding position.

Bryson Stott SS Born: 10/06/97 Age: 22 Bats: L Throws: R Height: 6'3" Weight: 200 Origin: Round 1, 2019 Draft (#14 overall)

YEAR	TEAM	LVL	AGE	PA	R	2B	3B	HR	RBI	BB	K	SB	CS	AVG/OBP/SLG	DRC+	VORP	BABIP	BRR	FRAA	WARP
2019	WPT	A-	21	182	27	8	2	5	24	22	39	5	3	.274/.370/.446	149	17.7	.336	1.1	SS(33): -1.0, 2B(2): -0.1	1.4
2020	PHI	MLB	22	251	24	12	1	7	27	16	71	2	1	.226/.282/.376	74	-0.3	.295	0.0	SS 0, 2B 0	0.0

Comparables: Tyler Greene, Brent Lillibridge, J.D. Davis

For the third consecutive year, the Phillies took a college hitter in the first round, selecting the UNLV product in the first round and quickly inking him to a $3.9 million signing bonus. Stott's polished, all-around game translated well to his professional debut, and he was one of the best hitters in the New York-Penn League right out of the gate. Stott isn't a high-end, tools-first prospect, but has the chance to excel because of his strong work ethic and a lack of any significant holes in his game. He has drawn comparison to Giants shortstop Brandon Crawford, and Stott - an avid viewer of baseball clips on YouTube - agrees it's a pretty accurate assessment. Stott should move quickly, giving the Phillies a Bryce/Bryson Las Vegas tandem for years to come.

Nick Williams LF Born: 09/08/93 Age: 26 Bats: L Throws: L Height: 6'3" Weight: 195 Origin: Round 2, 2012 Draft (#93 overall)

YEAR	TEAM	LVL	AGE	PA	R	2B	3B	HR	RBI	BB	K	SB	CS	AVG/OBP/SLG	DRC+	VORP	BABIP	BRR	FRAA	WARP
2017	LEH	AAA	23	306	43	16	2	15	44	16	90	5	4	.280/.328/.511	120	14.0	.358	0.4	RF(37): 6.2, LF(17): 1.5	1.9
2017	PHI	MLB	23	343	45	14	4	12	55	20	97	1	2	.288/.338/.473	93	18.5	.375	-0.8	RF(58): -5.9, CF(16): -2.0	-0.3
2018	PHI	MLB	24	448	53	12	3	17	50	32	111	3	2	.256/.324/.425	98	11.4	.312	-1.4	RF(95): -9.8, LF(19): -1.5	-0.4
2019	LEH	AAA	25	210	33	15	2	10	25	14	52	1	0	.316/.381/.574	130	17.4	.391	1.4	LF(20): 1.2, CF(16): 1.0	1.7
2019	PHI	MLB	25	112	9	4	0	2	5	4	43	0	0	.151/.196/.245	45	-4.6	.230	0.4	LF(23): 0.0, RF(5): -0.3	-0.4
2020	PHI	MLB	26	98	11	4	1	4	13	5	30	1	1	.241/.294/.432	87	1.1	.311	-0.1	LF 0, RF 0	0.1

Comparables: Gus Bell, Justin Upton, Bob Chance

Buried on the bench after the Bryce Harper signing, Williams struggled in a pinch-hitting/reserve role and couldn't get back on track even when regular playing time briefly materialized. It didn't help that after injuries ravaged the outfield, Philadelphia acquired Jay Bruce and Corey Dickerson with no interest in granting Williams an extended opportunity. It's hard to blame the Phillies for looking for better options than a poor defensive corner outfielder with a career 96 DRC+ entering 2019. It's also understandable that a 25-year-old with strong prospect pedigree and no clear shot at playing time got frustrated and started hacking at everything thrown his way. Williams needs a change of scenery badly but might not be good enough to get the opportunity.

PITCHERS

José Álvarez LHP Born: 05/06/89 Age: 31 Bats: L Throws: L Height: 5'11" Weight: 180 Origin: International Free Agent, 2005

YEAR	TEAM	LVL	AGE	W	L	SV	G	GS	IP	H	HR	BB/9	K/9	K	GB%	BABIP	WHIP	ERA	DRA	WARP	MPH	FB%	WHF	CSP
2017	SLC	AAA	28	0	0	0	9	0	11²	10	0	1.5	7.7	10	44%	.294	1.03	2.31	3.52	0.2				
2017	LAA	MLB	28	0	3	1	64	0	48²	50	7	2.2	8.3	45	39%	.309	1.27	3.88	4.35	0.4	93.2	55.9	12	45.6
2018	LAA	MLB	29	6	4	1	76	0	63	51	3	3.1	8.4	59	48%	.274	1.16	2.71	3.82	0.8	93.9	57	11.5	47.9
2019	PHI	MLB	30	3	4	1	67	1	59	66	8	2.7	7.8	51	50%	.328	1.42	3.36	4.90	0.3	93.7	52.6	11.8	48
2020	PHI	MLB	31	3	3	0	53	0	56	53	8	2.7	7.9	49	49%	.284	1.25	3.84	3.96	0.9	92.8	54.5	11.6	47.1

Comparables: Aaron Loup, Bobby Parnell, Rafael Perez

Acquired by the Phillies last winter to bolster their poor numbers against left-handed batters, Álvarez was competent enough as a LOOGY but struggled when asked to face right-handers. This became more of a problem as the season dragged on and Phillies relievers dropped faster than a hapless extra on The Walking Dead. The move from pitcher-friendly Angel Stadium to hitter-friendly Citizens Bank Park didn't do Álvarez any favors either, as his home run rate spiked despite an increase in grounders. It wasn't his fault, but Phillies relievers repeated as the fourth worst group in the majors in 2019 against lefties. Álvarez was fine, but there's only so much a complementary bullpen piece can do when the rest of the bullpen goes full zombie apocalypse.

Jake Arrieta RHP Born: 03/06/86 Age: 34 Bats: R Throws: R Height: 6'4" Weight: 225 Origin: Round 5, 2007 Draft (#159 overall)

YEAR	TEAM	LVL	AGE	W	L	SV	G	GS	IP	H	HR	BB/9	K/9	K	GB%	BABIP	WHIP	ERA	DRA	WARP	MPH	FB%	WHF	CSP
2017	CHN	MLB	31	14	10	0	30	30	168¹	150	23	2.9	8.7	163	46%	.279	1.22	3.53	4.09	2.8	94.1	64.3	9.3	49.1
2018	PHI	MLB	32	10	11	0	31	31	172²	165	21	3.0	7.2	138	52%	.289	1.29	3.96	4.08	2.4	95.2	55.8	8.8	50.1
2019	PHI	MLB	33	8	8	0	24	24	135²	149	21	3.4	7.3	110	53%	.316	1.47	4.64	5.45	0.5	94.6	56.2	7.9	46.9
2020	PHI	MLB	34	8	9	0	24	24	136	144	22	3.4	7.5	114	52%	.302	1.44	4.94	4.90	1.4	93.6	57.3	8.5	47.8

Comparables: Ian Kennedy, Jeff Samardzija, Jason Schmidt

If the 2017-2018 version of Arrieta was him slowly backsliding from his 2015 Cy Young form, the 2019 version was Wily E. Coyote falling hundreds of miles into a desert ravine. As Arrieta ages and his velocity gradually declines, he has relied more and more on guile and location to get hitters out. It seemed to work for a while at the start of the season, when he posted a decent 3.60 ERA in his first 11 starts but didn't work so well in his final 13 starts, when he was pummeled to the tune of a ghastly 5.76 ERA. Arrieta's season was cut short in mid-August, and officially ended later that month when he had surgery to remove bone spurs from his elbow. To what degree the injury was the culprit for Arrieta's performance decline is an open question, but a healthy Arrieta is a much better bet for success than a cartoon coyote and a kilo of Acme dynamite.

Enyel De Los Santos RHP   Born: 12/25/95   Age: 24   Bats: R   Throws: R   Height: 6'3"   Weight: 170   Origin: International Free Agent, 2014

YEAR	TEAM	LVL	AGE	W	L	SV	G	GS	IP	H	HR	BB/9	K/9	K	GB%	BABIP	WHIP	ERA	DRA	WARP	MPH	FB%	WHF	CSP
2017	SAN	AA	21	10	6	0	26	24	150	131	12	2.9	8.3	138	45%	.290	1.19	3.78	4.21	1.7				
2018	LEH	AAA	22	10	5	0	22	22	126²	104	12	3.1	7.8	110	42%	.264	1.16	2.63	3.60	2.8				
2018	PHI	MLB	22	1	0	0	7	2	19	19	2	3.8	7.1	15	51%	.309	1.42	4.74	4.97	0.0	97.4	60.3	10.8	50.2
2019	LEH	AAA	23	5	7	0	19	19	94	81	16	3.4	7.9	83	39%	.256	1.23	4.40	3.99	2.5				
2019	PHI	MLB	23	0	1	0	5	1	11	13	4	4.1	7.4	9	41%	.321	1.64	7.36	4.75	0.1	96.3	59.1	12.5	53.5
2020	PHI	MLB	24	3	4	0	24	8	57	57	10	3.1	7.6	48	40%	.286	1.34	4.68	4.74	0.6	96.7	61.6	11.8	53.6

Comparables: Jake Odorizzi, Brandon Maurer, Reynaldo López

It was telling that despite the Phillies' various needs in both their rotation and bullpen throughout the season that De Los Santos couldn't crack either and spent most of the year in the minors as an emergency option. The Dominican native has the same problem most pitchers who get stuck with the Quad-A label do. He has a strong, low-90s sinking fastball and a major-league-ready change but his neither of his breakers are anything special and there isn't enough separation between his slider and curve. De Los Santos' odds of making it as a back-end starter continue to diminish, and he looks more and more like a future bullpen piece.

Seranthony Domínguez RHP   Born: 11/25/94   Age: 25   Bats: R   Throws: R   Height: 6'1"   Weight: 185   Origin: International Free Agent, 2011

YEAR	TEAM	LVL	AGE	W	L	SV	G	GS	IP	H	HR	BB/9	K/9	K	GB%	BABIP	WHIP	ERA	DRA	WARP	MPH	FB%	WHF	CSP
2017	CLR	A+	22	4	4	0	15	13	62¹	51	6	4.3	10.8	75	45%	.306	1.30	3.61	4.59	0.5				
2018	REA	AA	23	1	2	0	8	0	13	8	0	1.4	12.5	18	52%	.296	0.77	2.08	1.65	0.5				
2018	PHI	MLB	23	2	5	16	53	0	58	32	4	3.4	11.5	74	56%	.220	0.93	2.95	3.00	1.3	99.7	66.6	16.3	49.1
2019	PHI	MLB	24	3	0	0	27	0	24²	24	3	4.4	10.6	29	56%	.323	1.46	4.01	4.20	0.3	99.3	61.2	14.4	46.9
2020	PHI	MLB	25	2	2	3	42	0	44	36	6	4.1	11.3	56	52%	.287	1.25	3.48	3.53	0.9	99.3	66.1	16	49

Comparables: Trevor Rosenthal, Hansel Robles, Ryan Helsley

Pity the poor folks in any professional team's marketing department. Unless you're talking about a bonafide superstar, it's difficult to build a promotional campaign around any player thanks to performance variability and the risk of injury in any given season. One of the most electrifying non-closing relievers in baseball in 2018, Domínguez wasn't nearly as effective last year before being shut down in June with an elbow injury. A partial UCL tear was discovered, and the Phillies won't know until spring training if he will be healed enough to pitch or if surgery will be required. Cancel the Knights of the Round Table giveaway. Send back the foam promotional swords for Jousting Competition Day (for the first 5,000 fans ages 14 and under only, please). This Seranthony might not be taking to the field of battle anytime soon.

Zach Eflin RHP   Born: 04/08/94   Age: 26   Bats: R   Throws: R   Height: 6'6"   Weight: 215   Origin: Round 1, 2012 Draft (#33 overall)

YEAR	TEAM	LVL	AGE	W	L	SV	G	GS	IP	H	HR	BB/9	K/9	K	GB%	BABIP	WHIP	ERA	DRA	WARP	MPH	FB%	WHF	CSP
2017	PHL	RK	23	0	0	0	2	2	7	5	0	0.0	7.7	6	55%	.250	0.71	1.29	2.56	0.3				
2017	LEH	AAA	23	1	4	0	8	7	43¹	48	3	3.1	7.9	38	41%	.346	1.45	4.57	4.57	0.5				
2017	PHI	MLB	23	1	5	0	11	11	64¹	79	16	1.7	4.9	35	46%	.297	1.41	6.16	5.62	0.0	95.8	68.1	7.6	51
2018	LEH	AAA	24	2	2	0	4	4	20	20	0	2.2	6.8	15	46%	.317	1.25	4.05	4.38	0.3				
2018	PHI	MLB	24	11	8	0	24	24	128	130	16	2.6	8.6	123	43%	.309	1.30	4.36	4.67	1.0	96.9	58.2	11.5	51.4
2019	PHI	MLB	25	10	13	0	32	28	163¹	172	28	2.6	7.1	129	46%	.291	1.35	4.13	5.13	1.1	95.7	55.5	9.7	48.5
2020	PHI	MLB	26	7	9	0	24	24	134	147	26	2.8	7.4	110	44%	.303	1.41	5.17	5.13	1.1	95.7	59.1	10.2	51

Comparables: Jeanmar Gómez, Blake Beavan, Jake Thompson

To a casual fan there might not seem to be a reason for Eflin's perennial inconsistency. He'll have a great month where it looks like everything is coming together, the cutter morphing into a devastating pitch, a move to a different side of the rubber making him virtually unhittable. Then it will all come crumbing down, and Eflin will look like the extremely hittable pitcher he was in early July before the Phils banished him to the bullpen. The reality is Eflin has worked diligently to find the right combination of pitch types and location that work for him, but hitters keep successfully adapting to the changes. There will come a time where Eflin settles in as the pitcher he is, the results are more consistent, and he's a starting pitcher who capably fills out the back-end of a rotation.

Jerad Eickhoff RHP   Born: 07/02/90   Age: 29   Bats: R   Throws: R   Height: 6'4"   Weight: 245   Origin: Round 15, 2011 Draft (#474 overall)

YEAR	TEAM	LVL	AGE	W	L	SV	G	GS	IP	H	HR	BB/9	K/9	K	GB%	BABIP	WHIP	ERA	DRA	WARP	MPH	FB%	WHF	CSP
2017	PHI	MLB	26	4	8	0	24	24	128	142	16	3.7	8.3	118	39%	.328	1.52	4.71	5.24	0.5	92.5	50.2	9.7	48.4
2018	CLR	A+	27	0	1	0	3	3	9	3	2	4.0	10.0	10	42%	.059	0.78	3.00	2.82	0.3				
2018	LEH	AAA	27	0	0	0	4	4	18²	17	1	3.9	4.8	10	52%	.267	1.34	2.41	4.30	0.3				
2018	PHI	MLB	27	0	1	0	3	1	5¹	10	1	0.0	18.6	11	20%	.643	1.88	6.75	3.07	0.1	92.4	52	19.4	49
2019	REA	AA	28	0	1	0	2	2	7¹	8	2	3.7	7.4	6	23%	.300	1.50	9.82	5.82	-0.1				
2019	LEH	AAA	28	3	1	0	4	4	17¹	13	3	4.2	8.3	16	27%	.222	1.21	4.67	4.14	0.4				
2019	PHI	MLB	28	3	4	1	12	10	58¹	58	18	2.8	7.9	51	38%	.256	1.30	5.71	6.14	-0.3	91.5	39.1	11.7	47.9
2020	PHI	MLB	29	2	2	0	33	0	35	35	7	3.0	8.1	32	35%	.286	1.33	4.79	4.90	0.2	91.4	45.6	10.8	48.4

Comparables: Tyler Duffey, Kevin Gausman, Deck McGuire

For a brief, shining moment, it appeared the tumblers had finally clicked into place for Eickhoff, and the injury demons that plagued him during previous seasons had been exorcised. Five major league starts into 2019, Eickhoff had a glittering 1.50 ERA, with 31 strikeouts in 30 innings. Alas, these five starts were a small sample mirage, and for the third year in a row injury dominated and ruined Eickhoff's season. His brief flirtation with success revolved around a shift away from a fastball that dropped below 90 mph last year and toward a biting, low-80s slider. The stuff is still good enough for Eickhoff to cobble together a decent career, but durability is a significant obstacle.

★ ★ ★ *2020 Top 101 Prospect* **#36** ★ ★ ★

Spencer Howard RHP Born: 07/28/96 Age: 23 Bats: R Throws: R Height: 6'2" Weight: 205 Origin: Round 2, 2017 Draft (#45 overall)

YEAR	TEAM	LVL	AGE	W	L	SV	G	GS	IP	H	HR	BB/9	K/9	K	GB%	BABIP	WHIP	ERA	DRA	WARP	MPH	FB%	WHF	CSP
2017	WPT	A-	20	1	1	0	9	9	28¹	22	0	5.7	12.7	40	48%	.349	1.41	4.45	4.13	0.4				
2018	LWD	A	21	9	8	0	23	23	112	101	6	3.2	11.8	147	40%	.349	1.26	3.78	3.87	1.8				
2019	CLR	A+	22	2	1	0	7	7	35	19	1	1.3	12.3	48	44%	.261	0.69	1.29	2.25	1.2				
2019	REA	AA	22	1	0	0	6	6	30²	20	2	2.6	11.2	38	42%	.242	0.95	2.35	2.93	0.8				
2020	PHI	MLB	23	2	2	0	33	0	35	34	5	3.3	10.8	42	41%	.327	1.35	4.33	4.45	0.4				

Comparables: Dylan Cease, Hunter Wood, José De León

Initially, the buzz surrounding Howard was muted after he missed the first two months of the season with shoulder pain. Not only did the top prospect not miss a beat when he returned from injury, but he elevated his game down the stretch, tightening his command and improving his already solid secondary offerings even further. Howard's filthy three-pitch arsenal includes a mid-90s fastball he can dial up to 7s and 8s, a splitter-esque plus change that's difficult for opposing hitters to pick up and a slider with some of the nastiest, late-breaking bite you're going to see in the minors. Howard is on the fast track to the majors. Regardless of whether he arrives on Opening Day or later in the year, he's going to have one of the more electrifying debuts of 2020 if his health permits.

Jared Hughes RHP Born: 07/04/85 Age: 34 Bats: R Throws: R Height: 6'7" Weight: 240 Origin: Round 4, 2006 Draft (#110 overall)

YEAR	TEAM	LVL	AGE	W	L	SV	G	GS	IP	H	HR	BB/9	K/9	K	GB%	BABIP	WHIP	ERA	DRA	WARP	MPH	FB%	WHF	CSP
2017	MIL	MLB	31	5	3	1	67	0	59²	49	4	3.6	7.2	48	63%	.278	1.22	3.02	5.86	-0.5	95.5	77.4	12.5	41.9
2018	CIN	MLB	32	4	3	7	72	0	78²	57	4	2.6	6.8	59	66%	.252	1.02	1.94	4.59	0.3	94.0	86	12.8	42.2
2019	PHI	MLB	33	2	1	0	25	0	23	16	7	3.1	7.8	20	55%	.164	1.04	3.91	4.55	0.2	93.3	80	12.1	36.9
2019	CIN	MLB	33	3	4	1	47	0	48¹	41	6	3.5	6.3	34	63%	.254	1.24	4.10	4.64	0.4	93.2	81.1	10.1	37.8
2020	PHI	MLB	34	2	2	0	33	0	35	33	4	3.5	7.4	29	61%	.284	1.33	4.06	4.15	0.5	92.9	80.6	11.7	39.6

Comparables: Jim Johnson, Pedro Beato, Rob Scahill

It doesn't matter how "juiced" the ball is, you can't allow home runs if you keep the ball on the ground. This makes eminent sense in theory, but in practice didn't serve Hughes well last season, a year that saw the grizzled sinkerballer nearly double his previous career high of seven homers allowed. What you see is what you get with Hughes, a pitcher managers love despite low strikeout rates because he hits the zone and typically keeps the ball in the yard. The Reds cut him after finding no takers at the trade deadline and the Phillies picked him up in mid-August for their failed playoff run. Hughes is a face that blends into the crowd of the modern eight-pitcher bullpen, but whose durability and flexibility makes him an essential cog for any team.

Damon Jones LHP Born: 09/30/94 Age: 25 Bats: L Throws: L Height: 6'5" Weight: 225 Origin: Round 18, 2017 Draft (#533 overall)

YEAR	TEAM	LVL	AGE	W	L	SV	G	GS	IP	H	HR	BB/9	K/9	K	GB%	BABIP	WHIP	ERA	DRA	WARP	MPH	FB%	WHF	CSP
2017	WPT	A-	22	2	3	3	13	0	26	23	0	6.9	13.2	38	52%	.377	1.65	4.85	5.67	-0.2				
2018	LWD	A	23	10	7	0	23	22	113¹	105	7	4.0	9.8	123	58%	.326	1.37	3.41	4.82	0.5				
2019	CLR	A+	24	4	3	0	11	11	58¹	38	3	3.7	13.6	88	61%	.310	1.06	1.54	3.12	1.4				
2019	REA	AA	24	1	0	0	4	4	22	9	0	3.7	12.7	31	52%	.225	0.82	0.82	2.63	0.6				
2019	LEH	AAA	24	0	1	0	8	8	34	27	4	6.9	8.7	33	52%	.258	1.56	6.62	5.03	0.6				
2020	PHI	MLB	25	2	2	0	33	0	35	34	5	3.9	10.6	41	46%	.321	1.42	4.70	4.64	0.3				

Comparables: Anthony Kay, Wei-Chieh Huang, Rico Garcia

A 18th round pick in the 2017 draft, Jones was a senior sign with nothing more than a hard fastball, poor control and no polish. The Phillies developmental team got their hands on him, and the combination of organizational patience and Jones' hard work unlocked a 91-94 mph heater with good movement, a solid changeup and a slurvy breaking ball that's eminently usable. The usual caveats about an older hurler dominating younger competition in the Florida State League apply but tall, hard throwing southpaws don't grow on trees. Jones has elevated himself significantly in the Philadelphia prospect pantheon and has put himself in the conversation for a potential major league debut in 2020.

Adonis Medina RHP Born: 12/18/96 Age: 23 Bats: R Throws: R Height: 6'1" Weight: 185 Origin: International Free Agent, 2014

YEAR	TEAM	LVL	AGE	W	L	SV	G	GS	IP	H	HR	BB/9	K/9	K	GB%	BABIP	WHIP	ERA	DRA	WARP	MPH	FB%	WHF	CSP
2017	LWD	A	20	4	9	0	22	22	119²	103	7	2.9	10.0	133	49%	.306	1.19	3.01	4.29	1.4				
2018	CLR	A+	21	10	4	0	22	21	111¹	103	11	2.9	9.9	123	51%	.316	1.25	4.12	4.73	0.8				
2019	REA	AA	22	7	7	0	22	21	105²	103	11	3.5	7.0	82	47%	.287	1.36	4.94	5.99	-1.3				
2020	PHI	MLB	23	1	2	0	5	5	24	25	4	3.9	6.4	17	44%	.278	1.45	5.30	5.22	0.2				

Comparables: Yennsy Diaz, Miguel Almonte, Paul Blackburn

It was more of the same in 2019 for Medina, a prospect whose stuff is tantalizingly great at its best and frustratingly inconsistent at its worst. When he's on, Medina hits 96-97 on the gun, throws a plus breaker, flashes an average change and looks like a future mid-tier starting pitcher. When he isn't the velocity disappears, the secondary pitches lack bite and consistency and his endurance is questionable. Reading is a tough place to pitch, and Medina's home ERA (6.14) was much worse than on the road (3.92) but his struggles weren't solely related to the venue. There was some talk of promoting Medina in September to help the big club's depleted pen, but the team decided rest was the better long-term option. A future as a multi-inning, Seranthony Domínguez type reliever is possible, but for now the Phillies are committed to seeing if Medina can make it as a starter.

Francisco Morales RHP   Born: 10/27/99   Age: 20   Bats: R   Throws: R   Height: 6'4"   Weight: 185   Origin: International Free Agent, 2016

YEAR	TEAM	LVL	AGE	W	L	SV	G	GS	IP	H	HR	BB/9	K/9	K	GB%	BABIP	WHIP	ERA	DRA	WARP	MPH	FB%	WHF	CSP
2017	PHL	RK	17	3	2	0	10	9	41¹	34	1	4.4	9.6	44	44%	.308	1.31	3.05	5.16	0.4				
2018	WPT	A-	18	4	5	0	13	13	56¹	54	6	5.3	10.9	68	42%	.324	1.54	5.27	6.11	-0.6				
2019	LWD	A	19	1	8	1	27	15	96²	82	8	4.3	12.0	129	46%	.325	1.32	3.82	4.39	0.7				
2020	PHI	MLB	20	2	2	0	33	0	35	36	6	4.0	9.4	37	40%	.313	1.47	5.10	5.08	0.1				

Comparables: JC Ramírez, Joel Payamps, Fabio Castillo

A teenage arm with a ton of talent and a lack of polish, Morales' large frame gives him the all-too-common combination of power and trouble repeating his delivery—which leads to a poor command profile. His fastball is an overpowering pitch that can get to the upper 90s on the gun and Morales has a slider he can throw at varying velocities and spin rates, but he lacks a quality third pitch. While his size and strength can easily overpower most hitters in the low minors, his inconsistency and inability to pitch in or near the zone will expose him against more advanced hitters. He'll only be 20 on Opening Day so there is plenty of time for things to click, but for these types of pitchers, turbulence is to be expected.

Adam Morgan LHP   Born: 02/27/90   Age: 30   Bats: L   Throws: L   Height: 6'1"   Weight: 200   Origin: Round 3, 2011 Draft (#120 overall)

YEAR	TEAM	LVL	AGE	W	L	SV	G	GS	IP	H	HR	BB/9	K/9	K	GB%	BABIP	WHIP	ERA	DRA	WARP	MPH	FB%	WHF	CSP
2017	LEH	AAA	27	0	1	0	12	0	17¹	19	1	2.6	7.3	14	44%	.340	1.38	4.67	4.25	0.2				
2017	PHI	MLB	27	3	3	0	37	0	54²	51	10	3.0	10.4	63	45%	.297	1.26	4.12	3.12	1.2	96.9	33.2	17.5	44.8
2018	PHI	MLB	28	0	2	1	67	0	49¹	49	5	4.0	9.1	50	54%	.324	1.44	3.83	4.31	0.4	96.2	34.9	13.1	48.5
2019	PHI	MLB	29	3	3	0	40	0	29²	20	4	3.0	8.8	29	41%	.216	1.01	3.94	4.26	0.4	94.8	28.1	16.6	47
2020	PHI	MLB	30	2	2	3	37	0	39	37	6	2.9	9.5	41	44%	.293	1.26	4.10	4.18	0.5	95.2	32.4	15.4	46.8

Comparables: T.J. McFarland, Vidal Nuño III, TJ House

Morgan's career has seen more second acts than the Off-Broadway production of The Fantasticks. The most recent incarnation of Morgan featured less velocity and fewer fastballs than ever, with more curves and changes supplementing a devastating slider. Morgan was effective across the board, but his best work came against his fellow southpaws, who struck out frequently and mostly generated weak contact on those rare occasions when they did put lumber on the ball. Injuries derailed Morgan's season; he tried pitching through a flexor strain in his elbow but was shut down in early August after posting a 7.15 ERA in his final 16 appearances. The injury didn't require surgery, and Morgan is on track to be ready for spring training.

Mike Morin RHP   Born: 05/03/91   Age: 29   Bats: R   Throws: R   Height: 6'4"   Weight: 220   Origin: Round 13, 2012 Draft (#417 overall)

YEAR	TEAM	LVL	AGE	W	L	SV	G	GS	IP	H	HR	BB/9	K/9	K	GB%	BABIP	WHIP	ERA	DRA	WARP	MPH	FB%	WHF	CSP
2017	SLC	AAA	26	0	1	1	22	1	39¹	34	5	1.6	5.7	25	34%	.252	1.04	3.20	3.29	0.9				
2017	LAA	MLB	26	0	0	0	10	0	14¹	21	3	1.3	6.3	10	54%	.367	1.60	6.91	2.88	0.4	93.0	47.3	13.7	43.3
2017	KCA	MLB	26	0	0	0	6	0	5²	8	0	4.8	9.5	6	42%	.421	1.94	7.94	4.32	0.1	91.9	47.3	14.6	49.5
2018	TAC	AAA	27	5	2	3	41	3	53²	51	3	2.2	8.7	52	43%	.308	1.19	3.86	3.62	1.0				
2018	SEA	MLB	27	0	0	0	3	0	4	6	0	2.2	13.5	6	27%	.545	1.75	6.75	7.63	-0.1	93.0	41.5	13.9	52.1
2019	ROC	AAA	28	0	1	1	8	1	12	11	1	2.2	9.0	12	37%	.294	1.17	2.25	3.40	0.3				
2019	MIN	MLB	28	0	0	1	23	0	22²	20	3	0.8	4.4	11	48%	.230	0.97	3.18	6.34	-0.2	93.4	49.1	12.6	53.1
2019	PHI	MLB	28	1	3	0	29	0	28	26	3	2.6	4.8	15	37%	.256	1.21	5.79	5.50	0.0	93.0	46.9	10.9	45.9
2020	PHI	MLB	29	2	2	0	33	0	35	34	6	2.4	7.3	28	43%	.276	1.24	4.17	4.37	0.4	92.4	47.4	12.2	49

Comparables: Kelvin Herrera, Kevin Jepsen, Tom Niedenfuer

It was logical to believe Morin's brief tenure in the majors was over after his excellent changeup disappeared three years ago, but he resurfaced in 2019 with the Twins before trading places with cash considerations and surfacing in Philly. Everything about Morin, from the lack of a quality offering outside of that cambio to an apparent pitch-to-contact strategy that led to a ludicrous dip in strikeouts, defied any kind of expectations. A mediocre ERA despite a low batting average against suggests Morin was unlucky but his DRA indicates Morin should have been tagged even harder by opposing batters. Relief arms can resurface at any given moment, so this is either the last time you'll read about Morin in this space or he'll find his way into the next 20 Baseball Prospectus annuals.

Héctor Neris RHP   Born: 06/14/89   Age: 31   Bats: R   Throws: R   Height: 6'2"   Weight: 215   Origin: International Free Agent, 2010

YEAR	TEAM	LVL	AGE	W	L	SV	G	GS	IP	H	HR	BB/9	K/9	K	GB%	BABIP	WHIP	ERA	DRA	WARP	MPH	FB%	WHF	CSP
2017	PHI	MLB	28	4	5	26	74	0	74²	68	9	3.1	10.4	86	35%	.306	1.26	3.01	4.25	0.8	96.2	48.6	17.8	48.3
2018	LEH	AAA	29	2	0	1	19	0	18²	9	0	3.4	14.9	31	46%	.257	0.86	1.45	1.86	0.7				
2018	PHI	MLB	29	1	3	11	53	0	47²	46	11	3.0	14.3	76	33%	.354	1.30	5.10	2.36	1.4	97.0	47.1	20.5	46.5
2019	PHI	MLB	30	3	6	28	68	0	67²	45	10	3.2	11.8	89	46%	.240	1.02	2.93	2.92	1.8	96.1	34.5	18.8	38.8
2020	PHI	MLB	31	3	3	32	53	0	56	44	8	4.2	12.7	79	42%	.297	1.25	3.73	3.75	1.0	95.5	41.7	18.8	43.4

Comparables: Erik Goeddel, Vinnie Pestano, Jacob Barnes

Few pitchers use a split-fingered fastball anymore, but in a world that has gone gluten free Neris' splitter is his bread-and-butter; he used it 67 percent of the time, far more than anyone else. Neris' big hands and thick, elongated fingers give him the unique ability to command a pitch that for most hurlers darts toward home plate with little if any precision. Neris has a solid fastball he can dial up to 95 mph, but it is his mastery of the splitter and ability to throw it for strikes when needed that makes him an asset. He is prone to the long ball when his signature pitch doesn't work, but Neris' one great skill has quietly made him one of the better relievers in the game.

Juan Nicasio RHP   Born: 08/31/86   Age: 33   Bats: R   Throws: R   Height: 6'4"   Weight: 252   Origin: International Free Agent, 2006

YEAR	TEAM	LVL	AGE	W	L	SV	G	GS	IP	H	HR	BB/9	K/9	K	GB%	BABIP	WHIP	ERA	DRA	WARP	MPH	FB%	WHF	CSP
2017	PIT	MLB	30	2	5	2	65	0	60	49	4	2.7	9.0	60	47%	.285	1.12	2.85	3.63	1.0	97.7	72.8	12	51.5
2017	PHI	MLB	30	1	0	0	2	0	1¹	0	0	0.0	6.8	1	100%	.000	0.00	0.00	5.22	0.0	98.3	45	20	59.7
2017	SLN	MLB	30	2	0	4	9	0	11	9	1	1.6	9.0	11	39%	.267	1.00	1.64	4.12	0.1	97.8	71.7	13.4	50.3
2018	SEA	MLB	31	1	6	1	46	0	42	53	6	1.1	11.4	53	37%	.402	1.38	6.00	2.73	1.1	96.6	70.7	12.2	51
2019	PHI	MLB	32	2	3	1	47	0	47¹	57	4	4.0	8.6	45	48%	.366	1.65	4.75	5.36	0.0	96.3	54.5	10.2	48.5
2020	PHI	MLB	33	2	2	0	33	0	35	36	6	3.1	8.8	34	44%	.307	1.36	4.61	4.68	0.3	95.8	64.2	11.3	49.5

Comparables: Carlos Villanueva, Zach McAllister, Bud Norris

Flipped to the Phillies from the Mariners as part of the Jean Segura/Carlos Santana swap, Nicasio had his worst season since 2015, the first year he switched to relieving full time. His believers pointed to his radical ERA/DRA differential in 2018 as a positive sign, but in retrospect a drop in fastball velocity was a harbinger of the ineffectiveness to come. Nicasio eventually adjusted by leaning heavily on his slider and for a brief stretch was somewhat effective but then the Injury Fairy that visited every Phillies reliever in 2019 sprinkled its magic dust on Nicasio in the form of rotator cuff tightness that cut his season short. No matter what happens from this point on for the 32-year-old, the greatest trick he'll ever pull isn't getting someone to chase his slider but earning nearly $30 million while being a replacement-level pitcher for his career.

Aaron Nola RHP   Born: 06/04/93   Age: 27   Bats: R   Throws: R   Height: 6'2"   Weight: 195   Origin: Round 1, 2014 Draft (#7 overall)

YEAR	TEAM	LVL	AGE	W	L	SV	G	GS	IP	H	HR	BB/9	K/9	K	GB%	BABIP	WHIP	ERA	DRA	WARP	MPH	FB%	WHF	CSP
2017	LEH	AAA	24	1	0	0	2	2	10¹	6	0	0.9	8.7	10	65%	.231	0.68	0.87	1.89	0.4				
2017	PHI	MLB	24	12	11	0	27	27	168	154	18	2.6	9.9	184	50%	.309	1.21	3.54	3.22	4.4	94.4	53.3	11.8	49.1
2018	PHI	MLB	25	17	6	0	33	33	212¹	149	17	2.5	9.5	224	52%	.251	0.97	2.37	2.60	6.6	94.9	49.5	13.1	48.4
2019	PHI	MLB	26	12	7	0	34	34	202¹	176	27	3.6	10.2	229	51%	.295	1.27	3.87	3.46	5.1	95.3	46.2	11.8	44.7
2020	PHI	MLB	27	11	9	0	29	29	172	153	22	3.3	10.1	194	51%	.298	1.25	3.67	3.75	3.9	94.5	49.4	12.4	47.6

Comparables: Gerrit Cole, Tommy Hanson, Luis Severino

It is a difficult feat to be a great player and fly under the proverbial radar, yet somehow Nola has managed to perform this magic trick with ease. Nola has been the seventh-best pitcher by WARP since 2016, yet inexplicably is a national nonentity. Even in Philadelphia, a city obsessed with its athletes to an unhealthy degree, Nola is frequently overlooked and overshadowed by more colorful superstars like Joel Embiid, Ben Simmons, Carson Wentz and teammate Bryce Harper. You can tick off all the obvious reasons: Nola's DRA is prettier than his ERA, he hasn't won a Cy Young award, has appeared in only one All-Star Game and hasn't tossed an inning in the playoffs. But most of this relative anonymity is because of the man himself. Nola is an unassuming athlete who goes about his business and stays off the back pages in a town where the media guzzles down controversy like a dog lapping up water on a scorching August afternoon. Locked up to a team-friendly contract through at least 2022, Nola is one of the most important components to the Phillies' present and future success.

Blake Parker RHP   Born: 06/19/85   Age: 35   Bats: R   Throws: R   Height: 6'3"   Weight: 225   Origin: Round 16, 2006 Draft (#479 overall)

YEAR	TEAM	LVL	AGE	W	L	SV	G	GS	IP	H	HR	BB/9	K/9	K	GB%	BABIP	WHIP	ERA	DRA	WARP	MPH	FB%	WHF	CSP
2017	LAA	MLB	32	3	3	8	71	0	67¹	40	7	2.1	11.5	86	48%	.229	0.83	2.54	2.26	2.2	95.5	60	15.1	44.7
2018	LAA	MLB	33	2	1	14	67	0	66¹	63	12	2.6	9.5	70	35%	.297	1.24	3.26	5.19	-0.2	94.5	57.5	11.6	46.5
2019	PHI	MLB	34	2	1	0	23	2	25	19	6	2.2	11.2	31	32%	.241	1.00	5.04	2.97	0.7	92.3	46.9	12.9	45.6
2019	MIN	MLB	34	1	2	10	37	0	36¹	34	7	4.0	8.4	34	45%	.276	1.38	4.21	5.29	0.0	93.4	46.9	11.4	44.6
2020	PHI	MLB	35	2	2	0	33	0	35	31	6	3.2	9.5	37	40%	.280	1.26	4.09	4.27	0.4	92.9	52.9	12.4	44.6

Comparables: Shawn Kelley, Chris Schroder, Fernando Salas

Parker is a rare member of a dying breed: a pitcher who relies on a split-fingered fastball as either his primary or secondary pitch. Parker's splitter is the slowest in the game, averaging under 80 miles-per-hour. Velocity isn't everything, but with Parker's fastball dropping a couple of ticks since his career year in 2017, if his splitter doesn't have enough bite and drop, it flies out of the park with ease. Parker started the year as Minnesota's closer, but by July was designated for assignment as the Twins looked to younger and harder throwing arms. He was fine for the Phillies in August, but the NL caught up to him quickly down the stretch and he gave up runs in six of his 11 September appearances. Parker is a useful middle relief cog, but the line between useful reliever and former major leaguer gets finer with each passing year.

Nick Pivetta RHP   Born: 02/14/93   Age: 27   Bats: R   Throws: R   Height: 6'5"   Weight: 220   Origin: Round 4, 2013 Draft (#136 overall)

YEAR	TEAM	LVL	AGE	W	L	SV	G	GS	IP	H	HR	BB/9	K/9	K	GB%	BABIP	WHIP	ERA	DRA	WARP	MPH	FB%	WHF	CSP
2017	LEH	AAA	24	5	0	0	5	5	32	25	1	0.6	10.4	37	40%	.293	0.84	1.41	2.03	1.3				
2017	PHI	MLB	24	8	10	0	26	26	133	144	25	3.9	9.5	140	45%	.332	1.51	6.02	4.66	1.4	96.8	66	10.1	50.2
2018	PHI	MLB	25	7	14	0	33	32	164	163	24	2.8	10.3	188	50%	.327	1.30	4.77	3.40	3.6	97.1	59	13.2	49.1
2019	LEH	AAA	26	5	1	0	9	6	41	23	2	4.8	12.7	58	52%	.253	1.10	3.07	1.99	1.9				
2019	PHI	MLB	26	4	6	1	30	13	93²	103	20	3.7	8.6	89	45%	.309	1.52	5.38	5.07	0.6	97.0	51.1	11.3	48.8
2020	PHI	MLB	27	3	4	0	47	5	66	67	12	3.8	9.0	67	46%	.303	1.43	4.96	4.88	0.5	96.5	59.2	11.9	49.8

Comparables: Jerad Eickhoff, Domingo Germán, Jakob Junis

Some buzzwords get bandied about so frequently they lose all meaning. Pivetta was rightfully praised in 2018 for picking up a new and improved curveball with an elite spin rate, but there was little else in his profile to support the notion that 2019 would be a big step forward. In hindsight, we should have seen the struggles Pivetta endured coming from a million miles away. He consistently dials his heater up into the mid-90s, but the pitch is too straight and too ordinary of an offering to fool most hitters. Pivetta tried all sorts of things to remedy this shortcoming—throwing more off-speed stuff early in the year and then throwing harder late in the season—but hitters adapted faster than the Borg to a gaggle of non-Enterprise Starfleet officers. Maybe there's something else Pivetta can try, but until he develops a third pitch, it matters very little how much spin his curveball has.

David Robertson **RHP** Born: 04/09/85 Age: 35 Bats: R Throws: R Height: 5'11" Weight: 195 Origin: Round 17, 2006 Draft (#524 overall)

YEAR	TEAM	LVL	AGE	W	L	SV	G	GS	IP	H	HR	BB/9	K/9	K	GB%	BABIP	WHIP	ERA	DRA	WARP	MPH	FB%	WHF	CSP
2017	CHA	MLB	32	4	2	13	31	0	33¹	21	4	3.0	12.7	47	43%	.250	0.96	2.70	1.98	1.2	93.6	56.1	16.5	46.9
2017	NYA	MLB	32	5	0	1	30	0	35	14	2	3.1	13.1	51	56%	.182	0.74	1.03	1.86	1.3	93.6	56.1	18.4	43.2
2018	NYA	MLB	33	8	3	5	69	0	69²	46	7	3.4	11.8	91	47%	.245	1.03	3.23	3.03	1.5	94.5	42.5	14.4	43.3
2019	PHI	MLB	34	0	1	0	7	0	6²	8	1	8.1	8.1	6	33%	.350	2.10	5.40	7.03	-0.1	94.1	57.4	11	42.7
2020	PHI	MLB	35	2	2	0	33	0	35	30	6	3.7	11.1	43	43%	.292	1.28	4.04	4.10	0.5	92.9	47.8	14.9	42.7

Comparables: Francisco Rodríguez, Greg Holland, Billy Wagner

Enlightened baseball fans in the 21st century don't care how much baseball players are paid by billionaire owners who could double their teams' payrolls and still have plenty to spare for a shiny, gold-plated yacht. On the other hand, TWO YEARS AND $23 MILLION FOR 6 2/3 INNINGS OF DAVID ROBERTSON? WHAT THE HELL? Advertised in the offseason as the lynchpin of the Phillies new-and-improved bullpen, Robertson made it as far as April 15 before being placed on the IL with elbow soreness. If you've followed baseball for any appreciable amount of time you know how this story usually ends. A flexor strain was discovered, a rehab attempt failed and Tommy John surgery in August knocked Robertson out of commission until 2021. It's a virtual impossibility the Phillies pick up their club option. D-Rob, we hardly knew ye.

JoJo Romero **LHP** Born: 09/09/96 Age: 23 Bats: L Throws: L Height: 5'11" Weight: 190 Origin: Round 4, 2016 Draft (#107 overall)

YEAR	TEAM	LVL	AGE	W	L	SV	G	GS	IP	H	HR	BB/9	K/9	K	GB%	BABIP	WHIP	ERA	DRA	WARP	MPH	FB%	WHF	CSP
2017	LWD	A	20	5	1	0	13	13	76²	61	2	2.5	9.3	79	60%	.299	1.07	2.11	3.77	1.4				
2017	CLR	A+	20	5	2	0	10	10	52¹	43	2	2.6	8.4	49	52%	.289	1.11	2.24	4.00	0.8				
2018	REA	AA	21	7	6	0	18	18	106²	97	13	3.5	8.4	100	53%	.286	1.29	3.80	4.23	1.4				
2019	REA	AA	22	4	4	0	11	11	57²	58	4	1.9	8.1	52	50%	.321	1.21	4.84	4.99	0.0				
2019	LEH	AAA	22	3	5	0	13	13	53²	68	8	5.9	6.7	40	50%	.345	1.92	6.88	7.96	-0.6				
2020	PHI	MLB	23	3	3	0	10	10	49	48	8	3.7	6.5	35	47%	.274	1.39	4.65	4.69	0.6				

Comparables: Steve Garrison, Yohander Méndez, Brock Burke

The stat line finally caught up with the cautious scouting reports, and 2019 was a big step back for Romero developmentally. His unorthodox, three-quarters arm action gave hitters difficulty in the low minors but hasn't been nearly as effective as Romero has moved up the ladder. He isn't missing many bats, and while his sinker/change combination does lead to a fair number of grounders it's not enough to stop more advanced batters from teeing off when he misses his spots. Romero could still fit in as a back-end starter, but like a lot of arms in the Phillies system is looking more and more like a future reliever.

Drew Smyly **LHP** Born: 06/13/89 Age: 31 Bats: L Throws: L Height: 6'3" Weight: 190 Origin: Round 2, 2010 Draft (#68 overall)

YEAR	TEAM	LVL	AGE	W	L	SV	G	GS	IP	H	HR	BB/9	K/9	K	GB%	BABIP	WHIP	ERA	DRA	WARP	MPH	FB%	WHF	CSP
2019	SAN	AAA	30	1	0	0	3	3	12²	10	2	2.1	12.8	18	31%	.296	1.03	4.97	2.50	0.5				
2019	TEX	MLB	30	1	5	1	13	9	51¹	64	19	6.0	9.1	52	29%	.310	1.91	8.42	9.68	-2.2	92.8	43.1	10	48.9
2019	PHI	MLB	30	3	2	0	12	12	62²	62	13	3.0	9.8	68	40%	.306	1.32	4.45	5.10	0.4	93.3	43.1	12.8	44.1
2020	PHI	MLB	31	2	2	0	33	0	35	35	8	3.6	8.9	35	34%	.291	1.41	5.13	5.17	0.1	92.2	42.9	11.3	46.2

Comparables: Steven Matz, David Price, Matt Moore

Recency bias is usually presented within a positive framework, part of a euphoric panacea that makes us collectively forget the bad times for a player or team that previously occurred. In Smyly's case, the past three years have been such a nightmarish rollercoaster that it's easy to forget he had a 3.24 ERA in his first 395 professional innings. Smyly finally stepped on a major-league mound after nearly two full years of recovery and rehab from Tommy John surgery, but was a punching bag in Texas before becoming a barely serviceable back-end starter in Philadelphia. Velocity was never Smyly's game, so slight uptick in his fastball did little if anything for his cause. Unfortunately, fly balls have always been a part of his game as well—which has been more of a bug than a feature in the rabbit ball era.

Ranger Suárez **LHP** Born: 08/26/95 Age: 24 Bats: L Throws: L Height: 6'1" Weight: 180 Origin: International Free Agent, 2012

YEAR	TEAM	LVL	AGE	W	L	SV	G	GS	IP	H	HR	BB/9	K/9	K	GB%	BABIP	WHIP	ERA	DRA	WARP	MPH	FB%	WHF	CSP
2017	LWD	A	21	6	2	0	14	14	85	52	4	2.5	9.5	90	58%	.233	0.89	1.59	2.96	2.3				
2017	CLR	A+	21	2	4	0	8	8	37²	43	1	2.6	9.1	38	50%	.382	1.43	3.82	5.54	-0.1				
2018	REA	AA	22	4	3	0	12	12	75	64	2	2.4	6.5	54	51%	.283	1.12	2.76	3.38	1.7				
2018	LEH	AAA	22	2	0	0	9	9	49¹	48	2	2.7	5.7	31	50%	.297	1.28	2.74	4.87	0.4				
2018	PHI	MLB	22	1	1	0	4	3	15	21	3	3.6	6.6	11	52%	.367	1.80	5.40	5.73	-0.1	94.1	60.4	7.6	51.1
2019	LEH	AAA	23	2	2	0	7	7	38	41	8	2.4	7.6	32	54%	.306	1.34	5.68	5.10	0.6				
2019	PHI	MLB	23	6	1	0	37	0	48²	52	6	2.2	7.8	42	57%	.319	1.32	3.14	4.21	0.6	94.3	52.6	10.2	43.6
2020	PHI	MLB	24	2	2	0	42	0	44	48	7	3.1	7.1	35	53%	.304	1.42	4.79	4.75	0.3	94.1	55.7	10	48.4

Comparables: Devin Smeltzer, Reynaldo López, Derek Holland

"Ranger Suárez" sounds like a weird, long forgotten spin-off to Chuck Norris' television drama smash hit *Walker, Texas Ranger*, not a Phillies pitching prospect who got his first significant taste of big-league action in 2019. Suárez didn't kick ass the way Norris did in his seminal 1990s CBS vehicle, but was effective, using a four-pitch mix that kept hitters off balance even though he didn't dial up his velocity in relief as anticipated. Suárez could arguably but use more seasoning, but sometimes you must rise to the challenge and defeat whatever is thrown your way, whether you're pitching in middle relief for the Phillies on a sweltering August day or thwarting a group of international terrorists who have traveled to Texas to stop a peace conference that could finally unify the Balkans.

Jason Vargas LHP Born: 02/02/83 Age: 37 Bats: L Throws: L Height: 6'0" Weight: 215 Origin: Round 2, 2004 Draft (#68 overall)

YEAR	TEAM	LVL	AGE	W	L	SV	G	GS	IP	H	HR	BB/9	K/9	K	GB%	BABIP	WHIP	ERA	DRA	WARP	MPH	FB%	WHF	CSP
2017	KCA	MLB	34	18	11	0	32	32	179²	181	27	2.9	6.7	134	41%	.289	1.33	4.16	4.48	2.2	87.9	46.8	10.2	45
2018	BRO	A-	35	0	0	0	2	2	12	7	2	0.0	14.2	19	30%	.238	0.58	1.50	1.72	0.5				
2018	NYN	MLB	35	7	9	0	20	20	92	100	18	2.9	8.2	84	42%	.307	1.41	5.77	4.11	1.3	88.7	54.4	11.7	47.3
2019	NYN	MLB	36	6	5	0	19	18	94¹	81	14	3.7	7.7	81	40%	.253	1.27	4.01	4.73	1.1	87.1	51.4	10.4	44.7
2019	PHI	MLB	36	1	4	0	11	11	55¹	60	7	3.9	7.0	43	40%	.312	1.52	5.37	6.15	-0.2	85.8	46.8	10.5	40.2
2020	PHI	MLB	37	2	2	0	33	0	35	35	7	3.1	7.3	28	39%	.276	1.36	4.88	4.98	0.2	86.2	48.6	10.4	43.8

Comparables: Bob Ojeda, Bruce Hurst, Frank Viola

Ignore the DRA and WARP that barely made a proverbial dent between the lines. Vargas had an amazing season, a journey that transcended statistics and, in many ways, not only baseball but life itself. Vargas' season was as inspirational as the fictitious *Rochelle, Rochelle's* erotic journey from Milan to Minsk. He scuffled with a New York beat reporter in the Mets clubhouse, was an associate professor at the City University of New York when he wasn't on the mound and was visited by a time traveler from the future during a postgame press conference. In between all these things that may have happened but may have also just been a series of ridiculous memes, Vargas pitched a complete-game shutout and somehow did more for the Mets by sabotaging the Phillies behind enemy lines than he did while he was still in Queens. It isn't easy to make your mark when your stat line is this bad but Vargas somehow managed to capture our hearts and minds, transcend the game and trip the light fantastic by the mere fact of his very existence.

Vince Velasquez RHP Born: 06/07/92 Age: 28 Bats: R Throws: R Height: 6'3" Weight: 205 Origin: Round 2, 2010 Draft (#58 overall)

YEAR	TEAM	LVL	AGE	W	L	SV	G	GS	IP	H	HR	BB/9	K/9	K	GB%	BABIP	WHIP	ERA	DRA	WARP	MPH	FB%	WHF	CSP
2017	PHI	MLB	25	2	7	0	15	15	72	74	15	4.2	8.5	68	45%	.303	1.50	5.12	5.66	-0.1	96.5	68.5	10.1	51.7
2018	PHI	MLB	26	9	12	0	31	30	146²	138	16	3.6	9.9	161	41%	.316	1.34	4.85	4.20	1.9	96.6	64	12.5	50.3
2019	PHI	MLB	27	7	8	0	33	23	117¹	120	26	3.3	10.0	130	36%	.305	1.39	4.91	5.46	0.4	96.6	66.7	12.7	46.8
2020	PHI	MLB	28	8	8	0	51	19	134	128	24	3.7	9.9	148	37%	.298	1.36	4.66	4.63	1.6	96.0	66.3	12.3	49.5

Comparables: Jon Gray, Luis Castillo, Bud Norris

It didn't happen until four seasons into his Phillies tenure, but the buzz and hope that once surrounded Velasquez has disappeared. Part of this is because 2019 didn't feature the sort of ace-level start Velasquez has delivered in the past that could make fans dream on him once again. Mostly, it is because it was his age-27 season and he has logged over 500 major-league innings with little if any tangible improvement. Velasquez is what he is. He still throws hard, but his secondary stuff has never played up and he still makes way too many mistakes in the meaty part of the zone. Velasquez abandoned his change and relied much more on a slider as his second pitch, which did him no favors. The raw ability and stuff could lead to a dominant season but given the track record if it happens it's more likely to be an anomaly than a breakout.

Nick Vincent RHP Born: 07/12/86 Age: 33 Bats: R Throws: R Height: 6'0" Weight: 185 Origin: Round 18, 2008 Draft (#555 overall)

YEAR	TEAM	LVL	AGE	W	L	SV	G	GS	IP	H	HR	BB/9	K/9	K	GB%	BABIP	WHIP	ERA	DRA	WARP	MPH	FB%	WHF	CSP
2017	SEA	MLB	30	3	3	0	69	0	64²	62	3	1.8	7.0	50	35%	.301	1.16	3.20	4.11	0.8	91.5	94.4	11.2	49.3
2018	SEA	MLB	31	4	4	0	62	1	56¹	50	7	2.4	8.9	56	31%	.272	1.15	3.99	3.55	0.9	91.3	96	13.2	50.9
2019	LEH	AAA	32	0	0	0	10	0	12¹	9	1	0.7	9.5	13	35%	.242	0.81	1.46	2.33	0.5				
2019	SFN	MLB	32	0	2	0	18	1	30²	36	7	2.3	8.8	30	39%	.322	1.43	5.58	5.66	-0.1	90.6	94.8	12.7	48.5
2019	PHI	MLB	32	1	2	0	14	0	14	11	1	2.6	10.9	17	35%	.303	1.07	1.93	4.00	0.2	90.2	94.8	11.1	51.9
2020	PHI	MLB	33	2	2	0	33	0	35	33	6	2.1	8.5	33	34%	.281	1.18	4.00	4.23	0.5	90.1	93.9	12.1	49.3

Comparables: Huston Street, Fernando Salas, Bruce Sutter

If necessity is the mother of invention, Philadelphia's front office was an old timey frontier doctor delivering little miracles in the back of the bullpen. The Phillies used 27 relievers in 2019, which doesn't even include the three position players the team trudged to the hill when games were well out of hand. Limited to 18 outings with the Giants due to a pectoral injury in May, the Phils signed Vincent as a free agent in August after the Giants cut him. Vincent was his usual effective albeit boring self, throwing a low-90s fastball and upper-80s cutter at the top of the zone and somehow getting results. In a season where the Phillies bullpen was more crowded than the Duggar household, Vincent was one of the forgotten middle children who seldom gets mentioned after Season 3.

Zack Wheeler RHP Born: 05/30/90 Age: 30 Bats: L Throws: R Height: 6'4" Weight: 195 Origin: Round 1, 2009 Draft (#6 overall)

YEAR	TEAM	LVL	AGE	W	L	SV	G	GS	IP	H	HR	BB/9	K/9	K	GB%	BABIP	WHIP	ERA	DRA	WARP	MPH	FB%	WHF	CSP
2017	NYN	MLB	27	3	7	0	17	17	86¹	97	15	4.2	8.4	81	48%	.332	1.59	5.21	5.30	0.3	97.1	61.7	10	49.5
2018	NYN	MLB	28	12	7	0	29	29	182¹	150	14	2.7	8.8	179	46%	.279	1.12	3.31	3.01	4.8	98.7	58.3	12	48.2
2019	NYN	MLB	29	11	8	0	31	31	195¹	196	22	2.3	9.0	195	45%	.312	1.26	3.96	3.80	4.2	98.9	59.1	11.6	50.6
2020	PHI	MLB	30	10	9	0	28	28	157	152	20	3.0	9.1	159	45%	.306	1.31	3.97	4.02	3.1	97.8	59	11.5	49.4

Comparables: Alex Cobb, Max Scherzer, Chris Archer

Wheeler and Carlos Gómez were teammates for a brief time after they were famously almost traded for each other in 2015, but it seemed that this was finally going to be the year that Wheeler would be on the move. The team shocked everyone and bought at the deadline instead of selling which meant that the righty finished the year in the orange and blue. Just like his rotation-mates, he featured elite velocity in his repertoire and had another encouragingly healthy season tossing a career-high number of innings. A strong showing in his walk year certainly did his wallet a bunch of good, as the Phillies inked the former sixth-overall pick to a five-year contract worth $118 million and are penciling him in as their second starter behind ace Aaron Nola. He earned it too, as Wheeler's 9.0 WARP over the last two seasons puts him in the top 10 of the National League.

LINEOUTS

Hitters

HITTER	POS	TEAM	LVL	AGE	PA	R	2B	3B	HR	RBI	BB	K	SB	CS	AVG/OBP/SLG	DRC+	VORP	BABIP	BRR	FRAA	WARP
Daniel Brito	2B	CLR	A+	21	379	37	14	1	4	32	22	73	6	10	.243/.296/.325	81	7.4	.293	3.5	2B(65): 7.9, SS(28): 4.3	2.4
Arquimedes Gamboa	SS	REA	AA	21	421	35	10	5	3	28	59	112	21	8	.188/.305/.270	73	5.7	.264	2.1	SS(101): -2.2, 3B(3): -0.2	0.6
Phil Gosselin	UT	PHI	MLB	30	68	5	3	0	0	7	3	16	0	0	.262/.294/.308	74	0.2	.347	0.3	LF(6): 0.0, SS(5): -0.5	0.0
	UT	LEH	AAA	30	353	54	20	5	8	47	46	61	3	2	.314/.405/.497	136	26.1	.365	-0.3	2B(57): 1.7, 1B(7): 0.4	2.5
Deivy Grullon	C	LEH	AAA	23	457	55	24	0	21	77	45	133	1	0	.283/.354/.496	115	23.8	.367	-0.9	C(85): -18.6, 1B(1): -0.3	0.9
	C	PHI	MLB	23	9	0	1	0	0	1	0	2	0	0	.111/.111/.222	93	0.4	.143	0.0	C(2): -0.1	0.0
Nick Hundley	C	LEH	AAA	35	36	2	1	0	1	3	2	17	0	0	.125/.167/.250	16	-3.1	.188	0.0	C(8): -1.3	-0.3
	C	OAK	MLB	35	73	5	3	1	2	5	2	18	0	1	.200/.233/.357	72	1.2	.240	-0.6	C(30): -3.3	-0.3
Andrew Knapp	C	PHI	MLB	27	160	12	9	0	2	8	18	51	0	0	.213/.318/.324	70	1.4	.325	1.4	C(43): -0.4, 1B(1): -0.1	0.2
Mikie Mahtook	CF	TOL	AAA	29	415	64	17	1	21	56	51	106	14	7	.260/.357/.492	119	17.5	.307	-0.7	RF(44): -1.6, LF(19): 1.9	1.6
	CF	DET	MLB	29	25	0	0	0	0	0	2	11	0	0	.000/.080/.000	52	-0.6	.000	-0.2	CF(7): 0.0, LF(1): 0.0	-0.1
Rafael Marchan	C	LWD	A	20	265	21	16	0	0	20	24	31	1	3	.271/.347/.339	130	15.2	.311	0.7	C(48): 1.8	2.1
	C	CLR	A+	20	86	6	4	0	0	3	6	8	1	2	.231/.291/.282	84	0.6	.254	-0.4	C(21): -0.3	0.2
Nick Maton	MI	CLR	A+	22	384	35	14	3	5	45	41	71	11	8	.276/.358/.380	127	14.7	.335	-5.9	SS(65): -2.0, 2B(14): -0.1	1.6
	MI	REA	AA	22	72	6	3	0	2	6	9	14	1	1	.210/.306/.355	94	1.6	.234	0.1	2B(11): -0.1, SS(8): -0.2	0.2
Logan Morrison	1B	PHI	MLB	31	38	5	1	0	2	3	3	10	0	0	.200/.263/.400	89	0.4	.217	0.0	1B(3): -0.3	0.0
	1B	LEH	AAA	31	69	7	5	0	3	12	7	12	0	0	.356/.435/.593	151	6.7	.400	0.0	1B(10): -0.7	1.4
	1B	SWB	AAA	31	164	29	11	0	15	37	8	26	0	1	.289/.341/.658	142	8.6	.261	0.4	1B(24): 0.5	1.4
Simon Muzziotti	CF	CLR	A+	20	465	52	21	3	3	28	32	60	21	12	.287/.337/.372	108	15.7	.327	2.1	CF(79): 0.0, RF(16): 0.8	2.2
Jhailyn Ortiz	RF	CLR	A+	20	478	57	15	3	19	65	36	149	2	3	.200/.272/.381	76	1.3	.252	0.5	RF(68): 7.9, CF(13): 2.3	1.1
Jose Pirela	OF	PHI	MLB	29	19	1	1	0	1	2	2	4	0	0	.235/.316/.471	78	0.0	.250	0.0	RF(3): -0.2, LF(3): -0.3	0.0
	OF	LEH	AAA	29	130	19	9	0	4	14	8	25	2	0	.281/.331/.455	105	3.3	.326	0.3	RF(26): 3.3, LF(6): 0.3	0.7
	OF	SDN	MLB	29	5	0	0	0	0	0	0	3	0	0	.000/.000/.000	70	0.0	.000	0.0	LF(1): 0.0	0.0
	OF	ELP	AAA	29	242	50	13	2	18	59	17	51	0	1	.353/.401/.674	126	25.2	.390	2.7	RF(46): -6.2, LF(4): -0.8	0.9
T.J. Rivera	INF	HAR	AA	30	41	4	3	0	0	4	3	8	0	0	.237/.293/.316	83	-1.2	.300	0.1	1B(6): -0.1, 3B(3): -0.1	0.0
Sean Rodríguez	INF	LEH	AAA	34	49	7	2	1	4	12	3	19	0	0	.267/.327/.622	84	2.7	.364	0.5	1B(5): -0.1, 3B(3): 0.1	0.0
	INF	PHI	MLB	34	139	24	5	0	4	12	19	41	1	1	.223/.348/.375	76	1.0	.309	-0.1	3B(24): 1.1, SS(11): -1.2	0.0
Johan Rojas	OF	PLL	Rk	18	84	13	6	5	0	4	9	12	3	2	.311/.393/.527	147	7.7	.371	-0.6	CF(16): 4.8, LF(1): -0.1	1.0
	OF	WPT	A-	18	172	17	5	6	2	11	5	29	11	4	.244/.273/.384	82	2.9	.284	-0.6	CF(17): -3.1, RF(13): 0.9	-0.1
Ronald Torreyes	UT	ROC	AAA	26	330	48	11	1	11	42	12	33	2	1	.256/.289/.406	73	3.7	.253	1.9	SS(63): -1.7, LF(7): -0.4	0.3
	UT	MIN	MLB	26	17	3	0	0	0	1	0	3	1	0	.188/.235/.188	83	0.4	.231	0.3	SS(6): -0.5, LF(1): 0.0	0.0

Daniel Brito has a pretty swing, but this aesthetic beauty hasn't manifested into raw results since his 2016 campaign in Rookie ball and 2020 will mark the third consecutive make-or-break year for the Phillies' second baseman. ⊕ **Arquimedes Gamboa** is the real deal defensively but his offense is so bad it doesn't even pass muster in Double-A. Perhaps he's young enough to develop some power, but realistically he profiles as a second-division starting shortstop in 1975. ⊕ Half of **Phil Gosselin**'s plate appearances in 2019 were as a pinch hitter, a role for which the light-hitting middle infielder seems a wee bit miscast. ⊕ A defensive specialist who has been praised in particular for his elite throwing skills, **Deivy Grullon** profiles as a backup catcher with decent power but too many flaws in his offensive game to make it as a starter. ⊕ The best swindlers know when it's time to go for the lump sum versus when it's better to milk someone dry over the long haul. **Nick Hundley** isn't a con man, but he's finished below replacement level in three of the last four seasons while clearing nearly $9 million. Even after a miserable 2019, which saw him released by the Phillies in August without so much as a big-league appearance, he's probably doing all right at doing all right. ⊕ In an era where most teams are electing to job share and split duties behind the plate, it's a cruel twist of fate that **Andrew Knapp** was buried on the bench behind the most durable and arguably the best catcher in baseball. ⊕ **Mikie Mahtook** became the eighth position player to finish at least 0-for-20 (23) in his fifth major league season or later. We knew Eugenio Velez, and you sir, are no Eugenio Velez. ⊕ One of the Phillies top prospects based mostly on projectability, **Rafael Marchan** made great strides with his defense behind the plate while displaying plus bat speed with a strong line-drive swing that hasn't translated into results just yet. ⊕ The younger brother of big-league reliever Phil, **Nick Maton** is an undersized middle infield prospect who has outperformed his modest scouting projection thus far on both sides of the ball and will get his first extended taste of the high minors this year. ⊕ A beneficiary of the juiced ball in 2017, **Logan Morrison** found himself a victim this time around, as younger and more talented hitters blocked his path to the majors. Morrison spent most of his time punishing Triple-A pitching, at least when he wasn't hurt or being DFA'd. ⊕ Scooped up by the Phillies in 2016 because the Red Sox couldn't follow international free agency rules, **Simon Muzziotti** has proven to be a solid all-around player whose lack of power limits his ceiling to average centerfielder but also squarely puts him at risk of being cast as a spare. ⊕ The Phillies have pushed **Jhailyn Ortiz** aggressively through their system, thus far with poor results. Ortiz's raw power and strong arm are plus-plus tools, but poor contact skills will bestow upon him the dreaded Quad-A label unless there is a significant change in approach. ⊕ Squeezed out of an overcrowded Padres outfield, **Jose Pirela** spent most of the year at Triple-A terrorizing PCL pitching. The Phillies acquired him as minor-league depth and later activated him as a barely used reserve down the stretch. ⊕ **T.J. Rivera** had an unusually tough road back from Tommy John surgery for a hitter, ending up where many former Met flashes in the pan go: the Long Island Ducks. Now back in affiliated ball, he seeks to recapture his form as a hit-first utility man. ⊕ **Sean Rodríguez** logged time at every position for the Phillies except catcher, but for the third year in a row was mostly replacement-level filler whose utility barely outweighed his lack of contributions across the board. ⊕ **Johan Rojas** plays center like his fanny is on fire and has speed and raw power to boot. Alas, the hit tool needs quite a bit of development. ⊕ **Ronald Torreyes** failed to bolster his case as a lucky charm. He logged just seven games down the stretch for an already-good Twins team before getting cast out into the flaming dumpster that is free agency for utility players.

Pitchers

PITCHER	TEAM	LVL	AGE	W	L	SV	G	GS	IP	H	HR	BB/9	K/9	K	GB%	BABIP	WHIP	ERA	DRA	WARP	MPH	FB%	WHF	CSP
Drew Anderson	LEH	AAA	25	0	6	0	11	11	48¹	48	9	5.0	7.4	40	41%	.273	1.55	5.77	4.81	0.9				
	PHI	MLB	25	0	0	0	2	0	6	6	1	9.0	9.0	6	44%	.294	2.00	7.50	5.54	0.0	94.8	55.8	15.4	39.7
Victor Arano	PHI	MLB	24	1	0	0	3	0	4²	2	1	3.9	13.5	7	29%	.167	0.86	3.86	4.99	0.0	96.3	38.8	28.4	39.6
Garrett Cleavinger	REA	AA	25	3	2	0	34	0	51²	32	2	5.9	14.5	83	46%	.294	1.28	3.66	3.97	0.4				
Austin Davis	LEH	AAA	26	4	1	3	37	0	52¹	43	2	4.1	11.0	64	40%	.318	1.28	2.75	3.29	1.5				
	PHI	MLB	26	0	0	0	14	0	20²	22	6	6.1	10.5	24	40%	.314	1.74	6.53	5.65	-0.1	96.2	58	11.8	50
Edgar Garcia	LEH	AAA	22	2	1	8	25	0	29	15	4	2.5	11.8	38	30%	.200	0.79	2.48	2.01	1.2				
	PHI	MLB	22	2	0	0	37	0	39	38	11	6.0	10.4	45	34%	.300	1.64	5.77	5.81	-0.2	95.8	49.7	13.8	38.9
JD Hammer	REA	AA	24	1	0	2	13	0	20¹	17	1	1.8	11.5	26	51%	.320	1.03	1.77	3.67	0.2				
	LEH	AAA	24	2	2	0	17	0	15²	20	4	8.6	9.2	16	26%	.310	2.23	12.64	8.29	-0.3				
	PHI	MLB	24	1	0	0	20	0	19	15	2	5.7	6.2	13	41%	.241	1.42	3.79	6.43	-0.2	96.2	54.1	9.1	44.6
Tommy Hunter	PHI	MLB	32	0	0	0	5	0	5¹	2	0	0.0	8.4	5	31%	.154	0.38	0.00	5.14	0.0	95.4	86.1	12.5	46.1
Cole Irvin	LEH	AAA	25	6	1	0	17	16	93²	113	13	1.3	6.2	65	42%	.326	1.36	3.94	4.54	1.9				
	PHI	MLB	25	2	1	1	16	3	41²	45	7	2.8	6.7	31	34%	.299	1.39	5.83	6.80	-0.6	93.6	50.5	10.5	48.7
Trevor Kelley	PAW	AAA	25	5	5	12	52	0	65¹	51	8	2.9	8.7	63	34%	.254	1.10	1.79	3.13	2.0				
	BOS	MLB	25	0	3	0	10	0	8¹	9	2	5.4	6.5	6	17%	.259	1.68	8.64	7.05	-0.2	90.3	60.1	6.8	53.1
Mauricio Llovera	REA	AA	23	3	4	0	14	12	65¹	60	7	3.9	9.9	72	43%	.306	1.35	4.55	4.70	0.2				
Erik Miller	WPT	A-	21	0	0	0	6	4	20	13	0	3.2	13.1	29	54%	.283	1.00	0.90	2.34	0.6				
	LWD	A	21	1	0	0	3	2	13	10	0	4.2	11.8	17	32%	.323	1.23	2.08	4.31	0.1				
Pat Neshek	PHI	MLB	38	0	1	3	20	0	18	23	5	1.0	4.5	9	41%	.286	1.39	5.00	6.40	-0.2	91.0	37.4	10.4	53.5
Cristopher Sanchez	BGR	A	22	3	1	2	11	4	40¹	28	3	2.5	8.3	37	56%	.231	0.97	2.01	3.02	0.9				
	PCH	A+	22	1	0	0	12	6	34	28	0	3.4	9.5	36	55%	.322	1.21	1.85	4.68	0.1				
Robert Stock	ELP	AAA	29	3	0	0	25	3	28¹	36	6	6.0	12.7	40	54%	.417	1.94	4.13	5.58	0.2				
	SDN	MLB	29	1	0	0	10	0	10²	14	2	6.8	12.7	15	50%	.400	2.06	10.12	3.86	0.2	100.1	54.7	11.1	39.5
Dan Straily	LEH	AAA	30	1	4	0	6	6	33	33	5	2.5	8.2	30	47%	.295	1.27	5.18	4.38	0.7				
	NOR	AAA	30	4	0	0	6	6	34	24	4	2.1	10.1	38	41%	.241	0.94	2.38	4.69	0.7				
	BAL	MLB	30	2	4	0	14	8	47²	73	22	4.2	6.2	33	27%	.325	1.99	9.82			92.9	52.3	8.4	48.1

A once promising prospect for the Phillies, **Drew Anderson**'s command and velocity disappeared, and he was unceremoniously released by the organization in early September. ⓧ Considered by some scouts to possess the best bullpen arm in the organization, **Victor Arano** had a bone spur removed from his elbow in May and missed nearly the entire season. ⓧ There are only so many jobs available in which having 'cleaving' in your name actually feels appropriate. Since Viking warrior is off the table as a career path, **Garrett Cleavinger** has turned to mowing down opposing hitters, an art he appeared to master at Double-A in 2019. ⓧ **Austin Davis** rode the Pennsylvania Turnpike Extension shuttle between Philadelphia and Lehigh Valley 14 times in 2019, making him the area's foremost expert on the pointless and neverending competition between local convenience store chains Wawa and Sheetz (they sell gasoline and sandwiches!). ⓧ An inconsistent two-pitch reliever, **Edgar Garcia** struggled in his major league debut as he suffered through an utter lack of command and was so inviting to left-handed batters that by September they were bring bottles of wine up to the plate. ⓧ MC Hammer was a rapper who rose to fame in 1990 for his rap single "U Can't Touch This." **J.D. Hammer** is a reliever for the Philadelphia Phillies. MC's signature look involved a pair of baggy pants. J.D.'s signature look is tied to his distinctive, dark-framed glasses. Hammer's stuff is good, but hitters can most definitely touch it. ⓧ **Tommy Hunter** was at the front of the injury parade of Phillies relievers, marching past the Liberty Bell and Independence Hall, up Benjamin Franklin Parkway to the Philadelphia Art Museum and Eastern State Penitentiary, ultimately disappearing into the bowels of The Mutter Museum to scavenge for new bones and sinews, as both team and city tradition demand of their fallen. ⓧ **Cole Irvin** was overmatched and hit hard in his major-league debut, although he quietly put up a strong September for the Phillies in a middle relief role, which might be where his future lies. ⓧ Generic low-leverage reliever **Trevor Kelley** continued his slow and steady ascent through the organization, earning his first cup of coffee in July. He was lit up by major leaguers in his limited exposure, proving that not every right-handed Kelley has Great Stuff™ ⓧ **Mauricio Llovera** possesses a three-pitch mix that could make him a future back-end starter, but his stuff plays up in the bullpen. He hails from El Tigre, Venezuela, which our dogeared Spanish/English dictionary informs us loosely translates to "The Tiger, Venezuela." ⓧ One of the most talented pitchers in the 2019 draft, **Erik Miller** slipped to the fourth round due to concerns about inconsistency and lack of command. The Phillies hope their track record with similar college pitchers gives them a future mid-tier starter. ⓧ Unless you're Doctor Who, time catches up to us all. **Pat Neshek** is not one of the 13 incarnations of the Gallifreyan Time Lord and found his offerings getting exterminated far too often by opposing batters in between stints on the IL that seemed to last an eternity. ⓧ The Phillies picked up promising pop-up arm **Cristopher Sanchez** from the Rays just before Rule 5 protects were due. He pitched well at both A-ball levels in 2019 and has mid-rotation potential as a three-pitch lefty. ⓧ After getting washed off the Padres roster by their incoming tide of high-octane arms, **Robert Stock** will try out his Three True Outcomes pitching act in Philadelphia this year. ⓧ The Orioles acquired **Dan Straily** to eat innings and save wear and tear on the team's young arms, but the cost of that many baseballs was just too much, even for the rebuilding Birds. Philadelphia acquired Straily in July, this time to devour those innings in Triple-A.

PITTSBURGH PIRATES

Essay by Emma Baccellieri

Player comments by Matt Sussman, Ben Spanier and BP staff

In the photo, Clint Hurdle is free. He smiles. He's dressed like a man of a certain age who wants to head out and have a little *fun*—slip-on shoes, button-down in a joyful plaid, glasses loose around his neck—and he rides on a cart driven by someone else. Getty Images provides context ("Former Pittsburgh Pirates manager Clint Hurdle leaves the clubhouse after being relieved of managerial duties...") but the picture doesn't need that. Hurdle's smile does it all.

The photo was taken about two hours before the start of Game 162, which is an odd time to be fired, given its proximity to the more reasonable alternatives of the night before or morning after or even just later that day. But to fire Hurdle at one of those times would have indicated a certain organizational competency, and these were the 2019 Pirates, so instead, it went like this. There was a report that Hurdle would stay in the job that he was under contract to do for two more years; Hurdle declared his desire to stay; the team said that there was no official decision; a few days passed with no clarity. Hurdle came to the stadium for Game 162. He held court with the media to discuss his plans for the future of the club. And then he was fired.

Moves like these are typically assessed on a binary. A firing feels certain or it feels like a shock. It is good or it is bad. There is not much gray area; by the time that a team has arrived at any discussion of these questions, much of the nuance has been beaten out of the situation, and the public isn't privy to detail that could add another dimension. These are definitive moves described in terms to match.

Which made the Pirates' dismissals—Hurdle, and then all the rest—unusual.

The Pirates did not come down on these binary lines. Instead, the team created a weird little place to live in between them. The moves felt certain—how could they *not*, after this season?—yet they were timed and handled in such a way that they came across in the moment as minor shocks. They were collectively necessary but with individually conflicted definitions of "need." They led to a different staff for a club that may not feel so very different at all. The 2020 Pirates now have as clean a slate as a team could ever ask for. They've torn out the roots of their issues from 2019, the

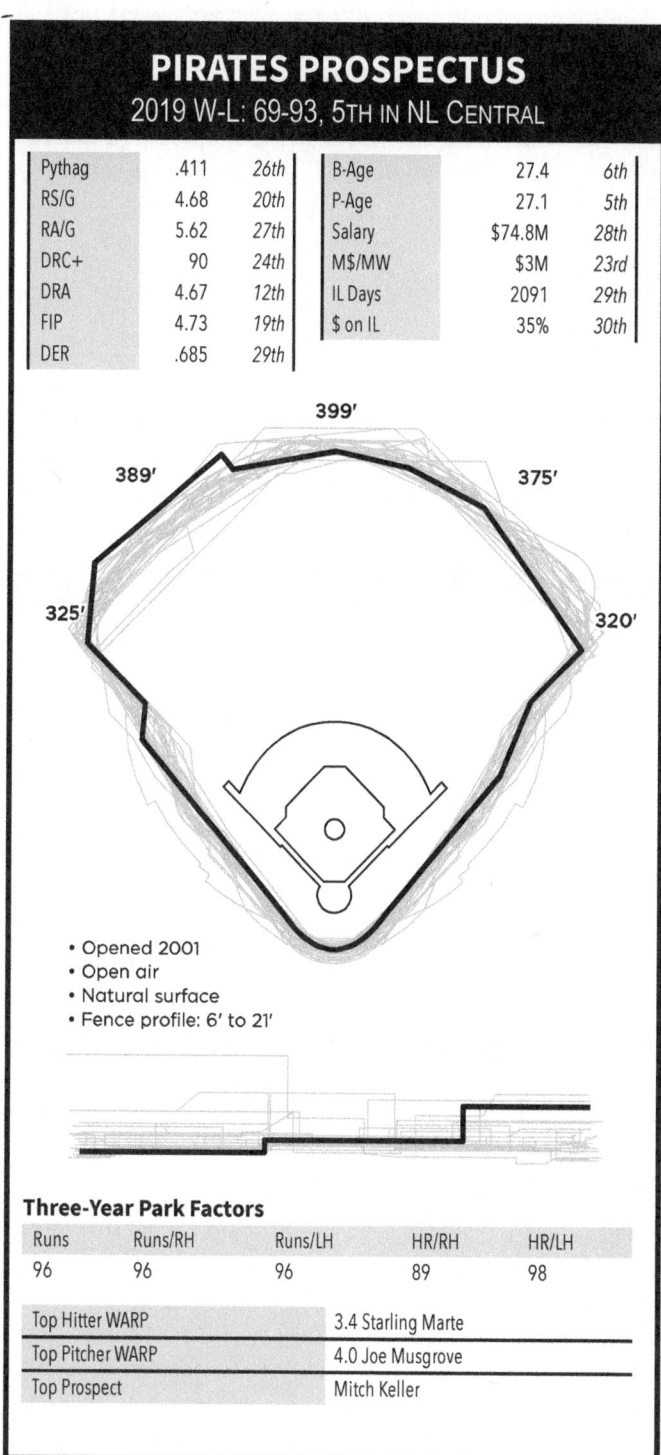

PIRATES PROSPECTUS
2019 W-L: 69-93, 5TH IN NL CENTRAL

Pythag	.411	26th	B-Age	27.4	6th
RS/G	4.68	20th	P-Age	27.1	5th
RA/G	5.62	27th	Salary	$74.8M	28th
DRC+	90	24th	M$/MW	$3M	23rd
DRA	4.67	12th	IL Days	2091	29th
FIP	4.73	19th	$ on IL	35%	30th
DER	.685	29th			

399'
389'
375'
325'
320'

- Opened 2001
- Open air
- Natural surface
- Fence profile: 6' to 21'

Three-Year Park Factors

Runs	Runs/RH	Runs/LH	HR/RH	HR/LH
96	96	96	89	98

Top Hitter WARP	3.4 Starling Marte
Top Pitcher WARP	4.0 Joe Musgrove
Top Prospect	Mitch Keller

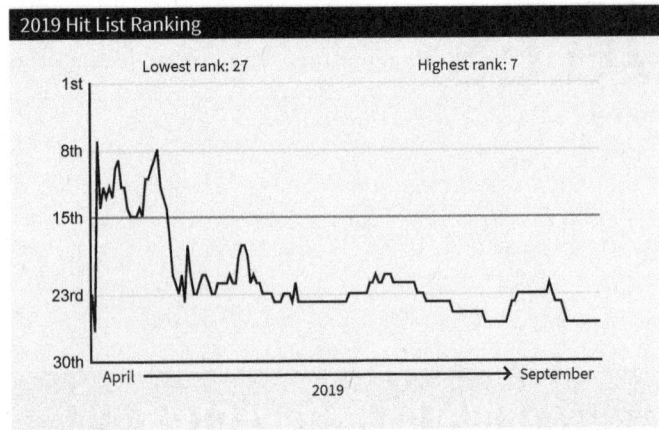

2019 Hit List Ranking

Lowest rank: 27   Highest rank: 7

April   2019   September

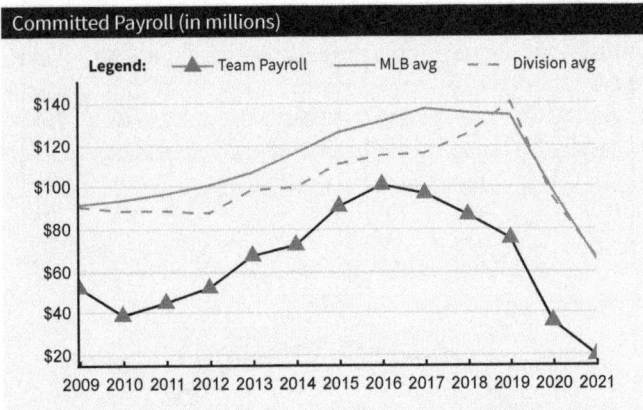

Committed Payroll (in millions)

Legend: Team Payroll — MLB avg — — Division avg

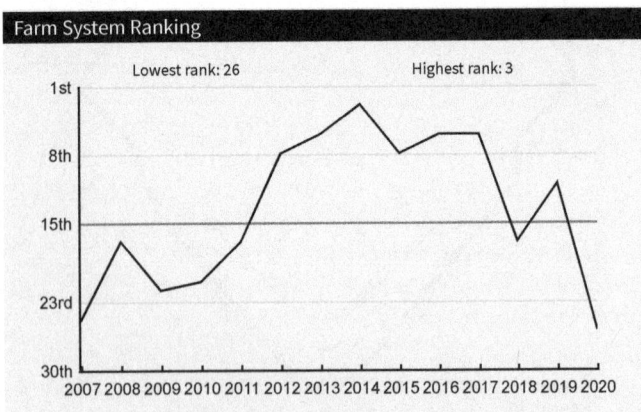

Farm System Ranking

Lowest rank: 26   Highest rank: 3

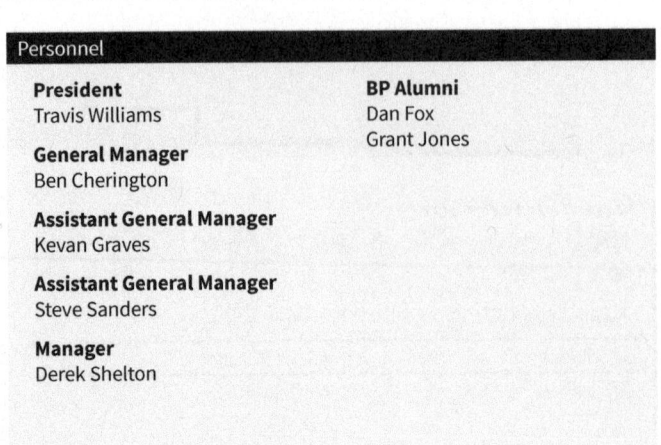

Personnel

President
Travis Williams

General Manager
Ben Cherington

Assistant General Manager
Kevan Graves

Assistant General Manager
Steve Sanders

Manager
Derek Shelton

BP Alumni
Dan Fox
Grant Jones

managerial staff, the front office, all of it. But their path to this fresh start was so torturous and ill-timed and simply *weird* that the fresh start itself may not matter much at all.

If you were trying to read this situation logically, Hurdle's dismissal communicated a particular set of priorities. *This was The Problem*, it said. He was fired by himself, without his coaches, without anyone from the front office. So if you were in search of reason—if you wanted to believe that there was a process, that the club had been evaluated holistically, that the motivation had been to locate the source of the issue here—Hurdle's departure looked like a reflection of the team's values. Just read the statement that announced it: "As an organization," GM Neal Huntington wrote, "we believe it was time for a managerial change to introduce a new voice and new leadership inside the clubhouse." It was not that he neatly placed himself inside the organizational "we" and outside the need for "new leadership"; it was that he was the one to make this statement in the first place. Huntington had signed his contract extension at the same time as Hurdle, back in 2017, and he trusted that he would see out his term—with good reason. Owner Bob Nutting issued his own statement: Huntington would not be fired. ("I strongly believe Neal Huntington and the leadership team that he has assembled are the right people…," a vote of confidence across the board.) There was no official word about other moves, not later that day, or the next one, or the next. It was just Hurdle.

If you were trying to read this situation logically, this demonstrated the team's assessment of The Problem. It was the manager, not the general manager, not his coaches. It was leadership. It was morale; it was the clubhouse fights and the other fights and the full-on second-half meltdown. This was a curiously partial read of the situation but not an incorrect one. (Those *were* problems, certainly, but they were not the only ones and arguably not close to the most pressing ones.) Yet there were no other moves for almost a week, and so if you were trying to read this situation logically, the conclusion stood: The Pirates had felt that Hurdle was the central source of the issue.

If you were trying to read this situation logically, if you really tried, you could find a coherent statement here. This was a team that seemed to believe in its process. It seemed to believe in its strategy and its roster construction and its organizational philosophy. Should it? That was almost beside the point. There was a direction, if (very) arguably not the most rational direction. The Pirates had delivered a clear affirmation of their commitment to Huntington & Co. They seemed to be firm; they knew what they valued and were not stuck on any hypothetical visions of Gerrit Cole and Tyler Glasnow. This was the size and substance of the problem, Pittsburgh said: Hurdle. They'd made a statement there. You could carry the coherence of that statement as they went on to fire pitching coach Ray Searage and bench coach Tim Prince—a little unusual that they hadn't done it with or immediately after Hurdle, but not so unusual, really—and as they went on to "part ways" with team president Frank

Coonelly, because how do you draw lines around the exact area of responsibility of the team president, anyway? The statement held. You could find extreme fault with the foundational beliefs of this statement, obviously. But you could see its internal coherence. Until you couldn't.

If you were trying to read this situation logically, on October 28, you had to stop trying. It was three days after the Red Sox, the only team with a vacancy at GM, had announced that they'd found their man after more than a month of searching. It was one day after Cole had thrown a phenomenal start in Game 5 of the World Series, his last appearance before he'd officially become the best pitcher in the history of free agency. And it was, of course, the day that the Pirates fired Neal Huntington.

It was not that it was illogical to fire him. (It can very easily be argued that the only logical choice was to fire him.) It was that to fire him *then* threw the team's entire endeavor into question. The coherence of the Pirates' initial statements broke. If Huntington had deserved a public vote of confidence on September 29, what changed in the period of relative inactivity that ran to his last day on October 28? If Huntington had been the one to fire Hurdle, what did this mean about his successor? (When Huntington was dismissed, most teams had already filled their managerial vacancies; the Angels, Cubs, Phillies and Padres were done, and within the week, they'd be joined by the Royals and Mets. The Pirates now had yet to even decide who would be in a position to hire for them, let alone who they'd hire.) What did this say about how the team saw its own situation? There was no good answer to any of these. The most generous reading of the situation was that the Pirates had clumsily stumbled through making the right moves in the wrong way at inconvenient times. A less generous reading was…far less generous.

This gave a wildly different view of The Problem. It was the leadership, it was the strategy, it was the roster, it was the vision. It required firing Hurdle, Searage, Prince, Coonelly, Huntington. The Problem was everything. Which—obviously. Obviously. The Problem had quite clearly been all of this all along. And the fact that it had ever been positioned as anything else demonstrated its own problem: *How could you fail to recognize The Problem?*

⚾   ⚾   ⚾

The Pirates went on to make a series of smart hires. (On a timeline that involved naming a manager almost a full month after the last one had been announced, and a GM weeks after the conclusion of the GM Meetings, but that's neither here

nor there.) Derek Shelton and Ben Cherington and the rest are well-positioned to make this team better. But in the context of how these hires were made, it feels relevant to look at who has stayed in place, rather than who has moved. And there is only one truly notable person who has stayed in place, and, of course, he's the only one who cannot easily be removed: Nutting, who oversaw all of this as chairman of the board, and who failed to recognize The Problem. Inasmuch as The Problem is everything, The Problem is Nutting. That will not be different.

It's not that the Pirates can't succeed under Nutting; they have, obviously, and they very well may do it again, maybe even this season. But with Nutting, their window for success is smaller and the conditions are narrower and it all demands far more delicate choreography than is the case for most teams. That's a matter of money, of course, but also of basic sense. It's one thing to have the Pirates' chronically low payroll. It's another to react to this season with this autumn, executed with such staggeringly poor timing and planning.

You should not try to read these situations logically. You can't. Who could?

⚾   ⚾   ⚾

In his media session before Game 162, when he still believed that he would not be fired, Hurdle said the typical things about believing in this group of men and being ready to put in the work for next season, and he also said this:

"I continue to hold fast when I evaluate things. I look at honest, realistic information, and then guarded and guided optimism that is fueled by belief, not hope."

Now, of course, Hurdle's views on the team are of limited use. But his comment here still feels relevant; even after the turmoil of the offseason, this read on the situation is sharp enough to cut through. It does not look like much, and, really, it's an increasingly common sentiment, in baseball and elsewhere. But under its drab cover of practicality, its stilted corporate cold, the statement's truth sits clear and shrill: *Hope has no place here.* It does not say that the situation is hopeless, of course, *that* would be bad. It simply notes that hope does not seem to be a useful instrument in this context.

This Pirates team is not that Pirates team. It's different. But if you look at honest, realistic information, and then guarded and guided optimism that is fueled by belief—if you try to read the situation logically—it could be fair to conclude, like Hurdle, that hope has no place here. ▪

—Emma Baccellieri is a staff writer at Sports Illustrated.

HITTERS

Josh Bell 1B   Born: 08/14/92   Age: 27   Bats: B   Throws: R   Height: 6'4"   Weight: 240   Origin: Round 2, 2011 Draft (#61 overall)

YEAR	TEAM	LVL	AGE	PA	R	2B	3B	HR	RBI	BB	K	SB	CS	AVG/OBP/SLG	DRC+	VORP	BABIP	BRR	FRAA	WARP
2017	PIT	MLB	24	620	75	26	6	26	90	66	117	2	4	.255/.334/.466	108	18.3	.278	-3.7	1B(147): -6.5	0.5
2018	PIT	MLB	25	583	74	31	4	12	62	77	104	2	5	.261/.357/.411	101	19.7	.305	-0.8	1B(137): -6.8	0.1
2019	PIT	MLB	26	613	94	37	3	37	116	74	118	0	1	.277/.367/.569	131	34.4	.288	-3.1	1B(134): -11.1	2.0
2020	PIT	MLB	27	630	81	33	4	29	91	74	119	4	3	.258/.348/.487	119	26.5	.281	-1.6	1B -6	2.1

Comparables: Justin Smoak, Steve Bilko, Freddie Freeman

Not only did Bell lead switch-hitters in home runs last year, his 37 dingers were most by a Bucco since Brian Giles hit 38 in 2002. He did all this with a better-than-average strikeout rate and a scant amount of lineup help. Though they feel as outdated as the rotary phone or Adobe Flash, burly first-base-only swatsmen might be making a comeback. (It's also possible it's just another level of irony foisted upon baseball.) Their return makes sense, what with everybody just swinging as hard as they can, positional flexibility be danged. Perhaps Bell and his counterparts will bring us back to the golden days, when the tragically slow were permitted to forego "defense" in favor of making small talk with the baserunner (now *those* were the original DMs). Of course, the other part of that social contract entails going yicketty with regularity. Bell, for his part, should have no problem upholding it.

Melky Cabrera RF   Born: 08/11/84   Age: 35   Bats: B   Throws: L   Height: 5'10"   Weight: 210   Origin: International Free Agent, 2001

YEAR	TEAM	LVL	AGE	PA	R	2B	3B	HR	RBI	BB	K	SB	CS	AVG/OBP/SLG	DRC+	VORP	BABIP	BRR	FRAA	WARP
2017	CHA	MLB	32	428	54	17	0	13	56	25	52	0	0	.295/.336/.436	97	9.2	.310	-2.2	LF(92): -5.7	0.1
2017	KCA	MLB	32	238	24	13	2	4	29	11	22	1	2	.269/.303/.399	98	0.0	.280	0.6	RF(46): -6.3, LF(12): -0.6	-0.2
2018	COH	AAA	33	80	7	6	1	0	8	2	10	2	0	.321/.338/.423	112	1.2	.368	-1.0	RF(10): 0.4, LF(6): 0.9	0.3
2018	CLE	MLB	33	278	28	17	0	6	39	20	38	1	1	.280/.335/.420	100	6.1	.303	-0.4	RF(68): 1.7, LF(4): 0.0	0.7
2019	PIT	MLB	34	397	43	22	1	7	47	17	41	2	0	.280/.313/.399	87	3.5	.300	-2.0	RF(74): -5.8, LF(24): -2.8	-0.7
2020	PIT	MLB	35	251	23	13	1	5	26	14	33	1	0	.264/.308/.389	84	2.4	.290	-0.5	RF -3, LF -1	-0.2

Comparables: Mark Kotsay, Darin Erstad, Johnny Damon

These days, the Melkman delivers to only the midwest. Since the start of the 2015 season, he's played for four teams, and all of them have been housed in a Central division. So far as we know, there's no rhyme or reason to Cabrera's employment choices. Maybe he just likes America's heartland? Or maybe the constant mediocrity of the AL Central has lent itself to his continued employment. After all, Cabrera has finished below replacement level in two of the past three seasons, and he has amassed all of 1.5 wins since the start of 2015. He's undoubtedly the most Remember Some Guys player left in the league. But shrinking benches and rising standards means it's about time for him to get on getting on with his post-playing days. First, however, he'll probably enjoy a year-long tour with the Tigers.

Rodolfo Castro MI   Born: 05/21/99   Age: 21   Bats: B   Throws: R   Height: 6'0"   Weight: 200   Origin: International Free Agent, 2015

YEAR	TEAM	LVL	AGE	PA	R	2B	3B	HR	RBI	BB	K	SB	CS	AVG/OBP/SLG	DRC+	VORP	BABIP	BRR	FRAA	WARP
2017	PIR	RK	18	211	27	12	4	6	32	16	47	4	3	.277/.344/.479	120	18.1	.338	0.5	SS(19): 1.3, 3B(17): -4.4	0.9
2018	WVA	A	19	426	47	19	4	12	50	26	100	6	3	.231/.278/.395	82	10.9	.276	2.9	2B(89): 4.3, SS(12): 1.6	1.4
2019	GRB	A	20	246	33	13	2	14	46	18	68	6	5	.242/.306/.516	127	20.7	.271	2.1	2B(34): -0.2, SS(17): -0.9	1.6
2019	BRD	A+	20	215	26	13	1	5	27	13	54	1	0	.243/.288/.391	105	8.0	.308	0.3	2B(36): 1.9, SS(16): -1.2	0.9
2020	PIT	MLB	21	251	22	12	1	6	26	17	81	1	0	.206/.265/.351	63	-4.4	.285	-0.3	2B 1, SS 0	-0.4

Comparables: Dilson Herrera, Abiatal Avelino, Michael Chavis

Say this, Castro looks the part. Indeed, he looks the part so well that he appears to have been summoned from central casting when contrasted with the workmanlike collegiates and the stalled-out international signings that populate much of A-ball. He has smooth actions at the various infield positions, and enough arm to cover the demands of the left side. At the plate, his loose and whippy swing produces beautiful line drives all over. Unfortunately, looks aren't all that matters. Castro is prone to swinging and missing at breaking balls, a combination that could make him a well-below-average hitter. The rest of his tool box is heavy on 5's and light on anything else, so he might end up being no more than a bench type (albeit one with a convincing look).

Will Craig 1B   Born: 11/16/94   Age: 25   Bats: R   Throws: R   Height: 6'3"   Weight: 212   Origin: Round 1, 2016 Draft (#22 overall)

YEAR	TEAM	LVL	AGE	PA	R	2B	3B	HR	RBI	BB	K	SB	CS	AVG/OBP/SLG	DRC+	VORP	BABIP	BRR	FRAA	WARP
2017	BRD	A+	22	542	59	26	1	6	61	62	106	1	3	.271/.373/.371	144	11.7	.335	-7.8	1B(93): 9.4	2.9
2018	ALT	AA	23	549	73	30	3	20	102	42	128	6	3	.248/.321/.448	111	28.6	.288	0.6	1B(122): 8.8	2.4
2019	IND	AAA	24	556	69	23	0	23	78	44	146	2	3	.249/.326/.435	94	3.2	.304	-0.4	1B(110): 0.7, RF(13): -1.1	0.2
2020	PIT	MLB	25	251	25	12	0	8	28	16	75	1	0	.223/.291/.381	78	0.4	.296	-0.5	1B 2, RF 0	0.3

Comparables: Travis Shaw, Christian Walker, Tyler Collins

Craig was a first-round pick in 2016 due to his offensive upside. He was never going to stick at third base, but the belief was that his strength, eye and feel for good contact would permit him to hit enough to survive a move across the diamond to first. Craig made the transition to the cold corner in 2018; his offensive acumen did not. Rather, he's walked less and struck out more in each of the past two seasons. He's remained a capable power threat, yet it's hard to see him being an above-average hitter in the majors when he can't be one in Triple-A. Maybe Craig turns the scooter around and becomes a Steve Pearce type; it seems more likely he's a Quad-A player.

★ ★ ★ *2020 Top 101 Prospect* **#55** ★ ★ ★

Oneil Cruz **SS** Born: 10/04/98 Age: 21 Bats: L Throws: R Height: 6'7" Weight: 175 Origin: International Free Agent, 2015

YEAR	TEAM	LVL	AGE	PA	R	2B	3B	HR	RBI	BB	K	SB	CS	AVG/OBP/SLG	DRC+	VORP	BABIP	BRR	FRAA	WARP
2017	GRL	A	18	375	51	9	1	8	36	28	110	8	7	.240/.293/.342	83	13.9	.323	3.2	3B(47): -9.3, SS(30): 0.2	-0.1
2017	WVA	A	18	63	9	2	1	2	8	8	22	0	0	.218/.317/.400	78	3.4	.323	1.0	3B(15): 0.6, SS(1): 0.0	0.2
2018	WVA	A	19	443	66	25	7	14	59	34	100	11	5	.286/.343/.488	130	37.7	.346	2.5	SS(102): -5.9	2.9
2019	BRD	A+	20	145	21	6	1	7	16	8	38	7	3	.301/.345/.515	152	14.8	.374	0.1	SS(35): 2.2	1.6
2019	ALT	AA	20	136	14	8	3	1	17	15	35	3	1	.269/.346/.412	121	10.1	.365	1.1	SS(34): 2.9	1.3
2020	PIT	MLB	21	251	24	12	1	7	27	18	80	3	1	.233/.290/.380	77	0.6	.327	-0.2	SS 1, 3B 0	0.1

Comparables: Yorman Rodriguez, Alex Liddi, Andrew Velazquez

Let's start by addressing the unusually tall elephant in the room: Cruz is indeed a 6-foot-7 shortstop. Normally, that's an elaborate way of saying "a future third baseman." In Cruz's case, he can play the position thanks to his strong arm and high-grade athleticism. There is a good amount of variability with regards to his speed and power projections. He's an above-average runner for the time being, but that seems likely to change as he adds strength to his frame—a development that will better position him to tap into his raw power. As such, there's no telling exactly how Cruz will mature. He is, nonetheless, among the most intriguing prospects in the minors. Put a star next to his name, for if all goes well that's what he'll become.

Elias Díaz **C** Born: 11/17/90 Age: 29 Bats: R Throws: R Height: 6'1" Weight: 220 Origin: International Free Agent, 2008

YEAR	TEAM	LVL	AGE	PA	R	2B	3B	HR	RBI	BB	K	SB	CS	AVG/OBP/SLG	DRC+	VORP	BABIP	BRR	FRAA	WARP
2017	IND	AAA	26	229	19	10	0	2	27	9	36	3	0	.266/.298/.339	88	2.1	.311	-1.2	C(50): 6.3	1.2
2017	PIT	MLB	26	200	18	14	0	1	19	11	38	1	0	.223/.265/.314	62	-4.8	.273	-0.9	C(55): -3.8	-0.4
2018	PIT	MLB	27	277	33	12	0	10	34	21	40	0	1	.286/.339/.452	113	21.2	.302	0.5	C(70): 0.6	1.9
2019	IND	AAA	28	30	5	3	0	0	4	1	5	0	0	.414/.433/.517	118	3.7	.500	0.0	C(6): 0.7	0.2
2019	PIT	MLB	28	332	31	14	0	2	28	23	56	0	0	.241/.296/.307	73	5.6	.286	1.3	C(96): -11.0	-0.4
2020	PIT	MLB	29	251	22	12	0	4	24	17	47	1	1	.240/.295/.350	72	-0.9	.285	0.3	C -2	-0.3

Comparables: Carlos Pèrez, Steve Clevenger, Yonder Alonso

George Carlin once said that somebody has to be the world's worst doctor, and that someone has an appointment with them tomorrow. Likewise, someone has to be the worst catcher in framing runs, and it happened to be Díaz—nearly four runs worse than anyone else. His wellspring of power from 2018 disappeared, and in the process his outlook downgraded from potential starter to backup at best. He did begin the season on the injured list with an unspecified viral illness. Maybe his poor effort can be blamed on office time with the world's worst doctor?

YEAR	TEAM	P. COUNT	FRM RUNS	BLK RUNS	THRW RUNS	TOT RUNS
2017	IND	7000	1.3	-0.4	0.8	1.2
2017	PIT	6832	-5.1	-0.7	0.2	-6.2
2018	PIT	9111	-1.2	-2.0	0.1	-3.2
2019	PIT	12591	-14.4	0.1	-0.1	-14.4
2020	PIT	9391	-4.6	-0.3	-0.3	-5.2

Adam Frazier **2B** Born: 12/14/91 Age: 28 Bats: L Throws: R Height: 5'10" Weight: 180 Origin: Round 6, 2013 Draft (#179 overall)

YEAR	TEAM	LVL	AGE	PA	R	2B	3B	HR	RBI	BB	K	SB	CS	AVG/OBP/SLG	DRC+	VORP	BABIP	BRR	FRAA	WARP
2017	PIT	MLB	25	454	55	20	6	6	53	36	57	9	5	.276/.344/.399	96	17.3	.306	1.3	LF(52): 2.8, 2B(42): -2.6	1.1
2018	IND	AAA	26	137	10	5	2	0	18	11	20	1	3	.223/.289/.298	71	-2.3	.262	-0.9	2B(17): 0.0, RF(7): -0.6	-0.2
2018	PIT	MLB	26	352	52	23	2	10	35	29	53	1	3	.277/.342/.456	104	21.7	.305	1.7	2B(55): 2.5, LF(14): 0.7	1.6
2019	PIT	MLB	27	608	80	33	7	10	50	40	75	5	5	.278/.336/.417	95	16.2	.306	1.0	2B(142): -6.4	1.1
2020	PIT	MLB	28	504	49	26	4	9	51	36	72	9	6	.260/.321/.391	91	15.5	.291	1.2	2B -2	1.4

Comparables: Whitey Lockman, Carl Yastrzemski, Chris Coghlan

Is Frazier what David Eckstein would have been had he played in this era? Of course not, Eckstein is his own gritty deity; however, if he had injected the (completely legal) wood nymph serum that caused the home-run spike, then he might have been able to crush 10 dingers a year as well. Frazier is the kind of undersized contact hitter who bats leadoff and has just enough power to justify playing exclusively second base rather than deploying as a utility type. Five of Frazier's 10 home runs were of the leadoff variety, so he left the park to begin a game as often as Kyle Schwarber did. For evidence concerning Frazier's protean nature, consider that he's one of the few (and presumably the proud) who can elicit comparisons to players as different as David Eckstein and Kyle Schwarber. Not bad, not bad at all.

Matt Gorski **CF** Born: 12/22/97 Age: 22 Bats: R Throws: R Height: 6'4" Weight: 198 Origin: Round 2, 2019 Draft (#57 overall)

YEAR	TEAM	LVL	AGE	PA	R	2B	3B	HR	RBI	BB	K	SB	CS	AVG/OBP/SLG	DRC+	VORP	BABIP	BRR	FRAA	WARP
2019	WEV	A-	21	202	32	9	2	3	22	19	48	11	3	.223/.297/.346	85	6.5	.282	2.2	CF(21): 0.2, LF(19): 2.9	0.8
2020	PIT	MLB	22	251	20	11	1	4	22	15	80	2	1	.200/.250/.312	50	-8.2	.282	0.0	CF 1, LF 1	-0.6

Comparables: Skye Bolt, Adam Haseley, Ryan Cordell

The surname Gorski has its roots in the Polish word for hill or mountain. Shamelessly, we must note that Gorski's path to Pittsburgh will be steep. His swing can get long and results in whiffs by the truck haul—hence his 24 percent K rate in his initial exposure to pro ball. Gorski does have a nice combination of power and athleticism going for him, but he's more of a project than you'd suspect for a collegiate second-round pick.

★ ★ ★ *2020 Top 101 Prospect* **#63** ★ ★ ★

Ke'Bryan Hayes **3B** Born: 01/28/97 Age: 23 Bats: R Throws: R Height: 6'1" Weight: 210 Origin: Round 1, 2015 Draft (#32 overall)

YEAR	TEAM	LVL	AGE	PA	R	2B	3B	HR	RBI	BB	K	SB	CS	AVG/OBP/SLG	DRC+	VORP	BABIP	BRR	FRAA	WARP
2017	BRD	A+	20	482	66	16	7	2	43	41	76	27	5	.278/.345/.363	124	18.8	.331	0.8	3B(108): 20.7	4.9
2018	ALT	AA	21	508	64	31	7	7	47	57	84	12	5	.293/.375/.444	133	38.7	.344	-0.8	3B(116): 9.0	4.5
2019	IND	AAA	22	480	64	30	2	10	53	43	90	12	1	.265/.336/.415	96	14.6	.311	2.3	3B(103): 8.2	2.3
2020	PIT	MLB	23	42	4	2	0	1	4	3	10	1	0	.231/.298/.356	74	-0.4	.290	0.0	3B 1	0.0

Comparables: Jefry Marte, Miguel Andújar, Rio Ruiz

Charlie's kid continued his methodical climb through the minors in 2019, as he spent the season at Triple-A. It's a little concerning that Hayes required the altered ball to reach double-digit home runs for the first time in his career, and it's a lot concerning that he graded as a below-average hitter overall. The optimistic projection here is the same—that he'll be an asset on both sides of the ball. But Hayes turned 23 in January and it's (still) fair to question if his bat is going to hold up its part of the bargain.

Kevin Kramer **2B** Born: 10/03/93 Age: 26 Bats: L Throws: R Height: 6'0" Weight: 200 Origin: Round 2, 2015 Draft (#62 overall)

YEAR	TEAM	LVL	AGE	PA	R	2B	3B	HR	RBI	BB	K	SB	CS	AVG/OBP/SLG	DRC+	VORP	BABIP	BRR	FRAA	WARP
2017	ALT	AA	23	234	31	17	3	6	27	17	50	7	2	.297/.380/.500	124	20.8	.362	1.7	2B(48): -1.6	1.3
2018	IND	AAA	24	527	73	35	3	15	59	38	127	13	5	.311/.365/.492	146	42.2	.392	1.7	2B(82): -6.3, 3B(19): 0.9	3.7
2018	PIT	MLB	24	40	5	0	0	0	4	2	20	0	0	.135/.175/.135	56	-3.3	.278	0.5	3B(7): -0.3, 2B(4): -0.6	-0.1
2019	IND	AAA	25	448	49	30	1	10	54	43	116	4	5	.260/.335/.417	102	11.9	.336	-2.2	2B(50): 1.2, LF(20): 0.6	1.0
2019	PIT	MLB	25	50	5	1	0	0	5	6	17	0	1	.167/.260/.190	66	-0.9	.259	0.7	RF(7): 0.0, LF(7): -0.9	-0.1
2020	PIT	MLB	26	105	10	5	0	2	10	8	31	1	1	.218/.284/.348	68	-1.5	.296	-0.2	2B 0, LF -1	-0.3

Comparables: Preston Tucker, Nick Solak, Ryan Adams

For a second consecutive season Kramer received a 20-something-game look, and for a second consecutive season Kramer failed to make his mark. In theory, he should be able to land on a bench thanks to a decent bat and the ability to stand on the dirt or grass alike; in practice, that hasn't been the case, leaving him another rough circle around the sun from hitting the waiver wire. The good news for Kramer—and for anyone who loves making easy *Seinfeld* jokes—is that there's a general manager named Jerry who would likely give him a spot if it comes to that.

Luke Maile **C** Born: 02/06/91 Age: 29 Bats: R Throws: R Height: 6'3" Weight: 225 Origin: Round 8, 2012 Draft (#272 overall)

YEAR	TEAM	LVL	AGE	PA	R	2B	3B	HR	RBI	BB	K	SB	CS	AVG/OBP/SLG	DRC+	VORP	BABIP	BRR	FRAA	WARP
2017	BUF	AAA	26	58	5	0	0	0	1	4	12	0	0	.167/.224/.167	36	-4.8	.214	0.4	C(13): 3.3	0.2
2017	TOR	MLB	26	136	10	5	0	2	7	3	35	1	0	.146/.176/.231	47	-7.1	.181	0.2	C(46): 4.3	0.2
2018	TOR	MLB	27	231	22	13	1	3	27	25	67	2	0	.248/.333/.366	85	8.6	.351	0.2	C(66): 9.5	1.7
2019	TOR	MLB	28	129	9	2	1	2	9	8	33	1	0	.151/.205/.235	55	-0.8	.190	-0.2	C(44): 7.2, P(2): 0.0	0.6
2020	PIT	MLB	29	259	21	11	1	5	23	19	70	1	0	.190/.256/.299	47	-6.0	.248	-0.1	C 7	0.2

Comparables: John Buck, Joel Skinner, Matt Wieters

Like many classic romantic comedies, *You've Got Mail* is formulaic and reflects, two decades after its release, some troubling gender attitudes. Luke Maile, well more than two decades after his own release, has also revealed some troubling tendencies that bog down his long-term staying power. A preternatural talent for framing, Maile (don't call him the Tom Hanks of it) has earned backup backstop duties almost on that ability alone. And I do mean alone—Maile's hitting is "two-thirds through a rom-com" grim, except with little hope of a happy ending. No matter the utility of frame jobs, a .556 career OPS will make it difficult for Maile to ever receive more than his career high of 231 plate appearances. Still,

YEAR	TEAM	P. COUNT	FRM RUNS	BLK RUNS	THRW RUNS	TOT RUNS
2017	BUF	1555	3.3	0.2	0.0	3.2
2017	TOR	5503	3.8	0.8	0.2	3.9
2018	TOR	9089	8.1	0.1	0.1	8.2
2019	TOR	5996	5.2	0.8	0.3	6.3
2020	PIT	11629	6.6	0.0	0.4	7.0

as long as it's available as a featured movie in the genre, *You've Got Mail* will be watched, and as long as he can steal bushels of strikes behind the plate, so will Maile.

Starling Marte **CF** Born: 10/09/88 Age: 31 Bats: R Throws: R Height: 6'1" Weight: 190 Origin: International Free Agent, 2007

YEAR	TEAM	LVL	AGE	PA	R	2B	3B	HR	RBI	BB	K	SB	CS	AVG/OBP/SLG	DRC+	VORP	BABIP	BRR	FRAA	WARP
2017	IND	AAA	28	40	4	1	0	1	3	2	8	3	0	.333/.400/.444	118	4.6	.407	0.9	LF(6): -0.4, CF(1): 0.1	0.2
2017	PIT	MLB	28	339	48	7	2	7	31	20	63	21	4	.275/.333/.379	91	10.2	.324	3.4	LF(56): 5.9, CF(25): 3.1	1.8
2018	PIT	MLB	29	606	81	32	5	20	72	35	109	33	14	.277/.327/.460	107	37.2	.312	0.1	CF(139): 7.0	3.4
2019	PIT	MLB	30	586	97	31	6	23	82	25	94	25	6	.295/.342/.503	108	28.1	.319	3.9	CF(130): 2.3	3.4
2020	PIT	MLB	31	595	68	30	3	19	72	30	108	32	10	.270/.326/.439	104	27.2	.306	1.9	CF 4	3.2

Comparables: Adam Lind, Allie Clark, Steve Henderson

Marte began his career as a dashing corner outfielder, was felled briefly by a PED suspension, and then returned to take departed Pittsburgh legend Andrew McCutchen's place in center. He's now reached the final and truest stage of development one can achieve as a Pirate: trade chit. The remade Pirates front office is likely to reimagine the roster sooner than later. Marte's team-friendly contract, meanwhile, has two years and $24 million remaining on it. One plus one equals two, and a good stick plus an established glove in a corner-outfield spot plus an affordable deal equals a marketable asset. If he's in Pittsburgh when you read this, it's probably just to visit some friends or to pack up his apartment.

Jason Martin CF   Born: 09/05/95   Age: 24   Bats: L   Throws: R   Height: 5'9"   Weight: 185   Origin: Round 8, 2013 Draft (#227 overall)

YEAR	TEAM	LVL	AGE	PA	R	2B	3B	HR	RBI	BB	K	SB	CS	AVG/OBP/SLG	DRC+	VORP	BABIP	BRR	FRAA	WARP
2017	BCA	A+	21	198	34	11	2	7	29	20	42	9	5	.287/.354/.494	142	13.1	.333	-1.6	LF(25): 1.1, CF(12): -2.2	1.0
2017	CCH	AA	21	320	38	24	3	11	37	19	82	7	6	.273/.319/.483	122	15.2	.343	1.1	LF(57): -6.9	0.7
2018	ALT	AA	22	289	49	13	5	9	34	28	61	7	8	.325/.392/.522	143	31.7	.396	-0.7	CF(62): -2.4, LF(6): -0.6	1.9
2018	IND	AAA	22	234	20	5	3	4	21	17	52	5	4	.211/.270/.319	63	-5.5	.261	-0.6	CF(53): -6.5, LF(6): -0.3	-0.8
2019	IND	AAA	23	406	47	25	5	8	50	29	79	9	6	.259/.312/.419	90	6.7	.307	0.8	CF(92): -4.1, LF(4): -0.7	0.5
2019	PIT	MLB	23	40	5	2	0	0	2	4	10	2	0	.250/.325/.306	73	-0.2	.346	0.5	LF(12): -0.6, CF(3): 0.1	0.0
2020	PIT	MLB	24	147	14	7	1	4	16	10	37	3	2	.223/.275/.378	69	-1.6	.275	-0.1	LF 0, CF 0	-0.2

Comparables: Dalton Pompey, Dick Williams, Willy García

The forgotten part of the Gerrit Cole trade, Martin actually attended the same high school as Cole—Orange Lutheran, in California. That's where the similarities end between the two. Martin is one of several outfielders in the system with a few decent characteristics: athleticism, speed, hit tool and glove (albeit just in a corner). He debuted in the majors last season and required shoulder surgery late in the year to repair a labral tear. Martin should get more big-league burn this season, but there's no reason to expect him to become more than a reserve type, if that.

Mason Martin 1B   Born: 06/02/99   Age: 21   Bats: L   Throws: R   Height: 6'0"   Weight: 201   Origin: Round 17, 2017 Draft (#508 overall)

YEAR	TEAM	LVL	AGE	PA	R	2B	3B	HR	RBI	BB	K	SB	CS	AVG/OBP/SLG	DRC+	VORP	BABIP	BRR	FRAA	WARP
2017	PIR	RK	18	166	37	8	0	11	22	32	41	2	2	.307/.457/.630	216	23.3	.368	-2.2	1B(26): 1.5, RF(9): -1.2	1.5
2018	BRI	RK	19	269	42	10	1	10	40	42	87	2	2	.233/.357/.422	109	8.1	.328	1.4	1B(52): -1.7	0.5
2018	WVA	A	19	173	16	8	0	4	18	18	62	1	1	.200/.302/.333	80	0.8	.310	0.0	1B(43): -3.0	-0.5
2019	GRB	A	20	355	58	19	3	23	83	46	103	8	2	.262/.361/.575	163	33.3	.311	-1.5	1B(77): 4.1	2.9
2019	BRD	A+	20	201	32	13	1	12	46	22	65	0	1	.239/.333/.528	130	8.8	.303	-0.8	1B(46): 3.4	1.1
2020	PIT	MLB	21	251	24	12	1	7	26	26	93	0	0	.189/.281/.339	67	-3.0	.287	-0.3	1B 2, RF 0	-0.1

Comparables: Tyler O'Neill, Matt Olson, Travis Demeritte

Yes, the Pirates have a Jason Martin *and* a Mason Martin. The wonders of the universe, y'all. This Martin is more interesting—provided you're into first-only prospects decimating the low-minors. He isn't going to wow you with athleticism in the field—obviously, he's a young first baseman—or even at the plate, but he has an excellent approach, adjusts well and does a nice job waiting for a pitch he can drive. Martin is far, far from a high-upside play, yet he's been effective so far in his young career and left-handed pop is always nice to have. Now, whom do we have to talk to about the Pirates landing a Cason Martin?

Cal Mitchell RF   Born: 03/08/99   Age: 21   Bats: L   Throws: L   Height: 6'0"   Weight: 209   Origin: Round 2, 2017 Draft (#50 overall)

YEAR	TEAM	LVL	AGE	PA	R	2B	3B	HR	RBI	BB	K	SB	CS	AVG/OBP/SLG	DRC+	VORP	BABIP	BRR	FRAA	WARP
2017	PIR	RK	18	185	17	11	0	2	20	24	35	2	3	.245/.351/.352	123	4.8	.303	-0.9	LF(35): 2.6, CF(3): 0.5	0.9
2018	WVA	A	19	495	55	29	3	10	65	41	109	4	5	.280/.344/.427	127	20.4	.347	-4.4	RF(100): 0.5, LF(11): -1.6	1.7
2019	BRD	A+	20	493	54	21	2	15	64	32	142	1	1	.251/.304/.406	104	8.5	.328	0.0	RF(110): -0.4	1.0
2020	PIT	MLB	21	251	25	12	1	7	28	20	81	0	0	.234/.299/.389	82	1.8	.328	-0.4	RF 0, LF 0	0.2

Comparables: Dalton Pompey, Willy García, Yorman Rodriguez

If there's one thing the Pirates have done well in recent years it's produce somewhat competent, ultimately underwhelming position players. Mitchell could be the next in the line—and hey, they do have value—provided he finds some balance in his game, but it's no sure thing. Mitchell is known primarily for a sweet swing (they always look nicer from the left side) and some hitting promise for a reason—that reason being he doesn't offer much secondary value. Mitchell doesn't offer heapings of primary value, either. His strikeout rate could bloat into the 30-percent range in Double-A, and he's unlikely to walk and bop enough to make up for it. We'll see how his age-21 season goes, but we'd feel better about Mitchell's overcoming the deficiencies in his profile if the strengths were stronger.

Colin Moran 3B   Born: 10/01/92   Age: 27   Bats: L   Throws: R   Height: 6'4"   Weight: 205   Origin: Round 1, 2013 Draft (#6 overall)

YEAR	TEAM	LVL	AGE	PA	R	2B	3B	HR	RBI	BB	K	SB	CS	AVG/OBP/SLG	DRC+	VORP	BABIP	BRR	FRAA	WARP
2017	FRE	AAA	24	338	53	15	1	18	63	31	55	0	3	.308/.373/.543	134	28.9	.323	-0.3	3B(57): 0.3, 1B(15): -1.7	2.3
2017	HOU	MLB	24	12	3	0	1	1	3	1	1	0	0	.364/.417/.818	97	2.5	.333	0.6	1B(4): -0.1, 3B(3): -0.2	0.0
2018	PIT	MLB	25	465	49	19	1	11	58	39	82	0	2	.277/.340/.407	100	22.7	.316	-1.5	3B(116): -2.7	1.2
2019	PIT	MLB	26	503	46	30	1	13	80	30	117	0	1	.277/.322/.429	84	8.1	.341	-0.7	3B(121): -18.7, 2B(11): 0.1	-1.1
2020	PIT	MLB	27	504	53	27	1	14	58	37	115	1	1	.259/.318/.415	93	7.9	.315	-0.2	3B -7	0.1

Comparables: Brandon Drury, Lonnie Chisenhall, Cheslor Cuthbert

WESTCHESTER, NY—Local man eyes bacon, egg and cheese on everything bagel, but can't bring himself to eat. Moran's lack of place in the world is troubling him. Sure, he's been successful all things considered. But he's seemingly plateaued, and a younger, more promising coworker is on the cusp of usurping him. Maybe he's just another millennial plagued with existential angst, tormented with thoughts of living up to his surname. After all, Moran's uncle played 19 years in the majors—and, to make matters worse, his brother debuted with the Marlins last season and struck him out for his first career punch out. He is fearful that conditions will continue to deteriorate. That's life, he reasons. He bites into the bagel. It's cold, and so is he.

Kevin Newman **SS** Born: 08/04/93 Age: 26 Bats: R Throws: R Height: 6'0" Weight: 195 Origin: Round 1, 2015 Draft (#19 overall)

YEAR	TEAM	LVL	AGE	PA	R	2B	3B	HR	RBI	BB	K	SB	CS	AVG/OBP/SLG	DRC+	VORP	BABIP	BRR	FRAA	WARP
2017	ALT	AA	23	375	42	18	2	4	30	22	40	4	2	.259/.310/.359	92	14.6	.282	1.4	SS(81): 0.6	1.6
2017	IND	AAA	23	178	23	11	2	0	11	7	22	7	1	.283/.314/.373	85	4.9	.324	-1.3	SS(38): 0.4	0.4
2018	IND	AAA	24	477	74	30	2	4	35	31	50	28	11	.302/.350/.407	126	32.8	.333	3.2	SS(83): 2.9, 2B(21): -0.6	3.7
2018	PIT	MLB	24	97	7	2	0	0	6	4	23	0	1	.209/.247/.231	62	-4.1	.275	-0.6	SS(24): -1.4, 2B(8): -0.7	-0.3
2019	IND	AAA	25	35	5	2	0	0	1	5	7	0	1	.233/.343/.300	85	0.1	.304	0.7	SS(4): -0.4, LF(2): -0.3	0.1
2019	PIT	MLB	25	531	61	20	6	12	64	28	62	16	8	.308/.353/.446	107	28.9	.333	0.9	SS(104): -1.3, 2B(23): 0.0	2.8
2020	PIT	MLB	26	560	53	27	3	9	55	33	75	11	4	.270/.320/.385	89	13.5	.302	0.7	SS -1, 2B 0	1.3

Comparables: Angel Berroa, Ramón Torres, Tony Kemp

A former first-round pick from Arizona acquitted himself well in the bigs, Newman showcased his plus (or thereabout) hit tool often enough to make up for the concerns about his glove. He has a limited profile at the plate since he doesn't walk much and entered the season with 15 home runs for his career. In other words, Newman will have to keep his average up to have value, so his path forward is a little more complicated than his rookie-year production indicates.

Jared Oliva **CF** Born: 11/27/95 Age: 24 Bats: R Throws: R Height: 6'3" Weight: 203 Origin: Round 7, 2017 Draft (#208 overall)

YEAR	TEAM	LVL	AGE	PA	R	2B	3B	HR	RBI	BB	K	SB	CS	AVG/OBP/SLG	DRC+	VORP	BABIP	BRR	FRAA	WARP
2017	WEV	A-	21	254	30	10	7	0	17	17	57	15	4	.266/.327/.374	97	9.3	.353	-0.4	CF(42): 0.6, LF(6): -0.2	0.7
2018	BRD	A+	22	454	75	24	4	9	47	40	91	33	8	.275/.354/.424	129	28.7	.332	4.3	CF(101): -7.6	2.4
2019	ALT	AA	23	507	70	24	6	6	42	42	104	36	10	.277/.352/.398	128	34.4	.347	4.2	CF(113): -1.2, LF(1): -0.1	3.4
2020	PIT	MLB	24	251	24	12	2	5	24	16	67	9	3	.236/.298/.362	76	1.4	.314	1.0	CF 0, LF 0	0.1

Comparables: Bryan Reynolds, Jake Marisnick, Tyler Naquin

Oliva is an average all-around player, which, if you think about it, translates to above-average in the general scheme of things. He's a pretty good runner, a pretty good defender in center with a pretty good arm, and he can hit a little more than a little. Not too shabby for a seventh rounder who could well bring his game to the Steel City before 2020 ends.

José Osuna **4C** Born: 12/12/92 Age: 27 Bats: R Throws: R Height: 6'2" Weight: 240 Origin: International Free Agent, 2009

YEAR	TEAM	LVL	AGE	PA	R	2B	3B	HR	RBI	BB	K	SB	CS	AVG/OBP/SLG	DRC+	VORP	BABIP	BRR	FRAA	WARP
2017	IND	AAA	24	41	6	5	0	0	1	5	9	1	1	.250/.341/.389	114	1.3	.333	0.1	1B(6): -0.2, RF(2): 0.0	0.1
2017	PIT	MLB	24	227	31	13	4	7	30	9	40	0	0	.233/.269/.428	78	-1.5	.254	-0.7	RF(25): -0.4, 1B(23): -1.1	-0.3
2018	IND	AAA	25	342	45	26	0	9	59	31	51	5	3	.321/.378/.497	163	30.5	.353	1.4	3B(47): 4.6, 1B(24): -0.7	3.8
2018	PIT	MLB	25	111	14	9	0	3	11	3	22	0	0	.226/.252/.396	80	0.7	.256	0.8	1B(12): 1.9, 3B(7): -0.2	0.3
2019	IND	AAA	26	83	13	7	1	2	13	9	22	2	0	.268/.361/.479	114	2.7	.354	0.2	RF(12): -2.6, LF(3): -0.2	0.1
2019	PIT	MLB	26	285	41	20	0	10	36	18	48	0	0	.264/.310/.456	94	4.7	.285	-1.1	1B(31): 1.2, RF(23): -0.5	0.6
2020	PIT	MLB	27	308	31	19	1	10	37	19	61	2	1	.236/.289/.412	82	-0.3	.267	-0.4	3B 1, RF 0	0.1

Comparables: C.J. Cron, Brett Wallace, Yonder Alonso

If we had to, we'd guess that Osuna is a proponent of the universal DH. The lack of a defensive home meant he received fewer plate appearances last season than various, less potent Pirates, like Elias Díaz (he can catch), Colin Moran (he can stand at third) and Melky Cabrera (web design is his passion). Osuna would benefit from the AL ruleset, under which all he would need to concern himself with is swinging through four or five plate appearances a game. He might be only a league-average stick, but sometimes that's enough to receive serious burn. Don't believe us? Ask Renato Nuñez.

Gregory Polanco **RF** Born: 09/14/91 Age: 28 Bats: L Throws: L Height: 6'5" Weight: 235 Origin: International Free Agent, 2009

YEAR	TEAM	LVL	AGE	PA	R	2B	3B	HR	RBI	BB	K	SB	CS	AVG/OBP/SLG	DRC+	VORP	BABIP	BRR	FRAA	WARP
2017	PIT	MLB	25	411	39	20	0	11	35	27	60	8	1	.251/.305/.391	87	2.8	.272	0.5	RF(68): 4.1, LF(25): -2.6	0.5
2018	PIT	MLB	26	535	75	32	6	23	81	61	117	12	2	.254/.340/.499	107	29.7	.287	0.7	RF(124): 1.3	1.8
2019	IND	AAA	27	54	5	4	0	1	11	9	16	2	0	.267/.389/.422	112	3.5	.393	1.0	RF(8): -1.1	0.2
2019	PIT	MLB	27	167	23	8	1	6	17	12	49	3	1	.242/.301/.425	80	-0.4	.316	0.5	RF(36): 0.4	0.0
2020	PIT	MLB	28	574	63	33	3	19	70	54	147	15	5	.241/.315/.425	93	8.9	.300	-0.1	RF 1, SS 0	1.0

Comparables: Jake Marisnick, Marcell Ozuna, Dave Winfield

Welcome back to El Coffee Talk with Linda Richman. Unfortunately the lines are not open, because this is a book. Our first topic, his injured shoulder. We all know it underwent surgery two autumns ago, but aggravating it a couple times, the poor kid, curbed all but a month of his 2019. That's his throwing arm, which used to be like buttah, but now it's just like matzah. The second topic, his rare combination of speed and power should return, but for how long? The thought of him passing his prime can make one a little verklempt. Talk amongst yourselves. Here's a topic. PECOTA projections are neither PECOTA nor a projection: Discuss.

Bryan Reynolds LF   Born: 01/27/95   Age: 25   Bats: B   Throws: R   Height: 6'3"   Weight: 205   Origin: Round 2, 2016 Draft (#59 overall)

YEAR	TEAM	LVL	AGE	PA	R	2B	3B	HR	RBI	BB	K	SB	CS	AVG/OBP/SLG	DRC+	VORP	BABIP	BRR	FRAA	WARP
2017	SJO	A+	22	541	72	26	9	10	63	37	106	5	3	.312/.364/.462	140	35.6	.376	-0.9	CF(50): -4.3, RF(42): -2.9	2.7
2018	ALT	AA	23	383	56	18	3	7	46	43	73	4	4	.302/.381/.438	136	33.4	.362	-0.2	CF(43): -3.2, LF(42): -3.6	2.0
2019	IND	AAA	24	57	10	1	1	5	11	7	11	3	2	.367/.446/.735	178	9.8	.394	-0.7	CF(13): -1.3	0.5
2019	PIT	MLB	24	546	83	37	4	16	68	46	121	3	2	.314/.377/.503	110	23.0	.387	1.5	LF(79): -0.4, RF(31): 0.1	2.2
2020	PIT	MLB	25	595	67	35	4	17	73	49	138	2	1	.283/.349/.458	113	27.5	.352	1.3	LF -2, RF 0	2.6

Comparables: Joe Adcock, Lance Berkman, Zoilo Almonte

Rookie of the Year predictions border on pseudoscience. The top challenge is guessing playing time, with deference given to players likely to make the team out of camp. Reynolds, the positional counterpart in the Andrew McCutchen deal, was one of those Swiss army knife outfielders (does a little bit of everything, and also your dad keeps telling you that you need one wherever you go) who rightfully began in Triple-A, yet injuries led to plenty of Pittsburgh-based reps. He not only held his own but nearly captured the league batting title and demonstrated a competent power game. We'd suggest he should be one of the favorites for Second Year Player of the Year—because of his play and because of his likely playing time—but that would be sophomoric.

Lolo Sanchez OF   Born: 04/23/99   Age: 21   Bats: R   Throws: R   Height: 5'11"   Weight: 168   Origin: International Free Agent, 2015

YEAR	TEAM	LVL	AGE	PA	R	2B	3B	HR	RBI	BB	K	SB	CS	AVG/OBP/SLG	DRC+	VORP	BABIP	BRR	FRAA	WARP
2017	PIR	RK	18	234	42	11	2	4	20	21	19	14	7	.284/.359/.417	126	14.9	.295	-0.9	CF(49): 7.6	1.9
2018	WVA	A	19	441	57	18	1	4	34	41	72	30	13	.243/.322/.328	97	14.2	.287	2.7	CF(88): 8.4, LF(19): -2.1	2.1
2019	GRB	A	20	263	43	10	6	4	26	17	28	20	10	.301/.377/.451	142	25.5	.327	2.1	CF(40): -3.7, LF(14): 0.5	1.8
2019	BRD	A+	20	195	21	3	3	1	9	18	31	13	5	.196/.300/.270	63	1.1	.233	2.4	LF(41): 0.3, CF(4): -0.8	-0.1
2020	PIT	MLB	21	251	21	11	1	3	21	18	46	7	4	.217/.287/.314	63	-4.1	.260	0.0	CF 1, LF -1	-0.3

Comparables: Abiatal Avelino, Abraham Almonte, Jason Martin

Sanchez is the kind of player that reminds you baseball is in the entertainment business. Daddy Yankee circa 2005 bumping as he settles into the box, a ball sliced down the third-base line, 12ish seconds and a slide into third. The A-ball crowd roars, probably the first and only time tonight everyone's eyes are fixed on the field. Did we mention he plays an excellent center field? All right, now that we've gotten you excited, we would be remiss if we didn't let you in on a few things; after all, if things were as rosy as portrayed over the first few sentences, you wouldn't be staring at a stat-line featuring an OPS under .600 post-promotion to Advanced-A. He has a quick bat but a questionable bat path—put another way, he is built like Rajai Davis but swings like Pete Alonso, which leads to more soft contact in the air than you'd like from the speedy dude bookending your lineup. He's had just one combined above-average offensive season in his pro career as a result, yet he's still young and armed with impressive tools and a great taste in music—that counts for something in this book.

Sammy Siani CF   Born: 12/14/00   Age: 19   Bats: L   Throws: L   Height: 6'0"   Weight: 195   Origin: Round 1, 2019 Draft (#37 overall)

YEAR	TEAM	LVL	AGE	PA	R	2B	3B	HR	RBI	BB	K	SB	CS	AVG/OBP/SLG	DRC+	VORP	BABIP	BRR	FRAA	WARP
2019	PIR	RK	18	164	21	3	3	0	9	26	41	5	0	.241/.372/.308	95	2.5	.340	-1.1	CF(21): -3.0, LF(16): 1.4	0.1
2020	PIT	MLB	19	251	21	11	1	3	20	23	85	3	1	.209/.287/.302	62	-4.2	.322	0.0	CF -1, LF 0	-0.5

Comparables: Derrick Robinson, Brett Phillips, Jason Martin

An overslot CBA selection from the other side of Pennsylvania, Sammy became the second Siani to forgo an ACC commitment to play pro ball: he skipped Duke after his brother Mike spurned Virginia to sign with Cincinnati. He isn't as overloaded with upside as some prep guys, but as a sweet-swinging lefty-hitting corner outfielder he shares some similarities with Mitchell.

Jacob Stallings C   Born: 12/22/89   Age: 30   Bats: R   Throws: R   Height: 6'4"   Weight: 220   Origin: Round 7, 2012 Draft (#226 overall)

YEAR	TEAM	LVL	AGE	PA	R	2B	3B	HR	RBI	BB	K	SB	CS	AVG/OBP/SLG	DRC+	VORP	BABIP	BRR	FRAA	WARP
2017	IND	AAA	27	243	35	16	0	4	38	17	30	1	2	.301/.358/.431	130	20.4	.330	1.2	C(60): -4.3, 1B(1): -0.1	1.5
2017	PIT	MLB	27	16	3	2	0	0	3	2	2	0	0	.357/.438/.500	83	3.0	.417	0.5	C(5): -0.1	0.1
2018	IND	AAA	28	278	37	22	1	3	40	15	51	1	2	.285/.335/.414	119	15.4	.343	-1.4	C(63): -4.7	1.2
2018	PIT	MLB	28	41	2	0	0	0	5	3	9	0	0	.216/.268/.216	74	-0.1	.276	0.5	C(13): 0.1	0.1
2019	IND	AAA	29	61	11	9	0	2	7	4	9	0	0	.275/.361/.569	116	2.4	.286	-3.2	C(15): 0.6	0.2
2019	PIT	MLB	29	210	26	5	0	6	13	16	40	0	0	.262/.325/.382	96	9.8	.303	0.6	C(61): 13.6, P(1): 0.0	2.3
2020	PIT	MLB	30	427	40	21	1	10	44	25	93	2	1	.235/.290/.365	74	6.7	.284	1.2	C 8	1.5

Comparables: Bryan Holaday, Brett Nicholas, Chad Moeller

We're just about there with pitchers, and so 25 years from now it's entirely possible we throw up our arms and implement a designated hitter for catchers, too. After all, rare is the pitch-caller who can do everything. Stallings certainly can't (and for that he is a backup), but he is developing a reputation as a savvy sequencer and elite framer. He doesn't exactly Mathis it at the plate but all of his value comes when he's wearing tons of padding. Are we saying he'd be an All-Star hitter if he batted in full catching gear? It'd be stupid not to try.

YEAR	TEAM	P. COUNT	FRM RUNS	BLK RUNS	THRW RUNS	TOT RUNS
2017	IND	8388	-4.6	-0.3	0.4	-5.2
2017	PIT	634	-0.2	0.2	0.0	-1.1
2018	IND	8927	-6.1	0.3	-0.1	-5.3
2018	PIT	1468	-0.7	0.5	0.0	0.9
2019	IND	2141	0.9	0.0	0.1	1.4
2019	PIT	7704	8.7	3.6	0.3	13.0
2020	PIT	16361	1.3	3.9	1.2	6.4

Travis Swaggerty CF   Born: 08/19/97   Age: 22   Bats: L   Throws: L   Height: 5'11"   Weight: 180   Origin: Round 1, 2018 Draft (#10 overall)

YEAR	TEAM	LVL	AGE	PA	R	2B	3B	HR	RBI	BB	K	SB	CS	AVG/OBP/SLG	DRC+	VORP	BABIP	BRR	FRAA	WARP
2018	WEV	A-	20	158	22	9	1	4	15	15	40	9	3	.288/.365/.453	151	12.5	.379	0.9	CF(36): -0.6	1.2
2018	WVA	A	20	71	6	1	1	1	5	7	18	0	0	.129/.225/.226	40	-1.2	.159	-0.6	CF(16): 0.7	-0.2
2019	BRD	A+	21	524	79	20	3	9	40	57	116	23	8	.265/.347/.381	124	25.2	.334	-0.2	CF(120): 7.4	3.7
2020	PIT	MLB	22	251	23	11	1	5	25	17	74	3	1	.223/.280/.347	67	-2.6	.302	0.2	CF 2	-0.1

Comparables: Daniel Fields, Zoilo Almonte, Kirk Nieuwenhuis

Swaggerty may seem familiar—not only because his name sounds like that of a character from *Deadwood*, but also because he's a former No. 10 pick who was the subject of a lot of chatter as he gained draft helium. Not hailing from South Dakota (rather South Alabama), Swaggerty is armed with a full set of tools. They're more fives and sixes than anything double-plus, but the overall package should be at least an above-average centerfielder in his early years plying power and speed as his trade.

Cole Tucker SS   Born: 07/03/96   Age: 23   Bats: B   Throws: R   Height: 6'3"   Weight: 205   Origin: Round 1, 2014 Draft (#24 overall)

YEAR	TEAM	LVL	AGE	PA	R	2B	3B	HR	RBI	BB	K	SB	CS	AVG/OBP/SLG	DRC+	VORP	BABIP	BRR	FRAA	WARP
2017	BRD	A+	20	316	46	15	6	4	32	34	70	36	12	.285/.364/.426	146	30.5	.368	1.5	SS(66): -0.4	2.7
2017	ALT	AA	20	194	25	4	5	2	18	21	31	11	3	.257/.349/.377	100	11.6	.304	1.3	SS(42): 0.9	1.1
2018	ALT	AA	21	589	77	21	7	5	44	55	104	35	12	.259/.333/.356	92	37.5	.310	3.4	SS(131): -0.6	2.4
2019	IND	AAA	22	353	51	15	4	8	28	38	73	11	3	.261/.346/.413	102	15.2	.319	1.2	SS(69): -4.7, 2B(6): 0.8	1.3
2019	PIT	MLB	22	159	16	10	3	2	13	10	40	0	0	.211/.266/.361	62	-0.3	.276	1.3	SS(45): -1.1	0.0
2020	PIT	MLB	23	189	17	8	2	3	17	14	47	6	3	.216/.280/.337	65	-0.9	.278	0.5	SS 0, 2B 0	-0.1

Comparables: Willi Castro, Jonathan Villar, Tyler Wade

Tucker's immediate impact at the big-league level may have convinced some that he was fit to be Pittsburgh's shortstop by the combination of his play (he recorded three hits, all for extra bases, in his first three games); his dynamic flow; and general bushy tailed optimism. Alas, the former first-round pick failed to capitalize on the opportunity, and instead spent most of the 2019 season in Triple-A, where he was fine. "Fine" is about the upshot here. Tucker runs and throws well, but he's never grown into power despite a 6-foot-3 frame. The rest of his tools are average or thereabout. There's still a big-league future here; after all, one needn't look further than Pittsburgh's recent history of shortstops for evidence that "fine" can result in a lengthy career. Even so, we would advise Pirates fans against looking at the 2014 draft—lest they remember that Tucker was selected right before the A's picked Matt Chapman, who, we can all agree, is a good bit better than "fine."

PITCHERS

Chris Archer RHP   Born: 09/26/88   Age: 31   Bats: R   Throws: R   Height: 6'2"   Weight: 195   Origin: Round 5, 2006 Draft (#161 overall)

YEAR	TEAM	LVL	AGE	W	L	SV	G	GS	IP	H	HR	BB/9	K/9	K	GB%	BABIP	WHIP	ERA	DRA	WARP	MPH	FB%	WHF	CSP
2017	TBA	MLB	28	10	12	0	34	34	201	193	27	2.7	11.1	249	43%	.325	1.26	4.07	3.53	4.6	97.8	47.4	14.6	47.4
2018	TBA	MLB	29	3	5	0	17	17	96	102	11	2.9	9.6	102	46%	.343	1.39	4.31	4.12	1.3	97.2	45.6	14.3	48.6
2018	PIT	MLB	29	3	3	0	10	10	52¹	53	8	3.1	10.3	60	48%	.328	1.36	4.30	4.30	0.6	96.9	49.3	13.2	45.6
2019	PIT	MLB	30	3	9	0	23	23	119²	114	25	4.1	10.8	143	38%	.298	1.41	5.19	4.42	1.8	96.1	50.5	13.5	45.2
2020	PIT	MLB	31	8	9	0	26	26	137	124	21	3.6	10.4	159	40%	.296	1.30	4.07	4.23	2.4	96.1	48	13.9	46.3

Comparables: Danny Salazar, Max Scherzer, Sonny Gray

Archer is suffering through the worst-case scenario Max Scherzer simulation. Five years ago, both seemed cut from the same cloth: fastball-slider dynamos who would rack up strikeouts if not complete games. Scherzer, of course, is a generational ace. Archer, conversely, wondering how both his ERA and FIP have crept above five. The easy answer is: the Pirates. The longer answer is...no, it's almost certainly the Pirates. Ex-pitching coach Ray Searage notoriously reintroduced Archer to the sinkerball, a tool he abandoned after 2014 to much success. But those were the types of decisions that cost Searage his job last year, so Archer would do well to return to the three-pitch mix that once made him a top-10 pitcher. And if that doesn't work, he may have to experience the extreme worst-case scenario for an old ace: life as a late-inning reliever.

Braxton Ashcraft RHP   Born: 10/05/99   Age: 20   Bats: L   Throws: R   Height: 6'5"   Weight: 195   Origin: Round 2, 2018 Draft (#51 overall)

YEAR	TEAM	LVL	AGE	W	L	SV	G	GS	IP	H	HR	BB/9	K/9	K	GB%	BABIP	WHIP	ERA	DRA	WARP	MPH	FB%	WHF	CSP
2018	PIR	RK	18	0	1	0	5	5	17²	16	2	2.5	6.1	12	52%	.259	1.19	4.58	3.27	0.5				
2019	WEV	A-	19	1	9	0	11	11	53	49	4	3.7	6.6	39	45%	.273	1.34	5.77	5.18	0.0				
2020	PIT	MLB	20	2	2	0	33	0	35	35	6	3.6	5.1	20	40%	.266	1.40	4.80	4.95	0.2				

Comparables: Alex Cobb, Jake Brigham, Peter Lambert

Ashcraft is a tall, projectable, former two-sport athlete from Texas who pairs a mid-90s fastball with some in-progress secondaries. You probably guessed he was a second-round pick just from reading that description. (He was.) There's a long time between now and when (if) Ashcraft debuts, so we'll save our jokes about how he'll one day be traded for Tyler Glasnow for 2021.

Osvaldo Bido RHP Born: 10/18/95 Age: 24 Bats: R Throws: R Height: 6'3" Weight: 175 Origin: International Free Agent, 2017

YEAR	TEAM	LVL	AGE	W	L	SV	G	GS	IP	H	HR	BB/9	K/9	K	GB%	BABIP	WHIP	ERA	DRA	WARP	MPH	FB%	WHF	CSP
2017	DPI	RK	21	1	8	0	15	13	50²	53	1	6.4	7.3	41	57%	.333	1.76	5.33	7.15	-0.6				
2018	WEV	A-	22	4	6	0	14	14	75¹	74	2	2.3	6.9	58	62%	.320	1.23	4.18	5.17	0.0				
2019	GRB	A	23	11	5	0	20	20	111²	94	9	2.3	7.3	90	42%	.267	1.10	3.55	4.54	0.8				
2019	BRD	A+	23	1	3	0	5	5	24	18	1	3.4	6.4	17	42%	.243	1.12	2.25	4.16	0.3				
2020	PIT	MLB	24	2	2	0	33	0	35	34	5	3.3	5.7	22	44%	.268	1.33	4.31	4.54	0.3				

Comparables: Tyson Brummett, James Marvel, Daniel Ponce de Leon

The long and lanky Bido has a pleasing ratio of vowels to syllables in his name. He also had a pleasing stretch of performance in his age-23 season. He's a somewhat late developer, having just been promoted to High-A to finish the season, but his stuff makes him a name worth watching. Bido touches the mid-90s with his heater and commands it well enough as well. His slider isn't quite there, and so if he's going to reach the majors it's likely to be as an arm-strength reliever.

Cody Bolton RHP Born: 06/19/98 Age: 22 Bats: R Throws: R Height: 6'3" Weight: 185 Origin: Round 6, 2017 Draft (#178 overall)

YEAR	TEAM	LVL	AGE	W	L	SV	G	GS	IP	H	HR	BB/9	K/9	K	GB%	BABIP	WHIP	ERA	DRA	WARP	MPH	FB%	WHF	CSP
2017	PIR	RK	19	0	2	0	9	9	25²	23	1	2.8	7.7	22	44%	.286	1.21	3.16	2.84	0.9				
2018	WVA	A	20	3	3	0	9	9	44¹	43	6	1.4	9.1	45	43%	.308	1.13	3.65	4.28	0.5				
2019	BRD	A+	21	6	3	0	12	12	61²	39	1	2.0	10.1	69	48%	.245	0.86	1.61	2.73	1.7				
2019	ALT	AA	21	2	3	0	9	9	40	37	6	3.6	7.4	33	35%	.277	1.33	5.85	4.31	0.3				
2020	PIT	MLB	22	2	2	0	33	0	35	35	6	3.8	8.1	32	37%	.296	1.43	4.78	4.89	0.2				

Comparables: Tyler Mahle, Edwin Díaz, Kyle Drabek

Bolton, a former sixth-round pick, has a lively fastball down in the zone and an advanced command profile—the combination of which made him lights out in the Florida State League. He scuffled a bit upon his promotion to Double-A, but it's important to remember that he won't turn 22 until next June. The more concerning matter is why he goes by "Cody" when his legal name is "Carl Donovan Bolton."

Steven Brault LHP Born: 04/29/92 Age: 28 Bats: L Throws: L Height: 6'0" Weight: 195 Origin: Round 11, 2013 Draft (#339 overall)

YEAR	TEAM	LVL	AGE	W	L	SV	G	GS	IP	H	HR	BB/9	K/9	K	GB%	BABIP	WHIP	ERA	DRA	WARP	MPH	FB%	WHF	CSP
2017	IND	AAA	25	10	5	0	21	20	120¹	85	5	3.3	8.2	109	53%	.252	1.07	1.94	2.85	3.8				
2017	PIT	MLB	25	1	0	1	11	4	34²	41	3	3.6	6.0	23	45%	.317	1.59	4.67	6.17	-0.3	93.9	72	8.8	46.8
2018	PIT	MLB	26	6	3	0	45	5	91²	84	10	5.6	8.1	82	50%	.289	1.54	4.61	5.66	-0.7	95.2	65	10.8	46.9
2019	PIT	MLB	27	4	6	0	25	19	113¹	117	15	4.2	7.9	100	45%	.310	1.50	5.16	4.40	1.6	94.1	64.3	10.5	47
2020	PIT	MLB	28	7	9	0	26	26	132	133	18	4.2	8.0	117	45%	.299	1.47	4.88	4.86	1.4	93.9	65.7	10.5	47.2

Comparables: Michael Kirkman, Adam Conley, André Rienzo

Brault wears his hobbies on his sleeve, or as part of his sleeve tattoo, anyway. He's a starter/swingman, a singer and a gamer, and he may soon become a two-way player after hitting .333/.349/.429 in 50 trips to the plate. (He's also a lefty, so add 10 more eclectic points.) Brault's athleticism makes the experiment worth the try even if he's likely to remain a hurler first and foremost. About his pitching: his pitches of choice are [Hank Hill voice] fastballs and fastball accessories. In one September start, Brault's first 69 pitches were all heaters. He's not good enough to stick in a rotation, and so leaning into his protean nature even more might be the difference between reaching arbitration and not.

Nick Burdi RHP Born: 01/19/93 Age: 27 Bats: R Throws: R Height: 6'3" Weight: 225 Origin: Round 2, 2014 Draft (#46 overall)

YEAR	TEAM	LVL	AGE	W	L	SV	G	GS	IP	H	HR	BB/9	K/9	K	GB%	BABIP	WHIP	ERA	DRA	WARP	MPH	FB%	WHF	CSP
2017	CHT	AA	24	2	0	1	14	0	17	9	1	2.1	10.6	20	46%	.222	0.76	0.53	2.61	0.4				
2018	PIT	MLB	25	0	0	0	2	0	1¹	3	1	13.5	13.5	2	33%	.400	3.75	20.25	1.82	0.0	99.0	71.4	14.3	46.9
2019	PIT	MLB	26	2	1	0	11	0	8²	11	1	3.1	17.7	17	20%	.526	1.62	9.35	2.67	0.3	98.6	45.3	18.9	49.5
2020	PIT	MLB	27	2	2	0	34	0	36	31	6	3.7	13.7	55	36%	.326	1.28	4.02	4.17	0.5	98.2	49.8	18.4	48.9

Comparables: Akeel Morris, Harvey Garcia, Mauricio Cabrera

It was a 1-0 pitch to Jarrod Dyson, a 97-mph fastball. Burdi released it, and then clutched his throwing arm and knelt to the ground in pain. He had been marked by a scalpel two winters ago for Tommy John reasons, and now this. Fortunately, in a sense, it wasn't the tendon but rather the nerve. He saw another surgeon, and this time they corrected his thoracic outlet syndrome (a procedure that should be called Chris Young surgery if we're going to name these things after players). Burdi ought to be ready to reaffirm his reputation for heat and high-leverage tolerance come spring. He'll try to throw more than 20 innings in a season for the first time since 2015.

Kyle Crick RHP Born: 11/30/92 Age: 27 Bats: L Throws: R Height: 6'4" Weight: 220 Origin: Round 1, 2011 Draft (#49 overall)

YEAR	TEAM	LVL	AGE	W	L	SV	G	GS	IP	H	HR	BB/9	K/9	K	GB%	BABIP	WHIP	ERA	DRA	WARP	MPH	FB%	WHF	CSP
2017	SAC	AAA	24	1	2	6	24	0	29¹	24	1	4.0	12.0	39	45%	.329	1.26	2.76	2.41	0.9				
2017	SFN	MLB	24	0	0	0	30	0	32¹	22	2	4.7	7.8	28	39%	.233	1.21	3.06	4.29	0.3	97.2	74.5	12.1	45.7
2018	PIT	MLB	25	3	2	2	64	0	60¹	45	3	3.4	9.7	65	43%	.268	1.13	2.39	4.41	0.4	97.8	72.9	12.6	47.9
2019	PIT	MLB	26	3	7	0	52	0	49	41	10	6.4	11.2	61	44%	.274	1.55	4.96	5.56	-0.1	96.7	62.3	13.3	46.4
2020	PIT	MLB	27	3	3	5	57	0	60	51	8	4.7	10.4	69	42%	.286	1.37	4.23	4.26	0.8	96.8	69.3	13	47.3

Comparables: Trevor May, Sam Tuivailala, Neftalí Feliz

Athletes always want to make a name for themselves and win ballgames, and sometimes that entails maintaining a high intensity level. Crick made a name for himself by playing a small role in that wild Pirates-Reds fight, in which he tried to further infuriate Yasiel Puig (who, it must be noted, had technically been traded to another team minutes earlier). Later in the season, Crick infuriated teammate Felipe Vásquez over clubhouse music, according to various reports, resulting in a fight that precipitated a season-ending injury. We're nearly out of space to discuss his pitching, but that's what happens when a Personality gets into altercations. His pitching was adequate, by the way.

Miguel Del Pozo LHP Born: 10/14/92 Age: 27 Bats: L Throws: L Height: 6'1" Weight: 180 Origin: International Free Agent, 2010

YEAR	TEAM	LVL	AGE	W	L	SV	G	GS	IP	H	HR	BB/9	K/9	K	GB%	BABIP	WHIP	ERA	DRA	WARP	MPH	FB%	WHF	CSP
2017	JUP	A+	24	2	0	0	12	0	16²	12	0	2.7	9.2	17	50%	.273	1.02	0.54	3.28	0.3				
2018	JAX	AA	25	5	0	1	28	0	34	37	3	4.0	9.0	34	39%	.343	1.53	3.97	5.30	-0.1				
2019	NAS	AAA	26	2	3	1	38	0	45²	53	5	4.1	12.8	65	37%	.432	1.62	5.12	3.88	1.0				
2019	LAA	MLB	26	1	1	0	17	0	9¹	10	3	7.7	10.6	11	27%	.304	1.93	10.61	6.58	-0.1	96.2	56.8	11.5	44.2
2020	PIT	MLB	27	2	2	0	33	0	35	33	6	4.4	8.7	34	36%	.281	1.42	4.75	4.76	0.3	95.7	57.5	11.6	44.7

Comparables: Adrian Houser, Steven Okert, Dustin Antolin

Through his rise up the ranks of the Marlins and Rangers systems, Del Pozo had two settings: too many walks, and *way* too many walks. At Triple-A Round Rock early in 2019, he was set to the former mode. After an August trade to, and subsequent call-up by, the Angels, he switched into the latter mode, with some extra home-run booster packs thrown in. Admittedly, this was a small sample, and Del Pozo is still a lefty whose whiff-inducing combination of a mid-90s heater and tumbling curve means that, though he was released by the Angels following the 2019 season, some team may want to keep tinkering under the hood.

Luis Escobar RHP Born: 05/30/96 Age: 24 Bats: R Throws: R Height: 6'1" Weight: 205 Origin: International Free Agent, 2013

YEAR	TEAM	LVL	AGE	W	L	SV	G	GS	IP	H	HR	BB/9	K/9	K	GB%	BABIP	WHIP	ERA	DRA	WARP	MPH	FB%	WHF	CSP
2017	WVA	A	21	10	7	0	26	25	131²	97	9	4.1	11.5	168	44%	.282	1.19	3.83	3.42	2.9				
2018	BRD	A+	22	7	6	0	17	16	92²	76	9	3.7	8.3	85	48%	.272	1.23	3.98	4.04	1.4				
2018	ALT	AA	22	4	0	0	7	7	35²	30	4	5.3	6.3	25	43%	.248	1.43	4.54	5.21	0.1				
2019	BRD	A+	23	0	0	3	10	0	13¹	6	0	4.1	10.1	15	58%	.194	0.90	0.00	3.34	0.2				
2019	IND	AAA	23	2	1	1	24	5	55	54	7	5.2	9.3	57	48%	.329	1.56	4.09	5.36	0.6				
2019	PIT	MLB	23	0	0	0	4	0	5²	10	1	6.4	3.2	2	46%	.429	2.47	7.94	4.72	0.0	96.6	68.3	9.6	45.5
2020	PIT	MLB	24	2	2	0	33	0	35	41	7	5.1	7.3	28	43%	.317	1.75	6.74	6.18	-0.3	96.4	70.3	9.9	46.9

Comparables: Merandy Gonzalez, Dylan Cease, Kendry Flores

The *Cartagenero* is your big-stuff pitcher with control issues *du jour* for the Pirates. Escobar has a primetime fastball with life and a real-deal curve, but his very eventful delivery causes the aforementioned sloppy geography. He's already a reliever as a result, though he should get more big-league duty come 2020. If the K rate ticks up and the walk rate ticks down, he could be fun.

Michael Feliz RHP Born: 06/28/93 Age: 27 Bats: R Throws: R Height: 6'4" Weight: 240 Origin: International Free Agent, 2010

YEAR	TEAM	LVL	AGE	W	L	SV	G	GS	IP	H	HR	BB/9	K/9	K	GB%	BABIP	WHIP	ERA	DRA	WARP	MPH	FB%	WHF	CSP
2017	HOU	MLB	24	4	2	0	46	0	48	53	8	4.1	13.1	70	31%	.381	1.56	5.62	3.18	1.1	98.6	71.9	15.4	50.4
2018	IND	AAA	25	2	1	2	9	0	10	13	2	0.9	10.8	12	40%	.393	1.40	7.20	5.76	-0.1				
2018	PIT	MLB	25	1	2	0	47	0	47²	49	6	4.3	10.4	55	33%	.331	1.51	5.66	5.20	-0.1	97.8	73.6	11	46.1
2019	IND	AAA	26	0	0	2	10	0	15	13	1	4.2	13.2	22	37%	.353	1.33	1.20	3.11	0.5				
2019	PIT	MLB	26	4	4	0	58	1	56¹	44	11	4.3	11.7	73	38%	.262	1.26	3.99	3.38	1.2	97.6	73.4	13.6	46.3
2020	PIT	MLB	27	3	3	2	57	0	60	50	9	4.1	11.4	76	36%	.291	1.29	3.88	4.00	0.9	97.4	74	13.3	47.8

Comparables: Adrian Houser, John Gant, Domingo Germán

You're probably familiar with the Tik Tok-featured song that goes something like, ahem, "don't be suspicious…don't be suspicious" and so on. (If not, ask the designated teenager in your life for assistance.) Feliz mutters a similar command on the mound: don't be too hittable…don't be too hittable. He strikes out a lot of batters, but walks a lot, too—and, despite the K rate, he's yielded 1.5 homers per nine through 225 big-league innings. It seems overzealous to conclude that he's maybe one more hit per nine away from being out of the league, yet our guess is that if that were to happen, his subsequent big-league career wouldn't be long enough to put in a bun.

Santiago Florez RHP Born: 05/09/00 Age: 20 Bats: R Throws: R Height: 6'5" Weight: 222 Origin: International Free Agent, 2016

YEAR	TEAM	LVL	AGE	W	L	SV	G	GS	IP	H	HR	BB/9	K/9	K	GB%	BABIP	WHIP	ERA	DRA	WARP	MPH	FB%	WHF	CSP
2017	DPI	RK	17	2	5	0	14	14	53¹	43	2	6.4	5.1	30	46%	.243	1.52	4.56	4.87	0.7				
2018	PIR	RK	18	5	2	0	10	10	43¹	37	0	4.8	7.3	35	55%	.289	1.38	4.15	5.09	0.5				
2019	BRI	RK+	19	2	2	0	10	10	41²	35	4	4.5	7.8	36	49%	.267	1.34	3.46	4.20	0.9				
2020													No projection											

Originally a low-money signing out of Colombia, Florez had himself a nice year. The opposition must experience some sensory overload when facing him due to his size and stuff—he has mid-90s heat and a promising curveball. Florez is years away from being years away, but if the Pirates are going to be praised for their international scouting prowess anytime soon, he figures to play a role.

Sam Howard **LHP**   Born: 03/05/93   Age: 27   Bats: R   Throws: L   Height: 6'3"   Weight: 170   Origin: Round 3, 2014 Draft (#82 overall)

YEAR	TEAM	LVL	AGE	W	L	SV	G	GS	IP	H	HR	BB/9	K/9	K	GB%	BABIP	WHIP	ERA	DRA	WARP	MPH	FB%	WHF	CSP
2017	HFD	AA	24	1	4	0	9	9	46¹	31	5	1.9	7.8	40	39%	.208	0.88	2.33	2.54	1.5				
2017	ABQ	AAA	24	4	4	0	15	14	81	82	6	3.7	7.1	64	41%	.309	1.42	3.89	3.82	1.6				
2018	ABQ	AAA	25	3	8	0	21	21	96	106	13	3.2	7.5	80	40%	.327	1.46	5.06	4.99	0.6				
2018	COL	MLB	25	0	0	0	4	0	4	5	0	6.8	2.2	1	53%	.333	2.00	2.25	8.49	-0.2	92.7	48.8	8.1	50.2
2019	ABQ	AAA	26	4	1	1	42	0	50²	50	5	4.1	11.0	62	44%	.363	1.44	3.91	3.01	1.6				
2019	COL	MLB	26	2	0	0	20	0	19	21	5	4.7	10.9	23	42%	.320	1.63	6.63	3.91	0.3	94.0	44.1	15.4	43
2020	PIT	MLB	27	1	1	0	23	0	24	20	4	3.8	9.0	24	40%	.268	1.28	3.89	4.07	0.4	93.3	45.4	14.5	46.7

Comparables: Steven Brault, Harrison Musgrave, Brian Johnson

Howard's problem wasn't his home park, like so many of his peers. Just three of the 14 earned runs he gave up came in Colorado. Quality lineups were his downfall instead. All but one of the remaining earned runs on his ledger came on the road, courtesy of three of the better offenses in baseball: the Dodgers, Nationals and Astros. Perhaps it's not surprising that the lefty's combination of solid-yet-unspectacular stuff and pitchability plays better against mediocre offenses than good ones. Perhaps it's just a small sample size fluke that his OPS allowed was over 500 points higher against teams with a winning record than against those who were sub-.500. For the first time in his career, Howard was exclusively a reliever, and it took him a little while to start leaning on the slider more heavily. The strikeouts certainly went up once he did, even if the results didn't match the peripherals. He ditched the lackluster change (Howard threw just six all season), and when he did locate the slider, hitters had real trouble with it. There might not be enough here for a great bullpen arm, but he has the potential to make a solid middle reliever.

Steven Jennings **RHP**   Born: 11/13/98   Age: 21   Bats: R   Throws: R   Height: 6'2"   Weight: 175   Origin: Round 2, 2017 Draft (#42 overall)

YEAR	TEAM	LVL	AGE	W	L	SV	G	GS	IP	H	HR	BB/9	K/9	K	GB%	BABIP	WHIP	ERA	DRA	WARP	MPH	FB%	WHF	CSP
2017	PIR	RK	18	0	2	0	10	10	26¹	31	2	3.4	4.4	13	57%	.305	1.56	4.10	5.98	0.0				
2018	BRI	RK	19	3	4	0	13	13	65¹	68	5	3.7	7.3	53	46%	.307	1.45	4.82	4.64	1.0				
2019	GRB	A	20	7	12	0	27	27	130	134	15	2.7	8.0	115	37%	.316	1.33	4.71	5.89	-1.1				
2020	PIT	MLB	21	2	2	0	33	0	35	36	6	3.9	6.2	24	34%	.278	1.47	5.13	5.17	0.1				

Comparables: Yennsy Diaz, Elvin Ramirez, Anthony Banda

A second-round pick three years ago out of a Tennessee high school, Jennings is a command pitcher who lacks command. His problem isn't with control—or, the ability most closely linked to walks—but with leaving too many of his pitches center-cut. That's a teensy weensy problem given he lacks the overpowering stuff required to cover up for his location-based deficiencies. Jennings is still young and athletic enough to envision growth on this front. But, as our friend Brendon Urie is prone to saying, it's best to face these kinds of things with a sense of poise and rationality. That's why we're concluding that Jennings probably won't make the gains he needs to become a mid-rotation starter like the Pirates' original projection.

Keone Kela **RHP**   Born: 04/16/93   Age: 27   Bats: R   Throws: R   Height: 6'1"   Weight: 210   Origin: Round 12, 2012 Draft (#396 overall)

YEAR	TEAM	LVL	AGE	W	L	SV	G	GS	IP	H	HR	BB/9	K/9	K	GB%	BABIP	WHIP	ERA	DRA	WARP	MPH	FB%	WHF	CSP
2017	TEX	MLB	24	4	1	2	39	0	38²	18	4	4.0	11.9	51	32%	.179	0.91	2.79	4.75	0.2	98.5	57.9	12.2	49.6
2018	TEX	MLB	25	3	3	24	38	0	36²	28	3	3.4	10.8	44	40%	.275	1.15	3.44	3.50	0.6	99.0	64.3	12.7	49.5
2018	PIT	MLB	25	0	1	0	16	0	15¹	10	2	2.9	12.9	22	27%	.258	0.98	2.93	2.37	0.5	98.7	58.7	16.1	50.3
2019	PIT	MLB	26	2	0	1	32	0	29²	19	3	3.3	10.0	33	36%	.225	1.01	2.12	3.83	0.5	98.2	53.5	11.7	46.7
2020	PIT	MLB	27	3	3	23	57	0	60	48	8	3.8	10.8	72	38%	.280	1.24	3.60	3.79	1.1	98.1	59.3	12.8	49

Comparables: Bruce Rondón, Neftalí Feliz, Cam Bedrosian

The best way to beat Kela's menacing fastball-curve combination is to catch him on the right day. Absences, both excused and unexcused, are everywhere. He missed three months to elbow inflammation; he also took a 10-game mandatory hiatus after that wild Reds-Pirates physical disagreement for being the one to throw over a batter's head; *and*, remarkably, he had yet another suspension, that one team-enforced for clashing with a coach. Kela was virtually unhittable in the second half, but his greatest enemy is himself (though his arm seems to be a tad self-loathing as well).

— ★ ★ ★ *2020 Top 101 Prospect* **#53** ★ ★ ★ —

Mitch Keller **RHP**   Born: 04/04/96   Age: 24   Bats: R   Throws: R   Height: 6'2"   Weight: 210   Origin: Round 2, 2014 Draft (#64 overall)

YEAR	TEAM	LVL	AGE	W	L	SV	G	GS	IP	H	HR	BB/9	K/9	K	GB%	BABIP	WHIP	ERA	DRA	WARP	MPH	FB%	WHF	CSP
2017	BRD	A+	21	6	3	0	15	15	77¹	57	5	2.3	7.4	64	55%	.248	1.00	3.14	3.14	1.9				
2017	ALT	AA	21	2	2	0	6	6	34²	25	2	2.9	11.7	45	48%	.280	1.04	3.12	2.41	1.1				
2018	ALT	AA	22	9	2	0	14	14	86	64	7	3.3	8.0	76	55%	.251	1.12	2.72	3.55	1.8				
2018	IND	AAA	22	3	2	0	10	10	52¹	59	3	3.8	9.8	57	35%	.366	1.55	4.82	6.93	-0.8				
2019	IND	AAA	23	7	5	0	19	19	103²	94	9	3.0	10.7	123	46%	.315	1.24	3.56	3.38	3.3				
2019	PIT	MLB	23	1	5	0	11	11	48	72	6	3.0	12.2	65	41%	.475	1.83	7.12	4.18	0.8	97.5	59.5	13.7	47.8
2020	PIT	MLB	24	7	7	0	23	23	113	108	13	3.3	10.0	127	43%	.315	1.32	4.00	4.12	2.1	97.3	61.3	14.1	49.3

Comparables: Jake Faria, Zack Littell, Lucas Sims

After consecutive years as one of our top 20 prospects, Keller finally received the call but not the response. That's because of either the worst luck or the worst tipping of his fastball in modern baseball. Check this. In recorded history, minimum 200 batters faced, nobody had a seasonal BABIP higher than .432 (Tim Lincecum's regrettable 2016 with the Angels) until Keller dropped a big ol' .475 right there for all to see. That's now the benchmark for standing on the mound and being witness to your own horror show. He's likely to be better this year without changing anything. And if his BABIP does, somehow, go up? Then he needs to tell his catcher to stop whispering to the batter, "wowie, watch this next fastball, it's the cat's pajamas," (or whatever catchers say these days) because that's the only explanation that makes sense for his struggles.

Chad Kuhl RHP   Born: 09/10/92   Age: 27   Bats: R   Throws: R   Height: 6'3"   Weight: 216   Origin: Round 9, 2013 Draft (#269 overall)

YEAR	TEAM	LVL	AGE	W	L	SV	G	GS	IP	H	HR	BB/9	K/9	K	GB%	BABIP	WHIP	ERA	DRA	WARP	MPH	FB%	WHF	CSP
2017	PIT	MLB	24	8	11	0	31	31	157¹	159	17	4.1	8.1	142	43%	.321	1.47	4.35	5.35	0.4	98.2	63.5	10.3	47.7
2018	PIT	MLB	25	5	5	0	16	16	85	89	14	3.5	8.6	81	41%	.311	1.44	4.55	4.24	1.0	97.8	59	10.3	49.3
2020	PIT	MLB	27	6	8	0	50	16	117	125	21	3.4	8.8	114	42%	.314	1.45	5.21	5.19	0.7	97.5	62.4	10.5	49.2

Comparables: Reynaldo López, Robert Gsellman, Sal Romano

Kuhl spent the year mending elbow scars and watching the world burn in front of him in the form of the self-immolations of the Pirates roster and front office. As hard as it is for a pitcher to sit out a season, he should be ready to partake in the latest New Era of Pirates Baseball come spring—and he'll do so without having that 2019 funk on him. Provided Kuhl can come back with his pitch gang intact—we're talking his mid-90s sinker and pair of breakers—then he has a chance to bring some peace to the universe, or, at least, the back of the rotation.

Francisco Liriano LHP   Born: 10/26/83   Age: 36   Bats: L   Throws: L   Height: 6'3"   Weight: 218   Origin: International Free Agent, 2000

YEAR	TEAM	LVL	AGE	W	L	SV	G	GS	IP	H	HR	BB/9	K/9	K	GB%	BABIP	WHIP	ERA	DRA	WARP	MPH	FB%	WHF	CSP
2017	TOR	MLB	33	6	5	0	18	18	82²	91	11	4.7	8.1	74	44%	.327	1.62	5.88	5.75	-0.2	95.0	49.3	10.1	42.2
2017	HOU	MLB	33	0	2	0	20	0	14¹	14	0	6.3	6.9	11	54%	.341	1.67	4.40	6.59	-0.2	96.4	54.6	10	44
2018	DET	MLB	34	5	12	0	27	26	133²	127	19	4.9	7.4	110	49%	.285	1.50	4.58	5.36	-0.1	94.4	46.7	10.5	43.8
2019	PIT	MLB	35	5	3	0	69	0	70	60	8	4.5	8.1	63	52%	.271	1.36	3.47	4.53	0.6	95.0	43.8	14.3	45.4
2020	PIT	MLB	36	2	2	0	33	0	35	32	5	4.6	9.1	36	50%	.289	1.44	4.63	4.61	0.3	93.5	45.8	11.2	43.2

Comparables: Jon Lester, Gio Gonzalez, Mark Langston

It didn't seem possible, but Liriano might have added a couple more years to his career by embracing the bullpen. Indeed, 2019 was the first time in his career he went an entire season without a start. His pitches had a skosh more zip, sure, and yet the real key to his success was avoiding all those mean right-handers: He faced lefties in 29 percent of his plate appearances, a new personal high. He also had the lowest BABIP of his long career—a career so long, in fact, he was once teammates with Terry freaking Mulholland. Liriano could probably use some pointers from Grandpa Terry, since that he was abysmal in back-to-back situations. If he can get that aspect figured out, though, he might pitch into his 40s, the way lefties were meant to.

Joe Musgrove RHP   Born: 12/04/92   Age: 27   Bats: R   Throws: R   Height: 6'5"   Weight: 230   Origin: Round 1, 2011 Draft (#46 overall)

YEAR	TEAM	LVL	AGE	W	L	SV	G	GS	IP	H	HR	BB/9	K/9	K	GB%	BABIP	WHIP	ERA	DRA	WARP	MPH	FB%	WHF	CSP
2017	FRE	AAA	24	1	0	0	1	1	7	1	0	2.6	9.0	7	54%	.077	0.43	0.00	2.94	0.2				
2017	HOU	MLB	24	7	8	2	38	15	109¹	117	18	2.3	8.1	98	46%	.316	1.33	4.77	4.49	1.2	96.1	48	13	51.6
2018	IND	AAA	25	1	1	0	2	2	10²	10	0	1.7	9.3	11	41%	.312	1.12	5.06	3.79	0.2				
2018	PIT	MLB	25	6	9	0	19	19	115¹	113	12	1.8	7.8	100	48%	.294	1.18	4.06	3.43	2.5	95.5	50.3	12.5	53.5
2019	PIT	MLB	26	11	12	0	32	31	170¹	168	21	2.1	8.3	157	45%	.299	1.22	4.44	3.59	4.0	94.7	49.5	12.7	49
2020	PIT	MLB	27	9	9	0	28	28	149	143	20	2.3	8.3	138	44%	.293	1.22	3.85	4.07	2.9	94.7	50	12.9	51.8

Comparables: Jameson Taillon, James Shields, Yonny Chirinos

Musgrove is a solid No. 4 starter who last season reached career-highs in innings and strikeouts, and who markedly outperformed FIP (the starting pitcher's mirror, mirror on the wall) for the second year in a row. For now, and perhaps for however long he's in Pittsburgh, fans are going to look at him as if he's sporting a tattoo that reads "Yes, I was traded for Gerrit Cole." First off, it's not his fault he was the positional counterpart in that trade. Second of all, why even get that tattoo, unless this is a *Memento* situation? Anyway, it's tough to disassociate from the player you were traded for, especially when said disembarking player is a top-five pitcher and said onboarding pitcher is a "mere" No. 4 starter (though he was top-30 by DRA in 2019). But one great piece of advice is to learn to let go; another is to be happy that the Pirates haven't turned the No. 4 they received for their No. 1 into a No. 7 with a large drink.

Héctor Noesi RHP   Born: 01/26/87   Age: 33   Bats: R   Throws: R   Height: 6'3"   Weight: 205   Origin: International Free Agent, 2004

YEAR	TEAM	LVL	AGE	W	L	SV	G	GS	IP	H	HR	BB/9	K/9	K	GB%	BABIP	WHIP	ERA	DRA	WARP	MPH	FB%	WHF	CSP
2019	NWO	AAA	32	11	4	0	21	21	125	112	27	2.2	9.6	133	41%	.271	1.14	3.82	3.21	4.2				
2019	MIA	MLB	32	0	3	0	12	4	27²	30	7	4.6	7.8	24	33%	.295	1.59	8.46	6.58	-0.3	94.8	44.1	13.3	46.3
2020	PIT	MLB	33	2	2	0	33	0	35	36	7	3.1	8.0	31	37%	.289	1.38	5.06	5.15	0.1	93.8	43.5	13.1	45.8

Comparables: Luis Cessa, Jason Bergmann, Chris Stratton

The curse conferred onto Noesí and Jesús Montero in 2012 when they were dealt to Seattle may have paid Noesí another visit, as new laws taxing foreign players in the Korean Baseball Organization apparently compelled Noesí and the Kia Tigers to part ways before 2019. Noesí had previously starred with the Tigers, winning 46 games and posting a 3.79 ERA over three seasons and winning the 2017 league championship. That success didn't carry over to Miami, where the 32-year-old pitcher struggled to replicate the mediocrity of his previous major league tenure. He can still eat some innings, but any utility beyond that starts with an "F".

Quinn Priester RHP   Born: 09/15/00   Age: 19   Bats: R   Throws: R   Height: 6'3"   Weight: 195   Origin: Round 1, 2019 Draft (#18 overall)

YEAR	TEAM	LVL	AGE	W	L	SV	G	GS	IP	H	HR	BB/9	K/9	K	GB%	BABIP	WHIP	ERA	DRA	WARP	MPH	FB%	WHF	CSP
2019	PIR	RK	18	1	1	0	8	7	32²	29	1	2.8	10.2	37	58%	.318	1.19	3.03	5.66	0.1				
2020	PIT	MLB	19	2	2	0	33	0	35	35	5	3.8	7.7	30	48%	.289	1.42	4.78	4.91	0.2				

Comparables: Domingo Germán, Sandy Baez, Alex Reyes

It may seem that your favorite team's chances of developing a front-end starter are the same an Umberto Eco character has at tracking down an apocryphal Christian king. Pirates fans know what we're talking about—Lord, do they—but they'll still dream on Priester, a first-round prep righty from the Chicago area who has two or three potential plus pitches in his fastballs (a four- and a two-seam version) and his curve. Priester was born on September 15, 2000. On that same day, the Pirates dropped a game to the Brewers. The losing pitcher was Matt Skrmetta, who feels as unreal as Prester John. We mention that to show quickly time moves, and how soon another failure to develop an ace could become just another minute in a sad fan's hour.

Richard Rodríguez RHP   Born: 03/04/90   Age: 30   Bats: R   Throws: R   Height: 6'4"   Weight: 230   Origin: International Free Agent, 2010

YEAR	TEAM	LVL	AGE	W	L	SV	G	GS	IP	H	HR	BB/9	K/9	K	GB%	BABIP	WHIP	ERA	DRA	WARP	MPH	FB%	WHF	CSP
2017	NOR	AAA	27	4	4	10	42	1	70²	56	5	2.3	10.2	80	29%	.285	1.05	2.42	3.06	1.7				
2017	BAL	MLB	27	0	0	0	5	0	5²	12	4	4.8	4.8	3	46%	.400	2.65	14.29	8.32	-0.2	95.1	65.8	6.7	50.2
2018	PIT	MLB	28	4	3	0	63	0	69¹	55	5	2.5	11.4	88	40%	.309	1.07	2.47	2.82	1.7	94.9	75.1	15.2	50.7
2019	PIT	MLB	29	4	5	1	72	0	65¹	65	14	3.2	8.7	63	44%	.280	1.35	3.72	4.70	0.5	95.0	85.2	11.6	48
2020	PIT	MLB	30	3	3	5	57	0	60	59	11	3.0	9.3	62	40%	.300	1.32	4.56	4.69	0.5	94.2	80	12.9	49.3

Comparables: Ben Rowen, Josh Lueke, Paul Sewald

Modern analytics have more or less replaced celestial numerology in sports, but consider: in his breakout 2018, Rodríguez and his low-90s fastball didn't allow a run in 17 straight games. In '19, he had a 19-game shutout appearance streak. Most of us can look at this and say, good for him, but no way he's going to have 22 straight shutout relief appearances in 2020. It's very hard to do in general, and especially for a pitcher equipped with a low-90s fastball and a declining strikeout rate. But there has to be some space left in athletic competition to believe that weird things can happen in radical sequence. Plus, you didn't have much of a reason to watch Rodríguez heading into the season. Now? You do.

Chris Stratton RHP   Born: 08/22/90   Age: 29   Bats: R   Throws: R   Height: 6'2"   Weight: 211   Origin: Round 1, 2012 Draft (#20 overall)

YEAR	TEAM	LVL	AGE	W	L	SV	G	GS	IP	H	HR	BB/9	K/9	K	GB%	BABIP	WHIP	ERA	DRA	WARP	MPH	FB%	WHF	CSP
2017	SAC	AAA	26	4	5	0	15	15	79¹	94	10	2.5	8.1	71	53%	.340	1.46	5.11	4.50	1.0				
2017	SFN	MLB	26	4	4	1	13	10	58²	59	5	4.3	7.8	51	46%	.316	1.48	3.68	4.62	0.6	93.7	62.4	9.9	45.5
2018	SAC	AAA	27	3	0	0	4	4	24	25	3	3.0	9.0	24	44%	.324	1.38	3.00	4.40	0.3				
2018	SFN	MLB	27	10	10	0	28	26	145	153	19	3.4	7.0	112	44%	.306	1.43	5.09	4.99	0.5	93.2	62.2	9.6	49.9
2019	PIT	MLB	28	1	1	0	28	0	46²	50	7	2.9	9.1	47	39%	.328	1.39	3.66	4.55	0.5	94.9	63.7	13.2	47.9
2019	LAA	MLB	28	0	2	0	7	5	29¹	43	6	5.5	6.8	22	43%	.378	2.08	8.59	8.60	-1.0	92.8	46.7	9.5	44.4
2020	PIT	MLB	29	2	2	0	45	0	48	50	7	3.6	7.7	41	43%	.305	1.44	4.73	4.78	0.3	92.9	60.5	10.4	47.4

Comparables: Drew VerHagen, Cody Martin, Sam Gaviglio

Stratton is among the myriad go-getters with Great Stuff who've yet to put it all together for a season. The aforementioned stuff encompasses two extremely spinny secondary moves: a curve that spins over 3,000 revolutions per minute, and a slider that falls just short of that mark. (That's fourth and 12th in the league, respectively.) Alas, his stint in the Angels rotation was a month of his getting spun around by opponents, and he finished the season in the Pirates bullpen, turning over lineups in a multi-inning relief role. For our money, that's where he should remain.

Jameson Taillon RHP   Born: 11/18/91   Age: 28   Bats: R   Throws: R   Height: 6'5"   Weight: 230   Origin: Round 1, 2010 Draft (#2 overall)

YEAR	TEAM	LVL	AGE	W	L	SV	G	GS	IP	H	HR	BB/9	K/9	K	GB%	BABIP	WHIP	ERA	DRA	WARP	MPH	FB%	WHF	CSP
2017	IND	AAA	25	0	1	0	2	2	11	12	0	1.6	12.3	15	58%	.387	1.27	4.09	3.59	0.3				
2017	PIT	MLB	25	8	7	0	25	25	133²	152	11	3.1	8.4	125	49%	.352	1.48	4.44	4.08	2.2	97.1	64.1	9.6	48
2018	PIT	MLB	26	14	10	0	32	32	191	179	20	2.2	8.4	179	48%	.298	1.18	3.20	3.41	4.2	97.3	57.3	11.8	48.6
2019	PIT	MLB	27	2	3	0	7	7	37¹	34	4	1.9	7.2	30	51%	.272	1.12	4.10	3.74	0.8	96.9	47.2	12.5	48.3
2020	PIT	MLB	28	2	2	0	33	0	35	34	4	2.5	8.2	32	48%	.296	1.25	3.86	4.08	0.5	96.6	58.6	11.2	48.6

Comparables: Joe Musgrove, James Shields, Ricky Nolasco

Best known for being drafted after Bryce Harper and before Manny Machado, Taillon has overcome a lot of adversity during his career—to the extent that slipping twice under the Tommy John knife somehow isn't the worst of it, even if it is the latest. There's no questioning his resiliency or his ability to bounce back—he's Flubber-esque in that regard—but it is fair to wonder how deleterious an effect the second operation will have on his often promising, ever frustrating career. We probably won't know the answer for a while. Taillon's operation occurred last August, meaning he might not reappear until the 2021 season. The way things are in baseball these days, let alone the world, it is hard to see anything beyond next season as guaranteed.

Tahnaj Thomas RHP   Born: 06/16/99   Age: 21   Bats: R   Throws: R   Height: 6'4"   Weight: 190   Origin: International Free Agent, 2016

YEAR	TEAM	LVL	AGE	W	L	SV	G	GS	IP	H	HR	BB/9	K/9	K	GB%	BABIP	WHIP	ERA	DRA	WARP	MPH	FB%	WHF	CSP
2017	CLE	RK	18	0	3	0	13	10	33	35	4	6.8	7.9	29	48%	.330	1.82	6.00	7.41	-0.5				
2018	CLE	RK	19	0	0	0	8	6	19²	13	2	4.6	12.4	27	60%	.275	1.17	4.58	2.13	0.8				
2019	BRI	RK+	20	2	3	0	12	12	48¹	40	5	2.6	11.0	59	42%	.292	1.12	3.17	3.77	1.3				
2020														No projection										

Writing that the Bahamas have become a destination for scouts feels like a cheeky quip, but it's true—and it's true in part because of pitchers like Thomas. Acquired from Cleveland in the blockbuster trade that saw Jordan Luplow and Erik González swap sides, Thomas is a good athlete with an excellent frame and some projection. He has a mid-90s heater and a touch for his breaking stuff. It's true his command isn't up to snuff; it's true he hasn't pitched above rookie ball; and it's, uh, also true that nitpicking 20-year-olds with this much potential is akin to complaining about an afternoon in the Bahamas because a cloud blocked out the sun for a few minutes.

Wei-Chung Wang LHP   Born: 04/25/92   Age: 28   Bats: L   Throws: L   Height: 6'1"   Weight: 160   Origin: International Free Agent, 2011

YEAR	TEAM	LVL	AGE	W	L	SV	G	GS	IP	H	HR	BB/9	K/9	K	GB%	BABIP	WHIP	ERA	DRA	WARP	MPH	FB%	WHF	CSP
2017	CSP	AAA	25	6	2	1	47	0	57	57	6	1.9	7.6	48	49%	.300	1.21	2.05	2.78	1.6				
2017	MIL	MLB	25	0	0	0	8	0	1¹	5	1	0.0	13.5	2	43%	.667	3.75	13.50	5.57	0.0	96.2	37.5	15.6	47.7
2019	LVG	AAA	27	1	1	1	19	0	26¹	29	5	2.7	8.2	24	46%	.308	1.41	4.78	3.74	0.6				
2019	OAK	MLB	27	1	0	0	20	0	27	22	4	3.7	5.3	16	30%	.231	1.22	3.33	7.42	-0.6	94.4	43.1	9.7	47.4
2019	PIT	MLB	27	2	0	0	5	0	4	5	0	6.8	4.5	2	71%	.357	2.00	6.75	1.94	0.1	94.0	47.4	5.1	41.4
2020	PIT	MLB	28	2	2	0	33	0	35	37	7	3.3	6.6	26	40%	.280	1.43	5.20	5.25	0.1	93.8	43.8	9.3	47.2

Comparables: Tyler Wilson, Tyler Duffey, Brent Suter

Left on the cutting floor of the Bee Gees' 1977 hit "Stayin' Alive" was the line "we can try to understand/the Rule 5 draft's effect on man." They were, of course, singing about Wang, some 37 years before the then-21-year-old Pirates prospect was taken straight from rookie ball by the Brewers in baseball's annual version of a yard sale. He survived the year in the Show, thanks in part to a lengthy stay on the shelf, and then proceeded directly to A-ball.

Wang has always had promising stuff (hence Milwaukee's calculated risk), and if you hold your thumb over his weird 2014 season, his ascent up the minor-league chain looks quite normal. But the Brewers cut ties after 2017 and he found his way to a contract in Korea, possibly chasing the money, or the playing time, or bulgogi, or the chance to be closer to his native Taiwan.

The story could have easily ended there, with a pitcher going through a severe case of the transactional bends. However the Athletics tend to confound such narratives and did so here by giving him a chance to join their bullpen, where he was permitted his first sustained major league utility. He was even in a pennant race. The A's once again became the A's, shedding him once they needed a spot for A.J. Puk and concluding his ERA was on borrowed time. Off to the waiver wire Wang went, before completing the circuit by returning to the Pirates.

There are transactional wormholes everywhere and Wang has nearly rolled a Yahtzee on the gamut of them. But, sometimes, part of being a curious talent is staying alive through them before eventually finding the correct fit. For Wang's sake, here's hoping he's found it.

Trevor Williams RHP   Born: 04/25/92   Age: 28   Bats: R   Throws: R   Height: 6'3"   Weight: 230   Origin: Round 2, 2013 Draft (#44 overall)

YEAR	TEAM	LVL	AGE	W	L	SV	G	GS	IP	H	HR	BB/9	K/9	K	GB%	BABIP	WHIP	ERA	DRA	WARP	MPH	FB%	WHF	CSP
2017	PIT	MLB	25	7	9	0	31	25	150¹	145	14	3.1	7.0	117	50%	.292	1.31	4.07	4.49	1.8	95.0	71.6	9.1	46.4
2018	PIT	MLB	26	14	10	0	31	31	170²	146	15	2.9	6.6	126	43%	.261	1.18	3.11	4.28	2.0	93.7	69.4	8.8	46
2019	PIT	MLB	27	7	9	0	26	26	145²	162	27	2.7	7.0	113	39%	.303	1.41	5.38	5.74	0.1	93.9	66.7	11.2	46.2
2020	PIT	MLB	28	9	10	0	28	28	154	157	24	2.9	7.0	121	40%	.289	1.35	4.58	4.72	1.9	93.5	69.3	9.9	46.5

Comparables: Jerad Eickhoff, Luis Cessa, Dillon Gee

An answer to a great trivia question no one will ever ask, Williams was acquired while he was a prospect as compensation for purported pitching guru Jim Benedict. (Benedict lasted all of two seasons in Miami.) His repertoire is low on frills—he hovers around the 20th percentile in fastball spin, curve spin and velocity—and he relies on contact management as opposed to missing bats. Williams used to be more of a ground-ball pitcher; in 2019, however, his batted-ball profile was tilted toward the air. In a sense, then, it's not too surprising that he had a shaky season the same year the ball was altered. Williams' stock was always going to be sensitive to external forces—that's the warp and the woof of the profile—and it'll be interesting to see what comes of his approach under the keen eye of new management.

LINEOUTS

Hitters

HITTER	POS	TEAM	LVL	AGE	PA	R	2B	3B	HR	RBI	BB	K	SB	CS	AVG/OBP/SLG	DRC+	VORP	BABIP	BRR	FRAA	WARP
Ji-Hwan Bae	MI	GRB	A	19	380	69	25	5	0	38	43	77	31	11	.323/.403/.430	158	38.0	.417	5.2	2B(44): 0.7, SS(32): -1.6	3.8
Steven Baron	C	PIT	MLB	28	10	0	1	0	0	1	0	6	0	0	.200/.200/.300	67	0.0	.500	0.0	C(5): 0.2	0.0
	C	IND	AAA	28	149	17	3	0	2	8	8	38	0	0	.180/.264/.248	46	-8.5	.237	-1.6	C(45): -0.7	-0.3
Sócrates Brito	OF	TOR	MLB	26	43	5	0	1	0	2	4	17	0	0	.077/.163/.128	53	-1.5	.136	0.0	RF(12): -0.8, CF(4): -0.2	-0.2
	OF	BUF	AAA	26	428	66	28	7	16	67	29	97	11	7	.282/.328/.510	107	13.9	.333	-1.4	LF(43): 1.8, RF(35): 4.8	1.6
Jake Elmore	UT	PIT	MLB	32	49	3	1	0	0	4	2	8	0	1	.213/.245/.234	87	0.7	.256	-1.4	LF(5): -0.5, 3B(4): 0.0	-0.1
	UT	IND	AAA	32	414	56	31	0	6	35	37	55	3	8	.322/.387/.455	127	34.1	.361	1.7	2B(43): -3.0, SS(29): -2.2	2.7
Erik González	SS	IND	AAA	27	81	6	3	1	1	10	3	29	1	1	.192/.222/.295	34	-5.3	.292	-2.0	SS(9): -0.7, 2B(8): 0.8	-0.5
	SS	PIT	MLB	27	156	15	4	1	1	6	9	37	4	1	.254/.301/.317	66	-0.3	.333	-0.1	SS(26): 1.4, 3B(16): 0.5	0.1
Jack Herman	RF	GRB	A	19	300	47	12	2	13	34	28	88	6	6	.257/.340/.464	125	17.9	.333	1.7	RF(35): 6.1, LF(34): 3.9	2.6
Corban Joseph	INF	SFN	MLB	30	17	0	0	0	0	2	1	6	0	0	.063/.118/.063	40	-0.8	.100	0.0	2B(3): 0.1, 3B(2): 0.2	-0.1
	INF	PIT	MLB	30	11	1	1	0	0	0	0	1	0	0	.182/.182/.273	95	0.3	.200	0.2	RF(1): 0.0, 2B(1): 0.0	0.0
	INF	OAK	MLB	30	40	4	2	0	1	5	2	5	0	0	.189/.225/.324	87	0.6	.188	0.2	2B(9): -1.8, 3B(1): 0.0	-0.1
	INF	LVG	AAA	30	425	63	35	4	13	73	33	46	0	0	.371/.421/.585	127	32.8	.392	-2.2	2B(55): -6.3, 1B(21): 0.9	1.7
Jung Ho Kang	3B	PIT	MLB	32	185	15	7	1	10	24	11	60	0	0	.169/.222/.395	75	1.5	.184	-2.1	3B(44): -0.3, SS(15): 0.3	-0.1
	3B	IND	AAA	32	31	4	3	0	1	6	4	8	0	0	.444/.516/.667	151	5.4	.611	0.1	3B(3): 0.1, SS(3): 0.1	0.3
Pablo Reyes	LF	PIT	MLB	25	157	18	7	2	2	19	13	36	1	1	.203/.274/.322	72	-0.9	.257	1.2	LF(19): -0.5, RF(19): -1.9	-0.1
	LF	IND	AAA	25	191	22	15	0	10	30	13	37	5	3	.286/.342/.543	123	12.9	.313	0.7	LF(20): 0.4, SS(15): -1.2	1.2
JB Shuck	OF	PIT	MLB	32	57	4	0	1	0	2	8	10	1	1	.213/.339/.255	84	0.4	.270	-0.1	RF(10): -0.2, LF(7): 0.1	0.0
	OF	IND	AAA	32	158	17	12	2	3	14	16	17	3	1	.268/.342/.444	110	7.0	.287	1.1	RF(19): 5.5, P(14): -0.3	1.4

Ji-Hwan Bae is a solid middle-infielder with good bat-to-ball skills and a lack of pop. He could be a player someday, but given his domestic violence conviction in Korea it might be fair to ask the Pirates if all this is really worth it. ⓧ Whatever playing time backup catcher **Steven Baron** gets will be better than the alternative, which is every pitch striking off the umpire or bouncing to the backstop. ⓧ Thrice cast off by the D'Backs, Padres and Jays before spending the majority of his season in Buffalo, **Sócrates Brito**'s chances seem to have dried up after injuries and underperformance in brief stints. "The unexamined life is not worth living," however, and Brito can only hope someone takes that to heart. ⓧ Let's not jump to conclusions and assume **Lonnie Chisenhall** really *missed* the 2019 Pirates season, but two calf strains and a broken finger left him pinin' for the fjords. He's played in 111 games over the last three seasons. ⓧ A little bit of truth in advertising for **Jake Elmore**, who made it back onto a 25-man after a two-year absence: having him in your lineup definitely helps you L more. ⓧ There's no statistic that accurately measures value added from a replacement player injuring themselves in an on-field collision, thereby resulting in missing most of the summer. Until we get to the blessed day when that changes, **Erik González** will have to settle for 50 Stanley nickels. ⓧ **Jack Herman** has become a favorite in prospect geek circles due to his low-minors performance as well as his bat speed and advanced approach. He's from Voorhees, New Jersey, but, thankfully, he was born on September 30—otherwise, we'd think he was born to be the Pumpkin King. ⓧ Yeoman infielder **Corban Joseph** had one of the more eventful transaction logs of the past year: after Oakland claimed him in the Rule 5 Draft, he made a handful of appearances for the Athletics, Giants, and Pirates during 2019. His at-bats, however, weren't nearly as interesting. ⓧ The collar-tugging decision for the Pirates to retain **Jung Ho Kang** last year looked even worse after an August release. He still has above-average exit velocity off the bat, but with a past sexual assault allegation (to say nothing of his other resolved legal issues), he probably shouldn't be playing sports right now. ⓧ Isn't it a modern baseball analysis faux pas to unironically label a player as scrappy? The algorithm is trying describe **Pablo Reyes**, an undersized utilityman with a can-do work ethic, and that's all it's spitting out. ⓧ Speedy outfield cameo artist **JB Shuck** is turning two-way. His fastball sits at 90 mph and struck out a mess of Triple-A batters in 20 innings alongside a ludicrous amount of walks.

Pitchers

PITCHER	TEAM	LVL	AGE	W	L	SV	G	GS	IP	H	HR	BB/9	K/9	K	GB%	BABIP	WHIP	ERA	DRA	WARP	MPH	FB%	WHF	CSP
JT Brubaker	WEV	A-	25	0	0	0	2	2	6²	5	0	5.4	5.4	4	42%	.263	1.35	1.35	5.47	0.0				
	IND	AAA	25	2	1	0	4	4	21	19	2	1.7	8.6	20	58%	.298	1.10	2.57	2.85	0.8				
Michael Burrows	WEV	A-	19	2	3	0	11	11	43²	44	2	4.1	8.9	43	44%	.363	1.47	4.33	7.40	-1.2				
Blake Cederlind	BRD	A+	23	0	0	2	7	0	7²	4	0	7.0	9.4	8	50%	.200	1.30	1.17	3.77	0.1				
	ALT	AA	23	5	1	2	31	0	45²	31	1	3.2	8.3	42	50%	.250	1.03	1.77	3.94	0.4				
	IND	AAA	23	0	1	0	3	0	6	11	1	3.0	7.5	5	54%	.435	2.17	7.50	8.09	-0.1				
Rookie Davis	IND	AAA	26	1	6	0	13	9	52²	61	9	3.8	6.8	40	31%	.325	1.58	5.64	6.73	0.0				
	PIT	MLB	26	0	1	0	5	1	10²	12	3	6.8	8.4	10	48%	.300	1.88	6.75	4.83	0.1	93.2	72.9	12.5	45.9
Montana DuRapau	IND	AAA	27	2	1	10	37	0	46¹	21	3	2.7	11.1	57	44%	.182	0.76	2.14	1.66	2.0				
	PIT	MLB	27	0	1	0	14	2	17¹	27	4	4.7	11.4	22	33%	.434	2.08	9.35	5.38	0.0	94.1	45.9	14.7	46
Geoff Hartlieb	IND	AAA	25	4	1	3	26	0	39²	31	0	3.4	11.3	50	64%	.316	1.16	2.50	2.59	1.4				
	PIT	MLB	25	0	1	0	29	0	35	52	8	4.6	9.8	38	46%	.411	2.00	9.00	5.11	0.1	98.2	70.4	11.6	49.2
Clay Holmes	IND	AAA	26	2	1	1	10	0	15²	17	1	8.6	7.5	13	55%	.320	2.04	6.32	6.00	0.0				
	PIT	MLB	26	1	2	0	35	0	50	45	5	6.5	10.1	56	60%	.301	1.62	5.58	4.16	0.6	96.5	62.8	9.5	45.2
Williams Jerez	SAC	AAA	27	4	4	2	47	0	56	46	6	2.6	9.8	61	44%	.268	1.11	3.86	2.18	2.2				
	PIT	MLB	27	0	0	0	6	0	3²	5	1	7.4	12.3	5	46%	.400	2.18	7.36	6.83	-0.1	96.0	49.3	8	45.8
	SFN	MLB	27	1	0	0	6	0	6²	7	1	8.1	5.4	4	53%	.333	1.95	2.70	4.77	0.0	96.4	61.2	9.5	44.1
Max Kranick	BRD	A+	21	6	7	0	20	20	109¹	100	11	2.5	6.4	78	45%	.276	1.19	3.79	4.81	0.3				
James Marvel	ALT	AA	25	9	5	0	17	17	101²	85	6	2.1	7.3	83	51%	.273	1.07	3.10	4.51	0.5				
	IND	AAA	25	7	0	0	11	11	60²	46	4	3.3	7.9	53	49%	.258	1.12	2.67	3.02	2.2				
	PIT	MLB	25	0	3	0	4	4	17¹	25	4	3.1	4.7	9	54%	.333	1.79	8.31	5.86	0.0	91.6	53.8	9.7	41.3
Alex McRae	IND	AAA	26	7	8	0	22	22	114¹	128	20	3.4	8.0	101	48%	.324	1.50	5.20	5.67	1.2				
	PIT	MLB	26	0	4	0	11	2	26²	36	9	5.4	6.4	19	43%	.318	1.95	8.77	7.12	-0.5	94.5	57.3	9	42.2
Dovydas Neverauskas	IND	AAA	26	3	4	9	36	0	52	51	8	3.8	12.6	73	37%	.364	1.40	5.02	4.37	0.9				
	PIT	MLB	26	0	0	0	10	0	9¹	15	2	6.8	9.6	10	35%	.406	2.36	10.61	6.29	-0.1	97.7	57.1	13.2	49.4
Cody Ponce	ALT	AA	25	0	0	1	3	1	6	3	1	1.5	9.0	6	33%	.091	0.67	6.00	3.11	0.1				
	BLX	AA	25	1	3	1	27	0	38¹	33	1	2.8	10.3	44	57%	.327	1.17	3.29	4.42	0.1				
	IND	AAA	25	1	3	0	4	4	18²	18	4	3.4	9.6	20	53%	.275	1.34	5.30	3.97	0.5				
Yefry Ramírez	NOR	AAA	25	1	1	0	4	4	18	11	2	4.5	12.0	24	29%	.250	1.11	1.50	5.54	0.2				
	IND	AAA	25	1	4	0	15	5	45	42	5	5.8	11.6	58	41%	.339	1.58	5.20	4.65	0.8				
	BAL	MLB	25	0	2	0	4	1	10¹	11	2	7.8	9.6	11	44%	.360	1.94	6.97	6.15	-0.1	95.7	52.5	11.6	42.1
	PIT	MLB	25	0	0	0	9	0	14	19	2	4.5	10.3	16	56%	.395	1.86	7.71	4.74	0.1	94.6	53	12.4	42.7
Yacksel Ríos	LEH	AAA	26	1	3	7	31	0	34	38	4	5.8	9.8	37	50%	.343	1.76	7.41	6.05	0.1				
	IND	AAA	26	0	0	1	9	0	15¹	19	2	2.3	7.0	12	42%	.354	1.50	2.35	6.21	0.0				
	PIT	MLB	26	1	0	0	10	0	10¹	10	2	4.4	8.7	10	45%	.296	1.45	5.23	7.55	-0.2	98.2	60.7	17.9	47.7
	PHI	MLB	26	0	0	0	4	0	2²	6	2	10.1	6.8	2	23%	.364	3.38	13.50	5.25	0.0	98.2	59.4	10.1	47.8
Felipe Vázquez	PIT	MLB	27	5	1	28	56	0	60	43	5	2.0	13.5	90	43%	.306	0.93	1.65	2.32	2.0	101.0	61.1	14.5	56.2

JT Brubaker missed most of 2019 with elbow woes. He's shown off enough fastball to be a potential factor in the bullpen or even the back of the rotation, and he's just about ready if healthy. ⓧ **Michael Burrows** is another overslot righty from the Northeast, with a pretty good feel and pitch mix. He'll make his full-season debut in 2020. ⓧ **Blake Cederlind** still hasn't managed to translate his triple-digit fastball into elite strikeout numbers. He did harness his control and develop his secondaries enough to move through three levels in 2019, so just a little more progress will take him to the Pittsburgh bullpen. ⓧ With only 10 2/3 innings for the Pirates last year, the most important thing about **Rookie Davis** held firm: he remained eligible for Rookie of the Year. His lack of control and penchant for getting lit up in those innings make it unlikely he gets there, but we can still dream. ⓧ He may be just organizational relief depth but **Montana DuRapau** is the first character from the *PaRappa The Rapper* series to reach the major leagues. ⓧ **Geoff Hartlieb** was the double-edged sword of feel-good stories: the former 29th-round pick made it to the Show after keeping the ball on the ground, but once there he pitched like a 29th-round pick. ⓧ **Clay Holmes** is a tall sinkerballer whose name summons images of adobe structures. Unlike mudbrick, Holmes doesn't appear to be worth building with. ⓧ The Pirates played with **Williams Jerez**'s pitch mix a little after acquiring him from the Giants late in the season, but hard-throwing lefty still looks like the quintessential taxi-squad LOOGY. ⓧ **Max Kranick** is a former overslot prep pick who was better than solid in Advanced-A with a good fastball combo and an emerging breaker, though his strikeout numbers are more Minimum Kranick. ⓧ **Travis MacGregor** has good stuff and was doing well before his elbow stopped working midway through 2018. The former second-rounder, now 22, will try and get it going again in 2020. ⚾ He's probably heard all the cinematic universe jokes in his lifetime, so we'll spare **James Marvel** and his September call-up the rod—unless he starts dating a Mrs. Maisel, then all bets are off. ⚾ **Alex McRae**'s stuff doesn't exactly play up in the bullpen, and so he'll work on winning a rotation spot in the same fashion that John Hickenlooper worked on winning the Democratic primary. ⚾ Never say never, but **Dovydas Neverauskas** is at best a sometimes pitcher: sometimes the pitch is high, sometimes it's outside. ⚾ A move to relief looked to be **Cody Ponce**'s ticket to the majors as his strikeouts spiked in his third attempt at Double-A. The Pirates had other ideas when they traded Jordan Lyles for him, putting Ponce back in the rotation and promoting him to Triple-A with mixed results. ⚾ Two pitches are enough to stick in the bullpen (fastball and changeup), just like two Y's are plenty for a first name. **Yefry Ramírez** can lay claim to both. ⚾ The Phillies waived **Yacksel Ríos** to the other side of the state last August because, despite his improved velocity, his walk rate wasn't up to the team's usual standard of yacksellence. ⚾ **Edgar Santana** might be the best reliever nobody talked about last year, but for good reason—Tommy John surgery. Expect him to return to some type of late-inning regimen, or at least the consciousness of the sport. ⚾ It's highly unlikely **Felipe Vázquez** will spend time on another professional baseball team. He was arrested and charged with the sexual assault of a 13-year-old.

SAN DIEGO PADRES

Essay by Jorge Arangure Jr.

Player comments by Ken Funck and BP staff

What does a color mean? For a sports team, mostly it's marketing; a way to sell merchandise. But if you step away from the cynicism for a moment, can it be more than that? Can a team's colors be representative of its soul?

In early November, the San Diego Padres held a ceremony at Petco Park to unveil a change that fans had wanted for more than a decade and the team finally agreed to and announced prior to the 2019 season: After nearly 20 years of dabbling in all kinds of blue-hued uniform color combinations—remember Ryan Klesko and Sean Burroughs running around the bases in cobalt and "sand" in the early aughts?—the team was finally going back to wearing brown.

For most baseball fans outside of San Diego, the hoopla surrounding the unveiling must have seemed ridiculous. Everyone could agree that the new uniforms looked good—the home ones, with brown pinstripes contrasted against a white background and gold trim, especially—but what was the big deal?

Why would thousands of fans head to Petco for a fashion show? Remember, this is a franchise that has ranked 10th or worse in attendance in the National League in 11 of the past 12 seasons. It takes a lot to get Padres fans to show up.

But in reality, it was about more than a uniform color. The Padres, a franchise that once proudly wore mustard and brown, had finally found their true selves again.

"This is going to be the uniform we select and win a championship in," Ron Fowler, the executive chairman of the Padres, said in a video that was shown before Fernando Tatis Jr., Manny Machado and Eric Hosmer walked onstage in the new uniforms. The new/old team colors were so well received that Padres fans couldn't even be bothered to boo Hosmer.

The ceremony felt like the start of something new—even though none of us Padres fans really know what that means—it just feels different. For the first time that I can remember, there are high expectations and a genuine enthusiasm, a sense that we're about to witness something special.

For one night, even the wonderful and wacked out collection of people who make up #PadresTwitter—I would argue as antagonistic a group of baseball fans that you'll find

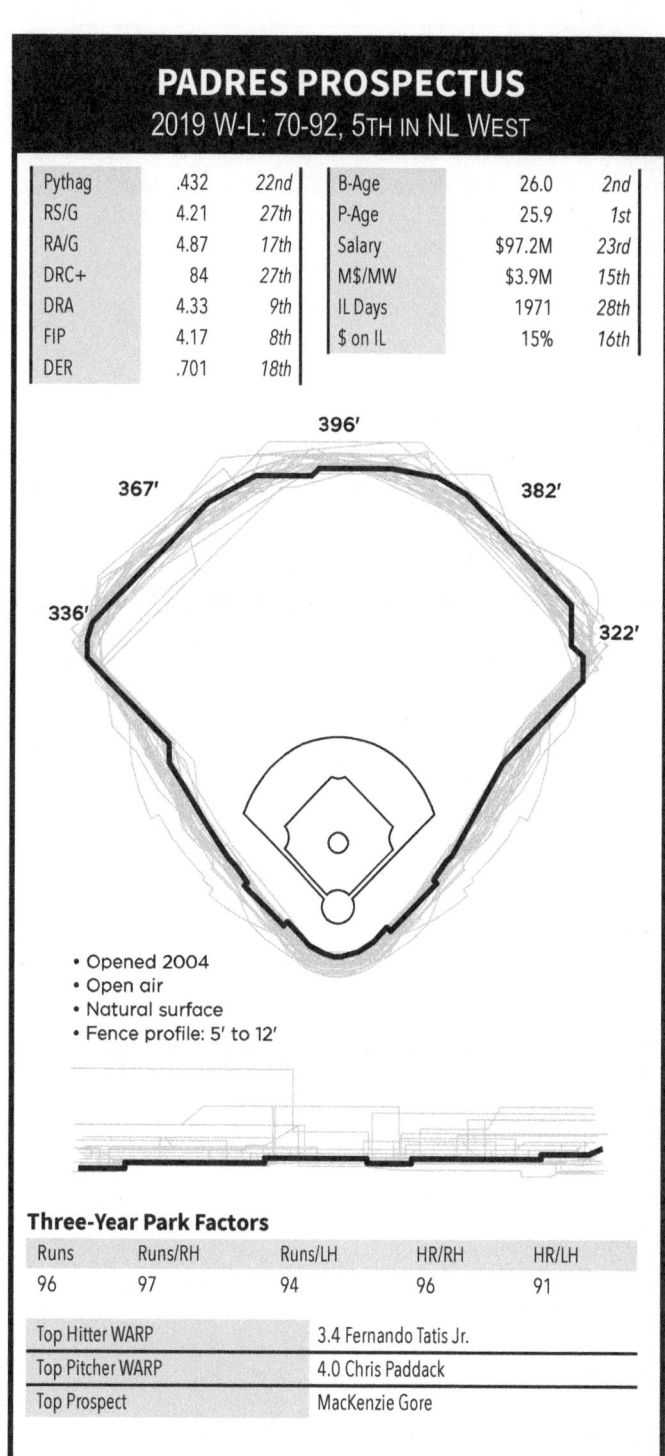

PADRES PROSPECTUS
2019 W-L: 70-92, 5TH IN NL WEST

Pythag	.432	22nd	B-Age	26.0	2nd
RS/G	4.21	27th	P-Age	25.9	1st
RA/G	4.87	17th	Salary	$97.2M	23rd
DRC+	84	27th	M$/MW	$3.9M	15th
DRA	4.33	9th	IL Days	1971	28th
FIP	4.17	8th	$ on IL	15%	16th
DER	.701	18th			

396'
367'
382'
336'
322'

- Opened 2004
- Open air
- Natural surface
- Fence profile: 5' to 12'

Three-Year Park Factors

Runs	Runs/RH	Runs/LH	HR/RH	HR/LH
96	97	94	96	91

Top Hitter WARP	3.4 Fernando Tatis Jr.
Top Pitcher WARP	4.0 Chris Paddack
Top Prospect	MacKenzie Gore

2019 Hit List Ranking

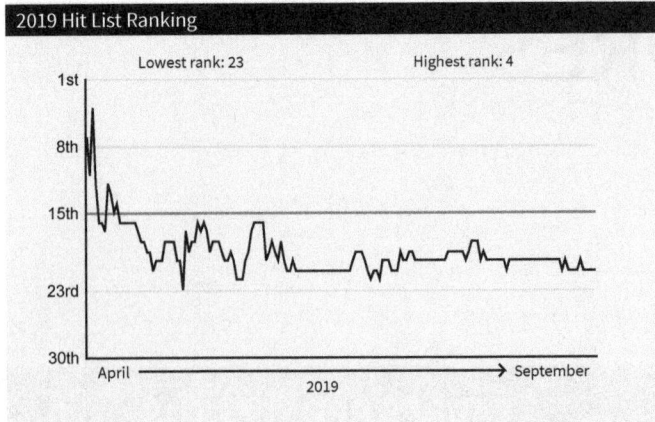

Lowest rank: 23   Highest rank: 4

Committed Payroll (in millions)

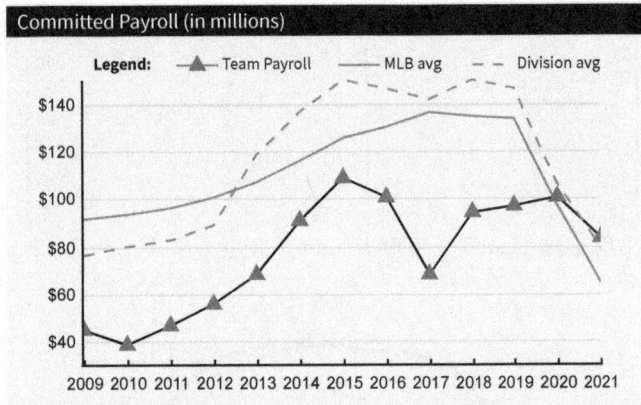

Legend: ▲ Team Payroll   — MLB avg   - - Division avg

Farm System Ranking

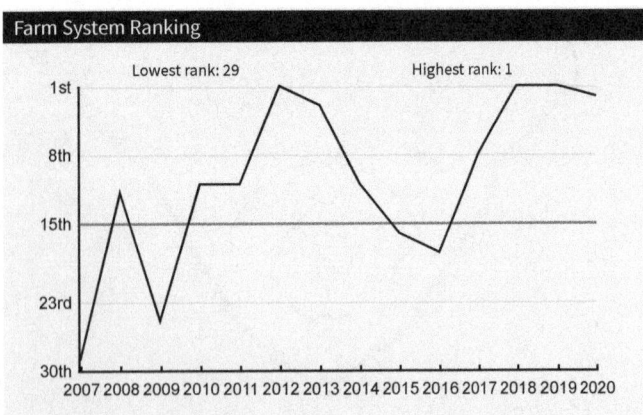

Lowest rank: 29   Highest rank: 1

Personnel

Executive Vice President, General Manager
A.J. Preller

Vice President, Assistant General Manager
Fred Uhlman, Jr.

Senior Advisor/Director of Player Personnel
Logan White

Assistant General Manager
Josh Stein

Manager
Jayce Tingler

BP Alumni
David Cameron

on social media—could agree on one thing: This was a good night! (This doesn't happen very often on #PadresTwitter. More often it's one part of #PadresTwitter ridiculing the other part because they think Luis Urías will eventually hit .280. He's #BrewersTwitter's problem now.)

Even if it doesn't turn out that San Diego is on the verge of success, just the sheer audacity of Fowler, and fans, to think in these ways—championships, MVPs and dynasties—belies an atmosphere that has never existed. The days of the passive Padres fan are over. Welcome to the win-at-all-costs era. We think this team should win, and if it doesn't, then we have all concluded that everyone in the front office should be fired.

Each Padres follower has a unique path into this particular fandom. It's hard to say that anyone in San Diego naturally becomes attached to the franchise. Who would choose to suffer through so many losing seasons?

But geography does play a part in why it's such a unique fanbase. Firstly, San Diego has always been known as a city of transplants. An analysis of 2017 census data published recently by the *Voice of San Diego* showed that more than half of all San Diegans were born outside of California. Also, only a third of those between the ages of 35 and 44 were born in state, they noted.

Such factors have helped to create a fractured fan base. For most of my time growing up in San Diego, and for the last several years, it was not uncommon for Padres games to be inundated with fans from the opposing team; it was natural since so many people in the city were from somewhere else. This was especially true of games against the Dodgers. Embarrassingly, Los Angeles fans almost always outnumber Padres fans at Petco.

But San Diego's demographics are changing at the same time the Padres' uniforms are changing. The article noted that the crash of the housing market has caused fewer people to move to San Diego. The percentage of San Diegans from San Diego is increasing. More people are considering themselves to be from San Diego than from elsewhere. They have a bigger attachment to the city.

And these demographic changes come at an opportune time. The Chargers moved to Los Angeles several years ago, leaving San Diego as a one-team town. But of course that one team has to be good in order to truly win over fans.

⚾   ⚾   ⚾

I became a Padres fan mostly because of proximity. I was born across the border in Tijuana, Mexico, and my family moved to San Diego when I was five years old. I grew up in San Ysidro, just a few miles away from the border crossing. I became a San Diegan.

And I loved baseball. But mostly, I loved the Padres. My parents have told me that I could recite the entire Padres lineup by the time I was four years old. (I'm not sure what it says about my parents that they were so proud that I could say "Terry Kennedy" at such a young age).

But even fandom-by-proximity can be tested. Around that time, Fernando Valenzuela was becoming an icon for the Dodgers. His immediate success coupled with his Mexican heritage made it natural for him to become my family's favorite player, and perhaps the Dodgers would become my family's new favorite team. It seemed like every other Mexican we knew was a Dodgers fan.

And it seemed we were headed that way too—before an unfortunate encounter changed everything.

This particular story has been told many times by different members of my family, each version slightly different than the previous, but it boils down to this: When I was very young, so young that I hardly remember any of this, my cousin and I staked out the players' exit after a Dodgers vs. Padres game at Jack Murphy Stadium (the former home of the Padres that was gloriously for many years named after a sportswriter and then was not so gloriously named for the telecommunications company Qualcomm and now is just named SDCCU Stadium because no one wants to pay money for the sponsorship rights), waiting for autographs.

In one version, we waited nearly an hour after the game. In other versions, it's much longer than that. None of the players were coming out, but we were not going to be denied. Eventually, several players emerged and signed our cards, but our real target was Fernando. So we continued to wait. And wait. And then we waited some more. Finally, Fernando emerged to a crowd that had been thinned by the long wait.

We shouted for Fernando to stop, pleading with him in English and Spanish, but he walked right past us. We didn't exist to him. He just walked away. That simple act of non-acknowledgement sealed the deal. After that, my family's fandom was unequivocally decided: We were Padres fans, and we hated the Dodgers.

It would be easy to say that this decision has turned out badly for us. But I wouldn't have wanted it to happen any other way.

Not too many years after the incident with Fernando, my father scored tickets to Game 4 of the 1984 National League Championship Series. We sat in the upper deck as Steve Garvey hit a walk-off home run against Lee Smith of the Chicago Cubs. I remember high fiving every person near us. Everyone seemed amused at my excitement. The Padres would eventually win that best-of-five series after having lost the first two games.

Unfortunately, the Detroit Tigers trounced them in the World Series. I wept for days afterward. Such is life as a Padres fan; some rare moments of excitement and a lot of crying.

There was perhaps more crying during the early-90s run of Tom Werner's ownership than any other. Werner oversaw trades that ended the tenures of players like Gary Sheffield and Fred McGriff, and despite a mere four-year term as majority owner, Werner nearly sunk the franchise with his actions. And that's not even accounting for his decision to introduce blue and orange into the Padres' color scheme in 1991; a decision the team didn't reverse until this coming season.

The most emblematic image of the Padres to that point, was of Tony Gwynn, already in his 10th season but still in the prime of his career, balanced as ever, stroking base hits through the 5.5 hole draped in a monk-ish brown. That he notched hit number 3,000 in a sparsely populated Olympic Stadium was unfortunate; that it happened in the drab, disaffecting grays and blues? Despicable.

I was lucky enough that in a previous life as a sportswriter—I'm currently an editor in news at *The New York Times*—that I was able to interview Gwynn after he had retired. We talked for about an hour in the Petco Park dugout. Of course, we talked hitting. But I also told him about how I used to attend his hitting camps when I was a kid, wearing that brown Padres hat. I told him how much his career had meant to me, and how much I loved his Padres teams as a kid. He seemed genuinely touched even though he'd probably had this similar conversation thousands of times.

Surprisingly, Werner's color legacy remained untouched for years after his disastrous era of ownership ended. The team's primary color stayed blue. In a sense, it seemed as though fans would never escape the Werner era.

But now here we are; the colors are brown again, and the team has the potential to really be exciting. In the last few years, they've spent significant money bringing in high-profile free agents, which is something they had never done. The farm system is stacked. This is the complete opposite of the Werner era.

And we're excited about it, even if we all show our excitement in different ways. Almost certainly, #PadresTwitter will debate the prognostications for Padres players that will follow this essay in the book, and bless them all. These are my people.

Many will argue that the Padres need to trade some of their young talent for established players. Others will call those people irrational and passionately argue the opposite. (For what it's worth, my thoughts after the 2019 season are to hold onto MacKenzie Gore, and to consider trading Luis Patiño in the right deal.) But at least we have something interesting to argue about. It seems so long ago that we wondered about whether Alexi Amarista was the second baseman of the future.

So when someone asks whether a uniform color really means anything, the answer is yes. Sure, the Padres are going to sell a lot of jerseys and hats because they're back in brown. And that was certainly part of the motivation. But we're all going to feel a lot better about spending some of our money on that merchandise. It won't feel like we've given away our soul to wear blue.

—Jorge Arangure Jr. is a senior editor at The New York Times.

HITTERS

★ ★ ★ *2020 Top 101 Prospect* **#33** ★ ★ ★

CJ Abrams SS Born: 10/03/00 Age: 19 Bats: L Throws: R Height: 6'2" Weight: 185 Origin: Round 1, 2019 Draft (#6 overall)

YEAR	TEAM	LVL	AGE	PA	R	2B	3B	HR	RBI	BB	K	SB	CS	AVG/OBP/SLG	DRC+	VORP	BABIP	BRR	FRAA	WARP
2019	PDR	RK	18	156	40	12	8	3	22	10	14	14	6	.401/.442/.662	199	24.1	.425	-0.7	SS(28): 6.9	2.5
2020	SDN	MLB	19	251	22	13	2	4	23	17	46	3	1	.240/.297/.360	77	0.5	.286	0.0	SS 2	0.2

Comparables: J.P. Crawford, Juan Soto, Justin Williams

The Padres' top pick in last summer's draft, Abrams burst onto the scene faster than a Hollywood studio green-lighting yet another uninspired sci-fi franchise reboot. The Georgia prep product has the type of raw speed that can warp space-time and a smooth lefty stroke that produces hit after hit, helping him bat over .400 en route to MVP honors in his rookie league debut. Abrams leverages his quick-twitch athleticism in the field and doesn't look lost at shortstop, but scouts worry that his funky throwing mechanics may precipitate a move to the keystone or center field, where his bat will more than play. His stroke is geared more for gappers than bombs so home run titles are an impossible mission, but Abrams makes consistent hard contact and there's a chance he could grow into at least league-average power while competing for batting and stolen base crowns. Coming soon to a ballpark near you.

★ ★ ★ *2020 Top 101 Prospect* **#67** ★ ★ ★

Luis Campusano C Born: 09/29/98 Age: 21 Bats: R Throws: R Height: 5'10" Weight: 215 Origin: Round 2, 2017 Draft (#39 overall)

YEAR	TEAM	LVL	AGE	PA	R	2B	3B	HR	RBI	BB	K	SB	CS	AVG/OBP/SLG	DRC+	VORP	BABIP	BRR	FRAA	WARP
2017	PDR	RK	18	98	3	4	0	1	13	6	14	0	1	.278/.327/.356	110	0.0	.316	-1.7	C(17): -0.3	0.3
2017	SDP	RK	18	53	5	0	0	3	12	9	11	0	1	.250/.377/.455	110	5.0	.267	0.3	C(10): -0.3	0.4
2018	FTW	A	19	284	26	11	0	3	40	19	43	0	1	.288/.345/.365	118	6.1	.335	-1.1	C(38): -0.8, 1B(4): 0.2	1.2
2019	LEL	A+	20	487	63	31	1	15	81	52	57	0	0	.325/.396/.509	168	44.6	.340	-4.4	C(76): -2.6, 1B(2): 0.0	3.9
2020	SDN	MLB	21	251	26	12	0	7	28	17	46	0	0	.255/.310/.400	88	3.8	.292	-0.5	C 0, 1B 0	0.4

Comparables: Chance Sisco, Christian Vázquez, Gorkys Hernández

For a catcher, Campusano carries a big stick—literally, as he often used a 40-ounce cudgel to whack horsehides around the yard while winning the California League batting title and co-MVP honors last summer. He has all the tools you would want in a catching prospect: plus athleticism, agility behind the plate, solid receiving skills and a strong, accurate arm to go along with a disciplined batting eye and obvious power potential. Dude even idolizes Salvy Pérez. Campusano isn't quite a unicorn, but two-way backstops with plus tools are harder to find than Shiny Magikarp and the Padres may have been lucky enough to catch one.

Franchy Cordero CF Born: 09/02/94 Age: 25 Bats: L Throws: R Height: 6'3" Weight: 175 Origin: International Free Agent, 2011

YEAR	TEAM	LVL	AGE	PA	R	2B	3B	HR	RBI	BB	K	SB	CS	AVG/OBP/SLG	DRC+	VORP	BABIP	BRR	FRAA	WARP
2017	ELP	AAA	22	419	68	21	18	17	64	23	118	15	4	.326/.369/.603	115	38.5	.431	1.7	CF(61): -2.5, LF(22): 1.5	2.2
2017	SDN	MLB	22	99	15	3	3	3	9	6	44	1	1	.228/.276/.424	54	3.8	.400	1.2	CF(25): 0.8, LF(1): -0.1	0.0
2018	ELP	AAA	23	31	3	1	0	1	1	4	10	3	0	.259/.355/.407	70	0.7	.375	0.6	CF(3): -0.8, LF(3): -0.4	-0.1
2018	SDN	MLB	23	154	19	5	1	7	19	14	55	5	2	.237/.307/.439	72	4.7	.338	0.6	LF(22): 0.4, CF(11): -1.3	-0.2
2019	ELP	AAA	24	51	7	2	1	3	8	4	19	0	0	.217/.294/.500	60	0.7	.292	0.5	CF(9): 0.6	0.0
2019	SDN	MLB	24	20	2	1	0	0	1	4	7	1	0	.333/.450/.400	75	0.0	.556	0.6	CF(5): -0.4, RF(4): -0.3	0.0
2020	SDN	MLB	25	287	28	12	3	8	31	19	112	7	3	.227/.285/.386	80	3.2	.362	1.0	CF -3, RF 0	0.0

Comparables: Byron Buxton, Wil Myers, Clint Frazier

"You could have all the talent in the world, but if you don't do the right thing, then nothing happens." DeNiro's bus-driving father character in *A Bronx Tale* could have been talking about Cordero, assuming you translate "the right thing" to mean focusing on defensive fundamentals and making more contact to help channel peerless natural athleticism, power and double-plus speed into consistent production. The only thing consistent in Franchy's game has been its inconsistency at the plate and in the field, and now that he's spent much of the last two seasons dealing with recurring elbow problems, we've seen a whole lot of "nothing happens" lately. Guys that whiff in over a third of their plate appearances rarely put it all together over the long haul, but a healthy Cordero could still tease out a .280/.330/.500 line in some future peak season and then draw years of paychecks from teams waiting in vain for him to repeat it.

Ty France 3B Born: 07/13/94 Age: 25 Bats: R Throws: R Height: 6'0" Weight: 205 Origin: Round 34, 2015 Draft (#1017 overall)

YEAR	TEAM	LVL	AGE	PA	R	2B	3B	HR	RBI	BB	K	SB	CS	AVG/OBP/SLG	DRC+	VORP	BABIP	BRR	FRAA	WARP
2017	LEL	A+	22	131	10	4	2	0	19	7	16	1	0	.288/.389/.360	113	3.8	.333	-0.9	1B(13): -0.2, 3B(4): 0.0	0.2
2017	SAN	AA	22	402	42	20	1	5	39	22	68	1	0	.275/.341/.377	103	15.4	.325	0.5	3B(85): -8.8, 1B(7): 0.2	0.5
2018	SAN	AA	23	479	66	22	2	17	77	33	70	3	4	.263/.349/.448	124	23.8	.276	1.3	3B(101): -7.7, 1B(1): 0.0	2.0
2018	ELP	AAA	23	110	18	8	0	5	19	13	19	0	0	.287/.382/.532	130	7.8	.310	0.6	3B(19): 2.8, 1B(9): 0.1	1.1
2019	ELP	AAA	24	348	83	27	1	27	89	30	51	1	0	.399/.477/.770	183	49.6	.410	1.0	3B(31): -1.8, 1B(29): -2.3	3.7
2019	SDN	MLB	24	201	20	8	1	7	24	9	49	0	2	.234/.294/.402	77	1.4	.279	0.4	3B(36): -0.6, 2B(21): 2.2	0.3
2020	SDN	MLB	25	112	14	5	0	5	15	7	26	0	0	.250/.325/.449	106	5.1	.289	0.3	2B 0, 3B 0	0.5

Comparables: Evan Longoria, Ed Sprague, Earl Robinson

France's El Paso numbers border on the ridiculous and are reminiscent of a total solar eclipse: they're stunningly beautiful, and if you stare at them too long their white-hot glare will burn your retinas, but don't hold your breath expecting to see them again any time soon. The former 34th-round pick laid waste to the juiced-ball PCL and earned two big-league call-ups where his solid power showed up but his contact skills and admirable walk rate disappeared. France is a good hitter, not a great one, especially in the context of major-league corner men. He's a second baseman in the same way Matt Carpenter is a second baseman, more out of necessity and willingness than a true talent for the position, which means he'll have a higher offensive bar to clear at third or first base. Truly elite batting talent will always make itself known, but at this point France looks more like a solid bench piece than a star in waiting.

Greg Garcia INF Born: 08/08/89 Age: 30 Bats: L Throws: R Height: 6'0" Weight: 190 Origin: Round 7, 2010 Draft (#229 overall)

YEAR	TEAM	LVL	AGE	PA	R	2B	3B	HR	RBI	BB	K	SB	CS	AVG/OBP/SLG	DRC+	VORP	BABIP	BRR	FRAA	WARP
2017	SLN	MLB	27	290	27	9	2	2	20	37	64	2	1	.253/.365/.332	80	13.4	.335	3.8	3B(41): 1.1, 2B(34): 0.5	0.8
2018	SLN	MLB	28	208	15	6	0	3	15	20	37	3	1	.221/.309/.304	81	0.2	.259	0.2	2B(31): -0.4, SS(17): 1.9	0.4
2019	SDN	MLB	29	372	52	13	4	4	31	53	83	0	2	.248/.364/.354	88	6.9	.323	2.4	2B(74): 2.1, 3B(13): -0.6	1.1
2020	SDN	MLB	30	280	27	10	1	3	23	35	62	4	1	.226/.335/.313	83	6.2	.292	1.6	2B -1, SS 0	0.6

Comparables: Desmond Jennings, Marv Throneberry, Joe Vitiello

The Practically Perfect Utility Infielder™ moved home to San Diego last year, where the Practically Perfect Weather™ clearly agreed with him. Injuries and the struggles of Luis Urías forced him into the lineup and Garcia proved he could be a passable platoon starter at the keystone when his usual menu of walks, singles and steady defense proved as tasty in the first inning as the seventh. Garcia sorts through pitches like a chef at a farmer's market, rarely offering at anything outside the zone, driving up pitch counts and making opposing hurlers work hard to retire him. He's never hit lefties and is a little stretched at shortstop, but Garcia should continue to bolster any team that employs him well into his 30s.

Trent Grisham OF Born: 11/01/96 Age: 23 Bats: L Throws: L Height: 6'0" Weight: 205 Origin: Round 1, 2015 Draft (#15 overall)

YEAR	TEAM	LVL	AGE	PA	R	2B	3B	HR	RBI	BB	K	SB	CS	AVG/OBP/SLG	DRC+	VORP	BABIP	BRR	FRAA	WARP
2017	CAR	A+	20	569	78	21	6	8	45	98	141	37	5	.223/.360/.348	106	14.2	.299	1.6	RF(52): 1.5, LF(40): -0.5	1.9
2018	BLX	AA	21	405	45	10	2	7	31	63	87	11	3	.233/.356/.337	110	7.1	.292	-1.8	RF(85): 3.5, LF(15): 1.1	1.8
2019	BLX	AA	22	283	34	14	3	13	41	44	50	6	4	.254/.371/.504	162	22.4	.269	-0.4	CF(59): 3.3	3.1
2019	SAN	AAA	22	158	37	8	3	13	30	23	22	6	1	.381/.471/.776	192	31.4	.384	0.3	CF(31): 3.3, LF(3): -0.1	2.6
2019	MIL	MLB	22	183	24	6	2	6	24	20	48	1	0	.231/.328/.410	90	3.2	.286	2.2	CF(21): -1.1, LF(17): -1.8	0.3
2020	SDN	MLB	23	350	40	14	2	12	42	40	88	9	3	.224/.318/.404	96	7.9	.273	0.4	RF -1, CF 0	0.7

Comparables: Billy McKinney, Victor Robles, Abraham Almonte

As if Grisham weren't already burdened with enough expectations—those of being a former top prospect and first-round pick—his misplay in the Wild Card Game added another layer to the onion. That reality is unfortunate for a number of reasons, in part because it obscured how hard he'd worked in order to reach the point of starting in a postseason game. Sure, Christian Yelich's injury was the main cause, but Grisham improved his approach and his power production in the minors, resuscitating an otherwise stalled career. If there's one thing that will help Grisham get over—you know—it's a fresh start in sunny San Diego.

Austin Hedges C Born: 08/18/92 Age: 27 Bats: R Throws: R Height: 6'1" Weight: 206 Origin: Round 2, 2011 Draft (#82 overall)

YEAR	TEAM	LVL	AGE	PA	R	2B	3B	HR	RBI	BB	K	SB	CS	AVG/OBP/SLG	DRC+	VORP	BABIP	BRR	FRAA	WARP
2017	SDN	MLB	24	417	36	17	0	18	55	23	122	4	1	.214/.262/.398	75	8.3	.260	0.6	C(115): 34.1	4.2
2018	ELP	AAA	25	31	7	3	0	3	11	3	9	0	0	.407/.452/.852	151	6.2	.500	0.0	C(6): 0.5	0.4
2018	SDN	MLB	25	326	29	14	2	14	37	21	90	3	0	.231/.282/.429	88	8.1	.280	-2.1	C(83): 11.8	2.1
2019	SDN	MLB	26	347	28	9	0	11	36	27	109	1	0	.176/.252/.311	61	0.7	.228	0.9	C(95): 28.2, 3B(2): 0.0	2.9
2020	SDN	MLB	27	315	32	12	0	13	39	20	93	2	1	.206/.262/.383	69	1.6	.254	-0.3	C 17	1.9

Comparables: Hank Conger, John Bateman, Steve Yeager

Last year Hedges was the worst hitter in the National League, whether you want to determine such a thing using classic rock (Batting Average), punk/new wave (OPS) or hip hop (DRC+) measures. Jarrod Dyson out-slugged him. Ten starting pitchers posted better offensive numbers than Hedges. Nonetheless, all of them would likely choose to have him behind the plate for their starts in a heartbeat. Hedges is a generational talent when it comes to catcher defense, a pitch-framing and game-calling savant with a cannon for an arm. Our metrics show he saved more runs with his glove than any player in baseball last

YEAR	TEAM	P. COUNT	FRM RUNS	BLK RUNS	THRW RUNS	TOT RUNS
2017	SDN	15353	28.0	1.3	2.2	30.3
2018	SDN	11915	13.0	0.1	-0.4	12.6
2019	SDN	13445	26.0	1.5	0.3	27.8
2020	SDN	12242	14.6	1.2	0.7	16.5

year. His season-long slump at the plate merely deepened his career-long rut, and we're beyond hoping that is ever going to change. The value Hedges provides is subtle and hard for fans to notice, but it continues to outweigh the more obvious dead weight of his bat. Until the robot umps arrive, of course.

Eric Hosmer 1B Born: 10/24/89 Age: 30 Bats: L Throws: L Height: 6'4" Weight: 225 Origin: Round 1, 2008 Draft (#3 overall)

YEAR	TEAM	LVL	AGE	PA	R	2B	3B	HR	RBI	BB	K	SB	CS	AVG/OBP/SLG	DRC+	VORP	BABIP	BRR	FRAA	WARP
2017	KCA	MLB	27	671	98	31	1	25	94	66	104	6	1	.318/.385/.498	126	35.9	.351	-1.3	1B(157): 0.6	3.0
2018	SDN	MLB	28	677	72	31	2	18	69	62	142	7	4	.253/.322/.398	84	-1.2	.302	-2.6	1B(157): 7.8	0.1
2019	SDN	MLB	29	667	72	29	2	22	99	40	163	0	3	.265/.310/.425	86	-1.9	.323	-0.2	1B(157): -3.9	-0.6
2020	SDN	MLB	30	630	67	26	2	20	74	48	145	5	2	.254/.313/.407	94	6.1	.307	-1.0	1B 0	0.6

Comparables: Paul Konerko, Torii Hunter, Casey Kotchman

If you're looking for a bright side in the $92 million Hosmer is still owed, well, at least his contract is no longer the largest in Padres history. If you were disappointed Hosmer didn't continue his career-long pattern of following up bad seasons with relatively good ones, well, maybe the pattern is just switching to two-off, one-on. If you thought Hosmer was still a Gold Glove-caliber first baseman, well, short-term defensive slumps are actually a thing. If you're disappointed that we don't have flying cars yet, well, at least we're on the verge of autonomous electric scooters. If you're horrified by Hosmer's woeful numbers against same-side pitching, well, at least lefties are in the minority. If you're worried that things will only get worse as Hosmer moves into his thirties, well, remember that the shape of the aging curve is a guideline, not a rule. If you tend to look for silver linings in even the darkest of clouds, well, we hope this has been of some help. Probably it hasn't.

Ian Kinsler 2B   Born: 06/22/82   Age: 38   Bats: R   Throws: R   Height: 6'0"   Weight: 200   Origin: Round 17, 2003 Draft (#496 overall)

YEAR	TEAM	LVL	AGE	PA	R	2B	3B	HR	RBI	BB	K	SB	CS	AVG/OBP/SLG	DRC+	VORP	BABIP	BRR	FRAA	WARP
2017	DET	MLB	35	613	90	25	3	22	52	55	86	14	5	.236/.313/.412	102	9.5	.244	4.7	2B(135): 1.0	2.6
2018	LAA	MLB	36	391	49	20	0	13	32	30	40	9	4	.239/.304/.406	97	7.8	.237	-0.9		1.4
2018	BOS	MLB	36	143	17	6	0	1	16	10	24	7	3	.242/.294/.311	97	-3.1	.287	0.6	2B(37): -1.3	0.3
2019	SDN	MLB	37	281	28	12	0	9	22	19	54	2	4	.217/.278/.368	75	0.5	.240	-2.7	2B(72): 3.1, P(1): 0.0	0.1
2020	SDN	MLB	38	251	26	11	1	8	29	16	47	5	2	.234/.290/.392	82	2.5	.261	0.3	2B 1	0.4

Comparables: Mark Ellis, Asdrúbal Cabrera, Jeff Kent

Kinsler made San Diego history last August when he became the first Padres pitcher (yes, you read that right) ever to hit a home run in the ninth inning. The veteran second-sacker took the mound in garbage time and allowed four baserunners but no runs before launching a meaningless two-run bomb in the bottom half. It was his last game of the season, as Kinsler awoke in pain two days later and spent the rest of the year on the injured list with a herniated disc in his neck. It was a fitting end to a disastrous year during which Kinsler's bat was dormant and age continued to erode his once-stellar speed and defensive range, continuing a three-year decline as he entered his late-30s. Kinsler could have hung on as a steady infield backup and veteran clubhouse presence. Instead, he'll end his career with four All-Star appearances, two Gold Gloves, 1,999 hits and likely enshrinement in the Hall of Very Good.

Manny Machado 3B   Born: 07/06/92   Age: 27   Bats: R   Throws: R   Height: 6'3"   Weight: 215   Origin: Round 1, 2010 Draft (#3 overall)

YEAR	TEAM	LVL	AGE	PA	R	2B	3B	HR	RBI	BB	K	SB	CS	AVG/OBP/SLG	DRC+	VORP	BABIP	BRR	FRAA	WARP
2017	BAL	MLB	24	690	81	33	1	33	95	50	115	9	4	.259/.310/.471	106	20.8	.265	-4.1	3B(156): -6.2	2.0
2018	BAL	MLB	25	413	48	21	1	24	65	45	51	8	1	.315/.387/.575	141	40.3	.311	-0.5	SS(96): -4.5	3.5
2018	LAN	MLB	25	296	36	14	2	13	42	25	53	6	1	.273/.338/.487	142	21.5	.296	1.4	SS(51): -4.5, 3B(16): 3.1	2.8
2019	SDN	MLB	26	661	81	21	2	32	85	65	128	5	3	.256/.334/.462	106	32.4	.274	-1.3	3B(119): -10.4, SS(37): -5.2	1.5
2020	SDN	MLB	27	630	81	29	1	31	92	58	119	9	4	.262/.334/.479	114	25.7	.282	-1.7	3B -5, SS -1	2.0

Comparables: Ryan Zimmerman, Adrián Beltré, Brandon Drury

Machado's first season cast as a generational talent accumulating generational wealth was not the rocket ride Padres fans had hoped for. The 300 Million Dollar Man was not an elite offensive force, as he was frequently bedeviled by breaking stuff and off-speed junk and posted disturbing platoon (.239/.315/.400 against righties) and home/road (.219/.297/.406 at Petco) splits. Machado's leatherwork at the hot corner was plus but not spectacular, and the month he spent Jetering his way around shortstop—hopefully for the last time—dragged his overall numbers down. This could be Machado's floor going forward, chalking up a down season to a random bad patch, difficulty adjusting to a run-suppressing ballpark and the pressure of earning his massive salary. Or ... he could be following the same trajectory as Hanley Ramírez, another prodigious infield talent accused of lethargy whose brilliant early career similarly began its decline just when he should have been entering his peak (aided, admittedly, by a nagging shoulder injury). A healthy Machado should be able to avoid that fate.

Manuel Margot CF   Born: 09/28/94   Age: 25   Bats: R   Throws: R   Height: 5'11"   Weight: 180   Origin: International Free Agent, 2011

YEAR	TEAM	LVL	AGE	PA	R	2B	3B	HR	RBI	BB	K	SB	CS	AVG/OBP/SLG	DRC+	VORP	BABIP	BRR	FRAA	WARP
2017	SDN	MLB	22	529	53	18	7	13	39	35	106	17	7	.263/.313/.409	90	23.8	.309	1.3	CF(123): -1.0	1.2
2018	SDN	MLB	23	519	50	26	8	8	51	32	88	11	10	.245/.292/.384	84	10.5	.281	0.9	CF(136): -4.9	0.4
2019	SDN	MLB	24	441	59	19	3	12	37	38	88	20	4	.234/.304/.387	80	4.8	.272	4.5	CF(135): -4.6	0.5
2020	SDN	MLB	25	294	28	14	2	7	30	21	58	10	4	.236/.295/.380	82	5.3	.278	1.1	CF -1	0.4

Comparables: Ruppert Jones, Lloyd Moseby, Andre Dawson

After three full seasons in Padres laundry, Margot continues to be a mixed bag. On the plus side, the turbo-charged Dominican did a better job of leveraging his plus speed on the bases and in the field, swiping bags with a high success rate and improving his jumps in center field. At the plate, he set a career high in home runs and lit up lefty pitching to the tune of .330/.420/.466. However, right-handers continued to work him over with all manner of fastballs, inducing weak contact and rendering Margot virtually unplayable against same-side pitching. Until that changes, Margot can capably man the short side of a platoon, pinch-run and play late-inning defense, but given his prospect pedigree, Padres fans had expected more than a SoCal version of Jake Marisnick.

Francisco Mejía C   Born: 10/27/95   Age: 24   Bats: B   Throws: R   Height: 5'10"   Weight: 180   Origin: International Free Agent, 2012

YEAR	TEAM	LVL	AGE	PA	R	2B	3B	HR	RBI	BB	K	SB	CS	AVG/OBP/SLG	DRC+	VORP	BABIP	BRR	FRAA	WARP
2017	AKR	AA	21	383	52	21	2	14	52	24	53	7	2	.297/.346/.490	133	32.6	.311	1.5	C(72): 1.6, 3B(1): -0.1	3.3
2017	CLE	MLB	21	14	1	0	0	0	1	1	3	0	0	.154/.214/.154	78	-1.7	.200	-0.3	C(3): 0.0	0.0
2018	COH	AAA	22	336	32	22	1	7	45	18	58	0	0	.279/.328/.426	102	9.4	.321	-1.2	C(41): 4.6, LF(22): -3.2	1.2
2018	ELP	AAA	22	132	22	8	1	7	23	7	25	0	0	.328/.364/.582	121	11.8	.359	0.7	C(26): 1.3	1.1
2018	CLE	MLB	22	4	0	0	0	0	0	2	0	0	0	.000/.500/.000	69	0.1	.000	0.0		0.0
2018	SDN	MLB	22	58	6	2	0	3	8	3	19	0	0	.185/.241/.389	73	-0.3	.219	0.2	C(10): -1.7	-0.1
2019	ELP	AAA	23	73	14	8	2	4	12	5	10	0	0	.365/.411/.746	136	9.3	.365	-1.0	C(16): 2.6	0.8
2019	SDN	MLB	23	244	27	11	2	8	22	13	56	1	1	.265/.316/.438	90	9.0	.319	2.0	C(60): -0.6, LF(4): 0.3	1.0
2020	SDN	MLB	24	364	39	16	1	14	46	20	82	1	0	.241/.293/.417	91	13.9	.278	1.3	C -2	1.3

Comparables: John Ryan Murphy, Ronald Guzmán, Dominic Smith

Mejía has been one of baseball's top prospects for years now, but at some point, a young player needs to start converting promise into production on a major-league diamond. For Mejía, that moment came in mid-June, when he was recalled from El Paso, where he had spent a month rehabbing a sore knee, working on defensive fundamentals and tattooing Triple-A pitchers. From that point on, the switch-hitting catcher with the rocket arm posted a .297/.349/.494 line, earning more and more playing time. His advanced contact skills, plus bat speed and power potential left few doubting the backstop would eventually hit big-league pitching. Just as importantly, Mejía seems more committed to improving on his poor play behind the dish, and the Padres seem convinced he has the tools to stay there. He graded out near average in our catching metrics last year, and if he can at least not be a liability back there, Mejía will be an All-Star.

YEAR	TEAM	P. COUNT	FRM RUNS	BLK RUNS	THRW RUNS	TOT RUNS
2017	AKR	9761	-0.5	-0.8	-0.1	0.7
2017	CLE	40	0.0	0.0	0.0	3.2
2018	COH	5559	2.6	0.7	0.3	3.8
2018	ELP	3547	0.0	0.0	0.2	0.6
2018	SDN	1484	-0.7	-0.8	0.0	-0.7
2019	ELP	2085	1.9	0.0	0.0	1.9
2019	SDN	7679	-0.8	0.1	-0.5	-1.3
2020	SDN	12848	-1.3	-1.1	-1.0	-3.4

Seth Mejias-Brean 3B
Born: 04/05/91 Age: 29 Bats: R Throws: R Height: 6'2" Weight: 216 Origin: Round 8, 2012 Draft (#262 overall)

YEAR	TEAM	LVL	AGE	PA	R	2B	3B	HR	RBI	BB	K	SB	CS	AVG/OBP/SLG	DRC+	VORP	BABIP	BRR	FRAA	WARP
2017	ARK	AA	26	323	31	8	2	3	42	22	71	4	1	.268/.328/.340	100	8.3	.339	-2.0	3B(69): -1.2, 1B(4): -0.4	0.7
2017	LOU	AAA	26	66	6	1	0	0	1	3	9	0	1	.262/.318/.279	89	-3.3	.308	-0.1	1B(11): 0.8, 3B(4): 1.6	0.3
2017	TAC	AAA	26	77	15	6	1	1	7	7	13	1	0	.271/.338/.429	91	3.0	.321	0.1	3B(19): 2.1	0.4
2018	ARK	AA	27	138	13	5	1	2	12	11	28	1	1	.238/.304/.341	88	4.6	.292	0.5	3B(28): 2.9, 1B(4): -0.6	0.6
2018	TAC	AAA	27	400	45	13	3	8	44	42	67	4	2	.266/.348/.389	94	16.2	.305	-0.9	3B(91): 6.5, 1B(6): -0.1	1.7
2019	ELP	AAA	28	448	69	18	3	11	66	33	79	4	2	.316/.371/.455	93	15.9	.370	-3.0	3B(56): -5.3, SS(55): 4.2	1.1
2019	SDN	MLB	28	33	3	2	0	2	5	3	9	0	0	.233/.303/.500	83	0.3	.263	0.2	1B(5): -0.1, SS(3): -0.1	0.0
2020	SDN	MLB	29	251	24	11	1	5	25	18	63	1	1	.244/.305/.367	79	1.1	.314	-0.3	3B 2, SS 1	0.4

Comparables: Travis Metcalf, Lane Adams, Chase d'Arnaud

"I just felt like I was floating. Running really fast, didn't know what happened. Just running the bases I was speechless. It was a dream come true." - *Seth Mejias-Brean, describing his first major-league home run*

Baseball is entertainment, joyful and beguiling. Major League Baseball is a business, cold and calculating. Time is a river, flowing and changing. They intertwine, shaping and coloring each other, and sometimes they conspire to bring us Mejias-Brean and his September call-up. The "career minor leaguer," as players who first reach the bigs in their late 20s are often called, acquitted himself well in San Diego, showing consistency at the plate and utility in the field. The odds are against Mejias-Brean and his .716 career Triple-A OPS ever gracing a major-league diamond again, but as fans we were happy to see and hear from him. When Fernando Tatís Jr. hit his first home run, it felt like destiny being fulfilled; when Mejias-Brean hit his, it felt like a wish being granted.

September rosters are slated to be reduced from 40 to 28 this year. Games will be faster, eyeballs and television remotes will have less chance to wander, and there will be fewer chances for players like Mejias-Brean to have their moment. The river gives, and the river takes away.

Wil Myers OF
Born: 12/10/90 Age: 29 Bats: R Throws: R Height: 6'3" Weight: 205 Origin: Round 3, 2009 Draft (#91 overall)

YEAR	TEAM	LVL	AGE	PA	R	2B	3B	HR	RBI	BB	K	SB	CS	AVG/OBP/SLG	DRC+	VORP	BABIP	BRR	FRAA	WARP
2017	SDN	MLB	26	649	80	29	3	30	74	70	180	20	6	.243/.328/.464	108	28.2	.297	1.1	1B(154): -1.8	1.4
2018	SDN	MLB	27	343	39	25	1	11	39	30	94	13	1	.253/.318/.446	91	14.7	.327	1.3	3B(36): -4.3, LF(31): 0.8	0.6
2019	SDN	MLB	28	490	58	22	1	18	53	51	168	16	7	.239/.321/.418	85	5.6	.344	-1.6	LF(98): -2.8, CF(66): -1.1	0.0
2020	SDN	MLB	29	301	35	13	1	11	37	31	99	9	3	.230/.313/.413	94	5.2	.318	-0.1	RF 4, CF 0	0.9

Comparables: Jay Bruce, Justin Upton, Jesse Barfield

New position. New hair. New teammates. Same result. Myers showed up this year sporting tinted Baywatch locks and looking ready to make a new start in left field, but struggled through his most disappointing season yet. Pitchers fed him a steady diet of high fastballs and sliders away and Myers kept swinging through them, helping his strikeout rate soar to a National League worst 34.4 percent while his power continued to dwindle. The Padres, perhaps thinking it would be easier to lower the floor than raise the stairs, tried him in center field but his misadventures there leaked so much value he ended the year as essentially a replacement-level player. Nearing 30 and set to earn $68.5 million over the next three years, Myers is as obvious a change-of-scenery candidate as there is in baseball.

Josh Naylor RF
Born: 06/22/97 Age: 23 Bats: L Throws: L Height: 5'11" Weight: 250 Origin: Round 1, 2015 Draft (#12 overall)

YEAR	TEAM	LVL	AGE	PA	R	2B	3B	HR	RBI	BB	K	SB	CS	AVG/OBP/SLG	DRC+	VORP	BABIP	BRR	FRAA	WARP
2017	LEL	A+	20	313	41	16	2	8	45	27	48	7	1	.297/.361/.452	135	14.5	.333	-0.1	1B(42): -0.6	1.4
2017	SAN	AA	20	175	18	9	0	2	19	16	36	2	1	.250/.320/.346	100	1.1	.308	-0.9	1B(40): 1.9	0.3
2018	SAN	AA	21	574	72	22	1	17	74	64	69	5	5	.297/.383/.447	142	27.3	.317	-5.1	LF(89): -20.4, 1B(29): 0.6	0.9
2019	ELP	AAA	22	252	51	20	1	10	42	28	30	1	0	.314/.389/.547	118	11.9	.326	0.0	RF(29): -2.2, LF(22): 1.0	1.0
2019	SDN	MLB	22	279	29	15	0	8	32	25	64	1	1	.249/.315/.403	82	0.5	.302	-0.2	LF(33): 0.7, RF(31): -4.1	-0.3
2020	SDN	MLB	23	273	28	14	1	7	30	22	56	1	1	.243/.308/.394	90	3.2	.286	0.0	RF -6, LF -1	-0.3

Comparables: Dominic Smith, Cole Tucker, Josh Vitters

Blocked at first base by Eric Hosmer's passbook, the Padres tried to get Naylor's estimable bat into the lineup some other way, with predictable results. The young Canuck is a Large Adult Son of the first order who should be taking pot shots at some AL stadium's short porch in right and spitting seeds between plate appearances, not shagging flies in Petco's vast expanses. Naylor has a preternatural feel for contact, an advanced approach and tremendous raw power that remains on back-order for game day but feels about ready to arrive.

Tommy Pham LF Born: 03/08/88 Age: 32 Bats: R Throws: R Height: 6'1" Weight: 215 Origin: Round 16, 2006 Draft (#496 overall)

YEAR	TEAM	LVL	AGE	PA	R	2B	3B	HR	RBI	BB	K	SB	CS	AVG/OBP/SLG	DRC+	VORP	BABIP	BRR	FRAA	WARP
2017	MEM	AAA	29	106	17	8	0	4	19	13	21	6	3	.283/.371/.500	125	9.1	.328	0.7	RF(15): 2.2, CF(9): -1.0	0.8
2017	SLN	MLB	29	530	95	22	2	23	73	71	117	25	7	.306/.411/.520	140	58.2	.368	4.6	LF(86): -2.6, CF(37): 0.1	4.3
2018	SLN	MLB	30	396	67	11	0	14	41	42	97	10	6	.248/.331/.399	122	18.6	.303	3.8	CF(91): -5.1	2.3
2018	TBA	MLB	30	174	35	7	6	7	22	25	43	5	1	.343/.448/.622	121	21.2	.442	0.9	LF(37): -0.5, CF(3): -0.2	0.9
2019	TBA	MLB	31	654	77	33	2	21	68	81	123	25	4	.273/.369/.450	116	30.6	.316	-0.2	LF(123): -9.6	2.0
2020	SDN	MLB	32	595	72	24	2	20	72	71	126	18	6	.254/.350/.424	109	24.8	.300	2.1	LF -8	1.7

Comparables: Matthew den Dekker, Brad Wilkerson, Marcus Thames

Pham was not as good as he was in the second half of 2018 for the Rays, but he was good nonetheless, and arguably the team's most consistent performer over the course of the year. At one point, he racked up a team-record, 48-game on-base streak that carried over from the 2018 season. For the second time over the last three campaigns, he reached the 20/20 plateau. In fact, he tallied the dubious distinction of going 20/20/20 if you add in the 22 times he grounded into double plays—the first player to do that since Ryan Braun in 2015. Defensively, he was limited to left field where he did not make an error. That said, it's hard to make errors on balls you don't get to. The outspoken outfielder took on more of a leadership role for the young Rays club and was often to the go-to guy for an opinion on things happening around the team. Of course, if they want that opinion in 2020, they'll have to dial long-distance as Pham was traded to San Diego just before the Winter Meetings.

Jurickson Profar 2B Born: 02/20/93 Age: 27 Bats: B Throws: R Height: 6'0" Weight: 190 Origin: International Free Agent, 2009

YEAR	TEAM	LVL	AGE	PA	R	2B	3B	HR	RBI	BB	K	SB	CS	AVG/OBP/SLG	DRC+	VORP	BABIP	BRR	FRAA	WARP
2017	ROU	AAA	24	383	50	25	0	7	45	43	33	5	0	.287/.383/.428	117	33.2	.302	2.9	SS(78): -6.6, 2B(3): -0.2	2.2
2017	TEX	MLB	24	70	8	2	0	0	5	9	14	1	1	.172/.294/.207	76	-0.8	.227	0.8	LF(12): 1.2, SS(4): -0.6	0.1
2018	TEX	MLB	25	594	82	35	6	20	77	54	88	10	0	.254/.335/.458	110	28.6	.269	2.2	SS(68): -8.6, 3B(51): -3.7	1.8
2019	OAK	MLB	26	518	65	24	2	20	67	48	75	9	1	.218/.301/.410	97	14.5	.218	0.4	2B(124): -12.5, LF(7): 0.0	0.2
2020	SDN	MLB	27	497	53	23	2	16	57	46	77	5	2	.222/.306/.390	90	12.0	.236	0.5	2B -8, 3B 0	0.4

Comparables: Dustin Ackley, Gordon Beckham, Rougned Odor

The nasty part about the yips is that practice can't really cure the disease. Much like stage fright, you simply can't simulate the conditions that produce the problem; Steve Sax could throw the ball to first just fine in practice, it was the game state that changed everything. Following an offseason trade and a positional switch, the yips came for Profar, who made six throwing errors in the first month of the season. Between those and many other unnatural looking tosses, it became clear what he was up against. From there, Profar battled. His throws were not always pretty: His arm slot changed, his release point came and went, the ball sometimes bounced on its way in. Ultimately though, his throws managed to find their destination more often than not. Whatever his DRS and DRC, that's a triumph, and hopefully it's one that clears the runway for bigger and better things going forward in San Diego.

Fernando Tatis Jr. SS Born: 01/02/99 Age: 21 Bats: R Throws: R Height: 6'3" Weight: 185 Origin: International Free Agent, 2015

YEAR	TEAM	LVL	AGE	PA	R	2B	3B	HR	RBI	BB	K	SB	CS	AVG/OBP/SLG	DRC+	VORP	BABIP	BRR	FRAA	WARP
2017	FTW	A	18	518	78	26	7	21	69	75	124	29	15	.281/.390/.520	151	52.3	.342	0.1	SS(109): -5.6	4.5
2017	SAN	AA	18	57	6	1	0	1	6	2	17	3	0	.255/.281/.327	70	0.5	.351	0.9	SS(9): -0.3, 3B(3): -0.5	0.0
2018	SAN	AA	19	394	77	22	4	16	43	33	109	16	5	.286/.355/.507	140	35.8	.370	3.0	SS(83): -1.9	3.4
2019	SDN	MLB	20	372	61	13	6	22	53	30	110	16	6	.317/.379/.590	118	26.9	.410	7.1	SS(83): 0.9	3.4
2020	SDN	MLB	21	595	72	26	4	26	81	43	175	17	7	.256/.316/.458	106	33.3	.331	6.1	SS 0	3.4

Comparables: Carlos Correa, Rougned Odor, Ronald Acuña Jr.

You know it when you see it, and you definitely saw it. Over 84 games last year Tatís unleashed his abundant talent, athleticism and exuberance in ballparks nationwide, stealing bases, smothering ground balls, skywalking to snag liners, blasting misplaced fastballs into orbit and generally acting like it was his game and everyone else was there to watch with mouths agape. We could point out his unsustainable BABIP and how his penchant to swing and miss will often keep him from reaching base at an elite rate, but why drop a Baby Ruth in the pool? It was 84 games of beach weather, and then ... ouch. Injuries are part of the game, and there's no reason Tatís shouldn't arrive at spring training with his back in fine fettle. The Padres have asked him to play a little more carefully, which of course they should, but was there any moment watching Tatís last year that made you think he possessed an on/off switch?

Luis Torrens C Born: 05/02/96 Age: 24 Bats: R Throws: R Height: 6'0" Weight: 175 Origin: International Free Agent, 2013

YEAR	TEAM	LVL	AGE	PA	R	2B	3B	HR	RBI	BB	K	SB	CS	AVG/OBP/SLG	DRC+	VORP	BABIP	BRR	FRAA	WARP
2017	SDN	MLB	21	139	7	3	1	0	7	12	30	0	0	.163/.243/.203	61	-6.3	.215	1.1	C(51): -9.0	-0.8
2018	LEL	A+	22	515	62	36	3	6	73	26	77	1	1	.280/.320/.406	100	26.2	.318	1.8	C(85): 1.0, 1B(3): 0.0	2.2
2019	AMA	AA	23	397	50	23	1	15	62	42	67	1	2	.300/.373/.500	135	27.2	.331	-2.6	C(84): 3.0, 1B(1): 0.2	3.1
2019	SDN	MLB	23	16	2	1	0	0	0	2	6	0	0	.214/.313/.286	75	0.2	.375	0.4	C(4): 0.4	0.1
2020	SDN	MLB	24	35	3	1	0	1	4	3	8	0	0	.223/.291/.351	74	0.4	.272	-0.1	C -1	-0.1

Comparables: Del Crandall, Vic Janowicz, Raudy Read

YEAR	TEAM	P. COUNT	FRM RUNS	BLK RUNS	THRW RUNS	TOT RUNS
2017	SDN	5274	-5.8	-2.5	0.0	-8.6
2019	AMA	12334	-2.8	0.0	5.2	2.2
2019	SDN	495	-0.1	0.4	0.0	1.0
2020	SDN	1331	-1.4	-0.2	0.2	-1.4

Two full years removed from his sacrificial season on San Diego's 25-man roster, Torrens is back on prospect radars in DayGlo color after a breakthrough year in the Texas League. Torrens continues to be a rock behind the plate and has the defensive chops to be a big-league backup as soon as brunch tomorrow. The big news, though, is the noise his bat made during his Sod Poodle sojourn. Torrens suddenly added power to his already advanced approach and bat-to-ball skills, posting a .304/.373/.546 line and going deep 12 times after the All-Star break. He now has the look of a potential starting catcher, validating the Friars' Rule 5 gambit.

★ ★ ★ *2020 Top 101 Prospect* **#69** ★ ★ ★

Taylor Trammell **OF** Born: 09/13/97 Age: 22 Bats: L Throws: L Height: 6'2" Weight: 215 Origin: Round 1, 2016 Draft (#35 overall)

YEAR	TEAM	LVL	AGE	PA	R	2B	3B	HR	RBI	BB	K	SB	CS	AVG/OBP/SLG	DRC+	VORP	BABIP	BRR	FRAA	WARP
2017	DYT	A	19	571	80	24	10	13	77	71	123	41	12	.281/.368/.450	127	43.1	.345	3.1	LF(104): -3.7, CF(17): -0.9	2.8
2018	DAY	A+	20	461	71	19	4	8	41	58	105	25	10	.277/.375/.406	128	26.4	.358	-0.8	CF(60): -1.7, LF(29): 4.5	2.6
2019	CHT	AA	21	381	47	8	3	6	33	54	86	17	4	.236/.349/.336	110	11.6	.299	2.1	LF(91): -0.7, CF(1): 0.1	1.5
2019	AMA	AA	21	133	14	4	1	4	10	13	36	3	4	.229/.316/.381	89	-0.9	.295	-0.6	CF(30): -1.4	0.1
2020	SDN	MLB	22	35	4	1	0	1	4	3	10	1	0	.226/.305/.364	84	0.6	.307	0.0	CF 0	0.1

Comparables: Jesse Winker, Clint Frazier, Trent Grisham

The Padres are hoping the Franmil Reyes Trade, much like what was once called the James Shields Trade, will someday be called the Taylor Trammell trade. The former Reds farmhand boasts paint-peeling speed, power potential and the plus makeup needed to translate his tools into everyday production. Last year in Double-A, Trammell focused on drawing more walks with fewer strikeouts, but his more contact-oriented approach cost him much of his power. This year's focus should be on maintaining an advanced approach and getting on base while working to unleash the power in his swing. Trammell will need to improve his arm and his defensive fundamentals to stay in center, but his speed and on-base skills give him a fourth outfielder's floor with a much higher ceiling.

PITCHERS

Lake Bachar **RHP** Born: 06/03/95 Age: 25 Bats: R Throws: R Height: 6'3" Weight: 215 Origin: Round 5, 2016 Draft (#144 overall)

YEAR	TEAM	LVL	AGE	W	L	SV	G	GS	IP	H	HR	BB/9	K/9	K	GB%	BABIP	WHIP	ERA	DRA	WARP	MPH	FB%	WHF	CSP
2017	PDR	RK	22	1	0	0	5	0	9	5	1	6.0	15.0	15	44%	.235	1.22	1.00	3.43	0.2				
2017	FTW	A	22	4	1	0	7	6	37²	33	6	1.4	6.7	28	43%	.252	1.04	4.06	3.67	0.7				
2018	LEL	A+	23	2	1	1	7	4	28¹	16	3	2.9	5.7	18	39%	.169	0.88	1.91	2.64	0.9				
2018	SAN	AA	23	3	7	1	20	14	87	99	15	3.9	6.4	62	33%	.315	1.57	5.59	6.70	-1.5				
2019	LEL	A+	24	0	0	0	1	1	6	6	0	3.0	10.5	7	62%	.375	1.33	3.00	5.48	0.0				
2019	AMA	AA	24	8	4	0	24	19	126²	121	18	4.1	9.0	126	39%	.314	1.41	3.98	5.03	-0.2				
2020	SDN	MLB	25	2	2	0	33	0	35	36	7	3.3	7.5	29	37%	.292	1.41	5.15	5.14	0.1				

Comparables: Drew Gagnon, Mario Hollands, Luis Santos

Bachar, once the punter and kicker for D-3 juggernaut Wisconsin-Whitewater's back-to-back NCAA championship squads, struck out more than a man per inning in the Amarillo rotation—an impressive feat given the obvious distraction of his father's cancer fight that prompted the Sod Poodles to hold a "Bachar Strong" fundraising promotion last August. He's not so much a prospect as a useful reminder that minor leaguers aren't tools and outcomes, but young men with lives, families, hopes and fears.

Michel Baez **RHP** Born: 01/21/96 Age: 24 Bats: R Throws: R Height: 6'8" Weight: 220 Origin: International Free Agent, 2016

YEAR	TEAM	LVL	AGE	W	L	SV	G	GS	IP	H	HR	BB/9	K/9	K	GB%	BABIP	WHIP	ERA	DRA	WARP	MPH	FB%	WHF	CSP
2017	FTW	A	21	6	2	0	10	10	58²	41	8	1.2	12.6	82	36%	.264	0.84	2.45	2.30	2.0				
2018	LEL	A+	22	4	7	0	17	17	86²	73	5	3.4	9.6	92	37%	.297	1.22	2.91	3.01	2.3				
2018	SAN	AA	22	0	3	0	4	4	18¹	22	4	5.9	10.3	21	31%	.375	1.85	7.36	7.00	-0.4				
2019	AMA	AA	23	3	2	1	15	0	27	22	1	3.7	12.7	38	38%	.333	1.22	2.00	3.42	0.4				
2019	SDN	MLB	23	1	1	0	24	1	29²	25	3	4.2	8.5	28	40%	.265	1.31	3.03	5.75	-0.1	97.4	58.7	11.7	41.9
2020	SDN	MLB	24	1	2	0	26	8	19	17	3	4.0	8.1	17	38%	.279	1.36	4.39	4.57	0.2	97.2	60.5	12.1	43.2

Comparables: Jorge Alcala, Vince Velasquez, Ryan Helsley

A *Gran Corona*-sized Cuban signee, Báez unleashed his powerful smoke in the San Diego 'pen last July with encouraging results. His four-seamer sits effortlessly at 96 and Báez supplements it with a solid changeup he can bury for swinging strikes, making it effective against both righties and lefties, though his curveball remains more of a show-me offering. He repeats his delivery surprisingly well for such a big man but will occasionally get out of sync, start issuing walks and lose command. Signed as a starter, Báez worked exclusively in relief last year and flashed late-inning upside but the Padres would be smart to stick him in the rotation to see if his flavor can satisfy all day.

José Castillo **LHP** Born: 01/10/96 Age: 24 Bats: L Throws: L Height: 6'5" Weight: 246 Origin: International Free Agent, 2012

YEAR	TEAM	LVL	AGE	W	L	SV	G	GS	IP	H	HR	BB/9	K/9	K	GB%	BABIP	WHIP	ERA	DRA	WARP	MPH	FB%	WHF	CSP
2017	LEL	A+	21	3	2	1	39	0	47	38	0	4.2	9.4	49	42%	.297	1.28	2.87	3.27	0.9				
2017	SAN	AA	21	1	0	0	8	0	9¹	8	1	3.9	9.6	10	28%	.292	1.29	2.89	4.36	0.0				
2018	SAN	AA	22	2	1	5	12	0	15	14	0	4.8	15.6	26	38%	.438	1.47	3.00	4.35	0.1				
2018	ELP	AAA	22	1	0	3	10	0	11¹	6	1	1.6	10.3	13	43%	.185	0.71	0.79	1.96	0.4				
2018	SDN	MLB	22	3	3	0	37	0	38¹	23	3	2.8	12.2	52	39%	.250	0.91	3.29	3.02	0.8	97.6	55.2	15.5	48.7
2019	SDN	MLB	23	0	0	0	1	0	0²	0	0	13.5	27.0	2	0%	.000	1.50	0.00	5.18	0.0	96.7	64.7	11.8	37.4
2020	SDN	MLB	24	2	1	0	30	0	32	24	3	5.0	9.9	35	37%	.269	1.32	3.79	3.88	0.5	97.4	57.2	15.8	43.7

Comparables: Mauricio Cabrera, Andrew Bellatti, Zack Littell

Castillo flashed nuclear stuff in his 2018 Padres debut, but cold, uncaring forces conspired to keep him off the mound last year. Forearm tightness in spring training limited him to infrequent minor-league rehab outings, a torn ligament in his hand ended his only Padres appearance and sanctions imposed by a very stable genius denied the lefty fireballer his annual Venezuelan Winter League stint. Castillo possesses a closer-level fastball/slider combo that can make big-league batsmen look silly, and if bad health doesn't intervene, he'll likely open another giant can of covfefe on them this summer.

Zach Davies RHP Born: 02/07/93 Age: 27 Bats: R Throws: R Height: 6'0" Weight: 155 Origin: Round 26, 2011 Draft (#785 overall)

YEAR	TEAM	LVL	AGE	W	L	SV	G	GS	IP	H	HR	BB/9	K/9	K	GB%	BABIP	WHIP	ERA	DRA	WARP	MPH	FB%	WHF	CSP
2017	MIL	MLB	24	17	9	0	33	33	191¹	204	20	2.6	5.8	124	51%	.302	1.35	3.90	4.77	1.7	91.6	57.8	7.6	44.9
2018	WIS	A	25	1	0	0	4	4	19	19	2	0.0	9.0	19	63%	.347	1.00	2.84	4.71	0.1				
2018	BLX	AA	25	1	1	0	2	2	11	7	1	3.3	9.8	12	54%	.240	1.00	4.09	3.43	0.2				
2018	CSP	AAA	25	0	3	0	5	5	17	18	0	6.4	6.9	13	44%	.333	1.76	6.35	5.92	-0.1				
2018	MIL	MLB	25	2	7	0	13	13	66	67	8	2.9	6.7	49	48%	.299	1.33	4.77	4.68	0.5	92.3	56.5	8.7	43.6
2019	MIL	MLB	26	10	7	0	31	31	159²	155	20	2.9	5.7	102	42%	.272	1.29	3.55	5.30	0.8	90.5	52.4	7.5	41.4
2020	SDN	MLB	27	7	9	0	24	24	126	130	20	3.0	5.9	84	43%	.281	1.37	4.71	4.93	1.3	90.7	55.5	7.8	43.5

Comparables: Jair Jurrjens, Art Mahaffey, Joe Ross

Davies continues to thrive as a pitch-to-contact pitcher in a strike-'em-out world. Brett Anderson and Iván Nova were the only starters with a lower strikeout-per-nine rate than Davies' 5.7, but he nonetheless posted the best ERA of his five-year career. (You may have noticed the wide discrepancy between his DRA and ERA—it is indeed one of the biggest in the league among starters.) While Davies will almost certainly not repeat his .272 BABIP from 2019, his lowest in four years by 27 points, his new digs in PETCO Park may just be the best place for a pitcher of his profile. The marine layer promises to keep fly balls from flying out of the yard and the deep power alleys should help Davies feel comfortable continuing to attack the zone and relying on his defense.

Miguel Diaz RHP Born: 11/28/94 Age: 25 Bats: R Throws: R Height: 6'0" Weight: 214 Origin: International Free Agent, 2011

YEAR	TEAM	LVL	AGE	W	L	SV	G	GS	IP	H	HR	BB/9	K/9	K	GB%	BABIP	WHIP	ERA	DRA	WARP	MPH	FB%	WHF	CSP
2017	LEL	A+	22	0	0	0	2	2	7¹	8	0	3.7	6.1	5	44%	.348	1.50	3.68	5.61	0.0				
2017	SDN	MLB	22	1	1	0	31	3	41²	44	11	5.4	7.1	33	41%	.275	1.66	7.34	7.15	-0.9	98.2	65.5	9.3	47.1
2018	SAN	AA	23	5	2	2	19	9	65	45	4	4.2	9.1	66	57%	.253	1.15	2.35	2.78	1.8				
2018	ELP	AAA	23	0	3	0	5	2	13¹	17	2	8.8	10.1	15	40%	.375	2.25	8.10	7.36	-0.3				
2018	SDN	MLB	23	1	0	0	11	0	18²	16	2	5.8	14.5	30	35%	.341	1.50	4.82	3.24	0.4	97.8	55.3	17.9	45.5
2019	AMA	AA	24	2	1	0	6	4	22²	21	9	3.2	13.1	33	30%	.255	1.28	4.37	4.35	0.1				
2019	ELP	AAA	24	0	1	0	4	4	7²	8	1	2.3	8.2	7	38%	.350	1.30	2.35	4.16	0.2				
2019	SDN	MLB	24	0	0	0	5	0	6¹	9	1	1.4	5.7	4	36%	.381	1.58	7.11	5.29	0.0	96.9	52.9	7.8	49
2020	SDN	MLB	25	2	2	0	33	0	35	38	9	4.1	10.0	39	38%	.317	1.55	6.23	6.12	-0.3	97.6	62.1	12.2	48.5

Comparables: Jose Cisnero, Dean Deetz, Elieser Hernandez

Three years after coming to the Padres as a Rule 5 draftee, Díaz remains a stereotypical relief pitching prospect. Like so many others, his fastball can reach the mid-90s but he doesn't command it well. His breaking ball and changeup have their moments, but with little consistency. He can miss bats with regularity, but he also misses targets. Díaz is coming off a season plagued by recurring knee problems, but after sanding some of the rough edges off his delivery, he posted a much-improved walk rate during his short time in the high minors. That bodes well for his potential future as a stereotypical middle reliever.

Robbie Erlin LHP Born: 10/08/90 Age: 29 Bats: R Throws: L Height: 6'0" Weight: 190 Origin: Round 3, 2009 Draft (#93 overall)

YEAR	TEAM	LVL	AGE	W	L	SV	G	GS	IP	H	HR	BB/9	K/9	K	GB%	BABIP	WHIP	ERA	DRA	WARP	MPH	FB%	WHF	CSP
2018	SDN	MLB	27	4	7	0	39	12	109	112	12	1.0	7.3	88	48%	.306	1.14	4.21	3.05	2.6	92.3	59.2	10.3	52
2019	ELP	AAA	28	0	1	1	10	0	15¹	26	2	1.2	8.2	14	51%	.453	1.83	8.80	5.83	0.1				
2019	SDN	MLB	28	0	1	0	37	1	55¹	72	6	2.4	8.5	52	46%	.373	1.57	5.37	5.17	0.1	92.1	50.7	11.3	46.3
2020	SDN	MLB	29	2	2	0	33	0	35	38	5	2.2	7.7	30	46%	.313	1.34	4.65	4.65	0.3	91.6	55.5	10.7	48.8

Comparables: Erasmo Ramírez, Jaime García, Brett Anderson

A soft-tossing lefty junkballer, Erlin spent last summer in the bullpen handing out hits like Halloween SweeTarts before earning his release at season's end. His peripherals weren't nearly as bad as his run prevention, however, as Erlin posted a career-high strikeout rate while keeping his walk rate low and inducing his share of ground balls. He's exactly the type of strike-thrower that Dave Duncan used to sprinkle with pixie dust and sinker shavings, as he gifts Cardinals fans another surprisingly successful starter reclamation. Erlin has enough pitchability to be a useful swingman, and could yet carve out a role at the back of a big-league rotation.

──────── ★ ★ ★ *2020 Top 101 Prospect* **#5** ★ ★ ★ ────────

MacKenzie Gore LHP Born: 02/24/99 Age: 21 Bats: L Throws: L Height: 6'3" Weight: 195 Origin: Round 1, 2017 Draft (#3 overall)

YEAR	TEAM	LVL	AGE	W	L	SV	G	GS	IP	H	HR	BB/9	K/9	K	GB%	BABIP	WHIP	ERA	DRA	WARP	MPH	FB%	WHF	CSP
2017	PDR	RK	18	0	1	0	7	7	21¹	14	0	3.0	14.3	34	69%	.333	0.98	1.27	0.48	1.3				
2018	FTW	A	19	2	5	0	16	16	60²	61	5	2.7	11.0	74	41%	.354	1.30	4.45	4.11	0.8				
2019	LEL	A+	20	7	1	0	15	15	79¹	36	4	2.3	12.5	110	38%	.211	0.71	1.02	1.70	3.2				
2019	AMA	AA	20	2	1	0	5	5	21²	20	3	3.3	10.4	25	40%	.308	1.29	4.15	4.20	0.2				
2020	SDN	MLB	21	2	3	0	8	8	38	37	6	4.1	11.6	49	40%	.335	1.43	4.83	4.91	0.4				

Comparables: Bryse Wilson, José Berríos, Henry Owens

Last summer's landmark case *Bush Leagues v. Gore, 1.02 ERA (2019)* ended in a unanimous ruling that the young left-hander is baseball's top pitching prospect. Gore laid waste to California League hitters with uncommon command of his lively mid-90s fastball, two quality breakers and a changeup that flashed plus. He's athletic, fluid, dynamic, poised, aggressive, confident, consistent, prepared, competitive, solidly built, blister-free and just barely old enough to order a Ballast Point Victory At Sea Imperial Porter. A few months building up his innings count and dominating more advanced Double-A hitters might be enough to land him in Petco, where a future at the front of the rotation awaits.

Javy Guerra RHP Born: 09/25/95 Age: 24 Bats: L Throws: R Height: 5'11" Weight: 155 Origin: International Free Agent, 2012

YEAR	TEAM	LVL	AGE	W	L	SV	G	GS	IP	H	HR	BB/9	K/9	K	GB%	BABIP	WHIP	ERA	DRA	WARP	MPH	FB%	WHF	CSP
2019	LEL	A+	23	0	0	1	17	0	17	13	2	2.6	12.2	23	34%	.306	1.06	3.71	3.67	0.2				
2019	SDN	MLB	23	0	0	0	8	0	8²	7	3	3.1	6.2	6	48%	.167	1.15	5.19	6.10	-0.1	100.2	76.9	8.2	52.6
2020	*SDN*	*MLB*	*24*	*1*	*2*	*0*	*30*	*0*	*32*	*35*	*5*	*3.3*	*7.8*	*27*	*46%*	*.314*	*1.47*	*5.36*	*5.45*	*0.0*	*100.0*	*79.2*	*8.5*	*54.2*

Comparables: Brandon Gomes, Drew Smith, Tony Gonsolin

Data Point #12,246 proving Baseball Is Cuh-RAY-Zee: Guerra, four years after being traded from Boston and four months after the former shortstop threw his first professional pitch, completed his September in the Padres 'pen with a better WARP than the superstar closer he was traded for, Craig Kimbrel. Sure, he was "better" only in the "not quite so far below replacement level" sense, but the fact Guerra showed enough in his minor-league debut to earn his call-up is a minor miracle. The young Panamanian's heavy fastball can reach triple-digits, his slider is workable and he can control them both surprisingly well. Improved command and pitchability are the next order of business, but Guerra has already proven to be a quick study, with all the tools needed to work high-leverage innings.

Dinelson Lamet RHP Born: 07/18/92 Age: 27 Bats: R Throws: R Height: 6'4" Weight: 187 Origin: International Free Agent, 2014

YEAR	TEAM	LVL	AGE	W	L	SV	G	GS	IP	H	HR	BB/9	K/9	K	GB%	BABIP	WHIP	ERA	DRA	WARP	MPH	FB%	WHF	CSP
2017	ELP	AAA	24	3	2	0	8	8	39	32	2	4.6	11.5	50	52%	.319	1.33	3.23	2.42	1.4				
2017	SDN	MLB	24	7	8	0	21	21	114¹	88	18	4.3	10.9	139	37%	.261	1.24	4.57	3.97	2.1	97.3	55.8	13	46.6
2019	LEL	A+	26	0	2	0	3	3	9	11	1	5.0	14.0	14	27%	.476	1.78	8.00	6.22	-0.1				
2019	ELP	AAA	26	1	0	0	3	3	15	10	3	2.4	11.4	19	51%	.219	0.93	4.80	1.99	0.7				
2019	SDN	MLB	26	3	5	0	14	14	73	62	12	3.7	12.9	105	38%	.311	1.26	4.07	3.19	2.0	97.9	54.8	14.6	45.9
2020	*SDN*	*MLB*	*27*	*8*	*7*	*0*	*23*	*23*	*122*	*99*	*17*	*4.1*	*12.2*	*166*	*39%*	*.299*	*1.26*	*3.79*	*3.97*	*2.5*	*97.1*	*55.9*	*14*	*46.7*

Comparables: Alex Meyer, Steven Matz, Justin Haley

Tommy John surgery has become so normalized that fans often mark a spot on their mental calendar, assuming the player will reappear unchanged in 18 months, as if they were returning from a 'round-the-world cruise. We often forget the physical and mental challenges they face during long hours spent in anonymous facilities, away from their teammates and the game they love, never sure if their career and livelihood will survive the crisis. Some never make it back at all, some are diminished and some take longer to regain what they've lost. And a handful, like Lamet, return on time, seemingly better than ever. When last we saw the bulldog right-hander, he had mid-90s heat and a wipeout slider, but the lack of a third pitch raised questions about his long-term viability in the rotation. Lamet 2.0, however, has added a tick to his fastball and some variation—a sinking fastball and a slurvy version of his breaking ball—to his repertoire, making it more likely he'll be able to hold his own against lefties and during multiple trips through the order. A healthy Lamet and his heavy dose of sliders will be an asset in the middle of the rotation.

Joey Lucchesi LHP Born: 06/06/93 Age: 27 Bats: L Throws: L Height: 6'5" Weight: 204 Origin: Round 4, 2016 Draft (#114 overall)

YEAR	TEAM	LVL	AGE	W	L	SV	G	GS	IP	H	HR	BB/9	K/9	K	GB%	BABIP	WHIP	ERA	DRA	WARP	MPH	FB%	WHF	CSP
2017	LEL	A+	24	6	4	0	14	14	78²	56	9	2.2	10.9	95	53%	.251	0.95	2.52	2.73	2.3				
2017	SAN	AA	24	5	3	1	10	9	60¹	46	3	2.1	7.9	53	50%	.259	0.99	1.79	2.91	1.6				
2018	SDN	MLB	25	8	9	0	26	26	130	125	23	3.0	10.0	145	47%	.307	1.29	4.08	3.79	2.3	92.8	64.1	11.5	49.9
2019	SDN	MLB	26	10	10	0	30	30	163²	144	23	3.1	8.7	158	49%	.271	1.22	4.18	4.16	2.9	92.6	64.9	11.5	46.9
2020	*SDN*	*MLB*	*27*	*8*	*8*	*0*	*24*	*24*	*134*	*123*	*22*	*3.3*	*9.0*	*133*	*47%*	*.282*	*1.29*	*4.21*	*4.45*	*2.0*	*92.2*	*65.4*	*11.6*	*48.8*

Comparables: Trevor Richards, Austin Davis, Brock Stewart

If you want to stick in the rotation as a league-average hurler, as Lucchesi was last summer, it helps to be an interesting one to watch. Old for his draft class and the first pitcher to reach the bigs (Lauer was second), Lucchesi is notable for his wind-up toy delivery, his groovy nickname (Joey Fuego) and his "churve," a changeup-curve hybrid which baffles opposing hitters and pitch classification algorithms with similar frequency. He favors his sinker over his four-seamer and gets his share of groundouts, but isn't a double-play machine. Already set to turn 27 this coming D-Day, Lucchesi isn't a star in waiting but has proven he has both the ability and the durability to munch innings at the back of a big-league rotation.

Nick Margevicius LHP Born: 06/18/96 Age: 24 Bats: L Throws: L Height: 6'5" Weight: 220 Origin: Round 7, 2017 Draft (#198 overall)

YEAR	TEAM	LVL	AGE	W	L	SV	G	GS	IP	H	HR	BB/9	K/9	K	GB%	BABIP	WHIP	ERA	DRA	WARP	MPH	FB%	WHF	CSP
2017	PDR	RK	21	1	1	1	5	4	19	19	0	1.9	14.2	30	61%	.413	1.21	1.42	2.48	0.7				
2017	TRI	A-	21	3	0	0	6	6	29	20	1	1.2	9.9	32	49%	.260	0.83	1.24	2.82	0.8				
2018	FTW	A	22	5	5	0	13	13	76¹	79	5	1.1	10.3	87	40%	.346	1.15	3.07	3.54	1.5				
2018	LEL	A+	22	5	3	0	10	9	58²	69	5	1.2	9.1	59	39%	.376	1.31	4.30	4.61	0.5				
2019	AMA	AA	23	4	4	0	12	12	69	75	14	1.7	6.9	53	44%	.296	1.28	4.30	5.33	-0.3				
2019	SDN	MLB	23	2	6	0	17	12	57	73	12	3.0	6.6	42	46%	.326	1.61	6.79	6.97	-0.8	90.5	54.1	10.5	49.6
2020	SDN	MLB	24	2	3	0	23	5	43	46	8	2.7	6.3	30	43%	.282	1.35	4.99	5.24	0.2	90.3	55.7	10.9	51

Comparables: Aaron Civale, Taylor Rogers, Cy Sneed

Although the Padres were clearly committed to their young rotation last year, it was a shock when Margevicius broke camp with the big club. Until then, he'd never thrown a pitch above High-A ball. He rewarded their faith by posting a 1.69 ERA with a 12:1 whiff-to-walk rate over his first three starts, then faded badly and spent most of the year in Double-A where he belonged. Margevicius (pronounced "cuh-MAND-spesh-list") rarely dents 90 with his well-placed fastballs but fools the kids in the bus leagues with an intoxicating blend of sliders, changeups and looping low-70s benders. The best hitters in the world are better equipped to wait the young lefty out and grind his mundane stuff into batting practice fodder, but Margevicius has plenty of time to improve his high-wire act and could eventually earn a swingman's salary.

★ ★ ★ *2020 Top 101 Prospect* **#75** ★ ★ ★

Adrian Morejon LHP Born: 02/27/99 Age: 21 Bats: L Throws: L Height: 6'0" Weight: 175 Origin: International Free Agent, 2016

YEAR	TEAM	LVL	AGE	W	L	SV	G	GS	IP	H	HR	BB/9	K/9	K	GB%	BABIP	WHIP	ERA	DRA	WARP	MPH	FB%	WHF	CSP
2017	TRI	A-	18	2	2	0	7	7	35¹	37	2	0.8	8.9	35	41%	.337	1.13	3.57	4.30	0.4				
2017	FTW	A	18	1	2	0	6	6	27²	28	2	4.2	7.5	23	34%	.321	1.48	4.23	5.57	-0.1				
2018	LEL	A+	19	4	4	0	13	13	62²	54	6	3.4	10.1	70	55%	.302	1.24	3.30	3.49	1.3				
2019	AMA	AA	20	0	4	0	16	16	36	29	3	3.8	11.0	44	51%	.292	1.22	4.25	2.75	1.0				
2019	SDN	MLB	20	0	0	0	5	2	8	15	1	3.4	10.1	9	37%	.483	2.25	10.12	5.09	0.0	97.9	53.9	9.7	50.7
2020	SDN	MLB	21	1	2	0	15	3	29	31	5	3.6	7.8	25	42%	.308	1.47	5.23	5.29	0.1	98.1	56.5	10.2	53.1

Comparables: Tyler Skaggs, Jenrry Mejia, Chris Tillman

Three years after signing with San Diego for $11 million, Morejon remains a top-flight starting prospect more in theory than practice. The young Cuban can unleash rare lefty heat that sits comfortably in the mid-90s and a changeup and curve which could both become quality offerings, but nagging injuries continue to limit his opportunities to polish them and fan the whispers that his frame won't hold up to a starter's workload. Morejon was knocked around during his brief July call-up, yet still tantalized with his swing-and-miss stuff. If Job One this year is proving he can take the ball every fifth day, Job Two is developing the command and consistency necessary for a big-league rotation spot.

Andres Munoz RHP Born: 01/16/99 Age: 21 Bats: R Throws: R Height: 6'2" Weight: 165 Origin: International Free Agent, 2015

YEAR	TEAM	LVL	AGE	W	L	SV	G	GS	IP	H	HR	BB/9	K/9	K	GB%	BABIP	WHIP	ERA	DRA	WARP	MPH	FB%	WHF	CSP
2017	TRI	A-	18	3	0	1	21	0	23²	15	2	6.1	13.3	35	71%	.265	1.31	3.80	3.97	0.3				
2018	SAN	AA	19	2	1	7	20	0	19	11	0	5.2	9.0	19	55%	.250	1.16	0.95	3.44	0.3				
2019	AMA	AA	20	0	2	4	16	0	16²	9	1	5.9	18.4	34	44%	.308	1.20	2.16	2.06	0.5				
2019	ELP	AAA	20	3	2	2	19	0	19	16	3	3.3	11.4	24	53%	.310	1.21	3.79	2.91	0.6				
2019	SDN	MLB	20	1	1	1	22	0	23	16	2	4.3	11.7	30	41%	.259	1.17	3.91	3.98	0.3	101.8	68	15.6	46.1
2020	SDN	MLB	21	2	2	2	42	0	45	37	5	4.2	11.9	59	43%	.304	1.29	3.77	3.91	0.7	102.0	71.2	16.4	48.3

Comparables: Joe Ortiz, Eduardo Sanchez, Mike Soroka

Munoz took the mound to face the Cubs on September 10th sporting a 1.69 ERA and .135/.238/.203 opponents' batting line, testaments to his almighty triple-digit fastball. With a man on, Kris Bryant ambushed a belt-high first-pitch hundo-ball and took Munoz deep for the first time, reminding us all that a misplaced fastball to a big-league hitter is unsafe at any speed. Munoz gave up another dinger to Jason Heyward that day, allowed three more runs in his next appearance and the Padres wisely shut down their fireballing prodigy before his arm and ego were put at further risk. Nevertheless, Munoz was a revelation last year, supplementing his blazing fastball with a sharp-breaking slider he can rush up in the low-90s. Only 21, Munoz has plenty of time to improve his command, take over the ninth inning and perhaps chase down Joakim Soria and Roberto Osuna to set the career saves record for players born in Mexico.

Chris Paddack RHP Born: 01/08/96 Age: 24 Bats: R Throws: R Height: 6'4" Weight: 195 Origin: Round 8, 2015 Draft (#236 overall)

YEAR	TEAM	LVL	AGE	W	L	SV	G	GS	IP	H	HR	BB/9	K/9	K	GB%	BABIP	WHIP	ERA	DRA	WARP	MPH	FB%	WHF	CSP
2018	LEL	A+	22	4	1	0	10	10	52¹	43	3	0.7	14.3	83	47%	.370	0.90	2.24	2.22	1.9				
2018	SAN	AA	22	3	2	0	7	7	37²	23	1	1.0	8.8	37	45%	.239	0.72	1.91	2.09	1.4				
2019	SDN	MLB	23	9	7	0	26	26	140²	107	23	2.0	9.8	153	41%	.237	0.98	3.33	3.18	4.0	96.2	61	12.9	50.5
2020	SDN	MLB	24	9	8	0	26	26	143	119	20	2.5	9.5	150	41%	.271	1.11	3.34	3.63	3.4	96.0	62.9	13.3	52

Comparables: Joe Musgrove, Daniel Hudson, Corbin Burnes

Black suit. Black hat. Dark shades. Lone Star boots, trimmed in … baby blue? Pink tie? Under Armour backpack? Mullet? Paddack arrived for his first big-league start sporting his own precocious take on Urban Cowboy, and the kid from suburban Austin ended the year pitching like the latest big thing from Texas. In between, Paddack displayed the confidence and tenacity that helped him return from Tommy John surgery, catapult up prospect lists and succeed in The Show after only 33 minor-league starts, and his strong finish after a mid-season slump speaks well of his ability to adjust on the fly. Paddack's fastball sits in the mid 90s and he commands it well, painting the black or drawing empty swings high out of the zone, while his changeup already ranks among the best in the game. Continued development of his inconsistent curveball may be the difference between Paddack becoming a true ace or a solid second starter, and this year there will be no innings restrictions to hold him back—just wide open skies, bluebonnet hillsides and a burble of ZZ Top floating on the breeze.

★ ★ ★ *2020 Top 101 Prospect* **#15** ★ ★ ★

Luis Patiño RHP Born: 10/26/99   Age: 20   Bats: R   Throws: R   Height: 6'0"   Weight: 192   Origin: International Free Agent, 2016

YEAR	TEAM	LVL	AGE	W	L	SV	G	GS	IP	H	HR	BB/9	K/9	K	GB%	BABIP	WHIP	ERA	DRA	WARP	MPH	FB%	WHF	CSP
2017	DPA	RK	17	2	1	0	4	4	16	11	0	1.1	8.4	15	58%	.256	0.81	1.69	1.90	0.7				
2017	PDR	RK	17	2	1	0	9	8	40	32	2	3.6	9.7	43	50%	.286	1.20	2.47	2.60	1.5				
2018	FTW	A	18	6	3	0	17	17	83¹	65	1	2.6	10.6	98	45%	.320	1.07	2.16	2.87	2.3				
2019	LEL	A+	19	6	8	0	18	17	87	61	4	3.5	11.7	113	40%	.278	1.09	2.69	2.71	2.4				
2019	AMA	AA	19	0	0	0	2	2	7²	8	0	4.7	11.7	10	19%	.381	1.57	1.17	4.52	0.0				
2020	*SDN*	*MLB*	*20*	*2*	*2*	*0*	*33*	*0*	*35*	*34*	*5*	*3.6*	*9.8*	*38*	*37%*	*.315*	*1.37*	*4.45*	*4.49*	*0.4*				

Comparables: Mike Soroka, Taijuan Walker, Jordan Lyles

The most impressive thing about Patiño's 2019 season wasn't how he breezed through the California League as a teenager; it was the way he matured throughout the year from thrower to pitcher. His darting slider misses bats, but his bread and butter is a lively high-90s fastball, which was enough to dominate lower leagues but couldn't stand on its own against more advanced hitters. As the year wore on, Patiño cut his walk rate, improved his command and worked on his changeup, which has grown into more than a show-me pitch. He'll be tested in Double-A this summer and has yet to shoulder a heavy innings load, but Patiño's raw stuff and improving pitchability gives him a Sistene ceiling.

Luis Perdomo RHP Born: 05/09/93   Age: 27   Bats: R   Throws: R   Height: 6'2"   Weight: 185   Origin: International Free Agent, 2003

YEAR	TEAM	LVL	AGE	W	L	SV	G	GS	IP	H	HR	BB/9	K/9	K	GB%	BABIP	WHIP	ERA	DRA	WARP	MPH	FB%	WHF	CSP
2017	SDN	MLB	24	8	11	0	29	29	163²	182	17	3.6	6.5	118	62%	.325	1.51	4.67	4.96	1.1	96.3	62.8	9.6	47.1
2018	ELP	AAA	25	6	3	0	13	13	75	72	12	2.5	7.3	61	57%	.284	1.24	3.72	3.38	1.8				
2018	SDN	MLB	25	1	6	0	12	10	44²	62	4	4.4	7.9	39	44%	.389	1.88	7.05	6.52	-0.6	95.6	63	8	47.1
2019	ELP	AAA	26	2	1	1	11	0	15	21	3	2.4	10.2	17	53%	.409	1.67	3.60	5.04	0.2				
2019	SDN	MLB	26	2	4	0	47	1	72	69	6	2.2	6.9	55	54%	.298	1.21	4.00	4.31	0.8	95.8	54.5	9.6	49.4
2020	*SDN*	*MLB*	*27*	*3*	*3*	*0*	*60*	*0*	*64*	*67*	*8*	*3.1*	*7.6*	*54*	*54%*	*.310*	*1.40*	*4.59*	*4.69*	*0.5*	*95.5*	*60.9*	*9.4*	*48.6*

Comparables: Jose Acevedo, James Baldwin, Jakob Junis

The Padres' commitment to the kiddie corps in their rotation sent Old Man Perdomo to the 'pen last year, with perfectly acceptable and mostly forgettable results. His sinker-slider mix featured less of the former and more of the latter, and while his stuff didn't exactly bloom, Perdomo showed improved command in shorter stints. He threw more strikes, cut his walk rate and continued to induce plenty of ground balls, providing his manager with a reliable multi-inning option to clean up someone else's messy start. His future as a mid-rotation stalwart has flown north with the butterflies, but Perdomo can take comfort from the fact that every bullpen needs a janitor.

Drew Pomeranz LHP Born: 11/22/88   Age: 31   Bats: R   Throws: L   Height: 6'6"   Weight: 240   Origin: Round 1, 2010 Draft (#5 overall)

YEAR	TEAM	LVL	AGE	W	L	SV	G	GS	IP	H	HR	BB/9	K/9	K	GB%	BABIP	WHIP	ERA	DRA	WARP	MPH	FB%	WHF	CSP
2017	BOS	MLB	28	17	6	0	32	32	173²	166	19	3.6	9.0	174	45%	.310	1.35	3.32	4.17	2.7	93.8	61.6	10.6	43.1
2018	PAW	AAA	29	0	2	0	5	5	19²	16	7	5.9	5.5	12	58%	.173	1.47	5.49	5.25	0.1				
2018	BOS	MLB	29	2	6	0	26	11	74	87	12	5.4	8.0	66	39%	.344	1.77	6.08	7.90	-2.3	91.8	58.9	7.9	43.7
2019	MIL	MLB	30	0	1	2	25	1	26¹	16	4	2.7	15.4	45	47%	.279	0.91	2.39	0.00	1.6	96.2	63.8	19.5	48.7
2019	SFN	MLB	30	2	9	0	21	17	77²	89	17	4.2	10.7	92	39%	.350	1.61	5.68	5.91	-0.2	94.5	63.8	10.4	48.8
2020	*SDN*	*MLB*	*31*	*3*	*3*	*4*	*60*	*0*	*64*	*59*	*9*	*3.9*	*10.5*	*75*	*41%*	*.306*	*1.36*	*4.30*	*4.45*	*0.7*	*93.0*	*61.4*	*10.6*	*45.4*

Comparables: Danny Duffy, Brian Matusz, Andrew Miller

Starting just isn't for Pomeranz. After another 17 mediocre starts for the Giants (and one spot-start following his midseason trade to Milwaukee), his career ERA in the role was 4.25. The sample size is much smaller for Pomeranz in the bullpen, but he has a career 2.72 ERA (and .596 OPS allowed) in 102 career relief appearances. The velocity increase out of the pen for Pomeranz tells much of the story—his average fastball rose from roughly 92 mph in the season's early months to 95-plus as in August and September. He leaned into it more, too, letting it eat. The Padres believed in Pomeranz's relief dominance enough to hand him a four-year deal worth $34 million.

Cal Quantrill RHP Born: 02/10/95   Age: 25   Bats: L   Throws: R   Height: 6'3"   Weight: 208   Origin: Round 1, 2016 Draft (#8 overall)

YEAR	TEAM	LVL	AGE	W	L	SV	G	GS	IP	H	HR	BB/9	K/9	K	GB%	BABIP	WHIP	ERA	DRA	WARP	MPH	FB%	WHF	CSP
2017	LEL	A+	22	6	5	0	14	14	73²	78	5	2.9	9.3	76	42%	.353	1.38	3.67	4.85	0.4				
2017	SAN	AA	22	1	5	0	8	8	42¹	52	5	3.4	7.2	34	39%	.341	1.61	4.04	6.11	-0.5				
2018	SAN	AA	23	6	5	0	22	22	117	135	12	2.9	7.8	101	45%	.336	1.48	5.15	5.74	-0.5				
2018	ELP	AAA	23	3	1	0	6	6	31	39	4	1.5	6.4	22	50%	.333	1.42	3.48	4.56	0.3				
2019	ELP	AAA	24	4	2	0	7	7	35²	38	3	3.0	8.3	33	52%	.324	1.40	4.54	3.78	1.0				
2019	SDN	MLB	24	6	8	0	23	18	103	106	15	2.4	7.8	89	45%	.295	1.30	5.16	4.34	1.5	96.2	56.7	10.8	44.6
2020	*SDN*	*MLB*	*25*	*4*	*4*	*0*	*28*	*10*	*70*	*68*	*10*	*2.9*	*7.5*	*58*	*45%*	*.285*	*1.29*	*4.20*	*4.45*	*1.0*	*95.9*	*58.1*	*11.1*	*45.7*

Comparables: Mike Mayers, Mike Wright, Trevor Williams

Quantrill's performance has consistently lagged behind his raw stuff and pedigree, ever since the Padres made him the eighth-overall pick in 2016, and his first spin through the senior circuit was more of the same. On the plus side, righties continually pounded his mid-90s fastball and sinker into the ground and swung through his slider and changeup en route to a miniscule .217/.243/.337 line with a 44:6 whiff-to-walk ratio. Unfortunately for Quantrill, his once-vaunted changeup did nothing to stop lefties from staging a nightly laser show. He doesn't have a true wipeout offering, but he keeps his walks in check, and if Quantrill can leverage some sort of voodoo to tame the lefties that have tortured him, he might be able to survive at the end of the rotation.

Gerardo Reyes RHP   Born: 05/13/93   Age: 27   Bats: R   Throws: R   Height: 5'11"   Weight: 160   Origin: Undrafted Free Agent, 2013

YEAR	TEAM	LVL	AGE	W	L	SV	G	GS	IP	H	HR	BB/9	K/9	K	GB%	BABIP	WHIP	ERA	DRA	WARP	MPH	FB%	WHF	CSP
2017	LEL	A+	24	3	3	5	47	0	61²	54	3	4.5	9.5	65	51%	.317	1.38	2.63	4.02	0.6				
2018	LEL	A+	25	0	1	1	14	0	16¹	11	0	6.6	11.0	20	43%	.297	1.41	2.20	3.30	0.3				
2018	SAN	AA	25	1	2	1	31	0	39	32	1	3.9	11.3	49	39%	.323	1.26	3.00	3.59	0.6				
2019	ELP	AAA	26	4	2	3	34	0	45¹	39	8	4.0	12.1	61	35%	.310	1.30	3.57	3.56	1.2				
2019	SDN	MLB	26	4	0	0	27	0	26	24	3	3.8	13.2	38	40%	.339	1.35	7.62	3.30	0.6	99.0	73.6	18.1	48.6
2020	SDN	MLB	27	2	2	0	36	0	38	31	5	4.3	12.4	52	37%	.299	1.28	3.95	4.08	0.6	98.5	74.5	18.3	49.2

Comparables: Colton Murray, Brandon Cunniff, Ryan Garton

Yet another San Diego bullpen centurion, Reyes is a joy to watch as he uncoils his short, slight frame and unleashes upper-90s heat from a sidearm slot with a windmill kick finish. When he's on, he fills the zone, and opposing righties have no chance to pick up the spin of his slider or catch up to his fastball; when he's off, he walks the yard and lefties take him to the woodshed. Reyes shuttled between El Paso and San Diego a half-dozen times last year and he never found a consistent groove, but the Padres will likely give the once-anonymous free agent from Galveston College every chance to make a name for himself in middle relief.

Garrett Richards RHP   Born: 05/27/88   Age: 32   Bats: R   Throws: R   Height: 6'3"   Weight: 210   Origin: Round 1, 2009 Draft (#42 overall)

YEAR	TEAM	LVL	AGE	W	L	SV	G	GS	IP	H	HR	BB/9	K/9	K	GB%	BABIP	WHIP	ERA	DRA	WARP	MPH	FB%	WHF	CSP
2017	LAA	MLB	29	0	2	0	6	6	27²	18	1	2.3	8.8	27	55%	.233	0.90	2.28	3.12	0.8	97.5	58.2	13.2	43.8
2018	LAA	MLB	30	5	4	0	16	16	76¹	64	11	4.0	10.3	87	50%	.277	1.28	3.66	3.73	1.4	97.8	50.4	12.3	47.5
2019	LEL	A+	31	0	1	0	3	3	6²	8	1	10.8	10.8	8	47%	.389	2.40	8.10	8.95	-0.3				
2019	SDN	MLB	31	0	1	0	3	3	8²	10	2	6.2	11.4	11	46%	.364	1.85	8.31	3.75	0.2	96.3	58	11.5	45
2020	SDN	MLB	32	8	8	0	24	24	134	116	16	3.7	9.9	147	46%	.291	1.28	3.81	3.98	2.7	96.6	52.1	12.2	45.1

Comparables: Tyson Ross, Bob Gibson, Andrew Cashner

The Padres signed Richards to a two-year, $15.5 million contract prior to last season, expecting the long-time, oft-injured Angels star to miss all of 2019 recovering from Tommy John surgery. That Richards was able to make three big-league starts was a bonus; that he struggled mightily with his control was unsurprising. The important thing is, his estimable stuff—a heavy mid-90s fastball, hard slider and usable curve—seems to have survived the knife. The idea has always been for Richards to return in 2020 and provide veteran leadership to the young Padres rotation, and with a normal offseason to regain his command and stretch out his arm, he'll likely post above-average numbers. That is, if he's healthy. Having lost most of the last four seasons to injury, that will always be the question with Richards.

Craig Stammen RHP   Born: 03/09/84   Age: 36   Bats: R   Throws: R   Height: 6'4"   Weight: 230   Origin: Round 12, 2005 Draft (#354 overall)

YEAR	TEAM	LVL	AGE	W	L	SV	G	GS	IP	H	HR	BB/9	K/9	K	GB%	BABIP	WHIP	ERA	DRA	WARP	MPH	FB%	WHF	CSP
2017	SDN	MLB	33	2	3	0	60	0	80¹	68	12	3.1	8.3	74	52%	.263	1.20	3.14	3.76	1.3	93.3	63.3	12.2	44.1
2018	SDN	MLB	34	8	3	0	73	0	79	65	3	1.9	10.0	88	51%	.301	1.04	2.73	2.86	1.9	94.0	67.6	14.6	47
2019	SDN	MLB	35	8	7	4	76	0	82	80	13	1.6	8.0	73	51%	.284	1.16	3.29	4.27	1.0	94.6	72.2	9.8	46
2020	SDN	MLB	36	3	3	0	60	0	64	58	8	2.3	8.3	59	51%	.282	1.16	3.44	3.74	1.2	92.8	67	11.7	44.9

Comparables: Matt Belisle, Chad Qualls, Tim Worrell

Middle relievers live and die by the vagaries of small sample sizes. A starter may struggle through 60 tough innings in April and May, but have the luxury of four more months to right the ship. For a middle reliever, those 60 innings are the full season on which you're judged and eventually compensated. That's what makes Stammen's ability to churn out 80-inning, 3.00 ERA, 1.2 WHIP seasons year after year after year so rare and valuable. His fastball/sinker/slider/curve repertoire is unremarkable, but he throws strikes, generates ground balls and keeps his teammates in games. There are a few warning signs, as Stammen is entering his late thirties with a swinging strike rate that has dropped below 10 percent for the first time in a decade, but betting against him still feels like betting against the sun rising.

Matt Strahm LHP   Born: 11/12/91   Age: 28   Bats: R   Throws: L   Height: 6'3"   Weight: 185   Origin: Round 21, 2012 Draft (#643 overall)

YEAR	TEAM	LVL	AGE	W	L	SV	G	GS	IP	H	HR	BB/9	K/9	K	GB%	BABIP	WHIP	ERA	DRA	WARP	MPH	FB%	WHF	CSP
2017	KCA	MLB	25	2	5	0	24	3	34²	30	6	5.7	9.6	37	42%	.279	1.50	5.45	5.80	-0.2	96.1	67.3	11.2	49.1
2018	SAN	AA	26	1	0	0	9	2	14¹	14	1	2.5	13.8	22	42%	.406	1.26	2.51	3.11	0.3				
2018	SDN	MLB	26	3	4	0	41	5	61¹	39	6	3.1	10.1	69	37%	.226	0.98	2.05	3.96	0.7	96.0	58	13.3	52.9
2019	SDN	MLB	27	6	11	0	46	16	114²	121	22	1.7	9.3	118	38%	.308	1.25	4.71	4.29	1.7	94.0	38.2	11.8	53.9
2020	SDN	MLB	28	2	2	0	48	0	51	45	8	2.5	9.2	52	38%	.276	1.16	3.77	4.06	0.8	94.2	47.7	12.2	52.7

Comparables: Hansel Robles, Brock Stewart, Mike Clevinger

Strahm struggled out of the gate in the San Diego rotation but once again proved electric in a relief role. After moving to the 'pen lefties were doomed when he was on the mound, posting a .137/.185/.294 line, and overall, batters lost 200 points of OPS facing PenStrahm compared to StartStrahm. The lean, leonine lefty possesses a broad four-pitch mix, but his stuff plays up in shorter stints and with certain matchups, making it likely his future lies in relief. It remains a bright one.

Trey Wingenter RHP Born: 04/15/94 Age: 26 Bats: R Throws: R Height: 6'7" Weight: 200 Origin: Round 17, 2015 Draft (#507 overall)

YEAR	TEAM	LVL	AGE	W	L	SV	G	GS	IP	H	HR	BB/9	K/9	K	GB%	BABIP	WHIP	ERA	DRA	WARP	MPH	FB%	WHF	CSP
2017	SAN	AA	23	2	1	20	49	0	47²	33	6	3.6	12.1	64	52%	.262	1.09	2.45	3.24	0.9				
2018	ELP	AAA	24	3	3	4	40	0	44¹	29	4	4.9	10.8	53	48%	.250	1.20	3.45	2.57	1.3				
2018	SDN	MLB	24	0	0	0	22	0	19	13	3	5.2	12.8	27	40%	.256	1.26	3.79	2.84	0.5	99.8	68.6	18.3	49.5
2019	SDN	MLB	25	1	3	1	51	1	51	34	5	4.9	12.7	72	37%	.269	1.22	5.65	3.55	1.0	98.1	55	16.7	45.2
2020	SDN	MLB	26	3	2	0	48	0	51	38	6	4.8	12.9	73	40%	.292	1.28	3.80	3.87	0.9	98.1	59.1	17.4	47.9

Comparables: Ryan Meisinger, Brad Boxberger, Ian Gibaut

Like the Padres as a whole, Wingenter flashed tremendous talent that never seemed to consistently produce strikes, outs and wins. As a young Padres reliever his high-90s heat is assured, and he abets it with a slider that flashes plus. But there's a lot of Wingenter to get moving in a coordinated fashion, and the young Alabaman can struggle with his mechanics and lose the plate. A few disasterpiece outings roughed up his overall numbers, but Wingenter's elite ability to miss bats will earn him plenty more chances to improve his command and become a late-inning leviathan.

Kirby Yates RHP Born: 03/25/87 Age: 33 Bats: L Throws: R Height: 5'10" Weight: 210 Origin: Round 26, 2005 Draft (#798 overall)

YEAR	TEAM	LVL	AGE	W	L	SV	G	GS	IP	H	HR	BB/9	K/9	K	GB%	BABIP	WHIP	ERA	DRA	WARP	MPH	FB%	WHF	CSP
2017	SLC	AAA	30	0	0	1	6	0	7	8	0	3.9	18.0	14	60%	.533	1.57	2.57	2.07	0.2				
2017	LAA	MLB	30	0	0	0	1	0	1	2	2	0.0	9.0	1	0%	.000	2.00	18.00	9.07	0.0	95.3	50	12.5	53.8
2017	SDN	MLB	30	4	5	1	61	0	55²	42	10	3.1	14.1	87	30%	.296	1.10	3.72	3.10	1.3	95.6	62.9	18.8	48.3
2018	SDN	MLB	31	5	3	12	65	0	63	41	6	2.4	12.9	90	43%	.263	0.92	2.14	1.92	2.2	95.8	58.3	18.6	43.2
2019	SDN	MLB	32	0	5	41	60	0	60²	41	2	1.9	15.0	101	48%	.325	0.89	1.19	2.03	2.2	94.8	57.1	17.1	44.4
2020	SDN	MLB	33	3	3	35	60	0	64	46	8	3.0	13.2	94	44%	.288	1.05	2.80	3.05	1.6	94.3	58.1	17.8	44.4

Comparables: Kevin Whelan, Zac Rosscup, Brandon Gomes

Ever since Bruce Sutter made the best hitters in the world look like they were swinging at an invisible feather, the splitter has been the most visually apt expression of a closer's dominance. Yates is the current split master, riding his tumbling terror to his first All-Star game last year and pacing the senior circuit in saves. The Kauai native upped his strikeout rate, cut his already low walk rate and kept the ball in the yard better than ever, leading to one of the top reliever seasons in baseball history by FIP and DRA. In a San Diego bullpen bursting with flame-throwing tyros, it's satisfying that the top dog is an undrafted, twice-sold, twice-released journeyman with a low-90s fastball who found success in his 30s with great command and a newfound pitch.

LINEOUTS

Hitters

HITTER	POS	TEAM	LVL	AGE	PA	R	2B	3B	HR	RBI	BB	K	SB	CS	AVG/OBP/SLG	DRC+	VORP	BABIP	BRR	FRAA	WARP
Gabriel Arias	SS	LEL	A+	19	511	62	21	4	17	75	25	128	8	4	.302/.339/.470	122	51.6	.378	1.5	SS(103): -11.4, 3B(10): 1.4	2.1
Allen Córdoba	UT	LEL	A+	23	470	68	20	6	5	43	31	77	32	11	.301/.367/.412	127	39.1	.357	7.2	3B(40): 4.4, LF(39): 2.5	4.0
Jake Cronenworth	UT	DUR	AAA	25	406	75	26	4	10	45	49	62	12	5	.334/.429/.520	138	39.6	.382	0.7	SS(64): -1.7, 2B(11): 1.3	3.4
Michael Gettys	CF	ELP	AAA	23	551	97	29	5	31	91	33	168	14	6	.256/.305/.517	79	11.3	.315	-0.9	CF(66): 2.6, LF(31): 1.9	1.0
Hudson Head	CF	PDR	Rk	18	141	19	7	3	1	12	15	29	3	3	.283/.383/.417	125	8.9	.363	-0.3	CF(26): -5.9	0.1
Tucupita Marcano	INF	FTW	A	19	504	55	19	3	2	45	35	45	15	16	.270/.323/.337	92	7.6	.293	-2.9	3B(42): -1.1, SS(40): -5.6	0.3
Owen Miller	INF	AMA	AA	22	560	76	28	2	13	68	46	86	5	5	.290/.355/.430	112	23.0	.328	1.3	SS(70): 5.1, 2B(48): 0.5	3.4
Edward Olivares	OF	AMA	AA	23	551	85	25	2	18	77	43	98	35	10	.283/.349/.453	114	25.3	.317	3.7	RF(104): 5.5, CF(19): -0.1	2.9
Jorge Oña	LF	AMA	AA	22	103	11	2	0	5	18	11	26	2	1	.348/.417/.539	170	8.0	.433	0.7	LF(15): -2.3	0.6
Tirso Ornelas	RF	LEL	A+	19	379	41	11	5	1	30	44	91	3	1	.220/.309/.292	67	-5.0	.296	-1.8	RF(75): -2.9, CF(3): 0.2	-0.9
	RF	PDR	Rk	19	97	6	2	0	0	11	9	22	4	0	.205/.278/.227	51	-5.5	.273	0.7	RF(19): -0.7, CF(1): 0.0	-0.2
Hudson Potts	INF	AMA	AA	20	448	56	23	1	16	59	32	128	3	1	.227/.290/.406	58	0.2	.288	-1.7	3B(85): -6.4, 2B(19): -0.7	-1.2
Boog Powell	CF	ELP	AAA	26	403	66	25	1	8	37	59	94	14	0	.288/.391/.438	94	12.4	.373	1.0	CF(51): -1.3, LF(33): 2.6	1.0
Esteban Quiroz	2B	ELP	AAA	27	366	64	25	0	19	66	52	82	3	1	.271/.384/.539	120	24.2	.309	0.7	2B(76): 0.0, SS(5): -1.1	2.0
Buddy Reed	OF	AMA	AA	24	441	49	15	2	14	50	42	126	23	8	.228/.310/.388	84	11.6	.294	4.7	CF(74): 2.7, LF(27): 2.7	2.0
Jeisson Rosario	CF	LEL	A+	19	525	67	14	4	3	35	87	114	11	4	.242/.372/.314	118	31.5	.322	4.3	CF(110): 0.6, LF(5): 1.7	3.3
Esteury Ruiz	2B	LEL	A+	20	380	45	18	2	6	36	26	101	34	11	.239/.300/.357	71	9.4	.319	3.7	2B(75): -7.9, LF(12): 0.2	-0.5

Last season's addition of power to his already superlative glove and cannon arm gives Venezuelan teenager **Gabriel Arias** a first-division shortstop's ceiling, but his free-swinging ways will likely keep him from reaching it. ⊗ Former Rule 5 martyr **Allen Córdoba** recovered from injury and a season's worth of big-league PTSD to post a bounce-back year in High-A; having moved from shortstop to left field while flashing speed and contact skills, his ceiling is late-career Lonnie Smith without the walks. ⊗ One of a new breed of "utility pitchers," **Jake Cronenworth** was the minor league player of the year for the Durham Bulls. ⊗ **Michael Gettys** has speed, plus range in center, a rifle arm and a newly-minted El Paso home run record; he may be the most powerful Chihuahua in history, but his career-long propensity to chase strike three makes it unlikely he'll spend much time playing with the big dogs. ⊗ Ambidextrous high school quarterback **Hudson Head** used both hands to dig into his $3 million bonus (a third-round record) while flashing speed, a strong arm, power potential and a surprisingly mature approach in his Rookie League debut; he has all the tools you look for in an All-Star center fielder. ⊗ Like most teenagers, **Tucupita Marcano** couldn't wait to get out of Fort Wayne and move to the coast, taking his high-contact speed game to Lake Elsinore for the High-A playoffs. He likely won't hit for power, but natural bat-to-ball skills and a high baseball IQ could earn him a utility infield spot some day. ⊗ From Ozaukee to Normal to Amarillo, **Owen Miller** has hit every place they bother to chalk lines, is a solid defender and held his own during an aggressive full-season debut in Double-A; his arm is stretched at shortstop and his line-drive stroke isn't geared for power, but the young Sconnie fits the profile of a bat-first second sacker. ⊗ **Edward Olivares** passed his Double-A weeder course last summer while setting career highs in batting average, OBP, home runs and steals. He's not a plus center fielder but has the arm for right and his power/speed combo will work well as a fourth outfielder. ⓧ Despite a season cut short by shoulder surgery, **Jorge Oña** hit so well it made watching Jorge Oña play defense seem palatable. Given the depth of the system and the roughness of his edges, the Padres gambled a bit when they added him to the 40-man, but the upside is sizable. ⓧ It's all about the projection for **Tirso Ornelas**, who cratered in his first full professional season but made strides at the plate after reworking his swing. The Tijuana native possesses the mature approach, athleticism, power potential and makeup to grow into a productive right fielder. ⓧ Former first-round pick **Hudson Potts** spent last summer too young to order a Shiner Bock in Amarillo, where he struggled to make contact but improved as the season wore on; a return Double-A engagement should help sort out whether his prospect buzz has gone flat or heady days as a hot corner power bat are in his future. ⓧ After cracking eight home runs in El Paso's launching pad last summer Boog The Younger is now only 371 dingers away from becoming the most powerful **Boog Powell** in the history of professional baseball. Then again, gentle reader, you yourself are only 399 away. ⓧ The sheer volume of 2019 PCL breakouts makes it difficult to sort the true-talent wheat from the ball-boosted chaff, but **Esteban Quiroz** has a good case to be considered among the former: namely, a knack for getting on base nearly 40 percent of the time. The time is ripe for the 28-year-old to see at least a grain of major-league experience in 2020. ⓧ His name may sound like he played drums with Charlie Parker, but **Buddy Reed** is actually a switch-hitting center fielder with elite speed and athleticism whose inability to find any consistent rhythm in the batter's box will likely keep him from bebopping his way to The Show. ⓧ Sure, signing a five-tool 16-year-old wunderkind like **Emmanuel Rodriguez** for $2.5 million is cool, but have you tried turning one of those guys into a productive big-leaguer in less than six years? ⓧ **Jeisson Rosario** showed off plus defensive chops in the center pasture and a surprisingly patient approach for a teenager in High-A, though he struggled to make consistent contact. The tools are here for him to grow into the top-of-the-order lefty pest every team craves. ⓧ Even in a Padres organization overstuffed with premium talent, **Esteury Ruiz** is notable for his speed and raw athleticism, but the young Dominican has shown a propensity to chase, struggles to make consistent contact and is a poor defender at the keystone; he's still only 21, but a slide down the defensive spectrum will make it even less likely his bat will play.

Pitchers

PITCHER	TEAM	LVL	AGE	W	L	SV	G	GS	IP	H	HR	BB/9	K/9	K	GB%	BABIP	WHIP	ERA	DRA	WARP	MPH	FB%	WHF	CSP
Pedro Avila	PDR	Rk	22	0	1	0	3	2	10	5	0	1.8	13.5	15	40%	.250	0.70	0.90	1.91	0.4				
	AMA	AA	22	0	2	0	3	3	12	14	4	4.5	9.8	13	33%	.312	1.67	8.25	6.37	-0.2				
	SDN	MLB	22	0	0	0	1	1	5¹	4	0	3.4	8.4	5	40%	.267	1.12	1.69	4.41	0.1	95.8	29.4	9.4	54
David Bednar	AMA	AA	24	2	5	14	44	0	58	49	4	2.8	13.3	86	50%	.349	1.16	2.95	3.36	0.9				
	SDN	MLB	24	0	2	0	13	0	11	10	3	4.1	11.5	14	34%	.269	1.36	6.55	4.50	0.1	96.5	43.4	15.3	50.4
Ronald Bolaños	LEL	A+	22	5	2	0	10	10	53²	37	4	3.9	9.1	54	50%	.244	1.12	2.85	3.37	1.1				
	AMA	AA	22	8	5	0	15	13	76²	71	7	3.5	10.3	88	48%	.335	1.32	4.23	4.88	0.0				
	SDN	MLB	22	0	2	0	5	3	19²	17	3	5.5	8.7	19	41%	.264	1.47	5.95	6.03	-0.1	97.9	62.7	9.8	44.5
Joey Cantillo	FTW	A	19	9	3	0	19	19	98	58	3	2.5	11.8	128	46%	.264	0.87	1.93	2.18	3.5				
	LEL	A+	19	1	1	0	3	3	13²	12	4	4.6	10.5	16	38%	.270	1.39	4.61	3.75	0.2				
Henry Henry	FTW	A	20	7	5	10	43	0	81¹	73	3	1.8	8.9	80	50%	.300	1.09	3.32	3.64	1.1				
Reggie Lawson	AMA	AA	21	3	1	0	6	6	27²	28	4	4.2	11.7	36	39%	.353	1.48	5.20	4.99	0.0				
Aaron Loup	SDN	MLB	31	0	0	0	4	0	3¹	2	0	2.7	13.5	5	57%	.286	0.90	0.00	4.43	0.0	93.6	43.4	15.1	48.5
Jacob Nix	LEL	A+	23	0	2	0	2	2	8²	10	1	3.1	11.4	11	63%	.346	1.50	3.12	3.90	0.1				
	ELP	AAA	23	1	0	0	2	2	11	7	1	0.8	9.8	12	42%	.240	0.73	0.82	2.22	0.5				
Franklin Van Gurp	AUG	A	23	2	0	4	16	0	28²	21	4	2.8	12.6	40	45%	.270	1.05	3.77	3.34	0.5				
	FTW	A	23	0	1	1	9	0	15²	16	0	2.9	9.2	16	49%	.372	1.34	2.87	4.47	0.1				
	LEL	A+	23	1	3	0	14	0	18¹	26	0	7.4	9.3	19	40%	.448	2.24	6.38	10.25	-1.2				
Ryan Weathers	FTW	A	19	3	7	0	22	22	96	101	6	1.7	8.4	90	46%	.347	1.24	3.84	5.46	-0.3				
Jimmy Yacabonis	NOR	AAA	27	2	2	2	17	0	24	26	2	5.6	8.2	22	51%	.316	1.71	4.50	6.07	0.0				
	BAL	MLB	27	1	2	0	29	4	41	51	9	5.3	7.2	33	36%	.336	1.83	6.80	8.17	-1.2	95.5	63.5	9.7	44

Over a 10-day span in April **Pedro Avila** experienced both the zenith and nadir of baseball prospectdom, baffling the Diamondbacks over five-plus innings in a triumphant debut before hurting his elbow in his next Texas League start; he'll spend 2020 recovering from last fall's Tommy John surgery. ⓧ Former 35th-round pick **David Bednar** has ridden a mid-90s fastball, a functional curve and a splitter he learned from Hideo Nomo all the way from Lafayette University to the San Diego 'pen; there's enough swing-and-miss here to envision a solid career in middle relief. ⓧ Live-armed Cuban **Ronald Bolaños** rode his mid-90s heat all the way from High-A to San Diego last year, but spotty control, indifferent secondaries and inconsistent mechanics may well send him to the bullpen. ⓧ A rare Padres pitching prospect who doesn't light up radar guns, **Joey Cantillo** dominated the Midwest League as a teenager with advanced pitchability and tremendous feel for his plus changeup; if the same tricks work this year against more advanced hitters he'll vault up prospect lists. ⓧ Another year, another setback for former top prospect **Anderson Espinoza**, as he underwent his second Tommy John procedure last April. ⓧ The Padres moved **Henry Henry** to the Fort Wayne bullpen last year, with encouraging results; his fastball/slider mix may not match the high octane stuff of so many other San Diego relief prospects, but he probably has a leg up on repeating his delivery. ⓧ **Brett Kennedy** wasn't particularly good for the Padres in 2018 and isn't particularly healthy now, as spring training arm fatigue that morphed into a bum shoulder kept him on the shelf all last season. ⓧ Long, lean **Reggie Lawson** only made six starts in Amarillo before experiencing elbow pain; he avoided surgery and resurfaced in the Arizona Fall League, where his mid-90s fastball and potentially plus curve delivered reasonable impersonations of big-league offerings. ⓧ Lefty sidearmer **Aaron Loup**'s first foray into free agency featured $1.4 million earned and 14 batters faced before his second elbow injury in as many years landed him on the shelf. ⓧ "There is only one thing in life worse than being talked about, and that is not being talked about," said Oscar Wilde. "Unless you're a fringy young starter in a loaded organization who just sat out a full year with a sore elbow and is making headlines after getting wasted, and allegedly trying to enter a stranger's house through the doggy door and getting yourself kicked, tased and arrested," added **Jacob Nix**. ⓧ **Franklin Van Gurp**, of the Saint Maarten Van Gurps, has completed his schooling at Chipola and Florida International and is pursuing a career in the entertainment industry. After his involvement in last June's Alex Dickerson trade, he summered in Lake Elsinore and Fort Wayne, where he spent his days tossing sinkers and sliders and handing out way too many free passes. ⓧ Top 2018 pick **Ryan Weathers** got off to a great start in his full-season debut before losing a month to a forearm issue and struggling through diminished velocity the rest of the way. ⓧ The twelfth time someone gets optioned, no matter how many different roles they've pitched in or how good their arm is, it can be considered the cost of doing business. But **Jimmy Yacabonis** was optioned a thirteenth time in August and the Orioles finally had enough, banishing him to Triple-A.

SAN FRANCISCO GIANTS

Essay by Eric Nusbaum

Player comments by Bryan Grosnick and BP staff

What is the difference between the San Francisco Giants and the Los Angeles Dodgers?

This is a dumb question.

Everything. The answer is everything. The Giants and Dodgers are complete opposites, and that opposition is, on the deepest particle level, what defines them, and it's been that way since the two franchises set out for California, hand-in-hand in the sunny spring of 1958. Hell, it may have been that way going back years earlier, to when they were sharing New York with the Yankees.

Manhattan and Brooklyn. San Francisco and LA. There are no Giants without Dodgers; there are no Dodgers without Giants. At least not like this. Black and orange. Pantone 294.

Just look at the previous decade. The Giants' story is one of highs and lows and inexplicable good vibes—of mediocrity punctuated by tremendous postseason success. Random misfits performing the feats of mythical heroes. Washed up Édgar Rentería and charmingly goofy Hunter Pence. A guy called, in all sincerity, Big Panda. The Giants' story is one of magic. The Dodgers' story, on the other hand, is one of cold and calculated and ruthless victory—and also, in that most crucial of ways—devastating futility.

I must confess here, that I was born and raised a Dodger fan. I once had a Coke thrown at me at Candlestick Park as a kid. But even I think it's good that things are this way. It's good that the Giants are the Giants and the Dodgers are the Dodgers. I wouldn't un-throw that Coke if I could. (I might send Alex Gordon in Game Seven of the 2014 World Series, though.)

One of the beautiful things about baseball is that every one of the 30 big league franchises has its own identity, and its own sensibility. But that version of the sport is fading away. We are entering a decade of same-ball. Of baseball by best practice. Thanks to the plentiful and increasing amount of data available to decision makers, everything from player evaluation practices to player development techniques is aligning. The search for an edge is becoming increasingly marginal, and increasingly distant from the actual game played on the field.

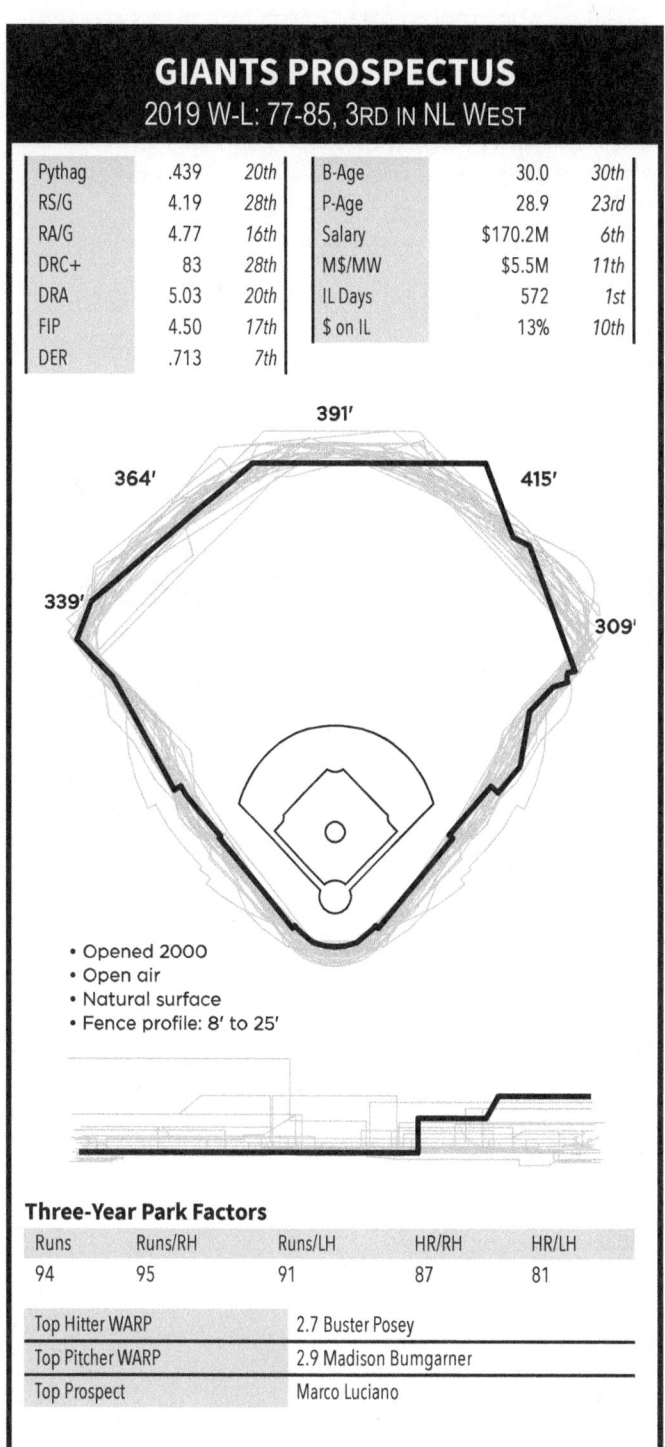

GIANTS PROSPECTUS
2019 W-L: 77-85, 3RD IN NL WEST

Pythag	.439	20th	B-Age	30.0	30th
RS/G	4.19	28th	P-Age	28.9	23rd
RA/G	4.77	16th	Salary	$170.2M	6th
DRC+	83	28th	M$/MW	$5.5M	11th
DRA	5.03	20th	IL Days	572	1st
FIP	4.50	17th	$ on IL	13%	10th
DER	.713	7th			

391'
364'
415'
339'
309'

- Opened 2000
- Open air
- Natural surface
- Fence profile: 8' to 25'

Three-Year Park Factors

Runs	Runs/RH	Runs/LH	HR/RH	HR/LH
94	95	91	87	81

Top Hitter WARP	2.7 Buster Posey
Top Pitcher WARP	2.9 Madison Bumgarner
Top Prospect	Marco Luciano

2019 Hit List Ranking

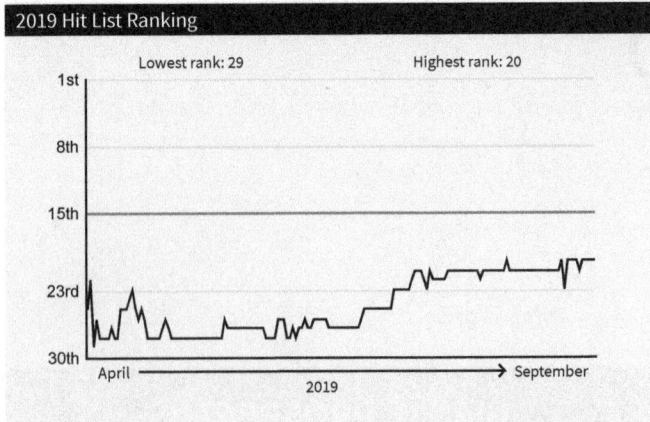

Lowest rank: 29   Highest rank: 20

April ——— 2019 ———→ September

Committed Payroll (in millions)

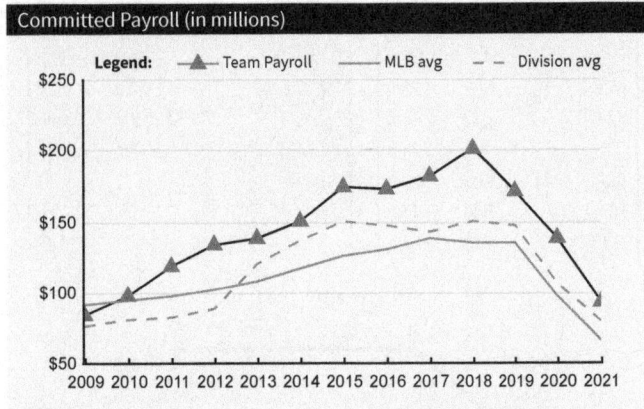

Legend: ▲ Team Payroll   —— MLB avg   - - - Division avg

Farm System Ranking

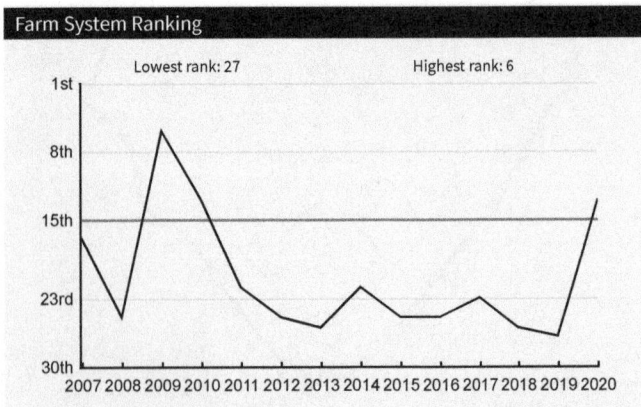

Lowest rank: 27   Highest rank: 6

Personnel

President, Baseball Operations
Farhan Zaidi

Executive Vice President of Baseball Operations
Brian Sabean

General Manager
Scott Harris

Vice President of Baseball Operations
Yeshayah Goldfarb

Manager
Gabe Kapler

The Giants of the early 2010s did not play that version of baseball. They were all angles, and no launch. In fact, they may have been the last great weird-ball dynasty. But that era is over. You don't even have to squint. Bruce Bochy is gone. Madison Bumgarner has gone to Arizona to literally tend his horses. Even Buster Posey is kind of just a guy now. The team's lack of success over the last five years might just have been one of those down cycles that even the greatest franchises can't avoid, it might just have been the result of a few bad breaks. Or maybe the Giants were getting left behind.

No longer. Before last season, the Giants hired Farhan Zaidi away from the Dodgers to run their baseball operations. Under Zaidi, they slowly began the process of remaking themselves as a hip, sleek data-driven franchise. They began to smooth out those angles. In some cases, this has been unceremonious. Joe Panik was quietly dismissed last August. Bochy was replaced by a man who seems, at least to relative outsiders, like his complete opposite in Gabe Kapler. But for the most part, the remaking of the Giants under Zaidi and his chosen general manager Scott Harris has been a quiet process.

To examine the list of transactions since Zaidi took office is the baseball equivalent of watching a time-lapse video of, like, a remote cliffside eroding over millennia. These transaction lists are their own form of quiet poetry. A roster gradually unmaking itself. The rhythmic crashing of waves, the rising and falling of tides, almost hypnotic in their smallness and their consistency. Aaron Altherr in and Aaron Altherr out. Tom Murphy in and Tom Murphy out. Hanser Alberto in and Hanser Alberto out. Yangervis Solarte. Connor Joe. Nick Vincent. Tyler Austin.

Jerry Dipoto has his trades. Farhan Zaidi has these quiet marginal moves. These tiny, intimate dramas. Sometimes the tides roll out. Sometimes you stumble on a Mike Yastrzemski. And in this way Zaidi has begun to unmake the Giants of Brian Sabean and Bobby Evans. Not in a sweeping way, but slowly, from the bottom up. One wave at a time until all that's left is Posey, standing on his tip toes, trying to keep his head above water.

The early offseason was more of the same. The Giants said goodbye to Bumgarner and Panda; to Bochy. They bought a nice prospect in Will Wilson by taking on the contract of injured Zack Cozart. This was exactly the kind of smart move that a wealthy franchise in a theoretical rebuilding state should be making. (By the way, even if he never plays a single inning in San Francisco Cozart is such a Giants guy.) But while it's a smart move, it's also a sort of clue. For the first time since before they signed Barry Bonds, the Giants franchise feels kind of small. This is not necessarily a bad thing—unless you're a Giants fan hoping for October glory right this minute.

They bring back a core of average-ish but established players. Joining Posey are Evan Longoria and Johnny Cueto and their contracts. Brandon Belt is still around, and for karmic reasons, it would be nice if he stayed healthy enough to enjoy the new dimensions at Oracle Park. Brandon Crawford is still around too, but barely. He was historically bad at the plate last year, and Kapler has already implied that he might not be an everyday player come 2020.

The rotation additions have been fine. Tyler Anderson and Kevin Gausman can and should eat innings alongside Cueto and Jeff Samardzija. They may even do a little better than that. Grant Brisbee, writing in The Athletic, implied that maybe Gausman could find his potential and morph into the next Jason Schmidt—and honestly, that seems plausible. There's upside!

But let's be honest, it would take a miracle for the Giants to actually compete. They are building toward some unspecified date in the future, when the coaching staff and player development apparatus are fully aligned, and that first wave of young controllable talent hits the big leagues. When they can become one of those unstoppable baseball machines with depth and maneuverability and players doing this and that. They are building toward becoming a Dodgers.

Even the manager they chose, Gabe Kapler, has his roots, like Zaidi, in the relatively recent Dodgers front office juggernaut. Before his short stint with the Phillies, Kapler was a player development director in LA, and the runner-up to Dave Roberts for that managerial opening after the 2015 season. Kapler comes with a bigger personality, and a more highly scrutinized history, than most managerial types. There's the lifestyle blog he had, there's the hyperenthusiastic personality, there's the embrace of nontraditional ideas (some of them are pretty normal; only in baseball would an executive be ridiculed for thinking it was a good idea for pro athletes to—gasp—eat healthy food); there's also the fact that he was accused of mishandling an assault case involving Dodger minor leaguers, and of firing Nick Francona for suffering from PTSD.

But if there *is* a miracle for the Giants, if they do compete ahead of schedule, it will probably have something to do with Kapler, and his, ahem, giant staff of coaches. The Giants will enter the season with at least three hitting coaches and three pitching coaches, including "pitching director" Brian Bannister who was lured away from the Red Sox. In his early interviews with San Francisco media, Kapler has stressed and restressed the idea of teaching at the major-league level. Those mediocre-to-solid old dudes who have been around forever don't necessarily have to stay mediocre or decline like we might expect them to; those fringe Zaidi pickups don't necessarily have to stay fringe. They may not all be Max Muncys, or even Mike Yastrzemskis—but they can contribute to a winning roster.

And this is it: a plausible, and somewhat interesting path forward for a franchise that has always seemed to find one; a successful end result of Zaidi's tinkering. The truth is, for all of the best practices they might share, and all their executive DNA they actually do share, it wouldn't be the worst thing for the Giants to start looking more like the Dodgers or vice versa; it would mean a competitive division year in and year out for the first time in a long time. It would mean a rivalry that pushes both teams to improve, to open their wallets, to nudge forward against whatever invisible forces are holding them back. Hell, it may force them to be creative, and find new ways to be different.

After all, these were the teams that brought baseball to the west coast. These were the teams that once upon a time, stretched the sport into its truly national form. The Giants never got the credit they deserved for that. But maybe the franchise that's been more stable than any—only 4 managers since 1993!—will be the one to shake things up.

—*Eric Nusbaum is a freelance writer and former editor at VICE Sports.*

HITTERS

Abiatal Avelino SS   Born: 02/14/95   Age: 25   Bats: R   Throws: R   Height: 5'11"   Weight: 195   Origin: International Free Agent, 2011

YEAR	TEAM	LVL	AGE	PA	R	2B	3B	HR	RBI	BB	K	SB	CS	AVG/OBP/SLG	DRC+	VORP	BABIP	BRR	FRAA	WARP
2017	TAM	A+	22	34	1	1	0	0	2	2	5	4	0	.219/.265/.250	64	-0.8	.259	0.6	3B(8): 0.5, 2B(2): 0.0	0.1
2017	TRN	AA	22	249	35	12	4	3	28	14	33	4	0	.270/.315/.396	92	12.6	.301	4.4	2B(39): 1.7, SS(16): 0.5	1.3
2017	SWB	AAA	22	68	5	1	1	0	6	5	10	3	1	.213/.284/.262	58	-1.6	.255	0.1	SS(11): 0.0, 3B(6): -0.4	-0.1
2018	TRN	AA	23	211	32	7	2	10	28	18	37	15	4	.337/.392/.553	161	26.5	.375	-0.2	SS(44): 3.4, 2B(2): 0.3	2.7
2018	SWB	AAA	23	290	33	6	6	5	38	14	61	10	2	.252/.291/.372	60	1.3	.308	1.7	SS(52): 3.4, 2B(16): 2.2	0.7
2018	SFN	MLB	23	11	1	0	0	0	0	0	3	0	0	.273/.273/.273	75	0.0	.375	0.2	SS(3): 0.0, 2B(1): -0.1	0.0
2019	SAC	AAA	24	502	70	24	8	12	62	23	84	17	5	.283/.315/.444	74	22.7	.321	4.9	SS(96): -2.8, 2B(11): -0.3	1.0
2019	SFN	MLB	24	8	0	0	0	0	1	1	3	0	0	.286/.375/.286	68	-0.1	.500	-0.9	LF(1): -0.2, SS(1): 0.1	-0.1
2020	SFN	MLB	25	70	6	3	0	1	6	3	15	2	1	.228/.268/.336	61	-1.2	.277	0.1	SS 0, LF 0	-0.1

Comparables: Yairo Muñoz, Eduardo Escobar, Tim Lopes

The most important thing about Avelino's 2019 season might be that he was able to hold onto some of his 2018 power surge, hitting a dozen homers at Triple-A and supplementing it with "tricky-speedster slugging": eight triples that belied his combination of gap power and foot speed. Here's a speedy, solid defensive infielder with versatility and a little pop on a team that struggled in the infield in 2019 so ... naturally Bruce Bochy gave plate appearances to veterans like Donovan Solano, Pablo Sandoval and Cristhian Adames instead. With the Giants perhaps drifting even further into rebuilding mode in 2020, perhaps Avelino will get more chances during this coming year, but he'll likely need to improve his on-base skills to endear himself to Gabe Kapler and establish himself as a regular.

─────────────── ★ ★ ★ *2020 Top 101 Prospect* **#25** ★ ★ ★ ───────────────

Joey Bart C Born: 12/15/96 Age: 23 Bats: R Throws: R Height: 6'3" Weight: 235 Origin: Round 1, 2018 Draft (#2 overall)

YEAR	TEAM	LVL	AGE	PA	R	2B	3B	HR	RBI	BB	K	SB	CS	AVG/OBP/SLG	DRC+	VORP	BABIP	BRR	FRAA	WARP
2018	GNT	RK	21	25	3	1	1	0	1	1	7	0	0	.261/.320/.391	85	0.6	.375	-0.1	C(4): -0.1	0.0
2018	SLO	A-	21	203	35	14	2	13	39	12	40	2	1	.298/.369/.613	149	21.6	.318	1.2	C(32): -1.0	1.7
2019	SJO	A+	22	251	37	10	2	12	37	14	50	5	2	.265/.315/.479	112	17.2	.291	1.0	C(50): -1.9	1.2
2019	RIC	AA	22	87	9	4	1	4	11	7	21	0	2	.316/.368/.544	164	8.0	.382	-1.2	C(15): 0.2	0.8
2020	*SFN*	*MLB*	*23*	*251*	*29*	*12*	*1*	*11*	*35*	*14*	*69*	*1*	*0*	*.245/.296/.450*	*94*	*5.8*	*.300*	*-0.3*	*C -4*	*0.2*

Comparables: Kevin Cron, Devin Mesoraco, Travis d'Arnaud

YEAR	TEAM	P. COUNT	FRM RUNS	BLK RUNS	THRW RUNS	TOT RUNS
2019	RIC	2187	0.4	0.0	0.1	0.9
2020	*SFN*	*9182*	*-2.3*	*-0.4*	*0.2*	*-2.5*

With all the violence that young Bart has done to baseballs from his time at Georgia Tech through his short time in the minors, is it any wonder that a few of them are jonesing for payback? Swaths of his runs in San Jose and in the Arizona Fall League were cut short thanks to pitches breaking bones in both of his hands, but it hasn't yet slowed down the Bart hype train or his propensity for brutalizing opposing pitching. The world is still waiting to see if upper-level movement might expose his hit tool or his approach, but if anyone not named Rutschman is a sure thing as a catching prospect, it's Bart. Of course, in San Francisco, anything less than the second coming of Buster Posey might be considered a disappointment ... though if his frame and skill set make him a poor man's Gary Sánchez instead, the Giants will have caught lightning in a bottle twice in a little over a decade.

Brandon Belt 1B Born: 04/20/88 Age: 32 Bats: L Throws: L Height: 6'4" Weight: 235 Origin: Round 5, 2009 Draft (#147 overall)

YEAR	TEAM	LVL	AGE	PA	R	2B	3B	HR	RBI	BB	K	SB	CS	AVG/OBP/SLG	DRC+	VORP	BABIP	BRR	FRAA	WARP
2017	SFN	MLB	29	451	63	27	3	18	51	66	104	3	2	.241/.355/.469	110	24.9	.284	0.3	1B(98): 9.0, LF(15): -0.3	2.1
2018	SFN	MLB	30	456	50	18	2	14	46	49	107	4	0	.253/.342/.414	108	14.9	.311	-0.6	1B(104): 9.9, LF(8): 0.3	2.1
2019	SFN	MLB	31	616	76	32	3	17	57	83	127	4	3	.234/.339/.403	106	14.8	.275	-2.2	1B(144): 7.2, LF(14): -0.5	1.9
2020	*SFN*	*MLB*	*32*	*602*	*66*	*25*	*4*	*17*	*67*	*78*	*135*	*5*	*3*	*.226/.332/.388*	*96*	*8.1*	*.273*	*-1.0*	*1B 11, LF 0*	*2.0*

Comparables: Carlos Pena, Justin Smoak, Steve Balboni

Everything eventually comes full circle. After almost a decade of being one of the most divisive players in baseball (not to mention the Bay Area), Belt could be nearing the end of his complicated run with the Giants. Early in his career he spawned the hashtags #FreeBelt and #Belted as the representation of a shift in how to value a modern first baseman; possessed of only moderate power but excellent on-base skills, he was hardly the model of the hulking slugger, and it led the Giants to work him into the team much more tentatively than many fans wished. Once established, he produced but also suffered through a litany of injuries, most notably concussion-related symptoms that kept him from playing full seasons. In 2019 his offensive skills continued to gently wane, keeping him an above-average hitter but also a veteran on the periphery of an incoming youth movement. This year, his name will consistently come up in trade rumors, so once again we may see #FreeBelt applied, only this time he'll be off to a change in scenery.

─────────────── ★ ★ ★ *2020 Top 101 Prospect* **#68** ★ ★ ★ ───────────────

Hunter Bishop CF Born: 06/25/98 Age: 22 Bats: L Throws: R Height: 6'5" Weight: 210 Origin: Round 1, 2019 Draft (#10 overall)

YEAR	TEAM	LVL	AGE	PA	R	2B	3B	HR	RBI	BB	K	SB	CS	AVG/OBP/SLG	DRC+	VORP	BABIP	BRR	FRAA	WARP
2019	GNT	RK	21	29	4	3	0	1	3	9	11	2	0	.250/.483/.550	113	3.6	.500	0.4	CF(4): -1.0	0.0
2019	SLO	A-	21	117	21	1	1	4	9	29	28	6	2	.224/.427/.400	177	9.2	.278	-0.3	CF(21): -2.2	0.7
2020	*SFN*	*MLB*	*22*	*251*	*23*	*11*	*1*	*6*	*24*	*25*	*87*	*2*	*1*	*.199/.287/.328*	*67*	*-2.6*	*.297*	*0.0*	*CF -1*	*-0.4*

Comparables: Dansby Swanson, Nolan Reimold, Christin Stewart

Selected 10th overall in the past year's draft out of Arizona State, Bishop has excellent power and speed tools. His 2019 debut seemed more focused on taking an advanced approach at the plate and reaching base, but he punished a few pitches in-game and seems primed to rise quickly through the system. His ceiling will be dictated by his ability to make contact, which wasn't always consistent in college, especially with breaking balls. But when it comes to raw athleticism and upside, Bishop is in a class above even the other talented young outfielders in San Francisco's system. And as for the inevitable other comparisons, let it be remembered that the last time the Giants brought in a mighty left-handed outfielder with speed from Arizona State, it worked out pretty well for all parties involved.

Alexander Canario OF Born: 05/07/00 Age: 20 Bats: R Throws: R Height: 6'1" Weight: 165 Origin: International Free Agent, 2016

YEAR	TEAM	LVL	AGE	PA	R	2B	3B	HR	RBI	BB	K	SB	CS	AVG/OBP/SLG	DRC+	VORP	BABIP	BRR	FRAA	WARP
2017	DGI	RK	17	274	42	17	4	5	45	33	40	18	10	.294/.391/.464	162	22.3	.335	-1.0	RF(50): 4.0, CF(7): 0.7	2.6
2018	GIA	RK	18	208	36	5	2	6	19	27	51	8	5	.250/.357/.403	113	13.2	.317	-0.5	CF(44): 1.0	1.0
2019	GNT	RK	19	46	13	3	1	7	14	2	9	1	0	.395/.435/1.000	285	11.7	.370	-0.3	CF(8): -0.7	0.8
2019	SLO	A-	19	219	38	17	1	9	40	18	71	3	1	.301/.365/.539	158	17.9	.419	-1.0	CF(26): -8.1, RF(16): -1.1	0.5
2020	*SFN*	*MLB*	*20*	*251*	*22*	*13*	*1*	*4*	*23*	*19*	*86*	*5*	*2*	*.212/.278/.332*	*63*	*-4.0*	*.318*	*-0.2*	*CF -2, RF 0*	*-0.6*

Comparables: José Martínez, Teoscar Hernández, Ronald Acuña Jr.

Ironically possessed of a surname that brings to mind a classic example of an early indicator, Canario is at the heart of an influx of talented young outfielders in the Giants' system. While he's not the best of the raw, toolsy bats the Giants are starting to cultivate, Canario is the type of player that can generate years of hype and hope based on raw power, athleticism, despite absolutely no strong indicators whether or not he will ever hit major-league pitching. Of course his MiLB numbers were promising last year—he played at Salem-Keiser, after all—but for now he's a beautiful cipher, more a riddle than an outfielder. In a few years, when he's facing advanced spin and crafty veterans, the truth will start to come out. Until then, we will simply wait for something to happen.

Zack Cozart 3B
Born: 08/12/85 Age: 34 Bats: R Throws: R Height: 6'0" Weight: 205 Origin: Round 2, 2007 Draft (#79 overall)

YEAR	TEAM	LVL	AGE	PA	R	2B	3B	HR	RBI	BB	K	SB	CS	AVG/OBP/SLG	DRC+	VORP	BABIP	BRR	FRAA	WARP
2017	CIN	MLB	31	507	80	24	7	24	63	62	78	3	0	.297/.385/.548	137	50.5	.312	-2.8	SS(112): 1.3	4.5
2018	LAA	MLB	32	253	29	13	2	5	18	19	42	0	0	.219/.296/.362	90	3.3	.244	-0.2		0.5
2019	LAA	MLB	33	107	4	2	0	0	7	5	16	0	0	.124/.178/.144	66	-0.4	.143	0.4		-0.1
2020	SFN	MLB	34	112	11	5	1	3	12	8	20	1	0	.219/.287/.367	76	-0.5	.246	-0.3	3B 0, 2B 0	-0.1

Comparables: Jordy Mercer, Brendan Ryan, Paul Janish

In 2017, Cozart may have had the contract year to end all contract years. After several steady-but-not-great seasons as the Reds' shortstop, Cozart caught that Joey Votto On-Base Fever, torqued it up with some long-ball power, and floated into free agency with the wind of a 4.5-win season beneath his wings. The Angels sidled up with a three-year deal, and shortly thereafter Cozart's shoulder decided to break down. It's hard to fly with a broken wing, and two surgeries later Cozart still hasn't taken flight. Even 2020 looks uncertain for the 34-year-old despite moving 400-odd miles north on I-5.

It is tempting to see this turn of events as a knock on the Angels' front office and a reinforcement of the perils of free agency. Confirmation that Cozart's signing was a "mistake" or a "bad contract." Another way to view the contract, though: it's unlikely a player who averaged 122 games a year over the prior six seasons would accumulate fewer than 100 the next two. It's clear Cozart's injuries have compromised his play, and that was a bummer for the Angels and their fans alike, but we can also appreciate that the former second-round pick made good and cashed in before misfortune struck.

Brandon Crawford SS
Born: 01/21/87 Age: 33 Bats: L Throws: R Height: 6'2" Weight: 227 Origin: Round 4, 2008 Draft (#117 overall)

YEAR	TEAM	LVL	AGE	PA	R	2B	3B	HR	RBI	BB	K	SB	CS	AVG/OBP/SLG	DRC+	VORP	BABIP	BRR	FRAA	WARP
2017	SFN	MLB	30	570	58	34	1	14	77	42	113	3	5	.253/.305/.403	84	23.6	.293	-1.4	SS(138): 4.1	1.7
2018	SFN	MLB	31	594	63	28	2	14	54	50	122	4	5	.254/.325/.394	95	27.1	.303	0.5	SS(146): 15.3	4.0
2019	SFN	MLB	32	560	58	24	2	11	59	53	117	3	2	.228/.304/.350	80	12.2	.274	-3.4	SS(142): 0.9	0.9
2020	SFN	MLB	33	595	57	26	3	13	60	54	133	6	3	.230/.306/.363	80	6.6	.284	-0.6	SS 1	0.8

Comparables: Trevor Plouffe, Stephen Drew, Hanley Ramirez

The reputation as a "defense-only" player can be a double-edged sword. For years, people could only see his wizardry, his quickness, and a silky smooth transition from glove to rifle arm—it shaded the fact that he was an improving offensive player worthy even of a Silver Slugger award, despite his lackluster OBP. This past season, perhaps due to his 2018 knee injury or his advancing age, his defensive prowess has slipped and he graded out as an average defender for the first time in his career. It's possible his vaunted reputation—or the fact that he's being paid $30 million over the next two years—will continue to make him a regular in the Giants' infield despite his fading skills. More than likely, it's the reputation that once caused people to undervalue his stick which may save him from becoming a utility infielder or worse in 2020.

Jaylin Davis RF
Born: 07/01/94 Age: 25 Bats: R Throws: R Height: 6'1" Weight: 190 Origin: Round 24, 2015 Draft (#710 overall)

YEAR	TEAM	LVL	AGE	PA	R	2B	3B	HR	RBI	BB	K	SB	CS	AVG/OBP/SLG	DRC+	VORP	BABIP	BRR	FRAA	WARP
2017	CDR	A	22	272	36	13	3	12	41	16	77	9	2	.267/.316/.486	105	13.6	.335	1.1	RF(60): 7.4	1.5
2017	FTM	A+	22	233	26	8	2	3	25	12	70	1	1	.237/.288/.335	65	-6.0	.333	-0.5	RF(45): 4.4, LF(10): 2.3	0.3
2018	FTM	A+	23	227	23	10	0	5	19	23	57	3	2	.271/.354/.397	126	12.4	.355	4.1	RF(50): -6.2, LF(2): -0.2	0.7
2018	CHT	AA	23	267	30	14	2	6	34	21	69	5	2	.275/.341/.425	111	7.9	.359	-0.2	RF(50): 2.5, CF(1): -0.1	1.1
2019	PEN	AA	24	251	34	9	0	10	25	36	64	7	3	.274/.382/.458	156	18.3	.345	-0.2	RF(42): -2.0, LF(8): 0.8	1.8
2019	ROC	AAA	24	173	39	11	1	15	42	15	46	2	0	.331/.405/.708	160	19.0	.387	0.3	RF(32): 2.8, CF(6): 0.5	1.8
2019	SAC	AAA	24	117	21	6	0	10	27	14	28	1	1	.333/.419/.686	138	13.6	.375	0.9	RF(15): 3.1, CF(7): 0.6	1.2
2019	SFN	MLB	24	47	2	0	0	1	3	3	11	1	2	.167/.255/.238	68	-0.8	.200	-0.7	RF(15): -0.5	-0.2
2020	SFN	MLB	26	105	11	4	0	4	12	9	34	1	0	.222/.296/.381	83	-0.3	.304	-0.2	RF 0	-0.1

Comparables: Brad Komminsk, Aaron Altherr, Johnny Lewis

From an oft-injured afterthought to a key piece in a deadline deal, Davis had a revelatory 2019, finally able to stay healthy and tap into his raw power. He launched dinger after dinger, no matter the minor-league level or organization, finishing the year with 35 minor-league bombs and a single emphatic walk-off homer in the big leagues to put an exclamation point on his year. It wasn't all home run trots and walk-off celebrations for him, as much of his debut consisted of ground ball outs, and he's still not rocketing up prospect lists ... but another hot start in Triple-A might force the issue and make the Giants push him into the big leagues for another chance to make a first impression.

Alex Dickerson LF
Born: 05/26/90 Age: 30 Bats: L Throws: L Height: 6'3" Weight: 235 Origin: Round 3, 2011 Draft (#91 overall)

YEAR	TEAM	LVL	AGE	PA	R	2B	3B	HR	RBI	BB	K	SB	CS	AVG/OBP/SLG	DRC+	VORP	BABIP	BRR	FRAA	WARP
2019	ELP	AAA	29	113	17	5	1	5	20	14	18	0	0	.372/.469/.606	126	10.1	.417	0.6	1B(6): -0.5, LF(6): 0.3	0.7
2019	SDN	MLB	29	19	1	0	0	0	2	0	7	0	0	.158/.158/.158	67	-0.2	.250	0.2	LF(6): -0.1	0.0
2019	SFN	MLB	29	171	28	13	3	6	26	13	35	1	1	.290/.351/.529	104	5.7	.339	0.5	LF(44): -4.5, RF(1): -0.2	0.1
2020	SFN	MLB	30	336	36	17	3	10	39	26	75	2	1	.253/.323/.422	100	9.4	.307	0.1	LF -1	0.8

Comparables: John Mayberry Jr., Seth Smith, Allen Craig

Two years off the field can be a lifetime, especially when you're establishing yourself as a major-league regular. But after recovering from back and elbow injuries, Dickerson returned to the majors with a vengeance last year, and was a major catalyst for the Giants' lineup through June and July. From a mid-season bit of transactional fluff to a regular role in the outfield, he promptly hit a grand slam in his first game with the Giants, and was one of the premier hitters in baseball—so long as the opposing pitcher was right-handed—right up until the time that the injury bug crept up again and hampered his performance as the season wore down. Nevertheless, Dickerson has proven that he could have serious value as a left-handed bat, as long as he's handled with kid gloves and not relied on to play 150 games a season. As a complement to the Austin Slaters of the world, he could likely outperform his $1.2 million contract for 2020.

Mauricio Dubón SS Born: 07/19/94   Age: 25   Bats: R   Throws: R   Height: 6'0"   Weight: 160   Origin: Round 26, 2013 Draft (#773 overall)

YEAR	TEAM	LVL	AGE	PA	R	2B	3B	HR	RBI	BB	K	SB	CS	AVG/OBP/SLG	DRC+	VORP	BABIP	BRR	FRAA	WARP
2017	BLX	AA	22	304	34	14	0	2	24	25	42	31	9	.276/.338/.351	101	6.0	.319	0.3	SS(53): 5.4, 2B(20): 3.0	2.3
2017	CSP	AAA	22	244	40	15	0	6	33	14	34	7	6	.272/.320/.420	76	0.4	.297	-0.4	SS(30): -1.0, 2B(27): 3.5	0.4
2018	CSP	AAA	23	114	18	9	2	4	18	2	19	6	3	.343/.348/.574	107	10.6	.379	1.5	SS(23): 0.3, 2B(4): 0.6	0.8
2019	SAN	AAA	24	427	59	22	1	16	47	18	59	9	6	.297/.333/.475	103	22.9	.316	-0.9	SS(83): 4.1, 2B(12): 0.7	2.4
2019	SAC	AAA	24	112	23	4	0	4	9	10	9	1	2	.323/.391/.485	103	8.4	.326	0.6	SS(17): -0.1, 2B(6): 0.3	0.9
2019	SFN	MLB	24	109	12	5	0	4	9	5	19	3	1	.279/.312/.442	88	2.4	.309	1.1	2B(22): 3.8, SS(9): -0.4	0.7
2019	MIL	MLB	24	2	0	0	0	0	0	0	1	0	0	.000/.000/.000	84	0.1	.000	0.0	SS(1): 0.0	0.0
2020	SFN	MLB	25	385	37	15	1	9	40	18	68	13	4	.250/.290/.375	78	4.5	.286	0.4	2B 9, SS 0	1.5

Comparables: Yairo Muñoz, Marwin Gonzalez, Didi Gregorius

Stop me if you've heard this one before, but it looks like a high-contact hitter with a solid defensive reputation may be stepping into the No. 2 spot in the order and the second base job with the Giants next year. After a solid start to his Giants career (and four homers in 109 plate appearances), Dubón might be an upgrade over the dear-but-departed Joe Panik. With Gabe Kapler manning the lineups instead of Bruce Bochy, it's likely that this solid-fielding rookie middle infielder will get first crack at the everyday second base job over the likes of Donovan Solano, but if there's a lack of power or consistency, Dubón is a perfect fit for a 2B/SS/CF utility role while providing offense against lefties. Entering his age-25 season and with little left to prove in the minors, it's finally time for MLB's first Honduran-born player to get an everyday role.

Steven Duggar RF Born: 11/04/93   Age: 26   Bats: L   Throws: R   Height: 6'2"   Weight: 189   Origin: Round 6, 2015 Draft (#186 overall)

YEAR	TEAM	LVL	AGE	PA	R	2B	3B	HR	RBI	BB	K	SB	CS	AVG/OBP/SLG	DRC+	VORP	BABIP	BRR	FRAA	WARP
2017	SJO	A+	23	133	22	11	0	4	20	17	42	7	0	.270/.361/.470	130	9.7	.386	2.0	RF(22): -2.3, CF(1): -0.2	0.6
2017	SAC	AAA	23	54	7	1	0	2	6	8	12	3	2	.261/.370/.413	95	3.0	.313	0.1	CF(12): 1.7	0.3
2018	SAC	AAA	24	356	52	27	4	4	21	39	103	11	4	.272/.354/.421	103	13.1	.392	-0.1	CF(74): 9.6	2.4
2018	SFN	MLB	24	152	20	11	1	2	17	10	44	5	1	.255/.303/.390	71	8.3	.354	3.6	CF(40): -3.4	0.0
2019	SAC	AAA	25	102	24	6	1	3	13	18	21	2	3	.337/.461/.542	138	13.1	.424	0.2	CF(19): 0.4	0.9
2019	SFN	MLB	25	281	29	12	2	4	28	16	78	1	4	.234/.278/.341	61	-5.6	.313	-1.4	CF(39): 2.1, RF(34): -0.8	-0.6
2020	SFN	MLB	26	490	44	20	3	8	45	42	134	8	4	.229/.299/.340	73	1.7	.310	1.5	CF 7, RF -1	0.9

Comparables: Bradley Zimmer, Kirk Nieuwenhuis, Chad Hermansen

On Opening Day, Duggar was "the promising one" out of the Giants' makeshift outfield crop. Flanked by Connor Joe and Michael Reed, Duggar stood out as the one player on the grass with a real possibility to be more than just a piece of Sporcle trivia in a few years. When the team acquired Kevin Pillar in April—a player who would've made Duggar redundant on most outfield depth charts—he moved to right field but battled back injuries and ineffectiveness at the plate before suffering a shoulder strain that will keep him rehabbing until spring training. There's still some potential that he can be the center of San Francisco's outfield, but now it seems as if he's merely the answer to the trivia question "Who played center field for the Giants before Heliot Ramos got called up?"

Aramis Garcia C Born: 01/12/93   Age: 27   Bats: R   Throws: R   Height: 6'2"   Weight: 220   Origin: Round 2, 2014 Draft (#52 overall)

YEAR	TEAM	LVL	AGE	PA	R	2B	3B	HR	RBI	BB	K	SB	CS	AVG/OBP/SLG	DRC+	VORP	BABIP	BRR	FRAA	WARP
2017	SJO	A+	24	347	43	20	1	17	65	15	73	0	0	.272/.314/.497	115	20.8	.301	-1.3	C(50): 0.7, 1B(17): 0.3	1.7
2017	RIC	AA	24	89	11	12	0	0	8	9	21	0	0	.282/.360/.436	120	6.5	.379	1.0	C(20): -0.5, 1B(2): 0.0	0.7
2018	RIC	AA	25	328	36	14	1	11	33	20	76	0	1	.233/.287/.395	92	10.4	.272	-2.0	C(69): 10.3, 1B(11): -0.5	2.0
2018	SAC	AAA	25	41	5	1	0	0	4	2	12	0	0	.237/.268/.263	62	-1.6	.333	0.3	C(10): 0.5	0.1
2018	SFN	MLB	25	65	8	1	0	4	9	2	31	0	0	.286/.308/.492	55	3.0	.500	0.2	1B(10): -0.6, C(7): 0.7	-0.2
2019	SAC	AAA	26	371	52	20	2	16	55	34	114	0	2	.271/.343/.488	89	14.6	.365	0.0	C(60): 6.6, 1B(23): -1.4	1.5
2019	SFN	MLB	26	46	5	1	0	2	5	4	21	0	0	.143/.217/.310	56	-0.7	.211	0.2	C(11): 0.8, 1B(5): 0.5	0.1
2020	SFN	MLB	27	322	30	12	1	10	35	21	117	0	0	.210/.268/.354	67	-0.3	.308	-0.5	C 7, 1B 0	0.6

Comparables: Grayson Greiner, Michael Perez, Lane Adams

At the risk of sounding like an amateur real estate agent, might we suggest Garcia invest in a home somewhere in Fairfield, or maybe Rio Vista? A cottage evenly set between San Francisco and Sacramento is the perfect spot for the team's likely third catcher, who should split time between Triple-A and the bigs in 2020. With only two dozen hits sprinkled across cups of coffee in two seasons, the FIU product hasn't yet translated his solid minor-league performance into acceptable lines in the majors. Even at 27, there's still some hope that he can align his strengths and shore up his weaknesses enough to be a solid regular, but until then he'll hang his hat in the spaces between.

YEAR	TEAM	P. COUNT	FRM RUNS	BLK RUNS	THRW RUNS	TOT RUNS
2017	RIC	2761	-0.4	0.2	-0.1	-0.7
2018	RIC	9457	13.6	-0.6	-1.5	11.3
2018	SAC	1487	-0.2	0.0	0.0	0.3
2018	SFN	874	0.4	0.3	0.0	0.7
2019	SAC	9165	3.7	-0.1	1.8	5.2
2019	SFN	1465	1.5	-1.0	0.0	0.5
2020	SFN	10438	7.9	-1.5	0.4	6.8

Evan Longoria 3B Born: 10/07/85   Age: 34   Bats: R   Throws: R   Height: 6'1"   Weight: 215   Origin: Round 1, 2006 Draft (#3 overall)

YEAR	TEAM	LVL	AGE	PA	R	2B	3B	HR	RBI	BB	K	SB	CS	AVG/OBP/SLG	DRC+	VORP	BABIP	BRR	FRAA	WARP
2017	TBA	MLB	31	677	71	36	2	20	86	46	109	6	1	.261/.313/.424	95	22.2	.282	-1.9	3B(142): 3.8	2.1
2018	SFN	MLB	32	512	51	25	4	16	54	22	101	3	1	.244/.281/.413	89	6.9	.274	-5.2	3B(123): -10.5	-0.5
2019	SFN	MLB	33	508	59	19	2	20	69	43	112	3	1	.254/.325/.437	100	19.7	.291	0.1	3B(119): 6.6	2.6
2020	SFN	MLB	34	567	61	27	2	19	68	42	130	3	1	.244/.308/.412	94	6.7	.291	-2.3	3B 0	0.7

Comparables: Eric Chavez, Mike Pagliarulo, Edwin Encarnación

Four years ago, this *Annual* compared Longoria's career to Joseph Campbell's monomyth, the hero's journey. Over the course of his career, the veteran third baseman overcame many trials, from being forced to play in the Trop to watching his skillset diminish with age, but none were as haunting as what he faced in his first season in San Francisco, an unmitigated disaster wherein both his defense and his patience evaporated. For a moment, it seemed as if this journey would never be completed, that he would fall into the abyss, and never receive his ultimate boon, be that a World Series ring or a call to the Hall of Fame. But while the future is yet unwritten, the 34-year-old still drives towards his apotheosis. Last year he was the Giants' second-best hitter among regulars, and his FRAA bounced back from his dismal 2018 numbers. It might be hard to see Longoria reaching the pinnacle of his journey wearing the orange and brown of a mid-tier Giants team, but the end of the journey has not come yet, and the end of his story is yet to be told.

★ ★ ★ *2020 Top 101 Prospect* **#14** ★ ★ ★

Marco Luciano SS Born: 09/10/01 Age: 18 Bats: R Throws: R Height: 6'2" Weight: 178 Origin: International Free Agent, 2018

YEAR	TEAM	LVL	AGE	PA	R	2B	3B	HR	RBI	BB	K	SB	CS	AVG/OBP/SLG	DRC+	VORP	BABIP	BRR	FRAA	WARP
2019	GNT	RK	17	178	46	9	2	10	38	27	39	8	6	.322/.438/.616	195	26.5	.378	1.2	SS(31): 1.6	2.4
2019	SLO	A-	17	38	6	4	0	0	4	5	6	1	0	.212/.316/.333	97	1.0	.259	-0.2	SS(9): -0.8	0.0
2020	SFN	MLB	18	251	22	12	1	4	22	26	77	3	1	.209/.300/.318	70	-1.7	.304	0.0	SS 1	-0.1

Comparables: *Gary Sánchez, Nomar Mazara, Oscar Hernández*

Few prospects in baseball are as purely thrilling as Luciano, whose prodigious bat speed evokes comparisons to the game's elite; he torched the AZL and flashed his signature bat-to-ball impact before even turning 18. Still growing into his frame, he may eventually have to move off shortstop, which can sometimes be a red flag for young infielders … but in Luciano's case it hints at even greater power to come; that power will play even if he has to move down the defensive spectrum. And though Luciano is young and yet to truly prove himself in the minors, his approach and raw physicality hints at a development track that will be swifter than many other prospects his age. Few minor leaguers in the game have Luciano's upside.

Kevin Pillar CF Born: 01/04/89 Age: 31 Bats: R Throws: R Height: 6'0" Weight: 210 Origin: Round 32, 2011 Draft (#979 overall)

YEAR	TEAM	LVL	AGE	PA	R	2B	3B	HR	RBI	BB	K	SB	CS	AVG/OBP/SLG	DRC+	VORP	BABIP	BRR	FRAA	WARP
2017	TOR	MLB	28	632	72	37	1	16	42	33	95	15	6	.256/.300/.404	87	8.0	.280	-1.1	CF(153): -6.2	0.5
2018	TOR	MLB	29	542	65	40	2	15	59	18	98	14	3	.252/.282/.426	94	16.1	.281	3.3	CF(142): 9.0	2.8
2019	TOR	MLB	30	17	1	0	0	0	1	0	3	0	0	.063/.059/.063	27	-0.7	.071	0.0	CF(4): 0.1	-0.1
2019	SFN	MLB	30	628	82	37	3	21	87	18	86	14	5	.264/.293/.442	87	10.9	.275	4.1	CF(129): -10.8, RF(27): 0.2	0.4
2020	SFN	MLB	31	400	36	21	1	9	41	16	61	10	3	.239/.278/.370	73	-0.2	.264	1.0	CF -1, RF 0	-0.2

Comparables: *Daniel Murphy, Elston Howard, Gerardo Parra*

On November 14th, 2019, it was revealed that San Francisco baseball writer Hank Schulman awarded Pillar with a 10th-place MVP vote, the first of his career. Was it possible that after Pillar's trade across leagues in early April, he could've posted a career year and emerged as one of the ten best players in his new league? Of course! After all, he had a reputation for stellar defense in center field, and enough power to light up scoreboards if he could ever resist the urge to swing at pitches outside the zone.

But that wasn't what *actually* happened in Pillar's sixth full major-league season. Yes, he only missed a fistful of games as the linchpin of San Francisco's mix-and-match outfield, but his once-lauded defense in center fell apart completely, and he provided negative offensive value thanks to his distressing .287 OBP (only surpassed in the race for the bottom by former teammate Randal Grichuk). His aggressiveness—he had the highest swing rate on pitches outside the zone and third-highest swing rate overall—works for elite bat-to-ball guys like Nick Castellanos and Jeff McNeil, but for Pillar it only resulted in him making outs 70 percent of the time. Alas, Pillar ended up outside even the 10 most valuable Giants position players for the 2019 season, and was non-tendered just weeks after the highest awards honor of his career.

Buster Posey C Born: 03/27/87 Age: 33 Bats: R Throws: R Height: 6'1" Weight: 210 Origin: Round 1, 2008 Draft (#5 overall)

YEAR	TEAM	LVL	AGE	PA	R	2B	3B	HR	RBI	BB	K	SB	CS	AVG/OBP/SLG	DRC+	VORP	BABIP	BRR	FRAA	WARP
2017	SFN	MLB	30	568	62	34	0	12	67	61	66	6	1	.320/.400/.462	129	49.2	.347	-1.5	C(99): 7.0, 1B(38): 3.5	5.2
2018	SFN	MLB	31	448	47	22	1	5	41	45	53	3	2	.284/.359/.382	107	20.6	.316	-1.3	C(88): 0.1, 1B(13): 1.5	2.4
2019	SFN	MLB	32	445	43	24	0	7	38	34	71	0	0	.257/.320/.368	86	14.4	.296	-1.4	C(101): 14.9, 1B(4): -0.1	2.7
2020	SFN	MLB	33	497	50	24	1	9	50	45	77	3	1	.263/.335/.380	93	15.9	.300	-1.2	C 12, 1B 2	3.2

Comparables: *Earl Battey, Ramon Hernández, Mike Piazza*

Unquestionably the most valuable Giants player of the decade, there's a great argument that Posey is the decade's signature player. After all, not only does he have three World Series rings with the decade's only true dynasty, but his position has been the center of a revolution in sabermetrics. (Posey himself is, undoubtedly, one of the greatest in the game at framing pitches for extra strikes.) He entered the league at an early age, one of the vanguards of the game's recent youth movement, where pre-free agency players have been providing more value than ever before as compared to their veteran counterparts. With the

YEAR	TEAM	P. COUNT	FRM RUNS	BLK RUNS	THRW RUNS	TOT RUNS
2017	SFN	13474	4.8	0.2	2.3	7.4
2018	SFN	12224	0.9	0.7	0.1	2.0
2019	SFN	13869	10.1	2.2	1.6	13.8
2020	SFN	19239	10.0	1.1	1.3	12.3

decade now complete, its signature player is one of those less-productive veterans, and hip surgery—*could there be a more old-player injury?*—appears to have robbed him of much of his offensive swagger. There's no chance he can be as great as he was during his prime, but now the Giants legend will look to stay behind the plate as long as he can, providing defensive value and leadership while looking to regain his stroke.

★ ★ ★ *2020 Top 101 Prospect* **#34** ★ ★ ★

Heliot Ramos OF Born: 09/07/99 Age: 20 Bats: R Throws: R Height: 6'0" Weight: 188 Origin: Round 1, 2017 Draft (#19 overall)

YEAR	TEAM	LVL	AGE	PA	R	2B	3B	HR	RBI	BB	K	SB	CS	AVG/OBP/SLG	DRC+	VORP	BABIP	BRR	FRAA	WARP
2017	GIA	RK	17	151	33	11	6	6	27	10	48	10	2	.348/.404/.645	163	21.0	.500	2.2	CF(29): -2.3	1.3
2018	AUG	A	18	535	61	24	8	11	52	35	136	8	7	.245/.313/.396	107	21.5	.319	1.8	CF(113): -4.5	1.7
2019	SJO	A+	19	338	51	18	0	13	40	32	85	6	7	.306/.385/.500	143	32.4	.385	0.1	CF(70): -5.1	1.7
2019	RIC	AA	19	106	13	6	1	3	15	10	33	2	3	.242/.321/.421	120	3.5	.339	-1.6	CF(19): -1.5	0.2
2020	*SFN*	*MLB*	*20*	*251*	*25*	*13*	*1*	*7*	*28*	*18*	*83*	*2*	*1*	*.235/.301/.389*	*83*	*2.2*	*.338*	*-0.4*	*CF -3*	*-0.1*

Comparables: Ronald Acuña Jr., Jesus Montero, Justin Upton

For years, people have gushed about Ramos' athleticism, his power, and his precociousness, and playing 25 games in the Eastern League before his 20th birthday really puts the whole package in perspective. He's already growing out of being a premium runner and defender in center, though all the signs point to him being an effective hitter even if his office is in right field. There's raw talent in spades thanks to his build and bat speed, and he's worked hard to develop an opposite-field approach, but Ramos is still fighting the urge to hack at too many pitches instead of waiting for his shot. Perhaps there's slightly less upside than there was a few years ago, but he still looks like he could grow into a good—perhaps great—major-league regular.

Joey Rickard OF Born: 05/21/91 Age: 29 Bats: R Throws: L Height: 6'1" Weight: 185 Origin: Round 9, 2012 Draft (#302 overall)

YEAR	TEAM	LVL	AGE	PA	R	2B	3B	HR	RBI	BB	K	SB	CS	AVG/OBP/SLG	DRC+	VORP	BABIP	BRR	FRAA	WARP
2017	NOR	AAA	26	58	8	1	0	1	4	11	9	0	0	.191/.345/.277	119	1.3	.216	1.2	LF(7): 0.5, RF(6): -1.0	0.3
2017	BAL	MLB	26	277	29	15	0	4	19	9	63	8	1	.241/.276/.345	65	-3.5	.303	0.9	RF(53): 2.8, LF(43): -1.4	-0.3
2018	NOR	AAA	27	185	25	13	1	2	27	26	28	3	0	.275/.384/.412	139	14.5	.317	-0.1	CF(32): 4.0, LF(8): 0.4	1.7
2018	BAL	MLB	27	230	27	10	1	8	23	15	55	4	2	.244/.300/.413	92	1.3	.293	-0.4	RF(40): 3.8, LF(36): -1.4	0.6
2019	SAC	AAA	28	195	45	15	2	6	23	18	27	0	2	.372/.431/.587	131	18.8	.408	2.1	LF(26): 0.0, CF(10): 0.3	1.4
2019	NOR	AAA	28	77	10	5	0	4	10	11	16	1	0	.203/.338/.469	107	2.6	.205	0.2	LF(8): 1.9, RF(5): 1.1	0.5
2019	BAL	MLB	28	135	10	7	2	2	6	14	33	3	2	.203/.304/.347	76	-0.2	.265	0.5	RF(23): -1.6, CF(16): -0.2	-0.1
2019	SFN	MLB	28	54	4	2	0	1	4	4	17	1	0	.280/.333/.380	60	-1.3	.406	0.7	LF(20): 0.0, RF(2): -0.1	-0.1
2020	*SFN*	*MLB*	*29*	*251*	*24*	*10*	*1*	*5*	*24*	*21*	*61*	*5*	*2*	*.227/.302/.347*	*76*	*0.7*	*.290*	*0.3*	*LF 0, RF 1*	*0.3*

Comparables: David Dellucci, Bob Borkowski, Pat Sheridan

Can you believe the things this guy can do? He is a superlative athlete, easily able to accelerate and run faster than most of the humans on this planet. His hand-eye coordination is marvelous, allowing him to make consistent hard contact on his swings off diving pitches moving upwards of 95 miles per hour. He's got the reflexes and cognitive abilities to excel as a defender, even as he tracks slicing liners off the bat and corrals them with relative ease. And when it comes to his 2020 outlook, the words we have to use are pernicious things like "fringy," "below-average," and "got non-tendered by the Giants after getting waived by the Orioles." Rickard's a top athlete in one of the hardest sports leagues in the world, and still he'll need a lucky break to make a 25-man roster as a platoon option and a defensive replacement. That's how hard professional baseball is.

Pablo Sandoval 3B Born: 08/11/86 Age: 33 Bats: B Throws: R Height: 5'11" Weight: 268 Origin: International Free Agent, 2003

YEAR	TEAM	LVL	AGE	PA	R	2B	3B	HR	RBI	BB	K	SB	CS	AVG/OBP/SLG	DRC+	VORP	BABIP	BRR	FRAA	WARP
2017	PAW	AAA	30	81	7	3	0	1	4	4	16	0	0	.221/.259/.299	68	-2.9	.267	-0.5	3B(15): -1.6	-0.2
2017	SAC	AAA	30	37	4	1	0	1	3	5	3	0	0	.207/.324/.345	81	1.4	.185	-0.1	3B(7): 1.2	0.1
2017	BOS	MLB	30	108	10	2	0	4	12	8	24	0	1	.212/.269/.354	81	-1.8	.236	-0.2	3B(29): -1.4, 2B(1): 0.0	0.0
2017	SFN	MLB	30	171	17	9	0	5	20	8	29	0	0	.225/.263/.375	80	-1.0	.242	-0.4	3B(38): -2.6, 1B(9): -0.1	-0.2
2018	SFN	MLB	31	252	22	10	1	9	40	19	52	0	0	.248/.310/.417	96	1.6	.282	-2.8	3B(36): -1.8, 1B(24): -1.4	-0.1
2019	SFN	MLB	32	296	42	23	0	14	41	18	67	1	0	.268/.313/.507	98	8.5	.304	0.0	3B(45): -4.1, 1B(23): 0.1	0.4
2020	*SFN*	*MLB*	*33*	*251*	*25*	*11*	*0*	*9*	*30*	*16*	*55*	*0*	*0*	*.223/.279/.386*	*74*	*-0.9*	*.256*	*-0.7*	*3B -4, 1B 0*	*-0.5*

Comparables: Adrián Beltré, Ryan Zimmerman, Mike Moustakas

Against long odds, the man they call Panda had his first above-replacement season since his previous Giants run, only this year didn't end with a parade. Instead of a fixture at a single position, he's now more of an instant-offense corner infield reserve, a switch-hitter especially effective against lefties but a liability in the field. Free agency should be … interesting for him, where he's likely to get something more like a minor-league invite than the nine-figure deal he wrapped the last time around. Although he's only going into his age-34 season, his (in)famous stature and conditioning, a late-season elbow surgery, and how downright terrible he was anywhere other than San Francisco might make teams hesitant to offer him anything more than a token contract to be a highly likable bench bat.

Chris Shaw LF Born: 10/20/93 Age: 26 Bats: L Throws: R Height: 6'3" Weight: 226 Origin: Round 1, 2015 Draft (#31 overall)

YEAR	TEAM	LVL	AGE	PA	R	2B	3B	HR	RBI	BB	K	SB	CS	AVG/OBP/SLG	DRC+	VORP	BABIP	BRR	FRAA	WARP
2017	RIC	AA	23	154	16	10	0	6	29	18	26	0	0	.301/.390/.511	154	10.1	.333	-1.5	1B(18): -0.9, LF(18): -1.1	0.8
2017	SAC	AAA	23	360	42	25	1	18	50	20	106	0	0	.289/.328/.530	99	14.0	.367	-5.3	LF(76): -14.5	-1.1
2018	SAC	AAA	24	422	55	21	2	24	65	21	144	0	0	.259/.308/.505	103	14.4	.345	-2.0	LF(86): -10.4	0.0
2018	SFN	MLB	24	62	2	2	0	1	7	7	23	1	0	.185/.274/.278	65	-1.8	.290	-0.1	LF(15): -1.9	-0.3
2019	RIC	AA	25	182	25	9	2	7	24	19	33	2	2	.288/.368/.500	149	15.2	.322	-1.4	LF(36): -4.7, 1B(1): -0.1	0.6
2019	SAC	AAA	25	310	52	18	1	21	70	20	78	0	0	.298/.355/.592	112	19.5	.341	0.3	1B(43): -4.4, LF(20): 1.7	0.8
2019	SFN	MLB	25	20	0	0	0	0	0	2	8	0	0	.056/.150/.056	63	-0.5	.100	0.0	1B(4): 0.1	0.0
2020	*SFN*	*MLB*	*26*	*147*	*16*	*6*	*0*	*6*	*19*	*9*	*43*	*0*	*0*	*.223/.281/.410*	*85*	*1.0*	*.278*	*-0.1*	*LF -3*	*-0.2*

Comparables: Preston Tucker, Bradley Zimmer, Ryan O'Hearn

For the third consecutive season, Shaw spent most of his time in Triple-A. For the fourth consecutive season, Shaw belted more than 20 homers. For the fifth consecutive season, Shaw was an MiLB.com Organizational All-Star. But after all this time, having this kind of sustained success in the minor leagues may say something about the possibility of sustained success in the major leagues. For all his accomplishments (and his might), the 26-year-old still hasn't proven that he can hit big-league movement and, for the second consecutive season, a cup of coffee led to minimal plate appearances and precious few of them could be called productive. With all the outfield talent rising in the Giants' system, it'll take a dramatic change for Shaw to hang onto the spot he's already struggling to keep.

Austin Slater UT Born: 12/13/92   Age: 27   Bats: R   Throws: R   Height: 6'2"   Weight: 197   Origin: Round 8, 2014 Draft (#238 overall)

YEAR	TEAM	LVL	AGE	PA	R	2B	3B	HR	RBI	BB	K	SB	CS	AVG/OBP/SLG	DRC+	VORP	BABIP	BRR	FRAA	WARP
2017	SAC	AAA	24	206	28	12	0	5	27	15	39	4	3	.321/.377/.467	116	9.5	.380	-2.7	RF(22): -0.9, LF(17): -0.1	0.7
2017	SFN	MLB	24	127	15	3	1	3	16	8	29	0	0	.282/.339/.402	84	4.6	.353	0.2	LF(30): -1.0, RF(3): -0.2	0.0
2018	SAC	AAA	25	223	32	24	2	5	32	21	39	8	2	.344/.417/.564	159	22.2	.405	1.4	RF(29): 0.6, 1B(13): -0.1	2.1
2018	SFN	MLB	25	225	21	6	1	1	23	20	69	7	0	.251/.333/.307	64	1.9	.377	1.3	LF(25): 1.8, 1B(21): 0.1	-0.2
2019	SAC	AAA	26	296	47	17	0	12	45	46	69	6	2	.308/.436/.529	139	30.0	.388	0.6	1B(38): 2.5, 3B(11): -1.4	2.1
2019	SFN	MLB	26	192	20	9	3	5	21	22	59	1	0	.238/.333/.417	73	-2.0	.337	-0.7	RF(46): -0.2, 1B(21): -0.8	-0.4
2020	SFN	MLB	27	413	44	16	1	10	44	42	120	5	2	.242/.329/.376	93	6.5	.332	-0.3	RF -1, LF 0	0.6

Comparables: Dick Williams, Junior Lake, Joe Adcock

Slater, a Jacksonville native who has spent his college and pro careers playing mostly in California, has picked up a trick or two since exiting Duval County. There's his opposite-field approach, adopted at Stanford and honed in the upper minors; this has caused him to wreak havoc on Triple-A pitching but hasn't yet translated into sustained big-league success. There's the collection of gloves he's picked up while trying out new positions; while best suited for the corners, he handled nearly every spot on the diamond last year and best profiles as a sort of super-utility hand. And then there's the advice from Barry Bonds that may have led to a dynamite August run for the big club: *only swing at pitches you can drive.* With everything he's learned along the way, a spot appears open for him as the soft side of a roving platoon, able to beat up lefties while spelling players all over the field.

Donovan Solano INF Born: 12/17/87   Age: 32   Bats: R   Throws: R   Height: 5'10"   Weight: 205   Origin: International Free Agent, 2005

YEAR	TEAM	LVL	AGE	PA	R	2B	3B	HR	RBI	BB	K	SB	CS	AVG/OBP/SLG	DRC+	VORP	BABIP	BRR	FRAA	WARP
2017	SWB	AAA	29	405	44	29	0	4	48	24	60	1	0	.282/.329/.391	108	6.2	.324	-0.8	2B(59): 2.3, 3B(28): 2.4	1.9
2018	DOD	RK	30	27	3	1	0	0	3	0	1	0	0	.440/.444/.480	189	3.6	.440	-0.1	SS(5): 1.6, 2B(1): 0.0	0.5
2018	OKL	AAA	30	340	38	21	1	4	43	16	40	4	1	.318/.353/.430	108	20.9	.348	-1.2	SS(65): -1.9, 2B(10): 0.7	1.6
2019	SAC	AAA	31	97	12	4	0	2	16	9	11	0	0	.322/.392/.437	112	4.1	.351	-0.9	2B(14): 0.4, 3B(10): 0.3	0.5
2019	SFN	MLB	31	228	27	13	1	4	23	10	49	0	1	.330/.360/.456	101	9.0	.409	1.7	2B(36): -2.6, SS(19): 0.5	0.9
2020	SFN	MLB	32	315	28	15	1	5	30	15	66	1	0	.268/.310/.371	83	6.3	.331	1.3	2B 0, SS 0	0.7

Comparables: Adam Kennedy, Emilio Bonifácio, Orlando Hudson

If you predicted Solano would be the most productive regular in the Giants' middle infield this year, we're checking your garage for a souped-up DeLorean. Never an exceptional defender or even an average hitter, the veteran utility man spent most of the past three seasons propping up the infields for various Triple-A squads since his few years as a regular on disappointing Marlins teams. A desperate San Francisco squad turned to the Colombian in May, and he finally showed out at the plate in the bigs during his age-31 season. There's reason to think that the surprising .330 batting average is a bit of a fluke, and that his flurry of doubles is more indicative of a jacked-up ball than a change in his skill level. But whether Solano returns to the upper minors or sticks around as a big-league bench piece, he's re-established himself as a reliable depth option with the potential to drop in a choice base hit.

Luis Toribio 3B Born: 09/28/00   Age: 19   Bats: L   Throws: R   Height: 6'1"   Weight: 165   Origin: International Free Agent, 2017

YEAR	TEAM	LVL	AGE	PA	R	2B	3B	HR	RBI	BB	K	SB	CS	AVG/OBP/SLG	DRC+	VORP	BABIP	BRR	FRAA	WARP
2018	DGI	RK	17	274	44	13	1	10	39	51	62	4	1	.270/.423/.479	155	23.9	.333	-1.8	3B(47): -5.6	1.6
2019	GNT	RK	18	234	45	15	3	3	33	45	54	4	5	.297/.436/.459	166	24.2	.400	-0.3	3B(41): -6.4	1.4
2020	SFN	MLB	19	251	22	13	1	3	22	28	85	0	0	.209/.302/.318	70	-2.0	.323	-0.4	3B -3	-0.6

Comparables: Victor Robles, Ronald Acuña Jr., Daniel Robertson

According to a popular story, for months Michaelangelo stared at a block of marble that would one day become the statue of David. Is that what it feels like to watch young Luis Toribio at this point in his career? He's big enough and powerful enough to disguise the fact that he's only 19, and he's rough and raw enough to only hint at a finished product. And is the comparison to a bit of stonework a little too on-the-nose? After all, while he's strong enough to put stones to shame, he carries the analogy a little too far with his defense at third base, threatening to end up on the opposite corner of the infield. Solid performances at both Rookie ball and Low-A keep us watching and waiting; are we looking at the beginning of a masterpiece, or just another brick in the wall?

Will Wilson SS Born: 07/21/98   Age: 21   Bats: R   Throws: R   Height: 6'0"   Weight: 184   Origin: Round 1, 2019 Draft (#15 overall)

YEAR	TEAM	LVL	AGE	PA	R	2B	3B	HR	RBI	BB	K	SB	CS	AVG/OBP/SLG	DRC+	VORP	BABIP	BRR	FRAA	WARP
2019	ORM	RK+	20	204	23	10	3	5	18	14	47	0	0	.275/.328/.439	94	5.3	.343	-0.8		0.6
2020	SFN	MLB	21	251	18	11	1	3	20	14	81	2	1	.205/.252/.298	48	-9.1	.299	0.0		-0.9

Comparables:

The Angels' first-round pick in the 2019 draft out of NC State, Wilson is the prototype of a polished college shortstop. But get the player out of those Friday Night ACC Lights, and what do you really have? A future second baseman who stands a good chance of making it to the majors and a less good chance of distinguishing himself once there. Turns out you also get collateral damage from the disastrous Zack Cozart contract, as the Giants got Wilson for the privilege of taking on the final year of that three-season pact.

Mike Yastrzemski LF Born: 08/23/90 Age: 29 Bats: L Throws: L Height: 5'11" Weight: 180 Origin: Round 14, 2013 Draft (#429 overall)

YEAR	TEAM	LVL	AGE	PA	R	2B	3B	HR	RBI	BB	K	SB	CS	AVG/OBP/SLG	DRC+	VORP	BABIP	BRR	FRAA	WARP
2017	BOW	AA	26	94	20	6	1	6	19	9	17	1	1	.386/.436/.699	183	13.8	.419	-0.5	RF(12): -0.3, CF(4): -0.2	0.9
2017	NOR	AAA	26	307	41	15	3	9	41	31	74	2	1	.240/.322/.417	109	11.3	.295	1.8	LF(36): 3.1, CF(30): 3.6	1.9
2018	BOW	AA	27	117	13	10	0	1	11	10	30	2	1	.202/.276/.327	75	1.2	.270	1.5	LF(14): 0.9, RF(7): 1.5	0.4
2018	NOR	AAA	27	374	48	18	6	9	49	44	75	6	4	.265/.359/.441	134	25.7	.320	4.3	LF(50): 8.7, CF(36): 2.2	4.0
2019	SAC	AAA	28	163	38	11	1	12	25	22	36	2	2	.316/.414/.676	145	23.7	.344	2.2	CF(21): -0.2, LF(8): -0.3	1.6
2019	SFN	MLB	28	411	64	22	3	21	55	32	107	2	4	.272/.334/.518	112	17.0	.325	0.5	LF(61): -0.5, RF(56): 0.3	1.7
2020	SFN	MLB	29	504	56	21	3	19	63	43	138	5	2	.230/.303/.416	93	11.1	.287	1.1	RF 6, CF 1	1.8

Comparables: George Shuba, John Andreoli, Brian Goodwin

Proof that even mid-season "organizational depth" trades can sometimes change everything, Yaz the Younger was the most visible bright spot for the 2019 Giants. Prior to this season, he was considered an upper-minors depth piece, an outfielder without the standout skills to hold down a regular job in the majors. But as a 28-year-old rookie, the Giants gave him the opportunity to play and he ran with it, displaying surprising newfound power and getting just a bit lucky with his batting average on balls in play. That power was on display during what might've been the signature moment of the 2019 Giants' season: On the road in Boston in September, Yaz III hung out with his grandfather before the game, patrolled grandad's old spot in left field during it, and then took Nate Eovaldi deep to help give the Giants their first win at Fenway in literally a century.

PITCHERS

Shaun Anderson RHP Born: 10/29/94 Age: 25 Bats: R Throws: R Height: 6'4" Weight: 225 Origin: Round 3, 2016 Draft (#88 overall)

YEAR	TEAM	LVL	AGE	W	L	SV	G	GS	IP	H	HR	BB/9	K/9	K	GB%	BABIP	WHIP	ERA	DRA	WARP	MPH	FB%	WHF	CSP
2017	GRN	A	22	3	0	0	7	7	38²	30	2	2.6	8.6	37	52%	.272	1.06	2.56	3.65	0.7				
2017	SLM	A+	22	3	3	0	11	11	58²	53	6	2.8	7.4	48	43%	.270	1.21	3.99	3.88	0.9				
2017	SJO	A+	22	3	3	0	6	5	25²	19	1	1.4	7.7	22	51%	.247	0.90	3.51	2.64	0.8				
2018	RIC	AA	23	6	5	0	17	16	94	93	9	2.1	8.9	93	49%	.316	1.22	3.45	4.21	1.2				
2018	SAC	AAA	23	2	2	0	8	8	47¹	48	5	2.1	6.5	34	47%	.287	1.25	4.18	4.11	0.8				
2019	SAC	AAA	24	2	1	0	8	8	38¹	36	3	3.1	9.6	41	54%	.317	1.28	3.76	2.92	1.4				
2019	SFN	MLB	24	3	5	2	28	16	96	111	13	3.6	6.6	70	43%	.322	1.55	5.44	6.51	-0.8	95.1	58.5	10	46.4
2020	SFN	MLB	25	2	3	17	50	0	53	57	7	3.3	6.7	40	44%	.301	1.44	4.46	5.00	0.3	94.8	59.9	10.3	47.5

Comparables: Justin Grimm, Cody Martin, Aaron Blair

A slider that gets missed 30 percent of the time it's swung at … that's a good pitch. You'd think with a pitch like that, Anderson might've gotten a few more strikeouts during his debut season. But instead of taking the league by storm, the former Gator had trouble putting hitters away, whether he was starting or ending games … it was pretty much a litany of troubles. After dropping out of the rotation, he got a crack at the closer job, but his first-inning struggles as a starter translated all too well to the first innings of his relief work too. After three years of posting solid numbers in the minors, the shock of struggles at the big-league level could have been a surprise, but there's still enough of a foundation to expect him to grow into a role as a back-end starter or late-inning reliever.

Tyler Anderson LHP Born: 12/30/89 Age: 30 Bats: L Throws: L Height: 6'3" Weight: 215 Origin: Round 1, 2011 Draft (#20 overall)

YEAR	TEAM	LVL	AGE	W	L	SV	G	GS	IP	H	HR	BB/9	K/9	K	GB%	BABIP	WHIP	ERA	DRA	WARP	MPH	FB%	WHF	CSP
2017	ABQ	AAA	27	0	2	0	4	2	12¹	14	0	2.9	9.5	13	35%	.412	1.46	4.38	4.12	0.2				
2017	COL	MLB	27	6	6	0	17	15	86	88	16	2.7	8.5	81	46%	.304	1.33	4.81	4.15	1.3	94.5	47.1	12.4	47.6
2018	COL	MLB	28	7	9	0	32	32	176	165	30	3.0	8.4	164	38%	.281	1.27	4.55	4.82	1.0	94.1	44.6	12.3	50
2019	COL	MLB	29	0	3	0	5	5	20²	33	8	4.8	10.0	23	42%	.391	2.13	11.76	5.69	0.0	93.2	47.6	12.3	50
2020	SFN	MLB	30	7	8	0	23	23	122	113	20	3.1	8.1	111	40%	.275	1.26	3.70	4.42	1.9	93.4	45.4	12.3	49.2

Comparables: Sam Gaviglio, Josh Outman, Steven Matz

Years of knee pain culminated in season-ending surgery in June for Anderson. The recovery period is almost as significant as the length of time that the former first-round pick has been suffering with the issue (a chondral defect in his left knee) with Anderson unlikely to be ready to begin the 2020 season. In hindsight, it's remarkable that the left-hander was able to make 32 starts the season prior. The extent to which the knee affected his performance may not become clear until, or if, he returns to full health. While the injury led Colorado to non-tender him, it does mean Anderson has the opportunity to get back on track in a rather more forgiving environment.

Tyler Beede RHP Born: 05/23/93 Age: 27 Bats: R Throws: R Height: 6'3" Weight: 211 Origin: Round 1, 2014 Draft (#14 overall)

YEAR	TEAM	LVL	AGE	W	L	SV	G	GS	IP	H	HR	BB/9	K/9	K	GB%	BABIP	WHIP	ERA	DRA	WARP	MPH	FB%	WHF	CSP
2017	SAC	AAA	24	6	7	0	19	19	109	121	14	3.2	6.9	83	52%	.316	1.47	4.79	4.96	0.9				
2018	SAC	AAA	25	4	9	0	33	10	74	82	10	6.8	9.1	75	41%	.346	1.86	7.05	6.99	-1.3				
2018	SFN	MLB	25	0	1	0	2	2	7²	9	0	9.4	10.6	9	46%	.409	2.22	8.22	4.22	0.1	95.3	51.8	11.5	41.3
2019	SAC	AAA	26	2	2	0	7	7	34²	24	3	3.6	12.7	49	35%	.296	1.10	2.34	2.42	1.4				
2019	SFN	MLB	26	5	10	0	24	22	117	127	22	3.5	8.7	113	45%	.312	1.48	5.08	5.24	0.7	96.0	56.2	12	45.3
2020	SFN	MLB	27	6	9	0	36	19	115	120	17	4.4	9.2	117	43%	.322	1.53	4.89	5.23	0.7	95.5	56.6	12.2	44.1

Comparables: Kyle McGowin, Chris Ellis, Rookie Davis

Finally.

The Giants faithful (and their team staff) have been waiting for the former first-round draft pick to step up and be a regular part of the team's rotation. After five consecutive years on our Giants Top 10 Prospects list, Beede finally surfaced as a regular part of the starting rotation and it was … mostly okay? There were flashes of excellence amidst an overall disappointing season. His command is still an open issue, and in trying to harness it, he gave up more home runs than he could safely absorb. However, he still has the swing-and-miss stuff that made him such a fascinating (if long-lasting) prospect, and he could stand to benefit from increased use of his bender; his curveball wasn't relied on too often, but when hitters swung at it, they missed it more than half the time. So far, the Giants stand with loads of back-of-the-rotation options, but Beede may have more upside than most of his competitors. Look for him to stick around the majors for a while longer, ceding the space on prospect lists once and for all.

Sam Coonrod RHP Born: 09/22/92 Age: 27 Bats: R Throws: R Height: 6'2" Weight: 225 Origin: Round 5, 2014 Draft (#148 overall)

YEAR	TEAM	LVL	AGE	W	L	SV	G	GS	IP	H	HR	BB/9	K/9	K	GB%	BABIP	WHIP	ERA	DRA	WARP	MPH	FB%	WHF	CSP
2017	RIC	AA	24	4	11	0	24	18	103²	96	7	3.6	8.2	94	47%	.302	1.33	4.69	4.79	0.4				
2018	SJO	A+	25	0	0	0	6	0	6¹	5	0	2.8	18.5	13	33%	.417	1.11	5.68	2.76	0.2				
2019	SAC	AAA	26	2	4	3	33	1	32¹	41	4	5.0	12.0	43	46%	.416	1.82	6.96	5.78	0.1				
2019	SFN	MLB	26	5	1	0	33	0	27²	19	3	4.9	6.5	20	51%	.222	1.23	3.58	4.71	0.2	98.5	65.3	10.4	47.4
2020	SFN	MLB	27	2	2	0	45	0	47	47	6	4.4	8.2	43	45%	.301	1.48	4.52	4.91	0.3	98.0	66.1	10.5	48

Comparables: Warwick Saupold, Ryne Stanek, Drew Gagnon

In theory, this rookie reliever has all the makings of a potential relief ace. A former starting prospect who blew out his elbow and moved to the bullpen, his return to pitching came with a bevy of strikeouts during his tour in Sacramento on the strength of his 96-mile per hour fastball and two viable secondaries. Command still seems to be an issue, both when in the minors and when promoted to San Francisco, but he survived last year on a steady diet of bad contact even when the whiffs failed him. The raw stuff is there, so a control upgrade could transform him from generic relief dude to bullpen stalwart.

Seth Corry LHP Born: 11/03/98 Age: 21 Bats: L Throws: L Height: 6'2" Weight: 195 Origin: Round 3, 2017 Draft (#96 overall)

YEAR	TEAM	LVL	AGE	W	L	SV	G	GS	IP	H	HR	BB/9	K/9	K	GB%	BABIP	WHIP	ERA	DRA	WARP	MPH	FB%	WHF	CSP
2017	GIA	RK	18	0	2	0	13	10	24¹	14	1	8.1	7.8	21	46%	.203	1.48	5.55	4.03	0.5				
2018	GNT	RK	19	3	1	0	9	9	38	38	1	4.0	9.9	42	46%	.349	1.45	2.61	5.01	0.5				
2018	SLO	A-	19	1	2	0	5	5	19²	14	1	6.9	7.8	17	54%	.245	1.47	5.49	4.42	0.2				
2019	AUG	A	20	9	3	0	27	26	122²	73	4	4.3	12.6	172	47%	.265	1.07	1.76	3.32	2.7				
2020	SFN	MLB	21	2	2	0	33	0	35	35	5	4.2	10.2	40	44%	.321	1.45	4.53	4.82	0.2				

Comparables: Darwinzon Hernandez, Matt Moore, Neftalí Feliz

It's almost impossible to have a better run than Corry did in the Sally League last year. The southpaw from Utah strung together 32 scoreless innings, struck out more than 12 batters per nine, and won the league's Most Outstanding Pitcher award in the process. There's a number of factors that seem to have played into his improvement—continued development of his changeup and two-seam fastball and improved focus on tunneling his pitches are two that his coaches credit—but like many young pitchers, mechanical consistency is still a bit of an issue. Corry's command profile still may paint him a late-inning reliever rather than a starting pitcher, but any repeat of his dominance in San Jose will have him rocketing towards the majors, walks or no.

Johnny Cueto RHP Born: 02/15/86 Age: 34 Bats: R Throws: R Height: 5'11" Weight: 229 Origin: International Free Agent, 2004

YEAR	TEAM	LVL	AGE	W	L	SV	G	GS	IP	H	HR	BB/9	K/9	K	GB%	BABIP	WHIP	ERA	DRA	WARP	MPH	FB%	WHF	CSP
2017	SJO	A+	31	0	1	0	2	2	6²	11	1	1.4	10.8	8	46%	.476	1.80	6.75	7.38	-0.2				
2017	SFN	MLB	31	8	8	0	25	25	147¹	160	22	3.2	8.3	136	41%	.322	1.45	4.52	4.57	1.7	93.8	51.2	11.4	42.7
2018	SAC	AAA	32	0	0	0	2	2	7²	5	0	1.2	11.7	10	39%	.278	0.78	0.00	2.50	0.3				
2018	SFN	MLB	32	3	2	0	9	9	53	46	8	2.2	6.5	38	45%	.253	1.11	3.23	4.56	0.5	92.7	46.8	10	46.4
2019	SJO	A+	33	0	1	0	2	2	7	8	1	1.3	6.4	5	56%	.318	1.29	6.43	5.72	-0.1				
2019	SFN	MLB	33	1	2	0	4	4	16	11	3	5.1	7.3	13	56%	.190	1.25	5.06	4.43	0.2	92.9	51.3	7.9	42.7
2020	SFN	MLB	34	7	9	0	24	24	134	124	19	3.0	8.0	119	47%	.280	1.26	3.61	4.28	2.3	92.3	49.3	10.5	43.3

Comparables: Aníbal Sánchez, Matt Garza, Zack Greinke

Instead of keeping us waiting until 2020, Johnny Beisbol returned ahead of schedule from his Tommy John surgery rehab to make four uneven starts as a test run for 2020. Not all the signs were positive, but the best news is that his velocity is right back to where it was in 2017 and 2018 before the injury. Of course, that's a touch slower than when he was at his peak, but Cueto is tricky enough to keep batters off balance despite below-average heat. Most notable was that for the first time in a decade the veteran had trouble finding the strike zone, walking nine batters in 16 innings. Historically, command returns last after these elbow surgeries, so the Giants will be hoping that Cueto finds his soon; they'd prefer that the $43 million committed to him at least pays for a middle-of-the-rotation starter with veteran wiles.

Kevin Gausman RHP Born: 01/06/91 Age: 29 Bats: L Throws: R Height: 6'3" Weight: 190 Origin: Round 1, 2012 Draft (#4 overall)

YEAR	TEAM	LVL	AGE	W	L	SV	G	GS	IP	H	HR	BB/9	K/9	K	GB%	BABIP	WHIP	ERA	DRA	WARP	MPH	FB%	WHF	CSP
2017	BAL	MLB	26	11	12	0	34	34	186²	208	29	3.4	8.6	179	44%	.336	1.49	4.68	4.91	1.4	97.7	64.3	12	44.9
2018	BAL	MLB	27	5	8	0	21	21	124	139	21	2.3	7.5	104	48%	.317	1.38	4.43	4.42	1.3	97.1	58.8	12.1	47.2
2018	ATL	MLB	27	5	3	0	10	10	59²	50	5	2.7	6.6	44	43%	.260	1.14	2.87	3.13	1.5	96.5	56.9	12.1	45.9
2019	GWN	AAA	28	0	1	0	1	1	7	6	1	1.3	12.9	10	69%	.333	1.00	2.57	2.62	0.3				
2019	ATL	MLB	28	3	7	0	16	16	80	92	12	3.0	9.6	85	40%	.345	1.49	6.19	5.17	0.4	96.7	56.6	14.8	46.1
2019	CIN	MLB	28	0	2	0	15	1	22¹	21	3	2.0	11.7	29	45%	.340	1.16	4.03	2.82	0.7	96.8	56.4	20.8	43.1
2020	SFN	MLB	29	6	8	0	23	23	113	111	15	3.1	9.4	119	44%	.311	1.32	3.78	4.37	1.8	96.4	59.8	13.1	45.8

Comparables: Joe Ross, Jake Odorizzi, Alex Cobb

Throughout Gausman's time with the Orioles, he generally performed like an above-average starter (making him an ace by Baltimore's low standards), but often flashed the potential for more. Freed from the Birds at the 2018 deadline, he pitched better during his initial run with the Braves. Yet Gausman found himself on the move again last season after a rough go at it that coincided with a foot injury, landing with the Reds via waiver claim. With Cincinnati, he essentially turned into a two-pitch reliever—an effective one at that. Granted, it was only 22 innings, but they were very good innings wherein he fiddled around with throwing his splitter close to 50 percent of the time. The thought of a full year of health and splitter-spamming enticed the Giants into signing him to an incentive-laden one-year deal.

Trevor Gott RHP Born: 08/26/92 Age: 27 Bats: R Throws: R Height: 6'0" Weight: 185 Origin: Round 6, 2013 Draft (#178 overall)

YEAR	TEAM	LVL	AGE	W	L	SV	G	GS	IP	H	HR	BB/9	K/9	K	GB%	BABIP	WHIP	ERA	DRA	WARP	MPH	FB%	WHF	CSP
2017	SYR	AAA	24	2	0	4	30	0	37¹	39	2	3.1	8.4	35	59%	.327	1.39	3.86	4.67	0.3				
2017	WAS	MLB	24	1	0	0	4	0	3	11	1	9.0	9.0	3	35%	.625	4.67	30.00	10.51	-0.2	96.6	67	9	42.5
2018	SYR	AAA	25	1	1	3	28	0	29¹	23	1	2.5	11.7	38	56%	.319	1.06	3.68	3.26	0.6				
2018	WAS	MLB	25	0	2	0	20	0	19	19	4	4.7	7.1	15	58%	.283	1.53	5.68	6.11	-0.3	96.9	74.8	6.6	52.6
2019	SFN	MLB	26	7	0	1	50	0	52²	41	4	2.9	9.7	57	44%	.276	1.10	4.44	3.86	0.9	96.3	77.2	11.6	49.1
2020	SFN	MLB	27	3	3	0	56	0	59	58	8	3.2	8.6	57	43%	.301	1.34	3.90	4.48	0.6	96.0	77.1	10.6	49.2

Comparables: *Andrew Bellatti, Sam Tuivailala, Jimmy Herget*

One of the hot "new" trends in baseball is the death of the sinker. Pitchers and teams are, en masse, leaving the pitch in the dust in favor of designed pitches that do not allow opposing hitters to elevate low pitches and park them in the bleachers. Gott, a castoff from a Nationals bullpen only charitably described as bad prior to the 2019 season, started his first year with the Giants throwing a four-seam fastball instead of a sinker, and the results were exciting. Now, instead of another year where he appears in this book only due to an eminently pun-able last name, Gott gets a chance to be a late-inning relief option if he can avoid the elbow troubles that sidelined him in August.

Jandel Gustave RHP Born: 10/12/92 Age: 27 Bats: R Throws: R Height: 6'2" Weight: 210 Origin: International Free Agent, 2010

YEAR	TEAM	LVL	AGE	W	L	SV	G	GS	IP	H	HR	BB/9	K/9	K	GB%	BABIP	WHIP	ERA	DRA	WARP	MPH	FB%	WHF	CSP
2017	HOU	MLB	24	0	0	0	6	0	5	5	0	12.6	3.6	2	50%	.312	2.40	5.40	6.53	-0.1	98.5	57	7.5	48.2
2019	SAC	AAA	26	2	2	7	29	1	26¹	28	5	4.1	8.5	25	46%	.307	1.52	6.15	4.59	0.4				
2019	SFN	MLB	26	0	0	1	23	0	24¹	18	1	3.3	5.2	14	45%	.227	1.11	2.96	5.76	-0.1	97.9	71.6	9.7	55.4
2020	SFN	MLB	27	2	2	0	45	0	47	50	7	3.7	7.6	40	45%	.308	1.47	4.82	5.25	0.1	97.5	70.2	9.5	53.3

Comparables: *Sam Tuivailala, Jake Barrett, Daniel Webb*

For relief pitchers these days, premium velocity is no longer a differentiator—it's the jump off. So while Gustave can touch triple digits and used that heat to find a place to settle after his 2018 Tommy John surgery rehab, he still needs to find another gear in order to nail down a definite bullpen role. His 2019 performance might've helped, but it also might have been a trick of the light; he hasn't yet converted his velo into whiffs, and his low ERA belies the three "unearned" runs he allowed in September. No, what he needs to stand out is consistency with his slider. If that offering goes back to being a plus pitch, he could find solid ground in the seventh or eighth inning; until then he's best suited to trying to force his heater past hitters in the fifth or the sixth frame.

Sean Hjelle RHP Born: 05/07/97 Age: 23 Bats: R Throws: R Height: 6'11" Weight: 225 Origin: Round 2, 2018 Draft (#45 overall)

YEAR	TEAM	LVL	AGE	W	L	SV	G	GS	IP	H	HR	BB/9	K/9	K	GB%	BABIP	WHIP	ERA	DRA	WARP	MPH	FB%	WHF	CSP
2018	SLO	A-	21	0	0	0	12	12	21¹	24	4	1.7	9.3	22	49%	.317	1.31	5.06	4.10	0.3				
2019	AUG	A	22	1	2	0	9	9	40²	41	3	2.0	9.7	44	63%	.333	1.23	2.66	5.32	-0.1				
2019	SJO	A+	22	5	5	0	14	14	77²	73	2	2.2	8.6	74	69%	.326	1.18	2.78	4.11	0.9				
2019	RIC	AA	22	1	2	0	5	5	25¹	38	1	3.2	7.5	21	48%	.430	1.86	6.04	7.44	-0.8				
2020	SFN	MLB	23	2	2	0	33	0	35	35	5	3.6	7.2	28	43%	.285	1.40	4.48	4.92	0.2				

Comparables: *David Phelps, Mike Wright, Shane Carle*

Probably the closest San Francisco has come to drafting a player who literally fits the team nickname, Hjelle's towering height allows him to release the ball closer to the plate than most pitchers. As such, his fastball becomes a near-plus offering despite less-than-premium velocity, and he uses it to get both strikeouts and balls on the ground. He earned two promotions over the course of 2019, thriving in both Augusta and San Jose before eventually securing an ill-fated Eastern League debut. There's still quite a lot of promise here, especially if he can add a little mass and refine his secondaries, as his command and stature both give him a solid foundation for an eventual rotation role.

Conner Menez LHP Born: 05/29/95 Age: 25 Bats: L Throws: L Height: 6'3" Weight: 205 Origin: Round 14, 2016 Draft (#425 overall)

YEAR	TEAM	LVL	AGE	W	L	SV	G	GS	IP	H	HR	BB/9	K/9	K	GB%	BABIP	WHIP	ERA	DRA	WARP	MPH	FB%	WHF	CSP
2017	SJO	A+	22	7	7	0	23	22	114¹	127	5	3.9	7.8	99	43%	.347	1.55	4.41	5.59	-0.4				
2018	SJO	A+	23	2	5	0	11	11	50¹	48	2	3.8	12.5	70	46%	.368	1.37	4.83	3.44	1.1				
2018	RIC	AA	23	6	4	0	15	15	74	73	1	4.1	11.2	92	39%	.375	1.45	4.38	4.72	0.5				
2018	SAC	AAA	23	1	1	0	2	2	11	6	0	4.1	7.4	9	50%	.214	1.00	3.27	3.10	0.3				
2019	RIC	AA	24	3	3	0	11	11	59²	37	5	3.0	10.6	70	39%	.237	0.96	2.72	3.47	1.1				
2019	SAC	AAA	24	3	1	0	12	11	61¹	60	12	4.4	12.3	84	33%	.340	1.47	4.84	3.82	1.7				
2019	SFN	MLB	24	0	1	0	8	3	17	13	4	6.4	11.6	22	31%	.257	1.47	5.29	4.07	0.3	92.8	61.2	12	48.5
2020	SFN	MLB	25	3	3	0	33	5	53	47	10	4.1	9.3	55	34%	.273	1.34	4.18	4.79	0.5	92.5	62.7	12.3	49.7

Comparables: *Matt Hall, Jeff Manship, Wes Parsons*

This grandson of a Plummer (former Reds catcher Bill Plummer, to be precise) appears more of a utility arm than a main event star, so the more appropriate comparison is to the hard-working Dustin Rhodes instead of the more flashy Cody. Despite his gaudy strikeout numbers, the lefty didn't have sustained success at the upper levels last season due to his enormous fly ball and walk rates. With a strong possibility he may move to the bullpen eventually (perhaps in a multi-inning relief role), he'll need to refine his command in order to hold down a regular job. Until then, it looks like he'll be forced to grapple with the rest of the contenders for a slot at the back-end of the Giants' rotation, or otherwise try to find some consistency at Triple-A this year.

Reyes Moronta RHP Born: 01/06/93 Age: 27 Bats: R Throws: R Height: 5'11" Weight: 241 Origin: International Free Agent, 2011

YEAR	TEAM	LVL	AGE	W	L	SV	G	GS	IP	H	HR	BB/9	K/9	K	GB%	BABIP	WHIP	ERA	DRA	WARP	MPH	FB%	WHF	CSP
2017	RIC	AA	24	0	1	5	19	0	18	15	1	6.0	13.0	26	42%	.333	1.50	4.00	3.72	0.2				
2017	SAC	AAA	24	3	0	0	13	0	17	13	1	4.2	9.0	17	33%	.273	1.24	2.12	3.16	0.4				
2017	SFN	MLB	24	0	0	0	7	0	6²	6	1	4.1	14.9	11	47%	.357	1.35	2.70	2.60	0.2	97.8	52.7	16.4	50.2
2018	SFN	MLB	25	5	2	1	69	0	65	34	4	5.1	10.9	79	43%	.211	1.09	2.49	3.09	1.4	99.0	51	14.8	47.2
2019	SFN	MLB	26	3	7	0	56	0	56²	41	4	5.2	11.1	70	39%	.272	1.31	2.86	4.10	0.8	98.9	58.3	12.5	45.4
2020	SFN	MLB	27	1	1	0	17	0	18	14	2	4.8	11.7	23	40%	.291	1.33	3.45	4.01	0.3	98.4	55.5	13.8	47.8

Comparables: Chris Withrow, Carl Edwards Jr., Domingo Germán

Plenty of things made Moronta an outlier in the Giants' bullpen; for one, he'd been fairly consistent through most of the past two seasons, an oddity in one of baseball's most volatile bullpen mixes. Of course there's his stature, with Moronta cutting a shorter and stouter profile than most relievers while still delivering the high-end velocity and a dynamic slider expected of late-inning arms. But more than most, what set Moronta apart was how exciting he was to watch. There was a bit of the cardiac-closer in him, but more Fernando Rodney than Armando Benítez; he tended to walk too many, but a strikeout and the end of an inning was always just a couple heaters away. Unfortunately labrum repair surgery has Moronta unlikely to return to the team until the very end of the 2020 season, so the Giants faithful will have to find another way to enjoy the late innings in the meantime.

Dereck Rodríguez RHP Born: 06/05/92 Age: 28 Bats: R Throws: R Height: 6'1" Weight: 215 Origin: Round 6, 2011 Draft (#208 overall)

YEAR	TEAM	LVL	AGE	W	L	SV	G	GS	IP	H	HR	BB/9	K/9	K	GB%	BABIP	WHIP	ERA	DRA	WARP	MPH	FB%	WHF	CSP
2017	FTM	A+	25	5	2	0	11	11	68	59	7	1.5	7.8	59	43%	.278	1.03	2.51	3.32	1.6				
2017	CHT	AA	25	5	4	0	15	13	75¹	74	9	3.2	7.4	62	41%	.294	1.34	3.94	5.39	-0.2				
2018	SAC	AAA	26	4	1	0	9	9	50¹	49	11	2.0	9.5	53	39%	.284	1.19	3.40	3.53	1.1				
2018	SFN	MLB	26	6	4	0	21	19	118¹	98	9	2.7	6.8	89	41%	.257	1.13	2.81	5.18	0.1	94.6	53.3	9.9	48
2019	SAC	AAA	27	3	0	0	6	6	29²	26	4	3.0	8.5	28	47%	.278	1.21	3.64	2.85	1.1				
2019	SFN	MLB	27	6	11	0	28	16	99	108	21	3.3	6.5	71	46%	.282	1.45	5.64	6.69	-1.1	93.2	48.6	9.5	46.7
2020	SFN	MLB	28	5	8	0	39	16	105	110	17	3.2	6.7	78	43%	.292	1.40	4.58	5.17	0.7	93.3	51.1	9.8	47.6

Comparables: Mark Leiter Jr., Brock Stewart, Luis Santos

Eyed as an obvious regression candidate from his solid 2018 rookie season, Rodríguez couldn't hang onto his starting rotation slot consistently last year, and was pushed to the bullpen and to Triple-A as the Giants looked to find ways to give others the shot Rodríguez made so much of once. In the end, it might be as simple as this: He just doesn't have the velocity or movement on his pitches to get outs consistently. Despite command and four pitches, he gets hammered when allowed to face hitters a second or third time, perhaps in part to all the pitches he has to throw his first time through. As one of the most ineffective semi-regular starting pitchers in baseball last year, he'll have to continue to work on refining his offerings and getting more movement, or else find himself resigned to a swingman role or toiling in the PCL.

Tyler Rogers RHP Born: 12/17/90 Age: 29 Bats: R Throws: R Height: 6'5" Weight: 187 Origin: Round 10, 2013 Draft (#312 overall)

YEAR	TEAM	LVL	AGE	W	L	SV	G	GS	IP	H	HR	BB/9	K/9	K	GB%	BABIP	WHIP	ERA	DRA	WARP	MPH	FB%	WHF	CSP
2017	SAC	AAA	26	4	4	10	55	0	76	65	2	3.3	5.1	43	63%	.268	1.22	2.37	3.43	1.6				
2018	SAC	AAA	27	3	2	3	51	0	67²	50	4	3.1	8.0	60	62%	.254	1.08	2.13	2.72	1.9				
2019	SAC	AAA	28	4	2	5	49	1	62	59	6	4.1	8.0	55	63%	.306	1.40	4.21	3.99	1.4				
2019	SFN	MLB	28	2	0	0	17	0	17²	12	0	1.5	8.2	16	70%	.240	0.85	1.02	3.96	0.3	83.7	67.1	8.2	55.2
2020	SFN	MLB	29	2	3	3	45	0	47	55	12	2.8	6.2	33	60%	.288	1.47	5.63	6.13	-0.4	83.1	67.1	8.2	55.2

Comparables: Colton Murray, Jose A. Valdez, Jorge Rondon

There's a dominant submariner in San Francisco, and no, Prince Namor hasn't conquered McCovey Cove. After two PCL All-Star game appearances, Rogers was a revelation when he joined the Giants late in 2019, shockingly effective against lefties and righties alike. Of course his unconventional delivery makes for a fan-favorite, but what's even more appealing was the fact that *he was actually pretty good*. Amidst the slapdash relief options the Giants have coming into 2020, Rogers is one of the most likely to worm(burn) his way into the late innings as well as fans' hearts. While there still isn't a huge sample size of major-league performance and his fastball would never get pulled over by CHiPs if it were cruising down I-80, the onus is now on management to let him sink or swim in the bigs.

Tyson Ross RHP Born: 04/22/87 Age: 33 Bats: R Throws: R Height: 6'6" Weight: 245 Origin: Round 2, 2008 Draft (#58 overall)

YEAR	TEAM	LVL	AGE	W	L	SV	G	GS	IP	H	HR	BB/9	K/9	K	GB%	BABIP	WHIP	ERA	DRA	WARP	MPH	FB%	WHF	CSP
2017	FRI	AA	30	1	1	0	2	2	11²	11	0	3.1	7.7	10	62%	.324	1.29	2.31	4.50	0.1				
2017	ROU	AAA	30	2	1	0	4	4	18²	23	3	5.3	5.3	11	46%	.345	1.82	7.71	7.55	-0.4				
2017	TEX	MLB	30	3	3	0	12	10	49	53	7	6.8	6.6	36	48%	.305	1.84	7.71	8.24	-1.5	94.1	57.1	7.7	41.1
2018	SDN	MLB	31	6	9	0	22	22	123¹	112	16	3.8	7.8	107	45%	.276	1.33	4.45	4.94	0.5	93.5	41.7	9.3	43.9
2018	SLN	MLB	31	2	0	0	9	1	26¹	20	1	3.4	5.1	15	58%	.244	1.14	2.73	5.50	-0.1	94.2	41.7	8.3	46.1
2019	DET	MLB	32	1	5	0	7	7	35¹	41	7	4.6	6.4	25	51%	.306	1.67	6.11	7.59	-0.7	92.1	46.3	7.2	46.1
2020	SFN	MLB	33	2	2	0	33	0	35	36	6	3.9	7.7	30	47%	.294	1.45	5.04	5.03	0.1	92.4	44.8	8.4	43.7

Comparables: Andrew Cashner, Lance Lynn, Jake Arrieta

A recent CareerBuilder survey said that 75 percent of hiring managers have found a lie on a résumé. The only one that slipped through the human resources fact-checkers was Ross claiming he was the All-Star representative for the Padres in 2014. Unfortunately, there is no way to verify that. An All-Star appearance, especially for a starting pitcher, gives you about five extra fliers for your career. Ross has a couple left after a tectonically turbulent Tigers season, missing his spots when he wasn't missing in action.

Jeff Samardzija RHP
Born: 01/23/85   Age: 35   Bats: R   Throws: R   Height: 6'5"   Weight: 240   Origin: Round 5, 2006 Draft (#149 overall)

YEAR	TEAM	LVL	AGE	W	L	SV	G	GS	IP	H	HR	BB/9	K/9	K	GB%	BABIP	WHIP	ERA	DRA	WARP	MPH	FB%	WHF	CSP
2017	SFN	MLB	32	9	15	0	32	32	207²	204	30	1.4	8.9	205	43%	.303	1.14	4.42	3.43	5.0	96.7	56.8	11.1	50.5
2018	SAC	AAA	33	0	2	0	4	4	17	17	5	1.6	10.6	20	40%	.286	1.18	5.29	4.27	0.2				
2018	SFN	MLB	33	1	5	0	10	10	44²	47	6	5.2	6.0	30	32%	.287	1.63	6.25	7.20	-1.0	96.0	63.2	9.2	46.3
2019	SFN	MLB	34	11	12	0	32	32	181¹	152	28	2.4	6.9	140	37%	.240	1.11	3.52	4.40	2.7	94.1	68.9	9.7	47.8
2020	SFN	MLB	35	8	10	0	26	26	148	144	25	2.4	7.2	118	37%	.276	1.25	3.94	4.69	1.9	94.0	62.9	9.9	47.1

Comparables: Jake Arrieta, Ian Kennedy, Wade Davis

While it's not fair to say that everything went right during Samardzija's bounceback season, the veteran righty did seem a bit charmed last year. For years he's been a serial home-run-allower, but this season only seven of the 28 he allowed plated more than one run. (His career solo homer percentage is 60 percent, so that's a marked improvement.) In addition, he had the second-lowest BABIP among qualified starting pitchers, behind only AL Cy Young Justin Verlander. All this helped keep his ERA tidy despite a strikeout rate that matched his ill-fated season on the South Side of Chicago. The Shark now swims into the final season of his contract as a useful member of the roster: a reliable mid-rotation starter who may be able to fetch a return in trade despite his hefty contract.

Sam Selman LHP
Born: 11/14/90   Age: 29   Bats: R   Throws: L   Height: 6'3"   Weight: 190   Origin: Round 2, 2012 Draft (#66 overall)

YEAR	TEAM	LVL	AGE	W	L	SV	G	GS	IP	H	HR	BB/9	K/9	K	GB%	BABIP	WHIP	ERA	DRA	WARP	MPH	FB%	WHF	CSP
2017	NWA	AA	26	4	3	5	24	0	39¹	21	1	4.3	13.5	59	38%	.260	1.02	2.97	2.34	1.2				
2017	OMA	AAA	26	0	1	3	18	0	28¹	13	1	6.0	12.1	38	35%	.214	1.13	2.22	2.81	0.8				
2018	NWA	AA	27	1	2	0	12	0	12¹	12	0	8.0	15.3	21	37%	.444	1.86	6.57	4.19	0.1				
2018	OMA	AAA	27	0	2	0	23	0	28¹	22	0	6.0	11.8	37	45%	.328	1.45	4.13	3.55	0.5				
2019	RIC	AA	28	0	0	0	4	0	7	3	0	1.3	16.7	13	58%	.250	0.57	0.00	2.23	0.2				
2019	SAC	AAA	28	3	2	0	39	1	48	25	4	3.0	15.2	81	41%	.253	0.85	2.06	0.69	2.6				
2019	SFN	MLB	28	0	0	0	10	0	10¹	6	2	5.2	8.7	10	38%	.167	1.16	4.35	5.45	0.0	92.2	42.5	12.4	43.1
2020	SFN	MLB	29	2	2	0	34	0	36	32	8	4.0	8.8	35	39%	.262	1.36	4.51	5.18	0.1	91.6	42.5	12.4	43.1

Comparables: Hunter Cervenka, Austin Adams, Ryan Mattheus

A move from Omaha to Sacramento—with a stop at Driveline Baseball to work on his mechanics—was just what Selman needed after years toiling in the upper minors for the Royals. He was a revelation for his new PCL squad, and appeared to have finally overcome his walk issues while posting the highest strikeout rate in the league among pitchers with more than 25 innings pitched. Called up after the Giants' post-deadline bullpen exodus, Selman might have forgotten to pack his control; he was beat up after being used almost equally against righties and lefties. If he can keep his mechanics consistent and, consequently, his pitches close to the zone, expect to see his vicious slider in high-leverage innings in 2020.

Tony Watson LHP
Born: 05/30/85   Age: 35   Bats: L   Throws: L   Height: 6'3"   Weight: 218   Origin: Round 9, 2007 Draft (#278 overall)

YEAR	TEAM	LVL	AGE	W	L	SV	G	GS	IP	H	HR	BB/9	K/9	K	GB%	BABIP	WHIP	ERA	DRA	WARP	MPH	FB%	WHF	CSP
2017	PIT	MLB	32	5	3	10	47	0	46²	57	7	2.7	6.8	35	46%	.333	1.52	3.66	5.55	-0.2	95.2	65.1	14	50.8
2017	LAN	MLB	32	2	1	0	24	0	20	15	2	2.7	8.1	18	62%	.241	1.05	2.70	5.14	0.0	95.4	64.9	13.3	46.7
2018	SFN	MLB	33	4	6	0	72	0	66	54	4	1.9	9.8	72	47%	.294	1.03	2.59	3.31	1.2	94.6	51.2	13.9	54.4
2019	SFN	MLB	34	2	2	0	60	0	54	56	9	2.0	6.8	41	46%	.287	1.26	4.17	5.57	-0.1	94.6	51.5	13.6	49
2020	SFN	MLB	35	3	3	13	56	0	59	57	9	2.4	8.3	55	47%	.289	1.23	3.63	4.32	0.7	93.5	54.1	13.5	50

Comparables: Fernando Abad, Mike Stanton, Jerry Blevins

Ironically dubbed an "especially nimble" reliever in last year's Annual due to his ability to thrive in almost any relief situation, Watson didn't look too agile breaking his wrist while diving to make a tag on Kolten Wong and preserve a win last September. (He'd later describe his move as "lay out like a 34-year-old dad," which was harsh but fair.) Paired with a disappointing '19 campaign, it's no big surprise that he exercised his player option to remain with the Giants instead of making another questionable leap, this time into free agency. Beyond his collection of talents which include adaptability, resilience, late-inning experience and a (mostly) functional left arm, the Giants should be especially glad to have a player who had the will to dive and sacrifice his arm to save (but not save) a meaningless September game. Players like Watson, more often than not, tend to land on their feet.

Logan Webb RHP
Born: 11/18/96   Age: 23   Bats: R   Throws: R   Height: 6'2"   Weight: 220   Origin: Round 4, 2014 Draft (#118 overall)

YEAR	TEAM	LVL	AGE	W	L	SV	G	GS	IP	H	HR	BB/9	K/9	K	GB%	BABIP	WHIP	ERA	DRA	WARP	MPH	FB%	WHF	CSP
2017	SLO	A-	20	2	0	0	15	0	28	26	1	2.2	10.0	31	68%	.325	1.18	2.89	3.49	0.5				
2018	SJO	A+	21	1	3	0	21	20	74	54	2	4.4	9.0	74	48%	.274	1.22	1.82	3.10	1.9				
2018	RIC	AA	21	1	2	0	6	6	30²	30	4	3.2	7.6	26	52%	.289	1.34	3.82	5.29	0.0				
2019	AUG	A	22	1	0	0	2	1	10	4	0	2.7	8.1	9	62%	.167	0.70	0.90	3.02	0.2				
2019	RIC	AA	22	1	4	0	8	7	41¹	41	2	2.6	10.2	47	66%	.333	1.28	2.18	4.35	0.3				
2019	SAC	AAA	22	0	0	0	1	1	7	7	0	0.0	9.0	7	63%	.368	1.00	1.29	3.15	0.2				
2019	SFN	MLB	22	2	3	0	8	8	39²	44	5	3.2	8.4	37	48%	.333	1.46	5.22	4.17	0.7	94.6	56.4	9.8	45.5
2020	SFN	MLB	23	5	7	0	18	18	89	94	12	3.6	7.7	76	52%	.309	1.45	4.40	4.93	0.9	94.5	58.4	10.1	47.1

Comparables: Tyler Mahle, Joe Ross, Zack Littell

To say that Webb's year was up-and-down might be underselling the dips and dives of his rookie season. After starting off hot in Double-A and building off his revitalized fastball velocity, Webb earned an 80-game PED suspension that seemed to tie a nice little bow on how his velo jumped up after his return from Tommy John surgery in 2017. After returning he picked up where he left off, posting great performances at *four* levels before finding his way to San Francisco to hold down a starting slot until the season's end. At 22 years old, Webb doesn't have the command or the secondaries (yet) to dominate as a starter, and that showed in his uneven performance at the big-league level. The Giants would probably prefer him to develop in the minors further before plunging him into the big-league fire, but he's already proven he can maintain starting pitcher status.

LINEOUTS

Hitters

HITTER	POS	TEAM	LVL	AGE	PA	R	2B	3B	HR	RBI	BB	K	SB	CS	AVG/OBP/SLG	DRC+	VORP	BABIP	BRR	FRAA	WARP
Sandro Fabian	OF	GIA	Rk	21	41	4	3	0	2	8	5	13	0	0	.219/.366/.500	124	2.7	.278	-0.8	LF(4): 0.1	0.1
	OF	SJO	A+	21	187	20	4	1	5	33	14	33	3	1	.287/.353/.413	121	10.4	.328	1.0	RF(36): 4.2	1.2
Scooter Gennett	2B	CIN	MLB	29	72	4	3	0	0	5	1	20	0	0	.217/.236/.261	68	-0.6	.300	-1.3	2B(19): -0.6	-0.2
	2B	SFN	MLB	29	67	11	4	0	2	6	1	21	0	0	.234/.254/.391	53	-1.9	.310	1.6	2B(17): -0.8	-0.1
Mike Gerber	OF	SAC	AAA	26	513	95	41	1	26	83	39	140	5	4	.308/.368/.569	108	32.5	.389	-0.6	CF(67): -8.7, RF(25): -4.4	0.7
	OF	SFN	MLB	26	26	0	1	0	0	0	2	15	0	0	.042/.115/.083	43	-1.2	.111	-0.6	LF(5): -0.2, RF(5): -0.3	-0.2
Jacob Gonzalez	3B	AUG	A	21	504	54	25	1	10	57	39	80	0	0	.241/.312/.367	104	16.8	.268	0.4	3B(66): -7.2, 1B(18): -1.6	0.5
Zach Green	3B	SFN	MLB	25	16	1	1	0	0	1	2	6	0	0	.143/.250/.214	65	-0.1	.250	-0.2	3B(5): -0.6	-0.1
	3B	SAC	AAA	25	297	43	18	1	25	64	39	99	1	0	.282/.380/.659	132	30.6	.351	-1.0	3B(57): -3.5, 1B(16): -0.1	1.7
Franklin Labour	OF	AUG	A	21	117	16	6	0	1	11	8	40	0	0	.215/.282/.299	61	-2.6	.333	0.5	RF(23): -2.3, LF(4): -0.4	-0.5
	OF	SLO	A-	21	189	37	9	2	14	34	18	43	2	1	.307/.392/.639	203	22.6	.339	-0.3	RF(34): -2.0, LF(3): 0.0	1.6
Hamlet Marte	C	SJO	A+	25	63	6	3	0	0	7	9	16	0	0	.245/.349/.302	101	2.2	.342	-1.4	C(16): -0.4	0.1
	C	RIC	AA	25	210	11	5	1	2	19	16	66	2	3	.187/.255/.257	52	-4.3	.270	-1.7	C(51): -6.2, 1B(4): -0.5	-1.0
Joe McCarthy	OF	SAC	AAA	25	89	10	3	0	1	4	8	30	0	0	.165/.247/.241	27	-6.5	.245	0.4	LF(10): 2.4, RF(10): -1.1	-0.4
	OF	DUR	AAA	25	182	24	6	2	6	23	29	54	1	0	.196/.335/.385	84	1.1	.256	0.3	RF(20): -1.5, CF(8): -1.0	-0.1
Jairo Pomares	OF	GIA	Rk	18	167	17	10	4	3	33	10	26	5	3	.368/.401/.542	169	15.9	.422	-3.6	RF(34): -0.2	1.0
	OF	SLO	A-	18	62	7	3	0	0	4	1	17	0	0	.207/.258/.259	42	-1.4	.293	0.4	LF(6): -0.1, RF(6): -1.1	-0.3
Kean Wong	2B	DUR	AAA	24	506	71	29	6	10	63	42	112	6	3	.307/.375/.464	110	21.7	.389	1.0	2B(47): -2.5, 3B(38): -2.9	2.0
	2B	LAA	MLB	24	4	1	0	0	0	0	0	1	0	0	.000/.000/.000	58	-0.1	.000	0.2		0.0
	2B	TBA	MLB	24	14	1	0	0	0	0	0	5	0	1	.214/.214/.214	72	-0.2	.333	-0.2	RF(2): -0.3, 2B(2): 0.0	-0.1
Logan Wyatt	1B	SLO	A-	21	78	10	2	0	2	12	10	9	0	1	.284/.385/.403	175	4.5	.304	-0.5	1B(16): -0.5	0.4
	1B	GIA	Rk	21	29	7	1	0	0	9	4	6	0	1	.375/.448/.417	113	2.8	.474	0.4	1B(6): 0.8	0.2
	1B	AUG	A	21	76	9	3	0	1	9	12	14	0	0	.233/.368/.333	108	0.8	.277	-1.4	1B(14): -0.4	-0.1

Injuries held back the toolsy and talented **Sandro Fabian** in 2019, but maybe that's for the best. Featuring one of the best outfield arms in the organization and potential for both power and contact ability, Fabian made some progress with his wildcat approach at the plate in his limited time on the field last year. ⏾ There was a time when **Scooter Gennett** was both a solid player and an answer to a trivia question about guys with four home runs in one game. Now, he's…an answer to a trivia question about guys with four home runs in one game. ⏾ Prototypical fourth-outfielder **Mike Gerber** was the first player Farhan Zaidi acquired after coming over to the Giants, but couldn't survive a full 12 months with the franchise after a 1-for-24 run in a brief call-up. ⏾ Repeating the Sally League didn't do more than provide very incremental improvements for **Jacob Gonzalez**. His fielding difficulties at third base should cause him to follow in his father's footsteps as a left fielder and/or first baseman, but he'd better hope his dad's game power comes along for the ride as well. ⏾ Third baseman **Zach Green** showed promising power in 2019 with the River Cats, but once he broached the big leagues he only drove pitches into the turf. ⏾ Labour power isn't just a central concept in the criticism of capitalism, it's also something the Giants discovered after outfield prospect **Franklin Labour** hit 14 homers in 41 games for Salem-Keizer. ⏾ Unfortunately it takes a quote from one Hamlet (Prince of Denmark) to describe another (**Hamlet Marte**)'s future outlook: "I must be cruel, only to be kind. Thus bad begins and worse remains behind." ⏾ Toolsy teenager **Luis Matos** already has incredible bat speed, but everything else is still a question mark. After making his stateside debut at the ripe old age of 17 in 2019, he quickly fell victim to an outfield collision, making us wait until 2020 for more looks at the promising youngster. ⏾ It's not all that cavalier to say that this University of Virginia product had a rough 2019. Once seen as a potential high-OBP corner guy with speed, **Joe McCarthy** hit .183 in the minors last year, which all the walks in the world can't make up for. ⏾ 2018 J2 pickup **Jairo Pomares** already has a solid approach at the plate and a dangerous hit tool. He might be a corner outfielder when all's said and done, but if he can develop his power profile, the Giants could have yet another high-test outfield prospect to go with Ramos, Bishop, Canario, and Matos. ⏾ **Kean Wong** plays for the San Francisco Giants after his brother complained about him not playing for the Rays. ⏾ Second-round draft pick **Logan Wyatt** flashed the skills at Louisville to make people think he could be the second coming of Brandon Belt. High-OBP, low-power first basemen are risky and unpopular even when they're successful, so we hope he's not counting on any endorsement deals.

Pitchers

PITCHER	TEAM	LVL	AGE	W	L	SV	G	GS	IP	H	HR	BB/9	K/9	K	GB%	BABIP	WHIP	ERA	DRA	WARP	MPH	FB%	WHF	CSP
Melvin Adon	RIC	AA	25	2	6	14	36	0	45	38	2	5.2	11.8	59	52%	.356	1.42	2.60	5.04	-0.2				
	SAC	AAA	25	0	1	0	12	0	10^1	16	1	7.0	15.7	18	50%	.517	2.32	13.94	5.19	0.1				
Kyle Barraclough	HAR	AA	29	0	1	0	7	0	9^2	4	0	4.7	13.0	14	44%	.222	0.93	1.86	3.03	0.2				
	WAS	MLB	29	1	2	0	33	0	25^2	33	8	4.2	10.5	30	36%	.347	1.75	6.66	5.69	-0.1	95.2	48.3	13	48.8
	SFN	MLB	29	0	0	0	10	0	8	5	1	10.1	11.2	10	57%	.200	1.75	2.25	5.93	-0.1	95.6	48.3	16.6	43
Tristan Beck	BRA	Rk	23	0	0	0	2	2	9	9	0	4.0	14.0	14	52%	.429	1.44	4.00	2.23	0.4				
	BRV	A+	23	2	2	0	8	8	36^2	45	2	3.4	9.6	39	53%	.413	1.61	5.65	7.05	-0.9				
	SJO	A+	23	3	2	0	6	6	35^2	33	1	3.3	9.3	37	44%	.337	1.29	2.27	4.38	0.3				
Enderson Franco	SAC	AAA	26	6	5	0	26	22	113	139	24	2.9	7.8	98	39%	.334	1.55	5.97	6.19	0.5				
	SFN	MLB	26	0	0	0	5	0	5^1	4	1	1.7	6.8	4	27%	.214	0.94	3.38	5.77	0.0	97.2	55.7	13.6	53.5
Matt Frisbee	AUG	A	22	0	1	0	4	2	16	11	3	3.4	12.9	23	30%	.267	1.06	2.81	2.81	0.4				
	SJO	A+	22	9	8	0	22	20	116^1	102	12	1.7	10.1	131	29%	.298	1.07	3.17	3.38	2.3				
Dany Jimenez	DUN	A+	25	5	1	4	20	0	25^1	23	2	3.2	16.7	47	45%	.429	1.26	3.55	3.37	0.4				
	NHP	AA	25	2	2	6	25	0	33^2	22	4	3.2	12.3	46	41%	.261	1.01	1.87	4.10	0.2				
Steven Okert	SAC	AAA	27	8	2	0	50	4	57^2	64	14	2.8	11.7	75	27%	.340	1.42	5.31	5.29	0.6				
Wandy Peralta	LOU	AAA	27	0	0	0	12	0	11	11	0	0.8	5.7	7	49%	.314	1.09	3.27	3.92	0.2				
	CIN	MLB	27	1	1	0	39	0	34	36	10	4.0	7.1	27	50%	.268	1.50	6.09	6.75	-0.5	97.2	34.6	15.7	42.5
	SFN	MLB	27	0	0	0	8	0	5^2	4	1	1.6	7.9	5	73%	.214	0.88	3.18	2.80	0.2	97.4	48.8	15.5	42.9
Aaron Phillips	SJO	A+	22	8	7	0	25	21	115	119	15	3.4	7.9	101	36%	.310	1.41	4.62	5.20	-0.3				
	SAC	AAA	22	1	0	0	1	1	6	3	0	1.5	10.5	7	47%	.200	0.67	1.50	2.05	0.3				
Ricardo Pinto	MNT	AA	25	2	1	0	4	2	18^2	20	2	3.9	7.2	15	26%	.327	1.50	4.82	6.34	-0.4				
	DUR	AAA	25	10	5	0	24	4	104^2	96	18	4.0	8.3	96	50%	.281	1.36	4.13	4.47	1.9				
	TBA	MLB	25	0	0	0	2	0	2^1	4	1	7.7	0.0	0	46%	.300	2.57	15.43	6.61	0.0	97.6	66.7	8.9	54.2
Blake Rivera	AUG	A	21	4	6	0	16	15	73	59	3	4.8	10.7	87	59%	.301	1.34	3.95	5.06	0.1				
Gregory Santos	AUG	A	19	1	5	0	8	8	34^2	34	4	2.3	6.8	26	56%	.288	1.24	2.86	5.64	-0.2				
Burch Smith	SAN	AAA	29	6	3	0	15	15	77^1	49	6	4.3	9.9	85	41%	.239	1.11	2.33	2.77	2.9				
	SAC	AAA	29	1	1	0	3	2	15	16	1	5.4	10.8	18	54%	.375	1.67	4.20	5.42	0.2				
	SFN	MLB	29	0	0	0	10	0	8^2	10	2	4.2	6.2	6	36%	.323	1.62	2.08	8.24	-0.3	95.6	66.5	8.2	48.6
	MIL	MLB	29	0	1	0	7	0	12^2	16	3	7.1	9.9	14	32%	.351	2.05	7.82	6.81	-0.2	95.2	66.5	14.7	48
Andrew Suárez	SAC	AAA	26	7	6	0	18	15	88	112	11	3.3	5.8	57	45%	.346	1.64	5.73	5.73	0.8				
	SFN	MLB	26	0	2	0	21	2	32^2	39	7	3.9	6.9	25	48%	.317	1.62	5.79	6.57	-0.4	94.3	56.5	8.4	49.8
Kai-Wei Teng	AUG	A	20	3	0	0	5	5	29	16	0	2.2	12.1	39	46%	.262	0.79	1.55	2.47	0.9				
	CDR	A	20	4	0	0	9	8	50^2	40	1	2.5	8.7	49	56%	.277	1.07	1.60	3.33	1.1				
Jake Wong	AUG	A	22	2	1	0	8	8	40^2	26	2	2.4	7.5	34	50%	.226	0.91	1.99	3.43	0.8				
	SJO	A+	22	3	2	0	15	15	72^1	76	6	3.0	8.3	67	43%	.345	1.38	4.98	5.78	-0.7				

Melvin Adon, like most relief prospects, can accurately be described by a series of Bad Religion album titles: *No Control, The Process of Belief, Into the Unknown*. Most guys with his profile add more BR album titles like *Suffer* or *No Substance* or *How Could Hell Be Any Worse?* but Adon has a chance to go *Against the Grain*. ⊗ Once the very definition of the term "effectively wild", **Kyle Barraclough** lost a little velocity this past season and the adverb from that clause went with it. His proven closer status will get him an invite to spring training somewhere, and he'll try to find a positive word to describe his status for the first time since 2017. ⊗ Acquired in exchange for Mark Melancon, **Tristan Beck** showed out as a starting pitcher after coming to the Giants. His strong performances in the AFL and in San Jose show glimmers of hope that his back issues could be, well, behind him, and soon there might be yet another Stanford alum gracing the 25-man roster. ⊗ It took 10 years for **Enderson Franco** to reach the majors, and there was an ovation after he finished mopping up the ninth. It was Bruce Bochy's 2,000th win. There were at least a couple people back in Venezuela cheering for a different reason, though. ⊗ The San Jose Giants' Pitcher of the Year, **Matt Frisbee**, racked up strikeouts and put the hammer down on opposing hitters. The starter's ultimate upside might be limited by his lack of plus pitches, but at least he's made it into the prospect disc-ussion. ⊗ Right-hander **Dany Jimenez** struck out billion percent of the batters he faced in Double-A, which is why the Giants stole him from Toronto in the Rule 5 draft. That's a tough break for all the Jays fans who named their kids "Dany" before waiting to see how this would all play out. ⊗ **Trevor Oaks** was one of four members of the Royals organization to miss the season due to injury, which is probably the worst Sporcle quiz ever conceived. He'll be throwing pitches into new dirt this year in San Francisco, and hoping that enough batters chase sinkers that he'll get to keep chasing his dreams. ⊗ **Steven Okert** allowed 14 homers in 50 appearances at Triple-A, couldn't crack the lefty specialist carousel in San Francisco, and remains the major-league player most likely to be confused with a Cardi B catchphrase. ⊗ Ground ball lefty **Wandy Peralta** was in the middle of another disappointing season for the Reds when they cast him aside. Lefties who top 95 miles per hour on their heater will always get a second look, and he showed enough in his late-season audition with the Giants to think he'll be some team's low-risk reclamation project this spring. ⊗ Young starter **Aaron Phillips**'s low-key velocity may keep him from prospect touts, but he still turned in two tremendous appearances in 2019. In July, he leapt up to Triple-A and threw a solid six-inning outing in a spot start, and in August threw the best pitching performance in the Giants system all season: a 93-pitch near-perfect game against Inland Empire. ⊗ After a horrific pair of late-season garbage-time appearances with the Rays, **Ricardo Pinto** and his mid-90s heater were stashed in Triple-A by the Giants in case of emergency. ⊗ Another starting pitching prospect who may eventually be destined for the bullpen, **Blake Rivera**'s curveball might make him the third pitcher from Wallace State Community College to make the majors (behind Craig Kimbrel and former-Giant Derek Holland). ⊗ Young **Gregory Santos** lost most of 2019 to shoulder issues, which takes much of the luster off his prospect hype. His future may be in the bullpen, where his fastball/slider combo can play up and he can focus on those two offerings, as well as staying healthy. ⊗ Every Murakami novel seems to involve the protagonist discovering an alternate reality. Every **Burch Smith** season involves him landing on a new team. He'll turn 30 soon, so he might want to go poking around wormholes—maybe there's a reality out there where he's more than an up-and-down arm. ⊗ Going to southpaw **Andrew Suárez** out of a major-league bullpen is a lot like hitting up your local gas station for dinner: there's plenty to choose from and you'll make it through the night, but none of the offerings are going to thrill you and you might wish you had made different choices later that night. ⊗ Acquired at the deadline as part of the Sam Dyson deal, **Kai-Wei Teng** is a thickly-built right-hander whose professional experience from Taiwan and pitchability allowed him to expose A-ball hitters all season long. He could rise to the level of a back-end starter even if he doesn't add velocity over time. ⊗ After rolling over the Sally League, including a stretch where he didn't allow a hit for 12 innings, **Jake Wong** struggled in his first taste of High-A. Nothing in the repertoire stands out as a signature, so it'll take more lines like he posted in Augusta to keep him on track to reach the bigs.

SEATTLE MARINERS

Essay by Graham MacAree

Player comments by Jordan Shusterman and BP staff

By the time of the Testicle Calamity, any goodwill from the Seattle Mariners' 13-2 start had disappeared. It was June 6th, the fans were thoroughly disengaged, Astros ace Justin Verlander was on the mound, the lineup was being efficiently mowed down, and Mariners were, to nobody's surprise, on the way to their 40th loss of the season.

Mitch Haniger, his teal uniform clashing horribly with T-Mobile Park's neon pink branding, stepped up in the third inning with the Mariners down 3-1. The 2018 All-Star had been expected to push on to new heights, but thanks mostly to a BABIP collapse, Haniger's season had failed to match the team's hopes. And that season was about to get much worse.

Verlander piped in two called strikes to put Haniger in a hole. He missed with the 0-2 pitch, leaving a 94 mph fastball up and in, inducing a defensive swing. Haniger made contact, just about. He quickly wished he hadn't. Rather than dribbling the pitch off to safety, he instead drilled it straight into his own crotch.

Haniger sagged to one knee in pain, touching home plate to steady himself. Somehow, he kept playing for another three innings, toughing his way through a pair of strikeouts before being replaced by Mac Williamson. The wince-inducing news emerged in full the next day: ruptured testicle, season over.

Haniger's loss was metaphor's gain. The Mariners are a self-inflicted ruptured testicle of a team, and four years into general manager Jerry Dipoto's tenure it's difficult to see how they'll contrive to end the longest playoff drought in American sports.

Dipoto's tenure had, until recently, been marked by abortive charges towards the American League Wild Card game. To their credit, the Mariners spent several years resisting the league-wide rebuilding spree, clinging stubbornly to the eroding middle ground and giving themselves a squint-and-*maybe* chance each season. But their repeated almost-contention was fueled by trading every minor leaguer of note for spare parts before the team inevitably fell apart just after each trade deadline, leaving the farm system on life support without anything to show for it at the major-league level.

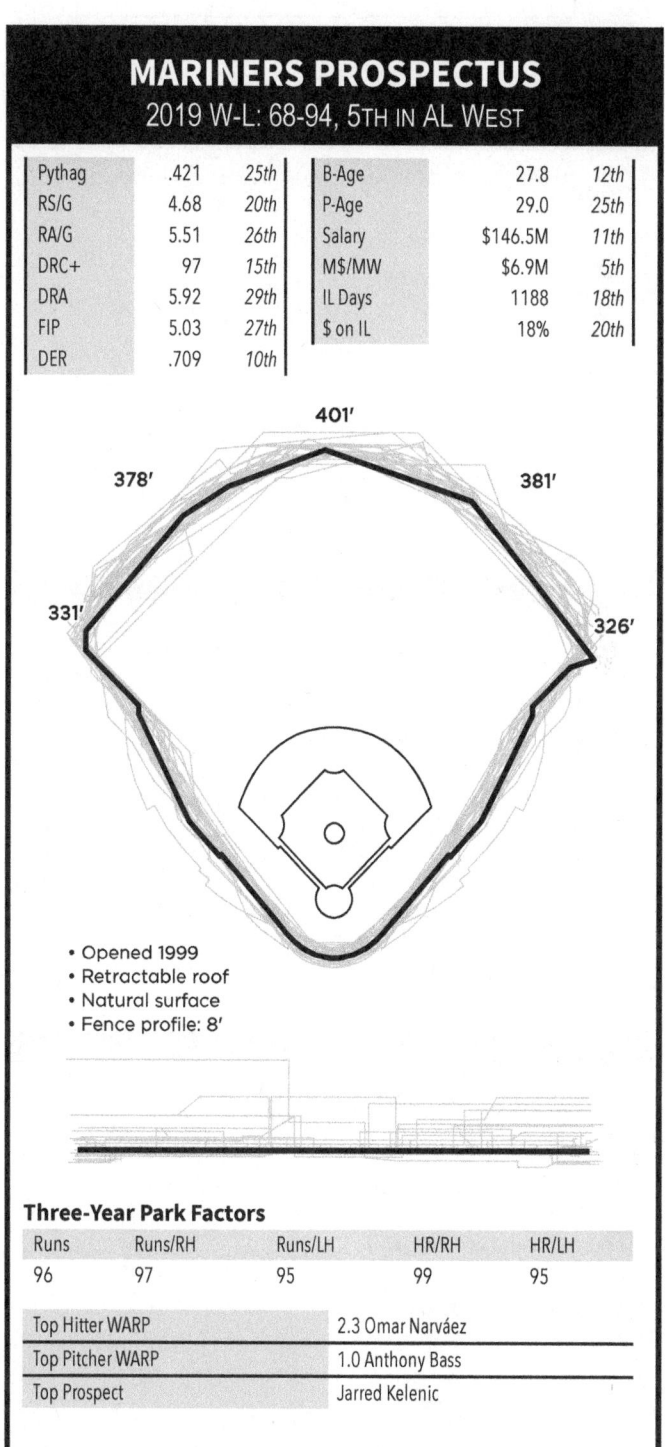

MARINERS PROSPECTUS
2019 W-L: 68-94, 5TH IN AL WEST

Pythag	.421	25th	B-Age	27.8	12th
RS/G	4.68	20th	P-Age	29.0	25th
RA/G	5.51	26th	Salary	$146.5M	11th
DRC+	97	15th	M$/MW	$6.9M	5th
DRA	5.92	29th	IL Days	1188	18th
FIP	5.03	27th	$ on IL	18%	20th
DER	.709	10th			

401'
378'
381'
331'
326'

- Opened 1999
- Retractable roof
- Natural surface
- Fence profile: 8'

Three-Year Park Factors

Runs	Runs/RH	Runs/LH	HR/RH	HR/LH
96	97	95	99	95

Top Hitter WARP	2.3 Omar Narváez
Top Pitcher WARP	1.0 Anthony Bass
Top Prospect	Jarred Kelenic

2019 Hit List Ranking

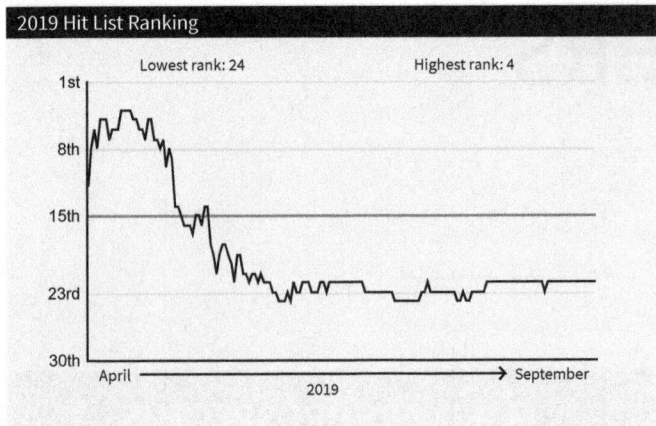

Committed Payroll (in millions)

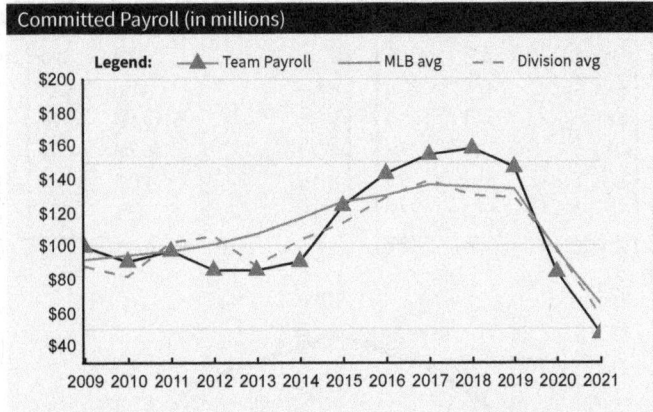

Farm System Ranking

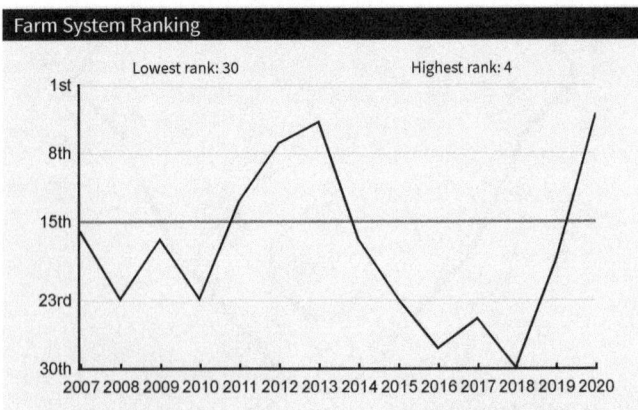

Personnel

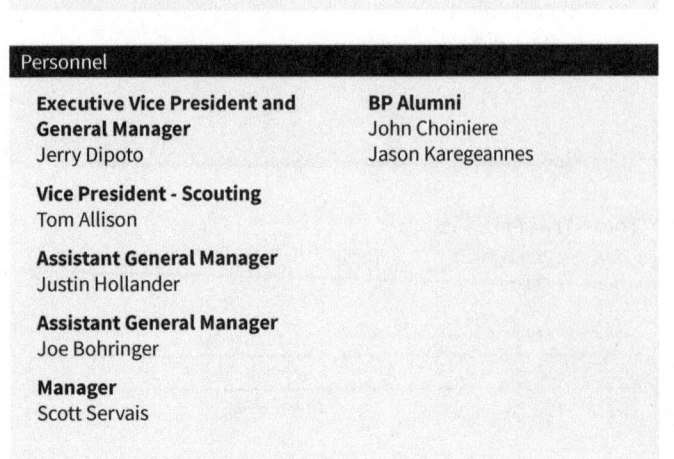

Executive Vice President and General Manager
Jerry Dipoto

Vice President - Scouting
Tom Allison

Assistant General Manager
Justin Hollander

Assistant General Manager
Joe Bohringer

Manager
Scott Servais

BP Alumni
John Choiniere
Jason Karegeannes

Three years in, Dipoto changed tack. The core was aging out, and the Wild Card not much of a prize anyway. A rebuild, however, might allow the Mariners to aim at the AL West crown. Granted, that rebuild was rendered more difficult by the fact that Dipoto had spent much of his time at the head of the org merrily torching his own farm system, but it wasn't impossible. In fact, he claimed, it could be achieved in two years. The Mariners would be duking it out with the Astros by 2021:

> "We believe that we have gotten younger, we've gotten more sustainable. And while we wouldn't anticipate that we are a threat to win the World Series in 2019 we do feel like we are better situated to do this come 2020, 2021.

> "We especially use 2021 as a target date just looking at the league around us and how their rosters are built. Looking at the Houston Astros specifically, the Boston Red Sox, Cleveland Indians, we felt that by 2021 either by free agency, age, or looking at their systems, that was the time on the calendar where maybe they would be more susceptible to being caught than they are right now…We view 2021 as that championship-type window if we did this the right way. Building around a group that was from an age perspective in a window that allowed us to crest in 2021."

That 2021 target was the only reason Haniger was on the team in the first place. In a traditional rebuild, he'd have been first out. Trading an All-Star outfielder under team control and heading right into his prime is an excellent way to restock the farm. But Dipoto, hoping that Haniger could anchor the 2021 lineup, kept him while his value was highest. So too Marco Gonzales, whose breakout 2018 would have made him a prime trade target for any team that wanted an upgrade to their starting rotation.

Out of the four club-controlled trade chips Dipoto had to play with: Haniger, Gonzales, James Paxton and Edwin Díaz, only two were dealt. This, naturally, limited Seattle's prospect haul. And the 2021 target influenced Dipoto's decision in other ways. When Robinson Canó (traded), Mike Zunino (traded), Jean Segura (traded), Nelson Cruz (free agent) and a slew of other minor names joined Paxton and Díaz in the Mariners' exodus, the return mostly focused on close-to-the-majors talent capable of plausibly helping the club compete in a short timeframe.

When that sort of player is available on the trade market for a non-stratospheric return, it's because they come with some warts. Take, for instance, Mallex Smith, who can play a premium defensive position and has a terrific batting eye but has serious problems making contact. Or J.P. Crawford, who…can play a premium defensive position (admittedly, better than Smith can) and has a terrific batting eye but has serious problems making contact. Or Domingo Santana, a ferocious hitter who cannot be said to play a defensive position at all. Or Omar Narváez, a wonderful hitter for a catcher but an atrocious receiver.

When the Mariners acquired that quartet, they presumably had plans to tweak their games and spark some sort of breakout. A year into the rebuild, it looks as though those plans have already failed. Crawford and Smith still can't hit, and it turns out Smith can't handle center field either. Narváez still can't catch, although his hitting has improved even further. Santana, meanwhile, had such a difficult time in left field that his tenure in Seattle is already over.

Those four, plus Japanese lefty Yusei Kikuchi, whose introduction to the major leagues fell out of the ugly tree and hit every piece of wood on the way down, constitute the young core meant to supplement the star-level talent in Haniger and Gonzales. Not only has that core failed to gel, but the supposed stars took a significant step back as well. Haniger's season was curtailed early, while Gonzales saw an alarming dip in both fastball velocity and strikeout rate.

So not only was the 2019 edition of the Mariners actively terrible (they ended the season at 64-98, the sixth-worst record in the majors), they displayed exactly none of the development they need in order to hit Dipoto's 2021 contention target. Meanwhile, their biggest obstacle in the AL West handed a debut to 22-year-old DH Yordan Álvarez, who spent four months absolutely torching the American League. The Astros lost Gerrit Cole to free agency, but Álvarez's performance should be a sobering reminder that they're miles ahead of Seattle in both major-league talent *and* player development. Houston's dominance followed a half-decade rebuilding process. The Mariners' attempt to match them on an accelerated schedule is already foundering.

There is, however, some good news. Dipoto's rebuild has managed to erase almost every significant contract from the Mariners' books. Dee Gordon, Kyle Seager and Kikuchi are the only players signed to multi-year deals, and the 2020 season is almost certainly Gordon's last. With so little payroll committed, Seattle is in a position—should they so choose, at any rate—to either go big in free agency themselves or to relieve other teams of problematic contracts in exchange for some prospect help.

Any such help would only make an already flourishing Mariners farm even stronger. Before the 2018 offseason, Dipoto had treated the minor-league system with the sort of cavalier disdain that Haniger apparently has for his own groin. Every ounce of value throughout the organization was squeezed out in exchange for marginal gains in Seattle itself. But now the tide has turned, and not entirely—or even mostly—via trade.

The big name is Jarred Kelenic, of course, who was shipped over from the New York Mets as part of the return for Díaz and Canó. Justin Dunn, Jake Fraley and Justus Sheffield all also arrived through Dipoto's offseason trade extravaganza. But the rest of the major prospects in the new-look Mariners farm are properly home-grown, and almost all took major steps forward last season.

Between Kelenic and 18-year-old wunderkind Julio Rodriguez, it's not impossible that Seattle has the two top outfield prospects in baseball by the end of the 2020 season. Evan White and Kyle Lewis went from best-in-system prospects to top-10s *despite* strong performances in 2019, which can only be a good sign, and both Logan Gilbert and Noelvi Marte had strong professional debuts (admittedly, at very different levels).

Sheffield's struggles aside, 2019 went almost perfectly in the minors, and this is now the sort of farm system that can take a team over the top. Those involved know it, too. When the Washington Nationals battered their way into and through the World Series, it left the Mariners as the only current major-league team to never have won themselves a pennant. That dismal fact spurred Kelenic, Rodriguez and Marte into making a perhaps unwise but nevertheless glorious promise: not for long.

It's easy to look at that promise and the talent piling up in the minor leagues as an indication that better days are ahead. Kelenic and Rodriguez are a prospect pairing worth savoring, one which can support big, even absurd dreams. Right now, however, the Mariners' project looks particularly absurd. The pieces are there on the minor-league level, but for Dipoto's plan to succeed he needs absolutely everything to go right above them.

So far, little has. That's not to say that the situation is irretrievable: one could look at, say, Crawford or Daniel Vogelbach and see a championship-caliber player waiting to be unlocked by making the right tweaks. But even the best player development staff in baseball would need to get very lucky to get the current version of the Mariners firing on all cylinders, and, anyway, results suggest that the Mariners do not have the best player development staff in baseball.

The task would have been much easier had Dipoto given himself more time. Focusing on the current minor-league talent as the giddy culmination of a championship project, rather than merely the opening salvo, has left Seattle building on wobbly foundations. Those foundations could set into something magical, of course, but right now they look like a hope-for-the-best rushed job.

When Kelenic and Rodriguez emerge—*if* they emerge, for we ought to remember that the last time that the Mariners had young players of this caliber around they were called "Dustin Ackley" and "Jesus Montero"—they're capable of catapulting the whole franchise to the next level. But unless Dipoto pulls off some miracles by the end of the 2020 season, the next level for this team looks like a return to soul- (and other-) crushing mediocrity. ▪

—Graham MacAree is an editor at SB Nation.

HITTERS

Tim Beckham SS   Born: 01/27/90   Age: 30   Bats: R   Throws: R   Height: 6'1"   Weight: 205   Origin: Round 1, 2008 Draft (#1 overall)

YEAR	TEAM	LVL	AGE	PA	R	2B	3B	HR	RBI	BB	K	SB	CS	AVG/OBP/SLG	DRC+	VORP	BABIP	BRR	FRAA	WARP
2017	TBA	MLB	27	345	31	5	3	12	36	24	110	5	4	.259/.314/.407	97	11.0	.357	-0.4	SS(70): -2.2, 2B(17): -0.8	1.0
2017	BAL	MLB	27	230	36	13	2	10	26	12	57	1	1	.306/.348/.523	98	18.8	.376	0.9	SS(49): 3.2	1.4
2018	BAL	MLB	28	402	45	17	0	12	35	27	100	1	2	.230/.287/.374	82	4.8	.282	0.8	SS(49): -3.7, 3B(40): -2.2	0.2
2019	SEA	MLB	29	328	39	21	1	15	47	21	102	1	3	.237/.293/.461	83	4.9	.305	0.9	SS(41): -1.3, LF(13): 1.4	0.6
2020	SEA	MLB	30	251	27	11	1	10	31	16	80	2	1	.229/.285/.412	81	2.6	.305	0.6	SS 0, 3B 0	0.2

Comparables: Nick Noonan, Robert Andino, Reid Brignac

There was big "Not Mad, Just Disappointed" energy surrounding the news of Beckham's 80-game suspension for the use of performance-enhancing drugs that ended his season in early August. Swaggy T was one of the most popular protagonists in the highly unrealistic April blockbuster, "13-2," punctuating some of its most dramatic scenes with a signature bat flip that even non-Mariners fans grew to recognize. Jerry Dipoto has long preached the value of acquiring former high draft picks, regardless of how sideways their careers may have gone. Had the Mariners struck gold with the former 1.1? Such fantasies were quickly quashed, as Beckham then played a prominent role in another film in the Mariners Cinematic Universe, "37 Errors in 31 Games," as the poster boy for the team's defensive ineptitude. The reality is, No. 1 picks tend to keep getting chances, so don't be surprised if Swaggy T has another supporting role left in the tank.

J.P. Crawford SS   Born: 01/11/95   Age: 25   Bats: L   Throws: R   Height: 6'2"   Weight: 180   Origin: Round 1, 2013 Draft (#16 overall)

YEAR	TEAM	LVL	AGE	PA	R	2B	3B	HR	RBI	BB	K	SB	CS	AVG/OBP/SLG	DRC+	VORP	BABIP	BRR	FRAA	WARP
2017	LEH	AAA	22	556	75	20	6	15	63	79	97	5	4	.243/.351/.405	114	27.5	.275	1.6	SS(113): -6.0, 3B(6): -0.7	2.5
2017	PHI	MLB	22	87	8	4	1	0	6	16	22	1	0	.214/.356/.300	85	2.9	.306	-0.2	3B(13): 2.3, SS(6): 0.4	0.4
2018	CLR	A+	23	49	8	1	0	1	4	7	14	0	0	.143/.265/.238	47	-1.5	.185	0.0	SS(8): -0.6, 3B(3): 0.5	-0.1
2018	LEH	AAA	23	68	6	2	1	1	7	5	17	1	0	.259/.358/.379	84	2.8	.350	-1.7	SS(16): 0.2	0.0
2018	PHI	MLB	23	138	17	6	3	3	12	13	37	2	0	.214/.319/.393	78	4.8	.286	0.2	SS(30): 0.6, 3B(13): -0.6	0.2
2019	TAC	AAA	24	138	20	7	0	3	15	19	25	3	0	.319/.420/.457	109	16.1	.382	2.6	SS(31): 0.1	1.0
2019	SEA	MLB	24	396	43	21	4	7	46	43	83	5	3	.226/.313/.371	84	10.9	.275	-1.9	SS(93): 4.6	1.3
2020	SEA	MLB	25	560	55	23	3	12	55	64	121	5	2	.223/.318/.354	82	6.8	.273	-1.3	SS 4	1.1

Comparables: Daniel Robertson, Nick Franklin, Tyler Wade

A combination of injury, poor performance and lack of opportunity had slowly taken Crawford out of the spotlight since debuting with the Phillies as one of the top prospects in baseball. A web gem helped him burst back into the national conversation in July, a sliding stop into a remix of the Jeter jump throw that robbed Jeimer Candelario of a hit and garnered millions of views on social media. Virality aside, his defense impressed all summer long. Extensive work with noted infield guru Perry Hill helped him translate his physical tools into what could be an easy plus glove moving forward. As for the bat, it came and went. The advanced approach he maintained in the minors remained, but Crawford did damage sparingly when he did choose to swing. Whether this version of Crawford amounts to the franchise shortstop the Mariners sought probably depends on your definition of a franchise shortstop.

Eric Filia OF   Born: 07/06/92   Age: 27   Bats: L   Throws: R   Height: 6'0"   Weight: 189   Origin: Round 20, 2016 Draft (#597 overall)

YEAR	TEAM	LVL	AGE	PA	R	2B	3B	HR	RBI	BB	K	SB	CS	AVG/OBP/SLG	DRC+	VORP	BABIP	BRR	FRAA	WARP
2017	MOD	A+	24	567	63	28	5	5	59	65	45	9	6	.326/.407/.434	150	39.8	.348	-0.6	RF(106): -11.7, 1B(12): -1.0	2.5
2018	ARK	AA	25	345	44	14	1	2	38	44	30	1	0	.274/.371/.348	109	5.1	.297	-1.1	RF(44): -0.9, LF(11): -0.8	0.6
2019	TAC	AAA	26	151	24	13	0	2	13	25	15	0	0	.331/.450/.488	144	10.0	.358	-1.5	RF(15): -1.4, 1B(14): -1.0	0.6
2020	SEA	MLB	27	251	25	12	1	4	25	27	34	1	0	.259/.345/.376	97	6.7	.290	-0.3	RF -1, 1B -1	0.5

Comparables: Daniel Robertson, Raffy Lopez, Nick Martini

On July 6, 1992, two future professional baseball players were born on opposite sides of the country: Filia, in Huntington Beach, California, and Manny Machado, in the Miami suburb of Hialeah. Since that summer day, Machado raced to the big leagues in a relative blink while Filia decided to take the route that Google Maps fails to mention includes some forest roads. Call it the scenic route, if you will. In 2012, Machado made his major-league debut at 20 years old while Filia was a bench bat at UCLA as a 19-year-old freshman. In 2015, Machado played in 162 Major League games while Filia played in 0 NCAA games due to an academic suspension. In 2019, Machado signed a $300 million free agent contract while Filia received a suspension for a "drug of abuse"—the second of his Minor League career—costing him the first 100 games of the season. And yet, thanks to an advanced hit tool that has remained throughout the bumpy, off-road journey, Filia still has the chance to share a big-league field with Machado one day.

Jake Fraley CF   Born: 05/25/95   Age: 25   Bats: L   Throws: L   Height: 6'0"   Weight: 195   Origin: Round 2, 2016 Draft (#77 overall)

YEAR	TEAM	LVL	AGE	PA	R	2B	3B	HR	RBI	BB	K	SB	CS	AVG/OBP/SLG	DRC+	VORP	BABIP	BRR	FRAA	WARP
2017	PCH	A+	22	105	6	3	1	1	12	7	24	1	3	.170/.238/.255	36	-5.0	.211	-0.6	CF(26): -3.6	-0.7
2018	PCH	A+	23	260	39	19	7	4	41	26	44	11	8	.347/.415/.547	169	26.4	.407	-2.2	LF(31): 2.6, CF(21): 2.1	2.7
2019	ARK	AA	24	259	40	15	2	11	47	23	55	16	5	.313/.386/.539	191	35.6	.370	-0.3	RF(21): -1.3, LF(12): -1.1	2.1
2019	TAC	AAA	24	168	28	12	3	8	33	11	34	6	2	.276/.333/.553	103	11.2	.304	-1.3	CF(21): 0.9, RF(9): -0.7	0.5
2019	SEA	MLB	24	41	3	2	0	0	1	0	14	0	0	.150/.171/.200	64	-0.6	.231	-0.7	CF(11): -1.5, RF(1): 0.0	-0.3
2020	SEA	MLB	25	350	39	14	3	13	43	22	92	14	7	.233/.291/.411	87	3.7	.285	0.7	CF 0, RF 1	0.4

Comparables: Rip Repulski, Roy Sievers, Anthony Gose

Upon acquiring Fraley from Tampa Bay in one of the team's ritual solstice exchanges, the Mariners organization remarked that the LSU product had made a mechanical tweak that piqued their interest, in the vein of Mitch Haniger. His mini-breakout in the Florida State League in 2018 became a much larger coming-out party in 2019, which saw Fraley absolutely torch the Texas League, and hit well enough in Tacoma to make his major-league debut in August. Injuries continued to haunt Fraley, as they have throughout his pro career, and appeared to hamper his first dozen big-league games before the Mariners shut him down for the season. If he can stay on the field, he may now be able to convincingly outplay the dreaded "fourth outfielder" label.

Dee Gordon 2B Born: 04/22/88 Age: 32 Bats: L Throws: R Height: 5'11" Weight: 170 Origin: Round 4, 2008 Draft (#127 overall)

YEAR	TEAM	LVL	AGE	PA	R	2B	3B	HR	RBI	BB	K	SB	CS	AVG/OBP/SLG	DRC+	VORP	BABIP	BRR	FRAA	WARP
2017	MIA	MLB	29	695	114	20	9	2	33	25	93	60	16	.308/.341/.375	87	26.4	.354	8.4	2B(153): -0.6, SS(3): 0.0	1.8
2018	SEA	MLB	30	588	62	17	8	4	36	9	80	30	12	.268/.288/.349	76	4.7	.304	4.2	2B(81): 2.5, CF(53): 0.7	0.9
2019	SEA	MLB	31	421	36	12	6	3	34	18	61	22	5	.275/.304/.359	78	2.1	.313	2.2	2B(111): 0.5, SS(2): 0.2	0.5
2020	SEA	MLB	32	560	51	18	5	5	47	23	88	38	12	.272/.306/.353	75	7.7	.318	3.3	2B 2	1.0

Comparables: Pat Meares, Garry Templeton, Jack Wilson

Gordon occupies a unique space on the Mariners roster, somehow simultaneously acting like everyone's older and younger brother while playing out his time on a team that probably wouldn't mind trading him before his contract is up. The center field experiment ended with Robinson Canó's departure, leaving Gordon to tend to his traditional second base, where he was far less likely to be GIF'd for everyone's amusement. His biggest offensive development was more than doubling his walk rate from 2018, which would be significant had he not been coming off the lowest single-season walk rate in nearly six decades—there was nowhere to go but up. Not even the juiced ball could help boost Gordon's offensive impact, unless you count skyrocketing from the first percentile in average exit velocity in 2018 to the second in 2019 as a marked improvement.

Mitch Haniger OF Born: 12/23/90 Age: 29 Bats: R Throws: R Height: 6'2" Weight: 215 Origin: Round 1, 2012 Draft (#38 overall)

YEAR	TEAM	LVL	AGE	PA	R	2B	3B	HR	RBI	BB	K	SB	CS	AVG/OBP/SLG	DRC+	VORP	BABIP	BRR	FRAA	WARP
2017	TAC	AAA	26	48	6	2	0	3	6	7	5	0	0	.256/.375/.538	123	6.5	.219	-1.0	RF(6): 1.4	0.3
2017	SEA	MLB	26	410	58	25	2	16	47	31	93	5	4	.282/.352/.491	115	16.8	.338	-1.4	RF(94): 4.7, CF(6): 0.2	2.0
2018	SEA	MLB	27	683	90	38	4	26	93	70	148	8	2	.285/.366/.493	129	48.6	.336	-3.5	RF(144): 5.0, CF(35): -2.8	3.9
2019	SEA	MLB	28	283	46	13	1	15	32	30	81	4	0	.220/.314/.463	102	8.5	.257	2.0	RF(43): 3.2, CF(24): 0.4	1.4
2020	SEA	MLB	29	560	73	24	2	29	83	53	157	7	3	.246/.330/.477	113	21.8	.300	-1.1	RF 5, CF 0	2.8

Comparables: Chris Young, Colby Rasmus, Kirk Gibson

When a hitter steps into the box against Justin Verlander, the odds of the plate appearance concluding in their favor are already rather low. But when Haniger faced off against the future Hall of Famer on June 6th, he would have been overjoyed to have merely escaped with a standard strikeout. Alas, Haniger swung at an inside fastball and fouled it off in the most unfortunate of directions—yeah, there—before flailing at strike three a couple pitches later. Somehow, Haniger played three more innings before being removed from the game, and shortly thereafter being diagnosed with a ruptured testicle. That fateful foul ball essentially ended Haniger's season, save for a few minor-league rehab games that never culminated in a return to the majors, with repeated setbacks and soreness along the way. It was surely a frustrating campaign for the outfielder whose breakout 2018 appeared to situate him as a potential cornerstone of the next good Mariners team. A healthy Haniger may still be just that, but he'll have to remind everyone in 2020.

─────────── ★ ★ ★ *2020 Top 101 Prospect* **#7** ★ ★ ★ ───────────

Jarred Kelenic OF Born: 07/16/99 Age: 20 Bats: L Throws: L Height: 6'0" Weight: 196 Origin: Round 1, 2018 Draft (#6 overall)

YEAR	TEAM	LVL	AGE	PA	R	2B	3B	HR	RBI	BB	K	SB	CS	AVG/OBP/SLG	DRC+	VORP	BABIP	BRR	FRAA	WARP
2018	MTS	RK	18	51	9	2	2	1	9	4	11	4	0	.413/.451/.609	183	8.0	.514	-0.1	CF(9): 2.0	0.7
2018	KNG	RK	18	200	33	8	4	5	33	22	39	11	1	.253/.350/.431	120	15.2	.300	2.5	CF(43): 5.8	1.9
2019	WVA	A	19	218	33	14	3	11	29	25	45	7	4	.309/.394/.586	181	25.6	.356	-0.5	CF(33): -1.8, RF(8): -0.1	2.3
2019	MOD	A+	19	190	36	13	1	6	22	17	49	10	3	.290/.353/.485	138	17.7	.368	1.4	CF(32): 1.1, RF(8): -1.2	1.3
2019	ARK	AA	19	92	11	4	1	6	17	8	17	3	0	.253/.315/.542	134	9.0	.246	0.6	CF(12): 0.6, RF(5): 0.6	0.7
2020	SEA	MLB	20	251	29	12	1	11	34	19	69	3	1	.245/.307/.453	99	8.1	.303	0.3	CF -1, RF -1	0.6

Comparables: Ronald Acuña Jr., Byron Buxton, Corey Seager

It all happened so fast. He wasn't even a Met long enough for the fans to know how to pronounce his name; "I can't believe we gave up kuh-LEH-nick" or "oh God, kel-nitch is going to be an All-Star, what is Brodie thinking?" (It's KELL-nick). And yet, for all the cries of front office malpractice when Kelenic was shipped to Seattle in the Robinson Canó/Edwin Díaz blockbuster, few could have foreseen how quickly the prospect huggers would chalk this up as a certified catastrophe for the Mets. Fans suffered through Canó injury updates and Díaz blown saves only to receive the frequent double whammy of opening Twitter to see the Wisconsin native's latest exploits, which included: participating in the All-Star Futures Game, reaching Double-A in his first full season and being the youngest player in the minors to go 20-20. Detractors may argue that Kelenic still doesn't have one plus-plus tool in his profile, but he's about as well-rounded of an outfield prospect as you're going to see. Even the most optimistic of big-league ETAs for high school hitters are rarely projected as any earlier than the player's first legal drink, but Kelenic doesn't appear to be constrained by traditional timetables. Service time games be damned; he could be knocking on the door ready to enter the major league party by the end of 2020.

Kyle Lewis OF Born: 07/13/95 Age: 24 Bats: R Throws: R Height: 6'4" Weight: 210 Origin: Round 1, 2016 Draft (#11 overall)

YEAR	TEAM	LVL	AGE	PA	R	2B	3B	HR	RBI	BB	K	SB	CS	AVG/OBP/SLG	DRC+	VORP	BABIP	BRR	FRAA	WARP
2017	MRN	RK	21	46	9	2	1	1	7	4	14	1	0	.263/.348/.447	80	4.0	.360	1.4	CF(8): -1.0	0.1
2017	MOD	A+	21	167	20	4	0	6	24	15	38	2	1	.255/.323/.403	110	1.9	.299	-1.5	CF(13): 0.1	0.3
2018	MOD	A+	22	211	21	18	0	5	32	11	55	0	0	.260/.303/.429	104	9.0	.333	0.3	CF(23): -3.1, RF(11): -0.7	0.2
2018	ARK	AA	22	152	18	8	0	4	20	17	32	1	0	.220/.309/.371	91	0.2	.255	-2.0	CF(29): -2.6, RF(1): 0.0	-0.2
2019	ARK	AA	23	517	61	25	2	11	62	56	152	3	2	.263/.342/.398	111	21.4	.367	-3.3	LF(48): 0.1, CF(36): -4.0	0.8
2019	SEA	MLB	23	75	10	5	0	6	13	3	29	0	0	.268/.293/.592	84	0.3	.351	0.8	RF(17): 0.0, CF(2): 0.1	0.1
2020	SEA	MLB	24	455	48	20	1	17	56	35	159	1	0	.230/.293/.405	85	1.2	.327	-0.7	LF -3, RF 0	-0.2

Comparables: Zoilo Almonte, Bubba Starling, Trayce Thompson

We were just about ready to close the book on the possibility of "Kyle Lewis, Transcendent Talent." The 2016 Golden Spikes winner who had his game-changing explosiveness sapped by Total Knee Disintegration followed by two rehab-filled and injury-plagued seasons was wrapping up an encouraging, if still unfulfilling, year in Double-A. The offensive tools continued to show up in spurts, and he was finally fully healthy, but the what ifs continued to linger, as if his career were somehow already dead and buried. Then, he became the latest 2019 dinger fun fact: the first player in major-league history to homer in six of his first 10 big-league games. So what in the world happened? Mariners officials cited Lewis as having hit the ball as hard as anyone in their system, but was it as simple as extracting him from Dickey-Stephens Park's bias against righties and adding a livelier baseball to produce these record-breaking results? A sample this small is not worth abandoning several years worth of post-ACL tear evaluations that more comfortably project Lewis as a solid everyday outfielder. But for 10 games in September, you didn't have to squint to see the game-changing player the Mariners fell in love with in 2016.

Shed Long 2B Born: 08/22/95 Age: 24 Bats: L Throws: R Height: 5'8" Weight: 184 Origin: Round 12, 2013 Draft (#375 overall)

YEAR	TEAM	LVL	AGE	PA	R	2B	3B	HR	RBI	BB	K	SB	CS	AVG/OBP/SLG	DRC+	VORP	BABIP	BRR	FRAA	WARP
2017	DAY	A+	21	279	37	16	1	13	36	27	63	6	3	.312/.380/.543	156	21.6	.368	-1.1	2B(62): 5.4	2.6
2017	PEN	AA	21	160	13	6	2	3	14	19	31	3	1	.227/.319/.362	102	1.8	.271	-2.4	2B(39): -1.7	0.1
2018	PEN	AA	22	522	75	22	5	12	56	57	123	19	6	.261/.353/.412	114	32.1	.333	3.7	2B(123): -1.9	2.6
2019	TAC	AAA	23	250	38	7	4	9	36	20	65	1	3	.274/.335/.460	75	8.7	.346	0.5	3B(21): -0.9, 2B(21): 0.2	0.2
2019	SEA	MLB	23	168	21	12	1	5	15	16	40	3	3	.263/.333/.454	91	3.2	.327	0.8	2B(24): 1.0, LF(16): -0.4	0.4
2020	SEA	MLB	24	385	41	16	2	13	46	30	104	5	2	.238/.303/.406	88	5.1	.301	0.0	LF -1, 2B 0	0.4

Comparables: Jeimer Candelario, Brandon Drury, Brett Phillips

Drafted and developed by Cincinnati, Long appeared destined for the Bronx as the primary return for Sonny Gray before Jerry Dipoto managed to wiggle his way into yet another trade (his 83rd as Mariners GM, to be exact). Whether or not he was invited, he managed to redirect the 5-foot-8 bat-first second baseman towards Seattle in exchange for 2018 second-rounder Josh Stowers. An injury to Dee Gordon rushed Long to the majors after just 32 games in Triple-A, and it showed: His first 19 major-league games featured some spark, but mostly struggle. Upon returning to the big leagues in September, Long looked far more comfortable, particularly once given the keys to the leadoff spot. His size and speed make him look the part of a leadoff hitter, but he sure doesn't swing like one, regularly unleashing what the kids so lovingly refer to as "big daddy hacks" when he gets his pitch. Legitimate thump rests in the bat, although the development of his on-base skills will more likely determine his staying power as an unorthodox leadoff man. Meanwhile, no pressure, but he also has to worry about whether he can handle the keystone; fortunately, the state of the franchise should give him plenty of time to make improvements.

Tom Murphy C Born: 04/03/91 Age: 29 Bats: R Throws: R Height: 6'1" Weight: 218 Origin: Round 3, 2012 Draft (#105 overall)

YEAR	TEAM	LVL	AGE	PA	R	2B	3B	HR	RBI	BB	K	SB	CS	AVG/OBP/SLG	DRC+	VORP	BABIP	BRR	FRAA	WARP
2017	ABQ	AAA	26	154	22	10	1	4	19	9	56	0	0	.255/.312/.426	69	1.6	.390	-0.7	C(34): 0.9	0.2
2017	COL	MLB	26	26	1	1	0	0	1	2	9	0	0	.042/.115/.083	54	-2.6	.067	0.2	C(8): 0.5	0.1
2018	ABQ	AAA	27	264	40	16	3	17	49	22	76	4	2	.258/.333/.568	107	18.0	.306	-0.9	C(52): 6.9	2.1
2018	COL	MLB	27	96	5	7	1	2	11	3	44	0	1	.226/.250/.387	45	-2.0	.404	-0.7	C(22): -0.3	-0.3
2019	SEA	MLB	28	281	32	12	1	18	40	19	87	2	0	.273/.324/.535	106	16.4	.340	-0.9	C(67): 4.7, P(3): 0.0	2.0
2020	SEA	MLB	29	455	55	21	2	24	67	30	155	3	1	.238/.295/.466	97	17.3	.315	-0.8	C 2	2.0

Comparables: Travis d'Arnaud, Yan Gomes, Stan Lopata

Murphy, a sentient bearded rectangle from upstate New York, gives off strong "hockey defenseman" vibes, a distant cousin of his actual professional sporting occupation of "baseball catcher and dinger smasher." Acquired for a minor-league pitcher at the end of Spring Training from San Francisco, Murphy ended up being the right-handed side of one of the most productive platoons in baseball. Among his surprises behind the plate, Murphy revealed a legitimate ability to frame pitches, particularly those at the lower half of the zone, giving him more opportunities to start games behind the plate, even when he didn't have the platoon advantage. Revelations aside, the bat is his calling card. While the plate discipline peripherals may hint at some incoming regression, his quality of contact suggests continued success: Murphy hit the ball harder on average than any other Mariner in 2019.

YEAR	TEAM	P. COUNT	FRM RUNS	BLK RUNS	THRW RUNS	TOT RUNS
2017	ABQ	4911	-0.8	0.1	0.4	-0.5
2017	COL	1031	-0.3	0.6	-0.1	0.1
2018	ABQ	7423	3.8	1.0	-0.2	4.6
2018	COL	2791	-0.3	0.0	0.0	-0.3
2019	SEA	9454	3.5	0.8	0.7	4.7
2020	SEA	16624	-1.7	0.4	1.4	0.1

Austin Nola C Born: 12/28/89 Age: 30 Bats: R Throws: R Height: 6'0" Weight: 195 Origin: Round 5, 2012 Draft (#167 overall)

YEAR	TEAM	LVL	AGE	PA	R	2B	3B	HR	RBI	BB	K	SB	CS	AVG/OBP/SLG	DRC+	VORP	BABIP	BRR	FRAA	WARP
2017	JAX	AA	27	197	21	7	0	2	25	25	26	3	2	.250/.352/.327	108	6.1	.284	-0.4	C(46): -2.1, 1B(1): -0.1	0.8
2017	NWO	AAA	27	105	7	4	0	1	6	10	16	0	0	.202/.287/.281	65	-2.4	.233	-1.0	C(29): -6.1	-0.6
2018	NWO	AAA	28	262	26	16	0	2	32	27	43	2	0	.279/.370/.376	111	17.0	.333	-2.2	C(68): 6.2	2.1
2019	TAC	AAA	29	229	36	15	1	7	37	29	40	4	1	.327/.415/.520	119	15.7	.377	-3.4	C(28): 2.8, 1B(24): -0.8	1.2
2019	SEA	MLB	29	267	37	12	1	10	31	23	63	1	0	.269/.342/.454	102	6.7	.325	-0.5	1B(59): 2.4, 2B(15): 1.0	0.9
2020	SEA	MLB	30	350	34	13	1	8	35	32	80	1	0	.229/.308/.351	79	2.1	.281	-0.3	C 3, 1B 0	0.5

Comparables: Chase d'Arnaud, Paul Janish, Sean Kazmar Jr.

YEAR	TEAM	P. COUNT	FRM RUNS	BLK RUNS	THRW RUNS	TOT RUNS
2017	JAX	5903	0.0	-2.5	0.1	-3.2
2017	NWO	4085	-6.9	-0.9	0.4	-7.7
2018	NWO	9352	3.9	0.0	1.0	4.5
2019	SEA	613	0.1	0.1	0.0	0.3
2019	TAC	4084	2.6	-0.1	0.3	2.8
2020	SEA	7638	1.4	0.4	-0.1	1.7

A minor-league free agent signing after seven seasons in the Marlins organization, Nola finally made his big-league debut at age 29 in Seattle, and quickly established himself as more than just a feel-good story. A half season of consistent playing time yielded an average DRC+ by definition, but a legitimate achievement when considering Nola's spotty track record of hitting in the minors. (It also would have ranked second among all Marlins hitters, which, well...you can decide whether that is a Nola compliment or a sick Marlins burn). He'll be a 30-year-old sophomore on Opening Day 2020, which isn't ordinarily a hallmark for success. With Omar Narváez in Milwaukee, however, the organization has discussed giving the versatile Nola a chunk of time behind the plate. If that's the case, and he's up to it (the metrics seem encouraging), he can have that obvious offensive regression and still be a valuable member of the ballclub.

Cal Raleigh C Born: 11/26/96 Age: 23 Bats: B Throws: R Height: 6'3" Weight: 215 Origin: Round 3, 2018 Draft (#90 overall)

YEAR	TEAM	LVL	AGE	PA	R	2B	3B	HR	RBI	BB	K	SB	CS	AVG/OBP/SLG	DRC+	VORP	BABIP	BRR	FRAA	WARP
2018	EVE	A-	21	167	25	10	1	8	29	18	29	1	1	.288/.367/.534	141	11.7	.309	0.3	C(25): -0.2	1.2
2019	MOD	A+	22	348	48	19	0	22	66	33	69	4	0	.261/.336/.535	151	33.4	.267	0.8	C(55): 0.9	3.1
2019	ARK	AA	22	159	16	6	0	7	16	14	47	0	0	.228/.296/.414	108	7.5	.286	-0.6	C(26): 0.0	0.6
2020	SEA	MLB	23	251	32	12	0	14	39	17	71	1	0	.239/.295/.481	101	7.9	.278	-0.5	C -3	0.5

Comparables: Chris Shaw, Josh Donaldson, Travis Shaw

YEAR	TEAM	P. COUNT	FRM RUNS	BLK RUNS	THRW RUNS	TOT RUNS
2019	ARK	3199	1.0	0.0	-1.4	-0.5
2020	SEA	9182	-1.7	-0.5	-1.3	-3.5

A fast-moving, highly-drafted, offensive catcher from a college baseball powerhouse in Florida who grew up in a baseball family? It's a familiar story for Mariners fans, but certainly an unfair comparison between how we should project Raleigh and the ultimately disappointing tenure of Mike Zunino. The expectations for a third-overall pick and third-round selection differ significantly, but the current front office may still keep Zunino's cautionary developmental tale in mind as they bring Raleigh along. The switch-hitting backstop's first full season gave even the most conservative of prospect observers a lot to love. He swatted more dingers than any other catcher in the minors, including a 9-in-11-games tear in July which essentially forced a promotion to Double-A. The bat cooled off in Arkansas, where it wouldn't be surprising to see him spend a considerable amount of time over the next season or two, getting more reps against left-handed pitching and continuing to improve his defense. With the team still a year or two away from really Going For It, Raleigh can take his sweet time.

───────────────── ★ ★ ★ *2020 Top 101 Prospect* **#10** ★ ★ ★ ─────────────────

Julio Rodriguez OF Born: 12/29/00 Age: 19 Bats: R Throws: R Height: 6'4" Weight: 225 Origin: International Free Agent, 2017

YEAR	TEAM	LVL	AGE	PA	R	2B	3B	HR	RBI	BB	K	SB	CS	AVG/OBP/SLG	DRC+	VORP	BABIP	BRR	FRAA	WARP
2018	DMR	RK	17	255	50	13	9	5	36	30	40	10	0	.315/.404/.525	163	34.0	.364	0.6	RF(45): 8.1, CF(6): -0.1	2.9
2019	WVA	A	18	295	50	20	1	10	50	20	66	1	3	.293/.359/.490	160	27.7	.353	0.0	RF(40): 4.7, CF(22): -0.2	2.8
2019	MOD	A+	18	72	13	6	3	2	19	5	10	0	0	.462/.514/.738	254	17.2	.528	0.5	CF(13): -3.4, RF(3): -0.5	0.9
2020	SEA	MLB	19	251	26	13	2	7	29	19	65	1	0	.254/.322/.414	98	7.4	.327	-0.2	RF 1, CF -1	0.8

Comparables: Nomar Mazara, Vladimir Guerrero Jr., Jon Singleton

It was a summer of hyperbole for Rodriguez, who began the year as one of the youngest players in full-season ball and finished it as the youngest player in the Arizona Fall League. Only a broken hand via hit-by-pitch that cost Rodriguez two months could slow him down, as his excellent, albeit abbreviated, South Atlantic League stint was convincing enough to earn an August promotion. He joined uber-prospect Wander Franco as the only 18-year-old in High-A, where he continued to show out. His listed height and weight undersell his gigantic frame, which will likely move out of center field eventually, though his athleticism and plus arm should make him above-average in a corner. Rodriguez endearingly toes the delicate line between confidence and cockiness, routinely hashtagging his own highlights on social media with #JRODshow. It's a nickname he's embraced to honor his favorite player, Alex Rodríguez, who dominated the sport in a way he unabashedly aspires to mirror one day. Phenoms like Juan Soto have shown that with the right combination of maturity, poise, and extraordinary raw ability, players can dictate their own timelines. So many things have to go right for a player to make his big-league debut as a teenager, but Rodriguez, who will play all of 2020 at 19, sure does check a lot of boxes. There is hardly any rush from the franchise's standpoint, but The J-Rod Show might be closer to airing on a major network sooner rather than later.

Domingo Santana OF Born: 08/05/92   Age: 27   Bats: R   Throws: R   Height: 6'5"   Weight: 220   Origin: International Free Agent, 2009

YEAR	TEAM	LVL	AGE	PA	R	2B	3B	HR	RBI	BB	K	SB	CS	AVG/OBP/SLG	DRC+	VORP	BABIP	BRR	FRAA	WARP
2017	MIL	MLB	24	607	88	29	0	30	85	73	178	15	4	.278/.371/.505	118	39.6	.363	0.2	RF(144): -7.7	2.0
2018	CSP	AAA	25	227	30	10	2	8	35	36	75	2	0	.283/.401/.487	122	10.8	.425	-2.6	RF(50): -10.4	-0.2
2018	MIL	MLB	25	235	21	14	1	5	20	20	77	1	1	.265/.328/.412	82	9.7	.386	-0.2	RF(55): -2.0	-0.2
2019	SEA	MLB	26	507	63	20	1	21	69	50	164	8	3	.253/.329/.441	102	13.5	.347	0.1	LF(59): -4.2, RF(42): -3.0	0.6
2020	SEA	MLB	27	251	31	11	0	10	33	28	81	3	1	.248/.336/.442	106	10.0	.343	-0.2	RF -3, LF 0	0.7

Comparables: Carlos Delgado, Pete Incaviglia, Melvin Nieves

The first of 154 regular-season grand slams, second-most in history, was hit at roughly 3:30 AM Seattle time, when Santana flicked an opposite-field fly over the 329-foot marker against the A's in the Tokyo Dome on March 20. He went on to contribute 20 more long balls to the cause, 17 of which came before the All-Star Break. A hot first half suggested that playing time was in fact all Santana needed to prove himself as a legitimate offensive weapon, recapturing the form he flashed in Milwaukee in 2017. Unfortunately, a mid-season elbow injury shelved the hulking outfielder for several weeks and continued to hamper him once he returned to action down the stretch. Once a promising young prospect himself, Santana found himself a victim of baseball's new fad of non-tendering players who might be eligible for raises in arbitration.

Kyle Seager 3B Born: 11/03/87   Age: 32   Bats: L   Throws: R   Height: 6'0"   Weight: 210   Origin: Round 3, 2009 Draft (#82 overall)

YEAR	TEAM	LVL	AGE	PA	R	2B	3B	HR	RBI	BB	K	SB	CS	AVG/OBP/SLG	DRC+	VORP	BABIP	BRR	FRAA	WARP
2017	SEA	MLB	29	650	72	33	1	27	88	58	110	2	1	.249/.323/.450	106	20.6	.262	-5.6	3B(154): 7.4	3.0
2018	SEA	MLB	30	630	62	36	1	22	78	38	138	2	2	.221/.273/.400	90	7.7	.251	-1.6	3B(154): 11.2, 2B(1): 0.0	2.5
2019	TAC	AAA	31	42	5	2	0	0	7	3	7	0	0	.256/.310/.308	71	-2.5	.313	-0.7	3B(5): 0.0	-0.1
2019	SEA	MLB	31	443	55	19	1	23	63	44	86	2	2	.239/.321/.468	113	24.9	.248	-2.4	3B(104): -0.2	2.2
2020	SEA	MLB	32	560	66	27	1	24	75	50	114	3	2	.241/.316/.441	99	10.0	.266	-2.5	3B 5	1.5

Comparables: Eric Chavez, Ron Santo, Matt Williams

Seager enters 2020 as the baseball version of the "Will Smith standing in an empty room at the end of Fresh Prince" meme, the last remaining player from the 40-man roster GM Jerry Dipoto inherited in September 2015. A relatively dismal 2018 prompted Seager to arrive to Spring Training in, you guessed it, the best shape of his life. Clichés aside, the veteran did report to Peoria leaner and more flexible than ever before, to the point where some teammates hardly recognized him from a distance and his uniforms weren't even fitting quite right. Hand surgery in March delayed the debut of his new physique until May, but after a slow start, Seager's bat started to look more familiar. A scorching hot August helped propel Seager to his eighth (!) consecutive 20-plus homer season, tied for the longest active streak in the majors alongside former Mariners Nelson Cruz, Edwin Encarnación, and decidedly non-former-Mariner Mike Trout. He appears to have staved off baseball hitter mortality for now, but the Grim Reaper (the shift) still looms large.

Mallex Smith CF Born: 05/06/93   Age: 27   Bats: L   Throws: R   Height: 5'10"   Weight: 180   Origin: Round 5, 2012 Draft (#165 overall)

YEAR	TEAM	LVL	AGE	PA	R	2B	3B	HR	RBI	BB	K	SB	CS	AVG/OBP/SLG	DRC+	VORP	BABIP	BRR	FRAA	WARP
2017	DUR	AAA	24	205	26	7	4	3	10	17	45	21	8	.263/.325/.392	90	5.1	.333	2.3	CF(33): 5.1, LF(7): 0.5	1.1
2017	TBA	MLB	24	282	33	8	4	2	12	23	62	16	5	.270/.329/.355	83	10.8	.347	2.1	CF(51): -5.2, LF(24): 0.2	0.1
2018	TBA	MLB	25	544	65	27	10	2	40	47	98	40	12	.296/.367/.406	99	28.3	.366	4.4	CF(71): -7.0, RF(47): -1.9	0.9
2019	TAC	AAA	26	48	8	3	0	1	6	3	4	7	0	.333/.375/.467	108	4.5	.350	0.6	CF(10): 0.2	0.3
2019	SEA	MLB	26	566	70	19	9	6	37	42	141	46	9	.227/.300/.335	73	-0.4	.302	6.8	CF(106): -5.9, RF(28): 2.5	0.3
2020	SEA	MLB	27	420	40	17	5	5	36	33	97	27	8	.243/.312/.350	78	6.2	.315	2.5	CF -5	0.1

Comparables: Herm Winningham, Dalton Pompey, Boog Powell

Smith's best party trick, his elite speed, can still elicit its fair share of oohs and aahs. He stole a major-league-best 46 bags, including a highly-entertaining "stolen base cycle" on May 28 against Texas. The overall production around his stolen base title, however, did not otherwise reflect a league leader. There's a difference between Rickey Henderson and Vince Coleman, but there's an even bigger one between Coleman and Brian L. Hunter. Concerns that his 2018 offensive breakout may have been a BABIP-fueled mirage were borne out, at one point even necessitating a tune-up in Triple-A, as Servais & Co. grew tired of the mental miscues that harmonized with the physical ones. As players and teams increasingly shift their focus away from stolen bases and small ball in favor of More Dingers, players like Smith will likely appeal more to fans than front offices. He can be just as delightful to watch as he is maddening to pencil into the lineup. Still just 26 on Opening Day 2020, Smith remains a good bet to be given a chance to bounce back.

Daniel Vogelbach DH Born: 12/17/92   Age: 27   Bats: L   Throws: R   Height: 6'0"   Weight: 250   Origin: Round 2, 2011 Draft (#68 overall)

YEAR	TEAM	LVL	AGE	PA	R	2B	3B	HR	RBI	BB	K	SB	CS	AVG/OBP/SLG	DRC+	VORP	BABIP	BRR	FRAA	WARP
2017	TAC	AAA	24	541	65	25	0	17	83	76	98	3	1	.290/.388/.455	120	22.5	.332	-7.3	1B(81): -8.3	0.6
2017	SEA	MLB	24	31	0	1	0	0	2	3	9	0	0	.214/.290/.250	82	-3.0	.316	-1.2	1B(7): -0.3	-0.2
2018	TAC	AAA	25	378	54	16	0	20	60	77	59	0	1	.290/.434/.545	161	27.8	.299	-6.0	1B(53): -2.9	2.4
2018	SEA	MLB	25	102	9	2	0	4	13	13	26	0	0	.207/.324/.368	92	0.9	.246	0.6	1B(20): -1.1	0.0
2019	SEA	MLB	26	558	73	17	0	30	76	92	149	0	0	.208/.341/.439	117	21.4	.232	-1.7	1B(57): -3.2	1.6
2020	SEA	MLB	27	595	82	22	1	31	88	95	155	1	0	.237/.363/.470	122	23.9	.280	-1.4	1B -2	2.3

Comparables: Mike Carp, Jeimer Candelario, Justin Smoak

Only Cody Bellinger and Christian Yelich posted a higher OPS in the first month of the season than Vogelbach, who appeared to be loudly answering the question that had followed him for his entire career: 'Will this Chris Farley impersonator actually hit enough to be an everyday designated hitter at the major-league level?' His popularity blossomed further with every home run. It seemed he was the next great chunky cult hero our beautiful game had to offer. Vogey cooled off after April, but his production held steady enough to earn a trip to the All-Star Game as the lone Mariners representative.

Post All-Star Break was an entirely different story. His already-low batting average plummeted to a measly .162 in the second half, severely limiting the opportunities for his prolific power to play. The final picture was that of a good hitter, albeit a rather extreme one: Nearly 49 percent of Vogelbach's plate appearances ended in a home run, walk, or strikeout, the highest Three True Outcome percentage among 135 qualified hitters in baseball. Off the field, he established himself as one of the most likable players in the Seattle clubhouse, creating a particularly special, if unlikely bond with Yusei Kikuchi. How special? Kikuchi's first son, Leo, born in July, was given the middle name "Daniel" in his teammate's honor. Out of options, Vogey's troubling second half may have shortened the leash on his future as the team's designated hitter. However, his beloved organizational presence may give him some breathing room to get his bat back on track.

Donnie Walton INF Born: 05/25/94 Age: 26 Bats: L Throws: R Height: 5'10" Weight: 184 Origin: Round 5, 2016 Draft (#147 overall)

YEAR	TEAM	LVL	AGE	PA	R	2B	3B	HR	RBI	BB	K	SB	CS	AVG/OBP/SLG	DRC+	VORP	BABIP	BRR	FRAA	WARP
2017	MOD	A+	23	272	37	16	1	2	24	27	49	6	6	.269/.349/.368	110	4.4	.330	-4.2	SS(47): 9.3, 2B(16): 1.7	2.0
2018	MOD	A+	24	256	35	12	3	3	19	30	37	8	3	.309/.402/.433	147	24.2	.358	-0.3	2B(36): -4.2, SS(19): 1.0	1.7
2018	ARK	AA	24	238	22	14	1	1	22	21	34	3	1	.236/.325/.327	83	1.8	.276	-1.4	2B(62): 6.2	0.8
2019	ARK	AA	25	558	72	22	3	11	50	63	72	10	13	.300/.390/.427	159	60.3	.333	-2.0	SS(102): 12.4, 2B(19): 1.6	6.6
2019	SEA	MLB	25	19	2	0	0	0	2	3	5	0	1	.188/.316/.188	83	0.5	.273	-0.2	SS(5): -0.7, 2B(2): -0.5	-0.1
2020	SEA	MLB	26	70	7	3	0	1	7	6	14	1	0	.247/.318/.365	85	1.2	.295	-0.2	2B 0, SS 1	0.2

Comparables: Dean Anna, Robinson Chirinos, J.P. Crawford

Pick your favorite platitude about gritty, scrappy, hard-nosed, **voice gets a bit more gravelly** BASEBALL PLAYERS and it has probably been ascribed to Walton at some point. You should expect nothing less for an undersized middle infielder whose dad, a former minor leaguer, coached him for four years (you're damn right he went back for his senior year) at Oklahoma State. It's honestly a miracle he doesn't play for the Cardinals. And yet, 2019 saw Walton take statistical strides beyond what you might expect from a player of his clichéd caliber, as he hit legitimately well in a full season in the Texas League, albeit as a 25-year-old in Double-A. Unlikely to be a core part of the Next Good Mariners Team, it's still easy to see Walton sticking around as a Triple-A shuttle bus utility infielder candidate.

───── ★ ★ ★ *2020 Top 101 Prospect* **#62** ★ ★ ★ ─────

Evan White 1B Born: 04/26/96 Age: 24 Bats: R Throws: L Height: 6'3" Weight: 205 Origin: Round 1, 2017 Draft (#17 overall)

YEAR	TEAM	LVL	AGE	PA	R	2B	3B	HR	RBI	BB	K	SB	CS	AVG/OBP/SLG	DRC+	VORP	BABIP	BRR	FRAA	WARP
2017	EVE	A-	21	55	6	1	1	3	12	6	6	1	1	.277/.345/.532	122	3.7	.250	-0.1	1B(8): -0.6	0.1
2018	MOD	A+	22	538	72	27	7	11	66	52	103	4	3	.303/.375/.458	143	38.4	.363	-0.5	1B(106): 5.5	3.5
2019	ARK	AA	23	400	61	13	2	18	55	29	92	2	0	.293/.350/.488	153	32.0	.346	1.1	1B(88): -5.3	1.9
2020	SEA	MLB	24	385	45	16	2	17	53	23	105	0	0	.261/.310/.457	103	8.3	.323	-0.6	1B -1	0.7

Comparables: Matt Clark, Rhys Hoskins, Kevin Cron

There's only so much you can do to make a first base prospect literally named "White" interesting. Give this one credit, though, as the 2017 first-round pick has managed to spice up his prospect profile beyond its vanilla exterior. To start, he has made first base defense look cooler than it has any right to be, with scouts consistently lauding his athleticism around the bag from stretches to scoops to plays you hadn't even thought possible. Of course, there is no level of first base defense that would actually carry a player to the big leagues, which makes White's continued progress with the bat all the more crucial. A minor swing tweak towards the end of 2018 carried over into his first go at Double-A, where he was one of the most productive hitters at the level, matching high exit velos with an increased proclivity for lifting the ball. He might not get the chance to replicate the achievement in Triple-A Tacoma: the Mariners signed White to a six-year, $24 million pact in late November, removing any concerns over service time, and have declared that he'll have every chance to win the first-base job in spring.

PITCHERS

Austin Adams RHP Born: 05/05/91 Age: 29 Bats: R Throws: R Height: 6'3" Weight: 225 Origin: Round 8, 2012 Draft (#267 overall)

YEAR	TEAM	LVL	AGE	W	L	SV	G	GS	IP	H	HR	BB/9	K/9	K	GB%	BABIP	WHIP	ERA	DRA	WARP	MPH	FB%	WHF	CSP
2017	SYR	AAA	26	6	2	5	44	0	59	44	2	5.6	13.9	91	49%	.321	1.37	2.14	3.12	1.4				
2017	WAS	MLB	26	0	0	0	6	0	5	4	0	14.4	18.0	10	40%	.400	2.40	3.60	2.01	0.2	96.5	52.7	14.5	43.7
2018	SYR	AAA	27	1	4	9	41	0	46¹	47	1	3.9	15.2	78	43%	.434	1.45	3.50	3.50	0.9				
2018	WAS	MLB	27	0	0	0	2	0	1	1	0	27.0	0.0	0	50%	.250	4.00	0.00	9.99	-0.1	97.2	58.3	4.2	44
2019	FRE	AAA	28	0	1	1	8	0	10	7	0	2.7	18.0	20	53%	.412	1.00	2.70	1.64	0.4				
2019	WAS	MLB	28	0	0	0	1	0	1	0	0	18.0	18.0	2	100%	.000	2.00	9.00	2.35	0.0	95.9	51.5	6.1	35.4
2019	SEA	MLB	28	2	2	0	29	2	31	20	4	4.1	14.8	51	49%	.291	1.10	3.77	2.65	0.9	97.0	35.2	18.6	45.6
2020	SEA	MLB	29	2	2	4	36	5	38	29	4	4.7	14.4	60	47%	.325	1.29	3.59	3.62	0.7	96.3	38.9	17	44.3

Comparables: Sam Selman, Jeff Stevens, Juan Jaime

Adams showed premium stuff coming up through the minors, but he had never harnessed it as effectively and efficiently as he did in his 31 innings with Seattle following an early-May DFA by the Nationals. Most good relievers have some kind of bizarro aesthetic; Adams pairs his bushy brown beard with an intense habit of vigorously chewing gum while on the mound. Frustratingly, the final chapter of his breakout season featured an ACL tear while covering first base in a September game against Baltimore. Adams' devastating injury in a meaningless late-season game will surely be held up as another example of why pitchers should never have to field their position. How many pitchers must get hurt doing Not Pitching Things before we realize that a designated fielder should be implemented universally? Hopefully Adams is the last.

Dan Altavilla RHP   Born: 09/08/92   Age: 27   Bats: R   Throws: R   Height: 5'11"   Weight: 200   Origin: Round 5, 2014 Draft (#141 overall)

YEAR	TEAM	LVL	AGE	W	L	SV	G	GS	IP	H	HR	BB/9	K/9	K	GB%	BABIP	WHIP	ERA	DRA	WARP	MPH	FB%	WHF	CSP
2017	TAC	AAA	24	2	0	6	20	0	23¹	17	1	5.8	13.9	36	44%	.340	1.37	1.54	2.74	0.7				
2017	SEA	MLB	24	1	1	0	41	0	46²	43	9	3.9	10.0	52	38%	.281	1.35	4.24	3.88	0.7	99.1	62.4	13.9	48.5
2018	TAC	AAA	25	0	2	0	9	1	6²	9	2	5.4	9.4	7	35%	.333	1.95	9.45	8.16	-0.2				
2018	SEA	MLB	25	3	2	0	22	0	20²	11	2	6.5	10.0	23	40%	.209	1.26	2.61	3.45	0.4	99.0	53.1	13.4	44.3
2019	ARK	AA	26	3	0	4	14	0	16¹	7	1	1.7	13.8	25	42%	.200	0.61	1.10	1.81	0.6				
2019	TAC	AAA	26	2	1	0	14	0	14	11	0	7.1	16.1	25	48%	.407	1.57	8.36	2.80	0.5				
2019	SEA	MLB	26	2	1	0	17	0	14²	9	1	7.4	11.0	18	47%	.242	1.43	5.52	4.53	0.1	98.9	59.3	13.6	46.5
2020	SEA	MLB	27	2	2	0	31	0	33	26	5	4.7	10.3	37	41%	.272	1.33	3.96	3.97	0.4	98.5	59.7	13.8	46.8

Comparables: Edubray Ramos, Dominic Leone, Sam Tuivailala

It was another injury-riddled season for the man they call Diesel Dan. The stuff remains appealing, but the infrequency with which it appears in the strike zone has made it difficult for the stunningly swole right-hander to grab hold of a clear-cut bullpen role, even when healthy. 2020 will be his fifth season appearing as a Mariner (an accomplishment in and of itself), but with so many stops and starts along the way, it doesn't feel like we are that much closer to knowing what Altavilla is or could be.

Gerson Bautista RHP   Born: 05/31/95   Age: 25   Bats: R   Throws: R   Height: 6'3"   Weight: 195   Origin: International Free Agent, 2013

YEAR	TEAM	LVL	AGE	W	L	SV	G	GS	IP	H	HR	BB/9	K/9	K	GB%	BABIP	WHIP	ERA	DRA	WARP	MPH	FB%	WHF	CSP
2017	SLM	A+	22	3	2	4	27	0	45¹	54	2	5.6	10.5	53	41%	.388	1.81	5.16	6.71	-1.0				
2017	SLU	A+	22	0	1	5	10	0	14¹	10	0	1.9	12.6	20	55%	.323	0.91	1.26	2.61	0.4				
2018	BIN	AA	23	1	0	0	6	0	9¹	12	0	0.0	14.5	15	42%	.500	1.29	4.82	3.66	0.1				
2018	LVG	AAA	23	3	1	3	31	0	39²	54	3	4.1	12.3	54	24%	.443	1.82	5.22	6.12	-0.4				
2018	NYN	MLB	23	0	1	0	5	0	4¹	8	2	10.4	6.2	3	35%	.400	3.00	12.46	7.18	-0.1	100.3	81.1	8.9	52
2019	TAC	AAA	24	0	0	1	21	0	23²	29	7	6.8	11.8	31	40%	.361	1.99	8.75	6.52	-0.1				
2019	SEA	MLB	24	0	1	0	8	2	9	13	2	9.0	7.0	7	33%	.355	2.44	11.00	6.96	-0.1	99.3	62.9	10.7	44.7
2020	SEA	MLB	25	1	2	0	31	0	33	37	6	5.2	8.4	31	34%	.317	1.69	6.34	5.91	-0.3	99.3	69.4	10.4	49.1

Comparables: Dean Deetz, Miguel Diaz, Lisalverto Bonilla

Sometimes a pitcher's high-octane velocity can be complimented for looking "easy," but in Bautista's case such velocity has also appeared easy for hitters to pick up. The least-heralded member of the Robinson Canó/Edwin Díaz return, Bautista entered 2019 with a clear path to big-league relief innings, but a pectoral strain in spring training delayed his Mariners debut until June. Further injuries and drastic ineffectiveness kept him away from major-league mounds the rest of the way. Bautista has a bazooka of a right arm, albeit one without a sight, and clearly requires additional refinement before being viewed as a useful bullpen piece. Regardless of his development as a pitcher, he remains an annual top candidate for Time Magazine's Gerson of the Year.

Brandon Brennan RHP   Born: 07/26/91   Age: 28   Bats: R   Throws: R   Height: 6'4"   Weight: 220   Origin: Round 4, 2012 Draft (#141 overall)

YEAR	TEAM	LVL	AGE	W	L	SV	G	GS	IP	H	HR	BB/9	K/9	K	GB%	BABIP	WHIP	ERA	DRA	WARP	MPH	FB%	WHF	CSP
2017	BIR	AA	25	2	2	9	28	0	42	47	1	4.3	8.4	39	54%	.362	1.60	5.36	6.14	-0.7				
2017	CHR	AAA	25	0	0	6	14	0	17²	16	0	4.6	8.2	16	56%	.333	1.42	3.06	5.10	0.0				
2018	BIR	AA	26	4	3	1	40	1	69²	54	4	2.7	9.0	70	53%	.266	1.08	3.10	3.32	1.3				
2019	TAC	AAA	27	1	0	0	9	0	8²	5	1	4.2	10.4	10	82%	.250	1.04	1.04	2.69	0.3				
2019	SEA	MLB	27	3	6	0	44	0	47¹	34	6	4.6	8.9	47	54%	.235	1.23	4.56	3.60	0.9	96.6	51.6	16.1	43.6
2020	SEA	MLB	28	3	2	7	50	0	53	46	6	4.2	10.6	62	54%	.298	1.34	3.93	3.98	0.7	96.0	51.9	16.2	43.9

Comparables: Kevin McGowan, Curtis Partch, Jed Bradley

One can only imagine how many opposing broadcasters referred to Brennan as Brendan Brannon, Brannon Branden or maybe even Brennan Boesch over the course of the Rule 5 pick's rookie campaign. Devastatingly challenging alliteration aside, the right-hander appeared to be quite the find through the first couple months of the season, showcasing a swing-and-miss changeup from a lower slot that gave right-handed hitters fits. Shoulder fatigue and unseemly dependability led to some less-than-stellar outings and some time on the injured list in the middle-third of the season, but Brennan finished the year strong. He already comfortably cleared the tremendously low bar of what is considered a Rule 5 success story, so any contribution from here on out is gravy.

Nestor Cortes Jr. LHP   Born: 12/10/94   Age: 25   Bats: R   Throws: L   Height: 5'11"   Weight: 210   Origin: Round 36, 2013 Draft (#1094 overall)

YEAR	TEAM	LVL	AGE	W	L	SV	G	GS	IP	H	HR	BB/9	K/9	K	GB%	BABIP	WHIP	ERA	DRA	WARP	MPH	FB%	WHF	CSP
2017	TRN	AA	22	5	0	0	18	7	52	35	3	3.5	7.8	45	31%	.235	1.06	2.60	3.14	1.2				
2017	SWB	AAA	22	2	4	0	11	6	48¹	40	0	2.0	10.6	57	41%	.317	1.06	1.49	2.50	1.6				
2018	SWB	AAA	23	6	6	0	23	18	111²	95	13	3.0	7.7	96	37%	.261	1.18	3.71	3.59	2.4				
2018	BAL	MLB	23	0	0	0	4	0	4²	10	2	7.7	5.8	3	47%	.471	3.00	7.71	4.30	0.0	90.9	62	10.2	49
2019	SWB	AAA	24	2	2	0	7	6	39²	29	3	2.5	9.5	42	38%	.260	1.01	3.86	2.61	1.6				
2019	NYA	MLB	24	5	1	0	33	1	66²	75	16	3.8	9.3	69	35%	.321	1.54	5.67	6.48	-0.8	91.8	52.3	11.4	47.9
2020	SEA	MLB	25	3	3	0	42	5	55	57	12	3.5	8.6	52	36%	.297	1.43	5.27	5.24	0.0	91.5	54.1	11.6	49.6

Comparables: Anthony Banda, Rafael Montero, Ryan Helsley

For a pitcher like Cortes Jr., deception is your best friend. He's a would-be lefty specialist who worked his way into an occasional opener and frequent bulk role. Whether or not his stuff is truly major-league caliber is up for debate, so he implemented every trick in the book to make up for it. A wise woman once said, "the rhythm is gonna get you" and Cortes Jr. took that to heart. Messing with a batter's rhythm was his go-to. One pitch would come from a standard three-quarters slot, the next a sidearm angle. His first delivery normal, then he's immediately quick pitching and the final pitch will come after a sudden hitch that feels minutes long. Replicating his season in Seattle after being traded for international slot money won't be easy with such fringy stuff, but Cortes Jr. isn't much for replication anyways.

Justin Dunn RHP Born: 09/22/95 Age: 24 Bats: R Throws: R Height: 6'2" Weight: 185 Origin: Round 1, 2016 Draft (#19 overall)

YEAR	TEAM	LVL	AGE	W	L	SV	G	GS	IP	H	HR	BB/9	K/9	K	GB%	BABIP	WHIP	ERA	DRA	WARP	MPH	FB%	WHF	CSP
2017	SLU	A+	21	5	6	0	20	16	95¹	101	5	4.5	7.1	75	44%	.322	1.56	5.00	6.27	-1.2				
2018	SLU	A+	22	2	3	0	9	9	45²	43	2	3.0	10.1	51	42%	.325	1.27	2.36	3.66	0.9				
2018	BIN	AA	22	6	5	0	15	15	89²	85	7	3.7	10.5	105	47%	.345	1.36	4.22	4.68	0.7				
2019	ARK	AA	23	9	5	0	25	25	131²	118	13	2.7	10.8	158	38%	.314	1.19	3.55	4.61	0.6				
2019	SEA	MLB	23	0	0	0	4	4	6²	2	0	12.1	6.8	5	44%	.125	1.65	2.70	5.32	0.0	94.3	58.8	7.3	42.2
2020	SEA	MLB	24	6	9	0	23	23	113	121	25	4.5	7.5	94	38%	.288	1.57	6.08	5.80	-0.2	94.1	60.6	7.6	43.5

Comparables: Robert Dugger, Ronald Bolaños, Hunter Wood

Many pitchers make the transition from starter to reliever. The reverse road is one far less-traveled, but Dunn has navigated a significant portion of his journey from skinny college reliever to sturdy big-league starter. A strong year as the horse of the prospect-laden Arkansas squad was soured only slightly by a major-league debut, in which he walked five batters and couldn't get out of the first inning. We'll chalk his dismal debut up to nerves, as control was something Dunn markedly improved upon in his first year with the organization. He hadn't walked more than three in any of the 25 starts leading up to his debut, and slashed his walk rate by a batter per inning compared to 2018. Questions remain about a usable changeup and his ability to brave a lineup three times through, but he's been trending in the right direction on both fronts.

Carl Edwards Jr. RHP Born: 09/03/91 Age: 28 Bats: R Throws: R Height: 6'3" Weight: 170 Origin: Round 48, 2011 Draft (#1464 overall)

YEAR	TEAM	LVL	AGE	W	L	SV	G	GS	IP	H	HR	BB/9	K/9	K	GB%	BABIP	WHIP	ERA	DRA	WARP	MPH	FB%	WHF	CSP
2017	CHN	MLB	25	5	4	0	73	0	66¹	29	6	5.2	12.8	94	46%	.193	1.01	2.98	3.05	1.6	97.1	70	16.1	42.8
2018	CHN	MLB	26	3	2	0	58	0	52	36	2	5.5	11.6	67	32%	.281	1.31	2.60	4.39	0.3	96.6	75.8	15.6	42.6
2019	IOW	AAA	27	2	0	0	14	0	14²	12	2	3.7	8.6	14	55%	.250	1.23	3.07	3.36	0.4				
2019	CHN	MLB	27	1	1	0	20	0	15¹	8	3	5.3	10.0	17	24%	.147	1.11	5.87	5.50	0.0	96.2	76.2	10.2	47.3
2019	SDN	MLB	27	0	0	0	2	0	1²	4	0	21.6	10.8	2	38%	.500	4.80	32.40	3.72	0.0	95.4	66.7	13.7	43.1
2020	SEA	MLB	28	3	3	4	56	0	59	44	8	4.7	11.1	73	38%	.262	1.27	3.63	3.73	0.9	96.1	73.8	14.9	44.6

Comparables: Corey Knebel, Brad Boxberger, Trevor Rosenthal

In major-league history, only Josh Hader has faced as many batters as Edwards and allowed a lower hit percentage. Then again, among active pitchers, only José Leclerc and Kyle Barraclough have allowed walks at a more alarming rate. Lately, the walks have outweighed the outs, leading to demotions, a change-of-scenery trade and his unceremonious release from San Diego at season's end. Edwards can still rack up whiffs, and his high-spin fastball remains notoriously difficult to square up, but he's seemingly lost all ability to control it and continued tinkering with his delivery hasn't helped his results or his headspace. The odds he'll ever reach his closer ceiling are slimmer than Edwards himself, but his still-intact raw stuff makes him a solid fixer-upper opportunity for Seattle.

————————————— ★ ★ ★ *2020 Top 101 Prospect* **#39** ★ ★ ★ —————————————

Logan Gilbert RHP Born: 05/05/97   Age: 23   Bats: R   Throws: R   Height: 6'6"   Weight: 225   Origin: Round 1, 2018 Draft (#14 overall)

YEAR	TEAM	LVL	AGE	W	L	SV	G	GS	IP	H	HR	BB/9	K/9	K	GB%	BABIP	WHIP	ERA	DRA	WARP	MPH	FB%	WHF	CSP
2019	WVA	A	22	1	0	0	5	5	22²	9	2	2.4	14.3	36	22%	.184	0.66	1.59	1.53	1.0				
2019	MOD	A+	22	5	3	0	12	12	62¹	52	3	1.7	10.5	73	47%	.320	1.03	1.73	3.20	1.4				
2019	ARK	AA	22	4	2	0	9	9	50	34	2	2.7	10.1	56	33%	.271	0.98	2.88	3.57	0.8				
2020	*SEA*	*MLB*	*23*	*2*	*2*	*0*	*33*	*0*	*35*	*35*	*5*	*3.4*	*10.0*	*39*	*36%*	*.319*	*1.37*	*4.57*	*4.61*	*0.2*				

Comparables: Ryan Helsley, Matt Harvey, Ben Lively

Gilbert appears to be on a faster track to the big leagues than the gradual routes taken by fellow Stetson University alumni Jacob deGrom and Corey Kluber, neither of whom cracked the majors until after their 25th birthdays. After a full-season debut that stretched across three levels, the latest hard-throwing Hatter may be primed to reach the bigs before he even turns 24. The mid-90s velocity that put him on the national radar in the Cape returned and held steady, he continued to throw a ton of strikes, and he stayed healthy. This is exactly what it's supposed to look like when you draft an advanced college pitcher, checking all the boxes of what would be considered a best case scenario for Year 1. Gilbert still tends to be labeled more starter than star, but as deGrom and Kluber have shown, there is a well-traveled road from DeLand to the Cy Young. Gilbert has taken all the right steps so far.

Marco Gonzales LHP Born: 02/16/92   Age: 28   Bats: L   Throws: L   Height: 6'1"   Weight: 195   Origin: Round 1, 2013 Draft (#19 overall)

YEAR	TEAM	LVL	AGE	W	L	SV	G	GS	IP	H	HR	BB/9	K/9	K	GB%	BABIP	WHIP	ERA	DRA	WARP	MPH	FB%	WHF	CSP
2017	PMB	A+	25	0	0	0	1	1	6	2	1	0.0	10.5	7	38%	.083	0.33	1.50	2.66	0.2				
2017	MEM	AAA	25	6	4	0	11	11	68¹	54	6	2.2	7.5	57	45%	.255	1.04	2.90	3.35	1.8				
2017	TAC	AAA	25	2	0	0	2	2	12	8	0	3.8	6.8	9	56%	.235	1.08	4.50	5.48	0.0				
2017	SLN	MLB	25	0	0	0	1	1	3¹	6	3	0.0	5.4	2	50%	.273	1.80	13.50	3.83	0.1	92.7	69	13.8	43
2017	SEA	MLB	25	1	1	0	10	7	36²	53	5	2.7	7.4	30	45%	.393	1.75	5.40	4.51	0.4	93.3	51	9.8	44.5
2018	SEA	MLB	26	13	9	0	29	29	166²	172	17	1.7	7.8	145	45%	.319	1.22	4.00	3.58	3.3	92.2	32.5	10.2	49.4
2019	SEA	MLB	27	16	13	0	34	34	203	210	23	2.5	6.5	147	42%	.295	1.31	3.99	5.78	0.0	90.3	39.6	8.5	51
2020	*SEA*	*MLB*	*28*	*11*	*11*	*0*	*29*	*29*	*175*	*189*	*30*	*2.5*	*6.8*	*133*	*42%*	*.297*	*1.36*	*4.86*	*4.96*	*1.2*	*90.7*	*38.2*	*9.3*	*49.1*

Comparables: Daniel Norris, Brian Matusz, Derek Holland

When manager Scott Servais named Gonzales the Opening Day starter ahead of the Japan Series, it broke Félix Hernández's 10-year streak of throwing the first pitch of the season for Seattle. It was an opportunity for the organization to demonstrate a changing of the guard, a not-so-subtle pass of the baton from the franchise icon to the young left-hander who has said and done all the right things since arriving via trade in 2017. But even Gonzales' most ardent supporters know that his profile has never been that of stuff-based domination, but rather one of dependable strike-throwing and consistent competency. In quarterback terms, he's a game-manager. The margin for error is small, however, for pitchers like Gonzales, for whom minor mistakes can snowball into big innings for opponents in a hurry. Staying healthy for another full season was encouraging—there will always be value in showing up for work every day—but chances are he'll start the third game of the year more often than the first from here on out.

Kendall Graveman RHP Born: 12/21/90   Age: 29   Bats: R   Throws: R   Height: 6'2"   Weight: 200   Origin: Round 8, 2013 Draft (#235 overall)

YEAR	TEAM	LVL	AGE	W	L	SV	G	GS	IP	H	HR	BB/9	K/9	K	GB%	BABIP	WHIP	ERA	DRA	WARP	MPH	FB%	WHF	CSP
2017	NAS	AAA	26	0	1	0	3	3	10	18	1	3.6	6.3	7	46%	.425	2.20	7.20	7.52	-0.2				
2017	OAK	MLB	26	6	4	0	19	19	105¹	114	12	2.7	6.0	70	52%	.313	1.39	4.19	5.42	1.4	95.8	68.9	7.4	43.4
2018	NAS	AAA	27	2	1	0	4	4	24	35	3	2.6	6.0	16	56%	.405	1.75	4.50	7.26	-0.5				
2018	OAK	MLB	27	1	5	0	7	7	34¹	44	9	3.4	7.1	27	57%	.324	1.66	7.60	5.38	0.0	96.2	57.2	8	44.4
2020	*SEA*	*MLB*	*29*	*5*	*7*	*0*	*19*	*19*	*87*	*104*	*18*	*3.0*	*6.9*	*67*	*52%*	*.315*	*1.53*	*5.92*	*5.73*	*-0.1*	*95.2*	*65*	*7.6*	*44*

Comparables: Joe Kelly, José Ureña, Jake Buchanan

Just for fun, picture Graveman walking into a room and boasting that he was once traded for prime Josh Donaldson. To this point—and likely to any point in the future—that's his claim to fame. The Cubs didn't see enough during his recovery from Tommy John surgery to justify picking up his option. The Mariners evidently did, signing Graveman to a big-league deal where he should get a crack at the majors, the way most every other pitcher in that system did in 2019.

Zac Grotz RHP Born: 02/17/93   Age: 27   Bats: R   Throws: R   Height: 6'2"   Weight: 195   Origin: Round 28, 2015 Draft (#829 overall)

YEAR	TEAM	LVL	AGE	W	L	SV	G	GS	IP	H	HR	BB/9	K/9	K	GB%	BABIP	WHIP	ERA	DRA	WARP	MPH	FB%	WHF	CSP
2018	COL	A	25	3	7	0	13	13	80	91	4	1.4	9.3	83	48%	.366	1.29	4.61	5.37	-0.2				
2019	ARK	AA	26	4	4	1	26	6	57¹	47	4	1.7	10.8	69	58%	.312	1.01	2.51	3.90	0.6				
2019	SEA	MLB	26	1	0	0	14	0	17¹	14	0	4.2	9.3	18	65%	.304	1.27	4.15	3.58	0.3	93.7	48.3	8.4	43.1
2020	*SEA*	*MLB*	*27*	*1*	*1*	*0*	*25*	*0*	*26*	*28*	*4*	*3.3*	*7.6*	*22*	*57%*	*.300*	*1.42*	*4.96*	*4.97*	*0.1*	*93.2*	*48.9*	*8.5*	*43.6*

Comparables: Cory Burns, Sam Tuivailala, Josh Roenicke

Of the 21 players to make their major-league debut with Seattle in 2019, perhaps none had more of a winding road to The Show than Grotz. His collegiate baseball journey alone had him zig-zagging across these United States: The right-hander pitched at a Division II school (Cal State Monterey Bay) as a freshman, a junior college (College of San Mateo) as a sophomore, an SEC school (Tennessee) as a junior and an NAIA powerhouse (Embry-Riddle Aeronautical University) as a senior. That academic adventure eventually earned him a call from the Astros in the 28th round of the 2015 Draft. The team gave him 22 professional innings before releasing him less than a year later. A couple minor-league contracts and multiple stints in Indy ball later, Grotz was scooped up by Seattle before the 2019 season and found success in Double-A immediately, prompting a big-league call-up in early August. We could speculate how Grotz fits into the Mariners' bullpen plans going forward, but does it really matter? He's here! He made it!

Taylor Guilbeau LHP   Born: 05/12/93   Age: 27   Bats: L   Throws: L   Height: 6'4"   Weight: 180   Origin: Round 10, 2015 Draft (#314 overall)

YEAR	TEAM	LVL	AGE	W	L	SV	G	GS	IP	H	HR	BB/9	K/9	K	GB%	BABIP	WHIP	ERA	DRA	WARP	MPH	FB%	WHF	CSP
2017	POT	A+	24	4	5	0	23	15	99¹	128	9	2.2	7.1	78	51%	.368	1.53	5.89	7.00	-2.1				
2018	POT	A+	25	1	0	0	28	0	35²	34	0	3.8	8.8	35	46%	.330	1.37	2.52	4.62	0.1				
2019	HAR	AA	26	1	2	0	27	0	35	27	1	2.6	11.3	44	61%	.310	1.06	2.31	3.74	0.4				
2019	FRE	AAA	26	2	0	0	7	0	8²	10	0	5.2	6.2	6	56%	.370	1.73	5.19	5.27	0.1				
2019	SEA	MLB	26	0	0	0	17	0	12¹	10	2	2.2	5.1	7	70%	.211	1.05	3.65	5.34	0.0	96.2	63.5	8.3	50.2
2020	SEA	MLB	27	1	1	0	25	0	26	31	5	3.6	7.3	21	59%	.326	1.59	6.05	5.77	-0.2	95.7	64.3	8.4	50.8

Comparables: Matt Dermody, Kyle Dowdy, Colt Hynes

Lefties that throw 96 mph may not grow on trees, but it's certainly a whole lot easier to find them than it used to be. A senior sign out of the University of Alabama, the Nationals gave Guilbeau a shot at starting for a couple seasons before shifting him to the bullpen in 2018. Sometimes "move him to the 'pen" is as simple as "just add water," and Guilbeau's transition had him looking like a future major leaguer in short order. The Mariners acquired him at the deadline and had him on their roster 18 days later.

Félix Hernández RHP   Born: 04/08/86   Age: 34   Bats: R   Throws: R   Height: 6'3"   Weight: 225   Origin: International Free Agent, 2002

YEAR	TEAM	LVL	AGE	W	L	SV	G	GS	IP	H	HR	BB/9	K/9	K	GB%	BABIP	WHIP	ERA	DRA	WARP	MPH	FB%	WHF	CSP
2017	TAC	AAA	31	2	0	0	3	3	13	9	1	2.1	11.1	16	42%	.267	0.92	4.15	2.32	0.5				
2017	SEA	MLB	31	6	5	0	16	16	86²	86	17	2.7	8.1	78	49%	.287	1.29	4.36	5.72	-0.1	92.5	44.5	10.2	46.5
2018	SEA	MLB	32	8	14	0	29	28	155²	159	27	3.4	7.2	125	48%	.286	1.40	5.55	5.30	0.0	91.6	43.3	8.8	45.3
2019	SEA	MLB	33	1	8	0	15	15	71²	85	17	3.1	7.2	57	49%	.309	1.53	6.40	7.10	-1.0	91.8	39.7	9.4	49.6
2020	SEA	MLB	34	2	2	0	33	0	35	38	7	3.1	7.8	30	48%	.301	1.42	5.40	5.29	0.0	90.7	41.8	9.1	46.7

Comparables: Dwight Gooden, Bert Blyleven, Matt Cain

"How many times do you think you cried tonight?" is not a question you'll hear often at a postgame press conference, but it was perfectly appropriate in the context: to Hernández, seated at the podium following his final start as a Mariner, smiling, but visibly drained. After mentioning a moment with his brother, Hernández paused in contemplation of the whole evening, before continuing: "It was fun!" On a night where a franchise said goodbye to its most loyal superstar, a borderline heartbreaking ending to wholly unfulfilled story, there was more than enough to be sad about. A team that had experienced strict disappointment over the King's 15-year tenure now had no choice but to let him go. And yet, here he was, beaming through the tears, proclaiming how much fun he had in his final, fitting act—a Mariners' defeat.

That, in many ways, was the beauty of Félix Hernández, Seattle Mariner. He was having fun when he was a 19-year-old baby-faced phenom. He was having fun at the peak of his powers, arguably the best pitcher on Earth. And he was still having fun at the end, a shell of the pitcher he once was. If Félix was having fun, we were having fun. He was as close to a one-man show as baseball can get, making every fifth day an event for a fan base that rarely had reason to care during the other four. Many pitied him. They couldn't fathom the endurance required to man the bilge pumps on a sinking ship. But he just wanted to perform his craft for the people that cheered him for his entire adult life. No matter the standings, no matter the score. That remained true all the way to the bitter end.

Hernández is 33 with an arm going on 40. It's possible he'll find a soft landing with a bad team in search of innings. Maybe he'll find somewhere else to have fun on a mound. But for now, Félix will move on, and the Mariners will march on without him, both still in search of October baseball. The drought is alive, but The King is dead. Long Live The King.

Yusei Kikuchi LHP   Born: 06/17/91   Age: 29   Bats: L   Throws: L   Height: 6'0"   Weight: 194   Origin: International Free Agent, 2019

YEAR	TEAM	LVL	AGE	W	L	SV	G	GS	IP	H	HR	BB/9	K/9	K	GB%	BABIP	WHIP	ERA	DRA	WARP	MPH	FB%	WHF	CSP
2019	SEA	MLB	28	6	11	0	32	32	161²	195	36	2.8	6.5	116	45%	.310	1.52	5.46	7.85	-3.6	95.5	49.1	9.5	50.8
2020	SEA	MLB	29	8	10	0	26	26	143	162	28	3.0	6.5	103	44%	.301	1.48	5.63	5.55	0.1	94.8	49.1	9.5	50.8

Comparables: Ryan Carpenter, Ryan Feierabend, Kei Igawa

A year after missing out on Shohei Ohtani, the Mariners managed to land a different prized Japanese free agent in Kikuchi. Simply not being Japanese Babe Ruth meant that he arrived with considerably less fanfare, but there were still high expectations for a 27-year-old who had already proven himself as one of the best arms in NPB. On its face, this was the type of pitcher profile whose stuff could translate seamlessly. To put it bluntly, it, uh, did not. His DRA was the worst among all qualified starting pitchers. The bright spots, save for an exquisite 96-pitch shutout in Toronto in August, were difficult to identify. Kikuchi also dealt with plenty off the field: his father passed away in March, and his first child was born in July, adding to the cultural assimilation he was already contending with. Optimists could reasonably point out that there are still mid-rotation starter ingredients present. Realists would say you'd be stretching to consider Kikuchi's rookie year anything but a rank disappointment.

George Kirby RHP   Born: 02/04/98   Age: 22   Bats: R   Throws: R   Height: 6'4"   Weight: 201   Origin: Round 1, 2019 Draft (#20 overall)

YEAR	TEAM	LVL	AGE	W	L	SV	G	GS	IP	H	HR	BB/9	K/9	K	GB%	BABIP	WHIP	ERA	DRA	WARP	MPH	FB%	WHF	CSP
2019	EVE	A-	21	0	0	0	9	8	23	24	1	0.0	9.8	25	48%	.355	1.04	2.35	3.50	0.5				
2020	SEA	MLB	22	2	2	0	33	0	35	35	5	3.5	7.4	29	42%	.286	1.38	4.65	4.75	0.2				

Comparables: Andrew Moore, Joe Musgrove, Pat Light

The Mariners went back to the mid-major college starter well for their first-round pick in 2019. A year after selecting Stetson's Logan Gilbert, Seattle popped Kirby out of Elon University with the 20th-overall selection. Kirby's first-round pedigree was built on a mid-90s fastball, a curveball that flashes plus, and an extreme propensity to not throw four balls during an at-bat. He allowed one free pass in his breakout summer on the Cape (to fellow 2019 first-rounder Michael Busch), just six walks next to 106 strikeouts in his draft spring at Elon, and zero in his first 23 pro innings after signing. There have been a fair share of highly-drafted collegiate no-walk artists in recent years, but their success levels in pro ball have varied from back-end emergency starter Tom Eshelman to All-Star Game MVP Shane Bieber. Kirby's raw stuff more closely resembles the latter's, but he'll have to show it plays against more than just the Colonial Athletic Association or the Northwest League before he sniffs any Top 100 lists.

Wade LeBlanc LHP Born: 08/07/84 Age: 35 Bats: L Throws: L Height: 6'3" Weight: 205 Origin: Round 2, 2006 Draft (#61 overall)

YEAR	TEAM	LVL	AGE	W	L	SV	G	GS	IP	H	HR	BB/9	K/9	K	GB%	BABIP	WHIP	ERA	DRA	WARP	MPH	FB%	WHF	CSP
2017	PIT	MLB	32	5	2	1	50	0	68	64	10	2.2	7.1	54	47%	.269	1.19	4.50	3.77	1.1	88.8	62.9	10.3	46.1
2018	SEA	MLB	33	9	5	0	32	27	162	151	24	2.2	7.2	130	37%	.273	1.18	3.72	5.07	0.4	88.0	61.1	10.1	47.7
2019	SEA	MLB	34	6	7	0	26	8	121¹	145	28	2.3	6.8	92	41%	.308	1.45	5.71	8.04	-3.4	87.6	58.1	10.5	47.9
2020	SEA	MLB	35	2	2	0	33	0	35	40	9	2.6	6.9	27	39%	.295	1.43	5.80	5.70	-0.2	86.8	59	10.1	46.5

Comparables: Clayton Richard, Jeff Francis, Tommy Milone

The peak of LeBlanc's season came before Opening Day, when he starred in the commercial "Arts and Crafty" alongside fellow left-handers Marco Gonzales and Yusei Kikuchi, a hilarious homage to the team's stockpile of soft-tossing southpaws. His 2018 renaissance was a delightful surprise for the popular veteran, but hitters tend not to be as nice to pitchers of LeBlanc's ilk for extended periods of time. The clock struck 2019, and LeBlanc was a pumpkin once again. The softest-tossing starter not named Jason Vargas was a lot worse than Vargas, which may be all you need to know.

Matt Magill RHP Born: 11/10/89 Age: 30 Bats: R Throws: R Height: 6'3" Weight: 210 Origin: Round 31, 2008 Draft (#937 overall)

YEAR	TEAM	LVL	AGE	W	L	SV	G	GS	IP	H	HR	BB/9	K/9	K	GB%	BABIP	WHIP	ERA	DRA	WARP	MPH	FB%	WHF	CSP
2017	ELP	AAA	27	6	5	0	19	17	95²	105	13	3.9	6.9	73	45%	.316	1.53	3.95	4.66	1.1				
2018	ROC	AAA	28	0	0	2	5	0	8²	5	0	2.1	13.5	13	28%	.278	0.81	0.00	2.68	0.2				
2018	MIN	MLB	28	3	3	0	40	0	56²	58	11	3.7	8.9	56	35%	.301	1.43	3.81	5.42	-0.3	96.7	60.9	11.8	46
2019	SEA	MLB	29	3	2	5	22	0	22¹	21	3	2.0	11.3	28	43%	.300	1.16	3.63	3.18	0.5	96.7	56.9	16.8	45.4
2019	MIN	MLB	29	2	0	0	28	0	28¹	30	4	4.8	11.4	36	36%	.342	1.59	4.45	6.11	-0.2	97.5	47.2	14.6	45.4
2020	SEA	MLB	30	3	3	14	56	0	59	54	8	3.8	10.3	67	40%	.302	1.34	4.26	4.34	0.5	96.2	55.7	13.7	45.5

Comparables: Michael Blazek, Allen Webster, Steve Johnson

It was hard to parse just what Seattle may have seen in Magill when they claimed him off waivers from Minnesota, other than a desire to add to their collection of Bullpen Matts. But the hard-throwing Magill halved his walk rate immediately upon arrival, a shocking development considering his decade-long professional track record. His newfound control and above-average whiff rate even earned him the few save opportunities of his career. It's quite possible this stretch with the M's was merely a misleading blip of competent control and he'll revert to his traditional wildness in due time. For now, he looks like he might belong.

Reggie McClain RHP Born: 11/16/92 Age: 27 Bats: R Throws: R Height: 6'2" Weight: 180 Origin: Round 13, 2016 Draft (#387 overall)

YEAR	TEAM	LVL	AGE	W	L	SV	G	GS	IP	H	HR	BB/9	K/9	K	GB%	BABIP	WHIP	ERA	DRA	WARP	MPH	FB%	WHF	CSP
2017	MOD	A+	24	12	9	0	27	27	153¹	164	15	2.1	7.5	127	50%	.323	1.30	4.75	4.76	0.9				
2018	MOD	A+	25	6	11	0	24	23	133	160	16	1.9	7.3	108	52%	.343	1.41	5.01	6.41	-1.7				
2019	MOD	A+	26	0	0	0	6	0	16	9	1	0.0	10.1	18	62%	.205	0.56	0.56	1.52	0.6				
2019	ARK	AA	26	0	0	0	6	2	15²	6	0	2.3	11.5	20	58%	.194	0.64	1.15	2.25	0.5				
2019	TAC	AAA	26	3	4	2	17	1	41	29	3	4.0	7.5	34	58%	.241	1.15	3.29	2.28	1.6				
2019	SEA	MLB	26	1	1	0	14	2	21	22	2	5.6	4.7	11	63%	.290	1.67	6.00	6.78	-0.3	96.4	76.6	6.8	47.6
2020	SEA	MLB	27	1	1	0	19	0	20	24	3	3.8	6.0	13	58%	.316	1.62	6.01	5.68	-0.1	95.9	77.5	6.9	48.2

Comparables: Joe Martinez, Cole Sulser, Jeff Brigham

McClain is the kind of new-age player dev success story that the best teams seem to replicate so frequently. After two straight nondescript years as an old-for-the-level college pitcher in the California League, he attended the Mariners' offseason "Gas Camp," where he saw his velocity and big-league prospects spike beyond what previously seemed possible. The third time was the charm for McClain in the Cal League—this time, as a reliever—where he dominated in six April appearances, kick-starting a race through the system that landed him in the Mariners bullpen come August. Eleven of those 14 earned runs came against the Astros, in Houston, across three appearances, one of which was his big-league debut. What happened to cracking down on rookie hazing?

Tommy Milone LHP Born: 02/16/87 Age: 33 Bats: L Throws: L Height: 6'0" Weight: 215 Origin: Round 10, 2008 Draft (#301 overall)

YEAR	TEAM	LVL	AGE	W	L	SV	G	GS	IP	H	HR	BB/9	K/9	K	GB%	BABIP	WHIP	ERA	DRA	WARP	MPH	FB%	WHF	CSP
2017	BIN	AA	30	1	0	0	4	4	20	26	8	0.9	4.9	11	27%	.273	1.40	4.95	6.48	-0.3				
2017	MIL	MLB	30	1	0	1	6	3	21	29	6	0.9	6.9	16	35%	.333	1.48	6.43	6.38	-0.2	89.8	65.2	8.3	43.8
2017	NYN	MLB	30	0	3	0	11	5	27¹	36	9	4.0	7.2	22	36%	.318	1.76	8.56	5.28	0.1	89.5	65.2	8.9	42.5
2018	SYR	AAA	31	7	4	0	20	20	109²	101	11	2.0	9.3	113	36%	.303	1.14	4.19	4.47	1.3				
2018	WAS	MLB	31	1	1	0	5	4	26¹	37	7	0.3	7.9	23	30%	.349	1.44	5.81	4.64	0.2	88.8	58.9	11.7	46.9
2019	TAC	AAA	32	4	2	0	9	8	49¹	49	7	2.2	7.8	43	39%	.286	1.24	3.83	3.06	1.7				
2019	SEA	MLB	32	4	10	0	23	6	111²	102	24	1.9	7.6	94	38%	.252	1.12	4.76	5.68	-0.3	88.6	43.7	10.5	45.8
2020	SEA	MLB	33	2	2	0	33	0	35	37	9	2.3	7.5	29	37%	.282	1.32	5.18	5.27	0.0	87.8	49.5	10.2	44.9

Comparables: Wade Miley, Wade LeBlanc, Jason Vargas

Each of Milone's Annual comments in recent years have read with a sense that this could be the last time his name was ever written in one of these hefty books. The notion that his mishmosh of meh pitches from the left side would return the next year to face major-league hitters is increasingly difficult to fathom. And yet, here we are again. 111 2/3 innings, only 108 1/3 more than PECOTA projected a year ago. At this point, Milone has become the baseball version of that friend in college you could always count on to show up to your intramural basketball game. "What's Tommy up to? He's definitely not doing anything and we're not just gonna play with 5 guys. We're gonna need someone to come off the bench." In the context of the 2019 Mariners, someone had to go out there and throw the baseball to the other team's hitters. Here's to another full Milone comment in next year's Annual, somehow, some way.

Justus Sheffield LHP Born: 05/13/96 Age: 24 Bats: L Throws: L Height: 6'0" Weight: 200 Origin: Round 1, 2014 Draft (#31 overall)

YEAR	TEAM	LVL	AGE	W	L	SV	G	GS	IP	H	HR	BB/9	K/9	K	GB%	BABIP	WHIP	ERA	DRA	WARP	MPH	FB%	WHF	CSP
2017	TRN	AA	21	7	6	0	17	17	93^1	94	14	3.2	7.9	82	48%	.293	1.36	3.18	5.33	-0.2				
2018	TRN	AA	22	1	2	0	5	5	28	16	1	4.5	12.5	39	44%	.259	1.07	2.25	3.54	0.6				
2018	SWB	AAA	22	6	4	0	20	15	88	66	3	3.7	8.6	84	46%	.264	1.16	2.56	3.41	2.1				
2018	NYA	MLB	22	0	0	0	3	0	2^2	4	1	10.1	0.0	0	55%	.300	2.62	10.12	6.56	-0.1	95.8	54.4	1.8	38.3
2019	ARK	AA	23	5	3	0	12	12	78	62	4	2.1	9.8	85	44%	.293	1.03	2.19	3.77	1.1				
2019	TAC	AAA	23	2	6	0	13	12	55	59	12	6.7	7.9	48	54%	.292	1.82	6.87	4.99	0.9				
2019	SEA	MLB	23	0	1	0	8	7	36	44	5	4.5	9.2	37	54%	.375	1.72	5.50	5.81	0.0	95.0	47.8	13.7	46.6
2020	SEA	MLB	24	9	10	0	62	24	161	167	23	4.2	9.2	164	47%	.321	1.50	5.02	4.93	1.0	94.9	49.6	13.3	44.2

Comparables: Jake Thompson, Zack Littell, Robert Stephenson

It's easy to imagine Sheffield feeling some semblance of relief when he found out in June he was being sent down to Double-A from Tacoma. The introduction of the hitter-friendly big-league baseball to the already hitter-friendly Pacific Coast League was less-than-friendly to the southpaw. Poor command and a bad habit of allowing the long ball added up to 6.87 ERA, which was unsettlingly close to league average but still troubling enough to warrant a demotion. The change of scenery helped: Sheffield absolutely carved in his return to Double-A, posting the best FIP among all starters in the Texas League during his 12-start rejuvenation. A return to the big leagues in August yielded middling results, as his wipeout slider continued to wipe out good hitters while his low-spin fastball rarely missed any bats. Everyone knows there is impact bullpen potential if all else fails, but there's no rush for Seattle to resort to that backup plan any time soon. Besides, depending on how the offseason goes, he might be the team's fifth starter by default.

Erik Swanson RHP Born: 09/04/93 Age: 26 Bats: R Throws: R Height: 6'3" Weight: 235 Origin: Round 8, 2014 Draft (#246 overall)

YEAR	TEAM	LVL	AGE	W	L	SV	G	GS	IP	H	HR	BB/9	K/9	K	GB%	BABIP	WHIP	ERA	DRA	WARP	MPH	FB%	WHF	CSP
2017	TAM	A+	23	7	3	0	20	20	100^1	115	10	1.3	7.5	84	42%	.344	1.29	3.95	4.53	0.9				
2018	STA	A-	24	0	0	0	2	2	6^2	8	0	0.0	8.1	6	48%	.381	1.20	4.05	4.42	0.1				
2018	TRN	AA	24	5	0	0	8	7	42^2	22	0	3.2	11.6	55	36%	.253	0.87	0.42	2.24	1.5				
2018	SWB	AAA	24	3	2	0	14	13	72^1	63	10	1.7	9.7	78	37%	.283	1.06	3.86	3.85	1.4				
2019	TAC	AAA	25	0	1	0	10	6	24^1	28	5	4.4	10.4	28	35%	.348	1.64	5.55	5.57	0.2				
2019	SEA	MLB	25	1	5	2	27	8	58	56	17	1.9	8.1	52	38%	.241	1.17	5.74	5.91	-0.2	95.2	67.9	11.2	49.2
2020	SEA	MLB	26	6	7	0	63	13	111	117	25	2.8	7.9	98	37%	.290	1.36	5.20	5.28	0.2	94.8	69.1	11.4	50.1

Comparables: Erick Fedde, Alec Mills, Brandon Workman

Forget worrying about getting through the order a third time—opponents that faced Swanson a *second* time in games he started posted a troubling 1.194 OPS, a scorching 554 points better than their first time facing the righty. The Mariners thought they may have starter ingredients in Swanson when they acquired him from the Yankees, but quickly changed course after his early-season struggles. Swanson had always pounded the zone throughout his career, but the high volume of strikes that minor-league hitters failed to take advantage of were getting absolutely pummeled by big leaguers, oftentimes over the fence. He remains dangerously homer-prone, but otherwise improved across the board once he moved to the bullpen, suggesting a respectable future as a decent middle-relief option.

Juan Then RHP Born: 02/07/00 Age: 20 Bats: R Throws: R Height: 6'1" Weight: 155 Origin: International Free Agent, 2016

YEAR	TEAM	LVL	AGE	W	L	SV	G	GS	IP	H	HR	BB/9	K/9	K	GB%	BABIP	WHIP	ERA	DRA	WARP	MPH	FB%	WHF	CSP
2017	DMR	RK	17	2	2	0	13	13	61^1	50	3	2.2	8.2	56	54%	.278	1.06	2.64	1.91	2.7				
2018	YAN	RK	18	0	3	0	11	11	50	38	2	2.0	7.6	42	48%	.259	0.98	2.70	2.07	2.1				
2019	EVE	A-	19	0	3	0	7	6	30^1	24	1	2.7	9.5	32	36%	.299	1.09	3.56	3.17	0.7				
2019	WVA	A	19	1	2	0	3	3	16	7	1	2.2	7.9	14	32%	.150	0.69	2.25	2.90	0.4				
2020	SEA	MLB	20	2	2	0	33	0	35	35	5	3.8	7.5	29	34%	.291	1.42	4.81	4.84	0.1				

Comparables: Felix Jorge, Jose Suarez, Huascar Ynoa

At first, Juan was a Mariner, signed as a promising 16-year-old right-hander out of the Dominican Republic. Then, Juan was a Yankee, traded away for Literally Nick Rumbelow. Then, Juan became a Mariner again, the return for half a season of Edwin Encarnación. This string of terrible puns falls apart when we inform you that it's actually pronounced 'ten.' But one *could* say that Juan Then made his full-season debut at Low-A West Virginia as one of the Then-youngest pitchers in the Sally League and more than held his own. We may never know what Then learned at Yankees summer camp but he clearly developed enough to warrant re-acquiring, and now looks like another name to monitor in a system suddenly flush with projectable arms. His improvements have already made him Juan-Thenth of a Mariners Top 10 list.

Sam Tuivailala RHP   Born: 10/19/92   Age: 27   Bats: R   Throws: R   Height: 6'3"   Weight: 225   Origin: Round 3, 2010 Draft (#106 overall)

YEAR	TEAM	LVL	AGE	W	L	SV	G	GS	IP	H	HR	BB/9	K/9	K	GB%	BABIP	WHIP	ERA	DRA	WARP	MPH	FB%	WHF	CSP
2017	MEM	AAA	24	1	0	6	18	0	21¹	13	2	1.3	8.9	21	42%	.216	0.75	1.27	1.77	0.8				
2017	SLN	MLB	24	3	3	0	37	0	42¹	35	4	2.3	7.2	34	49%	.258	1.09	2.55	3.86	0.6	97.8	61.8	11	54
2018	SLN	MLB	25	3	3	0	31	0	31²	35	3	3.1	7.4	26	50%	.314	1.45	3.69	4.77	0.1	97.6	58.7	10.6	52.3
2018	SEA	MLB	25	1	0	0	5	0	5¹	6	0	1.7	6.8	4	56%	.375	1.31	1.69	2.93	0.1	96.8	63	13.6	53.9
2019	MOD	A+	26	0	1	0	6	0	6	1	1	3.0	9.0	6	31%	.000	0.50	1.50	2.94	0.1				
2019	SEA	MLB	26	1	0	0	23	2	23	13	1	4.3	10.6	27	33%	.226	1.04	2.35	4.69	0.2	95.1	62	11.7	44
2020	SEA	MLB	27	3	3	7	53	3	56	53	8	3.6	9.0	56	42%	.292	1.34	4.38	4.46	0.5	96.4	61.5	11.4	49.9

Comparables: Neftalí Feliz, Shawn Armstrong, Bruce Rondón

Tuivailala arrived in the majors as a 21-year-old flamethrower in 2014. He arrived in Seattle with a fastball that can better be described as flame-licked. There is still some heat but it's never a good sign when a reliever's average velocity drops three miles per hour. Did we mention he used to throw his heater 65 percent of the time? This might feel like it's all trending in the wrong direction, but Tuivailala has shown an ability to compensate effectively, when he can get on the mound. He's thrown limited innings the last few years, and despite low ERAs, DRA hasn't taken kindly to him. still, he edged his K/9 part? "Still, even with decreased velocity, Tui might have carved a path forward in the majors on the back of a diversified pitch mix: he didn't throw any individual pitch over 35 percent of the time, and consequently edged his K/9 into the double digits for the first time since 2015.

Art Warren RHP   Born: 03/23/93   Age: 27   Bats: R   Throws: R   Height: 6'3"   Weight: 230   Origin: Round 23, 2015 Draft (#695 overall)

YEAR	TEAM	LVL	AGE	W	L	SV	G	GS	IP	H	HR	BB/9	K/9	K	GB%	BABIP	WHIP	ERA	DRA	WARP	MPH	FB%	WHF	CSP
2017	MOD	A+	24	3	1	8	43	0	64²	58	5	3.5	9.3	67	45%	.312	1.28	3.06	4.50	0.3				
2018	ARK	AA	25	1	2	2	14	0	15²	10	0	8.0	12.6	22	39%	.303	1.53	1.72	4.44	0.1				
2019	ARK	AA	26	2	1	15	29	0	31²	23	1	3.7	11.7	41	60%	.310	1.14	1.71	3.41	0.5				
2019	SEA	MLB	26	1	0	0	6	0	5¹	2	0	3.4	8.4	5	29%	.143	0.75	0.00	5.56	0.0	98.0	44.2	13	41.3
2020	SEA	MLB	27	1	1	0	25	0	26	28	5	4.8	7.0	20	45%	.293	1.60	5.89	5.66	-0.1	97.5	44.7	13.1	41.8

Comparables: Kyle Dowdy, Jon Meloan, Brad Wieck

Every day, Twitter users solicit the wisdom of @ArtDecider—an anonymous account that serves up definitive rulings on whether something is Art or Not Art—to determine whether various people, places, images, videos, memes, or otherwise are, indeed, Art. The account then renders a one- or two-word judgment that settles the inquiry once and for all. In the case of Warren, there isn't much to decide: his name is Art, so he is Art, not Arthur, and the first big-leaguer to go by Art since Art Howe in 1985. Whether Warren will be asked to fill the bona fide-closer role in which he has served throughout the minors or as a big-stuff middle reliever with fringy command isn't up to us. Check in with @ReliefRoleDecider. Or Scott Servais.

LINEOUTS

Hitters

HITTER	POS	TEAM	LVL	AGE	PA	R	2B	3B	HR	RBI	BB	K	SB	CS	AVG/OBP/SLG	DRC+	VORP	BABIP	BRR	FRAA	WARP
Carter Bins	C	EVE	A-	20	202	31	2	0	7	26	33	56	5	2	.208/.391/.357	127	14.7	.272	0.1	C(47): 1.1, P(1): 0.0	1.5
Braden Bishop	CF	MOD	A+	25	29	7	1	1	0	3	2	9	0	0	.240/.345/.360	56	2.3	.375	1.4	CF(3): 0.6	0.2
	CF	SEA	MLB	25	60	3	0	0	0	4	3	21	0	0	.107/.153/.107	45	-2.2	.171	0.2	CF(20): -0.6, LF(4): 0.2	-0.2
	CF	TAC	AAA	25	211	29	15	0	8	31	23	44	2	2	.276/.360/.486	92	10.7	.321	-0.2	CF(34): 0.7, RF(6): 1.0	0.6
Tim Lopes	2B	SEA	MLB	25	128	11	7	0	1	12	15	29	6	3	.270/.359/.360	91	2.0	.354	0.2	LF(33): -0.2, RF(3): -0.4	0.2
	2B	TAC	AAA	25	420	59	31	2	10	60	36	72	26	9	.302/.362/.476	99	28.6	.344	2.8	2B(63): -7.6, 3B(21): 0.8	0.9
Dylan Moore	UT	TAC	AAA	26	35	3	0	0	0	7	3	3	2	1	.172/.294/.172	49	-2.6	.192	0.3	SS(3): -0.1, 2B(2): 0.2	-0.1
	UT	SEA	MLB	26	282	31	14	2	9	28	25	93	11	9	.206/.302/.389	79	2.9	.290	-1.1	LF(31): 2.1, SS(31): 0.1	0.4
Brian O'Keefe	C	SFD	AA	25	346	36	9	0	13	40	37	71	1	1	.229/.319/.389	82	10.6	.255	-2.5	C(77): -0.7	0.6
Dom Thompson-Williams	OF	ARK	AA	24	479	46	24	4	12	41	35	152	15	2	.234/.298/.391	100	17.6	.327	0.9	CF(45): -2.3, RF(32): -0.4	0.8
Patrick Wisdom	3B	TEX	MLB	27	28	1	1	0	0	1	1	15	0	0	.154/.185/.192	48	-1.2	.364	-0.3	1B(5): -0.3, 3B(4): -0.1	-0.2
	3B	NAS	AAA	27	453	68	15	0	31	74	53	125	8	2	.240/.332/.513	111	28.1	.266	0.5	3B(56): 1.7, LF(15): -0.4	2.0

A reputation as an elite defensive catcher at Fresno State had some evaluators thinking **Carter Bins** could go early on Day 2 of the Draft. *Narrator*: He did not. Seattle scooped him up for $350K in the 11th round. ⓧ **Braden Bishop** suffered a lacerated spleen when he was hit by a pitch, threatening his health and derailing his season. His premier glove in center should secure him a bench spot in the majors when healthy. ⓧ If not for a brief study abroad experience with Toronto, **Tim Lopes**, Seattle's sixth-round selection in the 2012 Draft, would be the longest-tenured member of the Mariners organization this side of Kyle Seager. He'll enter 2020 just 376 home runs behind Jeff Kent on the all-time Edison High School alumni MLB home run list. ⓧ Could the Mariners have hit big in the international market for the second year in a row? Teenage shortstop **Noelvi Marte** followed up Julio Rodriguez's 2018 DSL MVP campaign with an MVP season of his own, thanks to a hot finish, posting a 1.221 OPS in his final 20 games. ⓧ **Dylan Moore** made at least one start at every position on the diamond other than pitcher and catcher, and he did manage to make some appearances on the mound. Impressive work for a player generated 15 seasons into your MLB: The Show franchise mode. ⓧ Either the Mariners selected **Brian O'Keefe** in the minor-league portion of the Rule 5 draft due to his offensive competency, or they confused him with the *Fortune* editor of the same name. We'd guess the former, but maybe Dipoto is cracking down on that "DiPoto" business. ⓧ Sharp home/road splits in favor of away games suggest **Dom Thompson-Williams** was another victim of the cavernous home park in Arkansas, but it's unclear if he did enough to avoid being sent back to Little Rock in 2020. ⓧ Despite his surname, **Patrick Wisdom** hasn't proven smart enough to avoid striking out in 40 percent of his career plate appearances. As such, he's exactly the type of Quad-A talent Jerry Dipoto swears he can stop collecting at any time, no really, he's in total control.

Pitchers

PITCHER	TEAM	LVL	AGE	W	L	SV	G	GS	IP	H	HR	BB/9	K/9	K	GB%	BABIP	WHIP	ERA	DRA	WARP	MPH	FB%	WHF	CSP
Elvis Alvarado	NAT	Rk	20	2	2	0	7	2	15	10	0	9.6	11.4	19	51%	.270	1.73	6.00	5.59	0.0				
	MRN	Rk	20	0	1	0	5	1	12	10	0	2.2	9.8	13	29%	.323	1.08	2.25	2.75	0.4				
Chasen Bradford	SEA	MLB	29	0	0	1	12	0	16²	17	6	2.2	5.9	11	52%	.229	1.26	4.86	5.16	0.0	92.8	51.4	11.7	50.1
Matt Carasiti	TAC	AAA	27	1	0	4	15	0	16¹	19	3	3.9	9.4	17	45%	.333	1.59	4.96	5.21	0.2				
	IOW	AAA	27	1	1	1	16	0	27	20	1	3.7	7.7	23	55%	.250	1.15	2.67	4.48	0.5				
	SEA	MLB	27	0	1	0	11	5	9²	11	2	4.7	9.3	10	50%	.346	1.66	4.66	4.36	0.1	97.2	57.8	13.5	48.8
Nabil Crismatt	ARK	AA	24	4	5	0	14	13	83²	57	6	1.2	9.6	89	44%	.242	0.81	1.94	2.70	2.3				
	TAC	AAA	24	0	5	0	13	8	46²	67	15	4.1	13.1	68	37%	.419	1.89	9.06	7.33	-0.3				
Sam Delaplane	MOD	A+	24	3	2	2	21	0	31²	22	2	4.0	17.6	62	40%	.417	1.14	4.26	3.03	0.6				
	ARK	AA	24	3	1	5	25	0	37	13	2	2.2	14.1	58	39%	.177	0.59	0.49	1.60	1.4				
Matt Festa	TAC	AAA	26	1	1	5	23	0	30²	23	3	4.1	9.7	33	36%	.260	1.21	2.64	2.81	1.0				
	SEA	MLB	26	0	2	0	20	0	22¹	20	5	4.8	8.5	21	40%	.250	1.43	5.64	5.57	-0.1	94.5	52.8	10.5	47.8
Aaron Fletcher	HAG	A	23	2	3	1	15	0	28	14	0	1.6	9.0	28	44%	.194	0.68	1.61	2.45	0.8				
	POT	A+	23	3	1	0	12	0	26	15	1	2.8	11.1	32	56%	.241	0.88	1.38	2.83	0.6				
	ARK	AA	23	0	0	0	9	0	13	14	0	2.1	10.4	15	54%	.371	1.31	3.46	5.57	-0.2				
	HAR	AA	23	0	0	0	5	0	6¹	7	0	2.8	12.8	9	62%	.438	1.42	4.26	4.67	0.0				
Joey Gerber	MOD	A+	22	0	2	8	25	0	26	17	0	4.2	13.5	39	39%	.304	1.12	3.46	2.41	0.7				
	ARK	AA	22	1	2	0	19	0	22²	21	2	2.8	11.9	30	41%	.352	1.24	1.59	4.30	0.1				
Wyatt Mills	ARK	AA	24	4	2	8	41	0	52²	43	2	2.9	11.3	66	55%	.320	1.14	4.27	4.29	0.2				
Anthony Misiewicz	ARK	AA	24	1	2	0	7	7	35²	36	0	1.8	9.1	36	51%	.360	1.21	2.52	4.45	0.2				
	TAC	AAA	24	8	6	0	19	17	95²	95	17	2.6	8.4	89	44%	.291	1.29	5.36	3.83	2.6				
Andrew Moore	ARK	AA	25	2	1	0	5	5	28	24	1	1.3	9.3	29	33%	.311	1.00	3.86	3.34	0.6				
	TAC	AAA	25	0	5	0	13	8	54	71	14	2.8	6.0	36	38%	.311	1.63	8.00	6.49	0.0				
	DUR	AAA	25	0	2	0	5	4	17¹	29	9	5.2	5.2	10	32%	.333	2.25	12.98	8.94	-0.4				
	SEA	MLB	25	0	0	0	1	1	4²	6	2	1.9	3.9	2	18%	.267	1.50	7.71	8.25	-0.1	93.5	48.7	5.1	50.8
Penn Murfee	MOD	A+	25	5	5	5	26	20	102²	95	3	2.0	10.7	122	49%	.347	1.15	3.07	3.93	1.3				
	TAC	AAA	25	0	0	0	5	0	8²	13	3	7.3	12.1	12	48%	.417	2.31	10.38	6.80	0.0				
Ljay Newsome	MOD	A+	22	6	6	0	18	18	100²	105	11	0.8	11.1	124	27%	.357	1.13	3.75	4.26	0.9				
	ARK	AA	22	3	4	0	9	9	48²	41	4	1.3	6.5	35	37%	.270	0.99	2.77	4.08	0.5				
Yohan Ramirez	BCA	A+	24	1	2	0	10	7	43²	22	0	4.5	14.2	69	55%	.262	1.01	2.89	2.73	1.2				
	CCH	AA	24	3	5	1	17	8	62¹	42	5	7.5	12.9	89	45%	.282	1.51	4.76	4.75	0.0				
Connor Sadzeck	SEA	MLB	27	0	1	1	20	0	23²	18	3	5.7	10.3	27	46%	.250	1.39	2.66	4.36	0.3	99.1	46.7	11.1	49.6
Ricardo Sánchez	ARK	AA	22	8	12	0	27	27	146	157	10	2.3	8.3	135	51%	.348	1.34	4.44	5.66	-1.2				
Phillips Valdez	NAS	AAA	27	1	7	1	26	14	78²	87	10	4.1	7.4	65	53%	.314	1.56	4.92	4.70	1.4				
	TEX	MLB	27	0	0	0	11	0	16	17	3	5.1	10.1	18	54%	.326	1.62	3.94	4.54	0.1	93.9	58.4	9.2	50.2
Arodys Vizcaíno	ATL	MLB	28	1	0	1	4	0	4	3	1	6.8	13.5	6	25%	.286	1.50	2.25	5.04	0.0	97.4	52.9	13.2	40.9
Brandon Williamson	EVE	A-	21	0	0	0	10	9	15¹	9	0	2.9	14.7	25	55%	.310	0.91	2.35	2.25	0.5				

Elvis Alvarado is a converted outfielder with premium velocity, the kind of quintessential low-level lottery ticket you tack onto a last-minute July deal, which is exactly what Seattle did when they acquired him from Washington minutes before the deadline. ⊕ A frequent perplexer in everyone's favorite trivia game, "Country Music Star or Relief Pitcher?" **Chasen Bradford** spent much of the season on the injured list before succumbing to Tommy John Surgery, which will keep him out of action until late 2020. More time to work on those songs. ⊕ After a long college season as the ace for Arkansas, **Isaiah Campbell** didn't throw a professional pitch after signing. If he climbs the ladder successfully, he could become the first Portuguese-born major leaguer since Frank Thompson debuted for the Brooklyn Atlantics. ⊕ In a bullpen chock full of anonymous 20-something-year-old right-handers named Matt, **Matt Carasiti** was the most anonymous of them all. Having spent 2018 in Japan, he returned to affiliated ball briefly with the Cubs before Seattle scooped him up in June. ⊕ The Mariners inked **Kristian Cardozo**, a Venezuelan right-hander, for a reported $595,000 bonus in July. He's shown the ability to hit the low 90s with his fastball and also shows a breaking ball and a changeup. ⊕ 2017 second-rounder **Sam Carlson** will look to improve upon his current career average of one inning pitched per season. Reports out of Peoria indicate that Carlson's fastball velocity has returned, and he should finally see the jump to A-ball this year. ⊕ There are only two A's in the name **Nabil Crismatt**, which may explain why he continues to dominate Double-A (2.82 ERA in 195 career Double-A innings) and get absolutely rocked in Triple-A (8.96 ERA in 85.1 career Triple-A innings). ⊕ No relief pitcher with at least 50 innings across the minors posted a higher strikeout rate than **Sam Delaplane**, who politely sat down 45.8 percent of the batters he faced across two levels; not bad for a 23rd-round senior sign. ⊕ It was a confounding year for reliever **Matt Festa**, who was good enough to make the Opening Day roster but apparently not valued enough to warrant a September call-up. He bounced between Tacoma and Seattle seven (!) times in the interim. ⊕ A big element of success is being in the right place at the right time. Meanwhile, **Aaron Fletcher** is a fastball/slider lefty in a league that just eliminated the LOOGY. The fastball has some bite to it, which is his inside straight draw for making it to the major leagues. ⊕ **Joey Gerber**'s streak of having never started a game in college or the pros will surely be broken whenever he is first asked to be an opener, a role that could fit his arsenal quite nicely. ⊕ It was another stellar statistical season for side-arming slinger **Wyatt Mills**. The Gonzaga product and Spokane native should spend much of 2020 back in the Evergreen State, whether it be in Tacoma or Seattle. ⊕ We're still waiting to find out what was so special about left-hander **Anthony Misiewicz** that the Mariners re-acquired him from the Rays just 16 months after trading him there in the first place. ⊕ It took less than a year for **Andrew Moore** to boomerang back to the organization that drafted him after being traded to Tampa Bay in 2018. He'll resume his lifelong quest to prove that crafty right-handers can be major leaguers too. ⊕ Penn Badgley is the guy in *Gossip Girl* and *Easy A*, Penn Jillette is the loud part of *Penn & Teller* and **Penn Murfee** is a 25-year-old who raced to Triple-A last year. The word on Murfee is that deception is part of the low-slot hurler's game and his breaking ball is an easy above-average offering, but turning a 33rd-rounder into a major leaguer? That's magic. ⊕ With peripherals that outpace his pure stuff, **Ljay Newsome** appears to have taken the organizational motto "Control the Zone" to heart. The right-hander posted a microscopic, MiLB-best 2.7 walk rate in 155 innings while striking out more than a batter per inning for the first time in his career. ⊕ A big dude with a big fastball. There's a lot to dream about, but an inconsistent delivery and below-average off-speed stuff have kept **Yohan Ramirez** from reaching his full potential. ⊕ Built like a small-ball power forward, the gigantic **Connor Sadzeck** is still chucking high-90s cheese with a vicious slider, but his continued inability to stay in the strike zone or on the field probably made it easier for Texas to ship him to the division rival M's. He got his second Tommy John surgery in October. ⊕ Once a prized teenage left-hander with mid-rotation upside, **Ricardo Sánchez** still has big league promise—he's just lost some luster. ⊕ **Phillips Valdez** followed in the footsteps of Austin Bibens-Dirkx and Brandon Mann to make his big-league debut with the Rangers after many years in the minors. He was good, but apparently not quite good enough to keep on the 40-man roster; the Mariners got him on a waiver claim not long after the end of the season. ⓧ **Arodys Vizcaíno**'s season was already over due to shoulder surgery when he was acquired by Seattle for salary purposes, so it's quite possible his tenure with the Mariners never even featured a single trip to T-Mobile Park. He'll either eventually return fully equipped with his tantalizing stuff, or he'll become the next electric arm to fall victim to its own nastiness, a sparkling blip in the long history of short-lived dynamite relievers. ⓧ "Welcome to the Big Leagues" could be a headline you see one day about 2019 second-round pick **Brandon Williamson**, a hard-throwing left-hander who grew up in the small rural town of Welcome, Minnesota.

ST. LOUIS CARDINALS

Essay by Manny Randhawa

Player comments by Ben Clemens and BP staff

We know better than to ever count out the Cardinals. But still, St. Louis' rise back to the top of the National League Central in 2019 over the Brewers and Cubs was mildly surprising given Chicago or Milwaukee had won the division in each of the previous three years. It was even more surprising considering that first baseman Paul Goldschmidt and third baseman Matt Carpenter—two of the Cardinals' best and most important hitters—had down seasons.

In his first season with the Cards, Goldschmidt got off to a very slow start. He eventually rebounded, but ended up posting the lowest full-season OPS of his career (.821). Carpenter, on the other hand, experienced an abrupt decline; just a year after setting career-highs in homers (36) and OPS (.897), he hit .226/.334/.392 and spent most of October on the bench.

Goldschmidt is about to enter his age-32 season, while Carpenter is going on his age-34 campaign. Given they didn't perform up to their normal standards in 2019 and St. Louis ended up in the National League Championship Series, it's fair to ask—are these two still instrumental in the Cardinals' success, or can the team win without significant contributions from them? And, on top of that: is there any reason to believe that rebound seasons could be in order?

⚾   ⚾   ⚾

The answer to the first pay may lie in how the Cardinals captured the division crown last year and how different things were from '18. That's because the two key areas in which the Cardinals significantly improved, somewhat mitigating the lineup's mediocre offensive performance, were the defense and the bullpen.

Let's start with the defensive improvement, because it actually has something to do with Goldschmidt. Adding the three-time Gold Glove first baseman in place of José Martínez, who made 84 starts at first in '18, drastically improved St. Louis' glovework at the cold corner. Consider that on a team level, the Cardinals converted 76.8 percent of grounders into outs in 2018—good for 11th in the majors. Last season, that percentage improved to 78.8 percent—or the second-highest mark in the majors.

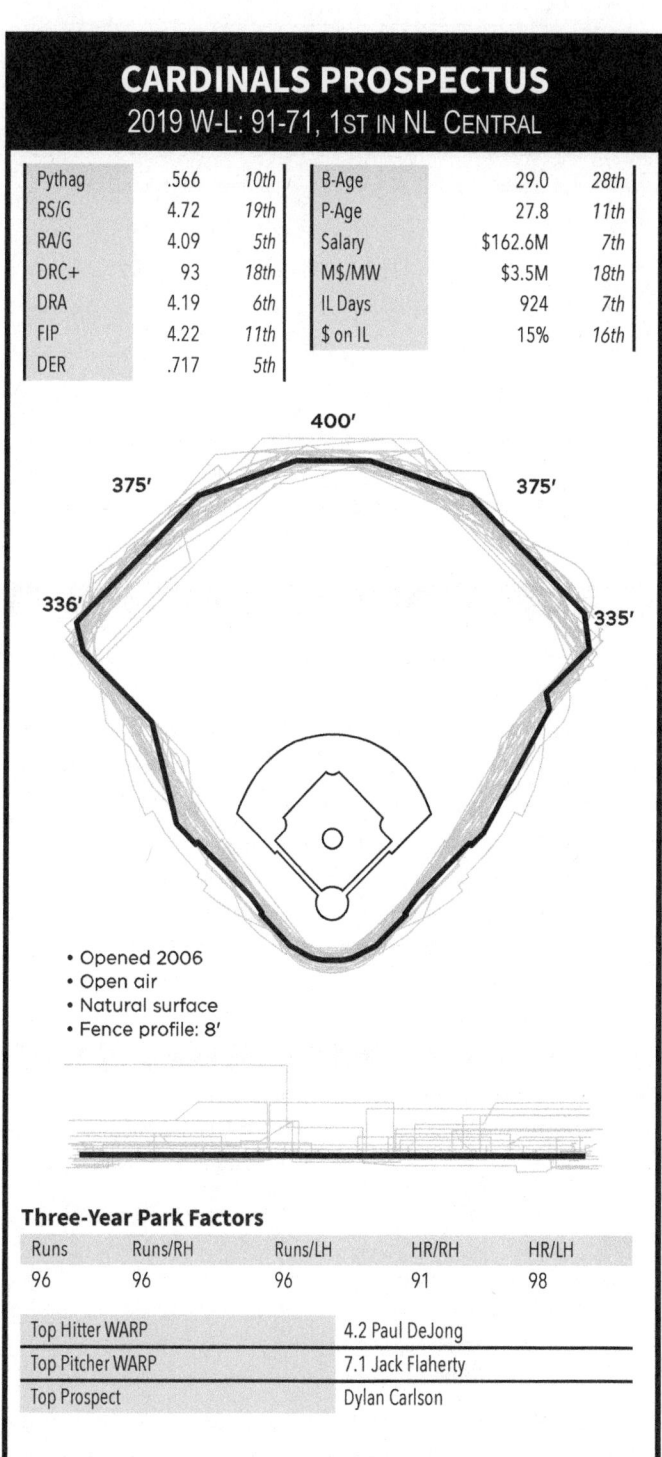

CARDINALS PROSPECTUS
2019 W-L: 91-71, 1ST IN NL CENTRAL

Pythag	.566	10th	B-Age	29.0	28th
RS/G	4.72	19th	P-Age	27.8	11th
RA/G	4.09	5th	Salary	$162.6M	7th
DRC+	93	18th	M$/MW	$3.5M	18th
DRA	4.19	6th	IL Days	924	7th
FIP	4.22	11th	$ on IL	15%	16th
DER	.717	5th			

400'

375'   375'

336'

335'

- Opened 2006
- Open air
- Natural surface
- Fence profile: 8'

Three-Year Park Factors

Runs	Runs/RH	Runs/LH	HR/RH	HR/LH
96	96	96	91	98

Top Hitter WARP	4.2 Paul DeJong
Top Pitcher WARP	7.1 Jack Flaherty
Top Prospect	Dylan Carlson

2019 Hit List Ranking

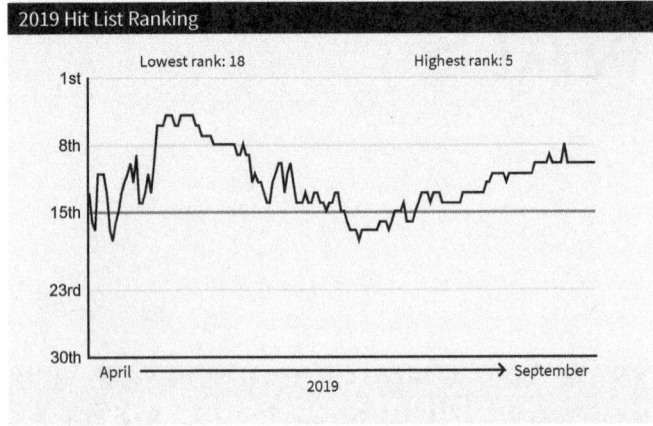

Lowest rank: 18   Highest rank: 5

April ——————→ September

2019

Committed Payroll (in millions)

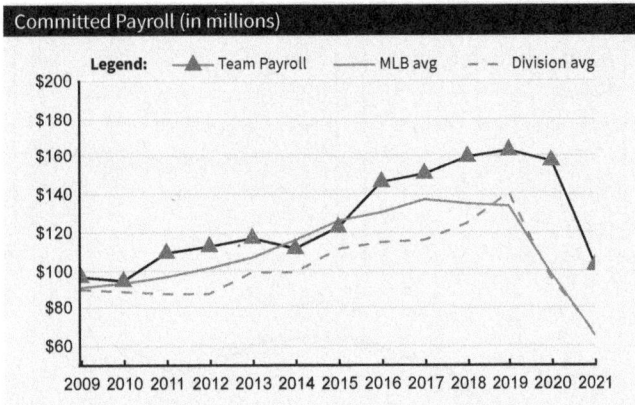

Legend: ▲ Team Payroll   — MLB avg   - - Division avg

2009 2010 2011 2012 2013 2014 2015 2016 2017 2018 2019 2020 2021

Farm System Ranking

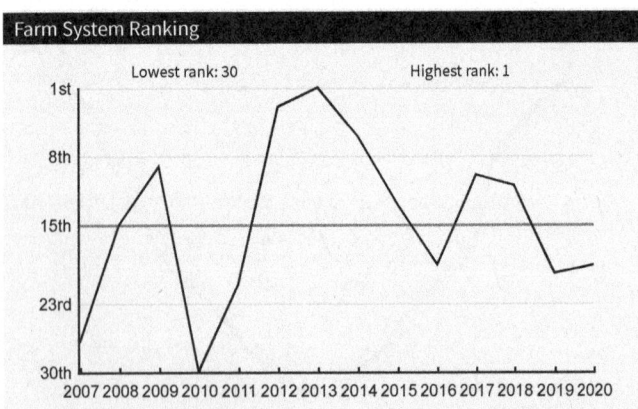

Lowest rank: 30   Highest rank: 1

2007 2008 2009 2010 2011 2012 2013 2014 2015 2016 2017 2018 2019 2020

Personnel

President of Baseball Operations
John Mozeliak

Vice President & General Manager
Mike Girsch

Assistant General Manager
Moises Rodriguez

Assistant General Manager & Director of Scouting
Randy Flores

Manager
Mike Shildt

BP Alumni
Zach Mortimer
Christopher Rodriguez
Mauricio Rubio

Goldschmidt undoubtedly played a role in that improvement, though he wasn't alone in that regard. Staying on the right side of the infield, better health and stronger production at the plate kept Kolten Wong at second base for 147 games, and it resulted in his first career Gold Glove Award. Meanwhile, the Cardinals received a boost from rookie Tommy Edman, who proved to be a defensive upgrade over Carpenter at the hot corner in his 55 appearances there. The difference between the two, per FRAA, was worth nearly 10 runs.

The Cardinals were better at turning balls hit in the air into outs, too, with the fleet-of-foot Harrison Bader playing in 48 more games in center field than he did in '18. Bader finished 10th in baseball (minimum 300 plate appearances) in FRAA, joining Wong (sixth) as the only pair of teammates to rank so high.

Defense certainly helps pitching, but so does…well, better pitching. The Cardinals' bullpen ranked second in the majors in DRA last season, a wide improvement over 2018, when they ranked 26th. That leap would have been impressive regardless, but it came during a season in which St. Louis received just 28 innings from closer Jordan Hicks before he was lost to injury.

The Cardinals received a huge lift foremost from Giovanny Gallegos, who was acquired from the Yankees in summer 2018 as part of the Luke Voit trade. He appeared more frequently in 2019, and for good reason: he posted a 2.31 ERA and struck out 33 percent of the batters he faced in 74 innings. Gallegos' unique mix of a slightly-above-average four-seam fastball with rise and a pitch he calls a slider but doesn't really act like one—it actually moves horizontally—can be tough for a hitter to distinguish. Hence the high K rate and excellent results when the ball was put in play against him—opposing batters hit .170.

The Cards made Carlos Martinez their closer after Hicks got hurt, and it worked—he finished with a 3.17 ERA over 48 relief appearances overall. Martinez will likely get a shot to return to the rotation in 2020, but between Gallegos and right-hander Ryan Helsley, who posted a 2.95 ERA over 24 appearances last season, and even Andrew Miller and John Brebbia, St. Louis has some late-inning options in throw out there ahead of Hicks' eventual return.

It would seem to bode well for the Cardinals that all the important actors in their run-prevention improvement—including the major one in the rotation we didn't address, in Jack Flaherty—will be in place for the 2020 season as well.

⚾   ⚾   ⚾

And then there are the two veteran sluggers we opened with, Goldschmidt and Carpenter. We've seen why the Cardinals were able to win despite subpar years from these two, but is there hope for a bounceback for either and/or both going into the 2020 season?

Let's start with a look at Goldschmidt. On July 1st of last season, he was hitting .246/.336/.405. He got red-hot in July, slugging 11 homers while slashing .308/.360/.725. He tapered off the rest of the way, posting a .259/.354/.472 line with nine homers over the final two months. But if you look at his quality of contact year-over-year from 2018-19, you'll find that while his surface-level stats were down significantly, his batted-ball profile wasn't far off from where it was when he turned in a more Goldy-like .922 OPS.

Goldschmidt's hard-hit rate, according to Statcast (percentage of batted balls with an exit velocity 95 mph or greater), was nearly identical to what it was in 2018—it was 43.8 percent then, and 42.4 percent last year. Likewise, while he barreled-up the baseball at a lower rate in '19, the discrepancy isn't super large—13.6 percent of batted balls to 11.3 percent.

Goldschmidt's DRC+ declined from 136 to 119, but while that gap certainly looks concerning, the differential in his Statcast expected weighted on-base average (based on launch angle and exit velocity of batted balls) wasn't as wretched (.384 to .361). And, while his .476 slugging percentage last year was the lowest for any full season of his career, his expected slugging percentage was 37 points higher.

Goldschmidt's average exit velocity was 90.1 mph in 2019, down 0.7 mph from '18. His average launch angle was nearly identical, at 15.3 degrees following a season in which it was 15.7. Now, that's all well and good when Goldschmidt makes contact—perhaps there is reason for optimism that 2019 was an aberration and not the start of a broader decline. But what about when he doesn't? His K rate was actually a smidge lower than in '18, down from 25.1 percent to 24.3 percent. He did walk a bit less, however, with his walk rate declining from 13.8 percent to 11.4 percent.

The quality of contact and plate-discipline figures indicate Goldschmidt lost his way early in his first season with a new club, but remains the hitter he had been in prior years—one who is regularly in the NL Most Valuable Player conversation (though he has yet to win). The Cardinals sure hope those indicators prove correct—after all, they inked Goldschmidt to a long-term extension that will run through the 2024 season before he'd even played a game with them.

⚾ ⚾ ⚾

So what about Carpenter, who had a career year at the plate in '18?

While Goldschmidt's quality of contact and strikeout rate suggest he did not fall off in his performance as much as his 101-point loss in OPS would indicate, the opposite appears to be true for Carpenter.

Carpenter's hard-hit rate was down drastically, from 44.7 percent to 31.1 percent, ranking 185th out of the 223 hitters who had put at least 250 balls in play last season. (He ranked 32nd out of 228 hitters in that category in 2018.) His barrel rate was sliced nearly in half, down from 13.7 percent to 7.8 percent. His groundball rate went from 28.3 percent to 34.5 percent. The strikeout rate went up from 23.3 percent to 26.1 percent, and the walk rate was down for the usually patient and discerning Carpenter, from 15.1 percent to 12.8 percent.

This is all bad. But wait, there's more.

As strong of a season as Carpenter had in 2018, there are some trends that suggest it was more likely an outlier than an indication of an output level he'll return to and sustain. Take, for example, his hard-hit rate in '17, before the big season at the plate—it was 37 percent, much more in line with what it was in '19 than the 44.7 percent from '18. And the barrel rate illustrates this point more vividly—it was 8.2 percent in '17, nearly the same as the 7.8 percent barrel rate in '19, with his big season sandwiched in the middle.

Furthermore, Carpenter's strikeout rate has been increasing progressively over the last three seasons, even including his career year in '18. It's climbed six percentage points. Predictably, his chase rate has also been rising, going from 14.3 percent in '17, to 18.4 percent in '18, to 20.7 percent last year. And before it jumped to 135 in '18, Carpenter's DRC+ was progressively declining, from 133 in 2015, to 126 in' 16, to 119 in '17. It was 96 last year. That dropped Carpenter from 14th in baseball among qualifiers in '18 to out of the top 100.

So, is this it for Carpenter? Have we seen his best baseball? At minimum, those trends aren't encouraging.

⚾ ⚾ ⚾

Even if things don't change with Carpenter and Goldschmidt, what the Cardinals have going for them is history; they've shown they can weather a subpar season from both and still win the division—that their balanced roster can overcome an absent or underperforming star.

In that sense, last season was the ultimate throwback season for the Cardinals, who we should once again be careful about counting out. ▪

—Manny Randhawa is a writer and Statcast researcher for MLB.com.

HITTERS

Randy Arozarena OF Born: 02/28/95 Age: 25 Bats: R Throws: R Height: 5'11" Weight: 170 Origin: International Free Agent, 2016

YEAR	TEAM	LVL	AGE	PA	R	2B	3B	HR	RBI	BB	K	SB	CS	AVG/OBP/SLG	DRC+	VORP	BABIP	BRR	FRAA	WARP
2017	PMB	A+	22	295	38	22	3	8	40	13	53	10	4	.275/.333/.472	144	24.3	.313	-2.5	LF(47): 4.3, CF(13): -0.5	2.2
2017	SFD	AA	22	195	34	10	1	3	9	27	34	8	3	.252/.366/.380	114	9.0	.299	2.7	LF(40): 0.1, CF(4): -0.9	0.9
2018	SFD	AA	23	102	22	5	0	7	21	6	25	9	3	.396/.455/.681	200	15.4	.492	1.0	RF(12): 1.6, CF(6): -0.4	1.5
2018	MEM	AAA	23	311	42	16	0	5	28	28	59	17	5	.232/.328/.348	83	9.3	.278	0.8	LF(49): -2.7, RF(18): 0.2	-0.1
2019	SFD	AA	24	116	14	7	2	3	15	13	23	8	5	.309/.422/.515	160	10.9	.380	-0.5	CF(13): 0.9, LF(5): 0.0	0.9
2019	MEM	AAA	24	283	51	18	2	12	38	24	48	9	7	.358/.435/.593	154	34.3	.404	-1.2	CF(25): -3.4, RF(20): 4.6	2.7
2019	SLN	MLB	24	23	4	1	0	1	2	2	4	2	1	.300/.391/.500	84	0.3	.333	-1.7	RF(6): -0.1, CF(5): 0.5	-0.1
2020	SLN	MLB	25	112	13	6	0	4	13	9	26	4	1	.258/.339/.431	110	4.9	.314	0.0	LF 0, CF 0	0.4

Comparables: Jack Daniels, Jordan Luplow, Joe Lefebvre

At some point, performance matters. After scuffling in Triple-A in 2018, the Cardinals sent Arozarena back to Double-A to start 2019, where he was simply too good for the competition. He returned to Memphis, and, again, posted preposterous marks—even in a high-offense environment. Arozarena's lack of power has always held back his otherwise polished offensive game, yet as his standout season shows, the socialization of home runs can help players with a tweener profile emerge from the pack. Though he doesn't have the pedigree or major-league reps of other young Cardinals outfielders, it's hard to ignore his offensive track record and his defensive skills. In other words, there may be three a's in Arozarena, but we think he's a big-league player.

Harrison Bader CF Born: 06/03/94 Age: 26 Bats: R Throws: R Height: 6'0" Weight: 195 Origin: Round 3, 2015 Draft (#100 overall)

YEAR	TEAM	LVL	AGE	PA	R	2B	3B	HR	RBI	BB	K	SB	CS	AVG/OBP/SLG	DRC+	VORP	BABIP	BRR	FRAA	WARP
2017	MEM	AAA	23	479	74	18	1	20	55	34	118	15	9	.283/.347/.469	117	41.2	.345	5.3	CF(111): 13.7, RF(3): 0.3	4.5
2017	SLN	MLB	23	92	10	3	0	3	10	5	24	2	1	.235/.283/.376	82	1.2	.288	0.3	CF(20): 2.0, LF(7): -0.1	0.3
2018	SLN	MLB	24	427	61	20	2	12	37	31	125	15	3	.264/.334/.422	90	25.1	.358	2.8	CF(74): 9.1, RF(38): 1.6	2.2
2019	MEM	AAA	25	75	23	3	0	7	15	8	16	3	0	.317/.427/.698	158	14.8	.325	1.4	CF(15): 1.7	1.0
2019	SLN	MLB	25	406	54	14	3	12	39	46	117	11	3	.205/.314/.366	84	6.6	.268	4.5	CF(122): 14.4	2.5
2020	SLN	MLB	26	427	51	17	2	17	55	36	125	11	5	.234/.317/.423	99	17.2	.301	1.7	CF 12	3.0

Comparables: Kirk Nieuwenhuis, Derek Fisher, Jackie Bradley Jr.

Outfield defense is hard to judge. Watching on TV, you never see the positioning or the jump, only the end of the play. Was that dive necessary, or did it make up for a bad jump? Was that ball uncatchable, or did the fielder take a bad route? That's all unknowable. And yet, watch Bader play outfield, and it's clear that he's superb. He takes protractor-straight routes, gets up to full speed quickly, and finishes plays with aplomb. He has a cannon arm, too, in case you judge outfielders by their assists. And yet, despite being maybe the best defensive outfielder in baseball, Bader's bat required a minor-league stint in 2019. He doesn't need to hit to be a valuable contributor, but the Cardinals are right to spend time working on his offense. If he can just flirt with a league-average line, he'd be one of the most valuable outfielders in the game.

Luken Baker 1B Born: 03/10/97 Age: 23 Bats: R Throws: R Height: 6'4" Weight: 265 Origin: Round 2C, 2018 Draft (#75 overall)

YEAR	TEAM	LVL	AGE	PA	R	2B	3B	HR	RBI	BB	K	SB	CS	AVG/OBP/SLG	DRC+	VORP	BABIP	BRR	FRAA	WARP
2018	CRD	RK	21	28	10	2	0	1	7	3	4	0	0	.500/.536/.708	212	3.9	.550	-0.7	1B(5): 0.1	0.2
2018	PEO	A	21	156	16	9	0	3	15	16	31	0	0	.288/.359/.417	148	2.7	.349	-1.4	1B(20): 0.3	0.8
2019	PMB	A+	22	496	47	32	1	10	53	52	112	1	1	.244/.327/.390	118	4.7	.304	-6.1	1B(96): -3.6	0.3
2020	SLN	MLB	23	251	25	13	0	8	29	17	71	1	0	.230/.286/.393	78	0.4	.296	-0.5	1B -1	-0.1

Comparables: Mark Trumbo, Nate Lowe, Matt Thaiss

When people make snide comments about baseball not requiring athleticism, they're thinking of players who look like Baker. He's listed at 6-foot-4 and 265 pounds, and plays just like it. He has light-tower power, a lot of swing-and-miss, and first-base-only defensive chops. And you know what? Watching someone of Baker's size play baseball is a *delight*. He doesn't quite look like Aaron Judge out there, but he still gives off the vibe an adult playing against children. Baker will have to keep hitting to make it to the majors. That means passing the Double-A test in 2020.

★ ★ ★ *2020 Top 101 Prospect* **#18** ★ ★ ★

Dylan Carlson OF Born: 10/23/98 Age: 21 Bats: B Throws: L Height: 6'3" Weight: 205 Origin: Round 1, 2016 Draft (#33 overall)

YEAR	TEAM	LVL	AGE	PA	R	2B	3B	HR	RBI	BB	K	SB	CS	AVG/OBP/SLG	DRC+	VORP	BABIP	BRR	FRAA	WARP
2017	PEO	A	18	451	63	18	1	7	42	52	116	6	6	.240/.342/.347	98	14.6	.323	2.6	RF(79): 0.8, CF(24): 0.1	1.4
2018	PEO	A	19	57	5	3	0	2	9	10	10	2	0	.234/.368/.426	137	1.4	.257	-0.7	RF(10): 2.3, CF(4): -0.3	0.5
2018	PMB	A+	19	441	63	19	3	9	53	52	78	6	3	.247/.345/.386	115	18.2	.286	1.7	RF(50): 4.7, LF(37): -0.1	2.1
2019	SFD	AA	20	483	81	24	6	21	59	52	98	18	7	.281/.364/.518	151	40.3	.315	3.1	CF(86): -10.2, RF(9): -0.3	2.7
2019	MEM	AAA	20	79	14	4	2	5	9	6	18	2	1	.361/.418/.681	142	10.9	.429	0.1	CF(8): -0.5, LF(7): 0.0	0.6
2020	SLN	MLB	21	140	16	6	1	5	18	12	38	0	0	.238/.312/.427	96	2.5	.297	0.0	LF 0, RF -1	0.2

Comparables: Nomar Mazara, Victor Robles, Yorman Rodriguez

Carslon feels like he's been in the Cardinals system for a decade. He hasn't—he just turned 21. As a young draft pick, he's been afforded the opportunity to partake in four professional seasons. Progress isn't always linear, but it has been here since each season has surpassed its predecessor. Last year, Carlson overwhelmed the Texas League before putting up even better numbers in a Triple-A cameo. Combine his high level of production against older competition with his plus physical skills—easy switch-hitting power and enough athleticism that he's stuck in center field much longer than scouts expected—and it stands to reason that he'll do more than knock on the big-league door in 2020, and that he might spend a decade on the Cards' 26-man roster.

Matt Carpenter 3B   Born: 11/26/85   Age: 34   Bats: L   Throws: R   Height: 6'3"   Weight: 205   Origin: Round 13, 2009 Draft (#399 overall)

YEAR	TEAM	LVL	AGE	PA	R	2B	3B	HR	RBI	BB	K	SB	CS	AVG/OBP/SLG	DRC+	VORP	BABIP	BRR	FRAA	WARP
2017	SLN	MLB	31	622	91	31	2	23	69	109	125	2	1	.241/.384/.451	119	34.8	.274	-2.4	1B(120): 2.1, 3B(16): 0.9	2.7
2018	SLN	MLB	32	677	111	42	0	36	81	102	158	4	1	.257/.374/.523	135	55.6	.291	-1.5	1B(95): -3.6, 3B(76): 4.8	4.6
2019	SLN	MLB	33	492	59	20	2	15	46	63	129	6	1	.226/.334/.392	96	15.9	.285	-1.9	3B(107): -6.5, 1B(4): -0.2	0.7
2020	SLN	MLB	34	469	56	21	2	17	58	65	122	3	1	.227/.342/.417	104	12.4	.283	-1.6	3B 0, 1B 0	1.3

Comparables: Brian Dozier, Dan Uggla, Kelly Johnson

Carpenter has continually reinvented himself; he came up as a high-contact, slap-hitting utility infielder and turned himself into an ultra-patient slugging first baseman. Last year's transformation (if you can call it that) was something new—he became a below-average hitter. It was a Frankenstein's monster of a season in reverse, or what would happen if an artist put out a *Worst Of...* record. The strikeout numbers from his walks-and-dingers years paired up with the walks and contact quality from his no-strikeout, no-power years. The only thing that didn't decline was Carpenter's salsa-making prowess, which is apparently still 80-grade. Until baseball starts awarding runs for perfectly-balanced mixes of flavor and spice, though, his contributions in the kitchen can't offset his on-field decline. Hopefully Carpenter has a jar of hard contact stored in a cabinet somewhere, because home runs are what will keep him in tomato money heading forward, even if that wasn't the case in 2019.

Paul DeJong SS   Born: 08/02/93   Age: 26   Bats: R   Throws: R   Height: 6'0"   Weight: 200   Origin: Round 4, 2015 Draft (#131 overall)

YEAR	TEAM	LVL	AGE	PA	R	2B	3B	HR	RBI	BB	K	SB	CS	AVG/OBP/SLG	DRC+	VORP	BABIP	BRR	FRAA	WARP
2017	MEM	AAA	23	190	27	9	0	13	34	9	46	0	2	.299/.339/.571	126	18.2	.336	-1.0	SS(39): -3.8, 2B(5): 0.4	1.0
2017	SLN	MLB	23	443	55	26	1	25	65	21	124	1	0	.285/.325/.532	115	33.3	.349	-3.9	SS(86): -0.3, 2B(20): -0.7	2.3
2018	SLN	MLB	24	490	68	25	1	19	68	36	123	1	1	.241/.313/.433	101	35.2	.288	3.1	SS(114): 0.3	2.7
2019	SLN	MLB	25	664	97	31	1	30	78	62	149	9	5	.233/.318/.444	104	35.4	.259	0.5	SS(157): 7.1	4.2
2020	SLN	MLB	26	595	69	26	1	26	80	46	139	4	2	.230/.303/.430	95	19.0	.262	0.0	SS 2	2.1

Comparables: Trevor Story, Matt Joyce, Brad Miller

Few players embody the trends of modern baseball more than DeJong. He has the kind of frame that traditionally screams infield corner, but advances in defensive positioning turned him into an above-average shortstop. His contact problems and low batting average would have left him shunned in prior eras, but his power and improving batting eye are enough to make him an above-average offensive player despite middling back-of-the-baseball-card stats. And he even signed that most modern of contracts—the pre-extension guaranteeing he'll be drastically underpaid for most of his career. People are often said to be the product of their environments. DeJong is the product of his era. He's one of the best players on the Cardinals, and he might never have even seen the majors if he'd played 20 years ago. Score one for modern player evaluation and development.

Tommy Edman INF   Born: 05/09/95   Age: 25   Bats: B   Throws: R   Height: 5'10"   Weight: 180   Origin: Round 6, 2016 Draft (#196 overall)

YEAR	TEAM	LVL	AGE	PA	R	2B	3B	HR	RBI	BB	K	SB	CS	AVG/OBP/SLG	DRC+	VORP	BABIP	BRR	FRAA	WARP
2017	PEO	A	22	174	24	8	5	2	18	15	19	8	2	.284/.347/.439	126	16.0	.309	2.1	SS(38): -0.6	1.4
2017	PMB	A+	22	82	7	2	1	1	11	7	18	0	1	.257/.338/.357	106	5.3	.327	-0.2	SS(15): -0.6, 2B(3): 0.1	0.3
2017	SFD	AA	22	239	20	12	2	2	26	16	34	5	2	.247/.298/.347	77	4.3	.281	0.7	SS(61): 1.0	0.7
2018	SFD	AA	23	498	71	23	3	6	36	35	76	27	5	.299/.350/.403	114	29.6	.345	3.4	SS(65): -1.4, 3B(22): 0.7	3.0
2018	MEM	AAA	23	76	13	0	1	1	5	8	11	3	0	.318/.382/.394	119	7.8	.357	1.0	2B(14): 1.4, SS(3): -0.1	0.7
2019	MEM	AAA	24	218	39	12	4	7	29	15	33	9	0	.305/.356/.513	102	19.1	.333	3.7	2B(25): 0.0, SS(10): -1.5	1.1
2019	SLN	MLB	24	349	59	17	7	11	36	16	61	15	1	.304/.350/.500	110	16.8	.346	4.7	3B(55): 0.3, 2B(29): 0.7	2.3
2020	SLN	MLB	25	595	59	25	7	14	64	33	109	13	4	.257/.306/.401	87	9.1	.297	3.2	3B 1, LF 0	1.2

Comparables: Greg Litton, Johan Camargo, Ed Brinkman

Somewhere in the eldritch past, Cardinals fan Frederick Bird made a terrible bargain. He would forever be forced to inhabit the body of a giant plush bird, unable to talk but forced to interact with children every day. In exchange, Lucifer promised a little help with the farm system. We may never know whether Fredbird is happy with his infernal deal, but Edman is surely pleased to be the most recent beneficiary of the Devil Magic. How else could a diminutive middle infielder who reached Triple-A only in August 2018 become one of the lineup's most valuable hitters in 2019? He'll probably be an under-appreciated cog in the next five good Cardinals teams before passing the baton to someone vaguely like him. Thanks to Fredbird, that's just how it works at this point.

Trejyn Fletcher OF   Born: 04/30/01   Age: 19   Bats: R   Throws: R   Height: 6'2"   Weight: 200   Origin: Round 2, 2019 Draft (#58 overall)

YEAR	TEAM	LVL	AGE	PA	R	2B	3B	HR	RBI	BB	K	SB	CS	AVG/OBP/SLG	DRC+	VORP	BABIP	BRR	FRAA	WARP
2019	CRD	RK	18	42	6	3	0	2	8	4	17	0	0	.297/.357/.541	92	2.1	.474	0.0	CF(7): 2.2	0.3
2019	JCY	RK+	18	133	9	4	1	2	18	7	59	7	1	.228/.271/.325	63	-3.3	.406	-0.2		-0.1
2020	SLN	MLB	19	251	21	11	1	4	22	19	128	2	1	.201/.266/.310	55	-6.8	.425	0.0	CF 1	-0.6

Comparables: Colby Rasmus, Addison Russell, Bo Bichette

Maine isn't a baseball hotbed, particularly at the prep level—only three Maine high schoolers have ever been taken in the first round in draft history. When Fletcher transferred to Portland and reclassified to the 2019 draft, scouts had to scramble to see him play. That led to him slipping to the second round, which could prove to be a steal on the Cardinals' part. He's a 6-foot-2 livewire on the field, with speed and strength to burn. His performance? Hey, we needn't discuss that more at this point than to acknowledge the learning curve that comes with transitioning from facing Maine pitching to professionals. It wasn't pretty, in other words, but Fletcher has the tools to make up for it over the coming years.

Dexter Fowler RF
Born: 03/22/86   Age: 34   Bats: B   Throws: R   Height: 6'5"   Weight: 195   Origin: Round 14, 2004 Draft (#410 overall)

YEAR	TEAM	LVL	AGE	PA	R	2B	3B	HR	RBI	BB	K	SB	CS	AVG/OBP/SLG	DRC+	VORP	BABIP	BRR	FRAA	WARP
2017	SLN	MLB	31	491	68	22	9	18	64	63	101	7	3	.264/.363/.488	118	37.8	.305	1.4	CF(109): -10.1	2.0
2018	SLN	MLB	32	334	40	10	0	8	31	38	75	5	2	.180/.278/.298	77	-1.4	.210	2.0	RF(75): -4.3	-0.4
2019	SLN	MLB	33	574	69	24	1	19	67	74	142	8	5	.238/.346/.409	100	16.4	.294	-0.5	RF(118): -0.3, CF(58): -3.4	1.2
2020	SLN	MLB	34	532	61	21	3	16	61	69	136	11	4	.232/.341/.398	99	14.5	.296	1.0	RF 0, CF -2	1.2

Comparables: Curtis Granderson, Peter Bourjos, B.J. Upton

After a down 2018 in which pretty much everything went wrong, perhaps no player in baseball was more in need of a bounceback than Fowler. He won't consider 2019 an unqualified success, but the results were encouraging: nearly two wins of improvement, an extended stay at the leadoff spot in the Cardinals lineup, much-improved defense, and the second-most plate appearances of his career. He's not likely to get better from here—34-year-old outfielders are hardly a good bet to improve in the modern game—but he's surely thrilled to have gone from pariah to useful contributor to a playoff team. The Cardinals have young outfielders coming, but Fowler doesn't look like he's ready to surrender his spot just yet.

Paul Goldschmidt 1B
Born: 09/10/87   Age: 32   Bats: R   Throws: R   Height: 6'3"   Weight: 225   Origin: Round 8, 2009 Draft (#246 overall)

YEAR	TEAM	LVL	AGE	PA	R	2B	3B	HR	RBI	BB	K	SB	CS	AVG/OBP/SLG	DRC+	VORP	BABIP	BRR	FRAA	WARP
2017	ARI	MLB	29	665	117	34	3	36	120	94	147	18	5	.297/.404/.563	140	57.2	.343	3.7	1B(151): 5.7	5.1
2018	ARI	MLB	30	690	95	35	5	33	83	90	173	7	4	.290/.389/.533	136	55.4	.359	-1.3	1B(155): 1.7	4.1
2019	SLN	MLB	31	682	97	25	1	34	97	78	166	3	1	.260/.346/.476	119	27.9	.303	-0.8	1B(159): -7.3	1.9
2020	SLN	MLB	32	630	85	27	2	29	89	82	160	14	4	.264/.364/.478	126	34.0	.323	0.4	1B 1	3.6

Comparables: Pat Burrell, Travis Hafner, Jonny Gomes

If you're looking for a silver lining in Goldschmidt's down 2019, there are plenty of places you could start. You could look at his plate-discipline numbers and say everything looks normal. You could look at his second-half numbers and say that after the break, Goldschmidt was almost back to his old self. You could look at his defensive prowess, which the team raves about, as a hard-to-quantify boost to St. Louis's excellent defense. But the truth is, those are just silver linings. The stormcloud that was 2019 is scary. Maybe it was fluky, and maybe he'll be as good as ever in 2020, but aging curves aren't always smooth declines from excellence to mediocrity. Sometimes decline comes fast and never reverses. That's not the most likely outcome, but the fact that it's even a question now tells you how haywire things went in 2019.

──────────────── ★ ★ ★ *2020 Top 101 Prospect* **#23** ★ ★ ★ ────────────────

Nolan Gorman 3B
Born: 05/10/00   Age: 20   Bats: L   Throws: R   Height: 6'1"   Weight: 210   Origin: Round 1, 2018 Draft (#19 overall)

YEAR	TEAM	LVL	AGE	PA	R	2B	3B	HR	RBI	BB	K	SB	CS	AVG/OBP/SLG	DRC+	VORP	BABIP	BRR	FRAA	WARP
2018	JCY	RK	18	167	41	10	1	11	28	24	37	1	3	.350/.443/.664	191	25.2	.411	-0.7	3B(33): 7.6	2.7
2018	PEO	A	18	107	8	3	0	6	16	10	39	0	2	.202/.280/.426	76	2.3	.255	-0.5	3B(25): 3.9	0.5
2019	PEO	A	19	282	41	14	3	10	41	32	79	2	0	.241/.344/.448	129	16.9	.312	0.4	3B(51): 8.4	2.6
2019	PMB	A+	19	230	24	16	3	5	21	13	73	0	1	.256/.304/.428	107	6.7	.365	-2.1	3B(48): -5.9	0.0
2020	SLN	MLB	20	251	26	12	1	8	29	24	86	1	0	.222/.302/.393	84	2.7	.320	-0.4	3B 1	0.4

Comparables: Miguel Sanó, Austin Riley, Gary Sánchez

Gorman has established a pattern. In 2018, he was simply too good for rookie ball, so the team challenged him with a promotion to Low-A, where he saw his strikeouts spike but hit for enough power to make the whole package work. He started in Low-A last year and cut his strikeouts while walking more, showing the team enough that they tasked him with the Florida State League…where he, as the youngest regular, struggled with strikeouts but hit for enough power to be an above-average hitter. (Note to the universe: Get more creative writers, won't you?) If the trend holds, Gorman will begin the year in Double-A, dominate, then try to slug enough to atone for his strikeout sins. The upside here is something like a lesser Joey Gallo if Joey Gallo liked playing third base. We think the old-timers called it "Russell Branyan."

Ivan Herrera C
Born: 06/01/00   Age: 20   Bats: R   Throws: R   Height: 6'0"   Weight: 180   Origin: International Free Agent, 2016

YEAR	TEAM	LVL	AGE	PA	R	2B	3B	HR	RBI	BB	K	SB	CS	AVG/OBP/SLG	DRC+	VORP	BABIP	BRR	FRAA	WARP
2017	DCA	RK	17	201	21	15	0	1	27	18	36	2	2	.335/.425/.441	144	19.5	.415	-0.5	C(49): 0.7	1.9
2018	CRD	RK	18	130	23	6	4	1	25	11	20	1	1	.348/.423/.500	154	11.6	.409	-1.9	C(20): 0.6	1.0
2019	PEO	A	19	291	41	10	0	8	42	35	56	1	1	.286/.381/.423	138	21.7	.337	-0.1	C(64): -1.0	2.4
2019	PMB	A+	19	65	7	0	0	1	5	5	16	0	0	.276/.338/.328	117	2.5	.357	-1.1	C(17): -0.1	0.3
2020	SLN	MLB	20	251	26	11	1	6	27	19	66	1	0	.258/.325/.392	92	5.3	.339	-0.3	C -1	0.5

Comparables: Victor Robles, J.P. Crawford, César Puello

The Arizona Fall League is purportedly a showcase for some of the best prospects in baseball, which means it provides a higher level of competition than younger players are accustomed to facing. So, when you go there and absolutely rake as a 19-year-old—a 19-year-old catcher, no less—it's bound to create waves. Herrera did just that, completing a season in which he also held his head above water in the Florida State League—notoriously a pitcher's paradise. Teenage catchers are always a high-variance quantity, and Herrera is a ways away from being a big-league ready defensive backstop. But his bat is promising and if he can do enough to stick behind the dish then he has a bright future ahead.

Andrew Knizner   C   Born: 02/03/95   Age: 25   Bats: R   Throws: R   Height: 6'1"   Weight: 200   Origin: Round 7, 2016 Draft (#226 overall)

YEAR	TEAM	LVL	AGE	PA	R	2B	3B	HR	RBI	BB	K	SB	CS	AVG/OBP/SLG	DRC+	VORP	BABIP	BRR	FRAA	WARP
2017	PEO	A	22	191	18	10	1	8	29	9	22	1	1	.279/.325/.480	124	13.5	.282	0.5	C(26): -0.3, 1B(3): -0.1	1.1
2017	SFD	AA	22	202	27	13	0	4	22	14	27	0	1	.324/.371/.462	145	18.7	.355	0.5	C(49): -3.5	1.5
2018	SFD	AA	23	313	39	13	0	7	41	23	40	0	1	.313/.365/.434	133	21.9	.339	-1.4	C(74): -7.3	1.6
2018	MEM	AAA	23	61	3	5	0	0	4	4	8	0	0	.315/.383/.407	115	3.8	.370	-0.1	C(16): 1.8	0.6
2019	MEM	AAA	24	280	41	10	0	12	34	24	37	2	0	.276/.357/.463	112	21.8	.281	-0.8	C(61): -17.2	0.2
2019	SLN	MLB	24	58	7	2	0	2	7	4	14	2	0	.226/.293/.377	82	1.7	.270	0.5	C(16): -4.4, 1B(1): 0.0	-0.2
2020	SLN	MLB	25	182	19	7	0	6	21	12	34	0	0	.242/.306/.388	88	5.2	.274	-0.4	C -10	-0.5

Comparables: AJ Hinch, Randy Knorr, Hal King

YEAR	TEAM	P. COUNT	FRM RUNS	BLK RUNS	THRW RUNS	TOT RUNS
2017	SFD	6878	-3.0	0.0	0.2	-3.9
2018	MEM	2067	1.9	0.2	-0.1	1.9
2018	SFD	10157	-3.7	-1.9	-0.1	-6.0
2019	MEM	9240	-18.8	-0.1	1.7	-17.1
2019	SLN	2077	-4.0	-0.4	0.1	-4.0
2020	SLN	6472	-9.6	-0.6	0.8	-9.4

With Carson Kelly dealt elsewhere, Knizner became the Cardinals' top catching prospect and the next young backstop to have his arrival delayed by Yadier Molina's remarkable durability. Knizer's offensive profile is unusual for a catcher, as it's all bat control and middling power. That combination has served him well in the minor leagues so far, but it's fair to be skeptical about anyone, let alone a slow-footed catcher, being able to sustain an offensive game based around singles. Without a huge offensive ceiling, defense—specifically framing—may decide whether Knizner is a regular or backup. While he's been up-and-down on that front since converting from third base, he'll get some more time in Triple-A to learn the trade before Molina's contract expires.

José Martínez   RF   Born: 07/25/88   Age: 31   Bats: R   Throws: R   Height: 6'6"   Weight: 215   Origin: International Free Agent, 2006

YEAR	TEAM	LVL	AGE	PA	R	2B	3B	HR	RBI	BB	K	SB	CS	AVG/OBP/SLG	DRC+	VORP	BABIP	BRR	FRAA	WARP
2017	SLN	MLB	28	307	47	13	1	14	46	32	60	4	0	.309/.379/.518	128	25.5	.350	0.1	1B(33): 0.0, LF(24): -2.8	1.4
2018	SLN	MLB	29	590	64	30	0	17	83	49	104	0	3	.305/.364/.457	119	30.3	.351	-3.6	1B(84): -10.4, RF(46): 0.2	0.9
2019	SLN	MLB	30	373	45	13	2	10	42	35	82	3	0	.269/.340/.410	94	6.2	.328	0.7	RF(75): -3.5, LF(7): 0.0	0.3
2020	SLN	MLB	31	245	27	11	1	7	29	23	51	2	1	.275/.345/.424	108	8.3	.330	-0.4	RF -1, LF -1	0.6

Comparables: Lee Stevens, Juan Lagares, Abraham Almonte

Martínez's immense height, Sideshow Bob-esque hairdo, and covered-in-bugs twitchiness make him one of the most distinctive-looking hitters in baseball. And, while his bat has slowed down, his contact skills and all-fields power enable him to remain an average or better hitter. Unfortunately, Martínez's baby-giraffe-learning-to-walk gait doesn't lend itself to glory in the field. His glove gives back most of the value his bat creates, leaving him best suited for DH—a position not afforded to the Cardinals or any other NL team. Eventually, we feel, Martínez will end up in the AL. When, where, how, and what he'll have left in his tank by then is to be determined.

Yadier Molina   C   Born: 07/13/82   Age: 37   Bats: R   Throws: R   Height: 5'11"   Weight: 205   Origin: Round 4, 2000 Draft (#113 overall)

YEAR	TEAM	LVL	AGE	PA	R	2B	3B	HR	RBI	BB	K	SB	CS	AVG/OBP/SLG	DRC+	VORP	BABIP	BRR	FRAA	WARP
2017	SLN	MLB	34	543	60	27	1	18	82	28	74	9	4	.273/.312/.439	102	21.3	.285	-4.5	C(133): 6.0, 1B(1): 0.0	3.0
2018	SLN	MLB	35	503	55	20	0	20	74	29	66	4	3	.261/.314/.436	111	28.1	.264	-2.3	C(121): 1.4, 1B(5): 0.0	3.1
2019	SLN	MLB	36	452	45	24	0	10	57	23	58	6	0	.270/.312/.399	92	19.0	.289	-2.4	C(111): 0.6, 1B(4): 0.0	1.7
2020	SLN	MLB	37	525	51	26	1	13	57	28	83	5	2	.257/.305/.392	85	11.4	.287	-2.8	C 5	1.6

Comparables: Jason Kendall, Russ Nixon, Tony Peña

YEAR	TEAM	P. COUNT	FRM RUNS	BLK RUNS	THRW RUNS	TOT RUNS
2017	SLN	18649	6.4	0.2	2.2	9.3
2018	SLN	17163	2.3	1.2	0.1	3.5
2019	SLN	15641	0.3	1.5	-0.1	1.5
2020	SLN	24468	6.2	0.4	-0.2	6.3

The year is 2063. Baseball franchises are worth more than ever despite average game length eclipsing four hours. Player salaries have remained stagnant since the Great Alex Rodríguez Riots of 2037. Baseball is still investigating whether the manufacturing process affects the aerodynamics of baseballs, an inquiry that peaked in urgency in 2035 when a 40-year-old Cody Bellinger hit 122 home runs (17 of which came on bunts). An automated strike-zone never took hold; instead, baseball cloned Joe West and Ángel Hernández to create a consistently ridiculous strike zone. And through it all, Molina has been catching 140 games a year for the Cardinals. Top prospect Andrew Knizner III, grandson of longtime backup Andrew Knizner, looks like a good bet to succeed Molina when he retires. (The day will never come, but don't tell Knizner that.)

Elehuris Montero   3B   Born: 08/17/98   Age: 21   Bats: R   Throws: R   Height: 6'3"   Weight: 215   Origin: International Free Agent, 2014

YEAR	TEAM	LVL	AGE	PA	R	2B	3B	HR	RBI	BB	K	SB	CS	AVG/OBP/SLG	DRC+	VORP	BABIP	BRR	FRAA	WARP
2017	CRD	RK	18	208	30	16	1	5	36	22	33	0	2	.277/.370/.468	141	10.8	.305	-0.5	3B(41): 2.8	1.5
2018	PEO	A	19	425	68	28	3	15	69	33	81	2	0	.322/.381/.529	169	39.7	.372	0.3	3B(77): 2.7	4.6
2018	PMB	A+	19	106	13	9	0	1	13	5	22	1	0	.286/.330/.408	118	5.7	.355	0.6	3B(20): 0.8	0.6
2019	SFD	AA	20	238	23	8	0	7	18	14	74	0	1	.188/.235/.317	34	-5.4	.245	-0.4	3B(51): -6.2	-1.4
2020	SLN	MLB	21	251	23	13	0	7	27	14	81	0	0	.221/.272/.370	70	-2.0	.306	-0.4	3B -3	-0.5

Comparables: Jorge Polanco, Miguel Andújar, Jonathan Schoop

If you're curious about why Double-A is considered the hardest step in the minor-league ladder, look no further than Montero. He was one of the hottest hitting prospects in baseball last year. He even held his own when promoted to the offense-suppressing Palm Beach affiliate. Montero started 2019 in Double-A, and baseball got very hard for him in no time at all. Pitchers knocked the bat out of his hands; he struck out almost a third of the time; he rarely walked; and he posted poor average and power numbers. His second year at the level will give him a chance to improve, but it's always perilous to project offensive performance based on A-ball stats. Montero's 2019 is an excellent example of why.

Yairo Muñoz INF   Born: 01/23/95   Age: 25   Bats: R   Throws: R   Height: 6'1"   Weight: 201   Origin: International Free Agent, 2012

YEAR	TEAM	LVL	AGE	PA	R	2B	3B	HR	RBI	BB	K	SB	CS	AVG/OBP/SLG	DRC+	VORP	BABIP	BRR	FRAA	WARP
2017	MID	AA	22	207	35	17	3	6	26	10	35	12	1	.316/.348/.532	120	19.0	.355	3.2	SS(22): -1.1, 3B(21): -0.3	1.3
2017	NAS	AAA	22	272	30	9	1	7	42	11	46	10	4	.289/.316/.414	92	7.7	.324	-2.9	SS(24): 2.4, CF(19): -1.9	0.7
2018	MEM	AAA	23	100	11	3	1	3	13	5	18	1	0	.287/.330/.436	104	7.2	.329	0.3	SS(13): 0.2, LF(4): -0.5	0.3
2018	SLN	MLB	23	329	39	16	0	8	42	30	71	5	6	.276/.350/.413	101	17.2	.338	-2.5	SS(40): -5.4, 2B(26): -0.8	0.2
2019	SLN	MLB	24	181	20	7	1	2	13	7	37	8	3	.267/.298/.355	73	0.3	.328	0.8	3B(21): -0.1, SS(17): 0.1	0.0
2020	SLN	MLB	25	161	16	8	1	4	17	9	35	2	1	.249/.294/.388	82	1.5	.298	-0.1	2B 0, SS 0	0.1

Comparables: Jorge Polanco, Eduardo Escobar, Didi Gregorius

When Muñoz debuted in 2018, the Citi Field scoreboard misspelled his name as "Yario." It was an honest mistake (or perhaps an homage to Mario's lesser-known nemesis?), but one that served as a harbinger for things to come. A quintessential utility infielder, Muñoz spent most of 2019 as out of position as the vowels in his name. For the first (and perhaps the last) time in his career, he saw considerable action in the outfield. Although his bat has never been outstanding, he hits lefties well enough to profile as either a spare infielder or the weak side of a platoon. The Cardinals haven't yet adhered to that evaluation, leaving his overall numbers to suffer as a result. Muñoz is the kind of complementary depth piece that most teams could find room for, and the kind that can be valuable (if not voluminous) with proper management. So far, the Cardinals have figured out that the "i" comes before the "r" in Yairo, they just need help realizing that "OF" should never come after "Muñoz."

Malcom Nunez 3B   Born: 03/09/01   Age: 19   Bats: R   Throws: R   Height: 5'11"   Weight: 205   Origin: International Free Agent, 2017

YEAR	TEAM	LVL	AGE	PA	R	2B	3B	HR	RBI	BB	K	SB	CS	AVG/OBP/SLG	DRC+	VORP	BABIP	BRR	FRAA	WARP
2018	DCA	RK	17	199	44	16	2	13	59	26	29	3	0	.415/.497/.774	225	37.1	.437	0.5	3B(30): -1.0, 1B(5): 1.2	3.2
2019	JCY	RK+	18	146	14	11	0	2	13	13	32	3	2	.254/.336/.385	108	4.1	.323	-0.4		0.6
2019	PEO	A	18	77	5	1	0	0	5	5	15	0	0	.183/.247/.197	56	-7.2	.232	-1.8	3B(8): 0.0	-0.4
2020	SLN	MLB	19	251	22	13	1	3	22	23	73	0	0	.222/.299/.328	71	-1.6	.312	-0.3	3B -1, 1B 0	-0.3

Comparables: Jefry Marte, Anthony Santander, Alex Liddi

Nunez was so good in the DSL that the Cardinals gave him an aggressive promotion to Low-A Peoria, where he was more than three years younger than the average player. He struggled there and the Cardinals moved him down, but it would be wise to cut him some slack. After all, within the past year he: moved to the U.S.; played a more grueling schedule; and faced far older opposition for the first time. Even with those caveats noted, Nunez's profile raises red flags for a player scouts see as an early bloomer. There's a chance he ends up as a first-base-only prospect given his build, in turn putting significant pressure on his bat. That's not disqualifying—his bat has a chance to be special, with plus feel for hit and power—but between his defensive limitations and his distance from the big leagues, it's premature to consider him the Cardinals' next big thing.

Tyler O'Neill LF   Born: 06/22/95   Age: 25   Bats: R   Throws: R   Height: 5'11"   Weight: 210   Origin: Round 3, 2013 Draft (#85 overall)

YEAR	TEAM	LVL	AGE	PA	R	2B	3B	HR	RBI	BB	K	SB	CS	AVG/OBP/SLG	DRC+	VORP	BABIP	BRR	FRAA	WARP
2017	TAC	AAA	22	396	54	21	2	19	56	44	108	9	2	.244/.328/.479	98	20.5	.295	0.3	LF(67): -1.8, RF(17): -0.9	0.6
2017	MEM	AAA	22	161	23	5	1	12	39	10	43	5	0	.253/.304/.548	104	7.1	.266	-0.6	RF(18): 1.0, LF(10): -0.3	0.8
2018	MEM	AAA	23	273	61	9	2	26	63	29	68	3	1	.311/.385/.693	159	40.8	.324	1.0	LF(33): -1.3, RF(21): 7.8	3.3
2018	SLN	MLB	23	142	29	5	0	9	23	7	57	2	0	.254/.303/.500	90	11.6	.364	2.2	RF(24): 0.7, LF(16): 1.1	0.5
2019	MEM	AAA	24	166	25	5	0	11	26	14	51	3	0	.265/.325/.517	104	10.8	.322	0.7	LF(25): 0.2, RF(11): 1.0	0.6
2019	SLN	MLB	24	151	18	6	0	5	16	10	53	1	0	.262/.311/.411	75	-0.5	.386	-0.9	LF(33): -3.3, RF(8): -0.2	-0.4
2020	SLN	MLB	25	301	36	13	1	14	41	23	110	4	1	.234/.299/.439	97	7.7	.332	0.5	LF -4	0.4

Comparables: Randal Grichuk, Clint Frazier, Matt Olson

It's a shame O'Neill is from Canada, because he's Texas personified: everything is bigger with O'Neill. The muscles, the speed, the power—the strikeouts, and the attrition risk. O'Neill's profile has always been extreme, and he did nothing to change that in 2019, as he struck out more than 30 percent of the time in both Triple-A and the majors. Those sky-high numbers would be the end for many players, but O'Neill theoretically has the power to make the overall package work—he just hasn't yet. It's tempting to shrug off his struggles last season as injury-related, but declining walk numbers and general plate-discipline struggles are a discouraging sign, given his batting average is always going to be suppressed by his contact woes. The Cardinals' pipeline includes a number of other promising outfielders, so O'Neill needs to start proving his stuff before he's sent out to pasture.

Marcell Ozuna LF   Born: 11/12/90   Age: 29   Bats: R   Throws: R   Height: 6'1"   Weight: 225   Origin: International Free Agent, 2008

YEAR	TEAM	LVL	AGE	PA	R	2B	3B	HR	RBI	BB	K	SB	CS	AVG/OBP/SLG	DRC+	VORP	BABIP	BRR	FRAA	WARP
2017	MIA	MLB	26	679	93	30	2	37	124	64	144	1	3	.312/.376/.548	134	55.1	.355	-3.5	LF(152): 4.9, CF(3): 0.0	4.8
2018	SLN	MLB	27	628	69	16	2	23	88	38	110	3	0	.280/.325/.433	109	30.9	.309	2.6	LF(147): -2.2	2.4
2019	SLN	MLB	28	549	80	23	1	29	89	62	114	12	2	.243/.330/.474	111	23.4	.259	3.1	LF(129): -11.2	1.5
2020	SLN	MLB	29	550	70	23	2	28	81	50	122	2	1	.258/.328/.477	109	11.3	.290	0.3	LF -2, CF 0	2.4

Comparables: Andruw Jones, Glenallen Hill, Kevin Kiermaier

Ozuna entered the winter possessing a rare pairing of qualities: he was young for a free agent, having just completed his age-28 season, and having already produced a star-level season in his past. Alas, that season was 2017 rather than 2019, and some of his value that year came from strong defense, which is emphatically no longer the case. But, despite those downsides, there's untapped potential here. Ozuna has crushed the ball the last two years, albeit without having the results to show for it. He graded well when judged by ball-tracking metrics in 2019, and posted a career-high walk rate and career-low chase rate. Has Ozuna peaked? Perhaps, but it seems like the baseball gods owe him a career year based on his under-the-hood numbers.

Rangel Ravelo 1B
Born: 04/24/92   Age: 28   Bats: R   Throws: R   Height: 6'1"   Weight: 225   Origin: Round 6, 2010 Draft (#188 overall)

YEAR	TEAM	LVL	AGE	PA	R	2B	3B	HR	RBI	BB	K	SB	CS	AVG/OBP/SLG	DRC+	VORP	BABIP	BRR	FRAA	WARP
2017	MEM	AAA	25	345	49	25	1	8	41	31	56	1	2	.314/.383/.480	131	20.9	.359	-2.9	1B(52): 0.0, RF(12): 0.2	1.6
2018	MEM	AAA	26	399	57	19	2	13	67	42	49	0	1	.308/.392/.487	135	29.0	.328	0.6	1B(54): 3.6, LF(36): -1.7	2.7
2019	MEM	AAA	27	381	50	20	1	12	56	37	61	0	1	.299/.383/.473	118	17.8	.336	-0.3	1B(43): 1.4, LF(36): 2.9	1.9
2019	SLN	MLB	27	43	4	2	0	2	7	3	12	0	0	.205/.256/.410	76	-0.3	.231	-0.1	1B(9): -0.5	-0.1
2020	SLN	MLB	28	49	5	2	0	1	6	4	10	0	0	.241/.316/.391	91	0.6	.285	-0.1	1B 0	0.1

Comparables: Ji-Man Choi, Joey Terdoslavich, José Osuna

Ravelo fits an interesting, oft-disregarded archetype: the right-right first baseman who puts up excellent offensive numbers despite middling power. The comparisons to Luke Voit are too easy to ignore. Like Voit, he's received few opportunities at the major-league level despite repeatedly performing in the minors. Unlike Voit, his batted-ball profile limits his ceiling—he hits too many grounders and, even with the altered ball in Triple-A this year, he could manage only 12 home runs. His low strikeout totals offset his lack of power, but the overall package isn't what you would hope for a player with his defensive limitations. As such, Ravelo's best chance is to be spun elsewhere, perhaps to a rebuilding team seeking a Voit of their own.

Jhon Torres OF
Born: 03/29/00   Age: 20   Bats: R   Throws: R   Height: 6'4"   Weight: 199   Origin: International Free Agent, 2016

YEAR	TEAM	LVL	AGE	PA	R	2B	3B	HR	RBI	BB	K	SB	CS	AVG/OBP/SLG	DRC+	VORP	BABIP	BRR	FRAA	WARP
2017	DIN	RK	17	226	25	7	3	5	35	28	41	4	4	.255/.363/.408	112	13.0	.290	-0.3	RF(29): -0.8, CF(22): -4.6	0.2
2018	CLT	RK	18	111	16	3	0	4	16	11	24	3	0	.273/.351/.424	123	3.6	.324	-0.3	RF(24): 5.6, CF(1): -0.1	1.0
2018	CRD	RK	18	75	11	6	0	4	18	8	13	1	1	.397/.493/.683	206	12.5	.457	0.2	RF(15): 5.2	1.3
2019	JCY	RK+	19	133	24	9	0	6	17	19	36	0	2	.286/.391/.527	151	11.8	.366	0.8		1.1
2019	PEO	A	19	75	4	3	0	0	8	7	29	0	1	.167/.240/.212	49	-4.5	.282	-0.6	RF(20): 3.8	0.1
2020	SLN	MLB	20	251	22	12	1	5	23	23	89	0	0	.211/.291/.329	67	-2.9	.326	-0.4	RF 4, CF 0	0.0

Comparables: José Martínez, Abraham Almonte, Dilson Herrera

Your eyes aren't deceiving you: that H in Torres' first name appears aggressively early. Also aggressively early: his offensive production. He overpowered Gulf Coast and Appy League pitching in 2018 and 2019, with his feel to hit, his patience, and his raw power—a trio that made him look like a potential middle-of-the-order bat. There is one red flag worth disclosing: the Cardinals briefly sent him to the Midwest League to start the season, and he looked like—well, a 19-year-old in a tough league. Provided Torres does better in his second tour in the Midwest League, he could be in the big-league picture sooner than expected. Players with his combination of production and projection don't tend to hang around in the minors for long.

Matt Wieters C
Born: 05/21/86   Age: 34   Bats: B   Throws: R   Height: 6'5"   Weight: 235   Origin: Round 1, 2007 Draft (#5 overall)

YEAR	TEAM	LVL	AGE	PA	R	2B	3B	HR	RBI	BB	K	SB	CS	AVG/OBP/SLG	DRC+	VORP	BABIP	BRR	FRAA	WARP
2017	WAS	MLB	31	465	43	20	0	10	52	38	94	1	0	.225/.288/.344	74	2.1	.264	-1.7	C(118): -10.4	-0.4
2018	WAS	MLB	32	271	24	8	0	8	30	30	45	0	1	.238/.330/.374	101	8.1	.261	-0.8	C(73): -4.0	0.9
2019	SLN	MLB	33	183	15	4	0	11	27	12	47	1	1	.214/.268/.435	97	8.6	.223	-0.8	C(54): -7.4	0.0
2020	SLN	MLB	34	251	27	11	0	9	31	20	61	1	0	.232/.297/.404	84	2.3	.276	-0.6	C -7	-0.5

Comparables: Jason Varitek, John Buck, Ryan Doumit

Wieters completed the transition from underqualified starter to adequately qualified backup last season. His framing was quite poor—his large frame has always been identified as part of the reason why—but he's a well-regarded veteran who can run into a mistake now and then. He'll probably keep getting jobs, even if he's a threat to finish below replacement level from here on out.

YEAR	TEAM	P. COUNT	FRM RUNS	BLK RUNS	THRW RUNS	TOT RUNS
2017	WAS	16476	-11.2	1.5	-0.7	-11.0
2018	WAS	9086	-3.7	1.1	0.3	-2.3
2019	SLN	6250	-8.7	1.2	0.3	-7.3
2020	SLN	12894	-8.1	0.5	1.0	-6.7

Justin Williams OF
Born: 08/20/95   Age: 24   Bats: L   Throws: R   Height: 6'2"   Weight: 215   Origin: Round 2, 2013 Draft (#52 overall)

YEAR	TEAM	LVL	AGE	PA	R	2B	3B	HR	RBI	BB	K	SB	CS	AVG/OBP/SLG	DRC+	VORP	BABIP	BRR	FRAA	WARP
2017	MNT	AA	21	409	53	21	3	14	72	37	69	6	2	.301/.364/.489	147	18.6	.334	-2.0	RF(80): -4.8, LF(7): 1.2	2.1
2018	DUR	AAA	22	386	41	18	0	8	46	25	81	4	3	.258/.313/.376	97	-4.9	.315	-2.7	RF(80): 13.7, LF(2): 1.0	1.8
2018	MEM	AAA	22	76	8	3	0	3	11	5	17	0	1	.217/.276/.391	86	-0.6	.240	-1.1	LF(10): 4.2, RF(7): 0.9	0.5
2018	TBA	MLB	22	1	0	0	0	0	0	0	0	0	0	.000/.000/.000	83	-0.5	.000	0.0	RF(1): 0.0	0.0
2019	SFD	AA	23	61	7	1	0	1	3	4	17	1	0	.193/.246/.263	56	-2.3	.256	-0.1	LF(12): -0.7, RF(2): -0.1	-0.2
2019	MEM	AAA	23	119	20	5	0	7	26	16	30	0	0	.353/.437/.608	146	14.2	.439	-0.5	RF(24): 3.9	1.2
2020	SLN	MLB	24	35	4	1	0	1	4	2	10	0	0	.235/.289/.379	76	-0.4	.301	-0.1	RF 0	0.0

Comparables: Xavier Avery, Gabriel Guerrero, Yorman Rodriguez

Thus far in his Cardinals career, Williams has a case of the second-bests. He was the second-best player the Birds received in return for Tommy Pham (after Génesis Cabrera), the second-best minor leaguer to hurt his hand punching something in frustration (after Alex Reyes), and is now the second-best lefty outfielder in Triple-A with Dylan Carlson also in tow. He doesn't do any one thing tremendously well, but he does a lot of things okay, which might earn him a swing role on the 2020 team—except, uh, Randy Arozarena does everything a little better, which makes Williams second-best there too. At least he's consistent?

Kolten Wong 2B Born: 10/10/90 Age: 29 Bats: L Throws: R Height: 5'9" Weight: 185 Origin: Round 1, 2011 Draft (#22 overall)

YEAR	TEAM	LVL	AGE	PA	R	2B	3B	HR	RBI	BB	K	SB	CS	AVG/OBP/SLG	DRC+	VORP	BABIP	BRR	FRAA	WARP
2017	SLN	MLB	26	411	55	27	3	4	42	41	60	8	2	.285/.376/.412	97	23.9	.331	1.6	2B(106): -4.6	0.8
2018	SLN	MLB	27	407	41	18	2	9	38	31	60	6	5	.249/.332/.388	91	11.8	.275	-2.0	2B(119): 6.0	1.2
2019	SLN	MLB	28	549	61	25	4	11	59	47	83	24	4	.285/.361/.423	102	20.0	.321	3.2	2B(147): 18.6	4.1
2020	SLN	MLB	29	595	62	27	4	13	62	48	100	12	4	.260/.337/.396	96	21.8	.299	0.6	2B 8	3.1

Comparables: Gordon Beckham, Bernie Allen, Cass Michaels

For as long as he's been in the majors, Wong has gone through stretches where he approaches stardom. He's been a great defender, shown sneaky power, reached base at an excellent clip, and provided value on the basepaths—just never all at the same time. In 2019, every thread came together to form his best season by far. You can't predict that for Wong going forward, of course, but his performance emphasizes his high floor. He strikes out less than average, walks (and gets hit by pitches) more than average, and plays excellent defense at second base. Those skills have always been there, which means he's roughly an average player even if some things go wrong, and a star-level performer when most things go right. Now entering the final season of the guaranteed portion of his contract, there's every reason to believe the Cardinals will be exercising their 2021 club option.

PITCHERS

John Brebbia RHP Born: 05/30/90 Age: 30 Bats: L Throws: R Height: 6'1" Weight: 185 Origin: Round 30, 2011 Draft (#929 overall)

YEAR	TEAM	LVL	AGE	W	L	SV	G	GS	IP	H	HR	BB/9	K/9	K	GB%	BABIP	WHIP	ERA	DRA	WARP	MPH	FB%	WHF	CSP
2017	MEM	AAA	27	1	1	3	15	1	26²	16	2	1.7	9.8	29	33%	.219	0.79	1.69	1.47	1.1				
2017	SLN	MLB	27	0	0	0	50	0	51²	37	8	1.9	8.9	51	26%	.216	0.93	2.44	4.60	0.3	96.4	56.7	13.5	49.2
2018	MEM	AAA	28	2	0	2	11	0	13²	16	3	2.6	15.8	24	6%	.433	1.46	4.61	3.60	0.2				
2018	SLN	MLB	28	3	3	2	45	0	50²	43	5	2.8	10.7	60	33%	.297	1.16	3.20	2.92	1.2	97.1	53.3	13.8	49.8
2019	SLN	MLB	29	3	4	0	66	0	72²	59	6	3.3	10.8	87	28%	.293	1.18	3.59	4.06	1.0	95.8	56.6	14.7	49.5
2020	SLN	MLB	30	3	3	0	58	0	61	51	9	2.7	10.3	70	28%	.276	1.12	3.25	3.68	1.2	95.5	55.5	14.1	49.4

Comparables: Erik Goeddel, Justin Grimm, Jacob Barnes

No one would have blamed Brebbia for calling it quits when the Yankees released him after the 2013 season. Instead, he spent two years in independent baseball, revamped his slider to better complement his fastball, and fought his way to the Show. Last season was his second year in a row of lights-out relief, and though the Cardinals still haven't used him in high-leverage roles very often, that's a reflection on the team's wide range of bullpen options rather than a lack of worthiness on his part. Brebbia will enter 2020 as an overqualified middle-relief arm, but if his career arc proves anything, it's that patience is often rewarded.

Génesis Cabrera LHP Born: 10/10/96 Age: 23 Bats: L Throws: L Height: 6'2" Weight: 190 Origin: International Free Agent, 2013

YEAR	TEAM	LVL	AGE	W	L	SV	G	GS	IP	H	HR	BB/9	K/9	K	GB%	BABIP	WHIP	ERA	DRA	WARP	MPH	FB%	WHF	CSP
2017	PCH	A+	20	4	5	0	13	12	69²	45	3	3.2	7.8	60	39%	.230	1.00	2.84	2.83	2.0				
2017	MNT	AA	20	5	4	0	12	12	64²	75	6	3.8	7.1	51	37%	.332	1.58	3.62	5.63	-0.4				
2018	MNT	AA	21	7	6	0	21	20	113²	90	11	4.5	9.8	124	35%	.282	1.29	4.12	4.27	1.4				
2018	SFD	AA	21	1	3	0	5	5	24²	24	3	4.7	7.7	21	37%	.300	1.50	4.74	5.19	0.0				
2019	MEM	AAA	22	5	6	0	20	18	99	107	20	3.5	9.6	106	42%	.330	1.47	5.91	5.11	1.5				
2019	SLN	MLB	22	0	2	1	13	2	20¹	23	2	4.9	8.4	19	39%	.323	1.67	4.87	5.53	0.0	98.5	61	8.1	49.5
2020	SLN	MLB	23	3	4	0	38	6	63	65	10	3.8	7.1	49	38%	.295	1.46	4.85	5.02	0.4	98.4	63.2	8.4	51.3

Comparables: Eduardo Rodriguez, Jake Thompson, Lucas Giolito

In the beginning, the Cardinals had Tommy Pham. Then John Mozeliak said, let there be light. At first, the rest of the front office was confused, but he eventually revealed that he meant he wanted to trade Pham for a package including Cabrera. And so, here we are. Cabrera is a power-armed lefty who is still struggling to find a pitch to pair with his 96 mph heater. His changeup is the best of his secondaries, yet it features minimal velocity separation despite otherwise excellent deception. He started a full complement of games last year, but without a stronger breaker his version of Revelations is likely to include the bullpen.

Seth Elledge RHP Born: 05/20/96 Age: 24 Bats: R Throws: R Height: 6'3" Weight: 240 Origin: Round 4, 2017 Draft (#123 overall)

YEAR	TEAM	LVL	AGE	W	L	SV	G	GS	IP	H	HR	BB/9	K/9	K	GB%	BABIP	WHIP	ERA	DRA	WARP	MPH	FB%	WHF	CSP
2017	CLN	A	21	3	0	5	15	0	21	14	1	2.6	15.0	35	40%	.310	0.95	3.00	2.21	0.7				
2018	MOD	A+	22	5	1	9	31	0	38¹	18	1	3.5	12.7	54	53%	.221	0.86	1.17	1.52	1.5				
2018	SFD	AA	22	3	1	4	13	0	16²	13	3	3.2	10.8	20	44%	.250	1.14	4.32	3.61	0.3				
2019	SFD	AA	23	3	3	3	26	0	33¹	34	3	3.5	11.6	43	44%	.383	1.41	3.78	5.22	-0.3				
2019	MEM	AAA	23	3	1	0	21	3	34¹	28	3	5.0	8.4	32	41%	.287	1.37	4.72	4.77	0.5				
2020	SLN	MLB	24	2	2	0	33	0	35	35	5	3.6	9.2	36	41%	.307	1.39	4.51	4.65	0.3				

Comparables: Akeel Morris, Heath Hembree, Eduardo Paredes

When Elledge joined the Cardinals in a 2018 trade, they showed what they thought of him by promoting him to Double-A. They continued to show their belief in him last year, pushing him to Triple-A midway through the season and then sending him to Fall League. Elledge didn't disappoint, striking out more than a batter an inning with a strikeout-to-walk ratio of 6.00 in the showcase league. His pitch mix, featuring a mid-90s fastball and cookie-cutter slider, doesn't jump off the page, but he has a deceptive, long-striding delivery that keeps batters off-balance and causes both pitches to play up. Plug him into the big league bullpen, and he'd be a younger, near-clone of Sam Tuivailala, the guy he was traded for.

Junior Fernandez RHP   Born: 03/02/97   Age: 23   Bats: R   Throws: R   Height: 6'1"   Weight: 180   Origin: International Free Agent, 2014

YEAR	TEAM	LVL	AGE	W	L	SV	G	GS	IP	H	HR	BB/9	K/9	K	GB%	BABIP	WHIP	ERA	DRA	WARP	MPH	FB%	WHF	CSP
2017	PMB	A+	20	5	3	0	16	16	90¹	82	5	3.9	5.8	58	45%	.281	1.34	3.69	4.91	0.4				
2018	PMB	A+	21	1	0	3	8	0	9²	9	0	1.9	6.5	7	43%	.321	1.14	0.00	4.69	0.0				
2018	SFD	AA	21	0	0	0	16	0	21	19	1	6.9	7.3	17	36%	.295	1.67	5.14	6.42	-0.4				
2019	PMB	A+	22	0	0	4	9	0	11²	8	0	6.2	8.5	11	45%	.258	1.37	1.54	4.57	0.0				
2019	SFD	AA	22	1	1	5	18	0	29	18	0	3.4	13.0	42	48%	.295	1.00	1.55	3.03	0.6				
2019	MEM	AAA	22	2	1	2	18	0	24¹	17	0	4.1	10.0	27	63%	.274	1.15	1.48	2.36	0.9				
2019	SLN	MLB	22	0	1	0	13	0	11²	9	2	4.6	12.3	16	50%	.269	1.29	5.40	3.34	0.3	99.0	41.7	19.7	39.7
2020	SLN	MLB	23	2	2	0	32	0	34	27	4	5.5	13.7	51	47%	.322	1.41	4.09	4.22	0.4	98.9	43.2	20.4	41.1

Comparables: Touki Toussaint, Jonathan Hernández, Tyrell Jenkins

The belief that every team could manufacture a good bullpen out of bubblegum and failed starters bouncing around the minors is tired. If it were that easy, there wouldn't be bad bullpens; there wouldn't be failed relief conversions. But, if you want to know why it's perpetually tempting, look no further than Fernandez. In 2017, he walked nearly as many batters as he struck out in A-ball. He was converted to relief thereafter, and he's since made it to the majors while posting an aggregate 2.52 ERA and striking out more than a quarter of opponents. Not all starters make excellent relievers; Fernandez might though.

Jack Flaherty RHP   Born: 10/15/95   Age: 24   Bats: R   Throws: R   Height: 6'4"   Weight: 205   Origin: Round 1, 2014 Draft (#34 overall)

YEAR	TEAM	LVL	AGE	W	L	SV	G	GS	IP	H	HR	BB/9	K/9	K	GB%	BABIP	WHIP	ERA	DRA	WARP	MPH	FB%	WHF	CSP
2017	SFD	AA	21	7	2	0	10	10	63¹	47	2	1.6	8.8	62	41%	.269	0.92	1.42	2.61	1.9				
2017	MEM	AAA	21	7	2	0	15	15	85¹	73	10	2.5	9.0	85	42%	.288	1.14	2.74	3.12	2.4				
2017	SLN	MLB	21	0	2	0	6	5	21¹	23	4	4.2	8.4	20	49%	.322	1.55	6.33	3.28	0.5	95.0	55.9	14	47.2
2018	MEM	AAA	22	4	1	0	5	5	31²	22	2	2.0	11.7	41	44%	.274	0.92	2.27	2.07	1.2				
2018	SLN	MLB	22	8	9	0	28	28	151	108	20	3.5	10.8	182	43%	.257	1.11	3.34	3.07	3.9	95.9	55.3	14.5	46
2019	SLN	MLB	23	11	8	0	33	33	196¹	135	25	2.5	10.6	231	41%	.242	0.97	2.75	2.44	7.1	96.7	57.7	14.9	46.2
2020	SLN	MLB	24	12	8	0	29	29	172	132	23	3.0	10.9	209	41%	.270	1.10	2.87	3.28	4.8	96.1	58.4	15.1	47.8

Comparables: Héctor Rondón, Yovani Gallardo, Luis Severino

It's generally quite hard to put yourself in a star athlete's shoes. They were the best kid in their class at every sport growing up, wunderkinds without equal, rarely failing at anything. Then they joined pro ball and outperformed older players at every turn. Stars arrive in the major leagues with a warped sense of reality—their world has always revolved around them, everyone else merely a prop in their play. But Flaherty doesn't quite fit this mold. Oh, he's a freak athlete, no doubt about that. But he pitched on the same high school team as Max Fried and Lucas Giolito, both of whom were first-round picks. Giolito was popping 100 mph as a prep, for crying out loud.

What could be more relatable than being excellent at a thing, only for someone at your school to outdo you? To call your friends to brag about your accomplishments, only to have them think "Lucas and Max did it better"—who among us hasn't told our parents what we accomplished this week, knowing that they're silently comparing us to that one person in our high school who was perfect? In a land populated mostly with unrelatable pillars of excellence, Flaherty represents a rare glimpse of humanity.

Of course, it's only a glimpse.

Flaherty is still very much unlike you. His career arc hasn't taken him the way most people go, leading a perfectly successful life that is nonetheless eclipsed by a frenemy. Instead of idling through life, content in his lot, he worked maniacally to get better. Instead of heading home after a day at work and sitting on the couch to watch TV, he started taking lessons in mound presence from Bob Gibson. While you got a "meets expectations" on your quarterly performance review, Flaherty posted a 0.91 ERA in the second half and crashed the Cy Young race, dragging the Cardinals into the playoffs in the process.

Just to emphasize the point, Flaherty won the series-deciding game against Fried's Braves, and even drove in a run with Fried on the mound. He's the unquestioned best of that trio now, one of the 15 or so best starters in baseball. So while in some sense Flaherty is just like us, in another sense his story is even more inconceivable. The star athlete who was always the best is so different from you that it's easy to believe you could accomplish the same thing, were you in their shoes. Flaherty was in your shoes—and he *still* ended up on top. What could be more unrelatable than that?

Giovanny Gallegos RHP   Born: 08/14/91   Age: 28   Bats: R   Throws: R   Height: 6'2"   Weight: 210   Origin: International Free Agent, 2011

YEAR	TEAM	LVL	AGE	W	L	SV	G	GS	IP	H	HR	BB/9	K/9	K	GB%	BABIP	WHIP	ERA	DRA	WARP	MPH	FB%	WHF	CSP
2017	SWB	AAA	25	4	2	5	28	0	43¹	28	4	2.3	14.3	69	32%	.286	0.90	2.08	1.60	1.8				
2017	NYA	MLB	25	0	1	0	16	0	20¹	21	3	2.2	9.7	22	37%	.316	1.28	4.87	3.15	0.5	95.6	63.5	15.3	49.6
2018	SWB	AAA	26	2	1	2	17	0	27²	24	1	2.3	13.3	41	39%	.354	1.12	3.90	2.95	0.7				
2018	MEM	AAA	26	0	0	1	13	0	16²	7	0	1.6	8.6	16	45%	.175	0.60	0.54	1.85	0.6				
2018	NYA	MLB	26	0	0	1	4	0	10	10	2	2.7	9.0	10	41%	.320	1.30	4.50	5.38	-0.1	95.7	58.6	8.9	50.5
2018	SLN	MLB	26	0	0	0	2	0	1¹	1	0	0.0	13.5	2	0%	.333	0.75	0.00	6.81	0.0	96.3	64	12	46.2
2019	SLN	MLB	27	3	2	1	66	0	74	44	9	1.9	11.3	93	34%	.222	0.81	2.31	2.82	2.0	95.3	55.2	17.4	46.5
2020	SLN	MLB	28	3	3	7	58	0	61	48	9	2.7	11.4	78	34%	.280	1.08	2.92	3.34	1.4	94.8	57.2	16.4	48.7

Comparables: Phil Maton, Jonathan Holder, Nick Wittgren

Believe it or not, Gallegos didn't start the year in the majors despite gaudy minor-league numbers. The Cardinals saw the light quickly enough, though, promoting Gallegos in April. From thereon, he accumulated more WARP than any other Cardinals reliever. His success wasn't startling—his minor-league strikeout and run-prevention numbers were excellent—but the timing was perfect for the Cardinals, whose patchwork starting rotation stacked a lot of pressure on a bullpen that had already lost Jordan Hicks earlier in the year. If he can keep it up, the Luke Voit trade—which was briefly known as the Chasen Shreve trade—might end up being remembered as the Giovanny Gallegos trade.

John Gant RHP Born: 08/06/92   Age: 27   Bats: R   Throws: R   Height: 6'3"   Weight: 200   Origin: Round 21, 2011 Draft (#642 overall)

YEAR	TEAM	LVL	AGE	W	L	SV	G	GS	IP	H	HR	BB/9	K/9	K	GB%	BABIP	WHIP	ERA	DRA	WARP	MPH	FB%	WHF	CSP
2017	MEM	AAA	24	6	5	0	18	18	103¹	109	10	2.2	8.6	99	47%	.334	1.30	3.83	4.06	1.9				
2017	SLN	MLB	24	0	1	0	7	2	17¹	17	4	5.2	5.7	11	54%	.260	1.56	4.67	5.03	0.1	95.8	65.2	11	46.1
2018	MEM	AAA	25	5	1	0	8	8	49	45	5	2.9	7.7	42	49%	.288	1.24	1.65	3.73	1.0				
2018	SLN	MLB	25	7	6	0	26	19	114	91	9	4.5	7.5	95	46%	.253	1.30	3.47	4.05	1.6	95.8	55.4	12.2	48.5
2019	SLN	MLB	26	11	1	3	64	0	66¹	51	4	4.6	8.1	60	46%	.275	1.28	3.66	4.32	0.7	98.0	55.7	13	48.4
2020	SLN	MLB	27	2	2	0	48	0	50	44	6	4.0	8.7	49	49%	.282	1.32	3.75	4.05	0.8	96.2	56.8	12.6	48.4

Comparables: Luis Cessa, Hunter Wood, Anthony Banda

It may feel weird to you that Gant didn't make the postseason roster; after all, he had an 11-1 record and a totally reasonable 3.66 ERA. Heck, even DRA liked his season well enough. What's not to love? Well, dig a little deeper, and it starts to get ugly. As the year wore on, his fastball velocity and command both dipped precipitously. How steep are we talking? In the first half of the season, he walked nine percent of the batters he faced. Over the subsequent months, that rate climbed to 11 percent, then 19 percent, then 29 percent in September (although, to be fair, that was against just 28 batters). Pretty much all of his other stats cratered as well, justifiably leaving him on the outside looking in. Here's hoping Gant can find a to avoid a similar trend in 2020.

Ryan Helsley RHP Born: 07/18/94   Age: 25   Bats: R   Throws: R   Height: 6'1"   Weight: 195   Origin: Round 5, 2015 Draft (#161 overall)

YEAR	TEAM	LVL	AGE	W	L	SV	G	GS	IP	H	HR	BB/9	K/9	K	GB%	BABIP	WHIP	ERA	DRA	WARP	MPH	FB%	WHF	CSP
2017	PMB	A+	22	8	2	0	17	16	93²	72	3	2.9	8.7	91	44%	.277	1.09	2.69	3.40	2.0				
2017	SFD	AA	22	3	1	0	6	6	33²	25	4	4.0	11.0	41	43%	.262	1.19	2.67	3.16	0.8				
2018	SFD	AA	23	3	2	0	7	7	41	30	5	4.4	9.7	44	49%	.243	1.22	4.39	3.52	0.9				
2018	MEM	AAA	23	2	1	0	5	5	26²	18	2	3.0	11.5	34	38%	.262	1.01	3.71	2.63	0.9				
2019	MEM	AAA	24	2	3	1	17	7	37¹	29	3	4.8	9.9	41	43%	.286	1.31	4.58	3.09	1.2				
2019	SLN	MLB	24	2	0	0	24	0	36²	34	5	2.9	7.9	32	35%	.279	1.25	2.95	5.04	0.1	100.2	56.6	11.3	51.7
2020	SLN	MLB	25	2	2	0	32	0	34	33	5	3.5	8.0	30	38%	.292	1.36	4.25	4.55	0.3	99.9	58	11.6	53

Comparables: Rafael Montero, Nestor Cortes Jr., Jakob Junis

If you didn't follow the Cardinals much in 2019, you might know Helsley only for his comments about how Atlanta's tomahawk chop chant devalues Native Americans. Brave is an overused adjective in sports, but it fits the bill here. No matter what he does the rest of his career, speaking up against a demeaning practice will define Helsley—there are few nobler things to be remembered for, in baseball or otherwise. This is purportedly a book about the game, so we'll note that he's a quality pitcher as well. His overpowering fastball and plus cutter and curve would look at home in the back of any bullpen, and it's possible the Cardinals are affording him the opportunity to win a rotation spot as you read this.

Jordan Hicks RHP Born: 09/06/96   Age: 23   Bats: R   Throws: R   Height: 6'2"   Weight: 185   Origin: Round SUP, 2015 Draft (#105 overall)

YEAR	TEAM	LVL	AGE	W	L	SV	G	GS	IP	H	HR	BB/9	K/9	K	GB%	BABIP	WHIP	ERA	DRA	WARP	MPH	FB%	WHF	CSP
2017	PEO	A	20	8	2	0	14	14	78	75	3	4.5	7.3	63	53%	.316	1.46	3.35	5.50	-0.2				
2017	PMB	A+	20	0	1	1	8	5	27	21	0	2.0	10.7	32	67%	.318	1.00	1.00	3.58	0.5				
2018	SLN	MLB	21	3	4	6	73	0	77²	59	2	5.2	8.1	70	62%	.266	1.34	3.59	6.03	-1.0	103.3	78	10.1	47.1
2019	SLN	MLB	22	2	2	14	29	0	28²	16	2	3.5	9.7	31	67%	.215	0.94	3.14	3.22	0.7	103.9	60.3	12.7	46
2020	SLN	MLB	23	1	1	0	11	0	11	10	1	5.2	10.4	13	62%	.319	1.50	4.38	4.44	0.1	103.4	75.3	11.3	48.2

Comparables: Clay Holmes, Jason García, Neil Ramírez

Hicks is best known for his blazing fastball, but he was developing into more than that before Tommy John surgery cut his season short. His slider, which averages around 87 mph and yet still sits 15 ticks below his heater, took a step forward and coerced whiffs on nearly 60 percent of the swings taken against it. He had also introduced a cromulent changeup to attack lefties. Those gains led him to post a better strikeout, walk, and groundball rate as compared to his rookie season. Hicks will likely return in the second half, and we can only hope he's as thrilling to watch as he was pre-injury.

Dakota Hudson RHP Born: 09/15/94   Age: 25   Bats: R   Throws: R   Height: 6'5"   Weight: 215   Origin: Round 1, 2016 Draft (#34 overall)

YEAR	TEAM	LVL	AGE	W	L	SV	G	GS	IP	H	HR	BB/9	K/9	K	GB%	BABIP	WHIP	ERA	DRA	WARP	MPH	FB%	WHF	CSP
2017	SFD	AA	22	9	4	0	18	18	114	111	5	2.7	6.1	77	58%	.296	1.27	2.53	4.47	0.9				
2017	MEM	AAA	22	1	1	0	7	7	38²	36	2	3.5	4.4	19	59%	.272	1.32	4.42	3.47	0.9				
2018	MEM	AAA	23	13	3	0	19	19	111²	107	1	3.1	7.0	87	59%	.313	1.30	2.50	3.63	2.4				
2018	SLN	MLB	23	4	1	0	26	0	27¹	19	0	5.9	6.3	19	64%	.237	1.35	2.63	6.41	-0.5	97.7	60.7	9.9	47.3
2019	SLN	MLB	24	16	7	1	33	32	174²	160	22	4.4	7.0	136	57%	.274	1.41	3.35	4.49	2.4	95.6	61.7	10.4	46.3
2020	SLN	MLB	25	9	9	0	26	26	143	137	17	3.9	7.2	114	57%	.286	1.40	4.29	4.53	2.1	95.5	63.1	10.6	47.8

Comparables: Jarred Cosart, Rob Whalen, Jake Odorizzi

Hudson is a glitch in the matrix—a groundball rate that must have been a transcription error, nearly as many walks as strikeouts, home runs on nearly 20 percent of his fly balls, easily exposed platoon issues against left-handed batters, and so on. Yet all that somehow adds up to a boring, slightly-better-than-average DRA? It all smacks of fiction. It's real life, though, and Hudson's particular brand of conflicting extremes works out to a serviceable starter, even if he doesn't get there in a normal way. Combine his worm-killing ways with the Cardinals' excellent infield defense, which makes his grounder-based game play up, and Hudson should again outperform his metrics as part of the rotation.

Connor Jones RHP   Born: 10/10/94   Age: 25   Bats: R   Throws: R   Height: 6'3"   Weight: 220   Origin: Round 2, 2016 Draft (#70 overall)

YEAR	TEAM	LVL	AGE	W	L	SV	G	GS	IP	H	HR	BB/9	K/9	K	GB%	BABIP	WHIP	ERA	DRA	WARP	MPH	FB%	WHF	CSP
2017	PMB	A+	22	8	5	1	24	21	113¹	120	3	3.9	6.0	76	69%	.321	1.49	3.97	5.58	-0.5				
2017	SFD	AA	22	1	0	0	1	1	6²	6	1	4.1	2.7	2	71%	.250	1.35	2.70	5.32	0.0				
2018	SFD	AA	23	5	5	0	22	17	94²	96	4	4.8	6.3	66	64%	.309	1.55	3.80	5.93	-0.7				
2018	MEM	AAA	23	1	0	0	4	4	15¹	20	1	8.2	9.4	16	62%	.388	2.22	6.46	7.78	-0.4				
2019	SFD	AA	24	1	1	9	42	0	48¹	54	5	6.5	9.1	49	63%	.353	1.84	4.66	6.78	-1.3				
2020	SLN	MLB	25	2	2	0	33	0	35	33	5	4.0	6.7	26	56%	.274	1.39	4.40	4.55	0.3				

Comparables: Pedro Payano, Jared Hughes, Chris Ellis

Jones made the switch from starting to relieving last season, an inevitable move given his spotty command. He was a lock for a few fastballs to the backstop and a few walks per game, as well as some nasty sinkers that batters couldn't square up. His first year of relief didn't go particularly well—he put on 15 percent of the batters he faced in Double-A—but he's a legitimate candidate to crack the big-league bullpen soon. His bowling-ball sinker continues to overpower batters, running into the upper-90s in short spurts and fueling a 63 percent groundball rate. Finding the strike zone with any regularity is the only thing standing between him and being a quality reliever.

Kwang-Hyun Kim LHP   Born: 07/02/88   Age: 31   Bats: L   Throws: L   Height: 6'2"   Weight: 185   Origin: International Free Agent, 2019

Depth and flexibility are two of the biggest buzzwords in baseball over the last few years, and the Cardinals acquired both when they signed Kim to a two-year, $8 million contract. The left-hander has the ability to start or relieve for a Cardinals team that could use some of both. He'll sit in the low-90s with an average slider, but Kim's best attribute is his ability to pound the zone. That alone might allow him to stick in the rotation, where he'll need to deploy his fringy changeup and get-me-over curve more frequently. The lack of a solid third pitch might have doomed him to the bullpen not so long ago, but Kim could find success as a two-time-through-the-order type in a starting role, now.

Evan Kruczynski LHP   Born: 03/31/95   Age: 25   Bats: L   Throws: L   Height: 6'5"   Weight: 215   Origin: Round 9, 2017 Draft (#274 overall)

YEAR	TEAM	LVL	AGE	W	L	SV	G	GS	IP	H	HR	BB/9	K/9	K	GB%	BABIP	WHIP	ERA	DRA	WARP	MPH	FB%	WHF	CSP
2017	PEO	A	22	4	3	0	14	13	68²	70	7	2.0	7.2	55	49%	.307	1.24	3.41	4.88	0.3				
2018	PMB	A+	23	5	3	0	15	15	76	74	6	2.5	8.8	74	49%	.309	1.25	4.03	4.40	0.8				
2018	SFD	AA	23	2	3	0	6	6	39²	27	1	2.3	7.5	33	36%	.255	0.93	2.50	2.80	1.2				
2019	SFD	AA	24	3	8	0	21	20	117¹	123	18	3.8	9.1	118	41%	.322	1.47	5.60	5.18	-0.4				
2019	MEM	AAA	24	1	2	0	7	6	30¹	44	3	5.0	8.3	28	33%	.414	2.01	8.01	7.56	-0.3				
2020	SLN	MLB	25	2	2	0	33	0	35	36	6	3.7	7.5	29	38%	.289	1.42	4.79	4.91	0.2				

Comparables: Brandon Workman, Jacob Waguespack, Thomas Pannone

With Gregg Popovich now coaching the U.S. Olympic basketball team, Kruczynski has some extra free time. Duke recruiting practically runs itself, and there are more things in the world than sitting on the sidelines and looking exactly the same as you did 20 years earlier. So, what did he do? Why he took to baseball. On the right day, he can be found tossing a low-90s fastball and array of passable secondary pitches that should grant him life as a low-end major leaguer. Not bad for a 73-year-old.

Carlos Martínez RHP   Born: 09/21/91   Age: 28   Bats: R   Throws: R   Height: 6'0"   Weight: 190   Origin: International Free Agent, 2009

YEAR	TEAM	LVL	AGE	W	L	SV	G	GS	IP	H	HR	BB/9	K/9	K	GB%	BABIP	WHIP	ERA	DRA	WARP	MPH	FB%	WHF	CSP
2017	SLN	MLB	25	12	11	0	32	32	205	179	27	3.1	9.5	217	52%	.285	1.22	3.64	3.43	4.9	99.1	56.3	11.6	50.8
2018	SFD	AA	26	0	0	0	3	1	7	6	3	0.0	7.7	6	29%	.167	0.86	3.86	4.58	0.0				
2018	SLN	MLB	26	8	6	5	33	18	118²	100	5	4.6	8.9	117	51%	.290	1.35	3.11	4.63	0.9	97.5	44.2	11.7	48.9
2019	SLN	MLB	27	4	2	24	48	0	48¹	39	2	3.4	9.9	53	59%	.298	1.18	3.17	3.29	1.1	98.6	51	14.3	47.4
2020	SLN	MLB	28	3	3	31	53	0	56	51	6	3.8	10.1	63	54%	.307	1.34	3.95	4.16	0.8	97.8	51.1	12.2	49

Comparables: Danny Salazar, Jaime García, Yovani Gallardo

Last season was another round of everyone's favorite game "What Should We Make of Martínez?" This spin, he became a full-time reliever for the first time since his rookie year and anchored an excellent bullpen. He also added velocity to every pitch, scrapped his cutter, and emphasized his slider and changeup, his two best pitches. That all sounds awesome—and while it was, the context makes it bittersweet. The Cardinals see Martínez as a top-end starter, but fate keeps conspiring against him, with injuries keeping him from ascending to the elite status that looked nearly guaranteed earlier in his career. The 2019 season was proof that even a diminished Martínez is an excellent pitcher. But make no mistake—it was a disappointing season, and one that put yet more distance between him and his desired destination.

Miles Mikolas RHP   Born: 08/23/88   Age: 31   Bats: R   Throws: R   Height: 6'5"   Weight: 220   Origin: Round 7, 2009 Draft (#204 overall)

YEAR	TEAM	LVL	AGE	W	L	SV	G	GS	IP	H	HR	BB/9	K/9	K	GB%	BABIP	WHIP	ERA	DRA	WARP	MPH	FB%	WHF	CSP
2018	SLN	MLB	29	18	4	0	32	32	200²	186	16	1.3	6.5	146	51%	.279	1.07	2.83	3.38	4.5	96.5	48.6	10.5	51.8
2019	SLN	MLB	30	9	14	0	32	32	184	193	27	1.6	7.0	144	49%	.302	1.22	4.16	4.14	3.3	96.0	51.5	10.7	48.8
2020	SLN	MLB	31	10	10	0	29	29	169	174	23	1.9	7.1	133	48%	.296	1.24	3.96	4.35	2.8	95.4	49.8	10.6	49.8

Comparables: Chase Whitley, Scott Feldman, Johnny Barbato

Mikolas was demoted from Lizard King to Lizard Prince last year, but his contract was boosted from princely to kingly, which means his season was a win on the whole. If you look past the royal nickname and blowout 2018, though, Mikolas makes a lot more sense. He's an above-average pitcher who gets there by keeping the ball on the ground and avoiding free passes. That kind of profile has a capped upside, but it also provides stability—potentially a high level. Mikolas isn't anyone's idea of an ace. He would be welcomed in every contender's rotation, however, and should be up to the challenge of validating his lucrative new deal over the coming seasons.

Andrew Miller LHP Born: 05/21/85 Age: 35 Bats: L Throws: L Height: 6'7" Weight: 205 Origin: Round 1, 2006 Draft (#6 overall)

YEAR	TEAM	LVL	AGE	W	L	SV	G	GS	IP	H	HR	BB/9	K/9	K	GB%	BABIP	WHIP	ERA	DRA	WARP	MPH	FB%	WHF	CSP
2017	CLE	MLB	32	4	3	2	57	0	62²	31	3	3.0	13.6	95	42%	.233	0.83	1.44	2.30	2.0	97.3	41.9	17.1	45.7
2018	CLE	MLB	33	2	4	2	37	0	34	31	3	4.2	11.9	45	50%	.329	1.38	4.24	3.08	0.7	95.9	43.3	13.7	50.2
2019	SLN	MLB	34	5	6	6	73	0	54²	45	11	4.4	11.5	70	38%	.283	1.32	4.45	3.73	1.0	95.6	38.6	13.7	48.7
2020	SLN	MLB	35	3	2	7	53	0	56	42	7	3.2	11.8	73	42%	.274	1.11	3.06	3.41	1.2	95.0	39.9	14.5	47.6

Comparables: Arthur Rhodes, Brian Matusz, J.P. Howell

It's a good thing the term "Andrew Miller-type role" never stuck to describe high-leverage firemen, because it would be all kinds of confusing now that Miller himself is no longer fit for the role. It's not that he's bad; he still struck out nearly 30 percent of opposing batters, still befuddled lefties, and still posted a better-than-average DRA. It's just that he's not the same anymore; not the guy who was nigh unhittable for two years, whose slider starred in the nightmares of AL Central opponents. That's how the passage of time works, but it's jarring to see a diminished Miller, and more unnerving still to picture him three years down the road, surviving at the back of a bullpen on sheer guile.

Alex Reyes RHP Born: 08/29/94 Age: 25 Bats: R Throws: R Height: 6'3" Weight: 175 Origin: International Free Agent, 2012

YEAR	TEAM	LVL	AGE	W	L	SV	G	GS	IP	H	HR	BB/9	K/9	K	GB%	BABIP	WHIP	ERA	DRA	WARP	MPH	FB%	WHF	CSP
2018	SFD	AA	23	1	0	0	1	1	7²	1	0	3.5	15.3	13	30%	.100	0.52	0.00	1.48	0.3				
2018	MEM	AAA	23	1	0	0	1	1	7	1	0	1.3	16.7	13	33%	.111	0.29	0.00	1.34	0.3				
2018	SLN	MLB	23	0	0	0	1	1	4	3	0	4.5	4.5	2	40%	.300	1.25	0.00	8.15	-0.1	97.4	57.5	4.1	43
2019	PMB	A+	24	0	1	0	2	2	9¹	9	0	2.9	10.6	11	54%	.346	1.29	1.93	3.65	0.2				
2019	MEM	AAA	24	1	3	0	10	7	28	27	5	7.7	12.2	38	41%	.344	1.82	7.39	5.18	0.4				
2019	SLN	MLB	24	0	1	0	4	0	3	2	1	18.0	3.0	1	30%	.111	2.67	15.00	6.67	0.0	99.1	59.4	5.8	42.2
2020	SLN	MLB	25	3	4	0	38	6	66	69	10	6.1	7.1	52	35%	.296	1.72	5.92	5.76	-0.1	97.9	60	5.1	43.6

Comparables: Rafael Montero, Aaron Sanchez, Neftalí Feliz

The wait for Reyes is threatening to eclipse that for Godot. He's been on the cusp of making it big since 2016, when he debuted in August and was electric in a hybrid role. From then on, it's been pratfalls and banana peels for Reyes; a UCL tear erased his 2017 season, and a shoulder injury he suffered while rehabbing spoke for 2018. Last season brought another mixture of injuries and ineffectiveness, including a two-for-one: Reyes broke his hand while punching a wall in frustration. The only silver lining for Reyes is that he was on the major-league roster for two of the last three seasons, accumulating service time and a major-league minimum salary. It's a small mercy, to be sure, but one that feels deserved after his poor run of luck.

Griffin Roberts RHP Born: 06/13/96 Age: 24 Bats: R Throws: R Height: 6'3" Weight: 205 Origin: Round 1, 2018 Draft (#43 overall)

YEAR	TEAM	LVL	AGE	W	L	SV	G	GS	IP	H	HR	BB/9	K/9	K	GB%	BABIP	WHIP	ERA	DRA	WARP	MPH	FB%	WHF	CSP
2018	CRD	RK	22	0	1	1	7	2	8²	6	0	4.2	11.4	11	55%	.300	1.15	6.23	2.47	0.3				
2019	PMB	A+	23	1	7	0	15	13	65²	79	3	4.8	4.9	36	49%	.338	1.74	6.44	8.09	-2.5				
2020	SLN	MLB	24	2	2	0	33	0	35	35	5	4.1	4.6	18	45%	.264	1.46	5.22	5.28	0.1				

Comparables: John Cornely, Jose A. Valdez, Mike Hauschild

It's high time the Cardinals start treating Roberts as an impact reliever rather than a starter. A summer spent weeding out some of the inconsistencies in his game explains his poor statline in High-A, but it can't explain the decreased velocity he showed, both there and in the Fall League. The fastball was down to around 90 mph as a starter after hitting the mid-90s in relief. While his dope slider bailed him out in Arizona, two-pitch starters without overpowering velocity tend to make a hash of things in the majors. The ideal situation for the Cardinals is probably Roberts and Alex Reyes in joint long relief roles, taking advantage of their starting history and allowing their velocity to play up in shorter, multi-inning stints.

Zack Thompson LHP Born: 10/28/97 Age: 22 Bats: L Throws: L Height: 6'2" Weight: 225 Origin: Round 1, 2019 Draft (#19 overall)

YEAR	TEAM	LVL	AGE	W	L	SV	G	GS	IP	H	HR	BB/9	K/9	K	GB%	BABIP	WHIP	ERA	DRA	WARP	MPH	FB%	WHF	CSP
2019	PMB	A+	21	0	0	0	11	0	13¹	16	0	2.7	12.8	19	48%	.455	1.50	4.05	6.71	-0.3				
2020	SLN	MLB	22	2	2	0	33	0	35	35	5	3.8	8.9	35	43%	.305	1.42	4.76	4.88	0.2				

Comparables: Tony Cingrani, Roman Mendez, Chasen Shreve

You know how sometimes when you're playing a board game, you keep using the same strategy, and it keeps working? You start to wonder if it's just you reading too much into luck, or if everyone else is just missing the obvious move. That's the Cardinals drafting college starters. Thompson slid in the draft due to a 2018 elbow injury and inconsistent command, but a four-pitch arsenal and fastball that tops out in the upper-90s give him at least mid-rotation upside. He was excellent in limited pro innings (he fanned nearly a third of the batters he faced in High-A), and he's likely to move quickly through the Cardinals system. In two years, when he's the number two starter on a Cardinals playoff team headlined by (digs into hat) Justin Williams and Max Schrock, we'll all wonder if the Cardinals cracked the code again, or—whether he's another Marco Gonzales or Michael Wacha or Dakota Hudson—if it's just luck.

Adam Wainwright RHP Born: 08/30/81   Age: 38   Bats: R   Throws: R   Height: 6'7"   Weight: 235   Origin: Round 1, 2000 Draft (#29 overall)

YEAR	TEAM	LVL	AGE	W	L	SV	G	GS	IP	H	HR	BB/9	K/9	K	GB%	BABIP	WHIP	ERA	DRA	WARP	MPH	FB%	WHF	CSP
2017	SLN	MLB	35	12	5	0	24	23	123¹	140	14	3.3	7.0	96	50%	.326	1.50	5.11	4.84	1.0	92.6	46.8	7.8	47.5
2018	SFD	AA	36	1	0	0	3	3	10	5	0	0.0	8.1	9	42%	.192	0.50	0.00	2.33	0.3				
2018	MEM	AAA	36	1	0	0	2	2	9	8	0	4.0	11.0	11	38%	.381	1.33	0.00	3.94	0.2				
2018	SLN	MLB	36	2	4	0	8	8	40¹	41	5	4.0	8.9	40	51%	.310	1.46	4.46	3.78	0.7	92.3	38	9.6	45.5
2019	SLN	MLB	37	14	10	0	31	31	171²	181	22	3.4	8.0	153	49%	.319	1.43	4.19	4.58	2.2	91.9	38.5	8.2	48.5
2020	SLN	MLB	38	9	9	0	26	26	143	147	20	2.9	7.7	122	48%	.303	1.36	4.34	4.62	1.9	90.7	39.6	8	46

Comparables: Jim Bunning, Gaylord Perry, Curt Schilling

If there's any justice in the world, Wainwright's 2019 will be remembered for his valiant effort in the playoffs, when he twice pitched into the eighth inning having allowed one or fewer runs. Unfortunately, the world isn't just: the Cardinals lost both of those games, and also lost the game where Wainwright pitched in relief on short rest. Even without the postseason heroics, however, 2019 would have been a satisfying bounceback for the Cardinals' former ace. He made 30 starts for only the second time in five years, adapting to his declining fastball velocity by throwing his curveball nearly 40 percent of the time, essentially a mirror image of his 2018 but over more innings. The end of the line isn't far away, but Wainwright's late-career renaissance is a welcome sight for the team and fans alike. He signed a one-year deal worth $5 million early in the offseason, and it shouldn't shock anyone if this is his farewell tour.

LINEOUTS

Hitters

HITTER	POS	TEAM	LVL	AGE	PA	R	2B	3B	HR	RBI	BB	K	SB	CS	AVG/OBP/SLG	DRC+	VORP	BABIP	BRR	FRAA	WARP
Conner Capel	OF	MEM	AAA	22	31	5	5	0	2	7	6	1	1	0	.433/.452/.800	145	6.1	.500	0.2	LF(6): 0.1, RF(1): 0.1	0.3
	OF	SFD	AA	22	368	39	12	1	9	40	23	84	9	4	.232/.283/.352	76	1.1	.280	2.1	LF(53): 3.7, CF(27): 5.5	1.4
Evan Mendoza	3B	SFD	AA	23	223	20	8	1	1	20	14	44	5	1	.248/.293/.311	71	1.3	.307	1.2	3B(31): 5.8, 1B(21): 1.7	1.0
Delvin Perez	SS	PEO	A	20	506	64	17	3	1	30	27	117	22	9	.269/.329/.325	101	16.0	.359	2.7	SS(111): -2.8	2.1
Max Schrock	INF	MEM	AAA	24	303	42	20	1	2	31	37	49	12	2	.275/.366/.381	103	10.3	.332	-1.6	3B(56): -4.8, 2B(10): 0.0	0.6
Edmundo Sosa	SS	MEM	AAA	23	496	70	18	5	17	62	17	96	2	3	.291/.335/.466	95	25.8	.332	0.7	SS(83): 4.0, 2B(17): 0.9	2.2
	SS	SLN	MLB	23	10	2	0	0	0	0	1	2	1	0	.250/.400/.250	85	0.1	.333	-0.1	2B(4): -0.1	0.0
Lane Thomas	CF	MEM	AAA	23	304	42	17	2	10	44	32	80	11	6	.268/.352/.460	98	16.3	.343	0.6	CF(37): 5.0, LF(32): -2.4	1.1
	CF	SLN	MLB	23	44	6	0	1	4	12	4	8	1	1	.316/.409/.684	111	2.1	.308	0.3	CF(19): 2.1, RF(5): 0.4	0.5
Ramón Urías	2B	MEM	AAA	25	375	51	24	0	9	52	44	71	4	1	.263/.369/.424	111	13.1	.310	-3.0	2B(63): 0.1, 3B(20): -0.9	1.4
Juan Yepez	1B	PMB	A+	21	115	16	4	0	4	20	10	21	1	0	.275/.351/.431	141	7.5	.312	0.2	RF(21): 0.2, 3B(5): 0.7	0.7
	1B	SFD	AA	21	59	8	2	0	2	10	5	14	0	0	.231/.288/.385	70	1.1	.263	0.3	LF(12): -1.5, 1B(5): 0.0	-0.2
	1B	PEO	A	21	101	14	7	0	4	13	11	24	2	1	.284/.366/.500	165	6.7	.344	-0.5	3B(11): 0.2, 1B(6): 0.5	0.9
Wadye Ynfante	OF	PEO	A	21	332	36	7	1	3	19	21	94	12	5	.219/.286/.279	72	-6.3	.306	-1.1	RF(50): 10.3, CF(27): 1.4	1.1
	OF	PMB	A+	21	34	4	0	0	0	0	3	7	0	0	.100/.206/.100	48	-4.7	.130	0.0	CF(11): 1.0	0.1

Conner Capel has the speed and arm to hold down any position in the outfield. It's a good thing, too, because his offensive production could play light. There's power there, but plenty of swing-and-miss as well. Think Harrison Bader with the volume turned down. ⊗ **Evan Mendoza** has the bad fortune to be a fringy prospect at the hot corner in a system filled with dynamic third basemen. He hit poorly in Double-A this year while former teammate Tommy Edman tore up the major leagues. In another universe that situation might be reversed, but in this one, Mendoza looks like bench depth. ⊗ **Delvin Perez** has hit only two home runs in nearly 1,100 plate appearances as a professional, and struck out 90 more times than he walked in what was—relatively—a good offensive year. We would note that he went just a few picks after Gavin Lux in the 2016 draft, but that would be mean. ⊗ **Max Schrock** is a high-contact, no-power infielder who would be voted most likely to become the new Stubby Clapp or Bo Hart if you polled fans whose only frame of reference was funnily named Cardinals spare infielders of the early aughts. ⊗ **Edmundo Sosa** combines the slick glove and defensive versatility of a utility infielder with the bat of … well, with the bat of a utility infielder. We'd say something more clever but we opted to practice the same amount of discipline with this comment that he displays at the plate. ⊗ **Lane Thomas** was one of the fastest players in the major leagues in limited opportunities, so you might say he can flat out fly. Jack Hanna, who attended the same high school as Thomas, would probably reserve that language for a hyacinth macaw rather than a fourth outfielder type. ⊗ **Ramón Urías** held his own in Memphis while developing a little patience at the plate, posting a career-high walk rate. Staple his 2018 power numbers to his 2019 walk rate, and that would be quite a spicy prospect. As is, he's merely a utility infielder in the Yairo Muñoz mold. ⊗ **Juan Yepez** will always be best known—if he's known at all—as the return for fan favorite Matt Adams. He performed well enough in Peoria and Palm Beach to earn a promotion to Double-A, where he predictably struggled. Adams, meanwhile, hit 20-plus homers for a third consecutive season and used Gary Clark Jr. as his walkup music. It's clear who won the trade. ⊗ **Wadye Ynfante** has nearly as many surprisingly placed Y's (two) as he had home runs in 2019 (three). He has the speed to play center field in the majors, but probably not the bat.

Pitchers

PITCHER	TEAM	LVL	AGE	W	L	SV	G	GS	IP	H	HR	BB/9	K/9	K	GB%	BABIP	WHIP	ERA	DRA	WARP	MPH	FB%	WHF	CSP
Tony Cingrani	OKL	AAA	29	1	0	0	7	0	6¹	5	0	5.7	7.1	5	62%	.312	1.42	2.84	4.34	0.1				
Austin Gomber	MEM	AAA	25	4	0	0	8	8	45¹	42	5	3.2	10.3	52	43%	.330	1.28	2.98	2.78	1.7				
Dominic Leone	MEM	AAA	27	1	0	0	23	0	31²	20	3	4.0	11.9	42	34%	.235	1.07	2.84	2.24	1.2				
	SLN	MLB	27	1	0	1	40	0	40²	39	9	4.9	10.2	46	39%	.291	1.50	5.53	5.69	-0.1	95.8	84	14.8	40
Tony Locey	PEO	A	20	1	2	0	10	0	15	15	1	6.0	16.8	28	37%	.483	1.67	6.00	5.21	-0.1				
Johan Oviedo	PMB	A+	21	5	0	0	6	5	33²	29	1	3.2	9.4	35	48%	.308	1.22	1.60	4.23	0.3				
	SFD	AA	21	7	8	0	23	23	113	120	9	5.1	10.2	128	44%	.366	1.63	5.65	6.32	-1.9				
Daniel Ponce de Leon	MEM	AAA	27	8	4	0	16	16	84¹	62	7	4.6	9.2	86	37%	.255	1.25	2.88	2.48	3.4				
	SLN	MLB	27	1	2	0	13	8	48²	36	6	4.8	9.6	52	46%	.256	1.27	3.70	3.54	1.1	95.6	70.6	13.1	45.1
Zac Rosscup	TOR	MLB	31	0	0	0	2	0	1	3	0	18.0	18.0	2	100%	.750	5.00	27.00	0.00	0.1	94.1	41	12.8	32.6
	SEA	MLB	31	2	0	0	19	0	14	13	1	9.0	12.9	20	54%	.353	1.93	3.21	3.47	0.3	94.5	38.4	17.5	36.8
	LAN	MLB	31	0	0	0	7	0	3	6	1	9.0	12.0	4	60%	.556	3.00	6.00	10.41	-0.2	93.5	45.7	18.6	27.5
Alvaro Seijas	PEO	A	20	4	5	0	14	14	80	73	6	3.2	8.0	71	46%	.300	1.26	2.92	5.67	-0.5				
	PMB	A+	20	4	1	0	10	10	54¹	54	2	4.3	7.1	43	48%	.313	1.47	2.65	5.98	-0.6				
Tyler Webb	MEM	AAA	28	0	1	0	5	0	6²	7	0	2.7	6.8	5	45%	.350	1.35	2.70	4.31	0.1				
	SLN	MLB	28	2	1	1	65	0	55	33	7	3.8	7.9	48	43%	.184	1.02	3.76	3.99	0.8	91.5	65.3	11	48.9
Kodi Whitley	SFD	AA	24	1	4	7	31	0	39¹	31	3	3.0	10.5	46	43%	.275	1.12	1.83	2.80	0.9				
	MEM	AAA	24	2	0	2	16	0	23²	21	0	1.5	10.3	27	28%	.323	1.06	1.52	2.21	0.9				
Jake Woodford	MEM	AAA	22	9	8	0	26	26	151²	124	22	4.5	7.8	131	37%	.242	1.31	4.15	3.38	4.9				

Brett Cecil didn't pitch in 2019. Given how his 2018 went, some Cardinals fans probably hope he won't pitch for the team in 2020, either. ⑂ **Tony Cingrani** didn't pitch in 2019 due to arthroscopic surgery on his throwing shoulder, but that didn't stop the Cardinals from acquiring him as financial ballast in July's Jedd Gyorko trade. If healthy, Cingrani should have no trouble overcoming the new three-batter minimum. ⑂ **Steven Gingery** has a killer changeup—or, he did before he missed the second half of 2018 and most of 2019 rehabbing from Tommy John surgery. This season will mark his first real opportunity to pitch as a professional. ⑂ Biceps and shoulder injuries led to a lost 2019 for **Austin Gomber**, whose combination of okay stuff and excellent command combine to create number three starter upside and journeyman downside. He'll have a place at the end of some roster as long as his health holds up, which is far from a given after this year. ⑂ **Dominic Leone** better hope he has a modified Saberhagen thing going on. He was excellent in '17, bad in '18, and ugly in '19. Maybe he's just a 33 percent shooter? ⑂ **Tony Locey** was a starter at Georgia, but the Cardinals took one look at his stuff (plus curveball, plus fastball) and his command (minus) and plugged him into the bullpen. He missed a ton of bats in limited action in 2019, and will likely rise quickly through the system, as college-age relief arms are wont to do. ⑂ **Johan Oviedo** boasts a mid-90s fastball and absolutely no idea where the ball is going. Tall pitchers often develop late, and he's posted good strikeout numbers even with command issues, but he's nothing more than a bullpen lottery ticket until he can control his delivery better. ⑂ **Daniel Ponce de Leon** would be more interesting if he could find the Fountain of Youth and reduce his age by a handful of years. Instead, he's entering his age-28 season and is probably a bad 20 innings away from falling down the waiver-wire well. ⑂ Just as his first name is missing a letter, **Zac Rosscup** has always had the ability to miss bats. Unfortunately, he also has trouble with missing the strike zone, which is why he played for three teams this year. ⑂ A surprising add to the 40-man roster in advance of the Rule 5 Draft, **Alvaro Seijas** took a step forward in harnessing his fastball that can run up to the mid-90s and his curveball that remains his best out pitch. ⑂ Southpaw **Tyler Webb** doesn't throw hard, impart good spin, or challenge the convention of what makes for a memorable name. He doesn't have job security weighing in his favor, either, since he's a quality LOOGY at a time when one-out appearances are newly outlawed. At least he'll always have 2019? ⑂ **Kodi Whitley** added velocity and spin to his fastball on his way to a dominant season across two levels of the minors. He struck out 28.3 percent of the batters he faced, and tweeted for the first time in nearly a year to thank his minor-league team for the happy birthday wishes. Both tidbits should endear him to Cardinals fans. ⑂ **Jake Woodford** generated a truckload of weak contact on his way to a solid season in the PCL. His stuff screams Edsel, but his command and age give him a chance of getting a test drive in the majors.

TAMPA BAY RAYS

Essay by Adam Sobsey

Player comments by Tommy Rancel and BP staff

"7*9. I reviewed the conventional means of attaining the castle."*

If you were trying to describe the indescribable Rays in a sentence, you might come close with this: They're the Astros without money. Brainiac front office. Indifference to the bad optics of bad characters. (Maybe not the Astros' sign-stealing techniques.) Cy Young Award winners—each team has had two over the past eight seasons. During last year's offseason, Tampa Bay signed Houston's fourth starter, Charlie Morton, to a free-agent deal that made him the Rays' costliest player for about half of what the Astros paid Justin Verlander. Verlander won the 2019 Cy Young Award; Morton finished third. The reader knows quite well how the ALDS turned out, of course.

In 2019, Tampa Bay had no four-win position players (the Astros had two) and only two top-100 BWARP finishers (the Astros had seven). They had the best pitching in baseball even though their two stellar young starters, including 2018 Cy Young winner Blake Snell, spent much of the year injured and ineffective; they improved the staff at midseason by trading their favorite "opener," former first-round pick Ryne Stanek, for a reliever no one ever heard of, Nick Anderson, who did not rate even a Lineout comment in last year's *Annual*—and who was nearly unhittable as a Ray.

Off the field, Tampa Bay's front office proposed playing half their "home" games in Montreal, an eccentric idea quite in line with their unusual ways on it. The Rays break baseball into parts, seeking more than the sum—they led the league in relief innings pitched, unsurprisingly—and they operate from bases on opposite sides of boundaries. They aspire to the highest goal in sports, winning, with their sport's lowest payroll. They suffer from brutally poor attendance and are always trying to run away from home (they had MLB's second-best road record in 2019), yet over the years have built one of the game's strongest organizational cultures, not around a place or players or people but around a way of thinking. The departure to Boston of Chaim Bloom, the Rays' Senior Vice President of Baseball Operations (who cut his sabermetric teeth as a Baseball Prospectus author in the early 2000s), will probably change very little in practice, as Andrew Friedman's to Los Angeles didn't in 2014.

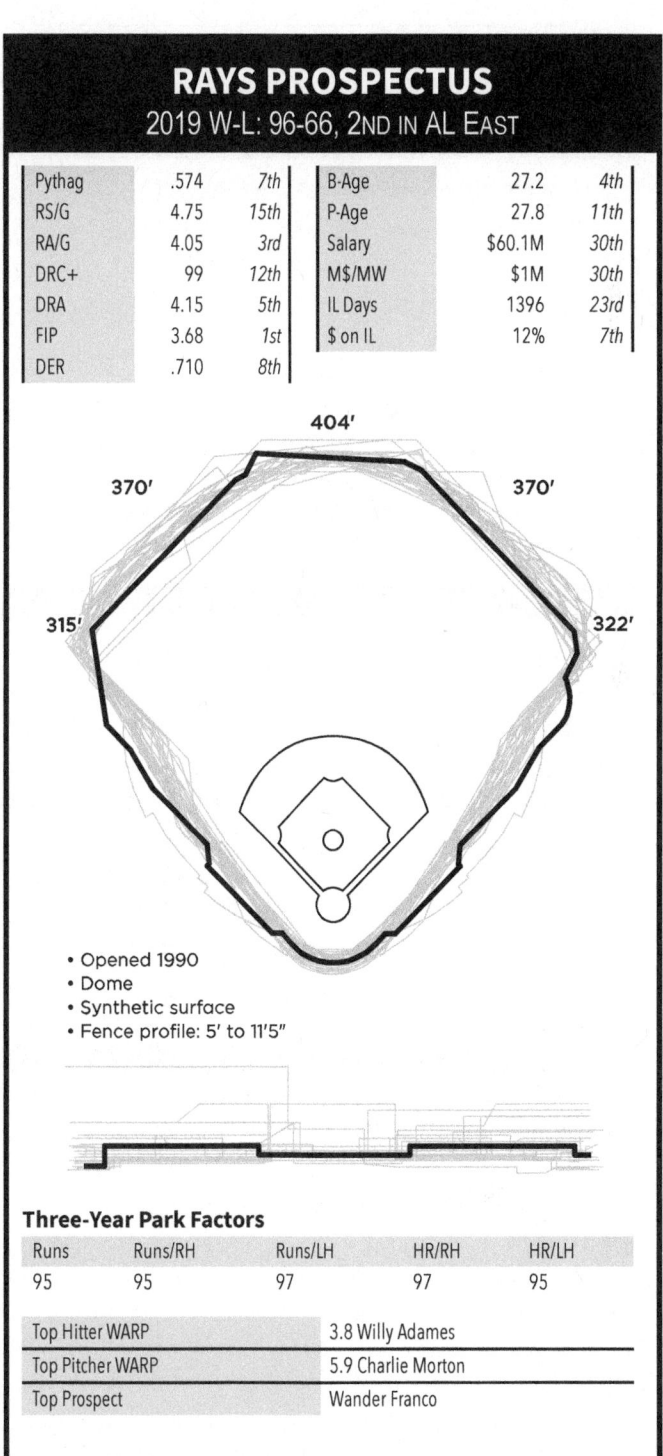

RAYS PROSPECTUS
2019 W-L: 96-66, 2ND IN AL EAST

Pythag	.574	7th	B-Age	27.2	4th
RS/G	4.75	15th	P-Age	27.8	11th
RA/G	4.05	3rd	Salary	$60.1M	30th
DRC+	99	12th	M$/MW	$1M	30th
DRA	4.15	5th	IL Days	1396	23rd
FIP	3.68	1st	$ on IL	12%	7th
DER	.710	8th			

404'

370'   370'

315'   322'

- Opened 1990
- Dome
- Synthetic surface
- Fence profile: 5' to 11'5"

Three-Year Park Factors

Runs	Runs/RH	Runs/LH	HR/RH	HR/LH
95	95	97	97	95

Top Hitter WARP	3.8 Willy Adames
Top Pitcher WARP	5.9 Charlie Morton
Top Prospect	Wander Franco

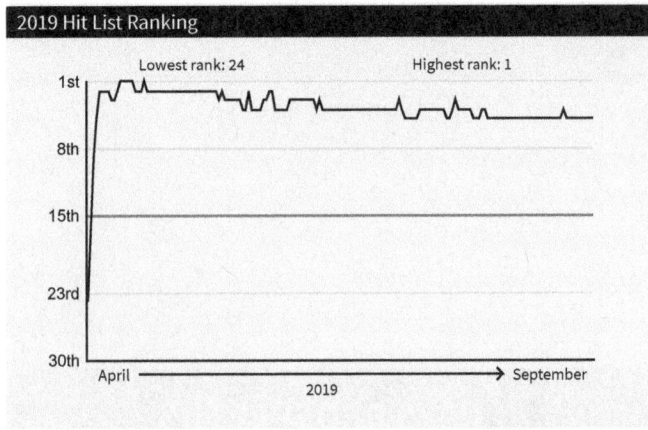

2019 Hit List Ranking

Lowest rank: 24   Highest rank: 1

April ———→ September

2019

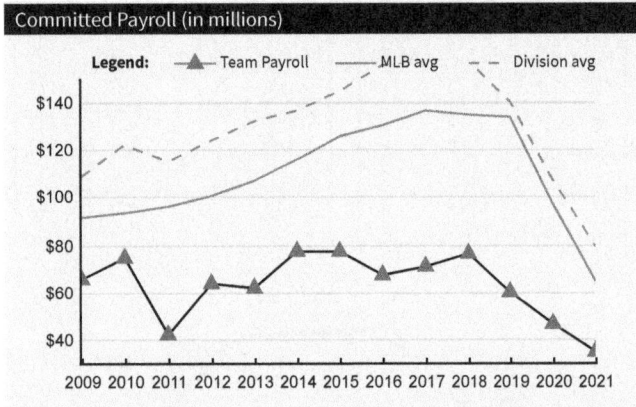

Committed Payroll (in millions)

Legend: ▲ Team Payroll — MLB avg -- Division avg

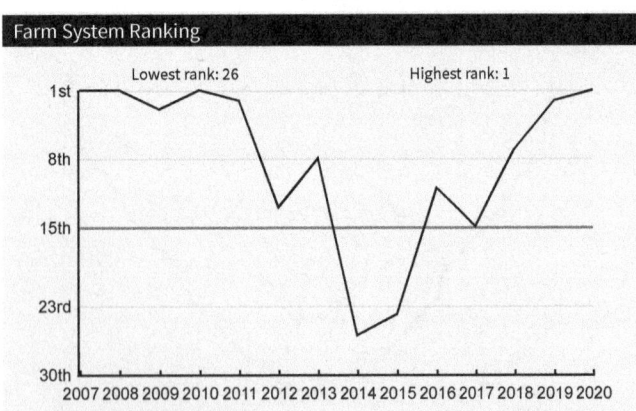

Farm System Ranking

Lowest rank: 26   Highest rank: 1

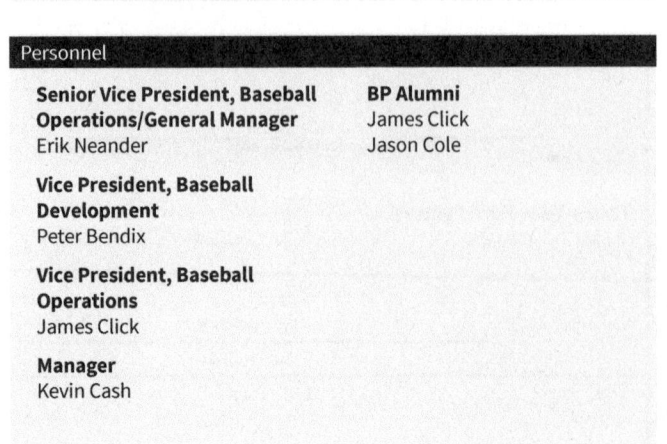

Personnel

Senior Vice President, Baseball Operations/General Manager
Erik Neander

Vice President, Baseball Development
Peter Bendix

Vice President, Baseball Operations
James Click

Manager
Kevin Cash

BP Alumni
James Click
Jason Cole

Yet that practice is remarkably adaptable. The franchise once known for homegrown talent has turned its approach inside out: by last season's end, nearly 70 percent of the roster originally came from outside the organization, a major-league high. Meanwhile, their 2013 fourth-round draftee, Kean Wong, was left to sandbag three full seasons and nearly 1,500 plate appearances in Triple-A, where he was an All-Star; he was finally called up in September 2019, got 14 big-league plate appearances, and was abruptly waived and claimed by another team. The Rays included Jesús Sánchez, the 32nd-best prospect in all of baseball, in the trade that brought Anderson from the Marlins. Just as Major League Baseball's franchises are now richer than ever, so too is its talent supply. (These are interdependent abundances.) There are more excellent players than any team can roster. The Rays know this, glean the field and thrive.

But how foolish it would be to continue on this way, writing conventionally about baseball's most unconventional franchise, applying practical craft to the work of prodigious theoreticians, and thinking organically where synthetics and bricolage obtain. Instead, the rest of this essay proceeds by compiling sentences from essays in last year's *Annual*, in adherence to the Rays' methods of breaking the game into parts and reappropriating other teams' assets. The assemblage includes at least one sentence from all but two of the essays in the 2019 Annual. Omitted are the essays about the Rays themselves, of course, and about Seattle because the Mariners are lately Tampa Bay's favorite trade partner and have been liberally acquired from already. The endnotes give authorship citations, along with other annotations where appropriate. Some sentences are fragments, breaking the game into parts. There are several ellipses, in the Rays' spirit of economy. Other sentences are taken out of context and placed in new ones in order to extract additional value; still others explore larger issues in the game and its business which the Rays' peculiar situation and approach exemplify or contradict, distort and critique. It is nearly impossible to consider the state of baseball without considering the Rays. Had they won the World Series, they'd have cleaved the very diamond as we've known it and forced front offices and fans to reexamine every facet.

Each sentence or string of sentences is given its own numbered paragraph. For background on this choice, the reader is referred to Donald Barthelme's short story, "The Glass Mountain," which provides the essay's epigraph.

⚾   ⚾   ⚾

1. How this team looks at any moment depends entirely on the light.[1]

2. The players are somewhere between incidental and academic. Mostly, of course, they are fungible.[2]

3. A sign that they had somehow transcended the usual pratfalls of modern baseball free agency signings.[3]

4. For a few weeks at the beginning of the season, they were a manifestation of the wildest dreams any baseball fan could have coming true.[4]

5. It's good to get to the party early in baseball.[5]

6. To leave the party early [...] in baseball, is far worse than arriving at the party too early.[6]

7. It's something of a cliché among wised-up sports fans that the worst place for a team to be is in the middle.[7]

8. The middle ground [...] is now considered baseball's Siberia.[8]

9. Winning without *really* winning.[9]

10. They became another team struggling with injury.[10,11]

11. No baseball team can fully protect itself against uncertainty.[12]

12. Trea Turner is just 25.[13,14]

13. In baseball, change is as inevitable as failure.[15]

14. In baseball, winning requires talent and strategy, but timing and luck cannot be discounted.[16]

15. (No one gets by without a little bit of luck in baseball).[17]

16. The best opportunity for certainty in baseball doesn't lie in a team's roster. It lies in a team's division.[18]

17. A team that looks fated to be stuck behind the same two teams in the division for the foreseeable future.[19]

18. In a world where sabermetric teams are always supposed to live for the future.[20]

19. The contention that had caught everyone by pleasant surprise.[21]

20. "Right up until it didn't work, it was great," Forst said.[22]

21. Maybe the 2015 Kansas City Royals are within dreaming distance.[23]

22. Baseball has experienced an influx of knowledge over the past 15 years.[24]

23. The waterfall of information pouring into every front office changes everything.[25]

24. It's no secret front offices, specifically analytical staffs, are more involved in the day-to-day operations than ever before.[26]

25. Some are hoping to improve without spending any money on improvements.[27]

26. You've all read *Moneyball*, right?[28]

27. We all read *Moneyball*, right?[29]

28. Did the "Moneyball" crew figure out some new market inefficiency?[30]

29. The A's took a page from Tampa Bay's handbook and started using an "opener."[31,32]

30. Lest we forget, what made Moneyball compelling as a sports narrative isn't that it's possible to build a cheaper, more efficient baseball team. What was compelling was seeing the possibility of winning from an apparent losing position through intelligence and cunning, and through finding what nobody else even thought to look for.[33]

31. In the past three years, the league's spending and competitive landscape has changed noticeably. The 2016 labor negotiations produced a joint bargaining agreement that, by nearly universal consensus, shifted power toward ownership. In the years since, teams have treated the luxury tax as a firm salary cap. Alongside, they have rushed to cut costs.[34]

32. Every owner ins baseball now has become an industrial strength scoundrel and acts as if the soft salary cap is a hard one.[35]

33. Because the owners have beaten the players as consistently in the court of public opinion as at the bargaining table, the partitions that separate business decisions from baseball decisions have all but disappeared. Teams have no problem whatsoever selling cynical financial choices to their fan bases as on-field choices merely focused on long-term competitiveness and analytics.[36]

34. Too many fans are willing to go along with it without any critical thinking.[37]

35. Contemporary baseball decision-makers have lured fans into the mindset that fuels amusement parks.[38]

36. There's usually an alternate source of entertainment.[39]

37. For [...] anyone who enjoys the game on the field more than the behind-the-scenes details of its production, they might be something of a bummer.[40]

38. The MLBPA has already started coming after clubs for failing to use their revenue-sharing checks for competitive purposes, namely the Rays, Marlins and Pirates. The Reds have only recently seen their payrolls reach similar lows

to those culprits, and they don't have the history of cynical behavior the Rays and Marlins have exhibited.[41]

39. Incentivized cynicism.[42]

40. It's the media culture that perpetrates it.[43]

41. Cynicism at the top [...] shows up with unpredictable toxicity downstream.[44]

42. The chronic and usually well-compensated cynics.[45]

43. Welcome to Econ 101, with Professor Friedman.[46]

44. Welcome to MLB, a magical world where failure is success.[47]

45. Whether the counterintuitive process will be talked about as a major breakthrough within the game 15 years from now.[48]

46. In late 2012, MLB rounded out its national television rights package for a total of $4.2 billion through 2021, an average annual per-team payout of more than $40 million [...] In early 2018, every MLB team received a one-time payment of $50 million for the share of the stake in MLBAM that the league sold to Disney. In November 2018, Fox extended its national television rights deal with MLB for $5.1 billion through 2028, locking in a rate hike of more than 20 percent.[49,50]

47. A staggering amount of that value is entirely independent of the product the Reds put on the field.[51]

48. Oh, wait, and you have to play baseball?[52]

49. Many other streams of revenue therefore negating the loyalty completely.[53]

50. The watchwords of the modern MLB team are "financial flexibility."[54]

51. They've achieved financial flexibility.[55]

52. Financial flexibility is only valuable insofar as it's used to stretch for anything.[56]

53. Having key cogs making deflated pre-free agency salaries, including several near the league minimum, goes a long way in keeping a team's payroll below the competitive balance threshold.[57]

54. A clear victory for the model of efficiency that now has even competitive teams selling off mid-career stars.[58]

55. Major-league salaries exchanged for minor-league talent.[59]

56. The cost-cutting, the empty stadiums, the focus on acquiring those sweet bargain-value prospects even absent a cohesive plan to turn them into major-league ballplayers. It's all here and it's all frustrating.[60]

57. A system where talent is passively distributed [...] is the ideal system for baseball owners—especially the small-market cohort.[61]

58. The shame is that it shouldn't have to be.[62]

59. It's happening all over the league. But baseball fandom is provincial, so it's being felt only as it happens to each team, one by one.[63]

60. It's a situation we'll see many more times in many more cities before the trend stops.[64]

61. An endlessly repeating cycle that can seemingly never be broken.[65]

62. It's the economics of certainty.[66]

63. Baseball especially encourages its participants towards steadiness.[67]

64. To turn fleeting success into something lasting.[68]

65. We perhaps even began to take them a bit for granted.[69]

66. Pure joy should permeate what is, at its core, still a simple game.[70]

67. Does any of this matter?[71]

68. The question of baseball's purpose. It's far too messy and existential to unpack with any real satisfaction.[72]

69. The question now is: where are the fans going to come from?[73,74]

70. You can't just slap a new roof on a dingy, dilapidated dome and call it good.[75]

-Adam Sobsey is an author of Baseball Prospectus.

---

1. Jesse Spector, "Colorado Rockies."

2. David Roth, "Pittsburgh Pirates."

3. Russell Carleton, "St. Louis Cardinals."

4. Rachael McDaniel, "Los Angeles Angels of Anaheim."

5. Craig Calcaterra, "Atlanta Braves."

6. Ibid.

7. Roth.

8. Craig Brown, "Kansas City Royals."

9. Zach Crizer, "Detroit Tigers."

10. McDaniel.

11. The Rays lost the tenth most injury days in the majors, and the second most among playoff teams behind the Yankees, who set the all-time record.

12. Emma Baccellieri, "Cleveland Indians."

13. Meg Rowley, "Washington Nationals."

14. In December 2014, the Rays traded Wil Myers to the San Diego Padres in a multiplayer deal. One of the players they received was Trea Turner, whom they immediately flipped to Washington for Steven Souza, Jr., fulfilling a prior agreement. Souza played three seasons for the Rays. He was the team MVP in 2017, after which he was traded to Arizona. He missed most of 2018 and all of 2019 with injuries. By the time Turner turns 27 at the end of June, barring injury he will have played more games at shortstop for Washington than any player has for Tampa Bay in the history of the franchise.

15. Justin Klugh, "Philadelphia Phillies."

16. Nick Offerman, "Chicago Cubs."

17. Carleton, "Milwaukee Brewers."

18. Baccellieri.

19. Whitney McIntosh, "Toronto Blue Jays."

20. Carleton, "Milwaukee Brewers."

21. Klugh.

22. Susan Slusser, "Oakland Athletics."

23. Eric Nusbaum, "San Diego Padres."

24. Chris Cwik, "Texas Rangers."

25. Grant Brisbee, "San Francisco Giants."

26. Mike Axisa, "New York Yankees."

27. Roth.

28. Carleton, "Milwaukee Brewers."

29. Axisa.

30. Slusser.

31. Ibid.

32. Before the 2019 season, the Rays traded for Oakland castoff Emilio Pagán, who became Tampa Bay's most valuable reliever and de facto closer.

33. Jack Moore, "Cincinnati Reds."

34. Brendan Gawlowski, "Chicago White Sox."

35. Roger Cormier, "New York Mets."

36. Matthew Trueblood, "Arizona Diamondbacks."

37. Chad Finn, "Boston Red Sox."

38. Crizer.

39. McIntosh.

40. Trueblood.

41. Moore.

42. Robert O'Connell, "Houston Astros."

43. Finn.

44. Roth.

45. Finn.

46. Eric Stephen, "Los Angeles Dodgers."

47. Moore.

48. Cwik.

49. Trueblood.

50. In 2019, the Rays and Fox Sports regional network Sun Sports reportedly reached an agreement on a 15-year broadcasting rights extension worth $1.23 billion, or $82 million per season.

51. Moore.

52. Cwik.

53. McIntosh.

54. Jonathan Bernhardt, "Baltimore Orioles."

55. Baccellieri.

56. Ibid.

57. Stephen.

58. O'Connell.

59. Baccellieri.

60. Gawlowski.

61. Moore.

62. Spector.

63. Trueblood.

64. McIntosh.

65. Michael Clair, "Miami Marlins."

66. Brown.

67. O'Connell.

68. Ibid.

69. Offerman.

70. McIntosh.

71. Cormier.

72. Baccellieri.

73. Clair.

74. The Rays had the second-lowest attendance in the major leagues in 2019. They have finished last or second-to-last in every season since 2011, when they drew 18,879 fans per game. In 2019, they drew 14,552 fans per game.

75. Nick Nelson, "Minnesota Twins."

HITTERS

Willy Adames SS   Born: 09/02/95   Age: 24   Bats: R   Throws: R   Height: 6'0"   Weight: 205   Origin: International Free Agent, 2015

YEAR	TEAM	LVL	AGE	PA	R	2B	3B	HR	RBI	BB	K	SB	CS	AVG/OBP/SLG	DRC+	VORP	BABIP	BRR	FRAA	WARP
2017	DUR	AAA	21	578	74	30	5	10	62	65	132	11	5	.277/.360/.415	123	34.5	.354	1.1	SS(117): 0.1, 2B(11): 0.5	3.9
2018	DUR	AAA	22	278	36	9	5	4	34	27	66	3	3	.286/.353/.412	110	15.0	.367	1.5	SS(62): 2.4	1.9
2018	TBA	MLB	22	323	43	7	0	10	34	31	95	6	5	.278/.348/.406	100	15.7	.378	2.3	SS(75): -6.7, 2B(10): 1.7	1.2
2019	TBA	MLB	23	584	69	25	1	20	52	46	153	4	2	.254/.317/.418	94	23.4	.320	2.9	SS(152): 12.2	3.8
2020	TBA	MLB	24	595	64	24	3	18	69	54	160	7	3	.242/.314/.400	90	17.5	.311	3.0	SS 5	2.3

Comparables: Milt Bolling, Jonathan Villar, Anthony Gose

If you are looking for an under-the-radar breakout candidate for the 2020 season, Adames is your guy. The sophomore struggled at the plate in the first half of the year, but after the All-Star Break he looked like a star in the making; his .278/.340/.467 line put him on par with players like Gleyber Torres and Amed Rosario down the stretch. Meanwhile, in the field, Adames had the highest FRAA among shortstops in 2019—a big step forward built on his range and an arm built for the left side. Still, at times those abilities get in his way. Of his 17 errors in 2019, 12 were on throws. Because he can get to balls most others may not, he tries to make every play even when the smart play is none at all. He's still rough around the edges, but Adames has all the makings of a dynamic two-way player that should hold down the six for the first half of the next decade.

Michael Brosseau   INF   Born: 03/15/94   Age: 26   Bats: R   Throws: R   Height: 5'10"   Weight: 215   Origin: Undrafted Free Agent, 2016

YEAR	TEAM	LVL	AGE	PA	R	2B	3B	HR	RBI	BB	K	SB	CS	AVG/OBP/SLG	DRC+	VORP	BABIP	BRR	FRAA	WARP
2017	BGR	A	23	344	50	21	2	6	32	26	48	5	7	.318/.393/.460	145	29.3	.361	2.6	3B(31): 4.8, 2B(30): 0.0	3.4
2017	PCH	A+	23	80	13	3	0	1	10	5	15	4	3	.333/.425/.420	157	5.2	.415	-2.2	3B(7): -0.3, 1B(3): 0.3	0.3
2018	MNT	AA	24	417	53	24	3	13	61	29	74	11	4	.262/.327/.449	116	31.8	.290	1.4	3B(64): 3.7, 2B(16): 0.0	2.5
2019	DUR	AAA	25	315	53	21	1	16	60	34	58	2	3	.304/.394/.567	135	24.8	.332	0.9	3B(32): -1.3, 1B(17): -1.1	2.0
2019	TBA	MLB	25	142	17	7	0	6	16	7	39	1	0	.273/.319/.462	93	3.7	.345	1.0	2B(26): -0.5, 3B(18): -0.6	0.3
2020	TBA	MLB	26	35	4	2	0	1	4	2	9	0	0	.243/.311/.425	96	0.6	.293	-0.1	3B 0	0.1

Comparables: Tyler White, Rougned Odor, Adam Engel

Undrafted out of the Oakland University in Rochester—not *that* Oakland or *that* Rochester either—Brosseau defied the odds and made his major-league debut in 2019. Despite the lack of draft status, the right-handed hitter has been productive at every level of the system and was able to contribute in the bigs as well. Brosseau packs solid pop for a player his size and demonstrated that he could carry that power over from Triple-A without missing a beat. Defensively, he offers flexibility with experience at all three bases and has played on the grass as well. His typical platoon splits—hitting .300/.329/.500 with four homers in 70 at-bats against southpaws—make him well-suited to be the short side of a platoon where he could spell Brandon Lowe or another left-handed hitting infielder.

------------- ★ ★ ★ *2020 Top 101 Prospect* **#73** ★ ★ ★ -------------

Vidal Brujan   2B   Born: 02/09/98   Age: 22   Bats: B   Throws: R   Height: 5'9"   Weight: 155   Origin: International Free Agent, 2014

YEAR	TEAM	LVL	AGE	PA	R	2B	3B	HR	RBI	BB	K	SB	CS	AVG/OBP/SLG	DRC+	VORP	BABIP	BRR	FRAA	WARP
2017	HUD	A-	19	302	51	15	5	3	20	34	36	16	8	.285/.378/.415	155	20.4	.321	-3.7	2B(65): 14.9	3.4
2018	BGR	A	20	434	86	18	5	5	41	48	53	43	15	.313/.395/.427	144	41.0	.351	8.2	2B(88): 4.4	4.6
2018	PCH	A+	20	114	26	7	2	4	12	15	15	12	4	.347/.434/.582	172	13.8	.380	1.0	2B(24): 4.5	1.7
2019	PCH	A+	21	196	28	8	3	1	15	17	26	24	5	.290/.357/.386	131	18.2	.333	5.5	2B(29): 0.7, SS(14): 0.7	2.0
2019	MNT	AA	21	233	28	9	4	3	25	20	35	24	8	.266/.336/.391	95	4.8	.304	-2.6	2B(33): 2.7, SS(14): -0.1	0.6
2020	TBA	MLB	22	35	3	2	0	1	3	3	6	1	1	.242/.305/.358	80	0.5	.284	0.0	2B 1	0.1

Comparables: Luis Valbuena, Corban Joseph, Thairo Estrada

In a system full of second-base prospects, Brujan stands out for multiple reasons. A switch-hitter signed for less than a waiver claim in 2014, he has easy plus speed and a plus hit tool that makes him an ideal candidate to top a lineup for a decade. His contact and plate discipline skills border on elite, and for his minor-league career he's struck out only 10 more times than he's walked. Brujan ended the 2019 season in Double-A and after a strong Arizona Fall League stint will be knocking on the door of the majors in 2020. The biggest question for the 22-year-old is where he'll end up defensively. He mostly mans the keystone not because of a lack of skill that would move him off short, but due to Willy Adames being ahead of him on the depth chart and Wander Franco peeking over his shoulder.

Ji-Man Choi   1B   Born: 05/19/91   Age: 29   Bats: L   Throws: R   Height: 6'1"   Weight: 250   Origin: International Free Agent, 2009

YEAR	TEAM	LVL	AGE	PA	R	2B	3B	HR	RBI	BB	K	SB	CS	AVG/OBP/SLG	DRC+	VORP	BABIP	BRR	FRAA	WARP
2017	SWB	AAA	26	338	42	25	1	15	69	39	86	3	1	.288/.373/.538	142	22.3	.351	1.7	1B(57): 4.3	2.4
2017	NYA	MLB	26	18	2	1	0	2	5	2	5	0	0	.267/.333/.733	100	1.2	.222	-0.3	1B(6): 0.2	0.0
2018	CSP	AAA	27	163	17	9	0	5	23	32	31	1	0	.302/.436/.488	139	12.3	.358	0.2	1B(38): -2.0, LF(1): 0.1	0.8
2018	DUR	AAA	27	86	9	4	0	2	14	11	18	0	0	.270/.360/.405	121	2.9	.327	-0.9	1B(18): 0.2, LF(2): 0.0	0.2
2018	MIL	MLB	27	32	4	2	0	2	5	2	14	0	0	.233/.281/.500	103	0.6	.357	0.3	1B(2): 0.0, LF(1): 0.0	0.1
2018	TBA	MLB	27	189	21	12	1	8	27	24	41	2	0	.269/.370/.506	110	12.6	.310	1.9	1B(1): 0.0	0.7
2019	TBA	MLB	28	487	54	20	2	19	63	64	108	2	3	.261/.363/.459	117	18.5	.303	-2.6	1B(103): -4.4	1.1
2020	TBA	MLB	29	525	66	25	1	22	70	66	125	5	2	.247/.348/.450	115	18.5	.295	-0.3	1B 0	1.9

Comparables: Bob Hamelin, Anthony Rizzo, Justin Smoak

They got options on my contract. I think they're sending me down. I can't believe this is happening in my own town. If I had wings I would fly, let me contemplate. I glanced in the box and I see my homie Nate (Lowe).

Now Nate got some pop and that's a known fact. We can both hit jacks 'bove the warning track. Back-to-back bombs cause it's on. N-A-T-E and me, the Choi-Man to the Ji.

Yandy Díaz 3B Born: 08/08/91 Age: 28 Bats: R Throws: R Height: 6'2" Weight: 215 Origin: International Free Agent, 2013

YEAR	TEAM	LVL	AGE	PA	R	2B	3B	HR	RBI	BB	K	SB	CS	AVG/OBP/SLG	DRC+	VORP	BABIP	BRR	FRAA	WARP
2017	COH	AAA	25	374	56	17	1	5	33	60	56	1	2	.350/.454/.460	181	34.1	.412	1.1	3B(42): -3.4, LF(21): 0.7	3.9
2017	CLE	MLB	25	179	25	8	1	0	13	21	35	2	0	.263/.352/.327	83	2.0	.336	-0.4	3B(40): -0.9, LF(3): -0.2	0.1
2018	COH	AAA	26	426	53	24	0	3	40	70	75	2	3	.293/.409/.388	150	26.0	.360	-2.6	3B(73): -9.6, 1B(12): 0.2	2.1
2018	CLE	MLB	26	120	15	5	2	1	15	11	19	0	0	.312/.375/.422	102	0.9	.371	-2.0	1B(9): 0.2, 3B(9): 0.2	0.1
2019	TBA	MLB	27	347	53	20	1	14	38	35	61	2	2	.267/.340/.476	108	13.6	.288	-0.5	3B(50): -0.9, 1B(22): -0.1	1.2
2020	TBA	MLB	28	420	46	21	2	10	46	48	80	2	1	.259/.346/.408	103	9.6	.305	-1.3	3B -3, 1B 0	0.7

Comparables: Ed Sprague, Trevor Crowe, Rob Refsnyder

EXIT VELOCITY. LAUNCH ANGLE. OK BOOMER. Díaz was the go-to guy for various buzz words in 2019. Although he looked very much like a slugger with bulging biceps and had good exit velocity, Díaz entered 2019 with one career home run in 299 plate appearances. The narrative that would follow is the Rays sprinkled their magic launch-angle dust on Díaz's hulking arms and the home runs came. Well, they did. The corner infielder slugged .476, a mark higher than any of his previous stateside assignments. That said, his launch angle only increased by a little over a degree. It turns out that Díaz simply just hit the ball with the barrel of the bat more often. Who knew that would work just as well?

Matt Duffy 3B Born: 01/15/91 Age: 29 Bats: R Throws: R Height: 6'2" Weight: 190 Origin: Round 18, 2012 Draft (#568 overall)

YEAR	TEAM	LVL	AGE	PA	R	2B	3B	HR	RBI	BB	K	SB	CS	AVG/OBP/SLG	DRC+	VORP	BABIP	BRR	FRAA	WARP
2018	TBA	MLB	27	560	59	22	1	4	44	47	93	12	6	.294/.361/.366	104	16.4	.353	-3.9	3B(125): 11.8, SS(1): 0.0	3.1
2019	DUR	AAA	28	36	4	1	0	1	9	1	5	0	0	.273/.306/.394	90	1.7	.286	0.4	3B(5): -0.5, LF(2): -0.1	0.1
2019	TBA	MLB	28	169	12	8	0	1	12	19	29	0	1	.252/.343/.327	88	3.9	.305	-0.3	3B(46): -1.7, SS(1): -0.1	0.2
2020	TBA	MLB	29	251	25	11	1	5	25	20	46	5	2	.258/.325/.376	89	3.6	.305	-0.8	3B 3, SS 0	0.7

Comparables: Chris Chambliss, Greg Colbrunn, Terrence Long

Ben Stein's voice personified, Duffy may be the league's least exciting man. He's a pretty good hitter with very little power. He is harmless defender and that is meant in the best way possible. The Rays have primarily played him at third, but he could also play at second, short in a pinch or a corner outfield spot if needed. It is a two-win package, but the problem lies in keeping him on the field long enough to accumulate such production. He has appeared in fewer than 200 games in three and a half seasons with Tampa Bay and did not make his 2019 debut until after the All-Star Break due to back and hamstring maladies. The Rays don't like paying healthy players money, so they really must have hated sending the ACH file with Duffy's direct deposit during his second year of arbitration; and in November they guaranteed they wouldn't have to for a third. If you like watching paint dry or water drip slowly from a faucet, Duff is your man.

───────── ★ ★ ★ *2020 Top 101 Prospect* **#95** ★ ★ ★ ─────────

Xavier Edwards SS Born: 08/09/99 Age: 20 Bats: B Throws: R Height: 5'10" Weight: 175 Origin: Round 1, 2018 Draft (#38 overall)

YEAR	TEAM	LVL	AGE	PA	R	2B	3B	HR	RBI	BB	K	SB	CS	AVG/OBP/SLG	DRC+	VORP	BABIP	BRR	FRAA	WARP
2018	PDR	RK	18	88	19	4	1	0	11	13	10	12	1	.384/.471/.466	187	13.5	.438	1.9	SS(15): 3.1	1.5
2018	TRI	A-	18	107	21	4	0	0	5	18	15	10	0	.314/.438/.360	181	9.9	.380	-0.3	SS(19): -1.1, 2B(5): 0.0	1.1
2019	FTW	A	19	344	44	13	4	1	30	30	35	20	9	.336/.392/.414	141	24.6	.371	0.2	2B(51): 4.1, SS(21): 3.1	3.4
2019	LEL	A+	19	217	32	5	4	0	13	14	19	14	2	.301/.349/.367	102	15.3	.331	3.5	2B(35): 0.2, SS(9): -1.2	0.9
2020	TBA	MLB	20	251	24	11	1	2	22	21	38	10	2	.278/.341/.367	92	6.1	.325	0.6	2B 2, SS 0	0.8

Comparables: José Ramírez, J.P. Crawford, Victor Robles

His full season debut couldn't have gone much better. Edwards flashed the speed and contact skills of an old-school switch-hitting table-setter and enough athleticism and arm strength to augur a future at shortstop that is more than a pipedream, with second base and center field listed as his safety schools. Edwards rarely swings and misses, sprays the ball to all fields and uses his wheels to beat out slow rollers and turn doubles into triples. His frame and swing aren't built for power, but Edwards isn't a slap-hitter. Instead, he plays within himself and doesn't sell out, focusing on putting the ball in play, reaching base and being an all-around pest once he gets there. Given his ability to avoid outs, produce runs with his legs and provide solid glovework at a premium defensive position, it's easy to dream on Edwards growing into the X-factor atop a big-league lineup.

───────── ★ ★ ★ *2020 Top 101 Prospect* **#1** ★ ★ ★ ─────────

Wander Franco SS Born: 03/01/01 Age: 19 Bats: B Throws: R Height: 5'10" Weight: 189 Origin: International Free Agent, 2017

YEAR	TEAM	LVL	AGE	PA	R	2B	3B	HR	RBI	BB	K	SB	CS	AVG/OBP/SLG	DRC+	VORP	BABIP	BRR	FRAA	WARP
2018	PRI	RK	17	273	46	10	7	11	57	27	19	4	3	.351/.418/.587	166	35.4	.346	-0.4	SS(53): -5.3	2.4
2019	BGR	A	18	272	42	16	5	6	29	30	20	14	9	.318/.390/.506	158	29.3	.318	0.1	SS(53): -1.0	2.6
2019	PCH	A+	18	223	40	11	2	3	24	26	15	4	5	.339/.408/.464	175	30.9	.346	4.3	SS(44): 8.1	3.9
2020	TBA	MLB	19	251	27	12	2	5	27	25	31	2	1	.271/.348/.412	106	10.0	.294	-0.3	SS 2	1.3

Comparables: Vladimir Guerrero Jr., Mike Trout, Manny Machado

Welcome to the 2020 Baseball Prospectus Annual, where Franco is rated as the top prospect in baseball. Despite being extremely young for his level, the teenager posted the third-highest DRC+ in the Florida State League while making dazzling plays in the field as a shortstop. He has a plus-plus hit tool from both sides with power that is already showing in games from the left—30 of his 36 extra-base hits came when facing right-handers. He can run. He can throw. He can play either shortstop or second base, though there's no reason to move him off the former yet. He is a superstar in waiting.

While we are here, let's just get next year's comment out of the way too. Welcome to the 2021 Baseball Prospectus Annual, where Franco is rated as the top prospect in baseball. Despite being young for his level, the teenager posted elite statistics while making dazzling plays in the field as a shortstop. He has a plus hit-tool from either side, and his power is already showing in games from the left. He can run. He can throw. He can play either shortstop or second base, though there's no reason to move him off the former yet. He is a superstar in waiting.

Guillermo Heredia CF   Born: 01/31/91   Age: 29   Bats: R   Throws: L   Height: 5'10"   Weight: 195   Origin: International Free Agent, 2016

YEAR	TEAM	LVL	AGE	PA	R	2B	3B	HR	RBI	BB	K	SB	CS	AVG/OBP/SLG	DRC+	VORP	BABIP	BRR	FRAA	WARP
2017	SEA	MLB	26	426	43	16	0	6	24	27	64	1	5	.249/.315/.337	88	2.0	.284	1.0	CF(63): 7.1, LF(62): 1.7	1.8
2018	TAC	AAA	27	38	4	1	0	0	2	4	3	2	1	.276/.421/.310	111	5.0	.296	0.9	LF(6): 1.0, CF(5): -0.5	0.3
2018	SEA	MLB	27	337	29	14	1	5	19	32	52	2	4	.236/.318/.342	89	7.8	.270	0.0	CF(89): -6.5, LF(32): 3.1	0.3
2019	DUR	AAA	28	30	3	1	0	1	4	1	10	0	1	.214/.267/.357	67	-2.1	.294	0.0	CF(8): -0.2	0.0
2019	TBA	MLB	28	231	31	13	0	5	20	18	60	2	2	.225/.306/.363	77	0.5	.293	2.0	CF(41): 0.5, RF(28): 0.8	0.4
2020	TBA	MLB	29	251	24	12	1	5	25	20	58	2	1	.233/.313/.361	83	3.6	.291	1.1	CF 1, LF 1	0.6

Comparables: Chris Magruder, Charles Gipson, Bob Watson

Heredia shifted coasts, moving from the Pacific Northwest to the west coast of Florida. Unfortunately, the change in team, division and time zone did not make him a better hitter. Heredia is a really good fourth outfielder. He has speed and can play all three outfield positions—an important skill when your center fielder injures himself on an annual basis. In an ideal world, Heredia would be on the short side of a platoon in center, but when your entire marketing plan revolves around ol' blue eyes, it would be a tough sell to have him miss a quarter of the games. Heredia's bat is only viable against lefties where he shows bat-to-ball skills and even a little punch. He will continue to have a role somewhere as a useful reserve outfielder and noted party starter in the dugout and clubhouse.

Ronaldo Hernandez C   Born: 11/11/97   Age: 22   Bats: R   Throws: R   Height: 6'1"   Weight: 185   Origin: International Free Agent, 2014

YEAR	TEAM	LVL	AGE	PA	R	2B	3B	HR	RBI	BB	K	SB	CS	AVG/OBP/SLG	DRC+	VORP	BABIP	BRR	FRAA	WARP
2017	PRI	RK	19	246	42	22	1	5	40	16	39	2	2	.332/.382/.507	150	24.4	.379	2.5	C(43): 1.1	2.6
2018	BGR	A	20	449	68	20	1	21	79	31	69	10	4	.284/.339/.494	136	39.2	.292	-0.8	C(85): 1.2	3.5
2019	PCH	A+	21	427	43	19	3	9	60	17	65	7	0	.265/.299/.397	105	20.3	.290	1.8	C(81): 1.9	2.3
2020	TBA	MLB	22	35	4	2	0	1	4	2	7	0	0	.254/.300/.435	94	1.3	.290	-0.1	C 0	0.1

Comparables: Meibrys Viloria, Abiatal Avelino, Dom Nuñez

A converted infielder out of Colombia, Hernandez continues to climb the organizational ladder as a catcher. He was named to the Futures Game in July and ended the season having provided a slightly above-average offensive performance. His raw power was a bit stifled in the humid air of the Florida State League, and he really would prefer not to walk, but his average bat combined with his plus arm makes him a potential starter at catcher. At present, there's no one in the depth chart that should stand in the way of him getting a shot at some point over the next two seasons.

Greg Jones SS   Born: 03/07/98   Age: 22   Bats: B   Throws: R   Height: 6'2"   Weight: 175   Origin: Round 1, 2019 Draft (#22 overall)

YEAR	TEAM	LVL	AGE	PA	R	2B	3B	HR	RBI	BB	K	SB	CS	AVG/OBP/SLG	DRC+	VORP	BABIP	BRR	FRAA	WARP
2019	HUD	A-	21	218	39	13	4	1	24	22	56	19	8	.335/.413/.461	174	25.2	.467	4.2	SS(21): 2.2	2.6
2020	TBA	MLB	22	251	22	12	1	4	23	16	84	3	1	.239/.295/.348	73	-0.9	.358	0.0	SS 1	0.0

Comparables: Mark Hamilton, J.D. Martinez, Alex Dickerson

The first player to ever be selected in the first round out of UNC-Wilmington, Jones saw his stock rise after a tremendous sophomore year. The shortstop can flat out fly. It is easy, 80-grade speed that will help keep him in the middle of the diamond. Jones might play the six in his current state, but some evaluators see his ultimate home in center field where his best tool can be put on display more regularly. A switch-hitter with pop from both sides, Jones still has to answer questions about his hit tool from both sides of the dish. This was evident in his pro debut at Hudson Valley, where despite good results, he struck out in a quarter of his plate appearances. Don't be surprised if the Rays are more aggressive with him than usual with assignments, as Jones will turn 22 before Opening Day.

Kevin Kiermaier CF   Born: 04/22/90   Age: 30   Bats: L   Throws: R   Height: 6'1"   Weight: 210   Origin: Round 31, 2010 Draft (#941 overall)

YEAR	TEAM	LVL	AGE	PA	R	2B	3B	HR	RBI	BB	K	SB	CS	AVG/OBP/SLG	DRC+	VORP	BABIP	BRR	FRAA	WARP
2017	PCH	A+	27	26	2	1	1	0	1	2	7	0	1	.125/.192/.250	15	-2.2	.176	0.3	CF(3): -0.3	-0.1
2017	TBA	MLB	27	421	56	15	3	15	39	31	99	16	7	.276/.338/.450	101	24.5	.337	2.9	CF(97): 7.6	2.6
2018	TBA	MLB	28	367	44	12	9	7	29	25	91	10	5	.217/.282/.370	76	6.1	.275	3.1	CF(88): 12.3	1.8
2019	TBA	MLB	29	480	60	20	7	14	55	26	104	19	5	.228/.278/.398	75	2.2	.267	1.9	CF(125): 6.0	1.0
2020	TBA	MLB	30	525	51	21	6	14	56	35	121	16	5	.225/.285/.380	77	6.7	.273	2.7	CF 9	1.6

Comparables: Kole Calhoun, Glenallen Hill, Ivan Calderon

Thank you to @baseballpro. Just checked my DRC+ is at an all-time high. People come up to me all the time and say, "Sir, you are the greatest Center Fielder of All-Time." Maybe I am. Who knows. What I do know is I hit DINGERS and have a very high average. Very, very high average...some say the highest, but I don't know. I draw huge crowds at Tropicana Stadium even though the not-so-nice media lies and says my attendance is very low. NOT TRUE. Some even say that I am not a good hitter and take poor routes in the outfield. WRONG! They also make up FAKE stories about me always being hurt. When am I hurt? I play 172 games a year. It is because they can't stand all the WARPING I am doing. OUTLAW!!! Don't believe me? Ask @cdgoldstein.

Brandon Lowe 2B Born: 07/06/94 Age: 25 Bats: L Throws: R Height: 5'10" Weight: 185 Origin: Round 3, 2015 Draft (#87 overall)

YEAR	TEAM	LVL	AGE	PA	R	2B	3B	HR	RBI	BB	K	SB	CS	AVG/OBP/SLG	DRC+	VORP	BABIP	BRR	FRAA	WARP
2017	PCH	A+	22	367	62	34	3	9	46	47	65	6	3	.311/.403/.524	178	39.6	.366	2.0	2B(75): -1.1, 3B(2): -0.2	3.6
2017	MNT	AA	22	101	8	5	1	2	12	2	26	1	1	.253/.270/.389	70	0.5	.319	-1.3	2B(24): 0.8	0.0
2018	MNT	AA	23	240	37	17	1	8	41	35	55	8	2	.291/.400/.508	161	25.7	.360	2.1	LF(26): 1.8, 2B(24): -3.2	2.2
2018	DUR	AAA	23	205	36	14	0	14	35	22	47	0	1	.304/.380/.613	183	24.3	.339	0.4	2B(31): 1.2, LF(13): 0.9	2.5
2018	TBA	MLB	23	148	16	6	2	6	25	16	38	2	1	.233/.324/.450	93	6.2	.279	0.8	2B(28): -0.6, LF(11): -0.3	0.3
2019	TBA	MLB	24	327	42	17	2	17	51	25	113	5	0	.270/.336/.514	107	13.2	.377	2.4	2B(69): 3.3, 1B(5): -0.8	1.7
2020	TBA	MLB	25	560	69	24	2	28	81	45	180	3	2	.242/.311/.462	104	24.9	.317	1.8	2B 0, LF 0	2.6

Comparables: Derek Dietrich, Danny Espinosa, Jack Dittmer

Not to be confused with the Lowe brothers—this Lowe rhymes with POW!—the second baseman received a six-year extension in the spring that should keep him in Tampa Bay's lineup for the foreseeable future. He has considerable power from the left side and was on his way to a 30-bomb season before the injury bug bit him twice in the summer. Soon after he was named to his first All-Star Game, he landed on the injured list after fouling a ball off his right leg. During his rehab assignment, he strained his left quad, which effectively ended his year at the halfway mark. Lowe did make it back to the lineup in late September for a handful of games and played in five of the team's six postseason games. Even if it's in a strong-side platoon role, Lowe should easily approach 30 home runs with a similar number of doubles. He's not a great runner and is a perfectly reasonable defender at the keystone with some flexibility to play elsewhere. The Zen Bobrist comp gets thrown around with scrappy white dudes that can play a few positions, but it seems more appropriate for Lowe since he is actually good at hitting baseballs.

Nate Lowe 1B Born: 07/07/95 Age: 24 Bats: L Throws: R Height: 6'4" Weight: 245 Origin: Round 13, 2016 Draft (#390 overall)

YEAR	TEAM	LVL	AGE	PA	R	2B	3B	HR	RBI	BB	K	SB	CS	AVG/OBP/SLG	DRC+	VORP	BABIP	BRR	FRAA	WARP
2017	BGR	A	21	269	34	13	0	5	35	36	53	0	1	.293/.387/.415	136	14.1	.356	-0.2	1B(49): 0.2	1.3
2017	PCH	A+	21	203	21	10	1	2	24	28	53	1	1	.249/.355/.353	109	1.0	.345	-0.5	1B(51): -1.5	0.2
2018	PCH	A+	22	220	39	15	0	10	44	25	33	0	0	.356/.432/.588	217	22.6	.391	-2.4	1B(35): -2.9	2.2
2018	MNT	AA	22	225	36	11	0	13	42	35	30	1	1	.340/.444/.606	218	33.7	.349	1.9	1B(39): -0.4	3.2
2018	DUR	AAA	22	110	18	6	1	4	16	8	27	0	1	.260/.327/.460	121	1.4	.319	-1.2	1B(25): -0.1	0.2
2019	DUR	AAA	23	406	63	24	0	16	63	72	82	1	0	.289/.421/.508	142	25.5	.341	-0.6	1B(71): -1.0, 3B(5): 0.3	2.3
2019	TBA	MLB	23	169	24	8	0	7	19	13	50	0	0	.263/.325/.454	88	0.2	.340	1.0	1B(21): 0.1, 3B(4): -0.2	0.1
2020	TBA	MLB	24	385	47	16	1	15	51	44	101	0	0	.252/.342/.440	111	11.6	.315	-0.6	1B 0	1.1

Comparables: Derek Fisher, Steve Bilko, Brandon Allen

Choi is on deck and I'm in the hole, Nate Lowe is about to make some pitchers turn cold. Now they dropping and yelling it's a tad bit late Nate Lowe and Ji-Man had to regulate.

Just like I thought, we had a wild card spot In need of some desperate help, but Nate Lowe and the Ji-child were in need of something else. One of the teams kept winning them games, I said "oooh, I like your spot." Billy Beane said "my ace got suspended and you seem real nice, would you let me ride?" I got a car full of banners and it's going real swell. The next stop is....taking first base full-time.

★ ★ ★ *2020 Top 101 Prospect* **#28** ★ ★ ★ ──────────

Brendan McKay LHP Born: 12/18/95 Age: 24 Bats: L Throws: L Height: 6'2" Weight: 212 Origin: Round 1, 2017 Draft (#4 overall)

YEAR	TEAM	LVL	AGE	PA	R	2B	3B	HR	RBI	BB	K	SB	CS	AVG/OBP/SLG	DRC+	VORP	BABIP	BRR	FRAA	WARP
2017	HUD	A-	21	149	16	4	1	4	22	21	33	2	0	.232/.349/.376	120	3.7	.281	-1.3	1B(21): -1.1, P(6): 0.1	0.2
2018	BGR	A	22	91	12	2	0	1	16	28	13	0	0	.254/.484/.333	180	1.0	.306	-3.1	1B(9): -0.3, P(6): 0.1	0.5
2018	PCH	A+	22	139	19	6	1	5	21	16	38	0	0	.210/.317/.403	97	1.5	.260	0.5	1B(18): -0.4, P(11): -0.3	0.1
2019	MNT	AA	23	90	8	2	0	0	8	7	27	0	1	.167/.256/.192	50	-4.2	.245	0.3	P(8): 0.5	-0.3
2019	DUR	AAA	23	78	11	2	0	5	11	10	24	1	0	.239/.346/.493	94	1.3	.289	-0.3	P(7): -0.2	0.0
2019	TBA	MLB	23	11	2	0	0	1	1	1	2	0	0	.200/.273/.500	57	0.2	.143	-0.1	P(13): -0.1	0.0
2020	TBA	MLB	24	35	3	1	0	1	4	4	11	0	0	.206/.297/.349	77	-1.2	.288	0.0	1B 0	-0.1

Comparables: Chris McGuiness, Chris Shaw, Pete Alonso

The Shohei Ohtani comps can stop for now as the Rays will have to settle for McKay just being a really good left-handed starter instead of a two-headed dragon. The Rays took away McKay's first base glove to start the season and then his bat somewhere along the way. He still may make the occasional start at designated hitter—and even with a 26-man roster, it will still be valuable to have a pitcher that can also hit a little—but McKay's on his way towards leaving that double life behind. He was nearly unhittable to start his career before the league caught up to him. By the end of the year, concerns about workload took over and he didn't throw over 65 pitches in an appearance after mid-August. Despite the ups and downs, McKay showed stuff and poise that makes him a potential number two or three starter. He has a four-pitch mix led by a low-to-mid 90s fastball and a true, plus curveball. Developing command led to some home run issues at the highest level, but he has the ability to repeat and turn that into a strength. The Rays may play some games early in the year with regards to service time and innings totals, but McKay should toss his most important pitches for Tampa Bay in 2020.

Austin Meadows RF Born: 05/03/95 Age: 25 Bats: L Throws: L Height: 6'3" Weight: 220 Origin: Round 1, 2013 Draft (#9 overall)

YEAR	TEAM	LVL	AGE	PA	R	2B	3B	HR	RBI	BB	K	SB	CS	AVG/OBP/SLG	DRC+	VORP	BABIP	BRR	FRAA	WARP
2017	IND	AAA	22	312	48	19	0	4	36	24	50	11	3	.250/.311/.359	92	9.0	.289	3.7	CF(33): -1.9, LF(24): -0.8	0.7
2018	IND	AAA	23	179	27	13	0	2	21	9	24	11	1	.279/.318/.394	154	8.3	.314	2.4	CF(22): -1.5, LF(18): 0.1	2.1
2018	DUR	AAA	23	106	19	11	0	10	22	8	13	1	1	.344/.396/.771	157	14.9	.311	-1.6	CF(17): -1.2, RF(4): -0.2	1.6
2018	PIT	MLB	23	165	16	8	2	5	13	8	35	4	1	.292/.327/.468	95	8.1	.345	-1.1	CF(15): -0.7, RF(13): -1.1	0.1
2018	TBA	MLB	23	26	3	1	0	1	4	2	5	1	0	.250/.308/.417	95	0.4	.278	-0.1	RF(7): -1.4, LF(1): 0.0	-0.1
2019	TBA	MLB	24	591	83	29	7	33	89	54	131	12	7	.291/.364/.558	135	40.3	.331	-3.5	RF(57): -3.5, LF(34): 4.6	3.7
2020	TBA	MLB	25	595	78	28	5	30	90	49	130	16	5	.272/.337/.507	122	30.0	.308	-2.3	RF -9, CF -1	2.1

Comparables: Michael Saunders, Clint Frazier, Cameron Maybin

Meadows' first full season in the big leagues went about as well as you could have hoped. He was the best player on a 96-win team and led the Rays in almost every offensive statistic. Meadows continued the power surge he showed late last season after his trade from Pittsburgh. His 33 home runs were the seventh most by a Ray in a single season. His .558 slugging percentage trailed just José Canseco and Carlos Peña for the highest team mark in a single year. Meadows also did something franchise cornerstone Evan Longoria was unable to do: post an OPS higher than .900 for a season. Considering his injury past and the home turf, the Rays limited him to just 86 starts in the field. The load management allowed him to play nearly a full season despite missing some time with a sprained thumb. In Meadows, Tampa Bay has an All-Star caliber hitter that should be worth between three and five wins a season and is under team control for most of his 20s.

Hunter Renfroe OF Born: 01/28/92 Age: 28 Bats: R Throws: R Height: 6'1" Weight: 220 Origin: Round 1, 2013 Draft (#13 overall)

YEAR	TEAM	LVL	AGE	PA	R	2B	3B	HR	RBI	BB	K	SB	CS	AVG/OBP/SLG	DRC+	VORP	BABIP	BRR	FRAA	WARP
2017	ELP	AAA	25	61	18	7	1	4	18	6	7	1	0	.509/.557/.891	236	17.2	.545	0.8	RF(12): 1.9	1.4
2017	SDN	MLB	25	479	51	25	1	26	58	27	140	3	0	.231/.284/.467	94	15.9	.275	-0.9	RF(120): -2.1	0.4
2018	ELP	AAA	26	43	6	1	0	2	4	2	10	0	0	.220/.256/.390	74	-0.8	.241	-0.1	RF(9): 2.4	0.2
2018	SDN	MLB	26	441	53	23	1	26	68	30	109	2	1	.248/.302/.504	110	18.9	.271	-1.2	LF(58): -1.3, RF(50): 6.6	2.0
2019	SDN	MLB	27	494	64	19	1	33	64	46	154	5	0	.216/.289/.489	98	11.9	.239	-2.2	RF(86): 6.5, LF(67): 0.7	1.6
2020	TBA	MLB	28	490	67	26	2	33	84	36	147	2	1	.245/.306/.529	114	20.2	.287	-1.5	LF 1, RF 1	2.4

Comparables: Jose Canseco, Jay Buhner, Bobby Bonds

For three months last summer the Padres finally saw the powerful, productive right fielder they thought they had popped with their first pick in the 2013 draft. Renfroe was not only playing excellent outfield defense and denting baseballs on his way to the first 30-bomb season by a Padres outfielder this century, but he ratcheted down his whiff and on-base rates from "Insufferable" to "Sufferable With Power." Then Renfroe augered in, possibly due to nagging foot and ankle pain, and his .252/.308/.613 first half gave way to a punchless and contact-free .161/.263/.299 denouement. Renfroe's hacktastic ways will always prevent stardom, but when healthy his combination of power and leather can make him a solid contributor. At least that's what the Rays were thinking when they acquired him in early December.

Daniel Robertson UT Born: 03/22/94 Age: 26 Bats: R Throws: R Height: 5'11" Weight: 200 Origin: Round 1, 2012 Draft (#34 overall)

YEAR	TEAM	LVL	AGE	PA	R	2B	3B	HR	RBI	BB	K	SB	CS	AVG/OBP/SLG	DRC+	VORP	BABIP	BRR	FRAA	WARP
2017	DUR	AAA	23	47	7	2	0	1	1	3	7	0	1	.372/.426/.488	143	3.1	.429	-1.0	SS(4): 0.3, 3B(3): -0.2	0.3
2017	TBA	MLB	23	254	22	7	2	5	19	29	73	1	1	.206/.308/.326	79	1.4	.282	-0.8	2B(41): -2.2, SS(24): 1.9	0.2
2018	TBA	MLB	24	340	46	16	0	9	34	43	77	2	2	.262/.382/.415	112	24.7	.328	1.8	2B(39): 3.1, SS(29): -0.3	2.1
2019	DUR	AAA	25	123	11	1	0	2	9	16	25	1	0	.260/.374/.327	89	0.4	.325	-0.7	SS(21): 0.7, 2B(4): 0.2	0.4
2019	TBA	MLB	25	237	23	9	1	2	19	24	59	2	2	.213/.312/.295	73	0.8	.288	-1.4	3B(43): 0.4, 2B(26): 0.5	0.1
2020	TBA	MLB	26	175	17	7	1	3	17	18	44	1	0	.227/.327/.349	85	2.6	.299	0.1	2B 1, 3B 0	0.5

Comparables: J.P. Crawford, Nick Franklin, Rio Ruiz

A year ago it looked as if Robertson was on the verge of a breakout year and earning an everyday role with the Rays. After an abysmal 2019, he is just looking to make the roster this spring. His discipline rates remained close enough to 2018 to offer some hope, but the biggest difference was a 50-point drop in BABIP and a huge drop in power output. Robertson underwent thumb surgery in late 2018 and then knee surgery in the middle of 2019, so there could be legitimate health reasons behind the decline as well as the rust from time off. A former top prospect with the A's, Robertson still has a leg up on some of the infield competition because he is a competent fielder who can fill in at shortstop—a skill many of the other Rays' infielders don't have.

Yoshitomo Tsutsugoh 3B/OF Born: 11/26/91 Age: 28 Bats: L Throws: R Height: 6'0" Weight: 210 Origin: International Free Agent, 2019

Every player in NPB has a cheer the crowd sings as they step up to the plate. "High into the Yokohama sky, hit a home run, Tsutsugo," were the first words of the Rays' newest import. (The Trop crowd might want to alter the lyrics to "hit the C-ring.") Predictably, Tsutsugo has impressive raw power, having walloped 185 home runs over his last six seasons in Japan, including 44 in 2016. He isn't a one-dimensional, pull-happy slugger, however. He'll take his fair share of walks, and he's willing to spray liners to all fields. Defensively, he's passable in left field (and has some history at third base), but an optimal deployment has him at DH. Tsutsugo is an especially rare surname in Japan, and the Rays hope his production proves as special.

Joey Wendle 2B   Born: 04/26/90   Age: 30   Bats: L   Throws: R   Height: 6'1"   Weight: 200   Origin: Round 6, 2012 Draft (#203 overall)

YEAR	TEAM	LVL	AGE	PA	R	2B	3B	HR	RBI	BB	K	SB	CS	AVG/OBP/SLG	DRC+	VORP	BABIP	BRR	FRAA	WARP
2017	NAS	AAA	27	510	67	29	8	8	54	19	82	13	4	.285/.327/.429	96	26.3	.329	0.6	2B(82): -0.7, 3B(24): 6.3	2.0
2017	OAK	MLB	27	14	3	1	0	1	5	1	3	0	0	.308/.357/.615	93	1.0	.333	-0.2	2B(5): -0.5	0.0
2018	TBA	MLB	28	545	62	33	6	7	61	37	96	16	4	.300/.354/.435	108	33.4	.353	3.7	2B(100): 5.8, 3B(20): 1.4	3.2
2019	TBA	MLB	29	263	32	13	2	3	19	14	47	8	3	.231/.293/.340	81	3.1	.272	-0.2	2B(48): 4.1, 3B(27): -1.1	0.6
2020	TBA	MLB	30	455	43	22	3	10	47	24	91	8	2	.243/.296/.382	82	5.2	.288	1.2	2B 3, 3B 3	1.2

Comparables: Bobby Young, Brandon Phillips, Wil Cordero

What do you get when you cross Ben Zobrist expectations with Sam Fuld's hitting ability? After unexpectedly placing as a finalist for the American League Rookie of the Year award in 2018, Wendle came crashing back to Earth hard. He was hit by a pitch in early April that resulted in a wrist fracture but was not effective even before that injury. Without much threat of power, opposing pitchers challenged him more often in the zone and yet Wendle took 41 percent of his hacks on balls compared to 36 percent the year prior. He remains an average-ish hitter against right-handed pitching and a solid defender up the middle with the ability to play short in a pinch and third base as well. As long as he remains cheap, he has a role with the Rays.

Mike Zunino C   Born: 03/25/91   Age: 29   Bats: R   Throws: R   Height: 6'2"   Weight: 235   Origin: Round 1, 2012 Draft (#3 overall)

YEAR	TEAM	LVL	AGE	PA	R	2B	3B	HR	RBI	BB	K	SB	CS	AVG/OBP/SLG	DRC+	VORP	BABIP	BRR	FRAA	WARP
2017	TAC	AAA	26	45	7	2	0	5	11	4	5	0	0	.293/.356/.707	135	9.1	.226	0.6	C(7): 0.8	0.5
2017	SEA	MLB	26	435	52	25	0	25	64	39	160	1	0	.251/.331/.509	109	27.4	.355	-1.4	C(120): 6.3	3.1
2018	SEA	MLB	27	405	37	18	0	20	44	24	150	0	0	.201/.259/.410	83	6.3	.268	-2.2	C(111): 6.4	1.6
2019	TBA	MLB	28	289	30	10	1	9	32	20	98	0	0	.165/.232/.312	57	-1.1	.220	-1.5	C(89): 8.3	0.5
2020	TBA	MLB	29	455	52	20	1	23	63	33	163	1	0	.207/.279/.423	82	9.2	.276	-1.7	C 14	2.4

Comparables: Bobby Estalella, Mike Napoli, Taylor Teagarden

YEAR	TEAM	P. COUNT	FRM RUNS	BLK RUNS	THRW RUNS	TOT RUNS
2017	SEA	16181	10.9	-3.1	-0.6	5.6
2018	SEA	14630	7.5	-1.1	0.4	6.6
2019	TBA	10964	7.0	1.7	1.1	9.8
2020	TBA	19437	12.4	0.0	2.3	14.7

Zunino came to the Rays from the Mariners in the annual winter trade between the two teams. Home cooking, however, did nothing for the Florida native, as his already abysmal bat sunk to a new low. Making things even worse, the 25-homer power that had previously propped up his overall offense also failed to make the trip back east. By the middle of the season, he had lost his starting gig to an older catcher that played for three different teams in the span of a month. There is always the hope that the former third-overall pick stops flailing at pitches out of the zone, but as he creeps toward 30 that grows more unlikely. The good news for Zunino is he remains a solid hand behind the plate. He is a very good framer and is a plus when it comes to blocking—what led to the Rays bringing him back on a one-year pact. Lesser catchers have had longer careers.

PITCHERS

José Alvarado LHP   Born: 05/21/95   Age: 25   Bats: L   Throws: L   Height: 6'2"   Weight: 245   Origin: International Free Agent, 2012

YEAR	TEAM	LVL	AGE	W	L	SV	G	GS	IP	H	HR	BB/9	K/9	K	GB%	BABIP	WHIP	ERA	DRA	WARP	MPH	FB%	WHF	CSP
2017	MNT	AA	22	2	1	0	9	0	11¹	4	1	4.0	11.1	14	78%	.136	0.79	2.38	2.70	0.3				
2017	DUR	AAA	22	0	2	1	16	0	18¹	11	1	6.4	12.8	26	43%	.244	1.31	3.93	3.32	0.4				
2017	TBA	MLB	22	0	3	0	35	0	29²	24	1	2.7	8.8	29	55%	.274	1.11	3.64	3.44	0.6	100.2	75.8	11.5	48.3
2018	TBA	MLB	23	1	6	8	70	0	64	42	1	4.1	11.2	80	57%	.270	1.11	2.39	2.65	1.7	100.0	70.5	13.6	49
2019	TBA	MLB	24	1	6	7	35	1	30	29	2	8.1	11.7	39	50%	.346	1.87	4.80	5.70	-0.1	100.5	79.5	12.6	42.5
2020	TBA	MLB	25	3	3	7	54	0	58	49	5	5.2	10.7	68	54%	.301	1.43	3.97	4.07	0.7	99.9	76.2	13.2	47.2

Comparables: Stephen Pryor, Eduardo Sanchez, Paco Rodríguez

Alvarado entered the season as the Rays de-facto closer. He saved four games by April 7 and looked poised for a monster season. The rest of the year sure was scary, but not for the same reasons. The big lefty lost sight of the strike zone and then the team lost sight of him. First, Alvarado left the club to return to Venezuela for personal reasons. He missed nearly a month there before returning in late June. A week later, he gave up eight runs in 3 1/3 innings before suffering an oblique injury. He returned once more only to give up eight walks in 3 1/3 innings before an elbow injury finally ended his season in August. Even with that cranky elbow, he was still pumping a consistent 98 mph until the end. The hope is 2019 was just an unexpected redshirt season presuming his elbow woes end at inflammation.

Nick Anderson   RHP   Born: 07/05/90   Age: 29   Bats: R   Throws: R   Height: 6'5"   Weight: 195   Origin: Round 32, 2012 Draft (#995 overall)

YEAR	TEAM	LVL	AGE	W	L	SV	G	GS	IP	H	HR	BB/9	K/9	K	GB%	BABIP	WHIP	ERA	DRA	WARP	MPH	FB%	WHF	CSP
2017	FTM	A+	26	2	0	2	15	0	20¹	13	0	1.3	8.9	20	50%	.250	0.79	0.89	2.39	0.6				
2017	CHT	AA	26	2	1	9	29	0	33²	19	0	1.9	9.9	37	39%	.237	0.77	1.07	2.17	1.1				
2018	ROC	AAA	27	8	2	4	39	4	60	49	8	2.8	13.2	88	31%	.323	1.13	3.30	3.62	1.1				
2019	TBA	MLB	28	3	0	0	23	0	21¹	12	3	0.8	17.3	41	32%	.290	0.66	2.11	0.75	1.1	98.0	69	26	53.8
2019	MIA	MLB	28	2	4	1	45	0	43²	40	5	3.3	14.2	69	28%	.368	1.28	3.92	3.41	0.9	97.5	55.9	18.2	48
2020	TBA	MLB	29	3	2	11	54	0	58	40	7	2.7	14.1	91	31%	.291	0.99	2.28	2.70	1.6	97.0	59.9	20.5	49.7

Comparables: Chris Smith, Tyler Sturdevant, Aaron Wilkerson

Anderson became the best reliever you never heard of prior to the 2019 season. A former farmhand of the Twins, he burst onto the scene with the Marlins early in the year. The right-hander works exclusively off of a high-90s fastball and a low-80s hook. The tandem was one of the best 1-2 punches out of the bullpen in all of baseball, as he struck out 42 percent of batters faced on the year. He was even better after the July trade north to the Rays. In 23 games for Tampa Bay, he struck out 41 of the 78 hitters that opposed him. Perhaps even more impressively, he walked just two during that stretch. Anderson may not have collected a save for the Rays, but he was the unquestioned relief ace as the team marched toward the playoffs and into the divisional series. Because he was such a late bloomer, he won't even reach arbitration eligibility until the 2022 season.

Anthony Banda   LHP   Born: 08/10/93   Age: 26   Bats: L   Throws: L   Height: 6'2"   Weight: 225   Origin: Round 10, 2012 Draft (#335 overall)

YEAR	TEAM	LVL	AGE	W	L	SV	G	GS	IP	H	HR	BB/9	K/9	K	GB%	BABIP	WHIP	ERA	DRA	WARP	MPH	FB%	WHF	CSP
2017	RNO	AAA	23	8	7	0	22	22	122	125	15	3.8	8.6	116	43%	.317	1.44	5.39	4.15	2.1				
2017	ARI	MLB	23	2	3	0	8	4	25²	26	1	3.5	8.8	25	39%	.329	1.40	5.96	4.21	0.4	96.7	63.4	11.7	45.1
2018	DUR	AAA	24	4	3	0	8	8	42	43	3	3.9	10.5	49	40%	.360	1.45	3.64	5.21	0.2				
2018	TBA	MLB	24	1	0	0	3	1	14²	12	1	1.8	6.1	10	49%	.262	1.02	3.68	4.75	0.1	96.6	77.8	10.6	57
2019	DUR	AAA	25	2	3	0	9	4	28¹	28	7	3.5	8.6	27	41%	.284	1.38	6.04	4.75	0.5				
2019	TBA	MLB	25	0	0	0	3	0	4	6	0	0.0	4.5	2	25%	.375	1.50	6.75	5.51	0.0	94.3	55.9	3.4	54.8
2020	TBA	MLB	26	1	1	0	3	3	13	15	3	3.4	6.3	9	39%	.298	1.52	6.02	5.89	0.0	96.0	68.4	10.5	54.1

Comparables: Jake Faria, Blake Snell, Dana Eveland

Acquired in 2018 in a trade with the Arizona Diamondbacks for Steven Souza, Banda has similarly struggled to stay on the field. After missing much of the last two seasons due to Tommy John surgery, the lefty returned to the mound but did little at the big-league level. He spent about six weeks in a hybrid starter/bulk guy role at Triple-A Durham before making a couple of mop-up appearances in Tampa Bay. That said, making it all the way back from injury is probably sufficient progress enough—though it's not ideal that he showed diminished velocity upon his return in relief. Banda still throws in the low-90s and can scrape higher with an above-average changeup and a sparingly-used slider. On the surface, Banda would fit nicely in a Jalen Beeks or Ryan Yarbrough type role, but he'll need to miss more bats to do so.

————————————   ★   ★   ★   *2020 Top 101 Prospect*   **#30**   ★   ★   ★   ————————————

Shane Baz   RHP   Born: 06/17/99   Age: 21   Bats: R   Throws: R   Height: 6'2"   Weight: 190   Origin: Round 1, 2017 Draft (#12 overall)

YEAR	TEAM	LVL	AGE	W	L	SV	G	GS	IP	H	HR	BB/9	K/9	K	GB%	BABIP	WHIP	ERA	DRA	WARP	MPH	FB%	WHF	CSP
2017	PIR	RK	18	0	3	0	10	10	23²	26	2	5.3	7.2	19	51%	.348	1.69	3.80	7.48	-0.4				
2018	BRI	RK	19	4	3	0	10	10	45¹	45	2	4.6	10.7	54	64%	.344	1.50	3.97	6.79	-0.3				
2018	PRI	RK	19	0	2	0	2	2	7	11	1	7.7	6.4	5	48%	.417	2.43	7.71	7.16	-0.1				
2019	BGR	A	20	3	2	0	17	17	81¹	63	5	4.1	9.6	87	39%	.279	1.23	2.99	3.88	1.2				
2020	TBA	MLB	21	2	2	0	33	0	35	35	6	4.0	7.8	30	37%	.294	1.45	4.97	5.00	0.1				

Comparables: Drew Anderson, Elvin Ramirez, Yennsy Diaz

With Austin Meadows' hitting and Tyler Glasnow's pitching, the Rays have already won the Chris Archer trade. Baz is just rubbing salt in the wound. The PTBNL in the mid-summer 2018 swap has the ability, and now the on-field production, to make this transaction one of the most lopsided moves of the decade. In his first full-season assignment, he struck out more than a batter per inning while keeping the ball in the yard. He struggled with control—let's not talk command yet—but that is a known issue and one that will ultimately define his ceiling. As is, he can reach the upper-90s with his fastball and has a pair of breaking balls that flash plus ability. Even his change projects to average and he has some room to fill out his naturally athletic frame. If he can clean up his delivery a bit to harness more of that command, Baz could be a dark horse for the top pitching prospect in baseball by the end of 2020.

Jalen Beeks   LHP   Born: 07/10/93   Age: 26   Bats: L   Throws: L   Height: 5'11"   Weight: 200   Origin: Round 12, 2014 Draft (#374 overall)

YEAR	TEAM	LVL	AGE	W	L	SV	G	GS	IP	H	HR	BB/9	K/9	K	GB%	BABIP	WHIP	ERA	DRA	WARP	MPH	FB%	WHF	CSP
2017	PME	AA	23	5	1	0	9	9	49¹	35	3	4.0	10.6	58	51%	.276	1.16	2.19	2.94	1.3				
2017	PAW	AAA	23	6	7	0	17	17	95²	86	10	3.1	9.1	97	45%	.291	1.24	3.86	4.17	1.6				
2018	PAW	AAA	24	5	5	0	16	16	87¹	70	10	2.6	12.1	117	41%	.299	1.09	2.89	3.33	2.2				
2018	BOS	MLB	24	0	1	0	2	1	6¹	11	1	5.7	7.1	5	33%	.435	2.37	12.79	7.48	-0.2	93.9	42.5	9.5	42.7
2018	TBA	MLB	24	5	0	0	12	0	44¹	41	5	4.1	7.5	37	51%	.288	1.38	4.47	5.18	-0.1	93.9	42.5	13.1	45
2019	DUR	AAA	25	0	1	0	3	3	10²	8	2	3.4	8.4	10	39%	.231	1.12	4.22	3.94	0.3				
2019	TBA	MLB	25	6	3	1	33	3	104¹	115	12	3.5	7.7	89	48%	.328	1.49	4.31	6.89	-1.7	94.6	43.6	11	46.3
2020	TBA	MLB	26	3	3	0	52	3	61	61	9	3.4	7.8	53	46%	.294	1.38	4.55	4.69	0.4	94.0	44.1	11.7	46.4

Comparables: John Gast, José Álvarez, Adalberto Mejía

Beeks threw the most anonymous 104 1/3 innings in history during 2019. Ask anyone. Go ahead. Nobody remembers a "Jalen Beeks moment." There is no "Jalen Beeks game." In fact, Beeks may be baseball's version of the Mandela Effect. People have heard of him, but is there proof he really exists? Sure, there are statistics above these words that say he does, but did you actually witness any of the "89 strikeouts" he is credited with? Who hit the 12 home runs he "allowed?" We need answers. If you have any vivid memories of Beeks actually being a major league player—or even better—visual evidence, please direct them to the estate of Robert Stack.

Diego Castillo RHP Born: 01/18/94 Age: 26 Bats: R Throws: R Height: 6'3" Weight: 250 Origin: International Free Agent, 2014

YEAR	TEAM	LVL	AGE	W	L	SV	G	GS	IP	H	HR	BB/9	K/9	K	GB%	BABIP	WHIP	ERA	DRA	WARP	MPH	FB%	WHF	CSP
2017	MNT	AA	23	1	3	8	21	0	29	20	1	2.2	9.9	32	61%	.250	0.93	1.86	2.44	0.8				
2017	DUR	AAA	23	3	2	7	30	1	42²	38	2	2.7	12.2	58	40%	.353	1.20	3.38	4.23	0.5				
2018	DUR	AAA	24	0	1	4	19	0	26¹	15	1	2.4	10.9	32	59%	.246	0.84	1.03	2.21	0.9				
2018	TBA	MLB	24	4	2	0	43	11	56²	36	6	2.9	10.3	65	46%	.229	0.95	3.18	3.70	0.9	101.0	54.1	14	48.9
2019	TBA	MLB	25	5	8	8	65	6	68²	59	8	3.4	10.6	81	56%	.300	1.24	3.41	3.41	1.5	100.2	48.5	14.8	48.2
2020	TBA	MLB	26	3	3	4	54	0	58	48	6	3.3	10.9	70	52%	.294	1.20	3.24	3.54	1.0	100.1	51.6	14.7	49.4

Comparables: Michael Tonkin, Chandler Shepherd, Jaye Chapman

Castillo entered the year as the setup man to José Alvarado. Both players were overworked early on and lost effectiveness, their health and ultimately their high-leverage roles. Alvarado never got his back, but Castillo did. It took time, but by September, the burly right-hander was back to pitching in key spots for the Rays. His six outs in the Wild Card Game were an integral part of the outcome as he bridged the gap from Charlie Morton to the new back-end tandem of Nick Anderson and Emilio Pagán. Castillo continued to pitch well against Houston in the divisional series including a "start" in Game 4. When he is on, few pitchers throw harder on average. The high-octane fastball is great, but his slider is even better and part of his resurgence was due to a month-over-month increase in breaking balls—peaking with a nice 69-percent usage rate in September. The big man will be counted on to get big outs once again this year.

Yonny Chirinos RHP Born: 12/26/93 Age: 26 Bats: R Throws: R Height: 6'2" Weight: 240 Origin: International Free Agent, 2012

YEAR	TEAM	LVL	AGE	W	L	SV	G	GS	IP	H	HR	BB/9	K/9	K	GB%	BABIP	WHIP	ERA	DRA	WARP	MPH	FB%	WHF	CSP
2017	MNT	AA	23	1	0	0	4	4	27¹	22	5	1.3	6.9	21	58%	.233	0.95	2.63	3.78	0.5				
2017	DUR	AAA	23	12	5	0	23	22	141	116	10	1.4	7.7	120	52%	.270	0.98	2.74	3.00	4.2				
2018	DUR	AAA	24	0	2	0	8	8	30²	35	7	2.1	9.1	31	50%	.326	1.37	5.28	5.92	-0.1				
2018	TBA	MLB	24	5	5	0	18	7	89²	84	7	2.5	7.5	75	45%	.298	1.22	3.51	4.23	0.9	96.4	63.1	12.2	49.8
2019	TBA	MLB	25	9	5	0	26	18	133¹	112	23	1.9	7.7	114	44%	.246	1.05	3.85	4.29	2.0	96.4	56.8	11.1	48.1
2020	TBA	MLB	26	8	7	0	44	19	131	122	18	2.5	8.0	116	45%	.282	1.21	3.66	4.00	2.2	96.0	60.1	11.7	49.7

Comparables: Joe Musgrove, Jordan Montgomery, Trevor Oaks

On a lot of teams Chirinos would have made 30 starts, pitched 175 innings and be set up to make a decent amount of money as a back-end of the rotation starter in arbitration. With Tampa Bay, he began the season as a hybrid before working his way into a more traditional role in June and July. Regardless of when he began pitching in a game, Chirinos was effective. He works in the low-90s with a slider, split-finger and solid control of the three-pitch mix. His biggest problem thus far has been home runs. This gets into the discussion of good control not being the same as good command. Some may look at the lack of strikeouts as a knock, but Chirinos pitches to contact and lives in the zone more than the average pitcher. This allowed him to average just under 15 pitches per inning. Effective and efficient aren't sexy, but it gets the job done most of the time. That's Chirinos in a honey nut shell.

Oliver Drake RHP Born: 01/13/87 Age: 33 Bats: R Throws: R Height: 6'4" Weight: 215 Origin: Round 43, 2008 Draft (#1286 overall)

YEAR	TEAM	LVL	AGE	W	L	SV	G	GS	IP	H	HR	BB/9	K/9	K	GB%	BABIP	WHIP	ERA	DRA	WARP	MPH	FB%	WHF	CSP
2017	BAL	MLB	30	0	0	0	3	0	3¹	6	0	8.1	8.1	3	67%	.500	2.70	8.10	6.84	-0.1	93.5	47.6	11	43.7
2017	MIL	MLB	30	3	5	1	61	0	52²	57	6	3.8	10.1	59	49%	.349	1.50	4.44	4.35	0.5	93.8	51.6	13	45.1
2018	SLC	AAA	31	0	0	0	6	0	7²	3	0	1.2	9.4	8	71%	.176	0.52	1.17	2.17	0.3				
2018	LAA	MLB	31	0	1	0	8	0	8²	15	2	1.0	8.3	8	39%	.448	1.85	5.19	3.11	0.2	94.4	47.1	15	49.1
2018	MIL	MLB	31	1	0	0	11	0	12²	14	0	5.7	10.7	15	57%	.400	1.74	6.39	2.52	0.4	94.6	49.3	13.5	50.5
2018	CLE	MLB	31	0	0	0	4	0	4¹	7	0	2.1	8.3	4	31%	.438	1.85	12.46	2.59	0.1	94.2	48.1	14.3	45.6
2018	TOR	MLB	31	0	0	0	2	0	1²	4	0	0.0	10.8	2	43%	.571	2.40	16.20	1.95	0.1	94.1	58.3	8.3	52.2
2018	MIN	MLB	31	0	0	0	19	0	20¹	12	2	3.1	9.7	22	55%	.204	0.93	2.21	3.40	0.4	93.9	40.6	13.6	45.5
2019	DUR	AAA	32	1	2	6	19	2	23²	20	2	2.7	15.2	40	51%	.400	1.14	4.94	2.46	0.9				
2019	TBA	MLB	32	5	2	2	50	0	56	36	9	3.1	11.2	70	52%	.225	0.98	3.21	3.12	1.4	95.1	40.7	17.7	48.3
2020	TBA	MLB	33	3	2	0	48	0	51	40	6	3.4	10.8	61	51%	.283	1.17	2.96	3.29	1.1	93.4	44.6	15	46.7

Comparables: Louis Coleman, Shawn Kelley, James Hoyt

Perhaps it was God's plan for Drake to pitch for the Rays. After all of his work around the league, and things going badly in other places, his 2019 season was the best he's ever had in the big leagues. Buying into the motto of throwing your best pitch more often, he relied on his splitter more than ever and just brutalized left-handed batters, who collectively hit .147/.163/.196 against him. Considering Tampa Bay's pitching philosophy requires the bullpen hotline to bling more than most teams, Drake was seemingly throwing nonstop and tied a career-high with 56 innings pitched despite making his first major-league appearance after Memorial Day. After passing through five other organizations in 2018, it looks like he's finally found a home and a role that suits him best in Tampa.

Tyler Glasnow RHP   Born: 08/23/93   Age: 26   Bats: L   Throws: R   Height: 6'8"   Weight: 230   Origin: Round 5, 2011 Draft (#152 overall)

YEAR	TEAM	LVL	AGE	W	L	SV	G	GS	IP	H	HR	BB/9	K/9	K	GB%	BABIP	WHIP	ERA	DRA	WARP	MPH	FB%	WHF	CSP
2017	IND	AAA	23	9	2	0	15	15	93¹	57	6	3.1	13.5	140	50%	.276	0.95	1.93	2.20	3.6				
2017	PIT	MLB	23	2	7	0	15	13	62	81	13	6.4	8.1	56	44%	.358	2.02	7.69	8.17	-1.8	97.6	64.7	8.6	46.9
2018	PIT	MLB	24	1	2	0	34	0	56	47	5	5.5	11.6	72	57%	.321	1.45	4.34	2.88	1.4	99.7	72.5	12.4	46.3
2018	TBA	MLB	24	1	5	0	11	11	55²	42	10	3.1	10.3	64	44%	.248	1.10	4.20	3.64	0.9	99.3	68.2	13.2	48.5
2019	TBA	MLB	25	6	1	0	12	12	60²	40	4	2.1	11.3	76	50%	.265	0.89	1.78	2.77	2.0	99.8	67.3	12.4	50.2
2020	*TBA*	*MLB*	*26*	*9*	*9*	*0*	*28*	*28*	*140*	*124*	*18*	*3.9*	*11.4*	*178*	*46%*	*.312*	*1.32*	*3.91*	*4.09*	*2.3*	*98.8*	*69.5*	*11.9*	*49.3*

Comparables: Archie Bradley, José Berríos, Jake Faria

At one point in the year, Glasnow was one of the best pitchers in the American League and perhaps all of baseball—sitting on a 6-0 record with a 1.47 ERA after throwing seven scoreless against the Orioles on May 3rd. That's a hell of a turnaround for the right-hander, who the Pirates gave up on as a starter just the year prior. Things got scary for a little bit as a forearm injury sidelined him from mid-May until September, though he looked very much like that same pitcher once again upon his return, albeit in much smaller doses. Even after the injury, Glasnow's stuff remained top notch with a triple-digit fastball and a hammer curveball. He was also the unintentional whistleblower for the Astros sign-stealing endeavor when it appeared as if the Astros knew was he was going to throw even before he did in the ALDS. He enters 2020 as one of three potential aces for a club looking to advance to the LCS for the first time in a dozen years.

Brent Honeywell Jr. RHP   Born: 03/31/95   Age: 25   Bats: R   Throws: R   Height: 6'2"   Weight: 180   Origin: Round 2, 2014 Draft (#72 overall)

YEAR	TEAM	LVL	AGE	W	L	SV	G	GS	IP	H	HR	BB/9	K/9	K	GB%	BABIP	WHIP	ERA	DRA	WARP	MPH	FB%	WHF	CSP
2017	MNT	AA	22	1	1	0	2	2	13	4	1	2.8	13.8	20	45%	.158	0.62	2.08	1.98	0.5				
2017	DUR	AAA	22	12	8	0	24	24	123²	130	11	2.3	11.1	152	42%	.366	1.30	3.64	4.26	2.0				
2020	*TBA*	*MLB*	*25*	*3*	*3*	*0*	*29*	*5*	*47*	*46*	*7*	*3.2*	*9.5*	*50*	*38%*	*.308*	*1.34*	*4.32*	*4.53*	*0.4*				

Comparables: Mitch Keller, Zack Littell, Stephen Gonsalves

Honeywell missed all of 2018 after undergoing Tommy John surgery. He was poised to make a mid-season debut in 2019 until he experienced a few minor setbacks and then a major one. The prized right-hander fractured his right elbow and has now gone two seasons without throwing a competitive pitch. Once again, the Rays are hoping for a mid-year return, but instead of the 23-year-old starter they thought they had in 2018, he will be a 25-year-old with more battlescars than pitches thrown at the major-league level. Honeywell has always been more of a pitcher than a thrower, so even with the arm ailments, he possesses the ceiling of an above-average starter because of his control, five-pitch mix and feel for the craft.

Andrew Kittredge RHP   Born: 03/17/90   Age: 30   Bats: R   Throws: R   Height: 6'1"   Weight: 235   Origin: Round 45, 2008 Draft (#1360 overall)

YEAR	TEAM	LVL	AGE	W	L	SV	G	GS	IP	H	HR	BB/9	K/9	K	GB%	BABIP	WHIP	ERA	DRA	WARP	MPH	FB%	WHF	CSP
2017	DUR	AAA	27	6	1	2	41	2	68¹	49	2	2.1	10.3	78	54%	.278	0.95	1.45	2.67	2.0				
2017	TBA	MLB	27	0	1	0	15	0	15¹	13	2	3.5	8.2	14	50%	.250	1.24	1.76	3.25	0.3	96.4	29	13.1	48.4
2018	DUR	AAA	28	6	0	2	21	1	46	41	3	2.3	11.3	58	39%	.317	1.15	2.74	3.39	0.9				
2018	TBA	MLB	28	3	2	0	33	3	38¹	54	7	4.0	7.0	30	51%	.373	1.85	7.75	6.06	-0.5	95.6	39.8	10.5	47.1
2019	DUR	AAA	29	2	1	6	27	1	37¹	24	3	1.4	13.3	55	51%	.276	0.80	1.93	1.32	1.8				
2019	TBA	MLB	29	1	0	0	37	7	49²	51	7	2.2	10.5	58	50%	.336	1.27	4.17	3.73	0.9	96.5	58.1	16.4	43.6
2020	*TBA*	*MLB*	*30*	*3*	*4*	*0*	*37*	*13*	*52*	*48*	*6*	*2.8*	*9.9*	*57*	*51%*	*.307*	*1.25*	*3.60*	*3.88*	*0.9*	*95.4*	*48.7*	*14*	*45.8*

Comparables: Josh Lueke, Rob Wooten, Chasen Bradford

Kittredge still looks like a sleepy fellow, but was a steady middle relief arm for the Rays. After throwing more sliders than fastballs in his first two partial seasons, the right-hander relied more on the heater to set up the slide piece to much better results. Leading with a mid-90s fastball, Kittredge threw a first-pitch strike 68 percent of the time. Getting ahead in the count allowed him to use his breaking ball as more of a chase pitch which resulted in a swinging strike rate about five percentage points higher than league average. The lack of a real changeup makes him susceptible to the platoon split, and he typically worked in low-to-medium leverage situations. That said, when you rely on the bullpen as much as Tampa Bay does, the 2019 version of Kittredge is a nice piece of an expanding puzzle.

★ ★ ★ *2020 Top 101 Prospect* **#50** ★ ★ ★

Matthew Liberatore LHP   Born: 11/06/99   Age: 20   Bats: L   Throws: L   Height: 6'5"   Weight: 200   Origin: Round 1, 2018 Draft (#16 overall)

YEAR	TEAM	LVL	AGE	W	L	SV	G	GS	IP	H	HR	BB/9	K/9	K	GB%	BABIP	WHIP	ERA	DRA	WARP	MPH	FB%	WHF	CSP
2018	RAY	RK	18	1	2	0	8	8	27²	16	0	3.6	10.4	32	45%	.258	0.98	0.98	2.03	1.2				
2019	BGR	A	19	6	2	0	16	15	78¹	70	2	3.6	8.7	76	58%	.311	1.29	3.10	4.78	0.4				
2020	*TBA*	*MLB*	*20*	*2*	*2*	*0*	*33*	*0*	*35*	*34*	*5*	*4.0*	*7.2*	*28*	*52%*	*.281*	*1.40*	*4.50*	*4.64*	*0.2*				

Comparables: Brad Hand, Jake Thompson, Eduardo Rodriguez

Arguably the top prep lefty in the 2018 draft, Liberatore made his full-season debut in 2019; a somewhat aggressive assignment by the conservative leaning Rays. He held up more than adequately as a 19-year-old in the Midwest League where most players are on average three years older than he was. He has a tall frame with the ability to fill out more as he matures. The southpaw tosses a four-pitch medley, led by a low-90s fastball that he can run higher when needed, a curveball that projects to be an out pitch, a changeup with similar projection to fend off the platoon split and a slider that he added along the way. He wraps it up with plus control that is solid enough to morph into plus command as he gains experience. He will likely spend most, if not all, of 2020 at the organization's spring training base in Port Charlotte, cutting his teeth in the muggy air of the Florida State League.

★ ★ ★ *2020 Top 101 Prospect* **#71** ★ ★ ★

Shane McClanahan LHP Born: 04/28/97 Age: 23 Bats: L Throws: L Height: 6'1" Weight: 200 Origin: Round 1C, 2018 Draft (#31 overall)

YEAR	TEAM	LVL	AGE	W	L	SV	G	GS	IP	H	HR	BB/9	K/9	K	GB%	BABIP	WHIP	ERA	DRA	WARP	MPH	FB%	WHF	CSP
2019	BGR	A	22	4	4	0	11	10	53	38	3	5.3	12.6	74	48%	.304	1.30	3.40	3.83	0.8				
2019	PCH	A+	22	6	1	0	9	8	49¹	33	1	1.5	10.8	59	44%	.250	0.83	1.46	2.48	1.5				
2019	MNT	AA	22	1	1	0	4	4	18¹	30	3	2.9	10.3	21	43%	.450	1.96	8.35	7.93	-0.7				
2020	TBA	MLB	23	2	2	0	33	0	35	34	5	3.4	9.4	37	41%	.308	1.36	4.37	4.48	0.3				

Comparables: *Greg Smith, Gregory Soto, Steven Matz*

Having already drafted arguably the best prep lefty pitcher in the 2018 draft, Matthew Liberatore, the Rays were ecstatic to see one of the best college southpaws—certainly the best in their backyard —sitting there for them with the 31st overall pick. The junior from the University of South Florida impressed during his first full-year in pro ball, making the wide trek from Bowling Green to Montgomery in a single season. In between his starting and ending point, he turned home briefly to dominate the Florida State League with nearly eight strikeouts versus every walk. He lives in the mid-90s with the strength to ramp up if needed. His changeup projects to be above-average and his curve is already there. There is some concern about his delivery, which is only heightened by the fact he already has Tommy John on his resume. The upside is a middle-of-the-rotation lefty. The Rays should let him continue on that path but find comfort in knowing they could turn him loose as a late-inning reliever at any time.

★ ★ ★ *2020 Top 101 Prospect* **#28** ★ ★ ★

Brendan McKay LHP Born: 12/18/95 Age: 24 Bats: L Throws: L Height: 6'2" Weight: 212 Origin: Round 1, 2017 Draft (#4 overall)

YEAR	TEAM	LVL	AGE	W	L	SV	G	GS	IP	H	HR	BB/9	K/9	K	GB%	BABIP	WHIP	ERA	DRA	WARP	MPH	FB%	WHF	CSP
2017	HUD	A-	21	1	0	0	6	6	20	10	3	2.2	9.4	21	53%	.159	0.75	1.80	2.68	0.6				
2018	RAY	RK	22	0	0	0	2	2	6	2	0	1.5	13.5	9	58%	.167	0.50	1.50	0.71	0.3				
2018	BGR	A	22	2	0	0	6	6	24²	8	1	0.7	14.6	40	63%	.167	0.41	1.09	1.44	1.1				
2018	PCH	A+	22	3	2	0	11	9	47²	45	2	2.1	10.2	54	39%	.350	1.17	3.21	3.90	0.7				
2019	MNT	AA	23	3	0	0	8	7	41²	25	2	1.9	13.4	62	44%	.280	0.82	1.30	2.51	1.2				
2019	DUR	AAA	23	3	0	0	7	6	32	17	1	2.5	11.2	40	49%	.229	0.81	0.84	1.54	1.6				
2019	TBA	MLB	23	2	4	0	13	11	49	53	8	2.9	10.3	56	37%	.331	1.41	5.14	5.79	0.0	95.6	57.1	11.6	50.4
2020	TBA	MLB	24	5	5	0	18	18	77	73	12	2.9	8.6	73	39%	.287	1.27	4.12	4.41	1.0	95.4	58.8	12	51.9

Comparables: *Dan Straily, Rogelio Armenteros, Joe Musgrove*

The Shohei Ohtani comps can stop for now as the Rays will have to settle for McKay just being a really good left-handed starter instead of a two-headed dragon. The Rays took away McKay's first base glove to start the season and then his bat somewhere along the way. He still may make the occasional start at designated hitter—and even with a 26-man roster, it will still be valuable to have a pitcher that can also hit a little—but McKay's on his way towards leaving that double life behind. He was nearly unhittable to start his career before the league caught up to him. By the end of the year, concerns about workload took over and he didn't throw over 65 pitches in an appearance after mid-August. Despite the ups and downs, McKay showed stuff and poise that makes him a potential number two or three starter. He has a four-pitch mix led by a low-to-mid 90s fastball and a true, plus curveball. Developing command led to some home run issues at the highest level, but he has the ability to repeat and turn that into a strength. The Rays may play some games early in the year with regards to service time and innings totals, but McKay should toss his most important pitches for Tampa Bay in 2020.

Charlie Morton RHP Born: 11/12/83 Age: 36 Bats: R Throws: R Height: 6'5" Weight: 215 Origin: Round 3, 2002 Draft (#95 overall)

YEAR	TEAM	LVL	AGE	W	L	SV	G	GS	IP	H	HR	BB/9	K/9	K	GB%	BABIP	WHIP	ERA	DRA	WARP	MPH	FB%	WHF	CSP
2017	FRE	AAA	33	0	1	0	2	2	6	4	1	3.0	4.5	3	71%	.188	1.00	1.50	4.31	0.1				
2017	HOU	MLB	33	14	7	0	25	25	146²	125	14	3.1	10.0	163	53%	.295	1.19	3.62	3.92	2.7	97.1	65.6	11.5	48.6
2018	HOU	MLB	34	15	3	0	30	30	167	130	18	3.4	10.8	201	49%	.284	1.16	3.13	3.68	3.1	97.9	63.4	12.8	48.3
2019	TBA	MLB	35	16	6	0	33	33	194²	154	15	2.6	11.1	240	48%	.298	1.08	3.05	2.96	5.9	96.4	50.2	14	50
2020	TBA	MLB	36	11	9	0	29	29	169	142	18	3.1	11.0	206	48%	.299	1.18	3.33	3.58	3.7	95.7	56.5	12.8	48

Comparables: *Jason Hammel, Todd Stottlemyre, Clay Buchholz*

Uncle Charlie. Chaz Moe. CFM. You can call him what you want, but make sure to also call him really freaking good. A finalist for the AL Cy Young Award, Morton was a rock for Tampa Bay in a rotation that sometimes featured just him and a few pebbles. Signed to a modest two-year deal because of durability and age concerns, the right-hander turned in a career year for the Rays. He set new high-water marks in games started, innings pitched, strikeouts, ERA and WHIP. Picking up where he left off in Philadelphia and Houston, Morton continued to pump mid-90s fastballs with arguably the best curveball in the game. In fact, the Rays encouraged the hammer so much, he threw it nearly 40 percent of the time. The former Braves' farmhand continued his recent run of postseason success by tossing 10 additional frames and allowing just one earned run in the process. Obviously, the Rays would prefer their younger arms to shoulder more of the load in 2020 with Cholly, Chip, Ground Chuck Morton being a solid pillar of support.

Emilio Pagán RHP Born: 05/07/91 Age: 29 Bats: L Throws: R Height: 6'3" Weight: 205 Origin: Round 10, 2013 Draft (#297 overall)

YEAR	TEAM	LVL	AGE	W	L	SV	G	GS	IP	H	HR	BB/9	K/9	K	GB%	BABIP	WHIP	ERA	DRA	WARP	MPH	FB%	WHF	CSP
2017	TAC	AAA	26	2	1	5	23	0	31²	19	0	2.3	10.2	36	29%	.241	0.85	2.56	1.55	1.3				
2017	SEA	MLB	26	2	3	0	34	0	50¹	39	7	1.4	10.0	56	23%	.258	0.93	3.22	3.68	0.8	95.8	68.7	15	54.7
2018	NAS	AAA	27	1	0	0	5	0	6	5	2	0.0	16.5	11	38%	.273	0.83	3.00	1.98	0.2				
2018	OAK	MLB	27	3	1	0	55	0	62	55	13	2.8	9.1	63	25%	.256	1.19	4.35	4.35	0.4	96.1	66.4	15.5	50.9
2019	DUR	AAA	28	0	0	2	4	1	6	2	0	6.0	15.0	10	46%	.182	1.00	0.00	1.74	0.3				
2019	TBA	MLB	28	4	2	20	66	0	70	45	12	1.7	12.3	96	35%	.228	0.83	2.31	2.91	1.9	97.4	61.5	19.3	50.2
2020	TBA	MLB	29	3	2	22	48	0	51	39	8	2.6	12.0	68	32%	.276	1.05	2.88	3.27	1.1	96.0	64.5	17.2	51.6

Comparables: Paul Sewald, Richard Rodríguez, Ryan Garton

Pagán did not make the Rays' Opening Day roster after losing the final spot to Adam Kolarek. By the end of the season, Kolarek was pitching in Los Angeles and Pagán was Tampa Bay's closer. It goes that way sometimes. Part of Pagán's ascent into the high-leverage life had to do with the failure of others. Jose Alvarado struggled as the closer and the committee approach was not much better. By the time the club acquired Nick Anderson, Pagán had established himself as a reliable reliever and allowed Anderson's fresh arm to get big outs in the seventh and eighth innings. A prototypical two-pitch reliever, Pagán got most of his outs with either a fastball or a slider. As a fly-ball pitcher, he can sometimes give up the big one, but he limits traffic on the bases with an elite walk rate. Anderson and Castillo are better pitchers, but Pagán won't sweat that little detail if he converts more saves and cashes those eventual arb-year checks.

Colin Poche LHP Born: 01/17/94 Age: 26 Bats: L Throws: L Height: 6'3" Weight: 235 Origin: Round 14, 2016 Draft (#419 overall)

YEAR	TEAM	LVL	AGE	W	L	SV	G	GS	IP	H	HR	BB/9	K/9	K	GB%	BABIP	WHIP	ERA	DRA	WARP	MPH	FB%	WHF	CSP
2017	KNC	A	23	2	0	1	13	0	24²	16	0	2.2	16.1	44	40%	.372	0.89	1.09	2.19	0.8				
2017	VIS	A+	23	1	1	2	18	0	25²	14	0	4.6	13.0	37	43%	.275	1.05	1.40	2.23	0.8				
2018	WTN	AA	24	0	0	1	9	0	11	3	0	1.6	18.8	23	8%	.250	0.45	0.00	2.25	0.3				
2018	DUR	AAA	24	5	0	1	28	2	50	29	2	3.1	14.0	78	28%	.297	0.92	1.08	2.33	1.6				
2019	DUR	AAA	25	2	2	0	20	2	27¹	32	4	3.0	15.8	48	35%	.459	1.50	6.26	3.62	0.7				
2019	TBA	MLB	25	5	5	2	51	0	51²	33	9	3.3	12.5	72	19%	.235	1.01	4.70	4.30	0.6	95.2	88.5	18.9	49.9
2020	TBA	MLB	26	3	3	0	54	0	58	42	9	3.3	12.2	78	24%	.267	1.10	3.07	3.42	1.1	94.8	90.1	19.2	50.8

Comparables: Phil Maton, James Pazos, Giovanny Gallegos

Poche tested his insane strikeout rate at the major-league level for the first time and for the most part it held up. After striking out just over 41 percent of the minor leaguers he faced in 2018, he punched out 35 percent of the big leaguers he danced with in 2019. Not bad for a dude that throws a 93-mph fastball nearly nine out of every 10 pitches. The strikeouts were good, but the location could use work; his extreme fly-ball approach means more homers when his command is substandard. Despite pitching with his left hand, Poche was platoon neutral in his first major-league run; a byproduct of not being reliant on a breaking pitch for outs. This will likely help him earn more high-leverage work in the future, especially if he can hone in on the location of his rising heater.

Austin Pruitt RHP Born: 08/31/89 Age: 30 Bats: R Throws: R Height: 5'10" Weight: 185 Origin: Round 9, 2013 Draft (#278 overall)

YEAR	TEAM	LVL	AGE	W	L	SV	G	GS	IP	H	HR	BB/9	K/9	K	GB%	BABIP	WHIP	ERA	DRA	WARP	MPH	FB%	WHF	CSP
2017	DUR	AAA	27	0	1	1	9	4	24²	17	2	0.7	12.0	33	58%	.273	0.77	2.55	2.06	0.9				
2017	TBA	MLB	27	7	5	1	30	8	83	103	11	2.4	7.2	66	46%	.345	1.51	5.31	4.81	0.5	93.2	43.3	10.4	47.1
2018	DUR	AAA	28	3	0	1	14	4	39²	26	2	1.6	11.1	49	49%	.261	0.83	2.95	2.35	1.3				
2018	TBA	MLB	28	2	3	4	23	0	69²	72	7	2.1	5.4	42	50%	.289	1.26	4.65	3.66	1.0	93.8	44	10.3	50.6
2019	DUR	AAA	29	3	3	0	18	6	48¹	61	9	2.2	9.5	51	49%	.364	1.51	5.40	5.09	0.6				
2019	TBA	MLB	29	3	0	0	14	2	47	47	7	2.3	7.5	39	55%	.296	1.26	4.40	4.76	0.3	93.5	44	11.9	46.9
2020	TBA	MLB	30	1	1	0	24	0	26	26	4	2.5	7.5	21	49%	.295	1.28	4.02	4.31	0.2	92.8	43.6	10.8	48

Comparables: Seth Lugo, Brent Suter, Josh Lueke

Do you know how some things are still around in 2020 and you do not know why? Things like wiping ourselves with paper, sending information via fax or Pruitt on a 40-man roster? Those type of things. If you had to endorse his best skill on LinkedIn, you would note his aptitude for traveling from Durham to St. Petersburg on short notice and throwing 50 meaningless pitches soon after. Meanwhile, there was a stretch when the Rays' staff was stretched so thin that Pruitt made two meaningful starts in late August and early September. He allowed just two runs across them combined, but then was used just twice the rest of the season when more dynamic arms were available. It has been a mystifying, magical ride thus far, but with 40-man roster spots becoming scarce this may be the last stop on the Pruitt Express.

Trevor Richards RHP Born: 05/15/93 Age: 27 Bats: R Throws: R Height: 6'2" Weight: 190 Origin: Undrafted Free Agent, 2016

YEAR	TEAM	LVL	AGE	W	L	SV	G	GS	IP	H	HR	BB/9	K/9	K	GB%	BABIP	WHIP	ERA	DRA	WARP	MPH	FB%	WHF	CSP
2017	JUP	A+	24	7	4	0	13	11	70²	54	2	1.5	10.3	81	62%	.284	0.93	2.17	2.90	1.9				
2017	JAX	AA	24	5	7	0	14	14	75¹	67	4	2.2	9.2	77	50%	.297	1.13	2.87	3.46	1.5				
2018	NWO	AAA	25	3	2	0	6	6	39¹	31	4	0.9	8.5	37	50%	.260	0.89	2.06	2.66	1.3				
2018	MIA	MLB	25	4	9	0	25	25	126¹	121	15	3.8	9.3	130	38%	.309	1.39	4.42	3.57	2.5	92.7	54.8	11.7	44.4
2019	MIA	MLB	26	3	12	0	23	20	112	104	16	4.1	8.3	103	38%	.286	1.38	4.50	5.69	0.1	92.3	42.3	12.8	45.9
2019	TBA	MLB	26	3	0	0	7	3	23¹	23	3	1.9	9.3	24	35%	.308	1.20	1.93	4.63	0.3	91.9	50	13	46.6
2020	TBA	MLB	27	3	2	0	33	3	48	43	7	3.3	8.5	45	38%	.278	1.27	3.98	4.22	0.6	92.2	49.1	12.5	45.9

Comparables: Brock Stewart, Domingo Germán, Mike Clevinger

When you google Richards' name, the first autocomplete is gray hair. It is true and he is only 26. The Rays acquired ol' pelo canoso at the trade deadline in an interstate swap with the Marlins. He was effective following the trade, but never made Tampa Bay's postseason roster. In a small sample size, he simplified his approach with his new club, leaning mostly on fastballs and changeups with breaking balls falling out of favor. The early returns were encouraging, with an increase in strikeout rate and a decrease in walks. Richards failed as a starter with Miami and there are too many talented arms ahead of him with the Rays to return to the rotation, but he also does not have the stuff that would allow him to dominate in short-relief, high-leverage situations. The bulk role that Tampa uses so effectively could be just what he needs to carve out a spot on the pitching staff going forward.

Chaz Roe RHP Born: 10/09/86 Age: 33 Bats: R Throws: R Height: 6'5" Weight: 190 Origin: Round 1, 2005 Draft (#32 overall)

YEAR	TEAM	LVL	AGE	W	L	SV	G	GS	IP	H	HR	BB/9	K/9	K	GB%	BABIP	WHIP	ERA	DRA	WARP	MPH	FB%	WHF	CSP
2017	DUR	AAA	30	0	3	4	17	0	21	18	1	2.1	15.0	35	43%	.370	1.10	3.00	3.49	0.4				
2017	ATL	MLB	30	0	0	0	3	0	2	3	0	9.0	4.5	1	67%	.333	2.50	9.00	7.60	-0.1	95.1	53.3	6.7	54.1
2017	TBA	MLB	30	0	0	0	9	0	8²	4	1	3.1	12.5	12	50%	.200	0.81	1.04	3.01	0.2	94.7	42.9	16.8	40.9
2018	TBA	MLB	31	1	3	1	61	0	50¹	35	6	2.9	9.5	53	48%	.242	1.01	3.58	3.71	0.7	94.5	47.4	11.7	49.4
2019	TBA	MLB	32	1	3	1	71	0	51	49	3	5.5	11.5	65	44%	.359	1.57	4.06	4.57	0.4	93.5	28.9	10.2	48.6
2020	TBA	MLB	33	2	2	0	48	0	51	44	7	3.5	9.8	56	46%	.285	1.26	3.84	4.07	0.6	93.0	36.4	10.8	47.3

Comparables: Brad Brach, Sam Freeman, Luis García

Chef Roe continues to serve up quality sliders out of his Chez Roe Cafe. The now St. Petersburg-based culinary artist forms his sliders by hand. Keeping his middle and index fingers close, he grips one side of the ball while keeping his ring finger on the other end and tucking his thumb below. This forms one of the most delicious offerings you will ever encounter. While the quality is fantastic in limited quantity, Chef Roe does not have the best track record when it comes to delivering large orders to the right location. He also struggles at times with trying to get the perfect slider out under pressure which can end up coming out flat. As for the rest of the menu, there is not much to it. Unless you like meatballs, of course.

Blake Snell LHP Born: 12/04/92 Age: 27 Bats: L Throws: L Height: 6'4" Weight: 215 Origin: Round 1, 2011 Draft (#52 overall)

YEAR	TEAM	LVL	AGE	W	L	SV	G	GS	IP	H	HR	BB/9	K/9	K	GB%	BABIP	WHIP	ERA	DRA	WARP	MPH	FB%	WHF	CSP
2017	DUR	AAA	24	5	0	0	7	7	44	43	5	3.1	12.5	61	46%	.362	1.32	2.66	3.78	0.9				
2017	TBA	MLB	24	5	7	0	24	24	129¹	113	15	4.1	8.3	119	45%	.278	1.33	4.04	4.05	2.2	96.5	55.1	11.4	40.4
2018	TBA	MLB	25	21	5	0	31	31	180²	112	16	3.2	11.0	221	46%	.241	0.97	1.89	2.44	6.0	98.2	51.5	15.7	44.5
2019	TBA	MLB	26	6	8	0	23	23	107	96	14	3.4	12.4	147	39%	.343	1.27	4.29	3.59	2.5	97.6	48.4	18.1	42.8
2020	TBA	MLB	27	10	8	0	28	28	154	125	18	4.1	12.8	220	41%	.315	1.27	3.42	3.62	3.3	97.1	51.9	15.7	43.3

Comparables: Anthony Banda, Matt Moore, Jake Faria

As expected, Snell was not as good as his award-winning season in 2018. However, the midseason elbow surgery that wiped out two months of his summer was unexpected. Snell returned in late September, but was never able to get back to full speed. Despite the two-and-a-half-run jump in ERA, the lanky lefty wasn't quite that far from pitcher he was a season ago. He still averaged 96 on the fastball with a hammer curveball to back it up. His changeup maintained about 10 mph of separation from the heater and he mixed in a hard slider/cutter when he wanted. He struck out even more batters on a percentage basis while keeping the walks static. So it comes down to two distinct possibilities: a rising fly-ball rate in a homer-happy environment or the weird goatee he attempted to pull off. All in all, a healthy Snell is one of the best pitchers in baseball. And with a team-friendly extension, he is also one of the most valuable pieces of a team built to win a lot over the next five seasons. Just don't tell him about trades while he's gaming.

Ryan Yarbrough LHP Born: 12/31/91 Age: 28 Bats: R Throws: L Height: 6'5" Weight: 210 Origin: Round 4, 2014 Draft (#111 overall)

YEAR	TEAM	LVL	AGE	W	L	SV	G	GS	IP	H	HR	BB/9	K/9	K	GB%	BABIP	WHIP	ERA	DRA	WARP	MPH	FB%	WHF	CSP
2017	DUR	AAA	25	13	6	0	26	26	157¹	144	20	2.2	9.1	159	47%	.296	1.16	3.43	4.46	2.1				
2018	TBA	MLB	26	16	6	0	38	6	147¹	140	18	3.1	7.8	128	39%	.288	1.29	3.91	4.82	0.3	91.7	63.9	10	50.6
2019	DUR	AAA	27	2	1	0	5	4	26	24	2	1.0	12.1	35	46%	.344	1.04	3.81	2.83	1.0				
2019	TBA	MLB	27	11	6	0	28	14	141²	121	15	1.3	7.4	117	44%	.264	1.00	4.13	3.97	2.5	89.9	61	11	49.2
2020	TBA	MLB	28	7	7	0	61	13	120	114	21	2.2	7.6	101	42%	.273	1.19	4.00	4.36	1.4	90.2	62.7	10.6	50.2

Comparables: Brent Suter, Tyler Anderson, Jarlin García

The Yarbrough arbitration case would be a fascinating one, and one it is doubtful the Rays will have. Tampa Bay has had impeccable timing with regards to moving some players before arbitration starts to at least modestly reward their production. Over the last two seasons, Yarbrough has shouldered a starter's workload, throwing 289 innings. Only 63 other pitchers have reached that threshold. That said, he has only made 20 official starts. No other pitcher on that list has made fewer than 35. The lefty did start more games in 2019 than 2018, yet half of his appearances still came in relief. His representation will likely point to innings and wins to get him paid like a starter. With all the public hearings on television over the past year, the one baseball fans would love to see is Yarbrough versus whatever employer he has at the time he is eligible.

Hitters

HITTER	POS	TEAM	LVL	AGE	PA	R	2B	3B	HR	RBI	BB	K	SB	CS	AVG/OBP/SLG	DRC+	VORP	BABIP	BRR	FRAA	WARP
Roberto Alvarez	C	BGR	A	19	406	30	13	3	3	42	17	70	2	0	.249/.291/.324	74	1.8	.295	-2.5	C(64): -2.5	-0.3
Emilio Bonifácio	UT	DUR	AAA	34	288	48	19	3	8	36	25	63	15	6	.286/.353/.475	102	14.9	.351	2.9	CF(31): -2.8, LF(22): 1.5	1.1
Dylan Cozens	OF	PHI	MLB	25	1	0	0	0	0	0	0	0	0	0	.000/.000/.000	82	0.0	.000	0.0		0.0
	OF	LEH	AAA	25	99	20	1	2	6	15	20	42	5	2	.167/.333/.462	96	3.9	.226	0.3	RF(13): 4.5, LF(4): 0.1	0.6
Johnny Davis	OF	TBA	MLB	29	4	5	0	1	0	0	0	2	0	0	.250/.250/.750	69	0.0	.500	0.1	CF(2): -0.2, LF(1): 0.0	0.0
Lucius Fox	MI	DUR	AAA	21	49	6	0	1	0	1	6	15	2	0	.143/.250/.190	47	0.1	.222	0.6	SS(12): 0.4, 2B(1): -0.1	0.0
	MI	MNT	AA	21	431	60	16	8	3	33	53	89	37	11	.230/.340/.342	106	16.6	.293	0.6	SS(79): -3.9, 2B(12): 1.4	2.0
Niko Hulsizer	OF	GRL	A	22	256	46	17	1	15	49	37	75	4	1	.268/.395/.574	186	28.8	.339	-3.3	LF(29): 4.2, RF(4): 1.0	2.9
	OF	RCU	A+	22	98	15	6	0	5	18	9	33	3	2	.259/.327/.506	100	7.2	.340	1.1	LF(15): 1.6	0.5
	OF	PCH	A+	22	39	4	2	0	1	4	4	11	0	1	.235/.308/.382	96	1.6	.304	-0.1	LF(5): 0.1, RF(3): 0.3	0.1
Josh Lowe	OF	MNT	AA	21	519	70	23	4	18	62	59	132	30	9	.252/.341/.442	128	38.1	.316	5.6	CF(110): -7.0, RF(8): 2.2	3.3
Brian O'Grady	1B	CIN	MLB	27	48	4	2	1	2	3	4	17	0	0	.190/.292/.429	76	0.0	.261	-0.5	CF(11): -0.2, LF(6): 0.1	-0.1
	1B	LOU	AAA	27	489	71	30	1	28	77	51	136	20	4	.280/.359/.550	111	31.6	.342	2.0	1B(64): -1.5, CF(32): 1.6	1.8
Kevin Padlo	INF	MNT	AA	22	277	39	20	0	12	35	47	70	11	4	.250/.383/.505	167	30.9	.299	0.2	3B(57): 7.1, 1B(6): -0.4	3.5
	INF	DUR	AAA	22	155	25	11	1	9	27	21	46	1	0	.290/.400/.595	128	11.7	.382	1.0	3B(30): 3.5, 2B(3): 0.2	1.3
Michael Perez	C	DUR	AAA	26	216	23	7	0	13	42	28	51	0	2	.245/.338/.495	116	13.2	.258	0.9	C(44): 1.2	1.5
	C	TBA	MLB	26	55	6	5	0	0	2	8	19	0	0	.217/.345/.326	74	1.0	.370	-1.2	C(20): 0.9, 1B(2): 0.0	0.1
Garrett Whitley	OF	PCH	A+	22	439	51	25	7	10	40	62	163	16	12	.226/.339/.412	119	23.0	.370	-3.6	LF(63): -2.8, CF(26): -2.5	1.1

One of these days, a catching prospect will work out for Tampa Bay. **Roberto Alvarez** is trying to be that one. ⚉ If **Emilio Bonifácio**'s rate stats on the diamond were anything like his confirmed 30-percent restaurant tipping practices, he'd have spent his season leaving gratuities in Tampa, Chicago and New York instead of Durham, Charlotte and Syracuse. ⚉ The Rays are paying **Dylan Cozens** to rehab from a foot injury. Meanwhile, the Buffalo Sabres selected him seventh overall in the 2019 NHL draft. ⚉ **Johnny Davis** came out of nowhere—well the Mexican League actually—to score some of the Rays' most important runs in September as a designated runner. ⚉ **Lucius Fox** will need to start hitting fast otherwise he will become lost in an ever-expanding middle infield depth chart. ⚉ Long-hair, don't care. **Niko Hulsizer** has the chance to be a solid hitting outfielder in the majors one day. ⚉ **Josh Lowe** is a former first-round pick with a lot of tools, and has a brother that raps with Ji-Man Choi. ⚉ **Brian O'Grady** is a 27-year-old who finally got a full look at Triple-A. To his credit, he hit just fine there; alas, it's hard to imagine him making enough contact in the majors to be more than an up-and-down guy—even if the power *is* legit. ⚉ After scuffling in the low minors over the last two years, **Kevin Padlo** hit the ol' UPGRADE button in Double-A and Triple-A, and now sits on the doorstep of the majors in 2020. ⚉ **Michael Perez** has some offensive chops, which is more than most catchers can say. He just needs an extended look to see how sharp his chops really are. ⚉ Ciara is married to Russell Wilson and has a child with rapper Future. **Garrett Whitley** currently looks like what you would get if Russell Wilson and Future had a child of their own. That is about the nicest thing you can say about this former first-round pick.

Pitchers

PITCHER	TEAM	LVL	AGE	W	L	SV	G	GS	IP	H	HR	BB/9	K/9	K	GB%	BABIP	WHIP	ERA	DRA	WARP	MPH	FB%	WHF	CSP
John Doxakis	HUD	A-	20	0	0	0	12	10	32²	20	0	3.0	8.5	31	51%	.235	0.95	1.93	3.07	0.8				
Peter Fairbanks	DEB	A+	25	1	0	2	11	0	12¹	10	0	2.9	10.9	15	59%	.312	1.14	2.92	3.64	0.2				
	FRI	AA	25	1	0	0	6	0	7¹	2	0	0.0	17.2	14	70%	.200	0.27	0.00	1.71	0.3				
	NAS	AAA	25	0	0	0	7	0	6¹	10	1	2.8	15.6	11	33%	.529	1.89	11.37	3.66	0.2				
	DUR	AAA	25	1	2	0	16	1	17²	15	3	3.1	15.3	30	44%	.333	1.19	5.09	2.49	0.6				
	TBA	MLB	25	2	1	2	13	0	12¹	17	1	2.2	9.5	13	43%	.390	1.62	5.11	4.77	0.1	99.7	38	13.9	51
	TEX	MLB	25	0	2	0	8	0	8²	8	4	7.3	15.6	15	42%	.267	1.73	9.35	3.79	0.1	99.3	51.5	18.7	44.2
JJ Goss	RAY	Rk	18	1	3	0	9	8	17	19	1	1.1	8.5	16	46%	.353	1.24	5.82	4.59	0.3				
Seth Johnson	RAY	Rk	20	0	0	0	5	5	10	7	0	1.8	6.3	7	43%	.233	0.90	0.00	2.02	0.4				
	PRI	Rk+	20	0	1	0	4	4	7	10	0	1.3	11.6	9	40%	.500	1.57	5.14	6.47	0.0				
Hoby Milner	DUR	AAA	28	3	3	12	50	0	61²	47	7	1.9	13.0	89	44%	.297	0.97	3.06	1.86	2.6				
	TBA	MLB	28	0	0	0	4	0	3²	4	0	2.5	7.4	3	25%	.333	1.36	7.36	5.33	0.0	89.6	68.6	5.7	52.5
Joe Ryan	BGR	A	23	2	2	0	6	6	27²	19	2	3.6	15.3	47	29%	.315	1.08	2.93	2.91	0.7				
	PCH	A+	23	7	2	0	15	13	82²	47	3	1.3	12.2	112	38%	.244	0.71	1.42	2.02	3.0				
	MNT	AA	23	0	0	0	3	3	13¹	11	2	2.7	16.2	24	27%	.375	1.12	3.38	4.14	0.1				
Phoenix Sanders	MNT	AA	24	3	3	15	37	1	49²	35	3	4.2	10.3	57	47%	.267	1.17	1.81	3.84	0.5				
	DUR	AAA	24	1	0	0	8	0	11¹	9	2	2.4	8.7	11	42%	.241	1.06	2.38	2.86	0.4				
Aaron Slegers	DUR	AAA	26	6	7	0	26	15	112¹	130	22	2.2	6.4	80	43%	.308	1.41	5.05	5.42	1.2				
	TBA	MLB	26	0	0	1	1	0	3	3	1	0.0	0.0	0	36%	.200	1.00	3.00	6.73	0.0	92.0	66.7	4.8	51.4

A second-round pick from Texas A&M, J to the Muah a.k.a. **John Doxakis** could be a mid-rotation lefty with more finesse than stuff or a reliever with more stuff than finesse. ⚉ **Peter Fairbanks** throws really hard toward a general area. Sometimes it works. Sometimes it doesn't. ⚉ The 36th selection in the 2019 draft, **J.J. Goss** is a projectable righty from Texas with a potential three-pitch mix and control. ⚉ **Seth Johnson** was a hitter in JUCO, but became a day-one draft pick as a pitcher who can throw in the upper-90s with two potential bat-missing secondaries. ⚉ After the war, Lt. **Hoby Milner** retired to the Tampa Bay area where he was diagnosed with a cervical nerve issue. ⚉ You know that meme where the cat looks into the mirror and sees a lion? That is **Joe Ryan**, the Rays' minor-league pitcher of the year. ⚉ **Phoenix Sanders** is a useful relief prospect from Augsburg, Germany and of the five players the Rays took out of the Tampa-based University of South Florida last decade, he's likely to make the majors first. ⚉ Here's a fun fact. Did you know **Aaron Slegers** is really tall? Oh, we said that for the last three years? Well, he still is. Check back next year for an update.

TEXAS RANGERS

Essay by Zach Crizer

Player comments by Levi Weaver and BP staff

The Rangers are opening a new ballpark this spring. It will be across the street from the old one, the one that opened 26 years ago and hosted the franchise's greatest period of success. Its very name—Globe Life Field—will give off a vibe that is more "spot-the-difference puzzle" than "heralding a new era." It will have a retractable roof to shelter the masses from sweltering summer heat; that's the big difference. Reading about it, you'd swear a law had been passed requiring the old, retiring stadium to be described as a "perfectly good ballpark." This is Texas, though; epicenter of a distinctive type of performative wealth—Southfork, oil barons, Mark Cuban, etc.

The thriving dad down the street replaces his SUV with the latest model every two years, without fail. A bigger swimming pool plants itself in the ground across the way. And yes, your instincts are right: Jerry Jones did build that other stadium in town at least partially as a monument to his personal largesse. Perfectly good isn't nearly as good as brand stinkin' new and declaratively expensive. Why live comfortably when you could live in luxury?

Pursuit of extravagance is not particularly stirring or sympathetic as life credos go, but within the context of sports fandom, it's the dream. Underlying the comfort and companionship of baseball's day-to-day grind is the same invitation other televised, professional athletic endeavors extend: A chance to fall back on our more base instincts, winners, losers. Champions. Count the wins, count the rings, and flaunt it. All the superiority for the cost of a T-shirt, a certain color cap, or the simple fact of being born in one town over the other.

Since baseball's current Collective Bargaining Agreement took effect in 2017 it has often felt that the league's owners are intentionally suppressing their own thirst for being the best, and depriving fans of the vicarious thrill of achieving it. Using a luxury tax, now known by the infinitely more bureaucratic and sinister Competitive Balance Tax as one important cudgel, those in power have made clear that there are (artificially) fewer things to spend on, fewer outwardly exciting investments worthy of a front office's attention and fewer incentives to vault past "perfectly good."

They have reframed success as the art of getting by.

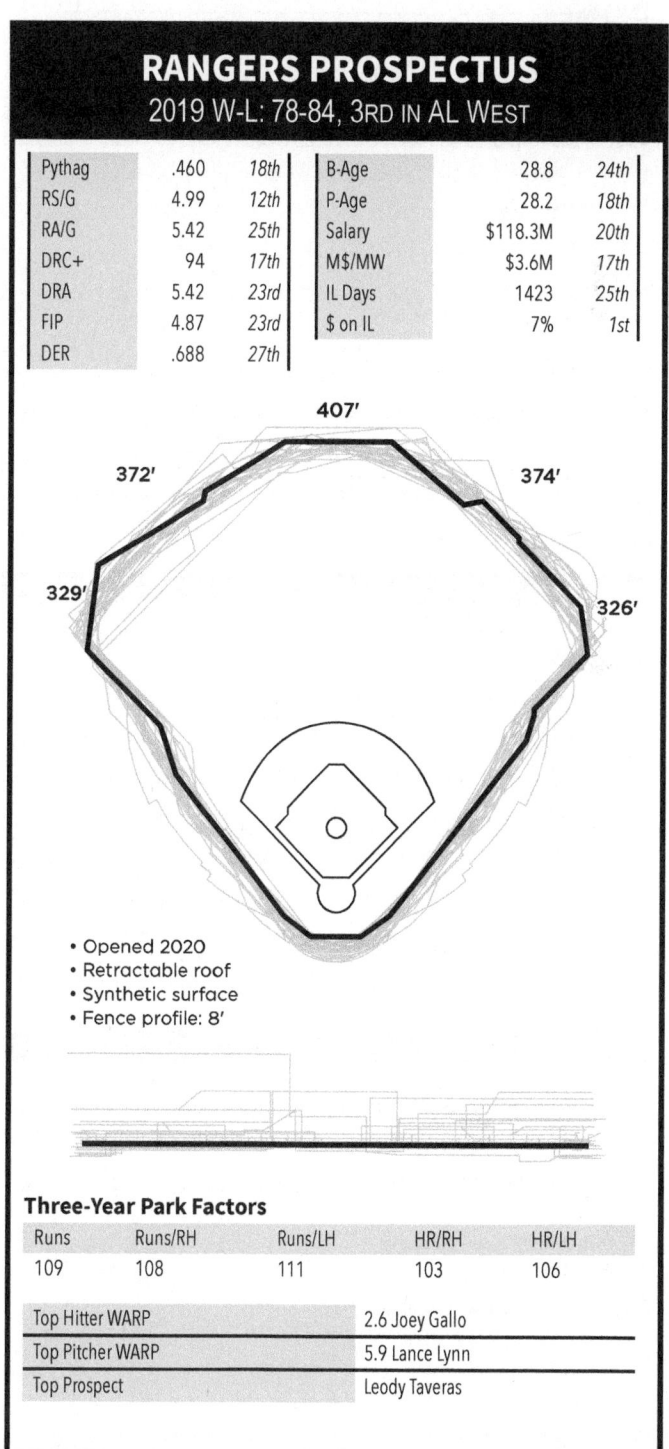

RANGERS PROSPECTUS
2019 W-L: 78-84, 3RD IN AL WEST

Pythag	.460	18th	B-Age	28.8	24th
RS/G	4.99	12th	P-Age	28.2	18th
RA/G	5.42	25th	Salary	$118.3M	20th
DRC+	94	17th	M$/MW	$3.6M	17th
DRA	5.42	23rd	IL Days	1423	25th
FIP	4.87	23rd	$ on IL	7%	1st
DER	.688	27th			

407'
372'
374'
329'
326'

- Opened 2020
- Retractable roof
- Synthetic surface
- Fence profile: 8'

Three-Year Park Factors

Runs	Runs/RH	Runs/LH	HR/RH	HR/LH
109	108	111	103	106

Top Hitter WARP	2.6 Joey Gallo
Top Pitcher WARP	5.9 Lance Lynn
Top Prospect	Leody Taveras

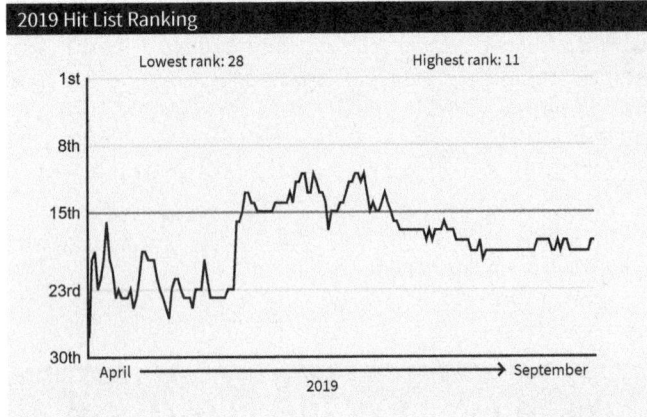

2019 Hit List Ranking

Lowest rank: 28   Highest rank: 11

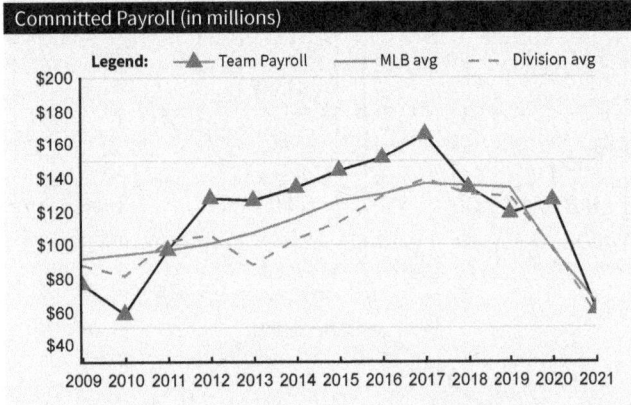

Committed Payroll (in millions)

Legend: ▲ Team Payroll — MLB avg - - Division avg

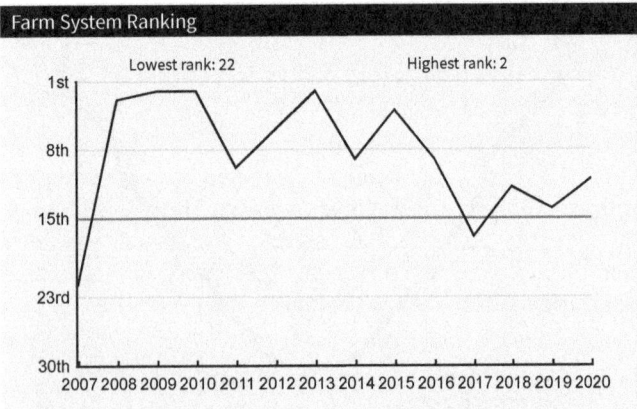

Farm System Ranking

Lowest rank: 22   Highest rank: 2

Personnel

President of Baseball Operations & General Manager
Jon Daniels

Assistant General Manager
Josh Boyd

Assistant General Manager
Mike Daly

Assistant General Manager
Shiraz Rehman

Manager
Chris Woodward

BP Alumni
Bradley Ankrom
Andrew Koo

And while some clubs have fielded more winners by diving headlong into this more arcane mode of building a team, the Rangers have not. Either by unfortunate circumstance or lacking aptitude, they have been slow to find precious stars in development and youth. Instead, they have constructed an urgent case for chasing the gaudy, luxurious new thing.

⚾   ⚾   ⚾

The Texas Rangers, once upon a time, backed up the Brinks truck to strike the first Alex Rodriguez deal. As defending American League champs after 2010, they saw franchise third baseman Michael Young and raised themselves Adrián Beltré to the tune of $96 million and great interpersonal strife. (Young requested a trade, feeling betrayed and marginalized, but ultimately remained with the club in 2011 and scratched out 689 plate appearances, a majors-leading 213 hits and one admittedly strange first-place MVP vote.)

That same summer, they spent $4.95 million to sign a 16-year-old international prospect of great promise named Nomar Mazara and another $3.45 million on a 16-year-old named Ronald Guzmán in a fit of what turned out to be transitional "extravagance"—Mazara's bonus alone would be larger than the average team's entire international pool, as dictated by the current CBA.

As Beltré's time in Texas unspooled, players like Mazara, Guzmán and international classmate Rougned Odor made it to the majors, as did 2012 draftee Joey Gallo. But with the last big splash fading into retirement, GM Jon Daniels' strong record of useful acquisitions has been largely overshadowed by the organization's struggle to turn those homegrown players into an actual winning core.

This is not to call them cheap or cynical. Even during a relatively clear stretch of rebuilding/retooling, the Rangers signed veterans to fill holes instead of letting open sores weep through the summer simply to accrue better draft picks.

Still, the young, sustainable, successful core has not come to fruition. Or maybe the young and sustainable has. The successful, not so much. At 6-foot-4 and not quite 21 years old, Mazara screamed promise when he arrived in 2016. Occasional 500-foot home runs into the now-defunct ballpark's steep right-field seats piled on to the aura of potential, but four seasons of slightly below average offensive lines—evidently very sustainable—from a corner outfield spot dampened that hope and weighed down the lineup.

Originally signed for less than one-tenth of Mazara's bonus, the fact that Rougned Odor reached the big leagues at all was a win. That he played a supporting role in perhaps the wildest inning in recent baseball history and later claimed the sport's pound-for-pound punching title counts as gravy, to be honest.

His ongoing presence in the order, however, is becoming hard to stomach. In only one of the last three seasons has he even sniffed average offensive production, and in 2017 and 2019 he logged "absolute wizard of a shortstop" level DRC+ numbers (75 and 87, respectively) despite hitting 30 homers in each season. Whether it's commitment to a still-young player who displayed promise as a 20-year-old rookie or something else, there are fewer and fewer arguments available in favor of Odor tallying 500 at-bats for a team trying to compete. At present, he's a walking, talking manifestation of a fact that baseball keeps teaching us: If you limit your choices to all or nothing, you'll usually wind up bitter and disillusioned that there is far more nothing in the world.

Still, in the midst of the nothing, there are often flickers. Every year, including this past one, Odor teases hopeful hearts and minds with a scorch-your-eyebrows-off hot streak. The 2019 version involved a .648 September slugging percentage, but the dark side of this streakiness is more prevalent. Just since the start of 2017, the Rangers have allowed Odor to slog through five different calendar months of at least 80 plate appearances with batting averages below .200—a terrifying display of faith only exceeded by his nemesis, José Bautista, in twilight, along with entrenched veterans Curtis Granderson and Kole Calhoun.

They won't stand accused of being too quick-tempered with their young, cost-controlled players. There is, of course, one tale of patience that appears to be paying off: Gallo—he of the prodigious power but flighty contact skills—legitimately took off under new manager Chris Woodward and a shifting coaching staff in 2019. He connected for 22 homers in only 70 games, yes. He also pared back his swing rate to about 40 percent, allowing more bad pitches to go by and bolster his on-base percentage to a star-level .389.

But even granting that they have pushed money into better player development practices that could produce further Gallo-like leaps, the present-day Rangers can't hang their hat there. Consider where their production came from in 2019.

2019 WARP DEVELOPED	2019 WARP ACQUIRED
1.5	16.1

PLAYER	2019 WARP	PLAYER	2019 WARP
Joey Gallo	2.6	Lance Lynn	5.9
Elvis Andrus	2.4	Mike Minor	3.9
José Leclerc	1.8	Danny Santana	2.1
Brad Martin	0.6	Shin-Soo Choo	2.0
Emmanuel Clase	0.4	Asdrúbal Cabrera	1.8
José Trevino	0.3	Hunter Pence	1.7
Ronald Guzmán	0.3	Delino DeShields	1.4
Peter Fairbanks	0.2	Willie Calhoun	1.1
Nomar Mazara	0.1	Chris Martin	0.9
Others	-7.2	Others	-4.7

Players acquired for immediate or near-immediate contributions in Arlington accumulated 16.1 WARP. The group of players whose development can be more reasonably credited to the Rangers was worth…1.5 WARP, and that's with Gallo alone notching 2.6 WARP. (Willie Calhoun is the one confusing case. If you're so inclined to grant his WARP to the development side, I won't argue.)

So even as much of the energy in the industry flows toward developing young talent, this team seems to be better the more directly and overtly Daniels and company assemble it from imported parts.

⚾　　⚾　　⚾

Even in the hole-plugging, water-treading days of 2019, outside additions thrived in Texas. In the second season of his three-year, $29 million deal, Mike Minor took off. Employing a four-pitch mix and amping up the usage of his bendy changeup, the lefty more than validated the decision to convert him back to the rotation.

Then there was Lance Lynn, who signed a three-year, $30 million deal that seemed to say, "Let's try the Mike Minor trick again!" This went about as well as it possibly could. Lynn found an extra gear of strikeout potential in his four-seamer and went from innings-eating starter to Cy Young contender.

Twin mini-risks on veteran arms—Lynn could certainly be called established while Minor was still ramping back up from an injury—turned into twin jackpots, and it's hard to overstate how bad the pitching would have been even if they were simply their old selves. Rangers starters had a 5.37 ERA despite 416 2/3 combined innings of stellar work from Minor and Lynn.

Other, even smaller moves also had strong enough hit rates for Daniels & Co. While Asdrúbal Cabrera and Logan Forsythe proved modest disappointments, the Hunter Pence flier netted a .910 OPS. Danny Santana (?) wound up churning out 511 plate appearances of an .857 OPS (?!).

All of which raised the question: Why not at least try to translate that hit rate into more ambitious upgrades?

In this winter of increased activity, the Rangers appear intent on doing that. They moved on from Mazara and opened a permanent space for Gallo. They continued with the $30 million-ish rotation filler bets that could turn into something more, adding Kyle Gibson, Jordan Lyles, and Joely Rodríguez. Crucially, they also swooped in for Corey Kluber via trade and appeared eager to spend elsewhere (though not eager enough to keep potential Beltré heir Anthony Rendon from joining a division rival).

The shorthand, as spring draws near, will go like this: The Rangers are gearing up to field a stronger product to capitalize on their new ballpark. Its roof will keep the air down to a more pleasant temperature in the upper 70s, even in the sweltering Texas summer. And the team will try to break its win total out of the less pleasant upper 70s purgatory of recent years.

For all the ways money spent on players is framed around the norms of investments and hard choices, fans can and should remember that their team is not in danger of going bankrupt over the baseball equivalent of splurging for a fancier car. Sports exist to free them of those concerns—not burden them with those of a shadowy billionaire or two (Ray Davis and Bob Simpson, in the Rangers' case).

Fact is: the degree to which Lynn exceeded expectations in year one isn't all that different from the degree to which Beltré exceeded expectations across the length of his deal, and perhaps the Rangers have some skill in identifying players who will surprise. But $30 million gets you an enjoyable, day-making pitcher who surges to a fifth-place finish in Cy Young voting, whereas $96 million might affirm a fan's allegiance for life, and offer them the chance to watch a star become a Hall of Famer in their colors.

These aren't the only ways to upgrade a team. A Kyle Gibson or Jordan Lyles doesn't need to exceed expectations, for instance, to improve upon the fledgling starters of 2019 Rangers vintage. A competitor for Odor's playing time at second base doesn't have to be a star to level out the dizzying highs and lows of the position. Money spent on the technologies and smart employees that could turn more draftees into Gallo-style success stories is still worthwhile. It just hasn't and won't replicate the satisfaction of going and getting the best players just because you want the best players.

What stands between those two things is, yes, mostly just a billionaire's willingness to throw money around. ▪

—Zach Crizer is an author of Baseball Prospectus.

HITTERS

Elvis Andrus SS Born: 08/26/88 Age: 31 Bats: R Throws: R Height: 6'0" Weight: 200 Origin: International Free Agent, 2005

YEAR	TEAM	LVL	AGE	PA	R	2B	3B	HR	RBI	BB	K	SB	CS	AVG/OBP/SLG	DRC+	VORP	BABIP	BRR	FRAA	WARP
2017	TEX	MLB	28	689	100	44	4	20	88	38	101	25	10	.297/.337/.471	108	37.7	.325	2.8	SS(157): 16.2	5.7
2018	TEX	MLB	29	428	53	20	3	6	33	28	66	5	3	.256/.308/.367	91	9.2	.292	0.5	SS(97): -6.4	0.8
2019	TEX	MLB	30	648	81	27	4	12	72	34	96	31	8	.275/.313/.393	89	21.8	.305	2.0	SS(146): 1.0	2.4
2020	TEX	MLB	31	630	62	30	4	11	63	40	97	20	8	.267/.318/.389	85	12.2	.304	1.1	SS 3	1.5

Comparables: Tomas Perez, Edgar Renteria, Jack Wilson

The Rangers' elder statesman—not by age, but as the last standing member of the team to have played in the 2011 World Series—Andrus overcame a heartbreaking end of the 2015 season to have career years in 2016 and 2017, only to miss a large portion of 2018 due to a broken bone in his right elbow. That was super terrible timing for Andrus, who had the first of two opt-outs in his career after that season. He wasn't bad in 2019 before his second (and final) opt-out, but his numbers were more in line with his inconsistent early-career totals. Whether or not Andrus was going to stay in Texas anyway, we may never know, but in this timeline, it made sense to stick around and take the remainder of his paycheck over the next three (or four, pending plate appearances in 2021-22) years. If he can somehow find that 2017-18 gear again, his contract will be an absolute steal for the Rangers.

Sherten Apostel 3B Born: 03/11/99 Age: 21 Bats: R Throws: R Height: 6'4" Weight: 200 Origin: International Free Agent, 2018

YEAR	TEAM	LVL	AGE	PA	R	2B	3B	HR	RBI	BB	K	SB	CS	AVG/OBP/SLG	DRC+	VORP	BABIP	BRR	FRAA	WARP
2017	DPI	RK	18	259	43	12	4	9	48	56	49	4	5	.258/.422/.495	158	37.7	.296	-0.6	3B(59): 8.9	2.9
2018	BRI	RK	19	175	28	7	0	7	26	32	42	3	1	.259/.406/.460	148	12.7	.319	-0.9	3B(35): 3.6	1.7
2018	SPO	A-	19	49	7	1	0	1	10	9	8	0	1	.351/.469/.459	203	9.0	.400	0.0	3B(8): -0.6	0.5
2019	HIC	A	20	319	38	13	1	15	43	28	71	2	1	.258/.332/.470	119	13.7	.290	-3.0	3B(70): 1.6, 1B(12): 0.0	1.4
2019	DEB	A+	20	159	18	5	1	4	16	23	49	0	0	.237/.352/.378	117	9.9	.341	1.6	3B(40): 1.4	1.1
2020	TEX	MLB	21	251	27	11	1	8	30	26	82	0	0	.228/.314/.397	87	3.4	.320	-0.4	3B 2, 1B 0	0.6

Comparables: Yairo Muñoz, Brett Phillips, Drew Robinson

Jamey Newberg of The Athletic brought up an interesting theory about Apostel's 2019 season, which started extremely slowly: "…the Curacao native had never played a pro game earlier than June, and some believe he was so unaccustomed to cool weather that it chilled his production." His output at Hickory definitely seemed to follow that pattern, switching gears mid-May and prompting a promotion to Down East. While the Josh Jung/Davis Wendzel question might be the easier minor league third base conundrum to identify from the outside (both Big 12 co-Players of the year were drafted by the Rangers in 2019), Apostel—who came from Pittsburgh as the PTBNL in the Keone Kela trade—is going to force the issue in 2020. In fact, with Wendzel missing time with a thumb injury, it's Apostel who will force the Rangers to make an interesting decision about which third baseman will start for the Wood Ducks and who will be elsewhere. For Apostel, that might mean Frisco—he was added to the 40-man roster over the offseason, and finished strong in Down East in 2019—or it might be first base.

Willie Calhoun LF   Born: 11/04/94   Age: 25   Bats: L   Throws: R   Height: 5'8"   Weight: 187   Origin: Round 4, 2015 Draft (#132 overall)

YEAR	TEAM	LVL	AGE	PA	R	2B	3B	HR	RBI	BB	K	SB	CS	AVG/OBP/SLG	DRC+	VORP	BABIP	BRR	FRAA	WARP
2017	OKL	AAA	22	414	64	24	5	23	67	36	49	3	2	.298/.357/.574	125	29.1	.289	-1.8	2B(74): 0.9, LF(12): -1.9	2.6
2017	ROU	AAA	22	120	16	3	1	8	26	6	12	1	0	.310/.345/.566	130	10.0	.290	-1.2	LF(24): 2.4, 2B(3): -0.7	2.5
2017	TEX	MLB	22	37	3	0	0	1	4	2	7	0	0	.265/.324/.353	87	1.0	.308	0.3	LF(11): -0.7	0.0
2018	ROU	AAA	23	470	66	32	0	9	47	32	47	4	0	.294/.351/.431	118	14.3	.314	-3.2	LF(91): -11.9	0.6
2018	TEX	MLB	23	108	8	5	0	2	11	6	24	0	0	.222/.269/.333	87	-2.5	.267	-0.7	LF(27): -2.8	-0.3
2019	NAS	AAA	24	172	23	8	0	8	28	32	24	1	1	.297/.433/.529	141	18.1	.311	-0.8	LF(33): -6.5, 2B(3): 0.2	0.6
2019	TEX	MLB	24	337	51	14	1	21	48	23	53	0	0	.269/.323/.524	119	17.3	.262	1.1	LF(71): -7.1	1.1
2020	TEX	MLB	25	560	73	28	1	30	87	46	99	1	0	.266/.331/.504	114	24.9	.277	0.5	LF -10	1.5

Comparables: Lonnie Chisenhall, Dave Collins, Kolten Wong

It's still unclear which was more shocking: Calhoun's off-season transformation that saw him report to spring training 26 pounds lighter than he left the team in 2018, or the fact that it (still) wasn't enough to land him a spot on the Opening Day roster. When he was recalled in May, it appeared the future had finally arrived—he hit .425 with an 1.197 OPS in his first six games—and then a strained left quad played the part of the evil plot twist. When Calhoun returned to action, he cooled a bit, but was still hitting .277 (.802) with only 19 strikeouts in 99 plate appearances when he was sent back to Triple-A yet again in July. That assignment was only about a week long, however, and Calhoun was an almost-every-day player upon returning. He tinkered a bit at second base while he was in Nashville, but with new acquisition Nick Solak now the primary competitor for Rougned Odor's job, it appears that Calhoun will be the team's regular left fielder/DH in 2020. Maybe. He technically does still have a minor-league option available, so let's not get ahead of ourselves.

Robinson Chirinos C   Born: 06/05/84   Age: 36   Bats: R   Throws: R   Height: 6'1"   Weight: 210   Origin: International Free Agent, 2000

YEAR	TEAM	LVL	AGE	PA	R	2B	3B	HR	RBI	BB	K	SB	CS	AVG/OBP/SLG	DRC+	VORP	BABIP	BRR	FRAA	WARP
2017	TEX	MLB	33	309	46	13	1	17	38	34	79	1	0	.255/.360/.506	121	20.7	.298	-1.7	C(85): -0.2	2.2
2018	TEX	MLB	34	426	48	15	1	18	65	45	140	2	0	.222/.338/.419	107	21.7	.304	-1.4	C(108): -10.8	1.2
2019	HOU	MLB	35	437	57	22	1	17	58	51	125	1	2	.238/.347/.443	100	23.3	.306	-0.1	C(112): 3.0	2.6
2020	TEX	MLB	36	350	40	14	1	14	44	34	104	1	0	.212/.312/.399	90	4.4	.271	-0.7	C -6	0.0

Comparables: Adam Hyzdu, Dan Johnson, Mike Hegan

No one would blame you if you didn't pay particularly close attention to the season Chirinos just had. But 30 games in, he looked like the steal of the off-season as he was was fourth on the Astros in DRC+ with a .278/.412/.567 slash line. For the rest of the season though he hit Extremely Not That. Still, he played 100+ games behind the plate for the second straight season. While he's not a standout framer, he was the second-best blocker in the game behind Roberto Pérez last year, a crucial skill for a team as breaking-ball heavy as Houston. As he enters his age-36 season, he'll look to get a few more one-year deals before riding off into the sunset, presumably after stopping a spiked curveball with a runner on third.

YEAR	TEAM	P. COUNT	FRM RUNS	BLK RUNS	THRW RUNS	TOT RUNS
2017	TEX	11679	-1.6	2.4	-0.9	0.2
2018	TEX	15072	-11.2	0.7	-0.8	-11.0
2019	HOU	15727	-3.5	5.8	-0.5	1.9
2020	TEX	17672	-13.2	2.8	-0.9	-11.2

Shin-Soo Choo OF   Born: 07/13/82   Age: 37   Bats: L   Throws: L   Height: 5'11"   Weight: 210   Origin: International Free Agent, 2000

YEAR	TEAM	LVL	AGE	PA	R	2B	3B	HR	RBI	BB	K	SB	CS	AVG/OBP/SLG	DRC+	VORP	BABIP	BRR	FRAA	WARP
2017	TEX	MLB	34	636	96	20	1	22	78	77	134	12	3	.261/.357/.423	105	11.0	.305	0.7	RF(77): -1.5	1.5
2018	TEX	MLB	35	665	83	30	1	21	62	92	156	6	1	.264/.377/.434	116	25.1	.330	-0.9	RF(34): -2.0, LF(26): -0.6	2.2
2019	TEX	MLB	36	660	93	31	2	24	61	78	165	15	1	.265/.371/.455	113	25.1	.333	-0.2	RF(42): -4.1, LF(40): -0.4	2.0
2020	TEX	MLB	37	560	68	24	1	19	69	64	147	7	3	.253/.355/.426	107	13.4	.325	-0.8	RF -1, LF 0	1.3

Comparables: Manny Ramirez, Reggie Sanders, Andre Ethier

This is perhaps the most remarkable statistic to come from the Rangers' 2019 season: Choo had 138 plate appearances leading off games for Texas. Here are his numbers in those plate appearances: .345/.449/.621 (1.070) with seven home runs. As Texas begins gearing up for contention with their newly turned-over roster, you'd think those numbers would be enough to get some team interested in Choo. Alas, one gets the sense that potential partners are instead concerned about two other numbers. The first—$21 million, which Choo is due in 2020—is daunting, but could be mitigated slightly by the fact that it's the last year of his contract (and Texas could offer to pay part of it). The other—37, which is the age Choo turned in 2019—has no cure, and will never become less concerning; such is the linear nature of a universe built with no reverse gear. If Texas can't find a trade partner, they're not going to be too upset about it; his clubhouse leadership and easy-going manner are huge assets on a team of guys who are just coming into their prime.

Joey Gallo OF   Born: 11/19/93   Age: 26   Bats: L   Throws: R   Height: 6'5"   Weight: 235   Origin: Round 1, 2012 Draft (#39 overall)

YEAR	TEAM	LVL	AGE	PA	R	2B	3B	HR	RBI	BB	K	SB	CS	AVG/OBP/SLG	DRC+	VORP	BABIP	BRR	FRAA	WARP
2017	TEX	MLB	23	532	85	18	3	41	80	75	196	7	2	.209/.333/.537	123	27.6	.250	0.5	3B(72): -1.8, 1B(59): 0.5	3.1
2018	TEX	MLB	24	577	82	24	1	40	92	74	207	3	4	.206/.312/.498	116	20.3	.249	1.9	LF(85): -6.3, 1B(35): 3.1	2.7
2019	TEX	MLB	25	297	54	15	1	22	49	52	114	4	2	.253/.389/.598	128	20.3	.368	1.7	CF(38): 0.8, LF(34): 4.1	2.6
2020	TEX	MLB	26	595	89	27	2	40	103	90	228	5	2	.227/.350/.533	126	35.6	.316	1.8	RF 4, CF 0	4.1

Comparables: Giancarlo Stanton, Dave Nicholson, Reggie Jackson

When Gallo went down with an oblique injury on June 1st, he was hitting .276/.421/.653 (1.074) with 17 home runs and whispers about an MVP candidacy were beginning to circulate around the league. It was the sort of breakout season that the Rangers had hoped was in there somewhere, and if there is one thing that should give Rangers fans hope for the future, it's what Gallo did in April and May. It's always been known that his power could play on Mercury, but the newly added ability to hit to the opposite field, find gaps for extra bases, and manage pitches on the inside corner of the plate are the sorts of additions that turn a fighter jet into a spaceship. Don't bother looking at his statistics after the oblique injury which gave way to a broken hamate bone that kept him out from July 24 through the end of the season. Those are not pretty and we do not enjoy looking at them. Put them under the sheet of shame and pretend they don't exist.

Ronald Guzmán 1B
Born: 10/20/94 Age: 25 Bats: L Throws: L Height: 6'5" Weight: 225 Origin: International Free Agent, 2011

YEAR	TEAM	LVL	AGE	PA	R	2B	3B	HR	RBI	BB	K	SB	CS	AVG/OBP/SLG	DRC+	VORP	BABIP	BRR	FRAA	WARP
2017	ROU	AAA	22	527	78	22	3	12	62	47	85	4	1	.298/.372/.434	115	20.8	.342	-0.3	1B(118): -1.6	1.5
2018	TEX	MLB	23	428	46	18	2	16	58	33	121	1	0	.235/.306/.416	92	2.6	.299	1.9	1B(117): 1.9	0.6
2019	NAS	AAA	24	135	22	8	0	5	16	17	31	0	0	.308/.400/.504	113	6.1	.383	-1.3	1B(22): 0.5	0.3
2019	TEX	MLB	24	295	34	20	0	10	36	32	87	1	2	.219/.308/.414	85	-1.0	.282	-2.5	1B(81): 6.2	0.3
2020	TEX	MLB	25	560	62	25	2	22	72	48	164	1	0	.234/.306/.422	87	0.8	.301	0.0	1B 4	0.5

Comparables: Dominic Smith, Rowdy Tellez, Steve Bilko

For all the mathematics involved in analyzing the sport, there's one major difference between math and baseball: When a problem is solved in math, it tends to stay solved. In baseball, all solutions are temporary. Such cat-herding of solutions is the case with first base in Texas, where it appeared after the 2018 season that Guzmán had the position locked up long-term with his exceptional defense and a bat that showed promise of improvement. By the middle of 2019, however, Guzmán was back in Triple-A Nashville, his bat a black hole in the lineup. He hit over .300 upon return to the big leagues, seemingly cured of the mechanical plague that had beset him, so the problem appears to be solved. Again. For now.

Scott Heineman OF
Born: 12/04/92 Age: 27 Bats: R Throws: R Height: 6'1" Weight: 215 Origin: Round 11, 2015 Draft (#318 overall)

YEAR	TEAM	LVL	AGE	PA	R	2B	3B	HR	RBI	BB	K	SB	CS	AVG/OBP/SLG	DRC+	VORP	BABIP	BRR	FRAA	WARP
2017	FRI	AA	24	529	82	26	7	9	44	50	121	12	9	.284/.363/.427	114	30.6	.365	6.8	LF(72): -8.5, CF(29): -2.9	1.3
2018	FRI	AA	25	31	6	2	0	1	10	7	5	2	1	.522/.613/.739	270	5.3	.611	-0.9	CF(5): -0.9, LF(2): 0.0	0.4
2018	ROU	AAA	25	469	68	20	2	11	57	32	93	16	8	.295/.355/.429	111	24.6	.353	4.0	RF(48): 1.7, CF(44): -3.3	2.1
2019	NAS	AAA	26	182	34	6	2	8	25	17	45	4	3	.340/.412/.553	139	14.9	.426	-1.1	RF(13): 0.8, LF(11): 1.6	1.3
2019	TEX	MLB	26	85	8	6	0	2	7	9	20	1	2	.213/.306/.373	87	1.0	.264	-0.5	CF(9): -0.5, RF(8): -0.5	-0.1
2020	TEX	MLB	27	280	32	11	2	9	34	21	74	7	3	.252/.321/.422	92	3.6	.320	0.0	LF -1, 1B -1	0.2

Comparables: Lorenzo Cain, Sócrates Brito, Matthew den Dekker

When the Rangers' crowded outfield seemed like it was going to block Heineman from a call-up, the team pulled a quick one and started having him play first base in Triple-A. The switch worked—he made his debut on August 2, logging a couple of hits in his first game, however he only ended up playing four games at first base in the big leagues, playing the remainder of his games in the outfield. Scott was the first "Heineman" in big-league history, narrowly edging out his big brother Tyler, who got his first big-league call-up with the Marlins on September 4, which just so happened to also be the night that Scott hit his first big-league home run, a solo shot in Yankee Stadium off Jonathan Loaisiga. Heineman will likely be a fourth outfielder with the Rangers in 2020, though the team will certainly allow him to provide competition for Delino DeShields in center field.

Sam Huff C
Born: 01/14/98 Age: 22 Bats: R Throws: R Height: 6'4" Weight: 230 Origin: Round 7, 2016 Draft (#219 overall)

YEAR	TEAM	LVL	AGE	PA	R	2B	3B	HR	RBI	BB	K	SB	CS	AVG/OBP/SLG	DRC+	VORP	BABIP	BRR	FRAA	WARP
2017	RNG	RK	19	225	34	9	2	9	31	24	66	3	2	.249/.329/.452	97	14.6	.320	0.7	C(30): -0.5	0.7
2018	HIC	A	20	448	53	22	3	18	55	23	140	9	1	.241/.292/.439	97	14.0	.317	-0.1	C(56): 1.9, 1B(11): -0.4	1.3
2019	HIC	A	21	114	22	5	0	15	29	6	37	4	1	.333/.368/.796	217	22.7	.375	0.8	C(14): 0.9	1.8
2019	DEB	A+	21	405	49	17	2	13	43	27	117	2	5	.262/.326/.425	110	18.4	.347	-2.7	C(50): 1.9, 1B(4): 0.1	1.5
2020	TEX	MLB	22	251	24	12	1	7	27	16	92	1	0	.219/.277/.364	68	-2.6	.328	-0.3	C 1, 1B 0	-0.2

Comparables: Eric Haase, Isan Díaz, Chris Carter

The question about Huff since forever has been if he'll be able to stick at catcher, since he's 6-foot-4 and getting down into the catcher's squat 150 times a game is like cramming a week's worth of clothes into a backpack and then zipping and unzipping it 150 times over the course of three hours. Huff has thus far proven to be stitched out of iron, wielding an arm made of gunpowder (48 percent caught-stealing rate) and a bat made of kerosene. His strikeout rate is still high enough to temper any legitimate push for the big leagues just yet, but he's still just 21. By catcher standards, that means he's only about 16 years old (and about nine feet tall). He'll likely see a lot of time in Double-A Frisco in 2020, hoping to arrive in Arlington right about the time the Rangers expect to be competitive again.

★ ★ ★ *2020 Top 101 Prospect* **#70** ★ ★ ★

Josh Jung 3B
Born: 02/12/98 Age: 22 Bats: R Throws: R Height: 6'2" Weight: 215 Origin: Round 1, 2019 Draft (#8 overall)

YEAR	TEAM	LVL	AGE	PA	R	2B	3B	HR	RBI	BB	K	SB	CS	AVG/OBP/SLG	DRC+	VORP	BABIP	BRR	FRAA	WARP
2019	HIC	A	21	179	18	13	0	1	23	16	29	4	1	.287/.363/.389	137	13.7	.341	0.6	3B(35): 2.5	1.5
2020	TEX	MLB	22	251	22	12	1	4	23	15	60	3	1	.233/.288/.343	70	-1.9	.297	0.0	3B 4	0.3

Comparables: Zelous Wheeler, Ty Kelly, Paul DeJong

You can certainly make an argument that the draft was the weakest of the five means of player acquisition (draft, trade, free agent, Latin American signings, waiver claims) for the Rangers in the early-to-mid 2010s. Sure, it's possible that player development could have been responsible for the busts of Dillon Tate, Chi Chi González, Travis Demeritte, Kevin Matthews, Kellin Deglan, and Jake Skole (all of whom were first-round picks for the Rangers this decade), but the last couple of years have (hopefully) turned the tide a bit. Bubba Thompson, Hans Crouse, Cole Ragans and others have populated the farm system with a hopeful crop of homegrowns.

Jung is the latest cause for optimism. Drafted out of Texas Tech, Jung shared Big 12 co-Player of the Year honors with Baylor's Davis Wendzel, also drafted by Texas in a nifty bit of synergy. He played just four games in the AZL before skipping straight to Low-A. At the end of his first month in Hickory, Jung was hitting over .300 with an on-base percentage of .358, prompting some to wonder if he would find himself in High-A by season's end. He cooled a bit, and his power is still in need of development, but he's still, ahem, Jung.

Isiah Kiner-Falefa UT Born: 03/23/95 Age: 25 Bats: R Throws: R Height: 5'10" Weight: 176 Origin: Round 4, 2013 Draft (#130 overall)

YEAR	TEAM	LVL	AGE	PA	R	2B	3B	HR	RBI	BB	K	SB	CS	AVG/OBP/SLG	DRC+	VORP	BABIP	BRR	FRAA	WARP
2017	FRI	AA	22	570	58	31	3	5	48	41	72	17	6	.288/.350/.390	121	36.8	.325	0.2	3B(50): 6.4, 2B(37): 4.2	4.4
2018	TEX	MLB	23	396	43	18	2	4	34	28	62	7	5	.261/.325/.357	86	3.8	.306	-0.6	3B(46): 3.4, C(35): -10.1	0.1
2019	FRI	AA	24	71	7	4	0	2	11	8	9	1	0	.283/.380/.450	152	6.9	.300	-0.1	C(9): -0.7, 3B(4): 1.5	0.7
2019	NAS	AAA	24	37	3	3	0	0	2	1	6	1	0	.147/.216/.235	34	-4.1	.179	-0.7	SS(4): 0.2, C(2): 0.0	-0.2
2019	TEX	MLB	24	222	23	12	1	1	21	14	49	3	0	.238/.299/.322	72	2.1	.307	1.8	C(38): -11.0, 3B(25): 1.7	-0.5
2020	TEX	MLB	25	280	25	14	1	4	25	19	55	3	2	.247/.313/.351	76	-1.1	.302	0.4	3B 7, 2B 0	0.6

Comparables: Marwin Gonzalez, Didi Gregorius, Jean Segura

YEAR	TEAM	P. COUNT	FRM RUNS	BLK RUNS	THRW RUNS	TOT RUNS
2017	FRI	4556	-1.1	-0.8	0.0	-1.7
2018	TEX	4896	-9.9	-1.0	0.0	-10.9
2019	FRI	1232	-0.8	0.0	0.0	-0.8
2019	TEX	5069	-9.1	-3.0	0.0	-12.3

There's super-utility, and then there's "No, he can even play catcher." In 2019, the Rangers tried to make Kiner-Falefa exclusively a catcher under the tutelage of Jeff Mathis. After a minor injury, that plan was abandoned. When he began his rehab assignment, he was back to playing around the infield. He's stuck in a bit of an in-between situation: his bat plays well enough for a catcher, but his defense didn't come along quite as quickly as the team hoped. His versatile defensive ability at other positions is more than sufficient to be an everyday player, but the bat has thus far not been potent enough to start anywhere but behind the plate. Round and round it goes. Kiner-Falefa's fate seems uniquely tied to that of Danny Santana—if Santana does win either the starting third base or center field jobs in 2020, Kiner-Falefa will likely slot into the super-utility role on the 2020 team.

Jeff Mathis C Born: 03/31/83 Age: 37 Bats: R Throws: R Height: 6'0" Weight: 205 Origin: Round 1, 2001 Draft (#33 overall)

YEAR	TEAM	LVL	AGE	PA	R	2B	3B	HR	RBI	BB	K	SB	CS	AVG/OBP/SLG	DRC+	VORP	BABIP	BRR	FRAA	WARP
2017	ARI	MLB	34	203	13	10	2	2	11	14	61	1	0	.215/.277/.323	59	-1.5	.309	0.4	C(58): 10.2	1.0
2018	ARI	MLB	35	218	15	9	1	1	20	20	66	0	0	.200/.272/.272	63	-3.3	.292	-0.4	C(63): 18.5, 2B(1): -0.1	2.0
2019	TEX	MLB	36	244	17	9	0	2	12	15	87	1	0	.158/.209/.224	41	-5.9	.243	0.7	C(86): -2.8, P(2): 0.0	-0.8
2020	TEX	MLB	37	315	24	12	1	5	27	20	111	1	0	.191/.247/.292	40	-10.0	.288	0.2	C 10	0.0

Comparables: Jason LaRue, Kelly Stinnett, Nick Hundley

YEAR	TEAM	P. COUNT	FRM RUNS	BLK RUNS	THRW RUNS	TOT RUNS
2017	ARI	7723	8.9	-0.7	1.1	8.9
2018	ARI	8583	11.8	2.3	0.0	14.1
2019	TEX	11104	-1.8	0.8	-1.0	-2.1
2020	TEX	8129	4.7	0.4	-0.5	4.6

It raised some eyebrows when the Rangers let Robinson Chirinos walk in free agency before the 2019 season, and those same eyebrows kept creeping toward the nearest hairline when Texas decided to replace Chirinos by signing Mathis to a two-year deal. After all, Mathis was a career backup—he hadn't caught more than 70 games since 2013. But with Isiah Kiner-Falefa and Jose Trevino on the verge of big-league catcherdom, his role would be something resembling player-coach. Mathis' defense was a major player in the decision, but his hitting was probably closer to what you might expect from a coach. Texas will almost undoubtedly return him to a backup role in 2020 as Trevino transitions into a more full-time role.

Rougned Odor 2B Born: 02/03/94 Age: 26 Bats: L Throws: R Height: 5'11" Weight: 195 Origin: International Free Agent, 2011

YEAR	TEAM	LVL	AGE	PA	R	2B	3B	HR	RBI	BB	K	SB	CS	AVG/OBP/SLG	DRC+	VORP	BABIP	BRR	FRAA	WARP
2017	TEX	MLB	23	651	79	21	3	30	75	32	162	15	6	.204/.252/.397	75	-9.7	.224	1.3	2B(158): 6.2	0.7
2018	TEX	MLB	24	535	76	23	2	18	63	43	127	12	12	.253/.326/.424	97	14.5	.305	1.0	2B(127): 7.5	2.4
2019	TEX	MLB	25	581	77	30	1	30	93	52	178	11	9	.205/.283/.439	87	9.3	.244	-2.8	2B(137): -12.8	-0.6
2020	TEX	MLB	26	595	70	26	3	30	84	39	170	11	6	.222/.283/.443	84	11.2	.264	0.4	2B 0	1.1

Comparables: Addison Russell, Jurickson Profar, Wilmer Flores

You put your finger on the page, didn't you? You put your index finger on the page and scrolled down, looking for this very name so that you could feel the potent energy of anger coursing through your veins. It's a powerful feeling, the superiority that comes from knowing more than a so-called expert. "I can't believe the media keeps buying this same old story," you think, shaking your head. "He's had hot streaks before. This won't last. It never lasts. He doesn't care. He's a problem. He needs to shave his beard and button up his shirt," you mutter, satisfied that if only the world would heed your advice, everything would make more sense. You're right, of course. It would make more sense, to you—maybe even to a sizable number of people. To this we say: you might be right! You should go apply for the GM job. Also, we have no idea what kind of player Rougned Odor is going to be in 2020, beyond this one small prediction: he will spectacularly either exceed or fall short of projections. But seriously, who even knows at this point?

Hunter Pence OF Born: 04/13/83 Age: 37 Bats: R Throws: R Height: 6'4" Weight: 230 Origin: Round 2, 2004 Draft (#64 overall)

YEAR	TEAM	LVL	AGE	PA	R	2B	3B	HR	RBI	BB	K	SB	CS	AVG/OBP/SLG	DRC+	VORP	BABIP	BRR	FRAA	WARP
2017	SFN	MLB	34	539	55	13	5	13	67	40	102	2	3	.260/.315/.385	89	16.4	.301	4.4	RF(125): 2.0	1.1
2018	SAC	AAA	35	111	11	4	0	1	13	6	24	0	0	.301/.342/.369	96	1.9	.380	-0.1	RF(12): 0.1, LF(11): 0.2	0.2
2018	SFN	MLB	35	248	19	11	1	4	24	11	59	5	1	.226/.258/.332	66	-2.6	.282	0.4	LF(44): -3.1, RF(12): -1.2	-0.8
2019	TEX	MLB	36	316	53	17	1	18	59	26	69	6	1	.297/.358/.552	122	15.3	.333	0.9	LF(16): 1.1, RF(8): 0.1	1.7
2020	TEX	MLB	37	251	29	12	1	10	33	18	60	2	1	.261/.317/.444	101	9.4	.314	1.0	RF 1, LF 1	1.1

Comparables: Jermaine Dye, Kendrys Morales, Glenallen Hill

The Rangers have employed some of the most beloved players in the game over the last few years: Adrián Beltré, Bartolo Colón, Tim Lincecum and now Hunter Pence. Pence spent the 2018-19 offseason revamping his swing, even going so far as to play in the Dominican Winter League to get the new swing a little in-game action. He signed a minor-league deal with his hometown Rangers and proceeded to make the Opening Day roster. To the untrained eye, the new swing still looked like a Tasmanian Devil trying to kill an aggressive pterodactyl, but the results didn't lie: by July, Pence had made one more roster, as he was named to his fourth career All-Star team. Injuries beset the veteran in the second half—he didn't play after August 22 due to a lower back injury—but his production was such that he seems likely to get another shot somewhere in 2020. If not (or if it's not Texas), Ranger fans were fortunate to get one season to cheer for one of the game's all-time good dudes.

Danny Santana CF   Born: 11/07/90   Age: 29   Bats: B   Throws: R   Height: 5'11"   Weight: 185   Origin: International Free Agent, 2007

YEAR	TEAM	LVL	AGE	PA	R	2B	3B	HR	RBI	BB	K	SB	CS	AVG/OBP/SLG	DRC+	VORP	BABIP	BRR	FRAA	WARP
2017	MIN	MLB	26	26	3	1	0	1	1	1	8	1	0	.200/.231/.360	59	-1.2	.250	0.2	LF(8): 0.8, RF(3): 0.0	0.0
2017	ATL	MLB	26	152	16	9	2	3	22	7	33	6	0	.203/.245/.357	62	-0.8	.243	2.0	LF(30): 2.7, 2B(7): -0.6	0.1
2018	GWN	AAA	27	342	57	21	3	16	40	15	80	12	5	.264/.294/.497	105	14.4	.301	1.5	CF(45): 1.1, 2B(14): 1.3	1.8
2018	ATL	MLB	27	32	4	3	0	0	2	3	11	1	1	.179/.281/.286	71	-1.0	.294	-0.7	LF(6): 0.1, CF(3): -0.1	-0.1
2019	NAS	AAA	28	40	4	4	1	0	6	4	10	1	1	.343/.425/.514	117	4.8	.480	1.1	RF(3): -0.2, SS(3): 0.8	0.3
2019	TEX	MLB	28	511	81	23	6	28	81	25	151	21	6	.283/.324/.534	106	18.0	.353	3.6	1B(44): 0.9, CF(27): 0.6	2.1
2020	TEX	MLB	29	595	68	26	6	25	80	28	176	20	8	.248/.289/.450	87	10.5	.315	1.6	CF -1, 1B 0	1.2

Comparables: Jacque Jones, Austin Jackson, Ender Inciarte

Santana had a breakout year in 2019 after signing a minor-league deal with the Rangers, finally living up to the high expectations he set for himself after a great rookie campaign preceded years of fumbled opportunities. So impressive was the performance that the Rangers opted to keep him in the system rather than take advantage of the buy low/sell high situation at the trade deadline. In the end, a full turn into adapting that fly-ball lifestyle—which he started in Atlanta and Gwinnett the prior year—led to him more than tripling his major-league home run total. A likely starting outfield job awaits Santana in 2020 and that in itself is a victory for the 29-year-old, even if it all comes crumbling down in a fit of swings and misses.

Chris Seise SS   Born: 01/06/99   Age: 21   Bats: R   Throws: R   Height: 6'2"   Weight: 175   Origin: Round 1, 2017 Draft (#29 overall)

YEAR	TEAM	LVL	AGE	PA	R	2B	3B	HR	RBI	BB	K	SB	CS	AVG/OBP/SLG	DRC+	VORP	BABIP	BRR	FRAA	WARP
2017	RNG	RK	18	129	23	5	3	3	27	9	30	5	0	.336/.395/.509	118	14.2	.429	1.4	SS(24): -3.6	0.5
2017	SPO	A-	18	104	10	3	1	0	9	4	30	1	1	.222/.250/.273	51	-1.4	.314	0.5	SS(23): -0.2	0.0
2019	HIC	A	20	92	12	4	3	0	6	3	33	6	5	.241/.272/.356	73	2.5	.382	-0.8	SS(18): -0.3	0.0
2020	TEX	MLB	21	251	20	11	2	4	22	13	96	3	1	.213/.260/.319	55	-6.6	.344	0.1	SS -1	-0.8

Comparables: Michael Chavis, Steven Moya, Deivy Grullon

If you're a Rangers prospect nerd who also plays guitar, this comment is for you: Have you had a Line 6 stomp box that was built after 2006? Sorry, let's re-phrase that: How many times have you had to replace your Line 6 stomp box that was built after 2006, after stupidly selling your old one that was still working? For the rest of you: the older pedals were made by a different manufacturer. The new ones broke about once a year if you were playing them regularly. Which was a shame: The Line 6 DL-4 was a fantastic delay/loop pedal! Anyway, if Chris Seise can stay healthy, he's probably going to be a fantastic shortstop. But he's going to need to stay healthy sometime in the near future or the Rangers might have to settle for one with a bit less functionality and a bit more durability.

—————————————— ★ ★ ★ *2020 Top 101 Prospect* **#74** ★ ★ ★ ——————————————

Nick Solak 2B   Born: 01/11/95   Age: 25   Bats: R   Throws: R   Height: 5'11"   Weight: 190   Origin: Round 2, 2016 Draft (#62 overall)

YEAR	TEAM	LVL	AGE	PA	R	2B	3B	HR	RBI	BB	K	SB	CS	AVG/OBP/SLG	DRC+	VORP	BABIP	BRR	FRAA	WARP
2017	TAM	A+	22	406	56	17	4	10	44	53	76	13	4	.301/.397/.460	173	39.3	.357	2.5	2B(92): 1.4	4.0
2017	TRN	AA	22	132	16	9	1	2	9	10	24	1	1	.286/.344/.429	108	8.1	.340	0.5	2B(30): 2.0	0.8
2018	MNT	AA	23	565	91	17	3	19	76	68	112	21	6	.282/.384/.450	141	46.4	.330	-0.5	2B(61): -6.9, 2B(40): -3.3	2.9
2019	DUR	AAA	24	349	56	13	1	17	47	39	80	3	2	.266/.353/.485	108	10.3	.303	-3.6	2B(61): -7.5, LF(17): 0.4	0.3
2019	NAS	AAA	24	128	23	6	0	10	27	6	25	2	0	.347/.386/.653	135	14.6	.369	0.7	2B(21): 0.4, RF(4): 0.3	1.0
2019	TEX	MLB	24	135	19	6	1	5	17	15	29	2	0	.293/.393/.491	109	5.1	.354	1.3	3B(11): -0.1, 2B(5): -0.7	0.6
2020	TEX	MLB	25	560	70	23	2	25	78	47	135	7	2	.267/.340/.469	110	20.1	.319	-0.2	3B -4, 2B 0	1.6

Comparables: Preston Tucker, Brandon Lowe, Logan Forsythe

When the Rangers traded Pete Fairbanks to the Tampa Bay Rays for Solak, the assessment was clear: the kid was going to hit, and he was going to work extremely hard. Shifting the conversation to defense, however, elicited a high-pitched and uncertain groan from scouts—the sort of sound when your car is telling you that you have 22 miles to empty and you're 22.5 miles from the nearest gas station and your spouse asks if you're going to make it. "*Ehhhhhhhhh,*" you reply in an upper register. "*Ehhhhhhh,*" because "It's a coin flip and I should have stopped at the last place" is too frank an admission, and "Yeah, no problem" sets you up to look like a fool. So you say "*Ehhhhhhh,*" simultaneously admitting that it's touch and go while also indicating that you don't really want to talk too much more about it. Can Solak play second base? *Ehhhhhh…* Third base? Left field? *Ehhhhhhh…* Solak will no doubt enter 2020 hoping to answer those doubts and change the first letter of that answer from an E to an S.

★ ★ ★ *2020 Top 101 Prospect* **#37** ★ ★ ★

Leody Taveras CF   Born: 09/08/98   Age: 21   Bats: B   Throws: R   Height: 6'1"   Weight: 171   Origin: International Free Agent, 2015

YEAR	TEAM	LVL	AGE	PA	R	2B	3B	HR	RBI	BB	K	SB	CS	AVG/OBP/SLG	DRC+	VORP	BABIP	BRR	FRAA	WARP
2017	HIC	A	18	577	73	20	7	8	50	47	92	20	6	.249/.312/.360	98	16.8	.287	3.3	CF(125): -3.7, LF(3): -0.1	1.6
2018	DEB	A+	19	580	65	16	7	5	48	51	96	19	11	.246/.312/.332	90	4.2	.292	0.3	CF(123): 7.0, RF(3): 0.0	2.0
2019	DEB	A+	20	290	44	7	4	2	25	31	62	21	5	.294/.368/.376	124	14.6	.378	-0.4	CF(34): -0.6, RF(23): 4.0	1.7
2019	FRI	AA	20	293	32	12	4	3	31	23	60	11	8	.265/.320/.375	97	9.2	.327	0.5	CF(64): 8.1	1.8
2020	TEX	MLB	21	210	18	8	2	3	19	14	53	4	2	.238/.291/.350	67	-1.1	.310	0.2	CF 1	0.0

Comparables: Engel Beltre, Carlos Tocci, Cheslor Cuthbert

When Taveras had an OPS of .644 in High-A in 2018, the Donald Harris alarm bells started going bonkers in the Rangers' front offices. The "can't miss" prospect was missing, a lot. He still missed a lot in 2019 (122 strikeouts in 519 plate appearances), but he started doing other things well, namely … hitting. He even held his own against Double-A pitching, so we can check that off the Will This Prospect Be Okay list. Furthermore, he just turned 21 in September, so even if the Texas League proves challenging in 2020, there's time for him to figure things out before the demand for his services in Arlington begins to over-ripen. As for his defense? Well that's never been an issue. He's probably ready to be a big-league center fielder right now, but unless he develops some completely unexpected power surge as he continues to grow into his body, he'll have to cut down on strikeouts before he's ready to face big-league pitching. You have to earn those kind of strikeout numbers by hitting mega-bombs in your other at-bats. Thus far, that does not appear to be the Taveras MO.

Anderson Tejeda SS   Born: 05/01/98   Age: 22   Bats: B   Throws: R   Height: 5'11"   Weight: 160   Origin: International Free Agent, 2014

YEAR	TEAM	LVL	AGE	PA	R	2B	3B	HR	RBI	BB	K	SB	CS	AVG/OBP/SLG	DRC+	VORP	BABIP	BRR	FRAA	WARP
2017	HIC	A	19	446	68	24	9	8	53	36	132	10	7	.247/.309/.411	93	21.4	.343	2.0	SS(82): -2.0, 2B(30): 0.0	1.4
2018	DEB	A+	20	522	76	17	5	19	74	49	142	11	4	.259/.331/.439	122	29.5	.330	3.0	SS(105): 2.9, 2B(12): 1.6	4.1
2019	DEB	A+	21	181	22	10	1	4	24	17	58	9	4	.234/.315/.386	84	11.5	.333	1.3	SS(39): 2.4	0.8
2020	TEX	MLB	22	251	24	12	2	8	29	15	92	2	1	.219/.270/.393	69	-1.8	.322	0.0	SS 0, 2B 1	-0.1

Comparables: Trevor Story, Yu Chang, Junior Lake

If all you have to go on is the numbers, it would be easy to look at Tejeda's 2019 season as a total bust. Not only did he repeat a level, but his numbers were worse than the previous season, all before a shoulder injury limited him to just 43 games. That's all true, and there's no mitigating the loss of playing time, but perhaps it helps to consider that he started switch-hitting in 2019 (which might have been part of the reason he started the season at High-A Down East). He's got good pop in his bat and is a great defender—enough so that Texas opted to add him to the 40-man roster rather than leave him susceptible to the Rule 5 draft—so assuming he's healthy in 2020, he'll probably get a fair amount of time in Frisco. A lot of the buzz about minor-league competition has been focused on third base, but there's a good chance that the competition for heir apparent to the Elvis Andrus throne will start to get extremely interesting in about two years' time when Tejeda and Chris Seise (not to mention Jonathan Ornelas and Eli White) could be contenders to take over the position in Arlington. Step one: they'll both need to stay healthy.

Bubba Thompson CF   Born: 06/09/98   Age: 22   Bats: R   Throws: R   Height: 6'1"   Weight: 180   Origin: Round 1, 2017 Draft (#26 overall)

YEAR	TEAM	LVL	AGE	PA	R	2B	3B	HR	RBI	BB	K	SB	CS	AVG/OBP/SLG	DRC+	VORP	BABIP	BRR	FRAA	WARP
2017	RNG	RK	19	123	23	7	2	3	12	6	28	5	5	.257/.317/.434	83	4.0	.317	0.8	CF(27): -4.0	-0.1
2018	HIC	A	20	363	52	18	5	8	42	23	104	32	7	.289/.344/.446	118	26.0	.396	6.1	CF(67): 1.1, LF(17): 0.7	2.6
2019	DEB	A+	21	228	24	8	2	5	21	21	72	12	3	.178/.261/.312	55	-2.9	.246	2.6	LF(33): 1.5, CF(20): -1.8	-0.2
2020	TEX	MLB	22	251	23	12	1	6	25	14	91	9	3	.205/.259/.344	57	-5.0	.307	0.9	CF -1, LF 2	-0.5

Comparables: Dexter Fowler, Keon Broxton, Darren Ford

There was a time (and that time was the end of the 2018 season) when some were beginning to wonder if Thompson was going to surpass Leody Taveras in the Rangers center field prospect rankings. Taveras was struggling to find himself at the plate and Thompson was exceeding expectations. Last season proved to be the great evening-out, though Thompson's step back was as much a result of bad luck as anything. First it was a hamate bone, then a foot injury cost him another month. The rest of the season was spent trying to overcome the rustiness that comes with missing a lot of time that would have otherwise been spent developing. Injuries are never "good news" but the ability to attribute Thompson's slow 2019 season to injuries does, in some way, provide a bit of hope that a simple "force-close and re-launch app" will be sufficient in 2020 for the 21-year-old.

Jose Trevino C   Born: 11/28/92   Age: 27   Bats: R   Throws: R   Height: 5'11"   Weight: 211   Origin: Round 6, 2014 Draft (#186 overall)

YEAR	TEAM	LVL	AGE	PA	R	2B	3B	HR	RBI	BB	K	SB	CS	AVG/OBP/SLG	DRC+	VORP	BABIP	BRR	FRAA	WARP
2017	FRI	AA	24	423	39	12	0	7	42	19	44	1	2	.241/.275/.323	66	-0.3	.256	-0.1	C(99): 32.1	4.0
2018	FRI	AA	25	201	18	7	1	3	16	13	27	0	1	.234/.284/.332	73	-0.7	.255	-0.8	C(38): 8.0	1.1
2018	TEX	MLB	25	8	0	0	0	0	3	0	1	0	0	.250/.250/.250	82	-0.6	.286	0.0	C(3): -0.5	0.0
2019	NAS	AAA	26	156	16	10	0	2	22	8	28	2	0	.226/.263/.336	46	-3.1	.263	0.7	C(40): 6.4	0.5
2019	TEX	MLB	26	126	18	9	0	2	13	3	27	0	0	.258/.272/.383	77	2.9	.312	-0.7	C(40): 0.5	0.3
2020	TEX	MLB	27	315	27	15	0	8	32	13	63	0	0	.231/.266/.359	61	-1.9	.269	-0.7	C 3	0.1

Comparables: Alberto Rosario, Bruce Maxwell, Gustavo Molina

A multiple minor-league Gold Glove winner and extraordinary clubhouse presence, Trevino's bat has always been the big question. By August of 2019, Trevino was in the big leagues and given a legitimate shot at proving he could stick. Before a rough final couple of weeks, the 26-year-old was hitting .282 with the Rangers. The next glaring deficiency is going to be selectivity at the plate—in 76 September plate appearances, Trevino worked just two walks (up from just one in 48 August PAs). According to the fine folks at Brooks Baseball, that's a result of two things: pitchers being very willing to throw him fastballs and changeups in the strike zone, and his willingness to swing at breaking pitches that are not in the zone. He should get another legitimate shot to show improvement at the plate in 2020, though Sam Huff's ascendant surge through the minor leagues could signal an ultimate fate for Trevino that resembles another defense-first catcher: career backup Jeff Mathis.

YEAR	TEAM	P. COUNT	FRM RUNS	BLK RUNS	THRW RUNS	TOT RUNS
2017	FRI	13448	24.9	4.7	0.5	30.2
2018	FRI	5456	6.0	0.5	0.6	6.7
2018	TEX	277	-0.2	-0.2	0.0	-0.6
2019	NAS	5534	7.3	0.2	0.0	7.0
2019	TEX	5125	0.8	0.0	0.0	0.6
2020	*TEX*	*2682*	*0.5*	*0.0*	*0.1*	*0.5*

Steele Walker OF Born: 07/30/96 Age: 23 Bats: L Throws: L Height: 5'11" Weight: 190 Origin: Round 2, 2018 Draft (#46 overall)

YEAR	TEAM	LVL	AGE	PA	R	2B	3B	HR	RBI	BB	K	SB	CS	AVG/OBP/SLG	DRC+	VORP	BABIP	BRR	FRAA	WARP
2018	GRF	RK	21	38	4	1	0	2	4	1	7	1	1	.206/.263/.412	74	0.9	.192	0.4	CF(8): -2.0	-0.2
2018	KAN	A	21	126	13	5	0	3	17	8	29	5	1	.186/.246/.310	55	-1.3	.214	0.3	CF(21): 1.2	-0.1
2019	KAN	A	22	87	6	10	3	0	11	8	15	4	2	.365/.437/.581	180	12.9	.443	-0.4	CF(16): -1.7, RF(4): -0.1	0.6
2019	WNS	A+	22	441	59	26	2	10	51	42	63	9	5	.269/.346/.426	126	18.1	.294	-1.0	CF(81): -2.5	2.0
2020	*TEX*	*MLB*	*23*	*251*	*25*	*13*	*1*	*7*	*28*	*14*	*55*	*5*	*2*	*.228/.280/.385*	*75*	*-0.1*	*.268*	*-0.1*	*CF -2, RF 0*	*-0.2*

Comparables: Lane Adams, Kevin Kiermaier, Dave Sappelt

Walker doesn't have top-end speed, so he can appear miscast as a center fielder. A ball stroked to the gap would typically provide a chance to assess an outfielder's ability to close and cover ground. But maybe Walker's hat pops off during his pursuit, his flowing blond locks flutter out like a fan, turned golden by the illumination of the sunlight. The Earth starts to slow, gentle pluckings of a Spanish guitar seem to waft in the air, and is Walker stopping in mid-pursuit to gaze into your eyes? Well…uh…so, the likelihood he ends up in an outfield corner puts more pressure on the bat—while the plate discipline has exceeded some college grades, his stout shorter frame needs to employ a bit more effort in his swing to tap into home-run power. Perhaps the added effort sends his batting helmet flying to the dirt, and revealing his hair again like a thousand glittering blades of dry grass in a meadow, bound together in a sumptuous wave. An appealing vision of a platoon-mashing left fielder comes into conceivable view, and…uh …um…what was the question?

Eli White SS Born: 06/26/94 Age: 26 Bats: R Throws: R Height: 6'2" Weight: 175 Origin: Round 11, 2016 Draft (#322 overall)

YEAR	TEAM	LVL	AGE	PA	R	2B	3B	HR	RBI	BB	K	SB	CS	AVG/OBP/SLG	DRC+	VORP	BABIP	BRR	FRAA	WARP
2017	STO	A+	23	502	71	32	6	4	36	41	121	12	5	.270/.342/.395	104	21.8	.360	-0.2	SS(92): -7.9, CF(8): -1.5	1.2
2018	MID	AA	24	578	81	30	8	9	55	62	116	18	9	.306/.388/.450	134	36.5	.379	3.2	2B(66): 2.8, SS(42): 2.6	4.6
2019	NAS	AAA	25	499	63	20	5	14	43	43	138	14	5	.253/.337/.418	80	17.4	.336	1.7	SS(91): -6.8, CF(22): -0.5	0.6
2020	*TEX*	*MLB*	*26*	*140*	*14*	*7*	*1*	*3*	*15*	*10*	*45*	*2*	*1*	*.242/.310/.388*	*81*	*1.5*	*.346*	*0.0*	*CF -1, 2B 0*	*0.1*

Comparables: Brian Bixler, Joey Butler, Joey Wendle

When the Rangers traded Jurickson Profar to Oakland in a three-way deal that netted them Brock Burke, Kyle Bird and Yoel Espinal from Tampa, White was a surprisingly valuable get from Oakland. The ability to play multiple positions well—including shortstop and center field—earned him an invitation to big-league camp, and he seemed to have an outside shot at making the club out of spring training. Instead, Logan Forsythe (and later Danny Santana) filled utility roles for Texas while White had a modestly successful season in Triple-A. The Rangers' coming horde of middle infielders made White a bit more expendable when roster-crunch time came in November, and Texas left him vulnerable to the Rule 5 draft.

PITCHERS

Kolby Allard LHP Born: 08/13/97 Age: 22 Bats: L Throws: L Height: 6'1" Weight: 190 Origin: Round 1, 2015 Draft (#14 overall)

YEAR	TEAM	LVL	AGE	W	L	SV	G	GS	IP	H	HR	BB/9	K/9	K	GB%	BABIP	WHIP	ERA	DRA	WARP	MPH	FB%	WHF	CSP
2017	MIS	AA	19	8	11	0	27	27	150	146	11	2.7	7.7	129	44%	.310	1.27	3.18	4.72	0.8				
2018	GWN	AAA	20	6	4	0	19	19	112¹	102	6	2.7	7.1	89	39%	.296	1.21	2.72	4.34	1.5				
2018	ATL	MLB	20	1	1	0	3	1	8	19	3	4.5	3.4	3	36%	.444	2.88	12.38	8.43	-0.3	91.1	62.7	5.6	46.5
2019	GWN	AAA	21	7	5	0	20	20	110	119	15	2.9	8.0	98	51%	.331	1.41	4.17	4.53	2.3				
2019	TEX	MLB	21	4	2	0	9	9	45¹	52	3	3.8	6.6	33	46%	.327	1.57	4.96	6.04	-0.1	93.7	46.4	8.6	52.5
2020	*TEX*	*MLB*	*22*	*3*	*3*	*0*	*10*	*10*	*51*	*60*	*9*	*3.3*	*6.0*	*34*	*46%*	*.312*	*1.54*	*5.65*	*5.28*	*0.2*	*93.4*	*50.6*	*8.5*	*51.9*

Comparables: Julio Teheran, Taijuan Walker, Mike Soroka

When Allard was 18, the Braves watched him breeze through rookie ball and A-Ball. At 19, he made quick work of Double-A opponents. Then in 2018, still just 20 and shrugging off Triple-A hitters, he was called up to the big leagues and that… did not go well. When he looked hittable at Triple-A Gwinnett at 21 in 2019, Atlanta traded him to the Rangers for relief pitcher Chris Martin. After Allard posted a sparkling 0.00 ERA in Nashville for, um, one game, the Rangers brought him up. It wasn't a dominant two months—he didn't strike many hitters out, and he walked too many—but Allard showed the ability to keep a cool head when waters got choppy. The Rangers won six and lost three with Allard on the mound. He'll battle about a half-dozen other young starters for a spot on the 25-man roster in 2020.

Kyle Bird LHP
Born: 04/12/93 Age: 27 Bats: L Throws: L Height: 6'2" Weight: 175 Origin: Round 35, 2014 Draft (#1057 overall)

YEAR	TEAM	LVL	AGE	W	L	SV	G	GS	IP	H	HR	BB/9	K/9	K	GB%	BABIP	WHIP	ERA	DRA	WARP	MPH	FB%	WHF	CSP
2017	MNT	AA	24	4	2	0	53	0	71¹	64	2	3.7	8.6	68	46%	.316	1.30	3.03	4.55	0.2				
2018	MNT	AA	25	0	2	4	16	1	19²	14	2	4.1	10.5	23	43%	.267	1.17	3.66	3.82	0.3				
2018	DUR	AAA	25	3	1	0	27	5	55²	38	4	4.2	10.5	65	40%	.264	1.15	1.94	3.15	1.3				
2019	NAS	AAA	26	5	1	2	29	0	34²	35	4	3.9	10.1	39	42%	.344	1.44	2.86	4.33	0.6				
2019	TEX	MLB	26	0	0	1	12	0	12²	11	5	10.7	7.1	10	42%	.182	2.05	7.82	7.33	-0.3	93.4	53.3	10	46.5
2020	TEX	MLB	27	2	2	0	31	0	33	33	6	4.4	7.2	26	40%	.277	1.49	5.50	5.21	0.0	92.9	54	10.1	47.1

Comparables: Buddy Baumann, Williams Jerez, Scott Alexander

There's an old saying about Nashville, that it's a "five-year town." The implication is that with so many musicians coming and going from their hometowns in hopes of making it big, it takes about five years before the locals will begin to trust that you're going to stick around—finally accepting you as one of them. After Kyle Bird's 2019 season, expect that number to go up. He spent five separate stints in Music City between big-league call-ups. Bird's performance in the bright lights of Nashville suggested that he was ready for the big stage, but—as many a country musician can tell you—if it doesn't play in Texas, it's not quite good enough yet.

Brock Burke LHP
Born: 08/04/96 Age: 23 Bats: L Throws: L Height: 6'4" Weight: 180 Origin: Round 3, 2014 Draft (#96 overall)

YEAR	TEAM	LVL	AGE	W	L	SV	G	GS	IP	H	HR	BB/9	K/9	K	GB%	BABIP	WHIP	ERA	DRA	WARP	MPH	FB%	WHF	CSP
2017	BGR	A	20	6	0	0	10	10	57¹	37	0	3.1	9.3	59	35%	.253	0.99	1.10	2.69	1.7				
2017	PCH	A+	20	5	6	0	13	13	66	75	6	2.2	6.7	49	47%	.329	1.38	4.64	5.46	-0.2				
2018	PCH	A+	21	3	5	0	16	13	82	85	4	3.3	9.5	87	48%	.343	1.40	3.84	4.77	0.5				
2018	MNT	AA	21	6	1	0	9	9	55¹	39	2	2.3	11.5	71	37%	.282	0.96	1.95	2.91	1.6				
2019	FRI	AA	22	3	5	0	9	9	45¹	34	2	2.4	9.7	49	50%	.262	1.01	3.18	2.73	1.2				
2019	NAS	AAA	22	0	0	0	2	2	8	12	1	6.8	12.4	11	50%	.478	2.25	7.88	6.74	0.0				
2019	TEX	MLB	22	0	2	0	6	6	26²	30	6	3.7	4.7	14	52%	.276	1.54	7.43	6.82	-0.3	94.3	61.3	5.7	51
2020	TEX	MLB	23	1	2	0	5	5	22	26	4	3.3	4.8	12	46%	.296	1.56	6.07	5.65	0.0	94.2	63.5	5.9	52.8

Comparables: Stephen Gonsalves, Robbie Ray, Lucas Sims

When Burke was first called up, his manager joked that the young left-hander was so unbothered by the big lights and pressure of the big leagues that it seemed like he was up there yawning between pitches. That statement became a bit more loaded when it came out that Burke had dealt with somnambulism (sleep walking) since childhood. Of all the young Rangers starters to make their big-league debuts in 2019, Burke might have the highest ceiling. He looked magnificent in his first couple of starts, but an illness and shoulder fatigue led to some performances that made his end-of-season stats look a bit bloated. Neither issue is expected to require anything more than rest over the offseason, and the Rangers hope that Burke will earn a rotation spot in spring training.

Jesse Chavez RHP
Born: 08/21/83 Age: 36 Bats: R Throws: R Height: 6'2" Weight: 175 Origin: Round 42, 2002 Draft (#1252 overall)

YEAR	TEAM	LVL	AGE	W	L	SV	G	GS	IP	H	HR	BB/9	K/9	K	GB%	BABIP	WHIP	ERA	DRA	WARP	MPH	FB%	WHF	CSP
2017	LAA	MLB	33	7	11	0	38	21	138	148	28	2.9	7.8	119	42%	.306	1.40	5.35	4.80	1.1	93.5	61	9.2	46
2018	TEX	MLB	34	3	1	1	30	0	56¹	58	10	1.9	8.0	50	45%	.296	1.24	3.51	3.20	1.1	94.7	92.9	11.7	53.6
2018	CHN	MLB	34	2	1	4	32	0	39	26	3	1.2	9.7	42	43%	.247	0.79	1.15	2.95	0.9	94.5	92.9	11.5	53
2019	TEX	MLB	35	3	5	1	48	9	78	82	12	2.5	8.3	72	42%	.310	1.33	4.85	5.07	0.4	92.8	70.8	7.8	48
2020	TEX	MLB	36	2	2	4	47	0	49	55	11	2.8	8.2	45	42%	.304	1.42	5.50	5.28	0.0	92.3	72.5	9.3	48.2

Comparables: Jay Howell, Dan Wheeler, Bob Howry

Fun with stats: Chavez as an opener in 2019: 4 games, 6 2/3 innings, 0 earned runs, 0 walks, 7 strikeouts. Chavez as a starter in 2019: 5 games, 23 1/3 innings, 20 earned runs (7.71 ERA), 5 walks, 21 strikeouts. Of course, there's context needed: Chavez "opened" against the Astros, Mariners, Mariners, and Reds, and started against the Tigers (0 ER), Rays (3 ER), Twins (4 ER), Astros (6 ER), and Diamondbacks (7 ER). Whether the decline in results came from the back-and-forth is the sort of thing that leads to speculation, as is the question of whether stretching him out led to the injuries that spiked the end of his season (surgery to remove loose bodies from his elbow). Side note: The best Chavez story of the season takes place on July 12. After home plate umpire Rob Drake had blown two ball/strike calls in the hitters' favor, Chavez exaggeratedly offered his prescription sunglasses to Drake as he walked off the field. After the game, he did not back down from the display. "I thought he needed 'em," Chavez shrugged.

Kyle Cody RHP
Born: 08/09/94 Age: 25 Bats: R Throws: R Height: 6'7" Weight: 245 Origin: Round 6, 2016 Draft (#189 overall)

YEAR	TEAM	LVL	AGE	W	L	SV	G	GS	IP	H	HR	BB/9	K/9	K	GB%	BABIP	WHIP	ERA	DRA	WARP	MPH	FB%	WHF	CSP
2017	HIC	A	22	6	6	0	18	18	95¹	77	4	3.1	9.5	101	47%	.286	1.15	2.83	3.54	1.9				
2017	DEB	A+	22	3	0	0	5	5	30²	25	0	2.9	10.3	35	51%	.325	1.14	2.05	3.79	0.5				
2020	TEX	MLB	25	2	2	0	33	0	35	35	5	3.7	8.9	35	45%	.308	1.43	4.84	4.73	0.2				

Comparables: Shaun Anderson, Christian Garcia, Alex Meyer

This is almost certainly the case in other organizations too, but there's a large faction of the Rangers' most interesting pitchers whose recent stats are pretty sparse due to, what else, Tommy John surgery. Cody is one of those. He won the Rangers' Minor League Pitcher of the Year in 2017, and it appeared that he was on the train to Arlington, ETA 2020. Instead, he has only pitched a total of five innings since receiving the award, and while he hasn't pitched above High-A the Rangers added him to the 40-man roster this winter.

Hans Crouse RHP   Born: 09/15/98   Age: 21   Bats: L   Throws: R   Height: 6'4"   Weight: 180   Origin: Round 2, 2017 Draft (#66 overall)

YEAR	TEAM	LVL	AGE	W	L	SV	G	GS	IP	H	HR	BB/9	K/9	K	GB%	BABIP	WHIP	ERA	DRA	WARP	MPH	FB%	WHF	CSP
2017	RNG	RK	18	0	0	0	10	6	20	7	1	3.2	13.5	30	60%	.176	0.70	0.45	0.00	1.3				
2018	SPO	A-	19	5	1	0	8	8	38	25	2	2.6	11.1	47	36%	.253	0.95	2.37	2.18	1.4				
2018	HIC	A	19	0	2	0	5	5	16²	18	1	4.3	8.1	15	40%	.333	1.56	2.70	5.31	0.0				
2019	HIC	A	20	6	1	0	19	19	87²	86	12	2.0	7.8	76	34%	.297	1.20	4.41	5.12	0.1				
2020	TEX	MLB	21	2	2	0	33	0	35	36	6	3.3	7.0	27	33%	.288	1.40	4.98	4.99	0.1				

Comparables: Joe Ross, Nate Adcock, Mike Foltynewicz

In the bright light of day, the little distractions can collectively stipple over the silence, making it seem like everything is copacetic beneath the white-noise surface. The promise of a silent night is perpetually inviting, like an old high school flame or a deceased relative—never aging, the memory always conjuring their best version. But the impossible promise is built on a static of little sounds and interactions. When the sun melts into the soil and the world yawns and flutters its eyelashes and blithely gives way to the night, the truth can no longer be glossed over. The universe shuts up and that's when you hear the howls—distant at first, then closer, then just outside your window until you can hear the breathing between the howls, the hot breath of the predator, sniffing at first, then pawing the walls for cracks, the scraping and howling building to a chilling roar that your radio cannot drown out. The danger is outside, yes, but you know that one of these nights it will find a crack you missed. It will come for you, and all the noises in the world cannot scream it into submission, cannot save you from its hunger, cannot add even one more second to your life.

You close the book and look at the wall with your head cocked to one side as if to imply "was that really necessary?" You scrunch your face slightly. That wasn't about Hans Crouse at all.

The book shakes in your lap and you are certain that you hear the beast again, just behind you, in a nearly imperceptible whisper… *"Wasn't it?"*

Kyle Gibson RHP   Born: 10/23/87   Age: 32   Bats: R   Throws: R   Height: 6'6"   Weight: 215   Origin: Round 1, 2009 Draft (#22 overall)

YEAR	TEAM	LVL	AGE	W	L	SV	G	GS	IP	H	HR	BB/9	K/9	K	GB%	BABIP	WHIP	ERA	DRA	WARP	MPH	FB%	WHF	CSP
2017	MIN	MLB	29	12	10	0	29	29	158	182	24	3.4	6.9	121	52%	.328	1.53	5.07	5.20	0.7	94.6	56.7	10.6	42.2
2018	MIN	MLB	30	10	13	0	32	32	196²	177	23	3.6	8.2	179	51%	.285	1.30	3.62	4.21	2.5	95.3	57.8	12.1	40.4
2019	MIN	MLB	31	13	7	0	34	29	160	175	23	3.2	9.0	160	52%	.331	1.44	4.84	5.60	0.3	95.4	50.3	13	38.5
2020	TEX	MLB	32	9	9	0	26	26	150	159	19	3.9	9.0	150	52%	.324	1.48	4.87	4.59	1.7	94.2	54.1	12	39.7

Comparables: Joe Kelly, Brandon McCarthy, Iván Nova

When you have a type, you have a type. Texas pounced on Gibson early in free agency, signing the now-former Twin to a three-year deal that mimicked the deals inked by Mike Minor and Lance Lynn, the club's most successful recent rotation reclamations. The healthy portions of Gibson's past two seasons have looked similar, but last year's final tallies were skewed after ulcerative colitis ripped 15 pounds off his frame and tanked his second half. His four-seamer continues to be highly problematic, but he finally started to get away from the pitch last year, giving in to the good deal of depth in the rest of his repertoire. If he pitches to his potential, he's a good bet to mark a third straight year of successful rotation bargain-binning by the Rangers.

Nick Goody RHP   Born: 07/06/91   Age: 28   Bats: R   Throws: R   Height: 5'11"   Weight: 200   Origin: Round 6, 2012 Draft (#217 overall)

YEAR	TEAM	LVL	AGE	W	L	SV	G	GS	IP	H	HR	BB/9	K/9	K	GB%	BABIP	WHIP	ERA	DRA	WARP	MPH	FB%	WHF	CSP
2017	CLE	MLB	25	1	2	0	56	0	54²	39	7	3.3	11.9	72	29%	.269	1.08	2.80	2.66	1.5	93.4	52.4	17.5	42.5
2018	CLE	MLB	26	0	2	0	12	0	11²	15	4	3.9	9.3	12	30%	.306	1.71	6.94	5.33	-0.1	93.4	54.8	14.4	40.7
2019	COH	AAA	27	0	1	0	21	0	24¹	28	8	4.8	12.6	34	26%	.345	1.68	7.77	6.41	0.0				
2019	CLE	MLB	27	3	2	0	39	0	40²	30	7	4.9	11.1	50	26%	.245	1.28	3.54	5.92	-0.3	94.1	51.1	16.4	44.1
2020	TEX	MLB	28	2	2	0	41	0	44	36	8	3.5	10.8	53	28%	.263	1.20	3.92	3.95	0.6	93.2	52.3	16.7	42.8

Comparables: Fernando Cabrera, Edubray Ramos, Dominic Leone

Entering the season's final weekend, Goody had a chance to finish with a 2.something ERA for the second time in three tries. If he was aware of that information, it didn't set well on him. Instead, Goody faced six batters and permitted four of them to reach (all four later scored). His ERA ended up at 3.54—an achievement, considering he'd appeared 39 times and departed with his seasonal ERA at least that high on just four occasions. What a grim, predictable surprise, seeing all that hard work wasted. It must be how the ants feel: always on the precipice of success, or, more often, existential dismay. Goody? No. Not quite.

Taylor Hearn LHP   Born: 08/30/94   Age: 25   Bats: L   Throws: L   Height: 6'5"   Weight: 210   Origin: Round 5, 2015 Draft (#164 overall)

YEAR	TEAM	LVL	AGE	W	L	SV	G	GS	IP	H	HR	BB/9	K/9	K	GB%	BABIP	WHIP	ERA	DRA	WARP	MPH	FB%	WHF	CSP
2017	BRD	A+	22	4	6	0	18	17	87¹	65	8	3.8	10.9	106	50%	.281	1.17	4.12	3.88	1.4				
2018	ALT	AA	23	3	6	0	19	19	104	75	6	3.3	9.3	107	41%	.256	1.09	3.12	3.02	2.8				
2018	FRI	AA	23	1	2	0	5	5	25	29	5	3.2	11.9	33	36%	.375	1.52	5.04	5.68	-0.1				
2019	NAS	AAA	24	1	3	0	4	4	20	14	3	4.5	11.7	26	29%	.262	1.20	4.05	2.90	0.7				
2019	TEX	MLB	24	0	1	0	1	1	0¹	3	0	108.0	0.0	0	50%	.750	21.00	108.00	1.88	0.0	93.9	69.2	2.6	43.8
2020	TEX	MLB	25	0	0	0	2	2	5	6	1	4.3	5.1	3	37%	.281	1.58	5.98	5.59	0.0	93.6	70.9	2.6	44.8

Comparables: Eric Skoglund, Taylor Rogers, Sean Nolin

Hang out with enough philosophy or astronomy majors and you're sure to get a lecture about how time is elastic. You don't have to explain that to Hearn—his big-league debut on April 25 was the answer to this question: When is an outing simultaneously brief and eternal? Yes, Hearn lasted just one-third of an inning. On the other hand, he threw 39 pitches and faced eight batters, eventually exiting the game only to learn that he had tweaked his elbow—called a "minor" injury at the time. When does a "a few weeks" mean "five-plus months"? Alas, while time is elastic, elbows are not: It was later reported that Hearn had also suffered an elbow fracture. The big lefty should be ready for 2020 and should get a shot at cracking the big-league rotation at some point, but it's hard to call 2019 anything but a lost season, an eternity squeezed into the first act of a play that will inevitably feel brief in retrospect.

Jimmy Herget RHP Born: 09/09/93 Age: 26 Bats: R Throws: R Height: 6'3" Weight: 170 Origin: Round 6, 2015 Draft (#175 overall)

YEAR	TEAM	LVL	AGE	W	L	SV	G	GS	IP	H	HR	BB/9	K/9	K	GB%	BABIP	WHIP	ERA	DRA	WARP	MPH	FB%	WHF	CSP
2017	PEN	AA	23	1	3	16	24	0	29²	22	1	3.6	13.3	44	32%	.323	1.15	2.73	2.76	0.7				
2017	LOU	AAA	23	3	1	9	28	0	32¹	30	4	2.5	7.8	28	38%	.283	1.21	3.06	3.94	0.5				
2018	LOU	AAA	24	1	3	0	50	0	59²	59	5	3.2	9.8	65	36%	.327	1.34	3.47	4.95	0.1				
2019	LOU	AAA	25	3	4	2	48	0	58²	41	7	5.5	10.4	68	37%	.246	1.31	2.91	3.12	1.8				
2019	CIN	MLB	25	0	0	0	5	0	6¹	8	2	4.3	0.0	0	22%	.286	1.74	4.26	8.49	-0.2	95.0	50.7	8.4	42.5
2020	TEX	MLB	26	1	2	0	33	0	35	54	12	5.1	8.9	34	35%	.382	2.11	10.09	6.94	-0.7	94.6	51.6	8.6	43.2

Comparables: Chandler Shepherd, Akeel Morris, Heath Hembree

Herget, a right-handed sidearmer who relies more on deception than stuff (though he sits around 93 mph, so he isn't without teeth), is going to have to prove he can handle lefties enough at the major-league level to be of greater use than in some specialist role. He'll need to do it affirmatively—and quickly—in order to survive, given the league's implementation of the three-batter minimum ahead of his rookie season. (He probably would've settled for a fruitcake or a simple "Welcome to the league, meat," y'all.) Herget's minor-league numbers suggest he could be up for the task.

Nate Jones RHP Born: 01/28/86 Age: 34 Bats: R Throws: R Height: 6'5" Weight: 220 Origin: Round 5, 2007 Draft (#179 overall)

YEAR	TEAM	LVL	AGE	W	L	SV	G	GS	IP	H	HR	BB/9	K/9	K	GB%	BABIP	WHIP	ERA	DRA	WARP	MPH	FB%	WHF	CSP
2017	CHA	MLB	31	1	0	0	11	0	11²	9	1	4.6	11.6	15	59%	.308	1.29	2.31	4.95	0.0	98.9	52.5	13	41.5
2018	CHA	MLB	32	2	2	5	33	0	30	28	4	4.5	9.6	32	41%	.289	1.43	3.00	4.55	0.1	99.0	64.7	15.2	47.1
2019	CHA	MLB	33	0	1	1	13	0	10¹	10	2	6.1	8.7	10	52%	.296	1.65	3.48	5.37	0.0	96.8	58.3	10.2	46.3
2020	TEX	MLB	34	2	2	0	33	0	35	32	5	3.7	10.4	41	44%	.306	1.33	4.35	4.38	0.3	97.3	60	13.2	44.7

Comparables: Robb Nen, Brad Brach, Pat Neshek

The Rangers have started doing this thing in recent years where they trade for an injured or underperforming player, absorbing his contract in exchange for some other included asset (see: eating Austin Jackson's contract to get Jason Bahr, or trading for Welington Castillo because he came with $250,000 in international slot money, subsequently paying Castillo $500,000 to buy out his 2020 option). Jones is another example of this trend. Texas traded minor leaguers Ray Castro, Joseph Jarneski and cash considerations to the White Sox for the reliever in 2019—a season in which it was highly unlikely that he would pitch—then chose not to exercise his 2020 option. Why? Because they also got $1 million in international slot money in return. It's worth a conversation about who is getting the short end of the paycheck if teams are willing to part with prospects and millions of actual dollars just to be allowed a larger pool of money that they can spend on Latin American players. One read would be that—since teams are paying X amount of additional dollars anyway—the market is telling us that those Latin American players are worth more money and the cap is artificially depressing their ability to earn a fair paycheck. Anyway, Nate Jones didn't throw a single pitch in a game at any level as a member of the Texas Rangers; yay capitalism!

Ariel Jurado RHP Born: 01/30/96 Age: 24 Bats: R Throws: R Height: 6'1" Weight: 180 Origin: International Free Agent, 2002

YEAR	TEAM	LVL	AGE	W	L	SV	G	GS	IP	H	HR	BB/9	K/9	K	GB%	BABIP	WHIP	ERA	DRA	WARP	MPH	FB%	WHF	CSP
2017	FRI	AA	21	9	11	0	27	27	157	188	16	2.1	5.4	95	53%	.335	1.43	4.59	5.64	-0.9				
2018	FRI	AA	22	5	3	0	16	16	101²	107	12	1.5	5.1	58	51%	.291	1.22	3.28	4.40	1.1				
2018	TEX	MLB	22	5	5	0	12	8	54²	66	7	3.0	3.6	22	52%	.304	1.54	5.93	6.97	-1.1	93.7	70.2	4.8	51.2
2019	NAS	AAA	23	3	0	0	4	4	22²	29	1	0.8	8.7	22	39%	.400	1.37	3.57	4.85	0.4				
2019	TEX	MLB	23	7	11	0	32	18	122¹	148	21	2.6	6.0	81	48%	.318	1.50	5.81	7.21	-2.0	94.5	64.2	8.3	48.9
2020	TEX	MLB	24	3	4	0	34	8	65	80	11	2.7	5.7	42	47%	.319	1.52	5.72	5.35	0.1	94.1	67.7	7.6	51.4

Comparables: Zach Eflin, Luis Ortiz, Jake Thompson

Once in awhile it's fun to use a player's comments section to write about something else entirely. This year, it's Jurado who gets the treatment. Today, we're going to highlight one way to know you're dating the wrong person. In any relationship, your significant other will inevitably do things that delight you and things that vex you; that's just how humanity works! We all have the capacity to annoy the &%#$ out of each other, to varying degrees, but the hope is that you eventually find someone who is worth the annoyances, someone who mostly behaves in a way that enhances your joy, and when they do something you don't like, it kind of comes as a surprise. When you're in a relationship with the wrong person, the opposite tends to occur: when they do something that delights you, you find that it comes as a surprise. "That was incredibly sweet," you exclaim, eyebrows furrowing as the entire realization sets in. "But…it was kind of out of character, wasn't it? What on earth does it mean that I'm surprised by them doing something good?" Eventually, if you pull the thread long enough, you'll reach the inevitable conclusion that the kind act was a surprise because it was out of character—a gesture, rather than a reflection of who they are.

And that's how you know.

Shawn Kelley RHP Born: 04/26/84 Age: 36 Bats: R Throws: R Height: 6'2" Weight: 237 Origin: Round 13, 2007 Draft (#405 overall)

YEAR	TEAM	LVL	AGE	W	L	SV	G	GS	IP	H	HR	BB/9	K/9	K	GB%	BABIP	WHIP	ERA	DRA	WARP	MPH	FB%	WHF	CSP
2017	WAS	MLB	33	3	2	4	33	0	26	29	12	3.8	8.7	25	26%	.236	1.54	7.27	6.11	-0.3	94.3	59.2	15.4	46.9
2018	WAS	MLB	34	1	0	0	35	0	32¹	26	7	1.4	8.9	32	28%	.229	0.96	3.34	4.51	0.2	94.5	52.8	12.4	50.7
2018	OAK	MLB	34	1	0	0	19	0	16²	7	0	3.2	9.7	18	40%	.184	0.78	2.16	3.22	0.3	93.1	50.6	12.4	50.1
2019	TEX	MLB	35	5	2	11	50	0	47¹	55	12	2.1	8.2	43	30%	.314	1.39	4.94	6.43	-0.6	94.3	39.7	12.4	49.8
2020	TEX	MLB	36	2	2	0	33	0	35	33	9	2.3	8.9	35	31%	.262	1.20	4.56	4.78	0.2	92.9	46.6	12.7	48.3

Comparables: Rafael Soriano, Blake Parker, Darren O'Day

A year ago, Kelley was the guy who power-slammed his glove in Washington and promptly traded to the A's. In Texas, he inherited a new role: closer. His 11 saves were a career high, probably giving the Rangers more value than they expected from the veteran. It wasn't enough to convince them to exercise his 2020 option, however. Kelley said during the season that if that option weren't picked up, he would retire rather than re-enter free agency. One might argue that throwing a still-functioning glove at the ground was some kind of predictive metaphor for this decision, but given the minor injuries he endured in 2019, it's also reasonable to accept that this 35-year-old is just ready to stop hurling things altogether and spend more time with his family.

Corey Kluber RHP   Born: 04/10/86   Age: 34   Bats: R   Throws: R   Height: 6'4"   Weight: 215   Origin: Round 4, 2007 Draft (#134 overall)

YEAR	TEAM	LVL	AGE	W	L	SV	G	GS	IP	H	HR	BB/9	K/9	K	GB%	BABIP	WHIP	ERA	DRA	WARP	MPH	FB%	WHF	CSP
2017	CLE	MLB	31	18	4	0	29	29	203²	141	21	1.6	11.7	265	46%	.267	0.87	2.25	2.28	7.5	94.2	42.4	16.4	47.2
2018	CLE	MLB	32	20	7	0	33	33	215	179	25	1.4	9.3	222	46%	.276	0.99	2.89	2.84	6.1	93.8	41.6	13	46.4
2019	CLE	MLB	33	2	3	0	7	7	35²	44	4	3.8	9.6	38	41%	.370	1.65	5.80	6.19	-0.2	93.4	39.8	13.4	43.7
2020	TEX	MLB	34	11	9	0	28	28	168	159	27	2.6	9.7	181	43%	.298	1.24	4.02	4.04	2.8	92.8	41.1	14.1	44.8

Comparables: Jeremy Hefner, Collin McHugh, Carlos Carrasco

Sustaining dominance ain't easy. That might seem obvious, but the sport is full of former All-Star hurlers who woke up one day and just didn't have It anymore. Our guess is that Kluber will rebound (even the best robots malfunction on occasion), but he's about to turn 34 and is coming off a rotten go. The two-time Cy Young winner saw his 2019 cut short by a fractured forearm and oblique strain, but he wasn't all that good before landing on the injured list; he walked more batters than ever, resulting in a WHIP—hey, stick with us here—that was more befitting of a swingman. After being traded to Texas in exchange for an intriguing relief arm and the ever-elusive financial flexibility, Kluber will look to be rebooted in a new ballpark and a new division. Here's hoping it's a good one, and that in a year we're writing about how easy the decision was to pick up his $18-million option for 2021.

José Leclerc RHP   Born: 12/19/93   Age: 26   Bats: R   Throws: R   Height: 6'0"   Weight: 190   Origin: International Free Agent, 2010

YEAR	TEAM	LVL	AGE	W	L	SV	G	GS	IP	H	HR	BB/9	K/9	K	GB%	BABIP	WHIP	ERA	DRA	WARP	MPH	FB%	WHF	CSP
2017	TEX	MLB	23	2	3	2	47	0	45²	23	4	7.9	11.8	60	40%	.204	1.38	3.94	4.65	0.3	97.6	50.9	16.6	39.3
2018	TEX	MLB	24	2	3	12	59	0	57²	24	1	3.9	13.3	85	34%	.211	0.85	1.56	2.87	1.4	97.8	47.8	19	44.2
2019	TEX	MLB	25	2	4	14	70	3	68²	52	7	5.1	13.1	100	38%	.306	1.33	4.33	3.00	1.8	98.8	50.2	14.5	43.4
2020	TEX	MLB	26	3	2	29	52	0	55	41	7	5.8	13.9	84	37%	.305	1.39	3.99	3.80	0.8	97.9	50.5	16.5	43.4

Comparables: Eduardo Sanchez, Armando Benitez, Matt Mantei

Leclerc was an absolute assassin after taking over the closer's role in 2018. Unfortunately, at least as far as experts have been able to guess, someone dropped Leclerc on the floor sometime in the offseason, knocking his sights slightly askew and morphing him into a rogue, unmanned fire hose to start 2019. After 10 games, Leclerc had a 7.88 ERA, and while he was still striking guys out (nine in eight innings), he also walked seven, including four Astros in two-thirds of an inning on April 26. That was his last night in the closer's role for awhile, as new manager Chris Woodward gave him a few months to get straightened out. He eventually did so, regaining the ninth inning by season's end, which makes him the presumptive favorite to start 2020 there again.

Jordan Lyles RHP   Born: 10/19/90   Age: 29   Bats: R   Throws: R   Height: 6'5"   Weight: 230   Origin: Round 1, 2008 Draft (#38 overall)

YEAR	TEAM	LVL	AGE	W	L	SV	G	GS	IP	H	HR	BB/9	K/9	K	GB%	BABIP	WHIP	ERA	DRA	WARP	MPH	FB%	WHF	CSP
2017	ELP	AAA	26	1	1	0	5	5	20	20	1	3.6	9.0	20	48%	.333	1.40	4.50	4.08	0.4				
2017	COL	MLB	26	0	2	0	33	0	46²	61	11	2.3	6.4	33	52%	.331	1.56	6.94	5.61	-0.2	96.4	56.7	10.1	48.5
2017	SDN	MLB	26	1	3	0	5	5	23	35	5	3.9	8.6	22	46%	.395	1.96	9.39	4.14	0.3	94.9	53.3	10.9	43.3
2018	SDN	MLB	27	2	4	0	24	8	71¹	71	12	2.4	7.8	62	47%	.286	1.26	4.29	5.91	-0.6	96.3	48.8	10.2	50.2
2018	MIL	MLB	27	1	0	0	11	0	16¹	12	0	5.0	12.1	22	42%	.316	1.29	3.31	2.57	0.5	96.7	47.6	14.5	46.6
2019	MIL	MLB	28	7	1	0	11	11	58²	43	9	3.4	8.6	56	41%	.225	1.11	2.45	3.83	1.2	94.3	50.6	10.2	44.8
2019	PIT	MLB	28	5	7	0	17	17	82¹	88	16	3.6	9.8	90	43%	.326	1.47	5.36	4.51	1.1	94.7	52.9	11.5	46
2020	TEX	MLB	29	7	7	0	47	16	114	119	19	3.7	9.1	115	42%	.314	1.45	5.06	4.81	0.8	94.6	51.7	10.9	47.1

Comparables: Jacob Turner, Chris Volstad, Martín Pérez

The seller's remorse kicked in quickly for the Brewers on Lyles, who was let go by Milwaukee after the curveball the club added to his repertoire failed to make a big impact on his results. Turned out all they had to do was wait a bit. Lyles' surface numbers with Pittsburgh were rough, but he flashed a great strikeout rate and was largely the victim of an elevated home-run rate. In acquiring him at the deadline, the Brewers made the correct bet that the home-run bug wouldn't bite him quite so hard in the second half of the season. Lyles will be just 29 in 2020, and the Rangers felt good enough about his chances of sustaining his new level of performance to hand him a two-year pact.

Lance Lynn RHP   Born: 05/12/87   Age: 33   Bats: B   Throws: R   Height: 6'5"   Weight: 280   Origin: Round 1, 2008 Draft (#39 overall)

YEAR	TEAM	LVL	AGE	W	L	SV	G	GS	IP	H	HR	BB/9	K/9	K	GB%	BABIP	WHIP	ERA	DRA	WARP	MPH	FB%	WHF	CSP
2017	SLN	MLB	30	11	8	0	33	33	186¹	151	27	3.8	7.4	153	45%	.244	1.23	3.43	4.98	1.2	94.4	81	10.1	46
2018	MIN	MLB	31	7	8	0	20	20	102¹	105	12	5.5	8.8	100	51%	.322	1.63	5.10	5.53	-0.3	95.8	77	10.8	42.6
2018	NYA	MLB	31	3	2	0	11	9	54¹	58	2	2.3	10.1	61	47%	.364	1.33	4.14	4.32	0.6	95.5	77	11.2	46.9
2019	TEX	MLB	32	16	11	0	33	33	208¹	195	21	2.5	10.6	246	41%	.322	1.22	3.67	3.15	5.9	96.6	71.5	13.9	49.4
2020	TEX	MLB	33	11	9	0	29	29	175	170	23	3.3	10.4	201	42%	.321	1.34	4.24	4.11	2.8	94.7	74.6	11.9	46.2

Comparables: Tyson Ross, Andrew Cashner, Ian Kennedy

Sometimes reclamation projects go the way of Drew Smyly (2019) or Shelby Miller (2019) or Tyson Ross (2017) or Tim Lincecum (2018) or Edinson Vólquez (2018-19) or Matt Moore (2018) or Kyle Lohse (2016) or Dillon Gee (2017) or Doug Fister (2018). Other times, they end up like Bartolo Colón (2018) or Yovani Gallardo (2018), and if you're lucky, you'll find the occasional Andrew Cashner (2017). But it's extremely rare to sign free agents who provide the sort of surprising value generated by Mike Minor (2018-19) and Lynn (2019). Both pitchers struck out over 200 batters in 2019, the first time Texas has had two

200-plus strikeout guys since Nolan Ryan and Bobby Witt in 1990, though they did it with two completely different styles: Minor is the finesse lefty, while Lynn would throw 200 fastballs per game if the manager allowed it. Fortunately for Lynn and the Rangers, the manager didn't allow it, and after a rough start, Lynn's improved pitch selection vaulted him to what should have been a Cy Young finalist nod.

Brett Martin LHP Born: 04/28/95 Age: 25 Bats: L Throws: L Height: 6'4" Weight: 190 Origin: Round 4, 2014 Draft (#126 overall)

YEAR	TEAM	LVL	AGE	W	L	SV	G	GS	IP	H	HR	BB/9	K/9	K	GB%	BABIP	WHIP	ERA	DRA	WARP	MPH	FB%	WHF	CSP
2017	DEB	A+	22	4	8	0	16	16	84¹	94	7	3.7	9.6	90	47%	.366	1.53	4.70	6.53	-1.3				
2018	FRI	AA	23	2	10	0	29	15	89	138	7	2.9	9.7	96	50%	.443	1.88	7.28	7.08	-1.9				
2019	NAS	AAA	24	0	0	1	10	0	12²	10	0	2.8	13.5	19	57%	.357	1.11	0.71	1.84	0.5				
2019	TEX	MLB	24	2	3	0	51	2	62¹	72	7	2.6	9.0	62	53%	.340	1.44	4.76	4.45	0.6	95.8	52.2	14.2	49.4
2020	TEX	MLB	25	2	2	0	41	0	44	44	5	3.0	8.9	43	51%	.316	1.34	4.19	4.10	0.5	95.5	53.4	14.5	50.6

Comparables: Jesus Tinoco, Elieser Hernandez, Keury Mella

One interesting thing about Martin's 2019 season was his home/away splits. While Globe Life Park was generally considered a hitter's park, Martin held opponents to a .676 OPS in Arlington. On the road, it was another story altogether, with opponents racking up a mark of .860 (Ironically, Martin had a win-loss record of 0-3 at home and 2-0 on the road. Yay, pitcher wins!). Jumble it together, and Martin was a microcosm of the 2019 Rangers: a few light-bulb moments of inspired progress sprinkled throughout the long, dark summer of learning (or "process", in the parlance of the day). Texas has a fairly left-handed herd of young starting pitchers (Kolby Allard, Taylor Hearn, Joe Palumbo, Brock Burke) but their up-and-coming relief corps are mostly starboard-side, so Martin will get every opportunity to succeed with the organization.

Yohander Méndez LHP Born: 01/17/95 Age: 25 Bats: L Throws: L Height: 6'5" Weight: 200 Origin: International Free Agent, 2011

YEAR	TEAM	LVL	AGE	W	L	SV	G	GS	IP	H	HR	BB/9	K/9	K	GB%	BABIP	WHIP	ERA	DRA	WARP	MPH	FB%	WHF	CSP
2017	FRI	AA	22	7	8	0	24	24	137²	114	23	2.8	8.1	124	46%	.256	1.14	3.79	4.07	1.8				
2017	TEX	MLB	22	0	1	0	7	0	12¹	13	3	2.2	5.1	7	37%	.263	1.30	5.11	7.67	-0.3	94.4	60.7	10	46.7
2018	DEB	A+	23	1	2	0	5	5	31	29	3	1.7	7.8	27	36%	.306	1.13	3.48	4.33	0.4				
2018	FRI	AA	23	1	1	0	6	6	33	33	6	2.7	8.7	32	32%	.300	1.30	4.91	4.82	0.2				
2018	ROU	AAA	23	0	7	0	12	12	58¹	65	13	3.7	7.7	50	40%	.310	1.53	5.25	6.19	-0.4				
2018	TEX	MLB	23	2	2	0	8	5	27²	28	4	4.9	5.9	18	40%	.286	1.55	5.53	7.02	-0.6	94.6	59.9	9.6	48.3
2019	FRI	AA	24	0	0	1	4	0	7¹	5	1	7.4	7.4	6	30%	.182	1.50	1.23	4.39	0.0				
2019	NAS	AAA	24	0	1	0	5	0	7¹	3	1	2.5	18.4	15	30%	.222	0.68	4.91	1.06	0.4				
2019	TEX	MLB	24	1	0	0	3	0	4²	4	2	9.6	15.4	8	25%	.333	1.93	5.79	4.81	0.0	95.4	41	13	35.8
2020	TEX	MLB	25	2	2	0	36	0	38	41	6	5.1	6.8	29	36%	.296	1.62	5.81	5.35	-0.1	94.4	58.3	10.5	43.7

Comparables: Stephen Gonsalves, Chase De Jong, Keyvius Sampson

Méndez has largely played the part of Wile E. Coyote in recent years. Every time it seems like he's about to succeed, something awful happens. He loses control of his inside fastball and discovers that he is hovering over the Grand Canyon, or takes the brunt of an organizational message about behavior and gets sent to High-A, or tweaks his elbow and rides a rocket ship into a tunnel that was just right there. Eventually, one must start to wonder if the creators of the narrative are cruel; if baseball is just some divine version of Calvinball, and the rules are that this man was built to be an object of scorn. But Méndez willed himself back to the big leagues by September, and while the results were mixed, there was a new twist: he was touching 97 with his fastball while working in relief. If the bullpen is where he's destined to land in 2020, perhaps he'll finally get to relax and sit down to a nice roadrunner dinner.

Mike Minor LHP Born: 12/26/87 Age: 32 Bats: R Throws: L Height: 6'4" Weight: 210 Origin: Round 1, 2009 Draft (#7 overall)

YEAR	TEAM	LVL	AGE	W	L	SV	G	GS	IP	H	HR	BB/9	K/9	K	GB%	BABIP	WHIP	ERA	DRA	WARP	MPH	FB%	WHF	CSP
2017	KCA	MLB	29	6	6	6	65	0	77²	57	5	2.5	10.2	88	43%	.272	1.02	2.55	2.96	1.9	96.5	45.7	13.5	46.5
2018	TEX	MLB	30	12	8	0	28	28	157	138	25	2.2	7.6	132	35%	.259	1.12	4.18	5.78	-0.9	95.2	49.5	10.9	50.5
2019	TEX	MLB	31	14	10	0	32	32	208¹	190	30	2.9	8.6	200	42%	.287	1.24	3.59	4.04	3.9	94.6	44.7	12.6	50
2020	TEX	MLB	32	11	10	0	29	29	175	172	30	2.9	8.6	167	40%	.293	1.30	4.36	4.31	2.5	94.1	46	12	48.9

Comparables: Jaime García, Alex Cobb, Denny Neagle

It's hard to mention Minor without Lance Lynn (or vice versa), since the tandem became the first two Rangers starters to strike out 200+ hitters in the same season since Nolan Ryan and Bobby Witt in 1990. Of course, Minor's 200th strikeout came after Ronald Guzmán intentionally let a foul ball drop in Minor's last inning, prompting the entire baseball world to lose their dang minds for awhile. "Ask me if I care, Pete" became a whole thing for a day (which is now the lifespan of these kinds of stories) and t-shirts were made. But it shouldn't be ignored that Minor's comeback is now firmly established. A year in the bullpen in Kansas City, a year with the reins pulled tight in Texas, and now a full season of dominance. Like Lynn, his pitch selection played a big part of his success in 2019—he became less predictable and relied on an inside-corner changeup that baffled right-handed hitters all season long. Why the Yankees didn't trade for him remains perhaps the greatest mystery of 2019.

Rafael Montero RHP Born: 10/17/90 Age: 29 Bats: R Throws: R Height: 6'0" Weight: 185 Origin: International Free Agent, 2011

YEAR	TEAM	LVL	AGE	W	L	SV	G	GS	IP	H	HR	BB/9	K/9	K	GB%	BABIP	WHIP	ERA	DRA	WARP	MPH	FB%	WHF	CSP
2017	LVG	AAA	26	0	2	0	5	5	29	18	3	3.7	11.5	37	52%	.238	1.03	2.48	1.87	1.2				
2017	NYN	MLB	26	5	11	0	34	18	119	141	12	5.1	8.6	114	50%	.366	1.75	5.52	4.67	1.1	95.7	55.5	10.9	44.2
2019	FRI	AA	28	0	0	0	5	2	9	15	0	2.0	15.0	15	26%	.556	1.89	7.00	6.24	-0.2				
2019	TEX	MLB	28	2	0	0	22	0	29	23	5	1.6	10.6	34	40%	.269	0.97	2.48	4.22	0.4	97.5	46.8	13.9	45.2
2020	TEX	MLB	29	2	2	5	41	0	44	42	6	4.1	10.3	50	42%	.314	1.41	4.43	4.23	0.5	95.5	53.3	11.7	44.8

Comparables: Kevin Gausman, Jake Faria, A.J. Cole

Fans in New York might remember Montero as the Hank Majewski of the Mets (since he never could quite cut it in the four seasons there (yes, this is a Frankie Valli and the Four Seasons reference, you can "okay boomer" us any time now)). After Tommy John surgery sidelined him for the entire 2018 season, Montero became a free agent, quietly signing a minor-league deal with the Rangers in January of 2019 to absolutely zero fanfare. By July 3, having completed a rehab assignment, he was in Double-A Frisco. By July 19, he was a member of the Nashville Sounds, and a mere three days later, he was called up to the big leagues, where he had his most successful season to date. By that time, the Rangers were out of contention, so there wasn't much buzz about his triumphant return to the majors, but the numbers were real, and so was his fastball.

Joe Palumbo LHP Born: 10/26/94 Age: 25 Bats: L Throws: L Height: 6'1" Weight: 168 Origin: Round 30, 2013 Draft (#910 overall)

YEAR	TEAM	LVL	AGE	W	L	SV	G	GS	IP	H	HR	BB/9	K/9	K	GB%	BABIP	WHIP	ERA	DRA	WARP	MPH	FB%	WHF	CSP
2017	DEB	A+	22	1	0	0	3	3	13²	4	0	2.6	14.5	22	58%	.167	0.59	0.66	1.48	0.6				
2018	DEB	A+	23	1	4	0	6	6	27	24	3	2.0	11.3	34	42%	.304	1.11	2.67	4.07	0.4				
2018	FRI	AA	23	1	0	0	2	2	9¹	6	0	2.9	9.6	10	39%	.261	0.96	1.93	3.31	0.2				
2019	FRI	AA	24	0	0	0	11	10	53²	43	5	4.2	11.6	69	41%	.309	1.27	3.19	3.60	0.9				
2019	NAS	AAA	24	3	0	0	6	6	27	13	4	3.3	13.0	39	40%	.188	0.85	2.67	1.78	1.3				
2019	TEX	MLB	24	0	3	0	7	4	16²	21	7	4.3	11.3	21	36%	.326	1.74	9.18	5.67	0.0	95.7	56.7	10	49.8
2020	TEX	MLB	25	2	3	0	34	3	45	47	9	3.4	7.9	39	38%	.294	1.42	5.30	5.11	0.1	95.4	58	10.2	51

Comparables: Thomas Pannone, Antonio Bastardo, Jarlin García

There's this weird sandwich happening with Palumbo's baseball career. One piece of bread is the kid who was drafted in the 30th round after an eligibility snafu left him pitching in a semi-pro men's league as a high school senior. Not exactly the recipe for an All-Star, right? A feel-good story, sure. An underdog? Absolutely. A can't-miss prospect? Ehhhh…The other piece of bread is Palumbo's 2019 season. Blisters and bats made it quite a lesson in—what was it that Calvin's dad used to call it in the comic strip—character building? Look at that line. That's a 30th-round draft pick's line if ever you've seen one. And yet, the meat of the sandwich is that Palumbo has become a for-real prospect who was laying waste to High-A batters in 2017 before the dreaded Tommy John surgery came to call, then worked his way back to enough success in 2018 that his major-league debut in 2019 was something of a foregone conclusion. Yeah, 2019 was an exercise in things going pear-shaped, but Palumbo has enough juice to make himself a starter of interest when pitchers and catchers report (and beyond).

Cole Ragans LHP Born: 12/12/97 Age: 22 Bats: L Throws: L Height: 6'4" Weight: 190 Origin: Round 1, 2016 Draft (#30 overall)

YEAR	TEAM	LVL	AGE	W	L	SV	G	GS	IP	H	HR	BB/9	K/9	K	GB%	BABIP	WHIP	ERA	DRA	WARP	MPH	FB%	WHF	CSP
2017	SPO	A-	19	3	2	0	13	13	57¹	50	5	5.5	13.7	87	42%	.369	1.48	3.61	3.71	1.1				
2020	TEX	MLB	22	2	2	0	33	0	35	36	6	4.2	9.3	36	38%	.312	1.48	5.14	5.11	0.0				

Comparables: Miguel Castro, Drew Anderson, Jake Brigham

Ragans is another of the Rangers' impressive all-Tommy-John-prospects rotation. In fact, he's the grizzled veteran of the bunch, having now undergone the procedure twice. When he's been able to stay healthy, he's been impressive, earning comparisons in his first spring training to another crafty left-hander named Cole (Hamels). 2020 is going to be a pivotal year for Ragans after missing so much action. The team isn't going to rush him through the system just to make up for lost time, but they will indubitably be watching closely to see how much rust has accumulated in the time off, and how his body responds to being in a competitive setting again after so long living in a red t-shirt. He's still just 21, but he does need to stay healthy.

Alex Speas RHP Born: 03/04/98 Age: 22 Bats: R Throws: R Height: 6'4" Weight: 180 Origin: Round 2, 2016 Draft (#63 overall)

YEAR	TEAM	LVL	AGE	W	L	SV	G	GS	IP	H	HR	BB/9	K/9	K	GB%	BABIP	WHIP	ERA	DRA	WARP	MPH	FB%	WHF	CSP
2017	SPO	A-	19	1	6	1	16	7	33²	29	5	6.7	12.0	45	42%	.282	1.60	6.15	4.28	0.3				
2018	HIC	A	20	2	0	6	20	0	28²	16	1	6.6	15.4	49	56%	.283	1.29	2.20	2.67	0.7				
2020	TEX	MLB	22	2	2	0	33	0	35	36	6	4.5	10.3	40	41%	.324	1.52	5.29	5.20	0.0				

Comparables: Darwinzon Hernandez, Brock Burke, Drew Anderson

Let's start with the bad news for Speas: 1. He has pitched in two games (one inning) since June 11, 2018, having undergone Tommy John surgery, because how else would you expect that phrase to end? It would be a much more interesting story to say that he had taken time off to study under a farce guru who promised to teach the lad how to hypnotize dolphins, in case he was ever on a cruise ship and a dolphin leapt aboard and began haranguing the passengers, but Speas discovered the grift and brought the fraud to justice. Heck of a story; most interesting player in the game, instantly. But no, it was just the same crappy surgery that steals years from pitchers with brutal regularity. 2. His name sounds like a combination of "soup" and "peas", like if you meant to say "pea soup" but you were distracted thinking about the logistics of how exactly the dolphin would go about haranguing passengers anyway, and your brain just slung the words out of your mouth carelessly. "Speeeaas". The good news? Dude is throwing 102mph in his side sessions now and might be a big-leaguer before the season is over.

Ricky Vanasco RHP Born: 10/13/98   Age: 21   Bats: R   Throws: R   Height: 6'3"   Weight: 180   Origin: Round 15, 2017 Draft (#464 overall)

YEAR	TEAM	LVL	AGE	W	L	SV	G	GS	IP	H	HR	BB/9	K/9	K	GB%	BABIP	WHIP	ERA	DRA	WARP	MPH	FB%	WHF	CSP
2017	RNG	RK	18	0	1	0	10	0	9	8	0	5.0	16.0	16	47%	.421	1.44	0.00	2.70	0.3				
2018	RNG	RK	19	3	3	0	7	3	24²	25	1	4.7	9.1	25	48%	.393	1.54	4.38	6.31	-0.1				
2019	SPO	A-	20	3	1	0	9	9	39	23	2	5.1	13.6	59	51%	.292	1.15	1.85	3.10	1.0				
2019	HIC	A	20	0	0	0	2	2	10²	5	0	2.5	13.5	16	47%	.263	0.75	1.69	2.70	0.3				
2020	TEX	MLB	21	2	2	0	33	0	35	35	5	3.8	10.9	42	44%	.328	1.41	4.68	4.73	0.2				

Comparables: Dylan Cease, Domingo Germán, Neftalí Feliz

If you're wondering "who the heck is Ricky Vanasco?" you're not alone. Unless you work for the Rangers, in which case, hoooo boy are you ever alone, and also you should probably update your resumé, because he went from relative unknown to organizational hot gossip in a very short amount of time. His previous anonymity was less to do with futility and more to do with bad luck—the 15th-round pick's first season in pro ball ended when catcher Sam Huff hit him in the back of the head while attempting to throw out a would-be base thief. After a long concussion recovery, Vanasco missed the end of the 2018 season with an elbow injury that did not require surgery. So imagine everyone's surprise when the 20-year-old took short-season Spokane by storm, then didn't miss a beat when he was promoted to Low-A. The helium year didn't just occur from being healthy; there was also the added benefit of his fastball hopping up into the mid-to-high 90s. It will be fascinating to see how aggressive the Rangers are in promoting him through the system.

Edinson Vólquez RHP Born: 07/03/83   Age: 36   Bats: R   Throws: R   Height: 6'0"   Weight: 220   Origin: International Free Agent, 2001

YEAR	TEAM	LVL	AGE	W	L	SV	G	GS	IP	H	HR	BB/9	K/9	K	GB%	BABIP	WHIP	ERA	DRA	WARP	MPH	FB%	WHF	CSP
2017	MIA	MLB	33	4	8	0	17	17	92¹	78	8	5.2	7.9	81	49%	.278	1.42	4.19	4.89	0.7	95.4	56.8	9.5	43.6
2019	TEX	MLB	35	0	1	0	11	4	16	20	3	6.8	5.6	10	45%	.340	2.00	6.75	6.50	-0.2	96.5	47.8	8.1	46.3
2020	TEX	MLB	36	2	2	0	33	0	35	37	5	4.4	7.8	30	47%	.311	1.56	5.41	5.19	0.0	94.3	53.4	9	44.3

Comparables: Ubaldo Jiménez, Bobby Witt, Edwin Jackson

The Rangers once traded Vólquez to the Cincinnati Reds for Josh Hamilton. That worked out great for them, but—while Vólquez wasn't quite as impactful as Hamilton's best years in Texas—he forged a pretty good big-league career in his own right. He eventually made it full-circle back to the Rangers, signing before the 2018 season while he was recovering from Tommy John surgery. Vólquez barely cleared the starting line in 2019 before going down with another elbow injury, and it would have been perfectly understandable if he had called it a career. Instead, the team asked him to stick around and help mentor some of their young pitchers. Vólquez did so, and eventually even made it back to the mound for the end of the season.

Cole Winn RHP Born: 11/25/99   Age: 20   Bats: R   Throws: R   Height: 6'2"   Weight: 190   Origin: Round 1, 2018 Draft (#15 overall)

YEAR	TEAM	LVL	AGE	W	L	SV	G	GS	IP	H	HR	BB/9	K/9	K	GB%	BABIP	WHIP	ERA	DRA	WARP	MPH	FB%	WHF	CSP
2019	HIC	A	19	4	4	0	18	18	68²	59	5	5.1	8.5	65	48%	.290	1.43	4.46	5.47	-0.2				
2020	TEX	MLB	20	2	2	0	33	0	35	35	6	4.1	6.7	26	44%	.280	1.45	4.95	4.94	0.1				

Comparables: Luke Jackson, Tyler Chatwood, Mauricio Cabrera

Everybody fails; that's the one lesson that the sport is better at teaching than any other. But not everyone finds the right levers to steady the ship before being dashed on the rocks. Winn spent the early part of 2019 taking on water at Low-A Hickory following his 2018 post-draft hiatus from pitching, which is part of the Rangers' de-load program. But as the season progressed, the starboard-side slinger gradually began weathering the storms a little better, using his four-pitch mix with increasing effectiveness. It's also important to remember that Winn was only 19 last season. At that age, most guys are still navigating rookie or short-season ball, and he was figuring it out in deeper waters. There's still a lot of sea to explore before Winn pulls into the big leagues, but…hey, we're going to just let you choose your own pun-adventure here. Circle one: "something something learn from the stars." / "something something prove he can Winn."

LINEOUTS

Hitters

HITTER	POS	TEAM	LVL	AGE	PA	R	2B	3B	HR	RBI	BB	K	SB	CS	AVG/OBP/SLG	DRC+	VORP	BABIP	BRR	FRAA	WARP
Tim Federowicz	C	COH	AAA	31	103	7	6	0	2	13	11	23	0	0	.278/.353/.411	98	2.0	.348	-2.6	C(22): 3.8, 3B(1): 0.0	0.5
	C	TEX	MLB	31	83	6	2	0	4	7	5	31	1	0	.160/.213/.347	69	1.0	.200	0.1	C(29): -0.6, P(1): 0.0	0.1
	C	NAS	AAA	31	63	5	0	0	1	8	4	16	0	0	.140/.190/.193	26	-7.2	.167	0.0	C(15): 1.0	-0.1
Logan Forsythe	INF	TEX	MLB	32	367	38	17	1	7	39	44	100	2	0	.227/.325/.353	87	4.8	.307	-0.6	1B(46): 0.3, 3B(33): 0.3	0.5
Adolis García	OF	MEM	AAA	26	529	96	22	6	32	96	22	159	14	10	.253/.301/.517	91	19.9	.305	1.6	RF(73): 11.7, CF(34): 4.9	2.4
Pedro Gonzalez	OF	HIC	A	21	459	69	13	5	23	67	39	129	14	6	.248/.317/.471	119	24.2	.300	-0.1	RF(55): 0.3, CF(37): -0.8	1.6
Julio Pablo Martinez	OF	HIC	A	23	44	7	1	1	1	5	3	12	4	1	.250/.295/.400	112	1.0	.321	-0.7	CF(7): -0.7, LF(3): 0.1	0.0
	OF	DEB	A+	23	456	59	21	4	14	58	39	144	28	12	.248/.319/.423	111	29.5	.344	6.0	CF(65): -5.0, LF(38): -3.0	1.6
Blake Swihart	LF	RNO	AAA	27	122	20	2	1	6	22	15	31	0	1	.189/.287/.396	68	-4.1	.200	0.3	RF(15): -2.9, LF(10): -0.6	-0.4
	LF	BOS	MLB	27	29	4	1	0	1	4	2	7	0	0	.231/.310/.385	98	1.1	.278	0.0	C(8): -0.7, LF(1): -0.1	0.0
	LF	ARI	MLB	27	70	9	0	0	3	9	4	29	0	0	.136/.186/.273	49	-2.5	.176	1.0	LF(10): -0.4, RF(9): 0.1	-0.2

Maximo Acosta has opened a few eyes in his short amount of time in the organization. Just 17, he's a bit further away from than some of the other Rangers' infield prospects, but it wouldn't be a major surprise if he ends up being the best among them. ⓧ Between Jeff Mathis and **Tim Federowicz**, last year's Rangers employed two of the seven worst hitting catchers in the majors dating back to the 2011 season. Jon Daniels should charge a small fee to pick people's HACKING MASS backstops for them. ⓧ At the onset of the season, it appeared that **Logan Forsythe** was on the Hunter Pence plan for career rejuvenation in Texas. Both had markedly worse second halves — Pence due to injury, and Forsythe due to regression (and then injury). ⓧ All strikeouts and no walks make **Adolis García** a dull prospect. All strikeouts and no walks make Adolis García a dull prospect. All strikeouts and no walks make Adolis

García a dull prospect.... ⓧ Much like your rich uncle who never fixes anything himself, **Pedro Gonzalez** has all the tools—you just haven't ever seen him use them. ⓧ It took until August for the Rangers to trade for enough international slot money to pay **Bayron Lora**'s $3.9 million bonus, but he's officially in Rangers gear now. Big gear. Some of the biggest gear they have, in fact, as the 16-year-old is listed at 6-foot-4, 200 pounds. ⓧ The Rangers hoped that **Julio Pablo Martinez** would be the next Cuban sensation when they signed him for $2.8 million in 2018. With 156 strikeouts in 447 at-bats in 2019 there seemed to be a Cuban *missing* crisis (get it?!), though he did finish the season strong. ⓧ In early September 2019, the Hubble Telescope captured stunning images of the star known as NGC 2371/2 dying in deep space. Scientists initially confused the image with that of former catching prospect **Blake Swihart**. ⓧ **Davis Wendzel** was Big 12 co-Player of the Year, then got drafted by the same organization that drafted the other guy (Josh Jung). Both play third base, but Wendzel is generally considered to be more versatile, and might end up as a Ben Zobrist-type.

Pitchers

PITCHER	TEAM	LVL	AGE	W	L	SV	G	GS	IP	H	HR	BB/9	K/9	K	GB%	BABIP	WHIP	ERA	DRA	WARP	MPH	FB%	WHF	CSP
Joe Barlow	DEB	A+	23	4	0	4	17	0	23^2	10	1	5.7	16.7	44	32%	.273	1.06	0.38	2.16	0.7				
	FRI	AA	23	1	1	0	13	0	16	6	1	3.4	15.2	27	42%	.217	0.75	1.12	2.01	0.5				
	NAS	AAA	23	1	1	0	19	0	17^1	23	1	10.9	11.4	22	37%	.440	2.54	8.83	8.07	-0.3				
Jesse Biddle	TEX	MLB	27	0	0	0	4	0	5^1	4	2	8.4	11.8	7	69%	.182	1.69	11.81	8.16	-0.2	94.6	41.7	10.4	49.3
	SEA	MLB	27	0	0	0	11	0	11	20	2	5.7	6.5	8	46%	.429	2.45	9.82	8.53	-0.4	95.8	64.6	6.7	47.3
	ATL	MLB	27	0	1	0	15	0	11^2	18	1	7.7	8.5	11	44%	.405	2.40	5.40	5.21	0.0	95.4	52.5	8.7	45.9
Tim Dillard	NAS	AAA	35	9	9	0	33	21	153^1	169	16	2.2	6.0	103	55%	.321	1.34	4.75	4.41	3.3				
Kyle Dowdy	AKR	AA	26	1	1	0	7	3	29	25	2	3.4	8.4	27	41%	.291	1.24	2.48	5.01	-0.1				
	NAS	AAA	26	1	1	0	8	1	12^1	13	0	7.3	8.0	11	50%	.361	1.86	6.57	4.87	0.2				
	TEX	MLB	26	2	1	0	13	1	22^1	26	4	7.3	6.9	17	45%	.314	1.97	7.25	6.68	-0.3	97.8	67.3	9.1	44.8
Demarcus Evans	DEB	A+	22	4	0	6	17	0	22^1	9	0	6.9	16.1	40	55%	.273	1.16	0.81	3.02	0.4				
	FRI	AA	22	2	0	6	30	0	37^2	14	2	5.3	14.3	60	37%	.203	0.96	0.96	2.36	1.0				
Luke Farrell	FRI	AA	28	0	0	0	5	0	8^2	2	0	4.2	12.5	12	43%	.143	0.69	1.04	2.28	0.2				
	TEX	MLB	28	1	0	0	9	1	13^1	6	3	2.0	8.1	12	27%	.100	0.68	2.70	5.15	0.0	93.1	52.4	9.4	46.8
Brian Flynn	OMA	AAA	29	4	4	0	11	5	43^1	47	7	3.7	8.7	42	44%	.312	1.50	4.78	4.08	1.0				
	KCA	MLB	29	2	2	0	11	1	29^1	38	2	5.2	6.8	22	46%	.379	1.88	5.22	8.32	-0.9	93.0	57	8.6	46.2
Ian Gibaut	DUR	AAA	25	1	0	4	11	1	10^1	7	0	8.7	13.9	16	41%	.318	1.65	3.48	4.33	0.2				
	TBA	MLB	25	0	0	0	1	0	2	1	0	9.0	9.0	2		.200	1.50	9.00	6.29	0.0	97.7	77.1	14.3	38.8
	TEX	MLB	25	1	1	0	9	0	12^1	11	1	5.8	10.2	14	50%	.323	1.54	5.11	4.35	0.1	97.0	53.4	11.1	48.9
Jeanmar Gómez	TEX	MLB	31	1	0	0	16	0	15^1	23	2	3.5	5.9	10	55%	.389	1.89	8.22	5.54	0.0	93.0	51.1	5.9	46.3
Taylor Guerrieri	NAS	AAA	26	1	3	0	23	2	36^1	36	1	3.7	9.7	39	58%	.365	1.40	3.47	3.05	1.1				
	TEX	MLB	26	0	0	0	20	0	26^1	26	3	7.5	9.2	27	56%	.333	1.82	5.81	5.97	-0.2	95.4	44.9	7.8	45.5
Ronny Henriquez	HIC	A	19	6	6	0	21	19	82	91	6	3.0	10.9	99	39%	.384	1.44	4.50	5.91	-0.7				
Jonathan Hernández	FRI	AA	22	5	9	0	22	16	96	100	11	3.6	8.9	95	48%	.331	1.44	5.16	5.72	-1.0				
	TEX	MLB	22	2	1	0	9	2	16^2	14	3	7.0	10.3	19	52%	.256	1.62	4.32	5.05	0.1	98.9	48.5	12.6	37.2
Wei-Chieh Huang	FRI	AA	25	1	0	0	6	1	9^2	7	2	1.9	13.0	14	24%	.263	0.93	1.86	3.25	0.2				
	NAS	AAA	25	1	2	0	18	3	31	24	5	7.3	12.2	42	29%	.292	1.58	6.10	4.30	0.6				
	TEX	MLB	25	0	0	0	4	0	5^2	8	0	7.9	3.2	2	40%	.333	2.29	3.18	5.11	0.0	95.1	52.6	5.3	46.2
Tyler Phillips	DEB	A+	21	2	2	0	6	6	37^2	28	1	1.4	6.7	28	57%	.260	0.90	1.19	3.46	0.7				
	FRI	AA	21	7	9	0	18	16	93^1	95	15	1.9	7.1	74	52%	.292	1.23	4.72	5.29	-0.4				
Adrian Sampson	TEX	MLB	27	6	8	0	35	15	125^1	156	29	2.6	7.3	101	42%	.327	1.53	5.89	7.49	-2.5	94.6	54	10.6	48.8
Jeffrey Springs	NAS	AAA	26	3	0	0	6	0	7	6	1	0.0	15.4	12	50%	.385	0.86	3.86	1.59	0.3				
	TEX	MLB	26	4	1	0	25	0	32^1	38	4	6.4	8.9	32	25%	.358	1.89	6.40	7.98	-0.9	94.0	58.1	13.8	50.2

A lot of folks were starting to wonder if **Joe Barlow** was going to get a call-up in 2019. Instead, his struggles with control returned when he got to Nashville. ⓧ **Jesse Biddle** was once famous for spinning a curveball that you could *hear* on the way to the plate. Now it's surprising whenever you hear he's on a 25-man roster. ⓧ You probably know **Tim Dillard** more for his social media presence than his on-field performance, but he bailed out the Nashville Sounds on multiple occasions when they desperately needed innings in 2019. Texas rewarded him with a flight to Arlington—he wasn't added to the big-league roster, but he did some sideline reporting, some player interviews, and ran in the Dot Race. ⓧ **Kyle Dowdy** should perhaps rebrand as BByle Dowdy, given that his unsightly 16 percent walk rate eclipsed his meager 15 percent strikeout rate in 22 1/3 big-league innings. ⓧ The Rangers decided that **Demarcus Evans** had too good a 2019 to be left vulnerable in the Rule 5 draft. If his 2020 is anything like his 2019, he'll pitch in the big leagues anyway (just probably not on Opening Day). ⓧ **Luke Farrell** spent most of 2019 recovering from a broken jaw he sustained in spring training when he was hit with a nasty line drive. Getting back to the big leagues at all was a success; the impressive numbers were a bonus. ⓧ Fun fact: **Brian Flynn** started one game for the Royals in 2019, and it was shorter than eight of his 10 relief appearances. Maybe it wasn't fun for Flynn. ⓧ Which number is higher: career big-league innings for **Ian Gibaut** through 2019 (14 1/3) or times he has had to politely pretend to chuckle at references to 1990s jeans brand Marithé + François Girbaud? We bet it's close. ⓧ In a small sample of innings, **Jeanmar Gómez** gave up a large sample of runs. He did manage to keep the ball on the ground, which might grant him a minor-league deal at some point. ⓧ **Taylor Guerrieri**: his pitches :: baseball writers : vowels in his last name. (a basic but imprecise idea of where they're going). Still, his curveball is good enough that he'll pitch somewhere in 2020. ⓧ It's a safe bet to say **Ronny Henriquez** will eventually end up in the bullpen, but perhaps only because it's always a safe bet to say that; a lot of pitchers end up there. To his credit, he skipped straight from the DSL to Low-A Hickory and held his own pretty well as a 19-year-old. ⓧ It's fun to play this game, so here: in **Jonathan Hernández**' big-league debut, he faced Albert Pujols and the game was won on a Hunter Pence walk-off single. For now that's not a super-fun fact, so it's up to Hernandez to stick around long enough to let it age into a fine vintage fun fact. ⓧ Speaking of debuts, **Wei-Chieh Huang** was another of the 13 pitchers to make their big-league debut with the Rangers in 2019. Unlucky numbers aren't real, but tell that to those guys, who had a combined ERA of 6.02. ⓧ After being named the Rangers' 2018 Minor League pitcher of the year, **Tyler Phillips** dominated again at High-A, then struggled when he got to Double-A. That doesn't really scream "ready for a full season in the majors," but the Rangers went ahead and added him to the 40-man roster to protect him from the Rule 5 draft anyway. ⓧ **Adrian Sampson** established himself as one of baseball's premier grumps when he bickered with the A's about bat flips, and one of baseball's more creative grumps when he stepped on Ramón Laureano's bat. Not cool, but definitely funny. He'll be playing in Korea in 2020. ⓧ **Jeffrey Springs** has done just that—he was not a highly-lauded prospect out of college, but his double-plus changeup has taken him much further than most would have expected. ⓧ If you read last year's essay, the demise of the Rangers' "de-load" program is probably not a huge surprise to you. **Owen White** is one of the pitchers for whom the program did not prevent a Tommy John surgery. As a result (of both the program and the surgery, which was done in May of 2019), the second-round pick from the 2018 draft still hasn't thrown a single pitch in his professional career, and likely won't until two full years after being drafted.

TORONTO BLUE JAYS

Essay by Drew Fairservice

Player comments by Ginny Searle and BP staff

In the bottom of the eighth inning of an otherwise meaningless September game, the 100-win juggernaut New York Yankees inserted Zack Britton to retire the bottom of the 96-loss Toronto Blue Jays' lineup. He did exactly that on 12 pitches, recording a pair of groundouts and a K. It was a routine outing for Britton, a dominant late-inning force, save for one particular moment.

The moment occurred as Britton readied to deliver a pitch to Teoscar Hernández. He came set with his hands held high near his chin, eyes locked on catcher Austin Romine's target. Even without runners on base, he paused in his set position, holding the baseball inside his glove with his left hand. As Britton stood motionless, a monarch butterfly flew over from the first base side of the diamond, coming to rest on his black leather glove.

Breaking his hands from the set position, Britton began his motion to the plate, just as he had more than 9,000 times in his big-league career. This time, however, the butterfly clung to his glove as he did so. The butterfly held on for an instant before fluttering away, presumably intending to put as much space as possible between itself and the hissing nightmare projectile that is a 95 mph big-league sinker. The pitch missed low for ball one to Hernández.

The Blue Jays broadcast crew caught the moment with their center-field camera, playing it back in super-slow motion after the half-inning ended. Calling the game for Rogers' Sportsnet, Dan Shulman insisted "You guys Photoshopped that in there, in the truck!" as his partner Buck Martínez offered his trademark guffaw: "That was awesome."

Later in the same game, the YES broadcast cameras caught a monarch at rest on an unidentified glove. The Blue Jays official Twitter account also shared video captured pregame, when several young Blue Jays were entertained by a butterfly involving itself in their pregame stretch by settling onto Vladimir Guerrero Jr.'s pant leg. Butterflies dominated the night.

Oddly, this was typical for Blue Jays home games in 2019. Butterflies were regularly spotted in the foreground of standard center-field camera shots by members of the viewing public inclined to notice such things. An anecdotal

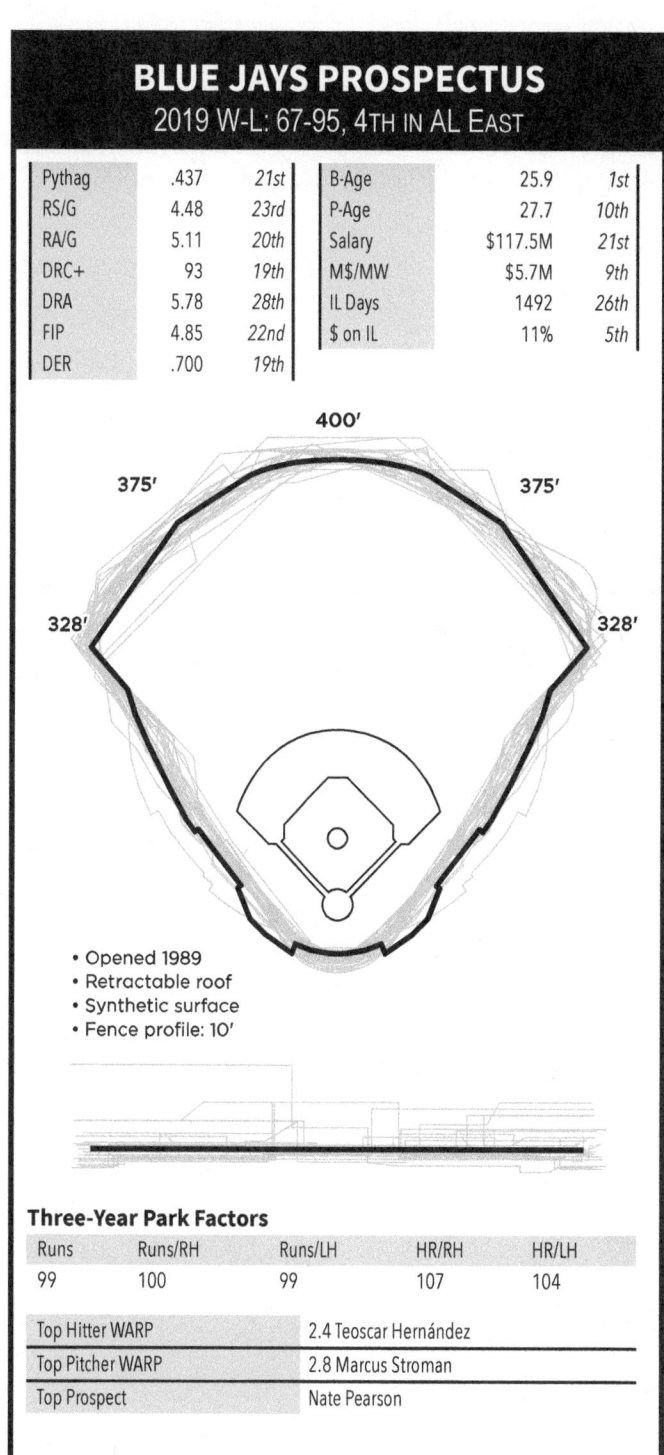

BLUE JAYS PROSPECTUS
2019 W-L: 67-95, 4TH IN AL EAST

Pythag	.437	21st	B-Age	25.9	1st
RS/G	4.48	23rd	P-Age	27.7	10th
RA/G	5.11	20th	Salary	$117.5M	21st
DRC+	93	19th	M$/MW	$5.7M	9th
DRA	5.78	28th	IL Days	1492	26th
FIP	4.85	22nd	$ on IL	11%	5th
DER	.700	19th			

400'

375'   375'

328'   328'

- Opened 1989
- Retractable roof
- Synthetic surface
- Fence profile: 10'

Three-Year Park Factors

Runs	Runs/RH	Runs/LH	HR/RH	HR/LH
99	100	99	107	104

Top Hitter WARP	2.4 Teoscar Hernández
Top Pitcher WARP	2.8 Marcus Stroman
Top Prospect	Nate Pearson

2019 Hit List Ranking

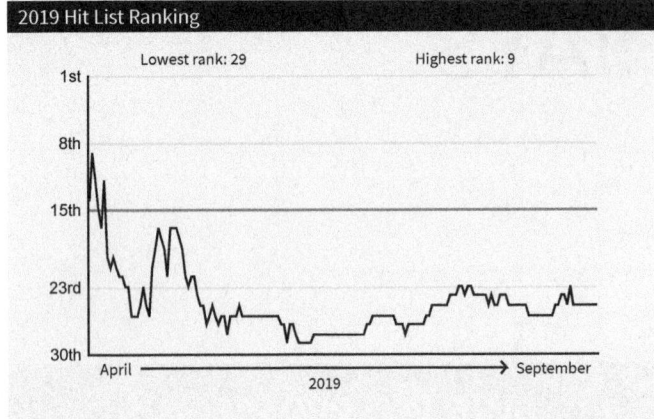

Lowest rank: 29   Highest rank: 9

April ——— 2019 ——→ September

Committed Payroll (in millions)

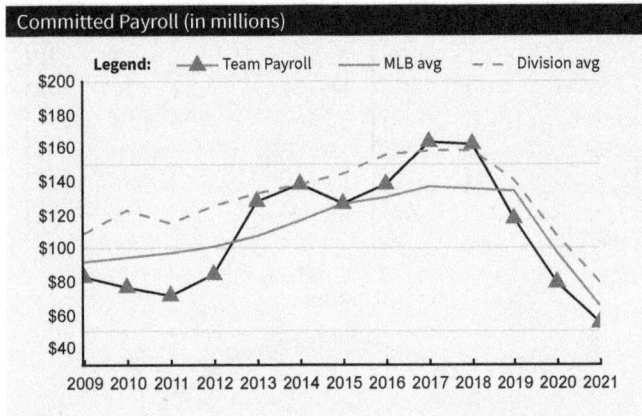

Legend: ▲ Team Payroll — MLB avg --- Division avg

Farm System Ranking

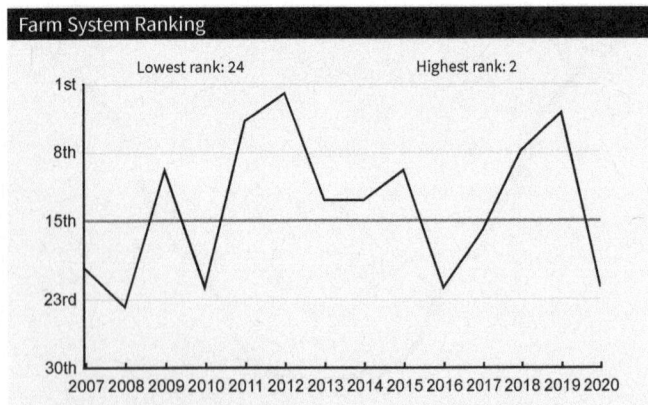

Lowest rank: 24   Highest rank: 2

Personnel

President & CEO
Mark A. Shapiro

**Executive Vice President,
Baseball Operations & General
Manager**
Ross Atkins

**Senior Vice President, Player
Personnel**
Tony Lacava

**Vice President, International
Scouting**
Andrew Tinnish

Assistant General Manager
Joe Sheehan

Manager
Charlie Montoyo

BP Alumni
Matt Bishoff

increase in on-field butterfly sightings is supported by observed science across North America: last year was a good one for monarch butterflies.

⚾   ⚾   ⚾

It was supposed to be a good year for prospects in Toronto, too.

Even though he raced to the big leagues at 21, Bo Bichette's progress through the minors was marked by a specific pattern: a short, post-promotion period of adjustment and then the proverbial flipping of the switch. That pattern didn't quite play out in the majors. Rather, rare were the moments that Bichette did not look the part of a big-league star. He hit, he fielded and ran the bases with exactly the right kind of reckless abandon. His debut was a 200-plate appearance shot of adrenaline in a Blue Jays season needing precisely that. Concerns about his swing and/or approach were set aside so quickly that finding them will be tricky when they're needed (sometime in early-to-mid 2020, during his first prolonged slump).

The role of human espresso was supposed to be played by the Blue Jays' other gifted second-generation stud: Guerrero Jr. His rookie season did not go according to script, however, and he was not the Blue Jays' best player, the way most scouts and analysts proposed he would be before his early-season promotion. On a rate basis, that distinction instead went to Bichette. To be clear: Guerrero was okay—he was a league-average hitter who wowed crowds at the Home Run Derby and during his patented hot streaks; he just appeared more mortal than anticipated, struggling mightily in the field and hitting grounders too frequently.

Last season was the time for the Blue Jays to give these players space to learn, fail, thrive and become accustomed to the life of big-league ballplaying. (The college experience they missed out on, basically.) Last season was also the time for the organization to reinstill confidence in the fan base by demonstrating competence and showcasing the so-called future. It was probably more successful than intended.

⚾   ⚾   ⚾

Over the last few years, monarch numbers have upticked across the continent, countering a 20-year downward trend. The gains made are still far from re-establishing their numbers to where they were in the early 1990s, but it's a start.

Monarchs face considerable hardship in their continent-spanning migration, as factors such as habitat loss and climate change make an already arduous journey even more difficult. As numbers dipped over the last decade, grassroots efforts encouraged ordinary people along the migration route to plant milkweed (a larvae host plant for monarch butterflies) in their yards, gardens or—in the case of heavily urbanized areas such as the tangle of high-rise buildings surrounding the Blue Jays' ballpark—on their balconies.

World Wildlife Fund-Canada's senior species specialist Emily Giles noted that the Rogers Centre is on the monarch's migration path as it makes its way to Mexico, where they congregate around the start of November. "Monarchs need a lot of local nectar sources, as the journey south is quite taxing, physiologically speaking, and they feed on nectar which gives them high-energy fuel for the long journey."

⚾ ⚾ ⚾

Whereas monarchs move south around November, the Blue Jays are southern residents during the early portion of the year. Sleepy Dunedin has been their only exhibition-season home since 1977 and—after some politicking in 2016—will as such for at least another 20 years.

Overhauling their spring complex has become a major passion point for president and CEO Mark Shapiro. The Blue Jays now believe their spring facility will provide them with a competitive advantage that will help the club overcome the financial gap between them and their American League East rivals.

During a quiet moment before a media appearance, Shapiro thumbed through photos and explained the work being done ahead of the park's grand opening. "Development isn't something you do to players," Shapiro explained on a 2019 podcast appearance. "Our job is to give them the best resources—mentally, physically and fundamentally, as well as tools like buildings, equipment and technology—to help give them a plan, and then work with them to be the best they can be."

The tools and equipment that the Blue Jays believe will help rise tide that floats all boats include three "sports labs," two "fuel bars," a "movement studio" as well as plunge pools, saunas and more. It is here they'll eat and train together, collaborate, share information and toil joyfully in pursuit of personal fulfillment and free-agent dollars. They'll swap hitting tips and create TikToks, increasing camaraderie and launch angles in equal measure.

Shapiro and the Blue Jays organization believe it is here they plan to go from last to first, initially in terms of complex quality with on-field results lining up soon thereafter. Why spend money on good players when you can just grow your own, yanking cloned babies out of a high-tech river like Adrian Veidt?

⚾ ⚾ ⚾

The Blue Jays of the present and the future exist concurrently. Much of the prospect food is on the table, with Guerrero Jr. and Bichette representing the main course and established as everyday players. Top pitching prospect Nate Pearson is knocking on the door with dessert, too.

But the ongoing austerity efforts and firm insistence that spending and revenues remain "aligned" means the Blue Jays need their big-name, high-ceiling young talent to fulfill their promise—with the club using its expensive redone complex as a lazarus pit of sorts, wherein instructors dip various mid-round picks until one surfaces as a valued asset.

Though the butterfly that landed on Britton's glove on the clear September night made for an unforgettable scene during an immensely forgettable baseball game, it wasn't likely to end well for the in-game field invader. Instead of being tackled by private security or ejected by an usher, any butterfly reaching the sickly green turf at the Rogers Centre was unlikely to ever taste the sweet nectar of freedom again, as WWF-Canada's Giles explains: "Once that individual butterfly made its way into the dome, it likely would've had trouble getting out as there's nothing but fake turf, pizza, and beer and no high-energy sources that a butterfly can readily use."

Getting good players to Toronto is one thing. Can the Blue Jays get them to become great players and, ideally, key parts of a great team? The test at this stage of the organization's trajectory is simple: grow something wonderful in a place historically hostile to the natural world. ▪

—Drew Fairservice is the co-host of the Birds All Day podcast.

HITTERS

Bo Bichette SS Born: 03/05/98 Age: 22 Bats: R Throws: R Height: 6'0" Weight: 185 Origin: Round 2, 2016 Draft (#66 overall)

YEAR	TEAM	LVL	AGE	PA	R	2B	3B	HR	RBI	BB	K	SB	CS	AVG/OBP/SLG	DRC+	VORP	BABIP	BRR	FRAA	WARP
2017	LNS	A	19	317	60	32	3	10	51	28	55	12	3	.384/.448/.623	210	49.2	.452	3.0	SS(51): 0.2, 2B(14): 0.3	5.5
2017	DUN	A+	19	182	28	9	1	4	23	14	26	10	4	.323/.379/.463	154	12.9	.360	-0.2	SS(35): -0.3	1.5
2018	NHP	AA	20	595	95	43	7	11	74	48	101	32	11	.286/.343/.453	127	40.6	.331	3.2	SS(116): -4.0, 2B(9): 0.6	4.2
2019	BUF	AAA	21	244	34	16	2	8	32	19	48	15	5	.275/.333/.473	103	10.7	.317	-2.0	SS(51): -1.4, 2B(1): 0.0	0.8
2019	TOR	MLB	21	212	32	18	0	11	21	14	50	4	4	.311/.358/.571	109	12.1	.368	-0.8	SS(42): 4.6	1.5
2020	TOR	MLB	22	595	68	33	3	23	78	40	137	15	6	.260/.314/.454	101	23.2	.308	0.1	SS 2	2.6

Comparables: Orlando Arcia, Francisco Lindor, Wilmer Flores

As everyone expected, in 2019 the son of a major leaguer took the league by storm after debuting at a young age with serious hype (though an injury delayed his debut). The surprising part was that the player whose bat electrified was not Vladimir Guerrero, Jr. but Bichette. After debuting on July 29th, the former second-round pick dropped an OPS that was more than fifty points clear of any Jay with at least four trips to the plate on the season (Trent Thornton disclaimer alert). His DRC+ lagged though, mostly due to the randomness of hitting doubles—had Bichette continued his pace of two-baggers for a full season, he'd have finished with the most since 1936. The 22-year-old won't be eligible for Rookie of the Year considerations in 2020, but the combined potency of his bat and his glove at a key defensive position should warrant All-Star, and maybe even MVP, votes.

Cavan Biggio 2B Born: 04/11/95 Age: 25 Bats: L Throws: R Height: 6'2" Weight: 200 Origin: Round 5, 2016 Draft (#162 overall)

YEAR	TEAM	LVL	AGE	PA	R	2B	3B	HR	RBI	BB	K	SB	CS	AVG/OBP/SLG	DRC+	VORP	BABIP	BRR	FRAA	WARP
2017	DUN	A+	22	556	75	17	5	11	60	74	140	11	7	.233/.342/.363	94	11.0	.304	1.1	2B(116): 6.4, 3B(6): -0.4	2.1
2018	NHP	AA	23	563	80	23	5	26	99	100	148	20	8	.252/.388/.499	137	44.8	.307	3.6	2B(68): 1.5, 3B(34): -1.1	4.4
2019	BUF	AAA	24	174	23	8	1	6	27	34	28	5	1	.312/.448/.514	150	19.7	.352	0.5	2B(22): 2.0, 1B(7): 0.2	1.7
2019	TOR	MLB	24	430	66	17	2	16	48	71	123	14	0	.234/.364/.429	112	20.5	.309	2.2	2B(85): 0.5, RF(8): -0.9	2.1
2020	TOR	MLB	25	595	79	25	3	26	82	90	162	10	4	.245/.365/.462	115	36.2	.309	0.2	2B 4	4.1

Comparables: Brandon Lowe, Nick Solak, Carlos Santana

You might get the sense Biggio is used to the shadows—a Hall of Fame dad, three teammates with better prospect cred whose fathers were also pros, a "next five" placement on the Blue Jays' 2019 prospect list. His first name comes from "the hollow" in Irish (*An Cabhán*), for goodness' sake. But if Biggio is acquainted with the shadows, he's surely used to carving out his own light, and got a start on that in a solid rookie season: his on-base percentage was the highest among his teammates with at least four plate appearances (Trent Thornton disclaimer alert), and he appears competent at second base. It's not the flashiest of profiles moving forward, but the same was true retrospectively, and there was certainly nothing hollow about his impressive 2019.

Griffin Conine RF Born: 07/11/97 Age: 22 Bats: L Throws: R Height: 6'1" Weight: 200 Origin: Round 2, 2018 Draft (#52 overall)

YEAR	TEAM	LVL	AGE	PA	R	2B	3B	HR	RBI	BB	K	SB	CS	AVG/OBP/SLG	DRC+	VORP	BABIP	BRR	FRAA	WARP
2018	VAN	A-	20	230	24	14	2	7	30	19	63	5	0	.238/.309/.427	92	2.2	.304	-1.5	RF(46): 10.1	1.1
2019	LNS	A	21	348	59	19	2	22	64	38	125	2	0	.283/.371/.576	155	32.8	.405	2.8	RF(73): 6.2	3.7
2020	TOR	MLB	22	251	21	12	1	6	25	16	103	0	0	.201/.259/.338	57	-6.2	.332	-0.3	RF 3	-0.3

Comparables: Austin Hays, Xavier Scruggs, Kennys Vargas

The mythological griffin is half of two animals: eagle and lion. Conine's season also mashed up two starkly different halves to head-scratching results: after being suspended at the end of 2018 for a banned substance used to treat ADHD, the 22-year-old sat out the first 50 games. After returning, Conine more than delivered on his second round bona fides in Low-A. The 22 home runs were enticing, the 36 percent strikeout rate worrisome. So it goes for a hybrid.

Brandon Drury 3B Born: 08/21/92 Age: 27 Bats: R Throws: R Height: 6'2" Weight: 215 Origin: Round 13, 2010 Draft (#404 overall)

YEAR	TEAM	LVL	AGE	PA	R	2B	3B	HR	RBI	BB	K	SB	CS	AVG/OBP/SLG	DRC+	VORP	BABIP	BRR	FRAA	WARP
2017	ARI	MLB	24	480	41	37	2	13	63	28	103	1	1	.267/.317/.447	83	9.8	.320	-3.9	2B(114): 2.5, 3B(1): -0.2	0.3
2018	TRN	AA	25	25	4	0	0	1	2	5	10	0	0	.263/.400/.421	109	3.3	.444	0.2	3B(4): -0.2	0.1
2018	SWB	AAA	25	235	30	13	1	5	30	32	58	3	1	.291/.400/.442	134	19.7	.390	-1.0	3B(45): 2.4, 1B(5): 0.7	1.7
2018	NYA	MLB	25	57	2	2	0	1	7	5	12	0	0	.176/.263/.275	78	-2.1	.211	0.1	3B(9): -0.7, 2B(5): -0.1	-0.1
2018	TOR	MLB	25	29	3	2	0	0	3	2	8	0	0	.154/.241/.231	80	-1.8	.222	0.0	3B(6): -0.1, 2B(2): -0.6	0.0
2019	TOR	MLB	26	447	43	21	1	15	41	25	113	0	1	.218/.262/.380	70	-2.6	.259	0.4	3B(65): -1.2, RF(18): -2.1	-0.7
2020	TOR	MLB	27	280	29	16	1	9	34	18	67	1	1	.235/.290/.408	81	-0.5	.281	-0.7	1B -3, 2B 0	-0.3

Comparables: Manny Machado, Aramis Ramirez, Jim Presley

Drury Lane is the protagonist of a quartet of 1930s detective novels published via a pseudonym-inside-a-synonym; in the books a retired actor quotes Hamlet and solves the cases no one else can, before in the fourth novel meeting a fittingly Shakespearean end. Now there's a mystery afoot in Toronto, namely how long they can sustain this sort of performance from their own Drury. It's no Hamlet, but it's been properly Shakespearean in tragedy. Forced into everyday play for much of the season due to pervasive injuries on the team, Drury was just abysmal with the bat (even by his standards) and squarely below-average in the field. Moving into his second of four swings at arbitration (it's probably for the best that Drury, who ran a 25-percent strikeout rate last year, gets an extra cut), one wonders if he will get another chance to make good on the J.A. Happ trade.

Derek Fisher OF   Born: 08/21/93   Age: 26   Bats: L   Throws: R   Height: 6'3"   Weight: 205   Origin: Round 1, 2014 Draft (#37 overall)

YEAR	TEAM	LVL	AGE	PA	R	2B	3B	HR	RBI	BB	K	SB	CS	AVG/OBP/SLG	DRC+	VORP	BABIP	BRR	FRAA	WARP
2017	FRE	AAA	23	384	63	26	1	21	66	35	74	16	10	.318/.384/.583	145	33.9	.352	-0.8	CF(53): -5.3, LF(17): 2.3	2.9
2017	HOU	MLB	23	166	21	4	1	5	17	17	54	3	3	.212/.307/.356	70	-1.2	.299	-0.5	LF(38): 1.2, RF(12): 0.0	-0.1
2018	FRE	AAA	24	281	44	12	1	10	34	39	85	11	1	.251/.363/.435	114	16.5	.347	2.2	CF(33): -2.7, LF(19): -0.7	1.1
2018	HOU	MLB	24	86	13	2	2	4	11	5	42	2	0	.165/.209/.392	48	1.6	.257	1.6	LF(26): -1.3, CF(9): -0.4	-0.3
2019	ROU	AAA	25	270	44	9	1	14	36	40	67	8	3	.286/.401/.522	122	24.3	.347	-0.5	CF(29): 1.5, RF(21): 1.5	1.7
2019	TOR	MLB	25	107	14	2	0	6	12	14	43	1	0	.161/.271/.376	67	-1.5	.205	-0.4	LF(27): 0.9, RF(4): -0.3	-0.1
2019	HOU	MLB	25	60	9	2	1	1	5	7	14	4	1	.226/.317/.358	83	0.2	.289	1.0	LF(11): 0.0, RF(5): 0.4	0.1
2020	TOR	MLB	26	315	42	12	1	17	47	36	107	9	3	.235/.328/.477	106	11.4	.312	0.8	RF 0, CF -1	1.1

Comparables: Kirk Nieuwenhuis, Brett Jackson, Matt Joyce

Long a bundle of kinetic energy ready to actualize, Fisher has just needed to get in motion. He ran out of time to do so, however, in Houston—regardless of his fourth consecutive year punishing the PCL—Fisher was unable to break into a defined role. With the blocks in front of his path concretizing, the Astros netted Aaron Sanchez, Joe Biagini, and prospect Cal Stevenson for the glimmer of possibility teams still saw in the 2014 first round pick. Conversely, the Blue Jays can offer nothing but time—likely something to do with the metric system. Still, another punishing performance (but not the good kind) in his Toronto debut will have Fisher on the hot seat this season, bereft of both minor league options and the expectations that come with nearly a half-decade of gracing team prospect lists.

Randal Grichuk RF   Born: 08/13/91   Age: 28   Bats: R   Throws: R   Height: 6'2"   Weight: 213   Origin: Round 1, 2009 Draft (#24 overall)

YEAR	TEAM	LVL	AGE	PA	R	2B	3B	HR	RBI	BB	K	SB	CS	AVG/OBP/SLG	DRC+	VORP	BABIP	BRR	FRAA	WARP
2017	MEM	AAA	25	67	11	3	0	6	9	3	20	0	0	.270/.313/.603	123	5.0	.297	0.0	LF(9): 3.6, CF(1): -0.1	0.7
2017	SLN	MLB	25	442	53	25	3	22	59	26	133	6	1	.238/.285/.473	95	11.9	.293	1.9	LF(58): -2.7, RF(55): 4.8	1.2
2018	TOR	MLB	26	462	60	32	1	25	61	27	122	3	2	.245/.301/.502	109	19.0	.282	2.5	RF(102): 2.4, CF(26): -2.3	1.9
2019	TOR	MLB	27	628	75	29	5	31	80	35	163	2	1	.232/.280/.457	90	9.7	.266	-0.2	RF(92): -3.2, CF(62): -4.9	0.1
2020	TOR	MLB	28	595	72	28	4	33	91	35	167	6	2	.230/.282/.475	91	11.8	.266	1.2	RF 1, CF -7	0.6

Comparables: Jay Bruce, Wil Myers, Jorge Soler

We can say one thing about Grichuk for certain: he is going to be around. With the signing of a five-year, $52 million contract at the start of 2019, Grichuk has security in spite of a season that otherwise would have seen him a likely DFA candidate. Like everyone else in 2019, the 28-year-old hit 31 home runs, but his OBP finally hit rock bottom and while his strikeout-to-walk rate would be elite for a pitcher, Grichuk does not pitch. Four years remain on the pact between the Blue Jays and their too-often center fielder (any amount of him there is too often), so it remains to be seen if Grichuk spends them as "guy on a bad contract" or reverts to "guy who was picked directly in front of Mike Trout."

★ ★ ★ *2020 Top 101 Prospect* **#43** ★ ★ ★

Jordan Groshans SS   Born: 11/10/99   Age: 20   Bats: R   Throws: R   Height: 6'3"   Weight: 205   Origin: Round 1, 2018 Draft (#12 overall)

YEAR	TEAM	LVL	AGE	PA	R	2B	3B	HR	RBI	BB	K	SB	CS	AVG/OBP/SLG	DRC+	VORP	BABIP	BRR	FRAA	WARP
2018	BLJ	RK	18	159	17	12	0	4	39	13	29	0	0	.331/.390/.500	147	14.7	.387	-0.8	3B(16): -1.2, SS(15): 0.6	1.1
2018	BLU	RK	18	48	4	1	0	1	4	2	8	0	0	.182/.229/.273	46	-0.6	.194	0.1	SS(6): 0.9, 3B(5): 0.0	0.0
2019	LNS	A	19	96	12	6	0	2	13	13	21	1	1	.337/.427/.482	169	10.6	.433	-0.4	SS(20): -1.8	0.9
2020	TOR	MLB	20	251	23	12	0	5	25	19	70	1	0	.238/.301/.363	78	0.4	.318	-0.5	SS 0, 3B 0	0.1

Comparables: Trevor Story, Brendan Rodgers, Alen Hanson

Groshans has a key distinction from many of the other recent top prospects the Jays have had—rather than following in the footsteps of a first baseball generation, he is the first generation leading the next. Sort of. The year after he was taken in the first round by the Jays, his older brother, Jaxx, was a fifth-round pick of the Red Sox. Limited to just 96 plate appearances before a stress injury in his foot kept him off the field and ultimately had him shut down, the teen took control of the Midwest League by hitting for average and power along with showing a discerning eye for his age. And though his future may be more hot corner than the six, even a brief glimpse was enough to leave fans and evaluators salivating for more. Whether he starts the year with a repeat engagement in Lansing or not, the big ballparks of the Florida State League await the second-best prospect in the Toronto system in 2020.

Vladimir Guerrero Jr. 3B   Born: 03/16/99   Age: 21   Bats: R   Throws: R   Height: 6'2"   Weight: 250   Origin: International Free Agent, 2015

YEAR	TEAM	LVL	AGE	PA	R	2B	3B	HR	RBI	BB	K	SB	CS	AVG/OBP/SLG	DRC+	VORP	BABIP	BRR	FRAA	WARP
2017	LNS	A	18	318	53	21	1	7	45	40	34	6	2	.316/.409/.480	172	27.5	.336	0.8	3B(61): -2.6	3.3
2017	DUN	A+	18	209	31	7	1	6	31	36	28	2	2	.333/.450/.494	196	17.7	.365	-2.4	3B(41): -1.5	2.0
2018	NHP	AA	19	266	48	19	1	14	60	21	27	3	3	.402/.449/.671	196	37.4	.402	-2.9	3B(53): 1.0	3.3
2018	BUF	AAA	19	128	15	7	0	6	16	15	10	0	0	.336/.414/.564	194	11.5	.323	-4.8	3B(25): 4.3	1.5
2019	BUF	AAA	20	34	7	1	0	3	8	4	2	1	0	.367/.441/.700	159	5.5	.320	-0.2	3B(7): 0.1	0.3
2019	TOR	MLB	20	514	52	26	2	15	69	46	91	0	1	.272/.339/.433	101	18.0	.308	-3.5	3B(96): -5.1	0.9
2020	TOR	MLB	21	630	77	33	2	26	87	53	105	4	2	.273/.339/.473	113	21.7	.295	-2.4	3B 0	2.3

Comparables: Carlos Correa, Ronald Acuña Jr., Ozzie Albies

Guerrero is the Prince That Was Promised, the one prophesied to fight the darkness and save the North. If you watched *Game of Thrones*, you probably know that didn't amount to all that much, and you'd be forgiven for feeling similarly about the debut season of the most hyped prospect of the last half of the 2010s. The 20-year-old wasn't bad by any means, but with a batting line that rated as basically average, he was neither the best rookie in the league nor on his own team. After the year-long waiting game of the Jays' service time manipulation, the landing was decidedly underwhelming. The defense was bad-to-untenable at third, where Vladito likely won't stick even 'til arbitration without serious improvement. Being one of the 25 worst runners in the league added another vector of disappointment.

In the disillusionment of a campaign that ultimately amounted to an average player, it's easy to forget Guerrero was just 20 years old, a year beyond the legal drinking age in Toronto but massively outstripping the huge majority of the league in his speed of development. It was the first chapter of a book that has yet to be written, and while it might not have immediately drawn in the readers, not every book must—especially when, as with Guerrero, a foundation is being built. He might still be the Prince That Was Promised, but rather than the *Game of Thrones'* version he will have to be the model from *A Song of Ice and Fire*. Like George R.R. Martin's series, the rest is not yet written. Even after seeing what we have on screen, audiences can immerse ourselves in the limitless possibility of Guerrero's potential, the dream that everything will be put to right when a new chapter is inked.

Lourdes Gurriel Jr. LF   Born: 10/10/93   Age: 26   Bats: R   Throws: R   Height: 6'3"   Weight: 215   Origin: International Free Agent, 2016

YEAR	TEAM	LVL	AGE	PA	R	2B	3B	HR	RBI	BB	K	SB	CS	AVG/OBP/SLG	DRC+	VORP	BABIP	BRR	FRAA	WARP
2017	DUN	A+	23	69	6	1	0	1	8	2	13	1	0	.197/.217/.258	57	-3.2	.226	0.3	SS(11): -0.2, 2B(1): 0.1	0.0
2017	NHP	AA	23	185	20	10	0	4	28	10	30	2	0	.241/.286/.371	73	4.0	.266	1.2	2B(22): 1.5, SS(17): 0.9	0.5
2018	NHP	AA	24	65	7	3	1	2	14	3	8	1	1	.322/.354/.508	129	6.7	.333	0.3	2B(7): -0.1, SS(5): -0.7	0.4
2018	BUF	AAA	24	156	20	8	0	5	30	4	34	3	2	.293/.321/.449	118	7.0	.345	-0.9	SS(23): 0.9, 2B(9): 0.2	0.9
2018	TOR	MLB	24	263	30	8	0	11	35	9	59	1	2	.281/.309/.446	104	8.8	.326	-1.7	SS(46): -0.8, 2B(24): -1.1	0.8
2019	BUF	AAA	25	130	18	13	0	4	26	3	23	0	2	.276/.308/.480	104	1.5	.309	-3.6	2B(12): -1.1, SS(7): -2.0	-0.2
2019	TOR	MLB	25	343	52	19	2	20	50	20	86	6	4	.277/.327/.541	113	14.9	.318	2.0	LF(63): -0.1, 2B(9): -1.3	1.5
2020	TOR	MLB	26	595	70	30	1	29	85	26	141	4	2	.251/.293/.463	96	11.5	.285	0.8	LF -10	0.2

Comparables: Troy Tulowitzki, José Rondón, Charlie Culberson

Son of a renowned ballplayer, the best hitter on the Blue Jays by DRC+: sorry, did you think this was someone other than Gurriel Jr.? While an imprecise arm at the keystone earned him an early-season demotion to figure out a new position and injuries kept the sophomore out for most of August and September, he improved at the plate in year two. The now left fielder (and not a bad one at that!) improved his walk rate and isolated power by more than 50 percent over his rookie campaign and even spiked his fly-ball rate by 10 percentage points on his way to 20 dingers. Hopefully in one of the four years remaining of Gurriel Jr.'s seven with the Jays, he will do more than flash tantalizing potential in brief stints. He'll be hard-pressed to best brother (and simultaneous Cuban defector) Yuli's career-high 31 homers from last season without a full campaign.

Teoscar Hernández OF   Born: 10/15/92   Age: 27   Bats: R   Throws: R   Height: 6'2"   Weight: 205   Origin: International Free Agent, 2011

YEAR	TEAM	LVL	AGE	PA	R	2B	3B	HR	RBI	BB	K	SB	CS	AVG/OBP/SLG	DRC+	VORP	BABIP	BRR	FRAA	WARP
2017	FRE	AAA	24	347	54	20	3	12	44	39	72	12	7	.279/.369/.485	122	22.7	.329	1.9	RF(44): 2.2, CF(22): 1.4	2.3
2017	BUF	AAA	24	109	14	6	2	6	22	8	30	4	1	.222/.294/.505	99	4.9	.254	0.8	RF(10): 0.8, CF(7): 1.0	0.9
2017	TOR	MLB	24	95	16	6	0	8	20	6	36	0	1	.261/.305/.602	101	8.5	.333	1.9	LF(18): -0.7, CF(5): 0.0	0.4
2018	TOR	MLB	25	523	67	29	7	22	57	41	163	5	5	.239/.302/.468	104	12.4	.313	-0.1	LF(87): -2.0, RF(35): 0.7	1.3
2019	BUF	AAA	26	83	11	0	1	5	11	6	21	3	0	.253/.313/.480	84	3.3	.280	0.8	CF(9): -1.5, LF(5): 0.3	0.0
2019	TOR	MLB	26	464	58	19	2	26	65	45	153	6	3	.230/.306/.472	100	16.0	.293	-0.4	CF(79): -0.8, LF(46): 9.6	2.4
2020	TOR	MLB	27	595	77	27	3	33	91	49	191	16	7	.235/.303/.481	101	16.6	.296	0.8	CF 4, LF 0	2.1

Comparables: Pete Incaviglia, Melvin Nieves, Aaron Cunningham

Hernández has long been a player around whom evaluators saw an uncertain future: not a solid enough defender to play center, unclear if the bat would support him as an everyday corner outfielder. The forecast only grew gloomier as Hernández distinguished himself with the glove in a negative sense in his first full campaign and showed only a league-average bat. This year the glove was markedly improved, but an extended slump to start the season led to a demotion to Buffalo. Upon his return Hernández put up an .873 OPS the rest of the way, and suddenly there's reason to think everything has come together for him—long something of a Magic Eye painting, the Blue Jays have finally stayed still long enough for them to see cohesion among mess.

Danny Jansen   C   Born: 04/15/95   Age: 25   Bats: R   Throws: R   Height: 6'2"   Weight: 230   Origin: Round 16, 2013 Draft (#475 overall)

YEAR	TEAM	LVL	AGE	PA	R	2B	3B	HR	RBI	BB	K	SB	CS	AVG/OBP/SLG	DRC+	VORP	BABIP	BRR	FRAA	WARP
2017	DUN	A+	22	136	19	6	0	5	18	8	14	0	0	.369/.422/.541	197	17.6	.385	-0.7	C(25): -2.0	1.4
2017	NHP	AA	22	210	23	15	1	2	20	22	19	1	0	.291/.378/.419	120	15.2	.311	-1.4	C(52): -0.9	1.2
2017	BUF	AAA	22	78	8	4	1	3	10	11	7	0	0	.328/.423/.552	170	11.2	.333	-0.1	C(21): -0.4	0.8
2018	BUF	AAA	23	360	45	21	1	12	58	44	49	5	1	.275/.390/.473	141	32.9	.292	0.2	C(56): -6.0	2.1
2018	TOR	MLB	23	95	12	6	0	3	8	9	17	0	0	.247/.347/.432	100	6.5	.274	0.9	C(29): 1.0	0.7
2019	TOR	MLB	24	384	41	12	1	13	43	31	79	0	1	.207/.279/.360	82	10.9	.230	-0.7	C(103): 11.9	2.2
2020	*TOR*	*MLB*	*25*	*280*	*32*	*13*	*0*	*11*	*36*	*25*	*56*	*1*	*0*	*.232/.313/.421*	*94*	*11.1*	*.256*	*0.2*	*C 7*	*1.8*

Comparables: Jim Pagliaroni, Chris Snyder, Max Kepler

Jansen's calling card was supposed to be the bat—not that he was considered a slouch from a defensive standpoint. His precipitous climb up the Toronto organizational rankings was sparked by a 2017 breakout season at the plate for which vision correction was credited. Yet, in a season where Jansen finally got his extended shot, it wasn't his work standing next to home plate but rather behind it that solidified him in the Blue Jays' plans for years to come. In fact, not only did Jansen finish sixth in the majors in CSAA, but the rookie was a finalist for a Gold Glove. He also made headlines in July for shaving his mustache mid-game after beginning the day hitless in three at-bats and then knocking in two during his next plate appearance. With a bat that grades as even average Jansen will be a top-10 catcher. Maybe it's just a matter of finding the right superstition.

YEAR	TEAM	P. COUNT	FRM RUNS	BLK RUNS	THRW RUNS	TOT RUNS
2017	BUF	2610	0.0	0.1	-0.1	0.2
2017	NHP	6546	-2.1	2.2	0.0	-0.8
2018	BUF	7393	-4.6	0.2	-0.1	-4.0
2018	TOR	3560	0.6	0.7	-0.2	1.8
2019	TOR	14774	10.9	2.1	0.4	13.4
2020	*TOR*	*10982*	*6.1*	*0.8*	*0.4*	*7.3*

Orelvis Martinez   SS   Born: 11/19/01   Age: 18   Bats: R   Throws: R   Height: 6'1"   Weight: 188   Origin: International Free Agent, 2018

YEAR	TEAM	LVL	AGE	PA	R	2B	3B	HR	RBI	BB	K	SB	CS	AVG/OBP/SLG	DRC+	VORP	BABIP	BRR	FRAA	WARP
2019	BLJ	RK	17	163	20	8	5	7	32	14	29	2	0	.275/.352/.549	140	18.2	.296	1.1	SS(26): -3.2, 3B(11): -2.0	0.8
2020	*TOR*	*MLB*	*18*	*251*	*21*	*11*	*2*	*4*	*22*	*19*	*72*	*2*	*1*	*.202/.272/.317*	*60*	*-5.1*	*.277*	*0.0*	*SS -1, 3B 0*	*-0.6*

Comparables: Franklin Barreto, Engel Beltre, Juan Lagares

Martinez was aggressively assigned to the Gulf Coast League last season, putting him against significantly older competition in his first affiliated showing. Despite being a minor for the entire season, the left-side infielder impressed enough to make the GCL All-Star team. In the box, Martinez has enough strength to show average power right now but projects for plus once he fills out a little more. On top of that, he's a natural hitter with quick bat speed—able to both pull the ball and go the other way with authority. The Adrián Beltré comparisons have not ceased, which, weighty or not, should indicate the degree to which the teenager has impressed since inking his $3.5 million bonus. No word as of yet on whether Martinez has a problem with people touching his head.

Reese McGuire   C   Born: 03/02/95   Age: 25   Bats: L   Throws: R   Height: 6'0"   Weight: 215   Origin: Round 1, 2013 Draft (#14 overall)

YEAR	TEAM	LVL	AGE	PA	R	2B	3B	HR	RBI	BB	K	SB	CS	AVG/OBP/SLG	DRC+	VORP	BABIP	BRR	FRAA	WARP
2017	BLJ	RK	22	26	4	2	0	0	7	3	1	0	1	.409/.462/.500	191	3.3	.409	-0.3	C(4): 0.0	0.2
2017	NHP	AA	22	136	19	5	1	6	20	16	19	2	1	.278/.366/.496	139	11.1	.283	-1.9	C(34): 5.0	1.6
2018	BUF	AAA	23	369	31	9	2	7	37	33	77	3	2	.233/.312/.339	94	8.6	.281	1.6	C(73): 15.0	2.9
2018	TOR	MLB	23	33	5	3	0	2	4	2	9	1	0	.290/.333/.581	95	3.3	.350	0.3	C(11): 0.7	0.2
2019	BUF	AAA	24	277	30	12	1	5	29	25	44	4	0	.247/.316/.366	77	3.4	.276	-3.8	C(71): 4.2	0.7
2019	TOR	MLB	24	105	14	7	0	5	11	7	18	0	0	.299/.346/.526	107	6.4	.324	0.6	C(30): 5.0	1.2
2020	*TOR*	*MLB*	*25*	*385*	*40*	*18*	*1*	*12*	*45*	*29*	*69*	*4*	*2*	*.241/.304/.400*	*83*	*9.2*	*.268*	*-0.4*	*C 13*	*2.3*

Comparables: Chance Sisco, L.J. Hoes, Tucker Barnhart

In an episode of the Disney Channel series *Lizzie McGuire*, Hilary Duff's titular character fears her athletic prowess will prevent boys from taking an interest in her, and that her skills are having her misrepresented. While this McGuire need not be concerned about his strong performance with the bat in two brief stints turning off teams, that he has a .539 slugging percentage through his first 44 career games is likely a sizable misrepresentation of a player who had otherwise never surpassed .500 in his various minor league stints. Still, he need not fret about teams perceiving him incorrectly: at the end of the TV episode, Lizzie learns that she should just be herself and not worry about what others think. Given his defensive chops, the Jays backstop could take the same lesson—whether this level of offensive performance in MLB is sustainable, McGuire has what it takes to stick in a sizable role.

YEAR	TEAM	P. COUNT	FRM RUNS	BLK RUNS	THRW RUNS	TOT RUNS
2017	NHP	4206	4.4	0.1	0.0	4.6
2018	BUF	9552	15.4	0.2	0.3	15.9
2018	TOR	1355	0.4	0.5	-0.1	1.0
2019	BUF	10029	7.0	0.0	-1.5	5.8
2019	TOR	4094	5.0	0.4	0.0	5.7
2020	*TOR*	*14758*	*13.8*	*1.2*	*-0.7*	*14.3*

Billy McKinney OF   Born: 08/23/94   Age: 25   Bats: L   Throws: L   Height: 6'1"   Weight: 205   Origin: Round 1, 2013 Draft (#24 overall)

YEAR	TEAM	LVL	AGE	PA	R	2B	3B	HR	RBI	BB	K	SB	CS	AVG/OBP/SLG	DRC+	VORP	BABIP	BRR	FRAA	WARP
2017	TRN	AA	22	276	34	16	4	6	29	30	45	2	1	.250/.339/.431	103	13.2	.277	0.3	RF(50): 12.3, LF(10): -1.1	2.2
2017	SWB	AAA	22	224	32	13	3	10	35	9	49	0	0	.306/.336/.541	128	12.6	.353	-0.7	LF(26): 0.1, RF(26): 1.6	1.2
2018	SWB	AAA	23	234	27	8	5	13	32	21	56	0	0	.226/.299/.495	99	7.5	.245	0.5	RF(32): -1.8, CF(12): 1.6	0.4
2018	BUF	AAA	23	72	10	3	2	3	8	8	16	0	0	.203/.292/.453	102	0.9	.222	0.4	RF(14): 3.3, 1B(4): 0.0	0.6
2018	NYA	MLB	23	4	0	0	0	0	0	0	1	0	0	.250/.250/.250	98	-0.1	.333	0.0	LF(2): -0.2	0.0
2018	TOR	MLB	23	128	14	7	0	6	13	11	32	1	0	.252/.320/.470	99	2.8	.295	-1.9	LF(26): -0.3, RF(13): -0.3	0.0
2019	BUF	AAA	24	154	17	8	4	4	20	22	25	1	1	.271/.383/.488	119	7.9	.307	-1.5	LF(16): 1.1, RF(8): 2.2	0.7
2019	TOR	MLB	24	276	37	14	1	12	28	19	73	0	2	.215/.274/.422	80	-0.4	.250	-0.3	RF(43): 0.0, LF(29): -2.2	-0.3
2020	TOR	MLB	25	175	21	9	1	8	25	15	44	0	0	.242/.314/.473	100	2.8	.282	-0.4	RF 1, LF -1	0.3

Comparables: Jorge Bonifacio, Clint Frazier, Wil Myers

William McKinley was the 25th U.S. President, assassinated in 1901 by anarchist Leon Czolgosz. As he succumbed to gangrene, his wife Ida is said to have cried, "I want to go too," to which McKinley replied, "we are all going" (and then went). Another William, McKinney's MLB career is still in its incipient stages, much as McKinley's presidency was when he was twice shot. It was the second bullet, which doctors could not locate in 25's abdomen, which sprung his mortal coil. After sputtering in his most extended opportunity yet, half the Jays' return for J.A. Happ is at risk of his career falling into sepsis—the two bullets acting on him are his lack of positional versatility and his below-average batting at the MLB level. In cases of sepsis, there is only so much time before the damage becomes irreversible, and the lefty's chances of healing his career are running sparse.

Travis Shaw 3B   Born: 04/16/90   Age: 30   Bats: L   Throws: R   Height: 6'4"   Weight: 230   Origin: Round 9, 2011 Draft (#292 overall)

YEAR	TEAM	LVL	AGE	PA	R	2B	3B	HR	RBI	BB	K	SB	CS	AVG/OBP/SLG	DRC+	VORP	BABIP	BRR	FRAA	WARP
2017	MIL	MLB	27	606	84	34	1	31	101	60	138	10	0	.273/.349/.513	114	40.9	.312	3.2	3B(143): 0.9, 1B(1): 0.0	3.7
2018	MIL	MLB	28	587	73	23	0	32	86	78	108	5	2	.241/.345/.480	120	43.5	.242	-0.7	3B(107): 1.8, 2B(39): -0.5	3.5
2019	SAN	AAA	29	174	27	4	0	12	33	36	37	3	1	.286/.437/.586	161	21.6	.299	-2.1	3B(23): 1.0, 1B(10): 0.4	1.6
2019	MIL	MLB	29	270	22	5	0	7	16	36	89	0	0	.157/.281/.270	71	-0.2	.216	0.1	3B(71): 2.3, 1B(6): 0.2	0.2
2020	TOR	MLB	30	455	62	19	1	26	71	54	132	4	1	.241/.337/.488	109	14.9	.291	0.3	1B 2, 3B 1	1.8

Comparables: Erubiel Durazo, Norm Zauchin, Freddie Freeman

The 10th percentile PECOTA projections on our website are as close as the system gets to providing a "worst-case scenario" for any given player. For Shaw, coming off a couple borderline All-Star seasons, his 10th percentile OPS was .678. You could talk yourself into it by envision his strikeout issues flaring up, or his power numbers dipping as his bat speed eroded, or some combination thereof. Both of those things (and more) happened, leaving him more than 100 points below that supposed floor. Shaw's approach also fell apart, and even a 42-game stint in the Pacific Coast League couldn't revive it. Power can be fickle, but a smart approach is supposed to transcend slumps. Shaw's didn't, and while he's been too good to give up on, it's possible that his collapse is indicative of a legitimate decline in skill.

Kevin Smith SS   Born: 07/04/96   Age: 23   Bats: R   Throws: R   Height: 5'11"   Weight: 188   Origin: Round 4, 2017 Draft (#129 overall)

YEAR	TEAM	LVL	AGE	PA	R	2B	3B	HR	RBI	BB	K	SB	CS	AVG/OBP/SLG	DRC+	VORP	BABIP	BRR	FRAA	WARP
2017	BLU	RK	20	283	43	25	1	8	43	16	70	9	0	.271/.312/.466	95	18.6	.337	3.9	SS(58): 8.3	2.2
2018	LNS	A	21	204	36	23	4	7	44	17	33	12	1	.355/.407/.639	196	33.7	.397	3.1	SS(24): 1.7, 3B(21): 0.7	3.5
2018	DUN	A+	21	371	57	8	2	18	49	23	88	17	5	.274/.332/.468	128	23.3	.319	4.6	SS(63): 6.9, 2B(13): 1.0	3.8
2019	NHP	AA	22	468	49	22	2	19	61	29	151	11	6	.209/.263/.402	91	9.8	.269	1.4	SS(86): 0.4, 3B(18): -1.1	1.5
2020	TOR	MLB	23	251	28	13	1	11	34	13	89	4	1	.225/.271/.433	80	1.8	.307	0.3	SS 3, 3B 0	0.5

Comparables: Ryan O'Hearn, Lane Thomas, Zach Walters

After reaching impressive heights in two levels in 2018, Smith came back to earth and then fell below at Double-A in 2019, posting a devilish .666 OPS and following it up with a hellacious AFL stint (38 strikeouts in 68 plate appearances). Looking like less of a sure thing at short and even slowing down on the basepaths from the previous season, it was a highly disappointing year all around. With the rest of the infield prospects around him improving and solidifying themselves in major-league roles, Smith tracks to be worthy of only a cameo and not someone who brings you lasagna at work.

Rowdy Tellez 1B   Born: 03/16/95   Age: 25   Bats: L   Throws: L   Height: 6'4"   Weight: 255   Origin: Round 30, 2013 Draft (#895 overall)

YEAR	TEAM	LVL	AGE	PA	R	2B	3B	HR	RBI	BB	K	SB	CS	AVG/OBP/SLG	DRC+	VORP	BABIP	BRR	FRAA	WARP
2017	BUF	AAA	22	501	45	29	1	6	56	47	94	6	1	.222/.295/.333	79	-11.6	.264	-0.6	1B(115): 1.8	-0.4
2018	BUF	AAA	23	444	43	22	0	13	50	40	74	7	4	.270/.340/.425	126	9.5	.298	-0.8	1B(107): -3.0	1.2
2018	TOR	MLB	23	73	10	9	0	4	14	2	21	0	0	.314/.329/.614	101	5.3	.391	-0.1	1B(17): -0.4	0.1
2019	BUF	AAA	24	109	20	9	0	7	21	14	25	0	0	.366/.450/.688	176	12.2	.435	-1.6	1B(25): 1.9	1.1
2019	TOR	MLB	24	409	49	19	0	21	54	29	116	1	1	.227/.293/.449	91	1.7	.267	-1.1	1B(57): 4.3	0.5
2020	TOR	MLB	25	385	51	17	0	23	61	32	104	2	1	.246/.316/.496	103	7.4	.284	-0.5	1B 1	0.8

Comparables: Ronald Guzmán, Steve Bilko, Dominic Smith

On September 25th, Tellez' biggest young fan, family friend Emmet Cooper, told him he had to hit a home run. Tellez hit two. Maybe this year, Cooper will tell the 25-year-old to take a walk. Tellez racked up one base on balls for every four strikeouts he tallied in 2019, putting him squarely below-average as a hitter despite his 21 long flies. To be more than a simple holdover until the next good edition of the Blue Jays, Tellez will need to bring more of the disciplined approach he's shown in the upper minors—or just keep hitting dingers on command.

Richard Ureña MI   Born: 02/26/96   Age: 24   Bats: B   Throws: R   Height: 6'0"   Weight: 195   Origin: International Free Agent, 2012

YEAR	TEAM	LVL	AGE	PA	R	2B	3B	HR	RBI	BB	K	SB	CS	AVG/OBP/SLG	DRC+	VORP	BABIP	BRR	FRAA	WARP
2017	NHP	AA	21	551	44	36	3	5	60	30	100	0	1	.247/.286/.359	74	6.0	.294	-1.9	SS(115): -4.6, 2B(11): 0.2	0.2
2017	TOR	MLB	21	75	6	4	0	1	4	6	28	1	0	.206/.270/.309	60	0.5	.333	1.4	SS(20): -2.0, 2B(1): 0.1	-0.1
2018	DUN	A+	22	29	2	0	0	0	2	1	6	0	0	.148/.172/.148	33	-3.3	.182	0.1	SS(3): 0.0, 2B(3): -0.4	-0.1
2018	BUF	AAA	22	268	28	11	3	5	29	12	48	2	3	.216/.250/.344	57	-4.7	.246	-0.6	SS(43): 1.8, 2B(17): 0.9	0.1
2018	TOR	MLB	22	108	10	4	0	1	6	7	32	2	1	.293/.340/.364	72	0.5	.424	-1.2	SS(20): -1.3, 2B(13): -1.0	-0.3
2019	BUF	AAA	23	403	43	18	4	6	52	23	85	3	2	.274/.314/.393	80	1.2	.336	1.2	SS(56): 4.8, 2B(39): -0.1	1.1
2019	TOR	MLB	23	80	4	6	0	0	4	2	23	0	0	.243/.273/.324	61	-0.7	.353	-0.8	SS(13): -1.1, 2B(9): -0.8	-0.3
2020	TOR	MLB	24	251	22	10	1	6	26	11	70	1	1	.230/.268/.363	63	-4.3	.300	-0.3	SS -1, 2B -1	-0.6

Comparables: Amed Rosario, Luis Sardiñas, Ketel Marte

Ureña is a genus of plants common in tropical and subtropical regions. By some the plants are considered weeds, though in other areas they are utilized for their fibers and as food. Ureña could hardly be called invasive, but his continued subtle presence on the Blue Jays—he has received between 75 and 108 plate appearances in each of the past three seasons—points to the organization's continued reliance on a player they might weed out were they in a better place. Strong, versatile defender or not (much like the plant), Ureña and his career .597 OPS do not provide the sustenance Toronto needs and it's only a matter of time before this sixth infielder gets excised from their plans for good.

PITCHERS

Jason Adam RHP   Born: 08/04/91   Age: 28   Bats: R   Throws: R   Height: 6'4"   Weight: 225   Origin: Round 5, 2010 Draft (#149 overall)

YEAR	TEAM	LVL	AGE	W	L	SV	G	GS	IP	H	HR	BB/9	K/9	K	GB%	BABIP	WHIP	ERA	DRA	WARP	MPH	FB%	WHF	CSP
2017	NWA	AA	25	0	0	0	5	0	6¹	3	0	5.7	15.6	11	27%	.273	1.11	7.11	3.41	0.1				
2018	NWA	AA	26	1	0	0	6	0	11¹	5	0	3.2	13.5	17	36%	.227	0.79	1.59	2.24	0.4				
2018	OMA	AAA	26	2	0	4	11	0	12²	6	0	5.0	10.7	15	34%	.207	1.03	1.42	3.06	0.3				
2018	KCA	MLB	26	0	3	0	31	0	32¹	30	9	4.2	10.3	37	29%	.269	1.39	6.12	7.04	-0.8	96.3	61.1	13.1	45.6
2019	BUF	AAA	27	1	3	1	11	0	14	10	2	3.2	12.9	20	19%	.276	1.07	2.57	3.33	0.4				
2019	TOR	MLB	27	3	0	0	23	0	21²	15	1	4.2	7.5	18	27%	.237	1.15	2.91	6.35	-0.2	96.2	61.5	12.4	41.8
2020	TOR	MLB	28	2	2	0	33	0	35	31	7	3.9	8.4	33	30%	.256	1.32	4.65	4.60	0.2	95.7	61.7	12.9	43.7

Comparables: Jesse Biddle, Brad Keller, JC Ramírez

Adam has the name of a low-rent knockoff of Jack Ryan–himself a low-rent knockoff of James Bond–like the kind of show you get when you take Jim from *the Office* and bulk him up like Spongebob with inflatable muscle arms, only for both seasons to be deluged by accusations of imperialism (and worse) in its plot and characterizations. Wait, sorry, that was *Jack Ryan*. Adam, though, was also in his second season in 2019, with much of his supporting staff turning over and in a new location. The Blue Jays picked up Adam for cash considerations before the season, and despite back-of-the-card stats that suggest a long-term bullpen piece, he had a gap between his ERA and DRA that the Red October could pass through with ease.

Chase Anderson RHP   Born: 11/30/87   Age: 32   Bats: R   Throws: R   Height: 6'1"   Weight: 200   Origin: Round 9, 2009 Draft (#276 overall)

YEAR	TEAM	LVL	AGE	W	L	SV	G	GS	IP	H	HR	BB/9	K/9	K	GB%	BABIP	WHIP	ERA	DRA	WARP	MPH	FB%	WHF	CSP
2017	MIL	MLB	29	12	4	0	25	25	141¹	113	14	2.6	8.5	133	41%	.265	1.09	2.74	4.13	2.3	95.4	52.5	11.5	47.6
2018	MIL	MLB	30	9	8	0	30	30	158	131	30	3.2	7.3	128	36%	.239	1.19	3.93	5.52	-0.4	94.5	53.5	10.3	46.9
2019	MIL	MLB	31	8	4	0	32	27	139	126	23	3.2	8.0	124	36%	.266	1.27	4.21	4.84	1.4	95.4	50.8	11.9	47.6
2020	TOR	MLB	32	8	7	0	23	23	120	117	25	3.4	8.0	107	36%	.275	1.35	4.96	4.89	0.9	94.1	51.7	11.1	47

Comparables: Chad Bettis, Joe Kelly, Kyle Gibson

Anderson has now surrendered 113 homers over the past five seasons, ranking him 23rd among big-league pitchers. (For reference, he's 43rd in innings during that span.) He has a tantalizing skillset, including a mid-90s fastball and four secondary pitches. The best one, the changeup, is a true swing-and-miss offering (16 percent whiff rate) and protects him from platoon-heavy lineups. But that home-run problem lingers, and has been the difference between a potential mid-rotation starter and somebody who has to scrap to hang onto a rotation spot. The Blue Jays hope a change of scenery can reverse his fortunes—at least long enough to drum up trade interest.

Anthony Bass RHP   Born: 11/01/87   Age: 32   Bats: R   Throws: R   Height: 6'2"   Weight: 200   Origin: Round 5, 2008 Draft (#165 overall)

YEAR	TEAM	LVL	AGE	W	L	SV	G	GS	IP	H	HR	BB/9	K/9	K	GB%	BABIP	WHIP	ERA	DRA	WARP	MPH	FB%	WHF	CSP
2017	RNG	RK	29	0	1	0	3	2	9	11	1	2.0	9.0	9	52%	.385	1.44	4.00	3.74	0.2				
2017	ROU	AAA	29	3	4	0	18	12	75¹	79	7	3.3	10.4	87	43%	.358	1.42	4.18	5.01	0.5				
2017	TEX	MLB	29	0	0	0	2	0	5²	14	1	0.0	1.6	1	47%	.448	2.47	14.29	7.65	-0.2	94.6	63.1	8.1	46.9
2018	IOW	AAA	30	0	3	3	27	0	32	34	3	1.7	7.0	25	53%	.307	1.25	3.38	4.36	0.3				
2018	CHN	MLB	30	0	0	0	16	0	15¹	18	1	1.8	8.2	14	53%	.386	1.37	2.93	4.77	0.0	96.1	68.4	8.6	48.4
2019	LOU	AAA	31	1	1	9	19	0	20¹	13	1	2.7	8.4	19	55%	.222	0.93	2.21	2.71	0.7				
2019	SEA	MLB	31	2	4	5	44	0	48	30	5	3.2	8.1	43	55%	.203	0.98	3.56	3.43	1.0	97.2	52.7	12.3	43
2020	TOR	MLB	32	3	3	7	58	0	62	63	9	3.3	8.3	57	55%	.304	1.38	4.50	4.52	0.5	95.9	56	11.2	45.4

Comparables: Brandon League, Al McBean, Neil Allen

In the sea of Anthony Bass-types that floated through the Mariners bullpen in 2019 was Bass himself, who quietly turned in a sufficient season for a team that surely appreciated even the slightest semblance of consistency. Bass' average fastball velocity sat north of 95 mph for the first time as a big leaguer, and he posted career-best marks in both WHIP and DRA. His multi-year journey to find a stable role in a big-league 'pen may actually have a happy ending after all, as he was scooped up by the Blue Jays in November. He'll compete for the role of setup man to Ken Giles.

Ryan Borucki LHP   Born: 03/31/94   Age: 26   Bats: L   Throws: L   Height: 6'4"   Weight: 215   Origin: Round 15, 2012 Draft (#475 overall)

YEAR	TEAM	LVL	AGE	W	L	SV	G	GS	IP	H	HR	BB/9	K/9	K	GB%	BABIP	WHIP	ERA	DRA	WARP	MPH	FB%	WHF	CSP
2017	DUN	A+	23	6	5	0	19	18	98	95	5	2.5	10.0	109	52%	.342	1.24	3.58	4.81	0.5				
2017	NHP	AA	23	2	3	0	7	7	46¹	31	2	1.6	8.2	42	58%	.236	0.84	1.94	2.20	1.6				
2017	BUF	AAA	23	0	0	0	1	1	6	6	0	1.5	9.0	6	50%	.375	1.17	0.00	3.93	0.1				
2018	BUF	AAA	24	6	5	0	13	13	77	62	6	3.3	6.8	58	52%	.255	1.17	3.27	3.57	1.7				
2018	TOR	MLB	24	4	6	0	17	17	97²	96	7	3.0	6.2	67	49%	.291	1.32	3.87	4.53	0.9	93.4	58.7	8.7	49.1
2019	BUF	AAA	25	1	0	0	2	2	11	11	4	2.5	7.4	9	42%	.241	1.27	4.91	5.11	0.2				
2019	TOR	MLB	25	0	1	0	2	2	6²	15	2	8.1	8.1	6	39%	.500	3.15	10.80	8.81	-0.2	94.2	52.3	9	44.1
2020	TOR	MLB	26	4	5	0	15	15	73	89	12	3.7	6.5	52	46%	.326	1.63	6.34	5.94	-0.3	93.1	59	8.9	47.2

Comparables: Steven Brault, Anthony Banda, Matt Hall

The story, once again with Borucki, was injuries. The 25-year-old has been racking up a health record that would make Mark Prior take note, and tossed fewer than 25 innings across four different levels last season. After elbow inflammation kept him out of roughly the season's first half, Borucki built up (and worked through various rehab stints) for two starts in the back half of July before his elbow again started acting up. One surgery for bone spurs later and the sophomore's season ended, a huge letdown after an encouraging debut and another contributing factor in the oft-pitiable Jays rotation. The lefty's elbow is purported to have a clean bill of health entering the new year, so here's to the rest of him staying healthy as well.

Buddy Boshers LHP   Born: 05/09/88   Age: 32   Bats: L   Throws: L   Height: 6'3"   Weight: 222   Origin: Round 4, 2008 Draft (#139 overall)

YEAR	TEAM	LVL	AGE	W	L	SV	G	GS	IP	H	HR	BB/9	K/9	K	GB%	BABIP	WHIP	ERA	DRA	WARP	MPH	FB%	WHF	CSP
2017	ROC	AAA	29	0	0	0	18	0	14²	16	1	4.9	9.2	15	52%	.366	1.64	3.68	5.75	-0.1				
2017	MIN	MLB	29	1	0	0	38	0	35	37	7	2.6	7.2	28	47%	.283	1.34	4.89	3.85	0.5	91.8	48.9	11.4	46.6
2018	FRE	AAA	30	2	1	4	41	0	51	48	5	2.6	9.7	55	49%	.319	1.24	3.18	3.78	0.8				
2018	IND	AAA	30	0	1	1	7	0	6	6	0	4.5	10.5	7	47%	.353	1.50	4.50	4.43	0.0				
2019	BUF	AAA	31	0	2	5	25	0	32¹	27	3	3.9	9.7	35	41%	.289	1.27	2.78	3.88	0.7				
2019	TOR	MLB	31	0	3	0	28	1	20	20	3	4.5	11.7	26	46%	.333	1.50	4.05	4.59	0.2	94.4	39.6	9.1	46.8
2020	TOR	MLB	32	2	2	0	33	0	35	35	6	3.7	9.5	37	45%	.308	1.40	4.68	4.66	0.2	92.1	43.5	10.1	46.3

Comparables: Lucas Luetge, Kevin Chapman, Sam Freeman

With a name that sounds less like an MLB reliever and more like a new character on the coming *Blue's Clues* reboot, Boshers has now pitched in four of the last seven seasons as a lefty specialist—he has faced 200 left-handed batters in his career compared to just 259 righties. Boshers actually posted a reverse split in his two months in Toronto, which would be more reason for concern had he not been league-average against right-handed batters (compared to his last MLB stint, when they posted a collective OPS of .904 against him). More pressing for his hopes of appearing in the bigs in back-to-back seasons, in 13 of Boshers' 28 appearances for Toronto he faced two batters or less. Still, the 32-year-old posted the best strikeout rate of his career and that will give him at least a fighting chance to avoid extinction.

Clay Buchholz RHP   Born: 08/14/84   Age: 35   Bats: L   Throws: R   Height: 6'3"   Weight: 190   Origin: Round 1, 2005 Draft (#42 overall)

YEAR	TEAM	LVL	AGE	W	L	SV	G	GS	IP	H	HR	BB/9	K/9	K	GB%	BABIP	WHIP	ERA	DRA	WARP	MPH	FB%	WHF	CSP
2017	PHI	MLB	32	0	1	0	2	2	7¹	16	1	3.7	6.1	5	31%	.484	2.59	12.27	6.77	-0.1	92.7	65.2	6.5	49.7
2018	VIS	A+	33	1	0	0	1	1	6	4	1	1.5	9.0	6	47%	.214	0.83	3.00	3.35	0.1				
2018	OMA	AAA	33	1	0	0	2	2	11¹	9	2	4.0	3.2	4	55%	.194	1.24	1.59	5.07	0.1				
2018	RNO	AAA	33	0	1	0	2	2	11²	12	0	3.9	7.7	10	40%	.324	1.46	5.40	4.73	0.1				
2018	ARI	MLB	33	7	2	0	16	16	98¹	80	9	2.0	7.4	81	43%	.256	1.04	2.01	3.74	1.8	92.0	65.9	10.5	50.4
2019	TOR	MLB	34	2	5	0	12	12	59	72	13	2.4	5.9	39	46%	.321	1.49	6.56	8.00	-1.4	91.8	62.8	9.7	47.5
2020	TOR	MLB	35	2	2	0	33	0	35	37	7	2.9	6.7	26	44%	.287	1.39	5.09	5.09	0.0	90.7	63.3	9.8	48.1

Comparables: Ervin Santana, Matt Garza, Jhoulys Chacín

"Man crafted from clay" is one of the most common creation myths, and humanity's fragility in relation to the gods an expected consequence. Buchholz has exemplified that fragility over the last three seasons, totaling just thirty starts and never crossing 100 innings after five consecutive seasons breaking that threshold. Still, even in a season again limited by injury, Buchholz played the Prometheus role, providing leadership and shelter to young charges—after a ball popped out of Billy McKinley's glove in a September game and led to several runs, Buchholz refused the outfielder's apology. Even as he struggled through season that must have felt like being chained to a rock and having his liver pecked out, the 34-year-old was an important presence to the developing squad.

Wilmer Font RHP Born: 05/24/90 Age: 30 Bats: R Throws: R Height: 6'4" Weight: 250 Origin: International Free Agent, 2006

YEAR	TEAM	LVL	AGE	W	L	SV	G	GS	IP	H	HR	BB/9	K/9	K	GB%	BABIP	WHIP	ERA	DRA	WARP	MPH	FB%	WHF	CSP
2017	OKL	AAA	27	10	8	0	25	25	134¹	114	11	2.3	11.9	178	39%	.315	1.11	3.42	2.03	5.4				
2017	LAN	MLB	27	0	0	0	3	0	3²	7	2	9.8	7.4	3	27%	.385	3.00	17.18	7.49	-0.1	97.0	68.1	11	44.3
2018	LAN	MLB	28	0	2	0	6	0	10¹	18	5	0.9	6.1	7	42%	.371	1.84	11.32	7.05	-0.2	97.0	69.5	8.9	51.7
2018	OAK	MLB	28	0	0	0	4	0	6²	13	5	5.4	12.1	9	33%	.421	2.55	14.85	3.80	0.1	97.7	68.5	13.6	41.8
2018	TBA	MLB	28	2	1	0	9	5	27	15	2	3.7	6.7	20	45%	.178	0.96	1.67	6.46	-0.4	98.0	63.6	9.7	49
2019	TBA	MLB	29	1	0	0	10	0	14	15	2	3.2	11.6	18	43%	.371	1.43	5.79	4.85	0.1	97.1	50.9	15	47.1
2019	TOR	MLB	29	2	3	0	23	14	39¹	34	7	2.5	12.1	53	35%	.300	1.14	3.66	3.58	0.8	97.1	61.8	14.6	47.2
2019	NYN	MLB	29	1	2	0	15	3	31	29	8	3.8	7.0	24	37%	.241	1.35	4.94	6.66	-0.4	97.0	58.5	11.2	47.9
2020	TOR	MLB	30	3	3	0	52	0	56	50	11	3.1	9.2	57	38%	.274	1.25	4.23	4.30	0.5	96.5	60.9	12.4	46.8

Comparables: Matt Magill, Jhan Mariñez, Christian Garcia

Font's three-team 2019, by fonts. Fourteen innings through early May in Tampa Bay were Futura: widely used, though mainly for advertisement. After a trade to the Mets, three disastrous starts and twelve *fine* relief appearances over two months were Papyrus: brash, but maybe indicative of those who don't quite know what they're doing. A final 23 appearances in Toronto after a DFA, though, were Times New Roman: not the flashiest, but reliable and solidly above average. It remains to be seen if Font can remain as ubiquitous moving forward after a mixed bag of a season, but then we always tend to turn back to our recently-used fonts, and perhaps the same is true of GMs.

Sam Gaviglio RHP Born: 05/22/90 Age: 30 Bats: R Throws: R Height: 6'2" Weight: 205 Origin: Round 5, 2011 Draft (#170 overall)

YEAR	TEAM	LVL	AGE	W	L	SV	G	GS	IP	H	HR	BB/9	K/9	K	GB%	BABIP	WHIP	ERA	DRA	WARP	MPH	FB%	WHF	CSP
2017	TAC	AAA	27	3	6	0	13	13	72	72	5	1.5	7.1	57	54%	.302	1.17	3.88	3.11	2.0				
2017	SEA	MLB	27	3	5	0	12	11	62¹	63	15	3.0	5.8	40	49%	.265	1.35	4.62	5.69	-0.1	90.6	56.6	7.3	50.3
2017	KCA	MLB	27	1	0	0	4	2	12	13	1	3.8	6.8	9	56%	.316	1.50	3.00	5.12	0.1	91.4	59.5	10	51.2
2018	BUF	AAA	28	0	0	0	5	5	29	21	4	1.2	9.0	29	46%	.243	0.86	1.86	3.12	0.8				
2018	TOR	MLB	28	3	10	0	26	24	123²	140	21	2.8	7.6	105	50%	.313	1.44	5.31	4.90	0.6	90.6	56	9.2	46.7
2019	TOR	MLB	29	4	2	0	52	0	95²	85	18	2.1	8.3	88	48%	.258	1.12	4.61	4.12	1.3	91.4	42.6	12.5	47.8
2020	TOR	MLB	30	3	3	0	64	0	68	71	13	2.6	8.2	62	48%	.297	1.34	4.84	4.82	0.3	90.2	50.9	10.2	48

Comparables: Chris Stratton, Brad Lincoln, Justin Haley

Having never been included in the massive pool of 21 starters Toronto used in 2019, you might assume his third big-league season was not a success. But actually, Gaviglio was worth five wins more than those 21 pitchers combined. The move to the bullpen agreed with the soft-tossing righty and the Blue Jays certainly got their money's worth out of him, as he was the only pitcher in baseball last year to throw 90 innings without making a start. For the first time using his slider more than his sinker, Gaviglio improved his strikeout rate without losing any of his low-walk, high-grounder profile. The rubber-armed righty who barely scratches 90 on the gun is not exactly a sought-after archetype in this era of a faceless and nameless legion of power arms, but as long as Gaviglio can work multiple innings at an above-average rate he'll have a home.

Ken Giles RHP Born: 09/20/90 Age: 29 Bats: R Throws: R Height: 6'3" Weight: 210 Origin: Round 7, 2011 Draft (#241 overall)

YEAR	TEAM	LVL	AGE	W	L	SV	G	GS	IP	H	HR	BB/9	K/9	K	GB%	BABIP	WHIP	ERA	DRA	WARP	MPH	FB%	WHF	CSP
2017	HOU	MLB	26	1	3	34	63	0	62²	44	4	3.0	11.9	83	45%	.290	1.04	2.30	2.85	1.6	100.1	52.8	17.2	49.1
2018	HOU	MLB	27	0	2	12	34	0	30²	36	2	0.9	9.1	31	37%	.366	1.27	4.99	3.42	0.5	99.3	57.7	16.9	51.8
2018	TOR	MLB	27	0	1	14	21	0	19²	18	4	1.8	10.1	22	54%	.269	1.12	4.12	3.18	0.4	99.1	61.3	16.3	48.9
2019	TOR	MLB	28	2	3	23	53	0	53	36	5	2.9	14.1	83	39%	.301	1.00	1.87	2.62	1.6	99.2	50.7	20.3	45.2
2020	TOR	MLB	29	3	2	38	52	0	56	41	7	3.2	13.2	82	41%	.296	1.10	2.81	3.03	1.3	98.8	53.9	18.3	48

Comparables: Cody Allen, Greg Holland, Francisco Rodríguez

Timing is a funny thing. It took a particular set of circumstances, including a sustained stretch pronouncedly worse than the rest of his career, for Giles to land in Toronto. And it took different circumstances—the need for a cortisone shot in his pitching elbow just before the trade deadline that reportedly influenced the Yankees to back out of a trade—for the closer to complete a full season as an expat. Despite some brief layoffs, it was perhaps Giles' finest year, with the highest strikeout rate and lowest ERA of his career. A year from free agency, it's anyone's guess how the Jays use their best trade chip they actually intend to move—teams will be less bullish on one season of a volatile reliever than they would be on two.

Anthony Kay LHP Born: 03/21/95 Age: 25 Bats: L Throws: L Height: 6'0" Weight: 218 Origin: Round 1, 2016 Draft (#31 overall)

YEAR	TEAM	LVL	AGE	W	L	SV	G	GS	IP	H	HR	BB/9	K/9	K	GB%	BABIP	WHIP	ERA	DRA	WARP	MPH	FB%	WHF	CSP
2018	COL	A	23	4	4	0	13	13	69¹	73	6	2.9	10.1	78	45%	.356	1.37	4.54	5.46	-0.2				
2018	SLU	A+	23	3	7	0	10	10	53¹	51	1	4.6	7.6	45	41%	.321	1.46	3.88	5.52	-0.1				
2019	BIN	AA	24	7	3	0	12	12	66¹	38	2	3.1	9.5	70	36%	.224	0.92	1.49	2.66	1.9				
2019	SYR	AAA	24	1	3	0	7	7	31¹	40	7	3.2	7.5	26	33%	.355	1.63	6.61	5.87	0.3				
2019	BUF	AAA	24	2	2	0	7	7	36	33	3	5.5	9.8	39	42%	.323	1.53	2.50	6.22	0.2				
2019	TOR	MLB	24	1	0	0	3	2	14	15	0	3.2	8.4	13	55%	.341	1.43	5.79	4.76	0.1	95.4	61.6	12.4	45
2020	TOR	MLB	25	4	4	0	17	11	63	60	11	3.8	7.7	54	39%	.273	1.37	4.71	4.66	0.6	95.1	63.1	12.7	46.1

Comparables: Pedro Figueroa, Pat Light, Amir Garrett

According to Kay Jewelers, their "Every Kiss Begins With Kay" slogan was first used in 1985 and is now utilized in each of the company's commercials, giving them a 98 percent brand awareness rate. After being packaged from the Mets to the Blue Jays and making his major league debut in 2019, MLB's Kay cannot boast that kind of consciousness, but he's trending in the right direction. After his post-draft Tommy John surgery in 2016, Kay worked at five different minor league affiliates across the past two seasons before debuting for a three-game stint with Toronto. It's likely a back-of-the-rotation profile, but Kay has a clear pathway to starts in a rotation as barren and empty as Winterfell during Robb Stark's campaign through the Riverlands.

Adam Kloffenstein RHP Born: 08/25/00 Age: 19 Bats: R Throws: R Height: 6'5" Weight: 243 Origin: Round 3, 2018 Draft (#88 overall)

YEAR	TEAM	LVL	AGE	W	L	SV	G	GS	IP	H	HR	BB/9	K/9	K	GB%	BABIP	WHIP	ERA	DRA	WARP	MPH	FB%	WHF	CSP
2019	VAN	A-	18	4	4	0	13	13	64¹	47	4	3.2	9.0	64	61%	.262	1.09	2.24	3.03	1.6				
2020	TOR	MLB	19	2	2	0	33	0	35	35	6	4.4	7.7	30	52%	.288	1.48	5.08	5.02	0.1				

Comparables: Jenrry Mejia, Arodys Vizcaíno, Jamie Callahan

Shortly after he was drafted two summers ago, Kloffenstein presented former burly right-handed pitching prospect Nate Pearson with an unusual proposal: "Hey man, I'm just gonna follow you around a little bit for the next couple days. Don't take it weird. I'm not gonna be wearing your shoes." Weird the phrasing might have been, but the then-17-year-old's willingness to put himself out there in the interest of furthering himself—in this case, via familiarizing himself with the rituals and routines of his new organization's most highly-regarded pitching prospect—portends well for the teenager's development. Kloffenstein impressed in short-season ball, albeit with slightly less punch to his heater than he showed as an amateur, giving reason to believe he can stick as a starter and potentially follow—metaphorically or not—the path Pearson's performance has blazed.

Derek Law RHP Born: 09/14/90 Age: 29 Bats: R Throws: R Height: 6'3" Weight: 215 Origin: Round 9, 2011 Draft (#297 overall)

YEAR	TEAM	LVL	AGE	W	L	SV	G	GS	IP	H	HR	BB/9	K/9	K	GB%	BABIP	WHIP	ERA	DRA	WARP	MPH	FB%	WHF	CSP
2017	SAC	AAA	26	1	1	10	25	0	32²	32	1	3.3	7.2	26	52%	.316	1.35	2.48	3.62	0.6				
2017	SFN	MLB	26	4	1	4	41	0	37¹	45	5	3.4	8.4	35	40%	.357	1.58	5.06	4.73	0.2	96.1	54	10.9	46.3
2018	SAC	AAA	27	1	3	8	33	0	40²	34	2	2.0	9.5	43	49%	.305	1.06	4.20	2.91	1.0				
2018	SFN	MLB	27	1	0	0	7	0	13¹	16	2	5.4	8.1	12	42%	.326	1.80	7.43	3.72	0.2	96.5	51.6	11.3	44.7
2019	BUF	AAA	28	2	1	2	8	0	10²	7	1	2.5	14.3	17	50%	.286	0.94	1.69	1.63	0.5				
2019	TOR	MLB	28	1	2	5	58	4	60²	61	8	5.9	9.9	67	51%	.317	1.66	4.90	5.48	-0.1	96.5	36.7	12.5	42.7
2020	TOR	MLB	29	2	2	0	33	0	35	32	4	3.9	9.2	36	49%	.291	1.34	4.04	4.06	0.4	95.7	42.1	12	44.2

Comparables: Evan Scribner, Nick Wittgren, Josh Lueke

Law and Order: Derek was never the most obvious spin-off, but it was hard to argue with the San Francisco-set series after seeing its performance in prime time upon its debut in 2016. Since then, ratings have faltered, and in April a surprise move to Toronto was announced in the hopes of enlivening flagging performance. Law (for short) appeared in 58 Toronto games (industry term for episodes), but following the series from San Francisco was inconsistent performance and shaky control. Just because channel Six didn't want to renew the series doesn't mean it's cancelled for good, but the pressure is on to do what so many shows couldn't: break out of old patterns.

Elvis Luciano RHP Born: 02/15/00 Age: 20 Bats: R Throws: R Height: 6'3" Weight: 200 Origin: International Free Agent, 2016

YEAR	TEAM	LVL	AGE	W	L	SV	G	GS	IP	H	HR	BB/9	K/9	K	GB%	BABIP	WHIP	ERA	DRA	WARP	MPH	FB%	WHF	CSP
2017	DDI	RK	17	3	1	0	11	6	48¹	42	2	2.8	7.6	41	56%	.294	1.18	2.98	3.47	1.2				
2017	DIA	RK	17	1	0	1	4	2	16¹	16	0	1.7	5.0	9	47%	.276	1.16	2.76	3.58	0.4				
2018	BNC	RK	18	3	5	0	11	11	56	55	4	3.2	9.0	56	49%	.327	1.34	4.66	4.11	1.2				
2018	IDA	RK	18	2	0	0	2	1	11	6	0	2.5	11.5	14	61%	.261	0.82	0.00	1.82	0.5				
2019	TOR	MLB	19	1	0	0	25	0	33²	36	4	6.4	7.2	27	38%	.317	1.78	5.35	8.66	-1.2	96.1	55.5	11.5	41.5
2020	TOR	MLB	20	1	1	0	23	0	25	24	4	4.5	7.3	20	39%	.281	1.48	5.19	5.05	0.0	96.5	58.5	12.1	43.8

Comparables: Pedro Araujo, Felix Jorge, Brandon Maurer

Do you know where you were when the clock struck midnight on January 1, 2000? If so, you'll be bummed to learn that Luciano was not yet born, becoming the first pitcher born after Y2K to make the majors. Take heart, at least, that Luciano was rostered by the Blue Jays all season because of his status as a Rule 5 pick, and now the team has his rights he'll very likely spend all of 2020 in the minors. With experience, Luciano will attack hitters with more variation—he was almost exclusively fastball/slider against righties and fastball/change against lefties—and hopefully more strikes.

★ ★ ★ *2020 Top 101 Prospect* **#83** ★ ★ ★

Alek Manoah RHP Born: 01/09/98 Age: 22 Bats: R Throws: R Height: 6'6" Weight: 260 Origin: Round 1, 2019 Draft (#11 overall)

YEAR	TEAM	LVL	AGE	W	L	SV	G	GS	IP	H	HR	BB/9	K/9	K	GB%	BABIP	WHIP	ERA	DRA	WARP	MPH	FB%	WHF	CSP
2019	VAN	A-	21	0	1	0	6	6	17	13	1	2.6	14.3	27	30%	.379	1.06	2.65	3.15	0.4				
2020	TOR	MLB	22	2	2	0	33	0	35	36	6	3.7	9.9	39	36%	.320	1.43	4.96	4.93	0.1				

Comparables: Radhames Liz, Michael Stutes, Jeremy Hefner

One of the most talented arms in the 2019 draft class, the 11th-overall pick has an impressive fastball-slider combo that bodes well for his chances of reaching and sticking at the highest level. Manoah is solidly built and throws hard, but is going to need to develop a pitch to keep lefties from tagging him as he climbs through the minors. Even if his abbreviated pro debut, he allowed an OPS more than 250 points higher when facing opposite-handed hitters. Having turned 22 at the start of the year, Manoah may also have the benefit of a bit more development time than most college arms are allotted—time he could use to find the feel for a change. It's also good to have long-term goals, as last May he told the Miami Herald he plans "to play 10 years in the big leagues, and then hop in the broadcast booth with Alex Rodriguez."

Tim Mayza LHP   Born: 01/15/92   Age: 28   Bats: L   Throws: L   Height: 6'3"   Weight: 220   Origin: Round 12, 2013 Draft (#355 overall)

YEAR	TEAM	LVL	AGE	W	L	SV	G	GS	IP	H	HR	BB/9	K/9	K	GB%	BABIP	WHIP	ERA	DRA	WARP	MPH	FB%	WHF	CSP
2017	NHP	AA	25	1	1	4	29	0	33¹	32	5	4.1	11.3	42	42%	.325	1.41	4.59	4.07	0.3				
2017	BUF	AAA	25	1	1	0	11	0	19¹	16	0	3.3	7.4	16	33%	.276	1.19	0.93	3.72	0.3				
2017	TOR	MLB	25	1	0	0	19	0	17	24	3	2.1	14.3	27	42%	.467	1.65	6.88	2.61	0.5	96.4	49.4	17.1	40.1
2018	BUF	AAA	26	6	2	1	20	0	25²	26	2	3.9	12.6	36	42%	.400	1.44	4.56	4.49	0.2				
2018	TOR	MLB	26	2	0	0	37	0	35²	33	3	3.5	10.1	40	46%	.326	1.32	3.28	3.76	0.5	96.1	56	15.1	43.6
2019	TOR	MLB	27	1	3	0	68	0	51¹	45	8	4.7	9.6	55	53%	.272	1.40	4.91	4.68	0.4	96.1	64.5	15.6	38.6
2020	TOR	MLB	28	2	2	0	33	0	35	29	4	4.1	10.1	39	50%	.279	1.28	3.65	3.76	0.5	95.6	60.4	15.7	40.9

Comparables: Austin Davis, Emilio Pagán, Sam Freeman

Mayza suffered one of 2019's worst on-field injuries, falling to his knees on the mound and gripping his elbow after sailing a pitch behind Didi Gregorius. The southpaw will spend all of 2020 on the shelf and ultimately return to a league that will no longer tolerate his LOOGY inclinations—one-fourth of Mayza's team-high 68 appearances in 2019 were against two batters or fewer. Still, despite getting worse in each of his three big league seasons as his workload grew, Mayza was a slightly above-average reliever in 2019, per DRA-, and even in two years it's safe to say the Jays will be in need of decent arms.

Thomas Pannone LHP   Born: 04/28/94   Age: 26   Bats: L   Throws: L   Height: 6'0"   Weight: 200   Origin: Round 9, 2013 Draft (#261 overall)

YEAR	TEAM	LVL	AGE	W	L	SV	G	GS	IP	H	HR	BB/9	K/9	K	GB%	BABIP	WHIP	ERA	DRA	WARP	MPH	FB%	WHF	CSP
2017	LYN	A+	23	2	0	0	5	5	27²	10	0	2.3	12.7	39	48%	.212	0.61	0.00	1.77	1.1				
2017	AKR	AA	23	6	1	0	14	14	82¹	67	5	2.3	8.9	81	37%	.281	1.07	2.62	4.05	1.1				
2017	NHP	AA	23	1	2	0	6	6	34²	31	9	2.1	7.5	29	38%	.232	1.12	3.63	5.27	0.0				
2018	NHP	AA	24	0	0	0	2	2	9	9	1	5.0	12.0	12	29%	.348	1.56	3.00	4.32	0.1				
2018	BUF	AAA	24	0	3	0	6	6	36²	40	8	1.7	9.8	40	24%	.327	1.28	4.91	5.49	0.0				
2018	TOR	MLB	24	4	1	0	12	6	43	37	7	3.1	6.1	29	36%	.234	1.21	4.19	5.89	-0.3	90.4	64.2	10.4	50.6
2019	BUF	AAA	25	3	1	0	8	6	33²	25	4	4.0	11.0	41	34%	.262	1.19	3.21	2.96	1.2				
2019	TOR	MLB	25	3	6	0	37	7	73	73	13	3.8	8.5	69	35%	.291	1.42	6.16	6.48	-0.8	92.3	61.7	11.9	46.2
2020	TOR	MLB	26	2	2	0	41	0	43	45	10	3.6	8.1	39	35%	.286	1.44	5.51	5.31	-0.1	91.3	63.6	11.6	49

Comparables: Jalen Beeks, Jharel Cotton, Tyler Wilson

Jumbo shrimp, spend'n'save, Pannone. All oxymorons, the prior trio each contain their opposites, presenting intriguing contradictions. Pannone lived up to his surname with his 2019 season a bevy of contradictions. In seven starts he took five losses and compiled an 11.54 ERA. In 30 relief appearances his ERA was 3.54. Less self-contradictory is Pannone's profile, and while the stark contrast between his success in Triple-A and his struggles in the majors present a conundrum, it's one we've all seen before, and one Pannone will need to overcome to dial his usage from 'none' to 'pan.'

Eric Pardinho RHP   Born: 01/05/01   Age: 19   Bats: R   Throws: R   Height: 5'10"   Weight: 155   Origin: International Free Agent, 2017

YEAR	TEAM	LVL	AGE	W	L	SV	G	GS	IP	H	HR	BB/9	K/9	K	GB%	BABIP	WHIP	ERA	DRA	WARP	MPH	FB%	WHF	CSP
2018	BLU	RK	17	4	3	0	11	11	50	37	5	2.9	11.5	64	47%	.274	1.06	2.88	1.45	2.5				
2019	LNS	A	18	1	1	0	7	7	33²	29	1	3.5	8.0	30	44%	.304	1.25	2.41	4.68	0.2				
2020	TOR	MLB	19	2	2	0	33	0	35	35	6	4.0	7.9	31	41%	.293	1.45	4.92	4.92	0.1				

Comparables: Jordan Lyles, Pedro Avila, Lewis Thorpe

The bad: Pardinho pitched fewer total innings in 2019 than the prior year after elbow soreness shut him down in spring training. The Jays took an extraordinarily cautious approach in handling the Brazilian sensation, keeping him out of action until June and then ending his season six weeks later. The good: the diminutive righty will not turn 20 until after the 2020 season, and he impressed in Low-A ball even with a compacted schedule. He'll need to add to his frame and show some extra durability to remain a starter, but there has been precious little to indicate Pardinho cannot deliver on the incredible promise he showed as a 15-year-old pitching in the World Baseball Classic.

────────────────── ★ ★ ★ *2020 Top 101 Prospect* **#19** ★ ★ ★ ──────────────────

Nate Pearson RHP   Born: 08/20/96   Age: 23   Bats: R   Throws: R   Height: 6'6"   Weight: 245   Origin: Round 1, 2017 Draft (#28 overall)

YEAR	TEAM	LVL	AGE	W	L	SV	G	GS	IP	H	HR	BB/9	K/9	K	GB%	BABIP	WHIP	ERA	DRA	WARP	MPH	FB%	WHF	CSP
2017	VAN	A-	20	0	0	0	7	7	19	6	0	2.4	11.4	24	40%	.158	0.58	0.95	1.01	0.9				
2019	DUN	A+	22	3	0	0	6	6	21	10	2	1.3	15.0	35	35%	.229	0.62	0.86	1.59	0.9				
2019	NHP	AA	22	1	4	0	16	16	62²	41	4	3.0	9.9	69	40%	.250	0.99	2.59	3.16	1.4				
2019	BUF	AAA	22	1	0	0	3	3	18	12	2	1.5	7.5	15	44%	.208	0.83	3.00	3.61	0.5				
2020	TOR	MLB	23	3	3	0	14	8	47	46	8	3.6	10.0	52	40%	.313	1.40	4.72	4.70	0.4				

Comparables: Clay Buchholz, Marco Gonzales, Daniel Hudson

Limited to just a single outing in the 2018 regular season, the impetus was on Pearson to perform last year, particularly with the system's best two prospects graduating and the organization having an obvious dearth of premiere or even reliable pitching. Pearson is not just a starter but an education company, though, and he did plenty of both learning and schooling in 2019. Hilariously overqualified for High-A, he steamrolled through Double-A as well, even acquitting himself well in three starts at Buffalo to finish the season. In the end, the year was a near-unqualified success; surpassing 100 innings put to rest any lingering concerns from the freak injury that cost Pearson 2018, and he appears on the cusp of breaking into the majors later this year—he gave evaluators little choice but to vaunt him to the top of org lists with his dominating season.

Sean Reid-Foley RHP Born: 08/30/95 Age: 24 Bats: R Throws: R Height: 6'3" Weight: 220 Origin: Round 2, 2014 Draft (#49 overall)

YEAR	TEAM	LVL	AGE	W	L	SV	G	GS	IP	H	HR	BB/9	K/9	K	GB%	BABIP	WHIP	ERA	DRA	WARP	MPH	FB%	WHF	CSP
2017	NHP	AA	21	10	11	0	27	27	132²	145	22	3.6	8.3	122	42%	.318	1.49	5.09	5.50	-0.5				
2018	NHP	AA	22	5	0	0	8	8	44¹	27	3	4.1	10.6	52	55%	.240	1.06	2.03	2.66	1.4				
2018	BUF	AAA	22	7	5	0	16	16	85¹	76	5	3.2	10.3	98	43%	.318	1.24	3.90	4.06	1.4				
2018	TOR	MLB	22	2	4	0	7	7	33¹	31	6	5.7	11.3	42	36%	.312	1.56	5.13	4.95	0.1	95.9	63.2	13.1	47.3
2019	BUF	AAA	23	3	5	0	20	19	89	78	13	6.6	10.6	105	44%	.293	1.61	6.47	4.95	1.5				
2019	TOR	MLB	23	2	4	0	9	6	31²	33	5	6.0	8.0	28	42%	.298	1.71	4.26	7.57	-0.6	95.1	50.2	11.2	46.2
2020	TOR	MLB	24	2	2	0	41	0	43	42	8	5.2	8.9	43	42%	.294	1.56	5.52	5.20	0.0	95.3	57.8	12.4	48.1

Comparables: Touki Toussaint, Zack Littell, Robert Stephenson

On August 14th, history was made as Reid-Foley pitched to the Rangers' Isiah Kiner-Falefa, creating MLB's first-ever pitcher-hitter matchup with two hyphenated last names. For those in the know, the factoid sparked a debate over whether this first was interesting-boring, or whether it was bad-worse. Entering the season as the Jays' seventh-ranked prospect, Reid-Foley's issues with command only intensified; he walked at least six per nine in both Triple-A and Toronto. Even more concerning, the 24-year-old's fastball dipped more than a full tick—things were so grim that the Blue Jays seemed perfectly justified not calling up Reid-Foley in September. At this point, Reid-Foley's development is clearly off-track, and there's little in his career to show that the command issues are a blip.

Tanner Roark RHP Born: 10/05/86 Age: 33 Bats: R Throws: R Height: 6'2" Weight: 240 Origin: Round 25, 2008 Draft (#753 overall)

YEAR	TEAM	LVL	AGE	W	L	SV	G	GS	IP	H	HR	BB/9	K/9	K	GB%	BABIP	WHIP	ERA	DRA	WARP	MPH	FB%	WHF	CSP
2017	WAS	MLB	30	13	11	0	32	30	181¹	178	23	3.2	8.2	166	49%	.300	1.33	4.67	3.89	3.4	94.6	56.2	10.7	45.3
2018	WAS	MLB	31	9	15	0	31	30	180¹	181	24	2.5	7.3	146	43%	.296	1.28	4.34	4.89	0.9	93.5	59.2	9.2	46.9
2019	CIN	MLB	32	6	7	0	21	21	110¹	119	14	3.1	8.8	108	38%	.333	1.42	4.24	5.27	0.6	94.3	61	9.9	44.9
2019	OAK	MLB	32	4	3	0	10	10	55	61	14	2.1	8.2	50	35%	.301	1.35	4.58	6.73	-0.6	93.7	61	9.5	48.7
2020	TOR	MLB	33	8	7	0	28	28	119	119	20	2.8	8.1	107	38%	.291	1.31	4.52	4.53	1.4	93.0	58.4	9.7	45.7

Comparables: Andrew Cashner, Daniel Hudson, Matt Shoemaker

Roark's numbers generally vacillate based on how well he suppresses homers. When the baseballs were normal in the early part of his career, Roark shined. In subsequent years, as hitters have benefited from a ball increasingly composed of the active ingredients in Silly Putty, his HR/FB rate soared and his performance commensurately dipped. Taken together, Roark's history as a strike-thrower capable of eating innings suggests he'll have his uses going forward. But free agency just isn't what it used to be, especially for sorta-athletic 33-year-old pitchers without a manifestly compelling explanation for his middling performance. Therefore, it was a pleasant surprise to see Roark get a two-year contract from the Blue Jays worth $24 million.

Jordan Romano RHP Born: 04/21/93 Age: 27 Bats: R Throws: R Height: 6'4" Weight: 200 Origin: Round 10, 2014 Draft (#294 overall)

YEAR	TEAM	LVL	AGE	W	L	SV	G	GS	IP	H	HR	BB/9	K/9	K	GB%	BABIP	WHIP	ERA	DRA	WARP	MPH	FB%	WHF	CSP
2017	DUN	A+	24	7	5	0	28	26	138	141	2	3.5	9.0	138	38%	.344	1.41	3.39	5.30	-0.1				
2018	NHP	AA	25	11	8	0	25	25	137¹	122	15	2.7	8.2	125	38%	.279	1.19	4.13	3.82	2.4				
2019	BUF	AAA	26	2	2	5	24	3	37²	37	8	3.3	12.7	53	40%	.333	1.35	5.73	4.27	0.8				
2019	TOR	MLB	26	0	2	0	17	0	15¹	17	4	5.3	12.3	21	51%	.351	1.70	7.63	4.07	0.2	97.2	63.7	14.1	45.8
2020	TOR	MLB	27	2	2	0	35	0	37	32	7	4.0	9.8	40	40%	.274	1.32	4.45	4.42	0.3	96.7	64.4	14.3	46.3

Comparables: Seth Lugo, Phillips Valdez, Mike Bolsinger

Selected in the Rule 5 Draft last winter and passing from the White Sox to Rangers before being returned after failing to scratch the Texas bullpen, Romano hit the bigs anyways in 2019. Finally completing a long-expected move to the bullpen, the flamethrower gave a number of reasons for confidence in the choice. The ERA was rough, both in Triple-A and his three stints as a Blue Jay, but bushels of strikeouts and grounders give fans license to dream on improvement. Romano may just be a two-pitch reliever at this point, but with a biting slider that can get whiffs against both righties and lefties, Romano has as good a chance as anyone to emerge as the heir to Ken Giles in the Great White North.

Hyun-Jin Ryu LHP Born: 03/25/87 Age: 33 Bats: R Throws: L Height: 6'3" Weight: 255 Origin: International Free Agent, 2013

YEAR	TEAM	LVL	AGE	W	L	SV	G	GS	IP	H	HR	BB/9	K/9	K	GB%	BABIP	WHIP	ERA	DRA	WARP	MPH	FB%	WHF	CSP
2017	LAN	MLB	30	5	9	1	25	24	126²	128	22	3.2	8.2	116	48%	.299	1.37	3.77	4.18	2.0	92.6	36.8	11.4	41
2018	LAN	MLB	31	7	3	0	15	15	82¹	68	9	1.6	9.7	89	47%	.281	1.01	1.97	2.45	2.7	92.4	37	12.6	49.8
2019	LAN	MLB	32	14	5	0	29	29	182²	160	17	1.2	8.0	163	53%	.280	1.01	2.32	3.03	5.4	92.5	40.6	12.4	47.5
2020	TOR	MLB	33	10	7	0	26	26	143	132	20	1.9	8.3	131	51%	.281	1.14	3.39	3.60	3.1	91.5	38.4	12	46.1

Comparables: Kris Medlen, Shane Reynolds, Ron Guidry

It's a wonder that Ryu is even pitching. Labrum tears have felled better pitchers than him, and Ryu's rehabilitation was complicated by an additional elbow surgery. Following a near two-year absence, the lefty re-established himself as an effective starter in 2017, found another gear in 2018, and authored a Cy-worthy season last year. Ryu wrote in black ink, too, leading the league in ERA and walks-per-nine, across 29 starts. A late-season swoon that saw him relent to the year of the homer paired with some "load management" from the Dodgers to ultimately sink his chances to take home the hardware.

Ryu accepted the qualifying offer last offseason, taking a chance on himself and his health. He won that gamble and headed into free agency looking for a more significant guarantee in both years and dollars. Despite what must have been a close eye on MRIs of his shoulder and groin, he got just that by signing a four-year deal with the Blue Jays worth $80 million. The underlying peripherals that say he's more of a fringe frontline arm than the ace he was in 2019, but the story of his climb back up the mountain is an inspiration.

Matt Shoemaker RHP   Born: 09/27/86   Age: 33   Bats: R   Throws: R   Height: 6'2"   Weight: 225   Origin: Undrafted Free Agent, 2008

YEAR	TEAM	LVL	AGE	W	L	SV	G	GS	IP	H	HR	BB/9	K/9	K	GB%	BABIP	WHIP	ERA	DRA	WARP	MPH	FB%	WHF	CSP
2017	LAA	MLB	30	6	3	0	14	14	77²	73	15	3.2	8.0	69	40%	.278	1.30	4.52	5.86	-0.2	94.4	49.5	12.4	45.6
2018	LAA	MLB	31	2	2	0	7	7	31	29	3	2.9	9.6	33	44%	.313	1.26	4.94	5.60	-0.1	94.1	47.1	13.4	46.2
2019	TOR	MLB	32	3	0	0	5	5	28²	16	3	2.8	7.5	24	51%	.183	0.87	1.57	4.57	0.4	93.2	46.7	13.9	40.9
2020	TOR	MLB	33	5	4	0	15	15	80	78	14	3.2	9.0	80	43%	.292	1.33	4.60	4.58	0.9	92.9	47.6	12.9	43.3

Comparables: Tanner Roark, Collin McHugh, Chris Rusin

Through the first four starts of Shoemaker's first run with a team based outside of Anaheim (and the United States), it seemed that he was back to the form that made him a valuable back-of-the-rotation piece for the Angels—or better, given the 1.75 ERA he entered start number five with. That one only lasted three (scoreless) frames, however, before Shoemaker suffered a nasty and demoralizing knee injury: a torn ACL that ended his seventh year and contributed to the 21 starters Toronto used in 2019. After three consecutive years throwing at least 135 innings with above-average DRAs, Shoemaker has had a more bedraggled trio of campaigns than, well, an oft-cobbled shoe. Entering his last year of arbitration eligibility, the 33-year-old will need to break this streak of injury-shortened seasons at three to find a guaranteed deal in free agency.

Trent Thornton RHP   Born: 09/30/93   Age: 26   Bats: R   Throws: R   Height: 6'0"   Weight: 195   Origin: Round 5, 2015 Draft (#139 overall)

YEAR	TEAM	LVL	AGE	W	L	SV	G	GS	IP	H	HR	BB/9	K/9	K	GB%	BABIP	WHIP	ERA	DRA	WARP	MPH	FB%	WHF	CSP
2017	CCH	AA	23	1	2	0	4	3	16¹	25	2	0.0	7.2	13	57%	.377	1.53	6.06	6.37	-0.3				
2017	FRE	AAA	23	8	4	0	21	20	115	137	12	1.8	6.9	88	47%	.338	1.39	5.09	5.02	0.8				
2018	FRE	AAA	24	9	8	0	24	22	124¹	118	13	2.2	8.8	122	42%	.304	1.20	4.42	4.08	2.0				
2019	TOR	MLB	25	6	9	0	32	29	154¹	156	24	3.6	8.7	149	34%	.301	1.41	4.84	6.08	-0.6	94.8	46.5	10.9	43.2
2020	TOR	MLB	26	6	5	0	32	15	91	90	16	3.6	8.5	87	35%	.292	1.38	4.76	4.71	0.8	94.4	47.3	11.1	44

Comparables: Andrew Moore, P.J. Walters, John Gant

Thornton, the 2018 Arizona Fall League roommate of Forrest Whitley before being dealt to Toronto, had a subsequent season in many ways on the opposite end of the spectrum from the top prospect. For one, Thornton not only debuted with Toronto but spent the entire season in the bigs and the rotation, leading the team in both starts and innings. The results were middling, but likely enough to earn the UNC product a spot this year in Toronto's depleted rotation. He also had the winter to continue working on the changeup and curve grips Clay Buchholz helped him develop. But ultimately, the biggest difference between the two former roommates is that Thornton is the kind of placeholder that gets moved aside when a prospect like Whitley is ready. Fortunately for the 25-year-old sophomore, that doesn't appear to be an imminent concern in this organization.

Jacob Waguespack RHP   Born: 11/05/93   Age: 26   Bats: R   Throws: R   Height: 6'6"   Weight: 235   Origin: Round 37, 2012 Draft (#1126 overall)

YEAR	TEAM	LVL	AGE	W	L	SV	G	GS	IP	H	HR	BB/9	K/9	K	GB%	BABIP	WHIP	ERA	DRA	WARP	MPH	FB%	WHF	CSP
2017	CLR	A+	23	6	5	1	24	10	68¹	63	3	3.2	9.6	73	46%	.321	1.27	3.29	4.35	0.6				
2017	REA	AA	23	3	2	0	7	6	37	37	2	3.9	8.5	35	50%	.327	1.43	3.65	3.94	0.5				
2018	REA	AA	24	1	1	0	7	7	29¹	31	0	4.9	9.5	31	59%	.352	1.60	3.99	4.90	0.1				
2018	LEH	AAA	24	3	5	1	14	8	53¹	54	4	3.4	8.1	48	52%	.323	1.39	5.06	5.81	-0.2				
2018	BUF	AAA	24	2	4	0	7	6	39¹	47	3	2.3	7.6	33	54%	.346	1.45	5.03	5.82	-0.2				
2019	BUF	AAA	25	2	6	0	12	11	52²	57	9	4.3	8.9	52	48%	.324	1.56	5.30	5.39	0.7				
2019	TOR	MLB	25	5	5	0	16	13	78	75	12	3.3	7.3	63	41%	.279	1.33	4.38	5.66	0.0	94.6	48.4	10.8	46.5
2020	TOR	MLB	26	3	3	0	38	3	53	55	10	3.9	7.4	44	44%	.289	1.46	5.22	5.06	0.2	94.2	49.2	11	47.3

Comparables: Brandon Workman, Erick Fedde, Charles Brewer

Waguespack made his MLB debut last season, the near dictionary definition of replacement level over his 78 innings, but still showed enough to get another look for the Jays rotation in 2020. If the big righty can bring his ground-ball rate back up after the bad sort of regression last season, he should be able to cement himself as a placeholder for Nate Pearson's eventual ascent. He lost more than two ticks of velocity between May and September, so it remains to be seen if the rigors of a full season agree with him. Though if he doesn't do a better job of keeping the ball in the yard, we may never truly find out.

Simeon Woods Richardson RHP   Born: 09/27/00   Age: 19   Bats: R   Throws: R   Height: 6'3"   Weight: 210   Origin: Round 2, 2018 Draft (#48 overall)

YEAR	TEAM	LVL	AGE	W	L	SV	G	GS	IP	H	HR	BB/9	K/9	K	GB%	BABIP	WHIP	ERA	DRA	WARP	MPH	FB%	WHF	CSP
2018	MTS	RK	17	1	0	1	5	2	11¹	9	0	3.2	11.9	15	50%	.321	1.15	0.00	1.39	0.6				
2018	KNG	RK	17	0	0	0	2	2	6	6	1	0.0	16.5	11	38%	.417	1.00	4.50	1.97	0.3				
2019	COL	A	18	3	8	0	20	20	78¹	78	5	2.0	11.1	97	50%	.356	1.21	4.25	5.04	0.1				
2019	DUN	A+	18	3	2	0	6	6	28¹	18	1	2.2	9.2	29	38%	.254	0.88	2.54	3.05	0.7				
2020	TOR	MLB	19	2	2	0	33	0	35	35	5	4.1	9.2	36	44%	.306	1.44	4.78	4.83	0.1				

Comparables: Jordan Lyles, Lewis Thorpe, Mike Soroka

In an interview before he was drafted in 2018, Woods Richardson said "I like being in control and making batters uncomfortable." Presumably, the 19-year-old and one-half of Toronto's return for Marcus Stroman is enjoying his new responsibility; taking control of the trade and making Brodie Van Wagenen uncomfortable. Anthony Kay may have the higher floor, but it's Woods Richardson with the vastly superior ceiling. After sputtering through a tough May, the Texan dominated both the South Atlantic and Florida State Leagues at the ripe age of 18, holding opposing batters to a .197/.246/.283 batting line over his last 70-plus innings of the season. Armed with a fastball that sits in the mid-90s but hit triple-digits from time to time and a curveball that gave hitters 4-5 years older than him fits, Woods Richardson has one of the most exciting one-two punches in the lower minors. The lack of a third pitch brings bullpen creep with it, but given he'll still be a teenager for the entirety of 2020, that concern can wait.

Shun Yamaguchi RHP   Born: 07/11/87   Age: 32   Bats: R   Throws: R   Height: 6'2"   Weight: 198   Origin: International Free Agent, 2019

The 2019 Blue Jays burned through rotation options more frequently than Emily Gilmore changed housemaids. Predictably, they spent the offseason tweaking their starting five. Yamaguchi might be the most unknown of the additions. His track record in Japan saw him serve as a frontline starter for much of the last seven years. He doesn't have great stuff—his fastball averages 90 mph and neither of his breaking balls are what you would classify as high-grade offerings—but his splitter is a legitimate weapon and he should serve as a useful reliever if nothing else.

LINEOUTS

Hitters

HITTER	POS	TEAM	LVL	AGE	PA	R	2B	3B	HR	RBI	BB	K	SB	CS	AVG/OBP/SLG	DRC+	VORP	BABIP	BRR	FRAA	WARP
Anthony Alford	CF	TOR	MLB	24	30	3	0	0	1	1	1	11	2	0	.179/.233/.286	66	-0.4	.250	0.3	LF(6): -0.3, RF(5): 0.0	0.0
	CF	BUF	AAA	24	319	46	16	3	7	37	31	94	22	8	.259/.343/.411	95	7.8	.365	1.4	RF(26): 3.8, CF(24): -4.4	0.8
Jonathan Davis	CF	TOR	MLB	27	95	8	1	0	2	6	5	24	3	1	.181/.266/.265	75	0.4	.224	0.3	CF(33): -2.8, RF(2): -0.1	-0.2
	CF	BUF	AAA	27	352	64	19	3	10	36	40	83	13	4	.262/.382/.449	122	18.4	.333	1.5	CF(48): 3.5, LF(22): -2.2	2.1
Santiago Espinal	MI	BUF	AAA	24	112	11	6	0	2	14	7	23	2	2	.317/.360/.433	101	4.8	.392	0.9	2B(18): 1.9, SS(11): -0.1	0.6
	MI	NHP	AA	24	409	46	21	1	5	57	35	50	10	11	.278/.343/.381	126	15.8	.310	-2.5	2B(51): 3.3, SS(22): 0.9	3.0
Alen Hanson	2B	BUF	AAA	26	180	19	3	1	3	18	9	39	7	2	.187/.232/.271	31	-13.1	.224	0.4	2B(22): -0.6, 3B(20): -0.5	-0.9
	2B	TOR	MLB	26	48	5	0	0	0	4	3	17	1	0	.163/.229/.163	59	-1.3	.259	-0.1	2B(8): -0.6, RF(5): 0.1	-0.2
Miguel Hiraldo	3B	BLU	Rk+	18	256	43	20	1	7	37	14	36	11	3	.300/.348/.481	125	20.5	.328	1.3		1.7
Leonardo Jimenez	SS	BLU	Rk+	18	245	34	13	2	0	22	21	42	2	1	.298/.377/.377	120	17.0	.368	1.5		1.6
Alejandro Kirk	C	DUN	A+	20	276	26	25	0	4	36	38	31	2	0	.288/.395/.446	154	18.4	.317	-3.4	C(67): 0.8	2.4
	C	LNS	A	20	96	15	6	1	3	8	18	8	1	0	.299/.427/.519	162	10.4	.299	0.9	C(17): 0.1	1.1
Gabriel Moreno	C	LNS	A	19	341	47	17	5	12	52	22	38	7	1	.280/.337/.485	130	23.6	.282	0.4	C(54): 1.0	2.5
Samad Taylor	2B	DUN	A+	20	384	48	20	3	7	38	49	107	26	10	.216/.325/.364	98	14.9	.292	2.9	2B(89): -2.9, 3B(13): 0.0	1.1
Breyvic Valera	INF	SWB	AAA	27	348	44	18	2	13	49	34	34	8	6	.315/.388/.515	130	21.7	.320	-2.1	SS(30): -3.1, 3B(28): -1.6	2.1
	INF	NYA	MLB	27	37	5	1	1	0	3	4	5	0	0	.219/.324/.313	91	0.7	.259	0.1	2B(12): 0.8	0.2
	INF	TOR	MLB	27	15	2	1	0	1	3	0	2	0	0	.267/.267/.533	102	0.7	.250	0.0	SS(2): -0.1, 2B(2): 0.0	0.0
	INF	SAC	AAA	27	92	10	3	0	1	7	16	10	2	1	.257/.396/.338	104	5.6	.286	-0.1	2B(16): 1.6, SS(8): 0.1	0.5
Forrest Wall	CF	BUF	AAA	23	53	9	3	0	2	4	6	14	1	0	.255/.340/.447	99	0.0	.323	-0.1	LF(12): 0.9	0.2
	CF	NHP	AA	23	469	70	27	4	9	41	49	109	13	8	.270/.353/.419	134	31.0	.347	2.6	CF(82): 4.0, LF(16): 0.0	3.8
Chavez Young	OF	DUN	A+	21	448	53	17	4	6	43	35	102	24	11	.247/.315/.354	85	5.5	.314	-0.4	CF(85): -0.5, RF(21): 3.6	0.9

"Injury-prone" is a label too hastily affixed, but applies to **Anthony Alford**, who has never reached 500 plate appearances in a season and looks overmatched in the majors. ⓧ **Jonathan Davis** made one of the catches of the year in his native center, ranging deep and to the left before making a full-extension Superman catch. Unfortunately the rest of the season was much more Clark Kent, with the slight right-handed outfielder failing to break .300 in any triple slash category. ⓧ **Santiago Espinal** made history in June as the first player in affiliated ball this century to steal home for a walk-off victory. He also impressed so much at Double-A that he was named an Eastern League All-Star and earned a promotion to Buffalo in August. ⓧ All anyone could talk about when discussing Triple-A in 2019 was offense, which must have been frustrating to **Alen Hanson** as he barely broke a .500 OPS in 180 plate appearances with Buffalo. ⓧ **Miguel Hiraldo** is not mimicking the meteoric path a few fellow Blue Jays prospects (and international signees) have, but there's still a lot to be encouraged by. The bat impressed in the Appalachian League, though a future at shortstop is looking less probable than at second base. ⓧ This teenage glove appears to have turned around enough to box out teammate Miguel Hiraldo at the six more often than not, qualifying as a mutation. At the plate, though, while he has the eye of a ninja, **Leonardo Jimenez** doesn't quite have that turtle power yet, as he still stands without a professional homer. ⓧ With a build more Kirk Gibson than romance novel, **Alejandro Kirk** will need to continue hitting and catching to prove his short and stout frame can succeed at the upper levels of affiliated ball. ⓧ Catchers who can hit are like Starburst: a juicy contradiction. **Gabriel Moreno** still has a ways to go before he'll have a chance to swat in the majors, but his 11 percent strikeout rate as a teen in the Midwest League was another indication this is an advanced bat in the making. ⓧ The second piece (after Thomas Pannone) Toronto acquired in the Joe Smith trade, the Blue Jays have moved **Samad Taylor** aggressively and the second baseman has rewarded their actions by holding his own despite his relative youth. ⓧ **Breyvic Valera** is destined to jump from team to team, filling in defensively whenever the injury bug strikes or a team is tanking as a switch-hitter who works his walks. ⓧ It's been a long road for **Forrest Wall**, the former Rockies first-round pick in 2014, but he finally reached Triple-A at the end of the 2019 season and the strides he's made with his center field defense give him a fighting chance at a fourth outfielder role. ⓧ Bearing the surnames of two former AL West All-Star infielders, **Chavez Young** plays against type in the outfield but he plays it well. However, the 39th-round pick struggled at the plate while attempting to navigate the better arms throughout the Florida State League.

Pitchers

PITCHER	TEAM	LVL	AGE	W	L	SV	G	GS	IP	H	HR	BB/9	K/9	K	GB%	BABIP	WHIP	ERA	DRA	WARP	MPH	FB%	WHF	CSP
Travis Bergen	SAC	AAA	25	0	0	1	15	0	16^2	13	2	5.4	8.1	15	46%	.250	1.38	3.78	4.24	0.3				
	SFN	MLB	25	2	0	0	21	0	19^2	18	4	4.1	8.2	18	39%	.264	1.37	5.49	5.27	0.0	92.4	68.9	7	47.8
Maximo Castillo	DUN	A+	20	11	5	0	24	24	130^1	115	8	1.9	7.9	114	39%	.290	1.10	2.69	3.81	1.9				
A.J. Cole	COH	AAA	27	0	1	2	13	0	17	10	2	2.6	11.1	21	36%	.235	0.88	3.18	2.73	0.6				
	CLE	MLB	27	3	1	1	25	0	26	31	4	2.8	10.4	30	31%	.355	1.50	3.81	6.45	-0.3	96.3	45	15.8	48.8
Yennsy Diaz	NHP	AA	22	11	9	0	26	24	144^1	125	12	3.3	7.2	116	42%	.270	1.23	3.74	4.82	0.2				
	TOR	MLB	22	0	0	0	1	0	0^2	1	0	54.0	0.0	0	33%	.333	7.50	27.00	10.53	0.0	98.4	66.7	9.1	30.6
Ryan Dull	SWB	AAA	29	1	0	0	4	0	6^2	3	1	1.4	5.4	4	22%	.118	0.60	2.70	3.19	0.2				
	LVG	AAA	29	1	4	4	30	0	39^2	43	6	2.9	11.3	50	37%	.356	1.41	5.45	3.73	1.0				
	TOR	MLB	29	0	0	0	1	0	1^1	1	1	0.0	20.2	3	0%	.000	0.75	6.75	3.35	0.0	91.4	40	20	43.7
	NYA	MLB	29	0	0	0	1	0	2^1	5	0	11.6	15.4	4	25%	.625	3.43	19.29	9.64	-0.1	92.8	46.7	8.3	39.4
	OAK	MLB	29	0	0	0	7	0	9	19	4	4.0	8.0	8	32%	.441	2.56	12.00	8.59	-0.3	93.1	57	10.5	46.5
Ryan Feierabend	BUF	AAA	33	6	5	0	14	12	68^1	77	19	2.8	7.0	53	38%	.286	1.43	5.53	5.79	0.6				
	TOR	MLB	33	0	1	0	2	1	5^2	11	2	1.6	6.4	4	42%	.409	2.12	11.12	6.35	0.0	88.0	23.1	13.5	23.2
Thomas Hatch	TEN	AA	24	4	10	0	21	21	100	104	13	3.3	8.4	93	38%	.322	1.41	4.59	5.63	-0.8				
	NHP	AA	24	2	3	0	6	6	35^1	25	5	0.5	8.7	34	52%	.235	0.76	2.80	3.71	0.5				
Kyle Johnston	POT	A+	22	9	9	0	20	20	105	92	7	3.2	8.6	100	44%	.293	1.23	4.03	4.93	0.1				
	DUN	A+	22	1	3	0	6	4	19^2	18	2	9.2	5.9	13	46%	.296	1.93	10.07	8.53	-0.8				
Nick Kingham	TOR	MLB	27	3	1	0	11	0	21	24	4	3.4	6.0	14	48%	.317	1.52	3.00	4.92	0.1	93.5	44.7	9.9	41.3
	PIT	MLB	27	1	1	1	14	4	34^2	54	7	4.4	8.3	32	40%	.412	2.05	9.87	8.39	-1.1	93.6	44.7	9.2	47.6
Jackson McClelland	NHP	AA	24	0	2	1	32	0	42^1	33	4	4.5	8.9	42	32%	.264	1.28	2.98	4.87	-0.1				
	BUF	AAA	24	0	0	0	11	0	15	12	2	6.6	8.4	14	28%	.270	1.53	6.00	4.41	0.3				
Justin Miller	FRE	AAA	32	0	0	0	9	0	12^2	9	3	2.1	11.4	16	23%	.214	0.95	2.84	3.25	0.4				
	WAS	MLB	32	1	0	0	17	0	15^2	16	5	2.3	6.3	11	23%	.256	1.28	4.02	7.34	-0.3	94.2	79.6	10.2	48.5
Patrick Murphy	NHP	AA	24	4	7	0	18	18	84	75	7	2.9	9.2	86	53%	.285	1.21	4.71	4.44	0.5				
Hector Perez	NHP	AA	23	7	6	0	26	24	121^1	130	9	5.0	8.7	117	40%	.349	1.62	4.60	6.70	-2.6				
Jackson Rees	LNS	A	24	2	0	2	14	0	25^1	13	0	1.4	15.6	44	68%	.295	0.67	0.36	1.79	0.9				
	DUN	A+	24	3	2	7	25	0	36^1	27	1	2.7	10.9	44	61%	.289	1.05	0.99	3.53	0.5				
Clayton Richard	TOR	MLB	35	1	5	0	10	10	45^1	53	9	3.6	4.4	22	55%	.297	1.57	5.96	7.11	-0.7	92.7	72.3	6.9	48.9
Brock Stewart	BUF	AAA	27	1	1	0	2	1	8^1	13	3	3.2	6.5	6	48%	.385	1.92	7.56	6.90	0.0				
	OKL	AAA	27	5	7	0	17	16	76	97	19	4.7	7.9	67	41%	.339	1.80	7.34	7.22	-0.4				
	TOR	MLB	27	4	0	0	10	0	21^2	28	9	2.5	6.6	16	35%	.275	1.57	8.31	9.65	-1.0	93.1	54.3	9.7	47.3
	LAN	MLB	27	0	0	0	3	0	4	9	2	4.5	6.8	3	44%	.500	2.75	18.00	4.57	0.0	94.2	53.5	8.1	44.8
Kendall Williams	BLJ	Rk	18	0	0	0	6	5	16	6	0	3.9	10.7	19	36%	.167	0.81	1.12	1.93	0.7				
Josh Winckowski	LNS	A	21	6	3	0	13	13	73^2	62	3	3.2	8.7	71	56%	.299	1.19	2.32	3.74	1.3				
	DUN	A+	21	4	5	1	11	10	53^2	48	5	2.9	6.2	37	50%	.259	1.21	3.19	3.98	0.7				
T.J. Zeuch	DUN	A+	23	0	0	0	2	2	8^2	7	0	2.1	12.5	12	43%	.143	1.04	4.15	2.19	0.3				
	BUF	AAA	23	4	3	0	13	13	78	70	6	3.7	4.5	39	58%	.256	1.31	3.69	3.95	2.1				
	TOR	MLB	23	1	2	0	5	3	22^2	22	2	4.4	7.9	20	48%	.303	1.46	4.76	5.30	0.1	94.0	52.5	9.9	41.3

A Rule 5 pick who spent most of his year in the Giants organization, **Travis Bergen** was returned to the Blue Jays. The 26-year-old southpaw has low-90s heat and leans on a curveball as his secondary offering. ⓧ **Maximo Castillo** came in third among Florida State League starters in both innings pitched and ERA and has progressed purposefully since his 2015 signing. ⓧ **A.J. Cole** didn't go platinum with no features, but he did utilize a new slider-heavy approach to strike out a quarter of the batters he faced before a shoulder impingement shortened his season. ⓧ **Yennsy Díaz** made his MLB debut on August 4th and recorded two outs of the seven batters he faced, but his four walks gave him 54.0 walks per nine in his abbreviated rookie season. He also topped out near 98, tossed a full season of average innings in Double A and is still just 23 years old, so he'll have opportunities to bring that egregious number down. ⓧ Americans have been been desensitized to violence by a variety of parameters but that doesn't mean we should feel good about shipping **Ryan Dull** to Canada just to see how they react to what batters do to his pitches. ⓧ It had been five years since **Ryan Feierabend** last appeared in the majors when the Jays added him to their roster last May. The knuckleballer was on the roster six days, but at least it got him his first comment in a decade! ⓧ A former rising prospect in the Cubs system with a big fastball, **Thomas Hatch** was sent up North when the Jays traded David Phelps to Chicago. No word on if the transition from Double-A Tennessee to his new affiliate in New Hampshire made Hatch chilly. ⓧ Toronto's return for Daniel Hudson, the Nationals' sixth-round pick from 2017, and perhaps the most tenuous of GM Ross Atkins' superior "42 years of team control" presumption, **Kyle Johnston** has yet to master High-A (4.97 ERA) in three separate stints dating back to 2018. ⓧ **Nick Kingham** finally met his fate in the bullpen last year, but the transition didn't take, and the 28-year-old was thrice designated. It appears the high end of his outcome range was taken by his 2015 Tommy John surgery, but the SK Wyverns have made a small bet that his fastball will look better in Korea. ⓧ **Jackson McClelland** could not maintain the sky-high punchout rates that earned him a promotion to Double-A at the end of 2018, but he still showed enough to be promoted to Triple-A for the end of 2019. If this pattern holds, expect to see the 25-year-old struggle to strike out six per nine and still be called up by year's end. ⓧ At 28, **Julian Merryweather** is not slightly older than the rest of the Blue Jays pitching prospects, but that's in part due to his elbow being a fairweather friend with Tommy John surgery costing him nearly all of the last two seasons. ⓧ Unmemorable is actually the highest compliment one can give a member of the Nationals bullpen in the first half. **Justin Miller** sure was there, featuring an unspectacular fastball-slider arsenal and posting boring numbers across the board before being sent into hibernation with the Fresno Grizzlies for the remainder of the season. ⓧ How unusual can a toe tap be? Extremely, in **Patrick Murphy**'s case—he's a pitcher. This quirk became a major problem in early June when Murphy was informed that his timing mechanism was illegal, representing a second step towards home. Those two steps forward became one step back: his ERA doubled amidst an emergency delivery overhaul. ⓧ As long as **Hector Perez** keeps putting up walk rates at or above five per nine innings, Annuals will keep forecasting a move to the bullpen. If the Blue Jays don't pull the plug soon, their paucity of starters might force Perez and his lack of control into an uncomfortable and possibly unwatchable situation. ⓧ In 2018, **Jackson Rees** was undrafted out of the University of Hawaii, signing with the Blue Jays a week after the draft for a lowly $1,000. A year later, he was one of the most dominant relievers in the low minors and a Fall Star in the AFL on the strength of his deception and a funky slider that hitters have trouble tracking. ⓧ Last September 12th, the Blue Jays official Twitter wished **Clayton Richard** a happy 36th birthday with the help of sponsor (and still-extant-in-Canada) Toys R Us, differentiable from the defunct US incarnation thanks to a handy maple leaf in the R's counter. That same day, the team released Richard, proving that classic Canadian hospitality does not translate to American-helmed front offices. ⓧ **Brock Stewart**'s 2019 featured two blue teams spread across a border, and he underwhelmed for both; the multi-inning role Toronto tried the onetime Dodgers product in took no better than his sporadic usage across four years in the valley. ⓧ **Kendall Williams**, Toronto's second-round pick in 2019, got nearly $150,000 over slot to spurn a commitment to Vanderbilt and hit the ground running in rookie ball with an unusually broad pitch mix (two fastballs, a curve, a slider and a change) for a starter of his age. ⓧ If **Josh Winckowski** continues his rapid ascent to the bump in Toronto, we could soon be following a Winck with a Giles, much to the delight of Harry Connick Jr fans everywhere. ⓧ He isn't the flashiest of former first-rounders, but **T.J. Zeuch** climbed to the majors despite striking out just a batter every other inning at Triple-A. Then again, one of those starts was a no-hitter in which the big right-hander struck out just three, so whatever works.

WASHINGTON NATIONALS

Essay by Kelsey McKinney

Player comments by Sydney Bergman, Jarrett Seidler and BP staff

Every year of my childhood just before the weather fully began to warm, I caught a mysterious, undiagnosable, 24-hour illness that absolutely demanded that I could not go to school or work. When I was in elementary school, my dad would pull me out of class in the morning. I was sick, you see. So sick. Very sick. I absolutely had to be taken to a sacred holy place that could cure me. It just so happened that the perfect remedy for my illness was the smell of freshly cut grass, and the rumble of a low-flying jet, and the taste of a hot dog. Weirdly, I always got very sick on the exact day when I could have all of these things: Opening Day.

My dad and I went together. We usually sat in the outfield, on flaming hot plastic seats, and we grinned. We nudged each other in the ribs and pointed: look at the new awnings; look at the old ladies with their scorebooks; look at our team. Every year, it was one of my best days. Every year there was the possibility that this could be The Year, our year. It vibrates in the air, the hope.

As an adult, I missed Opening Day. The city where I got my undergraduate degree didn't have a major league baseball team, and it never worked out for me to drive home. When I moved to Washington, D.C. after college, the season had already started, and I was miserable. It was summer. I had just started a new job that required me to work constantly. I was all alone in a big new city on a completely different coast and quickly acquired a healthy dose of culture shock. I had lived in Texas my entire life, and I was lonely. For the first time, I had coworkers, but I didn't have any friends. When I called home, I tried to play down how upset I was, how isolated, how even the light and the sky here looked different. When my dad updated me on the IL and the team's failures (they were always failing in new spectacular ways), I was jealous. I didn't get any of their games on my cable.

"You know," my dad said. "It wouldn't be so bad if you adopted the Nationals as your team." He had good reasons: I could learn about double-switches and the National League. I could watch all the games on TV. And plus, they were the home team. My dad himself grew up a Braves fan, and when he moved to Texas an adult, switched over to the Rangers.

NATIONALS PROSPECTUS
2019 W-L: 93-69, 2ND IN NL EAST

Pythag	.589	6th	B-Age	28.5	23rd
RS/G	5.39	6th	P-Age	30.7	29th
RA/G	4.47	9th	Salary	$197.2M	4th
DRC+	101	9th	M$/MW	$4.1M	13th
DRA	4.03	2nd	IL Days	1126	17th
FIP	4.08	6th	$ on IL	13%	10th
DER	.704	15th			

- Opened 2008
- Open air
- Natural surface
- Fence profile: 8' to 14'"

Three-Year Park Factors

Runs	Runs/RH	Runs/LH	HR/RH	HR/LH
104	104	105	108	107

Top Hitter WARP	6.3 Anthony Rendon
Top Pitcher WARP	8.3 Stephen Strasburg
Top Prospect	Carter Kieboom

2019 Hit List Ranking

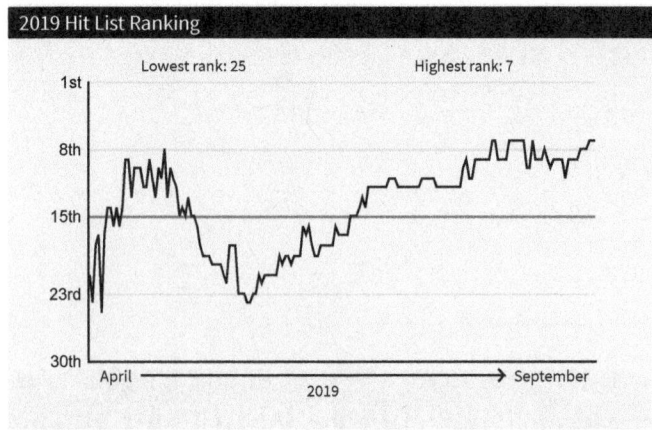

Lowest rank: 25   Highest rank: 7

Committed Payroll (in millions)

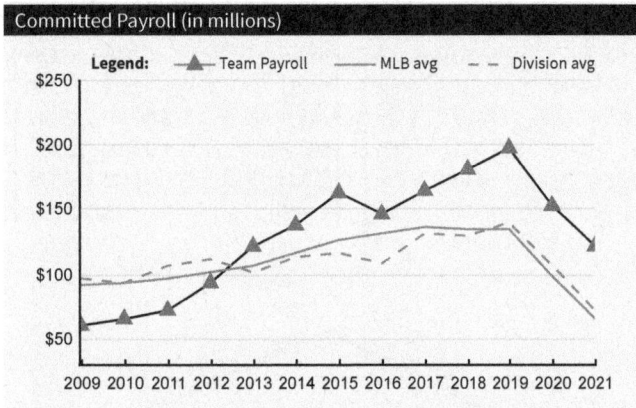

Legend: — Team Payroll   — MLB avg   – – Division avg

Farm System Ranking

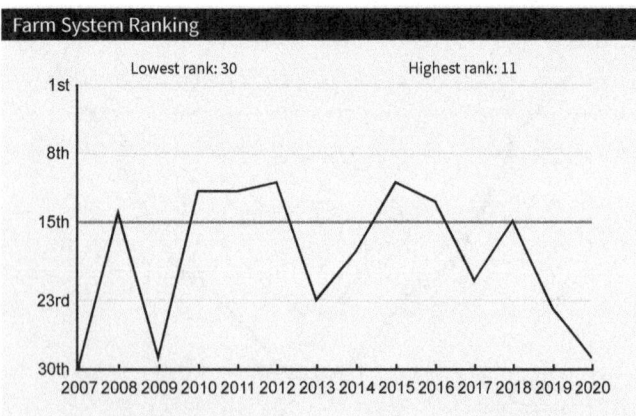

Lowest rank: 30   Highest rank: 11

Personnel

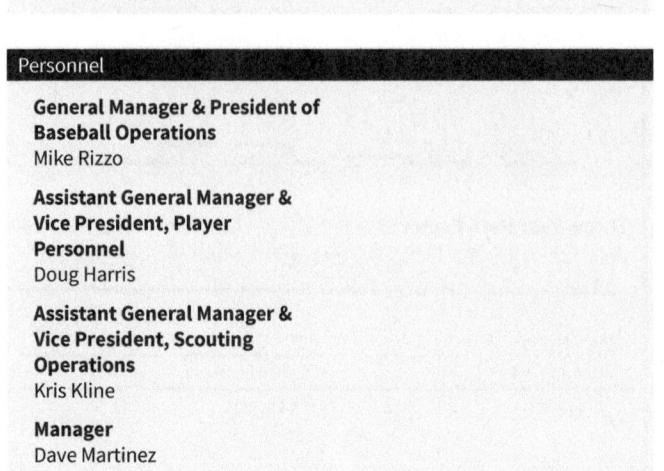

General Manager & President of Baseball Operations
Mike Rizzo

Assistant General Manager & Vice President, Player Personnel
Doug Harris

Assistant General Manager & Vice President, Scouting Operations
Kris Kline

Manager
Dave Martinez

So I began that summer to watch this new team who was all hyped up over their 10 year anniversary. It is hard to adjust to a new team, even one as newly minted as the Washington Nationals. There is a whole culture to adapt to; a history of inside jokes and truly inside baseball. So much of watching a baseball game is knowing the small things. Understanding which players have long-held grudges and which ones are hometown heroes takes time. And it was frustrating. Here I was with a team I didn't know anything about, in a city I hadn't learned yet how to love. On my birthday that year, as a special gift to me, the Washington Nationals played a franchise record breaking 5 hour and 34 minute game against the Dodgers, not yet a personal enemy, and won.

I had moved to Washington, D.C. blindly. I had a job offer and accepted it sight unseen. Whenever I told people I was moving here, to the capital city of our country, most wrinkled their noses. Why, my friends and family back home asked, would you want to live on the east coast? Why, my friends who had moved to New York asked, would you want to live in a city that only cares about politics? I quickly learned all the derogatory jokes made at the city's expense. A D.C. 8, people snickered, was a Los Angeles 3. Everyone wore suits from Brooks Brothers. No one, they said, stays there. If you outlive one administration, these people said, you can call yourself a native.

Almost six years later, I know that all of this is an ugly stereotype created by people who never had any intention of staying. Those people, I know now, are the ones who wear their childhood team's jerseys to the games, the ones who never bother to learn what this city really is. It is easy to believe them. Watching the broadcast, even, of this year's World Series games, the only parts of Washington, D.C. that got shown were the monuments and the White House and the Capitol. And while those are iconic landmarks that I, too, love to visit, they aren't the city. That is the federal district.

The city itself is as diverse and interesting and varied as any other metropolitan American city. There are independent bookstores and art galleries and Michelin-starred restaurants. There are bars near the Capitol with drink specials that accompany the C-SPAN showing of the impeachment trials and there are the bars I go to with sticky counters and a team wearing red (always red) playing on televisions. Washington, D.C. is home to both Georgetown University and Howard University. There are public schools and bus routes and almost 700,000 people who live and work here. In the spring, all of the trees bloom pink at once. It is the kind of city that makes a smart joke about its biggest issue on the license plates. They read at the bottom: "Taxation Without Representation."

At the third game of the World Series, activists stood on Half Street between still-forming condos, and handed out red flyers with the outline of the district on them. These were to advocate for D.C. statehood, something 79 percent of the residents of the city voted for in a 2016 ballot. Like Puerto Rico, the people who live in D.C. do not have any voting representation in Congress. United States citizens are entitled to representation in both the House and the Senate, and yet for decades the federal government has refused to acknowledge that living right under their noses are 700,000 people, more people than both Vermont and Wyoming, without that constitutional right. (Puerto Rico has a higher population than 20 states.)

The narrative that no one lives in D.C. for more than two years is intentional and perpetuated with purpose. That statement erases the people of color who have lived in Washington, D.C. for generations through one of the highest murder rates in America, a heroin epidemic, a basketball team named the Bullets, and a football team named something worse. Almost 50 percent of the population of D.C. is black. Residents of D.C., like Puerto Rico, have been denied their rights to vote via that erasure. When new transplants say that "no one lives in D.C. for long," they're only showing their own bias. No one *they know* stays for long. But plenty of people stay, and a lot of them call this place home. And when a place is your home, when you live there really, you root for its teams. You wear red.

I haven't been in D.C. for anywhere near as long as a lot of other Nationals fans. I sat next to an older gentleman down the first-base line at an August game who told me about the first game in the new stadium in 2008, about how he, then in his 60s, had cried real tears. He had waited for most of his life for Washington, D.C. to have a baseball team again. He'd been forced to grow up without a team to root for, and here they were, finally, back again just for him.

I learned to love D.C. because the Washington Nationals were easy to love. They gave me more first round of the playoffs flops to bemoan with my neighbors than anyone could have wanted. They gave me perfect games. They gave me racing presidents. They gave me a wunderkind outfielder with hair like Johnny Bravo, and then one who still had his round teenage face. The arms of the Washington Nationals were always open to me, and where they at first provided me freedom from my loneliness, they soon provided me with community.

That is the beauty of a team, any team. Investing in a sport emotionally gives us something to love that we don't have to do anything at all for. Turning on the game on our smartphones at our desks remind us that we're more than the job we get a paycheck for. Leaning over the bar to check the score reminds us that we're part of a bigger community than just the one that we've chosen for ourselves. At their best, sports teams remind us that it is okay to care about something with childlike enthusiasm even when we have absolutely no reason to. Sports, we often forget, are supposed to be fun. The investment in a team just for fun, not for any kind of gain, is what binds a community together, what causes strangers to tip a cap at another curly W on the street, or (in October) to raise a hand to high-five.

The 2019 Washington Nationals were something special. Despite a truly awful May, they refused to crumble into a sinkhole and never recover. I don't know what happened in that locker room over Memorial Day weekend, but whatever it was worked. The team figured out how to play baseball, but they also seemed to remember suddenly that this thing they were doing is a game. That it is supposed to be fun. Gerrardo Parra changed his walkup song for his daughter and suddenly the entire stadium was clapping along to "Baby Shark." Max Scherzer bunted a ball *into his own face* at practice and went out and pitched anyway with two black eyes, and his teammates made fun of him! They sang "Calma." They were, from June 1st on, a joy to watch.

But the most beautiful thing about this 2019 Washington Nationals team was watching them give that community to one another. When Daniel Hudson chose to support his wife through the birth of his child instead of pitching Game 1 of the NLCS, Sean Doolittle faced the press and reprimanded those who criticized him. When Scherzer's back cramped so badly he couldn't dress himself, every single one of his teammates gave statements about how impressed they were with him, how they knew he wouldn't sit if he didn't absolutely have to. They hugged Stephen Strasburg. They danced in the dugout. They snapped little baby sharks at each other from second base when they hit doubles, and whatever it is Brian Dozier is doing with his shirt off in the locker room seems to be shadily supported by them all.

This year, I begged my friends to go to Opening Day with me, but they all had to work, and were not able to be sick like me. As the day approached, I grew sadder and sadder. I hadn't been to Opening Day in ten years. It felt unjust, insane, heretical. So at the encouragement of a friend, I bought a ticket to go alone. I brought my scorebook and wore my hat, and showed up to Opening Day with a chest full of hope. That's a thing people don't tell you about Washington, D.C.: it has so much hope. Here is a city that is filled with people who voted for statehood recognition despite every barrier set in front of them. Here are some people who moved from another state to work on a campaign or in a congressional office or for an NGO because they believe that maybe, just maybe, the world can change. Here is a fanbase that despite never managing to get past the first round of the playoffs showed up on a chilly day in late March with Bryce Harper's name crossed out on their jerseys to say to one another quietly "This may be our year. This could finally be it."

When you go to a game alone, you remember how much of watching a sport is joining a community. It is human nature, even when alone, to turn to the person next to you with wide eyes when Trea Turner stretches his body out like a cat to snatch a ball out of the air. It is natural, to turn around to give high-fives when Juan Soto rockets a ball over the outfield fence. It is required that on the first day of the season, you ask the stranger next to you what he thinks the team's chances are and nod your head yes when he says, "Absolutely this is it, this will be our year," even if you don't know if he's right.

The 2019 Washington Nationals lost their first game of the season to the New York Mets 0-2. "It was a pleasure sitting next to you," my neighbor said to me when the game ended. "This may not be our year after all." For him and for myself and for all of Washington, D.C., I'm so glad he was wrong.

—Kelsey McKinney is a freelance reporter and former staff writer at Deadspin.

HITTERS

Matt Adams 1B Born: 08/31/88 Age: 31 Bats: L Throws: R Height: 6'3" Weight: 245 Origin: Round 23, 2009 Draft (#699 overall)

YEAR	TEAM	LVL	AGE	PA	R	2B	3B	HR	RBI	BB	K	SB	CS	AVG/OBP/SLG	DRC+	VORP	BABIP	BRR	FRAA	WARP
2017	SLN	MLB	28	53	4	2	0	1	7	4	17	0	0	.292/.340/.396	106	1.8	.419	-0.1	LF(6): -0.3, 1B(3): 0.1	0.2
2017	ATL	MLB	28	314	42	20	1	19	58	19	71	0	0	.271/.315/.543	109	13.6	.294	-0.6	1B(59): -3.3, LF(13): 0.5	0.6
2018	WAS	MLB	29	277	37	9	0	18	48	24	55	0	0	.257/.332/.510	110	10.8	.261	-2.3	1B(48): 0.3, LF(15): 0.7	0.7
2018	SLN	MLB	29	60	5	1	0	3	9	3	18	0	0	.158/.200/.333	115	-3.1	.167	0.0	1B(15): -0.5	0.2
2019	WAS	MLB	30	333	42	14	0	20	56	20	115	0	0	.226/.276/.465	85	-0.9	.284	-1.7	1B(79): -2.9	-0.5
2020	WAS	MLB	31	251	31	10	0	14	38	16	76	1	0	.233/.288/.463	93	5.0	.281	-0.9	1B 0, LF 0	0.5

Comparables: C.J. Cron, Mitch Moreland, Michael Cuddyer

At age 30, Adams was the youngest player to regularly play first base for the Nationals in 2019, shouldering the bulk of the season while Ryan Zimmerman recovered from a foot injury. Adams' at-bats played much younger, however, regressing to an astounding 35 percent strikeout rate, almost 10 percentage points higher than his previous career-high. A shoulder injury iced much of his August and September, and he remains who he's projected to be for much of his tenure in the majors: a bench player who can still manage to pop 20 home runs.

Asdrúbal Cabrera INF Born: 11/13/85 Age: 34 Bats: B Throws: R Height: 6'0" Weight: 205 Origin: International Free Agent, 2002

YEAR	TEAM	LVL	AGE	PA	R	2B	3B	HR	RBI	BB	K	SB	CS	AVG/OBP/SLG	DRC+	VORP	BABIP	BRR	FRAA	WARP
2017	NYN	MLB	31	540	66	32	0	14	59	50	83	3	2	.280/.351/.434	104	30.7	.310	-2.2	SS(45): -0.2, 3B(44): -1.1	1.8
2018	NYN	MLB	32	407	48	23	1	18	58	29	81	0	0	.277/.329/.488	105	29.3	.309	1.9	2B(90): -10.8	0.6
2018	PHI	MLB	32	185	20	13	0	5	17	12	38	0	0	.228/.286/.392	107	4.3	.266	0.5	SS(31): -0.6, 3B(22): -0.5	0.8
2019	WAS	MLB	33	146	24	10	1	6	40	19	18	0	0	.323/.404/.565	137	11.8	.330	-1.2	2B(31): -1.6, 3B(5): -0.3	0.9
2019	TEX	MLB	33	368	45	15	0	12	51	38	85	4	0	.235/.318/.393	95	11.7	.278	0.2	3B(93): 6.0	1.8
2020	WAS	MLB	34	294	35	17	1	12	40	26	62	2	1	.268/.339/.468	103	10.5	.311	-0.2	2B -3, 3B 0	0.9

Comparables: Cliff Pennington, Ian Kinsler, Delino DeShields

For an example of how little moves can pay off in unexpected ways, consider that the Nationals signed Cabrera in August following his release from the Rangers. Whereas he hadn't performed particularly well with Texas, instead looking like a 30-something-year-old infielder on his last legs, he dazzled with the Nationals during his second tour of duty in D.C. Cabrera hit, hit and hit some more, supplanting Brian Dozier on the depth chart by the time the postseason rolled around. He then drove in three runs in the World Series, a seven-game set in which the two teams were separated by—you guessed it—three runs. (The Astros actually outscored the Nationals by three runs, but never let facts interfere with vibes.) Every piece matters.

Starlin Castro SS Born: 03/24/90 Age: 30 Bats: R Throws: R Height: 6'2" Weight: 230 Origin: International Free Agent, 2006

YEAR	TEAM	LVL	AGE	PA	R	2B	3B	HR	RBI	BB	K	SB	CS	AVG/OBP/SLG	DRC+	VORP	BABIP	BRR	FRAA	WARP
2017	SWB	AAA	27	25	4	0	0	1	2	1	4	0	0	.333/.360/.458	123	1.3	.368	0.4	2B(4): 0.1	0.2
2017	NYA	MLB	27	473	66	18	1	16	63	23	93	2	0	.300/.338/.454	102	17.4	.347	0.5	2B(109): -4.9	1.1
2018	MIA	MLB	28	647	76	32	2	12	54	48	124	6	4	.278/.329/.400	102	32.0	.330	0.3	2B(150): -6.2	1.6
2019	MIA	MLB	29	676	68	31	4	22	86	28	111	2	2	.270/.300/.436	90	15.1	.293	-1.8	2B(117): -6.2, 3B(45): -0.3	0.6
2020	WAS	MLB	30	532	54	26	2	16	62	26	98	4	2	.264/.304/.416	86	9.7	.301	-0.1	2B -5, 3B 0	0.5

Comparables: Elvis Andrus, Jean Segura, Juan Uribe

It's hard to remember that there was a time when Castro was a top prospect; it's even harder to remember that he was once envisioned as a cornerstone of a budding Cubs juggernaut (some things do change a lot in a decade, huh?). Ten years into his major league career, and Castro managed to turn in another season of slightly below-average offense, while taking a step back in the plate discipline department. Considering Castro's other faults—he's a poor defender, he has middling power, he doesn't hit for a high average anymore—his walk rate plummeted again in 2019, sapping almost any offensive value he had. Castro's unique resilience has defined a truly bizarre march to 1600 career hits: No player above Castro on the list of active career hits leaders is younger than he is, or has played fewer seasons. Unfortunately for him, that robust career hit total is more likely to become a trivia question that an entry in the record books.

Brian Dozier 2B Born: 05/15/87 Age: 33 Bats: R Throws: R Height: 5'11" Weight: 200 Origin: Round 8, 2009 Draft (#252 overall)

YEAR	TEAM	LVL	AGE	PA	R	2B	3B	HR	RBI	BB	K	SB	CS	AVG/OBP/SLG	DRC+	VORP	BABIP	BRR	FRAA	WARP
2017	MIN	MLB	30	705	106	30	4	34	93	78	141	16	7	.271/.359/.498	123	37.9	.300	2.2	2B(152): 9.7	5.4
2018	MIN	MLB	31	462	65	21	2	16	52	46	96	8	3	.227/.307/.405	97	11.4	.256	1.6	2B(103): 1.9	1.6
2018	LAN	MLB	31	170	16	9	0	5	20	24	33	4	0	.182/.300/.350	97	-1.6	.196	-1.6	2B(45): 0.1	0.3
2019	WAS	MLB	32	482	54	20	0	20	50	61	105	3	4	.238/.340/.430	104	18.9	.271	-3.6	2B(123): -4.6, P(1): 0.0	1.0
2020	WAS	MLB	33	350	44	14	1	16	47	41	80	7	2	.230/.327/.436	101	8.4	.260	-0.1	2B 0	1.2

Comparables: Sean Rodríguez, Luis Valbuena, Kelly Johnson

Strip down Dozier's numbers for the season, and the bare fact remains that he was who he was last season: a below-average hitter with the ability to grind out at-bats by limiting his chases outside the zone. He's a dead pull hitter who—like so many of us—has only gotten entrenched in his ways as he's aged, as he's hit a total of one homer to the opposite field over the last two seasons. The history of second basemen entering their mid-30s looks a bit too much like the aftermath of a zombie apocalypse, and there's little in his profile that suggests Dozier has a second act that involves more than veteran leadership, professional at-bats and the ability to undress relievers with some late-inning power and pop.

Adam Eaton RF   Born: 12/06/88   Age: 31   Bats: L   Throws: L   Height: 5'9"   Weight: 176   Origin: Round 19, 2010 Draft (#571 overall)

YEAR	TEAM	LVL	AGE	PA	R	2B	3B	HR	RBI	BB	K	SB	CS	AVG/OBP/SLG	DRC+	VORP	BABIP	BRR	FRAA	WARP
2017	WAS	MLB	28	107	24	7	1	2	13	14	18	3	1	.297/.393/.462	100	9.4	.347	0.3	CF(20): -3.3, LF(5): 0.4	0.1
2018	WAS	MLB	29	370	55	18	1	5	33	38	64	9	1	.301/.394/.411	106	20.8	.364	0.4	RF(67): 5.7, LF(10): -0.5	1.7
2019	WAS	MLB	30	656	103	25	7	15	49	65	106	15	3	.279/.365/.428	102	17.3	.319	3.6	RF(139): 4.3, LF(7): 0.0	2.5
2020	WAS	MLB	31	595	68	28	5	15	68	58	103	13	5	.278/.362/.434	106	18.8	.322	0.9	RF 7, LF 0	2.7

Comparables: Dwight Smith, Cesar Geronimo, Bruce Aven

The truest sign of Eaton's recovery from last year's ankle injury is when he managed to stick his entire foot in his mouth concerning pay for minor league players in June. Eaton eventually walked those comments back, and showed himself to be a serviceable outfielder and a consistent hitter, and a pest in the NLCS and World Series. But one can't help but compare Eaton with a former National wunderkind, just not the one you're probably thinking of; he's a bit of subtraction by addition in light of Lucas Giolito's All-Star season. Maybe the Nationals should have tried paying him less.

Luis Garcia SS   Born: 05/16/00   Age: 20   Bats: L   Throws: R   Height: 6'2"   Weight: 190   Origin: International Free Agent, 2016

YEAR	TEAM	LVL	AGE	PA	R	2B	3B	HR	RBI	BB	K	SB	CS	AVG/OBP/SLG	DRC+	VORP	BABIP	BRR	FRAA	WARP
2017	NAT	RK	17	211	25	8	3	1	22	9	32	11	2	.302/.330/.387	97	7.5	.353	1.7	2B(25): -3.0, SS(17): 0.7	0.6
2018	HAG	A	18	323	48	14	4	3	31	19	49	8	5	.297/.335/.402	110	16.4	.343	0.7	3B(36): -4.6, SS(27): 0.4	1.0
2018	POT	A+	18	221	34	7	2	4	23	12	33	4	1	.299/.338/.412	118	9.8	.337	-0.3	SS(40): -2.7	0.9
2019	HAR	AA	19	553	66	22	4	4	30	17	86	11	5	.257/.280/.337	69	6.7	.299	3.1	SS(92): -3.9, 2B(38): 0.4	0.5
2020	WAS	MLB	20	251	21	11	1	4	23	11	50	2	1	.243/.279/.346	65	-3.6	.294	-0.1	SS 0, 2B 0	-0.4

Comparables: Jake Bauers, Mike Trout, Elvis Andrus

We measure baseball years from July 1st to June 30th, so last year was Garcia's "age-19 season." Playing the entirety of 2019 in Double-A at 19 would be an accomplishment enough, but because of his mid-May birthday, that season actually included six weeks on the front end where he was an 18-year-old in the high minors. Given that context of an incredibly—and perhaps needlessly—aggressive assignment, he held his own. It would be nice to see Garcia consolidate things offensively, and he might not have otherworldly upside. But you can do worse betting against teenagers with quick bats who are advanced enough to survive several levels higher than they should be.

Yan Gomes C   Born: 07/19/87   Age: 32   Bats: R   Throws: R   Height: 6'2"   Weight: 215   Origin: Round 10, 2009 Draft (#310 overall)

YEAR	TEAM	LVL	AGE	PA	R	2B	3B	HR	RBI	BB	K	SB	CS	AVG/OBP/SLG	DRC+	VORP	BABIP	BRR	FRAA	WARP
2017	CLE	MLB	29	383	43	15	0	14	56	31	99	0	0	.232/.309/.399	92	13.6	.283	1.7	C(103): 6.8	2.4
2018	CLE	MLB	30	435	52	26	0	16	48	21	119	0	0	.266/.313/.449	103	22.7	.336	-1.1	C(111): 9.1	3.1
2019	WAS	MLB	31	358	36	16	0	12	43	38	84	2	0	.223/.316/.389	91	14.7	.265	0.1	C(93): -1.6, 1B(1): 0.0	1.3
2020	WAS	MLB	32	350	37	16	0	13	43	25	92	1	0	.222/.287/.396	76	5.6	.268	0.1	C -1	0.4

Comparables: Matthew LeCroy, Miguel Montero, Welington Castillo

How's this for an exorcism? Gomes caught in two World Series Games 7, three years apart, the first being Cleveland's extra-innings loss to the Cubs and the second a late-inning pummeling of the Astros. The Nats acquired Gomes after taking the orthodox approach of sorting available catchers by OPS and then grabbing the best two not named Realmuto in an attempt to upgrade the position from Matt Wieters. Gomes posted a lower OPS this year than he did last season but with a career-high OBP. He emerged as a better defensive catcher than Suzuki (though who wouldn't have?), working as Pat Corbin's personal catcher and posting better numbers with Strasburg than Suzuki did in a comparable number of games.

YEAR	TEAM	P. COUNT	FRM RUNS	BLK RUNS	THRW RUNS	TOT RUNS
2017	CLE	13358	4.2	0.5	2.3	7.6
2018	CLE	15103	7.5	1.7	0.0	9.6
2019	WAS	13260	-4.3	2.8	0.7	-1.0
2020	WAS	14980	-2.0	0.5	0.4	-1.0

He also remained healthy all year, though in a diminished role, and remains a viable backup catcher now unburdened by the ghosts of 2016.

Howie Kendrick INF Born: 07/12/83 Age: 36 Bats: R Throws: R Height: 5'11" Weight: 220 Origin: Round 10, 2002 Draft (#294 overall)

YEAR	TEAM	LVL	AGE	PA	R	2B	3B	HR	RBI	BB	K	SB	CS	AVG/OBP/SLG	DRC+	VORP	BABIP	BRR	FRAA	WARP
2017	PHI	MLB	33	156	16	8	1	2	16	11	30	8	3	.340/.397/.454	108	10.4	.418	-0.7	LF(24): -0.4, 2B(10): 0.6	0.5
2017	WAS	MLB	33	178	24	8	2	7	25	11	38	4	2	.293/.343/.494	106	10.4	.342	0.6	LF(38): -3.0, 2B(5): -0.2	0.3
2018	WAS	MLB	34	160	17	14	0	4	12	5	29	1	1	.303/.331/.474	94	4.0	.350	-3.1	2B(33): -2.7, LF(6): -0.1	-0.2
2019	WAS	MLB	35	370	61	23	1	17	62	27	49	2	1	.344/.395/.572	132	24.9	.359	-2.6	1B(48): 1.8, 2B(23): 0.7	2.3
2020	WAS	MLB	36	560	63	29	2	17	68	37	98	10	4	.286/.340/.447	106	14.1	.325	-2.5	1B 7, 2B 0	2.2

Comparables: Robinson Canó, Adam Kennedy, Miguel Cairo

In another, worse universe, Kendrick would have been the last of the true DHs. He'll be in his late 30s this year, and is not a great first baseman, the last refuge of old men in the National League. But as every commentator, fellow player and likely, Joe Kelly, in a recurring nightmare he'll have for years, knows: The guy sure can hit. Age is in fact more than a number, and it wasn't clear if and how he'd recover from last year's season-ending Achilles rupture. Surely, he should diminish with time, the numbers said. Instead, he showed increased plate discipline, striking out a hair less than uber-disciplined teammate Anthony Rendon and posting a career-high exit velocity. Even in a juiced ball era, his talents lie in hitting screaming line drives to where fielders aren't. For the coming season, he'll continue providing that pop off the bench and be ready to DH when the rules allow, so long as DH stands for "Dodgers Hurter."

────────────── ★ ★ ★ *2020 Top 101 Prospect* **#11** ★ ★ ★ ──────────────

Carter Kieboom SS Born: 09/03/97 Age: 22 Bats: R Throws: R Height: 6'2" Weight: 190 Origin: Round 1, 2016 Draft (#28 overall)

YEAR	TEAM	LVL	AGE	PA	R	2B	3B	HR	RBI	BB	K	SB	CS	AVG/OBP/SLG	DRC+	VORP	BABIP	BRR	FRAA	WARP
2017	AUB	A-	19	29	4	1	0	1	4	1	2	1	0	.250/.276/.393	101	0.2	.240	0.2	SS(6): 1.1	0.2
2017	HAG	A	19	210	36	12	0	8	26	28	40	2	2	.296/.400/.497	163	20.0	.344	-0.7	SS(45): 1.4	2.3
2018	POT	A+	20	285	48	15	0	11	46	36	50	6	1	.298/.386/.494	159	31.4	.332	0.5	SS(56): -0.4	2.9
2018	HAR	AA	20	273	36	16	1	5	23	22	59	3	1	.262/.326/.395	108	13.3	.324	0.5	SS(62): 2.6	1.8
2019	FRE	AAA	21	494	79	24	3	16	79	68	100	5	2	.303/.409/.493	126	43.7	.362	1.4	SS(62): -3.7, 2B(40): 3.2	3.5
2019	WAS	MLB	21	43	4	0	0	2	2	4	16	0	0	.128/.209/.282	62	0.0	.143	0.1	SS(10): -1.0	-0.1
2020	WAS	MLB	22	420	46	19	1	14	50	38	114	1	1	.239/.316/.407	89	3.4	.305	-0.6	3B -3	0.0

Comparables: Corey Seager, Dilson Herrera, Victor Robles

The Nationals got pure magic early on in the 2018 season by utilizing the YOLO theory of player development and bringing stud prospect Juan Soto up to the majors before schedule. They went back to the well in 2019 by calling up Kieboom, one of baseball's top prospects, in late April. He lasted only ten completely overmatched games before being sent down. It was nevertheless a successful season for him on the whole; he put up a very fine campaign as a 21-year-old in his first run at Triple-A, and is still one of the top prospects in the game. But the Nats never gave him another run in The Show, even bypassing him for a seemingly deserved September call-up. He'll get another chance in 2020, one that he's actually ready for. Major League Baseball remains very, very hard, though.

Jake Noll 3B Born: 03/08/94 Age: 26 Bats: R Throws: R Height: 6'2" Weight: 195 Origin: Round 7, 2016 Draft (#214 overall)

YEAR	TEAM	LVL	AGE	PA	R	2B	3B	HR	RBI	BB	K	SB	CS	AVG/OBP/SLG	DRC+	VORP	BABIP	BRR	FRAA	WARP
2017	HAG	A	23	438	51	19	2	16	67	20	64	12	4	.270/.312/.448	124	18.0	.280	-1.5	2B(88): 0.8	2.1
2017	POT	A+	23	65	5	2	1	1	7	5	12	0	1	.190/.250/.310	52	-2.1	.217	-0.6	2B(16): -0.5	-0.2
2018	POT	A+	24	289	47	12	3	8	46	19	51	3	1	.302/.353/.460	135	20.1	.346	1.7	3B(42): 0.4, 1B(16): 0.4	2.0
2018	HAR	AA	24	260	35	8	1	3	26	14	39	4	1	.278/.328/.359	101	7.7	.318	1.8	3B(63): 8.5, 2B(1): 0.0	2.0
2019	FRE	AAA	25	489	69	24	0	11	54	26	89	5	2	.285/.327/.410	86	7.4	.331	4.6	3B(51): -1.3, 1B(50): -4.4	0.3
2019	WAS	MLB	25	13	1	1	0	0	2	1	4	0	0	.167/.231/.250	69	-0.2	.250	0.2	1B(2): 0.0, 3B(1): -0.1	0.0
2020	WAS	MLB	26	189	18	7	0	5	20	9	43	1	0	.237/.282/.365	68	-3.9	.285	-0.1	1B -2, 3B 0	-0.6

Comparables: Dale Long, Harry Agganis, Kelby Tomlinson

A little known addendum to the Saving America's Pastime Act legalized human cloning in exigent circumstances, such as when an MLB team has an MVP-caliber third baseman in a walk year. Enter Noll. Built using Ryan Zimmerman's DNA in a process known as somatic cell roster expansion and transplantation, Noll didn't match his progenitor's impressive 2005 minor league stint, instead posting respectable, but not explosive, numbers in Fresno. Still, he earned a cup of coffee look with the Nationals out of spring training, strolling into his first RBI as an off-brand Zimm—not as Mr. Walkoff but as Mr. Walkoff Walk.

Gerardo Parra OF Born: 05/06/87 Age: 33 Bats: L Throws: L Height: 5'11" Weight: 210 Origin: International Free Agent, 2004

YEAR	TEAM	LVL	AGE	PA	R	2B	3B	HR	RBI	BB	K	SB	CS	AVG/OBP/SLG	DRC+	VORP	BABIP	BRR	FRAA	WARP
2017	COL	MLB	30	425	56	24	1	10	71	20	67	2	5	.309/.341/.452	99	9.4	.343	-2.5	LF(82): 3.6, RF(22): -0.1	1.1
2018	COL	MLB	31	443	52	17	0	6	53	32	75	11	4	.284/.342/.372	96	11.2	.334	3.3	LF(111): 6.8, RF(10): 1.9	2.1
2019	SFN	MLB	32	97	8	3	0	1	6	8	18	2	1	.198/.278/.267	78	0.0	.235	0.6	LF(20): 2.2, RF(11): 3.5	0.6
2019	WAS	MLB	32	204	30	11	1	8	42	11	41	6	2	.250/.300/.447	84	1.0	.279	1.7	RF(23): 0.5, 1B(14): 0.6	0.4
2020	WAS	MLB	33	251	24	12	1	6	27	14	51	4	2	.240/.290/.378	75	0.7	.282	0.6	LF 3, RF 1	0.4

Comparables: Omar Infante, Carl Crawford, Thad Bosley

The dumbest, best split of the 2019 season has to be Parra's pre- and post-Baby Shark-as-walk-up-song one. Parra posted a barely-keeping-his-head-above-water slash line of .209/.276/.331 before June 19—the day of that fateful music change—and a .262/.314/.460 one after, enough to keep him swimming along in the majors, in addition to the chummier atmosphere he brought to the Nationals clubhouse. As a Nat, he matched offensive wits with Matt Adams and Victor Robles, provided some additional outfield depth and irritated the heck out of the Dodgers in the regular season, all of which might have made him the Nationals' least-expected most-valuable catch. His next stop? N-P-B, doo doo doo doo doo doo.

Raudy Read C Born: 10/29/93 Age: 26 Bats: R Throws: R Height: 6'0" Weight: 170 Origin: International Free Agent, 2011

YEAR	TEAM	LVL	AGE	PA	R	2B	3B	HR	RBI	BB	K	SB	CS	AVG/OBP/SLG	DRC+	VORP	BABIP	BRR	FRAA	WARP
2017	HAR	AA	23	442	44	25	1	17	61	27	79	2	0	.265/.312/.455	109	21.5	.290	-3.1	C(104): -24.7	-0.4
2017	WAS	MLB	23	11	1	0	0	0	0	0	3	0	0	.273/.273/.273	72	0.1	.375	-0.1	C(3): -0.4	0.0
2018	HAR	AA	24	161	14	9	2	3	24	11	30	0	0	.286/.335/.435	117	5.7	.336	-2.5	C(35): -7.8	0.0
2018	SYR	AAA	24	52	2	2	0	0	2	1	8	0	0	.260/.269/.300	79	0.0	.302	-0.1	C(10): -3.1	-0.2
2019	FRE	AAA	25	328	52	17	3	20	60	17	58	1	1	.275/.317/.546	105	15.0	.278	-0.7	C(66): -19.5, 1B(10): 1.5	0.0
2019	WAS	MLB	25	11	0	0	0	0	0	0	5	0	0	.091/.091/.091	69	0.1	.167	0.0	C(4): -0.4	0.0
2020	WAS	MLB	26	35	4	1	0	2	5	2	8	0	0	.225/.268/.419	74	0.4	.249	-0.1	C -1	-0.1

Comparables: Zoilo Almonte, Jose Lobaton, Josmil Pinto

Read came to hit balls and chew bubble gum, and unfortunately, he's not that great at one of those. The high point of his September call-up came when calling 5 2/3 innings of one-run ball for Austin Voth against Atlanta, a feat quickly (and rightly) forgotten after Charlie Culberson suffered a season-ending injury following a collision with a Fernando Rodney fastball. On the other side of the plate, Read—unlike other guys named Rowdy—cannot consistently deliver hits at the major-league level. A brutal framer who has already served one 80-game suspension for PED use, the 26-year-old truly is a callback to a different era.

YEAR	TEAM	P. COUNT	FRM RUNS	BLK RUNS	THRW RUNS	TOT RUNS
2017	HAR	13457	-28.1	1.5	0.4	-27.2
2017	WAS	211	-0.2	-0.1	0.0	-0.4
2018	HAR	4606	-8.1	0.0	-0.2	-8.4
2018	SYR	1432	-2.8	0.0	-0.1	-3.0
2019	FRE	9611	-18.9	0.0	0.7	-18.4
2019	WAS	378	-0.3	-0.1	0.0	0.1
2020	WAS	1299	-1.2	-0.2	0.1	-1.3

Victor Robles CF Born: 05/19/97 Age: 23 Bats: R Throws: R Height: 6'0" Weight: 190 Origin: International Free Agent, 2013

YEAR	TEAM	LVL	AGE	PA	R	2B	3B	HR	RBI	BB	K	SB	CS	AVG/OBP/SLG	DRC+	VORP	BABIP	BRR	FRAA	WARP
2017	POT	A+	20	338	49	25	7	7	33	25	62	16	7	.289/.377/.495	148	30.1	.345	0.7	CF(77): 16.1	4.5
2017	HAR	AA	20	158	24	12	1	3	14	12	22	11	3	.324/.394/.489	138	16.7	.368	2.7	CF(31): 4.1, LF(3): -0.1	1.9
2017	WAS	MLB	20	27	2	1	2	0	4	0	6	0	1	.250/.308/.458	79	-0.6	.333	-0.8	RF(6): 1.2, CF(3): -0.3	0.0
2018	NAT	RK	21	27	7	1	0	0	1	7	4	4	1	.333/.556/.389	199	4.7	.429	1.9	CF(7): -0.3	0.5
2018	SYR	AAA	21	182	25	9	1	2	10	18	26	14	6	.278/.356/.386	100	9.8	.318	1.2	CF(39): -0.8	0.6
2018	WAS	MLB	21	66	8	3	1	3	10	4	12	3	2	.288/.348/.525	103	5.3	.311	0.7	CF(14): 0.1, LF(2): 0.0	0.3
2019	WAS	MLB	22	617	86	33	3	17	65	35	140	28	9	.255/.326/.419	85	10.0	.310	5.6	CF(141): 6.6, RF(15): 1.1	2.3
2020	WAS	MLB	23	595	66	28	4	17	68	35	132	24	9	.247/.320/.410	91	18.4	.297	2.9	CF 9	2.8

Comparables: Manuel Margot, Justin Upton, Ruben Sierra

Let's all lean into Robles the way Robles leans into pitches. Robles would be the most exciting young gun on the Nationals if not for his younger, better counterpart in left field. He's a rookie in the way that young players (other than Soto) are: high speed, high energy, high swing rate on pitches outside the zone, who seems to learn throughout the course of each game only to reset the next. Still, his defense—a league-leading number of centerfield putouts and assists—makes it easier to forgive his tendency to get on base through soft contact when he hits the ball, and hard contact when the ball hits him.

Juan Soto LF Born: 10/25/98 Age: 21 Bats: L Throws: L Height: 6'1" Weight: 185 Origin: International Free Agent, 2015

YEAR	TEAM	LVL	AGE	PA	R	2B	3B	HR	RBI	BB	K	SB	CS	AVG/OBP/SLG	DRC+	VORP	BABIP	BRR	FRAA	WARP
2017	NAT	RK	18	27	3	1	1	0	4	2	1	0	0	.320/.370/.440	135	1.5	.333	0.0	RF(9): -1.1	0.0
2017	HAG	A	18	96	15	5	0	3	14	10	8	1	2	.360/.427/.523	181	8.0	.373	1.0	RF(19): -1.9, LF(2): -0.3	0.9
2018	HAG	A	19	74	12	5	3	5	24	14	13	2	0	.373/.486/.814	222	14.5	.405	0.3	RF(14): 1.1, CF(2): 0.2	1.2
2018	POT	A+	19	73	17	3	1	7	18	11	8	0	1	.371/.466/.790	260	15.4	.340	1.4	RF(14): 1.0, LF(1): 0.0	1.6
2018	HAR	AA	19	35	4	2	0	2	10	4	7	1	0	.323/.400/.581	113	3.6	.364	0.0	LF(4): 0.6, RF(4): -0.5	0.1
2018	WAS	MLB	19	494	77	25	1	22	70	79	99	5	2	.292/.406/.517	125	40.5	.338	-0.5	LF(114): 2.7	3.0
2019	WAS	MLB	20	659	110	32	5	34	110	108	132	12	1	.282/.401/.548	136	49.0	.312	1.4	LF(150): -0.8	4.9
2020	WAS	MLB	21	630	92	30	3	35	102	85	123	5	2	.284/.382/.543	133	43.6	.310	-0.1	LF 3	4.8

Comparables: Ronald Acuña Jr., Mike Trout, Tony Conigliaro

Talk about adjustments. Soto spent the year adjusting to pitchers who served him a steady diet of breaking stuff—with apologies to last year's Annual, sliders are one of the few things he doesn't routinely crush. To left field, improving his defense enough to get a Gold Glove nod. To a two-strike count with an expanded stance. To Josh Hader, who dished up a high fastball in the Wild Card game to a guy seemingly made to hit them. To Clayton Kershaw, who threw a slider that Soto demolished in NLDS Game 5. To Gerrit Cole, off whom he hit two home runs in the World Series. To the biggest stage in the world, talent seeming to grow to fill the ever-expanding container it's in.

Soto, as almost everyone who's watched him take a pitch knows, plays both older and somehow younger than he is. He's patient, with a swing profile that's more Rendon-ish than Robles-esque, watching balls go by with the excitement and enthusiasm of most guys hitting one over the fence. Younger too—when asked about the prospect of losing in the World Series, Soto remarked he'd experienced heartbreaking loss before...in Little League. A reminder that this is, after all, a kid's game; that when you strip away the pomp and ceremony, it's the transcendent feeling of pitcher versus batter, defense versus offense, that drives us to watch and to keep watching.

Andrew Stevenson LF Born: 06/01/94 Age: 26 Bats: L Throws: L Height: 6'0" Weight: 192 Origin: Round 2, 2015 Draft (#58 overall)

YEAR	TEAM	LVL	AGE	PA	R	2B	3B	HR	RBI	BB	K	SB	CS	AVG/OBP/SLG	DRC+	VORP	BABIP	BRR	FRAA	WARP
2017	HAR	AA	23	91	14	5	1	0	12	11	19	1	3	.350/.429/.438	140	7.9	.459	-0.4	CF(16): -3.1, LF(3): -0.3	0.3
2017	SYR	AAA	23	331	38	7	4	2	26	19	72	10	1	.252/.298/.320	68	-1.5	.323	2.2	CF(62): -0.2, LF(15): 1.9	0.3
2017	WAS	MLB	23	66	5	2	0	0	1	7	20	1	0	.158/.250/.193	54	-4.3	.243	0.5	RF(14): 0.1, LF(9): -0.5	-0.2
2018	SYR	AAA	24	331	40	10	1	6	28	31	75	12	6	.235/.318/.338	83	2.9	.296	-1.0	CF(49): -8.3, LF(25): 1.4	-0.4
2018	WAS	MLB	24	86	9	2	0	1	13	6	23	1	1	.253/.306/.320	70	1.8	.333	0.4	LF(16): -1.4, CF(3): -0.3	-0.2
2019	HAR	AA	25	88	12	4	0	1	5	3	24	3	0	.250/.284/.333	16	0.6	.339	1.1	LF(9): 2.5, CF(8): -0.9	-0.1
2019	FRE	AAA	25	333	50	17	8	6	44	24	76	10	4	.334/.383/.503	99	18.2	.428	1.5	CF(52): -10.5, LF(12): -1.1	0.3
2019	WAS	MLB	25	37	4	1	1	0	0	6	11	0	1	.367/.486/.467	75	0.0	.579	-0.2	LF(5): -0.7	-0.1
2020	WAS	MLB	26	133	13	5	1	2	13	9	38	4	2	.257/.312/.371	77	-0.2	.353	0.2	RF 1, LF 0	0.1

Comparables: Gus Bell, Mallex Smith, Jake Marisnick

Pity Old Man Andrew Stevenson. He's entering this season at the decrepit age of 26, having spent the previous relegated to Fresno, 2,800 miles and a world away from the majors. Stevenson proved a valuable call-up in September, but his perfectly normal development trajectory seems almost glacial compared with his fellow outfielders. Despite his advanced age, he'll continue to chase a dream—and hopefully fewer pitches out of the zone.

Kurt Suzuki C Born: 10/04/83 Age: 36 Bats: R Throws: R Height: 5'11" Weight: 210 Origin: Round 2, 2004 Draft (#67 overall)

YEAR	TEAM	LVL	AGE	PA	R	2B	3B	HR	RBI	BB	K	SB	CS	AVG/OBP/SLG	DRC+	VORP	BABIP	BRR	FRAA	WARP
2017	ATL	MLB	33	309	38	13	0	19	50	17	39	0	0	.283/.351/.536	129	27.1	.268	-2.8	C(77): 1.9	2.6
2018	ATL	MLB	34	388	45	24	0	12	50	22	43	0	0	.271/.332/.444	115	25.9	.275	-2.0	C(93): -5.5	1.8
2019	WAS	MLB	35	309	37	11	0	17	63	20	36	0	1	.264/.324/.486	115	22.3	.248	0.4	C(75): -8.6	1.4
2020	WAS	MLB	36	301	35	15	0	13	40	18	42	0	0	.256/.316/.448	96	11.8	.262	-0.9	C -8	0.4

Comparables: Rick Cerone, Ramon Hernandez, Brian Schneider

There's something to be said for distance. The sixty feet and six inches from the mound to the plate. The distance from the stands to the field. The distance between who we feel players are and who they ought to be. We could talk about Suzuki's offensive output; he posted the sixth-highest DRC+ among catchers who started more than 50 games. Or his work in game planning with Scherzer, Strasburg and Sánchez. His 2012 assurance to Doolittle to trust his fastball. But overshadowing all of that was the post-World Series trip to the White House, the seeming unawareness that his actions—donning a MAGA hat and literally being embraced by Trump—have consequences on others, one that left many Nationals fans feeling not just distant, but unmoored, adrift from a once-beloved fan favorite.

YEAR	TEAM	P. COUNT	FRM RUNS	BLK RUNS	THRW RUNS	TOT RUNS
2017	ATL	10594	-0.6	1.4	-0.9	-0.7
2018	ATL	12497	-7.5	1.5	-0.4	-6.6
2019	WAS	10602	-5.9	-1.7	-1.3	-9.3
2020	WAS	13270	-7.1	-0.1	-1.4	-8.6

Michael A. Taylor CF Born: 03/26/91 Age: 29 Bats: R Throws: R Height: 6'4" Weight: 212 Origin: Round 6, 2009 Draft (#172 overall)

YEAR	TEAM	LVL	AGE	PA	R	2B	3B	HR	RBI	BB	K	SB	CS	AVG/OBP/SLG	DRC+	VORP	BABIP	BRR	FRAA	WARP
2017	HAR	AA	26	28	3	2	0	1	4	2	8	3	0	.154/.214/.346	54	-0.9	.176	0.4	CF(5): 0.1	0.0
2017	WAS	MLB	26	432	55	23	3	19	53	29	137	17	7	.271/.320/.486	93	26.7	.363	3.1	CF(111): 12.6, RF(2): -0.2	2.7
2018	WAS	MLB	27	385	46	22	3	6	28	29	116	24	6	.227/.287/.357	67	1.4	.320	1.3	CF(113): 8.9, 1B(1): 0.0	0.8
2019	HAR	AA	28	247	36	16	2	9	35	25	69	10	6	.248/.324/.463	121	15.9	.315	3.9	CF(42): -1.2, RF(6): -0.1	1.5
2019	WAS	MLB	28	97	10	7	0	1	3	7	34	6	0	.250/.305/.364	58	-2.0	.396	-0.6	CF(25): 0.0, RF(7): -0.8	-0.3
2020	WAS	MLB	29	189	20	9	1	7	22	15	65	7	2	.228/.291/.401	78	0.8	.323	0.4	CF 2, RF 0	0.3

Comparables: Jackie Bradley Jr., Cameron Maybin, Dexter Fowler

Perhaps no other play exemplified the 2019 Washington Nationals more than Taylor catching the last out of NLDS Game 5 against the Dodgers—a pretty, desperate catch—followed by the centerfielder confusedly offering his teammates the ball as if to say, "What now?"

He spent much of his season as Michael AA. Taylor, buried in Harrisburg like so many former Pennsylvania governors. Gone, but not forgotten by the Nats faithful who remembered his tough performance in the 2017 NLDS, including a Game 4 grand slam into a Wrigley basket. Taylor's performance at the plate has always been his issue, striking out more than 30 percent of the time, though this year he at least hit the ball harder than his previous seasons, albeit over a small sample size. Now finally out of options, the 2009 draft pick still has two years left until free agency, and he's running out of time to show other teams he can be more than a defensive replacement who happens to heat up when the weather gets cold.

Eric Thames 1B Born: 11/10/86 Age: 33 Bats: L Throws: R Height: 6'0" Weight: 210 Origin: Round 7, 2008 Draft (#219 overall)

YEAR	TEAM	LVL	AGE	PA	R	2B	3B	HR	RBI	BB	K	SB	CS	AVG/OBP/SLG	DRC+	VORP	BABIP	BRR	FRAA	WARP
2017	MIL	MLB	30	551	83	26	4	31	63	75	163	4	2	.247/.359/.518	117	28.8	.309	-2.7	1B(108): -2.2, LF(25): -1.8	1.4
2018	MIL	MLB	31	278	41	10	3	16	37	29	97	7	0	.219/.306/.478	96	14.0	.284	2.3	RF(31): -0.3, 1B(29): -0.9	0.6
2019	MIL	MLB	32	459	67	23	2	25	61	51	140	3	2	.247/.346/.505	112	15.3	.313	1.8	1B(105): -1.4, RF(12): -0.1	1.5
2020	WAS	MLB	33	251	35	12	1	15	40	28	80	3	1	.249/.344/.517	114	13.0	.321	0.1	1B 0, RF 0	1.4

Comparables: Brandon Moss, Carlos Delgado, Brad Wilkerson

Three years into Thames's return to American baseball, we can safely say what you see is what you'll get. His swing features too many holes to avoid an abhorrent 30-percent strikeout rate, but he is disciplined enough to take his walks and has undeniable power. The biggest problem, honestly, is his defensive incompetence. His walk-and-bop stylings at the dish would enable him to start most days if he was a passable corner outfielder. But his bat loses some of its value when he's limited to either first base or DH. Is it any wonder, then, why the Brewers elected to bid him adieu?

Trea Turner SS Born: 06/30/93 Age: 27 Bats: R Throws: R Height: 6'2" Weight: 185 Origin: Round 1, 2014 Draft (#13 overall)

YEAR	TEAM	LVL	AGE	PA	R	2B	3B	HR	RBI	BB	K	SB	CS	AVG/OBP/SLG	DRC+	VORP	BABIP	BRR	FRAA	WARP
2017	WAS	MLB	24	447	75	24	6	11	45	30	80	46	8	.284/.338/.451	99	36.6	.329	6.8	SS(95): 0.2	2.7
2018	WAS	MLB	25	740	103	27	6	19	73	69	132	43	9	.271/.344/.416	107	46.5	.314	2.7	SS(159): 7.1	5.0
2019	WAS	MLB	26	569	96	37	5	19	57	43	113	35	5	.298/.353/.497	108	33.4	.348	4.1	SS(122): 3.8	4.0
2020	WAS	MLB	27	595	71	31	6	19	75	46	120	36	8	.281/.340/.465	109	32.4	.330	2.5	SS 6	3.9

Comparables: Juan Samuel, Gordon Beckham, Tony Batista

It turns out that 85 percent of Turner is still a good amount of Trea. The shortstop took a pitch off his hand on April 3rd, a bunt attempt on a ball that ran in on him, leaving one and a half of his fingers broken all season. He initially thought they were merely dislocated and allegedly told training staff to, "pop that [expletive] back in." So, operating at 85 percent would explain some of the defensive miscues, including an FRAA around half of his 2018 level. (Though not being next to a defensive black hole in the form of 2018 Daniel Murphy likely helped with that.) He didn't suffer as much on the other side of the plate, where he employed an 8.5-finger grip, trading a slightly elevated strikeout rate and chasing more out of the zone for an increase in both average and power. He'll have a shortened offseason in which to heal, but should consider retaining his altered grip, even at 100 percent.

Ryan Zimmerman 1B Born: 09/28/84 Age: 35 Bats: R Throws: R Height: 6'3" Weight: 215 Origin: Round 1, 2005 Draft (#4 overall)

YEAR	TEAM	LVL	AGE	PA	R	2B	3B	HR	RBI	BB	K	SB	CS	AVG/OBP/SLG	DRC+	VORP	BABIP	BRR	FRAA	WARP
2017	WAS	MLB	32	576	90	33	0	36	108	44	126	1	0	.303/.358/.573	130	39.4	.335	-0.3	1B(143): -11.4	1.8
2018	WAS	MLB	33	323	33	21	2	13	51	30	55	1	1	.264/.337/.486	111	14.5	.284	-0.5	1B(73): 1.4	1.0
2019	WAS	MLB	34	190	20	9	0	6	27	17	39	0	0	.257/.321/.415	93	1.4	.297	-0.9	1B(44): 1.2	0.2
2020	WAS	MLB	35	251	29	14	0	10	33	20	56	1	0	.249/.314/.443	98	7.3	.288	-0.3	1B 0	0.7

Comparables: Alex Gordon, Larry Parrish, Ed Sprague

There's a certain space in baseball mythology reserved not for the All-Stars or the has-beens, but something rarer and more fraught: the could-have-beens. Zimmerman's potential has been hanging over him like a cluster of grapes above Tantalus—something we all can see but that, frustratingly, remained just out of his grasp. He's been at this for 15 years, drafted when Soto was a kindergartener, a face-of-the-franchise player for a team that wasted six of his best years finding its footing. He missed much of the season with a foot injury, plantar fasciitis, that kind of nagging thing that sets in in your mid-30s and never really departs. But whatever gods or monsters control baseball's narrative, whatever forces decide who feasts and who stays hungry, wrote Zimmerman a happy ending—reaching up and grabbing hold of the success that had eluded him for so long.

PITCHERS

Fernando Abad LHP Born: 12/17/85 Age: 34 Bats: L Throws: L Height: 6'1" Weight: 220 Origin: International Free Agent, 2002

YEAR	TEAM	LVL	AGE	W	L	SV	G	GS	IP	H	HR	BB/9	K/9	K	GB%	BABIP	WHIP	ERA	DRA	WARP	MPH	FB%	WHF	CSP
2017	BOS	MLB	31	2	1	1	48	0	43²	40	4	2.9	7.6	37	46%	.286	1.24	3.30	5.11	0.0	94.4	53.7	7.7	43.2
2019	RIC	AA	33	1	0	0	3	0	6	3	0	1.5	9.0	6	27%	.200	0.67	0.00	3.08	0.1				
2019	SAC	AAA	33	2	3	13	38	0	44	49	3	0.8	10.0	49	47%	.357	1.20	3.07	3.04	1.4				
2019	SFN	MLB	33	0	2	0	21	0	13	9	2	2.1	6.2	9	62%	.200	0.92	4.15	4.28	0.2	95.1	57.9	10.5	48.3
2020	WAS	MLB	34	2	2	0	33	0	35	37	5	2.9	8.5	33	44%	.314	1.38	4.40	4.80	0.2	93.5	54	8.4	45.7

Comparables: Dan Jennings, Mike Stanton, Jerry Blevins

After a brief sojourn to rip up the Atlantic League in 2018, Abad picked up right where he left off in affiliated baseball this past season: he worked his way back up to the majors where he beat up left-handed hitters and barely skated by the righties. The stuff remains roughly the same as it always has, which means his profile does too: He's exactly the kind of relief pitcher teams want waiting in Triple-A, or on standby as the third left-hander out of the bullpen. Sure, they're constantly looking for an upgrade over guys like this, but every team needs a reliever or two like him, nominative determinism be damned.

Aaron Barrett RHP Born: 01/02/88 Age: 32 Bats: R Throws: R Height: 6'3" Weight: 230 Origin: Round 9, 2010 Draft (#266 overall)

YEAR	TEAM	LVL	AGE	W	L	SV	G	GS	IP	H	HR	BB/9	K/9	K	GB%	BABIP	WHIP	ERA	DRA	WARP	MPH	FB%	WHF	CSP
2018	AUB	A-	30	2	0	0	20	0	20²	13	0	3.5	11.3	26	60%	.250	1.02	1.74	3.67	0.3				
2019	HAR	AA	31	0	2	31	50	0	52¹	39	6	2.8	10.7	62	52%	.256	1.05	2.75	3.46	0.7				
2019	WAS	MLB	31	0	0	0	3	0	2¹	5	1	15.4	3.9	1	27%	.400	3.86	15.43	4.17	0.0	92.4	70.6	4.4	36.7
2020	WAS	MLB	32	1	1	0	25	0	26	28	6	5.0	8.1	23	43%	.293	1.64	6.50	5.97	-0.2	91.5	70	4.4	36.4

Comparables: Nate Karns, AJ Ramos, Nick Vincent

Baseball can be an unkind sport. Barrett missed almost four seasons after undergoing Tommy John surgery and then fracturing his arm so catastrophically that the team sequestered the video of the injury. After spending the season in Double-A, he returned to the majors as a September call-up and posted a hitless inning in his debut, including a strikeout looking to Ronald Acuña Jr. He's able to induce swings and misses with his secondary pitches, though the velocity was still low on the few pitches he got to throw. Unless the winter gives him time to find his fastball, Barrett will remain a feel-good story that fans may not feel so good about when he faces major-league hitting.

Tim Cate LHP Born: 09/30/97 Age: 22 Bats: L Throws: L Height: 6'0" Weight: 185 Origin: Round 2, 2018 Draft (#65 overall)

YEAR	TEAM	LVL	AGE	W	L	SV	G	GS	IP	H	HR	BB/9	K/9	K	GB%	BABIP	WHIP	ERA	DRA	WARP	MPH	FB%	WHF	CSP
2018	AUB	A-	20	2	3	0	9	8	31	34	1	2.9	7.5	26	45%	.333	1.42	4.65	5.74	-0.2				
2018	HAG	A	20	0	3	0	4	4	21	23	4	2.6	8.1	19	44%	.306	1.38	5.57	5.20	0.0				
2019	HAG	A	21	4	5	0	13	13	70¹	61	2	1.7	9.3	73	57%	.309	1.05	2.82	3.63	1.3				
2019	POT	A+	21	7	4	0	13	13	73¹	71	4	2.3	8.1	66	61%	.324	1.23	3.31	5.29	-0.3				
2020	WAS	MLB	22	2	2	0	33	0	35	34	5	3.8	7.0	27	50%	.277	1.39	4.35	4.57	0.3				

Comparables: Ranger Suárez, Jeff Locke, Patrick Sandoval

Cate is a southpaw who spins a mean, mean curveball. That alone is enough to net him a lot of per diems because lefty relievers with a wipeout breaker are pillars of the modern baseball architecture. The former UConn ace is going to need an extra something that he doesn't have right now to be effective in a big-league rotation, though. Options include a couple extra ticks on his fastball, a big improvement to a fringy change, a new third pitch like a cutter or invention of a time machine to travel back to the dead-ball era.

Patrick Corbin LHP Born: 07/19/89 Age: 30 Bats: L Throws: L Height: 6'3" Weight: 210 Origin: Round 2, 2009 Draft (#80 overall)

YEAR	TEAM	LVL	AGE	W	L	SV	G	GS	IP	H	HR	BB/9	K/9	K	GB%	BABIP	WHIP	ERA	DRA	WARP	MPH	FB%	WHF	CSP
2017	ARI	MLB	27	14	13	0	33	32	189²	208	26	2.9	8.4	178	52%	.326	1.42	4.03	4.92	1.4	94.5	53.3	11.9	43.8
2018	ARI	MLB	28	11	7	0	33	33	200	162	15	2.2	11.1	246	49%	.302	1.05	3.15	2.74	5.9	93.9	48.6	16.3	41.6
2019	WAS	MLB	29	14	7	0	33	33	202	169	24	3.1	10.6	238	51%	.290	1.18	3.25	3.09	5.9	94.3	53.6	14.9	42.2
2020	WAS	MLB	30	11	9	0	29	29	175	161	22	3.2	10.7	209	51%	.314	1.27	3.71	3.72	4.1	93.5	51.7	14.6	42.3

Comparables: Kevin Gausman, Travis Wood, Jaime García

If 2019 Nationals starting pitching was a gauntlet, specifically the Infinity Gauntlet, Corbin was the Soul Gem, seeming to steal, control and manipulate hitters' spirits. Corbin had a top-15 DRA, a top-10 WARP and was still the third-best starting pitcher on his own team. When his slider snaps, it's basically the Thanos of pitches—it generates more than a 50 percent whiff-per-swing rate, and he deploys it on a two-strike count more than half the time. The kind of put-away pitch that feels inevitable, and still brings hitters to their knees chasing it. He also threw a slow-as-you-please curve to righties this year, possible proof the soul of Liván Hernández remains in Nationals Park.

Wil Crowe RHP Born: 09/09/94 Age: 25 Bats: R Throws: R Height: 6'2" Weight: 240 Origin: Round 2, 2017 Draft (#65 overall)

YEAR	TEAM	LVL	AGE	W	L	SV	G	GS	IP	H	HR	BB/9	K/9	K	GB%	BABIP	WHIP	ERA	DRA	WARP	MPH	FB%	WHF	CSP
2017	AUB	A-	22	0	0	0	7	7	20²	18	3	1.3	6.5	15	52%	.250	1.02	2.61	3.71	0.4				
2018	POT	A+	23	11	0	0	16	15	87	71	6	3.1	8.1	78	47%	.267	1.16	2.69	4.17	1.2				
2018	HAR	AA	23	0	5	0	5	5	26¹	31	4	5.5	5.1	15	44%	.325	1.78	6.15	7.17	-0.6				
2019	HAR	AA	24	7	6	0	16	16	95¹	85	8	2.1	8.4	89	50%	.294	1.12	3.87	4.50	0.5				
2019	FRE	AAA	24	0	4	0	10	10	54	66	7	4.3	6.8	41	42%	.337	1.70	6.17	6.16	0.3				
2020	WAS	MLB	25	2	2	0	33	0	35	36	6	3.7	6.9	27	44%	.286	1.45	4.94	4.85	0.2				

Comparables: Erick Fedde, Dillon Tate, Mike Parisi

Crowe's quick path to the majors was sidetracked by an off-key decimette of starts in the Pacific Coast League. To be fair to the former Gamecock, the 2019 PCL frequently resembled what baseball would look like if played on the moon. Fresno gave up 6.57 runs per game as a team, and that was only fourth-worst in the league. In more normal conditions, he's just about ready to break into the majors, with a low-to-mid-90s fastball complemented by a slider, changeup and curveball. Altogether, it's your standard mid-rotation upside.

Sean Doolittle LHP Born: 09/26/86 Age: 33 Bats: L Throws: L Height: 6'2" Weight: 204 Origin: Round 1, 2007 Draft (#41 overall)

YEAR	TEAM	LVL	AGE	W	L	SV	G	GS	IP	H	HR	BB/9	K/9	K	GB%	BABIP	WHIP	ERA	DRA	WARP	MPH	FB%	WHF	CSP
2017	OAK	MLB	30	1	0	3	23	0	21¹	12	3	0.8	13.1	31	37%	.209	0.66	3.38	2.95	0.5	96.3	87.9	17.5	44.5
2017	WAS	MLB	30	1	0	21	30	0	30	22	2	2.4	9.3	31	28%	.260	1.00	2.40	3.71	0.5	96.5	87.5	16.8	48.3
2018	WAS	MLB	31	3	3	25	43	0	45	21	3	1.2	12.0	60	33%	.196	0.60	1.60	2.99	1.0	96.3	88.6	18.9	50.7
2019	WAS	MLB	32	6	5	29	63	0	60	63	11	2.2	9.9	66	27%	.313	1.30	4.05	4.88	0.3	95.6	88.2	13.9	50.8
2020	WAS	MLB	33	3	2	32	49	0	52	44	9	2.0	9.9	57	27%	.270	1.08	3.29	3.46	1.1	94.9	87.1	15.6	49.2

Comparables: Jake McGee, Nick Vincent, Rafael Soriano

If you're in DC and looking for a great lefty independent bookstore experience, look no further than Doolittle's. While other stores in the area floundered—Rosenthal's, for instance, held an early season fire-sale before closing to spend more time with its inventory—Doolittle's shouldered much of the workload, at times serving as the only reliable purveyor of outs in the area. This rapid expansion in role before the arrival of Rodney's, a traveling library, and Hudson's, which survived two renovations in its main wing, led to near-constant operating hours. After a much-needed rest and restock, the store has regained its reliable collection of high, unhittable fastballs. Also, as you'd expect, it's very pet friendly.

Roenis Elías LHP   Born: 08/01/88   Age: 31   Bats: L   Throws: L   Height: 6'1"   Weight: 205   Origin: International Free Agent, 2011

YEAR	TEAM	LVL	AGE	W	L	SV	G	GS	IP	H	HR	BB/9	K/9	K	GB%	BABIP	WHIP	ERA	DRA	WARP	MPH	FB%	WHF	CSP
2017	PAW	AAA	28	1	4	0	7	7	34	43	9	2.4	6.6	25	33%	.312	1.53	6.62	6.56	-0.3				
2017	BOS	MLB	28	0	0	0	1	0	0^1	0	0	27.0	27.0	1	0%	.000	3.00	0.00	1.45	0.0	93.6	54.6	18.2	36.5
2018	PAW	AAA	29	1	0	1	4	0	7^1	2	1	2.5	11.0	9	47%	.071	0.55	1.23	2.38	0.3				
2018	TAC	AAA	29	2	4	0	10	7	33^2	32	1	4.0	8.3	31	44%	.313	1.40	4.54	4.60	0.3				
2018	SEA	MLB	29	3	1	0	23	4	51	46	1	2.8	6.0	34	35%	.285	1.22	2.65	5.35	-0.2	96.0	55	9.8	46.9
2019	SEA	MLB	30	4	2	14	44	0	47	41	8	3.3	8.6	45	36%	.250	1.23	3.64	5.00	0.2	95.9	57.3	13	50.8
2019	WAS	MLB	30	0	0	0	4	0	3	5	2	3.0	6.0	2	30%	.375	2.00	9.00	12.80	-0.2	95.7	60	10	56.2
2020	*WAS*	*MLB*	*31*	*2*	*2*	*0*	*39*	*0*	*42*	*41*	*7*	*3.3*	*8.3*	*38*	*37%*	*.293*	*1.36*	*4.66*	*4.59*	*0.4*	*95.1*	*56*	*11.4*	*45.8*

Comparables: Shane Greene, Sean Gilmartin, Joe Kelly

The Nationals began the season with three bullpen lefties in Sipp, Grace and Doolittle. By September, only one remained. Elías was meant to be part of a solution to the chronic-lack-of-lefties woes. Instead, he posted bad reverse splits, a change from previous seasons, including an OPS above 1000 against left-handed batters mostly due to his curveball going from nigh unhittable by lefties to just nigh. Add to that his hamstring troubles—some brought on by attempting do something a former AL relief pitcher should never do: swing a bat—and the Nats had no choice but to leave him behind.

Erick Fedde RHP   Born: 02/25/93   Age: 27   Bats: R   Throws: R   Height: 6'4"   Weight: 195   Origin: Round 1, 2014 Draft (#18 overall)

YEAR	TEAM	LVL	AGE	W	L	SV	G	GS	IP	H	HR	BB/9	K/9	K	GB%	BABIP	WHIP	ERA	DRA	WARP	MPH	FB%	WHF	CSP
2017	HAR	AA	24	3	3	0	17	7	56^1	45	4	2.9	8.6	54	52%	.272	1.12	3.04	3.28	1.2				
2017	SYR	AAA	24	1	2	0	12	6	34	37	3	1.3	6.6	25	62%	.315	1.24	4.76	4.16	0.5				
2017	WAS	MLB	24	0	1	0	3	3	15^1	25	5	4.7	8.8	15	65%	.426	2.15	9.39	6.04	-0.1	95.6	61.1	6.7	47.8
2018	SYR	AAA	25	3	3	0	13	13	67^1	78	3	2.4	9.4	70	53%	.383	1.43	4.41	5.15	0.3				
2018	WAS	MLB	25	2	4	0	11	11	50^1	55	8	3.9	8.2	46	54%	.333	1.53	5.54	4.85	0.3	95.9	54.9	9.5	43.8
2019	HAR	AA	26	2	0	0	5	4	24^2	18	2	1.8	9.9	27	55%	.254	0.93	2.55	3.13	0.5				
2019	FRE	AAA	26	1	1	0	2	2	10	19	5	3.6	9.0	10	36%	.452	2.30	12.60	9.02	-0.2				
2019	WAS	MLB	26	4	2	0	21	12	78	81	11	3.8	4.7	41	52%	.283	1.46	4.50	6.27	-0.5	94.4	55.2	7.2	46.1
2020	*WAS*	*MLB*	*27*	*4*	*5*	*0*	*47*	*8*	*82*	*94*	*13*	*3.2*	*6.0*	*55*	*51%*	*.306*	*1.50*	*5.26*	*5.06*	*0.5*	*94.5*	*56.3*	*8.1*	*46.3*

Comparables: Brandon Workman, Daniel Barone, Charles Brewer

The year: 2265. The site: a resurrected Deadspin. An animatronic David Roth reaches into a box of baseball cards, fishing out such notables as Ross, McGowin, Voth, Hellickson and Fedde.

"Hey, let's remember some guys!" he beeps, holding up Fedde's card. "This guy! He threw six pitches. Well, five really. Four, if we're being honest. Look, he definitely throws a sinker, a cutter and a curve."

Across from him, the disembodied head of a staff writer sits in a bubble of isotonic solution adorned with wires delivering enough electrical current to keep it quote-unquote alive. "Interrogative," it displays. "What was his best pitch?"

Roth whirs as if searching for the abbreviated notion of 'best' as it pertains to a Nationals fifth starter and occasional bullpen piece. "Cutter?" he says after a minute.

"Is that an answer or a question?" the staff writer asks.

Roth considers the response, gears visibly turning. "Why not both?" he says, finally. "So is Fedde."

Matt Grace LHP   Born: 12/14/88   Age: 31   Bats: L   Throws: L   Height: 6'4"   Weight: 215   Origin: Round 8, 2010 Draft (#236 overall)

YEAR	TEAM	LVL	AGE	W	L	SV	G	GS	IP	H	HR	BB/9	K/9	K	GB%	BABIP	WHIP	ERA	DRA	WARP	MPH	FB%	WHF	CSP
2017	SYR	AAA	28	1	3	0	13	1	19^2	21	2	3.7	9.6	21	61%	.345	1.47	3.66	4.60	0.2				
2017	WAS	MLB	28	1	0	2	40	1	50	50	3	3.2	5.6	31	63%	.294	1.36	4.32	6.01	-0.5	92.8	72.2	7.9	50.9
2018	WAS	MLB	29	1	1	0	56	0	59^2	55	5	2.0	7.2	48	50%	.279	1.14	2.87	4.45	0.3	93.1	66.9	8.3	54.6
2019	WAS	MLB	30	1	2	0	51	1	46^2	61	11	1.9	6.8	35	50%	.338	1.52	6.36	5.96	-0.3	93.0	61.9	9.3	50.3
2020	*WAS*	*MLB*	*31*	*2*	*2*	*0*	*33*	*0*	*35*	*41*	*6*	*2.6*	*6.7*	*26*	*52%*	*.317*	*1.45*	*5.16*	*5.26*	*0.1*	*92.2*	*65.9*	*8.5*	*51.6*

Comparables: Scott Alexander, Robby Scott, Jeremy Horst

Not every garbage man can be promoted to garbage boss. Grace was given mostly garbage innings to throw, but managed to make even low-leverage situations high anxiety. Lefties hit over .400 against his sinker—his main pitch—this season while righties hit a measly .325. Grace eventually fell from it, DFA'd a few days before roster expansion, earning a trip down to Triple-A, and hopefully an opportunity to dump this season into the landfill of memory.

Javy Guerra RHP Born: 10/31/85 Age: 34 Bats: R Throws: R Height: 6'1" Weight: 216 Origin: Round 4, 2004 Draft (#118 overall)

YEAR	TEAM	LVL	AGE	W	L	SV	G	GS	IP	H	HR	BB/9	K/9	K	GB%	BABIP	WHIP	ERA	DRA	WARP	MPH	FB%	WHF	CSP
2017	NWO	AAA	31	2	4	2	35	0	51²	46	7	3.7	7.7	44	42%	.273	1.30	4.70	4.16	0.6				
2017	MIA	MLB	31	1	1	0	16	0	21	23	2	3.0	5.1	12	52%	.313	1.43	3.00	5.65	-0.1	94.4	54.9	6	51.7
2018	NWO	AAA	32	3	0	5	12	0	16²	9	0	1.6	13.0	24	61%	.273	0.72	0.00	1.65	0.7				
2018	MIA	MLB	32	1	1	1	32	0	35²	42	4	3.0	7.6	30	45%	.336	1.51	5.55	5.02	0.0	95.3	52.2	9.9	51.5
2019	BUF	AAA	33	0	1	1	5	0	7¹	4	0	4.9	7.4	6	28%	.222	1.09	2.45	4.91	0.1				
2019	WAS	MLB	33	3	1	1	40	0	53²	55	9	2.0	7.0	42	35%	.279	1.25	4.86	4.77	0.3	95.5	60	10.3	54.1
2019	TOR	MLB	33	0	0	1	11	0	14	12	1	3.2	9.6	15	29%	.297	1.21	3.86	6.77	-0.2	95.6	60	8	53.6
2020	WAS	MLB	34	2	2	0	33	0	35	36	6	3.0	7.1	28	38%	.292	1.37	4.62	4.57	0.3	94.2	56.4	9.3	51.8

Comparables: Hector Carrasco, Jay Powell, Joe Smith

If you predicted "Javy Guerra pitches in two (two!) World Series games" at the beginning of this season, congrats and go buy yourself a lottery ticket. The Nationals got Guerra mid-season in an effort to shore up their ailing bullpen with, well, any warm, semi-functional arm. Guerra turned out to be one such arm, less volatile than Rainey or Rodney, but with less-effective stuff. He was mainly deployed in low-leverage situations—a righty version of Matt Grace in terms of usage, which is about the meanest thing you can say about anyone.

Will Harris RHP Born: 08/28/84 Age: 35 Bats: R Throws: R Height: 6'4" Weight: 240 Origin: Round 9, 2006 Draft (#258 overall)

YEAR	TEAM	LVL	AGE	W	L	SV	G	GS	IP	H	HR	BB/9	K/9	K	GB%	BABIP	WHIP	ERA	DRA	WARP	MPH	FB%	WHF	CSP
2017	HOU	MLB	32	3	2	2	46	0	45¹	37	7	1.4	10.3	52	49%	.270	0.97	2.98	2.45	1.4	93.6	68.7	13.9	46.9
2018	HOU	MLB	33	5	3	0	61	0	56²	48	3	2.2	10.2	64	54%	.306	1.09	3.49	2.32	1.7	94.0	62.3	14.5	42.5
2019	HOU	MLB	34	4	1	4	68	0	60	42	6	2.1	9.3	62	54%	.245	0.93	1.50	3.45	1.2	93.0	58	12.6	45.2
2020	WAS	MLB	35	2	2	0	33	0	35	31	4	2.8	9.7	38	51%	.291	1.19	3.29	3.37	0.8	92.3	60.5	13.3	43.9

Comparables: Heath Bell, Fernando Salas, Mark Melancon

One of the best kept secrets of the Astros rebuild, it was a shame that the last memory Harris has in Houston is the ball that Howie Kendrick clanged off the right field foul pole in Game 7 of the World Series—though they'll now be able to reminisce about it over the post-game spread in Washington. The Astros selected him off of waivers when the Diamondbacks couldn't find room for him on their 40-man roster. All he's done since is sport a 2.36 ERA over 297 innings. Utilizing a two-pitch mix of cutter and curveball has been lethal to both lefties and righties, making Harris the perfect combination of high strikeout and weak contact that you would want in any arm trotting out of the bullpen. Maybe it's the baby face or the relatively low velocity, but he's never gotten the credit he deserves for being one of the more consistent bullpen arms in the game over the past few years.

Jeremy Hellickson RHP Born: 04/08/87 Age: 33 Bats: R Throws: R Height: 6'1" Weight: 190 Origin: Round 4, 2005 Draft (#118 overall)

YEAR	TEAM	LVL	AGE	W	L	SV	G	GS	IP	H	HR	BB/9	K/9	K	GB%	BABIP	WHIP	ERA	DRA	WARP	MPH	FB%	WHF	CSP
2017	PHI	MLB	30	6	5	0	20	20	112¹	111	22	2.4	5.2	65	37%	.255	1.26	4.73	5.99	-0.5	91.6	54.3	9.1	45.6
2017	BAL	MLB	30	2	6	0	10	10	51²	49	13	3.0	5.4	31	36%	.225	1.28	6.97	6.97	-0.8	92.0	54.3	8.5	43.9
2018	WAS	MLB	31	5	3	0	19	19	91¹	78	11	2.0	6.4	65	47%	.252	1.07	3.45	4.19	1.2	91.8	51.4	9	48.5
2019	NAT	RK	32	1	1	0	5	4	16²	11	1	1.1	11.9	22	49%	.250	0.78	2.16	0.55	1.0				
2019	WAS	MLB	32	2	3	0	9	8	39	47	9	4.6	6.9	30	39%	.309	1.72	6.23	6.84	-0.5	90.8	61.2	6.7	46.4
2020	WAS	MLB	33	2	2	0	33	0	35	40	9	3.0	6.7	26	41%	.288	1.47	6.04	6.01	-0.2	90.6	54.1	8.4	46.2

Comparables: Dillon Gee, Pedro Astacio, Clay Buchholz

The third time wasn't quite the charm. Hellickson returned to the Nationals after testing free agency in 2019, having previously been a reliable-ish fifth starter—at least the first two times through the order, before his batting average against ballooned to north of .400. In his return, the former AL Rookie of the Year diminished into the Nationals' fourth-best fifth starter before shoulder stiffness benched him for much of the season. After spending September warming a bullpen seat without pitching, Hellickson is unlikely to see another season in a Nationals uniform.

Daniel Hudson RHP Born: 03/09/87 Age: 33 Bats: R Throws: R Height: 6'3" Weight: 225 Origin: Round 5, 2008 Draft (#150 overall)

YEAR	TEAM	LVL	AGE	W	L	SV	G	GS	IP	H	HR	BB/9	K/9	K	GB%	BABIP	WHIP	ERA	DRA	WARP	MPH	FB%	WHF	CSP
2017	PIT	MLB	30	2	7	0	71	0	61²	57	7	4.8	9.6	66	44%	.312	1.46	4.38	4.74	0.3	97.1	60.2	12.8	47.3
2018	LAN	MLB	31	3	2	0	40	1	46	38	6	3.5	8.6	44	39%	.256	1.22	4.11	4.63	0.2	97.1	54.4	14	51.3
2019	TOR	MLB	32	6	3	2	45	1	48	38	5	4.3	9.0	48	42%	.258	1.27	3.00	5.10	0.1	97.5	70.2	11.1	47.5
2019	WAS	MLB	32	3	0	6	24	0	25	18	3	1.4	8.3	23	29%	.227	0.88	1.44	3.82	0.4	97.8	72.4	12	54.4
2020	WAS	MLB	33	2	2	0	44	0	47	44	7	3.7	9.3	49	39%	.292	1.34	4.34	4.28	0.6	96.3	63.4	12.2	49

Comparables: Wade Davis, Andrew Cashner, Jason Isringhausen

Someone should develop a bullpen phone with a defibrillator attachment. At the beginning of the season, the Nationals bullpen put the "cardiac" back in "cardiac Nats" in that they would and could break your heart. Hudson made less of a splash at the trade deadline than did Hunter Strickland, with whom the Nats had previous bad blood, an attempt to staunch the bleeding by a twice Tommy John'd starter-turned-reliever cut by the Angels in spring training. But Hudson became the beating heart of the Nationals bullpen, especially after Doolittle's workload led to an August stint on the IL. He was particularly effective in heart-palpitation-inducing situations, holding opponents to a .119 batting average with RISP and two outs, like in Game 2 of the NLDS when he punched Corey Seager out on a heartburn-generating, bases-loaded swinging strike. There are questions as to the sustainability of his efforts, notably the gap between his ERA and DRA, but as Damn Yankees reminds us, sometimes you just gotta have heart.

Kyle McGowin RHP   Born: 11/27/91   Age: 28   Bats: R   Throws: R   Height: 6'3"   Weight: 195   Origin: Round 5, 2013 Draft (#157 overall)

YEAR	TEAM	LVL	AGE	W	L	SV	G	GS	IP	H	HR	BB/9	K/9	K	GB%	BABIP	WHIP	ERA	DRA	WARP	MPH	FB%	WHF	CSP
2017	POT	A+	25	1	1	0	2	2	10	10	1	3.6	8.1	9	41%	.321	1.40	1.80	4.53	0.1				
2017	HAR	AA	25	1	5	0	8	8	42²	58	12	3.4	8.2	39	41%	.346	1.73	6.54	7.96	-1.4				
2017	SYR	AAA	25	1	6	0	9	9	45²	51	3	3.9	5.3	27	52%	.316	1.55	6.31	5.68	0.0				
2018	POT	A+	26	1	1	0	2	2	11	8	2	2.5	11.5	14	42%	.250	1.00	4.09	2.96	0.3				
2018	HAR	AA	26	4	3	0	13	13	78	62	7	2.2	10.8	94	50%	.281	1.04	3.69	2.54	2.5				
2018	SYR	AAA	26	3	2	0	8	8	52²	26	3	1.5	7.5	44	44%	.177	0.66	1.20	2.03	2.1				
2018	WAS	MLB	26	0	0	0	5	1	7²	6	2	5.9	9.4	8	33%	.211	1.43	5.87	4.65	0.0	92.5	59.2	12.3	38.9
2019	HAR	AA	27	1	1	0	6	6	32¹	22	2	2.5	10.0	36	40%	.263	0.96	2.51	3.24	0.7				
2019	FRE	AAA	27	7	2	0	11	11	60²	59	8	2.5	10.1	68	47%	.321	1.25	3.86	3.10	2.1				
2019	WAS	MLB	27	0	0	1	7	1	16	22	7	2.2	10.1	18	45%	.326	1.62	10.12	3.61	0.3	93.3	52.4	13.2	42
2020	WAS	MLB	28	3	3	0	26	6	53	56	10	3.2	9.5	56	44%	.316	1.40	4.96	4.83	0.5	92.5	54.5	13	40.8

Comparables: *Austin Voth, Tyler Beede, Mike Mayers*

May 24: A cloudy, rainless Friday night between two teams with the worst records in the NL—the scuffling Nationals and the limp Marlins. No one expected a season to pivot on a McGowin start, not when he gave up five runs on six hits, not when he was a pieced-together fifth-starter on a team that couldn't seem to piece together a win. Not when he was trying to do something as foolish as being a fly-ball pitcher in the juiced-ball, launch-angle era. The Nats won that game through the strange tactic of scoring more runs in the eighth than they surrendered, and McGowin would go on to make a handful of other relief appearances, an unspectacular component of one of baseball's least spectacular bullpens, who happened to be in the right place and time to witness a turnaround.

Tanner Rainey RHP   Born: 12/25/92   Age: 27   Bats: R   Throws: R   Height: 6'2"   Weight: 235   Origin: Round 2, 2015 Draft (#71 overall)

YEAR	TEAM	LVL	AGE	W	L	SV	G	GS	IP	H	HR	BB/9	K/9	K	GB%	BABIP	WHIP	ERA	DRA	WARP	MPH	FB%	WHF	CSP
2017	DAY	A+	24	2	2	9	39	0	45	21	4	4.4	15.4	77	47%	.230	0.96	3.80	1.74	1.7				
2017	PEN	AA	24	1	1	4	14	0	17	8	2	5.8	14.3	27	62%	.222	1.12	1.59	3.18	0.3				
2018	LOU	AAA	25	7	2	3	44	0	51	25	2	6.2	11.5	65	37%	.221	1.18	2.65	3.08	1.2				
2018	CIN	MLB	25	0	0	0	8	0	7	13	4	15.4	9.0	7	31%	.409	3.57	24.43	9.00	-0.3	100.1	71.4	12.2	38.9
2019	FRE	AAA	26	2	2	2	16	0	18	16	1	6.0	16.0	32	57%	.417	1.56	4.00	2.63	0.6				
2019	WAS	MLB	26	2	3	0	52	0	48¹	32	6	7.1	13.8	74	54%	.283	1.45	3.91	3.07	1.2	99.5	70.8	18.8	43.7
2020	WAS	MLB	27	3	2	4	49	0	52	41	6	6.2	14.2	82	47%	.327	1.48	4.29	4.11	0.7	99.1	71.7	18	42.1

Comparables: *Luke Farrell, Vic Black, Cody Carroll*

In pitching, real estate and life, sometimes all that matters is location, location, location. Rainey has stuff bordering on unfair—a fastball in the high-90s paired with a wicked slider in the high-80s—and he generated an incredible 41 percent swing-and-miss rate this season. But his issue was and is locating pitches. He allowed more walks than hits in 2019, cutting his previous season's WHIP in half, though still allowing for more on-base traffic than one would want from a potential late-inning reliever.

Fernando Rodney RHP   Born: 03/18/77   Age: 43   Bats: R   Throws: R   Height: 5'11"   Weight: 240   Origin: International Free Agent, 1997

YEAR	TEAM	LVL	AGE	W	L	SV	G	GS	IP	H	HR	BB/9	K/9	K	GB%	BABIP	WHIP	ERA	DRA	WARP	MPH	FB%	WHF	CSP
2017	ARI	MLB	40	5	4	39	61	0	55¹	40	3	4.2	10.6	65	54%	.274	1.19	4.23	3.63	1.0	96.9	59.5	13.2	45.4
2018	MIN	MLB	41	3	2	25	46	0	43²	42	5	3.9	10.3	50	45%	.319	1.40	3.09	3.85	0.5	97.0	71.8	13.1	46.8
2018	OAK	MLB	41	1	1	0	22	0	20²	20	2	5.7	8.7	20	46%	.316	1.60	3.92	4.52	0.1	97.1	68.7	9.5	43.9
2019	FRE	AAA	42	0	2	0	9	0	8	8	1	10.1	12.4	11	50%	.333	2.12	4.50	4.73	0.1				
2019	OAK	MLB	42	0	2	0	17	0	14¹	20	2	7.5	8.8	14	55%	.429	2.23	9.42	5.36	0.0	95.4	64.6	9.1	43.1
2019	WAS	MLB	42	0	3	2	38	0	33¹	29	3	4.3	9.4	35	48%	.302	1.35	4.05	4.32	0.4	96.7	69.4	13.2	45.7
2020	WAS	MLB	43	2	2	0	33	0	35	32	4	4.5	9.8	38	48%	.302	1.43	4.30	4.39	0.4	94.7	64.2	11.7	43.4

Comparables: *Al Reyes, Rudy Seanez, Santiago Casilla*

There are two Fernandos Rodney: One, Fernando Rodney, the oldest player in MLB. Thrower of a truly nasty changeup. Wearer of a terrific hat, and a reminder that, no matter your age, baseball is a kid's game. That despite everything, this is supposed to be *fun*. The other, Rodney Fernando, the oldest player in MLB. Hittable, over-the-hill, his glory days well behind him, a flat changeup and an imminent retirement. A relic, a fossil. Rodney has thrown more pitches than any active relief pitcher—some 16,500 of them since 2002. Some days, it seems he's feeling every one of those. Others are a reminder that there's value in youthful enthusiasm and that there's value in age and treachery. And that baseball should be wide enough to contain both.

Seth Romero LHP   Born: 04/19/96   Age: 24   Bats: L   Throws: L   Height: 6'3"   Weight: 240   Origin: Round 1, 2017 Draft (#25 overall)

YEAR	TEAM	LVL	AGE	W	L	SV	G	GS	IP	H	HR	BB/9	K/9	K	GB%	BABIP	WHIP	ERA	DRA	WARP	MPH	FB%	WHF	CSP
2017	AUB	A-	21	0	1	0	6	6	20	19	0	2.7	14.4	32	40%	.404	1.25	5.40	3.16	0.5				
2018	HAG	A	22	0	1	0	7	7	25¹	20	3	2.8	12.1	34	45%	.279	1.11	3.91	2.93	0.7				
2020	WAS	MLB	24	2	2	0	33	0	35	35	6	3.6	9.4	36	39%	.311	1.41	4.71	4.88	0.2				

Comparables: *Matt Hall, Caleb Smith, Steven Matz*

A career every bit as troubled as his arm is talented. Romero was dismissed from the University of Houston baseball team three years ago for decking a teammate, after a long list of prior infractions. The Nationals still drafted him in the first round, because when you're a lefty with the potential for three plus pitches, you can get away with quite a lot. He proceeded to get sent home during spring training in 2018 for staying out too late at night, and promptly blew out his elbow when he actually got on the mound later that summer. Romero missed the entire 2019 season recovering from Tommy John surgery; a year where he wasn't in the news counts as a win here. He enters his age-24 season with a whopping 47 1/3 pro innings, all at Low-A or below, and tons of injury and makeup concerns. But somewhere down there a wealth of talent remains too.

Joe Ross RHP Born: 05/21/93 Age: 27 Bats: R Throws: R Height: 6'4" Weight: 220 Origin: Round 1, 2011 Draft (#25 overall)

YEAR	TEAM	LVL	AGE	W	L	SV	G	GS	IP	H	HR	BB/9	K/9	K	GB%	BABIP	WHIP	ERA	DRA	WARP	MPH	FB%	WHF	CSP
2017	SYR	AAA	24	2	2	0	5	5	27²	33	3	2.6	7.2	22	37%	.341	1.48	4.88	6.15	-0.1				
2017	WAS	MLB	24	5	3	0	13	13	73²	88	16	2.4	8.3	68	41%	.332	1.47	5.01	4.19	1.1	94.1	54.8	11	48.9
2018	NAT	RK	25	0	0	0	2	2	6	0	0	4.5	12.0	8	56%	.000	0.50	0.00	1.05	0.3				
2018	SYR	AAA	25	2	0	0	2	2	11²	12	0	3.1	3.1	4	43%	.273	1.37	3.09	5.87	0.0				
2018	WAS	MLB	25	0	2	0	3	3	16	17	3	2.2	3.9	7	36%	.269	1.31	5.06	7.08	-0.3	94.9	56	9.2	44.9
2019	FRE	AAA	26	2	3	0	8	8	40	48	2	1.8	7.2	32	50%	.368	1.40	4.28	4.67	0.8				
2019	WAS	MLB	26	4	4	0	27	9	64	74	7	4.6	8.0	57	45%	.345	1.67	5.48	6.38	-0.5	96.0	62.8	11.2	45.3
2020	WAS	MLB	27	6	6	0	36	16	102	104	16	3.3	8.0	90	45%	.300	1.39	4.63	4.54	1.4	94.7	60.1	11.1	46.6

Comparables: Kevin Gausman, A.J. Cole, Alex Cobb

It would have been an epic story. Ross, coming back from Tommy John, occasional fifth starter and unspectacular long man, takes on the Houston Astros when a neck injury felled the mighty Max Scherzer in Game 5 of the World Series. It would have been epic, Homeric, an unlikely rise-from-the-ashes, workman-on-the-world's-largest-stage story, if only the Nationals' offense had shown up. Still, despite pitching well against baseball's best offense, Ross didn't quite rise to the occasion. His velocity has risen, though, his ground-ball-inducing sinker and four-seamer back up to their pre-surgery speeds, along with reworked, slurvier slider, all indications he'll return this year as a protagonist and not just a footnote.

Jackson Rutledge RHP Born: 04/01/99 Age: 21 Bats: R Throws: R Height: 6'8" Weight: 250 Origin: Round 1, 2019 Draft (#17 overall)

YEAR	TEAM	LVL	AGE	W	L	SV	G	GS	IP	H	HR	BB/9	K/9	K	GB%	BABIP	WHIP	ERA	DRA	WARP	MPH	FB%	WHF	CSP
2019	AUB	A-	20	0	0	0	3	3	9	4	2	3.0	6.0	6	42%	.091	0.78	3.00	3.55	0.2				
2019	HAG	A	20	2	0	0	6	6	27¹	14	0	3.6	10.2	31	46%	.222	0.91	2.30	3.40	0.6				
2020	WAS	MLB	21	2	2	0	33	0	35	35	5	3.8	7.8	30	41%	.292	1.43	4.75	4.91	0.2				

Comparables: Parker Markel, José Castillo, Keyvius Sampson

The Twitter account @J_Cheddar34 could only be run by a cheese-loving boomer or a pitcher who throws really hard like Rutledge does. The towering righty ended up in junior college after a hip injury sidetracked his career at Arkansas. He made the most of his newfound draft eligibility, mixing four-seamers and two-seamers ticking into the upper-90s with a new power slider that quickly projected out to plus, and adding the occasional curve and change. It's stuff that could front a rotation some day, although all the usual caveats about command and injuries apply.

Aníbal Sánchez RHP Born: 02/27/84 Age: 36 Bats: R Throws: R Height: 6'0" Weight: 205 Origin: International Free Agent, 2001

YEAR	TEAM	LVL	AGE	W	L	SV	G	GS	IP	H	HR	BB/9	K/9	K	GB%	BABIP	WHIP	ERA	DRA	WARP	MPH	FB%	WHF	CSP
2017	TOL	AAA	33	0	2	0	4	4	15²	17	3	2.9	11.5	20	46%	.350	1.40	4.60	4.68	0.2				
2017	DET	MLB	33	3	7	0	28	17	105¹	139	26	2.5	8.9	104	36%	.354	1.59	6.41	6.22	-0.8	93.2	49.6	10.9	49
2018	GWN	AAA	34	0	1	0	2	2	6²	9	2	5.4	12.1	9	37%	.412	1.95	10.80	7.00	-0.1				
2018	ATL	MLB	34	7	6	0	25	24	136²	106	15	2.8	8.9	135	47%	.255	1.08	2.83	2.75	4.0	92.7	37.6	11.5	46.2
2019	WAS	MLB	35	11	8	0	30	30	166	153	22	3.1	7.3	134	39%	.265	1.27	3.85	4.39	2.5	92.4	35.1	10.9	46
2020	WAS	MLB	36	8	9	0	26	26	137	137	27	2.9	7.4	113	40%	.277	1.32	4.54	4.52	2.0	91.3	38	10.8	45.9

Comparables: Johnny Cueto, Matt Garza, Ian Kennedy

A changeup like a butterfly
Eephus soft and gentle as a sigh
A multi-pitch arsenal like on satin wings
Cutter makes your heart feel strange inside
It flutters like soft wings in flight
Change up like a butterfly
A rare and lethal thing

It happened in St. Louis
That mariposa changeup
That slow and floating pitch that ties hitters up inside
Its touch is soft and gentle
Its velo cool and tender
Whenever he throws it, we think of butterflies

Max Scherzer RHP Born: 07/27/84 Age: 35 Bats: R Throws: R Height: 6'3" Weight: 215 Origin: Round 1, 2006 Draft (#11 overall)

YEAR	TEAM	LVL	AGE	W	L	SV	G	GS	IP	H	HR	BB/9	K/9	K	GB%	BABIP	WHIP	ERA	DRA	WARP	MPH	FB%	WHF	CSP
2017	WAS	MLB	32	16	6	0	31	31	200²	126	22	2.5	12.0	268	38%	.245	0.90	2.51	2.32	7.3	96.2	48.7	16.7	48.7
2018	WAS	MLB	33	18	7	0	33	33	220²	150	23	2.1	12.2	300	35%	.265	0.91	2.53	2.29	7.7	96.6	50.1	17.3	50
2019	WAS	MLB	34	11	7	0	27	27	172¹	144	18	1.7	12.7	243	41%	.322	1.03	2.92	2.48	6.2	97.1	48.3	17.8	49.2
2020	WAS	MLB	35	13	8	0	29	29	187	147	25	2.3	12.5	255	39%	.297	1.04	2.71	2.90	6.0	95.4	48.2	17	48.5

Comparables: Tim Lincecum, David Price, Pedro Martinez

Sing, Oh Writers, of the Wrath of Scherzer, Son of Missouri, that has brought countless ills upon the majors. Many a brave soul did he send hurrying back to the dugout, and many a hero did he yield as prey to yips and reporters, for so were the counsels of Rizzo fulfilled the day on which Bryce, new king of the city with brothers of love, and great Scherzer, fell out with one another.

And which of the owners was it that set them to quarrel? It was the son of Ted and Annette, for he was angry with Harper, and set deferred payments upon him to plague his people, because the new son of Philadelphia had dishonored his contract offer. Now the Phillies owner had come to the offices of Boras in free agency, and had brought with him a great ransom. Moreover, Bryce bore in his hands the slugger of Louisville, wreathed in pine tar, and he beset the Nationals but most of all Scherzer and Strasburg, who were their aces.

"Sons of Washington," Scherzer cried. "And all other Nationals. May the baseball gods who dwell in Cooperstown grant you strength to sack the City of the Liberty Bell. And that you reach home plate in safety. But earn me the Curly W, and offer run support, in reverence to Cy Young, father of pitcher wins."

Stephen Strasburg RHP Born: 07/20/88 Age: 31 Bats: R Throws: R Height: 6'5" Weight: 235 Origin: Round 1, 2009 Draft (#1 overall)

YEAR	TEAM	LVL	AGE	W	L	SV	G	GS	IP	H	HR	BB/9	K/9	K	GB%	BABIP	WHIP	ERA	DRA	WARP	MPH	FB%	WHF	CSP
2017	WAS	MLB	28	15	4	0	28	28	175¹	131	13	2.4	10.5	204	48%	.274	1.02	2.52	2.93	5.2	97.8	51.9	13.8	49.3
2018	POT	A+	29	0	1	0	2	2	9	7	1	1.0	12.0	12	50%	.261	0.89	1.00	2.56	0.3				
2018	WAS	MLB	29	10	7	0	22	22	130	118	18	2.6	10.8	156	45%	.309	1.20	3.74	2.97	3.5	97.5	52	13	47.2
2019	WAS	MLB	30	18	6	0	33	33	209	161	24	2.4	10.8	251	52%	.274	1.04	3.32	2.13	8.3	95.8	48.3	14.4	44.6
2020	WAS	MLB	31	12	9	0	29	29	178	154	23	2.6	10.9	216	50%	.300	1.16	3.24	3.34	4.9	95.9	49.8	13.8	46.3

Comparables: Pedro Martinez, Clayton Kershaw, Jake Peavy

A lot of talk about Strasburg has always been rooted in a place of toxic masculinity—he's been called "soft,", an "orchid." But he's a reminder that some orchids are epiphytic; they thrive best high up in the tree canopy, able to extract water from periodic rainfall, roots going from desiccated white to a sudden photosynthetic green under favorable environmental conditions. If Strasburg is an orchid, he's that kind. Gone are the days of the blazing fastball. Instead, he thrives on mixing his four-seamer with that devastating changeup, generating whiffs 45 percent of the times batters dare to swing. Perhaps unappreciated (if one could call anything about Strasburg's pitching unappreciated) is his curveball, his put-away pitch against righties, capable of its own kind of slow devastation—a reminder that it's often not the fastest, but the most adaptable, who are able to survive.

Hunter Strickland RHP Born: 09/24/88 Age: 31 Bats: R Throws: R Height: 6'3" Weight: 225 Origin: Round 18, 2007 Draft (#564 overall)

YEAR	TEAM	LVL	AGE	W	L	SV	G	GS	IP	H	HR	BB/9	K/9	K	GB%	BABIP	WHIP	ERA	DRA	WARP	MPH	FB%	WHF	CSP
2017	SFN	MLB	28	4	3	1	68	0	61¹	59	4	4.3	8.5	58	38%	.314	1.43	2.64	5.11	0.0	97.9	68.5	11.7	49.2
2018	SFN	MLB	29	3	5	14	49	0	45¹	43	5	4.2	7.3	37	40%	.277	1.41	3.97	4.49	0.2	97.5	64.3	11.8	46.9
2019	SEA	MLB	30	0	1	2	4	0	3¹	2	1	0.0	8.1	3	33%	.125	0.60	8.10	6.19	0.0	97.0	65.8	9.5	39.8
2019	WAS	MLB	30	2	0	0	24	0	21	20	5	3.4	6.4	15	33%	.242	1.33	5.14	6.72	-0.3	98.1	65.8	12.4	48.5
2020	WAS	MLB	31	2	2	0	39	0	42	38	6	3.2	8.2	38	36%	.274	1.26	3.93	3.97	0.7	96.9	65.8	11.8	47.7

Comparables: Blake Treinen, Kevin Quackenbush, Jeremy Jeffress

In a different timeline when the Nationals didn't win the World Series, Bryce Harper slapping a home run off Strickland two years after the brawl following a hit-by-pitch—and five years after Harper put a Strickland pitch into McCovey Cove—would have been enough #narrative for anyone. The 2019 home run came late in the game in which the Nationals clinched a postseason berth, one the Nats won 6-5 buoyed by a Trea Turner grand slam, a footnote that would have been a lede any other time.

The Nats acquired Strickland at the trade deadline in an attempt to find, if not something pleasant, at least something new, given their worst of all possible bullpens in the first half of the season. It was a move many decried not because of the pitch that hit Harper, but because of the downstream effects on fan-favorite former-National and now-former-Giant Michael Morse. Strickland did, in fact, become a member of the Nats bullpen, in all the damning ways that means, and it became evident that his habit of surrendering homers wasn't special to Harper but a symptom of broader concerns about injury recovery.

Wander Suero RHP Born: 09/15/91 Age: 28 Bats: R Throws: R Height: 6'4" Weight: 211 Origin: International Free Agent, 2010

YEAR	TEAM	LVL	AGE	W	L	SV	G	GS	IP	H	HR	BB/9	K/9	K	GB%	BABIP	WHIP	ERA	DRA	WARP	MPH	FB%	WHF	CSP
2017	HAR	AA	25	0	1	10	18	0	23	18	2	2.0	9.0	23	45%	.254	1.00	1.96	2.91	0.5				
2017	SYR	AAA	25	3	1	10	36	0	42¹	33	1	3.0	8.9	42	46%	.281	1.11	1.70	3.18	1.0				
2018	SYR	AAA	26	1	2	1	14	0	17	16	1	2.1	8.5	16	46%	.306	1.18	3.71	4.01	0.2				
2018	WAS	MLB	26	4	1	0	40	0	47²	43	4	2.8	8.9	47	36%	.300	1.22	3.59	4.29	0.3	94.2	79.9	11.9	51.1
2019	WAS	MLB	27	6	9	1	78	0	71¹	64	5	3.3	10.2	81	41%	.326	1.26	4.54	3.64	1.3	95.4	72.2	14.7	50.5
2020	WAS	MLB	28	3	2	4	49	0	52	47	7	3.1	9.8	57	40%	.296	1.24	3.68	3.70	1.0	94.4	75.3	13.8	51.1

Comparables: Lou Trivino, Dustin Antolin, Jeremy Horst

There are worse things for a bullpen arm with a wicked changeup who doesn't throw four-seamers than having Fernando Rodney sitting next to you for much of the year. Suero managed to put together a respectable, if unspectacular season, though that descriptor made him one of the better arms in the Nationals bullpen in the first half. Each success should be caveated with an asterisk: He had a career-high strikeout rate (though also had an increase in walk rate) and increased his ground-ball percentage (though also had a subsequent rise in BABIP), while retaining a non-elite but non-disastrous WHIP. Mostly, like his mentor, he should be kept away from left-handed hitters and out of high-leverage spots.

Austin Voth RHP Born: 06/26/92 Age: 28 Bats: R Throws: R Height: 6'2" Weight: 201 Origin: Round 5, 2013 Draft (#166 overall)

YEAR	TEAM	LVL	AGE	W	L	SV	G	GS	IP	H	HR	BB/9	K/9	K	GB%	BABIP	WHIP	ERA	DRA	WARP	MPH	FB%	WHF	CSP
2017	HAR	AA	25	3	4	0	10	10	54¹	63	8	2.2	7.3	44	44%	.320	1.40	5.13	5.01	0.1				
2017	SYR	AAA	25	1	7	0	13	13	66¹	85	12	4.6	5.7	42	45%	.329	1.79	6.38	7.08	-1.0				
2018	SYR	AAA	26	6	8	0	24	24	125²	119	13	2.9	8.4	117	42%	.295	1.27	4.37	3.92	2.3				
2018	WAS	MLB	26	1	1	0	4	2	12¹	12	3	4.4	8.0	11	45%	.257	1.46	6.57	5.14	0.0	93.1	62	9.3	51.7
2019	HAR	AA	27	1	1	0	3	3	11¹	11	1	1.6	8.7	11	37%	.345	1.15	4.76	5.54	-0.1				
2019	FRE	AAA	27	3	5	0	12	12	61¹	68	7	2.2	10.0	68	41%	.345	1.35	4.40	3.67	1.8				
2019	WAS	MLB	27	2	1	0	9	8	43²	33	5	2.7	9.1	44	38%	.257	1.05	3.30	4.08	0.8	94.7	60.5	13.7	49.5
2020	WAS	MLB	28	5	5	0	41	11	89	86	17	3.0	9.3	92	39%	.291	1.30	4.39	4.39	1.3	93.8	61.2	12.9	50.8

Comparables: Alec Mills, Kyle McGowin, William Cuevas

At a time when the game is moving away from having even a fourth starter, the Nationals improbably had three fifth starters—Ross, Fedde and Voth—the last of whom did not make the World Series roster despite having the best season of the three, albeit over a smaller number of games. His curveball, in particular, generated a whiff on nearly half of all swings, and he looked sharp in three losses to Atlanta, including a one-run gem that devolved into chaos following an errant Rodney fastball finding and injuring Charlie Culberson. Like his other fifth-starter counterparts, Voth may make an attractive trade piece as the Nationals attempt to restock their infield.

LINEOUTS

Hitters

HITTER	POS	TEAM	LVL	AGE	PA	R	2B	3B	HR	RBI	BB	K	SB	CS	AVG/OBP/SLG	DRC+	VORP	BABIP	BRR	FRAA	WARP
Tres Barrera	C	HAR	AA	24	403	42	23	0	8	46	36	69	1	2	.249/.323/.381	118	17.0	.285	-2.7	C(92): 3.4	2.7
	C	WAS	MLB	24	2	0	0	0	0	0	0	0	0	0	.000/.000/.000	96	0.1	.000	0.0	C(1): 0.0	0.0
Gage Canning	OF	HAG	A	22	44	7	1	0	1	5	3	13	6	0	.244/.295/.341	78	1.2	.333	-0.2	LF(6): -1.3, RF(3): -0.2	-0.2
	OF	POT	A+	22	410	44	17	6	3	40	32	114	8	4	.238/.310/.341	88	5.1	.337	0.7	RF(52): -1.0, CF(45): -3.6	0.0
Jeremy De La Rosa	OF	NAT	Rk	17	99	14	1	2	2	10	12	29	3	2	.232/.343/.366	85	0.6	.321	-0.8	RF(12): -0.2, LF(10): -0.2	-0.1
Wilmer Difo	INF	WAS	MLB	27	144	15	2	0	2	8	12	29	0	1	.252/.315/.313	74	1.8	.310	1.0	SS(33): -1.5, 3B(6): -0.3	0.1
	INF	FRE	AAA	27	261	48	14	3	4	30	25	51	13	5	.300/.369/.438	94	13.4	.369	3.7	SS(32): -1.9, 2B(20): 1.4	1.2
Cole Freeman	CF	POT	A+	24	534	82	27	3	3	49	53	60	31	6	.311/.394/.404	150	44.7	.351	6.9	2B(54): -1.6, CF(46): -0.2	4.5
Yadiel Hernandez	OF	FRE	AAA	31	508	87	22	1	33	90	63	106	7	5	.323/.406/.604	146	44.9	.357	-2.0	LF(52): -4.6, RF(44): -3.8	2.9
Spencer Kieboom	C	HAR	AA	28	188	12	7	0	1	14	18	35	0	0	.196/.271/.256	76	-2.6	.239	-0.6	C(42): 0.1, 1B(10): 1.1	0.4
Drew Mendoza	1B	HAG	A	21	239	23	12	0	4	25	34	57	3	0	.264/.377/.383	127	12.6	.348	0.8	1B(44): -3.5, 3B(6): 1.2	0.8
Viandel Pena	2B	NAT	Rk	18	154	27	10	3	0	15	21	31	6	3	.359/.455/.481	188	19.4	.470	2.1	2B(16): -2.0, SS(15): 0.7	1.8
Israel Pineda	C	HAG	A	19	411	48	12	0	7	35	30	102	1	2	.217/.278/.305	68	4.1	.276	0.9	C(83): 1.6	0.7
Matt Reynolds	UT	FRE	AAA	28	449	65	29	4	16	55	64	95	8	2	.295/.401/.521	119	33.5	.356	-1.9	SS(35): -2.9, 2B(30): 0.4	2.3
Adrián Sanchez	INF	WAS	MLB	28	32	3	0	0	0	1	1	10	0	0	.226/.250/.226	61	-0.5	.333	0.6	3B(6): 0.0, 2B(4): 0.0	0.0
	INF	HAR	AA	28	282	43	19	1	6	36	19	39	11	5	.316/.365/.469	157	24.3	.349	2.3	2B(33): -0.8, 3B(21): 0.3	3.0

Former $3.9 million bonus baby **Yasel Antuna** had a lost season on the road back from 2018 Tommy John surgery. He remains one of the system's top prospects, which is one part a nod to his upside and two parts damnation of the rest of the system. ⊗ Washington needed an emergency fourth catcher in September due to Kurt Suzuki's bad elbow and called up prospect **Tres Barrera**. He got into two games, both in the late innings of blowouts, and decades from now he will get to show his future grandchildren his World Series ring because of it. ⊗ If we had asked you before you opened this chapter whether **Gage Canning** was a white-shoe law firm that Sam Seaborn used to work at or a fourth outfielder prospect, would you have known? ⊗ He's a mile away from the majors, but the Nationals showed how much they like **Jeremy De La Rosa** by challenging him with a stateside assignment as a 17-year-old making his pro debut. He held his own. ⊗ Nothing says "juiced-ball era" like a **Wilmer Difo** second-deck home run against the Mets. In April. Somehow they kept playing baseball anyway. ⊗ No, we can't really explain what **Cole Freeman** was doing in the Carolina League long enough to contend for the batting title, either. He's speedy, puts the bat on the ball and can play both the infield and outfield, so the wheel is probably stopping on "utility player" here. ⊗ Former Cuban star **Yadiel Hernandez** had an absolute monster season in Triple A with the happy fun ball after taking a few years to adjust to the American minors. He deserves a shot at outfield time against righties on a bad team to be named later. ⊗ **Spencer Kieboom** belongs to an exclusive fraternity of marginal major-league catchers with less-marginal, middle-infielder brothers. It's actually just a table for two with Jhonatan Solano. Austin Romine used to be invited but is no longer welcome. ⊗ If you believe in nominative determinism, **Drew Mendoza** will only be a .200 hitter, which would be a real problem for his profile since he's actually a hulking college first baseman. ⊗ **Viandel Pena** is tiny—he is listed at 5-foot-8 and 148 pounds, and sometimes those listings are generous. You probably guessed that there isn't much power here, and you'd be right, but he has feel for the bat and can play the middle infield. ⊗ **Israel Pineda** is a glove-over-bat teenaged catching prospect, which means he could be anything from a minor-league coach to a major-league relief pitcher to an honorary Molina brother by the time he reaches his thirties. Oh, the possibilities of youth. ⊗ **Matt Reynolds** did everything he normally does and then some in 2019: played six positions in Triple A, set a new career high in homers and even pitched twice. But he failed to make the majors while doing so, breaking a four-year streak of being rostered that started when the Mets purchased his contract during the 2015 NLDS. ⊗ There's a cup of coffee, and then there's a caffeine overdose. **Adrián Sanchez** spent much of 2019 traversing the highway between DC and Harrisburg, serving as a replacement-level infielder when the Nats put up a crooked number or had one put up against them.

Pitchers

PITCHER	TEAM	LVL	AGE	W	L	SV	G	GS	IP	H	HR	BB/9	K/9	K	GB%	BABIP	WHIP	ERA	DRA	WARP	MPH	FB%	WHF	CSP
Joan Adon	HAG	A	20	11	3	0	22	21	105	93	8	3.8	7.7	90	46%	.289	1.30	3.86	5.27	-0.1				
Michael Blazek	FRE	AAA	30	2	2	1	34	1	38²	44	9	3.7	9.8	42	29%	.321	1.55	6.05	5.40	0.3				
	WAS	MLB	30	0	0	0	4	0	5	6	1	9.0	0.0	0	14%	.250	2.20	7.20	9.31	-0.2	96.8	72.1	4.7	48.4
James Bourque	HAR	AA	25	3	0	6	14	0	20¹	17	1	2.7	14.6	33	37%	.381	1.13	1.33	3.45	0.3				
	FRE	AAA	25	4	1	3	33	0	43²	41	6	6.2	10.9	53	47%	.318	1.63	5.56	3.93	1.0				
	WAS	MLB	25	0	0	0	1	0	0²	3	0	27.0	0.0	0	75%	.750	7.50	54.00	4.69	0.0	97.6	79.3	0	31.3
Ben Braymer	HAR	AA	25	4	4	0	13	13	79	56	7	2.4	7.9	69	34%	.225	0.97	2.51	3.29	1.6				
	FRE	AAA	25	0	6	0	13	13	60	81	18	5.2	7.1	47	33%	.346	1.93	7.20	9.19	-1.4				
Matt Cronin	HAG	A	21	0	0	1	17	0	22	11	1	4.5	16.8	41	20%	.345	1.00	0.82	2.34	0.6				
Mason Denaburg	NAT	Rk	19	1	1	0	7	4	20¹	23	1	6.2	8.4	19	48%	.361	1.82	7.52	8.54	-0.6				
Tyler Dyson	AUB	A-	21	2	1	0	8	8	31²	20	1	2.3	4.0	14	50%	.209	0.88	1.14	4.11	0.4				
Steven Fuentes	POT	A+	22	1	1	1	8	0	17	8	0	3.7	13.8	26	46%	.242	0.88	0.53	2.36	0.5				
	HAR	AA	22	5	4	0	15	11	63²	63	1	2.1	8.9	63	58%	.326	1.23	2.69	4.61	0.2				
David Hernandez	SWB	AAA	34	0	1	0	8	0	7	5	1	10.3	14.1	11	40%	.286	1.86	7.71	4.70	0.1				
	CIN	MLB	34	2	5	2	47	0	42²	53	7	4.2	11.2	53	32%	.393	1.71	8.02	6.09	-0.3	95.1	52.2	15.9	46.8
Tony Sipp	WAS	MLB	35	1	2	0	36	0	21	19	1	3.9	7.7	18	38%	.286	1.33	4.71	5.37	0.0	92.8	47.9	13	47.9
Jonny Venters	HAR	AA	34	0	0	0	10	0	7	6	0	7.7	5.1	4	74%	.261	1.71	1.29	6.46	-0.2				
	GWN	AAA	34	0	0	0	7	0	7	3	0	2.6	7.7	6	81%	.188	0.71	0.00	2.58	0.2				
	ATL	MLB	34	0	0	1	9	0	4²	9	3	15.4	13.5	7	50%	.462	3.64	17.36	5.41	0.0	94.9	79.1	7.5	42.5
	WAS	MLB	34	0	1	0	3	0	3¹	3	0	5.4	13.5	5	89%	.333	1.50	5.40	5.37	0.0	94.4	82.3	14.5	40.4
Austen Williams	WAS	MLB	26	0	0	0	2	0	0¹	5	2	27.0	27.0	1	40%	1.000	18.00	162.00	4.64	0.0	93.7	37.9	17.2	27
Eddy Yean	NAT	Rk	18	1	2	0	8	8	35¹	30	3	3.1	9.2	36	52%	.293	1.19	3.82	3.48	1.0				
	AUB	A-	18	1	1	0	2	2	11	7	0	4.1	5.7	7	44%	.219	1.09	2.45	4.35	0.1				

Joan Adon has always seemed destined to a future as a 95-and-a-slider reliever, but he stretched out into the rotation in Low-A during 2019 and held up just fine. ⊗ **Michael Blazek** was in spring training for the American Association's Lincoln Saltdogs when the Nationals purchased his contract. He would briefly and unsuccessfully pop up in the majors two months later. ⊗ **James Bourque** is memorable for his mustache and for posting worse numbers than Trevor Rosenthal, all within a span of a few depressing minutes. He, like Rosenthal, is likely to be shaved from a major-league roster soon. ⊗ **Ben Braymer** is just left-handed enough that the Nats opted to add him to their 40-man despite his poor showing in Fresno. That protected him from being eligible for the Rule 5 draft in which he would've had very little business being selected. ⊗ University of Arkansas closer **Matt Cronin** made a seamless transition to A-ball dominance after the Nationals popped him in the fourth round. He'll likely be one of the first players from the 2019 draft class to make the majors and projects as a future setup man or LOOGY, provided they still exist. ⊗ 2018 first-rounder **Mason Denaburg** has yet to make it out of the complex, and his season ended on August 3rd with shoulder problems. It's not what you want, especially when he originally fell in the draft due to injury concerns. ⊗ Fifth-round pick **Tyler Dyson** has extremely impressive raw stuff for a mid-round college pick. You can probably guess that he never really put it together in college because if you have big stuff and were actually good somewhere like the University of Florida you go a heck of a lot earlier in the draft than Dyson did. ⊗ Sleeper groundball specialist **Steven Fuentes** became a more interesting prospect when he continued to have success after a midseason conversion into the rotation. Unfortunately, the experiment came to an early end when he was hit with a suspension for stimulant usage in August. ⊗ Legend holds that if you stand in front of a bathroom mirror and recite, "It's only a forearm strain, how bad could it be?" three times, **Koda Glover** appears. Which he hasn't. All season. ⊗ **David Hernandez** has long seen his ERA balloon and contract based on how many homers he allows, and it shouldn't surprise that the rocket ball did him few favors. He can still rack up strikeouts, but between walks and hits allowed, he was quite the WHIPping boy last year. ⊗ **Andry Lara** was the highest-profile 2019 Nats international signing, and therefore is by default one of the top prospects in a system as thin as the branches of a cherry blossom tree. ⊗ If the Nationals wanted an older middle-inning reliever with inconsistent stuff, an above-4 ERA and a mediocre WHIP in **Tony Sipp**, well, Fernando Rodney was also right there. ⊗ Three games, three innings, three hits, three runs, and three-plus months on the IL (following three Tommy John surgeries): **Jonny Venters** stars in "Unearned Run: The 2019 Nationals Bullpen Story." ⊗ It is a truth universally acknowledged that a relief pitcher, in possession of a moderate slider, must be in want of the strike zone. Unfortunately for **Austen Williams**, like Lydia Bennet, he fell victim to many a rake last season before being rescued back into respectability with a long stint on the IL. ⊗ Projectable Dominican righty **Eddy Yean** was impressive in his stateside debut. He's a long way away, but intriguing.

MLB Managers

Brad Ausmus   wRM+: 95.5

TEAM	YEAR	W	L	Pythag +/-	Avg PC	100+ P	120+ P	QS	BQS	REL	REL w Zero R	IBB	PH	PH Avg	PH HR	SB2	CS2	SB3	CS3	SAC Att	SAC %	POS SAC	Squee-ze	Swing	In Play
DET	2014	90	72	3	101.0	103	3	90	9	473	367	34	71	.164	1	90	34	16	7	40	60.0	20	1	296	83
DET	2015	74	87	6	94.1	77	2	72	10	505	396	32	74	.121	1	66	44	17	5	43	53.5	23	1	293	86
DET	2016	86	75	2	94.5	61	1	50	3	476	375	25	79	.243	6	54	26	4	3	28	60.7	16	2	184	60
DET	2017	64	98	-1	94.1	68	2	45	1	510	372	42	83	.227	0	56	33	9	1	17	64.7	11	0	260	67
LAA	2019	72	90	1	74.2	15	0	8	1	589	422	11	94	.210	2	61	19	4	1	8	50.0	4	0	229	62

Rocco Baldelli   wRM+: 100.0

TEAM	YEAR	W	L	Pythag +/-	Avg PC	100+ P	120+ P	QS	BQS	REL	REL w Zero R	IBB	PH	PH Avg	PH HR	SB2	CS2	SB3	CS3	SAC Att	SAC %	POS SAC	Squee-ze	Swing	In Play
MIN	2019	101	61	3	89.5	33	0	28	3	524	419	10	75	.271	2	27	20	1	0	18	55.6	7	0	171	60

David Bell   wRM+: 98.7

TEAM	YEAR	W	L	Pythag +/-	Avg PC	100+ P	120+ P	QS	BQS	REL	REL w Zero R	IBB	PH	PH Avg	PH HR	SB2	CS2	SB3	CS3	SAC Att	SAC %	POS SAC	Squee-ze	Swing	In Play
CIN	2019	75	87	-5	91.6	47	0	29	2	535	407	31	311	.173	8	73	33	7	4	45	66.7	2	2	309	88

Bud Black   wRM+: 106.0

TEAM	YEAR	W	L	Pythag +/-	Avg PC	100+ P	120+ P	QS	BQS	REL	REL w Zero R	IBB	PH	PH Avg	PH HR	SB2	CS2	SB3	CS3	SAC Att	SAC %	POS SAC	Squee-ze	Swing	In Play
SDN	2007	89	74	-1	90.0	47	0	90	4	485	404	48	272	.188	3	50	16	5	7	93	68.8	28	1	246	90
SDN	2008	63	99	-3	90.9	49	3	76	4	490	348	61	285	.198	3	34	17	2	0	76	77.6	18	0	226	93
SDN	2009	75	87	9	91.0	46	1	77	3	528	412	58	263	.248	9	72	23	10	5	111	66.7	38	1	296	90
SDN	2010	90	72	-2	94.8	54	0	87	2	499	431	51	278	.206	9	114	47	10	1	111	71.2	44	1	359	97
SDN	2011	71	91	-8	96.7	65	1	91	4	489	416	56	283	.160	2	147	42	21	2	86	64.0	23	4	391	88
SDN	2012	76	86	2	92.2	49	1	75	5	529	449	48	278	.248	6	129	42	25	2	107	58.9	30	1	396	88
SDN	2013	76	86	5	93.9	59	2	87	2	488	402	31	266	.206	8	105	31	13	3	92	56.5	23	1	284	75
SDN	2014	77	85	2	94.4	52	1	91	2	481	417	32	311	.218	11	75	31	16	3	90	62.2	32	2	248	70
SDN	2015	32	35	0	97.7	33	0	43	0	206	160	16	119	.170	1	44	10	2	1	29	58.6	11	0	106	36
COL	2017	87	75	-1	90.0	28	1	34	1	549	424	20	261	.208	6	51	32	8	2	87	71.3	20	2	297	94
COL	2017	87	75	-1	90.0	28	1	34	1	549	424	20	261	.208	6	51	32	8	2	87	71.3	20	2	297	94
COL	2018	91	72	6	92.4	42	0	55	0	518	398	24	272	.242	8	91	33	4	0	76	55.3	11	1	267	71
COL	2019	71	91	1	87.8	24	0	26	2	590	422	33	296	.189	13	63	31	8	0	73	69.9	10	3	268	72

Bruce Bochy   wRM+: 94.5

TEAM	YEAR	W	L	Pythag +/-	Avg PC	100+ P	120+ P	QS	BQS	REL	REL w Zero R	IBB	PH	PH Avg	PH HR	SB2	CS2	SB3	CS3	SAC Att	SAC %	POS SAC	Squeeze	Swing	In Play
SDN	1995	70	74	-2				73	6	337	234	37	252	.243	10	96	40	27	5	73	76.7	19	0		
SDN	1996	91	71	0				80	8	411	335	47	280	.227	4	87	42	22	12	74	79.7	18	2		
SDN	1997	76	86	4				67	9	426	294	37	287	.247	7	117	50	22	7	82	76.8	22	2		
SDN	1998	98	64	4	90.0	59	9	99	5	369	309	45	272	.177	2	66	33	12	2	78	71.8	22	1		
SDN	1999	74	88	1	95.8	67	5	81	5	402	304	48	289	.204	7	141	56	28	9	63	57.1	8	0		
SDN	2000	76	86	2	98.5	78	16	75	7	443	334	50	275	.225	7	119	48	10	3	52	75.0	16	1		
SDN	2001	79	83	0	93.8	61	5	77	7	422	322	54	250	.227	2	111	35	18	3	43	67.4	9	1		
SDN	2002	66	96	2	91.5	47	2	74	5	459	355	61	235	.190	6	59	40	11	3	57	78.9	23	1		
SDN	2003	64	98	-1	93.6	67	2	74	3	473	339	52	288	.222	4	66	36	10	2	85	58.8	23	1	251	73
SDN	2004	87	75	-1	92.2	43	2	79	5	437	342	39	248	.204	5	45	20	7	5	86	60.5	22	0	251	90
SDN	2005	82	80	6	94.3	59	2	78	5	456	367	45	271	.211	4	94	36	4	6	108	66.7	36	0	316	118
SDN	2006	88	74	1	95.7	64	5	90	8	475	376	63	258	.260	8	111	26	12	4	86	68.6	19	0	358	114
SFN	2007	71	91	-6	98.7	78	8	86	3	497	380	41	261	.268	5	106	29	13	2	96	69.8	31	3	361	115
SFN	2008	72	90	5	99.7	90	8	86	7	479	366	59	273	.239	3	99	41	6	1	91	62.6	26	3	367	132
SFN	2009	88	74	1	97.4	74	5	84	4	457	370	49	230	.251	2	69	27	8	0	97	69.1	18	0	302	99
SFN	2010	92	70	-3	99.4	77	7	95	4	476	402	58	219	.262	6	49	28	6	3	106	71.7	28	0	264	85
SFN	2011	86	76	6	99.8	90	7	103	3	480	411	46	244	.212	4	76	42	7	6	86	72.1	29	2	395	118
SFN	2012	94	68	5	100.0	91	3	93	6	526	440	42	214	.217	3	111	35	6	2	100	69.0	27	2	382	123
SFN	2013	76	86	3	96.1	79	2	80	2	524	429	64	258	.213	4	64	24	3	1	86	76.7	25	2	329	119
SFN	2014	88	74	1	94.7	59	1	86	6	475	412	35	233	.222	4	52	24	4	2	66	68.2	20	5	268	97
SFN	2015	84	78	-5	90.8	37	0	78	3	557	474	28	224	.249	1	87	32	6	3	60	75.0	12	1	309	106
SFN	2016	87	75	-4	96.6	77	1	64	3	575	488	30	257	.225	4	70	33	9	3	64	65.6	18	3	305	104
SFN	2017	64	98	-1	96.0	66	0	59	2	502	392	42	292	.206	5	64	30	11	4	54	57.4	12	0	280	86
SFN	2018	73	89	4	89.5	33	0	37	1	549	441	37	297	.217	7	70	29	7	5	60	55.0	9	0	272	71
SFN	2019	77	85	7	87.9	29	0	26	2	586	460	26	354	.232	12	42	21	4	5	41	58.5	6	0	246	76

Aaron Boone   wRM+: 105.0

TEAM	YEAR	W	L	Pythag +/-	Avg PC	100+ P	120+ P	QS	BQS	REL	REL w Zero R	IBB	PH	PH Avg	PH HR	SB2	CS2	SB3	CS3	SAC Att	SAC %	POS SAC	Squeeze	Swing	In Play
NYA	2018	100	62	-0	88.1	33	0	27	3	508	408	9	63	.208	1	54	19	9	1	19	52.6	10	0	264	77
NYA	2019	103	59	3	79.1	20	0	25	1	545	404	12	54	.224	3	46	20	9	1	20	50.0	6	2	241	77

Mickey Callaway   wRM+: 101.9

TEAM	YEAR	W	L	Pythag +/-	Avg PC	100+ P	120+ P	QS	BQS	REL	REL w Zero R	IBB	PH	PH Avg	PH HR	SB2	CS2	SB3	CS3	SAC Att	SAC %	POS SAC	Squeeze	Swing	In Play
NYN	2018	77	85	-0	90.8	54	0	50	3	501	342	32	255	.220	7	60	33	11	6	44	63.6	9	1	253	74
NYN	2019	86	76	-1	94.9	72	0	55	3	502	359	40	267	.211	9	52	25	4	1	48	58.3	11	0	237	93

Kevin Cash   wRM+: 102.3

TEAM	YEAR	W	L	Pythag +/-	Avg PC	100+ P	120+ P	QS	BQS	REL	REL w Zero R	IBB	PH	PH Avg	PH HR	SB2	CS2	SB3	CS3	SAC Att	SAC %	POS SAC	Squeeze	Swing	In Play
TBA	2015	80	82	-1	90.6	46	1	68	3	530	416	23	179	.219	3	62	40	25	4	29	65.5	17	0	290	82
TBA	2016	68	94	-8	96.2	67	1	41	5	485	369	25	92	.128	1	48	33	12	3	31	58.1	18	1	306	86
TBA	2017	80	82	0	93.8	74	1	43	4	511	403	37	103	.191	2	66	28	22	5	35	45.7	14	1	292	72
TBA	2018	90	72	1	63.0	21	0	21	1	553	403	34	97	.200	1	116	44	11	4	53	52.8	28	5	371	107
TBA	2019	96	66	2	69.8	22	0	26	0	603	434	27	117	.219	3	82	30	10	4	15	53.3	8	1	343	107

Alex Cora   wRM+: 104.9

TEAM	YEAR	W	L	Pythag +/-	Avg PC	100+ P	120+ P	QS	BQS	REL	REL w Zero R	IBB	PH	PH Avg	PH HR	SB2	CS2	SB3	CS3	SAC Att	SAC %	POS SAC	Squeeze	Swing	In Play
BOS	2018	108	54	3	88.7	42	0	38	3	535	418	8	85	.205	2	109	25	16	4	10	70.0	7	0	366	113
BOS	2019	84	78	-4	86.5	48	0	26	1	632	467	22	111	.315	5	59	26	9	4	26	76.9	18	0	269	72

Craig Counsell   wRM+: 104.2

TEAM	YEAR	W	L	Pythag +/-	Avg PC	100+ P	120+ P	QS	BQS	REL	REL w Zero R	IBB	PH	PH Avg	PH HR	SB2	CS2	SB3	CS3	SAC Att	SAC %	POS SAC	Squeeze	Swing	In Play
MIL	2015	61	76	-3	92.4	40	0	53	6	424	338	30	244	.259	5	67	20	9	3	59	72.9	16	1	197	63
MIL	2016	73	89	-1	90.3	30	0	31	1	513	393	33	282	.178	7	144	46	35	10	87	60.9	21	2	371	76
MIL	2017	86	76	1	88.1	30	0	39	0	550	435	45	284	.219	8	98	32	30	7	68	61.8	12	3	336	94
MIL	2018	96	67	4	85.7	18	0	18	1	559	440	34	282	.246	10	96	25	28	7	48	60.4	6	0	331	74
MIL	2019	89	73	8	84.2	16	0	17	0	588	429	28	314	.190	8	79	18	22	5	32	62.5	5	1	297	76

Terry Francona   wRM+: 109.3

TEAM	YEAR	W	L	Pythag +/-	Avg PC	100+ P	120+ P	QS	BQS	REL	REL w Zero R	IBB	PH	PH Avg	PH HR	SB2	CS2	SB3	CS3	SAC Att	SAC %	POS SAC	Squeeze	Swing	In Play
PHI	1997	68	94	5				80	5	409	285	42	285	.184	3	79	48	11	6	98	75.5	29	0		
PHI	1998	75	87	4	95.8	74	20	77	9	386	273	27	255	.232	5	87	41	10	4	86	75.6	28	0		
PHI	1999	77	85	-4	96.9	79	14	73	10	441	333	24	237	.255	5	113	32	12	2	82	85.4	23	0		
PHI	2000	65	97	-3	102.6	106	23	87	10	413	273	32	271	.197	2	91	25	11	3	86	81.4	28	1		
BOS	2004	98	64	0	98.9	88	3	86	9	437	335	28	99	.264	2	64	27	4	2	24	50.0	10	0	263	78
BOS	2005	95	67	4	99.6	93	3	81	6	442	337	28	98	.221	1	42	12	3	0	25	56.0	13	0	252	98
BOS	2006	86	76	5	95.3	63	2	70	7	455	332	25	87	.222	0	46	22	5	1	38	57.9	22	0	273	106
BOS	2007	96	66	-7	97.6	66	3	84	10	451	379	20	73	.217	0	83	20	13	4	52	57.7	30	2	333	100
BOS	2008	95	67	-2	95.9	69	1	82	9	466	359	17	49	.250	2	99	32	21	2	47	59.6	27	0	310	90
BOS	2009	95	67	0	99.0	81	3	82	3	463	369	24	79	.221	0	106	35	19	4	32	59.4	17	0	309	97
BOS	2010	89	73	0	102.8	112	3	89	5	443	348	30	117	.260	2	56	14	11	2	38	76.3	24	0	340	108
BOS	2011	90	72	-5	96.8	78	4	71	5	443	359	11	83	.176	2	93	40	9	1	33	66.7	22	0	366	122
CLE	2013	92	70	1	94.9	68	0	73	5	540	454	26	58	.255	3	96	33	21	3	41	75.6	30	0	332	85
CLE	2014	85	77	2	94.6	61	0	78	5	573	507	51	103	.233	0	96	23	8	4	63	81.0	49	0	290	92
CLE	2015	81	80	-3	94.5	77	2	91	4	476	391	27	106	.240	4	79	26	7	1	65	72.3	45	0	274	58
CLE	2016	94	67	2	92.0	60	0	63	4	504	428	34	106	.143	1	104	25	29	6	48	64.6	27	0	294	71
CLE	2017	102	60	-8	93.7	72	1	60	4	497	430	15	86	.145	2	79	21	9	2	39	59.0	22	0	266	78
CLE	2018	91	71	-9	96.9	78	2	79	2	508	401	29	87	.234	2	118	32	15	3	45	55.6	23	0	344	78
CLE	2019	93	69	-1	93.5	75	3	54	3	522	409	19	91	.222	2	92	28	10	5	62	64.5	38	0	286	69

Ron Gardenhire   wRM+: 109.1

TEAM	YEAR	W	L	Pythag +/-	Avg PC	100+ P	120+ P	QS	BQS	REL	REL w Zero R	IBB	PH	PH Avg	PH HR	SB2	CS2	SB3	CS3	SAC Att	SAC %	POS SAC	Squeeze	Swing	In Play
MIN	2002	94	67	7	90.1	47	3	77	2	436	352	24	103	.283	3	66	50	12	12	45	75.6	33	0		
MIN	2003	90	72	5	92.2	54	2	80	7	399	311	35	102	.318	5	79	35	15	7	67	62.7	37	1	275	82
MIN	2004	92	70	4	93.8	61	1	83	7	436	333	27	112	.269	6	97	39	19	6	73	63.0	44	1	335	108
MIN	2005	83	79	-1	91.9	43	0	90	10	396	312	38	92	.300	2	85	39	17	4	67	62.7	40	1	352	116
MIN	2006	96	66	2	90.1	42	0	73	4	421	343	25	77	.145	1	88	36	13	6	55	56.4	28	0	369	146
MIN	2007	79	83	-1	93.5	46	0	80	3	438	352	33	82	.253	1	94	29	18	1	52	65.4	29	1	362	133
MIN	2008	88	75	-2	91.7	47	1	86	4	485	379	38	80	.224	3	86	37	16	5	88	59.1	47	3	340	117
MIN	2009	87	76	0	92.0	56	1	79	6	480	372	20	73	.333	4	74	28	11	2	77	66.2	46	1	368	127
MIN	2010	94	68	1	93.5	56	1	86	6	465	377	19	75	.156	2	60	23	8	5	50	76.0	33	0	272	101
MIN	2011	63	99	3	95.2	66	2	80	9	457	340	37	87	.175	0	86	33	6	4	52	59.6	31	1	361	135
MIN	2012	66	96	-1	88.0	29	0	62	3	499	390	43	59	.260	0	111	33	24	3	52	63.5	32	1	384	108
MIN	2013	66	96	5	91.1	44	0	62	6	511	415	31	97	.163	1	50	31	1	2	40	72.5	26	0	292	93
MIN	2014	70	92	-4	91.6	36	0	66	8	491	378	24	90	.210	0	84	33	15	2	34	73.5	25	0	307	98
DET	2018	64	98	2	86.3	20	0	29	2	542	415	20	66	.155	1	66	28	4	1	29	51.7	13	0	249	70
DET	2019	47	114	1	84.0	20	0	18	2	577	380	24	52	.286	2	54	20	3	0	20	45.0	9	0	248	64

Andy Green   wRM+: 109.9

TEAM	YEAR	W	L	Pythag +/-	Avg PC	100+ P	120+ P	QS	BQS	REL	REL w Zero R	IBB	PH	PH Avg	PH HR	SB2	CS2	SB3	CS3	SAC Att	SAC %	POS SAC	Squeeze	Swing	In Play
SDN	2016	68	94	-4	90.5	39	0	35	2	510	390	44	243	.208	4	103	40	18	5	60	60.0	11	2	304	79
SDN	2017	71	91	14	89.6	34	2	26	2	517	403	28	239	.164	6	76	28	11	3	80	65.0	21	2	247	69
SDN	2018	66	96	2	84.1	26	1	22	1	535	412	28	261	.171	4	87	32	8	3	76	46.1	14	2	233	59
SDN	2019	69	85	2	84.1	15	0	17	1	509	377	19	259	.226	10	58	29	9	4	52	67.3	7	1	259	82

A.J. Hinch   wRM+: 96.7

TEAM	YEAR	W	L	Pythag +/-	Avg PC	100+ P	120+ P	QS	BQS	REL	REL w Zero R	IBB	PH	PH Avg	PH HR	SB2	CS2	SB3	CS3	SAC Att	SAC %	POS SAC	Squeeze	Swing	In Play
ARI	2009	58	75	-4	98.8	79	0	73	5	392	281	24	220	.185	5	68	22	13	9	69	65.2	24	1	217	66
ARI	2010	31	48	-0	101.9	46	5	38	6	207	133	19	119	.213	0	42	11	3	2	21	81.0	7	0	151	48
HOU	2015	86	76	-8	98.0	74	4	94	4	482	412	17	114	.224	5	99	41	21	5	40	70.0	25	2	300	83
HOU	2016	84	78	0	93.7	52	0	51	3	500	403	19	98	.209	2	90	34	12	9	44	61.4	22	3	309	77
HOU	2017	101	61	0	92.0	31	0	32	2	519	399	17	68	.213	2	80	37	18	5	24	45.8	11	0	305	95
HOU	2018	103	59	-9	95.6	67	1	49	3	510	424	4	83	.169	0	63	22	8	3	22	63.6	14	6	329	124
HOU	2019	107	55	-2	91.6	55	0	41	4	492	377	0	77	.186	3	57	24	8	2	19	52.6	9	1	245	76

Clint Hurdle   wRM+: 94.8

TEAM	YEAR	W	L	Pythag +/-	Avg PC	100+ P	120+ P	QS	BQS	REL	REL w Zero R	IBB	PH	PH Avg	PH HR	SB2	CS2	SB3	CS3	SAC Att	SAC %	POS SAC	Squee-ze	Swing	In Play
COL	2002	67	73	5	93.1	45	1	61	7	437	322	38	244	.276	5	82	40	10	5	51	76.5	26	1		
COL	2003	74	88	-3	89.7	38	0	68	2	500	369	51	285	.260	5	57	34	6	3	103	53.4	28	1	238	85
COL	2004	68	94	-5	95.7	60	3	65	8	473	329	84	287	.253	11	36	31	8	2	148	65.5	55	0	258	87
COL	2005	67	95	-2	94.0	52	1	68	3	459	336	54	272	.224	4	61	26	4	5	131	67.2	52	2	334	116
COL	2006	76	86	-5	95.6	55	2	81	7	499	392	81	258	.215	6	80	44	4	3	167	71.3	64	0	325	112
COL	2007	90	73	-2	90.4	50	0	79	2	529	413	61	283	.216	4	98	31	2	0	130	63.8	37	2	354	104
COL	2008	74	88	1	92.2	53	0	68	3	484	370	49	250	.239	4	116	34	25	3	124	72.6	41	0	354	82
COL	2009	18	28	-3	92.5	19	0	26	2	135	96	11	73	.306	2	24	13	6	2	29	69.0	8	0	113	45
PIT	2011	72	90	3	89.5	26	0	78	2	549	452	65	275	.201	1	95	47	13	3	110	68.2	37	1	384	114
PIT	2012	79	83	1	90.4	42	0	83	2	483	398	30	266	.173	2	66	45	7	3	93	66.7	30	2	271	94
PIT	2013	94	68	5	89.7	41	0	83	2	465	395	26	285	.207	7	83	36	10	6	93	66.7	35	1	347	100
PIT	2014	88	74	1	93.7	44	0	90	3	452	361	43	317	.218	7	99	41	5	4	101	53.5	18	1	365	135
PIT	2015	98	64	4	94.2	46	0	92	7	500	431	38	267	.237	2	89	43	8	2	81	77.8	24	0	288	87
PIT	2016	78	84	0	87.4	27	0	28	0	525	405	28	290	.230	8	100	37	10	6	64	64.1	18	1	309	79
PIT	2017	75	87	1	90.6	37	0	35	4	502	383	32	276	.198	6	61	31	5	4	69	60.9	8	0	289	90
PIT	2018	82	79	2	88.0	20	0	37	1	480	369	43	264	.238	3	64	36	6	1	50	62.0	7	1	238	71
PIT	2019	69	92	3	84.8	22	0	22	1	548	396	22	281	.321	10	57	29	6	0	62	75.8	17	1	250	73

Brandon Hyde   wRM+: 104.3

TEAM	YEAR	W	L	Pythag +/-	Avg PC	100+ P	120+ P	QS	BQS	REL	REL w Zero R	IBB	PH	PH Avg	PH HR	SB2	CS2	SB3	CS3	SAC Att	SAC %	POS SAC	Squee-ze	Swing	In Play
BAL	2019	54	108	-4	85.0	17	0	20	0	533	341	11	120	.194	2	73	24	10	5	43	51.2	19	2	248	67

Gabe Kapler   wRM+: 97.5

TEAM	YEAR	W	L	Pythag +/-	Avg PC	100+ P	120+ P	QS	BQS	REL	REL w Zero R	IBB	PH	PH Avg	PH HR	SB2	CS2	SB3	CS3	SAC Att	SAC %	POS SAC	Squee-ze	Swing	In Play
PHI	2018	80	82	5	87.7	37	0	46	4	596	467	35	295	.207	5	64	20	3	5	53	60.4	6	0	198	50
PHI	2019	81	81	2	89.2	42	0	37	4	564	430	38	308	.202	9	65	15	12	1	55	61.8	11	1	261	55

Torey Lovullo   wRM+: 98.7

TEAM	YEAR	W	L	Pythag +/-	Avg PC	100+ P	120+ P	QS	BQS	REL	REL w Zero R	IBB	PH	PH Avg	PH HR	SB2	CS2	SB3	CS3	SAC Att	SAC %	POS SAC	Squee-ze	Swing	In Play
ARI	2017	93	69	-5	96.2	73	1	52	2	513	424	45	251	.223	7	77	24	25	6	56	69.6	8	0	265	73
ARI	2018	82	80	-5	92.4	36	0	44	2	574	474	43	256	.203	5	61	22	18	3	64	59.4	10	0	252	82
ARI	2018	82	80	-5	92.4	36	0	44	2	574	474	43	256	.203	5	61	22	18	3	64	59.4	10	0	252	82
ARI	2019	85	77	-3	89.0	32	0	36	2	557	431	38	254	.218	12	84	12	3	1	51	60.8	5	2	248	85

Joe Maddon   wRM+: 99.5

TEAM	YEAR	W	L	Pythag +/-	Avg PC	100+ P	120+ P	QS	BQS	REL	REL w Zero R	IBB	PH	PH Avg	PH HR	SB2	CS2	SB3	CS3	SAC Att	SAC %	POS SAC	Squee-ze	Swing	In Play
CAL	1996	6	16	-0				10	4	52	43	10	21	.235	0	7	7	0	0	11	36.4	4	0		
ANA	1999	19	10	2	96.3	13	3	11	1	85	72	3	27	.238	1	14	9	0	0	13	84.6	11	0		
TBA	2006	61	101	-3	92.8	48	1	65	6	444	303	39	76	.217	1	109	45	24	7	69	50.7	32	3	417	112
TBA	2007	66	96	0	96.9	77	0	73	8	484	320	31	68	.167	0	114	43	16	4	50	68.0	33	4	350	92
TBA	2008	97	65	5	95.9	71	0	82	3	448	365	29	90	.184	1	113	38	28	10	40	57.5	20	0	388	94
TBA	2009	84	78	-2	99.1	80	1	76	5	510	425	22	134	.164	7	167	49	26	11	41	61.0	24	6	404	101
TBA	2010	96	66	-2	98.9	90	2	95	5	491	412	34	154	.242	3	147	39	25	7	67	58.2	38	6	404	120
TBA	2011	91	71	-1	102.1	98	5	99	10	438	355	38	129	.252	1	134	54	20	8	63	58.7	35	5	441	138
TBA	2012	90	72	-6	99.9	91	7	90	2	471	415	35	135	.178	3	122	38	11	5	62	54.8	32	3	354	105
TBA	2013	92	71	4	94.9	65	2	80	2	485	399	38	169	.235	1	61	34	12	3	39	61.5	24	0	292	93
TBA	2014	77	85	-2	97.1	77	0	84	1	494	418	27	130	.218	1	52	24	11	2	73	58.9	42	3	313	106
CHN	2015	97	65	6	91.1	53	2	81	3	551	459	38	287	.201	5	82	32	13	3	53	60.4	15	2	330	105
CHN	2016	103	59	-7	94.5	56	1	66	2	502	407	24	234	.215	2	57	30	9	1	78	53.8	14	8	264	93
CHN	2017	92	70	-2	91.1	40	0	32	0	531	413	29	295	.241	5	56	25	5	6	65	73.8	22	5	263	75
CHN	2018	95	68	0	90.7	40	1	28	1	600	503	33	277	.242	6	53	31	11	6	71	56.3	14	4	280	85
CHN	2019	84	78	-7	90.4	40	0	38	0	576	444	16	240	.217	6	38	17	7	3	50	60.0	7	2	211	58

Dave Martinez   wRM+: 98.4

TEAM	YEAR	W	L	Pythag +/-	Avg PC	100+ P	120+ P	QS	BQS	REL	REL w Zero R	IBB	PH	PH Avg	PH HR	SB2	CS2	SB3	CS3	SAC Att	SAC %	POS SAC	Squee-ze	Swing	In Play
WAS	2018	82	80	-9	94.0	68	1	49	2	562	440	37	293	.176	4	98	31	20	2	78	52.6	13	0	299	68
WAS	2019	93	69	-3	94.8	66	0	44	3	530	384	41	252	.261	5	97	26	18	3	84	57.1	20	2	279	73

Don Mattingly   wRM+: 99.2

TEAM	YEAR	W	L	Pythag +/-	Avg PC	100+ P	120+ P	QS	BQS	REL	REL w Zero R	IBB	PH	PH Avg	PH HR	SB2	CS2	SB3	CS3	SAC Att	SAC %	POS SAC	Squeeze	Swing	In Play
LAN	2011	82	79	-3	97.8	66	3	94	4	461	369	48	229	.199	4	108	31	17	9	101	70.3	38	2	360	118
LAN	2012	86	76	-0	96.2	66	0	93	5	506	426	62	241	.281	2	93	39	10	2	122	67.2	33	2	329	97
LAN	2013	92	70	2	95.1	69	2	93	2	504	424	44	208	.209	4	74	22	4	5	113	62.8	32	0	283	93
LAN	2014	94	68	1	95.1	70	1	100	1	496	395	35	235	.231	1	123	46	14	3	82	57.3	15	1	340	104
LAN	2015	92	70	2	91.3	47	2	95	3	515	408	32	269	.215	8	51	26	8	8	69	71.0	15	1	250	76
MIA	2016	79	82	2	90.8	46	0	32	1	559	443	62	277	.215	6	61	25	10	3	76	60.5	15	2	240	74
MIA	2017	77	85	0	87.5	29	0	22	0	580	435	59	270	.262	6	82	22	9	6	84	59.5	15	3	275	80
MIA	2018	63	98	7	88.4	32	0	27	0	546	407	73	281	.177	6	40	29	5	2	58	55.2	12	0	251	80
MIA	2019	57	105	-2	91.8	36	0	31	1	539	389	52	290	.214	9	49	25	6	1	53	58.5	8	2	236	67

Bob Melvin   wRM+: 92.8

TEAM	YEAR	W	L	Pythag +/-	Avg PC	100+ P	120+ P	QS	BQS	REL	REL w Zero R	IBB	PH	PH Avg	PH HR	SB2	CS2	SB3	CS3	SAC Att	SAC %	POS SAC	Squeeze	Swing	In Play
SEA	2003	93	69	-6	101.9	108	6	94	8	366	305	24	62	.154	2	89	34	19	3	52	67.3	32	1	248	91
SEA	2004	63	99	-5	101.7	99	12	70	10	414	305	32	99	.276	4	92	33	18	9	63	73.0	45	0	355	112
ARI	2005	77	85	13	96.6	64	3	84	10	458	330	43	309	.232	9	64	21	3	4	107	66.4	30	1	281	86
ARI	2006	76	86	-3	94.9	68	3	81	8	461	349	44	274	.194	7	64	26	11	4	94	64.9	21	0	237	80
ARI	2007	90	72	11	94.7	68	4	84	5	469	367	38	239	.239	11	90	16	18	8	85	64.7	26	0	295	89
ARI	2008	82	80	-1	95.7	55	3	95	3	443	336	41	257	.226	3	46	16	12	5	95	71.6	29	1	261	89
ARI	2009	12	17	0	95.9	10	0	16	2	91	64	3	47	.209	3	16	7	5	1	18	50.0	6	0	61	17
OAK	2011	47	52	-0	100.4	51	1	55	3	282	220	9	30	.276	2	56	26	19	2	38	57.9	20	0	229	63
OAK	2012	94	68	1	92.5	52	0	90	4	462	386	34	93	.231	3	89	26	33	5	43	62.8	26	0	307	76
OAK	2013	96	66	-1	94.8	56	0	92	2	447	370	23	130	.135	5	58	24	17	3	37	56.8	21	2	253	87
OAK	2014	88	74	-12	96.0	61	1	102	5	441	380	28	161	.201	3	67	16	16	4	41	46.3	15	2	253	83
OAK	2015	68	94	-9	92.4	61	0	83	3	487	368	19	152	.252	0	65	25	13	3	24	58.3	12	1	268	90
OAK	2016	69	93	0	87.2	40	0	40	2	492	403	28	113	.185	2	44	23	6	0	24	54.2	10	1	205	61
OAK	2017	75	87	3	90.6	40	0	36	2	525	388	17	120	.217	1	47	20	9	2	23	56.5	9	1	226	59
OAK	2018	97	65	1	80.5	15	0	37	0	578	474	19	126	.239	3	31	20	3	1	10	60.0	6	1	225	75
OAK	2019	97	65	-1	88.5	30	1	36	0	547	435	19	107	.228	4	43	20	6	1	11	63.6	6	1	247	81

Charlie Montoyo   wRM+: 98.8

TEAM	YEAR	W	L	Pythag +/-	Avg PC	100+ P	120+ P	QS	BQS	REL	REL w Zero R	IBB	PH	PH Avg	PH HR	SB2	CS2	SB3	CS3	SAC Att	SAC %	POS SAC	Squeeze	Swing	In Play
TOR	2019	67	95	-3	75.9	19	0	15	0	591	409	25	70	.172	2	40	16	10	3	19	73.7	14		239	76

Rick Renteria   wRM+: 101.0

TEAM	YEAR	W	L	Pythag +/-	Avg PC	100+ P	120+ P	QS	BQS	REL	REL w Zero R	IBB	PH	PH Avg	PH HR	SB2	CS2	SB3	CS3	SAC Att	SAC %	POS SAC	Squeeze	Swing	In Play
CHN	2014	73	89	3	93.6	48	1	79	0	537	446	37	272	.185	1	58	37	7	3	93	61.3	25	3	246	82
CHA	2017	67	95	-2	93.2	52	0	32	1	520	397	36	77	.183	1	61	25	10	3	62	56.5	33	3	291	76
CHA	2018	62	100	1	92.9	49	0	47	4	553	430	25	79	.159	1	79	37	19	3	38	63.2	23	4	274	75
CHA	2018	62	100	1	92.9	49	0	47	4	553	430	25	79	.159	1	79	37	19	3	38	63.2	23	4	274	75
CHA	2019	72	89	4	89.0	50	0	24	1	536	401	30	72	.209	4	54	23	9	4	49	73.5	34	7	250	68

Dave Roberts   wRM+: 100.3

TEAM	YEAR	W	L	Pythag +/-	Avg PC	100+ P	120+ P	QS	BQS	REL	REL w Zero R	IBB	PH	PH Avg	PH HR	SB2	CS2	SB3	CS3	SAC Att	SAC %	POS SAC	Squeeze	Swing	In Play
LAN	2016	91	71	-0	87.6	29	0	32	2	606	503	50	323	.189	6	40	22	5	2	62	48.4	5	2	254	84
LAN	2017	104	58	1	86.6	21	0	38	1	536	428	33	341	.243	8	60	24	15	2	51	60.8	4	1	237	70
LAN	2018	92	71	-11	86.5	22	0	35	1	593	465	39	354	.238	9	57	20	18	1	65	60.0	9	3	248	63
LAN	2019	106	56	-4	85.8	24	0	50	1	545	413	24	302	.235	13	52	10	4	0	64	85.9	3	3	228	74

Scott Servais   wRM+: 105.5

TEAM	YEAR	W	L	Pythag +/-	Avg PC	100+ P	120+ P	QS	BQS	REL	REL w Zero R	IBB	PH	PH Avg	PH HR	SB2	CS2	SB3	CS3	SAC Att	SAC %	POS SAC	Squeeze	Swing	In Play
SEA	2016	86	76	-2	92.1	43	0	48	6	477	379	30	146	.254	4	48	26	8	1	43	55.8	21	0	268	83
SEA	2017	78	84	-1	88.2	32	0	31	0	526	405	28	87	.189	0	83	31	6	4	27	51.9	11	0	236	65
SEA	2018	89	73	12	86.4	31	0	40	1	537	417	21	97	.232	2	69	34	10	2	47	61.7	27	1	225	65
SEA	2019	68	94	0	75.8	20	0	32	1	537	354	25	69	.183	1	104	42	10	3	18	77.8	11	0	341	82

Brian Snitker   wRM+: 101.5

TEAM	YEAR	W	L	Pythag +/-	Avg PC	100+ P	120+ P	QS	BQS	REL	REL w Zero R	IBB	PH	PH Avg	PH HR	SB2	CS2	SB3	CS3	SAC Att	SAC %	POS SAC	Squeeze	Swing	In Play
ATL	2016	59	65	4	89.9	40	0	25	1	456	371	40	212	.226	4	48	21	11	3	78	61.5	14	1	208	74
ATL	2017	72	90	0	93.6	45	1	45	3	530	406	39	270	.234	10	64	29	13	2	87	67.8	18	0	312	92
ATL	2018	90	72	-3	90.8	41	1	28	3	552	427	43	247	.202	7	75	28	13	7	76	64.5	13	3	277	84
ATL	2019	97	65	5	88.3	27	0	30	0	575	433	33	260	.252	9	81	24	8	3	34	73.5	3	2	281	77

Chris Woodward   wRM+: 94.6

TEAM	YEAR	W	L	Pythag +/-	Avg PC	100+ P	120+ P	QS	BQS	REL	REL w Zero R	IBB	PH	PH Avg	PH HR	SB2	CS2	SB3	CS3	SAC Att	SAC %	POS SAC	Squeeze	Swing	In Play
TEX	2019	78	84	4	86.9	60	1	38	3	499	335	11	79	.206	4	107	34	20	4	25	68.0	16	0	319	69

Ned Yost   wRM+: 105.2

TEAM	YEAR	W	L	Pythag +/-	Avg PC	100+ P	120+ P	QS	BQS	REL	REL w Zero R	IBB	PH	PH Avg	PH HR	SB2	CS2	SB3	CS3	SAC Att	SAC %	POS SAC	Squeeze	Swing	In Play
MIL	2003	68	94	3	95.5	70	5	66	7	460	344	43	282	.220	6	89	34	9	5	98	63.3	29	1	267	82
MIL	2004	67	94	1	93.2	60	8	82	5	423	299	27	279	.205	7	124	35	14	2	96	58.3	28	1	358	101
MIL	2005	81	81	-3	99.3	86	4	91	5	396	292	52	253	.248	6	68	30	11	3	113	58.4	41	5	298	100
MIL	2006	75	87	5	94.5	67	3	81	7	427	306	34	235	.267	4	60	33	10	4	88	65.9	20	1	294	96
MIL	2007	83	79	-1	94.0	56	3	76	9	492	368	37	253	.224	6	86	25	9	4	81	74.1	22	0	321	100
MIL	2008	83	67	2	96.3	54	6	82	3	399	311	30	217	.208	7	85	27	20	7	66	69.7	17	3	333	108
KCA	2010	55	72	4	96.4	59	1	53	7	332	257	25	52	.214	2	73	35	12	4	45	66.7	25	0	281	78
KCA	2011	71	91	-7	96.9	74	0	75	5	420	339	42	36	.152	1	130	48	23	8	75	73.3	51	2	399	113
KCA	2012	72	90	-1	90.5	55	0	69	4	500	411	44	55	.208	3	109	34	22	4	42	61.9	25	1	334	97
KCA	2013	86	76	-1	98.6	79	2	95	5	427	374	21	74	.210	1	133	30	19	2	56	66.1	36	1	369	99
KCA	2014	89	73	5	98.6	90	2	95	4	451	399	14	43	.250	2	124	29	29	7	55	60.0	30	1	344	112
KCA	2015	95	67	4	92.8	52	0	71	3	493	418	10	36	.188	0	76	30	27	2	48	70.8	32	0	257	86
KCA	2016	81	81	4	93.2	61	0	42	6	472	391	8	47	.238	0	102	31	19	4	66	57.6	35	0	300	73
KCA	2017	80	82	9	88.7	26	0	38	3	538	423	24	41	.162	0	74	27	17	3	24	70.8	16	1	239	57
KCA	2018	58	104	-2	91.6	52	0	40	1	483	348	28	41	.314	1	85	31	32	5	47	51.1	23	0	287	73
KCA	2019	59	103	-4	89.5	37	1	30	4	520	365	25	56	.130	3	84	31	32	5	47	51.1	22	2	275	64

Top 101 Prospects

by Jeffrey Paternostro and Jarrett Seidler

1. Wander Franco, SS, Tampa Bay Rays

Franco is a switch-hitting shortstop who we think will either stay there or end up at second. He has a high chance at a plus hit/plus power outcome. He hit .327/.398/.487 as an 18-year-old playing at Low-A and High-A, and walked more than he struck out at both levels. If it wasn't for Nick Madrigal, we'd be talking about how he has the best bat-to-ball skills of any top prospect, despite his youth. He's been the best player in his age cohort for years now, with the signing bonus and past rankings to prove it. While he's not quite as toolsy as some of the players just below him on this list, he's still pretty toolsy, and he's blending it with dominant performance. He's the boring choice to be the best prospect in baseball, but clearly the right one.

2. Jo Adell, OF, Los Angeles Angels

Baseball is an entertainment business. That often gets lost beneath a haze of $/WARP analysis, four-and-a-half hour playoff games with picture-in-picture ads from Jaguar and arguments over whether the inconsistent seam height of baseballs has been purposeful. Now, generally speaking, good baseball is more entertaining than bad baseball, and good players more entertaining than bad. And Adell is going to be a very good baseball player. But he also gets that this is an entertainment business, and if that means staying past his allotted time in the batter's box during Futures Game batting practice to try and hit a ball off the scoreboard at Progressive Field—despite the wind blowing in—he's happy to oblige. Adell came up just a few rows short in the end, but it's one of our abiding memories of the 2019 season. And fair play, given his 70-grade raw power he had a shot at it. There's a potential plus hit tool that could carry that pop into major league games as soon as April 1st. And no foolin', while Franco has a better chance to be a very good player for a long time, Adell has the most upside of anyone on this list. He may not get there, but it sure will be entertaining to watch him try.

3. Gavin Lux, SS/2B, Los Angeles Dodgers

We have a lot of pithy little sayings here on the Baseball Prospectus prospect team. "Catchers are weird," "There's no such thing as a number three starter" and "Jo Adell is an icon" to name just a few. "Player development is not linear" is another one. It sure wasn't for Lux. He was in the mix for the back of our 2019 Top 101, but missed for merely being a polished middle infielder with a strong collection of average or solid-average tools. Very early in 2019, it became clear something had changed. He had grown into a stronger, but no less athletic frame. He looked more like a sure-shot shortstop, but with the flexibility to be above-average at other spots. The doubles power grew into over-the-fence power without giving up any plate coverage or sacrificing a patient approach. All of a sudden, Lux was slugging .719 in Triple-A and made the Dodgers playoff roster—where he mashed a pinch-hit home run in NLDS Game 1. We still think he's polished and high probability, but now he's probably going to make a few All-Star games. There wasn't a single tool breakout here, everything just got a little bit better. Put that mix of plus tools in a shortstop and, well, that's a heady brew.

4. Adley Rutschman, C, Baltimore Orioles

This is the highest the previous summer's 1-1 has landed on the 101 in quite some time. The circumstantial evidence from the draft process supports it; Rutschman was the consensus top player in the draft process from start to finish and set a record bonus number, under a system that incentivizes teams to shave money with the top pick to go after big-bonus preps later. Our looks at Rutschman after the draft flashed the expected offensive tools, led by two mirrored and near-perfect swings geared for power. We also saw a strong, polished base of defensive abilities, and we firmly believe that he will excel in the soft factors of catching as well. Will blowing up a highly-drafted switch-hitting Orioles catching prospect inevitably lead to Matt Wieters jokes? You bet. But Wieters is a four-time All-Star who has compiled over 20 WARP, so is that actually that bad?

5. MacKenzie Gore, LHP, San Diego Padres

As best pitching prospects in baseball go, Gore is not the most exciting example to write about. It's not his fault. He's a very good pitching prospect. We are literally saying he's the best pitching prospect. There just isn't an easy hook—although there is a very easy hook. Gore got a full, blister-free season under his belt, with the stipulation that "full" in our modern times means 20 judiciously spaced starts of 55-75 pitches, totaling 101 innings. So, it's still not clear exactly what the stuff will look like as a traditional 180-inning, every fifth day, starter. It's clear what it looks like now, though, and it's dang impressive. Gore boasts a deep arsenal of pitches led by a mid-90s fastball from the left side that he commands well for a 20-year-old with fewer than 200 pro innings under his belt. A plus-or-better curve—the aforementioned easy hook—and potentially above-average slider and change round out the repertoire. He gets good extension and deception from his funky delivery right out of the Ministry of Silly Walks. So there's no need to always look on the bright side of life to see that Gore is one of the elite pitching prospects in all of baseball.

6. Luis Robert, OF, Chicago White Sox

Professional baseball is a game for all shapes and sizes. Prospects on this list will range from 5-foot-7 (Nick Madrigal, allegedly) to 6-foot-7 (Oneil Cruz). There are beanpole pitchers and BIG BOY SZN corner mashers. There is no perfect baseball body. However, if there was a perfect baseball body, it might be Robert's. Built like an NFL wideout with the plus-plus run times to match, everything just looks easy when he's on the field or in the batter's box. The 21-year-old blitzed three levels to the tune of .328 and 32 home runs in 122 games, finishing the year on the doorstep of the South side. He looks like he should be a corner outfielder, but is perfectly fine roaming center. The offensive tools are All-Star level. The one question left: Can Robert's "see ball, hit ball" approach work against the best pitchers in the world? We'll find out in 2020.

7. Jarred Kelenic, OF, Seattle Mariners

We said last year that "in a year or two [Kelenic] might be the sort of prospect the Mets will sorely wish they still had." Well, here we go. The difference between projecting a player for a bunch of 55 tools and a bunch of 6 tools isn't huge. For hit and power, a half-grade jump is only one extra single and homer a month. And yet, that slight across-the-board uptick is the main difference driving Kelenic's 50-plus spot rise. That's not the whole story, of course; he's moving faster than we expected, subverting prior concerns about him being an older prep draftee into reaching Double-A less than a month after his 20th birthday and he's sticking in center, for now. He remains more likely to be a well-rounded star than a superstar, but every team in baseball could use this type of crown jewel prospect. Especially the Mets.

8. Dustin May, RHP, Los Angeles Dodgers

The "Gingergaard" sobriquet was supposed to stay between us, dear reader. It was meant mostly in jest, a nod to the long line of projectable Texas prep arms—with or without flowing locks—that get drafted every spring. But ESPN's Jeff Passan had to go and mention it in a column about May's call-up, and next it was on national broadcasts. Then both May and Syndergaard had to comment, and now it is just awkward for everyone. May can exist as his own pitcher sans glib comps, and he took another step forward in 2019. The velocity ticked up again into the high-90s without the fastball losing any of its frightening arm-side run. May added a hard cutter for a different glove-side look to pair with his aesthetically-

pleasing power curve. Okay, okay, perhaps this does sound a little bit familiar. May isn't quite there yet, as he struggled to command his offspeed stuff during his major-league cameo. But he announced his presence with all the fury of Heimdallr blowing the Gjallar-Horn. As for what shall come to pass afterward, "when all the world is burned, and dead are all the gods and all the champions and all mankind?" Well, probably a number two starter. Yeah, I mean anything was going to be an anti-climax after the apocalypse. But given all the postseason *Fimbulwinters* the Dodgers have gone through recently, May might be exactly the hero they need.

9. Jesus Luzardo, LHP, Oakland Athletics

Recency bias is a necessary evil in our line of work. Prospects can change rapidly, and the most recent look might be the most representative one of what they player can be. Watching Luzardo carve up major-league lineups down the stretch with a potent three-pitch mix could make one think they were watching the best pitching prospect in baseball. Upper-90s heat, a potential plus curve and change, enough command to make it all work—yeah that's a recipe for a top pitching prospect. Look a bit further back though, and you'll note Luzardo only threw 55 innings this year due to a lat issue, and missed a year after being drafted due to Tommy John surgery. And really the *most* recent version you saw was him dominating in relief. It would be awfully tempting to let Luzardo continue to rip off strikeouts with maxed out stuff in the late innings, but we'd like to see a full North American tour of 32 starts from The Jesus Lizard before consigning him to a supporting act in the bullpen.

10. Julio Rodriguez, OF, Seattle Mariners

For all we just waxed poetic about Jarred Kelenic, he's not even the highest-upside outfield prospect in Seattle's system. Forest Stulting saw Rodriguez's first series of the season in the South Atlantic League—literally Rodriguez's first stateside at-bats—and immediately sounded the claxons, stating he was one of the best outfield prospects in the game. By the end of the season, there was no debate about that, as Rodriguez laid waste to lower-minors pitching before holding his own in the Arizona Fall League, all as an 18-year-old. He has a quick, compact swing that is geared for hard contact, and already touts an advanced plate approach for a teenager with such limited experience. We expect that as he matures, he will start lifting the ball more and ultimately grow into significant game power. Simply put, he's a potential offensive monster in the making.

11. Carter Kieboom, IF, Washington Nationals

There are a few "prospect fatigue" entries every year on this list, and Kieboom will be the first. Development *isn't* always linear, but he's gone year-over-year from a late first-round pick with potential, to the 71st-best prospect in baseball after a strong full-season debut, to the 16th-best prospect in baseball upon reaching Double-A, to the 11th-best prospect in baseball after hitting .300 with some pop in Triple-A as a

21-year-old. Kieboom is a slow burn despite his top prospect status, who maintained his potential plus hit/power combo and strong approach at every minor-league stop, against better and better pitching. He's played all around the infield and should slot in somewhere on the dirt for the 2020 Nationals. This should be our last chance to write "Kieboom goes the dynamite," so let's get that in print at least.

12. Casey Mize, RHP, Detroit Tigers

Mize looked like the best pitching prospect in baseball early in 2019, breezing through the minors with four plus-or-better pitches. That version of Mize would rank no worse than fourth on this list. But from the moment he walked off the mound in mid-June with shoulder inflammation, he simply didn't look like a budding ace anymore. When he came back a month later, his full breadth of stuff didn't come back with him, and he got shelled until he was shut down in mid-August. If we were only considering that version of Mize, without his priors, he wouldn't be a candidate for this list at all. Shoulder injuries are notoriously tricky, and the delta is now massive even though he's something like a present No. 2 starter on talent. We're taking an optimistic line for now, hoping he's back to full form, or something close to it, come spring.

13. Nick Madrigal, 2B, Chicago White Sox

In an era where strikeouts are more prevalent than ever, Madrigal struck out just 16 times in 532 plate appearances across three levels of the minors, a ludicrous stat that you'd only expect to find in pre-war baseball. Unlike fellow unicorn Willians Astudillo, the only other hitter in affiliated baseball demonstrating anything close to this kind of contact ability, Madrigal combines his bat-to-ball skills with an excellent approach. This allows him to walk at a reasonable rate even though he makes contact with nearly everything he swings at. He also offers quality second base defense and plus speed which, combined with his unusual hitting abilities, gives him a high probability of being a solid regular or better. His reasonable ceiling involves multiple batting titles and endless "how did he square *that* up?" GIFs on Twitter.

14. Marco Luciano, SS, San Francisco Giants

This might feel aggressive for a player with nine games above complex ball, but it shouldn't. Luciano signed for $2.6 million last summer and already had heat on him when he landed in Arizona that fall for instructs. It's easy to point to seven-figure IFAs who flopped quickly once stateside. We've even ranked some of them in the Top 101 in the past, but organized baseball—even in the complex—will give you a better feel for these bonus babies. The Vlad Juniors and Wander Francos separate themselves out from the Kevin Maitans and Gilbert Laras quickly. Luciano looks closer to the former, with potential plus-plus raw power generated by a swing that's a leveraged blur through the zone. He's already pretty yoked up for a 17-year-old, and he could still grow off of shortstop. It's a potential power/speed combo that could play

anywhere on the diamond though. His path through the minors as an 18-year-old might not look all that different from Julio Rodriguez's and in some ways we have already baked that into this year's ranking. Like we said: it might feel aggressive, but it's justified.

15. Luis Patiño, RHP, San Diego Padres

There is a writer or two on staff that actually prefers Patiño to MacKenzie Gore among Padres prospects, and it's not crazy. Patiño is a bit less cerebral, a bit more visceral. While Gore's virtues require more focus as they unfurl over 90 or so minutes, like Schoenberg's *Erwartung*, Patiño is an easier scout. He has an explosive fastball/slider combo that announces itself early in starts, like Beethoven's Fifth Symphony—famously described by the composer as "the sound of fate knocking at the door." Patiño made it to Double-A as a 19-year-old, striking out over 30 percent of batters along the way; a Cal League batter's fate was often a quick return to the dugout. Like Gore, Patiño rounds out his arsenal with two more above-average secondaries, including a potentially impact changeup. On the other hand, Patiño hasn't even thrown 100 innings in a season yet and is a shorter righty as opposed to the tall, well-built, left-handed M Gore. Sometimes it does come down to a matter of taste, and this time we will side with the atonal opera buffs. Although we usually prefer five-tool-technique to 12-tone.

16. Kristian Robinson, OF, Arizona Diamondbacks

It wasn't an accident that Robinson snuck on the end of the 2019 101, but even we didn't think the profile would pay large dividends so quickly. He torched the Northwest League as an 18-year-old, earning a late-season promotion to the Midwest League where he hit a few bombs to dead center for Kane County on cool, late summer nights. There's plus raw power to all fields, a loose swing with plus-plus bat speed that stays in the zone, and an already advanced approach for a teenager. Robinson shows extreme athleticism both at the plate and in the field, although his large frame might end up better served in a corner outfield spot than center as it fills out. There's little question now that he will have the bat—and the arm—to carry a right field profile. Normally that would put a damper on the overall ceiling, as right fielders really have to hit. But, well, Robinson is really going to hit.

17. A.J. Puk, LHP, Oakland Athletics

The other oft-injured lefty prospect with huge stuff for Oakland, Puk's Tommy John "rehab" was storming through a few levels of the minors, and then taking a few relief innings for the Athletics in a playoff race. Like Jesus Luzardo, there's reliever risk here. In addition to the elbow scar, Puk has struggled with his control and command due to "tall pitcher problems" in his mechanics. But that delivery also gives him frightening extension on a fastball that can touch triple digits. It's a tough angle to pick up out of his hand as well, helping his upper-90s heat get on you faster than you'd think—and you'd think it would get there pretty fast. Puk pairs the fastball with a wipeout slider that sits around 90. He doesn't need much more than that to start—assuming his left elbow and command cooperate—but there's some feel for a changeup and a "slower" low-80s curve as well. There will always be the temptation to let him loose in the pen with the two 70-grade offerings as the next Andrew Miller or Josh Hader. But even if that happens, we ranked Hader around this spot a couple years ago and he's justified the ranking even in relief.

18. Dylan Carlson, OF, St. Louis Cardinals

In the interest of full disclosure, the signing scout on Carlson was Zach Mortimer, a former Baseball Prospectus prospect team member. With 20-plus alumni scattered among scouting and player development departments, this is going to happen more and more. It's easy to see why Mort got hired though, as his eye was dead on here. Carlson flashed big tools as a pro, but didn't consistently get them into games in 2018 during his time as a teenager in Peoria and Palm Beach. In 2019, everything popped. The plus raw power exploded into games. Then the Cardinals—being the Cardinals—decided he was a full-time center fielder now after playing mostly right in 2018. And wouldn't you know it, Carlson at worst could battle it to a draw, and there's above-average possibilities with more reps. You line up the updated reports—potential plus hit and power, solid arm, sneaky speed, improving glove, and all of a sudden you've got a five-tool center fielder and a top-20 prospect.

19. Nate Pearson, RHP, Toronto Blue Jays

Do you like big dudes that throw triple-digit gas with a wipeout slider? Is there anyone who doesn't? Pearson is famous as the hardest-throwing starting pitcher in baseball, and he is certainly that. He's also one of the best overall pitching prospects now, following a season of general dominance. He also finally logged a full season of innings after an injury-laden 2018, and we're a bit more confident that he can stick as a starter now. The "fallback" option here might be more fun, if not quite as valuable. Able to dump it out for a single inning in the 2019 Futures Game, Pearson sat a lively 99-101 and flashed an 80-grade slider, putting an alternate outcome where he ends up as an elite closer squarely in the mind's eye.

20. Michael Kopech, RHP, Chicago White Sox

After ranking 24th last year knowing he'd just had Tommy John surgery, this was a bit of a foregone conclusion. By all accounts, Kopech has had an uneventful rehab and should be a full go for spring training. Assuming full health—and there's always some risk with Tommy John rehabs until they're all the way back—Kopech possesses one of the most gifted arms around. Even the dialed back version of his fastball he was throwing in the majors in 2018 is a heavy pitch in the upper-90s, and he hit 100 multiple times for Steve Givarz while rehabbing in instructs last October. Command

often lags behind after elbow reconstructions, and Kopech's command was inconsistent before all this, so that's something to watch early this season.

21. Royce Lewis, SS, Minnesota Twins

Another bit of favored shorthand around the Prospect Team offices, er, Slack Channel, is "it just looks right." Eventually, most, if not all, of these prospects will make the majors and their performance will be laid bare for you in the preceding pages of this tome. Until then though, aesthetics can count for almost as much as stats. A lot of evaluation is running through a mental catalog of comparisons to major leaguers past and present, and we can't think of a major leaguer that makes Lewis' current swing work. The fact that he wasn't completely underwater statistically in 2019 is a testament to his hand/eye coordination and incredible hand speed, but he struggled mightily to stay in sync and get his bat through the zone last season, something chronicled in depth by Keanan Lamb out of the Florida State League. Lewis is a premium athlete, and he's maybe only a couple tweaks away from unlocking an All-Star upside. For right now, it doesn't look right.

22. Cristian Pache, OF, Atlanta Braves

Pache is the best defensive outfield prospect in the game, with plus-plus tools on the grass. That was true last year too, but what's changed in the interim is the offensive projection. Not all that long ago, Pache combined being a wild free swinger with limited strength; this led to a whole lot of off-balance, weak contact. He's added substantial upper-body strength over the past year while also gaining control over his swing. This has led to not just better present offensive outcomes but much better projection. If you combine his defensive profile with even an average offensive outcome, he's a first-division regular. If he's just a bit more than that with the stick, he's going to be a star, and that's firmly in play now.

23. Nolan Gorman, 3B, St. Louis Cardinals

Third-base profiles are tricky. The best third base prospects may be present shortstops—glance up to Kieboom, Luciano, or Royce Lewis above—and Gorman is a large enough human that there's going to be moderate concern he might slide further down the defensive spectrum in his 20s. But while third base is considered to be somewhere in the middle of the defensive spectrum, it carries a high offensive bar as well. In 2019 third basemen slugged .455, right in line with both corner outfield spots and first base. Wherever he ends up, the slugging should not be a problem for Gorman who has plus-plus raw power and should be able to get to all of it in major-league games given time to refine his swing and approach. At that point it's less important where he stands, but he's athletic for his size and passable at the hot corner with a plus arm. He may not end up the best third baseman on this list, but the present package is the best third base prospect in baseball.

24. Deivi Garcia, RHP, New York Yankees

As pitching roles in the majors have become amorphous, so too have role projections for pitching prospects. In the past, even the recent past, Garcia would've been consigned to a relief projection and likely been further down this list for it. He's extremely short—listed at 5-foot-9—and when ranking pitchers that short, it was largely assumed they'd be relievers until evidence proved otherwise. It's possible Garcia won't be able to handle a full starting workload as we envisioned it even a decade ago, but those workloads are petering out already. He threw over 110 innings in the minors last year, and even if he caps out around there, teams have gotten much more creative on how to leverage those innings. If he gets to much more than that, he's pretty close to a modern starting workload. Garcia certainly has the stuff, with a new slider combining with his explosive mid-90s fastball, sharp curve and developing change to give him four pitches that project to above-average or better.

25. Joey Bart, C, San Francisco Giants

Bart's reign as best catching prospect in baseball lasted for precisely one year, right up until Rob Manfred announced Adley Rutschman's name as the first-overall pick from the podium in Secaucus last summer. Mr. Congeniality acquitted himself well in 2019, although he missed time with a fracture on his left hand, and then had his AFL campaign ended early by a fractured thumb on his right. In between, he showcased plus power and promising defense behind the plate, the calling cards as an amateur that made him the second overall pick in 2018. There's some stiffness in the swing, and Bart is unlikely to contend for batting titles, but the offensive bar for catchers is low and he should easily hop over it via 20-plus bombs, while providing plus defense. Oh, and in case you didn't know, unlike Rutschman, he did call his own games in college.

26. Forrest Whitley, RHP, Houston Astros

A thorough albeit not exhaustive timeline of Whitley's last two seasons:

- Suspended 50 games for using a banned stimulant to help him drive back from a college basketball game during the 2017 offseason
- Suffers a left oblique injury a month into his delayed 2018 campaign, is limited to 26 1/3 innings overall
- Looks like the best pitching prospect in baseball in the Arizona Fall League
- Shut down with shoulder fatigue two months into a disastrous 2019 campaign
- Struggles on rehab in the GCL where his mechanics look like a mess

- Slowly rounds back into form in Double-A, although control and command issues continue
- Looks like the best pitching prospect in baseball in the Arizona Fall League...again

We held the line after 2018, but this is now two functionally lost seasons for Whitley, who has thrown a total of 138 innings over the last two calendar years, and has added arm issues to go with the inconsistent stuff. When he's right—usually in Arizona in front of half the baseball universe—he's got four plus-or-better pitches, not all that dissimilar from Casey Mize. We have our concerns about Mize as well, outlined above, but he's been better and healthier more recently than Whitley. With a pitcher this talented, you run it back again in 2020, but we really weren't expecting to still be writing about him at this point.

27. Sixto Sánchez, RHP, Miami Marlins

If you're going to give up the best catcher in baseball in his age-28 season for a short pitching prospect, it better be a hell of a short pitching prospect. The Marlins flipped J.T. Realmuto to the Phillies last February for a prospect package led by Sánchez, who is indeed a hell of a pitching prospect of any size. Sánchez sits in the high-90s and regularly gets into triple-digits with his fastball. He also throws a changeup, which he gives a few different looks to, and multiple breaking balls, all of which show as at least average offerings. Earlier in his career it looked like he'd be able to push one of those many offerings into plus-or-better territory. Instead, he's rounding into having a bundle of average-to-above-average offspeed pitches that confuse hitters without necessarily dominating them—that shows up in strikeout rates that have trended towards good instead of great. It's worth waiting another year or two to see if something jumps, because there's absolutely ace upside here. He maintains No. 2 starter or high-end closer potential even if the fastball velocity remains the flashiest part.

28. Brendan McKay, LHP/DH, Tampa Bay Rays

It has been obvious for a few years now that McKay was more promising as a pitcher than a hitter, but 2019 made Tampa Bay's intentions fully clear. He's major-league ready there, a polished lefty with a beautiful curveball and strong command. His velocity ticked up a notch or two in 2019, and he was more regularly hitting the mid-90s than he had in the past by the time he was in the majors. The Rays repossessed McKay's first base glove early in spring training, deciding to only use him as a pitcher and a designated hitter. While still in the minors, he was the DH around three or four times a week, on quiet days in his pitching cycle. While in the majors, he barely hit at all. He did get one spot start and a handful of appearances as a pinch-hitter, but for the most part he was used as a normal AL starting pitcher. For now, we'll consider McKay a ready, high-probability mid-rotation lefty with a touch of additional upside on the chance his bat catches up.

29. Bobby Witt Jr., SS, Kansas City Royals

Sometimes, baseball bloodlines manifest in profile similarities. There's exactly one shared trait between Bobby Witt, Jr. and his famous baseball father: draft pedigree. Bobby Witt, Sr. was the drafted third overall by the Texas Rangers in 1985, 34 years before his son went second overall to the Royals. Past that, well, there's not a lot in common. Senior was a college pitcher who quickly made The Show on his way to an itinerant career as a fourth starter type. Junior is a toolsy prep shortstop with plus power, a quick bat and the defensive chops for short. He's also raw, and is going to need substantial time in the minors to develop his hit tool. Senior never made the All-Star Game and while Junior has all the ability needed to reach that level and beyond, past prospect lists are littered with hitters who had everything else but never hit.

30. Shane Baz, RHP, Tampa Bay Rays

The Chris Archer trade is, uh, not working out well for the Pirates. Austin Meadows made the All-Star game, hitting .290 and swatting 33 home runs. The Rays waved a magic wand over Tyler Glasnow, which erased his control issues and left a dominant—when healthy—starter. Baz was the player to be named later in the deal, and all he managed in 2019 was a breakout season that places him just outside the top 10 pitching prospects in baseball. This was somewhat foreseeable: He was an intriguing power arm as a Texas prep that went 12th overall in the 2017 draft. On the back of mid-90s heat and a polished-for-his-age slider. The fastball bumps the upper 90s consistently now, and the slider is plus, flashing higher. His other offerings lag behind the first two, understandably, but his frame is that of a starting pitcher and he should be able to stick in the rotation if he can get a third pitch to the vicinity of average.

31. Andrew Vaughn, 1B, Chicago White Sox

Player development has been getting more scientific of late, with teams increasingly relying on data gathered from Trackman, Rapsodo, Edgertronic and the like as inputs. Evaluation has historically tended more towards art, but those same developmental systems are put to use for evaluation by analytics departments. Most of that information is not made public, and what is publicized is often lacking context. Vaughn is a short, hit-first, right-handed college first baseman, which is a profile that really has to hit to make it because there's no path to substantial secondary value. That he was drafted third overall despite the "limited" profile is a valuable bit of data. The expected leaks about elite exit velocity and batted ball profile have since come to fruition, and Ben Spanier projected him as a plus hit, plus power player in his Carolina League coverage following the draft. Hit tool projection is perhaps the last remaining art form when it comes to player evaluation, and even its days avoiding data are dwindling. Whether Vaughn ends up above-average, plus, or plus-plus will make a dramatic difference in his overall profile, but there's reason to be confident it will play despite the high baseline for his position.

32. Brusdar Graterol, RHP, Minnesota Twins

It's easy to look at the short, stocky right-hander with a checkered injury history—including a Tommy John as a teenager—and just chuck him in the reliever bin. The Twins thought as much and used him as a reliever after he came back from a shoulder impingement last summer. And, hey, Brusdar would likely be a dominant late-inning reliever. He boasts an easy upper-90s fastball with movement as a starter, and his sinker *sat* 99 in a late-season relief cameo in the Twin Cities. He pairs it with a firm, upper-80s slider that snaps off late on bewildered batters. The change is fringy but there's enough feel for it for it to at least keep lefties honest, and he's surprisingly athletic for a listed 265 pounds. So yeah, maybe he's just a reliever. We're still okay with ranking him here if that's the case, but we'd like to see what he can do with the ball in his hand every fifth day. And it's not like the 2020 Twins have a plethora of more interesting options.

33. CJ Abrams, SS, San Diego Padres

Abrams was one of the higher-variance prospects at the top of the 2019 Draft, and he slipped to the sixth pick, despite an insane athletic projection, due to concerns that he might not drive the ball enough against professional pitching. He proceeded to go out and hit over .400 with power in the Arizona League, and while complex league stats don't engender much faith, doing that is certainly better than not doing it. More importantly, our feedback from his time in the AZL indicated he was, indeed, driving the ball more and that some of the concerns from before the draft had already been allayed. Abrams might ultimately end up in center field a la Billy Hamilton, where he has some amateur experience, and we'd expect him to be quite good out there if it comes to pass. He doesn't quite have Hamilton's speed—nobody does—but he has a swing far more suited to gap power and perhaps a touch beyond.

34. Heliot Ramos, OF, San Francisco Giants

Prospect development isn't linear; often it isn't even unidirectional. Ramos has been a bit of a sine curve since being drafted. Strong post-draft reports in 2017—flagging all his tools as average-or-better—came quickly from the complex and an aggressive ranking for a late first-round draft pick followed. Ramos scuffled a bit in the South Atlantic League the following season as an 18-year-old, and the tools our staff saw were a bit more muted. The power/speed combo was still there, but so was an overly-aggressive approach exploited by full-season college arms. Everything also looked a little more corner outfield like. Something clicked in 2019 though, and from the first reports in the Cal League in April, the five tools were flashing again. Ramos is likely to end up in right field—although he should be quite good there—but with the volume turned back up, and possible 30-home-run pop to come, he sure looks like a Top 50 prospect in baseball. And we are happy to co-sign that.

35. JJ Bleday, OF, Miami Marlins

Bleday is the archetypal top college bat. A potential plus/hit power combo from a sweet lefty swing, experience up-the-middle in the NCAA, but athletic tools that fit better in a corner, and a long track record of mashing in a major conference. A middle-of-the-order stalwart for the College World Series champs, Vanderbilt, Bleday's junior year was marked by the raw power that was promised by his swing finding its way into games. There isn't as much upside as some of the prep bats drafted around him, but Bleday is very likely to be a high-quality player for five or six years, with a leisurely decline as an average starter, then bench bat. When David Roth is remembering some guys in 2045 or so, Bleday will be one of them, and the memories will be fond, perhaps Ryan Klesko-esque.

36. Spencer Howard, RHP, Philadelphia Phillies

Howard was one of the most painful cuts from this list last year. There is never enough room for all that could stick at the bottom: balancing high-upside players on the precipice of breaking out into national names and high-floor players likely to provide a significant contribution is a tricky one to strike. Howard certainly broke out in 2019, dominating two levels and the Arizona Fall League with a mid-to-high-90s fastball and a plus slider/changeup combo. Were it not for a shoulder injury that cost him a couple months in the early part of the summer, he probably would've reached the majors, and he might've anyway if the Phillies had been stronger contenders in September. He's close to ready on talent, but he might not have enough stamina built up to be a mid-rotation starter for the entirety of 2020.

37. Leody Taveras, OF, Texas Rangers

The Baseball Prospectus Top 101 List is a team effort generated by discussion amongst 20 or so writers and evaluators. This is not one writer's pref list. It is not beholden to industry consensus. It's the product of the prospect *team*. So we use "we" when writing these blurbs. However, Leody Taveras's spot—Top 50 prospect for three years running now—is mostly the doing of our Lead Prospect Writer, Jeffrey Paternostro. It's very likely he wrote the blurb you are reading now. The offensive performance has never been amazing, even after adjusting for how young Taveras has been for his levels. This year he got to Double-A as a 20-year-old and held his own, and there were accompanying good reports from our Texas League staffers. And even if he doesn't hit much more than he has so far, the defensive profile is strong. Taveras is a plus center fielder with a plus arm and foot speed to spare. Ender Inciarte has been worth almost 20 WARP for his career with slash lines that look similar to what Taveras has done so far. Perhaps the glove isn't quite *that* good, and maybe Inciarte isn't exactly what you are looking for in the

37th best prospect in baseball, but that outcome is above the median for this spot, and Taveras will still flash plus raw from both sides. It's getting less likely it will all click for him at the plate each year it doesn't. But we (I) am still going to hold out hope.

38. Ian Anderson, RHP, Atlanta Braves

For the second year in a row, Anderson was right on the border for our OFP (Overall Future Potential) grades, with our team debating whether he was a "soft 70" or a "hard 60." We have considered the OFP grade to represent a reasonable future ceiling projection, something akin to a 75th-percentile outcome for a projection system. (All of the prospects on the list this year are in the 70 OFP to 55 OFP band, and there are some 55s who didn't make it.) Translated from scout speak, a 70 for pitchers represents a No. 2 starter and a 60 represents a No. 3 starter. Anderson still has a shot for top-of-the-rotation outcomes, and we're not really down on him in any substantial way from last year. We just think he's a touch less likely to hit a top-of-the-rotation outcome (perhaps 20 percent instead of 25 percent) since he hasn't taken a major step forward in stuff and the command hasn't sharpened out yet. As our former Minor League Editor and current Editor-In-Chief Craig Goldstein has imparted on us many times: if you have to ask yourself this hard if a guy is a 70, he's probably a 60.

39. Logan Gilbert, RHP, Seattle Mariners

Have you ever heard of Stetson University? It's a private school nestled between Orlando and Daytona Beach—not a small school per se, but on the smaller side for Division I baseball. They play baseball in the mid-major Sun Belt Conference, and they've been pretty successful in recent years. In 2018, they made the NCAA World Series Super-Regionals for the first time ever behind staff ace Gilbert. He would soon become the highest draft pick in school history, 14th overall that year to the Mariners. He's a prototypical strong mid-rotation prospect: tall with advanced command and pitchability, moving through the minors quickly with a four pitch-mix. Despite being the best *prospect* the school has ever produced, Gilbert has next-to-no chance to be the best *pitcher* the school has produced, for the group of 10 Stetson alums that have made the majors includes both Jacob deGrom and Corey Kluber. Good luck living up to that legacy.

40. Alec Bohm, 3B, Philadelphia Phillies

Baseball teams have gotten better at fitting square pegs into round holes recently. Bohm has the body and defensive skills that would, under normal circumstances, best lend themselves to playing first base. Except the Phillies have Rhys Hoskins at first base, and they've already tried Hoskins in the outfield to dubious results. Bohm isn't great at third base either, and he has the limited range you'd expect from someone around his height (6-foot-5) who isn't named "Scott Rolen." But despite mediocre footwork, he projects to around fringe-average there thanks to a solid arm and improving instincts.That's exactly the kind of infielder you can hide with aggressive shifting and perhaps a defensive caddy, and he's athletic enough overall to make the corner outfield a future option if things become untenable at third. Bohm is a disciplined, advanced hitter on the verge of getting to all of his plus-plus raw power, and is going to force his way to the big leagues pretty soon.

41. Nico Hoerner, SS/2B/OF, Chicago Cubs

When Javier Baez broke his thumb at the beginning of September, the Cubs turned to Hoerner to man shortstop for the home stretch. He wasn't ready—he'd only had 375 professional plate appearances total, and he was putting up a 104 DRC+ in the Southern League, barely above league-average—but the Cubs lacked a shortstop on their 40-man in a desperate pennant race. Given the less-than-ideal circumstances, Hoerner performed with aplomb, giving the Cubs steady defense and competitive at-bats. He has a short swing with excellent bat-to-ball skills, projecting for a future plus hit tool, and those skills kept him above water in the majors. With Baez entrenched at short in Wrigley for the foreseeable future, the Cubs started working Hoerner at second base and center field in 2019, which are also good fits for his speed and athleticism. His power...well, the good news is that he hit as many homers in the majors as he did in a half-season in Double-A, and the bad news is that the number was three. He should be back in the bigs to stay at some point in 2020.

42. Drew Waters, OF, Atlanta Braves

"Waters or Pache?" has been a popular Braves prospect parlor game ever since Waters was drafted as a prep bat in 2017. They're both tools-laden center fielders who were born about a month apart, so it's an easy connection to make. Pache has pulled away for now, but that's no knock on Waters, who has done nothing but hit. Waters has blown through all four full-season minor-league levels, reaching Triple-A last August at just 20 years old. He has an advanced hit tool, especially from the left side, but we're still unsure if he's ever going to loft the ball enough to get above-average game power. He played almost all of the 2019 season alongside Pache, and they split time between center and the corners, with Pache spending a bit more time in center. Waters would have a chance to carry the position elsewhere, but in an organization with Ronald Acuña and Pache that defensive projection for center is going to be purely academic.

43. Jordan Groshans, SS, Toronto Blue Jays

Groshans was one of the big early-season breakout prospects of 2019. The 12th-overall pick in 2018 made the jump to full-season ball as a teenager and dominated in April, looking more like a college draftee than a 19-year-old prep. Then he suffered a foot injury in May and had a series of setbacks that ultimately ended his season. Groshans was already likely to

slide from shortstop to third base because of size and lack of foot speed, and we reckon that process will be sped up by the injury. He has a strong hit-and-power profile and surprising offensive polish for his age, but that he missed so much time is a bit alarming. The tools that he was flashing warrant a top-25 placement, if not higher, and he's expected to be ready for spring training, so some aggression is still warranted.

44. Sean Murphy, C, Oakland Athletics

The skillset of the major-league backstop is broad, and while traditionally they were evaluated on pop time and bat—framing and game calling are the current water cooler subjects—there's also a host of soft skills they need to manage a modern pitching staff. Murphy checks pretty much every catcher-skill box and he has a major-league cameo under his belt. There is, however, a top line concern remaining: We don't know if he's durable enough to handle the physical rigors of the everyday catcher. He is already dealing with knee issues in his mid-20s and, well, the job requires a lot of squatting. Murphy has never caught more than 91 games in a season, and this year managed only 53. If there was more certainty he could spend the next six to eight years catching 100-120 games a season, he'd be further up this list; the glove (an easy plus) and power (ditto) could land him on a few All-Star teams. Catcher can be a war of attrition, and Murphy has yet to fortify a Maginot Line.

45. Grayson Rodriguez, RHP, Baltimore Orioles

Rodriguez is straight off the touted assembly line of prep pitchers from Texas: a tall and sturdy righty flashing big stuff. He went a long way towards actualizing his projection in the 2019 season, showing marked improvement as the season wore on, sitting 94-97 and throwing five pitches in a late-August showing. There's still a bit of rawness present in the profile:, There's enough bleed between his curveball and slider to the point where he'd be best off picking one or the other, and a new hard cutter is only in the nascent stages of development. The late-season Rodriguez/Rutschman battery that the Orioles assembled in Delmarva points to a tantalizing future for a team that has little hope in the present.

46. Jasson Dominguez, OF, New York Yankees

The hype surrounding Dominguez is as out of this world as his nickname, "The Martian." He's billed as a five-tool outfielder, prodigiously advanced for his age. The Yankees dumped out nearly their entire 2019-20 international pool to sign him. The comps are lofty and colorful; Mike Trout was repeatedly brought up in an article by ESPN's Jeff Passan before Dominguez signed, and that's as lofty a comp as you can get in modern baseball. He's yet to play an official game, but he excelled in instructs, and the video we've reviewed supports the hype. Yet we just don't have the depth of information about Dominguez that we have about every other player on this list, and that makes him the trickiest player of all to rank. He doesn't have the extensive amateur foundation that similarly touted draftees do, let alone any significant pro foundation. It was only three years ago that we ranked Kevin Maitan at a similar stage of development and hype, and Maitan is perilously close to being an out-and-out bust. If Dominguez comes stateside this year and is as advertised, he'll surely be dozens of spots up the 101 next year. We're going to need to see it happen, though.

47. Matt Manning, RHP, Detroit Tigers

Another year, another step toward the majors. Manning passed the Double-A test with relative ease in 2019, although our in-person reports continue to be just a touch below the overall hype on him. He's a tall pitcher who extends well, which might cause the mid-90s fastball to play up a bit from the raw velocity. He throws a plus curveball already, an advanced pitch with true two-plane break. The changeup is coming along insomuch as it flashes usefulness—or even more—now, whereas in prior years it was a straight show-me pitch. In many ways, this is our first "plus fastball and breaking ball, but he needs to improve the changeup or command" third-starter entry of this list, although Manning has better command and less relief risk than most in that class. Which is why he's the highest-ranked of them.

48. Ronny Mauricio, SS, New York Mets

Mauricio's slash line in the South Atlantic League looks like a player just keeping his head above water, but our staff reports describe a projectable teenager with a potential plus hit/power combo due to good bat speed and enough hand-eye to cover for a presently raw approach. Mauricio may slide over to third as he ages, but he'd be above-average there with a plus arm, and it's not a lock he moves off the six. The overeager approach needs to be ironed out or he'll generate more bad contact than is ideal, making the power play down to average-or-a-tick-above. If the downside comp sounds a little like Wilmer Flores, well, that's a little lazy, but not wildly inaccurate, and Flores ranked in this range on prospect lists once upon a time.

49. Riley Greene, OF, Detroit Tigers

If there is a central casting office for "fifth-overall pick prep outfielder," Riley Greene would be the top headshot on the pile. He has a lean, projectable frame; one you can see growing into plus power, which he already flashes pull side in batting practice. There's also plus bat speed with lift and the contact makes *that* sound. He's an above-average runner, although his present routes in the outfield are crude and as he grows into his body he might be sliding to a corner, regardless. Greene showed some rawness against same-side spin, and he can get long with his swing, but that's all expected for a high schooler figuring things out during his first pro summer. There's nothing too loud here—if that were the case he'd be cast as "first overall prep outfielder"—but as 18-year-olds go, Greene is a high-probability regular with some first-division upside.

50. Matthew Liberatore, LHP, Tampa Bay Rays

In evaluating Liberatore's fortunes for 2019 we said he'd "shoot pretty far up the list with 120 healthy innings." He came up about 40 innings short. The Rays held him back in extended spring to start the season and abbreviated his outings late in the season, both in the name of load management. In between, he was one of the most advanced arms in the Low-A Midwest League, despite pitching the entire season as a 19-year-old. Liberatore possesses a full four-pitch arsenal and, as a smooth lefty with a plus overhand curve, he certainly has fine aesthetics for a pitching prospect. He lacks the high upside or certainty necessary to be higher than this, but a small jump in his stuff or continued strong performance and health would propel him into the top tier of pitching prospects.

51. Brandon Marsh, OF, Los Angeles Angels

The Angels have a type in the draft and it's "athletic high school football players." Marsh was a highly-recruited wide receiver out of Buford High School in Georgia, and although his long-term future was always likely on the diamond, he retains a lot of his football athleticism. The multi-sport prep prospect—Marsh played basketball as well—implies a certain amount of baseball rawness in this era of early specialization, but Marsh is already a polished hitter as well with advanced bat-to-ball skills. He's a plus runner of course, with a shot to stick in center field—although he's unlikely to man it in Angel Stadium. The one missing tool at the moment in game power, although Marsh is tall and strong, he doesn't consistently elevate the ball. If he can unlock some of his plus raw power in games, the 2022 *Angels in the Outfield* remake might feature a trio of All-Stars on the movie poster.

52. Jazz Chisholm, SS, Miami Marlins

Double-A can be a real Point of Departure for even good hitting prospects. The jump from the low minors is tricky; better velocity, better breaking stuff, older arms with major-league experience who knows exactly how to leave you feeling Kind of Blue. Jazz swings hard and often, and while his raw power can boom like Heavy Weather, Double-A pitchers figured out how to pitch to him on his Maiden Voyage at the level. Prospects always deserve Time Out to adjust though, and Chisholm hit .257/.340/.459 after June 1st. That will play, and gives a feel for what The Shape of Jazz to Come might look like. "Might" is doing some heavy lifting there though, as Double-A to the majors requires some Giant Steps. The shortstop glove is just about ready for the bigs though, and if the bat catches up in the next year or two, Marlins fans will be Moanin' in anticipation of his arrival in Miami. And I will Speak No Evil about Jazz either, because his power stroke is one of My Favorite Things. You've heard The Best of the Hot 5 and 7, and Jazz is a Hot 6.

53. Mitch Keller, RHP, Pittsburgh Pirates

Keller was two innings from graduating from this list, which would've saved a difficult discussion about how much we have to consider the context in which he's failing to blossom. His major-league performance was one part disastrous (the airplane ERA) and two parts okay (an above-average DRA and plenty of strikeouts). The fastball was still mid-90s and touching 98, but it got absolutely tattooed; opposing hitters hit .461 and slugged .719 off it. The curveball still flashes huge, but he didn't throw it all that much. Instead, Keller favored a slider that mostly replaced his underdeveloped and mediocre changeup, and it's not clear that's the right answer either. The Pirates have had long-standing issues developing pitchers and Keller's recent lack of progress sure looks like the latest manifestation of that. It may be overly cheeky to suggest that his most likely path to success is to end up on a smarter team, but... **[waves in the direction of Gerrit Cole and Tyler Glasnow]**

54. Alek Thomas, OF, Arizona Diamondbacks

Prospect writers love three things above all else: two-and-a-half hour games with no mid-inning pitching changes, a Panera Bread just off the interstate and sweet lefty swings. There's just something more aesthetically pleasing about the perfect southpaw swat. In Thomas' case, function follows form as everything is balanced and in sync, and his controlled aggression at the plate rips line drives from gap-to-gap. It's not an emphatic batting practice, punctuated by 400-foot bombs—and the power projection is fringy at present—but there's a pleasant rhythm at the plate, a Chopin piano concerto. Yeah, it just looks right (and just sounds right). The swing plays at seven o'clock too, as the 19-year-old hit .300 between two A-ball levels. Oh yeah, and Thomas is a potential plus center fielder with plus speed. It's an intriguing package of tools, but we are happy just to watch him take some hacks as the sun starts to set, the rest of the game blurring at the edges and then fading into the background, as he fires another ball to right-center to the strains of a faintly heard Steinway.

55. Oneil Cruz, SS, Pittsburgh Pirates

Cruz is 6-foot-7, about three inches taller than what we usually think of as the upper-bound for shortstop height. Athletically, he more resembles an ACC power forward or SEC defensive end than a shortstop prospect. Yet he's played every game over the past two seasons at short, and is fairly rangy and nimble at present. There is no real comp for where he might ultimately land defensively; there's never been a left-side infielder this tall, let alone a shortstop, and he's filling out as he ages. At the plate, he has long levers with titanic raw power and better natural feel for hitting than you'd otherwise expect. The most likely outcome by his mid-20s remains a power-hitting corner outfielder, but truly weird prospects are the ones that break the mold, and Cruz certainly qualifies.

56. Brendan Rodgers, SS, Colorado Rockies

Eons ago in prospect terms, when Taylor Swift's "Bad Blood" topped the charts, Rodgers was selected third overall in the draft behind fellow shortstops Dansby Swanson and Alex Bregman. Since then, Bregman won a World Series ring and scored himself a nine-figure contract extension. Swanson doesn't boast quite the same CV, but he's a solid regular with amazing hair. Rodgers is afforded a longer lead time as a prep product, but it's been a rocky road (sorry) even in the upper minors. He still touts a potential plus hit/power combination, but has been limited by an aggressive approach, and a labrum tear ended his 2019 early after a less-than-inspiring cup of coffee. There is probably some prospect fatigue, but it would be nice to see him dominate a level for an extended period of time. If that comes to pass, he won't be ranked here—or at all.

57. Ryan Mountcastle, 1B, Baltimore Orioles

Mountcastle has become a bit of a meme for our prospect team. Every list, midseason 50 or offseason 101, team or national, we end up staring at our final draft wondering how he ended up so high. Over five list cycles, he's moved from shortstop to third base—was there some outfield in there, we don't recall—and now finally, inevitably to first. And over the last few years he's ranked somewhere in this general range as a national prospect because every time we are finalizing a list, we look down at the names below him and ask "are they really going to hit more than Ryan Mountcastle?" The answer is inevitably no. Because wherever he stands on the field, he hits. Mountcastle capped off his minor league career by batting .312 with 25 bombs and 35 doubles as a 22-year-old in Triple-A. It's an effective swing from the right side, good bat speed, good feel for the barrel, some loft. And while we may roll our eyes internally every time he ends up ahead of a toolsy shortstop in A-ball or projectable draftee with a big fastball and hook, but there isn't really a better list-making strategy than "bet on the guy who you think will hit."

58. George Valera, OF, Cleveland Indians

Valera came stateside in 2018 after signing a $1.3 million dollar IFA deal the previous summer. He mashed for a week before promptly breaking his hamate bone, which ended his season. He struggled at times in 2019, following a tough assignment to the New York-Penn League. His swing features some moving parts—including a bit of waggle and a large step in to close his wide open stance—but he flashed more game power than you'd expect given the present frame and swing plane. The setup may be a bit unorthodox, but once Valera starts to move his hands forward, the bat speed is ferocious and...well, just looks right. There's enough hand-eye and barrel velocity that he can hang back on offspeed, although he's still developing an eye for spin generally. So while it's unusual to project a .300 hitter from a prospect that just hit .230 in short-season, Valera has a swing to dream on.

59. Nick Lodolo, LHP, Cincinnati Reds

A rare two-time first-rounder (unsigned in the compensatory first by the Pirates in 2016, signed as the seventh pick by the Reds last year), Lodolo was outrageously good in a small sample after signing, striking out 30 and walking none in 18 1/3 innings. Over the course of a three-year starting run at TCU, he grew from a tall, skinny kid with projection to a polished, well-rounded starting prospect that can hold velocity in the mid-90s and projects for two above-average-to-plus offspeed pitches. He was used lightly after the draft following a college campaign where he went over 100 innings, but he was far too good for hitters at the short-season or Low-A levels. Lodolo is a high probability No. 3 starter prospect, and is expected to move pretty quickly once stretched out as a pro.

60. Kyle Muller, LHP, Atlanta Braves

When drafted in 2016, Muller was your classic projectable prep arm with promising feel for spin, and he took a few seasons to get going in the minors. After several offseasons working with Driveline—one of the epicenters of rapid and significant change within player development—on velocity maximization, he's now consistently in the mid-to-high-90s from the left side with two average-or-better secondaries, a true power starter or closer in the making. Muller is not the only pitcher on this list who is affiliated with Driveline on this list, but he epitomizes current industry trends of players seeking to improve themselves outside of the team player development system and actually doing so.

61. Josiah Gray, RHP, Los Angeles Dodgers

Gray is the perfect pitching prospect to kick off a little game we like to call: future mid-rotation starter or closer? He has a plus fastball—mid-90s, heavy with run. He has a potential plus breaker too—a firm, mid-80s slider with sweep that can miss bats in the minors, but needs a bit more two-plane action to project as a bat misser in the majors. The change flashes, but is seldom used with less than ideal velocity separation off the heater. The command is actually okay, but he can have his rough patches. He's still a bit of a raw arm, as he converted from shortstop at small, cold-weather LeMoyne college, and was only a full-time pitcher his junior year. That might mean there's a bit more upside in his lightly-worn right arm. It also means there is a fair bit of bullpen risk. Same as it ever was.

62. Evan White, 1B, Seattle Mariners

The natural endgame to service time manipulation is the type of contract White signed last fall. The former first-rounder made significant gains at Double-A last year and now projects as an above-average hitter with unusual defensive prowess for the position. He's added game power over the past two seasons, getting to average from fringe, though average power is still not a lot for first base. He's almost ready, but the Mariners stood to claw back an extra year of team control by keeping him down just a few weeks

this spring. Instead, he signed a long-term contract that has options extending through 2028. The team gets a huge bargain if White becomes a star and a moderate one as long as he's a solid regular, and White locks in $24 million guaranteed before playing a game in Triple-A, much less the majors. That's generational wealth and financial security for his family, years before he'd have otherwise seen the money, and all of a sudden he has a strong shot at being the Opening Day first baseman. It's easy to understand all the motivations here, and it is a win/win deal, if only one ignores all the coercive factors of baseball's economic structure for young players.

63. Ke'Bryan Hayes, 3B, Pittsburgh Pirates

It felt like this was going to be the year Hayes started hitting for power and staked his claim as one of the best position player prospects in baseball. And that was before there were any signs that the Triple-A ball was going to travel like a V-2 rocket. Instead he went out and had another very Ke'Bryan Hayes season—plenty of doubles and great defense at third base, but not much over-the-fence power. That's a useful player, but as mentioned previously, there is a certain slugging standard for the hot corner. Hayes can make up the gap in other ways—that plus-plus glove certainly helps—but the wait continues to see if he can adjust the launch angle on those laser beams off his bat. Even if he doesn't, Hayes projects as a solid every day guy at third, but —fair or unfair—it feels a bit disappointing.

64. Brady Singer, RHP, Kansas City Royals

Singer is a bit of a different bird. Usually it's command and third pitch concerns keeping prospects in this range from the next tier up. Singer's stuff isn't quite as good as Gray or Muller's, but his command and ability to mix pitches makes everything play up. The stuff isn't fringy by any means, he can touch 95 and move the fastball this way and that, and there's a solid-average slider he can manipulate the action on. The change can be a bit fringy, so that fits with his list cohort at least. Singer has a good frame and a track record of durability. Nothing jumps off the scouting report, but it just all works. "He just knows how to pitch" is a meaningless cliche—nebulous and imprecise—but when you watch Singer, you get what it means.

65. Miguel Vargas, 3B, Los Angeles Dodgers

When you think of 14-year-old prodigies, you might think of Bobby Fisher or Samuel Barber or Jennifer Capriati. Fisher was a U.S. Chess Champion at 14, Barber was at the Curtis School of Music studying piano, Capriati made the semifinals of the French Open. Miguel Vargas was playing in the Cuban Serie Nacional de Béisbol, nearly 13 years younger than the average player. He went a fairly anemic 3-for-26, which might give him more in common with Joe Nuxhall, another famous teenaged baseball debutante. Nuxhall returned to the majors nine years later and carved out a 15-year career, even making a couple All-Star Games. It shouldn't take Vargas that long to find his way to Los Angeles. At 19, he hit .300 between two A-ball levels and the offensive prowess is every bit as precocious as that makes it sound. In fact every tool here grades out as average-or-better. Vargas is a smooth third baseman with soft hands and quick reflexes. He should grow into above-average power in his twenties to pair with the plus hit tool. He's a true two-way third-baseman, and he might make a couple All-Star Games himself.

66. Nolan Jones, 3B, Cleveland Indians

On the opposite side of the spectrum, Jones is not a true two-way third baseman. He might not even be a third baseman; he has a plus arm, but the hands have yet to improve enough to stick at the hot corner. His body is filling out such that he might end up just being a better fit in an outfield corner or even first base. He has the outer contours of an elite patience-and-power approach, with a vicious uppercut swing geared to tap into plus-plus raw and bat speed. The barrel control isn't there yet, and the resulting swing-and-miss both limits his hit tool projection and the ability to get to all of the raw power in games at present. There are building blocks here for stardom, but he's a few major adjustments away from actually getting there.

67. Luis Campusano, C, San Diego Padres

At present, any time we talk about the defensive skill set for a catcher, first and foremost is their ability to frame strikes. Robot umps, with which the MLB Umpires Association recently agreed to cooperate, obliterate the need for that skill set. This comes far too late for the Ryan Doumits of the world—perhaps just in time for the Zack Collinses—but Campusano might be a beneficiary, albeit in an indirect way. Although his defensive skills have been improving, he is an offensive-minded catcher with above-average hit and power tools. He's an athletic backstop and good at blocking balls, and will regularly pop 1.8 or 1.9 on throws. His throwing mechanics and actions can get out of sorts though, which has allowed baserunners in the minors to run a bit rampant on him. If he only had to focus on the man on first when the pitch is coming in, rather than his body and hand positions, it might allow him to clean up those caught-stealing rates, which are poised to become a bigger part of overall catching defense in our Post-Skynet world. This is all a hypothetical intellectual exercise, and either way, Campusano would be of the top catching prospects in baseball, but this could be a seismic change for catcher development and evaluation going forward.

68. Hunter Bishop, OF, San Francisco Giants

Bill James had a theory that the younger brother of a baseball-playing family disproportionately ended up with the most talent of his siblings. Hunter's older brother Braden never made a 101—although he has already debuted in the majors—but this one will take a while to play out. They certainly are very different kinds of baseball players though. Hunter has four inches and 20 pounds on his older sibling,

and smashed 22 home runs in 57 games for Arizona State this year, rocketing him up draft boards and making him a top-10 pick. He's got speed, but is still raw in the outfield, so he might end up in more of a corner slugger role, albeit with an intriguing power/speed combo. While Hunter may manage to take the baseball crown in the Bishop family, he is quite unlikely to be remembered as the best baseball player in his high school or college's history, as both institutions count Barry Bonds among their alumni.

69. Taylor Trammell, OF, San Diego Padres

"It is, moreover, evident from what has been said, that it is not the function of the poet to relate what has happened, but what may happen—what is possible according to the law of probability or necessity. The poet and the historian differ not by writing in verse or in prose. The work of Herodotus might be put into verse, and it would still be a species of history, with meter no less than without it. The true difference is that one relates what has happened, the other what may happen."

-Aristotle, Poetics

What happened: Trammell hit .234/.340/.349 in Double-A. His swing and approach were messy at the best of times. At others he looked more like a left fielder than a center fielder despite his easy plus speed. His game power remains mostly theoretical.

What may happen: It's a stretch to imply that a prospect writer is a poet, but by Aristotle's definition it seems to fit (and who are we to argue with Aristotle?). What is probable is not what is possible, and we are choosing to focus on what is possible for Trammell for another year—a two-way center fielder with above-average hit and power tools.

But the Greeks also knew that there is a real danger of falling into a well while gazing at the stars.

70. Josh Jung, 3B, Texas Rangers

A top-10 draft position presents a rebuttable presumption that the player will be on the following winter's 101. It means that smart, experienced player evaluators thought that the draftee was a 101-level prospect. Which brings us to Jung, who Texas popped with the eighth pick last June. He's basically what one would expect if all you knew about him was that he was a power conference third baseman drafted towards the back of the top 10: He has the potential to hit for average and power after he adjusts more to pro pitching and wood bats, solid defense but a touch unreliable, fairly polished. The presumption here that he's good hasn't been rebutted.

71. Shane McClanahan, LHP, Tampa Bay Rays

I'm hard-throwing but a little wild
I'm effort in the delivery but not too bad
I'm electric stuff but not always on, yeah

I'm a knee-buckling curve but not all the time
I'm a flashing change but inconsistent
I'm starting now but I might close

And what it all comes down to
Is that everything's gonna be fine, fine, fine
Cause I've got one outcome as a mid-rotation starter
And the other one is closin' games

72. Jordyn Adams, OF, Los Angeles Angels

Adams was a four-star wide receiver recruit signed to UNC, whom the Angels lured away with a first-round bonus in 2018. He has the extreme athleticism, speed, range and projection you'd expect to see in a top wide receiver recruit. He also showed off a fairly advanced approach for a teenager in full-season ball, with an all-fields approach suited for likely gap power. Adams is the third of four Angels in the outfield on this year's list, but his defensive prowess might ultimately be what knocks Mike Trout from center some years down the line.

73. Vidal Brujan, 2B, Tampa Bay Rays

Brujan is one of the fastest prospects around, in a system that picked up two more fellow notable speed demons last year, Xavier Edwards in the Tommy Pham trade and Greg Jones in the first round. He's a second baseman who is already picking up other positions; he played 29 games at short last year, his first appearances there since complex ball. We expect that at some point his speed will lend itself to picking up the outfield, although he hasn't seen game time there yet. And he has one of the best hit tool projections on this entire list. Steve Givarz gave it plus-plus potential last May, and if he ends up as a .300-plus hitter he's going to be a star (especially a fantasy one) despite lacking power. If he lands a bit below that projection, he'll still be quite useful. The Rays might be better than any other organization at maximizing the value of versatile players who do a few things very well, so he's in the right place.

74. Nick Solak, Hitter, Texas Rangers

We could list a bunch of positions for Solak, and they'd be correct in some technical sense. He played second and third in the majors, and also played all three outfield positions in the minors in 2019. Yet listing him as a 2B/3B/OF would imply a certain level of defensive value, wouldn't it? Well, he spent nearly half of his time in the majors as the DH. Like Willie Calhoun before him, picking a defensive home for Solak is more of a matter of where his glove would be acceptably hidden than finding somewhere for him to excel. The excelling part, that's going to be at the plate. He's long been a Professional Hitter with a short swing geared for hard contact that projected for strong average and on-base ability. In 2019, he suddenly showed up with plus game power, hitting 27 homers in 477 Triple-A plate appearances, all sandwiched around a rare midseason prospect-for-prospect challenge trade when he was swapped for pitcher Peter

Fairbanks. The rabbit ball conditions at Triple-A carry some cause for skepticism when it comes to sudden homer barrages there. But it kept looking right in the majors after his August promotion, and even if he caps out at a 20-home run bat, that's a heck of a hitter.

75. Adrian Morejon, LHP, San Diego Padres

Morejon has nearly every kind of prospect risk imaginable. He's never hit 70 innings in a season. He's undersized, listed at 6-foot-even (and few who are listed at that height actually are). He's had recurring shoulder problems. He only threw more than three innings three times in 2019, all in April. There's durability risk, there's injury risk, there's relief risk, there's command-and-control risk. There's one of the most talented lefty arms in baseball present and accounted for, too. Morejon is a dynamo with a strong chance for three plus pitches who reached the majors at the tender age of 20. Despite all the risks, we can't lose this thread: he might be really good.

76. Tarik Skubal, LHP, Detroit Tigers

One of the biggest debates about prospect rankings is how reactive we should be to new information. It's always a tightrope walk, comparing priors and past information to new things demonstrated in the present. Skubal was on the radar a year ago as a live-armed seventh-round pick who got well over slot but presented heavy risk because of command woes and a long Tommy John recovery. He broke out in 2019, slicing his way up to and through Double-A with a three-pitch mix that, when on, rivals nearly any lefty in the minors. In a vacuum, Skubal's 2019 would support a higher ranking than this, but it does not exist sans context. Prior command and injury risks factor in when assessing his overall future career path. The further he leaves those in the distance, the more confident we'll be. Right now, though, they're still in plain sight.

77. Shea Langeliers, C, Atlanta Braves

Of all the catchers on this list other than Rutschman, Langeliers projects for the highest floor thanks to a strong, well-rounded defensive profile. He has a strong arm, receives the ball well, has a solid frame and athleticism for the position and by reputation is a good leader and game caller. How much catcher defense evaluation is likely to change during this decade has already been discussed, and if we're this deep into a comment without mentioning a hitter's offense, that's pretty telling. Langeliers doesn't project to be useless with the bat, but he also doesn't project much above solid-average, and high floors for catchers are subject to cave in quickly due to the rigors of the position.

78. Miguel Amaya, C, Chicago Cubs

Amaya produced at roughly the same clip as he did last year, but did so at a level closer to the majors and in a tough home park to hit in. There were little improvements along the way for Amaya too. The batting practices were a little louder, and he's grown into plus raw power. The swing can be a bit short and upper-body heavy, so he might not get to all of it, but he should get to enough to be an average major-league hitter on balance. The defense is similarly competent if not spectacular. He's a solid receiver with an above-average arm. A collection of 50 and 55s on the scouting sheet usually isn't 101 worthy, but a catcher with this broad base of skills is rare, and Amaya already has a fair bit of polish for a 20-year-old backstop.

79. Keibert Ruiz, C, Los Angeles Dodgers

While Amaya took a small step forward in 2019, Ruiz scuffled. His aggressive approach outweighed his natural feel for the barrel, and, while he walked more than he struck out, he consistently made suboptimal contact. He continued to show good receiving skills and an above-average arm, but he struggles to move laterally and the athleticism has gone backwards a bit. He's also 21 now, which, while still young in prospect terms, is not as young as he used to be (and so it goes). Amaya and Ruiz went in different directions this year, but they now have similar profiles as catching prospects. That could end up meaning both just lack a carrying tool, but often just being able to don the tools of ignorance 115 times a year is the only one you need.

80. Jesus Sanchez, OF, Miami Marlins

Two years ago we wrote: "Sanchez is an A-ball left fielder…so he's going to have to hit. He's going to have to hit for average, and he's going to have to hit for power. So far, so good, and the underlying tools are there for a plus-hit/plus-power left fielder." Well, the underlying tools are still there, but they remain a little too underlying. The raw power is plus-plus, but he's yet to top 15 home runs in a season. His free-swinging ways haven't been tamed, either, and the hit tool now looks more average despite excellent hand-eye and bat control. A .260, 30-homer bat would fit nicely in any team's outfield corner, but until those offensive tools appear reliably in games, his stock will trend downward.

81. Tony Gonsolin, RHP, Los Angeles Dodgers

Gonsolin has a very good shot to be the most successful straight senior sign under the current capped draft bonus system. He was a two-way player at St. Mary's, primarily an outfielder who dabbled on the mound. The Dodgers selected him in the ninth round in 2016 as a soft-tossing senior reliever (read: a low-priority prospect) and signed him for $2,500. By 2018, he was a four-pitch starter with a mid-90s fastball and a ridiculous splitter that falls off the table as well as two distinct and usable breaking balls. He's an oddball profile, already entering his age-26 season but still improving rapidly, and he looked like he belonged in the majors last summer and fall.

82. Jose Urquidy, RHP, Houston Astros

Urquidy is among the most famous prospects on this list, thanks to his five shutout innings in Game 4 of the 2019 World Series. A year ago, you wouldn't have found him anywhere on here. For starters, he was known as Jose Luis Hernandez up until last spring, and under that name he was a middling prospect who passed through the Rule 5 draft after missing more than a season with Tommy John surgery. After changing his preferred presentation to his mother's family name, Urquidy quickly made major gains across his entire profile, and he was a key pitcher for the Astros down the stretch. He's ready to contribute now as a mid-rotation starter, and has one of the highest floors of any pitcher on the list since he's already had significant big-league success. Something to watch for early in the 2020 season: Urquidy started leaning heavily on his slider in the playoffs, and it was flashing plus, significantly better than earlier reports.

83. Alek Manoah, RHP, Toronto Blue Jays

Manoah is a hulking monster with a high-end fastball/slider combo that needs more changeup and command to stick in the rotation. Basically, he's a potential mid-rotation starter with caveats, just like a lot of his ranking brethren, which makes it tough to describe him in original terms. We'll just cut to the feeling: The macro outcomes for this kind of pitcher are good enough that they get ranked every year, but accurately predicting exactly which one is going to learn a new changeup grip or mesh with the right pitching guru is a river we may never ford.

84. Brailyn Marquez, LHP, Chicago Cubs

No prospect on this list shows just how good pitchers have gotten as a group more than Marquez. He's a tall and physically projectable lefty who regularly sits 100-plus with his fastball and supplements it with a potential wipeout slider and a usable changeup—oh, and he's already been successful in full-season ball. Even with significant command and relief risk, that's a profile that would've been much more touted, even in the fairly recent past. Marquez still possesses special arm talent—triple-digits from the left side is always going to be triple-digits from the left side and the slider is a second potential out pitch—but, at present, it's more likely than not that he's going to end up a reliever.

85. Trevor Larnach, OF, Minnesota Twins

Larnach hit more home runs in the third of the season he spent at Double-A than the two-thirds he spent in High-A, which is both a fun quirk and a testament to the difficulties hitters face in the Florida State League. He had a fine season adjusted for context, hitting well at both stops and starting to bring his plus-plus raw power into games. He's a big, maxed-out corner dude, so he's going to have to *hit* for it all to play, just like the next name on this list…

86. Alex Kirilloff, 1B/OF, Minnesota Twins

Hey, another Twin corner bat—sometimes it's nice to compare apples to apples instead of weighing them against kumquats. Like Larnoch, Kirilloff has a lot of offensive upside, driven by a tantalizing combination of advanced bat-to-ball skills and impressive raw power. His swing did get exploited more by upper-minors pitching, and it isn't geared to lift the ball enough, bringing into question whether he will ever maximize that raw. He's also sliding down the defensive spectrum towards first base, putting even more pressure on the bat to develop.

87. Daulton Varsho, C, Arizona Diamondbacks

Backstop prospects are tricky to rank, because defensive development can lag behind a major-league-ready bat, and because the rigors of catching everyday can grind down above-average offensive tools to fringy nubs. Varsho has hit and power to spare, mashing 18 home runs while batting .300 in just over 100 games in Double-A. The defensive development continues to, uh, develop though. Varsho is a good athlete—he'll post an average run time down the line—with the underlying actions to be a good receiver. But the catching is still rough around the edges, which brings us to the last problem with ranking catching prospects: We don't have great insight into the soft skills—game calling, pitcher management—that often makes or breaks "average" gloves. Should the worst-case scenario arise Varsho is athletic enough to handle a bit of third and corner outfield as well; even if he remains in the squat, he could benefit from some time spent elsewhere to give his knees a rest. And he, more than any other catching prospect on this list, might benefit from the robot umps.

88. Francisco Alvarez, C, New York Mets

Young catchers are the riskiest prospect demographic in the game, a horror show littered with examples of what John Sickels once dubbed "Young Catcher Offensive Stagnation Syndrome." While we're aware of the general risks of the profile, we *really* like Alvarez. He was one of the top prospects in the 2018 international free agent class, and he spent only seven games in complex ball last summer before being promoted to the Appy League. That's a brutal assignment for a 17-year-old adjusting to being a professional player in an unfamiliar country, yet Alvarez handled it with aplomb, showing off advanced and projectable hitting talent. He has the raw ability and frame to stay behind the plate, though a million little things can (and, perhaps) will happen to knock his course off track between here and the majors. Other than that, Alvarez is about as safe as a catching prospect below full-season ball can be.

89. Kyle Wright, RHP, Atlanta Braves

Wright was 42nd on this list two years ago and 58th last year. From a wide lens, he remains close to the ideal pitching prospect—a four-pitch starter with an optimal frame and classic motion. Zoomed in, he's shown less command than

hoped and there's been a concerning lack of development on his slower stuff. The relief risk is creeping, and while he'd be a good reliever—airing out the fastball and hard slider/cutter— he lacks the overwhelming stuff that would land a pure reliever on the101. Wright is still just some small gains away from a solid rotation outcome, but so are a lot of similar arms who end up pitching relief.

90. Andrés Giménez, SS, New York Mets

When swing changes are discussed in these pages, it is almost always in a positive context—"hey, this undersized middle infielder is launching the ball and now might hit 20 home runs." That was likely the intention when the Mets gave Giménez's stroke the ol' stomp-and-lift makeover, but he never really adjusted to it and instead scuffled in a repeat engagement in Double-A. The half-grade or so boost he saw in raw power negatively affected his hit tool, and he struggled to find a balance between the two. To make matters worse, he didn't even hit for that much power. The slick glove and plus speed are still present, which gives him a decent floor, and the reports from the AFL were improved enough to keep him on the back of this list. It's a bit confusing why they messed with a solid, if unspectacular offensive profile, but it's a reminder that not every swing change is a good one. You just don't usually find the bad ones on a top prospect list.

91. Geraldo Perdomo, SS, Arizona Diamondbacks

Last year's Giménez is a fairly good match for this year's Perdomo despite very different body types and approaches at the plate. Perdomo is a plus defender at the six with a polished hit tool and approach, though there is less power projection, and it might truly be a glove-driven profile. You don't have to hit much to be a decent shortstop prospect, especially when you have Perdomo's eye, but it would be nice to see Perdomo maintain his hitting line against Double-A arms or start filling out his lanky frame before projecting him as a plus regular. If he starts selling out for pull-side power in Jackson, we might have to worry we are in some sort of *Star Trek* temporal loop—or, perhaps it's just evidence that player-development staffs have become too infatuated with launch-angle swings.

92. Brennen Davis, OF, Chicago Cubs

Davis got held back in extended spring training for six weeks, and missed time after getting hit in the hand on two separate occasions, but he did enough in his 50 games on the field that necessitated a spot on this list. Davis was considered raw for a second-round prep outfielder, but he adjusted well to the Midwest League across the summer, flashing above-average hit and power tools. He's a plus runner who should maintain his speed as he ages, and he has enough speed to stick in center where he already shows advanced instincts.

This might look low in a year if Davis can avoid being plunked in the hand and continue to refine his swing and approach in the Carolina League.

93. Daniel Lynch, LHP, Kansas City Royals

Lefty heat
Ninety-nine, short relief?
Slider bites,
Change, all right
Command concerns, such great height
Third starter, repeat

94. Gabriel Arias, SS, San Diego Padres

Now, for the inverse of the Ryan Mountcastle principle: "Bet on the plus-plus shortstop and hope he hits a little bit." Arias has one of the best shortstop gloves in the minors and is a complete defender with a plus arm. He does everything well one needs to do at shortstop, and it's not a brief list of skills. And it isn't like he's an offensive zero, either. Arias, 19, hit .302/.339/.470 in the Cal League last season. Yes, it's the Cal League, filled with offensive paradises, but there's some real pop from the still-wiry Arias. The trade-off is his swing has some length and a lot of timing mechanisms. Couple that with a grip-it-and-rip-it approach at the plate, and the hit and power tools may play fringy against better competition. There's a fair bit of offensive upside, and if Arias keeps hitting in Double-A, then next year's blurb won't be in the 90s.

95. Xavier Edwards, 2B/SS, Tampa Bay Rays

If you're looking at this list to find out who the potential fantasy stars are, you need to know that Edwards possesses game-changing speed in the middle infield, and is extremely relevant to your interests, even if he doesn't develop much at the plate or in the field. For real baseball interests, Edwards is a bit more divisive as a prospect. He has good contact ability and some bat speed, so there are the makings for a plus hit outcome. We're concerned about his ability to get there because at present he's a slap hitter with minimal power projection. Our staff had a *lot* of looks on him between the Midwest and California Leagues, and is relatively split on his offensive upside, as is wont to happen when a hitting profile is hit tool-reliant. Defensively, Edwards has the physical ability to stay at short or second, but needs to develop greater reliability. He was playing both positions in the Padres system in 2019, and he's likely to continue expanding his versatility now that he's been traded to the Rays.

96. Kris Bubic, LHP, Kansas City Royals

Bubic is a potential mid-rotation starter who should stick there. His fastball has ticked up since the draft, now sitting low-90s more consistently. The breaking ball has improved as well, from a slurvy, show-me pitch to solid-average offering. The change is still plus, with huge velocity separation and good fade. There's deception due to his hitchy, stop-start delivery and high slot. His command profile is better than that description of his mechanics would lead one to believe. Bubic has an ideal starter's build and threw 150 highly effective innings in A-ball last year. And that's how you go from a back-of-the-rotation starting pitching prospect to a mid-rotation starting pitching prospect. Easy peasy, right? Double-A will be a test perhaps, but the only real finishing school for this combination of stuff and polish is major-league hitters.

97. Edward Cabrera, RHP, Miami Marlins

The Marlins system is dotted with boom-or-bust prospects. Cabrera perhaps has a higher floor, with a fastball that sits mid-90s and touched 100, plus two potential above-average secondary offerings. Like many pitching prospects nowadays, however, we don't know what he will look like fully stretched out. He's never thrown more than 100 innings in a season. Will the fastball really sit mid-90s across 100 pitches and 32 starts? Are the curve and change good enough to turn over a lineup a second time? These are the kind of questions that arise in regards to dozens of pitching prospects every offseason. But hey, if you are 6-foot-4 with three above-average pitches, you are probably going to make this list. We'll figure out the rest as we go.

98. Brayan Rocchio, SS, Cleveland Indians

Man, last year's Mahoning Valley team had a fun collection of prospects. In addition to Valera and Rocchio, they had two first-round picks in Ethan Hankins and Daniel Espino and a late-season appearance by seven-figure IFA second baseman Aaron Bracho. (Plus, the coolest alternate jersey in the minors, the Mahoning Valley Peppers in Oil, featuring an appropriately cranky-looking Italian *nonna* mascot.) Rocchio spent all of last summer about an hour away from Progessive Field, but if you had dropped him in The Cleve, he might have been able to handle the defensive responsibilities. Rocchio is as smooth a shortstop you will see in the low minors with good range and quick hands. The offensive stuff is going to be more of a slow burn. He's a switch-hitter with an approach and quick bat, although he's never going to show much in the way of pop. Rocchio is a good runner and canny on the bases though, and should add a bit of value that way. It might end up a bit of a glove-first profile, but it's a heckuva glove.

99. D'Shawn Knowles, OF, Los Angeles Angels

To promote the start of the 2019 season, MLB put together another "Let the kids play" commercial featuring some of the best young stars in baseball. There were World Series predictions, home run predictions, general trash talking and Francisco Lindor bat flipping a microphone. It was fun without being unserious. The 2019 season itself still featured the standard tension between on-field joy and the unwritten rules, moderated by the usual cranky coterie of columnists and color commentators with graying goatees. This is another reminder that baseball is an entertainment business, and Knowles is remarkably fun. He has the talent to someday be up on the dais with the stars, and he looks like a dude that has a mean microphone bat flip. Power isn't a huge part of the teenager's game yet, but he flashes plus bat speed from both sides. He makes it look easy in center field and is a joy to watch on the base paths. He's still pretty raw and spent all of last season as an 18-year-old in rookie ball, but we have a bit of a reputation for chasing upside, and Knowles doesn't lack for star potential. He's fun, but a serious talent.

100. Jeremy Pena, SS, Houston Astros

Dozens of prospects could credibly slot into this part of the list, where tiers are mushy and subjectivity plays a larger role than ever—101 is an arbitrary endpoint, and cuts off Jose Garcia or Brice Turang or Will Wilson, none of whom are that far off Pena as a prospect. Sometimes it comes down to a question as simple as "who do you want to get on the list?" We wanted Pena. It's not to get a marker down for 2020. His skillset is broad and solid on both sides of the ball, but he's unlikely to rocket up the 2021 edition. It's just that every member of the prospect team that has seen him—going back to college—likes him. There won't be much power coming, but he can hit a little, run a little and play a good everyday shortstop. You can move him around the infield if you like, and he will be a solid hand wherever he's positioned. Pena is unlikely to be a star, but sometimes you just want to nod in a prospect's general direction and say "we like the dude."

101. James Karinchak, RHP, Cleveland Indians

The term "video game pitcher" is used to describe pitchers whose repertoires resemble a maxed-out created player. Karinchak is more like a Super Baseball Simulator 1.000 pitcher throwing the ultra pitches; his arsenal is beyond belief on raw power stuff. He combines an explosive high-90s fastball with an absolutely ridiculous curveball that is a true 12-to-6 breaker at mid-80s velocity, and it all comes from an extreme overhand arm slot that is difficult to pick up. Because of that combination, he's posted nearly

unprecedented strikeout rates in the minors. He continued to absolutely baffle hitters in a September call-up, quickly becoming a Pitching Ninja favorite. There's enough uncertainty about command and injuries to stop us from running Karinchak any further up this list, and we'd be remiss to not mention once more that he's a two-pitch reliever. But it might be a better two pitches than anyone else on this list. That's the kind of overwhelming stuff that gets a pure reliever on the 101.

An additional note on Noah Song, RHP, Boston Red Sox

Song has one of the most unique backgrounds you'll ever see. He was a minor prospect coming out of high school, and his only Division I scholarship offer was from the Naval Academy. Over the course of his four years there, he unexpectedly developed into one of the best pitchers in college baseball and a serious pro prospect, with a fastball scraping the high-90s and a quality variety of other offerings. But he committed to serving in the Navy by staying until graduation. It was unclear at the time of the 2019 draft whether he'd be able to pursue a professional career; despite first-round talent, he slipped to the fourth round as a Red Sox priority senior sign. Song looked every bit the part of a top pitching prospect after the draft, and was so impressive that he would have ranked in the 80s if he received a deferral from his commitment. But as of press time, the likelihood is that he will miss some or all of the 2020 and 2021 seasons while serving as a flight officer. He's the best prospect to be facing years off for military service in recent memory, so it's quite an edge case for us as prospect evaluators. We feel comfortable saying it increases the chances he'll end up in the bullpen and substantially inflates his overall risk, enough to discourage us from placing him on the list proper.

Hit-by-Pitchers' Count

by Rob Mains

On March 20 last year, under the lights at the Tokyo Dome, the Mariners were threatening in the top of the third. The A's had taken a 2-0 lead in their half of the second, but a single, wild pitch, single and stolen base put a run across the plate and left the speedy Dee Gordon at second with two outs. Jay Bruce, who'd joined Seattle over the winter via the blockbuster Robinson Canó trade, stood in for his initial at-bat with his new club. Mike Fiers hit Bruce with his first offering.

On September 29, under sunny skies in Colorado, the Rockies scored a run each in the seventh, eighth and ninth innings to tie the visiting Brewers 3-3, sending the game into extra innings. In the top of the 11th, reliever Yency Almonte hit Brewers pinch-hitter Jacob Nottingham on a 1-0 pitch, loading the bases. Reliever DJ Johnson got out of the jam and the Rockies won in the 13th on a walkoff unearned run wild pitch.

In between, there were 1,982 batters hit by pitches. There were 461 batters, other than Bruce and Nottingham, who got hit—including Anthony Rizzo, who was plunked a majors-leading 27 times. The season total of 1,984 was the most in baseball history.

Of course, the gross number, compiled over 162 games played by each of 30 teams, isn't comparable to past years with fewer teams and fewer games per season. But the rate was the highest ever as well. For every five games last season, there were just over four hit batters, the first time since the formation of the American League in 1901 that the rate crested that round number. Put another way, there was a hit batter every 94 plate appearances, the most frequent rate in history.

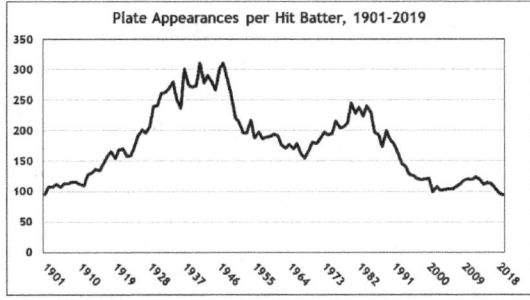

You hear that batters don't get hit as often as they used to because pitchers are afraid to pitch inside. Or that umpires, quick on the warning-both-benches-before-there's-a-beanball-war trigger, take the inside pitch out of pitchers' arsenals. Or that these players don't respect the game, why, in my day, if a guy stood there admiring a home run like that, he'd get one in the ribs, guaranteed.

It's all nonsense. The average pitcher in 2019, with a plunking per 94 plate appearances, hit batters far more frequently than Bob Gibson, who's remembered for pitching inside. (He hit one in 158.) The average pitcher in 2019 hit batters about as frequently as Don Drysdale, who really did hit a lot of batters (he led the National League five times)—one of every 92. Since 1901, there have been 1,127 pitchers to log at least 1,000 innings. Of the 25 with the highest rate of hitting batters, all but seven played in the 21st century. Four are still active: Charlie Morton (No. 2, he's hit one of 52 batters he's faced), Chris Sale (No. 13, one of 67), Johnny Cueto (No. 21, one of 74) and Oliver Perez (No. 23, one of 76).

We've established that pitchers are hitting batters at a record pace. The question is, why?

Part of the answer, you'd think, is pitch velocity. Interestingly, the average velocity on pitches that hit batters hasn't changed much. The average velocity on HBPs rose from 88.2 mph in 2008-10 to 88.4 mph in 2017-19. That's not much of a change. Batters are getting hit by both fast and slow pitches more often.

Perhaps pitchers are just coming inside more? Pitches intended to pass a foot or two away from the batter's body wind up sending the batter to first when the pitcher misses by an additional foot or two.

The problem with blaming the rise in hit batters on inside pitches is that pitchers aren't coming inside much more frequently. Pretend you're the catcher and there's a right-handed batter at the plate. Imagine a five-by-five grid representing where pitches cross the plate. The middle three-by-three area, comprising nine squares, is the strike zone. There are 16 squares surrounding it. The leftmost five represent inside pitches, the ones that can hit a batter.

In 2008, the first year of the pitch-tracking era, 13.4 percent of pitches were thrown inside, ranging from 10.3 percent of pitcher thrown by left-handed pitchers to left-handed batters to 17.2 percent thrown by lefties to righties. Last season the proportions had barely budged: 13.8 percent overall, a range of 10.8 percent to 17.7 percent. Here's the progression graphically.

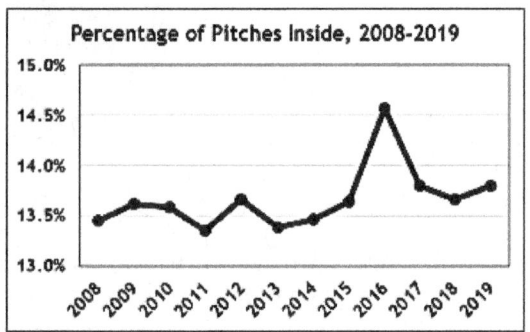

The trend is there, but it's pretty muted. Yes, the proportion of inside pitches has increased a bit. And it's up across most matchups: left-handed pitcher vs. batters on both sides of the plate, and right-handed pitchers against left-handed batters. (It's declined in recent years when right-handed pitchers face right-handed batters, but again, only modestly.)

Overall, the proportion of pitches inside has risen three percent from 2008 to 2019. The frequency with which batters were hit by pitches has increased 19 percent over that span. The slight uptick in inside pitches can't explain all the growth.

So let's look at when batters get hit. Some counts are more dangerous than others. Last year, for example, there were 12 batters hit on 3-0 counts. There were 209 hit on 0-2 counts. Even though 0-2 counts were only five times more frequent, there were more than 17 times more batters hit on 0-2 than on 3-0. Batters facing an 0-2 count were at greater risk of getting hit than those facing 3-0.

This chart displays the frequency with which batters were hit, by count, in 2019. Those 209 batters hit on 0-2 counts were drawn from 56,796 plate appearances during which the batter faced an 0-2 count at some point. Correspondingly, batters whose plate appearances included an 0-2 count were hit once in every 272 plate appearances. (The figure is lower than the 94 plate appearances per hit batter cited earlier because many 0-2 counts progressed to 1-2, 2-2 and 3-2.) The 12 batters hit on 3-0 counts occurred over 11,876 plate appearances, a ratio of one in 990.

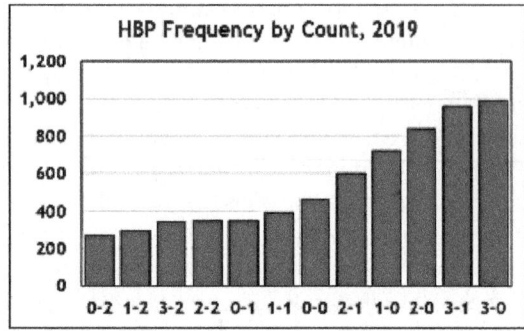

Batters were more likely to be hit on pitchers' counts than hitters' counts. They were hit the most often when pitchers had two strikes on them, followed by 0-1 counts. They were hit the least often when they had the advantage, with two or more balls than strikes.

You can figure out why. When the hitter's ahead 3-0, the pitcher has to throw within the strike zone. Excepting those 12 cases where the pitcher obviously was struggling with his control, batters don't get hit on those pitches. When the batter is ahead, the pitch is more likely to be in the zone.

Not so when the tables are turned. When the pitcher is ahead, he targets pitches at the periphery of, or a bit away from, the strike zone. They're trying to get the batter to chase in an attempt to induce a whiff or weak contact. If the batter lays off a pitch outside the zone, the pitcher is still in good shape.

That's reflected in the numbers. On 3-0 counts, pitchers threw inside on less than one percent of their pitches. On 0-2, they targeted the column in the five-by-five grid closest to the batter seven percent of the time. In total, they came inside, on average, on less than two percent of pitches on 2-0, 3-1 and 3-0. The corresponding figure for pitches on two-strike counts was nearly eight percent.

These ratios haven't changed much over the years. In the 12 years of pitch-tracking data, the percentage of pitches thrown inside the strike zone on batters with two strikes on them has averaged between 7.8 percent and 8.1 percent. The percentage for batters sitting 3-0, 3-1 and 2-0 has ranged between 1.6 and 1.8 percent. The percentage of pitches thrown inside—the type of pitches on which batters can be hit—hasn't changed much, either in aggregate or by count.

What's changed, though, is the counts.

As the bar graph above illustrates, the three counts on which batters are least likely to be hit are 3-0, 3-1 and 2-0. Here's the frequency of those counts since 1988.

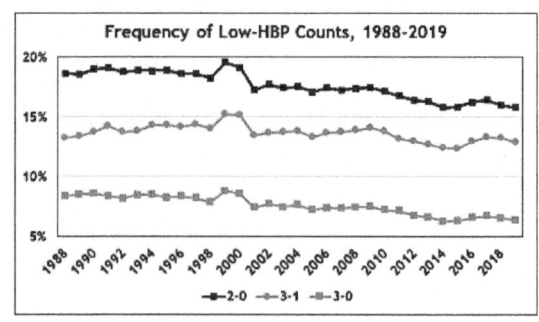

On the other hand, batters are most likely to be hit on 0-2, 1-2, 3-2, 2-2, and 0-1 counts.

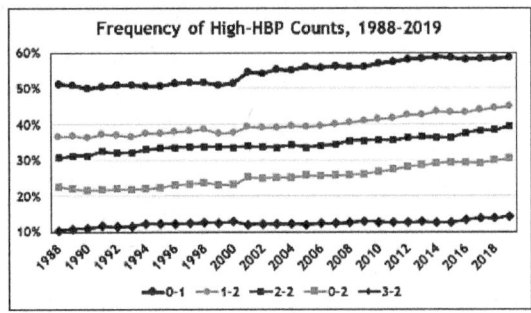

Frequency of High-HBP Counts, 1988-2019

-●- 0-1 -○- 1-2 -■- 2-2 -□- 0-2 -◆- 3-2

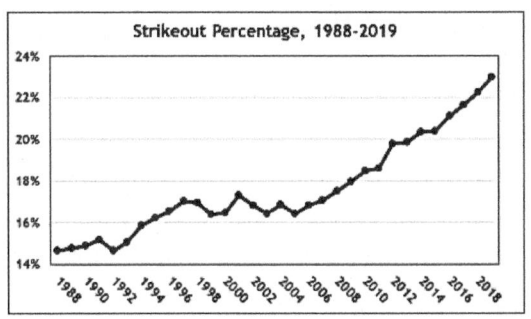

Strikeout Percentage, 1988-2019

These are not small changes. The two counts on which batters are most often hit are 0-2 and 1-2. The proportion of plate appearances that included a 0-2 count was 23 percent in 1988. It was 30 percent last year. In 1988, 37 percent of plate appearances had a 1-2 count. It rose to 45 percent last year.

And it's not just the pitcher's approach that changes depending on the count. The batter's does, too. When he's ahead of the count, he can be selective. We've all seen hitters stand up and step away from a pitch that's not to their liking on 3-0 as the umpire calls it a strike. The batter can wait for his pitch.

But when the pitcher is ahead, especially when there are two strikes, the batter has to be defensive. He's compelled to swing at anything that might be called a strike. He has to hang in at the plate, protecting against a strikeout, which also leaves him less time to avoid a pitch headed toward his body.

The counts on which batters are more likely to be hit, because pitchers are more likely to come inside and batters are less likely to get out of the way of the pitch, are rising. The counts on which batters are least likely to be hit, because pitchers are less likely to come inside and batters are more likely to get out of the way of the pitch, are declining.

Why are the counts changing? Last graph, promise.

You can't get to strike three other than via 0-2, 1-2, 3-2 or 2-2. And those counts rank first, second, third and fourth in likelihood for a batter to be hit.

There are more strikeouts in the game. We've set a new record 11 seasons in a row. More strikeouts mean more pitchers' counts; more pitchers' counts mean more pitchers targeting the fringes of the strike zone; and more hitters trying to defend the zone. And that means, when pitchers miss to the inside, more batters getting hit.

As strikeouts rise, batters face more pitchers' counts and fewer hitters' counts. They're more likely to get hit by pitches on pitchers' counts. They're less likely to get hit by pitchers on hitters' counts. The path to get hit by a pitch is on the upswing and the path to avoidance is receding.

It's not the velocity, though that plays a role. It's not the overall location of pitches, either, though that plays a role too. The biggest factor why pitchers got hit more frequently in 2019 than ever before? Strikeouts. The route to strikeouts puts batters in harm's way more often.

Since 1988, the frequency of strikeouts is up 57 percent. The frequency of batters getting hit by pitches is up 85 percent. Correlation isn't causation. Except when it is.

Thanks to Lucas Apostoleris for research assistance.

—*Rob Mains is an author of Baseball Prospectus.*

Collectively Bargained Acrimony

by Marc Normandin

"We voted unanimously to take a stand. We're not going to give them another goddamn cent! If they want to strike, let them strike."

So said Gussie Busch, then the owner of the St. Louis Cardinals, in 1972 in response to Major League Baseball's players wanting their pension to receive a cost of living adjustment. Busch's quote was, as the first executive director of the Major League Baseball Players Association, Marvin Miller, described it, a rallying cry for players that spring.[1] The players called the bluff of Busch, and the other owners, by striking rather than opening the '72 season. For that, they'd get their cost of living adjustment, while showing the owners that breaking the union wasn't going to be as simple as goading them into a strike they couldn't win—because the players could, in fact, win.

In 1994, then-interim commissioner Bud Selig—who was still an owner, and one who participated in the 1990 lockout, itself a reaction to owners (like Selig) colluding against the players in three consecutive offseasons in the '80s to weaken free agency and reduce spending—was ready to let the players strike. His plan, as decades of reporting on the subject has revealed, was to lure the players into a work stoppage by taking hardline, ridiculous stances—like introducing a hard salary cap and killing off collectively bargained rights like free agency and arbitration. Selig might have portrayed himself as disappointed that the 1994 World Series was canceled, but internally, and among his peers in MLB's ownership class, Selig was elated: he planned to hold out as long as it took to finally break the MLBPA. In his mind, canceling the World Series was a step toward this goal.

Like in 1972, the owners' plan didn't work. The players stood united as the owners overplayed their hand, attempting to unilaterally remove free agency and arbitration from the CBA while introducing replacement players—scabs—to spring training in 1995, effectively making it a lockout piled on top of a strike. This didn't fly with Judge Sonia Sotomayor, who issued an injunction against MLB's owners that brought things back to where they were under the previous CBA, ending both the attempt at replacement players and the strike.

Why the history lesson in a book about the 2020 season? Because the past is prologue: The MLBPA and MLB are set to fight in a way that they haven't in decades. Commissioner Rob Manfred—who began his journey to power by serving on the front lines for the owners in 1994 and 1995 as their outside counsel during the strike—has already reportedly thrown down the gauntlet to the Players Association.[2] Word is that, back in July during early negotiations between the owners and the players, Manfred told the union that there is "not going to be a deal where we pay you in economics to get labor peace," and that "maybe Marvin Miller's financial system doesn't work anymore."

"Marvin Miller's financial system," which gave the players a seat at the bargaining table, put to rest the lie that the commissioner was an impartial observer of MLB; won arbitration and free agency for the players; and changed the face of labor relations in baseball and the other major sports. Miller's system is what Selig and Co. were trying to upend in 1994. Stating that there won't be economic concessions in service of maintaining labor peace isn't quite as quotable as not "another goddamn cent," but the thinking and intention behind it are one and the same. Manfred, who has his position at the behest of the owners, is daring the union into action, and letting them know the owners are ready for some changes of their own. It's 1972 and 1994 (and '73, and '76, and '80, '81, '85 and 1990) all over again. Will the MLBPA prevail, as they (mostly) did in those instances? Or will this be the time that MLB's owners break the union and send the rights of labor into the past once more?

This is the story of Major League Baseball in 2020. Not what Anthony Rendon signed for, or when Gerrit Cole agreed to a deal, or how many players a normally inactive, losing team spent money on. It's the coming labor battle, the one that's imminent regardless of which free-agent contracts or attempts at Not Blatantly Tanking occurred between Manfred's statements and the time you're reading this essay. The only true business as usual in MLB is this: Labor peace is a lie, and it benefits management more than anyone else. Any interruption to this false peace is because management forced it into being: The players are simply trying to get what's rightfully theirs, what their existence in the league created in the first place. Whether it's a strike or a lockout that's coming after the 2021 season, it's going to come from the attitude Manfred already expressed to the union, an attitude passed on from those he works for to those who work for them.

You can see it in everything they do. Treating the luxury tax as a salary cap and discussing "flexibility" and "sustainability" as the reason for inaction, despite record annual revenues. Attempting to further weaken players' leverage and rights on the international market with a draft, claiming it's to fix problems and corruption in the system—even though corruption has flourished in large part due to MLB's unwillingness to enforce the rules already on its books. The threatened disaffiliation of 42 minor-league teams, which exists mostly to exert power over both Minor League Baseball's owners and, more importantly and sympathetically, its players—who earn sub-poverty-level wages and are limited to just 40 paid hours of work per week in-season, despite working far more than that, and for longer than just the length of the regular season. Everything done by MLB's owners is done to exert control and limit spending; their approach to negotiating the next CBA with the MLBPA is and will be no different.

It's going to cost us baseball in 2022. There will be a lockout because the owners won't stand for the players asking for structural changes, big or small, that will inhibit the slow strangulation of free agency, arbitration and players' choice that's been ongoing for a few offseasons now. The lockout will be blamed on the players, especially by segments of the media that haven't yet figured out that a strike and a lockout aren't the same thing, and MLB will wait for the union's solidarity to show cracks. Hell, they might even see if replacement players will work this time where they failed in 1994; the courts aren't exactly labor-friendly these days, and neither is the National Labor Relations Board that is, at least in theory, supposed to protect workers.

MLB is setting revenue records every year as they open up more and newer revenue streams—hello, new $1 billion Nike deal—but that money goes to minority investors and partners as a way to keep franchise valuations afloat: Investors raise the value of a franchise, and keeping investors happy and around means franchise value balloons even

further, which brings in more investors, and the process repeats. The on-field product is secondary to any potential profits: the Atlanta Braves have a real-estate guy *listed in their front office*, for Trout's sake. We've seen front offices evolve from observing "hey, maybe on-base percentage is valuable" to having soulless, efficiency-obsessed former McKinsey creeps dominate the sport and its thinking, putting us maybe two years away from teams hiring former Blackwater private military contractors in some capacity—maybe spring training facilities need APCs guarding the gates during a lockout, you don't know.

If you don't know about MLB's labor history, it's time you do. You're going to need to understand the past to know what's coming in the future and is already happening in the present. MLB's owners and front offices might hide their motivations behind being smarter, or advanced analytics or a workshop they attended at their old consulting firm that explained how women have pancake brains and men have the superior waffle brain.[3] But, ultimately, they're doing what they've always done. They're attacking the players and readying a "stop hitting yourself" defense that, sadly, convinces far too many—all while hoping tomorrow brings them closer to a return to baseball's feudalistic past.

MLB hasn't formally declared a labor war, but it's coming, and the result of its pitched battles at the bargaining table will have everything to do with how seriously the MLBPA knows they need to take this threat. There has already been a change in how the union's players perceive managements' action and inaction over the past few years; that feeling is going to need to carry them through the next negotiations and beyond to put MLB's owners on their heels for the first time since the last strike ended. ▪

—Marc Normandin is an author of Baseball Prospectus.

---

1. *A Whole Different Ball Game: The Inside Story of the Baseball Revolution*, p. 205

2. https://mlb.nbcsports.com/2019/11/20/rob-manfred-tells-mlbpa-there-will-be-no-economic-concessions-for-labor-peace/

3. https://www.huffpost.com/entry/women-ernst-young-how-to-dress-act-around-men_n_5da721eee4b002e33e78606a

A Relief for Relievers

by Gerald Schifman

Clinging to a one-run lead in their July 5th game against the Yankees last year, the Rays put in Emilio Pagan. Pagan was the breakout star of baseball's best bullpen, entering the game with a 1.64 ERA and one of the league's best strikeout rates. But pitching in a second consecutive game, he wouldn't be able to maintain the Rays' eighth-inning lead. On his second pitch, Pagan hung a slider that pinch-hitter Aaron Hicks hammered for a game-tying home run. Tampa Bay would go on to lose its second consecutive game to the Yankees, with this defeat proving to be particularly damaging.

Even though the Rays were 50-39 and had 73 games remaining, their probability of taking the American League East crown dwindled to 8.8 percent, per Baseball Prospectus' playoff odds. Meanwhile, the first-place Yankees' divisional lead rose to 8.5 games, their greatest advantage to date. New York's lead would never again fall below five games, and they spent months as a virtual lock to win the AL East. This cushion allowed the team to prepare for the postseason by resting key players.

The Yankees managed to complete the regular season without allowing any reliever to enter games on three consecutive days. Since pitch-tracking data became universal in Major League Baseball during the 2008 season, that feat has been matched by only one other team: the 2015 Yankees. But the two undertakings were not equal. The 2015 club made 497 total relief appearances, whereas the 2019 squad tallied 545 bullpen outings and 20 games in which short-stint openers were used in place of starters. The extra appearances created more opportunities to work relievers restlessly, yet the Yankees abstained to guard against injury and ineffectiveness.

"There's a recognition in the importance of trying to win games, but not at all expense," general manager Brian Cashman told the *New York Post* last summer about using relievers on three straight days. "If we can navigate that over the course of 162 [games], which is very difficult to pull off, you would be better for it."

This aversion has pushed the Yankees to the forefront of a leaguewide trend, as relievers are being asked to take the ball on consecutive days less often.

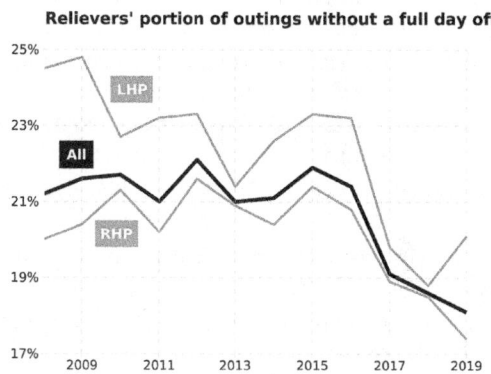

Relievers' portion of outings without a full day off

This chart (and this piece as a whole) doesn't look only at relief appearances, but at all regular-season outings from pitchers classified as relievers. The reliever distinction was assigned to pitchers who averaged fewer than three innings per game for the year. This cutoff makes standard relief outings the center of attention, while ensuring that openers are included.

From this universe, we find that the overall consecutive-game rate didn't often stray far from the 21.5 percent average posted in the 2008-15 period. But, ever since an excellent Royals relief core fueled a 2015 World Series victory, the league has posted decreases in each successive season. Last year, relievers' rate of consecutive outings was 18.1 percent, a drop of nearly four percentage points from 2015. This decrease emerges even as total reliever appearances rose 9.4 percent over the same span.

Even though teams are becoming more reliant on bullpens, they're managing to avoid an expansion of restless work. It may be a surprising result, given the prevailing narrative last year that bullpenning tactics burned out relievers. Roster turnover is one reason behind the trend. In analyses for BP in 2019, I found that teams have been ramping up on pitcher optional assignments and recalls, with the total number of trips between the minors and majors more than doubling over the past decade. Roster shuffling reached a high in 2017 and 2018, thanks to a rule change that reduced the minimum injured-list and optional-assignment stints from 15 to 10 days. That regular staff turnover has allowed teams to demote fatigued pitchers, recall fresher arms and sustain an abundance of able-bodied relievers.

The trend away from back-to-back outings appears for both lefties and righties, but there are differences between the two groups of pitchers. Breaking out the rates by handedness shows that lefties had consecutive outings in 20.1 percent of 2019 appearances, while righties came in at 17.4 percent. Southpaws' higher standing makes sense, given that they're often assigned to face a daily lineup's top lefty hitters. In recent years, though, the handedness gap has narrowed. In 2018, lefties posted an 18.8 percent consecutive-outing rate, which nearly matched righties' 18.5 percent clip.

This chart considers any span of consecutive games, leaving room for more examination. The majority of these outings come on a second straight day. Last year, relievers pitched on a second consecutive day in 16.7 percent of all appearances, a decrease of 2.1 percentage points from 2015. Taking it one step further, relievers threw on a third straight day in 1.4 percent of 2019 games—less than half the leaguewide rate from four years earlier.

Lengthy stretches of consecutive games are being eliminated. Earlier in the pitch-tracking era, there were dozens of outings annually in which a reliever threw on at least a fourth consecutive day. The count peaked at 58 in 2010, but the number has dropped since then. By 2016, only 14 appearances qualified, and last year the tally dwindled to five.

In the pitch-tracking era, the reliever with the most appearances on at least a fourth straight day was Pedro Feliciano. "Perpetual Pedro," as Mets broadcaster Gary Cohen nicknamed him, completed the maneuver 17 times in his four seasons in the data set. Feliciano would take the mound in 266 games over the 2008-10 seasons, ranking atop the appearance leaderboard in each campaign. Entering free agency as a top lefty specialist, the 34-year-old signed a two-year deal with the crosstown Yankees in January 2011.

Feliciano wouldn't ever pitch for the Yankees. He complained of left shoulder discomfort in spring training, and by April he was diagnosed with a torn capsule that required surgery and many months of recovery. When discussing the southpaw's injury with reporters that month, Cashman noted that the Mets' "use pattern [of Feliciano] was abusive."

⚾   ⚾   ⚾

Feliciano's extreme workload and eventual burnout may be a cautionary tale, but further analysis is needed to capture the pitfalls of restless usage. Rather than delve into amorphous injury concerns, this piece will assess how velocity and performance changes. If relievers wilt under the fatigue of pitching in consecutive games, that result should surface through velocity, strikeout, and walk numbers. Essentially, this tests an assertion made by former Yankees pitching coach Larry Rothschild in that same *New York Post* article from last year.

"If you put those guys into those situations [three days in a row] they are not going to perform to their peak, so why use them anyway?" Rothschild asked. "They are not the guy you are putting out on the third day that they were the first two."

For the velocity analysis, each pitcher's primary fastball was identified—this was either a four-seamer, sinker or hard cutter, depending on which offering was dominant in that season. Average velocity with those fastballs was drawn for every span of consecutive games in the 2008-19 period. Then the differences in velocity between a pitcher's first game following an off day and any appearances over the next two days were calculated. To emphasize larger sample sizes in the full velocity differences, every pair was weighted by the harmonic mean of fastballs thrown.

In a second consecutive appearance, relievers lose 0.22 miles per hour from the previous day's velocity. Pitching on a third straight day brings a similar 0.19-mph penalty. So slower fastball speeds emerge as expected, albeit in rather small magnitudes. Sample size shouldn't be an issue here, as many thousands of fastballs are coming into play over the dozen years studied.

Of course, velocity is only one dimension of a pitcher's stuff, as pitch movement, control and command are also important pieces of the puzzle. Rather than assess these additional attributes individually, a broader view at possible fatigue effects can be assessed through performance. The rates of strikeouts and walks per batter faced for every outing were tallied, with figures from a pitcher's first appearance following an off day compared to his successive games. Similar to the velocity look, pairs were weighted by the harmonic mean of batters faced.

On average, reliever strikeout rate drops 1.3 percentage points from Day 1 to Day 2, while walk rate rises 0.9 percentage points. On the third straight day, strikeout rate typically sinks 2.4 percentage points as walk rate climbs 1.5 percentage points. This round of results more strongly backs up the idea that pitchers' ability to perform is diminished in back-to-back outings.

⚾   ⚾   ⚾

Reduced effectiveness gives reason for curtailing consecutive outings. Parsing out the 2015-19 rates by team shows a broad spread, but a repeat of the trend away from these restless stretches.

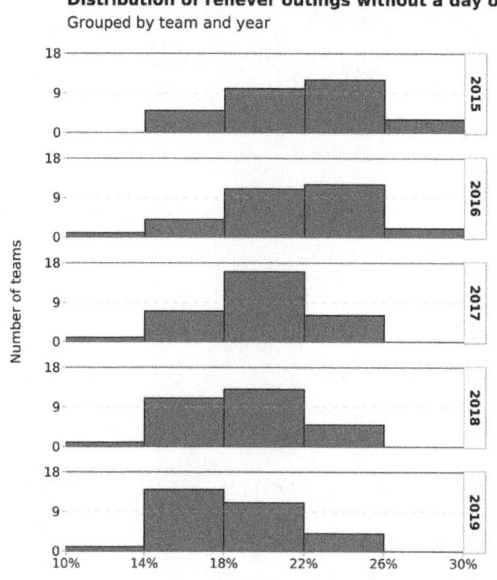

Distribution of reliever outings without a day off
Grouped by team and year

In 2015-16, the most common consecutive-outing rate for teams was between 22 and 26 percent. In later seasons, the distributions shift leftward. Last year, the most common rates were between 14 and 18 percent. Inspecting the 2019 season's low end shows that mainly noncompetitive teams avoided pushing pitchers to excess.

Relievers on the 94-loss Mariners posted a league-low 10.9 percent rate of consecutive outings. Ranking with them in the top five were the Orioles and Tigers, who finished with the worst records in the sport. In all, eight of the 10 teams with the lowest consecutive-game rates were below-.500 squads. But within that bunch of also-rans was the Yankees, who won 103 games despite having their relievers throw without a day off in just 14.6 percent of appearances. That clip was good enough for the No. 4 ranking. The other winning team placing in the league's top third was the National League East victor. The Braves were No. 10, thanks to a 16.4 percent consecutive-outing rate.

On the opposite end of the 2019 distribution was the Nationals, who had their relievers throw back-to-back games in a league-worst 25.4 percent of appearances. Washington's struggle to find reliable arms drove the restless work, worsening the club's bullpen issues. Compared with their first outing following a rest day, Nats relievers' strikeout rate dipped 1.2 percentage points and their walk rate surged 3.5 percentage points in outings on a second straight day. It was as though a prophecy from closer Sean Doolittle was fulfilled.

"It takes a different kind of toll on your body when night in, night out, you're asked to [get ready to pitch] at the drop of a hat," Doolittle said to *The Washington Post* last spring. "Over the course of a season, if your workload isn't managed properly, you may be able to get away with it for a few months, but at some point those innings are going to jump on your back and it can lead to ineffectiveness or injury risk that can derail your season or even your career."

Washington's poor relief corps became an afterthought in playoffs, as the team engineered a World Series victory with dominant starting pitchers. But even in the regular season, such heavy bullpen use isn't automatically a bad omen. That's because the team with the second-most back-to-back outings was Tampa Bay. The Rays had baseball's premier bullpen despite posting a consecutive-outing rate in one-quarter of reliever appearances. It raises the question of whether the Rays figured out how to make this usage viable—or if they merely succeeded in spite of these workloads.

⚾   ⚾   ⚾

There are several reasons to think that the leaguewide rate of back-to-back outings could rise next year. A rules revision by MLB will require that clubs wait 15 days before activating pitchers from the injured list and recalling pitchers from optional assignment in the minors. Additionally, teams will be limited in the number of pitchers they can carry on an active roster. With less flexibility, managers will need to rely on a more rigid group of relievers, which could lead to fewer days off.

Other changes could negate these effects. The league also announced that it will implement a three-batter minimum next season, which will eliminate brief mid-inning outings and discourage pitchers from taking on a Perpetual Pedro–like workload full of consecutive appearances. Plus, competitive clubs may seek to emulate the Yankees' strategy of avoiding back-to-back outings to fortify their bullpen for the playoffs.

But teams should recognize that this regular-season master plan won't make relievers capable to handle all matter of heavy workloads in October. The reins on Yankees relievers were loosened in last year's American League Championship Series, as they pitched half the innings against the high-powered Astros lineup. One quarter of their relievers' ALCS appearances were consecutive outings, and Zack Britton, Tommy Kahnle and Adam Ottavino pitched in five of the series' six games. Kahnle's final outing marked the first time in 2019 that a Yankee had thrown three games in a row. The previously formidable relief core seemed to wilt under the strain.

"I think everyone was running on fumes at the end," Britton told The Athletic after Yankees relievers allowed six runs in a series-ending ALCS Game 6 loss.

The expanded bullpen workload was a consequence of an unremarkable starting staff. That weakness was addressed in the offseason, as the Yankees signed Gerrit Cole to front their rotation. Maybe the luxury of having the 2019 AL Cy Young Award runner-up will reduce the responsibility on the

Yankees' relief corps. But, even with Cole, it will be challenging for the team to navigate another season without using any reliever on three consecutive days.

If next year's AL East race is tight, the Yankees might be compelled to push relievers beyond their de facto limits to capture short-term victories.

Thanks to Lucas Apostoleris and Pitch Info for supplying the game-logs data used in this piece.

—*Gerald Schifman is an author of Baseball Prospectus.*

PECOTA Leaderboards

Catcher DRC+

Rank	Name	Team	DRC+
1	Gary Sánchez	NYA	118
2	Will Smith	LAN	117
3	Willson Contreras	CHN	115
3	Mitch Garver	MIN	115
5	Yasmani Grandal	CHA	113
6	Omar Narváez	MIL	109
7	J.T. Realmuto	PHI	104
8	Alex Avila	MIN	101
8	Carson Kelly	ARI	101
10	Curt Casali	CIN	98

Catcher FRAA

Rank	Name	Team	FRAA
1	Yasmani Grandal	CHA	29.9
2	Roberto Pérez	CLE	25.0
3	Jeff Mathis	TEX	18.0
4	Austin Hedges	SDN	17.0
5	Christian Vázquez	BOS	16.0
6	Buster Posey	SFN	15.2
7	Mike Zunino	TBA	14.0
8	Jose Trevino	TEX	13.5
9	Reese McGuire	TOR	13.0
10	Tyler Flowers	ATL	12.3

Catcher WARP

Rank	Name	Team	WARP
1	Yasmani Grandal	CHA	6.0
2	J.T. Realmuto	PHI	4.1
2	Will Smith	LAN	4.1
4	Gary Sánchez	NYA	3.6
5	Roberto Pérez	CLE	3.5
6	Buster Posey	SFN	3.2
7	Willson Contreras	CHN	3.1
8	Christian Vázquez	BOS	2.7
9	Carson Kelly	ARI	2.6
10	Mike Zunino	TBA	2.4

First Base DRC+

Rank	Name	Team	DRC+
1	Pete Alonso	NYN	138
2	Freddie Freeman	ATL	135
3	Anthony Rizzo	CHN	132
4	Paul Goldschmidt	SLN	126
5	Carlos Santana	CLE	125
5	Luke Voit	NYA	125
5	Max Muncy	LAN	125
8	Matt Olson	OAK	121
9	Rhys Hoskins	PHI	120
10	Josh Bell	PIT	119
10	Trey Mancini	BAL	119

First Base FRAA

Rank	Name	Team	FRAA
1	Howie Kendrick	WAS	14.0
2	Brandon Belt	SFN	11.1
3	Joey Votto	CIN	11.0
4	Yuli Gurriel	HOU	9.0
5	Anthony Rizzo	CHN	8.0
6	C.J. Cron	DET	7.5
7	Pete Alonso	NYN	6.0
8	Daniel Murphy	COL	5.2
9	Matt Olson	OAK	5.0
10	Ronald Guzmán	TEX	4.3

First Base WARP

Rank	Name	Team	WARP
1	Pete Alonso	NYN	5.1
2	Anthony Rizzo	CHN	4.2
3	Freddie Freeman	ATL	4.1
4	Max Muncy	LAN	3.9
5	Paul Goldschmidt	SLN	3.6
6	Carlos Santana	CLE	3.3
6	Matt Olson	OAK	3.3
8	Joey Votto	CIN	2.9
8	Luke Voit	NYA	2.9
10	Rhys Hoskins	PHI	2.8

Second Base DRC+

Rank	Name	Team	DRC+
1	José Altuve	HOU	119
1	DJ LeMahieu	NYA	119
3	Cavan Biggio	TOR	115
4	Mike Moustakas	CIN	111
5	Gavin Lux	LAN	107
6	Brandon Lowe	TBA	104
7	Luis Arraez	MIN	103
8	Brian Dozier	WAS	101
8	Ozzie Albies	ATL	101
10	Keston Hiura	MIL	98

Second Base FRAA

Rank	Name	Team	FRAA
1	DJ LeMahieu	NYA	16.0
2	Mauricio Dubón	SFN	10.0
3	Kolten Wong	SLN	8.0
4	Ryan McMahon	COL	7.2
5	Nicky Lopez	KCA	7.0
6	Joey Wendle	TBA	6.0
7	Cavan Biggio	TOR	4.0
8	Jonathan Schoop	DET	3.0
8	David Fletcher	LAA	3.0
8	Danny Mendick	CHA	3.0
8	Nico Hoerner	CHN	3.0

Second Base WARP

Rank	Name	Team	WARP
1	DJ LeMahieu	NYA	5.7
2	Cavan Biggio	TOR	4.1
3	José Altuve	HOU	3.5
4	Kolten Wong	SLN	3.1
5	Ozzie Albies	ATL	3.0
6	Brandon Lowe	TBA	2.6
7	Luis Arraez	MIN	2.5
8	Mike Moustakas	CIN	2.4
9	Ryan McMahon	COL	2.3
10	Gavin Lux	LAN	2.0

Shortstop DRC+

Rank	Name	Team	DRC+
1	Xander Bogaerts	BOS	123
2	Carlos Correa	HOU	122
3	Francisco Lindor	CLE	117
4	Trevor Story	COL	115
5	Gleyber Torres	NYA	111
6	Marcus Semien	OAK	109
6	Trea Turner	WAS	109
8	Corey Seager	LAN	108
9	Fernando Tatis Jr.	SDN	106
10	Javier Báez	CHN	105

Shortstop FRAA

Rank	Name	Team	FRAA
1	Nick Ahmed	ARI	10.0
2	Niko Goodrum	DET	7.5
3	Andrelton Simmons	LAA	6.0
3	Marcus Semien	OAK	6.0
3	Trea Turner	WAS	6.0
3	Adalberto Mondesi	KCA	6.0
7	Willy Adames	TBA	5.0
8	J.P. Crawford	SEA	4.0
9	Elvis Andrus	TEX	3.0
9	Luis Urías	MIL	3.0

Shortstop WARP

Rank	Name	Team	WARP
1	Marcus Semien	OAK	4.0
2	Trea Turner	WAS	3.9
3	Francisco Lindor	CLE	3.8
4	Carlos Correa	HOU	3.6
5	Trevor Story	COL	3.5
6	Xander Bogaerts	BOS	3.4
6	Javier Báez	CHN	3.4
6	Gleyber Torres	NYA	3.4
6	Fernando Tatis Jr.	SDN	3.4
10	Corey Seager	LAN	3.1

Third Base DRC+

Rank	Name	Team	DRC+
1	Alex Bregman	HOU	152
2	Nolan Arenado	COL	133
3	Eugenio Suárez	CIN	130
3	Miguel Sanó	MIN	130
5	Kris Bryant	CHN	127
6	Anthony Rendon	LAA	125
7	Josh Donaldson	ATL	124
8	Justin Turner	LAN	122
9	Jeff McNeil	NYN	117
10	Manny Machado	SDN	114

Third Base FRAA

Rank	Name	Team	FRAA
1	Matt Chapman	OAK	17.0
2	Rafael Devers	BOS	8.0
3	Isiah Kiner-Falefa	TEX	7.0
4	Eric Sogard	MIL	6.1
5	Nolan Arenado	COL	6.0
5	Alex Bregman	HOU	6.0
7	Kyle Seager	SEA	5.0
8	Justin Turner	LAN	4.3
9	Yoán Moncada	CHA	4.2
10	Scott Kingery	PHI	4.1

Third Base WARP

Rank	Name	Team	WARP
1	Alex Bregman	HOU	6.6
2	Nolan Arenado	COL	5.0
3	Matt Chapman	OAK	4.1
4	Josh Donaldson	ATL	3.9
5	Kris Bryant	CHN	3.5
5	Anthony Rendon	LAA	3.5
7	Eugenio Suárez	CIN	3.4
7	Rafael Devers	BOS	3.4
9	Justin Turner	LAN	3.3
9	Miguel Sanó	MIN	3.3

Left Field DRC+

Rank	Name	Team	DRC+
1	Giancarlo Stanton	NYA	141
2	Juan Soto	WAS	133
3	Joc Pederson	LAN	124
4	Kyle Schwarber	CHN	123
5	Hunter Renfroe	TBA	114
5	Eloy Jiménez	CHA	114
5	Willie Calhoun	TEX	114
8	Andrew McCutchen	PHI	113
8	Justin Upton	LAA	113
8	Mark Canha	OAK	113
8	Jesse Winker	CIN	113
8	Bryan Reynolds	PIT	113

Left Field FRAA

Rank	Name	Team	FRAA
1	Justin Upton	LAA	10.7
2	Tyler Naquin	CLE	10.0
3	Anthony Santander	BAL	9.6
4	Corey Dickerson	MIA	9.3
5	Brett Gardner	NYA	6.0
6	Brett Phillips	KCA	5.0
7	Jake Bauers	CLE	3.5
8	Mark Canha	OAK	3.4
9	David Peralta	ARI	3.0
9	Hunter Renfroe	TBA	3.0
9	Juan Soto	WAS	3.0

Left Field WARP

Rank	Name	Team	WARP
1	Juan Soto	WAS	4.8
2	Giancarlo Stanton	NYA	4.0
3	Justin Upton	LAA	3.5
4	Mark Canha	OAK	3.1
5	Joc Pederson	LAN	3.0
6	Kyle Schwarber	CHN	2.9
7	Eloy Jiménez	CHA	2.7
8	Bryan Reynolds	PIT	2.6
9	Marcell Ozuna	SLN	2.4
9	Hunter Renfroe	TBA	2.4

Center Field DRC+

Rank	Name	Team	DRC+
1	Mike Trout	LAA	177
2	Cody Bellinger	LAN	141
3	George Springer	HOU	136
4	Ketel Marte	ARI	114
5	Brandon Nimmo	NYN	111
6	Ramón Laureano	OAK	110
7	Luis Robert	CHA	109
8	Starling Marte	PIT	104
9	A.J. Pollock	LAN	103
10	Teoscar Hernández	TOR	101

Center Field FRAA

Rank	Name	Team	FRAA
1	Byron Buxton	MIN	20.0
2	Harrison Bader	SLN	12.2
3	Kevin Kiermaier	TBA	9.0
3	Victor Robles	WAS	9.0
5	Harold Ramirez	MIA	8.5
6	Ender Inciarte	ATL	8.2
7	Lorenzo Cain	MIL	8.0
7	Luis Robert	CHA	8.0
9	Whit Merrifield	KCA	7.0
9	Steven Duggar	SFN	7.0

Center Field WARP

Rank	Name	Team	WARP
1	Mike Trout	LAA	8.6
2	Cody Bellinger	LAN	5.4
3	George Springer	HOU	5.1
4	Luis Robert	CHA	3.8
5	Ramón Laureano	OAK	3.4
6	Starling Marte	PIT	3.2
6	Ketel Marte	ARI	3.2
8	Byron Buxton	MIN	3.1
9	Harrison Bader	SLN	3.0
10	Brandon Nimmo	NYN	2.9

Right Field DRC+

Rank	Name	Team	DRC+
1	Christian Yelich	MIL	149
2	Aaron Judge	NYA	135
3	Mookie Betts	BOS	134
4	Bryce Harper	PHI	127
5	Joey Gallo	TEX	126
6	Ronald Acuña Jr.	ATL	125
7	Charlie Blackmon	COL	123
7	Michael Conforto	NYN	123
9	Austin Meadows	TBA	122
10	Aristides Aquino	CIN	118

Right Field FRAA

Rank	Name	Team	FRAA
1	Mookie Betts	BOS	16.0
2	Alex Verdugo	LAN	9.6
3	Michael Conforto	NYN	9.0
4	Mike Yastrzemski	SFN	7.2
5	Adam Eaton	WAS	7.0
6	Aaron Judge	NYA	6.4
7	Max Kepler	MIN	6.0
8	Mitch Haniger	SEA	5.3
9	Victor Reyes	DET	4.7
10	Joey Gallo	TEX	4.5

Right Field WARP

Rank	Name	Team	WARP
1	Mookie Betts	BOS	6.3
2	Christian Yelich	MIL	5.2
3	Aaron Judge	NYA	4.6
4	Joey Gallo	TEX	4.1
4	Michael Conforto	NYN	4.1
6	Ronald Acuña Jr.	ATL	3.5
7	Nicholas Castellanos	CHN	2.9
7	Max Kepler	MIN	2.9
9	Mitch Haniger	SEA	2.8
10	Adam Eaton	WAS	2.7

Batting Average

Rank	Name	Team	AVG
1	Nolan Arenado	COL	.308
2	DJ LeMahieu	NYA	.303
2	Luis Arraez	MIN	.303
4	Charlie Blackmon	COL	.301
5	Mike Trout	LAA	.298
6	Christian Yelich	MIL	.295
7	José Altuve	HOU	.292
7	Alex Bregman	HOU	.292
9	J.D. Martinez	BOS	.290
9	Ketel Marte	ARI	.290
11	Jeff McNeil	NYN	.287
12	Howie Kendrick	WAS	.286
12	Miguel Cabrera	DET	.286
12	Mookie Betts	BOS	.286
15	Freddie Freeman	ATL	.285
15	Xander Bogaerts	BOS	.285
17	Juan Soto	WAS	.284
17	Tim Anderson	CHA	.284
19	Bryan Reynolds	PIT	.283
19	Ronald Acuña Jr.	ATL	.283
19	Michael Brantley	HOU	.283

On-Base Percentage

Rank	Name	Team	OBP
1	Mike Trout	LAA	.435
2	Alex Bregman	HOU	.404
3	Christian Yelich	MIL	.387
4	Anthony Rizzo	CHN	.386
5	Juan Soto	WAS	.382
5	Freddie Freeman	ATL	.382
7	Carlos Santana	CLE	.376
8	Mookie Betts	BOS	.375
9	Joey Votto	CIN	.374
9	Bryce Harper	PHI	.374
11	Nolan Arenado	COL	.373
11	George Springer	HOU	.373
13	Anthony Rendon	LAA	.371
14	Kris Bryant	CHN	.369
15	Cody Bellinger	LAN	.367
15	Yordan Alvarez	HOU	.367
17	Aaron Judge	NYA	.366
18	J.D. Martinez	BOS	.365
18	Cavan Biggio	TOR	.365
20	Andrew McCutchen	PHI	.364
20	Paul Goldschmidt	SLN	.364
20	Josh Donaldson	ATL	.364

Slugging Percentage

Rank	Name	Team	SLG
1	Mike Trout	LAA	.645
2	Nolan Arenado	COL	.587
3	Yordan Alvarez	HOU	.576
4	Alex Bregman	HOU	.572
5	Pete Alonso	NYN	.570
6	Giancarlo Stanton	NYA	.563
6	Christian Yelich	MIL	.563
8	Cody Bellinger	LAN	.562
9	Nelson Cruz	MIN	.561
10	Aristides Aquino	CIN	.555
10	J.D. Martinez	BOS	.555
12	Eugenio Suárez	CIN	.544
13	Juan Soto	WAS	.543
14	Trevor Story	COL	.542
15	George Springer	HOU	.540
15	Miguel Sanó	MIN	.540
17	Joey Gallo	TEX	.533
18	Charlie Blackmon	COL	.530
19	Freddie Freeman	ATL	.529
19	Hunter Renfroe	TBA	.529

OPS

Rank	Name	Team	OPS
1	Mike Trout	LAA	1.080
2	Alex Bregman	HOU	.976
3	Nolan Arenado	COL	.960
4	Christian Yelich	MIL	.950
5	Yordan Alvarez	HOU	.943
6	Cody Bellinger	LAN	.929
7	Juan Soto	WAS	.925
8	J.D. Martinez	BOS	.920
8	Giancarlo Stanton	NYA	.920
10	Nelson Cruz	MIN	.919
10	Pete Alonso	NYN	.919
12	George Springer	HOU	.913
13	Freddie Freeman	ATL	.911
14	Eugenio Suárez	CIN	.897
15	Trevor Story	COL	.891
16	Charlie Blackmon	COL	.890
17	Mookie Betts	BOS	.889
17	Aaron Judge	NYA	.889
19	Joey Gallo	TEX	.883
20	Miguel Sanó	MIN	.881

Home Runs

Rank	Name	Team	HR
1	Mike Trout	LAA	48
1	Pete Alonso	NYN	48
3	Giancarlo Stanton	NYA	43
4	Eugenio Suárez	CIN	42
4	Yordan Alvarez	HOU	42
6	Joey Gallo	TEX	40
6	Cody Bellinger	LAN	40
8	Nelson Cruz	MIN	38
8	Nolan Arenado	COL	38
8	Miguel Sanó	MIN	38
11	Eloy Jiménez	CHA	37
11	J.D. Martinez	BOS	37
11	George Springer	HOU	37
14	Christian Yelich	MIL	36
14	Alex Bregman	HOU	36
14	Gary Sánchez	NYA	36
17	Matt Olson	OAK	35
17	Aristides Aquino	CIN	35
17	Aaron Judge	NYA	35
17	Juan Soto	WAS	35

Runs

Rank	Name	Team	R
1	Mike Trout	LAA	114
2	Pete Alonso	NYN	98
3	Alex Bregman	HOU	97
4	Eugenio Suárez	CIN	94
5	Yordan Alvarez	HOU	93
5	Nolan Arenado	COL	93
5	Giancarlo Stanton	NYA	93
8	Juan Soto	WAS	92
9	Christian Yelich	MIL	91
9	Cody Bellinger	LAN	91
11	George Springer	HOU	90
11	J.D. Martinez	BOS	90
13	Joey Gallo	TEX	89
14	Bryce Harper	PHI	86
15	Paul Goldschmidt	SLN	85
15	Mookie Betts	BOS	85
15	Max Muncy	LAN	85
18	Ronald Acuña Jr.	ATL	84
18	Freddie Freeman	ATL	84
18	Nelson Cruz	MIN	84

Isolated Power

Rank	Name	Team	ISO
1	Mike Trout	LAA	.347
2	Pete Alonso	NYN	.314
3	Joey Gallo	TEX	.306
4	Giancarlo Stanton	NYA	.302
5	Aristides Aquino	CIN	.300
6	Yordan Alvarez	HOU	.297
7	Miguel Sanó	MIN	.293
8	Cody Bellinger	LAN	.291
9	Hunter Renfroe	TBA	.284
10	Nelson Cruz	MIN	.282
11	Alex Bregman	HOU	.280
12	Nolan Arenado	COL	.279
13	Joc Pederson	LAN	.277
14	Eugenio Suárez	CIN	.275
14	Gary Sánchez	NYA	.275
16	Franmil Reyes	CLE	.269
16	Will Smith	LAN	.269
18	Edwin Encarnación	CHA	.268
18	Christian Yelich	MIL	.268
20	Aaron Judge	NYA	.267

Stolen Bases

Rank	Name	Team	SB
1	Jonathan Villar	MIA	38
1	Dee Gordon	SEA	38
3	Trea Turner	WAS	36
4	Starling Marte	PIT	32
4	Adalberto Mondesi	KCA	32
6	Oscar Mercado	CLE	29
7	Whit Merrifield	KCA	28
8	Mallex Smith	SEA	27
9	Tim Anderson	CHA	24
9	Victor Robles	WAS	24
11	Ronald Acuña Jr.	ATL	23
12	Yoán Moncada	CHA	22
12	Mookie Betts	BOS	22
14	José Altuve	HOU	21
14	Ramón Laureano	OAK	21
16	Elvis Andrus	TEX	20
16	Danny Santana	TEX	20
16	Jean Segura	PHI	20
16	Jon Berti	MIA	20
20	Lorenzo Cain	MIL	19
20	Mike Trout	LAA	19

Runs Batted In

Rank	Name	Team	RBI
1	Mike Trout	LAA	124
2	Pete Alonso	NYN	118
3	Nolan Arenado	COL	110
4	Eugenio Suárez	CIN	109
4	Giancarlo Stanton	NYA	109
6	Yordan Alvarez	HOU	108
7	Alex Bregman	HOU	106
8	J.D. Martinez	BOS	105
8	Cody Bellinger	LAN	105
10	Joey Gallo	TEX	103
11	Juan Soto	WAS	102
12	Christian Yelich	MIL	101
13	George Springer	HOU	100
14	Nelson Cruz	MIN	99
15	Miguel Sanó	MIN	98
15	Eloy Jiménez	CHA	98
17	Trevor Story	COL	95
18	Matt Chapman	OAK	94
18	Matt Olson	OAK	94
18	Max Muncy	LAN	94

Hitter Walk Rate

Rank	Name	Team	BB%
1	Mike Trout	LAA	17.5
2	Daniel Vogelbach	SEA	16.0
3	Carlos Santana	CLE	15.8
4	Yasmani Grandal	CHA	15.7
5	Bryce Harper	PHI	15.5
6	Joey Gallo	TEX	15.1
7	Cavan Biggio	TOR	15.1
8	Rhys Hoskins	PHI	14.8
9	Alex Bregman	HOU	14.6
10	Brandon Nimmo	NYN	14.5
11	Max Muncy	LAN	14.5
12	Josh Donaldson	ATL	14.2
13	Joey Votto	CIN	14.1
14	Andrew McCutchen	PHI	14.1
15	Matt Carpenter	SLN	13.9
16	Aaron Judge	NYA	13.9
17	Justin Smoak	MIL	13.5
18	Juan Soto	WAS	13.5
19	Dexter Fowler	SLN	13.0
20	Paul Goldschmidt	SLN	13.0

Strikeout Rate

Rank	Name	Team	SO%
1	Nick Madrigal	CHA	6.9
2	Andrelton Simmons	LAA	9.9
2	Luis Arraez	MIN	9.9
4	Hanser Alberto	BAL	11.4
5	Michael Brantley	HOU	11.6
5	David Fletcher	LAA	11.6
7	Tommy La Stella	LAA	11.9
8	Yuli Gurriel	HOU	12.6
8	Nicky Lopez	KCA	12.6
10	Miguel Rojas	MIA	12.9
11	José Iglesias	BAL	13.1
12	José Ramírez	CLE	13.4
12	Kevin Newman	PIT	13.4
14	Alex Bregman	HOU	13.8
15	Jean Segura	PHI	13.9
15	Jeff McNeil	NYN	13.9
17	Kurt Suzuki	WAS	14.0
18	Albert Pujols	LAA	14.3
18	Josh Reddick	HOU	14.3
18	Mookie Betts	BOS	14.3
18	Adam Frazier	PIT	14.3

DRC+

Rank	Name	Team	DRC+
1	Mike Trout	LAA	177
2	Alex Bregman	HOU	152
3	Christian Yelich	MIL	149
4	Giancarlo Stanton	NYA	141
4	Cody Bellinger	LAN	141
6	Yordan Alvarez	HOU	140
6	J.D. Martinez	BOS	140
8	Nelson Cruz	MIN	139
9	Pete Alonso	NYN	138
10	George Springer	HOU	136
11	Aaron Judge	NYA	135
11	Freddie Freeman	ATL	135
13	Mookie Betts	BOS	134
14	Nolan Arenado	COL	133
14	Juan Soto	WAS	133
16	Anthony Rizzo	CHN	132
17	Eugenio Suárez	CIN	130
17	Miguel Sanó	MIN	130
19	Kris Bryant	CHN	127
19	Bryce Harper	PHI	127

Hitter VORP

Rank	Name	Team	VORP
1	Mike Trout	LAA	85.6
2	Alex Bregman	HOU	57.7
3	Christian Yelich	MIL	51.1
4	George Springer	HOU	48.9
5	Cody Bellinger	LAN	47.9
6	Mookie Betts	BOS	45.1
7	Pete Alonso	NYN	43.8
8	Juan Soto	WAS	43.6
9	Giancarlo Stanton	NYA	43.2
10	Nolan Arenado	COL	41.8
11	Xander Bogaerts	BOS	41.2
12	Freddie Freeman	ATL	39.5
13	DJ LeMahieu	NYA	39.3
14	Yordan Alvarez	HOU	38.9
15	Josh Donaldson	ATL	38.5
15	Max Muncy	LAN	38.5
17	J.D. Martinez	BOS	38.3
18	José Altuve	HOU	38.2
19	Ronald Acuña Jr.	ATL	37.9
20	Aaron Judge	NYA	37.7

Base-Running Runs (BRR)

Rank	Name	Team	BRR
1	Fernando Tatis Jr.	SDN	6.1
2	Javier Báez	CHN	3.9
3	Byron Buxton	MIN	3.4
3	Ronald Acuña Jr.	ATL	3.4
5	Dee Gordon	SEA	3.3
5	Mookie Betts	BOS	3.3
5	Tim Anderson	CHA	3.3
8	Tommy Edman	SLN	3.2
9	Marcus Semien	OAK	3.0
9	Willy Adames	TBA	3.0
9	Ian Happ	CHN	3.0
12	Jon Berti	MIA	2.9
12	Victor Robles	WAS	2.9
14	Ozzie Albies	ATL	2.8
15	Kevin Kiermaier	TBA	2.7
16	José Iglesias	BAL	2.5
16	Mallex Smith	SEA	2.5
16	Trea Turner	WAS	2.5
16	Luis Arraez	MIN	2.5
20	Tony Wolters	COL	2.4

Hitter WARP

Rank	Name	Team	WARP
1	Mike Trout	LAA	8.6
2	Alex Bregman	HOU	6.6
3	Mookie Betts	BOS	6.3
4	Yasmani Grandal	CHA	6.0
5	DJ LeMahieu	NYA	5.7
6	Cody Bellinger	LAN	5.4
7	Christian Yelich	MIL	5.2
8	George Springer	HOU	5.1
8	Pete Alonso	NYN	5.1
10	Nolan Arenado	COL	5.0
11	Juan Soto	WAS	4.8
12	Aaron Judge	NYA	4.6
13	Anthony Rizzo	CHN	4.2
14	Freddie Freeman	ATL	4.1
14	J.T. Realmuto	PHI	4.1
14	Joey Gallo	TEX	4.1
14	Cavan Biggio	TOR	4.1
14	Michael Conforto	NYN	4.1
14	Matt Chapman	OAK	4.1
14	Will Smith	LAN	4.1

AL Hitter WARP

Rank	Name	Team	WARP
1	Mike Trout	LAA	8.6
2	Alex Bregman	HOU	6.6
3	Mookie Betts	BOS	6.3
4	Yasmani Grandal	CHA	6.0
5	DJ LeMahieu	NYA	5.7
6	George Springer	HOU	5.1
7	Aaron Judge	NYA	4.6
8	Joey Gallo	TEX	4.1
8	Cavan Biggio	TOR	4.1
8	Matt Chapman	OAK	4.1

NL Hitter WARP

Rank	Name	Team	WARP
1	Cody Bellinger	LAN	5.4
2	Christian Yelich	MIL	5.2
3	Pete Alonso	NYN	5.1
4	Nolan Arenado	COL	5.0
5	Juan Soto	WAS	4.8
6	Anthony Rizzo	CHN	4.2
7	Freddie Freeman	ATL	4.1
7	J.T. Realmuto	PHI	4.1
7	Michael Conforto	NYN	4.1
7	Will Smith	LAN	4.1

Deserved Run Average (DRA) - Starters

Rank	Name	Team	DRA
1	Jacob deGrom	NYN	2.90
1	Max Scherzer	WAS	2.90
3	Justin Verlander	HOU	2.95
4	Gerrit Cole	NYA	2.99
5	Chris Sale	BOS	3.00
6	Clayton Kershaw	LAN	3.18
7	Jack Flaherty	SLN	3.28
8	Stephen Strasburg	WAS	3.34
9	Noah Syndergaard	NYN	3.41
10	Walker Buehler	LAN	3.47
11	Luis Castillo	CIN	3.48
11	Zack Greinke	HOU	3.48
13	Luis Severino	NYA	3.52
14	Kenta Maeda	LAN	3.57
14	Mike Clevinger	CLE	3.57
16	Charlie Morton	TBA	3.58
17	Shane Bieber	CLE	3.60
17	Hyun-Jin Ryu	TOR	3.60
19	Blake Snell	TBA	3.62
20	Chris Paddack	SDN	3.63

Deserved Run Average (DRA) - Relievers

Rank	Name	Team	DRA
1	Dellin Betances	NYN	2.38
2	Nick Anderson	TBA	2.70
3	Josh Hader	MIL	2.85
4	Aroldis Chapman	NYA	2.90
5	Roberto Osuna	HOU	2.96
6	Ken Giles	TOR	3.03
6	Kenley Jansen	LAN	3.03
8	Kirby Yates	SDN	3.05
9	Edwin Díaz	NYN	3.10
10	Liam Hendriks	OAK	3.13
11	Will Smith	ATL	3.14
12	Zack Britton	NYA	3.27
12	Emilio Pagán	TBA	3.27
14	Víctor Arano	PHI	3.28
15	Oliver Drake	TBA	3.29
16	Tommy Kahnle	NYA	3.30
17	Ryan Pressly	HOU	3.33
18	Giovanny Gallegos	SLN	3.34
19	Oliver Pérez	CLE	3.36
20	Andrew Miller	SLN	3.41

Earned Run Average - Starters

Rank	Name	Team	ERA
1	Jacob deGrom	NYN	2.52
1	Gerrit Cole	NYA	2.52
3	Chris Sale	BOS	2.63
4	Clayton Kershaw	LAN	2.69
5	Max Scherzer	WAS	2.71
6	Justin Verlander	HOU	2.75
7	Jack Flaherty	SLN	2.87
8	Noah Syndergaard	NYN	3.07
9	Walker Buehler	LAN	3.08
10	Luis Severino	NYA	3.12
11	Kenta Maeda	LAN	3.17
12	Stephen Strasburg	WAS	3.24
13	Shane Bieber	CLE	3.26
14	Zack Greinke	HOU	3.33
14	Charlie Morton	TBA	3.33
16	Mike Clevinger	CLE	3.34
16	Chris Paddack	SDN	3.34
18	Luis Castillo	CIN	3.35
19	James Paxton	NYA	3.38
20	Hyun-Jin Ryu	TOR	3.39

Earned Run Average - Relievers

Rank	Name	Team	ERA
1	Dellin Betances	NYN	1.60
2	Nick Anderson	TBA	2.28
3	Aroldis Chapman	NYA	2.51
4	Kenley Jansen	LAN	2.54
5	Josh Hader	MIL	2.68
6	Liam Hendriks	OAK	2.70
7	Roberto Osuna	HOU	2.78
8	Kirby Yates	SDN	2.80
9	Ken Giles	TOR	2.81
10	Edwin Díaz	NYN	2.84
11	Will Smith	ATL	2.86
12	Emilio Pagán	TBA	2.88
13	Zack Britton	NYA	2.90
14	Giovanny Gallegos	SLN	2.92
15	Tommy Kahnle	NYA	2.95
16	Oliver Drake	TBA	2.96
17	Oliver Pérez	CLE	3.01
18	Chad Green	NYA	3.02
19	Andrew Miller	SLN	3.06
20	Víctor Arano	PHI	3.07
20	Colin Poche	TBA	3.07

Wins

Rank	Name	Team	W
1	Gerrit Cole	NYA	16
2	Justin Verlander	HOU	15
3	Zack Greinke	HOU	14
4	Jacob deGrom	NYN	13
4	Max Scherzer	WAS	13
4	Chris Sale	BOS	13
4	Clayton Kershaw	LAN	13
4	Walker Buehler	LAN	13
4	José Berríos	MIN	13
10	Jack Flaherty	SLN	12
10	Stephen Strasburg	WAS	12
10	Noah Syndergaard	NYN	12
10	Luis Severino	NYA	12
10	Shane Bieber	CLE	12
10	Lucas Giolito	CHA	12
10	Kyle Hendricks	CHN	12
10	Frankie Montas	OAK	12
10	Dallas Keuchel	CHA	12
19	Luis Castillo	CIN	11
19	Mike Clevinger	CLE	11
19	Charlie Morton	TBA	11
19	Brandon Woodruff	MIL	11
19	Patrick Corbin	WAS	11
19	James Paxton	NYA	11
19	Aaron Nola	PHI	11
19	David Price	BOS	11
19	Mike Soroka	ATL	11
19	Corey Kluber	TEX	11
19	Lance Lynn	TEX	11
19	Madison Bumgarner	ARI	11

Strikeouts

Rank	Name	Team	SO
1	Max Scherzer	WAS	255
1	Gerrit Cole	NYA	255
3	Justin Verlander	HOU	248
4	Chris Sale	BOS	237
5	Jacob deGrom	NYN	235
6	Blake Snell	TBA	220
7	Mike Clevinger	CLE	219
8	Stephen Strasburg	WAS	216
9	Shane Bieber	CLE	213
10	Luis Castillo	CIN	212
11	Walker Buehler	LAN	210
12	Jack Flaherty	SLN	209
12	Patrick Corbin	WAS	209
14	Charlie Morton	TBA	206
15	Lucas Giolito	CHA	204
15	Matthew Boyd	DET	204
17	Trevor Bauer	CIN	202
18	Lance Lynn	TEX	201
19	Aaron Nola	PHI	194
20	Yu Darvish	CHN	191

www.baseballprospectus.com

WHIP - Starters

Rank	Name	Team	WHIP
1	Justin Verlander	HOU	1.01
2	Chris Sale	BOS	1.02
3	Max Scherzer	WAS	1.04
4	Jacob deGrom	NYN	1.05
5	Gerrit Cole	NYA	1.06
6	Clayton Kershaw	LAN	1.07
7	Jack Flaherty	SLN	1.10
8	Zack Greinke	HOU	1.11
8	Chris Paddack	SDN	1.11
10	Noah Syndergaard	NYN	1.14
10	Hyun-Jin Ryu	TOR	1.14
12	Stephen Strasburg	WAS	1.16
12	Walker Buehler	LAN	1.16
12	Shane Bieber	CLE	1.16
15	Luis Severino	NYA	1.17
15	Kenta Maeda	LAN	1.17
17	Charlie Morton	TBA	1.18
17	Carlos Carrasco	CLE	1.18
17	David Price	BOS	1.18
17	Kyle Hendricks	CHN	1.18

Saves

Rank	Name	Team	SV
1	Aroldis Chapman	NYA	46
2	Roberto Osuna	HOU	44
3	Kenley Jansen	LAN	41
4	Ken Giles	TOR	38
4	Liam Hendriks	OAK	38
4	Taylor Rogers	MIN	38
7	Josh Hader	MIL	36
7	Craig Kimbrel	CHN	36
7	Alex Colomé	CHA	36
10	Kirby Yates	SDN	35
11	Brandon Workman	BOS	34
11	Brad Hand	CLE	34
11	Hansel Robles	LAA	34
14	Sean Doolittle	WAS	32
14	Héctor Neris	PHI	32
14	Archie Bradley	ARI	32
17	Carlos Martínez	SLN	31
18	Edwin Díaz	NYN	30
18	Raisel Iglesias	CIN	30
20	José Leclerc	TEX	29

Strikeout Rate

Rank	Name	Team	SO%
1	Josh Hader	MIL	45.3
2	Nick Anderson	TBA	39.9
3	Edwin Díaz	NYN	39.7
4	Aroldis Chapman	NYA	38.0
5	Craig Kimbrel	CHN	36.9
6	Kirby Yates	SDN	36.3
6	Ken Giles	TOR	36.3
8	Josh James	HOU	35.7
9	Matt Barnes	BOS	35.2
10	Tanner Rainey	WAS	35.0
11	Chris Sale	BOS	34.9
11	José Leclerc	TEX	34.9
13	Will Smith	ATL	34.8
14	Bryan Abreu	HOU	34.5
15	Dellin Betances	NYN	34.4
16	Justin Verlander	HOU	34.0
16	Max Scherzer	WAS	34.0
18	Blake Snell	TBA	33.7
19	Tommy Kahnle	NYA	33.3
19	Colin Poche	TBA	33.3
19	Héctor Neris	PHI	33.3
19	Trey Wingenter	SDN	33.3

Walk Rate

Rank	Name	Team	BB%
1	Richard Bleier	BAL	4.5
1	Mike Leake	ARI	4.5
3	Yusmeiro Petit	OAK	5.0
4	Miles Mikolas	SLN	5.1
5	Zack Greinke	HOU	5.2
6	Hyun-Jin Ryu	TOR	5.3
7	Kyle Hendricks	CHN	5.5
8	Brent Suter	MIL	5.6
9	Tyler Alexander	DET	5.7
9	Sean Doolittle	WAS	5.7
9	Jordan Zimmermann	DET	5.7
12	Ryan Yarbrough	TBA	5.8
12	Clayton Kershaw	LAN	5.8
14	Adam Cimber	CLE	6.0
14	Cole Irvin	PHI	6.0
14	Shane Bieber	CLE	6.0
14	Michael Pineda	MIN	6.0
14	Taylor Rogers	MIN	6.0
19	Rick Porcello	NYN	6.1
19	Craig Stammen	SDN	6.1
19	Madison Bumgarner	ARI	6.1

Fastball Velocity

Rank	Name	Team	FB Velo
1	Aroldis Chapman	NYA	100.90
2	Brusdar Graterol	MIN	100.61
3	Diego Castillo	TBA	99.72
4	José Alvarado	TBA	99.30
4	Ray Black	MIL	99.30
6	Shohei Ohtani	LAA	99.25
7	Hunter Harvey	BAL	99.23
8	Joe Kelly	LAN	99.18
9	Edwin Díaz	NYN	99.14
10	Luis Severino	NYA	98.99
11	Carlos Estévez	COL	98.98
12	Josh James	HOU	98.97
13	Dellin Betances	NYN	98.88
14	Tanner Rainey	WAS	98.87
15	Noah Syndergaard	NYN	98.80
16	A.J. Puk	OAK	98.78
17	Ryne Stanek	MIA	98.53
18	Ken Giles	TOR	98.45
19	Tyler Glasnow	TBA	98.39
19	Nathan Eovaldi	BOS	98.39

Ground-ball Rate

Rank	Name	Team	GB%
1	Zack Britton	NYA	74.4
2	Aaron Bummer	CHA	68.1
3	Framber Valdez	HOU	63.2
4	Adam Kolarek	LAN	62.9
5	Richard Bleier	BAL	60.3
6	Alex Claudio	MIL	59.5
7	Kevin McCarthy	KCA	58.4
8	Dallas Keuchel	CHA	58.2
9	Mark Melancon	ATL	57.2
10	Tim Hill	KCA	56.7
11	Dakota Hudson	SLN	56.6
12	Tyler Chatwood	CHN	56.2
13	Joe Kelly	LAN	56.0
13	Brett Anderson	MIL	56.0
15	Randy Dobnak	MIN	55.7
16	Marcus Stroman	NYN	55.3
17	Kyle Ryan	CHN	55.1
18	Adam Cimber	CLE	54.7
19	Anthony Bass	TOR	54.6
20	Luis Castillo	CIN	54.5

Pitcher WARP

Rank	Name	Team	WARP
1	Jacob deGrom	NYN	6.0
1	Max Scherzer	WAS	6.0
3	Gerrit Cole	NYA	5.7
4	Justin Verlander	HOU	5.3
5	Clayton Kershaw	LAN	5.0
6	Stephen Strasburg	WAS	4.9
7	Jack Flaherty	SLN	4.8
7	Chris Sale	BOS	4.8
9	Walker Buehler	LAN	4.6
10	Luis Castillo	CIN	4.5
10	Noah Syndergaard	NYN	4.5
12	Patrick Corbin	WAS	4.1
13	Zack Greinke	HOU	4.0
14	Aaron Nola	PHI	3.9
14	Brandon Woodruff	MIL	3.9
14	Shane Bieber	CLE	3.9
17	Charlie Morton	TBA	3.7
17	Sonny Gray	CIN	3.7
19	Mike Clevinger	CLE	3.6
20	Luis Severino	NYA	3.5
20	Yu Darvish	CHN	3.5
20	Kyle Hendricks	CHN	3.5
20	Trevor Bauer	CIN	3.5

AL Pitcher WARP

Rank	Name	Team	WARP
1	Gerrit Cole	NYA	5.7
2	Justin Verlander	HOU	5.3
3	Chris Sale	BOS	4.8
4	Zack Greinke	HOU	4.0
5	Shane Bieber	CLE	3.9
6	Charlie Morton	TBA	3.7
7	Mike Clevinger	CLE	3.6
8	Luis Severino	NYA	3.5
9	Blake Snell	TBA	3.3
10	Hyun-Jin Ryu	TOR	3.1

NL Pitcher WARP

Rank	Name	Team	WARP
1	Jacob deGrom	NYN	6.0
1	Max Scherzer	WAS	6.0
3	Clayton Kershaw	LAN	5.0
4	Stephen Strasburg	WAS	4.9
5	Jack Flaherty	SLN	4.8
6	Walker Buehler	LAN	4.6
7	Noah Syndergaard	NYN	4.5
7	Luis Castillo	CIN	4.5
9	Patrick Corbin	WAS	4.1
10	Brandon Woodruff	MIL	3.9
10	Aaron Nola	PHI	3.9

Catcher Framing Runs

Rank	Name	Team	Framing Runs
1	Yasmani Grandal	CHA	27.4
2	Christian Vázquez	BOS	18.5
3	Roberto Pérez	CLE	18.2
4	Tyler Flowers	ATL	15.2
5	Austin Hedges	SDN	14.6
6	Reese McGuire	TOR	13.8
7	Mike Zunino	TBA	12.4
8	Austin Barnes	LAN	10.4
9	Buster Posey	SFN	10.0
10	Travis d'Arnaud	ATL	9.5
11	Will Smith	LAN	8.3
11	Jason Castro	LAA	8.3
13	Aramis Garcia	SFN	7.9
14	Kyle Higashioka	NYA	7.8
15	Tony Wolters	COL	6.9
16	Luke Maile	PIT	6.6
17	Tomás Nido	NYN	6.5
18	Yadier Molina	SLN	6.2
19	Danny Jansen	TOR	6.1
20	Curt Casali	CIN	5.7

Catcher Blocking Runs

Rank	Name	Team	Blocking Runs
1	Roberto Pérez	CLE	4.6
2	Jacob Stallings	PIT	3.9
3	Juan Graterol	CIN	2.9
4	Robinson Chirinos	TEX	2.8
5	Bobby Wilson	DET	2.3
5	Tucker Barnhart	CIN	2.3
7	Steven Baron	PIT	2.2
8	J.T. Realmuto	PHI	1.8
9	Dom Nuñez	COL	1.4
10	Austin Barnes	LAN	1.3
10	Michael Perez	TBA	1.3
12	Carson Kelly	ARI	1.2
12	Austin Hedges	SDN	1.2
12	Seby Zavala	CHA	1.2
12	Reese McGuire	TOR	1.2
16	Buster Posey	SFN	1.1
16	Cam Gallagher	KCA	1.1
16	Willson Contreras	CHN	1.1
19	Martín Maldonado	HOU	1.0
19	Tomás Nido	NYN	1.0

Catcher Throwing Runs

Rank	Name	Team	Throwing Runs
1	J.T. Realmuto	PHI	4.8
2	Roberto Pérez	CLE	2.5
3	Mike Zunino	TBA	2.3
4	Jhon Nunez	BOS	2.1
5	Tony Wolters	COL	1.6
5	Christian Vázquez	BOS	1.6
7	Jesús Sucre	BAL	1.5
8	Tom Murphy	SEA	1.4
9	Buster Posey	SFN	1.3
10	Jacob Stallings	PIT	1.2
10	Salvador Perez	KCA	1.2
10	Alex Jackson	ATL	1.2
13	Alex Avila	MIN	1.1
13	Connor Wong	LAN	1.1
15	Matt Wieters	SLN	1.0
15	Yermin Mercedes	CHA	1.0
17	Carson Kelly	ARI	0.9
18	Wilkin Castillo	MIA	0.8
18	Jonah Heim	OAK	0.8
18	Andrew Knizner	SLN	0.8

AL Hitter Rookie WARP

Rank	Name	Team	ROOKIE WARP
1	Luis Robert	CHA	3.8
2	Reese McGuire	TOR	2.3
3	Austin Hays	BAL	1.6
3	Nick Solak	TEX	1.6
5	Myles Straw	HOU	1.3
6	Nick Madrigal	CHA	1.0
7	Austin Allen	OAK	0.8
7	Danny Mendick	CHA	0.8
9	Sean Murphy	OAK	0.7
9	Evan White	SEA	0.7

AL Pitcher Rookie WARP

Rank	Name	Team	ROOKIE WARP
1	Jose Urquidy	HOU	2.2
2	Jesus Luzardo	OAK	2.1
3	A.J. Puk	OAK	1.7
4	Patrick Sandoval	LAA	1.4
5	Dean Kremer	BAL	1.2
5	Bryan Abreu	HOU	1.2
7	Justus Sheffield	SEA	1.0
7	Randy Dobnak	MIN	1.0
7	Brendan McKay	TBA	1.0
7	Darwinzon Hernandez	BOS	1.0

NL Hitter Rookie WARP

Rank	Name	Team	ROOKIE WARP
1	Gavin Lux	LAN	2.0
2	Mauricio Dubón	SFN	1.5
3	Nico Hoerner	CHN	1.4
4	Dom Nuñez	COL	0.7
5	Kevin Cron	ARI	0.6
5	Aramis Garcia	SFN	0.6
7	Alec Bohm	PHI	0.5
8	Lane Thomas	SLN	0.4
8	Randy Arozarena	SLN	0.4
10	Esteban Quiroz	SDN	0.3
10	Cristian Pache	ATL	0.3
10	Andy Young	ARI	0.3
10	Daulton Varsho	ARI	0.3

NL Pitcher Rookie WARP

Rank	Name	Team	ROOKIE WARP
1	Mitch Keller	PIT	2.1
2	Dustin May	LAN	1.7
2	Tony Gonsolin	LAN	1.7
4	Rowan Wick	CHN	1.0
5	Ian Anderson	ATL	0.9
5	JT Brubaker	PIT	0.9
5	Logan Webb	SFN	0.9
8	Sixto Sanchez	MIA	0.8
8	Ray Black	MIL	0.8
10	Kevin Ginkel	ARI	0.7
10	Andres Munoz	SDN	0.7
10	Cole Irvin	PHI	0.7
10	Dennis Santana	LAN	0.7
10	José De León	CIN	0.7
10	José Quijada	MIA	0.7

Hitter WARP Declines

Rank	Name	Team	WARP 2019	WARP 2020	WARP DIFF
1	Marcus Semien	OAK	7.5	4.0	-3.5
2	Jorge Polanco	MIN	5.3	2.2	-3.1
3	Anthony Rendon	LAA	6.3	3.5	-2.8
4	Cody Bellinger	LAN	8.0	5.4	-2.6
4	Ronald Acuña Jr.	ATL	6.1	3.5	-2.6
4	Robinson Chirinos	TEX	2.6	0.0	-2.6
7	Yoán Moncada	CHA	5.1	2.6	-2.5
8	Gio Urshela	NYA	3.4	1.1	-2.3
8	Jonathan Villar	MIA	3.3	1.0	-2.3
8	Mitch Garver	MIN	4.4	2.1	-2.3
8	Jorge Soler	KCA	4.5	2.2	-2.3

Hitter WARP Improvements

Rank	Name	Team	WARP 2019	WARP 2020	WARP DIFF
1	Justin Upton	LAA	0.1	3.5	3.4
2	Will Smith	LAN	1.9	4.1	2.2
3	Brandon Nimmo	NYN	0.9	2.9	2.0
3	Cavan Biggio	TOR	2.1	4.1	2.0
5	Mike Zunino	TBA	0.5	2.4	1.9
6	José Abreu	CHA	0.2	1.9	1.7
6	Paul Goldschmidt	SLN	1.9	3.6	1.7
8	Travis Shaw	TOR	0.2	1.8	1.6
8	Luke Voit	NYA	1.3	2.9	1.6
10	Joey Gallo	TEX	2.6	4.1	1.5

Pitcher WARP Declines

Rank	Name	Team	WARP 2019	WARP 2020	WARP DIFF
1	Stephen Strasburg	WAS	8.3	4.9	-3.4
2	Lance Lynn	TEX	5.9	2.8	-3.1
3	Lucas Giolito	CHA	5.7	3.0	-2.7
4	Justin Verlander	HOU	7.9	5.3	-2.6
5	Yu Darvish	CHN	6.0	3.5	-2.5
6	Hyun-Jin Ryu	TOR	5.4	3.1	-2.3
6	Jack Flaherty	SLN	7.1	4.8	-2.3
8	Charlie Morton	TBA	5.9	3.7	-2.2
8	Gerrit Cole	NYA	7.9	5.7	-2.2
10	German Márquez	COL	4.7	2.8	-1.9

Pitcher WARP Improvements

Rank	Name	Team	WARP 2019	WARP 2020	WARP DIFF
1	Luis Severino	NYA	0.2	3.5	3.3
2	Garrett Richards	SDN	0.2	2.7	2.5
3	Carlos Carrasco	CLE	0.2	2.6	2.3
4	Johnny Cueto	SFN	0.2	2.3	2.0
5	Tyler Anderson	SFN	0.0	1.9	1.9
5	Jesus Luzardo	OAK	0.3	2.1	1.9
7	Trevor Williams	PIT	0.1	1.9	1.8
7	Dellin Betances	NYN	-0.0	1.8	1.8
9	Sean Manaea	OAK	0.6	2.2	1.7
10	David Price	BOS	1.3	2.8	1.6
10	Jose Urquidy	HOU	0.6	2.2	1.6

Team Codes

CODE	TEAM	LG	AFF.	Name
ABE	Aberdeen	NYP	Orioles	IronBirds
ABQ	Albuquerque	PCL	Rockies	Isotopes
AGO	AZL Athletics Gold	AZL	Athletics	-
AKR	Akron	EAS	Indians	RubberDucks
ALT	Altoona	EAS	Pirates	Curve
AMA	Amarillo	TEX	Padres	Sod Poodles
ARI	Arizona	NL	-	D-backs
ARK	Arkansas	TEX	Mariners	Travelers
ART	Artemisa	CNS	-	
ASH	Asheville	SAL	Rockies	Tourists
AST	GCL Astros	GCL	Astros	GCL Astros
ATH	AZL Athletics Green	AZL	Athletics	-
ATL	Atlanta	NL	-	Braves
AUB	Auburn	NYP	Nationals	Doubledays
AUG	Augusta	SAL	Giants	GreenJackets
BAL	Baltimore	AL	-	Orioles
BAT	Batavia	NYP	Marlins	Muckdogs
BCA	Fayetteville	CAR	Astros	Woodpeckers
BGR	Bowling Green	MID	Rays	Hot Rods
BIL	Billings	PIO	Reds	Mustangs
BIN	Binghamton	EAS	Mets	Rumble Ponies
BIR	Birmingham	SOU	White Sox	Barons
BLJ	GCL Blue Jays	GCL	Blue Jays	GCL Blue Jays
BLT	Beloit	MID	Athletics	Snappers
BLU	Bluefield	APP	Blue Jays	Blue Jays
BLX	Biloxi	SOU	Brewers	Shuckers
BNC	Burlington	APP	Royals	Royals
BOI	Boise	NWL	Rockies	Hawks
BOS	Boston	AL	-	Red Sox
BOW	Bowie	EAS	Orioles	Baysox
BRA	GCL Braves	GCL	Braves	GCL Braves
BRB	AZL Brewers Blue	AZL	Brewers	-
BRD	Bradenton	FSL	Pirates	Marauders
BRI	Bristol	APP	Pirates	Pirates
BRO	Brooklyn	NYP	Mets	Cyclones
BRR	AZL Brewers Gold	AZL	Brewers	-
BRV	Florida	FSL	Braves	Fire Frogs
BUF	Buffalo	INT	Blue Jays	Bisons
CAR	Carolina	CAR	Brewers	Mudcats
CCH	Corpus Christi	TEX	Astros	Hooks
CDR	Cedar Rapids	MID	Twins	Kernels
CFG	Cienfuegos	CNS	-	
CHA	Chicago	AL	-	White Sox
CHB	Chiba Lotte	NPB	-	Marines
CHN	Chicago	NL	-	Cubs
CHR	Charlotte	INT	White Sox	Knights
CHT	Chattanooga	SOU	Reds	Lookouts
CHU	Chunichi	NPB	-	Dragons
CIN	Cincinnati	NL	-	Reds
CIN	AZL Reds	AZL	Reds	-
CLE	Cleveland	AL	-	Indians
CLE	AZL Indians Red	AZL	Indians	-
CLN	Clinton	MID	Marlins	LumberKings
CLR	Clearwater	FSL	Phillies	Threshers
CLT	AZL Indians Blue	AZL	Indians	-

CODE	TEAM	LG	AFF.	Name
COH	Columbus	INT	Indians	Clippers
COL	Colorado	NL	-	Rockies
COL	Columbia	SAL	Mets	Fireflies
CRD	GCL Cardinals	GCL	Cardinals	GCL Cardinals
CSC	Charleston	SAL	Yankees	RiverDogs
CSP	Rocky Mountain	PIO	Brewers	Vibes
CUB	AZL Cubs 1	AZL	Cubs	-
CUT	AZL Cubs 2	AZL	Cubs	-
DAY	Daytona	FSL	Reds	Tortugas
DEB	Down East	CAR	Rangers	Wood Ducks
DEL	Delmarva	SAL	Orioles	Shorebirds
DET	Detroit	AL	-	Tigers
DIA	AZL D-backs	AZL	D-backs	-
DNV	Danville	APP	Braves	Braves
DOD	AZL Dodgers 1	AZL	Dodgers	-
DOT	AZL Dodgers 2	AZL	Dodgers	-
DUN	Dunedin	FSL	Blue Jays	Blue Jays
DUR	Durham	INT	Rays	Bulls
DYT	Dayton	MID	Reds	Dragons
ELP	El Paso	PCL	Padres	Chihuahuas
ELZ	Elizabethton	APP	Twins	Twins
ERI	Erie	EAS	Tigers	SeaWolves
EUG	Eugene	NWL	Cubs	Emeralds
EVE	Everett	NWL	Mariners	AquaSox
FKU	Fukuoka	NPB	-	Hawks
FRD	Frederick	CAR	Orioles	Keys
FRE	Fresno	PCL	Nationals	Grizzlies
FRI	Frisco	TEX	Rangers	RoughRiders
FTM	Fort Myers	FSL	Twins	Miracle
FTW	Fort Wayne	MID	Padres	TinCaps
GIA	AZL Giants Black	AZL	Giants	-
GJR	Grand Junction	PIO	Rockies	Rockies
GNT	AZL Giants Orange	AZL	Giants	-
GRB	Greensboro	SAL	Pirates	Grasshoppers
GRF	Great Falls	PIO	White Sox	Voyagers
GRL	Great Lakes	MID	Dodgers	Loons
GRN	Greenville	SAL	Red Sox	Drive
GRV	Greeneville	APP	Reds	Reds
GWN	Gwinnett	INT	Braves	Stripers
HAB	La Habana	CNS	-	
HAG	Hagerstown	SAL	Nationals	Suns
HAR	Harrisburg	EAS	Nationals	Senators
HFD	Hartford	EAS	Rockies	Yard Goats
HIC	Hickory	SAL	Rangers	Crawdads
HNS	Hanshin	NPB	-	Tigers
HOU	Houston	AL	-	Astros
HRO	Hiroshima Toyo	NPB	-	Carp
HUD	Hudson Valley	NYP	Rays	Renegades
IDA	Idaho Falls	PIO	Royals	Chukars
IND	Indianapolis	INT	Pirates	Indians
IOW	Iowa	PCL	Cubs	Cubs
JAX	Jacksonville	SOU	Marlins	Jumbo Shrimp
JCY	Johnson City	APP	Cardinals	Cardinals
JUP	Jupiter	FSL	Marlins	Hammerheads
KAN	Kannapolis	SAL	White Sox	Intimidators

CODE	TEAM	LG	AFF.	Name
KCA	Kansas City	AL	-	Royals
KNC	Kane County	MID	D-backs	Cougars
KNG	Kingsport	APP	Mets	Mets
LAK	Lakeland	FSL	Tigers	Flying Tigers
LAN	Los Angeles	NL	-	Dodgers
LEH	Lehigh Valley	INT	Phillies	IronPigs
LEL	Lake Elsinore	CAL	Padres	Storm
LEX	Lexington	SAL	Royals	Legends
LKC	Lake County	MID	Indians	Captains
LNC	Lancaster	CAL	Rockies	JetHawks
LNS	Lansing	MID	Blue Jays	Lugnuts
LOU	Louisville	INT	Reds	Bats
LOW	Lowell	NYP	Red Sox	Spinners
LTU	Las Tunas	CNS	-	
LVG	Las Vegas	PCL	Athletics	Aviators
LWD	Lakewood	SAL	Phillies	BlueClaws
LYN	Lynchburg	CAR	Indians	Hillcats
MEM	Memphis	PCL	Cardinals	Redbirds
MHV	Mahoning Valley	NYP	Indians	Scrappers
MIA	Miami	NL	-	Marlins
MID	Midland	TEX	Athletics	RockHounds
MIL	Milwaukee	NL	-	Brewers
MIN	Minnesota	AL	-	Twins
MIS	Mississippi	SOU	Braves	Braves
MNT	Montgomery	SOU	Rays	Biscuits
MOD	Modesto	CAL	Mariners	Nuts
MRL	GCL Marlins	GCL	Marlins	GCL Marlins
MRN	AZL Mariners	AZL	Mariners	-
MSO	Missoula	PIO	D-backs	Osprey
MTS	GCL Mets	GCL	Mets	GCL Mets
MYR	Myrtle Beach	CAR	Cubs	Pelicans
NAS	Nashville	PCL	Rangers	Sounds
NAT	GCL Nationals	GCL	Nationals	GCL Nationals
NHP	New Hampshire	EAS	Blue Jays	Fisher Cats
NIP	Nippon Ham	NPB	-	Fighters
NOR	Norfolk	INT	Orioles	Tides
NWA	NW Arkansas	TEX	Royals	Naturals
NWO	New Orleans	PCL	Marlins	Baby Cakes
NYA	New York	AL	-	Yankees
NYN	New York	NL	-	Mets
OAK	Oakland	AL	-	Athletics
OGD	Ogden	PIO	Dodgers	Raptors
OKL	Okla. City	PCL	Dodgers	Dodgers
OMA	Omaha	PCL	Royals	Storm Chasers
ONE	Connecticut	NYP	Tigers	Tigers
ORI	GCL Orioles	GCL	Orioles	GCL Orioles
ORX	Orix	NPB	-	Buffaloes
PAW	Pawtucket	INT	Red Sox	Red Sox
PCH	Charlotte	FSL	Rays	Stone Crabs
PDR	AZL Padres 1	AZL	Padres	-
PEN	Pensacola	SOU	Twins	Blue Wahoos
PEO	Peoria	MID	Cardinals	Chiefs
PHI	Philadelphia	NL	-	Phillies
PHL	GCL Phillies East	GCL	Phillies	GCL Phillies East
PIR	GCL Pirates	GCL	Pirates	GCL Pirates
PIT	Pittsburgh	NL	-	Pirates
PLL	GCL Phillies West	GCL	Phillies	GCL Phillies West
PMB	Palm Beach	FSL	Cardinals	Cardinals
PME	Portland	EAS	Red Sox	Sea Dogs
POT	Potomac	CAR	Nationals	Nationals
PRI	Princeton	APP	Rays	Rays
PUL	Pulaski	APP	Yankees	Yankees
QUD	Quad Cities	MID	Astros	River Bandits
RAK	Rakuten	NPB	-	Golden Eagles
RAY	GCL Rays	GCL	Rays	GCL Rays
RCU	Rancho Cucamonga	CAL	Dodgers	Quakes
REA	Reading	EAS	Phillies	Fightin Phils
RIC	Richmond	EAS	Giants	Flying Squirrels
RNG	AZL Rangers	AZL	Rangers	-
RNO	Reno	PCL	D-backs	Aces
ROC	Rochester	INT	Twins	Red Wings
ROM	Rome	SAL	Braves	Braves
ROU	Round Rock	PCL	Astros	Express
ROY	AZL Royals	AZL	Royals	-
RSX	GCL Red Sox	GCL	Red Sox	GCL Red Sox
SAC	Sacramento	PCL	Giants	River Cats
SAN	San Antonio	PCL	Brewers	Missions
SBN	South Bend	MID	Cubs	Cubs
SCO	State College	NYP	Cardinals	Spikes
SDN	San Diego	NL	-	Padres
SDP	AZL Padres 2	AZL	Padres	-
SEA	Seattle	AL	-	Mariners
SEI	Seibu	NPB	-	Lions
SFD	Springfield	TEX	Cardinals	Cardinals
SFN	San Francisco	NL	-	Giants
SJO	San Jose	CAL	Giants	Giants
SLM	Salem	CAR	Red Sox	Red Sox
SLN	St. Louis	NL	-	Cardinals
SLO	Salem-Keizer	NWL	Giants	Volcanoes
SLU	St. Lucie	FSL	Mets	Mets
SPO	Spokane	NWL	Rangers	Indians
STA	Staten Island	NYP	Yankees	Yankees
STO	Stockton	CAL	Athletics	Ports
SWB	Scranton/WB	INT	Yankees	RailRiders
SYR	Syracuse	INT	Mets	Mets
TAC	Tacoma	PCL	Mariners	Rainiers
TAM	Tampa	FSL	Yankees	Tarpons
TBA	Tampa Bay	AL	-	Rays
TCV	Tri-City	NYP	Astros	ValleyCats
TEN	Tennessee	SOU	Cubs	Smokies
TEX	Texas	AL	-	Rangers
TGR	GCL Tigers East	GCL	Tigers	GCL Tigers East
TGW	GCL Tigers West	GCL	Tigers	GCL Tigers West
TOL	Toledo	INT	Tigers	Mud Hens
TOR	Toronto	AL	-	Blue Jays
TRI	Tri-City	NWL	Padres	Dust Devils
TRN	Trenton	EAS	Yankees	Thunder
TUL	Tulsa	TEX	Dodgers	Drillers
TWI	GCL Twins	GCL	Twins	GCL Twins
VAN	Vancouver	NWL	Blue Jays	Canadians
VER	Vermont	NYP	Athletics	Lake Monsters
VIS	Visalia	CAL	D-backs	Rawhide
WAS	Washington	NL	-	Nationals
WEV	West Virginia	NYP	Pirates	Black Bears
WIL	Wilmington	CAR	Royals	Blue Rocks
WIS	Wisconsin	MID	Brewers	Timber Rattlers
WMI	West Michigan	MID	Tigers	Whitecaps
WNS	Winston-Salem	CAR	White Sox	Dash
WPT	Williamsport	NYP	Phillies	Crosscutters
WSX	AZL White Sox	AZL	White Sox	-
WTN	Jackson	SOU	D-backs	Generals
WVA	West Virginia	SAL	Mariners	Power
YAK	Hillsboro	NWL	D-backs	Hops
YAN	GCL Yankees East	GCL	Yankees	GCL Yankees East
YAT	GCL Yankees West	GCL	Yankees	GCL Yankees West
YKL	Yakult	NPB	-	Swallows
YKO	Yokohama DeNa	NPB	-	BayStars
YOM	Yomiuri	NPB	-	Giants

Contributors

R.J. Anderson has been a staff writer at CBS Sports since 2016. Previously, he contributed to Baseball Prospectus (and five Annuals) as an author. He lives in Washington, D.C., where he's developed disdain for the GEICO Gecko who resides at Nationals Park.

Jorge Arangure Jr. is a senior editor at The New York Times. He previously was a contributing editor at the Village Voice and the editor-in-chief of Vice Sports. In his previous life as a sportswriter, he was a senior writer at ESPN the Magazine and a staff writer at the Washington Post. He lives in Brooklyn.

Lucas Apostoleris lives in Miami, Florida, with his wife and their two cats. He is a full-time musician, and as of last year, he is also a writer and researcher at Baseball Prospectus. Before joining BPro, he had previously been published at ESPN, The Hardball Times, FanGraphs and Beyond The Box Score. As a musician, he performs regularly in the Miami area, and recently recorded his debut album of original compositions.

Robert Au is an occasional systems administrator and software developer, and a very recent addition to the BP stats team. He resides in the San Francisco Bay Area with a small cat and a somewhat larger piano.

Darius Austin writes for the fantasy team and updates the depth charts at Baseball Prospectus, which is exactly as glamorous as it sounds. As part of UK-based blog and podcast Bat Flips and Nerds, he is also one of many British baseball fans who very much enjoyed baseball in London in 2019, and is looking forward to doing it again in 2020.

Emma Baccellieri is a staff writer at *Sports Illustrated*. She lives in Washington, D.C., where she spent the majority of the 2019 baseball season trying to read *The Power Broker* and aims not to spend this season the same way.

Mark Barry is an author and fantasy writer at Baseball Prospectus. He lives in Los Angeles with his wife and two cats, and still dreams of a day (although this time wistfully) spent playing catch and talking about life with Francisco Lindor. Carlos Santana is there too.

Jordan Bastian has spent the past 15 seasons as a beat reporter for MLB.com, covering the Blue Jays (2005-10), Indians (2011-18) and Cubs (2019-present). Prior to MLB.com, he studied Journalism at Michigan State University.

Demetrius Bell is an Atlanta-based writer who focuses on the Atlanta Braves and sports uniforms and logos. You can find his deliberations on all things concerning the Braves at SB Nation's Talking Chop, while his opinions on sports fashion and iconography can be found on Forbes.com. He is also a weekly contributor to the Short Relief series here on Baseball Prospectus.

Jason Benetti is a TV play-by-play announcer for ESPN and the Chicago White Sox. He is a 2005 graduate of Syracuse University and a 2011 graduate of Wake Forest School of Law.

Sydney Bergman is a science educator and baseball podcaster. She worked as a high school science teacher in DC for 9 years before getting into the world of teacher education. Catch her podcast at https://www.restingpitchface.com/ or yell with her about Anthony Rendon on Twitter at @sydrpfp.

J.P. Breen is a long-time writer and podcaster about the Milwaukee Brewers and the Fantasy Editor for Baseball Prospectus. He also co-hosts the dynasty baseball podcast, There Is No Offseason, on the BP Podcast Network.

Grant Brisbee writes about the Giants and other things for The Athletic. Please subscribe, but only through one of his articles. He lives in a one-bedroom cottage on the internet that's filled with spiders, and while he's free to leave at any time, he never will. The spiders will eventually consume him.

Craig Brown is a member of the BBWAA and has been writing about the Royals at various stops along the internet since 2004. His words have been found at Baseball Prospectus, SB Nation, ESPN, Sports on Earth and The Hardball Times. This is his sixth year contributing to the Annual, and it remains a thrill to be involved. He thinks the next time you go to a baseball game, you should keep score.

Ben Carsley is a Senior Author at Baseball Prospectus. When he's not writing about baseball, Ben is generally cooking, drinking IPAs, losing NFL parlays or ignoring Malinowski's Law on Twitter. By day, he manages a team of SEO analysts and content writers who are fairly convinced he's Ron Swanson.

Ben Clemens is a writer for FanGraphs. His work has appeared at...well, pretty much just FanGraphs. A lifelong Cardinals fan, he now lives in San Francisco, where he's resisting the urge to get invested in the A's.

Zach Crizer is an editor at Yahoo Sports and a contributor to Baseball Prospectus. He lives in New York City and runs on Dr. Pepper.

Spring Marie Cullen is a prospect writer at Baseball Prospectus. When she's not writing, talking or fantasizing about baseball, she's mentally preparing her Academy Award acceptance speech and consuming all forms of pop culture. She considers herself part dog. Longs for more bunting.

Bradford William Davis is a columnist for the New York Daily News. He just wants your team to try harder. It's an honor to contribute to a publication that has shaped how the world understands our dumb, beautiful obsession.

Russell Dorsey is a reporter for MLB.com covering all of baseball and is based in Chicago. He has written for numerous publications including Baseball Prospectus, Forbes and the Chicago Tribune. He's currently a contributor on 670 The Score, La Vida Baseball and panelist on NBC Sports Chicago's Sports Talk Live. Follow him on Twitter @Russ_Dorsey1.

Patrick Dubuque is a former editor of BP and the annual, and founder of its whimsical baseball-adjacent Short Relief vertical. He lives in the Pacific Northwest with his wife Kjersten and his two garrulous children, Sylvie and Felix.

Drew Fairservice co-hosts the Birds All Day podcast and has written about baseball for theScore, Vice Sports, Fangraphs and his Vladimir Guerrero Jr. newsletters "Vlad Religion." If you, like him, hope to see all manner of birds on all manner of days, restore native plants in your area to support biodiversity.

James Fegan is a staff writer for The Athletic. His work has appeared in Baseball Prospectus, ESPN SweetSpot, NBC Sports Chicago, FanSided and Athlete's Quarterly. He lives and works in his hometown of Chicago with his wife Jacqueline Restrepo.

Anthony Fenech has worked as the *Detroit Free Press'* Tigers beat writer since 2015, placing as one of the top 10 beat writers by the Associated Press Sports Editors in 2017. In his tenure, Fenech has covered three last-place teams, two dead-last teams and one broadcasters' fight. He is ranked No. 93 in the world in MLB The Show's online home run derby.

Ken Funck has contributed to the Baseball Prospectus annual each year since 2009, during which time saplings became trees, children blossomed into adults and baseball analytics grew from nerdy outsider subculture to core organizational competency. Ken designs and manages Business Intelligence systems and lives outside Madison, Wisconsin with his wife and ideal travel companion Stephanie, a terrier named Jack, and a growing fear that the 2016 World Series was a one-off.

Brendan Gawlowski writes for FanGraphs. He lives in Seattle with his wife, Sierra, and new puppy, Yukon.

Mike Gianella is a senior writer at Baseball Prospectus. He lives in Pennsylvania with his wife, two awesome daughters and two annoying cats. He's still a Mets fan, for some stupid reason.

Craig Goldstein is the Editor-in-Chief of Baseball Prospectus. His work has appeared in Vice Sports, Baseball HQ, Fox Sports MLB/JABO and SB Nation MLB. He lives and works in Washington, DC, where he spends just the right amount of time thinking that cats can have a little salami as a treat.

Bryan Grosnick is an author of Baseball Prospectus and BP's Director of Reference and Training. This is his sixth consecutive appearance in the Annual, for which he's extremely grateful. He lives in New England with his remarkable wife, adorable son and two dogs.

Jon Hegglund is one of possibly 10-20 Giants fans currently residing in the state of Idaho. When he's not writing and podcasting about fantasy baseball, he thinks a lot about tacos, beer, the weather, cognitive narratology, late-stage capitalism, the end of the world and what comes after.

Christina Kahrl is a senior editor for MLB coverage at ESPN, a member of the Baseball Writers Association of America since 2009, and was one of the founding members of Baseball Prospectus back in 1995-1996. She also came out publicly as a transgender woman in 2003, become the first out trans woman working in sports journalism. She has been elected both to the Chicago LGBT Hall of Fame and the Gay and Lesbian Sports Hall of Fame. She lives in Connecticut with her wife.

Wilson Karaman is the Editor of Prospect Content at Baseball Prospectus, where he has hung his pen for a bunch of years now. When he's not writing about baseball he does his best to protect the Earth from humans and humans from facism. He's an East Coast migrant to the West Coast, last report had him living in Los Angeles still with his wife and some kids.

Justin Klugh is a contributing writer for FanGraphs, Baseball Prospectus, and various other outlets. He is a transplanted Philadelphian living in Baltimore, MD. If you name your beer after a baseball term, he will probably drink it.

David Lee is a former sports writer and current marketing coordinator who has been writing about prospects for Baseball Prospectus for five years. He has specifically followed the Braves system for half his life, hence the giddiness over Ronald Acuña Jr.

Ben Lindbergh is a staff writer for The Ringer. He also hosts the Effectively Wild podcast for FanGraphs. He is a former staff writer for FiveThirtyEight and Grantland, a former editor-in-chief of Baseball Prospectus, and the *New York Times* bestselling co-author of *The MVP Machine: How Baseball's New Nonconformists Are Using Data to Build Better Players* and *The Only Rule Is It Has to Work: Our Wild Experiment Building a New Kind of Baseball Team*. He lives in New York City.

Graham MacAree is a biological and structural engineer turned sports writer. He works for SB Nation and wishes that the Seattle Mariners would stop hurting him.

Rob Mains is a retired equities analyst living in upstate New York with his wife and too many bottles of Finger Lakes wine. A few years ago, someone posted a sabermetrics question on Twitter addressed to Bill James, Tom Tango, Neil Paine, and him, and I swear he's been insufferable ever since.

Allison McCague writes and podcasts about Mets baseball for Amazin' Avenue. She is also a contributor to Baseball Prospectus and The Hardball Times. When not expressing her deeply held beliefs about the designated hitter, Taylor ham, the nonexistence of Central Jersey, Harry Potter and Baltimore craft beers, she can be found utilizing her PhD training in genetics as a science policy professional.

Kelsey McKinney is a freelance reporter and writer in Washington, D.C. She is a former Deadspin staff writer and a famous hater of home runs.

Jon Meoli covers the Orioles for the *Baltimore Sun*, and is the head coach of the Loyola University Maryland women's ice hockey team. The former allows him to explore all the ways that players and teams can get better and write about it every day. The latter lets him live it. He lives in Baltimore with his wife, Meryl, and cat, Tom.

Ian Miller is one half of Productive Outs and a quarter of Puig Destroyer. He is a former BP columnist, and this is his 73rd year contributing to the Annual.

Jack Moore is a freelance writer and tutor living in Minneapolis, MN. His alter ego Jackie Peanuts can be heard on esports broadcasts across the Midwest.

Chad Moriyama writes about the Dodgers at a site called Dodgers Digest and tweet about them from @ChadMoriyama. Andy McCullough once called me a "a highly rational Internet troll" in the *Los Angeles Times*, so you know you're curious.

Marc Normandin is the former MLB Editor of SB Nation, and currently writes on baseball's labor issues and more for Patreon subscribers at marcnormandin.com. His baseball writing has appeared at Deadspin, Sports Illustrated, ESPN, Sports on Earth, The Guardian, The Nation, TalkPoverty and Baseball Prospectus, among others.

Sara Nović is the author of the books GIRL AT WAR and AMERICA IS IMMIGRANTS, both from Random House. She has an MFA in fiction and literary translation from Columbia, and lives with her family in Philly.

Eric Nusbaum is a writer and former editor at VICE. His first book, *Stealing Home: Los Angeles, the Dodgers, and the Lives Caught in Between* is available in bookstores everywhere.

Robert O'Connell is a writer in New York. His work has appeared in *The Atlantic*, *The New York Times*, *The Guardian*, among other outlets.

Jeffrey Paternostro is the Lead Prospect Writer and Multimedia Production Manager for Baseball Prospectus. He has written about prospects in his "The View From Behind the Backstop" column since 2015. He also produces the full range of shows on the Baseball Prospectus Podcast Network and co-hosts both "Three-Quarters Delivery," a prospect podcast, and "For All You Kids Out There," which is occasionally about the Mets. He primarily makes lists of things, despite finding High Fidelity kind of insipid.

Harry Pavlidis is the Director of Research & Development for Baseball Prospectus. His contributions to this year's edition are dedicated in loving memory of his wife, Kristine Melise Pavlidis.

Amy Pircher is a software engineer in Los Angeles, who helps send stuff to space by day, works for Baseball Prospectus by night, and is #1 cat mom at all times.

Manny Randhawa is a writer and Statcast researcher for MLB.com. He is a member of the Baseball Writers' Association of America and on the board of the Rocky Mountain Chapter of the Society for American Baseball Research. He is author of *The Blake Street Bombers*, chronicling the lives and careers of the most famous sluggers in Colorado Rockies history.

Tommy Rancel a.k.a. Pen Griffey Jr a.k.a. Nyce Harper a.k.a Mic Trout a.k.a Earn Me Banks a.k.a. Flow DiMaggio a.k.a Connie "Return of the" Mack a.k.a The One Marichal a.k.a Babe Truth a.k.a Trillie Stargell a.k.a Bread Williams a.k.a Drip Shumaker is a writer for ESPN and The Athletic. He has previously written for FanGraphs as well as contributing to the Baseball Prospectus Annual. He lives in the Tampa Bay area with his wife Jamie and their five children.

David Roth was an editor at Deadspin, and before that was an editor at Vice Sports, and before that was at SB Nation, and before that he co-founded The Classical. He has written for The New Republic and Slate and The Baffler and New York Magazine and GQ and Playboy and Dermatology Business Management. As of right now he's unemployed but he does do a podcast about Hallmark Channel movies.

Bret Sayre is the President of Baseball Prospectus. By day, he tells investment professionals what not to do. By night, he is a full-time family man and part-time nurse, cook, dynasty ranker, copy editor, musician and dog whisperer. As an eight-year-old boy, he was knocked over by a man in his thirties as he tried to catch a dead ball thrown by Kevin Mitchell at Shea Stadium. Now, he lives in New Jersey with his wife, Carolyn, their two children, Aly and Josh, a big-eyed bear named Hobbes, a fridge full of wine and more art supplies than a Michaels.

Nick Schaefer is a member of the massive contingent of baseball writers who also are afflicted with a license to practice law. He lives in New York with his wife Jane and his cat Chekhov.

Gerald Schifman works as a data editor and analyst in New York City. He joined Baseball Prospectus in late 2018 and writes the "Expanding the Zone" column. Previously, he wrote for The Hardball Times and FanGraphs.

Ginny Searle is a writer and editor at Baseball Prospectus. Her work has appeared at SB Nation, Allure, and Deadspin. She lives in southern California, where she is petulant about using "the" before freeway numbers and dismissive of the Shakespearean authorship question.

Jarrett Seidler is the Player Evaluation Coordinator and Senior Prospect Writer for Baseball Prospectus. He also co-hosts For All You Kids Out There, a weekly BP podcast that is occasionally about the Mets. As a lifelong New Jersey resident, he is hopeful that Bruce Springsteen and the E Street Band will tour in 2020.

Jordan Shusterman is one half of Cespedes Family BBQ. His work has appeared on Baseball Prospectus, Cut4, and MLB Pipeline. He lives and works in New York City, where he is one of the hosts of ChangeUp on DAZN. When he's not covering Major or Minor League Baseball, he's podcasting about Division-III baseball. No, seriously.

Matt Snyder has been with CBS Sports since February of 2011 and has covered every World Series since, though the 2016 World Series nearly made him pass out every inning all seven games. A die-hard Cubs fan since age six, he grew up wearing number eight in Little League after Andre Dawson's 1987 season. He's now angry at himself for knowing that was a dubious MVP selection.

Adam Sobsey has been writing for Baseball Prospectus since 2011. He covered the Durham Bulls as a beat writer from 2008-2013 and is the lead author of the baseball book *Bull City Summer* (Daylight Books, 2014). His biography of the rock musician Chrissie Hynde was published by University of Texas Press in 2017.

Ben Spanier grew up enjoying baseball amidst the humidity of the New York metro area and now writes about baseball amidst the humidity of the state of North Carolina. He happened upon the vast and diverse local Minor League scene after graduating from Guilford College with a degree in Economics.

Tyler Stafford lives outside of Houston where he is a good history teacher and a decent writer. His work has appeared on, among other places, Baseball Prospectus, The Athletic and his parent's refrigerator. You could, and dare we say should, follow him on Twitter @tylercstafford.

Linda Surovich is a children's librarian by day, Mets blogger and podcaster by night. In the summer you can usually find her at Citi Field questioning all of the life choices that led her there. The Grand-Slam single made her believe in miracles.

Matt Sussman writes for Baseball Prospectus/Short Relief and curls at the Black Swamp Curling Center in Bowling Green, Ohio. It would be risky to finish this line with a pun, so he will not, as it would present a bio hazard.

Jon Tayler is a former writer for Sports Illustrated whose work has also appeared in Baseball America, the Miami New Times, Lindy's Sports, and far too many issues of his college newspaper. He lives in New York and will go to his grave believing that Nomar Garciaparra was 10 times the shortstop Derek Jeter ever was. If you'd like a constant stream of his baseball insights intermixed with random Simpsons quotes and retweets of photos of ducks, follow him on Twitter: @JATayler.

Matt Trueblood writes for BP, about the Twins at Twins Daily, and in other places when editors get desperate. He lives in Minnesota, staring out the window and waiting for spring...training prices to come back from the stratosphere.

Levi Weaver is a former musician who became a baseball writer, because a career in day reading just wouldn't have been quiiiite risky enough. He likes predictably snotty music and has stronger Couch Opinions™? than he would have expected when he was young and his body and spirit were not yet splintered and waterlogged. Behold the pitiable wretch! Also, he didn't write this himself, Craig did it. Wow Craig what a jerk.

Holly M. Wendt is Director of Creative Writing and Assistant Professor of English at Lebanon Valley College and a regular contributor to Baseball Prospectus's Short Relief. Their writing (baseball-related and otherwise) has appeared in Sport Literate, The Rumpus, Barrelhouse, and elsewhere. They live in central Pennsylvania and have an illogical fondness for defensively gifted, offensively challenged middle infielders.

Collin Whitchurch has been an associate editor at Baseball Prospectus since 2019. He has been writing about baseball since 2013 and was previously the co-editor in chief of BP South Side. An Illinois native, he currently lives in Austin, TX, where he works full-time as a journalist in the newspaper industry. (Yes, those still exist).

Jeff Wiser is a professional in the world of public education, systems analysis and systems change for student achievement. He has written about baseball analytics for more than seven years now, often about the Arizona Diamondbacks.

Clarissa Young resides in Chicago, where she works in sports publishing for Triumph Books. She previously covered the Cubs for Baseball Prospectus and can be occasionally coaxed into new writing endeavors. When she was 10, Jason Giambi threw a ball to her at the Oakland Coliseum, but her dad made her "give it to a kid."

Acknowledgements

R.J. Anderson: Emma Baccellieri, Craig Goldstein, Bret Sayre, Patrick Dubuque, Tommy Rancel, Adam Sobsey and his CBS Sports colleagues. His parents and the rest of his family, forever and always.

Lucas Apostoleris: First and foremost, I would like to thank my family — most particularly my parents and my wife Kathleen — for their constant support. I also owe a lot to Harry Pavlidis, who brought me aboard at both Pitch Info and BP, and has always been there to answer my questions for the past decade. I'm grateful to Craig Goldstein, Aaron Gleeman, Patrick Dubuque and R.J. Anderson, who've all helped me become a better writer. To the friends I've made on the BP Stats team—you're all awesome, and each one of you has made me a bit smarter. And lastly, I need to thank Rob McQuown, who taught me so much and was always kind and gracious in sharing his wealth of knowledge. I miss him a lot.

Robert Au: Thanks to Craig and Harry for inviting me on board; to everyone else at BP for such a warm welcome; to my parents, for their love and support; and to Laura, Alexei, and Henry, for everything. My work on the annual is dedicated to the memory of my father.

Darius Austin: The phenomenal Depth Charts team: Ginny Searle, Randy Holt, Scott Orgera, Kazuto Yamazaki, Collin Whitchurch, Derek Albin and Rob Mains, for their tireless work on a never-ending task. The BP Fantasy team, for the camaraderie, support and feedback. Roger Cormier, for encouraging me to write things I otherwise would never have finished. Rob McQuown, for everything.

Emma Baccellieri: Editors, The Coven, Topo Chico, R.J.

Mark Barry: To the people that have given me a chance, most specifically Bret Sayre. To Craig Goldstein, Mike Gianella, JP Breen, Zach Steinhorn and R.J. Anderson. To my family most of all, Amanda, Kristen, Mom and Dad. You're all the best. And to Rob McQuown who was a pal that I only knew virtually, but one of my favorite people nonetheless and one whom I miss a lot. Fingers stay crossed for that Willy Adames Scoresheet push.

Jordan Bastian: Thank you to my amazing wife, Kelly, who has stuck by my side through the early years of covering preps and sleeping on air mattresses, while I promised better things were coming. And thank you to my kids, who think all I do is "type baseball" and live at the baseball stadium. All those hours I'm at the park or on the road are for you guys, and I will be forever grateful that you get it.

Demetrius Bell: Thank you to my parents and my immediate family for continuing to support me and also indulge me when I choose to rant about my nerdy interests. I'd also like to thank every rapper who has come out of Memphis since the early 90s. You provided the soundtrack for the words that are in this annual and I want you all to know that you're appreciated and to keep on doing what you're doing.

Jason Benetti: Thanks to all of the people who've helped make this career possible including the White Sox and ESPN. Specific thanks in this space to Adam Doster, a substantially more capable writer than I (he's actually been published a lot, you should read his stuff, it's excellent), for editing the first draft.

Sydney Bergman: I couldn't have done this without my podcast cohosts, Kay and Laura; the fine folks of Nats Twitter, particularly Jenn, Dara, and Noah; or her husband, Sam, who once asked where the 'longstop' was. A particular shout-out to my parents and sister, Hannah, an original Nats fan, as well as my new nephew, D.C., who will be the last great LOOGY once he learns to walk.

J.P. Breen: A massive thank you to R.J. Anderson, Craig Goldstein and everyone who graciously agreed to be interviewed for the Brewers' team essay.

Grant Brisbee: Amelia and Penelope for putting up with a cranky work-at-home dad. Lydia for putting up with me when I use Tom Waits, David Lee Roth, and David Bowie voices to sing that Traveling Wilburys song, which is often. Marc Normandin and Whitney McIntosh for continuing the spirit of the most important Slack room I'll ever have. Bryan Murphy and the rest of McCovey Chronicles for their fantastic, thankless work. And my coworker, Emma Baccellieri, for keeping me sane with pictures of her dog, Fisher.

Craig Brown: Thanks to R.J. Anderson, Craig Goldstein and Bret Sayre for inviting me back. Thanks to Scott Orgera invaluable assistance down the stretch. As always thanks to Joe Hamrahi, Steven Goldman, Clark Fosler, Jeff Zimmerman and Max Rieper. Can't forget Dave Brown, Alec Lewis, Jeff Passan, Rustin Dodd, and Jeffrey Flanagan. And Rob McQuown. Of course, thanks to my family who tolerates this baseball obsession. Finally, special thanks to C.E. Jones who taught me how to appreciate this game.

Ben Carsley: My Red Sox-crazed family, the ever-patient Allyson Clancy, Bret Sayre, Craig Goldstein, Sam Miller, R.J. Anderson, Patrick Dubuque, Mike Curtin, Xander Bogaerts, Mary Donovan, Daniel Ohman and the C-4 Content Team.

Ben Clemens: Thank you to my wife, Jenna, for encouraging me to pursue my dreams. Thanks also to my parents for giving me a lifelong love of baseball and writing, and to Ruby, though she'd probably prefer a chew toy to an acknowledgement in a book.

Zach Crizer: Thanks to Craig Goldstein, R.J. Anderson, Hannah Keyser, Stein, Jason, Jefe, Stin and Steph—who make following this game unquantifiably more interesting.

Spring Marie Cullen: To my parents, Joe and Jackie, for always supporting me no matter how wild my dreams. Bret Sayre, Jeff Paternostro, Wilson Karaman and Jarret Seidler for giving me this awesome opportunity and properly introducing me to the magical world of prospect writing. Craig Goldstein and Collin Whitchurch for all their help along the way, editorial and otherwise. And of course my dog Lucky, for constantly putting his paws on my computer when I'm about to type something lame and always wanting to go out when I've hit a groove.

Bradford William Davis: Thank you to everyone who ever thought I had something to say (even when I didn't know what that was), the colleagues who gave me gracious and necessary critiques to help me be the best writer I could be, the friends who prayed for me and encouraged me to trust in Christ—not the success of writing or the ebbs and flows of this cursed industry—and be everything He made me to be, the group texts who laughed with me through the nonsense of this again cursed industry and the readers who took time to offer timely encouragement. My wife who has done all the above and so much more. Mom, Dad, Johnny, Michael, DT, Tyler, Ray, Alex, Ekemini, CJ, Wit, Christian, Richard, Brent, Enoch, Wade, the Balan Bros, Kailyn, Morgan, Timothy, Tony, Sara, Dan, John, Huckabee (no relation), Sophia, Jason, Alan, Rich, Cray, Shakeia, Ese, Caryn, Claudia, Derek, Randy, Bobby, Jen, Dave, Gaby, Craig, Bob, Seth, Jason, Emma, Coley, Mirin, Julian, Paul, KP, Gluck, Lily, Ariana, Allison, Ashley, Nelson, Kyle, Kate, Dennis, Betty, Andy, Sarah, Laura, Grant and Didi—I'm grateful for you all.

Russell Dorsey: I've had several people give me an opportunity to share my thoughts on baseball at a young age and it's an honor. Being a part of this year's BP Annual is no different. BP was the first publication that allowed me to write about baseball when I was only a junior in college and has been a major part of my success in this business. For that, I am eternally grateful.

Patrick Dubuque: Thank you to everyone, but primarily to my indefatigable and unflappable wife, Kjersten, for the life that allows me to make this part of it.

Drew Fairservice: Thanks to Catherine, Lauren, Maddie and the little league coach who asked "are you afraid of the ball?" before sticking me behind the plate.

James Fegan: Thank you to John "Moon" Mullin, for tearing me down like no one had ever done up to that point, nor has done since, all for the express purpose of building me back up.

Anthony Fenech: Mike Clevinger.

Ken Funck: R.J. Anderson, Steph Bee, Patrick Dubuque, Aaron Gleeman, Steven Goldman, Craig Goldstein, Christina Kahrl, King Kaufman, Ben Lindbergh, Sam Miller, John Perrotto, Bret Sayre, Cecilia Tan, Jason Wojciechowski and anyone else who has worked their editorial magic on my behalf.

Brendan Gawlowski: I'd like to thank my family, particularly my dad Rich for encouraging my baseball career in whatever form it takes in any given year and my wife Sierra who is endlessly patient when I "need to write." Thank you to Patrick Dubuque, Nathan Bishop, Craig Goldstein, R.J. Anderson, Meg Rowley, Tom Eberlein and Jon Hegglund for always being there and willing to read over a draft.

Mike Gianella: My wife Colleen and daughters Lucy and Elise. Bret Sayre, Mark Barry, J.P. Breen and everyone on the awesome fantasy team at Baseball Prospectus. Alex Patton, Steve Gardner, Peter Kreutzer, Jeff Erickson, Eric Karabell, Tristan Cockcroft and so many others in the fantasy industry whose advice and contributions were instrumental along the way.

Craig Goldstein: Katherine Pappas, Laurie Gross, Harvey Goldstein, Alexis Goldstein, R.J. Anderson, Patrick Dubuque, Bret Sayre, Jason Wojciechowski, Sam Miller, Ginny Searle, Collin Whitchurch, Rob McQuown, Ben Carsley, Jacob Raim, Lucas Apostoleris, Harry Pavlidis, Kendall Guillemette, Jonathan Judge, Rob Mains, Jeffrey Paternostro, Jason Parks, Ben Lindbergh, The BP Prospect Team, Jarrett Seidler, Marc Normandin, Zach Mortimer, Tucker Blair, Ethan Purser, Mike Ferrin, Spike Lundberg, Tommy Rancel, Meg Rowley, James Fegan, Emma Baccellieri, Mauricio Rubio, J.P. Breen, Wilson Karaman, Zach Crizer, Jeffrey Wiser.

Bryan Grosnick: Sarah Grosnick, Luke Grosnick, Phil and Debbie Grosnick, Bret Sayre, Craig Goldstein, R.J. Anderson, Patrick Dubuque, Bryan Murphy and the staff of McCovey Chronicles, Jen Mac Ramos, Jonathan Judge, Jeffrey Paternostro, Jarrett Seidler, Aaron Gleeman, Jeff Long, Scott Orgera, Rich MacLeod, Rob Mains, the BP Stats Team, Ben Lindbergh, Sam Miller, Meg Rowley, and Jeff Sullivan of Effectively Wild, the data providers at Baseball-Reference, FanGraphs, Baseball Prospectus, Brooks Baseball and–of course–Rob McQuown.

Jon Hegglund: Thank you, thank you: Mike Gianella and Samuel Hale for all that is, and is not, on the podcast. Mark Barry for managing BP's fantasy office and letting me add minor-league pitchers to our TDGX team. J.P. Breen for meticulous, timely, and good-humored editing. Craig Goldstein for pretending not to be annoyed when I pester him at the worst possible times. Brendan Gawlowski for encouragement, support, and his strange obsession with the Kibbie Dome. Bret Sayre for being a kind and benevolent President Business. And, of course, Emily and Oscar, who make everything awesome.

Christina Kahrl: To Gary Huckabay, who made so many more things real than any knew possible at the time.

Wilson Karaman: I'm thankful for my family. My wife, my kids, my parents and everyone else I get to huddle up with in community. We are all of us gods, and curious ones at that. And I'll always be thankful to Rob McQuown for the research assistance.

Justin Klugh: I would like to thank my wife Aviva (she won't be my wife until around the World Series, but I'm jumping ahead), my impeccable mother and father, and my two massively intelligent sisters, Megan and Brittany, all just for being themselves. I would like to NOT thank Milkshake the cat for stealing my seat every time I stand up.

David Lee: I'd like to thank my fiancée for support, patience and joining in on my baseball obsession, as well as the rest of my family for always being a fan.

Graham MacAree: Mattie, Lucien and Théo.

Rob Mains: My mother, Rhoda Mains, for instilling a love of the game and my wife, Amy Durland, for encouraging me to pursue it and often not regretting having done so. Martín Alonso, José Hernández, Marco Gámez, Carlos Pérez, Pepe Latorre, and Carlos José Lugo for making BP en español, our daily Spanish language content, a reality. Rob McQuown, whose friendship, assistance, knowledge, patience, and dedication meant so much to so many of us, and for which I regret having not thanked him sufficiently during his too-short life. AM and PM, for everything else.

Allison McCague: I'd like to thank my dad, without whom I wouldn't be such a huge baseball-loving nerd. I'd like to thank my mom for putting up with my dad and I while we're watching Mets games. To my incredible support network of friends and family: I love you dearly. I owe an enormous amount of gratitude to Chris McShane and Brian Salvatore at Amazin' Avenue for believing in me and helping me grow immensely as a writer and podcaster. In a similar vein, I'd like to thank Jeff Paternostro and Jarrett Seidler for their friendship and helping me believe I could do this and Craig Goldstein, R.J. Anderson, and Bret Sayre for giving me the chance to do so. I'd like to thank my A Pod of Their Own co-hosts, Linda Surovich and Maggie Wiggin, for going on this podcast journey with me and making me a better person every day. I am so grateful for the Amazin' Avenue community, who I consider family and without whom I would not have met Michael, whose love and support is my tether.

Kelsey McKinney: Thank you to the Washington Nationals, first and foremost, for not letting me down on a week where I had to quit a job I loved. Thank you to every member of the Deadspin (RIP). Thank you to Trey, for learning to love baseball for me, and to my Dad who taught me to love it in the first place.

Jon Meoli: To my wife, Meryl: thanks for the support and understanding that makes this all possible. To my family: thanks for molding every part of me. To the SoxProspects crew: thanks for giving me a chance. To everyone that helped me grow over the years: thank you is not enough. But it's a start.

Ian Miller: Many thanks to Craig Goldstein for his incisive editing, to James Yasko and Kevin Goldstein for their invaluable feedback, and to Tracy Miller for her boundless support.

Chad Moriyama: Thanks to those who have helped me along the way, which is...everybody. I dunno I'm not good at these things.

Marc Normandin: Thank you to every reader and editor who has shown faith in me and in my work: you're the reason I get to keep writing.

Sara Nović: Thanks to the BP crew for giving me space to run away from sabermetrics, my grandma for teaching us all how to be Mets fans, and Zach, for holding the baby while I wrote this.

Eric Nusbaum: Shout out to Janelle, Clay, and Marco, to the city of Los Angeles and all my friends who are Giants fans.

Robert O'Connell: Mom and Dad.

Jeffrey Paternostro: My wife Jess for tolerating the ten mostly empty mugs of tea scattered around the office most days. Jarrett Seidler for being the elite. Nick Schaefer, Wilson Karaman, and the prospect team for keeping my word count manageable. Meg Rowley for always being able to pick the right Death Cab song to reference. David Roth for always being up to remember some guys. Kate Feldman for the dog photos. Allison McCague for the beer photos. The Amazin' Avenue folks. All of our patreon supporters, podcast listeners, group DMs and drinking buddies. And I guess Craig is back now, so Craig.

Harry Pavlidis: Rob McQuown.

Amy Pircher: Massive gratitude to the Python community for making such a great tool and making lives easier. Huge thanks to BP for giving me the opportunity and opening to pursue both of my passions, with special thanks to Harry Pavlidis and Matt Dennewitz for their mentorship and guidance. Additional kind folks at BP for their support includes but not limited to: Robert Au, Sean O'Rourke, Rob McQuown, Jen Ramos, Kendall Guillemette, and Beth Woerner. To Juan: much love and eternal gratitude.

Tommy Rancel: Jamie, Alexis, Vincent, Jarek, Brooklyn, Dakota, R.J. Anderson, Erik Hahmann, Bradley Ankrom, Craig Goldstein, Andrew Schulz, Alexxx Media, Kazeem Famuyide, Akaash Singh, Eddin DeTurkey Keith Law, Joel Martinez, Daniel Baker, LaJethro Jenkins, Dragonfly Jonez, Joset Kamali, Rebecca Basse, Carlos Alvarez, Randy Lemery, Harry Styles, Carl Reed, Daniel Goldman, Pubby Longway, Danny LoPriore Jr., Michael Castanos and Cordae Amari Dunston.

David Roth: Thank you to Kate and everyone else who puts up with my shit. It's awful, and you're great.

Bret Sayre: To Annie—Sometimes children are the best teachers, and it was one of the many ways you were special. We all are so accustomed to our fast paces that it feels impossible to slow down enough to make up a game where one doesn't exist, find a barely visible rainbow or bring out a smile in someone who can't find it for themselves. We met through a sport we both loved, and it will all forever be inseparable for me. I will play for you until we meet again.

To Rob—Every week or so, I'll still bring up our sprawling Slack DM history both so I can continue to learn from you and in the impossible hope that one day the light next to your name will turn green again. There's still so much I want to talk to you about, from Scoresheet advice to music to reliever projections. But above all else, I want the opportunity to say thank you. Not for the research assistance, but just for being you.

Nick Schaefer: Thank you to my family for their encouragement and to Bret, Craig, Jarrett, Jeff, Wilson, and Collin for their constant assistance.

Gerald Schifman: To my family for all their encouragement; to Craig Goldstein and Aaron Gleeman for enhancing and supporting my work; to Lucas Apostoleris, Rob McQuown, Harry Pavlidis and Martin Alonso for their research and data-querying assistance; to Dave Cameron, Paul Swydan and Mike McCormick for launching my baseball writing career.

Ginny Searle: Massive gratitude to all the kind folks at BP who tolerate my profoundly annoying ways, including but not limited to: Craig Goldstein, Collin Whitchurch, Rob Mains, Bret Sayre, Jeff Long, Kendall Guillemette, Steven Goldman. To Tori: love, forever and forever.

Jarrett Seidler: Jeffrey Paternostro, for always going double or nothing; Wilson Karaman and Nick Schaefer, for dealing with it when we do; Craig Goldstein and Bret Sayre, for being the best bosses I will ever have; Kate Feldman, for everything; the BP Prospect Team, for making me look smart; my friends and family, too many to name, for helping me become the best person and baseball writer I can be. In memory of Rob McQuown, one of those friends who passed far too soon.

Jordan Shusterman: Bailey Bowers, David Shusterman, Gila Shusterman, Alan Shusterman, Rebecca Shusterman, Jake Mintz, Kendall Guillemette, Gemma Kaneko, Craig Goldstein, Jeff Sullivan, Zach Mortimer, Mike Ferrin, Meg Rowley, Kiley McDaniel, Eric Longenhagen, Ben Lindbergh,

Sam Miller, Ryan Divish, Emma Baccellieri, Zach Crizer, Brent Honeywell, Kinza Baad, Lana Berry, Andrew Phillips, Ryan Mossman, Eric Mattera, Yige Sun, Jen Medyuk, Jamie Lackner.

Matt Snyder: First and foremost I have to thank my parents for instilling my love for baseball and the Chicago Cubs in me from a very young age. Upon birth I was given a glove—though it was for right-handers and I ended up left-handed—and a Cubs onesie. My brother and sister were huge contributors as well, with a special shout to my parents for having a brother just one year younger than myself, enabling us to always have someone to play baseball with. Every teammate I've ever had in football or baseball, you all helped shape me as a person and as a sportswriter. Speaking of teammates, my fellow CBS Sports MLB team members are amazing and I couldn't do my job without you. My two children light up my life everyday. As far as my wife, Sharla, there isn't really anything I could put into words to express how much every aspect of her means to me. Let's just say I'm Speechless.

Adam Sobsey: R.J. Anderson, Craig Goldstein, Heather Mallory.

Ben Spanier: My parents Jon and Jen for encouraging my foray into the let us say precarious world of baseball writing, and my friends Dave and Nick for listening to and interacting with my never-ending baseball kibitizing.

Tyler Stafford: Thank you to my wife, Alicia, who does not care for sports, but loves me enough to let me pretend to be a Real Writer sometimes. My entire family for always encouraging me to do the things I love most. James Yasko, whose blog Astros County made me realize there were people out there like me. Eno Sarris for inexplicably giving me a job that paid real American dollars, and Craig Goldstein who is responding to several dozen Gchats as you read this.

Linda Surovich: To my wonderful friends and family. Mom, Dad, Pauli, and Marie. Thank you for your support and belief in me, especially when I had none for myself. I would be nowhere without your encouragement, love, and also some slight chiding about my constant doubts. I love you all dearly. To my two amazing co-hosts Maggie and Allison, thank you for helping me find my voice and for your limitless knowledge. I am truly blessed to know you and you inspire me always. Finally #pizza. What a special group of people you all are and don't let anyone tell you otherwise. Your knowledge, support, and bad puns mean the world to me. No matter what I know I can always count on you for puppies and goofy JD Davis gifs. It's appreciated more than you know. To anyone who has ever offered a kind word thank you and of course #LFGM

Matt Sussman: Brit, Max and Mom.

Jon Tayler: First and foremost, thanks to Craig and R.J. for inviting me to be a part of this fun tradition and giving me a safe space to yell about the Red Sox, a team about which

I have lots of feelings. Thanks to my girlfriend, Lindsey, for insisting that I not be the last person to file my essay (in your face, whoever that was!) and also for being the best at all times. And thanks to my dog, Fisher, for repeatedly deciding that a more important thing than finishing my piece was for me to rub his stomach as much as possible. He knows what's truly important in this world.

Matt Trueblood: Maria: I hope I bring your empathy and passion for justice and equity to this. Sorkin: I hope I bring your roaring enthusiasm. Lincoln: I hope I write things at which you'll someday laugh that wonderful laugh. Anna: I hope I reflect your unbending conviction. Emerson: I hope my style and substance show the change you wrought in my heart. Readers, I hope I've absorbed and considered your feedback, and that I reflect your collected wisdom and varied perspectives. If I've done any of that, I've written the way I want to. You all make this worth my time.

Levi Weaver: My wife Heather who endured [sigh, meek waving at the past 13 years] just so much, honestly. Or Moyal, who took a risk and hired a musician to write about baseball. T.R. Sullivan who taught me not to change the subject, and The Athletic who took a risk and hired a writer as a reporter. And then just like honestly about 50 baseball writers to whom I owe any semblance of legitimacy I have.

Holly M. Wendt: Thanks immensely to Patrick Dubuque, Roger Cormier, Jason Wojciechowski, Craig Goldstein, R.J. Anderson, Bret Sayre, Sam Miller and all of the fantastic people I've been lucky enough to write beside at Short Relief. Thanks also to Bill Zeiders, my favorite person with whom to watch baseball.

Collin Whitchurch: I would like to thank Patrick Dubuque, Bret Sayre, and Craig Goldstein for deciding they liked my work as an editor enough to bring and keep me aboard the monolithic enterprise that is Baseball Prospectus. I'd like to thank James Fegan for once-upon-a-time not ignoring a random tweet from someone he'd never met that said "hey, are you looking for any contributors to your website?" I'd like to thank Nick Schaefer and all of the former BPSS crew for their friendship and camaraderie throughout the years. Lastly, I'd like to thank my parents for always supporting whatever I do, even if they often fail to fully understand exactly what that is.

Jeff Wiser: Thanks to my supportive wife, Annie, for her understanding and generous sharing of time (our household is a very uneven platoon situation). I would also like to thank Mike, Craig, Kendall, Zach, Nick, Jesse, Joshua and the WBtBS fantasy crew for ensuring that baseball remains just as fun as it should be.

Clarissa Young: R.J. Anderson, for the encouragement; Craig Goldstein, for the freedom; Rian Watt, for first taking a chance on me at BP. Brooke, Melissa, my colleagues and other enablers. Ricardo, who cares for me but doesn't care for baseball. Thank you to Oakland.

Index of Names

Experience all
Baseball Prospectus
has to offer!

 Subscriptions support the leaders in public research and analysis in an increasingly proprietary environment.

 Get regular updates from live views by our prospect team.

 Access premium editorial content year-round, from a talented stable of authors.

 Annual subscribers can access the **Player Forecast Manager** and the **PECOTA Weighted Means** spreadsheet.

 Super-Premium subscribers can access **The Bat Signal**, a service that answers any fantasy questions within 24 hours.

 Annual membership is a **45%** discount over monthly plans.

Sign up at
www.BaseballProspectus.com/subscriptions

2020 Major League Baseball Travel Routes

MLB teams are scheduled to travel over one million miles during the upcoming 2020 season. Geography, division alignment, and scheduling determine how far each team will travel. For example, the Mariners are geographically isolated while the Royals benefit from their central location; the Cubs and Cardinals will play a series in London, adding thousands of travel miles. Below are the visualized routes for each team and the total miles they are scheduled to travel.

For consistency, great-circle distances from ballpark to ballpark are used.   ✈ denotes international series travel.

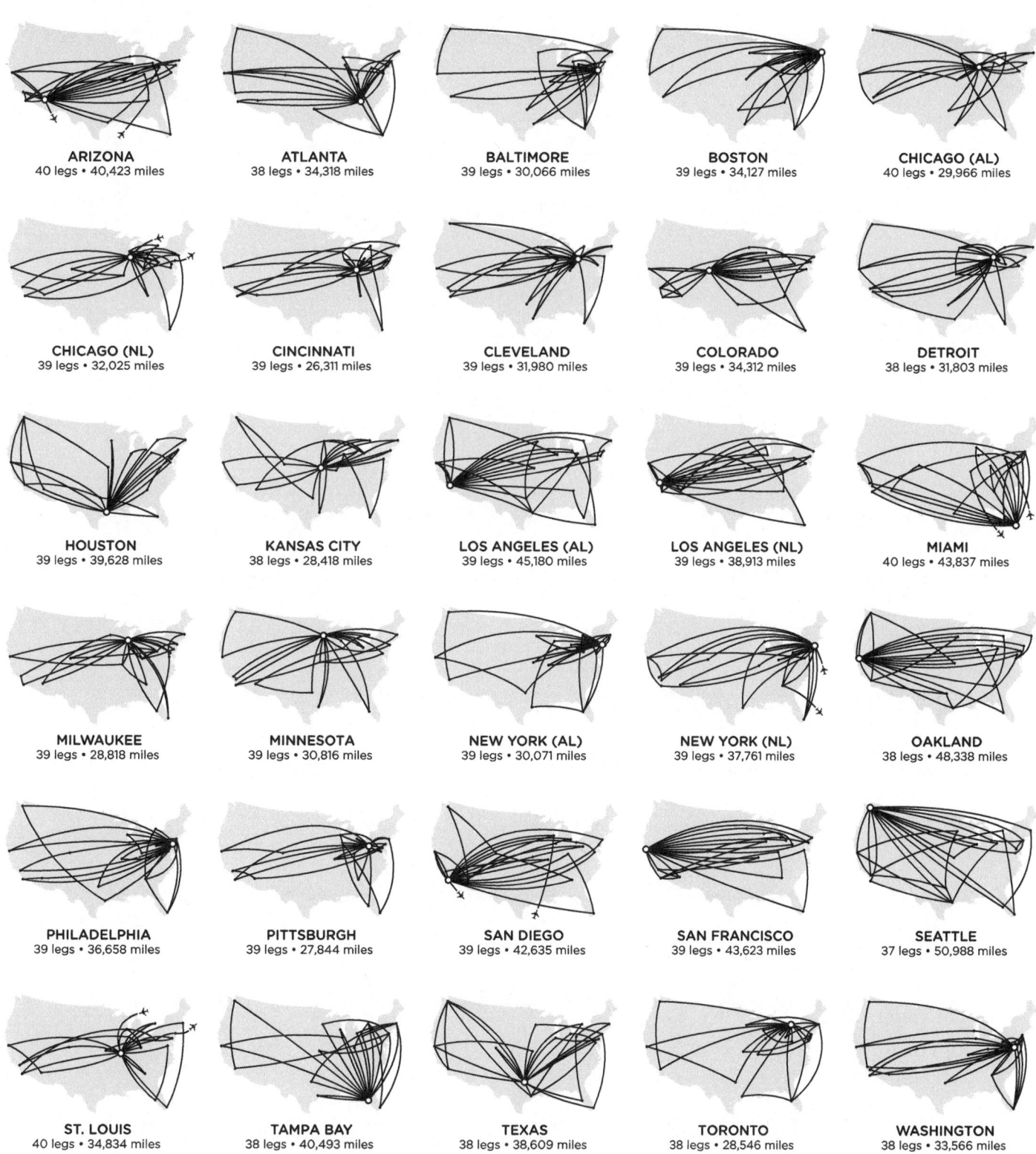

ARIZONA
40 legs • 40,423 miles

ATLANTA
38 legs • 34,318 miles

BALTIMORE
39 legs • 30,066 miles

BOSTON
39 legs • 34,127 miles

CHICAGO (AL)
40 legs • 29,966 miles

CHICAGO (NL)
39 legs • 32,025 miles

CINCINNATI
39 legs • 26,311 miles

CLEVELAND
39 legs • 31,980 miles

COLORADO
39 legs • 34,312 miles

DETROIT
38 legs • 31,803 miles

HOUSTON
39 legs • 39,628 miles

KANSAS CITY
38 legs • 28,418 miles

LOS ANGELES (AL)
39 legs • 45,180 miles

LOS ANGELES (NL)
39 legs • 38,913 miles

MIAMI
40 legs • 43,837 miles

MILWAUKEE
39 legs • 28,818 miles

MINNESOTA
39 legs • 30,816 miles

NEW YORK (AL)
39 legs • 30,071 miles

NEW YORK (NL)
39 legs • 37,761 miles

OAKLAND
38 legs • 48,338 miles

PHILADELPHIA
39 legs • 36,658 miles

PITTSBURGH
39 legs • 27,844 miles

SAN DIEGO
39 legs • 42,635 miles

SAN FRANCISCO
39 legs • 43,623 miles

SEATTLE
37 legs • 50,988 miles

ST. LOUIS
40 legs • 34,834 miles

TAMPA BAY
38 legs • 40,493 miles

TEXAS
38 legs • 38,609 miles

TORONTO
38 legs • 28,546 miles

WASHINGTON
38 legs • 33,566 miles

Adapted from the 2020 Travel Routes Poster and Calendar available at **thirty81project.com**.